TODAY'S LIGHT® BIBLE

A two year journey through the Bible

WITH DEVOTIONS BY

JANE L. FRYAR

This Bible has been developed and produced by The Livingstone Corporation. Project staff include Dr. James Galvin, Christopher D. Hudson, Jon Farrar, Jeannette Dall, Alan Sharrer, Thomas Ristow, Kathleen Ristow and Elizabeth Marchiori.

Interior design by Design Corps.
Cover design by Paetzold Design.

ISBN – Hard Cover
Soft Cover

Printed in the United States of America

5 6 7 8 9 10 11 12 13 14 18 17 16 15 14 13 12 11 10 09

Welcome

Welcome to the *Today's Light Bible*! Perhaps you've been a member of the *Today's Light* family for several years. Or maybe you've heard about *Today's Light* only recently. In either case, our Lord has wonderful plans in mind for you.

You see, God wants you to get to *know Him*. He's not so much interested in your learning facts *about* Him, though that's certainly part of the process. The holy, all-powerful, infinitely gracious God of the universe wants to reveal Himself to you. To you! As His Spirit works that deep, intimate knowledge in your heart of hearts, it will drive you to your knees in deep repentance at times. It will take you soaring to the heights of joy at times, the joy of the salvation Christ Jesus won for you on Calvary's cross.

And that knowledge will always change you. It will deepen your faith, and it will transform you into the image of the Savior-God whose love and goodness you will encounter in the Holy Scriptures.

The study helps in this Bible will take you from Genesis to Revelation in two years. The readings for Saturday and Sunday each week are combined, so you will have six days to do each week's readings. If your schedule causes you to skip a day, this arrangement gives you one make-up day each week.

If you find any reading too long, use the "If time is short" feature to decide what verses to focus on instead. In any case, the schedule should never drive you. Instead, let our Lord lead you into the pastures of His Word. Let Him feed your soul each day.

Those of us at Concordia Publishing House who worked on the *Today's Light Bible* are praying that He will do just that.

May you more and more fully *know* the only true God and Jesus Christ whom He has sent.

Joy in Jesus,
Jane L. Fryar

How to Use this Bible

1. Make an "appointment with Jesus." Ink it into your daily calendar. Choose a slot in which you will have about 20 minutes.
2. Forestall interruptions. Unplug the phone. Close your office door. Do whatever you need to do to get alone with your Lord.
3. Make the time pleasant for yourself. You may want to read at McDonald's over breakfast coffee. Choose a time and place you will be comfortable, relaxed, and open to the Holy Spirit's voice.
4. Start with prayer. Ask God to meet with you, to teach you, and to give you an open heart. Ask Him to personalize His Word to your circumstances today. Then talk with Him while you read.
5. Pray as you close. Ask God to bring His Word back to your mind as you need His help today.

Get the Big Picture: Gives you a helpful overview of the day's text before you read the passage.

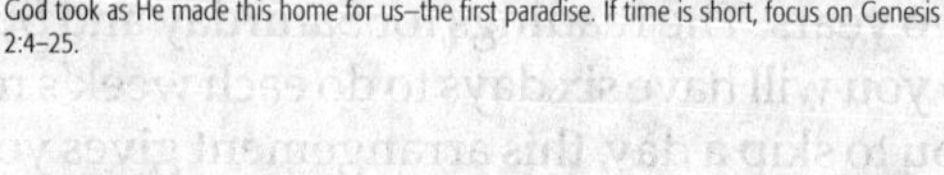

Genesis records many firsts—the first people, the first family, the first sin, the first city, the first musician, and more "firsts" besides. Today's reading zeroes in on the first week of our world's existence and on the first home God gave His human creatures. As you read, note the care God took as He made this home for us—the first paradise. If time is short, focus on Genesis 2:4–25.

Sharpen the Focus: Helps you clearly understand the passage and see its meaning for your life.

SHARPEN THE FOCUS

The Bible never attempts to prove that God exists. It simply asserts it: "In the beginning God . . ." (Genesis 1:1). Reading these four simple words, we take the first steps on an adventure of discovery. God gave us His Word—from Genesis through Revelation—to reveal to us what He is like. As we read, mark, learn, and think about His Word, our Lord will make Himself real to us. The Holy Spirit has promised to do this—in particular, He has promised to reveal to us His love and forgiveness for us in Christ.

As we read the account of the creation, for example, we see God's power, creativity, wisdom, and tender concern for His human creatures—His children. Take time to notice and to marvel at the creation around you today—the colors of the sky, the light of the sun or stars, the mosaic of leaves on the tree outside your window, or the snowflakes that drift down onto the front lawn. Praise the Creator who "richly provides us with everything for our enjoyment" (1 Timothy 6:17). You might want to use the words of Psalm 148 as you do so.

TABLE OF CONTENTS

tual criticism. Footnotes call attention to places where there was uncertainty about what the original text was. The best current printed texts of the Greek New Testament were used.

There is a sense in which the work of translation is never wholly finished. This applies to all great literature and uniquely so to the Bible. In 1973 the New Testament in the New International Version was published. Since then, suggestions for corrections and revisions have been received from various sources. The Committee on Bible Translation carefully considered the suggestions and adopted a number of them. These were incorporated in the first printing of the entire Bible in 1978. Additional revisions were made by the Committee on Bible Translation in 1983 and appear in printings after that date.

As in other ancient documents, the precise meaning of the biblical texts is sometimes uncertain. This is more often the case with the Hebrew and Aramaic texts than with the Greek text. Although archaeological and linguistic discoveries in this century aid in understanding difficult passages, some uncertainties remain. The more significant of these have been called to the reader's attention in the footnotes.

In regard to the divine name *YHWH*, commonly referred to as the *Tetragrammaton*, the translators adopted the device used in most English versions of rendering that name as in capital letters to distinguish it from *Adonai*, another Hebrew word rendered 'Lord,' for which small letters are used. Wherever the two names stand together in the Old Testament as a compound name of God, they are rendered "Sovereign LORD."

Because for most readers today the phrases "The LORD of hosts" and "the God of hosts" have little meaning, this version renders them "the LORD Almighty" and "God Almighty." These renderings convey the sense of the Hebrew, namely, "he who is sovereign over all the 'hosts' (powers) in heaven and on earth, especially over the 'hosts' (armies) of Israel." For readers unacquainted with Hebrew this does not make clear the distinction between *Sabaoth* ("hosts" or "Almighty") and *Shaddai* (which can also be translated "Almighty"), but the latter occurs infrequently and is always footnoted. When *Adonai* and *YHWH Sabaoth* occur together, they are rendered "the Lord, the LORD Almighty."

As for other proper nouns, the familiar spellings of the King James Version are generally retained. Names traditionally spelled with "ch," except where it is final, are usually spelled in this translation with " k" or "c," since the biblical languages do not have the sound that "ch" frequently indicates in English—for example, in *chant*. For well-known names such as Zechariah, however, the traditional spelling has been retained. Variation in the spelling of names in the original languages has usually not been indicated. Where a person or place has two or more different names in the Hebrew, Aramaic or Greek texts, the more familiar one has generally been used, with footnotes where needed.

To achieve clarity the translators sometimes supplied words not in the original texts but required by the context. If there was uncertainty about such material, it is enclosed in brackets. Also for the sake of clarity or style, nouns, including some proper nouns, are sometimes substituted for pronouns, and vice versa. And though the Hebrew writers often shifted back and forth between first, second and third personal pronouns without change of antecedent, this translation often makes them uniform, in accordance with English style and without the use of footnotes.

Poetical passages are printed as poetry, that is, with indentation of lines with separate stanzas. These are generally designed to reflect the structure of Hebrew poetry. This poetry is normally characterized by parallelism in balanced lines. Most of the poetry in the Bible is in the Old Testament, and scholars differ regarding the scansion of Hebrew lines. The translators determined the stanza divisions for the most part by analysis of the subject matter. The stanzas therefore poetic paragraphs.

As an aid to the reader, italicized sectional headings are inserted in most of the books. They are not to be regarded as part of the NIV text, are not for oral reading, and are not intended to dictate the interpretation of the sections they head.

The footnotes in this version are of several kinds, most of which need no explanation. Those giving alternative translations begin with "Or" and generally introduce the alternative with the word preceding it in the text, except when it is a single-word alternative; in poetry quoted in footnote a slant mark indicates a line division. Footnotes introduced by "Or" do not have uniform significance. In some cases two possible translations were considered to have about equal validity. In other cases, though the translators were convinced that the translation in the text was correct judged that another interpretation was possible and of sufficient importance to be represented in a footnote.

In the New Testament, footnotes that refer to uncertainty regarding the original text are introduced by "Some manuscripts" or similar expressions. In the Old Testament, evidence for the reading chosen is given first and evidence for the alternative is added after a semicolon (for the Septuagint; Hebrew *father*). In such notes the term "Hebrew" refers to the Masoretic Text.

It should be noted that minerals, flora and fauna, architectural details, articles of clothing jewelry, musical instruments and other articles cannot always be identified with decision. Also measures of capacity in the biblical period are particularly uncertain (see the table of weights measures following the text).

Like all translations of the Bible, made as they are by imperfect man, this one undoubtedly falls short of its goals. Yet we are grateful to God for the extent to which he has enabled us to realize these goals and for the strength he has given us and our colleagues to complete our task. We offer this version of the Bible to him in whose name and for whose glory it has been made. We pray that it will lead many into a better understanding of the Holy Scriptures and a fuller knowledge of Jesus Christ the incarnate Word, of whom the Scriptures so faithfully testify.

The Committee on Bible Translation

June 1978
(Revised Aug 1983)

Names of the translators and editors may be
secured from the International Bible Society
translation sponsors of the New International Version,
P .0. Box 62970, Colorado Springs, Colorado
80962-2970 U.S.A.

Old Testament

LORD God made all kinds of trees grow
out of the ground—trees that were
pleasing to the eye and good for food.
In the middle of the garden were the
tree of life and the tree of the knowledge
of good and evil.
10 A river watering the garden flowed
from Eden; from there it was separated
into four headwaters. 11 The name of the
first is the Pishon; it winds through the
entire land of Havilah, where there is
gold. 12 (The gold of that land is good;
aromatic resin[a] and onyx are also there.)
13 The name of the second river is the
Gihon; it winds through the entire land
of Cush.[b] 14 The name of the third river
is the Tigris; it runs along the east side
of Asshur. And the fourth river is the Euphrates.
15 The LORD God took the man and
put him in the Garden of Eden to work
it and take care of it. 16 And the LORD
God commanded the man, "You are free
to eat from any tree in the garden; 17 but
you must not eat from the tree of the
knowledge of good and evil, for when
you eat of it you will surely die."
18 The LORD God said, "It is not good
for the man to be alone. I will make a
helper suitable for him."
19 Now the LORD God had formed out
of the ground all the beasts of the field
and all the birds of the air. He brought
them to the man to see what he would
name them; and whatever the man
called each living creature, that was its
name. 20 So the man gave names to all
the livestock, the birds of the air and all
the beasts of the field.
But for Adam[c] no suitable helper was
found. 21 So the LORD God caused the
man to fall into a deep sleep; and while
he was sleeping, he took one of the
man's ribs[d] and closed up the place with
flesh. 22 Then the LORD God made a
woman from the rib[e] he had taken out
of the man, and he brought her to the
man.
23 The man said,

"This is now bone of my bones
  and flesh of my flesh;
she shall be called 'woman,'[f]
  for she was taken out of man."

24 For this reason a man will leave his father and mother and be united to his
wife, and they will become one flesh.
25 The man and his wife were both naked, and they felt no shame.

[a]12 Or *good; pearls* [b]13 Possibly southeast Mesopotamia [c]20 Or *the man* [d]21 Or *took part of the man's side* [e]22 Or *part* [f]23 The Hebrew for *woman* sounds like the Hebrew for *man.*

SHARPEN THE FOCUS

The Bible never attempts to prove that God exists. It simply asserts it: "In the beginning God . . ." (Genesis 1:1). Reading these four simple words, we take the first steps on an adventure of discovery. God gave us His Word—from Genesis through Revelation—to reveal to us what He is like. As we read, mark, learn, and think about His Word, our Lord will make Himself real to us. The Holy Spirit has promised to do this—in particular, He has promised to reveal to us His love and forgiveness for us in Christ.

As we read the account of the creation, for example, we see God's power, creativity, wisdom, and tender concern for His human creatures—His children. Take time to notice and to marvel at the creation around you today—the colors of the sky, the light of the sun or stars, the mosaic of leaves on the tree outside your window, or the snowflakes that drift down onto the front lawn. Praise the Creator who "richly provides us with everything for our enjoyment" (1 Timothy 6:17). You might want to use the words of Psalm 148 as you do so. ☼

WEEK 1 • TUESDAY

Genesis 3:1–24

GET THE BIG PICTURE

Our Creator built countless good gifts into the home He made for His first children. To these He added one last gift–the gift of worship. Luther called the tree of the knowledge of good and evil, "Adam's Altar." There Adam and Eve could return to God the worship of obedience. But Satan, "that ancient serpent" (Revelation 12:9), twisted God's blessing into a curse. If time is short, focus on Genesis 3:1–15.

The Fall of Man

3 Now the serpent was more
crafty than any of the wild animals the LORD God had made. He said
to the woman, "Did God really say, 'You
must not eat from any tree in the garden'?"
2 The woman said to the serpent, "We
may eat fruit from the trees in the garden, 3 but God did say, 'You must not eat
fruit from the tree that is in the middle
of the garden, and you must not touch
it, or you will die.' "
4 "You will not surely die," the serpent
said to the woman. 5 "For God knows
that when you eat of it your eyes will be
opened, and you will be like God,
knowing good and evil."
6 When the woman saw that the fruit
of the tree was good for food and pleasing to the eye, and also desirable for
gaining wisdom, she took some and ate
it. She also gave some to her husband,
who was with her, and he ate it. 7 Then
the eyes of both of them were opened,
and they realized they were naked; so
they sewed fig leaves together and
made coverings for themselves.
8 Then the man and his wife heard the
sound of the LORD God as he was walking in the garden in the cool of the day,
and they hid from the LORD God among
the trees of the garden. 9 But the LORD
God called to the man, "Where are
you?"
10 He answered, "I heard you in the
garden, and I was afraid because I was
naked; so I hid."
11 And he said, "Who told you that you
were naked? Have you eaten from the
tree that I commanded you not to eat
from?"
12 The man said, "The woman you put
here with me—she gave me some fruit
from the tree, and I ate it."
13 Then the LORD God said to the
woman, "What is this you have done?"
The woman said, "The serpent deceived me, and I ate."
14 So the LORD God said to the serpent,
"Because you have done this,

"Cursed are you above all the
livestock
and all the wild animals!
You will crawl on your belly
and you will eat dust
all the days of your life.
15 And I will put enmity
between you and the woman,
and between your offspring[a] and
hers;
he will crush[b] your head,
and you will strike his heel."

16 To the woman he said,

"I will greatly increase your pains in
childbearing;
with pain you will give birth to
children.

[a]15 Or *seed* [b]15 Or *strike*

Your desire will be for your husband,
and he will rule over you."

[17]To Adam he said, "Because you listened to your wife and ate from the tree about which I commanded you, 'You must not eat of it,'

"Cursed is the ground because
of you;
through painful toil you will eat
of it
all the days of your life.
[18]It will produce thorns and thistles
for you,
and you will eat the plants of the
field.
[19]By the sweat of your brow
you will eat your food
until you return to the ground,
since from it you were taken;
for dust you are
and to dust you will return."

[20]Adam[a] named his wife Eve,[b] because she would become the mother of all the living.
[21]The LORD God made garments of skin for Adam and his wife and clothed them. [22]And the LORD God said, "The man has now become like one of us, knowing good and evil. He must not be allowed to reach out his hand and take also from the tree of life and eat, and live forever." [23]So the LORD God banished him from the Garden of Eden to work the ground from which he had been taken. [24]After he drove the man out, he placed on the east side[c] of the Garden of Eden cherubim and a flaming sword flashing back and forth to guard the way to the tree of life.

[a]20 Or *The man* [b]20 *Eve* probably means *living.*
[c]24 Or *placed in front*

SHARPEN THE FOCUS

A perfect home. A perfect Father. A carefully crafted lie, and—disaster. Adam and Eve "made coverings for themselves" (Genesis 3:7) to camouflage their shame. They cowered in fear as they heard God approaching. Why? Because they knew instinctively that their kind and generous Father had now become their Judge. Found out in their hiding place, they began to make excuses and shift blame to one another—and even to God Himself (Genesis 3:12).

Still, Love would not give them up. The Father would not abandon His children to their guilt. Sin would bring consequences into human lives (Genesis 3:16–19). But God addressed His only words of rebuke to their enemy (and ours). The curse that day fell on Satan. And it brought hope to all of Adam's wandering sons and daughters (Genesis 3:15). A savior—*the* Savior—would come. He would crush the power of sin and of Satan forever.

Where in your life are you making excuses and shifting blame? Take a few moments now, empowered by Christ's cross, to make confession and accept responsibility instead. Then read your Father's promise to you from 1 John 1:8–9.

WEEK 1 • WEDNESDAY

Genesis 4:1—6:8

GET THE BIG PICTURE

The "firsts" of Genesis continue with the first human death–by murder. Genesis 5 tolls the somber note of sin's consequences through one generation after another–"And then he died." Even so, hope flickers in the darkness. As you read, look for evidence that God is active, calling sinners to come to Him for relief. If time is short, focus on Genesis 4:1–15.

Cain and Abel

4 Adam[a] lay with his wife Eve, and she became pregnant and gave birth to Cain.[b] She said, "With the help of the LORD I have brought forth[c] a man." 2Later she gave birth to his brother Abel.

Now Abel kept flocks, and Cain worked the soil. 3In the course of time Cain brought some of the fruits of the soil as an offering to the LORD. 4But Abel brought fat portions from some of the firstborn of his flock. The LORD looked with favor on Abel and his offering, 5but on Cain and his offering he did not look with favor. So Cain was very angry, and his face was downcast.

6Then the LORD said to Cain, "Why are you angry? Why is your face downcast? 7If you do what is right, will you not be accepted? But if you do not do what is right, sin is crouching at your door; it desires to have you, but you must master it."

8Now Cain said to his brother Abel, "Let's go out to the field."[d] And while they were in the field, Cain attacked his brother Abel and killed him.

9Then the LORD said to Cain, "Where is your brother Abel?"

"I don't know," he replied. "Am I my brother's keeper?"

10The LORD said, "What have you done? Listen! Your brother's blood cries out to me from the ground. 11Now you are under a curse and driven from the ground, which opened its mouth to receive your brother's blood from your hand. 12When you work the ground, it will no longer yield its crops for you. You will be a restless wanderer on the earth."

13Cain said to the LORD, "My punishment is more than I can bear. 14Today you are driving me from the land, and I will be hidden from your presence; I will be a restless wanderer on the earth, and whoever finds me will kill me."

15But the LORD said to him, "Not so[e]; if anyone kills Cain, he will suffer vengeance seven times over." Then the LORD put a mark on Cain so that no one who found him would kill him. 16So Cain went out from the LORD's presence and lived in the land of Nod,[f] east of Eden.

17Cain lay with his wife, and she became pregnant and gave birth to Enoch. Cain was then building a city, and he named it after his son Enoch. 18To Enoch was born Irad, and Irad was the father of Mehujael, and Mehujael was the father of Methushael, and Methushael was the father of Lamech.

19Lamech married two women, one named Adah and the other Zillah. 20Adah gave birth to Jabal; he was the father of those who live in tents and

[a]1 Or *The man* [b]1 *Cain* sounds like the Hebrew for *brought forth* or *acquired.* [c]1 Or *have acquired* [d]8 Samaritan Pentateuch, Septuagint, Vulgate and Syriac; Masoretic Text does not have *"Let's go out to the field."* [e]15 Septuagint, Vulgate and Syriac; Hebrew *Very well* [f]16 *Nod* means *wandering* (see verses 12 and 14).

raise livestock. [21]His brother's name was Jubal; he was the father of all who play the harp and flute. [22]Zillah also had a son, Tubal-Cain, who forged all kinds of tools out of[a] bronze and iron. Tubal-Cain's sister was Naamah.

[23]Lamech said to his wives,

"Adah and Zillah, listen to me;
  wives of Lamech, hear my words.
I have killed[b] a man for wounding me,
  a young man for injuring me.
[24]If Cain is avenged seven times,
  then Lamech seventy-seven
    times."

[25]Adam lay with his wife again, and she gave birth to a son and named him Seth,[c] saying, "God has granted me another child in place of Abel, since Cain killed him." [26]Seth also had a son, and he named him Enosh.

At that time men began to call on[d] the name of the LORD.

From Adam to Noah

5 This is the written account of Adam's line.

When God created man, he made him in the likeness of God. [2]He created them male and female and blessed them. And when they were created, he called them "man.[e]"

[3]When Adam had lived 130 years, he had a son in his own likeness, in his own image; and he named him Seth. [4]After Seth was born, Adam lived 800 years and had other sons and daughters. [5]Altogether, Adam lived 930 years, and then he died.

[6]When Seth had lived 105 years, he became the father[f] of Enosh. [7]And after he became the father of Enosh, Seth lived 807 years and had other sons and daughters. [8]Altogether, Seth lived 912 years, and then he died.

[9]When Enosh had lived 90 years, he became the father of Kenan. [10]And after he became the father of Kenan, Enosh lived 815 years and had other sons and daughters. [11]Altogether, Enosh lived 905 years, and then he died.

[12]When Kenan had lived 70 years, he became the father of Mahalalel. [13]And after he became the father of Mahalalel, Kenan lived 840 years and had other sons and daughters. [14]Altogether, Kenan lived 910 years, and then he died.

[15]When Mahalalel had lived 65 years, he became the father of Jared. [16]And after he became the father of Jared, Mahalalel lived 830 years and had other sons and daughters. [17]Altogether, Mahalalel lived 895 years, and then he died.

[18]When Jared had lived 162 years, he became the father of Enoch. [19]And after he became the father of Enoch, Jared lived 800 years and had other sons and daughters. [20]Altogether, Jared lived 962 years, and then he died.

[21]When Enoch had lived 65 years, he became the father of Methuselah. [22]And after he became the father of Methuselah, Enoch walked with God 300 years and had other sons and daughters. [23]Altogether, Enoch lived 365 years. [24]Enoch walked with God; then he was no more, because God took him away.

[25]When Methuselah had lived 187 years, he became the father of Lamech. [26]And after he became the father of Lamech, Methuselah lived 782 years and had other sons and daughters. [27]Altogether, Methuselah lived 969 years, and then he died.

[28]When Lamech had lived 182 years, he had a son. [29]He named him Noah[g] and said, "He will comfort us in the labor and painful toil of our hands caused by the ground the LORD has cursed." [30]After Noah was born, Lamech lived 595 years and had other sons and daughters. [31]Altogether, Lamech lived 777 years, and then he died.

[32]After Noah was 500 years old, he became the father of Shem, Ham and Japheth.

The Flood

6 When men began to increase in number on the earth and

[a]22 Or *who instructed all who work in* [b]23 Or *I will kill* [c]25 *Seth* probably means *granted.* [d]26 Or *to proclaim* [e]2 Hebrew *adam* [f]6 *Father* may mean *ancestor*; also in verses 7-26. [g]29 *Noah* sounds like the Hebrew for *comfort.*

daughters were born to them, 2the sons
of God saw that the daughters of men
were beautiful, and they married any of
them they chose. 3Then the LORD said,
"My Spirit will not contend with[a] man
forever, for he is mortal[b]; his days will be
a hundred and twenty years."
4The Nephilim were on the earth in
those days—and also afterward—when
the sons of God went to the daughters
of men and had children by them. They
were the heroes of old, men of renown.
5The LORD saw how great man's
wickedness on the earth had become,
and that every inclination of the
thoughts of his heart was only evil all
the time. 6The LORD was grieved that he
had made man on the earth, and his
heart was filled with pain. 7So the LORD
said, "I will wipe mankind, whom I
have created, from the face of the
earth—men and animals, and creatures
that move along the ground, and birds
of the air—for I am grieved that I have
made them." 8But Noah found favor in
the eyes of the LORD.

[a]3 Or *My spirit will not remain in* [b]3 Or *corrupt*

SHARPEN THE FOCUS

Once sin infects human hearts, it doesn't take long for it to begin its destructive work. "The wages of sin is death," Paul writes in Romans 6:23. This relentless paymaster stalks human beings, insisting that we cash our paycheck.

Cain found that out. A seemingly little sin—jealousy—wormed its way through his heart. He ignored God's pointed warning about the danger of his anger, killed his brother, lied to God about what he had done, and finally "went out from the Lord's presence" (Genesis 4:16). He walked away from his only source of pardon and hope.

Cain's descendants followed in their father's footsteps (Genesis 4:16–24). They attempted to fill their empty lives with all kinds of activities and accomplishments—power, possessions, polygamy, and even the arts. Their attempts bred only more violence and disregard for God's will about human life.

What little sin are you ignoring today? To what do you look to fill the emptiness in your heart? Take any sin you discover to your Lord, confident of His pardon and of His strength to free you from sin's power. ☼

WEEK 1 • THURSDAY

Genesis 6:9—8:22

GET THE BIG PICTURE

Today's reading describes a time when human wickedness became a tidal wave that threatened to drown out faith on the earth. God acts in mercy to rescue Noah and his family—eight believers in all—out of what may have been tens of thousands or even millions of people on earth. As you read, notice how the Lord's grace and His judgment form two sides of the same coin. If time is short, focus on Genesis 6:9–22.

separate light from darkness. And
God saw that it was good. 19And
there was evening, and there was
morning—the fourth day.
20And God said, "Let the water teem
with living creatures, and let birds
fly above the earth across the expanse of the sky." 21So God created
the great creatures of the sea and
every living and moving thing with
which the water teems, according to
their kinds, and every winged bird
according to its kind. And God saw
that it was good. 22God blessed them
and said, "Be fruitful and increase in
number and fill the water in the
seas, and let the birds increase on
the earth." 23And there was evening,
and there was morning—the fifth
day.
24And God said, "Let the land produce
living creatures according to their
kinds: livestock, creatures that
move along the ground, and wild
animals, each according to its kind."
And it was so. 25God made the wild
animals according to their kinds,
the livestock according to their
kinds, and all the creatures that
move along the ground according
to their kinds. And God saw that it
was good.
26Then God said, "Let us make
man in our image, in our likeness,
and let them rule over the fish of the
sea and the birds of the air, over the
livestock, over all the earth,[a] and
over all the creatures that move
along the ground."

27So God created man in his own
image,
in the image of God he created
him;
male and female he created them.

28God blessed them and said to
them, "Be fruitful and increase in
number; fill the earth and subdue it.
Rule over the fish of the sea and the
birds of the air and over every living creature that moves on the
ground."

29Then God said, "I give you
every seed-bearing plant on the
face of the whole earth and every
tree that has fruit with seed in it.
They will be yours for food. 30And to
all the beasts of the earth and all the
birds of the air and all the creatures
that move on the ground—everything that has the breath of life in
it—I give every green plant for
food." And it was so.
31God saw all that he had made,
and it was very good. And there
was evening, and there was morning—the sixth day.

2 Thus the heavens and the
earth were completed in all their
vast array.
2By the seventh day God had finished
the work he had been doing; so on
the seventh day he rested[b] from all
his work. 3And God blessed the seventh day and made it holy, because
on it he rested from all the work of
creating that he had done.

Adam and Eve

4This is the account of the heavens
and the earth when they were created.

When the LORD God made the earth
and the heavens— 5and no shrub of the
field had yet appeared on the earth[c] and
no plant of the field had yet sprung up,
for the LORD God had not sent rain on
the earth[c] and there was no man to
work the ground, 6but streams[d] came up
from the earth and watered the whole
surface of the ground— 7the LORD God
formed the man[e] from the dust of the
ground and breathed into his nostrils
the breath of life, and the man became
a living being.
8Now the LORD God had planted a
garden in the east, in Eden; and there he
put the man he had formed. 9And the

[a]26 Hebrew; Syriac *all the wild animals* [b]2 Or *ceased*; also in verse 3 [c]5 Or *land*; also in verse 6 [d]6 Or *mist* [e]7 The Hebrew for *man (adam)* sounds like and may be related to the Hebrew for *ground (adamah)*; it is also the name *Adam* (see Gen. 2:20).

GENESIS

WEEK 1 • MONDAY

Genesis 1:1—2:25

GET THE BIG PICTURE

Genesis records many firsts–the first people, the first family, the first sin, the first city, the first musician, and more "firsts" besides. Today's reading zeroes in on the first week of our world's existence and on the first home God gave His human creatures. As you read, note the care God took as He made this home for us–the first paradise. If time is short, focus on Genesis 2:4–25.

The Beginning

1 In the beginning God created the
heavens and the earth. [2]Now the
earth was[a] formless and empty,
darkness was over the surface of the
deep, and the Spirit of God was
hovering over the waters.

[3]And God said, "Let there be light," and
there was light. [4]God saw that the
light was good, and he separated
the light from the darkness. [5]God
called the light "day," and the darkness he called "night." And there
was evening, and there was morning—the first day.
[6]And God said, "Let there be an expanse
between the waters to separate water from water." [7]So God made the
expanse and separated the water
under the expanse from the water
above it. And it was so. [8]God called
the expanse "sky." And there was
evening, and there was morning—
the second day.
[9]And God said, "Let the water under the
sky be gathered to one place, and let
dry ground appear." And it was so.
[10]God called the dry ground "land,"
and the gathered waters he called
"seas." And God saw that it was
good.
[11]Then God said, "Let the land
produce vegetation: seed-bearing
plants and trees on the land that
bear fruit with seed in it, according
to their various kinds." And it was
so. [12]The land produced vegetation:
plants bearing seed according to
their kinds and trees bearing fruit
with seed in it according to their
kinds. And God saw that it was
good. [13]And there was evening, and
there was morning—the third day.
[14]And God said, "Let there be lights in
the expanse of the sky to separate
the day from the night, and let them
serve as signs to mark seasons and
days and years, [15]and let them be
lights in the expanse of the sky to
give light on the earth." And it was
so. [16]God made two great lights—
the greater light to govern the day
and the lesser light to govern the
night. He also made the stars. [17]God
set them in the expanse of the sky
to give light on the earth, [18]to govern the day and the night, and to

[a]2 Or possibly *became*

The first concern of the translators has been the accuracy of the translation and its fidelity to the thought of the biblical writers. They have weighed the significance of the lexical and grammatical details of the Hebrew, Aramaic and Greek texts. At the same time, they have striven for more than a word-for-word translation. Because thought patterns and syntax differ from language to language, faithful communication of the meaning of the writers of the Bible demands frequent modifications in sentence structure and constant regard for the contextual meanings of words.

A sensitive feeling for style does not always accompany scholarship. Accordingly the Committee on Bible Translation submitted the developing version to a number of stylistic consultants. Two of them read every book of both Old and New Testaments twice—once before and once after the last major revision—and made invaluable suggestions. Samples of the translation were tested for clarity and ease of reading by various kinds of people—young and old, highly educated and less well educated, ministers and laymen.

Concern for clear and natural English—that the New International Version should be idiomatic but not idiosyncratic, contemporary but not dated—motivated the translators and consultants. At the same time, they tried to reflect the differing styles of the biblical writers. In view of the international use of English, the translators sought to avoid obvious Americanisms on the one hand and obvious Anglicisms on the other. A British edition reflects the comparatively few differences of significant idiom and of spelling.

As for the traditional pronouns "thou," "thee" and "thine" in reference to the Deity, the translators judged that to use these archaisms (along with the old verb forms such as "doest," "wouldest" and "hadst") would violate accuracy in translation. Neither Hebrew, Aramaic nor Greek uses special pronouns for the persons of the Godhead. A present-day translation is not enhanced by forms that in the time of the King James Version were used in everyday speech, whether referring to God or man.

For the Old Testament the standard Hebrew text, the Masoretic Text as published in the latest editions of *Biblia Hebraica*, was used throughout. The Dead Sea Scrolls contain material bearing on an earlier stage of the Hebrew text. They were consulted, as were the Samaritan Pentateuch and the ancient scribal traditions relating to textual changes. Sometimes a variant Hebrew reading in the margin of the Masoretic Text was followed instead of the text itself. Such instances, being variants within the Masoretic tradition, are not specified by footnotes. In rare cases, words in the consonantal text were divided differently from the way they appear in the Masoretic Text. Footnotes indicate this. The translators also consulted the more important early versions—the Septuagint; Aquila, Symmachus and Theodotion; the Vulgate; the Syriac Peshitta; the Targums; and for the Psalms the *Juxta Hebraica* of Jerome. Readings from these versions were occasionally followed where the Masoretic Text seemed doubtful and where accepted principles of textual criticism showed that one or more of these textual witnesses appeared to provide the correct reading. Such instances are footnoted. Sometimes vowel letters and vowel signs did not, in the judgment of the translators, represent the correct vowels for the original consonantal text. Accordingly some words were read with a different set of vowels. These instances are usually not indicated by footnotes.

The Greek text used in translating the New Testament was an eclectic one. No other piece of ancient literature has such an abundance of manuscript witnesses as does the New Testament. Where existing manuscripts differ, the translators made their choice of readings according to accepted principles of New Testament tex-

PREFACE

THE NEW INTERNATIONAL VERSION is a completely new translation of the Holy Bible made by over a hundred scholars working directly from the best available Hebrew, Aramaic and Greek texts. It had its beginning in 1965 when, after several years of exploratory study by committees from the Christian Reformed Church and the National Association of Evangelicals, a group of scholars met at Palos Heights, Illinois, and concurred in the need for a new translation of the Bible in contemporary English. This group, though not made up of official church representatives, was transdenominational. Its conclusion was endorsed by a large number of leaders from many denominations who met in Chicago in 1966.

Responsibility for the new version was delegated by the Palos Heights group to a self-governing body of fifteen, the Committee on Bible Translation, composed for the most part of biblical scholars from colleges, universities and seminaries. In 1967 the New York Bible Society (now the International Bible Society) generously undertook the financial sponsorship of the project—a sponsorship that made it possible to enlist the help of many distinguished scholars. The fact that participants from the United States, Great Britain, Canada, Australia and New Zealand worked together gave the project its international scope. That they were from many denominations—including Anglican, Assemblies of God, Baptist, Brethren, Christian Reformed, Church of Christ, Evangelical free, Lutheran, Mennonite, Methodist, Nazarene, Presbyterian, Wesleyan and other churches—helped to safeguard the translation from sectarian bias.

How it was made helps to give the New International Version its distinctiveness. The translation of each book was assigned to a team of scholars. Next, one of the Intermediate Editorial Committees revised the initial translation, with constant reference to the Hebrew, Aramaic or Greek. Their work then went to one of the General Editorial Committees, which checked it in detail and made another thorough revision. This revision in turn was carefully reviewed by the Committee on Bible Translation, which made further changes and then released the final version for publication. In this way the entire Bible underwent three revisions, during each of which the translation was examined for its faithfulness to the original languages and for its English style.

All this involved many thousands of hours of research and discussion regarding the meaning of the texts and the precise way of putting them into English. It may well be that no other translation has been made by a more thorough process of review and revision from committee to committee than this one.

From the beginning of the project, the Committee on Bible Translation held to certain goals for the New International Version: that it would be an accurate translation and one that would rave clarity and literary quality and so prove suitable for public and private reading, teaching, preaching, memorizing and liturgical use. The Committee also sought to preserve some measure of continuity with the long tradition of translating the Scriptures into English.

In working toward these goals, the translators were united in their commitment to the authority and infallibility of the Bible as God's Word in written form. They believe that it contains the divine answer to the deepest needs of humanity, that it sheds unique light on our path in a dark world, and that it sets forth the way to our eternal well-being.

19They rose greatly on the earth, and all
the high mountains under the entire
heavens were covered. 20The waters
rose and covered the mountains to a
depth of more than twenty feet.[a,b] 21Ev-
ery living thing that moved on the earth
perished—birds, livestock, wild animals, all the creatures that swarm over
the earth, and all mankind. 22Everything
on dry land that had the breath of life in
its nostrils died. 23Every living thing on the
face of the earth was wiped out; men and
animals and the creatures that move
along the ground and the birds of the air
were wiped from the earth. Only Noah
was left, and those with him in the ark.

24The waters flooded the earth for a
hundred and fifty days.

8 But God remembered Noah and
all the wild animals and the livestock that were with him in the ark, and
he sent a wind over the earth, and the
waters receded. 2Now the springs of the
deep and the floodgates of the heavens
had been closed, and the rain had
stopped falling from the sky. 3The water
receded steadily from the earth. At the
end of the hundred and fifty days the
water had gone down, 4and on the seventeenth day of the seventh month the
ark came to rest on the mountains of Ararat. 5The waters continued to recede
until the tenth month, and on the first
day of the tenth month the tops of the
mountains became visible.

6After forty days Noah opened the
window he had made in the ark 7and
sent out a raven, and it kept flying back
and forth until the water had dried up
from the earth. 8Then he sent out a dove
to see if the water had receded from the
surface of the ground. 9But the dove
could find no place to set its feet because
there was water over all the surface of
the earth; so it returned to Noah in the
ark. He reached out his hand and took
the dove and brought it back to himself
in the ark. 10He waited seven more days
and again sent out the dove from the
ark. 11When the dove returned to him in
the evening, there in its beak was a
freshly plucked olive leaf! Then Noah
knew that the water had receded from
the earth. 12He waited seven more days
and sent the dove out again, but this
time it did not return to him.

13By the first day of the first month of
Noah's six hundred and first year, the
water had dried up from the earth.
Noah then removed the covering from
the ark and saw that the surface of the
ground was dry. 14By the twenty-
seventh day of the second month the
earth was completely dry.

15Then God said to Noah, 16"Come out
of the ark, you and your wife and your
sons and their wives. 17Bring out every
kind of living creature that is with you—
the birds, the animals, and all the creatures that move along the ground—so
they can multiply on the earth and be
fruitful and increase in number
upon it."

18So Noah came out, together with his
sons and his wife and his sons' wives.
19All the animals and all the creatures
that move along the ground and all the
birds—everything that moves on the
earth—came out of the ark, one kind after another.

20Then Noah built an altar to the LORD
and, taking some of all the clean animals
and clean birds, he sacrificed burnt offerings on it. 21The LORD smelled the
pleasing aroma and said in his heart:
"Never again will I curse the ground
because of man, even though[c] every inclination of his heart is evil from childhood. And never again will I destroy all
living creatures, as I have done.

22"As long as the earth endures,
seedtime and harvest,
cold and heat,
summer and winter,
day and night
will never cease."

[a]20 Hebrew *fifteen cubits* (about 6.9 meters)
[b]20 Or *rose more than twenty feet, and the mountains were covered* [c]21 Or *man, for*

9This is the account of Noah.

Noah was a righteous man, blameless among the people of his time, and he walked with God. 10Noah had three sons: Shem, Ham and Japheth.

11Now the earth was corrupt in God's sight and was full of violence. 12God saw how corrupt the earth had become, for all the people on earth had corrupted their ways. 13So God said to Noah, "I am going to put an end to all people, for the earth is filled with violence because of them. I am surely going to destroy both them and the earth. 14So make yourself an ark of cypress[a] wood; make rooms in it and coat it with pitch inside and out. 15This is how you are to build it: The ark is to be 450 feet long, 75 feet wide and 45 feet high.[b] 16Make a roof for it and finish[c] the ark to within 18 inches[d] of the top. Put a door in the side of the ark and make lower, middle and upper decks. 17I am going to bring floodwaters on the earth to destroy all life under the heavens, every creature that has the breath of life in it. Everything on earth will perish. 18But I will establish my covenant with you, and you will enter the ark—you and your sons and your wife and your sons' wives with you. 19You are to bring into the ark two of all living creatures, male and female, to keep them alive with you. 20Two of every kind of bird, of every kind of animal and of every kind of creature that moves along the ground will come to you to be kept alive. 21You are to take every kind of food that is to be eaten and store it away as food for you and for them."

22Noah did everything just as God commanded him.

7 The LORD then said to Noah, "Go into the ark, you and your whole family, because I have found you righteous in this generation. 2Take with you seven[e] of every kind of clean animal, a male and its mate, and two of every kind of unclean animal, a male and its mate, 3and also seven of every kind of bird, male and female, to keep their various kinds alive throughout the earth. 4Seven days from now I will send rain on the earth for forty days and forty nights, and I will wipe from the face of the earth every living creature I have made."

5And Noah did all that the LORD commanded him.

6Noah was six hundred years old when the floodwaters came on the earth. 7And Noah and his sons and his wife and his sons' wives entered the ark to escape the waters of the flood. 8Pairs of clean and unclean animals, of birds and of all creatures that move along the ground, 9male and female, came to Noah and entered the ark, as God had commanded Noah. 10And after the seven days the floodwaters came on the earth.

11In the six hundredth year of Noah's life, on the seventeenth day of the second month—on that day all the springs of the great deep burst forth, and the floodgates of the heavens were opened. 12And rain fell on the earth forty days and forty nights.

13On that very day Noah and his sons, Shem, Ham and Japheth, together with his wife and the wives of his three sons, entered the ark. 14They had with them every wild animal according to its kind, all livestock according to their kinds, every creature that moves along the ground according to its kind and every bird according to its kind, everything with wings. 15Pairs of all creatures that have the breath of life in them came to Noah and entered the ark. 16The animals going in were male and female of every living thing, as God had commanded Noah. Then the LORD shut him in.

17For forty days the flood kept coming on the earth, and as the waters increased they lifted the ark high above the earth. 18The waters rose and increased greatly on the earth, and the ark floated on the surface of the water.

[a]14 The meaning of the Hebrew for this word is uncertain. [b]15 Hebrew *300 cubits long, 50 cubits wide and 30 cubits high* (about 140 meters long, 23 meters wide and 13.5 meters high) [c]16 Or *Make an opening for light by finishing* [d]16 Hebrew *a cubit* (about 0.5 meter) [e]2 Or *seven pairs*; also in verse 3

SHARPEN THE FOCUS

Stand in Noah's shoes. Or Mrs. Noah's sandals. Imagine yourself a member of the only family of faith on the entire earth! What fears would you face–for yourself? your children? your grandchildren?

Perhaps from this perspective we see more clearly God's grace in the great flood. Not just here, but again and again in the Holy Scriptures we see God both judging sin and delivering His people in the same action. In fact, both occurred at the cross!

God's people since Noah's day have found themselves dismayed at the wickedness in the world around them. When you feel that way, when sin and senseless violence threaten to drown your courage and hope, remember that "the Lord knows how to rescue godly men from trials and to hold the unrighteous for the day of judgment" (2 Peter 2:9).

WEEK 1 • FRIDAY

Genesis 9:1—10:32

GET THE BIG PICTURE

The world system that tempted and ridiculed Noah's family had been washed away like so many dead leaves. When Noah walked off the ark, external temptations had vanished. Nevertheless, the eight survivors of the great flood faced an internal enemy just as treacherous: their own sin-stained nature. The Flood did not drown this enemy–not in Noah, nor in his descendants. If time is short, focus on Genesis 9:1–17.

God's Covenant With Noah

9 Then God blessed Noah and his
sons, saying to them, "Be fruitful
and increase in number and fill the
earth. 2The fear and dread of you will
fall upon all the beasts of the earth and
all the birds of the air, upon every creature that moves along the ground, and
upon all the fish of the sea; they are
given into your hands. 3Everything that
lives and moves will be food for you.
Just as I gave you the green plants, I
now give you everything.
4"But you must not eat meat that has
its lifeblood still in it. 5And for your lifeblood I will surely demand an accounting. I will demand an accounting from
every animal. And from each man, too,
I will demand an accounting for the life
of his fellow man.

6"Whoever sheds the blood of man,
by man shall his blood be shed;
for in the image of God
has God made man.

7As for you, be fruitful and increase in
number; multiply on the earth and increase upon it."
8Then God said to Noah and to his
sons with him: 9"I now establish my covenant with you and with your descendants after you 10and with every living
creature that was with you—the birds,
the livestock and all the wild animals, all
those that came out of the ark with
you—every living creature on earth. 11I
establish my covenant with you: Never
again will all life be cut off by the waters of a flood; never again will there be
a flood to destroy the earth."
12And God said, "This is the sign of the

covenant I am making between me and
you and every living creature with you,
a covenant for all generations to come:
[13]I have set my rainbow in the clouds,
and it will be the sign of the covenant
between me and the earth. [14]Whenever
I bring clouds over the earth and the
rainbow appears in the clouds, [15]I will
remember my covenant between me
and you and all living creatures of every
kind. Never again will the waters become a flood to destroy all life. [16]Whenever the rainbow appears in the clouds,
I will see it and remember the everlasting covenant between God and all living creatures of every kind on the
earth."

[17]So God said to Noah, "This is the sign of the covenant I have established between me and all life on the earth."

The Sons of Noah

[18]The sons of Noah who came out of
the ark were Shem, Ham and Japheth.
(Ham was the father of Canaan.) [19]These
were the three sons of Noah, and from
them came the people who were scattered over the earth.

[20]Noah, a man of the soil, proceeded[a]
to plant a vineyard. [21]When he drank
some of its wine, he became drunk and
lay uncovered inside his tent. [22]Ham, the
father of Canaan, saw his father's nakedness and told his two brothers outside. [23]But Shem and Japheth took a
garment and laid it across their shoulders; then they walked in backward and covered their father's nakedness. Their faces were turned the other way so that they would not see their father's nakedness.

[24]When Noah awoke from his wine
and found out what his youngest son
had done to him, [25]he said,

"Cursed be Canaan!
The lowest of slaves
will he be to his brothers."

[26]He also said,

"Blessed be the LORD, the God of
Shem!
May Canaan be the slave of Shem.[b]
[27]May God extend the territory of
Japheth[c];
may Japheth live in the tents of
Shem,
and may Canaan be his[d] slave."

[28]After the flood Noah lived 350 years.
[29]Altogether, Noah lived 950 years, and
then he died.

The Table of Nations

10 This is the account of Shem, Ham and Japheth, Noah's sons, who themselves had sons after the flood.

The Japhethites

[2]The sons[e] of Japheth:
Gomer, Magog, Madai, Javan,
Tubal, Meshech and Tiras.
[3]The sons of Gomer:
Ashkenaz, Riphath and Togarmah.
[4]The sons of Javan:
Elishah, Tarshish, the Kittim and
the Rodanim.[f] [5](From these the
maritime peoples spread out into
their territories by their clans
within their nations, each with
its own language.)

The Hamites

[6]The sons of Ham:
Cush, Mizraim,[g] Put and Canaan.
[7]The sons of Cush:
Seba, Havilah, Sabtah, Raamah
and Sabteca.
The sons of Raamah:
Sheba and Dedan.

[8]Cush was the father[h] of Nimrod, who
grew to be a mighty warrior on the
earth. [9]He was a mighty hunter before
the LORD; that is why it is said, "Like

[a]20 Or *soil, was the first* [b]26 Or *be his slave*
[c]27 *Japheth* sounds like the Hebrew for *extend.*
[d]27 Or *their* [e]2 *Sons* may mean *descendants* or *successors* or *nations*; also in verses 3, 4, 6, 7, 20-23, 29 and 31. [f]4 Some manuscripts of the Masoretic Text and Samaritan Pentateuch (see also Septuagint and 1 Chron. 1:7); most manuscripts of the Masoretic Text *Dodanim*
[g]6 That is, Egypt; also in verse 13 [h]8 *Father* may mean *ancestor* or *predecessor* or *founder*; also in verses 13, 15, 24 and 26.

Nimrod, a mighty hunter before the LORD." [10]The first centers of his kingdom were Babylon, Erech, Akkad and Calneh, in[a] Shinar.[b] [11]From that land he went to Assyria, where he built Nineveh, Rehoboth Ir,[c] Calah [12]and Resen, which is between Nineveh and Calah; that is the great city.

[13]Mizraim was the father of
the Ludites, Anamites, Lehabites, Naphtuhites, [14]Pathrusites, Casluhites (from whom the Philistines came) and Caphtorites.
[15]Canaan was the father of
Sidon his firstborn,[d] and of the Hittites, [16]Jebusites, Amorites, Girgashites, [17]Hivites, Arkites, Sinites, [18]Arvadites, Zemarites and Hamathites.

Later the Canaanite clans scattered [19]and the borders of Canaan reached from Sidon toward Gerar as far as Gaza, and then toward Sodom, Gomorrah, Admah and Zeboiim, as far as Lasha.

[20]These are the sons of Ham by their clans and languages, in their territories and nations.

The Semites

[21]Sons were also born to Shem, whose older brother was[e] Japheth; Shem was the ancestor of all the sons of Eber.

[22]The sons of Shem:
Elam, Asshur, Arphaxad, Lud and Aram.
[23]The sons of Aram:
Uz, Hul, Gether and Meshech.[f]
[24]Arphaxad was the father of[g] Shelah,
and Shelah the father of Eber.
[25]Two sons were born to Eber:
One was named Peleg,[h] because in his time the earth was divided; his brother was named Joktan.
[26]Joktan was the father of
Almodad, Sheleph, Hazarmaveth, Jerah, [27]Hadoram, Uzal, Diklah, [28]Obal, Abimael, Sheba, [29]Ophir, Havilah and Jobab. All these were sons of Joktan.

[30]The region where they lived stretched from Mesha toward Sephar, in the eastern hill country.

[31]These are the sons of Shem by their clans and languages, in their territories and nations.

[32]These are the clans of Noah's sons, according to their lines of descent, within their nations. From these the nations spread out over the earth after the flood.

[a]10 Or *Erech and Akkad—all of them in*
[b]10,2 That is, Babylonia [c]11 Or *Nineveh with its city squares* [d]15 Or *of the Sidonians, the foremost*
[e]21 Or *Shem, the older brother of* [f]23 See Septuagint and 1 Chron. 1:17; Hebrew *Mash*
[g]24 Hebrew; Septuagint *father of Cainan, and Cainan was the father of* [h]25 *Peleg* means *division.*

SHARPEN THE FOCUS

Try this thought experiment. Suppose Jesus appeared visibly on earth today and took everyone to live in a perfect environment. Suppose we arrived there just as we are right now, our sinful nature still intact. How long would it take for us to make that paradise a prison? How long before family members would start to hurt one another? How long before the hardware stores began to sell dead bolts and burglar alarms? We like to blame our lack of love on our environment. We might even think, "If only I didn't have to work with such impossible people, then I would live the kind of life my Lord wants me to live."

Really? Noah's experience proves otherwise. The old us trying hard to make life work won't succeed. We don't need guilt-driven motivation. We don't need self-propelled reformation. We need Spirit-led transformation. A transformation our Lord Himself will provide as we meditate on His Word (Romans 12:1–3).

That Word, particularly the Good News about the cross of our Savior, transforms us day by day. As we meditate on God's Word, our Lord changes us into the kind of Christ-like children who will bring joy to the Father and to one another in the heavenly home.

In the Bible, Babylon typifies the kingdom of darkness. We meet this kingdom for the first time today at the tower of Babel. Headed by Satan, this kingdom rebels against the Lord and wars against His people. Babylon will finally fall forever one day (Revelation 18). But for now the conflict continues. As the darkness deepens, the light of God's grace shines brightly still—as we see in today's reading. The Lord chooses Abram out of the darkness to become a blessing (Genesis 12:3). If time is short, focus on Genesis 12:1–9.

The Tower of Babel

11 Now the whole world had one language and a common speech. 2As men moved eastward,[a] they found a plain in Shinar[b] and settled there.

3They said to each other, "Come, let's make bricks and bake them thoroughly." They used brick instead of stone, and tar for mortar. 4Then they said, "Come, let us build ourselves a city, with a tower that reaches to the heavens, so that we may make a name for ourselves and not be scattered over the face of the whole earth."

5But the LORD came down to see the city and the tower that the men were building. 6The LORD said, "If as one people speaking the same language they have begun to do this, then nothing they plan to do will be impossible for them. 7Come, let us go down and confuse their language so they will not understand each other."

8So the LORD scattered them from there over all the earth, and they stopped building the city. 9That is why it was called Babel[c]—because there the LORD confused the language of the whole world. From there the LORD scattered them over the face of the whole earth.

From Shem to Abram

10This is the account of Shem.

Two years after the flood, when Shem was 100 years old, he became the father[d] of Arphaxad. 11And after he became the father of Arphaxad, Shem lived 500 years and had other sons and daughters.

12When Arphaxad had lived 35 years, he became the father of Shelah. 13And after he became the father of Shelah, Arphaxad lived 403 years and had other sons and daughters.[e]

14When Shelah had lived 30 years, he

[a]2 Or *from the east*; or *in the east* [b]2 That is, Babylonia [c]9 That is, Babylon; *Babel* sounds like the Hebrew for *confused*. [d]10 *Father* may mean *ancestor*; also in verses 11-25. [e]12,13 Hebrew; Septuagint (see also Luke 3:35, 36 and note at Gen. 10:24) *35 years, he became the father of Cainan. 13And after he became the father of Cainan, Arphaxad lived 430 years and had other sons and daughters, and then he died. When Cainan had lived 130 years, he became the father of Shelah. And after he became the father of Shelah, Cainan lived 330 years and had other sons and daughters*

became the father of Eber. [15]And after he became the father of Eber, Shelah lived 403 years and had other sons and daughters.

[16]When Eber had lived 34 years, he became the father of Peleg. [17]And after he became the father of Peleg, Eber lived 430 years and had other sons and daughters.

[18]When Peleg had lived 30 years, he became the father of Reu. [19]And after he became the father of Reu, Peleg lived 209 years and had other sons and daughters.

[20]When Reu had lived 32 years, he became the father of Serug. [21]And after he became the father of Serug, Reu lived 207 years and had other sons and daughters.

[22]When Serug had lived 30 years, he became the father of Nahor. [23]And after he became the father of Nahor, Serug lived 200 years and had other sons and daughters.

[24]When Nahor had lived 29 years, he became the father of Terah. [25]And after he became the father of Terah, Nahor lived 119 years and had other sons and daughters.

[26]After Terah had lived 70 years, he became the father of Abram, Nahor and Haran.

[27]This is the account of Terah.

Terah became the father of Abram, Nahor and Haran. And Haran became the father of Lot. [28]While his father Terah was still alive, Haran died in Ur of the Chaldeans, in the land of his birth. [29]Abram and Nahor both married. The name of Abram's wife was Sarai, and the name of Nahor's wife was Milcah; she was the daughter of Haran, the father of both Milcah and Iscah. [30]Now Sarai was barren; she had no children.

[31]Terah took his son Abram, his grandson Lot son of Haran, and his daughter-in-law Sarai, the wife of his son Abram, and together they set out from Ur of the Chaldeans to go to Canaan. But when they came to Haran, they settled there.

[32]Terah lived 205 years, and he died in Haran.

The Call of Abram

12 The LORD had said to Abram, "Leave your country, your people and your father's household and go to the land I will show you.

[2]"I will make you into a great nation
and I will bless you;
I will make your name great,
and you will be a blessing.
[3]I will bless those who bless you,
and whoever curses you I will curse;
and all peoples on earth
will be blessed through you."

[4]So Abram left, as the LORD had told him; and Lot went with him. Abram was seventy-five years old when he set out from Haran. [5]He took his wife Sarai, his nephew Lot, all the possessions they had accumulated and the people they had acquired in Haran, and they set out for the land of Canaan, and they arrived there.

[6]Abram traveled through the land as far as the site of the great tree of Moreh at Shechem. At that time the Canaanites were in the land. [7]The LORD appeared to Abram and said, "To your offspring[a] I will give this land." So he built an altar there to the LORD, who had appeared to him.

[8]From there he went on toward the hills east of Bethel and pitched his tent, with Bethel on the west and Ai on the east. There he built an altar to the LORD and called on the name of the LORD. [9]Then Abram set out and continued toward the Negev.

[a]7 Or *seed*

SHARPEN THE FOCUS

Maybe you know Howland Spencer's little poem:

How odd
Of God
To choose
The Jews.

From Joshua 24:2–3 we learn that Abram's ancestors worshiped idols—just like the people around them. Archaeologists have determined that the region in which Abram lived the first 75 years of his life was a center for the worship of Nanna, the moon-god. How odd of God to choose idolaters to receive His blessings. But not one bit odder than our Lord's choice of you and me—sinful as we know we are.

In love, God reached out to Abram. In that same love, God has called us too "out of darkness into His wonderful light" (1 Peter 2:9b). We belong to Him; we are His children, His heirs, sons and daughters of the mighty and merciful heavenly Father through Jesus Christ.

WEEK 2 • MONDAY

Genesis 12:10—13:18

GET THE BIG PICTURE

Side by side, the two main parts of today's reading show quite a contrast. In Genesis 12:10–20, we see Abram stumbling into gross doubt and unbelief. Then, in Genesis 13:5–18, we see him demonstrating great faith and self-sacrifice. As you read, think about times you have experienced the battle between fear and faith. If time is short, focus on Genesis 13:5–18.

Abram in Egypt

[10]Now there was a famine in the land,
and Abram went down to Egypt to live
there for a while because the famine
was severe. [11]As he was about to enter
Egypt, he said to his wife Sarai, "I know
what a beautiful woman you are.
[12]When the Egyptians see you, they will
say, 'This is his wife.' Then they will kill
me but will let you live. [13]Say you are my
sister, so that I will be treated well for
your sake and my life will be spared because of you."
[14]When Abram came to Egypt, the
Egyptians saw that she was a very beautiful woman. [15]And when Pharaoh's
officials saw her, they praised her to
Pharaoh, and she was taken into his palace. [16]He treated Abram well for her
sake, and Abram acquired sheep and
cattle, male and female donkeys, menservants and maidservants, and camels.
[17]But the LORD inflicted serious diseases on Pharaoh and his household
because of Abram's wife Sarai. [18]So Pharaoh summoned Abram. "What have
you done to me?" he said. "Why didn't
you tell me she was your wife? [19]Why
did you say, 'She is my sister,' so that I
took her to be my wife? Now then, here
is your wife. Take her and go!" [20]Then
Pharaoh gave orders about Abram to his
men, and they sent him on his way, with
his wife and everything he had.

Abram and Lot Separate

13 So Abram went up from
Egypt to the Negev, with his
wife and everything he had, and Lot
went with him. [2]Abram had become
very wealthy in livestock and in silver
and gold.
[3]From the Negev he went from place
to place until he came to Bethel, to the
place between Bethel and Ai where his
tent had been earlier [4]and where he had
first built an altar. There Abram called on
the name of the LORD.
[5]Now Lot, who was moving about
with Abram, also had flocks and herds
and tents. [6]But the land could not support them while they stayed together,
for their possessions were so great that
they were not able to stay together. [7]And
quarreling arose between Abram's
herdsmen and the herdsmen of Lot. The
Canaanites and Perizzites were also living in the land at that time.
[8]So Abram said to Lot, "Let's not have
any quarreling between you and me, or
between your herdsmen and mine, for
we are brothers. [9]Is not the whole land
before you? Let's part company. If you
go to the left, I'll go to the right; if you
go to the right, I'll go to the left."
[10]Lot looked up and saw that the
whole plain of the Jordan was well watered, like the garden of the LORD, like
the land of Egypt, toward Zoar. (This
was before the LORD destroyed Sodom
and Gomorrah.) [11]So Lot chose for himself the whole plain of the Jordan and
set out toward the east. The two men
parted company: [12]Abram lived in the
land of Canaan, while Lot lived among
the cities of the plain and pitched his
tents near Sodom. [13]Now the men of
Sodom were wicked and were sinning
greatly against the LORD.
[14]The LORD said to Abram after Lot
had parted from him, "Lift up your eyes
from where you are and look north and
south, east and west. [15]All the land that
you see I will give to you and your offspring[a] forever. [16]I will make your offspring like the dust of the earth, so that
if anyone could count the dust, then
your offspring could be counted. [17]Go,
walk through the length and breadth of
the land, for I am giving it to you."
[18]So Abram moved his tents and went
to live near the great trees of Mamre at
Hebron, where he built an altar to the
LORD.

[a]15 Or *seed*; also in verse 16

SHARPEN THE FOCUS

How do you react when you have to wait for God to fulfill His promises to you? That's the faith-challenge Abram faced. He had staked his future on God's promise that the land of Canaan would belong to him and his descendants. But he would not see the promise fulfilled in his lifetime.

Abram lived as a nomad, dependent on the good will of his neighbors for many things—including access to water. When drought struck, he found his flocks and herds in deep distress. So he journeyed to Egypt. There, Abram caved in to fear. His lies compromised his witness and endangered his wife.

How is it with us? We trust our Lord for the most important things in our lives—forgiveness of sins through Jesus and eternal life in heaven. But sometimes our faith falls apart when we face difficulties in everyday life. What happens when the car breaks down? The bills stack up? The kids have trouble in school?

In what one area of life do you find it hardest to trust God? Talk to Him about it. Then read Romans 8:31-32: "If God is for us, who can be against us? He who did not spare His own Son, but gave Him up for us all—how will he not also, along with Him, graciously give us all things?"

God had promised Abram many descendants and the land of Canaan as an inheritance for his descendants (Genesis 13:16). Genesis 14 recounts a military victory Abram won despite the odds. With this victory, God proved that He would keep his promises. The Lord gave Abram a vision upon his return from the battle to further assure Abram of His faithfulness. This vision looked over 400 years into the future and revealed the Lord's faithfulness to Abram's descendants from generation to generation. If time is short, focus on Genesis 15:1–6.

Abram Rescues Lot

14 At this time Amraphel king
of Shinar,[a] Arioch king of Ellasar, Kedorlaomer king of Elam and Tidal king of Goiim [2]went to war against
Bera king of Sodom, Birsha king of Gomorrah, Shinab king of Admah, Shem-
eber king of Zeboiim, and the king of
Bela (that is, Zoar). [3]All these latter kings
joined forces in the Valley of Siddim (the
Salt Sea[b]). [4]For twelve years they had
been subject to Kedorlaomer, but in the
thirteenth year they rebelled.
[5]In the fourteenth year, Kedorlaomer
and the kings allied with him went out
and defeated the Rephaites in Ashte-
roth Karnaim, the Zuzites in Ham, the
Emites in Shaveh Kiriathaim [6]and the
Horites in the hill country of Seir, as far
as El Paran near the desert. [7]Then they
turned back and went to En Mishpat
(that is, Kadesh), and they conquered
the whole territory of the Amalekites, as
well as the Amorites who were living in
Hazazon Tamar.
[8]Then the king of Sodom, the king of
Gomorrah, the king of Admah, the king
of Zeboiim and the king of Bela (that is,
Zoar) marched out and drew up their
battle lines in the Valley of Siddim
[9]against Kedorlaomer king of Elam,
Tidal king of Goiim, Amraphel king of
Shinar and Arioch king of Ellasar—four
kings against five. [10]Now the Valley of
Siddim was full of tar pits, and when the
kings of Sodom and Gomorrah fled,
some of the men fell into them and the
rest fled to the hills. [11]The four kings
seized all the goods of Sodom and Gomorrah and all their food; then they
went away. [12]They also carried off
Abram's nephew Lot and his possessions, since he was living in Sodom.
[13]One who had escaped came and reported this to Abram the Hebrew. Now
Abram was living near the great trees of
Mamre the Amorite, a brother[c] of Eshcol and Aner, all of whom were allied
with Abram. [14]When Abram heard that
his relative had been taken captive, he
called out the 318 trained men born in
his household and went in pursuit as far
as Dan. [15]During the night Abram divided his men to attack them and he routed them, pursuing them as far as
Hobah, north of Damascus. [16]He recovered all the goods and brought back his
relative Lot and his possessions, together with the women and the other
people.
[17]After Abram returned from defeating Kedorlaomer and the kings allied
with him, the king of Sodom came out
to meet him in the Valley of Shaveh (that
is, the King's Valley).
[18]Then Melchizedek king of Salem[a]
brought out bread and wine. He

[a]*1* That is, Babylonia; also in verse 9 [b]*3* That is, the Dead Sea [c]*13* Or *a relative*; or *an ally*

was priest of God Most High, 19and he
blessed Abram, saying,

"Blessed be Abram by God Most High,
Creator[b] of heaven and earth.
20 And blessed be[c] God Most High,
who delivered your enemies into
your hand."

Then Abram gave him a tenth of everything.
21The king of Sodom said to Abram,
"Give me the people and keep the goods
for yourself."
22But Abram said to the king of Sodom, "I have raised my hand to the LORD,
God Most High, Creator of heaven and
earth, and have taken an oath 23that I
will accept nothing belonging to you,
not even a thread or the thong of a sandal, so that you will never be able to say,
'I made Abram rich.' 24I will accept nothing but what my men have eaten and
the share that belongs to the men who
went with me—to Aner, Eshcol and
Mamre. Let them have their share."

God's Covenant With Abram

15 After this, the word of the
LORD came to Abram in a vision:

"Do not be afraid, Abram.
I am your shield,[d]
your very great reward.[e]"

2But Abram said, "O Sovereign LORD,
what can you give me since I remain
childless and the one who will inherit[f]
my estate is Eliezer of Damascus?" 3And
Abram said, "You have given me no children; so a servant in my household will
be my heir."
4Then the word of the LORD came to
him: "This man will not be your heir, but
a son coming from your own body will
be your heir." 5He took him outside and
said, "Look up at the heavens and count
the stars—if indeed you can count
them." Then he said to him, "So shall
your offspring be."
6Abram believed the LORD, and he
credited it to him as righteousness.
7He also said to him, "I am the LORD,
who brought you out of Ur of the Chaldeans to give you this land to take possession of it."
8But Abram said, "O Sovereign LORD,
how can I know that I will gain possession of it?"
9So the LORD said to him, "Bring me a
heifer, a goat and a ram, each three years
old, along with a dove and a young pigeon."
10Abram brought all these to him, cut
them in two and arranged the halves
opposite each other; the birds, however, he did not cut in half. 11Then birds of
prey came down on the carcasses, but
Abram drove them away.
12As the sun was setting, Abram fell
into a deep sleep, and a thick and dreadful darkness came over him. 13Then the
LORD said to him, "Know for certain that
your descendants will be strangers in a
country not their own, and they will be
enslaved and mistreated four hundred
years. 14But I will punish the nation they
serve as slaves, and afterward they will
come out with great possessions. 15You,
however, will go to your fathers in peace
and be buried at a good old age. 16In the
fourth generation your descendants
will come back here, for the sin of the
Amorites has not yet reached its full
measure."
17When the sun had set and darkness
had fallen, a smoking firepot with a
blazing torch appeared and passed between the pieces. 18On that day the
LORD made a covenant with Abram and
said, "To your descendants I give this
land, from the river[g] of Egypt to the
great river, the Euphrates— 19the land of
the Kenites, Kenizzites, Kadmonites,
20Hittites, Perizzites, Rephaites, 21Amo-
rites, Canaanites, Girgashites and Jebusites."

[a]18 That is, Jerusalem [b]19 Or *Possessor;* also in verse 22 [c]20 Or *And praise be to* [d]1 Or *sovereign* [e]1 Or *shield; / your reward will be very great* [f]2 The meaning of the Hebrew for this phrase is uncertain. [g]18 Or *Wadi*

SHARPEN THE FOCUS

The strongest oath Abram knew was the blood covenant practiced in the region of the Middle East, where he had lived before he immigrated to Canaan. In this ceremony, animals were killed, cut in two, and laid out on the ground. Two equal parties would walk solemnly between the bloody carcasses to seal an agreement they had reached. Breaking this kind of oath meant gory death at the hands of the other.

But note that in Abram's vision only a fiery, smoking torch (a symbol of God in His glory—see Exodus 13:21–22) passed between the sacrificial animals. The Lord alone took this oath. He made all the promises and Abram received all the blessings. Far from being two equal parties, the Lord and Abram enjoyed a relationship established solely by the Lord Most High. Abram, His humble servant, had only to believe—and it was "credited to him as righteousness" (Genesis 15:6). That righteousness is yours, too, in Jesus!

WEEK 2 • WEDNESDAY

Genesis 16:1—17:27

GET THE BIG PICTURE

Today's reading recounts yet another instance in which Abram's impatience drew down misery on himself and on those he loved. Still, God did not leave His servant alone in the darkness of doubt. Once again He repeated His promise (Genesis 17:5–8) and set a deadline for its fulfillment—one year. If time is short, focus on Genesis 17:1–17.

Hagar and Ishmael

16 Now Sarai, Abram's wife,
had borne him no children.
But she had an Egyptian maidservant
named Hagar; 2so she said to Abram,
"The LORD has kept me from having
children. Go, sleep with my maidservant; perhaps I can build a family
through her."
Abram agreed to what Sarai said. 3So
after Abram had been living in Canaan
ten years, Sarai his wife took her Egyptian maidservant Hagar and gave her to
her husband to be his wife. 4He slept
with Hagar, and she conceived.
When she knew she was pregnant,
she began to despise her mistress. 5Then
Sarai said to Abram, "You are responsible for the wrong I am suffering. I put
my servant in your arms, and now that
she knows she is pregnant, she despises
me. May the LORD judge between you
and me."
6"Your servant is in your hands,"
Abram said. "Do with her whatever you
think best." Then Sarai mistreated Hagar; so she fled from her.
7The angel of the LORD found Hagar
near a spring in the desert; it was the
spring that is beside the road to Shur.
8And he said, "Hagar, servant of Sarai,
where have you come from, and where
are you going?"
"I'm running away from my mistress
Sarai," she answered.
9Then the angel of the LORD told her,
"Go back to your mistress and submit to
her." 10The angel added, "I will so increase your descendants that they will
be too numerous to count."

11The angel of the LORD also said to her:

"You are now with child
and you will have a son.
You shall name him Ishmael,[a]
for the LORD has heard of your misery.
12He will be a wild donkey of a man;
his hand will be against everyone
and everyone's hand against him,
and he will live in hostility
toward[b] all his brothers."

13She gave this name to the LORD who spoke to her: "You are the God who sees me," for she said, "I have now seen[c] the One who sees me." 14That is why the well was called Beer Lahai Roi[d]; it is still there, between Kadesh and Bered.

15So Hagar bore Abram a son, and Abram gave the name Ishmael to the son she had borne. 16Abram was eighty-six years old when Hagar bore him Ishmael.

The Covenant of Circumcision

17 When Abram was ninety-nine years old, the LORD appeared to him and said, "I am God Almighty[e]; walk before me and be blameless. 2I will confirm my covenant between me and you and will greatly increase your numbers."

3Abram fell facedown, and God said to him, 4"As for me, this is my covenant with you: You will be the father of many nations. 5No longer will you be called Abram[f]; your name will be Abraham,[g] for I have made you a father of many nations. 6I will make you very fruitful; I will make nations of you, and kings will come from you. 7I will establish my covenant as an everlasting covenant between me and you and your descendants after you for the generations to come, to be your God and the God of your descendants after you. 8The whole land of Canaan, where you are now an alien, I will give as an everlasting possession to you and your descendants after you; and I will be their God."

9Then God said to Abraham, "As for you, you must keep my covenant, you and your descendants after you for the generations to come. 10This is my covenant with you and your descendants after you, the covenant you are to keep: Every male among you shall be circumcised. 11You are to undergo circumcision, and it will be the sign of the covenant between me and you. 12For the generations to come every male among you who is eight days old must be circumcised, including those born in your household or bought with money from a foreigner—those who are not your offspring. 13Whether born in your household or bought with your money, they must be circumcised. My covenant in your flesh is to be an everlasting covenant. 14Any uncircumcised male, who has not been circumcised in the flesh, will be cut off from his people; he has broken my covenant."

15God also said to Abraham, "As for Sarai your wife, you are no longer to call her Sarai; her name will be Sarah. 16I will bless her and will surely give you a son by her. I will bless her so that she will be the mother of nations; kings of peoples will come from her."

17Abraham fell facedown; he laughed and said to himself, "Will a son be born to a man a hundred years old? Will Sarah bear a child at the age of ninety?" 18And Abraham said to God, "If only Ishmael might live under your blessing!"

19Then God said, "Yes, but your wife Sarah will bear you a son, and you will call him Isaac.[h] I will establish my covenant with him as an everlasting covenant for his descendants after him. 20And as for Ishmael, I have heard you: I will surely bless him; I will make him fruitful and will greatly increase his numbers. He will be the father of twelve rulers, and I will make him into a great nation. 21But my covenant I will

[a]11 *Ishmael* means *God hears.* [b]12 Or *live to the east / of* [c]13 Or *seen the back of* [d]14 *Beer Lahai Roi* means *well of the Living One who sees me.*
[e]1 Hebrew *El-Shaddai* [f]5 *Abram* means *exalted father.* [g]5 *Abraham* means *father of many.*
[h]19 *Isaac* means *he laughs.*

establish with Isaac, whom Sarah will
bear to you by this time next year."
[22]When he had finished speaking with
Abraham, God went up from him.
[23]On that very day Abraham took his
son Ishmael and all those born in his
household or bought with his money,
every male in his household, and
circumcised them, as God told him.
[24]Abraham was ninety-nine years old
when he was circumcised, [25]and his
son Ishmael was thirteen; [26]Abraham
and his son Ishmael were both circumcised on that same day. [27]And every
male in Abraham's household, including those born in his household or
bought from a foreigner, was circumcised with him.

SHARPEN THE FOCUS

Abram and Sarai had been waiting 24 years for the Lord to give them the son He had promised. Abram was now 99, Sarai 89. They had done all they could to "help God out"—including Abram's tryst with Hagar (Genesis 16).

How like us—to think that somehow God can't or won't keep His Word, especially when we don't see Him fulfill His promises right away. How like God—to come to us, not with words of rebuke but of grace.

First, He reveals Himself to Abram as El Shaddai—loosely translated, "The [God] who acts in power." Perhaps we might say, "The God who is strong enough." Then the Lord repeats His promises and seals them with a visible sign—circumcision. Finally, God asserts a remarkable truth to Abram and Sarai by changing their names. These desert nomads with dust in their sandals were, in reality, His royal children. Kings would come from Abram, now Abraham. Sarai was now Sarah—"princess."

How do you see your God today? Is He the "God who is strong enough" to help in all times of need? And do you see yourself as the "royal priesthood" He has declared you to be in Christ (1 Peter 2:9)? If so, what difference does it make now, today?

WEEK 2 • THURSDAY

Genesis 18:1—19:38

GET THE BIG PICTURE

In today's reading, God visits Abraham in human form. He does this for two main reasons—to confirm His covenant promises to Sarah (Genesis 18:1–15) and to share with Abraham His plan to judge the cities of the plain for their wickedness (Genesis 18:16–33). As the events of Genesis 19 unfold, it becomes evident that Abraham's nephew, Lot, went to live in the city of Sodom, but soon the wickedness of Sodom came to live in him and in each member of his family. If time is short, focus on Genesis 19:1–29.

The Three Visitors

18 The LORD appeared to Abraham near the great trees of Mamre while he was sitting at the entrance to his tent in the heat of the day. 2Abraham looked up and saw three men standing nearby. When he saw them, he hurried from the entrance of his tent to meet them and bowed low to the ground.

3He said, "If I have found favor in your eyes, my lord,[a] do not pass your servant by. 4Let a little water be brought, and then you may all wash your feet and rest under this tree. 5Let me get you something to eat, so you can be refreshed and then go on your way—now that you have come to your servant."

"Very well," they answered, "do as you say."

6So Abraham hurried into the tent to Sarah. "Quick," he said, "get three seahs[b] of fine flour and knead it and bake some bread."

7Then he ran to the herd and selected a choice, tender calf and gave it to a servant, who hurried to prepare it. 8He then brought some curds and milk and the calf that had been prepared, and set these before them. While they ate, he stood near them under a tree.

9"Where is your wife Sarah?" they asked him.

"There, in the tent," he said.

10Then the LORD[c] said, "I will surely return to you about this time next year, and Sarah your wife will have a son."

Now Sarah was listening at the entrance to the tent, which was behind him. 11Abraham and Sarah were already old and well advanced in years, and Sarah was past the age of childbearing. 12So Sarah laughed to herself as she thought, "After I am worn out and my master[d] is old, will I now have this pleasure?"

13Then the LORD said to Abraham, "Why did Sarah laugh and say, 'Will I really have a child, now that I am old?' 14Is anything too hard for the LORD? I will return to you at the appointed time next year and Sarah will have a son."

15Sarah was afraid, so she lied and said, "I did not laugh."

But he said, "Yes, you did laugh."

Abraham Pleads for Sodom

16When the men got up to leave, they looked down toward Sodom, and Abraham walked along with them to see them on their way. 17Then the LORD said, "Shall I hide from Abraham what I am about to do? 18Abraham will surely become a great and powerful nation, and all nations on earth will be blessed through him. 19For I have chosen him, so that he will direct his children and his household after him to keep the way of the LORD by doing what is right and just, so that the LORD will bring about for Abraham what he has promised him."

20Then the LORD said, "The outcry against Sodom and Gomorrah is so great and their sin so grievous 21that I will go down and see if what they have done is as bad as the outcry that has reached me. If not, I will know."

22The men turned away and went toward Sodom, but Abraham remained standing before the LORD.[e] 23Then Abraham approached him and said: "Will you sweep away the righteous with the wicked? 24What if there are fifty righteous people in the city? Will you really sweep it away and not spare[f] the place for the sake of the fifty righteous people in it? 25Far be it from you to do such a thing—to kill the righteous with the wicked, treating the righteous and the wicked alike. Far be it from you! Will not the Judge[g] of all the earth do right?"

26The LORD said, "If I find fifty righteous people in the city of Sodom, I will spare the whole place for their sake."

27Then Abraham spoke up again: "Now that I have been so bold as to speak to the Lord, though I am nothing but dust and ashes, 28what if the

[a]3 Or *O Lord* [b]6 That is, probably about 20 quarts (about 22 liters) [c]10 Hebrew *Then he* [d]12 Or *husband* [e]22 Masoretic Text; an ancient Hebrew scribal tradition *but the LORD remained standing before Abraham* [f]24 Or *forgive;* also in verse 26 [g]25 Or *Ruler*

number of the righteous is five less than fifty? Will you destroy the whole city because of five people?"

"If I find forty-five there," he said, "I will not destroy it."

[29]Once again he spoke to him, "What if only forty are found there?"

He said, "For the sake of forty, I will not do it."

[30]Then he said, "May the Lord not be angry, but let me speak. What if only thirty can be found there?"

He answered, "I will not do it if I find thirty there."

[31]Abraham said, "Now that I have been so bold as to speak to the Lord, what if only twenty can be found there?"

He said, "For the sake of twenty, I will not destroy it."

[32]Then he said, "May the Lord not be angry, but let me speak just once more. What if only ten can be found there?"

He answered, "For the sake of ten, I will not destroy it."

[33]When the LORD had finished speaking with Abraham, he left, and Abraham returned home.

Sodom and Gomorrah Destroyed

19 The two angels arrived at Sodom in the evening, and Lot was sitting in the gateway of the city. When he saw them, he got up to meet them and bowed down with his face to the ground. [2]"My lords," he said, "please turn aside to your servant's house. You can wash your feet and spend the night and then go on your way early in the morning."

"No," they answered, "we will spend the night in the square."

[3]But he insisted so strongly that they did go with him and entered his house. He prepared a meal for them, baking bread without yeast, and they ate. [4]Before they had gone to bed, all the men from every part of the city of Sodom—both young and old—surrounded the house. [5]They called to Lot, "Where are the men who came to you tonight? Bring them out to us so that we can have sex with them."

[6]Lot went outside to meet them and shut the door behind him [7]and said, "No, my friends. Don't do this wicked thing. [8]Look, I have two daughters who have never slept with a man. Let me bring them out to you, and you can do what you like with them. But don't do anything to these men, for they have come under the protection of my roof."

[9]"Get out of our way," they replied. And they said, "This fellow came here as an alien, and now he wants to play the judge! We'll treat you worse than them." They kept bringing pressure on Lot and moved forward to break down the door.

[10]But the men inside reached out and pulled Lot back into the house and shut the door. [11]Then they struck the men who were at the door of the house, young and old, with blindness so that they could not find the door.

[12]The two men said to Lot, "Do you have anyone else here—sons-in-law, sons or daughters, or anyone else in the city who belongs to you? Get them out of here, [13]because we are going to destroy this place. The outcry to the LORD against its people is so great that he has sent us to destroy it."

[14]So Lot went out and spoke to his sons-in-law, who were pledged to marry[a] his daughters. He said, "Hurry and get out of this place, because the LORD is about to destroy the city!" But his sons-in-law thought he was joking.

[15]With the coming of dawn, the angels urged Lot, saying, "Hurry! Take your wife and your two daughters who are here, or you will be swept away when the city is punished."

[16]When he hesitated, the men grasped his hand and the hands of his wife and of his two daughters and led them safely out of the city, for the LORD was merciful to them. [17]As soon as they had brought them out, one of them said, "Flee for your lives! Don't look back, and don't stop anywhere in the plain!

[a]14 Or *were married to*

Flee to the mountains or you will be
swept away!"
18 But Lot said to them, "No, my lords,[a]
please! 19 Your[b] servant has found favor
in your[b] eyes, and you[b] have shown
great kindness to me in sparing my life.
But I can't flee to the mountains; this disaster will overtake me, and I'll die.
20 Look, here is a town near enough to
run to, and it is small. Let me flee to it—
it is very small, isn't it? Then my life will
be spared."
21 He said to him, "Very well, I will
grant this request too; I will not overthrow the town you speak of. 22 But flee
there quickly, because I cannot do anything until you reach it." (That is why
the town was called Zoar.[c])
23 By the time Lot reached Zoar, the
sun had risen over the land. 24 Then the
LORD rained down burning sulfur on
Sodom and Gomorrah—from the LORD
out of the heavens. 25 Thus he overthrew
those cities and the entire plain, including all those living in the cities—and
also the vegetation in the land. 26 But
Lot's wife looked back, and she became
a pillar of salt.
27 Early the next morning Abraham
got up and returned to the place where
he had stood before the LORD. 28 He
looked down toward Sodom and Gomorrah, toward all the land of the plain,
and he saw dense smoke rising from the
land, like smoke from a furnace.
29 So when God destroyed the cities of
the plain, he remembered Abraham,
and he brought Lot out of the catastrophe that overthrew the cities where Lot
had lived.

Lot and His Daughters

30 Lot and his two daughters left Zoar
and settled in the mountains, for he was
afraid to stay in Zoar. He and his two
daughters lived in a cave. 31 One day the
older daughter said to the younger,
"Our father is old, and there is no man
around here to lie with us, as is the custom all over the earth. 32 Let's get our father to drink wine and then lie with him
and preserve our family line through
our father."
33 That night they got their father to
drink wine, and the older daughter
went in and lay with him. He was not
aware of it when she lay down or when
she got up.
34 The next day the older daughter said
to the younger, "Last night I lay with my
father. Let's get him to drink wine again
tonight, and you go in and lie with him
so we can preserve our family line
through our father." 35 So they got their
father to drink wine that night also, and
the younger daughter went and lay
with him. Again he was not aware of it
when she lay down or when she got up.
36 So both of Lot's daughters became
pregnant by their father. 37 The older
daughter had a son, and she named him
Moab[d]; he is the father of the Moabites
of today. 38 The younger daughter also
had a son, and she named him Ben-
Ammi[e]; he is the father of the Ammonites of today.

[a] *18* Or *No, Lord;* or *No, my lord* [b] *19* The Hebrew is singular. [c] *22 Zoar* means *small.* [d] *37 Moab* sounds like the Hebrew for *from father.* [e] *38 Ben-Ammi* means *son of my people.*

SHARPEN THE FOCUS

How acute is your sense of morality? Are you grieved by the evils of our culture? Or has sin anesthetized you? For example:

Suppose Jesus sat with you as you watched TV tonight. Would you surf past the channel you usually choose?

What kind of example do you set for the members of your family and your neighbors as you model God's holy gift of sexuality?

How important are the material possessions God has given you? How important are they really? If God's angels took you by the hand tomorrow morning to take you to safety, how likely is it you would turn back in longing for one last look?

J. B. Phillips has paraphrased Romans 12:2 this way: "Don't let the world squeeze you into its own [mold]." But what if this has already happened? What if you're mangled, pressed and oppressed by the world system around you?

You know the answer—run to your Lord in penitent faith. Let Him assure you of His pardon in Christ. Let Him breathe on you the empowering breath of His grace. Let Him renew and fill you by His Spirit to become more like your Brother, His Son, our Lord Jesus.

WEEK 2 • FRIDAY

Genesis 20:1—21:34

Abraham and Sarah had less than a year to wait until God would keep His promise to send a son (Genesis 17:21). And yet we see them in today's reading plotting to repeat a sin that had once before led to the brink of disaster. (See Genesis 12:10–20.) Rescued once again by the God who remains faithful despite His children's faithlessness, Abraham and Sarah finally see the son for whom they have waited so long. If time is short, focus on Genesis 21:1–8.

Abraham and Abimelech

20 Now Abraham moved on
from there into the region
of the Negev and lived between Kadesh
and Shur. For a while he stayed in Gerar, [2]and there Abraham said of his wife
Sarah, "She is my sister." Then Abimelech king of Gerar sent for Sarah and
took her.
[3]But God came to Abimelech in a
dream one night and said to him, "You
are as good as dead because of the
woman you have taken; she is a married
woman."
[4]Now Abimelech had not gone near
her, so he said, "Lord, will you destroy
an innocent nation? [5]Did he not say to
me, 'She is my sister,' and didn't she also
say, 'He is my brother'? I have done this
with a clear conscience and clean
hands."
[6]Then God said to him in the dream,
"Yes, I know you did this with a clear
conscience, and so I have kept you from
sinning against me. That is why I did
not let you touch her. [7]Now return the
man's wife, for he is a prophet, and he
will pray for you and you will live. But
if you do not return her, you may be
sure that you and all yours will die."
[8]Early the next morning Abimelech
summoned all his officials, and when he
told them all that had happened, they
were very much afraid. [9]Then Abimelech called Abraham in and said, "What
have you done to us? How have I
wronged you that you have brought
such great guilt upon me and my kingdom? You have done things to me that
should not be done." [10]And Abimelech
asked Abraham, "What was your reason
for doing this?"
[11]Abraham replied, "I said to myself,
'There is surely no fear of God in this
place, and they will kill me because of
my wife.' [12]Besides, she really is my sister, the daughter of my father though
not of my mother; and she became my

wife. 13And when God had me wander from my father's household, I said to her, 'This is how you can show your love to me: Everywhere we go, say of me, "He is my brother." ' "

14Then Abimelech brought sheep and cattle and male and female slaves and gave them to Abraham, and he returned Sarah his wife to him. 15And Abimelech said, "My land is before you; live wherever you like."

16To Sarah he said, "I am giving your brother a thousand shekels[a] of silver. This is to cover the offense against you before all who are with you; you are completely vindicated."

17Then Abraham prayed to God, and God healed Abimelech, his wife and his slave girls so they could have children again, 18for the LORD had closed up every womb in Abimelech's household because of Abraham's wife Sarah.

The Birth of Isaac

21 Now the LORD was gracious to Sarah as he had said, and the LORD did for Sarah what he had promised. 2Sarah became pregnant and bore a son to Abraham in his old age, at the very time God had promised him. 3Abraham gave the name Isaac[b] to the son Sarah bore him. 4When his son Isaac was eight days old, Abraham circumcised him, as God commanded him. 5Abraham was a hundred years old when his son Isaac was born to him.

6Sarah said, "God has brought me laughter, and everyone who hears about this will laugh with me." 7And she added, "Who would have said to Abraham that Sarah would nurse children? Yet I have borne him a son in his old age."

Hagar and Ishmael Sent Away

8The child grew and was weaned, and on the day Isaac was weaned Abraham held a great feast. 9But Sarah saw that the son whom Hagar the Egyptian had borne to Abraham was mocking, 10and she said to Abraham, "Get rid of that slave woman and her son, for that slave woman's son will never share in the inheritance with my son Isaac."

11The matter distressed Abraham greatly because it concerned his son. 12But God said to him, "Do not be so distressed about the boy and your maidservant. Listen to whatever Sarah tells you, because it is through Isaac that your offspring[c] will be reckoned. 13I will make the son of the maidservant into a nation also, because he is your offspring."

14Early the next morning Abraham took some food and a skin of water and gave them to Hagar. He set them on her shoulders and then sent her off with the boy. She went on her way and wandered in the desert of Beersheba.

15When the water in the skin was gone, she put the boy under one of the bushes. 16Then she went off and sat down nearby, about a bowshot away, for she thought, "I cannot watch the boy die." And as she sat there nearby, she[d] began to sob.

17God heard the boy crying, and the angel of God called to Hagar from heaven and said to her, "What is the matter, Hagar? Do not be afraid; God has heard the boy crying as he lies there. 18Lift the boy up and take him by the hand, for I will make him into a great nation."

19Then God opened her eyes and she saw a well of water. So she went and filled the skin with water and gave the boy a drink.

20God was with the boy as he grew up. He lived in the desert and became an archer. 21While he was living in the Desert of Paran, his mother got a wife for him from Egypt.

The Treaty at Beersheba

22At that time Abimelech and Phicol the commander of his forces said to Abraham, "God is with you in everything you do. 23Now swear to me here before God that you will not deal falsely with me or my children or my

[a]16 That is, about 25 pounds (about 11.5 kilograms) [b]3 *Isaac* means *he laughs.* [c]12 Or *seed* [d]16 Hebrew; Septuagint *the child*

descendants. Show to me and the country where you are living as an alien the
same kindness I have shown to you."
[24]Abraham said, "I swear it."
[25]Then Abraham complained to Abimelech about a well of water that Abimelech's servants had seized. [26]But
Abimelech said, "I don't know who has
done this. You did not tell me, and I
heard about it only today."
[27]So Abraham brought sheep and
cattle and gave them to Abimelech, and
the two men made a treaty. [28]Abraham
set apart seven ewe lambs from the
flock, [29]and Abimelech asked Abraham,
"What is the meaning of these seven
ewe lambs you have set apart by themselves?"
[30]He replied, "Accept these seven
lambs from my hand as a witness that I
dug this well."
[31]So that place was called Beersheba,[a]
because the two men swore an oath
there.
[32]After the treaty had been made at
Beersheba, Abimelech and Phicol the
commander of his forces returned to the
land of the Philistines. [33]Abraham
planted a tamarisk tree in Beersheba,
and there he called upon the name of
the LORD, the Eternal God. [34]And Abraham stayed in the land of the Philistines
for a long time.

[a]*31 Beersheba* can mean *well of seven* or *well of the oath.*

SHARPEN THE FOCUS

Genesis 20:13 makes it clear that Abraham and Sarah had hatched their plan together in the clear light of day. No slip up under stress here. Their lie was deliberate, calculated, planned. The heathen King Abimelech acted with more integrity than God's covenant people!

We cannot help but see Satan lurking in between the lines, using human weakness to derail God's plan to save the world through Abraham's promised seed, our Lord Jesus.

Did Abraham realize this? Did Abraham and Sarah see their proposed lie as sin? Almost certainly not. They had fallen for the myth "heaven helps those who help themselves." After all, they were just taking responsible precautions. Right?

We've all failed to speak and act with integrity from time to time. We've all given a miserable witness in word and action on occasion. We've all failed to trust God's provision and care.

What good news, then, that Satan did not, could not stop God's plan to send a Savior! Abraham's seed (Galatians 3:16) has come, has died, has risen for us. Let Him fill you with the joy and power you need to defeat Satan's schemes and temptations today.

When the Emergency Broadcast System conducts a test, it announces it ahead of time. Maybe you've memorized these familiar words: "This is a test. For the next 60 seconds this station will conduct a test. . . ." As you read Genesis 22, try to stand in Abraham's sandals. Forget what you may already know about the outcome. What feelings engulf your heart as you take Abraham's test with him? If time is short, focus on Genesis 22:6-14.

Abraham Tested

22 Some time later God tested Abraham. He said to him, "Abraham!"

"Here I am," he replied.

[2]Then God said, "Take your son, your only son, Isaac, whom you love, and go to the region of Moriah. Sacrifice him there as a burnt offering on one of the mountains I will tell you about."

[3]Early the next morning Abraham got up and saddled his donkey. He took with him two of his servants and his son Isaac. When he had cut enough wood for the burnt offering, he set out for the place God had told him about. [4]On the third day Abraham looked up and saw the place in the distance. [5]He said to his servants, "Stay here with the donkey while I and the boy go over there. We will worship and then we will come back to you."

[6]Abraham took the wood for the burnt offering and placed it on his son Isaac, and he himself carried the fire and the knife. As the two of them went on together, [7]Isaac spoke up and said to his father Abraham, "Father?"

"Yes, my son?" Abraham replied.

"The fire and wood are here," Isaac said, "but where is the lamb for the burnt offering?"

[8]Abraham answered, "God himself will provide the lamb for the burnt offering, my son." And the two of them went on together.

[9]When they reached the place God had told him about, Abraham built an altar there and arranged the wood on it. He bound his son Isaac and laid him on the altar, on top of the wood. [10]Then he reached out his hand and took the knife to slay his son. [11]But the angel of the LORD called out to him from heaven, "Abraham! Abraham!"

"Here I am," he replied.

[12]"Do not lay a hand on the boy," he said. "Do not do anything to him. Now I know that you fear God, because you have not withheld from me your son, your only son."

[13]Abraham looked up and there in a thicket he saw a ram[a] caught by its horns. He went over and took the ram and sacrificed it as a burnt offering instead of his son. [14]So Abraham called that place The LORD Will Provide. And to this day it is said, "On the mountain of the LORD it will be provided."

[15]The angel of the LORD called to Abraham from heaven a second time [16]and said, "I swear by myself, declares the LORD, that because you have done this and have not withheld your son, your only son, [17]I will surely bless you and make your descendants as numerous as the stars in the sky and as the sand on the seashore. Your descendants will take possession of the cities of their enemies, [18]and through your offspring[b] all nations on earth will be blessed, because you have obeyed me."

[19]Then Abraham returned to his servants, and they set off together for Beersheba. And Abraham stayed in Beersheba.

Nahor's Sons

[20]Some time later Abraham was told, "Milcah is also a mother; she has borne sons to your brother Nahor: [21]Uz the firstborn, Buz his brother, Kemuel (the father of Aram), [22]Kesed, Hazo, Pildash, Jidlaph and Bethuel." [23]Bethuel became the father of Rebekah. Milcah bore these eight sons to Abraham's brother Nahor. [24]His concubine, whose name was Reumah, also had sons: Tebah, Gaham, Tahash and Maacah.

[a]*13* Many manuscripts of the Masoretic Text, Samaritan Pentateuch, Septuagint and Syriac; most manuscripts of the Masoretic Text *a ram behind* ⌞*him*⌟ [b]*18* Or *seed*

SHARPEN THE FOCUS

What was God up to? The Lord is omniscient, all-knowing. He knew beforehand how Abraham would respond. But—and this is the point—He wanted Abraham to know. Had Isaac become an idol? That danger certainly existed. Abraham and Sarah treasured their son Isaac born in their old age. Perhaps Abraham himself even consciously worried about the spiritual danger. And in grace, God gave His servant a chance to obey fully.

This test was the culmination of many tests Abraham had taken throughout his lifetime. While he had failed many, the Lord had graciously used His Word to build a faith in Abraham that would withstand trials and troubles. None of these experiences were pleasant, especially not the one you read about today. But all were productive, instructive, transforming.

Reflect on your own life. Looking back on some of the troubling circumstances you have faced, can you now see what God was up to—at least in some of them?

If so, thank Him for using His Word to strengthen and to teach you in them. And pray for grace to trust His wisdom and love for those trials you do not yet fully understand.

As Abraham's life here on earth wound to a close, he bought a cave and the surrounding field. Here he buried Sarah. It was the only land Abraham ever owned in Canaan. One final issue burned in Abraham's heart—finding a godly wife for Isaac. Genesis 24 tells how God continued to act through human beings to fulfill His promise to send the Savior through Abraham's descendants. If time is short, focus on Genesis 24:1–27.

The Death of Sarah

23 Sarah lived to be a hundred and twenty-seven
years old. 2She died at Kiriath Arba (that
is, Hebron) in the land of Canaan, and
Abraham went to mourn for Sarah and
to weep over her.
3Then Abraham rose from beside his
dead wife and spoke to the Hittites.[a] He
said, 4"I am an alien and a stranger
among you. Sell me some property for
a burial site here so I can bury my dead."
5The Hittites replied to Abraham,
6"Sir, listen to us. You are a mighty prince
among us. Bury your dead in the choicest of our tombs. None of us will refuse
you his tomb for burying your dead."
7Then Abraham rose and bowed
down before the people of the land, the
Hittites. 8He said to them, "If you are
willing to let me bury my dead, then listen to me and intercede with Ephron
son of Zohar on my behalf 9so he will
sell me the cave of Machpelah, which
belongs to him and is at the end of his
field. Ask him to sell it to me for the full
price as a burial site among you."
10Ephron the Hittite was sitting
among his people and he replied to

[a]3 Or *the sons of Heth*; also in verses 5, 7, 10, 16, 18 and 20

Abraham in the hearing of all the Hittites who had come to the gate of his city. [11]"No, my lord," he said. "Listen to me; I give[a] you the field, and I give[a] you the cave that is in it. I give[a] it to you in the presence of my people. Bury your dead."

[12]Again Abraham bowed down before the people of the land [13]and he said to Ephron in their hearing, "Listen to me, if you will. I will pay the price of the field. Accept it from me so I can bury my dead there."

[14]Ephron answered Abraham, [15]"Listen to me, my lord; the land is worth four hundred shekels[b] of silver, but what is that between me and you? Bury your dead."

[16]Abraham agreed to Ephron's terms and weighed out for him the price he had named in the hearing of the Hittites: four hundred shekels of silver, according to the weight current among the merchants.

[17]So Ephron's field in Machpelah near Mamre—both the field and the cave in it, and all the trees within the borders of the field—was deeded [18]to Abraham as his property in the presence of all the Hittites who had come to the gate of the city. [19]Afterward Abraham buried his wife Sarah in the cave in the field of Machpelah near Mamre (which is at Hebron) in the land of Canaan. [20]So the field and the cave in it were deeded to Abraham by the Hittites as a burial site.

Isaac and Rebekah

24 Abraham was now old and well advanced in years, and the LORD had blessed him in every way. [2]He said to the chief[c] servant in his household, the one in charge of all that he had, "Put your hand under my thigh. [3]I want you to swear by the LORD, the God of heaven and the God of earth, that you will not get a wife for my son from the daughters of the Canaanites, among whom I am living, [4]but will go to my country and my own relatives and get a wife for my son Isaac."

[5]The servant asked him, "What if the woman is unwilling to come back with me to this land? Shall I then take your son back to the country you came from?"

[6]"Make sure that you do not take my son back there," Abraham said. [7]"The LORD, the God of heaven, who brought me out of my father's household and my native land and who spoke to me and promised me on oath, saying, 'To your offspring[d] I will give this land'—he will send his angel before you so that you can get a wife for my son from there. [8]If the woman is unwilling to come back with you, then you will be released from this oath of mine. Only do not take my son back there." [9]So the servant put his hand under the thigh of his master Abraham and swore an oath to him concerning this matter.

[10]Then the servant took ten of his master's camels and left, taking with him all kinds of good things from his master. He set out for Aram Naharaim[e] and made his way to the town of Nahor. [11]He had the camels kneel down near the well outside the town; it was toward evening, the time the women go out to draw water.

[12]Then he prayed, "O LORD, God of my master Abraham, give me success today, and show kindness to my master Abraham. [13]See, I am standing beside this spring, and the daughters of the townspeople are coming out to draw water. [14]May it be that when I say to a girl, 'Please let down your jar that I may have a drink,' and she says, 'Drink, and I'll water your camels too'—let her be the one you have chosen for your servant Isaac. By this I will know that you have shown kindness to my master."

[15]Before he had finished praying, Rebekah came out with her jar on her shoulder. She was the daughter of Bethuel son of Milcah, who was the wife of Abraham's brother Nahor. [16]The girl was very beautiful, a virgin; no man had ever lain with her. She went down to the spring, filled her jar and came up again.

[a]*11* Or *sell* [b]*15* That is, about 10 pounds (about 4.5 kilograms) [c]*2* Or *oldest* [d]*7* Or *seed*
[e]*10* That is, Northwest Mesopotamia

[17]The servant hurried to meet her and said, "Please give me a little water from your jar."

[18]"Drink, my lord," she said, and quickly lowered the jar to her hands and gave him a drink.

[19]After she had given him a drink, she said, "I'll draw water for your camels too, until they have finished drinking." [20]So she quickly emptied her jar into the trough, ran back to the well to draw more water, and drew enough for all his camels. [21]Without saying a word, the man watched her closely to learn whether or not the LORD had made his journey successful.

[22]When the camels had finished drinking, the man took out a gold nose ring weighing a beka[a] and two gold bracelets weighing ten shekels.[b] [23]Then he asked, "Whose daughter are you? Please tell me, is there room in your father's house for us to spend the night?"

[24]She answered him, "I am the daughter of Bethuel, the son that Milcah bore to Nahor." [25]And she added, "We have plenty of straw and fodder, as well as room for you to spend the night."

[26]Then the man bowed down and worshiped the LORD, [27]saying, "Praise be to the LORD, the God of my master Abraham, who has not abandoned his kindness and faithfulness to my master. As for me, the LORD has led me on the journey to the house of my master's relatives."

[28]The girl ran and told her mother's household about these things. [29]Now Rebekah had a brother named Laban, and he hurried out to the man at the spring. [30]As soon as he had seen the nose ring, and the bracelets on his sister's arms, and had heard Rebekah tell what the man said to her, he went out to the man and found him standing by the camels near the spring. [31]"Come, you who are blessed by the LORD," he said. "Why are you standing out here? I have prepared the house and a place for the camels."

[32]So the man went to the house, and the camels were unloaded. Straw and fodder were brought for the camels, and water for him and his men to wash their feet. [33]Then food was set before him, but he said, "I will not eat until I have told you what I have to say."

"Then tell us," ⌞Laban⌟ said.

[34]So he said, "I am Abraham's servant. [35]The LORD has blessed my master abundantly, and he has become wealthy. He has given him sheep and cattle, silver and gold, menservants and maidservants, and camels and donkeys. [36]My master's wife Sarah has borne him a son in her[c] old age, and he has given him everything he owns. [37]And my master made me swear an oath, and said, 'You must not get a wife for my son from the daughters of the Canaanites, in whose land I live, [38]but go to my father's family and to my own clan, and get a wife for my son.'

[39]"Then I asked my master, 'What if the woman will not come back with me?'

[40]"He replied, 'The LORD, before whom I have walked, will send his angel with you and make your journey a success, so that you can get a wife for my son from my own clan and from my father's family. [41]Then, when you go to my clan, you will be released from my oath even if they refuse to give her to you—you will be released from my oath.'

[42]"When I came to the spring today, I said, 'O LORD, God of my master Abraham, if you will, please grant success to the journey on which I have come. [43]See, I am standing beside this spring; if a maiden comes out to draw water and I say to her, "Please let me drink a little water from your jar," [44]and if she says to me, "Drink, and I'll draw water for your camels too," let her be the one the LORD has chosen for my master's son.'

[45]"Before I finished praying in my heart, Rebekah came out, with her jar on her shoulder. She went down to the spring and drew water, and I said to her, 'Please give me a drink.'

[a]22 That is, about 1/5 ounce (about 5.5 grams)
[b]22 That is, about 4 ounces (about 110 grams)
[c]36 Or *his*

46“She quickly lowered her jar from
her shoulder and said, ‘Drink, and I’ll
water your camels too.’ So I drank, and
she watered the camels also.
47“I asked her, ‘Whose daughter are
you?’
“She said, ‘The daughter of Bethuel
son of Nahor, whom Milcah bore to
him.’
“Then I put the ring in her nose and
the bracelets on her arms, 48and I bowed
down and worshiped the LORD. I
praised the LORD, the God of my master Abraham, who had led me on the
right road to get the granddaughter of
my master’s brother for his son. 49Now
if you will show kindness and faithfulness to my master, tell me; and if not, tell
me, so I may know which way to turn.”
50Laban and Bethuel answered, “This
is from the LORD; we can say nothing to
you one way or the other. 51Here is Rebekah; take her and go, and let her become the wife of your master’s son, as
the LORD has directed.”
52When Abraham’s servant heard
what they said, he bowed down to the
ground before the LORD. 53Then the servant brought out gold and silver jewelry and articles of clothing and gave
them to Rebekah; he also gave costly
gifts to her brother and to her mother.
54Then he and the men who were with
him ate and drank and spent the night
there.
When they got up the next morning,
he said, “Send me on my way to my
master.”
55But her brother and her mother replied, “Let the girl remain with us ten
days or so; then you[a] may go.”
56But he said to them, “Do not detain
me, now that the LORD has granted success to my journey. Send me on my way
so I may go to my master.”
57Then they said, “Let’s call the girl
and ask her about it.” 58So they called
Rebekah and asked her, “Will you go
with this man?”
“I will go,” she said.
59So they sent their sister Rebekah on
her way, along with her nurse and
Abraham’s servant and his men. 60And
they blessed Rebekah and said to her,

“Our sister, may you increase
to thousands upon thousands;
may your offspring possess
the gates of their enemies.”

61Then Rebekah and her maids got
ready and mounted their camels and
went back with the man. So the servant
took Rebekah and left.
62Now Isaac had come from Beer Lahai Roi, for he was living in the Negev.
63He went out to the field one evening
to meditate,[b] and as he looked up, he
saw camels approaching. 64Rebekah also
looked up and saw Isaac. She got down
from her camel 65and asked the servant,
“Who is that man in the field coming
to meet us?”
“He is my master,” the servant answered. So she took her veil and covered herself.
66Then the servant told Isaac all he
had done. 67Isaac brought her into the
tent of his mother Sarah, and he married Rebekah. So she became his wife,
and he loved her; and Isaac was comforted after his mother’s death.

[a]55 Or *she* [b]63 The meaning of the Hebrew for this word is uncertain.

SHARPEN THE FOCUS

Funerals. Weddings. The stuff of everyday life. Trained and transformed by God for decades, Abraham had begun to live with the consistent, persistent faith the Holy Spirit worked into his life.

Canaan would be the home of Abraham’s descendants. God had said so, time and again over the past six decades and more. And so, of course, he and Sarah would be buried in Canaan. He bought the cave of Machpelah.

The Savior would come from Abraham's line. God had said so, time and again. And so, of course, Isaac would need a wife committed to the worship of the Lord. Abraham sent his servant to Haran to find her.

Most of us at one time or another have asked the question, "What will I be like when I grow older?" Someone has answered, "Just like you are now, only more so." The answer is probably right in most cases, because habits of thought and action build day by day. Together they form our character. Character is seldom easily changed.

What is God saying to you today about your thoughts? Your actions? Where do you need Christ's forgiveness? How can you more consistently follow your Savior? Remember, He's willing, anxious even, to help you in any way along that journey.

WEEK 3 • TUESDAY

Genesis 25:1—26:35

Abraham had learned what it meant to live by faith, and that's the way he died too (Genesis 25). It was a lesson that Isaac, like Abraham before him, would learn the hard way. Genesis 26 records the Lord's first appearance to Isaac. God assured him that the covenant promise belonged to him, just as it had belonged to his father Abraham. Despite God's grace, the events that then unfold, prove the adage, "The apple seldom falls far from the tree." If time is short, focus on Genesis 26:1–14.

The Death of Abraham

25 Abraham took[a] another
wife, whose name was
Keturah. 2She bore him Zimran, Jokshan, Medan, Midian, Ishbak and Shuah. 3Jokshan was the father of Sheba and
Dedan; the descendants of Dedan were
the Asshurites, the Letushites and the
Leummites. 4The sons of Midian were
Ephah, Epher, Hanoch, Abida and Eldaah. All these were descendants of Keturah.

5Abraham left everything he owned
to Isaac. 6But while he was still living, he
gave gifts to the sons of his concubines
and sent them away from his son Isaac
to the land of the east.

7Altogether, Abraham lived a hundred and seventy-five years. 8Then
Abraham breathed his last and died at
a good old age, an old man and full of
years; and he was gathered to his people. 9His sons Isaac and Ishmael buried
him in the cave of Machpelah near
Mamre, in the field of Ephron son of
Zohar the Hittite, 10the field Abraham
had bought from the Hittites.[b] There
Abraham was buried with his wife
Sarah. 11After Abraham's death, God
blessed his son Isaac, who then lived
near Beer Lahai Roi.

Ishmael's Sons

12This is the account of Abraham's
son Ishmael, whom Sarah's maidservant, Hagar the Egyptian, bore to
Abraham.

13These are the names of the sons of
Ishmael, listed in the order of their birth:
Nebaioth the firstborn of Ishmael, Ke-

[a]1 Or *had taken* [b]10 Or *the sons of Heth*

dar, Adbeel, Mibsam, [14]Mishma, Dumah, Massa, [15]Hadad, Tema, Jetur, Naphish and Kedemah. [16]These were the sons of Ishmael, and these are the names of the twelve tribal rulers according to their settlements and camps. [17]Altogether, Ishmael lived a hundred and thirty-seven years. He breathed his last and died, and he was gathered to his people. [18]His descendants settled in the area from Havilah to Shur, near the border of Egypt, as you go toward Asshur. And they lived in hostility toward[a] all their brothers.

Jacob and Esau

[19]This is the account of Abraham's son Isaac.

Abraham became the father of Isaac, [20]and Isaac was forty years old when he married Rebekah daughter of Bethuel the Aramean from Paddan Aram[b] and sister of Laban the Aramean.

[21]Isaac prayed to the LORD on behalf of his wife, because she was barren. The LORD answered his prayer, and his wife Rebekah became pregnant. [22]The babies jostled each other within her, and she said, "Why is this happening to me?" So she went to inquire of the LORD.

[23]The LORD said to her,

"Two nations are in your womb,
and two peoples from within you
will be separated;
one people will be stronger than the
other,
and the older will serve the
younger."

[24]When the time came for her to give birth, there were twin boys in her womb. [25]The first to come out was red, and his whole body was like a hairy garment; so they named him Esau.[c] [26]After this, his brother came out, with his hand grasping Esau's heel; so he was named Jacob.[d] Isaac was sixty years old when Rebekah gave birth to them.

[27]The boys grew up, and Esau became a skillful hunter, a man of the open country, while Jacob was a quiet man, staying among the tents. [28]Isaac, who had a taste for wild game, loved Esau, but Rebekah loved Jacob.

[29]Once when Jacob was cooking some stew, Esau came in from the open country, famished. [30]He said to Jacob, "Quick, let me have some of that red stew! I'm famished!" (That is why he was also called Edom.[e])

[31]Jacob replied, "First sell me your birthright."

[32]"Look, I am about to die," Esau said. "What good is the birthright to me?"

[33]But Jacob said, "Swear to me first." So he swore an oath to him, selling his birthright to Jacob.

[34]Then Jacob gave Esau some bread and some lentil stew. He ate and drank, and then got up and left.

So Esau despised his birthright.

Isaac and Abimelech

26 Now there was a famine in the land—besides the earlier famine of Abraham's time—and Isaac went to Abimelech king of the Philistines in Gerar. [2]The LORD appeared to Isaac and said, "Do not go down to Egypt; live in the land where I tell you to live. [3]Stay in this land for a while, and I will be with you and will bless you. For to you and your descendants I will give all these lands and will confirm the oath I swore to your father Abraham. [4]I will make your descendants as numerous as the stars in the sky and will give them all these lands, and through your offspring[f] all nations on earth will be blessed, [5]because Abraham obeyed me and kept my requirements, my commands, my decrees and my laws." [6]So Isaac stayed in Gerar.

[7]When the men of that place asked him about his wife, he said, "She is my sister," because he was afraid to say, "She is my wife." He thought, "The men of this place might kill me on account of Rebekah, because she is beautiful."

[a]18 Or *lived to the east of* [b]20 That is, Northwest Mesopotamia [c]25 *Esau* may mean *hairy;* he was also called Edom, which means *red.* [d]26 *Jacob* means *he grasps the heel* (figuratively, *he deceives*). [e]30 *Edom* means *red.* [f]4 Or *seed*

8When Isaac had been there a long time, Abimelech king of the Philistines looked down from a window and saw Isaac caressing his wife Rebekah. 9So Abimelech summoned Isaac and said, "She is really your wife! Why did you say, 'She is my sister'?"

Isaac answered him, "Because I thought I might lose my life on account of her."

10Then Abimelech said, "What is this you have done to us? One of the men might well have slept with your wife, and you would have brought guilt upon us."

11So Abimelech gave orders to all the people: "Anyone who molests this man or his wife shall surely be put to death."

12Isaac planted crops in that land and the same year reaped a hundredfold, because the LORD blessed him. 13The man became rich, and his wealth continued to grow until he became very wealthy. 14He had so many flocks and herds and servants that the Philistines envied him. 15So all the wells that his father's servants had dug in the time of his father Abraham, the Philistines stopped up, filling them with earth.

16Then Abimelech said to Isaac, "Move away from us; you have become too powerful for us."

17So Isaac moved away from there and encamped in the Valley of Gerar and settled there. 18Isaac reopened the wells that had been dug in the time of his father Abraham, which the Philistines had stopped up after Abraham died, and he gave them the same names his father had given them.

19Isaac's servants dug in the valley and discovered a well of fresh water there. 20But the herdsmen of Gerar quarreled with Isaac's herdsmen and said, "The water is ours!" So he named the well Esek,[a] because they disputed with him. 21Then they dug another well, but they quarreled over that one also; so he named it Sitnah.[b] 22He moved on from there and dug another well, and no one quarreled over it. He named it Rehoboth,[c] saying, "Now the LORD has given us room and we will flourish in the land."

23From there he went up to Beersheba. 24That night the LORD appeared to him and said, "I am the God of your father Abraham. Do not be afraid, for I am with you; I will bless you and will increase the number of your descendants for the sake of my servant Abraham."

25Isaac built an altar there and called on the name of the LORD. There he pitched his tent, and there his servants dug a well.

26Meanwhile, Abimelech had come to him from Gerar, with Ahuzzath his personal adviser and Phicol the commander of his forces. 27Isaac asked them, "Why have you come to me, since you were hostile to me and sent me away?"

28They answered, "We saw clearly that the LORD was with you; so we said, 'There ought to be a sworn agreement between us'—between us and you. Let us make a treaty with you 29that you will do us no harm, just as we did not molest you but always treated you well and sent you away in peace. And now you are blessed by the LORD."

30Isaac then made a feast for them, and they ate and drank. 31Early the next morning the men swore an oath to each other. Then Isaac sent them on their way, and they left him in peace.

32That day Isaac's servants came and told him about the well they had dug. They said, "We've found water!" 33He called it Shibah,[d] and to this day the name of the town has been Beersheba.[e]

34When Esau was forty years old, he married Judith daughter of Beeri the Hittite, and also Basemath daughter of Elon the Hittite. 35They were a source of grief to Isaac and Rebekah.

[a]20 *Esek* means *dispute*. [b]21 *Sitnah* means *opposition*. [c]22 *Rehoboth* means *room*. [d]33 *Shibah* can mean *oath* or *seven*. [e]33 *Beersheba* can mean *well of the oath* or *well of seven*.

SHARPEN THE FOCUS

God had established His covenant with Abraham. He now passes His promises on to Isaac. Reread the words of that covenant in Genesis 26:2–4. As you read, underline the "*I will*" phrases the Lord includes. Then note the culmination of the promise in Genesis 26:4, "Through your offspring [or seed] all nations on earth will be blessed."

Some have written about the "thin, blue line"—the police and other law enforcement officers—that keeps society from chaos and anarchy. Throughout the Old Testament Scriptures, we see what we might call a "thin, red line"—the continuing promise of God that He would send a Savior. That promise and its fulfillment in the cross of our Lord Jesus have kept the fires of God's judgment on human sin from falling on our planet and destroying each sinner—you and me too. That promise, now fulfilled, gives peace and meaning to our daily lives and hope for our eternity.

The Lord was faithful when His people were forgetful. God was faithful when His people were foolish. God was faithful when His people were faithless. And our Lord remains faithful even now.

WEEK 3 • WEDNESDAY

Genesis 27:1—28:22

GET THE BIG PICTURE

We got our first glimpse of Isaac's sons, Jacob and Esau, back in Genesis 25. There, they posed for a not-so-pious portrait. Now we meet up with them again, and find Jacob fully living up to his name—the deceitful one. Rebekah joins Jacob in his scheming (Genesis 27). Esau resents their plot so much, he threatens to murder Jacob. And so, in Genesis 28, we watch as Jacob starts out on a 500-mile journey to seek refuge with his uncle, Rebekah's brother, in Padan Aram—where Abraham had once lived. If time is short, focus on Genesis 28:1–9.

Jacob Gets Isaac's Blessing

27 When Isaac was old and his eyes were so weak that he could no longer see, he called for Esau his older son and said to him, "My son."

"Here I am," he answered.

[2]Isaac said, "I am now an old man and don't know the day of my death. [3]Now then, get your weapons—your quiver and bow—and go out to the open country to hunt some wild game for me. [4]Prepare me the kind of tasty food I like and bring it to me to eat, so that I may give you my blessing before I die."

[5]Now Rebekah was listening as Isaac spoke to his son Esau. When Esau left for the open country to hunt game and bring it back, [6]Rebekah said to her son Jacob, "Look, I overheard your father say to your brother Esau, [7]'Bring me some game and prepare me some tasty food to eat, so that I may give you my blessing in the presence of the LORD before I die.' [8]Now, my son, listen carefully and do what I tell you: [9]Go out to the flock and bring me two choice young goats, so I can prepare some tasty food for your father, just the way he likes it. [10]Then take it to your father to eat, so

that he may give you his blessing before
he dies."

11 Jacob said to Rebekah his mother,
"But my brother Esau is a hairy man,
and I'm a man with smooth skin. 12 What
if my father touches me? I would appear
to be tricking him and would bring
down a curse on myself rather than a
blessing."

13 His mother said to him, "My son, let
the curse fall on me. Just do what I say;
go and get them for me."

14 So he went and got them and
brought them to his mother, and she
prepared some tasty food, just the way
his father liked it. 15 Then Rebekah took
the best clothes of Esau her older son,
which she had in the house, and put
them on her younger son Jacob. 16 She
also covered his hands and the smooth
part of his neck with the goatskins.
17 Then she handed to her son Jacob the
tasty food and the bread she had made.

18 He went to his father and said, "My
father."

"Yes, my son," he answered. "Who
is it?"

19 Jacob said to his father, "I am Esau
your firstborn. I have done as you told
me. Please sit up and eat some of my
game so that you may give me your
blessing."

20 Isaac asked his son, "How did you
find it so quickly, my son?"

"The LORD your God gave me success," he replied.

21 Then Isaac said to Jacob, "Come near
so I can touch you, my son, to know
whether you really are my son Esau or
not."

22 Jacob went close to his father Isaac,
who touched him and said, "The voice
is the voice of Jacob, but the hands are
the hands of Esau." 23 He did not recognize him, for his hands were hairy like
those of his brother Esau; so he blessed
him. 24 "Are you really my son Esau?" he
asked.

"I am," he replied.

25 Then he said, "My son, bring me
some of your game to eat, so that I may
give you my blessing."

Jacob brought it to him and he ate;
and he brought some wine and he
drank. 26 Then his father Isaac said
to him, "Come here, my son, and kiss
me."

27 So he went to him and kissed him.
When Isaac caught the smell of his
clothes, he blessed him and said,

"Ah, the smell of my son
  is like the smell of a field
  that the LORD has blessed.
28 May God give you of heaven's dew
  and of earth's richness—
  an abundance of grain and new
    wine.
29 May nations serve you
  and peoples bow down to you.
Be lord over your brothers,
  and may the sons of your mother
    bow down to you.
May those who curse you be cursed
  and those who bless you be
    blessed."

30 After Isaac finished blessing him and
Jacob had scarcely left his father's presence, his brother Esau came in from
hunting. 31 He too prepared some tasty
food and brought it to his father. Then
he said to him, "My father, sit up and eat
some of my game, so that you may give
me your blessing."

32 His father Isaac asked him, "Who are
you?"

"I am your son," he answered, "your
firstborn, Esau."

33 Isaac trembled violently and said,
"Who was it, then, that hunted game
and brought it to me? I ate it just before
you came and I blessed him—and indeed he will be blessed!"

34 When Esau heard his father's
words, he burst out with a loud and bitter cry and said to his father, "Bless me—
me too, my father!"

35 But he said, "Your brother came deceitfully and took your blessing."

36 Esau said, "Isn't he rightly named
Jacob[a]? He has deceived me these two
times: He took my birthright, and now
he's taken my blessing!" Then he asked,

[a] *36 Jacob* means *he grasps the heel* (figuratively, *he deceives*).

"Haven't you reserved any blessing
for me?"
37Isaac answered Esau, "I have made
him lord over you and have made all his
relatives his servants, and I have sustained him with grain and new wine. So
what can I possibly do for you, my son?"
38Esau said to his father, "Do you have
only one blessing, my father? Bless me
too, my father!" Then Esau wept aloud.
39His father Isaac answered him,

"Your dwelling will be
away from the earth's richness,
away from the dew of heaven
above.
40You will live by the sword
and you will serve your brother.
But when you grow restless,
you will throw his yoke
from off your neck."

Jacob Flees to Laban

41Esau held a grudge against Jacob because of the blessing his father had
given him. He said to himself, "The days
of mourning for my father are near;
then I will kill my brother Jacob."
42When Rebekah was told what her
older son Esau had said, she sent for her
younger son Jacob and said to him,
"Your brother Esau is consoling himself
with the thought of killing you. 43Now
then, my son, do what I say: Flee at once
to my brother Laban in Haran. 44Stay
with him for a while until your
brother's fury subsides. 45When your
brother is no longer angry with you and
forgets what you did to him, I'll send
word for you to come back from there.
Why should I lose both of you in one
day?"
46Then Rebekah said to Isaac, "I'm dis-
gusted with living because of these Hittite women. If Jacob takes a wife from
among the women of this land, from
Hittite women like these, my life will
not be worth living."

28 So Isaac called for Jacob
and blessed[a] him and
commanded him: "Do not marry a Canaanite woman. 2Go at once to Paddan
Aram,[b] to the house of your mother's
father Bethuel. Take a wife for yourself
there, from among the daughters of Laban, your mother's brother. 3May God
Almighty[c] bless you and make you fruitful and increase your numbers until you
become a community of peoples. 4May
he give you and your descendants the
blessing given to Abraham, so that you
may take possession of the land where
you now live as an alien, the land God
gave to Abraham." 5Then Isaac sent Jacob on his way, and he went to Paddan
Aram, to Laban son of Bethuel the Aramean, the brother of Rebekah, who was
the mother of Jacob and Esau.
6Now Esau learned that Isaac had
blessed Jacob and had sent him to Paddan Aram to take a wife from there, and
that when he blessed him he commanded him, "Do not marry a Canaanite woman," 7and that Jacob had obeyed
his father and mother and had gone to
Paddan Aram. 8Esau then realized how
displeasing the Canaanite women were
to his father Isaac; 9so he went to Ishmael and married Mahalath, the sister of
Nebaioth and daughter of Ishmael son
of Abraham, in addition to the wives he
already had.

Jacob's Dream at Bethel

10Jacob left Beersheba and set out for
Haran. 11When he reached a certain
place, he stopped for the night because
the sun had set. Taking one of the stones
there, he put it under his head and lay
down to sleep. 12He had a dream in
which he saw a stairway[d] resting on the
earth, with its top reaching to heaven,
and the angels of God were ascending
and descending on it. 13There above it[e]
stood the LORD, and he said: "I am the
LORD, the God of your father Abraham
and the God of Isaac. I will give you and
your descendants the land on which
you are lying. 14Your descendants will be
like the dust of the earth, and you will
spread out to the west and to the east,

[a]1 Or *greeted* [b]2 That is, Northwest
Mesopotamia; also in verses 5, 6 and 7
[c]3 Hebrew *El-Shaddai* [d]12 Or *ladder*
[e]13 Or *There beside him*

to the north and to the south. All peoples on earth will be blessed through
you and your offspring. 15I am with you
and will watch over you wherever you
go, and I will bring you back to this land.
I will not leave you until I have done
what I have promised you."
16When Jacob awoke from his sleep,
he thought, "Surely the LORD is in
this place, and I was not aware of it."
17He was afraid and said, "How awesome is this place! This is none other
than the house of God; this is the gate
of heaven."
18Early the next morning Jacob took
the stone he had placed under his head
and set it up as a pillar and poured oil
on top of it. 19He called that place
Bethel,[a] though the city used to be called
Luz.
20Then Jacob made a vow, saying, "If
God will be with me and will watch
over me on this journey I am taking and
will give me food to eat and clothes to
wear 21so that I return safely to my
father's house, then the LORD[b] will be
my God 22and[c] this stone that I have set
up as a pillar will be God's house, and
of all that you give me I will give you a
tenth."

[a]*19 Bethel* means *house of God.* [b]*20,21* Or *Since God . . . father's house, the LORD* [c]*21,22* Or *house, and the LORD will be my God, 22then*

SHARPEN THE FOCUS

Jacob, "the deceiver," faced a journey that on foot must have taken nearly a month. Robbers. Wild animals. Storms. Desert heat. Who knew what lay ahead? How comforting then, Jacob must have found his dream.

In that dream, God's angels ascended and descended on a ladder or staircase. At the top stood the Lord Himself in majesty and power. The angels carried Jacob's prayers to heaven and brought God's gracious answers to earth.

Looking at the scene through New Testament eyes, we see our Lord Jesus Himself as the staircase, the ladder, the only bridge between a holy God and His sinful people. (See John 1:51.) God would not only protect Jacob's physical life, He would—through the coming Savior—forgive Jacob's sins.

What do you need right now? Forgiveness? Peace? Courage? Protection? Confidence? The humility to ask for pardon from a loved one you have hurt? Ask. The same grace that met Jacob on the road is available to you even now. Your Lord will meet your need, even as He met Jacob's.

WEEK 3 • THURSDAY

Genesis 29:1—30:43

GET THE BIG PICTURE

After receiving a warm welcome, Jacob makes himself useful around Uncle Laban's flocks and herds. Jacob falls in love with Laban's daughter Rachel. Tricked by Laban, Jacob ends up marrying both Rachel and her sister, Leah. Not only does God bless Jacob with 11 sons and one daughter, but Jacob also finds himself exceedingly prosperous in livestock and servants. If time is short, focus on Genesis 29:1–29.

Jacob Arrives in Paddan Aram

29 Then Jacob continued on
his journey and came to
the land of the eastern peoples. [2]There
he saw a well in the field, with three
flocks of sheep lying near it because the
flocks were watered from that well. The
stone over the mouth of the well was
large. [3]When all the flocks were gathered there, the shepherds would roll the
stone away from the well's mouth and
water the sheep. Then they would return the stone to its place over the
mouth of the well.

[4]Jacob asked the shepherds, "My
brothers, where are you from?"

"We're from Haran," they replied.

[5]He said to them, "Do you know Laban, Nahor's grandson?"

"Yes, we know him," they answered.

[6]Then Jacob asked them, "Is he well?"

"Yes, he is," they said, "and here
comes his daughter Rachel with the
sheep."

[7]"Look," he said, "the sun is still high;
it is not time for the flocks to be gathered. Water the sheep and take them
back to pasture."

[8]"We can't," they replied, "until all
the flocks are gathered and the stone
has been rolled away from the mouth
of the well. Then we will water the
sheep."

[9]While he was still talking with them,
Rachel came with her father's sheep, for
she was a shepherdess. [10]When Jacob
saw Rachel daughter of Laban, his
mother's brother, and Laban's sheep, he
went over and rolled the stone away
from the mouth of the well and watered
his uncle's sheep. [11]Then Jacob kissed
Rachel and began to weep aloud. [12]He
had told Rachel that he was a relative of
her father and a son of Rebekah. So she
ran and told her father.

[13]As soon as Laban heard the news
about Jacob, his sister's son, he hurried
to meet him. He embraced him and
kissed him and brought him to his
home, and there Jacob told him all these
things. [14]Then Laban said to him, "You
are my own flesh and blood."

Jacob Marries Leah and Rachel

After Jacob had stayed with him for a
whole month, [15]Laban said to him, "Just
because you are a relative of mine,
should you work for me for nothing?
Tell me what your wages should be."

[16]Now Laban had two daughters; the
name of the older was Leah, and the
name of the younger was Rachel. [17]Leah
had weak[a] eyes, but Rachel was lovely
in form, and beautiful. [18]Jacob was in
love with Rachel and said, "I'll work for
you seven years in return for your
younger daughter Rachel."

[19]Laban said, "It's better that I give her
to you than to some other man. Stay
here with me." [20]So Jacob served seven
years to get Rachel, but they seemed like
only a few days to him because of his
love for her.

[21]Then Jacob said to Laban, "Give me
my wife. My time is completed, and I
want to lie with her."

[22]So Laban brought together all the
people of the place and gave a feast.
[23]But when evening came, he took his
daughter Leah and gave her to Jacob,
and Jacob lay with her. [24]And Laban
gave his servant girl Zilpah to his
daughter as her maidservant.

[25]When morning came, there was
Leah! So Jacob said to Laban, "What is
this you have done to me? I served you
for Rachel, didn't I? Why have you deceived me?"

[26]Laban replied, "It is not our custom
here to give the younger daughter in
marriage before the older one. [27]Finish
this daughter's bridal week; then we
will give you the younger one also, in
return for another seven years of work."

[28]And Jacob did so. He finished the
week with Leah, and then Laban gave
him his daughter Rachel to be his
wife. [29]Laban gave his servant girl Bilhah to his daughter Rachel as her maidservant. [30]Jacob lay with Rachel also,
and he loved Rachel more than Leah.
And he worked for Laban another
seven years.

[a]17 Or *delicate*

Jacob's Children

31 When the LORD saw that Leah was
not loved, he opened her womb, but Rachel was barren. 32 Leah became pregnant and gave birth to a son. She named
him Reuben,[a] for she said, "It is because
the LORD has seen my misery. Surely my
husband will love me now."
33 She conceived again, and when she
gave birth to a son she said, "Because the
LORD heard that I am not loved, he gave
me this one too." So she named him
Simeon.[b]
34 Again she conceived, and when she
gave birth to a son she said, "Now at last
my husband will become attached to
me, because I have borne him three
sons." So he was named Levi.[c]
35 She conceived again, and when she
gave birth to a son she said, "This time I
will praise the LORD." So she named
him Judah.[d] Then she stopped having
children.

30 When Rachel saw that she
was not bearing Jacob any
children, she became jealous of her sister. So she said to Jacob, "Give me children, or I'll die!"
2 Jacob became angry with her and
said, "Am I in the place of God, who has
kept you from having children?"
3 Then she said, "Here is Bilhah, my
maidservant. Sleep with her so that she
can bear children for me and that
through her I too can build a family."
4 So she gave him her servant Bilhah
as a wife. Jacob slept with her, 5 and she
became pregnant and bore him a son.
6 Then Rachel said, "God has vindicated
me; he has listened to my plea and giv-
en me a son." Because of this she named
him Dan.[e]
7 Rachel's servant Bilhah conceived
again and bore Jacob a second son.
8 Then Rachel said, "I have had a great
struggle with my sister, and I have
won." So she named him Naphtali.[f]
9 When Leah saw that she had
stopped having children, she took her
maidservant Zilpah and gave her to
Jacob as a wife. 10 Leah's servant Zilpah bore Jacob a son. 11 Then Leah said,
"What good fortune!"[g] So she named
him Gad.[h]
12 Leah's servant Zilpah bore Jacob a
second son. 13 Then Leah said, "How
happy I am! The women will call me
happy." So she named him Asher.[i]
14 During wheat harvest, Reuben went
out into the fields and found some
mandrake plants, which he brought to
his mother Leah. Rachel said to Leah,
"Please give me some of your son's
mandrakes."
15 But she said to her, "Wasn't it
enough that you took away my husband? Will you take my son's mandrakes too?"
"Very well," Rachel said, "he can sleep
with you tonight in return for your
son's mandrakes."
16 So when Jacob came in from the
fields that evening, Leah went out to
meet him. "You must sleep with me,"
she said. "I have hired you with my
son's mandrakes." So he slept with her
that night.
17 God listened to Leah, and she became pregnant and bore Jacob a fifth
son. 18 Then Leah said, "God has rewarded me for giving my maidservant to my
husband." So she named him Issachar.[j]
19 Leah conceived again and bore Jacob a sixth son. 20 Then Leah said, "God
has presented me with a precious gift.
This time my husband will treat me
with honor, because I have borne him
six sons." So she named him Zebulun.[k]
21 Some time later she gave birth to a
daughter and named her Dinah.
22 Then God remembered Rachel; he
listened to her and opened her womb.
23 She became pregnant and gave birth
to a son and said, "God has taken away

[a] 32 *Reuben* sounds like the Hebrew for *he has seen my misery*; the name means *see, a son*.
[b] 33 *Simeon* probably means *one who hears*.
[c] 34 *Levi* sounds like and may be derived from the Hebrew for *attached*. [d] 35 *Judah* sounds like and may be derived from the Hebrew for *praise*.
[e] 6 *Dan* here means *he has vindicated*. [f] 8 *Naphtali* means *my struggle*. [g] 11 Or *"A troop is coming!"*
[h] 11 *Gad* can mean *good fortune* or *a troop*.
[i] 13 *Asher* means *happy*. [j] 18 *Issachar* sounds like the Hebrew for *reward*. [k] 20 *Zebulun* probably means *honor*.

my disgrace." [24]She named him Joseph,[a] and said, "May the LORD add to me another son."

Jacob's Flocks Increase

[25]After Rachel gave birth to Joseph, Jacob said to Laban, "Send me on my way so I can go back to my own homeland. [26]Give me my wives and children, for whom I have served you, and I will be on my way. You know how much work I've done for you."

[27]But Laban said to him, "If I have found favor in your eyes, please stay. I have learned by divination that[b] the LORD has blessed me because of you." [28]He added, "Name your wages, and I will pay them."

[29]Jacob said to him, "You know how I have worked for you and how your livestock has fared under my care. [30]The little you had before I came has increased greatly, and the LORD has blessed you wherever I have been. But now, when may I do something for my own household?"

[31]"What shall I give you?" he asked.

"Don't give me anything," Jacob replied. "But if you will do this one thing for me, I will go on tending your flocks and watching over them: [32]Let me go through all your flocks today and remove from them every speckled or spotted sheep, every dark-colored lamb and every spotted or speckled goat. They will be my wages. [33]And my honesty will testify for me in the future, whenever you check on the wages you have paid me. Any goat in my possession that is not speckled or spotted, or any lamb that is not dark-colored, will be considered stolen."

[34]"Agreed," said Laban. "Let it be as you have said." [35]That same day he removed all the male goats that were streaked or spotted, and all the speckled or spotted female goats (all that had white on them) and all the dark-colored lambs, and he placed them in the care of his sons. [36]Then he put a three-day journey between himself and Jacob, while Jacob continued to tend the rest of Laban's flocks.

[37]Jacob, however, took fresh-cut branches from poplar, almond and plane trees and made white stripes on them by peeling the bark and exposing the white inner wood of the branches. [38]Then he placed the peeled branches in all the watering troughs, so that they would be directly in front of the flocks when they came to drink. When the flocks were in heat and came to drink, [39]they mated in front of the branches. And they bore young that were streaked or speckled or spotted. [40]Jacob set apart the young of the flock by themselves, but made the rest face the streaked and dark-colored animals that belonged to Laban. Thus he made separate flocks for himself and did not put them with Laban's animals. [41]Whenever the stronger females were in heat, Jacob would place the branches in the troughs in front of the animals so they would mate near the branches, [42]but if the animals were weak, he would not place them there. So the weak animals went to Laban and the strong ones to Jacob. [43]In this way the man grew exceedingly prosperous and came to own large flocks, and maidservants and menservants, and camels and donkeys.

[a]24 *Joseph* means *may he add.* [b]27 Or possibly *have become rich and*

SHARPEN THE FOCUS

It's a truth that's hard to face—sometimes the faults we hate most in others are the very sins we ourselves most often commit! Note Jacob's angry words to Laban the morning after Jacob woke up to find himself married to Leah instead of Rachel: "Why have you deceived me?" (Genesis 29:25). The pot accuses the kettle!

Take a few moments to examine your own heart right now. Think about someone whose actions or attitudes irritate you. Ask yourself how often you act or think in the very ways you hate. Then ask the Lord's forgiveness, power, and patience as you deal with your sins and the sins of others.

WEEK 3 • FRIDAY

Genesis 31:1—33:20

Concerned about the growing jealousy of Laban and warned by God of the dangers, Jacob takes his family and flees. The holy angels, sent by God Himself, guard the way back to Canaan, back to Jacob's home and family. For 20 years, the Lord has been teaching Jacob what it means to live by faith. In Esau's peaceful greeting, we see evidence that God has been at work in his heart as well. If time is short, focus on Genesis 32:24–31.

Jacob Flees From Laban

31 Jacob heard that Laban's sons
were saying, "Jacob has taken
everything our father owned and has
gained all this wealth from what belonged to our father." [2]And Jacob noticed that Laban's attitude toward him
was not what it had been.
[3]Then the LORD said to Jacob, "Go
back to the land of your fathers and to
your relatives, and I will be with you."
[4]So Jacob sent word to Rachel and
Leah to come out to the fields where his
flocks were. [5]He said to them, "I see that
your father's attitude toward me is not
what it was before, but the God of my
father has been with me. [6]You know that
I've worked for your father with all my
strength, [7]yet your father has cheated
me by changing my wages ten times.
However, God has not allowed him to
harm me. [8]If he said, 'The speckled ones
will be your wages,' then all the flocks
gave birth to speckled young; and if he
said, 'The streaked ones will be your
wages,' then all the flocks bore streaked
young. [9]So God has taken away your
father's livestock and has given them
to me.
[10]"In breeding season I once had a
dream in which I looked up and saw
that the male goats mating with the
flock were streaked, speckled or spotted. [11]The angel of God said to me in the
dream, 'Jacob.' I answered, 'Here I am.'
[12]And he said, 'Look up and see that all
the male goats mating with the flock are
streaked, speckled or spotted, for I have
seen all that Laban has been doing to
you. [13]I am the God of Bethel, where you
anointed a pillar and where you made
a vow to me. Now leave this land at
once and go back to your native land.' "
[14]Then Rachel and Leah replied, "Do
we still have any share in the inheritance of our father's estate? [15]Does he
not regard us as foreigners? Not only
has he sold us, but he has used up what
was paid for us. [16]Surely all the wealth
that God took away from our father belongs to us and our children. So do
whatever God has told you."
[17]Then Jacob put his children and his
wives on camels, [18]and he drove all his
livestock ahead of him, along with all
the goods he had accumulated in Paddan Aram,[a] to go to his father Isaac in
the land of Canaan.

[a]18 That is, Northwest Mesopotamia

19When Laban had gone to shear his sheep, Rachel stole her father's household gods. 20Moreover, Jacob deceived Laban the Aramean by not telling him he was running away. 21So he fled with all he had, and crossing the River,[a] he headed for the hill country of Gilead.

Laban Pursues Jacob

22On the third day Laban was told that Jacob had fled. 23Taking his relatives with him, he pursued Jacob for seven days and caught up with him in the hill country of Gilead. 24Then God came to Laban the Aramean in a dream at night and said to him, "Be careful not to say anything to Jacob, either good or bad."

25Jacob had pitched his tent in the hill country of Gilead when Laban overtook him, and Laban and his relatives camped there too. 26Then Laban said to Jacob, "What have you done? You've deceived me, and you've carried off my daughters like captives in war. 27Why did you run off secretly and deceive me? Why didn't you tell me, so I could send you away with joy and singing to the music of tambourines and harps? 28You didn't even let me kiss my grandchildren and my daughters good-by. You have done a foolish thing. 29I have the power to harm you; but last night the God of your father said to me, 'Be careful not to say anything to Jacob, either good or bad.' 30Now you have gone off because you longed to return to your father's house. But why did you steal my gods?"

31Jacob answered Laban, "I was afraid, because I thought you would take your daughters away from me by force. 32But if you find anyone who has your gods, he shall not live. In the presence of our relatives, see for yourself whether there is anything of yours here with me; and if so, take it." Now Jacob did not know that Rachel had stolen the gods.

33So Laban went into Jacob's tent and into Leah's tent and into the tent of the two maidservants, but he found nothing. After he came out of Leah's tent, he entered Rachel's tent. 34Now Rachel had taken the household gods and put them inside her camel's saddle and was sitting on them. Laban searched through everything in the tent but found nothing.

35Rachel said to her father, "Don't be angry, my lord, that I cannot stand up in your presence; I'm having my period." So he searched but could not find the household gods.

36Jacob was angry and took Laban to task. "What is my crime?" he asked Laban. "What sin have I committed that you hunt me down? 37Now that you have searched through all my goods, what have you found that belongs to your household? Put it here in front of your relatives and mine, and let them judge between the two of us.

38"I have been with you for twenty years now. Your sheep and goats have not miscarried, nor have I eaten rams from your flocks. 39I did not bring you animals torn by wild beasts; I bore the loss myself. And you demanded payment from me for whatever was stolen by day or night. 40This was my situation: The heat consumed me in the daytime and the cold at night, and sleep fled from my eyes. 41It was like this for the twenty years I was in your household. I worked for you fourteen years for your two daughters and six years for your flocks, and you changed my wages ten times. 42If the God of my father, the God of Abraham and the Fear of Isaac, had not been with me, you would surely have sent me away empty-handed. But God has seen my hardship and the toil of my hands, and last night he rebuked you."

43Laban answered Jacob, "The women are my daughters, the children are my children, and the flocks are my flocks. All you see is mine. Yet what can I do today about these daughters of mine, or about the children they have borne? 44Come now, let's make a covenant, you and I, and let it serve as a witness between us."

45So Jacob took a stone and set it up as a pillar. 46He said to his relatives,

[a]*21* That is, the Euphrates

"Gather some stones." So they took
stones and piled them in a heap, and
they ate there by the heap. 47 Laban
called it Jegar Sahadutha,[a] and Jacob
called it Galeed.[b]
48 Laban said, "This heap is a witness
between you and me today." That is
why it was called Galeed. 49 It was also
called Mizpah,[c] because he said, "May
the LORD keep watch between you and
me when we are away from each other.
50 If you mistreat my daughters or if you
take any wives besides my daughters,
even though no one is with us, remember that God is a witness between you
and me."
51 Laban also said to Jacob, "Here is this
heap, and here is this pillar I have set up
between you and me. 52 This heap is a
witness, and this pillar is a witness, that
I will not go past this heap to your side
to harm you and that you will not go
past this heap and pillar to my side to
harm me. 53 May the God of Abraham
and the God of Nahor, the God of their
father, judge between us."
So Jacob took an oath in the name of
the Fear of his father Isaac. 54 He offered
a sacrifice there in the hill country and
invited his relatives to a meal. After they
had eaten, they spent the night there.
55 Early the next morning Laban kissed
his grandchildren and his daughters
and blessed them. Then he left and returned home.

Jacob Prepares to Meet Esau

32 Jacob also went on his
way, and the angels of
God met him. 2 When Jacob saw them,
he said, "This is the camp of God!" So he
named that place Mahanaim.[d]
3 Jacob sent messengers ahead of him
to his brother Esau in the land of Seir,
the country of Edom. 4 He instructed
them: "This is what you are to say to my
master Esau: 'Your servant Jacob says, I
have been staying with Laban and have
remained there till now. 5 I have cattle
and donkeys, sheep and goats, menservants and maidservants. Now I am
sending this message to my lord, that I
may find favor in your eyes.' "
6 When the messengers returned to Jacob, they said, "We went to your brother
Esau, and now he is coming to meet
you, and four hundred men are with
him."
7 In great fear and distress Jacob divided the people who were with him
into two groups,[e] and the flocks and
herds and camels as well. 8 He thought,
"If Esau comes and attacks one group,[f]
the group[f] that is left may escape."
9 Then Jacob prayed, "O God of my father Abraham, God of my father Isaac,
O LORD, who said to me, 'Go back to
your country and your relatives, and I
will make you prosper,' 10 I am unworthy
of all the kindness and faithfulness you
have shown your servant. I had only my
staff when I crossed this Jordan, but
now I have become two groups. 11 Save
me, I pray, from the hand of my brother
Esau, for I am afraid he will come and
attack me, and also the mothers with
their children. 12 But you have said, 'I will
surely make you prosper and will make
your descendants like the sand of the
sea, which cannot be counted.' "
13 He spent the night there, and from
what he had with him he selected a gift
for his brother Esau: 14 two hundred female goats and twenty male goats, two
hundred ewes and twenty rams, 15 thirty female camels with their young, forty cows and ten bulls, and twenty
female donkeys and ten male donkeys.
16 He put them in the care of his servants,
each herd by itself, and said to his servants, "Go ahead of me, and keep some
space between the herds."
17 He instructed the one in the lead:
"When my brother Esau meets you and
asks, 'To whom do you belong, and
where are you going, and who owns all
these animals in front of you?' 18 then
you are to say, 'They belong to your
servant Jacob. They are a gift sent to
my lord Esau, and he is coming behind
us.' "

[a]47 The Aramaic *Jegar Sahadutha* means *witness heap.* [b]47 The Hebrew *Galeed* means *witness heap.* [c]49 *Mizpah* means *watchtower.*
[d]2 *Mahanaim* means *two camps.* [e]7 Or *camps;* also in verse 10 [f]8 Or *camp*

19He also instructed the second, the third and all the others who followed the herds: "You are to say the same thing to Esau when you meet him. 20And be sure to say, 'Your servant Jacob is coming behind us.' " For he thought, "I will pacify him with these gifts I am sending on ahead; later, when I see him, perhaps he will receive me." 21So Jacob's gifts went on ahead of him, but he himself spent the night in the camp.

Jacob Wrestles With God

22That night Jacob got up and took his two wives, his two maidservants and his eleven sons and crossed the ford of the Jabbok. 23After he had sent them across the stream, he sent over all his possessions. 24So Jacob was left alone, and a man wrestled with him till daybreak. 25When the man saw that he could not overpower him, he touched the socket of Jacob's hip so that his hip was wrenched as he wrestled with the man. 26Then the man said, "Let me go, for it is daybreak."

But Jacob replied, "I will not let you go unless you bless me."

27The man asked him, "What is your name?"

"Jacob," he answered.

28Then the man said, "Your name will no longer be Jacob, but Israel,[a] because you have struggled with God and with men and have overcome."

29Jacob said, "Please tell me your name."

But he replied, "Why do you ask my name?" Then he blessed him there.

30So Jacob called the place Peniel,[b] saying, "It is because I saw God face to face, and yet my life was spared."

31The sun rose above him as he passed Peniel,[c] and he was limping because of his hip. 32Therefore to this day the Israelites do not eat the tendon attached to the socket of the hip, because the socket of Jacob's hip was touched near the tendon.

Jacob Meets Esau

33 Jacob looked up and there was Esau, coming with his four hundred men; so he divided the children among Leah, Rachel and the two maidservants. 2He put the maidservants and their children in front, Leah and her children next, and Rachel and Joseph in the rear. 3He himself went on ahead and bowed down to the ground seven times as he approached his brother.

4But Esau ran to meet Jacob and embraced him; he threw his arms around his neck and kissed him. And they wept. 5Then Esau looked up and saw the women and children. "Who are these with you?" he asked.

Jacob answered, "They are the children God has graciously given your servant."

6Then the maidservants and their children approached and bowed down. 7Next, Leah and her children came and bowed down. Last of all came Joseph and Rachel, and they too bowed down.

8Esau asked, "What do you mean by all these droves I met?"

"To find favor in your eyes, my lord," he said.

9But Esau said, "I already have plenty, my brother. Keep what you have for yourself."

10"No, please!" said Jacob. "If I have found favor in your eyes, accept this gift from me. For to see your face is like seeing the face of God, now that you have received me favorably. 11Please accept the present that was brought to you, for God has been gracious to me and I have all I need." And because Jacob insisted, Esau accepted it.

12Then Esau said, "Let us be on our way; I'll accompany you."

13But Jacob said to him, "My lord knows that the children are tender and that I must care for the ewes and cows that are nursing their young. If they are driven hard just one day, all the animals will die. 14So let my lord go on ahead of his servant, while I move along slowly at the pace of the droves before me and

[a]28 *Israel* means *he struggles with God.* [b]30 *Peniel* means *face of God.* [c]31 Hebrew *Penuel,* a variant of *Peniel*

that of the children, until I come to my
lord in Seir."
15Esau said, "Then let me leave some
of my men with you."
"But why do that?" Jacob asked. "Just
let me find favor in the eyes of my lord."
16So that day Esau started on his way
back to Seir. 17Jacob, however, went to
Succoth, where he built a place for himself and made shelters for his livestock.
That is why the place is called Succoth.[a]
18After Jacob came from Paddan
Aram,[b] he arrived safely at the[c] city of
Shechem in Canaan and camped with-
in sight of the city. 19For a hundred
pieces of silver,[d] he bought from the sons
of Hamor, the father of Shechem, the
plot of ground where he pitched his
tent. 20There he set up an altar and called
it El Elohe Israel.[e]

[a]*17 Succoth* means *shelters.* [b]18 That is, Northwest Mesopotamia [c]18 Or *arrived at Shalem, a* [d]19 Hebrew *hundred kesitahs*; a kesitah was a unit of money of unknown weight and value. [e]*20 El Elohe Israel* can mean *God, the God of Israel* or *mighty is the God of Israel.*

SHARPEN THE FOCUS

Throughout the Scriptures, we find the Lord telling His people about Himself as He reveals His names to them. Remember, for instance, El Shaddai? (Genesis 17:1.) Genesis 31:42 includes another divine name—"The Fear of Isaac."

What does the Bible mean when it commands us to fear God? Certainly not that we cower before Him. Certainly not that we cringe in terror. Certainly not that we expect Him to zap us at any moment for our wrongdoing.

Our Lord has revealed Himself as our compassionate Savior, our kind Father, our ever-present Helper. We see His limitless love for us clearly in Christ's gory cross and His open Easter tomb.

So then what about this fear of God the Scriptures command? This kind of fear involves reverence. It involves respect. It involves awe. But perhaps, most of all it includes an unwillingness of heart and mind to disobey the Lord, to do anything that would dishonor the one who has loved us enough to die for us.

Do you fear God in this sense? If you need more reverence, a heart filled with greater awe and honor for Him, ask Him to work it in you. He's promised to do that! (See Philippians 2:13.)

WEEK 3 • SATURDAY

Genesis 34:1—35:29

GET THE BIG PICTURE

When two of Jacob's older sons, Simeon and Levi, learn that their sister has been raped, they set up a scheme to get even. After they carry it out, Jacob doesn't so much as even rebuke them—for murder! Instead, he worries about his personal safety. At God's command, Jacob then moves his household to Bethel and worships there. In grace, God repeats His covenant promises and as a sign of that covenant, changes Jacob's name. If time is short, focus on Genesis 34:1–15.

Dinah and the Shechemites

34 Now Dinah, the daughter Leah had borne to Jacob, went out to visit the women of the land. 2 When Shechem son of Hamor the Hivite, the ruler of that area, saw her, he took her and violated her. 3 His heart was drawn to Dinah daughter of Jacob, and he loved the girl and spoke tenderly to her. 4 And Shechem said to his father Hamor, "Get me this girl as my wife."

5 When Jacob heard that his daughter Dinah had been defiled, his sons were in the fields with his livestock; so he kept quiet about it until they came home.

6 Then Shechem's father Hamor went out to talk with Jacob. 7 Now Jacob's sons had come in from the fields as soon as they heard what had happened. They were filled with grief and fury, because Shechem had done a disgraceful thing in[a] Israel by lying with Jacob's daughter—a thing that should not be done.

8 But Hamor said to them, "My son Shechem has his heart set on your daughter. Please give her to him as his wife. 9 Intermarry with us; give us your daughters and take our daughters for yourselves. 10 You can settle among us; the land is open to you. Live in it, trade[b] in it, and acquire property in it."

11 Then Shechem said to Dinah's father and brothers, "Let me find favor in your eyes, and I will give you whatever you ask. 12 Make the price for the bride and the gift I am to bring as great as you like, and I'll pay whatever you ask me. Only give me the girl as my wife."

13 Because their sister Dinah had been defiled, Jacob's sons replied deceitfully as they spoke to Shechem and his father Hamor. 14 They said to them, "We can't do such a thing; we can't give our sister to a man who is not circumcised. That would be a disgrace to us. 15 We will give our consent to you on one condition only: that you become like us by circumcising all your males. 16 Then we will give you our daughters and take your daughters for ourselves. We'll settle among you and become one people with you. 17 But if you will not agree to be circumcised, we'll take our sister[c] and go."

18 Their proposal seemed good to Hamor and his son Shechem. 19 The young man, who was the most honored of all his father's household, lost no time in doing what they said, because he was delighted with Jacob's daughter. 20 So Hamor and his son Shechem went to the gate of their city to speak to their fellow townsmen. 21 "These men are friendly toward us," they said. "Let them live in our land and trade in it; the land has plenty of room for them. We can marry their daughters and they can marry ours. 22 But the men will consent to live with us as one people only on the condition that our males be circumcised, as they themselves are. 23 Won't their livestock, their property and all their other animals become ours? So let us give our consent to them, and they will settle among us."

24 All the men who went out of the city gate agreed with Hamor and his son Shechem, and every male in the city was circumcised.

25 Three days later, while all of them were still in pain, two of Jacob's sons, Simeon and Levi, Dinah's brothers, took their swords and attacked the unsuspecting city, killing every male. 26 They put Hamor and his son Shechem to the sword and took Dinah from Shechem's house and left. 27 The sons of Jacob came upon the dead bodies and looted the city where[d] their sister had been defiled. 28 They seized their flocks and herds and donkeys and everything else of theirs in the city and out in the fields. 29 They carried off all their wealth and all their women and children, taking as plunder everything in the houses.

30 Then Jacob said to Simeon and Levi, "You have brought trouble on me by making me a stench to the Canaanites and Perizzites, the people living in this land. We are few in number, and if they join forces against me and attack

[a] 7 Or *against* [b] 10 Or *move about freely;* also in verse 21 [c] 17 Hebrew *daughter* [d] 27 Or *because*

me, I and my household will be destroyed."

[31]But they replied, "Should he have treated our sister like a prostitute?"

Jacob Returns to Bethel

35 Then God said to Jacob, "Go up to Bethel and settle there, and build an altar there to God, who appeared to you when you were fleeing from your brother Esau."

[2]So Jacob said to his household and to all who were with him, "Get rid of the foreign gods you have with you, and purify yourselves and change your clothes. [3]Then come, let us go up to Bethel, where I will build an altar to God, who answered me in the day of my distress and who has been with me wherever I have gone." [4]So they gave Jacob all the foreign gods they had and the rings in their ears, and Jacob buried them under the oak at Shechem. [5]Then they set out, and the terror of God fell upon the towns all around them so that no one pursued them.

[6]Jacob and all the people with him came to Luz (that is, Bethel) in the land of Canaan. [7]There he built an altar, and he called the place El Bethel,[a] because it was there that God revealed himself to him when he was fleeing from his brother.

[8]Now Deborah, Rebekah's nurse, died and was buried under the oak below Bethel. So it was named Allon Bacuth.[b]

[9]After Jacob returned from Paddan Aram,[c] God appeared to him again and blessed him. [10]God said to him, "Your name is Jacob,[d] but you will no longer be called Jacob; your name will be Israel.[e]" So he named him Israel.

[11]And God said to him, "I am God Almighty[f]; be fruitful and increase in number. A nation and a community of nations will come from you, and kings will come from your body. [12]The land I gave to Abraham and Isaac I also give to you, and I will give this land to your descendants after you." [13]Then God went up from him at the place where he had talked with him.

[14]Jacob set up a stone pillar at the place where God had talked with him, and he poured out a drink offering on it; he also poured oil on it. [15]Jacob called the place where God had talked with him Bethel.[g]

The Deaths of Rachel and Isaac

[16]Then they moved on from Bethel. While they were still some distance from Ephrath, Rachel began to give birth and had great difficulty. [17]And as she was having great difficulty in childbirth, the midwife said to her, "Don't be afraid, for you have another son." [18]As she breathed her last—for she was dying—she named her son Ben-Oni.[h] But his father named him Benjamin.[i]

[19]So Rachel died and was buried on the way to Ephrath (that is, Bethlehem). [20]Over her tomb Jacob set up a pillar, and to this day that pillar marks Rachel's tomb.

[21]Israel moved on again and pitched his tent beyond Migdal Eder. [22]While Israel was living in that region, Reuben went in and slept with his father's concubine Bilhah, and Israel heard of it.

Jacob had twelve sons:

[23]The sons of Leah:
Reuben the firstborn of Jacob,
Simeon, Levi, Judah, Issachar
and Zebulun.

[24]The sons of Rachel:
Joseph and Benjamin.

[25]The sons of Rachel's maidservant Bilhah:
Dan and Naphtali.

[26]The sons of Leah's maidservant Zilpah:
Gad and Asher.

These were the sons of Jacob, who were born to him in Paddan Aram.

[27]Jacob came home to his father Isaac in Mamre, near Kiriath Arba (that is,

[a]7 *El Bethel* means *God of Bethel.* [b]8 *Allon Bacuth* means *oak of weeping.* [c]9 That is, Northwest Mesopotamia; also in verse 26 [d]10 *Jacob* means *he grasps the heel* (figuratively, *he deceives*).
[e]10 *Israel* means *he struggles with God.*
[f]11 Hebrew *El-Shaddai* [g]15 *Bethel* means *house of God.* [h]18 *Ben-Oni* means *son of my trouble.*
[i]18 *Benjamin* means *son of my right hand.*

Hebron), where Abraham and Isaac had stayed. 28Isaac lived a hundred and eighty years. 29Then he breathed his last and died and was gathered to his people, old and full of years. And his sons Esau and Jacob buried him.

SHARPEN THE FOCUS

As we have already seen, the Bible places a good deal of significance on names. God's names tell us much about His character. Human names have significance, too. For example, Jacob living up to (or down to) his name—"the deceiver."

Sometimes God gives individuals new names as He did for Abram and Sarai (Genesis 17), and as He did for Jacob. "The deceitful one" was to be known as "the one who struggles with God." Jacob who had tried so hard to protect and promote himself was, by God's grace, learning to wrestle with the Lord in prayer instead.

Centuries later, Jesus changed Simon's name to Peter ("the rock"). At the time, Peter was anything but rock solid in his faith or in his leadership gifts. But the Holy Spirit would continue to work in Peter a stable faith. God would do this for Peter, even as He had kept His Word to make Abraham the "father of many nations" and Sarah "a princess" from whose descendants many kings would be born.

What new name has God given you? Saint or "holy one" (Psalm 116:15–16)? A royal priest (1 Peter 2:9)? His delight (Psalm 16:3)? Rest assured, He is at work through His Word even now bringing these things about—in you!

WEEK 4 • MONDAY

Genesis 36:1—37:36

GET THE BIG PICTURE

Moses records Esau's genealogy in Genesis 36. Then in Genesis 37, Moses again picks up the account of Israel's sons. Their plot against their brother Joseph shocks us, even more so because these men were God's chosen people! Their descendants were to become the twelve tribes of Israel, the nation from whom the Savior would be born. If time is short, focus on Genesis 37:1–36.

Esau's Descendants

36 This is the account of Esau
(that is, Edom).
2Esau took his wives from the
women of Canaan: Adah daughter
of Elon the Hittite, and Oholibamah
daughter of Anah and granddaughter
of Zibeon the Hivite—
3also Basemath daughter of Ishmael
and sister of Nebaioth.
4Adah bore Eliphaz to Esau, Basemath
bore Reuel, 5and Oholibamah
bore Jeush, Jalam and Korah.
These were the sons of Esau, who
were born to him in Canaan.
6Esau took his wives and sons
and daughters and all the members

of his household, as well as his livestock and all his other animals and all the goods he had acquired in Canaan, and moved to a land some distance from his brother Jacob.
7Their possessions were too great for them to remain together; the land where they were staying could not support them both because of their livestock.
8So Esau (that is, Edom) settled in the hill country of Seir.

9This is the account of Esau the father of the Edomites in the hill country of Seir.

10These are the names of Esau's sons:
Eliphaz, the son of Esau's wife Adah, and Reuel, the son of Esau's wife Basemath.
11The sons of Eliphaz:
Teman, Omar, Zepho, Gatam and Kenaz.
12Esau's son Eliphaz also had a concubine named Timna, who bore him Amalek. These were grandsons of Esau's wife Adah.
13The sons of Reuel:
Nahath, Zerah, Shammah and Mizzah. These were grandsons of Esau's wife Basemath.
14The sons of Esau's wife Oholibamah daughter of Anah and granddaughter of Zibeon, whom she bore to Esau:
Jeush, Jalam and Korah.

15These were the chiefs among Esau's descendants:
The sons of Eliphaz the firstborn of Esau:
Chiefs Teman, Omar, Zepho, Kenaz,
16Korah,[a] Gatam and Amalek. These were the chiefs descended from Eliphaz in Edom; they were grandsons of Adah.
17The sons of Esau's son Reuel:
Chiefs Nahath, Zerah, Shammah and Mizzah. These were the chiefs descended from Reuel in Edom; they were grandsons of Esau's wife Basemath.
18The sons of Esau's wife Oholibamah:
Chiefs Jeush, Jalam and Korah. These were the chiefs descended from Esau's wife Oholibamah daughter of Anah.
19These were the sons of Esau (that is, Edom), and these were their chiefs.

20These were the sons of Seir the Horite, who were living in the region:
Lotan, Shobal, Zibeon, Anah,
21Dishon, Ezer and Dishan. These sons of Seir in Edom were Horite chiefs.
22The sons of Lotan:
Hori and Homam.[b] Timna was Lotan's sister.
23The sons of Shobal:
Alvan, Manahath, Ebal, Shepho and Onam.
24The sons of Zibeon:
Aiah and Anah. This is the Anah who discovered the hot springs[c] in the desert while he was grazing the donkeys of his father Zibeon.
25The children of Anah:
Dishon and Oholibamah daughter of Anah.
26The sons of Dishon[d]:
Hemdan, Eshban, Ithran and Keran.
27The sons of Ezer:
Bilhan, Zaavan and Akan.
28The sons of Dishan:
Uz and Aran.
29These were the Horite chiefs:
Lotan, Shobal, Zibeon, Anah,
30Dishon, Ezer and Dishan. These were the Horite chiefs, according to their divisions, in the land of Seir.

The Rulers of Edom

31These were the kings who reigned in Edom before any Israelite king reigned[e]:

[a]*16* Masoretic Text; Samaritan Pentateuch (see also Gen. 36:11 and 1 Chron. 1:36) does not have *Korah.* [b]22 Hebrew *Hemam,* a variant of *Homam* (see 1 Chron. 1:39) [c]24 Vulgate; Syriac *discovered water;* the meaning of the Hebrew for this word is uncertain. [d]*26* Hebrew *Dishan,* a variant of *Dishon* [e]*31* Or *before an Israelite king reigned over them*

32 Bela son of Beor became king of
Edom. His city was named Dinhabah.
33 When Bela died, Jobab son of Zerah
from Bozrah succeeded him as
king.
34 When Jobab died, Husham from
the land of the Temanites succeeded him as king.
35 When Husham died, Hadad son of
Bedad, who defeated Midian in
the country of Moab, succeeded
him as king. His city was named
Avith.
36 When Hadad died, Samlah from
Masrekah succeeded him as
king.
37 When Samlah died, Shaul from Rehoboth on the river[a] succeeded
him as king.
38 When Shaul died, Baal-Hanan son
of Acbor succeeded him as king.
39 When Baal-Hanan son of Acbor
died, Hadad[b] succeeded him as
king. His city was named Pau,
and his wife's name was Mehetabel daughter of Matred, the
daughter of Me-Zahab.

40 These were the chiefs descended
from Esau, by name, according to their
clans and regions:
Timna, Alvah, Jetheth, 41 Oholibamah, Elah, Pinon, 42 Kenaz, Teman, Mibzar, 43 Magdiel and Iram.
These were the chiefs of Edom,
according to their settlements in
the land they occupied.

This was Esau the father of the Edomites.

Joseph's Dreams

37 Jacob lived in the land
where his father had stayed,
the land of Canaan.

2 This is the account of Jacob.

Joseph, a young man of seventeen,
was tending the flocks with his brothers, the sons of Bilhah and the sons of
Zilpah, his father's wives, and he
brought their father a bad report about
them.

3 Now Israel loved Joseph more than
any of his other sons, because he had
been born to him in his old age; and he
made a richly ornamented[c] robe for
him. 4 When his brothers saw that their
father loved him more than any of
them, they hated him and could not
speak a kind word to him.

5 Joseph had a dream, and when he
told it to his brothers, they hated him all
the more. 6 He said to them, "Listen to
this dream I had: 7 We were binding
sheaves of grain out in the field when
suddenly my sheaf rose and stood upright, while your sheaves gathered
around mine and bowed down to it."
8 His brothers said to him, "Do you intend to reign over us? Will you actually
rule us?" And they hated him all the
more because of his dream and what he
had said.

9 Then he had another dream, and he
told it to his brothers. "Listen," he said,
"I had another dream, and this time the
sun and moon and eleven stars were
bowing down to me."

10 When he told his father as well as his
brothers, his father rebuked him and
said, "What is this dream you had? Will
your mother and I and your brothers
actually come and bow down to the
ground before you?" 11 His brothers
were jealous of him, but his father kept
the matter in mind.

Joseph Sold by His Brothers

12 Now his brothers had gone to graze
their father's flocks near Shechem, 13 and
Israel said to Joseph, "As you know, your
brothers are grazing the flocks near
Shechem. Come, I am going to send you
to them."

"Very well," he replied.

14 So he said to him, "Go and see if all
is well with your brothers and with the
flocks, and bring word back to me."

[a] 37 Possibly the Euphrates [b] 39 Many manuscripts of the Masoretic Text, Samaritan Pentateuch and Syriac (see also 1 Chron. 1:50); most manuscripts of the Masoretic Text *Hadar*
[c] 3 The meaning of the Hebrew for *richly ornamented* is uncertain; also in verses 23 and 32.

Then he sent him off from the Valley of
Hebron.
When Joseph arrived at Shechem, [15]a
man found him wandering around in
the fields and asked him, "What are you
looking for?"
[16]He replied, "I'm looking for my
brothers. Can you tell me where they
are grazing their flocks?"
[17]"They have moved on from here,"
the man answered. "I heard them say,
'Let's go to Dothan.' "
So Joseph went after his brothers and
found them near Dothan. [18]But they saw
him in the distance, and before he
reached them, they plotted to kill him.
[19]"Here comes that dreamer!" they
said to each other. [20]"Come now, let's kill
him and throw him into one of these
cisterns and say that a ferocious animal
devoured him. Then we'll see what
comes of his dreams."
[21]When Reuben heard this, he tried to
rescue him from their hands. "Let's not
take his life," he said. [22]"Don't shed any
blood. Throw him into this cistern here
in the desert, but don't lay a hand on
him." Reuben said this to rescue him
from them and take him back to his father.
[23]So when Joseph came to his brothers, they stripped him of his robe—the
richly ornamented robe he was wearing— [24]and they took him and threw
him into the cistern. Now the cistern
was empty; there was no water in it.
[25]As they sat down to eat their meal,
they looked up and saw a caravan of
Ishmaelites coming from Gilead. Their
camels were loaded with spices, balm
and myrrh, and they were on their way
to take them down to Egypt.
[26]Judah said to his brothers, "What
will we gain if we kill our brother and
cover up his blood? [27]Come, let's sell
him to the Ishmaelites and not lay our
hands on him; after all, he is our brother, our own flesh and blood." His brothers agreed.
[28]So when the Midianite merchants
came by, his brothers pulled Joseph up
out of the cistern and sold him for
twenty shekels[a] of silver to the Ishmaelites, who took him to Egypt.
[29]When Reuben returned to the cistern and saw that Joseph was not there,
he tore his clothes. [30]He went back to his
brothers and said, "The boy isn't there!
Where can I turn now?"
[31]Then they got Joseph's robe, slaughtered a goat and dipped the robe in the
blood. [32]They took the ornamented robe
back to their father and said, "We found
this. Examine it to see whether it is your
son's robe."
[33]He recognized it and said, "It is my
son's robe! Some ferocious animal has
devoured him. Joseph has surely been
torn to pieces."
[34]Then Jacob tore his clothes, put on
sackcloth and mourned for his son
many days. [35]All his sons and daughters
came to comfort him, but he refused to
be comforted. "No," he said, "in mourning will I go down to the grave[b] to my
son." So his father wept for him.
[36]Meanwhile, the Midianites[c] sold Joseph in Egypt to Potiphar, one of Pharaoh's officials, the captain of the guard.

[a]*28* That is, about 8 ounces (about 0.2 kilogram)
[b]*35* Hebrew *Sheol* [c]*36* Samaritan Pentateuch,
Septuagint, Vulgate and Syriac (see also verse
28); Masoretic Text *Medanites*

SHARPEN THE FOCUS

Most brothers and sisters probably fantasize about selling each other—at least once or twice during childhood. Brothers and sisters often threaten one another with violence in the heat of argument. But youngsters seldom carry out their threats or find a way to make their fantasies come true.

Yet Jacob's sons did, and none of these men were children. Joseph, the youngest, was 17. Surely Jacob knew about the hatred mentioned in Genesis 37:4. Still, he did nothing to stop it.

Isaac, Jacob's father, never won the father-of-the-year award. But Jacob carried neglect of his family even further. We can't say why Jacob did not speak up. He was not evil. Perhaps he just hated conflict. Perhaps he was reluctant to confront sin. Perhaps he was too busy.

Ecclesiastes 3:7 tells us that there is a time to remain silent and there is a time to speak. Praise God that He forgives us in Christ for the times we have said too much. And praise Him, too, that He pardons those times we've been too timid, those times we've side-stepped our responsibilities to speak "the truth in love" to a son or daughter or to a brother or sister in the faith.

WEEK 4 • TUESDAY

Genesis 38:1—39:23

Genesis 38 interrupts the story of Joseph. The events in this chapter show us one of the reasons God took His people to Egypt. Intermarriage with the Canaanites had begun—and Judah, the very one whom God had chosen to be the ancestor of the Savior, had gotten involved. Genesis 39 picks up the Joseph narrative a series of seemingly random and unjust events in Joseph's life. But in reality, they are not random. God is working through Joseph's life to create a safe haven for the Israelites in Egypt. If time is short, focus on Genesis 39:1–23.

Judah and Tamar

38 At that time, Judah left his
brothers and went down
to stay with a man of Adullam named
Hirah. 2There Judah met the daughter
of a Canaanite man named Shua. He
married her and lay with her; 3she
became pregnant and gave birth to a
son, who was named Er. 4She conceived
again and gave birth to a son and
named him Onan. 5She gave birth to still
another son and named him Shelah. It
was at Kezib that she gave birth to him.
6Judah got a wife for Er, his firstborn,
and her name was Tamar. 7But Er,
Judah's firstborn, was wicked in the
LORD's sight; so the LORD put him to
death.
8Then Judah said to Onan, "Lie with
your brother's wife and fulfill your duty
to her as a brother-in-law to produce offspring for your brother." 9But Onan
knew that the offspring would not be
his; so whenever he lay with his
brother's wife, he spilled his semen on
the ground to keep from producing
offspring for his brother. 10What he did
was wicked in the LORD's sight; so he
put him to death also.
11Judah then said to his daughter-in-
law Tamar, "Live as a widow in your
father's house until my son Shelah
grows up." For he thought, "He may die
too, just like his brothers." So Tamar
went to live in her father's house.
12After a long time Judah's wife, the
daughter of Shua, died. When Judah
had recovered from his grief, he went
up to Timnah, to the men who were
shearing his sheep, and his friend Hirah
the Adullamite went with him.
13When Tamar was told, "Your father-
in-law is on his way to Timnah to shear
his sheep," 14she took off her widow's
clothes, covered herself with a veil to
disguise herself, and then sat down at

the entrance to Enaim, which is on the road to Timnah. For she saw that, though Shelah had now grown up, she had not been given to him as his wife.

15 When Judah saw her, he thought she was a prostitute, for she had covered her face. 16 Not realizing that she was his daughter-in-law, he went over to her by the roadside and said, "Come now, let me sleep with you."

"And what will you give me to sleep with you?" she asked.

17 "I'll send you a young goat from my flock," he said.

"Will you give me something as a pledge until you send it?" she asked.

18 He said, "What pledge should I give you?"

"Your seal and its cord, and the staff in your hand," she answered. So he gave them to her and slept with her, and she became pregnant by him. 19 After she left, she took off her veil and put on her widow's clothes again.

20 Meanwhile Judah sent the young goat by his friend the Adullamite in order to get his pledge back from the woman, but he did not find her. 21 He asked the men who lived there, "Where is the shrine prostitute who was beside the road at Enaim?"

"There hasn't been any shrine prostitute here," they said.

22 So he went back to Judah and said, "I didn't find her. Besides, the men who lived there said, 'There hasn't been any shrine prostitute here.' "

23 Then Judah said, "Let her keep what she has, or we will become a laughingstock. After all, I did send her this young goat, but you didn't find her."

24 About three months later Judah was told, "Your daughter-in-law Tamar is guilty of prostitution, and as a result she is now pregnant."

Judah said, "Bring her out and have her burned to death!"

25 As she was being brought out, she sent a message to her father-in-law. "I am pregnant by the man who owns these," she said. And she added, "See if you recognize whose seal and cord and staff these are."

26 Judah recognized them and said, "She is more righteous than I, since I wouldn't give her to my son Shelah." And he did not sleep with her again.

27 When the time came for her to give birth, there were twin boys in her womb. 28 As she was giving birth, one of them put out his hand; so the midwife took a scarlet thread and tied it on his wrist and said, "This one came out first." 29 But when he drew back his hand, his brother came out, and she said, "So this is how you have broken out!" And he was named Perez.[a] 30 Then his brother, who had the scarlet thread on his wrist, came out and he was given the name Zerah.[b]

Joseph and Potiphar's Wife

39 Now Joseph had been taken down to Egypt. Potiphar, an Egyptian who was one of Pharaoh's officials, the captain of the guard, bought him from the Ishmaelites who had taken him there.

2 The LORD was with Joseph and he prospered, and he lived in the house of his Egyptian master. 3 When his master saw that the LORD was with him and that the LORD gave him success in everything he did, 4 Joseph found favor in his eyes and became his attendant. Potiphar put him in charge of his household, and he entrusted to his care everything he owned. 5 From the time he put him in charge of his household and of all that he owned, the LORD blessed the household of the Egyptian because of Joseph. The blessing of the LORD was on everything Potiphar had, both in the house and in the field. 6 So he left in Joseph's care everything he had; with Joseph in charge, he did not concern himself with anything except the food he ate.

Now Joseph was well-built and handsome, 7 and after a while his master's wife took notice of Joseph and said, "Come to bed with me!"

8 But he refused. "With me in charge,"

[a] *29 Perez* means *breaking out.* [b] *30 Zerah* can mean *scarlet* or *brightness.*

he told her, "my master does not concern himself with anything in the
house; everything he owns he has entrusted to my care. 9No one is greater in
this house than I am. My master has
withheld nothing from me except you,
because you are his wife. How then
could I do such a wicked thing and
sin against God?" 10And though she
spoke to Joseph day after day, he
refused to go to bed with her or even be
with her.

11One day he went into the house to
attend to his duties, and none of the
household servants was inside. 12She
caught him by his cloak and said, "Come
to bed with me!" But he left his cloak in
her hand and ran out of the house.

13When she saw that he had left his
cloak in her hand and had run out of the
house, 14she called her household servants. "Look," she said to them, "this
Hebrew has been brought to us to make
sport of us! He came in here to sleep
with me, but I screamed. 15When he
heard me scream for help, he left his
cloak beside me and ran out of the
house."

16She kept his cloak beside her until
his master came home. 17Then she told
him this story: "That Hebrew slave you
brought us came to me to make sport of
me. 18But as soon as I screamed for help,
he left his cloak beside me and ran out
of the house."

19When his master heard the story his
wife told him, saying, "This is how your
slave treated me," he burned with anger. 20Joseph's master took him and put
him in prison, the place where the
king's prisoners were confined.

But while Joseph was there in the
prison, 21the LORD was with him; he
showed him kindness and granted him
favor in the eyes of the prison warden.
22So the warden put Joseph in charge of
all those held in the prison, and he was
made responsible for all that was done
there. 23The warden paid no attention to
anything under Joseph's care, because
the LORD was with Joseph and gave him
success in whatever he did.

SHARPEN THE FOCUS

Joseph found himself alone as a teenager in a land in which he did not even speak the language. He was cut off from his family. He had no written Scriptures. Idols filled the land of Egypt. The wealth and culture around Joseph probably left him wide-eyed for months.

Judah, on the other hand, had all the spiritual advantages. He was older. He doubtless had many opportunities to worship the Lord with his family on a regular basis. He had the support of family and could rely on their encouragement and advice.

Judah "left his brothers" (Genesis 38:1) intentionally and fell for temptation. Joseph was sold by his brothers involuntarily and by God's grace stood up under repeated temptation (Genesis 39:9–10).

In unusual circumstances, the Holy Spirit can and will sustain our faith without corporate worship or daily Bible reading. But if we deliberately choose to leave our brothers, to cut ourselves off from God's Word, from the power of the sacraments, from the encouragement of other believers, we leave ourselves wide open to Satan's schemes.

WEEK 4 • WEDNESDAY

Genesis 40:1–23

Joseph's integrity lands him in prison. Because God has given him favor with the captain of the prison guard, Joseph soon finds himself in charge. One night, two of the other prisoners, both high-ranking officials in Pharaoh's royal court, awaken from troubling dreams. By grace, Joseph interprets them. His interpretations come true. Still, he is forgotten, and must spend two more years in prison. If time is short, focus on Genesis 40:1–15.

The Cupbearer and the Baker

40 Some time later, the cupbearer and the baker of
the king of Egypt offended their master,
the king of Egypt. 2Pharaoh was angry
with his two officials, the chief cupbearer and the chief baker, 3and put them in
custody in the house of the captain of
the guard, in the same prison where Joseph was confined. 4The captain of the
guard assigned them to Joseph, and he
attended them.

After they had been in custody for
some time, 5each of the two men—the
cupbearer and the baker of the king of
Egypt, who were being held in prison—
had a dream the same night, and each
dream had a meaning of its own.

6When Joseph came to them the next
morning, he saw that they were dejected. 7So he asked Pharaoh's officials
who were in custody with him in his
master's house, "Why are your faces so
sad today?"

8"We both had dreams," they answered, "but there is no one to interpret
them."

Then Joseph said to them, "Do not interpretations belong to God? Tell me
your dreams."

9So the chief cupbearer told Joseph
his dream. He said to him, "In my dream
I saw a vine in front of me, 10and on the
vine were three branches. As soon as it
budded, it blossomed, and its clusters
ripened into grapes. 11Pharaoh's cup
was in my hand, and I took the grapes,
squeezed them into Pharaoh's cup and
put the cup in his hand."

12"This is what it means," Joseph said
to him. "The three branches are three
days. 13Within three days Pharaoh will
lift up your head and restore you to
your position, and you will put Pharaoh's cup in his hand, just as you used
to do when you were his cupbearer.
14But when all goes well with you, remember me and show me kindness;
mention me to Pharaoh and get me out
of this prison. 15For I was forcibly carried
off from the land of the Hebrews, and
even here I have done nothing to deserve being put in a dungeon."

16When the chief baker saw that Joseph had given a favorable interpretation, he said to Joseph, "I too had a
dream: On my head were three baskets
of bread.[a] 17In the top basket were all
kinds of baked goods for Pharaoh, but
the birds were eating them out of the
basket on my head."

18"This is what it means," Joseph said.
"The three baskets are three days.
19Within three days Pharaoh will lift off
your head and hang you on a tree.[b] And
the birds will eat away your flesh."

20Now the third day was Pharaoh's
birthday, and he gave a feast for all his
officials. He lifted up the heads of the

[a]16 Or *three wicker baskets* [b]19 Or *and impale you on a pole*

chief cupbearer and the chief baker
in the presence of his officials:
21He restored the chief cupbearer to
his position, so that he once again put
the cup into Pharaoh's hand, 22but he
hanged[a] the chief baker, just as Joseph
had said to them in his interpretation.
23The chief cupbearer, however, did
not remember Joseph; he forgot him.

SHARPEN THE FOCUS

What does it mean to "have favor" with someone? Simply speaking, it means that the other person thinks highly of us, respects us, trusts us, honors us, and wants to do anything possible to help us, to promote us.

We don't use this expression too often in daily life. But the Scriptures use it nearly 150 times. Most comforting are those passages that talk about our relationship with God in Christ being a position of favor. For instance:

> *Surely, O Lord, You bless the righteous;*
> *you surround them with Your favor as with a shield.* (Psalm 5:12)

In Christ, by faith in Him and in His life and death for us on the cross, we are "the righteous." We have right standing with God. Nothing will shake His love for us. Because this is true, He surrounds us with His favor. Psalm 139 assures us that our Lord is with us wherever we go and that He thinks about us all the time (Psalm 139:1–18).

God's favor, His high regard for us, shields us. It shields us from the fears and temptations Satan tries to use to intimidate us. It shields us from the guilt we have brought on ourselves by our past sins. It shields us from the fear of death itself.

WEEK 4 • THURSDAY

Genesis 41:1–40

GET THE BIG PICTURE

Joseph languished in prison two more years. Then God acted in a single day. God's plan to protect the people of Israel by providing a kind of "incubator in Egypt" is nearly ready. If time is short, focus on Genesis 41:1–16.

Pharaoh's Dreams

41 When two full years had
passed, Pharaoh had a
dream: He was standing by the Nile,
2when out of the river there came up
seven cows, sleek and fat, and they
grazed among the reeds. 3After them,
seven other cows, ugly and gaunt, came
up out of the Nile and stood beside
those on the riverbank. 4And the cows
that were ugly and gaunt ate up the
seven sleek, fat cows. Then Pharaoh
woke up.
5He fell asleep again and had a second
dream: Seven heads of grain, healthy
and good, were growing on a single

[a]22 Or *impaled*

stalk. 6After them, seven other heads of grain sprouted—thin and scorched by the east wind. 7The thin heads of grain swallowed up the seven healthy, full heads. Then Pharaoh woke up; it had been a dream.

8In the morning his mind was troubled, so he sent for all the magicians and wise men of Egypt. Pharaoh told them his dreams, but no one could interpret them for him.

9Then the chief cupbearer said to Pharaoh, "Today I am reminded of my shortcomings. 10Pharaoh was once angry with his servants, and he imprisoned me and the chief baker in the house of the captain of the guard. 11Each of us had a dream the same night, and each dream had a meaning of its own. 12Now a young Hebrew was there with us, a servant of the captain of the guard. We told him our dreams, and he interpreted them for us, giving each man the interpretation of his dream. 13And things turned out exactly as he interpreted them to us: I was restored to my position, and the other man was hanged.[a]"

14So Pharaoh sent for Joseph, and he was quickly brought from the dungeon. When he had shaved and changed his clothes, he came before Pharaoh.

15Pharaoh said to Joseph, "I had a dream, and no one can interpret it. But I have heard it said of you that when you hear a dream you can interpret it."

16"I cannot do it," Joseph replied to Pharaoh, "but God will give Pharaoh the answer he desires."

17Then Pharaoh said to Joseph, "In my dream I was standing on the bank of the Nile, 18when out of the river there came up seven cows, fat and sleek, and they grazed among the reeds. 19After them, seven other cows came up—scrawny and very ugly and lean. I had never seen such ugly cows in all the land of Egypt. 20The lean, ugly cows ate up the seven fat cows that came up first. 21But even after they ate them, no one could tell that they had done so; they looked just as ugly as before. Then I woke up.

22"In my dreams I also saw seven heads of grain, full and good, growing on a single stalk. 23After them, seven other heads sprouted—withered and thin and scorched by the east wind. 24The thin heads of grain swallowed up the seven good heads. I told this to the magicians, but none could explain it to me."

25Then Joseph said to Pharaoh, "The dreams of Pharaoh are one and the same. God has revealed to Pharaoh what he is about to do. 26The seven good cows are seven years, and the seven good heads of grain are seven years; it is one and the same dream. 27The seven lean, ugly cows that came up afterward are seven years, and so are the seven worthless heads of grain scorched by the east wind: They are seven years of famine.

28"It is just as I said to Pharaoh: God has shown Pharaoh what he is about to do. 29Seven years of great abundance are coming throughout the land of Egypt, 30but seven years of famine will follow them. Then all the abundance in Egypt will be forgotten, and the famine will ravage the land. 31The abundance in the land will not be remembered, because the famine that follows it will be so severe. 32The reason the dream was given to Pharaoh in two forms is that the matter has been firmly decided by God, and God will do it soon.

33"And now let Pharaoh look for a discerning and wise man and put him in charge of the land of Egypt. 34Let Pharaoh appoint commissioners over the land to take a fifth of the harvest of Egypt during the seven years of abundance. 35They should collect all the food of these good years that are coming and store up the grain under the authority of Pharaoh, to be kept in the cities for food. 36This food should be held in reserve for the country, to be used during the seven years of famine that will come upon Egypt, so that the country may not be ruined by the famine."

37The plan seemed good to Pharaoh and to all his officials. 38So Pharaoh

[a]13 Or *impaled*

asked them, "Can we find anyone like this man, one in whom is the spirit of God[a]?"

39Then Pharaoh said to Joseph, "Since God has made all this known to you, there is no one so discerning and wise as you. 40You shall be in charge of my palace, and all my people are to submit to your orders. Only with respect to the throne will I be greater than you."

SHARPEN THE FOCUS

For 13 years Joseph has found himself, as it were, enrolled in God's course "What It Means to Live by Faith." Now Joseph steps before Pharaoh. The first words out of his mouth are words of deep humility: "I cannot do it," Joseph replied to Pharaoh, "but God will give Pharaoh the answer he desires" (Genesis 41:16).

In God's school of faith, Joseph has learned to rely on the Lord—not on people, not on himself. Because the Holy Spirit has brought Joseph to this kind of spiritual maturity, we hear no edge of bitterness in Joseph's voice. He could have asked both the butler and the captain of Pharaoh's guard (Potiphar) some embarrassing questions—maybe in full view of the royal court. But we see no hardness of heart, no desire for revenge. Why not? Because the Lord has taught Joseph to live by faith. Joseph has learned to focus on His Savior-God, not on himself, nor on his difficulties.

What situations in your life today could be (or have already been) flash points for bitterness or vengefulness? What would happen to your attitude if you talked to your Lord about them? Ask Him to use His Word of comfort to teach you more about what it means to live by faith even in troubling situations.

WEEK 4 • FRIDAY

Genesis 41:41–57

GET THE BIG PICTURE

The Pharaoh does what he said he would do. He elevates Joseph to a position much more powerful than that of prime minister or president in our day. Joseph carries out the plan to save Egypt he outlined for Pharaoh in Genesis 41:33–36. As the years of plenty roll along, the Lord heals Joseph's personal pain. The names he gives his sons (Genesis 41:51–52) hint at how thorough this healing is. If time is short, focus on Genesis 41:46–52.

Joseph in Charge of Egypt

41So Pharaoh said to Joseph, "I hereby put you in charge of the whole land of Egypt." 42Then Pharaoh took his signet ring from his finger and put it on Joseph's finger. He dressed him in robes of fine linen and put a gold chain around his neck. 43He had him ride in a chariot as his second-in-command,[b] and men shouted before him, "Make way[c]!"

[a]38 Or *of the gods* [b]43 Or *in the chariot of his second-in-command*; or *in his second chariot*
[c]43 Or *Bow down*

Thus he put him in charge of the whole
land of Egypt.
44Then Pharaoh said to Joseph, "I am
Pharaoh, but without your word no one
will lift hand or foot in all Egypt." 45Phar-
aoh gave Joseph the name Zaphe-
nath-Paneah and gave him Asenath
daughter of Potiphera, priest of On,[a] to
be his wife. And Joseph went throughout the land of Egypt.
46Joseph was thirty years old when he
entered the service of Pharaoh king of
Egypt. And Joseph went out from Pharaoh's presence and traveled throughout
Egypt. 47During the seven years of
abundance the land produced plenti-
fully. 48Joseph collected all the food
produced in those seven years of abundance in Egypt and stored it in the cities. In each city he put the food grown
in the fields surrounding it. 49Joseph
stored up huge quantities of grain, like
the sand of the sea; it was so much that
he stopped keeping records because it
was beyond measure.
50Before the years of famine came, two
sons were born to Joseph by Asenath
daughter of Potiphera, priest of On. 51Jo-
seph named his firstborn Manasseh[b]
and said, "It is because God has made
me forget all my trouble and all my
father's household." 52The second son
he named Ephraim[c] and said, "It is because God has made me fruitful in the
land of my suffering."
53The seven years of abundance in
Egypt came to an end, 54and the seven
years of famine began, just as Joseph
had said. There was famine in all the
other lands, but in the whole land of
Egypt there was food. 55When all Egypt
began to feel the famine, the people
cried to Pharaoh for food. Then Pharaoh
told all the Egyptians, "Go to Joseph and
do what he tells you."
56When the famine had spread over
the whole country, Joseph opened the
storehouses and sold grain to the Egyptians, for the famine was severe
throughout Egypt. 57And all the countries came to Egypt to buy grain from
Joseph, because the famine was severe
in all the world.

[a]*45* That is, Heliopolis; also in verse 50
[b]*51 Manasseh* sounds like and may be derived from the Hebrew for *forget.* [c]*52 Ephraim* sounds like the Hebrew for *twice fruitful.*

SHARPEN THE FOCUS

The Lord gave Joseph two gifts—forgetfulness (Genesis 41:51) and fruitfulness (Genesis 41:52).

Forgetting is not always easy. Those biting words. That stinging accusation. The unjust decision. And the painful hours, days, or even years we've endured because of someone else's insensitivity or even wickedness. Maybe deep down, we don't even want to forget. Maybe we don't believe it's possible to pull off the knapsack of bitterness that's weighing us down. Maybe we think we'll never be able to leave it beside the road.

But for us, as for Joseph, fruitfulness follows forgetfulness. Knapsacks filled with resentment and revenge will keep us from running the race of faith with endurance (see Hebrews 12:1). But lest you believe forgetting is up to you, look carefully at Genesis 41:51–52 again. Note who is doing what: "God has made me forget . . . God has made me fruitful," Joseph says. And your Lord is willing to do the same thing for you today. Let Him lift from your shoulders any burdens of bitterness. Let Him carry the pain of your trouble. Invite Him to increase the harvest of spiritual fruit in your life. Then expect Him to do for you just what He has promised, just what He did for Joseph.

Today you will read three chapters in the continuing story of Joseph. As you read, notice the tests that Joseph sets up for his 10 brothers. Notice, too, how guilt's cold fist tightens until all the brothers realize their sin. Though more than 20 years have passed, time has not erased the debt they owe their Lord for their sins against Joseph. Note how God uses Joseph's tests to produce true repentance in the brothers' hearts. If time is short, focus on Genesis 42:1–26.

Joseph's Brothers Go to Egypt

42 When Jacob learned that there was grain in Egypt, he said to his sons, "Why do you just keep looking at each other?" [2]He continued, "I have heard that there is grain in Egypt. Go down there and buy some for us, so that we may live and not die."

[3]Then ten of Joseph's brothers went down to buy grain from Egypt. [4]But Jacob did not send Benjamin, Joseph's brother, with the others, because he was afraid that harm might come to him. [5]So Israel's sons were among those who went to buy grain, for the famine was in the land of Canaan also.

[6]Now Joseph was the governor of the land, the one who sold grain to all its people. So when Joseph's brothers arrived, they bowed down to him with their faces to the ground. [7]As soon as Joseph saw his brothers, he recognized them, but he pretended to be a stranger and spoke harshly to them. "Where do you come from?" he asked.

"From the land of Canaan," they replied, "to buy food."

[8]Although Joseph recognized his brothers, they did not recognize him. [9]Then he remembered his dreams about them and said to them, "You are spies! You have come to see where our land is unprotected."

[10]"No, my lord," they answered. "Your servants have come to buy food. [11]We are all the sons of one man. Your servants are honest men, not spies."

[12]"No!" he said to them. "You have come to see where our land is unprotected."

[13]But they replied, "Your servants were twelve brothers, the sons of one man, who lives in the land of Canaan. The youngest is now with our father, and one is no more."

[14]Joseph said to them, "It is just as I told you: You are spies! [15]And this is how you will be tested: As surely as Pharaoh lives, you will not leave this place unless your youngest brother comes here. [16]Send one of your number to get your brother; the rest of you will be kept in prison, so that your words may be tested to see if you are telling the truth. If you are not, then as surely as Pharaoh lives, you are spies!" [17]And he put them all in custody for three days.

[18]On the third day, Joseph said to them, "Do this and you will live, for I fear God: [19]If you are honest men, let one of your brothers stay here in prison, while the rest of you go and take grain back for your starving households. [20]But you must bring your youngest brother to me, so that your words may be verified and that you may not die." This they proceeded to do.

[21]They said to one another, "Surely we are being punished because of our brother. We saw how distressed he was when he pleaded with us for his life, but

we would not listen; that's why this distress has come upon us."

22Reuben replied, "Didn't I tell you not to sin against the boy? But you wouldn't listen! Now we must give an accounting for his blood." 23They did not realize that Joseph could understand them, since he was using an interpreter.

24He turned away from them and began to weep, but then turned back and spoke to them again. He had Simeon taken from them and bound before their eyes.

25Joseph gave orders to fill their bags with grain, to put each man's silver back in his sack, and to give them provisions for their journey. After this was done for them, 26they loaded their grain on their donkeys and left.

27At the place where they stopped for the night one of them opened his sack to get feed for his donkey, and he saw his silver in the mouth of his sack. 28"My silver has been returned," he said to his brothers. "Here it is in my sack."

Their hearts sank and they turned to each other trembling and said, "What is this that God has done to us?"

29When they came to their father Jacob in the land of Canaan, they told him all that had happened to them. They said, 30"The man who is lord over the land spoke harshly to us and treated us as though we were spying on the land. 31But we said to him, 'We are honest men; we are not spies. 32We were twelve brothers, sons of one father. One is no more, and the youngest is now with our father in Canaan.'

33"Then the man who is lord over the land said to us, 'This is how I will know whether you are honest men: Leave one of your brothers here with me, and take food for your starving households and go. 34But bring your youngest brother to me so I will know that you are not spies but honest men. Then I will give your brother back to you, and you can trade[a] in the land.' "

35As they were emptying their sacks, there in each man's sack was his pouch of silver! When they and their father saw the money pouches, they were frightened. 36Their father Jacob said to them, "You have deprived me of my children. Joseph is no more and Simeon is no more, and now you want to take Benjamin. Everything is against me!"

37Then Reuben said to his father, "You may put both of my sons to death if I do not bring him back to you. Entrust him to my care, and I will bring him back."

38But Jacob said, "My son will not go down there with you; his brother is dead and he is the only one left. If harm comes to him on the journey you are taking, you will bring my gray head down to the grave[b] in sorrow."

The Second Journey to Egypt

43 Now the famine was still severe in the land. 2So when they had eaten all the grain they had brought from Egypt, their father said to them, "Go back and buy us a little more food."

3But Judah said to him, "The man warned us solemnly, 'You will not see my face again unless your brother is with you.' 4If you will send our brother along with us, we will go down and buy food for you. 5But if you will not send him, we will not go down, because the man said to us, 'You will not see my face again unless your brother is with you.' "

6Israel asked, "Why did you bring this trouble on me by telling the man you had another brother?"

7They replied, "The man questioned us closely about ourselves and our family. 'Is your father still living?' he asked us. 'Do you have another brother?' We simply answered his questions. How were we to know he would say, 'Bring your brother down here'?"

8Then Judah said to Israel his father, "Send the boy along with me and we will go at once, so that we and you and our children may live and not die. 9I myself will guarantee his safety; you can hold me personally responsible for him. If I do not bring him back to you

[a]34 Or *move about freely* [b]38 Hebrew *Sheol*

and set him here before you, I will bear
the blame before you all my life. 10As it
is, if we had not delayed, we could have
gone and returned twice."

11Then their father Israel said to them,
"If it must be, then do this: Put some of
the best products of the land in your
bags and take them down to the man as
a gift—a little balm and a little honey,
some spices and myrrh, some pistachio
nuts and almonds. 12Take double the
amount of silver with you, for you must
return the silver that was put back into
the mouths of your sacks. Perhaps it was
a mistake. 13Take your brother also and
go back to the man at once. 14And may
God Almighty[a] grant you mercy before
the man so that he will let your other
brother and Benjamin come back with
you. As for me, if I am bereaved, I am
bereaved."

15So the men took the gifts and double
the amount of silver, and Benjamin also.
They hurried down to Egypt and presented themselves to Joseph. 16When Joseph saw Benjamin with them, he said
to the steward of his house, "Take these
men to my house, slaughter an animal
and prepare dinner; they are to eat with
me at noon."

17The man did as Joseph told him and
took the men to Joseph's house. 18Now
the men were frightened when they
were taken to his house. They thought,
"We were brought here because of the
silver that was put back into our sacks
the first time. He wants to attack us and
overpower us and seize us as slaves and
take our donkeys."

19So they went up to Joseph's steward
and spoke to him at the entrance to the
house. 20"Please, sir," they said, "we
came down here the first time to buy
food. 21But at the place where we
stopped for the night we opened our
sacks and each of us found his silver—
the exact weight—in the mouth of his
sack. So we have brought it back with
us. 22We have also brought additional silver with us to buy food. We don't know
who put our silver in our sacks."

23"It's all right," he said. "Don't be
afraid. Your God, the God of your father,
has given you treasure in your sacks; I
received your silver." Then he brought
Simeon out to them.

24The steward took the men into
Joseph's house, gave them water to
wash their feet and provided fodder for
their donkeys. 25They prepared their
gifts for Joseph's arrival at noon, because they had heard that they were to
eat there.

26When Joseph came home, they presented to him the gifts they had brought
into the house, and they bowed down
before him to the ground. 27He asked
them how they were, and then he said,
"How is your aged father you told me
about? Is he still living?"

28They replied, "Your servant our father is still alive and well." And they
bowed low to pay him honor.

29As he looked about and saw his
brother Benjamin, his own mother's
son, he asked, "Is this your youngest
brother, the one you told me about?"
And he said, "God be gracious to you,
my son." 30Deeply moved at the sight of
his brother, Joseph hurried out and
looked for a place to weep. He went into
his private room and wept there.

31After he had washed his face, he
came out and, controlling himself, said,
"Serve the food."

32They served him by himself, the
brothers by themselves, and the Egyptians who ate with him by themselves,
because Egyptians could not eat with
Hebrews, for that is detestable to Egyptians. 33The men had been seated before
him in the order of their ages, from the
firstborn to the youngest; and they
looked at each other in astonishment.
34When portions were served to them
from Joseph's table, Benjamin's portion
was five times as much as anyone else's.
So they feasted and drank freely with
him.

A Silver Cup in a Sack

44 Now Joseph gave these
instructions to the stew-
ard of his house: "Fill the men's sacks

[a]14 Hebrew *El-Shaddai*

with as much food as they can carry,
and put each man's silver in the mouth
of his sack. 2Then put my cup, the silver
one, in the mouth of the youngest one's
sack, along with the silver for his grain."
And he did as Joseph said.
3As morning dawned, the men were
sent on their way with their donkeys.
4They had not gone far from the city
when Joseph said to his steward, "Go
after those men at once, and when you
catch up with them, say to them, 'Why
have you repaid good with evil? 5Isn't
this the cup my master drinks from and
also uses for divination? This is a wicked
thing you have done.' "
6When he caught up with them, he
repeated these words to them. 7But they
said to him, "Why does my lord say
such things? Far be it from your servants
to do anything like that! 8We even
brought back to you from the land of
Canaan the silver we found inside the
mouths of our sacks. So why would we
steal silver or gold from your master's
house? 9If any of your servants is found
to have it, he will die; and the rest of us
will become my lord's slaves."
10"Very well, then," he said, "let it be
as you say. Whoever is found to have it
will become my slave; the rest of you
will be free from blame."
11Each of them quickly lowered his
sack to the ground and opened it.
12Then the steward proceeded to search,
beginning with the oldest and ending
with the youngest. And the cup was
found in Benjamin's sack. 13At this,
they tore their clothes. Then they all
loaded their donkeys and returned to
the city.
14Joseph was still in the house when
Judah and his brothers came in, and
they threw themselves to the ground
before him. 15Joseph said to them,
"What is this you have done? Don't you
know that a man like me can find things
out by divination?"
16"What can we say to my lord?" Judah replied. "What can we say? How
can we prove our innocence? God has
uncovered your servants' guilt. We are
now my lord's slaves—we ourselves
and the one who was found to have the
cup."
17But Joseph said, "Far be it from me
to do such a thing! Only the man who
was found to have the cup will become
my slave. The rest of you, go back to
your father in peace."
18Then Judah went up to him and
said: "Please, my lord, let your servant
speak a word to my lord. Do not be angry with your servant, though you are
equal to Pharaoh himself. 19My lord
asked his servants, 'Do you have a father or a brother?' 20And we answered,
'We have an aged father, and there is a
young son born to him in his old age.
His brother is dead, and he is the only
one of his mother's sons left, and his
father loves him.'
21"Then you said to your servants,
'Bring him down to me so I can see him
for myself.' 22And we said to my lord,
'The boy cannot leave his father; if he
leaves him, his father will die.' 23But you
told your servants, 'Unless your youngest brother comes down with you, you
will not see my face again.' 24When we
went back to your servant my father, we
told him what my lord had said.
25"Then our father said, 'Go back and
buy a little more food.' 26But we said,
'We cannot go down. Only if our youngest brother is with us will we go. We
cannot see the man's face unless our
youngest brother is with us.'
27"Your servant my father said to us,
'You know that my wife bore me two
sons. 28One of them went away from
me, and I said, "He has surely been torn
to pieces." And I have not seen him
since. 29If you take this one from me too
and harm comes to him, you will bring
my gray head down to the grave[a] in
misery.'
30"So now, if the boy is not with us
when I go back to your servant my father and if my father, whose life is closely bound up with the boy's life, 31sees
that the boy isn't there, he will die. Your
servants will bring the gray head of our
father down to the grave in sorrow.

[a]29 Hebrew *Sheol*; also in verse 31

32Your servant guaranteed the boy's
safety to my father. I said, 'If I do not
bring him back to you, I will bear
the blame before you, my father, all my
life!'
33"Now then, please let your servant
remain here as my lord's slave in place
of the boy, and let the boy return with
his brothers. 34How can I go back to my
father if the boy is not with me? No! Do
not let me see the misery that would
come upon my father."

SHARPEN THE FOCUS

Later in the Pentateuch (the first five Old Testament books) Moses would write, "You may be sure that your sin will find you out" (Numbers 32:23). We cannot escape the penalty for our sins when we try to run from them. No matter how many years we manage to put between our sins and ourselves, guilt will track us down. Relentlessly. We come by personal experience to realize that the curse of a guilty conscience truly is just that—a curse. We repeat with Judah, "How can we prove our innocence?" (Genesis 44:16).

In that moment of confession, St. Paul's words fall so gently and with such promise on our ears: "Christ redeemed us from the curse of the law, by becoming a curse for us" (Galatians 3:13).

Our sins will always "find us out," however faraway we look for refuge. But Christ has redeemed us—bought us back from the curse of guilt and of having to keep the Law. In Christ and His cross, we find favor with God. We need not hide any longer. We need not crouch in the bushes with Adam and Eve in naked despair. We can come home. We can fall into our kind Father's arms, there to receive total acceptance and full pardon.

Your Lord is waiting—for you—right now! What are you waiting for? ☼

WEEK 5 • MONDAY

Genesis 45:1—46:34

GET THE BIG PICTURE

Joseph dismisses everyone but his brothers and then makes a startling announcement: "I am Joseph." Then he makes preparations for his brothers to go back to Canaan and to return with their families. When they do return, Joseph and Jacob embrace in tears of joy—a joy Jacob never believed possible. If time is short, focus on Genesis 45:1–28.

Joseph Makes Himself Known

45 Then Joseph could no
longer control himself be-
fore all his attendants, and he cried out,
"Have everyone leave my presence!" So
there was no one with Joseph when he
made himself known to his brothers.
2And he wept so loudly that the Egyptians heard him, and Pharaoh's household heard about it.
3Joseph said to his brothers, "I am
Joseph! Is my father still living?" But his
brothers were not able to answer him,
because they were terrified at his presence.
4Then Joseph said to his brothers,
"Come close to me." When they had
done so, he said, "I am your brother Joseph, the one you sold into Egypt! 5And
now, do not be distressed and do not

be angry with yourselves for selling
me here, because it was to save lives
that God sent me ahead of you. 6For
two years now there has been famine
in the land, and for the next five years
there will not be plowing and reaping. 7But God sent me ahead of you
to preserve for you a remnant on earth
and to save your lives by a great deliverance.[a]

8"So then, it was not you who sent me
here, but God. He made me father to
Pharaoh, lord of his entire household
and ruler of all Egypt. 9Now hurry back
to my father and say to him, 'This is
what your son Joseph says: God has
made me lord of all Egypt. Come down
to me; don't delay. 10You shall live in the
region of Goshen and be near me—you,
your children and grandchildren, your
flocks and herds, and all you have. 11I
will provide for you there, because five
years of famine are still to come. Otherwise you and your household and all
who belong to you will become destitute.'

12"You can see for yourselves, and so
can my brother Benjamin, that it is
really I who am speaking to you. 13Tell
my father about all the honor accorded
me in Egypt and about everything you
have seen. And bring my father down
here quickly."

14Then he threw his arms around his
brother Benjamin and wept, and Benjamin embraced him, weeping. 15And he
kissed all his brothers and wept over
them. Afterward his brothers talked
with him.

16When the news reached Pharaoh's
palace that Joseph's brothers had come,
Pharaoh and all his officials were
pleased. 17Pharaoh said to Joseph, "Tell
your brothers, 'Do this: Load your animals and return to the land of Canaan,
18and bring your father and your families back to me. I will give you the best
of the land of Egypt and you can enjoy
the fat of the land.'

19"You are also directed to tell them,
'Do this: Take some carts from Egypt for
your children and your wives, and get
your father and come. 20Never mind
about your belongings, because the best
of all Egypt will be yours.' "

21So the sons of Israel did this. Joseph
gave them carts, as Pharaoh had commanded, and he also gave them provisions for their journey. 22To each of them
he gave new clothing, but to Benjamin
he gave three hundred shekels[b] of silver
and five sets of clothes. 23And this is
what he sent to his father: ten donkeys
loaded with the best things of Egypt,
and ten female donkeys loaded with
grain and bread and other provisions
for his journey. 24Then he sent his brothers away, and as they were leaving he
said to them, "Don't quarrel on the
way!"

25So they went up out of Egypt and
came to their father Jacob in the land of
Canaan. 26They told him, "Joseph is still
alive! In fact, he is ruler of all Egypt."
Jacob was stunned; he did not believe
them. 27But when they told him everything Joseph had said to them, and
when he saw the carts Joseph had sent
to carry him back, the spirit of their father Jacob revived. 28And Israel said,
"I'm convinced! My son Joseph is still
alive. I will go and see him before I die."

Jacob Goes to Egypt

46 So Israel set out with all
that was his, and when he
reached Beersheba, he offered sacrifices
to the God of his father Isaac.

2And God spoke to Israel in a vision
at night and said, "Jacob! Jacob!"

"Here I am," he replied.

3"I am God, the God of your father,"
he said. "Do not be afraid to go down to
Egypt, for I will make you into a great
nation there. 4I will go down to Egypt
with you, and I will surely bring you
back again. And Joseph's own hand will
close your eyes."

5Then Jacob left Beersheba, and
Israel's sons took their father Jacob and
their children and their wives in the
carts that Pharaoh had sent to transport

[a]7 Or *save you as a great band of survivors*
[b]22 That is, about 7 1/2 pounds (about 3.5 kilograms)

him. 6They also took with them their
livestock and the possessions they had
acquired in Canaan, and Jacob and all
his offspring went to Egypt. 7He took
with him to Egypt his sons and grandsons and his daughters and grand-
daughters—all his offspring.

8These are the names of the sons of Israel (Jacob and his descendants) who
went to Egypt:

Reuben the firstborn of Jacob.
9The sons of Reuben:
Hanoch, Pallu, Hezron and Carmi.
10The sons of Simeon:
Jemuel, Jamin, Ohad, Jakin, Zohar and Shaul the son of a Canaanite woman.
11The sons of Levi:
Gershon, Kohath and Merari.
12The sons of Judah:
Er, Onan, Shelah, Perez and Zerah (but Er and Onan had died in
the land of Canaan).
The sons of Perez:
Hezron and Hamul.
13The sons of Issachar:
Tola, Puah,[a] Jashub[b] and Shimron.
14The sons of Zebulun:
Sered, Elon and Jahleel.
15These were the sons Leah bore to Jacob in Paddan Aram,[c] besides his daughter Dinah. These sons and daughters of
his were thirty-three in all.

16The sons of Gad:
Zephon,[d] Haggi, Shuni, Ezbon,
Eri, Arodi and Areli.
17The sons of Asher:
Imnah, Ishvah, Ishvi and Beriah.
Their sister was Serah.
The sons of Beriah:
Heber and Malkiel.
18These were the children born to Ja-
cob by Zilpah, whom Laban had given
to his daughter Leah—sixteen in all.

19The sons of Jacob's wife Rachel:
Joseph and Benjamin. 20In Egypt,
Manasseh and Ephraim were
born to Joseph by Asenath
daughter of Potiphera, priest of
On.[e]
21The sons of Benjamin:
Bela, Beker, Ashbel, Gera, Naaman, Ehi, Rosh, Muppim, Hup-
pim and Ard.
22These were the sons of Rachel who
were born to Jacob—fourteen in all.

23The son of Dan:
Hushim.
24The sons of Naphtali:
Jahziel, Guni, Jezer and Shillem.
25These were the sons born to Jacob by
Bilhah, whom Laban had given to his
daughter Rachel—seven in all.

26All those who went to Egypt with
Jacob—those who were his direct descendants, not counting his sons'
wives—numbered sixty-six persons.
27With the two sons[f] who had been born
to Joseph in Egypt, the members of
Jacob's family, which went to Egypt,
were seventy[g] in all.

28Now Jacob sent Judah ahead of him
to Joseph to get directions to Goshen.
When they arrived in the region of Goshen, 29Joseph had his chariot made
ready and went to Goshen to meet his
father Israel. As soon as Joseph appeared before him, he threw his arms
around his father[h] and wept for a long
time.

30Israel said to Joseph, "Now I am
ready to die, since I have seen for myself that you are still alive."

31Then Joseph said to his brothers and
to his father's household, "I will go up
and speak to Pharaoh and will say to
him, 'My brothers and my father's
household, who were living in the land
of Canaan, have come to me. 32The men
are shepherds; they tend livestock, and

[a]*13* Samaritan Pentateuch and Syriac (see also 1 Chron. 7:1); Masoretic Text *Puvah*
[b]*13* Samaritan Pentateuch and some Septuagint manuscripts (see also Num. 26:24 and 1 Chron. 7:1); Masoretic Text *Iob* [c]*15* That is, Northwest Mesopotamia [d]*16* Samaritan Pentateuch and Septuagint (see also Num. 26:15); Masoretic Text *Ziphion* [e]*20* That is, Heliopolis [f]*27* Hebrew; Septuagint *the nine children* [g]*27* Hebrew (see also Exodus 1:5 and footnote); Septuagint (see also Acts 7:14) *seventy-five* [h]*29* Hebrew *around him*

they have brought along their flocks
and herds and everything they own.'
[33]When Pharaoh calls you in and asks,
'What is your occupation?' [34]you should
answer, 'Your servants have tended livestock from our boyhood on, just as our
fathers did.' Then you will be allowed
to settle in the region of Goshen, for all
shepherds are detestable to the Egyptians."

SHARPEN THE FOCUS

In Genesis 45:19–20, we read what we might call commands of grace. The Hebrew word for "commanded" in Genesis 45:19 comes from the same root as a word used for God's commands elsewhere in the Old Testament. But what commands! "Take wagons," Pharaoh says, "so your wives and children will have a comfortable ride. Don't worry about leaving some of your possessions behind; I will see to it that you have all you need. The best of Egypt is yours!" We hear in Pharaoh's words faint echoes of our Lord's urgent invitations, His commands of kindness:

> *Repent and be baptized every one of you, in the name of Jesus Christ for the forgiveness of your sins. And you will receive the gift of the Holy Spirit* (Acts 2:38).
>
> *Come to me, all you who are weary and burdened, and I will give you rest* (Matthew 11:28).
>
> *Let us then approach the throne of grace with confidence, so that we may receive mercy and find grace to help us in our time of need* (Hebrews 4:16).

Which of these "commands" would you most like to obey right now? ☼

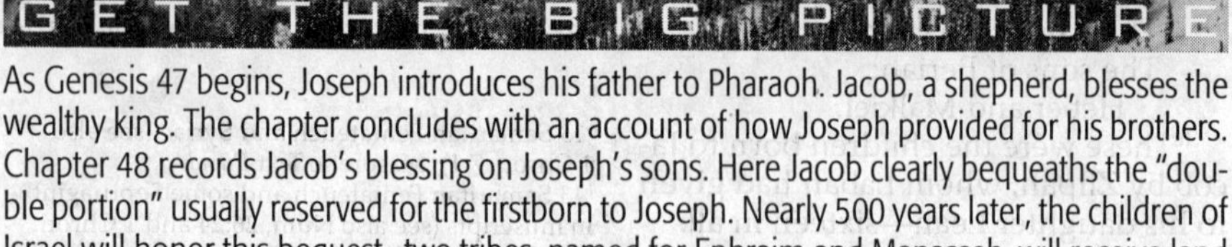

As Genesis 47 begins, Joseph introduces his father to Pharaoh. Jacob, a shepherd, blesses the wealthy king. The chapter concludes with an account of how Joseph provided for his brothers. Chapter 48 records Jacob's blessing on Joseph's sons. Here Jacob clearly bequeaths the "double portion" usually reserved for the firstborn to Joseph. Nearly 500 years later, the children of Israel will honor this bequest–two tribes, named for Ephraim and Manasseh, will receive land in Canaan in Joseph's place. If time is short, focus on Genesis 47:1–10.

47 Joseph went and told Pharaoh, "My father and brothers, with their flocks and herds and everything they own, have come from the land of Canaan and are now in Goshen." [2]He chose five of his brothers and presented them before Pharaoh.

[3]Pharaoh asked the brothers, "What is your occupation?"

"Your servants are shepherds," they replied to Pharaoh, "just as our fathers were." [4]They also said to him, "We have come to live here awhile, because the famine is severe in Canaan and your servants' flocks have no pasture. So now, please let your servants settle in Goshen."

[5]Pharaoh said to Joseph, "Your father and your brothers have come to you, [6]and the land of Egypt is before you; settle your father and your brothers in the best part of the land. Let them live in Goshen. And if you know of any among them with special ability, put them in charge of my own livestock."

[7]Then Joseph brought his father Jacob in and presented him before Pharaoh. After Jacob blessed[a] Pharaoh, [8]Pharaoh asked him, "How old are you?"

[9]And Jacob said to Pharaoh, "The years of my pilgrimage are a hundred and thirty. My years have been few and difficult, and they do not equal the years of the pilgrimage of my fathers." [10]Then Jacob blessed[b] Pharaoh and went out from his presence.

[11]So Joseph settled his father and his brothers in Egypt and gave them property in the best part of the land, the district of Rameses, as Pharaoh directed. [12]Joseph also provided his father and his brothers and all his father's household with food, according to the number of their children.

Joseph and the Famine

[13]There was no food, however, in the whole region because the famine was severe; both Egypt and Canaan wasted away because of the famine. [14]Joseph collected all the money that was to be found in Egypt and Canaan in payment for the grain they were buying, and he brought it to Pharaoh's palace. [15]When the money of the people of Egypt and Canaan was gone, all Egypt came to Joseph and said, "Give us food. Why should we die before your eyes? Our money is used up."

[16]"Then bring your livestock," said Joseph. "I will sell you food in exchange for your livestock, since your money is gone." [17]So they brought their livestock to Joseph, and he gave them food in exchange for their horses, their sheep and goats, their cattle and donkeys. And he brought them through that year with food in exchange for all their livestock.

[18]When that year was over, they came to him the following year and said, "We cannot hide from our lord the fact that since our money is gone and our livestock belongs to you, there is nothing left for our lord except our bodies and our land. [19]Why should we perish before your eyes—we and our land as well? Buy us and our land in exchange for food, and we with our land will be in bondage to Pharaoh. Give us seed so that we may live and not die, and that the land may not become desolate."

[20]So Joseph bought all the land in Egypt for Pharaoh. The Egyptians, one and all, sold their fields, because the famine was too severe for them. The land became Pharaoh's, [21]and Joseph reduced the people to servitude,[c] from one end of Egypt to the other. [22]However, he did not buy the land of the priests, because they received a regular allotment from Pharaoh and had food enough from the allotment Pharaoh gave them. That is why they did not sell their land.

[23]Joseph said to the people, "Now that I have bought you and your land today for Pharaoh, here is seed for you so you can plant the ground. [24]But when the crop comes in, give a fifth of it to Pharaoh. The other four-fifths you may keep as seed for the fields and as food for

[a]7 Or *greeted* [b]10 Or *said farewell to*
[c]21 Samaritan Pentateuch and Septuagint (see also Vulgate); Masoretic Text *and he moved the people into the cities*

yourselves and your households and
your children."
25"You have saved our lives," they
said. "May we find favor in the eyes of
our lord; we will be in bondage to Pharaoh."
26So Joseph established it as a law concerning land in Egypt—still in force today—that a fifth of the produce belongs
to Pharaoh. It was only the land of the
priests that did not become Pharaoh's.
27Now the Israelites settled in Egypt
in the region of Goshen. They acquired
property there and were fruitful and increased greatly in number.
28Jacob lived in Egypt seventeen
years, and the years of his life were a
hundred and forty-seven. 29When the
time drew near for Israel to die, he called
for his son Joseph and said to him, "If I
have found favor in your eyes, put your
hand under my thigh and promise that
you will show me kindness and faithfulness. Do not bury me in Egypt, 30but
when I rest with my fathers, carry me
out of Egypt and bury me where they
are buried."
"I will do as you say," he said.
31"Swear to me," he said. Then Joseph
swore to him, and Israel worshiped as
he leaned on the top of his staff.[a]

Manasseh and Ephraim

48 Some time later Joseph
was told, "Your father is
ill." So he took his two sons Manasseh
and Ephraim along with him. 2When
Jacob was told, "Your son Joseph has
come to you," Israel rallied his strength
and sat up on the bed.
3Jacob said to Joseph, "God Almighty[b]
appeared to me at Luz in the land of Canaan, and there he blessed me 4and said
to me, 'I am going to make you fruitful
and will increase your numbers. I will
make you a community of peoples, and
I will give this land as an everlasting
possession to your descendants after
you.'
5"Now then, your two sons born to
you in Egypt before I came to you here
will be reckoned as mine; Ephraim and
Manasseh will be mine, just as Reuben
and Simeon are mine. 6Any children
born to you after them will be yours; in
the territory they inherit they will be
reckoned under the names of their
brothers. 7As I was returning from Paddan,[c] to my sorrow Rachel died in the
land of Canaan while we were still on
the way, a little distance from Ephrath.
So I buried her there beside the road to
Ephrath" (that is, Bethlehem).
8When Israel saw the sons of Joseph,
he asked, "Who are these?"
9"They are the sons God has given me
here," Joseph said to his father.
Then Israel said, "Bring them to me so
I may bless them."
10Now Israel's eyes were failing because of old age, and he could hardly
see. So Joseph brought his sons close to
him, and his father kissed them and
embraced them.
11Israel said to Joseph, "I never expected to see your face again, and now
God has allowed me to see your children too."
12Then Joseph removed them from
Israel's knees and bowed down with his
face to the ground. 13And Joseph took
both of them, Ephraim on his right toward Israel's left hand and Manasseh on
his left toward Israel's right hand, and
brought them close to him. 14But Israel
reached out his right hand and put it on
Ephraim's head, though he was the
younger, and crossing his arms, he put
his left hand on Manasseh's head, even
though Manasseh was the firstborn.
15Then he blessed Joseph and said,

"May the God before whom my
fathers
Abraham and Isaac walked,
the God who has been my shepherd
all my life to this day,
16 the Angel who has delivered me
from all harm
—may he bless these boys.
May they be called by my name
and the names of my fathers
Abraham and Isaac,

[a]31 Or *Israel bowed down at the head of his bed*
[b]3 Hebrew *El-Shaddai* [c]7 That is, Northwest
Mesopotamia

and may they increase greatly
upon the earth."
17When Joseph saw his father placing
his right hand on Ephraim's head he was
displeased; so he took hold of his father's
hand to move it from Ephraim's head to
Manasseh's head. 18Joseph said to him,
"No, my father, this one is the firstborn;
put your right hand on his head."
19But his father refused and said, "I
know, my son, I know. He too will become a people, and he too will become
great. Nevertheless, his younger brother will be greater than he, and his descendants will become a group of
nations." 20He blessed them that day
and said,

"In your[a] name will Israel
pronounce this blessing:
'May God make you like Ephraim
and Manasseh.' "

So he put Ephraim ahead of Manasseh.
21Then Israel said to Joseph, "I am
about to die, but God will be with you[b]
and take you[b] back to the land of your[b]
fathers. 22And to you, as one who is over
your brothers, I give the ridge of land[c] I
took from the Amorites with my sword
and my bow."

[a]20 The Hebrew is singular. [b]21 The Hebrew is plural. [c]22 Or *And to you I give one portion more than to your brothers—the portion*

SHARPEN THE FOCUS

"Who do you think *you* are?" Often these words are spoken with a surly snap by someone who feels put down or humiliated. Take today's reading, for example. Who did Jacob think he was anyway, presuming to bless the mighty Pharaoh?

Only Israel—"the one who struggles with God." Only the one who had won in those struggles, the one who had triumphed when he had wrestled with God. The one who triumphed because the Lord in grace, had granted Israel victory. Israel knew himself to be the one whose seed, the Messiah, would be King of kings and Lord of lords. And so Jacob, Israel, walked in confidence—whether out to the sheep pen or into Pharaoh's throne room. Jacob had learned what it means to walk, by faith, with the Lord.

Who do you think *you* are? God's child, a son or daughter of the Sovereign of the universe? An heir of God and co-heir with Christ Jesus? A saint made holy by the blood of Jesus? A member of Christ's holy church? Let your identity in your Savior give you confidence and peace—no matter where your feet take you today.

WEEK 5 • WEDNESDAY

Genesis 49:1—50:26

GET THE BIG PICTURE

Jacob, on his deathbed, gathers his sons. Moved by the Holy Spirit, he both blesses them and prophesies about their futures. (Note especially the promises about the coming Savior in the blessing to Judah—Genesis 49:8–12.) Jacob then asks his sons to bury him in the Promised Land—the future homeland of his descendants. Genesis 50 concludes the history of the patriarchs. It records Jacob's burial and Joseph's death. If time is short, focus on Genesis 50:15–26.

Jacob Blesses His Sons

49 Then Jacob called for his sons and said: "Gather around so I can tell you what will happen to you in days to come.

[2]"Assemble and listen, sons of Jacob;
listen to your father Israel.

[3]"Reuben, you are my firstborn,
my might, the first sign of my strength,
excelling in honor, excelling in power.
[4]Turbulent as the waters, you will no longer excel,
for you went up onto your father's bed,
onto my couch and defiled it.

[5]"Simeon and Levi are brothers—
their swords[a] are weapons of violence.
[6]Let me not enter their council,
let me not join their assembly,
for they have killed men in their anger
and hamstrung oxen as they pleased.
[7]Cursed be their anger, so fierce,
and their fury, so cruel!
I will scatter them in Jacob
and disperse them in Israel.

[8]"Judah,[b] your brothers will praise you;
your hand will be on the neck of your enemies;
your father's sons will bow down to you.
[9]You are a lion's cub, O Judah;
you return from the prey, my son.
Like a lion he crouches and lies down,
like a lioness—who dares to rouse him?
[10]The scepter will not depart from Judah,
nor the ruler's staff from between his feet,
until he comes to whom it belongs[c]
and the obedience of the nations is his.
[11]He will tether his donkey to a vine,
his colt to the choicest branch;
he will wash his garments in wine,
his robes in the blood of grapes.
[12]His eyes will be darker than wine,
his teeth whiter than milk.[d]

[13]"Zebulun will live by the seashore
and become a haven for ships;
his border will extend toward Sidon.

[14]"Issachar is a rawboned[e] donkey
lying down between two saddlebags.[f]
[15]When he sees how good is his resting place
and how pleasant is his land,
he will bend his shoulder to the burden
and submit to forced labor.

[16]"Dan[g] will provide justice for his people
as one of the tribes of Israel.
[17]Dan will be a serpent by the roadside,
a viper along the path,
that bites the horse's heels
so that its rider tumbles backward.

[18]"I look for your deliverance,
O LORD.

[19]"Gad[h] will be attacked by a band of raiders,
but he will attack them at their heels.

[20]"Asher's food will be rich;
he will provide delicacies fit for a king.

[21]"Naphtali is a doe set free
that bears beautiful fawns.[i]

[22]"Joseph is a fruitful vine,
a fruitful vine near a spring,
whose branches climb over a wall.[j]

[a]5 The meaning of the Hebrew for this word is uncertain. [b]8 *Judah* sounds like and may be derived from the Hebrew for *praise*. [c]10 Or *until Shiloh comes*; or *until he comes to whom tribute belongs* [d]12 Or *will be dull from wine, / his teeth white from milk* [e]14 Or *strong* [f]14 Or *campfires* [g]16 *Dan* here means *he provides justice*. [h]19 *Gad* can mean *attack* and *band of raiders*. [i]21 Or *free; / he utters beautiful words* [j]22 Or *Joseph is a wild colt, / a wild colt near a spring, / a wild donkey on a terraced hill*

23 With bitterness archers attacked
him;
they shot at him with hostility.
24 But his bow remained steady,
his strong arms stayed[a] limber,
because of the hand of the Mighty
One of Jacob,
because of the Shepherd, the Rock
of Israel,
25 because of your father's God, who
helps you,
because of the Almighty,[b] who
blesses you
with blessings of the heavens above,
blessings of the deep that lies
below,
blessings of the breast and womb.
26 Your father's blessings are greater
than the blessings of the ancient
mountains,
than[c] the bounty of the age-old
hills.
Let all these rest on the head of
Joseph,
on the brow of the prince among[d]
his brothers.

27 "Benjamin is a ravenous wolf;
in the morning he devours the
prey,
in the evening he divides the
plunder."

28 All these are the twelve tribes of Israel, and this is what their father said to
them when he blessed them, giving
each the blessing appropriate to him.

The Death of Jacob

29 Then he gave them these instructions: "I am about to be gathered to my
people. Bury me with my fathers in the
cave in the field of Ephron the Hittite,
30 the cave in the field of Machpelah,
near Mamre in Canaan, which Abraham
bought as a burial place from Ephron
the Hittite, along with the field. 31 There
Abraham and his wife Sarah were buried, there Isaac and his wife Rebekah
were buried, and there I buried Leah.
32 The field and the cave in it were
bought from the Hittites.[e]"
33 When Jacob had finished giving instructions to his sons, he drew his feet
up into the bed, breathed his last and
was gathered to his people.

50 Joseph threw himself
upon his father and wept
over him and kissed him. 2 Then Joseph
directed the physicians in his service to
embalm his father Israel. So the physicians embalmed him, 3 taking a full forty days, for that was the time required
for embalming. And the Egyptians
mourned for him seventy days.
4 When the days of mourning had
passed, Joseph said to Pharaoh's court,
"If I have found favor in your eyes,
speak to Pharaoh for me. Tell him, 5 'My
father made me swear an oath and said,
"I am about to die; bury me in the tomb
I dug for myself in the land of Canaan."
Now let me go up and bury my father;
then I will return.' "
6 Pharaoh said, "Go up and bury your
father, as he made you swear to do."
7 So Joseph went up to bury his father.
All Pharaoh's officials accompanied
him—the dignitaries of his court and all
the dignitaries of Egypt— 8 besides all
the members of Joseph's household and
his brothers and those belonging to his
father's household. Only their children
and their flocks and herds were left in
Goshen. 9 Chariots and horsemen[f] also
went up with him. It was a very large
company.
10 When they reached the threshing
floor of Atad, near the Jordan, they la-
mented loudly and bitterly; and there
Joseph observed a seven-day period of
mourning for his father. 11 When the
Canaanites who lived there saw the
mourning at the threshing floor of Atad,
they said, "The Egyptians are holding a
solemn ceremony of mourning." That is
why that place near the Jordan is called
Abel Mizraim.[g]
12 So Jacob's sons did as he had commanded them: 13 They carried him to the
land of Canaan and buried him in the

[a] 23,24 Or *archers will attack . . . will shoot . . . will remain . . . will stay* [b] 25 Hebrew *Shaddai* [c] 26 Or *of my progenitors, / as great as* [d] 26 Or *the one separated from* [e] 32 Or *the sons of Heth* [f] 9 Or *charioteers* [g] 11 *Abel Mizraim* means *mourning of the Egyptians.*

cave in the field of Machpelah, near
Mamre, which Abraham had bought as
a burial place from Ephron the Hittite,
along with the field. 14After burying his
father, Joseph returned to Egypt, together with his brothers and all the others who had gone with him to bury his father.

Joseph Reassures His Brothers

15When Joseph's brothers saw that
their father was dead, they said, "What
if Joseph holds a grudge against us and
pays us back for all the wrongs we did
to him?" 16So they sent word to Joseph,
saying, "Your father left these instructions before he died: 17'This is what you
are to say to Joseph: I ask you to forgive
your brothers the sins and the wrongs
they committed in treating you so badly.' Now please forgive the sins of the
servants of the God of your father."
When their message came to him, Joseph wept.

18His brothers then came and threw
themselves down before him. "We are
your slaves," they said.

19But Joseph said to them, "Don't be
afraid. Am I in the place of God? 20You
intended to harm me, but God intended it for good to accomplish what is now
being done, the saving of many lives.
21So then, don't be afraid. I will provide
for you and your children." And he reassured them and spoke kindly to them.

The Death of Joseph

22Joseph stayed in Egypt, along with
all his father's family. He lived a hundred and ten years 23and saw the third
generation of Ephraim's children. Also
the children of Makir son of Manasseh
were placed at birth on Joseph's knees.[a]

24Then Joseph said to his brothers, "I
am about to die. But God will surely
come to your aid and take you up out
of this land to the land he promised on
oath to Abraham, Isaac and Jacob."
25And Joseph made the sons of Israel
swear an oath and said, "God will surely come to your aid, and then you must
carry my bones up from this place."

26So Joseph died at the age of a hundred and ten. And after they embalmed
him, he was placed in a coffin in Egypt.

[a]23 That is, were counted as his

SHARPEN THE FOCUS

How hard it sometimes is for us to receive forgiveness—from God or from those whom we have hurt. Only God knows how many tears have been shed, how many prayers of confession spoken, how many words of regret written—long after the original offense has already been forgiven and forgotten.

Joseph cried (Genesis 50:17) when he heard his brothers beg him for the pardon he had granted 50 years earlier. Joseph cried because he saw the pain and fear that guilty consciences had caused those whom he loved. The pain and fear that were so unnecessary!

In this account, Joseph is a picture or a "type" of Christ. He shows us what our Lord's forgiveness can do for us—reassuring us and speaking kindly to us about our past sins and our future hope (Genesis 50:21).

Do you find yourself confessing over and over again sins, which God has already forgiven? Then confess yet one more sin—the sin of not believing your Savior's word of grace. And ask His Spirit to build in you the confident faith to believe God's Word: "I will forgive their wickedness, and will remember their sins no more" (Jeremiah 31:34b).

Exodus

WEEK 5 • THURSDAY

Exodus 1:1–22

GET THE BIG PICTURE

Exodus 1 spans nearly 400 years of history. A few verses sweep us from the days of Joseph to the days of Moses. A change of dynasties in Egypt has radically changed Israel's circumstances. A new king "who did not know about Joseph" (Exodus 1:8) has risen to power. Driven by fear, this king and the Egyptians make slaves of God's people and begin the hellish practice of infanticide. If time is short, focus on Exodus 1:1–14.

The Israelites Oppressed

1 These are the names of the sons of
Israel who went to Egypt with Jacob, each with his family: 2Reuben, Simeon, Levi and Judah; 3Issachar, Zebulun
and Benjamin; 4Dan and Naphtali; Gad
and Asher. 5The descendants of Jacob
numbered seventy[a] in all; Joseph was already in Egypt.
6Now Joseph and all his brothers and
all that generation died, 7but the Israelites were fruitful and multiplied greatly
and became exceedingly numerous, so
that the land was filled with them.
8Then a new king, who did not know
about Joseph, came to power in Egypt.
9"Look," he said to his people, "the Israelites have become much too numerous
for us. 10Come, we must deal shrewdly
with them or they will become even
more numerous and, if war breaks out,
will join our enemies, fight against us
and leave the country."
11So they put slave masters over them
to oppress them with forced labor, and
they built Pithom and Rameses as store
cities for Pharaoh. 12But the more they
were oppressed, the more they multiplied and spread; so the Egyptians came
to dread the Israelites 13and worked
them ruthlessly. 14They made their lives
bitter with hard labor in brick and mortar and with all kinds of work in the
fields; in all their hard labor the Egyptians used them ruthlessly.
15The king of Egypt said to the Hebrew midwives, whose names were
Shiphrah and Puah, 16"When you help
the Hebrew women in childbirth and
observe them on the delivery stool, if it
is a boy, kill him; but if it is a girl, let her
live." 17The midwives, however, feared
God and did not do what the king of
Egypt had told them to do; they let the
boys live. 18Then the king of Egypt summoned the midwives and asked them,
"Why have you done this? Why have
you let the boys live?"
19The midwives answered Pharaoh,
"Hebrew women are not like Egyptian
women; they are vigorous and give
birth before the midwives arrive."
20So God was kind to the midwives
and the people increased and became
even more numerous. 21And because

[a]5 Masoretic Text (see also Gen. 46:27); Dead Sea Scrolls and Septuagint (see also Acts 7:14 and note at Gen. 46:27) *seventy-five*

the midwives feared God, he gave them
families of their own.
[22]Then Pharaoh gave this order to all
his people: "Every boy that is born[a] you
must throw into the Nile, but let every
girl live."

SHARPEN THE FOCUS

Have you ever felt used? put upon? Have the attitudes or actions of others evoked bitterness in your heart? Have your circumstances stolen your joy in the Lord?

The Egyptians appointed slave masters over God's people and oppressed them with forced labor (Exodus 1:11). The Egyptians "used [the Israelites] ruthlessly" (Exodus 1:14).

Things went from bad to worse, until hardships nearly suffocated the people of Israel. And then Pharaoh handed down his edict, sentencing all the boy babies to death.

Where *is* the God of Abraham? the God of Isaac? the God of Jacob? The people of Israel must have wondered. The people of Egypt must have snickered.

The Lord was where He had always been, doing what He has always done—planning a way to deliver and encourage, to save and to cheer His people. He was preparing Israel to see and receive His deliverance. He was planning to use Israel one day as the "cradle for Christ," our Savior from sin. And even now, He is planning a way to deliver you from your situation. He wants to encourage and cheer you while you wait for His deliverance.

WEEK 5 • FRIDAY

Exodus 2:1–25

GET THE BIG PICTURE

Moses, the writer of the Pentateuch (Genesis–Deuteronomy), now begins to tell of his role in the history of God's people. The Lord uses the courageous and creative plan of Moses' family to save the infant from murder at the hands of Pharaoh's soldiers. As the plan unfolds, Moses receives the best education available anywhere in the world at that time—in the palace of Pharaoh himself. When Moses foolishly tries to "speed up" the Lord's plan of deliverance, he must flee for his life. If time is short, focus on Exodus 2:1–10, 23–25.

The Birth of Moses

2 Now a man of the house of Levi
married a Levite woman, [2]and
she became pregnant and gave birth to
a son. When she saw that he was a fine
child, she hid him for three months. [3]But
when she could hide him no longer, she
got a papyrus basket for him and coat-
ed it with tar and pitch. Then she placed
the child in it and put it among the reeds
along the bank of the Nile. [4]His sister
stood at a distance to see what would
happen to him.
[5]Then Pharaoh's daughter went
down to the Nile to bathe, and her at-

[a]22 Masoretic Text; Samaritan Pentateuch, Septuagint and Targums *born to the Hebrews*

tendants were walking along the river
bank. She saw the basket among the
reeds and sent her slave girl to get it.
[6]She opened it and saw the baby. He was
crying, and she felt sorry for him. "This
is one of the Hebrew babies," she said.
[7]Then his sister asked Pharaoh's
daughter, "Shall I go and get one of the
Hebrew women to nurse the baby for
you?"
[8]"Yes, go," she answered. And the girl
went and got the baby's mother.
[9]Pharaoh's daughter said to her, "Take
this baby and nurse him for me, and I
will pay you." So the woman took the
baby and nursed him. [10]When the child
grew older, she took him to Pharaoh's
daughter and he became her son. She
named him Moses,[a] saying, "I drew him
out of the water."

Moses Flees to Midian

[11]One day, after Moses had grown up,
he went out to where his own people
were and watched them at their hard labor. He saw an Egyptian beating a Hebrew, one of his own people. [12]Glancing
this way and that and seeing no one, he
killed the Egyptian and hid him in the
sand. [13]The next day he went out and
saw two Hebrews fighting. He asked
the one in the wrong, "Why are you hit-
ting your fellow Hebrew?"
[14]The man said, "Who made you ruler
and judge over us? Are you thinking of
killing me as you killed the Egyptian?"
Then Moses was afraid and thought,
"What I did must have become known."
[15]When Pharaoh heard of this, he
tried to kill Moses, but Moses fled from
Pharaoh and went to live in Midian,
where he sat down by a well. [16]Now a
priest of Midian had seven daughters,
and they came to draw water and fill the
troughs to water their father's flock.
[17]Some shepherds came along and
drove them away, but Moses got up and
came to their rescue and watered their
flock.
[18]When the girls returned to Reuel
their father, he asked them, "Why have
you returned so early today?"
[19]They answered, "An Egyptian rescued us from the shepherds. He even
drew water for us and watered the
flock."
[20]"And where is he?" he asked his
daughters. "Why did you leave him? Invite him to have something to eat."
[21]Moses agreed to stay with the man,
who gave his daughter Zipporah to Moses in marriage. [22]Zipporah gave birth to
a son, and Moses named him Gershom,[b]
saying, "I have become an alien in a foreign land."
[23]During that long period, the king of
Egypt died. The Israelites groaned in
their slavery and cried out, and their cry
for help because of their slavery went
up to God. [24]God heard their groaning
and he remembered his covenant with
Abraham, with Isaac and with Jacob.
[25]So God looked on the Israelites and
was concerned about them.

[a]10 *Moses* sounds like the Hebrew for *draw out.*
[b]22 *Gershom* sounds like the Hebrew for *an alien there.*

SHARPEN THE FOCUS

Reread Exodus 2:23–25, pen in hand. Underline the verbs that tell what is happening in heaven as Israel groans under the burden of slavery.

This paragraph underscores the depth of God's concern for His people. The Lord longed—even more than Israel did—for their deliverance. The Hebrew text of Exodus 2:25, translated literally, says, "So God looked upon the children of Israel, and God knew." God knew!

The same paragraph could have been written about the day we call *Good Friday*. God heard His people groan under the bondage of their sins. Their cry went up to Him. He heard their groaning under the burden of guilt and shame. He remembered His covenant with Abraham, with Isaac, with Jacob. He thought about those covenant promises all the time. He looked on us with compassion. And He knew.

Still today, the paragraph from Exodus applies. Still today, God hears, God cares, God knows. In Christ Jesus, God has come to deliver us. From our bondage to sin. From our burdens of guilt. From our slavery to shame. From our fear of death.

Where are you burdened today? God hears. God knows. Take your needs to Him, confident in that truth.

Moses, now 80 years old, has learned humility during his 40 years of exile in the wilderness of Horeb. Now, God's work *in* him has reached a point where God can work *through* him. The Lord calls Moses in a most unusual way to his most unusual task. After several objections, Moses strikes out across the desert sands for Egypt. If time is short, focus on Exodus 3:1–15.

Moses and the Burning Bush

3 Now Moses was tending the
flock of Jethro his father-in-law,
the priest of Midian, and he led the flock
to the far side of the desert and came
to Horeb, the mountain of God. [2]There
the angel of the LORD appeared to him
in flames of fire from within a bush.
Moses saw that though the bush was on
fire it did not burn up. [3]So Moses
thought, "I will go over and see this
strange sight—why the bush does not
burn up."

[4]When the LORD saw that he had
gone over to look, God called to him
from within the bush, "Moses! Moses!"

And Moses said, "Here I am."

[5]"Do not come any closer," God said.
"Take off your sandals, for the place
where you are standing is holy ground."
[6]Then he said, "I am the God of your father, the God of Abraham, the God of
Isaac and the God of Jacob." At this,
Moses hid his face, because he was
afraid to look at God.

[7]The LORD said, "I have indeed seen
the misery of my people in Egypt. I have
heard them crying out because of their
slave drivers, and I am concerned about
their suffering. [8]So I have come down to
rescue them from the hand of the Egyptians and to bring them up out of that
land into a good and spacious land, a
land flowing with milk and honey—the
home of the Canaanites, Hittites, Amorites, Perizzites, Hivites and Jebusites.
[9]And now the cry of the Israelites has
reached me, and I have seen the way
the Egyptians are oppressing them. [10]So
now, go. I am sending you to Pharaoh
to bring my people the Israelites out of
Egypt."

[11]But Moses said to God, "Who am I,
that I should go to Pharaoh and bring
the Israelites out of Egypt?"

[12]And God said, "I will be with you.
And this will be the sign to you that it is
I who have sent you: When you have
brought the people out of Egypt, you[a]
will worship God on this mountain."

[a]12 The Hebrew is plural.

[13]Moses said to God, "Suppose I go to
the Israelites and say to them, 'The God
of your fathers has sent me to you,' and
they ask me, 'What is his name?' Then
what shall I tell them?"
[14]God said to Moses, "I AM WHO I AM.[a]
This is what you are to say to the Israelites: 'I AM has sent me to you.' "
[15]God also said to Moses, "Say to the
Israelites, 'The LORD,[b] the God of your
fathers—the God of Abraham, the God
of Isaac and the God of Jacob—has sent
me to you.' This is my name forever, the
name by which I am to be remembered
from generation to generation.
[16]"Go, assemble the elders of Israel
and say to them, 'The LORD, the God of
your fathers—the God of Abraham,
Isaac and Jacob—appeared to me and
said: I have watched over you and have
seen what has been done to you in
Egypt. [17]And I have promised to bring
you up out of your misery in Egypt into
the land of the Canaanites, Hittites,
Amorites, Perizzites, Hivites and Jebusites—a land flowing with milk and
honey.'
[18]"The elders of Israel will listen to
you. Then you and the elders are to go
to the king of Egypt and say to him, 'The
LORD, the God of the Hebrews, has met
with us. Let us take a three-day journey
into the desert to offer sacrifices to the
LORD our God.' [19]But I know that the
king of Egypt will not let you go unless
a mighty hand compels him. [20]So I will
stretch out my hand and strike the
Egyptians with all the wonders that I
will perform among them. After that, he
will let you go.
[21]"And I will make the Egyptians favorably disposed toward this people, so
that when you leave you will not go
empty-handed. [22]Every woman is to ask
her neighbor and any woman living in
her house for articles of silver and gold
and for clothing, which you will put on
your sons and daughters. And so you
will plunder the Egyptians."

Signs for Moses

4 Moses answered, "What if they
do not believe me or listen to me
and say, 'The LORD did not appear to
you'?"
[2]Then the LORD said to him, "What is
that in your hand?"
"A staff," he replied.
[3]The LORD said, "Throw it on the
ground."
Moses threw it on the ground and it
became a snake, and he ran from it.
[4]Then the LORD said to him, "Reach out
your hand and take it by the tail." So
Moses reached out and took hold of the
snake and it turned back into a staff in
his hand. [5]"This," said the LORD, "is so
that they may believe that the LORD, the
God of their fathers—the God of Abraham, the God of Isaac and the God of
Jacob—has appeared to you."
[6]Then the LORD said, "Put your hand
inside your cloak." So Moses put his
hand into his cloak, and when he took
it out, it was leprous,[c] like snow.
[7]"Now put it back into your cloak," he
said. So Moses put his hand back into
his cloak, and when he took it out, it was
restored, like the rest of his flesh.
[8]Then the LORD said, "If they do not
believe you or pay attention to the first
miraculous sign, they may believe the
second. [9]But if they do not believe these
two signs or listen to you, take some water from the Nile and pour it on the dry
ground. The water you take from the
river will become blood on the ground."
[10]Moses said to the LORD, "O Lord, I
have never been eloquent, neither in
the past nor since you have spoken to
your servant. I am slow of speech and
tongue."
[11]The LORD said to him, "Who gave
man his mouth? Who makes him deaf
or mute? Who gives him sight or makes
him blind? Is it not I, the LORD? [12]Now
go; I will help you speak and will teach
you what to say."
[13]But Moses said, "O Lord, please send
someone else to do it."

[a]*14* Or *I WILL BE WHAT I WILL BE* [b]*15* The Hebrew for *LORD* sounds like and may be derived from the Hebrew for *I AM* in verse 14.
[c]*6* The Hebrew word was used for various diseases affecting the skin—not necessarily leprosy.

14Then the LORD's anger burned
against Moses and he said, "What about
your brother, Aaron the Levite? I know
he can speak well. He is already on his
way to meet you, and his heart will be
glad when he sees you. 15You shall speak
to him and put words in his mouth; I
will help both of you speak and will
teach you what to do. 16He will speak to
the people for you, and it will be as if he
were your mouth and as if you were
God to him. 17But take this staff in your
hand so you can perform miraculous
signs with it."

Moses Returns to Egypt

18Then Moses went back to Jethro
his father-in-law and said to him, "Let
me go back to my own people in Egypt
to see if any of them are still alive."
Jethro said, "Go, and I wish you well."
19Now the LORD had said to Moses in
Midian, "Go back to Egypt, for all the
men who wanted to kill you are dead."
20So Moses took his wife and sons, put
them on a donkey and started back to
Egypt. And he took the staff of God in
his hand.
21The LORD said to Moses, "When you
return to Egypt, see that you perform
before Pharaoh all the wonders I have
given you the power to do. But I will
harden his heart so that he will not let
the people go. 22Then say to Pharaoh,
'This is what the LORD says: Israel is my
firstborn son, 23and I told you, "Let my
son go, so he may worship me." But you
refused to let him go; so I will kill your
firstborn son.' "
24At a lodging place on the way, the
LORD met ⌞Moses⌟[a] and was about to kill
him. 25But Zipporah took a flint knife,
cut off her son's foreskin and touched
⌞Moses'⌟ feet with it.[b] "Surely you are a
bridegroom of blood to me," she said.
26So the LORD let him alone. (At that time
she said "bridegroom of blood," referring to circumcision.)
27The LORD said to Aaron, "Go into the
desert to meet Moses." So he met
Moses at the mountain of God and
kissed him. 28Then Moses told Aaron
everything the LORD had sent him to
say, and also about all the miraculous
signs he had commanded him to perform.
29Moses and Aaron brought together
all the elders of the Israelites, 30and Aaron told them everything the LORD had
said to Moses. He also performed the
signs before the people, 31and they believed. And when they heard that the
LORD was concerned about them and
had seen their misery, they bowed
down and worshiped.

[a]24 Or *⌞Moses' son⌟*; Hebrew *him* [b]25 Or *and drew near ⌞Moses'⌟ feet*

SHARPEN THE FOCUS

So much in our faith-walk depends on our focus. When Moses took Israel's deliverance upon himself and murdered the Egyptian (Exodus 2:11–12), he counted on his own abilities and zeal. But when, from the burning bush, God called Moses to deliver Israel, Moses had lost all of his *self*-confidence. "Who am I," he asks, "that I should go to Pharaoh?" (Exodus 3:11).

At this point, the Lord focused Moses' attention away from himself. Instead, God calls Moses to focus on Him—the great I AM. The Lord, the Savior-God, was and is and always will be. He is the eternal, all-powerful ruler of the universe. He is King of kings and Lord of lords.

When we reach the end of our self-sufficiency, our Lord is there waiting for us. He takes us up in His arms and encourages us to rely on Him and on His love. When we focus on the cross of Christ and on what He has done for us, we can walk in confident faith. We can do with courage whatever He asks us to do.

WEEK 6 • MONDAY

Exodus 5:1—6:30

GET THE BIG PICTURE

In the previous chapter (Exodus 4:29–31), Moses and Aaron presented God's program to the leaders of Israel. Now, Moses and Aaron go to Pharaoh himself. The ruler mocks the Hebrews' God and makes life more miserable for them by increasing their already crushing workload. When the Israelites turn on Moses and Aaron in discouragement and anger, the Lord reassures Israel's leaders and then the people that He will perform what He has promised. If time is short, focus on Exodus 5:1–23.

Bricks Without Straw

5 Afterward Moses and Aaron went to Pharaoh and said, "This is what the LORD, the God of Israel, says: 'Let my people go, so that they may hold a festival to me in the desert.' "

[2]Pharaoh said, "Who is the LORD, that I should obey him and let Israel go? I do not know the LORD and I will not let Israel go."

[3]Then they said, "The God of the Hebrews has met with us. Now let us take a three-day journey into the desert to offer sacrifices to the LORD our God, or he may strike us with plagues or with the sword."

[4]But the king of Egypt said, "Moses and Aaron, why are you taking the people away from their labor? Get back to your work!" [5]Then Pharaoh said, "Look, the people of the land are now numerous, and you are stopping them from working."

[6]That same day Pharaoh gave this order to the slave drivers and foremen in charge of the people: [7]"You are no longer to supply the people with straw for making bricks; let them go and gather their own straw. [8]But require them to make the same number of bricks as before; don't reduce the quota. They are lazy; that is why they are crying out, 'Let us go and sacrifice to our God.' [9]Make the work harder for the men so that they keep working and pay no attention to lies."

[10]Then the slave drivers and the foremen went out and said to the people, "This is what Pharaoh says: 'I will not give you any more straw. [11]Go and get your own straw wherever you can find it, but your work will not be reduced at all.' " [12]So the people scattered all over Egypt to gather stubble to use for straw. [13]The slave drivers kept pressing them, saying, "Complete the work required of you for each day, just as when you had straw." [14]The Israelite foremen appointed by Pharaoh's slave drivers were beaten and were asked, "Why didn't you meet your quota of bricks yesterday or today, as before?"

[15]Then the Israelite foremen went and appealed to Pharaoh: "Why have you treated your servants this way? [16]Your servants are given no straw, yet we are told, 'Make bricks!' Your servants are being beaten, but the fault is with your own people."

[17]Pharaoh said, "Lazy, that's what you are—lazy! That is why you keep saying, 'Let us go and sacrifice to the LORD.' [18]Now get to work. You will not be given any straw, yet you must produce your full quota of bricks."

[19]The Israelite foremen realized they were in trouble when they were told, "You are not to reduce the number of bricks required of you for each day." [20]When they left Pharaoh, they found Moses and Aaron waiting to meet them, [21]and they said, "May the LORD look

upon you and judge you! You have made us a stench to Pharaoh and his officials and have put a sword in their hand to kill us."

God Promises Deliverance

[22]Moses returned to the LORD and said, "O Lord, why have you brought trouble upon this people? Is this why you sent me? [23]Ever since I went to Pharaoh to speak in your name, he has brought trouble upon this people, and you have not rescued your people at all."

6 Then the LORD said to Moses, "Now you will see what I will do to Pharaoh: Because of my mighty hand he will let them go; because of my mighty hand he will drive them out of his country."

[2]God also said to Moses, "I am the LORD. [3]I appeared to Abraham, to Isaac and to Jacob as God Almighty,[a] but by my name the LORD[b] I did not make myself known to them.[c] [4]I also established my covenant with them to give them the land of Canaan, where they lived as aliens. [5]Moreover, I have heard the groaning of the Israelites, whom the Egyptians are enslaving, and I have remembered my covenant.

[6]"Therefore, say to the Israelites: 'I am the LORD, and I will bring you out from under the yoke of the Egyptians. I will free you from being slaves to them, and I will redeem you with an outstretched arm and with mighty acts of judgment. [7]I will take you as my own people, and I will be your God. Then you will know that I am the LORD your God, who brought you out from under the yoke of the Egyptians. [8]And I will bring you to the land I swore with uplifted hand to give to Abraham, to Isaac and to Jacob. I will give it to you as a possession. I am the LORD.' "

[9]Moses reported this to the Israelites, but they did not listen to him because of their discouragement and cruel bondage.

[10]Then the LORD said to Moses, [11]"Go, tell Pharaoh king of Egypt to let the Israelites go out of his country."

[12]But Moses said to the LORD, "If the Israelites will not listen to me, why would Pharaoh listen to me, since I speak with faltering lips[d]?"

Family Record of Moses and Aaron

[13]Now the LORD spoke to Moses and Aaron about the Israelites and Pharaoh king of Egypt, and he commanded them to bring the Israelites out of Egypt.

[14]These were the heads of their families[e]:

The sons of Reuben the firstborn son of Israel were Hanoch and Pallu, Hezron and Carmi. These were the clans of Reuben.

[15]The sons of Simeon were Jemuel, Jamin, Ohad, Jakin, Zohar and Shaul the son of a Canaanite woman. These were the clans of Simeon.

[16]These were the names of the sons of Levi according to their records: Gershon, Kohath and Merari. Levi lived 137 years.

[17]The sons of Gershon, by clans, were Libni and Shimei.

[18]The sons of Kohath were Amram, Izhar, Hebron and Uzziel. Kohath lived 133 years.

[19]The sons of Merari were Mahli and Mushi.

These were the clans of Levi according to their records.

[20]Amram married his father's sister Jochebed, who bore him Aaron and Moses. Amram lived 137 years.

[21]The sons of Izhar were Korah, Nepheg and Zicri.

[22]The sons of Uzziel were Mishael, Elzaphan and Sithri.

[23]Aaron married Elisheba, daughter of Amminadab and sister of Nahshon, and she bore him Nadab and Abihu, Eleazar and Ithamar.

[24]The sons of Korah were Assir,

[a]3 Hebrew *El-Shaddai* [b]3 See note at Exodus 3:15. [c]3 Or *Almighty, and by my name the LORD did I not let myself be known to them?* [d]12 Hebrew *I am uncircumcised of lips*; also in verse 30
[e]14 The Hebrew for *families* here and in verse 25 refers to units larger than clans.

Elkanah and Abiasaph. These were
the Korahite clans.
25 Eleazar son of Aaron married
one of the daughters of Putiel, and
she bore him Phinehas.

These were the heads of the Levite families, clan by clan.

26 It was this same Aaron and Moses to
whom the LORD said, "Bring the Israelites out of Egypt by their divisions."
27 They were the ones who spoke to
Pharaoh king of Egypt about bringing
the Israelites out of Egypt. It was the
same Moses and Aaron.

Aaron to Speak for Moses

28 Now when the LORD spoke to Moses in Egypt, 29 he said to him, "I am the
LORD. Tell Pharaoh king of Egypt everything I tell you."
30 But Moses said to the LORD, "Since
I speak with faltering lips, why would
Pharaoh listen to me?"

SHARPEN THE FOCUS

When we walk by faith, we can expect opposition. Faith does not work like some kind of magic wand whose touch dissolves anything that stands in our way. No, when we walk by faith we can expect Satan and the world system around us to throw road blocks in our path.

At times it may look as though we will never get over, under, around, or through the obstacles. See what Exodus 6:9 says: the people felt so hopeless, they would not even listen to the Lord's plan to deliver them. Still, the Savior-God commanded Moses to stay on-track, to present another ultimatum to Pharaoh.

Though we, at times, may give up on God, He never gives up on us. Remember Romans 5:8: "God demonstrates His own love for us in this: While we were still sinners, Christ died for us." God acted to deliver us from our sins while we still lived as His enemies!

Our Lord will bring us through every one of our earthly troubles, whether or not we believe He will. He has promised—often—to do that (Romans 8:27–28; 2 Timothy 4:18). How much more peace, though, we can have along the way when we confess our sinful worries to Him and put our needs into His gracious hands.

WEEK 6 • TUESDAY

Exodus 7:1–24

GET THE BIG PICTURE

Moses and Aaron appear before Pharaoh once again to repeat God's command to let the Israelites go. Pharaoh does not listen to them. In the face of Pharaoh's unbelief, the Lord does not attempt to prove Himself to Moses. Instead, He simply repeats His word of promise and sends Moses and Aaron back to talk to Pharaoh. Once again Pharaoh refuses to listen. And so the first judgment, or "plague," begins. If time is short, focus on Exodus 7:1–7.

7 Then the LORD said to Moses, "See, I have made you like God to Pharaoh, and your brother Aaron will be your prophet. 2You are to say everything I command you, and your brother Aaron is to tell Pharaoh to let the Israelites go out of his country. 3But I will harden Pharaoh's heart, and though I multiply my miraculous signs and wonders in Egypt, 4he will not listen to you. Then I will lay my hand on Egypt and with mighty acts of judgment I will bring out my divisions, my people the Israelites. 5And the Egyptians will know that I am the LORD when I stretch out my hand against Egypt and bring the Israelites out of it."

6Moses and Aaron did just as the LORD commanded them. 7Moses was eighty years old and Aaron eighty-three when they spoke to Pharaoh.

Aaron's Staff Becomes a Snake

8The LORD said to Moses and Aaron, 9"When Pharaoh says to you, 'Perform a miracle,' then say to Aaron, 'Take your staff and throw it down before Pharaoh,' and it will become a snake."

10So Moses and Aaron went to Pharaoh and did just as the LORD commanded. Aaron threw his staff down in front of Pharaoh and his officials, and it became a snake. 11Pharaoh then summoned wise men and sorcerers, and the Egyptian magicians also did the same things by their secret arts: 12Each one threw down his staff and it became a snake. But Aaron's staff swallowed up their staffs. 13Yet Pharaoh's heart became hard and he would not listen to them, just as the LORD had said.

The Plague of Blood

14Then the LORD said to Moses, "Pharaoh's heart is unyielding; he refuses to let the people go. 15Go to Pharaoh in the morning as he goes out to the water. Wait on the bank of the Nile to meet him, and take in your hand the staff that was changed into a snake. 16Then say to him, 'The LORD, the God of the Hebrews, has sent me to say to you: Let my people go, so that they may worship me in the desert. But until now you have not listened. 17This is what the LORD says: By this you will know that I am the LORD: With the staff that is in my hand I will strike the water of the Nile, and it will be changed into blood. 18The fish in the Nile will die, and the river will stink; the Egyptians will not be able to drink its water.' "

19The LORD said to Moses, "Tell Aaron, 'Take your staff and stretch out your hand over the waters of Egypt—over the streams and canals, over the ponds and all the reservoirs'—and they will turn to blood. Blood will be everywhere in Egypt, even in the wooden buckets and stone jars."

20Moses and Aaron did just as the LORD had commanded. He raised his staff in the presence of Pharaoh and his officials and struck the water of the Nile, and all the water was changed into blood. 21The fish in the Nile died, and the river smelled so bad that the Egyptians could not drink its water. Blood was everywhere in Egypt.

22But the Egyptian magicians did the same things by their secret arts, and Pharaoh's heart became hard; he would not listen to Moses and Aaron, just as the LORD had said. 23Instead, he turned and went into his palace, and did not take even this to heart. 24And all the Egyptians dug along the Nile to get drinking water, because they could not drink the water of the river.

SHARPEN THE FOCUS

In Exodus 7:4, the Lord tells Moses that He intends to bring His "divisions" or "armies" out of Egypt. He will do this so the Egyptians will know that He is the Lord, the one and only Savior-God.

What an army—slaves and children! But God saw Israel quite differently than Pharaoh did. Israel was the Lord's pride, His joy. He saw His people with the 20/20 vision of love.

The "Israel of God" today is the one, holy Christian church. We belong to God's army of light. We may not think we have much power or exercise much influence. We often appear to ourselves and to those outside as merely spiritual children, playing at making a difference.

Our Lord sees quite another picture. He sees us as His army, equipped with His Word and the holy Sacraments. He has sent us to invade Satan's strongholds, to tear down the walls he's built. God empowers us to rescue those still in captivity to sin and death.

Sometime today, call a fellow believer who may feel discouraged about the church. Share Jesus' promise from Matthew 16:18 with one another. Then pray together for your church, pastor and other professional workers, lay leaders, and all the work of your congregation.

Exodus 8–9 recounts six of the ten plagues God visited on Egypt. The Lord intended each of these plagues to bring Pharaoh to repentance and to show the Egyptians that He was the one, true God. Pharaoh and most of his people rejected the Lord and hardened their hearts against His salvation. They did this in the face of overwhelming evidence and to their eternal destruction. If time is short, focus on Exodus 8:20–32.

The Plague of Frogs

[25]Seven days passed after the LORD
8 struck the Nile. [1]Then the
LORD said to Moses, "Go to Pharaoh and say to him, 'This is what the
LORD says: Let my people go, so that
they may worship me. [2]If you refuse to
let them go, I will plague your whole
country with frogs. [3]The Nile will teem
with frogs. They will come up into your
palace and your bedroom and onto
your bed, into the houses of your officials and on your people, and into your
ovens and kneading troughs. [4]The frogs
will go up on you and your people and
all your officials.' "
[5]Then the LORD said to Moses, "Tell
Aaron, 'Stretch out your hand with your
staff over the streams and canals and
ponds, and make frogs come up on the
land of Egypt.' "
[6]So Aaron stretched out his hand over
the waters of Egypt, and the frogs came
up and covered the land. [7]But the magicians did the same things by their secret arts; they also made frogs come up
on the land of Egypt.
[8]Pharaoh summoned Moses and Aaron and said, "Pray to the LORD to take
the frogs away from me and my people,
and I will let your people go to offer sacrifices to the LORD."
[9]Moses said to Pharaoh, "I leave to
you the honor of setting the time for me
to pray for you and your officials and
your people that you and your houses
may be rid of the frogs, except for those
that remain in the Nile."
[10]"Tomorrow," Pharaoh said.
Moses replied, "It will be as you say,
so that you may know there is no one
like the LORD our God. [11]The frogs will

leave you and your houses, your officials and your people; they will remain only in the Nile."

12 After Moses and Aaron left Pharaoh, Moses cried out to the LORD about the frogs he had brought on Pharaoh. 13 And the LORD did what Moses asked. The frogs died in the houses, in the courtyards and in the fields. 14 They were piled into heaps, and the land reeked of them. 15 But when Pharaoh saw that there was relief, he hardened his heart and would not listen to Moses and Aaron, just as the LORD had said.

The Plague of Gnats

16 Then the LORD said to Moses, "Tell Aaron, 'Stretch out your staff and strike the dust of the ground,' and throughout the land of Egypt the dust will become gnats." 17 They did this, and when Aaron stretched out his hand with the staff and struck the dust of the ground, gnats came upon men and animals. All the dust throughout the land of Egypt became gnats. 18 But when the magicians tried to produce gnats by their secret arts, they could not. And the gnats were on men and animals.

19 The magicians said to Pharaoh, "This is the finger of God." But Pharaoh's heart was hard and he would not listen, just as the LORD had said.

The Plague of Flies

20 Then the LORD said to Moses, "Get up early in the morning and confront Pharaoh as he goes to the water and say to him, 'This is what the LORD says: Let my people go, so that they may worship me. 21 If you do not let my people go, I will send swarms of flies on you and your officials, on your people and into your houses. The houses of the Egyptians will be full of flies, and even the ground where they are.

22 " 'But on that day I will deal differently with the land of Goshen, where my people live; no swarms of flies will be there, so that you will know that I, the LORD, am in this land. 23 I will make a distinction[a] between my people and your people. This miraculous sign will occur tomorrow.' "

24 And the LORD did this. Dense swarms of flies poured into Pharaoh's palace and into the houses of his officials, and throughout Egypt the land was ruined by the flies.

25 Then Pharaoh summoned Moses and Aaron and said, "Go, sacrifice to your God here in the land."

26 But Moses said, "That would not be right. The sacrifices we offer the LORD our God would be detestable to the Egyptians. And if we offer sacrifices that are detestable in their eyes, will they not stone us? 27 We must take a three-day journey into the desert to offer sacrifices to the LORD our God, as he commands us."

28 Pharaoh said, "I will let you go to offer sacrifices to the LORD your God in the desert, but you must not go very far. Now pray for me."

29 Moses answered, "As soon as I leave you, I will pray to the LORD, and tomorrow the flies will leave Pharaoh and his officials and his people. Only be sure that Pharaoh does not act deceitfully again by not letting the people go to offer sacrifices to the LORD."

30 Then Moses left Pharaoh and prayed to the LORD, 31 and the LORD did what Moses asked: The flies left Pharaoh and his officials and his people; not a fly remained. 32 But this time also Pharaoh hardened his heart and would not let the people go.

The Plague on Livestock

9 Then the LORD said to Moses, "Go to Pharaoh and say to him, 'This is what the LORD, the God of the Hebrews, says: "Let my people go, so that they may worship me." 2 If you refuse to let them go and continue to hold them back, 3 the hand of the LORD will bring a terrible plague on your livestock in the field—on your horses and donkeys and camels and on your cattle and sheep and goats. 4 But the LORD will

[a] 23 Septuagint and Vulgate; Hebrew *will put a deliverance*

make a distinction between the livestock of Israel and that of Egypt, so that
no animal belonging to the Israelites
will die.' "
5The LORD set a time and said, "Tomorrow the LORD will do this in the
land." 6And the next day the LORD did
it: All the livestock of the Egyptians
died, but not one animal belonging to
the Israelites died. 7Pharaoh sent men to
investigate and found that not even one
of the animals of the Israelites had died.
Yet his heart was unyielding and he
would not let the people go.

The Plague of Boils

8Then the LORD said to Moses and
Aaron, "Take handfuls of soot from a furnace and have Moses toss it into the air
in the presence of Pharaoh. 9It will become fine dust over the whole land of
Egypt, and festering boils will break out
on men and animals throughout the
land."
10So they took soot from a furnace and
stood before Pharaoh. Moses tossed it
into the air, and festering boils broke out
on men and animals. 11The magicians
could not stand before Moses because of
the boils that were on them and on all
the Egyptians. 12But the LORD hardened
Pharaoh's heart and he would not listen
to Moses and Aaron, just as the LORD
had said to Moses.

The Plague of Hail

13Then the LORD said to Moses, "Get
up early in the morning, confront Pharaoh and say to him, 'This is what the
LORD, the God of the Hebrews, says: Let
my people go, so that they may worship
me, 14or this time I will send the full
force of my plagues against you and
against your officials and your people,
so you may know that there is no one
like me in all the earth. 15For by now I
could have stretched out my hand and
struck you and your people with a
plague that would have wiped you off
the earth. 16But I have raised you up[a] for
this very purpose, that I might show
you my power and that my name might
be proclaimed in all the earth. 17You still
set yourself against my people and will
not let them go. 18Therefore, at this time
tomorrow I will send the worst hailstorm that has ever fallen on Egypt,
from the day it was founded till now.
19Give an order now to bring your livestock and everything you have in the
field to a place of shelter, because the
hail will fall on every man and animal
that has not been brought in and is still
out in the field, and they will die.' "
20Those officials of Pharaoh who
feared the word of the LORD hurried to
bring their slaves and their livestock inside. 21But those who ignored the word
of the LORD left their slaves and livestock in the field.
22Then the LORD said to Moses,
"Stretch out your hand toward the sky
so that hail will fall all over Egypt—on
men and animals and on everything
growing in the fields of Egypt." 23When
Moses stretched out his staff toward the
sky, the LORD sent thunder and hail, and
lightning flashed down to the ground.
So the LORD rained hail on the land of
Egypt; 24hail fell and lightning flashed
back and forth. It was the worst storm
in all the land of Egypt since it had become a nation. 25Throughout Egypt hail
struck everything in the fields—both
men and animals; it beat down everything growing in the fields and stripped
every tree. 26The only place it did not
hail was the land of Goshen, where the
Israelites were.
27Then Pharaoh summoned Moses
and Aaron. "This time I have sinned," he
said to them. "The LORD is in the right,
and I and my people are in the wrong.
28Pray to the LORD, for we have had
enough thunder and hail. I will let you
go; you don't have to stay any longer."
29Moses replied, "When I have gone
out of the city, I will spread out my
hands in prayer to the LORD. The thunder will stop and there will be no more
hail, so you may know that the earth is
the LORD's. 30But I know that you and
your officials still do not fear the LORD
God."

[a]16 Or *have spared you*

31(The flax and barley were destroyed,
since the barley had headed and the flax
was in bloom. 32The wheat and spelt,
however, were not destroyed, because
they ripen later.)
33Then Moses left Pharaoh and went
out of the city. He spread out his hands
toward the LORD; the thunder and hail
stopped, and the rain no longer poured
down on the land. 34When Pharaoh saw
that the rain and hail and thunder had
stopped, he sinned again: He and his
officials hardened their hearts. 35So
Pharaoh's heart was hard and he would
not let the Israelites go, just as the LORD
had said through Moses.

SHARPEN THE FOCUS

In the early 1980's, a prominent evangelist got into serious trouble with the press. He asserted that God hears only the prayers of His children, only the prayers of true Christians.

Several times in Exodus 8–10 we read that Pharaoh asked Moses and Aaron to intercede for him. Tragically, the hardened ruler did not want the Lord's forgiveness. Nor the gift of faith. Nor a repentant heart. He wanted a happy life, a carefree life, an easy life. And so, when the Lord stopped one plague, a new and more devastating one took its place.

Because the Lord knows and fully understands our deepest human needs, He waits to hear six short words from those who rebel against Him: "I've done wrong. Please forgive me." Unbelievers need to pray this prayer. But so do each of God's children when we become aware of sin in our lives.

How long has it been since you spoke the words of Psalm 139:23–24 with the psalmist? This process, done on a regular, or daily, basis, will prevent that most dangerous of all spiritual diseases—hardening of the heart. Let the Holy Spirit examine your heart, point out your sins, and assure you of His full forgiveness today.

WEEK 6 • THURSDAY

Exodus 10:1–29

GET THE BIG PICTURE

Plagues eight and nine fall upon the Egyptians in much the same way as the first seven plagues did. But we can begin to see changes in the hearts and minds of the people involved. As you read this chapter, note especially the statements by and about Pharaoh and his officials. If time is short, focus on Exodus 10:1–20.

The Plague of Locusts

10 Then the LORD said to Moses,
"Go to Pharaoh, for I have
hardened his heart and the hearts of his
officials so that I may perform these
miraculous signs of mine among them
2that you may tell your children and
grandchildren how I dealt harshly with the Egyptians and how I performed my signs among them, and

that you may know that I am the LORD."
3 So Moses and Aaron went to Pharaoh and said to him, "This is what the
LORD, the God of the Hebrews, says:
'How long will you refuse to humble
yourself before me? Let my people go,
so that they may worship me. 4 If you
refuse to let them go, I will bring locusts
into your country tomorrow. 5 They will
cover the face of the ground so that it
cannot be seen. They will devour what
little you have left after the hail, including every tree that is growing in your
fields. 6 They will fill your houses and
those of all your officials and all the
Egyptians—something neither your fathers nor your forefathers have ever
seen from the day they settled in this
land till now.' " Then Moses turned and
left Pharaoh.
7 Pharaoh's officials said to him, "How
long will this man be a snare to us? Let
the people go, so that they may worship
the LORD their God. Do you not yet realize that Egypt is ruined?"
8 Then Moses and Aaron were
brought back to Pharaoh. "Go, worship
the LORD your God," he said. "But just
who will be going?"
9 Moses answered, "We will go with
our young and old, with our sons and
daughters, and with our flocks and
herds, because we are to celebrate a festival to the LORD."
10 Pharaoh said, "The LORD be with
you—if I let you go, along with your
women and children! Clearly you are
bent on evil.[a] 11 No! Have only the men
go; and worship the LORD, since that's
what you have been asking for." Then
Moses and Aaron were driven out of
Pharaoh's presence.
12 And the LORD said to Moses,
"Stretch out your hand over Egypt so
that locusts will swarm over the land
and devour everything growing in the
fields, everything left by the hail."
13 So Moses stretched out his staff over
Egypt, and the LORD made an east
wind blow across the land all that day
and all that night. By morning the
wind had brought the locusts; 14 they
invaded all Egypt and settled down in
every area of the country in great
numbers. Never before had there been
such a plague of locusts, nor will there
ever be again. 15 They covered all the
ground until it was black. They devoured all that was left after the hail—
everything growing in the fields and the
fruit on the trees. Nothing green remained on tree or plant in all the land
of Egypt.
16 Pharaoh quickly summoned Moses
and Aaron and said, "I have sinned
against the LORD your God and against
you. 17 Now forgive my sin once more
and pray to the LORD your God to take
this deadly plague away from me."
18 Moses then left Pharaoh and prayed
to the LORD. 19 And the LORD changed
the wind to a very strong west wind,
which caught up the locusts and carried
them into the Red Sea.[b] Not a locust was
left anywhere in Egypt. 20 But the LORD
hardened Pharaoh's heart, and he
would not let the Israelites go.

The Plague of Darkness

21 Then the LORD said to Moses,
"Stretch out your hand toward the sky
so that darkness will spread over
Egypt—darkness that can be felt." 22 So
Moses stretched out his hand toward
the sky, and total darkness covered all
Egypt for three days. 23 No one could see
anyone else or leave his place for three
days. Yet all the Israelites had light in the
places where they lived.
24 Then Pharaoh summoned Moses
and said, "Go, worship the LORD. Even
your women and children may go with
you; only leave your flocks and herds
behind."
25 But Moses said, "You must allow us
to have sacrifices and burnt offerings to
present to the LORD our God. 26 Our
livestock too must go with us; not a hoof
is to be left behind. We have to use some
of them in worshiping the LORD our
God, and until we get there we will not
know what we are to use to worship the
LORD."

[a] *10* Or *Be careful, trouble is in store for you!*
[b] *19* Hebrew *Yam Suph*; that is, Sea of Reeds

27But the LORD hardened Pharaoh's
heart, and he was not willing to let them
go. 28Pharaoh said to Moses, "Get out of
my sight! Make sure you do not appear
before me again! The day you see my
face you will die."
29"Just as you say," Moses replied, "I
will never appear before you again."

SHARPEN THE FOCUS

The phrase *point of no return* has a unique meaning for airplane pilots. It's the point along the runway at which the plane must take off. Pilots who pass the point of no return will crash if they attempt to brake and taxi to a stop. They're out of runway.

Exodus 9:35 records Pharaoh's point of no return, spiritually speaking. Over and over again he had hardened his heart against the message that God, in grace and power, had tried to convey to him. Now there was no turning back. In Exodus 10:1, God confirms the decision Pharaoh had made for himself repeatedly.

Lest we think ourselves exempt from the temptation to hardness of heart, the Holy Spirit warns us:

> *See to it, brothers, that none of you has a sinful, unbelieving heart that turns away from the living God. But encourage one another daily, as long as it is called Today, so that none of you may be hardened by sin's deceitfulness.* (Hebrews 3:12–13)

Thank God today for other believers who encourage and warn you. Thank Him, too, for His gifts of repentance and faith. Pray for grace to be an encourager for others.

WEEK 6 • FRIDAY

Exodus 11:1—12:51

GET THE BIG PICTURE

One final plague, and Israel will be free. Chapter 11 includes this announcement to Pharaoh. Chapter 12 goes on to describe the tenth plague and the way in which the Savior-God spared His people. Exodus 12:14–28 and 42–49 come as parentheses in the story. These Exodus verses detail the Lord's instructions about the way Israel was to celebrate God's Passover victory in the coming years. If time is short, focus on Exodus 12:29–51.

The Plague on the Firstborn

11 Now the LORD had said to Moses, "I will bring one more
plague on Pharaoh and on Egypt. After
that, he will let you go from here, and
when he does, he will drive you out
completely. 2Tell the people that men
and women alike are to ask their neighbors for articles of silver and gold." 3(The
LORD made the Egyptians favorably disposed toward the people, and Moses
himself was highly regarded in Egypt

by Pharaoh's officials and by the people.)

4So Moses said, "This is what the LORD says: 'About midnight I will go throughout Egypt. 5Every firstborn son in Egypt will die, from the firstborn son of Pharaoh, who sits on the throne, to the firstborn son of the slave girl, who is at her hand mill, and all the firstborn of the cattle as well. 6There will be loud wailing throughout Egypt—worse than there has ever been or ever will be again. 7But among the Israelites not a dog will bark at any man or animal.' Then you will know that the LORD makes a distinction between Egypt and Israel. 8All these officials of yours will come to me, bowing down before me and saying, 'Go, you and all the people who follow you!' After that I will leave." Then Moses, hot with anger, left Pharaoh.

9The LORD had said to Moses, "Pharaoh will refuse to listen to you—so that my wonders may be multiplied in Egypt." 10Moses and Aaron performed all these wonders before Pharaoh, but the LORD hardened Pharaoh's heart, and he would not let the Israelites go out of his country.

The Passover

12 The LORD said to Moses and Aaron in Egypt, 2"This month is to be for you the first month, the first month of your year. 3Tell the whole community of Israel that on the tenth day of this month each man is to take a lamb[a] for his family, one for each household. 4If any household is too small for a whole lamb, they must share one with their nearest neighbor, having taken into account the number of people there are. You are to determine the amount of lamb needed in accordance with what each person will eat. 5The animals you choose must be year-old males without defect, and you may take them from the sheep or the goats. 6Take care of them until the fourteenth day of the month, when all the people of the community of Israel must slaughter them at twilight. 7Then they are to take some of the blood and put it on the sides and tops of the doorframes of the houses where they eat the lambs. 8That same night they are to eat the meat roasted over the fire, along with bitter herbs, and bread made without yeast. 9Do not eat the meat raw or cooked in water, but roast it over the fire—head, legs and inner parts. 10Do not leave any of it till morning; if some is left till morning, you must burn it. 11This is how you are to eat it: with your cloak tucked into your belt, your sandals on your feet and your staff in your hand. Eat it in haste; it is the LORD's Passover.

12"On that same night I will pass through Egypt and strike down every firstborn—both men and animals—and I will bring judgment on all the gods of Egypt. I am the LORD. 13The blood will be a sign for you on the houses where you are; and when I see the blood, I will pass over you. No destructive plague will touch you when I strike Egypt.

14"This is a day you are to commemorate; for the generations to come you shall celebrate it as a festival to the LORD—a lasting ordinance. 15For seven days you are to eat bread made without yeast. On the first day remove the yeast from your houses, for whoever eats anything with yeast in it from the first day through the seventh must be cut off from Israel. 16On the first day hold a sacred assembly, and another one on the seventh day. Do no work at all on these days, except to prepare food for everyone to eat—that is all you may do.

17"Celebrate the Feast of Unleavened Bread, because it was on this very day that I brought your divisions out of Egypt. Celebrate this day as a lasting ordinance for the generations to come. 18In the first month you are to eat bread made without yeast, from the evening of the fourteenth day until the evening of the twenty-first day. 19For seven days no yeast is to be found in your houses. And whoever eats anything with yeast in it must be cut off from the community

[a]3 The Hebrew word can mean *lamb* or *kid*; also in verse 4.

of Israel, whether he is an alien or native-born. [20]Eat nothing made with
yeast. Wherever you live, you must eat
unleavened bread."

[21]Then Moses summoned all the elders of Israel and said to them, "Go at
once and select the animals for your
families and slaughter the Passover
lamb. [22]Take a bunch of hyssop, dip it
into the blood in the basin and put some
of the blood on the top and on both
sides of the doorframe. Not one of you
shall go out the door of his house until
morning. [23]When the LORD goes
through the land to strike down the
Egyptians, he will see the blood on the
top and sides of the doorframe and will
pass over that doorway, and he will not
permit the destroyer to enter your
houses and strike you down.

[24]"Obey these instructions as a lasting
ordinance for you and your descendants. [25]When you enter the land that
the LORD will give you as he promised,
observe this ceremony. [26]And when
your children ask you, 'What does this
ceremony mean to you?' [27]then tell
them, 'It is the Passover sacrifice to the
LORD, who passed over the houses of
the Israelites in Egypt and spared our
homes when he struck down the Egyptians.' " Then the people bowed down
and worshiped. [28]The Israelites did just
what the LORD commanded Moses and
Aaron.

[29]At midnight the LORD struck down
all the firstborn in Egypt, from the
firstborn of Pharaoh, who sat on the
throne, to the firstborn of the prisoner,
who was in the dungeon, and the firstborn of all the livestock as well. [30]Phar-
aoh and all his officials and all the
Egyptians got up during the night, and
there was loud wailing in Egypt, for
there was not a house without someone
dead.

The Exodus

[31]During the night Pharaoh summoned Moses and Aaron and said, "Up!
Leave my people, you and the Israelites!
Go, worship the LORD as you have requested. [32]Take your flocks and herds,
as you have said, and go. And also
bless me."

[33]The Egyptians urged the people to
hurry and leave the country. "For otherwise," they said, "we will all die!" [34]So
the people took their dough before the
yeast was added, and carried it on
their shoulders in kneading troughs
wrapped in clothing. [35]The Israelites did
as Moses instructed and asked the
Egyptians for articles of silver and gold
and for clothing. [36]The LORD had made
the Egyptians favorably disposed toward the people, and they gave them
what they asked for; so they plundered
the Egyptians.

[37]The Israelites journeyed from Rameses to Succoth. There were about six
hundred thousand men on foot, besides
women and children. [38]Many other
people went up with them, as well as
large droves of livestock, both flocks
and herds. [39]With the dough they had
brought from Egypt, they baked cakes
of unleavened bread. The dough was
without yeast because they had been
driven out of Egypt and did not have
time to prepare food for themselves.

[40]Now the length of time the Israelite
people lived in Egypt[a] was 430 years.
[41]At the end of the 430 years, to the very
day, all the LORD's divisions left Egypt.
[42]Because the LORD kept vigil that night
to bring them out of Egypt, on this night
all the Israelites are to keep vigil to
honor the LORD for the generations to
come.

Passover Restrictions

[43]The LORD said to Moses and Aaron,
"These are the regulations for the Passover:

"No foreigner is to eat of it. [44]Any
slave you have bought may eat of it after you have circumcised him, [45]but a
temporary resident and a hired worker
may not eat of it.

[46]"It must be eaten inside one house;
take none of the meat outside the house.
Do not break any of the bones. [47]The

[a]40 Masoretic Text; Samaritan Pentateuch and Septuagint *Egypt and Canaan*

whole community of Israel must celebrate it.
48"An alien living among you who
wants to celebrate the LORD's Passover
must have all the males in his household
circumcised; then he may take part like
one born in the land. No uncircumcised
male may eat of it. 49The same law applies to the native-born and to the alien
living among you."

50All the Israelites did just what the
LORD had commanded Moses and
Aaron. 51And on that very day the LORD
brought the Israelites out of Egypt by
their divisions.

SHARPEN THE FOCUS

"Look, the Lamb of God, who takes away the sin of the world!"

This was the announcement of John the Baptizer to the crowd gathered one day as he saw Jesus coming toward him (John 1:29). Look carefully at Exodus 12—especially verses 1–13. Note how many similarities can be found between Jesus and the Passover lamb:

- The lamb had no defect. Jesus had no sin.
- The lamb died at an appointed time. Jesus' death was foretold by the prophets and occurred at the time appointed by the Father.
- The lamb was a sacrifice for the Israelites. Jesus was a sacrifice for all people.
- The blood of the lamb saved the Israelites from the tenth plague. Jesus' blood saved all people from damnation.
- The lamb's death made the Israelites realize that sin exacts a terrible price. Jesus' death was the price He paid for our sins.

WEEK 6 • SATURDAY

Exodus 13:1–22

GET THE BIG PICTURE

The Feast of Unleavened Bread (Exodus 13:3–10) and the law of the firstborn (Exodus 13:11–16) will come up later in Exodus. For now, note that both rituals spring from the same root concept—God had redeemed His people from slavery. Now they were free to live as His obedient "firstborn son." The nation's first hours and days of freedom (Exodus 13:17–22) conclude the chapter. If time is short, focus on Exodus 13:17–22.

Consecration of the Firstborn

13 The LORD said to Moses,
2"Consecrate to me every firstborn male. The first offspring of every
womb among the Israelites belongs to
me, whether man or animal."
3Then Moses said to the people,
"Commemorate this day, the day you
came out of Egypt, out of the land of
slavery, because the LORD brought you
out of it with a mighty hand. Eat nothing containing yeast. 4Today, in the

month of Abib, you are leaving. 5When
the LORD brings you into the land of the
Canaanites, Hittites, Amorites, Hivites
and Jebusites—the land he swore to
your forefathers to give you, a land
flowing with milk and honey—you are
to observe this ceremony in this month:
6For seven days eat bread made without
yeast and on the seventh day hold a festival to the LORD. 7Eat unleavened bread
during those seven days; nothing with
yeast in it is to be seen among you, nor
shall any yeast be seen anywhere within
your borders. 8On that day tell your son,
'I do this because of what the LORD did
for me when I came out of Egypt.' 9This
observance will be for you like a sign on
your hand and a reminder on your forehead that the law of the LORD is to be
on your lips. For the LORD brought you
out of Egypt with his mighty hand.
10You must keep this ordinance at the
appointed time year after year.
11"After the LORD brings you into the
land of the Canaanites and gives it to you,
as he promised on oath to you and your
forefathers, 12you are to give over to the
LORD the first offspring of every womb.
All the firstborn males of your livestock
belong to the LORD. 13Redeem with a
lamb every firstborn donkey, but if you
do not redeem it, break its neck. Redeem every firstborn among your sons.
14"In days to come, when your son
asks you, 'What does this mean?' say to
him, 'With a mighty hand the LORD
brought us out of Egypt, out of the land
of slavery. 15When Pharaoh stubbornly
refused to let us go, the LORD killed every firstborn in Egypt, both man and
animal. This is why I sacrifice to the
LORD the first male offspring of every
womb and redeem each of my firstborn
sons.' 16And it will be like a sign on your
hand and a symbol on your forehead
that the LORD brought us out of Egypt
with his mighty hand."

Crossing the Sea

17When Pharaoh let the people go,
God did not lead them on the road
through the Philistine country, though
that was shorter. For God said, "If they
face war, they might change their minds
and return to Egypt." 18So God led the
people around by the desert road toward the Red Sea.[a] The Israelites went
up out of Egypt armed for battle.
19Moses took the bones of Joseph with
him because Joseph had made the sons
of Israel swear an oath. He had said,
"God will surely come to your aid, and
then you must carry my bones up with
you from this place."[b]
20After leaving Succoth they camped
at Etham on the edge of the desert. 21By
day the LORD went ahead of them in a
pillar of cloud to guide them on their
way and by night in a pillar of fire to
give them light, so that they could travel
by day or night. 22Neither the pillar of
cloud by day nor the pillar of fire by
night left its place in front of the people.

[a]*18* Hebrew *Yam Suph*; that is, Sea of Reeds
[b]*19* See Gen. 50:25.

SHARPEN THE FOCUS

The psalmist summarizes Israel's escape from Egypt in these words:

> *[The LORD] brought out Israel, laden with silver and gold,*
> *and from among their tribes no one faltered. . . .*
> *He spread out a cloud as a covering,*
> *and a fire to give light at night.* (Psalm 105:37, 39)

God knew the Israelites had been through a lot. The 430 years of slavery, the last 9 months or so of plagues, the dark night of Passover in which they could not help but have overheard the wailing of the Egyptians for their dead. The whips, the terror, the bewilderment. God knew it all. And in compassion, He provided 400 years of back pay, physical healing and strength, shelter from the desert sun, light in the darkness, and best of all, His unfailing presence.

God knows what you're going through today too. Whatever your fear, or worry, or pain, He has compassion on you. He will meet every one of your needs and, best of all, give you His unfailing presence. ☼

WEEK 7 • MONDAY

Exodus 14:1–31

GET THE BIG PICTURE

The exodus of the Israelites from Egypt could be called the "Old Testament Easter." Again and again the Old Testament writers remind God's people of the Lord's plan and this decisive victory in the face of overwhelming odds. As you read about it, contrast Israel's fear with the Lord's faithfulness. If time is short, focus on Exodus 14:1–22, 29–31.

14 Then the LORD said to Moses, 2"Tell the Israelites to
turn back and encamp near Pi Hahiroth,
between Migdol and the sea. They are
to encamp by the sea, directly opposite
Baal Zephon. 3Pharaoh will think, 'The
Israelites are wandering around the
land in confusion, hemmed in by the
desert.' 4And I will harden Pharaoh's
heart, and he will pursue them. But I
will gain glory for myself through Pharaoh and all his army, and the Egyptians
will know that I am the LORD." So the
Israelites did this.
5When the king of Egypt was told that
the people had fled, Pharaoh and his officials changed their minds about them
and said, "What have we done? We
have let the Israelites go and have lost
their services!" 6So he had his chariot
made ready and took his army with
him. 7He took six hundred of the best
chariots, along with all the other chariots of Egypt, with officers over all of
them. 8The LORD hardened the heart of
Pharaoh king of Egypt, so that he
pursued the Israelites, who were marching out boldly. 9The Egyptians—all
Pharaoh's horses and chariots, horsemen[a] and troops—pursued the Israelites and overtook them as they camped
by the sea near Pi Hahiroth, opposite
Baal Zephon.
10As Pharaoh approached, the Israelites looked up, and there were the
Egyptians, marching after them. They
were terrified and cried out to the LORD.
11They said to Moses, "Was it because
there were no graves in Egypt that you
brought us to the desert to die? What
have you done to us by bringing us out
of Egypt? 12Didn't we say to you in
Egypt, 'Leave us alone; let us serve the
Egyptians'? It would have been better
for us to serve the Egyptians than to die
in the desert!"
13Moses answered the people, "Do not
be afraid. Stand firm and you will see
the deliverance the LORD will bring you
today. The Egyptians you see today you
will never see again. 14The LORD will
fight for you; you need only to be still."
15Then the LORD said to Moses, "Why
are you crying out to me? Tell the Israelites to move on. 16Raise your staff and

[a]9 Or *charioteers;* also in verses 17, 18, 23, 26 and 28

stretch out your hand over the sea to divide the water so that the Israelites can go through the sea on dry ground.
17I will harden the hearts of the Egyptians so that they will go in after them. And I will gain glory through Pharaoh and all his army, through his chariots and his horsemen. 18The Egyptians will know that I am the LORD when I gain glory through Pharaoh, his chariots and his horsemen."
19Then the angel of God, who had been traveling in front of Israel's army, withdrew and went behind them. The pillar of cloud also moved from in front and stood behind them, 20coming
between the armies of Egypt and Israel. Throughout the night the cloud brought darkness to the one side and light to the other side; so neither went near the other all night long.
21Then Moses stretched out his hand over the sea, and all that night the LORD drove the sea back with a strong east wind and turned it into dry land. The waters were divided, 22and the Israelites
went through the sea on dry ground, with a wall of water on their right and on their left.
23The Egyptians pursued them, and all Pharaoh's horses and chariots and horsemen followed them into the sea.
24During the last watch of the night the LORD looked down from the pillar of fire and cloud at the Egyptian army and threw it into confusion. 25He made the
wheels of their chariots come off[a] so that they had difficulty driving. And the Egyptians said, "Let's get away from the Israelites! The LORD is fighting for them against Egypt."
26Then the LORD said to Moses, "Stretch out your hand over the sea so that the waters may flow back over the Egyptians and their chariots and horsemen." 27Moses stretched out his hand
over the sea, and at daybreak the sea went back to its place. The Egyptians were fleeing toward[b] it, and the LORD swept them into the sea. 28The water flowed
back and covered the chariots and horsemen—the entire army of Pharaoh that had followed the Israelites into the sea. Not one of them survived.
29But the Israelites went through the sea on dry ground, with a wall of water on their right and on their left. 30That
day the LORD saved Israel from the hands of the Egyptians, and Israel saw the Egyptians lying dead on the shore.
31And when the Israelites saw the great power the LORD displayed against the Egyptians, the people feared the LORD and put their trust in him and in Moses his servant.

[a]25 Or *He jammed the wheels of their chariots* (see Samaritan Pentateuch, Septuagint and Syriac)
[b]27 Or *from*

SHARPEN THE FOCUS

No way! When did you last hear that expression? Or use it yourself? If you and I suddenly found ourselves trapped in the desert, with earth's best-equipped army behind us and, say, Lake Michigan ahead of us, we might find ourselves muttering "No Way!" and perhaps something stronger.

Reading Exodus 13:17–18 and 14:1–4, we can see that Israel's predicament was not a mistake which the Lord had to correct by shaking a miracle out of His sleeve. No. This had been His plan all along—to save Israel in such a way that they need never again doubt His commitment of love to them, nor His power to follow through on that commitment.

In Exodus 14:10, we see that Israel "looked up." They saw Pharaoh's army galloping down on them. They looked up, but they didn't look high enough. They forgot the pillar of cloud and fire, and the glorious Lord who led them and stood by to defend them.

Pray Psalm 121 today as you "look up" to the Lord. Think about the "No way!" situations in your life as you give them to Him in faith.

WEEK 7 • TUESDAY

Exodus 15:1–27

GET THE BIG PICTURE

God's people hadn't even gotten their feet muddy as they crossed the Red Sea! Their enemies had marched straight into the Lord's trap, and it snapped shut. To celebrate their freedom and the Lord's victory, the entire group sang and danced a hymn of praise to the Lord. Moving from worship to the wilderness, however, proved difficult. Israel worried and grumbled. In response, the Lord acted to help and gave His people another promise. If time is short, focus on Exodus 15:1–18.

The Song of Moses and Miriam

15 Then Moses and the Israelites sang this song to the LORD:

"I will sing to the LORD,
for he is highly exalted.
The horse and its rider
he has hurled into the sea.
2 The LORD is my strength and my song;
he has become my salvation.
He is my God, and I will praise him,
my father's God, and I will exalt him.
3 The LORD is a warrior;
the LORD is his name.
4 Pharaoh's chariots and his army
he has hurled into the sea.
The best of Pharaoh's officers
are drowned in the Red Sea.[a]
5 The deep waters have covered them;
they sank to the depths like a stone.

6 "Your right hand, O LORD,
was majestic in power.
Your right hand, O LORD,
shattered the enemy.
7 In the greatness of your majesty
you threw down those who opposed you.
You unleashed your burning anger;
it consumed them like stubble.
8 By the blast of your nostrils
the waters piled up.
The surging waters stood firm like a wall;
the deep waters congealed in the heart of the sea.

9 "The enemy boasted,
'I will pursue, I will overtake them.
I will divide the spoils;
I will gorge myself on them.
I will draw my sword
and my hand will destroy them.'
10 But you blew with your breath,
and the sea covered them.
They sank like lead
in the mighty waters.
11 "Who among the gods is like you,
O LORD?
Who is like you—
majestic in holiness,
awesome in glory,
working wonders?
12 You stretched out your right hand
and the earth swallowed them.

13 "In your unfailing love you will lead
the people you have redeemed.
In your strength you will guide them
to your holy dwelling.
14 The nations will hear and tremble;

[a]4 Hebrew *Yam Suph*; that is, Sea of Reeds; also in verse 22

anguish will grip the people of
Philistia.
15 The chiefs of Edom will be
terrified,
the leaders of Moab will be seized
with trembling,
the people[a] of Canaan will melt
away;
16 terror and dread will fall upon
them.
By the power of your arm
they will be as still as a stone—
until your people pass by, O LORD,
until the people you bought[b] pass
by.
17 You will bring them in and plant
them
on the mountain of your
inheritance—
the place, O LORD, you made for
your dwelling,
the sanctuary, O Lord, your hands
established.
18 The LORD will reign
for ever and ever."

19 When Pharaoh's horses, chariots
and horsemen[c] went into the sea, the
LORD brought the waters of the sea back
over them, but the Israelites walked
through the sea on dry ground. 20 Then
Miriam the prophetess, Aaron's sister,
took a tambourine in her hand, and all
the women followed her, with tambourines and dancing. 21 Miriam sang to
them:

"Sing to the LORD,
for he is highly exalted.
The horse and its rider
he has hurled into the sea."

The Waters of Marah and Elim

22 Then Moses led Israel from the Red
Sea and they went into the Desert of
Shur. For three days they traveled in the
desert without finding water. 23 When
they came to Marah, they could not
drink its water because it was bitter.
(That is why the place is called Marah.[d])
24 So the people grumbled against Moses, saying, "What are we to drink?"
25 Then Moses cried out to the LORD,
and the LORD showed him a piece of
wood. He threw it into the water, and
the water became sweet.

There the LORD made a decree and a
law for them, and there he tested them.
26 He said, "If you listen carefully to the
voice of the LORD your God and do
what is right in his eyes, if you pay attention to his commands and keep all
his decrees, I will not bring on you any
of the diseases I brought on the Egyptians, for I am the LORD, who heals
you."
27 Then they came to Elim, where
there were twelve springs and seventy
palm trees, and they camped there near
the water.

[a]15 Or *rulers* [b]16 Or *created* [c]19 Or *charioteers*
[d]23 *Marah* means *bitter.*

SHARPEN THE FOCUS

As yesterday's "Big Picture" pointed out, the exodus event was a kind of "Old Testament Easter." From here on, the Old Testament writers repeatedly pointed back to the deliverance of the Israelites at the Red Sea as proof that the Lord *could* and *would* deliver His people.

Take a few moments now to reread Moses' hymn of praise (Exodus 15:1–18). This time as you read, note some of these words and phrases that apply equally as well to the Easter victory of our Lord Jesus over sin, death, and Satan's power:

- "The LORD is my strength . . . ; He has become my salvation."
- "Your right hand, O LORD, shattered the enemy."
- "You will lead the people You have redeemed . . . You will guide them to Your holy dwelling."
- "The LORD will reign for ever and ever."

You might pray some of these words, praising our God for His great victory on Good Friday and Easter. Thank Him for the freedom we now enjoy as His sons and daughters in Christ. ☼

WEEK 7 • WEDNESDAY

Exodus 16:1—17:16

Thirty days after the Exodus, we see Israel tired, hot, and above all hungry. The people begin to complain. God meets their needs in a miraculous way. He shows His kindness in Exodus 17:1–7 and again in Exodus 17:8–16. As you read, note the Lord's care and patience. If time is short, focus on Exodus 17:1–16.

Manna and Quail

16 The whole Israelite community set out from Elim and
came to the Desert of Sin, which is between Elim and Sinai, on the fifteenth
day of the second month after they had
come out of Egypt. 2In the desert the
whole community grumbled against
Moses and Aaron. 3The Israelites said to
them, "If only we had died by the
LORD's hand in Egypt! There we sat
around pots of meat and ate all the food
we wanted, but you have brought us
out into this desert to starve this entire
assembly to death."
4Then the LORD said to Moses, "I will
rain down bread from heaven for you.
The people are to go out each day and
gather enough for that day. In this way
I will test them and see whether they
will follow my instructions. 5On the
sixth day they are to prepare what they
bring in, and that is to be twice as much
as they gather on the other days."
6So Moses and Aaron said to all the Israelites, "In the evening you will know
that it was the LORD who brought you
out of Egypt, 7and in the morning you
will see the glory of the LORD, because
he has heard your grumbling against
him. Who are we, that you should
grumble against us?" 8Moses also said,
"You will know that it was the LORD
when he gives you meat to eat in the
evening and all the bread you want in
the morning, because he has heard your
grumbling against him. Who are we?
You are not grumbling against us, but
against the LORD."
9Then Moses told Aaron, "Say to the
entire Israelite community, 'Come before the LORD, for he has heard your
grumbling.' "
10While Aaron was speaking to the
whole Israelite community, they looked
toward the desert, and there was the
glory of the LORD appearing in the
cloud.
11The LORD said to Moses, 12"I have
heard the grumbling of the Israelites.
Tell them, 'At twilight you will eat meat,
and in the morning you will be filled
with bread. Then you will know that I
am the LORD your God.' "
13That evening quail came and covered the camp, and in the morning
there was a layer of dew around the
camp. 14When the dew was gone, thin
flakes like frost on the ground appeared
on the desert floor. 15When the Israelites
saw it, they said to each other, "What is
it?" For they did not know what it was.
Moses said to them, "It is the bread
the LORD has given you to eat. 16This is
what the LORD has commanded: 'Each
one is to gather as much as he needs.

Take an omer[a] for each person you have
in your tent.' "
17The Israelites did as they were told;
some gathered much, some little. 18And
when they measured it by the omer, he
who gathered much did not have too
much, and he who gathered little did
not have too little. Each one gathered as
much as he needed.
19Then Moses said to them, "No one
is to keep any of it until morning."
20However, some of them paid no attention to Moses; they kept part of it
until morning, but it was full of maggots
and began to smell. So Moses was angry
with them.
21Each morning everyone gathered as
much as he needed, and when the sun
grew hot, it melted away. 22On the sixth
day, they gathered twice as much—two
omers[b] for each person—and the leaders of the community came and reported this to Moses. 23He said to them,
"This is what the LORD commanded:
'Tomorrow is to be a day of rest, a holy
Sabbath to the LORD. So bake what you
want to bake and boil what you want to
boil. Save whatever is left and keep it
until morning.' "
24So they saved it until morning, as
Moses commanded, and it did not stink
or get maggots in it. 25"Eat it today,"
Moses said, "because today is a Sabbath
to the LORD. You will not find any of it
on the ground today. 26Six days you are
to gather it, but on the seventh day, the
Sabbath, there will not be any."
27Nevertheless, some of the people
went out on the seventh day to gather
it, but they found none. 28Then the LORD
said to Moses, "How long will you[c] refuse to keep my commands and my instructions? 29Bear in mind that the LORD
has given you the Sabbath; that is why
on the sixth day he gives you bread for
two days. Everyone is to stay where he
is on the seventh day; no one is to go
out." 30So the people rested on the seventh day.
31The people of Israel called the bread
manna.[d] It was white like coriander seed
and tasted like wafers made with honey.
32Moses said, "This is what the LORD has
commanded: 'Take an omer of manna
and keep it for the generations to come,
so they can see the bread I gave you to
eat in the desert when I brought you out
of Egypt.' "
33So Moses said to Aaron, "Take a jar
and put an omer of manna in it. Then
place it before the LORD to be kept for
the generations to come."
34As the LORD commanded Moses,
Aaron put the manna in front of the Testimony, that it might be kept. 35The Israelites ate manna forty years, until they
came to a land that was settled; they ate
manna until they reached the border of
Canaan.
36(An omer is one tenth of an ephah.)

Water From the Rock

17 The whole Israelite community set out from the Desert of
Sin, traveling from place to place as the
LORD commanded. They camped at
Rephidim, but there was no water for
the people to drink. 2So they quarreled
with Moses and said, "Give us water to
drink."

Moses replied, "Why do you quarrel
with me? Why do you put the LORD to
the test?"
3But the people were thirsty for water there, and they grumbled against
Moses. They said, "Why did you bring
us up out of Egypt to make us and our
children and livestock die of thirst?"
4Then Moses cried out to the LORD,
"What am I to do with these people?
They are almost ready to stone me."
5The LORD answered Moses, "Walk on
ahead of the people. Take with you
some of the elders of Israel and take in
your hand the staff with which you
struck the Nile, and go. 6I will stand
there before you by the rock at Horeb.
Strike the rock, and water will come out
of it for the people to drink." So Moses
did this in the sight of the elders of Is-

[a] *16* That is, probably about 2 quarts (about 2 liters); also in verses 18, 32, 33 and 36
[b] 22 That is, probably about 4 quarts (about 4.5 liters) [c] *28* The Hebrew is plural. [d] *31 Manna* means *What is it?* (see verse 15).

rael. [7]And he called the place Massah[a] and
Meribah[b] because the Israelites quarreled and because they tested the LORD
saying, "Is the LORD among us or not?"

The Amalekites Defeated

[8]The Amalekites came and attacked
the Israelites at Rephidim. [9]Moses said
to Joshua, "Choose some of our men and
go out to fight the Amalekites. Tomorrow I will stand on top of the hill with
the staff of God in my hands."
[10]So Joshua fought the Amalekites as
Moses had ordered, and Moses, Aaron
and Hur went to the top of the hill. [11]As
long as Moses held up his hands, the Israelites were winning, but whenever he
lowered his hands, the Amalekites were
winning. [12]When Moses' hands grew
tired, they took a stone and put it under
him and he sat on it. Aaron and Hur
held his hands up—one on one side,
one on the other—so that his hands remained steady till sunset. [13]So Joshua
overcame the Amalekite army with the
sword.
[14]Then the LORD said to Moses, "Write
this on a scroll as something to be remembered and make sure that Joshua
hears it, because I will completely blot
out the memory of Amalek from under
heaven."
[15]Moses built an altar and called it The
LORD is my Banner. [16]He said, "For
hands were lifted up to the throne of the
LORD. The[c] LORD will be at war against
the Amalekites from generation to generation."

[a]7 *Massah* means *testing*. [b]7 *Meribah* means *quarreling*. [c]16 Or *"Because a hand was against the throne of the LORD, the*

SHARPEN THE FOCUS

Food. Rest. Water. Physical safety. Basic human needs. Remember Jesus' words about them?

> *I tell you, do not worry about your life, what you will eat or drink; or about your body, what you will wear. . . . your heavenly Father knows that you need [these things].* (Matthew 6:25, 32)

Don't worry, Jesus says. But we do. *I know God will come through, but. . . .* All of us can probably finish this sentence with our own favorite excuse for worry. No matter how good those excuses may sound, worry is still sin. At times, we like Israel of old, may even grumble. And at times, our grumbling may come dangerously close to blasphemy—accusing our Lord of things that Satan might do or plan (Exodus 17:3).

Israel's blasphemy justly deserved the death penalty. The eternal death penalty. But instead of striking the people dead, God told Moses to strike the rock. Instead of striking us for our own thoughts and words of unbelief, God struck His Son on Calvary. Now, instead of spiritual thirst, the water of life—the Holy Spirit—refreshes us (John 7:37–39). And that same Spirit strengthens us against the temptations to worry.

WEEK 7 • THURSDAY

Exodus 18:1–27

GET THE BIG PICTURE

Israel has arrived near the area where Moses had first met and married Zipporah. Moses' father-in-law, Jethro (also called "Reuel" in Exodus 2:18), comes to visit the Israelite camp. He hears and rejoices in what the Lord has done. Then he helps to resolve a major time-management problem in the making. If time is short, focus on Exodus 18:1–12.

Jethro Visits Moses

18 Now Jethro, the priest of Midian and father-in-law of Moses, heard of everything God had done for Moses and for his people Israel, and how the LORD had brought Israel out of Egypt.

2 After Moses had sent away his wife Zipporah, his father-in-law Jethro received her 3 and her two sons. One son was named Gershom,[a] for Moses said, "I have become an alien in a foreign land"; 4 and the other was named Eliezer,[b] for he said, "My father's God was my helper; he saved me from the sword of Pharaoh."

5 Jethro, Moses' father-in-law, together with Moses' sons and wife, came to him in the desert, where he was camped near the mountain of God. 6 Jethro had sent word to him, "I, your father-in-law Jethro, am coming to you with your wife and her two sons."

7 So Moses went out to meet his father-in-law and bowed down and kissed him. They greeted each other and then went into the tent. 8 Moses told his father-in-law about everything the LORD had done to Pharaoh and the Egyptians for Israel's sake and about all the hardships they had met along the way and how the LORD had saved them.

9 Jethro was delighted to hear about all the good things the LORD had done for Israel in rescuing them from the hand of the Egyptians. 10 He said, "Praise be to the LORD, who rescued you from the hand of the Egyptians and of Pharaoh, and who rescued the people from the hand of the Egyptians. 11 Now I know that the LORD is greater than all other gods, for he did this to those who had treated Israel arrogantly." 12 Then Jethro, Moses' father-in-law, brought a burnt offering and other sacrifices to God, and Aaron came with all the elders of Israel to eat bread with Moses' father-in-law in the presence of God.

13 The next day Moses took his seat to serve as judge for the people, and they stood around him from morning till evening. 14 When his father-in-law saw all that Moses was doing for the people, he said, "What is this you are doing for the people? Why do you alone sit as judge, while all these people stand around you from morning till evening?"

15 Moses answered him, "Because the people come to me to seek God's will. 16 Whenever they have a dispute, it is brought to me, and I decide between the parties and inform them of God's decrees and laws."

17 Moses' father-in-law replied, "What you are doing is not good. 18 You and these people who come to you will only wear yourselves out. The work is too heavy for you; you cannot handle it alone. 19 Listen now to me and I will give you some advice, and may God be with you. You must be the people's represen-

[a] 3 *Gershom* sounds like the Hebrew for *an alien there.* [b] 4 *Eliezer* means *my God is helper.*

tative before God and bring their disputes to him. 20Teach them the decrees
and laws, and show them the way to
live and the duties they are to perform.
21But select capable men from all the
people—men who fear God, trustworthy men who hate dishonest gain—and
appoint them as officials over thousands, hundreds, fifties and tens. 22Have
them serve as judges for the people at
all times, but have them bring every difficult case to you; the simple cases they
can decide themselves. That will make
your load lighter, because they will
share it with you. 23If you do this and
God so commands, you will be able to
stand the strain, and all these people
will go home satisfied."
24Moses listened to his father-in-law
and did everything he said. 25He chose
capable men from all Israel and made
them leaders of the people, officials over
thousands, hundreds, fifties and tens.
26They served as judges for the people
at all times. The difficult cases they
brought to Moses, but the simple ones
they decided themselves.
27Then Moses sent his father-in-law
on his way, and Jethro returned to his
own country.

SHARPEN THE FOCUS

We can imagine Jethro's eyes widening as Moses related all that the Lord had done for His people. The Bible records four specific responses:

- Jethro was delighted to hear about the deliverance and the care the Lord showed His people (Exodus 18:9).
- Jethro praised God for this deliverance (Exodus 18:10).
- Jethro witnessed to his faith—"Now I know that the LORD is greater than all other gods" (Exodus 18:11).
- Jethro offered a sacrifice in honor of God's goodness, and he fellowshiped with God's people (Exodus 18:12).

Think for a moment or two about the deliverance the Lord has worked for you on the cross of Jesus Christ and at His open tomb. In what specific ways will you respond today?

I will rejoice that . . .

I will praise God for . . .

I will witness to . . . by . . .

I will sacrifice and worship with other believers as . . .

WEEK 7 • FRIDAY

Exodus 19:1—20:26

GET THE BIG PICTURE

The Savior-God never, ever forces anyone to love Him. Instead, He draws people to Himself in kindness. In Exodus 19, it's almost as if the Lord asks permission to adopt the nation or to take

Israel as His bride. Then, in Exodus 20, we see the Lord's instructions. Commands? Yes, but each one is given in love with an eye toward everyone in the covenant relationship enjoying a "happy home life" with Him and with each other. If time is short, focus on Exodus 19:1–8; 20:1–17.

At Mount Sinai

19 In the third month after the Israelites left Egypt—on the very day—they came to the Desert of Sinai. [2]After they set out from Rephidim, they entered the Desert of Sinai, and Israel camped there in the desert in front of the mountain.

[3]Then Moses went up to God, and the LORD called to him from the mountain and said, "This is what you are to say to the house of Jacob and what you are to tell the people of Israel: [4]'You yourselves have seen what I did to Egypt, and how I carried you on eagles' wings and brought you to myself. [5]Now if you obey me fully and keep my covenant, then out of all nations you will be my treasured possession. Although the whole earth is mine, [6]you[a] will be for me a kingdom of priests and a holy nation.' These are the words you are to speak to the Israelites."

[7]So Moses went back and summoned the elders of the people and set before them all the words the LORD had commanded him to speak. [8]The people all responded together, "We will do everything the LORD has said." So Moses brought their answer back to the LORD.

[9]The LORD said to Moses, "I am going to come to you in a dense cloud, so that the people will hear me speaking with you and will always put their trust in you." Then Moses told the LORD what the people had said.

[10]And the LORD said to Moses, "Go to the people and consecrate them today and tomorrow. Have them wash their clothes [11]and be ready by the third day, because on that day the LORD will come down on Mount Sinai in the sight of all the people. [12]Put limits for the people around the mountain and tell them, 'Be careful that you do not go up the mountain or touch the foot of it. Whoever touches the mountain shall surely be put to death. [13]He shall surely be stoned or shot with arrows; not a hand is to be laid on him. Whether man or animal, he shall not be permitted to live.' Only when the ram's horn sounds a long blast may they go up to the mountain."

[14]After Moses had gone down the mountain to the people, he consecrated them, and they washed their clothes. [15]Then he said to the people, "Prepare yourselves for the third day. Abstain from sexual relations."

[16]On the morning of the third day there was thunder and lightning, with a thick cloud over the mountain, and a very loud trumpet blast. Everyone in the camp trembled. [17]Then Moses led the people out of the camp to meet with God, and they stood at the foot of the mountain. [18]Mount Sinai was covered with smoke, because the LORD descended on it in fire. The smoke billowed up from it like smoke from a furnace, the whole mountain[b] trembled violently, [19]and the sound of the trumpet grew louder and louder. Then Moses spoke and the voice of God answered him.[c]

[20]The LORD descended to the top of Mount Sinai and called Moses to the top of the mountain. So Moses went up [21]and the LORD said to him, "Go down and warn the people so they do not force their way through to see the LORD and many of them perish. [22]Even the priests, who approach the LORD, must consecrate themselves, or the LORD will break out against them."

[23]Moses said to the LORD, "The people cannot come up Mount Sinai, because you yourself warned us, 'Put limits

[a]5,6 Or *possession, for the whole earth is mine.* [6]*You* [b]18 Most Hebrew manuscripts; a few Hebrew manuscripts and Septuagint *all the people* [c]19 Or *and God answered him with thunder*

around the mountain and set it apart as holy.' "

24The LORD replied, "Go down and bring Aaron up with you. But the priests and the people must not force their way through to come up to the LORD, or he will break out against them."

25So Moses went down to the people and told them.

The Ten Commandments

20 And God spoke all these words:

2"I am the LORD your God, who brought you out of Egypt, out of the land of slavery.

3"You shall have no other gods before[a] me.

4"You shall not make for yourself an idol in the form of anything in heaven above or on the earth beneath or in the waters below. 5You shall not bow down to them or worship them; for I, the LORD your God, am a jealous God, punishing the children for the sin of the fathers to the third and fourth generation of those who hate me, 6but showing love to a thousand ⌞generations⌟ of those who love me and keep my commandments.

7"You shall not misuse the name of the LORD your God, for the LORD will not hold anyone guiltless who misuses his name.

8"Remember the Sabbath day by keeping it holy. 9Six days you shall labor and do all your work, 10but the seventh day is a Sabbath to the LORD your God. On it you shall not do any work, neither you, nor your son or daughter, nor your manservant or maidservant, nor your animals, nor the alien within your gates. 11For in six days the LORD made the heavens and the earth, the sea, and all that is in them, but he rested on the seventh day. Therefore the LORD blessed the Sabbath day and made it holy.

12"Honor your father and your mother, so that you may live long in the land the LORD your God is giving you.

13"You shall not murder.

14"You shall not commit adultery.

15"You shall not steal.

16"You shall not give false testimony against your neighbor.

17"You shall not covet your neighbor's house. You shall not covet your neighbor's wife, or his manservant or maidservant, his ox or donkey, or anything that belongs to your neighbor."

18When the people saw the thunder and lightning and heard the trumpet and saw the mountain in smoke, they trembled with fear. They stayed at a distance
19and said to Moses, "Speak to us yourself and we will listen. But do not have God speak to us or we will die."

20Moses said to the people, "Do not be afraid. God has come to test you, so that the fear of God will be with you to keep you from sinning."

21The people remained at a distance, while Moses approached the thick darkness where God was.

Idols and Altars

22Then the LORD said to Moses, "Tell the Israelites this: 'You have seen for yourselves that I have spoken to you from heaven:
23Do not make any gods to be alongside me; do not make for yourselves gods of silver or gods of gold.

24" 'Make an altar of earth for me and sacrifice on it your burnt offerings and fellowship offerings,[b] your sheep and goats and your cattle. Wherever I cause my name to be honored, I will come to

[a]3 Or *besides* [b]24 Traditionally *peace offerings*

you and bless you. 25If you make an altar of stones for me, do not build it with
dressed stones, for you will defile it if
you use a tool on it. 26And do not go up
to my altar on steps, lest your nakedness
be exposed on it.'

SHARPEN THE FOCUS

If you had stood at the foot of Mt. Sinai that day, what would you have felt? Which of these responses comes closest to your own?

- The Lord has "carried [us] on eagles' wings and brought [us] to [Himself]." I'm His "treasured possession" (Exodus 19:4–5). Wow!
- That trumpet is too scary! If I don't get out of here, I'm going to die from fright! (Exodus 20:18–19)
- Any minute now, that mountain is going to explode—with us under it! (Exodus 19:16–18)
- Why would the Lord choose us? Hasn't He already seen what we're like—all the complaints and grousing and unbelief? (Exodus 16–17)

The people of Israel probably thought and felt all these things and more. And we, like they, need to realize one more thing in our heart of hearts as we look at God's Law—"I can't *do* this." That thought is not pessimism. It's realism! We, like Israel, have tried. Hard. But in our own efforts, we always fail. And so we praise God for another "mountain"—Calvary, where Jesus bled and died for our failure. Praise God that in Christ we receive both forgiveness and renewed strength to obey.

The "moral law" is recorded in Exodus 20:1–17. Then the Lord goes on to explain various civil laws and penalties. Even though we no longer observe these civil laws today, they give us a glimpse into the heart of God. We see His deep concern for human life (Exodus 21:1–32). We see His justice and His concern for those who are victims of crime (Exodus 22:1–15). And we see His tender compassion for the weak and helpless in society (Exodus 22:16–27). If time is short, focus on Exodus 22:21–27.

21 "These are the laws you are
to set before them:

Hebrew Servants

2"If you buy a Hebrew servant, he is
to serve you for six years. But in the seventh year, he shall go free, without paying anything. 3If he comes alone, he is
to go free alone; but if he has a wife
when he comes, she is to go with
him. 4If his master gives him a wife and
she bears him sons or daughters, the

woman and her children shall belong to
her master, and only the man shall go
free.
5"But if the servant declares, 'I love
my master and my wife and children
and do not want to go free,' 6then his
master must take him before the
judges.[a] He shall take him to the door or
the doorpost and pierce his ear with an
awl. Then he will be his servant for life.
7"If a man sells his daughter as a servant, she is not to go free as menservants do. 8If she does not please the
master who has selected her for himself,[b] he must let her be redeemed. He
has no right to sell her to foreigners,
because he has broken faith with her. 9If
he selects her for his son, he must grant
her the rights of a daughter. 10If he marries another woman, he must not deprive the first one of her food, clothing
and marital rights. 11If he does not provide her with these three things, she is
to go free, without any payment of
money.

Personal Injuries

12"Anyone who strikes a man and kills
him shall surely be put to death. 13How-
ever, if he does not do it intentionally,
but God lets it happen, he is to flee to a
place I will designate. 14But if a man
schemes and kills another man deliberately, take him away from my altar and
put him to death.
15"Anyone who attacks[c] his father or
his mother must be put to death.
16"Anyone who kidnaps another and
either sells him or still has him when he
is caught must be put to death.
17"Anyone who curses his father or
mother must be put to death.
18"If men quarrel and one hits the other with a stone or with his fist[d] and he
does not die but is confined to bed, 19the
one who struck the blow will not be
held responsible if the other gets up and
walks around outside with his staff;
however, he must pay the injured man
for the loss of his time and see that he is
completely healed.
20"If a man beats his male or female
slave with a rod and the slave dies as a
direct result, he must be punished, 21but
he is not to be punished if the slave gets
up after a day or two, since the slave is
his property.
22"If men who are fighting hit a pregnant woman and she gives birth pre-
maturely[e] but there is no serious injury,
the offender must be fined whatever the
woman's husband demands and the
court allows. 23But if there is serious injury, you are to take life for life, 24eye for
eye, tooth for tooth, hand for hand, foot
for foot, 25burn for burn, wound for
wound, bruise for bruise.
26"If a man hits a manservant or maidservant in the eye and destroys it, he
must let the servant go free to compensate for the eye. 27And if he knocks out
the tooth of a manservant or maidservant, he must let the servant go free to
compensate for the tooth.
28"If a bull gores a man or a woman to
death, the bull must be stoned to death,
and its meat must not be eaten. But the
owner of the bull will not be held responsible. 29If, however, the bull has had
the habit of goring and the owner has
been warned but has not kept it penned
up and it kills a man or woman, the bull
must be stoned and the owner also must
be put to death. 30However, if payment
is demanded of him, he may redeem his
life by paying whatever is demanded.
31This law also applies if the bull gores a
son or daughter. 32If the bull gores a male
or female slave, the owner must pay
thirty shekels[f] of silver to the master of
the slave, and the bull must be stoned.
33"If a man uncovers a pit or digs one
and fails to cover it and an ox or a donkey falls into it, 34the owner of the pit
must pay for the loss; he must pay its
owner, and the dead animal will be his.
35"If a man's bull injures the bull of another and it dies, they are to sell the live
one and divide both the money and the
dead animal equally. 36However, if it was
known that the bull had the habit of

[a]6 Or *before God* [b]8 Or *master so that he does not choose her* [c]15 Or *kills* [d]18 Or *with a tool*
[e]22 Or *she has a miscarriage* [f]32 That is, about 12 ounces (about 0.3 kilogram)

goring, yet the owner did not keep it penned up, the owner must pay, animal for animal, and the dead animal will be his.

Protection of Property

22 "If a man steals an ox or a sheep and slaughters it or sells it, he must pay back five head of cattle for the ox and four sheep for the sheep.

2"If a thief is caught breaking in and is struck so that he dies, the defender is not guilty of bloodshed; 3but if it happens[a] after sunrise, he is guilty of bloodshed.

"A thief must certainly make restitution, but if he has nothing, he must be sold to pay for his theft.

4"If the stolen animal is found alive in his possession—whether ox or donkey or sheep—he must pay back double.

5"If a man grazes his livestock in a field or vineyard and lets them stray and they graze in another man's field, he must make restitution from the best of his own field or vineyard.

6"If a fire breaks out and spreads into thornbushes so that it burns shocks of grain or standing grain or the whole field, the one who started the fire must make restitution.

7"If a man gives his neighbor silver or goods for safekeeping and they are stolen from the neighbor's house, the thief, if he is caught, must pay back double. 8But if the thief is not found, the owner of the house must appear before the judges[b] to determine whether he has laid his hands on the other man's property. 9In all cases of illegal possession of an ox, a donkey, a sheep, a garment, or any other lost property about which somebody says, 'This is mine,' both parties are to bring their cases before the judges. The one whom the judges declare[c] guilty must pay back double to his neighbor.

10"If a man gives a donkey, an ox, a sheep or any other animal to his neighbor for safekeeping and it dies or is injured or is taken away while no one is looking, 11the issue between them will be settled by the taking of an oath before the LORD that the neighbor did not lay hands on the other person's property. The owner is to accept this, and no restitution is required. 12But if the animal was stolen from the neighbor, he must make restitution to the owner. 13If it was torn to pieces by a wild animal, he shall bring in the remains as evidence and he will not be required to pay for the torn animal.

14"If a man borrows an animal from his neighbor and it is injured or dies while the owner is not present, he must make restitution. 15But if the owner is with the animal, the borrower will not have to pay. If the animal was hired, the money paid for the hire covers the loss.

Social Responsibility

16"If a man seduces a virgin who is not pledged to be married and sleeps with her, he must pay the bride-price, and she shall be his wife. 17If her father absolutely refuses to give her to him, he must still pay the bride-price for virgins.

18"Do not allow a sorceress to live.

19"Anyone who has sexual relations with an animal must be put to death.

20"Whoever sacrifices to any god other than the LORD must be destroyed.[d]

21"Do not mistreat an alien or oppress him, for you were aliens in Egypt.

22"Do not take advantage of a widow or an orphan. 23If you do and they cry out to me, I will certainly hear their cry. 24My anger will be aroused, and I will kill you with the sword; your wives will become widows and your children fatherless.

25"If you lend money to one of my people among you who is needy, do not be like a moneylender; charge him no interest.[e] 26If you take your neighbor's cloak as a pledge, return it to him by sunset, 27because his cloak is the only covering he has for his body. What else

[a]3 Or *if he strikes him* [b]8 Or *before God;* also in verse 9 [c]9 Or *whom God declares* [d]20 The Hebrew term refers to the irrevocable giving over of things or persons to the LORD, often by totally destroying them. [e]25 Or *excessive interest*

will he sleep in? When he cries out to
me, I will hear, for I am compassionate.
28"Do not blaspheme God[a] or curse
the ruler of your people.
29"Do not hold back offerings from
your granaries or your vats.[b]
"You must give me the firstborn of
your sons. 30Do the same with your cattle and your sheep. Let them stay with
their mothers for seven days, but give
them to me on the eighth day.
31"You are to be my holy people. So do
not eat the meat of an animal torn by
wild beasts; throw it to the dogs.

SHARPEN THE FOCUS

Some of the laws recorded here may seem obscure, but one thing is clear—our God is a God of justice. Those in Israel who caused loss or hurt through simple carelessness had to make restitution. Those who caused loss or damage through evil intent had to restore it, plus pay hefty interest.

Today Christians tend to focus more on God's mercy than on His justice. But imagine yourself living in Israel as a refugee (Exodus 22:21) or as a widow (Exodus 22:22–24) or as a person caught up in the web of poverty (Exodus 22:25–27). Wouldn't God's justice have brought you comfort?

These verses also make clear God's will for us as we think about His people who are strangers, widows, orphans, or in poverty today. The Lord still hears their cry. Plan a way this week to show the heavenly Father's compassion to one of His people who feels helpless. Or find a way to speak our Savior's forgiveness to someone enduring the penalties justice demands.

WEEK 8 • MONDAY

Exodus 23:1—24:18

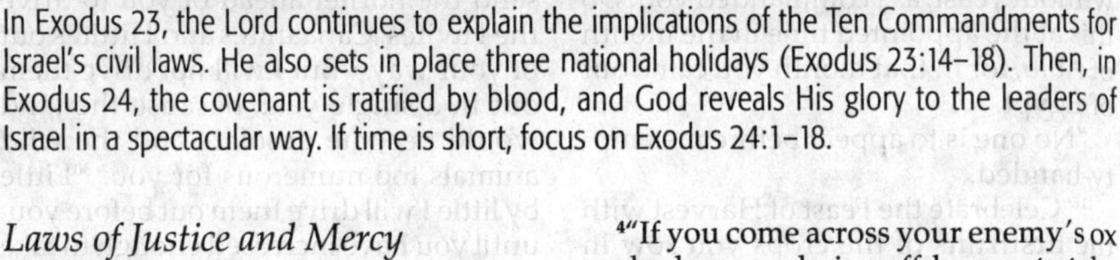

GET THE BIG PICTURE

In Exodus 23, the Lord continues to explain the implications of the Ten Commandments for Israel's civil laws. He also sets in place three national holidays (Exodus 23:14–18). Then, in Exodus 24, the covenant is ratified by blood, and God reveals His glory to the leaders of Israel in a spectacular way. If time is short, focus on Exodus 24:1–18.

Laws of Justice and Mercy

23 "Do not spread false reports. Do not help a
wicked man by being a malicious witness.
2"Do not follow the crowd in doing
wrong. When you give testimony in a
lawsuit, do not pervert justice by siding
with the crowd, 3and do not show favoritism to a poor man in his lawsuit.
4"If you come across your enemy's ox
or donkey wandering off, be sure to take
it back to him. 5If you see the donkey of
someone who hates you fallen down
under its load, do not leave it there; be
sure you help him with it.
6"Do not deny justice to your poor

[a]28 Or *Do not revile the judges* [b]29 The meaning of the Hebrew for this phrase is uncertain.

people in their lawsuits. 7Have nothing
to do with a false charge and do not put
an innocent or honest person to death,
for I will not acquit the guilty.

8"Do not accept a bribe, for a bribe
blinds those who see and twists the
words of the righteous.

9"Do not oppress an alien; you yourselves know how it feels to be aliens, because you were aliens in Egypt.

Sabbath Laws

10"For six years you are to sow your
fields and harvest the crops, 11but during the seventh year let the land lie unplowed and unused. Then the poor
among your people may get food from
it, and the wild animals may eat what
they leave. Do the same with your vineyard and your olive grove.

12"Six days do your work, but on the
seventh day do not work, so that your
ox and your donkey may rest and the
slave born in your household, and the
alien as well, may be refreshed.

13"Be careful to do everything I have
said to you. Do not invoke the names of
other gods; do not let them be heard on
your lips.

The Three Annual Festivals

14"Three times a year you are to celebrate a festival to me.

15"Celebrate the Feast of Unleavened
Bread; for seven days eat bread made
without yeast, as I commanded you. Do
this at the appointed time in the month
of Abib, for in that month you came out
of Egypt.

"No one is to appear before me empty-handed.

16"Celebrate the Feast of Harvest with
the firstfruits of the crops you sow in
your field.

"Celebrate the Feast of Ingathering at
the end of the year, when you gather in
your crops from the field.

17"Three times a year all the men are
to appear before the Sovereign LORD.

18"Do not offer the blood of a sacrifice
to me along with anything containing
yeast.

"The fat of my festival offerings must
not be kept until morning.

19"Bring the best of the firstfruits of
your soil to the house of the LORD your
God.

"Do not cook a young goat in its
mother's milk.

God's Angel to Prepare the Way

20"See, I am sending an angel ahead of
you to guard you along the way and to
bring you to the place I have prepared.
21Pay attention to him and listen to what
he says. Do not rebel against him; he
will not forgive your rebellion, since my
Name is in him. 22If you listen carefully
to what he says and do all that I say, I
will be an enemy to your enemies and
will oppose those who oppose you.
23My angel will go ahead of you and
bring you into the land of the Amorites,
Hittites, Perizzites, Canaanites, Hivites
and Jebusites, and I will wipe them out.
24Do not bow down before their gods or
worship them or follow their practices.
You must demolish them and break
their sacred stones to pieces. 25Worship
the LORD your God, and his blessing
will be on your food and water. I will
take away sickness from among you,
26and none will miscarry or be barren in
your land. I will give you a full life span.

27"I will send my terror ahead of you
and throw into confusion every nation
you encounter. I will make all your enemies turn their backs and run. 28I will
send the hornet ahead of you to drive
the Hivites, Canaanites and Hittites out
of your way. 29But I will not drive them
out in a single year, because the land
would become desolate and the wild
animals too numerous for you. 30Little
by little I will drive them out before you,
until you have increased enough to take
possession of the land.

31"I will establish your borders from
the Red Sea[a] to the Sea of the Philistines,[b] and from the desert to the River.[c]
I will hand over to you the people who

[a]*31* Hebrew *Yam Suph;* that is, Sea of Reeds
[b]*31* That is, the Mediterranean [c]*31* That is, the
Euphrates

live in the land and you will drive them
out before you. 32Do not make a covenant with them or with their gods. 33Do
not let them live in your land, or they
will cause you to sin against me, because
the worship of their gods will certainly
be a snare to you."

The Covenant Confirmed

24 Then he said to Moses,
"Come up to the LORD,
you and Aaron, Nadab and Abihu, and
seventy of the elders of Israel. You are
to worship at a distance, 2but Moses
alone is to approach the LORD; the others must not come near. And the people
may not come up with him."
3When Moses went and told the people all the LORD's words and laws, they
responded with one voice, "Everything
the LORD has said we will do." 4Moses
then wrote down everything the LORD
had said.

He got up early the next morning and
built an altar at the foot of the mountain
and set up twelve stone pillars representing the twelve tribes of Israel. 5Then
he sent young Israelite men, and they
offered burnt offerings and sacrificed
young bulls as fellowship offerings[a] to
the LORD. 6Moses took half of the blood
and put it in bowls, and the other half
he sprinkled on the altar. 7Then he took
the Book of the Covenant and read it to
the people. They responded, "We will
do everything the LORD has said; we
will obey."
8Moses then took the blood, sprinkled
it on the people and said, "This is the
blood of the covenant that the LORD has
made with you in accordance with all
these words."
9Moses and Aaron, Nadab and Abihu,
and the seventy elders of Israel went up
10and saw the God of Israel. Under his
feet was something like a pavement
made of sapphire,[b] clear as the sky itself.
11But God did not raise his hand against
these leaders of the Israelites; they saw
God, and they ate and drank.
12The LORD said to Moses, "Come up
to me on the mountain and stay here,
and I will give you the tablets of stone,
with the law and commands I have
written for their instruction."
13Then Moses set out with Joshua his
aide, and Moses went up on the mountain of God. 14He said to the elders, "Wait
here for us until we come back to you.
Aaron and Hur are with you, and anyone involved in a dispute can go to
them."
15When Moses went up on the mountain, the cloud covered it, 16and the
glory of the LORD settled on Mount
Sinai. For six days the cloud covered the
mountain, and on the seventh day the
LORD called to Moses from within
the cloud. 17To the Israelites the glory
of the LORD looked like a consuming
fire on top of the mountain. 18Then
Moses entered the cloud as he went
on up the mountain. And he stayed on
the mountain forty days and forty
nights.

[a]5 Traditionally *peace offerings* [b]10 Or *lapis lazuli*

SHARPEN THE FOCUS

At the institution of the Passover, the principle had been laid down: the lamb died so the people could live. Out of death came life. The writer to the Hebrews in the New Testament put it more precisely still: "Without the shedding of blood there is no forgiveness" (Hebrews 9:22).

As we continue in the Pentateuch, we will read about many different sacrifices. Most of them involved the shedding of blood. The sacrificial system offends many in our sophisticated, sanitized society. What a stinking mess it all must have been, they think. And they are right.

There's a deeper and even more offensive truth here. Israel sincerely promised, "Everything the LORD has said, we will do" (Exodus 24:3). But they—like we—did not do, could not do all the Law demanded. No one ever obeyed the holy God with 100 percent perfection.

And so the blood of the Old Testament sacrifices pointed toward that one gory sacrifice that would be offered on the altar of the cross. Twist and squirm as we may, we cannot wiggle out from under our need to be "sprinkled" with that blood, to rely on that sacrifice. In Christ's death alone we find forgiveness. In Him alone, God declares us righteous. ☼

WEEK 8 • TUESDAY

Exodus 25:1—27:21

GET THE BIG PICTURE

These chapters record the directions the Lord gave His people regarding the tabernacle, the place where Israel would worship Him. As you read, don't get bogged down in the details. Instead, meditate on the wonder that the almighty, holy God of Mt. Sinai would "pitch a tent" and make His home in the very center of His people's camp. If time is short, focus on Exodus 25:1–22.

Offerings for the Tabernacle

25 The LORD said to Moses,
2 "Tell the Israelites to bring
me an offering. You are to receive the
offering for me from each man whose
heart prompts him to give. 3 These are
the offerings you are to receive from
them: gold, silver and bronze; 4 blue,
purple and scarlet yarn and fine linen;
goat hair; 5 ram skins dyed red and hides
of sea cows[a]; acacia wood; 6 olive oil for
the light; spices for the anointing oil and
for the fragrant incense; 7 and onyx
stones and other gems to be mounted
on the ephod and breastpiece.
8 "Then have them make a sanctuary
for me, and I will dwell among them.
9 Make this tabernacle and all its furnishings exactly like the pattern I will show
you.

The Ark

10 "Have them make a chest of acacia
wood—two and a half cubits long, a cubit and a half wide, and a cubit and a
half high.[b] 11 Overlay it with pure gold,
both inside and out, and make a gold
molding around it. 12 Cast four gold rings
for it and fasten them to its four feet,
with two rings on one side and two
rings on the other. 13 Then make poles of
acacia wood and overlay them with
gold. 14 Insert the poles into the rings on
the sides of the chest to carry it. 15 The
poles are to remain in the rings of this
ark; they are not to be removed. 16 Then
put in the ark the Testimony, which I
will give you.
17 "Make an atonement cover[c] of pure
gold—two and a half cubits long and a
cubit and a half wide.[d] 18 And make two
cherubim out of hammered gold at the
ends of the cover. 19 Make one cherub on
one end and the second cherub on the
other; make the cherubim of one piece
with the cover, at the two ends. 20 The
cherubim are to have their wings spread
upward, overshadowing the cover with
them. The cherubim are to face each
other, looking toward the cover. 21 Place
the cover on top of the ark and put in
the ark the Testimony, which I will give

[a]5 That is, dugongs [b]10 That is, about 3 3/4 feet (about 1.1 meters) long and 2 1/4 feet (about 0.7 meter) wide and high [c]17 Traditionally *a mercy seat* [d]17 That is, about 3 3/4 feet (about 1.1 meters) long and 2 1/4 feet (about 0.7 meter) wide

you. 22There, above the cover between the two cherubim that are over the ark of the Testimony, I will meet with you and give you all my commands for the Israelites.

The Table

23"Make a table of acacia wood—two cubits long, a cubit wide and a cubit and a half high.[a] 24Overlay it with pure gold and make a gold molding around it. 25Also make around it a rim a handbreadth[b] wide and put a gold molding on the rim. 26Make four gold rings for the table and fasten them to the four corners, where the four legs are. 27The rings are to be close to the rim to hold the poles used in carrying the table. 28Make the poles of acacia wood, overlay them with gold and carry the table with them. 29And make its plates and dishes of pure gold, as well as its pitchers and bowls for the pouring out of offerings. 30Put the bread of the Presence on this table to be before me at all times.

The Lampstand

31"Make a lampstand of pure gold and hammer it out, base and shaft; its flowerlike cups, buds and blossoms shall be of one piece with it. 32Six branches are to extend from the sides of the lampstand—three on one side and three on the other. 33Three cups shaped like almond flowers with buds and blossoms are to be on one branch, three on the next branch, and the same for all six branches extending from the lampstand. 34And on the lampstand there are to be four cups shaped like almond flowers with buds and blossoms. 35One bud shall be under the first pair of branches extending from the lampstand, a second bud under the second pair, and a third bud under the third pair—six branches in all. 36The buds and branches shall all be of one piece with the lampstand, hammered out of pure gold.

37"Then make its seven lamps and set them up on it so that they light the space in front of it. 38Its wick trimmers and trays are to be of pure gold. 39A talent[c] of pure gold is to be used for the lampstand and all these accessories. 40See that you make them according to the pattern shown you on the mountain.

The Tabernacle

26 "Make the tabernacle with ten curtains of finely twisted linen and blue, purple and scarlet yarn, with cherubim worked into them by a skilled craftsman. 2All the curtains are to be the same size—twenty-eight cubits long and four cubits wide.[d] 3Join five of the curtains together, and do the same with the other five. 4Make loops of blue material along the edge of the end curtain in one set, and do the same with the end curtain in the other set. 5Make fifty loops on one curtain and fifty loops on the end curtain of the other set, with the loops opposite each other. 6Then make fifty gold clasps and use them to fasten the curtains together so that the tabernacle is a unit.

7"Make curtains of goat hair for the tent over the tabernacle—eleven altogether. 8All eleven curtains are to be the same size—thirty cubits long and four cubits wide.[e] 9Join five of the curtains together into one set and the other six into another set. Fold the sixth curtain double at the front of the tent. 10Make fifty loops along the edge of the end curtain in one set and also along the edge of the end curtain in the other set. 11Then make fifty bronze clasps and put them in the loops to fasten the tent together as a unit. 12As for the additional length of the tent curtains, the half curtain that is left over is to hang down at the rear of the tabernacle. 13The tent curtains will be a cubit[f] longer on both sides; what is left will hang over the

[a]23 That is, about 3 feet (about 0.9 meter) long and 1 1/2 feet (about 0.5 meter) wide and 2 1/4 feet (about 0.7 meter) high [b]25 That is, about 3 inches (about 8 centimeters) [c]39 That is, about 75 pounds (about 34 kilograms) [d]2 That is, about 42 feet (about 12.5 meters) long and 6 feet (about 1.8 meters) wide [e]8 That is, about 45 feet (about 13.5 meters) long and 6 feet (about 1.8 meters) wide [f]13 That is, about 1 1/2 feet (about 0.5 meter)

sides of the tabernacle so as to cover it.
[14]Make for the tent a covering of ram
skins dyed red, and over that a covering
of hides of sea cows.[a]
[15]"Make upright frames of acacia
wood for the tabernacle. [16]Each frame is
to be ten cubits long and a cubit and a
half wide,[b] [17]with two projections set
parallel to each other. Make all the
frames of the tabernacle in this way.
[18]Make twenty frames for the south side
of the tabernacle [19]and make forty silver
bases to go under them—two bases for
each frame, one under each projection.
[20]For the other side, the north side of the
tabernacle, make twenty frames [21]and
forty silver bases—two under each
frame. [22]Make six frames for the far
end, that is, the west end of the tabernacle, [23]and make two frames for the
corners at the far end. [24]At these two corners they must be double from the bottom all the way to the top, and fitted
into a single ring; both shall be like that.
[25]So there will be eight frames and sixteen silver bases—two under each
frame.
[26]"Also make crossbars of acacia wood:
five for the frames on one side of the
tabernacle, [27]five for those on the other
side, and five for the frames on the west,
at the far end of the tabernacle. [28]The
center crossbar is to extend from end to
end at the middle of the frames. [29]Over-
lay the frames with gold and make gold
rings to hold the crossbars. Also overlay
the crossbars with gold.
[30]"Set up the tabernacle according to
the plan shown you on the mountain.
[31]"Make a curtain of blue, purple and
scarlet yarn and finely twisted linen,
with cherubim worked into it by a
skilled craftsman. [32]Hang it with gold
hooks on four posts of acacia wood
overlaid with gold and standing on four
silver bases. [33]Hang the curtain from the
clasps and place the ark of the Testimony behind the curtain. The curtain
will separate the Holy Place from the
Most Holy Place. [34]Put the atonement
cover on the ark of the Testimony in the
Most Holy Place. [35]Place the table outside the curtain on the north side of the
tabernacle and put the lampstand opposite it on the south side.
[36]"For the entrance to the tent make a
curtain of blue, purple and scarlet yarn
and finely twisted linen—the work of
an embroiderer. [37]Make gold hooks for
this curtain and five posts of acacia
wood overlaid with gold. And cast five
bronze bases for them.

The Altar of Burnt Offering

27 "Build an altar of acacia
wood, three cubits[c] high; it
is to be square, five cubits long and five
cubits wide.[d] [2]Make a horn at each of the
four corners, so that the horns and the
altar are of one piece, and overlay
the altar with bronze. [3]Make all its utensils of bronze—its pots to remove the
ashes, and its shovels, sprinkling bowls,
meat forks and firepans. [4]Make a grating for it, a bronze network, and make
a bronze ring at each of the four corners
of the network. [5]Put it under the ledge
of the altar so that it is halfway up the
altar. [6]Make poles of acacia wood for the
altar and overlay them with bronze.
[7]The poles are to be inserted into the
rings so they will be on two sides of the
altar when it is carried. [8]Make the altar
hollow, out of boards. It is to be made
just as you were shown on the mountain.

The Courtyard

[9]"Make a courtyard for the tabernacle.
The south side shall be a hundred
cubits[e] long and is to have curtains of
finely twisted linen, [10]with twenty posts
and twenty bronze bases and with silver hooks and bands on the posts. [11]The
north side shall also be a hundred cubits
long and is to have curtains, with
twenty posts and twenty bronze bases
and with silver hooks and bands on the
posts.
[12]"The west end of the courtyard shall

[a]*14* That is, dugongs [b]*16* That is, about 15 feet (about 4.5 meters) long and 2 1/4 feet (about 0.7 meter) wide [c]*1* That is, about 4 1/2 feet (about 1.3 meters) [d]*1* That is, about 7 1/2 feet (about 2.3 meters) long and wide [e]*9* That is, about 150 feet (about 46 meters); also in verse 11

be fifty cubits[a] wide and have curtains, with ten posts and ten bases. [13]On the east end, toward the sunrise, the courtyard shall also be fifty cubits wide. [14]Curtains fifteen cubits[b] long are to be on one side of the entrance, with three posts and three bases, [15]and curtains fifteen cubits long are to be on the other side, with three posts and three bases.

[16]"For the entrance to the courtyard, provide a curtain twenty cubits[c] long, of blue, purple and scarlet yarn and finely twisted linen—the work of an embroiderer—with four posts and four bases. [17]All the posts around the courtyard are to have silver bands and hooks, and bronze bases. [18]The courtyard shall be a hundred cubits long and fifty cubits wide,[d] with curtains of finely twisted linen five cubits[e] high, and with bronze bases. [19]All the other articles used in the service of the tabernacle, whatever their function, including all the tent pegs for it and those for the courtyard, are to be of bronze.

Oil for the Lampstand

[20]"Command the Israelites to bring you clear oil of pressed olives for the light so that the lamps may be kept burning. [21]In the Tent of Meeting, outside the curtain that is in front of the Testimony, Aaron and his sons are to keep the lamps burning before the LORD from evening till morning. This is to be a lasting ordinance among the Israelites for the generations to come.

[a] *12* That is, about 75 feet (about 23 meters); also in verse 13 [b] *14* That is, about 22 1/2 feet (about 6.9 meters); also in verse 15 [c] *16* That is, about 30 feet (about 9 meters) [d] *18* That is, about 150 feet (about 46 meters) long and 75 feet (about 23 meters) wide [e] *18* That is, about 7 1/2 feet (about 2.3 meters)

SHARPEN THE FOCUS

Under the Old Covenant, the covenant of Sinai, God chose to reside on earth, as it were, in the tabernacle ("tent of meeting") and later on in the temple at Jerusalem.

When Jesus came, that changed. The apostle John tells us "the Word became flesh and made His dwelling [literally, 'tented'] among us" (John 1:14). In Jesus, God pitched His tent among His people to bring us His forgiveness, peace, healing, and grace.

More remarkable still, our Lord has now taken up residence in us! St. Paul asks, "Do you not know that your body is a temple of the Holy Spirit, who is in you?" (1 Corinthians 6:19) Jesus once said that He and the Father make their home in the hearts of those who love Him (John 14:23).

Think of it! The God of the universe has pitched His tent, made His home, in you! Just as the tabernacle served as a visible reminder of God's presence in Israel, so you are the sign of God's presence at your office, farm, shop; in your family; among your friends. How will you use the Spirit's power to bring Christ's forgiveness, peace, healing, and grace to those around you today?

WEEK 8 • WEDNESDAY

Exodus 28:1—29:46

GET THE BIG PICTURE

After the Lord describes the Tabernacle, He outlines the clothing and what we might today call the ordination ceremony for the priests who will serve God's people in the tabernacle. These chapters are rich with symbolism. As you read, note the honor and dignity the Lord gives His priests. Again today, avoid getting bogged down in the details. If time is short, focus on Exodus 28:1–12.

The Priestly Garments

28 "Have Aaron your brother
brought to you from among
the Israelites, along with his sons Nadab
and Abihu, Eleazar and Ithamar, so they
may serve me as priests. [2]Make sacred
garments for your brother Aaron, to
give him dignity and honor. [3]Tell all the
skilled men to whom I have given wisdom in such matters that they are to
make garments for Aaron, for his consecration, so he may serve me as priest.
[4]These are the garments they are to
make: a breastpiece, an ephod, a robe,
a woven tunic, a turban and a sash.
They are to make these sacred garments
for your brother Aaron and his sons, so
they may serve me as priests. [5]Have
them use gold, and blue, purple and
scarlet yarn, and fine linen.

The Ephod

[6]"Make the ephod of gold, and of
blue, purple and scarlet yarn, and of
finely twisted linen—the work of a
skilled craftsman. [7]It is to have two
shoulder pieces attached to two of its
corners, so it can be fastened. [8]Its skillfully woven waistband is to be like it—
of one piece with the ephod and made
with gold, and with blue, purple and
scarlet yarn, and with finely twisted
linen.
[9]"Take two onyx stones and engrave
on them the names of the sons of
Israel [10]in the order of their birth—six
names on one stone and the remaining
six on the other. [11]Engrave the names
of the sons of Israel on the two stones
the way a gem cutter engraves a seal.
Then mount the stones in gold filigree settings [12]and fasten them on
the shoulder pieces of the ephod as
memorial stones for the sons of Israel. Aaron is to bear the names on his
shoulders as a memorial before the
LORD. [13]Make gold filigree settings [14]and
two braided chains of pure gold, like a
rope, and attach the chains to the settings.

The Breastpiece

[15]"Fashion a breastpiece for making
decisions—the work of a skilled craftsman. Make it like the ephod: of gold,
and of blue, purple and scarlet yarn,
and of finely twisted linen. [16]It is to be
square—a span[a] long and a span wide—
and folded double. [17]Then mount four
rows of precious stones on it. In the first
row there shall be a ruby, a topaz and a
beryl; [18]in the second row a turquoise, a
sapphire[b] and an emerald; [19]in the third
row a jacinth, an agate and an amethyst;
[20]in the fourth row a chrysolite, an onyx
and a jasper.[c] Mount them in gold filigree settings. [21]There are to be twelve
stones, one for each of the names of the
sons of Israel, each engraved like a seal

[a]*16* That is, about 9 inches (about 22 centimeters) [b]*18* Or *lapis lazuli* [c]*20* The precise identification of some of these precious stones is uncertain.

with the name of one of the twelve tribes.

22"For the breastpiece make braided chains of pure gold, like a rope. 23Make two gold rings for it and fasten them to two corners of the breastpiece. 24Fasten the two gold chains to the rings at the corners of the breastpiece, 25and the other ends of the chains to the two settings, attaching them to the shoulder pieces of the ephod at the front. 26Make two gold rings and attach them to the other two corners of the breastpiece on the inside edge next to the ephod. 27Make two more gold rings and attach them to the bottom of the shoulder pieces on the front of the ephod, close to the seam just above the waistband of the ephod. 28The rings of the breastpiece are to be tied to the rings of the ephod with blue cord, connecting it to the waistband, so that the breastpiece will not swing out from the ephod.

29"Whenever Aaron enters the Holy Place, he will bear the names of the sons of Israel over his heart on the breastpiece of decision as a continuing memorial before the LORD. 30Also put the Urim and the Thummim in the breastpiece, so they may be over Aaron's heart whenever he enters the presence of the LORD. Thus Aaron will always bear the means of making decisions for the Israelites over his heart before the LORD.

Other Priestly Garments

31"Make the robe of the ephod entirely of blue cloth, 32with an opening for the head in its center. There shall be a woven edge like a collar[a] around this opening, so that it will not tear. 33Make pomegranates of blue, purple and scarlet yarn around the hem of the robe, with gold bells between them. 34The gold bells and the pomegranates are to alternate around the hem of the robe. 35Aaron must wear it when he ministers. The sound of the bells will be heard when he enters the Holy Place before the LORD and when he comes out, so that he will not die.

36"Make a plate of pure gold and engrave on it as on a seal: HOLY TO THE LORD. 37Fasten a blue cord to it to attach it to the turban; it is to be on the front of the turban. 38It will be on Aaron's forehead, and he will bear the guilt involved in the sacred gifts the Israelites consecrate, whatever their gifts may be. It will be on Aaron's forehead continually so that they will be acceptable to the LORD.

39"Weave the tunic of fine linen and make the turban of fine linen. The sash is to be the work of an embroiderer. 40Make tunics, sashes and headbands for Aaron's sons, to give them dignity and honor. 41After you put these clothes on your brother Aaron and his sons, anoint and ordain them. Consecrate them so they may serve me as priests.

42"Make linen undergarments as a covering for the body, reaching from the waist to the thigh. 43Aaron and his sons must wear them whenever they enter the Tent of Meeting or approach the altar to minister in the Holy Place, so that they will not incur guilt and die.

"This is to be a lasting ordinance for Aaron and his descendants.

Consecration of the Priests

29 "This is what you are to do to consecrate them, so they may serve me as priests: Take a young bull and two rams without defect. 2And from fine wheat flour, without yeast, make bread, and cakes mixed with oil, and wafers spread with oil. 3Put them in a basket and present them in it—along with the bull and the two rams. 4Then bring Aaron and his sons to the entrance to the Tent of Meeting and wash them with water. 5Take the garments and dress Aaron with the tunic, the robe of the ephod, the ephod itself and the breastpiece. Fasten the ephod on him by its skillfully woven waistband. 6Put the turban on his head and attach the sacred diadem to the turban. 7Take the anointing oil and anoint him by pouring it on his head. 8Bring his sons and dress them in tunics 9and put

[a]32 The meaning of the Hebrew for this word is uncertain.

headbands on them. Then tie sashes on Aaron and his sons.[a] The priesthood is theirs by a lasting ordinance. In this way you shall ordain Aaron and his sons.

10"Bring the bull to the front of the Tent of Meeting, and Aaron and his sons shall lay their hands on its head. 11Slaughter it in the LORD's presence at the entrance to the Tent of Meeting. 12Take some of the bull's blood and put it on the horns of the altar with your finger, and pour out the rest of it at the base of the altar. 13Then take all the fat around the inner parts, the covering of the liver, and both kidneys with the fat on them, and burn them on the altar. 14But burn the bull's flesh and its hide and its offal outside the camp. It is a sin offering.

15"Take one of the rams, and Aaron and his sons shall lay their hands on its head. 16Slaughter it and take the blood and sprinkle it against the altar on all sides. 17Cut the ram into pieces and wash the inner parts and the legs, putting them with the head and the other pieces. 18Then burn the entire ram on the altar. It is a burnt offering to the LORD, a pleasing aroma, an offering made to the LORD by fire.

19"Take the other ram, and Aaron and his sons shall lay their hands on its head. 20Slaughter it, take some of its blood and put it on the lobes of the right ears of Aaron and his sons, on the thumbs of their right hands, and on the big toes of their right feet. Then sprinkle blood against the altar on all sides. 21And take some of the blood on the altar and some of the anointing oil and sprinkle it on Aaron and his garments and on his sons and their garments. Then he and his sons and their garments will be consecrated.

22"Take from this ram the fat, the fat tail, the fat around the inner parts, the covering of the liver, both kidneys with the fat on them, and the right thigh. (This is the ram for the ordination.) 23From the basket of bread made without yeast, which is before the LORD, take a loaf, and a cake made with oil, and a wafer. 24Put all these in the hands of Aaron and his sons and wave them before the LORD as a wave offering. 25Then take them from their hands and burn them on the altar along with the burnt offering for a pleasing aroma to the LORD, an offering made to the LORD by fire. 26After you take the breast of the ram for Aaron's ordination, wave it before the LORD as a wave offering, and it will be your share.

27"Consecrate those parts of the ordination ram that belong to Aaron and his sons: the breast that was waved and the thigh that was presented. 28This is always to be the regular share from the Israelites for Aaron and his sons. It is the contribution the Israelites are to make to the LORD from their fellowship offerings.[b]

29"Aaron's sacred garments will belong to his descendants so that they can be anointed and ordained in them. 30The son who succeeds him as priest and comes to the Tent of Meeting to minister in the Holy Place is to wear them seven days.

31"Take the ram for the ordination and cook the meat in a sacred place. 32At the entrance to the Tent of Meeting, Aaron and his sons are to eat the meat of the ram and the bread that is in the basket. 33They are to eat these offerings by which atonement was made for their ordination and consecration. But no one else may eat them, because they are sacred. 34And if any of the meat of the ordination ram or any bread is left over till morning, burn it up. It must not be eaten, because it is sacred.

35"Do for Aaron and his sons everything I have commanded you, taking seven days to ordain them. 36Sacrifice a bull each day as a sin offering to make atonement. Purify the altar by making atonement for it, and anoint it to consecrate it. 37For seven days make atonement for the altar and consecrate it. Then the altar will be most holy, and whatever touches it will be holy.

38"This is what you are to offer on the altar regularly each day: two lambs a

[a]9 Hebrew; Septuagint *on them*
[b]28 Traditionally *peace offerings*

year old. 39Offer one in the morning and
the other at twilight. 40With the first
lamb offer a tenth of an ephah[a] of fine
flour mixed with a quarter of a hin[b] of
oil from pressed olives, and a quarter of
a hin of wine as a drink offering. 41Sac-
rifice the other lamb at twilight with the
same grain offering and its drink offering as in the morning—a pleasing aroma, an offering made to the LORD by
fire.

42"For the generations to come this
burnt offering is to be made regularly at
the entrance to the Tent of Meeting before the LORD. There I will meet you and
speak to you; 43there also I will meet
with the Israelites, and the place will be
consecrated by my glory.

44"So I will consecrate the Tent of
Meeting and the altar and will consecrate Aaron and his sons to serve me as
priests. 45Then I will dwell among the Israelites and be their God. 46They will
know that I am the LORD their God,
who brought them out of Egypt so that
I might dwell among them. I am the
LORD their God.

[a]*40* That is, probably about 2 quarts (about 2 liters) [b]*40* That is, probably about 1 quart (about 1 liter)

SHARPEN THE FOCUS

Peter tells all of God's New Covenant people, "You are . . . a royal priesthood." In ancient Israel, only the descendants of Aaron served as priests and intercessors. Now, all those who belong to God through Christ share these privileges. Note three similarities:

- God has given us, His priests, dignity and honor (Exodus 28:2; John 12:26).
- God has given us a crown of righteousness (Exodus 28:36; 2 Timothy 4:8).
- God has cleansed us from our sins, not with the blood of bulls and lambs but with the precious blood of Christ (Exodus 29:21; 1 Peter 1:18–19).

Exodus tells us that Aaron and his sons offered a burnt offering. The animal was completely burned up. This symbolized the total dedication of the worshiper to the Lord and to His service.

Because we have seen Christ's total dedication to us, because we have seen Him die for us, we want to give ourselves completely to Him. We want to live for Him (see Romans 12).

Ask the Holy Spirit to consecrate you anew, to set you aside once again for His service as His royal priest.

WEEK 8 • THURSDAY

Exodus 30:1—31:18

GET THE BIG PICTURE

Exodus 30 gives a few last details about tabernacle worship. We read of the altar of incense and the bronze basin where the priests will symbolically wash away their impurities before they approach the Lord. And we read recipes for the anointing oil and the incense. Chapter 31 goes on to designate oversight of tabernacle construction to two men whom God has gifted. The chapter closes with a reminder of the Sabbath rest and its importance to God's people. If time is short, focus on Exodus 31:12–18.

The Altar of Incense

30 "Make an altar of acacia
wood for burning incense.
2It is to be square, a cubit long and a
cubit wide, and two cubits high[a]—its
horns of one piece with it. 3Overlay the
top and all the sides and the horns with
pure gold, and make a gold molding
around it. 4Make two gold rings for the
altar below the molding—two on opposite sides—to hold the poles used to
carry it. 5Make the poles of acacia wood
and overlay them with gold. 6Put the
altar in front of the curtain that is before
the ark of the Testimony—before the
atonement cover that is over the Testimony—where I will meet with you.
7"Aaron must burn fragrant incense
on the altar every morning when he
tends the lamps. 8He must burn incense
again when he lights the lamps at twilight so incense will burn regularly before the LORD for the generations to
come. 9Do not offer on this altar any other incense or any burnt offering or grain
offering, and do not pour a drink offering on it. 10Once a year Aaron shall make
atonement on its horns. This annual
atonement must be made with the
blood of the atoning sin offering for the
generations to come. It is most holy to
the LORD."

Atonement Money

11Then the LORD said to Moses,
12"When you take a census of the Israelites to count them, each one must pay
the LORD a ransom for his life at the time
he is counted. Then no plague will come
on them when you number them.
13Each one who crosses over to those
already counted is to give a half shekel,[b]
according to the sanctuary shekel,
which weighs twenty gerahs. This half
shekel is an offering to the LORD. 14All
who cross over, those twenty years old
or more, are to give an offering to the
LORD. 15The rich are not to give more
than a half shekel and the poor are not
to give less when you make the offering
to the LORD to atone for your lives. 16Re-
ceive the atonement money from the Israelites and use it for the service of the
Tent of Meeting. It will be a memorial for
the Israelites before the LORD, making
atonement for your lives."

Basin for Washing

17Then the LORD said to Moses,
18"Make a bronze basin, with its bronze
stand, for washing. Place it between the
Tent of Meeting and the altar, and put
water in it. 19Aaron and his sons are to
wash their hands and feet with water
from it. 20Whenever they enter the Tent
of Meeting, they shall wash with water
so that they will not die. Also, when
they approach the altar to minister by
presenting an offering made to the
LORD by fire, 21they shall wash their
hands and feet so that they will not die.
This is to be a lasting ordinance for
Aaron and his descendants for the generations to come."

Anointing Oil

22Then the LORD said to Moses, 23"Take
the following fine spices: 500 shekels[c] of
liquid myrrh, half as much (that is, 250
shekels) of fragrant cinnamon, 250 shekels of fragrant cane, 24500 shekels of
cassia—all according to the sanctuary
shekel—and a hin[d] of olive oil. 25Make
these into a sacred anointing oil, a fragrant blend, the work of a perfumer. It
will be the sacred anointing oil. 26Then
use it to anoint the Tent of Meeting, the
ark of the Testimony, 27the table and all
its articles, the lampstand and its accessories, the altar of incense, 28the altar of

[a]2 That is, about 1 1/2 feet (about 0.5 meter) long and wide and about 3 feet (about 0.9 meter) high [b]13 That is, about 1/5 ounce (about 6 grams); also in verse 15 [c]23 That is, about 12 1/2 pounds (about 6 kilograms) [d]24 That is, probably about 4 quarts (about 4 liters)

burnt offering and all its utensils, and the basin with its stand. [29]You shall consecrate them so they will be most holy, and whatever touches them will be holy.

[30]"Anoint Aaron and his sons and consecrate them so they may serve me as priests. [31]Say to the Israelites, 'This is to be my sacred anointing oil for the generations to come. [32]Do not pour it on men's bodies and do not make any oil with the same formula. It is sacred, and you are to consider it sacred. [33]Whoever makes perfume like it and whoever puts it on anyone other than a priest must be cut off from his people.' "

Incense

[34]Then the LORD said to Moses, "Take fragrant spices—gum resin, onycha and galbanum—and pure frankincense, all in equal amounts, [35]and make a fragrant blend of incense, the work of a perfumer. It is to be salted and pure and sacred. [36]Grind some of it to powder and place it in front of the Testimony in the Tent of Meeting, where I will meet with you. It shall be most holy to you. [37]Do not make any incense with this formula for yourselves; consider it holy to the LORD. [38]Whoever makes any like it to enjoy its fragrance must be cut off from his people."

Bezalel and Oholiab

31 Then the LORD said to Moses, [2]"See, I have chosen Bezalel son of Uri, the son of Hur, of the tribe of Judah, [3]and I have filled him with the Spirit of God, with skill, ability and knowledge in all kinds of crafts— [4]to make artistic designs for work in gold, silver and bronze, [5]to cut and set stones, to work in wood, and to engage in all kinds of craftsmanship. [6]Moreover, I have appointed Oholiab son of Ahisamach, of the tribe of Dan, to help him. Also I have given skill to all the craftsmen to make everything I have commanded you: [7]the Tent of Meeting, the ark of the Testimony with the atonement cover on it, and all the other furnishings of the tent— [8]the table and its articles, the pure gold lampstand and all its accessories, the altar of incense, [9]the altar of burnt offering and all its utensils, the basin with its stand— [10]and also the woven garments, both the sacred garments for Aaron the priest and the garments for his sons when they serve as priests, [11]and the anointing oil and fragrant incense for the Holy Place. They are to make them just as I commanded you."

The Sabbath

[12]Then the LORD said to Moses, [13]"Say to the Israelites, 'You must observe my Sabbaths. This will be a sign between me and you for the generations to come, so you may know that I am the LORD, who makes you holy.[a]

[14]" 'Observe the Sabbath, because it is holy to you. Anyone who desecrates it must be put to death; whoever does any work on that day must be cut off from his people. [15]For six days, work is to be done, but the seventh day is a Sabbath of rest, holy to the LORD. Whoever does any work on the Sabbath day must be put to death. [16]The Israelites are to observe the Sabbath, celebrating it for the generations to come as a lasting covenant. [17]It will be a sign between me and the Israelites forever, for in six days the LORD made the heavens and the earth, and on the seventh day he abstained from work and rested.' "

[18]When the LORD finished speaking to Moses on Mount Sinai, he gave him the two tablets of the Testimony, the tablets of stone inscribed by the finger of God.

[a]13 Or *who sanctifies you;* or *who sets you apart as holy*

SHARPEN THE FOCUS

When was the last time you rested—really rested? Not fell into an exhausted sleep, but rested? The day of rest, the Sabbath day, distinguished God's Old Testament people from the nations round about. Other peoples at the time thought Israel lazy for taking one day off out of every seven.

Again and again God tells His people the Sabbath is His gift to them (see Exodus 16:23). "Take the day off," the Lord says. In fact, when Israel arrived in the Promised Land, they were to take one *year* out of every seven off (see Exodus 23:10–11)! They could trust their Lord to meet their needs. They could trust Him to provide. They need not slave day after dreary day for the gods of silver and gold.

Jesus has come to bring us rest, too. It is His gift to us. In Him, we have true peace, the peace of sins forgiven and the certainty of heaven. Knowing our Lord has provided all this, we can rest in the knowledge that He will meet our needs here on earth, too.

And so we praise God for our work, and as His children we work diligently. But we also praise God for the rest He has provided, and we relax in His love.

WEEK 8 • FRIDAY

Exodus 32:1–35

GET THE BIG PICTURE

As Exodus 32 opens, Moses has been on Mt. Sinai 40 days (Exodus 24:18). Convinced he will never return, Israel demands that Aaron fashion for them a new "god." Compelled by fear, Aaron gives in. As you read the infamous case of the golden calf, pay particular attention to Moses' words as he pleads with the Lord for His people (Exodus 32:30–33). If time is short, focus on Exodus 32:1–14.

The Golden Calf

32 When the people saw that
Moses was so long in com-
ing down from the mountain, they
gathered around Aaron and said,
"Come, make us gods[a] who will go before us. As for this fellow Moses who
brought us up out of Egypt, we don't
know what has happened to him."
2Aaron answered them, "Take off the
gold earrings that your wives, your sons
and your daughters are wearing, and
bring them to me." 3So all the people
took off their earrings and brought
them to Aaron. 4He took what they
handed him and made it into an idol
cast in the shape of a calf, fashioning it
with a tool. Then they said, "These are
your gods,[b] O Israel, who brought you
up out of Egypt."
5When Aaron saw this, he built an altar in front of the calf and announced,
"Tomorrow there will be a festival to the
LORD." 6So the next day the people rose
early and sacrificed burnt offerings and
presented fellowship offerings.[c] After-

[a]1 Or *a god;* also in verses 23 and 31 [b]4 Or *This is your god;* also in verse 8 [c]6 Traditionally *peace offerings*

ward they sat down to eat and drink
and got up to indulge in revelry.
7Then the LORD said to Moses, "Go
down, because your people, whom you
brought up out of Egypt, have become
corrupt. 8They have been quick to turn
away from what I commanded them
and have made themselves an idol cast
in the shape of a calf. They have bowed
down to it and sacrificed to it and have
said, 'These are your gods, O Israel, who
brought you up out of Egypt.'
9"I have seen these people," the LORD
said to Moses, "and they are a stiff-
necked people. 10Now leave me alone so
that my anger may burn against them
and that I may destroy them. Then I will
make you into a great nation."
11But Moses sought the favor of the
LORD his God. "O LORD," he said, "why
should your anger burn against your
people, whom you brought out of
Egypt with great power and a mighty
hand? 12Why should the Egyptians say,
'It was with evil intent that he brought
them out, to kill them in the mountains
and to wipe them off the face of the
earth'? Turn from your fierce anger; relent and do not bring disaster on your
people. 13Remember your servants
Abraham, Isaac and Israel, to whom you
swore by your own self: 'I will make
your descendants as numerous as the
stars in the sky and I will give your descendants all this land I promised them,
and it will be their inheritance forever.' "
14Then the LORD relented and did not
bring on his people the disaster he had
threatened.
15Moses turned and went down the
mountain with the two tablets of the
Testimony in his hands. They were inscribed on both sides, front and back.
16The tablets were the work of God; the
writing was the writing of God, engraved on the tablets.
17When Joshua heard the noise of the
people shouting, he said to Moses,
"There is the sound of war in the camp."
18Moses replied:

"It is not the sound of victory,
it is not the sound of defeat;
it is the sound of singing that I
hear."

19When Moses approached the camp
and saw the calf and the dancing, his
anger burned and he threw the tablets
out of his hands, breaking them to
pieces at the foot of the mountain. 20And
he took the calf they had made and
burned it in the fire; then he ground it
to powder, scattered it on the water and
made the Israelites drink it.
21He said to Aaron, "What did these
people do to you, that you led them into
such great sin?"
22"Do not be angry, my lord," Aaron
answered. "You know how prone these
people are to evil. 23They said to me,
'Make us gods who will go before us. As
for this fellow Moses who brought us up
out of Egypt, we don't know what has
happened to him.' 24So I told them,
'Whoever has any gold jewelry, take it
off.' Then they gave me the gold, and I
threw it into the fire, and out came this
calf!"
25Moses saw that the people were
running wild and that Aaron had let
them get out of control and so become
a laughingstock to their enemies. 26So he
stood at the entrance to the camp and
said, "Whoever is for the LORD, come to
me." And all the Levites rallied to him.
27Then he said to them, "This is what
the LORD, the God of Israel, says: 'Each
man strap a sword to his side. Go back
and forth through the camp from one
end to the other, each killing his brother
and friend and neighbor.' " 28The Levites
did as Moses commanded, and that day
about three thousand of the people
died. 29Then Moses said, "You have been
set apart to the LORD today, for you
were against your own sons and brothers, and he has blessed you this day."
30The next day Moses said to the people, "You have committed a great sin.
But now I will go up to the LORD; perhaps I can make atonement for your
sin."
31So Moses went back to the LORD and
said, "Oh, what a great sin these people have committed! They have made

themselves gods of gold. [32]But now,
please forgive their sin—but if not, then
blot me out of the book you have written."
[33]The LORD replied to Moses, "Whoever has sinned against me I will blot
out of my book. [34]Now go, lead the people to the place I spoke of, and my angel will go before you. However, when
the time comes for me to punish, I will
punish them for their sin."
[35]And the LORD struck the people
with a plague because of what they did
with the calf Aaron had made.

SHARPEN THE FOCUS

When was the last time you felt tempted to worship a statue or image of some kind? Few of us have experienced that kind of temptation. A god made out of stone? or wood? or even gold? It's laughable.

Maybe we can understand Israel's temptation better if we know that calf idols filled ancient Egypt and that the calf-god the Egyptians worshiped, Apis, symbolized power and sex. A culture that worshiped power and sex? The temptation to that kind of idolatry doesn't sound quite so foreign, does it?

Take some time to examine your own record with these temptations. Ask yourself:

- How often do I hurt myself by trying to control my own life instead of giving control over to the Lord?
- How often do I manipulate people or events to get my own way no matter who else is hurt by it?
- If my thoughts, actions, and motives were printed on the front page of tomorrow's newspaper, which of them would fail to honor God?

Frightening, isn't it? In the face of our failure, then, how good it is to remember that the Savior who died for us now pleads with us before God's throne of grace. Talk with God about your sin. Then read God's answer to your confession from Isaiah 55:6–7.

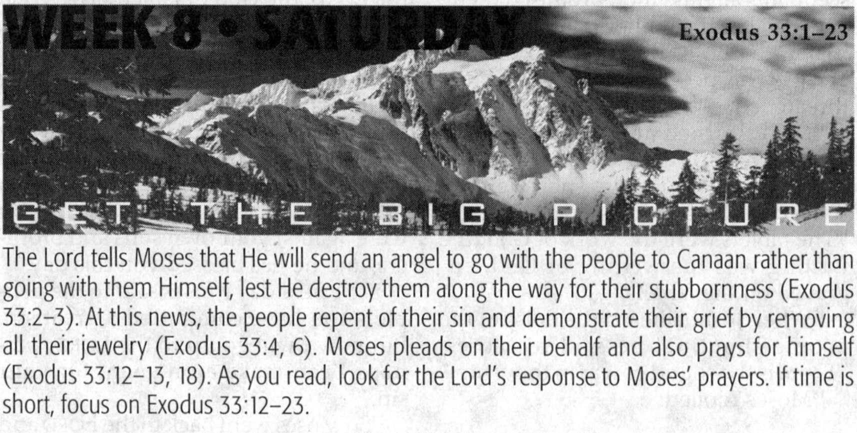

WEEK 8 • SATURDAY

Exodus 33:1–23

GET THE BIG PICTURE

The Lord tells Moses that He will send an angel to go with the people to Canaan rather than going with them Himself, lest He destroy them along the way for their stubbornness (Exodus 33:2–3). At this news, the people repent of their sin and demonstrate their grief by removing all their jewelry (Exodus 33:4, 6). Moses pleads on their behalf and also prays for himself (Exodus 33:12–13, 18). As you read, look for the Lord's response to Moses' prayers. If time is short, focus on Exodus 33:12–23.

33 Then the LORD said to
Moses, "Leave this place,
you and the people you brought up out
of Egypt, and go up to the land I promised on oath to Abraham, Isaac and Jacob, saying, 'I will give it to your
descendants.' 2I will send an angel before you and drive out the Canaanites,
Amorites, Hittites, Perizzites, Hivites
and Jebusites. 3Go up to the land flowing with milk and honey. But I will not
go with you, because you are a stiff-
necked people and I might destroy you
on the way."
4When the people heard these dis-
tressing words, they began to mourn
and no one put on any ornaments. 5For
the LORD had said to Moses, "Tell the Israelites, 'You are a stiff-necked people.
If I were to go with you even for a moment, I might destroy you. Now take off
your ornaments and I will decide what
to do with you.' " 6So the Israelites
stripped off their ornaments at Mount
Horeb.

The Tent of Meeting

7Now Moses used to take a tent and
pitch it outside the camp some distance
away, calling it the "tent of meeting."
Anyone inquiring of the LORD would go
to the tent of meeting outside the camp.
8And whenever Moses went out to the
tent, all the people rose and stood at the
entrances to their tents, watching Moses until he entered the tent. 9As Moses
went into the tent, the pillar of cloud
would come down and stay at the entrance, while the LORD spoke with Moses. 10Whenever the people saw the
pillar of cloud standing at the entrance
to the tent, they all stood and worshiped, each at the entrance to his tent.
11The LORD would speak to Moses face
to face, as a man speaks with his friend.
Then Moses would return to the camp,
but his young aide Joshua son of Nun
did not leave the tent.

Moses and the Glory of the LORD

12Moses said to the LORD, "You have
been telling me, 'Lead these people,' but
you have not let me know whom you will
send with me. You have said, 'I know you
by name and you have found favor with
me.' 13If you are pleased with me, teach
me your ways so I may know you and
continue to find favor with you. Remember that this nation is your people."
14The LORD replied, "My Presence will
go with you, and I will give you rest."
15Then Moses said to him, "If your
Presence does not go with us, do not
send us up from here. 16How will anyone know that you are pleased with me
and with your people unless you go
with us? What else will distinguish me
and your people from all the other
people on the face of the earth?"
17And the LORD said to Moses, "I will
do the very thing you have asked, because I am pleased with you and I know
you by name."
18Then Moses said, "Now show me
your glory."
19And the LORD said, "I will cause all
my goodness to pass in front of you, and
I will proclaim my name, the LORD, in
your presence. I will have mercy on
whom I will have mercy, and I will have
compassion on whom I will have compassion. 20But," he said, "you cannot see
my face, for no one may see me and
live."
21Then the LORD said, "There is a
place near me where you may stand on
a rock. 22When my glory passes by, I will
put you in a cleft in the rock and cover
you with my hand until I have passed
by. 23Then I will remove my hand and
you will see my back; but my face must
not be seen."

SHARPEN THE FOCUS

The "R word"—repentance. For many, it carries all the charm of a forced march in boot camp during a cold, April rainstorm. But in reality, it is one of God's best gifts to his children.

Moses devotes three chapters of Exodus to the idolatrous affair with the golden calf and the process of repentance that followed. By contrast the deliverance at the Red Sea takes up only two chapters. What makes the golden calf incident so important?

For one thing, it serves to remind us that sin involves much more than a few blotches on our record, more than two or ten or twenty-five demerits in God's book. Sin breaks fellowship. Most especially, sin—all sin—disrupts our relationship with the Lord. Not an insignificant matter.

In grace, the Lord wanted His people then—as He wants us now—to understand this critical concept. He did what He did and said what He said so they would see sin's seriousness.

God's forgiveness is free—but it's not cheap. It cost the lifeblood of His only Son. Our Savior-God always forgives us for Jesus' sake. But we dare not presume on His grace by shrugging off or winking at our sin.

WEEK 9 • MONDAY

Exodus 34:1–35

GET THE BIG PICTURE

The Lord reveals His glory to Moses (Exodus 34:5–7) just as He had promised (Exodus 33:18–23). He also renews the covenant promises He had made before the people's sin with the golden calf. When Moses returns to the camp, his face glows—he reflects the glory of the Lord! If time is short, focus on Exodus 34:1–9.

The New Stone Tablets

34 The LORD said to Moses,
"Chisel out two stone tab-
lets like the first ones, and I will write on
them the words that were on the first
tablets, which you broke. 2Be ready in
the morning, and then come up on
Mount Sinai. Present yourself to me
there on top of the mountain. 3No one
is to come with you or be seen anywhere on the mountain; not even the
flocks and herds may graze in front of
the mountain."
4So Moses chiseled out two stone tablets like the first ones and went up
Mount Sinai early in the morning, as the
LORD had commanded him; and he carried the two stone tablets in his hands.
5Then the LORD came down in the cloud
and stood there with him and proclaimed his name, the LORD. 6And he
passed in front of Moses, proclaiming,
"The LORD, the LORD, the compassionate and gracious God, slow to anger,
abounding in love and faithfulness,
7maintaining love to thousands, and
forgiving wickedness, rebellion and
sin. Yet he does not leave the guilty
unpunished; he punishes the children
and their children for the sin of the
fathers to the third and fourth generation."
8Moses bowed to the ground at once
and worshiped. 9"O Lord, if I have
found favor in your eyes," he said, "then
let the Lord go with us. Although this is
a stiff-necked people, forgive our wickedness and our sin, and take us as your
inheritance."
10Then the LORD said: "I am making a
covenant with you. Before all your people I will do wonders never before done
in any nation in all the world. The people you live among will see how awesome is the work that I, the LORD, will
do for you. 11Obey what I command you

today. I will drive out before you the Amorites, Canaanites, Hittites, Perizzites, Hivites and Jebusites. 12Be careful not to make a treaty with those who live in the land where you are going, or they will be a snare among you. 13Break down their altars, smash their sacred stones and cut down their Asherah poles.[a] 14Do not worship any other god, for the LORD, whose name is Jealous, is a jealous God.

15"Be careful not to make a treaty with those who live in the land; for when they prostitute themselves to their gods and sacrifice to them, they will invite you and you will eat their sacrifices. 16And when you choose some of their daughters as wives for your sons and those daughters prostitute themselves to their gods, they will lead your sons to do the same.

17"Do not make cast idols.

18"Celebrate the Feast of Unleavened Bread. For seven days eat bread made without yeast, as I commanded you. Do this at the appointed time in the month of Abib, for in that month you came out of Egypt.

19"The first offspring of every womb belongs to me, including all the firstborn males of your livestock, whether from herd or flock. 20Redeem the firstborn donkey with a lamb, but if you do not redeem it, break its neck. Redeem all your firstborn sons.

"No one is to appear before me empty-handed.

21"Six days you shall labor, but on the seventh day you shall rest; even during the plowing season and harvest you must rest.

22"Celebrate the Feast of Weeks with the firstfruits of the wheat harvest, and the Feast of Ingathering at the turn of the year.[b] 23Three times a year all your men are to appear before the Sovereign LORD, the God of Israel. 24I will drive out nations before you and enlarge your territory, and no one will covet your land when you go up three times each year to appear before the LORD your God.

25"Do not offer the blood of a sacrifice to me along with anything containing yeast, and do not let any of the sacrifice from the Passover Feast remain until morning.

26"Bring the best of the firstfruits of your soil to the house of the LORD your God.

"Do not cook a young goat in its mother's milk."

27Then the LORD said to Moses, "Write down these words, for in accordance with these words I have made a covenant with you and with Israel." 28Moses was there with the LORD forty days and forty nights without eating bread or drinking water. And he wrote on the tablets the words of the covenant—the Ten Commandments.

The Radiant Face of Moses

29When Moses came down from Mount Sinai with the two tablets of the Testimony in his hands, he was not aware that his face was radiant because he had spoken with the LORD. 30When Aaron and all the Israelites saw Moses, his face was radiant, and they were afraid to come near him. 31But Moses called to them; so Aaron and all the leaders of the community came back to him, and he spoke to them. 32Afterward all the Israelites came near him, and he gave them all the commands the LORD had given him on Mount Sinai.

33When Moses finished speaking to them, he put a veil over his face. 34But whenever he entered the LORD's presence to speak with him, he removed the veil until he came out. And when he came out and told the Israelites what he had been commanded, 35they saw that his face was radiant. Then Moses would put the veil back over his face until he went in to speak with the LORD.

[a]*13* That is, symbols of the goddess Asherah
[b]*22* That is, in the fall

SHARPEN THE FOCUS

Suppose someone asked you to describe yourself in 50 words or less. What words would you choose? Would they describe how you look, what you do, or your attitudes and beliefs? Would that choice change depending on who asked for the description?

Moses asks the Lord, "Show me Your glory" (Exodus 33:18). The Lord replies, "I will cause all My goodness to pass in front of you" (Exodus 33:19). God's glory *is* His goodness!

As we read about the events that followed, more details of God's goodness come to light. Reread Exodus 34:6–7. In fifty words or less, this is God's "autobiography"; these are the things for which He wants to be remembered forever. His description of Himself will never change—no matter who's asking.

On hearing God's Word, Moses "bowed to the ground at once and worshiped" (Exodus 34:8). How will *you* respond to God's goodness?

WEEK 9 • TUESDAY

Exodus 35:1—36:38

GET THE BIG PICTURE

Israel was given a second chance to turn their lives around and follow the Lord's commands. And they responded to that opportunity with joy. Forgiven and restored, Israel sets out with renewed zeal to build the tabernacle. The people offer not only their possessions, but themselves and their personal gifts and abilities to the Lord. If time is short, focus on Exodus 35:20–35.

Sabbath Regulations

35 Moses assembled the
whole Israelite commu-
nity and said to them, "These are the
things the LORD has commanded you to
do: [2]For six days, work is to be done, but
the seventh day shall be your holy day,
a Sabbath of rest to the LORD. Whoever
does any work on it must be put to
death. [3]Do not light a fire in any of your
dwellings on the Sabbath day."

Materials for the Tabernacle

[4]Moses said to the whole Israelite
community, "This is what the LORD has
commanded: [5]From what you have,
take an offering for the LORD. Everyone
who is willing is to bring to the LORD an
offering of gold, silver and bronze;
[6]blue, purple and scarlet yarn and fine
linen; goat hair; [7]ram skins dyed red and
hides of sea cows[a]; acacia wood; [8]olive
oil for the light; spices for the anointing
oil and for the fragrant incense; [9]and
onyx stones and other gems to be
mounted on the ephod and breastpiece.

[10]"All who are skilled among you are
to come and make everything the LORD
has commanded: [11]the tabernacle with
its tent and its covering, clasps, frames,
crossbars, posts and bases; [12]the ark with
its poles and the atonement cover and
the curtain that shields it; [13]the table
with its poles and all its articles and the
bread of the Presence; [14]the lampstand
that is for light with its accessories,
lamps and oil for the light; [15]the altar of
incense with its poles, the anointing oil

[a]7 That is, dugongs; also in verse 23

and the fragrant incense; the curtain for the doorway at the entrance to the tabernacle; 16the altar of burnt offering with its bronze grating, its poles and all its utensils; the bronze basin with its stand; 17the curtains of the courtyard with its posts and bases, and the curtain for the entrance to the courtyard; 18the tent pegs for the tabernacle and for the courtyard, and their ropes; 19the woven garments worn for ministering in the sanctuary—both the sacred garments for Aaron the priest and the garments for his sons when they serve as priests."

20Then the whole Israelite community withdrew from Moses' presence, 21and everyone who was willing and whose heart moved him came and brought an offering to the LORD for the work on the Tent of Meeting, for all its service, and for the sacred garments. 22All who were willing, men and women alike, came and brought gold jewelry of all kinds: brooches, earrings, rings and ornaments. They all presented their gold as a wave offering to the LORD. 23Everyone who had blue, purple or scarlet yarn or fine linen, or goat hair, ram skins dyed red or hides of sea cows brought them. 24Those presenting an offering of silver or bronze brought it as an offering to the LORD, and everyone who had acacia wood for any part of the work brought it. 25Every skilled woman spun with her hands and brought what she had spun—blue, purple or scarlet yarn or fine linen. 26And all the women who were willing and had the skill spun the goat hair. 27The leaders brought onyx stones and other gems to be mounted on the ephod and breastpiece. 28They also brought spices and olive oil for the light and for the anointing oil and for the fragrant incense. 29All the Israelite men and women who were willing brought to the LORD freewill offerings for all the work the LORD through Moses had commanded them to do.

Bezalel and Oholiab

30Then Moses said to the Israelites, "See, the LORD has chosen Bezalel son of Uri, the son of Hur, of the tribe of Judah, 31and he has filled him with the Spirit of God, with skill, ability and knowledge in all kinds of crafts— 32to make artistic designs for work in gold, silver and bronze, 33to cut and set stones, to work in wood and to engage in all kinds of artistic craftsmanship. 34And he has given both him and Oholiab son of Ahisamach, of the tribe of Dan, the ability to teach others. 35He has filled them with skill to do all kinds of work as craftsmen, designers, embroiderers in blue, purple and scarlet yarn and fine linen, and weavers—all of them master craftsmen and designers.

36 1So Bezalel, Oholiab and every skilled person to whom the LORD has given skill and ability to know how to carry out all the work of constructing the sanctuary are to do the work just as the LORD has commanded."

2Then Moses summoned Bezalel and Oholiab and every skilled person to whom the LORD had given ability and who was willing to come and do the work. 3They received from Moses all the offerings the Israelites had brought to carry out the work of constructing the sanctuary. And the people continued to bring freewill offerings morning after morning. 4So all the skilled craftsmen who were doing all the work on the sanctuary left their work 5and said to Moses, "The people are bringing more than enough for doing the work the LORD commanded to be done."

6Then Moses gave an order and they sent this word throughout the camp: "No man or woman is to make anything else as an offering for the sanctuary." And so the people were restrained from bringing more, 7because what they already had was more than enough to do all the work.

The Tabernacle

8All the skilled men among the workmen made the tabernacle with ten curtains of finely twisted linen and blue, purple and scarlet yarn, with cherubim worked into them by a skilled craftsman. 9All the curtains were the same size—twenty-eight cubits long and four cubits wide.[a] [10]They joined five of the curtains together and did the same with the other five. [11]Then they made loops of blue material along the edge of the end curtain in one set, and the same was done with the end curtain in the other set. [12]They also made fifty loops on one curtain and fifty loops on the end curtain of the other set, with the loops opposite each other. [13]Then they made fifty gold clasps and used them to fasten the two sets of curtains together so that the tabernacle was a unit.

[14]They made curtains of goat hair for the tent over the tabernacle—eleven altogether. [15]All eleven curtains were the same size—thirty cubits long and four cubits wide.[b] [16]They joined five of the curtains into one set and the other six into another set. [17]Then they made fifty loops along the edge of the end curtain in one set and also along the edge of the end curtain in the other set. [18]They made fifty bronze clasps to fasten the tent together as a unit. [19]Then they made for the tent a covering of ram skins dyed red, and over that a covering of hides of sea cows.[c]

[20]They made upright frames of acacia wood for the tabernacle. [21]Each frame was ten cubits long and a cubit and a half wide,[d] [22]with two projections set parallel to each other. They made all the frames of the tabernacle in this way. [23]They made twenty frames for the south side of the tabernacle [24]and made forty silver bases to go under them—two bases for each frame, one under each projection. [25]For the other side, the north side of the tabernacle, they made twenty frames [26]and forty silver bases—two under each frame. [27]They made six frames for the far end, that is, the west end of the tabernacle, [28]and two frames were made for the corners of the tabernacle at the far end. [29]At these two corners the frames were double from the bottom all the way to the top and fitted into a single ring; both were made alike. [30]So there were eight frames and sixteen silver bases—two under each frame.

[31]They also made crossbars of acacia wood: five for the frames on one side of the tabernacle, [32]five for those on the other side, and five for the frames on the west, at the far end of the tabernacle. [33]They made the center crossbar so that it extended from end to end at the middle of the frames. [34]They overlaid the frames with gold and made gold rings to hold the crossbars. They also overlaid the crossbars with gold.

[35]They made the curtain of blue, purple and scarlet yarn and finely twisted linen, with cherubim worked into it by a skilled craftsman. [36]They made four posts of acacia wood for it and overlaid them with gold. They made gold hooks for them and cast their four silver bases. [37]For the entrance to the tent they made a curtain of blue, purple and scarlet yarn and finely twisted linen—the work of an embroiderer; [38]and they made five posts with hooks for them. They overlaid the tops of the posts and their bands with gold and made their five bases of bronze.

[a] *9* That is, about 42 feet (about 12.5 meters) long and 6 feet (about 1.8 meters) wide [b] *15* That is, about 45 feet (about 13.5 meters) long and 6 feet (about 1.8 meters) wide [c] *19* That is, dugongs [d] *21* That is, about 15 feet (about 4.5 meters) long and 2 1/4 feet (about 0.7 meter) wide

SHARPEN THE FOCUS

We've all tried to carry out projects that failed to excite us. Tasks like that leave us feeling sluggish—exhausted even.

This can infect our relationships too. Even our relationship with the Lord. When we worship, serve, give half-heartedly, it exhausts our spirit. When "our hearts aren't in it," our service, giving, worship become drudgery rather than delight.

Israel was willing to give, to serve, to develop and create whole-heartedly. Because of Israel's willingness, these two chapters vibrate with delight and excitement. The Lord even reminds His people to rest on the Sabbath day. He doesn't want them to succumb to the temptation to work all weekend and miss the opportunity to be refreshed in a time of public worship.

God's mercy, pardon, and compassion motivated the Israelites. They knew these things were theirs despite their unworthiness, idolatry, and sin. Remembering God's goodness to them brought joy and turned their hearts toward Him. Think about your service, giving, and worship. What motivates it? Are you growing tired or bored or half-hearted in your worship? If so, ask your Savior-God to heal, refresh, and encourage your heart.

WEEK 9 • WEDNESDAY

Exodus 37:1—38:31

GET THE BIG PICTURE

These chapters continue the record of the careful way God's people followed the pattern He had given Moses as they constructed the tabernacle. The description concludes with an inventory of the vast wealth that went into the construction (Exodus 38:21–31). If time is short, focus on Exodus 37:1–7.

The Ark

37 Bezalel made the ark of
acacia wood—two and a
half cubits long, a cubit and a half wide,
and a cubit and a half high.[a] 2He overlaid it with pure gold, both inside and
out, and made a gold molding around
it. 3He cast four gold rings for it and
fastened them to its four feet, with
two rings on one side and two rings on
the other. 4Then he made poles of
acacia wood and overlaid them with
gold. 5And he inserted the poles into
the rings on the sides of the ark to
carry it.
6He made the atonement cover of
pure gold—two and a half cubits long
and a cubit and a half wide.[b] 7Then he
made two cherubim out of hammered
gold at the ends of the cover. 8He made
one cherub on one end and the second
cherub on the other; at the two ends he
made them of one piece with the cover.
9The cherubim had their wings spread
upward, overshadowing the cover with
them. The cherubim faced each other,
looking toward the cover.

The Table

10They[c] made the table of acacia
wood—two cubits long, a cubit wide,
and a cubit and a half high.[d] 11Then they
overlaid it with pure gold and made a
gold molding around it. 12They also
made around it a rim a handbreadth[e]
wide and put a gold molding on the rim.
13They cast four gold rings for the table
and fastened them to the four corners,
where the four legs were. 14The rings
were put close to the rim to hold the
poles used in carrying the table. 15The
poles for carrying the table were made

[a]*1* That is, about 3 3/4 feet (about 1.1 meters) long and 2 1/4 feet (about 0.7 meter) wide and high [b]*6* That is, about 3 3/4 feet (about 1.1 meters) long and 2 1/4 feet (about 0.7 meter) wide [c]*10* Or *He*; also in verses 11-29 [d]*10* That is, about 3 feet (about 0.9 meter) long, 1 1/2 feet (about 0.5 meter) wide, and 2 1/4 feet (about 0.7 meter) high [e]*12* That is, about 3 inches (about 8 centimeters)

of acacia wood and were overlaid with gold. 16And they made from pure gold the articles for the table—its plates and dishes and bowls and its pitchers for the pouring out of drink offerings.

The Lampstand

17They made the lampstand of pure gold and hammered it out, base and shaft; its flowerlike cups, buds and blossoms were of one piece with it. 18Six branches extended from the sides of the lampstand—three on one side and three on the other. 19Three cups shaped like almond flowers with buds and blossoms were on one branch, three on the next branch and the same for all six branches extending from the lampstand. 20And on the lampstand were four cups shaped like almond flowers with buds and blossoms. 21One bud was under the first pair of branches extending from the lampstand, a second bud under the second pair, and a third bud under the third pair—six branches in all. 22The buds and the branches were all of one piece with the lampstand, hammered out of pure gold.

23They made its seven lamps, as well as its wick trimmers and trays, of pure gold. 24They made the lampstand and all its accessories from one talent[a] of pure gold.

The Altar of Incense

25They made the altar of incense out of acacia wood. It was square, a cubit long and a cubit wide, and two cubits high[b]—its horns of one piece with it. 26They overlaid the top and all the sides and the horns with pure gold, and made a gold molding around it. 27They made two gold rings below the molding—two on opposite sides—to hold the poles used to carry it. 28They made the poles of acacia wood and overlaid them with gold.

29They also made the sacred anointing oil and the pure, fragrant incense—the work of a perfumer.

The Altar of Burnt Offering

38 They[c] built the altar of burnt offering of acacia wood, three cubits[d] high; it was square, five cubits long and five cubits wide.[e] 2They made a horn at each of the four corners, so that the horns and the altar were of one piece, and they overlaid the altar with bronze. 3They made all its utensils of bronze—its pots, shovels, sprinkling bowls, meat forks and firepans. 4They made a grating for the altar, a bronze network, to be under its ledge, halfway up the altar. 5They cast bronze rings to hold the poles for the four corners of the bronze grating. 6They made the poles of acacia wood and overlaid them with bronze. 7They inserted the poles into the rings so they would be on the sides of the altar for carrying it. They made it hollow, out of boards.

Basin for Washing

8They made the bronze basin and its bronze stand from the mirrors of the women who served at the entrance to the Tent of Meeting.

The Courtyard

9Next they made the courtyard. The south side was a hundred cubits[f] long and had curtains of finely twisted linen, 10with twenty posts and twenty bronze bases, and with silver hooks and bands on the posts. 11The north side was also a hundred cubits long and had twenty posts and twenty bronze bases, with silver hooks and bands on the posts.

12The west end was fifty cubits[g] wide and had curtains, with ten posts and ten bases, with silver hooks and bands on the posts. 13The east end, toward the sunrise, was also fifty cubits wide. 14Curtains fifteen cubits[h] long were on one side of the entrance, with three posts and three bases, 15and curtains fifteen

[a] *24* That is, about 75 pounds (about 34 kilograms) [b] *25* That is, about 1 1/2 feet (about 0.5 meter) long and wide, and about 3 feet (about 0.9 meter) high [c] *1* Or *He*; also in verses 2-9
[d] *1* That is, about 4 1/2 feet (about 1.3 meters)
[e] *1* That is, about 7 1/2 feet (about 2.3 meters) long and wide [f] *9* That is, about 150 feet (about 46 meters) [g] *12* That is, about 75 feet (about 23 meters) [h] *14* That is, about 22 1/2 feet (about 6.9 meters)

cubits long were on the other side of the entrance to the courtyard, with three posts and three bases. [16]All the curtains around the courtyard were of finely twisted linen. [17]The bases for the posts were bronze. The hooks and bands on the posts were silver, and their tops were overlaid with silver; so all the posts of the courtyard had silver bands.

[18]The curtain for the entrance to the courtyard was of blue, purple and scarlet yarn and finely twisted linen—the work of an embroiderer. It was twenty cubits[a] long and, like the curtains of the courtyard, five cubits[b] high, [19]with four posts and four bronze bases. Their hooks and bands were silver, and their tops were overlaid with silver. [20]All the tent pegs of the tabernacle and of the surrounding courtyard were bronze.

The Materials Used

[21]These are the amounts of the materials used for the tabernacle, the tabernacle of the Testimony, which were recorded at Moses' command by the Levites under the direction of Ithamar son of Aaron, the priest. [22](Bezalel son of Uri, the son of Hur, of the tribe of Judah, made everything the LORD commanded Moses; [23]with him was Oholiab son of Ahisamach, of the tribe of Dan—a craftsman and designer, and an embroiderer in blue, purple and scarlet yarn and fine linen.) [24]The total amount of the gold from the wave offering used for all the work on the sanctuary was 29 talents and 730 shekels,[c] according to the sanctuary shekel.

[25]The silver obtained from those of the community who were counted in the census was 100 talents and 1,775 shekels,[d] according to the sanctuary shekel—[26]one beka per person, that is, half a shekel,[e] according to the sanctuary shekel, from everyone who had crossed over to those counted, twenty years old or more, a total of 603,550 men. [27]The 100 talents[f] of silver were used to cast the bases for the sanctuary and for the curtain—100 bases from the 100 talents, one talent for each base. [28]They used the 1,775 shekels[g] to make the hooks for the posts, to overlay the tops of the posts, and to make their bands.

[29]The bronze from the wave offering was 70 talents and 2,400 shekels.[h] [30]They used it to make the bases for the entrance to the Tent of Meeting, the bronze altar with its bronze grating and all its utensils, [31]the bases for the surrounding courtyard and those for its entrance and all the tent pegs for the tabernacle and those for the surrounding courtyard.

[a] *18* That is, about 30 feet (about 9 meters)
[b] *18* That is, about 7 1/2 feet (about 2.3 meters)
[c] *24* The weight of the gold was a little over one ton (about 1 metric ton).
[d] *25* The weight of the silver was a little over 3 3/4 tons (about 3.4 metric tons).
[e] *26* That is, about 1/5 ounce (about 5.5 grams)
[f] *27* That is, about 3 3/4 tons (about 3.4 metric tons)
[g] *28* That is, about 45 pounds (about 20 kilograms)
[h] *29* The weight of the bronze was about 2 1/2 tons (about 2.4 metric tons).

SHARPEN THE FOCUS

Each piece of furniture in the tabernacle symbolized part of God's covenant promise to His people. Each was also a temporary "shadow" of a reality that stands forever in heaven (Hebrews 8–10). Here is a brief list of some of these items and what they symbolized:

The mercy seat (atonement cover)–Here Christ presented His own blood as a once-for-all-time atonement for sin (Romans 3:25).

The golden lampstand–Christ, "the light of the world" (John 9:5), and the church, "the light of the world" (Matthew 5:14), burning with the oil of the Holy Spirit and displaying the light of Christ to those lost in the darkness of sin.

The bread of the presence–The Word of God is often symbolized by bread (see

Matthew 4:3–4). In particular, Jesus Himself, the eternal Word, is the bread of life (John 6:35). "Whoever eats [Jesus'] flesh and drinks [His] blood has eternal life" (John 6:54).

The altar of incense–On the cross, Christ "gave Himself up for us as a fragrant offering and sacrifice to God" (Ephesians 5:2). The prayers of God's people are also a sweet aroma that rise before Him like incense (Revelation 5:8).

Today's reading begins with a description of the clothing the people furnished for the priests. Each article was made just as the Lord had commanded Moses earlier (Exodus 28). The chapter then closes with Moses' "inspection tour" of the completed Tabernacle furnishings. Having approved the work, Moses blessed the people and led them in dedicating their place of public worship. If time is short, focus on Exodus 39:1–14; 40:34–38.

The Priestly Garments

39 From the blue, purple and scarlet yarn they made woven garments for ministering in the sanctuary. They also made sacred garments for Aaron, as the LORD commanded Moses.

The Ephod

2 They[a] made the ephod of gold, and of blue, purple and scarlet yarn, and of finely twisted linen. 3 They hammered out thin sheets of gold and cut strands to be worked into the blue, purple and scarlet yarn and fine linen—the work of a skilled craftsman. 4 They made shoulder pieces for the ephod, which were attached to two of its corners, so it could be fastened. 5 Its skillfully woven waistband was like it—of one piece with the ephod and made with gold, and with blue, purple and scarlet yarn, and with finely twisted linen, as the LORD commanded Moses.

6 They mounted the onyx stones in gold filigree settings and engraved them like a seal with the names of the sons of Israel. 7 Then they fastened them on the shoulder pieces of the ephod as memorial stones for the sons of Israel, as the LORD commanded Moses.

The Breastpiece

8 They fashioned the breastpiece—the work of a skilled craftsman. They made it like the ephod: of gold, and of blue, purple and scarlet yarn, and of finely twisted linen. 9 It was square—a span[b] long and a span wide—and folded double. 10 Then they mounted four rows of precious stones on it. In the first row there was a ruby, a topaz and a beryl; 11 in the second row a turquoise, a sapphire[c] and an emerald; 12 in the third row a jacinth, an agate and an amethyst; 13 in the fourth row a chrysolite, an onyx and a jasper.[d] They were mounted in gold filigree settings. 14 There were twelve stones, one for each of the names of the sons of Israel, each engraved like a seal with the name of one of the twelve tribes.

[a] 2 Or *He;* also in verses 7, 8 and 22 [b] 9 That is, about 9 inches (about 22 centimeters) [c] *11* Or *lapis lazuli* [d] *13* The precise identification of some of these precious stones is uncertain.

15For the breastpiece they made braided chains of pure gold, like a rope.
16They made two gold filigree settings
and two gold rings, and fastened the
rings to two of the corners of the breastpiece. 17They fastened the two gold
chains to the rings at the corners of the
breastpiece, 18and the other ends of the
chains to the two settings, attaching
them to the shoulder pieces of the
ephod at the front. 19They made two
gold rings and attached them to the other two corners of the breastpiece on the
inside edge next to the ephod. 20Then
they made two more gold rings and attached them to the bottom of the shoulder pieces on the front of the ephod,
close to the seam just above the waistband of the ephod. 21They tied the rings
of the breastpiece to the rings of the
ephod with blue cord, connecting it to
the waistband so that the breastpiece
would not swing out from the ephod—
as the LORD commanded Moses.

Other Priestly Garments

22They made the robe of the ephod
entirely of blue cloth—the work of a
weaver— 23with an opening in the center of the robe like the opening of a
collar,[a] and a band around this opening,
so that it would not tear. 24They made
pomegranates of blue, purple and scarlet yarn and finely twisted linen around
the hem of the robe. 25And they made
bells of pure gold and attached them
around the hem between the pomegranates. 26The bells and pomegranates
alternated around the hem of the robe
to be worn for ministering, as the LORD
commanded Moses.

27For Aaron and his sons, they made
tunics of fine linen—the work of a
weaver— 28and the turban of fine linen,
the linen headbands and the undergarments of finely twisted linen. 29The sash
was of finely twisted linen and blue,
purple and scarlet yarn—the work of an
embroiderer—as the LORD commanded
Moses.

30They made the plate, the sacred diadem, out of pure gold and engraved on
it, like an inscription on a seal: HOLY TO
THE LORD. 31Then they fastened a blue
cord to it to attach it to the turban, as the
LORD commanded Moses.

Moses Inspects the Tabernacle

32So all the work on the tabernacle,
the Tent of Meeting, was completed.
The Israelites did everything just as the
LORD commanded Moses. 33Then they
brought the tabernacle to Moses: the
tent and all its furnishings, its clasps,
frames, crossbars, posts and bases; 34the
covering of ram skins dyed red, the covering of hides of sea cows[b] and the
shielding curtain; 35the ark of the Testimony with its poles and the atonement
cover; 36the table with all its articles and
the bread of the Presence; 37the pure
gold lampstand with its row of lamps
and all its accessories, and the oil for the
light; 38the gold altar, the anointing oil,
the fragrant incense, and the curtain for
the entrance to the tent; 39the bronze
altar with its bronze grating, its poles
and all its utensils; the basin with its
stand; 40the curtains of the courtyard
with its posts and bases, and the curtain
for the entrance to the courtyard; the
ropes and tent pegs for the courtyard;
all the furnishings for the tabernacle,
the Tent of Meeting; 41and the woven
garments worn for ministering in the
sanctuary, both the sacred garments for
Aaron the priest and the garments for
his sons when serving as priests.

42The Israelites had done all the work
just as the LORD had commanded Moses. 43Moses inspected the work and saw
that they had done it just as the LORD
had commanded. So Moses blessed
them.

Setting Up the Tabernacle

40 Then the LORD said to
Moses: 2"Set up the taber-
nacle, the Tent of Meeting, on the first
day of the first month. 3Place the ark of
the Testimony in it and shield the ark
with the curtain. 4Bring in the table and
set out what belongs on it. Then bring

[a]23 The meaning of the Hebrew for this word is uncertain. [b]34 That is, dugongs

in the lampstand and set up its lamps. 5Place the gold altar of incense in front of the ark of the Testimony and put the curtain at the entrance to the tabernacle.

6"Place the altar of burnt offering in front of the entrance to the tabernacle, the Tent of Meeting; 7place the basin between the Tent of Meeting and the altar and put water in it. 8Set up the courtyard around it and put the curtain at the entrance to the courtyard.

9"Take the anointing oil and anoint the tabernacle and everything in it; consecrate it and all its furnishings, and it will be holy. 10Then anoint the altar of burnt offering and all its utensils; consecrate the altar, and it will be most holy. 11Anoint the basin and its stand and consecrate them.

12"Bring Aaron and his sons to the entrance to the Tent of Meeting and wash them with water. 13Then dress Aaron in the sacred garments, anoint him and consecrate him so he may serve me as priest. 14Bring his sons and dress them in tunics. 15Anoint them just as you anointed their father, so they may serve me as priests. Their anointing will be to a priesthood that will continue for all generations to come." 16Moses did everything just as the LORD commanded him.

17So the tabernacle was set up on the first day of the first month in the second year. 18When Moses set up the tabernacle, he put the bases in place, erected the frames, inserted the crossbars and set up the posts. 19Then he spread the tent over the tabernacle and put the covering over the tent, as the LORD commanded him.

20He took the Testimony and placed it in the ark, attached the poles to the ark and put the atonement cover over it. 21Then he brought the ark into the tabernacle and hung the shielding curtain and shielded the ark of the Testimony, as the LORD commanded him.

22Moses placed the table in the Tent of Meeting on the north side of the tabernacle outside the curtain 23and set out the bread on it before the LORD, as the LORD commanded him.

24He placed the lampstand in the Tent of Meeting opposite the table on the south side of the tabernacle 25and set up the lamps before the LORD, as the LORD commanded him.

26Moses placed the gold altar in the Tent of Meeting in front of the curtain 27and burned fragrant incense on it, as the LORD commanded him. 28Then he put up the curtain at the entrance to the tabernacle.

29He set the altar of burnt offering near the entrance to the tabernacle, the Tent of Meeting, and offered on it burnt offerings and grain offerings, as the LORD commanded him.

30He placed the basin between the Tent of Meeting and the altar and put water in it for washing, 31and Moses and Aaron and his sons used it to wash their hands and feet. 32They washed whenever they entered the Tent of Meeting or approached the altar, as the LORD commanded Moses.

33Then Moses set up the courtyard around the tabernacle and altar and put up the curtain at the entrance to the courtyard. And so Moses finished the work.

The Glory of the LORD

34Then the cloud covered the Tent of Meeting, and the glory of the LORD filled the tabernacle. 35Moses could not enter the Tent of Meeting because the cloud had settled upon it, and the glory of the LORD filled the tabernacle.

36In all the travels of the Israelites, whenever the cloud lifted from above the tabernacle, they would set out; 37but if the cloud did not lift, they did not set out—until the day it lifted. 38So the cloud of the LORD was over the tabernacle by day, and fire was in the cloud by night, in the sight of all the house of Israel during all their travels.

SHARPEN THE FOCUS

As Aaron and the high priests who served after him ministered, they wore a breastplate. Twelve precious stones, one for each tribe of Israel, were sown into this breastplate. It was worn over the heart of the high priest.

Each Old Testament high priest represented Christ, the Messiah, who was to come. Jesus now serves us forever as our final, great High Priest and intercessor.

As the high priests of old, Jesus carries His people and their needs on His heart as He prays for us before the Father. Our Savior-God considers us infinitely more precious than any sapphires or rubies or emeralds to be found on earth. No amount of silver nor gold could have secured our redemption. And so Lord Jesus purchased it with His own blood.

Think of how precious you are to your God! Then pray with confidence today, knowing that Christ has gone into God's presence ahead of you to pray with and for you.

LEVITICUS

WEEK 9 • FRIDAY

Leviticus 1:1–17

GET THE BIG PICTURE

As you read Leviticus 1 and following chapters in coming days, keep in mind the purpose behind all the rituals and laws the Lord gave His people. He used these "visual aids" to make them aware of the insidious and destructive nature of sin and to point them toward the coming Savior who would die in their place for their sins. As you read today, ask yourself, "What picture of Christ does the burnt offering of Leviticus 1 paint?" Hint: Circle the word *all* in Leviticus 1:9, 13. If time is short, focus on Leviticus 1:1–9.

The Burnt Offering

1 The LORD called to Moses and
spoke to him from the Tent of Meeting. He said, 2"Speak to the Israelites
and say to them: 'When any of you
brings an offering to the LORD, bring as
your offering an animal from either the
herd or the flock.
3" 'If the offering is a burnt offering
from the herd, he is to offer a male without defect. He must present it at the entrance to the Tent of Meeting so that it[a]
will be acceptable to the LORD. 4He is to
lay his hand on the head of the burnt offering, and it will be accepted on his behalf to make atonement for him. 5He is
to slaughter the young bull before the
LORD, and then Aaron's sons the priests
shall bring the blood and sprinkle it
against the altar on all sides at the entrance to the Tent of Meeting. 6He is to
skin the burnt offering and cut it into
pieces. 7The sons of Aaron the priest are
to put fire on the altar and arrange
wood on the fire. 8Then Aaron's sons
the priests shall arrange the pieces, including the head and the fat, on the
burning wood that is on the altar. 9He is
to wash the inner parts and the legs
with water, and the priest is to burn all
of it on the altar. It is a burnt offering, an
offering made by fire, an aroma pleasing to the LORD.
10" 'If the offering is a burnt offering
from the flock, from either the sheep or
the goats, he is to offer a male without
defect. 11He is to slaughter it at the north
side of the altar before the LORD, and
Aaron's sons the priests shall sprinkle its
blood against the altar on all sides. 12He
is to cut it into pieces, and the priest
shall arrange them, including the head
and the fat, on the burning wood that
is on the altar. 13He is to wash the inner
parts and the legs with water, and the
priest is to bring all of it and burn it on
the altar. It is a burnt offering, an offering made by fire, an aroma pleasing to
the LORD.
14" 'If the offering to the LORD is a
burnt offering of birds, he is to offer a
dove or a young pigeon. 15The priest
shall bring it to the altar, wring off the
head and burn it on the altar; its blood
shall be drained out on the side of the

[a]3 Or *he*

altar. 16He is to remove the crop with its contents[a] and throw it to the east side of the altar, where the ashes are. 17He shall tear it open by the wings, not severing it completely, and then the priest shall burn it on the wood that is on the fire on the altar. It is a burnt offering, an offering made by fire, an aroma pleasing to the LORD.

[a]16 Or *crop and the feathers*; the meaning of the Hebrew for this word is uncertain.

SHARPEN THE FOCUS

Francis Havergal penned the well-loved hymn:

Take my life, O Lord, renew,
Consecrate my heart to You;
Take my moments and my days;
Let them sing Your ceaseless praise. (*Lutheran Worship* 404)

In the burnt offering God's Old Testament people said: "All that I am, all that I have, belongs to You, Lord. As I place my hand on the head of this animal, I identify myself with it. As the flames burn it up completely, I ask that I might be consumed with love and zeal for You."

A beautiful thought. A lovely song. Both we and our Old Testament brothers and sisters have sung the refrain again and again. We've meant it with all our hearts. And yet, that kind of zeal so often evaporates in the heat of trouble or the sunshine of pleasure. Sometimes, even before the chords of the melody have died away, we find ourselves less than thrilled with doing what our Lord asks of us.

That's why it's helpful, even necessary, to see in the burnt offering a picture of our Savior. He dedicated Himself totally to the heavenly Father, obeying the Father's will fully in our place. And then He laid down on the altar of the cross, consumed with zeal and love for God—and for you!

WEEK 9 • SATURDAY

Leviticus 2:1—3:17

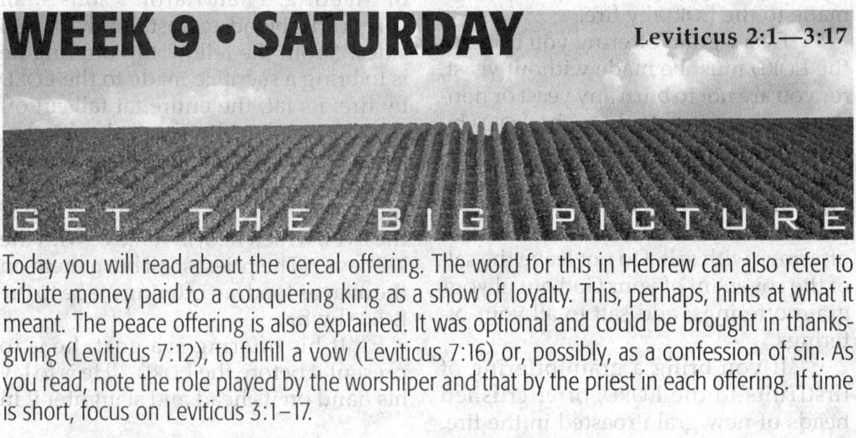

GET THE BIG PICTURE

Today you will read about the cereal offering. The word for this in Hebrew can also refer to tribute money paid to a conquering king as a show of loyalty. This, perhaps, hints at what it meant. The peace offering is also explained. It was optional and could be brought in thanksgiving (Leviticus 7:12), to fulfill a vow (Leviticus 7:16) or, possibly, as a confession of sin. As you read, note the role played by the worshiper and that by the priest in each offering. If time is short, focus on Leviticus 3:1–17.

The Grain Offering

2 " 'When someone brings a grain
offering to the LORD, his offering
is to be of fine flour. He is to pour oil
on it, put incense on it 2and take it to
Aaron's sons the priests. The priest shall
take a handful of the fine flour and oil,
together with all the incense, and burn
this as a memorial portion on the altar,
an offering made by fire, an aroma
pleasing to the LORD. 3The rest of the
grain offering belongs to Aaron and his
sons; it is a most holy part of the offerings made to the LORD by fire.
4" 'If you bring a grain offering baked
in an oven, it is to consist of fine flour:
cakes made without yeast and mixed
with oil, or[a] wafers made without yeast
and spread with oil. 5If your grain offering is prepared on a griddle, it is to be
made of fine flour mixed with oil, and
without yeast. 6Crumble it and pour oil
on it; it is a grain offering. 7If your grain
offering is cooked in a pan, it is to be
made of fine flour and oil. 8Bring the
grain offering made of these things to
the LORD; present it to the priest, who
shall take it to the altar. 9He shall take out
the memorial portion from the grain
offering and burn it on the altar as an
offering made by fire, an aroma pleasing to the LORD. 10The rest of the grain
offering belongs to Aaron and his sons;
it is a most holy part of the offerings
made to the LORD by fire.
11" 'Every grain offering you bring to
the LORD must be made without yeast,
for you are not to burn any yeast or honey in an offering made to the LORD by
fire. 12You may bring them to the LORD
as an offering of the firstfruits, but they
are not to be offered on the altar as a
pleasing aroma. 13Season all your grain
offerings with salt. Do not leave the salt
of the covenant of your God out of your
grain offerings; add salt to all your offerings.
14" 'If you bring a grain offering of
firstfruits to the LORD, offer crushed
heads of new grain roasted in the fire.
15Put oil and incense on it; it is a grain
offering. 16The priest shall burn the
memorial portion of the crushed grain
and the oil, together with all the incense, as an offering made to the LORD
by fire.

The Fellowship Offering

3 " 'If someone's offering is a fellowship offering,[b] and he offers
an animal from the herd, whether male
or female, he is to present before the
LORD an animal without defect. 2He is
to lay his hand on the head of his offering and slaughter it at the entrance to
the Tent of Meeting. Then Aaron's sons
the priests shall sprinkle the blood
against the altar on all sides. 3From the
fellowship offering he is to bring a sacrifice made to the LORD by fire: all the
fat that covers the inner parts or is connected to them, 4both kidneys with the
fat on them near the loins, and the covering of the liver, which he will remove
with the kidneys. 5Then Aaron's sons
are to burn it on the altar on top of the
burnt offering that is on the burning
wood, as an offering made by fire, an
aroma pleasing to the LORD.
6" 'If he offers an animal from the
flock as a fellowship offering to the
LORD, he is to offer a male or female
without defect. 7If he offers a lamb, he
is to present it before the LORD. 8He is
to lay his hand on the head of his offering and slaughter it in front of the Tent
of Meeting. Then Aaron's sons shall
sprinkle its blood against the altar on all
sides. 9From the fellowship offering he
is to bring a sacrifice made to the LORD
by fire: its fat, the entire fat tail cut off
close to the backbone, all the fat that
covers the inner parts or is connected to
them, 10both kidneys with the fat on
them near the loins, and the covering of
the liver, which he will remove with the
kidneys. 11The priest shall burn them on
the altar as food, an offering made to the
LORD by fire.
12" 'If his offering is a goat, he is to
present it before the LORD. 13He is to lay
his hand on its head and slaughter it in

[a]4 Or *and* [b]1 Traditionally *peace offering*; also in verses 3, 6 and 9

front of the Tent of Meeting. Then
Aaron's sons shall sprinkle its blood
against the altar on all sides. 14From
what he offers he is to make this offering to the LORD by fire: all the fat that
covers the inner parts or is connected to
them, 15both kidneys with the fat on
them near the loins, and the covering of
the liver, which he will remove with the
kidneys. 16The priest shall burn them on
the altar as food, an offering made by
fire, a pleasing aroma. All the fat is the
LORD's.
17" 'This is a lasting ordinance for the
generations to come, wherever you live:
You must not eat any fat or any blood.' "

SHARPEN THE FOCUS

Few people who lived through the late 1980s will ever forget where they were when the Berlin Wall came down. The snapshots of freedom have been burned into our memories: young people dancing in the streets; men and women with sledge hammers slamming away at the symbol of their captivity; East German soldiers, machine guns slung over their shoulders, watching it all, numbness masking their faces. For decades the wall separated families, loved ones. Then, finally, the wall fell.

Sin separates, alienates, as certainly as any physical barrier. It's no wonder then that the Scriptures often picture Jesus' work in words like these:

> *For [Christ] Himself is our peace, who has . . . destroyed the barrier, the dividing wall of hostility.* (Ephesians 2:14)

In Christ Jesus, through His blood shed on the cross, the wall that stood between us and the holy God has fallen. In Christ, we have peace with God. And in Christ, we have the courage to work toward peace with one another in our families, neighborhoods, and churches.

Where are the walls in your relationships? Ask the Lord for courage and for the wisdom you need to bring peace into those situations today.

WEEK 10 • MONDAY

Leviticus 4:1—6:30

GET THE BIG PICTURE

Moses spells out the rituals that Israel had to perform when sin polluted their hearts and lives. Depending on the community standing of the lawbreaker, the sin offering involved one of several different animals. The trespass offering included provisions for making restitution to one's neighbor in addition to the sacrifice offered to God. Most of Leviticus 6, then, reviews the regulations concerning the burnt offering, the grain offering, and the sin offering. If time is short, focus on Leviticus 4:27–35.

The Sin Offering

4 The LORD said to Moses, 2"Say to the Israelites: 'When anyone sins unintentionally and does what is forbidden in any of the LORD's commands—

3" 'If the anointed priest sins, bringing guilt on the people, he must bring to the LORD a young bull without defect as a sin offering for the sin he has committed. 4He is to present the bull at the entrance to the Tent of Meeting before the LORD. He is to lay his hand on its head and slaughter it before the LORD. 5Then the anointed priest shall take some of the bull's blood and carry it into the Tent of Meeting. 6He is to dip his finger into the blood and sprinkle some of it seven times before the LORD, in front of the curtain of the sanctuary. 7The priest shall then put some of the blood on the horns of the altar of fragrant incense that is before the LORD in the Tent of Meeting. The rest of the bull's blood he shall pour out at the base of the altar of burnt offering at the entrance to the Tent of Meeting. 8He shall remove all the fat from the bull of the sin offering—the fat that covers the inner parts or is connected to them, 9both kidneys with the fat on them near the loins, and the covering of the liver, which he will remove with the kidneys— 10just as the fat is removed from the ox[a] sacrificed as a fellowship offering.[b] Then the priest shall burn them on the altar of burnt offering. 11But the hide of the bull and all its flesh, as well as the head and legs, the inner parts and offal— 12that is, all the rest of the bull—he must take outside the camp to a place ceremonially clean, where the ashes are thrown, and burn it in a wood fire on the ash heap.

13" 'If the whole Israelite community sins unintentionally and does what is forbidden in any of the LORD's commands, even though the community is unaware of the matter, they are guilty. 14When they become aware of the sin they committed, the assembly must bring a young bull as a sin offering and present it before the Tent of Meeting. 15The elders of the community are to lay their hands on the bull's head before the LORD, and the bull shall be slaughtered before the LORD. 16Then the anointed priest is to take some of the bull's blood into the Tent of Meeting. 17He shall dip his finger into the blood and sprinkle it before the LORD seven times in front of the curtain. 18He is to put some of the blood on the horns of the altar that is before the LORD in the Tent of Meeting. The rest of the blood he shall pour out at the base of the altar of burnt offering at the entrance to the Tent of Meeting. 19He shall remove all the fat from it and burn it on the altar, 20and do with this bull just as he did with the bull for the sin offering. In this way the priest will make atonement for them, and they will be forgiven. 21Then he shall take the bull outside the camp and burn it as he burned the first bull. This is the sin offering for the community.

22" 'When a leader sins unintentionally and does what is forbidden in any of the commands of the LORD his God, he is guilty. 23When he is made aware of the sin he committed, he must bring as his offering a male goat without defect. 24He is to lay his hand on the goat's head and slaughter it at the place where the burnt offering is slaughtered before the LORD. It is a sin offering. 25Then the priest shall take some of the blood of the sin offering with his finger and put it on the horns of the altar of burnt offering and pour out the rest of the blood at the base of the altar. 26He shall burn all the fat on the altar as he burned the fat of the fellowship offering. In this way the priest will make atonement for the man's sin, and he will be forgiven.

27" 'If a member of the community sins unintentionally and does what is forbidden in any of the LORD's commands, he is guilty. 28When he is made aware of the sin he committed, he must

[a]*10* The Hebrew word can include both male and female. [b]*10* Traditionally *peace offering;* also in verses 26, 31 and 35

bring as his offering for the sin he committed a female goat without defect. 29 He is to lay his hand on the head of the sin offering and slaughter it at the place of the burnt offering. 30 Then the priest is to take some of the blood with his finger and put it on the horns of the altar of burnt offering and pour out the rest of the blood at the base of the altar. 31 He shall remove all the fat, just as the fat is removed from the fellowship offering, and the priest shall burn it on the altar as an aroma pleasing to the LORD. In this way the priest will make atonement for him, and he will be forgiven.

32 " 'If he brings a lamb as his sin offering, he is to bring a female without defect. 33 He is to lay his hand on its head and slaughter it for a sin offering at the place where the burnt offering is slaughtered. 34 Then the priest shall take some of the blood of the sin offering with his finger and put it on the horns of the altar of burnt offering and pour out the rest of the blood at the base of the altar. 35 He shall remove all the fat, just as the fat is removed from the lamb of the fellowship offering, and the priest shall burn it on the altar on top of the offerings made to the LORD by fire. In this way the priest will make atonement for him for the sin he has committed, and he will be forgiven.

5 " 'If a person sins because he does not speak up when he hears a public charge to testify regarding something he has seen or learned about, he will be held responsible.

2 " 'Or if a person touches anything ceremonially unclean—whether the carcasses of unclean wild animals or of unclean livestock or of unclean creatures that move along the ground—even though he is unaware of it, he has become unclean and is guilty.

3 " 'Or if he touches human uncleanness—anything that would make him unclean—even though he is unaware of it, when he learns of it he will be guilty.

4 " 'Or if a person thoughtlessly takes an oath to do anything, whether good or evil—in any matter one might carelessly swear about—even though he is unaware of it, in any case when he learns of it he will be guilty.

5 " 'When anyone is guilty in any of these ways, he must confess in what way he has sinned 6 and, as a penalty for the sin he has committed, he must bring to the LORD a female lamb or goat from the flock as a sin offering; and the priest shall make atonement for him for his sin.

7 " 'If he cannot afford a lamb, he is to bring two doves or two young pigeons to the LORD as a penalty for his sin—one for a sin offering and the other for a burnt offering. 8 He is to bring them to the priest, who shall first offer the one for the sin offering. He is to wring its head from its neck, not severing it completely, 9 and is to sprinkle some of the blood of the sin offering against the side of the altar; the rest of the blood must be drained out at the base of the altar. It is a sin offering. 10 The priest shall then offer the other as a burnt offering in the prescribed way and make atonement for him for the sin he has committed, and he will be forgiven.

11 " 'If, however, he cannot afford two doves or two young pigeons, he is to bring as an offering for his sin a tenth of an ephah[a] of fine flour for a sin offering. He must not put oil or incense on it, because it is a sin offering. 12 He is to bring it to the priest, who shall take a handful of it as a memorial portion and burn it on the altar on top of the offerings made to the LORD by fire. It is a sin offering. 13 In this way the priest will make atonement for him for any of these sins he has committed, and he will be forgiven. The rest of the offering will belong to the priest, as in the case of the grain offering.' "

The Guilt Offering

14 The LORD said to Moses: 15 "When a person commits a violation and sins unintentionally in regard to any of the LORD's holy things, he is to bring to the

[a] *11* That is, probably about 2 quarts (about 2 liters)

LORD as a penalty a ram from the flock, one without defect and of the proper value in silver, according to the sanctuary shekel.[a] It is a guilt offering. 16He must make restitution for what he has failed to do in regard to the holy things, add a fifth of the value to that and give it all to the priest, who will make atonement for him with the ram as a guilt offering, and he will be forgiven.

17"If a person sins and does what is forbidden in any of the LORD's commands, even though he does not know it, he is guilty and will be held responsible. 18He is to bring to the priest as a guilt offering a ram from the flock, one without defect and of the proper value. In this way the priest will make atonement for him for the wrong he has committed unintentionally, and he will be forgiven. 19It is a guilt offering; he has been guilty of[b] wrongdoing against the LORD."

6 The LORD said to Moses: 2"If anyone sins and is unfaithful to the LORD by deceiving his neighbor about something entrusted to him or left in his care or stolen, or if he cheats him, 3or if he finds lost property and lies about it, or if he swears falsely, or if he commits any such sin that people may do— 4when he thus sins and becomes guilty, he must return what he has stolen or taken by extortion, or what was entrusted to him, or the lost property he found, 5or whatever it was he swore falsely about. He must make restitution in full, add a fifth of the value to it and give it all to the owner on the day he presents his guilt offering. 6And as a penalty he must bring to the priest, that is, to the LORD, his guilt offering, a ram from the flock, one without defect and of the proper value. 7In this way the priest will make atonement for him before the LORD, and he will be forgiven for any of these things he did that made him guilty."

The Burnt Offering

8The LORD said to Moses: 9"Give Aaron and his sons this command: 'These are the regulations for the burnt offering: The burnt offering is to remain on the altar hearth throughout the night, till morning, and the fire must be kept burning on the altar. 10The priest shall then put on his linen clothes, with linen undergarments next to his body, and shall remove the ashes of the burnt offering that the fire has consumed on the altar and place them beside the altar. 11Then he is to take off these clothes and put on others, and carry the ashes outside the camp to a place that is ceremonially clean. 12The fire on the altar must be kept burning; it must not go out. Every morning the priest is to add firewood and arrange the burnt offering on the fire and burn the fat of the fellowship offerings[c] on it. 13The fire must be kept burning on the altar continuously; it must not go out.

The Grain Offering

14" 'These are the regulations for the grain offering: Aaron's sons are to bring it before the LORD, in front of the altar. 15The priest is to take a handful of fine flour and oil, together with all the incense on the grain offering, and burn the memorial portion on the altar as an aroma pleasing to the LORD. 16Aaron and his sons shall eat the rest of it, but it is to be eaten without yeast in a holy place; they are to eat it in the courtyard of the Tent of Meeting. 17It must not be baked with yeast; I have given it as their share of the offerings made to me by fire. Like the sin offering and the guilt offering, it is most holy. 18Any male descendant of Aaron may eat it. It is his regular share of the offerings made to the LORD by fire for the generations to come. Whatever touches them will become holy.[d]' "

19The LORD also said to Moses, 20"This is the offering Aaron and his sons are to bring to the LORD on the day he[e] is anointed: a tenth of an ephah[f] of fine

[a]15 That is, about 2/5 ounce (about 11.5 grams)
[b]19 Or *has made full expiation for his*
[c]12 Traditionally *peace offerings* [d]18 Or *Whoever touches them must be holy*; similarly in verse 27
[e]20 Or *each* [f]20 That is, probably about 2 quarts (about 2 liters)

flour as a regular grain offering, half of
it in the morning and half in the evening. [21]Prepare it with oil on a griddle;
bring it well-mixed and present the
grain offering broken[a] in pieces as an
aroma pleasing to the LORD. [22]The son
who is to succeed him as anointed priest
shall prepare it. It is the LORD's regular
share and is to be burned completely.
[23]Every grain offering of a priest shall be
burned completely; it must not be
eaten."

The Sin Offering

[24]The LORD said to Moses, [25]"Say to
Aaron and his sons: 'These are the regulations for the sin offering: The sin offering is to be slaughtered before the
LORD in the place the burnt offering is
slaughtered; it is most holy. [26]The priest
who offers it shall eat it; it is to be eaten
in a holy place, in the courtyard of the
Tent of Meeting. [27]Whatever touches
any of the flesh will become holy, and if
any of the blood is spattered on a garment, you must wash it in a holy place.
[28]The clay pot the meat is cooked in
must be broken; but if it is cooked in a
bronze pot, the pot is to be scoured and
rinsed with water. [29]Any male in a
priest's family may eat it; it is most holy.
[30]But any sin offering whose blood is
brought into the Tent of Meeting to
make atonement in the Holy Place must
not be eaten; it must be burned.

[a]*21* The meaning of the Hebrew for this word is uncertain.

SHARPEN THE FOCUS

Think of the mess. The cost. The physical work. The inconvenience. The Old Testament sacrificial system must have been a burden in every way. Nothing about it was microwave quick or ATM easy.

"Why?" We may well ask. "What point was the Lord trying to drive home to His people?" For one thing, the system taught them the seriousness of sin. The holy God had taken up residence among this group of sinners. As we shall see in future readings, when holiness touched sinfulness, death snapped its jaws shut on the guilty. If the Lord was to continue His presence among them, the pollution of sin had to be cleansed, eliminated.

The worshiper could make the sacrifice, but only God could grant the pardon. And so, again and again, Moses repeats the refrain of hope: "and he will be forgiven" (Leviticus 4:20, 26, 31, 35). Not because the blood of bulls or goats had any cleansing power. But because the blood of Christ would be shed for human sin.

WEEK 10 • TUESDAY

Leviticus 7:1—9:24

GET THE BIG PICTURE

Chapter 7 continues the review that began in chapter 6. Both of these chapters add some instructions not previously given. Chapter 7 concentrates on the trespass offering and the peace offering. Chapters 8 and 9 then report the rite in which Aaron and his sons were consecrated (set apart) for their special work as priests in Israel. If time is short, focus on Leviticus 8:1–36.

The Guilt Offering

7 " 'These are the regulations for the guilt offering, which is most holy: [2]The guilt offering is to be slaughtered in the place where the burnt offering is slaughtered, and its blood is to be sprinkled against the altar on all sides. [3]All its fat shall be offered: the fat tail and the fat that covers the inner parts, [4]both kidneys with the fat on them near the loins, and the covering of the liver, which is to be removed with the kidneys. [5]The priest shall burn them on the altar as an offering made to the LORD by fire. It is a guilt offering. [6]Any male in a priest's family may eat it, but it must be eaten in a holy place; it is most holy.

[7]" 'The same law applies to both the sin offering and the guilt offering: They belong to the priest who makes atonement with them. [8]The priest who offers a burnt offering for anyone may keep its hide for himself. [9]Every grain offering baked in an oven or cooked in a pan or on a griddle belongs to the priest who offers it, [10]and every grain offering, whether mixed with oil or dry, belongs equally to all the sons of Aaron.

The Fellowship Offering

[11]" 'These are the regulations for the fellowship offering[a] a person may present to the LORD:

[12]" 'If he offers it as an expression of thankfulness, then along with this thank offering he is to offer cakes of bread made without yeast and mixed with oil, wafers made without yeast and spread with oil, and cakes of fine flour well-kneaded and mixed with oil. [13]Along with his fellowship offering of thanksgiving he is to present an offering with cakes of bread made with yeast. [14]He is to bring one of each kind as an offering, a contribution to the LORD; it belongs to the priest who sprinkles the blood of the fellowship offerings. [15]The meat of his fellowship offering of thanksgiving must be eaten on the day it is offered; he must leave none of it till morning.

[16]" 'If, however, his offering is the result of a vow or is a freewill offering, the sacrifice shall be eaten on the day he offers it, but anything left over may be eaten on the next day. [17]Any meat of the sacrifice left over till the third day must be burned up. [18]If any meat of the fellowship offering is eaten on the third day, it will not be accepted. It will not be credited to the one who offered it, for it is impure; the person who eats any of it will be held responsible.

[19]" 'Meat that touches anything ceremonially unclean must not be eaten; it must be burned up. As for other meat, anyone ceremonially clean may eat it. [20]But if anyone who is unclean eats any meat of the fellowship offering belonging to the LORD, that person must be cut off from his people. [21]If anyone touches something unclean—whether human uncleanness or an unclean animal or any unclean, detestable thing—and then eats any of the meat of the fellowship offering belonging to the LORD, that person must be cut off from his people.' "

Eating Fat and Blood Forbidden

[22]The LORD said to Moses, [23]"Say to the Israelites: 'Do not eat any of the fat of cattle, sheep or goats. [24]The fat of an animal found dead or torn by wild animals may be used for any other purpose, but you must not eat it. [25]Anyone who eats the fat of an animal from which an offering by fire may be[b] made to the LORD must be cut off from his people. [26]And wherever you live, you must not eat the blood of any bird or animal. [27]If anyone eats blood, that person must be cut off from his people.' "

The Priests' Share

[28]The LORD said to Moses, [29]"Say to the Israelites: 'Anyone who brings a fellowship offering to the LORD is to bring part of it as his sacrifice to the LORD. [30]With his own hands he is to bring the offering made to the LORD by fire; he is to bring the fat, together with the breast,

[a]11 Traditionally *peace offering*; also in verses 13-37
[b]25 Or *fire is*

and wave the breast before the LORD as a wave offering. [31]The priest shall burn the fat on the altar, but the breast belongs to Aaron and his sons. [32]You are to give the right thigh of your fellowship offerings to the priest as a contribution. [33]The son of Aaron who offers the blood and the fat of the fellowship offering shall have the right thigh as his share. [34]From the fellowship offerings of the Israelites, I have taken the breast that is waved and the thigh that is presented and have given them to Aaron the priest and his sons as their regular share from the Israelites.' "

[35]This is the portion of the offerings made to the LORD by fire that were allotted to Aaron and his sons on the day they were presented to serve the LORD as priests. [36]On the day they were anointed, the LORD commanded that the Israelites give this to them as their regular share for the generations to come.

[37]These, then, are the regulations for the burnt offering, the grain offering, the sin offering, the guilt offering, the ordination offering and the fellowship offering, [38]which the LORD gave Moses on Mount Sinai on the day he commanded the Israelites to bring their offerings to the LORD, in the Desert of Sinai.

The Ordination of Aaron and His Sons

8 The LORD said to Moses, [2]"Bring Aaron and his sons, their garments, the anointing oil, the bull for the sin offering, the two rams and the basket containing bread made without yeast, [3]and gather the entire assembly at the entrance to the Tent of Meeting." [4]Moses did as the LORD commanded him, and the assembly gathered at the entrance to the Tent of Meeting.

[5]Moses said to the assembly, "This is what the LORD has commanded to be done." [6]Then Moses brought Aaron and his sons forward and washed them with water. [7]He put the tunic on Aaron, tied the sash around him, clothed him with the robe and put the ephod on him. He also tied the ephod to him by its skillfully woven waistband; so it was fastened on him. [8]He placed the breastpiece on him and put the Urim and Thummim in the breastpiece. [9]Then he placed the turban on Aaron's head and set the gold plate, the sacred diadem, on the front of it, as the LORD commanded Moses.

[10]Then Moses took the anointing oil and anointed the tabernacle and everything in it, and so consecrated them. [11]He sprinkled some of the oil on the altar seven times, anointing the altar and all its utensils and the basin with its stand, to consecrate them. [12]He poured some of the anointing oil on Aaron's head and anointed him to consecrate him. [13]Then he brought Aaron's sons forward, put tunics on them, tied sashes around them and put headbands on them, as the LORD commanded Moses.

[14]He then presented the bull for the sin offering, and Aaron and his sons laid their hands on its head. [15]Moses slaughtered the bull and took some of the blood, and with his finger he put it on all the horns of the altar to purify the altar. He poured out the rest of the blood at the base of the altar. So he consecrated it to make atonement for it. [16]Moses also took all the fat around the inner parts, the covering of the liver, and both kidneys and their fat, and burned it on the altar. [17]But the bull with its hide and its flesh and its offal he burned up outside the camp, as the LORD commanded Moses.

[18]He then presented the ram for the burnt offering, and Aaron and his sons laid their hands on its head. [19]Then Moses slaughtered the ram and sprinkled the blood against the altar on all sides. [20]He cut the ram into pieces and burned the head, the pieces and the fat. [21]He washed the inner parts and the legs with water and burned the whole ram on the altar as a burnt offering, a pleasing aroma, an offering made to the LORD by fire, as the LORD commanded Moses.

[22]He then presented the other ram,

the ram for the ordination, and Aaron
and his sons laid their hands on its head.
23Moses slaughtered the ram and took
some of its blood and put it on the lobe
of Aaron's right ear, on the thumb of his
right hand and on the big toe of his right
foot. 24Moses also brought Aaron's sons
forward and put some of the blood on
the lobes of their right ears, on the
thumbs of their right hands and on the
big toes of their right feet. Then he
sprinkled blood against the altar on all
sides. 25He took the fat, the fat tail, all the
fat around the inner parts, the covering
of the liver, both kidneys and their fat
and the right thigh. 26Then from the
basket of bread made without yeast,
which was before the LORD, he took a
cake of bread, and one made with oil,
and a wafer; he put these on the fat
portions and on the right thigh. 27He put
all these in the hands of Aaron and his
sons and waved them before the LORD
as a wave offering. 28Then Moses took
them from their hands and burned
them on the altar on top of the burnt
offering as an ordination offering, a
pleasing aroma, an offering made to the
LORD by fire. 29He also took the breast—
Moses' share of the ordination ram—
and waved it before the LORD as a wave
offering, as the LORD commanded
Moses.

30Then Moses took some of the
anointing oil and some of the blood
from the altar and sprinkled them on
Aaron and his garments and on his sons
and their garments. So he consecrated
Aaron and his garments and his sons
and their garments.

31Moses then said to Aaron and his
sons, "Cook the meat at the entrance to
the Tent of Meeting and eat it there with
the bread from the basket of ordination
offerings, as I commanded, saying,[a]
'Aaron and his sons are to eat it.' 32Then
burn up the rest of the meat and the
bread. 33Do not leave the entrance to the
Tent of Meeting for seven days, until the
days of your ordination are completed,
for your ordination will last seven days.
34What has been done today was commanded by the LORD to make atonement for you. 35You must stay at the entrance to the Tent of Meeting day and
night for seven days and do what the
LORD requires, so you will not die; for
that is what I have been commanded."
36So Aaron and his sons did everything
the LORD commanded through Moses.

The Priests Begin Their Ministry

9 On the eighth day Moses summoned Aaron and his sons and
the elders of Israel. 2He said to Aaron,
"Take a bull calf for your sin offering and
a ram for your burnt offering, both
without defect, and present them before
the LORD. 3Then say to the Israelites:
'Take a male goat for a sin offering, a calf
and a lamb—both a year old and without defect—for a burnt offering, 4and an
ox[b] and a ram for a fellowship offering[c]
to sacrifice before the LORD, together
with a grain offering mixed with oil. For
today the LORD will appear to you.' "

5They took the things Moses commanded to the front of the Tent of Meeting, and the entire assembly came near
and stood before the LORD. 6Then Moses said, "This is what the LORD has
commanded you to do, so that the glory
of the LORD may appear to you."

7Moses said to Aaron, "Come to the altar and sacrifice your sin offering and
your burnt offering and make atonement for yourself and the people; sacrifice the offering that is for the people
and make atonement for them, as the
LORD has commanded."

8So Aaron came to the altar and
slaughtered the calf as a sin offering for
himself. 9His sons brought the blood to
him, and he dipped his finger into the
blood and put it on the horns of the altar; the rest of the blood he poured out
at the base of the altar. 10On the altar he
burned the fat, the kidneys and the covering of the liver from the sin offering,
as the LORD commanded Moses; 11the
flesh and the hide he burned up outside
the camp.

[a]31 Or *I was commanded:* [b]4 The Hebrew word can include both male and female; also in verses 18 and 19. [c]4 Traditionally *peace offering;* also in verses 18 and 22

12 Then he slaughtered the burnt offering. His sons handed him the blood, and
he sprinkled it against the altar on all
sides. 13 They handed him the burnt offering piece by piece, including the
head, and he burned them on the altar.
14 He washed the inner parts and the legs
and burned them on top of the burnt
offering on the altar.

15 Aaron then brought the offering
that was for the people. He took the
goat for the people's sin offering and
slaughtered it and offered it for a sin
offering as he did with the first one.

16 He brought the burnt offering and
offered it in the prescribed way. 17 He
also brought the grain offering, took a
handful of it and burned it on the altar
in addition to the morning's burnt offering.

18 He slaughtered the ox and the ram
as the fellowship offering for the people. His sons handed him the blood, and
he sprinkled it against the altar on all
sides. 19 But the fat portions of the ox and
the ram—the fat tail, the layer of fat, the
kidneys and the covering of the liver—
20 these they laid on the breasts, and then
Aaron burned the fat on the altar.
21 Aaron waved the breasts and the right
thigh before the LORD as a wave offering, as Moses commanded.

22 Then Aaron lifted his hands toward
the people and blessed them. And having sacrificed the sin offering, the burnt
offering and the fellowship offering, he
stepped down.

23 Moses and Aaron then went into the
Tent of Meeting. When they came out,
they blessed the people; and the glory
of the LORD appeared to all the people.
24 Fire came out from the presence of the
LORD and consumed the burnt offering
and the fat portions on the altar. And
when all the people saw it, they shouted
for joy and fell facedown.

SHARPEN THE FOCUS

It's only natural to think of Jesus' work as we read the "worship handbook" of Old Testament Israel. In Leviticus, we see Jesus as the one perfect sacrifice for our sins and as our faithful and eternal High Priest.

But the work of the Holy Spirit comes through loud and clear in Leviticus too. In today's reading for instance, we see again the role oil played in Old Testament worship life. Anointing oil, symbolic of the Spirit's presence and work, was poured over Aaron's head. Psalm 133 pictures this anointing process and connects it with unity among God's people.

The New Testament talks about the "unity of the Spirit" too, and it ties this unique kind of unity to the work of the apostles, prophets, evangelists, pastors, and teachers in Christ's church (Ephesians 4:3, 11–13) as they teach the Word of God.

Whenever God's Word is proclaimed, the Holy Spirit works to produce faith. True faith leads to love for God and for others around us. This love shows itself in words and actions of concern and kindness—especially toward other believers.

WEEK 10 • WEDNESDAY

Lev. 10:1—11:47

GET THE BIG PICTURE

Leviticus 10 illustrates the Scriptural truth that those "who teach will be judged more strictly" (James 3:1). Leviticus 11, then, outlines the dietary laws Israel was to observe. By following these, Israel would demonstrate to the nations around her the unique relationship she enjoyed with her Savior-God. This outreach (evangelistic) purpose lay behind many of the regulations that you will read about today. If time is short, focus on Leviticus 10:1–20.

The Death of Nadab and Abihu

10 Aaron's sons Nadab and
Abihu took their censers, put
fire in them and added incense; and
they offered unauthorized fire before
the LORD, contrary to his command. 2So
fire came out from the presence of the
LORD and consumed them, and they
died before the LORD. 3Moses then said
to Aaron, "This is what the LORD spoke
of when he said:

" 'Among those who approach me
I will show myself holy;
in the sight of all the people
I will be honored.' "

Aaron remained silent.

4Moses summoned Mishael and Elzaphan, sons of Aaron's uncle Uzziel, and
said to them, "Come here; carry your
cousins outside the camp, away from the
front of the sanctuary." 5So they came
and carried them, still in their tunics,
outside the camp, as Moses ordered.

6Then Moses said to Aaron and his
sons Eleazar and Ithamar, "Do not let
your hair become unkempt,[a] and do not
tear your clothes, or you will die and the
LORD will be angry with the whole community. But your relatives, all the house
of Israel, may mourn for those the LORD
has destroyed by fire. 7Do not leave the
entrance to the Tent of Meeting or you
will die, because the LORD's anointing
oil is on you." So they did as Moses said.
8Then the LORD said to Aaron, 9"You
and your sons are not to drink wine or
other fermented drink whenever you
go into the Tent of Meeting, or you will
die. This is a lasting ordinance for the
generations to come. 10You must distinguish between the holy and the common, between the unclean and the
clean, 11and you must teach the Israelites all the decrees the LORD has given
them through Moses."

12Moses said to Aaron and his remaining sons, Eleazar and Ithamar, "Take the
grain offering left over from the offerings made to the LORD by fire and eat it
prepared without yeast beside the altar,
for it is most holy. 13Eat it in a holy place,
because it is your share and your sons'
share of the offerings made to the LORD
by fire; for so I have been commanded.
14But you and your sons and your
daughters may eat the breast that was
waved and the thigh that was presented. Eat them in a ceremonially clean
place; they have been given to you and
your children as your share of the Israelites' fellowship offerings.[b] 15The thigh
that was presented and the breast that
was waved must be brought with the fat
portions of the offerings made by fire,
to be waved before the LORD as a wave
offering. This will be the regular share
for you and your children, as the LORD
has commanded."

[a]6 Or *Do not uncover your heads*
[b]14 Traditionally *peace offerings*

16 When Moses inquired about the goat of the sin offering and found that it had been burned up, he was angry with Eleazar and Ithamar, Aaron's remaining sons, and asked, 17 "Why didn't you eat the sin offering in the sanctuary area? It is most holy; it was given to you to take away the guilt of the community by making atonement for them before the LORD. 18 Since its blood was not taken into the Holy Place, you should have eaten the goat in the sanctuary area, as I commanded."

19 Aaron replied to Moses, "Today they sacrificed their sin offering and their burnt offering before the LORD, but such things as this have happened to me. Would the LORD have been pleased if I had eaten the sin offering today?" 20 When Moses heard this, he was satisfied.

Clean and Unclean Food

11 The LORD said to Moses and Aaron, 2 "Say to the Israelites: 'Of all the animals that live on land, these are the ones you may eat: 3 You may eat any animal that has a split hoof completely divided and that chews the cud.

4 " 'There are some that only chew the cud or only have a split hoof, but you must not eat them. The camel, though it chews the cud, does not have a split hoof; it is ceremonially unclean for you. 5 The coney,[a] though it chews the cud, does not have a split hoof; it is unclean for you. 6 The rabbit, though it chews the cud, does not have a split hoof; it is unclean for you. 7 And the pig, though it has a split hoof completely divided, does not chew the cud; it is unclean for you. 8 You must not eat their meat or touch their carcasses; they are unclean for you.

9 " 'Of all the creatures living in the water of the seas and the streams, you may eat any that have fins and scales. 10 But all creatures in the seas or streams that do not have fins and scales—whether among all the swarming things or among all the other living creatures in the water—you are to detest. 11 And since you are to detest them, you must not eat their meat and you must detest their carcasses. 12 Anything living in the water that does not have fins and scales is to be detestable to you.

13 " 'These are the birds you are to detest and not eat because they are detestable: the eagle, the vulture, the black vulture, 14 the red kite, any kind of black kite, 15 any kind of raven, 16 the horned owl, the screech owl, the gull, any kind of hawk, 17 the little owl, the cormorant, the great owl, 18 the white owl, the desert owl, the osprey, 19 the stork, any kind of heron, the hoopoe and the bat.[b]

20 " 'All flying insects that walk on all fours are to be detestable to you. 21 There are, however, some winged creatures that walk on all fours that you may eat: those that have jointed legs for hopping on the ground. 22 Of these you may eat any kind of locust, katydid, cricket or grasshopper. 23 But all other winged creatures that have four legs you are to detest.

24 " 'You will make yourselves unclean by these; whoever touches their carcasses will be unclean till evening. 25 Whoever picks up one of their carcasses must wash his clothes, and he will be unclean till evening.

26 " 'Every animal that has a split hoof not completely divided or that does not chew the cud is unclean for you; whoever touches ⌊the carcass of⌋ any of them will be unclean. 27 Of all the animals that walk on all fours, those that walk on their paws are unclean for you; whoever touches their carcasses will be unclean till evening. 28 Anyone who picks up their carcasses must wash his clothes, and he will be unclean till evening. They are unclean for you.

29 " 'Of the animals that move about on the ground, these are unclean for you: the weasel, the rat, any kind of great lizard, 30 the gecko, the monitor lizard, the wall lizard, the skink and the chameleon. 31 Of all those that move along the ground, these are unclean for you.

[a] *5* That is, the hyrax or rock badger [b] *19* The precise identification of some of the birds, insects and animals in this chapter is uncertain.

Whoever touches them when they are
dead will be unclean till evening.
32 When one of them dies and falls on
something, that article, whatever its use,
will be unclean, whether it is made of
wood, cloth, hide or sackcloth. Put it in
water; it will be unclean till evening,
and then it will be clean. 33 If one of them
falls into a clay pot, everything in it will
be unclean, and you must break the pot.
34 Any food that could be eaten but has
water on it from such a pot is unclean,
and any liquid that could be drunk from
it is unclean. 35 Anything that one of their
carcasses falls on becomes unclean; an
oven or cooking pot must be broken up.
They are unclean, and you are to regard
them as unclean. 36 A spring, however, or
a cistern for collecting water remains
clean, but anyone who touches one of
these carcasses is unclean. 37 If a carcass
falls on any seeds that are to be planted,
they remain clean. 38 But if water has
been put on the seed and a carcass falls
on it, it is unclean for you.

39 " 'If an animal that you are allowed
to eat dies, anyone who touches the carcass will be unclean till evening. 40 Anyone who eats some of the carcass must
wash his clothes, and he will be unclean
till evening. Anyone who picks up the
carcass must wash his clothes, and he
will be unclean till evening.

41 " 'Every creature that moves about
on the ground is detestable; it is not to
be eaten. 42 You are not to eat any creature that moves about on the ground,
whether it moves on its belly or walks
on all fours or on many feet; it is detestable. 43 Do not defile yourselves by any
of these creatures. Do not make yourselves unclean by means of them or be
made unclean by them. 44 I am the LORD
your God; consecrate yourselves and be
holy, because I am holy. Do not make
yourselves unclean by any creature that
moves about on the ground. 45 I am the
LORD who brought you up out of Egypt
to be your God; therefore be holy, because I am holy.

46 " 'These are the regulations concerning animals, birds, every living thing
that moves in the water and every creature that moves about on the ground.
47 You must distinguish between the unclean and the clean, between living
creatures that may be eaten and those
that may not be eaten.' "

SHARPEN THE FOCUS

What attitude should we, as God's people, have towards ourselves? On the one hand, we enjoy the honor of being a holy, royal priesthood (1 Peter 2:9–10) and that's as it should be, for our Lord *has* truly honored us. On the other hand, the Scriptures everywhere warn against the dangers of pride and presumption—self-reliance.

Nadab and Abihu learned the hard way that "among those who approach [the Lord], [He] will show [Himself] holy" (Leviticus 10:3). We dare not swagger into our Lord's presence, cocky in our own innate acceptability. We have none of our own. Instead, we honor and glorify our Lord for the righteous standing He has provided for us in Jesus Christ.

On balance, it may be better not to think about ourselves too much at all. The writer to the Hebrews encourages us instead to fix our eyes (continually) on Jesus, the one who began and who will complete the work of saving us (Hebrews 12:1–2). Keeping Him and His cross always in mind, we will by His grace avoid spiritual arrogance. We will also avoid tiring out under our burdens and giving up in our struggles (Hebrews 12:2–3) as we serve Him.

WEEK 10 • THURSDAY

Leviticus 12:1—15:33

GET THE BIG PICTURE

You may well want to skim today's reading, but as you do, note the meticulous attention to detail the Lord asked of His people as they dealt with the ceremonial uncleanness in their lives. Also note the social and spiritual consequences of outward uncleanness in any individual's life (Leviticus 13:45–46). If time is short, focus on Leviticus 13:38–46.

Purification After Childbirth

12 The LORD said to Moses, 2"Say to the Israelites: 'A woman who becomes pregnant and gives birth to a son will be ceremonially unclean for seven days, just as she is unclean during her monthly period. 3On the eighth day the boy is to be circumcised. 4Then the woman must wait thirty-three days to be purified from her bleeding. She must not touch anything sacred or go to the sanctuary until the days of her purification are over. 5If she gives birth to a daughter, for two weeks the woman will be unclean, as during her period. Then she must wait sixty-six days to be purified from her bleeding.

6" 'When the days of her purification for a son or daughter are over, she is to bring to the priest at the entrance to the Tent of Meeting a year-old lamb for a burnt offering and a young pigeon or a dove for a sin offering. 7He shall offer them before the LORD to make atonement for her, and then she will be ceremonially clean from her flow of blood.

" 'These are the regulations for the woman who gives birth to a boy or a girl. 8If she cannot afford a lamb, she is to bring two doves or two young pigeons, one for a burnt offering and the other for a sin offering. In this way the priest will make atonement for her, and she will be clean.' "

Regulations About Infectious Skin Diseases

13 The LORD said to Moses and Aaron, 2"When anyone has a swelling or a rash or a bright spot on his skin that may become an infectious skin disease,[a] he must be brought to Aaron the priest or to one of his sons[b] who is a priest. 3The priest is to examine the sore on his skin, and if the hair in the sore has turned white and the sore appears to be more than skin deep,[c] it is an infectious skin disease. When the priest examines him, he shall pronounce him ceremonially unclean. 4If the spot on his skin is white but does not appear to be more than skin deep and the hair in it has not turned white, the priest is to put the infected person in isolation for seven days. 5On the seventh day the priest is to examine him, and if he sees that the sore is unchanged and has not spread in the skin, he is to keep him in isolation another seven days. 6On the seventh day the priest is to examine him again, and if the sore has faded and has not spread in the skin, the priest shall pronounce him clean; it is only a rash. The man must wash his clothes, and he will be clean. 7But if the rash does spread in his skin after he has shown himself to

[a]2 Traditionally *leprosy*; the Hebrew word was used for various diseases affecting the skin—not necessarily leprosy; also elsewhere in this chapter. [b]2 Or *descendants* [c]3 Or *be lower than the rest of the skin*; also elsewhere in this chapter

the priest to be pronounced clean, he must appear before the priest again. 8The priest is to examine him, and if the rash has spread in the skin, he shall pronounce him unclean; it is an infectious disease.

9"When anyone has an infectious skin disease, he must be brought to the priest. 10The priest is to examine him, and if there is a white swelling in the skin that has turned the hair white and if there is raw flesh in the swelling, 11it is a chronic skin disease and the priest shall pronounce him unclean. He is not to put him in isolation, because he is already unclean.

12"If the disease breaks out all over his skin and, so far as the priest can see, it covers all the skin of the infected person from head to foot, 13the priest is to examine him, and if the disease has covered his whole body, he shall pronounce that person clean. Since it has all turned white, he is clean. 14But whenever raw flesh appears on him, he will be unclean. 15When the priest sees the raw flesh, he shall pronounce him unclean. The raw flesh is unclean; he has an infectious disease. 16Should the raw flesh change and turn white, he must go to the priest. 17The priest is to examine him, and if the sores have turned white, the priest shall pronounce the infected person clean; then he will be clean.

18"When someone has a boil on his skin and it heals, 19and in the place where the boil was, a white swelling or reddish-white spot appears, he must present himself to the priest. 20The priest is to examine it, and if it appears to be more than skin deep and the hair in it has turned white, the priest shall pronounce him unclean. It is an infectious skin disease that has broken out where the boil was. 21But if, when the priest examines it, there is no white hair in it and it is not more than skin deep and has faded, then the priest is to put him in isolation for seven days. 22If it is spreading in the skin, the priest shall pronounce him unclean; it is infectious. 23But if the spot is unchanged and has not spread, it is only a scar from the boil, and the priest shall pronounce him clean.

24"When someone has a burn on his skin and a reddish-white or white spot appears in the raw flesh of the burn, 25the priest is to examine the spot, and if the hair in it has turned white, and it appears to be more than skin deep, it is an infectious disease that has broken out in the burn. The priest shall pronounce him unclean; it is an infectious skin disease. 26But if the priest examines it and there is no white hair in the spot and if it is not more than skin deep and has faded, then the priest is to put him in isolation for seven days. 27On the seventh day the priest is to examine him, and if it is spreading in the skin, the priest shall pronounce him unclean; it is an infectious skin disease. 28If, however, the spot is unchanged and has not spread in the skin but has faded, it is a swelling from the burn, and the priest shall pronounce him clean; it is only a scar from the burn.

29"If a man or woman has a sore on the head or on the chin, 30the priest is to examine the sore, and if it appears to be more than skin deep and the hair in it is yellow and thin, the priest shall pronounce that person unclean; it is an itch, an infectious disease of the head or chin. 31But if, when the priest examines this kind of sore, it does not seem to be more than skin deep and there is no black hair in it, then the priest is to put the infected person in isolation for seven days. 32On the seventh day the priest is to examine the sore, and if the itch has not spread and there is no yellow hair in it and it does not appear to be more than skin deep, 33he must be shaved except for the diseased area, and the priest is to keep him in isolation another seven days. 34On the seventh day the priest is to examine the itch, and if it has not spread in the skin and appears to be no more than skin deep, the priest shall pronounce him clean. He must wash his clothes, and he will be clean. 35But if the itch does spread in the skin after he is pronounced clean, 36the priest is to examine him, and if the itch has spread in

the skin, the priest does not need to look
for yellow hair; the person is unclean.
[37]If, however, in his judgment it is unchanged and black hair has grown in it,
the itch is healed. He is clean, and the
priest shall pronounce him clean.
[38]"When a man or woman has white
spots on the skin, [39]the priest is to examine them, and if the spots are dull white,
it is a harmless rash that has broken out
on the skin; that person is clean.
[40]"When a man has lost his hair and
is bald, he is clean. [41]If he has lost his hair
from the front of his scalp and has a bald
forehead, he is clean. [42]But if he has a
reddish-white sore on his bald head or
forehead, it is an infectious disease
breaking out on his head or forehead.
[43]The priest is to examine him, and if the
swollen sore on his head or forehead is
reddish-white like an infectious skin
disease, [44]the man is diseased and is unclean. The priest shall pronounce him
unclean because of the sore on his head.
[45]"The person with such an infectious
disease must wear torn clothes, let his
hair be unkempt,[a] cover the lower part
of his face and cry out, 'Unclean! Unclean!' [46]As long as he has the infection
he remains unclean. He must live alone;
he must live outside the camp.

Regulations About Mildew

[47]"If any clothing is contaminated
with mildew—any woolen or linen
clothing, [48]any woven or knitted material of linen or wool, any leather or anything made of leather— [49]and if the
contamination in the clothing, or
leather, or woven or knitted material, or
any leather article, is greenish or reddish, it is a spreading mildew and must
be shown to the priest. [50]The priest is to
examine the mildew and isolate the affected article for seven days. [51]On the
seventh day he is to examine it, and if
the mildew has spread in the clothing,
or the woven or knitted material, or the
leather, whatever its use, it is a destructive mildew; the article is unclean. [52]He
must burn up the clothing, or the woven or knitted material of wool or linen,
or any leather article that has the contamination in it, because the mildew
is destructive; the article must be
burned up.
[53]"But if, when the priest examines it,
the mildew has not spread in the clothing, or the woven or knitted material, or
the leather article, [54]he shall order that
the contaminated article be washed.
Then he is to isolate it for another seven
days. [55]After the affected article has been
washed, the priest is to examine it, and
if the mildew has not changed its appearance, even though it has not
spread, it is unclean. Burn it with fire,
whether the mildew has affected one
side or the other. [56]If, when the priest
examines it, the mildew has faded after
the article has been washed, he is to tear
the contaminated part out of the clothing, or the leather, or the woven or knitted material. [57]But if it reappears in the
clothing, or in the woven or knitted material, or in the leather article, it is
spreading, and whatever has the mildew must be burned with fire. [58]The
clothing, or the woven or knitted material, or any leather article that has been
washed and is rid of the mildew, must
be washed again, and it will be clean."
[59]These are the regulations concerning contamination by mildew in woolen
or linen clothing, woven or knitted material, or any leather article, for pronouncing them clean or unclean.

Cleansing From Infectious Skin Diseases

14 The LORD said to Moses,
[2]"These are the regulations
for the diseased person at the time of his
ceremonial cleansing, when he is
brought to the priest: [3]The priest is to go
outside the camp and examine him. If
the person has been healed of his infectious skin disease,[b] [4]the priest shall order
that two live clean birds and some cedar
wood, scarlet yarn and hyssop be
brought for the one to be cleansed.

[a]45 Or *clothes, uncover his head* [b]3 Traditionally *leprosy*; the Hebrew word was used for various diseases affecting the skin—not necessarily leprosy; also elsewhere in this chapter.

[5]Then the priest shall order that one of the birds be killed over fresh water in a clay pot. [6]He is then to take the live bird and dip it, together with the cedar wood, the scarlet yarn and the hyssop, into the blood of the bird that was killed over the fresh water. [7]Seven times he shall sprinkle the one to be cleansed of the infectious disease and pronounce him clean. Then he is to release the live bird in the open fields.

[8]"The person to be cleansed must wash his clothes, shave off all his hair and bathe with water; then he will be ceremonially clean. After this he may come into the camp, but he must stay outside his tent for seven days. [9]On the seventh day he must shave off all his hair; he must shave his head, his beard, his eyebrows and the rest of his hair. He must wash his clothes and bathe himself with water, and he will be clean.

[10]"On the eighth day he must bring two male lambs and one ewe lamb a year old, each without defect, along with three-tenths of an ephah[a] of fine flour mixed with oil for a grain offering, and one log[b] of oil. [11]The priest who pronounces him clean shall present both the one to be cleansed and his offerings before the LORD at the entrance to the Tent of Meeting.

[12]"Then the priest is to take one of the male lambs and offer it as a guilt offering, along with the log of oil; he shall wave them before the LORD as a wave offering. [13]He is to slaughter the lamb in the holy place where the sin offering and the burnt offering are slaughtered. Like the sin offering, the guilt offering belongs to the priest; it is most holy. [14]The priest is to take some of the blood of the guilt offering and put it on the lobe of the right ear of the one to be cleansed, on the thumb of his right hand and on the big toe of his right foot. [15]The priest shall then take some of the log of oil, pour it in the palm of his own left hand, [16]dip his right forefinger into the oil in his palm, and with his finger sprinkle some of it before the LORD seven times. [17]The priest is to put some of the oil remaining in his palm on the lobe of the right ear of the one to be cleansed, on the thumb of his right hand and on the big toe of his right foot, on top of the blood of the guilt offering. [18]The rest of the oil in his palm the priest shall put on the head of the one to be cleansed and make atonement for him before the LORD.

[19]"Then the priest is to sacrifice the sin offering and make atonement for the one to be cleansed from his uncleanness. After that, the priest shall slaughter the burnt offering [20]and offer it on the altar, together with the grain offering, and make atonement for him, and he will be clean.

[21]"If, however, he is poor and cannot afford these, he must take one male lamb as a guilt offering to be waved to make atonement for him, together with a tenth of an ephah[c] of fine flour mixed with oil for a grain offering, a log of oil, [22]and two doves or two young pigeons, which he can afford, one for a sin offering and the other for a burnt offering.

[23]"On the eighth day he must bring them for his cleansing to the priest at the entrance to the Tent of Meeting, before the LORD. [24]The priest is to take the lamb for the guilt offering, together with the log of oil, and wave them before the LORD as a wave offering. [25]He shall slaughter the lamb for the guilt offering and take some of its blood and put it on the lobe of the right ear of the one to be cleansed, on the thumb of his right hand and on the big toe of his right foot. [26]The priest is to pour some of the oil into the palm of his own left hand, [27]and with his right forefinger sprinkle some of the oil from his palm seven times before the LORD. [28]Some of the oil in his palm he is to put on the same places he put the blood of the guilt offering—on the lobe of the right ear of the one to be cleansed, on the thumb of his right hand and on the big toe of his right foot. [29]The rest of

[a]*10* That is, probably about 6 quarts (about 6.5 liters) [b]*10* That is, probably about 2/3 pint (about 0.3 liter); also in verses 12, 15, 21 and 24 [c]*21* That is, probably about 2 quarts (about 2 liters)

the oil in his palm the priest shall put on the head of the one to be cleansed, to make atonement for him before the LORD. 30Then he shall sacrifice the doves or the young pigeons, which the person can afford, 31one[a] as a sin offering and the other as a burnt offering, together with the grain offering. In this way the priest will make atonement before the LORD on behalf of the one to be cleansed."

32These are the regulations for anyone who has an infectious skin disease and who cannot afford the regular offerings for his cleansing.

Cleansing From Mildew

33The LORD said to Moses and Aaron, 34"When you enter the land of Canaan, which I am giving you as your possession, and I put a spreading mildew in a house in that land, 35the owner of the house must go and tell the priest, 'I have seen something that looks like mildew in my house.' 36The priest is to order the house to be emptied before he goes in to examine the mildew, so that nothing in the house will be pronounced unclean. After this the priest is to go in and inspect the house. 37He is to examine the mildew on the walls, and if it has greenish or reddish depressions that appear to be deeper than the surface of the wall, 38the priest shall go out the doorway of the house and close it up for seven days. 39On the seventh day the priest shall return to inspect the house. If the mildew has spread on the walls, 40he is to order that the contaminated stones be torn out and thrown into an unclean place outside the town. 41He must have all the inside walls of the house scraped and the material that is scraped off dumped into an unclean place outside the town. 42Then they are to take other stones to replace these and take new clay and plaster the house.

43"If the mildew reappears in the house after the stones have been torn out and the house scraped and plastered, 44the priest is to go and examine it and, if the mildew has spread in the house, it is a destructive mildew; the house is unclean. 45It must be torn down—its stones, timbers and all the plaster—and taken out of the town to an unclean place.

46"Anyone who goes into the house while it is closed up will be unclean till evening. 47Anyone who sleeps or eats in the house must wash his clothes.

48"But if the priest comes to examine it and the mildew has not spread after the house has been plastered, he shall pronounce the house clean, because the mildew is gone. 49To purify the house he is to take two birds and some cedar wood, scarlet yarn and hyssop. 50He shall kill one of the birds over fresh water in a clay pot. 51Then he is to take the cedar wood, the hyssop, the scarlet yarn and the live bird, dip them into the blood of the dead bird and the fresh water, and sprinkle the house seven times. 52He shall purify the house with the bird's blood, the fresh water, the live bird, the cedar wood, the hyssop and the scarlet yarn. 53Then he is to release the live bird in the open fields outside the town. In this way he will make atonement for the house, and it will be clean."

54These are the regulations for any infectious skin disease, for an itch, 55for mildew in clothing or in a house, 56and for a swelling, a rash or a bright spot, 57to determine when something is clean or unclean.

These are the regulations for infectious skin diseases and mildew.

Discharges Causing Uncleanness

15 The LORD said to Moses and Aaron, 2"Speak to the Israelites and say to them: 'When any man has a bodily discharge, the discharge is unclean. 3Whether it continues flowing from his body or is blocked, it will make him unclean. This is how his discharge will bring about uncleanness:

4" 'Any bed the man with a discharge lies on will be unclean, and anything he

[a]*31* Septuagint and Syriac; Hebrew *31such as the person can afford, one*

sits on will be unclean. [5]Anyone who
touches his bed must wash his clothes
and bathe with water, and he will be unclean till evening. [6]Whoever sits on anything that the man with a discharge sat
on must wash his clothes and bathe
with water, and he will be unclean till
evening.

[7]" 'Whoever touches the man who
has a discharge must wash his clothes
and bathe with water, and he will be
unclean till evening.

[8]" 'If the man with the discharge spits
on someone who is clean, that person
must wash his clothes and bathe with
water, and he will be unclean till evening.

[9]" 'Everything the man sits on when
riding will be unclean, [10]and whoever
touches any of the things that were under him will be unclean till evening;
whoever picks up those things must
wash his clothes and bathe with water,
and he will be unclean till evening.

[11]" 'Anyone the man with a discharge
touches without rinsing his hands with
water must wash his clothes and bathe
with water, and he will be unclean till
evening.

[12]" 'A clay pot that the man touches
must be broken, and any wooden article
is to be rinsed with water.

[13]" 'When a man is cleansed from his
discharge, he is to count off seven days
for his ceremonial cleansing; he must
wash his clothes and bathe himself with
fresh water, and he will be clean. [14]On
the eighth day he must take two doves
or two young pigeons and come before
the LORD to the entrance to the Tent of
Meeting and give them to the priest.
[15]The priest is to sacrifice them, the one
for a sin offering and the other for a
burnt offering. In this way he will make
atonement before the LORD for the man
because of his discharge.

[16]" 'When a man has an emission of
semen, he must bathe his whole body
with water, and he will be unclean till
evening. [17]Any clothing or leather that
has semen on it must be washed with
water, and it will be unclean till evening.
[18]When a man lies with a woman and
there is an emission of semen, both must
bathe with water, and they will be unclean till evening.

[19]" 'When a woman has her regular
flow of blood, the impurity of her
monthly period will last seven days, and
anyone who touches her will be unclean till evening.

[20]" 'Anything she lies on during her
period will be unclean, and anything
she sits on will be unclean. [21]Whoever
touches her bed must wash his clothes
and bathe with water, and he will be unclean till evening. [22]Whoever touches
anything she sits on must wash his
clothes and bathe with water, and he
will be unclean till evening. [23]Whether
it is the bed or anything she was sitting
on, when anyone touches it, he will be
unclean till evening.

[24]" 'If a man lies with her and her
monthly flow touches him, he will be
unclean for seven days; any bed he lies
on will be unclean.

[25]" 'When a woman has a discharge of
blood for many days at a time other
than her monthly period or has a discharge that continues beyond her period, she will be unclean as long as she
has the discharge, just as in the days of
her period. [26]Any bed she lies on while
her discharge continues will be unclean,
as is her bed during her monthly period, and anything she sits on will be
unclean, as during her period. [27]Who-
ever touches them will be unclean; he
must wash his clothes and bathe with
water, and he will be unclean till evening.

[28]" 'When she is cleansed from her
discharge, she must count off seven
days, and after that she will be ceremonially clean. [29]On the eighth day she
must take two doves or two young pigeons and bring them to the priest at the
entrance to the Tent of Meeting. [30]The
priest is to sacrifice one for a sin offering and the other for a burnt offering.
In this way he will make atonement for
her before the LORD for the uncleanness
of her discharge.

[31]" 'You must keep the Israelites separate from things that make them un-

clean, so they will not die in their uncleanness for defiling my dwelling
place,[a] which is among them.' "
32These are the regulations for a man
with a discharge, for anyone made unclean by an emission of semen, 33for a
woman in her monthly period, for a
man or a woman with a discharge, and
for a man who lies with a woman who
is ceremonially unclean.

SHARPEN THE FOCUS

"Every time we turn around, we're unclean again. Another ritual. Another bath. Another sacrifice. Where will it all end?" If ancient Israelites felt this way, who could blame them? The burden of staying ceremonially clean must have weighed heavily on their hearts. And if outward uncleanness caused so much trouble, then how much heavier the burden of unclean hearts and lips and lives—for us as well as Old Testament Israel!

Maybe our Lord's expectation that you live a life of holiness, a life set-apart for Him, weighs you down at times, too. Maybe you catch yourself thinking, "Every time I turn around, I've missed the mark, stepped over the line, spoiled God's purpose for this part of my life again. Where will it all end?"

If you feel like that—a failure like that—remember this: it ended at the baptismal font. There you died with Christ. There you were raised with Christ. Now, you live in Christ. In Christ, you are holy.

Someone has said, "Holiness is not the way to Christ; Christ is the way to holiness." Look to Him to supply the strength—all the strength—you need to keep walking toward a more holy lifestyle. He is *your* holiness. And He is your way to a holier life.

WEEK 10 • FRIDAY

Leviticus 16:1—17:16

GET THE BIG PICTURE

Once each year the high priest entered the Most Holy Place. He took with him blood to "atone for" his own sins and the sins of the people. The great Day of Atonement was Israel's most solemn observance, corresponding roughly to our Good Friday. In fact, it did point forward to Christ's cross and the victory He won for us there. As you read, look for parallels and differences between Aaron and Jesus. If time is short, focus on Leviticus 16:1–34.

The Day of Atonement

16 The LORD spoke to Moses
after the death of the two
sons of Aaron who died when they approached the LORD. 2The LORD said to
Moses: "Tell your brother Aaron not to
come whenever he chooses into the
Most Holy Place behind the curtain in
front of the atonement cover on the ark,
or else he will die, because I appear in
the cloud over the atonement cover.
3"This is how Aaron is to enter the

[a]31 Or *my tabernacle*

sanctuary area: with a young bull for a
sin offering and a ram for a burnt offering. 4He is to put on the sacred linen tunic, with linen undergarments next to
his body; he is to tie the linen sash
around him and put on the linen turban. These are sacred garments; so he
must bathe himself with water before he
puts them on. 5From the Israelite community he is to take two male goats for
a sin offering and a ram for a burnt offering.

6"Aaron is to offer the bull for his own
sin offering to make atonement for himself and his household. 7Then he is to
take the two goats and present them
before the LORD at the entrance to the
Tent of Meeting. 8He is to cast lots for the
two goats—one lot for the LORD and the
other for the scapegoat.[a] 9Aaron shall
bring the goat whose lot falls to the
LORD and sacrifice it for a sin offering.
10But the goat chosen by lot as the scapegoat shall be presented alive before the
LORD to be used for making atonement
by sending it into the desert as a scapegoat.

11"Aaron shall bring the bull for his
own sin offering to make atonement for
himself and his household, and he is to
slaughter the bull for his own sin offering. 12He is to take a censer full of burning coals from the altar before the LORD
and two handfuls of finely ground fragrant incense and take them behind the
curtain. 13He is to put the incense on the
fire before the LORD, and the smoke of
the incense will conceal the atonement
cover above the Testimony, so that he
will not die. 14He is to take some of the
bull's blood and with his finger sprinkle
it on the front of the atonement cover;
then he shall sprinkle some of it with his
finger seven times before the atonement
cover.

15"He shall then slaughter the goat for
the sin offering for the people and take
its blood behind the curtain and do with
it as he did with the bull's blood: He
shall sprinkle it on the atonement cover
and in front of it. 16In this way he will
make atonement for the Most Holy
Place because of the uncleanness and
rebellion of the Israelites, whatever their
sins have been. He is to do the same for
the Tent of Meeting, which is among
them in the midst of their uncleanness.
17No one is to be in the Tent of Meeting
from the time Aaron goes in to make
atonement in the Most Holy Place until
he comes out, having made atonement
for himself, his household and the
whole community of Israel.

18"Then he shall come out to the altar
that is before the LORD and make atonement for it. He shall take some of the
bull's blood and some of the goat's
blood and put it on all the horns of the
altar. 19He shall sprinkle some of the
blood on it with his finger seven times
to cleanse it and to consecrate it from
the uncleanness of the Israelites.

20"When Aaron has finished making
atonement for the Most Holy Place, the
Tent of Meeting and the altar, he shall
bring forward the live goat. 21He is to lay
both hands on the head of the live goat
and confess over it all the wickedness
and rebellion of the Israelites—all their
sins—and put them on the goat's head.
He shall send the goat away into the
desert in the care of a man appointed for
the task. 22The goat will carry on itself all
their sins to a solitary place; and the
man shall release it in the desert.

23"Then Aaron is to go into the Tent of
Meeting and take off the linen garments
he put on before he entered the Most
Holy Place, and he is to leave them
there. 24He shall bathe himself with water in a holy place and put on his regular garments. Then he shall come out
and sacrifice the burnt offering for himself and the burnt offering for the
people, to make atonement for himself
and for the people. 25He shall also burn
the fat of the sin offering on the altar.

26"The man who releases the goat as
a scapegoat must wash his clothes and
bathe himself with water; afterward he
may come into the camp. 27The bull and
the goat for the sin offerings, whose
blood was brought into the Most Holy

[a]8 That is, the goat of removal; Hebrew *azazel*; also in verses 10 and 26

Place to make atonement, must be taken outside the camp; their hides, flesh and offal are to be burned up. 28 The man who burns them must wash his clothes and bathe himself with water; afterward he may come into the camp.

29 "This is to be a lasting ordinance for you: On the tenth day of the seventh month you must deny yourselves[a] and not do any work—whether native-born or an alien living among you— 30 because on this day atonement will be made for you, to cleanse you. Then, before the LORD, you will be clean from all your sins. 31 It is a sabbath of rest, and you must deny yourselves; it is a lasting ordinance. 32 The priest who is anointed and ordained to succeed his father as high priest is to make atonement. He is to put on the sacred linen garments 33 and make atonement for the Most Holy Place, for the Tent of Meeting and the altar, and for the priests and all the people of the community.

34 "This is to be a lasting ordinance for you: Atonement is to be made once a year for all the sins of the Israelites."

And it was done, as the LORD commanded Moses.

Eating Blood Forbidden

17 The LORD said to Moses, 2 "Speak to Aaron and his sons and to all the Israelites and say to them: 'This is what the LORD has commanded: 3 Any Israelite who sacrifices an ox,[b] a lamb or a goat in the camp or outside of it 4 instead of bringing it to the entrance to the Tent of Meeting to present it as an offering to the LORD in front of the tabernacle of the LORD—that man shall be considered guilty of bloodshed; he has shed blood and must be cut off from his people. 5 This is so the Israelites will bring to the LORD the sacrifices they are now making in the open fields. They must bring them to the priest, that is, to the LORD, at the entrance to the Tent of Meeting and sacrifice them as fellowship offerings.[c] 6 The priest is to sprinkle the blood against the altar of the LORD at the entrance to the Tent of Meeting and burn the fat as an aroma pleasing to the LORD. 7 They must no longer offer any of their sacrifices to the goat idols[d] to whom they prostitute themselves. This is to be a lasting ordinance for them and for the generations to come.'

8 "Say to them: 'Any Israelite or any alien living among them who offers a burnt offering or sacrifice 9 and does not bring it to the entrance to the Tent of Meeting to sacrifice it to the LORD—that man must be cut off from his people.

10 " 'Any Israelite or any alien living among them who eats any blood—I will set my face against that person who eats blood and will cut him off from his people. 11 For the life of a creature is in the blood, and I have given it to you to make atonement for yourselves on the altar; it is the blood that makes atonement for one's life. 12 Therefore I say to the Israelites, "None of you may eat blood, nor may an alien living among you eat blood."

13 " 'Any Israelite or any alien living among you who hunts any animal or bird that may be eaten must drain out the blood and cover it with earth, 14 because the life of every creature is its blood. That is why I have said to the Israelites, "You must not eat the blood of any creature, because the life of every creature is its blood; anyone who eats it must be cut off."

15 " 'Anyone, whether native-born or alien, who eats anything found dead or torn by wild animals must wash his clothes and bathe with water, and he will be ceremonially unclean till evening; then he will be clean. 16 But if he does not wash his clothes and bathe himself, he will be held responsible.' "

[a] 29 Or *must fast*; also in verse 31 [b] 3 The Hebrew word can include both male and female. [c] 5 Traditionally *peace offerings* [d] 7 Or *demons*

SHARPEN THE FOCUS

I lay my sins on Jesus
The spotless Lamb of God.
He bears them all and frees us
From the accursed load . . . (*Lutheran Worship* 366)

When Aaron and the high priests who followed him laid their hands on the "scapegoat" (Leviticus 16:21), they confessed the sins of God's people. Symbolically, they transferred these sins to the goat that was then taken far into the wilderness and released.

Later on, the Old Testament picks up this idea of God sending His people's sins far away from them and from His own sight. Remember these comforting words?

As far as the east is from the west,
so far has He removed our transgressions from us. (Psalm 103:12)

The most common New Testament word for forgiveness means "to send away." Soldiers used this word to dismiss those of a lower rank.

Still today we can trust our Lord to remove our burden of sin and to send it far away from us and from His remembrance. What the Day of Atonement only pictured, Good Friday fulfilled. Spend some time today praising your Savior for His mighty deliverance.

WEEK 10 • SATURDAY

Leviticus 18:1—19:37

GET THE BIG PICTURE

In Leviticus 18, the Lord warns His people against sexual sins, particularly incest. These sins pollute the land (Leviticus 18:24–25) and destroy lives and families. Chapter 19, then, goes on to repeat the Ten Commandments in expanded form. How many of them can you identify? If time is short, focus on Leviticus 19:1–37.

Unlawful Sexual Relations

18 The LORD said to Moses,
2"Speak to the Israelites and
say to them: 'I am the LORD your God.
3You must not do as they do in Egypt,
where you used to live, and you must
not do as they do in the land of Canaan,
where I am bringing you. Do not follow
their practices. 4You must obey my laws
and be careful to follow my decrees. I
am the LORD your God. 5Keep my decrees and laws, for the man who obeys
them will live by them. I am the LORD.
6" 'No one is to approach any close
relative to have sexual relations. I am the
LORD.
7" 'Do not dishonor your father by
having sexual relations with your mother. She is your mother; do not have relations with her.

[8]" 'Do not have sexual relations with your father's wife; that would dishonor your father.

[9]" 'Do not have sexual relations with your sister, either your father's daughter or your mother's daughter, whether she was born in the same home or elsewhere.

[10]" 'Do not have sexual relations with your son's daughter or your daughter's daughter; that would dishonor you.

[11]" 'Do not have sexual relations with the daughter of your father's wife, born to your father; she is your sister.

[12]" 'Do not have sexual relations with your father's sister; she is your father's close relative.

[13]" 'Do not have sexual relations with your mother's sister, because she is your mother's close relative.

[14]" 'Do not dishonor your father's brother by approaching his wife to have sexual relations; she is your aunt.

[15]" 'Do not have sexual relations with your daughter-in-law. She is your son's wife; do not have relations with her.

[16]" 'Do not have sexual relations with your brother's wife; that would dishonor your brother.

[17]" 'Do not have sexual relations with both a woman and her daughter. Do not have sexual relations with either her son's daughter or her daughter's daughter; they are her close relatives. That is wickedness.

[18]" 'Do not take your wife's sister as a rival wife and have sexual relations with her while your wife is living.

[19]" 'Do not approach a woman to have sexual relations during the uncleanness of her monthly period.

[20]" 'Do not have sexual relations with your neighbor's wife and defile yourself with her.

[21]" 'Do not give any of your children to be sacrificed[a] to Molech, for you must not profane the name of your God. I am the LORD.

[22]" 'Do not lie with a man as one lies with a woman; that is detestable.

[23]" 'Do not have sexual relations with an animal and defile yourself with it. A woman must not present herself to an animal to have sexual relations with it; that is a perversion.

[24]" 'Do not defile yourselves in any of these ways, because this is how the nations that I am going to drive out before you became defiled. [25]Even the land was defiled; so I punished it for its sin, and the land vomited out its inhabitants. [26]But you must keep my decrees and my laws. The native-born and the aliens living among you must not do any of these detestable things, [27]for all these things were done by the people who lived in the land before you, and the land became defiled. [28]And if you defile the land, it will vomit you out as it vomited out the nations that were before you.

[29]" 'Everyone who does any of these detestable things—such persons must be cut off from their people. [30]Keep my requirements and do not follow any of the detestable customs that were practiced before you came and do not defile yourselves with them. I am the LORD your God.' "

Various Laws

19 The LORD said to Moses, [2]"Speak to the entire assembly of Israel and say to them: 'Be holy because I, the LORD your God, am holy.

[3]" 'Each of you must respect his mother and father, and you must observe my Sabbaths. I am the LORD your God.

[4]" 'Do not turn to idols or make gods of cast metal for yourselves. I am the LORD your God.

[5]" 'When you sacrifice a fellowship offering[b] to the LORD, sacrifice it in such a way that it will be accepted on your behalf. [6]It shall be eaten on the day you sacrifice it or on the next day; anything left over until the third day must be burned up. [7]If any of it is eaten on the third day, it is impure and will not be accepted. [8]Whoever eats it will be held responsible because he has desecrated what is holy to the LORD; that person must be cut off from his people.

[9]" 'When you reap the harvest of your

[a]21 Or *to be passed through* ⌞*the fire*⌟
[b]5 Traditionally *peace offering*

land, do not reap to the very edges of your field or gather the gleanings of your harvest. [10]Do not go over your vineyard a second time or pick up the grapes that have fallen. Leave them for the poor and the alien. I am the LORD your God.

[11]" 'Do not steal.

" 'Do not lie.

" 'Do not deceive one another.

[12]" 'Do not swear falsely by my name and so profane the name of your God. I am the LORD.

[13]" 'Do not defraud your neighbor or rob him.

" 'Do not hold back the wages of a hired man overnight.

[14]" 'Do not curse the deaf or put a stumbling block in front of the blind, but fear your God. I am the LORD.

[15]" 'Do not pervert justice; do not show partiality to the poor or favoritism to the great, but judge your neighbor fairly.

[16]" 'Do not go about spreading slander among your people.

" 'Do not do anything that endangers your neighbor's life. I am the LORD.

[17]" 'Do not hate your brother in your heart. Rebuke your neighbor frankly so you will not share in his guilt.

[18]" 'Do not seek revenge or bear a grudge against one of your people, but love your neighbor as yourself. I am the LORD.

[19]" 'Keep my decrees.

" 'Do not mate different kinds of animals.

" 'Do not plant your field with two kinds of seed.

" 'Do not wear clothing woven of two kinds of material.

[20]" 'If a man sleeps with a woman who is a slave girl promised to another man but who has not been ransomed or given her freedom, there must be due punishment. Yet they are not to be put to death, because she had not been freed. [21]The man, however, must bring a ram to the entrance to the Tent of Meeting for a guilt offering to the LORD. [22]With the ram of the guilt offering the priest is to make atonement for him before the LORD for the sin he has committed, and his sin will be forgiven.

[23]" 'When you enter the land and plant any kind of fruit tree, regard its fruit as forbidden.[a] For three years you are to consider it forbidden[a]; it must not be eaten. [24]In the fourth year all its fruit will be holy, an offering of praise to the LORD. [25]But in the fifth year you may eat its fruit. In this way your harvest will be increased. I am the LORD your God.

[26]" 'Do not eat any meat with the blood still in it.

" 'Do not practice divination or sorcery.

[27]" 'Do not cut the hair at the sides of your head or clip off the edges of your beard.

[28]" 'Do not cut your bodies for the dead or put tattoo marks on yourselves. I am the LORD.

[29]" 'Do not degrade your daughter by making her a prostitute, or the land will turn to prostitution and be filled with wickedness.

[30]" 'Observe my Sabbaths and have reverence for my sanctuary. I am the LORD.

[31]" 'Do not turn to mediums or seek out spiritists, for you will be defiled by them. I am the LORD your God.

[32]" 'Rise in the presence of the aged, show respect for the elderly and revere your God. I am the LORD.

[33]" 'When an alien lives with you in your land, do not mistreat him. [34]The alien living with you must be treated as one of your native-born. Love him as yourself, for you were aliens in Egypt. I am the LORD your God.

[35]" 'Do not use dishonest standards when measuring length, weight or quantity. [36]Use honest scales and honest weights, an honest ephah[b] and an honest hin.[c] I am the LORD your God, who brought you out of Egypt.

[37]" 'Keep all my decrees and all my laws and follow them. I am the LORD.' "

[a]23 Hebrew *uncircumcised* [b]36 An ephah was a dry measure. [c]36 A hin was a liquid measure.

SHARPEN THE FOCUS

Even if "just getting by" is your goal as you think about keeping the Ten Commandments, you can't help but despair at Leviticus 19. The examples God gives here illustrate Leviticus 19:18: "Love your neighbor as yourself." This principle of love requires, among other things, that we:

- renounce greed; care for the poor (Leviticus 19:9–10);
- practice complete honesty (Leviticus 19:11–12);
- give up gossip and the desire for revenge (Leviticus 19:16, 18);
- refuse to harbor ill will against anyone (Leviticus 19:17);
- practice total purity in our sexual behavior (Leviticus 19:20, 29) and total honesty in our work relationships (Leviticus 19:11, 13, 35–36).
- never consult a horoscope or dabble in the occult (Leviticus 19:26–29, 31).

No wonder Paul concluded, "No one will be declared righteous in [God's] sight by observing the law" (Romans 3:20). Does this mean we're off the hook? After all, God knows we can't keep His Law. So can we just ignore it?

Far from it! Rather, we cling by faith to Christ Jesus who kept the Law of love in our place. In love, He hung on our hook—the hook of the cross—to take our punishment. Looking to Him, we receive forgiveness. And we receive motivation and power to walk in love—step by step.

WEEK 11 • MONDAY

Leviticus 20:1—22:33

GET THE BIG PICTURE

In Leviticus 20, God places a high priority on relationships—those between Himself and His people and those between individuals among His people. This contrasts sharply with the laws of most pagan cultures of that day (and oftentimes our own), which placed first priority on property and possessions. Chapters 21 and 22 reveal the Lord's concern that His priests accurately represent the Savior—our perfect Priest and the perfect Sacrifice for our sin—the Savior who was to come. If time is short, focus on Leviticus 20:1–27.

Punishments for Sin

20 The LORD said to Moses,
[2]"Say to the Israelites: 'Any
Israelite or any alien living in Israel who
gives[a] any of his children to Molech
must be put to death. The people of the
community are to stone him. [3]I will set
my face against that man and I will cut
him off from his people; for by giving
his children to Molech, he has defiled
my sanctuary and profaned my holy
name. [4]If the people of the community
close their eyes when that man gives
one of his children to Molech and they
fail to put him to death, [5]I will set my
face against that man and his family and

[a]2 Or *sacrifices;* also in verses 3 and 4

will cut off from their people both him
and all who follow him in prostituting
themselves to Molech.
[6]" 'I will set my face against the person who turns to mediums and spiritists to prostitute himself by following
them, and I will cut him off from his
people.
[7]" 'Consecrate yourselves and be holy,
because I am the LORD your God. [8]Keep
my decrees and follow them. I am the
LORD, who makes you holy.[a]
[9]" 'If anyone curses his father or
mother, he must be put to death. He has
cursed his father or his mother, and his
blood will be on his own head.
[10]" 'If a man commits adultery with
another man's wife—with the wife of
his neighbor—both the adulterer and
the adulteress must be put to death.
[11]" 'If a man sleeps with his father's
wife, he has dishonored his father. Both
the man and the woman must be put to
death; their blood will be on their own
heads.
[12]" 'If a man sleeps with his daughter-
in-law, both of them must be put to
death. What they have done is a perversion; their blood will be on their own
heads.
[13]" 'If a man lies with a man as one lies
with a woman, both of them have done
what is detestable. They must be put to
death; their blood will be on their own
heads.
[14]" 'If a man marries both a woman
and her mother, it is wicked. Both he
and they must be burned in the fire,
so that no wickedness will be among
you.
[15]" 'If a man has sexual relations with
an animal, he must be put to death, and
you must kill the animal.
[16]" 'If a woman approaches an animal
to have sexual relations with it, kill both
the woman and the animal. They must
be put to death; their blood will be on
their own heads.
[17]" 'If a man marries his sister, the
daughter of either his father or his
mother, and they have sexual relations,
it is a disgrace. They must be cut off before the eyes of their people. He has dishonored his sister and will be held responsible.
[18]" 'If a man lies with a woman during
her monthly period and has sexual relations with her, he has exposed the
source of her flow, and she has also uncovered it. Both of them must be cut off
from their people.
[19]" 'Do not have sexual relations with
the sister of either your mother or your
father, for that would dishonor a close
relative; both of you would be held responsible.
[20]" 'If a man sleeps with his aunt, he
has dishonored his uncle. They will be
held responsible; they will die childless.
[21]" 'If a man marries his brother's
wife, it is an act of impurity; he has dishonored his brother. They will be childless.
[22]" 'Keep all my decrees and laws and
follow them, so that the land where I am
bringing you to live may not vomit you
out. [23]You must not live according to the
customs of the nations I am going to
drive out before you. Because they did
all these things, I abhorred them. [24]But
I said to you, "You will possess their
land; I will give it to you as an inheritance, a land flowing with milk and
honey." I am the LORD your God, who
has set you apart from the nations.
[25]" 'You must therefore make a distinction between clean and unclean animals and between unclean and clean
birds. Do not defile yourselves by any
animal or bird or anything that moves
along the ground—those which I have
set apart as unclean for you. [26]You are to
be holy to me[b] because I, the LORD, am
holy, and I have set you apart from the
nations to be my own.
[27]" 'A man or woman who is a medium or spiritist among you must be put
to death. You are to stone them; their
blood will be on their own heads.' "

Rules for Priests

21 The LORD said to Moses,
"Speak to the priests, the sons

[a]8 Or *who sanctifies you*; or *who sets you apart as holy* [b]26 Or *be my holy ones*

of Aaron, and say to them: 'A priest must
not make himself ceremonially unclean
for any of his people who die, 2except
for a close relative, such as his mother
or father, his son or daughter, his
brother, 3or an unmarried sister who is
dependent on him since she has no husband—for her he may make himself unclean. 4He must not make himself
unclean for people related to him by
marriage,[a] and so defile himself.
5" 'Priests must not shave their heads
or shave off the edges of their beards or
cut their bodies. 6They must be holy to
their God and must not profane the
name of their God. Because they
present the offerings made to the LORD
by fire, the food of their God, they are
to be holy.
7" 'They must not marry women defiled by prostitution or divorced from
their husbands, because priests are holy
to their God. 8Regard them as holy, because they offer up the food of your
God. Consider them holy, because I the
LORD am holy—I who make you holy.[b]
9" 'If a priest's daughter defiles herself
by becoming a prostitute, she disgraces
her father; she must be burned in the
fire.
10" 'The high priest, the one among
his brothers who has had the anointing
oil poured on his head and who has
been ordained to wear the priestly garments, must not let his hair become
unkempt[c] or tear his clothes. 11He must
not enter a place where there is a dead
body. He must not make himself unclean, even for his father or mother,
12nor leave the sanctuary of his God or
desecrate it, because he has been dedicated by the anointing oil of his God. I
am the LORD.
13" 'The woman he marries must be a
virgin. 14He must not marry a widow, a
divorced woman, or a woman defiled
by prostitution, but only a virgin from
his own people, 15so he will not defile his
offspring among his people. I am the
LORD, who makes him holy.[d] ' "
16The LORD said to Moses, 17"Say to
Aaron: 'For the generations to come
none of your descendants who has a
defect may come near to offer the food
of his God. 18No man who has any defect may come near: no man who is
blind or lame, disfigured or deformed;
19no man with a crippled foot or hand,
20or who is hunchbacked or dwarfed, or
who has any eye defect, or who has festering or running sores or damaged testicles. 21No descendant of Aaron the
priest who has any defect is to come
near to present the offerings made to
the LORD by fire. He has a defect; he
must not come near to offer the food of
his God. 22He may eat the most holy
food of his God, as well as the holy food;
23yet because of his defect, he must not
go near the curtain or approach the altar, and so desecrate my sanctuary. I am
the LORD, who makes them holy.[e] ' "
24So Moses told this to Aaron and his
sons and to all the Israelites.

22 The LORD said to Moses,
2"Tell Aaron and his sons
to treat with respect the sacred offerings
the Israelites consecrate to me, so they
will not profane my holy name. I am the
LORD.
3"Say to them: 'For the generations to
come, if any of your descendants is ceremonially unclean and yet comes near
the sacred offerings that the Israelites
consecrate to the LORD, that person
must be cut off from my presence. I am
the LORD.
4" 'If a descendant of Aaron has an infectious skin disease[f] or a bodily discharge, he may not eat the sacred
offerings until he is cleansed. He will
also be unclean if he touches something
defiled by a corpse or by anyone who
has an emission of semen, 5or if he
touches any crawling thing that makes
him unclean, or any person who makes
him unclean, whatever the uncleanness
may be. 6The one who touches any such

[a]4 Or *unclean as a leader among his people* [b]8 Or *who sanctify you*; or *who set you apart as holy* [c]10 Or *not uncover his head* [d]15 Or *who sanctifies him*; or *who sets him apart as holy* [e]23 Or *who sanctifies them*; or *who sets them apart as holy* [f]4 Traditionally *leprosy*; the Hebrew word was used for various diseases affecting the skin—not necessarily leprosy.

thing will be unclean till evening. He must not eat any of the sacred offerings unless he has bathed himself with water. [7]When the sun goes down, he will be clean, and after that he may eat the sacred offerings, for they are his food. [8]He must not eat anything found dead or torn by wild animals, and so become unclean through it. I am the LORD.

[9]" 'The priests are to keep my requirements so that they do not become guilty and die for treating them with contempt. I am the LORD, who makes them holy.[a]

[10]" 'No one outside a priest's family may eat the sacred offering, nor may the guest of a priest or his hired worker eat it. [11]But if a priest buys a slave with money, or if a slave is born in his household, that slave may eat his food. [12]If a priest's daughter marries anyone other than a priest, she may not eat any of the sacred contributions. [13]But if a priest's daughter becomes a widow or is divorced, yet has no children, and she returns to live in her father's house as in her youth, she may eat of her father's food. No unauthorized person, however, may eat any of it.

[14]" 'If anyone eats a sacred offering by mistake, he must make restitution to the priest for the offering and add a fifth of the value to it. [15]The priests must not desecrate the sacred offerings the Israelites present to the LORD [16]by allowing them to eat the sacred offerings and so bring upon them guilt requiring payment. I am the LORD, who makes them holy.' "

Unacceptable Sacrifices

[17]The LORD said to Moses, [18]"Speak to Aaron and his sons and to all the Israelites and say to them: 'If any of you—either an Israelite or an alien living in Israel—presents a gift for a burnt offering to the LORD, either to fulfill a vow or as a freewill offering, [19]you must present a male without defect from the cattle, sheep or goats in order that it may be accepted on your behalf. [20]Do not bring anything with a defect, because it will not be accepted on your behalf. [21]When anyone brings from the herd or flock a fellowship offering[b] to the LORD to fulfill a special vow or as a freewill offering, it must be without defect or blemish to be acceptable. [22]Do not offer to the LORD the blind, the injured or the maimed, or anything with warts or festering or running sores. Do not place any of these on the altar as an offering made to the LORD by fire. [23]You may, however, present as a freewill offering an ox[c] or a sheep that is deformed or stunted, but it will not be accepted in fulfillment of a vow. [24]You must not offer to the LORD an animal whose testicles are bruised, crushed, torn or cut. You must not do this in your own land, [25]and you must not accept such animals from the hand of a foreigner and offer them as the food of your God. They will not be accepted on your behalf, because they are deformed and have defects.' "

[26]The LORD said to Moses, [27]"When a calf, a lamb or a goat is born, it is to remain with its mother for seven days. From the eighth day on, it will be acceptable as an offering made to the LORD by fire. [28]Do not slaughter a cow or a sheep and its young on the same day.

[29]"When you sacrifice a thank offering to the LORD, sacrifice it in such a way that it will be accepted on your behalf. [30]It must be eaten that same day; leave none of it till morning. I am the LORD.

[31]"Keep my commands and follow them. I am the LORD. [32]Do not profane my holy name. I must be acknowledged as holy by the Israelites. I am the LORD, who makes[d] you holy[e] [33]and who brought you out of Egypt to be your God. I am the LORD."

[a]9 Or *who sanctifies them;* or *who sets them apart as holy;* also in verse 16 [b]21 Traditionally *peace offering* [c]23 The Hebrew word can include both male and female. [d]32 Or *made* [e]32 Or *who sanctifies you;* or *who sets you apart as holy*

SHARPEN THE FOCUS

Heinous crimes often take neighbors and even family members by surprise. No one sees the warning signs for months or even years. Then, suddenly, the police show up.

Sometimes there's a fine line between not knowing and not wanting to know. For instance, when we see our brothers and sisters in the faith continually breaking God's Law, we're often tempted to pretend it's not happening. How easily we convince ourselves to turn away. How readily we decide not to get involved in "other people's business." That's the tendency the Lord addresses in Leviticus 20:1–5.

"Am I my brother's keeper?" a belligerent Cain asked God (Genesis 4:9). Much of Scripture answers that question—with a resounding, *yes!* Christ's love in us leads us to bear patiently with each other's sins of weakness. But Christ's love also leads us to share our honest concern when we see another believer drifting in the wrong direction or sliding down sin's slippery slope toward disaster.

As Christ empowers us, we don't turn our heads; instead, we bow them in prayer for ourselves and for our wandering brother or sister. And then we speak the truth, in love and concern.

WEEK 11 • TUESDAY

Leviticus 23:1—25:55

GET THE BIG PICTURE

Leviticus 23 summarizes the holy days the Lord commanded His people to observe. In chapter 25, Israel's Father-God gives His people Sabbath years and, twice in every century, the Year of Jubilee. As you read, try to imagine the joy of that year. If time is short, focus on Leviticus 25:1–43.

23 The LORD said to Moses,
2"Speak to the Israelites
and say to them: 'These are my appointed feasts, the appointed feasts of the LORD, which you are to proclaim as sacred assemblies.

The Sabbath

3" 'There are six days when you may work, but the seventh day is a Sabbath of rest, a day of sacred assembly. You are not to do any work; wherever you live, it is a Sabbath to the LORD.

The Passover and Unleavened Bread

4" 'These are the LORD's appointed feasts, the sacred assemblies you are to proclaim at their appointed times:
5The LORD's Passover begins at twilight on the fourteenth day of the first month.
6On the fifteenth day of that month the LORD's Feast of Unleavened Bread begins; for seven days you must eat bread made without yeast.
7On the first day hold a sacred assembly and do no regular work.
8For seven days present an offering made to the LORD by fire. And on the seventh day hold a sacred assembly and do no regular work.' "

Firstfruits

9The LORD said to Moses,
10"Speak to the Israelites and say to them: 'When you enter the land I am going to give

you and you reap its harvest, bring to
the priest a sheaf of the first grain you
harvest. [11]He is to wave the sheaf before
the LORD so it will be accepted on your
behalf; the priest is to wave it on the day
after the Sabbath. [12]On the day you
wave the sheaf, you must sacrifice as a
burnt offering to the LORD a lamb a year
old without defect, [13]together with its
grain offering of two-tenths of an
ephah[a] of fine flour mixed with oil—an
offering made to the LORD by fire, a
pleasing aroma—and its drink offering
of a quarter of a hin[b] of wine. [14]You must
not eat any bread, or roasted or new
grain, until the very day you bring this
offering to your God. This is to be a lasting ordinance for the generations to
come, wherever you live.

Feast of Weeks

[15]" 'From the day after the Sabbath,
the day you brought the sheaf of the
wave offering, count off seven full
weeks. [16]Count off fifty days up to the
day after the seventh Sabbath, and then
present an offering of new grain to the
LORD. [17]From wherever you live, bring
two loaves made of two-tenths of an
ephah of fine flour, baked with yeast, as
a wave offering of firstfruits to the
LORD. [18]Present with this bread seven
male lambs, each a year old and without defect, one young bull and two
rams. They will be a burnt offering to
the LORD, together with their grain offerings and drink offerings—an offering
made by fire, an aroma pleasing to the
LORD. [19]Then sacrifice one male goat for
a sin offering and two lambs, each a year
old, for a fellowship offering.[c] [20]The
priest is to wave the two lambs before
the LORD as a wave offering, together
with the bread of the firstfruits. They are
a sacred offering to the LORD for the
priest. [21]On that same day you are to
proclaim a sacred assembly and do no
regular work. This is to be a lasting ordinance for the generations to come,
wherever you live.

[22]" 'When you reap the harvest of
your land, do not reap to the very edges
of your field or gather the gleanings of
your harvest. Leave them for the poor
and the alien. I am the LORD your
God.' "

Feast of Trumpets

[23]The LORD said to Moses, [24]"Say to
the Israelites: 'On the first day of the
seventh month you are to have a day of
rest, a sacred assembly commemorated
with trumpet blasts. [25]Do no regular
work, but present an offering made to
the LORD by fire.' "

Day of Atonement

[26]The LORD said to Moses, [27]"The
tenth day of this seventh month is the
Day of Atonement. Hold a sacred assembly and deny yourselves,[d] and
present an offering made to the LORD
by fire. [28]Do no work on that day, because it is the Day of Atonement, when
atonement is made for you before the
LORD your God. [29]Anyone who does not
deny himself on that day must be cut off
from his people. [30]I will destroy from
among his people anyone who does any
work on that day. [31]You shall do no work
at all. This is to be a lasting ordinance for
the generations to come, wherever you
live. [32]It is a sabbath of rest for you, and
you must deny yourselves. From the
evening of the ninth day of the month
until the following evening you are to
observe your sabbath."

Feast of Tabernacles

[33]The LORD said to Moses, [34]"Say to
the Israelites: 'On the fifteenth day of
the seventh month the LORD's Feast of
Tabernacles begins, and it lasts for seven
days. [35]The first day is a sacred assembly; do no regular work. [36]For seven
days present offerings made to the LORD
by fire, and on the eighth day hold a sacred assembly and present an offering
made to the LORD by fire. It is the closing assembly; do no regular work.

[37](" 'These are the LORD's appointed

[a]*13* That is, probably about 4 quarts (about 4.5 liters); also in verse 17 [b]*13* That is, probably about 1 quart (about 1 liter) [c]*19* Traditionally *peace offering* [d]*27* Or *and fast*; also in verses 29 and 32

feasts, which you are to proclaim as sacred assemblies for bringing offerings
made to the LORD by fire—the burnt offerings and grain offerings, sacrifices
and drink offerings required for each
day. 38These offerings are in addition to
those for the LORD's Sabbaths and[a] in
addition to your gifts and whatever you
have vowed and all the freewill offerings you give to the LORD.)

39" 'So beginning with the fifteenth
day of the seventh month, after you
have gathered the crops of the land, celebrate the festival to the LORD for seven
days; the first day is a day of rest, and
the eighth day also is a day of rest. 40On
the first day you are to take choice fruit
from the trees, and palm fronds, leafy
branches and poplars, and rejoice before the LORD your God for seven days.
41Celebrate this as a festival to the LORD
for seven days each year. This is to be a
lasting ordinance for the generations to
come; celebrate it in the seventh month.
42Live in booths for seven days: All native-born Israelites are to live in booths
43so your descendants will know that I
had the Israelites live in booths when I
brought them out of Egypt. I am the
LORD your God.' "

44So Moses announced to the Israelites the appointed feasts of the LORD.

Oil and Bread Set Before the LORD

24 The LORD said to Moses,
2"Command the Israelites
to bring you clear oil of pressed olives
for the light so that the lamps may be
kept burning continually. 3Outside the
curtain of the Testimony in the Tent of
Meeting, Aaron is to tend the lamps
before the LORD from evening till morning, continually. This is to be a lasting ordinance for the generations to come.
4The lamps on the pure gold lampstand
before the LORD must be tended continually.

5"Take fine flour and bake twelve
loaves of bread, using two-tenths of an
ephah[b] for each loaf. 6Set them in two
rows, six in each row, on the table of
pure gold before the LORD. 7Along each
row put some pure incense as a memorial portion to represent the bread and
to be an offering made to the LORD by
fire. 8This bread is to be set out before
the LORD regularly, Sabbath after Sabbath, on behalf of the Israelites, as a lasting covenant. 9It belongs to Aaron and
his sons, who are to eat it in a holy place,
because it is a most holy part of their
regular share of the offerings made to
the LORD by fire."

A Blasphemer Stoned

10Now the son of an Israelite mother
and an Egyptian father went out among
the Israelites, and a fight broke out in
the camp between him and an Israelite.
11The son of the Israelite woman blasphemed the Name with a curse; so they
brought him to Moses. (His mother's
name was Shelomith, the daughter of
Dibri the Danite.) 12They put him in custody until the will of the LORD should
be made clear to them.

13Then the LORD said to Moses: 14"Take
the blasphemer outside the camp. All
those who heard him are to lay their
hands on his head, and the entire assembly is to stone him. 15Say to the Israelites: 'If anyone curses his God, he will
be held responsible; 16anyone who blasphemes the name of the LORD must be
put to death. The entire assembly must
stone him. Whether an alien or native-
born, when he blasphemes the Name,
he must be put to death.

17" 'If anyone takes the life of a human
being, he must be put to death. 18Any-
one who takes the life of someone's animal must make restitution—life for life.
19If anyone injures his neighbor, whatever he has done must be done to him:
20fracture for fracture, eye for eye, tooth
for tooth. As he has injured the other, so
he is to be injured. 21Whoever kills an
animal must make restitution, but whoever kills a man must be put to death.
22You are to have the same law for the
alien and the native-born. I am the
LORD your God.' "

[a]38 Or *These feasts are in addition to the LORD's Sabbaths, and these offerings are* [b]5 That is, probably about 4 quarts (about 4.5 liters)

23Then Moses spoke to the Israelites,
and they took the blasphemer outside
the camp and stoned him. The Israelites
did as the LORD commanded Moses.

The Sabbath Year

25 The LORD said to Moses
on Mount Sinai, 2"Speak
to the Israelites and say to them: 'When
you enter the land I am going to give
you, the land itself must observe a sabbath to the LORD. 3For six years sow
your fields, and for six years prune your
vineyards and gather their crops. 4But in
the seventh year the land is to have a
sabbath of rest, a sabbath to the LORD.
Do not sow your fields or prune your
vineyards. 5Do not reap what grows of
itself or harvest the grapes of your untended vines. The land is to have a year
of rest. 6Whatever the land yields during the sabbath year will be food for
you—for yourself, your manservant
and maidservant, and the hired worker
and temporary resident who live
among you, 7as well as for your livestock
and the wild animals in your land.
Whatever the land produces may be
eaten.

The Year of Jubilee

8" 'Count off seven sabbaths of
years—seven times seven years—so
that the seven sabbaths of years amount
to a period of forty-nine years. 9Then
have the trumpet sounded everywhere
on the tenth day of the seventh month;
on the Day of Atonement sound the
trumpet throughout your land. 10Conse-
crate the fiftieth year and proclaim liberty throughout the land to all its
inhabitants. It shall be a jubilee for you;
each one of you is to return to his family property and each to his own clan.
11The fiftieth year shall be a jubilee for
you; do not sow and do not reap what
grows of itself or harvest the untended
vines. 12For it is a jubilee and is to be holy
for you; eat only what is taken directly
from the fields.

13" 'In this Year of Jubilee everyone is
to return to his own property.

14" 'If you sell land to one of your
countrymen or buy any from him, do
not take advantage of each other. 15You
are to buy from your countryman on the
basis of the number of years since the
Jubilee. And he is to sell to you on the
basis of the number of years left for harvesting crops. 16When the years are
many, you are to increase the price, and
when the years are few, you are to decrease the price, because what he is
really selling you is the number of crops.
17Do not take advantage of each other,
but fear your God. I am the LORD your
God.

18" 'Follow my decrees and be careful
to obey my laws, and you will live safely
in the land. 19Then the land will yield its
fruit, and you will eat your fill and live
there in safety. 20You may ask, "What
will we eat in the seventh year if we do
not plant or harvest our crops?" 21I will
send you such a blessing in the sixth
year that the land will yield enough for
three years. 22While you plant during
the eighth year, you will eat from the old
crop and will continue to eat from it
until the harvest of the ninth year
comes in.

23" 'The land must not be sold perma-
nently, because the land is mine and
you are but aliens and my tenants.
24Throughout the country that you hold
as a possession, you must provide for
the redemption of the land.

25" 'If one of your countrymen becomes poor and sells some of his property, his nearest relative is to come and
redeem what his countryman has sold.
26If, however, a man has no one to redeem it for him but he himself prospers
and acquires sufficient means to redeem
it, 27he is to determine the value for the
years since he sold it and refund the
balance to the man to whom he sold it;
he can then go back to his own property.
28But if he does not acquire the means to
repay him, what he sold will remain in
the possession of the buyer until the
Year of Jubilee. It will be returned in the
Jubilee, and he can then go back to his
property.

29" 'If a man sells a house in a walled
city, he retains the right of redemption

a full year after its sale. During that time
he may redeem it. 30If it is not redeemed
before a full year has passed, the house
in the walled city shall belong perma-
nently to the buyer and his descendants. It is not to be returned in the
Jubilee. 31But houses in villages without
walls around them are to be considered
as open country. They can be redeemed, and they are to be returned in
the Jubilee.

32" 'The Levites always have the right
to redeem their houses in the Levitical
towns, which they possess. 33So the
property of the Levites is redeemable—
that is, a house sold in any town they
hold—and is to be returned in the Jubilee, because the houses in the towns of
the Levites are their property among
the Israelites. 34But the pastureland belonging to their towns must not be sold;
it is their permanent possession.

35" 'If one of your countrymen becomes poor and is unable to support
himself among you, help him as you
would an alien or a temporary resident,
so he can continue to live among you.
36Do not take interest of any kind[a] from
him, but fear your God, so that your
countryman may continue to live
among you. 37You must not lend him
money at interest or sell him food at a
profit. 38I am the LORD your God, who
brought you out of Egypt to give you
the land of Canaan and to be your God.

39" 'If one of your countrymen becomes poor among you and sells himself to you, do not make him work as a
slave. 40He is to be treated as a hired
worker or a temporary resident among
you; he is to work for you until the Year
of Jubilee. 41Then he and his children are
to be released, and he will go back to his
own clan and to the property of his forefathers. 42Because the Israelites are my
servants, whom I brought out of Egypt,
they must not be sold as slaves. 43Do not
rule over them ruthlessly, but fear your
God.

44" 'Your male and female slaves are to
come from the nations around you;
from them you may buy slaves. 45You
may also buy some of the temporary
residents living among you and members of their clans born in your country,
and they will become your property.
46You can will them to your children as
inherited property and can make them
slaves for life, but you must not rule
over your fellow Israelites ruthlessly.

47" 'If an alien or a temporary resident
among you becomes rich and one of
your countrymen becomes poor and
sells himself to the alien living among
you or to a member of the alien's clan,
48he retains the right of redemption after he has sold himself. One of his relatives may redeem him: 49An uncle or a
cousin or any blood relative in his clan
may redeem him. Or if he prospers, he
may redeem himself. 50He and his buyer
are to count the time from the year he
sold himself up to the Year of Jubilee.
The price for his release is to be based
on the rate paid to a hired man for that
number of years. 51If many years remain, he must pay for his redemption a
larger share of the price paid for him. 52If
only a few years remain until the Year
of Jubilee, he is to compute that and pay
for his redemption accordingly. 53He is
to be treated as a man hired from year
to year; you must see to it that his owner
does not rule over him ruthlessly.

54" 'Even if he is not redeemed in any
of these ways, he and his children are to
be released in the Year of Jubilee, 55for
the Israelites belong to me as servants.
They are my servants, whom I brought
out of Egypt. I am the LORD your God.

[a]36 Or *take excessive interest*; similarly in verse 37

SHARPEN THE FOCUS

Imagine the anticipation as the Day of Atonement drew to a close and the Year of Jubilee began. As the evening sacrifice concluded, the unmistakable blast of the ram's horn would sound.

Imagine the people of God walking home, arm-in-arm, to break their fast and to revel in the Lord's fantastic generosity toward them:

- They had, not a day or a week, but a *year* to rest and enjoy their relationships (Leviticus 25:11–22).
- All their debts were cancelled (Leviticus 25:25–28).
- All who had sold land once again held title to their family's property (Leviticus 25:23–28).
- All who had been slaves went free (Leviticus 25:40–41).

Freedom. Joy. Relief. Rest. The Year of Jubilee represented all of these and more. More, in that it symbolized what the Savior would accomplish one day for all of God's people. He would:

- give us rest from the burden of having to save ourselves (Hebrews 4:1–3, 8–9);
- cancel the debt we, by our sins, had incurred (Matthew 18:21–27);
- free us from slavery to sin and to the Law (John 8:34–36);
- make it possible for us to return home to our Father and to stay there forever (Luke 15:11–24; John 14:1–3).

Jesus is our Jubilee! Celebrate Him today! ☼

WEEK 11 • WEDNESDAY

Lev. 26:1—27:34

GET THE BIG PICTURE

Leviticus concludes with promises from God and some possible responses by His people. The Lord pledges Himself to bless the obedient (Leviticus 26:1–13), to punish the disobedient (Leviticus 26:14–39), and to restore the repentant (Leviticus 26:40–46). Chapter 27 brings Leviticus to a close by explaining ways God's people can respond to His goodness. If time is short, focus on Leviticus 26:1–13.

Reward for Obedience

26 " 'Do not make idols or set
up an image or a sacred
stone for yourselves, and do not place
a carved stone in your land to bow
down before it. I am the LORD your God.
2" 'Observe my Sabbaths and have
reverence for my sanctuary. I am the
LORD.
3" 'If you follow my decrees and are
careful to obey my commands, 4I will
send you rain in its season, and the
ground will yield its crops and the trees
of the field their fruit. 5Your threshing
will continue until grape harvest and
the grape harvest will continue until
planting, and you will eat all the food
you want and live in safety in your land.
6" 'I will grant peace in the land, and
you will lie down and no one will make

you afraid. I will remove savage beasts from the land, and the sword will not pass through your country. [7]You will pursue your enemies, and they will fall by the sword before you. [8]Five of you will chase a hundred, and a hundred of you will chase ten thousand, and your enemies will fall by the sword before you.

[9]" 'I will look on you with favor and make you fruitful and increase your numbers, and I will keep my covenant with you. [10]You will still be eating last year's harvest when you will have to move it out to make room for the new. [11]I will put my dwelling place[a] among you, and I will not abhor you. [12]I will walk among you and be your God, and you will be my people. [13]I am the LORD your God, who brought you out of Egypt so that you would no longer be slaves to the Egyptians; I broke the bars of your yoke and enabled you to walk with heads held high.

Punishment for Disobedience

[14]" 'But if you will not listen to me and carry out all these commands, [15]and if you reject my decrees and abhor my laws and fail to carry out all my commands and so violate my covenant, [16]then I will do this to you: I will bring upon you sudden terror, wasting diseases and fever that will destroy your sight and drain away your life. You will plant seed in vain, because your enemies will eat it. [17]I will set my face against you so that you will be defeated by your enemies; those who hate you will rule over you, and you will flee even when no one is pursuing you.

[18]" 'If after all this you will not listen to me, I will punish you for your sins seven times over. [19]I will break down your stubborn pride and make the sky above you like iron and the ground beneath you like bronze. [20]Your strength will be spent in vain, because your soil will not yield its crops, nor will the trees of the land yield their fruit.

[21]" 'If you remain hostile toward me and refuse to listen to me, I will multiply your afflictions seven times over, as your sins deserve. [22]I will send wild animals against you, and they will rob you of your children, destroy your cattle and make you so few in number that your roads will be deserted.

[23]" 'If in spite of these things you do not accept my correction but continue to be hostile toward me, [24]I myself will be hostile toward you and will afflict you for your sins seven times over. [25]And I will bring the sword upon you to avenge the breaking of the covenant. When you withdraw into your cities, I will send a plague among you, and you will be given into enemy hands. [26]When I cut off your supply of bread, ten women will be able to bake your bread in one oven, and they will dole out the bread by weight. You will eat, but you will not be satisfied.

[27]" 'If in spite of this you still do not listen to me but continue to be hostile toward me, [28]then in my anger I will be hostile toward you, and I myself will punish you for your sins seven times over. [29]You will eat the flesh of your sons and the flesh of your daughters. [30]I will destroy your high places, cut down your incense altars and pile your dead bodies on the lifeless forms of your idols, and I will abhor you. [31]I will turn your cities into ruins and lay waste your sanctuaries, and I will take no delight in the pleasing aroma of your offerings. [32]I will lay waste the land, so that your enemies who live there will be appalled. [33]I will scatter you among the nations and will draw out my sword and pursue you. Your land will be laid waste, and your cities will lie in ruins. [34]Then the land will enjoy its sabbath years all the time that it lies desolate and you are in the country of your enemies; then the land will rest and enjoy its sabbaths. [35]All the time that it lies desolate, the land will have the rest it did not have during the sabbaths you lived in it.

[36]" 'As for those of you who are left, I will make their hearts so fearful in the lands of their enemies that the sound of a windblown leaf will put them to flight.

[a]11 Or *my tabernacle*

They will run as though fleeing from
the sword, and they will fall, even
though no one is pursuing them. 37They
will stumble over one another as
though fleeing from the sword, even
though no one is pursuing them. So you
will not be able to stand before your
enemies. 38You will perish among the
nations; the land of your enemies will
devour you. 39Those of you who are left
will waste away in the lands of their
enemies because of their sins; also because of their fathers' sins they will
waste away.

40" 'But if they will confess their sins
and the sins of their fathers—their
treachery against me and their hostility
toward me, 41which made me hostile toward them so that I sent them into the
land of their enemies—then when their
uncircumcised hearts are humbled and
they pay for their sin, 42I will remember
my covenant with Jacob and my covenant with Isaac and my covenant with
Abraham, and I will remember the land.
43For the land will be deserted by them
and will enjoy its sabbaths while it lies
desolate without them. They will pay
for their sins because they rejected my
laws and abhorred my decrees. 44Yet in
spite of this, when they are in the land
of their enemies, I will not reject them
or abhor them so as to destroy them
completely, breaking my covenant with
them. I am the LORD their God. 45But for
their sake I will remember the covenant
with their ancestors whom I brought
out of Egypt in the sight of the nations
to be their God. I am the LORD.' "

46These are the decrees, the laws and
the regulations that the LORD established on Mount Sinai between himself
and the Israelites through Moses.

Redeeming What Is the LORD's

27 The LORD said to Moses,
2"Speak to the Israelites
and say to them: 'If anyone makes a
special vow to dedicate persons to the
LORD by giving equivalent values, 3set
the value of a male between the ages of
twenty and sixty at fifty shekels[a] of silver, according to the sanctuary shekel[b];
4and if it is a female, set her value at
thirty shekels.[c] 5If it is a person between
the ages of five and twenty, set the value
of a male at twenty shekels[d] and of a
female at ten shekels.[e] 6If it is a person
between one month and five years, set
the value of a male at five shekels[f] of
silver and that of a female at three
shekels[g] of silver. 7If it is a person sixty
years old or more, set the value of a male
at fifteen shekels[h] and of a female at ten
shekels. 8If anyone making the vow is
too poor to pay the specified amount, he
is to present the person to the priest,
who will set the value for him according to what the man making the vow
can afford.

9" 'If what he vowed is an animal that
is acceptable as an offering to the LORD,
such an animal given to the LORD becomes holy. 10He must not exchange it or
substitute a good one for a bad one, or
a bad one for a good one; if he should
substitute one animal for another, both
it and the substitute become holy. 11If
what he vowed is a ceremonially unclean animal—one that is not acceptable
as an offering to the LORD—the animal
must be presented to the priest, 12who
will judge its quality as good or bad.
Whatever value the priest then sets, that
is what it will be. 13If the owner wishes
to redeem the animal, he must add a
fifth to its value.

14" 'If a man dedicates his house as
something holy to the LORD, the priest
will judge its quality as good or bad.
Whatever valuc the priest then sets, so
it will remain. 15If the man who dedicates his house redeems it, he must add
a fifth to its value, and the house will
again become his.

16" 'If a man dedicates to the LORD
part of his family land, its value is to be

[a]3 That is, about 1 1/4 pounds (about 0.6 kilogram); also in verse 16 [b]3 That is, about 2/5 ounce (about 11.5 grams); also in verse 25
[c]4 That is, about 12 ounces (about 0.3 kilogram)
[d]5 That is, about 8 ounces (about 0.2 kilogram)
[e]5 That is, about 4 ounces (about 110 grams); also in verse 7 [f]6 That is, about 2 ounces (about 55 grams) [g]6 That is, about 1 1/4 ounces (about 35 grams) [h]7 That is, about 6 ounces (about 170 grams)

set according to the amount of seed required for it—fifty shekels of silver to a homer[a] of barley seed. 17If he dedicates his field during the Year of Jubilee, the value that has been set remains. 18But if he dedicates his field after the Jubilee, the priest will determine the value according to the number of years that remain until the next Year of Jubilee, and its set value will be reduced. 19If the man who dedicates the field wishes to redeem it, he must add a fifth to its value, and the field will again become his. 20If, however, he does not redeem the field, or if he has sold it to someone else, it can never be redeemed. 21When the field is released in the Jubilee, it will become holy, like a field devoted to the LORD; it will become the property of the priests.[b]

22" 'If a man dedicates to the LORD a field he has bought, which is not part of his family land, 23the priest will determine its value up to the Year of Jubilee, and the man must pay its value on that day as something holy to the LORD. 24In the Year of Jubilee the field will revert to the person from whom he bought it, the one whose land it was. 25Every value is to be set according to the sanctuary shekel, twenty gerahs to the shekel.

26" 'No one, however, may dedicate the firstborn of an animal, since the firstborn already belongs to the LORD; whether an ox[c] or a sheep, it is the LORD's. 27If it is one of the unclean animals, he may buy it back at its set value, adding a fifth of the value to it. If he does not redeem it, it is to be sold at its set value.

28" 'But nothing that a man owns and devotes[d] to the LORD—whether man or animal or family land—may be sold or redeemed; everything so devoted is most holy to the LORD.

29" 'No person devoted to destruction[e] may be ransomed; he must be put to death.

30" 'A tithe of everything from the land, whether grain from the soil or fruit from the trees, belongs to the LORD; it is holy to the LORD. 31If a man redeems any of his tithe, he must add a fifth of the value to it. 32The entire tithe of the herd and flock—every tenth animal that passes under the shepherd's rod—will be holy to the LORD. 33He must not pick out the good from the bad or make any substitution. If he does make a substitution, both the animal and its substitute become holy and cannot be redeemed.' "

34These are the commands the LORD gave Moses on Mount Sinai for the Israelites.

[a]*16* That is, probably about 6 bushels (about 220 liters) [b]*21* Or *priest* [c]*26* The Hebrew word can include both male and female. [d]*28* The Hebrew term refers to the irrevocable giving over of things or persons to the LORD. [e]*29* The Hebrew term refers to the irrevocable giving over of things or persons to the LORD, often by totally destroying them.

SHARPEN THE FOCUS

If . . . then. Much of life revolves around if . . . then transactions. If you clean your room, we'll go get ice cream. If you do a good job on this project, you'll get a raise and a bonus. If you pay the bills, I'll cook the dinner.

The covenant God set up with Israel on Mt. Sinai (the "Old Covenant") includes many "if . . . then" features. Today you read one of them.

"If . . . then" promises appeal to us. They're familiar. We coax ourselves into thinking, "I can do that." But the Old Covenant could not accomplish our salvation. Not because it was defective. But because Israel was. And so are we.

Paul tells us what was in God's heart in giving the conditional promises and threats of the Old Covenant; "The law was put in charge to lead us to Christ that we might be justified by faith" (Galatians 3:24). The Law teaches one thing–our need for something besides the Law. And in Christ, God has replaced "if . . . then" with "but now . . . ":

> *But now a righteousness from God, apart from law, has been made known . . . This righteousness from God comes through faith in Jesus Christ to all who believe.* (Romans 3:21–22)

NUMBERS

WEEK 11 • THURSDAY

Numbers 1:1—3:51

As Numbers opens, Israel is still camped at Mt. Sinai. The Lord will soon give the order to move out–toward the Promised Land. Before He does so, He orders a census taken of all the men over the age of 20 who are "able to serve in the army" (Numbers 1:3). The Levites are not counted here; instead, they are to be set aside to help Aaron and the other priests in the service of the tabernacle (Numbers 3:1–51). If time is short, focus on Numbers 2:1–34.

The Census

1 The LORD spoke to Moses in the
Tent of Meeting in the Desert of Sinai on the first day of the second month
of the second year after the Israelites
came out of Egypt. He said: 2"Take a
census of the whole Israelite community
by their clans and families, listing every
man by name, one by one. 3You and
Aaron are to number by their divisions
all the men in Israel twenty years old or
more who are able to serve in the army.
4One man from each tribe, each the
head of his family, is to help you. 5These
are the names of the men who are to
assist you:

from Reuben, Elizur son of Shedeur;
6 from Simeon, Shelumiel son of Zurishaddai;
7 from Judah, Nahshon son of Amminadab;
8 from Issachar, Nethanel son of Zuar;
9 from Zebulun, Eliab son of Helon;
10 from the sons of Joseph:
from Ephraim, Elishama son of Ammihud;
from Manasseh, Gamaliel son of Pedahzur;
11 from Benjamin, Abidan son of Gideoni;
12 from Dan, Ahiezer son of Ammishaddai;
13 from Asher, Pagiel son of Ocran;
14 from Gad, Eliasaph son of Deuel;
15 from Naphtali, Ahira son of Enan."

16These were the men appointed from
the community, the leaders of their ancestral tribes. They were the heads of
the clans of Israel.

17Moses and Aaron took these men
whose names had been given, 18and
they called the whole community together on the first day of the second
month. The people indicated their ancestry by their clans and families, and
the men twenty years old or more were
listed by name, one by one, 19as the
LORD commanded Moses. And so he
counted them in the Desert of Sinai:

20From the descendants of Reuben the
firstborn son of Israel:

All the men twenty years old or more who were able to serve in the army were listed by name, one by one, according to the records of their clans and families. 21The number from the tribe of Reuben was 46,500.

22From the descendants of Simeon:
All the men twenty years old or more who were able to serve in the army were counted and listed by name, one by one, according to the records of their clans and families. 23The number from the tribe of Simeon was 59,300.

24From the descendants of Gad:
All the men twenty years old or more who were able to serve in the army were listed by name, according to the records of their clans and families. 25The number from the tribe of Gad was 45,650.

26From the descendants of Judah:
All the men twenty years old or more who were able to serve in the army were listed by name, according to the records of their clans and families. 27The number from the tribe of Judah was 74,600.

28From the descendants of Issachar:
All the men twenty years old or more who were able to serve in the army were listed by name, according to the records of their clans and families. 29The number from the tribe of Issachar was 54,400.

30From the descendants of Zebulun:
All the men twenty years old or more who were able to serve in the army were listed by name, according to the records of their clans and families. 31The number from the tribe of Zebulun was 57,400.

32From the sons of Joseph:
From the descendants of Ephraim:
All the men twenty years old or more who were able to serve in the army were listed by name, according to the records of their clans and families. 33The number from the tribe of Ephraim was 40,500.

34From the descendants of Manasseh:
All the men twenty years old or more who were able to serve in the army were listed by name, according to the records of their clans and families. 35The number from the tribe of Manasseh was 32,200.

36From the descendants of Benjamin:
All the men twenty years old or more who were able to serve in the army were listed by name, according to the records of their clans and families. 37The number from the tribe of Benjamin was 35,400.

38From the descendants of Dan:
All the men twenty years old or more who were able to serve in the army were listed by name, according to the records of their clans and families. 39The number from the tribe of Dan was 62,700.

40From the descendants of Asher:
All the men twenty years old or more who were able to serve in the army were listed by name, according to the records of their clans and families. 41The number from the tribe of Asher was 41,500.

42From the descendants of Naphtali:
All the men twenty years old or more who were able to serve in the army were listed by name, according to the records of their clans and families. 43The number from the tribe of Naphtali was 53,400.

44These were the men counted by Moses and Aaron and the twelve leaders of Israel, each one representing his family. 45All the Israelites twenty years old or more who were able to serve in Israel's army were counted according to their families. 46The total number was 603,550.

47The families of the tribe of Levi,

however, were not counted along with the others. [48]The LORD had said to Moses: [49]"You must not count the tribe of Levi or include them in the census of the other Israelites. [50]Instead, appoint the Levites to be in charge of the tabernacle of the Testimony—over all its furnishings and everything belonging to it. They are to carry the tabernacle and all its furnishings; they are to take care of it and encamp around it. [51]Whenever the tabernacle is to move, the Levites are to take it down, and whenever the tabernacle is to be set up, the Levites shall do it. Anyone else who goes near it shall be put to death. [52]The Israelites are to set up their tents by divisions, each man in his own camp under his own standard. [53]The Levites, however, are to set up their tents around the tabernacle of the Testimony so that wrath will not fall on the Israelite community. The Levites are to be responsible for the care of the tabernacle of the Testimony."

[54]The Israelites did all this just as the LORD commanded Moses.

The Arrangement of the Tribal Camps

2 The LORD said to Moses and Aaron: [2]"The Israelites are to camp around the Tent of Meeting some distance from it, each man under his standard with the banners of his family."

[3]On the east, toward the sunrise, the divisions of the camp of Judah are to encamp under their standard. The leader of the people of Judah is Nahshon son of Amminadab. [4]His division numbers 74,600.

[5]The tribe of Issachar will camp next to them. The leader of the people of Issachar is Nethanel son of Zuar. [6]His division numbers 54,400.

[7]The tribe of Zebulun will be next. The leader of the people of Zebulun is Eliab son of Helon. [8]His division numbers 57,400.

[9]All the men assigned to the camp of Judah, according to their divisions, number 186,400. They will set out first.

[10]On the south will be the divisions of the camp of Reuben under their standard. The leader of the people of Reuben is Elizur son of Shedeur. [11]His division numbers 46,500.

[12]The tribe of Simeon will camp next to them. The leader of the people of Simeon is Shelumiel son of Zurishaddai. [13]His division numbers 59,300.

[14]The tribe of Gad will be next. The leader of the people of Gad is Eliasaph son of Deuel.[a] [15]His division numbers 45,650.

[16]All the men assigned to the camp of Reuben, according to their divisions, number 151,450. They will set out second.

[17]Then the Tent of Meeting and the camp of the Levites will set out in the middle of the camps. They will set out in the same order as they encamp, each in his own place under his standard.

[18]On the west will be the divisions of the camp of Ephraim under their standard. The leader of the people of Ephraim is Elishama son of Ammihud. [19]His division numbers 40,500.

[20]The tribe of Manasseh will be next to them. The leader of the people of Manasseh is Gamaliel son of Pedahzur. [21]His division numbers 32,200.

[22]The tribe of Benjamin will be next. The leader of the people of Benjamin is Abidan son of Gideoni. [23]His division numbers 35,400.

[24]All the men assigned to the camp of Ephraim, according to their divisions, number 108,100. They will set out third.

[a]*14* Many manuscripts of the Masoretic Text, Samaritan Pentateuch and Vulgate (see also Num. 1:14); most manuscripts of the Masoretic Text *Reuel*

[25]On the north will be the divisions of the camp of Dan, under their standard. The leader of the people of Dan is Ahiezer son of Ammishaddai. [26]His division numbers 62,700.

[27]The tribe of Asher will camp next to them. The leader of the people of Asher is Pagiel son of Ocran. [28]His division numbers 41,500.

[29]The tribe of Naphtali will be next. The leader of the people of Naphtali is Ahira son of Enan. [30]His division numbers 53,400.

[31]All the men assigned to the camp of Dan number 157,600. They will set out last, under their standards.

[32]These are the Israelites, counted according to their families. All those in the camps, by their divisions, number 603,550. [33]The Levites, however, were not counted along with the other Israelites, as the LORD commanded Moses.

[34]So the Israelites did everything the LORD commanded Moses; that is the way they encamped under their standards, and that is the way they set out, each with his clan and family.

The Levites

3 This is the account of the family of Aaron and Moses at the time the LORD talked with Moses on Mount Sinai.

[2]The names of the sons of Aaron were Nadab the firstborn and Abihu, Eleazar and Ithamar. [3]Those were the names of Aaron's sons, the anointed priests, who were ordained to serve as priests. [4]Nadab and Abihu, however, fell dead before the LORD when they made an offering with unauthorized fire before him in the Desert of Sinai. They had no sons; so only Eleazar and Ithamar served as priests during the lifetime of their father Aaron.

[5]The LORD said to Moses, [6]"Bring the tribe of Levi and present them to Aaron the priest to assist him. [7]They are to perform duties for him and for the whole community at the Tent of Meeting by doing the work of the tabernacle. [8]They are to take care of all the furnishings of the Tent of Meeting, fulfilling the obligations of the Israelites by doing the work of the tabernacle. [9]Give the Levites to Aaron and his sons; they are the Israelites who are to be given wholly to him.[a] [10]Appoint Aaron and his sons to serve as priests; anyone else who approaches the sanctuary must be put to death."

[11]The LORD also said to Moses, [12]"I have taken the Levites from among the Israelites in place of the first male offspring of every Israelite woman. The Levites are mine, [13]for all the firstborn are mine. When I struck down all the firstborn in Egypt, I set apart for myself every firstborn in Israel, whether man or animal. They are to be mine. I am the LORD."

[14]The LORD said to Moses in the Desert of Sinai, [15]"Count the Levites by their families and clans. Count every male a month old or more." [16]So Moses counted them, as he was commanded by the word of the LORD.

[17]These were the names of the sons of Levi:
Gershon, Kohath and Merari.
[18]These were the names of the Gershonite clans:
Libni and Shimei.
[19]The Kohathite clans:
Amram, Izhar, Hebron and Uzziel.
[20]The Merarite clans:
Mahli and Mushi.

These were the Levite clans, according to their families.

[21]To Gershon belonged the clans of the Libnites and Shimeites; these were the Gershonite clans. [22]The number of all the males a month old or more who were counted was 7,500. [23]The Gershonite clans were to camp on the west, behind the tabernacle. [24]The leader of

[a]9 Most manuscripts of the Masoretic Text; some manuscripts of the Masoretic Text, Samaritan Pentateuch and Septuagint (see also Num. 8:16) *to me*

the families of the Gershonites was Eliasaph son of Lael. [25]At the Tent of Meeting the Gershonites were responsible for the care of the tabernacle and tent, its coverings, the curtain at the entrance to the Tent of Meeting, [26]the curtains of the courtyard, the curtain at the entrance to the courtyard surrounding the tabernacle and altar, and the ropes—and everything related to their use.

[27]To Kohath belonged the clans of the Amramites, Izharites, Hebronites and Uzzielites; these were the Kohathite clans. [28]The number of all the males a month old or more was 8,600.[a] The Kohathites were responsible for the care of the sanctuary. [29]The Kohathite clans were to camp on the south side of the tabernacle. [30]The leader of the families of the Kohathite clans was Elizaphan son of Uzziel. [31]They were responsible for the care of the ark, the table, the lampstand, the altars, the articles of the sanctuary used in ministering, the curtain, and everything related to their use. [32]The chief leader of the Levites was Eleazar son of Aaron, the priest. He was appointed over those who were responsible for the care of the sanctuary.

[33]To Merari belonged the clans of the Mahlites and the Mushites; these were the Merarite clans. [34]The number of all the males a month old or more who were counted was 6,200. [35]The leader of the families of the Merarite clans was Zuriel son of Abihail; they were to camp on the north side of the tabernacle. [36]The Merarites were appointed to take care of the frames of the tabernacle, its crossbars, posts, bases, all its equipment, and everything related to their use, [37]as well as the posts of the surrounding courtyard with their bases, tent pegs and ropes.

[38]Moses and Aaron and his sons were to camp to the east of the tabernacle, toward the sunrise, in front of the Tent of Meeting. They were responsible for the care of the sanctuary on behalf of the Israelites. Anyone else who approached the sanctuary was to be put to death.

[39]The total number of Levites counted at the LORD's command by Moses and Aaron according to their clans, including every male a month old or more, was 22,000.

[40]The LORD said to Moses, "Count all the firstborn Israelite males who are a month old or more and make a list of their names. [41]Take the Levites for me in place of all the firstborn of the Israelites, and the livestock of the Levites in place of all the firstborn of the livestock of the Israelites. I am the LORD."

[42]So Moses counted all the firstborn of the Israelites, as the LORD commanded him. [43]The total number of firstborn males a month old or more, listed by name, was 22,273.

[44]The LORD also said to Moses, [45]"Take the Levites in place of all the firstborn of Israel, and the livestock of the Levites in place of their livestock. The Levites are to be mine. I am the LORD. [46]To redeem the 273 firstborn Israelites who exceed the number of the Levites, [47]collect five shekels[b] for each one, according to the sanctuary shekel, which weighs twenty gerahs. [48]Give the money for the redemption of the additional Israelites to Aaron and his sons."

[49]So Moses collected the redemption money from those who exceeded the number redeemed by the Levites. [50]From the firstborn of the Israelites he collected silver weighing 1,365 shekels,[c] according to the sanctuary shekel. [51]Moses gave the redemption money to Aaron and his sons, as he was commanded by the word of the LORD.

[a]28 Hebrew; some Septuagint manuscripts *8,300*
[b]47 That is, about 2 ounces (about 55 grams)
[c]50 That is, about 35 pounds (about 15.5 kilograms)

SHARPEN THE FOCUS

Imagine Israel camped in the early morning, the banners of each of the 12 tribes snapping like flags in the sunshine above the camp. The tabernacle lay at the very center, and the people of God pitched their tents around it on all four sides. It must have made quite an impressive sight. Not unlike C. S. Lewis's picture of the holy Christian church in *The Screwtape Letters*:

> *. . . spread out through all time and space and rooted in eternity, terrible as an army with banners.*

Many times the people of God seem, to all outward appearance, to be weak and irrelevant. Nevertheless, we are our Lord's "divisions," His troops. He marches with us into the world as heart-by-heart, we touch lives with the precious Gospel of our Lord Jesus. The victory is already ours because He has won it for us.

Our Deliverer has sounded the trumpet; He has called us to share His life and peace, wholeness and joy, with a world that is dead in sin and at war with the One who is their only hope. He has hung His banner over us—His love (Song of Songs 2:4). Lift that banner high over your life today.

WEEK 11 • FRIDAY

Numbers 4:1—6:27

GET THE BIG PICTURE

Each of the three chapters in today's reading deals with separateness of one kind or another, for one purpose or another. How many kinds of separation or "set-apartness" can you find? Try to determine the purpose that may lie behind each one. If time is short, focus on Numbers 6:1–27.

The Kohathites

4 The LORD said to Moses and Aaron: [2]"Take a census of the Kohathite branch of the Levites by their clans and families. [3]Count all the men from thirty to fifty years of age who come to serve in the work in the Tent of Meeting.

[4]"This is the work of the Kohathites in the Tent of Meeting: the care of the most holy things. [5]When the camp is to move, Aaron and his sons are to go in and take down the shielding curtain and cover the ark of the Testimony with it. [6]Then they are to cover this with hides of sea cows,[a] spread a cloth of solid blue over that and put the poles in place.

[7]"Over the table of the Presence they are to spread a blue cloth and put on it the plates, dishes and bowls, and the jars for drink offerings; the bread that is continually there is to remain on it. [8]Over these they are to spread a scarlet cloth, cover that with hides of sea cows and put its poles in place.

[a]6 That is, dugongs; also in verses 8, 10, 11, 12, 14 and 25

9"They are to take a blue cloth and cover the lampstand that is for light, together with its lamps, its wick trimmers and trays, and all its jars for the oil used to supply it. 10Then they are to wrap it and all its accessories in a covering of hides of sea cows and put it on a carrying frame.

11"Over the gold altar they are to spread a blue cloth and cover that with hides of sea cows and put its poles in place.

12"They are to take all the articles used for ministering in the sanctuary, wrap them in a blue cloth, cover that with hides of sea cows and put them on a carrying frame.

13"They are to remove the ashes from the bronze altar and spread a purple cloth over it. 14Then they are to place on it all the utensils used for ministering at the altar, including the firepans, meat forks, shovels and sprinkling bowls. Over it they are to spread a covering of hides of sea cows and put its poles in place.

15"After Aaron and his sons have finished covering the holy furnishings and all the holy articles, and when the camp is ready to move, the Kohathites are to come to do the carrying. But they must not touch the holy things or they will die. The Kohathites are to carry those things that are in the Tent of Meeting.

16"Eleazar son of Aaron, the priest, is to have charge of the oil for the light, the fragrant incense, the regular grain offering and the anointing oil. He is to be in charge of the entire tabernacle and everything in it, including its holy furnishings and articles."

17The LORD said to Moses and Aaron, 18"See that the Kohathite tribal clans are not cut off from the Levites. 19So that they may live and not die when they come near the most holy things, do this for them: Aaron and his sons are to go into the sanctuary and assign to each man his work and what he is to carry. 20But the Kohathites must not go in to look at the holy things, even for a moment, or they will die."

The Gershonites

21The LORD said to Moses, 22"Take a census also of the Gershonites by their families and clans. 23Count all the men from thirty to fifty years of age who come to serve in the work at the Tent of Meeting.

24"This is the service of the Gershonite clans as they work and carry burdens: 25They are to carry the curtains of the tabernacle, the Tent of Meeting, its covering and the outer covering of hides of sea cows, the curtains for the entrance to the Tent of Meeting, 26the curtains of the courtyard surrounding the tabernacle and altar, the curtain for the entrance, the ropes and all the equipment used in its service. The Gershonites are to do all that needs to be done with these things. 27All their service, whether carrying or doing other work, is to be done under the direction of Aaron and his sons. You shall assign to them as their responsibility all they are to carry. 28This is the service of the Gershonite clans at the Tent of Meeting. Their duties are to be under the direction of Ithamar son of Aaron, the priest.

The Merarites

29"Count the Merarites by their clans and families. 30Count all the men from thirty to fifty years of age who come to serve in the work at the Tent of Meeting. 31This is their duty as they perform service at the Tent of Meeting: to carry the frames of the tabernacle, its crossbars, posts and bases, 32as well as the posts of the surrounding courtyard with their bases, tent pegs, ropes, all their equipment and everything related to their use. Assign to each man the specific things he is to carry. 33This is the service of the Merarite clans as they work at the Tent of Meeting under the direction of Ithamar son of Aaron, the priest."

The Numbering of the Levite Clans

34Moses, Aaron and the leaders of the community counted the Kohathites by their clans and families. 35All the men from thirty to fifty years of age who came to serve in the work in the Tent of Meeting, 36 counted by clans, were 2,750. 37 This was the total of all those in the Kohathite clans who served in the Tent of Meeting. Moses and Aaron counted them according to the LORD's command through Moses.

38 The Gershonites were counted by their clans and families. 39 All the men from thirty to fifty years of age who came to serve in the work at the Tent of Meeting, 40 counted by their clans and families, were 2,630. 41 This was the total of those in the Gershonite clans who served at the Tent of Meeting. Moses and Aaron counted them according to the LORD's command.

42 The Merarites were counted by their clans and families. 43 All the men from thirty to fifty years of age who came to serve in the work at the Tent of Meeting, 44 counted by their clans, were 3,200. 45 This was the total of those in the Merarite clans. Moses and Aaron counted them according to the LORD's command through Moses.

46 So Moses, Aaron and the leaders of Israel counted all the Levites by their clans and families. 47 All the men from thirty to fifty years of age who came to do the work of serving and carrying the Tent of Meeting 48 numbered 8,580. 49 At the LORD's command through Moses, each was assigned his work and told what to carry.

Thus they were counted, as the LORD commanded Moses.

The Purity of the Camp

5 The LORD said to Moses, 2 "Command the Israelites to send away from the camp anyone who has an infectious skin disease[a] or a discharge of any kind, or who is ceremonially unclean because of a dead body. 3 Send away male and female alike; send them outside the camp so they will not defile their camp, where I dwell among them." 4 The Israelites did this; they sent them outside the camp. They did just as the LORD had instructed Moses.

Restitution for Wrongs

5 The LORD said to Moses, 6 "Say to the Israelites: 'When a man or woman wrongs another in any way[b] and so is unfaithful to the LORD, that person is guilty 7 and must confess the sin he has committed. He must make full restitution for his wrong, add one fifth to it and give it all to the person he has wronged. 8 But if that person has no close relative to whom restitution can be made for the wrong, the restitution belongs to the LORD and must be given to the priest, along with the ram with which atonement is made for him. 9 All the sacred contributions the Israelites bring to a priest will belong to him. 10 Each man's sacred gifts are his own, but what he gives to the priest will belong to the priest.' "

The Test for an Unfaithful Wife

11 Then the LORD said to Moses, 12 "Speak to the Israelites and say to them: 'If a man's wife goes astray and is unfaithful to him 13 by sleeping with another man, and this is hidden from her husband and her impurity is undetected (since there is no witness against her and she has not been caught in the act), 14 and if feelings of jealousy come over her husband and he suspects his wife and she is impure—or if he is jealous and suspects her even though she is not impure— 15 then he is to take his wife to the priest. He must also take an offering of a tenth of an ephah[c] of barley flour on her behalf. He must not pour oil on it or put incense on it, because it is a grain offering for jealousy, a reminder offering to draw attention to guilt.

16 " 'The priest shall bring her and have her stand before the LORD. 17 Then he shall take some holy water in a clay jar and put some dust from the tabernacle floor into the water. 18 After the priest

[a]2 Traditionally *leprosy;* the Hebrew word was used for various diseases affecting the skin—not necessarily leprosy. [b]6 Or *woman commits any wrong common to mankind* [c]15 That is, probably about 2 quarts (about 2 liters)

has had the woman stand before the LORD, he shall loosen her hair and place in her hands the reminder offering, the grain offering for jealousy, while he himself holds the bitter water that brings a curse. 19Then the priest shall put the woman under oath and say to her, "If no other man has slept with you and you have not gone astray and become impure while married to your husband, may this bitter water that brings a curse not harm you. 20But if you have gone astray while married to your husband and you have defiled yourself by sleeping with a man other than your husband"— 21here the priest is to put the woman under this curse of the oath—"may the LORD cause your people to curse and denounce you when he causes your thigh to waste away and your abdomen to swell.[a] 22May this water that brings a curse enter your body so that your abdomen swells and your thigh wastes away.[b]"

" 'Then the woman is to say, "Amen. So be it."

23" 'The priest is to write these curses on a scroll and then wash them off into the bitter water. 24He shall have the woman drink the bitter water that brings a curse, and this water will enter her and cause bitter suffering. 25The priest is to take from her hands the grain offering for jealousy, wave it before the LORD and bring it to the altar. 26The priest is then to take a handful of the grain offering as a memorial offering and burn it on the altar; after that, he is to have the woman drink the water. 27If she has defiled herself and been unfaithful to her husband, then when she is made to drink the water that brings a curse, it will go into her and cause bitter suffering; her abdomen will swell and her thigh waste away,[c] and she will become accursed among her people. 28If, however, the woman has not defiled herself and is free from impurity, she will be cleared of guilt and will be able to have children.

29" 'This, then, is the law of jealousy when a woman goes astray and defiles herself while married to her husband, 30or when feelings of jealousy come over a man because he suspects his wife. The priest is to have her stand before the LORD and is to apply this entire law to her. 31The husband will be innocent of any wrongdoing, but the woman will bear the consequences of her sin.' "

The Nazirite

6 The LORD said to Moses, 2"Speak to the Israelites and say to them: 'If a man or woman wants to make a special vow, a vow of separation to the LORD as a Nazirite, 3he must abstain from wine and other fermented drink and must not drink vinegar made from wine or from other fermented drink. He must not drink grape juice or eat grapes or raisins. 4As long as he is a Nazirite, he must not eat anything that comes from the grapevine, not even the seeds or skins.

5" 'During the entire period of his vow of separation no razor may be used on his head. He must be holy until the period of his separation to the LORD is over; he must let the hair of his head grow long. 6Throughout the period of his separation to the LORD he must not go near a dead body. 7Even if his own father or mother or brother or sister dies, he must not make himself ceremonially unclean on account of them, because the symbol of his separation to God is on his head. 8Throughout the period of his separation he is consecrated to the LORD.

9" 'If someone dies suddenly in his presence, thus defiling the hair he has dedicated, he must shave his head on the day of his cleansing—the seventh day. 10Then on the eighth day he must bring two doves or two young pigeons to the priest at the entrance to the Tent of Meeting. 11The priest is to offer one as a sin offering and the other as a burnt offering to make atonement for him because he sinned by being in the

[a]21 Or *causes you to have a miscarrying womb and barrenness* [b]22 Or *body and cause you to be barren and have a miscarrying womb* [c]27 Or *suffering; she will have barrenness and a miscarrying womb*

presence of the dead body. That same day he is to consecrate his head. [12]He must dedicate himself to the LORD for the period of his separation and must bring a year-old male lamb as a guilt offering. The previous days do not count, because he became defiled during his separation.

[13]" 'Now this is the law for the Nazirite when the period of his separation is over. He is to be brought to the entrance to the Tent of Meeting. [14]There he is to present his offerings to the LORD: a year-old male lamb without defect for a burnt offering, a year-old ewe lamb without defect for a sin offering, a ram without defect for a fellowship offering,[a] [15]together with their grain offerings and drink offerings, and a basket of bread made without yeast—cakes made of fine flour mixed with oil, and wafers spread with oil.

[16]" 'The priest is to present them before the LORD and make the sin offering and the burnt offering. [17]He is to present the basket of unleavened bread and is to sacrifice the ram as a fellowship offering to the LORD, together with its grain offering and drink offering.

[18]" 'Then at the entrance to the Tent of Meeting, the Nazirite must shave off the hair that he dedicated. He is to take the hair and put it in the fire that is under the sacrifice of the fellowship offering.

[19]" 'After the Nazirite has shaved off the hair of his dedication, the priest is to place in his hands a boiled shoulder of the ram, and a cake and a wafer from the basket, both made without yeast. [20]The priest shall then wave them before the LORD as a wave offering; they are holy and belong to the priest, together with the breast that was waved and the thigh that was presented. After that, the Nazirite may drink wine.

[21]" 'This is the law of the Nazirite who vows his offering to the LORD in accordance with his separation, in addition to whatever else he can afford. He must fulfill the vow he has made, according to the law of the Nazirite.' "

The Priestly Blessing

[22]The LORD said to Moses, [23]"Tell Aaron and his sons, 'This is how you are to bless the Israelites. Say to them:

[24]" ' "The LORD bless you
and keep you;
[25]the LORD make his face shine upon you
and be gracious to you;
[26]the LORD turn his face toward you
and give you peace." '

[27]"So they will put my name on the Israelites, and I will bless them."

[a]14 Traditionally *peace offering;* also in verses 17 and 18

SHARPEN THE FOCUS

Week after week since the time of Moses, God's representatives have spoken the Lord's blessings over His people (Numbers 6:22–27). In all those centuries, the words have been translated into hundreds of languages, but not changed in meaning at all:

The LORD bless you and keep you—preserve your body and your soul with every good and perfect gift you need for your total well-being.

The LORD make His face shine upon you and be gracious to you—smile in love and forgiveness toward you and show you His compassion for all your distresses and hurts.

The LORD turn His face toward you and give you peace—give you His peace *(shalom)*, the sum total of all the good things He establishes for His people, especially in Christ, our Savior.

All these benefits can be summed up in the name of the Lord—the Savior-God, Yahweh (Jehovah). In His name, in His Word, and by His promises in Christ Jesus, each and every one of these blessings come to us and remain on us. We are blessed!

While most Nazirites dedicated themselves to God for a specific period of time, several biblical characters lived as Nazirites their whole lives. Samson may well have been the most famous (Judges 13:1–7, 14, 24). John the Baptizer also lived as a Nazirite (Luke 1:11–17). Samuel, too, likely lived this set-apart lifestyle (1 Samuel 1:11). While not priests, Nazirites dedicated themselves to God's service and to a lifestyle of purity.

Each tribe gave the same exact offerings for the use of the Levites as they served in the tabernacle and in transporting it (Numbers 7). Nevertheless, the Lord in grace noted and recorded each gift separately. Each came as an offering from the hearts of His precious children! The Levites, in turn, were His gifts back to Aaron and the priests who could not do all the work of worship themselves (Numbers 8:18), and to the nation as a whole. If time is short, focus on Numbers 8:1–20.

Offerings at the Dedication of the Tabernacle

7 When Moses finished setting up
the tabernacle, he anointed it
and consecrated it and all its furnishings. He also anointed and consecrated
the altar and all its utensils. 2Then the
leaders of Israel, the heads of families
who were the tribal leaders in charge of
those who were counted, made offerings. 3They brought as their gifts before
the LORD six covered carts and twelve
oxen—an ox from each leader and a cart
from every two. These they presented
before the tabernacle.
4The LORD said to Moses, 5"Accept
these from them, that they may be used
in the work at the Tent of Meeting. Give
them to the Levites as each man's work
requires."
6So Moses took the carts and oxen and
gave them to the Levites. 7He gave two
carts and four oxen to the Gershonites,
as their work required, 8and he gave
four carts and eight oxen to the Merarites, as their work required. They were
all under the direction of Ithamar son of
Aaron, the priest. 9But Moses did not
give any to the Kohathites, because they
were to carry on their shoulders the
holy things, for which they were responsible.
10When the altar was anointed, the
leaders brought their offerings for its
dedication and presented them before
the altar. 11For the LORD had said to Moses, "Each day one leader is to bring his
offering for the dedication of the altar."
12The one who brought his offering on
the first day was Nahshon son of Amminadab of the tribe of Judah.
13His offering was one silver plate
weighing a hundred and thirty
shekels,[a] and one silver sprinkling
bowl weighing seventy shekels,[b]
both according to the sanctuary
shekel, each filled with fine flour

[a]13 That is, about 3 1/4 pounds (about 1.5 kilograms); also elsewhere in this chapter
[b]13 That is, about 1 3/4 pounds (about 0.8 kilogram); also elsewhere in this chapter

mixed with oil as a grain offering;
14 one gold dish weighing ten
shekels,[a] filled with incense; 15 one
young bull, one ram and one male
lamb a year old, for a burnt offering; 16 one male goat for a sin offering; 17 and two oxen, five rams, five
male goats and five male lambs a
year old, to be sacrificed as a
fellowship offering.[b] This was the
offering of Nahshon son of Amminadab.

18 On the second day Nethanel son of
Zuar, the leader of Issachar, brought his
offering.
19 The offering he brought was one
silver plate weighing a hundred
and thirty shekels, and one silver
sprinkling bowl weighing seventy
shekels, both according to the sanctuary shekel, each filled with fine
flour mixed with oil as a grain offering; 20 one gold dish weighing ten
shekels, filled with incense; 21 one
young bull, one ram and one male
lamb a year old, for a burnt offering; 22 one male goat for a sin offering; 23 and two oxen, five rams, five
male goats and five male lambs a
year old, to be sacrificed as a fellowship offering. This was the offering
of Nethanel son of Zuar.

24 On the third day, Eliab son of Helon,
the leader of the people of Zebulun,
brought his offering.
25 His offering was one silver plate
weighing a hundred and thirty
shekels, and one silver sprinkling
bowl weighing seventy shekels,
both according to the sanctuary
shekel, each filled with fine flour
mixed with oil as a grain offering;
26 one gold dish weighing ten shekels, filled with incense; 27 one young
bull, one ram and one male lamb a
year old, for a burnt offering; 28 one
male goat for a sin offering; 29 and
two oxen, five rams, five male goats
and five male lambs a year old, to
be sacrificed as a fellowship offering. This was the offering of Eliab
son of Helon.

30 On the fourth day Elizur son of Shedeur, the leader of the people of Reuben,
brought his offering.
31 His offering was one silver plate
weighing a hundred and thirty
shekels, and one silver sprinkling
bowl weighing seventy shekels,
both according to the sanctuary
shekel, each filled with fine flour
mixed with oil as a grain offering;
32 one gold dish weighing ten shekels, filled with incense; 33 one young
bull, one ram and one male lamb a
year old, for a burnt offering; 34 one
male goat for a sin offering; 35 and
two oxen, five rams, five male goats
and five male lambs a year old, to
be sacrificed as a fellowship offering. This was the offering of Elizur
son of Shedeur.

36 On the fifth day Shelumiel son of Zurishaddai, the leader of the people of
Simeon, brought his offering.
37 His offering was one silver plate
weighing a hundred and thirty
shekels, and one silver sprinkling
bowl weighing seventy shekels,
both according to the sanctuary
shekel, each filled with fine flour
mixed with oil as a grain offering;
38 one gold dish weighing ten shekels, filled with incense; 39 one young
bull, one ram and one male lamb a
year old, for a burnt offering; 40 one
male goat for a sin offering; 41 and
two oxen, five rams, five male goats
and five male lambs a year old, to
be sacrificed as a fellowship offering. This was the offering of Shelumiel son of Zurishaddai.

42 On the sixth day Eliasaph son of Deuel, the leader of the people of Gad,
brought his offering.
43 His offering was one silver plate
weighing a hundred and thirty
shekels, and one silver sprinkling
bowl weighing seventy shekels,
both according to the sanctuary

[a] *14* That is, about 4 ounces (about 110 grams); also elsewhere in this chapter [b] *17* Traditionally *peace offering*; also elsewhere in this chapter

shekel, each filled with fine flour
mixed with oil as a grain offering;
44one gold dish weighing ten shekels, filled with incense; 45one young
bull, one ram and one male lamb a
year old, for a burnt offering; 46one
male goat for a sin offering; 47and
two oxen, five rams, five male goats
and five male lambs a year old, to
be sacrificed as a fellowship offering. This was the offering of Eliasaph son of Deuel.

48On the seventh day Elishama son of
Ammihud, the leader of the people of
Ephraim, brought his offering.

49His offering was one silver plate
weighing a hundred and thirty
shekels, and one silver sprinkling
bowl weighing seventy shekels,
both according to the sanctuary
shekel, each filled with fine flour
mixed with oil as a grain offering;
50one gold dish weighing ten shekels, filled with incense; 51one young
bull, one ram and one male lamb a
year old, for a burnt offering; 52one
male goat for a sin offering; 53and
two oxen, five rams, five male goats
and five male lambs a year old, to
be sacrificed as a fellowship offering. This was the offering of Elishama son of Ammihud.

54On the eighth day Gamaliel son of Pedahzur, the leader of the people of Manasseh, brought his offering.

55His offering was one silver plate
weighing a hundred and thirty
shekels, and one silver sprinkling
bowl weighing seventy shekels,
both according to the sanctuary
shekel, each filled with fine flour
mixed with oil as a grain offering;
56one gold dish weighing ten shekels, filled with incense; 57one young
bull, one ram and one male lamb a
year old, for a burnt offering; 58one
male goat for a sin offering; 59and
two oxen, five rams, five male goats
and five male lambs a year old, to
be sacrificed as a fellowship offering. This was the offering of Gamaliel son of Pedahzur.

60On the ninth day Abidan son of Gideoni, the leader of the people of Benjamin, brought his offering.

61His offering was one silver plate
weighing a hundred and thirty
shekels, and one silver sprinkling
bowl weighing seventy shekels,
both according to the sanctuary
shekel, each filled with fine flour
mixed with oil as a grain offering;
62one gold dish weighing ten shekels, filled with incense; 63one young
bull, one ram and one male lamb a
year old, for a burnt offering; 64one
male goat for a sin offering; 65and
two oxen, five rams, five male goats
and five male lambs a year old, to
be sacrificed as a fellowship offering. This was the offering of Abidan
son of Gideoni.

66On the tenth day Ahiezer son of Ammishaddai, the leader of the people of
Dan, brought his offering.

67His offering was one silver plate
weighing a hundred and thirty
shekels, and one silver sprinkling
bowl weighing seventy shekels,
both according to the sanctuary
shekel, each filled with fine flour
mixed with oil as a grain offering;
68one gold dish weighing ten shekels, filled with incense; 69one young
bull, one ram and one male lamb a
year old, for a burnt offering; 70one
male goat for a sin offering; 71and
two oxen, five rams, five male goats
and five male lambs a year old, to
be sacrificed as a fellowship offering. This was the offering of Ahiezer son of Ammishaddai.

72On the eleventh day Pagiel son of Ocran, the leader of the people of Asher,
brought his offering.

73His offering was one silver plate
weighing a hundred and thirty
shekels, and one silver sprinkling
bowl weighing seventy shekels,
both according to the sanctuary
shekel, each filled with fine flour
mixed with oil as a grain offering;
74one gold dish weighing ten shekels, filled with incense; 75one young

bull, one ram and one male lamb a year old, for a burnt offering; 76one male goat for a sin offering; 77and two oxen, five rams, five male goats and five male lambs a year old, to be sacrificed as a fellowship offering. This was the offering of Pagiel son of Ocran.

78On the twelfth day Ahira son of Enan, the leader of the people of Naphtali, brought his offering.

79His offering was one silver plate weighing a hundred and thirty shekels, and one silver sprinkling bowl weighing seventy shekels, both according to the sanctuary shekel, each filled with fine flour mixed with oil as a grain offering; 80one gold dish weighing ten shekels, filled with incense; 81one young bull, one ram and one male lamb a year old, for a burnt offering; 82one male goat for a sin offering; 83and two oxen, five rams, five male goats and five male lambs a year old, to be sacrificed as a fellowship offering. This was the offering of Ahira son of Enan.

84These were the offerings of the Israelite leaders for the dedication of the altar when it was anointed: twelve silver plates, twelve silver sprinkling bowls and twelve gold dishes. 85Each silver plate weighed a hundred and thirty shekels, and each sprinkling bowl seventy shekels. Altogether, the silver dishes weighed two thousand four hundred shekels,[a] according to the sanctuary shekel. 86The twelve gold dishes filled with incense weighed ten shekels each, according to the sanctuary shekel. Altogether, the gold dishes weighed a hundred and twenty shekels.[b] 87The total number of animals for the burnt offering came to twelve young bulls, twelve rams and twelve male lambs a year old, together with their grain offering. Twelve male goats were used for the sin offering. 88The total number of animals for the sacrifice of the fellowship offering came to twenty-four oxen, sixty rams, sixty male goats and sixty male lambs a year old. These were the offerings for the dedication of the altar after it was anointed.

89When Moses entered the Tent of Meeting to speak with the LORD, he heard the voice speaking to him from between the two cherubim above the atonement cover on the ark of the Testimony. And he spoke with him.

Setting Up the Lamps

8 The LORD said to Moses, 2"Speak to Aaron and say to him, 'When you set up the seven lamps, they are to light the area in front of the lampstand.' "

3Aaron did so; he set up the lamps so that they faced forward on the lampstand, just as the LORD commanded Moses. 4This is how the lampstand was made: It was made of hammered gold—from its base to its blossoms. The lampstand was made exactly like the pattern the LORD had shown Moses.

The Setting Apart of the Levites

5The LORD said to Moses: 6"Take the Levites from among the other Israelites and make them ceremonially clean. 7To purify them, do this: Sprinkle the water of cleansing on them; then have them shave their whole bodies and wash their clothes, and so purify themselves. 8Have them take a young bull with its grain offering of fine flour mixed with oil; then you are to take a second young bull for a sin offering. 9Bring the Levites to the front of the Tent of Meeting and assemble the whole Israelite community. 10You are to bring the Levites before the LORD, and the Israelites are to lay their hands on them. 11Aaron is to present the Levites before the LORD as a wave offering from the Israelites, so that they may be ready to do the work of the LORD.

12"After the Levites lay their hands on the heads of the bulls, use the one for a sin offering to the LORD and the other

[a]*85* That is, about 60 pounds (about 28 kilograms) [b]*86* That is, about 3 pounds (about 1.4 kilograms)

for a burnt offering, to make atonement
for the Levites. 13Have the Levites stand
in front of Aaron and his sons and then
present them as a wave offering to the
LORD. 14In this way you are to set the Levites apart from the other Israelites, and
the Levites will be mine.
15"After you have purified the Levites
and presented them as a wave offering,
they are to come to do their work at the
Tent of Meeting. 16They are the Israelites
who are to be given wholly to me. I have
taken them as my own in place of the
firstborn, the first male offspring from
every Israelite woman. 17Every firstborn
male in Israel, whether man or animal,
is mine. When I struck down all the firstborn in Egypt, I set them apart for myself. 18And I have taken the Levites in
place of all the firstborn sons in Israel.
19Of all the Israelites, I have given the
Levites as gifts to Aaron and his sons to
do the work at the Tent of Meeting on
behalf of the Israelites and to make
atonement for them so that no plague
will strike the Israelites when they go
near the sanctuary."
20Moses, Aaron and the whole Israelite community did with the Levites just
as the LORD commanded Moses. 21The
Levites purified themselves and
washed their clothes. Then Aaron presented them as a wave offering before
the LORD and made atonement for them
to purify them. 22After that, the Levites
came to do their work at the Tent of
Meeting under the supervision of Aaron
and his sons. They did with the Levites
just as the LORD commanded Moses.
23The LORD said to Moses, 24"This applies to the Levites: Men twenty-five
years old or more shall come to take part
in the work at the Tent of Meeting, 25but
at the age of fifty, they must retire from
their regular service and work no longer.
26They may assist their brothers in performing their duties at the Tent of Meeting, but they themselves must not do the
work. This, then, is how you are to assign the responsibilities of the Levites."

SHARPEN THE FOCUS

"He thinks he's God's gift to humanity." Most often, we say words like these in disgust, offended by an arrogant or otherwise obnoxious attitude in someone we dislike. That can't change the fact, however, that the Lord *does* give some of His gifts to us in the form of people:

> *It was [Christ] who gave some to be apostles, some to be prophets, some to be evangelists, and some to be pastors and teachers, to prepare God's people for works of service, so that the body of Christ may be built up.* (Ephesians 4:11–12)

For which particular people-gifts in the church do you feel most thankful? Why not jot a note or pick up the phone to thank those people-gifts today? Don't stop with a general "thank you" statement; instead give one or two examples of ways you've been strengthened through the ministry you've received.

WEEK 12 • MONDAY

Numbers 9:1—10:36

GET THE BIG PICTURE

Israel has been camped at the base of Mt. Sinai for about a year. As the people prepare to break camp, they celebrate the Passover. Then the pillar of cloud lifts, and the nation marches out toward the Promised Land. The tribe of Judah leads the way–its standard (banner) shining in the sun (Numbers 10:14). If time is short, focus on Numbers 10:11-36.

The Passover

9 The LORD spoke to Moses in the Desert of Sinai in the first month of the second year after they came out of Egypt. He said, [2]"Have the Israelites celebrate the Passover at the appointed time. [3]Celebrate it at the appointed time, at twilight on the fourteenth day of this month, in accordance with all its rules and regulations."

[4]So Moses told the Israelites to celebrate the Passover, [5]and they did so in the Desert of Sinai at twilight on the fourteenth day of the first month. The Israelites did everything just as the LORD commanded Moses.

[6]But some of them could not celebrate the Passover on that day because they were ceremonially unclean on account of a dead body. So they came to Moses and Aaron that same day [7]and said to Moses, "We have become unclean because of a dead body, but why should we be kept from presenting the LORD's offering with the other Israelites at the appointed time?"

[8]Moses answered them, "Wait until I find out what the LORD commands concerning you."

[9]Then the LORD said to Moses, [10]"Tell the Israelites: 'When any of you or your descendants are unclean because of a dead body or are away on a journey, they may still celebrate the LORD's Passover. [11]They are to celebrate it on the fourteenth day of the second month at twilight. They are to eat the lamb, together with unleavened bread and bitter herbs. [12]They must not leave any of it till morning or break any of its bones. When they celebrate the Passover, they must follow all the regulations. [13]But if a man who is ceremonially clean and not on a journey fails to celebrate the Passover, that person must be cut off from his people because he did not present the LORD's offering at the appointed time. That man will bear the consequences of his sin.

[14]" 'An alien living among you who wants to celebrate the LORD's Passover must do so in accordance with its rules and regulations. You must have the same regulations for the alien and the native-born.' "

The Cloud Above the Tabernacle

[15]On the day the tabernacle, the Tent of the Testimony, was set up, the cloud covered it. From evening till morning the cloud above the tabernacle looked like fire. [16]That is how it continued to be; the cloud covered it, and at night it looked like fire. [17]Whenever the cloud lifted from above the Tent, the Israelites set out; wherever the cloud settled, the Israelites encamped. [18]At the LORD's command the Israelites set out, and at his command they encamped. As long as the cloud stayed over the tabernacle, they remained in camp. [19]When the cloud remained over the tabernacle a long time, the Israelites obeyed the LORD's order and did not set out.

20Sometimes the cloud was over the tabernacle only a few days; at the LORD's
command they would encamp, and
then at his command they would set
out. 21Sometimes the cloud stayed only
from evening till morning, and when it
lifted in the morning, they set out.
Whether by day or by night, whenever
the cloud lifted, they set out. 22Whether
the cloud stayed over the tabernacle for
two days or a month or a year, the Israelites would remain in camp and not set
out; but when it lifted, they would set
out. 23At the LORD's command they encamped, and at the LORD's command
they set out. They obeyed the LORD's
order, in accordance with his command
through Moses.

The Silver Trumpets

10 The LORD said to Moses:
2"Make two trumpets of
hammered silver, and use them for calling the community together and for
having the camps set out. 3When both
are sounded, the whole community is to
assemble before you at the entrance to
the Tent of Meeting. 4If only one is
sounded, the leaders—the heads of the
clans of Israel—are to assemble before
you. 5When a trumpet blast is sounded,
the tribes camping on the east are to set
out. 6At the sounding of a second blast,
the camps on the south are to set out.
The blast will be the signal for setting
out. 7To gather the assembly, blow the
trumpets, but not with the same signal.
8"The sons of Aaron, the priests, are to
blow the trumpets. This is to be a lasting ordinance for you and the generations to come. 9When you go into battle
in your own land against an enemy who
is oppressing you, sound a blast on the
trumpets. Then you will be remembered by the LORD your God and rescued from your enemies. 10Also at your
times of rejoicing—your appointed
feasts and New Moon festivals—you are
to sound the trumpets over your burnt
offerings and fellowship offerings,[a]
and they will be a memorial for you
before your God. I am the LORD your
God."

The Israelites Leave Sinai

11On the twentieth day of the second
month of the second year, the cloud lifted from above the tabernacle of the Testimony. 12Then the Israelites set out from
the Desert of Sinai and traveled from
place to place until the cloud came to
rest in the Desert of Paran. 13They set
out, this first time, at the LORD's command through Moses.
14The divisions of the camp of Judah
went first, under their standard. Nahshon son of Amminadab was in command. 15Nethanel son of Zuar was over
the division of the tribe of Issachar, 16and
Eliab son of Helon was over the division
of the tribe of Zebulun. 17Then the tabernacle was taken down, and the Gershonites and Merarites, who carried it,
set out.
18The divisions of the camp of Reuben
went next, under their standard. Elizur
son of Shedeur was in command. 19She-
lumiel son of Zurishaddai was over the
division of the tribe of Simeon, 20and Eliasaph son of Deuel was over the division of the tribe of Gad. 21Then the
Kohathites set out, carrying the holy
things. The tabernacle was to be set up
before they arrived.
22The divisions of the camp of Ephraim went next, under their standard.
Elishama son of Ammihud was in command. 23Gamaliel son of Pedahzur was
over the division of the tribe of Manasseh, 24and Abidan son of Gideoni was
over the division of the tribe of Benjamin.
25Finally, as the rear guard for all the
units, the divisions of the camp of Dan
set out, under their standard. Ahiezer
son of Ammishaddai was in command.
26Pagiel son of Ocran was over the division of the tribe of Asher, 27and Ahira son
of Enan was over the division of the
tribe of Naphtali. 28This was the order of
march for the Israelite divisions as they
set out.
29Now Moses said to Hobab son of
Reuel the Midianite, Moses' father-in-

[a]10 Traditionally *peace offerings*

law, "We are setting out for the place
about which the LORD said, 'I will give
it to you.' Come with us and we will
treat you well, for the LORD has promised good things to Israel."
30He answered, "No, I will not go; I
am going back to my own land and my
own people."
31But Moses said, "Please do not leave
us. You know where we should camp in
the desert, and you can be our eyes. 32If
you come with us, we will share with
you whatever good things the LORD
gives us."
33So they set out from the mountain
of the LORD and traveled for three days.
The ark of the covenant of the LORD
went before them during those three
days to find them a place to rest. 34The
cloud of the LORD was over them by day
when they set out from the camp.
35Whenever the ark set out, Moses
said,

"Rise up, O LORD!
May your enemies be scattered;
may your foes flee before you."

36Whenever it came to rest, he said,

"Return, O LORD,
to the countless thousands of
Israel."

SHARPEN THE FOCUS

As you begin new tasks, face new challenges, take up new opportunities, do you begin with praise to the Lord, the One who has chosen, delivered, and forgiven you? the One who has, in His cross, given you a new life and a reason to live? The name *Judah* means "praise." In a very literal sense, praise led the way, as Israel marched through the desert to Canaan. Focused on the cloud of God's glory that sheltered them from the desert sun, the people had every reason to praise their Savior-God. He had, after all, "promised good things to Israel" (Numbers 10:29). And, what He promised, He was able to perform (see Romans 4:21).

What new project lies ahead of you right now? Maybe your new beginning involves something as simple as a new day. Or maybe you're beginning a new career, a new family, or life in a new city. Regardless, you can begin in confidence and praise because your Lord is faithful.

WEEK 12 • TUESDAY

Numbers 11:1—12:16

GET THE BIG PICTURE

The people tire of God's provision and grumble because He has not—in their opinion—done a good job in caring for them. Moses takes these complaints personally and goes to the Lord in near despair. In love, the Lord helps Moses and feeds His people in a miraculous way. As the reading closes, He also reaffirms His choice of Moses to lead Israel despite the jealousies of Miriam and Aaron. If time is short, focus on Numbers 11:1–35.

Fire From the LORD

11 Now the people complained about their hardships in the hearing of the LORD, and when he heard them his anger was aroused. Then fire from the LORD burned among them and consumed some of the outskirts of the camp. 2When the people cried out to Moses, he prayed to the LORD and the fire died down. 3So that place was called Taberah,[a] because fire from the LORD had burned among them.

Quail From the LORD

4The rabble with them began to crave other food, and again the Israelites started wailing and said, "If only we had meat to eat! 5We remember the fish we ate in Egypt at no cost—also the cucumbers, melons, leeks, onions and garlic. 6But now we have lost our appetite; we never see anything but this manna!"

7The manna was like coriander seed and looked like resin. 8The people went around gathering it, and then ground it in a handmill or crushed it in a mortar. They cooked it in a pot or made it into cakes. And it tasted like something made with olive oil. 9When the dew settled on the camp at night, the manna also came down.

10Moses heard the people of every family wailing, each at the entrance to his tent. The LORD became exceedingly angry, and Moses was troubled. 11He asked the LORD, "Why have you brought this trouble on your servant? What have I done to displease you that you put the burden of all these people on me? 12Did I conceive all these people? Did I give them birth? Why do you tell me to carry them in my arms, as a nurse carries an infant, to the land you promised on oath to their forefathers? 13Where can I get meat for all these people? They keep wailing to me, 'Give us meat to eat!' 14I cannot carry all these people by myself; the burden is too heavy for me. 15If this is how you are going to treat me, put me to death right now—if I have found favor in your eyes—and do not let me face my own ruin."

16The LORD said to Moses: "Bring me seventy of Israel's elders who are known to you as leaders and officials among the people. Have them come to the Tent of Meeting, that they may stand there with you. 17I will come down and speak with you there, and I will take of the Spirit that is on you and put the Spirit on them. They will help you carry the burden of the people so that you will not have to carry it alone.

18"Tell the people: 'Consecrate yourselves in preparation for tomorrow, when you will eat meat. The LORD heard you when you wailed, "If only we had meat to eat! We were better off in Egypt!" Now the LORD will give you meat, and you will eat it. 19You will not eat it for just one day, or two days, or five, ten or twenty days, 20but for a whole month—until it comes out of your nostrils and you loathe it—because you have rejected the LORD, who is among you, and have wailed before him, saying, "Why did we ever leave Egypt?"'"

21But Moses said, "Here I am among six hundred thousand men on foot, and you say, 'I will give them meat to eat for a whole month!' 22Would they have enough if flocks and herds were slaughtered for them? Would they have enough if all the fish in the sea were caught for them?"

23The LORD answered Moses, "Is the LORD's arm too short? You will now see whether or not what I say will come true for you."

24So Moses went out and told the people what the LORD had said. He brought together seventy of their elders and had them stand around the Tent. 25Then the LORD came down in the cloud and spoke with him, and he took of the Spirit that was on him and put the Spirit on the seventy elders. When the Spirit rested on them, they prophesied, but they did not do so again.[b]

[a]3 *Taberah* means *burning.* [b]25 Or *prophesied and continued to do so*

26However, two men, whose names
were Eldad and Medad, had remained
in the camp. They were listed among
the elders, but did not go out to the Tent.
Yet the Spirit also rested on them, and
they prophesied in the camp. 27A young
man ran and told Moses, "Eldad and
Medad are prophesying in the camp."
28Joshua son of Nun, who had been
Moses' aide since youth, spoke up and
said, "Moses, my lord, stop them!"
29But Moses replied, "Are you jealous
for my sake? I wish that all the LORD's
people were prophets and that the
LORD would put his Spirit on them!"
30Then Moses and the elders of Israel
returned to the camp.
31Now a wind went out from the
LORD and drove quail in from the sea.
It brought them[a] down all around the
camp to about three feet[b] above the
ground, as far as a day's walk in any direction. 32All that day and night and all
the next day the people went out and
gathered quail. No one gathered less
than ten homers.[c] Then they spread
them out all around the camp. 33But
while the meat was still between their
teeth and before it could be consumed,
the anger of the LORD burned against
the people, and he struck them with a
severe plague. 34Therefore the place was
named Kibroth Hattaavah,[d] because
there they buried the people who had
craved other food.
35From Kibroth Hattaavah the people
traveled to Hazeroth and stayed there.

Miriam and Aaron Oppose Moses

12 Miriam and Aaron began to
talk against Moses because of
his Cushite wife, for he had married a
Cushite. 2"Has the LORD spoken only
through Moses?" they asked. "Hasn't he
also spoken through us?" And the LORD
heard this.
3(Now Moses was a very humble
man, more humble than anyone else on
the face of the earth.)
4At once the LORD said to Moses, Aaron and Miriam, "Come out to the Tent
of Meeting, all three of you." So the
three of them came out. 5Then the LORD
came down in a pillar of cloud; he stood
at the entrance to the Tent and summoned Aaron and Miriam. When both
of them stepped forward, 6he said, "Listen to my words:

"When a prophet of the LORD is
among you,
I reveal myself to him in visions,
I speak to him in dreams.
7But this is not true of my servant
Moses;
he is faithful in all my house.
8With him I speak face to face,
clearly and not in riddles;
he sees the form of the LORD.
Why then were you not afraid
to speak against my servant
Moses?"

9The anger of the LORD burned
against them, and he left them.
10When the cloud lifted from above
the Tent, there stood Miriam—leprous,[e]
like snow. Aaron turned toward her and
saw that she had leprosy; 11and he said
to Moses, "Please, my lord, do not hold
against us the sin we have so foolishly
committed. 12Do not let her be like a stillborn infant coming from its mother's
womb with its flesh half eaten away."
13So Moses cried out to the LORD, "O
God, please heal her!"
14The LORD replied to Moses, "If her
father had spit in her face, would she
not have been in disgrace for seven
days? Confine her outside the camp for
seven days; after that she can be
brought back." 15So Miriam was confined outside the camp for seven days,
and the people did not move on till she
was brought back.
16After that, the people left Hazeroth
and encamped in the Desert of Paran.

[a]31 Or *They flew* [b]31 Hebrew *two cubits* (about 1 meter) [c]32 That is, probably about 60 bushels (about 2.2 kiloliters) [d]34 *Kibroth Hattaavah* means *graves of craving.* [e]10 The Hebrew word was used for various diseases affecting the skin—not necessarily leprosy.

SHARPEN THE FOCUS

Will God's Word come true for *me* or not? When we find ourselves in humanly impossible situations, that's the question that can flit through our minds—or come home to roost there.

As Moses faced the anger and disappointment of the people, he found himself overwhelmed. He threw up his arms in dismay and said, in effect, to God, "This is out of my hands. It's too much for me. Kill me now if You don't intend to help us" (Numbers 11:10–15).

Maybe you've been there. Maybe you've felt as helpless or desperate as Moses did. If so, the Lord's response to Moses can encourage you. Moses heard not one word of rebuke from heaven. Instead, the Lord granted some immediate, practical help (Numbers 11:16–17). He gave Moses His solemn promise to provide an answer to calm the crisis (Numbers 11:18–20). And when Moses couldn't quite believe that promise, God repeated it and personalized it: "You will now see whether or not what I say will come true for you" (Numbers 11:23).

What doubts or fears flood your heart today? Take them to your Lord in prayer and hear His Word of grace. His promises *will* come true for you. Rest in His love until you see His deliverance.

WEEK 12 • WEDNESDAY

Num. 13:1—15:41

GET THE BIG PICTURE

At the Lord's command, Moses sends out 12 spies, one from each of the 12 tribes, to scout out the land of Canaan. Ten of the spies report news that provokes terror in Israel. But Joshua and Caleb try to reassure the people and encourage them to trust in the Lord. Faithless and rebellious, the people pay the price for their unbelief. If time is short, focus on Numbers 14:1–35.

Exploring Canaan

13 The LORD said to Moses,
2"Send some men to explore
the land of Canaan, which I am giving
to the Israelites. From each ancestral
tribe send one of its leaders."
3So at the LORD's command Moses
sent them out from the Desert of Paran.
All of them were leaders of the Israelites.
4These are their names:

from the tribe of Reuben, Shammua son of Zaccur;
5from the tribe of Simeon, Shaphat son of Hori;
6from the tribe of Judah, Caleb son of Jephunneh;
7from the tribe of Issachar, Igal son of Joseph;
8from the tribe of Ephraim, Hoshea son of Nun;
9from the tribe of Benjamin, Palti son of Raphu;
10from the tribe of Zebulun, Gaddiel son of Sodi;
11from the tribe of Manasseh (a tribe of Joseph), Gaddi son of Susi;
12from the tribe of Dan, Ammiel son of Gemalli;
13from the tribe of Asher, Sethur son of Michael;

14 from the tribe of Naphtali, Nahbi
son of Vophsi;
15 from the tribe of Gad, Geuel son of
Maki.

16 These are the names of the men Moses
sent to explore the land. (Moses gave
Hoshea son of Nun the name Joshua.)
17 When Moses sent them to explore
Canaan, he said, "Go up through the
Negev and on into the hill country. 18 See
what the land is like and whether the
people who live there are strong or
weak, few or many. 19 What kind of land
do they live in? Is it good or bad? What
kind of towns do they live in? Are they
unwalled or fortified? 20 How is the soil?
Is it fertile or poor? Are there trees on it
or not? Do your best to bring back some
of the fruit of the land." (It was the season for the first ripe grapes.)
21 So they went up and explored the
land from the Desert of Zin as far as
Rehob, toward Lebo[a] Hamath. 22 They
went up through the Negev and came
to Hebron, where Ahiman, Sheshai and
Talmai, the descendants of Anak, lived.
(Hebron had been built seven years
before Zoan in Egypt.) 23 When they
reached the Valley of Eshcol,[b] they cut
off a branch bearing a single cluster of
grapes. Two of them carried it on a pole
between them, along with some pomegranates and figs. 24 That place was
called the Valley of Eshcol because of the
cluster of grapes the Israelites cut off
there. 25 At the end of forty days they returned from exploring the land.

Report on the Exploration

26 They came back to Moses and Aaron
and the whole Israelite community at
Kadesh in the Desert of Paran. There
they reported to them and to the whole
assembly and showed them the fruit of
the land. 27 They gave Moses this account: "We went into the land to which
you sent us, and it does flow with milk
and honey! Here is its fruit. 28 But the
people who live there are powerful, and
the cities are fortified and very large. We
even saw descendants of Anak there.
29 The Amalekites live in the Negev; the
Hittites, Jebusites and Amorites live
in the hill country; and the Canaanites
live near the sea and along the Jordan."
30 Then Caleb silenced the people before Moses and said, "We should go up
and take possession of the land, for we
can certainly do it."
31 But the men who had gone up with
him said, "We can't attack those people;
they are stronger than we are." 32 And
they spread among the Israelites a bad
report about the land they had explored. They said, "The land we explored devours those living in it. All the
people we saw there are of great size.
33 We saw the Nephilim there (the descendants of Anak come from the
Nephilim). We seemed like grasshoppers in our own eyes, and we looked the
same to them."

The People Rebel

14 That night all the people of
the community raised their
voices and wept aloud. 2 All the Israelites
grumbled against Moses and Aaron,
and the whole assembly said to them,
"If only we had died in Egypt! Or in this
desert! 3 Why is the LORD bringing us to
this land only to let us fall by the sword?
Our wives and children will be taken as
plunder. Wouldn't it be better for us to
go back to Egypt?" 4 And they said to
each other, "We should choose a leader
and go back to Egypt."
5 Then Moses and Aaron fell facedown
in front of the whole Israelite assembly
gathered there. 6 Joshua son of Nun and
Caleb son of Jephunneh, who were
among those who had explored the
land, tore their clothes 7 and said to the
entire Israelite assembly, "The land we
passed through and explored is exceedingly good. 8 If the LORD is pleased with
us, he will lead us into that land, a land
flowing with milk and honey, and will
give it to us. 9 Only do not rebel against
the LORD. And do not be afraid of the
people of the land, because we will
swallow them up. Their protection is

[a] 21 Or *toward the entrance to* [b] 23 *Eshcol* means *cluster;* also in verse 24.

gone, but the LORD is with us. Do not be afraid of them."

[10]But the whole assembly talked about stoning them. Then the glory of the LORD appeared at the Tent of Meeting to all the Israelites. [11]The LORD said to Moses, "How long will these people treat me with contempt? How long will they refuse to believe in me, in spite of all the miraculous signs I have performed among them? [12]I will strike them down with a plague and destroy them, but I will make you into a nation greater and stronger than they."

[13]Moses said to the LORD, "Then the Egyptians will hear about it! By your power you brought these people up from among them. [14]And they will tell the inhabitants of this land about it. They have already heard that you, O LORD, are with these people and that you, O LORD, have been seen face to face, that your cloud stays over them, and that you go before them in a pillar of cloud by day and a pillar of fire by night. [15]If you put these people to death all at one time, the nations who have heard this report about you will say, [16]'The LORD was not able to bring these people into the land he promised them on oath; so he slaughtered them in the desert.'

[17]"Now may the Lord's strength be displayed, just as you have declared: [18]'The LORD is slow to anger, abounding in love and forgiving sin and rebellion. Yet he does not leave the guilty unpunished; he punishes the children for the sin of the fathers to the third and fourth generation.' [19]In accordance with your great love, forgive the sin of these people, just as you have pardoned them from the time they left Egypt until now."

[20]The LORD replied, "I have forgiven them, as you asked. [21]Nevertheless, as surely as I live and as surely as the glory of the LORD fills the whole earth, [22]not one of the men who saw my glory and the miraculous signs I performed in Egypt and in the desert but who disobeyed me and tested me ten times— [23]not one of them will ever see the land I promised on oath to their forefathers. No one who has treated me with contempt will ever see it. [24]But because my servant Caleb has a different spirit and follows me wholeheartedly, I will bring him into the land he went to, and his descendants will inherit it. [25]Since the Amalekites and Canaanites are living in the valleys, turn back tomorrow and set out toward the desert along the route to the Red Sea.[a]"

[26]The LORD said to Moses and Aaron: [27]"How long will this wicked community grumble against me? I have heard the complaints of these grumbling Israelites. [28]So tell them, 'As surely as I live, declares the LORD, I will do to you the very things I heard you say: [29]In this desert your bodies will fall—every one of you twenty years old or more who was counted in the census and who has grumbled against me. [30]Not one of you will enter the land I swore with uplifted hand to make your home, except Caleb son of Jephunneh and Joshua son of Nun. [31]As for your children that you said would be taken as plunder, I will bring them in to enjoy the land you have rejected. [32]But you—your bodies will fall in this desert. [33]Your children will be shepherds here for forty years, suffering for your unfaithfulness, until the last of your bodies lies in the desert. [34]For forty years—one year for each of the forty days you explored the land—you will suffer for your sins and know what it is like to have me against you.' [35]I, the LORD, have spoken, and I will surely do these things to this whole wicked community, which has banded together against me. They will meet their end in this desert; here they will die."

[36]So the men Moses had sent to explore the land, who returned and made the whole community grumble against him by spreading a bad report about it— [37]these men responsible for spreading the bad report about the land were struck down and died of a plague before the LORD. [38]Of the men who went to explore the land, only Joshua son of Nun and Caleb son of Jephunneh survived.

[39]When Moses reported this to all the

[a]25 Hebrew *Yam Suph;* that is, Sea of Reeds

Israelites, they mourned bitterly. [40]Early
the next morning they went up toward
the high hill country. "We have sinned,"
they said. "We will go up to the place the
LORD promised."

[41]But Moses said, "Why are you disobeying the LORD's command? This will
not succeed! [42]Do not go up, because the
LORD is not with you. You will be defeated by your enemies, [43]for the Amalekites
and Canaanites will face you there. Because you have turned away from the
LORD, he will not be with you and you
will fall by the sword."

[44]Nevertheless, in their presumption
they went up toward the high hill country, though neither Moses nor the ark of
the LORD's covenant moved from the
camp. [45]Then the Amalekites and Canaanites who lived in that hill country
came down and attacked them and beat
them down all the way to Hormah.

Supplementary Offerings

15 The LORD said to Moses,
[2]"Speak to the Israelites and
say to them: 'After you enter the land I
am giving you as a home [3]and you
present to the LORD offerings made by
fire, from the herd or the flock, as an
aroma pleasing to the LORD—whether
burnt offerings or sacrifices, for special
vows or freewill offerings or festival offerings— [4]then the one who brings his
offering shall present to the LORD a
grain offering of a tenth of an ephah[a] of
fine flour mixed with a quarter of a hin[b]
of oil. [5]With each lamb for the burnt offering or the sacrifice, prepare a quarter
of a hin of wine as a drink offering.

[6]" 'With a ram prepare a grain offering of two-tenths of an ephah[c] of fine
flour mixed with a third of a hin[d] of oil,
[7]and a third of a hin of wine as a drink
offering. Offer it as an aroma pleasing
to the LORD.

[8]" 'When you prepare a young bull as
a burnt offering or sacrifice, for a special
vow or a fellowship offering[e] to the
LORD, [9]bring with the bull a grain offering of three-tenths of an ephah[f] of fine
flour mixed with half a hin[g] of oil. [10]Also
bring half a hin of wine as a drink offering. It will be an offering made by fire,
an aroma pleasing to the LORD. [11]Each
bull or ram, each lamb or young goat, is
to be prepared in this manner. [12]Do this
for each one, for as many as you prepare.

[13]" 'Everyone who is native-born
must do these things in this way when
he brings an offering made by fire as an
aroma pleasing to the LORD. [14]For the
generations to come, whenever an alien
or anyone else living among you presents an offering made by fire as an
aroma pleasing to the LORD, he must do
exactly as you do. [15]The community is to
have the same rules for you and for the
alien living among you; this is a lasting
ordinance for the generations to come.
You and the alien shall be the same before the LORD: [16]The same laws and regulations will apply both to you and to
the alien living among you.' "

[17]The LORD said to Moses, [18]"Speak to
the Israelites and say to them: 'When
you enter the land to which I am taking
you [19]and you eat the food of the land,
present a portion as an offering to the
LORD. [20]Present a cake from the first of
your ground meal and present it as an
offering from the threshing floor.
[21]Throughout the generations to come
you are to give this offering to the LORD
from the first of your ground meal.

Offerings for Unintentional Sins

[22]" 'Now if you unintentionally fail to
keep any of these commands the LORD
gave Moses— [23]any of the LORD's commands to you through him, from the
day the LORD gave them and continuing through the generations to come—
[24]and if this is done unintentionally
without the community being aware of
it, then the whole community is to of-

[a]4 That is, probably about 2 quarts (about 2 liters) [b]4 That is, probably about 1 quart (about 1 liter); also in verse 5 [c]6 That is, probably about 4 quarts (about 4.5 liters) [d]6 That is, probably about 1 1/4 quarts (about 1.2 liters); also in verse 7 [e]8 Traditionally *peace offering* [f]9 That is, probably about 6 quarts (about 6.5 liters) [g]9 That is, probably about 2 quarts (about 2 liters); also in verse 10

fer a young bull for a burnt offering as
an aroma pleasing to the LORD, along
with its prescribed grain offering and
drink offering, and a male goat for a sin
offering. 25The priest is to make atonement for the whole Israelite community,
and they will be forgiven, for it was not
intentional and they have brought to
the LORD for their wrong an offering
made by fire and a sin offering. 26The
whole Israelite community and the
aliens living among them will be forgiven, because all the people were involved in the unintentional wrong.
27" 'But if just one person sins unintentionally, he must bring a year-old
female goat for a sin offering. 28The
priest is to make atonement before the
LORD for the one who erred by sinning
unintentionally, and when atonement
has been made for him, he will be forgiven. 29One and the same law applies
to everyone who sins unintentionally,
whether he is a native-born Israelite or
an alien.
30" 'But anyone who sins defiantly,
whether native-born or alien, blasphemes the LORD, and that person must
be cut off from his people. 31Because he
has despised the LORD's word and broken
his commands, that person must surely
be cut off; his guilt remains on him.' "

The Sabbath-Breaker Put to Death

32While the Israelites were in the
desert, a man was found gathering
wood on the Sabbath day. 33Those who
found him gathering wood brought
him to Moses and Aaron and the whole
assembly, 34and they kept him in custody, because it was not clear what
should be done to him. 35Then the LORD
said to Moses, "The man must die. The
whole assembly must stone him outside
the camp." 36So the assembly took him
outside the camp and stoned him to
death, as the LORD commanded Moses.

Tassels on Garments

37The LORD said to Moses, 38"Speak to
the Israelites and say to them:
'Throughout the generations to come
you are to make tassels on the corners
of your garments, with a blue cord on
each tassel. 39You will have these tassels
to look at and so you will remember all
the commands of the LORD, that you
may obey them and not prostitute yourselves by going after the lusts of your
own hearts and eyes. 40Then you will remember to obey all my commands and
will be consecrated to your God. 41I am
the LORD your God, who brought you
out of Egypt to be your God. I am the
LORD your God.' "

SHARPEN THE FOCUS

Someone once asked General Patton, "Have you ever been afraid in battle?"

"I experience fear," the general replied, "but I never take counsel from my fears."

How often in your own life have you taken counsel from your fears and missed out on blessings God wanted you to have? Does fear keep you from taking on some task in your congregation or community God might want you to do for His glory? Does fear keep you from speaking about Christ to that someone who needs Him so much? Does fear padlock your wallet and keep you from supporting God's mission in Panama, Russia, China, or Mexico?

There's a remedy for that kind of fear. The apostle John wrote, "Perfect love drives out fear" (1 John 4:18). This is not our effort in drumming up perfect love for God in our own hearts, but rather His already perfect (complete) love for us in Christ! God showed us that love by sending Jesus to die for us while we were still living in rebellion, still acting in hatred toward Him.

If you struggle with fear, set aside some time to meditate on your Savior's perfect love for you. Let His Spirit counsel your heart, using His powerful Word. Let His grace strengthen you as you face the "giants" of your life.

WEEK 12 • THURSDAY

Numbers 16:1—18:32

GET THE BIG PICTURE

These chapters tell of challenges and confirmation. Take note of the difference of opinion between some in Israel and the Lord concerning the authority of Aaron and the Levites who served God and the people in the tabernacle. If time is short, focus on Numbers 16:1–40.

Korah, Dathan and Abiram

16 Korah son of Izhar, the son of Kohath, the son of Levi, and certain Reubenites—Dathan and Abiram, sons of Eliab, and On son of Peleth—became insolent[a] [2]and rose up against Moses. With them were 250 Israelite men, well-known community leaders who had been appointed members of the council. [3]They came as a group to oppose Moses and Aaron and said to them, "You have gone too far! The whole community is holy, every one of them, and the LORD is with them. Why then do you set yourselves above the LORD's assembly?"

[4]When Moses heard this, he fell facedown. [5]Then he said to Korah and all his followers: "In the morning the LORD will show who belongs to him and who is holy, and he will have that person come near him. The man he chooses he will cause to come near him. [6]You, Korah, and all your followers are to do this: Take censers [7]and tomorrow put fire and incense in them before the LORD. The man the LORD chooses will be the one who is holy. You Levites have gone too far!"

[8]Moses also said to Korah, "Now listen, you Levites! [9]Isn't it enough for you that the God of Israel has separated you from the rest of the Israelite community and brought you near himself to do the work at the LORD's tabernacle and to stand before the community and minister to them? [10]He has brought you and all your fellow Levites near himself, but now you are trying to get the priesthood too. [11]It is against the LORD that you and all your followers have banded together. Who is Aaron that you should grumble against him?"

[12]Then Moses summoned Dathan and Abiram, the sons of Eliab. But they said, "We will not come! [13]Isn't it enough that you have brought us up out of a land flowing with milk and honey to kill us in the desert? And now you also want to lord it over us? [14]Moreover, you haven't brought us into a land flowing with milk and honey or given us an inheritance of fields and vineyards. Will you gouge out the eyes of[b] these men? No, we will not come!"

[15]Then Moses became very angry and said to the LORD, "Do not accept their offering. I have not taken so much as a donkey from them, nor have I wronged any of them."

[16]Moses said to Korah, "You and all your followers are to appear before the LORD tomorrow—you and they and Aaron. [17]Each man is to take his censer and put incense in it—250 censers in all—and present it before the LORD. You and Aaron are to present your censers also." [18]So each man took his censer, put fire and incense in it, and stood with Moses and Aaron at the entrance to the Tent of Meeting. [19]When Korah had gathered all his followers in opposition to them at the entrance to the Tent of

[a]1 Or *Peleth—took* ⌞*men*⌟ [b]14 Or *you make slaves of;* or *you deceive*

Meeting, the glory of the LORD appeared to the entire assembly. [20]The
LORD said to Moses and Aaron, [21]"Separate yourselves from this assembly so I
can put an end to them at once."

[22]But Moses and Aaron fell facedown
and cried out, "O God, God of the spirits of all mankind, will you be angry
with the entire assembly when only one
man sins?"

[23]Then the LORD said to Moses, [24]"Say
to the assembly, 'Move away from the
tents of Korah, Dathan and Abiram.' "

[25]Moses got up and went to Dathan
and Abiram, and the elders of Israel followed him. [26]He warned the assembly,
"Move back from the tents of these
wicked men! Do not touch anything belonging to them, or you will be swept
away because of all their sins." [27]So they
moved away from the tents of Korah,
Dathan and Abiram. Dathan and Abiram had come out and were standing
with their wives, children and little ones
at the entrances to their tents.

[28]Then Moses said, "This is how you
will know that the LORD has sent me to
do all these things and that it was not
my idea: [29]If these men die a natural
death and experience only what usually
happens to men, then the LORD has not
sent me. [30]But if the LORD brings about
something totally new, and the earth
opens its mouth and swallows them,
with everything that belongs to them,
and they go down alive into the grave,[a]
then you will know that these men have
treated the LORD with contempt."

[31]As soon as he finished saying all this,
the ground under them split apart [32]and
the earth opened its mouth and swallowed them, with their households and
all Korah's men and all their possessions. [33]They went down alive into the
grave, with everything they owned; the
earth closed over them, and they perished and were gone from the community. [34]At their cries, all the Israelites
around them fled, shouting, "The earth
is going to swallow us too!"

[35]And fire came out from the LORD
and consumed the 250 men who were
offering the incense.

[36]The LORD said to Moses, [37]"Tell Eleazar son of Aaron, the priest, to take the
censers out of the smoldering remains
and scatter the coals some distance
away, for the censers are holy— [38]the
censers of the men who sinned at the
cost of their lives. Hammer the censers
into sheets to overlay the altar, for they
were presented before the LORD and
have become holy. Let them be a sign to
the Israelites."

[39]So Eleazar the priest collected the
bronze censers brought by those who
had been burned up, and he had them
hammered out to overlay the altar, [40]as
the LORD directed him through Moses.
This was to remind the Israelites that no
one except a descendant of Aaron
should come to burn incense before the
LORD, or he would become like Korah
and his followers.

[41]The next day the whole Israelite
community grumbled against Moses
and Aaron. "You have killed the LORD's
people," they said.

[42]But when the assembly gathered in
opposition to Moses and Aaron and
turned toward the Tent of Meeting, suddenly the cloud covered it and the glory
of the LORD appeared. [43]Then Moses
and Aaron went to the front of the Tent
of Meeting, [44]and the LORD said to Moses, [45]"Get away from this assembly so I
can put an end to them at once." And
they fell facedown.

[46]Then Moses said to Aaron, "Take
your censer and put incense in it, along
with fire from the altar, and hurry to the
assembly to make atonement for them.
Wrath has come out from the LORD; the
plague has started." [47]So Aaron did as
Moses said, and ran into the midst of the
assembly. The plague had already
started among the people, but Aaron
offered the incense and made atonement for them. [48]He stood between the
living and the dead, and the plague
stopped. [49]But 14,700 people died from
the plague, in addition to those who
had died because of Korah. [50]Then
Aaron returned to Moses at the

[a]30 Hebrew *Sheol;* also in verse 33

entrance to the Tent of Meeting, for the plague had stopped.

The Budding of Aaron's Staff

17 The LORD said to Moses, 2"Speak to the Israelites and get twelve staffs from them, one from the leader of each of their ancestral tribes. Write the name of each man on his staff. 3On the staff of Levi write Aaron's name, for there must be one staff for the head of each ancestral tribe. 4Place them in the Tent of Meeting in front of the Testimony, where I meet with you. 5The staff belonging to the man I choose will sprout, and I will rid myself of this constant grumbling against you by the Israelites."

6So Moses spoke to the Israelites, and their leaders gave him twelve staffs, one for the leader of each of their ancestral tribes, and Aaron's staff was among them. 7Moses placed the staffs before the LORD in the Tent of the Testimony.

8The next day Moses entered the Tent of the Testimony and saw that Aaron's staff, which represented the house of Levi, had not only sprouted but had budded, blossomed and produced almonds. 9Then Moses brought out all the staffs from the LORD's presence to all the Israelites. They looked at them, and each man took his own staff.

10The LORD said to Moses, "Put back Aaron's staff in front of the Testimony, to be kept as a sign to the rebellious. This will put an end to their grumbling against me, so that they will not die." 11Moses did just as the LORD commanded him.

12The Israelites said to Moses, "We will die! We are lost, we are all lost! 13Anyone who even comes near the tabernacle of the LORD will die. Are we all going to die?"

Duties of Priests and Levites

18 The LORD said to Aaron, "You, your sons and your father's family are to bear the responsibility for offenses against the sanctuary, and you and your sons alone are to bear the responsibility for offenses against the priesthood. 2Bring your fellow Levites from your ancestral tribe to join you and assist you when you and your sons minister before the Tent of the Testimony. 3They are to be responsible to you and are to perform all the duties of the Tent, but they must not go near the furnishings of the sanctuary or the altar, or both they and you will die. 4They are to join you and be responsible for the care of the Tent of Meeting—all the work at the Tent—and no one else may come near where you are.

5"You are to be responsible for the care of the sanctuary and the altar, so that wrath will not fall on the Israelites again. 6I myself have selected your fellow Levites from among the Israelites as a gift to you, dedicated to the LORD to do the work at the Tent of Meeting. 7But only you and your sons may serve as priests in connection with everything at the altar and inside the curtain. I am giving you the service of the priesthood as a gift. Anyone else who comes near the sanctuary must be put to death."

Offerings for Priests and Levites

8Then the LORD said to Aaron, "I myself have put you in charge of the offerings presented to me; all the holy offerings the Israelites give me I give to you and your sons as your portion and regular share. 9You are to have the part of the most holy offerings that is kept from the fire. From all the gifts they bring me as most holy offerings, whether grain or sin or guilt offerings, that part belongs to you and your sons. 10Eat it as something most holy; every male shall eat it. You must regard it as holy.

11"This also is yours: whatever is set aside from the gifts of all the wave offerings of the Israelites. I give this to you and your sons and daughters as your regular share. Everyone in your household who is ceremonially clean may eat it.

12"I give you all the finest olive oil and all the finest new wine and grain they give the LORD as the firstfruits of their harvest. 13All the land's firstfruits that they bring to the LORD will be yours. Ev-

eryone in your household who is ceremonially clean may eat it.
14"Everything in Israel that is devoted[a] to the LORD is yours. 15The first offspring of every womb, both man and
animal, that is offered to the LORD is
yours. But you must redeem every firstborn son and every firstborn male of
unclean animals. 16When they are a
month old, you must redeem them at
the redemption price set at five shekels[b]
of silver, according to the sanctuary
shekel, which weighs twenty gerahs.
17"But you must not redeem the firstborn of an ox, a sheep or a goat; they are
holy. Sprinkle their blood on the altar
and burn their fat as an offering made
by fire, an aroma pleasing to the LORD.
18Their meat is to be yours, just as the
breast of the wave offering and the right
thigh are yours. 19Whatever is set aside
from the holy offerings the Israelites
present to the LORD I give to you and
your sons and daughters as your regular share. It is an everlasting covenant of
salt before the LORD for both you and
your offspring."
20The LORD said to Aaron, "You will
have no inheritance in their land, nor
will you have any share among them; I
am your share and your inheritance
among the Israelites.
21"I give to the Levites all the tithes in
Israel as their inheritance in return for
the work they do while serving at the
Tent of Meeting. 22From now on the Israelites must not go near the Tent of
Meeting, or they will bear the consequences of their sin and will die. 23It is
the Levites who are to do the work at
the Tent of Meeting and bear the responsibility for offenses against it. This
is a lasting ordinance for the generations to come. They will receive no
inheritance among the Israelites. 24In-
stead, I give to the Levites as their inheritance the tithes that the Israelites
present as an offering to the LORD. That
is why I said concerning them: 'They
will have no inheritance among the Israelites.' "
25The LORD said to Moses, 26"Speak to
the Levites and say to them: 'When you
receive from the Israelites the tithe I
give you as your inheritance, you must
present a tenth of that tithe as the
LORD's offering. 27Your offering will be
reckoned to you as grain from the
threshing floor or juice from the winepress. 28In this way you also will present
an offering to the LORD from all the
tithes you receive from the Israelites.
From these tithes you must give the
LORD's portion to Aaron the priest. 29You
must present as the LORD's portion the
best and holiest part of everything giv-
en to you.'
30"Say to the Levites: 'When you
present the best part, it will be reckoned
to you as the product of the threshing
floor or the winepress. 31You and your
households may eat the rest of it anywhere, for it is your wages for your
work at the Tent of Meeting. 32By presenting the best part of it you will not
be guilty in this matter; then you will
not defile the holy offerings of the Israelites, and you will not die.' "

[a]*14* The Hebrew term refers to the irrevocable giving over of things or persons to the LORD.
[b]*16* That is, about 2 ounces (about 55 grams)

SHARPEN THE FOCUS

How easily we can come to blame others for our own sins:

- If she hadn't gotten angry first . . .
- If they would have done what they promised . . .
- If he had been more helpful . . .

Today's reading from Numbers quickly convinces us that blame-shifting is not a new trend in the human race. Note Numbers 16:12–14, 41. Dathan and his followers blamed Moses for consequences they had brought on themselves. They, not Moses, had swallowed the fear-provoking report of the 10 spies. They, not Moses, had refused to believe Joshua and Caleb's report based on God's faithfulness. Moses and Aaron hadn't made the earth open up! The Lord had! And in anger against just this sort of disrespect.

How do you deal with the sin in your own heart? Do you acknowledge it for what it is and open yourself to the Holy Spirit's examination, forgiveness, and cleansing? Or do you hide behind excuses, blaming circumstances or other people for your own ungodly attitudes, words, and actions?

Read 1 John 1:5–9 prayerfully, perhaps several times. Let God's love chase away your fears as you talk with Him about your failure and His forgiveness in Jesus Christ.

WEEK 12 • FRIDAY

Numbers 19:1—20:29

GET THE BIG PICTURE

Because death is a consequence of sin, death defiled and polluted those Old Covenant believers who came into contact with it. By His own death, Christ has purified us from this pollution. The sacrifice of the red heifer symbolized this (Numbers 19). Chapter 20 records the deaths of Miriam (Numbers 20:1) and Aaron (Numbers 20:22–29). If time is short, focus on Numbers 20:1–13.

The Water of Cleansing

19 The LORD said to Moses and
Aaron: 2"This is a require-
ment of the law that the LORD has commanded: Tell the Israelites to bring you
a red heifer without defect or blemish
and that has never been under a yoke.
3Give it to Eleazar the priest; it is to be
taken outside the camp and slaughtered
in his presence. 4Then Eleazar the priest
is to take some of its blood on his finger
and sprinkle it seven times toward the
front of the Tent of Meeting. 5While he
watches, the heifer is to be burned—its
hide, flesh, blood and offal. 6The priest
is to take some cedar wood, hyssop and
scarlet wool and throw them onto the
burning heifer. 7After that, the priest
must wash his clothes and bathe himself
with water. He may then come into the
camp, but he will be ceremonially unclean till evening. 8The man who burns
it must also wash his clothes and bathe
with water, and he too will be unclean
till evening.
9"A man who is clean shall gather up
the ashes of the heifer and put them in
a ceremonially clean place outside the
camp. They shall be kept by the Israelite community for use in the water of
cleansing; it is for purification from sin.
10The man who gathers up the ashes of
the heifer must also wash his clothes,
and he too will be unclean till evening.
This will be a lasting ordinance both for
the Israelites and for the aliens living
among them.
11"Whoever touches the dead body of
anyone will be unclean for seven days.
12He must purify himself with the water on the third day and on the seventh
day; then he will be clean. But if he does

not purify himself on the third and seventh days, he will not be clean. 13Who-
ever touches the dead body of anyone
and fails to purify himself defiles the
LORD's tabernacle. That person must be
cut off from Israel. Because the water of
cleansing has not been sprinkled on
him, he is unclean; his uncleanness remains on him.

14"This is the law that applies when a
person dies in a tent: Anyone who enters the tent and anyone who is in it will
be unclean for seven days, 15and every
open container without a lid fastened
on it will be unclean.

16"Anyone out in the open who
touches someone who has been killed
with a sword or someone who has died
a natural death, or anyone who touches
a human bone or a grave, will be unclean for seven days.

17"For the unclean person, put some
ashes from the burned purification offering into a jar and pour fresh water
over them. 18Then a man who is ceremonially clean is to take some hyssop, dip
it in the water and sprinkle the tent and
all the furnishings and the people who
were there. He must also sprinkle anyone who has touched a human bone or
a grave or someone who has been killed
or someone who has died a natural
death. 19The man who is clean is to
sprinkle the unclean person on the third
and seventh days, and on the seventh
day he is to purify him. The person being cleansed must wash his clothes and
bathe with water, and that evening he
will be clean. 20But if a person who is unclean does not purify himself, he must
be cut off from the community, because he
has defiled the sanctuary of the LORD.
The water of cleansing has not been
sprinkled on him, and he is unclean.
21This is a lasting ordinance for them.

"The man who sprinkles the water of
cleansing must also wash his clothes,
and anyone who touches the water of
cleansing will be unclean till evening.
22Anything that an unclean person
touches becomes unclean, and anyone
who touches it becomes unclean till evening."

Water From the Rock

20 In the first month the
whole Israelite commu-
nity arrived at the Desert of Zin, and
they stayed at Kadesh. There Miriam
died and was buried.

2Now there was no water for the community, and the people gathered in opposition to Moses and Aaron. 3They
quarreled with Moses and said, "If only
we had died when our brothers fell
dead before the LORD! 4Why did you
bring the LORD's community into
this desert, that we and our livestock
should die here? 5Why did you bring us
up out of Egypt to this terrible place? It
has no grain or figs, grapevines or
pomegranates. And there is no water to
drink!"

6Moses and Aaron went from the assembly to the entrance to the Tent of
Meeting and fell facedown, and the glory of the LORD appeared to them. 7The
LORD said to Moses, 8"Take the staff, and
you and your brother Aaron gather the
assembly together. Speak to that rock
before their eyes and it will pour out its
water. You will bring water out of the
rock for the community so they and
their livestock can drink."

9So Moses took the staff from the
LORD's presence, just as he commanded
him. 10He and Aaron gathered the assembly together in front of the rock and
Moses said to them, "Listen, you rebels,
must we bring you water out of this
rock?" 11Then Moses raised his arm and
struck the rock twice with his staff. Water gushed out, and the community and
their livestock drank.

12But the LORD said to Moses and Aaron, "Because you did not trust in
me enough to honor me as holy in the
sight of the Israelites, you will not bring
this community into the land I give
them."

13These were the waters of Meribah,[a]
where the Israelites quarreled with the
LORD and where he showed himself
holy among them.

[a] *13 Meribah* means *quarreling*.

Edom Denies Israel Passage

14 Moses sent messengers from Kadesh to the king of Edom, saying:

"This is what your brother Israel says: You know about all the hardships that have come upon us.
15 Our forefathers went down into Egypt, and we lived there many years. The Egyptians mistreated us and our fathers,
16 but when we cried out to the LORD, he heard our cry and sent an angel and brought us out of Egypt.

"Now we are here at Kadesh, a town on the edge of your territory.
17 Please let us pass through your country. We will not go through any field or vineyard, or drink water from any well. We will travel along the king's highway and not turn to the right or to the left until we have passed through your territory."

18 But Edom answered:

"You may not pass through here; if you try, we will march out and attack you with the sword."

19 The Israelites replied:

"We will go along the main road, and if we or our livestock drink any of your water, we will pay for it. We only want to pass through on foot—nothing else."

20 Again they answered:

"You may not pass through."

Then Edom came out against them with a large and powerful army.
21 Since Edom refused to let them go through their territory, Israel turned away from them.

The Death of Aaron

22 The whole Israelite community set out from Kadesh and came to Mount Hor.
23 At Mount Hor, near the border of Edom, the LORD said to Moses and Aaron,
24 "Aaron will be gathered to his people. He will not enter the land I give the Israelites, because both of you rebelled against my command at the waters of Meribah.
25 Get Aaron and his son Eleazar and take them up Mount Hor.
26 Remove Aaron's garments and put them on his son Eleazar, for Aaron will be gathered to his people; he will die there."

27 Moses did as the LORD commanded: They went up Mount Hor in the sight of the whole community.
28 Moses removed Aaron's garments and put them on his son Eleazar. And Aaron died there on top of the mountain. Then Moses and Eleazar came down from the mountain,
29 and when the whole community learned that Aaron had died, the entire house of Israel mourned for him thirty days.

SHARPEN THE FOCUS

Who could blame Moses and Aaron for feeling exasperated? They had faced rebellion, hardship, and leadership crises for nearly 40 years. Both were over 100 years old, well past the time most people want to put up with constant hardships and grumbling people. No wonder Moses fell prey to the temptation to "lay down the Law" (Numbers 20:10).

And yet it seems that the Lord intended to induce repentance and trust through an act of kindness (Numbers 20:8; cf. Romans 2:4). Much as He had provided water for their parents in a similar situation (Exodus 17:1–7), He now would display His grace to this generation. And to keep them from turning Aaron's staff itself into an object of worship, Moses was simply to speak to the rock.

Instead, Moses scolds the people and beats the rock—actions that paint for Israel a portrait of the Lord just the opposite of what He Himself had intended.

Distinguishing Law from Gospel is fairly easy. Speaking each at the right time is often not. Ask the Lord for grace to learn to know Him better through His Word. Ask that you more appropriately discern and apply His Law and His grace to your own heart and to those lives your life touches. ☼

WEEK 12 • SATURDAY

Numbers 21:1–35

GET THE BIG PICTURE

As Israel moves toward the outskirts of Canaan, she faces several enemies—not the least of which is the nation's own tendency toward discouragement and complaining. In grace, God makes victory possible, providing all that the people need. If time is short, focus on Numbers 21:1–9.

Arad Destroyed

21 When the Canaanite king of
Arad, who lived in the Neg-
ev, heard that Israel was coming along
the road to Atharim, he attacked the Israelites and captured some of them.
2Then Israel made this vow to the LORD:
"If you will deliver these people into our
hands, we will totally destroy[a] their cities." 3The LORD listened to Israel's plea
and gave the Canaanites over to them.
They completely destroyed them and
their towns; so the place was named
Hormah.[b]

The Bronze Snake

4They traveled from Mount Hor along
the route to the Red Sea,[c] to go around
Edom. But the people grew impatient
on the way; 5they spoke against God
and against Moses, and said, "Why have
you brought us up out of Egypt to die
in the desert? There is no bread! There
is no water! And we detest this miserable food!"
6Then the LORD sent venomous
snakes among them; they bit the people
and many Israelites died. 7The people
came to Moses and said, "We sinned
when we spoke against the LORD and
against you. Pray that the LORD will take
the snakes away from us." So Moses
prayed for the people.
8The LORD said to Moses, "Make a
snake and put it up on a pole; anyone
who is bitten can look at it and live." 9So
Moses made a bronze snake and put it
up on a pole. Then when anyone was
bitten by a snake and looked at the
bronze snake, he lived.

The Journey to Moab

10The Israelites moved on and
camped at Oboth. 11Then they set out
from Oboth and camped in Iye Abarim,
in the desert that faces Moab toward the
sunrise. 12From there they moved on
and camped in the Zered Valley. 13They
set out from there and camped alongside the Arnon, which is in the desert extending into Amorite territory. The
Arnon is the border of Moab, between
Moab and the Amorites. 14That is why
the Book of the Wars of the LORD says:

[a]2 The Hebrew term refers to the irrevocable giving over of things or persons to the LORD, often by totally destroying them; also in verse 3. [b]3 *Hormah* means *destruction.* [c]4 Hebrew *Yam Suph*; that is, Sea of Reeds

"... Waheb in Suphah[a] and the
ravines,
the Arnon [15]and[b] the slopes of the
ravines
that lead to the site of Ar
and lie along the border of Moab."

[16]From there they continued on to Beer, the well where the LORD said to Moses, "Gather the people together and I will give them water."

[17]Then Israel sang this song:

"Spring up, O well!
Sing about it,
[18]about the well that the princes dug,
that the nobles of the people
sank—
the nobles with scepters and
staffs."

Then they went from the desert to Mattanah, [19]from Mattanah to Nahaliel,
from Nahaliel to Bamoth, [20]and from Bamoth to the valley in Moab where the
top of Pisgah overlooks the wasteland.

Defeat of Sihon and Og

[21]Israel sent messengers to say to Sihon king of the Amorites:

[22]"Let us pass through your
country. We will not turn aside into
any field or vineyard, or drink water from any well. We will travel
along the king's highway until we
have passed through your territory."

[23]But Sihon would not let Israel pass
through his territory. He mustered his
entire army and marched out into the
desert against Israel. When he reached
Jahaz, he fought with Israel. [24]Israel,
however, put him to the sword and took
over his land from the Arnon to the Jabbok, but only as far as the Ammonites,
because their border was fortified. [25]Is-
rael captured all the cities of the Amorites and occupied them, including
Heshbon and all its surrounding settlements. [26]Heshbon was the city of Sihon
king of the Amorites, who had fought against the former king of Moab and had taken from him all his land as far as the Arnon.

[27]That is why the poets say:

"Come to Heshbon and let it be
rebuilt;
let Sihon's city be restored.

[28]"Fire went out from Heshbon,
a blaze from the city of Sihon.
It consumed Ar of Moab,
the citizens of Arnon's heights.
[29]Woe to you, O Moab!
You are destroyed, O people of
Chemosh!
He has given up his sons as fugitives
and his daughters as captives
to Sihon king of the Amorites.

[30]"But we have overthrown them;
Heshbon is destroyed all the way
to Dibon.
We have demolished them as far as
Nophah,
which extends to Medeba."

[31]So Israel settled in the land of the Amorites.

[32]After Moses had sent spies to Jazer,
the Israelites captured its surrounding
settlements and drove out the Amorites
who were there. [33]Then they turned and
went up along the road toward Bashan,
and Og king of Bashan and his whole
army marched out to meet them in battle at Edrei.

[34]The LORD said to Moses, "Do not be
afraid of him, for I have handed him
over to you, with his whole army and
his land. Do to him what you did to Sihon king of the Amorites, who reigned
in Heshbon."

[35]So they struck him down, together
with his sons and his whole army, leaving them no survivors. And they took
possession of his land.

[a]14 The meaning of the Hebrew for this phrase is uncertain. [b]14,15 Or *"I have been given from Suphah and the ravines / of the Arnon [15]to*

SHARPEN THE FOCUS

The New Testament word for *confess* means literally "to say the same thing" or "to speak together." When we confess our sins, we say what God says:

- I did it.
- It was wrong.
- I have no excuse.
- I deserve punishment.

Compare Numbers 21:5 with Numbers 21:7 and notice how Israel handles the sins of disrespect and rebellion this time. They do not make excuses. They do not try to shift blame. "We did it," they confess simply. "We were wrong. We have sinned."

The Lord has been at work in their hearts. He has made a difference there. By His grace, the nation is growing up spiritually. Of course ideally, the people of Israel (and we ourselves) will avoid wrongdoing in the first place. Nevertheless, the willingness to make honest confession and to admit the need for forgiveness is one signpost along the road of spiritual growth.

Where do you see this sign of the Lord's work in your own life? In what situations do you still tend to make excuses instead of making confession? Why not talk to the Lord about that right now? ☼

WEEK 13 • MONDAY

Numbers 22:1—25:18

GET THE BIG PICTURE

These four chapters detail the encounter of Israel with Balaam. Terrified that no human army can stop the Lord's divisions from conquering Canaan, the king of Moab (Balak) chooses a superhuman weapon: he asks the pagan magician Balaam to conjure up a curse against Israel. But what God has blessed, Balaam *cannot* curse. And so, in the end, Israel's enemies get the people to bring God's wrath down upon themselves—by committing spiritual adultery (Numbers 25:1–3). If time is short, focus on Numbers 22:1–41.

Balak Summons Balaam

22 Then the Israelites traveled to the plains of Moab
and camped along the Jordan across
from Jericho.[a]
2 Now Balak son of Zippor saw all that
Israel had done to the Amorites, 3 and
Moab was terrified because there were
so many people. Indeed, Moab was
filled with dread because of the Israelites.
4 The Moabites said to the elders of
Midian, "This horde is going to lick up
everything around us, as an ox licks up
the grass of the field."

[a]1 Hebrew *Jordan of Jericho;* possibly an ancient name for the Jordan River

So Balak son of Zippor, who was king
of Moab at that time, 5sent messengers
to summon Balaam son of Beor, who
was at Pethor, near the River,[a] in his native land. Balak said:

"A people has come out of Egypt;
they cover the face of the land and
have settled next to me. 6Now come
and put a curse on these people, because they are too powerful for me.
Perhaps then I will be able to defeat
them and drive them out of the
country. For I know that those you
bless are blessed, and those you
curse are cursed."

7The elders of Moab and Midian left,
taking with them the fee for divination.
When they came to Balaam, they told
him what Balak had said.
8"Spend the night here," Balaam said
to them, "and I will bring you back the
answer the LORD gives me." So the Moabite princes stayed with him.
9God came to Balaam and asked,
"Who are these men with you?"
10Balaam said to God, "Balak son of
Zippor, king of Moab, sent me this message: 11'A people that has come out of
Egypt covers the face of the land. Now
come and put a curse on them for me.
Perhaps then I will be able to fight them
and drive them away.' "
12But God said to Balaam, "Do not
go with them. You must not put a curse
on those people, because they are
blessed."
13The next morning Balaam got up
and said to Balak's princes, "Go back to
your own country, for the LORD has refused to let me go with you."
14So the Moabite princes returned to
Balak and said, "Balaam refused to come
with us."
15Then Balak sent other princes, more
numerous and more distinguished than
the first. 16They came to Balaam and
said:

"This is what Balak son of Zippor
says: Do not let anything keep you
from coming to me, 17because I will
reward you handsomely and do
whatever you say. Come and put a
curse on these people for me."

18But Balaam answered them, "Even
if Balak gave me his palace filled with
silver and gold, I could not do anything
great or small to go beyond the command of the LORD my God. 19Now stay
here tonight as the others did, and I will
find out what else the LORD will
tell me."
20That night God came to Balaam and
said, "Since these men have come to
summon you, go with them, but do only
what I tell you."

Balaam's Donkey

21Balaam got up in the morning, saddled his donkey and went with the
princes of Moab. 22But God was very angry when he went, and the angel of the
LORD stood in the road to oppose him.
Balaam was riding on his donkey, and
his two servants were with him. 23When
the donkey saw the angel of the LORD
standing in the road with a drawn
sword in his hand, she turned off the
road into a field. Balaam beat her to get
her back on the road.
24Then the angel of the LORD stood in
a narrow path between two vineyards,
with walls on both sides. 25When the
donkey saw the angel of the LORD, she
pressed close to the wall, crushing
Balaam's foot against it. So he beat her
again.
26Then the angel of the LORD moved
on ahead and stood in a narrow place
where there was no room to turn, either
to the right or to the left. 27When the
donkey saw the angel of the LORD, she
lay down under Balaam, and he was angry and beat her with his staff. 28Then
the LORD opened the donkey's mouth,
and she said to Balaam, "What have I
done to you to make you beat me these
three times?"
29Balaam answered the donkey, "You
have made a fool of me! If I had a sword
in my hand, I would kill you right now."
30The donkey said to Balaam, "Am I not

[a]5 That is, the Euphrates

your own donkey, which you have always ridden, to this day? Have I been in
the habit of doing this to you?"
"No," he said.
31Then the LORD opened Balaam's
eyes, and he saw the angel of the LORD
standing in the road with his sword
drawn. So he bowed low and fell facedown.
32The angel of the LORD asked him,
"Why have you beaten your donkey
these three times? I have come here to
oppose you because your path is a reckless one before me.[a] 33The donkey saw
me and turned away from me these
three times. If she had not turned away,
I would certainly have killed you by
now, but I would have spared her."
34Balaam said to the angel of the
LORD, "I have sinned. I did not realize
you were standing in the road to oppose
me. Now if you are displeased, I will go
back."
35The angel of the LORD said to Balaam, "Go with the men, but speak only
what I tell you." So Balaam went with
the princes of Balak.
36When Balak heard that Balaam was
coming, he went out to meet him at the
Moabite town on the Arnon border, at
the edge of his territory. 37Balak said to
Balaam, "Did I not send you an urgent
summons? Why didn't you come to me?
Am I really not able to reward you?"
38"Well, I have come to you now," Balaam replied. "But can I say just anything? I must speak only what God puts
in my mouth."
39Then Balaam went with Balak to Kiriath Huzoth. 40Balak sacrificed cattle and
sheep, and gave some to Balaam and
the princes who were with him. 41The
next morning Balak took Balaam up to
Bamoth Baal, and from there he saw
part of the people.

Balaam's First Oracle

23 Balaam said, "Build me
seven altars here, and prepare seven bulls and seven rams for
me." 2Balak did as Balaam said, and the
two of them offered a bull and a ram on
each altar.
3Then Balaam said to Balak, "Stay
here beside your offering while I go
aside. Perhaps the LORD will come to
meet with me. Whatever he reveals
to me I will tell you." Then he went off
to a barren height.
4God met with him, and Balaam said,
"I have prepared seven altars, and on
each altar I have offered a bull and a
ram."
5The LORD put a message in Balaam's
mouth and said, "Go back to Balak and
give him this message."
6So he went back to him and found
him standing beside his offering, with
all the princes of Moab. 7Then Balaam
uttered his oracle:

"Balak brought me from Aram,
the king of Moab from the eastern
mountains.
'Come,' he said, 'curse Jacob for me;
come, denounce Israel.'
8 How can I curse
those whom God has not cursed?
How can I denounce
those whom the LORD has not
denounced?
9 From the rocky peaks I see them,
from the heights I view them.
I see a people who live apart
and do not consider themselves
one of the nations.
10 Who can count the dust of Jacob
or number the fourth part of
Israel?
Let me die the death of the
righteous,
and may my end be like theirs!"

11Balak said to Balaam, "What have
you done to me? I brought you to curse
my enemies, but you have done nothing but bless them!"
12He answered, "Must I not speak
what the LORD puts in my mouth?"

Balaam's Second Oracle

13Then Balak said to him, "Come with
me to another place where you can see
them; you will see only a part but not all

[a]32 The meaning of the Hebrew for this clause is uncertain.

of them. And from there, curse them for
me." 14So he took him to the field of Zo-
phim on the top of Pisgah, and there he
built seven altars and offered a bull and
a ram on each altar.

15Balaam said to Balak, "Stay here beside your offering while I meet with him
over there."

16The LORD met with Balaam and put
a message in his mouth and said, "Go
back to Balak and give him this message."

17So he went to him and found him
standing beside his offering, with the
princes of Moab. Balak asked him,
"What did the LORD say?"

18Then he uttered his oracle:

"Arise, Balak, and listen;
hear me, son of Zippor.
19 God is not a man, that he should lie,
nor a son of man, that he should change his mind.
Does he speak and then not act?
Does he promise and not fulfill?
20 I have received a command to bless;
he has blessed, and I cannot change it.
21 "No misfortune is seen in Jacob,
no misery observed in Israel.[a]
The LORD their God is with them;
the shout of the King is among them.
22 God brought them out of Egypt;
they have the strength of a wild ox.
23 There is no sorcery against Jacob,
no divination against Israel.
It will now be said of Jacob
and of Israel, 'See what God has done!'
24 The people rise like a lioness;
they rouse themselves like a lion
that does not rest till he devours his prey
and drinks the blood of his victims."

25Then Balak said to Balaam, "Neither
curse them at all nor bless them at all!"

26Balaam answered, "Did I not tell you
I must do whatever the LORD says?"

Balaam's Third Oracle

27Then Balak said to Balaam, "Come,
let me take you to another place. Perhaps it will please God to let you curse
them for me from there." 28And Balak
took Balaam to the top of Peor, overlooking the wasteland.

29Balaam said, "Build me seven altars
here, and prepare seven bulls and seven
rams for me." 30Balak did as Balaam had
said, and offered a bull and a ram on
each altar.

24 Now when Balaam saw
that it pleased the LORD to
bless Israel, he did not resort to sorcery
as at other times, but turned his face
toward the desert. 2When Balaam
looked out and saw Israel encamped
tribe by tribe, the Spirit of God came
upon him 3and he uttered his oracle:

"The oracle of Balaam son of Beor,
the oracle of one whose eye sees clearly,
4 the oracle of one who hears the words of God,
who sees a vision from the Almighty,[b]
who falls prostrate, and whose eyes are opened:

5 "How beautiful are your tents, O Jacob,
your dwelling places, O Israel!

6 "Like valleys they spread out,
like gardens beside a river,
like aloes planted by the LORD,
like cedars beside the waters.
7 Water will flow from their buckets;
their seed will have abundant water.

"Their king will be greater than Agag;
their kingdom will be exalted.

8 "God brought them out of Egypt;
they have the strength of a wild ox.
They devour hostile nations

[a]21 Or *He has not looked on Jacob's offenses / or on the wrongs found in Israel.* [b]4 Hebrew *Shaddai;* also in verse 16

and break their bones in pieces;
with their arrows they pierce
them.
9 Like a lion they crouch and lie
down,
like a lioness—who dares to rouse
them?

"May those who bless you be
blessed
and those who curse you be
cursed!"

10 Then Balak's anger burned against
Balaam. He struck his hands together
and said to him, "I summoned you to
curse my enemies, but you have blessed
them these three times. 11 Now leave at
once and go home! I said I would reward you handsomely, but the LORD
has kept you from being rewarded."
12 Balaam answered Balak, "Did I not
tell the messengers you sent me, 13 'Even
if Balak gave me his palace filled with
silver and gold, I could not do anything
of my own accord, good or bad, to go
beyond the command of the LORD—
and I must say only what the LORD
says'? 14 Now I am going back to my
people, but come, let me warn you of
what this people will do to your people
in days to come."

Balaam's Fourth Oracle

15 Then he uttered his oracle:

"The oracle of Balaam son of Beor,
the oracle of one whose eye sees
clearly,
16 the oracle of one who hears the
words of God,
who has knowledge from the
Most High,
who sees a vision from the Almighty,
who falls prostrate, and whose
eyes are opened:

17 "I see him, but not now;
I behold him, but not near.
A star will come out of Jacob;
a scepter will rise out of Israel.
He will crush the foreheads of
Moab,
the skulls[a] of[b] all the sons of
Sheth.[c]
18 Edom will be conquered;
Seir, his enemy, will be conquered,
but Israel will grow strong.
19 A ruler will come out of Jacob
and destroy the survivors of the
city."

Balaam's Final Oracles

20 Then Balaam saw Amalek and uttered his oracle:

"Amalek was first among the nations,
but he will come to ruin at last."

21 Then he saw the Kenites and uttered
his oracle:

"Your dwelling place is secure,
your nest is set in a rock;
22 yet you Kenites will be destroyed
when Asshur takes you captive."

23 Then he uttered his oracle:

"Ah, who can live when God does
this?[d]
24 Ships will come from the shores of
Kittim;
they will subdue Asshur and Eber,
but they too will come to ruin."

25 Then Balaam got up and returned
home and Balak went his own way.

Moab Seduces Israel

25 While Israel was staying
in Shittim, the men began
to indulge in sexual immorality with
Moabite women, 2 who invited them to
the sacrifices to their gods. The people
ate and bowed down before these gods.
3 So Israel joined in worshiping the Baal
of Peor. And the LORD's anger burned
against them.
4 The LORD said to Moses, "Take all the
leaders of these people, kill them and
expose them in broad daylight before
the LORD, so that the LORD's fierce anger may turn away from Israel."

[a]17 Samaritan Pentateuch (see also Jer. 48:45); the meaning of the word in the Masoretic Text is uncertain. [b]17 Or possibly *Moab, / batter* [c]17 Or *all the noisy boasters* [d]23 Masoretic Text; with a different word division of the Hebrew *A people will gather from the north.*

[5]So Moses said to Israel's judges,
"Each of you must put to death those of
your men who have joined in worshiping the Baal of Peor."
[6]Then an Israelite man brought to his
family a Midianite woman right before
the eyes of Moses and the whole assembly of Israel while they were weeping at
the entrance to the Tent of Meeting.
[7]When Phinehas son of Eleazar, the son
of Aaron, the priest, saw this, he left the
assembly, took a spear in his hand [8]and
followed the Israelite into the tent. He
drove the spear through both of them—
through the Israelite and into the
woman's body. Then the plague against
the Israelites was stopped; [9]but those
who died in the plague numbered
24,000.
[10]The LORD said to Moses, [11]"Phinehas
son of Eleazar, the son of Aaron, the
priest, has turned my anger away from
the Israelites; for he was as zealous as I
am for my honor among them, so that
in my zeal I did not put an end to them.
[12]Therefore tell him I am making my
covenant of peace with him. [13]He and
his descendants will have a covenant of
a lasting priesthood, because he was
zealous for the honor of his God and
made atonement for the Israelites."
[14]The name of the Israelite who was
killed with the Midianite woman was
Zimri son of Salu, the leader of a Sime-
onite family. [15]And the name of the Midianite woman who was put to death was
Cozbi daughter of Zur, a tribal chief of
a Midianite family.
[16]The LORD said to Moses, [17]"Treat the
Midianites as enemies and kill them,
[18]because they treated you as enemies
when they deceived you in the affair of
Peor and their sister Cozbi, the daughter of a Midianite leader, the woman
who was killed when the plague came
as a result of Peor."

SHARPEN THE FOCUS

Someone has said, "God made man in His own image, and man has since returned the favor." How tempted we often are to characterize God in human terms, to assume He thinks and will act just as we sinful human beings do. The Lord Himself once rebuked this notion: "You thought I was altogether like you" (Psalm 50:21). Balaam prophesied against this idea, too:

God is not a man, that He should lie,
nor a son of man, that He should change His mind.
Does He speak and then not act?
Does He promise and not fulfill? (Numbers 23:19)

Unlike sinful, imperfect human beings, God always keeps His Word. He acts with perfect integrity. He is always true to Himself and to His people. Through the cross of Christ He has sworn to bless His repentant people. And He will never change His mind. How can this truth comfort you today?

WEEK 13 • TUESDAY

Numbers 26:1—27:23

As he did before the people broke camp at Sinai (Numbers 1–4), Moses takes a census now, 40 years later. Nearly all the people from the previous generation have died, and Israel is preparing to enter and conquer Canaan itself. Moses knows he will not go with them, and so he prayerfully appoints Joshua to lead the people in their conquest. If time is short, focus on Numbers 27:15–23.

The Second Census

26 After the plague the LORD said to Moses and Eleazar son of Aaron, the priest, 2"Take a census of the whole Israelite community by families—all those twenty years old or more who are able to serve in the army of Israel." 3So on the plains of Moab by the Jordan across from Jericho,[a] Moses and Eleazar the priest spoke with them and said, 4"Take a census of the men twenty years old or more, as the LORD commanded Moses."

These were the Israelites who came out of Egypt:

5The descendants of Reuben, the firstborn son of Israel, were:
through Hanoch, the Hanochite clan;
through Pallu, the Palluite clan;
6through Hezron, the Hezronite clan;
through Carmi, the Carmite clan.
7These were the clans of Reuben; those numbered were 43,730.

8The son of Pallu was Eliab, 9and the sons of Eliab were Nemuel, Dathan and Abiram. The same Dathan and Abiram were the community officials who rebelled against Moses and Aaron and were among Korah's followers when they rebelled against the LORD. 10The earth opened its mouth and swallowed them along with Korah, whose followers died when the fire devoured the 250 men. And they served as a warning sign. 11The line of Korah, however, did not die out.

12The descendants of Simeon by their clans were:
through Nemuel, the Nemuelite clan;
through Jamin, the Jaminite clan;
through Jakin, the Jakinite clan;
13through Zerah, the Zerahite clan;
through Shaul, the Shaulite clan.
14These were the clans of Simeon; there were 22,200 men.

15The descendants of Gad by their clans were:
through Zephon, the Zephonite clan;
through Haggi, the Haggite clan;
through Shuni, the Shunite clan;
16through Ozni, the Oznite clan;
through Eri, the Erite clan;
17through Arodi,[b] the Arodite clan;
through Areli, the Arelite clan.
18These were the clans of Gad; those numbered were 40,500.

19Er and Onan were sons of Judah, but they died in Canaan.
20The descendants of Judah by their clans were:
through Shelah, the Shelanite clan;

[a]3 Hebrew *Jordan of Jericho*; possibly an ancient name for the Jordan River; also in verse 63
[b]17 Samaritan Pentateuch and Syriac (see also Gen. 46:16); Masoretic Text *Arod*

through Perez, the Perezite clan;
through Zerah, the Zerahite clan.
21 The descendants of Perez were:
through Hezron, the Hezronite clan;
through Hamul, the Hamulite clan.
22 These were the clans of Judah; those numbered were 76,500.

23 The descendants of Issachar by their clans were:
through Tola, the Tolaite clan;
through Puah, the Puite[a] clan;
24 through Jashub, the Jashubite clan;
through Shimron, the Shimronite clan.
25 These were the clans of Issachar; those numbered were 64,300.

26 The descendants of Zebulun by their clans were:
through Sered, the Seredite clan;
through Elon, the Elonite clan;
through Jahleel, the Jahleelite clan.
27 These were the clans of Zebulun; those numbered were 60,500.

28 The descendants of Joseph by their clans through Manasseh and Ephraim were:

29 The descendants of Manasseh:
through Makir, the Makirite clan (Makir was the father of Gilead);
through Gilead, the Gileadite clan.
30 These were the descendants of Gilead:
through Iezer, the Iezerite clan;
through Helek, the Helekite clan;
31 through Asriel, the Asrielite clan;
through Shechem, the Shechemite clan;
32 through Shemida, the Shemidaite clan;
through Hepher, the Hepherite clan.
33 (Zelophehad son of Hepher had no sons; he had only daughters, whose names were Mahlah, Noah, Hoglah, Milcah and Tirzah.)
34 These were the clans of Manasseh; those numbered were 52,700.

35 These were the descendants of Ephraim by their clans:
through Shuthelah, the Shuthelahite clan;
through Beker, the Bekerite clan;
through Tahan, the Tahanite clan.
36 These were the descendants of Shuthelah:
through Eran, the Eranite clan.
37 These were the clans of Ephraim; those numbered were 32,500.

These were the descendants of Joseph by their clans.

38 The descendants of Benjamin by their clans were:
through Bela, the Belaite clan;
through Ashbel, the Ashbelite clan;
through Ahiram, the Ahiramite clan;
39 through Shupham,[b] the Shuphamite clan;
through Hupham, the Huphamite clan.
40 The descendants of Bela through Ard and Naaman were:
through Ard,[c] the Ardite clan;
through Naaman, the Naamite clan.
41 These were the clans of Benjamin; those numbered were 45,600.

42 These were the descendants of Dan by their clans:
through Shuham, the Shuhamite clan.
These were the clans of Dan: 43 All of them were Shuhamite clans; and those numbered were 64,400.

44 The descendants of Asher by their clans were:
through Imnah, the Imnite clan;
through Ishvi, the Ishvite clan;
through Beriah, the Beriite clan;

[a] 23 Samaritan Pentateuch, Septuagint, Vulgate and Syriac (see also 1 Chron. 7:1); Masoretic Text *through Puvah, the Punite* [b] 39 A few manuscripts of the Masoretic Text, Samaritan Pentateuch, Vulgate and Syriac (see also Septuagint); most manuscripts of the Masoretic Text *Shephupham* [c] 40 Samaritan Pentateuch and Vulgate (see also Septuagint); Masoretic Text does not have *through Ard*.

[45] and through the descendants of
Beriah:
through Heber, the Heberite
clan;
through Malkiel, the Malkielite
clan.
[46] (Asher had a daughter named Serah.)
[47] These were the clans of Asher; those
numbered were 53,400.

[48] The descendants of Naphtali by their
clans were:
through Jahzeel, the Jahzeelite
clan;
through Guni, the Gunite clan;
[49] through Jezer, the Jezerite clan;
through Shillem, the Shillemite
clan.
[50] These were the clans of Naphtali;
those numbered were 45,400.

[51] The total number of the men of Israel
was 601,730.

[52] The LORD said to Moses, [53] "The land
is to be allotted to them as an inheritance
based on the number of names.
[54] To a larger group give a larger inheritance,
and to a smaller group a smaller
one; each is to receive its inheritance
according to the number of those listed.
[55] Be sure that the land is distributed by
lot. What each group inherits will be according
to the names for its ancestral
tribe. [56] Each inheritance is to be distributed
by lot among the larger and smaller
groups."

[57] These were the Levites who were
counted by their clans:
through Gershon, the Gershonite
clan;
through Kohath, the Kohathite
clan;
through Merari, the Merarite clan.
[58] These also were Levite clans:
the Libnite clan,
the Hebronite clan,
the Mahlite clan,
the Mushite clan,
the Korahite clan.
(Kohath was the forefather of Amram;
[59] the name of Amram's wife
was Jochebed, a descendant of
Levi, who was born to the Levites[a]
in Egypt. To Amram she bore Aaron,
Moses and their sister Miriam.
[60] Aaron was the father of Nadab
and Abihu, Eleazar and Ithamar.
[61] But Nadab and Abihu died when
they made an offering before the
LORD with unauthorized fire.)

[62] All the male Levites a month old or
more numbered 23,000. They were not
counted along with the other Israelites
because they received no inheritance
among them.

[63] These are the ones counted by Moses
and Eleazar the priest when they
counted the Israelites on the plains of
Moab by the Jordan across from Jericho.
[64] Not one of them was among those
counted by Moses and Aaron the priest
when they counted the Israelites in the
Desert of Sinai. [65] For the LORD had told
those Israelites they would surely die in
the desert, and not one of them was left
except Caleb son of Jephunneh and
Joshua son of Nun.

Zelophehad's Daughters

27 The daughters of Zelophehad son of Hepher, the
son of Gilead, the son of Makir, the son
of Manasseh, belonged to the clans of
Manasseh son of Joseph. The names of
the daughters were Mahlah, Noah,
Hoglah, Milcah and Tirzah. They approached
[2] the entrance to the Tent of
Meeting and stood before Moses, Eleazar
the priest, the leaders and the whole
assembly, and said, [3] "Our father died in
the desert. He was not among Korah's
followers, who banded together against
the LORD, but he died for his own sin
and left no sons. [4] Why should our
father's name disappear from his clan
because he had no son? Give us property
among our father's relatives."
[5] So Moses brought their case before
the LORD [6] and the LORD said to him,
[7] "What Zelophehad's daughters are

[a] 59 Or *Jochebed, a daughter of Levi, who was born to Levi*

saying is right. You must certainly give
them property as an inheritance among
their father's relatives and turn their
father's inheritance over to them.
8"Say to the Israelites, 'If a man dies
and leaves no son, turn his inheritance
over to his daughter. 9If he has no
daughter, give his inheritance to his
brothers. 10If he has no brothers, give his
inheritance to his father's brothers. 11If
his father had no brothers, give his inheritance to the nearest relative in his
clan, that he may possess it. This is to be
a legal requirement for the Israelites, as
the LORD commanded Moses.' "

Joshua to Succeed Moses

12Then the LORD said to Moses, "Go
up this mountain in the Abarim range
and see the land I have given the Israelites. 13After you have seen it, you too
will be gathered to your people, as your
brother Aaron was, 14for when the community rebelled at the waters in the
Desert of Zin, both of you disobeyed my
command to honor me as holy before
their eyes." (These were the waters of
Meribah Kadesh, in the Desert of Zin.)
15Moses said to the LORD, 16"May the
LORD, the God of the spirits of all mankind, appoint a man over this community 17to go out and come in before
them, one who will lead them out and
bring them in, so the LORD's people
will not be like sheep without a shepherd."
18So the LORD said to Moses, "Take
Joshua son of Nun, a man in whom is
the spirit,[a] and lay your hand on him.
19Have him stand before Eleazar the
priest and the entire assembly and commission him in their presence. 20Give
him some of your authority so the
whole Israelite community will obey
him. 21He is to stand before Eleazar the
priest, who will obtain decisions for him
by inquiring of the Urim before the
LORD. At his command he and the entire community of the Israelites will
go out, and at his command they will
come in."
22Moses did as the LORD commanded
him. He took Joshua and had him stand
before Eleazar the priest and the whole
assembly. 23Then he laid his hands on
him and commissioned him, as the
LORD instructed through Moses.

[a]*18* Or *Spirit*

SHARPEN THE FOCUS

Clearly, Moses mentored Joshua at the battle with Amalek (Exodus 17:8–13); on Sinai (Exodus 24:13); and at Kadesh Barnea (Numbers 13:1–2; 14:6–10).

Moses also made Joshua his assistant (Exodus 24:13). This position prepared Joshua for later leadership. Yet, the Lord led Joshua in a personal, spiritual preparation too:

> *The LORD would speak to Moses face to face, as a man speaks with his friend. Then Moses would return to the camp, but his young aide Joshua the son of Nun did not leave the tent.* (Exodus 33:11)

What did Joshua do there? Undoubtedly, he meditated on the Lord's Word, on the Lord's goodness, and on the Lord's promise. He prayed for himself and for his people and praised and thanked the Lord.

The Lord drew Joshua to Himself—just as He wants to draw you to Himself. We can enjoy all the experiences, mentoring, and previous service for Christ in the world, but these things cannot replace the time we spend with our Lord in His Word. We do not (and need not) know what plans He has in mind for our future service to Him. For now, we need only let Him bring us closer to Himself through the cross of His Son.

WEEK 13 • WEDNESDAY

Num. 28:1—30:16

For a new generation, Moses once again repeats and summarizes Israel's regular sacrifices and yearly observances. Numbers 30 then gives explicit case by case instructions about the oaths the Lord's people take. God stresses His intention that their word be as certain as His. If time is short, focus on Numbers 28:1–31.

Daily Offerings

28 The LORD said to Moses,
2"Give this command to
the Israelites and say to them: 'See that
you present to me at the appointed time
the food for my offerings made by fire,
as an aroma pleasing to me.' 3Say to
them: 'This is the offering made by fire
that you are to present to the LORD: two
lambs a year old without defect, as a
regular burnt offering each day. 4Pre-
pare one lamb in the morning and the
other at twilight, 5together with a grain
offering of a tenth of an ephah[a] of fine
flour mixed with a quarter of a hin[b] of
oil from pressed olives. 6This is the
regular burnt offering instituted at
Mount Sinai as a pleasing aroma, an
offering made to the LORD by fire. 7The
accompanying drink offering is to be a
quarter of a hin of fermented drink
with each lamb. Pour out the drink offering to the LORD at the sanctuary.
8Prepare the second lamb at twilight,
along with the same kind of grain
offering and drink offering that you
prepare in the morning. This is an offering made by fire, an aroma pleasing to
the LORD.

Sabbath Offerings

9" 'On the Sabbath day, make an offering of two lambs a year old without defect, together with its drink offering and
a grain offering of two-tenths of an
ephah[c] of fine flour mixed with oil.
10This is the burnt offering for every
Sabbath, in addition to the regular burnt
offering and its drink offering.

Monthly Offerings

11" 'On the first of every month,
present to the LORD a burnt offering of
two young bulls, one ram and seven
male lambs a year old, all without defect. 12With each bull there is to be a
grain offering of three-tenths of an
ephah[d] of fine flour mixed with oil; with
the ram, a grain offering of two-tenths
of an ephah of fine flour mixed with oil;
13and with each lamb, a grain offering of
a tenth of an ephah of fine flour mixed
with oil. This is for a burnt offering, a
pleasing aroma, an offering made to the
LORD by fire. 14With each bull there is to
be a drink offering of half a hin[e] of wine;
with the ram, a third of a hin[f]; and with
each lamb, a quarter of a hin. This is the
monthly burnt offering to be made at
each new moon during the year.
15Besides the regular burnt offering
with its drink offering, one male goat is
to be presented to the LORD as a sin offering.

[a]*5* That is, probably about 2 quarts (about 2 liters); also in verses 13, 21 and 29 [b]*5* That is, probably about 1 quart (about 1 liter); also in verses 7 and 14 [c]*9* That is, probably about 4 quarts (about 4.5 liters); also in verses 12, 20 and 28 [d]*12* That is, probably about 6 quarts (about 6.5 liters); also in verses 20 and 28 [e]*14* That is, probably about 2 quarts (about 2 liters) [f]*14* That is, probably about 1 1/4 quarts (about 1.2 liters)

The Passover

16" 'On the fourteenth day of the first month the LORD's Passover is to be held. 17On the fifteenth day of this month there is to be a festival; for seven days eat bread made without yeast. 18On the first day hold a sacred assembly and do no regular work. 19Present to the LORD an offering made by fire, a burnt offering of two young bulls, one ram and seven male lambs a year old, all without defect. 20With each bull prepare a grain offering of three-tenths of an ephah of fine flour mixed with oil; with the ram, two-tenths; 21and with each of the seven lambs, one-tenth. 22Include one male goat as a sin offering to make atonement for you. 23Prepare these in addition to the regular morning burnt offering. 24In this way prepare the food for the offering made by fire every day for seven days as an aroma pleasing to the LORD; it is to be prepared in addition to the regular burnt offering and its drink offering. 25On the seventh day hold a sacred assembly and do no regular work.

Feast of Weeks

26" 'On the day of firstfruits, when you present to the LORD an offering of new grain during the Feast of Weeks, hold a sacred assembly and do no regular work. 27Present a burnt offering of two young bulls, one ram and seven male lambs a year old as an aroma pleasing to the LORD. 28With each bull there is to be a grain offering of three-tenths of an ephah of fine flour mixed with oil; with the ram, two-tenths; 29and with each of the seven lambs, one-tenth. 30Include one male goat to make atonement for you. 31Prepare these together with their drink offerings, in addition to the regular burnt offering and its grain offering. Be sure the animals are without defect.

Feast of Trumpets

29 " 'On the first day of the seventh month hold a sacred assembly and do no regular work. It is a day for you to sound the trumpets. 2As an aroma pleasing to the LORD, prepare a burnt offering of one young bull, one ram and seven male lambs a year old, all without defect. 3With the bull prepare a grain offering of three-tenths of an ephah[a] of fine flour mixed with oil; with the ram, two-tenths[b]; 4and with each of the seven lambs, one-tenth.[c] 5Include one male goat as a sin offering to make atonement for you. 6These are in addition to the monthly and daily burnt offerings with their grain offerings and drink offerings as specified. They are offerings made to the LORD by fire—a pleasing aroma.

Day of Atonement

7" 'On the tenth day of this seventh month hold a sacred assembly. You must deny yourselves[d] and do no work. 8Present as an aroma pleasing to the LORD a burnt offering of one young bull, one ram and seven male lambs a year old, all without defect. 9With the bull prepare a grain offering of three-tenths of an ephah of fine flour mixed with oil; with the ram, two-tenths; 10and with each of the seven lambs, one-tenth. 11Include one male goat as a sin offering, in addition to the sin offering for atonement and the regular burnt offering with its grain offering, and their drink offerings.

Feast of Tabernacles

12" 'On the fifteenth day of the seventh month, hold a sacred assembly and do no regular work. Celebrate a festival to the LORD for seven days. 13Present an offering made by fire as an aroma pleasing to the LORD, a burnt offering of thirteen young bulls, two rams and fourteen male lambs a year old, all without defect. 14With each of the thirteen bulls prepare a grain offering of three-tenths of an ephah of fine flour mixed with oil; with each of the two rams, two-

[a]3 That is, probably about 6 quarts (about 6.5 liters); also in verses 9 and 14 [b]3 That is, probably about 4 quarts (about 4.5 liters); also in verses 9 and 14 [c]4 That is, probably about 2 quarts (about 2 liters); also in verses 10 and 15 [d]7 Or *must fast*

tenths; 15and with each of the fourteen
lambs, one-tenth. 16Include one male
goat as a sin offering, in addition to the
regular burnt offering with its grain offering and drink offering.
17" 'On the second day prepare twelve
young bulls, two rams and fourteen
male lambs a year old, all without defect. 18With the bulls, rams and lambs,
prepare their grain offerings and drink
offerings according to the number specified. 19Include one male goat as a sin
offering, in addition to the regular burnt
offering with its grain offering, and their
drink offerings.
20" 'On the third day prepare eleven
bulls, two rams and fourteen male
lambs a year old, all without defect.
21With the bulls, rams and lambs, prepare their grain offerings and drink
offerings according to the number specified. 22Include one male goat as a sin
offering, in addition to the regular burnt
offering with its grain offering and
drink offering.
23" 'On the fourth day prepare ten
bulls, two rams and fourteen male
lambs a year old, all without defect.
24With the bulls, rams and lambs, prepare their grain offerings and drink
offerings according to the number specified. 25Include one male goat as a sin
offering, in addition to the regular burnt
offering with its grain offering and
drink offering.
26" 'On the fifth day prepare nine
bulls, two rams and fourteen male
lambs a year old, all without defect.
27With the bulls, rams and lambs, prepare their grain offerings and drink offerings according to the number
specified. 28Include one male goat as a
sin offering, in addition to the regular
burnt offering with its grain offering
and drink offering.
29" 'On the sixth day prepare eight
bulls, two rams and fourteen male
lambs a year old, all without defect.
30With the bulls, rams and lambs, prepare their grain offerings and drink
offerings according to the number specified. 31Include one male goat as a sin
offering, in addition to the regular burnt
offering with its grain offering and
drink offering.
32" 'On the seventh day prepare seven
bulls, two rams and fourteen male
lambs a year old, all without defect.
33With the bulls, rams and lambs, prepare their grain offerings and drink
offerings according to the number specified. 34Include one male goat as a sin
offering, in addition to the regular burnt
offering with its grain offering and
drink offering.
35" 'On the eighth day hold an assembly and do no regular work. 36Present an
offering made by fire as an aroma pleasing to the LORD, a burnt offering of one
bull, one ram and seven male lambs a
year old, all without defect. 37With the
bull, the ram and the lambs, prepare
their grain offerings and drink offerings
according to the number specified. 38In-
clude one male goat as a sin offering, in
addition to the regular burnt offering
with its grain offering and drink offering.
39" 'In addition to what you vow and
your freewill offerings, prepare these
for the LORD at your appointed feasts:
your burnt offerings, grain offerings,
drink offerings and fellowship offerings.[a]' "
40Moses told the Israelites all that the
LORD commanded him.

Vows

30 Moses said to the heads of
the tribes of Israel: "This is
what the LORD commands: 2When a
man makes a vow to the LORD or takes
an oath to obligate himself by a pledge,
he must not break his word but must do
everything he said.
3"When a young woman still living in
her father's house makes a vow to the
LORD or obligates herself by a pledge
4and her father hears about her vow or
pledge but says nothing to her, then all
her vows and every pledge by which
she obligated herself will stand. 5But if
her father forbids her when he hears
about it, none of her vows or the
pledges by which she obligated herself

[a]39 Traditionally *peace offerings*

will stand; the LORD will release her
because her father has forbidden her.
6"If she marries after she makes a vow
or after her lips utter a rash promise by
which she obligates herself 7and her
husband hears about it but says nothing
to her, then her vows or the pledges by
which she obligated herself will stand.
8But if her husband forbids her when he
hears about it, he nullifies the vow that
obligates her or the rash promise by
which she obligates herself, and the
LORD will release her.
9"Any vow or obligation taken by a
widow or divorced woman will be binding on her.
10"If a woman living with her husband makes a vow or obligates herself
by a pledge under oath 11and her husband hears about it but says nothing to
her and does not forbid her, then all her
vows or the pledges by which she obligated herself will stand. 12But if her husband nullifies them when he hears
about them, then none of the vows or
pledges that came from her lips will
stand. Her husband has nullified them,
and the LORD will release her. 13Her husband may confirm or nullify any vow
she makes or any sworn pledge to deny
herself. 14But if her husband says nothing to her about it from day to day, then
he confirms all her vows or the pledges
binding on her. He confirms them by
saying nothing to her when he hears
about them. 15If, however, he nullifies
them some time after he hears about
them, then he is responsible for her
guilt."
16These are the regulations the LORD
gave Moses concerning relationships
between a man and his wife, and between a father and his young daughter
still living in his house.

SHARPEN THE FOCUS

An elderly lady waited all afternoon for a plumber to arrive. Late in the day, she gave up and headed for the grocery store. Sure enough, the plumber drove up 10 minutes later. He rapped on the door. "Who is it?" croaked the lady's parrot from inside the house.

"It's the plumber."

"Who is it?" insisted the voice from inside the house.

"It's the plumber!" hollered the repairman.

"Who is it?" insisted the voice again.

The veins stuck out on his neck as he bellowed at the top of his lungs, "It's the plumber!" Whereupon he suffered a heart attack and died on the spot. The lady of the house returned shortly thereafter. "Who is it?" she wondered aloud, seeing the fallen repairman on her front steps.

"It's the plumber," croaked the parrot from the living room.

As any teacher can tell us, parrots aren't the only creatures that learn through repetition. In today's reading from Numbers, the Lord may seem to repeat Himself once too often. After all, haven't we heard most of these worship regulations detail by detail many times by now?

Yes. But our Lord knows how easily we humans forget. And so He tells us again and again about our sin and the work of our Savior, Jesus.

WEEK 13 • THURSDAY

Numbers 31:1–54

GET THE BIG PICTURE

If Canaan is to serve as a kind of "spiritual incubator" for the infant nation Israel, the dangerous virus of idolatry must be neutralized. The people of Midian, allied with Moab, have already tempted Israel into this sin. At that time 24,000 Israelites died (Numbers 25:1–9). Thus, the Lord declares the "holy war" you will read about today. If time is short, focus on Numbers 31:1–8.

Vengeance on the Midianites

31 The LORD said to Moses, [2]"Take vengeance on the Midianites for the Israelites. After that, you will be gathered to your people."

[3]So Moses said to the people, "Arm some of your men to go to war against the Midianites and to carry out the LORD's vengeance on them. [4]Send into battle a thousand men from each of the tribes of Israel." [5]So twelve thousand men armed for battle, a thousand from each tribe, were supplied from the clans of Israel. [6]Moses sent them into battle, a thousand from each tribe, along with Phinehas son of Eleazar, the priest, who took with him articles from the sanctuary and the trumpets for signaling.

[7]They fought against Midian, as the LORD commanded Moses, and killed every man. [8]Among their victims were Evi, Rekem, Zur, Hur and Reba—the five kings of Midian. They also killed Balaam son of Beor with the sword. [9]The Israelites captured the Midianite women and children and took all the Midianite herds, flocks and goods as plunder. [10]They burned all the towns where the Midianites had settled, as well as all their camps. [11]They took all the plunder and spoils, including the people and animals, [12]and brought the captives, spoils and plunder to Moses and Eleazar the priest and the Israelite assembly at their camp on the plains of Moab, by the Jordan across from Jericho.[a]

[13]Moses, Eleazar the priest and all the leaders of the community went to meet them outside the camp. [14]Moses was angry with the officers of the army—the commanders of thousands and commanders of hundreds—who returned from the battle.

[15]"Have you allowed all the women to live?" he asked them. [16]"They were the ones who followed Balaam's advice and were the means of turning the Israelites away from the LORD in what happened at Peor, so that a plague struck the LORD's people. [17]Now kill all the boys. And kill every woman who has slept with a man, [18]but save for yourselves every girl who has never slept with a man.

[19]"All of you who have killed anyone or touched anyone who was killed must stay outside the camp seven days. On the third and seventh days you must purify yourselves and your captives. [20]Purify every garment as well as everything made of leather, goat hair or wood."

[21]Then Eleazar the priest said to the soldiers who had gone into battle, "This is the requirement of the law that the LORD gave Moses: [22]Gold, silver, bronze, iron, tin, lead [23]and anything else that

[a]12 Hebrew *Jordan of Jericho;* possibly an ancient name for the Jordan River

can withstand fire must be put through
the fire, and then it will be clean. But it
must also be purified with the water of
cleansing. And whatever cannot withstand fire must be put through that water. 24On the seventh day wash your
clothes and you will be clean. Then you
may come into the camp."

Dividing the Spoils

25The LORD said to Moses, 26"You and
Eleazar the priest and the family heads
of the community are to count all the
people and animals that were captured.
27Divide the spoils between the soldiers
who took part in the battle and the rest
of the community. 28From the soldiers
who fought in the battle, set apart as
tribute for the LORD one out of every
five hundred, whether persons, cattle,
donkeys, sheep or goats. 29Take this tribute from their half share and give it to
Eleazar the priest as the LORD's part.
30From the Israelites' half, select one out
of every fifty, whether persons, cattle,
donkeys, sheep, goats or other animals.
Give them to the Levites, who are responsible for the care of the LORD's
tabernacle." 31So Moses and Eleazar the
priest did as the LORD commanded Moses.

32The plunder remaining from the
spoils that the soldiers took was 675,000
sheep, 3372,000 cattle, 3461,000 donkeys
35and 32,000 women who had never
slept with a man.

36The half share of those who fought
in the battle was:

337,500 sheep, 37of which the tribute for the LORD was 675;
38 36,000 cattle, of which the tribute
for the LORD was 72;
39 30,500 donkeys, of which the tribute for the LORD was 61;
40 16,000 people, of which the tribute
for the LORD was 32.

41Moses gave the tribute to Eleazar the
priest as the LORD's part, as the LORD
commanded Moses.

42The half belonging to the Israelites,
which Moses set apart from that of the
fighting men— 43the community's
half—was 337,500 sheep, 4436,000 cattle,
4530,500 donkeys 46and 16,000 people.
47From the Israelites' half, Moses selected one out of every fifty persons and
animals, as the LORD commanded him,
and gave them to the Levites, who were
responsible for the care of the LORD's
tabernacle.

48Then the officers who were over the
units of the army—the commanders of
thousands and commanders of hundreds—went to Moses 49and said to
him, "Your servants have counted the
soldiers under our command, and not
one is missing. 50So we have brought as
an offering to the LORD the gold articles
each of us acquired—armlets, bracelets,
signet rings, earrings and necklaces—to
make atonement for ourselves before
the LORD."

51Moses and Eleazar the priest accepted from them the gold—all the crafted
articles. 52All the gold from the commanders of thousands and commanders of hundreds that Moses and Eleazar
presented as a gift to the LORD weighed
16,750 shekels.[a] 53Each soldier had tak-
en plunder for himself. 54Moses and Eleazar the priest accepted the gold from
the commanders of thousands and commanders of hundreds and brought it
into the Tent of Meeting as a memorial
for the Israelites before the LORD.

[a]52 That is, about 420 pounds (about 190 kilograms)

SHARPEN THE FOCUS

Because we read Balaam's story three days ago, it would be easy to miss the tie-in with today's account. Numbers 31:8b and 16 serve as flares, flagging us down so we don't miss the point.

Unable to curse Israel, the soothsayer Balaam signed on with Israel's enemies as an unholy consultant. He apparently knew the Lord's attitude toward idolatry. And he knew enough about sinful human nature to guess what might result if Israel met up with a strong enough temptation. His motive? Greed, pure and simple.

Well, perhaps simple, but not so pure. Within weeks or, at most, a few months, Balaam's sin caught up with him. His love of money destroyed him.

The love of money—and the comforts and trinkets money can buy—creep into even Christian hearts. Greed can insert itself so quietly so that it leaves not so much as a ripple on the surface of our lives to betray its presence. We need not have money to love it. And if we do love it, no amount, however large, will leave us feeling content and secure. Only in Jesus—the wisdom of God and the power of God—can we find forgiveness for our greed and the strength to look to the Lord for true security.

The leaders of the tribes of Gad and Reuben come to Moses with a request that makes him throw up his hands and say, in essence, "Here we go again!" But once they explain their reasoning and volunteer their help to the other 10 tribes, Moses relents. Chapter 33 chronicles the nation's physical journey from Egypt to Canaan, and in chapter 34 the Lord lays out the boundaries of the land He intends His people to have. If time is short, focus on Numbers 32:1–27.

The Transjordan Tribes

32 The Reubenites and Gadites, who had very large
herds and flocks, saw that the lands of
Jazer and Gilead were suitable for livestock. 2So they came to Moses and Eleazar the priest and to the leaders of the
community, and said, 3"Ataroth, Dibon,
Jazer, Nimrah, Heshbon, Elealeh, Se-
bam, Nebo and Beon— 4the land the
LORD subdued before the people of Israel—are suitable for livestock, and
your servants have livestock. 5If we
have found favor in your eyes," they
said, "let this land be given to your servants as our possession. Do not make us
cross the Jordan."

6Moses said to the Gadites and Reubenites, "Shall your countrymen go to
war while you sit here? 7Why do you
discourage the Israelites from going
over into the land the LORD has given
them? 8This is what your fathers did
when I sent them from Kadesh Barnea
to look over the land. 9After they went
up to the Valley of Eshcol and viewed
the land, they discouraged the Israelites
from entering the land the LORD had
given them. 10The LORD's anger was
aroused that day and he swore this
oath: 11'Because they have not followed
me wholeheartedly, not one of the men
twenty years old or more who came up
out of Egypt will see the land I promised
on oath to Abraham, Isaac and Jacob—
12not one except Caleb son of Jephunneh the Kenizzite and Joshua
son of Nun, for they followed the
LORD wholeheartedly.' 13The LORD's
anger burned against Israel and he
made them wander in the desert forty
years, until the whole generation of

those who had done evil in his sight was
gone.
[14]“And here you are, a brood of sinners, standing in the place of your fathers and making the LORD even more
angry with Israel. [15]If you turn away
from following him, he will again leave
all this people in the desert, and you will
be the cause of their destruction.”
[16]Then they came up to him and said,
“We would like to build pens here for
our livestock and cities for our women
and children. [17]But we are ready to arm
ourselves and go ahead of the Israelites
until we have brought them to their
place. Meanwhile our women and children will live in fortified cities, for protection from the inhabitants of the land.
[18]We will not return to our homes until
every Israelite has received his inheritance. [19]We will not receive any inheritance with them on the other side of the
Jordan, because our inheritance has
come to us on the east side of the Jordan.”
[20]Then Moses said to them, “If you
will do this—if you will arm yourselves
before the LORD for battle, [21]and if all of
you will go armed over the Jordan before the LORD until he has driven his enemies out before him— [22]then when the
land is subdued before the LORD, you
may return and be free from your obligation to the LORD and to Israel. And
this land will be your possession before
the LORD.
[23]“But if you fail to do this, you will be
sinning against the LORD; and you may
be sure that your sin will find you out.
[24]Build cities for your women and children, and pens for your flocks, but do
what you have promised.”
[25]The Gadites and Reubenites said to
Moses, “We your servants will do as our
lord commands. [26]Our children and
wives, our flocks and herds will remain
here in the cities of Gilead. [27]But your
servants, every man armed for battle,
will cross over to fight before the LORD,
just as our lord says.”
[28]Then Moses gave orders about them
to Eleazar the priest and Joshua son of
Nun and to the family heads of the Israelite tribes. [29]He said to them, “If the
Gadites and Reubenites, every man
armed for battle, cross over the Jordan
with you before the LORD, then when
the land is subdued before you, give
them the land of Gilead as their possession. [30]But if they do not cross over with
you armed, they must accept their possession with you in Canaan.”
[31]The Gadites and Reubenites answered, “Your servants will do what the
LORD has said. [32]We will cross over before the LORD into Canaan armed, but
the property we inherit will be on this
side of the Jordan.”
[33]Then Moses gave to the Gadites, the
Reubenites and the half-tribe of Manasseh son of Joseph the kingdom of Sihon
king of the Amorites and the kingdom
of Og king of Bashan—the whole land
with its cities and the territory around
them.
[34]The Gadites built up Dibon, Ataroth,
Aroer, [35]Atroth Shophan, Jazer, Jogbehah, [36]Beth Nimrah and Beth Haran as
fortified cities, and built pens for their
flocks. [37]And the Reubenites rebuilt
Heshbon, Elealeh and Kiriathaim, [38]as
well as Nebo and Baal Meon (these names
were changed) and Sibmah. They gave
names to the cities they rebuilt.
[39]The descendants of Makir son of
Manasseh went to Gilead, captured it
and drove out the Amorites who were
there. [40]So Moses gave Gilead to the Makirites, the descendants of Manasseh,
and they settled there. [41]Jair, a descendant of Manasseh, captured their settlements and called them Havvoth Jair.[a]
[42]And Nobah captured Kenath and its
surrounding settlements and called it
Nobah after himself.

Stages in Israel's Journey

33 Here are the stages in the
journey of the Israelites
when they came out of Egypt by divisions under the leadership of Moses and
Aaron. [2]At the LORD's command Moses
recorded the stages in their journey.
This is their journey by stages:

[a]41 Or *them the settlements of Jair*

[3]The Israelites set out from Rameses on the fifteenth day of the
first month, the day after the Passover. They marched out boldly
in full view of all the Egyptians,
[4]who were burying all their firstborn, whom the LORD had struck
down among them; for the LORD
had brought judgment on their
gods.
[5]The Israelites left Rameses and
camped at Succoth.
[6]They left Succoth and camped at
Etham, on the edge of the desert.
[7]They left Etham, turned back to
Pi Hahiroth, to the east of Baal Zephon, and camped near Migdol.
[8]They left Pi Hahiroth[a] and
passed through the sea into the
desert, and when they had traveled
for three days in the Desert of
Etham, they camped at Marah.
[9]They left Marah and went to
Elim, where there were twelve
springs and seventy palm trees,
and they camped there.
[10]They left Elim and camped by
the Red Sea.[b]
[11]They left the Red Sea and
camped in the Desert of Sin.
[12]They left the Desert of Sin and
camped at Dophkah.
[13]They left Dophkah and camped
at Alush.
[14]They left Alush and camped at
Rephidim, where there was no water for the people to drink.
[15]They left Rephidim and
camped in the Desert of Sinai.
[16]They left the Desert of Sinai and
camped at Kibroth Hattaavah.
[17]They left Kibroth Hattaavah
and camped at Hazeroth.
[18]They left Hazeroth and camped
at Rithmah.
[19]They left Rithmah and camped
at Rimmon Perez.
[20]They left Rimmon Perez and
camped at Libnah.
[21]They left Libnah and camped at
Rissah.
[22]They left Rissah and camped at
Kehelathah.
[23]They left Kehelathah and
camped at Mount Shepher.
[24]They left Mount Shepher and
camped at Haradah.
[25]They left Haradah and camped
at Makheloth.
[26]They left Makheloth and
camped at Tahath.
[27]They left Tahath and camped at
Terah.
[28]They left Terah and camped at
Mithcah.
[29]They left Mithcah and camped
at Hashmonah.
[30]They left Hashmonah and
camped at Moseroth.
[31]They left Moseroth and camped
at Bene Jaakan.
[32]They left Bene Jaakan and
camped at Hor Haggidgad.
[33]They left Hor Haggidgad and
camped at Jotbathah.
[34]They left Jotbathah and
camped at Abronah.
[35]They left Abronah and camped
at Ezion Geber.
[36]They left Ezion Geber and
camped at Kadesh, in the Desert of
Zin.
[37]They left Kadesh and camped
at Mount Hor, on the border of
Edom. [38]At the LORD's command
Aaron the priest went up Mount
Hor, where he died on the first day
of the fifth month of the fortieth
year after the Israelites came out of
Egypt. [39]Aaron was a hundred and
twenty-three years old when he
died on Mount Hor.
[40]The Canaanite king of Arad,
who lived in the Negev of Canaan,
heard that the Israelites were coming.
[41]They left Mount Hor and
camped at Zalmonah.
[42]They left Zalmonah and
camped at Punon.

[a]*8* Many manuscripts of the Masoretic Text, Samaritan Pentateuch and Vulgate; most manuscripts of the Masoretic Text *left from before Hahiroth* [b]*10* Hebrew *Yam Suph*; that is, Sea of Reeds; also in verse 11

[43]They left Punon and camped at Oboth.

[44]They left Oboth and camped at Iye Abarim, on the border of Moab.

[45]They left Iyim[a] and camped at Dibon Gad.

[46]They left Dibon Gad and camped at Almon Diblathaim.

[47]They left Almon Diblathaim and camped in the mountains of Abarim, near Nebo.

[48]They left the mountains of Abarim and camped on the plains of Moab by the Jordan across from Jericho.[b] [49]There on the plains of Moab they camped along the Jordan from Beth Jeshimoth to Abel Shittim.

[50]On the plains of Moab by the Jordan across from Jericho the LORD said to Moses, [51]"Speak to the Israelites and say to them: 'When you cross the Jordan into Canaan, [52]drive out all the inhabitants of the land before you. Destroy all their carved images and their cast idols, and demolish all their high places. [53]Take possession of the land and settle in it, for I have given you the land to possess. [54]Distribute the land by lot, according to your clans. To a larger group give a larger inheritance, and to a smaller group a smaller one. Whatever falls to them by lot will be theirs. Distribute it according to your ancestral tribes.

[55]" 'But if you do not drive out the inhabitants of the land, those you allow to remain will become barbs in your eyes and thorns in your sides. They will give you trouble in the land where you will live. [56]And then I will do to you what I plan to do to them.' "

Boundaries of Canaan

34 The LORD said to Moses, [2]"Command the Israelites and say to them: 'When you enter Canaan, the land that will be allotted to you as an inheritance will have these boundaries:

[3]" 'Your southern side will include some of the Desert of Zin along the border of Edom. On the east, your southern boundary will start from the end of the Salt Sea,[c] [4]cross south of Scorpion[d] Pass, continue on to Zin and go south of Kadesh Barnea. Then it will go to Hazar Addar and over to Azmon, [5]where it will turn, join the Wadi of Egypt and end at the Sea.[e]

[6]" 'Your western boundary will be the coast of the Great Sea. This will be your boundary on the west.

[7]" 'For your northern boundary, run a line from the Great Sea to Mount Hor [8]and from Mount Hor to Lebo[f] Hamath. Then the boundary will go to Zedad, [9]continue to Ziphron and end at Hazar Enan. This will be your boundary on the north.

[10]" 'For your eastern boundary, run a line from Hazar Enan to Shepham. [11]The boundary will go down from Shepham to Riblah on the east side of Ain and continue along the slopes east of the Sea of Kinnereth.[g] [12]Then the boundary will go down along the Jordan and end at the Salt Sea.

" 'This will be your land, with its boundaries on every side.' "

[13]Moses commanded the Israelites: "Assign this land by lot as an inheritance. The LORD has ordered that it be given to the nine and a half tribes, [14]because the families of the tribe of Reuben, the tribe of Gad and the half-tribe of Manasseh have received their inheritance. [15]These two and a half tribes have received their inheritance on the east side of the Jordan of Jericho,[h] toward the sunrise."

[16]The LORD said to Moses, [17]"These are the names of the men who are to assign the land for you as an inheritance: Eleazar the priest and Joshua son of Nun. [18]And appoint one leader from each tribe to help assign the land. [19]These are their names:

[a]45 That is, Iye Abarim [b]48 Hebrew *Jordan of Jericho*; possibly an ancient name for the Jordan River; also in verse 50 [c]3 That is, the Dead Sea; also in verse 12 [d]4 Hebrew *Akrabbim* [e]5 That is, the Mediterranean; also in verses 6 and 7 [f]8 Or *to the entrance to* [g]11 That is, Galilee [h]15 *Jordan of Jericho* was possibly an ancient name for the Jordan River.

Caleb son of Jephunneh,
from the tribe of Judah;
20 Shemuel son of Ammihud,
from the tribe of Simeon;
21 Elidad son of Kislon,
from the tribe of Benjamin;
22 Bukki son of Jogli,
the leader from the tribe of Dan;
23 Hanniel son of Ephod,
the leader from the tribe of Manasseh son of Joseph;
24 Kemuel son of Shiphtan,
the leader from the tribe of Ephraim son of Joseph;
25 Elizaphan son of Parnach,
the leader from the tribe of Zebulun;
26 Paltiel son of Azzan,
the leader from the tribe of Issachar;
27 Ahihud son of Shelomi,
the leader from the tribe of Asher;
28 Pedahel son of Ammihud,
the leader from the tribe of Naphtali."
29 These are the men the LORD commanded to assign the inheritance to the Israelites in the land of Canaan.

SHARPEN THE FOCUS

The Bible clearly teaches that sin against other people is, first and foremost, sin against God. Note Moses' words to Reuben and Gad:

> *If you fail to [help the other 10 tribes conquer Canaan], you will be sinning against the LORD; and you may be sure that your sin will find you out.* (Numbers 32:23)

When we think nasty thoughts about our employees or our supervisor, when we snap at others in our family, when we drive carelessly, when we fail to help those who hurt, when we use racial slurs even in jest—these sins all offend God and add to the wall that divides us from Him.

God's plans for us include relationships with other people. His will for us includes the joy of harmony and self-forgetful love in our relationships. When we sin against others, we delay His plan, we subvert His purpose for our lives. And when we do these things we can be sure that our sins will find us out. That fact would drive us to despair if it weren't for one other fact—the Lord Jesus lived and died and rose again for each of us. Cling by faith to Him as you pray the prayer of Ephesians 3:14–21 for yourself and your family.

WEEK 13 • SATURDAY

Numbers 35:1—36:13

GET THE BIG PICTURE

A nation of former slaves that lived as wandering shepherds for 40 years is now about to inherit land, cities, farms, and villages. As Israel settles in Canaan, the Lord will prosper them as He promised. Prosperity will bring new problems and temptations: spiritual forgetfulness, a rising crime rate, the desire for the power that can come with wealth. The Lord gave Israel safeguards to protect them against these temptations. Can you identify the two pictures of Christ in these chapters? If time is short, focus on Numbers 35:9–34.

Towns for the Levites

35 On the plains of Moab by the Jordan across from Jericho,[a] the LORD said to Moses, 2"Command the Israelites to give the Levites towns to live in from the inheritance the Israelites will possess. And give them pasturelands around the towns. 3Then they will have towns to live in and pasturelands for their cattle, flocks and all their other livestock.

4"The pasturelands around the towns that you give the Levites will extend out fifteen hundred feet[b] from the town wall. 5Outside the town, measure three thousand feet[c] on the east side, three thousand on the south side, three thousand on the west and three thousand on the north, with the town in the center. They will have this area as pastureland for the towns.

Cities of Refuge

6"Six of the towns you give the Levites will be cities of refuge, to which a person who has killed someone may flee. In addition, give them forty-two other towns. 7In all you must give the Levites forty-eight towns, together with their pasturelands. 8The towns you give the Levites from the land the Israelites possess are to be given in proportion to the inheritance of each tribe: Take many towns from a tribe that has many, but few from one that has few."

9Then the LORD said to Moses: 10"Speak to the Israelites and say to them: 'When you cross the Jordan into Canaan, 11select some towns to be your cities of refuge, to which a person who has killed someone accidentally may flee. 12They will be places of refuge from the avenger, so that a person accused of murder may not die before he stands trial before the assembly. 13These six towns you give will be your cities of refuge. 14Give three on this side of the Jordan and three in Canaan as cities of refuge. 15These six towns will be a place of refuge for Israelites, aliens and any other people living among them, so that anyone who has killed another accidentally can flee there.

16" 'If a man strikes someone with an iron object so that he dies, he is a murderer; the murderer shall be put to death. 17Or if anyone has a stone in his hand that could kill, and he strikes someone so that he dies, he is a murderer; the murderer shall be put to death. 18Or if anyone has a wooden object in his hand that could kill, and he hits someone so that he dies, he is a murderer; the murderer shall be put to death. 19The avenger of blood shall put the murderer to death; when he meets him, he shall put him to death. 20If anyone with malice aforethought shoves another or throws something at him intentionally so that he dies 21or if in hostility he hits him with his fist so that he dies, that person shall be put to death; he is a murderer. The avenger of blood shall put the murderer to death when he meets him.

22" 'But if without hostility someone suddenly shoves another or throws something at him unintentionally 23or, without seeing him, drops a stone on him that could kill him, and he dies, then since he was not his enemy and he did not intend to harm him, 24the assembly must judge between him and the avenger of blood according to these regulations. 25The assembly must protect the one accused of murder from the avenger of blood and send him back to the city of refuge to which he fled. He must stay there until the death of the high priest, who was anointed with the holy oil.

26" 'But if the accused ever goes out-

[a]1 Hebrew *Jordan of Jericho*; possibly an ancient name for the Jordan River [b]4 Hebrew *a thousand cubits* (about 450 meters) [c]5 Hebrew *two thousand cubits* (about 900 meters)

side the limits of the city of refuge to
which he has fled 27and the avenger of
blood finds him outside the city, the
avenger of blood may kill the accused
without being guilty of murder. 28The
accused must stay in his city of refuge
until the death of the high priest; only
after the death of the high priest may he
return to his own property.
29" 'These are to be legal requirements
for you throughout the generations to
come, wherever you live.
30" 'Anyone who kills a person is to be
put to death as a murderer only on the
testimony of witnesses. But no one is to
be put to death on the testimony of only
one witness.
31" 'Do not accept a ransom for the life
of a murderer, who deserves to die. He
must surely be put to death.
32" 'Do not accept a ransom for anyone who has fled to a city of refuge and
so allow him to go back and live on his
own land before the death of the high
priest.
33" 'Do not pollute the land where you
are. Bloodshed pollutes the land, and
atonement cannot be made for the land
on which blood has been shed, except
by the blood of the one who shed it. 34Do
not defile the land where you live and
where I dwell, for I, the LORD, dwell
among the Israelites.' "

Inheritance of Zelophehad's Daughters

36 The family heads of the
clan of Gilead son of Ma-
kir, the son of Manasseh, who were from
the clans of the descendants of Joseph,
came and spoke before Moses and the
leaders, the heads of the Israelite families. 2They said, "When the LORD commanded my lord to give the land as an
inheritance to the Israelites by lot, he ordered you to give the inheritance of our
brother Zelophehad to his daughters.
3Now suppose they marry men from
other Israelite tribes; then their inheritance will be taken from our ancestral
inheritance and added to that of the
tribe they marry into. And so part of the
inheritance allotted to us will be taken
away. 4When the Year of Jubilee for the
Israelites comes, their inheritance will
be added to that of the tribe into which
they marry, and their property will be
taken from the tribal inheritance of our
forefathers."
5Then at the LORD's command Moses
gave this order to the Israelites: "What
the tribe of the descendants of Joseph is
saying is right. 6This is what the LORD
commands for Zelophehad's daughters:
They may marry anyone they please as
long as they marry within the tribal clan
of their father. 7No inheritance in Israel
is to pass from tribe to tribe, for every
Israelite shall keep the tribal land inherited from his forefathers. 8Every daughter who inherits land in any Israelite
tribe must marry someone in her
father's tribal clan, so that every Israelite will possess the inheritance of his
fathers. 9No inheritance may pass from
tribe to tribe, for each Israelite tribe is to
keep the land it inherits."
10So Zelophehad's daughters did as
the LORD commanded Moses. 11Zelo-
phehad's daughters—Mahlah, Tirzah,
Hoglah, Milcah and Noah—married
their cousins on their father's side.
12They married within the clans of the
descendants of Manasseh son of Joseph,
and their inheritance remained in their
father's clan and tribe.
13These are the commands and regulations the LORD gave through Moses to
the Israelites on the plains of Moab by
the Jordan across from Jericho.[a]

[a] 13 Hebrew *Jordan of Jericho;* possibly an ancient name for the Jordan River

SHARPEN THE FOCUS

What pictures come to your mind when you hear the word *refuge*? A cave in a cliff where a hiker can hide in a hailstorm? A family whose members provide emotional comfort for one another? A home where neighborhood teens can spend time after school and on weekends and relax, safe from the crime in the streets and maybe even the alcohol or drug abuse in their own homes?

The Bible often calls the Lord our "refuge." In Jesus, we can hide in safety when Satan's accusations roar in our ears and when the hurricane of death threatens to carry us away. He is our hiding place from sin and Satan, hell and death. He is our "city of refuge." He died for our offenses in our place.

Think about that as you read one or more of these psalms which describe the Lord as our refuge: Psalms 14; 46; 57; 62; 91.

From what do you seek refuge today? Find it–in Him! ☼

DEUTERONOMY

WEEK 14 • MONDAY

Deuteronomy 1:1–46

The book of Deuteronomy is made up of three sermons. Moses preached them on the Plain of Moab as he prepared to turn his leadership responsibilities over to Joshua. In sermon one (Deuteronomy 1:1–4:40), Moses recalls the nation's history from its roots to the present. As you read, look for his themes–faith and unbelief, obedience and disobedience. But above all, look for evidence of the Lord's faithfulness even when His people were faithless. If time is short, focus on Deuteronomy 1:1–5.

The Command to Leave Horeb

1 These are the words Moses spoke to
all Israel in the desert east of the Jordan—that is, in the Arabah—opposite
Suph, between Paran and Tophel, Laban, Hazeroth and Dizahab. 2(It takes
eleven days to go from Horeb to Kadesh
Barnea by the Mount Seir road.)
3In the fortieth year, on the first day
of the eleventh month, Moses proclaimed to the Israelites all that the
LORD had commanded him concerning
them. 4This was after he had defeated
Sihon king of the Amorites, who
reigned in Heshbon, and at Edrei had
defeated Og king of Bashan, who
reigned in Ashtaroth.
5East of the Jordan in the territory of
Moab, Moses began to expound this law,
saying:

6The LORD our God said to us at Horeb, "You have stayed long enough at
this mountain. 7Break camp and advance into the hill country of the Amorites; go to all the neighboring peoples
in the Arabah, in the mountains, in the
western foothills, in the Negev and
along the coast, to the land of the Canaanites and to Lebanon, as far as the
great river, the Euphrates. 8See, I have
given you this land. Go in and take possession of the land that the LORD swore
he would give to your fathers—to Abraham, Isaac and Jacob—and to their descendants after them."

The Appointment of Leaders

9At that time I said to you, "You are too
heavy a burden for me to carry alone.
10The LORD your God has increased
your numbers so that today you are as
many as the stars in the sky. 11May the
LORD, the God of your fathers, increase
you a thousand times and bless you as
he has promised! 12But how can I bear
your problems and your burdens and
your disputes all by myself? 13Choose
some wise, understanding and respected men from each of your tribes, and I
will set them over you."
14You answered me, "What you propose to do is good."
15So I took the leading men of your
tribes, wise and respected men, and appointed them to have authority over
you—as commanders of thousands, of
hundreds, of fifties and of tens and as

tribal officials. 16And I charged your
judges at that time: Hear the disputes
between your brothers and judge fairly,
whether the case is between brother Israelites or between one of them and an
alien. 17Do not show partiality in judging; hear both small and great alike. Do
not be afraid of any man, for judgment
belongs to God. Bring me any case too
hard for you, and I will hear it. 18And at
that time I told you everything you
were to do.

Spies Sent Out

19Then, as the LORD our God commanded us, we set out from Horeb and
went toward the hill country of the Amorites through all that vast and dreadful desert that you have seen, and so we
reached Kadesh Barnea. 20Then I said to
you, "You have reached the hill country
of the Amorites, which the LORD our
God is giving us. 21See, the LORD your
God has given you the land. Go up and
take possession of it as the LORD, the
God of your fathers, told you. Do not be
afraid; do not be discouraged."

22Then all of you came to me and said,
"Let us send men ahead to spy out the
land for us and bring back a report
about the route we are to take and the
towns we will come to."

23The idea seemed good to me; so I selected twelve of you, one man from each
tribe. 24They left and went up into the
hill country, and came to the Valley of
Eshcol and explored it. 25Taking with
them some of the fruit of the land, they
brought it down to us and reported, "It
is a good land that the LORD our God is
giving us."

Rebellion Against the LORD

26But you were unwilling to go up;
you rebelled against the command of
the LORD your God. 27You grumbled in
your tents and said, "The LORD hates us;
so he brought us out of Egypt to deliver
us into the hands of the Amorites to destroy us. 28Where can we go? Our brothers have made us lose heart. They say,
'The people are stronger and taller than
we are; the cities are large, with walls up
to the sky. We even saw the Anakites
there.' "

29Then I said to you, "Do not be terrified; do not be afraid of them. 30The
LORD your God, who is going before
you, will fight for you, as he did for you
in Egypt, before your very eyes, 31and in
the desert. There you saw how the
LORD your God carried you, as a father
carries his son, all the way you went
until you reached this place."

32In spite of this, you did not trust in
the LORD your God, 33who went ahead
of you on your journey, in fire by night
and in a cloud by day, to search out
places for you to camp and to show you
the way you should go.

34When the LORD heard what you
said, he was angry and solemnly swore:
35"Not a man of this evil generation shall
see the good land I swore to give your
forefathers, 36except Caleb son of Jephunneh. He will see it, and I will give
him and his descendants the land he set
his feet on, because he followed the
LORD wholeheartedly."

37Because of you the LORD became angry with me also and said, "You shall not
enter it, either. 38But your assistant,
Joshua son of Nun, will enter it. Encourage him, because he will lead Israel to
inherit it. 39And the little ones that you
said would be taken captive, your children who do not yet know good from
bad—they will enter the land. I will give
it to them and they will take possession
of it. 40But as for you, turn around and
set out toward the desert along the
route to the Red Sea.[a]"

41Then you replied, "We have sinned
against the LORD. We will go up and
fight, as the LORD our God commanded
us." So every one of you put on his
weapons, thinking it easy to go up into
the hill country.

42But the LORD said to me, "Tell them,
'Do not go up and fight, because I will
not be with you. You will be defeated by
your enemies.' "

43So I told you, but you would not lis-

[a]40 Hebrew *Yam Suph*; that is, Sea of Reeds

ten. You rebelled against the LORD's
command and in your arrogance you
marched up into the hill country. 44The
Amorites who lived in those hills came
out against you; they chased you like a
swarm of bees and beat you down from
Seir all the way to Hormah. 45You came
back and wept before the LORD, but he
paid no attention to your weeping and
turned a deaf ear to you. 46And so you
stayed in Kadesh many days—all the
time you spent there.

SHARPEN THE FOCUS

Suppose you loaded up a moving van in Bangor, Maine, and headed for Walla Walla, Washington. You might expect the journey to take about 10 unhurried days or so.

But suppose your arrival was slightly delayed? delayed by, say, 40 years? That scenario parallels Israel's history quite closely (Deuteronomy 1:2–3).

"What took you so long?" concerned relatives or angry employers might ask. And we might ask the same question of ancient Israel. Today's reading begins to answer that question. Moses paints an answer so classic, so typical of human beings, that we might consider his sermon a paint-by-number project.

If we're honest, we recognize in Israel's unbelief our own. Failure to trust. Failure to obey. The story of Israel's life. And of ours. Still, in all of those 40 years of wandering, the faithful Lord did not abandon His children in the desert. He did not shake the dust from His sandals and walk away. Instead He continued to guide, forgive, strengthen, and protect them. The story of Israel's life, and of ours. Thank God!

WEEK 14 • TUESDAY

Deuteronomy 2:1–37

GET THE BIG PICTURE

Moses continues to review Israel's wilderness wanderings. As he does so, he makes it clear that the Lord will give Israel the land He promised to Abraham, Isaac and Jacob, but *only* that land. Some of the territory surrounding them will belong to others: the area around Mt. Seir to Esau's descendants, (Deuteronomy 2:4) and the area of Moab and Ammon to Lot's descendants (Deuteronomy 2:9–10). As you read, note the Lord's constant faithfulness toward His people and His promises. If time is short, focus on Deuteronomy 2:1–8.

Wanderings in the Desert

2 Then we turned back and set out
toward the desert along the
route to the Red Sea,[a] as the LORD had
directed me. For a long time we made
our way around the hill country of Seir.
2Then the LORD said to me, 3"You
have made your way around this hill
country long enough; now turn north.
4Give the people these orders: 'You are
about to pass through the territory of
your brothers the descendants of Esau,
who live in Seir. They will be afraid of
you, but be very careful. 5Do not pro-

[a]1 Hebrew *Yam Suph*; that is, Sea of Reeds

voke them to war, for I will not give you
any of their land, not even enough to
put your foot on. I have given Esau the
hill country of Seir as his own. [6]You are
to pay them in silver for the food you eat
and the water you drink.' "

[7]The LORD your God has blessed you
in all the work of your hands. He has
watched over your journey through
this vast desert. These forty years the
LORD your God has been with you, and
you have not lacked anything.

[8]So we went on past our brothers the
descendants of Esau, who live in Seir.
We turned from the Arabah road, which
comes up from Elath and Ezion Geber,
and traveled along the desert road of
Moab.

[9]Then the LORD said to me, "Do not
harass the Moabites or provoke them to
war, for I will not give you any part of
their land. I have given Ar to the descendants of Lot as a possession."

[10](The Emites used to live there—a
people strong and numerous, and as tall
as the Anakites. [11]Like the Anakites, they
too were considered Rephaites, but the
Moabites called them Emites. [12]Horites
used to live in Seir, but the descendants
of Esau drove them out. They destroyed
the Horites from before them and
settled in their place, just as Israel did in
the land the LORD gave them as their
possession.)

[13]And the LORD said, "Now get up
and cross the Zered Valley." So we
crossed the valley.

[14]Thirty-eight years passed from the
time we left Kadesh Barnea until we
crossed the Zered Valley. By then, that
entire generation of fighting men had
perished from the camp, as the LORD
had sworn to them. [15]The LORD's hand
was against them until he had completely eliminated them from the
camp.

[16]Now when the last of these fighting
men among the people had died, [17]the
LORD said to me, [18]"Today you are to
pass by the region of Moab at Ar. [19]When
you come to the Ammonites, do not
harass them or provoke them to war, for
I will not give you possession of any
land belonging to the Ammonites. I
have given it as a possession to the descendants of Lot."

[20](That too was considered a land of
the Rephaites, who used to live there;
but the Ammonites called them Zam-
zummites. [21]They were a people strong
and numerous, and as tall as the Anakites. The LORD destroyed them from
before the Ammonites, who drove them
out and settled in their place. [22]The
LORD had done the same for the descendants of Esau, who lived in Seir, when
he destroyed the Horites from before
them. They drove them out and have
lived in their place to this day. [23]And as
for the Avvites who lived in villages as
far as Gaza, the Caphtorites coming out
from Caphtor[a] destroyed them and
settled in their place.)

Defeat of Sihon King of Heshbon

[24]"Set out now and cross the Arnon
Gorge. See, I have given into your hand
Sihon the Amorite, king of Heshbon,
and his country. Begin to take possession of it and engage him in battle. [25]This
very day I will begin to put the terror
and fear of you on all the nations under
heaven. They will hear reports of you
and will tremble and be in anguish because of you."

[26]From the desert of Kedemoth I sent
messengers to Sihon king of Heshbon
offering peace and saying, [27]"Let us pass
through your country. We will stay on
the main road; we will not turn aside to
the right or to the left. [28]Sell us food to
eat and water to drink for their price in
silver. Only let us pass through on
foot— [29]as the descendants of Esau, who
live in Seir, and the Moabites, who live
in Ar, did for us—until we cross the Jordan into the land the LORD our God is
giving us." [30]But Sihon king of Heshbon
refused to let us pass through. For the
LORD your God had made his spirit
stubborn and his heart obstinate in order to give him into your hands, as he
has now done.

[31]The LORD said to me, "See, I have be-

[a]23 That is, Crete

gun to deliver Sihon and his country over to you. Now begin to conquer and possess his land."

[32]When Sihon and all his army came out to meet us in battle at Jahaz, [33]the LORD our God delivered him over to us and we struck him down, together with his sons and his whole army. [34]At that time we took all his towns and completely destroyed[a] them—men, women and children. We left no survivors. [35]But the livestock and the plunder from the towns we had captured we carried off for ourselves. [36]From Aroer on the rim of the Arnon Gorge, and from the town in the gorge, even as far as Gilead, not one town was too strong for us. The LORD our God gave us all of them. [37]But in accordance with the command of the LORD our God, you did not encroach on any of the land of the Ammonites, neither the land along the course of the Jabbok nor that around the towns in the hills.

[a]*34* The Hebrew term refers to the irrevocable giving over of things or persons to the LORD, often by totally destroying them.

SHARPEN THE FOCUS

Take a moment right now and take a long look at your hands. What work do they do?

Maybe your hands type on computer keys or grip power tools or diaper babies or direct choirs or swing a baseball bat or write traffic tickets. Most of us use our hands to make a living. But we also use our hands to make a life. Maybe your hands insert stamps into a collector's album or bake cookies or pick apples or paint the railing on the front stairs. Maybe your hands dry someone's tears or write a lonely relative a letter or pat a child on the back in recognition of a job well done.

Moses told Israel, "The LORD your God has blessed you in all the work of your hands" (Deuteronomy 2:7). Israel's hands did much the same work as yours do–they prepared food, repaired their dwellings, washed their clothes, comforted one another, and worshiped the Lord.

Before you end your time with your Savior today, fold your hands. Thank Him for stretching out His hands on the cross to receive the nails–for you. Thank Him that because He did, the Father can bless all the work of your hands. Then think of one way you will use your hands to bless someone who needs the touch of the Savior's love.

WEEK 14 • WEDNESDAY

Deuteronomy 3:1–29

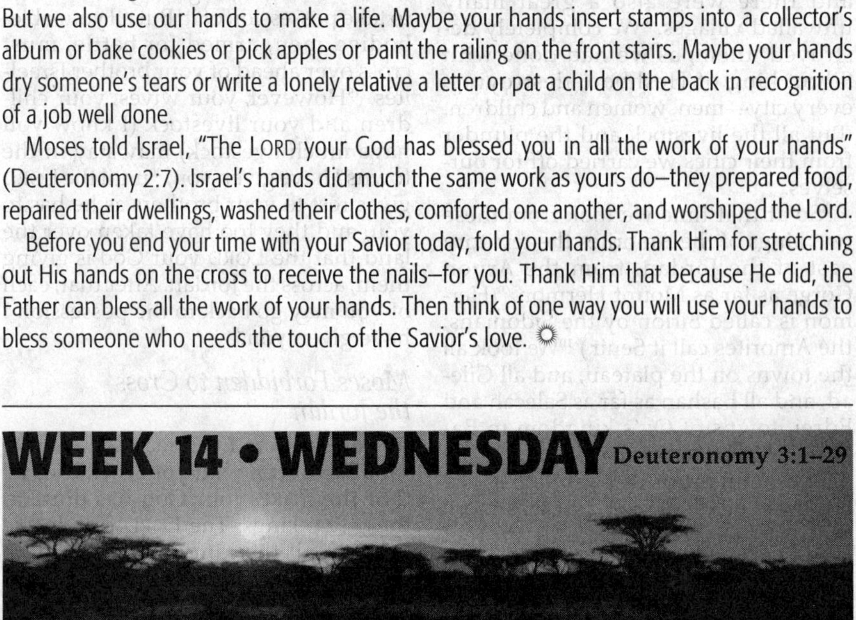

GET THE BIG PICTURE

Moses continues his first sermon, reviewing Israel's history, including the victory over King Og of Bashan and Moses' agreement to give land east of the Jordan River to Reuben, Gad, and Manasseh. The chapter concludes with the Lord's appointment of Joshua as Moses' successor. If time is short, focus on Deuteronomy 3:21–29.

Defeat of Og King of Bashan

3 Next we turned and went up along the road toward Bashan, and Og king of Bashan with his whole army marched out to meet us in battle at Edrei. [2]The LORD said to me, "Do not be afraid of him, for I have handed him over to you with his whole army and his land. Do to him what you did to Sihon king of the Amorites, who reigned in Heshbon."

[3]So the LORD our God also gave into our hands Og king of Bashan and all his army. We struck them down, leaving no survivors. [4]At that time we took all his cities. There was not one of the sixty cities that we did not take from them—the whole region of Argob, Og's kingdom in Bashan. [5]All these cities were fortified with high walls and with gates and bars, and there were also a great many unwalled villages. [6]We completely destroyed[a] them, as we had done with Sihon king of Heshbon, destroying[a] every city—men, women and children. [7]But all the livestock and the plunder from their cities we carried off for ourselves.

[8]So at that time we took from these two kings of the Amorites the territory east of the Jordan, from the Arnon Gorge as far as Mount Hermon. [9](Hermon is called Sirion by the Sidonians; the Amorites call it Senir.) [10]We took all the towns on the plateau, and all Gilead, and all Bashan as far as Salecah and Edrei, towns of Og's kingdom in Bashan. [11](Only Og king of Bashan was left of the remnant of the Rephaites. His bed[b] was made of iron and was more than thirteen feet long and six feet wide.[c] It is still in Rabbah of the Ammonites.)

Division of the Land

[12]Of the land that we took over at that time, I gave the Reubenites and the Gadites the territory north of Aroer by the Arnon Gorge, including half the hill country of Gilead, together with its towns. [13]The rest of Gilead and also all of Bashan, the kingdom of Og, I gave to the half tribe of Manasseh. (The whole region of Argob in Bashan used to be known as a land of the Rephaites. [14]Jair, a descendant of Manasseh, took the whole region of Argob as far as the border of the Geshurites and the Maacathites; it was named after him, so that to this day Bashan is called Havvoth Jair.[d]) [15]And I gave Gilead to Makir. [16]But to the Reubenites and the Gadites I gave the territory extending from Gilead down to the Arnon Gorge (the middle of the gorge being the border) and out to the Jabbok River, which is the border of the Ammonites. [17]Its western border was the Jordan in the Arabah, from Kinnereth to the Sea of the Arabah (the Salt Sea[e]), below the slopes of Pisgah.

[18]I commanded you at that time: "The LORD your God has given you this land to take possession of it. But all your able-bodied men, armed for battle, must cross over ahead of your brother Israelites. [19]However, your wives, your children and your livestock (I know you have much livestock) may stay in the towns I have given you, [20]until the LORD gives rest to your brothers as he has to you, and they too have taken over the land that the LORD your God is giving them, across the Jordan. After that, each of you may go back to the possession I have given you."

Moses Forbidden to Cross the Jordan

[21]At that time I commanded Joshua: "You have seen with your own eyes all that the LORD your God has done to these two kings. The LORD will do the same to all the kingdoms over there where you are going. [22]Do not be afraid of them; the LORD your God himself will fight for you."

[23]At that time I pleaded with the

[a]6 The Hebrew term refers to the irrevocable giving over of things or persons to the LORD, often by totally destroying them. [b]11 Or *sarcophagus* [c]11 Hebrew *nine cubits long and four cubits wide* (about 4 meters long and 1.8 meters wide) [d]14 Or *called the settlements of Jair*
[e]17 That is, the Dead Sea

LORD: 24"O Sovereign LORD, you have begun to show to your servant your greatness and your strong hand. For what god is there in heaven or on earth who can do the deeds and mighty works you do? 25Let me go over and see the good land beyond the Jordan—that fine hill country and Lebanon."

26But because of you the LORD was angry with me and would not listen to me. "That is enough," the LORD said. "Do not speak to me anymore about this matter. 27Go up to the top of Pisgah and look west and north and south and east. Look at the land with your own eyes, since you are not going to cross this Jordan. 28But commission Joshua, and encourage and strengthen him, for he will lead this people across and will cause them to inherit the land that you will see." 29So we stayed in the valley near Beth Peor.

SHARPEN THE FOCUS

Our Father in heaven,
hallowed be Your name,
Your kingdom come,
Your will be done on earth as it is in heaven . . .

In one way or another, each of these petitions of the Lord's Prayer ask that our Lord would preserve and extend His kingdom. We ask that:

- we would be enabled to live, speak, and teach in such a way that those around us would see our Father's majesty, grace, power, purity, holiness and that seeing it, many would fall on their knees in worship to Him;
- the Lord would bring many into His family, His kingdom–the church, and that He will bring His family safely home to Himself when our mission–His mission–here on earth ends;
- we would receive His power to do His will as gladly and willingly as the angels in heaven, especially that He would use us to bring the message of the salvation Christ won on the cross to those who do not yet know or love Him.

Our warfare–the spiritual battles to which our Lord calls us–differ from those ancient Israel fought. In essence, though, we wrestle with the same ultimate enemy–Satan. We face no less danger. And like Israel before us, we know the outcome. Victory already belongs to us because of Christ's cross.

WEEK 14 • THURSDAY

Deuteronomy 4:1–49

GET THE BIG PICTURE

Moses closes the first of his three sermons in Deuteronomy by summarizing the covenant the Lord had made with Israel. Moses warns the people especially about the dangers of idolatry as he points them to the Lord's greatness. As you read, look for the evidence Moses cites to prove the uniqueness of our God and His worthiness of our praise. If time is short, focus on Deuteronomy 4:1–39.

Obedience Commanded

4 Hear now, O Israel, the decrees and laws I am about to teach you. Follow them so that you may live and may go in and take possession of the land that the LORD, the God of your fathers, is giving you. 2 Do not add to what I command you and do not subtract from it, but keep the commands of the LORD your God that I give you.

3 You saw with your own eyes what the LORD did at Baal Peor. The LORD your God destroyed from among you everyone who followed the Baal of Peor, 4 but all of you who held fast to the LORD your God are still alive today.

5 See, I have taught you decrees and laws as the LORD my God commanded me, so that you may follow them in the land you are entering to take possession of it. 6 Observe them carefully, for this will show your wisdom and understanding to the nations, who will hear about all these decrees and say, "Surely this great nation is a wise and understanding people." 7 What other nation is so great as to have their gods near them the way the LORD our God is near us whenever we pray to him? 8 And what other nation is so great as to have such righteous decrees and laws as this body of laws I am setting before you today?

9 Only be careful, and watch yourselves closely so that you do not forget the things your eyes have seen or let them slip from your heart as long as you live. Teach them to your children and to their children after them. 10 Remember the day you stood before the LORD your God at Horeb, when he said to me, "Assemble the people before me to hear my words so that they may learn to revere me as long as they live in the land and may teach them to their children." 11 You came near and stood at the foot of the mountain while it blazed with fire to the very heavens, with black clouds and deep darkness. 12 Then the LORD spoke to you out of the fire. You heard the sound of words but saw no form; there was only a voice. 13 He declared to you his covenant, the Ten Commandments, which he commanded you to follow and then wrote them on two stone tablets. 14 And the LORD directed me at that time to teach you the decrees and laws you are to follow in the land that you are crossing the Jordan to possess.

Idolatry Forbidden

15 You saw no form of any kind the day the LORD spoke to you at Horeb out of the fire. Therefore watch yourselves very carefully, 16 so that you do not become corrupt and make for yourselves an idol, an image of any shape, whether formed like a man or a woman, 17 or like any animal on earth or any bird that flies in the air, 18 or like any creature that moves along the ground or any fish in the waters below. 19 And when you look up to the sky and see the sun, the moon and the stars—all the heavenly array—do not be enticed into bowing down to them and worshiping things the LORD your God has apportioned to all the nations under heaven. 20 But as for you, the LORD took you and brought you out of the iron-smelting furnace, out of Egypt, to be the people of his inheritance, as you now are.

21 The LORD was angry with me because of you, and he solemnly swore that I would not cross the Jordan and enter the good land the LORD your God is giving you as your inheritance. 22 I will die in this land; I will not cross the Jordan; but you are about to cross over and take possession of that good land. 23 Be careful not to forget the covenant of the LORD your God that he made with you; do not make for yourselves an idol in the form of anything the LORD your God has forbidden. 24 For the LORD your God is a consuming fire, a jealous God.

25 After you have had children and

grandchildren and have lived in the land a long time—if you then become corrupt and make any kind of idol, doing evil in the eyes of the LORD your God and provoking him to anger, [26]I call heaven and earth as witnesses against you this day that you will quickly perish from the land that you are crossing the Jordan to possess. You will not live there long but will certainly be destroyed. [27]The LORD will scatter you among the peoples, and only a few of you will survive among the nations to which the LORD will drive you. [28]There you will worship man-made gods of wood and stone, which cannot see or hear or eat or smell. [29]But if from there you seek the LORD your God, you will find him if you look for him with all your heart and with all your soul. [30]When you are in distress and all these things have happened to you, then in later days you will return to the LORD your God and obey him. [31]For the LORD your God is a merciful God; he will not abandon or destroy you or forget the covenant with your forefathers, which he confirmed to them by oath.

The LORD Is God

[32]Ask now about the former days, long before your time, from the day God created man on the earth; ask from one end of the heavens to the other. Has anything so great as this ever happened, or has anything like it ever been heard of? [33]Has any other people heard the voice of God[a] speaking out of fire, as you have, and lived? [34]Has any god ever tried to take for himself one nation out of another nation, by testings, by miraculous signs and wonders, by war, by a mighty hand and an outstretched arm, or by great and awesome deeds, like all the things the LORD your God did for you in Egypt before your very eyes?

[35]You were shown these things so that you might know that the LORD is God; besides him there is no other. [36]From heaven he made you hear his voice to discipline you. On earth he showed you his great fire, and you heard his words from out of the fire. [37]Because he loved your forefathers and chose their descendants after them, he brought you out of Egypt by his Presence and his great strength, [38]to drive out before you nations greater and stronger than you and to bring you into their land to give it to you for your inheritance, as it is today.

[39]Acknowledge and take to heart this day that the LORD is God in heaven above and on the earth below. There is no other. [40]Keep his decrees and commands, which I am giving you today, so that it may go well with you and your children after you and that you may live long in the land the LORD your God gives you for all time.

Cities of Refuge

[41]Then Moses set aside three cities east of the Jordan, [42]to which anyone who had killed a person could flee if he had unintentionally killed his neighbor without malice aforethought. He could flee into one of these cities and save his life. [43]The cities were these: Bezer in the desert plateau, for the Reubenites; Ramoth in Gilead, for the Gadites; and Golan in Bashan, for the Manassites.

Introduction to the Law

[44]This is the law Moses set before the Israelites. [45]These are the stipulations, decrees and laws Moses gave them when they came out of Egypt [46]and were in the valley near Beth Peor east of the Jordan, in the land of Sihon king of the Amorites, who reigned in Heshbon and was defeated by Moses and the Israelites as they came out of Egypt. [47]They took possession of his land and the land of Og king of Bashan, the two Amorite kings east of the Jordan. [48]This land extended from Aroer on the rim of the Arnon Gorge to Mount Siyon[b] (that is, Hermon), [49]and included all the Arabah east of the Jordan, as far as the Sea of the Arabah,[c] below the slopes of Pisgah.

[a]33 Or *of a god* [b]48 Hebrew; Syriac (see also Deut. 3:9) *Sirion* [c]49 That is, the Dead Sea

SHARPEN THE FOCUS

"Has anything so great as this ever happened?" Moses asked Israel (Deuteronomy 4:32). "Has any god ever tried to take for himself one nation out of another nation . . . like all the things the LORD your God did for you in Egypt" (Deuteronomy 4:34)?

Moses' audience would have had to answer, "No. Never. Nothing so great as the exodus has ever happened."

But if Moses were to ask these questions today, he would hear a different response. He would hear us say words like these: "The exodus was a great thing. God's rescue of His people from Egypt and all the wonders He performed were great things. But we've seen something even greater. We've seen the Son of God—who is God Himself—die for us and rise again from death! And we've received new life from Him by His grace through faith in what He has done!"

God's Old Testament people saw the shadow of God's mercy; we see the Son in all His blazing glory. God's Old Testament people had a foretaste of God's love; we feast on a magnificent banquet of His grace and truth.

No other group of people have ever been so highly blessed as we—God's New Testament children. As He was for Israel, so He is—in full—to us.

WEEK 14 • FRIDAY

Deuteronomy 5:1–33

GET THE BIG PICTURE

With today's reading we begin Moses' second (and longest) sermon in Deuteronomy. Having reviewed the past, Moses moves to Israel's present. In chapters 5–26, Moses will review for the people what the Lord expects of them *now*. And He will again tell them of His unfailing present commitment to the covenant He made with Abraham, Isaac, and Jacob over 400 years before. If time is short, focus on Deuteronomy 5:28–33.

The Ten Commandments

5 Moses summoned all Israel and said:

Hear, O Israel, the decrees and laws I declare in your hearing today. Learn
them and be sure to follow them. 2The
LORD our God made a covenant with us
at Horeb. 3It was not with our fathers
that the LORD made this covenant, but
with us, with all of us who are alive here
today. 4The LORD spoke to you face to
face out of the fire on the mountain. 5(At
that time I stood between the LORD and
you to declare to you the word of the LORD, because you were afraid of the fire and did not go up the mountain.) And he said:

6"I am the LORD your God, who brought you out of Egypt, out of the land of slavery.

7"You shall have no other gods before[a] me.

8"You shall not make for yourself an idol in the form of any-

[a]7 Or *besides*

thing in heaven above or on
the earth beneath or in the
waters below. 9You shall not
bow down to them or worship them; for I, the LORD
your God, am a jealous God,
punishing the children for
the sin of the fathers to the
third and fourth generation
of those who hate me, 10but
showing love to a thousand
⌞generations⌟ of those who
love me and keep my commandments.
11"You shall not misuse the name of the LORD your God, for the LORD will not hold anyone guiltless who misuses his name.
12"Observe the Sabbath day by
keeping it holy, as the LORD your God has commanded
you. 13Six days you shall labor
and do all your work, 14but
the seventh day is a Sabbath to the LORD your God. On it you shall not do any work, neither you, nor your son or daughter, nor your manservant or maidservant, nor your ox, your donkey or any of your animals, nor the alien within your gates, so that your manservant and maidservant may rest, as you do.
15Remember that you were slaves in Egypt and that the LORD your God brought you out of there with a mighty hand and an outstretched arm. Therefore the LORD your God has commanded you to observe the Sabbath day.
16"Honor your father and your mother, as the LORD your God has commanded you, so that you may live long and that it may go well with you in the land the LORD your God is giving you.
17"You shall not murder.
18"You shall not commit adultery.
19"You shall not steal.
20"You shall not give false testimony against your neighbor.
21"You shall not covet your neighbor's wife. You shall not set your desire on your neighbor's house or land, his manservant or maidservant, his ox or donkey, or anything that belongs to your neighbor."

22These are the commandments the LORD proclaimed in a loud voice to your whole assembly there on the mountain from out of the fire, the cloud and the deep darkness; and he added nothing more. Then he wrote them on two stone tablets and gave them to me.
23When you heard the voice out of the
darkness, while the mountain was ablaze with fire, all the leading men of your tribes and your elders came to me.
24And you said, "The LORD our God has shown us his glory and his majesty, and we have heard his voice from the fire. Today we have seen that a man can live even if God speaks with him. 25But now,
why should we die? This great fire will consume us, and we will die if we hear the voice of the LORD our God any longer. 26For what mortal man has ever heard
the voice of the living God speaking out of fire, as we have, and survived? 27Go
near and listen to all that the LORD our God says. Then tell us whatever the LORD our God tells you. We will listen and obey."
28The LORD heard you when you spoke to me and the LORD said to me, "I have heard what this people said to you. Everything they said was good.
29Oh, that their hearts would be inclined to fear me and keep all my commands always, so that it might go well with them and their children forever!
30"Go, tell them to return to their
tents. 31But you stay here with me so that I may give you all the commands, decrees and laws you are to teach them to follow in the land I am giving them to possess."
32So be careful to do what the LORD

your God has commanded you; do not
turn aside to the right or to the left.
33Walk in all the way that the LORD your
God has commanded you, so that you
may live and prosper and prolong your
days in the land that you will possess.

SHARPEN THE FOCUS

You've probably heard the expression, "Everything I love is either illegal, immoral, or fattening." Maybe you've jokingly said it yourself. And maybe, sometimes, you've found yourself wondering if it might not be true—especially when your eyes and nose met up with a freshly baked cherry cheesecake!

Since Eden, human beings have been suspicious that God is holding out on us, that He takes pleasure in tantalizing us with good things and then denying them to us.

In Deuteronomy 5:29, 33 we see God's heart. He *wants* to bless His people! He *wants* us to have good things. But, as the Ten Commandments make so clear, He doesn't want our good things to have us. And so, He fences off our greed (Deuteronomy 5:19, 21). He commands us to balance work, leisure, and worship (Deuteronomy 5:12–15). He tells us how to have happy families (Deuteronomy 5:16, 18). He prohibits us from hurting one another (Deuteronomy 5:17, 20). And, most of all, He commands us to do the things that maintain a healthy relationship with Him (Deuteronomy 5:6–12).

The Lord who rescued Israel, the Lord who bled and died for our transgressions on the cross—this same Lord offers us the power we need that we will fear Him and always keep all His commandments.

The family is the primary building block of society. And so the Lord, through Moses, gives His people specific directions for sharing His covenant and its promises with their children. As you read, think about the children and young people in whose lives you are a person of influence. If time is short, focus on Deuteronomy 6:1–12.

Love the LORD Your God

6 These are the commands, decrees and laws the LORD your
God directed me to teach you to observe
in the land that you are crossing the Jordan to possess, 2so that you, your children and their children after them may
fear the LORD your God as long as you
live by keeping all his decrees and commands that I give you, and so that you
may enjoy long life. 3Hear, O Israel, and
be careful to obey so that it may go well
with you and that you may increase
greatly in a land flowing with milk and
honey, just as the LORD, the God of your
fathers, promised you.

[4]Hear, O Israel: The LORD our God,
the LORD is one.[a] [5]Love the LORD your
God with all your heart and with all
your soul and with all your strength.
[6]These commandments that I give you
today are to be upon your hearts. [7]Im-
press them on your children. Talk about
them when you sit at home and when
you walk along the road, when you lie
down and when you get up. [8]Tie them
as symbols on your hands and bind
them on your foreheads. [9]Write them on
the doorframes of your houses and on
your gates.
[10]When the LORD your God brings
you into the land he swore to your fathers, to Abraham, Isaac and Jacob, to
give you—a land with large, flourishing
cities you did not build, [11]houses filled
with all kinds of good things you did
not provide, wells you did not dig, and
vineyards and olive groves you did not
plant—then when you eat and are satisfied, [12]be careful that you do not forget the LORD, who brought you out of
Egypt, out of the land of slavery.
[13]Fear the LORD your God, serve him
only and take your oaths in his name.
[14]Do not follow other gods, the gods of
the peoples around you; [15]for the LORD
your God, who is among you, is a jealous God and his anger will burn against
you, and he will destroy you from the
face of the land. [16]Do not test the LORD
your God as you did at Massah. [17]Be
sure to keep the commands of the LORD
your God and the stipulations and decrees he has given you. [18]Do what is
right and good in the LORD's sight, so
that it may go well with you and you
may go in and take over the good land
that the LORD promised on oath to your
forefathers, [19]thrusting out all your enemies before you, as the LORD said.
[20]In the future, when your son asks
you, "What is the meaning of the stipulations, decrees and laws the LORD our
God has commanded you?" [21]tell him:
"We were slaves of Pharaoh in Egypt,
but the LORD brought us out of Egypt
with a mighty hand. [22]Before our eyes
the LORD sent miraculous signs and
wonders—great and terrible—upon
Egypt and Pharaoh and his whole
household. [23]But he brought us out from
there to bring us in and give us the land
that he promised on oath to our forefathers. [24]The LORD commanded us to
obey all these decrees and to fear the
LORD our God, so that we might always
prosper and be kept alive, as is the case
today. [25]And if we are careful to obey all
this law before the LORD our God, as he
has commanded us, that will be our
righteousness."

[a]4 Or *The LORD our God is one LORD*; or *The LORD is our God, the LORD is one*; or *The LORD is our God, the LORD alone*

SHARPEN THE FOCUS

A careful reading of Matthew, Mark, Luke, and John shows that the Lord Jesus memorized a great many verses from the book of Deuteronomy. Compare Deuteronomy 6:5 with Matthew 22:37, for instance. When do you suppose Jesus learned these words? Probably at the feet of Mary and Joseph as they obeyed the commands of Deuteronomy 6:6–9, 20–25. And no doubt Jesus' parents taught Him the rest of God's Law as well, the Law He was even then keeping in our place.

Several recent studies have shown the power that parents have over the spiritual lives of their children. One study revealed that a parent who shares with his or her child a conversation from the heart about "what Jesus means to me" has more impact on whether or not that young person continues in the Christian faith than if the parent were to send that child to church every week for a year! Of course, Christian parents will want both to witness to and worship with their children.

Praise God that in Christ's cross He has already forgiven our past failures to witness in our families. And praise Him that He promises to empower our witness in the future.

WEEK 15 • MONDAY

Deuteronomy 7:1–26

Moses' second sermon continues. He's repeated the covenant (chapter 5) and commanded Israel to teach it to their children (chapter 6). Now he moves to God's command that Israel should conquer Canaan and utterly destroy the gross idolatry practiced by the Canaanites. If time is short, focus on Deuteronomy 7:1–15.

Driving Out the Nations

7 When the LORD your God brings you into the land you are entering to possess and drives out before you many nations—the Hittites, Girgashites, Amorites, Canaanites, Perizzites, Hivites and Jebusites, seven nations larger and stronger than you— 2and when the LORD your God has delivered them over to you and you have defeated them, then you must destroy them totally.[a] Make no treaty with them, and show them no mercy. 3Do not intermarry with them. Do not give your daughters to their sons or take their daughters for your sons, 4for they will turn your sons away from following me to serve other gods, and the LORD's anger will burn against you and will quickly destroy you. 5This is what you are to do to them: Break down their altars, smash their sacred stones, cut down their Asherah poles[b] and burn their idols in the fire. 6For you are a people holy to the LORD your God. The LORD your God has chosen you out of all the peoples on the face of the earth to be his people, his treasured possession.

7The LORD did not set his affection on you and choose you because you were more numerous than other peoples, for you were the fewest of all peoples. 8But it was because the LORD loved you and kept the oath he swore to your forefathers that he brought you out with a mighty hand and redeemed you from the land of slavery, from the power of Pharaoh king of Egypt. 9Know therefore that the LORD your God is God; he is the faithful God, keeping his covenant of love to a thousand generations of those who love him and keep his commands. 10But

those who hate him he will repay to
    their face by destruction;
he will not be slow to repay to
    their face those who hate
    him.

11Therefore, take care to follow the commands, decrees and laws I give you today.

12If you pay attention to these laws and are careful to follow them, then the LORD your God will keep his covenant of love with you, as he swore to your forefathers. 13He will love you and bless you and increase your numbers. He will bless the fruit of your womb, the crops

[a]2 The Hebrew term refers to the irrevocable giving over of things or persons to the LORD, often by totally destroying them; also in verse 26.
[b]5 That is, symbols of the goddess Asherah; here and elsewhere in Deuteronomy

of your land—your grain, new wine
and oil—the calves of your herds and
the lambs of your flocks in the land that
he swore to your forefathers to give you.
14You will be blessed more than any other people; none of your men or women
will be childless, nor any of your livestock without young. 15The LORD will
keep you free from every disease. He
will not inflict on you the horrible diseases you knew in Egypt, but he will inflict them on all who hate you. 16You
must destroy all the peoples the LORD
your God gives over to you. Do not
look on them with pity and do not serve
their gods, for that will be a snare to
you.
17You may say to yourselves, "These
nations are stronger than we are. How
can we drive them out?" 18But do not be
afraid of them; remember well what the
LORD your God did to Pharaoh and to
all Egypt. 19You saw with your own eyes
the great trials, the miraculous signs and
wonders, the mighty hand and outstretched arm, with which the LORD
your God brought you out. The LORD
your God will do the same to all the
peoples you now fear. 20Moreover, the
LORD your God will send the hornet
among them until even the survivors
who hide from you have perished. 21Do
not be terrified by them, for the LORD
your God, who is among you, is a great
and awesome God. 22The LORD your
God will drive out those nations before
you, little by little. You will not be allowed to eliminate them all at once, or
the wild animals will multiply around
you. 23But the LORD your God will deliver them over to you, throwing them
into great confusion until they are destroyed. 24He will give their kings into
your hand, and you will wipe out their
names from under heaven. No one will
be able to stand up against you; you will
destroy them. 25The images of their gods
you are to burn in the fire. Do not covet
the silver and gold on them, and do not
take it for yourselves, or you will be ensnared by it, for it is detestable to the
LORD your God. 26Do not bring a detestable thing into your house or you, like
it, will be set apart for destruction. Utterly abhor and detest it, for it is set apart
for destruction.

SHARPEN THE FOCUS

A friend of mine tells that when he was a teenager his father set very few rules. The two enjoyed a balanced, healthy relationship, a remarkable relationship. Whenever the son would leave on a date or to attend a ballgame or concert, his dad would hug him and say, "Remember, you're my son." Those words, my friend says, echoed in his ears and kept him from giving into temptation more than a few times.

That's what our Lord says to us in today's Bible reading, too. "Remember, you're My sons and daughters. Remember, I love you. Remember, you're My treasure; My special, chosen, holy people" (see Deuteronomy 7:6–8).

God's treasure. God's jewel. How can you be sure of that? Because the Lord says so, and because He has backed His Word of promise by giving up *the* crown jewel of His kingdom, His one and only Son, to ransom you from the enemies that held you hostage—sin and Satan, hell and death.

Think for a few moments about the fact that *you* are precious to your Lord, His unique treasure. How does remembering that change your purpose for living? your attitude toward others? your approach to problems and temptations? ☼

WEEK 15 • TUESDAY

Deuteronomy 8:1–20

GET THE BIG PICTURE

Perils or prosperity—each brings its own spiritual dangers. As you read today, study especially what Moses says about each. Recall what you know about Israel's wilderness wanderings and the people's reactions to their circumstances. Then ask yourself how peril and prosperity each affect your spiritual health. If time is short, focus on Deuteronomy 8:6–20.

Do Not Forget the LORD

8 Be careful to follow every command I am giving you today, so
that you may live and increase and may
enter and possess the land that the
LORD promised on oath to your forefathers. 2Remember how the LORD your
God led you all the way in the desert
these forty years, to humble you and to
test you in order to know what was in
your heart, whether or not you would
keep his commands. 3He humbled you,
causing you to hunger and then feeding
you with manna, which neither you nor
your fathers had known, to teach you
that man does not live on bread alone
but on every word that comes from the
mouth of the LORD. 4Your clothes did
not wear out and your feet did not swell
during these forty years. 5Know then in
your heart that as a man disciplines his
son, so the LORD your God disciplines
you.
6Observe the commands of the LORD
your God, walking in his ways and re-
vering him. 7For the LORD your God is
bringing you into a good land—a land
with streams and pools of water, with
springs flowing in the valleys and hills;
8a land with wheat and barley, vines and
fig trees, pomegranates, olive oil and
honey; 9a land where bread will not be
scarce and you will lack nothing; a land
where the rocks are iron and you can
dig copper out of the hills.
10When you have eaten and are satisfied, praise the LORD your God for the
good land he has given you. 11Be careful that you do not forget the LORD your
God, failing to observe his commands,
his laws and his decrees that I am giving you this day. 12Otherwise, when you
eat and are satisfied, when you build
fine houses and settle down, 13and
when your herds and flocks grow large
and your silver and gold increase and all
you have is multiplied, 14then your heart
will become proud and you will forget
the LORD your God, who brought you
out of Egypt, out of the land of slavery.
15He led you through the vast and
dreadful desert, that thirsty and waterless land, with its venomous snakes and
scorpions. He brought you water out of
hard rock. 16He gave you manna to eat
in the desert, something your fathers
had never known, to humble and to test
you so that in the end it might go well
with you. 17You may say to yourself, "My
power and the strength of my hands
have produced this wealth for me."
18But remember the LORD your God, for
it is he who gives you the ability to produce wealth, and so confirms his covenant, which he swore to your
forefathers, as it is today.
19If you ever forget the LORD your
God and follow other gods and worship
and bow down to them, I testify against
you today that you will surely be destroyed. 20Like the nations the LORD
destroyed before you, so you will be
destroyed for not obeying the LORD
your God.

SHARPEN THE FOCUS

Troubles and blessings, each of us have an equal share of both in our lives. How do you handle these circumstances when they occur? Do troubles drive you to your Savior? Or do they tend to drive a wedge between you and Him? Do blessings drive you to your Savior? Or when things go well do you tend to wander, to forget the Lord?

As you think today about your own "wilderness wanderings"—caused by both the trials and triumphs of life—thank Him for His faithfulness and forgiveness in Jesus during your times of unfaithfulness and forgetfulness. You may find the words of this hymn helpful as you ask Him to help you grow in trusting Him:

The God of Abr'am praise,
Whose all sufficient grace
Shall guide me all my pilgrim days
In all my ways.
He deigns to call me friend;
He calls Himself my God.
And He shall save me to the end
Through Jesus' blood. (*Lutheran Worship* 450)

WEEK 15 • WEDNESDAY

Deut. 9:1—10:22

GET THE BIG PICTURE

As Moses' second sermon continues, so does his theme: what the Lord expects of Israel right now—in the present. As you read, look for evidence that instead of mere outward compliance to His will, the Lord wants inward commitment to it. If time is short, focus on Deuteronomy 10:12–21.

Not Because of Israel's Righteousness

9 Hear, O Israel. You are now about
to cross the Jordan to go in and
dispossess nations greater and stronger
than you, with large cities that have
walls up to the sky. 2The people are
strong and tall—Anakites! You know
about them and have heard it said:
"Who can stand up against the Anakites?"
3But be assured today that the
LORD your God is the one who goes
across ahead of you like a devouring
fire. He will destroy them; he will subdue
them before you. And you will
drive them out and annihilate them
quickly, as the LORD has promised you.
4After the LORD your God has driven
them out before you, do not say to yourself,
"The LORD has brought me here to
take possession of this land because of
my righteousness." No, it is on account

of the wickedness of these nations that the LORD is going to drive them out before you. 5It is not because of your righteousness or your integrity that you are going in to take possession of their land; but on account of the wickedness of these nations, the LORD your God will drive them out before you, to accomplish what he swore to your fathers, to Abraham, Isaac and Jacob. 6Understand, then, that it is not because of your righteousness that the LORD your God is giving you this good land to possess, for you are a stiff-necked people.

The Golden Calf

7Remember this and never forget how you provoked the LORD your God to anger in the desert. From the day you left Egypt until you arrived here, you have been rebellious against the LORD. 8At Horeb you aroused the LORD's wrath so that he was angry enough to destroy you. 9When I went up on the mountain to receive the tablets of stone, the tablets of the covenant that the LORD had made with you, I stayed on the mountain forty days and forty nights; I ate no bread and drank no water. 10The LORD gave me two stone tablets inscribed by the finger of God. On them were all the commandments the LORD proclaimed to you on the mountain out of the fire, on the day of the assembly.

11At the end of the forty days and forty nights, the LORD gave me the two stone tablets, the tablets of the covenant. 12Then the LORD told me, "Go down from here at once, because your people whom you brought out of Egypt have become corrupt. They have turned away quickly from what I commanded them and have made a cast idol for themselves."

13And the LORD said to me, "I have seen this people, and they are a stiff-necked people indeed! 14Let me alone, so that I may destroy them and blot out their name from under heaven. And I will make you into a nation stronger and more numerous than they."

15So I turned and went down from the mountain while it was ablaze with fire. And the two tablets of the covenant were in my hands.[a] 16When I looked, I saw that you had sinned against the LORD your God; you had made for yourselves an idol cast in the shape of a calf. You had turned aside quickly from the way that the LORD had commanded you. 17So I took the two tablets and threw them out of my hands, breaking them to pieces before your eyes.

18Then once again I fell prostrate before the LORD for forty days and forty nights; I ate no bread and drank no water, because of all the sin you had committed, doing what was evil in the LORD's sight and so provoking him to anger. 19I feared the anger and wrath of the LORD, for he was angry enough with you to destroy you. But again the LORD listened to me. 20And the LORD was angry enough with Aaron to destroy him, but at that time I prayed for Aaron too. 21Also I took that sinful thing of yours, the calf you had made, and burned it in the fire. Then I crushed it and ground it to powder as fine as dust and threw the dust into a stream that flowed down the mountain.

22You also made the LORD angry at Taberah, at Massah and at Kibroth Hattaavah.

23And when the LORD sent you out from Kadesh Barnea, he said, "Go up and take possession of the land I have given you." But you rebelled against the command of the LORD your God. You did not trust him or obey him. 24You have been rebellious against the LORD ever since I have known you.

25I lay prostrate before the LORD those forty days and forty nights because the LORD had said he would destroy you. 26I prayed to the LORD and said, "O Sovereign LORD, do not destroy your people, your own inheritance that you redeemed by your great power and brought out of Egypt with a mighty hand. 27Remember your servants Abraham, Isaac and Jacob. Overlook the stubbornness of this people, their wick-

[a]15 Or *And I had the two tablets of the covenant with me, one in each hand*

edness and their sin. [28]Otherwise, the country from which you brought us will say, 'Because the LORD was not able to take them into the land he had promised them, and because he hated them, he brought them out to put them to death in the desert.' [29]But they are your people, your inheritance that you brought out by your great power and your outstretched arm."

Tablets Like the First Ones

10 At that time the LORD said to me, "Chisel out two stone tablets like the first ones and come up to me on the mountain. Also make a wooden chest.[a] [2]I will write on the tablets the words that were on the first tablets, which you broke. Then you are to put them in the chest."

[3]So I made the ark out of acacia wood and chiseled out two stone tablets like the first ones, and I went up on the mountain with the two tablets in my hands. [4]The LORD wrote on these tablets what he had written before, the Ten Commandments he had proclaimed to you on the mountain, out of the fire, on the day of the assembly. And the LORD gave them to me. [5]Then I came back down the mountain and put the tablets in the ark I had made, as the LORD commanded me, and they are there now.

[6](The Israelites traveled from the wells of the Jaakanites to Moserah. There Aaron died and was buried, and Eleazar his son succeeded him as priest. [7]From there they traveled to Gudgodah and on to Jotbathah, a land with streams of water. [8]At that time the LORD set apart the tribe of Levi to carry the ark of the covenant of the LORD, to stand before the LORD to minister and to pronounce blessings in his name, as they still do today. [9]That is why the Levites have no share or inheritance among their brothers; the LORD is their inheritance, as the LORD your God told them.)

[10]Now I had stayed on the mountain forty days and nights, as I did the first time, and the LORD listened to me at this time also. It was not his will to destroy you. [11]"Go," the LORD said to me, "and lead the people on their way, so that they may enter and possess the land that I swore to their fathers to give them."

Fear the LORD

[12]And now, O Israel, what does the LORD your God ask of you but to fear the LORD your God, to walk in all his ways, to love him, to serve the LORD your God with all your heart and with all your soul, [13]and to observe the LORD's commands and decrees that I am giving you today for your own good?

[14]To the LORD your God belong the heavens, even the highest heavens, the earth and everything in it. [15]Yet the LORD set his affection on your forefathers and loved them, and he chose you, their descendants, above all the nations, as it is today. [16]Circumcise your hearts, therefore, and do not be stiff-necked any longer. [17]For the LORD your God is God of gods and Lord of lords, the great God, mighty and awesome, who shows no partiality and accepts no bribes. [18]He defends the cause of the fatherless and the widow, and loves the alien, giving him food and clothing. [19]And you are to love those who are aliens, for you yourselves were aliens in Egypt. [20]Fear the LORD your God and serve him. Hold fast to him and take your oaths in his name. [21]He is your praise; he is your God, who performed for you those great and awesome wonders you saw with your own eyes. [22]Your forefathers who went down into Egypt were seventy in all, and now the LORD your God has made you as numerous as the stars in the sky.

[a] *1* That is, an ark

SHARPEN THE FOCUS

"Circumcise your hearts," the Lord says (Deuteronomy 10:16). What radical surgery! What can this mean?

There's a New Testament passage with a similar word picture. The crowd around Peter on Pentecost heard God's Word accusing them of grave sin—they had killed their Messiah, the Christ! Convicted of their responsibility, the people "were cut to the heart and said . . . 'What shall we do?' " (Acts 2:37).

Israel and the Jews of Jesus' day often fell for Satan's lie that following the rules and obeying the outward regulations of God's Law were enough. What else could God expect?

The Lord could and did expect much more—circumcision of the heart. A heart broken before God in repentance and humbly dependent on Him for right standing before the throne of judgment.

Are we ever satisfied with mere outward obedience? with following the rules? Are we content to go through the motions of church attendance, Bible reading, and a respectable lifestyle? Even if we are, our Lord is not.

No earthly doctor can cut our hearts to reveal our sins, our needs. Only our Savior-God can. No earthly doctor can heal the wounds those sins have caused. Only Christ and His cross can. ☼

WEEK 15 • THURSDAY

Deut. 11:1—12:32

GET THE BIG PICTURE

Moses reminds the people of times they have seen the Lord act in love and power on their behalf. Now, as they continue to obey Him, He will bless them with victory. In response, they are to worship their Lord in joy. If time is short, focus on Deuteronomy 12:1–12.

Love and Obey the LORD

11 Love the LORD your God and
keep his requirements, his decrees, his laws and his commands always. [2]Remember today that your
children were not the ones who saw
and experienced the discipline of the
LORD your God: his majesty, his mighty
hand, his outstretched arm; [3]the signs
he performed and the things he did in
the heart of Egypt, both to Pharaoh king
of Egypt and to his whole country;
[4]what he did to the Egyptian army, to its
horses and chariots, how he overwhelmed them with the waters of the
Red Sea[a] as they were pursuing you,
and how the LORD brought lasting ruin
on them. [5]It was not your children who
saw what he did for you in the desert
until you arrived at this place, [6]and what
he did to Dathan and Abiram, sons of
Eliab the Reubenite, when the earth
opened its mouth right in the middle of
all Israel and swallowed them up with
their households, their tents and every
living thing that belonged to them. [7]But
it was your own eyes that saw all these
great things the LORD has done.

[a]4 Hebrew *Yam Suph;* that is, Sea of Reeds

8Observe therefore all the commands
I am giving you today, so that you may
have the strength to go in and take over
the land that you are crossing the Jordan to possess, 9and so that you may live
long in the land that the LORD swore to
your forefathers to give to them and
their descendants, a land flowing with
milk and honey. 10The land you are entering to take over is not like the land of
Egypt, from which you have come,
where you planted your seed and irri-
gated it by foot as in a vegetable garden.
11But the land you are crossing the Jordan to take possession of is a land of
mountains and valleys that drinks rain
from heaven. 12It is a land the LORD your
God cares for; the eyes of the LORD your
God are continually on it from the beginning of the year to its end.
13So if you faithfully obey the commands I am giving you today—to love
the LORD your God and to serve him
with all your heart and with all your
soul— 14then I will send rain on your
land in its season, both autumn and
spring rains, so that you may gather in
your grain, new wine and oil. 15I will
provide grass in the fields for your
cattle, and you will eat and be satisfied.
16Be careful, or you will be enticed to
turn away and worship other gods and
bow down to them. 17Then the LORD's
anger will burn against you, and he will
shut the heavens so that it will not rain
and the ground will yield no produce,
and you will soon perish from the good
land the LORD is giving you. 18Fix these
words of mine in your hearts and
minds; tie them as symbols on your
hands and bind them on your foreheads. 19Teach them to your children,
talking about them when you sit at
home and when you walk along the
road, when you lie down and when you
get up. 20Write them on the doorframes
of your houses and on your gates, 21so
that your days and the days of your children may be many in the land that the
LORD swore to give your forefathers, as
many as the days that the heavens are
above the earth.
22If you carefully observe all these
commands I am giving you to follow—
to love the LORD your God, to walk in
all his ways and to hold fast to him—
23then the LORD will drive out all these
nations before you, and you will dispossess nations larger and stronger than
you. 24Every place where you set your
foot will be yours: Your territory will
extend from the desert to Lebanon, and
from the Euphrates River to the western
sea.[a] 25No man will be able to stand
against you. The LORD your God, as he
promised you, will put the terror and
fear of you on the whole land, wherever
you go.
26See, I am setting before you today a
blessing and a curse— 27the blessing if
you obey the commands of the LORD
your God that I am giving you today;
28the curse if you disobey the commands
of the LORD your God and turn from the
way that I command you today by following other gods, which you have not
known. 29When the LORD your God has
brought you into the land you are entering to possess, you are to proclaim on
Mount Gerizim the blessings, and on
Mount Ebal the curses. 30As you know,
these mountains are across the Jordan,
west of the road,[b] toward the setting
sun, near the great trees of Moreh, in the
territory of those Canaanites living in
the Arabah in the vicinity of Gilgal. 31You
are about to cross the Jordan to enter
and take possession of the land the
LORD your God is giving you. When
you have taken it over and are living
there, 32be sure that you obey all the decrees and laws I am setting before you
today.

The One Place of Worship

12 These are the decrees and
laws you must be careful to
follow in the land that the LORD, the
God of your fathers, has given you to
possess—as long as you live in the land.
2Destroy completely all the places on the
high mountains and on the hills and
under every spreading tree where the

[a]24 That is, the Mediterranean [b]30 Or *Jordan, westward*

nations you are dispossessing worship their gods. 3Break down their altars, smash their sacred stones and burn their Asherah poles in the fire; cut down the idols of their gods and wipe out their names from those places.

4You must not worship the LORD your God in their way. 5But you are to seek the place the LORD your God will choose from among all your tribes to put his Name there for his dwelling. To that place you must go; 6there bring your burnt offerings and sacrifices, your tithes and special gifts, what you have vowed to give and your freewill offerings, and the firstborn of your herds and flocks. 7There, in the presence of the LORD your God, you and your families shall eat and shall rejoice in everything you have put your hand to, because the LORD your God has blessed you.

8You are not to do as we do here today, everyone as he sees fit, 9since you have not yet reached the resting place and the inheritance the LORD your God is giving you. 10But you will cross the Jordan and settle in the land the LORD your God is giving you as an inheritance, and he will give you rest from all your enemies around you so that you will live in safety. 11Then to the place the LORD your God will choose as a dwelling for his Name—there you are to bring everything I command you: your burnt offerings and sacrifices, your tithes and special gifts, and all the choice possessions you have vowed to the LORD. 12And there rejoice before the LORD your God, you, your sons and daughters, your menservants and maidservants, and the Levites from your towns, who have no allotment or inheritance of their own. 13Be careful not to sacrifice your burnt offerings anywhere you please. 14Offer them only at the place the LORD will choose in one of your tribes, and there observe everything I command you.

15Nevertheless, you may slaughter your animals in any of your towns and eat as much of the meat as you want, as if it were gazelle or deer, according to the blessing the LORD your God gives you. Both the ceremonially unclean and the clean may eat it. 16But you must not eat the blood; pour it out on the ground like water. 17You must not eat in your own towns the tithe of your grain and new wine and oil, or the firstborn of your herds and flocks, or whatever you have vowed to give, or your freewill offerings or special gifts. 18Instead, you are to eat them in the presence of the LORD your God at the place the LORD your God will choose—you, your sons and daughters, your menservants and maidservants, and the Levites from your towns—and you are to rejoice before the LORD your God in everything you put your hand to. 19Be careful not to neglect the Levites as long as you live in your land.

20When the LORD your God has enlarged your territory as he promised you, and you crave meat and say, "I would like some meat," then you may eat as much of it as you want. 21If the place where the LORD your God chooses to put his Name is too far away from you, you may slaughter animals from the herds and flocks the LORD has given you, as I have commanded you, and in your own towns you may eat as much of them as you want. 22Eat them as you would gazelle or deer. Both the ceremonially unclean and the clean may eat. 23But be sure you do not eat the blood, because the blood is the life, and you must not eat the life with the meat. 24You must not eat the blood; pour it out on the ground like water. 25Do not eat it, so that it may go well with you and your children after you, because you will be doing what is right in the eyes of the LORD.

26But take your consecrated things and whatever you have vowed to give, and go to the place the LORD will choose. 27Present your burnt offerings on the altar of the LORD your God, both the meat and the blood. The blood of your sacrifices must be poured beside the altar of the LORD your God, but you may eat the meat. 28Be careful to obey all these regulations I am giving you, so that it may always go well with you and

your children after you, because you
will be doing what is good and right in
the eyes of the LORD your God.
[29]The LORD your God will cut off before you the nations you are about to
invade and dispossess. But when you
have driven them out and settled in
their land, [30]and after they have been
destroyed before you, be careful not to
be ensnared by inquiring about their
gods, saying, "How do these nations
serve their gods? We will do the same."
[31]You must not worship the LORD your
God in their way, because in worshiping their gods, they do all kinds of detestable things the LORD hates. They
even burn their sons and daughters in
the fire as sacrifices to their gods.
[32]See that you do all I command you;
do not add to it or take away from it.

SHARPEN THE FOCUS

"Rejoice in the Lord always. I will say it again: Rejoice!" (Philippians 4:4).

Paul echoes the command of Moses (Deuteronomy 12:7, 12, 18). "Rejoice!" If it's payday or the first day of a vacation, that may be easy to do. On the other hand, if the kids are sick or the car needs $600 worth of repairs, rejoicing could be the last thing on your agenda.

Paul's phrase, "in the Lord" changes a command into a possibility. These words remind us of our potential as forgiven children of God. Our Lord doesn't say, "I know you've had a bad week, but try hard to rejoice in Me anyway."

Paul reminds us that we are "in the Lord." He has joined us to Himself, to His righteousness, to His resurrected life in our Baptism. We are in Him, and nothing can separate us from Him. This relationship forms the foundation from which we can grow more and more fully into a lifestyle marked by love, joy, peace, patience, and all the other fruit the Spirit produces in us. (Galatians 5:22–23).

You may be laughing today—rejoice in the Lord. You may be weeping today—let your Savior hold you, and rejoice in the Lord. Ask the Holy Spirit to comfort you with His presence and promise that you are His.

WEEK 15 • FRIDAY

Deuteronomy 13:1–18

GET THE BIG PICTURE

Today's reading of Deuteronomy 13 reveals the Lord's anger at attempted murder—spiritual murder. As you read, think about why the Lord prescribed the death penalty for this crime under Old Testament Law. If time is short, focus on Deuteronomy 13:1–5.

Worshiping Other Gods

13 If a prophet, or one who foretells by dreams, appears
among you and announces to you a
miraculous sign or wonder, [2]and if the
sign or wonder of which he has spoken
takes place, and he says, "Let us follow
other gods" (gods you have not known)
"and let us worship them," [3]you must
not listen to the words of that prophet

or dreamer. The LORD your God is testing you to find out whether you love
him with all your heart and with all
your soul. 4It is the LORD your God you
must follow, and him you must revere.
Keep his commands and obey him;
serve him and hold fast to him. 5That
prophet or dreamer must be put to
death, because he preached rebellion
against the LORD your God, who
brought you out of Egypt and redeemed you from the land of slavery;
he has tried to turn you from the way
the LORD your God commanded you to
follow. You must purge the evil from
among you.
6If your very own brother, or your son
or daughter, or the wife you love, or
your closest friend secretly entices you,
saying, "Let us go and worship other
gods" (gods that neither you nor your
fathers have known, 7gods of the peoples around you, whether near or far,
from one end of the land to the other),
8do not yield to him or listen to him.
Show him no pity. Do not spare him or
shield him. 9You must certainly put him
to death. Your hand must be the first in
putting him to death, and then the
hands of all the people. 10Stone him to
death, because he tried to turn you
away from the LORD your God, who
brought you out of Egypt, out of the
land of slavery. 11Then all Israel will hear
and be afraid, and no one among you
will do such an evil thing again.
12If you hear it said about one of the
towns the LORD your God is giving you
to live in 13that wicked men have arisen
among you and have led the people of
their town astray, saying, "Let us go and
worship other gods" (gods you have not
known), 14then you must inquire, probe
and investigate it thoroughly. And if it
is true and it has been proved that this
detestable thing has been done among
you, 15you must certainly put to the
sword all who live in that town. Destroy
it completely,[a] both its people and its
livestock. 16Gather all the plunder of the
town into the middle of the public
square and completely burn the town
and all its plunder as a whole burnt offering to the LORD your God. It is to remain a ruin forever, never to be rebuilt.
17None of those condemned things[a]
shall be found in your hands, so that the
LORD will turn from his fierce anger; he
will show you mercy, have compassion
on you, and increase your numbers, as
he promised on oath to your forefathers, 18because you obey the LORD your
God, keeping all his commands that I
am giving you today and doing what is
right in his eyes.

[a] *15,17* The Hebrew term refers to the irrevocable giving over of things or persons to the LORD, often by totally destroying them.

SHARPEN THE FOCUS

False prophets hardly ever wear a sign saying, "False prophet—beware!" Wolves come into the flock disguised as sheep, Jesus warns (Matthew 7:15). They may even perform miracles; their forecasts about the future may materialize, Moses adds (Deuteronomy 13:1–2).

Jesus echoes Moses' warning:

> *False Christs and false prophets will appear and perform great signs and miracles to deceive even the elect—if that were possible.* (Matthew 24:24)

So how are we to know the truth? Not by following our hearts—our feelings can deceive us. Not by following our heads—our minds have been warped by sin and can lead us astray. Not by following the opinion or ideas of other people—our friends and even members of our own family may be blind and confused without even knowing it.

We follow Christ. We use His Word as our compass. We align our thoughts with His truth.

How important for us, then, to know the Scriptures well! To be steeped in them. To let God's Word have its way in us as it transforms our mind and our feelings so thoroughly that we know the mind and will of the Father. In this way, the Lord's forgiven children escape the spiritual and intellectual traps Satan has set for us.

WEEK 15 • SATURDAY Deuteronomy 14:1—15:23

Continuing his sermon on what the Lord requires of Israel as the nation enters the Promised Land, Moses repeats and expands several of the laws we've encountered before. As you read, take note of any new information you find. If time is short, focus on Deuteronomy 15:12–18.

Clean and Unclean Food

14 You are the children of the LORD your God. Do not cut yourselves or shave the front of your heads for the dead, 2for you are a people holy to the LORD your God. Out of all the peoples on the face of the earth, the LORD has chosen you to be his treasured possession.

3Do not eat any detestable thing. 4These are the animals you may eat: the ox, the sheep, the goat, 5the deer, the gazelle, the roe deer, the wild goat, the ibex, the antelope and the mountain sheep.[a] 6You may eat any animal that has a split hoof divided in two and that chews the cud. 7However, of those that chew the cud or that have a split hoof completely divided you may not eat the camel, the rabbit or the coney.[b] Although they chew the cud, they do not have a split hoof; they are ceremonially unclean for you. 8The pig is also unclean; although it has a split hoof, it does not chew the cud. You are not to eat their meat or touch their carcasses.

9Of all the creatures living in the water, you may eat any that has fins and scales. 10But anything that does not have fins and scales you may not eat; for you it is unclean.

11You may eat any clean bird. 12But these you may not eat: the eagle, the vulture, the black vulture, 13the red kite, the black kite, any kind of falcon, 14any kind of raven, 15the horned owl, the screech owl, the gull, any kind of hawk, 16the little owl, the great owl, the white owl, 17the desert owl, the osprey, the cormorant, 18the stork, any kind of heron, the hoopoe and the bat.

19All flying insects that swarm are unclean to you; do not eat them. 20But any winged creature that is clean you may eat.

21Do not eat anything you find already dead. You may give it to an alien living in any of your towns, and he may eat it, or you may sell it to a foreigner. But you are a people holy to the LORD your God.

Do not cook a young goat in its mother's milk.

Tithes

22Be sure to set aside a tenth of all that your fields produce each year. 23Eat the tithe of your grain, new wine and oil, and the firstborn of your herds and

[a]5 The precise identification of some of the birds and animals in this chapter is uncertain.
[b]7 That is, the hyrax or rock badger

flocks in the presence of the LORD your God at the place he will choose as a dwelling for his Name, so that you may learn to revere the LORD your God always. 24But if that place is too distant and you have been blessed by the LORD your God and cannot carry your tithe (because the place where the LORD will choose to put his Name is so far away), 25then exchange your tithe for silver, and take the silver with you and go to the place the LORD your God will choose. 26Use the silver to buy whatever you like: cattle, sheep, wine or other fermented drink, or anything you wish. Then you and your household shall eat there in the presence of the LORD your God and rejoice. 27And do not neglect the Levites living in your towns, for they have no allotment or inheritance of their own.

28At the end of every three years, bring all the tithes of that year's produce and store it in your towns, 29so that the Levites (who have no allotment or inheritance of their own) and the aliens, the fatherless and the widows who live in your towns may come and eat and be satisfied, and so that the LORD your God may bless you in all the work of your hands.

The Year for Canceling Debts

15 At the end of every seven years you must cancel debts. 2This is how it is to be done: Every creditor shall cancel the loan he has made to his fellow Israelite. He shall not require payment from his fellow Israelite or brother, because the LORD's time for canceling debts has been proclaimed. 3You may require payment from a foreigner, but you must cancel any debt your brother owes you. 4However, there should be no poor among you, for in the land the LORD your God is giving you to possess as your inheritance, he will richly bless you, 5if only you fully obey the LORD your God and are careful to follow all these commands I am giving you today. 6For the LORD your God will bless you as he has promised, and you will lend to many nations but will borrow from none. You will rule over many nations but none will rule over you.

7If there is a poor man among your brothers in any of the towns of the land that the LORD your God is giving you, do not be hardhearted or tightfisted toward your poor brother. 8Rather be openhanded and freely lend him whatever he needs. 9Be careful not to harbor this wicked thought: "The seventh year, the year for canceling debts, is near," so that you do not show ill will toward your needy brother and give him nothing. He may then appeal to the LORD against you, and you will be found guilty of sin. 10Give generously to him and do so without a grudging heart; then because of this the LORD your God will bless you in all your work and in everything you put your hand to. 11There will always be poor people in the land. Therefore I command you to be openhanded toward your brothers and toward the poor and needy in your land.

Freeing Servants

12If a fellow Hebrew, a man or a woman, sells himself to you and serves you six years, in the seventh year you must let him go free. 13And when you release him, do not send him away emptyhanded. 14Supply him liberally from your flock, your threshing floor and your winepress. Give to him as the LORD your God has blessed you. 15Remember that you were slaves in Egypt and the LORD your God redeemed you. That is why I give you this command today.

16But if your servant says to you, "I do not want to leave you," because he loves you and your family and is well off with you, 17then take an awl and push it through his ear lobe into the door, and he will become your servant for life. Do the same for your maidservant.

18Do not consider it a hardship to set your servant free, because his service to you these six years has been worth twice as much as that of a hired hand. And the LORD your God will bless you in everything you do.

The Firstborn Animals

[19]Set apart for the LORD your God every firstborn male of your herds and
flocks. Do not put the firstborn of your
oxen to work, and do not shear the firstborn of your sheep. [20]Each year you and
your family are to eat them in the presence of the LORD your God at the place
he will choose. [21]If an animal has a defect, is lame or blind, or has any serious
flaw, you must not sacrifice it to the
LORD your God. [22]You are to eat it in
your own towns. Both the ceremonially
unclean and the clean may eat it, as if it
were gazelle or deer. [23]But you must not
eat the blood; pour it out on the ground
like water.

SHARPEN THE FOCUS

Every seventh year Hebrew servants were freed. Their debts paid and duty done. But suppose a servant didn't want to go! He might think, "My life is better than it's ever been. Living here is the best thing that's ever happened to me. I don't want my freedom. My service is not a burden, but a blessing." What then?

Deuteronomy 15:17 tells the story. The process poses some questions for us:

- Do you see your service for Christ as a burden or a blessing?
- Have you said, in love, to your Master, "Pierce my ear"?
- Sometimes, deep down to your heart, do you ever regret that request?

We all serve halfheartedly at times. Usually it happens when we forget the poverty, the spiritual emptiness, from which Christ Jesus has rescued us. We forget the crushing sin-debt our Savior has lifted from our shoulders and carried to His cross.

If you find yourself burdened by your service for the Lord Jesus or even resentful about it, back off a bit. Take time to remember your former slavery to Satan and to the Law. Take time to remember the freedom from guilt and sin that are now yours in Jesus. Let your Savior's love shine from His cross into your heart and melt the hardness there.

WEEK 16 • MONDAY

Deuteronomy 16:1—17:20

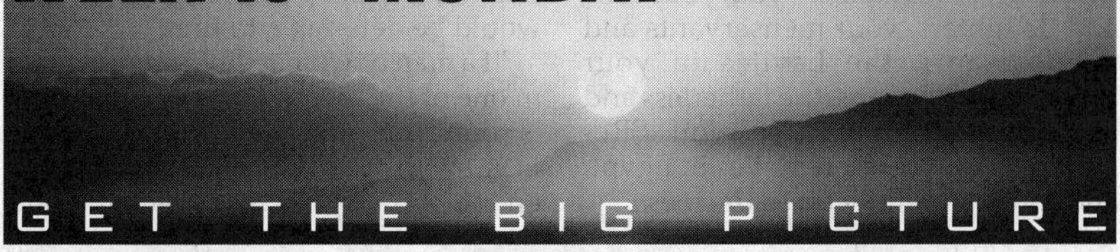

GET THE BIG PICTURE

As Moses continues to prepare Israel for life in Canaan, he reminds them of the three observances the Lord requires each year. He reviews the authority and responsibilities of the priests and Levites in judging legal questions. And he provides for the day when Israel will ask for an earthly king. If time is short, focus on Deuteronomy 17:14–20.

Passover

16 Observe the month of Abib
and celebrate the Passover of
the LORD your God, because in the
month of Abib he brought you out of
Egypt by night. [2]Sacrifice as the Passover to the LORD your God an animal
from your flock or herd at the place the

LORD will choose as a dwelling for his Name. [3]Do not eat it with bread made with yeast, but for seven days eat unleavened bread, the bread of affliction, because you left Egypt in haste—so that all the days of your life you may remember the time of your departure from Egypt. [4]Let no yeast be found in your possession in all your land for seven days. Do not let any of the meat you sacrifice on the evening of the first day remain until morning.

[5]You must not sacrifice the Passover in any town the LORD your God gives you [6]except in the place he will choose as a dwelling for his Name. There you must sacrifice the Passover in the evening, when the sun goes down, on the anniversary[a] of your departure from Egypt. [7]Roast it and eat it at the place the LORD your God will choose. Then in the morning return to your tents. [8]For six days eat unleavened bread and on the seventh day hold an assembly to the LORD your God and do no work.

Feast of Weeks

[9]Count off seven weeks from the time you begin to put the sickle to the standing grain. [10]Then celebrate the Feast of Weeks to the LORD your God by giving a freewill offering in proportion to the blessings the LORD your God has given you. [11]And rejoice before the LORD your God at the place he will choose as a dwelling for his Name—you, your sons and daughters, your menservants and maidservants, the Levites in your towns, and the aliens, the fatherless and the widows living among you. [12]Remember that you were slaves in Egypt, and follow carefully these decrees.

Feast of Tabernacles

[13]Celebrate the Feast of Tabernacles for seven days after you have gathered the produce of your threshing floor and your winepress. [14]Be joyful at your Feast—you, your sons and daughters, your menservants and maidservants, and the Levites, the aliens, the fatherless and the widows who live in your towns. [15]For seven days celebrate the Feast to the LORD your God at the place the LORD will choose. For the LORD your God will bless you in all your harvest and in all the work of your hands, and your joy will be complete.

[16]Three times a year all your men must appear before the LORD your God at the place he will choose: at the Feast of Unleavened Bread, the Feast of Weeks and the Feast of Tabernacles. No man should appear before the LORD empty-handed: [17]Each of you must bring a gift in proportion to the way the LORD your God has blessed you.

Judges

[18]Appoint judges and officials for each of your tribes in every town the LORD your God is giving you, and they shall judge the people fairly. [19]Do not pervert justice or show partiality. Do not accept a bribe, for a bribe blinds the eyes of the wise and twists the words of the righteous. [20]Follow justice and justice alone, so that you may live and possess the land the LORD your God is giving you.

Worshiping Other Gods

[21]Do not set up any wooden Asherah pole[b] beside the altar you build to the LORD your God, [22]and do not erect a sacred stone, for these the LORD your God hates.

17 Do not sacrifice to the LORD your God an ox or a sheep that has any defect or flaw in it, for that would be detestable to him.

[2]If a man or woman living among you in one of the towns the LORD gives you is found doing evil in the eyes of the LORD your God in violation of his covenant, [3]and contrary to my command has worshiped other gods, bowing down to them or to the sun or the moon or the stars of the sky, [4]and this has been brought to your attention, then you must investigate it thoroughly. If it is true and it has been proved that this detestable thing has been done in Israel, [5]take the man or woman who has done

[a]6 Or *down, at the time of day* [b]21 Or *Do not plant any tree dedicated to Asherah*

this evil deed to your city gate and stone
that person to death. 6On the testimony of two or three witnesses a man shall
be put to death, but no one shall be put
to death on the testimony of only one
witness. 7The hands of the witnesses
must be the first in putting him to death,
and then the hands of all the people.
You must purge the evil from among you.

Law Courts

8If cases come before your courts that
are too difficult for you to judge—
whether bloodshed, lawsuits or assaults—take them to the place the LORD
your God will choose. 9Go to the priests,
who are Levites, and to the judge who
is in office at that time. Inquire of them
and they will give you the verdict. 10You
must act according to the decisions they
give you at the place the LORD will
choose. Be careful to do everything they
direct you to do. 11Act according to the
law they teach you and the decisions
they give you. Do not turn aside from
what they tell you, to the right or to the
left. 12The man who shows contempt for
the judge or for the priest who stands
ministering there to the LORD your God
must be put to death. You must purge
the evil from Israel. 13All the people will
hear and be afraid, and will not be contemptuous again.

The King

14When you enter the land the LORD
your God is giving you and have taken
possession of it and settled in it, and you
say, "Let us set a king over us like all the
nations around us," 15be sure to appoint
over you the king the LORD your God
chooses. He must be from among your
own brothers. Do not place a foreigner
over you, one who is not a brother Israelite. 16The king, moreover, must not acquire great numbers of horses for
himself or make the people return to
Egypt to get more of them, for the LORD
has told you, "You are not to go back
that way again." 17He must not take
many wives, or his heart will be led
astray. He must not accumulate large
amounts of silver and gold.
18When he takes the throne of his
kingdom, he is to write for himself on a
scroll a copy of this law, taken from that
of the priests, who are Levites. 19It is to
be with him, and he is to read it all the
days of his life so that he may learn to
revere the LORD his God and follow
carefully all the words of this law and
these decrees 20and not consider himself
better than his brothers and turn from
the law to the right or to the left. Then
he and his descendants will reign a long
time over his kingdom in Israel.

SHARPEN THE FOCUS

Pomp. Power. Wealth. So often people push for leadership positions because of the perks that come along with that leadership. We've all probably known someone who wanted authority while skirting the responsibility that went along with it. Maybe you've even picked up the pieces after such a person.

God made His will for Israel's kings crystal clear; only one thing mattered–knowing the Lord and obeying Him (Deuteronomy 17:18–19). Not wealth. Not the web of political alliances that could be had with multiple marriages to foreign princesses. Not power.

Knowing God. Obeying God. That's where God-pleasing leadership begins. That's where authority links up with responsibility and a servant's heart is born.

Think of those you lead today–in your family, at your church, on the job, in the community. Ask the Holy Spirit to point out any self-seeking motives that keep you from servant-leadership. Then, repentant and relying on your Lord's forgiveness in Jesus, move forward in His power toward more Christlike service as you lead.

WEEK 16 • TUESDAY

Deuteronomy 18:1—19:21

GET THE BIG PICTURE

Israel is to avoid false teachers and the false gods they proclaim, and the nation is to administer justice with an even hand. Our Lord Himself and the apostle Peter quoted verses from the chapters you will read today. See if you can spot the "quotable quotes" as you read. If time is short, focus on Deuteronomy 18:15–22.

Offerings for Priests and Levites

18 The priests, who are
Levites—indeed the whole
tribe of Levi—are to have no allotment
or inheritance with Israel. They shall
live on the offerings made to the LORD
by fire, for that is their inheritance.
[2]They shall have no inheritance among
their brothers; the LORD is their inheritance, as he promised them.
[3]This is the share due the priests from
the people who sacrifice a bull or a
sheep: the shoulder, the jowls and the
inner parts. [4]You are to give them the
firstfruits of your grain, new wine and
oil, and the first wool from the shearing
of your sheep, [5]for the LORD your God
has chosen them and their descendants
out of all your tribes to stand and minister in the LORD's name always.
[6]If a Levite moves from one of your
towns anywhere in Israel where he is
living, and comes in all earnestness to
the place the LORD will choose, [7]he may
minister in the name of the LORD his
God like all his fellow Levites who serve
there in the presence of the LORD. [8]He
is to share equally in their benefits, even
though he has received money from the
sale of family possessions.

Detestable Practices

[9]When you enter the land the LORD
your God is giving you, do not learn to
imitate the detestable ways of the nations there. [10]Let no one be found
among you who sacrifices his son or
daughter in[a] the fire, who practices divination or sorcery, interprets omens, en-
gages in witchcraft, [11]or casts spells, or
who is a medium or spiritist or who consults the dead. [12]Anyone who does these
things is detestable to the LORD, and because of these detestable practices the
LORD your God will drive out those nations before you. [13]You must be blameless before the LORD your God.

The Prophet

[14]The nations you will dispossess listen to those who practice sorcery or
divination. But as for you, the LORD
your God has not permitted you to do
so. [15]The LORD your God will raise up
for you a prophet like me from among
your own brothers. You must listen to
him. [16]For this is what you asked of the
LORD your God at Horeb on the day of
the assembly when you said, "Let us not
hear the voice of the LORD our God nor
see this great fire anymore, or we will
die."
[17]The LORD said to me: "What they
say is good. [18]I will raise up for them a
prophet like you from among their
brothers; I will put my words in his
mouth, and he will tell them everything
I command him. [19]If anyone does not
listen to my words that the prophet
speaks in my name, I myself will call
him to account. [20]But a prophet who
presumes to speak in my name anything I have not commanded him to say,

[a]10 Or *who makes his son or daughter pass through*

or a prophet who speaks in the name of
other gods, must be put to death."
21You may say to yourselves, "How
can we know when a message has not
been spoken by the LORD?" 22If what a
prophet proclaims in the name of the
LORD does not take place or come true,
that is a message the LORD has not spoken. That prophet has spoken presump-
tuously. Do not be afraid of him.

Cities of Refuge

19 When the LORD your God
has destroyed the nations
whose land he is giving you, and when
you have driven them out and settled in
their towns and houses, 2then set aside
for yourselves three cities centrally lo-
cated in the land the LORD your God is
giving you to possess. 3Build roads to
them and divide into three parts the
land the LORD your God is giving you
as an inheritance, so that anyone who
kills a man may flee there.
4This is the rule concerning the man
who kills another and flees there to save
his life—one who kills his neighbor
unintentionally, without malice aforethought. 5For instance, a man may go
into the forest with his neighbor to cut
wood, and as he swings his ax to fell a
tree, the head may fly off and hit his
neighbor and kill him. That man may
flee to one of these cities and save his
life. 6Otherwise, the avenger of blood
might pursue him in a rage, overtake
him if the distance is too great, and kill
him even though he is not deserving of
death, since he did it to his neighbor
without malice aforethought. 7This is
why I command you to set aside for
yourselves three cities.
8If the LORD your God enlarges your
territory, as he promised on oath to your
forefathers, and gives you the whole
land he promised them, 9because you
carefully follow all these laws I command you today—to love the LORD
your God and to walk always in his
ways—then you are to set aside three
more cities. 10Do this so that innocent
blood will not be shed in your land,
which the LORD your God is giving you
as your inheritance, and so that you will
not be guilty of bloodshed.
11But if a man hates his neighbor and
lies in wait for him, assaults and kills
him, and then flees to one of these cities, 12the elders of his town shall send for
him, bring him back from the city, and
hand him over to the avenger of blood
to die. 13Show him no pity. You must
purge from Israel the guilt of shedding
innocent blood, so that it may go well
with you.
14Do not move your neighbor's
boundary stone set up by your prede-
cessors in the inheritance you receive in
the land the LORD your God is giving
you to possess.

Witnesses

15One witness is not enough to convict a man accused of any crime or offense he may have committed. A matter
must be established by the testimony of
two or three witnesses.
16If a malicious witness takes the stand
to accuse a man of a crime, 17the two
men involved in the dispute must stand
in the presence of the LORD before the
priests and the judges who are in office
at the time. 18The judges must make a
thorough investigation, and if the witness proves to be a liar, giving false testimony against his brother, 19then do to
him as he intended to do to his brother.
You must purge the evil from among
you. 20The rest of the people will hear of
this and be afraid, and never again will
such an evil thing be done among you.
21Show no pity: life for life, eye for eye,
tooth for tooth, hand for hand, foot for
foot.

SHARPEN THE FOCUS

In Deuteronomy 18:15–19 we read another Old Testament "job description" for the coming Messiah. Moses calls God's promised Savior a *prophet*. In fact, the Messiah would serve God's people as prophet in many of the same ways the prophet Moses did.

Most often we think of prophets as foretelling future events. Moses certainly did that. (See Deuteronomy 30:1–10.) And so did Jesus. (See Matthew 24:4–31.)

But the prophets' main task involved declaring God's Word, God's will, with power to God's people. Moses did that–today's reading is one example. And so did Jesus. In fact, Jesus was Himself the Word of God, the Word made flesh as the apostle John wrote (John 1:1, 14). "You must listen to Him," Moses says (Deuteronomy 18:15).

Are you a good listener? Do you hear and obey? Or hear and forget God's Law? Do you hear the Gospel, the truth that God in Christ forgives and loves you? Do you rely on it wholeheartedly? Or do you beat on yourself for your failures and insist on trying to earn more of God's love with good behaviors?

Talk to Jesus, your great Prophet today. Ask for His grace to hear and believe the Good News more firmly. Ask for open ears and a willing, obedient heart.

WEEK 16 • WEDNESDAY

Deut. 20:1—21:23

GET THE BIG PICTURE

Moses now turns to specific situations apt to occur after Israel settles in Canaan. Some of the issues were: Who can be drafted for military service? What do we do with incorrigible criminals? What if there's a serious crime, but no suspect? Remember, the Lord gave these laws to people of another time, another culture. Nevertheless, they reveal much about God–His justice and His mercy. The Lord intended His people to benefit through these civil laws. If time is short, focus on Deuteronomy 20:1–9.

Going to War

20 When you go to war against your enemies and
see horses and chariots and an army
greater than yours, do not be afraid of
them, because the LORD your God, who
brought you up out of Egypt, will be
with you. 2When you are about to go
into battle, the priest shall come forward
and address the army. 3He shall say:
"Hear, O Israel, today you are going into
battle against your enemies. Do not be
fainthearted or afraid; do not be terrified or give way to panic before them.
4For the LORD your God is the one who
goes with you to fight for you against
your enemies to give you victory."
5The officers shall say to the army:
"Has anyone built a new house and not
dedicated it? Let him go home, or he
may die in battle and someone else may
dedicate it. 6Has anyone planted a vineyard and not begun to enjoy it? Let him
go home, or he may die in battle and
someone else enjoy it. 7Has anyone become pledged to a woman and not mar-

ried her? Let him go home, or he may die in battle and someone else marry her." [8]Then the officers shall add, "Is any man afraid or fainthearted? Let him go home so that his brothers will not become disheartened too." [9]When the officers have finished speaking to the army, they shall appoint commanders over it.

[10]When you march up to attack a city, make its people an offer of peace. [11]If they accept and open their gates, all the people in it shall be subject to forced labor and shall work for you. [12]If they refuse to make peace and they engage you in battle, lay siege to that city. [13]When the LORD your God delivers it into your hand, put to the sword all the men in it. [14]As for the women, the children, the livestock and everything else in the city, you may take these as plunder for yourselves. And you may use the plunder the LORD your God gives you from your enemies. [15]This is how you are to treat all the cities that are at a distance from you and do not belong to the nations nearby.

[16]However, in the cities of the nations the LORD your God is giving you as an inheritance, do not leave alive anything that breathes. [17]Completely destroy[a] them—the Hittites, Amorites, Canaanites, Perizzites, Hivites and Jebusites—as the LORD your God has commanded you. [18]Otherwise, they will teach you to follow all the detestable things they do in worshiping their gods, and you will sin against the LORD your God.

[19]When you lay siege to a city for a long time, fighting against it to capture it, do not destroy its trees by putting an ax to them, because you can eat their fruit. Do not cut them down. Are the trees of the field people, that you should besiege them?[b] [20]However, you may cut down trees that you know are not fruit trees and use them to build siege works until the city at war with you falls.

Atonement for an Unsolved Murder

21 If a man is found slain, lying in a field in the land the LORD your God is giving you to possess, and it is not known who killed him, [2]your elders and judges shall go out and measure the distance from the body to the neighboring towns. [3]Then the elders of the town nearest the body shall take a heifer that has never been worked and has never worn a yoke [4]and lead her down to a valley that has not been plowed or planted and where there is a flowing stream. There in the valley they are to break the heifer's neck. [5]The priests, the sons of Levi, shall step forward, for the LORD your God has chosen them to minister and to pronounce blessings in the name of the LORD and to decide all cases of dispute and assault. [6]Then all the elders of the town nearest the body shall wash their hands over the heifer whose neck was broken in the valley, [7]and they shall declare: "Our hands did not shed this blood, nor did our eyes see it done. [8]Accept this atonement for your people Israel, whom you have redeemed, O LORD, and do not hold your people guilty of the blood of an innocent man." And the bloodshed will be atoned for. [9]So you will purge from yourselves the guilt of shedding innocent blood, since you have done what is right in the eyes of the LORD.

Marrying a Captive Woman

[10]When you go to war against your enemies and the LORD your God delivers them into your hands and you take captives, [11]if you notice among the captives a beautiful woman and are attracted to her, you may take her as your wife. [12]Bring her into your home and have her shave her head, trim her nails [13]and put aside the clothes she was wearing when captured. After she has lived in your house and mourned her father and mother for a full month, then you may go to her and be her husband and she shall be your wife. [14]If you are not pleased with her, let her go wherever she wishes. You must not sell her

[a]17 The Hebrew term refers to the irrevocable giving over of things or persons to the LORD, often by totally destroying them. [b]19 Or *down to use in the siege, for the fruit trees are for the benefit of man.*

or treat her as a slave, since you have
dishonored her.

The Right of the Firstborn

[15]If a man has two wives, and he loves
one but not the other, and both bear him
sons but the firstborn is the son of the
wife he does not love, [16]when he wills
his property to his sons, he must not
give the rights of the firstborn to the son
of the wife he loves in preference to his
actual firstborn, the son of the wife he
does not love. [17]He must acknowledge
the son of his unloved wife as the firstborn by giving him a double share of all
he has. That son is the first sign of his
father's strength. The right of the firstborn belongs to him.

A Rebellious Son

[18]If a man has a stubborn and rebellious son who does not obey his father
and mother and will not listen to them
when they discipline him, [19]his father
and mother shall take hold of him and
bring him to the elders at the gate of his
town. [20]They shall say to the elders,
"This son of ours is stubborn and rebellious. He will not obey us. He is a prof-
ligate and a drunkard." [21]Then all the
men of his town shall stone him to
death. You must purge the evil from
among you. All Israel will hear of it and
be afraid.

Various Laws

[22]If a man guilty of a capital offense is
put to death and his body is hung on a
tree, [23]you must not leave his body on
the tree overnight. Be sure to bury him
that same day, because anyone who is
hung on a tree is under God's curse. You
must not desecrate the land the LORD
your God is giving you as an inheritance.

SHARPEN THE FOCUS

Think about the last time you felt truly afraid. The doctor's verdict: surgery. The police officer's voice: "We're holding your son." The siren's wail: tornado. The newscaster's announcement: "A massive explosion leveled several buildings downtown today." How did you get the courage you needed to walk through your own time of fear?

Each time Israel went to war, the people were to pause and remember the truth—the truth about the Lord's love and faithfulness to them. Reread the words of encouragement the priests were to speak (Deuteronomy 20:1–4). As you do, think about the "enemies" you battle today, the fears you face.

Then remind yourself that since God Himself is for you, since He freely gave His Son into death in your place, nothing and no one can stand against you. In Jesus, you are safe. You can face life (or death) confident in His love.

WEEK 16 • THURSDAY

Deut. 22:1—23:25

GET THE BIG PICTURE

Today's reading includes regulations about everything from personal property to personal hygiene. One thread runs through both chapters: Israel belongs to the Lord. They are His holy people, set apart from the nations to serve Him and to display His goodness to the world. If time is short, focus on Deuteronomy 22:1–4.

22 If you see your brother's ox or sheep straying, do not ignore it but be sure to take it back to him. [2]If the brother does not live near you or if you do not know who he is, take it home with you and keep it until he comes looking for it. Then give it back to him. [3]Do the same if you find your brother's donkey or his cloak or anything he loses. Do not ignore it.

[4]If you see your brother's donkey or his ox fallen on the road, do not ignore it. Help him get it to its feet.

[5]A woman must not wear men's clothing, nor a man wear women's clothing, for the LORD your God detests anyone who does this.

[6]If you come across a bird's nest beside the road, either in a tree or on the ground, and the mother is sitting on the young or on the eggs, do not take the mother with the young. [7]You may take the young, but be sure to let the mother go, so that it may go well with you and you may have a long life.

[8]When you build a new house, make a parapet around your roof so that you may not bring the guilt of bloodshed on your house if someone falls from the roof.

[9]Do not plant two kinds of seed in your vineyard; if you do, not only the crops you plant but also the fruit of the vineyard will be defiled.[a]

[10]Do not plow with an ox and a donkey yoked together.

[11]Do not wear clothes of wool and linen woven together.

[12]Make tassels on the four corners of the cloak you wear.

Marriage Violations

[13]If a man takes a wife and, after lying with her, dislikes her [14]and slanders her and gives her a bad name, saying, "I married this woman, but when I approached her, I did not find proof of her virginity," [15]then the girl's father and mother shall bring proof that she was a virgin to the town elders at the gate. [16]The girl's father will say to the elders, "I gave my daughter in marriage to this man, but he dislikes her. [17]Now he has slandered her and said, 'I did not find your daughter to be a virgin.' But here is the proof of my daughter's virginity." Then her parents shall display the cloth before the elders of the town, [18]and the elders shall take the man and punish him. [19]They shall fine him a hundred shekels of silver[b] and give them to the girl's father, because this man has given an Israelite virgin a bad name. She shall continue to be his wife; he must not divorce her as long as he lives.

[20]If, however, the charge is true and no proof of the girl's virginity can be found, [21]she shall be brought to the door of her father's house and there the men of her town shall stone her to death. She has done a disgraceful thing in Israel by being promiscuous while still in her father's house. You must purge the evil from among you.

[22]If a man is found sleeping with another man's wife, both the man who slept with her and the woman must die. You must purge the evil from Israel.

[23]If a man happens to meet in a town a virgin pledged to be married and he sleeps with her, [24]you shall take both of them to the gate of that town and stone them to death—the girl because she was in a town and did not scream for help, and the man because he violated another man's wife. You must purge the evil from among you.

[25]But if out in the country a man happens to meet a girl pledged to be married and rapes her, only the man who has done this shall die. [26]Do nothing to the girl; she has committed no sin deserving death. This case is like that of someone who attacks and murders his neighbor, [27]for the man found the girl

[a]9 Or *be forfeited to the sanctuary* [b]19 That is, about 2 1/2 pounds (about 1 kilogram)

out in the country, and though the betrothed girl screamed, there was no one to rescue her.

[28]If a man happens to meet a virgin who is not pledged to be married and rapes her and they are discovered, [29]he shall pay the girl's father fifty shekels of silver.[a] He must marry the girl, for he has violated her. He can never divorce her as long as he lives.

[30]A man is not to marry his father's wife; he must not dishonor his father's bed.

Exclusion From the Assembly

23 No one who has been emasculated by crushing or cutting may enter the assembly of the LORD.

[2]No one born of a forbidden marriage[b] nor any of his descendants may enter the assembly of the LORD, even down to the tenth generation.

[3]No Ammonite or Moabite or any of his descendants may enter the assembly of the LORD, even down to the tenth generation. [4]For they did not come to meet you with bread and water on your way when you came out of Egypt, and they hired Balaam son of Beor from Pethor in Aram Naharaim[c] to pronounce a curse on you. [5]However, the LORD your God would not listen to Balaam but turned the curse into a blessing for you, because the LORD your God loves you. [6]Do not seek a treaty of friendship with them as long as you live.

[7]Do not abhor an Edomite, for he is your brother. Do not abhor an Egyptian, because you lived as an alien in his country. [8]The third generation of children born to them may enter the assembly of the LORD.

Uncleanness in the Camp

[9]When you are encamped against your enemies, keep away from everything impure. [10]If one of your men is unclean because of a nocturnal emission, he is to go outside the camp and stay there. [11]But as evening approaches he is to wash himself, and at sunset he may return to the camp.

[12]Designate a place outside the camp where you can go to relieve yourself. [13]As part of your equipment have something to dig with, and when you relieve yourself, dig a hole and cover up your excrement. [14]For the LORD your God moves about in your camp to protect you and to deliver your enemies to you. Your camp must be holy, so that he will not see among you anything indecent and turn away from you.

Miscellaneous Laws

[15]If a slave has taken refuge with you, do not hand him over to his master. [16]Let him live among you wherever he likes and in whatever town he chooses. Do not oppress him.

[17]No Israelite man or woman is to become a shrine prostitute. [18]You must not bring the earnings of a female prostitute or of a male prostitute[d] into the house of the LORD your God to pay any vow, because the LORD your God detests them both.

[19]Do not charge your brother interest, whether on money or food or anything else that may earn interest. [20]You may charge a foreigner interest, but not a brother Israelite, so that the LORD your God may bless you in everything you put your hand to in the land you are entering to possess.

[21]If you make a vow to the LORD your God, do not be slow to pay it, for the LORD your God will certainly demand it of you and you will be guilty of sin. [22]But if you refrain from making a vow, you will not be guilty. [23]Whatever your lips utter you must be sure to do, because you made your vow freely to the LORD your God with your own mouth.

[24]If you enter your neighbor's vineyard, you may eat all the grapes you want, but do not put any in your basket. [25]If you enter your neighbor's grainfield, you may pick kernels with your hands, but you must not put a sickle to his standing grain.

[a]29 That is, about 1 1/4 pounds (about 0.6 kilogram) [b]2 Or *one of illegitimate birth*
[c]4 That is, Northwest Mesopotamia
[d]18 Hebrew *of a dog*

SHARPEN THE FOCUS

A wallet is left in the shopping cart. Someone's dog wanders onto your property, hot and in distress. You find a pair of glasses or a day timer on the plane or train seat next to you. What do you do?

Ignoring needs like these hardly seems like a major offense. We lead hectic lives. Someone may sue us if we get involved. The bother irritates us. Besides, with all the crime in the world what difference can our one little act of kindness make?

Deuteronomy 22:1–2 sets a God-given principle for His people. When a neighbor's property is at risk, we are not to look the other way.

The book *Random Acts of Kindness* was quite popular a few years ago. The title gives away the content: do kind things at random throughout your day—and you'll find your life is happier. This shouldn't have been a new idea to God's people. Part of becoming like our Savior involves growth in demonstrating Christlike kindness.

When we hold our own lives up next to Christ's life, we see how far short we often fall. We see how much we need His kindness and mercy—and how richly He offers it! Rejoice in that today, child of God, and draw from it the strength you need to grow in His kindness.

WEEK 16 • FRIDAY

Deuteronomy 24:1–22

GET THE BIG PICTURE

This part of Moses' sermon continues the recitation of miscellaneous laws, which regulated specific situations His people would encounter in Canaan. As you read, note the Lord's concern for the dignity of persons, His compassion for the poor, and His commitment to justice for the innocent. If time is short, focus on Deuteronomy 24:18–22.

24 If a man marries a woman
who becomes displeasing
to him because he finds something indecent about her, and he writes her a
certificate of divorce, gives it to her and
sends her from his house, 2and if after
she leaves his house she becomes the
wife of another man, 3and her second
husband dislikes her and writes her a
certificate of divorce, gives it to her and
sends her from his house, or if he dies,
4then her first husband, who divorced
her, is not allowed to marry her again
after she has been defiled. That would
be detestable in the eyes of the LORD. Do
not bring sin upon the land the LORD
your God is giving you as an inheritance.
5If a man has recently married, he
must not be sent to war or have any other duty laid on him. For one year he is
to be free to stay at home and bring happiness to the wife he has married.
6Do not take a pair of millstones—not
even the upper one—as security for a
debt, because that would be taking a
man's livelihood as security.
7If a man is caught kidnapping one of
his brother Israelites and treats him as
a slave or sells him, the kidnapper must

die. You must purge the evil from
among you.
[8]In cases of leprous[a] diseases be very
careful to do exactly as the priests, who
are Levites, instruct you. You must follow carefully what I have commanded
them. [9]Remember what the LORD your
God did to Miriam along the way after
you came out of Egypt.
[10]When you make a loan of any kind
to your neighbor, do not go into his
house to get what he is offering as a
pledge. [11]Stay outside and let the man to
whom you are making the loan bring
the pledge out to you. [12]If the man is
poor, do not go to sleep with his pledge
in your possession. [13]Return his cloak to
him by sunset so that he may sleep in it.
Then he will thank you, and it will be
regarded as a righteous act in the sight
of the LORD your God.
[14]Do not take advantage of a hired
man who is poor and needy, whether he
is a brother Israelite or an alien living in
one of your towns. [15]Pay him his wages
each day before sunset, because he is
poor and is counting on it. Otherwise he
may cry to the LORD against you, and
you will be guilty of sin.
[16]Fathers shall not be put to death for
their children, nor children put to death
for their fathers; each is to die for his
own sin.
[17]Do not deprive the alien or the fatherless of justice, or take the cloak of
the widow as a pledge. [18]Remember that
you were slaves in Egypt and the LORD
your God redeemed you from there.
That is why I command you to do this.
[19]When you are harvesting in your
field and you overlook a sheaf, do not
go back to get it. Leave it for the alien,
the fatherless and the widow, so that the
LORD your God may bless you in all the
work of your hands. [20]When you beat
the olives from your trees, do not go
over the branches a second time. Leave
what remains for the alien, the fatherless and the widow. [21]When you harvest
the grapes in your vineyard, do not go
over the vines again. Leave what remains for the alien, the fatherless and
the widow. [22]Remember that you were
slaves in Egypt. That is why I command
you to do this.

[a]*8* The Hebrew word was used for various diseases affecting the skin—not necessarily leprosy.

SHARPEN THE FOCUS

Over and over again we read the familiar formula found in Deuteronomy 24:22: "Remember who you were," the Lord says to His people. "Remember where you've come from," He commands. In saying this, the Lord is not trying to be manipulative or threatening. Neither is He trying to shame His people into action they don't really want to take.

Instead, God wants to help the people of Israel find joy and motivation for the obedience that brings peace and fulfillment. He wants to help them grow up–to become spiritually mature. In the New Testament, we see writers, inspired by the Holy Spirit, offering us the same joy and motivation Moses held out to ancient Israel. Read Ephesians 2:1–10, and think about the "before" and "after" picture Paul paints:

> I was *dead in sin, followed the ways of the world and my sinful nature, and disobedient.*
>
> I came from *the world with all its sin and evil desires.*
>
> Now I am *alive with Christ, forgiven and saved, and seated in the heavenly realms.*

Moses concludes his second sermon by highlighting the Lord's goodness to Israel. Moses also reminds the people of Israel of the covenant the Lord has made with them and that God's people are just and generous. If time is short, focus on Deuteronomy 26:1–19.

25 When men have a dis-
pute, they are to take it to
court and the judges will decide the
case, acquitting the innocent and condemning the guilty. [2]If the guilty man
deserves to be beaten, the judge shall
make him lie down and have him
flogged in his presence with the number of lashes his crime deserves, [3]but he
must not give him more than forty
lashes. If he is flogged more than that,
your brother will be degraded in your
eyes.
[4]Do not muzzle an ox while it is treading out the grain.
[5]If brothers are living together and
one of them dies without a son, his widow must not marry outside the family.
Her husband's brother shall take her
and marry her and fulfill the duty of a
brother-in-law to her. [6]The first son she
bears shall carry on the name of the
dead brother so that his name will not
be blotted out from Israel.
[7]However, if a man does not want to
marry his brother's wife, she shall go to
the elders at the town gate and say, "My
husband's brother refuses to carry on
his brother's name in Israel. He will not
fulfill the duty of a brother-in-law to
me." [8]Then the elders of his town shall
summon him and talk to him. If he per-
sists in saying, "I do not want to marry
her," [9]his brother's widow shall go up to
him in the presence of the elders, take
off one of his sandals, spit in his face and
say, "This is what is done to the man
who will not build up his brother's family line." [10]That man's line shall be
known in Israel as The Family of the
Unsandaled.
[11]If two men are fighting and the wife
of one of them comes to rescue her husband from his assailant, and she reaches
out and seizes him by his private parts,
[12]you shall cut off her hand. Show her
no pity.
[13]Do not have two differing weights
in your bag—one heavy, one light. [14]Do
not have two differing measures in your
house—one large, one small. [15]You must
have accurate and honest weights and
measures, so that you may live long in
the land the LORD your God is giving
you. [16]For the LORD your God detests
anyone who does these things, anyone
who deals dishonestly.
[17]Remember what the Amalekites did
to you along the way when you came
out of Egypt. [18]When you were weary
and worn out, they met you on your
journey and cut off all who were lag-
ging behind; they had no fear of God.
[19]When the LORD your God gives you
rest from all the enemies around you in
the land he is giving you to possess as
an inheritance, you shall blot out the
memory of Amalek from under heaven.
Do not forget!

Firstfruits and Tithes

26 When you have entered
the land the LORD your
God is giving you as an inheritance and
have taken possession of it and settled
in it, [2]take some of the firstfruits of all
that you produce from the soil of the
land the LORD your God is giving you

and put them in a basket. Then go to the place the LORD your God will choose as a dwelling for his Name [3]and say to the priest in office at the time, "I declare today to the LORD your God that I have come to the land the LORD swore to our forefathers to give us." [4]The priest shall take the basket from your hands and set it down in front of the altar of the LORD your God. [5]Then you shall declare before the LORD your God: "My father was a wandering Aramean, and he went down into Egypt with a few people and lived there and became a great nation, powerful and numerous. [6]But the Egyptians mistreated us and made us suffer, putting us to hard labor. [7]Then we cried out to the LORD, the God of our fathers, and the LORD heard our voice and saw our misery, toil and oppression. [8]So the LORD brought us out of Egypt with a mighty hand and an outstretched arm, with great terror and with miraculous signs and wonders. [9]He brought us to this place and gave us this land, a land flowing with milk and honey; [10]and now I bring the firstfruits of the soil that you, O LORD, have given me." Place the basket before the LORD your God and bow down before him. [11]And you and the Levites and the aliens among you shall rejoice in all the good things the LORD your God has given to you and your household.

[12]When you have finished setting aside a tenth of all your produce in the third year, the year of the tithe, you shall give it to the Levite, the alien, the fatherless and the widow, so that they may eat in your towns and be satisfied. [13]Then say to the LORD your God: "I have removed from my house the sacred portion and have given it to the Levite, the alien, the fatherless and the widow, according to all you commanded. I have not turned aside from your commands nor have I forgotten any of them. [14]I have not eaten any of the sacred portion while I was in mourning, nor have I removed any of it while I was unclean, nor have I offered any of it to the dead. I have obeyed the LORD my God; I have done everything you commanded me. [15]Look down from heaven, your holy dwelling place, and bless your people Israel and the land you have given us as you promised on oath to our forefathers, a land flowing with milk and honey."

Follow the LORD's Commands

[16]The LORD your God commands you this day to follow these decrees and laws; carefully observe them with all your heart and with all your soul. [17]You have declared this day that the LORD is your God and that you will walk in his ways, that you will keep his decrees, commands and laws, and that you will obey him. [18]And the LORD has declared this day that you are his people, his treasured possession as he promised, and that you are to keep all his commands. [19]He has declared that he will set you in praise, fame and honor high above all the nations he has made and that you will be a people holy to the LORD your God, as he promised.

SHARPEN THE FOCUS

What do you think of the church? Maybe you grew up in a congregation that supported and encouraged you. Maybe your present congregation is like your spiritual family. On the other hand, maybe you've seen too many scandals, politics, and hypocrisy. Maybe you've become hardened, even cynical.

Some Christians get so down on their spiritual leaders and fellow church members that they refuse to have any more to do with God's family. They drop out. Others attend worship services only. Believers caught in this trap act more like distant cousins than like brothers and sisters in Christ.

Christ's church on earth is imperfect. But Jesus loves the church! (Deuteronomy 26:19). These words describe the high view the Lord has of His sons and daughters, His people: "in praise, fame, and honor high above all the nations." In Jesus, the heavenly Father has set us apart for such a privilege.

While we live and work in the church on earth, we live and work with sinners. Still, while we live and work in the church on earth, we live and work with God's saints, too. If we ignore that fact or doubt it, we will miss out on opportunities to be blessed and to bless others in the family of our Father. ☼

WEEK 17 • MONDAY

Deuteronomy 27:1–26

This chapter begins Moses' third and final sermon. In it he arranges for a permanent "billboard" display of the covenant to be set up in Canaan (Deuteronomy 27:1–8). And he arranges an "audiovisual" demonstration as well (Deuteronomy 27:9–26). As you read, note especially the Lord's concern for the spiritual well-being of His people and His compassion for the poor and weak. If time is short, focus on Deuteronomy 27:1–10.

The Altar on Mount Ebal

27 Moses and the elders of
Israel commanded the
people: "Keep all these commands that
I give you today. 2When you have
crossed the Jordan into the land the
LORD your God is giving you, set up
some large stones and coat them with
plaster. 3Write on them all the words of
this law when you have crossed over to
enter the land the LORD your God is giving you, a land flowing with milk and
honey, just as the LORD, the God of your
fathers, promised you. 4And when you
have crossed the Jordan, set up these
stones on Mount Ebal, as I command
you today, and coat them with plaster.
5Build there an altar to the LORD your
God, an altar of stones. Do not use any
iron tool upon them. 6Build the altar of
the LORD your God with fieldstones and
offer burnt offerings on it to the LORD
your God. 7Sacrifice fellowship offerings[a] there, eating them and rejoicing in
the presence of the LORD your God.
8And you shall write very clearly all the
words of this law on these stones you
have set up."

Curses From Mount Ebal

9Then Moses and the priests, who are
Levites, said to all Israel, "Be silent, O
Israel, and listen! You have now become
the people of the LORD your God.
10Obey the LORD your God and follow
his commands and decrees that I give
you today."

11On the same day Moses commanded the people:

12When you have crossed the Jordan,
these tribes shall stand on Mount Gerizim to bless the people: Simeon, Levi,
Judah, Issachar, Joseph and Benjamin.
13And these tribes shall stand on Mount
Ebal to pronounce curses: Reuben, Gad,
Asher, Zebulun, Dan and Naphtali.

[a]7 Traditionally *peace offerings*

[14]The Levites shall recite to all the people of Israel in a loud voice:

[15]"Cursed is the man who carves an image or casts an idol—a thing detestable to the LORD, the work of the craftsman's hands—and sets it up in secret."

Then all the people shall say, "Amen!"

[16]"Cursed is the man who dishonors his father or his mother."

Then all the people shall say, "Amen!"

[17]"Cursed is the man who moves his neighbor's boundary stone."

Then all the people shall say, "Amen!"

[18]"Cursed is the man who leads the blind astray on the road."

Then all the people shall say, "Amen!"

[19]"Cursed is the man who withholds justice from the alien, the fatherless or the widow."

Then all the people shall say, "Amen!"

[20]"Cursed is the man who sleeps with his father's wife, for he dishonors his father's bed."

Then all the people shall say, "Amen!"

[21]"Cursed is the man who has sexual relations with any animal."

Then all the people shall say, "Amen!"

[22]"Cursed is the man who sleeps with his sister, the daughter of his father or the daughter of his mother."

Then all the people shall say, "Amen!"

[23]"Cursed is the man who sleeps with his mother-in-law."

Then all the people shall say, "Amen!"

[24]"Cursed is the man who kills his neighbor secretly."

Then all the people shall say, "Amen!"

[25]"Cursed is the man who accepts a bribe to kill an innocent person."

Then all the people shall say, "Amen!"

[26]"Cursed is the man who does not uphold the words of this law by carrying them out."

Then all the people shall say, "Amen!"

SHARPEN THE FOCUS

The Old Covenant—the one given first at Sinai and ratified by Israel just before they entered Canaan—was a good and glorious thing. The Lord intended it to bless His people—but the people did not receive the fullness of God's blessing through it. Not because it was flawed, but because they were. Neither they nor we could "keep all these commands" (Deuteronomy 27:1). The Law written on stone tablets or on stone billboards could only bring sinful human beings under a curse.

Speaking for God centuries later, the prophet Ezekiel offered a solution—a new and better covenant, the covenant that is ours in Christ's cross:

> *I will give you a new heart and put a new spirit in you; I will remove from you your heart of stone and give you a heart of flesh. And I will put My Spirit in you and move you to follow My decrees and be careful to keep My laws.* (Ezekiel 36:26–27)

If you belong to Christ, that new heart is yours today. Your "heart of stone" has been removed. Your God has replaced it with a "heart of flesh." The Spirit of God Himself has taken up residence in you. And now God "works in you to will and to act according to His good purpose" (Philippians 2:13). In what specific way will you use that power today?

WEEK 17 • TUESDAY

Deuteronomy 28:1–68

Imagine the scene: The priests standing between Mt. Gerizim and Mt. Ebal with the ark of the covenant; the people of six tribes of Israel on Gerizim, the people of the other six tribes on Ebal. As the priests pronounce the blessings and curses, the people reply, "Amen!" In this way, the covenant was to be ratified. If time is short, focus on Deuteronomy 28:1–14.

Blessings for Obedience

28 If you fully obey the LORD
your God and carefully
follow all his commands I give you today, the LORD your God will set you
high above all the nations on earth. 2All
these blessings will come upon you and
accompany you if you obey the LORD
your God:

3You will be blessed in the city
and blessed in the country.
4The fruit of your womb will be
blessed, and the crops of your land
and the young of your livestock—
the calves of your herds and the
lambs of your flocks.
5Your basket and your kneading
trough will be blessed.
6You will be blessed when you
come in and blessed when you go
out.

7The LORD will grant that the enemies
who rise up against you will be defeated
before you. They will come at you from
one direction but flee from you in
seven.
8The LORD will send a blessing on
your barns and on everything you put
your hand to. The LORD your God will
bless you in the land he is giving you.
9The LORD will establish you as his
holy people, as he promised you on
oath, if you keep the commands of the
LORD your God and walk in his ways.
10Then all the peoples on earth will see
that you are called by the name of the
LORD, and they will fear you. 11The
LORD will grant you abundant prosperity—in the fruit of your womb, the
young of your livestock and the crops of
your ground—in the land he swore to
your forefathers to give you.
12The LORD will open the heavens, the
storehouse of his bounty, to send rain on
your land in season and to bless all the
work of your hands. You will lend to
many nations but will borrow from
none. 13The LORD will make you the
head, not the tail. If you pay attention
to the commands of the LORD your God
that I give you this day and carefully
follow them, you will always be at the
top, never at the bottom. 14Do not turn
aside from any of the commands I give
you today, to the right or to the left, following other gods and serving them.

Curses for Disobedience

15However, if you do not obey the
LORD your God and do not carefully follow all his commands and decrees I am
giving you today, all these curses will
come upon you and overtake you:

16You will be cursed in the city
and cursed in the country.
17Your basket and your kneading
trough will be cursed.
18The fruit of your womb will be
cursed, and the crops of your land,
and the calves of your herds and
the lambs of your flocks.
19You will be cursed when you

come in and cursed when you go out.

20 The LORD will send on you curses, confusion and rebuke in everything you put your hand to, until you are destroyed and come to sudden ruin because of the evil you have done in forsaking him.[a] 21 The LORD will plague you with diseases until he has destroyed you from the land you are entering to possess. 22 The LORD will strike you with wasting disease, with fever and inflammation, with scorching heat and drought, with blight and mildew, which will plague you until you perish. 23 The sky over your head will be bronze, the ground beneath you iron. 24 The LORD will turn the rain of your country into dust and powder; it will come down from the skies until you are destroyed.

25 The LORD will cause you to be defeated before your enemies. You will come at them from one direction but flee from them in seven, and you will become a thing of horror to all the kingdoms on earth. 26 Your carcasses will be food for all the birds of the air and the beasts of the earth, and there will be no one to frighten them away. 27 The LORD will afflict you with the boils of Egypt and with tumors, festering sores and the itch, from which you cannot be cured. 28 The LORD will afflict you with madness, blindness and confusion of mind. 29 At midday you will grope about like a blind man in the dark. You will be unsuccessful in everything you do; day after day you will be oppressed and robbed, with no one to rescue you.

30 You will be pledged to be married to a woman, but another will take her and ravish her. You will build a house, but you will not live in it. You will plant a vineyard, but you will not even begin to enjoy its fruit. 31 Your ox will be slaughtered before your eyes, but you will eat none of it. Your donkey will be forcibly taken from you and will not be returned. Your sheep will be given to your enemies, and no one will rescue them. 32 Your sons and daughters will be given to another nation, and you will wear out your eyes watching for them day after day, powerless to lift a hand. 33 A people that you do not know will eat what your land and labor produce, and you will have nothing but cruel oppression all your days. 34 The sights you see will drive you mad. 35 The LORD will afflict your knees and legs with painful boils that cannot be cured, spreading from the soles of your feet to the top of your head.

36 The LORD will drive you and the king you set over you to a nation unknown to you or your fathers. There you will worship other gods, gods of wood and stone. 37 You will become a thing of horror and an object of scorn and ridicule to all the nations where the LORD will drive you.

38 You will sow much seed in the field but you will harvest little, because locusts will devour it. 39 You will plant vineyards and cultivate them but you will not drink the wine or gather the grapes, because worms will eat them. 40 You will have olive trees throughout your country but you will not use the oil, because the olives will drop off. 41 You will have sons and daughters but you will not keep them, because they will go into captivity. 42 Swarms of locusts will take over all your trees and the crops of your land.

43 The alien who lives among you will rise above you higher and higher, but you will sink lower and lower. 44 He will lend to you, but you will not lend to him. He will be the head, but you will be the tail.

45 All these curses will come upon you. They will pursue you and overtake you until you are destroyed, because you did not obey the LORD your God and observe the commands and decrees he gave you. 46 They will be a sign and a wonder to you and your descendants forever. 47 Because you did not serve the LORD your God joyfully and gladly in the time of prosperity, 48 therefore in

[a] 20 Hebrew *me*

hunger and thirst, in nakedness and
dire poverty, you will serve the enemies
the LORD sends against you. He will put
an iron yoke on your neck until he has
destroyed you.
49The LORD will bring a nation against
you from far away, from the ends of the
earth, like an eagle swooping down, a
nation whose language you will not understand, 50a fierce-looking nation without respect for the old or pity for the
young. 51They will devour the young of
your livestock and the crops of your
land until you are destroyed. They will
leave you no grain, new wine or oil, nor
any calves of your herds or lambs of
your flocks until you are ruined. 52They
will lay siege to all the cities throughout
your land until the high fortified
walls in which you trust fall down.
They will besiege all the cities throughout the land the LORD your God is giving you.
53Because of the suffering that your
enemy will inflict on you during the
siege, you will eat the fruit of the womb,
the flesh of the sons and daughters the
LORD your God has given you. 54Even
the most gentle and sensitive man
among you will have no compassion on
his own brother or the wife he loves or
his surviving children, 55and he will not
give to one of them any of the flesh of
his children that he is eating. It will be
all he has left because of the suffering
your enemy will inflict on you during
the siege of all your cities. 56The most
gentle and sensitive woman among
you—so sensitive and gentle that she
would not venture to touch the ground
with the sole of her foot—will begrudge
the husband she loves and her own son
or daughter 57the afterbirth from her
womb and the children she bears. For
she intends to eat them secretly during
the siege and in the distress that your
enemy will inflict on you in your cities.
58If you do not carefully follow all the
words of this law, which are written in
this book, and do not revere this glorious and awesome name—the LORD
your God— 59the LORD will send fearful
plagues on you and your descendants,
harsh and prolonged disasters, and severe and lingering illnesses. 60He will
bring upon you all the diseases of Egypt
that you dreaded, and they will cling to
you. 61The LORD will also bring on you
every kind of sickness and disaster not
recorded in this Book of the Law, until
you are destroyed. 62You who were as
numerous as the stars in the sky will be
left but few in number, because you did
not obey the LORD your God. 63Just as it
pleased the LORD to make you prosper
and increase in number, so it will please
him to ruin and destroy you. You will be
uprooted from the land you are entering to possess.
64Then the LORD will scatter you
among all nations, from one end of the
earth to the other. There you will worship other gods—gods of wood and
stone, which neither you nor your fathers have known. 65Among those nations you will find no repose, no resting
place for the sole of your foot. There the
LORD will give you an anxious mind,
eyes weary with longing, and a despairing heart. 66You will live in constant
suspense, filled with dread both night
and day, never sure of your life. 67In the
morning you will say, "If only it were
evening!" and in the evening, "If only it
were morning!"—because of the terror
that will fill your hearts and the sights
that your eyes will see. 68The LORD will
send you back in ships to Egypt on a
journey I said you should never make
again. There you will offer yourselves
for sale to your enemies as male and female slaves, but no one will buy you.

SHARPEN THE FOCUS

One of the most powerful verses describing the curse that would fall on those who disobeyed the covenant contains these words:

You will live in constant suspense, filled with dread both night and day, never sure of your life. (Deuteronomy 28:66)

Commenting on these words, the Reformer Martin Luther wrote, "I have never seen a passage which describes more clearly the misery of a guilty conscience, in words or thoughts so fitting or appropriate. For this is just the way in which a [person] is affected who knows God is offended, i.e., who is harassed with the consciousness of sin."

Maybe you've known the curse, the misery of a guilty conscience. Maybe you've felt the fear that chills human hearts when we realize how greatly our sins offend the holy God. Maybe that chill sends shivers up your spine today. If so, thank God that on the cross Jesus suffered the punishment you deserve. Then read the sure and certain promise of Galatians 3:13–14. Know for sure that in Christ you are set free from the Law's curse. You have now inherited all of God's magnificent blessings, best of all, forgiveness and life in Jesus!

WEEK 17 • WEDNESDAY

Deut. 29:1–29

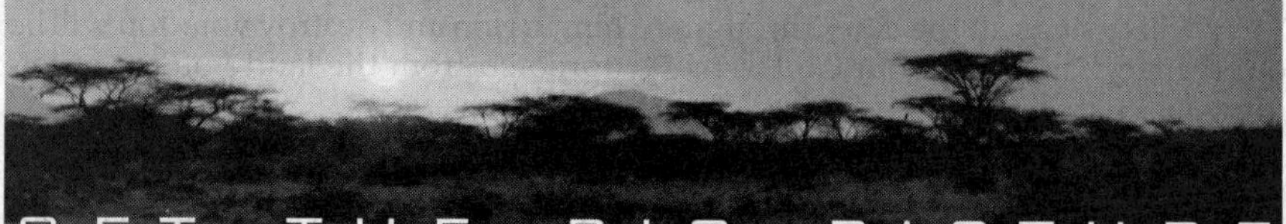

GET THE BIG PICTURE

Once again Moses reminds the entire nation of who they are and of what the Lord has done for them. Then he invites them to enter fully, personally, and wholeheartedly into the covenant God wants to give them (Deuteronomy 29:12). But if they refuse—individually or as a group—the curse will most certainly fall. If time is short, focus on Deuteronomy 29:1–15.

Renewal of the Covenant

29 These are the terms of the
covenant the LORD commanded Moses to make with the Israelites in Moab, in addition to the covenant
he had made with them at Horeb.
2Moses summoned all the Israelites
and said to them:

Your eyes have seen all that the LORD
did in Egypt to Pharaoh, to all his officials and to all his land. 3With your own
eyes you saw those great trials, those
miraculous signs and great wonders.
4But to this day the LORD has not given
you a mind that understands or eyes
that see or ears that hear. 5During the
forty years that I led you through the
desert, your clothes did not wear out,
nor did the sandals on your feet. 6You
ate no bread and drank no wine or other
fermented drink. I did this so that you
might know that I am the LORD your
God.
7When you reached this place, Sihon
king of Heshbon and Og king of Bashan
came out to fight against us, but we defeated them. 8We took their land and
gave it as an inheritance to the Reubenites, the Gadites and the half-tribe of
Manasseh.
9Carefully follow the terms of this
covenant, so that you may prosper in
everything you do. 10All of you are
standing today in the presence of the
LORD your God—your leaders and chief
men, your elders and officials, and all
the other men of Israel, 11together with
your children and your wives, and the
aliens living in your camps who chop

your wood and carry your water. 12You
are standing here in order to enter into
a covenant with the LORD your God, a
covenant the LORD is making with you
this day and sealing with an oath, 13to
confirm you this day as his people, that
he may be your God as he promised you
and as he swore to your fathers, Abraham, Isaac and Jacob. 14I am making this
covenant, with its oath, not only with
you 15who are standing here with us today in the presence of the LORD our
God but also with those who are not
here today.

16You yourselves know how we lived
in Egypt and how we passed through
the countries on the way here. 17You saw
among them their detestable images
and idols of wood and stone, of silver
and gold. 18Make sure there is no man
or woman, clan or tribe among you today whose heart turns away from the
LORD our God to go and worship the
gods of those nations; make sure there
is no root among you that produces
such bitter poison.

19When such a person hears the
words of this oath, he invokes a blessing on himself and therefore thinks, "I
will be safe, even though I persist in going my own way." This will bring disaster on the watered land as well as the
dry.[a] 20The LORD will never be willing to
forgive him; his wrath and zeal will
burn against that man. All the curses
written in this book will fall upon him,
and the LORD will blot out his name
from under heaven. 21The LORD will
single him out from all the tribes of Israel for disaster, according to all the
curses of the covenant written in this
Book of the Law.

22Your children who follow you in later generations and foreigners who come
from distant lands will see the calamities that have fallen on the land and the
diseases with which the LORD has afflicted it. 23The whole land will be a
burning waste of salt and sulfur—nothing planted, nothing sprouting, no vegetation growing on it. It will be like the
destruction of Sodom and Gomorrah,
Admah and Zeboiim, which the LORD
overthrew in fierce anger. 24All the nations will ask: "Why has the LORD done
this to this land? Why this fierce, burning anger?"

25And the answer will be: "It is because this people abandoned the covenant of the LORD, the God of their
fathers, the covenant he made with
them when he brought them out of
Egypt. 26They went off and worshiped
other gods and bowed down to them,
gods they did not know, gods he had
not given them. 27Therefore the LORD's
anger burned against this land, so that
he brought on it all the curses written in
this book. 28In furious anger and in great
wrath the LORD uprooted them from
their land and thrust them into another
land, as it is now."

29The secret things belong to the LORD
our God, but the things revealed belong to us and to our children forever,
that we may follow all the words of this
law.

[a]19 Or *way, in order to add drunkenness to thirst."*

SHARPEN THE FOCUS

The Christian life is a process of continual repentance and renewal. From our Lord's side, the covenant is never broken. His promises stand forever sure. Yet every day we break faith with our promise to love and obey Him. Our faithlessness need never be fatal, though. His Word of love reaches out to us in our unfaithfulness:

> *Return to the LORD your God,*
> *for He is gracious and compassionate,*
> *slow to anger and abounding in love.* (Joel 2:13)

The New Covenant began on Calvary. It was sealed to you personally at your Baptism. No sin is so great or terrible, no number of sins are too many, as to cause that Covenant to be canceled. We can always go home to our heavenly Father. We can always return to His outstretched waiting arms. Don't hesitate. Don't put it off. Remember:

In repentance and rest is your salvation,
in quietness and trust is your strength. (Isaiah 30:15)

WEEK 17 • THURSDAY

Deuteronomy 30:1–20

How well the Lord knows human hearts! Despite the spiritual growth He had brought about in the hearts of the people of that generation during their wilderness wanderings, times of unbelief and sin lay ahead. Future generations would wander from the covenant and from the Covenant-Maker, their Lord. As you read today, look for the message of Law (judgment on sin) and the message of Gospel (grace for the repentant sinner). If time is short, focus on Deuteronomy 30:11–20.

Prosperity After Turning to the LORD

30 When all these blessings
and curses I have set be-
fore you come upon you and you take
them to heart wherever the LORD your
God disperses you among the nations,
2and when you and your children return to the LORD your God and obey
him with all your heart and with all
your soul according to everything I
command you today, 3then the LORD
your God will restore your fortunes[a]
and have compassion on you and
gather you again from all the nations
where he scattered you. 4Even if you
have been banished to the most distant
land under the heavens, from there the
LORD your God will gather you and
bring you back. 5He will bring you to the
land that belonged to your fathers, and
you will take possession of it. He will
make you more prosperous and numerous than your fathers. 6The LORD your
God will circumcise your hearts and the
hearts of your descendants, so that you
may love him with all your heart and
with all your soul, and live. 7The LORD
your God will put all these curses on
your enemies who hate and persecute
you. 8You will again obey the LORD and
follow all his commands I am giving you
today. 9Then the LORD your God will
make you most prosperous in all the
work of your hands and in the fruit of
your womb, the young of your livestock
and the crops of your land. The LORD
will again delight in you and make you
prosperous, just as he delighted in your
fathers, 10if you obey the LORD your God
and keep his commands and decrees
that are written in this Book of the Law
and turn to the LORD your God with all
your heart and with all your soul.

The Offer of Life or Death

11Now what I am commanding you
today is not too difficult for you or beyond your reach. 12It is not up in heaven,

[a]3 Or *will bring you back from captivity*

so that you have to ask, "Who will ascend into heaven to get it and proclaim it to us so we may obey it?" [13]Nor is it beyond the sea, so that you have to ask, "Who will cross the sea to get it and proclaim it to us so we may obey it?" [14]No, the word is very near you; it is in your mouth and in your heart so you may obey it.

[15]See, I set before you today life and prosperity, death and destruction. [16]For I command you today to love the LORD your God, to walk in his ways, and to keep his commands, decrees and laws; then you will live and increase, and the LORD your God will bless you in the land you are entering to possess.

[17]But if your heart turns away and you are not obedient, and if you are drawn away to bow down to other gods and worship them, [18]I declare to you this day that you will certainly be destroyed. You will not live long in the land you are crossing the Jordan to enter and possess.

[19]This day I call heaven and earth as witnesses against you that I have set before you life and death, blessings and curses. Now choose life, so that you and your children may live [20]and that you may love the LORD your God, listen to his voice, and hold fast to him. For the LORD is your life, and he will give you many years in the land he swore to give to your fathers, Abraham, Isaac and Jacob.

SHARPEN THE FOCUS

Some people think of life as a pie—one wedge for family, another wedge for the job. Hobbies, entertainment, chores, a special project—all get a slice. And of course, the Lord gets the biggest slice.

But as life's pressures mount, the slices get thinner. The joy almost disappears. Deuteronomy 30:20 cues us in to the true nature of the problem: "The LORD is your life." Paul uses almost the same words in Colossians 3:4: "When Christ, who is your life, appears, then you also will appear with Him in glory."

Christ *is* our life. Not a part of it. In Christ we have eternal life, an eternal relationship with the Father. His life in us transforms our earthly life into something significant, beautiful, joyful.

We who know Christ as our life have a choice. We can relegate Him to an hour on Sunday, 20 minutes of Bible reading a day, brief prayers before and after meals. Or we can ask Him to keep us mindful of His presence, strength, and direction each minute of every day. We can rely on His Spirit to help us see the people around us with His eyes. We can live our life as an adventure of receiving God's grace and of letting that grace flow through us into the lives of others.

WEEK 17 • FRIDAY

Deuteronomy 31:1–30

GET THE BIG PICTURE

Moses concludes his third sermon by inaugurating Joshua as Israel's new leader. After Moses' death the people are to review the covenant regularly and teach it to their children. Nevertheless, Moses warns them, this covenant will fail. Not because the Lord will break it, but because human beings cannot fulfill it. We are, by nature, rebels. If time is short, focus on Deuteronomy 31:1–13.

Joshua to Succeed Moses

31 Then Moses went out and spoke these words to all Israel: 2"I am now a hundred and twenty years old and I am no longer able to lead you. The LORD has said to me, 'You shall not cross the Jordan.' 3The LORD your God himself will cross over ahead of you. He will destroy these nations before you, and you will take possession of their land. Joshua also will cross over ahead of you, as the LORD said. 4And the LORD will do to them what he did to Sihon and Og, the kings of the Amorites, whom he destroyed along with their land. 5The LORD will deliver them to you, and you must do to them all that I have commanded you. 6Be strong and courageous. Do not be afraid or terrified because of them, for the LORD your God goes with you; he will never leave you nor forsake you."

7Then Moses summoned Joshua and said to him in the presence of all Israel, "Be strong and courageous, for you must go with this people into the land that the LORD swore to their forefathers to give them, and you must divide it among them as their inheritance. 8The LORD himself goes before you and will be with you; he will never leave you nor forsake you. Do not be afraid; do not be discouraged."

The Reading of the Law

9So Moses wrote down this law and gave it to the priests, the sons of Levi, who carried the ark of the covenant of the LORD, and to all the elders of Israel. 10Then Moses commanded them: "At the end of every seven years, in the year for canceling debts, during the Feast of Tabernacles, 11when all Israel comes to appear before the LORD your God at the place he will choose, you shall read this law before them in their hearing. 12Assemble the people—men, women and children, and the aliens living in your towns—so they can listen and learn to fear the LORD your God and follow carefully all the words of this law. 13Their children, who do not know this law, must hear it and learn to fear the LORD your God as long as you live in the land you are crossing the Jordan to possess."

Israel's Rebellion Predicted

14The LORD said to Moses, "Now the day of your death is near. Call Joshua and present yourselves at the Tent of Meeting, where I will commission him." So Moses and Joshua came and presented themselves at the Tent of Meeting.

15Then the LORD appeared at the Tent in a pillar of cloud, and the cloud stood over the entrance to the Tent. 16And the LORD said to Moses: "You are going to rest with your fathers, and these people will soon prostitute themselves to the foreign gods of the land they are entering. They will forsake me and break the covenant I made with them. 17On that day I will become angry with them and forsake them; I will hide my face from them, and they will be destroyed. Many disasters and difficulties will come upon them, and on that day they will ask, 'Have not these disasters come upon us because our God is not with us?' 18And I will certainly hide my face on that day because of all their wickedness in turning to other gods.

19"Now write down for yourselves this song and teach it to the Israelites and have them sing it, so that it may be a witness for me against them. 20When I have brought them into the land flowing with milk and honey, the land I promised on oath to their forefathers, and when they eat their fill and thrive, they will turn to other gods and worship them, rejecting me and breaking my covenant. 21And when many disasters and difficulties come upon them, this song will testify against them, because it will not be forgotten by their de-

scendants. I know what they are disposed to do, even before I bring them
into the land I promised them on oath."
22So Moses wrote down this song that
day and taught it to the Israelites.
23The LORD gave this command to
Joshua son of Nun: "Be strong and courageous, for you will bring the Israelites
into the land I promised them on oath,
and I myself will be with you."
24After Moses finished writing in a
book the words of this law from beginning to end, 25he gave this command to
the Levites who carried the ark of the
covenant of the LORD: 26"Take this Book
of the Law and place it beside the ark of
the covenant of the LORD your God.
There it will remain as a witness against
you. 27For I know how rebellious and
stiff-necked you are. If you have been
rebellious against the LORD while I am
still alive and with you, how much more
will you rebel after I die! 28Assemble before me all the elders of your tribes and
all your officials, so that I can speak
these words in their hearing and call
heaven and earth to testify against
them. 29For I know that after my death
you are sure to become utterly corrupt
and to turn from the way I have commanded you. In days to come, disaster
will fall upon you because you will do
evil in the sight of the LORD and provoke him to anger by what your hands
have made."

The Song of Moses

30And Moses recited the words of this
song from beginning to end in the hearing of the whole assembly of Israel:

SHARPEN THE FOCUS

Why set up an elaborate system of laws, rules, directives that can't be obeyed, followed, or practiced? Why did the Lord even bother with the Old Covenant? Moses saw that Israel was made up of lawbreakers.

The Lord intended His Law to serve His Old Covenant people in much the same way it serves us, His New Covenant people. He wanted Old Testament Israel to throw up their hands in despair. God intended His Law to show Israel their utter powerlessness to do and be what He wanted them to do and be. He intended it to show them their sin and their need for a Savior.

Has God's Law done that for you as you've read the Pentateuch (Genesis–Deuteronomy)? Have you stood in Israel's sandals and seen your plight? Do you realize your problem isn't your circumstances? that it isn't the people around you? Do you see your own personal need for that "heart transplant" Ezekiel wrote about (Ezekiel 36:26–27)?

If so, know that the Lord's mercy in Jesus is here for you now. Remember the New Covenant He put into effect at Calvary. His body was given there—for you! His blood was spilled there—for you! Rest in His unchanging, forgiving love. ☼

Did you ever get the words and tune of a song caught in your mind? When that happens, often against our will, we hear the lyrics over and over. Moses taught Israel such a song. Years and even centuries later, the people would find their minds playing these lyrics over and over. Caught in their sin and its consequences, they would remember—often seemingly against their will—the Lord, His Law, His covenant promises to Abraham, and His invitation to return to Him. If time is short, focus on Deuteronomy 32:1–43.

32 Listen, O heavens, and I will speak;
hear, O earth, the words of my mouth.
2 Let my teaching fall like rain
and my words descend like dew,
like showers on new grass,
like abundant rain on tender plants.

3 I will proclaim the name of the LORD.
Oh, praise the greatness of our God!
4 He is the Rock, his works are perfect,
and all his ways are just.
A faithful God who does no wrong,
upright and just is he.
5 They have acted corruptly toward him;
to their shame they are no longer his children,
but a warped and crooked generation.[a]
6 Is this the way you repay the LORD,
O foolish and unwise people?
Is he not your Father, your Creator,[b]
who made you and formed you?
7 Remember the days of old;
consider the generations long past.
Ask your father and he will tell you,
your elders, and they will explain to you.
8 When the Most High gave the nations their inheritance,
when he divided all mankind,
he set up boundaries for the peoples
according to the number of the sons of Israel.[c]
9 For the LORD's portion is his people,
Jacob his allotted inheritance.

10 In a desert land he found him,
in a barren and howling waste.
He shielded him and cared for him;
he guarded him as the apple of his eye,
11 like an eagle that stirs up its nest
and hovers over its young,
that spreads its wings to catch them
and carries them on its pinions.
12 The LORD alone led him;
no foreign god was with him.

13 He made him ride on the heights of the land
and fed him with the fruit of the fields.
He nourished him with honey from the rock,
and with oil from the flinty crag,
14 with curds and milk from herd and flock
and with fattened lambs and goats,
with choice rams of Bashan
and the finest kernels of wheat.
You drank the foaming blood of the grape.

15 Jeshurun[d] grew fat and kicked;
filled with food, he became heavy and sleek.
He abandoned the God who made him
and rejected the Rock his Savior.
16 They made him jealous with their foreign gods
and angered him with their detestable idols.
17 They sacrificed to demons, which are not God—
gods they had not known,
gods that recently appeared,
gods your fathers did not fear.
18 You deserted the Rock, who fathered you;

[a]5 Or *Corrupt are they and not his children, / a generation warped and twisted to their shame*
[b]6 Or *Father, who bought you* [c]8 Masoretic Text; Dead Sea Scrolls (see also Septuagint) *sons of God*
[d]15 *Jeshurun* means *the upright one*, that is, Israel.

you forgot the God who gave you
birth.
19 The LORD saw this and rejected them
because he was angered by his
sons and daughters.
20 "I will hide my face from them," he
said,
"and see what their end will be;
for they are a perverse generation,
children who are unfaithful.
21 They made me jealous by what is no
god
and angered me with their
worthless idols.
I will make them envious by those
who are not a people;
I will make them angry by a
nation that has no
understanding.
22 For a fire has been kindled by my
wrath,
one that burns to the realm of
death[a] below.
It will devour the earth and its
harvests
and set afire the foundations of
the mountains.

23 "I will heap calamities upon them
and spend my arrows against
them.
24 I will send wasting famine against
them,
consuming pestilence and deadly
plague;
I will send against them the fangs of
wild beasts,
the venom of vipers that glide in
the dust.
25 In the street the sword will make
them childless;
in their homes terror will reign.
Young men and young women will
perish,
infants and gray-haired men.
26 I said I would scatter them
and blot out their memory from
mankind,
27 but I dreaded the taunt of the
enemy,
lest the adversary misunderstand
and say, 'Our hand has triumphed;
the LORD has not done all this.' "
28 They are a nation without sense,
there is no discernment in them.
29 If only they were wise and would
understand this
and discern what their end will
be!
30 How could one man chase a
thousand,
or two put ten thousand to flight,
unless their Rock had sold them,
unless the LORD had given them
up?
31 For their rock is not like our Rock,
as even our enemies concede.
32 Their vine comes from the vine of
Sodom
and from the fields of Gomorrah.
Their grapes are filled with poison,
and their clusters with bitterness.
33 Their wine is the venom of serpents,
the deadly poison of cobras.

34 "Have I not kept this in reserve
and sealed it in my vaults?
35 It is mine to avenge; I will repay.
In due time their foot will slip;
their day of disaster is near
and their doom rushes upon
them."

36 The LORD will judge his people
and have compassion on his
servants
when he sees their strength is gone
and no one is left, slave or free.
37 He will say: "Now where are their
gods,
the rock they took refuge in,
38 the gods who ate the fat of their
sacrifices
and drank the wine of their drink
offerings?
Let them rise up to help you!
Let them give you shelter!

39 "See now that I myself am He!
There is no god besides me.
I put to death and I bring to life,
I have wounded and I will heal,
and no one can deliver out of my
hand.
40 I lift my hand to heaven and
declare:

[a]22 Hebrew *to Sheol*

As surely as I live forever,
41 when I sharpen my flashing sword
and my hand grasps it in judgment,
I will take vengeance on my adversaries
and repay those who hate me.
42 I will make my arrows drunk with blood,
while my sword devours flesh:
the blood of the slain and the captives,
the heads of the enemy leaders."
43 Rejoice, O nations, with his people,[a,b]
for he will avenge the blood of his servants;
he will take vengeance on his enemies
and make atonement for his land and people.

44 Moses came with Joshua[c] son of
Nun and spoke all the words of this
song in the hearing of the people.
45 When Moses finished reciting all these
words to all Israel, 46 he said to them,
"Take to heart all the words I have solemnly declared to you this day, so that
you may command your children to
obey carefully all the words of this law.
47 They are not just idle words for you—
they are your life. By them you will live
long in the land you are crossing the Jordan to possess."

Moses to Die on Mount Nebo

48 On that same day the LORD told Moses, 49 "Go up into the Abarim Range to
Mount Nebo in Moab, across from Jericho, and view Canaan, the land I am
giving the Israelites as their own possession. 50 There on the mountain that you
have climbed you will die and be gathered to your people, just as your brother
Aaron died on Mount Hor and was
gathered to his people. 51 This is because
both of you broke faith with me in the
presence of the Israelites at the waters
of Meribah Kadesh in the Desert of Zin
and because you did not uphold my
holiness among the Israelites. 52 Therefore, you will see the land only from a
distance; you will not enter the land I
am giving to the people of Israel."

[a]43 Or *Make his people rejoice, O nations*
[b]43 Masoretic Text; Dead Sea Scrolls (see also Septuagint) *people, / and let all the angels worship him /* [c]44 Hebrew *Hoshea*, a variant of *Joshua*

SHARPEN THE FOCUS

Like many songs today, Moses' song is chock-full of powerful word pictures. Take verse 10 for example. Imagine yourself exhausted, dirty, hot, dressed in rags, and marooned in a wilderness. That's the picture of our plight Moses paints here. Our sins had made us outcasts. We wandered alone and helpless.

But look at the rest of the picture! The Lord *found* us! He came after His runaway children. He shielded us. He cared for us. He guarded us as carefully as we guard the pupil of our eyes.

- Having read the first five Old Testament books, you can see specific ways the Lord did those things for Abraham and for ancient Israel.
- Having seen God's love in Jesus, you can see how our Savior accomplished these things for us in an even more powerful way through His cross and open tomb.
- Having come to faith in Him by His grace you can see how He continues to shield you from sin and Satan, hell and eternal death. You know how He cares for your needs and how faithfully He stands guard over your life.

Why not find a hymnal or put on a compact disc and sing a song of praise to Him for His faithful mercy right now? Maybe your praises will even replay in your mind and heart all day long!

WEEK 18 • MONDAY

Deuteronomy 33:1–29

GET THE BIG PICTURE

In his last official act as the leader of the people of Israel, Moses blesses them. For 40 years he has led them as they wandered in the desert. As you read, zero in on the details of the Lord's goodness Moses mentions. If time is short, focus on Deuteronomy 33:1–5, 26–29.

Moses Blesses the Tribes

33 This is the blessing that Moses the man of God pronounced on the Israelites before his death. 2 He said:

"The LORD came from Sinai
and dawned over them from Seir;
he shone forth from Mount Paran.
He came with[a] myriads of holy ones
from the south, from his mountain slopes.[b]
3 Surely it is you who love the people;
all the holy ones are in your hand.
At your feet they all bow down,
and from you receive instruction,
4 the law that Moses gave us,
the possession of the assembly of Jacob.
5 He was king over Jeshurun[c]
when the leaders of the people assembled,
along with the tribes of Israel.

6 "Let Reuben live and not die,
nor[d] his men be few."

7 And this he said about Judah:

"Hear, O LORD, the cry of Judah;
bring him to his people.
With his own hands he defends his cause.
Oh, be his help against his foes!"

8 About Levi he said:

"Your Thummim and Urim belong
to the man you favored.
You tested him at Massah;
you contended with him at the waters of Meribah.
9 He said of his father and mother,
'I have no regard for them.'
He did not recognize his brothers
or acknowledge his own children,
but he watched over your word
and guarded your covenant.
10 He teaches your precepts to Jacob
and your law to Israel.
He offers incense before you
and whole burnt offerings on your altar.
11 Bless all his skills, O LORD,
and be pleased with the work of his hands.
Smite the loins of those who rise up against him;
strike his foes till they rise no more."

12 About Benjamin he said:

"Let the beloved of the LORD rest secure in him,
for he shields him all day long,
and the one the LORD loves rests between his shoulders."

13 About Joseph he said:

"May the LORD bless his land
with the precious dew from heaven above
and with the deep waters that lie below;
14 with the best the sun brings forth
and the finest the moon can yield;

[a]2 Or *from* [b]2 The meaning of the Hebrew for this phrase is uncertain. [c]5 *Jeshurun* means *the upright one,* that is, Israel; also in verse 26.
[d]6 Or *but let*

15 with the choicest gifts of the ancient
mountains
and the fruitfulness of the
everlasting hills;
16 with the best gifts of the earth and
its fullness
and the favor of him who dwelt in
the burning bush.
Let all these rest on the head of
Joseph,
on the brow of the prince among[a]
his brothers.
17 In majesty he is like a firstborn bull;
his horns are the horns of a wild
ox.
With them he will gore the nations,
even those at the ends of the
earth.
Such are the ten thousands of
Ephraim;
such are the thousands of
Manasseh."

18 About Zebulun he said:

"Rejoice, Zebulun, in your going
out,
and you, Issachar, in your tents.
19 They will summon peoples to the
mountain
and there offer sacrifices of
righteousness;
they will feast on the abundance of
the seas,
on the treasures hidden in the
sand."

20 About Gad he said:

"Blessed is he who enlarges Gad's
domain!
Gad lives there like a lion,
tearing at arm or head.
21 He chose the best land for himself;
the leader's portion was kept for
him.
When the heads of the people
assembled,
he carried out the LORD's
righteous will,
and his judgments concerning
Israel."

22 About Dan he said:

"Dan is a lion's cub,
springing out of Bashan."

23 About Naphtali he said:

"Naphtali is abounding with the
favor of the LORD
and is full of his blessing;
he will inherit southward to the
lake."

24 About Asher he said:

"Most blessed of sons is Asher;
let him be favored by his brothers,
and let him bathe his feet in oil.
25 The bolts of your gates will be iron
and bronze,
and your strength will equal your
days.

26 "There is no one like the God of
Jeshurun,
who rides on the heavens to help
you
and on the clouds in his majesty.
27 The eternal God is your refuge,
and underneath are the
everlasting arms.
He will drive out your enemy before
you,
saying, 'Destroy him!'
28 So Israel will live in safety alone;
Jacob's spring is secure
in a land of grain and new wine,
where the heavens drop dew.
29 Blessed are you, O Israel!
Who is like you,
a people saved by the LORD?
He is your shield and helper
and your glorious sword.
Your enemies will cower before you,
and you will trample down their
high places.[b]"

[a]16 Or *of the one separated from* [b]29 Or *will tread upon their bodies*

SHARPEN THE FOCUS

Suppose you found yourself in big trouble. Falsely accused of a crime and jailed. Or your home burned to the ground with all your earthly possessions inside. Or standing at the bedside of someone you dearly love who is dying.

None of us wants to face situations like those alone. Suppose you phoned your dearest friend, a friend who lives across the continent or even across the ocean. Suppose that friend said, "I'll be on the next jet. I'm headed for the airport right now." It's hard to imagine more comforting words, isn't it? To have a friend who cares enough to come.

That's the truth behind Deuteronomy 33:26. Our God "rides on the heavens to help [us]." When we cry out to Him, nothing can keep Him from racing to our side. To be with us, support us, shelter and strengthen us.

Moses calls God's people *Jeshurun* (Deuteronomy 33:5, 26). It means "the upright one." In the Messiah who was to come, Israel was righteous. In Jesus, the Savior who has come, you and I are righteous, too. We're "all right" with God. We have right standing with Him, because in Jesus "[our] guilt is taken away and [our] sin is atoned for" (Isaiah 6:7).

WEEK 18 • TUESDAY

Deuteronomy 34:1–12

GET THE BIG PICTURE

Before taking Moses to the Promised Land of heaven, the Lord shows Moses the full extent of the Promised Land of Canaan on earth. After Moses' death, the people of Israel willingly follow Joshua, the Lord's newly appointed leader. If time is short, focus on Deuteronomy 34:1–6.

The Death of Moses

34 Then Moses climbed
Mount Nebo from the
plains of Moab to the top of Pisgah,
across from Jericho. There the LORD
showed him the whole land—from Gilead to Dan, 2all of Naphtali, the territory
of Ephraim and Manasseh, all the land
of Judah as far as the western sea,[a] 3the
Negev and the whole region from the
Valley of Jericho, the City of Palms, as far
as Zoar. 4Then the LORD said to him,
"This is the land I promised on oath to
Abraham, Isaac and Jacob when I said,
'I will give it to your descendants.' I
have let you see it with your eyes, but
you will not cross over into it."
5And Moses the servant of the LORD
died there in Moab, as the LORD had
said. 6He buried him[b] in Moab, in the
valley opposite Beth Peor, but to this day
no one knows where his grave is. 7Mo-
ses was a hundred and twenty years old
when he died, yet his eyes were not
weak nor his strength gone. 8The Israelites grieved for Moses in the plains of
Moab thirty days, until the time of
weeping and mourning was over.
9Now Joshua son of Nun was filled
with the spirit[c] of wisdom because Moses had laid his hands on him. So the

[a]2 That is, the Mediterranean [b]6 Or *He was buried* [c]9 Or *Spirit*

Israelites listened to him and did what the LORD had commanded Moses.
[10]Since then, no prophet has risen in Israel like Moses, whom the LORD knew face to face, [11]who did all those miraculous signs and wonders the LORD sent him to do in Egypt—to Pharaoh and to all his officials and to his whole land.
[12]For no one has ever shown the mighty power or performed the awesome deeds that Moses did in the sight of all Israel.

SHARPEN THE FOCUS

At what age can a person best serve the Lord? Moses didn't begin until he was 80. He spent the first 40 years of his life in Pharaoh's court and the second 40 years in the desert of Sinai herding sheep.

Moses was 80, but Josiah was 8. This boy became king during a time of spiritual crisis among God's people, and at age 20 he began a religious reformation in his nation (2 Kings 22:1–23:25).

Our Lord can provide opportunities to serve Him at any age. He can provide the physical strength, wisdom, and spiritual insight. He must provide these things, because we cannot produce them in ourselves.

Are you reluctant to answer and obey the Lord's call–like Moses at the burning bush? The Scriptures constantly repeat the principle that God's people are to serve Him. And we are to serve with a willing attitude, "with gladness" (Psalm 100:2).

But what if we're not willing to do whatever our Lord gives us to do at the moment? Then read Joel 2:13 and let the Holy Spirit burn God's Word of law and of grace into your heart. Remember His compassion and love. Then let Him fill you with His holy desires. He wants to do that–no matter how many years young you are.

JOSHUA

As today's reading begins, Moses has died. Joshua, probably in his 80's, steps into leadership. Made willing by the Holy Spirit, the people submit to that leadership. As you read, watch for some of the recurring themes of this book: God's promised presence; God's Word and the importance of Israel's obedience to it; and the nation of Israel as one people, under God. If time is short, focus on Joshua 1:1–9.

The LORD Commands Joshua

1 After the death of Moses the servant of the LORD, the LORD said to
Joshua son of Nun, Moses' aide: [2]"Moses my servant is dead. Now then, you
and all these people, get ready to cross
the Jordan River into the land I am
about to give to them—to the Israelites.
[3]I will give you every place where you
set your foot, as I promised Moses. [4]Your
territory will extend from the desert to
Lebanon, and from the great river, the
Euphrates—all the Hittite country—to
the Great Sea[a] on the west. [5]No one will
be able to stand up against you all the
days of your life. As I was with Moses,
so I will be with you; I will never leave
you nor forsake you.
[6]"Be strong and courageous, because
you will lead these people to inherit the
land I swore to their forefathers to give
them. [7]Be strong and very courageous.
Be careful to obey all the law my servant
Moses gave you; do not turn from it
to the right or to the left, that you may
be successful wherever you go. [8]Do
not let this Book of the Law depart
from your mouth; meditate on it day
and night, so that you may be careful to
do everything written in it. Then you
will be prosperous and successful.
[9]Have I not commanded you? Be strong
and courageous. Do not be terrified;
do not be discouraged, for the LORD
your God will be with you wherever
you go."
[10]So Joshua ordered the officers of the
people: [11]"Go through the camp and tell
the people, 'Get your supplies ready.
Three days from now you will cross the
Jordan here to go in and take possession
of the land the LORD your God is giving
you for your own.' "
[12]But to the Reubenites, the Gadites
and the half-tribe of Manasseh, Joshua
said, [13]"Remember the command that
Moses the servant of the LORD gave
you: 'The LORD your God is giving you
rest and has granted you this land.'
[14]Your wives, your children and your
livestock may stay in the land that Moses gave you east of the Jordan, but all
your fighting men, fully armed, must
cross over ahead of your brothers. You
are to help your brothers [15]until the
LORD gives them rest, as he has done for
you, and until they too have taken possession of the land that the LORD your

[a]4 That is, the Mediterranean

God is giving them. After that, you may
go back and occupy your own land,
which Moses the servant of the LORD
gave you east of the Jordan toward the
sunrise."
16Then they answered Joshua, "Whatever you have commanded us we will
do, and wherever you send us we will
go. 17Just as we fully obeyed Moses, so
we will obey you. Only may the LORD
your God be with you as he was with
Moses. 18Whoever rebels against your
word and does not obey your words,
whatever you may command them, will
be put to death. Only be strong and courageous!"

SHARPEN THE FOCUS

What activities and interests do you really get into? Gardening? Basketball? Italian cooking? Maybe you've noticed that the things we get into eventually get into us. Once gardening or carpentry or jogging get "into our blood," they change us—our outlook, our self-image, and sometimes even the course of our lives.

The Lord urged Joshua to get into His Word so that the Word could get into Joshua. According to Joshua 1:8, Joshua's immersion in the Word was to be:

- Permanent—"Do not let this Book of the Law depart from your mouth."
- Pervasive—"Meditate on it day and night."
- Purposeful—"So that you may be careful to do everything written in it."
- Powerful—"Then you will be prosperous and successful."

The Lord wants this from us today, too. But for us, as for Joshua of old, getting into the Word in this thoroughgoing way will prove impossible every time.

Except, that is, for one thing. The Word—the Word made flesh, our Savior Jesus Christ—has come to us. His Spirit has given us the gift of faith, and Christ Himself has made His home in our hearts. His blood covers our failures to obey, and His love empowers our new obedience.

WEEK 18 • THURSDAY

Joshua 2:1—3:17

GET THE BIG PICTURE

Today you will read about two miracles, miracles made possible only by the grace of the Lord: the faith of the prostitute, Rahab, and Israel's crossing of the River Jordan. As you read, look for evidence that the Lord's reputation had preceded Israel into Canaan. If time is short, focus on Joshua 2:1–24.

Rahab and the Spies

2 Then Joshua son of Nun secretly
sent two spies from Shittim. "Go,
look over the land," he said, "especially
Jericho." So they went and entered the
house of a prostitute[a] named Rahab and
stayed there.

[a]1 Or possibly *an innkeeper*

2The king of Jericho was told, "Look!
Some of the Israelites have come here
tonight to spy out the land." 3So the king
of Jericho sent this message to Rahab:
"Bring out the men who came to you
and entered your house, because they
have come to spy out the whole land."
4But the woman had taken the two
men and hidden them. She said, "Yes,
the men came to me, but I did not know
where they had come from. 5At dusk,
when it was time to close the city gate,
the men left. I don't know which way
they went. Go after them quickly. You
may catch up with them." 6(But she had
taken them up to the roof and hidden
them under the stalks of flax she had
laid out on the roof.) 7So the men set out
in pursuit of the spies on the road that
leads to the fords of the Jordan, and as
soon as the pursuers had gone out, the
gate was shut.
8Before the spies lay down for the
night, she went up on the roof 9and said
to them, "I know that the LORD has
given this land to you and that a great
fear of you has fallen on us, so that all
who live in this country are melting in
fear because of you. 10We have heard
how the LORD dried up the water of the
Red Sea[a] for you when you came out of
Egypt, and what you did to Sihon and
Og, the two kings of the Amorites east
of the Jordan, whom you completely
destroyed.[b] 11When we heard of it, our
hearts melted and everyone's courage
failed because of you, for the LORD your
God is God in heaven above and on the
earth below. 12Now then, please swear
to me by the LORD that you will show
kindness to my family, because I have
shown kindness to you. Give me a sure
sign 13that you will spare the lives of my
father and mother, my brothers and sisters, and all who belong to them, and
that you will save us from death."
14"Our lives for your lives!" the men
assured her. "If you don't tell what we
are doing, we will treat you kindly and
faithfully when the LORD gives us the
land."
15So she let them down by a rope
through the window, for the house she
lived in was part of the city wall. 16Now
she had said to them, "Go to the hills so
the pursuers will not find you. Hide
yourselves there three days until they
return, and then go on your way."
17The men said to her, "This oath you
made us swear will not be binding on us
18unless, when we enter the land, you
have tied this scarlet cord in the window through which you let us down,
and unless you have brought your father and mother, your brothers and all
your family into your house. 19If anyone
goes outside your house into the street,
his blood will be on his own head; we
will not be responsible. As for anyone
who is in the house with you, his blood
will be on our head if a hand is laid on
him. 20But if you tell what we are doing,
we will be released from the oath you
made us swear."
21"Agreed," she replied. "Let it be as
you say." So she sent them away and
they departed. And she tied the scarlet
cord in the window.
22When they left, they went into the
hills and stayed there three days, until
the pursuers had searched all along the
road and returned without finding
them. 23Then the two men started back.
They went down out of the hills, ford-
ed the river and came to Joshua son of
Nun and told him everything that had
happened to them. 24They said to
Joshua, "The LORD has surely given the
whole land into our hands; all the people are melting in fear because of us."

Crossing the Jordan

3 Early in the morning Joshua and
all the Israelites set out from
Shittim and went to the Jordan, where
they camped before crossing over. 2Af-
ter three days the officers went throughout the camp, 3giving orders to the
people: "When you see the ark of the
covenant of the LORD your God, and
the priests, who are Levites, carrying it,

[a]10 Hebrew *Yam Suph*; that is, Sea of Reeds
[b]10 The Hebrew term refers to the irrevocable giving over of things or persons to the LORD, often by totally destroying them.

you are to move out from your positions
and follow it. [4]Then you will know which
way to go, since you have never been this
way before. But keep a distance of about
a thousand yards[a] between you and the
ark; do not go near it."
[5]Joshua told the people, "Consecrate
yourselves, for tomorrow the LORD will
do amazing things among you."
[6]Joshua said to the priests, "Take up
the ark of the covenant and pass on
ahead of the people." So they took it up
and went ahead of them.
[7]And the LORD said to Joshua, "Today
I will begin to exalt you in the eyes of
all Israel, so they may know that I am
with you as I was with Moses. [8]Tell the
priests who carry the ark of the covenant: 'When you reach the edge of the
Jordan's waters, go and stand in the
river.' "
[9]Joshua said to the Israelites, "Come
here and listen to the words of the LORD
your God. [10]This is how you will know
that the living God is among you and
that he will certainly drive out before
you the Canaanites, Hittites, Hivites,
Perizzites, Girgashites, Amorites and
Jebusites. [11]See, the ark of the covenant
of the Lord of all the earth will go into
the Jordan ahead of you. [12]Now then,
choose twelve men from the tribes of Israel, one from each tribe. [13]And as soon
as the priests who carry the ark of the
LORD—the Lord of all the earth—set
foot in the Jordan, its waters flowing
downstream will be cut off and stand up
in a heap."
[14]So when the people broke camp to
cross the Jordan, the priests carrying the
ark of the covenant went ahead of them.
[15]Now the Jordan is at flood stage all
during harvest. Yet as soon as the priests
who carried the ark reached the Jordan
and their feet touched the water's edge,
[16]the water from upstream stopped
flowing. It piled up in a heap a great
distance away, at a town called Adam in
the vicinity of Zarethan, while the water flowing down to the Sea of the Arabah (the Salt Sea[b]) was completely cut
off. So the people crossed over opposite
Jericho. [17]The priests who carried the ark
of the covenant of the LORD stood firm
on dry ground in the middle of the Jordan, while all Israel passed by until the
whole nation had completed the crossing on dry ground.

[a]4 Hebrew *about two thousand cubits* (about 900 meters) [b]16 That is, the Dead Sea

SHARPEN THE FOCUS

Repeatedly in the Old Testament we read that the Lord is the "living God" (Joshua 3:10). Looking at this phrase in its context, we soon see that it means "the God who acts." In everyday language we might say "the God who does stuff" for His people.

We know the truth of this, yet we often act as though our Lord is anything but living. We don't see His activity in our lives. We "forget" His Law when it's convenient. And we burden ourselves with unnecessary worries.

The Lord always remains the living God. Rahab turned to Him in repentance and faith. And she received from Him forgiveness, deliverance, peace, and a place among God's people. The living God acted at the Jordan in order to keep His promise to give the land, and more importantly, the Savior, through the family tree of Abraham, Isaac, and Jacob.

Where in your life do you need to see the Lord as the "living God," the God who acts on your behalf to give you repentance, forgiveness, deliverance, or peace? Remember what the Lord Jesus told the apostle John, "I am the Living One; I was dead, and behold I am alive for ever and ever!" (Revelation 1:18).

WEEK 18 • FRIDAY

Joshua 4:1—5:12

GET THE BIG PICTURE

Israel has landed safely in Canaan. We might expect everyone immediately to throw themselves into final preparations for conquering the land. But not so. As you read today, note the first-things-first attitude of the people. If time is short, focus on Joshua 4:1–24.

4 When the whole nation had finished crossing the Jordan, the
LORD said to Joshua, 2"Choose twelve
men from among the people, one from
each tribe, 3and tell them to take up
twelve stones from the middle of the
Jordan from right where the priests
stood and to carry them over with you
and put them down at the place where
you stay tonight."
4So Joshua called together the twelve
men he had appointed from the Israelites, one from each tribe, 5and said to
them, "Go over before the ark of the
LORD your God into the middle of the
Jordan. Each of you is to take up a stone
on his shoulder, according to the number of the tribes of the Israelites, 6to
serve as a sign among you. In the future,
when your children ask you, 'What do
these stones mean?' 7tell them that the
flow of the Jordan was cut off before the
ark of the covenant of the LORD. When
it crossed the Jordan, the waters of the
Jordan were cut off. These stones are to
be a memorial to the people of Israel
forever."
8So the Israelites did as Joshua commanded them. They took twelve stones
from the middle of the Jordan, according to the number of the tribes of the Israelites, as the LORD had told Joshua;
and they carried them over with them
to their camp, where they put them
down. 9Joshua set up the twelve stones
that had been[a] in the middle of the Jordan at the spot where the priests who
carried the ark of the covenant had
stood. And they are there to this day.
10Now the priests who carried the ark
remained standing in the middle of the
Jordan until everything the LORD had
commanded Joshua was done by the
people, just as Moses had directed Joshua. The people hurried over, 11and as
soon as all of them had crossed, the ark
of the LORD and the priests came to the
other side while the people watched.
12The men of Reuben, Gad and the half-
tribe of Manasseh crossed over, armed,
in front of the Israelites, as Moses had
directed them. 13About forty thousand
armed for battle crossed over before the
LORD to the plains of Jericho for war.
14That day the LORD exalted Joshua in
the sight of all Israel; and they revered
him all the days of his life, just as they
had revered Moses.
15Then the LORD said to Joshua,
16"Command the priests carrying the ark
of the Testimony to come up out of the
Jordan."
17So Joshua commanded the priests,
"Come up out of the Jordan."
18And the priests came up out of the
river carrying the ark of the covenant of
the LORD. No sooner had they set their
feet on the dry ground than the waters
of the Jordan returned to their place and
ran at flood stage as before.
19On the tenth day of the first month
the people went up from the Jordan and
camped at Gilgal on the eastern border
of Jericho. 20And Joshua set up at Gilgal
the twelve stones they had taken out of
the Jordan. 21He said to the Israelites, "In

[a]9 Or *Joshua also set up twelve stones*

the future when your descendants ask
their fathers, 'What do these stones
mean?' 22tell them, 'Israel crossed the
Jordan on dry ground.' 23For the LORD
your God dried up the Jordan before
you until you had crossed over. The
LORD your God did to the Jordan just
what he had done to the Red Sea[a] when
he dried it up before us until we had
crossed over. 24He did this so that all the
peoples of the earth might know that
the hand of the LORD is powerful and
so that you might always fear the LORD
your God."

Circumcision at Gilgal

5 Now when all the Amorite kings
west of the Jordan and all the
Canaanite kings along the coast heard
how the LORD had dried up the Jordan
before the Israelites until we had
crossed over, their hearts melted and
they no longer had the courage to face
the Israelites.
2At that time the LORD said to Joshua,
"Make flint knives and circumcise the Israelites again." 3So Joshua made flint
knives and circumcised the Israelites at
Gibeath Haaraloth.[b]
4Now this is why he did so: All those
who came out of Egypt—all the men of
military age—died in the desert on the
way after leaving Egypt. 5All the people
that came out had been circumcised, but
all the people born in the desert during
the journey from Egypt had not. 6The Israelites had moved about in the desert
forty years until all the men who were
of military age when they left Egypt had
died, since they had not obeyed the
LORD. For the LORD had sworn to them
that they would not see the land that he
had solemnly promised their fathers to
give us, a land flowing with milk and
honey. 7So he raised up their sons in
their place, and these were the ones
Joshua circumcised. They were still uncircumcised because they had not been
circumcised on the way. 8And after the
whole nation had been circumcised,
they remained where they were in
camp until they were healed.
9Then the LORD said to Joshua, "Today I have rolled away the reproach of
Egypt from you." So the place has been
called Gilgal[c] to this day.
10On the evening of the fourteenth
day of the month, while camped at Gilgal on the plains of Jericho, the Israelites celebrated the Passover. 11The day
after the Passover, that very day, they ate
some of the produce of the land: unleavened bread and roasted grain. 12The
manna stopped the day after[d] they ate
this food from the land; there was no
longer any manna for the Israelites, but
that year they ate of the produce of Canaan.

[a]23 Hebrew *Yam Suph*; that is, Sea of Reeds
[b]3 *Gibeath Haaraloth* means *hill of foreskins.*
[c]9 *Gilgal* sounds like the Hebrew for *roll.*
[d]12 Or *the day*

SHARPEN THE FOCUS

Gilgal became a rallying place for God's people. For over 400 years after Israel built the memorial there, Gilgal served as a place where the nation gathered to recall God's mercy.

The name Gilgal means "circle" or "wheel." The Lord had now truly "rolled away" Israel's shame (Joshua 5:9). The people were no longer slaves. Instead, they were the Lord's own sons and daughters (see Galatians 4:7). As further reminder of the Lord's willingness to do what He had sworn to Abraham, the nation celebrated what we might call Old Testament sacraments—circumcision and the Passover (Joshua 5:7–10).

What or where is your "Gilgal"? When you need a reminder that the Lord has "rolled away" the shame of your slavery to sin by placing that shame on the shoulders of His Son, to what do you look?

As you worship in church, take special note of the baptismal font. Remember that in your

Baptism the Lord circumcised your heart (Romans 2:28; Colossians 3:11–12). And as you receive the body and blood of Christ in the Lord's Supper, praise Him that He is your Passover Lamb. He has been sacrificed for you (1 Corinthians 5:7–8).

WEEK 18 • SATURDAY

Joshua 5:13—7:26

GET THE BIG PICTURE

Some in Jericho must have jeered from the walls. Others inside must have trembled in dismay at the eerie battle plan Israel followed. As you read, remember God's purpose for the conquest of Canaan: to fulfill the covenant promise He had made with Abraham to give his descendants the land. In keeping that promise, the Lord was making a down payment on another promise of that covenant–He was providing a homeland for the people through whom the Messiah would come. If time is short, focus on Joshua 6:1–17.

The Fall of Jericho

[13]Now when Joshua was near Jericho,
he looked up and saw a man standing
in front of him with a drawn sword in
his hand. Joshua went up to him and
asked, "Are you for us or for our enemies?"
[14]"Neither," he replied, "but as commander of the army of the LORD I have
now come." Then Joshua fell facedown
to the ground in reverence, and asked
him, "What message does my Lord[a]
have for his servant?"
[15]The commander of the LORD's army
replied, "Take off your sandals, for the
place where you are standing is holy."
And Joshua did so.

6 Now Jericho was tightly shut up
because of the Israelites. No one
went out and no one came in.
[2]Then the LORD said to Joshua, "See,
I have delivered Jericho into your
hands, along with its king and its fighting men. [3]March around the city once
with all the armed men. Do this for six
days. [4]Have seven priests carry trumpets of rams' horns in front of the ark.
On the seventh day, march around the
city seven times, with the priests blowing the trumpets. [5]When you hear them
sound a long blast on the trumpets,
have all the people give a loud shout;
then the wall of the city will collapse
and the people will go up, every man
straight in."
[6]So Joshua son of Nun called the
priests and said to them, "Take up the
ark of the covenant of the LORD and
have seven priests carry trumpets in
front of it." [7]And he ordered the people,
"Advance! March around the city, with
the armed guard going ahead of the ark
of the LORD."
[8]When Joshua had spoken to the people, the seven priests carrying the seven
trumpets before the LORD went forward, blowing their trumpets, and the
ark of the LORD's covenant followed
them. [9]The armed guard marched
ahead of the priests who blew the trumpets, and the rear guard followed the
ark. All this time the trumpets were
sounding. [10]But Joshua had commanded the people, "Do not give a war
cry, do not raise your voices, do not say
a word until the day I tell you to shout.

[a]14 Or *lord*

Then shout!" 11So he had the ark of the
LORD carried around the city, circling it
once. Then the people returned to camp
and spent the night there.
12Joshua got up early the next morning and the priests took up the ark of the
LORD. 13The seven priests carrying the
seven trumpets went forward, marching before the ark of the LORD and blowing the trumpets. The armed men went
ahead of them and the rear guard followed the ark of the LORD, while the
trumpets kept sounding. 14So on the second day they marched around the city
once and returned to the camp. They
did this for six days.
15On the seventh day, they got up at
daybreak and marched around the city
seven times in the same manner, except
that on that day they circled the city sev-
en times. 16The seventh time around,
when the priests sounded the trumpet
blast, Joshua commanded the people,
"Shout! For the LORD has given you the
city! 17The city and all that is in it are to
be devoted[a] to the LORD. Only Rahab
the prostitute[b] and all who are with her
in her house shall be spared, because
she hid the spies we sent. 18But keep
away from the devoted things, so that
you will not bring about your own destruction by taking any of them. Otherwise you will make the camp of Israel
liable to destruction and bring trouble
on it. 19All the silver and gold and the
articles of bronze and iron are sacred to
the LORD and must go into his treasury."
20When the trumpets sounded, the
people shouted, and at the sound of the
trumpet, when the people gave a loud
shout, the wall collapsed; so every man
charged straight in, and they took the
city. 21They devoted the city to the LORD
and destroyed with the sword every living thing in it—men and women,
young and old, cattle, sheep and donkeys.
22Joshua said to the two men who had
spied out the land, "Go into the prostitute's house and bring her out and all
who belong to her, in accordance with
your oath to her." 23So the young men
who had done the spying went in and
brought out Rahab, her father and
mother and brothers and all who belonged to her. They brought out her entire family and put them in a place
outside the camp of Israel.
24Then they burned the whole city
and everything in it, but they put the silver and gold and the articles of bronze
and iron into the treasury of the LORD's
house. 25But Joshua spared Rahab the
prostitute, with her family and all who
belonged to her, because she hid the
men Joshua had sent as spies to Jericho—and she lives among the Israelites
to this day.
26At that time Joshua pronounced this
solemn oath: "Cursed before the LORD
is the man who undertakes to rebuild
this city, Jericho:

"At the cost of his firstborn son
  will he lay its foundations;
at the cost of his youngest
  will he set up its gates."

27So the LORD was with Joshua, and
his fame spread throughout the land.

Achan's Sin

7 But the Israelites acted unfaithfully in regard to the devoted
things[c]; Achan son of Carmi, the son of
Zimri,[d] the son of Zerah, of the tribe of
Judah, took some of them. So the LORD's
anger burned against Israel.
2Now Joshua sent men from Jericho to
Ai, which is near Beth Aven to the east
of Bethel, and told them, "Go up and
spy out the region." So the men went up
and spied out Ai.
3When they returned to Joshua, they
said, "Not all the people will have to go
up against Ai. Send two or three thousand men to take it and do not weary all
the people, for only a few men are

[a]*17* The Hebrew term refers to the irrevocable giving over of things or persons to the LORD, often by totally destroying them; also in verses 18 and 21. [b]*17* Or possibly *innkeeper*; also in verses 22 and 25 [c]*1* The Hebrew term refers to the irrevocable giving over of things or persons to the LORD, often by totally destroying them; also in verses 11, 12, 13 and 15. [d]*1* See Septuagint and 1 Chron. 2:6; Hebrew *Zabdi*; also in verses 17 and 18.

there." 4So about three thousand men
went up; but they were routed by the
men of Ai, 5who killed about thirty-six
of them. They chased the Israelites from
the city gate as far as the stone quarries[a]
and struck them down on the slopes. At
this the hearts of the people melted and
became like water.
6Then Joshua tore his clothes and fell
facedown to the ground before the ark
of the LORD, remaining there till evening. The elders of Israel did the same,
and sprinkled dust on their heads. 7And
Joshua said, "Ah, Sovereign LORD, why
did you ever bring this people across the
Jordan to deliver us into the hands of
the Amorites to destroy us? If only we
had been content to stay on the other
side of the Jordan! 8O Lord, what can I
say, now that Israel has been routed by
its enemies? 9The Canaanites and the
other people of the country will hear
about this and they will surround us
and wipe out our name from the earth.
What then will you do for your own
great name?"
10The LORD said to Joshua, "Stand up!
What are you doing down on your face?
11Israel has sinned; they have violated
my covenant, which I commanded
them to keep. They have taken some of
the devoted things; they have stolen,
they have lied, they have put them with
their own possessions. 12That is why the
Israelites cannot stand against their enemies; they turn their backs and run because they have been made liable to
destruction. I will not be with you anymore unless you destroy whatever
among you is devoted to destruction.
13"Go, consecrate the people. Tell
them, 'Consecrate yourselves in preparation for tomorrow; for this is what the
LORD, the God of Israel, says: That
which is devoted is among you, O Israel.
You cannot stand against your enemies
until you remove it.
14" 'In the morning, present yourselves tribe by tribe. The tribe that the
LORD takes shall come forward clan by
clan; the clan that the LORD takes shall
come forward family by family; and the
family that the LORD takes shall come
forward man by man. 15He who is
caught with the devoted things shall be
destroyed by fire, along with all that belongs to him. He has violated the covenant of the LORD and has done a
disgraceful thing in Israel!' "
16Early the next morning Joshua had
Israel come forward by tribes, and Judah was taken. 17The clans of Judah
came forward, and he took the Zerahites. He had the clan of the Zerahites
come forward by families, and Zimri
was taken. 18Joshua had his family come
forward man by man, and Achan son of
Carmi, the son of Zimri, the son of Zerah, of the tribe of Judah, was taken.
19Then Joshua said to Achan, "My son,
give glory to the LORD,[b] the God of Israel, and give him the praise.[c] Tell me
what you have done; do not hide it
from me."
20Achan replied, "It is true! I have
sinned against the LORD, the God of Israel. This is what I have done: 21When I
saw in the plunder a beautiful robe from
Babylonia,[d] two hundred shekels[e] of silver and a wedge of gold weighing fifty
shekels,[f] I coveted them and took them.
They are hidden in the ground inside
my tent, with the silver underneath."
22So Joshua sent messengers, and they
ran to the tent, and there it was, hidden
in his tent, with the silver underneath.
23They took the things from the tent,
brought them to Joshua and all the Israelites and spread them out before the
LORD.
24Then Joshua, together with all Israel, took Achan son of Zerah, the silver,
the robe, the gold wedge, his sons and
daughters, his cattle, donkeys and
sheep, his tent and all that he had, to the
Valley of Achor. 25Joshua said, "Why
have you brought this trouble on us?
The LORD will bring trouble on you today."
Then all Israel stoned him, and after
they had stoned the rest, they burned

[a]5 Or *as far as Shebarim* [b]19 A solemn charge to tell the truth [c]19 Or *and confess to him* [d]21 Hebrew *Shinar* [e]21 That is, about 5 pounds (about 2.3 kilograms) [f]21 That is, about 1 1/4 pounds (about 0.6 kilogram)

them. 26Over Achan they heaped up a large pile of rocks, which remains to this day. Then the LORD turned from his fierce anger. Therefore that place has been called the Valley of Achor[a] ever since.

SHARPEN THE FOCUS

The people of Israel camped beside the Jordan River for five days; then they crossed. The people of Israel marched around the walls of Jericho for seven days; then the walls fell. Why the delay? Couldn't the Lord have parted the Jordan or toppled Jericho on day one?

Of course. But in waiting to act, the living God gave His people a gift—time to reflect and refocus. Time to get their eyes off themselves and their own weakness. Time to remember His promises, His love, and His strength.

We, too, often find ourselves waiting—for the river to part, for a wall to fall, for help to come. We can chafe in impatience while we wait. Or we can thank our Lord for His gift of time. We can—by His grace—spend it in His presence, asking Him to strengthen us in His Word of promise.

Whenever you check the time today, remember that in the Lord's time you will receive every victory Christ won for you on Calvary.

WEEK 19 • MONDAY

Joshua 8:1—9:27

GET THE BIG PICTURE

The Lord will now reverse the defeat Achan brought on Israel. The people follow their Commander's strategy to the letter, and He gives them total victory. The nation celebrates this victory by worshiping their Lord as Moses had commanded earlier. But just when things are going well, a major lapse mars Joshua's leadership record. He and the rulers of Israel fail to "inquire of the LORD" (Joshua 9:14) and commit the nation to a treaty they never should have made. If time is short, focus on Joshua 9:1–27.

Ai Destroyed

8 Then the LORD said to Joshua, "Do not be afraid; do not be discouraged. Take the whole army with you, and go up and attack Ai. For I have delivered into your hands the king of
Ai, his people, his city and his land. 2You
shall do to Ai and its king as you did to Jericho and its king, except that you may carry off their plunder and livestock for yourselves. Set an ambush behind the city."
3So Joshua and the whole army moved out to attack Ai. He chose thirty thousand of his best fighting men and sent them out at night 4with these orders: "Listen carefully. You are to set an ambush behind the city. Don't go very far from it. All of you be on the alert. 5I
and all those with me will advance on the city, and when the men come out against us, as they did before, we will flee from them. 6They will pursue us until we have lured them away from the

[a]26 *Achor* means *trouble.*

city, for they will say, 'They are running away from us as they did before.' So when we flee from them, 7you are to rise up from ambush and take the city. The LORD your God will give it into your hand. 8When you have taken the city, set it on fire. Do what the LORD has commanded. See to it; you have my orders."

9Then Joshua sent them off, and they went to the place of ambush and lay in wait between Bethel and Ai, to the west of Ai—but Joshua spent that night with the people.

10Early the next morning Joshua mustered his men, and he and the leaders of Israel marched before them to Ai. 11The entire force that was with him marched up and approached the city and arrived in front of it. They set up camp north of Ai, with the valley between them and the city. 12Joshua had taken about five thousand men and set them in ambush between Bethel and Ai, to the west of the city. 13They had the soldiers take up their positions—all those in the camp to the north of the city and the ambush to the west of it. That night Joshua went into the valley.

14When the king of Ai saw this, he and all the men of the city hurried out early in the morning to meet Israel in battle at a certain place overlooking the Arabah. But he did not know that an ambush had been set against him behind the city. 15Joshua and all Israel let themselves be driven back before them, and they fled toward the desert. 16All the men of Ai were called to pursue them, and they pursued Joshua and were lured away from the city. 17Not a man remained in Ai or Bethel who did not go after Israel. They left the city open and went in pursuit of Israel.

18Then the LORD said to Joshua, "Hold out toward Ai the javelin that is in your hand, for into your hand I will deliver the city." So Joshua held out his javelin toward Ai. 19As soon as he did this, the men in the ambush rose quickly from their position and rushed forward. They entered the city and captured it and quickly set it on fire.

20The men of Ai looked back and saw the smoke of the city rising against the sky, but they had no chance to escape in any direction, for the Israelites who had been fleeing toward the desert had turned back against their pursuers. 21For when Joshua and all Israel saw that the ambush had taken the city and that smoke was going up from the city, they turned around and attacked the men of Ai. 22The men of the ambush also came out of the city against them, so that they were caught in the middle, with Israelites on both sides. Israel cut them down, leaving them neither survivors nor fugitives. 23But they took the king of Ai alive and brought him to Joshua.

24When Israel had finished killing all the men of Ai in the fields and in the desert where they had chased them, and when every one of them had been put to the sword, all the Israelites returned to Ai and killed those who were in it. 25Twelve thousand men and women fell that day—all the people of Ai. 26For Joshua did not draw back the hand that held out his javelin until he had destroyed[a] all who lived in Ai. 27But Israel did carry off for themselves the livestock and plunder of this city, as the LORD had instructed Joshua.

28So Joshua burned Ai and made it a permanent heap of ruins, a desolate place to this day. 29He hung the king of Ai on a tree and left him there until evening. At sunset, Joshua ordered them to take his body from the tree and throw it down at the entrance of the city gate. And they raised a large pile of rocks over it, which remains to this day.

The Covenant Renewed at Mount Ebal

30Then Joshua built on Mount Ebal an altar to the LORD, the God of Israel, 31as Moses the servant of the LORD had commanded the Israelites. He built it according to what is written in the Book of the Law of Moses—an altar of uncut stones, on which no iron tool had been

[a]26 The Hebrew term refers to the irrevocable giving over of things or persons to the LORD, often by totally destroying them.

used. On it they offered to the LORD burnt offerings and sacrificed fellowship offerings.[a] [32]There, in the presence of the Israelites, Joshua copied on stones the law of Moses, which he had written. [33]All Israel, aliens and citizens alike, with their elders, officials and judges, were standing on both sides of the ark of the covenant of the LORD, facing those who carried it—the priests, who were Levites. Half of the people stood in front of Mount Gerizim and half of them in front of Mount Ebal, as Moses the servant of the LORD had formerly commanded when he gave instructions to bless the people of Israel.

[34]Afterward, Joshua read all the words of the law—the blessings and the curses—just as it is written in the Book of the Law. [35]There was not a word of all that Moses had commanded that Joshua did not read to the whole assembly of Israel, including the women and children, and the aliens who lived among them.

The Gibeonite Deception

9 Now when all the kings west of the Jordan heard about these things—those in the hill country, in the western foothills, and along the entire coast of the Great Sea[b] as far as Lebanon (the kings of the Hittites, Amorites, Canaanites, Perizzites, Hivites and Jebusites)— [2]they came together to make war against Joshua and Israel.

[3]However, when the people of Gibeon heard what Joshua had done to Jericho and Ai, [4]they resorted to a ruse: They went as a delegation whose donkeys were loaded[c] with worn-out sacks and old wineskins, cracked and mended. [5]The men put worn and patched sandals on their feet and wore old clothes. All the bread of their food supply was dry and moldy. [6]Then they went to Joshua in the camp at Gilgal and said to him and the men of Israel, "We have come from a distant country; make a treaty with us."

[7]The men of Israel said to the Hivites, "But perhaps you live near us. How then can we make a treaty with you?"

[8]"We are your servants," they said to Joshua.

But Joshua asked, "Who are you and where do you come from?"

[9]They answered: "Your servants have come from a very distant country because of the fame of the LORD your God. For we have heard reports of him: all that he did in Egypt, [10]and all that he did to the two kings of the Amorites east of the Jordan—Sihon king of Heshbon, and Og king of Bashan, who reigned in Ashtaroth. [11]And our elders and all those living in our country said to us, 'Take provisions for your journey; go and meet them and say to them, "We are your servants; make a treaty with us."' [12]This bread of ours was warm when we packed it at home on the day we left to come to you. But now see how dry and moldy it is. [13]And these wineskins that we filled were new, but see how cracked they are. And our clothes and sandals are worn out by the very long journey."

[14]The men of Israel sampled their provisions but did not inquire of the LORD. [15]Then Joshua made a treaty of peace with them to let them live, and the leaders of the assembly ratified it by oath.

[16]Three days after they made the treaty with the Gibeonites, the Israelites heard that they were neighbors, living near them. [17]So the Israelites set out and on the third day came to their cities: Gibeon, Kephirah, Beeroth and Kiriath Jearim. [18]But the Israelites did not attack them, because the leaders of the assembly had sworn an oath to them by the LORD, the God of Israel.

The whole assembly grumbled against the leaders, [19]but all the leaders answered, "We have given them our oath by the LORD, the God of Israel, and we cannot touch them now. [20]This is what we will do to them: We will let them live, so that wrath will not fall on us for breaking the oath we swore to them." [21]They continued, "Let them

[a]31 Traditionally *peace offerings* [b]1 That is, the Mediterranean [c]4 Most Hebrew manuscripts; some Hebrew manuscripts, Vulgate and Syriac (see also Septuagint) *They prepared provisions and loaded their donkeys*

live, but let them be woodcutters and
water carriers for the entire community." So the leaders' promise to them was
kept.
[22]Then Joshua summoned the Gibeonites and said, "Why did you deceive
us by saying, 'We live a long way from
you,' while actually you live near us?
[23]You are now under a curse: You will
never cease to serve as woodcutters and
water carriers for the house of my God."
[24]They answered Joshua, "Your servants were clearly told how the LORD
your God had commanded his servant
Moses to give you the whole land and
to wipe out all its inhabitants from before you. So we feared for our lives because of you, and that is why we did
this. [25]We are now in your hands. Do to
us whatever seems good and right to
you."
[26]So Joshua saved them from the Israelites, and they did not kill them. [27]That
day he made the Gibeonites woodcutters and water carriers for the community and for the altar of the LORD at the
place the LORD would choose. And that
is what they are to this day.

SHARPEN THE FOCUS

Failure brings pain. But success brings its own unique temptations. The temptation to rely on ourselves. The temptation to "believe our own publicity." The temptation to think the Lord should be thankful to have us and our abilities on His side.

We might never say these things out loud. But the attitude can lie there, just under the surface of our hearts.

Maybe that's what happened to Joshua and the elders. Their decision to make a treaty with the Gibeonites made good sense. And so Joshua signed on the dotted line. He swore "by the LORD, the God of Israel" (Joshua 9:18). Three days later the whole congregation heard the truth. The Gibeonites who said they had come from a far country (Joshua 9:6) really lived only 20 miles or so from Israel's camp. And, worse, they were Hivites—condemned for destruction by the Lord so that they would not lead His people into the spiritual death of idolatry (Exodus 23:28–33).

What decisions do you face? Certainly the Lord expects you to use common sense to gather the facts, to apply your best logic. But even then, He invites you to ask for His counsel, counsel He has promised to provide. Turn to your Savior-God for grace to cover the ungodly decisions that lie in the past. Trust in Him for guidance as you face your future.

WEEK 19 • TUESDAY

Joshua 10:1–43

GET THE BIG PICTURE

Joshua and the nation he leads soon have a chance to keep their word to Gibeon. Angered and frightened by Gibeon's treaty with Israel, five nearby city-states declare war on Gibeon. True to his oath, Joshua sends his troops into battle to defend Gibeon. Once on the attack, Israel's army sweeps through most of the southern third of Canaan, and the Lord gives every enemy into their hands. If time is short, focus on Joshua 10:1–14.

The Sun Stands Still

10 Now Adoni-Zedek king of Jerusalem heard that Joshua had taken Ai and totally destroyed[a] it, doing to Ai and its king as he had done to Jericho and its king, and that the people of Gibeon had made a treaty of peace with Israel and were living near them. [2]He and his people were very much alarmed at this, because Gibeon was an important city, like one of the royal cities; it was larger than Ai, and all its men were good fighters. [3]So Adoni-Zedek king of Jerusalem appealed to Hoham king of Hebron, Piram king of Jarmuth, Japhia king of Lachish and Debir king of Eglon. [4]"Come up and help me attack Gibeon," he said, "because it has made peace with Joshua and the Israelites."

[5]Then the five kings of the Amorites—the kings of Jerusalem, Hebron, Jarmuth, Lachish and Eglon—joined forces. They moved up with all their troops and took up positions against Gibeon and attacked it.

[6]The Gibeonites then sent word to Joshua in the camp at Gilgal: "Do not abandon your servants. Come up to us quickly and save us! Help us, because all the Amorite kings from the hill country have joined forces against us."

[7]So Joshua marched up from Gilgal with his entire army, including all the best fighting men. [8]The LORD said to Joshua, "Do not be afraid of them; I have given them into your hand. Not one of them will be able to withstand you."

[9]After an all-night march from Gilgal, Joshua took them by surprise. [10]The LORD threw them into confusion before Israel, who defeated them in a great victory at Gibeon. Israel pursued them along the road going up to Beth Horon and cut them down all the way to Azekah and Makkedah. [11]As they fled before Israel on the road down from Beth Horon to Azekah, the LORD hurled large hailstones down on them from the sky, and more of them died from the hailstones than were killed by the swords of the Israelites.

[12]On the day the LORD gave the Amorites over to Israel, Joshua said to the LORD in the presence of Israel:

"O sun, stand still over Gibeon,
O moon, over the Valley of Aijalon."
[13]So the sun stood still,
and the moon stopped,
till the nation avenged itself on[b] its enemies,

as it is written in the Book of Jashar.

The sun stopped in the middle of the sky and delayed going down about a full day. [14]There has never been a day like it before or since, a day when the LORD listened to a man. Surely the LORD was fighting for Israel!

[15]Then Joshua returned with all Israel to the camp at Gilgal.

Five Amorite Kings Killed

[16]Now the five kings had fled and hidden in the cave at Makkedah. [17]When Joshua was told that the five kings had been found hiding in the cave at Makkedah, [18]he said, "Roll large rocks up to the mouth of the cave, and post some men there to guard it. [19]But don't stop! Pursue your enemies, attack them from the rear and don't let them reach their cities, for the LORD your God has given them into your hand."

[20]So Joshua and the Israelites destroyed them completely—almost to a man—but the few who were left reached their fortified cities. [21]The whole army then returned safely to Joshua in the camp at Makkedah, and no one uttered a word against the Israelites.

[22]Joshua said, "Open the mouth of the cave and bring those five kings out to me." [23]So they brought the five kings out of the cave—the kings of Jerusalem, Hebron, Jarmuth, Lachish and Eglon. [24]When they had brought these kings to

[a]1 The Hebrew term refers to the irrevocable giving over of things or persons to the LORD, often by totally destroying them; also in verses 28, 35, 37, 39 and 40. [b]13 Or *nation triumphed over*

Joshua, he summoned all the men of Israel and said to the army commanders
who had come with him, "Come here
and put your feet on the necks of these
kings." So they came forward and
placed their feet on their necks.
25Joshua said to them, "Do not be
afraid; do not be discouraged. Be strong
and courageous. This is what the LORD
will do to all the enemies you are going
to fight." 26Then Joshua struck and
killed the kings and hung them on five
trees, and they were left hanging on the
trees until evening.
27At sunset Joshua gave the order and
they took them down from the trees and
threw them into the cave where they
had been hiding. At the mouth of the
cave they placed large rocks, which are
there to this day.
28That day Joshua took Makkedah. He
put the city and its king to the sword
and totally destroyed everyone in it. He
left no survivors. And he did to the king
of Makkedah as he had done to the king
of Jericho.

Southern Cities Conquered

29Then Joshua and all Israel with him
moved on from Makkedah to Libnah
and attacked it. 30The LORD also gave
that city and its king into Israel's hand.
The city and everyone in it Joshua put
to the sword. He left no survivors there.
And he did to its king as he had done to
the king of Jericho.
31Then Joshua and all Israel with him
moved on from Libnah to Lachish; he
took up positions against it and attacked
it. 32The LORD handed Lachish over to
Israel, and Joshua took it on the second
day. The city and everyone in it he put
to the sword, just as he had done to Libnah. 33Meanwhile, Horam king of Gezer
had come up to help Lachish, but
Joshua defeated him and his army—until no survivors were left.
34Then Joshua and all Israel with him
moved on from Lachish to Eglon; they
took up positions against it and attacked
it. 35They captured it that same day and
put it to the sword and totally destroyed
everyone in it, just as they had done to
Lachish.
36Then Joshua and all Israel with him
went up from Eglon to Hebron and attacked it. 37They took the city and put it
to the sword, together with its king, its
villages and everyone in it. They left no
survivors. Just as at Eglon, they totally
destroyed it and everyone in it.
38Then Joshua and all Israel with him
turned around and attacked Debir.
39They took the city, its king and its villages, and put them to the sword. Everyone in it they totally destroyed. They
left no survivors. They did to Debir and
its king as they had done to Libnah and
its king and to Hebron.
40So Joshua subdued the whole region, including the hill country, the
Negev, the western foothills and the
mountain slopes, together with all their
kings. He left no survivors. He totally
destroyed all who breathed, just as the
LORD, the God of Israel, had commanded. 41Joshua subdued them from Kadesh
Barnea to Gaza and from the whole region of Goshen to Gibeon. 42All these
kings and their lands Joshua conquered
in one campaign, because the LORD, the
God of Israel, fought for Israel.
43Then Joshua returned with all Israel
to the camp at Gilgal.

SHARPEN THE FOCUS

How big is your vision? How bold are your prayers?

Joshua knew that he and the army he commanded would be victorious. He had God's word on that (Joshua 10:8). Nothing would stop them–not even approaching darkness. Clinging by grace to the Lord's gracious promise, Joshua spoke to the Lord and then to the sun (Joshua 10:12).

The result? Total victory. Overwhelming victory. The nations fall one by one, because God fights for His people. The wicked are judged and displaced. The land of Canaan falls into the hands of the people from whom the Seed of Abraham, our Lord Jesus, would come. Jesus would rightly inherit all the covenant promises God had made to Abraham.

Now that same covenant-making, covenant-keeping God says to Christ:

> *Ask of me,*
> *and I will make*
> *the nations your inheritance,*
> *the ends of the earth your possession.* (Psalm 2:8)

And Christ says to us:

> *Therefore go and make disciples of all nations, baptizing them in the name of the Father and of the Son and of the Holy Spirit, and teaching them to obey everything I have commanded you.* (Matthew 28:19–20)

WEEK 19 • WEDNESDAY

Joshua 11:1—12:24

The Lord's armies march north in a campaign that probably lasted nearly seven years. Just as southern Canaan fell under the sword of Joshua, so do all the cities of the north. As chapter 11 ends, none of the remaining Canaanite kings have any desire to attack God's people. Israel has rest. If time is short, focus on Joshua 12:7–24.

Northern Kings Defeated

11 When Jabin king of Hazor heard
of this, he sent word to Jobab
king of Madon, to the kings of Shimron
and Acshaph, 2and to the northern
kings who were in the mountains, in the
Arabah south of Kinnereth, in the western foothills and in Naphoth Dor[a] on
the west; 3to the Canaanites in the east
and west; to the Amorites, Hittites, Perizzites and Jebusites in the hill country;
and to the Hivites below Hermon in the
region of Mizpah. 4They came out with
all their troops and a large number of
horses and chariots—a huge army, as
numerous as the sand on the seashore.
5All these kings joined forces and made
camp together at the Waters of Merom,
to fight against Israel.
6The LORD said to Joshua, "Do not be
afraid of them, because by this time tomorrow I will hand all of them over to
Israel, slain. You are to hamstring their
horses and burn their chariots."
7So Joshua and his whole army came
against them suddenly at the Waters of
Merom and attacked them, 8and the
LORD gave them into the hand of Israel.
They defeated them and pursued them
all the way to Greater Sidon, to Misrephoth Maim, and to the Valley of Mizpah on the east, until no survivors were
left. 9Joshua did to them as the LORD
had directed: He hamstrung their
horses and burned their chariots.
10At that time Joshua turned back and
captured Hazor and put its king to the
sword. (Hazor had been the head of all

[a]2 Or *in the heights of Dor*

these kingdoms.) [11]Everyone in it they put to the sword. They totally destroyed[a] them, not sparing anything that breathed, and he burned up Hazor itself.

[12]Joshua took all these royal cities and their kings and put them to the sword. He totally destroyed them, as Moses the servant of the LORD had commanded. [13]Yet Israel did not burn any of the cities built on their mounds—except Hazor, which Joshua burned. [14]The Israelites carried off for themselves all the plunder and livestock of these cities, but all the people they put to the sword until they completely destroyed them, not sparing anyone that breathed. [15]As the LORD commanded his servant Moses, so Moses commanded Joshua, and Joshua did it; he left nothing undone of all that the LORD commanded Moses.

[16]So Joshua took this entire land: the hill country, all the Negev, the whole region of Goshen, the western foothills, the Arabah and the mountains of Israel with their foothills, [17]from Mount Halak, which rises toward Seir, to Baal Gad in the Valley of Lebanon below Mount Hermon. He captured all their kings and struck them down, putting them to death. [18]Joshua waged war against all these kings for a long time. [19]Except for the Hivites living in Gibeon, not one city made a treaty of peace with the Israelites, who took them all in battle. [20]For it was the LORD himself who hardened their hearts to wage war against Israel, so that he might destroy them totally, exterminating them without mercy, as the LORD had commanded Moses.

[21]At that time Joshua went and destroyed the Anakites from the hill country: from Hebron, Debir and Anab, from all the hill country of Judah, and from all the hill country of Israel. Joshua totally destroyed them and their towns. [22]No Anakites were left in Israelite territory; only in Gaza, Gath and Ashdod did any survive. [23]So Joshua took the entire land, just as the LORD had directed Moses, and he gave it as an inheritance to Israel according to their tribal divisions.

Then the land had rest from war.

List of Defeated Kings

12 These are the kings of the land whom the Israelites had defeated and whose territory they took over east of the Jordan, from the Arnon Gorge to Mount Hermon, including all the eastern side of the Arabah:

[2]Sihon king of the Amorites,
who reigned in Heshbon. He ruled from Aroer on the rim of the Arnon Gorge—from the middle of the gorge—to the Jabbok River, which is the border of the Ammonites. This included half of Gilead. [3]He also ruled over the eastern Arabah from the Sea of Kinnereth[b] to the Sea of the Arabah (the Salt Sea[c]), to Beth Jeshimoth, and then southward below the slopes of Pisgah.

[4]And the territory of Og king of Bashan,
one of the last of the Rephaites, who reigned in Ashtaroth and Edrei. [5]He ruled over Mount Hermon, Salecah, all of Bashan to the border of the people of Geshur and Maacah, and half of Gilead to the border of Sihon king of Heshbon.

[6]Moses, the servant of the LORD, and the Israelites conquered them. And Moses the servant of the LORD gave their land to the Reubenites, the Gadites and the half-tribe of Manasseh to be their possession.

[7]These are the kings of the land that Joshua and the Israelites conquered on the west side of the Jordan, from Baal Gad in the Valley of Lebanon to Mount Halak, which rises toward Seir (their lands Joshua gave as an inheritance to the tribes of Israel according to their tribal divisions— [8]the hill country, the western foothills, the Arabah, the mountain slopes, the desert and the Negev—the lands of the Hittites, Amorites, Canaanites, Perizzites, Hivites and Jebusites):

[a]*11* The Hebrew term refers to the irrevocable giving over of things or persons to the LORD, often by totally destroying them; also in verses 12, 20 and 21. [b]*3* That is, Galilee [c]*3* That is, the Dead Sea

9 the king of Jericho	one
the king of Ai (near Bethel)	one
10 the king of Jerusalem	one
the king of Hebron	one
11 the king of Jarmuth	one
the king of Lachish	one
12 the king of Eglon	one
the king of Gezer	one
13 the king of Debir	one
the king of Geder	one
14 the king of Hormah	one
the king of Arad	one
15 the king of Libnah	one
the king of Adullam	one
16 the king of Makkedah	one
the king of Bethel	one
17 the king of Tappuah	one
the king of Hepher	one
18 the king of Aphek	one
the king of Lasharon	one
19 the king of Madon	one
the king of Hazor	one
20 the king of Shimron Meron	one
the king of Acshaph	one
21 the king of Taanach	one
the king of Megiddo	one
22 the king of Kedesh	one
the king of Jokneam in Carmel	one
23 the king of Dor (in Naphoth Dor[a])	one
the king of Goyim in Gilgal	one
24 the king of Tirzah	one

thirty-one kings in all.

[a]23 Or *in the heights of Dor*

SHARPEN THE FOCUS

The Holy Spirit could have inspired the holy writer to condense Joshua 12 into perhaps just one verse something like this: "The LORD gave Israel many victories under the leadership of Moses and Joshua." Instead, we read 24 verses, verses which name specific kings, one by one.

Why might that be? Here's one possibility. Perhaps the Lord wants to use these verses to show us the importance of remembering the victories He's given us one by one. Perhaps, too, we see a hint here of the best way to carry out the tasks He gives us—one step at a time.

Take some time to think back over the past few years of your own life. If you were to make a list of the victories your Lord has won for you, what would you name?

- What specific fears or sins have fallen, by grace, to the lordship of Christ?
- What individuals have experienced, by grace, Jesus' love in you or heard about that love from you?
- What sins has He wiped from your record for the sake of Christ's cross?

Go ahead. Make your own list of victories. Then praise your victorious Savior for each triumph—one by one.

WEEK 19 • THURSDAY

Joshua 13:1—15:63

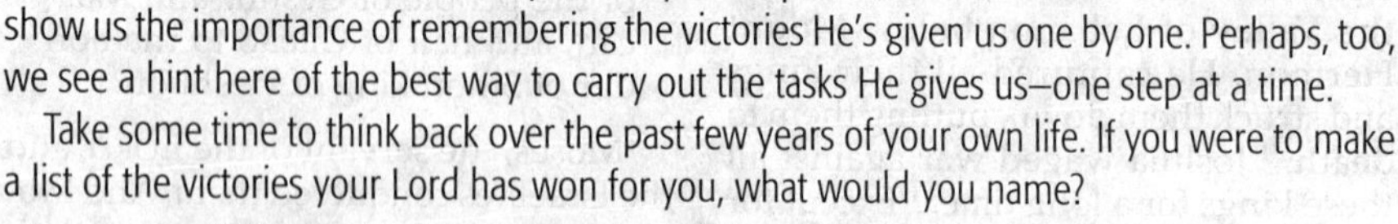

GET THE BIG PICTURE

Today's reading (and the ones for the next several days) outlines the boundaries of the land each tribe will inherit. As you read, note how often the word *inheritance* appears. As Abraham's heirs, the people of Israel received the land as God's gift to them, not something they earned. If time is short, focus on Joshua 14:6–15.

Land Still to Be Taken

13 When Joshua was old and well advanced in years, the LORD said to him, "You are very old, and there are still very large areas of land to be taken over.

2"This is the land that remains: all the regions of the Philistines and Geshurites: 3from the Shihor River on the east of Egypt to the territory of Ekron on the north, all of it counted as Canaanite (the territory of the five Philistine rulers in Gaza, Ashdod, Ashkelon, Gath and Ekron—that of the Avvites); 4from the south, all the land of the Canaanites, from Arah of the Sidonians as far as Aphek, the region of the Amorites, 5the area of the Gebalites[a]; and all Lebanon to the east, from Baal Gad below Mount Hermon to Lebo[b] Hamath.

6"As for all the inhabitants of the mountain regions from Lebanon to Misrephoth Maim, that is, all the Sidonians, I myself will drive them out before the Israelites. Be sure to allocate this land to Israel for an inheritance, as I have instructed you, 7and divide it as an inheritance among the nine tribes and half of the tribe of Manasseh."

Division of the Land East of the Jordan

8The other half of Manasseh,[c] the Reubenites and the Gadites had received the inheritance that Moses had given them east of the Jordan, as he, the servant of the LORD, had assigned it to them.

9It extended from Aroer on the rim of the Arnon Gorge, and from the town in the middle of the gorge, and included the whole plateau of Medeba as far as Dibon, 10and all the towns of Sihon king of the Amorites, who ruled in Heshbon, out to the border of the Ammonites. 11It also included Gilead, the territory of the people of Geshur and Maacah, all of Mount Hermon and all Bashan as far as Salecah— 12that is, the whole kingdom of Og in Bashan, who had reigned in Ashtaroth and Edrei and had survived as one of the last of the Rephaites. Moses had defeated them and taken over their land. 13But the Israelites did not drive out the people of Geshur and Maacah, so they continue to live among the Israelites to this day.

14But to the tribe of Levi he gave no inheritance, since the offerings made by fire to the LORD, the God of Israel, are their inheritance, as he promised them.

15This is what Moses had given to the tribe of Reuben, clan by clan:

16The territory from Aroer on the rim of the Arnon Gorge, and from the town in the middle of the gorge, and the whole plateau past Medeba 17to Heshbon and all its towns on the plateau, including Dibon, Bamoth Baal, Beth Baal Meon, 18Jahaz, Kedemoth, Mephaath, 19Kiriathaim, Sibmah, Zereth Shahar on the hill in the valley, 20Beth Peor, the slopes of Pisgah, and Beth Jeshimoth 21—all the towns on the plateau and the entire realm of Sihon king of the Amorites, who ruled at Heshbon. Moses had defeated him and the Midianite chiefs, Evi, Rekem, Zur, Hur and Reba—princes allied with Sihon—who lived in that country. 22In addition to those slain in battle, the Israelites had put to the sword Balaam son of Beor, who practiced divination. 23The boundary of the

[a]5 That is, the area of Byblos [b]5 Or *to the entrance to* [c]8 Hebrew *With it* (that is, with the other half of Manasseh)

Reubenites was the bank of the Jordan. These towns and their villages were the inheritance of the Reubenites, clan by clan.

24This is what Moses had given to the tribe of Gad, clan by clan:

25The territory of Jazer, all the towns of Gilead and half the Ammonite country as far as Aroer, near Rabbah; 26and from Heshbon to Ramath Mizpah and Betonim, and from Mahanaim to the territory of Debir; 27and in the valley, Beth Haram, Beth Nimrah, Succoth and Zaphon with the rest of the realm of Sihon king of Heshbon (the east side of the Jordan, the territory up to the end of the Sea of Kinnereth[a]). 28These towns and their villages were the inheritance of the Gadites, clan by clan.

29This is what Moses had given to the half-tribe of Manasseh, that is, to half the family of the descendants of Manasseh, clan by clan:

30The territory extending from Mahanaim and including all of Bashan, the entire realm of Og king of Bashan—all the settlements of Jair in Bashan, sixty towns, 31half of Gilead, and Ashtaroth and Edrei (the royal cities of Og in Bashan). This was for the descendants of Makir son of Manasseh—for half of the sons of Makir, clan by clan.

32This is the inheritance Moses had given when he was in the plains of Moab across the Jordan east of Jericho. 33But to the tribe of Levi, Moses had given no inheritance; the LORD, the God of Israel, is their inheritance, as he promised them.

Division of the Land West of the Jordan

14 Now these are the areas the Israelites received as an inheritance in the land of Canaan, which Eleazar the priest, Joshua son of Nun and the heads of the tribal clans of Israel allotted to them. 2Their inheritances were assigned by lot to the nine-and-a-half tribes, as the LORD had commanded through Moses. 3Moses had granted the two-and-a-half tribes their inheritance east of the Jordan but had not granted the Levites an inheritance among the rest, 4for the sons of Joseph had become two tribes—Manasseh and Ephraim. The Levites received no share of the land but only towns to live in, with pasturelands for their flocks and herds. 5So the Israelites divided the land, just as the LORD had commanded Moses.

Hebron Given to Caleb

6Now the men of Judah approached Joshua at Gilgal, and Caleb son of Jephunneh the Kenizzite said to him, "You know what the LORD said to Moses the man of God at Kadesh Barnea about you and me. 7I was forty years old when Moses the servant of the LORD sent me from Kadesh Barnea to explore the land. And I brought him back a report according to my convictions, 8but my brothers who went up with me made the hearts of the people melt with fear. I, however, followed the LORD my God wholeheartedly. 9So on that day Moses swore to me, 'The land on which your feet have walked will be your inheritance and that of your children forever, because you have followed the LORD my God wholeheartedly.'[b]

10"Now then, just as the LORD promised, he has kept me alive for forty-five years since the time he said this to Moses, while Israel moved about in the desert. So here I am today, eighty-five years old! 11I am still as strong today as the day Moses sent me out; I'm just as vigorous to go out to battle now as I was then. 12Now give me this hill country that the LORD promised me that day. You yourself heard then that the Anakites were there and their cities were large and fortified, but, the LORD helping me, I will drive them out just as he said."

13Then Joshua blessed Caleb son of Je-

[a]27 That is, Galilee [b]9 Deut. 1:36

phunneh and gave him Hebron as his
inheritance. 14So Hebron has belonged
to Caleb son of Jephunneh the Kenizzite
ever since, because he followed the
LORD, the God of Israel, wholeheartedly. 15(Hebron used to be called Kiriath
Arba after Arba, who was the greatest
man among the Anakites.)

Then the land had rest from war.

Allotment for Judah

15 The allotment for the tribe of
Judah, clan by clan, extended
down to the territory of Edom, to the
Desert of Zin in the extreme south.

2Their southern boundary started from the bay at the southern
end of the Salt Sea,[a] 3crossed south
of Scorpion[b] Pass, continued on to
Zin and went over to the south of
Kadesh Barnea. Then it ran past
Hezron up to Addar and curved
around to Karka. 4It then passed
along to Azmon and joined the
Wadi of Egypt, ending at the sea.
This is their[c] southern boundary.

5The eastern boundary is the Salt
Sea as far as the mouth of the Jordan.

The northern boundary started
from the bay of the sea at the
mouth of the Jordan, 6went up to
Beth Hoglah and continued north
of Beth Arabah to the Stone of Bohan son of Reuben. 7The boundary
then went up to Debir from the Valley of Achor and turned north to
Gilgal, which faces the Pass of
Adummim south of the gorge. It
continued along to the waters of En
Shemesh and came out at En Rogel.
8Then it ran up the Valley of Ben
Hinnom along the southern slope
of the Jebusite city (that is, Jerusalem). From there it climbed to the
top of the hill west of the Hinnom
Valley at the northern end of the
Valley of Rephaim. 9From the hilltop the boundary headed toward
the spring of the waters of Nephtoah, came out at the towns of Mount
Ephron and went down toward Baalah (that is, Kiriath Jearim). 10Then
it curved westward from Baalah to
Mount Seir, ran along the northern
slope of Mount Jearim (that is, Kes-
alon), continued down to Beth Shemesh and crossed to Timnah. 11It
went to the northern slope of Ekron, turned toward Shikkeron,
passed along to Mount Baalah and
reached Jabneel. The boundary
ended at the sea.

12The western boundary is the
coastline of the Great Sea.[d]

These are the boundaries around the
people of Judah by their clans.

13In accordance with the LORD's command to him, Joshua gave to Caleb son
of Jephunneh a portion in Judah—Kiriath Arba, that is, Hebron. (Arba was the
forefather of Anak.) 14From Hebron Caleb drove out the three Anakites—Sheshai, Ahiman and Talmai—descendants
of Anak. 15From there he marched
against the people living in Debir (formerly called Kiriath Sepher). 16And Caleb said, "I will give my daughter Acsah
in marriage to the man who attacks and
captures Kiriath Sepher." 17Othniel son
of Kenaz, Caleb's brother, took it; so
Caleb gave his daughter Acsah to him in
marriage.

18One day when she came to Othni-
el, she urged him[e] to ask her father for a
field. When she got off her donkey, Caleb asked her, "What can I do for you?"

19She replied, "Do me a special favor.
Since you have given me land in the
Negev, give me also springs of water."
So Caleb gave her the upper and lower
springs.

20This is the inheritance of the tribe of
Judah, clan by clan:

21The southernmost towns of the tribe of
Judah in the Negev toward the boundary of Edom were:

Kabzeel, Eder, Jagur, 22Kinah, Di-

[a]2 That is, the Dead Sea; also in verse 5
[b]3 Hebrew *Akrabbim* [c]4 Hebrew *your*
[d]12 That is, the Mediterranean; also in verse 47
[e]18 Hebrew and some Septuagint manuscripts; other Septuagint manuscripts (see also note at Judges 1:14) *Othniel, he urged her*

monah, Adadah, [23]Kedesh, Hazor,
Ithnan, [24]Ziph, Telem, Bealoth,
[25]Hazor Hadattah, Kerioth Hezron
(that is, Hazor), [26]Amam, Shema,
Moladah, [27]Hazar Gaddah, Hesh-
mon, Beth Pelet, [28]Hazar Shual, Beersheba, Biziothiah, [29]Baalah, Iim,
Ezem, [30]Eltolad, Kesil, Hormah,
[31]Ziklag, Madmannah, Sansannah,
[32]Lebaoth, Shilhim, Ain and Rimmon—a total of twenty-nine towns
and their villages.

[33]In the western foothills:

Eshtaol, Zorah, Ashnah, [34]Zano-
ah, En Gannim, Tappuah, Enam,
[35]Jarmuth, Adullam, Socoh, Azekah, [36]Shaaraim, Adithaim and
Gederah (or Gederothaim)[a]—fourteen towns and their villages.

[37]Zenan, Hadashah, Migdal Gad,
[38]Dilean, Mizpah, Joktheel, [39]La-
chish, Bozkath, Eglon, [40]Cabbon,
Lahmas, Kitlish, [41]Gederoth, Beth
Dagon, Naamah and Makkedah—
sixteen towns and their villages.

[42]Libnah, Ether, Ashan, [43]Iphtah,
Ashnah, Nezib, [44]Keilah, Aczib and
Mareshah—nine towns and their
villages.

[45]Ekron, with its surrounding
settlements and villages; [46]west of
Ekron, all that were in the vicinity
of Ashdod, together with their villages; [47]Ashdod, its surrounding
settlements and villages; and Gaza,
its settlements and villages, as far as
the Wadi of Egypt and the coastline
of the Great Sea.

[48]In the hill country:

Shamir, Jattir, Socoh, [49]Dannah,
Kiriath Sannah (that is, Debir),
[50]Anab, Eshtemoh, Anim, [51]Goshen,
Holon and Giloh—eleven towns
and their villages.

[52]Arab, Dumah, Eshan, [53]Janim,
Beth Tappuah, Aphekah, [54]Hum-
tah, Kiriath Arba (that is, Hebron)
and Zior—nine towns and their villages.

[55]Maon, Carmel, Ziph, Juttah,
[56]Jezreel, Jokdeam, Zanoah, [57]Kain,
Gibeah and Timnah—ten towns
and their villages.

[58]Halhul, Beth Zur, Gedor, [59]Ma-
arath, Beth Anoth and Eltekon—six
towns and their villages.

[60]Kiriath Baal (that is, Kiriath Jearim) and Rabbah—two towns and
their villages.

[61]In the desert:

Beth Arabah, Middin, Secacah,
[62]Nibshan, the City of Salt and En
Gedi—six towns and their villages.

[63]Judah could not dislodge the Jebusites, who were living in Jerusalem; to
this day the Jebusites live there with the
people of Judah.

[a]36 Or *Gederah and Gederothaim*

SHARPEN THE FOCUS

Can't you just see the twinkle in Caleb's eye as he presents his case to Joshua? The two went way back. They had served in the first spy patrol that Moses sent into Canaan nearly 50 years before. The other 10 spies saw only giants and defeat, but Joshua and Caleb focused on the faithful Lord who had given His promise of victory.

Now at age 85 and with vision as clear as ever, Caleb stood before Joshua. "Give me this hill country that the LORD promised me," he says. And before long Caleb finds himself chasing the giants (Joshua 14:12; 15:14) up and down those hills–and defeating them.

Years later the psalmist would plead with the Lord "Give me an undivided heart, that I may fear Your name" (Psalm 86:11). The Lord had given Caleb an undivided heart. It was the secret of Caleb's success. While the hearts of everyone else melted, Caleb followed the Lord wholeheartedly (Joshua 14:8).

What parts of your heart remain unconquered by your Lord and His love? Where do you serve Him halfheartedly? Pray the psalmist's prayer for a whole heart. Then serve the Lord with holy boldness, claiming His promises of forgiveness and cleansing.

Today's reading provides more details about the borders of two tribes of Israel. As you skim it, note the hints the holy writer drops about Israel's failure to drive the Canaanites completely from the land. Note also the possible reasons for this failure. If time is short, focus on Joshua 17:7–18.

Allotment for Ephraim and Manasseh

16 The allotment for Joseph
began at the Jordan of
Jericho,[a] east of the waters of Jericho, and went up from there
through the desert into the hill
country of Bethel. [2]It went on from
Bethel (that is, Luz),[b] crossed over
to the territory of the Arkites in Ataroth, [3]descended westward to the
territory of the Japhletites as far as
the region of Lower Beth Horon
and on to Gezer, ending at the sea.
[4]So Manasseh and Ephraim, the descendants of Joseph, received their inheritance.

[5]This was the territory of Ephraim, clan
by clan:
The boundary of their inheritance went from Ataroth Addar in
the east to Upper Beth Horon [6]and
continued to the sea. From Micmethath on the north it curved eastward to Taanath Shiloh, passing by
it to Janoah on the east. [7]Then it
went down from Janoah to Ataroth
and Naarah, touched Jericho and
came out at the Jordan. [8]From Tappuah the border went west to the
Kanah Ravine and ended at the
sea. This was the inheritance of the
tribe of the Ephraimites, clan by
clan. [9]It also included all the towns
and their villages that were set
aside for the Ephraimites within
the inheritance of the Manassites.
[10]They did not dislodge the Canaanites
living in Gezer; to this day the Canaanites live among the people of Ephraim
but are required to do forced labor.

17 This was the allotment for the
tribe of Manasseh as Joseph's
firstborn, that is, for Makir, Manasseh's
firstborn. Makir was the ancestor of the
Gileadites, who had received Gilead
and Bashan because the Makirites were
great soldiers. [2]So this allotment was for
the rest of the people of Manasseh—the
clans of Abiezer, Helek, Asriel, Shechem,
Hepher and Shemida. These are the
other male descendants of Manasseh
son of Joseph by their clans.
[3]Now Zelophehad son of Hepher, the
son of Gilead, the son of Makir, the son
of Manasseh, had no sons but only
daughters, whose names were Mahlah,
Noah, Hoglah, Milcah and Tirzah. [4]They
went to Eleazar the priest, Joshua son of

[a]1 *Jordan of Jericho* was possibly an ancient name for the Jordan River. [b]2 Septuagint; Hebrew *Bethel to Luz*

Nun, and the leaders and said, "The
LORD commanded Moses to give us an
inheritance among our brothers." So
Joshua gave them an inheritance along
with the brothers of their father, according to the LORD's command. 5Manas-
seh's share consisted of ten tracts of land
besides Gilead and Bashan east of the
Jordan, 6because the daughters of the
tribe of Manasseh received an inheritance among the sons. The land of
Gilead belonged to the rest of the descendants of Manasseh.
7The territory of Manasseh extended from Asher to Micmethath
east of Shechem. The boundary ran
southward from there to include
the people living at En Tappuah.
8(Manasseh had the land of Tappuah, but Tappuah itself, on the
boundary of Manasseh, belonged
to the Ephraimites.) 9Then the
boundary continued south to the
Kanah Ravine. There were towns
belonging to Ephraim lying among
the towns of Manasseh, but the
boundary of Manasseh was the
northern side of the ravine and
ended at the sea. 10On the south the
land belonged to Ephraim, on the
north to Manasseh. The territory of
Manasseh reached the sea and bor-
dered Asher on the north and Issachar on the east.
11Within Issachar and Asher, Manasseh also had Beth Shan, Ibleam
and the people of Dor, Endor, Taanach and Megiddo, together with
their surrounding settlements (the
third in the list is Naphoth[a]).
12Yet the Manassites were not able to occupy these towns, for the Canaanites
were determined to live in that region.
13However, when the Israelites grew
stronger, they subjected the Canaanites
to forced labor but did not drive them
out completely.
14The people of Joseph said to Joshua,
"Why have you given us only one
allotment and one portion for an inheritance? We are a numerous people
and the LORD has blessed us abundantly."
15"If you are so numerous," Joshua answered, "and if the hill country of
Ephraim is too small for you, go up into
the forest and clear land for yourselves
there in the land of the Perizzites and
Rephaites."
16The people of Joseph replied, "The
hill country is not enough for us, and all
the Canaanites who live in the plain
have iron chariots, both those in Beth
Shan and its settlements and those in
the Valley of Jezreel."
17But Joshua said to the house of Joseph—to Ephraim and Manasseh—
"You are numerous and very powerful.
You will have not only one allotment
18but the forested hill country as well.
Clear it, and its farthest limits will be
yours; though the Canaanites have iron
chariots and though they are strong,
you can drive them out."

[a] *11* That is, Naphoth Dor

SHARPEN THE FOCUS

"I'm responsible." "I did it." "It's my fault." Admissions like these often take us aback. So seldom do we hear individuals own up to their behavior. Instead, we hear excuses or blame-shifting or bold-faced denial in the face of fact.

Are we today the most irresponsible people in all history? Hardly. Human beings back to Adam have made excuses, have hidden out in the bushes, and have tried to cover themselves with a patchwork of fig leaves.

Think about Israel's excuse for disobeying the Lord's command to drive the Canaanites out of the Promised Land: "[They] have iron chariots" (Joshua 17:18). These words imply an attitude something like this: "Look here, Joshua, the Lord left out some critical details. We know His command. We've heard His promises. But the Canaanites have iron chariots!"

And so they use their logic to cover up their unbelief, to excuse their inaction. Drowning in doubt, they delay and disobey.

As we face the sinful doubt and disobedience in our own lives, we can make excuses. Or we can make confession. We can pile up "logical" reasons to justify our failure. Or we can meet our Savior at the foot of His cross. What do you need to say to Him today?

WEEK 19 • SATURDAY

Joshua 18:1—19:51

Joshua moves his headquarters and the tabernacle to Shiloh. A large part of Canaan remains to be occupied. Seven tribes have no land yet. After some brief words of reprimand and encouragement, Joshua sends representatives from each tribe to survey the rest of the land. When the surveyors return, Joshua completes the land division. If time is short, focus on Joshua 19:49–51.

Division of the Rest of the Land

18 The whole assembly of the Israelites gathered at Shiloh
and set up the Tent of Meeting there.
The country was brought under their
control, 2but there were still seven Israelite tribes who had not yet received
their inheritance.
3So Joshua said to the Israelites: "How
long will you wait before you begin to
take possession of the land that the
LORD, the God of your fathers, has
given you? 4Appoint three men from
each tribe. I will send them out to make
a survey of the land and to write a description of it, according to the inheritance of each. Then they will return to
me. 5You are to divide the land into
seven parts. Judah is to remain in its territory on the south and the house of
Joseph in its territory on the north. 6Af-
ter you have written descriptions of the
seven parts of the land, bring them here
to me and I will cast lots for you in the
presence of the LORD our God. 7The Levites, however, do not get a portion
among you, because the priestly service
of the LORD is their inheritance. And
Gad, Reuben and the half-tribe of Manasseh have already received their inheritance on the east side of the Jordan. Moses the servant of the LORD gave it to them."
8As the men started on their way to
map out the land, Joshua instructed
them, "Go and make a survey of the
land and write a description of it. Then
return to me, and I will cast lots for you
here at Shiloh in the presence of the
LORD." 9So the men left and went
through the land. They wrote its description on a scroll, town by town, in
seven parts, and returned to Joshua in
the camp at Shiloh. 10Joshua then cast
lots for them in Shiloh in the presence
of the LORD, and there he distributed
the land to the Israelites according to
their tribal divisions.

Allotment for Benjamin

11The lot came up for the tribe of Benjamin, clan by clan. Their allotted territory lay between the tribes of Judah and
Joseph:
12On the north side their boundary began at the Jordan, passed the

northern slope of Jericho and headed west into the hill country, coming out at the desert of Beth Aven.
13From there it crossed to the south slope of Luz (that is, Bethel) and went down to Ataroth Addar on the hill south of Lower Beth Horon.

14From the hill facing Beth Horon on the south the boundary turned south along the western side and came out at Kiriath Baal (that is, Kiriath Jearim), a town of the people of Judah. This was the western side.

15The southern side began at the outskirts of Kiriath Jearim on the west, and the boundary came out at the spring of the waters of Nephtoah.
16The boundary went down to the foot of the hill facing the Valley of Ben Hinnom, north of the Valley of Rephaim. It continued down the Hinnom Valley along the southern slope of the Jebusite city and so to En Rogel.
17It then curved north, went to En Shemesh, continued to Geliloth, which faces the Pass of Adummim, and ran down to the Stone of Bohan son of Reuben.
18It continued to the northern slope of Beth Arabah[a] and on down into the Arabah.
19It then went to the northern slope of Beth Hoglah and came out at the northern bay of the Salt Sea,[b] at the mouth of the Jordan in the south. This was the southern boundary.

20The Jordan formed the boundary on the eastern side.
These were the boundaries that marked out the inheritance of the clans of Benjamin on all sides.

21The tribe of Benjamin, clan by clan, had the following cities:

Jericho, Beth Hoglah, Emek Keziz,
22Beth Arabah, Zemaraim, Bethel,
23Avvim, Parah, Ophrah,
24Kephar Ammoni, Ophni and Geba—twelve towns and their villages.

25Gibeon, Ramah, Beeroth,
26Mizpah, Kephirah, Mozah,
27Rekem, Irpeel, Taralah,
28Zelah, Haeleph, the Jebusite city (that is, Jerusalem), Gibeah and Kiriath—fourteen towns and their villages.

This was the inheritance of Benjamin for its clans.

Allotment for Simeon

19 The second lot came out for the tribe of Simeon, clan by clan. Their inheritance lay within the territory of Judah.
2It included:

Beersheba (or Sheba),[c] Moladah,
3Hazar Shual, Balah, Ezem,
4Eltolad, Bethul, Hormah,
5Ziklag, Beth Marcaboth, Hazar Susah,
6Beth Lebaoth and Sharuhen—thirteen towns and their villages;

7Ain, Rimmon, Ether and Ashan—four towns and their villages—
8and all the villages around these towns as far as Baalath Beer (Ramah in the Negev).

This was the inheritance of the tribe of the Simeonites, clan by clan.
9The inheritance of the Simeonites was taken from the share of Judah, because Judah's portion was more than they needed. So the Simeonites received their inheritance within the territory of Judah.

Allotment for Zebulun

10The third lot came up for Zebulun, clan by clan:

The boundary of their inheritance went as far as Sarid.
11Going west it ran to Maralah, touched Dabbesheth, and extended to the ravine near Jokneam.
12It turned east from Sarid toward the sunrise to the territory of Kisloth Tabor and went on to Daberath and up to Japhia.
13Then it continued eastward to Gath Hepher and Eth Kazin; it came out at Rimmon and turned toward Neah.
14There the boundary went around on the north to Hannathon and ended at the Valley of Iphtah El.
15Included were Kat-

[a]18 Septuagint; Hebrew *slope facing the Arabah*
[b]19 That is, the Dead Sea [c]2 Or *Beersheba, Sheba;* 1 Chron. 4:28 does not have *Sheba.*

tath, Nahalal, Shimron, Idalah and
Bethlehem. There were twelve
towns and their villages.
16These towns and their villages were
the inheritance of Zebulun, clan by clan.

Allotment for Issachar

17The fourth lot came out for Issachar,
clan by clan. 18Their territory included:
Jezreel, Kesulloth, Shunem,
19Hapharaim, Shion, Anaharath,
20Rabbith, Kishion, Ebez, 21Remeth,
En Gannim, En Haddah and Beth
Pazzez. 22The boundary touched
Tabor, Shahazumah and Beth Shemesh, and ended at the Jordan.
There were sixteen towns and their
villages.
23These towns and their villages were
the inheritance of the tribe of Issachar,
clan by clan.

Allotment for Asher

24The fifth lot came out for the tribe of
Asher, clan by clan. 25Their territory included:
Helkath, Hali, Beten, Acshaph,
26Allammelech, Amad and Mishal.
On the west the boundary touched
Carmel and Shihor Libnath. 27It
then turned east toward Beth Dagon, touched Zebulun and the Valley of Iphtah El, and went north to
Beth Emek and Neiel, passing Cabul on the left. 28It went to Abdon,[a]
Rehob, Hammon and Kanah, as far
as Greater Sidon. 29The boundary
then turned back toward Ramah
and went to the fortified city of
Tyre, turned toward Hosah and
came out at the sea in the region of
Aczib, 30Ummah, Aphek and Rehob. There were twenty-two towns
and their villages.
31These towns and their villages were
the inheritance of the tribe of Asher, clan
by clan.

Allotment for Naphtali

32The sixth lot came out for Naphtali,
clan by clan:
33Their boundary went from He-
leph and the large tree in Zaanannim, passing Adami Nekeb and Jabneel to Lakkum and ending at the
Jordan. 34The boundary ran west
through Aznoth Tabor and came
out at Hukkok. It touched Zebulun
on the south, Asher on the west
and the Jordan[b] on the east. 35The
fortified cities were Ziddim, Zer,
Hammath, Rakkath, Kinnereth,
36Adamah, Ramah, Hazor, 37Kedesh,
Edrei, En Hazor, 38Iron, Migdal El,
Horem, Beth Anath and Beth Shemesh. There were nineteen towns
and their villages.
39These towns and their villages were
the inheritance of the tribe of Naphtali,
clan by clan.

Allotment for Dan

40The seventh lot came out for the tribe
of Dan, clan by clan. 41The territory of
their inheritance included:
Zorah, Eshtaol, Ir Shemesh,
42Shaalabbin, Aijalon, Ithlah, 43Elon,
Timnah, Ekron, 44Eltekeh, Gibbethon, Baalath, 45Jehud, Bene Berak,
Gath Rimmon, 46Me Jarkon and
Rakkon, with the area facing Joppa.
47(But the Danites had difficulty taking possession of their territory, so they
went up and attacked Leshem, took it,
put it to the sword and occupied it. They
settled in Leshem and named it Dan
after their forefather.)
48These towns and their villages were
the inheritance of the tribe of Dan, clan
by clan.

Allotment for Joshua

49When they had finished dividing
the land into its allotted portions, the Israelites gave Joshua son of Nun an inheritance among them, 50as the LORD
had commanded. They gave him the
town he asked for—Timnath Serah[c] in
the hill country of Ephraim. And he
built up the town and settled there.
51These are the territories that Eleazar

[a] *28* Some Hebrew manuscripts (see also Joshua 21:30); most Hebrew manuscripts *Ebron*
[b] *34* Septuagint; Hebrew *west, and Judah, the Jordan,* [c] *50* Also known as *Timnath Heres* (see Judges 2:9)

the priest, Joshua son of Nun and the heads of the tribal clans of Israel assigned by lot at Shiloh in the presence of the LORD at the entrance to the Tent of Meeting. And so they finished dividing the land.

SHARPEN THE FOCUS

Children very often have a hard time understanding that the food they eat, the clothes they wear, and the house or apartment in which they live come to them as gifts of God. After all, doesn't Dad write our rent check? Didn't Mom wrap up my new jacket and give it to me for my birthday?

The connection between what Israel had to do to take Canaan and God's blessing that gave Canaan to Israel seems much less far-fetched when we remember where the people of Israel started out—in the clay pits of Egypt. Only the grace of God can account for the change in their circumstances—they were once slaves of Pharaoh; now they had become sons of the Lord. They had been property, the possessions of the Egyptians. Now they had begun to enjoy prosperity. And it was all by God's grace.

And only by that same amazing grace in Jesus have we come out of the slavery to sin and into the freedom of our heavenly Father's love. That love will continue to supply all we need—spiritually and materially—for our lives now and as we march on toward the Promised Land for which we wait in hope.

WEEK 20 • MONDAY

Joshua 20:1—21:45

GET THE BIG PICTURE

As the Lord had commanded through Moses, the nation now establishes the cities of refuge to which those accused of capital crimes may flee and receive a fair hearing. Cities were also allotted to people from the tribe of Levi because they received no land of their own. As you read, review for yourself the ways that Jesus is *your* city of refuge and also think about the high standing you enjoy as the Lord's New Testament priest. If time is short, focus on Joshua 21:43–45.

Cities of Refuge

20 Then the LORD said to
Joshua: 2"Tell the Israelites
to designate the cities of refuge, as I instructed you through Moses, 3so that
anyone who kills a person accidentally
and unintentionally may flee there and
find protection from the avenger of
blood.
4"When he flees to one of these cities,
he is to stand in the entrance of the city
gate and state his case before the elders
of that city. Then they are to admit him
into their city and give him a place to
live with them. 5If the avenger of blood
pursues him, they must not surrender
the one accused, because he killed his
neighbor unintentionally and without
malice aforethought. 6He is to stay in
that city until he has stood trial before
the assembly and until the death of
the high priest who is serving at that

time. Then he may go back to his
own home in the town from which he
fled."
7So they set apart Kedesh in Galilee in
the hill country of Naphtali, Shechem in
the hill country of Ephraim, and Kiriath
Arba (that is, Hebron) in the hill country of Judah. 8On the east side of the
Jordan of Jericho[a] they designated Bezer in the desert on the plateau in the
tribe of Reuben, Ramoth in Gilead in
the tribe of Gad, and Golan in Bashan
in the tribe of Manasseh. 9Any of the Israelites or any alien living among them
who killed someone accidentally could
flee to these designated cities and not be
killed by the avenger of blood prior to
standing trial before the assembly.

Towns for the Levites

21 Now the family heads of the
Levites approached Eleazar
the priest, Joshua son of Nun, and the
heads of the other tribal families of Israel 2at Shiloh in Canaan and said to
them, "The LORD commanded through
Moses that you give us towns to live in,
with pasturelands for our livestock."
3So, as the LORD had commanded, the
Israelites gave the Levites the following
towns and pasturelands out of their
own inheritance:
4The first lot came out for the Kohathites, clan by clan. The Levites who were
descendants of Aaron the priest were
allotted thirteen towns from the tribes
of Judah, Simeon and Benjamin. 5The
rest of Kohath's descendants were allotted ten towns from the clans of the
tribes of Ephraim, Dan and half of Manasseh.
6The descendants of Gershon were allotted thirteen towns from the clans of
the tribes of Issachar, Asher, Naphtali
and the half-tribe of Manasseh in Bashan.
7The descendants of Merari, clan by
clan, received twelve towns from the
tribes of Reuben, Gad and Zebulun.
8So the Israelites allotted to the Levites these towns and their pasturelands, as the LORD had commanded
through Moses.
9From the tribes of Judah and Simeon
they allotted the following towns by
name 10(these towns were assigned to
the descendants of Aaron who were
from the Kohathite clans of the Levites,
because the first lot fell to them):
11They gave them Kiriath Arba
(that is, Hebron), with its surrounding pastureland, in the hill country
of Judah. (Arba was the forefather
of Anak.) 12But the fields and villages around the city they had giv-
en to Caleb son of Jephunneh as his
possession.
13So to the descendants of Aaron
the priest they gave Hebron (a city
of refuge for one accused of murder), Libnah, 14Jattir, Eshtemoa,
15Holon, Debir, 16Ain, Juttah and
Beth Shemesh, together with their
pasturelands—nine towns from
these two tribes.
17And from the tribe of Benjamin
they gave them Gibeon, Geba, 18An-
athoth and Almon, together with
their pasturelands—four towns.
19All the towns for the priests, the descendants of Aaron, were thirteen, together with their pasturelands.
20The rest of the Kohathite clans of the
Levites were allotted towns from the
tribe of Ephraim:
21In the hill country of Ephraim
they were given Shechem (a city of
refuge for one accused of murder)
and Gezer, 22Kibzaim and Beth Horon, together with their pasturelands—four towns.
23Also from the tribe of Dan they
received Eltekeh, Gibbethon, 24Aija-
lon and Gath Rimmon, together
with their pasturelands—four
towns.
25From half the tribe of Manasseh
they received Taanach and Gath
Rimmon, together with their pasturelands—two towns.
26All these ten towns and their pasturelands were given to the rest of the Kohathite clans.

[a] *8 Jordan of Jericho* was possibly an ancient name for the Jordan River.

[27]The Levite clans of the Gershonites were given:
from the half-tribe of Manasseh,
Golan in Bashan (a city of refuge for one accused of murder) and Be Eshtarah, together with their pasturelands—two towns;
[28]from the tribe of Issachar,
Kishion, Daberath, [29]Jarmuth and En Gannim, together with their pasturelands—four towns;
[30]from the tribe of Asher,
Mishal, Abdon, [31]Helkath and Rehob, together with their pasturelands—four towns;
[32]from the tribe of Naphtali,
Kedesh in Galilee (a city of refuge for one accused of murder), Hammoth Dor and Kartan, together with their pasturelands—three towns.
[33]All the towns of the Gershonite clans were thirteen, together with their pasturelands.

[34]The Merarite clans (the rest of the Levites) were given:
from the tribe of Zebulun,
Jokneam, Kartah, [35]Dimnah and Nahalal, together with their pasturelands—four towns;
[36]from the tribe of Reuben,
Bezer, Jahaz, [37]Kedemoth and Mephaath, together with their pasturelands—four towns;
[38]from the tribe of Gad,
Ramoth in Gilead (a city of refuge for one accused of murder), Mahanaim, [39]Heshbon and Jazer, together with their pasturelands—four towns in all.
[40]All the towns allotted to the Merarite clans, who were the rest of the Levites, were twelve.
[41]The towns of the Levites in the territory held by the Israelites were forty-eight in all, together with their pasturelands. [42]Each of these towns had pasturelands surrounding it; this was true for all these towns.

[43]So the LORD gave Israel all the land he had sworn to give their forefathers, and they took possession of it and settled there. [44]The LORD gave them rest on every side, just as he had sworn to their forefathers. Not one of their enemies withstood them; the LORD handed all their enemies over to them. [45]Not one of all the LORD's good promises to the house of Israel failed; every one was fulfilled.

SHARPEN THE FOCUS

Through all the long years of wandering, fighting battles, and finally settling in Canaan, God kept every promise He made to Israel. "Not one of all the LORD's good promises to the house of Israel failed; every one was fulfilled" (Joshua 21:45). These words are also stamped over our lives as members of God's New Testament Israel.

The Lord has made "good promises" to us and continues to fulfill them every day. God promises to take care of us and give us what we need; He promises to hear our prayers and to help us in time of trouble. Most importantly, God promised to send a Savior to rescue us from our sins, the power of Satan, and eternal damnation. Jesus is that Savior who died on the cross and shed His blood for us. Now we are God's forgiven children who will live eternally with the Lord. Thank God for His faithfulness in keeping all His "good promises."

WEEK 20 • TUESDAY

Joshua 22:1–34

GET THE BIG PICTURE

With thanks and the Lord's blessing Joshua sends the armies of Reuben, Gad, and half the tribe of Manasseh back home to the east side of the Jordan. They have carried out their duties to their brothers and sisters in Israel just as Moses commanded (see Numbers 32). The chapter continues with a short story about zeal for the Lord that results in a terrible misunderstanding and a near disaster. If time is short, focus on Joshua 22:11–34.

Eastern Tribes Return Home

22 Then Joshua summoned
the Reubenites, the Gad-
ites and the half-tribe of Manasseh 2and
said to them, "You have done all that
Moses the servant of the LORD commanded, and you have obeyed me in
everything I commanded. 3For a long
time now—to this very day—you have
not deserted your brothers but have
carried out the mission the LORD your
God gave you. 4Now that the LORD your
God has given your brothers rest as he
promised, return to your homes in the
land that Moses the servant of the LORD
gave you on the other side of the Jordan.
5But be very careful to keep the commandment and the law that Moses the
servant of the LORD gave you: to love
the LORD your God, to walk in all his
ways, to obey his commands, to hold
fast to him and to serve him with all
your heart and all your soul."
6Then Joshua blessed them and sent
them away, and they went to their
homes. 7(To the half-tribe of Manasseh
Moses had given land in Bashan, and to
the other half of the tribe Joshua gave
land on the west side of the Jordan with
their brothers.) When Joshua sent them
home, he blessed them, 8saying, "Return
to your homes with your great wealth—
with large herds of livestock, with silver,
gold, bronze and iron, and a great quantity of clothing—and divide with your
brothers the plunder from your enemies."
9So the Reubenites, the Gadites and
the half-tribe of Manasseh left the Israelites at Shiloh in Canaan to return to
Gilead, their own land, which they had
acquired in accordance with the command of the LORD through Moses.
10When they came to Geliloth near the
Jordan in the land of Canaan, the Reubenites, the Gadites and the half-tribe of
Manasseh built an imposing altar there
by the Jordan. 11And when the Israelites
heard that they had built the altar on the
border of Canaan at Geliloth near the
Jordan on the Israelite side, 12the whole
assembly of Israel gathered at Shiloh to
go to war against them.
13So the Israelites sent Phinehas son of
Eleazar, the priest, to the land of Gilead—to Reuben, Gad and the half-tribe
of Manasseh. 14With him they sent ten
of the chief men, one for each of the
tribes of Israel, each the head of a family division among the Israelite clans.
15When they went to Gilead—to Reuben, Gad and the half-tribe of Manasseh—they said to them: 16"The whole
assembly of the LORD says: 'How could
you break faith with the God of Israel
like this? How could you turn away
from the LORD and build yourselves
an altar in rebellion against him now?
17Was not the sin of Peor enough for us?
Up to this very day we have not
cleansed ourselves from that sin, even
though a plague fell on the community
of the LORD! 18And are you now turning
away from the LORD?

" 'If you rebel against the LORD today, tomorrow he will be angry with the whole community of Israel.
19 If the land you possess is defiled, come over to the LORD's land, where the LORD's tabernacle stands, and share the land with us. But do not rebel against the LORD or against us by building an altar for yourselves, other than the altar of the LORD our God.
20 When Achan son of Zerah acted unfaithfully regarding the devoted things,[a] did not wrath come upon the whole community of Israel? He was not the only one who died for his sin.' "

21 Then Reuben, Gad and the half-tribe of Manasseh replied to the heads of the clans of Israel:
22 "The Mighty One, God, the LORD! The Mighty One, God, the LORD! He knows! And let Israel know! If this has been in rebellion or disobedience to the LORD, do not spare us this day.
23 If we have built our own altar to turn away from the LORD and to offer burnt offerings and grain offerings, or to sacrifice fellowship offerings[b] on it, may the LORD himself call us to account.

24 "No! We did it for fear that some day your descendants might say to ours, 'What do you have to do with the LORD, the God of Israel?
25 The LORD has made the Jordan a boundary between us and you—you Reubenites and Gadites! You have no share in the LORD.' So your descendants might cause ours to stop fearing the LORD.

26 "That is why we said, 'Let us get ready and build an altar—but not for burnt offerings or sacrifices.'
27 On the contrary, it is to be a witness between us and you and the generations that follow, that we will worship the LORD at his sanctuary with our burnt offerings, sacrifices and fellowship offerings. Then in the future your descendants will not be able to say to ours, 'You have no share in the LORD.'

28 "And we said, 'If they ever say this to us, or to our descendants, we will answer: Look at the replica of the LORD's altar, which our fathers built, not for burnt offerings and sacrifices, but as a witness between us and you.'

29 "Far be it from us to rebel against the LORD and turn away from him today by building an altar for burnt offerings, grain offerings and sacrifices, other than the altar of the LORD our God that stands before his tabernacle."

30 When Phinehas the priest and the leaders of the community—the heads of the clans of the Israelites—heard what Reuben, Gad and Manasseh had to say, they were pleased.
31 And Phinehas son of Eleazar, the priest, said to Reuben, Gad and Manasseh, "Today we know that the LORD is with us, because you have not acted unfaithfully toward the LORD in this matter. Now you have rescued the Israelites from the LORD's hand."

32 Then Phinehas son of Eleazar, the priest, and the leaders returned to Canaan from their meeting with the Reubenites and Gadites in Gilead and reported to the Israelites.
33 They were glad to hear the report and praised God. And they talked no more about going to war against them to devastate the country where the Reubenites and the Gadites lived.

34 And the Reubenites and the Gadites gave the altar this name: A Witness Between Us that the LORD is God.

[a]20 The Hebrew term refers to the irrevocable giving over of things or persons to the LORD, often by totally destroying them.
[b]23 Traditionally *peace offerings;* also in verse 27

SHARPEN THE FOCUS

Everyone on both sides wanted to do the right thing—and because of it, the nation teetered on the brink of civil war. Does this story warn us of the dangers of zeal? Should we avoid caring too much about our Lord's commands and His honor? Not at all. The Lord commands and rewards wholehearted devotion to Him and to His kingdom. Jesus Himself was consumed with zeal for the Lord's house (John 2:17). Even so, at those times when we experience the most zeal, we need to listen very carefully to our brothers and sisters in the Lord.

What if the western tribes had rushed into battle half-cocked and ill-informed? What if they had asked no questions and taken no prisoners? By the same token, what if the eastern tribes had taken immediate offense to the questions they were asked? What if they had told the western tribes to mind their own spiritual business?

Only as God's Spirit works His patience and kindness in our hearts can we temper our godly zeal with Christlike love. Ask Him to do that for you so that the next time you're confronted and the next time you need to confront, you will speak and act for the good of your family in Christ.

WEEK 20 • WEDNESDAY

Joshua 23:1–16

Today's chapter records the second of three meetings Joshua calls with the people of Israel shortly before his death. (The first came in Joshua 22:1–9, and the third is recorded in Joshua 24:1–28.) As you read, picture Joshua at about age 110. He knows he will soon die. What concerns are uppermost in his mind? Why? If time is short, focus on Joshua 23:1–11.

Joshua's Farewell to the Leaders

23 After a long time had
passed and the LORD had
given Israel rest from all their enemies
around them, Joshua, by then old and
well advanced in years, [2]summoned all
Israel—their elders, leaders, judges and
officials—and said to them: "I am old
and well advanced in years. [3]You yourselves have seen everything the LORD
your God has done to all these nations
for your sake; it was the LORD your God
who fought for you. [4]Remember how I
have allotted as an inheritance for your
tribes all the land of the nations that
remain—the nations I conquered—between the Jordan and the Great Sea[a] in
the west. [5]The LORD your God himself
will drive them out of your way. He will
push them out before you, and you will
take possession of their land, as the
LORD your God promised you.
[6]"Be very strong; be careful to obey all
that is written in the Book of the Law of
Moses, without turning aside to the
right or to the left. [7]Do not associate with
these nations that remain among you;
do not invoke the names of their gods
or swear by them. You must not serve
them or bow down to them. [8]But you
are to hold fast to the LORD your God,
as you have until now.
[9]"The LORD has driven out before you
great and powerful nations; to this day
no one has been able to withstand you.
[10]One of you routs a thousand, because
the LORD your God fights for you, just
as he promised. [11]So be very careful to
love the LORD your God.
[12]"But if you turn away and ally yourselves with the survivors of these nations that remain among you and if you
intermarry with them and associate
with them, [13]then you may be sure that

[a]4 That is, the Mediterranean

the LORD your God will no longer drive
out these nations before you. Instead,
they will become snares and traps for
you, whips on your backs and thorns in
your eyes, until you perish from this
good land, which the LORD your God
has given you.
14"Now I am about to go the way of all
the earth. You know with all your heart
and soul that not one of all the good
promises the LORD your God gave you
has failed. Every promise has been fulfilled; not one has failed. 15But just as
every good promise of the LORD your
God has come true, so the LORD will
bring on you all the evil he has threatened, until he has destroyed you from
this good land he has given you. 16If you
violate the covenant of the LORD your
God, which he commanded you, and go
and serve other gods and bow down to
them, the LORD's anger will burn
against you, and you will quickly perish
from the good land he has given you."

SHARPEN THE FOCUS

The author of *Debt of Honor,* Tom Clancy, begins to tie up the loose ends of his plot near the end of the book. The breakneck pace of the story slows and the reader begins to relax. Then one seemingly small subplot explodes. The danger that has posed the greatest threat from the start finally appears.

The book of Joshua has a similar ending. The Canaanite kings and their armies seemed to pose the greatest threat to Israel. But the last few pages of the book make the *real* danger clear. It's actually Canaan's gods that threaten the security of the Lord's people.

False gods can quickly rob us of the security our Lord freely gives us in Jesus. Toward which false gods do you bow? What takes first place as you set your priorities? Would your calendar and your check stubs verify the answers you just gave?

If you find yourself squirming as you answer, be encouraged! The Lord has brought you closer to a remedy. Recognizing your need, you can take it to Him. Ask for help in rooting out the idolatry that keeps you from being the person that, in Christ, God intends you to be. Freed from the guilt of the past through Christ's cross, you can rely on Him in the present for power.

WEEK 20 • THURSDAY

Joshua 24:1–33

GET THE BIG PICTURE

In his farewell sermon, Joshua focuses on what the Lord has done for His people from the time of Abraham onward. Then he calls for a response of love from the people. As you read, note the *I's* with which the Lord refers to Himself. Then notice the action words that follow each *I.* These tell of specific ways in which the Lord acted to deliver His people and to prepare the way for the Savior He had promised to send. If time is short, focus on Joshua 24:1–15.

The Covenant Renewed at Shechem

24 Then Joshua assembled
all the tribes of Israel at
Shechem. He summoned the elders,
leaders, judges and officials of Israel,
and they presented themselves before
God.
2Joshua said to all the people, "This is
what the LORD, the God of Israel, says:
'Long ago your forefathers, including
Terah the father of Abraham and Nahor,
lived beyond the River[a] and worshiped
other gods. 3But I took your father Abraham from the land beyond the River
and led him throughout Canaan and
gave him many descendants. I gave him
Isaac, 4and to Isaac I gave Jacob and
Esau. I assigned the hill country of Seir
to Esau, but Jacob and his sons went
down to Egypt.
5" 'Then I sent Moses and Aaron, and
I afflicted the Egyptians by what I did
there, and I brought you out. 6When I
brought your fathers out of Egypt, you
came to the sea, and the Egyptians pursued them with chariots and horsemen[b]
as far as the Red Sea.[c] 7But they cried to
the LORD for help, and he put darkness
between you and the Egyptians; he
brought the sea over them and covered
them. You saw with your own eyes
what I did to the Egyptians. Then you
lived in the desert for a long time.
8" 'I brought you to the land of the
Amorites who lived east of the Jordan.
They fought against you, but I gave
them into your hands. I destroyed them
from before you, and you took possession of their land. 9When Balak son of
Zippor, the king of Moab, prepared to
fight against Israel, he sent for Balaam
son of Beor to put a curse on you. 10But
I would not listen to Balaam, so he
blessed you again and again, and I delivered you out of his hand.
11" 'Then you crossed the Jordan and
came to Jericho. The citizens of Jericho
fought against you, as did also the Amorites, Perizzites, Canaanites, Hittites,
Girgashites, Hivites and Jebusites, but I
gave them into your hands. 12I sent the
hornet ahead of you, which drove them
out before you—also the two Amorite
kings. You did not do it with your own
sword and bow. 13So I gave you a land
on which you did not toil and cities you
did not build; and you live in them and
eat from vineyards and olive groves that
you did not plant.'
14"Now fear the LORD and serve him
with all faithfulness. Throw away the
gods your forefathers worshiped beyond the River and in Egypt, and serve
the LORD. 15But if serving the LORD
seems undesirable to you, then choose
for yourselves this day whom you will
serve, whether the gods your forefathers served beyond the River, or the
gods of the Amorites, in whose land you
are living. But as for me and my household, we will serve the LORD."
16Then the people answered, "Far be
it from us to forsake the LORD to serve
other gods! 17It was the LORD our God
himself who brought us and our fathers
up out of Egypt, from that land of slavery, and performed those great signs
before our eyes. He protected us on our
entire journey and among all the nations through which we traveled. 18And
the LORD drove out before us all the
nations, including the Amorites, who
lived in the land. We too will serve the
LORD, because he is our God."
19Joshua said to the people, "You are
not able to serve the LORD. He is a holy
God; he is a jealous God. He will not forgive your rebellion and your sins. 20If
you forsake the LORD and serve foreign
gods, he will turn and bring disaster on
you and make an end of you, after he
has been good to you."
21But the people said to Joshua, "No!
We will serve the LORD."
22Then Joshua said, "You are witnesses against yourselves that you have
chosen to serve the LORD."
"Yes, we are witnesses," they replied.
23"Now then," said Joshua, "throw
away the foreign gods that are among
you and yield your hearts to the LORD,
the God of Israel."

[a]2 That is, the Euphrates; also in verses 3, 14 and 15 [b]6 Or *charioteers* [c]6 Hebrew *Yam Suph*; that is, Sea of Reeds

[24]And the people said to Joshua, "We will serve the LORD our God and obey him."

[25]On that day Joshua made a covenant for the people, and there at Shechem he drew up for them decrees and laws. [26]And Joshua recorded these things in the Book of the Law of God. Then he took a large stone and set it up there under the oak near the holy place of the LORD.

[27]"See!" he said to all the people. "This stone will be a witness against us. It has heard all the words the LORD has said to us. It will be a witness against you if you are untrue to your God."

Buried in the Promised Land

[28]Then Joshua sent the people away, each to his own inheritance.

[29]After these things, Joshua son of Nun, the servant of the LORD, died at the age of a hundred and ten. [30]And they buried him in the land of his inheritance, at Timnath Serah[a] in the hill country of Ephraim, north of Mount Gaash.

[31]Israel served the LORD throughout the lifetime of Joshua and of the elders who outlived him and who had experienced everything the LORD had done for Israel.

[32]And Joseph's bones, which the Israelites had brought up from Egypt, were buried at Shechem in the tract of land that Jacob bought for a hundred pieces of silver[b] from the sons of Hamor, the father of Shechem. This became the inheritance of Joseph's descendants.

[33]And Eleazar son of Aaron died and was buried at Gibeah, which had been allotted to his son Phinehas in the hill country of Ephraim.

[a]30 Also known as *Timnath Heres* (see Judges 2:9)
[b]32 Hebrew *hundred kesitahs*; a kesitah was a unit of money of unknown weight and value.

SHARPEN THE FOCUS

"As for me and my household, we will serve the LORD" (Joshua 24:15). Familiar words. Maybe you even have a plaque or poster in your home which makes Joshua's declaration your own. Can you speak this declaration with conviction?

If so, and I pray you can, the reason you are able to say these words and mean them goes back to the God of Joshua, Abraham, Isaac, and Jacob.

The Lord took Abraham out of idolatry. The Lord afflicted the Egyptian slavemasters. The Lord gave Israel's enemies into their hands. The Lord delivered. The Lord saved.

And the story of your life and of mine sounds remarkably similar. The Lord called us out of the darkness of sin. The Lord put His name on us in our Baptism. The Lord strengthens us as we fight Satan's temptations. The Lord delivers us out of our difficulties. The Lord gives. The Lord saves.

"We love because He first loved us" (1 John 4:19). That love, love that shines its brightest from the darkness that settled on Calvary, makes our love possible—love for the Lord, love for one another. Soak up that love today. Then, loved, serve.

JUDGES

Joshua is dead. The relatively bright 30 years of conquest he led in Canaan is about to be eclipsed by 350 years of spiritual failure in Israel. The time of the judges was truly a dark age for God's people. In Judges 1, we meet this darkness. As you read, note evidence that the Lord has not withdrawn His presence or His promises. What, then, *has* changed? If time is short, focus on Judges 1:1–20.

Israel Fights the Remaining Canaanites

1 After the death of Joshua, the Israelites asked the LORD, "Who will be
the first to go up and fight for us against
the Canaanites?"
[2]The LORD answered, "Judah is to go;
I have given the land into their hands."
[3]Then the men of Judah said to the
Simeonites their brothers, "Come up
with us into the territory allotted to us,
to fight against the Canaanites. We in
turn will go with you into yours." So the
Simeonites went with them.
[4]When Judah attacked, the LORD gave
the Canaanites and Perizzites into their
hands and they struck down ten thousand men at Bezek. [5]It was there that
they found Adoni-Bezek and fought
against him, putting to rout the Canaanites and Perizzites. [6]Adoni-Bezek fled,
but they chased him and caught him,
and cut off his thumbs and big toes.
[7]Then Adoni-Bezek said, "Seventy
kings with their thumbs and big toes cut
off have picked up scraps under my
table. Now God has paid me back for
what I did to them." They brought him
to Jerusalem, and he died there.
[8]The men of Judah attacked Jerusalem
also and took it. They put the city to the
sword and set it on fire.
[9]After that, the men of Judah went
down to fight against the Canaanites
living in the hill country, the Negev and
the western foothills. [10]They advanced
against the Canaanites living in Hebron
(formerly called Kiriath Arba) and defeated Sheshai, Ahiman and Talmai.
[11]From there they advanced against
the people living in Debir (formerly
called Kiriath Sepher). [12]And Caleb said,
"I will give my daughter Acsah in marriage to the man who attacks and captures Kiriath Sepher." [13]Othniel son of
Kenaz, Caleb's younger brother, took it;
so Caleb gave his daughter Acsah to him
in marriage.
[14]One day when she came to Othniel, she urged him[a] to ask her father for a
field. When she got off her donkey, Caleb asked her, "What can I do for you?"
[15]She replied, "Do me a special favor.
Since you have given me land in the
Negev, give me also springs of water."
Then Caleb gave her the upper and lower springs.

[a]14 Hebrew; Septuagint and Vulgate *Othniel, he urged her*

16 The descendants of Moses' father-
in-law, the Kenite, went up from the
City of Palms[a] with the men of Judah to
live among the people of the Desert of
Judah in the Negev near Arad.
17 Then the men of Judah went with
the Simeonites their brothers and attacked the Canaanites living in Ze-
phath, and they totally destroyed[b] the
city. Therefore it was called Hormah.[c]
18 The men of Judah also took[d] Gaza,
Ashkelon and Ekron—each city with its
territory.
19 The LORD was with the men of Judah. They took possession of the hill
country, but they were unable to drive
the people from the plains, because they
had iron chariots. 20 As Moses had promised, Hebron was given to Caleb, who
drove from it the three sons of Anak.
21 The Benjamites, however, failed to dislodge the Jebusites, who were living in
Jerusalem; to this day the Jebusites live
there with the Benjamites.
22 Now the house of Joseph attacked
Bethel, and the LORD was with them.
23 When they sent men to spy out Bethel (formerly called Luz), 24 the spies saw
a man coming out of the city and they
said to him, "Show us how to get into
the city and we will see that you are
treated well." 25 So he showed them, and
they put the city to the sword but
spared the man and his whole family.
26 He then went to the land of the Hittites, where he built a city and called it
Luz, which is its name to this day.
27 But Manasseh did not drive out the
people of Beth Shan or Taanach or Dor
or Ibleam or Megiddo and their surrounding settlements, for the Canaanites were determined to live in that land.
28 When Israel became strong, they
pressed the Canaanites into forced labor but never drove them out completely. 29 Nor did Ephraim drive out the
Canaanites living in Gezer, but the Canaanites continued to live there among
them. 30 Neither did Zebulun drive out
the Canaanites living in Kitron or Naha-
lol, who remained among them; but
they did subject them to forced labor.
31 Nor did Asher drive out those living in
Acco or Sidon or Ahlab or Aczib or Hel-
bah or Aphek or Rehob, 32 and because
of this the people of Asher lived among
the Canaanite inhabitants of the land.
33 Neither did Naphtali drive out those
living in Beth Shemesh or Beth Anath;
but the Naphtalites too lived among the
Canaanite inhabitants of the land, and
those living in Beth Shemesh and Beth
Anath became forced laborers for them.
34 The Amorites confined the Danites to
the hill country, not allowing them to
come down into the plain. 35 And the
Amorites were determined also to hold
out in Mount Heres, Aijalon and Shaalbim, but when the power of the house
of Joseph increased, they too were
pressed into forced labor. 36 The boundary of the Amorites was from Scorpion[e]
Pass to Sala and beyond.

[a] *16* That is, Jericho [b] *17* The Hebrew term refers to the irrevocable giving over of things or persons to the LORD, often by totally destroying them. [c] *17* *Hormah* means *destruction.*
[d] *18* Hebrew; Septuagint *Judah did not take*
[e] *36* Hebrew *Akrabbim*

SHARPEN THE FOCUS

Under Joshua, Israel had broken the will of the Canaanites to mount any more massive campaigns against them. But dozens of pockets of resistance still lay in the land. The strongholds of idol worshipers pockmarked it. These had to be rooted out.

Joshua had warned the people what would happen if they compromised with evil and failed to expel the pagans of Canaan:

> *They will become snares and traps for you, whips on your backs and thorns in your eyes, until you perish from this good land, which the LORD your God has given you.* (Joshua 23:13)

Israel knew God's will but refused to do it. They were satisfied with the progress they had already made in conquering Canaan and decided to make peace with evil. Compromise seemed like a good solution.

What areas of your heart lay yet unconquered by the King of kings? Invite Him to raise His cross over that territory today. Ask Him to set up His banner of love there. He will not make peace with our sin, because He knows that every sin hurts us. He will not compromise, and neither should we. ☼

WEEK 20 • SATURDAY

Judges 2:1–23

GET THE BIG PICTURE

In the chapter you will read today, the writer links the passing of the generation Joshua led with the spiritual history of that generation's children and grandchildren. It also gives a general description of the cycle of judgment that the nation would live again and again and again over the next three and a half centuries. If time is short, focus on Judges 2:11–19.

The Angel of the LORD at Bokim

2 The angel of the LORD went up
from Gilgal to Bokim and said, "I
brought you up out of Egypt and led
you into the land that I swore to give to
your forefathers. I said, 'I will never
break my covenant with you, [2]and you
shall not make a covenant with the
people of this land, but you shall break
down their altars.' Yet you have disobeyed me. Why have you done this?
[3]Now therefore I tell you that I will not
drive them out before you; they will be
⌊thorns⌋ in your sides and their gods will
be a snare to you."
[4]When the angel of the LORD had spoken these things to all the Israelites, the
people wept aloud, [5]and they called that
place Bokim.[a] There they offered sacrifices to the LORD.

Disobedience and Defeat

[6]After Joshua had dismissed the Israelites, they went to take possession of
the land, each to his own inheritance.
[7]The people served the LORD throughout the lifetime of Joshua and of the elders who outlived him and who had
seen all the great things the LORD had
done for Israel.
[8]Joshua son of Nun, the servant of the
LORD, died at the age of a hundred and
ten. [9]And they buried him in the land of
his inheritance, at Timnath Heres[b] in the
hill country of Ephraim, north of Mount
Gaash.
[10]After that whole generation had
been gathered to their fathers, another
generation grew up, who knew neither
the LORD nor what he had done for Israel. [11]Then the Israelites did evil in the
eyes of the LORD and served the Baals.
[12]They forsook the LORD, the God of
their fathers, who had brought them
out of Egypt. They followed and worshiped various gods of the peoples
around them. They provoked the LORD
to anger [13]because they forsook him and
served Baal and the Ashtoreths. [14]In his
anger against Israel the LORD handed
them over to raiders who plundered

[a]5 *Bokim* means *weepers.* [b]9 Also known as *Timnath Serah* (see Joshua 19:50 and 24:30)

them. He sold them to their enemies all around, whom they were no longer able to resist.
15Whenever Israel went out to fight, the hand of the LORD was against them to defeat them, just as he had sworn to them. They were in great distress.
16Then the LORD raised up judges,[a] who saved them out of the hands of these raiders.
17Yet they would not listen to their judges but prostituted themselves to other gods and worshiped them. Unlike their fathers, they quickly turned from the way in which their fathers had walked, the way of obedience to the LORD's commands.
18Whenever the LORD raised up a judge for them, he was with the judge and saved them out of the hands of their enemies as long as the judge lived; for the LORD had compassion on them as they groaned under those who oppressed and afflicted them.
19But when the judge died, the people returned to ways even more corrupt than those of their fathers, following other gods and serving and worshiping them. They refused to give up their evil practices and stubborn ways.
20Therefore the LORD was very angry with Israel and said, "Because this nation has violated the covenant that I laid down for their forefathers and has not listened to me,
21I will no longer drive out before them any of the nations Joshua left when he died.
22I will use them to test Israel and see whether they will keep the way of the LORD and walk in it as their forefathers did."
23The LORD had allowed those nations to remain; he did not drive them out at once by giving them into the hands of Joshua.

[a]16 Or *leaders*; similarly in verses 17-19

SHARPEN THE FOCUS

Stop. Look. Listen. Parents teaching their children how to cross the street often use these three steps as guidelines.

The writer of Judges says that the people of Israel "would not listen" to their spiritual leaders (Judges 2:17). As a result, they found themselves run down by God's judgment again and again.

Even so, the Lord never gave them up. No matter how far away from Him they walked (or even ran), when they got to the end of the road and to the end of themselves, He heard them cry. He "had compassion on them as they groaned under those who oppressed and afflicted them" (Judges 2:18).

We can dare to imagine our God taking us back, in mercy, the first time and maybe the second or third or fourth. We cannot comprehend the love of a God whose "compassions never fail. They are new every morning" (Lamentations 3:22–23). This Good News seems too good to be true. But it is. His faithfulness went all the way to the cross to bring us forgiveness and peace.

Stop. Look to that cross and to the Savior who bled there for you. Listen and believe His Word: "My peace I give you" (John 14:27).

WEEK 21 • MONDAY

Judges 3:1–30

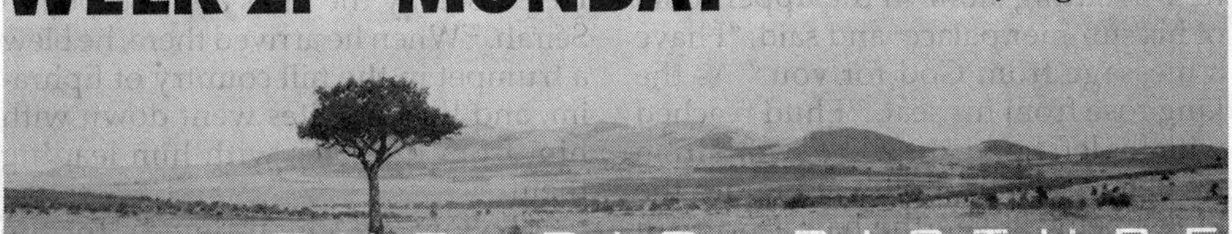

GET THE BIG PICTURE

Many, perhaps most, of the "judges" would have fit in quite readily with the guests on any of the seediest daytime TV talk shows. Some, of course, lived godly lives and served with godly zeal. Some others, though, definitely reflected the depravity that infected Israel at the time. As you read, ask yourself whether God still uses less-than-perfect people to do His work today. If time is short, focus on Judges 3:5–11.

3 These are the nations the LORD
left to test all those Israelites who
had not experienced any of the wars in
Canaan 2(he did this only to teach warfare to the descendants of the Israelites
who had not had previous battle experience): 3the five rulers of the Philistines,
all the Canaanites, the Sidonians, and
the Hivites living in the Lebanon mountains from Mount Baal Hermon to Lebo[a]
Hamath. 4They were left to test the Israelites to see whether they would obey
the LORD's commands, which he had
given their forefathers through Moses.
5The Israelites lived among the Canaanites, Hittites, Amorites, Perizzites,
Hivites and Jebusites. 6They took their
daughters in marriage and gave their
own daughters to their sons, and served
their gods.

Othniel

7The Israelites did evil in the eyes of
the LORD; they forgot the LORD their
God and served the Baals and the
Asherahs. 8The anger of the LORD
burned against Israel so that he sold
them into the hands of Cushan-Risha-
thaim king of Aram Naharaim,[b] to
whom the Israelites were subject for
eight years. 9But when they cried out to
the LORD, he raised up for them a deliverer, Othniel son of Kenaz, Caleb's
younger brother, who saved them. 10The
Spirit of the LORD came upon him, so
that he became Israel's judge[c] and went
to war. The LORD gave Cushan-Risha-
thaim king of Aram into the hands of
Othniel, who overpowered him. 11So
the land had peace for forty years, until
Othniel son of Kenaz died.

Ehud

12Once again the Israelites did evil in
the eyes of the LORD, and because they
did this evil the LORD gave Eglon king
of Moab power over Israel. 13Getting the
Ammonites and Amalekites to join him,
Eglon came and attacked Israel, and
they took possession of the City of
Palms.[d] 14The Israelites were subject to
Eglon king of Moab for eighteen years.
15Again the Israelites cried out to the
LORD, and he gave them a deliverer—
Ehud, a left-handed man, the son of
Gera the Benjamite. The Israelites sent
him with tribute to Eglon king of Moab.
16Now Ehud had made a double-edged
sword about a foot and a half[e] long,
which he strapped to his right thigh under his clothing. 17He presented the tribute to Eglon king of Moab, who was a
very fat man. 18After Ehud had presented the tribute, he sent on their way the
men who had carried it. 19At the idols[f]
near Gilgal he himself turned back and
said, "I have a secret message for you,
O king."

The king said, "Quiet!" And all his attendants left him.

[a]3 Or *to the entrance to* [b]8 That is, Northwest Mesopotamia [c]10 Or *leader* [d]13 That is, Jericho [e]16 Hebrew *a cubit* (about 0.5 meter) [f]19 Or *the stone quarries*; also in verse 26

20Ehud then approached him while
he was sitting alone in the upper room
of his summer palace[a] and said, "I have
a message from God for you." As the
king rose from his seat, 21Ehud reached
with his left hand, drew the sword from
his right thigh and plunged it into the
king's belly. 22Even the handle sank in
after the blade, which came out his back.
Ehud did not pull the sword out, and
the fat closed in over it. 23Then Ehud
went out to the porch[b]; he shut the
doors of the upper room behind him
and locked them.

24After he had gone, the servants
came and found the doors of the upper
room locked. They said, "He must be re-
lieving himself in the inner room of the
house." 25They waited to the point of
embarrassment, but when he did not
open the doors of the room, they took a
key and unlocked them. There they saw
their lord fallen to the floor, dead.

26While they waited, Ehud got away.
He passed by the idols and escaped to
Seirah. 27When he arrived there, he blew
a trumpet in the hill country of Ephraim, and the Israelites went down with
him from the hills, with him leading
them.

28"Follow me," he ordered, "for the
LORD has given Moab, your enemy, into
your hands." So they followed him
down and, taking possession of the
fords of the Jordan that led to Moab,
they allowed no one to cross over.
29At that time they struck down about
ten thousand Moabites, all vigorous
and strong; not a man escaped. 30That
day Moab was made subject to Israel,
and the land had peace for eighty
years.

[a]20 The meaning of the Hebrew for this phrase is uncertain. [b]23 The meaning of the Hebrew for this word is uncertain.

SHARPEN THE FOCUS

As Jesus once pointed out, the road to hell is broad, easy to find, easy to follow. It slopes gradually downward as it lulls us into a spiritual sleepiness. The last thing our enemy wants to hear is the clang of a wake-up call from heaven.

Judges 3:5–7 records Israel's drift into spiritual numbness. First the people settled among the Canaanites. Then they intermarried with them. Then they added the idols of Canaan to their worship of the Lord. Finally, they forgot Him entirely and served only the Canaanite idols.

That's when the alarm rang. The Lord's anger burned. Why? Because He hated Israel? Not at all. In fact, just the opposite. Have you ever noticed that we get angriest at those we care most about? When something threatens our most treasured relationships we act, and speak—firmly. So does our Lord.

That is what the cross was all about. There, God punished human sin so that He could welcome sinful humans into His family. Forever. There's security in that cross. And there's security in knowing that love that refuses to let us go, the love that will come after us, even in—especially in—our sins.

Again we encounter the sin-and-repentance cycle that recurs so often in Judges. We see again Israel's sin, God's judgment and the people's prayer for help. At Israel's cry, the Lord raises up the "judge" Deborah. Note that throughout both the account of a military victory and the hymn of praise that follows that the Lord receives credit. If time is short, focus on Judges 4:1–34.

Shamgar

31After Ehud came Shamgar son of
Anath, who struck down six hundred
Philistines with an oxgoad. He too
saved Israel.

Deborah

4 After Ehud died, the Israelites
once again did evil in the eyes of
the LORD. 2So the LORD sold them into
the hands of Jabin, a king of Canaan,
who reigned in Hazor. The commander
of his army was Sisera, who lived in
Harosheth Haggoyim. 3Because he had
nine hundred iron chariots and had
cruelly oppressed the Israelites for
twenty years, they cried to the LORD for
help.
4Deborah, a prophetess, the wife of
Lappidoth, was leading[a] Israel at that
time. 5She held court under the Palm of
Deborah between Ramah and Bethel in
the hill country of Ephraim, and the Israelites came to her to have their disputes decided. 6She sent for Barak son
of Abinoam from Kedesh in Naphtali
and said to him, "The LORD, the God of
Israel, commands you: 'Go, take with
you ten thousand men of Naphtali and
Zebulun and lead the way to Mount Tabor. 7I will lure Sisera, the commander of
Jabin's army, with his chariots and his
troops to the Kishon River and give him
into your hands.' "
8Barak said to her, "If you go with me,
I will go; but if you don't go with me, I
won't go."
9"Very well," Deborah said, "I will go
with you. But because of the way you
are going about this,[b] the honor will not
be yours, for the LORD will hand Sisera
over to a woman." So Deborah went
with Barak to Kedesh, 10where he summoned Zebulun and Naphtali. Ten
thousand men followed him, and Deborah also went with him.
11Now Heber the Kenite had left the
other Kenites, the descendants of Hobab, Moses' brother-in-law,[c] and pitched
his tent by the great tree in Zaanannim
near Kedesh.
12When they told Sisera that Barak
son of Abinoam had gone up to Mount
Tabor, 13Sisera gathered together his nine
hundred iron chariots and all the men
with him, from Harosheth Haggoyim to
the Kishon River.
14Then Deborah said to Barak, "Go!
This is the day the LORD has given Sisera into your hands. Has not the LORD
gone ahead of you?" So Barak went
down Mount Tabor, followed by ten
thousand men. 15At Barak's advance, the
LORD routed Sisera and all his chariots
and army by the sword, and Sisera
abandoned his chariot and fled on foot.
16But Barak pursued the chariots and
army as far as Harosheth Haggoyim. All
the troops of Sisera fell by the sword;
not a man was left.
17Sisera, however, fled on foot to the
tent of Jael, the wife of Heber the Kenite,
because there were friendly relations

[a]4 Traditionally *judging* [b]9 Or *But on the expedition you are undertaking* [c]11 Or *father-in-law*

between Jabin king of Hazor and the
clan of Heber the Kenite.
18 Jael went out to meet Sisera and said
to him, "Come, my lord, come right in.
Don't be afraid." So he entered her tent,
and she put a covering over him.
19 "I'm thirsty," he said. "Please give
me some water." She opened a skin of
milk, gave him a drink, and covered
him up.
20 "Stand in the doorway of the tent,"
he told her. "If someone comes by and
asks you, 'Is anyone here?' say 'No.' "
21 But Jael, Heber's wife, picked up a
tent peg and a hammer and went quietly to him while he lay fast asleep, exhausted. She drove the peg through his
temple into the ground, and he died.
22 Barak came by in pursuit of Sisera,
and Jael went out to meet him. "Come,"
she said, "I will show you the man
you're looking for." So he went in with
her, and there lay Sisera with the tent
peg through his temple—dead.
23 On that day God subdued Jabin, the
Canaanite king, before the Israelites.
24 And the hand of the Israelites grew
stronger and stronger against Jabin, the
Canaanite king, until they destroyed
him.

The Song of Deborah

5 On that day Deborah and Barak
son of Abinoam sang this song:

2 "When the princes in Israel take the
lead,
when the people willingly offer
themselves—
praise the LORD!

3 "Hear this, you kings! Listen, you
rulers!
I will sing to[a] the LORD, I will sing;
I will make music to[b] the LORD,
the God of Israel.

4 "O LORD, when you went out from
Seir,
when you marched from the land
of Edom,
the earth shook, the heavens
poured,
the clouds poured down water.
5 The mountains quaked before the
LORD, the One of Sinai,
before the LORD, the God of Israel.

6 "In the days of Shamgar son of
Anath,
in the days of Jael, the roads were
abandoned;
travelers took to winding paths.
7 Village life[c] in Israel ceased,
ceased until I,[d] Deborah, arose,
arose a mother in Israel.
8 When they chose new gods,
war came to the city gates,
and not a shield or spear was seen
among forty thousand in Israel.
9 My heart is with Israel's princes,
with the willing volunteers among
the people.
Praise the LORD!

10 "You who ride on white donkeys,
sitting on your saddle blankets,
and you who walk along the road,
consider 11 the voice of the singers[e] at
the watering places.
They recite the righteous acts of
the LORD,
the righteous acts of his warriors[f]
in Israel.

"Then the people of the LORD
went down to the city gates.
12 'Wake up, wake up, Deborah!
Wake up, wake up, break out in
song!
Arise, O Barak!
Take captive your captives, O son
of Abinoam.'

13 "Then the men who were left
came down to the nobles;
the people of the LORD
came to me with the mighty.
14 Some came from Ephraim, whose
roots were in Amalek;
Benjamin was with the people
who followed you.
From Makir captains came down,
from Zebulun those who bear a
commander's staff.

[a]3 Or *of* [b]3 Or / *with song I will praise* [c]7 Or *Warriors* [d]7 Or *you* [e]11 Or *archers*; the meaning of the Hebrew for this word is uncertain. [f]11 Or *villagers*

[15]"The princes of Issachar were with
Deborah;
yes, Issachar was with Barak,
rushing after him into the valley.
In the districts of Reuben
there was much searching of
heart.
[16]Why did you stay among the
campfires[a]
to hear the whistling for the
flocks?
In the districts of Reuben
there was much searching of
heart.
[17]Gilead stayed beyond the Jordan.
And Dan, why did he linger by
the ships?
Asher remained on the coast
and stayed in his coves.
[18]The people of Zebulun risked their
very lives;
so did Naphtali on the heights of
the field.

[19]"Kings came, they fought;
the kings of Canaan fought
at Taanach by the waters of Megiddo,
but they carried off no silver, no
plunder.
[20]From the heavens the stars fought,
from their courses they fought
against Sisera.
[21]The river Kishon swept them away,
the age-old river, the river Kishon.
March on, my soul; be strong!
[22]Then thundered the horses' hoofs—
galloping, galloping go his mighty
steeds.
[23]'Curse Meroz,' said the angel of the
LORD.
'Curse its people bitterly,
because they did not come to help
the LORD,
to help the LORD against the
mighty.'

[24]"Most blessed of women be Jael,
the wife of Heber the Kenite,
most blessed of tent-dwelling
women.
[25]He asked for water, and she gave
him milk;
in a bowl fit for nobles she
brought him curdled milk.
[26]Her hand reached for the tent peg,
her right hand for the workman's
hammer.
She struck Sisera, she crushed his
head,
she shattered and pierced his
temple.
[27]At her feet he sank,
he fell; there he lay.
At her feet he sank, he fell;
where he sank, there he fell—
dead.

[28]"Through the window peered
Sisera's mother;
behind the lattice she cried out,
'Why is his chariot so long in
coming?
Why is the clatter of his chariots
delayed?'
[29]The wisest of her ladies answer her;
indeed, she keeps saying to
herself,
[30]'Are they not finding and dividing
the spoils:
a girl or two for each man,
colorful garments as plunder for
Sisera,
colorful garments embroidered,
highly embroidered garments for
my neck—
all this as plunder?'

[31]"So may all your enemies perish,
O LORD!
But may they who love you be
like the sun
when it rises in its strength."

Then the land had peace forty years.

[a]16 Or *saddlebags*

SHARPEN THE FOCUS

How remarkable! The Creator of the universe notices what happens on earth. How much more remarkable still that He cares! But He does.

Israel had made her own bed. Her Lord could have said, "Now lie in it." Instead, He knelt on one knee, as it were, and opened His arms wide to welcome His tearful, sinful children back to Himself.

He still holds His arms wide to His tearful, fearful, sinful children today. Psalm 35 says, "Who is like you, O LORD? You rescue the poor from those too strong for them, the poor and needy from those who rob them" (Psalm 35:10).

Satan comes against us again and again "to steal and kill and destroy" (John 10:10). But our Lord is for us, He's on our side. "He who did not spare His own Son, but gave Him up for us all—how will He not also, along with Him, graciously give us all things?" (Romans 8:32). The victory is ours in Christ Jesus.

If the last time you heard the story of Gideon was in Sunday school, hold on to your seat and prepare for an adventure. This judge was outstanding—at first for his doubt and unbelief, then for his faith and valor, and finally for his temper and idolatry. He was far from a paragon of virtue. And yet, all that the New Testament records about him is his faithfulness (Hebrews 11:32). If time is short, focus on Judges 7:1–25.

Gideon

6 Again the Israelites did evil in
the eyes of the LORD, and for
seven years he gave them into the
hands of the Midianites. 2Because the
power of Midian was so oppressive, the
Israelites prepared shelters for themselves in mountain clefts, caves and
strongholds. 3Whenever the Israelites
planted their crops, the Midianites, Amalekites and other eastern peoples invaded the country. 4They camped on
the land and ruined the crops all the
way to Gaza and did not spare a living
thing for Israel, neither sheep nor cattle
nor donkeys. 5They came up with their
livestock and their tents like swarms of
locusts. It was impossible to count the
men and their camels; they invaded the
land to ravage it. 6Midian so impoverished the Israelites that they cried out to
the LORD for help.

7When the Israelites cried to the LORD
because of Midian, 8he sent them a
prophet, who said, "This is what the
LORD, the God of Israel, says: I brought
you up out of Egypt, out of the land of
slavery. 9I snatched you from the power
of Egypt and from the hand of all your
oppressors. I drove them from before
you and gave you their land. 10I said to
you, 'I am the LORD your God; do not
worship the gods of the Amorites, in
whose land you live.' But you have not
listened to me."

11The angel of the LORD came and sat
down under the oak in Ophrah that belonged to Joash the Abiezrite, where his
son Gideon was threshing wheat in a
winepress to keep it from the Midianites. 12When the angel of the LORD appeared to Gideon, he said, "The LORD is
with you, mighty warrior."

13"But sir," Gideon replied, "if the

LORD is with us, why has all this happened to us? Where are all his wonders
that our fathers told us about when they
said, 'Did not the LORD bring us up out
of Egypt?' But now the LORD has abandoned us and put us into the hand of
Midian."
14 The LORD turned to him and said,
"Go in the strength you have and save
Israel out of Midian's hand. Am I not
sending you?"
15 "But Lord,[a]" Gideon asked, "how
can I save Israel? My clan is the weak-
est in Manasseh, and I am the least in
my family."
16 The LORD answered, "I will be with
you, and you will strike down all the
Midianites together."
17 Gideon replied, "If now I have
found favor in your eyes, give me a sign
that it is really you talking to me.
18 Please do not go away until I come
back and bring my offering and set it
before you."
And the LORD said, "I will wait until
you return."
19 Gideon went in, prepared a young
goat, and from an ephah[b] of flour he
made bread without yeast. Putting the
meat in a basket and its broth in a pot,
he brought them out and offered them
to him under the oak.
20 The angel of God said to him, "Take
the meat and the unleavened bread,
place them on this rock, and pour out
the broth." And Gideon did so. 21 With
the tip of the staff that was in his hand,
the angel of the LORD touched the meat
and the unleavened bread. Fire flared
from the rock, consuming the meat and
the bread. And the angel of the LORD
disappeared. 22 When Gideon realized
that it was the angel of the LORD, he exclaimed, "Ah, Sovereign LORD! I have
seen the angel of the LORD face to
face!"
23 But the LORD said to him, "Peace! Do
not be afraid. You are not going to die."
24 So Gideon built an altar to the LORD
there and called it The LORD is Peace.
To this day it stands in Ophrah of the
Abiezrites.
25 That same night the LORD said to
him, "Take the second bull from your
father's herd, the one seven years old.[c]
Tear down your father's altar to Baal
and cut down the Asherah pole[d] beside
it. 26 Then build a proper kind of[e] altar to
the LORD your God on the top of this
height. Using the wood of the Asherah
pole that you cut down, offer the
second[f] bull as a burnt offering."
27 So Gideon took ten of his servants
and did as the LORD told him. But because he was afraid of his family and the
men of the town, he did it at night
rather than in the daytime.
28 In the morning when the men of the
town got up, there was Baal's altar, demolished, with the Asherah pole beside
it cut down and the second bull sacrificed on the newly built altar!
29 They asked each other, "Who did
this?"
When they carefully investigated,
they were told, "Gideon son of Joash
did it."
30 The men of the town demanded of
Joash, "Bring out your son. He must die,
because he has broken down Baal's altar and cut down the Asherah pole
beside it."
31 But Joash replied to the hostile crowd
around him, "Are you going to plead
Baal's cause? Are you trying to save him?
Whoever fights for him shall be put to
death by morning! If Baal really is a god,
he can defend himself when someone
breaks down his altar." 32 So that day
they called Gideon "Jerub-Baal,[g]" saying, "Let Baal contend with him," because he broke down Baal's altar.
33 Now all the Midianites, Amalekites
and other eastern peoples joined forces
and crossed over the Jordan and
camped in the Valley of Jezreel. 34 Then
the Spirit of the LORD came upon Gideon, and he blew a trumpet, summoning
the Abiezrites to follow him. 35 He sent

[a] 15 Or *sir* [b] 19 That is, probably about 3/5 bushel (about 22 liters) [c] 25 Or *Take a full-grown, mature bull from your father's herd* [d] 25 That is, a symbol of the goddess Asherah; here and elsewhere in Judges [e] 26 Or *build with layers of stone an* [f] 26 Or *full-grown*; also in verse 28 [g] 32 *Jerub-Baal* means *let Baal contend.*

messengers throughout Manasseh, calling them to arms, and also into Asher,
Zebulun and Naphtali, so that they too
went up to meet them.
36 Gideon said to God, "If you will save
Israel by my hand as you have promised— 37 look, I will place a wool fleece
on the threshing floor. If there is dew
only on the fleece and all the ground is
dry, then I will know that you will save
Israel by my hand, as you said." 38 And
that is what happened. Gideon rose early the next day; he squeezed the fleece
and wrung out the dew—a bowlful of
water.
39 Then Gideon said to God, "Do not
be angry with me. Let me make just one
more request. Allow me one more test
with the fleece. This time make the
fleece dry and the ground covered with
dew." 40 That night God did so. Only the
fleece was dry; all the ground was covered with dew.

Gideon Defeats the Midianites

7 Early in the morning, Jerub-Baal
(that is, Gideon) and all his men
camped at the spring of Harod. The
camp of Midian was north of them in
the valley near the hill of Moreh. 2 The
LORD said to Gideon, "You have too
many men for me to deliver Midian into
their hands. In order that Israel may not
boast against me that her own strength
has saved her, 3 announce now to the
people, 'Anyone who trembles with fear
may turn back and leave Mount Gilead.' " So twenty-two thousand men left,
while ten thousand remained.
4 But the LORD said to Gideon, "There
are still too many men. Take them down
to the water, and I will sift them for you
there. If I say, 'This one shall go with
you,' he shall go; but if I say, 'This one
shall not go with you,' he shall not go."
5 So Gideon took the men down to the
water. There the LORD told him, "Separate those who lap the water with their
tongues like a dog from those who kneel
down to drink." 6 Three hundred men
lapped with their hands to their
mouths. All the rest got down on their
knees to drink.
7 The LORD said to Gideon, "With the
three hundred men that lapped I will
save you and give the Midianites into
your hands. Let all the other men go,
each to his own place." 8 So Gideon sent
the rest of the Israelites to their tents but
kept the three hundred, who took over
the provisions and trumpets of the
others.
Now the camp of Midian lay below
him in the valley. 9 During that night the
LORD said to Gideon, "Get up, go down
against the camp, because I am going to
give it into your hands. 10 If you are
afraid to attack, go down to the camp
with your servant Purah 11 and listen to
what they are saying. Afterward, you
will be encouraged to attack the camp."
So he and Purah his servant went down
to the outposts of the camp. 12 The Midianites, the Amalekites and all the other
eastern peoples had settled in the valley, thick as locusts. Their camels could
no more be counted than the sand on
the seashore.
13 Gideon arrived just as a man was
telling a friend his dream. "I had a
dream," he was saying. "A round loaf of
barley bread came tumbling into the
Midianite camp. It struck the tent with
such force that the tent overturned and
collapsed."
14 His friend responded, "This can be
nothing other than the sword of Gideon son of Joash, the Israelite. God has
given the Midianites and the whole
camp into his hands."
15 When Gideon heard the dream and
its interpretation, he worshiped God.
He returned to the camp of Israel and
called out, "Get up! The LORD has given
the Midianite camp into your hands."
16 Dividing the three hundred men into
three companies, he placed trumpets
and empty jars in the hands of all of
them, with torches inside.
17 "Watch me," he told them. "Follow
my lead. When I get to the edge of the
camp, do exactly as I do. 18 When I and
all who are with me blow our trumpets,
then from all around the camp blow
yours and shout, 'For the LORD and for
Gideon.' "

[19]Gideon and the hundred men with him reached the edge of the camp at the beginning of the middle watch, just after they had changed the guard. They blew their trumpets and broke the jars that were in their hands. [20]The three companies blew the trumpets and smashed the jars. Grasping the torches in their left hands and holding in their right hands the trumpets they were to blow, they shouted, "A sword for the LORD and for Gideon!" [21]While each man held his position around the camp, all the Midianites ran, crying out as they fled.

[22]When the three hundred trumpets sounded, the LORD caused the men throughout the camp to turn on each other with their swords. The army fled to Beth Shittah toward Zererah as far as the border of Abel Meholah near Tabbath. [23]Israelites from Naphtali, Asher and all Manasseh were called out, and they pursued the Midianites. [24]Gideon sent messengers throughout the hill country of Ephraim, saying, "Come down against the Midianites and seize the waters of the Jordan ahead of them as far as Beth Barah."

So all the men of Ephraim were called out and they took the waters of the Jordan as far as Beth Barah. [25]They also captured two of the Midianite leaders, Oreb and Zeeb. They killed Oreb at the rock of Oreb, and Zeeb at the winepress of Zeeb. They pursued the Midianites and brought the heads of Oreb and Zeeb to Gideon, who was by the Jordan.

Zebah and Zalmunna

8 Now the Ephraimites asked Gideon, "Why have you treated us like this? Why didn't you call us when you went to fight Midian?" And they criticized him sharply.

[2]But he answered them, "What have I accomplished compared to you? Aren't the gleanings of Ephraim's grapes better than the full grape harvest of Abiezer? [3]God gave Oreb and Zeeb, the Midianite leaders, into your hands. What was I able to do compared to you?" At this, their resentment against him subsided.

[4]Gideon and his three hundred men, exhausted yet keeping up the pursuit, came to the Jordan and crossed it. [5]He said to the men of Succoth, "Give my troops some bread; they are worn out, and I am still pursuing Zebah and Zalmunna, the kings of Midian."

[6]But the officials of Succoth said, "Do you already have the hands of Zebah and Zalmunna in your possession? Why should we give bread to your troops?"

[7]Then Gideon replied, "Just for that, when the LORD has given Zebah and Zalmunna into my hand, I will tear your flesh with desert thorns and briers."

[8]From there he went up to Peniel[a] and made the same request of them, but they answered as the men of Succoth had. [9]So he said to the men of Peniel, "When I return in triumph, I will tear down this tower."

[10]Now Zebah and Zalmunna were in Karkor with a force of about fifteen thousand men, all that were left of the armies of the eastern peoples; a hundred and twenty thousand swordsmen had fallen. [11]Gideon went up by the route of the nomads east of Nobah and Jogbehah and fell upon the unsuspecting army. [12]Zebah and Zalmunna, the two kings of Midian, fled, but he pursued them and captured them, routing their entire army.

[13]Gideon son of Joash then returned from the battle by the Pass of Heres. [14]He caught a young man of Succoth and questioned him, and the young man wrote down for him the names of the seventy-seven officials of Succoth, the elders of the town. [15]Then Gideon came and said to the men of Succoth, "Here are Zebah and Zalmunna, about whom you taunted me by saying, 'Do you already have the hands of Zebah and Zalmunna in your possession? Why should we give bread to your exhausted men?' " [16]He took the elders of the town and taught the men of Succoth a lesson by punishing them with desert thorns and briers. [17]He also pulled down the

[a]8 Hebrew *Penuel,* a variant of *Peniel;* also in verses 9 and 17

tower of Peniel and killed the men of the
town.
18Then he asked Zebah and Zalmunna, "What kind of men did you kill at
Tabor?"
"Men like you," they answered, "each
one with the bearing of a prince."
19Gideon replied, "Those were my
brothers, the sons of my own mother. As
surely as the LORD lives, if you had
spared their lives, I would not kill you."
20Turning to Jether, his oldest son, he
said, "Kill them!" But Jether did not
draw his sword, because he was only a
boy and was afraid.
21Zebah and Zalmunna said, "Come,
do it yourself. 'As is the man, so is his
strength.' " So Gideon stepped forward
and killed them, and took the ornaments off their camels' necks.

Gideon's Ephod

22The Israelites said to Gideon, "Rule
over us—you, your son and your grandson—because you have saved us out of
the hand of Midian."
23But Gideon told them, "I will not
rule over you, nor will my son rule over
you. The LORD will rule over you."
24And he said, "I do have one request,
that each of you give me an earring
from your share of the plunder." (It was
the custom of the Ishmaelites to wear
gold earrings.)
25They answered, "We'll be glad to
give them." So they spread out a garment, and each man threw a ring from
his plunder onto it. 26The weight of the
gold rings he asked for came to seventeen hundred shekels,[a] not counting the
ornaments, the pendants and the purple garments worn by the kings of Midian or the chains that were on their
camels' necks. 27Gideon made the gold
into an ephod, which he placed in
Ophrah, his town. All Israel prostituted
themselves by worshiping it there, and
it became a snare to Gideon and his
family.

Gideon's Death

28Thus Midian was subdued before
the Israelites and did not raise its head
again. During Gideon's lifetime, the
land enjoyed peace forty years.
29Jerub-Baal son of Joash went back
home to live. 30He had seventy sons of
his own, for he had many wives. 31His
concubine, who lived in Shechem, also
bore him a son, whom he named Abimelech. 32Gideon son of Joash died at a
good old age and was buried in the
tomb of his father Joash in Ophrah of
the Abiezrites.
33No sooner had Gideon died than the
Israelites again prostituted themselves
to the Baals. They set up Baal-Berith as
their god and 34did not remember the
LORD their God, who had rescued them
from the hands of all their enemies on
every side. 35They also failed to show
kindness to the family of Jerub-Baal
(that is, Gideon) for all the good things
he had done for them.

[a]*26* That is, about 43 pounds (about 19.5 kilograms)

SHARPEN THE FOCUS

To come face to face with God. We would not easily forget such an encounter. Most of us would, I suspect, find our hearts flooding with despair just as Gideon's heart did (Judges 6:21–22). We, like Gideon, live among a nation of idolaters, and we cherish the gods of comfort or position or possessions just as he did. Gideon felt afraid in God's presence. And so do we when we see our true condition: The sin in which we swim. Daily. The good we fail to do. Daily.

But, praise God, His Word to us is peace. He reveals Himself to us, as to Gideon, in one of His covenant names—"The LORD is Peace" (Judges 6:24). When the Law has revealed our sin to us, the Holy Spirit is quick to leap to our defense with the Gospel. Our Savior's words soothe our souls:

Peace I leave with you; My peace I give you . . . . Do not let your hearts be troubled and do not be afraid. (John 14:27)

May the Lord, who is peace, hold you in His care today as He comforts you with His pardon for all your sins and with His presence in all your trials.

WEEK 21 • THURSDAY

Judges 9:1—10:18

GET THE BIG PICTURE

After Gideon (also called Jerub-Baal) died, one of his 70 sons—Abimelech—forges an alliance with the Israelites who live in Shechem. Chaos and divine judgment follow. The bleak picture brightens as the Lord leads His people to true repentance. If time is short, focus on Judges 10:1–18.

Abimelech

9 Abimelech son of Jerub-Baal
went to his mother's brothers in
Shechem and said to them and to all his
mother's clan, 2"Ask all the citizens of
Shechem, 'Which is better for you: to
have all seventy of Jerub-Baal's sons
rule over you, or just one man?' Remember, I am your flesh and blood."
3When the brothers repeated all this
to the citizens of Shechem, they were inclined to follow Abimelech, for they
said, "He is our brother." 4They gave him
seventy shekels[a] of silver from the
temple of Baal-Berith, and Abimelech
used it to hire reckless adventurers, who
became his followers. 5He went to his
father's home in Ophrah and on one
stone murdered his seventy brothers,
the sons of Jerub-Baal. But Jotham, the
youngest son of Jerub-Baal, escaped by
hiding. 6Then all the citizens of Shechem and Beth Millo gathered beside
the great tree at the pillar in Shechem to
crown Abimelech king.
7When Jotham was told about this, he
climbed up on the top of Mount Gerizim and shouted to them, "Listen to me,
citizens of Shechem, so that God may
listen to you. 8One day the trees went
out to anoint a king for themselves.
They said to the olive tree, 'Be our king.'
9"But the olive tree answered, 'Should
I give up my oil, by which both gods
and men are honored, to hold sway
over the trees?'
10"Next, the trees said to the fig tree,
'Come and be our king.'
11"But the fig tree replied, 'Should I
give up my fruit, so good and sweet, to
hold sway over the trees?'
12"Then the trees said to the vine,
'Come and be our king.'
13"But the vine answered, 'Should I
give up my wine, which cheers both
gods and men, to hold sway over the
trees?'
14"Finally all the trees said to the
thornbush, 'Come and be our king.'
15"The thornbush said to the trees, 'If
you really want to anoint me king over
you, come and take refuge in my shade;
but if not, then let fire come out of the
thornbush and consume the cedars of
Lebanon!'
16"Now if you have acted honorably
and in good faith when you made
Abimelech king, and if you have been

[a]4 That is, about 1 3/4 pounds (about 0.8 kilogram)

fair to Jerub-Baal and his family, and if you have treated him as he deserves— 17and to think that my father fought for you, risked his life to rescue you from the hand of Midian 18(but today you have revolted against my father's family, murdered his seventy sons on a single stone, and made Abimelech, the son of his slave girl, king over the citizens of Shechem because he is your brother)— 19if then you have acted honorably and in good faith toward Jerub-Baal and his family today, may Abimelech be your joy, and may you be his, too! 20But if you have not, let fire come out from Abimelech and consume you, citizens of Shechem and Beth Millo, and let fire come out from you, citizens of Shechem and Beth Millo, and consume Abimelech!"

21Then Jotham fled, escaping to Beer, and he lived there because he was afraid of his brother Abimelech.

22After Abimelech had governed Israel three years, 23God sent an evil spirit between Abimelech and the citizens of Shechem, who acted treacherously against Abimelech. 24God did this in order that the crime against Jerub-Baal's seventy sons, the shedding of their blood, might be avenged on their brother Abimelech and on the citizens of Shechem, who had helped him murder his brothers. 25In opposition to him these citizens of Shechem set men on the hilltops to ambush and rob everyone who passed by, and this was reported to Abimelech.

26Now Gaal son of Ebed moved with his brothers into Shechem, and its citizens put their confidence in him. 27After they had gone out into the fields and gathered the grapes and trodden them, they held a festival in the temple of their god. While they were eating and drinking, they cursed Abimelech. 28Then Gaal son of Ebed said, "Who is Abimelech, and who is Shechem, that we should be subject to him? Isn't he Jerub-Baal's son, and isn't Zebul his deputy? Serve the men of Hamor, Shechem's father! Why should we serve Abimelech? 29If only this people were under my command! Then I would get rid of him. I would say to Abimelech, 'Call out your whole army!' "[a]

30When Zebul the governor of the city heard what Gaal son of Ebed said, he was very angry. 31Under cover he sent messengers to Abimelech, saying, "Gaal son of Ebed and his brothers have come to Shechem and are stirring up the city against you. 32Now then, during the night you and your men should come and lie in wait in the fields. 33In the morning at sunrise, advance against the city. When Gaal and his men come out against you, do whatever your hand finds to do."

34So Abimelech and all his troops set out by night and took up concealed positions near Shechem in four companies. 35Now Gaal son of Ebed had gone out and was standing at the entrance to the city gate just as Abimelech and his soldiers came out from their hiding place.

36When Gaal saw them, he said to Zebul, "Look, people are coming down from the tops of the mountains!"

Zebul replied, "You mistake the shadows of the mountains for men."

37But Gaal spoke up again: "Look, people are coming down from the center of the land, and a company is coming from the direction of the soothsayers' tree."

38Then Zebul said to him, "Where is your big talk now, you who said, 'Who is Abimelech that we should be subject to him?' Aren't these the men you ridiculed? Go out and fight them!"

39So Gaal led out[b] the citizens of Shechem and fought Abimelech. 40Abimelech chased him, and many fell wounded in the flight—all the way to the entrance to the gate. 41Abimelech stayed in Arumah, and Zebul drove Gaal and his brothers out of Shechem.

42The next day the people of Shechem went out to the fields, and this was reported to Abimelech. 43So he took his

[a]29 Septuagint; Hebrew *him." Then he said to Abimelech, "Call out your whole army!"* [b]39 Or *Gaal went out in the sight of*

men, divided them into three companies and set an ambush in the fields.
When he saw the people coming out of
the city, he rose to attack them. 44Abim-
elech and the companies with him
rushed forward to a position at the entrance to the city gate. Then two companies rushed upon those in the fields
and struck them down. 45All that day
Abimelech pressed his attack against
the city until he had captured it and
killed its people. Then he destroyed the
city and scattered salt over it.
46On hearing this, the citizens in the
tower of Shechem went into the stronghold of the temple of El-Berith. 47When
Abimelech heard that they had assembled there, 48he and all his men went up
Mount Zalmon. He took an ax and cut
off some branches, which he lifted to his
shoulders. He ordered the men with
him, "Quick! Do what you have seen
me do!" 49So all the men cut branches
and followed Abimelech. They piled
them against the stronghold and set it
on fire over the people inside. So all
the people in the tower of Shechem,
about a thousand men and women, also
died.
50Next Abimelech went to Thebez and
besieged it and captured it. 51Inside the
city, however, was a strong tower, to
which all the men and women—all the
people of the city—fled. They locked
themselves in and climbed up on the
tower roof. 52Abimelech went to the
tower and stormed it. But as he approached the entrance to the tower to
set it on fire, 53a woman dropped an upper millstone on his head and cracked
his skull.
54Hurriedly he called to his armor-
bearer, "Draw your sword and kill me,
so that they can't say, 'A woman killed
him.' " So his servant ran him through,
and he died. 55When the Israelites saw
that Abimelech was dead, they went
home.
56Thus God repaid the wickedness
that Abimelech had done to his father
by murdering his seventy brothers.
57God also made the men of Shechem
pay for all their wickedness. The curse
of Jotham son of Jerub-Baal came on
them.

Tola

10 After the time of Abimelech a
man of Issachar, Tola son of
Puah, the son of Dodo, rose to save
Israel. He lived in Shamir, in the hill
country of Ephraim. 2He led[a] Israel
twenty-three years; then he died, and
was buried in Shamir.

Jair

3He was followed by Jair of Gilead,
who led Israel twenty-two years. 4He
had thirty sons, who rode thirty donkeys. They controlled thirty towns in
Gilead, which to this day are called Havvoth Jair.[b] 5When Jair died, he was buried in Kamon.

Jephthah

6Again the Israelites did evil in the
eyes of the LORD. They served the Baals and the Ashtoreths, and the gods of
Aram, the gods of Sidon, the gods of
Moab, the gods of the Ammonites and
the gods of the Philistines. And because
the Israelites forsook the LORD and no
longer served him, 7he became angry
with them. He sold them into the hands
of the Philistines and the Ammonites,
8who that year shattered and crushed
them. For eighteen years they oppressed all the Israelites on the east side
of the Jordan in Gilead, the land of the
Amorites. 9The Ammonites also crossed
the Jordan to fight against Judah, Benjamin and the house of Ephraim; and
Israel was in great distress. 10Then the Israelites cried out to the LORD, "We have
sinned against you, forsaking our God
and serving the Baals."
11The LORD replied, "When the Egyptians, the Amorites, the Ammonites, the
Philistines, 12the Sidonians, the Amalekites and the Maonites[c] oppressed you
and you cried to me for help, did I not
save you from their hands? 13But you

[a]2 Traditionally *judged*; also in verse 3 [b]4 Or *called the settlements of Jair* [c]12 Hebrew; some Septuagint manuscripts *Midianites*

have forsaken me and served other
gods, so I will no longer save you. [14]Go
and cry out to the gods you have chosen. Let them save you when you are in
trouble!"
[15]But the Israelites said to the LORD,
"We have sinned. Do with us whatever
you think best, but please rescue us
now." [16]Then they got rid of the foreign
gods among them and served the LORD.
And he could bear Israel's misery no
longer.
[17]When the Ammonites were called to
arms and camped in Gilead, the Israelites assembled and camped at Mizpah.
[18]The leaders of the people of Gilead
said to each other, "Whoever will launch
the attack against the Ammonites
will be the head of all those living in Gilead."

SHARPEN THE FOCUS

Robert Louis Stevenson once told of a time in his childhood when he misbehaved and then hid from his father. He ducked inside a closet and shut the door. In seconds, the darkness closed in. Panicked, the boy screamed and pushed against the door. But it was locked.

When his father finally came, and a locksmith released the latch, father and son fell into one another's arms. What a relief—for both of them!

Again and again in the book of Judges we see the people of Israel running to hide from their heavenly Father. They know what to do with sin—confess it and, with the power of God's pardon, forsake it. Yet the pull of idolatry is so strong.

In Judges 10:10, we hear them mouth the magic words: We're sorry God! Forgive us just this once and we'll be good. But God is not some sleepy, indulgent grandfather in the sky. Their pretense does not fool Him. He confronts them in their rebellion with some of the sternest Law in all the Scriptures (Judges 10:11–14). This, too, harsh as it may seem, is really evidence of His concern for them. And the Law does its holy work—it drives them out of the closet and into their Father's arms, weeping (Judges 10:16).

WEEK 21 • FRIDAY

Judges 11:1—12:15

GET THE BIG PICTURE

The sordid history of Israel during the time of the judges rolls on. The Lord uses Jephthah and an Israelite named Gilead, to deliver His people from oppression by the armies of Ammon. Even though he's a social outcast, Jephthah knows the Lord, knows His Word, and knows the history of His dealings with Israel (Judges 11:15–27). Through Jephthah, the Lord works to preserve the land and His other covenant promises to Israel. If time is short, focus on Judges 11:1–11.

11 Jephthah the Gileadite was a
mighty warrior. His father was
Gilead; his mother was a prostitute.
[2]Gilead's wife also bore him sons, and
when they were grown up, they drove
Jephthah away. "You are not going to

get any inheritance in our family," they
said, "because you are the son of another woman." 3So Jephthah fled from
his brothers and settled in the land of
Tob, where a group of adventurers gathered around him and followed him.
4Some time later, when the Ammonites made war on Israel, 5the elders of
Gilead went to get Jephthah from the
land of Tob. 6"Come," they said, "be our
commander, so we can fight the Ammonites."
7Jephthah said to them, "Didn't you
hate me and drive me from my father's
house? Why do you come to me now,
when you're in trouble?"
8The elders of Gilead said to him,
"Nevertheless, we are turning to you
now; come with us to fight the Ammonites, and you will be our head over all
who live in Gilead."
9Jephthah answered, "Suppose you
take me back to fight the Ammonites
and the LORD gives them to me—will I
really be your head?"
10The elders of Gilead replied, "The
LORD is our witness; we will certainly do
as you say." 11So Jephthah went with the
elders of Gilead, and the people made
him head and commander over them.
And he repeated all his words before the
LORD in Mizpah.
12Then Jephthah sent messengers to
the Ammonite king with the question:
"What do you have against us that you
have attacked our country?"
13The king of the Ammonites answered Jephthah's messengers, "When
Israel came up out of Egypt, they took
away my land from the Arnon to the
Jabbok, all the way to the Jordan. Now
give it back peaceably."
14Jephthah sent back messengers to
the Ammonite king, 15saying:

"This is what Jephthah says: Israel
did not take the land of Moab or the
land of the Ammonites. 16But when
they came up out of Egypt, Israel
went through the desert to the Red
Sea[a] and on to Kadesh. 17Then Israel
sent messengers to the king of
Edom, saying, 'Give us permission
to go through your country,' but
the king of Edom would not listen.
They sent also to the king of Moab,
and he refused. So Israel stayed at
Kadesh.
18"Next they traveled through
the desert, skirted the lands of
Edom and Moab, passed along the
eastern side of the country of
Moab, and camped on the other
side of the Arnon. They did not enter the territory of Moab, for the
Arnon was its border.
19"Then Israel sent messengers to
Sihon king of the Amorites, who
ruled in Heshbon, and said to him,
'Let us pass through your country
to our own place.' 20Sihon, however, did not trust Israel[b] to pass
through his territory. He mustered
all his men and encamped at Jahaz
and fought with Israel.
21"Then the LORD, the God of Israel, gave Sihon and all his men
into Israel's hands, and they defeated them. Israel took over all the
land of the Amorites who lived in
that country, 22capturing all of it
from the Arnon to the Jabbok and
from the desert to the Jordan.
23"Now since the LORD, the God
of Israel, has driven the Amorites
out before his people Israel, what
right have you to take it over? 24Will
you not take what your god Chemosh gives you? Likewise, whatever the LORD our God has given us,
we will possess. 25Are you better
than Balak son of Zippor, king of
Moab? Did he ever quarrel with Israel or fight with them? 26For three
hundred years Israel occupied
Heshbon, Aroer, the surrounding
settlements and all the towns along
the Arnon. Why didn't you retake
them during that time? 27I have not
wronged you, but you are doing
me wrong by waging war against
me. Let the LORD, the Judge,[c] de-

[a]16 Hebrew *Yam Suph*; that is, Sea of Reeds
[b]20 Or *however, would not make an agreement for Israel* [c]27 Or *Ruler*

cide the dispute this day between
the Israelites and the Ammonites."

[28]The king of Ammon, however, paid no
attention to the message Jephthah sent
him.

[29]Then the Spirit of the LORD came
upon Jephthah. He crossed Gilead and
Manasseh, passed through Mizpah of
Gilead, and from there he advanced
against the Ammonites. [30]And Jephthah
made a vow to the LORD: "If you give
the Ammonites into my hands, [31]what-
ever comes out of the door of my house
to meet me when I return in triumph
from the Ammonites will be the LORD's,
and I will sacrifice it as a burnt offering."

[32]Then Jephthah went over to fight
the Ammonites, and the LORD gave
them into his hands. [33]He devastated
twenty towns from Aroer to the vicinity of Minnith, as far as Abel Keramim.
Thus Israel subdued Ammon.

[34]When Jephthah returned to his
home in Mizpah, who should come out
to meet him but his daughter, dancing
to the sound of tambourines! She was
an only child. Except for her he had neither son nor daughter. [35]When he saw
her, he tore his clothes and cried, "Oh!
My daughter! You have made me miserable and wretched, because I have
made a vow to the LORD that I cannot
break."

[36]"My father," she replied, "you have
given your word to the LORD. Do to me
just as you promised, now that the
LORD has avenged you of your enemies,
the Ammonites. [37]But grant me this one
request," she said. "Give me two months
to roam the hills and weep with my
friends, because I will never marry."

[38]"You may go," he said. And he let
her go for two months. She and the girls
went into the hills and wept because she
would never marry. [39]After the two
months, she returned to her father and
he did to her as he had vowed. And she
was a virgin.

From this comes the Israelite custom
[40]that each year the young women of
Israel go out for four days to commemorate the daughter of Jephthah the Gileadite.

Jephthah and Ephraim

12 The men of Ephraim called
out their forces, crossed over
to Zaphon and said to Jephthah, "Why
did you go to fight the Ammonites without calling us to go with you? We're going to burn down your house over your
head."

[2]Jephthah answered, "I and my people were engaged in a great struggle
with the Ammonites, and although I
called, you didn't save me out of their
hands. [3]When I saw that you wouldn't
help, I took my life in my hands and
crossed over to fight the Ammonites,
and the LORD gave me the victory over
them. Now why have you come up today to fight me?"

[4]Jephthah then called together the
men of Gilead and fought against
Ephraim. The Gileadites struck them
down because the Ephraimites had
said, "You Gileadites are renegades
from Ephraim and Manasseh." [5]The
Gileadites captured the fords of the Jordan leading to Ephraim, and whenever
a survivor of Ephraim said, "Let me
cross over," the men of Gilead asked
him, "Are you an Ephraimite?" If he replied, "No," [6]they said, "All right, say
'Shibboleth.'" If he said, "Sibboleth,"
because he could not pronounce the
word correctly, they seized him and
killed him at the fords of the Jordan.
Forty-two thousand Ephraimites were
killed at that time.

[7]Jephthah led[a] Israel six years. Then
Jephthah the Gileadite died, and was
buried in a town in Gilead.

Ibzan, Elon and Abdon

[8]After him, Ibzan of Bethlehem led Israel. [9]He had thirty sons and thirty
daughters. He gave his daughters away
in marriage to those outside his clan,
and for his sons he brought in thirty
young women as wives from outside his
clan. Ibzan led Israel seven years. [10]Then

[a]7 Traditionally *judged*; also in verses 8-14

Ibzan died, and was buried in Bethlehem.
11After him, Elon the Zebulunite led
Israel ten years. 12Then Elon died, and was
buried in Aijalon in the land of Zebulun.
13After him, Abdon son of Hillel, from
Pirathon, led Israel. 14He had forty sons
and thirty grandsons, who rode on seventy donkeys. He led Israel eight years.
15Then Abdon son of Hillel died, and
was buried at Pirathon in Ephraim, in
the hill country of the Amalekites.

SHARPEN THE FOCUS

Knowledge is power. This adage proved itself true in Jephthah's life. The king of Ammon tried to claim ownership of a large tract of land in Canaan (Judges 11:13). But Jephthah knew the truth. He didn't need title insurance to protect his people's 300-year-old claim. He had something more secure—the Lord was on his side (Judges 11:27). And he rendered a just verdict in Israel's favor.

Repeatedly the Scriptures urge us to know the Lord. This kind of knowledge involves more than knowing facts *about* Him. It includes knowing how He's treated His people down through all generations and relying on His promises to protect and deliver.

Most of all, it involves knowing that our Judge is also our Savior. He who will render the verdict on our lives on Judgment Day has adopted us into His family. He has placed an indelible mark on us in our Baptism—the sign of His cross.

The people around us may think highly of us. Or they may reject us, ridiculing our family, our race, or our social standing—as they did Jephthah's. Even so, we can walk confident in God's opinion of us. He frees us to serve Him as His holy priests, His representatives on earth. That's who—in Christ—we are!

WEEK 21 • SATURDAY

Judges 13:1—16:31

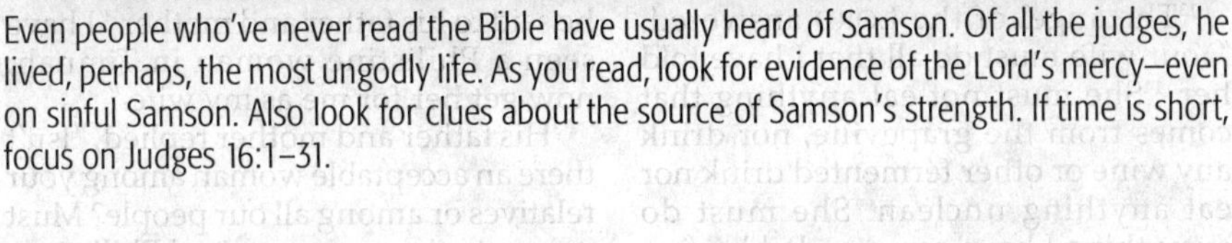

GET THE BIG PICTURE

Even people who've never read the Bible have usually heard of Samson. Of all the judges, he lived, perhaps, the most ungodly life. As you read, look for evidence of the Lord's mercy—even on sinful Samson. Also look for clues about the source of Samson's strength. If time is short, focus on Judges 16:1–31.

The Birth of Samson

13 Again the Israelites did evil in
the eyes of the LORD, so the
LORD delivered them into the hands of
the Philistines for forty years.
2A certain man of Zorah, named Manoah, from the clan of the Danites, had
a wife who was sterile and remained
childless. 3The angel of the LORD appeared to her and said, "You are sterile
and childless, but you are going to conceive and have a son. 4Now see to it that
you drink no wine or other fermented
drink and that you do not eat anything

unclean, 5because you will conceive and
give birth to a son. No razor may be
used on his head, because the boy is to
be a Nazirite, set apart to God from
birth, and he will begin the deliverance
of Israel from the hands of the Philistines."
6Then the woman went to her husband and told him, "A man of God came
to me. He looked like an angel of God,
very awesome. I didn't ask him where
he came from, and he didn't tell me his
name. 7But he said to me, 'You will conceive and give birth to a son. Now then,
drink no wine or other fermented drink
and do not eat anything unclean,
because the boy will be a Nazirite of
God from birth until the day of his
death.' "
8Then Manoah prayed to the LORD:
"O Lord, I beg you, let the man of God
you sent to us come again to teach us
how to bring up the boy who is to be
born."
9God heard Manoah, and the angel of
God came again to the woman while
she was out in the field; but her husband Manoah was not with her. 10The
woman hurried to tell her husband,
"He's here! The man who appeared to
me the other day!"
11Manoah got up and followed his
wife. When he came to the man, he said,
"Are you the one who talked to my
wife?"
"I am," he said.
12So Manoah asked him, "When your
words are fulfilled, what is to be the rule
for the boy's life and work?"
13The angel of the LORD answered,
"Your wife must do all that I have told
her. 14She must not eat anything that
comes from the grapevine, nor drink
any wine or other fermented drink nor
eat anything unclean. She must do
everything I have commanded her."
15Manoah said to the angel of the
LORD, "We would like you to stay until
we prepare a young goat for you."
16The angel of the LORD replied,
"Even though you detain me, I will not
eat any of your food. But if you prepare
a burnt offering, offer it to the LORD."
(Manoah did not realize that it was the
angel of the LORD.)
17Then Manoah inquired of the angel
of the LORD, "What is your name, so
that we may honor you when your
word comes true?"
18He replied, "Why do you ask my
name? It is beyond understanding.[a]"
19Then Manoah took a young goat, together with the grain offering, and sacrificed it on a rock to the LORD. And the
LORD did an amazing thing while Manoah and his wife watched: 20As the
flame blazed up from the altar toward
heaven, the angel of the LORD ascended
in the flame. Seeing this, Manoah and
his wife fell with their faces to the
ground. 21When the angel of the LORD
did not show himself again to Manoah
and his wife, Manoah realized that it
was the angel of the LORD.
22"We are doomed to die!" he said to
his wife. "We have seen God!"
23But his wife answered, "If the LORD
had meant to kill us, he would not have
accepted a burnt offering and grain offering from our hands, nor shown us all
these things or now told us this."
24The woman gave birth to a boy and
named him Samson. He grew and the
LORD blessed him, 25and the Spirit of the
LORD began to stir him while he was in
Mahaneh Dan, between Zorah and Eshtaol.

Samson's Marriage

14 Samson went down to Timnah and saw there a young
Philistine woman. 2When he returned,
he said to his father and mother, "I have
seen a Philistine woman in Timnah;
now get her for me as my wife."
3His father and mother replied, "Isn't
there an acceptable woman among your
relatives or among all our people? Must
you go to the uncircumcised Philistines
to get a wife?"
But Samson said to his father, "Get her
for me. She's the right one for me." 4(His
parents did not know that this was from
the LORD, who was seeking an occasion

[a]18 Or *is wonderful*

to confront the Philistines; for at that
time they were ruling over Israel.) 5Sam-
son went down to Timnah together
with his father and mother. As they approached the vineyards of Timnah, suddenly a young lion came roaring toward
him. 6The Spirit of the LORD came upon
him in power so that he tore the lion
apart with his bare hands as he might
have torn a young goat. But he told neither his father nor his mother what he
had done. 7Then he went down and
talked with the woman, and he liked
her.
8Some time later, when he went back
to marry her, he turned aside to look at
the lion's carcass. In it was a swarm of
bees and some honey, 9which he
scooped out with his hands and ate as
he went along. When he rejoined his
parents, he gave them some, and they
too ate it. But he did not tell them that
he had taken the honey from the lion's
carcass.
10Now his father went down to see
the woman. And Samson made a feast
there, as was customary for bride-
grooms. 11When he appeared, he was
given thirty companions.
12"Let me tell you a riddle," Samson
said to them. "If you can give me the answer within the seven days of the feast,
I will give you thirty linen garments and
thirty sets of clothes. 13If you can't tell
me the answer, you must give me thirty
linen garments and thirty sets of
clothes."
"Tell us your riddle," they said. "Let's
hear it."
14He replied,

"Out of the eater, something to eat;
out of the strong, something
sweet."

For three days they could not give the
answer.
15On the fourth[a] day, they said to
Samson's wife, "Coax your husband
into explaining the riddle for us, or we
will burn you and your father's household to death. Did you invite us here to
rob us?"
16Then Samson's wife threw herself
on him, sobbing, "You hate me! You
don't really love me. You've given my
people a riddle, but you haven't told me
the answer."
"I haven't even explained it to my father or mother," he replied, "so why
should I explain it to you?" 17She cried
the whole seven days of the feast. So on
the seventh day he finally told her, because she continued to press him. She
in turn explained the riddle to her people.
18Before sunset on the seventh day
the men of the town said to him,

"What is sweeter than honey?
What is stronger than a lion?"

Samson said to them,

"If you had not plowed with my
heifer,
you would not have solved my
riddle."

19Then the Spirit of the LORD came
upon him in power. He went down to
Ashkelon, struck down thirty of their
men, stripped them of their belongings
and gave their clothes to those who had
explained the riddle. Burning with anger, he went up to his father's house.
20And Samson's wife was given to the
friend who had attended him at his
wedding.

Samson's Vengeance on the Philistines

15 Later on, at the time of wheat
harvest, Samson took a
young goat and went to visit his wife.
He said, "I'm going to my wife's room."
But her father would not let him
go in.
2"I was so sure you thoroughly hated
her," he said, "that I gave her to your
friend. Isn't her younger sister more attractive? Take her instead."
3Samson said to them, "This time I
have a right to get even with the Philistines; I will really harm them." 4So he
went out and caught three hundred fox-

[a]*15* Some Septuagint manuscripts and Syriac; Hebrew *seventh*

es and tied them tail to tail in pairs. He
then fastened a torch to every pair of
tails, 5lit the torches and let the foxes
loose in the standing grain of the Philistines. He burned up the shocks and
standing grain, together with the vineyards and olive groves.
6When the Philistines asked, "Who
did this?" they were told, "Samson, the
Timnite's son-in-law, because his wife
was given to his friend."

So the Philistines went up and
burned her and her father to death.
7Samson said to them, "Since you've
acted like this, I won't stop until I get
my revenge on you." 8He attacked them
viciously and slaughtered many of
them. Then he went down and stayed
in a cave in the rock of Etam.
9The Philistines went up and camped
in Judah, spreading out near Lehi. 10The
men of Judah asked, "Why have you
come to fight us?"

"We have come to take Samson prisoner," they answered, "to do to him as
he did to us."
11Then three thousand men from
Judah went down to the cave in the
rock of Etam and said to Samson,
"Don't you realize that the Philistines
are rulers over us? What have you done
to us?"

He answered, "I merely did to them
what they did to me."
12They said to him, "We've come to tie
you up and hand you over to the Philistines."

Samson said, "Swear to me that you
won't kill me yourselves."
13"Agreed," they answered. "We will
only tie you up and hand you over to
them. We will not kill you." So they
bound him with two new ropes and led
him up from the rock. 14As he approached Lehi, the Philistines came toward him shouting. The Spirit of the
LORD came upon him in power. The
ropes on his arms became like charred
flax, and the bindings dropped from his
hands. 15Finding a fresh jawbone of a
donkey, he grabbed it and struck down
a thousand men.
16Then Samson said,

"With a donkey's jawbone
  I have made donkeys of them.[a]
With a donkey's jawbone
  I have killed a thousand men."

17When he finished speaking, he threw
away the jawbone; and the place was
called Ramath Lehi.[b]
18Because he was very thirsty, he cried
out to the LORD, "You have given your
servant this great victory. Must I now
die of thirst and fall into the hands of the
uncircumcised?" 19Then God opened up
the hollow place in Lehi, and water
came out of it. When Samson drank, his
strength returned and he revived. So
the spring was called En Hakkore,[c] and
it is still there in Lehi.
20Samson led[d] Israel for twenty years
in the days of the Philistines.

Samson and Delilah

16 One day Samson went to
Gaza, where he saw a prosti-
tute. He went in to spend the night with
her. 2The people of Gaza were told,
"Samson is here!" So they surrounded
the place and lay in wait for him all
night at the city gate. They made no
move during the night, saying, "At dawn
we'll kill him."
3But Samson lay there only until the
middle of the night. Then he got up and
took hold of the doors of the city gate,
together with the two posts, and tore
them loose, bar and all. He lifted them
to his shoulders and carried them to the
top of the hill that faces Hebron.
4Some time later, he fell in love with a
woman in the Valley of Sorek whose
name was Delilah. 5The rulers of the
Philistines went to her and said, "See if
you can lure him into showing you the
secret of his great strength and how we
can overpower him so we may tie him
up and subdue him. Each one of us will
give you eleven hundred shekels[e] of silver."

[a]16 Or *made a heap or two;* the Hebrew for *donkey* sounds like the Hebrew for *heap.* [b]17 *Ramath Lehi* means *jawbone hill.* [c]19 *En Hakkore* means *caller's spring.* [d]20 Traditionally *judged* [e]5 That is, about 28 pounds (about 13 kilograms)

6So Delilah said to Samson, "Tell me
the secret of your great strength and
how you can be tied up and subdued."
7Samson answered her, "If anyone ties
me with seven fresh thongs[a] that have
not been dried, I'll become as weak as
any other man."
8Then the rulers of the Philistines
brought her seven fresh thongs that had
not been dried, and she tied him with
them. 9With men hidden in the room,
she called to him, "Samson, the Philistines are upon you!" But he snapped the
thongs as easily as a piece of string
snaps when it comes close to a flame. So
the secret of his strength was not discovered.
10Then Delilah said to Samson, "You
have made a fool of me; you lied to me.
Come now, tell me how you can be
tied."
11He said, "If anyone ties me securely
with new ropes that have never been
used, I'll become as weak as any other
man."
12So Delilah took new ropes and tied
him with them. Then, with men hidden
in the room, she called to him, "Samson,
the Philistines are upon you!" But he
snapped the ropes off his arms as if they
were threads.
13Delilah then said to Samson, "Until
now, you have been making a fool of me
and lying to me. Tell me how you can be
tied."
He replied, "If you weave the seven
braids of my head into the fabric ⌞on the
loom⌟ and tighten it with the pin, I'll become as weak as any other man." So
while he was sleeping, Delilah took the
seven braids of his head, wove them
into the fabric 14and[b] tightened it with
the pin.
Again she called to him, "Samson, the
Philistines are upon you!" He awoke
from his sleep and pulled up the pin
and the loom, with the fabric.
15Then she said to him, "How can you
say, 'I love you,' when you won't con-
fide in me? This is the third time you
have made a fool of me and haven't told
me the secret of your great strength."
16With such nagging she prodded him
day after day until he was tired to death.
17So he told her everything. "No razor
has ever been used on my head," he
said, "because I have been a Nazirite set
apart to God since birth. If my head
were shaved, my strength would leave
me, and I would become as weak as any
other man."
18When Delilah saw that he had told
her everything, she sent word to the rulers of the Philistines, "Come back once
more; he has told me everything." So
the rulers of the Philistines returned
with the silver in their hands. 19Having
put him to sleep on her lap, she called a
man to shave off the seven braids of his
hair, and so began to subdue him.[c] And
his strength left him.
20Then she called, "Samson, the Philistines are upon you!"
He awoke from his sleep and
thought, "I'll go out as before and shake
myself free." But he did not know that
the LORD had left him.
21Then the Philistines seized him,
gouged out his eyes and took him down
to Gaza. Binding him with bronze
shackles, they set him to grinding in
the prison. 22But the hair on his head
began to grow again after it had been
shaved.

The Death of Samson

23Now the rulers of the Philistines
assembled to offer a great sacrifice to
Dagon their god and to celebrate, saying, "Our god has delivered Samson,
our enemy, into our hands."
24When the people saw him, they
praised their god, saying,

"Our god has delivered our enemy
into our hands,
the one who laid waste our land
and multiplied our slain."

25While they were in high spirits, they
shouted, "Bring out Samson to entertain

[a]7 Or *bowstrings*; also in verses 8 and 9
[b]13,14 Some Septuagint manuscripts; Hebrew "*⌞I can, if you weave the seven braids of my head into the fabric ⌞on the loom⌟.*" [14]*So she* [c]19 Hebrew; some Septuagint manuscripts *and he began to weaken*

us." So they called Samson out of the
prison, and he performed for them.
When they stood him among the pillars, 26Samson said to the servant who
held his hand, "Put me where I can feel
the pillars that support the temple, so
that I may lean against them." 27Now the
temple was crowded with men and
women; all the rulers of the Philistines
were there, and on the roof were about
three thousand men and women
watching Samson perform. 28Then Samson prayed to the LORD, "O Sovereign
LORD, remember me. O God, please
strengthen me just once more, and let
me with one blow get revenge on the
Philistines for my two eyes." 29Then
Samson reached toward the two central
pillars on which the temple stood. Brac-
ing himself against them, his right hand
on the one and his left hand on the other, 30Samson said, "Let me die with the
Philistines!" Then he pushed with all his
might, and down came the temple on
the rulers and all the people in it. Thus
he killed many more when he died than
while he lived.
31Then his brothers and his father's
whole family went down to get him.
They brought him back and buried him
between Zorah and Eshtaol in the tomb
of Manoah his father. He had led[a] Israel
twenty years.

[a]31 Traditionally *judged*

SHARPEN THE FOCUS

Three different times we read that "the Spirit of the LORD came upon him [Samson] in power" (Judges 14:6; 14:19; 15:14). Filled with the Spirit, Samson accomplished mighty things. Then, by way of contrast, we read these sad words, "[Samson] did not know that the LORD had left him" (Judges 16:20).

Samson grieved the Holy Spirit again and again by his impenitent lifestyle. Unwelcome, the Spirit finally left. In the end, Samson did come back to the Lord in humility and faith. And God received him in grace just as He always receives His penitent children. But think of what the Lord might have been able to accomplish in Israel through Samson had he been willing to live a life "worthy of the calling you have received" (Ephesians 4:1).

Samson's bad example prods us to examine our own hearts. Even if we see ourselves doing great things for God and His kingdom, we need continually to invite the Spirit of God to cleanse us. We need to listen when He points out thoughts or choices in lifestyle that cause Him grief. The Lord has promised never to leave us or forsake us. But He will not stay forever where He is not welcome or where His warnings continually fall on deaf ears.

WEEK 22 • MONDAY

Judges 17:1—18:31

GET THE BIG PICTURE

The 350-year downward spiral continues in Israel. As you read today, note as the evidence of that is presented: Exhibit A—Micah the idol worshiper. Exhibit B—the greedy Levite. Exhibit C—the idolatrous tribe of Dan. If time is short, focus on Judges 17:1–13.

Micah's Idols

17 Now a man named Micah
from the hill country of
Ephraim 2said to his mother, "The
eleven hundred shekels[a] of silver that
were taken from you and about which
I heard you utter a curse—I have that
silver with me; I took it."
Then his mother said, "The LORD
bless you, my son!"
3When he returned the eleven hundred shekels of silver to his mother, she
said, "I solemnly consecrate my silver to
the LORD for my son to make a carved
image and a cast idol. I will give it back
to you."
4So he returned the silver to his mother, and she took two hundred shekels[b] of
silver and gave them to a silversmith,
who made them into the image and the
idol. And they were put in Micah's house.
5Now this man Micah had a shrine,
and he made an ephod and some idols
and installed one of his sons as his
priest. 6In those days Israel had no king;
everyone did as he saw fit.
7A young Levite from Bethlehem in
Judah, who had been living within the
clan of Judah, 8left that town in search
of some other place to stay. On his way[c]
he came to Micah's house in the hill
country of Ephraim.
9Micah asked him, "Where are you
from?"
"I'm a Levite from Bethlehem in Judah," he said, "and I'm looking for a
place to stay."
10Then Micah said to him, "Live with
me and be my father and priest, and I'll
give you ten shekels[d] of silver a year, your
clothes and your food." 11So the Levite
agreed to live with him, and the young
man was to him like one of his sons.
12Then Micah installed the Levite, and the
young man became his priest and lived
in his house. 13And Micah said, "Now I
know that the LORD will be good to me,
since this Levite has become my priest."

Danites Settle in Laish

18 In those days Israel had no
king.
And in those days the tribe of the
Danites was seeking a place of their own
where they might settle, because they
had not yet come into an inheritance
among the tribes of Israel. 2So the Danites sent five warriors from Zorah and
Eshtaol to spy out the land and explore
it. These men represented all their clans.
They told them, "Go, explore the land."
The men entered the hill country of
Ephraim and came to the house of Micah, where they spent the night. 3When
they were near Micah's house, they recognized the voice of the young Levite;
so they turned in there and asked him,
"Who brought you here? What are you
doing in this place? Why are you here?"
4He told them what Micah had done
for him, and said, "He has hired me and
I am his priest."
5Then they said to him, "Please inquire of God to learn whether our journey will be successful."
6The priest answered them, "Go in
peace. Your journey has the LORD's approval."
7So the five men left and came to Laish, where they saw that the people
were living in safety, like the Sidonians,
unsuspecting and secure. And since
their land lacked nothing, they were
prosperous.[e] Also, they lived a long way
from the Sidonians and had no relationship with anyone else.[f]
8When they returned to Zorah and
Eshtaol, their brothers asked them,
"How did you find things?"
9They answered, "Come on, let's attack them! We have seen that the land
is very good. Aren't you going to do
something? Don't hesitate to go there
and take it over. 10When you get there,
you will find an unsuspecting people
and a spacious land that God has put
into your hands, a land that lacks nothing whatever."

[a]2 That is, about 28 pounds (about 13 kilograms)
[b]4 That is, about 5 pounds (about 2.3 kilograms)
[c]8 Or *To carry on his profession* [d]10 That is, about 4 ounces (about 110 grams) [e]7 The meaning of the Hebrew for this clause is uncertain. [f]7 Hebrew; some Septuagint manuscripts *with the Arameans*

[11]Then six hundred men from the clan of the Danites, armed for battle, set out from Zorah and Eshtaol. [12]On their way they set up camp near Kiriath Jearim in Judah. This is why the place west of Kiriath Jearim is called Mahaneh Dan[a] to this day. [13]From there they went on to the hill country of Ephraim and came to Micah's house.

[14]Then the five men who had spied out the land of Laish said to their brothers, "Do you know that one of these houses has an ephod, other household gods, a carved image and a cast idol? Now you know what to do." [15]So they turned in there and went to the house of the young Levite at Micah's place and greeted him. [16]The six hundred Danites, armed for battle, stood at the entrance to the gate. [17]The five men who had spied out the land went inside and took the carved image, the ephod, the other household gods and the cast idol while the priest and the six hundred armed men stood at the entrance to the gate.

[18]When these men went into Micah's house and took the carved image, the ephod, the other household gods and the cast idol, the priest said to them, "What are you doing?"

[19]They answered him, "Be quiet! Don't say a word. Come with us, and be our father and priest. Isn't it better that you serve a tribe and clan in Israel as priest rather than just one man's household?" [20]Then the priest was glad. He took the ephod, the other household gods and the carved image and went along with the people. [21]Putting their little children, their livestock and their possessions in front of them, they turned away and left.

[22]When they had gone some distance from Micah's house, the men who lived near Micah were called together and overtook the Danites. [23]As they shouted after them, the Danites turned and said to Micah, "What's the matter with you that you called out your men to fight?"

[24]He replied, "You took the gods I made, and my priest, and went away. What else do I have? How can you ask, 'What's the matter with you?' "

[25]The Danites answered, "Don't argue with us, or some hot-tempered men will attack you, and you and your family will lose your lives." [26]So the Danites went their way, and Micah, seeing that they were too strong for him, turned around and went back home.

[27]Then they took what Micah had made, and his priest, and went on to Laish, against a peaceful and unsuspecting people. They attacked them with the sword and burned down their city. [28]There was no one to rescue them because they lived a long way from Sidon and had no relationship with anyone else. The city was in a valley near Beth Rehob.

The Danites rebuilt the city and settled there. [29]They named it Dan after their forefather Dan, who was born to Israel—though the city used to be called Laish. [30]There the Danites set up for themselves the idols, and Jonathan son of Gershom, the son of Moses,[b] and his sons were priests for the tribe of Dan until the time of the captivity of the land. [31]They continued to use the idols Micah had made, all the time the house of God was in Shiloh.

[a]*12 Mahaneh Dan* means *Dan's camp.* [b]*30* An ancient Hebrew scribal tradition, some Septuagint manuscripts and Vulgate; Masoretic Text *Manasseh*

SHARPEN THE FOCUS

The dark history of Israel stands as stark testimony to human nature. This nation lived in an ideal environment. The Lord had given them fields they hadn't cleared, houses they hadn't built, wealth they hadn't earned, vineyards and orchards they hadn't planted.

On top of that, He had given them His Word, His commandments, His promises, and His love. He had marched with them into battle and had utterly demolished their enemies before their eyes.

If *any* human beings in all of recorded history had been able to trust and obey the Lord, these people should have been. But they didn't. They couldn't. They—like we had zero ability to walk in God's ways. They proved Paul's verdict in Romans 3:20—"Therefore no one will be declared righteous [right with God] . . . by observing the law."

God did not give up on Israel. He had promised Abraham that the Savior would be born from this people in this land. And He intended—fully—to keep His Word.

You and I have dark histories of our own. Still, God has not given up on us. Why not? For the sake of the Savior whom He has indeed sent for the world and for us.

WEEK 22 • TUESDAY

Judges 19:1—20:48

Maybe you thought the events of Judges couldn't get any worse! But today's reading plunges us into the sewer of human depravity. It records the actions of people whose hearts have hardened beyond flint. Even the idol-worshipers in Israel are shocked—and they become the agents of the Lord's judgment. If time is short, focus on Judges 19:1–30.

A Levite and His Concubine

19 In those days Israel had no
king.
Now a Levite who lived in a remote
area in the hill country of Ephraim took
a concubine from Bethlehem in Judah.
2But she was unfaithful to him. She left
him and went back to her father's house
in Bethlehem, Judah. After she had been
there four months, 3her husband went
to her to persuade her to return. He had
with him his servant and two donkeys.
She took him into her father's house,
and when her father saw him, he gladly welcomed him. 4His father-in-law, the
girl's father, prevailed upon him to stay;
so he remained with him three days,
eating and drinking, and sleeping there.
5On the fourth day they got up early
and he prepared to leave, but the girl's
father said to his son-in-law, "Refresh
yourself with something to eat; then
you can go." 6So the two of them sat
down to eat and drink together. Afterward the girl's father said, "Please stay
tonight and enjoy yourself." 7And when
the man got up to go, his father-in-law
persuaded him, so he stayed there that
night. 8On the morning of the fifth day,
when he rose to go, the girl's father said,
"Refresh yourself. Wait till afternoon!"
So the two of them ate together.
9Then when the man, with his concubine and his servant, got up to leave, his
father-in-law, the girl's father, said,
"Now look, it's almost evening. Spend
the night here; the day is nearly over.
Stay and enjoy yourself. Early tomorrow morning you can get up and be on
your way home." 10But, unwilling to
stay another night, the man left and
went toward Jebus (that is, Jerusalem),
with his two saddled donkeys and his
concubine.
11When they were near Jebus and the
day was almost gone, the servant said
to his master, "Come, let's stop at this
city of the Jebusites and spend the
night."
12His master replied, "No. We won't

go into an alien city, whose people are not Israelites. We will go on to Gibeah." 13He added, "Come, let's try to reach Gibeah or Ramah and spend the night in one of those places." 14So they went on, and the sun set as they neared Gibeah in Benjamin. 15There they stopped to spend the night. They went and sat in the city square, but no one took them into his home for the night.

16That evening an old man from the hill country of Ephraim, who was living in Gibeah (the men of the place were Benjamites), came in from his work in the fields. 17When he looked and saw the traveler in the city square, the old man asked, "Where are you going? Where did you come from?"

18He answered, "We are on our way from Bethlehem in Judah to a remote area in the hill country of Ephraim where I live. I have been to Bethlehem in Judah and now I am going to the house of the LORD. No one has taken me into his house. 19We have both straw and fodder for our donkeys and bread and wine for ourselves your servants—me, your maidservant, and the young man with us. We don't need anything."

20"You are welcome at my house," the old man said. "Let me supply whatever you need. Only don't spend the night in the square." 21So he took him into his house and fed his donkeys. After they had washed their feet, they had something to eat and drink.

22While they were enjoying themselves, some of the wicked men of the city surrounded the house. Pounding on the door, they shouted to the old man who owned the house, "Bring out the man who came to your house so we can have sex with him."

23The owner of the house went outside and said to them, "No, my friends, don't be so vile. Since this man is my guest, don't do this disgraceful thing. 24Look, here is my virgin daughter, and his concubine. I will bring them out to you now, and you can use them and do to them whatever you wish. But to this man, don't do such a disgraceful thing."

25But the men would not listen to him. So the man took his concubine and sent her outside to them, and they raped her and abused her throughout the night, and at dawn they let her go. 26At daybreak the woman went back to the house where her master was staying, fell down at the door and lay there until daylight.

27When her master got up in the morning and opened the door of the house and stepped out to continue on his way, there lay his concubine, fallen in the doorway of the house, with her hands on the threshold. 28He said to her, "Get up; let's go." But there was no answer. Then the man put her on his donkey and set out for home.

29When he reached home, he took a knife and cut up his concubine, limb by limb, into twelve parts and sent them into all the areas of Israel. 30Everyone who saw it said, "Such a thing has never been seen or done, not since the day the Israelites came up out of Egypt. Think about it! Consider it! Tell us what to do!"

Israelites Fight the Benjamites

20 Then all the Israelites from Dan to Beersheba and from the land of Gilead came out as one man and assembled before the LORD in Mizpah. 2The leaders of all the people of the tribes of Israel took their places in the assembly of the people of God, four hundred thousand soldiers armed with swords. 3(The Benjamites heard that the Israelites had gone up to Mizpah.) Then the Israelites said, "Tell us how this awful thing happened."

4So the Levite, the husband of the murdered woman, said, "I and my concubine came to Gibeah in Benjamin to spend the night. 5During the night the men of Gibeah came after me and surrounded the house, intending to kill me. They raped my concubine, and she died. 6I took my concubine, cut her into pieces and sent one piece to each region of Israel's inheritance, because they committed this lewd and disgraceful act in Israel. 7Now, all you Israelites, speak up and give your verdict."

8All the people rose as one man, saying, "None of us will go home. No, not one of us will return to his house. 9But now this is what we'll do to Gibeah: We'll go up against it as the lot directs. 10We'll take ten men out of every hundred from all the tribes of Israel, and a hundred from a thousand, and a thousand from ten thousand, to get provisions for the army. Then, when the army arrives at Gibeah[a] in Benjamin, it can give them what they deserve for all this vileness done in Israel." 11So all the men of Israel got together and united as one man against the city.

12The tribes of Israel sent men throughout the tribe of Benjamin, saying, "What about this awful crime that was committed among you? 13Now surrender those wicked men of Gibeah so that we may put them to death and purge the evil from Israel."

But the Benjamites would not listen to their fellow Israelites. 14From their towns they came together at Gibeah to fight against the Israelites. 15At once the Benjamites mobilized twenty-six thousand swordsmen from their towns, in addition to seven hundred chosen men from those living in Gibeah. 16Among all these soldiers there were seven hundred chosen men who were left-handed, each of whom could sling a stone at a hair and not miss.

17Israel, apart from Benjamin, mustered four hundred thousand swordsmen, all of them fighting men.

18The Israelites went up to Bethel[b] and inquired of God. They said, "Who of us shall go first to fight against the Benjamites?"

The LORD replied, "Judah shall go first."

19The next morning the Israelites got up and pitched camp near Gibeah. 20The men of Israel went out to fight the Benjamites and took up battle positions against them at Gibeah. 21The Benjamites came out of Gibeah and cut down twenty-two thousand Israelites on the battlefield that day. 22But the men of Israel encouraged one another and again took up their positions where they had stationed themselves the first day. 23The Israelites went up and wept before the LORD until evening, and they inquired of the LORD. They said, "Shall we go up again to battle against the Benjamites, our brothers?"

The LORD answered, "Go up against them."

24Then the Israelites drew near to Benjamin the second day. 25This time, when the Benjamites came out from Gibeah to oppose them, they cut down another eighteen thousand Israelites, all of them armed with swords.

26Then the Israelites, all the people, went up to Bethel, and there they sat weeping before the LORD. They fasted that day until evening and presented burnt offerings and fellowship offerings[c] to the LORD. 27And the Israelites inquired of the LORD. (In those days the ark of the covenant of God was there, 28with Phinehas son of Eleazar, the son of Aaron, ministering before it.) They asked, "Shall we go up again to battle with Benjamin our brother, or not?"

The LORD responded, "Go, for tomorrow I will give them into your hands."

29Then Israel set an ambush around Gibeah. 30They went up against the Benjamites on the third day and took up positions against Gibeah as they had done before. 31The Benjamites came out to meet them and were drawn away from the city. They began to inflict casualties on the Israelites as before, so that about thirty men fell in the open field and on the roads—the one leading to Bethel and the other to Gibeah.

32While the Benjamites were saying, "We are defeating them as before," the Israelites were saying, "Let's retreat and draw them away from the city to the roads."

33All the men of Israel moved from their places and took up positions at Baal Tamar, and the Israelite ambush

[a]10 One Hebrew manuscript; most Hebrew manuscripts *Geba,* a variant of *Gibeah* [b]18 Or *to the house of God;* also in verse 26
[c]26 Traditionally *peace offerings*

charged out of its place on the west[a] of Gibeah.[b] 34 Then ten thousand of Israel's finest men made a frontal attack on Gibeah. The fighting was so heavy that the Benjamites did not realize how near disaster was. 35 The LORD defeated Benjamin before Israel, and on that day the Israelites struck down 25,100 Benjamites, all armed with swords. 36 Then the Benjamites saw that they were beaten.

Now the men of Israel had given way before Benjamin, because they relied on the ambush they had set near Gibeah. 37 The men who had been in ambush made a sudden dash into Gibeah, spread out and put the whole city to the sword. 38 The men of Israel had arranged with the ambush that they should send up a great cloud of smoke from the city, 39 and then the men of Israel would turn in the battle.

The Benjamites had begun to inflict casualties on the men of Israel (about thirty), and they said, "We are defeating them as in the first battle." 40 But when the column of smoke began to rise from the city, the Benjamites turned and saw the smoke of the whole city going up into the sky. 41 Then the men of Israel turned on them, and the men of Benjamin were terrified, because they realized that disaster had come upon them. 42 So they fled before the Israelites in the direction of the desert, but they could not escape the battle. And the men of Israel who came out of the towns cut them down there. 43 They surrounded the Benjamites, chased them and easily[c] overran them in the vicinity of Gibeah on the east. 44 Eighteen thousand Benjamites fell, all of them valiant fighters. 45 As they turned and fled toward the desert to the rock of Rimmon, the Israelites cut down five thousand men along the roads. They kept pressing after the Benjamites as far as Gidom and struck down two thousand more.

46 On that day twenty-five thousand Benjamite swordsmen fell, all of them valiant fighters. 47 But six hundred men turned and fled into the desert to the rock of Rimmon, where they stayed four months. 48 The men of Israel went back to Benjamin and put all the towns to the sword, including the animals and everything else they found. All the towns they came across they set on fire.

[a]33 Some Septuagint manuscripts and Vulgate; the meaning of the Hebrew for this word is uncertain. [b]33 Hebrew *Geba,* a variant of *Gibeah* [c]43 The meaning of the Hebrew for this word is uncertain.

SHARPEN THE FOCUS

Gang rape. Sodomy. Murder. Dismemberment. Are we reading some pornographic magazine from today's newsstand? You know the answer. Human nature hasn't changed. We're sinners. Then. And now.

But maybe as you read today's account or as you see the news on TV each evening, you find a thought tickling your mind that goes something like this: "I would *never* do such a thing. How awful those people are!"

The moment we entertain that thought, the trap snaps shut. Satan has us. The truth is that any of us are capable of the most heinous crimes. Given the right set of circumstances, you and I could find ourselves acting just like the residents of Gibeah. That truth may be hard to believe, even to fathom. Scriptures make it plain—apart from the grace of God in Christ, we cannot claim to be any different than the worst sinners.

But we need not despair. In fact, we can find eternal comfort in the "no difference" truths of Scripture. Yes, all have sinned. And yet Christ also died for all! My self-righteousness. Your greed or selfishness. Someone else's adultery or homicide. God nailed all of it to Christ's cross.

There *is* no difference. And we can thank God for that!

WEEK 22 • WEDNESDAY

Judges 21:1–25

GET THE BIG PICTURE

Justice demanded that all Israel hold the tribe of Benjamin accountable. But the civil war Israel started went far beyond justice—almost to the point of genocide.

Now Israel had a problem. How could they let this tribe disappear? Rather than repent of their foolish oath, they schemed until they had concocted a two-pronged solution. Chapter 21 reports it. If time is short, focus on Judges 21:1–15.

Wives for the Benjamites

21 The men of Israel had taken
an oath at Mizpah: "Not one
of us will give his daughter in marriage
to a Benjamite."
2The people went to Bethel,[a] where
they sat before God until evening, raising their voices and weeping bitterly.
3"O LORD, the God of Israel," they cried,
"why has this happened to Israel? Why
should one tribe be missing from Israel
today?"
4Early the next day the people built an
altar and presented burnt offerings and
fellowship offerings.[b]
5Then the Israelites asked, "Who from
all the tribes of Israel has failed to assemble before the LORD?" For they had taken
a solemn oath that anyone who failed to
assemble before the LORD at Mizpah
should certainly be put to death.
6Now the Israelites grieved for their
brothers, the Benjamites. "Today one
tribe is cut off from Israel," they said.
7"How can we provide wives for those
who are left, since we have taken an
oath by the LORD not to give them any
of our daughters in marriage?" 8Then
they asked, "Which one of the tribes of
Israel failed to assemble before the LORD
at Mizpah?" They discovered that no
one from Jabesh Gilead had come to the
camp for the assembly. 9For when they
counted the people, they found that
none of the people of Jabesh Gilead
were there.
10So the assembly sent twelve thousand fighting men with instructions to
go to Jabesh Gilead and put to the
sword those living there, including the
women and children. 11"This is what
you are to do," they said. "Kill every
male and every woman who is not a
virgin." 12They found among the people
living in Jabesh Gilead four hundred
young women who had never slept
with a man, and they took them to the
camp at Shiloh in Canaan.
13Then the whole assembly sent an offer of peace to the Benjamites at the rock
of Rimmon. 14So the Benjamites returned at that time and were given the
women of Jabesh Gilead who had been
spared. But there were not enough for
all of them.
15The people grieved for Benjamin,
because the LORD had made a gap in the
tribes of Israel. 16And the elders of the
assembly said, "With the women of Benjamin destroyed, how shall we provide
wives for the men who are left? 17The
Benjamite survivors must have heirs,"
they said, "so that a tribe of Israel will
not be wiped out. 18We can't give them
our daughters as wives, since we Israelites have taken this oath: 'Cursed be
anyone who gives a wife to a Benjamite.' 19But look, there is the annual festival of the LORD in Shiloh, to the north
of Bethel, and east of the road that goes

[a]2 Or *to the house of God* [b]4 Traditionally *peace offerings*

from Bethel to Shechem, and to the
south of Lebonah."
20So they instructed the Benjamites,
saying, "Go and hide in the vineyards
21and watch. When the girls of Shiloh
come out to join in the dancing, then
rush from the vineyards and each of
you seize a wife from the girls of Shiloh
and go to the land of Benjamin. 22When
their fathers or brothers complain to us,
we will say to them, 'Do us a kindness
by helping them, because we did not get
wives for them during the war, and you
are innocent, since you did not give
your daughters to them.' "
23So that is what the Benjamites did.
While the girls were dancing, each man
caught one and carried her off to be his
wife. Then they returned to their inheritance and rebuilt the towns and settled
in them.
24At that time the Israelites left that
place and went home to their tribes and
clans, each to his own inheritance.
25In those days Israel had no king;
everyone did as he saw fit.

SHARPEN THE FOCUS

Sooner or later in childhood most of us begin to notice that one lie often leads to another lie which then leads to a third. The cover-up can leave us dizzy as we try to remember what we told whom when.

Other sins work that way, too, as Israel found out in the incident you read about today. Instead of seeing their oath for what it was—a statement forged in the fires of fury and a desire for revenge—the Israelites decided to follow through. Instead of asking God for forgiveness and trusting in His mercy to grant it, they bulldozed their way through on their original course. Who knows how much suffering followed in who knows how many families. The Bible promises:

He who conceals his sins does not prosper,
but whoever confesses and renounces them finds mercy. (Proverbs 28:13)

May God grant us His grace to do just that—for our own good and for the good of those around us.

RUTH

WEEK 22 • THURSDAY

Ruth 1:1—2:23

GET THE BIG PICTURE

The contrast, desert versus oasis, pictures quite accurately the differences between the book of Judges and the book of Ruth. We've been walking through a spiritual desert for the past few weeks. Now it's time to take off our sandals and let the Lord refresh us with the story of His faithful love at work. If time is short, focus on Ruth 1:1–2:12.

Naomi and Ruth

1 In the days when the judges ruled,[a]
there was a famine in the land, and
a man from Bethlehem in Judah, together with his wife and two sons, went
to live for a while in the country of
Moab. 2The man's name was Elimelech,
his wife's name Naomi, and the names
of his two sons were Mahlon and Kilion. They were Ephrathites from Bethlehem, Judah. And they went to Moab
and lived there.
3Now Elimelech, Naomi's husband,
died, and she was left with her two sons.
4They married Moabite women, one
named Orpah and the other Ruth. After they had lived there about ten years,
5both Mahlon and Kilion also died, and
Naomi was left without her two sons
and her husband.
6When she heard in Moab that the
LORD had come to the aid of his people
by providing food for them, Naomi and
her daughters-in-law prepared to return home from there. 7With her two
daughters-in-law she left the place
where she had been living and set out
on the road that would take them back
to the land of Judah.
8Then Naomi said to her two daughters-in-law, "Go back, each of you, to
your mother's home. May the LORD
show kindness to you, as you have
shown to your dead and to me. 9May
the LORD grant that each of you will find
rest in the home of another husband."
Then she kissed them and they wept
aloud 10and said to her, "We will go back
with you to your people."
11But Naomi said, "Return home, my
daughters. Why would you come with
me? Am I going to have any more sons,
who could become your husbands?
12Return home, my daughters; I am too
old to have another husband. Even if I
thought there was still hope for me—
even if I had a husband tonight and
then gave birth to sons— 13would you
wait until they grew up? Would you remain unmarried for them? No, my
daughters. It is more bitter for me than
for you, because the LORD's hand has
gone out against me!"
14At this they wept again. Then Orpah
kissed her mother-in-law good-by, but
Ruth clung to her.

[a]1 Traditionally *judged*

15"Look," said Naomi, "your sister-in-law is going back to her people and her gods. Go back with her."

16But Ruth replied, "Don't urge me to leave you or to turn back from you. Where you go I will go, and where you stay I will stay. Your people will be my people and your God my God. 17Where you die I will die, and there I will be buried. May the LORD deal with me, be it ever so severely, if anything but death separates you and me." 18When Naomi realized that Ruth was determined to go with her, she stopped urging her.

19So the two women went on until they came to Bethlehem. When they arrived in Bethlehem, the whole town was stirred because of them, and the women exclaimed, "Can this be Naomi?"

20"Don't call me Naomi,[a]" she told them. "Call me Mara,[b] because the Almighty[c] has made my life very bitter. 21I went away full, but the LORD has brought me back empty. Why call me Naomi? The LORD has afflicted[d] me; the Almighty has brought misfortune upon me."

22So Naomi returned from Moab accompanied by Ruth the Moabitess, her daughter-in-law, arriving in Bethlehem as the barley harvest was beginning.

Ruth Meets Boaz

2 Now Naomi had a relative on her husband's side, from the clan of Elimelech, a man of standing, whose name was Boaz.

2And Ruth the Moabitess said to Naomi, "Let me go to the fields and pick up the leftover grain behind anyone in whose eyes I find favor."

Naomi said to her, "Go ahead, my daughter." 3So she went out and began to glean in the fields behind the harvesters. As it turned out, she found herself working in a field belonging to Boaz, who was from the clan of Elimelech.

4Just then Boaz arrived from Bethlehem and greeted the harvesters, "The LORD be with you!"

"The LORD bless you!" they called back.

5Boaz asked the foreman of his harvesters, "Whose young woman is that?"

6The foreman replied, "She is the Moabitess who came back from Moab with Naomi. 7She said, 'Please let me glean and gather among the sheaves behind the harvesters.' She went into the field and has worked steadily from morning till now, except for a short rest in the shelter."

8So Boaz said to Ruth, "My daughter, listen to me. Don't go and glean in another field and don't go away from here. Stay here with my servant girls. 9Watch the field where the men are harvesting, and follow along after the girls. I have told the men not to touch you. And whenever you are thirsty, go and get a drink from the water jars the men have filled."

10At this, she bowed down with her face to the ground. She exclaimed, "Why have I found such favor in your eyes that you notice me—a foreigner?"

11Boaz replied, "I've been told all about what you have done for your mother-in-law since the death of your husband—how you left your father and mother and your homeland and came to live with a people you did not know before. 12May the LORD repay you for what you have done. May you be richly rewarded by the LORD, the God of Israel, under whose wings you have come to take refuge."

13"May I continue to find favor in your eyes, my lord," she said. "You have given me comfort and have spoken kindly to your servant—though I do not have the standing of one of your servant girls."

14At mealtime Boaz said to her, "Come over here. Have some bread and dip it in the wine vinegar."

When she sat down with the harvesters, he offered her some roasted grain. She ate all she wanted and had some left over. 15As she got up to glean, Boaz gave orders to his men, "Even if she gathers

[a]20 *Naomi* means *pleasant*; also in verse 21. [b]20 *Mara* means *bitter*. [c]20 Hebrew *Shaddai*; also in verse 21 [d]21 Or *has testified against*

among the sheaves, don't embarrass her. [16]Rather, pull out some stalks for her from the bundles and leave them for her to pick up, and don't rebuke her."

[17]So Ruth gleaned in the field until evening. Then she threshed the barley she had gathered, and it amounted to about an ephah.[a] [18]She carried it back to town, and her mother-in-law saw how much she had gathered. Ruth also brought out and gave her what she had left over after she had eaten enough.

[19]Her mother-in-law asked her, "Where did you glean today? Where did you work? Blessed be the man who took notice of you!"

Then Ruth told her mother-in-law about the one at whose place she had been working. "The name of the man I worked with today is Boaz," she said.

[20]"The LORD bless him!" Naomi said to her daughter-in-law. "He has not stopped showing his kindness to the living and the dead." She added, "That man is our close relative; he is one of our kinsman-redeemers."

[21]Then Ruth the Moabitess said, "He even said to me, 'Stay with my workers until they finish harvesting all my grain.' "

[22]Naomi said to Ruth her daughter-in-law, "It will be good for you, my daughter, to go with his girls, because in someone else's field you might be harmed."

[23]So Ruth stayed close to the servant girls of Boaz to glean until the barley and wheat harvests were finished. And she lived with her mother-in-law.

[a]17 That is, probably about 3/5 bushel (about 22 liters)

SHARPEN THE FOCUS

"I'm disappointed in God." Few Christians will say those words right out loud. They sound so harsh. But Naomi admitted her disappointment without flinching. "Call me Bitter [Mara] from now on," she said in essence.

Life had dealt Naomi a cruel hand. Maybe at some time or another you've felt as bitter as Naomi. Maybe you're tempted to feel that way right now. The education you wanted but couldn't afford. The child or spouse who walked away. The friend who betrayed you. The job you wanted but couldn't land. The illness that won't respond to treatment.

These are all serious disappointments. Not even pious words can stop the pain or ease the anguish. Sometimes they make the hurt worse. Sometimes they may even deepen the bitterness.

It's worth noting though, that even while Naomi suffers, even while she rails against the Lord, He is still on her side. Not her honesty, not her doubt, not even her bitterness can stop His care for her. First through Ruth, then through Boaz, God provides for His beloved daughter. And, as we will see in chapter 4, God provides the ultimate care for us and for her through her great-great-great-great . . . grandson, the Lord Jesus.

The book of Ruth takes on new meaning when you keep in mind the concept of kinsman-redeemer. Boaz was Ruth's kinsman-redeemer. As such, he is a picture or, more strictly speaking, a "type" of Christ. Before you read from Ruth, review the Law regarding the "kinsman-redeemer" from Leviticus 25:25. If time is short, focus on Ruth 4:1–22.

Ruth and Boaz at the Threshing Floor

3 One day Naomi her mother-in-
law said to her, "My daughter,
should I not try to find a home[a] for you,
where you will be well provided for? 2Is
not Boaz, with whose servant girls you
have been, a kinsman of ours? Tonight
he will be winnowing barley on the
threshing floor. 3Wash and perfume
yourself, and put on your best clothes.
Then go down to the threshing floor,
but don't let him know you are there
until he has finished eating and drinking. 4When he lies down, note the place
where he is lying. Then go and uncover
his feet and lie down. He will tell you
what to do."
5"I will do whatever you say," Ruth
answered. 6So she went down to the
threshing floor and did everything her
mother-in-law told her to do.
7When Boaz had finished eating and
drinking and was in good spirits, he
went over to lie down at the far end of
the grain pile. Ruth approached quietly,
uncovered his feet and lay down. 8In the
middle of the night something startled
the man, and he turned and discovered
a woman lying at his feet.
9"Who are you?" he asked.
"I am your servant Ruth," she said.
"Spread the corner of your garment
over me, since you are a kinsman-redeemer."
10"The LORD bless you, my daughter,"
he replied. "This kindness is greater
than that which you showed earlier:
You have not run after the younger
men, whether rich or poor. 11And now,
my daughter, don't be afraid. I will do
for you all you ask. All my fellow townsmen know that you are a woman of
noble character. 12Although it is true that
I am near of kin, there is a kinsman-
redeemer nearer than I. 13Stay here for
the night, and in the morning if he
wants to redeem, good; let him redeem.
But if he is not willing, as surely as the
LORD lives I will do it. Lie here until
morning."
14So she lay at his feet until morning,
but got up before anyone could be recognized; and he said, "Don't let it be
known that a woman came to the
threshing floor."
15He also said, "Bring me the shawl
you are wearing and hold it out." When
she did so, he poured into it six measures of barley and put it on her. Then
he[b] went back to town.
16When Ruth came to her mother-in-
law, Naomi asked, "How did it go, my
daughter?"
Then she told her everything Boaz
had done for her 17and added, "He gave
me these six measures of barley, saying,
'Don't go back to your mother-in-law
empty-handed.' "
18Then Naomi said, "Wait, my daughter, until you find out what happens. For

[a]*1* Hebrew *find rest* (see Ruth 1:9) [b]*15* Most Hebrew manuscripts; many Hebrew manuscripts, Vulgate and Syriac *she*

the man will not rest until the matter is
settled today."

Boaz Marries Ruth

4 Meanwhile Boaz went up to the
town gate and sat there. When
the kinsman-redeemer he had mentioned came along, Boaz said, "Come
over here, my friend, and sit down." So
he went over and sat down.
[2]Boaz took ten of the elders of the
town and said, "Sit here," and they did
so. [3]Then he said to the kinsman-
redeemer, "Naomi, who has come back
from Moab, is selling the piece of land
that belonged to our brother Elimelech.
[4]I thought I should bring the matter to
your attention and suggest that you buy
it in the presence of these seated here
and in the presence of the elders of my
people. If you will redeem it, do so. But
if you[a] will not, tell me, so I will know.
For no one has the right to do it except
you, and I am next in line."
"I will redeem it," he said.
[5]Then Boaz said, "On the day you buy
the land from Naomi and from Ruth the
Moabitess, you acquire[b] the dead man's
widow, in order to maintain the name
of the dead with his property."
[6]At this, the kinsman-redeemer said,
"Then I cannot redeem it because I
might endanger my own estate. You redeem it yourself. I cannot do it."
[7](Now in earlier times in Israel, for the
redemption and transfer of property to
become final, one party took off his sandal and gave it to the other. This was the
method of legalizing transactions in Israel.)
[8]So the kinsman-redeemer said to
Boaz, "Buy it yourself." And he removed
his sandal.
[9]Then Boaz announced to the elders
and all the people, "Today you are witnesses that I have bought from Naomi
all the property of Elimelech, Kilion and
Mahlon. [10]I have also acquired Ruth the
Moabitess, Mahlon's widow, as my wife,
in order to maintain the name of the
dead with his property, so that his name
will not disappear from among his family or from the town records. Today you
are witnesses!"
[11]Then the elders and all those at the
gate said, "We are witnesses. May the
LORD make the woman who is coming
into your home like Rachel and Leah,
who together built up the house of Israel. May you have standing in Ephrathah and be famous in Bethlehem.
[12]Through the offspring the LORD gives
you by this young woman, may your
family be like that of Perez, whom Tamar
bore to Judah."

The Genealogy of David

[13]So Boaz took Ruth and she became
his wife. Then he went to her, and the
LORD enabled her to conceive, and she
gave birth to a son. [14]The women said to
Naomi: "Praise be to the LORD, who this
day has not left you without a kinsman-
redeemer. May he become famous
throughout Israel! [15]He will renew your
life and sustain you in your old age. For
your daughter-in-law, who loves you
and who is better to you than seven
sons, has given him birth."
[16]Then Naomi took the child, laid him
in her lap and cared for him. [17]The wom-
en living there said, "Naomi has a son."
And they named him Obed. He was the
father of Jesse, the father of David.
[18]This, then, is the family line of Perez:

Perez was the father of Hezron,
[19]Hezron the father of Ram,
Ram the father of Amminadab,
[20]Amminadab the father of Nahshon,
Nahshon the father of Salmon,[c]
[21]Salmon the father of Boaz,
Boaz the father of Obed,
[22]Obed the father of Jesse,
and Jesse the father of David.

[a]4 Many Hebrew manuscripts, Septuagint, Vulgate and Syriac; most Hebrew manuscripts *he*
[b]5 Hebrew; Vulgate and Syriac *Naomi, you acquire Ruth the Moabitess,* [c]20 A few Hebrew manuscripts, some Septuagint manuscripts and Vulgate (see also verse 21 and Septuagint of 1 Chron. 2:11); most Hebrew manuscripts *Salma*

SHARPEN THE FOCUS

Have you ever needed someone to champion your cause? the cavalry to ride to your rescue? an ally to speak up in your defense? Did the help you needed materialize? If so, you have some idea of what Ruth and Naomi experienced in Boaz.

Boaz, the kinsman-redeemer is like our Lord Jesus in many ways. Here are a few. Maybe you can think of others:

- The kinsman-redeemer had to be a close family member. Jesus is our Brother. (Hebrews 2:14–17)
- The kinsman-redeemer had to be *able* to pay the price of redemption. The price Jesus paid to redeem us was His own blood. (1 Peter 1:18–19)
- The kinsman-redeemer had to be *willing* to pay the price of redemption. Jesus loved us so much that He died to redeem us. (John 17:24)

The women in Bethlehem blessed Naomi. You can claim that same blessing today:

> *Praise be to the LORD, who this day has not left you without a kinsman-redeemer. May he become famous!* (Ruth 4:14)

1 SAMUEL

WEEK 22 • SATURDAY

1 Samuel 1:1–28

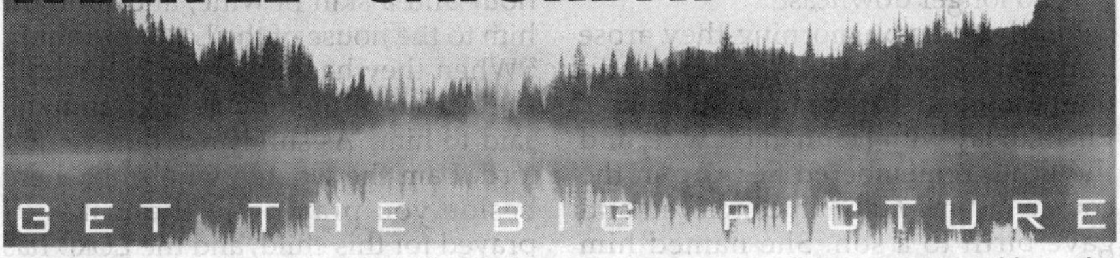

Not since the prayer of Abraham for Sodom have we read such an earnest petition. The person you will meet today came before heaven's throne with a heavy heart. But she left rejoicing. As you read, ask yourself what accounts for her change of attitude. If time is short, focus on 1 Samuel 1:1–18.

The Birth of Samuel

1 There was a certain man from
Ramathaim, a Zuphite[a] from the hill
country of Ephraim, whose name was
Elkanah son of Jeroham, the son of Elihu, the son of Tohu, the son of Zuph, an
Ephraimite. 2He had two wives; one
was called Hannah and the other Peninnah. Peninnah had children, but Hannah had none.
3Year after year this man went up
from his town to worship and sacrifice
to the LORD Almighty at Shiloh, where
Hophni and Phinehas, the two sons of
Eli, were priests of the LORD. 4Whenever
the day came for Elkanah to sacrifice, he
would give portions of the meat to his
wife Peninnah and to all her sons and
daughters. 5But to Hannah he gave a
double portion because he loved her,
and the LORD had closed her womb.
6And because the LORD had closed her
womb, her rival kept provoking her in
order to irritate her. 7This went on year
after year. Whenever Hannah went up
to the house of the LORD, her rival provoked her till she wept and would not
eat. 8Elkanah her husband would say to
her, "Hannah, why are you weeping?
Why don't you eat? Why are you down-
hearted? Don't I mean more to you than
ten sons?"
9Once when they had finished eating
and drinking in Shiloh, Hannah stood
up. Now Eli the priest was sitting on a
chair by the doorpost of the LORD's
temple.[b] 10In bitterness of soul Hannah
wept much and prayed to the LORD.
11And she made a vow, saying, "O LORD
Almighty, if you will only look upon
your servant's misery and remember
me, and not forget your servant but give
her a son, then I will give him to the
LORD for all the days of his life, and no
razor will ever be used on his head."
12As she kept on praying to the LORD,
Eli observed her mouth. 13Hannah was
praying in her heart, and her lips were
moving but her voice was not heard. Eli
thought she was drunk 14and said to her,
"How long will you keep on getting
drunk? Get rid of your wine."
15"Not so, my lord," Hannah replied,
"I am a woman who is deeply troubled.
I have not been drinking wine or beer;
I was pouring out my soul to the LORD.
16Do not take your servant for a wicked

[a]1 Or *from Ramathaim Zuphim* [b]9 That is, tabernacle

woman; I have been praying here out of
my great anguish and grief."
17Eli answered, "Go in peace, and may
the God of Israel grant you what you
have asked of him."
18She said, "May your servant find favor in your eyes." Then she went her
way and ate something, and her face
was no longer downcast.
19Early the next morning they arose
and worshiped before the LORD and
then went back to their home at Ramah.
Elkanah lay with Hannah his wife, and
the LORD remembered her. 20So in the
course of time Hannah conceived and
gave birth to a son. She named him
Samuel,[a] saying, "Because I asked the
LORD for him."

Hannah Dedicates Samuel

21When the man Elkanah went up
with all his family to offer the annual
sacrifice to the LORD and to fulfill his
vow, 22Hannah did not go. She said to
her husband, "After the boy is weaned,
I will take him and present him before
the LORD, and he will live there always."
23"Do what seems best to you," Elkanah her husband told her. "Stay here
until you have weaned him; only may
the LORD make good his[b] word." So the
woman stayed at home and nursed her
son until she had weaned him.
24After he was weaned, she took the
boy with her, young as he was, along
with a three-year-old bull,[c] an ephah[d] of
flour and a skin of wine, and brought
him to the house of the LORD at Shiloh.
25When they had slaughtered the bull,
they brought the boy to Eli, 26and she
said to him, "As surely as you live, my
lord, I am the woman who stood here
beside you praying to the LORD. 27I
prayed for this child, and the LORD has
granted me what I asked of him. 28So
now I give him to the LORD. For his
whole life he will be given over to the
LORD." And he worshiped the LORD
there.

[a]20 *Samuel* sounds like the Hebrew for *heard of God.* [b]23 Masoretic Text; Dead Sea Scrolls, Septuagint and Syriac *your* [c]24 Dead Sea Scrolls, Septuagint and Syriac; Masoretic Text *with three bulls* [d]24 That is, probably about 3/5 bushel (about 22 liters)

SHARPEN THE FOCUS

Childlessness carried a special stigma in Old Testament Israel. Many couples today share Hannah's pain. It hurt then, just as it hurts now.

Maybe Hannah had brought her problem to the Lord many times before. Or maybe this prayer was her first about this need. What matters is that while she prayed, the Lord took her burden and gave her His peace in exchange. He did this *before* Hannah knew whether or not He would do what she had asked about a son. His Spirit filled her heart with the faith to believe that the Lord was her Savior-God. He would make good things happen for her.

When we take our burdens to our Lord, we can be sure He hears and will answer us. He has only two responses to our requests. He may say, "Yes, your petition is granted." Or, "I have something even better in mind for you."

Hannah's prayer for a son is an example of the first kind of answer. Abraham's prayer for Sodom was answered in the second way—the Lord spared Lot's life and at the same time got Lot and his family out of the unholy culture in which they had chosen to live (Genesis 18:16–19:29).

What burden will you bring in prayer before your heavenly King today?

The Savior-God gave Hannah peace, and He also granted her request for a son. Her song of praise sounds much like Mary's song in Luke 1:46–55. But Hannah's response to the Lord's kindness stands in sharp contrast against the faithlessness in Israel at the time. As you will read today, even the priests despised the Lord and His worship! If time is short, focus on 1 Samuel 2:1–11.

Hannah's Prayer

2 Then Hannah prayed and said:

"My heart rejoices in the LORD;
in the LORD my horn[a] is lifted high.
My mouth boasts over my enemies,
for I delight in your deliverance.

2 "There is no one holy[b] like the LORD;
there is no one besides you;
there is no Rock like our God.

3 "Do not keep talking so proudly
or let your mouth speak such arrogance,
for the LORD is a God who knows,
and by him deeds are weighed.

4 "The bows of the warriors are broken,
but those who stumbled are armed with strength.
5 Those who were full hire themselves out for food,
but those who were hungry hunger no more.
She who was barren has borne seven children,
but she who has had many sons pines away.

6 "The LORD brings death and makes alive;
he brings down to the grave[c] and raises up.
7 The LORD sends poverty and wealth;
he humbles and he exalts.
8 He raises the poor from the dust
and lifts the needy from the ash heap;
he seats them with princes
and has them inherit a throne of honor.

"For the foundations of the earth are the LORD's;
upon them he has set the world.
9 He will guard the feet of his saints,
but the wicked will be silenced in darkness.

"It is not by strength that one prevails;
10 those who oppose the LORD will be shattered.
He will thunder against them from heaven;
the LORD will judge the ends of the earth.

"He will give strength to his king
and exalt the horn of his anointed."

11 Then Elkanah went home to Ramah,
but the boy ministered before the LORD
under Eli the priest.

Eli's Wicked Sons

12 Eli's sons were wicked men; they
had no regard for the LORD. 13 Now it
was the practice of the priests with the
people that whenever anyone offered a
sacrifice and while the meat was being

[a] 1 *Horn* here symbolizes strength; also in verse 10. [b] 2 Or *no Holy One* [c] 6 Hebrew *Sheol*

boiled, the servant of the priest would
come with a three-pronged fork in his
hand. 14He would plunge it into the
pan or kettle or caldron or pot, and the
priest would take for himself whatever
the fork brought up. This is how they
treated all the Israelites who came to
Shiloh. 15But even before the fat was
burned, the servant of the priest would
come and say to the man who was sacrificing, "Give the priest some meat to
roast; he won't accept boiled meat from
you, but only raw."

16If the man said to him, "Let the fat
be burned up first, and then take whatever you want," the servant would then
answer, "No, hand it over now; if you
don't, I'll take it by force."

17This sin of the young men was very
great in the LORD's sight, for they[a] were
treating the LORD's offering with contempt.

18But Samuel was ministering before
the LORD—a boy wearing a linen
ephod. 19Each year his mother made
him a little robe and took it to him when
she went up with her husband to offer
the annual sacrifice. 20Eli would bless
Elkanah and his wife, saying, "May the
LORD give you children by this woman
to take the place of the one she prayed
for and gave to the LORD." Then they
would go home. 21And the LORD was
gracious to Hannah; she conceived and
gave birth to three sons and two daughters. Meanwhile, the boy Samuel grew
up in the presence of the LORD.

22Now Eli, who was very old, heard
about everything his sons were doing to
all Israel and how they slept with the
women who served at the entrance to
the Tent of Meeting. 23So he said to them,
"Why do you do such things? I hear
from all the people about these wicked
deeds of yours. 24No, my sons; it is not a
good report that I hear spreading
among the LORD's people. 25If a man
sins against another man, God[b] may me-
diate for him; but if a man sins against
the LORD, who will intercede for him?"
His sons, however, did not listen to their
father's rebuke, for it was the LORD's
will to put them to death.

26And the boy Samuel continued to
grow in stature and in favor with the
LORD and with men.

Prophecy Against the House of Eli

27Now a man of God came to Eli and
said to him, "This is what the LORD says:
'Did I not clearly reveal myself to your
father's house when they were in Egypt
under Pharaoh? 28I chose your father
out of all the tribes of Israel to be my
priest, to go up to my altar, to burn incense, and to wear an ephod in my presence. I also gave your father's house all
the offerings made with fire by the Israelites. 29Why do you[c] scorn my sacrifice and offering that I prescribed for my
dwelling? Why do you honor your sons
more than me by fattening yourselves
on the choice parts of every offering
made by my people Israel?'

30"Therefore the LORD, the God of Israel, declares: 'I promised that your
house and your father's house would
minister before me forever.' But now the
LORD declares: 'Far be it from me! Those
who honor me I will honor, but those
who despise me will be disdained. 31The
time is coming when I will cut short
your strength and the strength of
your father's house, so that there will
not be an old man in your family line
32and you will see distress in my dwelling. Although good will be done to Israel, in your family line there will never
be an old man. 33Every one of you that I
do not cut off from my altar will be
spared only to blind your eyes with
tears and to grieve your heart, and all
your descendants will die in the prime
of life.

34" 'And what happens to your two
sons, Hophni and Phinehas, will be a
sign to you—they will both die on the
same day. 35I will raise up for myself a
faithful priest, who will do according to
what is in my heart and mind. I will
firmly establish his house, and he will
minister before my anointed one al-

[a]17 Or *men* [b]25 Or *the judges* [c]29 The Hebrew is plural.

ways. 36Then everyone left in your family line will come and bow down before
him for a piece of silver and a crust of
bread and plead, "Appoint me to some
priestly office so I can have food to
eat." ' "

SHARPEN THE FOCUS

Suppose God were willing to answer our prayers, but was incapable of doing so. That kind of God would be loving, but impotent. And prayer would be a joke.

On the other hand, suppose God were capable of answering our prayers, but was not willing to do it. That kind of God would be almighty, but unloving. And prayer would be futile.

Our heavenly Father is both willing and able to answer when His children call to Him. Hannah's hymn of praise recounts evidence for both aspects of our Lord's character.

At Christ's cross and open tomb the love and might of our Savior-God shine most brightly of all. In the cross we have unshakable proof that the God who controls the universe will always act for the good of His children.

Look for an opportunity today to share the kindness and power of God with someone who needs His help. Then assure that person of your prayers for him or her.

WEEK 23 • TUESDAY

1 Samuel 3:1–21

GET THE BIG PICTURE

Again today we read of a heart made faithful to God by His grace—in the boy Samuel. We also read an account of almost unbelievable impenitence. Eli decides to "let nature take its course." His heart had hardened in fear, in fatalism, and perhaps in just plain laziness. As you read, notice the comments the chapter makes about the "Word of the Lord" and what God intends that His Word do in us. If time is short, focus on 1 Samuel 3:1–10.

The LORD Calls Samuel

3 The boy Samuel ministered before the LORD under Eli. In those
days the word of the LORD was rare;
there were not many visions.
2One night Eli, whose eyes were becoming so weak that he could barely
see, was lying down in his usual place.
3The lamp of God had not yet gone out,
and Samuel was lying down in the
temple[a] of the LORD, where the ark of
God was. 4Then the LORD called Samuel.
Samuel answered, "Here I am." 5And
he ran to Eli and said, "Here I am; you
called me."
But Eli said, "I did not call; go back
and lie down." So he went and lay
down.
6Again the LORD called, "Samuel!"
And Samuel got up and went to Eli and
said, "Here I am; you called me."
"My son," Eli said, "I did not call; go
back and lie down."
7Now Samuel did not yet know the
LORD: The word of the LORD had not
yet been revealed to him.

[a]3 That is, tabernacle

8 The LORD called Samuel a third time,
and Samuel got up and went to Eli and
said, "Here I am; you called me."
Then Eli realized that the LORD was
calling the boy. 9 So Eli told Samuel, "Go
and lie down, and if he calls you, say,
'Speak, LORD, for your servant is listening.' " So Samuel went and lay down in
his place.
10 The LORD came and stood there,
calling as at the other times, "Samuel!
Samuel!"
Then Samuel said, "Speak, for your
servant is listening."
11 And the LORD said to Samuel: "See,
I am about to do something in Israel that
will make the ears of everyone who
hears of it tingle. 12 At that time I will carry out against Eli everything I spoke
against his family—from beginning to
end. 13 For I told him that I would judge
his family forever because of the sin he
knew about; his sons made themselves
contemptible,[a] and he failed to restrain
them. 14 Therefore, I swore to the house
of Eli, 'The guilt of Eli's house will never
be atoned for by sacrifice or offering.' "
15 Samuel lay down until morning and
then opened the doors of the house of
the LORD. He was afraid to tell Eli the vision, 16 but Eli called him and said, "Samuel, my son."
Samuel answered, "Here I am."
17 "What was it he said to you?" Eli
asked. "Do not hide it from me. May
God deal with you, be it ever so severely,
if you hide from me anything he told
you." 18 So Samuel told him everything,
hiding nothing from him. Then Eli said,
"He is the LORD; let him do what is good
in his eyes."
19 The LORD was with Samuel as he
grew up, and he let none of his words
fall to the ground. 20 And all Israel from
Dan to Beersheba recognized that Samuel was attested as a prophet of the
LORD. 21 The LORD continued to appear
at Shiloh, and there he revealed himself
to Samuel through his word.

[a] *13* Masoretic Text; an ancient Hebrew scribal tradition and Septuagint *sons blasphemed God*

SHARPEN THE FOCUS

Could we say that "the Word of the Lord" is rare in our day, too? Oh, we have plenty of printed Scriptures in western society. Version piles upon version, translation upon translation. And yet even those of us who read the Bible every day may miss what God wants to do for us and in us.

More than anything else, our Lord gave the Holy Scriptures to reveal Himself to us. He wants us to know *about* Him, surely. But He also wants us to *know Him*. Intimately. Personally. Remember Paul's powerful life-vision?

> *I want to know Christ and the power of His resurrection and the fellowship of sharing in His sufferings, becoming like Him in His death, and so, somehow, to attain to the resurrection from the dead. Not that I have already obtained all this, or have already been made perfect, but I press on to take hold of that for which Christ Jesus took hold of me.* (Philippians 3:10–12)

To know Christ, become like Christ, and share Christ. Those are God's goals for His people. God's grace will accomplish that in us. What a vision for life! What a reason to live!

WEEK 23 • WEDNESDAY

1 Samuel 4:1–22

Religion without relationship. That's the point to which Israel's sin had taken the nation under the judges. As you read today, note the way the Israelite army uses the ark of the covenant—as a kind of good luck charm. If time is short, focus on 1 Samuel 4:1–10.

4 And Samuel's word came to all Israel.

The Philistines Capture the Ark

Now the Israelites went out to fight
against the Philistines. The Israelites
camped at Ebenezer, and the Philistines
at Aphek. 2The Philistines deployed
their forces to meet Israel, and as the
battle spread, Israel was defeated by the
Philistines, who killed about four thousand of them on the battlefield. 3When
the soldiers returned to camp, the elders
of Israel asked, "Why did the LORD
bring defeat upon us today before the
Philistines? Let us bring the ark of the
LORD's covenant from Shiloh, so that it[a]
may go with us and save us from the
hand of our enemies."
4So the people sent men to Shiloh,
and they brought back the ark of the
covenant of the LORD Almighty, who is
enthroned between the cherubim. And
Eli's two sons, Hophni and Phinehas,
were there with the ark of the covenant
of God.
5When the ark of the LORD's covenant
came into the camp, all Israel raised
such a great shout that the ground
shook. 6Hearing the uproar, the Philistines asked, "What's all this shouting in
the Hebrew camp?"

When they learned that the ark of the
LORD had come into the camp, 7the Philistines were afraid. "A god has come
into the camp," they said. "We're in
trouble! Nothing like this has happened
before. 8Woe to us! Who will deliver us
from the hand of these mighty gods?
They are the gods who struck the Egyptians with all kinds of plagues in the
desert. 9Be strong, Philistines! Be men,
or you will be subject to the Hebrews,
as they have been to you. Be men, and
fight!"
10So the Philistines fought, and the Israelites were defeated and every man
fled to his tent. The slaughter was very
great; Israel lost thirty thousand foot
soldiers. 11The ark of God was captured,
and Eli's two sons, Hophni and Phinehas, died.

Death of Eli

12That same day a Benjamite ran from
the battle line and went to Shiloh, his
clothes torn and dust on his head.
13When he arrived, there was Eli sitting
on his chair by the side of the road,
watching, because his heart feared for
the ark of God. When the man entered
the town and told what had happened,
the whole town sent up a cry.
14Eli heard the outcry and asked,
"What is the meaning of this uproar?"

The man hurried over to Eli, 15who
was ninety-eight years old and whose
eyes were set so that he could not see.
16He told Eli, "I have just come from
the battle line; I fled from it this very
day."

Eli asked, "What happened, my son?"
17The man who brought the news
replied, "Israel fled before the Philistines, and the army has suffered heavy
losses. Also your two sons, Hophni and

[a]3 Or *he*

Phinehas, are dead, and the ark of God
has been captured."
18When he mentioned the ark of God,
Eli fell backward off his chair by the side
of the gate. His neck was broken and he
died, for he was an old man and heavy.
He had led[a] Israel forty years.
19His daughter-in-law, the wife of
Phinehas, was pregnant and near the
time of delivery. When she heard the
news that the ark of God had been captured and that her father-in-law and her
husband were dead, she went into labor
and gave birth, but was overcome by
her labor pains. 20As she was dying, the
women attending her said, "Don't despair; you have given birth to a son." But
she did not respond or pay any attention.
21She named the boy Ichabod,[b] saying,
"The glory has departed from Israel"—
because of the capture of the ark of God
and the deaths of her father-in-law and
her husband. 22She said, "The glory has
departed from Israel, for the ark of God
has been captured."

[a]18 Traditionally *judged* [b]21 *Ichabod* means *no glory.*

SHARPEN THE FOCUS

The Little Leaguer's socks nearly stood up by themselves, but he wouldn't let Mom wash them. He had worn them the day he pitched the no-hitter, and he didn't want to change his luck.

Sports involve many superstitions, but they're also found in religion. We easily substitute form for reality. We come to rely on things in the creation rather than trusting the Creator.

Our Lord has always tied His Word to things we can touch, see, and taste. The ark of the covenant was one of those things. But the Lord intended that it point beyond itself to His presence among His people. Our Lord still ties His Word to physical elements—water, bread, and wine. He speaks to us when we read our Bible. But He intends that these means point beyond themselves to Him, the One who gave them to us.

Likewise, any of our Lord's wonderful gifts can become magical amulets. Prayer, our hymnal, the altar at which we worship, even our pastor—can come to mean more than the One who gave them to us. Ask your Lord to point out any ways Satan has seduced you into this kind of religious idolatry. Then, certain of the forgiveness He freely grants in Jesus, worship Him in more freedom.

WEEK 23 • THURSDAY

1 Samuel 5:1—6:21

GET THE BIG PICTURE

No doubt the Philistines thought they had scored a touchdown when they managed to capture the ark of the covenant. But they were soon to find out they had the proverbial tiger by the tail. The Lord defended Himself and His holiness. If time is short, focus on 1 Samuel 5:1–6:9.

The Ark in Ashdod and Ekron

5 After the Philistines had captured the ark of God, they took it from Ebenezer to Ashdod. [2]Then they carried the ark into Dagon's temple and set it beside Dagon. [3]When the people of Ashdod rose early the next day, there was Dagon, fallen on his face on the ground before the ark of the LORD! They took Dagon and put him back in his place. [4]But the following morning when they rose, there was Dagon, fallen on his face on the ground before the ark of the LORD! His head and hands had been broken off and were lying on the threshold; only his body remained. [5]That is why to this day neither the priests of Dagon nor any others who enter Dagon's temple at Ashdod step on the threshold.

[6]The LORD's hand was heavy upon the people of Ashdod and its vicinity; he brought devastation upon them and afflicted them with tumors.[a] [7]When the men of Ashdod saw what was happening, they said, "The ark of the god of Israel must not stay here with us, because his hand is heavy upon us and upon Dagon our god." [8]So they called together all the rulers of the Philistines and asked them, "What shall we do with the ark of the god of Israel?"

They answered, "Have the ark of the god of Israel moved to Gath." So they moved the ark of the God of Israel.

[9]But after they had moved it, the LORD's hand was against that city, throwing it into a great panic. He afflicted the people of the city, both young and old, with an outbreak of tumors.[b] [10]So they sent the ark of God to Ekron.

As the ark of God was entering Ekron, the people of Ekron cried out, "They have brought the ark of the god of Israel around to us to kill us and our people." [11]So they called together all the rulers of the Philistines and said, "Send the ark of the god of Israel away; let it go back to its own place, or it[c] will kill us and our people." For death had filled the city with panic; God's hand was very heavy upon it. [12]Those who did not die were afflicted with tumors, and the outcry of the city went up to heaven.

The Ark Returned to Israel

6 When the ark of the LORD had been in Philistine territory seven months, [2]the Philistines called for the priests and the diviners and said, "What shall we do with the ark of the LORD? Tell us how we should send it back to its place."

[3]They answered, "If you return the ark of the god of Israel, do not send it away empty, but by all means send a guilt offering to him. Then you will be healed, and you will know why his hand has not been lifted from you."

[4]The Philistines asked, "What guilt offering should we send to him?"

They replied, "Five gold tumors and five gold rats, according to the number of the Philistine rulers, because the same plague has struck both you and your rulers. [5]Make models of the tumors and of the rats that are destroying the country, and pay honor to Israel's god. Perhaps he will lift his hand from you and your gods and your land. [6]Why do you harden your hearts as the Egyptians and Pharaoh did? When he[d] treated them harshly, did they not send the Israelites out so they could go on their way?

[7]"Now then, get a new cart ready, with two cows that have calved and have never been yoked. Hitch the cows to the cart, but take their calves away and pen them up. [8]Take the ark of the LORD and put it on the cart, and in a chest beside it put the gold objects you are sending back to him as a guilt offering. Send it on its way, [9]but keep watching it. If it goes up to its own territory, toward Beth Shemesh, then the LORD has brought this great disaster on us. But if it does not, then we will know that it was not his hand that struck us and that it happened to us by chance."

[a]6 Hebrew; Septuagint and Vulgate *tumors. And rats appeared in their land, and death and destruction were throughout the city* [b]9 Or *with tumors in the groin* (see Septuagint) [c]11 Or *he* [d]6 That is, God

[10]So they did this. They took two such
cows and hitched them to the cart and
penned up their calves. [11]They placed
the ark of the LORD on the cart and
along with it the chest containing the
gold rats and the models of the tumors.
[12]Then the cows went straight up toward Beth Shemesh, keeping on the
road and lowing all the way; they did
not turn to the right or to the left. The
rulers of the Philistines followed them
as far as the border of Beth Shemesh.
[13]Now the people of Beth Shemesh
were harvesting their wheat in the valley, and when they looked up and saw
the ark, they rejoiced at the sight. [14]The
cart came to the field of Joshua of Beth
Shemesh, and there it stopped beside a
large rock. The people chopped up the
wood of the cart and sacrificed the cows
as a burnt offering to the LORD. [15]The
Levites took down the ark of the LORD,
together with the chest containing the
gold objects, and placed them on the
large rock. On that day the people of
Beth Shemesh offered burnt offerings
and made sacrifices to the LORD. [16]The
five rulers of the Philistines saw all this
and then returned that same day to
Ekron.
[17]These are the gold tumors the Philistines sent as a guilt offering to the
LORD—one each for Ashdod, Gaza,
Ashkelon, Gath and Ekron. [18]And the
number of the gold rats was according
to the number of Philistine towns belonging to the five rulers—the fortified
towns with their country villages. The
large rock, on which[a] they set the ark of
the LORD, is a witness to this day in the
field of Joshua of Beth Shemesh.
[19]But God struck down some of the
men of Beth Shemesh, putting seventy[b]
of them to death because they had
looked into the ark of the LORD. The
people mourned because of the heavy
blow the LORD had dealt them, [20]and
the men of Beth Shemesh asked, "Who
can stand in the presence of the LORD,
this holy God? To whom will the ark go
up from here?"
[21]Then they sent messengers to the
people of Kiriath Jearim, saying, "The
Philistines have returned the ark of the
LORD. Come down and take it up to
your place."

[a]*18* A few Hebrew manuscripts (see also Septuagint); most Hebrew manuscripts *villages as far as Greater Abel, where* [b]*19* A few Hebrew manuscripts; most Hebrew manuscripts and Septuagint *50,070*

SHARPEN THE FOCUS

Maybe you've seen or even played the comparison game *I, You, He*. Each round includes three sentences, like these:

I am concerned about a potentially serious problem.
You are worried over a minor issue.
He's given himself ulcers over nothing.

I am detail-oriented.
You are fussy.
He is a paranoid control freak.

I have the courage of my convictions.
You are stubborn.
He is a pig-headed oaf.

In 1 Samuel 6:6, we hear a warning against the dangers of stubbornness. Good advice from pagan priests! Yet stubbornness isn't as easy to spot in ourselves as it is in others. We, it's clear, "have the courage of our convictions."

Several times in the pages of 1 Samuel we will see different people fall into the trap of nursing stubborn and impenitent hearts. It always results in problems, sometimes in disaster. Our Lord does want us to stand up for Him and for the cross of His Son. But He also wants to work in us hearts that are soft and open to His gentle leading. Let His forgiveness begin that process in you right now.

Finally! Israel has a leader who will tell them the truth—God's truth—whether they want to hear it or not. And this same leader intercedes for them. Unlike Eli. Unlike many of the judges who came before. And the people respond. As you read today, look for ways in which Samuel is a "type," or picture, of Christ Jesus. If time is short, focus on 1 Samuel 7:7–17.

7 1So the men of Kiriath Jearim
came and took up the ark of the
LORD. They took it to Abinadab's house
on the hill and consecrated Eleazar his
son to guard the ark of the LORD.

Samuel Subdues the Philistines at Mizpah

2It was a long time, twenty years in all,
that the ark remained at Kiriath Jearim,
and all the people of Israel mourned
and sought after the LORD. 3And Samuel said to the whole house of Israel, "If
you are returning to the LORD with all
your hearts, then rid yourselves of the
foreign gods and the Ashtoreths and
commit yourselves to the LORD and
serve him only, and he will deliver
you out of the hand of the Philistines."
4So the Israelites put away their Baals
and Ashtoreths, and served the LORD
only.
5Then Samuel said, "Assemble all Israel at Mizpah and I will intercede with
the LORD for you." 6When they had assembled at Mizpah, they drew water
and poured it out before the LORD. On
that day they fasted and there they confessed, "We have sinned against the
LORD." And Samuel was leader[a] of Israel
at Mizpah.
7When the Philistines heard that Israel had assembled at Mizpah, the rulers
of the Philistines came up to attack
them. And when the Israelites heard
of it, they were afraid because of the
Philistines. 8They said to Samuel, "Do
not stop crying out to the LORD our
God for us, that he may rescue us from
the hand of the Philistines." 9Then Samuel took a suckling lamb and offered it
up as a whole burnt offering to the
LORD. He cried out to the LORD on
Israel's behalf, and the LORD answered
him.
10While Samuel was sacrificing the
burnt offering, the Philistines drew near
to engage Israel in battle. But that day
the LORD thundered with loud thunder
against the Philistines and threw them
into such a panic that they were routed
before the Israelites. 11The men of Israel
rushed out of Mizpah and pursued the
Philistines, slaughtering them along the
way to a point below Beth Car.
12Then Samuel took a stone and set it

[a]6 Traditionally *judge*

up between Mizpah and Shen. He
named it Ebenezer,[a] saying, "Thus far
has the LORD helped us." 13So the Philistines were subdued and did not invade Israelite territory again.
Throughout Samuel's lifetime, the
hand of the LORD was against the Philistines. 14The towns from Ekron to Gath
that the Philistines had captured from
Israel were restored to her, and Israel delivered the neighboring territory
from the power of the Philistines. And
there was peace between Israel and the
Amorites.
15Samuel continued as judge over Israel all the days of his life. 16From year
to year he went on a circuit from Bethel
to Gilgal to Mizpah, judging Israel in all
those places. 17But he always went back
to Ramah, where his home was, and
there he also judged Israel. And he built
an altar there to the LORD.

[a]12 *Ebenezer* means *stone of help.*

SHARPEN THE FOCUS

They are some of the most beautiful words that the church on earth has ever sung. We sing them still. Usually just before we approach the altar to receive the Holy Supper:

Lamb of God,
You take away the sin of the world,
Have mercy on us . . . grant us Your peace.

We hear echoes of that prayer from Israel's lips in 1 Samuel 7:8: "Do not stop crying out to the LORD our God for us, that He may rescue us."

God's people can pray that prayer—we have always been able to pray that prayer—because we already know our Lord's answer. He *is* merciful. We've seen His mercy enfleshed in Christ Jesus.

One Hebrew word translated "mercy" means "faithful love." The love that never changes. The love of God that makes and keeps His covenant with His people. The burnt sacrifice Samuel offered the day the Philistines met defeat pointed forward to Christ's total sacrifice of Himself to God for us and our sin. He truly is our Savior, our one and only God, the One who defeats sin and death for us.

So when we pray, "Lord, have mercy," we're in effect saying, "Lord, remember Your covenant—with Abraham, with Isaac, with Jacob, with me." In Christ, we inherit that mercy, that covenant-love as surely as did the patriarchs.

WEEK 23 • SATURDAY

1 Samuel 8:1–22

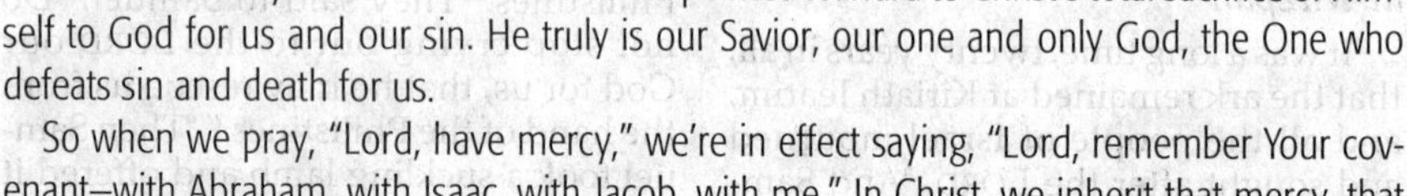

GET THE BIG PICTURE

Until now the Lord has led Israel into battle. He has given them victory. But the people have tired of this arrangement. They covet the prestige and pomp of a royal court. They want to be "like all the other nations" (1 Samuel 8:20). In doing so, they reject not only Samuel, but also the Lord. If time is short, focus on 1 Samuel 8:1–9.

Israel Asks for a King

8 When Samuel grew old, he appointed his sons as judges for Israel. [2]The name of his firstborn was Joel and the name of his second was Abijah, and they served at Beersheba. [3]But his sons did not walk in his ways. They turned aside after dishonest gain and accepted bribes and perverted justice.

[4]So all the elders of Israel gathered together and came to Samuel at Ramah. [5]They said to him, "You are old, and your sons do not walk in your ways; now appoint a king to lead[a] us, such as all the other nations have."

[6]But when they said, "Give us a king to lead us," this displeased Samuel; so he prayed to the LORD. [7]And the LORD told him: "Listen to all that the people are saying to you; it is not you they have rejected, but they have rejected me as their king. [8]As they have done from the day I brought them up out of Egypt until this day, forsaking me and serving other gods, so they are doing to you. [9]Now listen to them; but warn them solemnly and let them know what the king who will reign over them will do."

[10]Samuel told all the words of the LORD to the people who were asking him for a king. [11]He said, "This is what the king who will reign over you will do: He will take your sons and make them serve with his chariots and horses, and they will run in front of his chariots. [12]Some he will assign to be commanders of thousands and commanders of fifties, and others to plow his ground and reap his harvest, and still others to make weapons of war and equipment for his chariots. [13]He will take your daughters to be perfumers and cooks and bakers. [14]He will take the best of your fields and vineyards and olive groves and give them to his attendants. [15]He will take a tenth of your grain and of your vintage and give it to his officials and attendants. [16]Your menservants and maidservants and the best of your cattle[b] and donkeys he will take for his own use. [17]He will take a tenth of your flocks, and you yourselves will become his slaves. [18]When that day comes, you will cry out for relief from the king you have chosen, and the LORD will not answer you in that day."

[19]But the people refused to listen to Samuel. "No!" they said. "We want a king over us. [20]Then we will be like all the other nations, with a king to lead us and to go out before us and fight our battles."

[21]When Samuel heard all that the people said, he repeated it before the LORD. [22]The LORD answered, "Listen to them and give them a king."

Then Samuel said to the men of Israel, "Everyone go back to his town."

[a]5 Traditionally *judge*; also in verses 6 and 20
[b]16 Septuagint; Hebrew *young men*

SHARPEN THE FOCUS

Mentoring has been one of the "big ideas" in business for several decades. Actually the concept has been around since Old Testament times.

Mentoring has always been easier said than done. Samuel didn't raise up anyone to take his place in Israel. Nor did Eli nor the judges before them. The last time we encountered anything like it was the relationship between Joshua and Moses. (See Exodus 17:8–15.)

Under whose teaching do you sit as you seek to grow in your own discipleship? And who will learn to teach or witness or encourage or make decisions from you?

If you feel a bit intimidated by those questions, take heart. In and of ourselves we have neither the humility to be discipled nor the ability to disciple others. Remember Paul's words?

> *Such confidence as this is ours through Christ before God. Not that we are competent in ourselves to claim anything for ourselves, but our competence comes from God. He has made us competent as ministers of a new covenant.* (2 Corinthians 3:4–6)

Cleansed by Christ's blood, the blood of the new covenant, we have been made competent to serve others and to grow ourselves in Christian maturity.

WEEK 24 • MONDAY

1 Samuel 9:1—10:27

Jesus once told His disciples "Your Father in heaven give[s] good gifts to those who ask Him" (Matthew 7:11). Even though Israel's motive in asking for a king had been sinful, still the Lord loved His people. He wanted them to have good leadership. As you read today, list the qualities you see in Saul that would have made him a blessing to those whom he ruled. If time is short, focus on 1 Samuel 10:1–16.

Samuel Anoints Saul

9 There was a Benjamite, a man of
standing, whose name was Kish
son of Abiel, the son of Zeror, the son of
Becorath, the son of Aphiah of Benjamin. 2He had a son named Saul, an impressive young man without equal
among the Israelites—a head taller than
any of the others.
3Now the donkeys belonging to Saul's
father Kish were lost, and Kish said to
his son Saul, "Take one of the servants
with you and go and look for the donkeys." 4So he passed through the hill
country of Ephraim and through the
area around Shalisha, but they did not
find them. They went on into the district of Shaalim, but the donkeys were
not there. Then he passed through the
territory of Benjamin, but they did not
find them.
5When they reached the district of
Zuph, Saul said to the servant who was
with him, "Come, let's go back, or my father will stop thinking about the donkeys and start worrying about us."
6But the servant replied, "Look, in this
town there is a man of God; he is highly
respected, and everything he says
comes true. Let's go there now. Perhaps
he will tell us what way to take."
7Saul said to his servant, "If we go,
what can we give the man? The food in
our sacks is gone. We have no gift to take
to the man of God. What do we have?"
8The servant answered him again.
"Look," he said, "I have a quarter of a
shekel[a] of silver. I will give it to the man
of God so that he will tell us what way
to take." 9(Formerly in Israel, if a man
went to inquire of God, he would say,
"Come, let us go to the seer," because the
prophet of today used to be called a
seer.)
10"Good," Saul said to his servant.
"Come, let's go." So they set out for the
town where the man of God was.
11As they were going up the hill to the
town, they met some girls coming out
to draw water, and they asked them, "Is
the seer here?"

[a]8 That is, about 1/10 ounce (about 3 grams)

12“He is,” they answered. “He’s ahead
of you. Hurry now; he has just come to
our town today, for the people have a
sacrifice at the high place. 13As soon as
you enter the town, you will find him
before he goes up to the high place to
eat. The people will not begin eating until he comes, because he must bless the
sacrifice; afterward, those who are invited will eat. Go up now; you should find
him about this time.”

14They went up to the town, and as
they were entering it, there was Samuel,
coming toward them on his way up to
the high place.

15Now the day before Saul came, the
LORD had revealed this to Samuel:
16“About this time tomorrow I will send
you a man from the land of Benjamin.
Anoint him leader over my people Israel; he will deliver my people from the
hand of the Philistines. I have looked
upon my people, for their cry has
reached me.”

17When Samuel caught sight of Saul,
the LORD said to him, “This is the man I
spoke to you about; he will govern my
people.”

18Saul approached Samuel in the gateway and asked, “Would you please tell
me where the seer’s house is?”

19“I am the seer,” Samuel replied. “Go
up ahead of me to the high place, for today you are to eat with me, and in the
morning I will let you go and will tell
you all that is in your heart. 20As for the
donkeys you lost three days ago, do not
worry about them; they have been
found. And to whom is all the desire of
Israel turned, if not to you and all your
father’s family?”

21Saul answered, “But am I not a Benjamite, from the smallest tribe of Israel,
and is not my clan the least of all the
clans of the tribe of Benjamin? Why do
you say such a thing to me?”

22Then Samuel brought Saul and his
servant into the hall and seated them at
the head of those who were invited—
about thirty in number. 23Samuel said to
the cook, “Bring the piece of meat I gave
you, the one I told you to lay aside.”

24So the cook took up the leg with
what was on it and set it in front of Saul.
Samuel said, “Here is what has been
kept for you. Eat, because it was set
aside for you for this occasion, from the
time I said, ‘I have invited guests.’ ” And
Saul dined with Samuel that day.

25After they came down from the high
place to the town, Samuel talked with
Saul on the roof of his house. 26They rose
about daybreak and Samuel called to
Saul on the roof, “Get ready, and I will
send you on your way.” When Saul got
ready, he and Samuel went outside together. 27As they were going down to
the edge of the town, Samuel said to
Saul, “Tell the servant to go on ahead of
us”—and the servant did so—“but you
stay here awhile, so that I may give you
a message from God.”

10 Then Samuel took a flask of
oil and poured it on Saul’s
head and kissed him, saying, “Has not
the LORD anointed you leader over his
inheritance?[a] 2When you leave me today, you will meet two men near
Rachel’s tomb, at Zelzah on the border
of Benjamin. They will say to you, ‘The
donkeys you set out to look for have
been found. And now your father has
stopped thinking about them and is
worried about you. He is asking, “What
shall I do about my son?” ’

3“Then you will go on from there until you reach the great tree of Tabor.
Three men going up to God at Bethel
will meet you there. One will be carrying three young goats, another three
loaves of bread, and another a skin of
wine. 4They will greet you and offer you
two loaves of bread, which you will accept from them.

5“After that you will go to Gibeah of
God, where there is a Philistine outpost.
As you approach the town, you will
meet a procession of prophets coming
down from the high place with lyres,
tambourines, flutes and harps being
played before them, and they will be

[a]1 Hebrew; Septuagint and Vulgate *over his people Israel? You will reign over the LORD’s people and save them from the power of their enemies round about. And this will be a sign to you that the LORD has anointed you leader over his inheritance:*

prophesying. [6]The Spirit of the LORD will come upon you in power, and you will prophesy with them; and you will be changed into a different person. [7]Once these signs are fulfilled, do whatever your hand finds to do, for God is with you.

[8]"Go down ahead of me to Gilgal. I will surely come down to you to sacrifice burnt offerings and fellowship offerings,[a] but you must wait seven days until I come to you and tell you what you are to do."

Saul Made King

[9]As Saul turned to leave Samuel, God changed Saul's heart, and all these signs were fulfilled that day. [10]When they arrived at Gibeah, a procession of prophets met him; the Spirit of God came upon him in power, and he joined in their prophesying. [11]When all those who had formerly known him saw him prophesying with the prophets, they asked each other, "What is this that has happened to the son of Kish? Is Saul also among the prophets?"

[12]A man who lived there answered, "And who is their father?" So it became a saying: "Is Saul also among the prophets?" [13]After Saul stopped prophesying, he went to the high place.

[14]Now Saul's uncle asked him and his servant, "Where have you been?"

"Looking for the donkeys," he said. "But when we saw they were not to be found, we went to Samuel."

[15]Saul's uncle said, "Tell me what Samuel said to you."

[16]Saul replied, "He assured us that the donkeys had been found." But he did not tell his uncle what Samuel had said about the kingship.

[17]Samuel summoned the people of Israel to the LORD at Mizpah [18]and said to them, "This is what the LORD, the God of Israel, says: 'I brought Israel up out of Egypt, and I delivered you from the power of Egypt and all the kingdoms that oppressed you.' [19]But you have now rejected your God, who saves you out of all your calamities and distresses. And you have said, 'No, set a king over us.' So now present yourselves before the LORD by your tribes and clans."

[20]When Samuel brought all the tribes of Israel near, the tribe of Benjamin was chosen. [21]Then he brought forward the tribe of Benjamin, clan by clan, and Matri's clan was chosen. Finally Saul son of Kish was chosen. But when they looked for him, he was not to be found. [22]So they inquired further of the LORD, "Has the man come here yet?"

And the LORD said, "Yes, he has hidden himself among the baggage."

[23]They ran and brought him out, and as he stood among the people he was a head taller than any of the others. [24]Samuel said to all the people, "Do you see the man the LORD has chosen? There is no one like him among all the people."

Then the people shouted, "Long live the king!"

[25]Samuel explained to the people the regulations of the kingship. He wrote them down on a scroll and deposited it before the LORD. Then Samuel dismissed the people, each to his own home.

[26]Saul also went to his home in Gibeah, accompanied by valiant men whose hearts God had touched. [27]But some troublemakers said, "How can this fellow save us?" They despised him and brought him no gifts. But Saul kept silent.

[a]8 Traditionally *peace offerings*

SHARPEN THE FOCUS

Most often in the Old Testament when we encounter the Holy Spirit, we see Him filling prophets, priests, or kings, empowering them for the work God had given them. The psalmist promised that the Savior whom God would send—the King of kings—would be anointed with the Holy Spirit, "the oil of joy," in a fuller way than any king before Him (Psalm 45:6–7).

In the New Testament, all of God's people have become royalty (1 Peter 2:9). We are kings and priests who serve our God and Father (Revelation 1:6). We, too, need the anointing power of the Holy Spirit as we worship our Lord, as we represent Him to the world, and as we intercede for those around us.

And that "oil of joy" has anointed us. In Baptism, the Holy Spirit came to dwell in us. The Father continues to pour that holy oil into our hearts as we have need of Him.

Read Jesus' promise about that from Luke 11:11–13. Then ask for a fresh flood of peace, power, and joy. Confident in it, then, be who you are today—Christ's royal priest, forgiven and reigning with Him!

WEEK 24 • TUESDAY

1 Samuel 11:1–15

GET THE BIG PICTURE

Despite his having been anointed king, Saul seems to have gone back home to farm. As chapter 11 opens, the town of Jabesh Gilead is under attack by an Ammonite tribal chieftain. As you read, note Saul's response to the troubles his people face. If time is short, focus on 1 Samuel 11:1–9.

Saul Rescues the City of Jabesh

11 Nahash the Ammonite went up
and besieged Jabesh Gilead. And
all the men of Jabesh said to him, "Make
a treaty with us, and we will be subject
to you."
2But Nahash the Ammonite replied, "I
will make a treaty with you only on the
condition that I gouge out the right eye
of every one of you and so bring disgrace on all Israel."
3The elders of Jabesh said to him,
"Give us seven days so we can send
messengers throughout Israel; if no one
comes to rescue us, we will surrender to
you."
4When the messengers came to Gibeah of Saul and reported these terms to
the people, they all wept aloud. 5Just
then Saul was returning from the fields,
behind his oxen, and he asked, "What is
wrong with the people? Why are they
weeping?" Then they repeated to him
what the men of Jabesh had said.
6When Saul heard their words, the
Spirit of God came upon him in power,
and he burned with anger. 7He took a
pair of oxen, cut them into pieces, and
sent the pieces by messengers throughout Israel, proclaiming, "This is what
will be done to the oxen of anyone who
does not follow Saul and Samuel." Then
the terror of the LORD fell on the people,
and they turned out as one man. 8When
Saul mustered them at Bezek, the men
of Israel numbered three hundred thousand and the men of Judah thirty thousand.
9They told the messengers who had
come, "Say to the men of Jabesh Gilead,
'By the time the sun is hot tomorrow,
you will be delivered.' " When the messengers went and reported this to the
men of Jabesh, they were elated. 10They
said to the Ammonites, "Tomorrow we
will surrender to you, and you can do
to us whatever seems good to you."
11The next day Saul separated his men

into three divisions; during the last
watch of the night they broke into the
camp of the Ammonites and slaughtered them until the heat of the day.
Those who survived were scattered, so
that no two of them were left together.

Saul Confirmed as King

12The people then said to Samuel,
"Who was it that asked, 'Shall Saul reign
over us?' Bring these men to us and we
will put them to death."
13But Saul said, "No one shall be put
to death today, for this day the LORD has
rescued Israel."
14Then Samuel said to the people,
"Come, let us go to Gilgal and there reaffirm the kingship." 15So all the people
went to Gilgal and confirmed Saul as
king in the presence of the LORD. There
they sacrificed fellowship offerings[a] before the LORD, and Saul and all the Israelites held a great celebration.

[a]15 Traditionally *peace offerings*

SHARPEN THE FOCUS

Anger is a powerful emotion. Some consider it a negative one. And indeed anger that runs out of control or anger used toward evil ends displeases God.

Yet, as we think about God's goal to make us more like Christ, we need to remember that our Lord does indeed become angry. In today's reading King Saul shows a righteous response to his people's plight. His righteous anger moves him to act in godly ways. (In this case, he defends his people.)

Saul's feelings and his response look a lot like those of our Lord Himself in Psalm 18. Here one of God's children is in distress and cries to the Lord for help. The Lord hears. And as a result:

The earth trembled and quaked,
and the foundations of the mountains shook;
they trembled because he was angry. (Psalm 18:7)

The psalm goes on to describe the Lord riding on the clouds of a thunderstorm to help His child. Have you ever imagined your prayers for help evoking such a strong response in your Lord? They do, you know. He cares that much about you.

What a challenge as we think about our own anger: What evokes it? How can we use it as a force for helping others and furthering the kingdom of our Savior?

WEEK 24 • WEDNESDAY

1 Samuel 12:1–25

GET THE BIG PICTURE

Israel has gathered at Gilgal to "reaffirm the kingship" (1 Samuel 11:14). They are ready to unite under Saul against the Philistines and the other enemies they face. As they worship there (1 Samuel 11:14–15), Samuel stands to speak. Note the "pastor's heart" the Lord has placed within him—what he says, he says only for the nation's good, not for his own gain. If time is short, focus on 1 Samuel 12:1–15.

Samuel's Farewell Speech

12 Samuel said to all Israel, "I have listened to everything you said to me and have set a king over you. 2 Now you have a king as your leader. As for me, I am old and gray, and my sons are here with you. I have been your leader from my youth until this day. 3 Here I stand. Testify against me in the presence of the LORD and his anointed. Whose ox have I taken? Whose donkey have I taken? Whom have I cheated? Whom have I oppressed? From whose hand have I accepted a bribe to make me shut my eyes? If I have done any of these, I will make it right."

4 "You have not cheated or oppressed us," they replied. "You have not taken anything from anyone's hand."

5 Samuel said to them, "The LORD is witness against you, and also his anointed is witness this day, that you have not found anything in my hand."

"He is witness," they said.

6 Then Samuel said to the people, "It is the LORD who appointed Moses and Aaron and brought your forefathers up out of Egypt. 7 Now then, stand here, because I am going to confront you with evidence before the LORD as to all the righteous acts performed by the LORD for you and your fathers.

8 "After Jacob entered Egypt, they cried to the LORD for help, and the LORD sent Moses and Aaron, who brought your forefathers out of Egypt and settled them in this place.

9 "But they forgot the LORD their God; so he sold them into the hand of Sisera, the commander of the army of Hazor, and into the hands of the Philistines and the king of Moab, who fought against them. 10 They cried out to the LORD and said, 'We have sinned; we have forsaken the LORD and served the Baals and the Ashtoreths. But now deliver us from the hands of our enemies, and we will serve you.' 11 Then the LORD sent Jerub-Baal,[a] Barak,[b] Jephthah and Samuel,[c] and he delivered you from the hands of your enemies on every side, so that you lived securely.

12 "But when you saw that Nahash king of the Ammonites was moving against you, you said to me, 'No, we want a king to rule over us'—even though the LORD your God was your king. 13 Now here is the king you have chosen, the one you asked for; see, the LORD has set a king over you. 14 If you fear the LORD and serve and obey him and do not rebel against his commands, and if both you and the king who reigns over you follow the LORD your God—good! 15 But if you do not obey the LORD, and if you rebel against his commands, his hand will be against you, as it was against your fathers.

16 "Now then, stand still and see this great thing the LORD is about to do before your eyes! 17 Is it not wheat harvest now? I will call upon the LORD to send thunder and rain. And you will realize what an evil thing you did in the eyes of the LORD when you asked for a king."

18 Then Samuel called upon the LORD, and that same day the LORD sent thunder and rain. So all the people stood in awe of the LORD and of Samuel.

19 The people all said to Samuel, "Pray to the LORD your God for your servants so that we will not die, for we have added to all our other sins the evil of asking for a king."

20 "Do not be afraid," Samuel replied. "You have done all this evil; yet do not turn away from the LORD, but serve the LORD with all your heart. 21 Do not turn away after useless idols. They can do you no good, nor can they rescue you, because they are useless. 22 For the sake of his great name the LORD will not reject his people, because the LORD was

[a] *11* Also called *Gideon* [b] *11* Some Septuagint manuscripts and Syriac; Hebrew *Bedan*
[c] *11* Hebrew; some Septuagint manuscripts and Syriac *Samson*

pleased to make you his own. 23As for
me, far be it from me that I should sin
against the LORD by failing to pray for
you. And I will teach you the way that
is good and right. 24But be sure to fear
the LORD and serve him faithfully with
all your heart; consider what great
things he has done for you. 25Yet if you
persist in doing evil, both you and your
king will be swept away."

SHARPEN THE FOCUS

Israel might have expected a rousing "get the Philistines" pep talk from their prophet-priest-pastor Samuel. But he scarcely mentions external enemies at all. The real threat, he reminds them, comes from right inside their own hearts. Then he strikes a single, familiar note: Repent. And he punctuates it with a lengthy audio-visual demonstration (1 Samuel 12:17–18).

The Law does its holy work in the people's hearts. They turn in true repentance and faith toward their gracious Lord. They had forgotten Him and forsaken His covenant relationship with them. But He had never forgotten. Nor would He ever forsake that covenant.

What a blessing from God to have people around us who will tell us the truth. What a blessing when our pastor or a godly Bible class teacher points out God's law—specifically and in all its severity. And how sweet the comfort of the Gospel when it comes to soothe our fearful, guilty hearts.

Reread Samuel's Gospel message from 1 Samuel 12:20–24. Then think of a way to thank your pastor for speaking the truth in love to you and to your congregation.

WEEK 24 • THURSDAY

1 Samuel 13:1–23

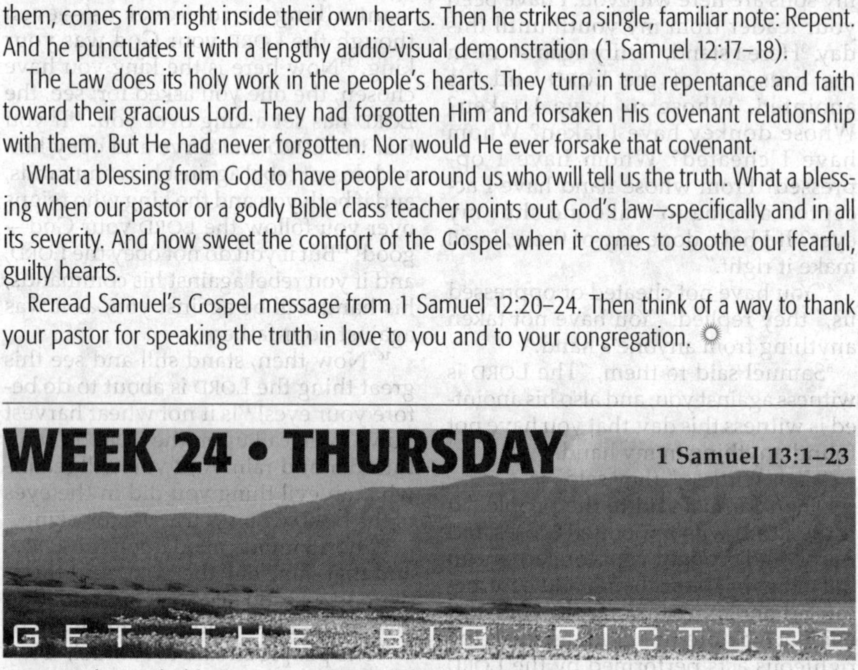

GET THE BIG PICTURE

Anyone who reads this chapter of 1 Samuel from a merely human viewpoint won't get it. What did Saul do wrong? His army was melting away. He took "sensible" action. Viewed, though, from the Lord's perspective, Saul's unbelief can't be denied or explained away. If time is short, focus on 1 Samuel 13:1–14.

Samuel Rebukes Saul

13 Saul was ⌞thirty⌟[a] years old
when he became king, and
he reigned over Israel ⌞forty-⌟[b] two years.
2Saul[c] chose three thousand men
from Israel; two thousand were with
him at Micmash and in the hill country
of Bethel, and a thousand were with
Jonathan at Gibeah in Benjamin. The
rest of the men he sent back to their
homes.
3Jonathan attacked the Philistine outpost at Geba, and the Philistines heard
about it. Then Saul had the trumpet
blown throughout the land and said,
"Let the Hebrews hear!" 4So all Israel
heard the news: "Saul has attacked the

[a]1 A few late manuscripts of the Septuagint; Hebrew does not have *thirty.* [b]1 See the round number in Acts 13:21; Hebrew does not have *forty-.* [c]1,2 Or *and when he had reigned over Israel two years,* 2*he*

Philistine outpost, and now Israel has become a stench to the Philistines." And the people were summoned to join Saul at Gilgal.

[5]The Philistines assembled to fight Israel, with three thousand[a] chariots, six thousand charioteers, and soldiers as numerous as the sand on the seashore. They went up and camped at Micmash, east of Beth Aven. [6]When the men of Israel saw that their situation was critical and that their army was hard pressed, they hid in caves and thickets, among the rocks, and in pits and cisterns. [7]Some Hebrews even crossed the Jordan to the land of Gad and Gilead.

Saul remained at Gilgal, and all the troops with him were quaking with fear. [8]He waited seven days, the time set by Samuel; but Samuel did not come to Gilgal, and Saul's men began to scatter. [9]So he said, "Bring me the burnt offering and the fellowship offerings.[b]" And Saul offered up the burnt offering. [10]Just as he finished making the offering, Samuel arrived, and Saul went out to greet him.

[11]"What have you done?" asked Samuel.

Saul replied, "When I saw that the men were scattering, and that you did not come at the set time, and that the Philistines were assembling at Micmash, [12]I thought, 'Now the Philistines will come down against me at Gilgal, and I have not sought the LORD's favor.' So I felt compelled to offer the burnt offering."

[13]"You acted foolishly," Samuel said. "You have not kept the command the LORD your God gave you; if you had, he would have established your kingdom over Israel for all time. [14]But now your kingdom will not endure; the LORD has sought out a man after his own heart and appointed him leader of his people, because you have not kept the LORD's command."

[15]Then Samuel left Gilgal[c] and went up to Gibeah in Benjamin, and Saul counted the men who were with him. They numbered about six hundred.

Israel Without Weapons

[16]Saul and his son Jonathan and the men with them were staying in Gibeah[d] in Benjamin, while the Philistines camped at Micmash. [17]Raiding parties went out from the Philistine camp in three detachments. One turned toward Ophrah in the vicinity of Shual, [18]another toward Beth Horon, and the third toward the borderland overlooking the Valley of Zeboim facing the desert.

[19]Not a blacksmith could be found in the whole land of Israel, because the Philistines had said, "Otherwise the Hebrews will make swords or spears!" [20]So all Israel went down to the Philistines to have their plowshares, mattocks, axes and sickles[e] sharpened. [21]The price was two thirds of a shekel[f] for sharpening plowshares and mattocks, and a third of a shekel[g] for sharpening forks and axes and for repointing goads.

[22]So on the day of the battle not a soldier with Saul and Jonathan had a sword or spear in his hand; only Saul and his son Jonathan had them.

Jonathan Attacks the Philistines

[23]Now a detachment of Philistines had gone out to the pass at Micmash.

[a]5 Some Septuagint manuscripts and Syriac; Hebrew *thirty thousand* [b]9 Traditionally *peace offerings* [c]15 Hebrew; Septuagint *Gilgal and went his way; the rest of the people went after Saul to meet the army, and they went out of Gilgal*
[d]16 Two Hebrew manuscripts; most Hebrew manuscripts *Geba*, a variant of *Gibeah*
[e]20 Septuagint; Hebrew *plowshares* [f]21 Hebrew *pim*; that is, about 1/4 ounce (about 8 grams)
[g]21 That is, about 1/8 ounce (about 4 grams)

SHARPEN THE FOCUS

What do you battle? Deadlines? Child-care arrangements? Creditors? Discouragement? Coworkers? In-laws? Chronic pain? A fear or worry of some kind? Pick out one battle that is really the worst right now.

Think about Saul's choices when his soldiers began to melt away into the caves and thickets of Canaan. He could decide to fight a human war or a holy war. He could depend upon human strength or divine strength. He could rely on his own wisdom, or he could count on the Lord's covenant.

We can see what he should have done. But it wasn't easy. Remember the terrible struggle Gideon had with his doubts? Remember all the signs for which he asked?

The "holy wars" waged by God's Old Testament people had several things in common. But the premier characteristic was the fact that the Savior-God fought and won victory for His people. He did for them what they could never have done for themselves.

In this sense, *the* holy war of all time took place on Calvary. There, Jesus defeated the overwhelming forces of hell, sin, and death for us.

Forgiven in His cross for our failures of faith, we receive the power we need to stand victorious in our daily battles, too.

WEEK 24 • FRIDAY

1 Samuel 14:1–52

GET THE BIG PICTURE

In chapter 10 we saw Saul filled with the power of God's Spirit and relying on Him. But more and more as the story continues we see Saul trying to maintain his authority in Israel by creating the outward appearance of closeness to the Lord. Appearance versus reality. As you read, notice the outwardly "religious" actions Saul takes. Contrast these with the true faithfulness to the Lord shown by Jonathan. If time is short, focus on 1 Samuel 14:1–23.

14 1One day Jonathan son of
Saul said to the young man
bearing his armor, "Come, let's go over
to the Philistine outpost on the other
side." But he did not tell his father.
2Saul was staying on the outskirts of
Gibeah under a pomegranate tree in
Migron. With him were about six hundred men, 3among whom was Ahijah,
who was wearing an ephod. He was a
son of Ichabod's brother Ahitub son of
Phinehas, the son of Eli, the LORD's
priest in Shiloh. No one was aware that
Jonathan had left.
4On each side of the pass that Jonathan intended to cross to reach the Philistine outpost was a cliff; one was called
Bozez, and the other Seneh. 5One cliff
stood to the north toward Micmash, the
other to the south toward Geba.
6Jonathan said to his young armor-
bearer, "Come, let's go over to the outpost of those uncircumcised fellows.
Perhaps the LORD will act in our behalf.
Nothing can hinder the LORD from saving, whether by many or by few."
7"Do all that you have in mind," his armor-bearer said. "Go ahead; I am with
you heart and soul."
8Jonathan said, "Come, then; we will
cross over toward the men and let them
see us. 9If they say to us, 'Wait there until we come to you,' we will stay where
we are and not go up to them. 10But if
they say, 'Come up to us,' we will climb
up, because that will be our sign that the

LORD has given them into our hands."
11So both of them showed themselves
to the Philistine outpost. "Look!" said
the Philistines. "The Hebrews are crawling out of the holes they were hiding
in." 12The men of the outpost shouted to
Jonathan and his armor-bearer, "Come
up to us and we'll teach you a lesson."

So Jonathan said to his armor-bearer, "Climb up after me; the LORD has given them into the hand of Israel."

13Jonathan climbed up, using his
hands and feet, with his armor-bearer
right behind him. The Philistines fell
before Jonathan, and his armor-bearer
followed and killed behind him. 14In
that first attack Jonathan and his armor-
bearer killed some twenty men in an
area of about half an acre.[a]

Israel Routs the Philistines

15Then panic struck the whole army—
those in the camp and field, and those
in the outposts and raiding parties—
and the ground shook. It was a panic
sent by God.[b]

16Saul's lookouts at Gibeah in Benjamin saw the army melting away in all
directions. 17Then Saul said to the men
who were with him, "Muster the forces
and see who has left us." When they
did, it was Jonathan and his armor-
bearer who were not there.

18Saul said to Ahijah, "Bring the ark of
God." (At that time it was with the
Israelites.)[c] 19While Saul was talking to
the priest, the tumult in the Philistine
camp increased more and more. So Saul
said to the priest, "Withdraw your
hand."

20Then Saul and all his men assembled
and went to the battle. They found the
Philistines in total confusion, striking
each other with their swords. 21Those
Hebrews who had previously been with
the Philistines and had gone up with
them to their camp went over to the Israelites who were with Saul and Jonathan. 22When all the Israelites who had
hidden in the hill country of Ephraim
heard that the Philistines were on the
run, they joined the battle in hot pursuit. 23So the LORD rescued Israel that
day, and the battle moved on beyond
Beth Aven.

Jonathan Eats Honey

24Now the men of Israel were in distress that day, because Saul had bound
the people under an oath, saying,
"Cursed be any man who eats food before evening comes, before I have
avenged myself on my enemies!" So
none of the troops tasted food.

25The entire army[d] entered the woods,
and there was honey on the ground.
26When they went into the woods, they
saw the honey oozing out, yet no one
put his hand to his mouth, because they
feared the oath. 27But Jonathan had not
heard that his father had bound the
people with the oath, so he reached out
the end of the staff that was in his hand
and dipped it into the honeycomb. He
raised his hand to his mouth, and his
eyes brightened.[e] 28Then one of the soldiers told him, "Your father bound the
army under a strict oath, saying, 'Cursed
be any man who eats food today!' That
is why the men are faint."

29Jonathan said, "My father has made
trouble for the country. See how my
eyes brightened[f] when I tasted a little of
this honey. 30How much better it would
have been if the men had eaten today
some of the plunder they took from
their enemies. Would not the slaughter of
the Philistines have been even greater?"

31That day, after the Israelites had
struck down the Philistines from Micmash to Aijalon, they were exhausted.
32They pounced on the plunder and,
taking sheep, cattle and calves, they
butchered them on the ground and ate
them, together with the blood. 33Then
someone said to Saul, "Look, the men
are sinning against the LORD by eating
meat that has blood in it."

"You have broken faith," he said. "Roll

[a]14 Hebrew *half a yoke*; a "yoke" was the land plowed by a yoke of oxen in one day. [b]15 Or *a terrible panic* [c]18 Hebrew; Septuagint *"Bring the ephod." (At that time he wore the ephod before the Israelites.)* [d]25 Or *Now all the people of the land* [e]27 Or *his strength was renewed* [f]29 Or *my strength was renewed*

a large stone over here at once." [34]Then he said, "Go out among the men and tell them, 'Each of you bring me your cattle and sheep, and slaughter them here and eat them. Do not sin against the LORD by eating meat with blood still in it.' "

So everyone brought his ox that night and slaughtered it there. [35]Then Saul built an altar to the LORD; it was the first time he had done this.

[36]Saul said, "Let us go down after the Philistines by night and plunder them till dawn, and let us not leave one of them alive."

"Do whatever seems best to you," they replied.

But the priest said, "Let us inquire of God here."

[37]So Saul asked God, "Shall I go down after the Philistines? Will you give them into Israel's hand?" But God did not answer him that day.

[38]Saul therefore said, "Come here, all you who are leaders of the army, and let us find out what sin has been committed today. [39]As surely as the LORD who rescues Israel lives, even if it lies with my son Jonathan, he must die." But not one of the men said a word.

[40]Saul then said to all the Israelites, "You stand over there; I and Jonathan my son will stand over here."

"Do what seems best to you," the men replied.

[41]Then Saul prayed to the LORD, the God of Israel, "Give me the right answer."[a] And Jonathan and Saul were taken by lot, and the men were cleared. [42]Saul said, "Cast the lot between me and Jonathan my son." And Jonathan was taken.

[43]Then Saul said to Jonathan, "Tell me what you have done."

So Jonathan told him, "I merely tasted a little honey with the end of my staff. And now must I die?"

[44]Saul said, "May God deal with me, be it ever so severely, if you do not die, Jonathan."

[45]But the men said to Saul, "Should Jonathan die—he who has brought about this great deliverance in Israel? Never! As surely as the LORD lives, not a hair of his head will fall to the ground, for he did this today with God's help." So the men rescued Jonathan, and he was not put to death.

[46]Then Saul stopped pursuing the Philistines, and they withdrew to their own land.

[47]After Saul had assumed rule over Israel, he fought against their enemies on every side: Moab, the Ammonites, Edom, the kings[b] of Zobah, and the Philistines. Wherever he turned, he inflicted punishment on them.[c] [48]He fought valiantly and defeated the Amalekites, delivering Israel from the hands of those who had plundered them.

Saul's Family

[49]Saul's sons were Jonathan, Ishvi and Malki-Shua. The name of his older daughter was Merab, and that of the younger was Michal. [50]His wife's name was Ahinoam daughter of Ahimaaz. The name of the commander of Saul's army was Abner son of Ner, and Ner was Saul's uncle. [51]Saul's father Kish and Abner's father Ner were sons of Abiel.

[52]All the days of Saul there was bitter war with the Philistines, and whenever Saul saw a mighty or brave man, he took him into his service.

[a]41 Hebrew; Septuagint *"Why have you not answered your servant today? If the fault is in me or my son Jonathan, respond with Urim, but if the men of Israel are at fault, respond with Thummim."*
[b]47 Masoretic Text; Dead Sea Scrolls and Septuagint *king* [c]47 Hebrew; Septuagint *he was victorious*

SHARPEN THE FOCUS

Outward show or inward authenticity? Pretense or reality? This issue in our spiritual lives will never go away this side of heaven. Of course, we don't confront the question as an either/or choice. At any given point, we fall somewhere along a continuum. And, at any given point, our Lord invites us to let Him draw us closer to Himself, closer to reality and away from pretense.

Jonathan's words in 1 Samuel 14:6 glow with warmth of a close, personal, faith-relationship with the Lord. He refers to the Philistines as "uncircumcised." These enemies do not have a covenant relationship with Israel's God. Jonathan literally stakes his life on the covenant promises of his God. And he is not disappointed.

Your Lord has established His covenant with you in your Baptism. Your God has sworn His faithfulness to you through that covenant which was ratified on Calvary. He invites you to fuller faith in every one of His promises. He calls you to deeper dimensions of worship. He empowers you for more willing obedience.

Ask yourself—and your Savior—in which direction you are moving along the pretense-reality continuum. Then rely on His forgiving grace to draw you closer to Himself.

WEEK 24 • SATURDAY

1 Samuel 15:1–35

A tragedy. The dictionary defines it as a "dramatic composition which evokes pity and terror by a succession of unhappy events bringing the lead character to catastrophe through some fatal flaw." Keep this definition in mind today as you continue to read the account of Saul's reign. What made the story of Saul's life tragic? If time is short, focus on 1 Samuel 15:1–23.

The LORD Rejects Saul as King

15 Samuel said to Saul, "I am the
one the LORD sent to anoint
you king over his people Israel; so listen
now to the message from the LORD.
2This is what the LORD Almighty says:
'I will punish the Amalekites for what
they did to Israel when they waylaid
them as they came up from Egypt.
3Now go, attack the Amalekites and totally destroy[a] everything that belongs to
them. Do not spare them; put to death
men and women, children and infants,
cattle and sheep, camels and donkeys.' "
4So Saul summoned the men and
mustered them at Telaim—two hundred thousand foot soldiers and ten
thousand men from Judah. 5Saul went
to the city of Amalek and set an ambush
in the ravine. 6Then he said to the Kenites, "Go away, leave the Amalekites so
that I do not destroy you along with
them; for you showed kindness to all
the Israelites when they came up out of
Egypt." So the Kenites moved away
from the Amalekites.
7Then Saul attacked the Amalekites all
the way from Havilah to Shur, to the
east of Egypt. 8He took Agag king of the
Amalekites alive, and all his people he
totally destroyed with the sword. 9But
Saul and the army spared Agag and the
best of the sheep and cattle, the fat
calves[b] and lambs—everything that was

[a]3 The Hebrew term refers to the irrevocable giving over of things or persons to the LORD, often by totally destroying them; also in verses 8, 9, 15, 18, 20 and 21. [b]9 Or *the grown bulls*; the meaning of the Hebrew for this phrase is uncertain.

good. These they were unwilling to destroy completely, but everything that was despised and weak they totally destroyed.

10 Then the word of the LORD came to Samuel: 11 "I am grieved that I have made Saul king, because he has turned away from me and has not carried out my instructions." Samuel was troubled, and he cried out to the LORD all that night.

12 Early in the morning Samuel got up and went to meet Saul, but he was told, "Saul has gone to Carmel. There he has set up a monument in his own honor and has turned and gone on down to Gilgal."

13 When Samuel reached him, Saul said, "The LORD bless you! I have carried out the LORD's instructions."

14 But Samuel said, "What then is this bleating of sheep in my ears? What is this lowing of cattle that I hear?"

15 Saul answered, "The soldiers brought them from the Amalekites; they spared the best of the sheep and cattle to sacrifice to the LORD your God, but we totally destroyed the rest."

16 "Stop!" Samuel said to Saul. "Let me tell you what the LORD said to me last night."

"Tell me," Saul replied.

17 Samuel said, "Although you were once small in your own eyes, did you not become the head of the tribes of Israel? The LORD anointed you king over Israel. 18 And he sent you on a mission, saying, 'Go and completely destroy those wicked people, the Amalekites; make war on them until you have wiped them out.' 19 Why did you not obey the LORD? Why did you pounce on the plunder and do evil in the eyes of the LORD?"

20 "But I did obey the LORD," Saul said. "I went on the mission the LORD assigned me. I completely destroyed the Amalekites and brought back Agag their king. 21 The soldiers took sheep and cattle from the plunder, the best of what was devoted to God, in order to sacrifice them to the LORD your God at Gilgal."

22 But Samuel replied:

"Does the LORD delight in burnt
    offerings and sacrifices
  as much as in obeying the voice of
    the LORD?
To obey is better than sacrifice,
  and to heed is better than the fat
    of rams.
23 For rebellion is like the sin of
    divination,
  and arrogance like the evil of
    idolatry.
Because you have rejected the word
    of the LORD,
  he has rejected you as king."

24 Then Saul said to Samuel, "I have sinned. I violated the LORD's command and your instructions. I was afraid of the people and so I gave in to them. 25 Now I beg you, forgive my sin and come back with me, so that I may worship the LORD."

26 But Samuel said to him, "I will not go back with you. You have rejected the word of the LORD, and the LORD has rejected you as king over Israel!"

27 As Samuel turned to leave, Saul caught hold of the hem of his robe, and it tore. 28 Samuel said to him, "The LORD has torn the kingdom of Israel from you today and has given it to one of your neighbors—to one better than you. 29 He who is the Glory of Israel does not lie or change his mind; for he is not a man, that he should change his mind."

30 Saul replied, "I have sinned. But please honor me before the elders of my people and before Israel; come back with me, so that I may worship the LORD your God." 31 So Samuel went back with Saul, and Saul worshiped the LORD.

32 Then Samuel said, "Bring me Agag king of the Amalekites."

Agag came to him confidently,[a] thinking, "Surely the bitterness of death is past."

33 But Samuel said,

"As your sword has made women
    childless,

[a] 32 Or *him trembling, yet*

so will your mother be childless
among women."

And Samuel put Agag to death before
the LORD at Gilgal.
34Then Samuel left for Ramah, but
Saul went up to his home in Gibeah of
Saul. 35Until the day Samuel died, he did
not go to see Saul again, though Samuel
mourned for him. And the LORD was
grieved that he had made Saul king
over Israel.

SHARPEN THE FOCUS

If we mapped Saul's spiritual journey, we would find it studded with crossroads after crossroads at which he took the wrong turn. Samuel's words, Jonathan's godly example, even Israel's army's sensible reaction to their king's foolish oath (1 Samuel 14:45) called for a confession and a U-turn in Saul's direction. The potential that we saw as Saul's reign began make the story just that much sadder.

But what exactly was Saul's "fatal flaw"? Verse 23 gives us several clues. These two key words stand out: *rebellion* and *arrogance.* And note this phrase: "you have rejected the Word of the LORD." Saul placed himself above the Word of God and made himself his own, final authority.

That thought-pattern is the essence of rebellion. And how easily we, too, fall into it. Our sinful nature pulls us downward with a force far stronger than gravity. We praise God that He never abandons us to free-fall. Even given the state of Saul's heart, the Lord's grace called and called and kept on calling to him.

That same grace calls to you and me today. Saul denied the problem and rejected the grace. What is your response?

WEEK 25 • MONDAY

1 Samuel 16:1–23

GET THE BIG PICTURE

Samuel secretly anoints David as Israel's next king. But outwardly nothing much changes in Israel. Saul still sits on the throne. David still tends his flocks in between stints at the royal court. Nonetheless God is at work. And even now, we see the sharp contrast between the one whom God has chosen and the one who has rejected God. If time is short, focus on 1 Samuel 16:1–13.

Samuel Anoints David

16 The LORD said to Samuel,
"How long will you mourn
for Saul, since I have rejected him as
king over Israel? Fill your horn with oil
and be on your way; I am sending you
to Jesse of Bethlehem. I have chosen one
of his sons to be king."
2But Samuel said, "How can I go? Saul
will hear about it and kill me."
The LORD said, "Take a heifer with
you and say, 'I have come to sacrifice
to the LORD.' 3Invite Jesse to the sacrifice, and I will show you what to do.
You are to anoint for me the one I indicate."

[4]Samuel did what the LORD said. When he arrived at Bethlehem, the elders of the town trembled when they met him. They asked, "Do you come in peace?"

[5]Samuel replied, "Yes, in peace; I have come to sacrifice to the LORD. Consecrate yourselves and come to the sacrifice with me." Then he consecrated Jesse and his sons and invited them to the sacrifice.

[6]When they arrived, Samuel saw Eliab and thought, "Surely the LORD's anointed stands here before the LORD."

[7]But the LORD said to Samuel, "Do not consider his appearance or his height, for I have rejected him. The LORD does not look at the things man looks at. Man looks at the outward appearance, but the LORD looks at the heart."

[8]Then Jesse called Abinadab and had him pass in front of Samuel. But Samuel said, "The LORD has not chosen this one either." [9]Jesse then had Shammah pass by, but Samuel said, "Nor has the LORD chosen this one." [10]Jesse had seven of his sons pass before Samuel, but Samuel said to him, "The LORD has not chosen these." [11]So he asked Jesse, "Are these all the sons you have?"

"There is still the youngest," Jesse answered, "but he is tending the sheep."

Samuel said, "Send for him; we will not sit down[a] until he arrives."

[12]So he sent and had him brought in. He was ruddy, with a fine appearance and handsome features.

Then the LORD said, "Rise and anoint him; he is the one."

[13]So Samuel took the horn of oil and anointed him in the presence of his brothers, and from that day on the Spirit of the LORD came upon David in power. Samuel then went to Ramah.

David in Saul's Service

[14]Now the Spirit of the LORD had departed from Saul, and an evil[b] spirit from the LORD tormented him.

[15]Saul's attendants said to him, "See, an evil spirit from God is tormenting you. [16]Let our lord command his servants here to search for someone who can play the harp. He will play when the evil spirit from God comes upon you, and you will feel better."

[17]So Saul said to his attendants, "Find someone who plays well and bring him to me."

[18]One of the servants answered, "I have seen a son of Jesse of Bethlehem who knows how to play the harp. He is a brave man and a warrior. He speaks well and is a fine-looking man. And the LORD is with him."

[19]Then Saul sent messengers to Jesse and said, "Send me your son David, who is with the sheep." [20]So Jesse took a donkey loaded with bread, a skin of wine and a young goat and sent them with his son David to Saul.

[21]David came to Saul and entered his service. Saul liked him very much, and David became one of his armor-bearers. [22]Then Saul sent word to Jesse, saying, "Allow David to remain in my service, for I am pleased with him."

[23]Whenever the spirit from God came upon Saul, David would take his harp and play. Then relief would come to Saul; he would feel better, and the evil spirit would leave him.

[a] *11* Some Septuagint manuscripts; Hebrew *not gather around* [b] *14* Or *injurious*; also in verses 15, 16 and 23

SHARPEN THE FOCUS

Fifteen years passed between David's anointing and his coronation. During this time, the Lord wanted to extend to Saul further opportunities to repent. And the Lord had much to teach David about what it means to live as His servant-son. David needed the kind of wisdom that comes only through experience. Like Moses before him, David would receive training both in the royal court and in the sheep pen.

Take time to reflect on the fact that in your Baptism the Lord has chosen and anointed you with the Holy Spirit as surely as He chose and anointed David. Think about your current opportunities to serve and about those things He might be preparing you to do.

Then remember that only as the Spirit of God moves to prepare you will you find yourself ready for fuller service. Ask for His grace to complete that class or that degree, to live through that trying experience, to work on that troubled relationship—with patience and endurance. And maybe even do this with joy as you consider your high standing in His opinion and the potential He sees in you because you are united with His Son, your Savior.

WEEK 25 • TUESDAY

1 Samuel 17:1–58

GET THE BIG PICTURE

As you read today's familiar account note especially the war of words involved. While both Goliath and King Saul focused on the outward appearance of Israel's weakness, David relied on the promise and power of the Lord. Also think about the ways Satan wages a similar war of words with you as you face the "giants" in your own life. If time is short, focus on 1 Samuel 17:1–11, 32–51.

David and Goliath

17 Now the Philistines gathered their forces for war and assembled at Socoh in Judah. They pitched camp at Ephes Dammim, between Socoh and Azekah. 2 Saul and the Israelites assembled and camped in the Valley of Elah and drew up their battle line to meet the Philistines. 3 The Philistines occupied one hill and the Israelites another, with the valley between them.

4 A champion named Goliath, who was from Gath, came out of the Philistine camp. He was over nine feet[a] tall. 5 He had a bronze helmet on his head and wore a coat of scale armor of bronze weighing five thousand shekels[b]; 6 on his legs he wore bronze greaves, and a bronze javelin was slung on his back. 7 His spear shaft was like a weaver's rod, and its iron point weighed six hundred shekels.[c] His shield bearer went ahead of him.

8 Goliath stood and shouted to the ranks of Israel, "Why do you come out and line up for battle? Am I not a Philistine, and are you not the servants of Saul? Choose a man and have him come down to me. 9 If he is able to fight and kill me, we will become your subjects; but if I overcome him and kill him, you will become our subjects and serve us." 10 Then the Philistine said, "This day I defy the ranks of Israel! Give me a man and let us fight each other." 11 On hearing the Philistine's words, Saul and all the Israelites were dismayed and terrified.

12 Now David was the son of an Ephrathite named Jesse, who was from Bethlehem in Judah. Jesse had eight sons, and in Saul's time he was old and well advanced in years. 13 Jesse's three oldest sons had followed Saul to the war: The firstborn was Eliab; the second, Abinadab; and the third, Shammah. 14 David was the youngest. The

[a]4 Hebrew *was six cubits and a span* (about 3 meters) [b]5 That is, about 125 pounds (about 57 kilograms) [c]7 That is, about 15 pounds (about 7 kilograms)

three oldest followed Saul, 15 but David
went back and forth from Saul to tend
his father's sheep at Bethlehem.
16 For forty days the Philistine came
forward every morning and evening
and took his stand.
17 Now Jesse said to his son David,
"Take this ephah[a] of roasted grain and
these ten loaves of bread for your brothers and hurry to their camp. 18 Take along
these ten cheeses to the commander of
their unit.[b] See how your brothers are
and bring back some assurance[c] from
them. 19 They are with Saul and all the
men of Israel in the Valley of Elah, fighting against the Philistines."
20 Early in the morning David left the
flock with a shepherd, loaded up and
set out, as Jesse had directed. He
reached the camp as the army was going out to its battle positions, shouting
the war cry. 21 Israel and the Philistines
were drawing up their lines facing each
other. 22 David left his things with the
keeper of supplies, ran to the battle lines
and greeted his brothers. 23 As he was
talking with them, Goliath, the Philistine champion from Gath, stepped out
from his lines and shouted his usual
defiance, and David heard it. 24 When
the Israelites saw the man, they all ran
from him in great fear.
25 Now the Israelites had been saying,
"Do you see how this man keeps coming out? He comes out to defy Israel.
The king will give great wealth to the
man who kills him. He will also give him
his daughter in marriage and will exempt his father's family from taxes in
Israel."
26 David asked the men standing near
him, "What will be done for the man
who kills this Philistine and removes
this disgrace from Israel? Who is this uncircumcised Philistine that he should
defy the armies of the living God?"
27 They repeated to him what they had
been saying and told him, "This is what
will be done for the man who kills him."
28 When Eliab, David's oldest brother,
heard him speaking with the men, he
burned with anger at him and asked,
"Why have you come down here? And
with whom did you leave those few
sheep in the desert? I know how conceited you are and how wicked your
heart is; you came down only to watch
the battle."
29 "Now what have I done?" said
David. "Can't I even speak?" 30 He then
turned away to someone else and
brought up the same matter, and the
men answered him as before. 31 What
David said was overheard and reported
to Saul, and Saul sent for him.
32 David said to Saul, "Let no one lose
heart on account of this Philistine; your
servant will go and fight him."
33 Saul replied, "You are not able to go
out against this Philistine and fight him;
you are only a boy, and he has been a
fighting man from his youth."
34 But David said to Saul, "Your servant
has been keeping his father's sheep.
When a lion or a bear came and carried
off a sheep from the flock, 35 I went after
it, struck it and rescued the sheep from
its mouth. When it turned on me, I
seized it by its hair, struck it and killed
it. 36 Your servant has killed both the lion
and the bear; this uncircumcised Philistine will be like one of them, because he
has defied the armies of the living God.
37 The LORD who delivered me from the
paw of the lion and the paw of the bear
will deliver me from the hand of this
Philistine."
Saul said to David, "Go, and the LORD
be with you."
38 Then Saul dressed David in his own
tunic. He put a coat of armor on him and
a bronze helmet on his head. 39 David
fastened on his sword over the tunic
and tried walking around, because he
was not used to them.
"I cannot go in these," he said to Saul,
"because I am not used to them." So he
took them off. 40 Then he took his staff
in his hand, chose five smooth stones
from the stream, put them in the pouch
of his shepherd's bag and, with his sling
in his hand, approached the Philistine.

[a]17 That is, probably about 3/5 bushel (about 22 liters) [b]18 Hebrew *thousand* [c]18 Or *some token;* or *some pledge of spoils*

[41]Meanwhile, the Philistine, with his shield bearer in front of him, kept coming closer to David. [42]He looked David over and saw that he was only a boy, ruddy and handsome, and he despised him. [43]He said to David, "Am I a dog, that you come at me with sticks?" And the Philistine cursed David by his gods. [44]"Come here," he said, "and I'll give your flesh to the birds of the air and the beasts of the field!"

[45]David said to the Philistine, "You come against me with sword and spear and javelin, but I come against you in the name of the LORD Almighty, the God of the armies of Israel, whom you have defied. [46]This day the LORD will hand you over to me, and I'll strike you down and cut off your head. Today I will give the carcasses of the Philistine army to the birds of the air and the beasts of the earth, and the whole world will know that there is a God in Israel. [47]All those gathered here will know that it is not by sword or spear that the LORD saves; for the battle is the LORD's, and he will give all of you into our hands."

[48]As the Philistine moved closer to attack him, David ran quickly toward the battle line to meet him. [49]Reaching into his bag and taking out a stone, he slung it and struck the Philistine on the forehead. The stone sank into his forehead, and he fell facedown on the ground.

[50]So David triumphed over the Philistine with a sling and a stone; without a sword in his hand he struck down the Philistine and killed him.

[51]David ran and stood over him. He took hold of the Philistine's sword and drew it from the scabbard. After he killed him, he cut off his head with the sword.

When the Philistines saw that their hero was dead, they turned and ran. [52]Then the men of Israel and Judah surged forward with a shout and pursued the Philistines to the entrance of Gath[a] and to the gates of Ekron. Their dead were strewn along the Shaaraim road to Gath and Ekron. [53]When the Israelites returned from chasing the Philistines, they plundered their camp. [54]David took the Philistine's head and brought it to Jerusalem, and he put the Philistine's weapons in his own tent.

[55]As Saul watched David going out to meet the Philistine, he said to Abner, commander of the army, "Abner, whose son is that young man?"

Abner replied, "As surely as you live, O king, I don't know."

[56]The king said, "Find out whose son this young man is."

[57]As soon as David returned from killing the Philistine, Abner took him and brought him before Saul, with David still holding the Philistine's head.

[58]"Whose son are you, young man?" Saul asked him.

David said, "I am the son of your servant Jesse of Bethlehem."

[a]52 Some Septuagint manuscripts; Hebrew *a valley*

SHARPEN THE FOCUS

Our hero is the Lord, our Savior-God. Scripture makes it clear that in all of history and in each of our individual lives as well, only the Lord can save, only He can deliver.

When we realize this, we can throw up our hands in fatalism and apathy. We can say with faithless Eli, "He is the LORD. Let Him do what is good in His eyes" (1 Samuel 3:18). Or we can see ourselves as the covenant children of a mighty Lord. We can use the power of His Word as the mighty Word it is—the Word that carries "divine power to demolish strongholds" (2 Corinthians 10:4). We can "take captive every thought to make it obedient to Christ" (2 Corinthians 10:5). We can speak God's promises to ourselves and to those around us—as David did. We can remind ourselves of the personal ways God has delivered us in the past—as David did. And we can rid ourselves of the timidity and fear that Satan wants to plant in our hearts.

If David sat with you reading his story today, he would be the first to say it: "The LORD won the victory over Goliath. The LORD is our hero." Live today in the shadow of your Lord's protecting presence.

WEEK 25 • WEDNESDAY

1 Sam. 18:1—19:24

GET THE BIG PICTURE

While David becomes more and more popular with the people, Saul eyes him with more and more suspicion. Today's reading tells of six attempts Saul made on David's life (1 Samuel 20 describes a seventh such attempt). If time is short, focus on 1 Samuel 18:1–16.

Saul's Jealousy of David

18 After David had finished
talking with Saul, Jonathan
became one in spirit with David, and he
loved him as himself. 2From that day
Saul kept David with him and did not
let him return to his father's house.
3And Jonathan made a covenant with
David because he loved him as himself.
4Jonathan took off the robe he was wearing and gave it to David, along with his
tunic, and even his sword, his bow and
his belt.
5Whatever Saul sent him to do, David
did it so successfully[a] that Saul gave
him a high rank in the army. This
pleased all the people, and Saul's officers as well.
6When the men were returning home
after David had killed the Philistine, the
women came out from all the towns of
Israel to meet King Saul with singing
and dancing, with joyful songs and with
tambourines and lutes. 7As they danced,
they sang:

"Saul has slain his thousands,
and David his tens of thousands."

8Saul was very angry; this refrain
galled him. "They have credited David
with tens of thousands," he thought,
"but me with only thousands. What
more can he get but the kingdom?"
9And from that time on Saul kept a jealous eye on David.
10The next day an evil[b] spirit from God
came forcefully upon Saul. He was
prophesying in his house, while David
was playing the harp, as he usually did.
Saul had a spear in his hand 11and he
hurled it, saying to himself, "I'll pin David to the wall." But David eluded him
twice.
12Saul was afraid of David, because
the LORD was with David but had left
Saul. 13So he sent David away from him
and gave him command over a thousand men, and David led the troops in
their campaigns. 14In everything he did
he had great success,[c] because the LORD
was with him. 15When Saul saw how
successful[d] he was, he was afraid of
him. 16But all Israel and Judah loved David, because he led them in their campaigns.
17Saul said to David, "Here is my older
daughter Merab. I will give her to you
in marriage; only serve me bravely and
fight the battles of the LORD." For Saul
said to himself, "I will not raise a hand
against him. Let the Philistines do that!"

[a]5 Or *wisely* [b]10 Or *injurious* [c]14 Or *he was very wise* [d]15 Or *wise*

18But David said to Saul, "Who am I,
and what is my family or my father's
clan in Israel, that I should become the
king's son-in-law?" 19So[a] when the time
came for Merab, Saul's daughter, to be
given to David, she was given in marriage to Adriel of Meholah.
20Now Saul's daughter Michal was in
love with David, and when they told
Saul about it, he was pleased. 21"I will
give her to him," he thought, "so that
she may be a snare to him and so that
the hand of the Philistines may be
against him." So Saul said to David,
"Now you have a second opportunity to
become my son-in-law."
22Then Saul ordered his attendants:
"Speak to David privately and say,
'Look, the king is pleased with you, and
his attendants all like you; now become
his son-in-law.' "
23They repeated these words to David. But David said, "Do you think it is
a small matter to become the king's son-
in-law? I'm only a poor man and little
known."
24When Saul's servants told him what
David had said, 25Saul replied, "Say to
David, 'The king wants no other price
for the bride than a hundred Philistine
foreskins, to take revenge on his enemies.' " Saul's plan was to have David
fall by the hands of the Philistines.
26When the attendants told David
these things, he was pleased to become
the king's son-in-law. So before the allotted time elapsed, 27David and his men
went out and killed two hundred Philistines. He brought their foreskins and
presented the full number to the king so
that he might become the king's son-in-
law. Then Saul gave him his daughter
Michal in marriage.
28When Saul realized that the LORD
was with David and that his daughter
Michal loved David, 29Saul became still
more afraid of him, and he remained his
enemy the rest of his days.
30The Philistine commanders continued to go out to battle, and as often as
they did, David met with more success[b]
than the rest of Saul's officers, and his
name became well known.

Saul Tries to Kill David

19 Saul told his son Jonathan
and all the attendants to kill
David. But Jonathan was very fond of
David 2and warned him, "My father
Saul is looking for a chance to kill you.
Be on your guard tomorrow morning;
go into hiding and stay there. 3I will go
out and stand with my father in the field
where you are. I'll speak to him about
you and will tell you what I find out."
4Jonathan spoke well of David to Saul
his father and said to him, "Let not the
king do wrong to his servant David; he
has not wronged you, and what he has
done has benefited you greatly. 5He
took his life in his hands when he killed
the Philistine. The LORD won a great
victory for all Israel, and you saw it and
were glad. Why then would you do
wrong to an innocent man like David by
killing him for no reason?"
6Saul listened to Jonathan and took
this oath: "As surely as the LORD lives,
David will not be put to death."
7So Jonathan called David and told
him the whole conversation. He
brought him to Saul, and David was
with Saul as before.
8Once more war broke out, and David
went out and fought the Philistines. He
struck them with such force that they
fled before him.
9But an evil[c] spirit from the LORD
came upon Saul as he was sitting in his
house with his spear in his hand. While
David was playing the harp, 10Saul tried
to pin him to the wall with his spear, but
David eluded him as Saul drove the
spear into the wall. That night David
made good his escape.
11Saul sent men to David's house to
watch it and to kill him in the morning.
But Michal, David's wife, warned him,
"If you don't run for your life tonight,
tomorrow you'll be killed." 12So Michal
let David down through a window, and
he fled and escaped. 13Then Michal took
an idol[d] and laid it on the bed, covering

[a]19 Or *However,* [b]30 Or *David acted more wisely*
[c]9 Or *injurious* [d]13 Hebrew *teraphim;* also in verse 16

it with a garment and putting some goats' hair at the head.
14When Saul sent the men to capture David, Michal said, "He is ill."
15Then Saul sent the men back to see David and told them, "Bring him up to me in his bed so that I may kill him."
16But when the men entered, there was the idol in the bed, and at the head was some goats' hair.
17Saul said to Michal, "Why did you deceive me like this and send my enemy away so that he escaped?"

Michal told him, "He said to me, 'Let me get away. Why should I kill you?' "
18When David had fled and made his escape, he went to Samuel at Ramah and told him all that Saul had done to him. Then he and Samuel went to Naioth and stayed there.
19Word came to Saul: "David is in Naioth at Ramah";
20so he sent men to capture him. But when they saw a group of prophets prophesying, with Samuel standing there as their leader, the Spirit of God came upon Saul's men and they also prophesied.
21Saul was told about it, and he sent more men, and they prophesied too. Saul sent men a third time, and they also prophesied.
22Finally, he himself left for Ramah and went to the great cistern at Secu. And he asked, "Where are Samuel and David?"

"Over in Naioth at Ramah," they said.
23So Saul went to Naioth at Ramah. But the Spirit of God came even upon him, and he walked along prophesying until he came to Naioth.
24He stripped off his robes and also prophesied in Samuel's presence. He lay that way all that day and night. This is why people say, "Is Saul also among the prophets?"

SHARPEN THE FOCUS

Have you ever worked or lived with someone who hated you, who set out to get you? What does our Lord ask of us during times like those? Reflect upon these principles:

- That we act with the wisdom revealed in His Word regardless of what others say or do (1 Samuel 18:14; Proverbs 2:10–13).
- That we do good to those who sin against us (1 Samuel 19:4; Proverbs 25:21–22; Matthew 5:44).
- That we do what we can to protect and care for ourselves, and that we share our feelings and needs with Him and with other believers who can support us (1 Samuel 19:18; Philippians 4:4–7).
- That we keep our focus on the tasks He has given us and that we do them to the best of our ability (1 Samuel 18:30; 1 Thessalonians 4:11–12).
- That we trust Him for justice and resist the temptation to take revenge (Romans 12:17–21; 1 Peter 4:17–19).

An impossible order, if we're honest with ourselves and with God. Impossible, that is, if He hadn't promised to provide the faith we need to do what He has commanded.

Jesus knew the burden and pain of abuse from enemies. Trust Him for the forgiveness you need for failures to act in love toward your own enemies. Then rely on Him for daily power to make a fresh start.

WEEK 25 • THURSDAY

1 Samuel 20:1—21:15

GET THE BIG PICTURE

Reluctant to believe his father's insane jealousy, Jonathan finally faces the truth when Saul hurls a spear at him for defending David. David leaves Saul's court to hide, first at Nob and then in Gath with the Philistines. As you read, notice especially the comfort the Lord gave David in Jonathan his friend. If time is short, focus on 1 Samuel 20:1–17.

David and Jonathan

20 Then David fled from Naioth at Ramah and went to
Jonathan and asked, "What have I
done? What is my crime? How have I
wronged your father, that he is trying to
take my life?"
2"Never!" Jonathan replied. "You are
not going to die! Look, my father
doesn't do anything, great or small,
without confiding in me. Why would he
hide this from me? It's not so!"
3But David took an oath and said,
"Your father knows very well that I have
found favor in your eyes, and he has
said to himself, 'Jonathan must not
know this or he will be grieved.' Yet as
surely as the LORD lives and as you live,
there is only a step between me and
death."
4Jonathan said to David, "Whatever
you want me to do, I'll do for you."
5So David said, "Look, tomorrow is
the New Moon festival, and I am supposed to dine with the king; but let me
go and hide in the field until the evening of the day after tomorrow. 6If your
father misses me at all, tell him, 'David
earnestly asked my permission to hurry to Bethlehem, his hometown, because an annual sacrifice is being made
there for his whole clan.' 7If he says,
'Very well,' then your servant is safe.
But if he loses his temper, you can be
sure that he is determined to harm me.
8As for you, show kindness to your servant, for you have brought him into a
covenant with you before the LORD. If I
am guilty, then kill me yourself! Why
hand me over to your father?"
9"Never!" Jonathan said. "If I had the
least inkling that my father was determined to harm you, wouldn't I tell
you?"
10David asked, "Who will tell me if
your father answers you harshly?"
11"Come," Jonathan said, "let's go out
into the field." So they went there together.
12Then Jonathan said to David: "By
the LORD, the God of Israel, I will surely
sound out my father by this time the
day after tomorrow! If he is favorably
disposed toward you, will I not send
you word and let you know? 13But if my
father is inclined to harm you, may the
LORD deal with me, be it ever so severely, if I do not let you know and send
you away safely. May the LORD be with
you as he has been with my father. 14But
show me unfailing kindness like that of
the LORD as long as I live, so that I may
not be killed, 15and do not ever cut off
your kindness from my family—not
even when the LORD has cut off every
one of David's enemies from the face of
the earth."
16So Jonathan made a covenant with
the house of David, saying, "May the
LORD call David's enemies to account."
17And Jonathan had David reaffirm his
oath out of love for him, because he
loved him as he loved himself.
18Then Jonathan said to David: "Tomorrow is the New Moon festival. You
will be missed, because your seat will be

empty. 19The day after tomorrow, toward evening, go to the place where you hid when this trouble began, and wait by the stone Ezel. 20I will shoot three arrows to the side of it, as though I were shooting at a target. 21Then I will send a boy and say, 'Go, find the arrows.' If I say to him, 'Look, the arrows are on this side of you; bring them here,' then come, because, as surely as the LORD lives, you are safe; there is no danger. 22But if I say to the boy, 'Look, the arrows are beyond you,' then you must go, because the LORD has sent you away. 23And about the matter you and I discussed—remember, the LORD is witness between you and me forever."

24So David hid in the field, and when the New Moon festival came, the king sat down to eat. 25He sat in his customary place by the wall, opposite Jonathan,[a] and Abner sat next to Saul, but David's place was empty. 26Saul said nothing that day, for he thought, "Something must have happened to David to make him ceremonially unclean—surely he is unclean." 27But the next day, the second day of the month, David's place was empty again. Then Saul said to his son Jonathan, "Why hasn't the son of Jesse come to the meal, either yesterday or today?"

28Jonathan answered, "David earnestly asked me for permission to go to Bethlehem. 29He said, 'Let me go, because our family is observing a sacrifice in the town and my brother has ordered me to be there. If I have found favor in your eyes, let me get away to see my brothers.' That is why he has not come to the king's table."

30Saul's anger flared up at Jonathan and he said to him, "You son of a perverse and rebellious woman! Don't I know that you have sided with the son of Jesse to your own shame and to the shame of the mother who bore you? 31As long as the son of Jesse lives on this earth, neither you nor your kingdom will be established. Now send and bring him to me, for he must die!"

32"Why should he be put to death? What has he done?" Jonathan asked his father. 33But Saul hurled his spear at him to kill him. Then Jonathan knew that his father intended to kill David.

34Jonathan got up from the table in fierce anger; on that second day of the month he did not eat, because he was grieved at his father's shameful treatment of David.

35In the morning Jonathan went out to the field for his meeting with David. He had a small boy with him, 36and he said to the boy, "Run and find the arrows I shoot." As the boy ran, he shot an arrow beyond him. 37When the boy came to the place where Jonathan's arrow had fallen, Jonathan called out after him, "Isn't the arrow beyond you?" 38Then he shouted, "Hurry! Go quickly! Don't stop!" The boy picked up the arrow and returned to his master. 39(The boy knew nothing of all this; only Jonathan and David knew.) 40Then Jonathan gave his weapons to the boy and said, "Go, carry them back to town."

41After the boy had gone, David got up from the south side ⌞of the stone⌟ and bowed down before Jonathan three times, with his face to the ground. Then they kissed each other and wept together—but David wept the most.

42Jonathan said to David, "Go in peace, for we have sworn friendship with each other in the name of the LORD, saying, 'The LORD is witness between you and me, and between your descendants and my descendants forever.' " Then David left, and Jonathan went back to the town.

David at Nob

21 David went to Nob, to Ahimelech the priest. Ahimelech trembled when he met him, and asked, "Why are you alone? Why is no one with you?"

2David answered Ahimelech the priest, "The king charged me with a certain matter and said to me, 'No one is to know anything about your mission and your instructions.' As for my men, I have told them to meet me at a certain

[a]25 Septuagint; Hebrew *wall. Jonathan arose*

place. 3Now then, what do you have on
hand? Give me five loaves of bread, or
whatever you can find."
4But the priest answered David, "I
don't have any ordinary bread on hand;
however, there is some consecrated
bread here—provided the men have
kept themselves from women."
5David replied, "Indeed women have
been kept from us, as usual whenever[a]
I set out. The men's things[b] are holy
even on missions that are not holy. How
much more so today!" 6So the priest
gave him the consecrated bread, since
there was no bread there except the
bread of the Presence that had been removed from before the LORD and replaced by hot bread on the day it was
taken away.
7Now one of Saul's servants was there
that day, detained before the LORD; he
was Doeg the Edomite, Saul's head
shepherd.
8David asked Ahimelech, "Don't you
have a spear or a sword here? I haven't
brought my sword or any other weapon, because the king's business was
urgent."
9The priest replied, "The sword of Goliath the Philistine, whom you killed in
the Valley of Elah, is here; it is wrapped
in a cloth behind the ephod. If you want
it, take it; there is no sword here but that
one."

David said, "There is none like it; give
it to me."

David at Gath

10That day David fled from Saul and
went to Achish king of Gath. 11But the
servants of Achish said to him, "Isn't this
David, the king of the land? Isn't he the
one they sing about in their dances:

" 'Saul has slain his thousands,
and David his tens of
thousands'?"

12David took these words to heart and
was very much afraid of Achish king of
Gath. 13So he pretended to be insane
in their presence; and while he was
in their hands he acted like a madman, making marks on the doors of the
gate and letting saliva run down his
beard.
14Achish said to his servants, "Look at
the man! He is insane! Why bring him
to me? 15Am I so short of madmen that
you have to bring this fellow here to carry on like this in front of me? Must this
man come into my house?"

[a]5 Or *from us in the past few days since* [b]5 Or *bodies*

SHARPEN THE FOCUS

Even hardened criminals will testify to the fact that people were created for relationships. When prison officials need to punish an inmate severely, they put that prisoner in solitary confinement. On the other hand, we can endure almost anything if we have the support of even one good friend. And it's even more helpful if our friend is also a friend of Jesus.

We need not hide our feelings nor even our sins from such a friend. And as we share both worries and joys with a friend like that, we encourage one another in the Lord.

That's what Jonathan did for David. In 1 Samuel 23:16 we read, "Saul's son Jonathan went to David at Horesh and helped him find strength in God." All believers, men and women alike, need those kinds of relationships.

If you enjoy one or more strong, Christian friendships, thank God (and your friend) today! If you have an opportunity to be a friend like that for another believer, ask your Savior for His grace to love that person with His love. If you need such a friendship yourself, ask your Lord to provide it. Remember, He has promised to "meet all your needs according to His glorious riches in Christ Jesus" (Philippians 4:19).

We continue to see the contrasts between David and Saul. While David feigns insanity (1 Samuel 21:10–15), Saul has reached the point of true paranoia. Insanely jealous of David, he imagines everyone is plotting against him—even those in his own personal bodyguard! As you read today, take special note of Doeg, Saul's chief herdsman. What motivates him? If time is short, focus on 1 Samuel 22:11–23.

David at Adullam and Mizpah

22 David left Gath and
escaped to the cave of
Adullam. When his brothers and his
father's household heard about it, they
went down to him there. [2]All those who
were in distress or in debt or discon-
tented gathered around him, and he became their leader. About four hundred
men were with him.
[3]From there David went to Mizpah in
Moab and said to the king of Moab,
"Would you let my father and mother
come and stay with you until I learn
what God will do for me?" [4]So he left
them with the king of Moab, and they
stayed with him as long as David was in
the stronghold.
[5]But the prophet Gad said to David,
"Do not stay in the stronghold. Go into
the land of Judah." So David left and
went to the forest of Hereth.

Saul Kills the Priests of Nob

[6]Now Saul heard that David and his
men had been discovered. And Saul,
spear in hand, was seated under the
tamarisk tree on the hill at Gibeah, with
all his officials standing around him.
[7]Saul said to them, "Listen, men of Benjamin! Will the son of Jesse give all of
you fields and vineyards? Will he make
all of you commanders of thousands
and commanders of hundreds? [8]Is that
why you have all conspired against me?
No one tells me when my son makes a
covenant with the son of Jesse. None of
you is concerned about me or tells me
that my son has incited my servant to lie
in wait for me, as he does today."
[9]But Doeg the Edomite, who was
standing with Saul's officials, said, "I
saw the son of Jesse come to Ahimelech
son of Ahitub at Nob. [10]Ahimelech inquired of the LORD for him; he also gave
him provisions and the sword of Goliath the Philistine."
[11]Then the king sent for the priest
Ahimelech son of Ahitub and his
father's whole family, who were the
priests at Nob, and they all came to the
king. [12]Saul said, "Listen now, son of
Ahitub."
"Yes, my lord," he answered.
[13]Saul said to him, "Why have you
conspired against me, you and the son
of Jesse, giving him bread and a sword
and inquiring of God for him, so that he
has rebelled against me and lies in wait
for me, as he does today?"
[14]Ahimelech answered the king,
"Who of all your servants is as loyal as
David, the king's son-in-law, captain of
your bodyguard and highly respected
in your household? [15]Was that day the
first time I inquired of God for him? Of
course not! Let not the king accuse your
servant or any of his father's family, for
your servant knows nothing at all about
this whole affair."
[16]But the king said, "You will surely
die, Ahimelech, you and your father's
whole family."
[17]Then the king ordered the guards at

his side: "Turn and kill the priests of the
LORD, because they too have sided with
David. They knew he was fleeing, yet
they did not tell me."
But the king's officials were not willing to raise a hand to strike the priests
of the LORD.
18The king then ordered Doeg, "You
turn and strike down the priests." So
Doeg the Edomite turned and struck
them down. That day he killed eighty-
five men who wore the linen ephod.
19He also put to the sword Nob, the
town of the priests, with its men and
women, its children and infants, and its
cattle, donkeys and sheep.
20But Abiathar, a son of Ahimelech son
of Ahitub, escaped and fled to join
David. 21He told David that Saul had
killed the priests of the LORD. 22Then
David said to Abiathar: "That day, when
Doeg the Edomite was there, I knew he
would be sure to tell Saul. I am responsible for the death of your father's
whole family. 23Stay with me; don't be
afraid; the man who is seeking your life
is seeking mine also. You will be safe
with me."

SHARPEN THE FOCUS

Some of the most knotty moral dilemmas we face involve questions of when to obey those in authority and when to oppose them. For instance:

- When does disagreeing with the position of an elected official cross the line into defaming that official (Romans 13:1–7)?
- When does asserting your position on an issue at work become disrespect to those in authority over you on the job (Ephesians 6:5–8)?
- When does arguing for an action that you believe is in your congregation's best interests become gossip, divisiveness, and rebellion against your pastor and the other spiritual authorities whom the Lord has placed over you (Hebrews 13:17)?

Doeg bowed and scraped and did what King Saul told him to do—to the point of multiple murder! Maybe he feared Saul's power. Maybe he thought God's command to obey human authority was absolute. Or maybe he saw a chance for personal promotion.

What attitudes motivate your relationships with those in authority? Ask your Lord to create a right heart within you in this regard. Then, cleansed by Christ and empowered by His Spirit, write a note of encouragement to someone in authority over you today.

WEEK 25 • SATURDAY

1 Samuel 23:1–29

GET THE BIG PICTURE

Saul chases and harasses David at every turn. As you read today, put yourself in David's place. What would you have been thinking about your lifestyle? about King Saul? about the Lord's promises to you? If time is short, focus on 1 Samuel 23:1–12.

David Saves Keilah

23 When David was told,
"Look, the Philistines are
fighting against Keilah and are looting
the threshing floors," [2]he inquired of the
LORD, saying, "Shall I go and attack
these Philistines?"
The LORD answered him, "Go, attack
the Philistines and save Keilah."
[3]But David's men said to him, "Here
in Judah we are afraid. How much
more, then, if we go to Keilah against
the Philistine forces!"
[4]Once again David inquired of the
LORD, and the LORD answered him, "Go
down to Keilah, for I am going to give
the Philistines into your hand." [5]So David and his men went to Keilah, fought
the Philistines and carried off their livestock. He inflicted heavy losses on the
Philistines and saved the people of Keilah. [6](Now Abiathar son of Ahimelech
had brought the ephod down with him
when he fled to David at Keilah.)

Saul Pursues David

[7]Saul was told that David had gone to
Keilah, and he said, "God has handed
him over to me, for David has imprisoned himself by entering a town with
gates and bars." [8]And Saul called up all
his forces for battle, to go down to Keilah to besiege David and his men.
[9]When David learned that Saul was
plotting against him, he said to Abiathar
the priest, "Bring the ephod." [10]David
said, "O LORD, God of Israel, your servant has heard definitely that Saul plans
to come to Keilah and destroy the town
on account of me. [11]Will the citizens of
Keilah surrender me to him? Will Saul
come down, as your servant has heard?
O LORD, God of Israel, tell your servant."
And the LORD said, "He will."
[12]Again David asked, "Will the citizens
of Keilah surrender me and my men to
Saul?"
And the LORD said, "They will."
[13]So David and his men, about six
hundred in number, left Keilah and kept
moving from place to place. When Saul
was told that David had escaped from
Keilah, he did not go there.
[14]David stayed in the desert strongholds and in the hills of the Desert of
Ziph. Day after day Saul searched for
him, but God did not give David into his
hands.
[15]While David was at Horesh in the
Desert of Ziph, he learned that Saul had
come out to take his life. [16]And Saul's son
Jonathan went to David at Horesh and
helped him find strength in God.
[17]"Don't be afraid," he said. "My father
Saul will not lay a hand on you. You will
be king over Israel, and I will be second
to you. Even my father Saul knows
this." [18]The two of them made a covenant before the LORD. Then Jonathan
went home, but David remained at
Horesh.
[19]The Ziphites went up to Saul at
Gibeah and said, "Is not David hiding
among us in the strongholds at Horesh,
on the hill of Hakilah, south of Jeshimon? [20]Now, O king, come down
whenever it pleases you to do so, and
we will be responsible for handing him
over to the king."
[21]Saul replied, "The LORD bless you
for your concern for me. [22]Go and make
further preparation. Find out where
David usually goes and who has seen
him there. They tell me he is very crafty.
[23]Find out about all the hiding places he
uses and come back to me with definite
information.[a] Then I will go with you; if
he is in the area, I will track him down
among all the clans of Judah."
[24]So they set out and went to Ziph
ahead of Saul. Now David and his men
were in the Desert of Maon, in the Arabah south of Jeshimon. [25]Saul and his
men began the search, and when David
was told about it, he went down to the
rock and stayed in the Desert of Maon.
When Saul heard this, he went into the
Desert of Maon in pursuit of David.
[26]Saul was going along one side of
the mountain, and David and his men
were on the other side, hurrying to get
away from Saul. As Saul and his forces

[a]23 Or *me at Nacon*

were closing in on David and his men to capture them, 27 a messenger came to Saul, saying, "Come quickly! The Philistines are raiding the land." 28 Then Saul broke off his pursuit of David and went to meet the Philistines. That is why they call this place Sela Hammahlekoth.[a] 29 And David went up from there and lived in the strongholds of En Gedi.

SHARPEN THE FOCUS

We know what David was thinking at this time. Even more important, we know what he was praying. We know these things because David recorded his thoughts and prayers in several psalms written—literally—on the run.

Psalm 54 carries a title that ties it specifically to 1 Samuel 23:19–20. Turn to this short psalm and read it twice now with the following thoughts in mind:

- During the first reading, think of David circling the mountain to avoid capture by Saul.
- During the second reading, think of yourself harassed by your own sinful nature, by Satan, and by the ungodly world-system around you. Make David's prayer your prayer.

Take comfort that even as the Lord proved Himself to be David's helper, so also He will be that for you. Even before David saw a resolution of his hassles, he could pray the words of Psalm 54:7. So, in Christ's cross, can you.

WEEK 26 • MONDAY

1 Samuel 24:1–22

GET THE BIG PICTURE

Saul selects 3,000 crack troops and takes off after David's ragtag band of 400 or so (see 1 Samuel 22:2; 25:13). Despite the odds, David gets what looks like a heaven-sent chance to resolve his problems with Saul. But he obeys the Word of God instead of doing what the circumstances might suggest. As you read, ask yourself how David was able to make decisions that pleased the Lord so consistently. If time is short, focus on 1 Samuel 24:1–13.

David Spares Saul's Life

24 After Saul returned from pursuing the Philistines, he was told, "David is in the Desert of En Gedi." 2 So Saul took three thousand chosen men from all Israel and set out to look for David and his men near the Crags of the Wild Goats.

3 He came to the sheep pens along the way; a cave was there, and Saul went in to relieve himself. David and his men were far back in the cave. 4 The men said, "This is the day the LORD spoke of when he said[b] to you, 'I will give your enemy into your hands for you to deal with as

[a] 28 *Sela Hammahlekoth* means *rock of parting.*
[b] 4 Or *"Today the LORD is saying*

you wish.' " Then David crept up unnoticed and cut off a corner of Saul's robe.

[5]Afterward, David was conscience-stricken for having cut off a corner of his robe. [6]He said to his men, "The LORD forbid that I should do such a thing to my master, the LORD's anointed, or lift my hand against him; for he is the anointed of the LORD." [7]With these words David rebuked his men and did not allow them to attack Saul. And Saul left the cave and went his way.

[8]Then David went out of the cave and called out to Saul, "My lord the king!" When Saul looked behind him, David bowed down and prostrated himself with his face to the ground. [9]He said to Saul, "Why do you listen when men say, 'David is bent on harming you'? [10]This day you have seen with your own eyes how the LORD delivered you into my hands in the cave. Some urged me to kill you, but I spared you; I said, 'I will not lift my hand against my master, because he is the LORD's anointed.' [11]See, my father, look at this piece of your robe in my hand! I cut off the corner of your robe but did not kill you. Now understand and recognize that I am not guilty of wrongdoing or rebellion. I have not wronged you, but you are hunting me down to take my life. [12]May the LORD judge between you and me. And may the LORD avenge the wrongs you have done to me, but my hand will not touch you. [13]As the old saying goes, 'From evildoers come evil deeds,' so my hand will not touch you.

[14]"Against whom has the king of Israel come out? Whom are you pursuing? A dead dog? A flea? [15]May the LORD be our judge and decide between us. May he consider my cause and uphold it; may he vindicate me by delivering me from your hand."

[16]When David finished saying this, Saul asked, "Is that your voice, David my son?" And he wept aloud. [17]"You are more righteous than I," he said. "You have treated me well, but I have treated you badly. [18]You have just now told me of the good you did to me; the LORD delivered me into your hands, but you did not kill me. [19]When a man finds his enemy, does he let him get away unharmed? May the LORD reward you well for the way you treated me today. [20]I know that you will surely be king and that the kingdom of Israel will be established in your hands. [21]Now swear to me by the LORD that you will not cut off my descendants or wipe out my name from my father's family."

[22]So David gave his oath to Saul. Then Saul returned home, but David and his men went up to the stronghold.

SHARPEN THE FOCUS

Jesus said, "Every good tree bears good fruit, but a bad tree bears bad fruit." (Matthew 7:17). His words elaborated on David's words in 1 Samuel 24:13—"From evildoers come evil deeds."

Who we are inside often shows on the outside. If we see a need for a change in our actions, we need to recognize that first we need a change in heart.

Maybe you've noticed already that David is a "type" of Christ. As we continue to read David's story, we will see many points of comparison between the two. But today, think about David's compassion for his enemy, Saul. That compassion forgave, but it also confronted Saul's sin. How like Christ's compassion for the scribes and Pharisees!

But unlike the sinner David, our Lord Jesus lived a completely consistent lifestyle of compassion. He lived that life obedient to His Father's will in every detail. He lived it in David's place and in ours. When our hearts trouble us, as David's troubled him (1 Samuel 24:5), we can remember that because of what Jesus did for us our record is clean. No charges are pending against us in heaven's court. Our Judge already has declared us "not guilty" and has credited Christ's own righteous life to our account.

WEEK 26 • TUESDAY

1 Samuel 25:1–44

GET THE BIG PICTURE

In addition to the dangers posed by King Saul, David faced the challenges of finding provisions for the 600 or so men who had by this time joined him in the wilderness. Today's chapter shows a little of what that must have been like. As you read, notice David's aggravation and the means the Lord used to keep him from taking justice into his own hands. If time is short, focus on 1 Samuel 25:1–33.

David, Nabal and Abigail

25 Now Samuel died, and all
Israel assembled and
mourned for him; and they buried him
at his home in Ramah.
Then David moved down into the
Desert of Maon.[a] [2]A certain man in
Maon, who had property there at Carmel, was very wealthy. He had a thousand goats and three thousand sheep,
which he was shearing in Carmel. [3]His
name was Nabal and his wife's name
was Abigail. She was an intelligent and
beautiful woman, but her husband, a
Calebite, was surly and mean in his
dealings.
[4]While David was in the desert, he
heard that Nabal was shearing sheep.
[5]So he sent ten young men and said to
them, "Go up to Nabal at Carmel and
greet him in my name. [6]Say to him:
'Long life to you! Good health to you
and your household! And good health
to all that is yours!
[7]" 'Now I hear that it is sheep-shearing
time. When your shepherds were with
us, we did not mistreat them, and the
whole time they were at Carmel nothing of theirs was missing. [8]Ask your own
servants and they will tell you. Therefore be favorable toward my young men,
since we come at a festive time. Please
give your servants and your son David
whatever you can find for them.' "
[9]When David's men arrived, they
gave Nabal this message in David's
name. Then they waited.
[10]Nabal answered David's servants,
"Who is this David? Who is this son of
Jesse? Many servants are breaking away
from their masters these days. [11]Why
should I take my bread and water, and
the meat I have slaughtered for my
shearers, and give it to men coming
from who knows where?"
[12]David's men turned around and
went back. When they arrived, they reported every word. [13]David said to his
men, "Put on your swords!" So they put
on their swords, and David put on his.
About four hundred men went up with
David, while two hundred stayed with
the supplies.
[14]One of the servants told Nabal's
wife Abigail: "David sent messengers
from the desert to give our master his
greetings, but he hurled insults at them.
[15]Yet these men were very good to us.
They did not mistreat us, and the whole
time we were out in the fields near them
nothing was missing. [16]Night and day
they were a wall around us all the time
we were herding our sheep near them.
[17]Now think it over and see what you
can do, because disaster is hanging over
our master and his whole household.
He is such a wicked man that no one can
talk to him."
[18]Abigail lost no time. She took two
hundred loaves of bread, two skins of
wine, five dressed sheep, five seahs[b] of

[a]1 Some Septuagint manuscripts; Hebrew *Paran*
[b]18 That is, probably about a bushel (about 37 liters)

roasted grain, a hundred cakes of raisins
and two hundred cakes of pressed figs,
and loaded them on donkeys. [19]Then
she told her servants, "Go on ahead; I'll
follow you." But she did not tell her
husband Nabal.

[20]As she came riding her donkey into
a mountain ravine, there were David
and his men descending toward her,
and she met them. [21]David had just said,
"It's been useless—all my watching over
this fellow's property in the desert so
that nothing of his was missing. He has
paid me back evil for good. [22]May God
deal with David,[a] be it ever so severely,
if by morning I leave alive one male of
all who belong to him!"

[23]When Abigail saw David, she quickly got off her donkey and bowed down
before David with her face to the
ground. [24]She fell at his feet and said:
"My lord, let the blame be on me alone.
Please let your servant speak to you;
hear what your servant has to say. [25]May
my lord pay no attention to that wicked
man Nabal. He is just like his name—his
name is Fool, and folly goes with him.
But as for me, your servant, I did not see
the men my master sent.

[26]"Now since the LORD has kept you,
my master, from bloodshed and from
avenging yourself with your own
hands, as surely as the LORD lives and
as you live, may your enemies and all
who intend to harm my master be like
Nabal. [27]And let this gift, which your
servant has brought to my master, be
given to the men who follow you.
[28]Please forgive your servant's offense,
for the LORD will certainly make a
lasting dynasty for my master, because
he fights the LORD's battles. Let no
wrongdoing be found in you as long as
you live. [29]Even though someone is
pursuing you to take your life, the life
of my master will be bound securely in
the bundle of the living by the LORD
your God. But the lives of your enemies
he will hurl away as from the pocket of
a sling. [30]When the LORD has done
for my master every good thing he
promised concerning him and has appointed him leader over Israel, [31]my
master will not have on his conscience
the staggering burden of needless
bloodshed or of having avenged himself. And when the LORD has brought
my master success, remember your servant."

[32]David said to Abigail, "Praise be to
the LORD, the God of Israel, who has
sent you today to meet me. [33]May you
be blessed for your good judgment and
for keeping me from bloodshed this day
and from avenging myself with my own
hands. [34]Otherwise, as surely as the
LORD, the God of Israel, lives, who has
kept me from harming you, if you had
not come quickly to meet me, not one
male belonging to Nabal would have
been left alive by daybreak."

[35]Then David accepted from her hand
what she had brought him and said, "Go
home in peace. I have heard your words
and granted your request."

[36]When Abigail went to Nabal, he was
in the house holding a banquet like that
of a king. He was in high spirits and
very drunk. So she told him nothing
until daybreak. [37]Then in the morning,
when Nabal was sober, his wife told him
all these things, and his heart failed him
and he became like a stone. [38]About ten
days later, the LORD struck Nabal and he
died.

[39]When David heard that Nabal was
dead, he said, "Praise be to the LORD,
who has upheld my cause against Nabal for treating me with contempt. He
has kept his servant from doing wrong
and has brought Nabal's wrongdoing
down on his own head."

Then David sent word to Abigail, asking her to become his wife. [40]His servants went to Carmel and said to
Abigail, "David has sent us to you to
take you to become his wife."

[41]She bowed down with her face to
the ground and said, "Here is your
maidservant, ready to serve you and
wash the feet of my master's servants."
[42]Abigail quickly got on a donkey and,
attended by her five maids, went with

[a]22 Some Septuagint manuscripts; Hebrew *with David's enemies*

David's messengers and became his
wife. 43David had also married Ahinoam
of Jezreel, and they both were his wives.
44But Saul had given his daughter Michal, David's wife, to Paltiel[a] son of Laish, who was from Gallim.

SHARPEN THE FOCUS

"You don't have to avenge yourself," Abigail told David. "Remember who you are. The LORD has promised to give you an enduring dynasty. You fight the LORD's battles, David. And He will fight yours" (1 Samuel 25:28).

Abigail's words of godly advice turned David from a course he would have regretted when he became king. At Abigail's reminder of who he was and *whose* he was, David put the injustice he had received at Nabal's hands on to the Lord. And God took care of the situation.

Whose battles are you fighting? Where do you focus your energies? On getting even? On making sure you get your fair share? Or on being about your Father's business? On advancing His kingdom here on earth? On growing in Christlikeness, by His gracious power at work in you?

Won't a self-forgetful attitude like that turn us into doormats? Not unless David was a doormat. Not unless our Lord Jesus was a doormat. In the end, the heavenly Father vindicated the wisdom of David and of David's greater Son, Jesus. He will vindicate you, too.

Read 1 Peter 2:19–24 prayerfully today. Ask your Lord for grace to believe and to act on His word of wisdom.

WEEK 26 • WEDNESDAY

1 Samuel 26:1–25

Someone has said, "The trouble with life is that it's so daily!" After awhile the day-after-day life of a fugitive had to grate on David. Maybe he began to rethink some of the choices he had made earlier. In today's reading, we see him confront an old temptation. Note the subtle ways it differs from last time we read about it. Note, too, the subtle clues that the Lord is maturing David day by day. If time is short, focus on 1 Samuel 26:1–11.

David Again Spares Saul's Life

26 The Ziphites went to Saul
at Gibeah and said, "Is not
David hiding on the hill of Hakilah,
which faces Jeshimon?"
2So Saul went down to the Desert of
Ziph, with his three thousand chosen
men of Israel, to search there for David.
3Saul made his camp beside the road on
the hill of Hakilah facing Jeshimon, but
David stayed in the desert. When he
saw that Saul had followed him there,
4he sent out scouts and learned that Saul
had definitely arrived.[b]
5Then David set out and went to the

[a]44 Hebrew *Palti*, a variant of *Paltiel* [b]4 Or *had come to Nacon*

place where Saul had camped. He saw where Saul and Abner son of Ner, the commander of the army, had lain down. Saul was lying inside the camp, with the army encamped around him.

[6]David then asked Ahimelech the Hittite and Abishai son of Zeruiah, Joab's brother, "Who will go down into the camp with me to Saul?"

"I'll go with you," said Abishai.

[7]So David and Abishai went to the army by night, and there was Saul, lying asleep inside the camp with his spear stuck in the ground near his head. Abner and the soldiers were lying around him.

[8]Abishai said to David, "Today God has delivered your enemy into your hands. Now let me pin him to the ground with one thrust of my spear; I won't strike him twice."

[9]But David said to Abishai, "Don't destroy him! Who can lay a hand on the LORD's anointed and be guiltless? [10]As surely as the LORD lives," he said, "the LORD himself will strike him; either his time will come and he will die, or he will go into battle and perish. [11]But the LORD forbid that I should lay a hand on the LORD's anointed. Now get the spear and water jug that are near his head, and let's go."

[12]So David took the spear and water jug near Saul's head, and they left. No one saw or knew about it, nor did anyone wake up. They were all sleeping, because the LORD had put them into a deep sleep.

[13]Then David crossed over to the other side and stood on top of the hill some distance away; there was a wide space between them. [14]He called out to the army and to Abner son of Ner, "Aren't you going to answer me, Abner?"

Abner replied, "Who are you who calls to the king?"

[15]David said, "You're a man, aren't you? And who is like you in Israel? Why didn't you guard your lord the king? Someone came to destroy your lord the king. [16]What you have done is not good. As surely as the LORD lives, you and your men deserve to die, because you did not guard your master, the LORD's anointed. Look around you. Where are the king's spear and water jug that were near his head?"

[17]Saul recognized David's voice and said, "Is that your voice, David my son?"

David replied, "Yes it is, my lord the king." [18]And he added, "Why is my lord pursuing his servant? What have I done, and what wrong am I guilty of? [19]Now let my lord the king listen to his servant's words. If the LORD has incited you against me, then may he accept an offering. If, however, men have done it, may they be cursed before the LORD! They have now driven me from my share in the LORD's inheritance and have said, 'Go, serve other gods.' [20]Now do not let my blood fall to the ground far from the presence of the LORD. The king of Israel has come out to look for a flea—as one hunts a partridge in the mountains."

[21]Then Saul said, "I have sinned. Come back, David my son. Because you considered my life precious today, I will not try to harm you again. Surely I have acted like a fool and have erred greatly."

[22]"Here is the king's spear," David answered. "Let one of your young men come over and get it. [23]The LORD rewards every man for his righteousness and faithfulness. The LORD delivered you into my hands today, but I would not lay a hand on the LORD's anointed. [24]As surely as I valued your life today, so may the LORD value my life and deliver me from all trouble."

[25]Then Saul said to David, "May you be blessed, my son David; you will do great things and surely triumph."

So David went on his way, and Saul returned home.

SHARPEN THE FOCUS

"Let me assassinate Saul," Abishai begged. His words hint at the thought, "You can blame it on me. I'll take the blame and you take the throne." David doesn't even stop to think it over. He acts based on a decision he has already settled in his heart. "The Lord—the living God, the God who acts on behalf of His people—will bring about justice for me," David says in essence (1 Samuel 26:10). Confident in the Lord's promise to give him a lasting dynasty, David spares Saul's life a second time.

As life becomes "daily" for you, with what does Satan tempt you? What choices does he present to you a second, third, or fourth time? How does he sugarcoat them to make them more palatable, less seemingly sinful?

When we notice a pattern, a series of temptations repeated for us as they were for David, we do well to settle the matter once and for all in our minds. Then, when Satan attacks, we already know what our response will be.

Of course, only God's power at work in us through His Word and the Sacraments can make such a choice possible. And such power is already yours in Jesus—day after day.

WEEK 26 • THURSDAY

1 Samuel 27:1—29:11

GET THE BIG PICTURE

Life in Saul's kingdom finally grows so dangerous that David takes refuge in Goliath's hometown, Gath! He cleverly keeps on attacking Israel's enemies while tricking the ruler of Gath into thinking he has committed treason in Israel. Saul, meanwhile, continues in his steep downward spiral—even consulting demons when the Lord won't answer him. If time is short, focus on 1 Samuel 28:1–25.

David Among the Philistines

27 But David thought to himself, "One of these days I
will be destroyed by the hand of Saul.
The best thing I can do is to escape to the
land of the Philistines. Then Saul will
give up searching for me anywhere in
Israel, and I will slip out of his hand."
2So David and the six hundred men
with him left and went over to Achish
son of Maoch king of Gath. 3David and
his men settled in Gath with Achish.
Each man had his family with him, and
David had his two wives: Ahinoam of
Jezreel and Abigail of Carmel, the widow of Nabal. 4When Saul was told that
David had fled to Gath, he no longer
searched for him.
5Then David said to Achish, "If I have
found favor in your eyes, let a place be
assigned to me in one of the country
towns, that I may live there. Why
should your servant live in the royal city
with you?"
6So on that day Achish gave him Ziklag, and it has belonged to the kings of
Judah ever since. 7David lived in Philistine territory a year and four months.
8Now David and his men went up
and raided the Geshurites, the Girzites

and the Amalekites. (From ancient times
these peoples had lived in the land extending to Shur and Egypt.) [9]Whenever
David attacked an area, he did not leave
a man or woman alive, but took sheep
and cattle, donkeys and camels, and
clothes. Then he returned to Achish.
[10]When Achish asked, "Where did
you go raiding today?" David would
say, "Against the Negev of Judah" or
"Against the Negev of Jerahmeel" or
"Against the Negev of the Kenites." [11]He
did not leave a man or woman alive to
be brought to Gath, for he thought,
"They might inform on us and say, 'This
is what David did.' " And such was his
practice as long as he lived in Philistine
territory. [12]Achish trusted David and
said to himself, "He has become so odi-
ous to his people, the Israelites, that he
will be my servant forever."

Saul and the Witch of Endor

28 In those days the Philistines gathered their forces
to fight against Israel. Achish said to
David, "You must understand that you
and your men will accompany me in the
army."
[2]David said, "Then you will see for
yourself what your servant can do."
Achish replied, "Very well, I will make
you my bodyguard for life."
[3]Now Samuel was dead, and all Israel
had mourned for him and buried him
in his own town of Ramah. Saul had expelled the mediums and spiritists from
the land.
[4]The Philistines assembled and came
and set up camp at Shunem, while Saul
gathered all the Israelites and set up
camp at Gilboa. [5]When Saul saw the
Philistine army, he was afraid; terror
filled his heart. [6]He inquired of the
LORD, but the LORD did not answer him
by dreams or Urim or prophets. [7]Saul
then said to his attendants, "Find me a
woman who is a medium, so I may go
and inquire of her."
"There is one in Endor," they said.
[8]So Saul disguised himself, putting on
other clothes, and at night he and two
men went to the woman. "Consult a
spirit for me," he said, "and bring up for
me the one I name."
[9]But the woman said to him, "Surely
you know what Saul has done. He has
cut off the mediums and spiritists from
the land. Why have you set a trap for my
life to bring about my death?"
[10]Saul swore to her by the LORD, "As
surely as the LORD lives, you will not be
punished for this."
[11]Then the woman asked, "Whom
shall I bring up for you?"
"Bring up Samuel," he said.
[12]When the woman saw Samuel, she
cried out at the top of her voice and said
to Saul, "Why have you deceived me?
You are Saul!"
[13]The king said to her, "Don't be
afraid. What do you see?"
The woman said, "I see a spirit[a] coming up out of the ground."
[14]"What does he look like?" he asked.
"An old man wearing a robe is coming
up," she said.
Then Saul knew it was Samuel, and
he bowed down and prostrated himself
with his face to the ground.
[15]Samuel said to Saul, "Why have you
disturbed me by bringing me up?"
"I am in great distress," Saul said.
"The Philistines are fighting against me,
and God has turned away from me. He
no longer answers me, either by prophets or by dreams. So I have called on you
to tell me what to do."
[16]Samuel said, "Why do you consult
me, now that the LORD has turned away
from you and become your enemy?
[17]The LORD has done what he predicted
through me. The LORD has torn the
kingdom out of your hands and given
it to one of your neighbors—to David.
[18]Because you did not obey the LORD or
carry out his fierce wrath against the
Amalekites, the LORD has done this to
you today. [19]The LORD will also hand over
both Israel and you to the Philistines,
and tomorrow you and your sons will
be with me. The LORD will also hand
over the army of Israel to the Philistines."

[a]*13* Or *see spirits;* or *see gods*

[20]Immediately Saul fell full length on the ground, filled with fear because of Samuel's words. His strength was gone, for he had eaten nothing all that day and night.

[21]When the woman came to Saul and saw that he was greatly shaken, she said, "Look, your maidservant has obeyed you. I took my life in my hands and did what you told me to do. [22]Now please listen to your servant and let me give you some food so you may eat and have the strength to go on your way."

[23]He refused and said, "I will not eat."

But his men joined the woman in urging him, and he listened to them. He got up from the ground and sat on the couch.

[24]The woman had a fattened calf at the house, which she butchered at once. She took some flour, kneaded it and baked bread without yeast. [25]Then she set it before Saul and his men, and they ate. That same night they got up and left.

Achish Sends David Back to Ziklag

29 The Philistines gathered all their forces at Aphek, and Israel camped by the spring in Jezreel. [2]As the Philistine rulers marched with their units of hundreds and thousands, David and his men were marching at the rear with Achish. [3]The commanders of the Philistines asked, "What about these Hebrews?"

Achish replied, "Is this not David, who was an officer of Saul king of Israel? He has already been with me for over a year, and from the day he left Saul until now, I have found no fault in him."

[4]But the Philistine commanders were angry with him and said, "Send the man back, that he may return to the place you assigned him. He must not go with us into battle, or he will turn against us during the fighting. How better could he regain his master's favor than by taking the heads of our own men? [5]Isn't this the David they sang about in their dances:

" 'Saul has slain his thousands,
and David his tens of
thousands'?"

[6]So Achish called David and said to him, "As surely as the LORD lives, you have been reliable, and I would be pleased to have you serve with me in the army. From the day you came to me until now, I have found no fault in you, but the rulers don't approve of you. [7]Turn back and go in peace; do nothing to displease the Philistine rulers."

[8]"But what have I done?" asked David. "What have you found against your servant from the day I came to you until now? Why can't I go and fight against the enemies of my lord the king?"

[9]Achish answered, "I know that you have been as pleasing in my eyes as an angel of God; nevertheless, the Philistine commanders have said, 'He must not go up with us into battle.' [10]Now get up early, along with your master's servants who have come with you, and leave in the morning as soon as it is light."

[11]So David and his men got up early in the morning to go back to the land of the Philistines, and the Philistines went up to Jezreel.

SHARPEN THE FOCUS

Romance. Money. Job. Family. All problems solved!

So read signs, yellow page ads, and TV spots touting professional psychics and various psychic networks available on 900 numbers.

Today's reading makes it plain that this abomination is nothing new. Sometimes it even works! Whether the witch at Endor really conjured up the soul of Samuel or whether a demon disguised as Samuel makes little difference. The incident reveals the depravity of Saul's heart. He knew that dabbling in the occult incurred the death penalty (Leviticus 20:6). Saul took this final step in his rebellion against the Lord—siding with the enemy, Satan himself.

Saul's disobedience stands as a warning to us. Spirituality outside our relationship with God through Christ is indeed spirituality. But the spirits involved are demons. We who are filled with the Holy Spirit renounced the devil—all his works and all his ways—in our Baptism. We have, by God's grace, taken our stand with the holy angels who serve our Lord day and night before His throne. Read Revelation 12:7–11 as you ask the Lord Jesus to keep your allegiance to Him and His kingdom ever strong.

Today's chapter records one final set of contrasts between David and King Saul. As we saw last time, the Lord refused to answer Saul. But 1 Samuel 30 shows David asking for direction and receiving it from the Lord. Today we also see David victorious in battle. Tomorrow we will read the witch's prediction of defeat and death come true for Saul. As you read today, ask yourself what accounts for David's strength. If time is short, focus on 1 Samuel 30:1–20.

David Destroys the Amalekites

30 David and his men reached Ziklag on the third day. Now the Amalekites had raided the Negev and Ziklag. They had attacked Ziklag and burned it,
2and had taken captive the women and all who were in it, both young and old. They killed none of them, but carried them off as they went on their way.
3When David and his men came to Ziklag, they found it destroyed by fire and their wives and sons and daughters taken captive.
4So David and his men wept aloud until they had no strength left to weep.
5David's two wives had been captured—Ahinoam of Jezreel and Abigail, the widow of Nabal of Carmel.
6David was greatly distressed because the men were talking of stoning him; each one was bitter in spirit because of his sons and daughters. But David found strength in the LORD his God.
7Then David said to Abiathar the priest, the son of Ahimelech, "Bring me the ephod." Abiathar brought it to him,
8and David inquired of the LORD, "Shall I pursue this raiding party? Will I overtake them?"

"Pursue them," he answered. "You will certainly overtake them and succeed in the rescue."
9David and the six hundred men with him came to the Besor Ravine, where some stayed behind,
10for two hundred men were too exhausted to cross the ravine. But David and four hundred men continued the pursuit.
11They found an Egyptian in a field and brought him to David. They gave him water to drink and food to eat—
12part of a cake of pressed figs and two cakes of raisins. He ate and was revived, for he had not eaten any food or drunk any water for three days and three nights.
13David asked him, "To whom do you belong, and where do you come from?"

He said, "I am an Egyptian, the slave of an Amalekite. My master abandoned me when I became ill three days ago. 14 We raided the Negev of the Kerethites and the territory belonging to Judah and the Negev of Caleb. And we burned Ziklag."

15 David asked him, "Can you lead me down to this raiding party?"

He answered, "Swear to me before God that you will not kill me or hand me over to my master, and I will take you down to them."

16 He led David down, and there they were, scattered over the countryside, eating, drinking and reveling because of the great amount of plunder they had taken from the land of the Philistines and from Judah. 17 David fought them from dusk until the evening of the next day, and none of them got away, except four hundred young men who rode off on camels and fled. 18 David recovered everything the Amalekites had taken, including his two wives. 19 Nothing was missing: young or old, boy or girl, plunder or anything else they had taken. David brought everything back. 20 He took all the flocks and herds, and his men drove them ahead of the other livestock, saying, "This is David's plunder."

21 Then David came to the two hundred men who had been too exhausted to follow him and who were left behind at the Besor Ravine. They came out to meet David and the people with him. As David and his men approached, he greeted them. 22 But all the evil men and troublemakers among David's followers said, "Because they did not go out with us, we will not share with them the plunder we recovered. However, each man may take his wife and children and go."

23 David replied, "No, my brothers, you must not do that with what the LORD has given us. He has protected us and handed over to us the forces that came against us. 24 Who will listen to what you say? The share of the man who stayed with the supplies is to be the same as that of him who went down to the battle. All will share alike." 25 David made this a statute and ordinance for Israel from that day to this.

26 When David arrived in Ziklag, he sent some of the plunder to the elders of Judah, who were his friends, saying, "Here is a present for you from the plunder of the LORD's enemies."

27 He sent it to those who were in Bethel, Ramoth Negev and Jattir; 28 to those in Aroer, Siphmoth, Eshtemoa 29 and Racal; to those in the towns of the Jerahmeelites and the Kenites; 30 to those in Hormah, Bor Ashan, Athach 31 and Hebron; and to those in all the other places where David and his men had roamed.

SHARPEN THE FOCUS

On a scale of 1 to 10 how would you rate yourself in spiritual strength during trials? How would you rate yourself in taking God at His word, believing and acting on His promises?

The two traits are closely related. In ourselves, we have zero spiritual strength. Jesus once cautioned His disciples, "Apart from Me, you can do nothing" (John 15:5). Not the easy things. Not a few things. But nothing!

We can demonstrate the kind of faith under fire David showed only as the Holy Spirit strengthens our faith. Our strength comes from our Lord and not from inside us.

Which brings us to taking God at His word—knowing, trusting, and acting in line with what our Lord has promised to do for us in Christ Jesus. David "found strength in the LORD his God" (1 Samuel 30:6). He rehearsed what God had said and done in the past. He mulled over the covenant promises God had confirmed to him personally. That word strengthened David's heart.

Find one or more of God's promises that has proven meaningful and comforting in the past. Write it down. Carry it with you and roll it over and over in your mind today as you let your Lord strengthen you.

WEEK 26 • SATURDAY

1 Samuel 31:1–13

GET THE BIG PICTURE

King Saul's life draws to a bloody close. His three sons, including Jonathan, die along with him. Loyal citizens of Jabesh Gilead travel all night to recover Saul's body and give it a proper burial. If time is short, focus on 1 Samuel 31:1–6.

Saul Takes His Life

31 Now the Philistines fought
against Israel; the Israelites
fled before them, and many fell slain on
Mount Gilboa. 2The Philistines pressed
hard after Saul and his sons, and they
killed his sons Jonathan, Abinadab and
Malki-Shua. 3The fighting grew fierce
around Saul, and when the archers
overtook him, they wounded him criti-
cally.
4Saul said to his armor-bearer, "Draw
your sword and run me through, or
these uncircumcised fellows will come
and run me through and abuse me."
But his armor-bearer was terrified
and would not do it; so Saul took his
own sword and fell on it. 5When the
armor-bearer saw that Saul was dead,
he too fell on his sword and died with
him. 6So Saul and his three sons and
his armor-bearer and all his men died
together that same day.
7When the Israelites along the valley
and those across the Jordan saw that the
Israelite army had fled and that Saul
and his sons had died, they abandoned
their towns and fled. And the Philistines
came and occupied them.
8The next day, when the Philistines
came to strip the dead, they found Saul
and his three sons fallen on Mount Gilboa. 9They cut off his head and stripped
off his armor, and they sent messengers
throughout the land of the Philistines to
proclaim the news in the temple of their
idols and among their people. 10They
put his armor in the temple of the Ashtoreths and fastened his body to the
wall of Beth Shan.
11When the people of Jabesh Gilead
heard of what the Philistines had done
to Saul, 12all their valiant men journeyed
through the night to Beth Shan. They
took down the bodies of Saul and his
sons from the wall of Beth Shan and
went to Jabesh, where they burned
them. 13Then they took their bones and
buried them under a tamarisk tree at
Jabesh, and they fasted seven days.

SHARPEN THE FOCUS

Perhaps at some time you've studied God's attributes. Such a list includes characteristics like graciousness, kindness, omnipotence, holiness, faithfulness, and unchangeableness.

Each one of these attributes comforts those who live by grace through faith in Christ Jesus and the blood of His cross.

The Bible teaches that God is omniscient—He knows everything. Nothing was, or ever will be, hidden from Him. Unlike the Philistines, we don't need to tell our God about our defeats or victories (1 Samuel 31:9). He already knows "the end from the beginning" (Isaiah 46:10).

This makes all the difference in the world if you link His omniscience with His love for you and His kindness toward you. It means that all along He knows all about your sin. And knowing that, He made provision for the cross of Christ where that sin would be nailed and would lose its power over you.

God also knows already the troubles and temptations you'll face today. He's known all along. And knowing that, He's made provision to strengthen you by His Spirit through His Word so that He can "keep you from falling and to present you before His glorious presence without fault and with great joy" (Jude 24).

2 Samuel

WEEK 27 • MONDAY

2 Samuel 1:1—2:32

The book of 2 Samuel continues the history began in 1 Samuel, the two books forming a seamless story of God's mercy to His people, especially through David. As you read, note the humility, honesty, and wisdom the Lord has worked in David's character during his years as a fugitive. If time is short, focus on 2 Samuel 1:1–27.

David Hears of Saul's Death

1 After the death of Saul, David returned from defeating the Amalekites and stayed in Ziklag two days. 2On
the third day a man arrived from Saul's
camp, with his clothes torn and with
dust on his head. When he came to David, he fell to the ground to pay him
honor.

3"Where have you come from?"
David asked him.

He answered, "I have escaped from
the Israelite camp."

4"What happened?" David asked.
"Tell me."

He said, "The men fled from the battle. Many of them fell and died. And
Saul and his son Jonathan are dead."

5Then David said to the young man
who brought him the report, "How do
you know that Saul and his son Jonathan are dead?"

6"I happened to be on Mount Gilboa,"
the young man said, "and there was
Saul, leaning on his spear, with the
chariots and riders almost upon him.
7When he turned around and saw me,
he called out to me, and I said, 'What
can I do?'

8"He asked me, 'Who are you?'

" 'An Amalekite,' I answered.

9"Then he said to me, 'Stand over me
and kill me! I am in the throes of death,
but I'm still alive.'

10"So I stood over him and killed him,
because I knew that after he had fallen
he could not survive. And I took the
crown that was on his head and the
band on his arm and have brought them
here to my lord."

11Then David and all the men with
him took hold of their clothes and tore
them. 12They mourned and wept and
fasted till evening for Saul and his son
Jonathan, and for the army of the LORD
and the house of Israel, because they
had fallen by the sword.

13David said to the young man who
brought him the report, "Where are you
from?"

"I am the son of an alien, an Amalekite," he answered.

14David asked him, "Why were you
not afraid to lift your hand to destroy
the LORD's anointed?"

15Then David called one of his men
and said, "Go, strike him down!" So he
struck him down, and he died. 16For David had said to him, "Your blood be on
your own head. Your own mouth testified against you when you said, 'I killed
the LORD's anointed.' "

David's Lament for Saul and Jonathan

17David took up this lament concerning Saul and his son Jonathan, 18and ordered that the men of Judah be taught this lament of the bow (it is written in the Book of Jashar):

19"Your glory, O Israel, lies slain on your heights.
How the mighty have fallen!

20"Tell it not in Gath,
proclaim it not in the streets of Ashkelon,
lest the daughters of the Philistines be glad,
lest the daughters of the uncircumcised rejoice.

21"O mountains of Gilboa,
may you have neither dew nor rain,
nor fields that yield offerings ⌞of grain⌟.
For there the shield of the mighty was defiled,
the shield of Saul—no longer rubbed with oil.
22From the blood of the slain,
from the flesh of the mighty,
the bow of Jonathan did not turn back,
the sword of Saul did not return unsatisfied.

23"Saul and Jonathan—
in life they were loved and gracious,
and in death they were not parted.
They were swifter than eagles,
they were stronger than lions.

24"O daughters of Israel,
weep for Saul,
who clothed you in scarlet and finery,
who adorned your garments with ornaments of gold.

25"How the mighty have fallen in battle!
Jonathan lies slain on your heights.

26I grieve for you, Jonathan my brother;
you were very dear to me.
Your love for me was wonderful,
more wonderful than that of women.

27"How the mighty have fallen!
The weapons of war have perished!"

David Anointed King Over Judah

2 In the course of time, David inquired of the LORD. "Shall I go up to one of the towns of Judah?" he asked.

The LORD said, "Go up."

David asked, "Where shall I go?"

"To Hebron," the LORD answered.

2So David went up there with his two wives, Ahinoam of Jezreel and Abigail, the widow of Nabal of Carmel. 3David also took the men who were with him, each with his family, and they settled in Hebron and its towns. 4Then the men of Judah came to Hebron and there they anointed David king over the house of Judah.

When David was told that it was the men of Jabesh Gilead who had buried Saul, 5he sent messengers to the men of Jabesh Gilead to say to them, "The LORD bless you for showing this kindness to Saul your master by burying him. 6May the LORD now show you kindness and faithfulness, and I too will show you the same favor because you have done this. 7Now then, be strong and brave, for Saul your master is dead, and the house of Judah has anointed me king over them."

War Between the Houses of David and Saul

8Meanwhile, Abner son of Ner, the commander of Saul's army, had taken Ish-Bosheth son of Saul and brought him over to Mahanaim. 9He made him king over Gilead, Ashuri[a] and Jezreel, and also over Ephraim, Benjamin and all Israel.

[a]9 Or *Asher*

[10]Ish-Bosheth son of Saul was forty years old when he became king over Israel, and he reigned two years. The house of Judah, however, followed David. [11]The length of time David was king in Hebron over the house of Judah was seven years and six months.

[12]Abner son of Ner, together with the men of Ish-Bosheth son of Saul, left Mahanaim and went to Gibeon. [13]Joab son of Zeruiah and David's men went out and met them at the pool of Gibeon. One group sat down on one side of the pool and one group on the other side.

[14]Then Abner said to Joab, "Let's have some of the young men get up and fight hand to hand in front of us."

"All right, let them do it," Joab said.

[15]So they stood up and were counted off—twelve men for Benjamin and Ish-Bosheth son of Saul, and twelve for David. [16]Then each man grabbed his opponent by the head and thrust his dagger into his opponent's side, and they fell down together. So that place in Gibeon was called Helkath Hazzurim.[a]

[17]The battle that day was very fierce, and Abner and the men of Israel were defeated by David's men.

[18]The three sons of Zeruiah were there: Joab, Abishai and Asahel. Now Asahel was as fleet-footed as a wild gazelle. [19]He chased Abner, turning neither to the right nor to the left as he pursued him. [20]Abner looked behind him and asked, "Is that you, Asahel?"

"It is," he answered.

[21]Then Abner said to him, "Turn aside to the right or to the left; take on one of the young men and strip him of his weapons." But Asahel would not stop chasing him.

[22]Again Abner warned Asahel, "Stop chasing me! Why should I strike you down? How could I look your brother Joab in the face?"

[23]But Asahel refused to give up the pursuit; so Abner thrust the butt of his spear into Asahel's stomach, and the spear came out through his back. He fell there and died on the spot. And every man stopped when he came to the place where Asahel had fallen and died.

[24]But Joab and Abishai pursued Abner, and as the sun was setting, they came to the hill of Ammah, near Giah on the way to the wasteland of Gibeon. [25]Then the men of Benjamin rallied behind Abner. They formed themselves into a group and took their stand on top of a hill.

[26]Abner called out to Joab, "Must the sword devour forever? Don't you realize that this will end in bitterness? How long before you order your men to stop pursuing their brothers?"

[27]Joab answered, "As surely as God lives, if you had not spoken, the men would have continued the pursuit of their brothers until morning.[b]"

[28]So Joab blew the trumpet, and all the men came to a halt; they no longer pursued Israel, nor did they fight anymore.

[29]All that night Abner and his men marched through the Arabah. They crossed the Jordan, continued through the whole Bithron[c] and came to Mahanaim.

[30]Then Joab returned from pursuing Abner and assembled all his men. Besides Asahel, nineteen of David's men were found missing. [31]But David's men had killed three hundred and sixty Benjamites who were with Abner. [32]They took Asahel and buried him in his father's tomb at Bethlehem. Then Joab and his men marched all night and arrived at Hebron by daybreak.

[a]*16 Helkath Hazzurim* means *field of daggers* or *field of hostilities.* [b]*27* Or *spoken this morning, the men would not have taken up the pursuit of their brothers;* or *spoken, the men would have given up the pursuit of their brothers by morning* [c]29 Or *morning;* or *ravine;* the meaning of the Hebrew for this word is uncertain.

SHARPEN THE FOCUS

Had David been self-focused, his camp would have celebrated the death of Saul and David's certain, imminent promotion to the throne.

Had David been focused on other's opinions, he would have put up a strong front at the loss of his friend Jonathan. He would have grieved in private or suppressed his grief entirely for the good of his career.

But by God's grace, David lived a life focused on his Lord and on the Lord's coming kingdom. God's people had been defeated. Saul and Jonathan had died violent deaths. David and the nation had suffered a great loss, and the Lord's enemies had won a temporary, but real victory. Strong in faith and in love for God's people, David wept—unashamed and in public.

As you face life's challenges, where's your focus? On what the swirl of events will mean for your life or career? On how to best control the fallout or contain your own emotions? Or on the kingdom of God and His righteousness?

That righteousness—right standing before God—belongs to you in Christ's cross. By His grace, you can claim it. In His strength you can find ways to extend the kingdom of His righteousness even in the most challenging circumstances.

WEEK 27 • TUESDAY

2 Samuel 3:1—4:12

GET THE BIG PICTURE

Chapter 3 introduces a seven-year civil war between David in Judah and Ish-Bosheth, Saul's son in Israel. As you read, note how, again and again, David acts with integrity and justice despite the opportunity to seize the crown and to take vengeance on his enemies. If time is short, focus on 2 Samuel 4:1–12.

3 The war between the house of
Saul and the house of David
lasted a long time. David grew stronger
and stronger, while the house of Saul
grew weaker and weaker.
2 Sons were born to David in Hebron:
His firstborn was Amnon the son of Ahinoam of Jezreel;
3 his second, Kileab the son of Abigail the widow of Nabal of Carmel;
the third, Absalom the son of Maacah daughter of Talmai king of Geshur;
4 the fourth, Adonijah the son of Haggith;
the fifth, Shephatiah the son of Abital;
5 and the sixth, Ithream the son of David's wife Eglah.
These were born to David in Hebron.

Abner Goes Over to David

6 During the war between the house of
Saul and the house of David, Abner had
been strengthening his own position in
the house of Saul. 7 Now Saul had had a
concubine named Rizpah daughter of

Aiah. And Ish-Bosheth said to Abner, "Why did you sleep with my father's concubine?"

8Abner was very angry because of what Ish-Bosheth said and he answered, "Am I a dog's head—on Judah's side? This very day I am loyal to the house of your father Saul and to his family and friends. I haven't handed you over to David. Yet now you accuse me of an offense involving this woman! 9May God deal with Abner, be it ever so severely, if I do not do for David what the LORD promised him on oath 10and transfer the kingdom from the house of Saul and establish David's throne over Israel and Judah from Dan to Beersheba." 11Ish-Bosheth did not dare to say another word to Abner, because he was afraid of him.

12Then Abner sent messengers on his behalf to say to David, "Whose land is it? Make an agreement with me, and I will help you bring all Israel over to you."

13"Good," said David. "I will make an agreement with you. But I demand one thing of you: Do not come into my presence unless you bring Michal daughter of Saul when you come to see me." 14Then David sent messengers to Ish-Bosheth son of Saul, demanding, "Give me my wife Michal, whom I betrothed to myself for the price of a hundred Philistine foreskins."

15So Ish-Bosheth gave orders and had her taken away from her husband Paltiel son of Laish. 16Her husband, however, went with her, weeping behind her all the way to Bahurim. Then Abner said to him, "Go back home!" So he went back.

17Abner conferred with the elders of Israel and said, "For some time you have wanted to make David your king. 18Now do it! For the LORD promised David, 'By my servant David I will rescue my people Israel from the hand of the Philistines and from the hand of all their enemies.' "

19Abner also spoke to the Benjamites in person. Then he went to Hebron to tell David everything that Israel and the whole house of Benjamin wanted to do. 20When Abner, who had twenty men with him, came to David at Hebron, David prepared a feast for him and his men. 21Then Abner said to David, "Let me go at once and assemble all Israel for my lord the king, so that they may make a compact with you, and that you may rule over all that your heart desires." So David sent Abner away, and he went in peace.

Joab Murders Abner

22Just then David's men and Joab returned from a raid and brought with them a great deal of plunder. But Abner was no longer with David in Hebron, because David had sent him away, and he had gone in peace. 23When Joab and all the soldiers with him arrived, he was told that Abner son of Ner had come to the king and that the king had sent him away and that he had gone in peace.

24So Joab went to the king and said, "What have you done? Look, Abner came to you. Why did you let him go? Now he is gone! 25You know Abner son of Ner; he came to deceive you and observe your movements and find out everything you are doing."

26Joab then left David and sent messengers after Abner, and they brought him back from the well of Sirah. But David did not know it. 27Now when Abner returned to Hebron, Joab took him aside into the gateway, as though to speak with him privately. And there, to avenge the blood of his brother Asahel, Joab stabbed him in the stomach, and he died.

28Later, when David heard about this, he said, "I and my kingdom are forever innocent before the LORD concerning the blood of Abner son of Ner. 29May his blood fall upon the head of Joab and upon all his father's house! May Joab's house never be without someone who has a running sore or leprosy[a] or who

[a]29 The Hebrew word was used for various diseases affecting the skin—not necessarily leprosy.

leans on a crutch or who falls by the sword or who lacks food."

30(Joab and his brother Abishai murdered Abner because he had killed their brother Asahel in the battle at Gibeon.)

31Then David said to Joab and all the people with him, "Tear your clothes and put on sackcloth and walk in mourning in front of Abner." King David himself walked behind the bier. 32They buried Abner in Hebron, and the king wept aloud at Abner's tomb. All the people wept also.

33The king sang this lament for Abner:

"Should Abner have died as the
    lawless die?
34 Your hands were not bound,
    your feet were not fettered.
You fell as one falls before wicked
    men."

And all the people wept over him again.

35Then they all came and urged David to eat something while it was still day; but David took an oath, saying, "May God deal with me, be it ever so severely, if I taste bread or anything else before the sun sets!"

36All the people took note and were pleased; indeed, everything the king did pleased them. 37So on that day all the people and all Israel knew that the king had no part in the murder of Abner son of Ner.

38Then the king said to his men, "Do you not realize that a prince and a great man has fallen in Israel this day? 39And today, though I am the anointed king, I am weak, and these sons of Zeruiah are too strong for me. May the LORD repay the evildoer according to his evil deeds!"

Ish-Bosheth Murdered

4 When Ish-Bosheth son of Saul heard that Abner had died in Hebron, he lost courage, and all Israel became alarmed. 2Now Saul's son had two men who were leaders of raiding bands. One was named Baanah and the other Recab; they were sons of Rimmon the Beerothite from the tribe of Benjamin—Beeroth is considered part of Benjamin, 3because the people of Beeroth fled to Gittaim and have lived there as aliens to this day.

4(Jonathan son of Saul had a son who was lame in both feet. He was five years old when the news about Saul and Jonathan came from Jezreel. His nurse picked him up and fled, but as she hurried to leave, he fell and became crippled. His name was Mephibosheth.)

5Now Recab and Baanah, the sons of Rimmon the Beerothite, set out for the house of Ish-Bosheth, and they arrived there in the heat of the day while he was taking his noonday rest. 6They went into the inner part of the house as if to get some wheat, and they stabbed him in the stomach. Then Recab and his brother Baanah slipped away.

7They had gone into the house while he was lying on the bed in his bedroom. After they stabbed and killed him, they cut off his head. Taking it with them, they traveled all night by way of the Arabah. 8They brought the head of Ish-Bosheth to David at Hebron and said to the king, "Here is the head of Ish-Bosheth son of Saul, your enemy, who tried to take your life. This day the LORD has avenged my lord the king against Saul and his offspring."

9David answered Recab and his brother Baanah, the sons of Rimmon the Beerothite, "As surely as the LORD lives, who has delivered me out of all trouble, 10when a man told me, 'Saul is dead,' and thought he was bringing good news, I seized him and put him to death in Ziklag. That was the reward I gave him for his news! 11How much more—when wicked men have killed an innocent man in his own house and on his own bed—should I not now demand his blood from your hand and rid the earth of you!"

12So David gave an order to his men, and they killed them. They cut off their hands and feet and hung the bodies by the pool in Hebron. But they took the head of Ish-Bosheth and buried it in Abner's tomb at Hebron.

SHARPEN THE FOCUS

Think about *integration*—the complete meshing of different parts to make a unified whole. Or consider *disintegration*. When something disintegrates, it falls apart.

Now think about the concept of *integrity*. A person of integrity has one worldview. People of integrity speak and act predictably, whether they find themselves in church or at the office or in a canoe on a weekend float trip. Such people have a personal center. They know who they are—deep down, where it counts.

Now, of course, Al Capone and Adolf Hitler would arguably fit this definition of integrity. That's why our center, the focus of our lives, matters so much. If Jesus Christ isn't the integrating force in our lives, we may live "true to ourselves," but we are not true to our Lord. Nor are we true to the life-vision He wants to give us.

Do you ever feel yourself falling apart? running in 100 directions at once? If so, let your Lord draw you back to your center—your Redeemer. Remember that your life is anchored in His cross. Then ask your Savior to integrate your worldview in the forgiveness He won for you there.

WEEK 27 • WEDNESDAY

2 Samuel 5:1–25

GET THE BIG PICTURE

The Lord works through people and events to establish David as king over all 12 tribes. As this happens, we begin to see David more and more as a "type of Christ." As you read, note that David is portrayed as a shepherd for Israel (2 Samuel 5:2), the ruler of Zion (2 Samuel 5:7), and the king over Israel (2 Samuel 5:12). If time is short, focus on 2 Samuel 5:1–16.

David Becomes King Over Israel

5 All the tribes of Israel came to
David at Hebron and said, "We
are your own flesh and blood. 2In the
past, while Saul was king over us, you
were the one who led Israel on their
military campaigns. And the LORD said
to you, 'You will shepherd my people Israel, and you will become their ruler.' "
3When all the elders of Israel had
come to King David at Hebron, the king
made a compact with them at Hebron
before the LORD, and they anointed David king over Israel.
4David was thirty years old when he
became king, and he reigned forty
years. 5In Hebron he reigned over Judah
seven years and six months, and in Jerusalem he reigned over all Israel and
Judah thirty-three years.

David Conquers Jerusalem

6The king and his men marched to
Jerusalem to attack the Jebusites, who
lived there. The Jebusites said to David,
"You will not get in here; even the blind
and the lame can ward you off." They
thought, "David cannot get in here."
7Nevertheless, David captured the fortress of Zion, the City of David.
8On that day, David said, "Anyone
who conquers the Jebusites will have to

use the water shaft[a] to reach those 'lame
and blind' who are David's enemies.[b]"
That is why they say, "The 'blind and
lame' will not enter the palace."

9David then took up residence in the
fortress and called it the City of David.
He built up the area around it, from the
supporting terraces[c] inward. 10And he
became more and more powerful, because the LORD God Almighty was with
him.

11Now Hiram king of Tyre sent messengers to David, along with cedar logs
and carpenters and stonemasons, and
they built a palace for David. 12And David knew that the LORD had established
him as king over Israel and had exalted
his kingdom for the sake of his people
Israel.

13After he left Hebron, David took
more concubines and wives in Jerusalem, and more sons and daughters were
born to him. 14These are the names of
the children born to him there: Shammua, Shobab, Nathan, Solomon, 15Ibhar,
Elishua, Nepheg, Japhia, 16Elishama,
Eliada and Eliphelet.

David Defeats the Philistines

17When the Philistines heard that David had been anointed king over Israel,
they went up in full force to search for
him, but David heard about it and went
down to the stronghold. 18Now the Philistines had come and spread out in the
Valley of Rephaim; 19so David inquired
of the LORD, "Shall I go and attack the
Philistines? Will you hand them over
to me?"

The LORD answered him, "Go, for I
will surely hand the Philistines over to
you."

20So David went to Baal Perazim, and
there he defeated them. He said, "As waters break out, the LORD has broken out
against my enemies before me." So that
place was called Baal Perazim.[d] 21The
Philistines abandoned their idols there,
and David and his men carried them off.

22Once more the Philistines came up
and spread out in the Valley of Rephaim; 23so David inquired of the LORD, and
he answered, "Do not go straight up,
but circle around behind them and attack them in front of the balsam trees.
24As soon as you hear the sound of
marching in the tops of the balsam trees,
move quickly, because that will mean
the LORD has gone out in front of you
to strike the Philistine army." 25So David
did as the LORD commanded him, and
he struck down the Philistines all the
way from Gibeon[e] to Gezer.

[a]8 Or *use scaling hooks* [b]8 Or *are hated by David* [c]9 Or *the Millo* [d]20 *Baal Perazim* means *the lord who breaks out.* [e]25 Septuagint (see also 1 Chron. 14:16); Hebrew *Geba*

SHARPEN THE FOCUS

Frank Peretti's first novel, *This Present Darkness,* took the world of Christian publishing by storm. Regardless of what else we may think of Peretti's work, he made the doctrines of angels, demons, and spiritual warfare real for tens of thousands of Christians, often for the first time.

In 2 Samuel 5:10, the holy writer tells us that David became great because "the LORD God Almighty was with him." God's angel army fought for David, beside David's earthly army. Our Lord used David to establish Israel in the land as a great nation so that from this nation He could bless the entire world in the Seed of Abraham—our Savior, the Lord Christ (Genesis 12:1–3; Galatians 3:7–14).

The heavenly Father went about fulfilling His covenant with Abraham with single-minded determination. He marshaled heaven's armies to accomplish His purpose.

With this in mind, we can read 2 Samuel 5:12 in two ways. Certainly the words apply to King David and the nation of Israel 1,000 years or so before Christ. But the words also prophesy of

"David's Greater Son": "The LORD had established him as king over Israel and had exalted his Kingdom for the sake of His people Israel." ☼

WEEK 27 • THURSDAY

2 Samuel 6:1–23

The Lord had given His people specific directions about the proper way to carry the ark of the covenant (Exodus 25:10–14; Numbers 4:15). In their excitement, David and his people had "a better idea." It ended in tragedy. In fear and anger, David left the ark outside Jerusalem for three months. Then, convicted of his sin, David brought the ark of the covenant into Jerusalem with an unforgettable demonstration of joy and worship. If time is short, focus on 2 Samuel 6:12–23.

The Ark Brought to Jerusalem

6 David again brought together
out of Israel chosen men, thirty
thousand in all. 2He and all his men set
out from Baalah of Judah[a] to bring up
from there the ark of God, which is
called by the Name,[b] the name of the
LORD Almighty, who is enthroned between the cherubim that are on the ark.
3They set the ark of God on a new cart
and brought it from the house of Abinadab, which was on the hill. Uzzah and
Ahio, sons of Abinadab, were guiding
the new cart 4with the ark of God on it,[c]
and Ahio was walking in front of it. 5Da-
vid and the whole house of Israel were
celebrating with all their might before
the LORD, with songs[d] and with harps,
lyres, tambourines, sistrums and cymbals.
6When they came to the threshing
floor of Nacon, Uzzah reached out and
took hold of the ark of God, because
the oxen stumbled. 7The LORD's anger
burned against Uzzah because of his ir-
reverent act; therefore God struck him
down and he died there beside the ark
of God.
8Then David was angry because the
LORD's wrath had broken out against
Uzzah, and to this day that place is
called Perez Uzzah.[e]
9David was afraid of the LORD that
day and said, "How can the ark of the
LORD ever come to me?" 10He was not
willing to take the ark of the LORD to be
with him in the City of David. Instead,
he took it aside to the house of Obed-
Edom the Gittite. 11The ark of the LORD
remained in the house of Obed-Edom
the Gittite for three months, and the
LORD blessed him and his entire household.
12Now King David was told, "The
LORD has blessed the household of
Obed-Edom and everything he has,
because of the ark of God." So David
went down and brought up the ark of
God from the house of Obed-Edom to
the City of David with rejoicing. 13When

[a]2 That is, Kiriath Jearim; Hebrew *Baale Judah*, a variant of *Baalah of Judah* [b]2 Hebrew; Septuagint and Vulgate do not have *the Name.* [c]3,4 Dead Sea Scrolls and some Septuagint manuscripts; Masoretic Text *cart* [4]*and they brought it with the ark of God from the house of Abinadab, which was on the hill* [d]5 See Dead Sea Scrolls, Septuagint and 1 Chronicles 13:8; Masoretic Text *celebrating before the LORD with all kinds of instruments made of pine.* [e]8 *Perez Uzzah* means *outbreak against Uzzah.*

those who were carrying the ark of the
LORD had taken six steps, he sacrificed
a bull and a fattened calf. 14 David, wearing a linen ephod, danced before the
LORD with all his might, 15 while he and
the entire house of Israel brought up the
ark of the LORD with shouts and the
sound of trumpets.

16 As the ark of the LORD was entering
the City of David, Michal daughter of
Saul watched from a window. And
when she saw King David leaping and
dancing before the LORD, she despised
him in her heart.

17 They brought the ark of the LORD
and set it in its place inside the tent that
David had pitched for it, and David
sacrificed burnt offerings and fellowship offerings[a] before the LORD. 18 After
he had finished sacrificing the burnt
offerings and fellowship offerings, he
blessed the people in the name of
the LORD Almighty. 19 Then he gave a
loaf of bread, a cake of dates and a cake
of raisins to each person in the whole
crowd of Israelites, both men and wom-
en. And all the people went to their
homes.

20 When David returned home to bless
his household, Michal daughter of Saul
came out to meet him and said, "How
the king of Israel has distinguished himself today, disrobing in the sight of the
slave girls of his servants as any vulgar
fellow would!"

21 David said to Michal, "It was before
the LORD, who chose me rather than
your father or anyone from his house
when he appointed me ruler over the
LORD's people Israel—I will celebrate
before the LORD. 22 I will become even
more undignified than this, and I will be
humiliated in my own eyes. But by
these slave girls you spoke of, I will be
held in honor."

23 And Michal daughter of Saul had no
children to the day of her death.

[a]17 Traditionally *peace offerings;* also in verse 18

SHARPEN THE FOCUS

True worship explodes from hearts touched by the goodness of God. Again and again in the Old Testament we see the Lord's people dance and shout as they worship Him. When we lose ourselves in worship like David did, not everyone will approve. But look at David's response to those kinds of criticism (2 Samuel 6:21–22). "I will celebrate before the LORD," he says. As you think about your own worship life, does your heart more resemble David's or Michal's? More often than we'd probably like to admit, our worship is cold, and our hearts are numb. What then?

The solution doesn't lie in more flares and fireworks in the worship service, though well-planned services are important. The solution doesn't lie in trying harder or resolving to worship more fervently. Rather, we ask God for what we need.

We bring our coldness, our numbness to our Lord. We ask for His forgiveness and His help. We ask for a fresh in-filling of His Holy Spirit, a renewed realization of His goodness to us in Christ. And we wait, expectantly, for Him to give us just that.

WEEK 27 • FRIDAY

2 Samuel 7:1–29

Moved by a thankful heart, David proposes to build a "house" for Yahweh, the Lord. But through the prophet Nathan, the Lord promises to establish a house of a different kind for David: a dynasty that would last forever. As you read, note all of God's specific "I will . . ." promises to David. If time is short, focus on 2 Samuel 7:1–17.

God's Promise to David

7 After the king was settled in his
palace and the LORD had given
him rest from all his enemies around
him, [2]he said to Nathan the prophet,
"Here I am, living in a palace of cedar,
while the ark of God remains in a tent."
[3]Nathan replied to the king, "Whatever you have in mind, go ahead and do
it, for the LORD is with you."
[4]That night the word of the LORD
came to Nathan, saying:

[5]"Go and tell my servant David,
'This is what the LORD says: Are
you the one to build me a house to
dwell in? [6]I have not dwelt in a
house from the day I brought the
Israelites up out of Egypt to this
day. I have been moving from
place to place with a tent as my
dwelling. [7]Wherever I have moved
with all the Israelites, did I ever say
to any of their rulers whom I commanded to shepherd my people
Israel, "Why have you not built me
a house of cedar?" '
[8]"Now then, tell my servant David, 'This is what the LORD Almighty says: I took you from the
pasture and from following the
flock to be ruler over my people
Israel. [9]I have been with you wherever you have gone, and I have cut
off all your enemies from before
you. Now I will make your name
great, like the names of the greatest men of the earth. [10]And I will
provide a place for my people Israel
and will plant them so that they can
have a home of their own and no
longer be disturbed. Wicked people
will not oppress them anymore, as
they did at the beginning [11]and
have done ever since the time I
appointed leaders[a] over my people
Israel. I will also give you rest from
all your enemies.
" 'The LORD declares to you that
the LORD himself will establish a
house for you: [12]When your days
are over and you rest with your fathers, I will raise up your offspring
to succeed you, who will come
from your own body, and I will
establish his kingdom. [13]He is the
one who will build a house for my
Name, and I will establish the
throne of his kingdom forever. [14]I
will be his father, and he will be my
son. When he does wrong, I will
punish him with the rod of men,
with floggings inflicted by men.
[15]But my love will never be taken
away from him, as I took it away
from Saul, whom I removed from
before you. [16]Your house and your
kingdom will endure forever before me[b]; your throne will be established forever.' "

[17]Nathan reported to David all the
words of this entire revelation.

[a]11 Traditionally *judges* [b]16 Some Hebrew manuscripts and Septuagint; most Hebrew manuscripts *you*

David's Prayer

18Then King David went in and sat before the LORD, and he said:

"Who am I, O Sovereign LORD,
and what is my family, that you
have brought me this far? 19And as
if this were not enough in your
sight, O Sovereign LORD, you have
also spoken about the future of the
house of your servant. Is this your
usual way of dealing with man, O
Sovereign LORD?
20"What more can David say to
you? For you know your servant,
O Sovereign LORD. 21For the sake of
your word and according to your
will, you have done this great thing
and made it known to your servant.
22"How great you are, O Sovereign LORD! There is no one like you,
and there is no God but you, as we
have heard with our own ears.
23And who is like your people Israel—the one nation on earth that
God went out to redeem as a people for himself, and to make a name
for himself, and to perform great
and awesome wonders by driving
out nations and their gods from
before your people, whom you redeemed from Egypt?[a] 24You have
established your people Israel as
your very own forever, and you,
O LORD, have become their God.
25"And now, LORD God, keep forever the promise you have made
concerning your servant and his
house. Do as you promised, 26so
that your name will be great forever. Then men will say, 'The LORD
Almighty is God over Israel!' And
the house of your servant David
will be established before you.
27"O LORD Almighty, God of Israel, you have revealed this to your
servant, saying, 'I will build a house
for you.' So your servant has found
courage to offer you this prayer.
28O Sovereign LORD, you are God!
Your words are trustworthy, and
you have promised these good
things to your servant. 29Now be
pleased to bless the house of your
servant, that it may continue forever in your sight; for you, O Sovereign LORD, have spoken, and
with your blessing the house of
your servant will be blessed forever."

[a]23 See Septuagint and 1 Chron. 17:21; Hebrew *wonders for your land and before your people, whom you redeemed from Egypt, from the nations and their gods.*

SHARPEN THE FOCUS

When you hear the word *dynasty*, what comes to mind? The ruthless Egyptian pharaoh? The Russian Czars who lived in luxury at the expense of their people? It's hard to name examples of compassionate dynasties. Yet, today's reading tells of one. The Lord promises to establish David's throne forever (2 Samuel 7:16). He kept this promise fully in Jesus, who came from "the house and line of David" (Luke 2:4).

Jesus' kingdom would be a kingdom of peace, of justice, of righteousness. Jesus would sit on David's throne and rule His Israel, His church—forever.

Justice was served at the cross where Jesus took the punishment you and I deserve for our sins. Righteousness—right standing before God—now belongs to us, because God has credited Christ's own righteousness to our account. This kind of justice and this declaration of righteousness bring us peace now and forever.

A compassionate dynasty. How will you walk in the righteousness and enjoy the peace today?

WEEK 27 • SATURDAY

2 Samuel 8:1—10:19

It would be easy to think of David only as a conquering warrior. But if we let ourselves picture him in this one-dimensional way, we miss many other aspects of his character. As you read today, note how the strength God gave David showed itself in kindness, in sensitivity to the feelings of others, and in a heart of worship toward the Lord. If time is short, focus on 2 Samuel 9:1–13.

David's Victories

8 In the course of time, David defeated the Philistines and subdued them, and he took Metheg Ammah from the control of the Philistines.
[2]David also defeated the Moabites. He
made them lie down on the ground and
measured them off with a length of
cord. Every two lengths of them were
put to death, and the third length was
allowed to live. So the Moabites became
subject to David and brought tribute.
[3]Moreover, David fought Hadadezer
son of Rehob, king of Zobah, when he
went to restore his control along the
Euphrates River. [4]David captured a
thousand of his chariots, seven thousand charioteers[a] and twenty thousand
foot soldiers. He hamstrung all but a
hundred of the chariot horses.
[5]When the Arameans of Damascus
came to help Hadadezer king of Zobah,
David struck down twenty-two thousand of them. [6]He put garrisons in the
Aramean kingdom of Damascus, and
the Arameans became subject to him
and brought tribute. The LORD gave David victory wherever he went.
[7]David took the gold shields that belonged to the officers of Hadadezer and
brought them to Jerusalem. [8]From
Tebah[b] and Berothai, towns that belonged to Hadadezer, King David took
a great quantity of bronze.
[9]When Tou[c] king of Hamath heard
that David had defeated the entire army
of Hadadezer, [10]he sent his son Joram[d] to
King David to greet him and congratulate him on his victory in battle over
Hadadezer, who had been at war with
Tou. Joram brought with him articles of
silver and gold and bronze.
[11]King David dedicated these articles
to the LORD, as he had done with the silver and gold from all the nations he had
subdued: [12]Edom[e] and Moab, the Ammonites and the Philistines, and Amalek. He also dedicated the plunder taken
from Hadadezer son of Rehob, king of
Zobah.
[13]And David became famous after he
returned from striking down eighteen
thousand Edomites[f] in the Valley of Salt.
[14]He put garrisons throughout Edom,
and all the Edomites became subject to
David. The LORD gave David victory
wherever he went.

David's Officials

[15]David reigned over all Israel, doing
what was just and right for all his people. [16]Joab son of Zeruiah was over the

[a]4 Septuagint (see also Dead Sea Scrolls and 1 Chron. 18:4); Masoretic Text *captured seventeen hundred of his charioteers* [b]8 See some Septuagint manuscripts (see also 1 Chron. 18:8); Hebrew *Betah.* [c]9 Hebrew *Toi,* a variant of *Tou;* also in verse 10 [d]10 A variant of *Hadoram* [e]12 Some Hebrew manuscripts, Septuagint and Syriac (see also 1 Chron. 18:11); most Hebrew manuscripts *Aram* [f]13 A few Hebrew manuscripts, Septuagint and Syriac (see also 1 Chron. 18:12); most Hebrew manuscripts *Aram* (that is, Arameans)

army; Jehoshaphat son of Ahilud was recorder; [17]Zadok son of Ahitub and Ahimelech son of Abiathar were priests; Seraiah was secretary; [18]Benaiah son of Jehoiada was over the Kerethites and Pelethites; and David's sons were royal advisers.[a]

David and Mephibosheth

9 David asked, "Is there anyone still left of the house of Saul to whom I can show kindness for Jonathan's sake?"

[2]Now there was a servant of Saul's household named Ziba. They called him to appear before David, and the king said to him, "Are you Ziba?"

"Your servant," he replied.

[3]The king asked, "Is there no one still left of the house of Saul to whom I can show God's kindness?"

Ziba answered the king, "There is still a son of Jonathan; he is crippled in both feet."

[4]"Where is he?" the king asked.

Ziba answered, "He is at the house of Makir son of Ammiel in Lo Debar."

[5]So King David had him brought from Lo Debar, from the house of Makir son of Ammiel.

[6]When Mephibosheth son of Jonathan, the son of Saul, came to David, he bowed down to pay him honor.

David said, "Mephibosheth!"

"Your servant," he replied.

[7]"Don't be afraid," David said to him, "for I will surely show you kindness for the sake of your father Jonathan. I will restore to you all the land that belonged to your grandfather Saul, and you will always eat at my table."

[8]Mephibosheth bowed down and said, "What is your servant, that you should notice a dead dog like me?"

[9]Then the king summoned Ziba, Saul's servant, and said to him, "I have given your master's grandson everything that belonged to Saul and his family. [10]You and your sons and your servants are to farm the land for him and bring in the crops, so that your master's grandson may be provided for. And Mephibosheth, grandson of your master, will always eat at my table." (Now Ziba had fifteen sons and twenty servants.)

[11]Then Ziba said to the king, "Your servant will do whatever my lord the king commands his servant to do." So Mephibosheth ate at David's[b] table like one of the king's sons.

[12]Mephibosheth had a young son named Mica, and all the members of Ziba's household were servants of Mephibosheth. [13]And Mephibosheth lived in Jerusalem, because he always ate at the king's table, and he was crippled in both feet.

David Defeats the Ammonites

10 In the course of time, the king of the Ammonites died, and his son Hanun succeeded him as king. [2]David thought, "I will show kindness to Hanun son of Nahash, just as his father showed kindness to me." So David sent a delegation to express his sympathy to Hanun concerning his father.

When David's men came to the land of the Ammonites, [3]the Ammonite nobles said to Hanun their lord, "Do you think David is honoring your father by sending men to you to express sympathy? Hasn't David sent them to you to explore the city and spy it out and overthrow it?" [4]So Hanun seized David's men, shaved off half of each man's beard, cut off their garments in the middle at the buttocks, and sent them away.

[5]When David was told about this, he sent messengers to meet the men, for they were greatly humiliated. The king said, "Stay at Jericho till your beards have grown, and then come back."

[6]When the Ammonites realized that they had become a stench in David's nostrils, they hired twenty thousand Aramean foot soldiers from Beth Rehob and Zobah, as well as the king of Maacah with a thousand men, and also twelve thousand men from Tob.

[a]18 Or *were priests* [b]11 Septuagint; Hebrew *my*

[7]On hearing this, David sent Joab out
with the entire army of fighting men.
[8]The Ammonites came out and drew up
in battle formation at the entrance to
their city gate, while the Arameans of
Zobah and Rehob and the men of Tob
and Maacah were by themselves in the
open country.
[9]Joab saw that there were battle lines
in front of him and behind him; so he
selected some of the best troops in Israel and deployed them against the Arameans. [10]He put the rest of the men
under the command of Abishai his
brother and deployed them against the
Ammonites. [11]Joab said, "If the Arameans are too strong for me, then you are
to come to my rescue; but if the Ammonites are too strong for you, then I
will come to rescue you. [12]Be strong and
let us fight bravely for our people and
the cities of our God. The LORD will do
what is good in his sight."
[13]Then Joab and the troops with him
advanced to fight the Arameans, and
they fled before him. [14]When the Ammonites saw that the Arameans were
fleeing, they fled before Abishai and
went inside the city. So Joab returned
from fighting the Ammonites and came
to Jerusalem.
[15]After the Arameans saw that they
had been routed by Israel, they re-
grouped. [16]Hadadezer had Arameans
brought from beyond the River[a]; they
went to Helam, with Shobach the commander of Hadadezer's army leading
them.
[17]When David was told of this, he
gathered all Israel, crossed the Jordan
and went to Helam. The Arameans
formed their battle lines to meet David
and fought against him. [18]But they fled
before Israel, and David killed seven
hundred of their charioteers and forty
thousand of their foot soldiers.[b] He also
struck down Shobach the commander
of their army, and he died there. [19]When
all the kings who were vassals of Hadadezer saw that they had been defeated
by Israel, they made peace with the Israelites and became subject to them.

So the Arameans were afraid to help the Ammonites anymore.

[a]*16* That is, the Euphrates [b]*18* Some Septuagint manuscripts (see also 1 Chron. 19:18); Hebrew *horsemen*

SHARPEN THE FOCUS

It often takes courage to act in kindness. It's easier to turn a cold shoulder to someone who's hurt us. Or to pretend not to see the needs of those all around us.

Put yourself in this picture. You and your family have stopped for milk. At the far end of the parking lot sits a car, held together, it appears, by rust and wire. Two toddlers hang out the windows, crying. Dad pokes around with a greasy rag under the hood.

What would kindness do? What excuses come immediately to mind? Why is courage required?

The Scriptures never gloss over the riskiness of Christ-like living. In a few days, we will read about the apparent disloyalty Mephibosheth returns for David's kindness. His actions are at best confusing and at worst treasonous. Yet David continues to show him kindness because of the pact of peace he had made with Jonathan (1 Samuel 20:42).

David could live out risky kindness. He lived in the confidence that the Lord would preserve and keep him (2 Samuel 8:6b, 14b).

In our lives, too, kindness grows from confidence in Christ's love for us, from the courage His love creates in our hearts. In what relationship do you need the courage to act in kindness today?

WEEK 28 • MONDAY

2 Samuel 11:1—12:31

"In the spring, at the time when kings go off to war" David remained in Jerusalem (2 Samuel 11:1). One, seemingly insignificant, wrong turn. Followed by another. Then another. And soon David found himself mired so deeply in the swamp of sin that there was no way out. Or so it appeared. As you read today, notice Satan's subtle snares. And notice also the Lord's tender mercy toward David, His wandering son. If time is short, focus on 2 Samuel 12:1–14.

David and Bathsheba

11 In the spring, at the time when kings go off to war, David sent Joab out with the king's men and the whole Israelite army. They destroyed the Ammonites and besieged Rabbah. But David remained in Jerusalem.

2 One evening David got up from his bed and walked around on the roof of the palace. From the roof he saw a woman bathing. The woman was very beautiful, 3 and David sent someone to find out about her. The man said, "Isn't this Bathsheba, the daughter of Eliam and the wife of Uriah the Hittite?" 4 Then David sent messengers to get her. She came to him, and he slept with her. (She had purified herself from her uncleanness.) Then[a] she went back home. 5 The woman conceived and sent word to David, saying, "I am pregnant."

6 So David sent this word to Joab: "Send me Uriah the Hittite." And Joab sent him to David. 7 When Uriah came to him, David asked him how Joab was, how the soldiers were and how the war was going. 8 Then David said to Uriah, "Go down to your house and wash your feet." So Uriah left the palace, and a gift from the king was sent after him. 9 But Uriah slept at the entrance to the palace with all his master's servants and did not go down to his house.

10 When David was told, "Uriah did not go home," he asked him, "Haven't you just come from a distance? Why didn't you go home?"

11 Uriah said to David, "The ark and Israel and Judah are staying in tents, and my master Joab and my lord's men are camped in the open fields. How could I go to my house to eat and drink and lie with my wife? As surely as you live, I will not do such a thing!"

12 Then David said to him, "Stay here one more day, and tomorrow I will send you back." So Uriah remained in Jerusalem that day and the next. 13 At David's invitation, he ate and drank with him, and David made him drunk. But in the evening Uriah went out to sleep on his mat among his master's servants; he did not go home.

14 In the morning David wrote a letter to Joab and sent it with Uriah. 15 In it he wrote, "Put Uriah in the front line where the fighting is fiercest. Then withdraw from him so he will be struck down and die."

16 So while Joab had the city under siege, he put Uriah at a place where he knew the strongest defenders were. 17 When the men of the city came out and fought against Joab, some of the men in David's army fell; moreover, Uriah the Hittite died.

18 Joab sent David a full account of the battle. 19 He instructed the messenger: "When you have finished giving the king this account of the battle, 20 the king's anger may flare up, and he may

[a]4 Or *with her. When she purified herself from her uncleanness,*

ask you, 'Why did you get so close to the
city to fight? Didn't you know they
would shoot arrows from the wall?
21Who killed Abimelech son of Jerub-
Besheth[a]? Didn't a woman throw an
upper millstone on him from the wall,
so that he died in Thebez? Why did you
get so close to the wall?' If he asks you
this, then say to him, 'Also, your servant
Uriah the Hittite is dead.' "
22The messenger set out, and when he
arrived he told David everything Joab
had sent him to say. 23The messenger
said to David, "The men overpowered
us and came out against us in the open,
but we drove them back to the entrance
to the city gate. 24Then the archers shot
arrows at your servants from the wall,
and some of the king's men died. Moreover, your servant Uriah the Hittite is
dead."
25David told the messenger, "Say this
to Joab: 'Don't let this upset you; the
sword devours one as well as another.
Press the attack against the city and destroy it.' Say this to encourage Joab."
26When Uriah's wife heard that her
husband was dead, she mourned for
him. 27After the time of mourning was
over, David had her brought to his
house, and she became his wife and
bore him a son. But the thing David had
done displeased the LORD.

Nathan Rebukes David

12 The LORD sent Nathan to
David. When he came to him,
he said, "There were two men in a certain town, one rich and the other poor.
2The rich man had a very large number
of sheep and cattle, 3but the poor man
had nothing except one little ewe lamb
he had bought. He raised it, and it grew
up with him and his children. It shared
his food, drank from his cup and even
slept in his arms. It was like a daughter
to him.
4"Now a traveler came to the rich
man, but the rich man refrained from
taking one of his own sheep or cattle to
prepare a meal for the traveler who had
come to him. Instead, he took the ewe
lamb that belonged to the poor man and
prepared it for the one who had come
to him."
5David burned with anger against the
man and said to Nathan, "As surely as
the LORD lives, the man who did this deserves to die! 6He must pay for that lamb
four times over, because he did such a
thing and had no pity."
7Then Nathan said to David, "You are
the man! This is what the LORD, the God
of Israel, says: 'I anointed you king over
Israel, and I delivered you from the
hand of Saul. 8I gave your master's
house to you, and your master's wives
into your arms. I gave you the house of
Israel and Judah. And if all this had been
too little, I would have given you even
more. 9Why did you despise the word
of the LORD by doing what is evil in his
eyes? You struck down Uriah the Hittite
with the sword and took his wife to be
your own. You killed him with the
sword of the Ammonites. 10Now, therefore, the sword will never depart from
your house, because you despised me
and took the wife of Uriah the Hittite to
be your own.'
11"This is what the LORD says: 'Out of
your own household I am going to bring
calamity upon you. Before your very
eyes I will take your wives and give
them to one who is close to you, and he
will lie with your wives in broad daylight. 12You did it in secret, but I will do
this thing in broad daylight before all
Israel.' "
13Then David said to Nathan, "I have
sinned against the LORD."
Nathan replied, "The LORD has taken
away your sin. You are not going to die.
14But because by doing this you have
made the enemies of the LORD show utter contempt,[b] the son born to you will
die."
15After Nathan had gone home, the
LORD struck the child that Uriah's wife
had borne to David, and he became ill.
16David pleaded with God for the child.
He fasted and went into his house and

[a]21 Also known as *Jerub-Baal* (that is, Gideon)
[b]14 Masoretic Text; an ancient Hebrew scribal tradition *this you have shown utter contempt for the LORD*

spent the nights lying on the ground.
17The elders of his household stood beside him to get him up from the ground,
but he refused, and he would not eat
any food with them.
18On the seventh day the child died.
David's servants were afraid to tell him
that the child was dead, for they
thought, "While the child was still living, we spoke to David but he would
not listen to us. How can we tell him the
child is dead? He may do something
desperate."
19David noticed that his servants were
whispering among themselves and he
realized the child was dead. "Is the child
dead?" he asked.
"Yes," they replied, "he is dead."
20Then David got up from the ground.
After he had washed, put on lotions and
changed his clothes, he went into the
house of the LORD and worshiped. Then
he went to his own house, and at his request they served him food, and he ate.
21His servants asked him, "Why are
you acting this way? While the child
was alive, you fasted and wept, but now
that the child is dead, you get up and
eat!"
22He answered, "While the child was
still alive, I fasted and wept. I thought,
'Who knows? The LORD may be gracious to me and let the child live.' 23But
now that he is dead, why should I fast?
Can I bring him back again? I will go to
him, but he will not return to me."
24Then David comforted his wife
Bathsheba, and he went to her and lay
with her. She gave birth to a son, and
they named him Solomon. The LORD
loved him; 25and because the LORD
loved him, he sent word through
Nathan the prophet to name him Jedidiah.[a]
26Meanwhile Joab fought against Rabbah of the Ammonites and captured the
royal citadel. 27Joab then sent messengers to David, saying, "I have fought
against Rabbah and taken its water supply. 28Now muster the rest of the troops
and besiege the city and capture it. Otherwise I will take the city, and it will be
named after me."
29So David mustered the entire army
and went to Rabbah, and attacked and
captured it. 30He took the crown from
the head of their king[b]—its weight was
a talent[c] of gold, and it was set with precious stones—and it was placed on
David's head. He took a great quantity
of plunder from the city 31and brought
out the people who were there, consigning them to labor with saws and
with iron picks and axes, and he made
them work at brickmaking.[d] He did this
to all the Ammonite towns. Then David
and his entire army returned to Jerusalem.

[a]25 *Jedidiah* means *loved by the LORD*. [b]30 Or *of Milcom* (that is, Molech) [c]30 That is, about 75 pounds (about 34 kilograms) [d]31 The meaning of the Hebrew for this clause is uncertain.

SHARPEN THE FOCUS

Duty demanded that David defend his people against the army of Ammon. But David sent Joab instead (2 Samuel 11:1). Idle hands. An evening stroll. A stolen glance. The rest, as they say, is history. A sad history, one full of regret.

The Scripture never hides the failures and foibles of the people in its pages. The Bible's *only* hero is the Lord Himself. The Lord who confronts His people with their sin; who works godly contrition, sorrow for sin, in human hearts; who wipes away all tears and purges away all guilt.

The jaws of sin snapped shut when David least expected it. And so it can easily happen for us. That's why St. Paul warns, "So, if you think you are standing firm, be careful that you don't fall" (1 Corinthians 10:12). To all outward appearances, David towered as a spiritual giant. But he stood on feet of clay.

With what "little sin" has Satan baited his hook for you? What duty are you tempted to neglect? What corners have you already cut?

Whether you are standing, slipping, or looking up from a muddy fall right now, turn to the Lord for His help. He is gracious and merciful, slow to anger and abounding in steadfast love. *Abounding* in steadfast love (Joel 2:13)!

WEEK 28 • TUESDAY

2 Samuel 13:1—14:24

The incident with Bathsheba marks a turning point in David's life and reign. The Lord had fully forgiven him, yet the earthly consequences of his sins would continue until the day he died. Quite possibly David felt that by his sin he had lost his moral authority. As you read today, look for opportunities David missed—as a father and as a king in Israel. If time is short, focus on 2 Samuel 13:1–39.

Amnon and Tamar

13 In the course of time, Amnon son of David fell in love with Tamar, the beautiful sister of Absalom son of David.

2 Amnon became frustrated to the point of illness on account of his sister Tamar, for she was a virgin, and it seemed impossible for him to do anything to her.

3 Now Amnon had a friend named Jonadab son of Shimeah, David's brother. Jonadab was a very shrewd man. 4 He asked Amnon, "Why do you, the king's son, look so haggard morning after morning? Won't you tell me?"

Amnon said to him, "I'm in love with Tamar, my brother Absalom's sister."

5 "Go to bed and pretend to be ill," Jonadab said. "When your father comes to see you, say to him, 'I would like my sister Tamar to come and give me something to eat. Let her prepare the food in my sight so I may watch her and then eat it from her hand.' "

6 So Amnon lay down and pretended to be ill. When the king came to see him, Amnon said to him, "I would like my sister Tamar to come and make some special bread in my sight, so I may eat from her hand."

7 David sent word to Tamar at the palace: "Go to the house of your brother Amnon and prepare some food for him." 8 So Tamar went to the house of her brother Amnon, who was lying down. She took some dough, kneaded it, made the bread in his sight and baked it. 9 Then she took the pan and served him the bread, but he refused to eat.

"Send everyone out of here," Amnon said. So everyone left him. 10 Then Amnon said to Tamar, "Bring the food here into my bedroom so I may eat from your hand." And Tamar took the bread she had prepared and brought it to her brother Amnon in his bedroom. 11 But when she took it to him to eat, he grabbed her and said, "Come to bed with me, my sister."

12 "Don't, my brother!" she said to him. "Don't force me. Such a thing should not be done in Israel! Don't do this wicked thing. 13 What about me? Where could I get rid of my disgrace? And what about you? You would be like one of the

wicked fools in Israel. Please speak to the king; he will not keep me from being married to you." 14But he refused to listen to her, and since he was stronger than she, he raped her.

15Then Amnon hated her with intense hatred. In fact, he hated her more than he had loved her. Amnon said to her, "Get up and get out!"

16"No!" she said to him. "Sending me away would be a greater wrong than what you have already done to me."

But he refused to listen to her. 17He called his personal servant and said, "Get this woman out of here and bolt the door after her." 18So his servant put her out and bolted the door after her. She was wearing a richly ornamented[a] robe, for this was the kind of garment the virgin daughters of the king wore. 19Tamar put ashes on her head and tore the ornamented[b] robe she was wearing. She put her hand on her head and went away, weeping aloud as she went.

20Her brother Absalom said to her, "Has that Amnon, your brother, been with you? Be quiet now, my sister; he is your brother. Don't take this thing to heart." And Tamar lived in her brother Absalom's house, a desolate woman.

21When King David heard all this, he was furious. 22Absalom never said a word to Amnon, either good or bad; he hated Amnon because he had disgraced his sister Tamar.

Absalom Kills Amnon

23Two years later, when Absalom's sheepshearers were at Baal Hazor near the border of Ephraim, he invited all the king's sons to come there. 24Absalom went to the king and said, "Your servant has had shearers come. Will the king and his officials please join me?"

25"No, my son," the king replied. "All of us should not go; we would only be a burden to you." Although Absalom urged him, he still refused to go, but gave him his blessing.

26Then Absalom said, "If not, please let my brother Amnon come with us."

The king asked him, "Why should he go with you?" 27But Absalom urged him, so he sent with him Amnon and the rest of the king's sons.

28Absalom ordered his men, "Listen! When Amnon is in high spirits from drinking wine and I say to you, 'Strike Amnon down,' then kill him. Don't be afraid. Have not I given you this order? Be strong and brave." 29So Absalom's men did to Amnon what Absalom had ordered. Then all the king's sons got up, mounted their mules and fled.

30While they were on their way, the report came to David: "Absalom has struck down all the king's sons; not one of them is left." 31The king stood up, tore his clothes and lay down on the ground; and all his servants stood by with their clothes torn.

32But Jonadab son of Shimeah, David's brother, said, "My lord should not think that they killed all the princes; only Amnon is dead. This has been Absalom's expressed intention ever since the day Amnon raped his sister Tamar. 33My lord the king should not be concerned about the report that all the king's sons are dead. Only Amnon is dead."

34Meanwhile, Absalom had fled.

Now the man standing watch looked up and saw many people on the road west of him, coming down the side of the hill. The watchman went and told the king, "I see men in the direction of Horonaim, on the side of the hill."[c]

35Jonadab said to the king, "See, the king's sons are here; it has happened just as your servant said."

36As he finished speaking, the king's sons came in, wailing loudly. The king, too, and all his servants wept very bitterly.

37Absalom fled and went to Talmai son of Ammihud, the king of Geshur. But King David mourned for his son every day.

38After Absalom fled and went to Geshur, he stayed there three years. 39And

[a] *18* The meaning of the Hebrew for this phrase is uncertain. [b] *19* The meaning of the Hebrew for this word is uncertain. [c] *34* Septuagint; Hebrew does not have this sentence.

the spirit of the king[a] longed to go to Absalom, for he was consoled concerning Amnon's death.

Absalom Returns to Jerusalem

14 Joab son of Zeruiah knew that the king's heart longed for Absalom. [2]So Joab sent someone to Tekoa and had a wise woman brought from there. He said to her, "Pretend you are in mourning. Dress in mourning clothes, and don't use any cosmetic lotions. Act like a woman who has spent many days grieving for the dead. [3]Then go to the king and speak these words to him." And Joab put the words in her mouth.

[4]When the woman from Tekoa went[b] to the king, she fell with her face to the ground to pay him honor, and she said, "Help me, O king!"

[5]The king asked her, "What is troubling you?"

She said, "I am indeed a widow; my husband is dead. [6]I your servant had two sons. They got into a fight with each other in the field, and no one was there to separate them. One struck the other and killed him. [7]Now the whole clan has risen up against your servant; they say, 'Hand over the one who struck his brother down, so that we may put him to death for the life of his brother whom he killed; then we will get rid of the heir as well.' They would put out the only burning coal I have left, leaving my husband neither name nor descendant on the face of the earth."

[8]The king said to the woman, "Go home, and I will issue an order in your behalf."

[9]But the woman from Tekoa said to him, "My lord the king, let the blame rest on me and on my father's family, and let the king and his throne be without guilt."

[10]The king replied, "If anyone says anything to you, bring him to me, and he will not bother you again."

[11]She said, "Then let the king invoke the LORD his God to prevent the avenger of blood from adding to the destruction, so that my son will not be destroyed."

"As surely as the LORD lives," he said, "not one hair of your son's head will fall to the ground."

[12]Then the woman said, "Let your servant speak a word to my lord the king."

"Speak," he replied.

[13]The woman said, "Why then have you devised a thing like this against the people of God? When the king says this, does he not convict himself, for the king has not brought back his banished son? [14]Like water spilled on the ground, which cannot be recovered, so we must die. But God does not take away life; instead, he devises ways so that a banished person may not remain estranged from him.

[15]"And now I have come to say this to my lord the king because the people have made me afraid. Your servant thought, 'I will speak to the king; perhaps he will do what his servant asks. [16]Perhaps the king will agree to deliver his servant from the hand of the man who is trying to cut off both me and my son from the inheritance God gave us.'

[17]"And now your servant says, 'May the word of my lord the king bring me rest, for my lord the king is like an angel of God in discerning good and evil. May the LORD your God be with you.' "

[18]Then the king said to the woman, "Do not keep from me the answer to what I am going to ask you."

"Let my lord the king speak," the woman said.

[19]The king asked, "Isn't the hand of Joab with you in all this?"

The woman answered, "As surely as you live, my lord the king, no one can turn to the right or to the left from anything my lord the king says. Yes, it was your servant Joab who instructed me to do this and who put all these words into the mouth of your servant. [20]Your servant Joab did this to change the present

[a]39 Dead Sea Scrolls and some Septuagint manuscripts; Masoretic Text *But the spirit of David the king* [b]4 Many Hebrew manuscripts, Septuagint, Vulgate and Syriac; most Hebrew manuscripts *spoke*

situation. My lord has wisdom like that
of an angel of God—he knows everything that happens in the land."
21 The king said to Joab, "Very well, I
will do it. Go, bring back the young man
Absalom."
22 Joab fell with his face to the ground
to pay him honor, and he blessed the
king. Joab said, "Today your servant
knows that he has found favor in your
eyes, my lord the king, because the king
has granted his servant's request."
23 Then Joab went to Geshur and
brought Absalom back to Jerusalem.
24 But the king said, "He must go to his
own house; he must not see my face."
So Absalom went to his own house and
did not see the face of the king.
25 In all Israel there was not a man so
highly praised for his handsome appearance as Absalom. From the top of
his head to the sole of his foot there was
no blemish in him. 26 Whenever he cut
the hair of his head—he used to cut his
hair from time to time when it became
too heavy for him—he would weigh it,
and its weight was two hundred
shekels[a] by the royal standard.
27 Three sons and a daughter were
born to Absalom. The daughter's name
was Tamar, and she became a beautiful
woman.
28 Absalom lived two years in Jerusalem without seeing the king's face.
29 Then Absalom sent for Joab in order to
send him to the king, but Joab refused
to come to him. So he sent a second
time, but he refused to come. 30 Then he
said to his servants, "Look, Joab's field
is next to mine, and he has barley there.
Go and set it on fire." So Absalom's servants set the field on fire.
31 Then Joab did go to Absalom's
house and he said to him, "Why have
your servants set my field on fire?"
32 Absalom said to Joab, "Look, I sent
word to you and said, 'Come here so I
can send you to the king to ask, "Why
have I come from Geshur? It would be
better for me if I were still there!" ' Now
then, I want to see the king's face, and
if I am guilty of anything, let him put me
to death."
33 So Joab went to the king and told
him this. Then the king summoned Absalom, and he came in and bowed down
with his face to the ground before the
king. And the king kissed Absalom.

[a] 26 That is, about 5 pounds (about 2.3 kilograms)

SHARPEN THE FOCUS

A vehicle that sits just so, beside and behind ours, won't show up in the rearview mirror. It's in our blind spot. Unless we deliberately turn around to look, we'll be deceived into thinking we're alone on the highway. It can be a deadly mistake.

Today's reading places David in just such a spiritual blind spot. Disaster edges ever closer to the royal family. But David doesn't see it.

To this point in both 1 and 2 Samuel, we've seen David's strength and his weakness. In today's narrative, we've seen him react in weakness toward Amnon when he should have acted strongly and in justice. Today we've also seen David act in too much strength, refusing to show Absalom either mercy or justice. David should have tried Absalom for murder. Or, perhaps, he should have pardoned him. Instead, David's inaction imprisoned Absalom in a kind of gray world, outside the reach of either justice or mercy.

As you think about your own relationships, particularly family relationships right now, ask the Lord to show you any blind spots that keep you from representing the Lord Jesus as fully as you and He would like. Ask Him for grace to balance justice and strength with mercy and pardon.

WEEK 28 • WEDNESDAY

2 Sam. 14:25—16:23

Rejected by his father, Absalom began to curry favor with those who came to David with legal complaints. Year after year, Absalom lived just outside the shadow of his father's love. Finally, Absalom's anger exploded into a rebellion that nearly toppled David from Israel's throne. If time is short, focus on 2 Samuel 15:7–37.

Absalom's Conspiracy

15 In the course of time,
Absalom provided himself
with a chariot and horses and with fifty
men to run ahead of him. 2He would get
up early and stand by the side of the
road leading to the city gate. Whenever
anyone came with a complaint to be
placed before the king for a decision,
Absalom would call out to him, "What
town are you from?" He would answer,
"Your servant is from one of the tribes
of Israel." 3Then Absalom would say to
him, "Look, your claims are valid and
proper, but there is no representative of
the king to hear you." 4And Absalom
would add, "If only I were appointed
judge in the land! Then everyone who
has a complaint or case could come to
me and I would see that he gets justice."
5Also, whenever anyone approached
him to bow down before him, Absalom
would reach out his hand, take hold of
him and kiss him. 6Absalom behaved in
this way toward all the Israelites who
came to the king asking for justice, and
so he stole the hearts of the men of Israel.
7At the end of four[a] years, Absalom
said to the king, "Let me go to Hebron
and fulfill a vow I made to the LORD.
8While your servant was living at Geshur in Aram, I made this vow: 'If the
LORD takes me back to Jerusalem, I will
worship the LORD in Hebron.[b]' "
9The king said to him, "Go in peace."
So he went to Hebron.
10Then Absalom sent secret messengers throughout the tribes of Israel to
say, "As soon as you hear the sound of
the trumpets, then say, 'Absalom is king
in Hebron.' " 11Two hundred men from
Jerusalem had accompanied Absalom.
They had been invited as guests and
went quite innocently, knowing nothing about the matter. 12While Absalom
was offering sacrifices, he also sent for
Ahithophel the Gilonite, David's counselor, to come from Giloh, his hometown. And so the conspiracy gained
strength, and Absalom's following kept
on increasing.

David Flees

13A messenger came and told David,
"The hearts of the men of Israel are with
Absalom."
14Then David said to all his officials
who were with him in Jerusalem,
"Come! We must flee, or none of us will
escape from Absalom. We must leave
immediately, or he will move quickly to
overtake us and bring ruin upon us and
put the city to the sword."
15The king's officials answered him,
"Your servants are ready to do whatever
our lord the king chooses."
16The king set out, with his entire
household following him; but he left ten
concubines to take care of the palace.
17So the king set out, with all the people

[a]7 Some Septuagint manuscripts, Syriac and Josephus; Hebrew *forty* [b]8 Some Septuagint manuscripts; Hebrew does not have *in Hebron.*

following him, and they halted at a
place some distance away. [18]All his men
marched past him, along with all the
Kerethites and Pelethites; and all the six
hundred Gittites who had accompanied
him from Gath marched before the king.
[19]The king said to Ittai the Gittite,
"Why should you come along with us?
Go back and stay with King Absalom.
You are a foreigner, an exile from your
homeland. [20]You came only yesterday.
And today shall I make you wander
about with us, when I do not know
where I am going? Go back, and take
your countrymen. May kindness and
faithfulness be with you."
[21]But Ittai replied to the king, "As surely as the LORD lives, and as my lord the
king lives, wherever my lord the king
may be, whether it means life or death,
there will your servant be."
[22]David said to Ittai, "Go ahead, march
on." So Ittai the Gittite marched on with
all his men and the families that were
with him.
[23]The whole countryside wept aloud
as all the people passed by. The king also
crossed the Kidron Valley, and all the
people moved on toward the desert.
[24]Zadok was there, too, and all the Levites who were with him were carrying
the ark of the covenant of God. They set
down the ark of God, and Abiathar offered sacrifices[a] until all the people had
finished leaving the city.
[25]Then the king said to Zadok, "Take
the ark of God back into the city. If I find
favor in the LORD's eyes, he will bring
me back and let me see it and his
dwelling place again. [26]But if he says, 'I
am not pleased with you,' then I am
ready; let him do to me whatever seems
good to him."
[27]The king also said to Zadok the
priest, "Aren't you a seer? Go back to the
city in peace, with your son Ahimaaz
and Jonathan son of Abiathar. You and
Abiathar take your two sons with you.
[28]I will wait at the fords in the desert
until word comes from you to inform
me." [29]So Zadok and Abiathar took the
ark of God back to Jerusalem and stayed
there.
[30]But David continued up the Mount
of Olives, weeping as he went; his head
was covered and he was barefoot. All
the people with him covered their
heads too and were weeping as they
went up. [31]Now David had been told,
"Ahithophel is among the conspirators
with Absalom." So David prayed,
"O LORD, turn Ahithophel's counsel
into foolishness."
[32]When David arrived at the summit,
where people used to worship God, Hushai the Arkite was there to meet him,
his robe torn and dust on his head. [33]Da-
vid said to him, "If you go with me, you
will be a burden to me. [34]But if you return to the city and say to Absalom, 'I
will be your servant, O king; I was your
father's servant in the past, but now I
will be your servant,' then you can help
me by frustrating Ahithophel's advice.
[35]Won't the priests Zadok and Abiathar
be there with you? Tell them anything
you hear in the king's palace. [36]Their
two sons, Ahimaaz son of Zadok and
Jonathan son of Abiathar, are there with
them. Send them to me with anything
you hear."
[37]So David's friend Hushai arrived at
Jerusalem as Absalom was entering the
city.

David and Ziba

16 When David had gone a
short distance beyond the
summit, there was Ziba, the steward of
Mephibosheth, waiting to meet him. He
had a string of donkeys saddled and
loaded with two hundred loaves of
bread, a hundred cakes of raisins, a hundred cakes of figs and a skin of wine.
[2]The king asked Ziba, "Why have you
brought these?"
Ziba answered, "The donkeys are for
the king's household to ride on, the
bread and fruit are for the men to eat,
and the wine is to refresh those who become exhausted in the desert."
[3]The king then asked, "Where is your
master's grandson?"
Ziba said to him, "He is staying in

[a]24 Or *Abiathar went up*

Jerusalem, because he thinks, 'Today the
house of Israel will give me back my
grandfather's kingdom.' "
4Then the king said to Ziba, "All that
belonged to Mephibosheth is now
yours."
"I humbly bow," Ziba said. "May I
find favor in your eyes, my lord the
king."

Shimei Curses David

5As King David approached Bahurim,
a man from the same clan as Saul's family came out from there. His name was
Shimei son of Gera, and he cursed as he
came out. 6He pelted David and all the
king's officials with stones, though all
the troops and the special guard were
on David's right and left. 7As he cursed,
Shimei said, "Get out, get out, you man
of blood, you scoundrel! 8The LORD has
repaid you for all the blood you shed in
the household of Saul, in whose place
you have reigned. The LORD has
handed the kingdom over to your son
Absalom. You have come to ruin because you are a man of blood!"
9Then Abishai son of Zeruiah said to
the king, "Why should this dead dog
curse my lord the king? Let me go over
and cut off his head."
10But the king said, "What do you and
I have in common, you sons of Zeruiah?
If he is cursing because the LORD said to
him, 'Curse David,' who can ask, 'Why
do you do this?' "
11David then said to Abishai and all
his officials, "My son, who is of my own
flesh, is trying to take my life. How
much more, then, this Benjamite! Leave
him alone; let him curse, for the LORD
has told him to. 12It may be that the
LORD will see my distress and repay me
with good for the cursing I am receiving today."
13So David and his men continued
along the road while Shimei was going
along the hillside opposite him, cursing
as he went and throwing stones at him
and showering him with dirt. 14The king
and all the people with him arrived at
their destination exhausted. And there
he refreshed himself.

The Advice of Hushai and Ahithophel

15Meanwhile, Absalom and all the
men of Israel came to Jerusalem, and
Ahithophel was with him. 16Then Hushai the Arkite, David's friend, went to
Absalom and said to him, "Long live the
king! Long live the king!"
17Absalom asked Hushai, "Is this the
love you show your friend? Why didn't
you go with your friend?"
18Hushai said to Absalom, "No, the
one chosen by the LORD, by these
people, and by all the men of Israel—
his I will be, and I will remain with
him. 19Furthermore, whom should I
serve? Should I not serve the son? Just
as I served your father, so I will serve
you."
20Absalom said to Ahithophel, "Give
us your advice. What should we do?"
21Ahithophel answered, "Lie with
your father's concubines whom he left
to take care of the palace. Then all Israel
will hear that you have made yourself
a stench in your father's nostrils, and
the hands of everyone with you will be
strengthened." 22So they pitched a tent
for Absalom on the roof, and he lay with
his father's concubines in the sight of all
Israel.
23Now in those days the advice Ahithophel gave was like that of one who in-
quires of God. That was how both
David and Absalom regarded all of
Ahithophel's advice.

SHARPEN THE FOCUS

A sore that isn't properly cleaned and treated with antiseptic festers. A fire that isn't properly extinguished can smolder for days and then burst into flame without warning. Unresolved anger and resentment are like that. A relationship may look fine on the surface, while underneath an angry infection poisons the person's entire system.

As you think about what today's Scripture means for you, you may want to ask yourself questions like these:

- Am I withholding acceptance or love from someone who doesn't deserve it, but who really needs it?
- Am I harboring resentment or bitterness toward anyone, particularly anyone in authority over me?
- Have I let the sun go down on my anger and thereby given Satan a foothold in my heart (Ephesians 4:26)?

If you feel uncomfortable with your answers to any of these questions, talk with your Savior about it. He's more than willing to give you His forgiveness, peace, and the strength you need.

WEEK 28 • THURSDAY

2 Samuel 17:1—18:33

Problems that we ignore seldom disappear. Especially relationship problems. Absalom's resentment and frustration have led him to rape and pillage his way through David's palace. Intoxicated by power, he ignores the wise advice Ahithophel gives. Instead of pursuing David and killing him that very night, Absalom holds off his attack until David's armies have a chance to regroup. If time is short, focus on 2 Samuel 18:1–16.

17 Ahithophel said to Absalom,
"I would[a] choose twelve
thousand men and set out tonight in
pursuit of David. 2 I would[b] attack him
while he is weary and weak. I would[b]
strike him with terror, and then all the
people with him will flee. I would[b] strike
down only the king 3 and bring all the
people back to you. The death of the
man you seek will mean the return of
all; all the people will be unharmed."
4 This plan seemed good to Absalom and
to all the elders of Israel.
5 But Absalom said, "Summon also
Hushai the Arkite, so we can hear what
he has to say." 6 When Hushai came to
him, Absalom said, "Ahithophel has given this advice. Should we do what he
says? If not, give us your opinion."
7 Hushai replied to Absalom, "The advice Ahithophel has given is not good
this time. 8 You know your father and his
men; they are fighters, and as fierce as
a wild bear robbed of her cubs. Besides,
your father is an experienced fighter; he
will not spend the night with the troops.
9 Even now, he is hidden in a cave or
some other place. If he should attack
your troops first,[c] whoever hears about
it will say, 'There has been a slaughter
among the troops who follow Absalom.'
10 Then even the bravest soldier, whose
heart is like the heart of a lion, will melt
with fear, for all Israel knows that your
father is a fighter and that those with
him are brave.
11 "So I advise you: Let all Israel, from
Dan to Beersheba—as numerous as the
sand on the seashore—be gathered to

[a]1 Or *Let me* [b]2 Or *will* [c]9 Or *When some of the men fall at the first attack*

you, with you yourself leading them
into battle. 12Then we will attack him
wherever he may be found, and we will
fall on him as dew settles on the ground.
Neither he nor any of his men will be
left alive. 13If he withdraws into a city,
then all Israel will bring ropes to that
city, and we will drag it down to the
valley until not even a piece of it can be
found."

14Absalom and all the men of Israel
said, "The advice of Hushai the Arkite
is better than that of Ahithophel." For
the LORD had determined to frustrate
the good advice of Ahithophel in order
to bring disaster on Absalom.

15Hushai told Zadok and Abiathar, the
priests, "Ahithophel has advised Absalom and the elders of Israel to do such
and such, but I have advised them to do
so and so. 16Now send a message immediately and tell David, 'Do not spend the
night at the fords in the desert; cross
over without fail, or the king and all the
people with him will be swallowed
up.' "

17Jonathan and Ahimaaz were staying
at En Rogel. A servant girl was to go and
inform them, and they were to go and
tell King David, for they could not risk
being seen entering the city. 18But a
young man saw them and told Absalom. So the two of them left quickly and
went to the house of a man in Bahurim.
He had a well in his courtyard, and they
climbed down into it. 19His wife took a
covering and spread it out over the
opening of the well and scattered grain
over it. No one knew anything about it.

20When Absalom's men came to the
woman at the house, they asked,
"Where are Ahimaaz and Jonathan?"

The woman answered them, "They
crossed over the brook."[a] The men
searched but found no one, so they returned to Jerusalem.

21After the men had gone, the two
climbed out of the well and went to inform King David. They said to him, "Set
out and cross the river at once; Ahithophel has advised such and such against
you." 22So David and all the people with
him set out and crossed the Jordan. By
daybreak, no one was left who had not
crossed the Jordan.

23When Ahithophel saw that his advice had not been followed, he saddled
his donkey and set out for his house in
his hometown. He put his house in order and then hanged himself. So he died
and was buried in his father's tomb.

24David went to Mahanaim, and Absalom crossed the Jordan with all the
men of Israel. 25Absalom had appointed
Amasa over the army in place of Joab.
Amasa was the son of a man named
Jether,[b] an Israelite[c] who had married
Abigail,[d] the daughter of Nahash and
sister of Zeruiah the mother of Joab.
26The Israelites and Absalom camped in
the land of Gilead.

27When David came to Mahanaim,
Shobi son of Nahash from Rabbah of the
Ammonites, and Makir son of Ammiel
from Lo Debar, and Barzillai the Gileadite from Rogelim 28brought bedding and
bowls and articles of pottery. They also
brought wheat and barley, flour and
roasted grain, beans and lentils,[e] 29hon-
ey and curds, sheep, and cheese from
cows' milk for David and his people to
eat. For they said, "The people have
become hungry and tired and thirsty in
the desert."

Absalom's Death

18 David mustered the men
who were with him and ap-
pointed over them commanders of
thousands and commanders of hundreds. 2David sent the troops out—a
third under the command of Joab, a
third under Joab's brother Abishai son
of Zeruiah, and a third under Ittai the
Gittite. The king told the troops, "I myself will surely march out with you."

3But the men said, "You must not go
out; if we are forced to flee, they won't

[a]20 Or *"They passed by the sheep pen toward the water."* [b]25 Hebrew *Ithra,* a variant of *Jether* [c]25 Hebrew and some Septuagint manuscripts; other Septuagint manuscripts (see also 1 Chron. 2:17) *Ishmaelite* or *Jezreelite* [d]25 Hebrew *Abigal,* a variant of *Abigail* [e]28 Most Septuagint manuscripts and Syriac; Hebrew *lentils, and roasted grain*

care about us. Even if half of us die, they
won't care; but you are worth ten thousand of us.[a] It would be better now for
you to give us support from the city."
4The king answered, "I will do whatever seems best to you."
So the king stood beside the gate
while all the men marched out in units
of hundreds and of thousands. 5The
king commanded Joab, Abishai and Ittai, "Be gentle with the young man Absalom for my sake." And all the troops
heard the king giving orders concerning
Absalom to each of the commanders.
6The army marched into the field to
fight Israel, and the battle took place in
the forest of Ephraim. 7There the army
of Israel was defeated by David's men,
and the casualties that day were great—
twenty thousand men. 8The battle
spread out over the whole countryside,
and the forest claimed more lives that
day than the sword.
9Now Absalom happened to meet
David's men. He was riding his mule,
and as the mule went under the thick
branches of a large oak, Absalom's head
got caught in the tree. He was left hanging in midair, while the mule he was riding kept on going.
10When one of the men saw this, he
told Joab, "I just saw Absalom hanging
in an oak tree."
11Joab said to the man who had told
him this, "What! You saw him? Why
didn't you strike him to the ground
right there? Then I would have had to
give you ten shekels[b] of silver and a
warrior's belt."
12But the man replied, "Even if a thousand shekels[c] were weighed out into
my hands, I would not lift my hand
against the king's son. In our hearing
the king commanded you and Abishai
and Ittai, 'Protect the young man Absalom for my sake.[d]' 13And if I had put my
life in jeopardy[e]—and nothing is hidden
from the king—you would have kept
your distance from me."
14Joab said, "I'm not going to wait like
this for you." So he took three javelins
in his hand and plunged them into
Absalom's heart while Absalom was still
alive in the oak tree. 15And ten of Joab's
armor-bearers surrounded Absalom,
struck him and killed him.
16Then Joab sounded the trumpet,
and the troops stopped pursuing Israel,
for Joab halted them. 17They took Absalom, threw him into a big pit in the forest and piled up a large heap of rocks
over him. Meanwhile, all the Israelites
fled to their homes.
18During his lifetime Absalom had
taken a pillar and erected it in the King's
Valley as a monument to himself, for he
thought, "I have no son to carry on the
memory of my name." He named the
pillar after himself, and it is called Absalom's Monument to this day.

David Mourns

19Now Ahimaaz son of Zadok said,
"Let me run and take the news to the
king that the LORD has delivered him
from the hand of his enemies."
20"You are not the one to take the
news today," Joab told him. "You may
take the news another time, but you
must not do so today, because the king's
son is dead."
21Then Joab said to a Cushite, "Go, tell
the king what you have seen." The Cushite bowed down before Joab and ran off.
22Ahimaaz son of Zadok again said to
Joab, "Come what may, please let me
run behind the Cushite."
But Joab replied, "My son, why do
you want to go? You don't have any
news that will bring you a reward."
23He said, "Come what may, I want to
run."
So Joab said, "Run!" Then Ahimaaz
ran by way of the plain[f] and outran the
Cushite.
24While David was sitting between

[a]3 Two Hebrew manuscripts, some Septuagint manuscripts and Vulgate; most Hebrew manuscripts *care; for now there are ten thousand like us* [b]11 That is, about 4 ounces (about 115 grams) [c]12 That is, about 25 pounds (about 11 kilograms) [d]12 A few Hebrew manuscripts, Septuagint, Vulgate and Syriac; most Hebrew manuscripts may be translated *Absalom, whoever you may be.* [e]13 Or *Otherwise, if I had acted treacherously toward him* [f]23 That is, the plain of the Jordan

the inner and outer gates, the watchman went up to the roof of the gateway by the wall. As he looked out, he saw a man running alone. [25]The watchman called out to the king and reported it.

The king said, "If he is alone, he must have good news." And the man came closer and closer.

[26]Then the watchman saw another man running, and he called down to the gatekeeper, "Look, another man running alone!"

The king said, "He must be bringing good news, too."

[27]The watchman said, "It seems to me that the first one runs like Ahimaaz son of Zadok."

"He's a good man," the king said. "He comes with good news."

[28]Then Ahimaaz called out to the king, "All is well!" He bowed down before the king with his face to the ground and said, "Praise be to the LORD your God! He has delivered up the men who lifted their hands against my lord the king."

[29]The king asked, "Is the young man Absalom safe?"

Ahimaaz answered, "I saw great confusion just as Joab was about to send the king's servant and me, your servant, but I don't know what it was."

[30]The king said, "Stand aside and wait here." So he stepped aside and stood there.

[31]Then the Cushite arrived and said, "My lord the king, hear the good news! The LORD has delivered you today from all who rose up against you."

[32]The king asked the Cushite, "Is the young man Absalom safe?"

The Cushite replied, "May the enemies of my lord the king and all who rise up to harm you be like that young man."

[33]The king was shaken. He went up to the room over the gateway and wept. As he went, he said: "O my son Absalom! My son, my son Absalom! If only I had died instead of you—O Absalom, my son, my son!"

SHARPEN THE FOCUS

This whole, sad series of events could become just another moral lesson like "Obey those in authority," or "Don't harbor bitterness in your heart." Unless we pay close attention to clues in the text. Like 2 Samuel 17:14, for example: "The LORD had determined . . ."

None of these events surprised the Lord. Remember His promise to build an eternal dynasty for David? Much water has flowed beneath the proverbial bridge since that promise:

- David's own tears of repentance for his sins of adultery and murder.
- Tamar's tears of anguish and shame.
- Absalom's tears of loneliness and frustration.

But the Lord's word of promise to David stood firm. Not even the hatred of a rebellious son would snuff out the flickering flame of that promise. Through the obedience of His Son, the eternal King, the heavenly Father would bring all His rebellious sons and daughters back to Himself.

Standing where we do in the stream of history, we know the eternal King whom the Lord brought through David's line. We have seen that King die a cruel and bloody death so sins like those of Absalom, of David, of Amnon, of you, and of me could be forgiven.

Absalom's death plunged David into deep grief. So much so that his troops, though victorious, sneak back from the battlefield in shame. Joab's sharp words bring David back to reality. He acts decisively to regain his crown in both Judah and Israel. His enemies receive mercy, and his allies rewards. If time is short, focus on 2 Samuel 19:1–7.

19 Joab was told, "The king is weeping and mourning for Absalom." 2And for the whole army the victory that day was turned into mourning, because on that day the troops heard it said, "The king is grieving for his son." 3The men stole into the city that day as men steal in who are ashamed when they flee from battle. 4The king covered his face and cried aloud, "O my son Absalom! O Absalom, my son, my son!"

5Then Joab went into the house to the king and said, "Today you have humiliated all your men, who have just saved your life and the lives of your sons and daughters and the lives of your wives and concubines. 6You love those who hate you and hate those who love you. You have made it clear today that the commanders and their men mean nothing to you. I see that you would be pleased if Absalom were alive today and all of us were dead. 7Now go out and encourage your men. I swear by the LORD that if you don't go out, not a man will be left with you by nightfall. This will be worse for you than all the calamities that have come upon you from your youth till now."

8So the king got up and took his seat in the gateway. When the men were told, "The king is sitting in the gateway," they all came before him.

David Returns to Jerusalem

Meanwhile, the Israelites had fled to their homes. 9Throughout the tribes of Israel, the people were all arguing with each other, saying, "The king delivered us from the hand of our enemies; he is the one who rescued us from the hand of the Philistines. But now he has fled the country because of Absalom; 10and Absalom, whom we anointed to rule over us, has died in battle. So why do you say nothing about bringing the king back?"

11King David sent this message to Zadok and Abiathar, the priests: "Ask the elders of Judah, 'Why should you be the last to bring the king back to his palace, since what is being said throughout Israel has reached the king at his quarters? 12You are my brothers, my own flesh and blood. So why should you be the last to bring back the king?' 13And say to Amasa, 'Are you not my own flesh and blood? May God deal with me, be it ever so severely, if from now on you are not the commander of my army in place of Joab.' "

14He won over the hearts of all the men of Judah as though they were one man. They sent word to the king, "Return, you and all your men." 15Then the king returned and went as far as the Jordan.

Now the men of Judah had come to Gilgal to go out and meet the king and bring him across the Jordan. 16Shimei son of Gera, the Benjamite from Bahurim, hurried down with the men of Judah to meet King David. 17With him were a thousand Benjamites, along with Ziba, the steward of Saul's household,

and his fifteen sons and twenty servants. They rushed to the Jordan, where
the king was. 18They crossed at the ford
to take the king's household over and to
do whatever he wished.

When Shimei son of Gera crossed the
Jordan, he fell prostrate before the king
19and said to him, "May my lord not
hold me guilty. Do not remember how
your servant did wrong on the day my
lord the king left Jerusalem. May the
king put it out of his mind. 20For I your
servant know that I have sinned, but today I have come here as the first of the
whole house of Joseph to come down
and meet my lord the king."

21Then Abishai son of Zeruiah said,
"Shouldn't Shimei be put to death for
this? He cursed the LORD's anointed."

22David replied, "What do you and I
have in common, you sons of Zeruiah?
This day you have become my adversaries! Should anyone be put to death in Israel today? Do I not know that today I
am king over Israel?" 23So the king said
to Shimei, "You shall not die." And the
king promised him on oath.

24Mephibosheth, Saul's grandson,
also went down to meet the king. He
had not taken care of his feet or trimmed
his mustache or washed his clothes
from the day the king left until the day
he returned safely. 25When he came
from Jerusalem to meet the king, the
king asked him, "Why didn't you go
with me, Mephibosheth?"

26He said, "My lord the king, since I
your servant am lame, I said, 'I will have
my donkey saddled and will ride on it,
so I can go with the king.' But Ziba my
servant betrayed me. 27And he has slandered your servant to my lord the king.
My lord the king is like an angel of God;
so do whatever pleases you. 28All my
grandfather's descendants deserved
nothing but death from my lord the
king, but you gave your servant a place
among those who eat at your table. So
what right do I have to make any more
appeals to the king?"

29The king said to him, "Why say
more? I order you and Ziba to divide the
fields."

30Mephibosheth said to the king, "Let
him take everything, now that my lord
the king has arrived home safely."

31Barzillai the Gileadite also came
down from Rogelim to cross the Jordan
with the king and to send him on his
way from there. 32Now Barzillai was a
very old man, eighty years of age. He
had provided for the king during his
stay in Mahanaim, for he was a very
wealthy man. 33The king said to Barzillai, "Cross over with me and stay with
me in Jerusalem, and I will provide for
you."

34But Barzillai answered the king,
"How many more years will I live, that
I should go up to Jerusalem with the
king? 35I am now eighty years old. Can
I tell the difference between what is
good and what is not? Can your servant
taste what he eats and drinks? Can I still
hear the voices of men and women singers? Why should your servant be an
added burden to my lord the king?
36Your servant will cross over the Jordan
with the king for a short distance, but
why should the king reward me in this
way? 37Let your servant return, that I
may die in my own town near the tomb
of my father and mother. But here is
your servant Kimham. Let him cross
over with my lord the king. Do for him
whatever pleases you."

38The king said, "Kimham shall cross
over with me, and I will do for him
whatever pleases you. And anything
you desire from me I will do for you."

39So all the people crossed the Jordan,
and then the king crossed over. The king
kissed Barzillai and gave him his blessing, and Barzillai returned to his home.
40When the king crossed over to Gilgal, Kimham crossed with him. All the
troops of Judah and half the troops of
Israel had taken the king over.

41Soon all the men of Israel were coming to the king and saying to him, "Why
did our brothers, the men of Judah, steal
the king away and bring him and his
household across the Jordan, together
with all his men?"

42All the men of Judah answered the
men of Israel, "We did this because the

king is closely related to us. Why are
you angry about it? Have we eaten any
of the king's provisions? Have we taken
anything for ourselves?"
43Then the men of Israel answered the
men of Judah, "We have ten shares in
the king; and besides, we have a greater
claim on David than you have. So why
do you treat us with contempt? Were we
not the first to speak of bringing back
our king?"
But the men of Judah responded even
more harshly than the men of Israel.

Sheba Rebels Against David

20 Now a troublemaker named
Sheba son of Bicri, a Benjamite, happened to be there. He sounded the trumpet and shouted,

"We have no share in David,
no part in Jesse's son!
Every man to his tent, O Israel!"

2So all the men of Israel deserted David to follow Sheba son of Bicri. But the
men of Judah stayed by their king all the
way from the Jordan to Jerusalem.
3When David returned to his palace
in Jerusalem, he took the ten concubines
he had left to take care of the palace and
put them in a house under guard. He
provided for them, but did not lie with
them. They were kept in confinement
till the day of their death, living as widows.
4Then the king said to Amasa, "Summon the men of Judah to come to me
within three days, and be here yourself." 5But when Amasa went to summon Judah, he took longer than the
time the king had set for him.
6David said to Abishai, "Now Sheba
son of Bicri will do us more harm than
Absalom did. Take your master's men
and pursue him, or he will find fortified
cities and escape from us." 7So Joab's
men and the Kerethites and Pelethites
and all the mighty warriors went out
under the command of Abishai. They
marched out from Jerusalem to pursue
Sheba son of Bicri.
8While they were at the great rock in
Gibeon, Amasa came to meet them. Joab
was wearing his military tunic, and
strapped over it at his waist was a belt
with a dagger in its sheath. As he
stepped forward, it dropped out of its
sheath.
9Joab said to Amasa, "How are you,
my brother?" Then Joab took Amasa by
the beard with his right hand to kiss
him. 10Amasa was not on his guard
against the dagger in Joab's hand, and
Joab plunged it into his belly, and his
intestines spilled out on the ground.
Without being stabbed again, Amasa
died. Then Joab and his brother Abishai pursued Sheba son of Bicri.
11One of Joab's men stood beside Amasa and said, "Whoever favors Joab, and
whoever is for David, let him follow
Joab!" 12Amasa lay wallowing in his
blood in the middle of the road, and the
man saw that all the troops came to a
halt there. When he realized that everyone who came up to Amasa stopped, he
dragged him from the road into a field
and threw a garment over him. 13After
Amasa had been removed from the
road, all the men went on with Joab to
pursue Sheba son of Bicri.
14Sheba passed through all the tribes
of Israel to Abel Beth Maacah[a] and
through the entire region of the Berites,
who gathered together and followed
him. 15All the troops with Joab came and
besieged Sheba in Abel Beth Maacah.
They built a siege ramp up to the city,
and it stood against the outer fortifica-
tions. While they were battering the
wall to bring it down, 16a wise woman
called from the city, "Listen! Listen! Tell
Joab to come here so I can speak to him."
17He went toward her, and she asked,
"Are you Joab?"
"I am," he answered.
She said, "Listen to what your servant
has to say."
"I'm listening," he said.
18She continued, "Long ago they used
to say, 'Get your answer at Abel,' and
that settled it. 19We are the peaceful and
faithful in Israel. You are trying to destroy a city that is a mother in Israel.

[a]14 Or *Abel, even Beth Maacah*; also in verse 15

Why do you want to swallow up the
LORD's inheritance?"
20"Far be it from me!" Joab replied,
"Far be it from me to swallow up or destroy! 21That is not the case. A man
named Sheba son of Bicri, from the hill
country of Ephraim, has lifted up his
hand against the king, against David.
Hand over this one man, and I'll withdraw from the city."
The woman said to Joab, "His
head will be thrown to you from the
wall."
22Then the woman went to all the
people with her wise advice, and they
cut off the head of Sheba son of Bicri
and threw it to Joab. So he sounded the
trumpet, and his men dispersed from
the city, each returning to his home.
And Joab went back to the king in Jerusalem.
23Joab was over Israel's entire army;
Benaiah son of Jehoiada was over the
Kerethites and Pelethites; 24Adoniram[a]
was in charge of forced labor; Jehoshaphat son of Ahilud was recorder; 25She-
va was secretary; Zadok and Abiathar
were priests; 26and Ira the Jairite was
David's priest.

[a]24 Some Septuagint manuscripts (see also 1 Kings 4:6 and 5:14); Hebrew *Adoram*

SHARPEN THE FOCUS

Rebuke a wise man and he will love you. (Proverbs 9:8)

The book of Proverbs includes at least two dozen verses that encourage God's people to seek out wise counsel, to listen to godly advice, and to act on it. Had David rejected Joab's admonition, who knows what would have happened to David's kingdom. God had indeed promised to give the world an eternal King through David's line. And He would still have kept that promise. But had David not listened to Joab, how much more grief might David and his people have endured?

How responsive are you to godly counsel? Do you cultivate relationships with other believers who will "[speak] the truth in love" (Ephesians 4:15) when you need to hear it? How do you respond when your pastor or your spouse or your best friend points out sin in your heart or words or lifestyle?

Such people are God's gifts to us. They are allies in our battle against sin and Satan. If we are wise, we will treasure people like that. We will thank our Savior for them, and we will carefully consider their words in light of the Scriptures and our own actions.

WEEK 28 • SATURDAY

2 Samuel 21:1—22:51

GET THE BIG PICTURE

The holy writer recounts several instances from King David's reign which illustrate the ways in which he righted the wrongs done by King Saul and also showed respect for Saul and Jonathan even after their death. Chapter 22 then records a song written by King David in praise to the Lord for His faithfulness throughout David's life. If time is short, focus on 2 Samuel 22:1–25.

The Gibeonites Avenged

21 During the reign of David,
there was a famine for three
successive years; so David sought the
face of the LORD. The LORD said, "It is
on account of Saul and his blood-
stained house; it is because he put the
Gibeonites to death."
[2]The king summoned the Gibeonites
and spoke to them. (Now the Gibeonites were not a part of Israel but were
survivors of the Amorites; the Israelites
had sworn to ⌞spare⌟ them, but Saul in
his zeal for Israel and Judah had tried to
annihilate them.) [3]David asked the Gibeonites, "What shall I do for you? How
shall I make amends so that you will
bless the LORD's inheritance?"
[4]The Gibeonites answered him, "We
have no right to demand silver or gold
from Saul or his family, nor do we have
the right to put anyone in Israel to
death."
"What do you want me to do for
you?" David asked.
[5]They answered the king, "As for the
man who destroyed us and plotted
against us so that we have been deci-
mated and have no place anywhere in
Israel, [6]let seven of his male descendants
be given to us to be killed and exposed
before the LORD at Gibeah of Saul—the
LORD's chosen one."
So the king said, "I will give them to
you."
[7]The king spared Mephibosheth son
of Jonathan, the son of Saul, because of
the oath before the LORD between
David and Jonathan son of Saul. [8]But
the king took Armoni and Mephibosheth, the two sons of Aiah's daughter
Rizpah, whom she had borne to Saul,
together with the five sons of Saul's
daughter Merab,[a] whom she had borne
to Adriel son of Barzillai the Mehola-
thite. [9]He handed them over to the Gibeonites, who killed and exposed them
on a hill before the LORD. All seven of
them fell together; they were put to
death during the first days of the harvest, just as the barley harvest was beginning.
[10]Rizpah daughter of Aiah took sackcloth and spread it out for herself on a
rock. From the beginning of the harvest
till the rain poured down from the heavens on the bodies, she did not let the
birds of the air touch them by day or the
wild animals by night. [11]When David
was told what Aiah's daughter Rizpah,
Saul's concubine, had done, [12]he went
and took the bones of Saul and his son
Jonathan from the citizens of Jabesh
Gilead. (They had taken them secretly
from the public square at Beth Shan,
where the Philistines had hung them after they struck Saul down on Gilboa.)
[13]David brought the bones of Saul and
his son Jonathan from there, and the
bones of those who had been killed and
exposed were gathered up.
[14]They buried the bones of Saul and
his son Jonathan in the tomb of Saul's
father Kish, at Zela in Benjamin, and did
everything the king commanded. After
that, God answered prayer in behalf of
the land.

Wars Against the Philistines

[15]Once again there was a battle between the Philistines and Israel. David
went down with his men to fight
against the Philistines, and he became
exhausted. [16]And Ishbi-Benob, one of
the descendants of Rapha, whose
bronze spearhead weighed three hundred shekels[b] and who was armed with
a new ⌞sword⌟, said he would kill David.
[17]But Abishai son of Zeruiah came to
David's rescue; he struck the Philistine
down and killed him. Then David's
men swore to him, saying, "Never again
will you go out with us to battle, so that
the lamp of Israel will not be extinguished."
[18]In the course of time, there was another battle with the Philistines, at Gob.
At that time Sibbecai the Hushathite
killed Saph, one of the descendants of
Rapha.

[a]*8* Two Hebrew manuscripts, some Septuagint manuscripts and Syriac (see also 1 Samuel 18:19); most Hebrew and Septuagint manuscripts *Michal* [b]*16* That is, about 7 1/2 pounds (about 3.5 kilograms)

[19]In another battle with the Philistines at Gob, Elhanan son of Jaare-Oregim[a] the Bethlehemite killed Goliath[b] the Gittite, who had a spear with a shaft like a weaver's rod.

[20]In still another battle, which took place at Gath, there was a huge man with six fingers on each hand and six toes on each foot—twenty-four in all. He also was descended from Rapha. [21]When he taunted Israel, Jonathan son of Shimeah, David's brother, killed him.

[22]These four were descendants of Rapha in Gath, and they fell at the hands of David and his men.

David's Song of Praise

22 David sang to the LORD the words of this song when the LORD delivered him from the hand of all his enemies and from the hand of Saul. [2]He said:

"The LORD is my rock, my fortress
and my deliverer;
[3] my God is my rock, in whom I
take refuge,
my shield and the horn[c] of my
salvation.
He is my stronghold, my refuge and
my savior—
from violent men you save me.
[4]I call to the LORD, who is worthy of
praise,
and I am saved from my enemies.

[5]"The waves of death swirled about
me;
the torrents of destruction
overwhelmed me.
[6]The cords of the grave[d] coiled around
me;
the snares of death confronted
me.
[7]In my distress I called to the LORD;
I called out to my God.
From his temple he heard my voice;
my cry came to his ears.

[8]"The earth trembled and quaked,
the foundations of the heavens[e]
shook;
they trembled because he was
angry.
[9]Smoke rose from his nostrils;
consuming fire came from his
mouth,
burning coals blazed out of it.
[10]He parted the heavens and came
down;
dark clouds were under his feet.
[11]He mounted the cherubim and flew;
he soared[f] on the wings of the
wind.
[12]He made darkness his canopy
around him—
the dark[g] rain clouds of the sky.
[13]Out of the brightness of his presence
bolts of lightning blazed forth.
[14]The LORD thundered from heaven;
the voice of the Most High
resounded.
[15]He shot arrows and scattered ⌞the
enemies⌟,
bolts of lightning and routed them.
[16]The valleys of the sea were exposed
and the foundations of the earth
laid bare
at the rebuke of the LORD,
at the blast of breath from his
nostrils.

[17]"He reached down from on high
and took hold of me;
he drew me out of deep waters.
[18]He rescued me from my powerful
enemy,
from my foes, who were too
strong for me.
[19]They confronted me in the day of
my disaster,
but the LORD was my support.
[20]He brought me out into a spacious
place;
he rescued me because he
delighted in me.

[21]"The LORD has dealt with me
according to my
righteousness;

[a]19 Or *son of Jair the weaver* [b]19 Hebrew and Septuagint; 1 Chron. 20:5 *son of Jair killed Lahmi the brother of Goliath* [c]3 *Horn* here symbolizes strength. [d]6 Hebrew *Sheol* [e]8 Hebrew; Vulgate and Syriac (see also Psalm 18:7) *mountains* [f]11 Many Hebrew manuscripts (see also Psalm 18:10); most Hebrew manuscripts *appeared* [g]12 Septuagint and Vulgate (see also Psalm 18:11); Hebrew *massed*

according to the cleanness of my
hands he has rewarded me.
22 For I have kept the ways of the LORD;
I have not done evil by turning
from my God.
23 All his laws are before me;
I have not turned away from his
decrees.
24 I have been blameless before him
and have kept myself from sin.
25 The LORD has rewarded me according
to my righteousness,
according to my cleanness[a] in his
sight.
26 "To the faithful you show yourself
faithful,
to the blameless you show
yourself blameless,
27 to the pure you show yourself pure,
but to the crooked you show
yourself shrewd.
28 You save the humble,
but your eyes are on the haughty
to bring them low.
29 You are my lamp, O LORD;
the LORD turns my darkness into
light.
30 With your help I can advance
against a troop[b];
with my God I can scale a wall.

31 "As for God, his way is perfect;
the word of the LORD is flawless.
He is a shield
for all who take refuge in him.
32 For who is God besides the LORD?
And who is the Rock except our
God?
33 It is God who arms me with
strength[c]
and makes my way perfect.
34 He makes my feet like the feet of a
deer;
he enables me to stand on the
heights.
35 He trains my hands for battle;
my arms can bend a bow of
bronze.
36 You give me your shield of victory;
you stoop down to make me
great.
37 You broaden the path beneath me,
so that my ankles do not turn.

38 "I pursued my enemies and crushed
them;
I did not turn back till they were
destroyed.
39 I crushed them completely, and they
could not rise;
they fell beneath my feet.
40 You armed me with strength for
battle;
you made my adversaries bow at
my feet.
41 You made my enemies turn their
backs in flight,
and I destroyed my foes.
42 They cried for help, but there was
no one to save them—
to the LORD, but he did not answer.
43 I beat them as fine as the dust of the
earth;
I pounded and trampled them like
mud in the streets.

44 "You have delivered me from the
attacks of my people;
you have preserved me as the
head of nations.
People I did not know are subject to
me,
45 and foreigners come cringing to
me;
as soon as they hear me, they
obey me.
46 They all lose heart;
they come trembling[d] from their
strongholds.

47 "The LORD lives! Praise be to my
Rock!
Exalted be God, the Rock, my
Savior!
48 He is the God who avenges me,
who puts the nations under me,
49 who sets me free from my
enemies.
You exalted me above my foes;
from violent men you rescued me.

[a]25 Hebrew; Septuagint and Vulgate (see also Psalm 18:24) *to the cleanness of my hands* [b]30 Or *can run through a barricade* [c]33 Dead Sea Scrolls, some Septuagint manuscripts, Vulgate and Syriac (see also Psalm 18:32); Masoretic Text *who is my strong refuge* [d]46 Some Septuagint manuscripts and Vulgate (see also Psalm 18:45); Masoretic Text *they arm themselves.*

50 Therefore I will praise you, O LORD,
among the nations;
I will sing praises to your name.
51 He gives his king great victories;
he shows unfailing kindness to his
anointed,
to David and his descendants
forever."

SHARPEN THE FOCUS

The God of personal pronouns. That's who our Lord is. Look back at 2 Samuel 22:1–3 and count all the *my's.* David knew the Lord, not as some impersonal cosmic force or anonymous, unknowable deity, but rather as the Savior-Lord who knew him intimately and cared for his every need.

Think back on a few of the descriptors David used in his hymn of praise and what each of them means for you today. Jot your thoughts on a piece of paper and look at them frequently. Here are some of David's *my's:*

The LORD is my rock (2 Samuel 22:2). How is the Lord your rock? Your hiding place? You are protected in God's loving care and tender mercy.

The LORD is my fortress (2 Samuel 22:2). How is the Lord your fortress? The only true "fortress" is the Lord because true security can only be found in Him.

The LORD is my Savior (2 Samuel 22:3). What a wonderful joyous statement for David and for you. God sent His Son, Jesus, as the Savior of all people. By His death on the cross, all the sins of all people are forgiven, and the gift of eternal life belongs to all of God's children.

As David looks back over his career, he focuses on the goodness of the Lord and on the covenant promises God has made to him. The chapter goes on to summarize the contributions made by several of David's supporters. As you read, think of all the saints who have served their Lord down through history, doing "mighty deeds" without looking for any reward except the honor of bringing glory to Christ. If time is short, focus on 2 Samuel 23:8–17.

The Last Words of David

23 These are the last words of David:

"The oracle of David son of Jesse,
the oracle of the man exalted by
the Most High,
the man anointed by the God of
Jacob,
Israel's singer of songs[a]:
2 "The Spirit of the LORD spoke
through me;
his word was on my tongue.
3 The God of Israel spoke,
the Rock of Israel said to me:
'When one rules over men in
righteousness,
when he rules in the fear of God,

[a]1 Or *Israel's beloved singer*

4he is like the light of morning at
sunrise
on a cloudless morning,
like the brightness after rain
that brings the grass from the
earth.'

5"Is not my house right with God?
Has he not made with me an
everlasting covenant,
arranged and secured in every
part?
Will he not bring to fruition my
salvation
and grant me my every
desire?
6But evil men are all to be cast aside
like thorns,
which are not gathered with the
hand.
7Whoever touches thorns
uses a tool of iron or the shaft of a
spear;
they are burned up where they
lie."

David's Mighty Men

8These are the names of David's mighty men:

Josheb-Basshebeth,[a] a Tahkemonite,[b] was chief of the Three; he raised his spear against eight hundred men, whom he killed[c] in one encounter.

9Next to him was Eleazar son of Dodai the Ahohite. As one of the three mighty men, he was with David when they taunted the Philistines gathered ⌞at Pas Dammim⌟[d] for battle. Then the men of Israel retreated, 10but he stood his ground and struck down the Philistines till his hand grew tired and froze to the sword. The LORD brought about a great victory that day. The troops returned to Eleazar, but only to strip the dead.

11Next to him was Shammah son of Agee the Hararite. When the Philistines banded together at a place where there was a field full of lentils, Israel's troops fled from them. 12But Shammah took his stand in the middle of the field. He defended it and struck the Philistines down, and the LORD brought about a great victory.

13During harvest time, three of the thirty chief men came down to David at the cave of Adullam, while a band of Philistines was encamped in the Valley of Rephaim. 14At that time David was in the stronghold, and the Philistine garrison was at Bethlehem. 15David longed for water and said, "Oh, that someone would get me a drink of water from the well near the gate of Bethlehem!" 16So the three mighty men broke through the Philistine lines, drew water from the well near the gate of Bethlehem and carried it back to David. But he refused to drink it; instead, he poured it out before the LORD. 17"Far be it from me, O LORD, to do this!" he said. "Is it not the blood of men who went at the risk of their lives?" And David would not drink it.

Such were the exploits of the three mighty men.

18Abishai the brother of Joab son of Zeruiah was chief of the Three.[e] He raised his spear against three hundred men, whom he killed, and so he became as famous as the Three. 19Was he not held in greater honor than the Three? He became their commander, even though he was not included among them.

20Benaiah son of Jehoiada was a valiant fighter from Kabzeel, who performed great exploits. He struck down two of Moab's best men. He also went down into a pit on a snowy day and killed a lion. 21And he struck down a huge Egyptian. Although the Egyptian had a spear in his hand, Benaiah went against him with a club. He snatched the spear from the Egyptian's hand and killed him with his own spear. 22Such were the exploits of Benaiah son of

[a]*8* Hebrew; some Septuagint manuscripts suggest *Ish-Bosheth,* that is, *Esh-Baal* (see also 1 Chron. 11:11 *Jashobeam*). [b]*8* Probably a variant of *Hacmonite* (see 1 Chron. 11:11) [c]*8* Some Septuagint manuscripts (see also 1 Chron. 11:11); Hebrew and other Septuagint manuscripts *Three; it was Adino the Eznite who killed eight hundred men* [d]*9* See 1 Chron. 11:13; Hebrew *gathered there.* [e]*18* Most Hebrew manuscripts (see also 1 Chron. 11:20); two Hebrew manuscripts and Syriac *Thirty*

Jehoiada; he too was as famous as the three mighty men. 23He was held in greater honor than any of the Thirty, but he was not included among the Three. And David put him in charge of his bodyguard.

24 Among the Thirty were:
Asahel the brother of Joab,
Elhanan son of Dodo from Bethlehem,
25 Shammah the Harodite,
Elika the Harodite,
26 Helez the Paltite,
Ira son of Ikkesh from Tekoa,
27 Abiezer from Anathoth,
Mebunnai[a] the Hushathite,
28 Zalmon the Ahohite,
Maharai the Netophathite,
29 Heled[b] son of Baanah the Netophathite,
Ithai son of Ribai from Gibeah in Benjamin,
30 Benaiah the Pirathonite,
Hiddai[c] from the ravines of Gaash,
31 Abi-Albon the Arbathite,
Azmaveth the Barhumite,
32 Eliahba the Shaalbonite,
the sons of Jashen,
Jonathan 33son of[d] Shammah the Hararite,
Ahiam son of Sharar[e] the Hararite,
34 Eliphelet son of Ahasbai the Maacathite,
Eliam son of Ahithophel the Gilonite,
35 Hezro the Carmelite,
Paarai the Arbite,
36 Igal son of Nathan from Zobah,
the son of Hagri,[f]
37 Zelek the Ammonite,
Naharai the Beerothite, the armor-bearer of Joab son of Zeruiah,
38 Ira the Ithrite,
Gareb the Ithrite
39 and Uriah the Hittite.
There were thirty-seven in all.

[a]27 Hebrew; some Septuagint manuscripts (see also 1 Chron. 11:29) *Sibbecai* [b]29 Some Hebrew manuscripts and Vulgate (see also 1 Chron. 11:30); most Hebrew manuscripts *Heleb* [c]30 Hebrew; some Septuagint manuscripts (see also 1 Chron. 11:32) *Hurai* [d]33 Some Septuagint manuscripts (see also 1 Chron. 11:34); Hebrew does not have *son of.* [e]33 Hebrew; some Septuagint manuscripts (see also 1 Chron. 11:35) *Sacar* [f]36 Some Septuagint manuscripts (see also 1 Chron. 11:38); Hebrew *Haggadi*

SHARPEN THE FOCUS

Josheb-Basshebeth. Eleazar son of Dodai. Shammah son of Agee. It's a safe bet that few believers would recognize these names. Fewer still could identify any of their exploits. And yet, God the Holy Spirit saw fit to inspire the holy writer to record both their names and their deeds.

Confident of God's love and concerned about His people, these ordinary people did extraordinary things. None of them probably gave their service a second thought. But the Lord saw and remembered.

Perhaps you fail to see your own service for the Lord and His people as anything extraordinary. Or perhaps you're discouraged in your service. Maybe your hand is so tired it's "[frozen] to the sword." Or maybe you find yourself defending a "field of lentils." Or maybe you have "only a cup of cold water" to offer today. If so, take heart. Let your Lord encourage you. He sees. He remembers. He knows your love for Him and for His people. Your service matters. And *you* matter to the One who died for you.

WEEK 29 • TUESDAY

2 Samuel 24:1–25

GET THE BIG PICTURE

Many times in our walk with the Lord, our specific actions matter much less than our motives. Today's reading includes just such an incident in the life of King David. As you read, ask yourself how David would have answered Joab's question at the end of 2 Samuel 24:3 had he stopped to think it through. If time is short, focus on 2 Samuel 24:18–25.

David Counts the Fighting Men

24 Again the anger of the
LORD burned against Is-
rael, and he incited David against them,
saying, "Go and take a census of Israel
and Judah."
2So the king said to Joab and the army
commanders[a] with him, "Go throughout the tribes of Israel from Dan to Beersheba and enroll the fighting men, so
that I may know how many there are."
3But Joab replied to the king, "May
the LORD your God multiply the troops
a hundred times over, and may the eyes
of my lord the king see it. But why does
my lord the king want to do such a
thing?"
4The king's word, however, overruled
Joab and the army commanders; so they
left the presence of the king to enroll the
fighting men of Israel.
5After crossing the Jordan, they
camped near Aroer, south of the town
in the gorge, and then went through
Gad and on to Jazer. 6They went to Gilead and the region of Tahtim Hodshi,
and on to Dan Jaan and around toward
Sidon. 7Then they went toward the fortress of Tyre and all the towns of the
Hivites and Canaanites. Finally, they
went on to Beersheba in the Negev of
Judah.
8After they had gone through the entire land, they came back to Jerusalem
at the end of nine months and twenty
days.
9Joab reported the number of the
fighting men to the king: In Israel there
were eight hundred thousand able-bodied men who could handle a sword, and
in Judah five hundred thousand.
10David was conscience-stricken after
he had counted the fighting men, and
he said to the LORD, "I have sinned
greatly in what I have done. Now,
O LORD, I beg you, take away the guilt
of your servant. I have done a very foolish thing."
11Before David got up the next morning, the word of the LORD had come to
Gad the prophet, David's seer: 12"Go
and tell David, 'This is what the LORD
says: I am giving you three options.
Choose one of them for me to carry out
against you.' "
13So Gad went to David and said to
him, "Shall there come upon you three[b]
years of famine in your land? Or three
months of fleeing from your enemies
while they pursue you? Or three days
of plague in your land? Now then, think
it over and decide how I should answer
the one who sent me."
14David said to Gad, "I am in deep distress. Let us fall into the hands of the
LORD, for his mercy is great; but do not
let me fall into the hands of men."
15So the LORD sent a plague on Israel
from that morning until the end of the
time designated, and seventy thousand
of the people from Dan to Beersheba
died. 16When the angel stretched out his

[a]2 Septuagint (see also verse 4 and 1 Chron. 21:2); Hebrew *Joab the army commander*
[b]13 Septuagint (see also 1 Chron. 21:12); Hebrew *seven*

hand to destroy Jerusalem, the LORD was grieved because of the calamity and said to the angel who was afflicting the people, "Enough! Withdraw your hand." The angel of the LORD was then at the threshing floor of Araunah the Jebusite.
17When David saw the angel who was striking down the people, he said to the LORD, "I am the one who has sinned and done wrong. These are but sheep. What have they done? Let your hand fall upon me and my family."

David Builds an Altar

18On that day Gad went to David and said to him, "Go up and build an altar to the LORD on the threshing floor of Araunah the Jebusite." 19So David went
up, as the LORD had commanded through Gad. 20When Araunah looked
and saw the king and his men coming toward him, he went out and bowed down before the king with his face to the ground.
21Araunah said, "Why has my lord the king come to his servant?"

"To buy your threshing floor," David answered, "so I can build an altar to the LORD, that the plague on the people may be stopped."
22Araunah said to David, "Let my lord the king take whatever pleases him and offer it up. Here are oxen for the burnt offering, and here are threshing sledges and ox yokes for the wood. 23O king,
Araunah gives all this to the king." Araunah also said to him, "May the LORD your God accept you."
24But the king replied to Araunah, "No, I insist on paying you for it. I will not sacrifice to the LORD my God burnt offerings that cost me nothing."
So David bought the threshing floor and the oxen and paid fifty shekels[a] of silver for them. 25David built an altar to
the LORD there and sacrificed burnt offerings and fellowship offerings.[b] Then the LORD answered prayer in behalf of the land, and the plague on Israel was stopped.

[a]24 That is, about 1 1/4 pounds (about 0.6 kilogram) [b]25 Traditionally *peace offerings*

SHARPEN THE FOCUS

Joab's question, "Why do you want to do this?" is a great diagnostic. Of course, we can overdo it. Nevertheless, it's with good reason that the Scriptures urge us:

> *Examine yourselves to see whether you are in the faith; test yourselves. Do you not realize that Christ Jesus is in you—unless, of course, you fail the test?* (2 Corinthians 13:5)

Had David stopped to listen to Joab and his commanders (2 Samuel 24:4), perhaps the Holy Spirit would have been able to get through to him. Perhaps king and people together could have repented before their sins brought the Lord's judgment on them. As it was, judgment fell (2 Samuel 24:15).

But the Lord acted in mercy and accepted David's confession. The plague stopped.

Have you set your heart on a course of action without examining your motives? If so, stop. Reread Joab's words to David in 2 Samuel 24:3. Ask the Holy Spirit to do a quick heart-check for you. Then talk with Him about what He shows you.

Assured that Christ Jesus is truly in you, you can make decisions in repentant faith. Whether you choose to turn around or to go ahead, you can move forward in your faith-walk as the Holy Spirit Himself guides your steps.

1 Kings

WEEK 29 • WEDNESDAY

1 Kings 1:1—2:46

Yet another rebellion arises from inside King David's own household. Adonijah, one of David's sons and a half-brother of Solomon conspires with Joab and Abiathar. Clued in by the prophet Nathan and Bathsheba, David arranges for Solomon's coronation. After David's death, Solomon follows David's last instructions and in doing so makes his throne more and more secure against the treachery and treason of several power-hungry rivals. If time is short, focus on 1 Kings 1:1–40.

Adonijah Sets Himself Up as King

1 When King David was old and well
advanced in years, he could not
keep warm even when they put covers
over him. 2So his servants said to him,
"Let us look for a young virgin to attend
the king and take care of him. She can
lie beside him so that our lord the king
may keep warm."
3Then they searched throughout Israel for a beautiful girl and found Abishag, a Shunammite, and brought her to
the king. 4The girl was very beautiful;
she took care of the king and waited on
him, but the king had no intimate relations with her.
5Now Adonijah, whose mother was
Haggith, put himself forward and said,
"I will be king." So he got chariots and
horses[a] ready, with fifty men to run
ahead of him. 6(His father had never interfered with him by asking, "Why do
you behave as you do?" He was also
very handsome and was born next after
Absalom.)
7Adonijah conferred with Joab son of
Zeruiah and with Abiathar the priest,
and they gave him their support. 8But
Zadok the priest, Benaiah son of Jehoiada, Nathan the prophet, Shimei and
Rei[b] and David's special guard did not
join Adonijah.
9Adonijah then sacrificed sheep, cattle and fattened calves at the Stone of
Zoheleth near En Rogel. He invited all
his brothers, the king's sons, and all the
men of Judah who were royal officials,
10but he did not invite Nathan the
prophet or Benaiah or the special guard
or his brother Solomon.
11Then Nathan asked Bathsheba, Solomon's mother, "Have you not heard
that Adonijah, the son of Haggith, has
become king without our lord David's
knowing it? 12Now then, let me advise
you how you can save your own life and
the life of your son Solomon. 13Go in to
King David and say to him, 'My lord the
king, did you not swear to me your servant: "Surely Solomon your son shall be
king after me, and he will sit on my
throne"? Why then has Adonijah become king?' 14While you are still there
talking to the king, I will come in and
confirm what you have said."
15So Bathsheba went to see the aged

[a]5 Or *charioteers* [b]8 Or *and his friends*

king in his room, where Abishag the Shunammite was attending him. [16]Bathsheba bowed low and knelt before the king.

"What is it you want?" the king asked.

[17]She said to him, "My lord, you yourself swore to me your servant by the LORD your God: 'Solomon your son shall be king after me, and he will sit on my throne.' [18]But now Adonijah has become king, and you, my lord the king, do not know about it. [19]He has sacrificed great numbers of cattle, fattened calves, and sheep, and has invited all the king's sons, Abiathar the priest and Joab the commander of the army, but he has not invited Solomon your servant. [20]My lord the king, the eyes of all Israel are on you, to learn from you who will sit on the throne of my lord the king after him. [21]Otherwise, as soon as my lord the king is laid to rest with his fathers, I and my son Solomon will be treated as criminals."

[22]While she was still speaking with the king, Nathan the prophet arrived. [23]And they told the king, "Nathan the prophet is here." So he went before the king and bowed with his face to the ground.

[24]Nathan said, "Have you, my lord the king, declared that Adonijah shall be king after you, and that he will sit on your throne? [25]Today he has gone down and sacrificed great numbers of cattle, fattened calves, and sheep. He has invited all the king's sons, the commanders of the army and Abiathar the priest. Right now they are eating and drinking with him and saying, 'Long live King Adonijah!' [26]But me your servant, and Zadok the priest, and Benaiah son of Jehoiada, and your servant Solomon he did not invite. [27]Is this something my lord the king has done without letting his servants know who should sit on the throne of my lord the king after him?"

David Makes Solomon King

[28]Then King David said, "Call in Bathsheba." So she came into the king's presence and stood before him.

[29]The king then took an oath: "As surely as the LORD lives, who has delivered me out of every trouble, [30]I will surely carry out today what I swore to you by the LORD, the God of Israel: Solomon your son shall be king after me, and he will sit on my throne in my place."

[31]Then Bathsheba bowed low with her face to the ground and, kneeling before the king, said, "May my lord King David live forever!"

[32]King David said, "Call in Zadok the priest, Nathan the prophet and Benaiah son of Jehoiada." When they came before the king, [33]he said to them: "Take your lord's servants with you and set Solomon my son on my own mule and take him down to Gihon. [34]There have Zadok the priest and Nathan the prophet anoint him king over Israel. Blow the trumpet and shout, 'Long live King Solomon!' [35]Then you are to go up with him, and he is to come and sit on my throne and reign in my place. I have appointed him ruler over Israel and Judah."

[36]Benaiah son of Jehoiada answered the king, "Amen! May the LORD, the God of my lord the king, so declare it. [37]As the LORD was with my lord the king, so may he be with Solomon to make his throne even greater than the throne of my lord King David!"

[38]So Zadok the priest, Nathan the prophet, Benaiah son of Jehoiada, the Kerethites and the Pelethites went down and put Solomon on King David's mule and escorted him to Gihon. [39]Zadok the priest took the horn of oil from the sacred tent and anointed Solomon. Then they sounded the trumpet and all the people shouted, "Long live King Solomon!" [40]And all the people went up after him, playing flutes and rejoicing greatly, so that the ground shook with the sound.

[41]Adonijah and all the guests who were with him heard it as they were finishing their feast. On hearing the sound of the trumpet, Joab asked, "What's the meaning of all the noise in the city?"

[42]Even as he was speaking, Jonathan son of Abiathar the priest arrived. Adonijah said, "Come in. A worthy man like you must be bringing good news."

43 "Not at all!" Jonathan answered. "Our lord King David has made Solomon king. 44 The king has sent with him Zadok the priest, Nathan the prophet, Benaiah son of Jehoiada, the Kerethites and the Pelethites, and they have put him on the king's mule, 45 and Zadok the priest and Nathan the prophet have anointed him king at Gihon. From there they have gone up cheering, and the city resounds with it. That's the noise you hear. 46 Moreover, Solomon has taken his seat on the royal throne. 47 Also, the royal officials have come to congratulate our lord King David, saying, 'May your God make Solomon's name more famous than yours and his throne greater than yours!' And the king bowed in worship on his bed 48 and said, 'Praise be to the LORD, the God of Israel, who has allowed my eyes to see a successor on my throne today.' "

49 At this, all Adonijah's guests rose in alarm and dispersed. 50 But Adonijah, in fear of Solomon, went and took hold of the horns of the altar. 51 Then Solomon was told, "Adonijah is afraid of King Solomon and is clinging to the horns of the altar. He says, 'Let King Solomon swear to me today that he will not put his servant to death with the sword.' "

52 Solomon replied, "If he shows himself to be a worthy man, not a hair of his head will fall to the ground; but if evil is found in him, he will die." 53 Then King Solomon sent men, and they brought him down from the altar. And Adonijah came and bowed down to King Solomon, and Solomon said, "Go to your home."

David's Charge to Solomon

2 When the time drew near for David to die, he gave a charge to Solomon his son.

2 "I am about to go the way of all the earth," he said. "So be strong, show yourself a man, 3 and observe what the LORD your God requires: Walk in his ways, and keep his decrees and commands, his laws and requirements, as written in the Law of Moses, so that you may prosper in all you do and wherever you go, 4 and that the LORD may keep his promise to me: 'If your descendants watch how they live, and if they walk faithfully before me with all their heart and soul, you will never fail to have a man on the throne of Israel.'

5 "Now you yourself know what Joab son of Zeruiah did to me—what he did to the two commanders of Israel's armies, Abner son of Ner and Amasa son of Jether. He killed them, shedding their blood in peacetime as if in battle, and with that blood stained the belt around his waist and the sandals on his feet. 6 Deal with him according to your wisdom, but do not let his gray head go down to the grave[a] in peace.

7 "But show kindness to the sons of Barzillai of Gilead and let them be among those who eat at your table. They stood by me when I fled from your brother Absalom.

8 "And remember, you have with you Shimei son of Gera, the Benjamite from Bahurim, who called down bitter curses on me the day I went to Mahanaim. When he came down to meet me at the Jordan, I swore to him by the LORD: 'I will not put you to death by the sword.' 9 But now, do not consider him innocent. You are a man of wisdom; you will know what to do to him. Bring his gray head down to the grave in blood."

10 Then David rested with his fathers and was buried in the City of David. 11 He had reigned forty years over Israel—seven years in Hebron and thirty-three in Jerusalem. 12 So Solomon sat on the throne of his father David, and his rule was firmly established.

Solomon's Throne Established

13 Now Adonijah, the son of Haggith, went to Bathsheba, Solomon's mother. Bathsheba asked him, "Do you come peacefully?"

He answered, "Yes, peacefully." 14 Then he added, "I have something to say to you."

"You may say it," she replied.

15 "As you know," he said, "the king-

[a]6 Hebrew *Sheol*; also in verse 9

dom was mine. All Israel looked to me
as their king. But things changed, and
the kingdom has gone to my brother;
for it has come to him from the LORD.
16Now I have one request to make of
you. Do not refuse me."
"You may make it," she said.
17So he continued, "Please ask King
Solomon—he will not refuse you—to
give me Abishag the Shunammite as my
wife."
18"Very well," Bathsheba replied, "I
will speak to the king for you."
19When Bathsheba went to King Solomon to speak to him for Adonijah, the
king stood up to meet her, bowed down
to her and sat down on his throne. He
had a throne brought for the king's mother, and she sat down at his right hand.
20"I have one small request to make of
you," she said. "Do not refuse me."
The king replied, "Make it, my mother; I will not refuse you."
21So she said, "Let Abishag the Shunammite be given in marriage to your
brother Adonijah."
22King Solomon answered his mother,
"Why do you request Abishag the Shunammite for Adonijah? You might as
well request the kingdom for him—after all, he is my older brother—yes, for
him and for Abiathar the priest and Joab
son of Zeruiah!"
23Then King Solomon swore by the
LORD: "May God deal with me, be it
ever so severely, if Adonijah does not
pay with his life for this request! 24And
now, as surely as the LORD lives—he
who has established me securely on the
throne of my father David and has
founded a dynasty for me as he promised—Adonijah shall be put to death
today!" 25So King Solomon gave orders
to Benaiah son of Jehoiada, and he
struck down Adonijah and he died.
26To Abiathar the priest the king said,
"Go back to your fields in Anathoth. You
deserve to die, but I will not put you to
death now, because you carried the ark
of the Sovereign LORD before my father
David and shared all my father's hardships." 27So Solomon removed Abiathar
from the priesthood of the LORD, fulfilling the word the LORD had spoken at
Shiloh about the house of Eli.
28When the news reached Joab, who
had conspired with Adonijah though
not with Absalom, he fled to the tent of
the LORD and took hold of the horns of
the altar. 29King Solomon was told that
Joab had fled to the tent of the LORD and
was beside the altar. Then Solomon ordered Benaiah son of Jehoiada, "Go,
strike him down!"
30So Benaiah entered the tent of the
LORD and said to Joab, "The king says,
'Come out!' "
But he answered, "No, I will die
here."
Benaiah reported to the king, "This is
how Joab answered me."
31Then the king commanded Benaiah,
"Do as he says. Strike him down and
bury him, and so clear me and my
father's house of the guilt of the innocent blood that Joab shed. 32The LORD
will repay him for the blood he shed,
because without the knowledge of my
father David he attacked two men and
killed them with the sword. Both of
them—Abner son of Ner, commander of
Israel's army, and Amasa son of Jether,
commander of Judah's army—were better men and more upright than he.
33May the guilt of their blood rest on the
head of Joab and his descendants forever. But on David and his descendants,
his house and his throne, may there be
the LORD's peace forever."
34So Benaiah son of Jehoiada went up
and struck down Joab and killed him,
and he was buried on his own land[a] in
the desert. 35The king put Benaiah son
of Jehoiada over the army in Joab's
position and replaced Abiathar with
Zadok the priest.
36Then the king sent for Shimei and
said to him, "Build yourself a house in
Jerusalem and live there, but do not go
anywhere else. 37The day you leave and
cross the Kidron Valley, you can be sure
you will die; your blood will be on your
own head."
38Shimei answered the king, "What

[a]34 Or *buried in his tomb*

you say is good. Your servant will do as
my lord the king has said." And Shimei
stayed in Jerusalem for a long time.
39But three years later, two of Shimei's
slaves ran off to Achish son of Maacah,
king of Gath, and Shimei was told,
"Your slaves are in Gath." 40At this, he
saddled his donkey and went to Achish
at Gath in search of his slaves. So Shimei went away and brought the slaves
back from Gath.
41When Solomon was told that Shimei had gone from Jerusalem to Gath and
had returned, 42the king summoned
Shimei and said to him, "Did I not make
you swear by the LORD and warn you,
'On the day you leave to go anywhere
else, you can be sure you will die'? At
that time you said to me, 'What you say
is good. I will obey.' 43Why then did you
not keep your oath to the LORD and
obey the command I gave you?"
44The king also said to Shimei, "You
know in your heart all the wrong you
did to my father David. Now the LORD
will repay you for your wrongdoing.
45But King Solomon will be blessed, and
David's throne will remain secure before the LORD forever."
46Then the king gave the order to Benaiah son of Jehoiada, and he went out
and struck Shimei down and killed him.

The kingdom was now firmly established in Solomon's hands.

SHARPEN THE FOCUS

We can draw several parallels between King Solomon and King Jesus:

- Both came from David's line and received from God the right to rule His people.
- Both came to their people humbly, riding not on a war horse, but on a lowly donkey or mule.
- Solomon's name means *peace* or *peaceable;* the Lord Jesus is our Prince of Peace.

Perhaps you can think of other connections between the two. But one point is clear: Solomon did not ascend the throne by accident or by human design. The Lord intended to place Solomon on the throne of his father, David, and eventually to bring the Savior, Jesus, from this royal line.

While the two books of Kings tell of intrigue and sin, victories and idolatry of Israel's earthly kings, these books are not just about human affairs. They are instead the story of how the Lord preserved a people for Himself, through whom the King of kings would come. This King brings peace–true peace–to those heartbroken by sin. Through this King, you and I receive peace with God and with one another. Live in the peace and victory of His kingdom today.

As you read 1 Kings 3 and 4, take particular note of the heart-attitude of King Solomon and his people. Such an attitude comes to God's people as His gift of grace and brings with it peace and contentment. If time is short, focus on 1 Kings 3:1–15.

Solomon Asks for Wisdom

3 Solomon made an alliance with
Pharaoh king of Egypt and married his daughter. He brought her to the
City of David until he finished building
his palace and the temple of the LORD,
and the wall around Jerusalem. 2The
people, however, were still sacrificing at
the high places, because a temple had
not yet been built for the Name of the
LORD. 3Solomon showed his love for the
LORD by walking according to the statutes of his father David, except that he
offered sacrifices and burned incense on
the high places.
4The king went to Gibeon to offer sacrifices, for that was the most important
high place, and Solomon offered a thousand burnt offerings on that altar. 5At
Gibeon the LORD appeared to Solomon
during the night in a dream, and God
said, "Ask for whatever you want me to
give you."
6Solomon answered, "You have
shown great kindness to your servant,
my father David, because he was faithful to you and righteous and upright in
heart. You have continued this great
kindness to him and have given him a
son to sit on his throne this very day.
7"Now, O LORD my God, you have
made your servant king in place of my
father David. But I am only a little child
and do not know how to carry out my
duties. 8Your servant is here among the
people you have chosen, a great people,
too numerous to count or number. 9So
give your servant a discerning heart to
govern your people and to distinguish
between right and wrong. For who is
able to govern this great people of
yours?"
10The Lord was pleased that Solomon
had asked for this. 11So God said to him,
"Since you have asked for this and not
for long life or wealth for yourself, nor
have asked for the death of your enemies but for discernment in administering justice, 12I will do what you have
asked. I will give you a wise and discerning heart, so that there will never
have been anyone like you, nor will
there ever be. 13Moreover, I will give you
what you have not asked for—both
riches and honor—so that in your lifetime you will have no equal among
kings. 14And if you walk in my ways and
obey my statutes and commands as
David your father did, I will give you a
long life." 15Then Solomon awoke—and
he realized it had been a dream.
He returned to Jerusalem, stood before the ark of the Lord's covenant and
sacrificed burnt offerings and fellowship offerings.[a] Then he gave a feast for
all his court.

A Wise Ruling

16Now two prostitutes came to the
king and stood before him. 17One of
them said, "My lord, this woman and I
live in the same house. I had a baby
while she was there with me. 18The third
day after my child was born, this woman also had a baby. We were alone; there
was no one in the house but the two of us.
19"During the night this woman's son

[a]15 Traditionally *peace offerings*

died because she lay on him. 20So she got
up in the middle of the night and took
my son from my side while I your servant was asleep. She put him by her
breast and put her dead son by my
breast. 21The next morning, I got up to
nurse my son—and he was dead! But
when I looked at him closely in the
morning light, I saw that it wasn't the
son I had borne."

22The other woman said, "No! The living one is my son; the dead one is
yours."

But the first one insisted, "No! The dead one is yours; the living one is mine." And so they argued before the king.

23The king said, "This one says, 'My
son is alive and your son is dead,' while
that one says, 'No! Your son is dead and
mine is alive.' "

24Then the king said, "Bring me a
sword." So they brought a sword for the
king. 25He then gave an order: "Cut the
living child in two and give half to one
and half to the other."

26The woman whose son was alive
was filled with compassion for her son
and said to the king, "Please, my lord,
give her the living baby! Don't kill him!"

But the other said, "Neither I nor you shall have him. Cut him in two!"

27Then the king gave his ruling: "Give
the living baby to the first woman. Do
not kill him; she is his mother."

28When all Israel heard the verdict the
king had given, they held the king in
awe, because they saw that he had wisdom from God to administer justice.

Solomon's Officials and Governors

4 So King Solomon ruled over all
Israel. 2And these were his chief
officials:

Azariah son of Zadok—the priest;
3Elihoreph and Ahijah, sons of Shisha—secretaries;
Jehoshaphat son of Ahilud—recorder;
4Benaiah son of Jehoiada—commander in chief;
Zadok and Abiathar—priests;
5Azariah son of Nathan—in charge of the district officers;
Zabud son of Nathan—a priest and personal adviser to the king;
6Ahishar—in charge of the palace;
Adoniram son of Abda—in charge of forced labor.

7Solomon also had twelve district
governors over all Israel, who supplied
provisions for the king and the royal
household. Each one had to provide
supplies for one month in the year.
8These are their names:

Ben-Hur—in the hill country of Ephraim;
9Ben-Deker—in Makaz, Shaalbim, Beth Shemesh and Elon Bethhanan;
10Ben-Hesed—in Arubboth (Socoh and all the land of Hepher were his);
11Ben-Abinadab—in Naphoth Dor[a] (he was married to Taphath daughter of Solomon);
12Baana son of Ahilud—in Taanach and Megiddo, and in all of Beth Shan next to Zarethan below Jezreel, from Beth Shan to Abel Meholah across to Jokmeam;
13Ben-Geber—in Ramoth Gilead (the settlements of Jair son of Manasseh in Gilead were his, as well as the district of Argob in Bashan and its sixty large walled cities with bronze gate bars);
14Ahinadab son of Iddo—in Mahanaim;
15Ahimaaz—in Naphtali (he had married Basemath daughter of Solomon);
16Baana son of Hushai—in Asher and in Aloth;
17Jehoshaphat son of Paruah—in Issachar;
18Shimei son of Ela—in Benjamin;
19Geber son of Uri—in Gilead (the country of Sihon king of the Amorites and the country of Og king of Bashan). He was the only governor over the district.

[a]11 Or *in the heights of Dor*

Solomon's Daily Provisions

[20]The people of Judah and Israel were
as numerous as the sand on the seashore; they ate, they drank and they
were happy. [21]And Solomon ruled over
all the kingdoms from the River[a] to the
land of the Philistines, as far as the border of Egypt. These countries brought
tribute and were Solomon's subjects all
his life.

[22]Solomon's daily provisions were
thirty cors[b] of fine flour and sixty cors[c]
of meal, [23]ten head of stall-fed cattle,
twenty of pasture-fed cattle and a hundred sheep and goats, as well as deer,
gazelles, roebucks and choice fowl. [24]For
he ruled over all the kingdoms west of
the River, from Tiphsah to Gaza, and
had peace on all sides. [25]During Solomon's lifetime Judah and Israel, from
Dan to Beersheba, lived in safety, each
man under his own vine and fig tree.

[26]Solomon had four[d] thousand stalls
for chariot horses, and twelve thousand
horses.[e]

[27]The district officers, each in his
month, supplied provisions for King
Solomon and all who came to the king's
table. They saw to it that nothing was
lacking. [28]They also brought to the proper place their quotas of barley and straw
for the chariot horses and the other
horses.

Solomon's Wisdom

[29]God gave Solomon wisdom and
very great insight, and a breadth of understanding as measureless as the sand
on the seashore. [30]Solomon's wisdom
was greater than the wisdom of all the
men of the East, and greater than all the
wisdom of Egypt. [31]He was wiser than
any other man, including Ethan the Ezrahite—wiser than Heman, Calcol and
Darda, the sons of Mahol. And his fame
spread to all the surrounding nations.
[32]He spoke three thousand proverbs
and his songs numbered a thousand
and five. [33]He described plant life, from
the cedar of Lebanon to the hyssop that
grows out of walls. He also taught about
animals and birds, reptiles and fish.
[34]Men of all nations came to listen to
Solomon's wisdom, sent by all the kings
of the world, who had heard of his wisdom.

[a]*21* That is, the Euphrates; also in verse 24
[b]*22* That is, probably about 185 bushels (about 6.6 kiloliters) [c]*22* That is, probably about 375 bushels (about 13.2 kiloliters) [d]*26* Some Septuagint manuscripts (see also 2 Chron. 9:25); Hebrew *forty* [e]*26* Or *charioteers*

SHARPEN THE FOCUS

A kind heart. A big heart. A hard heart. A wounded heart. A faithful heart. We use similar expressions as short-hand descriptions of the character and attitude of others.

Solomon prayed for a hearing heart (1 Kings 3:9); that's the literal translation of the Hebrew words in his prayer. He wanted to hear God's Word and truth, the Lord's voice. Hearing *that* would equip Solomon to rule in justice and enable him to reign righteously over the people of God.

The Lord answered Solomon's prayer. He gave Solomon "a wise and discerning heart" (1 Kings 3:12). Solomon would hear, understand, and put God's Word into practice.

Do we ask our Lord for hearing hearts? And once we've heard, do we treasure and obey the Word? As we'll see, Solomon failed just as we fail. But God's Word of forgiveness, comfort, and strength doesn't fail. When "we are faithless, He will remain faithful, for He cannot disown Himself" (2 Timothy 2:13).

Ask your Lord for a heart that hears, receives, and truly believes this precious Gospel. It's yours in Christ! Then rely on the power that comes to us through that Word to prize God's wisdom and to practice it more completely in your life.

It sometimes happens: the son fulfills his father's dream. Today you will read about Solomon constructing the temple David had planned before his death. As you read, recall Israel's joy as they built the tabernacle some 480 years earlier. Why did both projects bring God's people such joy? If time is short, focus on 1 Kings 5:1–18; 6:7–14.

Preparations for Building the Temple

5 When Hiram king of Tyre heard
that Solomon had been anointed
king to succeed his father David, he sent
his envoys to Solomon, because he had
always been on friendly terms with
David. 2Solomon sent back this message
to Hiram:

3"You know that because of the
wars waged against my father David from all sides, he could not
build a temple for the Name of the
LORD his God until the LORD put
his enemies under his feet. 4But
now the LORD my God has given
me rest on every side, and there is
no adversary or disaster. 5I intend,
therefore, to build a temple for the
Name of the LORD my God, as the
LORD told my father David, when
he said, 'Your son whom I will put
on the throne in your place will
build the temple for my Name.'

6"So give orders that cedars of
Lebanon be cut for me. My men
will work with yours, and I will pay
you for your men whatever wages
you set. You know that we have no
one so skilled in felling timber as
the Sidonians."

7When Hiram heard Solomon's message, he was greatly pleased and said,
"Praise be to the LORD today, for he has
given David a wise son to rule over this
great nation."
8So Hiram sent word to Solomon:

"I have received the message you
sent me and will do all you want in
providing the cedar and pine logs.
9My men will haul them down
from Lebanon to the sea, and I will
float them in rafts by sea to the
place you specify. There I will separate them and you can take them
away. And you are to grant my
wish by providing food for my
royal household."

10In this way Hiram kept Solomon
supplied with all the cedar and pine
logs he wanted, 11and Solomon gave Hiram twenty thousand cors[a] of wheat as
food for his household, in addition to
twenty thousand baths[b,c] of pressed olive oil. Solomon continued to do this for
Hiram year after year. 12The LORD gave
Solomon wisdom, just as he had promised him. There were peaceful relations
between Hiram and Solomon, and the
two of them made a treaty.
13King Solomon conscripted laborers
from all Israel—thirty thousand men.
14He sent them off to Lebanon in shifts
of ten thousand a month, so that they
spent one month in Lebanon and two
months at home. Adoniram was in
charge of the forced labor. 15Solomon
had seventy thousand carriers and
eighty thousand stonecutters in the

[a]*11* That is, probably about 125,000 bushels (about 4,400 kiloliters) [b]*11* Septuagint (see also 2 Chron. 2:10); Hebrew *twenty cors* [c]*11* That is, about 115,000 gallons (about 440 kiloliters)

hills, 16as well as thirty-three hundred[a]
foremen who supervised the project
and directed the workmen. 17At the
king's command they removed from
the quarry large blocks of quality stone
to provide a foundation of dressed
stone for the temple. 18The craftsmen of
Solomon and Hiram and the men of
Gebal[b] cut and prepared the timber and
stone for the building of the temple.

Solomon Builds the Temple

6 In the four hundred and
eightieth[c] year after the Israelites
had come out of Egypt, in the fourth
year of Solomon's reign over Israel, in
the month of Ziv, the second month, he
began to build the temple of the LORD.
2The temple that King Solomon built
for the LORD was sixty cubits long,
twenty wide and thirty high.[d] 3The portico at the front of the main hall of the
temple extended the width of the
temple, that is twenty cubits,[e] and pro-
jected ten cubits[f] from the front of the
temple. 4He made narrow clerestory
windows in the temple. 5Against the
walls of the main hall and inner sanctuary he built a structure around the
building, in which there were side
rooms. 6The lowest floor was five cubits[g]
wide, the middle floor six cubits[h] and
the third floor seven.[i] He made offset
ledges around the outside of the temple
so that nothing would be inserted into
the temple walls.
7In building the temple, only blocks
dressed at the quarry were used, and no
hammer, chisel or any other iron tool
was heard at the temple site while it was
being built.
8The entrance to the lowest[j] floor was
on the south side of the temple; a stairway led up to the middle level and from
there to the third. 9So he built the temple and completed it, roofing it with
beams and cedar planks. 10And he built
the side rooms all along the temple. The
height of each was five cubits, and they
were attached to the temple by beams
of cedar.
11The word of the LORD came to Solomon: 12"As for this temple you are
building, if you follow my decrees, carry
out my regulations and keep all my
commands and obey them, I will fulfill
through you the promise I gave to
David your father. 13And I will live
among the Israelites and will not abandon my people Israel."
14So Solomon built the temple and
completed it. 15He lined its interior walls
with cedar boards, paneling them from
the floor of the temple to the ceiling, and
covered the floor of the temple with
planks of pine. 16He partitioned off
twenty cubits[k] at the rear of the temple
with cedar boards from floor to ceiling
to form within the temple an inner sanctuary, the Most Holy Place. 17The main
hall in front of this room was forty
cubits[l] long. 18The inside of the temple
was cedar, carved with gourds and open
flowers. Everything was cedar; no stone
was to be seen.
19He prepared the inner sanctuary
within the temple to set the ark of the
covenant of the LORD there. 20The inner
sanctuary was twenty cubits long, twenty wide and twenty high.[m] He overlaid
the inside with pure gold, and he also
overlaid the altar of cedar. 21Solomon
covered the inside of the temple with
pure gold, and he extended gold chains
across the front of the inner sanctuary,
which was overlaid with gold. 22So he
overlaid the whole interior with gold.
He also overlaid with gold the altar that
belonged to the inner sanctuary.
23In the inner sanctuary he made a
pair of cherubim of olive wood, each ten
cubits[n] high. 24One wing of the first

[a]*16* Hebrew; some Septuagint manuscripts (see also 2 Chron. 2:2, 18) *thirty-six hundred* [b]*18* That is, Byblos [c]*1* Hebrew; Septuagint *four hundred and fortieth* [d]*2* That is, about 90 feet (about 27 meters) long and 30 feet (about 9 meters) wide and 45 feet (about 13.5 meters) high [e]*3* That is, about 30 feet (about 9 meters) [f]*3* That is, about 15 feet (about 4.5 meters) [g]*6* That is, about 7 1/2 feet (about 2.3 meters); also in verses 10 and 24 [h]*6* That is, about 9 feet (about 2.7 meters) [i]*6* That is, about 10 1/2 feet (about 3.1 meters) [j]*8* Septuagint; Hebrew *middle* [k]*16* That is, about 30 feet (about 9 meters) [l]*17* That is, about 60 feet (about 18 meters) [m]*20* That is, about 30 feet (about 9 meters) long, wide and high [n]*23* That is, about 15 feet (about 4.5 meters)

cherub was five cubits long, and the other wing five cubits—ten cubits from
wing tip to wing tip. [25]The second cherub also measured ten cubits, for the two
cherubim were identical in size and
shape. [26]The height of each cherub was
ten cubits. [27]He placed the cherubim inside the innermost room of the temple,
with their wings spread out. The wing
of one cherub touched one wall, while
the wing of the other touched the other
wall, and their wings touched each other in the middle of the room. [28]He overlaid the cherubim with gold.

[29]On the walls all around the temple,
in both the inner and outer rooms, he
carved cherubim, palm trees and open
flowers. [30]He also covered the floors of
both the inner and outer rooms of the
temple with gold.

[31]For the entrance of the inner sanctuary he made doors of olive wood with
five-sided jambs. [32]And on the two olive
wood doors he carved cherubim, palm
trees and open flowers, and overlaid the
cherubim and palm trees with beaten
gold. [33]In the same way he made four-
sided jambs of olive wood for the entrance to the main hall. [34]He also made
two pine doors, each having two leaves
that turned in sockets. [35]He carved cherubim, palm trees and open flowers on
them and overlaid them with gold hammered evenly over the carvings.

[36]And he built the inner courtyard of
three courses of dressed stone and one
course of trimmed cedar beams.

[37]The foundation of the temple of the
LORD was laid in the fourth year, in the
month of Ziv. [38]In the eleventh year in
the month of Bul, the eighth month, the
temple was finished in all its details
according to its specifications. He had
spent seven years building it.

Solomon Builds His Palace

7 It took Solomon thirteen years,
however, to complete the construction of his palace. [2]He built the Palace of the Forest of Lebanon a hundred
cubits long, fifty wide and thirty high,[a]
with four rows of cedar columns supporting trimmed cedar beams. [3]It was
roofed with cedar above the beams that
rested on the columns—forty-five
beams, fifteen to a row. [4]Its windows
were placed high in sets of three, facing
each other. [5]All the doorways had rectangular frames; they were in the front
part in sets of three, facing each other.[b]

[6]He made a colonnade fifty cubits
long and thirty wide.[c] In front of it was
a portico, and in front of that were pillars and an overhanging roof.

[7]He built the throne hall, the Hall of
Justice, where he was to judge, and he
covered it with cedar from floor to
ceiling.[d] [8]And the palace in which he
was to live, set farther back, was similar
in design. Solomon also made a palace
like this hall for Pharaoh's daughter,
whom he had married.

[9]All these structures, from the outside
to the great courtyard and from foundation to eaves, were made of blocks of
high-grade stone cut to size and
trimmed with a saw on their inner and
outer faces. [10]The foundations were laid
with large stones of good quality, some
measuring ten cubits[e] and some eight.[f]
[11]Above were high-grade stones, cut to
size, and cedar beams. [12]The great courtyard was surrounded by a wall of three
courses of dressed stone and one course
of trimmed cedar beams, as was the inner courtyard of the temple of the LORD
with its portico.

The Temple's Furnishings

[13]King Solomon sent to Tyre and
brought Huram,[g] [14]whose mother was a
widow from the tribe of Naphtali and
whose father was a man of Tyre and a
craftsman in bronze. Huram was highly
skilled and experienced in all kinds of
bronze work. He came to King Solomon
and did all the work assigned to him.

[a]2 That is, about 150 feet (about 46 meters) long, 75 feet (about 23 meters) wide and 45 feet (about 13.5 meters) high [b]5 The meaning of the Hebrew for this verse is uncertain. [c]6 That is, about 75 feet (about 23 meters) long and 45 feet (about 13.5 meters) wide [d]7 Vulgate and Syriac; Hebrew *floor* [e]10 That is, about 15 feet (about 4.5 meters) [f]10 That is, about 12 feet (about 3.6 meters) [g]13 Hebrew *Hiram,* a variant of *Huram;* also in verses 40 and 45

[15]He cast two bronze pillars, each eighteen cubits high and twelve cubits around,[a] by line. [16]He also made two capitals of cast bronze to set on the tops of the pillars; each capital was five cubits[b] high. [17]A network of interwoven chains festooned the capitals on top of the pillars, seven for each capital. [18]He made pomegranates in two rows[c] encircling each network to decorate the capitals on top of the pillars.[d] He did the same for each capital. [19]The capitals on top of the pillars in the portico were in the shape of lilies, four cubits[e] high. [20]On the capitals of both pillars, above the bowl-shaped part next to the network, were the two hundred pomegranates in rows all around. [21]He erected the pillars at the portico of the temple. The pillar to the south he named Jakin[f] and the one to the north Boaz.[g] [22]The capitals on top were in the shape of lilies. And so the work on the pillars was completed.

[23]He made the Sea of cast metal, circular in shape, measuring ten cubits[h] from rim to rim and five cubits high. It took a line of thirty cubits[i] to measure around it. [24]Below the rim, gourds encircled it—ten to a cubit. The gourds were cast in two rows in one piece with the Sea.

[25]The Sea stood on twelve bulls, three facing north, three facing west, three facing south and three facing east. The Sea rested on top of them, and their hindquarters were toward the center. [26]It was a handbreadth[j] in thickness, and its rim was like the rim of a cup, like a lily blossom. It held two thousand baths.[k]

[27]He also made ten movable stands of bronze; each was four cubits long, four wide and three high.[l] [28]This is how the stands were made: They had side panels attached to uprights. [29]On the panels between the uprights were lions, bulls and cherubim—and on the uprights as well. Above and below the lions and bulls were wreaths of hammered work. [30]Each stand had four bronze wheels with bronze axles, and each had a basin resting on four supports, cast with wreaths on each side. [31]On the inside of the stand there was an opening that had a circular frame one cubit[m] deep. This opening was round, and with its basework it measured a cubit and a half.[n] Around its opening there was engraving. The panels of the stands were square, not round. [32]The four wheels were under the panels, and the axles of the wheels were attached to the stand. The diameter of each wheel was a cubit and a half. [33]The wheels were made like chariot wheels; the axles, rims, spokes and hubs were all of cast metal.

[34]Each stand had four handles, one on each corner, projecting from the stand. [35]At the top of the stand there was a circular band half a cubit[o] deep. The supports and panels were attached to the top of the stand. [36]He engraved cherubim, lions and palm trees on the surfaces of the supports and on the panels, in every available space, with wreaths all around. [37]This is the way he made the ten stands. They were all cast in the same molds and were identical in size and shape.

[38]He then made ten bronze basins, each holding forty baths[p] and measuring four cubits across, one basin to go on each of the ten stands. [39]He placed five of the stands on the south side of the

[a] *15* That is, about 27 feet (about 8.1 meters) high and 18 feet (about 5.4 meters) around [b] *16* That is, about 7 1/2 feet (about 2.3 meters); also in verse 23 [c] *18* Two Hebrew manuscripts and Septuagint; most Hebrew manuscripts *made the pillars, and there were two rows* [d] *18* Many Hebrew manuscripts and Syriac; most Hebrew manuscripts *pomegranates* [e] *19* That is, about 6 feet (about 1.8 meters); also in verse 38
[f] *21 Jakin* probably means *he establishes.*
[g] *21 Boaz* probably means *in him is strength.*
[h] *23* That is, about 15 feet (about 4.5 meters)
[i] *23* That is, about 45 feet (about 13.5 meters)
[j] *26* That is, about 3 inches (about 8 centimeters)
[k] *26* That is, probably about 11,500 gallons (about 44 kiloliters); the Septuagint does not have this sentence. [l] *27* That is, about 6 feet (about 1.8 meters) long and wide and about 4 1/2 feet (about 1.3 meters) high [m] *31* That is, about 1 1/2 feet (about 0.5 meter) [n] *31* That is, about 2 1/4 feet (about 0.7 meter); also in verse 32 [o] *35* That is, about 3/4 foot (about 0.2 meter) [p] *38* That is, about 230 gallons (about 880 liters)

temple and five on the north. He placed the Sea on the south side, at the southeast corner of the temple. [40]He also made the basins and shovels and sprinkling bowls.

So Huram finished all the work he had undertaken for King Solomon in the temple of the LORD:

[41] the two pillars;
the two bowl-shaped capitals on top of the pillars;
the two sets of network decorating the two bowl-shaped capitals on top of the pillars;
[42] the four hundred pomegranates for the two sets of network (two rows of pomegranates for each network, decorating the bowl-shaped capitals on top of the pillars);
[43] the ten stands with their ten basins;
[44] the Sea and the twelve bulls under it;
[45] the pots, shovels and sprinkling bowls.

All these objects that Huram made for King Solomon for the temple of the LORD were of burnished bronze. [46]The king had them cast in clay molds in the plain of the Jordan between Succoth and Zarethan. [47]Solomon left all these things unweighed, because there were so many; the weight of the bronze was not determined.

[48]Solomon also made all the furnishings that were in the LORD's temple:

the golden altar;
the golden table on which was the bread of the Presence;
[49] the lampstands of pure gold (five on the right and five on the left, in front of the inner sanctuary);
the gold floral work and lamps and tongs;
[50] the pure gold basins, wick trimmers, sprinkling bowls, dishes and censers;
and the gold sockets for the doors of the innermost room, the Most Holy Place, and also for the doors of the main hall of the temple.

[51]When all the work King Solomon had done for the temple of the LORD was finished, he brought in the things his father David had dedicated—the silver and gold and the furnishings—and he placed them in the treasuries of the LORD's temple.

SHARPEN THE FOCUS

God chose to dwell among His people in the tabernacle and later in the temple. When Jesus came to earth, He "tented" among His people (as the Greek of John 1:14 literally tells us). Today Christ lives in each of us. Those who belong to Him are "being built together to become a dwelling in which God lives by His Spirit" (Ephesians 2:22).

Solomon's workers chiseled the stone at the quarry. They shaped and dressed it so that each block was ready to slip into place. By the time a stone arrived at the temple, no more was needed (1 Kings 6:7).

We live now "in the quarry." We are being shaped–into the image of Christ Himself (Romans 8:29)! Often, the process hurts. Sometimes, we get discouraged at the slowness of the Workman's progress. We wish the chisel didn't dig so deeply and the hammer didn't have to land so many times or with so much force.

Remember where we're headed. Together with our brothers and sisters in the faith, we're "being built together" to form "a dwelling in which God lives." Throughout all eternity, we will enjoy His presence, experience His love, and bring Him honor. The pain past, the chiseling done, we will live with our Savior forever.

Construction on the temple lasted seven years. Finally the time came for its dedication. As you read about that today, think about the place where *you* worship. While God is everywhere, why is it good for us to set aside special times and special places to meet with Him? If time is short, focus on 1 Kings 8:22–43.

The Ark Brought to the Temple

8 Then King Solomon summoned
into his presence at Jerusalem
the elders of Israel, all the heads of the
tribes and the chiefs of the Israelite families, to bring up the ark of the LORD's
covenant from Zion, the City of David.
2All the men of Israel came together to
King Solomon at the time of the festival
in the month of Ethanim, the seventh
month.
3When all the elders of Israel had arrived, the priests took up the ark, 4and
they brought up the ark of the LORD
and the Tent of Meeting and all the sacred furnishings in it. The priests and
Levites carried them up, 5and King Solomon and the entire assembly of Israel
that had gathered about him were before the ark, sacrificing so many sheep
and cattle that they could not be recorded or counted.
6The priests then brought the ark of
the LORD's covenant to its place in the
inner sanctuary of the temple, the Most
Holy Place, and put it beneath the
wings of the cherubim. 7The cherubim
spread their wings over the place of the
ark and overshadowed the ark and its
carrying poles. 8These poles were so
long that their ends could be seen from
the Holy Place in front of the inner sanctuary, but not from outside the Holy
Place; and they are still there today.
9There was nothing in the ark except the
two stone tablets that Moses had placed
in it at Horeb, where the LORD made a
covenant with the Israelites after they
came out of Egypt.
10When the priests withdrew from the
Holy Place, the cloud filled the temple
of the LORD. 11And the priests could not
perform their service because of the
cloud, for the glory of the LORD filled his
temple.
12Then Solomon said, "The LORD has
said that he would dwell in a dark
cloud; 13I have indeed built a magnificent temple for you, a place for you to
dwell forever."
14While the whole assembly of Israel
was standing there, the king turned
around and blessed them. 15Then he
said:

"Praise be to the LORD, the God
of Israel, who with his own hand
has fulfilled what he promised
with his own mouth to my father
David. For he said, 16'Since the day
I brought my people Israel out of
Egypt, I have not chosen a city in
any tribe of Israel to have a temple
built for my Name to be there, but
I have chosen David to rule my
people Israel.'
17"My father David had it in his
heart to build a temple for the
Name of the LORD, the God of Israel. 18But the LORD said to my father David, 'Because it was in your
heart to build a temple for my
Name, you did well to have this in
your heart. 19Nevertheless, you are

not the one to build the temple, but your son, who is your own flesh and blood—he is the one who will build the temple for my Name.'

20"The LORD has kept the promise he made: I have succeeded David my father and now I sit on the throne of Israel, just as the LORD promised, and I have built the temple for the Name of the LORD, the God of Israel. 21I have provided a place there for the ark, in which is the covenant of the LORD that he made with our fathers when he brought them out of Egypt."

Solomon's Prayer of Dedication

22Then Solomon stood before the altar of the LORD in front of the whole assembly of Israel, spread out his hands toward heaven 23and said:

"O LORD, God of Israel, there is no God like you in heaven above or on earth below—you who keep your covenant of love with your servants who continue wholeheartedly in your way. 24You have kept your promise to your servant David my father; with your mouth you have promised and with your hand you have fulfilled it—as it is today.

25"Now LORD, God of Israel, keep for your servant David my father the promises you made to him when you said, 'You shall never fail to have a man to sit before me on the throne of Israel, if only your sons are careful in all they do to walk before me as you have done.' 26And now, O God of Israel, let your word that you promised your servant David my father come true.

27"But will God really dwell on earth? The heavens, even the highest heaven, cannot contain you. How much less this temple I have built! 28Yet give attention to your servant's prayer and his plea for mercy, O LORD my God. Hear the cry and the prayer that your servant is praying in your presence this day. 29May your eyes be open toward this temple night and day, this place of which you said, 'My Name shall be there,' so that you will hear the prayer your servant prays toward this place. 30Hear the supplication of your servant and of your people Israel when they pray toward this place. Hear from heaven, your dwelling place, and when you hear, forgive.

31"When a man wrongs his neighbor and is required to take an oath and he comes and swears the oath before your altar in this temple, 32then hear from heaven and act. Judge between your servants, condemning the guilty and bringing down on his own head what he has done. Declare the innocent not guilty, and so establish his innocence.

33"When your people Israel have been defeated by an enemy because they have sinned against you, and when they turn back to you and confess your name, praying and making supplication to you in this temple, 34then hear from heaven and forgive the sin of your people Israel and bring them back to the land you gave to their fathers.

35"When the heavens are shut up and there is no rain because your people have sinned against you, and when they pray toward this place and confess your name and turn from their sin because you have afflicted them, 36then hear from heaven and forgive the sin of your servants, your people Israel. Teach them the right way to live, and send rain on the land you gave your people for an inheritance.

37"When famine or plague comes to the land, or blight or mildew, locusts or grasshoppers, or when an enemy besieges them in any of their cities, whatever disaster or disease may come, 38and when a prayer or plea is made by any of

your people Israel—each one
aware of the afflictions of his own
heart, and spreading out his hands
toward this temple— 39then hear
from heaven, your dwelling place.
Forgive and act; deal with each
man according to all he does, since
you know his heart (for you alone
know the hearts of all men), 40so
that they will fear you all the time
they live in the land you gave our
fathers.

41"As for the foreigner who does
not belong to your people Israel but
has come from a distant land
because of your name— 42for men
will hear of your great name and
your mighty hand and your outstretched arm—when he comes and
prays toward this temple, 43then
hear from heaven, your dwelling
place, and do whatever the foreigner asks of you, so that all the
peoples of the earth may know
your name and fear you, as do your
own people Israel, and may know
that this house I have built bears
your Name.

44"When your people go to war
against their enemies, wherever
you send them, and when they
pray to the LORD toward the city
you have chosen and the temple I
have built for your Name, 45then
hear from heaven their prayer and
their plea, and uphold their cause.

46"When they sin against you—
for there is no one who does not
sin—and you become angry with
them and give them over to the enemy, who takes them captive to his
own land, far away or near; 47and if
they have a change of heart in the
land where they are held captive,
and repent and plead with you in
the land of their conquerors and
say, 'We have sinned, we have done
wrong, we have acted wickedly';
48and if they turn back to you with
all their heart and soul in the land
of their enemies who took them
captive, and pray to you toward the
land you gave their fathers, toward
the city you have chosen and the
temple I have built for your Name;
49then from heaven, your dwelling
place, hear their prayer and their
plea, and uphold their cause. 50And
forgive your people, who have
sinned against you; forgive all the
offenses they have committed
against you, and cause their conquerors to show them mercy; 51for
they are your people and your inheritance, whom you brought out
of Egypt, out of that iron-smelting
furnace.

52"May your eyes be open to your
servant's plea and to the plea of
your people Israel, and may you listen to them whenever they cry out
to you. 53For you singled them out
from all the nations of the world to
be your own inheritance, just as
you declared through your servant
Moses when you, O Sovereign
LORD, brought our fathers out of
Egypt."

54When Solomon had finished all
these prayers and supplications to the
LORD, he rose from before the altar of
the LORD, where he had been kneeling
with his hands spread out toward heav-
en. 55He stood and blessed the whole assembly of Israel in a loud voice, saying:

56"Praise be to the LORD, who has
given rest to his people Israel just
as he promised. Not one word has
failed of all the good promises he
gave through his servant Moses.
57May the LORD our God be with us
as he was with our fathers; may he
never leave us nor forsake us. 58May
he turn our hearts to him, to walk
in all his ways and to keep the commands, decrees and regulations he
gave our fathers. 59And may these
words of mine, which I have
prayed before the LORD, be near to
the LORD our God day and night,
that he may uphold the cause of his
servant and the cause of his people
Israel according to each day's need,
60so that all the peoples of the earth
may know that the LORD is God

and that there is no other. 61But
your hearts must be fully committed to the LORD our God, to live by
his decrees and obey his commands, as at this time."

The Dedication of the Temple

62Then the king and all Israel with him
offered sacrifices before the LORD. 63Sol-
omon offered a sacrifice of fellowship
offerings[a] to the LORD: twenty-two
thousand cattle and a hundred and
twenty thousand sheep and goats. So
the king and all the Israelites dedicated
the temple of the LORD.
64On that same day the king consecrated the middle part of the courtyard
in front of the temple of the LORD, and
there he offered burnt offerings, grain
offerings and the fat of the fellowship
offerings, because the bronze altar before the LORD was too small to hold the
burnt offerings, the grain offerings and
the fat of the fellowship offerings.
65So Solomon observed the festival at
that time, and all Israel with him—a vast
assembly, people from Lebo[b] Hamath to
the Wadi of Egypt. They celebrated it before the LORD our God for seven days
and seven days more, fourteen days in
all. 66On the following day he sent the
people away. They blessed the king and
then went home, joyful and glad in
heart for all the good things the LORD
had done for his servant David and his
people Israel.

[a]63 Traditionally *peace offerings;* also in verse 64
[b]65 Or *from the entrance to*

SHARPEN THE FOCUS

Hear from heaven, Your dwelling place, and when You hear, forgive.
(1 Kings 8:30)

Over and over Solomon prayed this refrain. Over and over he, like we today, stood in need of forgiveness. Over and over, we sin against our neighbors (1 Kings 8:31) and against our God (1 Kings 8:33). Over and over, we become aware of the burden of our guilt, the "afflictions," the "plague" of our own hearts. We experience our need individually and with others in our family and our church. And we bring our burden to our Lord.

God never tires of this refrain. He has promised to remove the burden of guilt from us, "as far as the east is from the west" (Psalm 103:12).

But what about sins we commit again and again? Even about these sins, the Lord promises, "I will forgive their wickedness and will remember their sins no more" (Hebrews 8:12).

None of God's people *want* to disobey Him; none of us sins with "a high hand"—defiant of God and in rebellion against His kind, wise rule of our lives. Yet when we fall into the pit of sin, even when it's the same sin, over and over again, our Savior is there to pull us out. So gracious and compassionate is His love for us in His cross!

WEEK 30 • MONDAY

1 Kings 9:1—10:29

Before you read from 1 Kings today, turn back to Deuteronomy 17:14–20. About halfway into his reign, Solomon started down the slippery slope of disobedience—despite his wisdom. As you read, note the specific ways Solomon violated the clear instructions found in Deuteronomy. If time is short, focus on 1 Kings 10:1–29.

The LORD Appears to Solomon

9 When Solomon had finished
building the temple of the LORD
and the royal palace, and had achieved
all he had desired to do, [2]the LORD appeared to him a second time, as he had
appeared to him at Gibeon. [3]The LORD
said to him:

"I have heard the prayer and
plea you have made before me; I
have consecrated this temple,
which you have built, by putting
my Name there forever. My eyes
and my heart will always be there.
[4]"As for you, if you walk before
me in integrity of heart and uprightness, as David your father did,
and do all I command and observe
my decrees and laws, [5]I will establish your royal throne over Israel
forever, as I promised David your
father when I said, 'You shall never
fail to have a man on the throne of
Israel.'
[6]"But if you[a] or your sons turn
away from me and do not observe
the commands and decrees I have
given you[a] and go off to serve other gods and worship them, [7]then I
will cut off Israel from the land I
have given them and will reject this
temple I have consecrated for my
Name. Israel will then become a byword and an object of ridicule
among all peoples. [8]And though
this temple is now imposing, all
who pass by will be appalled and
will scoff and say, 'Why has the
LORD done such a thing to this land
and to this temple?' [9]People will
answer, 'Because they have forsak-
en the LORD their God, who
brought their fathers out of Egypt,
and have embraced other gods,
worshiping and serving them—
that is why the LORD brought all
this disaster on them.' "

Solomon's Other Activities

[10]At the end of twenty years, during
which Solomon built these two buildings—the temple of the LORD and the
royal palace— [11]King Solomon gave
twenty towns in Galilee to Hiram king
of Tyre, because Hiram had supplied
him with all the cedar and pine and gold
he wanted. [12]But when Hiram went
from Tyre to see the towns that Solomon
had given him, he was not pleased with
them. [13]"What kind of towns are these
you have given me, my brother?" he
asked. And he called them the Land of
Cabul,[b] a name they have to this day.
[14]Now Hiram had sent to the king 120
talents[c] of gold.
[15]Here is the account of the forced labor King Solomon conscripted to build
the LORD's temple, his own palace, the
supporting terraces,[d] the wall of Jerusalem, and Hazor, Megiddo and Gezer.

[a]6 The Hebrew is plural. [b]13 *Cabul* sounds like the Hebrew for *good-for-nothing.* [c]14 That is, about 4 1/2 tons (about 4 metric tons) [d]15 Or *the Millo;* also in verse 24

[16](Pharaoh king of Egypt had attacked and captured Gezer. He had set it on fire. He killed its Canaanite inhabitants and then gave it as a wedding gift to his daughter, Solomon's wife. [17]And Solomon rebuilt Gezer.) He built up Lower Beth Horon, [18]Baalath, and Tadmor[a] in the desert, within his land, [19]as well as all his store cities and the towns for his chariots and for his horses[b]—whatever he desired to build in Jerusalem, in Lebanon and throughout all the territory he ruled.

[20]All the people left from the Amorites, Hittites, Perizzites, Hivites and Jebusites (these peoples were not Israelites), [21]that is, their descendants remaining in the land, whom the Israelites could not exterminate[c]—these Solomon conscripted for his slave labor force, as it is to this day. [22]But Solomon did not make slaves of any of the Israelites; they were his fighting men, his government officials, his officers, his captains, and the commanders of his chariots and charioteers. [23]They were also the chief officials in charge of Solomon's projects—550 officials supervising the men who did the work.

[24]After Pharaoh's daughter had come up from the City of David to the palace Solomon had built for her, he constructed the supporting terraces.

[25]Three times a year Solomon sacrificed burnt offerings and fellowship offerings[d] on the altar he had built for the LORD, burning incense before the LORD along with them, and so fulfilled the temple obligations.

[26]King Solomon also built ships at Ezion Geber, which is near Elath in Edom, on the shore of the Red Sea.[e] [27]And Hiram sent his men—sailors who knew the sea—to serve in the fleet with Solomon's men. [28]They sailed to Ophir and brought back 420 talents[f] of gold, which they delivered to King Solomon.

The Queen of Sheba Visits Solomon

10 When the queen of Sheba heard about the fame of Solomon and his relation to the name of the LORD, she came to test him with hard questions. [2]Arriving at Jerusalem with a very great caravan—with camels carrying spices, large quantities of gold, and precious stones—she came to Solomon and talked with him about all that she had on her mind. [3]Solomon answered all her questions; nothing was too hard for the king to explain to her. [4]When the queen of Sheba saw all the wisdom of Solomon and the palace he had built, [5]the food on his table, the seating of his officials, the attending servants in their robes, his cupbearers, and the burnt offerings he made at[g] the temple of the LORD, she was overwhelmed.

[6]She said to the king, "The report I heard in my own country about your achievements and your wisdom is true. [7]But I did not believe these things until I came and saw with my own eyes. Indeed, not even half was told me; in wisdom and wealth you have far exceeded the report I heard. [8]How happy your men must be! How happy your officials, who continually stand before you and hear your wisdom! [9]Praise be to the LORD your God, who has delighted in you and placed you on the throne of Israel. Because of the LORD's eternal love for Israel, he has made you king, to maintain justice and righteousness."

[10]And she gave the king 120 talents[h] of gold, large quantities of spices, and precious stones. Never again were so many spices brought in as those the queen of Sheba gave to King Solomon.

[11](Hiram's ships brought gold from Ophir; and from there they brought great cargoes of almugwood[i] and precious stones. [12]The king used the almugwood to make supports for the temple of the LORD and for the royal palace, and to make harps and lyres for the

[a]*18* The Hebrew may also be read *Tamar.*
[b]*19* Or *charioteers* [c]*21* The Hebrew term refers to the irrevocable giving over of things or persons to the LORD, often by totally destroying them. [d]*25* Traditionally *peace offerings*
[e]*26* Hebrew *Yam Suph;* that is, Sea of Reeds
[f]*28* That is, about 16 tons (about 14.5 metric tons)
[g]*5* Or *the ascent by which he went up to* [h]*10* That is, about 4 1/2 tons (about 4 metric tons)
[i]*11* Probably a variant of *algumwood;* also in verse 12

musicians. So much almugwood has never been imported or seen since that day.)

13King Solomon gave the queen of Sheba all she desired and asked for, besides what he had given her out of his royal bounty. Then she left and returned with her retinue to her own country.

Solomon's Splendor

14The weight of the gold that Solomon received yearly was 666 talents,[a] 15not including the revenues from merchants and traders and from all the Arabian kings and the governors of the land.

16King Solomon made two hundred large shields of hammered gold; six hundred bekas[b] of gold went into each shield. 17He also made three hundred small shields of hammered gold, with three minas[c] of gold in each shield. The king put them in the Palace of the Forest of Lebanon.

18Then the king made a great throne inlaid with ivory and overlaid with fine gold. 19The throne had six steps, and its back had a rounded top. On both sides of the seat were armrests, with a lion standing beside each of them. 20Twelve lions stood on the six steps, one at either end of each step. Nothing like it had ever been made for any other kingdom. 21All King Solomon's goblets were gold, and all the household articles in the Palace of the Forest of Lebanon were pure gold. Nothing was made of silver, because silver was considered of little value in Solomon's days. 22The king had a fleet of trading ships[d] at sea along with the ships of Hiram. Once every three years it returned, carrying gold, silver and ivory, and apes and baboons.

23King Solomon was greater in riches and wisdom than all the other kings of the earth. 24The whole world sought audience with Solomon to hear the wisdom God had put in his heart. 25Year after year, everyone who came brought a gift—articles of silver and gold, robes, weapons and spices, and horses and mules.

26Solomon accumulated chariots and horses; he had fourteen hundred chariots and twelve thousand horses,[e] which he kept in the chariot cities and also with him in Jerusalem. 27The king made silver as common in Jerusalem as stones, and cedar as plentiful as sycamore-fig trees in the foothills. 28Solomon's horses were imported from Egypt[f] and from Kue[g]—the royal merchants purchased them from Kue. 29They imported a chariot from Egypt for six hundred shekels[h] of silver, and a horse for a hundred and fifty.[i] They also exported them to all the kings of the Hittites and of the Arameans.

[a] *14* That is, about 25 tons (about 23 metric tons) [b] *16* That is, about 7 1/2 pounds (about 3.5 kilograms) [c] *17* That is, about 3 3/4 pounds (about 1.7 kilograms) [d] *22* Hebrew *of ships of Tarshish* [e] *26* Or *charioteers* [f] *28* Or possibly *Muzur*, a region in Cilicia; also in verse 29 [g] *28* Probably *Cilicia* [h] *29* That is, about 15 pounds (about 7 kilograms) [i] *29* That is, about 3 3/4 pounds (about 1.7 kilograms)

SHARPEN THE FOCUS

Mission congregations often notice–their life together is never quite the same after they move out of the storefront and into their first, permanent church building.

Young couples may notice–their life together changes after they pass the years of financial struggle and exchange the one-bedroom apartment for a new home in the suburbs.

Solomon evidently noticed–his life somehow changed after he completed his building projects. Maybe the challenge evaporated and he got bored. Maybe his God-given wisdom made him self-confident.

We need to pay attention to our own hearts. Achievement, arriving on a plateau after a long, upward climb–these things can prove treacherous. We may relax our commitment to the vision God has given us for service in His kingdom. We may subtly shift our focus, looking for joy in the gifts God has given instead of in the Giver.

Are you climbing, building, and pressing on? Or are you self-satisfied and bored? However you answer those questions, talk with your Savior about them. Let Him forgive any wrong attitudes. Then let Him sharpen your focus on His kingdom and His righteousness so that you can move forward toward His next goals for your life.

Today's chapter outlines the decline and fall of King Solomon. Despite the Lord's warnings, rebukes, and the consequence He imposes, Solomon continues down the slippery slope of idolatry. Worst of all, he takes his people—God's people—down that slope with him. If time is short, focus on 1 Kings 11:1–13.

Solomon's Wives

11 King Solomon, however, loved
many foreign women besides
Pharaoh's daughter—Moabites, Ammonites, Edomites, Sidonians and Hittites. [2]They were from nations about
which the LORD had told the Israelites,
"You must not intermarry with them,
because they will surely turn your
hearts after their gods." Nevertheless,
Solomon held fast to them in love. [3]He
had seven hundred wives of royal birth
and three hundred concubines, and his
wives led him astray. [4]As Solomon grew
old, his wives turned his heart after other gods, and his heart was not fully devoted to the LORD his God, as the heart
of David his father had been. [5]He followed Ashtoreth the goddess of the Sidonians, and Molech[a] the detestable
god of the Ammonites. [6]So Solomon did
evil in the eyes of the LORD; he did not
follow the LORD completely, as David
his father had done.

[7]On a hill east of Jerusalem, Solomon
built a high place for Chemosh the detestable god of Moab, and for Molech
the detestable god of the Ammonites.
[8]He did the same for all his foreign
wives, who burned incense and offered
sacrifices to their gods.

[9]The LORD became angry with Solomon because his heart had turned away
from the LORD, the God of Israel, who
had appeared to him twice. [10]Although
he had forbidden Solomon to follow
other gods, Solomon did not keep the
LORD's command. [11]So the LORD said to
Solomon, "Since this is your attitude
and you have not kept my covenant and
my decrees, which I commanded you, I
will most certainly tear the kingdom
away from you and give it to one of
your subordinates. [12]Nevertheless, for
the sake of David your father, I will not
do it during your lifetime. I will tear it
out of the hand of your son. [13]Yet I will
not tear the whole kingdom from him,
but will give him one tribe for the sake
of David my servant and for the sake of
Jerusalem, which I have chosen."

Solomon's Adversaries

[14]Then the LORD raised up against
Solomon an adversary, Hadad the
Edomite, from the royal line of Edom.

[a]5 Hebrew *Milcom;* also in verse 33

[15]Earlier when David was fighting with Edom, Joab the commander of the army, who had gone up to bury the dead, had struck down all the men in Edom. [16]Joab and all the Israelites stayed there for six months, until they had destroyed all the men in Edom. [17]But Hadad, still only a boy, fled to Egypt with some Edomite officials who had served his father. [18]They set out from Midian and went to Paran. Then taking men from Paran with them, they went to Egypt, to Pharaoh king of Egypt, who gave Hadad a house and land and provided him with food.

[19]Pharaoh was so pleased with Hadad that he gave him a sister of his own wife, Queen Tahpenes, in marriage. [20]The sister of Tahpenes bore him a son named Genubath, whom Tahpenes brought up in the royal palace. There Genubath lived with Pharaoh's own children.

[21]While he was in Egypt, Hadad heard that David rested with his fathers and that Joab the commander of the army was also dead. Then Hadad said to Pharaoh, "Let me go, that I may return to my own country."

[22]"What have you lacked here that you want to go back to your own country?" Pharaoh asked.

"Nothing," Hadad replied, "but do let me go!"

[23]And God raised up against Solomon another adversary, Rezon son of Eliada, who had fled from his master, Hadadezer king of Zobah. [24]He gathered men around him and became the leader of a band of rebels when David destroyed the forces[a] ⌞of Zobah⌟; the rebels went to Damascus, where they settled and took control. [25]Rezon was Israel's adversary as long as Solomon lived, adding to the trouble caused by Hadad. So Rezon ruled in Aram and was hostile toward Israel.

Jeroboam Rebels Against Solomon

[26]Also, Jeroboam son of Nebat rebelled against the king. He was one of Solomon's officials, an Ephraimite from Zeredah, and his mother was a widow named Zeruah.

[27]Here is the account of how he rebelled against the king: Solomon had built the supporting terraces[b] and had filled in the gap in the wall of the city of David his father. [28]Now Jeroboam was a man of standing, and when Solomon saw how well the young man did his work, he put him in charge of the whole labor force of the house of Joseph.

[29]About that time Jeroboam was going out of Jerusalem, and Ahijah the prophet of Shiloh met him on the way, wearing a new cloak. The two of them were alone out in the country, [30]and Ahijah took hold of the new cloak he was wearing and tore it into twelve pieces. [31]Then he said to Jeroboam, "Take ten pieces for yourself, for this is what the LORD, the God of Israel, says: 'See, I am going to tear the kingdom out of Solomon's hand and give you ten tribes. [32]But for the sake of my servant David and the city of Jerusalem, which I have chosen out of all the tribes of Israel, he will have one tribe. [33]I will do this because they have[c] forsaken me and worshiped Ashtoreth the goddess of the Sidonians, Chemosh the god of the Moabites, and Molech the god of the Ammonites, and have not walked in my ways, nor done what is right in my eyes, nor kept my statutes and laws as David, Solomon's father, did.

[34]" 'But I will not take the whole kingdom out of Solomon's hand; I have made him ruler all the days of his life for the sake of David my servant, whom I chose and who observed my commands and statutes. [35]I will take the kingdom from his son's hands and give you ten tribes. [36]I will give one tribe to his son so that David my servant may always have a lamp before me in Jerusalem, the city where I chose to put my Name. [37]However, as for you, I will take you, and you will rule over all that your heart desires; you will be king over Israel. [38]If you do whatever I command you and walk in my ways and do what is right in my eyes by keeping my statutes and com-

[a]24 Hebrew *destroyed them* [b]27 Or *the Millo* [c]33 Hebrew; Septuagint, Vulgate and Syriac *because he has*

mands, as David my servant did, I will
be with you. I will build you a dynasty
as enduring as the one I built for David
and will give Israel to you. [39]I will humble David's descendants because of this,
but not forever.' "
[40]Solomon tried to kill Jeroboam, but
Jeroboam fled to Egypt, to Shishak the
king, and stayed there until Solomon's
death.

Solomon's Death

[41]As for the other events of Solomon's
reign—all he did and the wisdom he
displayed—are they not written in the
book of the annals of Solomon? [42]Solo-
mon reigned in Jerusalem over all Israel
forty years. [43]Then he rested with his fathers and was buried in the city of David his father. And Rehoboam his son
succeeded him as king.

SHARPEN THE FOCUS

Early in his reign, Solomon had prayed for a hearing heart (1 Kings 3:9). Late in life, Solomon refused to listen. The holy writer tells us that "his heart was not fully devoted to the LORD His God" (1 Kings 11:4). Literally the Hebrew here says that Solomon's heart "was not at peace with the LORD."

Solomon tried to "keep a foot in each camp," so to speak. He showed up for worship at the temple to praise the Lord, and then he went with his wives to bow before Chemosh and Molech, the gods of Moab and Ammon.

One prayer of confession begins, "I have lived as if God didn't matter and as if I mattered most." We may not kneel in front of a statue carved from a tree stump, but we all can think of times in which we have lived "as if God didn't matter."

The Good News is that Jesus is our peace (Ephesians 2:14). His death in our place brings peace to hearts made uneasy by guilt. Even when "the great god self" has interfered with our devotion to our Lord, Jesus is still our peace. He removes our sins and gives us the desire and the ability to start over.

WEEK 30 • WEDNESDAY

1 Kings 12:1–33

GET THE BIG PICTURE

A "no confidence" public opinion poll. The murder of the head of IRS (Israel's Revenue Service). A nation divided. Today's reading includes all of this and more. As you read, notice how God used human ambition, frustration, and even sin to accomplish what He had foretold (1 Kings 11:30–37). If time is short, focus on 1 Kings 12:1–24.

Israel Rebels Against Rehoboam

12 Rehoboam went to Shechem,
for all the Israelites had gone
there to make him king. [2]When Jeroboam son of Nebat heard this (he was still
in Egypt, where he had fled from King
Solomon), he returned from[a] Egypt. [3]So
they sent for Jeroboam, and he and the
whole assembly of Israel went to Reho-

[a]2 Or *he remained in*

boam and said to him: 4“Your father put a heavy yoke on us, but now lighten the harsh labor and the heavy yoke he put on us, and we will serve you.”

5Rehoboam answered, “Go away for three days and then come back to me.” So the people went away.

6Then King Rehoboam consulted the elders who had served his father Solomon during his lifetime. “How would you advise me to answer these people?” he asked.

7They replied, “If today you will be a servant to these people and serve them and give them a favorable answer, they will always be your servants.”

8But Rehoboam rejected the advice the elders gave him and consulted the young men who had grown up with him and were serving him. 9He asked them, “What is your advice? How should we answer these people who say to me, ‘Lighten the yoke your father put on us’?”

10The young men who had grown up with him replied, “Tell these people who have said to you, ‘Your father put a heavy yoke on us, but make our yoke lighter’—tell them, ‘My little finger is thicker than my father’s waist. 11My father laid on you a heavy yoke; I will make it even heavier. My father scourged you with whips; I will scourge you with scorpions.’ ”

12Three days later Jeroboam and all the people returned to Rehoboam, as the king had said, “Come back to me in three days.” 13The king answered the people harshly. Rejecting the advice given him by the elders, 14he followed the advice of the young men and said, “My father made your yoke heavy; I will make it even heavier. My father scourged you with whips; I will scourge you with scorpions.” 15So the king did not listen to the people, for this turn of events was from the LORD, to fulfill the word the LORD had spoken to Jeroboam son of Nebat through Ahijah the Shilonite.

16When all Israel saw that the king refused to listen to them, they answered the king:

“What share do we have in David,
what part in Jesse’s son?
To your tents, O Israel!
Look after your own house,
O David!”

So the Israelites went home. 17But as for the Israelites who were living in the towns of Judah, Rehoboam still ruled over them.

18King Rehoboam sent out Adoniram,[a] who was in charge of forced labor, but all Israel stoned him to death. King Rehoboam, however, managed to get into his chariot and escape to Jerusalem. 19So Israel has been in rebellion against the house of David to this day.

20When all the Israelites heard that Jeroboam had returned, they sent and called him to the assembly and made him king over all Israel. Only the tribe of Judah remained loyal to the house of David.

21When Rehoboam arrived in Jerusalem, he mustered the whole house of Judah and the tribe of Benjamin—a hundred and eighty thousand fighting men—to make war against the house of Israel and to regain the kingdom for Rehoboam son of Solomon.

22But this word of God came to Shemaiah the man of God: 23“Say to Rehoboam son of Solomon king of Judah, to the whole house of Judah and Benjamin, and to the rest of the people, 24‘This is what the LORD says: Do not go up to fight against your brothers, the Israelites. Go home, every one of you, for this is my doing.’ ” So they obeyed the word of the LORD and went home again, as the LORD had ordered.

Golden Calves at Bethel and Dan

25Then Jeroboam fortified Shechem in the hill country of Ephraim and lived there. From there he went out and built up Peniel.[b]

26Jeroboam thought to himself, “The kingdom will now likely revert to the house of David. 27If these people go up

[a] *18* Some Septuagint manuscripts and Syriac (see also 1 Kings 4:6 and 5:14); Hebrew *Adoram*
[b] *25* Hebrew *Penuel,* a variant of *Peniel*

to offer sacrifices at the temple of the
LORD in Jerusalem, they will again give
their allegiance to their lord, Rehoboam
king of Judah. They will kill me and return to King Rehoboam."
28After seeking advice, the king made
two golden calves. He said to the people, "It is too much for you to go up to
Jerusalem. Here are your gods, O Israel,
who brought you up out of Egypt."
29One he set up in Bethel, and the other
in Dan. 30And this thing became a sin;
the people went even as far as Dan to
worship the one there.
31Jeroboam built shrines on high
places and appointed priests from all
sorts of people, even though they were
not Levites. 32He instituted a festival on
the fifteenth day of the eighth month,
like the festival held in Judah, and offered sacrifices on the altar. This he did
in Bethel, sacrificing to the calves he had
made. And at Bethel he also installed
priests at the high places he had made.
33On the fifteenth day of the eighth
month, a month of his own choosing, he
offered sacrifices on the altar he had
built at Bethel. So he instituted the festival for the Israelites and went up to the
altar to make offerings.

SHARPEN THE FOCUS

Charles Schultz, the cartoonist of *Peanuts* fame, once pictured Lucy standing alone and shouting in her best fuss-budget voice, "All I want is my just desserts! All I want is what I have coming to me!"

King Rehoboam got "what was coming to him." Still today "logical consequences" for sin continue to land in people's laps. As we watch that happen, we can be tempted, in "love," to intervene. It's difficult to watch a son or daughter fail an exam for not studying or for cheating. It's wrenching to watch an alcoholic lose his job for failing to show up at work.

Commenting on the consequence of Rehoboam's choices, God says, "This is My doing" (1 Kings 12:24). To his credit, Rehoboam humbled himself enough—this time (1 Kings 12:22–24)—to listen to wise counsel and to turn back from the war he intended to start.

It's encouraging to know that God can and does teach people through circumstances. More encouraging still is the truth that at the cross Jesus "got what was coming to us" because of our sins. For those who believe in Him, all "logical consequences" are temporary. Our Lord forgives every misdeed and helps His penitent children walk through even the worst earthly effects of sin.

WEEK 30 • THURSDAY

1 Kings 13:1—14:31

GET THE BIG PICTURE

Like a split-screen TV tuned-in to two different disasters, 1 Kings 13 and 14 show us the end of kings Jeroboam (Northern Kingdom) and Rehoboam (Southern Kingdom). As you read, note that God's grace called and called and kept on calling for repentance. But those calls fell on deaf ears. If time is short, focus on 1 Kings 14:21–31.

The Man of God From Judah

13 By the word of the LORD a
man of God came from Judah
to Bethel, as Jeroboam was standing by
the altar to make an offering. 2He cried
out against the altar by the word of the
LORD: "O altar, altar! This is what the
LORD says: 'A son named Josiah will be
born to the house of David. On you he
will sacrifice the priests of the high
places who now make offerings here,
and human bones will be burned on
you.' " 3That same day the man of God
gave a sign: "This is the sign the LORD
has declared: The altar will be split apart
and the ashes on it will be poured out."
4When King Jeroboam heard what
the man of God cried out against the
altar at Bethel, he stretched out his hand
from the altar and said, "Seize him!" But
the hand he stretched out toward the
man shriveled up, so that he could not
pull it back. 5Also, the altar was split
apart and its ashes poured out according to the sign given by the man of God
by the word of the LORD.
6Then the king said to the man of
God, "Intercede with the LORD your
God and pray for me that my hand may
be restored." So the man of God inter-
ceded with the LORD, and the king's
hand was restored and became as it was
before.
7The king said to the man of God,
"Come home with me and have something to eat, and I will give you a gift."
8But the man of God answered the
king, "Even if you were to give me half
your possessions, I would not go with
you, nor would I eat bread or drink water here. 9For I was commanded by the
word of the LORD: 'You must not eat
bread or drink water or return by the
way you came.' " 10So he took another
road and did not return by the way he
had come to Bethel.
11Now there was a certain old prophet
living in Bethel, whose sons came and
told him all that the man of God had
done there that day. They also told their
father what he had said to the king.
12Their father asked them, "Which way
did he go?" And his sons showed him
which road the man of God from Judah
had taken. 13So he said to his sons, "Saddle the donkey for me." And when they
had saddled the donkey for him, he
mounted it 14and rode after the man of
God. He found him sitting under an oak
tree and asked, "Are you the man of God
who came from Judah?"
"I am," he replied.
15So the prophet said to him, "Come
home with me and eat."
16The man of God said, "I cannot turn
back and go with you, nor can I eat
bread or drink water with you in this
place. 17I have been told by the word of
the LORD: 'You must not eat bread or
drink water there or return by the way
you came.' "
18The old prophet answered, "I too
am a prophet, as you are. And an angel
said to me by the word of the LORD:
'Bring him back with you to your house
so that he may eat bread and drink water.' " (But he was lying to him.) 19So the
man of God returned with him and ate
and drank in his house.
20While they were sitting at the table,
the word of the LORD came to the old
prophet who had brought him back.
21He cried out to the man of God who
had come from Judah, "This is what the
LORD says: 'You have defied the word of
the LORD and have not kept the command the LORD your God gave you.
22You came back and ate bread and
drank water in the place where he told
you not to eat or drink. Therefore your
body will not be buried in the tomb of
your fathers.' "
23When the man of God had finished
eating and drinking, the prophet who
had brought him back saddled his donkey for him. 24As he went on his way, a
lion met him on the road and killed him,
and his body was thrown down on the
road, with both the donkey and the lion
standing beside it. 25Some people who
passed by saw the body thrown down
there, with the lion standing beside the
body, and they went and reported it in
the city where the old prophet lived.
26When the prophet who had brought

him back from his journey heard of it, he said, "It is the man of God who defied the word of the LORD. The LORD has given him over to the lion, which has mauled him and killed him, as the word of the LORD had warned him."

27The prophet said to his sons, "Saddle the donkey for me," and they did so. 28Then he went out and found the body thrown down on the road, with the donkey and the lion standing beside it. The lion had neither eaten the body nor mauled the donkey. 29So the prophet picked up the body of the man of God, laid it on the donkey, and brought it back to his own city to mourn for him and bury him. 30Then he laid the body in his own tomb, and they mourned over him and said, "Oh, my brother!"

31After burying him, he said to his sons, "When I die, bury me in the grave where the man of God is buried; lay my bones beside his bones. 32For the message he declared by the word of the LORD against the altar in Bethel and against all the shrines on the high places in the towns of Samaria will certainly come true."

33Even after this, Jeroboam did not change his evil ways, but once more appointed priests for the high places from all sorts of people. Anyone who wanted to become a priest he consecrated for the high places. 34This was the sin of the house of Jeroboam that led to its downfall and to its destruction from the face of the earth.

Ahijah's Prophecy Against Jeroboam

14 At that time Abijah son of Jeroboam became ill, 2and Jeroboam said to his wife, "Go, disguise yourself, so you won't be recognized as the wife of Jeroboam. Then go to Shiloh. Ahijah the prophet is there—the one who told me I would be king over this people. 3Take ten loaves of bread with you, some cakes and a jar of honey, and go to him. He will tell you what will happen to the boy." 4So Jeroboam's wife did what he said and went to Ahijah's house in Shiloh.

Now Ahijah could not see; his sight was gone because of his age. 5But the LORD had told Ahijah, "Jeroboam's wife is coming to ask you about her son, for he is ill, and you are to give her such and such an answer. When she arrives, she will pretend to be someone else."

6So when Ahijah heard the sound of her footsteps at the door, he said, "Come in, wife of Jeroboam. Why this pretense? I have been sent to you with bad news. 7Go, tell Jeroboam that this is what the LORD, the God of Israel, says: 'I raised you up from among the people and made you a leader over my people Israel. 8I tore the kingdom away from the house of David and gave it to you, but you have not been like my servant David, who kept my commands and followed me with all his heart, doing only what was right in my eyes. 9You have done more evil than all who lived before you. You have made for yourself other gods, idols made of metal; you have provoked me to anger and thrust me behind your back.

10" 'Because of this, I am going to bring disaster on the house of Jeroboam. I will cut off from Jeroboam every last male in Israel—slave or free. I will burn up the house of Jeroboam as one burns dung, until it is all gone. 11Dogs will eat those belonging to Jeroboam who die in the city, and the birds of the air will feed on those who die in the country. The LORD has spoken!'

12"As for you, go back home. When you set foot in your city, the boy will die. 13All Israel will mourn for him and bury him. He is the only one belonging to Jeroboam who will be buried, because he is the only one in the house of Jeroboam in whom the LORD, the God of Israel, has found anything good.

14"The LORD will raise up for himself a king over Israel who will cut off the family of Jeroboam. This is the day! What? Yes, even now.[a] 15And the LORD will strike Israel, so that it will be like a reed swaying in the water. He will uproot Israel from this good land that he

[a] *14* The meaning of the Hebrew for this sentence is uncertain.

gave to their forefathers and scatter them beyond the River,[a] because they provoked the LORD to anger by making Asherah poles.[b] 16And he will give Israel up because of the sins Jeroboam has committed and has caused Israel to commit."

17Then Jeroboam's wife got up and left and went to Tirzah. As soon as she stepped over the threshold of the house, the boy died. 18They buried him, and all Israel mourned for him, as the LORD had said through his servant the prophet Ahijah.

19The other events of Jeroboam's reign, his wars and how he ruled, are written in the book of the annals of the kings of Israel. 20He reigned for twenty-two years and then rested with his fathers. And Nadab his son succeeded him as king.

Rehoboam King of Judah

21Rehoboam son of Solomon was king in Judah. He was forty-one years old when he became king, and he reigned seventeen years in Jerusalem, the city the LORD had chosen out of all the tribes of Israel in which to put his Name. His mother's name was Naamah; she was an Ammonite.

22Judah did evil in the eyes of the LORD. By the sins they committed they stirred up his jealous anger more than their fathers had done. 23They also set up for themselves high places, sacred stones and Asherah poles on every high hill and under every spreading tree. 24There were even male shrine prostitutes in the land; the people engaged in all the detestable practices of the nations the LORD had driven out before the Israelites.

25In the fifth year of King Rehoboam, Shishak king of Egypt attacked Jerusalem. 26He carried off the treasures of the temple of the LORD and the treasures of the royal palace. He took everything, including all the gold shields Solomon had made. 27So King Rehoboam made bronze shields to replace them and assigned these to the commanders of the guard on duty at the entrance to the royal palace. 28Whenever the king went to the LORD's temple, the guards bore the shields, and afterward they returned them to the guardroom.

29As for the other events of Rehoboam's reign, and all he did, are they not written in the book of the annals of the kings of Judah? 30There was continual warfare between Rehoboam and Jeroboam. 31And Rehoboam rested with his fathers and was buried with them in the City of David. His mother's name was Naamah; she was an Ammonite. And Abijah[c] his son succeeded him as king.

[a]*15* That is, the Euphrates [b]*15* That is, symbols of the goddess Asherah; here and elsewhere in 1 Kings [c]*31* Some Hebrew manuscripts and Septuagint (see also 2 Chron. 12:16); most Hebrew manuscripts *Abijam*

SHARPEN THE FOCUS

We're used to people in power breaking the law and trying to hide it from us. Today you read about a cover-up from long ago (1 Kings 14:25–28). The king of Egypt plundered Jerusalem. He took the gold-plated shields that had been used on state occasions. Rehoboam replaced the gold shields with bronze ones. If you polished them enough, they shone like gold.

God wasn't fooled. The gold had symbolized the spiritual blessings and the earthly wealth the Lord had given to King Solomon. But Rehoboam worshiped "gods" that were as counterfeit as his shields.

We may fool people with a pretense of piety for awhile. We can assure them of our prayers for them—without really praying. We can attend worship services—without really worshiping. We can give and work—without intending to serve Christ. But going through the motions doesn't fool God.

If your walk of faith has become a parade of mostly outward show, do what Rehoboam should have done. Go to your Lord and ask Him to replace the pretense with repentance. He promises His penitent people "the LORD will be your everlasting light, and your God will be your glory" (Isaiah 60:19).

WEEK 30 • FRIDAY

1 Kings 15:1—16:34

As you read today, don't worry about remembering (or pronouncing) the kings' names. If fact, it won't be necessary to do that through all of 2 Kings and both books of Chronicles. Focus instead on the character and conduct of the kings and their people. Ask yourself what was going on in their hearts. Remember, too, the Lord's promise to bring the Messiah from the people of Judah. Watch to see how He worked with His people to prepare them to receive this gift. If time is short, focus on 1 Kings 16:29–34.

Abijah King of Judah

15 In the eighteenth year of the
reign of Jeroboam son of Ne-
bat, Abijah[a] became king of Judah, 2and
he reigned in Jerusalem three years. His
mother's name was Maacah daughter
of Abishalom.[b]
3He committed all the sins his father
had done before him; his heart was not
fully devoted to the LORD his God, as
the heart of David his forefather had
been. 4Nevertheless, for David's sake
the LORD his God gave him a lamp in
Jerusalem by raising up a son to succeed
him and by making Jerusalem strong.
5For David had done what was right in
the eyes of the LORD and had not failed
to keep any of the LORD's commands all
the days of his life—except in the case
of Uriah the Hittite.
6There was war between Rehoboam[c]
and Jeroboam throughout ⌊Abijah's⌋
lifetime. 7As for the other events of
Abijah's reign, and all he did, are they
not written in the book of the annals of
the kings of Judah? There was war between Abijah and Jeroboam. 8And Abijah rested with his fathers and was
buried in the City of David. And Asa his
son succeeded him as king.

Asa King of Judah

9In the twentieth year of Jeroboam
king of Israel, Asa became king of Judah,
10and he reigned in Jerusalem forty-one
years. His grandmother's name was
Maacah daughter of Abishalom.
11Asa did what was right in the eyes
of the LORD, as his father David had
done. 12He expelled the male shrine
prostitutes from the land and got rid of
all the idols his fathers had made. 13He
even deposed his grandmother Maacah
from her position as queen mother, because she had made a repulsive Asherah pole. Asa cut the pole down and
burned it in the Kidron Valley. 14Al-
though he did not remove the high
places, Asa's heart was fully committed
to the LORD all his life. 15He brought into

[a]*1* Some Hebrew manuscripts and Septuagint (see also 2 Chron. 12:16); most Hebrew manuscripts *Abijam;* also in verses 7 and 8
[b]*2* A variant of *Absalom;* also in verse 10
[c]*6* Most Hebrew manuscripts; some Hebrew manuscripts and Syriac *Abijam* (that is, Abijah)

the temple of the LORD the silver and
gold and the articles that he and his father had dedicated.
16There was war between Asa and
Baasha king of Israel throughout their
reigns. 17Baasha king of Israel went up
against Judah and fortified Ramah to
prevent anyone from leaving or entering the territory of Asa king of Judah.
18Asa then took all the silver and gold
that was left in the treasuries of the
LORD's temple and of his own palace.
He entrusted it to his officials and sent
them to Ben-Hadad son of Tabrimmon,
the son of Hezion, the king of Aram,
who was ruling in Damascus. 19"Let
there be a treaty between me and you,"
he said, "as there was between my father and your father. See, I am sending
you a gift of silver and gold. Now break
your treaty with Baasha king of Israel so
he will withdraw from me."
20Ben-Hadad agreed with King Asa
and sent the commanders of his forces
against the towns of Israel. He conquered Ijon, Dan, Abel Beth Maacah
and all Kinnereth in addition to Naphtali. 21When Baasha heard this, he
stopped building Ramah and withdrew
to Tirzah. 22Then King Asa issued an
order to all Judah—no one was exempt—and they carried away from Ramah the stones and timber Baasha had
been using there. With them King Asa
built up Geba in Benjamin, and also
Mizpah.
23As for all the other events of Asa's
reign, all his achievements, all he did
and the cities he built, are they not written in the book of the annals of the kings
of Judah? In his old age, however, his
feet became diseased. 24Then Asa rested
with his fathers and was buried with
them in the city of his father David. And
Jehoshaphat his son succeeded him as
king.

Nadab King of Israel

25Nadab son of Jeroboam became king
of Israel in the second year of Asa king
of Judah, and he reigned over Israel two
years. 26He did evil in the eyes of the
LORD, walking in the ways of his father
and in his sin, which he had caused Israel to commit.
27Baasha son of Ahijah of the house of
Issachar plotted against him, and he
struck him down at Gibbethon, a Philistine town, while Nadab and all Israel
were besieging it. 28Baasha killed Nadab
in the third year of Asa king of Judah
and succeeded him as king.
29As soon as he began to reign, he
killed Jeroboam's whole family. He did
not leave Jeroboam anyone that
breathed, but destroyed them all,
according to the word of the LORD
given through his servant Ahijah the
Shilonite— 30because of the sins Jeroboam had committed and had caused
Israel to commit, and because he provoked the LORD, the God of Israel, to
anger.
31As for the other events of Nadab's
reign, and all he did, are they not written in the book of the annals of the kings
of Israel? 32There was war between Asa
and Baasha king of Israel throughout
their reigns.

Baasha King of Israel

33In the third year of Asa king of Judah, Baasha son of Ahijah became king
of all Israel in Tirzah, and he reigned
twenty-four years. 34He did evil in the
eyes of the LORD, walking in the ways
of Jeroboam and in his sin, which he
had caused Israel to commit.

16 Then the word of the LORD
came to Jehu son of Hanani
against Baasha: 2"I lifted you up from
the dust and made you leader of my
people Israel, but you walked in the
ways of Jeroboam and caused my
people Israel to sin and to provoke me
to anger by their sins. 3So I am about to
consume Baasha and his house, and I
will make your house like that of Jeroboam son of Nebat. 4Dogs will eat those
belonging to Baasha who die in the city,
and the birds of the air will feed on
those who die in the country."
5As for the other events of Baasha's
reign, what he did and his achievements, are they not written in the book
of the annals of the kings of Israel? 6Ba-

asha rested with his fathers and was
buried in Tirzah. And Elah his son succeeded him as king.
7Moreover, the word of the LORD
came through the prophet Jehu son of
Hanani to Baasha and his house, because of all the evil he had done in the
eyes of the LORD, provoking him to anger by the things he did, and becoming
like the house of Jeroboam—and also
because he destroyed it.

Elah King of Israel

8In the twenty-sixth year of Asa king
of Judah, Elah son of Baasha became
king of Israel, and he reigned in Tirzah
two years.
9Zimri, one of his officials, who had
command of half his chariots, plotted
against him. Elah was in Tirzah at the
time, getting drunk in the home of Arza,
the man in charge of the palace at Tirzah. 10Zimri came in, struck him down
and killed him in the twenty-seventh
year of Asa king of Judah. Then he succeeded him as king.
11As soon as he began to reign and
was seated on the throne, he killed off
Baasha's whole family. He did not spare
a single male, whether relative or friend.
12So Zimri destroyed the whole family of
Baasha, in accordance with the word
of the LORD spoken against Baasha
through the prophet Jehu— 13because
of all the sins Baasha and his son Elah
had committed and had caused Israel
to commit, so that they provoked the
LORD, the God of Israel, to anger by
their worthless idols.
14As for the other events of Elah's
reign, and all he did, are they not written in the book of the annals of the kings
of Israel?

Zimri King of Israel

15In the twenty-seventh year of Asa
king of Judah, Zimri reigned in Tirzah
seven days. The army was encamped
near Gibbethon, a Philistine town.
16When the Israelites in the camp heard
that Zimri had plotted against the king
and murdered him, they proclaimed
Omri, the commander of the army, king
over Israel that very day there in the
camp. 17Then Omri and all the Israelites
with him withdrew from Gibbethon
and laid siege to Tirzah. 18When Zimri
saw that the city was taken, he went into
the citadel of the royal palace and set the
palace on fire around him. So he died,
19because of the sins he had committed,
doing evil in the eyes of the LORD and
walking in the ways of Jeroboam and in
the sin he had committed and had
caused Israel to commit.
20As for the other events of Zimri's
reign, and the rebellion he carried out,
are they not written in the book of the
annals of the kings of Israel?

Omri King of Israel

21Then the people of Israel were split
into two factions; half supported Tibni
son of Ginath for king, and the other
half supported Omri. 22But Omri's followers proved stronger than those of
Tibni son of Ginath. So Tibni died and
Omri became king.
23In the thirty-first year of Asa king of
Judah, Omri became king of Israel, and
he reigned twelve years, six of them in
Tirzah. 24He bought the hill of Samaria
from Shemer for two talents[a] of silver
and built a city on the hill, calling it Samaria, after Shemer, the name of the former owner of the hill.
25But Omri did evil in the eyes of the
LORD and sinned more than all those
before him. 26He walked in all the ways
of Jeroboam son of Nebat and in his sin,
which he had caused Israel to commit,
so that they provoked the LORD, the
God of Israel, to anger by their worthless idols.
27As for the other events of Omri's
reign, what he did and the things he
achieved, are they not written in the
book of the annals of the kings of Israel? 28Omri rested with his fathers and
was buried in Samaria. And Ahab his
son succeeded him as king.

[a]24 That is, about 150 pounds (about 70 kilograms)

Ahab Becomes King of Israel

[29]In the thirty-eighth year of Asa king
of Judah, Ahab son of Omri became
king of Israel, and he reigned in Samaria over Israel twenty-two years. [30]Ahab
son of Omri did more evil in the eyes of
the LORD than any of those before him.
[31]He not only considered it trivial to
commit the sins of Jeroboam son of Nebat, but he also married Jezebel daughter of Ethbaal king of the Sidonians, and
began to serve Baal and worship him.
[32]He set up an altar for Baal in the temple of Baal that he built in Samaria.
[33]Ahab also made an Asherah pole and
did more to provoke the LORD, the God
of Israel, to anger than did all the kings
of Israel before him.

[34]In Ahab's time, Hiel of Bethel rebuilt
Jericho. He laid its foundations at the
cost of his firstborn son Abiram, and he
set up its gates at the cost of his youngest son Segub, in accordance with the
word of the LORD spoken by Joshua son
of Nun.

SHARPEN THE FOCUS

The fall of the Northern Kingdom (the Kingdom of Israel) was no accident. Note the progression:

- Jeroboam felt fearful that if his people went to Jerusalem (in the Southern Kingdom) to worship, his power would never be secure. So he set up golden calves on each end of his territory (at Dan and Bethel) to make worshiping the Lord more "convenient" for his people (1 Kings 12:28–30).
- A phony priesthood, phony festivals, and phony temples became "traditions" (1 Kings 12:31–33).
- The people gradually added worship of the pagan gods of Canaan who represented power, pleasure, and possessions.
- Ahab made Baal worship official (1 Kings 16:30–31).

Little by little worship of the Creator was replaced by devotion to things He created. Power. Pleasure. Possessions. Which are you most tempted to serve? Ask your Lord to light up any dark corners of your heart where these things may be encroaching. Receive from Him the forgiveness and strength you need to worship Him from a pure heart.

WEEK 30 • SATURDAY

1 Kings 17:1—18:46

GET THE BIG PICTURE

Despite the dreary disobedience we've read about in the palaces of Israel and Judah, the Lord had not abandoned His people! Elijah. The widow of Zarephath. Obadiah. These all took their place among God's people of faith. As you read today, note all the remarkable things the Lord accomplished through them! If time is short, focus on 1 Kings 18:20–40.

Elijah Fed by Ravens

17 Now Elijah the Tishbite, from
Tishbe[a] in Gilead, said to
Ahab, "As the LORD, the God of Israel,
lives, whom I serve, there will be neither
dew nor rain in the next few years except at my word."
2 Then the word of the LORD came to
Elijah: 3 "Leave here, turn eastward and
hide in the Kerith Ravine, east of the Jordan. 4 You will drink from the brook, and
I have ordered the ravens to feed you
there."
5 So he did what the LORD had told
him. He went to the Kerith Ravine, east
of the Jordan, and stayed there. 6 The
ravens brought him bread and meat in
the morning and bread and meat in the
evening, and he drank from the brook.

The Widow at Zarephath

7 Some time later the brook dried up
because there had been no rain in the
land. 8 Then the word of the LORD came
to him: 9 "Go at once to Zarephath of Sidon and stay there. I have commanded
a widow in that place to supply you
with food." 10 So he went to Zarephath.
When he came to the town gate, a
widow was there gathering sticks. He
called to her and asked, "Would you
bring me a little water in a jar so I may
have a drink?" 11 As she was going to get
it, he called, "And bring me, please, a
piece of bread."
12 "As surely as the LORD your God
lives," she replied, "I don't have any
bread—only a handful of flour in a jar
and a little oil in a jug. I am gathering a
few sticks to take home and make a meal
for myself and my son, that we may eat
it—and die."
13 Elijah said to her, "Don't be afraid.
Go home and do as you have said. But
first make a small cake of bread for me
from what you have and bring it to me,
and then make something for yourself
and your son. 14 For this is what the
LORD, the God of Israel, says: 'The jar of
flour will not be used up and the jug of
oil will not run dry until the day the
LORD gives rain on the land.' "
15 She went away and did as Elijah had
told her. So there was food every day for
Elijah and for the woman and her family. 16 For the jar of flour was not used up
and the jug of oil did not run dry, in
keeping with the word of the LORD spoken by Elijah.
17 Some time later the son of the woman who owned the house became ill. He
grew worse and worse, and finally
stopped breathing. 18 She said to Elijah,
"What do you have against me, man of
God? Did you come to remind me of my
sin and kill my son?"
19 "Give me your son," Elijah replied.
He took him from her arms, carried him
to the upper room where he was staying, and laid him on his bed. 20 Then he
cried out to the LORD, "O LORD my
God, have you brought tragedy also
upon this widow I am staying with, by
causing her son to die?" 21 Then he
stretched himself out on the boy three
times and cried to the LORD, "O LORD
my God, let this boy's life return to
him!"
22 The LORD heard Elijah's cry, and the
boy's life returned to him, and he lived.
23 Elijah picked up the child and carried
him down from the room into the
house. He gave him to his mother and
said, "Look, your son is alive!"
24 Then the woman said to Elijah,
"Now I know that you are a man of God
and that the word of the LORD from
your mouth is the truth."

Elijah and Obadiah

18 After a long time, in the third
year, the word of the LORD
came to Elijah: "Go and present yourself
to Ahab, and I will send rain on the
land." 2 So Elijah went to present himself
to Ahab.

Now the famine was severe in Samaria, 3 and Ahab had summoned Obadiah,
who was in charge of his palace. (Obadiah was a devout believer in the LORD.
4 While Jezebel was killing off the LORD's
prophets, Obadiah had taken a hundred prophets and hidden them in two

[a]1 Or *Tishbite, of the settlers*

caves, fifty in each, and had supplied them with food and water.) 5Ahab had said to Obadiah, "Go through the land to all the springs and valleys. Maybe we can find some grass to keep the horses and mules alive so we will not have to kill any of our animals." 6So they divided the land they were to cover, Ahab going in one direction and Obadiah in another.

7As Obadiah was walking along, Elijah met him. Obadiah recognized him, bowed down to the ground, and said, "Is it really you, my lord Elijah?"

8"Yes," he replied. "Go tell your master, 'Elijah is here.'"

9"What have I done wrong," asked Obadiah, "that you are handing your servant over to Ahab to be put to death? 10As surely as the LORD your God lives, there is not a nation or kingdom where my master has not sent someone to look for you. And whenever a nation or kingdom claimed you were not there, he made them swear they could not find you. 11But now you tell me to go to my master and say, 'Elijah is here.' 12I don't know where the Spirit of the LORD may carry you when I leave you. If I go and tell Ahab and he doesn't find you, he will kill me. Yet I your servant have worshiped the LORD since my youth. 13Haven't you heard, my lord, what I did while Jezebel was killing the prophets of the LORD? I hid a hundred of the LORD's prophets in two caves, fifty in each, and supplied them with food and water. 14And now you tell me to go to my master and say, 'Elijah is here.' He will kill me!"

15Elijah said, "As the LORD Almighty lives, whom I serve, I will surely present myself to Ahab today."

Elijah on Mount Carmel

16So Obadiah went to meet Ahab and told him, and Ahab went to meet Elijah. 17When he saw Elijah, he said to him, "Is that you, you troubler of Israel?"

18"I have not made trouble for Israel," Elijah replied. "But you and your father's family have. You have abandoned the LORD's commands and have followed the Baals. 19Now summon the people from all over Israel to meet me on Mount Carmel. And bring the four hundred and fifty prophets of Baal and the four hundred prophets of Asherah, who eat at Jezebel's table."

20So Ahab sent word throughout all Israel and assembled the prophets on Mount Carmel. 21Elijah went before the people and said, "How long will you waver between two opinions? If the LORD is God, follow him; but if Baal is God, follow him."

But the people said nothing.

22Then Elijah said to them, "I am the only one of the LORD's prophets left, but Baal has four hundred and fifty prophets. 23Get two bulls for us. Let them choose one for themselves, and let them cut it into pieces and put it on the wood but not set fire to it. I will prepare the other bull and put it on the wood but not set fire to it. 24Then you call on the name of your god, and I will call on the name of the LORD. The god who answers by fire—he is God."

Then all the people said, "What you say is good."

25Elijah said to the prophets of Baal, "Choose one of the bulls and prepare it first, since there are so many of you. Call on the name of your god, but do not light the fire." 26So they took the bull given them and prepared it.

Then they called on the name of Baal from morning till noon. "O Baal, answer us!" they shouted. But there was no response; no one answered. And they danced around the altar they had made.

27At noon Elijah began to taunt them. "Shout louder!" he said. "Surely he is a god! Perhaps he is deep in thought, or busy, or traveling. Maybe he is sleeping and must be awakened." 28So they shouted louder and slashed themselves with swords and spears, as was their custom, until their blood flowed. 29Midday passed, and they continued their frantic prophesying until the time for the evening sacrifice. But there was no response, no one answered, no one paid attention.

30Then Elijah said to all the people,

"Come here to me." They came to him,
and he repaired the altar of the LORD,
which was in ruins. 31Elijah took twelve
stones, one for each of the tribes descended from Jacob, to whom the word
of the LORD had come, saying, "Your
name shall be Israel." 32With the stones
he built an altar in the name of the
LORD, and he dug a trench around it
large enough to hold two seahs[a] of seed.
33He arranged the wood, cut the bull
into pieces and laid it on the wood.
Then he said to them, "Fill four large jars
with water and pour it on the offering
and on the wood."
34"Do it again," he said, and they did
it again.
"Do it a third time," he ordered, and
they did it the third time. 35The water
ran down around the altar and even
filled the trench.
36At the time of sacrifice, the prophet
Elijah stepped forward and prayed:
"O LORD, God of Abraham, Isaac and
Israel, let it be known today that you are
God in Israel and that I am your servant
and have done all these things at your
command. 37Answer me, O LORD, answer me, so these people will know that
you, O LORD, are God, and that you are
turning their hearts back again."
38Then the fire of the LORD fell and
burned up the sacrifice, the wood, the
stones and the soil, and also licked up
the water in the trench.
39When all the people saw this, they
fell prostrate and cried, "The LORD—he
is God! The LORD—he is God!"
40Then Elijah commanded them,
"Seize the prophets of Baal. Don't let anyone get away!" They seized them, and
Elijah had them brought down to the
Kishon Valley and slaughtered there.
41And Elijah said to Ahab, "Go, eat and
drink, for there is the sound of a heavy
rain." 42So Ahab went off to eat and
drink, but Elijah climbed to the top of
Carmel, bent down to the ground and
put his face between his knees.
43"Go and look toward the sea," he
told his servant. And he went up and
looked.
"There is nothing there," he said.
Seven times Elijah said, "Go back."
44The seventh time the servant reported, "A cloud as small as a man's hand is
rising from the sea."
So Elijah said, "Go and tell Ahab,
'Hitch up your chariot and go down before the rain stops you.'"
45Meanwhile, the sky grew black with
clouds, the wind rose, a heavy rain came
on and Ahab rode off to Jezreel. 46The
power of the LORD came upon Elijah
and, tucking his cloak into his belt,
he ran ahead of Ahab all the way to
Jezreel.

[a]32 That is, probably about 13 quarts (about 15 liters)

SHARPEN THE FOCUS

From Satan's point of view, Israel lay in a spiritual coma and would soon slip off into spiritual death. What difference could Elijah's few words or few prayers make? What difference could the widow's pitiful flour-cake make (1 Kings 17:9–16)? What difference could Obadiah's secret "meals-on-wheels" plan make (1 Kings 18:3–4)? But the Lord used each of these three people in a unique way in His plan to turn the hearts of His people back to Himself.

The power of one. It's really the power of the One who works His work through us. Do your words of witness, your prayers of faith, your faithful giving, your secret acts of courage make any difference? Oh, yes. You have, by our Lord's grace, a part in His holy work of turning troubled, sin-darkened hearts to Him who is our peace and the light of the world:

- What words of faith, of Law, of Gospel will you get to speak today?
- What prayers of faith will you get to pray?
- What acts of kindness or even courage will you get to do?

WEEK 31 • MONDAY

1 Kings 19:1–21

GET THE BIG PICTURE

The apostle James tells us that Elijah was a human being "just like us" (James 5:17). Today as you read you will see how true that is. And you will see the Lord's compassion and concern for His children whenever they feel discouraged. As you read, look at the ways our Wonderful Counselor (Isaiah 9:6) brought healing to His servant's heart. If time is short, focus on 1 Kings 19:1–18.

Elijah Flees to Horeb

19 Now Ahab told Jezebel everything Elijah had done and
how he had killed all the prophets with
the sword. [2]So Jezebel sent a messenger
to Elijah to say, "May the gods deal with
me, be it ever so severely, if by this time
tomorrow I do not make your life like
that of one of them."
[3]Elijah was afraid[a] and ran for his life.
When he came to Beersheba in Judah,
he left his servant there, [4]while he
himself went a day's journey into the
desert. He came to a broom tree, sat
down under it and prayed that he might
die. "I have had enough, LORD," he said.
"Take my life; I am no better than my
ancestors." [5]Then he lay down under
the tree and fell asleep.
All at once an angel touched him and
said, "Get up and eat." [6]He looked
around, and there by his head was a
cake of bread baked over hot coals, and
a jar of water. He ate and drank and
then lay down again.
[7]The angel of the LORD came back a
second time and touched him and said,
"Get up and eat, for the journey is too
much for you." [8]So he got up and ate
and drank. Strengthened by that food,
he traveled forty days and forty nights
until he reached Horeb, the mountain of
God. [9]There he went into a cave and
spent the night.

The LORD Appears to Elijah

And the word of the LORD came to
him: "What are you doing here, Elijah?"
[10]He replied, "I have been very zealous for the LORD God Almighty. The Israelites have rejected your covenant,
broken down your altars, and put your
prophets to death with the sword. I am
the only one left, and now they are trying to kill me too."
[11]The LORD said, "Go out and stand on
the mountain in the presence of the
LORD, for the LORD is about to pass by."
Then a great and powerful wind tore
the mountains apart and shattered the
rocks before the LORD, but the LORD
was not in the wind. After the wind
there was an earthquake, but the LORD
was not in the earthquake. [12]After the
earthquake came a fire, but the LORD
was not in the fire. And after the fire
came a gentle whisper. [13]When Elijah
heard it, he pulled his cloak over his face
and went out and stood at the mouth of
the cave.
Then a voice said to him, "What are
you doing here, Elijah?"
[14]He replied, "I have been very zealous for the LORD God Almighty. The Israelites have rejected your covenant,
broken down your altars, and put your
prophets to death with the sword. I am
the only one left, and now they are trying to kill me too."
[15]The LORD said to him, "Go back the
way you came, and go to the Desert of
Damascus. When you get there, anoint
Hazael king over Aram. [16]Also, anoint
Jehu son of Nimshi king over Israel, and

[a]3 Or *Elijah saw*

anoint Elisha son of Shaphat from Abel
Meholah to succeed you as prophet.
[17]Jehu will put to death any who escape
the sword of Hazael, and Elisha will put
to death any who escape the sword of
Jehu. [18]Yet I reserve seven thousand in
Israel—all whose knees have not bowed
down to Baal and all whose mouths
have not kissed him."

The Call of Elisha

[19]So Elijah went from there and found
Elisha son of Shaphat. He was plowing
with twelve yoke of oxen, and he himself was driving the twelfth pair. Elijah
went up to him and threw his cloak
around him. [20]Elisha then left his oxen
and ran after Elijah. "Let me kiss my father and mother good-by," he said, "and
then I will come with you."

"Go back," Elijah replied. "What have
I done to you?"

[21]So Elisha left him and went back. He
took his yoke of oxen and slaughtered
them. He burned the plowing equipment to cook the meat and gave it to the
people, and they ate. Then he set out to
follow Elijah and became his attendant.

SHARPEN THE FOCUS

Maybe you find yourself really "down in the dumps" and discouraged today, just as Elijah did. Perhaps life just doesn't seem worth the effort. Why not just give up and feel sorry for yourself? Instead of having a "pity party," compare yourself to Elijah and think about what your Lord might, in compassion, prescribe for you.

The Lord gave Elijah nourishing food (1 Kings 19:6–8). What ordinary and extraordinary things might the Lord want to give you?

The Lord listened to Elijah's anger and fear (1 Kings 19:10, 14). What angers, fears, and discouragements do you want to tell the Lord about today? He is listening.

The Lord revealed Himself in His word (1 Kings 19:11–12). The Lord has revealed Himself as Jesus your Savior. He will reveal His grace to you in Christ as you read and study the Scriptures. Are you ready for His wonderful revelations?

The Lord gave Elijah a new mission (1 Kings 19:15). What mission might the Lord have in mind for you? The possibilities are endless.

The Lord gave Elijah a student and friend (1 Kings 19:16). How might the Lord use your special friend to help and encourage you? Get in contact with that friend today.

WEEK 31 • TUESDAY

1 Kings 20:1–43

GET THE BIG PICTURE

The more we learn to know God, the more we see that His ways are not our ways, nor His thoughts our thoughts (Isaiah 55:8). We, for instance, would probably have rained down punishment on King Ahab and his idolatrous people. Instead, the Lord delivered and blessed them. Romans 2:4 says that God's kindness leads us to repentance. Look for that kindness as you read today's accounts. If time is short, focus on 1 Kings 20:1–21.

Ben-Hadad Attacks Samaria

20 Now Ben-Hadad king of Aram mustered his entire army. Accompanied by thirty-two kings with their horses and chariots, he went up and besieged Samaria and attacked it. [2]He sent messengers into the city to Ahab king of Israel, saying, "This is what Ben-Hadad says: [3]'Your silver and gold are mine, and the best of your wives and children are mine.' "

[4]The king of Israel answered, "Just as you say, my lord the king. I and all I have are yours."

[5]The messengers came again and said, "This is what Ben-Hadad says: 'I sent to demand your silver and gold, your wives and your children. [6]But about this time tomorrow I am going to send my officials to search your palace and the houses of your officials. They will seize everything you value and carry it away.' "

[7]The king of Israel summoned all the elders of the land and said to them, "See how this man is looking for trouble! When he sent for my wives and my children, my silver and my gold, I did not refuse him."

[8]The elders and the people all answered, "Don't listen to him or agree to his demands."

[9]So he replied to Ben-Hadad's messengers, "Tell my lord the king, 'Your servant will do all you demanded the first time, but this demand I cannot meet.' " They left and took the answer back to Ben-Hadad.

[10]Then Ben-Hadad sent another message to Ahab: "May the gods deal with me, be it ever so severely, if enough dust remains in Samaria to give each of my men a handful."

[11]The king of Israel answered, "Tell him: 'One who puts on his armor should not boast like one who takes it off.' "

[12]Ben-Hadad heard this message while he and the kings were drinking in their tents,[a] and he ordered his men: "Prepare to attack." So they prepared to attack the city.

Ahab Defeats Ben-Hadad

[13]Meanwhile a prophet came to Ahab king of Israel and announced, "This is what the LORD says: 'Do you see this vast army? I will give it into your hand today, and then you will know that I am the LORD.' "

[14]"But who will do this?" asked Ahab.

The prophet replied, "This is what the LORD says: 'The young officers of the provincial commanders will do it.' "

"And who will start the battle?" he asked.

The prophet answered, "You will."

[15]So Ahab summoned the young officers of the provincial commanders, 232 men. Then he assembled the rest of the Israelites, 7,000 in all. [16]They set out at noon while Ben-Hadad and the 32 kings allied with him were in their tents getting drunk. [17]The young officers of the provincial commanders went out first.

Now Ben-Hadad had dispatched scouts, who reported, "Men are advancing from Samaria."

[18]He said, "If they have come out for peace, take them alive; if they have come out for war, take them alive."

[19]The young officers of the provincial commanders marched out of the city with the army behind them [20]and each one struck down his opponent. At that, the Arameans fled, with the Israelites in pursuit. But Ben-Hadad king of Aram escaped on horseback with some of his horsemen. [21]The king of Israel advanced and overpowered the horses and chariots and inflicted heavy losses on the Arameans.

[22]Afterward, the prophet came to the king of Israel and said, "Strengthen your position and see what must be done, because next spring the king of Aram will attack you again."

[23]Meanwhile, the officials of the king of Aram advised him, "Their gods are gods of the hills. That is why they were too strong for us. But if we fight them on the plains, surely we will be stronger than they. [24]Do this: Remove all the kings from their commands and replace

[a]12 Or *in Succoth;* also in verse 16

them with other officers. [25]You must also raise an army like the one you lost—horse for horse and chariot for chariot—so we can fight Israel on the plains. Then surely we will be stronger than they." He agreed with them and acted accordingly.

[26]The next spring Ben-Hadad mustered the Arameans and went up to Aphek to fight against Israel. [27]When the Israelites were also mustered and given provisions, they marched out to meet them. The Israelites camped opposite them like two small flocks of goats, while the Arameans covered the countryside.

[28]The man of God came up and told the king of Israel, "This is what the LORD says: 'Because the Arameans think the LORD is a god of the hills and not a god of the valleys, I will deliver this vast army into your hands, and you will know that I am the LORD.' "

[29]For seven days they camped opposite each other, and on the seventh day the battle was joined. The Israelites inflicted a hundred thousand casualties on the Aramean foot soldiers in one day. [30]The rest of them escaped to the city of Aphek, where the wall collapsed on twenty-seven thousand of them. And Ben-Hadad fled to the city and hid in an inner room.

[31]His officials said to him, "Look, we have heard that the kings of the house of Israel are merciful. Let us go to the king of Israel with sackcloth around our waists and ropes around our heads. Perhaps he will spare your life."

[32]Wearing sackcloth around their waists and ropes around their heads, they went to the king of Israel and said, "Your servant Ben-Hadad says: 'Please let me live.' "

The king answered, "Is he still alive? He is my brother."

[33]The men took this as a good sign and were quick to pick up his word. "Yes, your brother Ben-Hadad!" they said.

"Go and get him," the king said. When Ben-Hadad came out, Ahab had him come up into his chariot.

[34]"I will return the cities my father took from your father," Ben-Hadad offered. "You may set up your own market areas in Damascus, as my father did in Samaria."

⌞Ahab said,⌟ "On the basis of a treaty I will set you free." So he made a treaty with him, and let him go.

A Prophet Condemns Ahab

[35]By the word of the LORD one of the sons of the prophets said to his companion, "Strike me with your weapon," but the man refused.

[36]So the prophet said, "Because you have not obeyed the LORD, as soon as you leave me a lion will kill you." And after the man went away, a lion found him and killed him.

[37]The prophet found another man and said, "Strike me, please." So the man struck him and wounded him. [38]Then the prophet went and stood by the road waiting for the king. He disguised himself with his headband down over his eyes. [39]As the king passed by, the prophet called out to him, "Your servant went into the thick of the battle, and someone came to me with a captive and said, 'Guard this man. If he is missing, it will be your life for his life, or you must pay a talent[a] of silver.' [40]While your servant was busy here and there, the man disappeared."

"That is your sentence," the king of Israel said. "You have pronounced it yourself."

[41]Then the prophet quickly removed the headband from his eyes, and the king of Israel recognized him as one of the prophets. [42]He said to the king, "This is what the LORD says: 'You have set free a man I had determined should die.[b] Therefore it is your life for his life, your people for his people.' " [43]Sullen and angry, the king of Israel went to his palace in Samaria.

[a]*39* That is, about 75 pounds (about 34 kilograms) [b]*42* The Hebrew term refers to the irrevocable giving over of things or persons to the LORD, often by totally destroying them.

SHARPEN THE FOCUS

Have you ever defended a helpless pet against a dangerous predator? Have you ever stood up for a small child being taunted by a bully? Or comforted an infant racked by a raging fever?

If so, you know something of the compassion, the sense of outrage, the commitment to care and to help expressed in 1 Kings 20:27. The Lord saw Ben-Hadad's army spread out like a blanket over the countryside. And He saw His people huddled together in fear "like two small flocks of goats." The Good Shepherd saw the wolves circling. And He came to His people's rescue.

Still today the Lord watches over us as our Good Shepherd. At His cross, Jesus gave up His life for us. He pulled the teeth of Satan who "prowls around like a roaring lion looking for someone to devour" (1 Peter 5:8). Despite its roar, death can no longer destroy us. And when we're in danger—any kind of danger—our Savior runs to our rescue. He stays right beside us. In Him we are safe.

WEEK 31 • WEDNESDAY

1 Kings 21:1—22:53

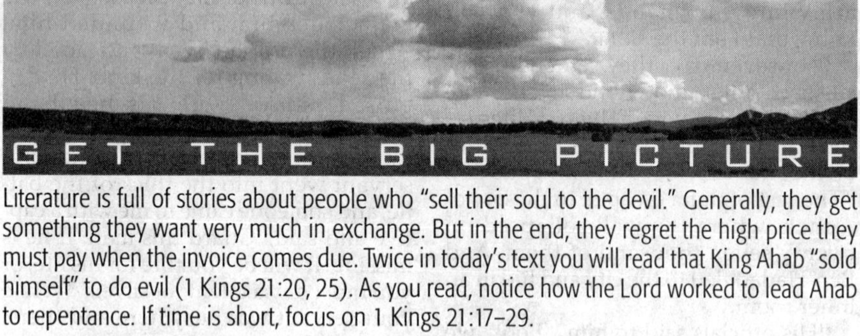

GET THE BIG PICTURE

Literature is full of stories about people who "sell their soul to the devil." Generally, they get something they want very much in exchange. But in the end, they regret the high price they must pay when the invoice comes due. Twice in today's text you will read that King Ahab "sold himself" to do evil (1 Kings 21:20, 25). As you read, notice how the Lord worked to lead Ahab to repentance. If time is short, focus on 1 Kings 21:17–29.

Naboth's Vineyard

21 Some time later there was an
incident involving a vineyard
belonging to Naboth the Jezreelite. The
vineyard was in Jezreel, close to the
palace of Ahab king of Samaria. 2Ahab
said to Naboth, "Let me have your vineyard to use for a vegetable garden, since
it is close to my palace. In exchange I will
give you a better vineyard or, if you prefer, I will pay you whatever it is worth."
3But Naboth replied, "The LORD forbid that I should give you the inheritance of my fathers."
4So Ahab went home, sullen and angry because Naboth the Jezreelite had
said, "I will not give you the inheritance
of my fathers." He lay on his bed sulk-
ing and refused to eat.
5His wife Jezebel came in and asked
him, "Why are you so sullen? Why
won't you eat?"
6He answered her, "Because I said to
Naboth the Jezreelite, 'Sell me your
vineyard; or if you prefer, I will give you
another vineyard in its place.' But he
said, 'I will not give you my vineyard.' "
7Jezebel his wife said, "Is this how you
act as king over Israel? Get up and eat!
Cheer up. I'll get you the vineyard of
Naboth the Jezreelite."
8So she wrote letters in Ahab's name,
placed his seal on them, and sent them
to the elders and nobles who lived in

Naboth's city with him. 9In those letters
she wrote:

> "Proclaim a day of fasting and
> seat Naboth in a prominent place
> among the people. 10But seat two
> scoundrels opposite him and have
> them testify that he has cursed both
> God and the king. Then take him
> out and stone him to death."

11So the elders and nobles who lived
in Naboth's city did as Jezebel directed
in the letters she had written to them.
12They proclaimed a fast and seated Naboth in a prominent place among the
people. 13Then two scoundrels came
and sat opposite him and brought
charges against Naboth before the
people, saying, "Naboth has cursed
both God and the king." So they took
him outside the city and stoned him to
death. 14Then they sent word to Jezebel:
"Naboth has been stoned and is dead."

15As soon as Jezebel heard that Naboth had been stoned to death, she said
to Ahab, "Get up and take possession of
the vineyard of Naboth the Jezreelite
that he refused to sell you. He is no
longer alive, but dead." 16When Ahab
heard that Naboth was dead, he got up
and went down to take possession of
Naboth's vineyard.

17Then the word of the LORD came to
Elijah the Tishbite: 18"Go down to meet
Ahab king of Israel, who rules in Samaria. He is now in Naboth's vineyard,
where he has gone to take possession of
it. 19Say to him, 'This is what the LORD
says: Have you not murdered a man
and seized his property?' Then say to
him, 'This is what the LORD says: In the
place where dogs licked up Naboth's
blood, dogs will lick up your blood—
yes, yours!' "

20Ahab said to Elijah, "So you have
found me, my enemy!"

"I have found you," he answered,
"because you have sold yourself to do
evil in the eyes of the LORD. 21'I am going to bring disaster on you. I will consume your descendants and cut off from
Ahab every last male in Israel—slave or
free. 22I will make your house like that
of Jeroboam son of Nebat and that of Baasha son of Ahijah, because you have
provoked me to anger and have caused
Israel to sin.'

23"And also concerning Jezebel the
LORD says: 'Dogs will devour Jezebel by
the wall of[a] Jezreel.'

24"Dogs will eat those belonging to
Ahab who die in the city, and the birds
of the air will feed on those who die in
the country."

25(There was never a man like Ahab,
who sold himself to do evil in the eyes
of the LORD, urged on by Jezebel his
wife. 26He behaved in the vilest manner
by going after idols, like the Amorites
the LORD drove out before Israel.)

27When Ahab heard these words, he
tore his clothes, put on sackcloth and
fasted. He lay in sackcloth and went
around meekly.

28Then the word of the LORD came to
Elijah the Tishbite: 29"Have you noticed
how Ahab has humbled himself before
me? Because he has humbled himself, I
will not bring this disaster in his day, but
I will bring it on his house in the days
of his son."

Micaiah Prophesies Against Ahab

22 For three years there was
no war between Aram and
Israel. 2But in the third year Jehoshaphat
king of Judah went down to see the king
of Israel. 3The king of Israel had said to
his officials, "Don't you know that Ramoth Gilead belongs to us and yet we
are doing nothing to retake it from the
king of Aram?"

4So he asked Jehoshaphat, "Will you
go with me to fight against Ramoth Gilead?"

Jehoshaphat replied to the king of Israel, "I am as you are, my people as your
people, my horses as your horses." 5But
Jehoshaphat also said to the king of Israel, "First seek the counsel of the
LORD."

6So the king of Israel brought together

[a]23 Most Hebrew manuscripts; a few Hebrew manuscripts, Vulgate and Syriac (see also 2 Kings 9:26) *the plot of ground at*

the prophets—about four hundred
men—and asked them, "Shall I go to
war against Ramoth Gilead, or shall I refrain?"
"Go," they answered, "for the Lord
will give it into the king's hand."
7But Jehoshaphat asked, "Is there not
a prophet of the LORD here whom we
can inquire of?"
8The king of Israel answered Jehoshaphat, "There is still one man through
whom we can inquire of the LORD, but
I hate him because he never prophesies
anything good about me, but always
bad. He is Micaiah son of Imlah."
"The king should not say that," Jehoshaphat replied.
9So the king of Israel called one of his
officials and said, "Bring Micaiah son of
Imlah at once."
10Dressed in their royal robes, the king
of Israel and Jehoshaphat king of Judah
were sitting on their thrones at the
threshing floor by the entrance of the
gate of Samaria, with all the prophets
prophesying before them. 11Now Zedekiah son of Kenaanah had made iron
horns and he declared, "This is what
the LORD says: 'With these you will
gore the Arameans until they are destroyed.' "
12All the other prophets were prophesying the same thing. "Attack Ramoth
Gilead and be victorious," they said, "for
the LORD will give it into the king's
hand."
13The messenger who had gone to
summon Micaiah said to him, "Look, as
one man the other prophets are predicting success for the king. Let your word
agree with theirs, and speak favorably."
14But Micaiah said, "As surely as the
LORD lives, I can tell him only what the
LORD tells me."
15When he arrived, the king asked
him, "Micaiah, shall we go to war
against Ramoth Gilead, or shall I refrain?"
"Attack and be victorious," he answered, "for the LORD will give it into
the king's hand."
16The king said to him, "How many
times must I make you swear to tell me
nothing but the truth in the name of the
LORD?"
17Then Micaiah answered, "I saw all
Israel scattered on the hills like sheep
without a shepherd, and the LORD said,
'These people have no master. Let each
one go home in peace.' "
18The king of Israel said to Jehoshaphat, "Didn't I tell you that he never
prophesies anything good about me,
but only bad?"
19Micaiah continued, "Therefore hear
the word of the LORD: I saw the LORD
sitting on his throne with all the host of
heaven standing around him on his
right and on his left. 20And the LORD
said, 'Who will entice Ahab into attacking Ramoth Gilead and going to his
death there?'
"One suggested this, and another
that. 21Finally, a spirit came forward,
stood before the LORD and said, 'I will
entice him.'
22" 'By what means?' the LORD asked.
" 'I will go out and be a lying spirit in
the mouths of all his prophets,' he said.
" 'You will succeed in enticing him,'
said the LORD. 'Go and do it.'
23"So now the LORD has put a lying
spirit in the mouths of all these prophets of yours. The LORD has decreed disaster for you."
24Then Zedekiah son of Kenaanah
went up and slapped Micaiah in the
face. "Which way did the spirit from[a]
the LORD go when he went from me to
speak to you?" he asked.
25Micaiah replied, "You will find out
on the day you go to hide in an inner
room."
26The king of Israel then ordered,
"Take Micaiah and send him back to
Amon the ruler of the city and to Joash
the king's son 27and say, 'This is what the
king says: Put this fellow in prison and
give him nothing but bread and water
until I return safely.' "
28Micaiah declared, "If you ever return safely, the LORD has not spoken
through me." Then he added, "Mark my
words, all you people!"

[a]24 Or *Spirit of*

Ahab Killed at Ramoth Gilead

[29]So the king of Israel and Jehoshaphat king of Judah went up to Ramoth
Gilead. [30]The king of Israel said to Jehoshaphat, "I will enter the battle in disguise, but you wear your royal robes."
So the king of Israel disguised himself
and went into battle.
[31]Now the king of Aram had ordered
his thirty-two chariot commanders, "Do
not fight with anyone, small or great,
except the king of Israel." [32]When the
chariot commanders saw Jehoshaphat,
they thought, "Surely this is the king of
Israel." So they turned to attack him, but
when Jehoshaphat cried out, [33]the
chariot commanders saw that he was
not the king of Israel and stopped pursuing him.
[34]But someone drew his bow at random and hit the king of Israel between
the sections of his armor. The king told
his chariot driver, "Wheel around and
get me out of the fighting. I've been
wounded." [35]All day long the battle
raged, and the king was propped up in
his chariot facing the Arameans. The
blood from his wound ran onto the floor
of the chariot, and that evening he died.
[36]As the sun was setting, a cry spread
through the army: "Every man to his
town; everyone to his land!"
[37]So the king died and was brought to
Samaria, and they buried him there.
[38]They washed the chariot at a pool in
Samaria (where the prostitutes bathed),[a]
and the dogs licked up his blood, as the
word of the LORD had declared.
[39]As for the other events of Ahab's
reign, including all he did, the palace he
built and inlaid with ivory, and the cities he fortified, are they not written in
the book of the annals of the kings of Israel? [40]Ahab rested with his fathers. And
Ahaziah his son succeeded him as king.

Jehoshaphat King of Judah

[41]Jehoshaphat son of Asa became king
of Judah in the fourth year of Ahab king
of Israel. [42]Jehoshaphat was thirty-five
years old when he became king, and he
reigned in Jerusalem twenty-five years.
His mother's name was Azubah daughter of Shilhi. [43]In everything he walked
in the ways of his father Asa and did
not stray from them; he did what was
right in the eyes of the LORD. The high
places, however, were not removed, and
the people continued to offer sacrifices
and burn incense there. [44]Jehosha-
phat was also at peace with the king of
Israel.
[45]As for the other events of Jehoshaphat's reign, the things he achieved
and his military exploits, are they not
written in the book of the annals of the
kings of Judah? [46]He rid the land of the
rest of the male shrine prostitutes who
remained there even after the reign of
his father Asa. [47]There was then no king
in Edom; a deputy ruled.
[48]Now Jehoshaphat built a fleet of
trading ships[b] to go to Ophir for gold,
but they never set sail—they were
wrecked at Ezion Geber. [49]At that time
Ahaziah son of Ahab said to Jehoshaphat, "Let my men sail with your men,"
but Jehoshaphat refused.
[50]Then Jehoshaphat rested with his fathers and was buried with them in the
city of David his father. And Jehoram his
son succeeded him.

Ahaziah King of Israel

[51]Ahaziah son of Ahab became king of
Israel in Samaria in the seventeenth
year of Jehoshaphat king of Judah, and
he reigned over Israel two years. [52]He
did evil in the eyes of the LORD, because
he walked in the ways of his father and
mother and in the ways of Jeroboam son
of Nebat, who caused Israel to sin. [53]He
served and worshiped Baal and provoked the LORD, the God of Israel, to
anger, just as his father had done.

[a]38 Or *Samaria and cleaned the weapons*
[b]48 Hebrew *of ships of Tarshish*

SHARPEN THE FOCUS

The Lord waged a long intense spiritual battle to win Ahab. All the scriptural evidence suggests He lost. Ahab repeatedly resisted God's grace. God called and kept on calling. But in Ahab's case it seems the darkness won.

Ahab came close to true repentance. He grieved over his murder of Naboth (1 Kings 21:27–29). But his grief involved only what Paul would later call "worldly sorrow" (2 Corinthians 7:10). For awhile, Ahab dropped his arrogant attitude. But as 1 Kings 22 shows, he soon returned to his disrespectful disregard for God's Word and God's prophets.

Godly sorrow focuses on the Lord—on His will, His pain at our sins, and His love and kindness that make us want to avoid anything that damages our relationship with Him. But worldly sorrow focuses on us. It sees the painful consequences of sin coming and regrets having to bear them.

Godly sorrow comes to us as God's gift. We can ask Him for it and be certain we will receive it for Jesus' sake. This contrition then leads to confession and to the Spirit's assurance that God fully forgives, again for Jesus' sake. With our Lord's forgiveness we receive the power to walk away from sin and toward greater Christlikeness.

2 Kings

WEEK 31 • THURSDAY

2 Kings 1:1—2:25

As you begin today's reading, recall that our books of 1 Kings and 2 Kings were originally one volume in the Hebrew Bible. The saga of sin and grace, Law and Gospel, continues. As you read, also notice the contrast between godless King Ahaziah and the godly prophets Elijah and Elisha. If time is short, focus on 2 Kings 2:1–18.

The LORD's Judgment on Ahaziah

1 After Ahab's death, Moab rebelled
against Israel. 2Now Ahaziah had
fallen through the lattice of his upper
room in Samaria and injured himself. So
he sent messengers, saying to them, "Go
and consult Baal-Zebub, the god of Ekron, to see if I will recover from this injury."
3But the angel of the LORD said to Elijah the Tishbite, "Go up and meet the
messengers of the king of Samaria and
ask them, 'Is it because there is no God
in Israel that you are going off to consult Baal-Zebub, the god of Ekron?'
4Therefore this is what the LORD says:
'You will not leave the bed you are lying on. You will certainly die!' " So Elijah went.
5When the messengers returned to
the king, he asked them, "Why have
you come back?"
6"A man came to meet us," they replied. "And he said to us, 'Go back to the
king who sent you and tell him, "This is
what the LORD says: Is it because there
is no God in Israel that you are sending
men to consult Baal-Zebub, the god of
Ekron? Therefore you will not leave the
bed you are lying on. You will certainly
die!" ' "
7The king asked them, "What kind of
man was it who came to meet you and
told you this?"
8They replied, "He was a man with a
garment of hair and with a leather belt
around his waist."
The king said, "That was Elijah the
Tishbite."
9Then he sent to Elijah a captain with
his company of fifty men. The captain
went up to Elijah, who was sitting on
the top of a hill, and said to him, "Man
of God, the king says, 'Come down!' "
10Elijah answered the captain, "If I am
a man of God, may fire come down from
heaven and consume you and your fifty
men!" Then fire fell from heaven and
consumed the captain and his men.
11At this the king sent to Elijah another captain with his fifty men. The
captain said to him, "Man of God, this
is what the king says, 'Come down at
once!' "
12"If I am a man of God," Elijah replied, "may fire come down from heav-
en and consume you and your fifty
men!" Then the fire of God fell from
heaven and consumed him and his fifty
men.
13So the king sent a third captain with
his fifty men. This third captain went up

and fell on his knees before Elijah. "Man
of God," he begged, "please have respect for my life and the lives of these
fifty men, your servants! 14See, fire has
fallen from heaven and consumed the
first two captains and all their men. But
now have respect for my life!"
15The angel of the LORD said to Elijah,
"Go down with him; do not be afraid of
him." So Elijah got up and went down
with him to the king.
16He told the king, "This is what the
LORD says: Is it because there is no God
in Israel for you to consult that you have
sent messengers to consult Baal-Zebub,
the god of Ekron? Because you have
done this, you will never leave the bed
you are lying on. You will certainly die!"
17So he died, according to the word of
the LORD that Elijah had spoken.
Because Ahaziah had no son, Joram[a]
succeeded him as king in the second
year of Jehoram son of Jehoshaphat
king of Judah. 18As for all the other
events of Ahaziah's reign, and what he
did, are they not written in the book of
the annals of the kings of Israel?

Elijah Taken Up to Heaven

2 When the LORD was about to
take Elijah up to heaven in a
whirlwind, Elijah and Elisha were on
their way from Gilgal. 2Elijah said to Elisha, "Stay here; the LORD has sent me
to Bethel."
But Elisha said, "As surely as the LORD
lives and as you live, I will not leave
you." So they went down to Bethel.
3The company of the prophets at
Bethel came out to Elisha and asked,
"Do you know that the LORD is going to
take your master from you today?"
"Yes, I know," Elisha replied, "but do
not speak of it."
4Then Elijah said to him, "Stay here,
Elisha; the LORD has sent me to Jericho."
And he replied, "As surely as the LORD
lives and as you live, I will not leave
you." So they went to Jericho.
5The company of the prophets at Jericho went up to Elisha and asked him,
"Do you know that the LORD is going to
take your master from you today?"
"Yes, I know," he replied, "but do not
speak of it."
6Then Elijah said to him, "Stay here;
the LORD has sent me to the Jordan."
And he replied, "As surely as the LORD
lives and as you live, I will not leave
you." So the two of them walked on.
7Fifty men of the company of the
prophets went and stood at a distance,
facing the place where Elijah and Elisha
had stopped at the Jordan. 8Elijah took
his cloak, rolled it up and struck the water with it. The water divided to the
right and to the left, and the two of them
crossed over on dry ground.
9When they had crossed, Elijah said to
Elisha, "Tell me, what can I do for you
before I am taken from you?"
"Let me inherit a double portion of
your spirit," Elisha replied.
10"You have asked a difficult thing,"
Elijah said, "yet if you see me when I am
taken from you, it will be yours—otherwise not."
11As they were walking along and
talking together, suddenly a chariot of
fire and horses of fire appeared and separated the two of them, and Elijah went
up to heaven in a whirlwind. 12Elisha
saw this and cried out, "My father! My
father! The chariots and horsemen of
Israel!" And Elisha saw him no more.
Then he took hold of his own clothes
and tore them apart.
13He picked up the cloak that had
fallen from Elijah and went back and
stood on the bank of the Jordan. 14Then
he took the cloak that had fallen from
him and struck the water with it.
"Where now is the LORD, the God of Elijah?" he asked. When he struck the water, it divided to the right and to the left,
and he crossed over.
15The company of the prophets from
Jericho, who were watching, said, "The
spirit of Elijah is resting on Elisha." And
they went to meet him and bowed to
the ground before him. 16"Look," they
said, "we your servants have fifty able
men. Let them go and look for your
master. Perhaps the Spirit of the LORD

[a]17 Hebrew *Jehoram,* a variant of *Joram*

has picked him up and set him down on
some mountain or in some valley."

"No," Elisha replied, "do not send
them."

17But they persisted until he was too
ashamed to refuse. So he said, "Send
them." And they sent fifty men, who
searched for three days but did not find
him. 18When they returned to Elisha,
who was staying in Jericho, he said to
them, "Didn't I tell you not to go?"

Healing of the Water

19The men of the city said to Elisha,
"Look, our lord, this town is well situated, as you can see, but the water is bad
and the land is unproductive."

20"Bring me a new bowl," he said,
"and put salt in it." So they brought it to
him.

21Then he went out to the spring and
threw the salt into it, saying, "This is
what the LORD says: 'I have healed this
water. Never again will it cause death or
make the land unproductive.' " 22And
the water has remained wholesome to
this day, according to the word Elisha
had spoken.

Elisha Is Jeered

23From there Elisha went up to Bethel. As he was walking along the road,
some youths came out of the town and
jeered at him. "Go on up, you bald-
head!" they said. "Go on up, you bald-
head!" 24He turned around, looked at
them and called down a curse on them
in the name of the LORD. Then two
bears came out of the woods and
mauled forty-two of the youths. 25And
he went on to Mount Carmel and from
there returned to Samaria.

SHARPEN THE FOCUS

A few years ago a song popular on Christian radio included a refrain that began, "When I leave, I want to go out like Elijah . . ."

How did Elijah "go out"? Perhaps we can best answer that question by contrasting his last days with those of Ahaziah:

- The king confided in his idols; Elijah clung to the Savior-God.
- The king rejected the word of the Lord; Elijah remained faithful to God's Law and His Gospel promises.
- Ahaziah's "god" rewarded him with eternal death; the Lord gave Elijah the crown of life.

Whether we like to think about our own death or not, someday we will die. We probably won't enter heaven in a whirlwind, but we will see our Savior face to face. What a day that will be! A day that even now fills us with "inexpressible and glorious joy" (1 Peter 1:8).

Have you thought about the legacy you will leave behind on that day? Is your testimony as bold and clear as you would like it to be? If not, talk it over with your Lord right now. Ask for His grace to see your life and your potential as He sees it and then to live it out with holy joy.

A familiar motto says: "Don't sweat the small stuff." And its corollary: "It's *all* small stuff." That's what the Lord through His servant, Elisha, tells the kings of Israel and Judah today as they face the fear of battle with Moab ("This is an easy thing . . ." 2 Kings 3:18). The Lord has the situation under control. Debt, drought, and even death pose no problem for the Lord who provides, protects, and resurrects His children. If time is short, focus on 2 Kings 4:8–37.

Moab Revolts

3 Joram[a] son of Ahab became king
of Israel in Samaria in the eighteenth year of Jehoshaphat king of Judah, and he reigned twelve years. 2He
did evil in the eyes of the LORD, but not
as his father and mother had done. He
got rid of the sacred stone of Baal that
his father had made. 3Nevertheless he
clung to the sins of Jeroboam son of
Nebat, which he had caused Israel to
commit; he did not turn away from
them.
4Now Mesha king of Moab raised
sheep, and he had to supply the king of
Israel with a hundred thousand lambs
and with the wool of a hundred thousand rams. 5But after Ahab died, the
king of Moab rebelled against the king
of Israel. 6So at that time King Joram
set out from Samaria and mobilized
all Israel. 7He also sent this message
to Jehoshaphat king of Judah: "The
king of Moab has rebelled against me.
Will you go with me to fight against
Moab?"
"I will go with you," he replied. "I am
as you are, my people as your people,
my horses as your horses."
8"By what route shall we attack?" he
asked.
"Through the Desert of Edom," he
answered.
9So the king of Israel set out with the
king of Judah and the king of Edom.
After a roundabout march of seven
days, the army had no more water for
themselves or for the animals with
them.
10"What!" exclaimed the king of Israel.
"Has the LORD called us three kings together only to hand us over to Moab?"
11But Jehoshaphat asked, "Is there no
prophet of the LORD here, that we may
inquire of the LORD through him?"
An officer of the king of Israel answered, "Elisha son of Shaphat is here.
He used to pour water on the hands of
Elijah.[b]"
12Jehoshaphat said, "The word of the
LORD is with him." So the king of Israel
and Jehoshaphat and the king of Edom
went down to him.
13Elisha said to the king of Israel,
"What do we have to do with each other? Go to the prophets of your father
and the prophets of your mother."
"No," the king of Israel answered,
"because it was the LORD who called us
three kings together to hand us over to
Moab."
14Elisha said, "As surely as the LORD
Almighty lives, whom I serve, if I did
not have respect for the presence of Jehoshaphat king of Judah, I would not
look at you or even notice you. 15But
now bring me a harpist."
While the harpist was playing, the

[a]*1* Hebrew *Jehoram,* a variant of *Joram;* also in verse 6 [b]*11* That is, he was Elijah's personal servant.

hand of the LORD came upon Elisha 16and he said, "This is what the LORD says: Make this valley full of ditches. 17For this is what the LORD says: You will see neither wind nor rain, yet this valley will be filled with water, and you, your cattle and your other animals will drink. 18This is an easy thing in the eyes of the LORD; he will also hand Moab over to you. 19You will overthrow every fortified city and every major town. You will cut down every good tree, stop up all the springs, and ruin every good field with stones."

20The next morning, about the time for offering the sacrifice, there it was—water flowing from the direction of Edom! And the land was filled with water.

21Now all the Moabites had heard that the kings had come to fight against them; so every man, young and old, who could bear arms was called up and stationed on the border. 22When they got up early in the morning, the sun was shining on the water. To the Moabites across the way, the water looked red—like blood. 23"That's blood!" they said. "Those kings must have fought and slaughtered each other. Now to the plunder, Moab!"

24But when the Moabites came to the camp of Israel, the Israelites rose up and fought them until they fled. And the Israelites invaded the land and slaughtered the Moabites. 25They destroyed the towns, and each man threw a stone on every good field until it was covered. They stopped up all the springs and cut down every good tree. Only Kir Hareseth was left with its stones in place, but men armed with slings surrounded it and attacked it as well.

26When the king of Moab saw that the battle had gone against him, he took with him seven hundred swordsmen to break through to the king of Edom, but they failed. 27Then he took his firstborn son, who was to succeed him as king, and offered him as a sacrifice on the city wall. The fury against Israel was great; they withdrew and returned to their own land.

The Widow's Oil

4 The wife of a man from the company of the prophets cried out to Elisha, "Your servant my husband is dead, and you know that he revered the LORD. But now his creditor is coming to take my two boys as his slaves."

2Elisha replied to her, "How can I help you? Tell me, what do you have in your house?"

"Your servant has nothing there at all," she said, "except a little oil."

3Elisha said, "Go around and ask all your neighbors for empty jars. Don't ask for just a few. 4Then go inside and shut the door behind you and your sons. Pour oil into all the jars, and as each is filled, put it to one side."

5She left him and afterward shut the door behind her and her sons. They brought the jars to her and she kept pouring. 6When all the jars were full, she said to her son, "Bring me another one."

But he replied, "There is not a jar left." Then the oil stopped flowing.

7She went and told the man of God, and he said, "Go, sell the oil and pay your debts. You and your sons can live on what is left."

The Shunammite's Son Restored to Life

8One day Elisha went to Shunem. And a well-to-do woman was there, who urged him to stay for a meal. So whenever he came by, he stopped there to eat. 9She said to her husband, "I know that this man who often comes our way is a holy man of God. 10Let's make a small room on the roof and put in it a bed and a table, a chair and a lamp for him. Then he can stay there whenever he comes to us."

11One day when Elisha came, he went up to his room and lay down there. 12He said to his servant Gehazi, "Call the Shunammite." So he called her, and she stood before him. 13Elisha said to him, "Tell her, 'You have gone to all this trouble for us. Now what can be done for you? Can we speak on your behalf

to the king or the commander of the
army?' "
She replied, "I have a home among
my own people."
14"What can be done for her?" Elisha
asked.
Gehazi said, "Well, she has no son and
her husband is old."
15Then Elisha said, "Call her." So he
called her, and she stood in the doorway. 16"About this time next year," Elisha
said, "you will hold a son in your arms."
"No, my lord," she objected. "Don't
mislead your servant, O man of God!"
17But the woman became pregnant,
and the next year about that same time
she gave birth to a son, just as Elisha had
told her.
18The child grew, and one day he went
out to his father, who was with the reap-
ers. 19"My head! My head!" he said to his
father.
His father told a servant, "Carry him
to his mother." 20After the servant had
lifted him up and carried him to his
mother, the boy sat on her lap until
noon, and then he died. 21She went up
and laid him on the bed of the man of
God, then shut the door and went out.
22She called her husband and said,
"Please send me one of the servants and
a donkey so I can go to the man of God
quickly and return."
23"Why go to him today?" he asked.
"It's not the New Moon or the Sabbath."
"It's all right," she said.
24She saddled the donkey and said to
her servant, "Lead on; don't slow down
for me unless I tell you." 25So she set out
and came to the man of God at Mount
Carmel.
When he saw her in the distance, the
man of God said to his servant Gehazi,
"Look! There's the Shunammite! 26Run
to meet her and ask her, 'Are you all
right? Is your husband all right? Is your
child all right?' "
"Everything is all right," she said.
27When she reached the man of God
at the mountain, she took hold of his
feet. Gehazi came over to push her
away, but the man of God said, "Leave
her alone! She is in bitter distress, but
the LORD has hidden it from me and has
not told me why."
28"Did I ask you for a son, my lord?"
she said. "Didn't I tell you, 'Don't raise
my hopes'?"
29Elisha said to Gehazi, "Tuck your
cloak into your belt, take my staff in
your hand and run. If you meet anyone,
do not greet him, and if anyone greets
you, do not answer. Lay my staff on the
boy's face."
30But the child's mother said, "As surely as the LORD lives and as you live, I will
not leave you." So he got up and followed her.
31Gehazi went on ahead and laid the
staff on the boy's face, but there was no
sound or response. So Gehazi went back
to meet Elisha and told him, "The boy
has not awakened."
32When Elisha reached the house,
there was the boy lying dead on his
couch. 33He went in, shut the door on
the two of them and prayed to the
LORD. 34Then he got on the bed and lay
upon the boy, mouth to mouth, eyes to
eyes, hands to hands. As he stretched
himself out upon him, the boy's body
grew warm. 35Elisha turned away and
walked back and forth in the room and
then got on the bed and stretched out
upon him once more. The boy sneezed
seven times and opened his eyes.
36Elisha summoned Gehazi and said,
"Call the Shunammite." And he did.
When she came, he said, "Take your
son." 37She came in, fell at his feet and
bowed to the ground. Then she took her
son and went out.

Death in the Pot

38Elisha returned to Gilgal and there
was a famine in that region. While the
company of the prophets was meeting
with him, he said to his servant, "Put on
the large pot and cook some stew for
these men."
39One of them went out into the fields
to gather herbs and found a wild vine.
He gathered some of its gourds and
filled the fold of his cloak. When he returned, he cut them up into the pot of
stew, though no one knew what they

were. 40The stew was poured out for the
men, but as they began to eat it, they
cried out, "O man of God, there is death
in the pot!" And they could not eat it.
41Elisha said, "Get some flour." He put
it into the pot and said, "Serve it to the
people to eat." And there was nothing
harmful in the pot.

Feeding of a Hundred

42A man came from Baal Shalishah,
bringing the man of God twenty loaves
of barley bread baked from the first ripe
grain, along with some heads of new
grain. "Give it to the people to eat," Elisha said.
43"How can I set this before a hundred
men?" his servant asked.
But Elisha answered, "Give it to the
people to eat. For this is what the LORD
says: 'They will eat and have some left
over.' " 44Then he set it before them, and
they ate and had some left over, according to the word of the LORD.

SHARPEN THE FOCUS

The crises of daily life can loom so large. The debt that hangs overhead. The worries about how we'll provide for ourselves or for our family if this or that emergency should arise. The sickness or death of someone we love.

In the concerns we face, we hear the Shunammite's confession of faith echo down the corridors of time: "It's all right. . . . Everything is all right," she says (2 Kings 4:23, 26). How can she say that? And, more to the point, how can *we* say that in our times of trouble and grief?

She and we can say it, because our Lord has already said it. Remember His gentle words of rebuke to Abraham and Sarah: "Is anything too hard for the LORD?" (Genesis 18:14).

In the cross of Jesus Christ and in His open tomb we see the ultimate proof that nothing is too difficult, nothing is impossible for our God. The One who could erase our sins, the One who could defeat Satan, the One who could die our death and rise again can also now take care of His children's other needs and concerns.

Roll your worries—big or small—onto His strong shoulders today. Then tell yourself and the world, with confidence, "It's all right. Everything is all right!"

WEEK 31 • SATURDAY

2 Kings 5:1–27

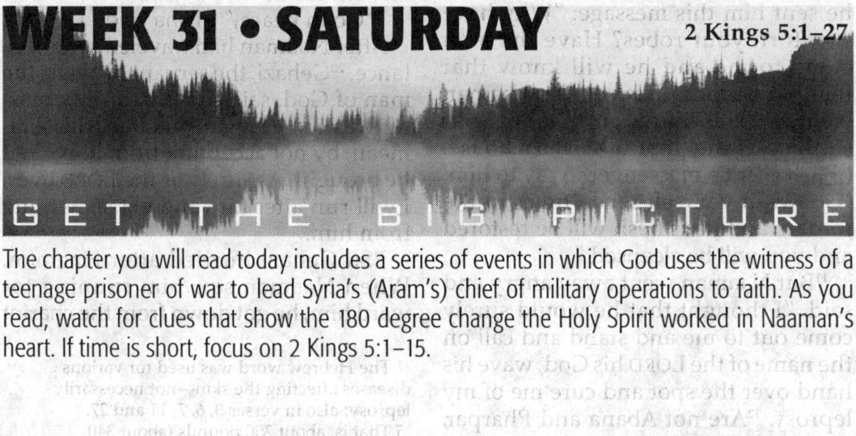

GET THE BIG PICTURE

The chapter you will read today includes a series of events in which God uses the witness of a teenage prisoner of war to lead Syria's (Aram's) chief of military operations to faith. As you read, watch for clues that show the 180 degree change the Holy Spirit worked in Naaman's heart. If time is short, focus on 2 Kings 5:1–15.

Naaman Healed of Leprosy

5 Now Naaman was commander of the army of the king of Aram. He was a great man in the sight of his master and highly regarded, because through him the LORD had given victory to Aram. He was a valiant soldier, but he had leprosy.[a]

2Now bands from Aram had gone out and had taken captive a young girl from Israel, and she served Naaman's wife. 3She said to her mistress, "If only my master would see the prophet who is in Samaria! He would cure him of his leprosy."

4Naaman went to his master and told him what the girl from Israel had said. 5"By all means, go," the king of Aram replied. "I will send a letter to the king of Israel." So Naaman left, taking with him ten talents[b] of silver, six thousand shekels[c] of gold and ten sets of clothing. 6The letter that he took to the king of Israel read: "With this letter I am sending my servant Naaman to you so that you may cure him of his leprosy."

7As soon as the king of Israel read the letter, he tore his robes and said, "Am I God? Can I kill and bring back to life? Why does this fellow send someone to me to be cured of his leprosy? See how he is trying to pick a quarrel with me!"

8When Elisha the man of God heard that the king of Israel had torn his robes, he sent him this message: "Why have you torn your robes? Have the man come to me and he will know that there is a prophet in Israel." 9So Naaman went with his horses and chariots and stopped at the door of Elisha's house. 10Elisha sent a messenger to say to him, "Go, wash yourself seven times in the Jordan, and your flesh will be restored and you will be cleansed."

11But Naaman went away angry and said, "I thought that he would surely come out to me and stand and call on the name of the LORD his God, wave his hand over the spot and cure me of my leprosy. 12Are not Abana and Pharpar, the rivers of Damascus, better than any of the waters of Israel? Couldn't I wash in them and be cleansed?" So he turned and went off in a rage.

13Naaman's servants went to him and said, "My father, if the prophet had told you to do some great thing, would you not have done it? How much more, then, when he tells you, 'Wash and be cleansed'!" 14So he went down and dipped himself in the Jordan seven times, as the man of God had told him, and his flesh was restored and became clean like that of a young boy.

15Then Naaman and all his attendants went back to the man of God. He stood before him and said, "Now I know that there is no God in all the world except in Israel. Please accept now a gift from your servant."

16The prophet answered, "As surely as the LORD lives, whom I serve, I will not accept a thing." And even though Naaman urged him, he refused.

17"If you will not," said Naaman, "please let me, your servant, be given as much earth as a pair of mules can carry, for your servant will never again make burnt offerings and sacrifices to any other god but the LORD. 18But may the LORD forgive your servant for this one thing: When my master enters the temple of Rimmon to bow down and he is leaning on my arm and I bow there also—when I bow down in the temple of Rimmon, may the LORD forgive your servant for this."

19"Go in peace," Elisha said.

After Naaman had traveled some distance, 20Gehazi, the servant of Elisha the man of God, said to himself, "My master was too easy on Naaman, this Aramean, by not accepting from him what he brought. As surely as the LORD lives, I will run after him and get something from him."

21So Gehazi hurried after Naaman. When Naaman saw him running toward him, he got down from the chariot

[a]*1* The Hebrew word was used for various diseases affecting the skin—not necessarily leprosy; also in verses 3, 6, 7, 11 and 27.
[b]*5* That is, about 750 pounds (about 340 kilograms) [c]*5* That is, about 150 pounds (about 70 kilograms)

to meet him. "Is everything all right?" he asked.

22"Everything is all right," Gehazi answered. "My master sent me to say, 'Two young men from the company of the prophets have just come to me from the hill country of Ephraim. Please give them a talent[a] of silver and two sets of clothing.' "

23"By all means, take two talents," said Naaman. He urged Gehazi to accept them, and then tied up the two talents of silver in two bags, with two sets of clothing. He gave them to two of his servants, and they carried them ahead of Gehazi. 24When Gehazi came to the hill, he took the things from the servants and put them away in the house. He sent the men away and they left. 25Then he went in and stood before his master Elisha.

"Where have you been, Gehazi?" Elisha asked.

"Your servant didn't go anywhere," Gehazi answered.

26But Elisha said to him, "Was not my spirit with you when the man got down from his chariot to meet you? Is this the time to take money, or to accept clothes, olive groves, vineyards, flocks, herds, or menservants and maidservants? 27Naaman's leprosy will cling to you and to your descendants forever." Then Gehazi went from Elisha's presence and he was leprous, as white as snow.

[a]22 That is, about 75 pounds (about 34 kilograms)

SHARPEN THE FOCUS

Do you ever find yourself intimidated or even overwhelmed by something you believe the Lord is asking you to do? It's one of the most uncomfortable positions a Christian can be in—knowing that the Lord wants you to do *x* or *y*, and struggling with the fears and feelings of inadequacy that would keep you from obeying your Lord.

The king of Israel in 2 Kings 5:5–8 didn't experience that fight. He simply tore his robe in dismay and declared the task impossible.

We will find ourselves engulfed by that same dismay if we let ourselves believe what Israel's king believed—that he needed to generate within himself the power to do the work the Lord was asking him to do. Elisha did not heal Naaman. The Lord did. The little slave girl did not bring Naaman to faith. The Lord did. The Lord's servants did what they could do. Then they left the rest to Him.

What is it that your Lord wants to do in the lives of those whom your life touches today? You need not feel inadequate or afraid. He is faithful to empower you and to do those things only He can do. ☼

WEEK 32 • MONDAY

2 Kings 6:1—7:20

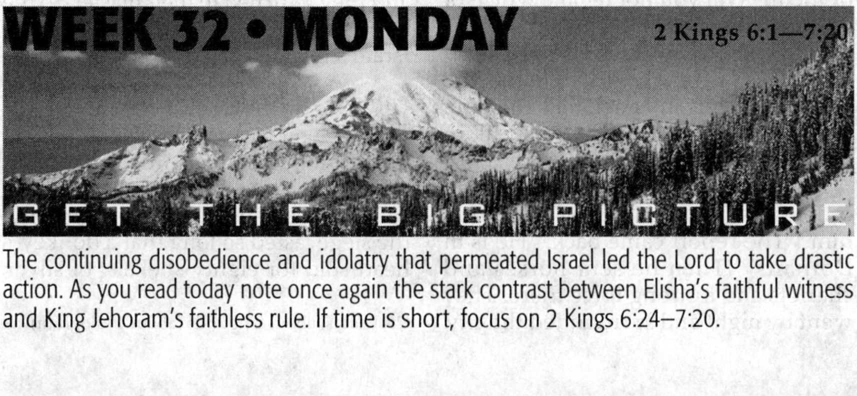

GET THE BIG PICTURE

The continuing disobedience and idolatry that permeated Israel led the Lord to take drastic action. As you read today note once again the stark contrast between Elisha's faithful witness and King Jehoram's faithless rule. If time is short, focus on 2 Kings 6:24–7:20.

An Axhead Floats

6 The company of the prophets
said to Elisha, "Look, the place
where we meet with you is too small for
us. 2Let us go to the Jordan, where each
of us can get a pole; and let us build a
place there for us to live."
And he said, "Go."
3Then one of them said, "Won't you
please come with your servants?"
"I will," Elisha replied. 4And he went
with them.
They went to the Jordan and began to
cut down trees. 5As one of them was cutting down a tree, the iron axhead fell
into the water. "Oh, my lord," he cried
out, "it was borrowed!"
6The man of God asked, "Where did
it fall?" When he showed him the place,
Elisha cut a stick and threw it there, and
made the iron float. 7"Lift it out," he said.
Then the man reached out his hand and
took it.

Elisha Traps Blinded Arameans

8Now the king of Aram was at war
with Israel. After conferring with his officers, he said, "I will set up my camp in
such and such a place."
9The man of God sent word to the
king of Israel: "Beware of passing that
place, because the Arameans are going
down there." 10So the king of Israel
checked on the place indicated by the
man of God. Time and again Elisha
warned the king, so that he was on his
guard in such places.
11This enraged the king of Aram. He
summoned his officers and demanded
of them, "Will you not tell me which of
us is on the side of the king of Israel?"
12"None of us, my lord the king," said
one of his officers, "but Elisha, the
prophet who is in Israel, tells the king
of Israel the very words you speak in
your bedroom."
13"Go, find out where he is," the king
ordered, "so I can send men and capture
him." The report came back: "He is in
Dothan." 14Then he sent horses and
chariots and a strong force there. They
went by night and surrounded the city.
15When the servant of the man of God
got up and went out early the next
morning, an army with horses and chariots had surrounded the city. "Oh, my
lord, what shall we do?" the servant
asked.
16"Don't be afraid," the prophet answered. "Those who are with us are
more than those who are with them."
17And Elisha prayed, "O LORD, open
his eyes so he may see." Then the LORD
opened the servant's eyes, and he
looked and saw the hills full of horses
and chariots of fire all around Elisha.
18As the enemy came down toward
him, Elisha prayed to the LORD, "Strike
these people with blindness." So he
struck them with blindness, as Elisha
had asked.
19Elisha told them, "This is not the
road and this is not the city. Follow me,
and I will lead you to the man you are
looking for." And he led them to Samaria.
20After they entered the city, Elisha
said, "LORD, open the eyes of these men
so they can see." Then the LORD opened
their eyes and they looked, and there
they were, inside Samaria.
21When the king of Israel saw them,
he asked Elisha, "Shall I kill them, my father? Shall I kill them?"
22"Do not kill them," he answered.
"Would you kill men you have captured
with your own sword or bow? Set food
and water before them so that they may
eat and drink and then go back to their
master." 23So he prepared a great feast
for them, and after they had finished
eating and drinking, he sent them away,
and they returned to their master. So the
bands from Aram stopped raiding
Israel's territory.

Famine in Besieged Samaria

24Some time later, Ben-Hadad king of
Aram mobilized his entire army and
marched up and laid siege to Samaria.
25There was a great famine in the city;
the siege lasted so long that a donkey's
head sold for eighty shekels[a] of silver,

[a]25 That is, about 2 pounds (about 1 kilogram)

and a quarter of a cab[a] of seed pods[b] for five shekels.[c]

26As the king of Israel was passing by on the wall, a woman cried to him, "Help me, my lord the king!"

27The king replied, "If the LORD does not help you, where can I get help for you? From the threshing floor? From the winepress?" 28Then he asked her, "What's the matter?"

She answered, "This woman said to me, 'Give up your son so we may eat him today, and tomorrow we'll eat my son.' 29So we cooked my son and ate him. The next day I said to her, 'Give up your son so we may eat him,' but she had hidden him."

30When the king heard the woman's words, he tore his robes. As he went along the wall, the people looked, and there, underneath, he had sackcloth on his body. 31He said, "May God deal with me, be it ever so severely, if the head of Elisha son of Shaphat remains on his shoulders today!"

32Now Elisha was sitting in his house, and the elders were sitting with him. The king sent a messenger ahead, but before he arrived, Elisha said to the elders, "Don't you see how this murderer is sending someone to cut off my head? Look, when the messenger comes, shut the door and hold it shut against him. Is not the sound of his master's footsteps behind him?"

33While he was still talking to them, the messenger came down to him. And ⌊the king⌋ said, "This disaster is from the LORD. Why should I wait for the LORD any longer?"

7 Elisha said, "Hear the word of the LORD. This is what the LORD says: About this time tomorrow, a seah[d] of flour will sell for a shekel[e] and two seahs[f] of barley for a shekel at the gate of Samaria."

2The officer on whose arm the king was leaning said to the man of God, "Look, even if the LORD should open the floodgates of the heavens, could this happen?"

"You will see it with your own eyes," answered Elisha, "but you will not eat any of it!"

The Siege Lifted

3Now there were four men with leprosy[g] at the entrance of the city gate. They said to each other, "Why stay here until we die? 4If we say, 'We'll go into the city'—the famine is there, and we will die. And if we stay here, we will die. So let's go over to the camp of the Arameans and surrender. If they spare us, we live; if they kill us, then we die."

5At dusk they got up and went to the camp of the Arameans. When they reached the edge of the camp, not a man was there, 6for the Lord had caused the Arameans to hear the sound of chariots and horses and a great army, so that they said to one another, "Look, the king of Israel has hired the Hittite and Egyptian kings to attack us!" 7So they got up and fled in the dusk and abandoned their tents and their horses and donkeys. They left the camp as it was and ran for their lives.

8The men who had leprosy reached the edge of the camp and entered one of the tents. They ate and drank, and carried away silver, gold and clothes, and went off and hid them. They returned and entered another tent and took some things from it and hid them also.

9Then they said to each other, "We're not doing right. This is a day of good news and we are keeping it to ourselves. If we wait until daylight, punishment will overtake us. Let's go at once and report this to the royal palace."

10So they went and called out to the city gatekeepers and told them, "We went into the Aramean camp and not a man was there—not a sound of anyone—only tethered horses and donkeys, and the tents left just as they

[a]25 That is, probably about 1/2 pint (about 0.3 liter) [b]25 Or *of dove's dung* [c]25 That is, about 2 ounces (about 55 grams) [d]1 That is, probably about 7 quarts (about 7.3 liters); also in verses 16 and 18 [e]1 That is, about 2/5 ounce (about 11 grams); also in verses 16 and 18 [f]1 That is, probably about 13 quarts (about 15 liters); also in verses 16 and 18 [g]3 The Hebrew word is used for various diseases affecting the skin—not necessarily leprosy; also in verse 8.

were." 11The gatekeepers shouted the news, and it was reported within the palace.

12The king got up in the night and said to his officers, "I will tell you what the Arameans have done to us. They know we are starving; so they have left the camp to hide in the countryside, thinking, 'They will surely come out, and then we will take them alive and get into the city.' "

13One of his officers answered, "Have some men take five of the horses that are left in the city. Their plight will be like that of all the Israelites left here—yes, they will only be like all these Israelites who are doomed. So let us send them to find out what happened."

14So they selected two chariots with their horses, and the king sent them after the Aramean army. He commanded the drivers, "Go and find out what has happened." 15They followed them as far as the Jordan, and they found the whole road strewn with the clothing and equipment the Arameans had thrown away in their headlong flight. So the messengers returned and reported to the king. 16Then the people went out and plundered the camp of the Arameans. So a seah of flour sold for a shekel, and two seahs of barley sold for a shekel, as the LORD had said.

17Now the king had put the officer on whose arm he leaned in charge of the gate, and the people trampled him in the gateway, and he died, just as the man of God had foretold when the king came down to his house. 18It happened as the man of God had said to the king: "About this time tomorrow, a seah of flour will sell for a shekel and two seahs of barley for a shekel at the gate of Samaria."

19The officer had said to the man of God, "Look, even if the LORD should open the floodgates of the heavens, could this happen?" The man of God had replied, "You will see it with your own eyes, but you will not eat any of it!" 20And that is exactly what happened to him, for the people trampled him in the gateway, and he died.

SHARPEN THE FOCUS

The Old Testament often calls prophets "seers." God's prophets *saw* realities that escaped the notice of ordinary people such as Elisha's servant (2 Kings 6:14–17) or King Jehoram's deputy (2 Kings 7:1–2). Their fear and unbelief limited their vision.

When you listen to the evening news does Psalm 2 echo in your ears? When you think about what's going on at your workplace, city government, or even in your own family, do you stop to consider what your Lord might be up to, and the part your prayers, words, and actions might play in the war with the kingdom of darkness?

Moses once sighed, "I wish that all the LORD's people were prophets and that the LORD would put His Spirit on them!" (Numbers 11:29). The Holy Spirit also desires that. The apostle Paul pleads for his readers:

> *I keep asking that the God of our Lord Jesus Christ, the glorious Father, may give you the Spirit of wisdom and revelation, so that you may know Him better. I pray also that the eyes of your heart may be enlightened in order that you may know the hope to which He has called you, the riches of His glorious inheritance in the saints, and His incomparably great power for us who believe.* (Ephesians 1:17–19)

WEEK 32 • TUESDAY

2 Kings 8:1–29

GET THE BIG PICTURE

The Lord continues His faithful love to His people, protecting the Shunammite woman whose son Elisha had raised from the dead (2 Kings 8:1–6). The rest of the chapter details affairs of state in Aram (Syria), Israel, and Judah. As you read, note particularly 2 Kings 8:19, a reminder of the covenant the Lord has established with David. If time is short, focus on 2 Kings 8:1–6.

The Shunammite's Land Restored

8 Now Elisha had said to the woman whose son he had restored to
life, "Go away with your family and stay
for a while wherever you can, because
the LORD has decreed a famine in the
land that will last seven years." [2]The
woman proceeded to do as the man of
God said. She and her family went away
and stayed in the land of the Philistines
seven years.
[3]At the end of the seven years she
came back from the land of the Philistines and went to the king to beg for her
house and land. [4]The king was talking
to Gehazi, the servant of the man of
God, and had said, "Tell me about all the
great things Elisha has done." [5]Just as
Gehazi was telling the king how Elisha
had restored the dead to life, the woman whose son Elisha had brought back
to life came to beg the king for her house
and land.
Gehazi said, "This is the woman, my
lord the king, and this is her son whom
Elisha restored to life." [6]The king asked
the woman about it, and she told him.
Then he assigned an official to her
case and said to him, "Give back everything that belonged to her, including all
the income from her land from the day
she left the country until now."

Hazael Murders Ben-Hadad

[7]Elisha went to Damascus, and Ben-
Hadad king of Aram was ill. When the
king was told, "The man of God has
come all the way up here," [8]he said to
Hazael, "Take a gift with you and go to
meet the man of God. Consult the LORD
through him; ask him, 'Will I recover
from this illness?' "
[9]Hazael went to meet Elisha, taking
with him as a gift forty camel-loads of
all the finest wares of Damascus. He
went in and stood before him, and said,
"Your son Ben-Hadad king of Aram has
sent me to ask, 'Will I recover from this
illness?' "
[10]Elisha answered, "Go and say to
him, 'You will certainly recover'; but[a]
the LORD has revealed to me that he will
in fact die." [11]He stared at him with a
fixed gaze until Hazael felt ashamed.
Then the man of God began to weep.
[12]"Why is my lord weeping?" asked
Hazael.
"Because I know the harm you will do
to the Israelites," he answered. "You will
set fire to their fortified places, kill their
young men with the sword, dash their
little children to the ground, and rip
open their pregnant women."
[13]Hazael said, "How could your servant, a mere dog, accomplish such a
feat?"
"The LORD has shown me that you
will become king of Aram," answered
Elisha.
[14]Then Hazael left Elisha and returned to his master. When Ben-Hadad
asked, "What did Elisha say to you?"
Hazael replied, "He told me that you

[a]10 The Hebrew may also be read *Go and say, 'You will certainly not recover,' for.*

would certainly recover." 15But the next day he took a thick cloth, soaked it in water and spread it over the king's face, so that he died. Then Hazael succeeded him as king.

Jehoram King of Judah

16In the fifth year of Joram son of Ahab king of Israel, when Jehoshaphat was king of Judah, Jehoram son of Jehoshaphat began his reign as king of Judah. 17He was thirty-two years old when he became king, and he reigned in Jerusalem eight years. 18He walked in the ways of the kings of Israel, as the house of Ahab had done, for he married a daughter of Ahab. He did evil in the eyes of the LORD. 19Nevertheless, for the sake of his servant David, the LORD was not willing to destroy Judah. He had promised to maintain a lamp for David and his descendants forever.

20In the time of Jehoram, Edom rebelled against Judah and set up its own king. 21So Jehoram[a] went to Zair with all his chariots. The Edomites surrounded him and his chariot commanders, but he rose up and broke through by night; his army, however, fled back home. 22To this day Edom has been in rebellion against Judah. Libnah revolted at the same time.

23As for the other events of Jehoram's reign, and all he did, are they not written in the book of the annals of the kings of Judah? 24Jehoram rested with his fathers and was buried with them in the City of David. And Ahaziah his son succeeded him as king.

Ahaziah King of Judah

25In the twelfth year of Joram son of Ahab king of Israel, Ahaziah son of Jehoram king of Judah began to reign. 26Ahaziah was twenty-two years old when he became king, and he reigned in Jerusalem one year. His mother's name was Athaliah, a granddaughter of Omri king of Israel. 27He walked in the ways of the house of Ahab and did evil in the eyes of the LORD, as the house of Ahab had done, for he was related by marriage to Ahab's family.

28Ahaziah went with Joram son of Ahab to war against Hazael king of Aram at Ramoth Gilead. The Arameans wounded Joram; 29so King Joram returned to Jezreel to recover from the wounds the Arameans had inflicted on him at Ramoth[b] in his battle with Hazael king of Aram.

Then Ahaziah son of Jehoram king of Judah went down to Jezreel to see Joram son of Ahab, because he had been wounded.

[a]21 Hebrew *Joram,* a variant of *Jehoram;* also in verses 23 and 24 [b]29 Hebrew *Ramah,* a variant of *Ramoth*

SHARPEN THE FOCUS

Wouldn't it be thrilling if we could sit and chat with the unnamed Shunammite woman who graces the pages of 2 Kings? While idolatry grew and spread, while pagan armies marched back and forth across the map of the Mideast, while Satan schemed to snuff out the light of the Lord's covenant promise, the Savior-God kept on caring for His own.

What would Elisha's friend, by now probably a widow, say to us if she could speak? Without doubt, she would echo the words of the hymn writer:

If you but trust in God to guide you
And place your confidence in Him,
You'll find Him always there beside you
To give you hope and strength within.
For those who trust God's changeless love
Build on the rock that will not move.

Sing, pray, and keep His ways unswerving,
Offer your service faithfully,
And trust His Word; though undeserving,
You'll find His promise true to be.
God never will forsake in need
The soul that trusts in Him indeed. (*Lutheran Worship* 420; stanzas 1, 4)

WEEK 32 • WEDNESDAY

2 Kings 9:1—10:36

A thorough housecleaning fulfills the prophecies Elijah had made before his death. Jehu acts as God's agent in taking revenge on the wicked king of Israel, Joram, and the wicked king of Judah, Ahaziah. Despite Jehu's zeal for the Lord in the bloody coup described in 2 Kings 9–10, he fails to go far enough in ridding the land of idol worship (2 Kings 10:29–31). As you read, note once again the terrible dangers of half-hearted obedience to the Lord. If time is short, focus on 2 Kings 10:1–31.

Jehu Anointed King of Israel

9 The prophet Elisha summoned a
man from the company of the
prophets and said to him, "Tuck your
cloak into your belt, take this flask of oil
with you and go to Ramoth Gilead.
[2]When you get there, look for Jehu son
of Jehoshaphat, the son of Nimshi. Go
to him, get him away from his companions and take him into an inner room.
[3]Then take the flask and pour the oil on
his head and declare, 'This is what the
LORD says: I anoint you king over Israel.' Then open the door and run; don't
delay!"
[4]So the young man, the prophet, went
to Ramoth Gilead. [5]When he arrived, he
found the army officers sitting together. "I have a message for you, commander," he said.
"For which of us?" asked Jehu.
"For you, commander," he replied.
[6]Jehu got up and went into the house.
Then the prophet poured the oil on
Jehu's head and declared, "This is what
the LORD, the God of Israel, says: 'I
anoint you king over the LORD's people
Israel. [7]You are to destroy the house of
Ahab your master, and I will avenge the
blood of my servants the prophets and
the blood of all the LORD's servants shed
by Jezebel. [8]The whole house of Ahab
will perish. I will cut off from Ahab every last male in Israel—slave or free. [9]I
will make the house of Ahab like the
house of Jeroboam son of Nebat and like
the house of Baasha son of Ahijah. [10]As
for Jezebel, dogs will devour her on the
plot of ground at Jezreel, and no one
will bury her.'" Then he opened the
door and ran.
[11]When Jehu went out to his fellow officers, one of them asked him, "Is everything all right? Why did this madman
come to you?"
"You know the man and the sort of
things he says," Jehu replied.
[12]"That's not true!" they said. "Tell us."
Jehu said, "Here is what he told me:
'This is what the LORD says: I anoint you
king over Israel.'"
[13]They hurried and took their cloaks

and spread them under him on the bare
steps. Then they blew the trumpet and
shouted, "Jehu is king!"

Jehu Kills Joram and Ahaziah

14So Jehu son of Jehoshaphat, the son
of Nimshi, conspired against Joram.
(Now Joram and all Israel had been defending Ramoth Gilead against Hazael
king of Aram, 15but King Joram[a] had returned to Jezreel to recover from the
wounds the Arameans had inflicted on
him in the battle with Hazael king of
Aram.) Jehu said, "If this is the way you
feel, don't let anyone slip out of the city
to go and tell the news in Jezreel."
16Then he got into his chariot and rode
to Jezreel, because Joram was resting
there and Ahaziah king of Judah had
gone down to see him.
17When the lookout standing on the
tower in Jezreel saw Jehu's troops approaching, he called out, "I see some
troops coming."
"Get a horseman," Joram ordered.
"Send him to meet them and ask, 'Do
you come in peace?' "
18The horseman rode off to meet Jehu
and said, "This is what the king says:
'Do you come in peace?' "
"What do you have to do with
peace?" Jehu replied. "Fall in behind
me."
The lookout reported, "The messenger has reached them, but he isn't coming back."
19So the king sent out a second horseman. When he came to them he said,
"This is what the king says: 'Do you
come in peace?' "
Jehu replied, "What do you have to
do with peace? Fall in behind me."
20The lookout reported, "He has
reached them, but he isn't coming back
either. The driving is like that of Jehu
son of Nimshi—he drives like a madman."
21"Hitch up my chariot," Joram ordered. And when it was hitched up, Joram king of Israel and Ahaziah king of
Judah rode out, each in his own chariot,
to meet Jehu. They met him at the plot
of ground that had belonged to Naboth
the Jezreelite. 22When Joram saw Jehu
he asked, "Have you come in peace,
Jehu?"
"How can there be peace," Jehu replied, "as long as all the idolatry and
witchcraft of your mother Jezebel
abound?"
23Joram turned about and fled, calling
out to Ahaziah, "Treachery, Ahaziah!"
24Then Jehu drew his bow and shot
Joram between the shoulders. The arrow pierced his heart and he slumped
down in his chariot. 25Jehu said to Bid-
kar, his chariot officer, "Pick him up and
throw him on the field that belonged to
Naboth the Jezreelite. Remember how
you and I were riding together in chariots behind Ahab his father when the
LORD made this prophecy about him:
26'Yesterday I saw the blood of Naboth
and the blood of his sons, declares the
LORD, and I will surely make you pay
for it on this plot of ground, declares the
LORD.'[b] Now then, pick him up and
throw him on that plot, in accordance
with the word of the LORD."
27When Ahaziah king of Judah saw
what had happened, he fled up the road
to Beth Haggan.[c] Jehu chased him,
shouting, "Kill him too!" They wounded
him in his chariot on the way up to Gur
near Ibleam, but he escaped to Megiddo and died there. 28His servants took
him by chariot to Jerusalem and buried
him with his fathers in his tomb in the
City of David. 29(In the eleventh year of
Joram son of Ahab, Ahaziah had become king of Judah.)

Jezebel Killed

30Then Jehu went to Jezreel. When
Jezebel heard about it, she painted her
eyes, arranged her hair and looked out
of a window. 31As Jehu entered the
gate, she asked, "Have you come in
peace, Zimri, you murderer of your
master?"[d]
32He looked up at the window and

[a]15 Hebrew *Jehoram*, a variant of *Joram*; also in verses 17 and 21-24 [b]26 See 1 Kings 21:19. [c]27 Or *fled by way of the garden house* [d]31 Or *"Did Zimri have peace, who murdered his master?"*

called out, "Who is on my side? Who?"
Two or three eunuchs looked down at
him. 33"Throw her down!" Jehu said. So
they threw her down, and some of her
blood spattered the wall and the horses
as they trampled her underfoot.
34Jehu went in and ate and drank.
"Take care of that cursed woman," he
said, "and bury her, for she was a king's
daughter." 35But when they went out to
bury her, they found nothing except her
skull, her feet and her hands. 36They
went back and told Jehu, who said,
"This is the word of the LORD that he
spoke through his servant Elijah the
Tishbite: On the plot of ground at Jezreel dogs will devour Jezebel's flesh.[a]
37Jezebel's body will be like refuse on the
ground in the plot at Jezreel, so that no
one will be able to say, 'This is Jezebel.' "

Ahab's Family Killed

10 Now there were in Samaria
seventy sons of the house of
Ahab. So Jehu wrote letters and sent
them to Samaria: to the officials of
Jezreel,[b] to the elders and to the guardians of Ahab's children. He said, 2"As
soon as this letter reaches you, since
your master's sons are with you and
you have chariots and horses, a fortified
city and weapons, 3choose the best and
most worthy of your master's sons and
set him on his father's throne. Then
fight for your master's house."
4But they were terrified and said, "If
two kings could not resist him, how can
we?"
5So the palace administrator, the city
governor, the elders and the guardians
sent this message to Jehu: "We are your
servants and we will do anything you
say. We will not appoint anyone as king;
you do whatever you think best."
6Then Jehu wrote them a second letter, saying, "If you are on my side and
will obey me, take the heads of your
master's sons and come to me in Jezreel by this time tomorrow."
Now the royal princes, seventy of
them, were with the leading men of the
city, who were rearing them. 7When the
letter arrived, these men took the
princes and slaughtered all seventy of
them. They put their heads in baskets
and sent them to Jehu in Jezreel. 8When
the messenger arrived, he told Jehu,
"They have brought the heads of the
princes."
Then Jehu ordered, "Put them in two
piles at the entrance of the city gate until morning."
9The next morning Jehu went out. He
stood before all the people and said,
"You are innocent. It was I who conspired against my master and killed
him, but who killed all these? 10Know
then, that not a word the LORD has spoken against the house of Ahab will fail.
The LORD has done what he promised
through his servant Elijah." 11So Jehu
killed everyone in Jezreel who remained of the house of Ahab, as well as
all his chief men, his close friends and
his priests, leaving him no survivor.
12Jehu then set out and went toward
Samaria. At Beth Eked of the Shepherds,
13he met some relatives of Ahaziah king
of Judah and asked, "Who are you?"
They said, "We are relatives of Ahaziah, and we have come down to greet the
families of the king and of the queen
mother."
14"Take them alive!" he ordered. So
they took them alive and slaughtered
them by the well of Beth Eked—forty-
two men. He left no survivor.
15After he left there, he came upon Jehonadab son of Recab, who was on his
way to meet him. Jehu greeted him and
said, "Are you in accord with me, as I am
with you?"
"I am," Jehonadab answered.
"If so," said Jehu, "give me your
hand." So he did, and Jehu helped him
up into the chariot. 16Jehu said, "Come
with me and see my zeal for the LORD."
Then he had him ride along in his chariot.
17When Jehu came to Samaria, he
killed all who were left there of Ahab's
family; he destroyed them, according to
the word of the LORD spoken to Elijah.

[a]36 See 1 Kings 21:23. [b]1 Hebrew; some Septuagint manuscripts and Vulgate *of the city*

Ministers of Baal Killed

18Then Jehu brought all the people together and said to them, "Ahab served
Baal a little; Jehu will serve him much.
19Now summon all the prophets of Baal,
all his ministers and all his priests. See
that no one is missing, because I am going to hold a great sacrifice for Baal.
Anyone who fails to come will no longer
live." But Jehu was acting deceptively in
order to destroy the ministers of Baal.
20Jehu said, "Call an assembly in hon-
or of Baal." So they proclaimed it. 21Then
he sent word throughout Israel, and all
the ministers of Baal came; not one
stayed away. They crowded into the
temple of Baal until it was full from one
end to the other. 22And Jehu said to the
keeper of the wardrobe, "Bring robes for
all the ministers of Baal." So he brought
out robes for them.
23Then Jehu and Jehonadab son of Recab went into the temple of Baal. Jehu
said to the ministers of Baal, "Look
around and see that no servants of the
LORD are here with you—only ministers
of Baal." 24So they went in to make sacrifices and burnt offerings. Now Jehu
had posted eighty men outside with this
warning: "If one of you lets any of the
men I am placing in your hands escape,
it will be your life for his life."
25As soon as Jehu had finished making the burnt offering, he ordered the
guards and officers: "Go in and kill
them; let no one escape." So they cut
them down with the sword. The guards
and officers threw the bodies out and
then entered the inner shrine of the
temple of Baal. 26They brought the sacred stone out of the temple of Baal and
burned it. 27They demolished the sacred
stone of Baal and tore down the temple
of Baal, and people have used it for a la-
trine to this day.
28So Jehu destroyed Baal worship in
Israel. 29However, he did not turn away
from the sins of Jeroboam son of Nebat,
which he had caused Israel to commit—
the worship of the golden calves at
Bethel and Dan.
30The LORD said to Jehu, "Because you
have done well in accomplishing what
is right in my eyes and have done to the
house of Ahab all I had in mind to do,
your descendants will sit on the throne
of Israel to the fourth generation." 31Yet
Jehu was not careful to keep the law of
the LORD, the God of Israel, with all his
heart. He did not turn away from the
sins of Jeroboam, which he had caused
Israel to commit.
32In those days the LORD began to reduce the size of Israel. Hazael overpowered the Israelites throughout their
territory 33east of the Jordan in all the
land of Gilead (the region of Gad, Reuben and Manasseh), from Aroer by the
Arnon Gorge through Gilead to Bashan.
34As for the other events of Jehu's
reign, all he did, and all his achievements, are they not written in the book
of the annals of the kings of Israel?
35Jehu rested with his fathers and was
buried in Samaria. And Jehoahaz his son
succeeded him as king. 36The time that
Jehu reigned over Israel in Samaria was
twenty-eight years.

SHARPEN THE FOCUS

Parents and teachers sometimes follow a threat with yet a second and third and fourth in an effort to change children's behavior. It doesn't take youngsters long to figure out that "right now" means "after I've scolded a few more times."

Human threats are often empty threats. But our Lord says what He means and means what He says. When He speaks, each word of Law or Gospel, comes true. We see this most clearly of all in Christ's cross. There God's threat came true: "The soul who sins is the one who will die" (Ezekiel 18:20). At the cross God's just anger at human sin—at your sin and mine—fell on Christ. Jesus died our death. We shudder in recognition of what we by our sins had deserved.

But the cross also quiets our fears. It assures us, "This sacrifice, this death, ends your guilt. Your sin is taken away; your guilt is atoned for. Christ, the sinless Lamb of God, is your substitute." And we poor sinners relax and rejoice in the face of such incredible grace.

WEEK 32 • THURSDAY

2 Kings 11:1—12:21

GET THE BIG PICTURE

In his *Chronicles of Narnia,* C. S. Lewis paints quite a nasty picture of the White Witch, a creature who symbolizes Satan. Today you will read about the reign of the wicked queen, Athaliah. In sheer nastiness and lust for power, Lewis's fictional White Witch has a hard time keeping up with the historical Queen Athaliah. Today you will read about her plans for God's people. But the Lord had other plans. If time is short, focus on 2 Kings 11:1–12:3.

Athaliah and Joash

11 When Athaliah the mother of Ahaziah saw that her son was dead, she proceeded to destroy the whole royal family. [2]But Jehosheba, the daughter of King Jehoram[a] and sister of Ahaziah, took Joash son of Ahaziah and stole him away from among the royal princes, who were about to be murdered. She put him and his nurse in a bedroom to hide him from Athaliah; so he was not killed. [3]He remained hidden with his nurse at the temple of the LORD for six years while Athaliah ruled the land.

[4]In the seventh year Jehoiada sent for the commanders of units of a hundred, the Carites and the guards and had them brought to him at the temple of the LORD. He made a covenant with them and put them under oath at the temple of the LORD. Then he showed them the king's son. [5]He commanded them, saying, "This is what you are to do: You who are in the three companies that are going on duty on the Sabbath—a third of you guarding the royal palace, [6]a third at the Sur Gate, and a third at the gate behind the guard, who take turns guarding the temple— [7]and you who are in the other two companies that normally go off Sabbath duty are all to guard the temple for the king. [8]Station yourselves around the king, each man with his weapon in his hand. Anyone who approaches your ranks[b] must be put to death. Stay close to the king wherever he goes."

[9]The commanders of units of a hundred did just as Jehoiada the priest ordered. Each one took his men—those who were going on duty on the Sabbath and those who were going off duty—and came to Jehoiada the priest. [10]Then he gave the commanders the spears and shields that had belonged to King David and that were in the temple of the LORD. [11]The guards, each with his weapon in his hand, stationed themselves around the king—near the altar and the temple, from the south side to the north side of the temple.

[12]Jehoiada brought out the king's son and put the crown on him; he presented him with a copy of the covenant and proclaimed him king. They anointed him, and the people clapped their

[a]2 Hebrew *Joram,* a variant of *Jehoram*
[b]8 Or *approaches the precincts*

hands and shouted, "Long live the
king!"
13When Athaliah heard the noise
made by the guards and the people, she
went to the people at the temple of the
LORD. 14She looked and there was the
king, standing by the pillar, as the custom was. The officers and the trumpeters
were beside the king, and all the people
of the land were rejoicing and blowing
trumpets. Then Athaliah tore her robes
and called out, "Treason! Treason!"
15Jehoiada the priest ordered the commanders of units of a hundred, who
were in charge of the troops: "Bring her
out between the ranks[a] and put to the
sword anyone who follows her." For the
priest had said, "She must not be put
to death in the temple of the LORD."
16So they seized her as she reached the
place where the horses enter the palace grounds, and there she was put to
death.
17Jehoiada then made a covenant between the LORD and the king and
people that they would be the LORD's
people. He also made a covenant between the king and the people. 18All the
people of the land went to the temple
of Baal and tore it down. They smashed
the altars and idols to pieces and killed
Mattan the priest of Baal in front of the
altars.

Then Jehoiada the priest posted
guards at the temple of the LORD. 19He
took with him the commanders of hundreds, the Carites, the guards and all the
people of the land, and together they
brought the king down from the temple
of the LORD and went into the palace,
entering by way of the gate of the
guards. The king then took his place on
the royal throne, 20and all the people of
the land rejoiced. And the city was
quiet, because Athaliah had been slain
with the sword at the palace.
21Joash[b] was seven years old when he
began to reign.

Joash Repairs the Temple

12 In the seventh year of Jehu,
Joash[c] became king, and he
reigned in Jerusalem forty years. His
mother's name was Zibiah; she was
from Beersheba. 2Joash did what was
right in the eyes of the LORD all the
years Jehoiada the priest instructed
him. 3The high places, however, were
not removed; the people continued to
offer sacrifices and burn incense there.
4Joash said to the priests, "Collect all
the money that is brought as sacred offerings to the temple of the LORD—the
money collected in the census, the money received from personal vows and the
money brought voluntarily to the temple. 5Let every priest receive the money
from one of the treasurers, and let it be
used to repair whatever damage is
found in the temple."
6But by the twenty-third year of King
Joash the priests still had not repaired
the temple. 7Therefore King Joash summoned Jehoiada the priest and the other priests and asked them, "Why aren't
you repairing the damage done to the
temple? Take no more money from your
treasurers, but hand it over for repairing
the temple." 8The priests agreed that
they would not collect any more money from the people and that they would
not repair the temple themselves.
9Jehoiada the priest took a chest and
bored a hole in its lid. He placed it beside the altar, on the right side as one
enters the temple of the LORD. The
priests who guarded the entrance put
into the chest all the money that was
brought to the temple of the LORD.
10Whenever they saw that there was a
large amount of money in the chest, the
royal secretary and the high priest
came, counted the money that had been
brought into the temple of the LORD
and put it into bags. 11When the amount
had been determined, they gave the
money to the men appointed to supervise the work on the temple. With it
they paid those who worked on the
temple of the LORD—the carpenters and
builders, 12the masons and stonecutters.
They purchased timber and dressed

[a]15 Or *out from the precincts* [b]21 Hebrew *Jehoash,* a variant of *Joash* [c]1 Hebrew *Jehoash,* a variant of *Joash;* also in verses 2, 4, 6, 7 and 18

stone for the repair of the temple of the LORD, and met all the other expenses of restoring the temple.

13The money brought into the temple was not spent for making silver basins, wick trimmers, sprinkling bowls, trumpets or any other articles of gold or silver for the temple of the LORD; 14it was paid to the workmen, who used it to repair the temple. 15They did not require an accounting from those to whom they gave the money to pay the workers, because they acted with complete honesty. 16The money from the guilt offerings and sin offerings was not brought into the temple of the LORD; it belonged to the priests.

17About this time Hazael king of Aram went up and attacked Gath and captured it. Then he turned to attack Jerusalem. 18But Joash king of Judah took all the sacred objects dedicated by his fathers—Jehoshaphat, Jehoram and Ahaziah, the kings of Judah—and the gifts he himself had dedicated and all the gold found in the treasuries of the temple of the LORD and of the royal palace, and he sent them to Hazael king of Aram, who then withdrew from Jerusalem.

19As for the other events of the reign of Joash, and all he did, are they not written in the book of the annals of the kings of Judah? 20His officials conspired against him and assassinated him at Beth Millo, on the road down to Silla. 21The officials who murdered him were Jozabad son of Shimeath and Jehozabad son of Shomer. He died and was buried with his fathers in the City of David. And Amaziah his son succeeded him as king.

SHARPEN THE FOCUS

Humanistic thinkers tend to pooh-pooh the reality of original sin, the "bentness" passed down from one generation to the next like some horrific genetic defect. Yet the case study we've been reading the past several weeks testifies to sin's reality. As C. S. Lewis pointed out, we're not sinners so much because we commit sins; rather, we commit sins because we are, at heart, sinners. We are inclined away from our Creator, bent toward disrespect for Him and disobedience to Him.

Even Joash's reforms were only skin-deep. When the boy-king's mentor, the priest Jehoiada, died these reforms fell by the wayside. The people and their king reverted to the sins of their ancestors.

Lest we throw up our hands in despair, though, we need to remember the new life we have received in Christ our Savior. "If anyone is in Christ," Paul writes, "he is a new creation; the old has gone, the new has come!" (2 Corinthians 5:17). By God's grace we have been reborn to eternal salvation; we are even now, by that same grace, being transformed into the character of Christ Himself (Romans 8:29–30)! Rejoice in the relief your new identity brings and look for ways to live it out today.

As you read today, you may hear Joe Garigiola shouting from the press box, "It's déjà vu all over again!" All the way back to the time of the judges the history of Israel and Judah repeated itself. As you read, don't just look for the sins of the people and their leaders, though. Also look for evidences of their Lord's continuing compassion for His straying children. If time is short, focus on 2 Kings 13:14–25.

Jehoahaz King of Israel

13 In the twenty-third year of Joash son of Ahaziah king of Judah, Jehoahaz son of Jehu became king of Israel in Samaria, and he reigned seventeen years. 2He did evil in the eyes of the LORD by following the sins of Jeroboam son of Nebat, which he had caused Israel to commit, and he did not turn away from them. 3So the LORD's anger burned against Israel, and for a long time he kept them under the power of Hazael king of Aram and Ben-Hadad his son.

4Then Jehoahaz sought the LORD's favor, and the LORD listened to him, for he saw how severely the king of Aram was oppressing Israel. 5The LORD provided a deliverer for Israel, and they escaped from the power of Aram. So the Israelites lived in their own homes as they had before. 6But they did not turn away from the sins of the house of Jeroboam, which he had caused Israel to commit; they continued in them. Also, the Asherah pole[a] remained standing in Samaria.

7Nothing had been left of the army of Jehoahaz except fifty horsemen, ten chariots and ten thousand foot soldiers, for the king of Aram had destroyed the rest and made them like the dust at threshing time.

8As for the other events of the reign of Jehoahaz, all he did and his achievements, are they not written in the book of the annals of the kings of Israel? 9Jehoahaz rested with his fathers and was buried in Samaria. And Jehoash[b] his son succeeded him as king.

Jehoash King of Israel

10In the thirty-seventh year of Joash king of Judah, Jehoash son of Jehoahaz became king of Israel in Samaria, and he reigned sixteen years. 11He did evil in the eyes of the LORD and did not turn away from any of the sins of Jeroboam son of Nebat, which he had caused Israel to commit; he continued in them.

12As for the other events of the reign of Jehoash, all he did and his achievements, including his war against Amaziah king of Judah, are they not written in the book of the annals of the kings of Israel? 13Jehoash rested with his fathers, and Jeroboam succeeded him on the throne. Jehoash was buried in Samaria with the kings of Israel.

14Now Elisha was suffering from the illness from which he died. Jehoash king of Israel went down to see him and wept over him. "My father! My father!" he cried. "The chariots and horsemen of Israel!"

15Elisha said, "Get a bow and some arrows," and he did so. 16"Take the bow in your hands," he said to the king of Isra-

[a]6 That is, a symbol of the goddess Asherah; here and elsewhere in 2 Kings [b]9 Hebrew *Joash,* a variant of *Jehoash*; also in verses 12-14 and 25

el. When he had taken it, Elisha put his
hands on the king's hands.
17"Open the east window," he said,
and he opened it. "Shoot!" Elisha said,
and he shot. "The LORD's arrow of victory, the arrow of victory over Aram!"
Elisha declared. "You will completely
destroy the Arameans at Aphek."
18Then he said, "Take the arrows," and
the king took them. Elisha told him,
"Strike the ground." He struck it three
times and stopped. 19The man of God was
angry with him and said, "You should
have struck the ground five or six times;
then you would have defeated Aram
and completely destroyed it. But now
you will defeat it only three times."
20Elisha died and was buried.
Now Moabite raiders used to enter
the country every spring. 21Once while
some Israelites were burying a man,
suddenly they saw a band of raiders; so
they threw the man's body into Elisha's
tomb. When the body touched Elisha's
bones, the man came to life and stood
up on his feet.
22Hazael king of Aram oppressed Israel throughout the reign of Jehoahaz.
23But the LORD was gracious to them
and had compassion and showed concern for them because of his covenant
with Abraham, Isaac and Jacob. To this
day he has been unwilling to destroy
them or banish them from his presence.
24Hazael king of Aram died, and Ben-
Hadad his son succeeded him as king.
25Then Jehoash son of Jehoahaz recap-
tured from Ben-Hadad son of Hazael
the towns he had taken in battle from
his father Jehoahaz. Three times Jehoash defeated him, and so he recovered
the Israelite towns.

Amaziah King of Judah

14 In the second year of Jehoash[a] son of Jehoahaz king
of Israel, Amaziah son of Joash king of
Judah began to reign. 2He was twenty-
five years old when he became king,
and he reigned in Jerusalem twenty-
nine years. His mother's name was Jehoaddin; she was from Jerusalem. 3He
did what was right in the eyes of the
LORD, but not as his father David had
done. In everything he followed the example of his father Joash. 4The high
places, however, were not removed; the
people continued to offer sacrifices and
burn incense there.
5After the kingdom was firmly in his
grasp, he executed the officials who had
murdered his father the king. 6Yet he did
not put the sons of the assassins to
death, in accordance with what is written in the Book of the Law of Moses
where the LORD commanded: "Fathers
shall not be put to death for their children, nor children put to death for their
fathers; each is to die for his own sins."[b]
7He was the one who defeated ten
thousand Edomites in the Valley of Salt
and captured Sela in battle, calling it
Joktheel, the name it has to this day.
8Then Amaziah sent messengers to
Jehoash son of Jehoahaz, the son of
Jehu, king of Israel, with the challenge:
"Come, meet me face to face."
9But Jehoash king of Israel replied to
Amaziah king of Judah: "A thistle in
Lebanon sent a message to a cedar in
Lebanon, 'Give your daughter to my
son in marriage.' Then a wild beast in
Lebanon came along and trampled the
thistle underfoot. 10You have indeed defeated Edom and now you are arrogant.
Glory in your victory, but stay at home!
Why ask for trouble and cause your
own downfall and that of Judah also?"
11Amaziah, however, would not listen,
so Jehoash king of Israel attacked. He
and Amaziah king of Judah faced each
other at Beth Shemesh in Judah. 12Judah
was routed by Israel, and every man
fled to his home. 13Jehoash king of Israel
captured Amaziah king of Judah, the
son of Joash, the son of Ahaziah, at Beth
Shemesh. Then Jehoash went to Jerusalem and broke down the wall of Jerusalem from the Ephraim Gate to the
Corner Gate—a section about six hundred feet long.[c] 14He took all the gold
and silver and all the articles found in

[a]1 Hebrew *Joash,* a variant of *Jehoash;* also in verses 13, 23 and 27 [b]6 Deut. 24:16
[c]13 Hebrew *four hundred cubits* (about 180 meters)

the temple of the LORD and in the treasuries of the royal palace. He also took
hostages and returned to Samaria.
15 As for the other events of the reign
of Jehoash, what he did and his achievements, including his war against Amaziah king of Judah, are they not written
in the book of the annals of the kings of
Israel? 16 Jehoash rested with his fathers
and was buried in Samaria with the
kings of Israel. And Jeroboam his son
succeeded him as king.
17 Amaziah son of Joash king of Judah
lived for fifteen years after the death of
Jehoash son of Jehoahaz king of Israel.
18 As for the other events of Amaziah's
reign, are they not written in the book
of the annals of the kings of Judah?
19 They conspired against him in Jerusalem, and he fled to Lachish, but they
sent men after him to Lachish and killed
him there. 20 He was brought back by
horse and was buried in Jerusalem with
his fathers, in the City of David.
21 Then all the people of Judah took
Azariah,[a] who was sixteen years old,
and made him king in place of his father
Amaziah. 22 He was the one who rebuilt
Elath and restored it to Judah after Amaziah rested with his fathers.

Jeroboam II King of Israel

23 In the fifteenth year of Amaziah son
of Joash king of Judah, Jeroboam son of
Jehoash king of Israel became king in
Samaria, and he reigned forty-one
years. 24 He did evil in the eyes of the
LORD and did not turn away from any
of the sins of Jeroboam son of Nebat,
which he had caused Israel to commit.
25 He was the one who restored the
boundaries of Israel from Lebo[b] Hamath
to the Sea of the Arabah,[c] in accordance
with the word of the LORD, the God of
Israel, spoken through his servant Jonah son of Amittai, the prophet from
Gath Hepher.
26 The LORD had seen how bitterly everyone in Israel, whether slave or free,
was suffering; there was no one to help
them. 27 And since the LORD had not said
he would blot out the name of Israel
from under heaven, he saved them by
the hand of Jeroboam son of Jehoash.
28 As for the other events of Jeroboam's reign, all he did, and his military
achievements, including how he recovered for Israel both Damascus and Hamath, which had belonged to Yaudi,[d]
are they not written in the book of the
annals of the kings of Israel? 29 Jeroboam
rested with his fathers, the kings of Israel. And Zechariah his son succeeded
him as king.

[a]21 Also called *Uzziah* [b]25 Or *from the entrance to* [c]25 That is, the Dead Sea [d]28 Or *Judah*

SHARPEN THE FOCUS

In an effort to feel secure, most countries of the world set up defense systems. Sophisticated radar. A network of spies world-wide. Submarines armed with nuclear warheads. Still, when we think it through, we know we're not secure. One terrorist with a death wish can defeat the most sophisticated security plan.

Jehoash (Joash) of Israel knew that. He despairs at Elisha's imminent death (2 Kings 13:14): "My father! My father! The chariots and horsemen of Israel!" Elisha's servant had seen God's angel army surround Elisha! Jehoash feared that if Elisha died, Israel would lose her true defense—the Lord's protecting care.

To what do you look for security? Your nation's armies? Your city's police force? Your family's history of sticking together? All these things come to us as God's gifts.

But in the end, our security rests in the One whose "chariots and horsemen" surrounded Elisha. We need never doubt His ability nor His willingness to help us. We see that power and that love in our Savior's cross and open tomb. Jesus Christ is, forever, our sure defense.

WEEK 32 • SATURDAY

2 Kings 15:1—16:20

The sad litany of idolatry continues in both Judah and Israel. The Lord continues to keep His word (2 Kings 15:8–12); His people continue to ignore it or, at best, to obey it only partially (2 Kings 15:3–4, 17–18). As you read 2 Kings 16, keep in mind God's command from Exodus 10:24–25. If time is short, focus on 2 Kings 16:10–20.

Azariah King of Judah

15 In the twenty-seventh year
of Jeroboam king of Israel,
Azariah son of Amaziah king of Judah
began to reign. 2 He was sixteen years
old when he became king, and he
reigned in Jerusalem fifty-two years. His
mother's name was Jecoliah; she was
from Jerusalem. 3 He did what was right
in the eyes of the LORD, just as his father
Amaziah had done. 4 The high places,
however, were not removed; the people
continued to offer sacrifices and burn
incense there.
5 The LORD afflicted the king with
leprosy[a] until the day he died, and he
lived in a separate house.[b] Jotham the
king's son had charge of the palace and
governed the people of the land.
6 As for the other events of Azariah's
reign, and all he did, are they not written in the book of the annals of the kings
of Judah? 7 Azariah rested with his fathers and was buried near them in the
City of David. And Jotham his son succeeded him as king.

Zechariah King of Israel

8 In the thirty-eighth year of Azariah
king of Judah, Zechariah son of Jeroboam became king of Israel in Samaria,
and he reigned six months. 9 He did evil
in the eyes of the LORD, as his fathers
had done. He did not turn away from
the sins of Jeroboam son of Nebat,
which he had caused Israel to commit.
10 Shallum son of Jabesh conspired
against Zechariah. He attacked him in
front of the people,[c] assassinated him
and succeeded him as king. 11 The other
events of Zechariah's reign are written
in the book of the annals of the kings of
Israel. 12 So the word of the LORD spoken
to Jehu was fulfilled: "Your descendants
will sit on the throne of Israel to the
fourth generation."[d]

Shallum King of Israel

13 Shallum son of Jabesh became king
in the thirty-ninth year of Uzziah king
of Judah, and he reigned in Samaria one
month. 14 Then Menahem son of Gadi
went from Tirzah up to Samaria. He attacked Shallum son of Jabesh in Samaria, assassinated him and succeeded him
as king.
15 The other events of Shallum's reign,
and the conspiracy he led, are written
in the book of the annals of the kings of
Israel.
16 At that time Menahem, starting out
from Tirzah, attacked Tiphsah and everyone in the city and its vicinity, because they refused to open their gates.
He sacked Tiphsah and ripped open all
the pregnant women.

Menahem King of Israel

17 In the thirty-ninth year of Azariah
king of Judah, Menahem son of Gadi became king of Israel, and he reigned in

[a]5 The Hebrew word was used for various diseases affecting the skin—not necessarily leprosy. [b]5 Or *in a house where he was relieved of responsibility* [c]10 Hebrew; some Septuagint manuscripts *in Ibleam* [d]12 2 Kings 10:30

Samaria ten years. [18]He did evil in the eyes of the LORD. During his entire reign he did not turn away from the sins of Jeroboam son of Nebat, which he had caused Israel to commit.

[19]Then Pul[a] king of Assyria invaded the land, and Menahem gave him a thousand talents[b] of silver to gain his support and strengthen his own hold on the kingdom. [20]Menahem exacted this money from Israel. Every wealthy man had to contribute fifty shekels[c] of silver to be given to the king of Assyria. So the king of Assyria withdrew and stayed in the land no longer.

[21]As for the other events of Menahem's reign, and all he did, are they not written in the book of the annals of the kings of Israel? [22]Menahem rested with his fathers. And Pekahiah his son succeeded him as king.

Pekahiah King of Israel

[23]In the fiftieth year of Azariah king of Judah, Pekahiah son of Menahem became king of Israel in Samaria, and he reigned two years. [24]Pekahiah did evil in the eyes of the LORD. He did not turn away from the sins of Jeroboam son of Nebat, which he had caused Israel to commit. [25]One of his chief officers, Pekah son of Remaliah, conspired against him. Taking fifty men of Gilead with him, he assassinated Pekahiah, along with Argob and Arieh, in the citadel of the royal palace at Samaria. So Pekah killed Pekahiah and succeeded him as king.

[26]The other events of Pekahiah's reign, and all he did, are written in the book of the annals of the kings of Israel.

Pekah King of Israel

[27]In the fifty-second year of Azariah king of Judah, Pekah son of Remaliah became king of Israel in Samaria, and he reigned twenty years. [28]He did evil in the eyes of the LORD. He did not turn away from the sins of Jeroboam son of Nebat, which he had caused Israel to commit.

[29]In the time of Pekah king of Israel, Tiglath-Pileser king of Assyria came and took Ijon, Abel Beth Maacah, Janoah, Kedesh and Hazor. He took Gilead and Galilee, including all the land of Naphtali, and deported the people to Assyria. [30]Then Hoshea son of Elah conspired against Pekah son of Remaliah. He attacked and assassinated him, and then succeeded him as king in the twentieth year of Jotham son of Uzziah.

[31]As for the other events of Pekah's reign, and all he did, are they not written in the book of the annals of the kings of Israel?

Jotham King of Judah

[32]In the second year of Pekah son of Remaliah king of Israel, Jotham son of Uzziah king of Judah began to reign. [33]He was twenty-five years old when he became king, and he reigned in Jerusalem sixteen years. His mother's name was Jerusha daughter of Zadok. [34]He did what was right in the eyes of the LORD, just as his father Uzziah had done. [35]The high places, however, were not removed; the people continued to offer sacrifices and burn incense there. Jotham rebuilt the Upper Gate of the temple of the LORD.

[36]As for the other events of Jotham's reign, and what he did, are they not written in the book of the annals of the kings of Judah? [37](In those days the LORD began to send Rezin king of Aram and Pekah son of Remaliah against Judah.) [38]Jotham rested with his fathers and was buried with them in the City of David, the city of his father. And Ahaz his son succeeded him as king.

Ahaz King of Judah

16 In the seventeenth year of Pekah son of Remaliah, Ahaz son of Jotham king of Judah began to reign. [2]Ahaz was twenty years old when he became king, and he reigned in Jerusalem sixteen years. Unlike David his father, he did not do what was right in the eyes of the LORD his God. [3]He

[a]*19* Also called *Tiglath-Pileser* [b]*19* That is, about 37 tons (about 34 metric tons) [c]*20* That is, about 1 1/4 pounds (about 0.6 kilogram)

walked in the ways of the kings of Israel and even sacrificed his son in[a] the fire, following the detestable ways of the nations the LORD had driven out before the Israelites. 4He offered sacrifices and burned incense at the high places, on the hilltops and under every spreading tree.

5Then Rezin king of Aram and Pekah son of Remaliah king of Israel marched up to fight against Jerusalem and besieged Ahaz, but they could not overpower him. 6At that time, Rezin king of Aram recovered Elath for Aram by driving out the men of Judah. Edomites then moved into Elath and have lived there to this day.

7Ahaz sent messengers to say to Tiglath-Pileser king of Assyria, "I am your servant and vassal. Come up and save me out of the hand of the king of Aram and of the king of Israel, who are attacking me." 8And Ahaz took the silver and gold found in the temple of the LORD and in the treasuries of the royal palace and sent it as a gift to the king of Assyria. 9The king of Assyria complied by attacking Damascus and capturing it. He deported its inhabitants to Kir and put Rezin to death.

10Then King Ahaz went to Damascus to meet Tiglath-Pileser king of Assyria. He saw an altar in Damascus and sent to Uriah the priest a sketch of the altar, with detailed plans for its construction. 11So Uriah the priest built an altar in accordance with all the plans that King Ahaz had sent from Damascus and finished it before King Ahaz returned. 12When the king came back from Damascus and saw the altar, he approached it and presented offerings[b] on it. 13He offered up his burnt offering and grain offering, poured out his drink offering, and sprinkled the blood of his fellowship offerings[c] on the altar. 14The bronze altar that stood before the LORD he brought from the front of the temple—from between the new altar and the temple of the LORD—and put it on the north side of the new altar.

15King Ahaz then gave these orders to Uriah the priest: "On the large new altar, offer the morning burnt offering and the evening grain offering, the king's burnt offering and his grain offering, and the burnt offering of all the people of the land, and their grain offering and their drink offering. Sprinkle on the altar all the blood of the burnt offerings and sacrifices. But I will use the bronze altar for seeking guidance." 16And Uriah the priest did just as King Ahaz had ordered.

17King Ahaz took away the side panels and removed the basins from the movable stands. He removed the Sea from the bronze bulls that supported it and set it on a stone base. 18He took away the Sabbath canopy[d] that had been built at the temple and removed the royal entryway outside the temple of the LORD, in deference to the king of Assyria.

19As for the other events of the reign of Ahaz, and what he did, are they not written in the book of the annals of the kings of Judah? 20Ahaz rested with his fathers and was buried with them in the City of David. And Hezekiah his son succeeded him as king.

[a]3 Or *even made his son pass through* [b]12 Or *and went up* [c]13 Traditionally *peace offerings* [d]18 Or *the dais of his throne* (see Septuagint)

SHARPEN THE FOCUS

The Lord places great importance on worship, because He cares so much about our relationship with Him. He comes to meet with us during our times of worship to strengthen that relationship.

That's why the phony altar of Ahaz (2 Kings 16:10–16) was such an abomination. From earliest times the Lord had told His people not to craft elaborate altars for their sacrifices. He didn't want them to believe that their effort, skill, or diligence earned His favor. They approached His throne by His gracc. He welcomed them because of His tender mercy.

We approach our Lord on the same basis. Not because we've taught Sunday school for 30 years. Not because the choir would fall apart without us. Not because the money we give covers half the pastor's salary. All these things, offered in thanksgiving, do honor and please Him. But if we mingle our gifts or service with self-righteousness or spiritual pride, we sin Ahaz's sin—idolatry.

That's why we praise God for another altar, the cross on which our Savior willingly offered up His life for us. Through His sacrifice we have been cleansed from all sin to become the Lord's holy priests. Let that gift stir your heart to deeper worship.

WEEK 33 • MONDAY

2 Kings 17:1–41

Throughout most of Old Testament history, when nations attacked one another the loser paid the winner tribute. Assyria changed all that. When Assyria won a war, Assyria's army rounded up the population and forcibly relocated them in another land. Virtually the whole nation became prisoners of war. As you read today, count the formal charges the righteous Judge makes against His people, Israel. If time is short, focus on 2 Kings 17:7–23.

Hoshea Last King of Israel

17 In the twelfth year of Ahaz
king of Judah, Hoshea son of
Elah became king of Israel in Samaria,
and he reigned nine years. [2]He did evil
in the eyes of the LORD, but not like the
kings of Israel who preceded him.
[3]Shalmaneser king of Assyria came up
to attack Hoshea, who had been Shalmaneser's vassal and had paid him tribute. [4]But the king of Assyria discovered
that Hoshea was a traitor, for he had
sent envoys to So[a] king of Egypt, and he
no longer paid tribute to the king of
Assyria, as he had done year by year.
Therefore Shalmaneser seized him and
put him in prison. [5]The king of Assyria
invaded the entire land, marched
against Samaria and laid siege to it for
three years. [6]In the ninth year of Hoshea, the king of Assyria captured Samaria and deported the Israelites to
Assyria. He settled them in Halah, in
Gozan on the Habor River and in the
towns of the Medes.

Israel Exiled Because of Sin

[7]All this took place because the Israelites had sinned against the LORD their
God, who had brought them up out of
Egypt from under the power of Pharaoh
king of Egypt. They worshiped other
gods [8]and followed the practices of the
nations the LORD had driven out before
them, as well as the practices that the
kings of Israel had introduced. [9]The Israelites secretly did things against the
LORD their God that were not right.
From watchtower to fortified city they
built themselves high places in all their
towns. [10]They set up sacred stones and
Asherah poles on every high hill and

[a]4 Or *to Sais, to the; So* is possibly an abbreviation for *Osorkon*.

under every spreading tree. 11At every
high place they burned incense, as the
nations whom the LORD had driven out
before them had done. They did wicked
things that provoked the LORD to anger.
12They worshiped idols, though the
LORD had said, "You shall not do this."[a]
13The LORD warned Israel and Judah
through all his prophets and seers:
"Turn from your evil ways. Observe my
commands and decrees, in accordance
with the entire Law that I commanded
your fathers to obey and that I delivered
to you through my servants the prophets."
14But they would not listen and were
as stiff-necked as their fathers, who did
not trust in the LORD their God. 15They
rejected his decrees and the covenant he
had made with their fathers and the
warnings he had given them. They followed worthless idols and themselves
became worthless. They imitated the
nations around them although the
LORD had ordered them, "Do not do as
they do," and they did the things the
LORD had forbidden them to do.
16They forsook all the commands of
the LORD their God and made for
themselves two idols cast in the shape
of calves, and an Asherah pole. They
bowed down to all the starry hosts, and
they worshiped Baal. 17They sacrificed
their sons and daughters in[b] the fire.
They practiced divination and sorcery
and sold themselves to do evil in the
eyes of the LORD, provoking him to anger.
18So the LORD was very angry with Israel and removed them from his presence. Only the tribe of Judah was left,
19and even Judah did not keep the commands of the LORD their God. They
followed the practices Israel had introduced. 20Therefore the LORD rejected all
the people of Israel; he afflicted them
and gave them into the hands of plunderers, until he thrust them from his
presence.
21When he tore Israel away from the
house of David, they made Jeroboam
son of Nebat their king. Jeroboam enticed Israel away from following the
LORD and caused them to commit a
great sin. 22The Israelites persisted in all
the sins of Jeroboam and did not turn
away from them 23until the LORD removed them from his presence, as he
had warned through all his servants the
prophets. So the people of Israel were
taken from their homeland into exile in
Assyria, and they are still there.

Samaria Resettled

24The king of Assyria brought people
from Babylon, Cuthah, Avva, Hamath
and Sepharvaim and settled them in the
towns of Samaria to replace the Israelites. They took over Samaria and lived
in its towns. 25When they first lived
there, they did not worship the LORD;
so he sent lions among them and they
killed some of the people. 26It was reported to the king of Assyria: "The
people you deported and resettled in
the towns of Samaria do not know what
the god of that country requires. He has
sent lions among them, which are killing them off, because the people do not
know what he requires."
27Then the king of Assyria gave this
order: "Have one of the priests you took
captive from Samaria go back to live
there and teach the people what the god
of the land requires." 28So one of the
priests who had been exiled from Samaria came to live in Bethel and taught
them how to worship the LORD.
29Nevertheless, each national group
made its own gods in the several towns
where they settled, and set them up in
the shrines the people of Samaria had
made at the high places. 30The men from
Babylon made Succoth Benoth, the men
from Cuthah made Nergal, and the men
from Hamath made Ashima; 31the Avvites made Nibhaz and Tartak, and the
Sepharvites burned their children in the
fire as sacrifices to Adrammelech and
Anammelech, the gods of Sepharvaim.
32They worshiped the LORD, but they
also appointed all sorts of their own
people to officiate for them as priests in

[a]12 Exodus 20:4, 5 [b]17 Or *They made their sons and daughters pass through*

the shrines at the high places. [33]They
worshiped the LORD, but they also
served their own gods in accordance
with the customs of the nations from
which they had been brought.
[34]To this day they persist in their former practices. They neither worship the
LORD nor adhere to the decrees and ordinances, the laws and commands that
the LORD gave the descendants of Jacob,
whom he named Israel. [35]When the
LORD made a covenant with the Israelites, he commanded them: "Do not worship any other gods or bow down to
them, serve them or sacrifice to them.
[36]But the LORD, who brought you up out
of Egypt with mighty power and outstretched arm, is the one you must worship. To him you shall bow down and to
him offer sacrifices. [37]You must always
be careful to keep the decrees and ordinances, the laws and commands he
wrote for you. Do not worship other
gods. [38]Do not forget the covenant I
have made with you, and do not worship other gods. [39]Rather, worship the
LORD your God; it is he who will deliver you from the hand of all your
enemies."
[40]They would not listen, however, but
persisted in their former practices.
[41]Even while these people were worshiping the LORD, they were serving
their idols. To this day their children and
grandchildren continue to do as their
fathers did.

SHARPEN THE FOCUS

Suppose your Lord would indict you as He indicted ancient Israel. Suppose He were to spell out the specific charges against you. What would His indictment include?

If you find yourself shuddering, think again. Remember the Good News of Romans 8:1? "Therefore, there is now no condemnation for those who are in Christ Jesus." Your page in heaven's hall of records contains no charges at all. The record has been expunged.

But that doesn't mean your page is blank. Actually, your file is quite full—full of the record of righteous acts you have, by the grace of Christ, had the privilege of doing. Paul reminds us:

> *We are God's workmanship, created in Christ Jesus to do good works, which God prepared in advance for us to do.* (Ephesians 2:10)

The word "workmanship" was used in classical Greek to mean "poem." Your life is now, in Christ, a poem of praise to your Savior-God. He sees your love, your faith, your witness, and He smiles the smile of a father pleased with his child. Is that hard for you to believe? Then ask the Holy Spirit to deepen your appreciation for His grace toward you in Christ. ☼

WEEK 33 • TUESDAY

2 Kings 18:1—19:37

GET THE BIG PICTURE

Today's narrative is so rich, it deserves a second reading. (And you will read it again—in Isaiah 36–37.) As you read, note the battle that plays itself out on two planes—on earth and in heaven. And note the outcome of that battle as you pray, in your own circumstances, a prayer similar to Hezekiah's prayer in 2 Kings 19:19. If time is short, focus on 2 Kings 18:5–16.

Hezekiah King of Judah

18 In the third year of Hoshea son of Elah king of Israel, Hezekiah son of Ahaz king of Judah began to reign.
2He was twenty-five years old when he became king, and he reigned in Jerusalem twenty-nine years. His mother's name was Abijah[a] daughter of Zechariah.
3He did what was right in the eyes of the LORD, just as his father David had done.
4He removed the high places, smashed the sacred stones and cut down the Asherah poles. He broke into pieces the bronze snake Moses had made, for up to that time the Israelites had been burning incense to it. (It was called[b] Nehushtan.[c])

5Hezekiah trusted in the LORD, the God of Israel. There was no one like him among all the kings of Judah, either before him or after him.
6He held fast to the LORD and did not cease to follow him; he kept the commands the LORD had given Moses.
7And the LORD was with him; he was successful in whatever he undertook. He rebelled against the king of Assyria and did not serve him.
8From watchtower to fortified city, he defeated the Philistines, as far as Gaza and its territory.

9In King Hezekiah's fourth year, which was the seventh year of Hoshea son of Elah king of Israel, Shalmaneser king of Assyria marched against Samaria and laid siege to it.
10At the end of three years the Assyrians took it. So Samaria was captured in Hezekiah's sixth year, which was the ninth year of Hoshea king of Israel.
11The king of Assyria deported Israel to Assyria and settled them in Halah, in Gozan on the Habor River and in towns of the Medes.
12This happened because they had not obeyed the LORD their God, but had violated his covenant—all that Moses the servant of the LORD commanded. They neither listened to the commands nor carried them out.

13In the fourteenth year of King Hezekiah's reign, Sennacherib king of Assyria attacked all the fortified cities of Judah and captured them.
14So Hezekiah king of Judah sent this message to the king of Assyria at Lachish: "I have done wrong. Withdraw from me, and I will pay whatever you demand of me." The king of Assyria exacted from Hezekiah king of Judah three hundred talents[d] of silver and thirty talents[e] of gold.
15So Hezekiah gave him all the silver that was found in the temple of the LORD and in the treasuries of the royal palace.

16At this time Hezekiah king of Judah stripped off the gold with which he had covered the doors and doorposts of the temple of the LORD, and gave it to the king of Assyria.

Sennacherib Threatens Jerusalem

17The king of Assyria sent his supreme commander, his chief officer and his field commander with a large army, from Lachish to King Hezekiah at Jerusalem. They came up to Jerusalem and stopped at the aqueduct of the Upper Pool, on the road to the Washerman's Field.
18They called for the king; and Eliakim son of Hilkiah the palace administrator, Shebna the secretary, and Joah son of Asaph the recorder went out to them.

19The field commander said to them, "Tell Hezekiah:

> " 'This is what the great king, the king of Assyria, says: On what are you basing this confidence of yours?
> 20You say you have strategy and military strength—but you speak only empty words. On whom are you depending, that you rebel against me?
> 21Look now, you

[a]2 Hebrew *Abi,* a variant of *Abijah* [b]4 Or *He called it* [c]4 *Nehushtan* sounds like the Hebrew for *bronze* and *snake* and *unclean thing.*
[d]14 That is, about 11 tons (about 10 metric tons)
[e]14 That is, about 1 ton (about 1 metric ton)

are depending on Egypt, that splintered reed of a staff, which pierces
a man's hand and wounds him if
he leans on it! Such is Pharaoh king
of Egypt to all who depend on him.
22And if you say to me, "We are depending on the LORD our God"—
isn't he the one whose high places
and altars Hezekiah removed, saying to Judah and Jerusalem, "You
must worship before this altar in Jerusalem"?
23" 'Come now, make a bargain
with my master, the king of Assyria: I will give you two thousand
horses—if you can put riders on
them! 24How can you repulse one
officer of the least of my master's
officials, even though you are depending on Egypt for chariots and
horsemen[a]? 25Furthermore, have I
come to attack and destroy this
place without word from the
LORD? The LORD himself told me
to march against this country and
destroy it.' "

26Then Eliakim son of Hilkiah, and
Shebna and Joah said to the field commander, "Please speak to your servants
in Aramaic, since we understand it.
Don't speak to us in Hebrew in the hearing of the people on the wall."
27But the commander replied, "Was it
only to your master and you that my
master sent me to say these things, and
not to the men sitting on the wall—who,
like you, will have to eat their own filth
and drink their own urine?"
28Then the commander stood and
called out in Hebrew: "Hear the word of
the great king, the king of Assyria! 29This
is what the king says: Do not let Hezekiah deceive you. He cannot deliver you
from my hand. 30Do not let Hezekiah
persuade you to trust in the LORD when
he says, 'The LORD will surely deliver
us; this city will not be given into the
hand of the king of Assyria.'
31"Do not listen to Hezekiah. This is
what the king of Assyria says: Make
peace with me and come out to me.
Then every one of you will eat from his
own vine and fig tree and drink water
from his own cistern, 32until I come and
take you to a land like your own, a land
of grain and new wine, a land of bread
and vineyards, a land of olive trees and
honey. Choose life and not death!
"Do not listen to Hezekiah, for he is
misleading you when he says, 'The
LORD will deliver us.' 33Has the god of
any nation ever delivered his land from
the hand of the king of Assyria? 34Where
are the gods of Hamath and Arpad?
Where are the gods of Sepharvaim,
Hena and Ivvah? Have they rescued
Samaria from my hand? 35Who of all the
gods of these countries has been able to
save his land from me? How then can
the LORD deliver Jerusalem from my
hand?"
36But the people remained silent and
said nothing in reply, because the king
had commanded, "Do not answer him."
37Then Eliakim son of Hilkiah the palace administrator, Shebna the secretary
and Joah son of Asaph the recorder
went to Hezekiah, with their clothes
torn, and told him what the field commander had said.

Jerusalem's Deliverance Foretold

19 When King Hezekiah heard
this, he tore his clothes and
put on sackcloth and went into the
temple of the LORD. 2He sent Eliakim
the palace administrator, Shebna the
secretary and the leading priests, all
wearing sackcloth, to the prophet Isaiah
son of Amoz. 3They told him, "This is
what Hezekiah says: This day is a day
of distress and rebuke and disgrace, as
when children come to the point of
birth and there is no strength to deliver
them. 4It may be that the LORD your
God will hear all the words of the field
commander, whom his master, the king
of Assyria, has sent to ridicule the living
God, and that he will rebuke him for the
words the LORD your God has heard.
Therefore pray for the remnant that still
survives."
5When King Hezekiah's officials came

[a]24 Or *charioteers*

to Isaiah, [6]Isaiah said to them, "Tell your
master, 'This is what the LORD says: Do
not be afraid of what you have heard—
those words with which the underlings
of the king of Assyria have blasphemed
me. [7]Listen! I am going to put such a
spirit in him that when he hears a certain report, he will return to his own
country, and there I will have him cut
down with the sword.' "
[8]When the field commander heard
that the king of Assyria had left Lachish,
he withdrew and found the king fighting against Libnah.
[9]Now Sennacherib received a report
that Tirhakah, the Cushite[a] king ⌞of
Egypt⌟, was marching out to fight
against him. So he again sent messengers to Hezekiah with this word: [10]"Say
to Hezekiah king of Judah: Do not let
the god you depend on deceive you
when he says, 'Jerusalem will not be
handed over to the king of Assyria.'
[11]Surely you have heard what the kings
of Assyria have done to all the countries,
destroying them completely. And will
you be delivered? [12]Did the gods of the
nations that were destroyed by my forefathers deliver them: the gods of Gozan,
Haran, Rezeph and the people of Eden
who were in Tel Assar? [13]Where is the
king of Hamath, the king of Arpad, the
king of the city of Sepharvaim, or of
Hena or Ivvah?"

Hezekiah's Prayer

[14]Hezekiah received the letter from
the messengers and read it. Then he
went up to the temple of the LORD and
spread it out before the LORD. [15]And
Hezekiah prayed to the LORD: "O LORD,
God of Israel, enthroned between the
cherubim, you alone are God over all
the kingdoms of the earth. You have
made heaven and earth. [16]Give ear,
O LORD, and hear; open your eyes,
O LORD, and see; listen to the words
Sennacherib has sent to insult the living
God.
[17]"It is true, O LORD, that the Assyrian
kings have laid waste these nations and
their lands. [18]They have thrown their
gods into the fire and destroyed them,
for they were not gods but only wood
and stone, fashioned by men's hands.
[19]Now, O LORD our God, deliver us from
his hand, so that all kingdoms on earth
may know that you alone, O LORD, are
God."

Isaiah Prophesies Sennacherib's Fall

[20]Then Isaiah son of Amoz sent a message to Hezekiah: "This is what the
LORD, the God of Israel, says: I have
heard your prayer concerning Sennacherib king of Assyria. [21]This is the word
that the LORD has spoken against him:

" 'The Virgin Daughter of Zion
  despises you and mocks you.
The Daughter of Jerusalem
  tosses her head as you flee.
[22]Who is it you have insulted and
    blasphemed?
  Against whom have you raised
    your voice
and lifted your eyes in pride?
  Against the Holy One of Israel!
[23]By your messengers
  you have heaped insults on the
    Lord.
And you have said,
  "With my many chariots
I have ascended the heights of the
    mountains,
  the utmost heights of Lebanon.
I have cut down its tallest cedars,
  the choicest of its pines.
I have reached its remotest parts,
  the finest of its forests.
[24]I have dug wells in foreign lands
  and drunk the water there.
With the soles of my feet
  I have dried up all the streams of
    Egypt."

[25]" 'Have you not heard?
  Long ago I ordained it.
In days of old I planned it;
  now I have brought it to pass,
that you have turned fortified cities
  into piles of stone.
[26]Their people, drained of power,
  are dismayed and put to shame.
They are like plants in the field,

[a]9 That is, from the upper Nile region

like tender green shoots,
like grass sprouting on the roof,
scorched before it grows up.
27 " 'But I know where you stay
and when you come and go
and how you rage against me.
28 Because you rage against me
and your insolence has reached
my ears,
I will put my hook in your nose
and my bit in your mouth,
and I will make you return
by the way you came.'

29 "This will be the sign for you,
O Hezekiah:

"This year you will eat what grows
by itself,
and the second year what springs
from that.
But in the third year sow and reap,
plant vineyards and eat their
fruit.
30 Once more a remnant of the house
of Judah
will take root below and bear fruit
above.
31 For out of Jerusalem will come a
remnant,
and out of Mount Zion a band of
survivors.
The zeal of the LORD Almighty will accomplish this.

32 "Therefore this is what the LORD
says concerning the king of Assyria:

"He will not enter this city
or shoot an arrow here.
He will not come before it with
shield
or build a siege ramp against it.
33 By the way that he came he will
return;
he will not enter this city,
declares the LORD.
34 I will defend this city and save it,
for my sake and for the sake of
David my servant."

35 That night the angel of the LORD
went out and put to death a hundred
and eighty-five thousand men in the
Assyrian camp. When the people got up
the next morning—there were all the
dead bodies!
36 So Sennacherib king of
Assyria broke camp and withdrew. He
returned to Nineveh and stayed there.
37 One day, while he was worshiping
in the temple of his god Nisroch, his
sons Adrammelech and Sharezer cut
him down with the sword, and they
escaped to the land of Ararat. And Esarhaddon his son succeeded him as king.

SHARPEN THE FOCUS

Do you see the irony in the transition between 2 Kings 18:8 and 18:9? For the first time since the reign of David, Judah's king whole-heartedly obeyed God. The holy writer says: "He did what was right in the eyes of the LORD" (2 Kings 18:3). He did what was right–and, wham! Assyria attacked, demanding tribute. Then Assyria attacked again, demanding surrender.

What are we to make of this? Even if our life is running smoothly, it doesn't mean for certain that our walk with the Lord pleases Him in every respect. He may be blessing us with peace and prosperity to bring us to repentance! (Romans 2:4) But, if we've hit some bumps it doesn't mean for certain that our walk with the Lord has gotten off track. We may simply have attracted Satan's attention as Hezekiah surely did.

How *do* we then evaluate our Christian walk? By allowing the Holy Spirit to point out from Scripture anything in us that needs to be changed. And then by asking the Spirit to point us to Christ, the only source of pardon, and for power to make the changes that need to occur. If you haven't done so in awhile, pray Psalm 139:23–24 now. Then spend some time in your Lord's presence to be cleansed and re-empowered for His service.

WEEK 33 • WEDNESDAY

2 Kings 20:1–21

GET THE BIG PICTURE

Today's reading begins with another example of the deep prayer life the Lord gave King Hezekiah. As you read, think about the Lord's invitation to come to Him in prayer with all your needs. How confident are you in His willingness to hear and respond? If time is short, focus on 2 Kings 20:1–11.

Hezekiah's Illness

20 In those days Hezekiah
became ill and was at the
point of death. The prophet Isaiah son
of Amoz went to him and said, "This is
what the LORD says: Put your house in
order, because you are going to die; you
will not recover."
2 Hezekiah turned his face to the wall
and prayed to the LORD, 3 "Remember,
O LORD, how I have walked before you
faithfully and with wholehearted devotion and have done what is good in your
eyes." And Hezekiah wept bitterly.
4 Before Isaiah had left the middle
court, the word of the LORD came to
him: 5 "Go back and tell Hezekiah, the
leader of my people, 'This is what the
LORD, the God of your father David,
says: I have heard your prayer and seen
your tears; I will heal you. On the third
day from now you will go up to the
temple of the LORD. 6 I will add fifteen
years to your life. And I will deliver you
and this city from the hand of the king
of Assyria. I will defend this city for my
sake and for the sake of my servant
David.'"
7 Then Isaiah said, "Prepare a poultice
of figs." They did so and applied it to the
boil, and he recovered.
8 Hezekiah had asked Isaiah, "What
will be the sign that the LORD will heal
me and that I will go up to the temple
of the LORD on the third day from
now?"
9 Isaiah answered, "This is the LORD's
sign to you that the LORD will do what
he has promised: Shall the shadow go
forward ten steps, or shall it go back ten
steps?"
10 "It is a simple matter for the shadow
to go forward ten steps," said Hezekiah.
"Rather, have it go back ten steps."
11 Then the prophet Isaiah called upon
the LORD, and the LORD made the
shadow go back the ten steps it had
gone down on the stairway of Ahaz.

Envoys From Babylon

12 At that time Merodach-Baladan son
of Baladan king of Babylon sent Hezekiah letters and a gift, because he had
heard of Hezekiah's illness. 13 Hezekiah
received the messengers and showed
them all that was in his storehouses—
the silver, the gold, the spices and the
fine oil—his armory and everything
found among his treasures. There was
nothing in his palace or in all his
kingdom that Hezekiah did not show
them.
14 Then Isaiah the prophet went to
King Hezekiah and asked, "What did
those men say, and where did they
come from?"
"From a distant land," Hezekiah replied. "They came from Babylon."
15 The prophet asked, "What did they
see in your palace?"
"They saw everything in my palace,"
Hezekiah said. "There is nothing among
my treasures that I did not show them."
16 Then Isaiah said to Hezekiah, "Hear

the word of the LORD: 17The time will
surely come when everything in your
palace, and all that your fathers have
stored up until this day, will be carried
off to Babylon. Nothing will be left, says
the LORD. 18And some of your descendants, your own flesh and blood, that
will be born to you, will be taken away,
and they will become eunuchs in the
palace of the king of Babylon."
19"The word of the LORD you have
spoken is good," Hezekiah replied. For
he thought, "Will there not be peace and
security in my lifetime?"
20As for the other events of Hezekiah's
reign, all his achievements and how he
made the pool and the tunnel by which
he brought water into the city, are they
not written in the book of the annals of
the kings of Judah? 21Hezekiah rested
with his fathers. And Manasseh his son
succeeded him as king.

SHARPEN THE FOCUS

One of the cardinal rules of customer satisfaction: *Always give customers more than they expect to get.* Getting more than we expect pleases us and it's good business. Companies that are best at it do it because the people there genuinely care about their customers.

Consider Hezekiah's prayer and the Lord's reply. The king came to God distraught, but before he left God's presence, the Lord had given Isaiah His answer. Hezekiah would fully recover in only 3 days. And the Lord would add 15 years to his life. And God would defend him and His people from the Assyrian threat. And to illustrate His power to keep His promise, the shadow on the sundial would move backward 10 degrees.

The Lord will still move heaven and earth for the good of His children. But even so, sometimes, we pray, "Thy will be done," fatalistically. We expect the worst, or at least, something less than the best.

But the best is exactly what God wants for you. If you doubt that, look toward Calvary. God gave His one and only Son into death—for you! Since He gave His best, He won't withhold the rest. His will for you is gracious, good, and perfect. You can trust that gracious will today.

WEEK 33 • THURSDAY

2 Kings 21:1–26

GET THE BIG PICTURE

The trouble with cleaning house or caring for a lawn is that the job is never finished. Just about the time you think it is, the dust settles or the grass grows, seemingly overnight. As you read today, you'll see that King Hezekiah's spiritual "housecleaning" was short-lived. As you read, notice how thorough Judah's relapse was. If time is short, focus on 2 Kings 21:1–16.

Manasseh King of Judah

21 Manasseh was twelve years
old when he became king,
and he reigned in Jerusalem fifty-five
years. His mother's name was Hephzibah. 2He did evil in the eyes of the LORD,
following the detestable practices of the
nations the LORD had driven out before

the Israelites. 3He rebuilt the high places
his father Hezekiah had destroyed; he
also erected altars to Baal and made an
Asherah pole, as Ahab king of Israel had
done. He bowed down to all the starry
hosts and worshiped them. 4He built altars in the temple of the LORD, of which
the LORD had said, "In Jerusalem I will
put my Name." 5In both courts of the
temple of the LORD, he built altars to all
the starry hosts. 6He sacrificed his own
son in[a] the fire, practiced sorcery and
divination, and consulted mediums and
spiritists. He did much evil in the eyes
of the LORD, provoking him to anger.
7He took the carved Asherah pole he
had made and put it in the temple, of
which the LORD had said to David and
to his son Solomon, "In this temple and
in Jerusalem, which I have chosen out
of all the tribes of Israel, I will put my
Name forever. 8I will not again make the
feet of the Israelites wander from the
land I gave their forefathers, if only they
will be careful to do everything I commanded them and will keep the whole
Law that my servant Moses gave them."
9But the people did not listen. Manasseh
led them astray, so that they did more
evil than the nations the LORD had destroyed before the Israelites.
10The LORD said through his servants
the prophets: 11"Manasseh king of Judah has committed these detestable
sins. He has done more evil than the
Amorites who preceded him and has
led Judah into sin with his idols. 12There-
fore this is what the LORD, the God of
Israel, says: I am going to bring such disaster on Jerusalem and Judah that the
ears of everyone who hears of it will
tingle. 13I will stretch out over Jerusalem
the measuring line used against Samaria and the plumb line used against the
house of Ahab. I will wipe out Jerusalem
as one wipes a dish, wiping it and turning it upside down. 14I will forsake the
remnant of my inheritance and hand
them over to their enemies. They will be
looted and plundered by all their foes,
15because they have done evil in my
eyes and have provoked me to anger
from the day their forefathers came out
of Egypt until this day."
16Moreover, Manasseh also shed so
much innocent blood that he filled Jerusalem from end to end—besides the
sin that he had caused Judah to commit,
so that they did evil in the eyes of the
LORD.
17As for the other events of Manasseh's reign, and all he did, including the
sin he committed, are they not written
in the book of the annals of the kings of
Judah? 18Manasseh rested with his fathers and was buried in his palace garden, the garden of Uzza. And Amon his
son succeeded him as king.

Amon King of Judah

19Amon was twenty-two years old
when he became king, and he reigned
in Jerusalem two years. His mother's
name was Meshullemeth daughter of
Haruz; she was from Jotbah. 20He did
evil in the eyes of the LORD, as his father
Manasseh had done. 21He walked in all
the ways of his father; he worshiped the
idols his father had worshiped, and
bowed down to them. 22He forsook the
LORD, the God of his fathers, and did
not walk in the way of the LORD.
23Amon's officials conspired against
him and assassinated the king in his palace. 24Then the people of the land killed
all who had plotted against King Amon,
and they made Josiah his son king in his
place.
25As for the other events of Amon's
reign, and what he did, are they not
written in the book of the annals of the
kings of Judah? 26He was buried in his
grave in the garden of Uzza. And Josiah his son succeeded him as king.

[a]6 Or *He made his own son pass through*

SHARPEN THE FOCUS

Have you ever played "Crack the Whip"? In this game, children hold hands in a long line and run wherever the lead child takes them. At times the leader increases speed and then suddenly changes directions. The child at the end of the line finds herself jerked and whipped violently by centripetal force.

During the reigns of Hezekiah, Manasseh, Amon, and Josiah the people of Judah found themselves whip-sawed by the spiritual forces around them. Reformations began and were revoked. Godly rulers removed the sites of idol worship; ungodly rulers reinstated them.

Elijah's challenge (1 Kings 18:21) to Israel in the north surely fit Judah in the south as well: "How long will you waver between two opinions? If the LORD is God, follow Him; but if Baal is God, follow him." Judah, like Israel before her, had become spiritually rootless. Not firmly anchored in the Word of God, the people drifted in whichever direction the political wind was blowing.

Our Lord wants His people to be "rooted and established" in our Savior's love for us (Ephesians 3:17). When that happens, by His grace at work in us through His Word, we can stand firm against the temptations to drift or to doubt.

WEEK 33 • FRIDAY

2 Kings 22:1—23:37

GET THE BIG PICTURE

Josiah, about whom you will read today, was the last of Judah's godly rulers. He wanted—with all his heart—to bring his people to true repentance. But by this point, the people had sealed their own fate. Their idolatrous hearts had hardened. As you read today, think about this truth: "It is a dreadful thing to fall into the hands of the living God" (Hebrews 10:31). If time is short, focus on 2 Kings 22:1–20.

The Book of the Law Found

22 Josiah was eight years old
when he became king,
and he reigned in Jerusalem thirty-one
years. His mother's name was Jedidah
daughter of Adaiah; she was from Bozkath. 2He did what was right in the eyes
of the LORD and walked in all the ways
of his father David, not turning aside to
the right or to the left.
3In the eighteenth year of his reign,
King Josiah sent the secretary, Shaphan
son of Azaliah, the son of Meshullam, to
the temple of the LORD. He said: 4"Go up
to Hilkiah the high priest and have him
get ready the money that has been
brought into the temple of the LORD,
which the doorkeepers have collected
from the people. 5Have them entrust it to
the men appointed to supervise the
work on the temple. And have these men
pay the workers who repair the temple
of the LORD— 6the carpenters, the builders and the masons. Also have them
purchase timber and dressed stone to repair the temple. 7But they need not account for the money entrusted to them,
because they are acting faithfully."

8 Hilkiah the high priest said to Shaphan the secretary, "I have found the
Book of the Law in the temple of the
LORD." He gave it to Shaphan, who read
it. 9 Then Shaphan the secretary went to
the king and reported to him: "Your officials have paid out the money that was
in the temple of the LORD and have entrusted it to the workers and supervisors at the temple." 10 Then Shaphan the
secretary informed the king, "Hilkiah
the priest has given me a book." And
Shaphan read from it in the presence of
the king.
11 When the king heard the words of
the Book of the Law, he tore his robes.
12 He gave these orders to Hilkiah the
priest, Ahikam son of Shaphan, Acbor
son of Micaiah, Shaphan the secretary
and Asaiah the king's attendant: 13 "Go
and inquire of the LORD for me and for
the people and for all Judah about what
is written in this book that has been
found. Great is the LORD's anger that
burns against us because our fathers
have not obeyed the words of this book;
they have not acted in accordance with
all that is written there concerning us."
14 Hilkiah the priest, Ahikam, Acbor,
Shaphan and Asaiah went to speak to
the prophetess Huldah, who was the
wife of Shallum son of Tikvah, the son
of Harhas, keeper of the wardrobe. She
lived in Jerusalem, in the Second District.
15 She said to them, "This is what the
LORD, the God of Israel, says: Tell the
man who sent you to me, 16 'This is what
the LORD says: I am going to bring disaster on this place and its people, according to everything written in the
book the king of Judah has read. 17 Because they have forsaken me and
burned incense to other gods and provoked me to anger by all the idols their
hands have made,[a] my anger will burn
against this place and will not be
quenched.' 18 Tell the king of Judah, who
sent you to inquire of the LORD, 'This is
what the LORD, the God of Israel, says
concerning the words you heard: 19 Because your heart was responsive and
you humbled yourself before the LORD
when you heard what I have spoken
against this place and its people, that
they would become accursed and laid
waste, and because you tore your robes
and wept in my presence, I have heard
you, declares the LORD. 20 Therefore I
will gather you to your fathers, and you
will be buried in peace. Your eyes will
not see all the disaster I am going to
bring on this place.'"
So they took her answer back to the
king.

Josiah Renews the Covenant

23 Then the king called together all the elders of Ju-
dah and Jerusalem. 2 He went up to the
temple of the LORD with the men of Judah, the people of Jerusalem, the priests
and the prophets—all the people from
the least to the greatest. He read in their
hearing all the words of the Book of the
Covenant, which had been found in the
temple of the LORD. 3 The king stood by
the pillar and renewed the covenant in
the presence of the LORD—to follow the
LORD and keep his commands, regulations and decrees with all his heart and
all his soul, thus confirming the words
of the covenant written in this book.
Then all the people pledged themselves
to the covenant.
4 The king ordered Hilkiah the high
priest, the priests next in rank and the
doorkeepers to remove from the temple
of the LORD all the articles made for Baal
and Asherah and all the starry hosts. He
burned them outside Jerusalem in the
fields of the Kidron Valley and took the
ashes to Bethel. 5 He did away with the
pagan priests appointed by the kings of
Judah to burn incense on the high
places of the towns of Judah and on
those around Jerusalem—those who
burned incense to Baal, to the sun and
moon, to the constellations and to all the
starry hosts. 6 He took the Asherah pole
from the temple of the LORD to the
Kidron Valley outside Jerusalem and
burned it there. He ground it to powder
and scattered the dust over the graves

[a]17 Or *by everything they have done*

of the common people. [7]He also tore
down the quarters of the male shrine
prostitutes, which were in the temple of
the LORD and where women did weav-
ing for Asherah.
[8]Josiah brought all the priests from
the towns of Judah and desecrated the
high places, from Geba to Beersheba,
where the priests had burned incense.
He broke down the shrines[a] at the
gates—at the entrance to the Gate of
Joshua, the city governor, which is on
the left of the city gate. [9]Although the
priests of the high places did not serve
at the altar of the LORD in Jerusalem,
they ate unleavened bread with their
fellow priests.
[10]He desecrated Topheth, which was
in the Valley of Ben Hinnom, so no one
could use it to sacrifice his son or daughter in[b] the fire to Molech. [11]He removed
from the entrance to the temple of the
LORD the horses that the kings of Judah
had dedicated to the sun. They were in
the court near the room of an official
named Nathan-Melech. Josiah then
burned the chariots dedicated to the
sun.
[12]He pulled down the altars the kings
of Judah had erected on the roof near
the upper room of Ahaz, and the altars
Manasseh had built in the two courts of
the temple of the LORD. He removed
them from there, smashed them to
pieces and threw the rubble into the
Kidron Valley. [13]The king also desecrated the high places that were east of Jerusalem on the south of the Hill of
Corruption—the ones Solomon king of
Israel had built for Ashtoreth the vile
goddess of the Sidonians, for Chemosh
the vile god of Moab, and for Molech[c]
the detestable god of the people of
Ammon. [14]Josiah smashed the sacred
stones and cut down the Asherah poles
and covered the sites with human
bones.
[15]Even the altar at Bethel, the high
place made by Jeroboam son of Nebat,
who had caused Israel to sin—even that
altar and high place he demolished. He
burned the high place and ground it to
powder, and burned the Asherah pole
also. [16]Then Josiah looked around, and
when he saw the tombs that were there
on the hillside, he had the bones removed from them and burned on the
altar to defile it, in accordance with
the word of the LORD proclaimed by
the man of God who foretold these
things.
[17]The king asked, "What is that tomb-
stone I see?"
The men of the city said, "It marks the
tomb of the man of God who came from
Judah and pronounced against the altar
of Bethel the very things you have done
to it."
[18]"Leave it alone," he said. "Don't let
anyone disturb his bones." So they
spared his bones and those of the
prophet who had come from Samaria.
[19]Just as he had done at Bethel, Josiah
removed and defiled all the shrines at
the high places that the kings of Israel
had built in the towns of Samaria that
had provoked the LORD to anger. [20]Josi-
ah slaughtered all the priests of those
high places on the altars and burned
human bones on them. Then he went
back to Jerusalem.
[21]The king gave this order to all the
people: "Celebrate the Passover to the
LORD your God, as it is written in this
Book of the Covenant." [22]Not since the
days of the judges who led Israel, nor
throughout the days of the kings of Israel and the kings of Judah, had any
such Passover been observed. [23]But in
the eighteenth year of King Josiah, this
Passover was celebrated to the LORD in
Jerusalem.
[24]Furthermore, Josiah got rid of the
mediums and spiritists, the household
gods, the idols and all the other detestable things seen in Judah and Jerusalem. This he did to fulfill the
requirements of the law written in the
book that Hilkiah the priest had discovered in the temple of the LORD. [25]Nei-
ther before nor after Josiah was there a
king like him who turned to the LORD
as he did—with all his heart and with all

[a]8 Or *high places* [b]10 Or *to make his son or daughter pass through* [c]13 Hebrew *Milcom*

his soul and with all his strength, in accordance with all the Law of Moses.

[26]Nevertheless, the LORD did not turn away from the heat of his fierce anger, which burned against Judah because of all that Manasseh had done to provoke him to anger. [27]So the LORD said, "I will remove Judah also from my presence as I removed Israel, and I will reject Jerusalem, the city I chose, and this temple, about which I said, 'There shall my Name be.'[a]"

[28]As for the other events of Josiah's reign, and all he did, are they not written in the book of the annals of the kings of Judah?

[29]While Josiah was king, Pharaoh Neco king of Egypt went up to the Euphrates River to help the king of Assyria. King Josiah marched out to meet him in battle, but Neco faced him and killed him at Megiddo. [30]Josiah's servants brought his body in a chariot from Megiddo to Jerusalem and buried him in his own tomb. And the people of the land took Jehoahaz son of Josiah and anointed him and made him king in place of his father.

Jehoahaz King of Judah

[31]Jehoahaz was twenty-three years old when he became king, and he reigned in Jerusalem three months. His mother's name was Hamutal daughter of Jeremiah; she was from Libnah. [32]He did evil in the eyes of the LORD, just as his fathers had done. [33]Pharaoh Neco put him in chains at Riblah in the land of Hamath[b] so that he might not reign in Jerusalem, and he imposed on Judah a levy of a hundred talents[c] of silver and a talent[d] of gold. [34]Pharaoh Neco made Eliakim son of Josiah king in place of his father Josiah and changed Eliakim's name to Jehoiakim. But he took Jehoahaz and carried him off to Egypt, and there he died. [35]Jehoiakim paid Pharaoh Neco the silver and gold he demanded. In order to do so, he taxed the land and exacted the silver and gold from the people of the land according to their assessments.

Jehoiakim King of Judah

[36]Jehoiakim was twenty-five years old when he became king, and he reigned in Jerusalem eleven years. His mother's name was Zebidah daughter of Pedaiah; she was from Rumah. [37]And he did evil in the eyes of the LORD, just as his fathers had done.

[a]27 1 Kings 8:29 [b]33 Hebrew; Septuagint (see also 2 Chron. 36:3) *Neco at Riblah in Hamath removed him* [c]33 That is, about 3 3/4 tons (about 3.4 metric tons) [d]33 That is, about 75 pounds (about 34 kilograms)

SHARPEN THE FOCUS

"It's all in the Lord's hands." Some people say these words in resignation. Some say them in hope and confidence. Judah was about to fall into those hands. And it was for the nation a dreadful thing. The Lord is a God of justice. The living God judges sin.

Isaiah called this the Lord's foreign or "alien" work (Isaiah 28:21). Why? Because He longs to show mercy to sinners. His anger at the impenitent is the anger of grief. For centuries, He opened His heart and His arms wide to Judah. He commanded, invited, urged, and warned them to come to Him in penitent faith. He withdrew His protection so that perhaps their need would drive them back to Him. All to no avail. When Josiah died, his reforms died with him.

The writer to the Hebrews got it right. It *is* a dreadful thing for sinners to fall into the hands of the living God. But those who have received from the living God a tender, repentant heart, have nothing to fear. We remember the nail prints that still today scar the hands of our Lord Jesus, and we gladly throw ourselves and all we have into those hands—the hands of mercy.

WEEK 33 • SATURDAY

2 Kings 24:1—25:30

GET THE BIG PICTURE

As 2 Kings 25 begins, Jerusalem is under siege and about to fall. This disaster comes at the end of a series of trend-setting events: Jehoiakim's refusal to pay Nebuchadnezzar's tribute (2 Kings 24:1–4); Egypt's refusal to enter into an alliance to protect Judah (2 Kings 24:5–7); and previous deportation of Judah's "best and brightest" (2 Kings 24:8–20). If time is short, focus on 2 Kings 25:1–30.

24 During Jehoiakim's reign,
Nebuchadnezzar king of
Babylon invaded the land, and Jehoiakim became his vassal for three years.
But then he changed his mind and rebelled against Nebuchadnezzar. [2]The
LORD sent Babylonian,[a] Aramean, Moabite and Ammonite raiders against
him. He sent them to destroy Judah, in
accordance with the word of the LORD
proclaimed by his servants the prophets. [3]Surely these things happened to
Judah according to the LORD's command, in order to remove them from his
presence because of the sins of Manasseh and all he had done, [4]including the
shedding of innocent blood. For he had
filled Jerusalem with innocent blood,
and the LORD was not willing to forgive.
[5]As for the other events of Jehoiakim's
reign, and all he did, are they not written in the book of the annals of the kings
of Judah? [6]Jehoiakim rested with his fathers. And Jehoiachin his son succeeded him as king.
[7]The king of Egypt did not march out
from his own country again, because
the king of Babylon had taken all his territory, from the Wadi of Egypt to the
Euphrates River.

Jehoiachin King of Judah

[8]Jehoiachin was eighteen years old
when he became king, and he reigned
in Jerusalem three months. His mother's name was Nehushta daughter of
Elnathan; she was from Jerusalem. [9]He
did evil in the eyes of the LORD, just as
his father had done.
[10]At that time the officers of Nebuchadnezzar king of Babylon advanced
on Jerusalem and laid siege to it, [11]and
Nebuchadnezzar himself came up to
the city while his officers were besieging it. [12]Jehoiachin king of Judah, his
mother, his attendants, his nobles and
his officials all surrendered to him.
In the eighth year of the reign of the
king of Babylon, he took Jehoiachin
prisoner. [13]As the LORD had declared,
Nebuchadnezzar removed all the treasures from the temple of the LORD and
from the royal palace, and took away all
the gold articles that Solomon king of Israel had made for the temple of the
LORD. [14]He carried into exile all Jerusalem: all the officers and fighting men,
and all the craftsmen and artisans—a
total of ten thousand. Only the poorest
people of the land were left.
[15]Nebuchadnezzar took Jehoiachin
captive to Babylon. He also took from
Jerusalem to Babylon the king's mother,
his wives, his officials and the leading
men of the land. [16]The king of Babylon
also deported to Babylon the entire
force of seven thousand fighting men,
strong and fit for war, and a thousand
craftsmen and artisans. [17]He made Mattaniah, Jehoiachin's uncle, king in his
place and changed his name to Zedekiah.

[a]2 Or *Chaldean*

Zedekiah King of Judah

18 Zedekiah was twenty-one years old when he became king, and he reigned in Jerusalem eleven years. His mother's name was Hamutal daughter of Jeremiah; she was from Libnah. 19 He did evil in the eyes of the LORD, just as Jehoiakim had done. 20 It was because of the LORD's anger that all this happened to Jerusalem and Judah, and in the end he thrust them from his presence.

The Fall of Jerusalem

Now Zedekiah rebelled against the king of Babylon.

25 So in the ninth year of Zedekiah's reign, on the tenth day of the tenth month, Nebuchadnezzar king of Babylon marched against Jerusalem with his whole army. He encamped outside the city and built siege works all around it. 2 The city was kept under siege until the eleventh year of King Zedekiah. 3 By the ninth day of the ⌞fourth⌟[a] month the famine in the city had become so severe that there was no food for the people to eat. 4 Then the city wall was broken through, and the whole army fled at night through the gate between the two walls near the king's garden, though the Babylonians[b] were surrounding the city. They fled toward the Arabah,[c] 5 but the Babylonian[d] army pursued the king and overtook him in the plains of Jericho. All his soldiers were separated from him and scattered, 6 and he was captured. He was taken to the king of Babylon at Riblah, where sentence was pronounced on him. 7 They killed the sons of Zedekiah before his eyes. Then they put out his eyes, bound him with bronze shackles and took him to Babylon.

8 On the seventh day of the fifth month, in the nineteenth year of Nebuchadnezzar king of Babylon, Nebuzaradan commander of the imperial guard, an official of the king of Babylon, came to Jerusalem. 9 He set fire to the temple of the LORD, the royal palace and all the houses of Jerusalem. Every important building he burned down. 10 The whole Babylonian army, under the commander of the imperial guard, broke down the walls around Jerusalem. 11 Nebuzaradan the commander of the guard carried into exile the people who remained in the city, along with the rest of the populace and those who had gone over to the king of Babylon. 12 But the commander left behind some of the poorest people of the land to work the vineyards and fields.

13 The Babylonians broke up the bronze pillars, the movable stands and the bronze Sea that were at the temple of the LORD and they carried the bronze to Babylon. 14 They also took away the pots, shovels, wick trimmers, dishes and all the bronze articles used in the temple service. 15 The commander of the imperial guard took away the censers and sprinkling bowls—all that were made of pure gold or silver.

16 The bronze from the two pillars, the Sea and the movable stands, which Solomon had made for the temple of the LORD, was more than could be weighed. 17 Each pillar was twenty-seven feet[e] high. The bronze capital on top of one pillar was four and a half feet[f] high and was decorated with a network and pomegranates of bronze all around. The other pillar, with its network, was similar.

18 The commander of the guard took as prisoners Seraiah the chief priest, Zephaniah the priest next in rank and the three doorkeepers. 19 Of those still in the city, he took the officer in charge of the fighting men and five royal advisers. He also took the secretary who was chief officer in charge of conscripting the people of the land and sixty of his men who were found in the city. 20 Nebuzaradan the commander took them all and brought them to the king of Babylon at Riblah. 21 There at Riblah, in the land of Hamath, the king had them executed.

[a]3 See Jer. 52:6. [b]4 Or *Chaldeans;* also in verses 13, 25 and 26 [c]4 Or *the Jordan Valley* [d]5 Or *Chaldean;* also in verses 10 and 24 [e]17 Hebrew *eighteen cubits* (about 8.1 meters) [f]17 Hebrew *three cubits* (about 1.3 meters)

So Judah went into captivity, away
from her land.
[22]Nebuchadnezzar king of Babylon
appointed Gedaliah son of Ahikam, the
son of Shaphan, to be over the people
he had left behind in Judah. [23]When all
the army officers and their men heard
that the king of Babylon had appointed
Gedaliah as governor, they came to
Gedaliah at Mizpah—Ishmael son of
Nethaniah, Johanan son of Kareah,
Seraiah son of Tanhumeth the Netophathite, Jaazaniah the son of the Maacathite, and their men. [24]Gedaliah took an
oath to reassure them and their men.
"Do not be afraid of the Babylonian officials," he said. "Settle down in the land
and serve the king of Babylon, and it
will go well with you."
[25]In the seventh month, however, Ishmael son of Nethaniah, the son of Elishama, who was of royal blood, came with
ten men and assassinated Gedaliah and
also the men of Judah and the Babylonians who were with him at Mizpah.
[26]At this, all the people from the least to
the greatest, together with the army officers, fled to Egypt for fear of the Babylonians.

Jehoiachin Released

[27]In the thirty-seventh year of the exile of Jehoiachin king of Judah, in the
year Evil-Merodach[a] became king of
Babylon, he released Jehoiachin from
prison on the twenty-seventh day of the
twelfth month. [28]He spoke kindly to him
and gave him a seat of honor higher
than those of the other kings who were
with him in Babylon. [29]So Jehoiachin put
aside his prison clothes and for the rest
of his life ate regularly at the king's table. [30]Day by day the king gave Jehoiachin a regular allowance as long as he
lived.

[a]27 Also called *Amel-Marduk*

SHARPEN THE FOCUS

As you have no doubt noticed by now, the Lord wove a bright red covenant thread through the fabric of Old Testament history. Maybe you missed that thread today, hidden as it was behind the sadness of Jerusalem's destruction. If so, look again at 2 Kings 25:27–30 and compare the names there with those listed in Matthew 1:8–11, part of Jesus' genealogy. (Jeconiah is Jehoiachin.) Despite all odds, the line of David would continue. The Lord would build David an eternal house, just as He had promised.

Perhaps to this point your day or your week hasn't seemed too bright. Maybe your mood is shrouded in the grays of guilt or fear or in a heavy cloak of responsibilities. If so, your Lord wants to give you a "change of clothes." Just as Jehoiachin shed his prison garments (2 Kings 25:29) by the Lord's grace, so you too have a Savior-God sent to do what He promised in Isaiah 61:3. Read that promise and rejoice in that Savior and in His mercy toward you—personally—today!

1 Chronicles

WEEK 34 • MONDAY

1 Chronicles 1:1—4:43

Today's reading can be as long and involved or as short and sweet as you like. If you skim all four chapters, make note of the names you recognize. If you pause briefly to reflect after each familiar name, you will have reviewed most of the Old Testament history you have read since Week 1. If time is short, focus on 1 Chronicles 3:10–16.

Historical Records From Adam to Abraham

To Noah's Sons

1 Adam, Seth, Enosh, [2]Kenan, Mahalalel, Jared, [3]Enoch, Methuselah, Lamech, Noah.

[4]The sons of Noah:[a]
Shem, Ham and Japheth.

The Japhethites

[5]The sons[b] of Japheth:
Gomer, Magog, Madai, Javan, Tubal, Meshech and Tiras.
[6]The sons of Gomer:
Ashkenaz, Riphath[c] and Togarmah.
[7]The sons of Javan:
Elishah, Tarshish, the Kittim and the Rodanim.

The Hamites

[8]The sons of Ham:
Cush, Mizraim,[d] Put and Canaan.
[9]The sons of Cush:
Seba, Havilah, Sabta, Raamah and Sabteca.
The sons of Raamah:
Sheba and Dedan.
[10]Cush was the father[e] of
Nimrod, who grew to be a mighty warrior on earth.
[11]Mizraim was the father of
the Ludites, Anamites, Lehabites, Naphtuhites, [12]Pathrusites, Casluhites (from whom the Philistines came) and Caphtorites.
[13]Canaan was the father of
Sidon his firstborn,[f] and of the Hittites, [14]Jebusites, Amorites, Girgashites, [15]Hivites, Arkites, Sinites, [16]Arvadites, Zemarites and Hamathites.

The Semites

[17]The sons of Shem:
Elam, Asshur, Arphaxad, Lud and Aram.
The sons of Aram[g]:
Uz, Hul, Gether and Meshech.

[a]4 Septuagint; Hebrew does not have *The sons of Noah:* [b]5 *Sons* may mean *descendants* or *successors* or *nations*; also in verses 6-10, 17 and 20. [c]6 Many Hebrew manuscripts and Vulgate (see also Septuagint and Gen. 10:3); most Hebrew manuscripts *Diphath* [d]8 That is, Egypt; also in verse 11 [e]10 *Father* may mean *ancestor* or *predecessor* or *founder*; also in verses 11, 13, 18 and 20. [f]13 Or *of the Sidonians, the foremost* [g]17 One Hebrew manuscript and some Septuagint manuscripts (see also Gen. 10:23); most Hebrew manuscripts do not have this line.

[18] Arphaxad was the father of Shelah,
and Shelah the father of Eber.
[19] Two sons were born to Eber:
One was named Peleg,[a] because in his time the earth was divided; his brother was named Joktan.
[20] Joktan was the father of
Almodad, Sheleph, Hazarmaveth, Jerah, [21] Hadoram, Uzal, Diklah, [22] Obal,[b] Abimael, Sheba, [23] Ophir, Havilah and Jobab. All these were sons of Joktan.

[24] Shem, Arphaxad,[c] Shelah,
[25] Eber, Peleg, Reu,
[26] Serug, Nahor, Terah
[27] and Abram (that is, Abraham).

The Family of Abraham

[28] The sons of Abraham:
Isaac and Ishmael.

Descendants of Hagar

[29] These were their descendants:
Nebaioth the firstborn of Ishmael, Kedar, Adbeel, Mibsam, [30] Mishma, Dumah, Massa, Hadad, Tema, [31] Jetur, Naphish and Kedemah. These were the sons of Ishmael.

Descendants of Keturah

[32] The sons born to Keturah, Abraham's concubine:
Zimran, Jokshan, Medan, Midian, Ishbak and Shuah.
The sons of Jokshan:
Sheba and Dedan.
[33] The sons of Midian:
Ephah, Epher, Hanoch, Abida and Eldaah.
All these were descendants of Keturah.

Descendants of Sarah

[34] Abraham was the father of Isaac.
The sons of Isaac:
Esau and Israel.

Esau's Sons

[35] The sons of Esau:
Eliphaz, Reuel, Jeush, Jalam and Korah.
[36] The sons of Eliphaz:
Teman, Omar, Zepho,[d] Gatam and Kenaz;
by Timna: Amalek.[e]
[37] The sons of Reuel:
Nahath, Zerah, Shammah and Mizzah.

The People of Seir in Edom

[38] The sons of Seir:
Lotan, Shobal, Zibeon, Anah, Dishon, Ezer and Dishan.
[39] The sons of Lotan:
Hori and Homam. Timna was Lotan's sister.
[40] The sons of Shobal:
Alvan,[f] Manahath, Ebal, Shepho and Onam.
The sons of Zibeon:
Aiah and Anah.
[41] The son of Anah:
Dishon.
The sons of Dishon:
Hemdan,[g] Eshban, Ithran and Keran.
[42] The sons of Ezer:
Bilhan, Zaavan and Akan.[h]
The sons of Dishan[i]:
Uz and Aran.

The Rulers of Edom

[43] These were the kings who reigned in Edom before any Israelite king reigned[j]:
Bela son of Beor, whose city was named Dinhabah.

[a] *19 Peleg* means *division.* [b] 22 Some Hebrew manuscripts and Syriac (see also Gen. 10:28); most Hebrew manuscripts *Ebal* [c] 24 Hebrew; some Septuagint manuscripts *Arphaxad, Cainan* (see also note at Gen. 11:10) [d] *36* Many Hebrew manuscripts, some Septuagint manuscripts and Syriac (see also Gen. 36:11); most Hebrew manuscripts *Zephi* [e] *36* Some Septuagint manuscripts (see also Gen. 36:12); Hebrew *Gatam, Kenaz, Timna and Amalek* [f] *40* Many Hebrew manuscripts and some Septuagint manuscripts (see also Gen. 36:23); most Hebrew manuscripts *Alian* [g] *41* Many Hebrew manuscripts and some Septuagint manuscripts (see also Gen. 36:26); most Hebrew manuscripts *Hamran* [h] 42 Many Hebrew and Septuagint manuscripts (see also Gen. 36:27); most Hebrew manuscripts *Zaavan, Jaakan* [i] 42 Hebrew *Dishon,* a variant of *Dishan* [j] 43 Or *before an Israelite king reigned over them*

44 When Bela died, Jobab son of Zerah from Bozrah succeeded him as king.
45 When Jobab died, Husham from the land of the Temanites succeeded him as king.
46 When Husham died, Hadad son of Bedad, who defeated Midian in the country of Moab, succeeded him as king. His city was named Avith.
47 When Hadad died, Samlah from Masrekah succeeded him as king.
48 When Samlah died, Shaul from Rehoboth on the river[a] succeeded him as king.
49 When Shaul died, Baal-Hanan son of Acbor succeeded him as king.
50 When Baal-Hanan died, Hadad succeeded him as king. His city was named Pau,[b] and his wife's name was Mehetabel daughter of Matred, the daughter of Me-
Zahab. 51 Hadad also died.

The chiefs of Edom were:
Timna, Alvah, Jetheth, 52 Oholibamah, Elah, Pinon, 53 Kenaz, Teman, Mibzar, 54 Magdiel and Iram.
These were the chiefs of Edom.

Israel's Sons

2 These were the sons of Israel:
Reuben, Simeon, Levi, Judah,
Issachar, Zebulun, 2 Dan, Joseph,
Benjamin, Naphtali, Gad and Asher.

Judah

To Hezron's Sons

3 The sons of Judah:
Er, Onan and Shelah. These three were born to him by a Canaanite woman, the daughter of Shua. Er, Judah's firstborn, was wicked in the LORD's sight; so the LORD put
him to death. 4 Tamar, Judah's daughter-in-law, bore him Perez and Zerah. Judah had five sons in all.

5 The sons of Perez:
Hezron and Hamul.
6 The sons of Zerah:
Zimri, Ethan, Heman, Calcol and Darda[c]—five in all.
7 The son of Carmi:
Achar,[d] who brought trouble on Israel by violating the ban on taking devoted things.[e]
8 The son of Ethan:
Azariah.
9 The sons born to Hezron were:
Jerahmeel, Ram and Caleb.[f]

From Ram Son of Hezron

10 Ram was the father of
Amminadab, and Amminadab the father of Nahshon, the leader of the people of Judah. 11 Nah-
shon was the father of Salmon,[g]
Salmon the father of Boaz, 12 Boaz
the father of Obed and Obed the father of Jesse.
13 Jesse was the father of
Eliab his firstborn; the second son was Abinadab, the third
Shimea, 14 the fourth Nethanel,
the fifth Raddai, 15 the sixth Ozem
and the seventh David. 16 Their
sisters were Zeruiah and Abigail. Zeruiah's three sons were Abishai, Joab and Asahel. 17 Abigail was
the mother of Amasa, whose father was Jether the Ishmaelite.

Caleb Son of Hezron

18 Caleb son of Hezron had children by his wife Azubah (and by Jeri-
oth). These were her sons: Jesher,
Shobab and Ardon. 19 When Azubah died, Caleb married Ephrath, who bore him Hur. 20 Hur

[a] *48* Possibly the Euphrates [b] *50* Many Hebrew manuscripts, some Septuagint manuscripts, Vulgate and Syriac (see also Gen. 36:39); most Hebrew manuscripts *Pai* [c] *6* Many Hebrew manuscripts, some Septuagint manuscripts and Syriac (see also 1 Kings 4:31); most Hebrew manuscripts *Dara* [d] *7 Achar* means *trouble*; *Achar* is called *Achan* in Joshua. [e] *7* The Hebrew term refers to the irrevocable giving over of things or persons to the LORD, often by totally destroying them. [f] *9* Hebrew *Kelubai,* a variant of *Caleb* [g] *11* Septuagint (see also Ruth 4:21); Hebrew *Salma*

was the father of Uri, and Uri the
father of Bezalel.
21 Later, Hezron lay with the daughter of Makir the father of Gilead
(he had married her when he
was sixty years old), and she bore
him Segub. 22 Segub was the father of Jair, who controlled twenty-three towns in Gilead. 23 (But
Geshur and Aram captured Havvoth Jair,[a] as well as Kenath with
its surrounding settlements—
sixty towns.) All these were descendants of Makir the father of
Gilead.

24 After Hezron died in Caleb Ephrathah, Abijah the wife of Hezron
bore him Ashhur the father[b] of
Tekoa.

Jerahmeel Son of Hezron

25 The sons of Jerahmeel the firstborn
of Hezron:
Ram his firstborn, Bunah, Oren,
Ozem and[c] Ahijah. 26 Jerahmeel
had another wife, whose name
was Atarah; she was the mother
of Onam.
27 The sons of Ram the firstborn of
Jerahmeel:
Maaz, Jamin and Eker.
28 The sons of Onam:
Shammai and Jada.
The sons of Shammai:
Nadab and Abishur.
29 Abishur's wife was named Abihail,
who bore him Ahban and Molid.
30 The sons of Nadab:
Seled and Appaim. Seled died
without children.
31 The son of Appaim:
Ishi, who was the father of Sheshan.
Sheshan was the father of Ahlai.
32 The sons of Jada, Shammai's brother:
Jether and Jonathan. Jether died
without children.
33 The sons of Jonathan:
Peleth and Zaza.
These were the descendants of
Jerahmeel.

34 Sheshan had no sons—only
daughters.
He had an Egyptian servant
named Jarha. 35 Sheshan gave his
daughter in marriage to his
servant Jarha, and she bore him
Attai.
36 Attai was the father of Nathan,
Nathan the father of Zabad,
37 Zabad the father of Ephlal,
Ephlal the father of Obed,
38 Obed the father of Jehu,
Jehu the father of Azariah,
39 Azariah the father of Helez,
Helez the father of Eleasah,
40 Eleasah the father of Sismai,
Sismai the father of Shallum,
41 Shallum the father of Jekamiah,
and Jekamiah the father of Elishama.

The Clans of Caleb

42 The sons of Caleb the brother of
Jerahmeel:
Mesha his firstborn, who was the
father of Ziph, and his son
Mareshah,[d] who was the father
of Hebron.
43 The sons of Hebron:
Korah, Tappuah, Rekem and Shema. 44 Shema was the father of
Raham, and Raham the father of
Jorkeam. Rekem was the father
of Shammai. 45 The son of Shammai was Maon, and Maon was
the father of Beth Zur.
46 Caleb's concubine Ephah was the
mother of Haran, Moza and
Gazez. Haran was the father of
Gazez.
47 The sons of Jahdai:
Regem, Jotham, Geshan, Pelet,
Ephah and Shaaph.
48 Caleb's concubine Maacah was the
mother of Sheber and Tirhanah.
49 She also gave birth to Shaaph
the father of Madmannah and to
Sheva the father of Macbenah

[a]23 Or *captured the settlements of Jair* [b]24 *Father* may mean *civic leader* or *military leader*; also in verses 42, 45, 49-52 and possibly elsewhere. [c]25 Or *Oren and Ozem, by* [d]42 The meaning of the Hebrew for this phrase is uncertain.

and Gibea. Caleb's daughter was Acsah. [50]These were the descendants of Caleb.

The sons of Hur the firstborn of Ephrathah:
Shobal the father of Kiriath Jearim, [51]Salma the father of Bethlehem, and Hareph the father of Beth Gader.
[52]The descendants of Shobal the father of Kiriath Jearim were:
Haroeh, half the Manahathites, [53]and the clans of Kiriath Jearim: the Ithrites, Puthites, Shumathites and Mishraites. From these descended the Zorathites and Eshtaolites.
[54]The descendants of Salma:
Bethlehem, the Netophathites, Atroth Beth Joab, half the Manahathites, the Zorites, [55]and the clans of scribes[a] who lived at Jabez: the Tirathites, Shimeathites and Sucathites. These are the Kenites who came from Hammath, the father of the house of Recab.[b]

The Sons of David

3 These were the sons of David born to him in Hebron:
The firstborn was Amnon the son of Ahinoam of Jezreel;
the second, Daniel the son of Abigail of Carmel;
[2]the third, Absalom the son of Maacah daughter of Talmai king of Geshur;
the fourth, Adonijah the son of Haggith;
[3]the fifth, Shephatiah the son of Abital;
and the sixth, Ithream, by his wife Eglah.
[4]These six were born to David in Hebron, where he reigned seven years and six months.
David reigned in Jerusalem thirty-three years, [5]and these were the children born to him there:
Shammua,[c] Shobab, Nathan and Solomon. These four were by Bathsheba[d] daughter of Ammiel.
[6]There were also Ibhar, Elishua,[e] Eliphelet, [7]Nogah, Nepheg, Japhia, [8]Elishama, Eliada and Eliphelet—nine in all. [9]All these were the sons of David, besides his sons by his concubines. And Tamar was their sister.

The Kings of Judah

[10]Solomon's son was Rehoboam,
Abijah his son,
Asa his son,
Jehoshaphat his son,
[11]Jehoram[f] his son,
Ahaziah his son,
Joash his son,
[12]Amaziah his son,
Azariah his son,
Jotham his son,
[13]Ahaz his son,
Hezekiah his son,
Manasseh his son,
[14]Amon his son,
Josiah his son.
[15]The sons of Josiah:
Johanan the firstborn,
Jehoiakim the second son,
Zedekiah the third,
Shallum the fourth.
[16]The successors of Jehoiakim:
Jehoiachin[g] his son,
and Zedekiah.

The Royal Line After the Exile

[17]The descendants of Jehoiachin the captive:
Shealtiel his son, [18]Malkiram, Pedaiah, Shenazzar, Jekamiah, Hoshama and Nedabiah.
[19]The sons of Pedaiah:
Zerubbabel and Shimei.
The sons of Zerubbabel:
Meshullam and Hananiah.
Shelomith was their sister.

[a]55 Or *of the Sopherites* [b]55 Or *father of Beth Recab* [c]5 Hebrew *Shimea,* a variant of *Shammua* [d]5 One Hebrew manuscript and Vulgate (see also Septuagint and 2 Samuel 11:3); most Hebrew manuscripts *Bathshua* [e]6 Two Hebrew manuscripts (see also 2 Samuel 5:15 and 1 Chron. 14:5); most Hebrew manuscripts *Elishama* [f]11 Hebrew *Joram,* a variant of *Jehoram* [g]16 Hebrew *Jeconiah,* a variant of *Jehoiachin;* also in verse 17

[20] There were also five others:
Hashubah, Ohel, Berekiah, Hasadiah and Jushab-Hesed.
[21] The descendants of Hananiah:
Pelatiah and Jeshaiah, and the sons of Rephaiah, of Arnan, of Obadiah and of Shecaniah.
[22] The descendants of Shecaniah:
Shemaiah and his sons:
Hattush, Igal, Bariah, Neariah and Shaphat—six in all.
[23] The sons of Neariah:
Elioenai, Hizkiah and Azrikam—three in all.
[24] The sons of Elioenai:
Hodaviah, Eliashib, Pelaiah, Akkub, Johanan, Delaiah and Anani—seven in all.

Other Clans of Judah

4 The descendants of Judah:
Perez, Hezron, Carmi, Hur and Shobal.
[2] Reaiah son of Shobal was the father of Jahath, and Jahath the father of Ahumai and Lahad. These were the clans of the Zorathites.
[3] These were the sons[a] of Etam:
Jezreel, Ishma and Idbash. Their sister was named Hazzelelponi.
[4] Penuel was the father of Gedor, and Ezer the father of Hushah.
These were the descendants of Hur, the firstborn of Ephrathah and father[b] of Bethlehem.
[5] Ashhur the father of Tekoa had two wives, Helah and Naarah.
[6] Naarah bore him Ahuzzam, Hepher, Temeni and Haahashtari. These were the descendants of Naarah.
[7] The sons of Helah:
Zereth, Zohar, Ethnan, [8] and Koz, who was the father of Anub and Hazzobebah and of the clans of Aharhel son of Harum.

[9] Jabez was more honorable than his
brothers. His mother had named him
Jabez,[c] saying, "I gave birth to him in
pain." [10] Jabez cried out to the God of Israel, "Oh, that you would bless me and
enlarge my territory! Let your hand be
with me, and keep me from harm so
that I will be free from pain." And God
granted his request.

[11] Kelub, Shuhah's brother, was the father of Mehir, who was the father of Eshton.
[12] Eshton was the father of Beth Rapha, Paseah and Tehinnah the father of Ir Nahash.[d] These were the men of Recah.
[13] The sons of Kenaz:
Othniel and Seraiah.
The sons of Othniel:
Hathath and Meonothai.[e]
[14] Meonothai was the father of Ophrah.
Seraiah was the father of Joab, the father of Ge Harashim.[f] It was called this because its people were craftsmen.
[15] The sons of Caleb son of Jephunneh:
Iru, Elah and Naam.
The son of Elah:
Kenaz.
[16] The sons of Jehallelel:
Ziph, Ziphah, Tiria and Asarel.
[17] The sons of Ezrah:
Jether, Mered, Epher and Jalon. One of Mered's wives gave birth to Miriam, Shammai and Ishbah the father of Eshtemoa.
[18] (His Judean wife gave birth to Jered the father of Gedor, Heber the father of Soco, and Jekuthiel the father of Zanoah.) These were the children of Pharaoh's daughter Bithiah, whom Mered had married.
[19] The sons of Hodiah's wife, the sister of Naham:
the father of Keilah the Garmite, and Eshtemoa the Maacathite.

[a] 3 Some Septuagint manuscripts (see also Vulgate); Hebrew *father* [b] 4 *Father* may mean *civic leader* or *military leader*; also in verses 12, 14, 17, 18 and possibly elsewhere. [c] 9 *Jabez* sounds like the Hebrew for *pain.* [d] 12 Or *of the city of Nahash* [e] 13 Some Septuagint manuscripts and Vulgate; Hebrew does not have *and Meonothai.* [f] 14 *Ge Harashim* means *valley of craftsmen.*

[20]The sons of Shimon:
Amnon, Rinnah, Ben-Hanan and Tilon.
The descendants of Ishi:
Zoheth and Ben-Zoheth.
[21]The sons of Shelah son of Judah:
Er the father of Lecah, Laadah
the father of Mareshah and the
clans of the linen workers at Beth
Ashbea, [22]Jokim, the men of Co-
zeba, and Joash and Saraph, who
ruled in Moab and Jashubi Lehem. (These records are from
ancient times.) [23]They were the
potters who lived at Netaim and
Gederah; they stayed there and
worked for the king.

Simeon

[24]The descendants of Simeon:
Nemuel, Jamin, Jarib, Zerah and Shaul;
[25]Shallum was Shaul's son, Mibsam his son and Mishma his son.
[26]The descendants of Mishma:
Hammuel his son, Zaccur his son and Shimei his son.

[27]Shimei had sixteen sons and six
daughters, but his brothers did not have
many children; so their entire clan did
not become as numerous as the people
of Judah. [28]They lived in Beersheba,
Moladah, Hazar Shual, [29]Bilhah, Ezem,
Tolad, [30]Bethuel, Hormah, Ziklag, [31]Beth
Marcaboth, Hazar Susim, Beth Biri and
Shaaraim. These were their towns until
the reign of David. [32]Their surrounding
villages were Etam, Ain, Rimmon, Token
and Ashan—five towns— [33]and all the
villages around these towns as far as
Baalath.[a] These were their settlements.
And they kept a genealogical record.

[34]Meshobab, Jamlech, Joshah son of
Amaziah, [35]Joel, Jehu son of Joshi-
biah, the son of Seraiah, the son of
Asiel, [36]also Elioenai, Jaakobah,
Jeshohaiah, Asaiah, Adiel, Jesimiel,
Benaiah, [37]and Ziza son of Shiphi,
the son of Allon, the son of Jedaiah,
the son of Shimri, the son of Shemaiah.

[38]The men listed above by name were
leaders of their clans. Their families increased greatly, [39]and they went to the
outskirts of Gedor to the east of the valley in search of pasture for their flocks.
[40]They found rich, good pasture, and the
land was spacious, peaceful and quiet.
Some Hamites had lived there formerly.
[41]The men whose names were listed
came in the days of Hezekiah king of
Judah. They attacked the Hamites in
their dwellings and also the Meunites
who were there and completely destroyed[b] them, as is evident to this day.
Then they settled in their place, because
there was pasture for their flocks. [42]And
five hundred of these Simeonites, led by
Pelatiah, Neariah, Rephaiah and Uzziel, the sons of Ishi, invaded the hill
country of Seir. [43]They killed the remaining Amalekites who had escaped, and
they have lived there to this day.

[a]*33* Some Septuagint manuscripts (see also Joshua 19:8); Hebrew *Baal* [b]*41* The Hebrew term refers to the irrevocable giving over of things or persons to the LORD, often by totally destroying them.

SHARPEN THE FOCUS

What may at first appear to be ashes of a history long past, the genealogy of 1 Chronicles 1–4, can come to life in the light of the Lord's grace. Remember Adam? Seth? Enoch? Noah? Abraham? Isaac? Esau? Jacob? Reuben? Levi? Judah? Joseph?

The list goes on and on. Through Boaz, Obed, Jesse, David, Hezekiah, Josiah. Each life marked by grace. Each life touched, transformed by the Lord's unfailing love. Each life a link in the chain of salvation history.

Before you close your Bible today, turn ahead to Hebrews 11. The holy writer there recorded the results of his own Spirit-led meditation on the lives of some of the individual people of God chronicled in the Old Testament. Read a few of those verses in the light of the cross. Then think about your own life in the light of the grace and pardon that belong to you in Jesus.

Like yesterday's reading, today's genealogies include brief historical notes sprinkled through the text. Pay particular attention to 1 Chronicles 6:1–49. It's the genealogy of Israel's priesthood. Keep in mind that the books of Chronicles repeat Old Testament history, but this time from the perspective of the nation's faithful spiritual leaders. If time is short, focus on 1 Chronicles 6:1–49.

Reuben

5 The sons of Reuben the firstborn
of Israel (he was the firstborn,
but when he defiled his father's marriage bed, his rights as firstborn were
given to the sons of Joseph son of Israel;
so he could not be listed in the genealogical record in accordance with his
birthright, 2and though Judah was the
strongest of his brothers and a ruler
came from him, the rights of the firstborn belonged to Joseph)— 3the sons of
Reuben the firstborn of Israel:
Hanoch, Pallu, Hezron and Carmi.
4The descendants of Joel:
Shemaiah his son, Gog his son,
Shimei his son, 5Micah his son,
Reaiah his son, Baal his son,
6and Beerah his son, whom Tiglath-Pileser[a] king of Assyria took
into exile. Beerah was a leader of
the Reubenites.
7Their relatives by clans, listed
according to their genealogical
records:
Jeiel the chief, Zechariah, 8and
Bela son of Azaz, the son of Shema, the son of Joel. They settled
in the area from Aroer to Nebo
and Baal Meon. 9To the east they
occupied the land up to the edge
of the desert that extends to the
Euphrates River, because their
livestock had increased in Gilead.
10During Saul's reign they waged
war against the Hagrites, who were
defeated at their hands; they occupied the dwellings of the Hagrites
throughout the entire region east of
Gilead.

Gad

11The Gadites lived next to them in
Bashan, as far as Salecah:
12Joel was the chief, Shapham the
second, then Janai and Shaphat,
in Bashan.
13Their relatives, by families, were:
Michael, Meshullam, Sheba, Jo-
rai, Jacan, Zia and Eber—seven
in all.
14These were the sons of Abihail
son of Huri, the son of Jaroah, the
son of Gilead, the son of Michael, the son of Jeshishai, the son of
Jahdo, the son of Buz.

[a]6 Hebrew *Tilgath-Pilneser,* a variant of *Tiglath-Pileser*; also in verse 26

[15] Ahi son of Abdiel, the son of
Guni, was head of their family.
[16] The Gadites lived in Gilead, in Bashan and its outlying villages, and on all the pasturelands of Sharon as far as they extended.

[17] All these were entered in the genealogical records during the reigns of Jotham king of Judah and Jeroboam king of Israel.

[18] The Reubenites, the Gadites and the half-tribe of Manasseh had 44,760 men ready for military service—able-bodied men who could handle shield and sword, who could use a bow, and who
were trained for battle. [19] They waged
war against the Hagrites, Jetur, Naphish
and Nodab. [20] They were helped in fighting them, and God handed the Hagrites and all their allies over to them, because they cried out to him during the battle. He answered their prayers, because
they trusted in him. [21] They seized the
livestock of the Hagrites—fifty thousand camels, two hundred fifty thousand sheep and two thousand donkeys. They also took one hundred thousand
people captive, [22] and many others fell
slain, because the battle was God's. And they occupied the land until the exile.

The Half-Tribe of Manasseh

[23] The people of the half-tribe of Manasseh were numerous; they settled in the land from Bashan to Baal Hermon, that is, to Senir (Mount Hermon).

[24] These were the heads of their families: Epher, Ishi, Eliel, Azriel, Jeremiah, Hodaviah and Jahdiel. They were brave warriors, famous men, and heads of
their families. [25] But they were unfaithful to the God of their fathers and prostituted themselves to the gods of the peoples of the land, whom God had de-
stroyed before them. [26] So the God of Israel stirred up the spirit of Pul king of Assyria (that is, Tiglath-Pileser king of Assyria), who took the Reubenites, the Gadites and the half-tribe of Manasseh into exile. He took them to Halah, Habor, Hara and the river of Gozan, where they are to this day.

Levi

6 The sons of Levi:
Gershon, Kohath and Merari.
[2] The sons of Kohath:
Amram, Izhar, Hebron and Uzziel.
[3] The children of Amram:
Aaron, Moses and Miriam.
The sons of Aaron:
Nadab, Abihu, Eleazar and Ithamar.
[4] Eleazar was the father of Phinehas,
Phinehas the father of Abishua,
[5] Abishua the father of Bukki,
Bukki the father of Uzzi,
[6] Uzzi the father of Zerahiah,
Zerahiah the father of Meraioth,
[7] Meraioth the father of Amariah,
Amariah the father of Ahitub,
[8] Ahitub the father of Zadok,
Zadok the father of Ahimaaz,
[9] Ahimaaz the father of Azariah,
Azariah the father of Johanan,
[10] Johanan the father of Azariah (it was he who served as priest in the temple Solomon built in Jerusalem),
[11] Azariah the father of Amariah,
Amariah the father of Ahitub,
[12] Ahitub the father of Zadok,
Zadok the father of Shallum,
[13] Shallum the father of Hilkiah,
Hilkiah the father of Azariah,
[14] Azariah the father of Seraiah,
and Seraiah the father of Jehozadak.
[15] Jehozadak was deported when the LORD sent Judah and Jerusalem into exile by the hand of Nebuchadnezzar.

[16] The sons of Levi:
Gershon,[a] Kohath and Merari.
[17] These are the names of the sons of Gershon:
Libni and Shimei.
[18] The sons of Kohath:
Amram, Izhar, Hebron and Uzziel.

[a] *16* Hebrew *Gershom,* a variant of *Gershon;* also in verses 17, 20, 43, 62 and 71

19 The sons of Merari:
Mahli and Mushi.
These are the clans of the Levites
listed according to their fathers:
20 Of Gershon:
Libni his son, Jehath his son,
Zimmah his son, 21 Joah his son,
Iddo his son, Zerah his son
and Jeatherai his son.
22 The descendants of Kohath:
Amminadab his son, Korah his son,
Assir his son, 23 Elkanah his son,
Ebiasaph his son, Assir his son,
24 Tahath his son, Uriel his son,
Uzziah his son and Shaul his son.
25 The descendants of Elkanah:
Amasai, Ahimoth,
26 Elkanah his son,[a] Zophai his son,
Nahath his son, 27 Eliab his son,
Jeroham his son, Elkanah his son
and Samuel his son.[b]
28 The sons of Samuel:
Joel[c] the firstborn
and Abijah the second son.
29 The descendants of Merari:
Mahli, Libni his son,
Shimei his son, Uzzah his son,
30 Shimea his son, Haggiah his son
and Asaiah his son.

The Temple Musicians

31 These are the men David put in
charge of the music in the house of the
LORD after the ark came to rest there.
32 They ministered with music before the
tabernacle, the Tent of Meeting, until
Solomon built the temple of the LORD in
Jerusalem. They performed their duties
according to the regulations laid down
for them.
33 Here are the men who served, together with their sons:
From the Kohathites:
Heman, the musician,
the son of Joel, the son of Samuel,
34 the son of Elkanah, the son of Jeroham,
the son of Eliel, the son of Toah,
35 the son of Zuph, the son of Elkanah,
the son of Mahath, the son of Amasai,
36 the son of Elkanah, the son of Joel,
the son of Azariah, the son of Zephaniah,
37 the son of Tahath, the son of Assir,
the son of Ebiasaph, the son of Korah,
38 the son of Izhar, the son of Kohath,
the son of Levi, the son of Israel;
39 and Heman's associate Asaph, who served at his right hand:
Asaph son of Berekiah, the son of Shimea,
40 the son of Michael, the son of Baaseiah,[d]
the son of Malkijah, 41 the son of Ethni,
the son of Zerah, the son of Adaiah,
42 the son of Ethan, the son of Zimmah,
the son of Shimei, 43 the son of Jahath,
the son of Gershon, the son of Levi;
44 and from their associates, the Merarites, at his left hand:
Ethan son of Kishi, the son of Abdi,
the son of Malluch, 45 the son of Hashabiah,
the son of Amaziah, the son of Hilkiah,
46 the son of Amzi, the son of Bani,
the son of Shemer, 47 the son of Mahli,
the son of Mushi, the son of Merari,
the son of Levi.

48 Their fellow Levites were assigned
to all the other duties of the tabernacle,

[a]26 Some Hebrew manuscripts, Septuagint and Syriac; most Hebrew manuscripts *Ahimoth* [26]*and Elkanah. The sons of Elkanah:* [b]27 Some Septuagint manuscripts (see also 1 Samuel 1:19,20 and 1 Chron. 6:33,34); Hebrew does not have *and Samuel his son.* [c]28 Some Septuagint manuscripts and Syriac (see also 1 Samuel 8:2 and 1 Chron. 6:33); Hebrew does not have *Joel.* [d]40 Most Hebrew manuscripts; some Hebrew manuscripts, one Septuagint manuscript and Syriac *Maaseiah*

the house of God. 49 But Aaron and his
descendants were the ones who presented offerings on the altar of burnt
offering and on the altar of incense in
connection with all that was done in the
Most Holy Place, making atonement for
Israel, in accordance with all that Moses
the servant of God had commanded.

50 These were the descendants of
Aaron:
Eleazar his son, Phinehas his son,
Abishua his son, 51 Bukki his son,
Uzzi his son, Zerahiah his son,
52 Meraioth his son, Amariah his
son,
Ahitub his son, 53 Zadok his son
and Ahimaaz his son.

54 These were the locations of their
settlements allotted as their territory
(they were assigned to the descendants
of Aaron who were from the Kohathite
clan, because the first lot was for them):
55 They were given Hebron in Judah with its surrounding pasturelands. 56 But the fields and villages
around the city were given to Caleb son of Jephunneh.
57 So the descendants of Aaron
were given Hebron (a city of refuge), and Libnah,[a] Jattir, Eshtemoa,
58 Hilen, Debir, 59 Ashan, Juttah[b] and
Beth Shemesh, together with their
pasturelands. 60 And from the tribe
of Benjamin they were given Gibeon,[c] Geba, Alemeth and Anathoth,
together with their pasturelands.
These towns, which were distributed among the Kohathite clans,
were thirteen in all.
61 The rest of Kohath's descendants
were allotted ten towns from the clans
of half the tribe of Manasseh.
62 The descendants of Gershon, clan
by clan, were allotted thirteen towns
from the tribes of Issachar, Asher and
Naphtali, and from the part of the tribe
of Manasseh that is in Bashan.
63 The descendants of Merari, clan by
clan, were allotted twelve towns from
the tribes of Reuben, Gad and Zebulun.
64 So the Israelites gave the Levites
these towns and their pasturelands.
65 From the tribes of Judah, Simeon and
Benjamin they allotted the previously
named towns.
66 Some of the Kohathite clans were
given as their territory towns from the
tribe of Ephraim.
67 In the hill country of Ephraim
they were given Shechem (a city of
refuge), and Gezer,[d] 68 Jokmeam,
Beth Horon, 69 Aijalon and Gath
Rimmon, together with their pasturelands.
70 And from half the tribe of Manasseh the Israelites gave Aner and
Bileam, together with their pasturelands, to the rest of the Kohathite clans.

71 The Gershonites received the following:
From the clan of the half-tribe of
Manasseh
they received Golan in Bashan
and also Ashtaroth, together
with their pasturelands;
72 from the tribe of Issachar
they received Kedesh, Daberath,
73 Ramoth and Anem, together
with their pasturelands;
74 from the tribe of Asher
they received Mashal, Abdon,
75 Hukok and Rehob, together
with their pasturelands;
76 and from the tribe of Naphtali
they received Kedesh in Galilee,
Hammon and Kiriathaim, together with their pasturelands.

77 The Merarites (the rest of the Levites) received the following:
From the tribe of Zebulun
they received Jokneam, Kartah,[e]
Rimmono and Tabor, together
with their pasturelands;
78 from the tribe of Reuben across the
Jordan east of Jericho

[a] 57 See Joshua 21:13; Hebrew *given the cities of refuge: Hebron, Libnah.* [b] 59 Syriac (see also Septuagint and Joshua 21:16); Hebrew does not have *Juttah.* [c] 60 See Joshua 21:17; Hebrew does not have *Gibeon.* [d] 67 See Joshua 21:21; Hebrew *given the cities of refuge: Shechem, Gezer.* [e] 77 See Septuagint and Joshua 21:34; Hebrew does not have *Jokneam, Kartah.*

they received Bezer in the desert,
Jahzah, [79]Kedemoth and Mephaath, together with their pasturelands;
[80]and from the tribe of Gad
they received Ramoth in Gilead,
Mahanaim, [81]Heshbon and Jazer,
together with their pasturelands.

Issachar

7 The sons of Issachar:
Tola, Puah, Jashub and Shimron—four in all.
[2]The sons of Tola:
Uzzi, Rephaiah, Jeriel, Jahmai,
Ibsam and Samuel—heads of
their families. During the reign of
David, the descendants of Tola
listed as fighting men in their genealogy numbered 22,600.
[3]The son of Uzzi:
Izrahiah.
The sons of Izrahiah:
Michael, Obadiah, Joel and Isshiah. All five of them were
chiefs. [4]According to their family genealogy, they had 36,000
men ready for battle, for they
had many wives and children.
[5]The relatives who were fighting
men belonging to all the clans of
Issachar, as listed in their genealogy, were 87,000 in all.

Benjamin

[6]Three sons of Benjamin:
Bela, Beker and Jediael.
[7]The sons of Bela:
Ezbon, Uzzi, Uzziel, Jerimoth
and Iri, heads of families—five in
all. Their genealogical record
listed 22,034 fighting men.
[8]The sons of Beker:
Zemirah, Joash, Eliezer, Elioenai,
Omri, Jeremoth, Abijah, Anathoth and Alemeth. All these
were the sons of Beker. [9]Their genealogical record listed the heads
of families and 20,200 fighting
men.
[10]The son of Jediael:
Bilhan.
The sons of Bilhan:
Jeush, Benjamin, Ehud, Kenaanah, Zethan, Tarshish and Ahish-
ahar. [11]All these sons of Jediael
were heads of families. There
were 17,200 fighting men ready
to go out to war.
[12]The Shuppites and Huppites were
the descendants of Ir, and the
Hushites the descendants of
Aher.

Naphtali

[13]The sons of Naphtali:
Jahziel, Guni, Jezer and Shillem[a]—the descendants of Bilhah.

Manasseh

[14]The descendants of Manasseh:
Asriel was his descendant
through his Aramean concubine.
She gave birth to Makir the father
of Gilead. [15]Makir took a wife from
among the Huppites and Shuppites. His sister's name was Maacah.
Another descendant was named
Zelophehad, who had only daughters.
[16]Makir's wife Maacah gave birth
to a son and named him Peresh. His
brother was named Sheresh, and
his sons were Ulam and Rakem.
[17]The son of Ulam:
Bedan.
These were the sons of Gilead son
of Makir, the son of Manasseh.
[18]His sister Hammoleketh gave
birth to Ishhod, Abiezer and
Mahlah.
[19]The sons of Shemida were:
Ahian, Shechem, Likhi and Ani-
am.

Ephraim

[20]The descendants of Ephraim:
Shuthelah, Bered his son,
Tahath his son, Eleadah his son,
Tahath his son, [21]Zabad his son
and Shuthelah his son.

[a]*13* Some Hebrew and Septuagint manuscripts (see also Gen. 46:24 and Num. 26:49); most Hebrew manuscripts *Shallum*

Ezer and Elead were killed by the
native-born men of Gath, when
they went down to seize their
livestock. 22Their father Ephraim
mourned for them many days, and
his relatives came to comfort him.
23Then he lay with his wife again,
and she became pregnant and gave
birth to a son. He named him
Beriah,[a] because there had been
misfortune in his family. 24His
daughter was Sheerah, who built
Lower and Upper Beth Horon as
well as Uzzen Sheerah.

25 Rephah was his son, Resheph his son,[b]
Telah his son, Tahan his son,
26 Ladan his son, Ammihud his son,
Elishama his son, 27Nun his son
and Joshua his son.

28Their lands and settlements included Bethel and its surrounding villages,
Naaran to the east, Gezer and its villages
to the west, and Shechem and its villages all the way to Ayyah and its villages. 29Along the borders of Manasseh
were Beth Shan, Taanach, Megiddo and
Dor, together with their villages. The descendants of Joseph son of Israel lived
in these towns.

Asher

30 The sons of Asher:
Imnah, Ishvah, Ishvi and Beriah.
Their sister was Serah.
31 The sons of Beriah:
Heber and Malkiel, who was the father of Birzaith.
32 Heber was the father of Japhlet,
Shomer and Hotham and of their sister Shua.
33 The sons of Japhlet:
Pasach, Bimhal and Ashvath.
These were Japhlet's sons.
34 The sons of Shomer:
Ahi, Rohgah,[c] Hubbah and Aram.
35 The sons of his brother Helem:
Zophah, Imna, Shelesh and Amal.
36 The sons of Zophah:
Suah, Harnepher, Shual, Beri,
Imrah, 37Bezer, Hod, Shamma,
Shilshah, Ithran[d] and Beera.
38 The sons of Jether:
Jephunneh, Pispah and Ara.
39 The sons of Ulla:
Arah, Hanniel and Rizia.

40All these were descendants of Asher—heads of families, choice men, brave
warriors and outstanding leaders. The
number of men ready for battle, as listed in their genealogy, was 26,000.

The Genealogy of Saul the Benjamite

8 Benjamin was the father of Bela his firstborn,
Ashbel the second son, Aharah the third,
2 Nohah the fourth and Rapha the fifth.
3 The sons of Bela were:
Addar, Gera, Abihud,[e] 4Abishua,
Naaman, Ahoah, 5Gera, Shephu-
phan and Huram.
6 These were the descendants of Ehud, who were heads of families of those living in Geba and were deported to Manahath:
7 Naaman, Ahijah, and Gera, who deported them and who was the father of Uzza and Ahihud.
8 Sons were born to Shaharaim in
Moab after he had divorced his
wives Hushim and Baara. 9By his
wife Hodesh he had Jobab, Zib-
ia, Mesha, Malcam, 10Jeuz, Sakia
and Mirmah. These were his
sons, heads of families. 11By Hushim he had Abitub and Elpaal.
12 The sons of Elpaal:
Eber, Misham, Shemed (who
built Ono and Lod with its surrounding villages), 13and Beriah
and Shema, who were heads of
families of those living in Aijalon
and who drove out the inhabitants of Gath.
14 Ahio, Shashak, Jeremoth, 15Zeba-
diah, Arad, Eder, 16Michael, Ish-
pah and Joha were the sons of
Beriah.

[a]23 *Beriah* sounds like the Hebrew for *misfortune.* [b]25 Some Septuagint manuscripts; Hebrew does not have *his son.* [c]34 Or *of his brother Shomer: Rohgah* [d]37 Possibly a variant of *Jether* [e]3 Or *Gera the father of Ehud*

17 Zebadiah, Meshullam, Hizki, Heber, 18 Ishmerai, Izliah and Jobab were the sons of Elpaal.

19 Jakim, Zicri, Zabdi, 20 Elienai, Zillethai, Eliel, 21 Adaiah, Beraiah and Shimrath were the sons of Shimei.

22 Ishpan, Eber, Eliel, 23 Abdon, Zicri, Hanan, 24 Hananiah, Elam, Anthothijah, 25 Iphdeiah and Penuel were the sons of Shashak.

26 Shamsherai, Shehariah, Athaliah, 27 Jaareshiah, Elijah and Zicri were the sons of Jeroham.

28 All these were heads of families, chiefs as listed in their genealogy, and they lived in Jerusalem.

29 Jeiel[a] the father[b] of Gibeon lived in Gibeon.
His wife's name was Maacah, 30 and his firstborn son was Abdon, followed by Zur, Kish, Baal, Ner,[c] Nadab, 31 Gedor, Ahio, Zeker 32 and Mikloth, who was the father of Shimeah. They too lived near their relatives in Jerusalem.

33 Ner was the father of Kish, Kish the father of Saul, and Saul the father of Jonathan, Malki-Shua, Abinadab and Esh-Baal.[d]

34 The son of Jonathan:
Merib-Baal,[e] who was the father of Micah.

35 The sons of Micah:
Pithon, Melech, Tarea and Ahaz.
36 Ahaz was the father of Jehoaddah, Jehoaddah was the father of Alemeth, Azmaveth and Zimri, and Zimri was the father of Moza. 37 Moza was the father of Binea; Raphah was his son, Eleasah his son and Azel his son.

38 Azel had six sons, and these were their names:
Azrikam, Bokeru, Ishmael, Sheariah, Obadiah and Hanan. All these were the sons of Azel.

39 The sons of his brother Eshek:
Ulam his firstborn, Jeush the second son and Eliphelet the third.
40 The sons of Ulam were brave warriors who could handle the bow. They had many sons and grandsons—150 in all.
All these were the descendants of Benjamin.

[a]29 Some Septuagint manuscripts (see also 1 Chron. 9:35); Hebrew does not have *Jeiel.* [b]29 *Father* may mean *civic leader* or *military leader.* [c]30 Some Septuagint manuscripts (see also 1 Chron. 9:36); Hebrew does not have *Ner.* [d]33 Also known as *Ish-Bosheth* [e]34 Also known as *Mephibosheth*

SHARPEN THE FOCUS

Classical? Rock? R and B? Country Western? What style of music most relaxes, enlivens, or entertains you? Even though we may debate the merits of a particular song or genre of music, no one would debate music's power.

Because this is so, those who serve God's people by planning and providing music for our worship have a unique privilege and carry a special responsibility. Like Korah and Asaph before them (1 Chronicles 6:37, 39), church musicians direct God's people to their Lord and help us to open up our hearts to Him in worship.

The psalms of Korah and Asaph betray their hearts—they had fallen hopelessly in love with the Lord. They so treasured His grace that it spilled over into lives filled with praise. (See Psalms 42 and 50.)

Of course, our Savior-God is worthy of our best. But far more important than excellent technical performance is excellence of heart, the undivided worship of a heart made righteous by the blood of Christ and in the process of being transformed by the Holy Spirit into the image of Christ.

Pray today for all those who lead your congregation in worship. Ask for grace so that you and all your brothers and sisters worship from righteous, thankful hearts.

WEEK 34 • WEDNESDAY

1 Chr. 9:1—12:40

GET THE BIG PICTURE

Again today's reading begins with a genealogy that at first blush looks like just another list of unpronounceable names. But in reality it's the genealogy of the people of Judah, including the priests, who returned after the exile. This list of names chronicles the Lord's grace in bringing His people back from captivity and moving ahead on His promise to send the Savior—our Savior! If time is short, focus on 1 Chronicles 12:1–22.

9 All Israel was listed in the genealogies recorded in the book of
the kings of Israel.

The People in Jerusalem

The people of Judah were taken captive to Babylon because of their unfaithfulness. [2]Now the first to resettle on
their own property in their own towns
were some Israelites, priests, Levites
and temple servants.
[3]Those from Judah, from Benjamin,
and from Ephraim and Manasseh who
lived in Jerusalem were:
[4]Uthai son of Ammihud, the son of
Omri, the son of Imri, the son of
Bani, a descendant of Perez son
of Judah.
[5]Of the Shilonites:
Asaiah the firstborn and his sons.
[6]Of the Zerahites:
Jeuel.
The people from Judah numbered 690.
[7]Of the Benjamites:
Sallu son of Meshullam, the son
of Hodaviah, the son of Hassenuah;
[8]Ibneiah son of Jeroham; Elah son
of Uzzi, the son of Micri; and Meshullam son of Shephatiah, the
son of Reuel, the son of Ibnijah.
[9]The people from Benjamin, as
listed in their genealogy, numbered 956. All these men were
heads of their families.
[10]Of the priests:
Jedaiah; Jehoiarib; Jakin;
[11]Azariah son of Hilkiah, the son of
Meshullam, the son of Zadok,
the son of Meraioth, the son of
Ahitub, the official in charge of
the house of God;
[12]Adaiah son of Jeroham, the son
of Pashhur, the son of Malkijah;
and Maasai son of Adiel, the son
of Jahzerah, the son of Meshullam, the son of Meshillemith, the
son of Immer.
[13]The priests, who were heads of
families, numbered 1,760. They
were able men, responsible for
ministering in the house of God.
[14]Of the Levites:
Shemaiah son of Hasshub, the
son of Azrikam, the son of Hashabiah, a Merarite; [15]Bakbakkar,
Heresh, Galal and Mattaniah son
of Mica, the son of Zicri, the son
of Asaph; [16]Obadiah son of Shemaiah, the son of Galal, the son
of Jeduthun; and Berekiah son of

Asa, the son of Elkanah, who
lived in the villages of the Netophathites.
[17]The gatekeepers:
Shallum, Akkub, Talmon, Ahiman and their brothers, Shallum
their chief [18]being stationed at
the King's Gate on the east, up to
the present time. These were the
gatekeepers belonging to the
camp of the Levites. [19]Shallum
son of Kore, the son of Ebiasaph,
the son of Korah, and his fellow
gatekeepers from his family (the
Korahites) were responsible for
guarding the thresholds of the
Tent[a] just as their fathers had
been responsible for guarding
the entrance to the dwelling of
the LORD. [20]In earlier times Phinehas son of Eleazar was in charge
of the gatekeepers, and the LORD
was with him. [21]Zechariah son of
Meshelemiah was the gatekeeper at the entrance to the Tent of
Meeting.
[22]Altogether, those chosen to be gatekeepers at the thresholds numbered
212. They were registered by genealogy
in their villages. The gatekeepers had
been assigned to their positions of trust
by David and Samuel the seer. [23]They
and their descendants were in charge of
guarding the gates of the house of the
LORD—the house called the Tent. [24]The
gatekeepers were on the four sides: east,
west, north and south. [25]Their brothers
in their villages had to come from time
to time and share their duties for seven-
day periods. [26]But the four principal
gatekeepers, who were Levites, were
entrusted with the responsibility for the
rooms and treasuries in the house of
God. [27]They would spend the night stationed around the house of God, because they had to guard it; and they had
charge of the key for opening it each
morning.
[28]Some of them were in charge of the
articles used in the temple service; they
counted them when they were brought
in and when they were taken out. [29]Oth-
ers were assigned to take care of the furnishings and all the other articles of the
sanctuary, as well as the flour and wine,
and the oil, incense and spices. [30]But
some of the priests took care of mixing
the spices. [31]A Levite named Mattithiah,
the firstborn son of Shallum the Korahite, was entrusted with the responsibility for baking the offering bread. [32]Some
of their Kohathite brothers were in
charge of preparing for every Sabbath
the bread set out on the table.
[33]Those who were musicians, heads of
Levite families, stayed in the rooms of
the temple and were exempt from other duties because they were responsible
for the work day and night.
[34]All these were heads of Levite families, chiefs as listed in their genealogy,
and they lived in Jerusalem.

The Genealogy of Saul

[35]Jeiel the father[b] of Gibeon lived in
Gibeon.
His wife's name was Maacah,
[36]and his firstborn son was Abdon, followed by Zur, Kish, Baal,
Ner, Nadab, [37]Gedor, Ahio, Zechariah and Mikloth. [38]Mikloth was
the father of Shimeam. They too
lived near their relatives in Jerusalem.
[39]Ner was the father of Kish, Kish the
father of Saul, and Saul the father
of Jonathan, Malki-Shua, Abinadab and Esh-Baal.[c]
[40]The son of Jonathan:
Merib-Baal,[d] who was the father
of Micah.
[41]The sons of Micah:
Pithon, Melech, Tahrea and
Ahaz.[e]
[42]Ahaz was the father of Jadah,
Jadah[f] was the father of Alemeth,
Azmaveth and Zimri, and Zimri
was the father of Moza. [43]Moza

[a]*19* That is, the temple; also in verses 21 and 23
[b]*35* *Father* may mean *civic leader* or *military leader.*
[c]*39* Also known as *Ish-Bosheth* [d]*40* Also known as *Mephibosheth* [e]*41* Vulgate and Syriac (see also Septuagint and 1 Chron. 8:35); Hebrew does not have *and Ahaz.* [f]*42* Some Hebrew manuscripts and Septuagint (see also 1 Chron. 8:36); most Hebrew manuscripts *Jarah, Jarah*

was the father of Binea; Rephaiah was his son, Eleasah his son
and Azel his son.
44Azel had six sons, and these were
their names:
Azrikam, Bokeru, Ishmael, Sheariah, Obadiah and Hanan. These
were the sons of Azel.

Saul Takes His Life

10 Now the Philistines fought
against Israel; the Israelites
fled before them, and many fell slain on
Mount Gilboa. 2The Philistines pressed
hard after Saul and his sons, and they
killed his sons Jonathan, Abinadab and
Malki-Shua. 3The fighting grew fierce
around Saul, and when the archers
overtook him, they wounded him.
4Saul said to his armor-bearer, "Draw
your sword and run me through, or
these uncircumcised fellows will come
and abuse me."
But his armor-bearer was terrified
and would not do it; so Saul took his
own sword and fell on it. 5When the
armor-bearer saw that Saul was dead,
he too fell on his sword and died. 6So
Saul and his three sons died, and all his
house died together.
7When all the Israelites in the valley
saw that the army had fled and that Saul
and his sons had died, they abandoned
their towns and fled. And the Philistines
came and occupied them.
8The next day, when the Philistines
came to strip the dead, they found Saul
and his sons fallen on Mount Gilboa.
9They stripped him and took his head
and his armor, and sent messengers
throughout the land of the Philistines to
proclaim the news among their idols
and their people. 10They put his armor
in the temple of their gods and hung up
his head in the temple of Dagon.
11When all the inhabitants of Jabesh
Gilead heard of everything the Philistines had done to Saul, 12all their valiant
men went and took the bodies of Saul
and his sons and brought them to Jabesh. Then they buried their bones under the great tree in Jabesh, and they
fasted seven days.
13Saul died because he was unfaithful
to the LORD; he did not keep the word
of the LORD and even consulted a medium for guidance, 14and did not inquire
of the LORD. So the LORD put him to
death and turned the kingdom over to
David son of Jesse.

David Becomes King Over Israel

11 All Israel came together to
David at Hebron and said, "We
are your own flesh and blood. 2In the
past, even while Saul was king, you
were the one who led Israel on their
military campaigns. And the LORD your
God said to you, 'You will shepherd my
people Israel, and you will become their
ruler.' "
3When all the elders of Israel had
come to King David at Hebron, he made
a compact with them at Hebron before
the LORD, and they anointed David king
over Israel, as the LORD had promised
through Samuel.

David Conquers Jerusalem

4David and all the Israelites marched
to Jerusalem (that is, Jebus). The Jebusites who lived there 5said to David,
"You will not get in here." Nevertheless,
David captured the fortress of Zion, the
City of David.
6David had said, "Whoever leads the
attack on the Jebusites will become com-
mander-in-chief." Joab son of Zeruiah
went up first, and so he received the
command.
7David then took up residence in the
fortress, and so it was called the City of
David. 8He built up the city around it,
from the supporting terraces[a] to the surrounding wall, while Joab restored the
rest of the city. 9And David became more
and more powerful, because the LORD
Almighty was with him.

David's Mighty Men

10These were the chiefs of David's
mighty men—they, together with all Israel, gave his kingship strong support to
extend it over the whole land, as the

[a]8 Or *the Millo*

LORD had promised— 11this is the list of
David's mighty men:
Jashobeam,[a] a Hacmonite, was chief
of the officers[b]; he raised his spear
against three hundred men, whom he
killed in one encounter.
12Next to him was Eleazar son of Dodai the Ahohite, one of the three mighty
men. 13He was with David at Pas Dammim when the Philistines gathered
there for battle. At a place where there
was a field full of barley, the troops fled
from the Philistines. 14But they took
their stand in the middle of the field.
They defended it and struck the Philistines down, and the LORD brought
about a great victory.
15Three of the thirty chiefs came down
to David to the rock at the cave of Adullam, while a band of Philistines was
encamped in the Valley of Rephaim. 16At
that time David was in the stronghold,
and the Philistine garrison was at Bethlehem. 17David longed for water and
said, "Oh, that someone would get me
a drink of water from the well near the
gate of Bethlehem!" 18So the Three
broke through the Philistine lines, drew
water from the well near the gate of
Bethlehem and carried it back to David.
But he refused to drink it; instead, he
poured it out before the LORD. 19"God
forbid that I should do this!" he said.
"Should I drink the blood of these men
who went at the risk of their lives?" Because they risked their lives to bring it
back, David would not drink it.
Such were the exploits of the three
mighty men.
20Abishai the brother of Joab was chief
of the Three. He raised his spear against
three hundred men, whom he killed,
and so he became as famous as the
Three. 21He was doubly honored above
the Three and became their commander, even though he was not included
among them.
22Benaiah son of Jehoiada was a valiant fighter from Kabzeel, who performed great exploits. He struck down
two of Moab's best men. He also went
down into a pit on a snowy day and
killed a lion. 23And he struck down an
Egyptian who was seven and a half feet[c]
tall. Although the Egyptian had a spear
like a weaver's rod in his hand, Benaiah went against him with a club. He
snatched the spear from the Egyptian's
hand and killed him with his own spear.
24Such were the exploits of Benaiah son
of Jehoiada; he too was as famous as the
three mighty men. 25He was held in
greater honor than any of the Thirty, but
he was not included among the Three.
And David put him in charge of his
bodyguard.

26The mighty men were:
Asahel the brother of Joab,
Elhanan son of Dodo from Bethlehem,
27Shammoth the Harorite,
Helez the Pelonite,
28Ira son of Ikkesh from Tekoa,
Abiezer from Anathoth,
29Sibbecai the Hushathite,
Ilai the Ahohite,
30Maharai the Netophathite,
Heled son of Baanah the Netophathite,
31Ithai son of Ribai from Gibeah in
Benjamin,
Benaiah the Pirathonite,
32Hurai from the ravines of Gaash,
Abiel the Arbathite,
33Azmaveth the Baharumite,
Eliahba the Shaalbonite,
34the sons of Hashem the Gizonite,
Jonathan son of Shagee the Hararite,
35Ahiam son of Sacar the Hararite,
Eliphal son of Ur,
36Hepher the Mekerathite,
Ahijah the Pelonite,
37Hezro the Carmelite,
Naarai son of Ezbai,
38Joel the brother of Nathan,
Mibhar son of Hagri,
39Zelek the Ammonite,
Naharai the Berothite, the armor-
bearer of Joab son of Zeruiah,
40Ira the Ithrite,

[a]*11* Possibly a variant of *Jashob-Baal* [b]*11* Or *Thirty*; some Septuagint manuscripts *Three* (see also 2 Samuel 23:8) [c]*23* Hebrew *five cubits* (about 2.3 meters)

Gareb the Ithrite,
41 Uriah the Hittite,
Zabad son of Ahlai,
42 Adina son of Shiza the Reubenite, who was chief of the Reubenites, and the thirty with him,
43 Hanan son of Maacah,
Joshaphat the Mithnite,
44 Uzzia the Ashterathite,
Shama and Jeiel the sons of Hotham the Aroerite,
45 Jediael son of Shimri,
his brother Joha the Tizite,
46 Eliel the Mahavite,
Jeribai and Joshaviah the sons of Elnaam,
Ithmah the Moabite,
47 Eliel, Obed and Jaasiel the Mezobaite.

Warriors Join David

12 These were the men who came to David at Ziklag, while
he was banished from the presence of
Saul son of Kish (they were among
the warriors who helped him in battle;
2 they were armed with bows and were
able to shoot arrows or to sling stones
right-handed or left-handed; they were
kinsmen of Saul from the tribe of Benjamin):

3 Ahiezer their chief and Joash the
sons of Shemaah the Gibeathite;
Jeziel and Pelet the sons of Azmaveth; Beracah, Jehu the Anathothite, 4 and Ishmaiah the Gibeonite, a
mighty man among the Thirty, who
was a leader of the Thirty; Jeremiah, Jahaziel, Johanan, Jozabad the
Gederathite, 5 Eluzai, Jerimoth, Bealiah, Shemariah and Shephatiah
the Haruphite; 6 Elkanah, Isshiah,
Azarel, Joezer and Jashobeam the
Korahites; 7 and Joelah and Zebadiah
the sons of Jeroham from Gedor.

8 Some Gadites defected to David at
his stronghold in the desert. They were
brave warriors, ready for battle and able
to handle the shield and spear. Their
faces were the faces of lions, and they
were as swift as gazelles in the mountains.

9 Ezer was the chief,
Obadiah the second in command,
Eliab the third,
10 Mishmannah the fourth, Jeremiah the fifth,
11 Attai the sixth, Eliel the seventh,
12 Johanan the eighth, Elzabad the ninth,
13 Jeremiah the tenth and Macbannai the eleventh.

14 These Gadites were army commanders; the least was a match for a hundred,
and the greatest for a thousand. 15 It was
they who crossed the Jordan in the first
month when it was overflowing all its
banks, and they put to flight everyone
living in the valleys, to the east and to
the west.

16 Other Benjamites and some men
from Judah also came to David in his
stronghold. 17 David went out to meet
them and said to them, "If you have
come to me in peace, to help me, I am
ready to have you unite with me. But if
you have come to betray me to my enemies when my hands are free from violence, may the God of our fathers see it
and judge you."
18 Then the Spirit came upon Amasai,
chief of the Thirty, and he said:

"We are yours, O David!
We are with you, O son of Jesse!
Success, success to you,
and success to those who help you,
for your God will help you."

So David received them and made them leaders of his raiding bands.
19 Some of the men of Manasseh defected to David when he went with the
Philistines to fight against Saul. (He and
his men did not help the Philistines because, after consultation, their rulers
sent him away. They said, "It will cost us
our heads if he deserts to his master
Saul.") 20 When David went to Ziklag,
these were the men of Manasseh who
defected to him: Adnah, Jozabad, Jediael, Michael, Jozabad, Elihu and Zillethai, leaders of units of a thousand in
Manasseh. 21 They helped David against
raiding bands, for all of them were
brave warriors, and they were com-

manders in his army. 22 Day after day men came to help David, until he had a great army, like the army of God.[a]

Others Join David at Hebron

23 These are the numbers of the men armed for battle who came to David at Hebron to turn Saul's kingdom over to him, as the LORD had said:

24 men of Judah, carrying shield and spear—6,800 armed for battle;
25 men of Simeon, warriors ready for battle—7,100;
26 men of Levi—4,600, 27 including Jehoiada, leader of the family of Aaron, with 3,700 men, 28 and Zadok, a brave young warrior, with 22 officers from his family;
29 men of Benjamin, Saul's kinsmen—3,000, most of whom had remained loyal to Saul's house until then;
30 men of Ephraim, brave warriors, famous in their own clans—20,800;
31 men of half the tribe of Manasseh, designated by name to come and make David king—18,000;
32 men of Issachar, who understood the times and knew what Israel should do—200 chiefs, with all their relatives under their command;
33 men of Zebulun, experienced soldiers prepared for battle with every type of weapon, to help David with undivided loyalty—50,000;
34 men of Naphtali—1,000 officers, together with 37,000 men carrying shields and spears;
35 men of Dan, ready for battle—28,600;
36 men of Asher, experienced soldiers prepared for battle—40,000;
37 and from east of the Jordan, men of Reuben, Gad and the half-tribe of Manasseh, armed with every type of weapon—120,000.

38 All these were fighting men who
volunteered to serve in the ranks. They
came to Hebron fully determined to
make David king over all Israel. All the
rest of the Israelites were also of one
mind to make David king. 39 The men
spent three days there with David, eating and drinking, for their families had
supplied provisions for them. 40 Also,
their neighbors from as far away as Issachar, Zebulun and Naphtali came
bringing food on donkeys, camels,
mules and oxen. There were plentiful
supplies of flour, fig cakes, raisin cakes,
wine, oil, cattle and sheep, for there was
joy in Israel.

[a]22 Or *a great and mighty army*

SHARPEN THE FOCUS

Did you notice the comic note in 1 Chronicles 10:9? The Philistines had to send messengers to let their "god" know what they had done in battle!

We may smile at the notion, but all the while act as though the Lord is limited in the same way. For example, as you set your budget, does the Lord guide your decisions—not just about the percentage that you'll give to Him, but also about the percentage that you'll spend, save, or invest? As you walk into church to worship Him, do you come expecting to hear Him speak to you—to you personally—in the service? In short, is your Lord a part of your daily existence? Or is He enthroned in heaven as a kindly grandfather whom you visit once a week to exchange sweet sentiments?

When David's army met Amasai (1 Chronicles 12:16–18), Amasai reminded David that God was helping him and would continue to do so. David was encouraged because he knew the Lord to be the living God—the God who speaks and acts on behalf of His people.

That same God is "our God for ever and ever; He will be our guide even to the end" (Psalm 48:14).

The Ark Brought to Jerusalem

15 After David had constructed buildings for himself in the City of David, he prepared a place for the ark of God and pitched a tent for it. 2Then David said, "No one but the Levites may carry the ark of God, because the LORD chose them to carry the ark of the LORD and to minister before him forever."

3David assembled all Israel in Jerusalem to bring up the ark of the LORD to the place he had prepared for it. 4He called together the descendants of Aaron and the Levites:

5From the descendants of Kohath,
Uriel the leader and 120 relatives;
6from the descendants of Merari,
Asaiah the leader and 220 relatives;
7from the descendants of Gershon,[a]
Joel the leader and 130 relatives;
8from the descendants of Elizaphan,
Shemaiah the leader and 200 relatives;
9from the descendants of Hebron,
Eliel the leader and 80 relatives;
10from the descendants of Uzziel,
Amminadab the leader and 112 relatives.

11Then David summoned Zadok and Abiathar the priests, and Uriel, Asaiah, Joel, Shemaiah, Eliel and Amminadab the Levites. 12He said to them, "You are the heads of the Levitical families; you and your fellow Levites are to consecrate yourselves and bring up the ark of the LORD, the God of Israel, to the place I have prepared for it. 13It was because you, the Levites, did not bring it up the first time that the LORD our God broke out in anger against us. We did not inquire of him about how to do it in the prescribed way." 14So the priests and Levites consecrated themselves in order to bring up the ark of the LORD, the God of Israel. 15And the Levites carried the ark of God with the poles on their shoulders, as Moses had commanded in accordance with the word of the LORD.

16David told the leaders of the Levites to appoint their brothers as singers to sing joyful songs, accompanied by musical instruments: lyres, harps and cymbals.

17So the Levites appointed Heman son of Joel; from his brothers, Asaph son of Berekiah; and from their brothers the Merarites, Ethan son of Kushaiah; 18and with them their brothers next in rank: Zechariah,[b] Jaaziel, Shemiramoth, Jehiel, Unni, Eliab, Benaiah, Maaseiah, Mattithiah, Eliphelehu, Mikneiah, Obed-Edom and Jeiel,[c] the gatekeepers.

19The musicians Heman, Asaph and Ethan were to sound the bronze cymbals; 20Zechariah, Aziel, Shemiramoth, Jehiel, Unni, Eliab, Maaseiah and Benaiah were to play the lyres according to *alamoth*,[d] 21and Mattithiah, Eliphelehu, Mikneiah, Obed-Edom, Jeiel and Azaziah were to play the harps, directing according to *sheminith*.[d] 22Kenaniah the head Levite was in charge of the singing; that was his responsibility because he was skillful at it.

23Berekiah and Elkanah were to be doorkeepers for the ark. 24Shebaniah, Joshaphat, Nethanel, Amasai, Zechariah, Benaiah and Eliezer the priests were to blow trumpets before the ark of God. Obed-Edom and Jehiah were also to be doorkeepers for the ark.

25So David and the elders of Israel and the commanders of units of a thousand went to bring up the ark of the covenant of the LORD from the house of Obed-Edom, with rejoicing. 26Because God had helped the Levites who were carrying the ark of the covenant of the LORD, seven bulls and seven rams were sacrificed. 27Now David was clothed in a robe of fine linen, as were all the Levites who were carrying the ark, and as were the singers, and Kenaniah, who was in charge of the singing of the choirs. David also wore a linen ephod. 28So all Israel brought up the ark of the

[a]7 Hebrew *Gershom,* a variant of *Gershon*
[b]18 Three Hebrew manuscripts and most Septuagint manuscripts (see also verse 20 and 1 Chron. 16:5); most Hebrew manuscripts *Zechariah son and* or *Zechariah, Ben and*
[c]18 Hebrew; Septuagint (see also verse 21) *Jeiel and Azaziah* [d]20,21 Probably a musical term

covenant of the LORD with shouts, with
the sounding of rams' horns and trumpets, and of cymbals, and the playing of
lyres and harps.
29 As the ark of the covenant of the
LORD was entering the City of David,
Michal daughter of Saul watched from
a window. And when she saw King
David dancing and celebrating, she despised him in her heart.

16 They brought the ark of God
and set it inside the tent that
David had pitched for it, and they presented burnt offerings and fellowship
offerings[a] before God. 2 After David had
finished sacrificing the burnt offerings
and fellowship offerings, he blessed the
people in the name of the LORD. 3 Then
he gave a loaf of bread, a cake of dates
and a cake of raisins to each Israelite
man and woman.
4 He appointed some of the Levites to
minister before the ark of the LORD, to
make petition, to give thanks, and to
praise the LORD, the God of Israel:
5 Asaph was the chief, Zechariah second,
then Jeiel, Shemiramoth, Jehiel, Mattithiah, Eliab, Benaiah, Obed-Edom and
Jeiel. They were to play the lyres and
harps, Asaph was to sound the cymbals,
6 and Benaiah and Jahaziel the priests
were to blow the trumpets regularly before the ark of the covenant of God.

David's Psalm of Thanks

7 That day David first committed to
Asaph and his associates this psalm of
thanks to the LORD:

8 Give thanks to the LORD, call on his
name;
make known among the nations
what he has done.
9 Sing to him, sing praise to him;
tell of all his wonderful acts.
10 Glory in his holy name;
let the hearts of those who seek
the LORD rejoice.
11 Look to the LORD and his strength;
seek his face always.
12 Remember the wonders he has done,
his miracles, and the judgments
he pronounced,
13 O descendants of Israel his servant,
O sons of Jacob, his chosen ones.

14 He is the LORD our God;
his judgments are in all the earth.
15 He remembers[b] his covenant forever,
the word he commanded, for a
thousand generations,
16 the covenant he made with
Abraham,
the oath he swore to Isaac.
17 He confirmed it to Jacob as a decree,
to Israel as an everlasting
covenant:
18 "To you I will give the land of Canaan
as the portion you will inherit."

19 When they were but few in number,
few indeed, and strangers in it,
20 they[c] wandered from nation to
nation,
from one kingdom to another.
21 He allowed no man to oppress
them;
for their sake he rebuked kings:
22 "Do not touch my anointed ones;
do my prophets no harm."

23 Sing to the LORD, all the earth;
proclaim his salvation day after
day.
24 Declare his glory among the nations,
his marvelous deeds among all
peoples.
25 For great is the LORD and most
worthy of praise;
he is to be feared above all gods.
26 For all the gods of the nations are
idols,
but the LORD made the heavens.
27 Splendor and majesty are before
him;
strength and joy in his dwelling
place.
28 Ascribe to the LORD, O families of
nations,
ascribe to the LORD glory and
strength,

[a] *1* Traditionally *peace offerings*; also in verse 2
[b] *15* Some Septuagint manuscripts (see also Psalm 105:8); Hebrew *Remember*
[c] *18-20* One Hebrew manuscript, Septuagint and Vulgate (see also Psalm 105:12); most Hebrew manuscripts *inherit, / 19 though you are but few in number, / few indeed, and strangers in it." / 20 They*

[29] ascribe to the LORD the glory due his name.
Bring an offering and come before him;
worship the LORD in the splendor of his[a] holiness.
[30] Tremble before him, all the earth!
The world is firmly established; it cannot be moved.
[31] Let the heavens rejoice, let the earth be glad;
let them say among the nations, "The LORD reigns!"
[32] Let the sea resound, and all that is in it;
let the fields be jubilant, and everything in them!
[33] Then the trees of the forest will sing,
they will sing for joy before the LORD,
for he comes to judge the earth.

[34] Give thanks to the LORD, for he is good;
his love endures forever.
[35] Cry out, "Save us, O God our Savior;
gather us and deliver us from the nations,
that we may give thanks to your holy name,
that we may glory in your praise."
[36] Praise be to the LORD, the God of Israel,
from everlasting to everlasting.

Then all the people said "Amen" and "Praise the LORD."

[37] David left Asaph and his associates before the ark of the covenant of the LORD to minister there regularly, according to each day's requirements.
[38] He also left Obed-Edom and his sixty-eight associates to minister with them. Obed-Edom son of Jeduthun, and also Hosah, were gatekeepers.
[39] David left Zadok the priest and his fellow priests before the tabernacle of the LORD at the high place in Gibeon
[40] to present burnt offerings to the LORD on the altar of burnt offering regularly, morning and evening, in accordance with everything written in the Law of the LORD, which he had given Israel.
[41] With them were Heman and Jeduthun and the rest of those chosen and designated by name to give thanks to the LORD, "for his love endures forever."
[42] Heman and Jeduthun were responsible for the sounding of the trumpets and cymbals and for the playing of the other instruments for sacred song. The sons of Jeduthun were stationed at the gate.
[43] Then all the people left, each for his own home, and David returned home to bless his family.

[a]29 Or *LORD with the splendor of*

SHARPEN THE FOCUS

Have you ever known someone whose smile made your life worth living? Someone with whom you longed to spend time—not doing anything special, just *being* together?

The ark of the covenant represented God's presence among His people in a unique way. It was, in a sense, His throne on earth. King David, passionately in love with the Lord, found his heart moved to unspeakable joy in the Lord's presence. He worshiped with abandon, so much so that his wife accused him of undignified behavior for a man of David's rank.

King David once wrote:

> *You have made known to me the path of life;*
> *You will fill me with joy in Your presence,*
> *with eternal pleasures at Your right hand.* (Psalm 16:11)

To be with Jesus—now and forever. It's every believer's fervent desire, our best and highest joy. The cross radiates the love that draws us to Him and lavishes the pardon that creates our peace in His presence. The cross conveys the righteousness that fills our hearts with joy in His presence.

No wonder David danced as He saw Christ's deliverance from afar! Let David's Lord put a spring in your step today, too, as you live more conscious of His presence with you.

WEEK 34 • SATURDAY

1 Chronicles 17:1–27

In today's reading, the Lord promises to build an eternal house for David. This promise is a prophecy of the Messiah who would come. The promise is so big that it seemingly knocks David off his feet; the king sits down as he responds to the Lord's Word. As you read, ask yourself, "Do I fully realize the uniqueness and the fullness of God's love—for me?" If time is short, focus on 1 Chronicles 17:16–27.

God's Promise to David

17 After David was settled in his
palace, he said to Nathan the
prophet, "Here I am, living in a palace
of cedar, while the ark of the covenant
of the LORD is under a tent."
[2]Nathan replied to David, "Whatever
you have in mind, do it, for God is with
you."
[3]That night the word of God came to
Nathan, saying:

[4]"Go and tell my servant David,
'This is what the LORD says: You are
not the one to build me a house to
dwell in. [5]I have not dwelt in a
house from the day I brought Israel
up out of Egypt to this day. I have
moved from one tent site to another, from one dwelling place to another. [6]Wherever I have moved
with all the Israelites, did I ever say
to any of their leaders[a] whom I
commanded to shepherd my
people, "Why have you not built
me a house of cedar?"'
[7]"Now then, tell my servant David, 'This is what the LORD Almighty says: I took you from the
pasture and from following the
flock, to be ruler over my people
Israel. [8]I have been with you wherever you have gone, and I have cut
off all your enemies from before
you. Now I will make your name
like the names of the greatest men
of the earth. [9]And I will provide a
place for my people Israel and will
plant them so that they can have a
home of their own and no longer
be disturbed. Wicked people will
not oppress them anymore, as they
did at the beginning [10]and have
done ever since the time I appointed leaders over my people Israel. I will also subdue all your
enemies.
"'I declare to you that the LORD
will build a house for you: [11]When
your days are over and you go to be
with your fathers, I will raise up
your offspring to succeed you, one
of your own sons, and I will establish his kingdom. [12]He is the one
who will build a house for me, and
I will establish his throne forever. [13]I

[a]6 Traditionally *judges;* also in verse 10

will be his father, and he will be my
son. I will never take my love away
from him, as I took it away from
your predecessor. [14]I will set him
over my house and my kingdom
forever; his throne will be established forever.' "

[15]Nathan reported to David all the
words of this entire revelation.

David's Prayer

[16]Then King David went in and sat before the LORD, and he said:

"Who am I, O LORD God, and
what is my family, that you have
brought me this far? [17]And as if this
were not enough in your sight, O
God, you have spoken about the
future of the house of your servant.
You have looked on me as though
I were the most exalted of men, O
LORD God.

[18]"What more can David say to
you for honoring your servant? For
you know your servant, [19]O LORD.
For the sake of your servant and
according to your will, you have
done this great thing and made
known all these great promises.

[20]"There is no one like you, O
LORD, and there is no God but you,
as we have heard with our own
ears. [21]And who is like your people
Israel—the one nation on earth
whose God went out to redeem a
people for himself, and to make a
name for yourself, and to perform
great and awesome wonders by
driving out nations from before
your people, whom you redeemed
from Egypt? [22]You made your people Israel your very own forever,
and you, O LORD, have become
their God.

[23]"And now, LORD, let the promise you have made concerning your
servant and his house be established forever. Do as you promised,
[24]so that it will be established and
that your name will be great forever. Then men will say, 'The LORD
Almighty, the God over Israel, is
Israel's God!' And the house of
your servant David will be established before you.

[25]"You, my God, have revealed to
your servant that you will build a
house for him. So your servant has
found courage to pray to you. [26]O
LORD, you are God! You have
promised these good things to your
servant. [27]Now you have been
pleased to bless the house of your
servant, that it may continue forever in your sight; for you, O LORD,
have blessed it, and it will be
blessed forever."

SHARPEN THE FOCUS

Had human beings thought for centuries, never would any of us have imagined the kind of God revealed to us in the Scriptures. Yahweh, the Lord:

- is kind, gentle, good;
- longs for a personal relationship with each of His human creations;
- makes and keeps promises to His people;
- chooses to create a family—Israel, His church—to live with Him forever.

No wonder David exclaimed:

There is no one like You, O LORD, and there is no God but You, as we have heard with our own ears. (1 Chronicles 17:20)

In another psalm David wrote of the Lord, "You stoop down to make me great" (Psalm 18:35). As New Testament believers we see this gentleness even more clearly than did King David. We've seen Jesus, the God of heaven and earth, take a towel and kneel to wash the dirt-caked feet of his disciples. We've seen Jesus, the King of heaven, kneel in agonized prayer in Gethsemane. We've seen Jesus, the Lord of lords, fall to His knees beneath the weight of His own cross. All for you. All for me. Awesome! There truly is none like Him, nor is there any God beside Him.

Miscellaneous victories. That's what you'll see if you disconnect 1 Chronicles 18–20 from 1 Chronicles 17:25–27. If you do that, you'll miss the real point of the Word of God you'll read today. So review 1 Chronicles 17:25–27 as you begin. If time is short, focus on 1 Chronicles 18:1–11.

David's Victories

18 In the course of time, David defeated the Philistines and subdued them, and he took Gath and its surrounding villages from the control of the Philistines.
2David also defeated the Moabites, and they became subject to him and brought tribute.
3Moreover, David fought Hadadezer king of Zobah, as far as Hamath, when he went to establish his control along
the Euphrates River. 4David captured a
thousand of his chariots, seven thousand charioteers and twenty thousand foot soldiers. He hamstrung all but a hundred of the chariot horses.
5When the Arameans of Damascus came to help Hadadezer king of Zobah, David struck down twenty-two thou-
sand of them. 6He put garrisons in the
Aramean kingdom of Damascus, and the Arameans became subject to him and brought tribute. The LORD gave David victory everywhere he went.
7David took the gold shields carried by the officers of Hadadezer and
brought them to Jerusalem. 8From
Tebah[a] and Cun, towns that belonged to Hadadezer, David took a great quantity of bronze, which Solomon used to make the bronze Sea, the pillars and various bronze articles.
9When Tou king of Hamath heard that David had defeated the entire army of
Hadadezer king of Zobah, 10he sent his
son Hadoram to King David to greet him and congratulate him on his victory in battle over Hadadezer, who had been at war with Tou. Hadoram brought all kinds of articles of gold and silver and bronze.
11King David dedicated these articles to the LORD, as he had done with the silver and gold he had taken from all these nations: Edom and Moab, the Ammonites and the Philistines, and Amalek.
12Abishai son of Zeruiah struck down eighteen thousand Edomites in the Val-
ley of Salt. 13He put garrisons in Edom,

[a]8 Hebrew *Tibhath,* a variant of *Tebah*

and all the Edomites became subject to David. The LORD gave David victory everywhere he went.

David's Officials

14David reigned over all Israel, doing what was just and right for all his people. 15Joab son of Zeruiah was over the army; Jehoshaphat son of Ahilud was recorder; 16Zadok son of Ahitub and Ahimelech[a] son of Abiathar were priests; Shavsha was secretary; 17Benaiah son of Jehoiada was over the Kerethites and Pelethites; and David's sons were chief officials at the king's side.

The Battle Against the Ammonites

19 In the course of time, Nahash king of the Ammonites died, and his son succeeded him as king. 2David thought, "I will show kindness to Hanun son of Nahash, because his father showed kindness to me." So David sent a delegation to express his sympathy to Hanun concerning his father.

When David's men came to Hanun in the land of the Ammonites to express sympathy to him, 3the Ammonite nobles said to Hanun, "Do you think David is honoring your father by sending men to you to express sympathy? Haven't his men come to you to explore and spy out the country and overthrow it?" 4So Hanun seized David's men, shaved them, cut off their garments in the middle at the buttocks, and sent them away.

5When someone came and told David about the men, he sent messengers to meet them, for they were greatly humiliated. The king said, "Stay at Jericho till your beards have grown, and then come back."

6When the Ammonites realized that they had become a stench in David's nostrils, Hanun and the Ammonites sent a thousand talents[b] of silver to hire chariots and charioteers from Aram Naharaim,[c] Aram Maacah and Zobah. 7They hired thirty-two thousand chariots and charioteers, as well as the king of Maacah with his troops, who came and camped near Medeba, while the Ammonites were mustered from their towns and moved out for battle.

8On hearing this, David sent Joab out with the entire army of fighting men. 9The Ammonites came out and drew up in battle formation at the entrance to their city, while the kings who had come were by themselves in the open country.

10Joab saw that there were battle lines in front of him and behind him; so he selected some of the best troops in Israel and deployed them against the Arameans. 11He put the rest of the men under the command of Abishai his brother, and they were deployed against the Ammonites. 12Joab said, "If the Arameans are too strong for me, then you are to rescue me; but if the Ammonites are too strong for you, then I will rescue you. 13Be strong and let us fight bravely for our people and the cities of our God. The LORD will do what is good in his sight."

14Then Joab and the troops with him advanced to fight the Arameans, and they fled before him. 15When the Ammonites saw that the Arameans were fleeing, they too fled before his brother Abishai and went inside the city. So Joab went back to Jerusalem.

16After the Arameans saw that they had been routed by Israel, they sent messengers and had Arameans brought from beyond the River,[d] with Shophach the commander of Hadadezer's army leading them.

17When David was told of this, he gathered all Israel and crossed the Jordan; he advanced against them and formed his battle lines opposite them. David formed his lines to meet the Arameans in battle, and they fought against him. 18But they fled before Israel, and David killed seven thousand of their charioteers and forty thousand of their foot soldiers. He also killed Shophach the commander of their army.

19When the vassals of Hadadezer saw

[a]*16* Some Hebrew manuscripts, Vulgate and Syriac (see also 2 Samuel 8:17); most Hebrew manuscripts *Abimelech* [b]*6* That is, about 37 tons (about 34 metric tons) [c]*6* That is, Northwest Mesopotamia [d]*16* That is, the Euphrates

that they had been defeated by Israel, they made peace with David and became subject to him.

So the Arameans were not willing to help the Ammonites anymore.

The Capture of Rabbah

20 In the spring, at the time when kings go off to war, Joab led out the armed forces. He laid waste the land of the Ammonites and went to Rabbah and besieged it, but David remained in Jerusalem. Joab attacked Rabbah and left it in ruins.
[2]David took the crown from the head of their king[a]—its weight was found to be a talent[b] of gold, and it was set with precious stones—and it was placed on David's head. He took a great quantity of plunder from the city [3]and brought out the people who were there, consigning them to labor with saws and with iron picks and axes. David did this to all the Ammonite towns. Then David and his entire army returned to Jerusalem.

War With the Philistines

[4]In the course of time, war broke out with the Philistines, at Gezer. At that time Sibbecai the Hushathite killed Sippai, one of the descendants of the Rephaites, and the Philistines were subjugated.

[5]In another battle with the Philistines, Elhanan son of Jair killed Lahmi the brother of Goliath the Gittite, who had a spear with a shaft like a weaver's rod.

[6]In still another battle, which took place at Gath, there was a huge man with six fingers on each hand and six toes on each foot—twenty-four in all. He also was descended from Rapha.
[7]When he taunted Israel, Jonathan son of Shimea, David's brother, killed him.

[8]These were descendants of Rapha in Gath, and they fell at the hands of David and his men.

[a]2 Or *of Milcom,* that is, Molech [b]2 That is, about 75 pounds (about 34 kilograms)

SHARPEN THE FOCUS

Suppose your doctor diagnosed you with a fatal disease, but somehow you knew from the beginning the treatment would cure you.

Suppose an important relationship in your life hit some bumps, but somehow you could be sure from the beginning that reconciliation would occur.

What difference would foreknowledge like this make? It would not erase the need to live with the side effects of the drugs or to talk through the relationship glitches. Still, it would help whittle them down to size. It would be much easier to live in joy in times of hardship if we knew the end when we began.

King David knew the final outcome of his battles. He knew, because the Lord had promised to make him great and to give him an eternal dynasty. Still, David had to strap on his sword and ride off to war.

In a sense, we are like David. Because of the cross and open tomb of Jesus, we know the outcome of our struggles. God has promised to give us the crown of life (Revelation 2:10).

But now, at times, we must fight. We fight fear; we battle temptation; we confront injustice and wickedness. But when the dust clears, we will be standing–on the Rock who is Christ.

WEEK 35 • TUESDAY

1 Chronicles 21:1–30

Maybe it was pride. Maybe it was wrong-headed confidence in the size of the militia he was able to muster. Either way, David's sin brought the Lord's judgment down around the ears of all Israel. Nonetheless, the account you are about to read shows once again that God's mercy triumphs over judgment for His repentant people. If time is short, focus on 1 Chronicles 21:18–30.

David Numbers the Fighting Men

21 Satan rose up against Israel
and incited David to take a
census of Israel. 2So David said to Joab
and the commanders of the troops, "Go
and count the Israelites from Beersheba to Dan. Then report back to me so
that I may know how many there are."
3But Joab replied, "May the LORD
multiply his troops a hundred times
over. My lord the king, are they not all
my lord's subjects? Why does my lord
want to do this? Why should he bring
guilt on Israel?"
4The king's word, however, overruled
Joab; so Joab left and went throughout
Israel and then came back to Jerusalem.
5Joab reported the number of the fighting men to David: In all Israel there
were one million one hundred thousand men who could handle a sword,
including four hundred and seventy
thousand in Judah.
6But Joab did not include Levi and
Benjamin in the numbering, because
the king's command was repulsive to
him. 7This command was also evil in the
sight of God; so he punished Israel.
8Then David said to God, "I have
sinned greatly by doing this. Now, I beg
you, take away the guilt of your servant.
I have done a very foolish thing."
9The LORD said to Gad, David's seer,
10"Go and tell David, 'This is what the
LORD says: I am giving you three options. Choose one of them for me to
carry out against you.' "
11So Gad went to David and said to
him, "This is what the LORD says: 'Take
your choice: 12three years of famine,
three months of being swept away[a] before your enemies, with their swords
overtaking you, or three days of the
sword of the LORD—days of plague in
the land, with the angel of the LORD ravaging every part of Israel.' Now then,
decide how I should answer the one
who sent me."
13David said to Gad, "I am in deep distress. Let me fall into the hands of the
LORD, for his mercy is very great; but do
not let me fall into the hands of men."
14So the LORD sent a plague on Israel,
and seventy thousand men of Israel fell
dead. 15And God sent an angel to destroy Jerusalem. But as the angel was
doing so, the LORD saw it and was
grieved because of the calamity and said
to the angel who was destroying the
people, "Enough! Withdraw your
hand." The angel of the LORD was then
standing at the threshing floor of
Araunah[b] the Jebusite.
16David looked up and saw the angel
of the LORD standing between heaven
and earth, with a drawn sword in his
hand extended over Jerusalem. Then
David and the elders, clothed in sackcloth, fell facedown.
17David said to God, "Was it not I who

[a]12 Hebrew; Septuagint and Vulgate (see also 2 Samuel 24:13) *of fleeing* [b]15 Hebrew *Ornan,* a variant of *Araunah;* also in verses 18-28

ordered the fighting men to be counted? I am the one who has sinned and done wrong. These are but sheep. What have they done? O LORD my God, let your hand fall upon me and my family, but do not let this plague remain on your people."

[18]Then the angel of the LORD ordered Gad to tell David to go up and build an altar to the LORD on the threshing floor of Araunah the Jebusite. [19]So David went up in obedience to the word that Gad had spoken in the name of the LORD.

[20]While Araunah was threshing wheat, he turned and saw the angel; his four sons who were with him hid themselves. [21]Then David approached, and when Araunah looked and saw him, he left the threshing floor and bowed down before David with his face to the ground.

[22]David said to him, "Let me have the site of your threshing floor so I can build an altar to the LORD, that the plague on the people may be stopped. Sell it to me at the full price."

[23]Araunah said to David, "Take it! Let my lord the king do whatever pleases him. Look, I will give the oxen for the burnt offerings, the threshing sledges for the wood, and the wheat for the grain offering. I will give all this."

[24]But King David replied to Araunah, "No, I insist on paying the full price. I will not take for the LORD what is yours, or sacrifice a burnt offering that costs me nothing."

[25]So David paid Araunah six hundred shekels[a] of gold for the site. [26]David built an altar to the LORD there and sacrificed burnt offerings and fellowship offerings.[b] He called on the LORD, and the LORD answered him with fire from heaven on the altar of burnt offering.

[27]Then the LORD spoke to the angel, and he put his sword back into its sheath. [28]At that time, when David saw that the LORD had answered him on the threshing floor of Araunah the Jebusite, he offered sacrifices there. [29]The tabernacle of the LORD, which Moses had made in the desert, and the altar of burnt offering were at that time on the high place at Gibeon. [30]But David could not go before it to inquire of God, because he was afraid of the sword of the angel of the LORD.

[a]25 That is, about 15 pounds (about 7 kilograms)
[b]26 Traditionally *peace offerings*

SHARPEN THE FOCUS

Imagine standing on Araunah's threshing floor. Picture the angel of the Lord in the sky above Jerusalem. Imagine His sword, unsheathed, glistening in the sun. Picture the angel poised to descend on the city. Frightening, isn't it?

But the sword did not destroy David and all Israel with him that day. Why not? Was it because David pacified a holy God by bribery, by buying a tract of land on which the temple would later be built? No. We've seen ample evidence in Scripture that the Lord has no need of land or cattle nor of the puny worship of sinful human beings.

So why did the angel sheathe His sword (1 Chronicles 21:27)? Because the burnt offering David sacrificed (1 Chronicles 21:25–26) that day stood as a memorial—a reminder—of that one perfect Sacrifice that was to come. God would punish Jesus for David's sinful pride and self-reliance. All Israel's sins would be incinerated in the white-hot wrath of God when that wrath fell on Christ at Calvary.

Your sins and mine were burned to cinders on Christ's cross, too. What a relief to know that! What a relief to rely on the One who died for us and rose again so that we need never fear His judgment. With whom will you share this Good News today?

WEEK 35 • WEDNESDAY

1 Chr. 22:1–19

David had one duty, Solomon another. David conquered the land. Solomon constructed the temple. Given the tendency of human beings to hold a grudge, the same person could not have handled both tasks (1 Chronicles 22:8). As you read today, look for evidence that God's heart of love reached out beyond Israel to people of *all* nations. If time is short, focus on 1 Chronicles 22:1–5.

22 Then David said, "The
house of the LORD God is
to be here, and also the altar of burnt
offering for Israel."

Preparations for the Temple

2So David gave orders to assemble the
aliens living in Israel, and from among
them he appointed stonecutters to prepare dressed stone for building the
house of God. 3He provided a large
amount of iron to make nails for the
doors of the gateways and for the fit-
tings, and more bronze than could be
weighed. 4He also provided more cedar
logs than could be counted, for the Sidonians and Tyrians had brought large
numbers of them to David.
5David said, "My son Solomon is
young and inexperienced, and the
house to be built for the LORD should be
of great magnificence and fame and
splendor in the sight of all the nations.
Therefore I will make preparations for
it." So David made extensive preparations before his death.
6Then he called for his son Solomon
and charged him to build a house for
the LORD, the God of Israel. 7David said
to Solomon: "My son, I had it in my
heart to build a house for the Name of
the LORD my God. 8But this word of the
LORD came to me: 'You have shed much
blood and have fought many wars. You
are not to build a house for my Name,
because you have shed much blood on
the earth in my sight. 9But you will have
a son who will be a man of peace and
rest, and I will give him rest from all his
enemies on every side. His name will be
Solomon,[a] and I will grant Israel peace
and quiet during his reign. 10He is the
one who will build a house for my
Name. He will be my son, and I will
be his father. And I will establish the
throne of his kingdom over Israel forever.'
11"Now, my son, the LORD be with
you, and may you have success and
build the house of the LORD your God,
as he said you would. 12May the LORD
give you discretion and understanding
when he puts you in command over Israel, so that you may keep the law of the
LORD your God. 13Then you will have
success if you are careful to observe the
decrees and laws that the LORD gave
Moses for Israel. Be strong and courageous. Do not be afraid or discouraged.
14"I have taken great pains to provide
for the temple of the LORD a hundred
thousand talents[b] of gold, a million
talents[c] of silver, quantities of bronze
and iron too great to be weighed, and
wood and stone. And you may add to
them. 15You have many workmen: stonecutters, masons and carpenters, as well
as men skilled in every kind of work
16in gold and silver, bronze and iron—
craftsmen beyond number. Now begin

[a] *9 Solomon* sounds like and may be derived from the Hebrew for *peace.* [b] *14* That is, about 3,750 tons (about 3,450 metric tons) [c] *14* That is, about 37,500 tons (about 34,500 metric tons)

the work, and the LORD be with you."
17Then David ordered all the leaders
of Israel to help his son Solomon. 18He
said to them, "Is not the LORD your God
with you? And has he not granted you
rest on every side? For he has handed
the inhabitants of the land over to me,
and the land is subject to the LORD and
to his people. 19Now devote your heart
and soul to seeking the LORD your God.
Begin to build the sanctuary of the LORD
God, so that you may bring the ark of
the covenant of the LORD and the sacred
articles belonging to God into the
temple that will be built for the Name
of the LORD."

SHARPEN THE FOCUS

It's a Christian cliché: Our God is a missionary God. The fact that the statement is a cliché doesn't change its truthfulness.

From the time of Adam, Eve, Abel, and Cain, the Lord has drawn people to Himself so that He could give them His gift of forgiveness and the benefits that flow from it—that package we know as salvation.

Under the Old Covenant, the Lord picked a people, set them down at the crossroads of the world, and gave them a unique system of worship, unique promises, and a knowledge of Himself. Then He drew people to Israel. They came. They saw. And many believed.

Under the New Covenant, God's people have themselves become the temple of the Holy Spirit. God has made His home in our hearts. Now the direction of His missionary activity has reversed. Where once He drew people from the world to a specific location, now He sends us to the world.

He sends us with the same message His Old Covenant people carried: the Good News that no one need live alienated from God by sin, no one need live in terror or rebellion. The war has ended. All of the Father's wayward children can go home. His Messiah has brought all of us peace.

WEEK 35 • THURSDAY

1 Chronicles 23:1—27:34

GET THE BIG PICTURE

You may want to skim today's reading; it is quite lengthy. On the other hand, the text includes many gems to be mined—a phrase or two, a sentence or two that provoke thought and nearly beg us to apply them to our lives. (See, for instance, 1 Chronicles 23:13; 25:1–23; 25:5–7.) If time is short, focus on 1 Chronicles 26:1–19.

The Levites

23 When David was old and
full of years, he made his
son Solomon king over Israel.
2He also gathered together all the
leaders of Israel, as well as the priests
and Levites. 3The Levites thirty years
old or more were counted, and the to-

tal number of men was thirty-eight
thousand. 4David said, "Of these,
twenty-four thousand are to supervise
the work of the temple of the LORD and
six thousand are to be officials and
judges. 5Four thousand are to be gatekeepers and four thousand are to praise
the LORD with the musical instruments
I have provided for that purpose."

6David divided the Levites into
groups corresponding to the sons of
Levi: Gershon, Kohath and Merari.

Gershonites

7Belonging to the Gershonites:
Ladan and Shimei.
8The sons of Ladan:
Jehiel the first, Zetham and Joel—three in all.
9The sons of Shimei:
Shelomoth, Haziel and Haran—three in all.
These were the heads of the families of Ladan.
10And the sons of Shimei:
Jahath, Ziza,[a] Jeush and Beriah.
These were the sons of Shimei—four in all.
11Jahath was the first and Ziza the second, but Jeush and Beriah did not have many sons; so they were counted as one family with one assignment.

Kohathites

12The sons of Kohath:
Amram, Izhar, Hebron and Uzziel—four in all.
13The sons of Amram:
Aaron and Moses.
Aaron was set apart, he and his descendants forever, to consecrate the most holy things, to offer sacrifices before the LORD, to minister before him and to pronounce blessings in his name for-
ever. 14The sons of Moses the man of God were counted as part of the tribe of Levi.
15The sons of Moses:
Gershom and Eliezer.
16The descendants of Gershom:
Shubael was the first.
17The descendants of Eliezer:
Rehabiah was the first.
Eliezer had no other sons, but the sons of Rehabiah were very numerous.
18The sons of Izhar:
Shelomith was the first.
19The sons of Hebron:
Jeriah the first, Amariah the second, Jahaziel the third and Jekameam the fourth.
20The sons of Uzziel:
Micah the first and Isshiah the second.

Merarites

21The sons of Merari:
Mahli and Mushi.
The sons of Mahli:
Eleazar and Kish.
22Eleazar died without having sons: he had only daughters. Their cousins, the sons of Kish, married them.
23The sons of Mushi:
Mahli, Eder and Jerimoth—three in all.

24These were the descendants of Levi
by their families—the heads of families
as they were registered under their
names and counted individually, that is,
the workers twenty years old or more
who served in the temple of the LORD.
25For David had said, "Since the LORD,
the God of Israel, has granted rest to his
people and has come to dwell in Jerusalem forever, 26the Levites no longer
need to carry the tabernacle or any of
the articles used in its service." 27Accord-
ing to the last instructions of David, the
Levites were counted from those
twenty years old or more.

28The duty of the Levites was to help
Aaron's descendants in the service of
the temple of the LORD: to be in charge
of the courtyards, the side rooms, the
purification of all sacred things and the
performance of other duties at the
house of God. 29They were in charge of

[a]*10* One Hebrew manuscript, Septuagint and Vulgate (see also verse 11); most Hebrew manuscripts *Zina*

the bread set out on the table, the flour
for the grain offerings, the unleavened
wafers, the baking and the mixing, and
all measurements of quantity and size.
30They were also to stand every morning to thank and praise the LORD. They
were to do the same in the evening
31and whenever burnt offerings were
presented to the LORD on Sabbaths and
at New Moon festivals and at appointed feasts. They were to serve before the
LORD regularly in the proper number
and in the way prescribed for them.
32And so the Levites carried out their
responsibilities for the Tent of Meeting,
for the Holy Place and, under their
brothers the descendants of Aaron, for
the service of the temple of the LORD.

The Divisions of Priests

24 These were the divisions of the sons of Aaron:

The sons of Aaron were Nadab, Abihu, Eleazar and Ithamar. 2But Nadab
and Abihu died before their father did,
and they had no sons; so Eleazar and
Ithamar served as the priests. 3With the
help of Zadok a descendant of Eleazar
and Ahimelech a descendant of Ithamar,
David separated them into divisions for
their appointed order of ministering. 4A
larger number of leaders were found
among Eleazar's descendants than
among Ithamar's, and they were divided accordingly: sixteen heads of
families from Eleazar's descendants and
eight heads of families from Ithamar's
descendants. 5They divided them impartially by drawing lots, for there were
officials of the sanctuary and officials of
God among the descendants of both
Eleazar and Ithamar.

6The scribe Shemaiah son of Nethanel, a Levite, recorded their names in the
presence of the king and of the officials:
Zadok the priest, Ahimelech son of Abiathar and the heads of families of the
priests and of the Levites—one family
being taken from Eleazar and then one
from Ithamar.

7The first lot fell to Jehoiarib,
the second to Jedaiah,
8the third to Harim,
the fourth to Seorim,
9the fifth to Malkijah,
the sixth to Mijamin,
10the seventh to Hakkoz,
the eighth to Abijah,
11the ninth to Jeshua,
the tenth to Shecaniah,
12the eleventh to Eliashib,
the twelfth to Jakim,
13the thirteenth to Huppah,
the fourteenth to Jeshebeab,
14the fifteenth to Bilgah,
the sixteenth to Immer,
15the seventeenth to Hezir,
the eighteenth to Happizzez,
16the nineteenth to Pethahiah,
the twentieth to Jehezkel,
17the twenty-first to Jakin,
the twenty-second to Gamul,
18the twenty-third to Delaiah
and the twenty-fourth to Maaziah.

19This was their appointed order of
ministering when they entered the temple of the LORD, according to the regulations prescribed for them by their
forefather Aaron, as the LORD, the God
of Israel, had commanded him.

The Rest of the Levites

20As for the rest of the descendants of
Levi:
from the sons of Amram: Shubael;
from the sons of Shubael: Jehdeiah.
21As for Rehabiah, from his sons:
Isshiah was the first.
22From the Izharites: Shelomoth;
from the sons of Shelomoth: Jahath.
23The sons of Hebron: Jeriah the
first,[a] Amariah the second, Jahaziel the third and Jekameam the
fourth.
24The son of Uzziel: Micah;
from the sons of Micah: Shamir.
25The brother of Micah: Isshiah;
from the sons of Isshiah: Zechariah.

[a]23 Two Hebrew manuscripts and some Septuagint manuscripts (see also 1 Chron. 23:19); most Hebrew manuscripts *The sons of Jeriah:*

26 The sons of Merari: Mahli and Mushi.
The son of Jaaziah: Beno.
27 The sons of Merari:
from Jaaziah: Beno, Shoham, Zaccur and Ibri.
28 From Mahli: Eleazar, who had no sons.
29 From Kish: the son of Kish: Jerahmeel.
30 And the sons of Mushi: Mahli, Eder and Jerimoth.

These were the Levites, according to
their families. 31They also cast lots, just
as their brothers the descendants of
Aaron did, in the presence of King David and of Zadok, Ahimelech, and the
heads of families of the priests and of
the Levites. The families of the oldest
brother were treated the same as those
of the youngest.

The Singers

25 David, together with the
commanders of the army,
set apart some of the sons of Asaph,
Heman and Jeduthun for the ministry
of prophesying, accompanied by harps,
lyres and cymbals. Here is the list of the
men who performed this service:

2 From the sons of Asaph:
Zaccur, Joseph, Nethaniah and Asarelah. The sons of Asaph were under the supervision of Asaph, who prophesied under the king's supervision.
3 As for Jeduthun, from his sons:
Gedaliah, Zeri, Jeshaiah, Shimei,[a] Hashabiah and Mattithiah, six in all, under the supervision of their father Jeduthun, who prophesied, using the harp in thanking and praising the LORD.
4 As for Heman, from his sons:
Bukkiah, Mattaniah, Uzziel, Shubael and Jerimoth; Hananiah,
Hanani, Eliathah, Giddalti and Romamti-Ezer; Joshbekashah, Mallothi, Hothir and Mahazioth. 5All
these were sons of Heman the
king's seer. They were given him
through the promises of God to
exalt him.[b] God gave Heman fourteen sons and three daughters.

6 All these men were under the supervision of their fathers for the music of
the temple of the LORD, with cymbals,
lyres and harps, for the ministry at the
house of God. Asaph, Jeduthun and Heman were under the supervision of the
king. 7Along with their relatives—all of
them trained and skilled in music for
the LORD—they numbered 288. 8Young
and old alike, teacher as well as student,
cast lots for their duties.

9 The first lot, which was for
Asaph, fell to Joseph,
his sons and relatives,[c] 12[d]
the second to Gedaliah,
he and his relatives
and sons, 12
10 the third to Zaccur,
his sons and relatives, 12
11 the fourth to Izri,[e]
his sons and relatives, 12
12 the fifth to Nethaniah,
his sons and relatives, 12
13 the sixth to Bukkiah,
his sons and relatives, 12
14 the seventh to Jesarelah,[f]
his sons and relatives, 12
15 the eighth to Jeshaiah,
his sons and relatives, 12
16 the ninth to Mattaniah,
his sons and relatives, 12
17 the tenth to Shimei,
his sons and relatives, 12
18 the eleventh to Azarel,[g]
his sons and relatives, 12
19 the twelfth to Hashabiah,
his sons and relatives, 12
20 the thirteenth to Shubael,
his sons and relatives, 12
21 the fourteenth to Mattithiah,
his sons and relatives, 12
22 the fifteenth to Jerimoth,
his sons and relatives, 12

[a]3 One Hebrew manuscript and some Septuagint manuscripts (see also verse 17); most Hebrew manuscripts do not have *Shimei.*
[b]5 Hebrew *exalt the horn* [c]9 See Septuagint; Hebrew does not have *his sons and relatives.*
[d]9 See the total in verse 7; Hebrew does not have *twelve.* [e]11 A variant of *Zeri* [f]14 A variant of *Asarelah* [g]18 A variant of *Uzziel*

[23] the sixteenth to Hananiah,
his sons and relatives, 12
[24] the seventeenth to Joshbekashah,
his sons and relatives, 12
[25] the eighteenth to Hanani,
his sons and relatives, 12
[26] the nineteenth to Mallothi,
his sons and relatives, 12
[27] the twentieth to Eliathah,
his sons and relatives, 12
[28] the twenty-first to Hothir,
his sons and relatives, 12
[29] the twenty-second to Giddalti,
his sons and relatives, 12
[30] the twenty-third to Mahazioth,
his sons and relatives, 12
[31] the twenty-fourth to Romamti-Ezer,
his sons and relatives, 12

The Gatekeepers

26 The divisions of the gatekeepers:

From the Korahites: Meshelemiah son of Kore, one of the sons of Asaph.
[2] Meshelemiah had sons:
Zechariah the firstborn,
Jediael the second,
Zebadiah the third,
Jathniel the fourth,
[3] Elam the fifth,
Jehohanan the sixth
and Eliehoenai the seventh.
[4] Obed-Edom also had sons:
Shemaiah the firstborn,
Jehozabad the second,
Joah the third,
Sacar the fourth,
Nethanel the fifth,
[5] Ammiel the sixth,
Issachar the seventh
and Peullethai the eighth.
(For God had blessed Obed-Edom.)

[6] His son Shemaiah also had sons, who were leaders in their father's family because they were very capable men. [7] The sons of Shemaiah: Othni, Rephael, Obed and Elzabad; his relatives Elihu and Semakiah were also able men. [8] All these were descendants of Obed-Edom; they and their sons and their relatives were capable men with the strength to do the work—descendants of Obed-Edom, 62 in all.
[9] Meshelemiah had sons and relatives, who were able men—18 in all.

[10] Hosah the Merarite had sons: Shimri the first (although he was not the firstborn, his father had appointed him the first), [11] Hilkiah the second, Tabaliah the third and Zechariah the fourth. The sons and relatives of Hosah were 13 in all.

[12] These divisions of the gatekeepers, through their chief men, had duties for ministering in the temple of the LORD, just as their relatives had. [13] Lots were cast for each gate, according to their families, young and old alike.

[14] The lot for the East Gate fell to Shelemiah.[a] Then lots were cast for his son Zechariah, a wise counselor, and the lot for the North Gate fell to him. [15] The lot for the South Gate fell to Obed-Edom, and the lot for the storehouse fell to his sons. [16] The lots for the West Gate and the Shalleketh Gate on the upper road fell to Shuppim and Hosah.

Guard was alongside of guard: [17] There were six Levites a day on the east, four a day on the north, four a day on the south and two at a time at the storehouse. [18] As for the court to the west, there were four at the road and two at the court itself.

[19] These were the divisions of the gatekeepers who were descendants of Korah and Merari.

The Treasurers and Other Officials

[20] Their fellow Levites were[b] in charge of the treasuries of the house of God

[a] 14 A variant of *Meshelemiah* [b] 20 Septuagint; Hebrew *As for the Levites, Ahijah was*

and the treasuries for the dedicated things.
21 The descendants of Ladan, who were Gershonites through Ladan and who were heads of families belonging to Ladan the Gershonite, were Jehieli,
22 the sons of Jehieli, Zetham and his brother Joel. They were in charge of the treasuries of the temple of the LORD.
23 From the Amramites, the Izharites, the Hebronites and the Uzzielites:
24 Shubael, a descendant of Gershom son of Moses, was the officer in charge of the treasuries.
25 His relatives through Eliezer: Rehabiah his son, Jeshaiah his son, Joram his son, Zicri his son and Shelomith his son.
26 Shelomith and his relatives were in charge of all the treasuries for the things dedicated by King David, by the heads of families who were the commanders of thousands and commanders of hundreds, and by the other army commanders.
27 Some of the plunder taken in battle they dedicated for the repair of the temple of the LORD.
28 And everything dedicated by Samuel the seer and by Saul son of Kish, Abner son of Ner and Joab son of Zeruiah, and all the other dedicated things were in the care of Shelomith and his relatives.
29 From the Izharites: Kenaniah and his sons were assigned duties away from the temple, as officials and judges over Israel.
30 From the Hebronites: Hashabiah and his relatives—seventeen hundred able men—were responsible in Israel west of the Jordan for all the work of the LORD and for the king's service.
31 As for the Hebronites, Jeriah was their chief according to the genealogical records of their families. In the fortieth year of David's reign a search was made in the records, and capable men among the Hebronites were found at Jazer in Gilead.
32 Jeriah had twenty-seven hundred relatives, who were able men and heads of families, and King David put them in charge of the Reubenites, the Gadites and the half-tribe of Manasseh for every matter pertaining to God and for the affairs of the king.

Army Divisions

27 This is the list of the Israelites—heads of families, commanders of thousands and commanders of hundreds, and their officers, who served the king in all that concerned the army divisions that were on duty month by month throughout the year. Each division consisted of 24,000 men.
2 In charge of the first division, for the first month, was Jashobeam son of Zabdiel. There were 24,000 men in his division.
3 He was a descendant of Perez and chief of all the army officers for the first month.
4 In charge of the division for the second month was Dodai the Ahohite; Mikloth was the leader of his division. There were 24,000 men in his division.
5 The third army commander, for the third month, was Benaiah son of Jehoiada the priest. He was chief and there were 24,000 men in his division.
6 This was the Benaiah who was a mighty man among the Thirty and was over the Thirty. His son Ammizabad was in charge of his division.
7 The fourth, for the fourth month, was Asahel the brother of Joab; his son Zebadiah was his successor. There were 24,000 men in his division.
8 The fifth, for the fifth month, was the commander Shamhuth the Izrahite. There were 24,000 men in his division.
9 The sixth, for the sixth month, was Ira the son of Ikkesh the Tekoite. There were 24,000 men in his division.
10 The seventh, for the seventh month, was Helez the Pelonite, an Ephra-

imite. There were 24,000 men in his
division.
11The eighth, for the eighth month, was
Sibbecai the Hushathite, a Zerahite.
There were 24,000 men in his division.
12The ninth, for the ninth month, was
Abiezer the Anathothite, a Benjamite. There were 24,000 men in his
division.
13The tenth, for the tenth month, was
Maharai the Netophathite, a Zerahite. There were 24,000 men in his
division.
14The eleventh, for the eleventh month,
was Benaiah the Pirathonite, an
Ephraimite. There were 24,000 men
in his division.
15The twelfth, for the twelfth month,
was Heldai the Netophathite, from
the family of Othniel. There were
24,000 men in his division.

Officers of the Tribes

16The officers over the tribes of Israel:

over the Reubenites: Eliezer son of Zicri;
over the Simeonites: Shephatiah son of Maacah;
17over Levi: Hashabiah son of Kemuel;
over Aaron: Zadok;
18over Judah: Elihu, a brother of David;
over Issachar: Omri son of Michael;
19over Zebulun: Ishmaiah son of Obadiah;
over Naphtali: Jerimoth son of Azriel;
20over the Ephraimites: Hoshea son of Azaziah;
over half the tribe of Manasseh: Joel son of Pedaiah;
21over the half-tribe of Manasseh in Gilead: Iddo son of Zechariah;
over Benjamin: Jaasiel son of Abner;
22over Dan: Azarel son of Jeroham.

These were the officers over the tribes
of Israel.

23David did not take the number of
the men twenty years old or less, because the LORD had promised to make
Israel as numerous as the stars in the sky.
24Joab son of Zeruiah began to count the
men but did not finish. Wrath came on
Israel on account of this numbering, and
the number was not entered in the
book[a] of the annals of King David.

The King's Overseers

25Azmaveth son of Adiel was in
charge of the royal storehouses.

Jonathan son of Uzziah was in charge of the storehouses in the outlying districts, in the towns, the villages and the watchtowers.

26Ezri son of Kelub was in charge of
the field workers who farmed the land.
27Shimei the Ramathite was in charge
of the vineyards.

Zabdi the Shiphmite was in charge of the produce of the vineyards for the wine vats.

28Baal-Hanan the Gederite was in
charge of the olive and sycamore-fig
trees in the western foothills.

Joash was in charge of the supplies of olive oil.

29Shitrai the Sharonite was in charge
of the herds grazing in Sharon.

Shaphat son of Adlai was in charge of the herds in the valleys.

30Obil the Ishmaelite was in charge of
the camels.

Jehdeiah the Meronothite was in charge of the donkeys.

31Jaziz the Hagrite was in charge of
the flocks.

All these were the officials in charge of King David's property.

32Jonathan, David's uncle, was a
counselor, a man of insight and a scribe.
Jehiel son of Hacmoni took care of the
king's sons.
33Ahithophel was the king's counselor.

Hushai the Arkite was the king's
friend. 34Ahithophel was succeeded by
Jehoiada son of Benaiah and by Abiathar.

Joab was the commander of the royal army.

[a]24 Septuagint; Hebrew *number*

SHARPEN THE FOCUS

Authors. Musicians. Actors. People who pursue these careers care what the critics say. A bad review can pitch an author into the depths of despair. A good review, especially one by a respected commentator, can catapult an artist into the stratosphere.

With that in mind, pretend you are one of the sons of Shemaiah and read the "review" in 1 Chronicles 26:6. Or pretend you are Elihu or Semakiah as you read 1 Chronicles 26:7. Or pretend you are Zechariah as you read 1 Chronicles 26:14.

"But," you may protest, "I'm not Elihu or Zechariah or any of the others. So what does this snapshot of holy history have to do with me?"

The Lord knew each of these, His children, by name. He knew exactly where to place them in service so they could use the abilities He had given them for the good of their brothers and sisters in the faith. He noticed their faithful service and recorded His verdict: These people were capable, wise, strong. Even when other people failed to appreciate them, God knew what they had done.

Note that no review contains a sour note. The Lord kept track of their service, not their slip-ups. What an encouragement for us as we serve the One who died for us and rose again!

Because the nation of Israel was to be the "cradle of Christ" in human history, Israel's history mattered. A lot! As you read today, remember that these are some of David's last official words as Israel's ruler. Ask yourself why David did and said all these things as he looked forward to the Lord's promised Messiah. If time is short, focus on 1 Chronicles 28:11–21.

David's Plans for the Temple

28 David summoned all the officials of Israel to assemble at Jerusalem: the officers over the tribes, the commanders of the divisions in the service of the king, the commanders of thousands and commanders of hundreds, and the officials in charge of all the property and livestock belonging to the king and his sons, together with the palace officials, the mighty men and all the brave warriors.
2 King David rose to his feet and said: "Listen to me, my brothers and my people. I had it in my heart to build a house as a place of rest for the ark of the covenant of the LORD, for the footstool of our God, and I made plans to build it.
3 But God said to me, 'You are not to build a house for my Name, because you are a warrior and have shed blood.'
4 "Yet the LORD, the God of Israel, chose me from my whole family to be king over Israel forever. He chose Judah as leader, and from the house of Judah he chose my family, and from my father's sons he was pleased to make me king over all Israel.
5 Of all my sons—and the LORD has given me many—he has

chosen my son Solomon to sit on the throne of the kingdom of the LORD over Israel. 6He said to me: 'Solomon your son is the one who will build my house and my courts, for I have chosen him to be my son, and I will be his father. 7I will establish his kingdom forever if he is unswerving in carrying out my commands and laws, as is being done at this time.'

8"So now I charge you in the sight of all Israel and of the assembly of the LORD, and in the hearing of our God: Be careful to follow all the commands of the LORD your God, that you may possess this good land and pass it on as an inheritance to your descendants forever.

9"And you, my son Solomon, acknowledge the God of your father, and serve him with wholehearted devotion and with a willing mind, for the LORD searches every heart and understands every motive behind the thoughts. If you seek him, he will be found by you; but if you forsake him, he will reject you forever. 10Consider now, for the LORD has chosen you to build a temple as a sanctuary. Be strong and do the work."

11Then David gave his son Solomon the plans for the portico of the temple, its buildings, its storerooms, its upper parts, its inner rooms and the place of atonement. 12He gave him the plans of all that the Spirit had put in his mind for the courts of the temple of the LORD and all the surrounding rooms, for the treasuries of the temple of God and for the treasuries for the dedicated things. 13He gave him instructions for the divisions of the priests and Levites, and for all the work of serving in the temple of the LORD, as well as for all the articles to be used in its service. 14He designated the weight of gold for all the gold articles to be used in various kinds of service, and the weight of silver for all the silver articles to be used in various kinds of service: 15the weight of gold for the gold lampstands and their lamps, with the weight for each lampstand and its lamps; and the weight of silver for each silver lampstand and its lamps, according to the use of each lampstand; 16the weight of gold for each table for consecrated bread; the weight of silver for the silver tables; 17the weight of pure gold for the forks, sprinkling bowls and pitchers; the weight of gold for each gold dish; the weight of silver for each silver dish; 18and the weight of the refined gold for the altar of incense. He also gave him the plan for the chariot, that is, the cherubim of gold that spread their wings and shelter the ark of the covenant of the LORD.

19"All this," David said, "I have in writing from the hand of the LORD upon me, and he gave me understanding in all the details of the plan."

20David also said to Solomon his son, "Be strong and courageous, and do the work. Do not be afraid or discouraged, for the LORD God, my God, is with you. He will not fail you or forsake you until all the work for the service of the temple of the LORD is finished. 21The divisions of the priests and Levites are ready for all the work on the temple of God, and every willing man skilled in any craft will help you in all the work. The officials and all the people will obey your every command."

SHARPEN THE FOCUS

The Seven Wonders of the Ancient World—people still today recognize the achievements of the architects who conceived the Great Pyramids of Egypt, the Hanging Gardens of Babylon, and the Temple of Diana in Ephesus.

We owe much more honor to the Architect of the Universe. Our Creator-God not only designed our universe, He designed the tabernacle and, later on, Solomon's temple. (See 1 Chronicles 28:12, 19.) Compared to the universe, these buildings may seem to pale. How could they equal the miracle of comets, mountain ranges and tropical forests?

These building not only equal them, they surpass them in majesty. Both the tabernacle and the temple, designed by the Holy Spirit Himself, shouted this awesome truth: The God of the universe wanted a relationship with human beings, with sinners like you and me! The fixtures and ceremonies performed there foreshadowed the fact that our Creator-God would clear the way for people like us to belong to His very own family.

Now, He has done that. The builder of the universe has become salvation's architect. His building materials were the wood of Christ's manger and the beams of His cross. What an awesome God we serve!

WEEK 35 • SATURDAY

1 Chronicles 29:1–30

If a reader had to choose one word to summarize the mood of 1 Chronicles 29, that word would have to be *joy*. As you read, particularly as you read David's prayer in 1 Chronicles 29:10–15, ask the Holy Spirit to work an attitude of joy and thanksgiving in your own heart. If time is short, focus on 1 Chronicles 29:10–25.

Gifts for Building the Temple

29 Then King David said to
the whole assembly: "My
son Solomon, the one whom God has
chosen, is young and inexperienced.
The task is great, because this palatial
structure is not for man but for the LORD
God. 2With all my resources I have provided for the temple of my God—gold
for the gold work, silver for the silver,
bronze for the bronze, iron for the iron
and wood for the wood, as well as onyx
for the settings, turquoise,[a] stones of
various colors, and all kinds of fine
stone and marble—all of these in large
quantities. 3Besides, in my devotion to
the temple of my God I now give my
personal treasures of gold and silver for
the temple of my God, over and above
everything I have provided for this holy
temple: 4three thousand talents[b] of gold
(gold of Ophir) and seven thousand
talents[c] of refined silver, for the overlay-
ing of the walls of the buildings, 5for the
gold work and the silver work, and for
all the work to be done by the craftsmen. Now, who is willing to consecrate
himself today to the LORD?"
6Then the leaders of families, the
officers of the tribes of Israel, the commanders of thousands and commanders of hundreds, and the officials in
charge of the king's work gave willingly. 7They gave toward the work on the
temple of God five thousand talents[d]
and ten thousand darics[e] of gold, ten
thousand talents[f] of silver, eighteen
thousand talents[g] of bronze and a hundred thousand talents[h] of iron. 8Any
who had precious stones gave them to
the treasury of the temple of the LORD
in the custody of Jehiel the Gershonite.

[a]2 The meaning of the Hebrew for this word is uncertain. [b]4 That is, about 110 tons (about 100 metric tons) [c]4 That is, about 260 tons (about 240 metric tons) [d]7 That is, about 190 tons (about 170 metric tons) [e]7 That is, about 185 pounds (about 84 kilograms) [f]7 That is, about 375 tons (about 345 metric tons) [g]7 That is, about 675 tons (about 610 metric tons) [h]7 That is, about 3,750 tons (about 3,450 metric tons)

9 The people rejoiced at the willing response of their leaders, for they had
given freely and wholeheartedly to the
LORD. David the king also rejoiced
greatly.

David's Prayer

10 David praised the LORD in the presence of the whole assembly, saying,

"Praise be to you, O LORD,
God of our father Israel,
from everlasting to everlasting.
11 Yours, O LORD, is the greatness and the power
and the glory and the majesty and the splendor,
for everything in heaven and earth is yours.
Yours, O LORD, is the kingdom;
you are exalted as head over all.
12 Wealth and honor come from you;
you are the ruler of all things.
In your hands are strength and power
to exalt and give strength to all.
13 Now, our God, we give you thanks,
and praise your glorious name.

14 "But who am I, and who are my
people, that we should be able to give
as generously as this? Everything comes
from you, and we have given you only
what comes from your hand. 15 We are
aliens and strangers in your sight, as
were all our forefathers. Our days on
earth are like a shadow, without hope.
16 O LORD our God, as for all this abundance that we have provided for building you a temple for your Holy Name,
it comes from your hand, and all of it belongs to you. 17 I know, my God, that you
test the heart and are pleased with integrity. All these things have I given
willingly and with honest intent. And
now I have seen with joy how willingly
your people who are here have given to
you. 18 O LORD, God of our fathers Abraham, Isaac and Israel, keep this desire in
the hearts of your people forever, and
keep their hearts loyal to you. 19 And give
my son Solomon the wholehearted devotion to keep your commands, requirements and decrees and to do everything
to build the palatial structure for which
I have provided."

20 Then David said to the whole assembly, "Praise the LORD your God." So
they all praised the LORD, the God of
their fathers; they bowed low and fell
prostrate before the LORD and the king.

Solomon Acknowledged as King

21 The next day they made sacrifices to
the LORD and presented burnt offerings
to him: a thousand bulls, a thousand
rams and a thousand male lambs, together with their drink offerings, and
other sacrifices in abundance for all Israel. 22 They ate and drank with great joy
in the presence of the LORD that day.

Then they acknowledged Solomon
son of David as king a second time,
anointing him before the LORD to be ruler and Zadok to be priest. 23 So Solomon
sat on the throne of the LORD as king in
place of his father David. He prospered
and all Israel obeyed him. 24 All the officers and mighty men, as well as all of
King David's sons, pledged their submission to King Solomon.

25 The LORD highly exalted Solomon in
the sight of all Israel and bestowed on
him royal splendor such as no king over
Israel ever had before.

The Death of David

26 David son of Jesse was king over all
Israel. 27 He ruled over Israel forty
years—seven in Hebron and thirty-
three in Jerusalem. 28 He died at a good
old age, having enjoyed long life,
wealth and honor. His son Solomon succeeded him as king.

29 As for the events of King David's
reign, from beginning to end, they are
written in the records of Samuel the
seer, the records of Nathan the prophet
and the records of Gad the seer, 30 together with the details of his reign and
power, and the circumstances that surrounded him and Israel and the kingdoms of all the other lands.

SHARPEN THE FOCUS

When the ushers pass the offering plates are you tempted to applaud?

Maybe that thought seems a bit radical. But the attitude of expressive, explosive joy that erupts in applause radiates from the Scripture portion you just read.

Reread 1 Chronicles 29:14. We can certainly put ourselves in this part of David's praise-prayer. Who are *we* that God should have given us the privilege of giving and the grace to give willingly, generously? But He has.

Our walk with the Lord began with a gift—"God so loved the world that He *gave* . . ." (John 3:16). Our Lord loved, and that love spilled over in an incredibly generous gift—the life, death, and resurrection of His one and only Son. The tag on that gift included your name and mine.

Gifted, we give. Blessed, we bless. By the power of the cross that became ours in Baptism, we grow in love and in the gift of giving. We grow more like our big Brother, more like our Father, the greatest Giver of all.

2 CHRONICLES

WEEK 36 • MONDAY

2 Chronicles 1:1—2:18

The book of 2 Chronicles picks up Israel's history where 1 Chronicles left off. We first see King Solomon, David's son and successor, worshiping. As you review his prayer in chapter 1 and his plans in chapter 2, ask yourself what it means to have true wisdom. If time is short, focus on 2 Chronicles 2:1–18.

Solomon Asks for Wisdom

1 Solomon son of David established
himself firmly over his kingdom,
for the LORD his God was with him and
made him exceedingly great.
2Then Solomon spoke to all Israel—to
the commanders of thousands and commanders of hundreds, to the judges and
to all the leaders in Israel, the heads of
families— 3and Solomon and the whole
assembly went to the high place at Gibeon, for God's Tent of Meeting was
there, which Moses the LORD's servant
had made in the desert. 4Now David
had brought up the ark of God from
Kiriath Jearim to the place he had prepared for it, because he had pitched a
tent for it in Jerusalem. 5But the bronze
altar that Bezalel son of Uri, the son of
Hur, had made was in Gibeon in front
of the tabernacle of the LORD; so Solomon and the assembly inquired of him
there. 6Solomon went up to the bronze
altar before the LORD in the Tent of
Meeting and offered a thousand burnt
offerings on it.
7That night God appeared to Solomon and said to him, "Ask for whatever
you want me to give you."
8Solomon answered God, "You have
shown great kindness to David my father and have made me king in his place.
9Now, LORD God, let your promise to my
father David be confirmed, for you have
made me king over a people who are as
numerous as the dust of the earth.
10Give me wisdom and knowledge, that
I may lead this people, for who is able
to govern this great people of yours?"
11God said to Solomon, "Since this is
your heart's desire and you have not
asked for wealth, riches or honor, nor for
the death of your enemies, and since
you have not asked for a long life but for
wisdom and knowledge to govern my
people over whom I have made you
king, 12therefore wisdom and knowledge will be given you. And I will also
give you wealth, riches and honor, such
as no king who was before you ever had
and none after you will have."
13Then Solomon went to Jerusalem
from the high place at Gibeon, from
before the Tent of Meeting. And he
reigned over Israel.
14Solomon accumulated chariots and
horses; he had fourteen hundred chariots and twelve thousand horses,[a] which

[a]14 Or *charioteers*

he kept in the chariot cities and also
with him in Jerusalem. 15The king made
silver and gold as common in Jerusalem
as stones, and cedar as plentiful as sycamore-fig trees in the foothills. 16Solo-
mon's horses were imported from
Egypt[a] and from Kue[b]—the royal merchants purchased them from Kue.
17They imported a chariot from Egypt
for six hundred shekels[c] of silver, and a
horse for a hundred and fifty.[d] They also
exported them to all the kings of the
Hittites and of the Arameans.

Preparations for Building the Temple

2 Solomon gave orders to build a
temple for the Name of the LORD
and a royal palace for himself. 2He
conscripted seventy thousand men as
carriers and eighty thousand as stonecutters in the hills and thirty-six hundred as foremen over them.
3Solomon sent this message to Hiram[e]
king of Tyre:

"Send me cedar logs as you did
for my father David when you sent
him cedar to build a palace to live
in. 4Now I am about to build a temple for the Name of the LORD my
God and to dedicate it to him for
burning fragrant incense before
him, for setting out the consecrated bread regularly, and for making
burnt offerings every morning and
evening and on Sabbaths and New
Moons and at the appointed feasts
of the LORD our God. This is a lasting ordinance for Israel.
5"The temple I am going to build
will be great, because our God is
greater than all other gods. 6But
who is able to build a temple for
him, since the heavens, even the
highest heavens, cannot contain
him? Who then am I to build a temple for him, except as a place to
burn sacrifices before him?
7"Send me, therefore, a man
skilled to work in gold and silver,
bronze and iron, and in purple,
crimson and blue yarn, and experienced in the art of engraving, to
work in Judah and Jerusalem with
my skilled craftsmen, whom my father David provided.
8"Send me also cedar, pine and
algum[f] logs from Lebanon, for I
know that your men are skilled in
cutting timber there. My men will
work with yours 9to provide me
with plenty of lumber, because the
temple I build must be large and
magnificent. 10I will give your servants, the woodsmen who cut the
timber, twenty thousand cors[g] of
ground wheat, twenty thousand
cors of barley, twenty thousand
baths[h] of wine and twenty thousand baths of olive oil."

11Hiram king of Tyre replied by letter
to Solomon:

"Because the LORD loves his people, he has made you their king."

12And Hiram added:

"Praise be to the LORD, the God
of Israel, who made heaven and
earth! He has given King David a
wise son, endowed with intelligence and discernment, who will
build a temple for the LORD and a
palace for himself.
13"I am sending you Huram-Abi,
a man of great skill, 14whose mother was from Dan and whose father
was from Tyre. He is trained to
work in gold and silver, bronze and
iron, stone and wood, and with
purple and blue and crimson yarn
and fine linen. He is experienced in
all kinds of engraving and can execute any design given to him. He
will work with your craftsmen and
with those of my lord, David your
father.

[a] *16* Or possibly *Muzur,* a region in Cilicia; also in verse 17 [b] *16* Probably Cilicia [c] *17* That is, about 15 pounds (about 7 kilograms) [d] *17* That is, about 3 3/4 pounds (about 1.7 kilograms) [e] *3* Hebrew *Huram,* a variant of *Hiram;* also in verses 11 and 12 [f] *8* Probably a variant of *almug;* possibly juniper [g] *10* That is, probably about 125,000 bushels (about 4,400 kiloliters) [h] *10* That is, probably about 115,000 gallons (about 440 kiloliters)

15"Now let my lord send his servants the wheat and barley and the
olive oil and wine he promised,
16and we will cut all the logs from
Lebanon that you need and will
float them in rafts by sea down to
Joppa. You can then take them up
to Jerusalem."

17Solomon took a census of all the
aliens who were in Israel, after the census his father David had taken; and
they were found to be 153,600. 18He assigned 70,000 of them to be carriers and
80,000 to be stonecutters in the hills,
with 3,600 foremen over them to keep
the people working.

SHARPEN THE FOCUS

How big is your picture of God? Moses caught a glimpse of the Lord's majesty as the Red Sea parted. In response, he sang:

> *Who among the gods is like You, O LORD?*
> *Who is like You—*
> *majestic in holiness*
> *awesome in glory,*
> *working wonders?* (Exodus 15:11)

How big is your picture of God? Solomon caught a glimpse of the Lord's majesty as he worshiped with God's people at the Tent of Meeting (2 Chronicles 1:3). In response, he offered a thousand burnt offerings (2 Chronicles 1:6). And he made his father's decision to build a temple his own (2 Chronicles 2:1).

How big is your picture of God? Once we begin to see His glory, particularly His goodness to us in our Savior, Jesus Christ, we have begun to walk the path of wisdom. And as we begin to realize His glorious goodness toward us in our Savior, our hearts well up in song with Moses and in self-sacrificial lives with Solomon.

Do you need a bigger picture of God today? You need only ask Him for it (see James 1:5). The Holy One who gave Solomon wisdom will freely supply it to you—for Christ's sake—as well.

WEEK 36 • TUESDAY

2 Chronicles 3:1—5:14

GET THE BIG PICTURE

The dedication of Solomon's temple probably brought heaven closer to earth than any other Old Testament event. Think of the choir—led by 120 trumpets, not to mention all the other instruments. As you read, focus on both the solemnity and the joy of this occasion. If time is short, focus on 2 Chronicles 5:1–2, 11–14.

Solomon Builds the Temple

3 Then Solomon began to build the
temple of the LORD in Jerusalem
on Mount Moriah, where the LORD had
appeared to his father David. It was on
the threshing floor of Araunah[a] the Jebusite, the place provided by David. 2He
began building on the second day of the
second month in the fourth year of his
reign.
3The foundation Solomon laid for
building the temple of God was sixty cubits long and twenty cubits wide[b] (using
the cubit of the old standard). 4The portico at the front of the temple was twenty cubits[c] long across the width of the
building and twenty cubits[d] high.
He overlaid the inside with pure gold.
5He paneled the main hall with pine and
covered it with fine gold and decorated
it with palm tree and chain designs. 6He
adorned the temple with precious
stones. And the gold he used was gold
of Parvaim. 7He overlaid the ceiling
beams, doorframes, walls and doors of
the temple with gold, and he carved
cherubim on the walls.
8He built the Most Holy Place, its
length corresponding to the width of
the temple—twenty cubits long and
twenty cubits wide. He overlaid the inside with six hundred talents[e] of fine
gold. 9The gold nails weighed fifty
shekels.[f] He also overlaid the upper
parts with gold.
10In the Most Holy Place he made a
pair of sculptured cherubim and overlaid them with gold. 11The total wing-
span of the cherubim was twenty cubits.
One wing of the first cherub was five
cubits[g] long and touched the temple
wall, while its other wing, also five cubits long, touched the wing of the other
cherub. 12Similarly one wing of the second cherub was five cubits long and
touched the other temple wall, and its
other wing, also five cubits long,
touched the wing of the first cherub.
13The wings of these cherubim extended
twenty cubits. They stood on their feet,
facing the main hall.[h]
14He made the curtain of blue, purple
and crimson yarn and fine linen, with
cherubim worked into it.
15In the front of the temple he made
two pillars, which ⌊together⌋ were thirty-
five cubits[i] long, each with a capital on
top measuring five cubits. 16He made interwoven chains[j] and put them on top
of the pillars. He also made a hundred
pomegranates and attached them to the
chains. 17He erected the pillars in the
front of the temple, one to the south and
one to the north. The one to the south
he named Jakin[k] and the one to the
north Boaz.[l]

The Temple's Furnishings

4 He made a bronze altar twenty
cubits long, twenty cubits wide
and ten cubits high.[m] 2He made the Sea
of cast metal, circular in shape, measuring ten cubits from rim to rim and five
cubits[n] high. It took a line of thirty
cubits[o] to measure around it. 3Below the
rim, figures of bulls encircled it—ten to
a cubit.[p] The bulls were cast in two rows
in one piece with the Sea.
4The Sea stood on twelve bulls, three
facing north, three facing west, three
facing south and three facing east. The
Sea rested on top of them, and their
hindquarters were toward the center. 5It
was a handbreadth[q] in thickness, and its
rim was like the rim of a cup, like a lily
blossom. It held three thousand baths.[r]

[a]1 Hebrew *Ornan,* a variant of *Araunah* [b]3 That is, about 90 feet (about 27 meters) long and 30 feet (about 9 meters) wide [c]4 That is, about 30 feet (about 9 meters); also in verses 8, 11 and 13 [d]4 Some Septuagint and Syriac manuscripts; Hebrew *and a hundred and twenty* [e]8 That is, about 23 tons (about 21 metric tons) [f]9 That is, about 1 1/4 pounds (about 0.6 kilogram) [g]11 That is, about 7 1/2 feet (about 2.3 meters); also in verse 15 [h]13 Or *facing inward* [i]15 That is, about 52 feet (about 16 meters) [j]16 Or possibly *made chains in the inner sanctuary*; the meaning of the Hebrew for this phrase is uncertain. [k]17 *Jakin* probably means *he establishes.* [l]17 *Boaz* probably means *in him is strength.* [m]1 That is, about 30 feet (about 9 meters) long and wide, and about 15 feet (about 4.5 meters) high
[n]2 That is, about 7 1/2 feet (about 2.3 meters)
[o]2 That is, about 45 feet (about 13.5 meters)
[p]3 That is, about 1 1/2 feet (about 0.5 meter)
[q]5 That is, about 3 inches (about 8 centimeters)
[r]5 That is, about 17,500 gallons (about 66 kiloliters)

[6]He then made ten basins for washing
and placed five on the south side and
five on the north. In them the things to
be used for the burnt offerings were
rinsed, but the Sea was to be used by the
priests for washing.
[7]He made ten gold lampstands according to the specifications for them
and placed them in the temple, five on
the south side and five on the north.
[8]He made ten tables and placed them
in the temple, five on the south side and
five on the north. He also made a hundred gold sprinkling bowls.
[9]He made the courtyard of the priests,
and the large court and the doors for the
court, and overlaid the doors with
bronze. [10]He placed the Sea on the south
side, at the southeast corner.
[11]He also made the pots and shovels
and sprinkling bowls.
So Huram finished the work he had
undertaken for King Solomon in the
temple of God:

[12]the two pillars;
the two bowl-shaped capitals on
top of the pillars;
the two sets of network decorating
the two bowl-shaped capitals on
top of the pillars;
[13]the four hundred pomegranates for
the two sets of network (two
rows of pomegranates for each
network, decorating the bowl-
shaped capitals on top of the pillars);
[14]the stands with their basins;
[15]the Sea and the twelve bulls
under it;
[16]the pots, shovels, meat forks and all
related articles.

All the objects that Huram-Abi made
for King Solomon for the temple of the
LORD were of polished bronze. [17]The
king had them cast in clay molds in the
plain of the Jordan between Succoth
and Zarethan.[a] [18]All these things that
Solomon made amounted to so much
that the weight of the bronze was not
determined.
[19]Solomon also made all the furnishings that were in God's temple:

the golden altar;
the tables on which was the bread
of the Presence;
[20]the lampstands of pure gold with
their lamps, to burn in front of
the inner sanctuary as prescribed;
[21]the gold floral work and lamps and
tongs (they were solid gold);
[22]the pure gold wick trimmers, sprinkling bowls, dishes and censers;
and the gold doors of the temple:
the inner doors to the Most Holy
Place and the doors of the main
hall.

5 When all the work Solomon had
done for the temple of the LORD
was finished, he brought in the things
his father David had dedicated—the silver and gold and all the furnishings—
and he placed them in the treasuries of
God's temple.

The Ark Brought to the Temple

[2]Then Solomon summoned to Jerusalem the elders of Israel, all the heads of
the tribes and the chiefs of the Israelite
families, to bring up the ark of the
LORD's covenant from Zion, the City of
David. [3]And all the men of Israel came
together to the king at the time of the
festival in the seventh month.
[4]When all the elders of Israel had arrived, the Levites took up the ark, [5]and
they brought up the ark and the Tent of
Meeting and all the sacred furnishings
in it. The priests, who were Levites, carried them up; [6]and King Solomon and
the entire assembly of Israel that had
gathered about him were before the ark,
sacrificing so many sheep and cattle that
they could not be recorded or counted.
[7]The priests then brought the ark of
the LORD's covenant to its place in the
inner sanctuary of the temple, the Most
Holy Place, and put it beneath the
wings of the cherubim. [8]The cherubim
spread their wings over the place of the
ark and covered the ark and its carrying
poles. [9]These poles were so long that

[a]17 Hebrew *Zeredatha,* a variant of *Zarethan*

their ends, extending from the ark,
could be seen from in front of the inner
sanctuary, but not from outside the
Holy Place; and they are still there today. 10There was nothing in the ark except the two tablets that Moses had
placed in it at Horeb, where the LORD
made a covenant with the Israelites after they came out of Egypt.
11The priests then withdrew from the
Holy Place. All the priests who were
there had consecrated themselves, regardless of their divisions. 12All the
Levites who were musicians—Asaph,
Heman, Jeduthun and their sons and
relatives—stood on the east side of the
altar, dressed in fine linen and playing
cymbals, harps and lyres. They were accompanied by 120 priests sounding
trumpets. 13The trumpeters and singers
joined in unison, as with one voice, to
give praise and thanks to the LORD.
Accompanied by trumpets, cymbals
and other instruments, they raised
their voices in praise to the LORD and
sang:

"He is good;
his love endures forever."

Then the temple of the LORD was
filled with a cloud, 14and the priests
could not perform their service because
of the cloud, for the glory of the LORD
filled the temple of God.

SHARPEN THE FOCUS

If you had been at the temple's dedication, for what would you have thanked the Lord? Doubtless everyone there had experienced countless blessings. But the priests and people that day primarily glorified their God for another specific and precious gift–the gift of worship. He had now given them a place in which they could praise Him. Solomon's prayer (2 Chronicles 6:4–42) reflects this focus.

Our Lord didn't *need* Israel's worship any more than He *needs* ours. But *we* need to worship. When we lose ourselves in the presence, in the power, in the goodness and mercy of God, we see our lives in proper perspective. Our Lord reminds us of His willingness and His ability to help us. The Holy Spirit assures us that in Jesus we stand before God as His forgiven, righteous children.

Of course, like any good earthly father, our Lord smiles with pleasure when He hears our expressions of love and trust. He's glad when He sees the work His Spirit has done in our hearts to transform us into more appreciative, generous, and obedient sons and daughters. But primarily our Lord invites us to worship so that we will grow in our ability to love and trust in Him.

WEEK 36 • WEDNESDAY

2 Chr. 6:1—7:22

GET THE BIG PICTURE

The temple dedication service continues. The Lord has come into the midst of His people (2 Chronicles 5:14), and they worship Him. As you read, note carefully the connection between what God *says* and what he *does*. If time is short, focus on 2 Chronicles 6:12–21.

6 Then Solomon said, "The LORD
has said that he would dwell in
a dark cloud; 2I have built a magnificent
temple for you, a place for you to dwell
forever."
3While the whole assembly of Israel
was standing there, the king turned
around and blessed them. 4Then he
said:

"Praise be to the LORD, the God
of Israel, who with his hands has
fulfilled what he promised with his
mouth to my father David. For he
said, 5'Since the day I brought my
people out of Egypt, I have not chosen a city in any tribe of Israel to
have a temple built for my Name to
be there, nor have I chosen anyone
to be the leader over my people Israel. 6But now I have chosen Jerusalem for my Name to be there, and
I have chosen David to rule my
people Israel.'
7"My father David had it in his
heart to build a temple for the
Name of the LORD, the God of Israel. 8But the LORD said to my father David, 'Because it was in your
heart to build a temple for my
Name, you did well to have this in
your heart. 9Nevertheless, you are
not the one to build the temple, but
your son, who is your own flesh
and blood—he is the one who will
build the temple for my Name.'
10"The LORD has kept the promise he made. I have succeeded
David my father and now I sit on
the throne of Israel, just as the
LORD promised, and I have built
the temple for the Name of the
LORD, the God of Israel. 11There I
have placed the ark, in which is the
covenant of the LORD that he made
with the people of Israel."

Solomon's Prayer of Dedication

12Then Solomon stood before the altar of the LORD in front of the whole assembly of Israel and spread out his
hands. 13Now he had made a bronze
platform, five cubits[a] long, five cubits
wide and three cubits[b] high, and had
placed it in the center of the outer court.
He stood on the platform and then knelt
down before the whole assembly of Israel and spread out his hands toward
heaven. 14He said:

"O LORD, God of Israel, there is
no God like you in heaven or on
earth—you who keep your covenant of love with your servants
who continue wholeheartedly in
your way. 15You have kept your
promise to your servant David my
father; with your mouth you have
promised and with your hand you
have fulfilled it—as it is today.
16"Now LORD, God of Israel, keep
for your servant David my father
the promises you made to him
when you said, 'You shall never fail
to have a man to sit before me on
the throne of Israel, if only your
sons are careful in all they do to
walk before me according to my
law, as you have done.' 17And now,
O LORD, God of Israel, let your
word that you promised your servant David come true.
18"But will God really dwell on
earth with men? The heavens, even
the highest heavens, cannot contain you. How much less this temple I have built! 19Yet give attention
to your servant's prayer and his
plea for mercy, O LORD my God.
Hear the cry and the prayer that
your servant is praying in your
presence. 20May your eyes be open
toward this temple day and night,
this place of which you said you
would put your Name there. May
you hear the prayer your servant
prays toward this place. 21Hear the
supplications of your servant and
of your people Israel when they
pray toward this place. Hear from
heaven, your dwelling place; and
when you hear, forgive.
22"When a man wrongs his
neighbor and is required to take an

[a]13 That is, about 7 1/2 feet (about 2.3 meters)
[b]13 That is, about 4 1/2 feet (about 1.3 meters)

oath and he comes and swears the
oath before your altar in this
temple, 23 then hear from heaven
and act. Judge between your servants, repaying the guilty by bringing down on his own head what he
has done. Declare the innocent not
guilty and so establish his innocence.
24 "When your people Israel have
been defeated by an enemy because they have sinned against you
and when they turn back and confess your name, praying and making supplication before you in this
temple, 25 then hear from heaven
and forgive the sin of your people
Israel and bring them back to the
land you gave to them and their fathers.
26 "When the heavens are shut up
and there is no rain because your
people have sinned against you,
and when they pray toward this
place and confess your name and
turn from their sin because you
have afflicted them, 27 then hear
from heaven and forgive the sin of
your servants, your people Israel.
Teach them the right way to live,
and send rain on the land you gave
your people for an inheritance.
28 "When famine or plague comes
to the land, or blight or mildew, locusts or grasshoppers, or when enemies besiege them in any of their
cities, whatever disaster or disease
may come, 29 and when a prayer or
plea is made by any of your people
Israel—each one aware of his afflictions and pains, and spreading out
his hands toward this temple—
30 then hear from heaven, your
dwelling place. Forgive, and deal
with each man according to all he
does, since you know his heart (for
you alone know the hearts of men),
31 so that they will fear you and walk
in your ways all the time they live
in the land you gave our fathers.
32 "As for the foreigner who does
not belong to your people Israel but
has come from a distant land because of your great name and your
mighty hand and your out-
stretched arm—when he comes
and prays toward this temple,
33 then hear from heaven, your
dwelling place, and do whatever
the foreigner asks of you, so that all
the peoples of the earth may know
your name and fear you, as do your
own people Israel, and may know
that this house I have built bears
your Name.
34 "When your people go to war
against their enemies, wherever
you send them, and when they
pray to you toward this city you
have chosen and the temple I have
built for your Name, 35 then hear
from heaven their prayer and their
plea, and uphold their cause.
36 "When they sin against you—
for there is no one who does not
sin—and you become angry with
them and give them over to the enemy, who takes them captive to a
land far away or near; 37 and if they
have a change of heart in the land
where they are held captive, and
repent and plead with you in the
land of their captivity and say, 'We
have sinned, we have done wrong
and acted wickedly'; 38 and if they
turn back to you with all their heart
and soul in the land of their captivity where they were taken, and
pray toward the land you gave
their fathers, toward the city you
have chosen and toward the temple I have built for your Name;
39 then from heaven, your dwelling
place, hear their prayer and their
pleas, and uphold their cause. And
forgive your people, who have
sinned against you.
40 "Now, my God, may your eyes
be open and your ears attentive to
the prayers offered in this place.

41 "Now arise, O LORD God, and
come to your resting
place,
you and the ark of your
might.

May your priests, O LORD God,
be clothed with salvation,
may your saints rejoice in
your goodness.
42 O LORD God, do not reject our
anointed one.
Remember the great love
promised to David your
servant."

The Dedication of the Temple

7 When Solomon finished praying,
fire came down from
heaven and consumed the burnt offering
and the sacrifices, and the glory of
the LORD filled the temple. 2 The priests
could not enter the temple of the LORD
because the glory of the LORD filled it.
3 When all the Israelites saw the fire coming
down and the glory of the LORD
above the temple, they knelt on the
pavement with their faces to the
ground, and they worshiped and gave
thanks to the LORD, saying,

"He is good;
his love endures forever."

4 Then the king and all the people offered
sacrifices before the LORD. 5 And
King Solomon offered a sacrifice of
twenty-two thousand head of cattle and
a hundred and twenty thousand sheep
and goats. So the king and all the people
dedicated the temple of God. 6 The
priests took their positions, as did the
Levites with the LORD's musical instruments,
which King David had made for
praising the LORD and which were used
when he gave thanks, saying, "His love
endures forever." Opposite the Levites,
the priests blew their trumpets, and all
the Israelites were standing.

7 Solomon consecrated the middle
part of the courtyard in front of the temple
of the LORD, and there he offered
burnt offerings and the fat of the fellowship
offerings,[a] because the bronze altar
he had made could not hold the burnt
offerings, the grain offerings and the fat
portions.

8 So Solomon observed the festival at
that time for seven days, and all Israel
with him—a vast assembly, people from
Lebo[b] Hamath to the Wadi of Egypt. 9 On
the eighth day they held an assembly,
for they had celebrated the dedication
of the altar for seven days and the festival
for seven days more. 10 On the
twenty-third day of the seventh month
he sent the people to their homes, joyful
and glad in heart for the good things
the LORD had done for David and Solomon
and for his people Israel.

The LORD Appears to Solomon

11 When Solomon had finished the
temple of the LORD and the royal palace,
and had succeeded in carrying out all he
had in mind to do in the temple of the
LORD and in his own palace, 12 the LORD
appeared to him at night and said:

"I have heard your prayer and
have chosen this place for myself as
a temple for sacrifices.

13 "When I shut up the heavens so
that there is no rain, or command
locusts to devour the land or send
a plague among my people, 14 if my
people, who are called by my
name, will humble themselves and
pray and seek my face and turn
from their wicked ways, then will I
hear from heaven and will forgive
their sin and will heal their land.
15 Now my eyes will be open and
my ears attentive to the prayers
offered in this place. 16 I have chosen
and consecrated this temple so
that my Name may be there forever.
My eyes and my heart will always
be there.

17 "As for you, if you walk before
me as David your father did, and
do all I command, and observe my
decrees and laws, 18 I will establish
your royal throne, as I covenanted
with David your father when I said,
'You shall never fail to have a man
to rule over Israel.'

19 "But if you[c] turn away and forsake
the decrees and commands I
have given you[c] and go off to serve

[a]7 Traditionally *peace offerings* [b]8 Or *from the entrance to* [c]19 The Hebrew is plural.

other gods and worship them,
[20]then I will uproot Israel from my
land, which I have given them, and
will reject this temple I have consecrated for my Name. I will make it
a byword and an object of ridicule
among all peoples. [21]And though
this temple is now so imposing, all
who pass by will be appalled and
say, 'Why has the LORD done such
a thing to this land and to this temple?' [22]People will answer, 'Because
they have forsaken the LORD, the
God of their fathers, who brought
them out of Egypt, and have embraced other gods, worshiping and
serving them—that is why he
brought all this disaster on them.' "

SHARPEN THE FOCUS

When people list God's characteristics, they use words like *merciful, gracious, just, omnipotent,* and so on. Hardly ever does the term *integrity* appear, but it certainly could. First and foremost, a person of integrity *does* what he or she *says*. Such a person's words and actions match up.

Our Lord acts with perfect integrity, an integrity unimaginable from sinful human beings. Several times Solomon's prayer reflects the Lord's integrity (2 Chronicles 6:4, 15), and the Lord's words in response to Solomon's prayer also reflect it (2 Chronicles 7:1–22). God's people could trust that as they turned to Him in repentance and faith, He would hear and help. No sin, no drought, no famine, no war, no national disaster could separate them from His love.

In fact, Solomon's list (2 Chronicles 6:22–40) sounds a bit like one penned by the apostle Paul centuries later:

> *Who shall separate us from the love of Christ? Shall trouble or hardship or persecution or famine or nakedness or danger or sword?* (Romans 8:35)

Whatever is happening in your life today, whatever may happen tomorrow, you can rest in God's integrity. He will do what He has said. You are His redeemed child in Jesus Christ.

WEEK 36 • THURSDAY

2 Chronicles 8:1—9:31

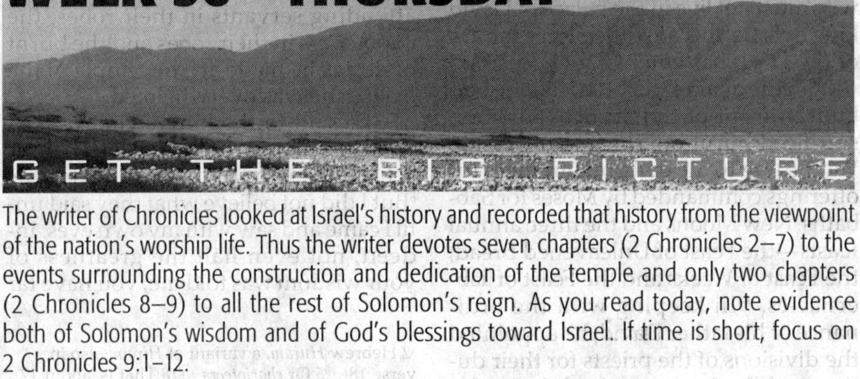

GET THE BIG PICTURE

The writer of Chronicles looked at Israel's history and recorded that history from the viewpoint of the nation's worship life. Thus the writer devotes seven chapters (2 Chronicles 2–7) to the events surrounding the construction and dedication of the temple and only two chapters (2 Chronicles 8–9) to all the rest of Solomon's reign. As you read today, note evidence both of Solomon's wisdom and of God's blessings toward Israel. If time is short, focus on 2 Chronicles 9:1–12.

Solomon's Other Activities

8 At the end of twenty years, during which Solomon built the
temple of the LORD and his own palace,
2Solomon rebuilt the villages that
Hiram[a] had given him, and settled Israelites in them. 3Solomon then went to
Hamath Zobah and captured it. 4He also
built up Tadmor in the desert and all the
store cities he had built in Hamath. 5He
rebuilt Upper Beth Horon and Lower
Beth Horon as fortified cities, with walls
and with gates and bars, 6as well as Baalath and all his store cities, and all the
cities for his chariots and for his
horses[b]—whatever he desired to build
in Jerusalem, in Lebanon and throughout all the territory he ruled.
7All the people left from the Hittites,
Amorites, Perizzites, Hivites and Jebusites (these peoples were not Israelites),
8that is, their descendants remaining in
the land, whom the Israelites had not
destroyed—these Solomon conscripted
for his slave labor force, as it is to this
day. 9But Solomon did not make slaves
of the Israelites for his work; they were
his fighting men, commanders of his
captains, and commanders of his chariots and charioteers. 10They were also
King Solomon's chief officials—two
hundred and fifty officials supervising
the men.
11Solomon brought Pharaoh's daughter up from the City of David to the palace he had built for her, for he said, "My
wife must not live in the palace of David
king of Israel, because the places the ark
of the LORD has entered are holy."
12On the altar of the LORD that he had
built in front of the portico, Solomon
sacrificed burnt offerings to the LORD,
13according to the daily requirement for
offerings commanded by Moses for Sabbaths, New Moons and the three annual
feasts—the Feast of Unleavened Bread,
the Feast of Weeks and the Feast of Tabernacles. 14In keeping with the ordinance of his father David, he appointed
the divisions of the priests for their duties, and the Levites to lead the praise
and to assist the priests according to
each day's requirement. He also appointed the gatekeepers by divisions for
the various gates, because this was what
David the man of God had ordered.
15They did not deviate from the king's
commands to the priests or to the Levites in any matter, including that of the
treasuries.
16All Solomon's work was carried out,
from the day the foundation of the temple of the LORD was laid until its completion. So the temple of the LORD was
finished.
17Then Solomon went to Ezion Geber
and Elath on the coast of Edom. 18And
Hiram sent him ships commanded by
his own officers, men who knew the sea.
These, with Solomon's men, sailed to
Ophir and brought back four hundred
and fifty talents[c] of gold, which they delivered to King Solomon.

The Queen of Sheba Visits Solomon

9 When the queen of Sheba heard
of Solomon's fame, she came to
Jerusalem to test him with hard questions. Arriving with a very great caravan—with camels carrying spices, large
quantities of gold, and precious
stones—she came to Solomon and
talked with him about all she had on her
mind. 2Solomon answered all her questions; nothing was too hard for him to
explain to her. 3When the queen of Sheba saw the wisdom of Solomon, as well
as the palace he had built, 4the food on
his table, the seating of his officials, the
attending servants in their robes, the
cupbearers in their robes and the burnt
offerings he made at[d] the temple of the
LORD, she was overwhelmed.
5She said to the king, "The report I
heard in my own country about your
achievements and your wisdom is true.
6But I did not believe what they said until I came and saw with my own eyes. Indeed, not even half the greatness of
your wisdom was told me; you have far

[a]2 Hebrew *Huram,* a variant of *Hiram;* also in verse 18 [b]6 Or *charioteers* [c]18 That is, about 17 tons (about 16 metric tons) [d]4 Or *the ascent by which he went up to*

exceeded the report I heard. 7 How happy your men must be! How happy your officials, who continually stand before you and hear your wisdom! 8 Praise be to the LORD your God, who has delighted in you and placed you on his throne as king to rule for the LORD your God. Because of the love of your God for Israel and his desire to uphold them forever, he has made you king over them, to maintain justice and righteousness."

9 Then she gave the king 120 talents[a] of gold, large quantities of spices, and precious stones. There had never been such spices as those the queen of Sheba gave to King Solomon.

10 (The men of Hiram and the men of Solomon brought gold from Ophir; they also brought algumwood[b] and precious stones. 11 The king used the algumwood to make steps for the temple of the LORD and for the royal palace, and to make harps and lyres for the musicians. Nothing like them had ever been seen in Judah.)

12 King Solomon gave the queen of Sheba all she desired and asked for; he gave her more than she had brought to him. Then she left and returned with her retinue to her own country.

Solomon's Splendor

13 The weight of the gold that Solomon received yearly was 666 talents,[c] 14 not including the revenues brought in by merchants and traders. Also all the kings of Arabia and the governors of the land brought gold and silver to Solomon.

15 King Solomon made two hundred large shields of hammered gold; six hundred bekas[d] of hammered gold went into each shield. 16 He also made three hundred small shields of hammered gold, with three hundred bekas[e] of gold in each shield. The king put them in the Palace of the Forest of Lebanon.

17 Then the king made a great throne inlaid with ivory and overlaid with pure gold. 18 The throne had six steps, and a footstool of gold was attached to it. On both sides of the seat were armrests, with a lion standing beside each of them. 19 Twelve lions stood on the six steps, one at either end of each step. Nothing like it had ever been made for any other kingdom. 20 All King Solomon's goblets were gold, and all the household articles in the Palace of the Forest of Lebanon were pure gold. Nothing was made of silver, because silver was considered of little value in Solomon's day. 21 The king had a fleet of trading ships[f] manned by Hiram's[g] men. Once every three years it returned, carrying gold, silver and ivory, and apes and baboons.

22 King Solomon was greater in riches and wisdom than all the other kings of the earth. 23 All the kings of the earth sought audience with Solomon to hear the wisdom God had put in his heart. 24 Year after year, everyone who came brought a gift—articles of silver and gold, and robes, weapons and spices, and horses and mules.

25 Solomon had four thousand stalls for horses and chariots, and twelve thousand horses,[h] which he kept in the chariot cities and also with him in Jerusalem. 26 He ruled over all the kings from the River[i] to the land of the Philistines, as far as the border of Egypt. 27 The king made silver as common in Jerusalem as stones, and cedar as plentiful as sycamore-fig trees in the foothills. 28 Solomon's horses were imported from Egypt[j] and from all other countries.

Solomon's Death

29 As for the other events of Solomon's reign, from beginning to end, are they not written in the records of Nathan the prophet, in the prophecy of Ahijah the Shilonite and in the visions of Iddo the

[a] *9* That is, about 4 1/2 tons (about 4 metric tons)
[b] *10* Probably a variant of *almugwood* [c] *13* That is, about 25 tons (about 23 metric tons)
[d] *15* That is, about 7 1/2 pounds (about 3.5 kilograms) [e] *16* That is, about 3 3/4 pounds (about 1.7 kilograms) [f] *21* Hebrew *of ships that could go to Tarshish* [g] *21* Hebrew *Huram,* a variant of *Hiram* [h] *25* Or *charioteers* [i] *26* That is, the Euphrates [j] *28* Or possibly *Muzur,* a region in Cilicia

seer concerning Jeroboam son of Nebat?
30 Solomon reigned in Jerusalem over all
Israel forty years. 31 Then he rested with
his fathers and was buried in the city of
David his father. And Rehoboam his son
succeeded him as king.

SHARPEN THE FOCUS

Why did God make Solomon king and give him such wisdom? The Queen of Sheba tells us–the Lord loved Israel (2 Chronicles 9:8). Not just Israel then, but those of us who belong to Israel today–His people of all time (Galatians 6:14–16). The Savior would come from David's line, and that covenant promise passed like a baton in a relay race from David to Solomon. Think of it: God loved *you,* so He made Solomon king!

When those who don't know the Lord look at your life and at your Christian congregation, what do they say? Do they shake their heads in amazement at your wisdom, as did the Queen of Sheba after she had seen the ways which the Lord had blessed Israel under Solomon? Do they exclaim, "How they *love* one another!" as did the pagans who came into contact with the early Christians?

Solomon's fame had preceded him (2 Chronicles 9:6). And, like it or not, many people in our world derive their ideas about God from what they see in those of us who claim to be His people.

Then and now, our Lord wants the people of His kingdom to focus on the King, on trusting and obeying Him. Ask your Savior to point out any ways your priorities or your witness are being compromised today. Ask too that He show you new ways to reinforce your church's witness in your community. Then, confident in His forgiveness, walk in the wisdom He will supply.

WEEK 36 • FRIDAY

2 Chronicles 10:1—11:23

GET THE BIG PICTURE

In 1 Kings 12:1–19 we first read about the split that divided the Northern Kingdom (Israel) from the Southern Kingdom (Judah). The writer of Chronicles records the events that led up to this split and the fallout from the split, as did the writer of Kings. But today's account describes in more detail the spiritual division that also took place. Take special note of that description as you read. If time is short, focus on 2 Chronicles 10:1–19; 11:13–17.

Israel Rebels Against Rehoboam

10 Rehoboam went to Shechem,
for all the Israelites had gone
there to make him king. 2 When Jeroboam son of Nebat heard this (he was in
Egypt, where he had fled from King Solomon), he returned from Egypt. 3 So
they sent for Jeroboam, and he and all
Israel went to Rehoboam and said to
him: 4 "Your father put a heavy yoke on
us, but now lighten the harsh labor and
the heavy yoke he put on us, and we
will serve you."
5 Rehoboam answered, "Come back to

me in three days." So the people went
away.
[6]Then King Rehoboam consulted the
elders who had served his father Solomon during his lifetime. "How would
you advise me to answer these people?"
he asked.
[7]They replied, "If you will be kind to
these people and please them and give
them a favorable answer, they will always be your servants."
[8]But Rehoboam rejected the advice
the elders gave him and consulted the
young men who had grown up with
him and were serving him. [9]He asked
them, "What is your advice? How
should we answer these people who say
to me, 'Lighten the yoke your father put
on us'?"
[10]The young men who had grown up
with him replied, "Tell the people who
have said to you, 'Your father put a
heavy yoke on us, but make our yoke
lighter'—tell them, 'My little finger is
thicker than my father's waist. [11]My father laid on you a heavy yoke; I will
make it even heavier. My father
scourged you with whips; I will scourge
you with scorpions.' "
[12]Three days later Jeroboam and all
the people returned to Rehoboam, as
the king had said, "Come back to me in
three days." [13]The king answered them
harshly. Rejecting the advice of the elders, [14]he followed the advice of the
young men and said, "My father made
your yoke heavy; I will make it even
heavier. My father scourged you with
whips; I will scourge you with scorpions." [15]So the king did not listen to the
people, for this turn of events was from
God, to fulfill the word the LORD had
spoken to Jeroboam son of Nebat
through Ahijah the Shilonite.
[16]When all Israel saw that the king refused to listen to them, they answered
the king:

"What share do we have in David,
what part in Jesse's son?
To your tents, O Israel!
Look after your own house,
O David!"

So all the Israelites went home. [17]But as
for the Israelites who were living in the
towns of Judah, Rehoboam still ruled
over them.
[18]King Rehoboam sent out Adoniram,[a]
who was in charge of forced labor, but
the Israelites stoned him to death. King
Rehoboam, however, managed to get
into his chariot and escape to Jerusalem.
[19]So Israel has been in rebellion against
the house of David to this day.

11 When Rehoboam arrived in Jerusalem, he mustered the house
of Judah and Benjamin—a hundred and
eighty thousand fighting men—to make
war against Israel and to regain the
kingdom for Rehoboam.
[2]But this word of the LORD came to
Shemaiah the man of God: [3]"Say to Rehoboam son of Solomon king of Judah
and to all the Israelites in Judah and
Benjamin, [4]'This is what the LORD says:
Do not go up to fight against your
brothers. Go home, every one of you,
for this is my doing.' " So they obeyed
the words of the LORD and turned back
from marching against Jeroboam.

Rehoboam Fortifies Judah

[5]Rehoboam lived in Jerusalem and
built up towns for defense in Judah:
[6]Bethlehem, Etam, Tekoa, [7]Beth Zur,
Soco, Adullam, [8]Gath, Mareshah, Ziph,
[9]Adoraim, Lachish, Azekah, [10]Zorah, Aijalon and Hebron. These were fortified
cities in Judah and Benjamin. [11]He
strengthened their defenses and put
commanders in them, with supplies of
food, olive oil and wine. [12]He put shields
and spears in all the cities, and made
them very strong. So Judah and Benjamin were his.
[13]The priests and Levites from all their
districts throughout Israel sided with
him. [14]The Levites even abandoned
their pasturelands and property, and
came to Judah and Jerusalem because
Jeroboam and his sons had rejected
them as priests of the LORD. [15]And he
appointed his own priests for the high
places and for the goat and calf idols he

[a]*18* Hebrew *Hadoram,* a variant of *Adoniram*

had made. [16]Those from every tribe of
Israel who set their hearts on seeking
the LORD, the God of Israel, followed
the Levites to Jerusalem to offer sacrifices to the LORD, the God of their fathers. [17]They strengthened the kingdom
of Judah and supported Rehoboam son
of Solomon three years, walking in the
ways of David and Solomon during this
time.

Rehoboam's Family

[18]Rehoboam married Mahalath, who
was the daughter of David's son Jerimoth and of Abihail, the daughter of
Jesse's son Eliab. [19]She bore him sons:
Jeush, Shemariah and Zaham. [20]Then he
married Maacah daughter of Absalom,
who bore him Abijah, Attai, Ziza and
Shelomith. [21]Rehoboam loved Maacah
daughter of Absalom more than any of
his other wives and concubines. In all,
he had eighteen wives and sixty concubines, twenty-eight sons and sixty
daughters.

[22]Rehoboam appointed Abijah son of
Maacah to be the chief prince among his
brothers, in order to make him king.
[23]He acted wisely, dispersing some of
his sons throughout the districts of Judah and Benjamin, and to all the fortified cities. He gave them abundant
provisions and took many wives for
them.

SHARPEN THE FOCUS

Solomon once wrote:

> *Righteousness exalts a nation,*
> *but sin is a disgrace to any people.* (Proverbs 14:34)

The life of Solomon's son, Rehoboam, illustrates the truth of Solomon's proverb in an unmistakable way. When Rehoboam acted in arrogant power, Israel suffered. God's people came to the brink of civil war. But when the priests and Levites left the Northern Kingdom, rallying to Rehoboam's side and intent on worshiping only their one, true Savior-God, Judah prospered (2 Chronicles 11:14–17).

As God's people today, we no longer live in a theocracy. No nation on earth can claim to be "God's nation." Under the New Covenant Jesus died to bring us (the new Israel) forgiveness, peace, and hope. People of every language and nation on earth belong to this "Israel" by virtue of their faith in Christ Jesus, our Messiah. Nonetheless, Solomon's proverb still holds true. Knowing that sin shames our nation and brings much trouble, we pray and work for just laws. Knowing that righteousness will exalt our nation and will bring with it the Lord's blessing, we pray and witness so that more and more of our fellow citizens come to know and to trust the righteousness that comes by faith in Christ Jesus.

WEEK 36 • SATURDAY

2 Chronicles 12:1–16

GET THE BIG PICTURE

As 2 Chronicles 12 opens, King Rehoboam's stubborn arrogance has led Judah to the edge of disaster. But the Lord sends His word through the prophet Shemaiah, and that word leads king and people alike to repentance. As you read, note the various references in the text to godly humility. Ask yourself what it means to be humble in a God-pleasing way. If time is short, focus on 2 Chronicles 12:1–12.

Shishak Attacks Jerusalem

12 After Rehoboam's position as
king was established and he
had become strong, he and all Israel[a]
with him abandoned the law of the
LORD. 2Because they had been unfaithful to the LORD, Shishak king of Egypt
attacked Jerusalem in the fifth year of
King Rehoboam. 3With twelve hundred
chariots and sixty thousand horsemen
and the innumerable troops of Libyans,
Sukkites and Cushites[b] that came with
him from Egypt, 4he captured the fortified cities of Judah and came as far as
Jerusalem.
5Then the prophet Shemaiah came to
Rehoboam and to the leaders of Judah
who had assembled in Jerusalem for
fear of Shishak, and he said to them,
"This is what the LORD says, 'You have
abandoned me; therefore, I now abandon you to Shishak.' "
6The leaders of Israel and the king
humbled themselves and said, "The
LORD is just."
7When the LORD saw that they humbled themselves, this word of the LORD
came to Shemaiah: "Since they have
humbled themselves, I will not destroy
them but will soon give them deliverance. My wrath will not be poured out
on Jerusalem through Shishak. 8They
will, however, become subject to him, so
that they may learn the difference between serving me and serving the kings
of other lands."
9When Shishak king of Egypt attacked Jerusalem, he carried off the treasures of the temple of the LORD and the
treasures of the royal palace. He took
everything, including the gold shields
Solomon had made. 10So King Rehoboam made bronze shields to replace them
and assigned these to the commanders
of the guard on duty at the entrance to
the royal palace. 11Whenever the king
went to the LORD's temple, the guards
went with him, bearing the shields, and
afterward they returned them to the
guardroom.
12Because Rehoboam humbled himself, the LORD's anger turned from him,
and he was not totally destroyed. Indeed, there was some good in Judah.
13King Rehoboam established himself
firmly in Jerusalem and continued as
king. He was forty-one years old when
he became king, and he reigned seventeen years in Jerusalem, the city the
LORD had chosen out of all the tribes of
Israel in which to put his Name. His
mother's name was Naamah; she was
an Ammonite. 14He did evil because he
had not set his heart on seeking the
LORD.
15As for the events of Rehoboam's
reign, from beginning to end, are they
not written in the records of Shemaiah
the prophet and of Iddo the seer that

[a]1 That is, Judah, as frequently in 2 Chronicles
[b]3 That is, people from the upper Nile region

deal with genealogies? There was continual warfare between Rehoboam and
Jeroboam. [16]Rehoboam rested with his
fathers and was buried in the City of
David. And Abijah his son succeeded
him as king.

SHARPEN THE FOCUS

Most athletes need a coach, because few individuals will push themselves hard enough to reach peak performance. Most students need a teacher to grade their homework, because few individuals will study hard enough on their own to master any given subject matter. Given a choice, most people would prefer an easy life.

Rehoboam's problem, though, was that "he had not set his heart on seeking the LORD" (2 Chronicles 12:14). He chose to live for himself and for the perks of power life held out to him.

In Proverbs 13:15, King Solomon warned, "The way of the unfaithful is hard." On the other hand, "The path of the upright is a highway" (Proverbs 15:19). It seldom looks it at the time, but the easiest path through life is to do the godly things.

We believe this. But still we sometimes wake up to find ourselves in the same ditch as Rehoboam. What then? Our Lord will seek us out, just as He sought out Rehoboam. He will give us the courage we need to acknowledge our sinfulness. He will forgive, for Jesus' sake, and after dusting us off, He will set us back upon the highway of the righteous. He will even give us strength to put one foot in front of the other on that path. We need only ask.

WEEK 37 • MONDAY

2 Chronicles 13:1—14:15

GET THE BIG PICTURE

As you read 2 Chronicles 13–14 today, note the source of the confidence, the holy boldness with which King Abijah and later King Asa confront the enemies of God's people. If time is short, focus on 2 Chronicles 13:1–22.

Abijah King of Judah

13 In the eighteenth year of the
reign of Jeroboam, Abijah became king of Judah, [2]and he reigned in
Jerusalem three years. His mother's
name was Maacah,[a] a daughter[b] of Uriel of Gibeah.

There was war between Abijah and
Jeroboam. [3]Abijah went into battle with
a force of four hundred thousand able
fighting men, and Jeroboam drew up a
battle line against him with eight hundred thousand able troops.

[4]Abijah stood on Mount Zemaraim, in
the hill country of Ephraim, and said,
"Jeroboam and all Israel, listen to me!
[5]Don't you know that the LORD, the
God of Israel, has given the kingship of
Israel to David and his descendants forever by a covenant of salt? [6]Yet Jeroboam son of Nebat, an official of Solomon
son of David, rebelled against his master. [7]Some worthless scoundrels gath-

[a]2 Most Septuagint manuscripts and Syriac (see also 2 Chron. 11:20 and 1 Kings 15:2); Hebrew *Micaiah* [b]2 Or *granddaughter*

ered around him and opposed Rehoboam son of Solomon when he was young
and indecisive and not strong enough
to resist them.
[8]"And now you plan to resist the kingdom of the LORD, which is in the hands
of David's descendants. You are indeed
a vast army and have with you the gold-
en calves that Jeroboam made to be your
gods. [9]But didn't you drive out the
priests of the LORD, the sons of Aaron,
and the Levites, and make priests of
your own as the peoples of other lands
do? Whoever comes to consecrate himself with a young bull and seven rams
may become a priest of what are not gods.
[10]"As for us, the LORD is our God, and
we have not forsaken him. The priests
who serve the LORD are sons of Aaron,
and the Levites assist them. [11]Every
morning and evening they present
burnt offerings and fragrant incense to
the LORD. They set out the bread on the
ceremonially clean table and light the
lamps on the gold lampstand every evening. We are observing the requirements of the LORD our God. But you
have forsaken him. [12]God is with us; he
is our leader. His priests with their trumpets will sound the battle cry against
you. Men of Israel, do not fight against
the LORD, the God of your fathers, for
you will not succeed."
[13]Now Jeroboam had sent troops
around to the rear, so that while he was
in front of Judah the ambush was behind them. [14]Judah turned and saw that
they were being attacked at both front
and rear. Then they cried out to the
LORD. The priests blew their trumpets
[15]and the men of Judah raised the battle
cry. At the sound of their battle cry, God
routed Jeroboam and all Israel before
Abijah and Judah. [16]The Israelites fled
before Judah, and God delivered them
into their hands. [17]Abijah and his men
inflicted heavy losses on them, so that
there were five hundred thousand casualties among Israel's able men. [18]The
men of Israel were subdued on that occasion, and the men of Judah were victorious because they relied on the LORD,
the God of their fathers.
[19]Abijah pursued Jeroboam and took
from him the towns of Bethel, Jeshanah
and Ephron, with their surrounding villages. [20]Jeroboam did not regain power
during the time of Abijah. And the LORD
struck him down and he died.
[21]But Abijah grew in strength. He
married fourteen wives and had
twenty-two sons and sixteen daughters.
[22]The other events of Abijah's reign,
what he did and what he said, are written in the annotations of the prophet
Iddo.
14 And Abijah rested with his
fathers and was buried in the
City of David. Asa his son succeeded
him as king, and in his days the country was at peace for ten years.

Asa King of Judah

[2]Asa did what was good and right in
the eyes of the LORD his God. [3]He removed the foreign altars and the high
places, smashed the sacred stones and
cut down the Asherah poles.[a] [4]He commanded Judah to seek the LORD, the
God of their fathers, and to obey his
laws and commands. [5]He removed the
high places and incense altars in every
town in Judah, and the kingdom was at
peace under him. [6]He built up the fortified cities of Judah, since the land was
at peace. No one was at war with him
during those years, for the LORD gave
him rest.
[7]"Let us build up these towns," he
said to Judah, "and put walls around
them, with towers, gates and bars. The
land is still ours, because we have
sought the LORD our God; we sought
him and he has given us rest on every
side." So they built and prospered.
[8]Asa had an army of three hundred
thousand men from Judah, equipped
with large shields and with spears, and
two hundred and eighty thousand from
Benjamin, armed with small shields and
with bows. All these were brave fighting men.
[9]Zerah the Cushite marched out

[a]3 That is, symbols of the goddess Asherah; here
and elsewhere in 2 Chronicles

against them with a vast army[a] and
three hundred chariots, and came as far
as Mareshah. [10]Asa went out to meet
him, and they took up battle positions
in the Valley of Zephathah near Mareshah.
[11]Then Asa called to the LORD his God
and said, "LORD, there is no one like you
to help the powerless against the
mighty. Help us, O LORD our God, for
we rely on you, and in your name we
have come against this vast army. O
LORD, you are our God; do not let man
prevail against you."
[12]The LORD struck down the Cushites
before Asa and Judah. The Cushites
fled, [13]and Asa and his army pursued
them as far as Gerar. Such a great number of Cushites fell that they could not
recover; they were crushed before the
LORD and his forces. The men of Judah
carried off a large amount of plunder.
[14]They destroyed all the villages around
Gerar, for the terror of the LORD had fall-
en upon them. They plundered all these
villages, since there was much booty
there. [15]They also attacked the camps of
the herdsmen and carried off droves of
sheep and goats and camels. Then they
returned to Jerusalem.

[a]9 Hebrew *with an army of a thousand thousands* or *with an army of thousands upon thousands*

SHARPEN THE FOCUS

A familiar piece of advice says, "Be sure you're right, then go ahead." Maybe you've relied on this advice or some like it. Abijah and later Asa took the proverb a step further. In brief the tack they followed went, "Be sure you're righteous, then go ahead."

Both kings walked through the battles of 2 Chronicles 13 and 14, knowing their Lord counted them righteous. Not that they claimed to be perfect; they weren't. But they knew and relied on the covenant the Lord had made with Abraham, Isaac, Jacob, and David. They knew they enjoyed right standing before the King of kings because of what their coming Messiah would do. And so they rested all of their trust in Him—come life or death. They were not disappointed.

As you face life's challenges, how confident are you of that same righteousness? Spend a few moments meditating on Romans 3:21–28, focusing especially on the truth that in Jesus you are right with God. Then continue your day in the holy confidence His righteousness brings.

WEEK 37 • TUESDAY

2 Chronicles 15:1—16:14

Scripture never shies away from painting an accurate portrait of the persons that people its pages. In today's reading, for example, you will see King Asa at his best—and at his worst. As you read, note the contrast between 2 Chronicles 15 and 16. Ask yourself what accounts for Asa's defection. If time is short, focus on 2 Chronicles 15:1–19.

Asa's Reform

15 The Spirit of God came upon
Azariah son of Oded. 2He
went out to meet Asa and said to him,
"Listen to me, Asa and all Judah and
Benjamin. The LORD is with you when
you are with him. If you seek him, he
will be found by you, but if you forsake
him, he will forsake you. 3For a long
time Israel was without the true God,
without a priest to teach and without
the law. 4But in their distress they
turned to the LORD, the God of Israel,
and sought him, and he was found by
them. 5In those days it was not safe to
travel about, for all the inhabitants of
the lands were in great turmoil. 6One
nation was being crushed by another
and one city by another, because God
was troubling them with every kind of
distress. 7But as for you, be strong and
do not give up, for your work will be rewarded."
8When Asa heard these words and the
prophecy of Azariah son of[a] Oded the
prophet, he took courage. He removed
the detestable idols from the whole land
of Judah and Benjamin and from the
towns he had captured in the hills of
Ephraim. He repaired the altar of the
LORD that was in front of the portico of
the LORD's temple.
9Then he assembled all Judah and
Benjamin and the people from Ephraim, Manasseh and Simeon who had settled among them, for large numbers had
come over to him from Israel when they
saw that the LORD his God was with
him.
10They assembled at Jerusalem in the
third month of the fifteenth year of
Asa's reign. 11At that time they sacrificed
to the LORD seven hundred head of
cattle and seven thousand sheep and
goats from the plunder they had
brought back. 12They entered into a covenant to seek the LORD, the God of their
fathers, with all their heart and soul.
13All who would not seek the LORD, the
God of Israel, were to be put to death,
whether small or great, man or woman.
14They took an oath to the LORD with
loud acclamation, with shouting and
with trumpets and horns. 15All Judah rejoiced about the oath because they had
sworn it wholeheartedly. They sought
God eagerly, and he was found by them.
So the LORD gave them rest on every
side.
16King Asa also deposed his grandmother Maacah from her position as
queen mother, because she had made a
repulsive Asherah pole. Asa cut the pole
down, broke it up and burned it in the
Kidron Valley. 17Although he did not remove the high places from Israel, Asa's
heart was fully committed ⌊to the LORD⌋
all his life. 18He brought into the temple
of God the silver and gold and the articles that he and his father had dedicated.
19There was no more war until the
thirty-fifth year of Asa's reign.

Asa's Last Years

16 In the thirty-sixth year of
Asa's reign Baasha king of
Israel went up against Judah and fortified Ramah to prevent anyone from
leaving or entering the territory of Asa
king of Judah.
2Asa then took the silver and gold out
of the treasuries of the LORD's temple
and of his own palace and sent it to Ben-
Hadad king of Aram, who was ruling in
Damascus. 3"Let there be a treaty between me and you," he said, "as there
was between my father and your father.
See, I am sending you silver and gold.
Now break your treaty with Baasha
king of Israel so he will withdraw
from me."
4Ben-Hadad agreed with King Asa
and sent the commanders of his forces
against the towns of Israel. They conquered Ijon, Dan, Abel Maim[b] and all
the store cities of Naphtali. 5When Baasha heard this, he stopped building Ramah and abandoned his work. 6Then
King Asa brought all the men of Judah,
and they carried away from Ramah the

[a]8 Vulgate and Syriac (see also Septuagint and verse 1); Hebrew does not have *Azariah son of.*
[b]4 Also known as *Abel Beth Maacah*

stones and timber Baasha had been using. With them he built up Geba and
Mizpah.
7At that time Hanani the seer came to
Asa king of Judah and said to him: "Because you relied on the king of Aram
and not on the LORD your God, the
army of the king of Aram has escaped
from your hand. 8Were not the Cushites[a]
and Libyans a mighty army with great
numbers of chariots and horsemen[b]? Yet
when you relied on the LORD, he delivered them into your hand. 9For the eyes
of the LORD range throughout the earth
to strengthen those whose hearts are
fully committed to him. You have done
a foolish thing, and from now on you
will be at war."
10Asa was angry with the seer because
of this; he was so enraged that he put
him in prison. At the same time Asa
brutally oppressed some of the people.
11The events of Asa's reign, from beginning to end, are written in the book
of the kings of Judah and Israel. 12In the
thirty-ninth year of his reign Asa was
afflicted with a disease in his feet.
Though his disease was severe, even in
his illness he did not seek help from the
LORD, but only from the physicians.
13Then in the forty-first year of his reign
Asa died and rested with his fathers.
14They buried him in the tomb that he
had cut out for himself in the City of
David. They laid him on a bier covered
with spices and various blended perfumes, and they made a huge fire in his
honor.

[a]8 That is, people from the upper Nile region
[b]8 Or *charioteers*

SHARPEN THE FOCUS

Think back to the last time you tried to do something very challenging. Suppose you could have been absolutely sure, as you began, that you would succeed. How would that confidence have changed your attitude? your actions? With that in mind, reread 2 Chronicles 15:7–8. When Asa heard God's word, he acted decisively. He knew the Lord would do what He had promised. And so, in confidence, Asa set about the difficult task of spiritual reform in his nation (2 Chronicles 15:9–15) and even in his own family (2 Chronicles 15:16)!

As we face our own challenges, we can have the same kind of confidence that so mightily encouraged King Asa. Especially as we witness, as we love the unlovely, as we teach our children or grandchildren the Word of God, we can rely on the Lord's promise to King Asa:

> *But as for you, be strong and do not give up, for your work will be rewarded.* (2 Chronicles 15:7)

The apostle Paul, several centuries later, said in the light of our Savior's death and resurrection victory:

> *Therefore, my dear brothers, stand firm. Let nothing move you. Always give yourselves fully to the work of the Lord, because you know that your labor in the Lord is not in vain.* (1 Corinthians 15:58)

WEEK 37 • WEDNESDAY

2 Chr. 17:1—18:34

GET THE BIG PICTURE

In 2 Chronicles 16:9 the Lord made a wonderful promise, one King Asa ignored: "The eyes of the Lord range throughout the earth, to strengthen those whose hearts are fully committed to Him." As you read about King Jehoshaphat's reign in Judah, look for evidence that the Lord kept this promise. If time is short, focus on 2 Chronicles 17:1–9.

Jehoshaphat King of Judah

17 Jehoshaphat his son succeeded him as king and strengthened himself against Israel. 2He stationed troops in all the fortified cities of
Judah and put garrisons in Judah and in
the towns of Ephraim that his father Asa
had captured.
3The LORD was with Jehoshaphat because in his early years he walked in the
ways his father David had followed. He
did not consult the Baals 4but sought the
God of his father and followed his
commands rather than the practices of
Israel. 5The LORD established the kingdom under his control; and all Judah
brought gifts to Jehoshaphat, so that he
had great wealth and honor. 6His heart
was devoted to the ways of the LORD;
furthermore, he removed the high
places and the Asherah poles from
Judah.
7In the third year of his reign he sent
his officials Ben-Hail, Obadiah, Zechariah, Nethanel and Micaiah to teach in
the towns of Judah. 8With them were
certain Levites—Shemaiah, Nethaniah,
Zebadiah, Asahel, Shemiramoth, Jehonathan, Adonijah, Tobijah and Tob-Ado-
nijah—and the priests Elishama and
Jehoram. 9They taught throughout Judah, taking with them the Book of the
Law of the LORD; they went around to
all the towns of Judah and taught the
people.
10The fear of the LORD fell on all the
kingdoms of the lands surrounding
Judah, so that they did not make war
with Jehoshaphat. 11Some Philistines
brought Jehoshaphat gifts and silver as
tribute, and the Arabs brought him
flocks: seven thousand seven hundred
rams and seven thousand seven hundred goats.
12Jehoshaphat became more and more
powerful; he built forts and store cities
in Judah 13and had large supplies in the
towns of Judah. He also kept experienced fighting men in Jerusalem. 14Their
enrollment by families was as follows:

From Judah, commanders of units of 1,000:
Adnah the commander, with 300,000 fighting men;
15next, Jehohanan the commander, with 280,000;
16next, Amasiah son of Zicri, who volunteered himself for the service of the LORD, with 200,000.
17From Benjamin:
Eliada, a valiant soldier, with 200,000 men armed with bows and shields;
18next, Jehozabad, with 180,000 men armed for battle.

19These were the men who served the
king, besides those he stationed in the
fortified cities throughout Judah.

Micaiah Prophesies Against Ahab

18 Now Jehoshaphat had great
wealth and honor, and he allied himself with Ahab by marriage.
2Some years later he went down to visit

Ahab in Samaria. Ahab slaughtered many sheep and cattle for him and the people with him and urged him to attack Ramoth Gilead. 3Ahab king of Israel asked Jehoshaphat king of Judah, "Will you go with me against Ramoth Gilead?"

Jehoshaphat replied, "I am as you are, and my people as your people; we will join you in the war." 4But Jehoshaphat also said to the king of Israel, "First seek the counsel of the LORD."

5So the king of Israel brought together the prophets—four hundred men—and asked them, "Shall we go to war against Ramoth Gilead, or shall I refrain?"

"Go," they answered, "for God will give it into the king's hand."

6But Jehoshaphat asked, "Is there not a prophet of the LORD here whom we can inquire of?"

7The king of Israel answered Jehoshaphat, "There is still one man through whom we can inquire of the LORD, but I hate him because he never prophesies anything good about me, but always bad. He is Micaiah son of Imlah."

"The king should not say that," Jehoshaphat replied.

8So the king of Israel called one of his officials and said, "Bring Micaiah son of Imlah at once."

9Dressed in their royal robes, the king of Israel and Jehoshaphat king of Judah were sitting on their thrones at the threshing floor by the entrance to the gate of Samaria, with all the prophets prophesying before them. 10Now Zedekiah son of Kenaanah had made iron horns, and he declared, "This is what the LORD says: 'With these you will gore the Arameans until they are destroyed.' "

11All the other prophets were prophesying the same thing. "Attack Ramoth Gilead and be victorious," they said, "for the LORD will give it into the king's hand."

12The messenger who had gone to summon Micaiah said to him, "Look, as one man the other prophets are predicting success for the king. Let your word agree with theirs, and speak favorably."

13But Micaiah said, "As surely as the LORD lives, I can tell him only what my God says."

14When he arrived, the king asked him, "Micaiah, shall we go to war against Ramoth Gilead, or shall I refrain?"

"Attack and be victorious," he answered, "for they will be given into your hand."

15The king said to him, "How many times must I make you swear to tell me nothing but the truth in the name of the LORD?"

16Then Micaiah answered, "I saw all Israel scattered on the hills like sheep without a shepherd, and the LORD said, 'These people have no master. Let each one go home in peace.' "

17The king of Israel said to Jehoshaphat, "Didn't I tell you that he never prophesies anything good about me, but only bad?"

18Micaiah continued, "Therefore hear the word of the LORD: I saw the LORD sitting on his throne with all the host of heaven standing on his right and on his left. 19And the LORD said, 'Who will entice Ahab king of Israel into attacking Ramoth Gilead and going to his death there?'

"One suggested this, and another that. 20Finally, a spirit came forward, stood before the LORD and said, 'I will entice him.'

" 'By what means?' the LORD asked.

21" 'I will go and be a lying spirit in the mouths of all his prophets,' he said.

" 'You will succeed in enticing him,' said the LORD. 'Go and do it.'

22"So now the LORD has put a lying spirit in the mouths of these prophets of yours. The LORD has decreed disaster for you."

23Then Zedekiah son of Kenaanah went up and slapped Micaiah in the face. "Which way did the spirit from[a] the LORD go when he went from me to speak to you?" he asked.

24Micaiah replied, "You will find out

[a]23 Or *Spirit of*

on the day you go to hide in an inner
room."
[25]The king of Israel then ordered,
"Take Micaiah and send him back to
Amon the ruler of the city and to Joash
the king's son, [26]and say, 'This is what
the king says: Put this fellow in prison
and give him nothing but bread and water until I return safely.' "
[27]Micaiah declared, "If you ever return safely, the LORD has not spoken
through me." Then he added, "Mark my
words, all you people!"

Ahab Killed at Ramoth Gilead

[28]So the king of Israel and Jehoshaphat king of Judah went up to Ramoth
Gilead. [29]The king of Israel said to Jehoshaphat, "I will enter the battle in disguise, but you wear your royal robes."
So the king of Israel disguised himself
and went into battle.
[30]Now the king of Aram had ordered
his chariot commanders, "Do not fight
with anyone, small or great, except the
king of Israel." [31]When the chariot
commanders saw Jehoshaphat, they
thought, "This is the king of Israel." So
they turned to attack him, but Jehoshaphat cried out, and the LORD helped
him. God drew them away from him,
[32]for when the chariot commanders saw
that he was not the king of Israel, they
stopped pursuing him.
[33]But someone drew his bow at random and hit the king of Israel between
the sections of his armor. The king told
the chariot driver, "Wheel around and
get me out of the fighting. I've been
wounded." [34]All day long the battle
raged, and the king of Israel propped
himself up in his chariot facing the Arameans until evening. Then at sunset he
died.

SHARPEN THE FOCUS

Think of it! God continually looks for ways to "strengthen" you.

"But wait a minute," you may say, "My heart isn't always fully committed to Him. I sometimes give in to the temptation to live for idols of gold and silver, just as the citizens of ancient Judah did. I don't always keep my priorities straight. My mind wanders in worship and my heart follows it. How could God's promise apply to me?"

If you've said that, you're absolutely right. You've stated the truth, but not quite enough truth. Like King Jehoshaphat of old, we've all allied ourselves with our Lord's enemies on occasion. But the Lord doesn't give up on us any more than He gave up on Jehoshaphat. At the cross God nailed Jesus for Jehoshaphat's disloyalty—and for our own. There, Jesus' heart broke with the guilt of our disloyal words and actions. Then Jesus walked out of Joseph's garden tomb as our victorious and reigning Savior.

Our Lord truly has taken sides with His repentant children. Touched by His grace, our hearts are transformed again and again as He works in them. He creates within us more loyalty to Him, to His kingdom, to His Word.

WEEK 37 • THURSDAY

2 Chronicles 19:1—20:37

GET THE BIG PICTURE

Today's reading, especially chapter 20, can raise goose bumps for even the most casual Bible student. As you work through the text, note King Jehoshaphat's honest cries for help and the Lord's powerful and compassionate answer. If time is short, focus on 2 Chronicles 20:1–25.

19 When Jehoshaphat king of
Judah returned safely to his
palace in Jerusalem, 2Jehu the seer, the
son of Hanani, went out to meet him
and said to the king, "Should you help
the wicked and love[a] those who hate the
LORD? Because of this, the wrath of the
LORD is upon you. 3There is, however,
some good in you, for you have rid the
land of the Asherah poles and have set
your heart on seeking God."

Jehoshaphat Appoints Judges

4Jehoshaphat lived in Jerusalem, and
he went out again among the people
from Beersheba to the hill country of
Ephraim and turned them back to the
LORD, the God of their fathers. 5He appointed judges in the land, in each of the
fortified cities of Judah. 6He told them,
"Consider carefully what you do, because you are not judging for man but
for the LORD, who is with you whenever you give a verdict. 7Now let the fear
of the LORD be upon you. Judge carefully, for with the LORD our God there is no
injustice or partiality or bribery."

8In Jerusalem also, Jehoshaphat appointed some of the Levites, priests and
heads of Israelite families to administer
the law of the LORD and to settle disputes. And they lived in Jerusalem. 9He
gave them these orders: "You must
serve faithfully and wholeheartedly in
the fear of the LORD. 10In every case that
comes before you from your fellow
countrymen who live in the cities—
whether bloodshed or other concerns of
the law, commands, decrees or ordinances—you are to warn them not to
sin against the LORD; otherwise his
wrath will come on you and your brothers. Do this, and you will not sin.

11"Amariah the chief priest will be over
you in any matter concerning the LORD,
and Zebadiah son of Ishmael, the leader
of the tribe of Judah, will be over you in
any matter concerning the king, and the
Levites will serve as officials before you.
Act with courage, and may the LORD be
with those who do well."

Jehoshaphat Defeats Moab and Ammon

20 After this, the Moabites
and Ammonites with
some of the Meunites[b] came to make
war on Jehoshaphat.

2Some men came and told Jehoshaphat, "A vast army is coming against you
from Edom,[c] from the other side of the
Sea.[d] It is already in Hazazon Tamar"
(that is, En Gedi). 3Alarmed, Jehoshaphat resolved to inquire of the LORD,
and he proclaimed a fast for all Judah.
4The people of Judah came together to
seek help from the LORD; indeed, they
came from every town in Judah to seek
him.

5Then Jehoshaphat stood up in the assembly of Judah and Jerusalem at the
temple of the LORD in the front of the
new courtyard 6and said:

[a]2 Or *and make alliances with* [b]1 Some Septuagint manuscripts; Hebrew *Ammonites*
[c]2 One Hebrew manuscript; most Hebrew manuscripts, Septuagint and Vulgate *Aram*
[d]2 That is, the Dead Sea

"O LORD, God of our fathers, are
you not the God who is in heaven?
You rule over all the kingdoms of
the nations. Power and might are in
your hand, and no one can withstand you. 7O our God, did you not
drive out the inhabitants of this
land before your people Israel and
give it forever to the descendants of
Abraham your friend? 8They have
lived in it and have built in it a sanctuary for your Name, saying, 9'If calamity comes upon us, whether the
sword of judgment, or plague or
famine, we will stand in your presence before this temple that bears
your Name and will cry out to you
in our distress, and you will hear us
and save us.'

10"But now here are men from
Ammon, Moab and Mount Seir,
whose territory you would not allow Israel to invade when they
came from Egypt; so they turned
away from them and did not destroy them. 11See how they are repaying us by coming to drive us out
of the possession you gave us as an
inheritance. 12O our God, will you
not judge them? For we have no
power to face this vast army that is
attacking us. We do not know what
to do, but our eyes are upon you."

13All the men of Judah, with their
wives and children and little ones, stood
there before the LORD.

14Then the Spirit of the LORD came
upon Jahaziel son of Zechariah, the son
of Benaiah, the son of Jeiel, the son of
Mattaniah, a Levite and descendant of
Asaph, as he stood in the assembly.

15He said: "Listen, King Jehoshaphat
and all who live in Judah and Jerusalem!
This is what the LORD says to you: 'Do
not be afraid or discouraged because of
this vast army. For the battle is not
yours, but God's. 16Tomorrow march
down against them. They will be climbing up by the Pass of Ziz, and you will
find them at the end of the gorge in the
Desert of Jeruel. 17You will not have to
fight this battle. Take up your positions;
stand firm and see the deliverance the
LORD will give you, O Judah and Jerusalem. Do not be afraid; do not be discouraged. Go out to face them
tomorrow, and the LORD will be with
you.'"

18Jehoshaphat bowed with his face to
the ground, and all the people of Judah
and Jerusalem fell down in worship before the LORD. 19Then some Levites from
the Kohathites and Korahites stood up
and praised the LORD, the God of Israel,
with very loud voice.

20Early in the morning they left for the
Desert of Tekoa. As they set out, Jehoshaphat stood and said, "Listen to me, Judah and people of Jerusalem! Have faith
in the LORD your God and you will be
upheld; have faith in his prophets and
you will be successful." 21After consulting the people, Jehoshaphat appointed
men to sing to the LORD and to praise
him for the splendor of his[a] holiness as
they went out at the head of the army,
saying:

"Give thanks to the LORD,
for his love endures forever."

22As they began to sing and praise, the
LORD set ambushes against the men of
Ammon and Moab and Mount Seir who
were invading Judah, and they were defeated. 23The men of Ammon and Moab
rose up against the men from Mount
Seir to destroy and annihilate them.
After they finished slaughtering the
men from Seir, they helped to destroy
one another.

24When the men of Judah came to the
place that overlooks the desert and
looked toward the vast army, they saw
only dead bodies lying on the ground;
no one had escaped. 25So Jehoshaphat
and his men went to carry off their
plunder, and they found among them a
great amount of equipment and
clothing[b] and also articles of value—
more than they could take away. There
was so much plunder that it took three

[a]21 Or *him with the splendor of* [b]25 Some Hebrew manuscripts and Vulgate; most Hebrew manuscripts *corpses*

days to collect it. [26]On the fourth day
they assembled in the Valley of Beracah,
where they praised the LORD. This is
why it is called the Valley of Beracah[a] to
this day.
[27]Then, led by Jehoshaphat, all the
men of Judah and Jerusalem returned
joyfully to Jerusalem, for the LORD had
given them cause to rejoice over their
enemies. [28]They entered Jerusalem and
went to the temple of the LORD with
harps and lutes and trumpets.
[29]The fear of God came upon all the
kingdoms of the countries when they
heard how the LORD had fought against
the enemies of Israel. [30]And the kingdom of Jehoshaphat was at peace, for
his God had given him rest on every
side.

The End of Jehoshaphat's Reign

[31]So Jehoshaphat reigned over Judah.
He was thirty-five years old when he
became king of Judah, and he reigned
in Jerusalem twenty-five years. His
mother's name was Azubah daughter
of Shilhi. [32]He walked in the ways of his
father Asa and did not stray from them;
he did what was right in the eyes of the
LORD. [33]The high places, however, were
not removed, and the people still had
not set their hearts on the God of their
fathers.
[34]The other events of Jehoshaphat's
reign, from beginning to end, are written in the annals of Jehu son of Hanani,
which are recorded in the book of the
kings of Israel.
[35]Later, Jehoshaphat king of Judah
made an alliance with Ahaziah king of
Israel, who was guilty of wickedness.
[36]He agreed with him to construct a fleet
of trading ships.[b] After these were built
at Ezion Geber, [37]Eliezer son of Dodava-
hu of Mareshah prophesied against Jehoshaphat, saying, "Because you have
made an alliance with Ahaziah, the
LORD will destroy what you have
made." The ships were wrecked and
were not able to set sail to trade.[c]

[a]26 *Beracah* means *praise.* [b]36 Hebrew *of ships that could go to Tarshish* [c]37 Hebrew *sail for Tarshish*

SHARPEN THE FOCUS

What does it mean for you that your Lord acts in compassion toward you? It means He looks on you and on your fears, sadness, and problems with tender concern. As we read 2 Chronicles 20:13, we catch a glimpse of Judah through the Lord's compassionate eyes:

> *All the men of Judah, with their wives and children and little ones, stood there before the LORD.*

The enemy thundered down. God's people stood in His presence, powerless to help themselves against such an overwhelming force. But their prayers rose to heaven. God saw and heard. As He had done so many times before, God came to help. Israel didn't need to fight this battle (2 Chronicles 20:17). They simply stood and watched their Lord prove Himself strong on their behalf.

Do you see your Lord's compassion toward you? You can, you know. If you doubt it, look toward Calvary. Remember that the heavenly Father turned His face of compassion away from His own dear Son so that He could, in compassion, forgive and rescue you. Then pray Jehoshaphat's prayer about the troubles and emergencies of your own life:

> *O our God . . . we have no power . . . . We do not know what to do,*
> *but our eyes are upon You.* (2 Chronicles 20:12)

As we read these two sorry chapters in Judah's history, we can't help but shake our heads in dismay over the depths to which the house of David had sunk. Still, the Lord's covenant with David's house was unshakable. Look for evidence of this as you read. If time is short, focus on 2 Chronicles 21:1–20.

21 Then Jehoshaphat rested with his fathers and was buried with them in the City of David. And Jehoram his son succeeded him as king. 2Jehoram's brothers, the sons of Jehoshaphat, were Azariah, Jehiel, Zechariah, Azariahu, Michael and Shephatiah. All these were sons of Jehoshaphat king of Israel.[a] 3Their father had given them many gifts of silver and gold and articles of value, as well as fortified cities in Judah, but he had given the kingdom to Jehoram because he was his firstborn son.

Jehoram King of Judah

4When Jehoram established himself firmly over his father's kingdom, he put all his brothers to the sword along with some of the princes of Israel. 5Jehoram was thirty-two years old when he became king, and he reigned in Jerusalem eight years. 6He walked in the ways of the kings of Israel, as the house of Ahab had done, for he married a daughter of Ahab. He did evil in the eyes of the LORD. 7Nevertheless, because of the covenant the LORD had made with David, the LORD was not willing to destroy the house of David. He had promised to maintain a lamp for him and his descendants forever.

8In the time of Jehoram, Edom rebelled against Judah and set up its own king. 9So Jehoram went there with his officers and all his chariots. The Edomites surrounded him and his chariot commanders, but he rose up and broke through by night. 10To this day Edom has been in rebellion against Judah.

Libnah revolted at the same time, because Jehoram had forsaken the LORD, the God of his fathers. 11He had also built high places on the hills of Judah and had caused the people of Jerusalem to prostitute themselves and had led Judah astray.

12Jehoram received a letter from Elijah the prophet, which said:

> "This is what the LORD, the God of your father David, says: 'You have not walked in the ways of your father Jehoshaphat or of Asa king of Judah. 13But you have walked in the ways of the kings of Israel, and you have led Judah and the people of Jerusalem to prostitute themselves, just as the house of Ahab did. You have also murdered your own brothers, members of your father's house, men who were better than you. 14So now the LORD is about to strike your people, your sons, your wives and everything that is yours, with a heavy blow. 15You yourself will be very ill with a lingering disease of the bowels, until the disease causes your bowels to come out.' "

16The LORD aroused against Jehoram the hostility of the Philistines and of the Arabs who lived near the Cushites. 17They attacked Judah, invaded it and

[a]2 That is, Judah, as frequently in 2 Chronicles

carried off all the goods found in the
king's palace, together with his sons and
wives. Not a son was left to him except
Ahaziah,[a] the youngest.
18After all this, the LORD afflicted Jehoram with an incurable disease of the
bowels. 19In the course of time, at the
end of the second year, his bowels came
out because of the disease, and he died
in great pain. His people made no fire
in his honor, as they had for his fathers.
20Jehoram was thirty-two years old
when he became king, and he reigned
in Jerusalem eight years. He passed
away, to no one's regret, and was buried in the City of David, but not in the
tombs of the kings.

Ahaziah King of Judah

22 The people of Jerusalem
made Ahaziah, Jehoram's
youngest son, king in his place, since the
raiders, who came with the Arabs into
the camp, had killed all the older sons.
So Ahaziah son of Jehoram king of Judah began to reign.
2Ahaziah was twenty-two[b] years old
when he became king, and he reigned
in Jerusalem one year. His mother's
name was Athaliah, a granddaughter of
Omri.
3He too walked in the ways of the
house of Ahab, for his mother encouraged him in doing wrong. 4He did evil
in the eyes of the LORD, as the house of
Ahab had done, for after his father's
death they became his advisers, to his
undoing. 5He also followed their counsel when he went with Joram[c] son of
Ahab king of Israel to war against Hazael king of Aram at Ramoth Gilead. The
Arameans wounded Joram; 6so he returned to Jezreel to recover from the
wounds they had inflicted on him at
Ramoth[d] in his battle with Hazael king
of Aram.
Then Ahaziah[e] son of Jehoram king of
Judah went down to Jezreel to see Joram son of Ahab because he had been
wounded.
7Through Ahaziah's visit to Joram,
God brought about Ahaziah's downfall.
When Ahaziah arrived, he went out
with Joram to meet Jehu son of Nimshi,
whom the LORD had anointed to destroy the house of Ahab. 8While Jehu
was executing judgment on the house
of Ahab, he found the princes of Judah
and the sons of Ahaziah's relatives, who
had been attending Ahaziah, and he
killed them. 9He then went in search of
Ahaziah, and his men captured him
while he was hiding in Samaria. He was
brought to Jehu and put to death. They
buried him, for they said, "He was a son
of Jehoshaphat, who sought the LORD
with all his heart." So there was no one
in the house of Ahaziah powerful
enough to retain the kingdom.

Athaliah and Joash

10When Athaliah the mother of Ahaziah saw that her son was dead, she proceeded to destroy the whole royal
family of the house of Judah. 11But
Jehosheba,[f] the daughter of King Jehoram, took Joash son of Ahaziah and stole
him away from among the royal princes
who were about to be murdered and
put him and his nurse in a bedroom.
Because Jehosheba,[f] the daughter of
King Jehoram and wife of the priest Jehoiada, was Ahaziah's sister, she hid the
child from Athaliah so she could not kill
him. 12He remained hidden with them
at the temple of God for six years while
Athaliah ruled the land.

[a]17 Hebrew *Jehoahaz,* a variant of *Ahaziah*
[b]2 Some Septuagint manuscripts and Syriac (see also 2 Kings 8:26); Hebrew *forty-two*
[c]5 Hebrew *Jehoram,* a variant of *Joram;* also in verses 6 and 7
[d]6 Hebrew *Ramah,* a variant of *Ramoth*
[e]6 Some Hebrew manuscripts, Septuagint, Vulgate and Syriac (see also 2 Kings 8:29); most Hebrew manuscripts *Azariah*
[f]11 Hebrew *Jehoshabeath,* a variant of *Jehosheba*

SHARPEN THE FOCUS

Each of us today will add a bit more to the legacy we will leave behind. Whether that legacy is one of regret or rejoicing depends largely on how we live today.

Take a look at Jehoram's legacy (2 Chronicles 21:18–20). No one mourned his death or shed a tear. No one even regretted his passing! Or look at Athaliah's legacy (2 Chronicles 22:2–3). Her son followed her advice, and he lived out her values—to his destruction.

Will those who come behind us find a legacy of faithfulness to Christ and to His priorities? Maybe that question makes us squirm. We're well aware of the unfaithfulness of our hearts. We've watched ourselves blow chances to leave a holy legacy for our children or our church.

But praise God that He remains faithful. The Lord "was not willing to destroy the house of David. He had promised to maintain a lamp for him and his descendants forever" (2 Chronicles 21:7). The Lord refuses to give up on us for the same reason—the new covenant He has made with us in the Son of David, Christ our Lord.

In Jesus, our past faithlessness is gone and we receive power to begin anew each morning. Certain of that, ask yourself, "What will I add to the legacy of my life in Christ today?"

WEEK 37 • SATURDAY

2 Chronicles 23:1—24:27

GET THE BIG PICTURE

Despite Queen Athaliah's wicked schemes, the Lord preserves one of David's descendants, Joash. Mentored by a godly priest, Jehoiada, Joash institutes a reformation in Judah. But when Jehoiada dies, Joash and his people revert back to the worship of pagan gods. As you read, note Jehoiada's remarkable courage. If time is short, focus on 2 Chronicles 24:1–27.

23 In the seventh year Jehoiada showed his
strength. He made a covenant with the
commanders of units of a hundred: Azariah son of Jeroham, Ishmael son of
Jehohanan, Azariah son of Obed, Maaseiah son of Adaiah, and Elishaphat son
of Zicri. 2They went throughout Judah
and gathered the Levites and the heads
of Israelite families from all the towns.
When they came to Jerusalem, 3the
whole assembly made a covenant with
the king at the temple of God.

Jehoiada said to them, "The king's son
shall reign, as the LORD promised concerning the descendants of David. 4Now
this is what you are to do: A third of you
priests and Levites who are going on
duty on the Sabbath are to keep watch
at the doors, 5a third of you at the royal
palace and a third at the Foundation
Gate, and all the other men are to be in
the courtyards of the temple of the
LORD. 6No one is to enter the temple of
the LORD except the priests and Levites
on duty; they may enter because they
are consecrated, but all the other men
are to guard what the LORD has assigned to them.[a] 7The Levites are to station themselves around the king, each
man with his weapons in his hand. Anyone who enters the temple must be put

[a]6 Or *to observe the LORD's command* ⌊*not to enter*⌋

to death. Stay close to the king wherever he goes."
[8]The Levites and all the men of Judah
did just as Jehoiada the priest ordered.
Each one took his men—those who
were going on duty on the Sabbath and
those who were going off duty—for Jehoiada the priest had not released any
of the divisions. [9]Then he gave the commanders of units of a hundred the
spears and the large and small shields
that had belonged to King David and
that were in the temple of God. [10]He stationed all the men, each with his
weapon in his hand, around the king—
near the altar and the temple, from the
south side to the north side of the temple.
[11]Jehoiada and his sons brought out
the king's son and put the crown on
him; they presented him with a copy of
the covenant and proclaimed him king.
They anointed him and shouted, "Long
live the king!"
[12]When Athaliah heard the noise of
the people running and cheering the
king, she went to them at the temple of
the LORD. [13]She looked, and there was
the king, standing by his pillar at the entrance. The officers and the trumpeters
were beside the king, and all the people
of the land were rejoicing and blowing
trumpets, and singers with musical instruments were leading the praises.
Then Athaliah tore her robes and shouted, "Treason! Treason!"
[14]Jehoiada the priest sent out the commanders of units of a hundred, who
were in charge of the troops, and said
to them: "Bring her out between the
ranks[a] and put to the sword anyone
who follows her." For the priest had
said, "Do not put her to death at the
temple of the LORD." [15]So they seized
her as she reached the entrance of the
Horse Gate on the palace grounds, and
there they put her to death.
[16]Jehoiada then made a covenant that
he and the people and the king[b] would
be the LORD's people. [17]All the people
went to the temple of Baal and tore it
down. They smashed the altars and
idols and killed Mattan the priest of Baal
in front of the altars.
[18]Then Jehoiada placed the oversight
of the temple of the LORD in the hands
of the priests, who were Levites, to
whom David had made assignments in
the temple, to present the burnt offerings of the LORD as written in the Law
of Moses, with rejoicing and singing, as
David had ordered. [19]He also stationed
doorkeepers at the gates of the LORD's
temple so that no one who was in any
way unclean might enter.
[20]He took with him the commanders
of hundreds, the nobles, the rulers of
the people and all the people of the land
and brought the king down from the
temple of the LORD. They went into the
palace through the Upper Gate and
seated the king on the royal throne,
[21]and all the people of the land rejoiced.
And the city was quiet, because Athaliah had been slain with the sword.

Joash Repairs the Temple

24 Joash was seven years old
when he became king,
and he reigned in Jerusalem forty years.
His mother's name was Zibiah; she was
from Beersheba. [2]Joash did what was
right in the eyes of the LORD all the
years of Jehoiada the priest. [3]Jehoiada
chose two wives for him, and he had
sons and daughters.
[4]Some time later Joash decided to restore the temple of the LORD. [5]He called
together the priests and Levites and said
to them, "Go to the towns of Judah and
collect the money due annually from all
Israel, to repair the temple of your God.
Do it now." But the Levites did not act
at once.
[6]Therefore the king summoned Jehoiada the chief priest and said to him,
"Why haven't you required the Levites
to bring in from Judah and Jerusalem
the tax imposed by Moses the servant of
the LORD and by the assembly of Israel
for the Tent of the Testimony?"
[7]Now the sons of that wicked woman
Athaliah had broken into the temple of

[a]14 Or *out from the precincts* [b]16 Or *covenant between ⌞the LORD⌟ and the people and the king that they* (see 2 Kings 11:17)

God and had used even its sacred objects for the Baals.
[8]At the king's command, a chest was made and placed outside, at the gate of the temple of the LORD. [9]A proclamation was then issued in Judah and Jerusalem that they should bring to the LORD the tax that Moses the servant of God had required of Israel in the desert. [10]All the officials and all the people brought their contributions gladly, dropping them into the chest until it was full. [11]Whenever the chest was brought in by the Levites to the king's officials and they saw that there was a large amount of money, the royal secretary and the officer of the chief priest would come and empty the chest and carry it back to its place. They did this regularly and collected a great amount of money. [12]The king and Jehoiada gave it to the men who carried out the work required for the temple of the LORD. They hired masons and carpenters to restore the LORD's temple, and also workers in iron and bronze to repair the temple.
[13]The men in charge of the work were diligent, and the repairs progressed under them. They rebuilt the temple of God according to its original design and reinforced it. [14]When they had finished, they brought the rest of the money to the king and Jehoiada, and with it were made articles for the LORD's temple: articles for the service and for the burnt offerings, and also dishes and other objects of gold and silver. As long as Jehoiada lived, burnt offerings were presented continually in the temple of the LORD.
[15]Now Jehoiada was old and full of years, and he died at the age of a hundred and thirty. [16]He was buried with the kings in the City of David, because of the good he had done in Israel for God and his temple.

The Wickedness of Joash

[17]After the death of Jehoiada, the officials of Judah came and paid homage to the king, and he listened to them. [18]They abandoned the temple of the LORD, the God of their fathers, and worshiped Asherah poles and idols. Because of their guilt, God's anger came upon Judah and Jerusalem. [19]Although the LORD sent prophets to the people to bring them back to him, and though they testified against them, they would not listen.
[20]Then the Spirit of God came upon Zechariah son of Jehoiada the priest. He stood before the people and said, "This is what God says: 'Why do you disobey the LORD's commands? You will not prosper. Because you have forsaken the LORD, he has forsaken you.' "
[21]But they plotted against him, and by order of the king they stoned him to death in the courtyard of the LORD's temple. [22]King Joash did not remember the kindness Zechariah's father Jehoiada had shown him but killed his son, who said as he lay dying, "May the LORD see this and call you to account."
[23]At the turn of the year,[a] the army of Aram marched against Joash; it invaded Judah and Jerusalem and killed all the leaders of the people. They sent all the plunder to their king in Damascus. [24]Although the Aramean army had come with only a few men, the LORD delivered into their hands a much larger army. Because Judah had forsaken the LORD, the God of their fathers, judgment was executed on Joash. [25]When the Arameans withdrew, they left Joash severely wounded. His officials conspired against him for murdering the son of Jehoiada the priest, and they killed him in his bed. So he died and was buried in the City of David, but not in the tombs of the kings.
[26]Those who conspired against him were Zabad,[b] son of Shimeath an Ammonite woman, and Jehozabad, son of Shimrith[c] a Moabite woman. [27]The account of his sons, the many prophecies about him, and the record of the restoration of the temple of God are written in the annotations on the book of the kings. And Amaziah his son succeeded him as king.

[a]23 Probably in the spring [b]26 A variant of *Jozabad* [c]26 A variant of *Shomer*

SHARPEN THE FOCUS

Walk into any video store, look in any direction, and chances are 100 percent you'll spot a film built around a hero who ferrets out the crooks or rescues the kidnapped victim or finds a way to save the company and give everyone's job back. At least in fiction, our heroes usually work single-handedly.

Jehoiada could seem to be that kind of hero—the lone figure who pulls his nation back from the brink of disaster. No question—his actions took courage and plenty of it. But Jehoiada was no single-handed hero. His courage grew out of his conviction that his people were called to be the Lord's people (2 Chronicles 23:16) and that his Savior was from David's line.

For us, too, courage comes not from a decision to take a deep breath and plunge ahead single-handedly. Rather it comes from the confidence that our Savior-God holds our hand and will help us do what we need to do with single-hearted devotion to Him.

WEEK 38 • MONDAY

2 Chronicles 25:1—26:23

GET THE BIG PICTURE

King Amaziah lived an outwardly obedient life, at least during the early years of his reign. But his heart wasn't in it (2 Chronicles 25:2). King Uzziah likewise began his reign in obedience, but found his heart corrupted by the arrogance of his position as king. As you read, notice the power disobedience has—the power to destroy. If time is short, focus on 2 Chronicles 26:1–21.

Amaziah King of Judah

25 Amaziah was twenty-five
years old when he be-
came king, and he reigned in Jerusalem
twenty-nine years. His mother's name
was Jehoaddin[a]; she was from Jerusalem. 2 He did what was right in the eyes
of the LORD, but not wholeheartedly.
3 After the kingdom was firmly in his
control, he executed the officials who
had murdered his father the king. 4 Yet
he did not put their sons to death, but
acted in accordance with what is written in the Law, in the Book of Moses,
where the LORD commanded: "Fathers
shall not be put to death for their children, nor children put to death for their
fathers; each is to die for his own sins."[b]
5 Amaziah called the people of Judah
together and assigned them according
to their families to commanders of thousands and commanders of hundreds for
all Judah and Benjamin. He then mustered those twenty years old or more
and found that there were three hundred thousand men ready for military
service, able to handle the spear and
shield. 6 He also hired a hundred thousand fighting men from Israel for a hundred talents[c] of silver.
7 But a man of God came to him and
said, "O king, these troops from Israel
must not march with you, for the LORD
is not with Israel—not with any of the
people of Ephraim. 8 Even if you go and
fight courageously in battle, God will
overthrow you before the enemy, for

[a]1 Hebrew *Jehoaddan,* a variant of *Jehoaddin*
[b]4 Deut. 24:16 [c]6 That is, about 3 3/4 tons (about 3.4 metric tons); also in verse 9

God has the power to help or to overthrow."
[9]Amaziah asked the man of God, "But
what about the hundred talents I paid
for these Israelite troops?"
The man of God replied, "The LORD
can give you much more than that."
[10]So Amaziah dismissed the troops
who had come to him from Ephraim
and sent them home. They were furious
with Judah and left for home in a great
rage.
[11]Amaziah then marshaled his
strength and led his army to the Valley
of Salt, where he killed ten thousand
men of Seir. [12]The army of Judah also
captured ten thousand men alive, took
them to the top of a cliff and threw them
down so that all were dashed to pieces.
[13]Meanwhile the troops that Amaziah
had sent back and had not allowed to
take part in the war raided Judean
towns from Samaria to Beth Horon.
They killed three thousand people and
carried off great quantities of plunder.
[14]When Amaziah returned from
slaughtering the Edomites, he brought
back the gods of the people of Seir. He
set them up as his own gods, bowed
down to them and burned sacrifices to
them. [15]The anger of the LORD burned
against Amaziah, and he sent a prophet
to him, who said, "Why do you consult
this people's gods, which could not save
their own people from your hand?"
[16]While he was still speaking, the king
said to him, "Have we appointed you an
adviser to the king? Stop! Why be struck
down?"
So the prophet stopped but said, "I
know that God has determined to destroy you, because you have done this
and have not listened to my counsel."
[17]After Amaziah king of Judah consulted his advisers, he sent this challenge to Jehoash[a] son of Jehoahaz, the
son of Jehu, king of Israel: "Come, meet
me face to face."
[18]But Jehoash king of Israel replied to
Amaziah king of Judah: "A thistle in
Lebanon sent a message to a cedar in
Lebanon, 'Give your daughter to my
son in marriage.' Then a wild beast in
Lebanon came along and trampled the
thistle underfoot. [19]You say to yourself
that you have defeated Edom, and now
you are arrogant and proud. But stay at
home! Why ask for trouble and cause
your own downfall and that of Judah
also?"
[20]Amaziah, however, would not listen,
for God so worked that he might hand
them over to ⌞Jehoash⌟, because they
sought the gods of Edom. [21]So Jehoash
king of Israel attacked. He and Amaziah king of Judah faced each other at
Beth Shemesh in Judah. [22]Judah was
routed by Israel, and every man fled to
his home. [23]Jehoash king of Israel captured Amaziah king of Judah, the son of
Joash, the son of Ahaziah,[b] at Beth Shemesh. Then Jehoash brought him to Jerusalem and broke down the wall of
Jerusalem from the Ephraim Gate to the
Corner Gate—a section about six hundred feet[c] long. [24]He took all the gold
and silver and all the articles found in
the temple of God that had been in the
care of Obed-Edom, together with the
palace treasures and the hostages, and
returned to Samaria.
[25]Amaziah son of Joash king of Judah
lived for fifteen years after the death of
Jehoash son of Jehoahaz king of Israel.
[26]As for the other events of Amaziah's
reign, from beginning to end, are they
not written in the book of the kings of
Judah and Israel? [27]From the time that
Amaziah turned away from following
the LORD, they conspired against him in
Jerusalem and he fled to Lachish, but
they sent men after him to Lachish and
killed him there. [28]He was brought back
by horse and was buried with his fathers in the City of Judah.

Uzziah King of Judah

26 Then all the people of
Judah took Uzziah,[d] who
was sixteen years old, and made him
king in place of his father Amaziah. [2]He

[a]17 Hebrew *Joash,* a variant of *Jehoash*; also in verses 18, 21, 23 and 25 [b]23 Hebrew *Jehoahaz,* a variant of *Ahaziah* [c]23 Hebrew *four hundred cubits* (about 180 meters) [d]1 Also called *Azariah*

was the one who rebuilt Elath and restored it to Judah after Amaziah rested with his fathers.

[3]Uzziah was sixteen years old when he became king, and he reigned in Jerusalem fifty-two years. His mother's name was Jecoliah; she was from Jerusalem. [4]He did what was right in the eyes of the LORD, just as his father Amaziah had done. [5]He sought God during the days of Zechariah, who instructed him in the fear[a] of God. As long as he sought the LORD, God gave him success.

[6]He went to war against the Philistines and broke down the walls of Gath, Jabneh and Ashdod. He then rebuilt towns near Ashdod and elsewhere among the Philistines. [7]God helped him against the Philistines and against the Arabs who lived in Gur Baal and against the Meunites. [8]The Ammonites brought tribute to Uzziah, and his fame spread as far as the border of Egypt, because he had become very powerful.

[9]Uzziah built towers in Jerusalem at the Corner Gate, at the Valley Gate and at the angle of the wall, and he fortified them. [10]He also built towers in the desert and dug many cisterns, because he had much livestock in the foothills and in the plain. He had people working his fields and vineyards in the hills and in the fertile lands, for he loved the soil.

[11]Uzziah had a well-trained army, ready to go out by divisions according to their numbers as mustered by Jeiel the secretary and Maaseiah the officer under the direction of Hananiah, one of the royal officials. [12]The total number of family leaders over the fighting men was 2,600. [13]Under their command was an army of 307,500 men trained for war, a powerful force to support the king against his enemies. [14]Uzziah provided shields, spears, helmets, coats of armor, bows and slingstones for the entire army. [15]In Jerusalem he made machines designed by skillful men for use on the towers and on the corner defenses to shoot arrows and hurl large stones. His fame spread far and wide, for he was greatly helped until he became powerful.

[16]But after Uzziah became powerful, his pride led to his downfall. He was unfaithful to the LORD his God, and entered the temple of the LORD to burn incense on the altar of incense. [17]Azariah the priest with eighty other courageous priests of the LORD followed him in. [18]They confronted him and said, "It is not right for you, Uzziah, to burn incense to the LORD. That is for the priests, the descendants of Aaron, who have been consecrated to burn incense. Leave the sanctuary, for you have been unfaithful; and you will not be honored by the LORD God."

[19]Uzziah, who had a censer in his hand ready to burn incense, became angry. While he was raging at the priests in their presence before the incense altar in the LORD's temple, leprosy[b] broke out on his forehead. [20]When Azariah the chief priest and all the other priests looked at him, they saw that he had leprosy on his forehead, so they hurried him out. Indeed, he himself was eager to leave, because the LORD had afflicted him.

[21]King Uzziah had leprosy until the day he died. He lived in a separate house[c]—leprous, and excluded from the temple of the LORD. Jotham his son had charge of the palace and governed the people of the land.

[22]The other events of Uzziah's reign, from beginning to end, are recorded by the prophet Isaiah son of Amoz. [23]Uzziah rested with his fathers and was buried near them in a field for burial that belonged to the kings, for people said, "He had leprosy." And Jotham his son succeeded him as king.

[a]5 Many Hebrew manuscripts, Septuagint and Syriac; other Hebrew manuscripts *vision*
[b]19 The Hebrew word was used for various diseases affecting the skin—not necessarily leprosy; also in verses 20, 21 and 23. [c]21 Or *in a house where he was relieved of responsibilities*

SHARPEN THE FOCUS

If someone were to accuse you of being prosperous, would you plead guilty? Most of us probably equate prosperity with financial stability. We think of a prosperous person as one who can afford to buy what the family needs and still have enough left over to invest, to give to the needy, and to enjoy some of life's luxuries.

The Scriptures portray prosperity in a different light. Notice 2 Chronicles 24:20–"Why do you disobey the LORD's commands? You will not prosper. Because you have forsaken the LORD, He has forsaken you." Outwardly, at least for awhile, Uzziah's financial circumstances did not change. But his disobedience had robbed him of the ability to truly prosper.

True prosperity lies in knowing God's mercy toward us in Jesus. The prophet Isaiah tells us that the will of the Lord prospered in Christ's hands (Isaiah 53:10). Think of it! God's will prospered in the hands that were outstretched and nailed to Calvary's cross–for Amaziah's disobedience, for Uzziah's foolish arrogance, for your transgressions and for mine. In mercy like that lies our true prosperity.

WEEK 38 • TUESDAY

2 Chronicles 27:1—28:27

GET THE BIG PICTURE

The two kings about whom you will read today come from opposite ends of the spectrum. Jotham loved and obeyed the Lord. Ahaz "promoted wickedness" (2 Chronicles 28:19). As you read, notice just how low Judah actually went. If time is short, focus on 2 Chronicles 28:19–27.

Jotham King of Judah

27 Jotham was twenty-five years old when he became king, and he reigned in Jerusalem sixteen years. His mother's name was Jerusha daughter of Zadok. [2]He did what was right in the eyes of the LORD, just as his father Uzziah had done, but unlike him he did not enter the temple of the LORD. The people, however, continued their corrupt practices. [3]Jotham rebuilt the Upper Gate of the temple of the LORD and did extensive work on the wall at the hill of Ophel. [4]He built towns in the Judean hills and forts and towers in the wooded areas.

[5]Jotham made war on the king of the Ammonites and conquered them. That year the Ammonites paid him a hundred talents[a] of silver, ten thousand cors[b] of wheat and ten thousand cors of barley. The Ammonites brought him the same amount also in the second and third years.

[6]Jotham grew powerful because he walked steadfastly before the LORD his God.

[7]The other events in Jotham's reign, including all his wars and the other things he did, are written in the book of the kings of Israel and Judah. [8]He was twenty-five years old when he became king, and he reigned in Jerusalem

[a]5 That is, about 3 3/4 tons (about 3.4 metric tons) [b]5 That is, probably about 62,000 bushels (about 2,200 kiloliters)

sixteen years. 9Jotham rested with his fathers and was buried in the City of David. And Ahaz his son succeeded him as
king.

Ahaz King of Judah

28 Ahaz was twenty years
old when he became king,
and he reigned in Jerusalem sixteen
years. Unlike David his father, he did
not do what was right in the eyes of the
LORD. 2He walked in the ways of the
kings of Israel and also made cast idols
for worshiping the Baals. 3He burned
sacrifices in the Valley of Ben Hinnom
and sacrificed his sons in the fire, following the detestable ways of the nations
the LORD had driven out before the Israelites. 4He offered sacrifices and
burned incense at the high places, on
the hilltops and under every spreading
tree.

5Therefore the LORD his God handed
him over to the king of Aram. The Arameans defeated him and took many of
his people as prisoners and brought
them to Damascus.

He was also given into the hands of
the king of Israel, who inflicted heavy
casualties on him. 6In one day Pekah son
of Remaliah killed a hundred and twenty thousand soldiers in Judah—because
Judah had forsaken the LORD, the God
of their fathers. 7Zicri, an Ephraimite
warrior, killed Maaseiah the king's son,
Azrikam the officer in charge of the palace, and Elkanah, second to the king.
8The Israelites took captive from their
kinsmen two hundred thousand wives,
sons and daughters. They also took a
great deal of plunder, which they carried back to Samaria.

9But a prophet of the LORD named
Oded was there, and he went out to
meet the army when it returned to Samaria. He said to them, "Because the
LORD, the God of your fathers, was angry with Judah, he gave them into your
hand. But you have slaughtered them in
a rage that reaches to heaven. 10And
now you intend to make the men and
women of Judah and Jerusalem your
slaves. But aren't you also guilty of sins
against the LORD your God? 11Now listen to me! Send back your fellow countrymen you have taken as prisoners, for
the LORD's fierce anger rests on you."

12Then some of the leaders in Ephraim—Azariah son of Jehohanan, Berekiah son of Meshillemoth, Jehizkiah son
of Shallum, and Amasa son of Hadlai—
confronted those who were arriving
from the war. 13"You must not bring
those prisoners here," they said, "or we
will be guilty before the LORD. Do you
intend to add to our sin and guilt? For
our guilt is already great, and his fierce
anger rests on Israel."

14So the soldiers gave up the prisoners and plunder in the presence of the
officials and all the assembly. 15The men
designated by name took the prisoners,
and from the plunder they clothed all
who were naked. They provided them
with clothes and sandals, food and
drink, and healing balm. All those who
were weak they put on donkeys. So
they took them back to their fellow
countrymen at Jericho, the City of
Palms, and returned to Samaria.

16At that time King Ahaz sent to the
king[a] of Assyria for help. 17The Edomites
had again come and attacked Judah and
carried away prisoners, 18while the Philistines had raided towns in the foothills
and in the Negev of Judah. They captured and occupied Beth Shemesh, Aijalon and Gederoth, as well as Soco,
Timnah and Gimzo, with their surrounding villages. 19The LORD had humbled Judah because of Ahaz king of
Israel,[b] for he had promoted wickedness
in Judah and had been most unfaithful
to the LORD. 20Tiglath-Pileser[c] king of
Assyria came to him, but he gave him
trouble instead of help. 21Ahaz took
some of the things from the temple of
the LORD and from the royal palace and
from the princes and presented them to
the king of Assyria, but that did not help
him.

[a]*16* One Hebrew manuscript, Septuagint and Vulgate (see also 2 Kings 16:7); most Hebrew manuscripts *kings* [b]*19* That is, Judah, as frequently in 2 Chronicles [c]*20* Hebrew *Tilgath-Pilneser,* a variant of *Tiglath-Pileser*

[22]In his time of trouble King Ahaz became even more unfaithful to the LORD.
[23]He offered sacrifices to the gods of
Damascus, who had defeated him; for
he thought, "Since the gods of the kings
of Aram have helped them, I will sacrifice to them so they will help me." But
they were his downfall and the downfall of all Israel.
[24]Ahaz gathered together the furnishings from the temple of God and took
them away.[a] He shut the doors of the
LORD's temple and set up altars at every
street corner in Jerusalem. [25]In every
town in Judah he built high places to
burn sacrifices to other gods and provoked the LORD, the God of his fathers,
to anger.
[26]The other events of his reign and all
his ways, from beginning to end, are
written in the book of the kings of Judah
and Israel. [27]Ahaz rested with his fathers
and was buried in the city of Jerusalem,
but he was not placed in the tombs of
the kings of Israel. And Hezekiah his
son succeeded him as king.

[a]24 Or *and cut them up*

SHARPEN THE FOCUS

Several years ago audiences roared over a movie called *The Money Pit*. The story line involved a young couple who bought their dream home that needed only "a few improvements." The remodeling began and before long, it sucked up time, money, and effort like a gigantic sponge. The dream home became a nightmare that never ended.

The false gods we worship are often like that. We honestly believe they will fulfill our dreams. The job for which we long, the vacation that we "must" put on credit cards, the person whose affection and love we can't live without. Sometimes we get what we think we want. But if we count on things or on other people to fulfill our lives, we will find our dreams turning to nightmares.

As Ahaz's idols gripped his heart more and more tightly, disaster fell again and again. And as his stress multiplied, so did his unfaithfulness to the Lord.

What false gods inhabit your heart? Ask your Lord to help you face the answer to that question with His courage and honesty today. Then talk with Him about what He shows you. As you finish your prayer, read His absolution from Joel 2:13.

WEEK 38 • WEDNESDAY

2 Chr. 29:1–36

GET THE BIG PICTURE

Night and day. That's the contrast we see as we compare the lives of King Ahaz (about whom we read yesterday) and Ahaz's son, King Hezekiah (about whom we will read today). Look for evidence in the text about the goals Hezekiah had for Judah under his reign. If time is short, focus on 2 Chronicles 29:1–19.

Hezekiah Purifies the Temple

29 Hezekiah was twenty-five years old when he became king, and he reigned in Jerusalem twenty-nine years. His mother's name was Abijah daughter of Zechariah. [2]He did what was right in the eyes of the LORD, just as his father David had done.
[3]In the first month of the first year of his reign, he opened the doors of the temple of the LORD and repaired them.
[4]He brought in the priests and the Levites, assembled them in the square on
the east side [5]and said: "Listen to me, Levites! Consecrate yourselves now and consecrate the temple of the LORD, the God of your fathers. Remove all defilement from the sanctuary. [6]Our fathers were unfaithful; they did evil in the eyes of the LORD our God and forsook him. They turned their faces away from the LORD's dwelling place and turned their backs on him. [7]They also shut the doors of the portico and put out the lamps. They did not burn incense or present any burnt offerings at the sanctuary to the God of Israel. [8]Therefore, the anger of the LORD has fallen on Judah and Jerusalem; he has made them an object of dread and horror and scorn, as you can see with your own eyes. [9]This is why our fathers have fallen by the sword and why our sons and daughters and our wives are in captivity. [10]Now I intend to make a covenant with the LORD, the God of Israel, so that his fierce anger will turn away from us. [11]My sons, do not be negligent now, for the LORD has chosen you to stand before him and serve him, to minister before him and to burn incense."

[12]Then these Levites set to work:
from the Kohathites,
Mahath son of Amasai and Joel son of Azariah;
from the Merarites,
Kish son of Abdi and Azariah son of Jehallelel;
from the Gershonites,
Joah son of Zimmah and Eden son of Joah;
[13]from the descendants of Elizaphan,
Shimri and Jeiel;
from the descendants of Asaph,
Zechariah and Mattaniah;
[14]from the descendants of Heman,
Jehiel and Shimei;
from the descendants of Jeduthun,
Shemaiah and Uzziel.

[15]When they had assembled their brothers and consecrated themselves, they went in to purify the temple of the LORD, as the king had ordered, following the word of the LORD. [16]The priests went into the sanctuary of the LORD to purify it. They brought out to the courtyard of the LORD's temple everything unclean that they found in the temple of the LORD. The Levites took it and carried it out to the Kidron Valley. [17]They began the consecration on the first day of the first month, and by the eighth day of the month they reached the portico of the LORD. For eight more days they consecrated the temple of the LORD itself, finishing on the sixteenth day of the first month.

[18]Then they went in to King Hezekiah and reported: "We have purified the entire temple of the LORD, the altar of burnt offering with all its utensils, and the table for setting out the consecrated bread, with all its articles. [19]We have prepared and consecrated all the articles that King Ahaz removed in his unfaithfulness while he was king. They are now in front of the LORD's altar."

[20]Early the next morning King Hezekiah gathered the city officials together and went up to the temple of the LORD. [21]They brought seven bulls, seven rams, seven male lambs and seven male goats as a sin offering for the kingdom, for the sanctuary and for Judah. The king commanded the priests, the descendants of Aaron, to offer these on the altar of the LORD. [22]So they slaughtered the bulls, and the priests took the blood and sprinkled it on the altar; next they slaughtered the rams and sprinkled their blood on the altar; then they slaughtered the lambs and sprinkled their blood on the altar. [23]The goats for the sin offering were brought before the king and the assembly, and they laid

their hands on them. 24The priests then slaughtered the goats and presented their blood on the altar for a sin offering to atone for all Israel, because the king had ordered the burnt offering and the sin offering for all Israel.

25He stationed the Levites in the temple of the LORD with cymbals, harps and lyres in the way prescribed by David and Gad the king's seer and Nathan the prophet; this was commanded by the LORD through his prophets. 26So the Levites stood ready with David's instruments, and the priests with their trumpets.

27Hezekiah gave the order to sacrifice the burnt offering on the altar. As the offering began, singing to the LORD began also, accompanied by trumpets and the instruments of David king of Israel. 28The whole assembly bowed in worship, while the singers sang and the trumpeters played. All this continued until the sacrifice of the burnt offering was completed.

29When the offerings were finished, the king and everyone present with him knelt down and worshiped. 30King Hezekiah and his officials ordered the Levites to praise the LORD with the words of David and of Asaph the seer. So they sang praises with gladness and bowed their heads and worshiped.

31Then Hezekiah said, "You have now dedicated yourselves to the LORD. Come and bring sacrifices and thank offerings to the temple of the LORD." So the assembly brought sacrifices and thank offerings, and all whose hearts were willing brought burnt offerings.

32The number of burnt offerings the assembly brought was seventy bulls, a hundred rams and two hundred male lambs—all of them for burnt offerings to the LORD. 33The animals consecrated as sacrifices amounted to six hundred bulls and three thousand sheep and goats. 34The priests, however, were too few to skin all the burnt offerings; so their kinsmen the Levites helped them until the task was finished and until other priests had been consecrated, for the Levites had been more conscientious in consecrating themselves than the priests had been. 35There were burnt offerings in abundance, together with the fat of the fellowship offerings[a] and the drink offerings that accompanied the burnt offerings.

So the service of the temple of the LORD was reestablished. 36Hezekiah and all the people rejoiced at what God had brought about for his people, because it was done so quickly.

[a]35 Traditionally *peace offerings*

SHARPEN THE FOCUS

"What will you do during your first week in office?" That's a great question to ask political candidates. First actions reflect a candidate's priorities. They often set the tone of an official's entire term of office.

By that standard, King Hezekiah left no unanswered questions about the goals of his administration. Year one, month one he opened the temple that Ahaz had boarded up. He called the priests and Levites together and charged them with renovating Judah's place of worship (2 Chronicles 29:3–5). The celebration on earth was doubtless mirrored by joy in heaven.

Today may be your first day on the job. Or your first day as a parent. Or your first day of school. On the other hand, it may be day 17 or 86 or 3,721. Whatever day it is according to the calendar, it can be the first day of a fresh start. After all, God's mercies and His forgiving love are "new every morning" (Lamentations 3:23).

So, what will you do with your "first day," your "first week"? Ask your Savior to so fill and empower you that His "first things" become your own "first things"—today and every new day He, in grace, gives.

"Come home! Celebrate Passover! The Lord forgives!" That's the message Hezekiah sent out, not only to his own people but also to the people of Israel, the Northern Kingdom (many of whose citizens had been taken into exile). As you read, look for the response that invitation received in both kingdoms. Notice, too, how the grace of God took precedence over the letter of the law. If time is short, focus on 2 Chronicles 30:1–27.

Hezekiah Celebrates the Passover

30 Hezekiah sent word to all
Israel and Judah and also
wrote letters to Ephraim and Manasseh,
inviting them to come to the temple of
the LORD in Jerusalem and celebrate the
Passover to the LORD, the God of Israel.
2The king and his officials and the whole
assembly in Jerusalem decided to celebrate the Passover in the second
month. 3They had not been able to celebrate it at the regular time because not
enough priests had consecrated themselves and the people had not assembled in Jerusalem. 4The plan seemed
right both to the king and to the whole
assembly. 5They decided to send a proclamation throughout Israel, from Beersheba to Dan, calling the people to come
to Jerusalem and celebrate the Passover
to the LORD, the God of Israel. It had not
been celebrated in large numbers according to what was written.
6At the king's command, couriers
went throughout Israel and Judah with
letters from the king and from his officials, which read:

"People of Israel, return to the
LORD, the God of Abraham, Isaac
and Israel, that he may return to
you who are left, who have escaped from the hand of the kings of
Assyria. 7Do not be like your fathers
and brothers, who were unfaithful
to the LORD, the God of their fathers, so that he made them an object of horror, as you see. 8Do not be
stiff-necked, as your fathers were;
submit to the LORD. Come to the
sanctuary, which he has consecrated forever. Serve the LORD your
God, so that his fierce anger will
turn away from you. 9If you return
to the LORD, then your brothers
and your children will be shown
compassion by their captors and
will come back to this land, for the
LORD your God is gracious and
compassionate. He will not turn his
face from you if you return to him."

10The couriers went from town to
town in Ephraim and Manasseh, as far
as Zebulun, but the people scorned and
ridiculed them. 11Nevertheless, some
men of Asher, Manasseh and Zebulun
humbled themselves and went to Jerusalem. 12Also in Judah the hand of God
was on the people to give them unity of
mind to carry out what the king and his
officials had ordered, following the
word of the LORD.
13A very large crowd of people assembled in Jerusalem to celebrate the Feast
of Unleavened Bread in the second
month. 14They removed the altars in Jerusalem and cleared away the incense
altars and threw them into the Kidron
Valley.
15They slaughtered the Passover lamb
on the fourteenth day of the second
month. The priests and the Levites were
ashamed and consecrated themselves

and brought burnt offerings to the temple of the LORD. [16]Then they took up
their regular positions as prescribed in
the Law of Moses the man of God. The
priests sprinkled the blood handed to
them by the Levites. [17]Since many in
the crowd had not consecrated themselves, the Levites had to kill the Passover lambs for all those who were not
ceremonially clean and could not consecrate ⌞their lambs⌟ to the LORD. [18]Al-
though most of the many people who
came from Ephraim, Manasseh, Issachar
and Zebulun had not purified themselves, yet they ate the Passover, contrary to what was written. But Hezekiah
prayed for them, saying, "May the
LORD, who is good, pardon everyone
[19]who sets his heart on seeking God—
the LORD, the God of his fathers—even
if he is not clean according to the rules
of the sanctuary." [20]And the LORD heard
Hezekiah and healed the people.

[21]The Israelites who were present in
Jerusalem celebrated the Feast of Unleavened Bread for seven days with
great rejoicing, while the Levites and
priests sang to the LORD every day, accompanied by the LORD's instruments
of praise.[a]

[22]Hezekiah spoke encouragingly to all
the Levites, who showed good understanding of the service of the LORD. For
the seven days they ate their assigned
portion and offered fellowship offerings[b] and praised the LORD, the God of
their fathers.

[23]The whole assembly then agreed to
celebrate the festival seven more days;
so for another seven days they celebrated joyfully. [24]Hezekiah king of Judah
provided a thousand bulls and seven
thousand sheep and goats for the assembly, and the officials provided them
with a thousand bulls and ten thousand
sheep and goats. A great number of
priests consecrated themselves. [25]The
entire assembly of Judah rejoiced, along
with the priests and Levites and all who
had assembled from Israel, including
the aliens who had come from Israel
and those who lived in Judah. [26]There
was great joy in Jerusalem, for since the
days of Solomon son of David king of
Israel there had been nothing like this
in Jerusalem. [27]The priests and the Levites stood to bless the people, and God
heard them, for their prayer reached
heaven, his holy dwelling place.

31 When all this had ended, the
Israelites who were there went
out to the towns of Judah, smashed the
sacred stones and cut down the Asherah poles. They destroyed the high
places and the altars throughout Judah
and Benjamin and in Ephraim and
Manasseh. After they had destroyed
all of them, the Israelites returned to
their own towns and to their own property.

Contributions for Worship

[2]Hezekiah assigned the priests and
Levites to divisions—each of them according to their duties as priests or Levites—to offer burnt offerings and
fellowship offerings,[b] to minister, to give
thanks and to sing praises at the gates
of the LORD's dwelling. [3]The king contributed from his own possessions for
the morning and evening burnt offerings and for the burnt offerings on the
Sabbaths, New Moons and appointed
feasts as written in the Law of the LORD.
[4]He ordered the people living in Jerusalem to give the portion due the priests
and Levites so they could devote themselves to the Law of the LORD. [5]As soon
as the order went out, the Israelites generously gave the firstfruits of their grain,
new wine, oil and honey and all that the
fields produced. They brought a great
amount, a tithe of everything. [6]The men
of Israel and Judah who lived in the
towns of Judah also brought a tithe of
their herds and flocks and a tithe of the
holy things dedicated to the LORD their
God, and they piled them in heaps.
[7]They began doing this in the third
month and finished in the seventh
month. [8]When Hezekiah and his officials came and saw the heaps, they

[a]21 Or *priests praised the LORD every day with resounding instruments belonging to the LORD*
[b]22,2 Traditionally *peace offerings*

praised the LORD and blessed his people
Israel.
[9]Hezekiah asked the priests and Levites about the heaps; [10]and Azariah the
chief priest, from the family of Zadok,
answered, "Since the people began to
bring their contributions to the temple
of the LORD, we have had enough to eat
and plenty to spare, because the LORD
has blessed his people, and this great
amount is left over."
[11]Hezekiah gave orders to prepare
storerooms in the temple of the LORD,
and this was done. [12]Then they faithfully brought in the contributions, tithes
and dedicated gifts. Conaniah, a Levite,
was in charge of these things, and his
brother Shimei was next in rank. [13]Jehi-
el, Azaziah, Nahath, Asahel, Jerimoth,
Jozabad, Eliel, Ismakiah, Mahath and
Benaiah were supervisors under Conaniah and Shimei his brother, by appointment of King Hezekiah and
Azariah the official in charge of the temple of God.
[14]Kore son of Imnah the Levite, keeper of the East Gate, was in charge of the
freewill offerings given to God, distributing the contributions made to the
LORD and also the consecrated gifts.
[15]Eden, Miniamin, Jeshua, Shemaiah,
Amariah and Shecaniah assisted him
faithfully in the towns of the priests, distributing to their fellow priests according to their divisions, old and young
alike.
[16]In addition, they distributed to the
males three years old or more whose
names were in the genealogical records—all who would enter the temple
of the LORD to perform the daily duties
of their various tasks, according to their
responsibilities and their divisions.
[17]And they distributed to the priests enrolled by their families in the genealogical records and likewise to the Levites
twenty years old or more, according to
their responsibilities and their divisions.
[18]They included all the little ones, the
wives, and the sons and daughters of
the whole community listed in these
genealogical records. For they were
faithful in consecrating themselves.
[19]As for the priests, the descendants of
Aaron, who lived on the farm lands
around their towns or in any other
towns, men were designated by name
to distribute portions to every male
among them and to all who were recorded in the genealogies of the Levites.
[20]This is what Hezekiah did throughout Judah, doing what was good and
right and faithful before the LORD his
God. [21]In everything that he undertook
in the service of God's temple and in
obedience to the law and the commands, he sought his God and worked
wholeheartedly. And so he prospered.

SHARPEN THE FOCUS

King Arthur's quest, to gather the most virtuous knights at Camelot, symbolizes the end of the Dark Ages, and in some sense, the transition from paganism to Christianity in Britain. But the movie version of the legend ends with Arthur in tears, his vision for a renewed society about to dissolve in the fury of war. He laments the passing of that "one, brief, shining moment that was known as Camelot."

King Hezekiah presided over a similarly brief, but shining, moment in Judah's history. The darkness brought by Canaan's fertility gods evaporated in the light of the Lord and His renewed covenant promises. The chapters describing the revival God brought during Hezekiah's reign ring with joy.

Our Lord still brings spiritual renewal to His people. The renewal the Holy Spirit gives, through His gifts of repentance and faith, produces joy. As the apostle Paul lists the fruit of the Spirit, he mentions joy second, right after love (Galatians 5:22). True repentance brings with it true joy—the full confidence in our Lord that laughs at death and sings even when Satan has done his worst. May that laughter and that song fill your heart today and forever.

As you read the account of the Assyrian invasion today, note the verses that tell what Hezekiah did to prepare for battle and what the Lord did to protect His people. Also note the propaganda war Assyria waged. Listen carefully, for behind the human words you'll hear Satan's lies. If time is short, focus on 2 Chronicles 32:1–23.

Sennacherib Threatens Jerusalem

32 After all that Hezekiah
had so faithfully done,
Sennacherib king of Assyria came and
invaded Judah. He laid siege to the fortified cities, thinking to conquer them
for himself. 2When Hezekiah saw that
Sennacherib had come and that he intended to make war on Jerusalem, 3he
consulted with his officials and military
staff about blocking off the water from
the springs outside the city, and they
helped him. 4A large force of men assembled, and they blocked all the
springs and the stream that flowed
through the land. "Why should the
kings[a] of Assyria come and find plenty
of water?" they said. 5Then he worked
hard repairing all the broken sections of
the wall and building towers on it. He
built another wall outside that one and
reinforced the supporting terraces[b] of
the City of David. He also made large
numbers of weapons and shields.
6He appointed military officers over
the people and assembled them before
him in the square at the city gate and encouraged them with these words: 7"Be
strong and courageous. Do not be afraid
or discouraged because of the king of
Assyria and the vast army with him, for
there is a greater power with us than
with him. 8With him is only the arm of
flesh, but with us is the LORD our God
to help us and to fight our battles." And
the people gained confidence from
what Hezekiah the king of Judah said.
9Later, when Sennacherib king of Assyria and all his forces were laying siege
to Lachish, he sent his officers to Jerusalem with this message for Hezekiah
king of Judah and for all the people of
Judah who were there:
10"This is what Sennacherib king
of Assyria says: On what are you
basing your confidence, that you
remain in Jerusalem under siege?
11When Hezekiah says, 'The LORD
our God will save us from the hand
of the king of Assyria,' he is misleading you, to let you die of hunger and thirst. 12Did not Hezekiah
himself remove this god's high
places and altars, saying to Judah
and Jerusalem, 'You must worship
before one altar and burn sacrifices
on it'?
13"Do you not know what I and
my fathers have done to all the
peoples of the other lands? Were
the gods of those nations ever able

[a]4 Hebrew; Septuagint and Syriac *king* [b]5 Or *the Millo*

to deliver their land from my hand?
[14]Who of all the gods of these nations that my fathers destroyed has
been able to save his people from
me? How then can your god deliver you from my hand? [15]Now do
not let Hezekiah deceive you and
mislead you like this. Do not believe him, for no god of any nation
or kingdom has been able to deliver
his people from my hand or the
hand of my fathers. How much less
will your god deliver you from my
hand!"

[16]Sennacherib's officers spoke further
against the LORD God and against his
servant Hezekiah. [17]The king also wrote
letters insulting the LORD, the God of Israel, and saying this against him: "Just
as the gods of the peoples of the other
lands did not rescue their people from
my hand, so the god of Hezekiah will
not rescue his people from my hand."
[18]Then they called out in Hebrew to the
people of Jerusalem who were on the
wall, to terrify them and make them
afraid in order to capture the city. [19]They
spoke about the God of Jerusalem as
they did about the gods of the other
peoples of the world—the work of
men's hands.

[20]King Hezekiah and the prophet Isaiah son of Amoz cried out in prayer to
heaven about this. [21]And the LORD sent
an angel, who annihilated all the fighting men and the leaders and officers in
the camp of the Assyrian king. So he
withdrew to his own land in disgrace.
And when he went into the temple of
his god, some of his sons cut him down
with the sword.

[22]So the LORD saved Hezekiah and
the people of Jerusalem from the hand
of Sennacherib king of Assyria and from
the hand of all others. He took care of
them[a] on every side. [23]Many brought offerings to Jerusalem for the LORD and
valuable gifts for Hezekiah king of Judah. From then on he was highly regarded by all the nations.

Hezekiah's Pride, Success and Death

[24]In those days Hezekiah became ill
and was at the point of death. He
prayed to the LORD, who answered him
and gave him a miraculous sign. [25]But
Hezekiah's heart was proud and he did
not respond to the kindness shown him;
therefore the LORD's wrath was on him
and on Judah and Jerusalem. [26]Then
Hezekiah repented of the pride of his
heart, as did the people of Jerusalem;
therefore the LORD's wrath did not
come upon them during the days of
Hezekiah.

[27]Hezekiah had very great riches and
honor, and he made treasuries for his silver and gold and for his precious stones,
spices, shields and all kinds of valuables.
[28]He also made buildings to store the
harvest of grain, new wine and oil; and
he made stalls for various kinds of cattle,
and pens for the flocks. [29]He built villages and acquired great numbers of
flocks and herds, for God had given him
very great riches.

[30]It was Hezekiah who blocked the
upper outlet of the Gihon spring and
channeled the water down to the west
side of the City of David. He succeeded
in everything he undertook. [31]But when
envoys were sent by the rulers of Babylon to ask him about the miraculous
sign that had occurred in the land, God
left him to test him and to know everything that was in his heart.

[32]The other events of Hezekiah's reign
and his acts of devotion are written in
the vision of the prophet Isaiah son
of Amoz in the book of the kings of Judah and Israel. [33]Hezekiah rested with
his fathers and was buried on the hill
where the tombs of David's descendants are. All Judah and the people of
Jerusalem honored him when he died.
And Manasseh his son succeeded him
as king.

[a]22 Hebrew; Septuagint and Vulgate *He gave them rest*

SHARPEN THE FOCUS

God takes it personally when His children come under attack. Our enemies may poke fun at us or insult us. Satan may ridicule or tempt or try to deceive us. But our Savior-God so identifies with His people that He counts those insults as if they were leveled directly at Him.

So it was when Assyria poured out the war of words against Hezekiah and the citizens of Jerusalem (2 Chronicles 32:16). And so it is today.

The prophet Zechariah put the principle this way: "Whoever touches you touches the apple of His eye" (Zechariah 2:8). Those who harm God's children "poke God in the eye," so to speak. That's how much He cares for us and how concerned He is about our welfare.

What lies is Satan telling you today? What insults is he hurling about your Lord or about His ability or willingness to help you? What propaganda is he preaching about your past sins or about your weaknesses or about your worth in the Redeemer's eyes?

Consider the source. Then rest in the truth your Lord has revealed in His Word about who He is, about whose you are, and about whom you serve. Fill your heart with His gracious word of truth. Then stand firm in your Savior's forgiving love.

WEEK 38 • SATURDAY

2 Chronicles 33:1–25

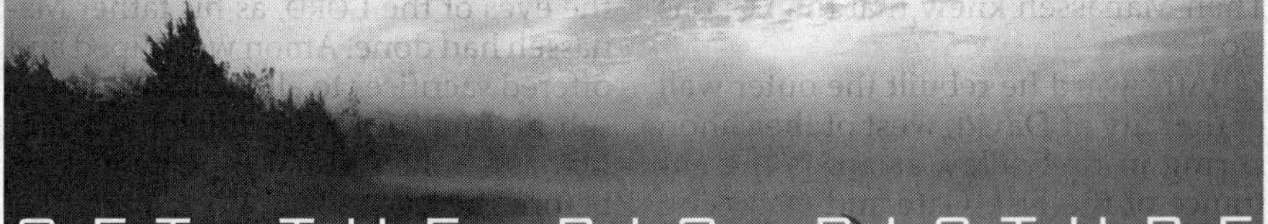

GET THE BIG PICTURE

Today's reading includes the history of two more kings of Judah—one who finally caught on to the Lord's message through His prophets (the "seers") and one who never did. Read prayerfully, asking the Holy Spirit to preserve you against stubbornness. If time is short, focus on 2 Chronicles 33:1–20.

Manasseh King of Judah

33 Manasseh was twelve
years old when he became
king, and he reigned in Jerusalem fifty-
five years. 2He did evil in the eyes of the
LORD, following the detestable practices
of the nations the LORD had driven out
before the Israelites. 3He rebuilt the high
places his father Hezekiah had demolished; he also erected altars to the Baals
and made Asherah poles. He bowed
down to all the starry hosts and worshiped them. 4He built altars in the
temple of the LORD, of which the LORD
had said, "My Name will remain in Jerusalem forever." 5In both courts of the
temple of the LORD, he built altars to all
the starry hosts. 6He sacrificed his sons
in[a] the fire in the Valley of Ben Hinnom,
practiced sorcery, divination and witchcraft, and consulted mediums and spiritists. He did much evil in the eyes of the
LORD, provoking him to anger.

7He took the carved image he had
made and put it in God's temple, of
which God had said to David and to his
son Solomon, "In this temple and in Jerusalem, which I have chosen out of all
the tribes of Israel, I will put my Name
forever. 8I will not again make the feet

[a]6 Or *He made his sons pass through*

of the Israelites leave the land I assigned
to your forefathers, if only they will be
careful to do everything I commanded
them concerning all the laws, decrees
and ordinances given through Moses."
9 But Manasseh led Judah and the
people of Jerusalem astray, so that they
did more evil than the nations the LORD
had destroyed before the Israelites.
10 The LORD spoke to Manasseh and
his people, but they paid no attention.
11 So the LORD brought against them the
army commanders of the king of Assyria, who took Manasseh prisoner, put a
hook in his nose, bound him with
bronze shackles and took him to Babylon. 12 In his distress he sought the favor of the LORD his God and humbled
himself greatly before the God of his fathers. 13 And when he prayed to him, the
LORD was moved by his entreaty and
listened to his plea; so he brought him
back to Jerusalem and to his kingdom.
Then Manasseh knew that the LORD is
God.
14 Afterward he rebuilt the outer wall
of the City of David, west of the Gihon
spring in the valley, as far as the entrance of the Fish Gate and encircling
the hill of Ophel; he also made it much
higher. He stationed military commanders in all the fortified cities in Judah.
15 He got rid of the foreign gods and
removed the image from the temple of
the LORD, as well as all the altars he had
built on the temple hill and in Jerusalem; and he threw them out of the city.
16 Then he restored the altar of the LORD
and sacrificed fellowship offerings[a] and
thank offerings on it, and told Judah to
serve the LORD, the God of Israel. 17 The
people, however, continued to sacrifice
at the high places, but only to the LORD
their God.
18 The other events of Manasseh's
reign, including his prayer to his God
and the words the seers spoke to him in
the name of the LORD, the God of Israel,
are written in the annals of the kings of
Israel.[b] 19 His prayer and how God was
moved by his entreaty, as well as all his
sins and unfaithfulness, and the sites
where he built high places and set up
Asherah poles and idols before he humbled himself—all are written in the
records of the seers.[c] 20 Manasseh rested
with his fathers and was buried in his
palace. And Amon his son succeeded
him as king.

Amon King of Judah

21 Amon was twenty-two years old
when he became king, and he reigned
in Jerusalem two years. 22 He did evil in
the eyes of the LORD, as his father Manasseh had done. Amon worshiped and
offered sacrifices to all the idols Manasseh had made. 23 But unlike his father
Manasseh, he did not humble himself
before the LORD; Amon increased his
guilt.
24 Amon's officials conspired against
him and assassinated him in his palace.
25 Then the people of the land killed all
who had plotted against King Amon,
and they made Josiah his son king in his
place.

[a] *16* Traditionally *peace offerings* [b] *18* That is, Judah, as frequently in 2 Chronicles [c] *19* One Hebrew manuscript and Septuagint; most Hebrew manuscripts *of Hozai*

SHARPEN THE FOCUS

A farmer bought a mule from his friend. The seller told the buyer, "Just tell it what to do, and it'll do it!" But the buyer found that no matter what he said or did, the mule refused to get up off its haunches. He confronted the seller who agreed to stop by and appraise the situation.

When he arrived, there sat the mule, determined not to move. The former owner picked up a two-by-four and whacked the mule across the forehead three times. Then he gave a verbal command. The mule hopped up and began to pull its load.

"I thought all I had to do was speak," said the new owner. "Yeah," drawled his friend, "but first you have to get its attention."

It took a "big stick" of sorts to get King Manasseh's attention. But troubles and hardships are never our Lord's preferred methods for dealing with His people. Like any good earthly father, He would rather simply speak to us and then honor our obedience to His words. Still, His kindness will not leave us alone in our sins. Why not? Because the end of *that* road is death—now and forever.

Read Proverbs 4:10–13. Ask the Holy Spirit to soften any hard spots in your heart and to open your ears so that you will always hear and obey His Word.

WEEK 39 • MONDAY

2 Chronicles 34:1—35:27

Because God loved the world, He sent yet another time of renewal to Judah. King Josiah led this revival and kept Judah true to the Lord, at least outwardly, throughout his reign. The Savior would come from the tribe of Judah, from the house (dynasty) of David. The Lord had promised that. And so He patiently worked in and through the lives of Judah's kings. As you read, look for evidence of that holy work. If time is short, focus on 2 Chronicles 34:1–28.

Josiah's Reforms

34 Josiah was eight years old
when he became king,
and he reigned in Jerusalem thirty-one
years. 2He did what was right in the eyes
of the LORD and walked in the ways of
his father David, not turning aside to
the right or to the left.
3In the eighth year of his reign, while
he was still young, he began to seek the
God of his father David. In his twelfth
year he began to purge Judah and Jerusalem
of high places, Asherah poles,
carved idols and cast images. 4Under his
direction the altars of the Baals were
torn down; he cut to pieces the incense
altars that were above them, and
smashed the Asherah poles, the idols
and the images. These he broke to
pieces and scattered over the graves of
those who had sacrificed to them. 5He
burned the bones of the priests on their
altars, and so he purged Judah and Jerusalem.
6In the towns of Manasseh,
Ephraim and Simeon, as far as Naphtali,
and in the ruins around them, 7he tore
down the altars and the Asherah poles
and crushed the idols to powder and cut
to pieces all the incense altars throughout
Israel. Then he went back to Jerusalem.
8In the eighteenth year of Josiah's
reign, to purify the land and the temple,
he sent Shaphan son of Azaliah and Maaseiah
the ruler of the city, with Joah son
of Joahaz, the recorder, to repair the
temple of the LORD his God.
9They went to Hilkiah the high priest
and gave him the money that had been
brought into the temple of God, which
the Levites who were the doorkeepers
had collected from the people of Manasseh,
Ephraim and the entire remnant of
Israel and from all the people of Judah
and Benjamin and the inhabitants of Jerusalem.
10Then they entrusted it to the

men appointed to supervise the work
on the LORD's temple. These men paid
the workers who repaired and restored
the temple. 11 They also gave money to
the carpenters and builders to purchase
dressed stone, and timber for joists
and beams for the buildings that the
kings of Judah had allowed to fall into
ruin.
12 The men did the work faithfully.
Over them to direct them were Jahath
and Obadiah, Levites descended from
Merari, and Zechariah and Meshullam,
descended from Kohath. The Levites—
all who were skilled in playing musical
instruments— 13 had charge of the laborers and supervised all the workers from
job to job. Some of the Levites were secretaries, scribes and doorkeepers.

The Book of the Law Found

14 While they were bringing out the
money that had been taken into the
temple of the LORD, Hilkiah the priest
found the Book of the Law of the LORD
that had been given through Moses.
15 Hilkiah said to Shaphan the secretary,
"I have found the Book of the Law in the
temple of the LORD." He gave it to Shaphan.
16 Then Shaphan took the book to the
king and reported to him: "Your officials
are doing everything that has been committed to them. 17 They have paid out the
money that was in the temple of the
LORD and have entrusted it to the supervisors and workers." 18 Then Shaphan the secretary informed the king,
"Hilkiah the priest has given me a
book." And Shaphan read from it in the
presence of the king.
19 When the king heard the words of
the Law, he tore his robes. 20 He gave
these orders to Hilkiah, Ahikam son of
Shaphan, Abdon son of Micah,[a] Shaphan the secretary and Asaiah the
king's attendant: 21 "Go and inquire of
the LORD for me and for the remnant in
Israel and Judah about what is written
in this book that has been found. Great
is the LORD's anger that is poured out on
us because our fathers have not kept the
word of the LORD; they have not acted
in accordance with all that is written in
this book."
22 Hilkiah and those the king had sent
with him[b] went to speak to the prophetess Huldah, who was the wife of Shallum son of Tokhath,[c] the son of Hasrah,[d]
keeper of the wardrobe. She lived in Jerusalem, in the Second District.
23 She said to them, "This is what the
LORD, the God of Israel, says: Tell the
man who sent you to me, 24 'This is what
the LORD says: I am going to bring disaster on this place and its people—all
the curses written in the book that has
been read in the presence of the king of
Judah. 25 Because they have forsaken me
and burned incense to other gods and
provoked me to anger by all that their
hands have made,[e] my anger will be
poured out on this place and will not be
quenched.' 26 Tell the king of Judah, who
sent you to inquire of the LORD, 'This is
what the LORD, the God of Israel, says
concerning the words you heard: 27 Because your heart was responsive and
you humbled yourself before God when
you heard what he spoke against this
place and its people, and because you
humbled yourself before me and tore
your robes and wept in my presence, I
have heard you, declares the LORD.
28 Now I will gather you to your fathers,
and you will be buried in peace. Your
eyes will not see all the disaster I am
going to bring on this place and on
those who live here.' "
So they took her answer back to the
king.
29 Then the king called together all the
elders of Judah and Jerusalem. 30 He
went up to the temple of the LORD with
the men of Judah, the people of Jerusalem, the priests and the Levites—all the
people from the least to the greatest. He
read in their hearing all the words of the
Book of the Covenant, which had been
found in the temple of the LORD. 31 The
king stood by his pillar and renewed the

[a]20 Also called *Acbor son of Micaiah* [b]22 One Hebrew manuscript, Vulgate and Syriac; most Hebrew manuscripts do not have *had sent with him.* [c]22 Also called *Tikvah* [d]22 Also called *Harhas* [e]25 Or *by everything they have done*

covenant in the presence of the LORD—
to follow the LORD and keep his commands, regulations and decrees with all
his heart and all his soul, and to obey the
words of the covenant written in this
book.
32Then he had everyone in Jerusalem
and Benjamin pledge themselves to it;
the people of Jerusalem did this in accordance with the covenant of God, the
God of their fathers.
33Josiah removed all the detestable
idols from all the territory belonging to
the Israelites, and he had all who were
present in Israel serve the LORD their
God. As long as he lived, they did not
fail to follow the LORD, the God of their
fathers.

Josiah Celebrates the Passover

35 Josiah celebrated the Passover to the LORD in Jerusa-
lem, and the Passover lamb was slaughtered on the fourteenth day of the first
month. 2He appointed the priests to
their duties and encouraged them in the
service of the LORD's temple. 3He said to
the Levites, who instructed all Israel
and who had been consecrated to the
LORD: "Put the sacred ark in the temple
that Solomon son of David king of Israel
built. It is not to be carried about on your
shoulders. Now serve the LORD your
God and his people Israel. 4Prepare
yourselves by families in your divisions,
according to the directions written by
David king of Israel and by his son Solomon.
5"Stand in the holy place with a group
of Levites for each subdivision of the
families of your fellow countrymen, the
lay people. 6Slaughter the Passover
lambs, consecrate yourselves and prepare ⌊the lambs⌋ for your fellow countrymen, doing what the LORD commanded
through Moses."
7Josiah provided for all the lay people
who were there a total of thirty thousand sheep and goats for the Passover
offerings, and also three thousand cattle—all from the king's own possessions.
8His officials also contributed voluntarily to the people and the priests and
Levites. Hilkiah, Zechariah and Jehiel,
the administrators of God's temple,
gave the priests twenty-six hundred
Passover offerings and three hundred
cattle. 9Also Conaniah along with Shemaiah and Nethanel, his brothers, and
Hashabiah, Jeiel and Jozabad, the leaders of the Levites, provided five thousand Passover offerings and five
hundred head of cattle for the Levites.
10The service was arranged and the
priests stood in their places with the
Levites in their divisions as the king had
ordered. 11The Passover lambs were
slaughtered, and the priests sprinkled
the blood handed to them, while the Levites skinned the animals. 12They set
aside the burnt offerings to give them to
the subdivisions of the families of the
people to offer to the LORD, as is written in the Book of Moses. They did the
same with the cattle. 13They roasted the
Passover animals over the fire as prescribed, and boiled the holy offerings in
pots, caldrons and pans and served
them quickly to all the people. 14After
this, they made preparations for themselves and for the priests, because the
priests, the descendants of Aaron, were
sacrificing the burnt offerings and the
fat portions until nightfall. So the Levites made preparations for themselves
and for the Aaronic priests.
15The musicians, the descendants of
Asaph, were in the places prescribed by
David, Asaph, Heman and Jeduthun
the king's seer. The gatekeepers at each
gate did not need to leave their posts,
because their fellow Levites made the
preparations for them.
16So at that time the entire service of
the LORD was carried out for the celebration of the Passover and the offering
of burnt offerings on the altar of the
LORD, as King Josiah had ordered. 17The
Israelites who were present celebrated
the Passover at that time and observed
the Feast of Unleavened Bread for seven
days. 18The Passover had not been observed like this in Israel since the days
of the prophet Samuel; and none of the
kings of Israel had ever celebrated such

a Passover as did Josiah, with the priests,
the Levites and all Judah and Israel who
were there with the people of Jerusalem. [19]This Passover was celebrated in
the eighteenth year of Josiah's reign.

The Death of Josiah

[20]After all this, when Josiah had set the
temple in order, Neco king of Egypt
went up to fight at Carchemish on the
Euphrates, and Josiah marched out to
meet him in battle. [21]But Neco sent messengers to him, saying, "What quarrel is
there between you and me, O king of
Judah? It is not you I am attacking at this
time, but the house with which I am at
war. God has told me to hurry; so stop
opposing God, who is with me, or he
will destroy you."

[22]Josiah, however, would not turn
away from him, but disguised himself to
engage him in battle. He would not listen to what Neco had said at God's command but went to fight him on the plain
of Megiddo.

[23]Archers shot King Josiah, and he
told his officers, "Take me away; I am
badly wounded." [24]So they took him out
of his chariot, put him in the other chariot he had and brought him to Jerusalem, where he died. He was buried in
the tombs of his fathers, and all Judah
and Jerusalem mourned for him.

[25]Jeremiah composed laments for Josiah, and to this day all the men and
women singers commemorate Josiah in
the laments. These became a tradition in
Israel and are written in the Laments.

[26]The other events of Josiah's reign
and his acts of devotion, according to
what is written in the Law of the
LORD— [27]all the events, from beginning
to end, are written in the book of the
kings of Israel and Judah.

SHARPEN THE FOCUS

Sometimes spiritual direction comes from an unlikely source. Maybe the character on a TV sitcom hits us between the eyes with an off-handed comment that nails our pet sin. Or maybe our preschool son or granddaughter asks us to share his or her bedtime prayers, and we find ourselves dissolved to tears by the childlike faith we witness.

King Josiah was about 16 when he began to break down Jerusalem's pagan altars (2 Chronicles 34:3–4). The Bible tells us that wickedness continually grew during the reign of Josiah's father, Amon (2 Chronicles 33:23). But as Josiah reached the age at which most teens today are perfecting their football skills or percussion techniques, the youthful ruler was leading his nation to repentance.

Remarkable. And yet Josiah served a remarkable God, a God who loved His people with remarkable love. Remarkable, surely. And also reassuring, because the same God is at work in our lives today. He can and will use us to do remarkable things. Not because we're so worthy, but because He's made us wholly His in Jesus. And He has promised to continue His holy work in and through us.

The nation of Judah entered a long, dark tunnel after the death of Josiah. Four wicked kings followed him. The reigns of the last three were punctuated by an invasion of Babylonians who carried the people off to exile. Nonetheless, the exile in Babylon did not cancel the Lord's promises. The last two verses of today's chapter chronicle the way the Lord brought His people back to the land He had promised them. If time is short, focus on 2 Chronicles 36:11–23.

36 1 And the people of the
land took Jehoahaz son of
Josiah and made him king in Jerusalem
in place of his father.

Jehoahaz King of Judah

2 Jehoahaz[a] was twenty-three years
old when he became king, and he
reigned in Jerusalem three months. 3 The
king of Egypt dethroned him in Jerusalem and imposed on Judah a levy of a
hundred talents[b] of silver and a talent[c]
of gold. 4 The king of Egypt made Eliakim, a brother of Jehoahaz, king over
Judah and Jerusalem and changed
Eliakim's name to Jehoiakim. But Neco
took Eliakim's brother Jehoahaz and
carried him off to Egypt.

Jehoiakim King of Judah

5 Jehoiakim was twenty-five years old
when he became king, and he reigned
in Jerusalem eleven years. He did evil in
the eyes of the LORD his God. 6 Nebuchadnezzar king of Babylon attacked
him and bound him with bronze shackles to take him to Babylon. 7 Nebuchadnezzar also took to Babylon articles from
the temple of the LORD and put them in
his temple[d] there.
8 The other events of Jehoiakim's
reign, the detestable things he did and
all that was found against him, are written in the book of the kings of Israel and
Judah. And Jehoiachin his son succeeded him as king.

Jehoiachin King of Judah

9 Jehoiachin was eighteen[e] years old
when he became king, and he reigned
in Jerusalem three months and ten days.
He did evil in the eyes of the LORD. 10 In
the spring, King Nebuchadnezzar sent
for him and brought him to Babylon, together with articles of value from the
temple of the LORD, and he made
Jehoiachin's uncle,[f] Zedekiah, king over
Judah and Jerusalem.

Zedekiah King of Judah

11 Zedekiah was twenty-one years old
when he became king, and he reigned
in Jerusalem eleven years. 12 He did evil
in the eyes of the LORD his God and did
not humble himself before Jeremiah the
prophet, who spoke the word of the
LORD. 13 He also rebelled against King
Nebuchadnezzar, who had made him
take an oath in God's name. He became
stiff-necked and hardened his heart and
would not turn to the LORD, the God of
Israel. 14 Furthermore, all the leaders of
the priests and the people became more
and more unfaithful, following all the
detestable practices of the nations and

[a] 2 Hebrew *Joahaz,* a variant of *Jehoahaz;* also in verse 4 [b] 3 That is, about 3 3/4 tons (about 3.4 metric tons) [c] 3 That is, about 75 pounds (about 34 kilograms) [d] 7 Or *palace* [e] 9 One Hebrew manuscript, some Septuagint manuscripts and Syriac (see also 2 Kings 24:8); most Hebrew manuscripts *eight* [f] 10 Hebrew *brother,* that is, relative (see 2 Kings 24:17)

defiling the temple of the LORD, which
he had consecrated in Jerusalem.

The Fall of Jerusalem

15The LORD, the God of their fathers,
sent word to them through his messengers again and again, because he had
pity on his people and on his dwelling
place. 16But they mocked God's messengers, despised his words and scoffed at
his prophets until the wrath of the LORD
was aroused against his people and
there was no remedy. 17He brought up
against them the king of the Babylonians,[a] who killed their young men
with the sword in the sanctuary, and
spared neither young man nor young
woman, old man or aged. God handed
all of them over to Nebuchadnezzar.
18He carried to Babylon all the articles
from the temple of God, both large and
small, and the treasures of the LORD's
temple and the treasures of the king and
his officials. 19They set fire to God's
temple and broke down the wall of Jerusalem; they burned all the palaces
and destroyed everything of value
there.

20He carried into exile to Babylon the
remnant, who escaped from the sword,
and they became servants to him and
his sons until the kingdom of Persia
came to power. 21The land enjoyed its
sabbath rests; all the time of its desolation it rested, until the seventy years
were completed in fulfillment of the
word of the LORD spoken by Jeremiah.

22In the first year of Cyrus king of Persia, in order to fulfill the word of the
LORD spoken by Jeremiah, the LORD
moved the heart of Cyrus king of Persia
to make a proclamation throughout his
realm and to put it in writing:

23"This is what Cyrus king of Persia
says:

"'The LORD, the God of heaven, has given me all the kingdoms of the earth and he has appointed me to build a temple for him at Jerusalem in Judah. Anyone of his people among you—may the LORD his God be with him, and let him go up.'"

[a]17 Or *Chaldeans*

SHARPEN THE FOCUS

There's no known cure. Chilling words, whether we're speaking about a new killer virus or a progressive, debilitating illness. And how much more chilling if the patient has refused previous remedies the doctor has prescribed.

Yet that's exactly the scenario described in 2 Chronicles 36:15–16. The Lord sent His word through His servants, the prophets. But His people would not listen. They rejected their Doctor's diagnosis and His medicine. Then only the most drastic measures would suffice.

Judah was repeatedly invaded by the Babylonian army—a ruthless enemy that had managed to conquer even the fierce Assyrian army. Finally, during King Zedekiah's reign, Nebuchadnezzar attacked for the last time and completed the deportations that had begun a few years earlier. For 70 years thereafter the temple lay in ruins, just as God had foretold through the prophet Jeremiah.

But God did not reject His covenant people. They would return to Jerusalem—chastened, but healed. Through David's line would come the Cure that would wipe out the plague of sin. Isaiah put it this way:

By [Christ's] wounds we are healed. (Isaiah 53:5)

EZRA

Ezra's book recounts the return of the exiles to Palestine after about 70 years in captivity (dating from the first deportation in 605 B.C.). As you read, note the miraculous way in which the Lord used a heathen ruler, Cyrus, to accomplish His ultimate purpose–sending the world's Messiah who would be born, not in Babylon but in Bethlehem as the prophet had foretold (Micah 5:2). If time is short, focus on Ezra 1:1–11.

Cyrus Helps the Exiles to Return

1 In the first year of Cyrus king of Persia, in order to fulfill the word of the
LORD spoken by Jeremiah, the LORD
moved the heart of Cyrus king of Persia
to make a proclamation throughout his
realm and to put it in writing:

2 "This is what Cyrus king of Persia
says:
" 'The LORD, the God of heaven,
has given me all the kingdoms of
the earth and he has appointed me
to build a temple for him at Jerusalem in Judah. 3 Anyone of his people among you—may his God be
with him, and let him go up to Jerusalem in Judah and build the
temple of the LORD, the God of Israel, the God who is in Jerusalem.
4 And the people of any place where
survivors may now be living are to
provide him with silver and gold,
with goods and livestock, and with
freewill offerings for the temple of
God in Jerusalem.' "

5 Then the family heads of Judah and
Benjamin, and the priests and Levites—
everyone whose heart God had
moved—prepared to go up and build
the house of the LORD in Jerusalem. 6 All
their neighbors assisted them with articles of silver and gold, with goods and
livestock, and with valuable gifts, in
addition to all the freewill offerings.
7 Moreover, King Cyrus brought out the
articles belonging to the temple of the
LORD, which Nebuchadnezzar had carried away from Jerusalem and had
placed in the temple of his god.[a] 8 Cyrus
king of Persia had them brought by
Mithredath the treasurer, who counted
them out to Sheshbazzar the prince of
Judah.
9 This was the inventory:

gold dishes	30
silver dishes	1,000
silver pans[b]	29
10 gold bowls	30
matching silver bowls	410
other articles	1,000

11 In all, there were 5,400 articles of
gold and of silver. Sheshbazzar brought
all these along when the exiles came up
from Babylon to Jerusalem.

[a] 7 Or *gods* [b] 9 The meaning of the Hebrew for this word is uncertain.

The List of the Exiles Who Returned

2 Now these are the people of the
province who came up from the
captivity of the exiles, whom Nebuchadnezzar king of Babylon had taken
captive to Babylon (they returned to
Jerusalem and Judah, each to his own
town, 2 in company with Zerubbabel,
Jeshua, Nehemiah, Seraiah, Reelaiah,
Mordecai, Bilshan, Mispar, Bigvai, Rehum and Baanah):

The list of the men of the people of Israel:

3 the descendants of Parosh 2,172
4 of Shephatiah 372
5 of Arah 775
6 of Pahath-Moab (through the line of Jeshua and Joab) 2,812
7 of Elam 1,254
8 of Zattu 945
9 of Zaccai 760
10 of Bani 642
11 of Bebai 623
12 of Azgad 1,222
13 of Adonikam 666
14 of Bigvai 2,056
15 of Adin 454
16 of Ater (through Hezekiah) 98
17 of Bezai 323
18 of Jorah 112
19 of Hashum 223
20 of Gibbar 95

21 the men of Bethlehem 123
22 of Netophah 56
23 of Anathoth 128
24 of Azmaveth 42
25 of Kiriath Jearim,[a] Kephirah and Beeroth 743
26 of Ramah and Geba 621
27 of Micmash 122
28 of Bethel and Ai 223
29 of Nebo 52
30 of Magbish 156
31 of the other Elam 1,254
32 of Harim 320
33 of Lod, Hadid and Ono 725
34 of Jericho 345
35 of Senaah 3,630

36 The priests:

the descendants of Jedaiah (through the family of Jeshua) 973
37 of Immer 1,052
38 of Pashhur 1,247
39 of Harim 1,017

40 The Levites:

the descendants of Jeshua and Kadmiel (through the line of Hodaviah) 74

41 The singers:

the descendants of Asaph 128

42 The gatekeepers of the temple:

the descendants of
Shallum, Ater, Talmon,
Akkub, Hatita and Shobai 139

43 The temple servants:

the descendants of
Ziha, Hasupha, Tabbaoth,
44 Keros, Siaha, Padon,
45 Lebanah, Hagabah, Akkub,
46 Hagab, Shalmai, Hanan,
47 Giddel, Gahar, Reaiah,
48 Rezin, Nekoda, Gazzam,
49 Uzza, Paseah, Besai,
50 Asnah, Meunim, Nephussim,
51 Bakbuk, Hakupha, Harhur,
52 Bazluth, Mehida, Harsha,
53 Barkos, Sisera, Temah,
54 Neziah and Hatipha

55 The descendants of the servants of Solomon:

the descendants of
Sotai, Hassophereth, Peruda,
56 Jaala, Darkon, Giddel,
57 Shephatiah, Hattil,
Pokereth-Hazzebaim and Ami

58 The temple servants and the descendants of the servants of Solomon 392

59 The following came up from
the towns of Tel Melah, Tel Harsha,
Kerub, Addon and Immer, but they

[a]25 See Septuagint (see also Neh. 7:29); Hebrew *Kiriath Arim.*

could not show that their families were descended from Israel:

[60]The descendants of
Delaiah, Tobiah and
Nekoda 652

[61]And from among the priests:

The descendants of
Hobaiah, Hakkoz and Barzillai (a man who had married a daughter of Barzillai the Gileadite and was called by that name).

[62]These searched for their family records, but they could not find them and so were excluded from the priesthood as unclean. [63]The governor ordered them not to eat any of the most sacred food until there was a priest ministering with the Urim and Thummim.

[64]The whole company numbered 42,360, [65]besides their 7,337 menservants and maidservants; and they also had 200 men and women singers. [66]They had 736 horses, 245 mules, [67]435 camels and 6,720 donkeys.

[68]When they arrived at the house of the LORD in Jerusalem, some of the heads of the families gave freewill offerings toward the rebuilding of the house of God on its site. [69]According to their ability they gave to the treasury for this work 61,000 drachmas[a] of gold, 5,000 minas[b] of silver and 100 priestly garments.

[70]The priests, the Levites, the singers, the gatekeepers and the temple servants settled in their own towns, along with some of the other people, and the rest of the Israelites settled in their towns.

[a]*69* That is, about 1,100 pounds (about 500 kilograms) [b]*69* That is, about 3 tons (about 2.9 metric tons)

SHARPEN THE FOCUS

Night after night. Morning after morning. The headlines scream out the same news—nearly all of it bad. A new war in a country with yet another unpronounceable name. A child-pornography ring no one can crack. A renaissance in the use of heroin or cocaine. The world hurtles along in the darkness of space toward an ever deeper darkness. Or so it seems.

God's people in Babylon lived through seven dark decades. Some, no doubt, lost hope of returning home. For them, the Lord's promises turned to the ashes of bitterness. They turned their hearts toward creating peace for themselves in property and possessions.

That may be why, of perhaps two to three million Jews in Babylon, less than 50,000 returned to Jerusalem—even when Cyrus blessed that return and helped to fund it. Even so, the Lord was at work. His promises hadn't died. The story of His people and His plan of salvation wasn't finished.

As we read today's headlines, we can have that same assurance. The resurrected Jesus ascended to heaven to rule this earth for the good of His church. He is even now King of this earth's kings, Lord of this earth's lords. And He is *your* kind, good Savior.

WEEK 39 • THURSDAY

Ezra 3:1—4:24

GET THE BIG PICTURE

Despite their fears about the dangers, the former exiles, led by Zerubbabel, began to rebuild the temple. Sure enough, as soon as the foundation was laid, opposition began to heat up. Chapter 4 gives three examples of this opposition. As you read today, ask yourself how you would have responded to the opposition had you been among the returning exiles. If time is short, focus on Ezra 3:1–13.

Rebuilding the Altar

3 When the seventh month came
and the Israelites had settled in
their towns, the people assembled as
one man in Jerusalem. 2Then Jeshua son
of Jozadak and his fellow priests and Zerubbabel son of Shealtiel and his associates began to build the altar of the God
of Israel to sacrifice burnt offerings on
it, in accordance with what is written in
the Law of Moses the man of God. 3De-
spite their fear of the peoples around
them, they built the altar on its foundation and sacrificed burnt offerings on it
to the LORD, both the morning and evening sacrifices. 4Then in accordance
with what is written, they celebrated
the Feast of Tabernacles with the required number of burnt offerings prescribed for each day. 5After that, they
presented the regular burnt offerings,
the New Moon sacrifices and the sacrifices for all the appointed sacred feasts
of the LORD, as well as those brought as
freewill offerings to the LORD. 6On the
first day of the seventh month they began to offer burnt offerings to the LORD,
though the foundation of the LORD's
temple had not yet been laid.

Rebuilding the Temple

7Then they gave money to the masons
and carpenters, and gave food and
drink and oil to the people of Sidon and
Tyre, so that they would bring cedar logs
by sea from Lebanon to Joppa, as authorized by Cyrus king of Persia.
8In the second month of the second
year after their arrival at the house of
God in Jerusalem, Zerubbabel son of
Shealtiel, Jeshua son of Jozadak and the
rest of their brothers (the priests and the
Levites and all who had returned from
the captivity to Jerusalem) began the
work, appointing Levites twenty years
of age and older to supervise the building of the house of the LORD. 9Jeshua
and his sons and brothers and Kadmiel
and his sons (descendants of Hodaviah[a]) and the sons of Henadad and
their sons and brothers—all Levites—
joined together in supervising those
working on the house of God.
10When the builders laid the foundation of the temple of the LORD, the
priests in their vestments and with
trumpets, and the Levites (the sons of
Asaph) with cymbals, took their places
to praise the LORD, as prescribed by David king of Israel. 11With praise and
thanksgiving they sang to the LORD:

"He is good;
his love to Israel endures forever."

And all the people gave a great shout of
praise to the LORD, because the foundation of the house of the LORD was laid.
12But many of the older priests and Levites and family heads, who had seen
the former temple, wept aloud when
they saw the foundation of this temple

[a]9 Hebrew *Yehudah,* probably a variant of *Hodaviah*

being laid, while many others shouted
for joy. 13No one could distinguish the
sound of the shouts of joy from the
sound of weeping, because the people
made so much noise. And the sound
was heard far away.

Opposition to the Rebuilding

4 When the enemies of Judah and
Benjamin heard that the exiles
were building a temple for the LORD,
the God of Israel, 2they came to Zerubbabel and to the heads of the families
and said, "Let us help you build because, like you, we seek your God and
have been sacrificing to him since the
time of Esarhaddon king of Assyria,
who brought us here."

3But Zerubbabel, Jeshua and the rest
of the heads of the families of Israel answered, "You have no part with us in
building a temple to our God. We alone
will build it for the LORD, the God of Israel, as King Cyrus, the king of Persia,
commanded us."

4Then the peoples around them set
out to discourage the people of Judah
and make them afraid to go on
building.[a] 5They hired counselors to
work against them and frustrate their
plans during the entire reign of Cyrus
king of Persia and down to the reign of
Darius king of Persia.

Later Opposition Under Xerxes and Artaxerxes

6At the beginning of the reign of
Xerxes,[b] they lodged an accusation
against the people of Judah and Jerusalem.

7And in the days of Artaxerxes king of
Persia, Bishlam, Mithredath, Tabeel and
the rest of his associates wrote a letter to
Artaxerxes. The letter was written in
Aramaic script and in the Aramaic
language.[c,d]

8Rehum the commanding officer and
Shimshai the secretary wrote a letter
against Jerusalem to Artaxerxes the king
as follows:

9Rehum the commanding officer
and Shimshai the secretary, together with the rest of their associates—
the judges and officials over the
men from Tripolis, Persia,[e] Erech
and Babylon, the Elamites of Susa,
10and the other people whom the
great and honorable Ashurbanipal[f]
deported and settled in the city of
Samaria and elsewhere in Trans-
Euphrates.

11(This is a copy of the letter they sent
him.)

To King Artaxerxes,

From your servants, the men of
Trans-Euphrates:

12The king should know that the
Jews who came up to us from you
have gone to Jerusalem and are rebuilding that rebellious and wicked
city. They are restoring the walls
and repairing the foundations.
13Furthermore, the king should
know that if this city is built and its
walls are restored, no more taxes,
tribute or duty will be paid, and the
royal revenues will suffer. 14Now
since we are under obligation to the
palace and it is not proper for us to
see the king dishonored, we are
sending this message to inform the
king, 15so that a search may be
made in the archives of your prede-
cessors. In these records you will
find that this city is a rebellious city,
troublesome to kings and provinces, a place of rebellion from ancient times. That is why this city
was destroyed. 16We inform the
king that if this city is built and its
walls are restored, you will be left
with nothing in Trans-Euphrates.

17The king sent this reply:

To Rehum the commanding officer,
Shimshai the secretary and the

[a]4 Or *and troubled them as they built* [b]6 Hebrew *Ahasuerus,* a variant of Xerxes' Persian name [c]7 Or *written in Aramaic and translated* [d]7 The text of Ezra 4:8—6:18 is in Aramaic. [e]9 Or *officials, magistrates and governors over the men from* [f]10 Aramaic *Osnappar,* a variant of *Ashurbanipal*

rest of their associates living in
Samaria and elsewhere in Trans-
Euphrates:

Greetings.

18The letter you sent us has been
read and translated in my presence.
19I issued an order and a search was
made, and it was found that this
city has a long history of revolt
against kings and has been a place
of rebellion and sedition. 20Jerusa-
lem has had powerful kings ruling
over the whole of Trans-Euphrates,
and taxes, tribute and duty were
paid to them. 21Now issue an order
to these men to stop work, so that
this city will not be rebuilt until I so
order. 22Be careful not to neglect this
matter. Why let this threat grow, to
the detriment of the royal interests?

23As soon as the copy of the letter of
King Artaxerxes was read to Rehum and
Shimshai the secretary and their asso-
ciates, they went immediately to the
Jews in Jerusalem and compelled them
by force to stop.

24Thus the work on the house of God
in Jerusalem came to a standstill until
the second year of the reign of Darius
king of Persia.

SHARPEN THE FOCUS

Think about the most meaningful worship service you've ever attended. When did it happen? Where? Who led the service? What was the occasion? Why does the service stand out in your mind?

Had you asked the repatriated Jews those questions, undoubtedly most would have talked about the service described in Ezra 3:10–13. No one who attended came from force of habit. No one simply went through the motions. Many wept, their tears pouring from hearts that realized anew the depth of the Lord's mercy. Many others wept tears of repentance and of sorrow over what might have been. Many shouted for the sheer joy of seeing what God had done.

That day was surely "the day the LORD [had] made" (Psalm 118:24), and the temple was just as surely a place of worship He would construct, albeit by human hands.

Still today our Lord is building His church. It's not an edifice of stone or cedar, but the place wherein He dwells by His Spirit, just as He has promised (Ephesians 3:19–22). That building's cornerstone is Jesus Christ Himself (Psalm 118:22–23).

WEEK 39 • FRIDAY

Ezra 5:1—6:22

GET THE BIG PICTURE

Twenty years after the exiles' return, the temple still had not been completed. The Lord acts on His people's behalf in the government of King Darius. And He sends His prophets to His people. As you read, note the role they played in the temple's completion. If time is short, focus on Ezra 6:1–18.

Tattenai's Letter to Darius

5 Now Haggai the prophet and Zechariah the prophet, a descendant of Iddo, prophesied to the Jews in Judah and Jerusalem in the name of the God of Israel, who was over them. 2Then Zerubbabel son of Shealtiel and Jeshua son of Jozadak set to work to rebuild the house of God in Jerusalem. And the prophets of God were with them, helping them.

3At that time Tattenai, governor of Trans-Euphrates, and Shethar-Bozenai and their associates went to them and asked, "Who authorized you to rebuild this temple and restore this structure?" 4They also asked, "What are the names of the men constructing this building?"[a] 5But the eye of their God was watching over the elders of the Jews, and they were not stopped until a report could go to Darius and his written reply be received.

6This is a copy of the letter that Tattenai, governor of Trans-Euphrates, and Shethar-Bozenai and their associates, the officials of Trans-Euphrates, sent to King Darius. 7The report they sent him read as follows:

To King Darius:

Cordial greetings.

8The king should know that we went to the district of Judah, to the temple of the great God. The people are building it with large stones and placing the timbers in the walls. The work is being carried on with diligence and is making rapid progress under their direction.

9We questioned the elders and asked them, "Who authorized you to rebuild this temple and restore this structure?" 10We also asked them their names, so that we could write down the names of their leaders for your information.

11This is the answer they gave us:

"We are the servants of the God of heaven and earth, and we are rebuilding the temple that was built many years ago, one that a great king of Israel built and finished. 12But because our fathers angered the God of heaven, he handed them over to Nebuchadnezzar the Chaldean, king of Babylon, who destroyed this temple and deported the people to Babylon.

13"However, in the first year of Cyrus king of Babylon, King Cyrus issued a decree to rebuild this house of God. 14He even removed from the temple[b] of Babylon the gold and silver articles of the house of God, which Nebuchadnezzar had taken from the temple in Jerusalem and brought to the temple[b] in Babylon.

"Then King Cyrus gave them to a man named Sheshbazzar, whom he had appointed governor, 15and he told him, 'Take these articles and go and deposit them in the temple in Jerusalem. And rebuild the house of God on its site.' 16So this Sheshbazzar came and laid the foundations of the house of God in Jerusalem. From that day to the present it has been under construction but is not yet finished."

17Now if it pleases the king, let a search be made in the royal archives of Babylon to see if King Cyrus did in fact issue a decree to rebuild this house of God in Jerusalem. Then let the king send us his decision in this matter.

The Decree of Darius

6 King Darius then issued an order, and they searched in the archives stored in the treasury at Babylon. 2A scroll was found in the citadel of Ecbatana in the province of Media, and this was written on it:

Memorandum:

[a]4 See Septuagint; Aramaic 4*We told them the names of the men constructing this building.*
[b]14 Or *palace*

[3]In the first year of King Cyrus, the king issued a decree concerning the temple of God in Jerusalem:

Let the temple be rebuilt as a place to present sacrifices, and let its foundations be laid. It is to be ninety feet[a] high and ninety feet wide, [4]with three courses of large stones and one of timbers. The costs are to be paid by the royal treasury. [5]Also, the gold and silver articles of the house of God, which Nebuchadnezzar took from the temple in Jerusalem and brought to Babylon, are to be returned to their places in the temple in Jerusalem; they are to be deposited in the house of God.

[6]Now then, Tattenai, governor of Trans-Euphrates, and Shethar-Bozenai and you, their fellow officials of that province, stay away from there. [7]Do not interfere with the work on this temple of God. Let the governor of the Jews and the Jewish elders rebuild this house of God on its site.

[8]Moreover, I hereby decree what you are to do for these elders of the Jews in the construction of this house of God:

The expenses of these men are to be fully paid out of the royal treasury, from the revenues of Trans-Euphrates, so that the work will not stop. [9]Whatever is needed—young bulls, rams, male lambs for burnt offerings to the God of heaven, and wheat, salt, wine and oil, as requested by the priests in Jerusalem—must be given them daily without fail, [10]so that they may offer sacrifices pleasing to the God of heaven and pray for the well-being of the king and his sons.

[11]Furthermore, I decree that if anyone changes this edict, a beam is to be pulled from his house and he is to be lifted up and impaled on it. And for this crime his house is to be made a pile of rubble. [12]May God, who has caused his Name to dwell there, overthrow any king or people who lifts a hand to change this decree or to destroy this temple in Jerusalem.

I Darius have decreed it. Let it be carried out with diligence.

Completion and Dedication of the Temple

[13]Then, because of the decree King Darius had sent, Tattenai, governor of Trans-Euphrates, and Shethar-Bozenai and their associates carried it out with diligence. [14]So the elders of the Jews continued to build and prosper under the preaching of Haggai the prophet and Zechariah, a descendant of Iddo. They finished building the temple according to the command of the God of Israel and the decrees of Cyrus, Darius and Artaxerxes, kings of Persia. [15]The temple was completed on the third day of the month Adar, in the sixth year of the reign of King Darius.

[16]Then the people of Israel—the priests, the Levites and the rest of the exiles—celebrated the dedication of the house of God with joy. [17]For the dedication of this house of God they offered a hundred bulls, two hundred rams, four hundred male lambs and, as a sin offering for all Israel, twelve male goats, one for each of the tribes of Israel. [18]And they installed the priests in their divisions and the Levites in their groups for the service of God at Jerusalem, according to what is written in the Book of Moses.

The Passover

[19]On the fourteenth day of the first month, the exiles celebrated the Passover. [20]The priests and Levites had purified themselves and were all ceremonially clean. The Levites slaughtered the Passover lamb for all the exiles, for their brothers the priests and for themselves. [21]So the Israelites who had returned from the exile ate it, together with all who had separated themselves from the unclean practices of their Gen-

[a]3 Aramaic *sixty cubits* (about 27 meters)

tile neighbors in order to seek the LORD,
the God of Israel. 22For seven days they
celebrated with joy the Feast of Unleavened Bread, because the LORD had filled
them with joy by changing the attitude
of the king of Assyria, so that he assisted
them in the work on the house of God,
the God of Israel.

SHARPEN THE FOCUS

Suppose a remodeling project stalled at your house, and everyone just got used to living without a shower or a kitchen sink. That was the situation in Jerusalem a few years after the exiles' return. Enthused at first, the people soon got used to life without a temple when construction was delayed. They denied themselves the blessings the Lord wanted for them.

The entire Bible testifies to the fact that God wants His people to enjoy a rich, full relationship with Him. But we can rob ourselves of that by settling down, comfortable and content with where we find ourselves in our spiritual walk.

The Lord sent His prophets, Haggai and Zechariah, to help His people see that while *they* might be satisfied with their partially finished place of worship, *He* was not. The people listened, repented, and prospered (Ezra 6:14).

How about you? Are you satisfied with your spiritual growth, maybe even complacent about it? Why not talk to your Lord right now about the renovations He has in mind for your heart and life. Then, confident of His forgiveness in Christ, invite Him to continue His work in you. Ask too that you will prosper through the Word His servants speak to you.

WEEK 39 • SATURDAY

Ezra 7:1—8:36

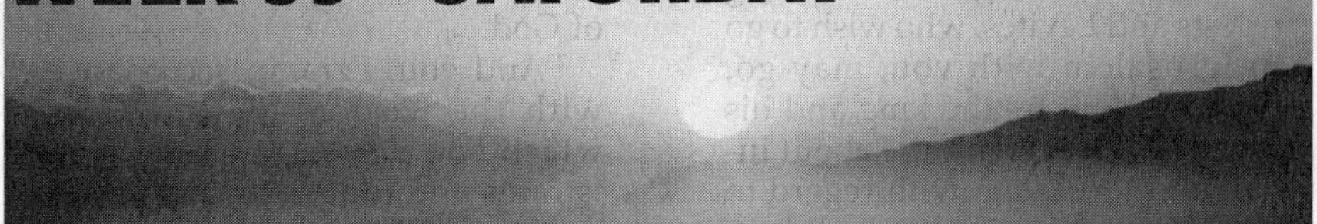

GET THE BIG PICTURE

A gap of about 58 years lies between Ezra 6 and 7. The events recorded in the book of Esther occurred during this gap. Ezra has to this point in his book related events as they had been told to him. Now, the book becomes an autobiography. Ezra tells more about himself and how he came to lead the second large group of exiles back to Jerusalem. As you read, notice the phrase "the hand of the LORD my God was on me" (Ezra 7:28). If time is short, focus on Ezra 8:1–32.

Ezra Comes to Jerusalem

7 After these things, during the
reign of Artaxerxes king of Persia, Ezra son of Seraiah, the son of Azariah, the son of Hilkiah, 2the son of
Shallum, the son of Zadok, the son of
Ahitub, 3the son of Amariah, the son
of Azariah, the son of Meraioth, 4the son
of Zerahiah, the son of Uzzi, the son of
Bukki, 5the son of Abishua, the son of
Phinehas, the son of Eleazar, the son
of Aaron the chief priest— 6this Ezra
came up from Babylon. He was a teacher well versed in the Law of Moses,
which the LORD, the God of Israel, had
given. The king had granted him everything he asked, for the hand of the LORD
his God was on him. 7Some of the Israelites, including priests, Levites, singers,
gatekeepers and temple servants, also

came up to Jerusalem in the seventh
year of King Artaxerxes.
8Ezra arrived in Jerusalem in the fifth
month of the seventh year of the king.
9He had begun his journey from Babylon on the first day of the first month,
and he arrived in Jerusalem on the first
day of the fifth month, for the gracious
hand of his God was on him. 10For Ezra
had devoted himself to the study and
observance of the Law of the LORD, and
to teaching its decrees and laws in
Israel.

King Artaxerxes' Letter to Ezra

11This is a copy of the letter King Artaxerxes had given to Ezra the priest and
teacher, a man learned in matters concerning the commands and decrees of
the LORD for Israel:

12[a]Artaxerxes, king of kings,

To Ezra the priest, a teacher of the
Law of the God of heaven:

Greetings.

13Now I decree that any of the Israelites in my kingdom, including
priests and Levites, who wish to go
to Jerusalem with you, may go.
14You are sent by the king and his
seven advisers to inquire about Judah and Jerusalem with regard to
the Law of your God, which is in
your hand. 15Moreover, you are to
take with you the silver and gold
that the king and his advisers have
freely given to the God of Israel,
whose dwelling is in Jerusalem,
16together with all the silver and
gold you may obtain from the province of Babylon, as well as the freewill offerings of the people and
priests for the temple of their God
in Jerusalem. 17With this money be
sure to buy bulls, rams and male
lambs, together with their grain offerings and drink offerings, and
sacrifice them on the altar of the
temple of your God in Jerusalem.
18You and your brother Jews may
then do whatever seems best with
the rest of the silver and gold, in accordance with the will of your God.
19Deliver to the God of Jerusalem all
the articles entrusted to you for
worship in the temple of your God.
20And anything else needed for the
temple of your God that you may
have occasion to supply, you may
provide from the royal treasury.
21Now I, King Artaxerxes, order
all the treasurers of Trans-Euphrates to provide with diligence whatever Ezra the priest, a teacher of the
Law of the God of heaven, may ask
of you— 22up to a hundred talents[b]
of silver, a hundred cors[c] of wheat,
a hundred baths[d] of wine, a hundred baths[d] of olive oil, and salt
without limit. 23Whatever the God
of heaven has prescribed, let it be
done with diligence for the temple
of the God of heaven. Why should
there be wrath against the realm of
the king and of his sons? 24You are
also to know that you have no authority to impose taxes, tribute or
duty on any of the priests, Levites,
singers, gatekeepers, temple servants or other workers at this house
of God.
25And you, Ezra, in accordance
with the wisdom of your God,
which you possess, appoint magistrates and judges to administer
justice to all the people of Trans-
Euphrates—all who know the laws
of your God. And you are to teach
any who do not know them.
26Whoever does not obey the law of
your God and the law of the king
must surely be punished by death,
banishment, confiscation of property, or imprisonment.

27Praise be to the LORD, the God of our
fathers, who has put it into the king's
heart to bring honor to the house of the
LORD in Jerusalem in this way 28and
who has extended his good favor to me

[a]12 The text of Ezra 7:12-26 is in Aramaic.
[b]22 That is, about 3 3/4 tons (about 3.4 metric tons) [c]22 That is, probably about 600 bushels (about 22 kiloliters) [d]22 That is, probably about 600 gallons (about 2.2 kiloliters)

before the king and his advisers and all
the king's powerful officials. Because
the hand of the LORD my God was on
me, I took courage and gathered leading men from Israel to go up with me.

List of the Family Heads Returning With Ezra

8 These are the family heads and
those registered with them who
came up with me from Babylon during
the reign of King Artaxerxes:

2 of the descendants of Phinehas,
Gershom;
of the descendants of Ithamar, Daniel;
of the descendants of David, Hattush 3 of the descendants of Shecaniah;

of the descendants of Parosh, Zechariah, and with him were registered 150 men;
4 of the descendants of Pahath-
Moab, Eliehoenai son of Zerahiah, and with him 200 men;
5 of the descendants of Zattu,[a] Shecaniah son of Jahaziel, and with
him 300 men;
6 of the descendants of Adin, Ebed
son of Jonathan, and with him 50
men;
7 of the descendants of Elam, Jeshaiah son of Athaliah, and with him
70 men;
8 of the descendants of Shephatiah,
Zebadiah son of Michael, and
with him 80 men;
9 of the descendants of Joab, Obadiah son of Jehiel, and with him
218 men;
10 of the descendants of Bani,[b] Shelomith son of Josiphiah, and with
him 160 men;
11 of the descendants of Bebai, Zechariah son of Bebai, and with him
28 men;
12 of the descendants of Azgad, Johanan son of Hakkatan, and with
him 110 men;
13 of the descendants of Adonikam,
the last ones, whose names were
Eliphelet, Jeuel and Shemaiah,
and with them 60 men;
14 of the descendants of Bigvai, Uthai
and Zaccur, and with them 70
men.

The Return to Jerusalem

15 I assembled them at the canal that
flows toward Ahava, and we camped
there three days. When I checked
among the people and the priests, I
found no Levites there. 16 So I summoned Eliezer, Ariel, Shemaiah, Elnathan, Jarib, Elnathan, Nathan, Zechariah and Meshullam, who were leaders,
and Joiarib and Elnathan, who were
men of learning, 17 and I sent them to
Iddo, the leader in Casiphia. I told them
what to say to Iddo and his kinsmen, the
temple servants in Casiphia, so that they
might bring attendants to us for the
house of our God. 18 Because the gracious hand of our God was on us, they
brought us Sherebiah, a capable man,
from the descendants of Mahli son of
Levi, the son of Israel, and Sherebiah's
sons and brothers, 18 men; 19 and Hashabiah, together with Jeshaiah from the
descendants of Merari, and his brothers
and nephews, 20 men. 20 They also
brought 220 of the temple servants—a
body that David and the officials had established to assist the Levites. All were
registered by name.
21 There, by the Ahava Canal, I proclaimed a fast, so that we might humble
ourselves before our God and ask him
for a safe journey for us and our children, with all our possessions. 22 I was
ashamed to ask the king for soldiers and
horsemen to protect us from enemies on
the road, because we had told the king,
"The gracious hand of our God is on everyone who looks to him, but his great
anger is against all who forsake him."
23 So we fasted and petitioned our God
about this, and he answered our prayer.
24 Then I set apart twelve of the leading

[a] 5 Some Septuagint manuscripts (also 1 Esdras 8:32); Hebrew does not have *Zattu*. [b] 10 Some Septuagint manuscripts (also 1 Esdras 8:36); Hebrew does not have *Bani*.

priests, together with Sherebiah, Hashabiah and ten of their brothers, 25and I
weighed out to them the offering of silver and gold and the articles that the
king, his advisers, his officials and all
Israel present there had donated for the
house of our God. 26I weighed out to
them 650 talents[a] of silver, silver articles
weighing 100 talents,[b] 100 talents[b] of
gold, 2720 bowls of gold valued at 1,000
darics,[c] and two fine articles of polished
bronze, as precious as gold.
28I said to them, "You as well as these
articles are consecrated to the LORD. The
silver and gold are a freewill offering to
the LORD, the God of your fathers.
29Guard them carefully until you weigh
them out in the chambers of the house
of the LORD in Jerusalem before the
leading priests and the Levites and the
family heads of Israel." 30Then the
priests and Levites received the silver
and gold and sacred articles that had
been weighed out to be taken to the
house of our God in Jerusalem.
31On the twelfth day of the first
month we set out from the Ahava Canal to go to Jerusalem. The hand of our
God was on us, and he protected us
from enemies and bandits along the
way. 32So we arrived in Jerusalem,
where we rested three days.
33On the fourth day, in the house of
our God, we weighed out the silver and
gold and the sacred articles into the
hands of Meremoth son of Uriah, the
priest. Eleazar son of Phinehas was with
him, and so were the Levites Jozabad
son of Jeshua and Noadiah son of Binnui. 34Everything was accounted for by
number and weight, and the entire
weight was recorded at that time.
35Then the exiles who had returned
from captivity sacrificed burnt offerings
to the God of Israel: twelve bulls for all
Israel, ninety-six rams, seventy-seven
male lambs and, as a sin offering, twelve
male goats. All this was a burnt offering
to the LORD. 36They also delivered the
king's orders to the royal satraps and to
the governors of Trans-Euphrates, who
then gave assistance to the people and
to the house of God.

[a]26 That is, about 25 tons (about 22 metric tons) [b]26 That is, about 3 3/4 tons (about 3.4 metric tons) [c]27 That is, about 19 pounds (about 8.5 kilograms)

SHARPEN THE FOCUS

Some people picture God as heavy-handed. They read His Law and see how far short they fall of fulfilling His demands. Knowing instinctively that it "is a dreadful thing to fall into the hands of the living God" (Hebrews 10:31), they spend their lives in a sorry race to avoid Him, to deny He exists or that He has any proper claim on them.

Contrast this with Ezra. He continually reminded himself and his readers that the Lord's hand rested upon him and those whom he led. Ezra did not see the Lord as heavy-handed; rather he took comfort in God's strength and mercy.

God's Law sometimes weighs heavily on our hearts. We recognize, by the power of the Holy Spirit, that we fall into the pits of spiritual pride or selfishness or lust or greed.

How wonderful to realize that even then, perhaps even especially then, the hand of our Lord is on us. You see, Jesus' hands still bear the scars of Calvary. And now He stretches those hands out to us in pardon, in protection, in peace. Relax in His grace today.

WEEK 40 • MONDAY

Ezra 9:1—10:44

Appointed as governor by King Artaxerxes, Ezra safely led a second large group of exiles home to Jerusalem. But shortly after they arrived, gross disobedience to the Lord's Law came to Ezra's attention. Note the forceful way Ezra deals with the nation's sins and also the solidarity with which he identifies with his people. If time is short, focus on Ezra 9:1–15.

Ezra's Prayer About Intermarriage

9 After these things had been
done, the leaders came to me
and said, "The people of Israel, including the priests and the Levites, have not
kept themselves separate from the
neighboring peoples with their detestable practices, like those of the Canaanites, Hittites, Perizzites, Jebusites,
Ammonites, Moabites, Egyptians and
Amorites. [2]They have taken some of
their daughters as wives for themselves
and their sons, and have mingled the
holy race with the peoples around
them. And the leaders and officials have
led the way in this unfaithfulness."
[3]When I heard this, I tore my tunic
and cloak, pulled hair from my head
and beard and sat down appalled.
[4]Then everyone who trembled at the
words of the God of Israel gathered
around me because of this unfaithfulness of the exiles. And I sat there appalled until the evening sacrifice.
[5]Then, at the evening sacrifice, I rose
from my self-abasement, with my tunic
and cloak torn, and fell on my knees
with my hands spread out to the LORD
my God [6]and prayed:

"O my God, I am too ashamed
and disgraced to lift up my face to
you, my God, because our sins are
higher than our heads and our guilt
has reached to the heavens. [7]From
the days of our forefathers until
now, our guilt has been great. Because of our sins, we and our kings
and our priests have been subjected to the sword and captivity, to
pillage and humiliation at the hand
of foreign kings, as it is today.
[8]"But now, for a brief moment,
the LORD our God has been gracious in leaving us a remnant and
giving us a firm place in his sanctuary, and so our God gives light to
our eyes and a little relief in our
bondage. [9]Though we are slaves,
our God has not deserted us in our
bondage. He has shown us kindness in the sight of the kings of Persia: He has granted us new life to
rebuild the house of our God and
repair its ruins, and he has given us
a wall of protection in Judah and
Jerusalem.
[10]"But now, O our God, what can
we say after this? For we have disregarded the commands [11]you gave
through your servants the prophets when you said: 'The land you
are entering to possess is a land
polluted by the corruption of its
peoples. By their detestable practices they have filled it with their
impurity from one end to the other. [12]Therefore, do not give your
daughters in marriage to their sons
or take their daughters for your
sons. Do not seek a treaty of friendship with them at any time, that
you may be strong and eat the good
things of the land and leave it to
your children as an everlasting inheritance.'

13“What has happened to us is a
result of our evil deeds and our
great guilt, and yet, our God, you
have punished us less than our sins
have deserved and have given us a
remnant like this. 14Shall we again
break your commands and intermarry with the peoples who commit such detestable practices?
Would you not be angry enough
with us to destroy us, leaving us no
remnant or survivor? 15O LORD,
God of Israel, you are righteous! We
are left this day as a remnant. Here
we are before you in our guilt,
though because of it not one of us
can stand in your presence.”

The People's Confession of Sin

10 While Ezra was praying and
confessing, weeping and
throwing himself down before the
house of God, a large crowd of Israelites—men, women and children—gathered around him. They too wept
bitterly. 2Then Shecaniah son of Jehiel,
one of the descendants of Elam, said to
Ezra, “We have been unfaithful to our
God by marrying foreign women from
the peoples around us. But in spite of
this, there is still hope for Israel. 3Now
let us make a covenant before our God
to send away all these women and their
children, in accordance with the counsel of my lord and of those who fear the
commands of our God. Let it be done according to the Law. 4Rise up; this matter is in your hands. We will support
you, so take courage and do it.”

5So Ezra rose up and put the leading
priests and Levites and all Israel under
oath to do what had been suggested.
And they took the oath. 6Then Ezra
withdrew from before the house of God
and went to the room of Jehohanan son
of Eliashib. While he was there, he ate
no food and drank no water, because he
continued to mourn over the unfaithfulness of the exiles.

7A proclamation was then issued
throughout Judah and Jerusalem for all
the exiles to assemble in Jerusalem.
8Anyone who failed to appear within
three days would forfeit all his property, in accordance with the decision of
the officials and elders, and would himself be expelled from the assembly of the
exiles.

9Within the three days, all the men of
Judah and Benjamin had gathered in Jerusalem. And on the twentieth day of
the ninth month, all the people were sitting in the square before the house of
God, greatly distressed by the occasion
and because of the rain. 10Then Ezra the
priest stood up and said to them, “You
have been unfaithful; you have married
foreign women, adding to Israel's guilt.
11Now make confession to the LORD, the
God of your fathers, and do his will.
Separate yourselves from the peoples
around you and from your foreign
wives.”

12The whole assembly responded
with a loud voice: “You are right! We
must do as you say. 13But there are many
people here and it is the rainy season;
so we cannot stand outside. Besides, this
matter cannot be taken care of in a day
or two, because we have sinned greatly
in this thing. 14Let our officials act for the
whole assembly. Then let everyone in
our towns who has married a foreign
woman come at a set time, along with
the elders and judges of each town, until the fierce anger of our God in this
matter is turned away from us.” 15Only
Jonathan son of Asahel and Jahzeiah
son of Tikvah, supported by Meshullam
and Shabbethai the Levite, opposed
this.

16So the exiles did as was proposed.
Ezra the priest selected men who were
family heads, one from each family division, and all of them designated by
name. On the first day of the tenth
month they sat down to investigate the
cases, 17and by the first day of the first
month they finished dealing with all the
men who had married foreign women.

Those Guilty of Intermarriage

18Among the descendants of the
priests, the following had married foreign women:

From the descendants of Jeshua
son of Jozadak, and his brothers:
Maaseiah, Eliezer, Jarib and Gedaliah. [19](They all gave their hands
in pledge to put away their
wives, and for their guilt they
each presented a ram from the
flock as a guilt offering.)
[20] From the descendants of Immer:
Hanani and Zebadiah.
[21] From the descendants of Harim:
Maaseiah, Elijah, Shemaiah, Jehiel and Uzziah.
[22] From the descendants of Pashhur:
Elioenai, Maaseiah, Ishmael, Nethanel, Jozabad and Elasah.

[23] Among the Levites:

Jozabad, Shimei, Kelaiah (that is,
Kelita), Pethahiah, Judah and El-
iezer.
[24] From the singers:
Eliashib.
From the gatekeepers:
Shallum, Telem and Uri.

[25] And among the other Israelites:

From the descendants of Parosh:
Ramiah, Izziah, Malkijah, Mijamin, Eleazar, Malkijah and Benaiah.
[26] From the descendants of Elam:
Mattaniah, Zechariah, Jehiel,
Abdi, Jeremoth and Elijah.
[27] From the descendants of Zattu:
Elioenai, Eliashib, Mattaniah, Jeremoth, Zabad and Aziza.
[28] From the descendants of Bebai:
Jehohanan, Hananiah, Zabbai
and Athlai.
[29] From the descendants of Bani:
Meshullam, Malluch, Adaiah, Jashub, Sheal and Jeremoth.
[30] From the descendants of Pahath-
Moab:
Adna, Kelal, Benaiah, Maaseiah,
Mattaniah, Bezalel, Binnui and
Manasseh.
[31] From the descendants of Harim:
Eliezer, Ishijah, Malkijah, Shema-
iah, Shimeon, [32]Benjamin, Mal-
luch and Shemariah.
[33] From the descendants of Hashum:
Mattenai, Mattattah, Zabad,
Eliphelet, Jeremai, Manasseh
and Shimei.
[34] From the descendants of Bani:
Maadai, Amram, Uel, [35]Benaiah,
Bedeiah, Keluhi, [36]Vaniah, Mer-
emoth, Eliashib, [37]Mattaniah,
Mattenai and Jaasu.
[38] From the descendants of Binnui:[a]
Shimei, [39]Shelemiah, Nathan,
Adaiah, [40]Macnadebai, Shashai,
Sharai, [41]Azarel, Shelemiah,
Shemariah, [42]Shallum, Amariah
and Joseph.
[43] From the descendants of Nebo:
Jeiel, Mattithiah, Zabad, Zebina,
Jaddai, Joel and Benaiah.

[44]All these had married foreign women, and some of them had children by these wives.[b]

[a]37,38 See Septuagint (also 1 Esdras 9:34); Hebrew *Jaasu* [38]*and Bani and Binnui,* [b]44 Or *and they sent them away with their children*

SHARPEN THE FOCUS

They sat as the rain drenched them, wondering: *What would God do to them?* Like children who have finally come to their senses, Israel knew the penalty for failing to obey would—and should—be heavy indeed.

Knowing the mercy of God as we do, we may find ourselves tempted to take sin lightly. Our culture has decayed to the point that scarcely any sin shocks—or even surprises—us anymore. So what made Israel's intermarriage with Canaanite wives so awful? God forgives. No big deal. Right?

Dead wrong. Israel's disobedience put God's plan to save the world in jeopardy. Israel was to be a kind of spiritual incubator into which the Messiah would be born. Intermarriage with those practicing the Canaanite religion would compromise or even destroy that incubator. Over and over the Lord's prophets had warned of this danger. The exile itself had resulted from idolatry that grew out of disobedience to God's Law. God forgave ancient Israel, as He forgives us–in the promised Messiah.

But in Israel's experience lies a stern warning for us. Who knows what plans of God's grace we may compromise by toying with sin? In firm love, our God says to us today, "This is the one I esteem: he who is humble and contrite in spirit, and trembles at my Word" (Isaiah 66:2).

NEHEMIAH

WEEK 40 • TUESDAY

Nehemiah 1:1–11

GET THE BIG PICTURE

Nehemiah's book begins about 12 years after Ezra's reformation in Jerusalem (Ezra 9–10). As the king's cupbearer, Nehemiah holds a position of honor and responsibility in Persia. Nonetheless, Nehemiah remembers his spiritual roots and identifies with his people—God's covenant people. Look for evidence of this as you read. If time is short, focus on Nehemiah 1:1–9.

Nehemiah's Prayer

1 The words of Nehemiah son of
Hacaliah:

In the month of Kislev in the twentieth year, while I was in the citadel of
Susa, 2Hanani, one of my brothers, came
from Judah with some other men, and
I questioned them about the Jewish
remnant that survived the exile, and
also about Jerusalem.
3They said to me, "Those who survived the exile and are back in the province are in great trouble and disgrace.
The wall of Jerusalem is broken down,
and its gates have been burned with
fire."
4When I heard these things, I sat
down and wept. For some days I
mourned and fasted and prayed before
the God of heaven. 5Then I said:

"O LORD, God of heaven, the
great and awesome God, who
keeps his covenant of love with
those who love him and obey his
commands, 6let your ear be attentive and your eyes open to hear the
prayer your servant is praying before you day and night for your servants, the people of Israel. I confess
the sins we Israelites, including myself and my father's house, have
committed against you. 7We have
acted very wickedly toward you.
We have not obeyed the commands, decrees and laws you gave
your servant Moses.
8"Remember the instruction you
gave your servant Moses, saying, 'If
you are unfaithful, I will scatter you
among the nations, 9but if you return to me and obey my commands, then even if your exiled
people are at the farthest horizon,
I will gather them from there and
bring them to the place I have chosen as a dwelling for my Name.'
10"They are your servants and
your people, whom you redeemed
by your great strength and your
mighty hand. 11O Lord, let your ear
be attentive to the prayer of this
your servant and to the prayer of
your servants who delight in rever-
ing your name. Give your servant
success today by granting him favor in the presence of this man."

I was cupbearer to the king.

SHARPEN THE FOCUS

Catch a group of children in some rule-breaking activity and usually fingers will point in all directions. *She* started it. *I* just watched. *We* just got here. *He* did it too. Even adults sometimes squirm as we wrestle with the temptation to avoid responsibility for our actions.

In light of this tendency, then, how much more amazing Nehemiah's prayer becomes. So far as we know, Nehemiah had never even been in Jerusalem. But notice his confession:

- I confess the sins we . . . have committed (Nehemiah 1:6).
- We have acted very wickedly . . . (Nehemiah 1:7).
- We have not obeyed . . . (Nehemiah 1:7).

Like Moses before him. Like Samuel and Daniel and Ezra. And like Jesus Himself! Nehemiah stands beside his brothers and sisters in the faith, not to accuse or shame them, but to share their grief and to ask for pardon.

As we grow in Christlikeness, we will find the Holy Spirit nudging us to pray the same kind of prayers for our congregation and for His church throughout the world. Not from arrogant hearts, but from hearts broken by the pain sin brings into the lives of those whom God loves.

WEEK 40 • WEDNESDAY Nehemiah 2:1—3:32

GET THE BIG PICTURE

Four months after Nehemiah had begun to pray for the people of Judah, he got a chance to present the problem and a proposal to King Artaxerxes. As you read, note the evidence that Nehemiah relied, not on himself, but on the Lord. If time is short, focus on Nehemiah 2:1–20.

Artaxerxes Sends Nehemiah to Jerusalem

2 In the month of Nisan in the
twentieth year of King Artaxerxes, when wine was brought for him,
I took the wine and gave it to the king.
I had not been sad in his presence before; 2so the king asked me, "Why does
your face look so sad when you are not
ill? This can be nothing but sadness of
heart."

I was very much afraid, 3but I said to
the king, "May the king live forever!
Why should my face not look sad when
the city where my fathers are buried lies
in ruins, and its gates have been destroyed by fire?"

4The king said to me, "What is it you
want?"

Then I prayed to the God of heaven,
5and I answered the king, "If it pleases
the king and if your servant has found
favor in his sight, let him send me to the
city in Judah where my fathers are buried so that I can rebuild it."

6Then the king, with the queen sitting
beside him, asked me, "How long will
your journey take, and when will you
get back?" It pleased the king to send
me; so I set a time.

7I also said to him, "If it pleases the
king, may I have letters to the governors
of Trans-Euphrates, so that they will
provide me safe-conduct until I arrive in

Judah? [8]And may I have a letter to
Asaph, keeper of the king's forest, so he
will give me timber to make beams for
the gates of the citadel by the temple
and for the city wall and for the residence I will occupy?" And because the
gracious hand of my God was upon me,
the king granted my requests. [9]So I went
to the governors of Trans-Euphrates
and gave them the king's letters. The
king had also sent army officers and
cavalry with me.
[10]When Sanballat the Horonite and
Tobiah the Ammonite official heard
about this, they were very much disturbed that someone had come to promote the welfare of the Israelites.

Nehemiah Inspects Jerusalem's Walls

[11]I went to Jerusalem, and after staying there three days [12]I set out during
the night with a few men. I had not told
anyone what my God had put in my
heart to do for Jerusalem. There were no
mounts with me except the one I was
riding on.
[13]By night I went out through the Valley Gate toward the Jackal[a] Well and the
Dung Gate, examining the walls of Jerusalem, which had been broken down,
and its gates, which had been destroyed
by fire. [14]Then I moved on toward the
Fountain Gate and the King's Pool, but
there was not enough room for my
mount to get through; [15]so I went up the
valley by night, examining the wall. Finally, I turned back and reentered
through the Valley Gate. [16]The officials
did not know where I had gone or what
I was doing, because as yet I had said
nothing to the Jews or the priests or
nobles or officials or any others who
would be doing the work.
[17]Then I said to them, "You see the
trouble we are in: Jerusalem lies in ruins, and its gates have been burned
with fire. Come, let us rebuild the wall
of Jerusalem, and we will no longer
be in disgrace." [18]I also told them
about the gracious hand of my God
upon me and what the king had said
to me.
They replied, "Let us start rebuilding." So they began this good work.
[19]But when Sanballat the Horonite,
Tobiah the Ammonite official and Geshem the Arab heard about it, they
mocked and ridiculed us. "What is this
you are doing?" they asked. "Are you
rebelling against the king?"
[20]I answered them by saying, "The
God of heaven will give us success. We
his servants will start rebuilding, but as
for you, you have no share in Jerusalem
or any claim or historic right to it."

Builders of the Wall

3 Eliashib the high priest and his
fellow priests went to work and
rebuilt the Sheep Gate. They dedicated
it and set its doors in place, building as
far as the Tower of the Hundred, which
they dedicated, and as far as the Tower
of Hananel. [2]The men of Jericho built
the adjoining section, and Zaccur son of
Imri built next to them.

[3]The Fish Gate was rebuilt by the sons
of Hassenaah. They laid its beams and
put its doors and bolts and bars in place.
[4]Meremoth son of Uriah, the son of Hakkoz, repaired the next section. Next to
him Meshullam son of Berekiah, the son
of Meshezabel, made repairs, and next
to him Zadok son of Baana also made
repairs. [5]The next section was repaired
by the men of Tekoa, but their nobles
would not put their shoulders to the
work under their supervisors.[b]

[6]The Jeshanah[c] Gate was repaired by
Joiada son of Paseah and Meshullam
son of Besodeiah. They laid its beams
and put its doors and bolts and bars in
place. [7]Next to them, repairs were made
by men from Gibeon and Mizpah—
Melatiah of Gibeon and Jadon of
Meronoth—places under the authority
of the governor of Trans-Euphrates.
[8]Uzziel son of Harhaiah, one of the
goldsmiths, repaired the next section;
and Hananiah, one of the perfume-
makers, made repairs next to that. They

[a]13 Or *Serpent* or *Fig* [b]5 Or *their Lord* or *the governor* [c]6 Or *Old*

restored[a] Jerusalem as far as the Broad
Wall. 9Rephaiah son of Hur, ruler of a
half-district of Jerusalem, repaired the
next section. 10Adjoining this, Jedaiah
son of Harumaph made repairs opposite his house, and Hattush son of Hashabneiah made repairs next to him.
11Malkijah son of Harim and Hasshub
son of Pahath-Moab repaired another
section and the Tower of the Ovens.
12Shallum son of Hallohesh, ruler of a
half-district of Jerusalem, repaired the
next section with the help of his daughters.

13The Valley Gate was repaired by Hanun and the residents of Zanoah. They
rebuilt it and put its doors and bolts and
bars in place. They also repaired five
hundred yards[b] of the wall as far as the
Dung Gate.

14The Dung Gate was repaired by
Malkijah son of Recab, ruler of the district of Beth Hakkerem. He rebuilt it and
put its doors and bolts and bars in place.

15The Fountain Gate was repaired by
Shallun son of Col-Hozeh, ruler of the
district of Mizpah. He rebuilt it, roofing
it over and putting its doors and bolts
and bars in place. He also repaired the
wall of the Pool of Siloam,[c] by the King's
Garden, as far as the steps going down
from the City of David. 16Beyond him,
Nehemiah son of Azbuk, ruler of a half-
district of Beth Zur, made repairs up to
a point opposite the tombs[d] of David, as
far as the artificial pool and the House
of the Heroes.

17Next to him, the repairs were made
by the Levites under Rehum son of
Bani. Beside him, Hashabiah, ruler of
half the district of Keilah, carried out
repairs for his district. 18Next to him, the
repairs were made by their countrymen
under Binnui[e] son of Henadad, ruler of
the other half-district of Keilah. 19Next to
him, Ezer son of Jeshua, ruler of Mizpah, repaired another section, from a
point facing the ascent to the armory as
far as the angle. 20Next to him, Baruch
son of Zabbai zealously repaired another section, from the angle to the entrance of the house of Eliashib the high
priest. 21Next to him, Meremoth son of
Uriah, the son of Hakkoz, repaired another section, from the entrance of
Eliashib's house to the end of it.

22The repairs next to him were made
by the priests from the surrounding region. 23Beyond them, Benjamin and
Hasshub made repairs in front of their
house; and next to them, Azariah son of
Maaseiah, the son of Ananiah, made repairs beside his house. 24Next to him,
Binnui son of Henadad repaired another section, from Azariah's house to
the angle and the corner, 25and Palal son
of Uzai worked opposite the angle and
the tower projecting from the upper
palace near the court of the guard. Next
to him, Pedaiah son of Parosh 26and the
temple servants living on the hill of
Ophel made repairs up to a point opposite the Water Gate toward the east and
the projecting tower. 27Next to them, the
men of Tekoa repaired another section,
from the great projecting tower to the
wall of Ophel.

28Above the Horse Gate, the priests
made repairs, each in front of his own
house. 29Next to them, Zadok son of Immer made repairs opposite his house.
Next to him, Shemaiah son of Shecaniah, the guard at the East Gate, made repairs. 30Next to him, Hananiah son of
Shelemiah, and Hanun, the sixth son of
Zalaph, repaired another section. Next
to them, Meshullam son of Berekiah
made repairs opposite his living quarters. 31Next to him, Malkijah, one of
the goldsmiths, made repairs as far
as the house of the temple servants
and the merchants, opposite the Inspection Gate, and as far as the room above
the corner; 32and between the room
above the corner and the Sheep Gate
the goldsmiths and merchants made
repairs.

[a]8 Or *They left out part of* [b]13 Hebrew *a thousand cubits* (about 450 meters) [c]15 Hebrew *Shelah,* a variant of *Shiloah,* that is, Siloam
[d]16 Hebrew; Septuagint, some Vulgate manuscripts and Syriac *tomb* [e]18 Two Hebrew manuscripts and Syriac (see also Septuagint and verse 24); most Hebrew manuscripts *Bavvai*

SHARPEN THE FOCUS

More often than you might think, God uses us as part of His answer to our own prayers:

- We may ask God to strengthen a friend who is ill, and find Him sending us to visit that person with words of encouragement.
- We may pray that people in a specific foreign place hear the Gospel, and find God moving us to support work in that country with our financial gifts.
- We may intercede for a coworker who is out of fellowship with the Lord or His church, and find Him prompting us to express our concern and to show His love to that person.

Nehemiah prayed for the settlers in Judah, and soon the Lord sent him to help them. The disciples prayed for workers in Christ's harvest fields (Matthew 9:37–38), and Jesus sent them to minister in His name (Matthew 10). If you're wondering what your Lord might want you to do today, examine the direction your prayers have taken in recent weeks. Ask for your Savior's direction. And get ready for an adventure!

WEEK 40 • THURSDAY

Nehemiah 4:1—6:19

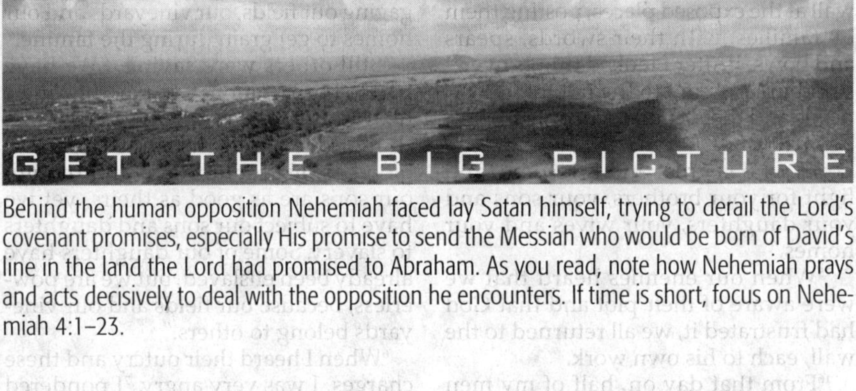

GET THE BIG PICTURE

Behind the human opposition Nehemiah faced lay Satan himself, trying to derail the Lord's covenant promises, especially His promise to send the Messiah who would be born of David's line in the land the Lord had promised to Abraham. As you read, note how Nehemiah prays and acts decisively to deal with the opposition he encounters. If time is short, focus on Nehemiah 4:1–23.

Opposition to the Rebuilding

4 When Sanballat heard that we
were rebuilding the wall, he became angry and was greatly incensed.
He ridiculed the Jews, 2and in the presence of his associates and the army of
Samaria, he said, "What are those feeble
Jews doing? Will they restore their wall?
Will they offer sacrifices? Will they finish in a day? Can they bring the stones
back to life from those heaps of rubble—
burned as they are?"
3Tobiah the Ammonite, who was at his
side, said, "What they are building—if
even a fox climbed up on it, he would
break down their wall of stones!"

4Hear us, O our God, for we are despised. Turn their insults back on their
own heads. Give them over as plunder
in a land of captivity. 5Do not cover up
their guilt or blot out their sins from
your sight, for they have thrown insults
in the face of[a] the builders.

6So we rebuilt the wall till all of it
reached half its height, for the people
worked with all their heart.

[a]5 Or *have provoked you to anger before*

7But when Sanballat, Tobiah, the
Arabs, the Ammonites and the men of
Ashdod heard that the repairs to
Jerusalem's walls had gone ahead and
that the gaps were being closed, they
were very angry. 8They all plotted together to come and fight against Jerusalem and stir up trouble against it. 9But
we prayed to our God and posted a
guard day and night to meet this threat.
10Meanwhile, the people in Judah
said, "The strength of the laborers is giving out, and there is so much rubble that
we cannot rebuild the wall."
11Also our enemies said, "Before they
know it or see us, we will be right there
among them and will kill them and put
an end to the work."
12Then the Jews who lived near them
came and told us ten times over, "Wherever you turn, they will attack us."
13Therefore I stationed some of the
people behind the lowest points of the
wall at the exposed places, posting them
by families, with their swords, spears
and bows. 14After I looked things over, I
stood up and said to the nobles, the officials and the rest of the people, "Don't
be afraid of them. Remember the
Lord, who is great and awesome, and
fight for your brothers, your sons and
your daughters, your wives and your
homes."
15When our enemies heard that we
were aware of their plot and that God
had frustrated it, we all returned to the
wall, each to his own work.
16From that day on, half of my men
did the work, while the other half were
equipped with spears, shields, bows
and armor. The officers posted themselves behind all the people of Judah
17who were building the wall. Those
who carried materials did their work
with one hand and held a weapon in
the other, 18and each of the builders
wore his sword at his side as he worked.
But the man who sounded the trumpet
stayed with me.
19Then I said to the nobles, the officials
and the rest of the people, "The work is
extensive and spread out, and we are
widely separated from each other along
the wall. 20Wherever you hear the sound
of the trumpet, join us there. Our God
will fight for us!"
21So we continued the work with half
the men holding spears, from the first
light of dawn till the stars came out.
22At that time I also said to the people,
"Have every man and his helper stay
inside Jerusalem at night, so they can
serve us as guards by night and workmen by day." 23Neither I nor my brothers nor my men nor the guards with me
took off our clothes; each had his weapon, even when he went for water.[a]

Nehemiah Helps the Poor

5 Now the men and their wives
raised a great outcry against
their Jewish brothers. 2Some were saying, "We and our sons and daughters
are numerous; in order for us to eat and
stay alive, we must get grain."
3Others were saying, "We are mort-
gaging our fields, our vineyards and our
homes to get grain during the famine."
4Still others were saying, "We have
had to borrow money to pay the king's
tax on our fields and vineyards. 5Al-
though we are of the same flesh and
blood as our countrymen and though
our sons are as good as theirs, yet we
have to subject our sons and daughters
to slavery. Some of our daughters have
already been enslaved, but we are powerless, because our fields and our vineyards belong to others."
6When I heard their outcry and these
charges, I was very angry. 7I pondered
them in my mind and then accused the
nobles and officials. I told them, "You
are exacting usury from your own countrymen!" So I called together a large
meeting to deal with them 8and said: "As
far as possible, we have bought back our
Jewish brothers who were sold to the
Gentiles. Now you are selling your
brothers, only for them to be sold back
to us!" They kept quiet, because they
could find nothing to say.
9So I continued, "What you are doing

[a]23 The meaning of the Hebrew for this clause is uncertain.

is not right. Shouldn't you walk in the
fear of our God to avoid the reproach of
our Gentile enemies? [10]I and my brothers and my men are also lending the
people money and grain. But let the exacting of usury stop! [11]Give back to them
immediately their fields, vineyards, olive groves and houses, and also the
usury you are charging them—the hundredth part of the money, grain, new
wine and oil."

[12]"We will give it back," they said.
"And we will not demand anything
more from them. We will do as you say."

Then I summoned the priests and
made the nobles and officials take an
oath to do what they had promised. [13]I
also shook out the folds of my robe and
said, "In this way may God shake out of
his house and possessions every man
who does not keep this promise. So may
such a man be shaken out and emptied!"

At this the whole assembly said,
"Amen," and praised the LORD. And the
people did as they had promised.

[14]Moreover, from the twentieth year
of King Artaxerxes, when I was appointed to be their governor in the land of
Judah, until his thirty-second year—
twelve years—neither I nor my brothers
ate the food allotted to the governor.
[15]But the earlier governors—those preceding me—placed a heavy burden on
the people and took forty shekels[a] of silver from them in addition to food and
wine. Their assistants also lorded it over
the people. But out of reverence for God
I did not act like that. [16]Instead, I devoted myself to the work on this wall.
All my men were assembled there for
the work; we[b] did not acquire any land.

[17]Furthermore, a hundred and fifty
Jews and officials ate at my table, as well
as those who came to us from the surrounding nations. [18]Each day one ox, six
choice sheep and some poultry were
prepared for me, and every ten days an
abundant supply of wine of all kinds. In
spite of all this, I never demanded the
food allotted to the governor, because
the demands were heavy on these
people.

[19]Remember me with favor, O my
God, for all I have done for these people.

Further Opposition to the Rebuilding

6 When word came to Sanballat,
Tobiah, Geshem the Arab and
the rest of our enemies that I had rebuilt
the wall and not a gap was left in it—
though up to that time I had not set the
doors in the gates— [2]Sanballat and Geshem sent me this message: "Come, let
us meet together in one of the villages[c]
on the plain of Ono."

But they were scheming to harm me;
[3]so I sent messengers to them with this
reply: "I am carrying on a great project
and cannot go down. Why should the
work stop while I leave it and go down
to you?" [4]Four times they sent me the
same message, and each time I gave
them the same answer.

[5]Then, the fifth time, Sanballat sent
his aide to me with the same message,
and in his hand was an unsealed letter
[6]in which was written:

> "It is reported among the na-
> tions—and Geshem[d] says it is
> true—that you and the Jews are
> plotting to revolt, and therefore
> you are building the wall. More-
> over, according to these reports you
> are about to become their king [7]and
> have even appointed prophets to
> make this proclamation about you
> in Jerusalem: 'There is a king in
> Judah!' Now this report will get
> back to the king; so come, let us
> confer together."

[8]I sent him this reply: "Nothing like
what you are saying is happening; you
are just making it up out of your head."

[9]They were all trying to frighten us,
thinking, "Their hands will get too
weak for the work, and it will not be
completed."

[a]*15* That is, about 1 pound (about 0.5 kilogram)
[b]*16* Most Hebrew manuscripts; some Hebrew manuscripts, Septuagint, Vulgate and Syriac *I*
[c]*2* Or *in Kephirim* [d]*6* Hebrew *Gashmu,* a variant of *Geshem*

⌞But I prayed,⌟ "Now strengthen my hands."

[10]One day I went to the house of Shemaiah son of Delaiah, the son of Mehetabel, who was shut in at his home. He said, "Let us meet in the house of God, inside the temple, and let us close the temple doors, because men are coming to kill you—by night they are coming to kill you."

[11]But I said, "Should a man like me run away? Or should one like me go into the temple to save his life? I will not go!" [12]I realized that God had not sent him, but that he had prophesied against me because Tobiah and Sanballat had hired him. [13]He had been hired to intimidate me so that I would commit a sin by doing this, and then they would give me a bad name to discredit me.

[14]Remember Tobiah and Sanballat, O my God, because of what they have done; remember also the prophetess Noadiah and the rest of the prophets who have been trying to intimidate me.

The Completion of the Wall

[15]So the wall was completed on the twenty-fifth of Elul, in fifty-two days. [16]When all our enemies heard about this, all the surrounding nations were afraid and lost their self-confidence, because they realized that this work had been done with the help of our God.

[17]Also, in those days the nobles of Judah were sending many letters to Tobiah, and replies from Tobiah kept coming to them. [18]For many in Judah were under oath to him, since he was son-in-law to Shecaniah son of Arah, and his son Jehohanan had married the daughter of Meshullam son of Berekiah. [19]Moreover, they kept reporting to me his good deeds and then telling him what I said. And Tobiah sent letters to intimidate me.

SHARPEN THE FOCUS

The Lord's work done in any way other than the Lord's way is not the Lord's work. The end will never justify the means, not even when the ends are the Lord's ends.

Think of the many alternative ways Nehemiah could have faced his challenges. He could have looked for allies among the idol worshipers in Palestine. He could have abandoned the construction project and tried to wait out Sanballat. He could have downplayed the seriousness of his people's greed in an effort to keep the most influential people in Judah on his side. He could have raised taxes instead of spending his own resources on the construction site. Instead, Nehemiah kept praying, and plugging away at the gaps in Jerusalem's walls.

Where are you tempted to take shortcuts or to use quick fixes to do the tasks God has given you? Do not fall for Satan's lie that heaven helps those who help themselves. Instead, "Remember the Lord, who is great and awesome" (Nehemiah 4:14). Remember that your "God will fight for [you]" (Nehemiah 4:20). Ask a brother or sister in the faith to stand "on the wall" beside you to encourage you. Then continue to do the Lord's work the Lord's way in the power He provides.

Nehemiah intended all along to resettle Jerusalem. Now that the city walls are finished and the gates hung, he takes a census of the people. From the list he will select families to repopulate the city. Nehemiah 8–10 tells how Ezra, Nehemiah, and the other leaders rebuild the "spiritual walls" in Israel that have fallen into disrepair. Then the resettlement can occur. If time is short, focus on Nehemiah 8:1–18.

7 After the wall had been rebuilt
and I had set the doors in place,
the gatekeepers and the singers and the
Levites were appointed. [2]I put in charge
of Jerusalem my brother Hanani, along
with[a] Hananiah the commander of the
citadel, because he was a man of integrity and feared God more than most
men do. [3]I said to them, "The gates of Jerusalem are not to be opened until the
sun is hot. While the gatekeepers are
still on duty, have them shut the doors
and bar them. Also appoint residents of
Jerusalem as guards, some at their posts
and some near their own houses."

The List of the Exiles Who Returned

[4]Now the city was large and spacious,
but there were few people in it, and the
houses had not yet been rebuilt. [5]So my
God put it into my heart to assemble the
nobles, the officials and the common
people for registration by families. I
found the genealogical record of those
who had been the first to return. This is
what I found written there:

[6]These are the people of the
province who came up from the
captivity of the exiles whom Nebuchadnezzar king of Babylon had
taken captive (they returned to
Jerusalem and Judah, each to his
own town, [7]in company with
Zerubbabel, Jeshua, Nehemiah,
Azariah, Raamiah, Nahamani,
Mordecai, Bilshan, Mispereth, Bigvai, Nehum and Baanah):

The list of the men of Israel:

[8]the descendants of Parosh	2,172
[9]of Shephatiah	372
[10]of Arah	652
[11]of Pahath-Moab (through the line of Jeshua and Joab)	2,818
[12]of Elam	1,254
[13]of Zattu	845
[14]of Zaccai	760
[15]of Binnui	648
[16]of Bebai	628
[17]of Azgad	2,322
[18]of Adonikam	667
[19]of Bigvai	2,067
[20]of Adin	655
[21]of Ater (through Hezekiah)	98
[22]of Hashum	328
[23]of Bezai	324
[24]of Hariph	112
[25]of Gibeon	95
[26]the men of Bethlehem and Netophah	188
[27]of Anathoth	128
[28]of Beth Azmaveth	42
[29]of Kiriath Jearim, Kephirah and Beeroth	743
[30]of Ramah and Geba	621
[31]of Micmash	122
[32]of Bethel and Ai	123
[33]of the other Nebo	52

[a]2 Or *Hanani, that is,*

34 of the other Elam	1,254
35 of Harim	320
36 of Jericho	345
37 of Lod, Hadid and Ono	721
38 of Senaah	3,930

39 The priests:

the descendants of Jedaiah (through the family of Jeshua)	973
40 of Immer	1,052
41 of Pashhur	1,247
42 of Harim	1,017

43 The Levites:

the descendants of Jeshua (through Kadmiel through the line of Hodaviah)	74

44 The singers:

the descendants of Asaph	148

45 The gatekeepers:

the descendants of Shallum, Ater, Talmon, Akkub, Hatita and Shobai	138

46 The temple servants:

the descendants of
Ziha, Hasupha, Tabbaoth,
47 Keros, Sia, Padon,
48 Lebana, Hagaba, Shalmai,
49 Hanan, Giddel, Gahar,
50 Reaiah, Rezin, Nekoda,
51 Gazzam, Uzza, Paseah,
52 Besai, Meunim, Nephussim,
53 Bakbuk, Hakupha, Harhur,
54 Bazluth, Mehida, Harsha,
55 Barkos, Sisera, Temah,
56 Neziah and Hatipha

57 The descendants of the servants of Solomon:

the descendants of
Sotai, Sophereth, Perida,
58 Jaala, Darkon, Giddel,
59 Shephatiah, Hattil,
Pokereth-Hazzebaim and
Amon

60 The temple servants and the descendants of the servants of Solomon	392

61 The following came up from the towns of Tel Melah, Tel Harsha, Kerub, Addon and Immer, but they could not show that their families were descended from Israel:

62 the descendants of Delaiah, Tobiah and Nekoda	642

63 And from among the priests:

the descendants of
Hobaiah, Hakkoz and Barzillai (a man who had married a daughter of Barzillai the Gileadite and was called by that name).

64 These searched for their family records, but they could not find them and so were excluded from the priesthood as unclean. 65 The governor, therefore, ordered them not to eat any of the most sacred food until there should be a priest ministering with the Urim and Thummim.

66 The whole company numbered 42,360, 67 besides their 7,337 menservants and maidservants; and they also had 245 men and women singers. 68 There were 736 horses, 245 mules,[a] 69 435 camels and 6,720 donkeys.

70 Some of the heads of the families contributed to the work. The governor gave to the treasury 1,000 drachmas[b] of gold, 50 bowls and 530 garments for priests. 71 Some of the heads of the families gave to the treasury for the work 20,000 drachmas[c] of gold and 2,200 minas[d] of silver. 72 The total given by the rest of the people was 20,000 drachmas of gold, 2,000 minas[e] of silver and 67 garments for priests.

73 The priests, the Levites, the gatekeepers, the singers and the

[a] *68* Some Hebrew manuscripts (see also Ezra 2:66); most Hebrew manuscripts do not have this verse. [b] *70* That is, about 19 pounds (about 8.5 kilograms) [c] *71* That is, about 375 pounds (about 170 kilograms); also in verse 72 [d] *71* That is, about 1 1/3 tons (about 1.2 metric tons)
[e] *72* That is, about 1 1/4 tons (about 1.1 metric tons)

temple servants, along with certain
of the people and the rest of the Israelites, settled in their own towns.

Ezra Reads the Law

When the seventh month came and
the Israelites had settled in their towns,
8 1 all the people assembled as one
man in the square before the
Water Gate. They told Ezra the scribe to
bring out the Book of the Law of Moses,
which the LORD had commanded for Israel.
2 So on the first day of the seventh
month Ezra the priest brought the Law
before the assembly, which was made
up of men and women and all who
were able to understand. 3 He read it
aloud from daybreak till noon as he
faced the square before the Water Gate
in the presence of the men, women and
others who could understand. And all
the people listened attentively to the
Book of the Law.
4 Ezra the scribe stood on a high wood-
en platform built for the occasion. Beside him on his right stood Mattithiah,
Shema, Anaiah, Uriah, Hilkiah and
Maaseiah; and on his left were Pedaiah,
Mishael, Malkijah, Hashum, Hashbad-
danah, Zechariah and Meshullam.
5 Ezra opened the book. All the people
could see him because he was standing
above them; and as he opened it, the
people all stood up. 6 Ezra praised the
LORD, the great God; and all the people
lifted their hands and responded,
"Amen! Amen!" Then they bowed down
and worshiped the LORD with their
faces to the ground.
7 The Levites—Jeshua, Bani, Sherebiah, Jamin, Akkub, Shabbethai, Hodiah,
Maaseiah, Kelita, Azariah, Jozabad, Hanan and Pelaiah—instructed the people
in the Law while the people were standing there. 8 They read from the Book of
the Law of God, making it clear[a] and
giving the meaning so that the people
could understand what was being read.
9 Then Nehemiah the governor, Ezra
the priest and scribe, and the Levites
who were instructing the people said to
them all, "This day is sacred to the LORD
your God. Do not mourn or weep." For
all the people had been weeping as they
listened to the words of the Law.
10 Nehemiah said, "Go and enjoy
choice food and sweet drinks, and send
some to those who have nothing prepared. This day is sacred to our Lord. Do
not grieve, for the joy of the LORD is
your strength."
11 The Levites calmed all the people,
saying, "Be still, for this is a sacred day.
Do not grieve."
12 Then all the people went away to eat
and drink, to send portions of food and
to celebrate with great joy, because they
now understood the words that had
been made known to them.
13 On the second day of the month, the
heads of all the families, along with the
priests and the Levites, gathered
around Ezra the scribe to give attention
to the words of the Law. 14 They found
written in the Law, which the LORD had
commanded through Moses, that the Israelites were to live in booths during the
feast of the seventh month 15 and that
they should proclaim this word and
spread it throughout their towns and in
Jerusalem: "Go out into the hill country
and bring back branches from olive
and wild olive trees, and from myr-
tles, palms and shade trees, to make
booths"—as it is written.[b]
16 So the people went out and brought
back branches and built themselves
booths on their own roofs, in their
courtyards, in the courts of the house of
God and in the square by the Water Gate
and the one by the Gate of Ephraim.
17 The whole company that had returned
from exile built booths and lived in
them. From the days of Joshua son of
Nun until that day, the Israelites had not
celebrated it like this. And their joy was
very great.
18 Day after day, from the first day to
the last, Ezra read from the Book of the
Law of God. They celebrated the feast
for seven days, and on the eighth day,
in accordance with the regulation, there
was an assembly.

[a]8 Or *God, translating it* [b]15 See Lev. 23:37-40.

SHARPEN THE FOCUS

Ezra opened the book. The people stood. People and leaders together honored the Lord who had given them His Word of life.

Notice the two things the Word of God did in His people:

- It brought conviction and sorrow over sin (Nehemiah 8:9).
- It brought joy (Nehemiah 8:12).

The Holy Spirit is always at work when God's Word is proclaimed. And the Spirit's aim is always to bring God's people to repentance and to work in them the joy that comes from sins forgiven and from the realization of the Lord's faithful love.

As you read the Scriptures, do you expect to receive information or transformation?

Christianity is rooted in history, and our Lord has taken great care to record for us the facts of His work down through the centuries. However, His goal for us is our total transformation into the image of Christ Jesus! He is at work in us—right now—to accomplish that, and He will "carry it on to completion until the day of Christ Jesus" (Philippians 1:6).

As you read the Scriptures for yourself, as you hear the Word of God proclaimed and taught, remember: You're changing. You're becoming more like Jesus. God's power is at work in you!

WEEK 40 • SATURDAY

Nehemiah 9:1—10:39

GET THE BIG PICTURE

Most of Nehemiah 9 records the prayer Israel prayed on a day set aside for repentance and for the renewal of the covenant. As you read, note the truth of the people's confession in Nehemiah 9:33. If time is short, focus on Nehemiah 9:32–38.

The Israelites Confess Their Sins

9 On the twenty-fourth day of the
same month, the Israelites gathered together, fasting and wearing sackcloth and having dust on their heads.
2Those of Israelite descent had separated themselves from all foreigners.
They stood in their places and confessed
their sins and the wickedness of their fathers. 3They stood where they were and
read from the Book of the Law of the
LORD their God for a quarter of the day,
and spent another quarter in confession
and in worshiping the LORD their God.
4Standing on the stairs were the Levites—Jeshua, Bani, Kadmiel, Shebaniah, Bunni, Sherebiah, Bani and Ke-
nani—who called with loud voices to
the LORD their God. 5And the Levites—
Jeshua, Kadmiel, Bani, Hashabneiah,
Sherebiah, Hodiah, Shebaniah and
Pethahiah—said: "Stand up and praise
the LORD your God, who is from everlasting to everlasting.[a]"

"Blessed be your glorious name,
and may it be exalted above all
blessing and praise. 6You alone are
the LORD. You made the heavens,
even the highest heavens, and all
their starry host, the earth and all

[a]5 Or *God for ever and ever*

that is on it, the seas and all that is
in them. You give life to everything,
and the multitudes of heaven worship you.
7"You are the LORD God, who
chose Abram and brought him out
of Ur of the Chaldeans and named
him Abraham. 8You found his heart
faithful to you, and you made a
covenant with him to give to his
descendants the land of the Canaanites, Hittites, Amorites, Perizzites, Jebusites and Girgashites. You
have kept your promise because
you are righteous.
9"You saw the suffering of our
forefathers in Egypt; you heard
their cry at the Red Sea.[a] 10You sent
miraculous signs and wonders
against Pharaoh, against all his officials and all the people of his land,
for you knew how arrogantly the
Egyptians treated them. You made
a name for yourself, which remains
to this day. 11You divided the sea
before them, so that they passed
through it on dry ground, but you
hurled their pursuers into the
depths, like a stone into mighty
waters. 12By day you led them with
a pillar of cloud, and by night with
a pillar of fire to give them light on
the way they were to take.
13"You came down on Mount
Sinai; you spoke to them from
heaven. You gave them regulations
and laws that are just and right,
and decrees and commands that
are good. 14You made known to
them your holy Sabbath and gave
them commands, decrees and laws
through your servant Moses. 15In
their hunger you gave them bread
from heaven and in their thirst you
brought them water from the rock;
you told them to go in and take
possession of the land you had
sworn with uplifted hand to give
them.
16"But they, our forefathers, became arrogant and stiff-necked,
and did not obey your commands.
17They refused to listen and failed
to remember the miracles you performed among them. They became
stiff-necked and in their rebellion
appointed a leader in order to return to their slavery. But you are a
forgiving God, gracious and compassionate, slow to anger and
abounding in love. Therefore you
did not desert them, 18even when
they cast for themselves an image
of a calf and said, 'This is your god,
who brought you up out of Egypt,'
or when they committed awful
blasphemies.
19"Because of your great compassion you did not abandon them in
the desert. By day the pillar of
cloud did not cease to guide them
on their path, nor the pillar of fire
by night to shine on the way they
were to take. 20You gave your good
Spirit to instruct them. You did not
withhold your manna from their
mouths, and you gave them water
for their thirst. 21For forty years you
sustained them in the desert; they
lacked nothing, their clothes did
not wear out nor did their feet become swollen.
22"You gave them kingdoms and
nations, allotting to them even the
remotest frontiers. They took over
the country of Sihon[b] king of Heshbon and the country of Og king of
Bashan. 23You made their sons as
numerous as the stars in the sky,
and you brought them into the
land that you told their fathers to
enter and possess. 24Their sons
went in and took possession of the
land. You subdued before them the
Canaanites, who lived in the land;
you handed the Canaanites over to
them, along with their kings and
the peoples of the land, to deal
with them as they pleased. 25They
captured fortified cities and fertile
land; they took possession of
houses filled with all kinds of good

[a]9 Hebrew *Yam Suph*; that is, Sea of Reeds
[b]22 One Hebrew manuscript and Septuagint; most Hebrew manuscripts *Sihon, that is, the country of the*

things, wells already dug, vineyards, olive groves and fruit trees in
abundance. They ate to the full and
were well-nourished; they reveled
in your great goodness.
26"But they were disobedient and
rebelled against you; they put your
law behind their backs. They killed
your prophets, who had admon-
ished them in order to turn them
back to you; they committed awful
blasphemies. 27So you handed them
over to their enemies, who oppressed them. But when they were
oppressed they cried out to you.
From heaven you heard them, and
in your great compassion you gave
them deliverers, who rescued them
from the hand of their enemies.
28"But as soon as they were at
rest, they again did what was evil
in your sight. Then you abandoned
them to the hand of their enemies
so that they ruled over them. And
when they cried out to you again,
you heard from heaven, and in
your compassion you delivered
them time after time.
29"You warned them to return to
your law, but they became arrogant
and disobeyed your commands.
They sinned against your ordinances, by which a man will live if
he obeys them. Stubbornly they
turned their backs on you, became
stiff-necked and refused to listen.
30For many years you were patient
with them. By your Spirit you ad-
monished them through your
prophets. Yet they paid no attention, so you handed them over to
the neighboring peoples. 31But in
your great mercy you did not put
an end to them or abandon them,
for you are a gracious and merciful
God.
32"Now therefore, O our God, the
great, mighty and awesome God,
who keeps his covenant of love, do
not let all this hardship seem tri-
fling in your eyes—the hardship
that has come upon us, upon our
kings and leaders, upon our priests
and prophets, upon our fathers and
all your people, from the days of
the kings of Assyria until today. 33In
all that has happened to us, you
have been just; you have acted
faithfully, while we did wrong.
34Our kings, our leaders, our priests
and our fathers did not follow your
law; they did not pay attention to
your commands or the warnings
you gave them. 35Even while they
were in their kingdom, enjoying
your great goodness to them in the
spacious and fertile land you gave
them, they did not serve you or
turn from their evil ways.
36"But see, we are slaves today,
slaves in the land you gave our
forefathers so they could eat its
fruit and the other good things it
produces. 37Because of our sins, its
abundant harvest goes to the kings
you have placed over us. They rule
over our bodies and our cattle as
they please. We are in great distress.

The Agreement of the People

38"In view of all this, we are making
a binding agreement, putting it in
writing, and our leaders, our Levites
and our priests are affixing their seals
to it."

10 Those who sealed it were:

Nehemiah the governor, the son of Hacaliah.

Zedekiah, 2Seraiah, Azariah, Jeremiah,
3Pashhur, Amariah, Malkijah,
4Hattush, Shebaniah, Malluch,
5Harim, Meremoth, Obadiah,
6Daniel, Ginnethon, Baruch,
7Meshullam, Abijah, Mijamin,
8Maaziah, Bilgai and Shemaiah.
These were the priests.

9The Levites:

Jeshua son of Azaniah, Binnui of the sons of Henadad, Kadmiel,
10and their associates: Shebaniah,
Hodiah, Kelita, Pelaiah, Hanan,

11 Mica, Rehob, Hashabiah,
12 Zaccur, Sherebiah, Shebaniah,
13 Hodiah, Bani and Beninu.

14 The leaders of the people:
Parosh, Pahath-Moab, Elam, Zattu,
Bani,
15 Bunni, Azgad, Bebai,
16 Adonijah, Bigvai, Adin,
17 Ater, Hezekiah, Azzur,
18 Hodiah, Hashum, Bezai,
19 Hariph, Anathoth, Nebai,
20 Magpiash, Meshullam, Hezir,
21 Meshezabel, Zadok, Jaddua,
22 Pelatiah, Hanan, Anaiah,
23 Hoshea, Hananiah, Hasshub,
24 Hallohesh, Pilha, Shobek,
25 Rehum, Hashabnah, Maaseiah,
26 Ahiah, Hanan, Anan,
27 Malluch, Harim and Baanah.

28 "The rest of the people—
priests, Levites, gatekeepers, singers, temple servants and all who
separated themselves from the
neighboring peoples for the sake of
the Law of God, together with their
wives and all their sons and daughters who are able to understand—
29 all these now join their brothers
the nobles, and bind themselves
with a curse and an oath to follow
the Law of God given through
Moses the servant of God and to
obey carefully all the commands,
regulations and decrees of the
LORD our Lord.
30 "We promise not to give our
daughters in marriage to the peoples around us or take their daughters for our sons.
31 "When the neighboring peoples bring merchandise or grain to
sell on the Sabbath, we will not buy
from them on the Sabbath or on
any holy day. Every seventh year
we will forgo working the land and
will cancel all debts.
32 "We assume the responsibility
for carrying out the commands to
give a third of a shekel[a] each year
for the service of the house of our
God: 33 for the bread set out on the
table; for the regular grain offerings
and burnt offerings; for the offerings on the Sabbaths, New Moon
festivals and appointed feasts; for
the holy offerings; for sin offerings
to make atonement for Israel; and
for all the duties of the house of our
God.
34 "We—the priests, the Levites
and the people—have cast lots to
determine when each of our families is to bring to the house of our
God at set times each year a contribution of wood to burn on the altar of the LORD our God, as it is
written in the Law.
35 "We also assume responsibility
for bringing to the house of the
LORD each year the firstfruits of our
crops and of every fruit tree.
36 "As it is also written in the Law,
we will bring the firstborn of our
sons and of our cattle, of our herds
and of our flocks to the house of
our God, to the priests ministering
there.
37 "Moreover, we will bring to the
storerooms of the house of our
God, to the priests, the first of our
ground meal, of our ⌞grain⌟ offerings, of the fruit of all our trees and
of our new wine and oil. And we
will bring a tithe of our crops to the
Levites, for it is the Levites who
collect the tithes in all the towns
where we work. 38 A priest descended from Aaron is to accompany the Levites when they receive
the tithes, and the Levites are to
bring a tenth of the tithes up to the
house of our God, to the storerooms of the treasury. 39 The people
of Israel, including the Levites, are
to bring their contributions of
grain, new wine and oil to the
storerooms where the articles for
the sanctuary are kept and where
the ministering priests, the gatekeepers and the singers stay.
"We will not neglect the house of
our God."

[a]32 That is, about 1/8 ounce (about 4 grams)

SHARPEN THE FOCUS

Take a few moments right now to compose your own prayer; structure it in a way similar to the one you just read. You can mentally make notes or jot the prayer down on a piece of paper. That way, you can refer to your prayer again at a later date. You may want to use some of the ideas below to get you started:

- God's goodness to my family and me in the past includes . . .
- God's faithful love to me despite my unfaithfulness includes . . .
- Present sins I want to confess include . . .
- Present distresses with which I need God's help include . . .

Now pray your prayer. Remember that the "blood of the New Covenant" which Jesus shed on the cross has completely cleansed you from all sin. Next time you celebrate the Lord's Supper, let your Savior assure you of His covenant love for you.

WEEK 41 • MONDAY

Nehemiah 11:1—13:31

GET THE BIG PICTURE

We leave the last chapters of Nehemiah on a (literal) note of praise. God has preserved a remnant, a small group of true believers, from whose descendants He will bring the world's Savior, just as He had promised Abraham. When Nehemiah returns to Persia, the people fall back into their former sins. So, when Nehemiah comes back again to Jerusalem, he leads yet another spiritual "housecleaning." If time is short, focus on Nehemiah 12:27–47.

The New Residents of Jerusalem

11 Now the leaders of the people
settled in Jerusalem, and the rest
of the people cast lots to bring one out
of every ten to live in Jerusalem, the
holy city, while the remaining nine were
to stay in their own towns. 2The people
commended all the men who volunteered to live in Jerusalem.

3These are the provincial leaders who
settled in Jerusalem (now some Israelites, priests, Levites, temple servants
and descendants of Solomon's servants
lived in the towns of Judah, each on his
own property in the various towns,
4while other people from both Judah
and Benjamin lived in Jerusalem):

From the descendants of Judah:

Athaiah son of Uzziah, the son of
Zechariah, the son of Amariah, the
son of Shephatiah, the son of Mahalalel, a descendant of Perez; 5and
Maaseiah son of Baruch, the son of
Col-Hozeh, the son of Hazaiah, the
son of Adaiah, the son of Joiarib, the
son of Zechariah, a descendant of
Shelah. 6The descendants of Perez
who lived in Jerusalem totaled 468
able men.

7From the descendants of Benjamin:

Sallu son of Meshullam, the son of
Joed, the son of Pedaiah, the son of

Kolaiah, the son of Maaseiah, the
son of Ithiel, the son of Jeshaiah,
8and his followers, Gabbai and Sal-
lai—928 men. 9Joel son of Zicri was
their chief officer, and Judah son of
Hassenuah was over the Second
District of the city.

10From the priests:

Jedaiah; the son of Joiarib; Jakin;
11Seraiah son of Hilkiah, the son of
Meshullam, the son of Zadok, the
son of Meraioth, the son of Ahitub,
supervisor in the house of God,
12and their associates, who carried
on work for the temple—822 men;
Adaiah son of Jeroham, the son of
Pelaliah, the son of Amzi, the son of
Zechariah, the son of Pashhur, the
son of Malkijah, 13and his associates, who were heads of families—
242 men; Amashsai son of Azarel,
the son of Ahzai, the son of Meshillemoth, the son of Immer, 14and his[a]
associates, who were able men—
128. Their chief officer was Zabdiel
son of Haggedolim.

15From the Levites:

Shemaiah son of Hasshub, the son
of Azrikam, the son of Hashabiah,
the son of Bunni; 16Shabbethai and
Jozabad, two of the heads of the
Levites, who had charge of the outside work of the house of God;
17Mattaniah son of Mica, the son of
Zabdi, the son of Asaph, the director who led in thanksgiving and
prayer; Bakbukiah, second among
his associates; and Abda son of
Shammua, the son of Galal, the son
of Jeduthun. 18The Levites in the
holy city totaled 284.

19The gatekeepers:

Akkub, Talmon and their associates,
who kept watch at the gates—172
men.

20The rest of the Israelites, with the
priests and Levites, were in all the
towns of Judah, each on his ancestral
property.

21The temple servants lived on the hill
of Ophel, and Ziha and Gishpa were in
charge of them.

22The chief officer of the Levites in Jerusalem was Uzzi son of Bani, the son
of Hashabiah, the son of Mattaniah, the
son of Mica. Uzzi was one of Asaph's descendants, who were the singers responsible for the service of the house of
God. 23The singers were under the
king's orders, which regulated their daily activity.

24Pethahiah son of Meshezabel, one of
the descendants of Zerah son of Judah,
was the king's agent in all affairs relating to the people.

25As for the villages with their fields,
some of the people of Judah lived in Kiriath Arba and its surrounding settlements, in Dibon and its settlements, in
Jekabzeel and its villages, 26in Jeshua, in
Moladah, in Beth Pelet, 27in Hazar Shual, in Beersheba and its settlements, 28in
Ziklag, in Meconah and its settlements,
29in En Rimmon, in Zorah, in Jarmuth,
30Zanoah, Adullam and their villages, in
Lachish and its fields, and in Azekah
and its settlements. So they were living
all the way from Beersheba to the Valley of Hinnom.

31The descendants of the Benjamites
from Geba lived in Micmash, Aija, Bethel and its settlements, 32in Anathoth,
Nob and Ananiah, 33in Hazor, Ramah
and Gittaim, 34in Hadid, Zeboim and
Neballat, 35in Lod and Ono, and in the
Valley of the Craftsmen.

36Some of the divisions of the Levites
of Judah settled in Benjamin.

Priests and Levites

12 These were the priests and
Levites who returned with
Zerubbabel son of Shealtiel and with
Jeshua:

Seraiah, Jeremiah, Ezra,
2Amariah, Malluch, Hattush,
3Shecaniah, Rehum, Meremoth,
4Iddo, Ginnethon,[b] Abijah,

[a]*14* Most Septuagint manuscripts; Hebrew *their*
[b]*4* Many Hebrew manuscripts and Vulgate (see also Neh. 12:16); most Hebrew manuscripts *Ginnethoi*

5Mijamin,[a] Moadiah, Bilgah,
6Shemaiah, Joiarib, Jedaiah,
7Sallu, Amok, Hilkiah and Jedaiah.
These were the leaders of the priests
and their associates in the days of
Jeshua.
8The Levites were Jeshua, Binnui,
Kadmiel, Sherebiah, Judah, and also
Mattaniah, who, together with his associates, was in charge of the songs of
thanksgiving. 9Bakbukiah and Unni,
their associates, stood opposite them in
the services.
10Jeshua was the father of Joiakim,
Joiakim the father of Eliashib, Eliashib
the father of Joiada, 11Joiada the father
of Jonathan, and Jonathan the father of
Jaddua.
12In the days of Joiakim, these were
the heads of the priestly families:
of Seraiah's family, Meraiah;
of Jeremiah's, Hananiah;
13of Ezra's, Meshullam;
of Amariah's, Jehohanan;
14of Malluch's, Jonathan;
of Shecaniah's,[b] Joseph;
15of Harim's, Adna;
of Meremoth's,[c] Helkai;
16of Iddo's, Zechariah;
of Ginnethon's, Meshullam;
17of Abijah's, Zicri;
of Miniamin's and of Moadiah's,
Piltai;
18of Bilgah's, Shammua;
of Shemaiah's, Jehonathan;
19of Joiarib's, Mattenai;
of Jedaiah's, Uzzi;
20of Sallu's, Kallai;
of Amok's, Eber;
21of Hilkiah's, Hashabiah;
of Jedaiah's, Nethanel.
22The family heads of the Levites in
the days of Eliashib, Joiada, Johanan
and Jaddua, as well as those of the
priests, were recorded in the reign of
Darius the Persian. 23The family heads
among the descendants of Levi up to
the time of Johanan son of Eliashib
were recorded in the book of the annals.
24And the leaders of the Levites were
Hashabiah, Sherebiah, Jeshua son of
Kadmiel, and their associates, who
stood opposite them to give praise and
thanksgiving, one section responding to
the other, as prescribed by David the
man of God.
25Mattaniah, Bakbukiah, Obadiah,
Meshullam, Talmon and Akkub were
gatekeepers who guarded the storerooms at the gates. 26They served in the
days of Joiakim son of Jeshua, the son of
Jozadak, and in the days of Nehemiah
the governor and of Ezra the priest and
scribe.

Dedication of the Wall of Jerusalem

27At the dedication of the wall of Jerusalem, the Levites were sought out from
where they lived and were brought to
Jerusalem to celebrate joyfully the dedication with songs of thanksgiving and
with the music of cymbals, harps and
lyres. 28The singers also were brought
together from the region around Jerusalem—from the villages of the Netophathites, 29from Beth Gilgal, and from the
area of Geba and Azmaveth, for the
singers had built villages for themselves
around Jerusalem. 30When the priests
and Levites had purified themselves
ceremonially, they purified the people,
the gates and the wall.
31I had the leaders of Judah go up on
top[d] of the wall. I also assigned two large
choirs to give thanks. One was to proceed on top[e] of the wall to the right, toward the Dung Gate. 32Hoshaiah and
half the leaders of Judah followed them,
33along with Azariah, Ezra, Meshullam,
34Judah, Benjamin, Shemaiah, Jeremiah,
35as well as some priests with trumpets,
and also Zechariah son of Jonathan, the
son of Shemaiah, the son of Mattaniah,
the son of Micaiah, the son of Zaccur, the
son of Asaph, 36and his associates—Shemaiah, Azarel, Milalai, Gilalai, Maai,
Nethanel, Judah and Hanani—with
musical instruments ⌞prescribed by⌟
David the man of God. Ezra the scribe

[a]5 A variant of *Miniamin* [b]14 Very many Hebrew manuscripts, some Septuagint manuscripts and Syriac (see also Neh. 12:3); most Hebrew manuscripts *Shebaniah's* [c]15 Some Septuagint manuscripts (see also Neh. 12:3); Hebrew *Meraioth's* [d]31 Or *go alongside* [e]31 Or *proceed alongside*

led the procession. [37]At the Fountain
Gate they continued directly up the
steps of the City of David on the ascent
to the wall and passed above the house
of David to the Water Gate on the east.
[38]The second choir proceeded in the
opposite direction. I followed them on
top[a] of the wall, together with half
the people—past the Tower of the Ovens to the Broad Wall, [39]over the Gate of
Ephraim, the Jeshanah[b] Gate, the Fish
Gate, the Tower of Hananel and the
Tower of the Hundred, as far as the
Sheep Gate. At the Gate of the Guard
they stopped.
[40]The two choirs that gave thanks
then took their places in the house of
God; so did I, together with half the officials, [41]as well as the priests—Eliakim,
Maaseiah, Miniamin, Micaiah, Elioenai,
Zechariah and Hananiah with their
trumpets— [42]and also Maaseiah, Shemaiah, Eleazar, Uzzi, Jehohanan, Malkijah, Elam and Ezer. The choirs sang
under the direction of Jezrahiah. [43]And
on that day they offered great sacrifices,
rejoicing because God had given them
great joy. The women and children also
rejoiced. The sound of rejoicing in Jerusalem could be heard far away.
[44]At that time men were appointed to
be in charge of the storerooms for the
contributions, firstfruits and tithes.
From the fields around the towns they
were to bring into the storerooms the
portions required by the Law for the
priests and the Levites, for Judah was
pleased with the ministering priests and
Levites. [45]They performed the service of
their God and the service of purification, as did also the singers and gatekeepers, according to the commands of
David and his son Solomon. [46]For long
ago, in the days of David and Asaph,
there had been directors for the singers
and for the songs of praise and thanksgiving to God. [47]So in the days of Zerubbabel and of Nehemiah, all Israel
contributed the daily portions for the
singers and gatekeepers. They also set
aside the portion for the other Levites,
and the Levites set aside the portion for
the descendants of Aaron.

Nehemiah's Final Reforms

13 On that day the Book of
Moses was read aloud in the
hearing of the people and there it was
found written that no Ammonite or
Moabite should ever be admitted into
the assembly of God, [2]because they had
not met the Israelites with food and
water but had hired Balaam to call a
curse down on them. (Our God, however, turned the curse into a blessing.)
[3]When the people heard this law, they
excluded from Israel all who were of
foreign descent.
[4]Before this, Eliashib the priest had
been put in charge of the storerooms of
the house of our God. He was closely associated with Tobiah, [5]and he had provided him with a large room formerly
used to store the grain offerings and
incense and temple articles, and also the
tithes of grain, new wine and oil prescribed for the Levites, singers and gatekeepers, as well as the contributions for
the priests.
[6]But while all this was going on, I was
not in Jerusalem, for in the thirty-second year of Artaxerxes king of Babylon
I had returned to the king. Some time
later I asked his permission [7]and came
back to Jerusalem. Here I learned about
the evil thing Eliashib had done in providing Tobiah a room in the courts of the
house of God. [8]I was greatly displeased
and threw all Tobiah's household goods
out of the room. [9]I gave orders to purify
the rooms, and then I put back into
them the equipment of the house of
God, with the grain offerings and the
incense.
[10]I also learned that the portions assigned to the Levites had not been given
to them, and that all the Levites and
singers responsible for the service had
gone back to their own fields. [11]So I rebuked the officials and asked them,
"Why is the house of God neglected?"
Then I called them together and stationed them at their posts.
[12]All Judah brought the tithes of grain,

[a]38 Or *them alongside* [b]39 Or *Old*

new wine and oil into the storerooms. 13I put Shelemiah the priest, Zadok the scribe, and a Levite named Pedaiah in charge of the storerooms and made Hanan son of Zaccur, the son of Mattaniah, their assistant, because these men were considered trustworthy. They were made responsible for distributing the supplies to their brothers.

14Remember me for this, O my God, and do not blot out what I have so faithfully done for the house of my God and its services.

15In those days I saw men in Judah treading winepresses on the Sabbath and bringing in grain and loading it on donkeys, together with wine, grapes, figs and all other kinds of loads. And they were bringing all this into Jerusalem on the Sabbath. Therefore I warned them against selling food on that day. 16Men from Tyre who lived in Jerusalem were bringing in fish and all kinds of merchandise and selling them in Jerusalem on the Sabbath to the people of Judah. 17I rebuked the nobles of Judah and said to them, "What is this wicked thing you are doing—desecrating the Sabbath day? 18Didn't your forefathers do the same things, so that our God brought all this calamity upon us and upon this city? Now you are stirring up more wrath against Israel by desecrating the Sabbath."

19When evening shadows fell on the gates of Jerusalem before the Sabbath, I ordered the doors to be shut and not opened until the Sabbath was over. I stationed some of my own men at the gates so that no load could be brought in on the Sabbath day. 20Once or twice the merchants and sellers of all kinds of goods spent the night outside Jerusalem. 21But I warned them and said, "Why do you spend the night by the wall? If you do this again, I will lay hands on you." From that time on they no longer came on the Sabbath. 22Then I commanded the Levites to purify themselves and go and guard the gates in order to keep the Sabbath day holy.

Remember me for this also, O my God, and show mercy to me according to your great love.

23Moreover, in those days I saw men of Judah who had married women from Ashdod, Ammon and Moab. 24Half of their children spoke the language of Ashdod or the language of one of the other peoples, and did not know how to speak the language of Judah. 25I rebuked them and called curses down on them. I beat some of the men and pulled out their hair. I made them take an oath in God's name and said: "You are not to give your daughters in marriage to their sons, nor are you to take their daughters in marriage for your sons or for yourselves. 26Was it not because of marriages like these that Solomon king of Israel sinned? Among the many nations there was no king like him. He was loved by his God, and God made him king over all Israel, but even he was led into sin by foreign women. 27Must we hear now that you too are doing all this terrible wickedness and are being unfaithful to our God by marrying foreign women?"

28One of the sons of Joiada son of Eliashib the high priest was son-in-law to Sanballat the Horonite. And I drove him away from me.

29Remember them, O my God, because they defiled the priestly office and the covenant of the priesthood and of the Levites.

30So I purified the priests and the Levites of everything foreign, and assigned them duties, each to his own task. 31I also made provision for contributions of wood at designated times, and for the firstfruits.

Remember me with favor, O my God.

SHARPEN THE FOCUS

Suppose you were to make a "top ten" list of influences in your life. What would appear on that list?

Israel found herself influenced toward disobedience and idolatry by an unlikely "leader." During the 12 years Nehemiah was away from Jerusalem, Israel's most persistent enemy took up residence within the holy temple itself! From there (Nehemiah 13:4–9), Tobiah evidently exercised control over Israel's family and worship life. He probably had no real political power, but he used his powers of persuasion deftly.

Within a few years, Tobiah had succeeded in derailing the reforms Ezra, Nehemiah, and other faithful servants of the Lord had begun. The Lord still held Israel accountable for her disobedience. No one in Israel could blame Tobiah for sins they themselves had committed. We can learn from this account and take warning from it.

Ask your Lord to help you accurately discern any ungodly influences in your life. After you've identified them, talk to Him about any sins you've committed while under those influences. Then, cleansed by the blood of His Son, walk in the freedom and righteousness His forgiveness brings.

ESTHER

WEEK 41 • TUESDAY

Esther 1:1—2:23

GET THE BIG PICTURE

Before you read today, remember that the account of Esther takes place between the events recorded in Ezra 6 and those recorded in Ezra 7. While some Jews have returned to Jerusalem with the blessing of King Cyrus some years before, most have chosen to remain in voluntary exile. This undoubtedly grieved the Lord, but it did not stop His love toward them. If time is short, focus on Esther 2:1–23.

Queen Vashti Deposed

1 This is what happened during the
time of Xerxes,[a] the Xerxes who
ruled over 127 provinces stretching
from India to Cush[b]: [2]At that time King
Xerxes reigned from his royal throne in
the citadel of Susa, [3]and in the third year
of his reign he gave a banquet for all his
nobles and officials. The military leaders of Persia and Media, the princes, and
the nobles of the provinces were
present.
[4]For a full 180 days he displayed the
vast wealth of his kingdom and the
splendor and glory of his majesty.
[5]When these days were over, the king
gave a banquet, lasting seven days, in
the enclosed garden of the king's palace, for all the people from the least to
the greatest, who were in the citadel of
Susa. [6]The garden had hangings of
white and blue linen, fastened with
cords of white linen and purple material to silver rings on marble pillars.
There were couches of gold and silver
on a mosaic pavement of porphyry,
marble, mother-of-pearl and other
costly stones. [7]Wine was served in goblets of gold, each one different from the
other, and the royal wine was abundant,
in keeping with the king's liberality. [8]By
the king's command each guest was allowed to drink in his own way, for the
king instructed all the wine stewards to
serve each man what he wished.
[9]Queen Vashti also gave a banquet for
the women in the royal palace of King
Xerxes.
[10]On the seventh day, when King Xerxes was in high spirits from wine, he
commanded the seven eunuchs who
served him—Mehuman, Biztha, Harbona, Bigtha, Abagtha, Zethar and Carcas— [11]to bring before him Queen
Vashti, wearing her royal crown, in order to display her beauty to the people
and nobles, for she was lovely to look
at. [12]But when the attendants delivered
the king's command, Queen Vashti refused to come. Then the king became
furious and burned with anger.
[13]Since it was customary for the king
to consult experts in matters of law and
justice, he spoke with the wise men who
understood the times [14]and were closest
to the king—Carshena, Shethar, Admatha, Tarshish, Meres, Marsena and Me-

[a]*1* Hebrew *Ahasuerus,* a variant of Xerxes' Persian name; here and throughout Esther [b]*1* That is, the upper Nile region

mucan, the seven nobles of Persia and Media who had special access to the king and were highest in the kingdom.
15"According to law, what must be done to Queen Vashti?" he asked. "She has not obeyed the command of King Xerxes that the eunuchs have taken to her."
16Then Memucan replied in the presence of the king and the nobles, "Queen Vashti has done wrong, not only against the king but also against all the nobles and the peoples of all the provinces of King Xerxes. 17For the queen's conduct will become known to all the women, and so they will despise their husbands and say, 'King Xerxes commanded Queen Vashti to be brought before him, but she would not come.' 18This very day the Persian and Median women of the nobility who have heard about the queen's conduct will respond to all the king's nobles in the same way. There will be no end of disrespect and discord.
19"Therefore, if it pleases the king, let him issue a royal decree and let it be written in the laws of Persia and Media, which cannot be repealed, that Vashti is never again to enter the presence of King Xerxes. Also let the king give her royal position to someone else who is better than she. 20Then when the king's edict is proclaimed throughout all his vast realm, all the women will respect their husbands, from the least to the greatest."
21The king and his nobles were pleased with this advice, so the king did as Memucan proposed. 22He sent dispatches to all parts of the kingdom, to each province in its own script and to each people in its own language, proclaiming in each people's tongue that every man should be ruler over his own household.

Esther Made Queen

2 Later when the anger of King Xerxes had subsided, he remembered Vashti and what she had done and what he had decreed about her. 2Then the king's personal attendants proposed, "Let a search be made for beautiful young virgins for the king. 3Let the king appoint commissioners in every province of his realm to bring all these beautiful girls into the harem at the citadel of Susa. Let them be placed under the care of Hegai, the king's eunuch, who is in charge of the women; and let beauty treatments be given to them. 4Then let the girl who pleases the king be queen instead of Vashti." This advice appealed to the king, and he followed it.
5Now there was in the citadel of Susa a Jew of the tribe of Benjamin, named Mordecai son of Jair, the son of Shimei, the son of Kish, 6who had been carried into exile from Jerusalem by Nebuchadnezzar king of Babylon, among those taken captive with Jehoiachin[a] king of Judah. 7Mordecai had a cousin named Hadassah, whom he had brought up because she had neither father nor mother. This girl, who was also known as Esther, was lovely in form and features, and Mordecai had taken her as his own daughter when her father and mother died.
8When the king's order and edict had been proclaimed, many girls were brought to the citadel of Susa and put under the care of Hegai. Esther also was taken to the king's palace and entrusted to Hegai, who had charge of the harem. 9The girl pleased him and won his favor. Immediately he provided her with her beauty treatments and special food. He assigned to her seven maids selected from the king's palace and moved her and her maids into the best place in the harem.
10Esther had not revealed her nationality and family background, because Mordecai had forbidden her to do so. 11Every day he walked back and forth near the courtyard of the harem to find out how Esther was and what was happening to her.
12Before a girl's turn came to go in to King Xerxes, she had to complete twelve months of beauty treatments prescribed for the women, six months with oil of

[a]6 Hebrew *Jeconiah,* a variant of *Jehoiachin*

myrrh and six with perfumes and cosmetics. 13And this is how she would go to the king: Anything she wanted was given her to take with her from the harem to the king's palace. 14In the evening she would go there and in the morning return to another part of the harem to the care of Shaashgaz, the king's eunuch who was in charge of the concubines. She would not return to the king unless he was pleased with her and summoned her by name.

15When the turn came for Esther (the girl Mordecai had adopted, the daughter of his uncle Abihail) to go to the king, she asked for nothing other than what Hegai, the king's eunuch who was in charge of the harem, suggested. And Esther won the favor of everyone who saw her. 16She was taken to King Xerxes in the royal residence in the tenth month, the month of Tebeth, in the seventh year of his reign.

17Now the king was attracted to Esther more than to any of the other women, and she won his favor and approval more than any of the other virgins. So he set a royal crown on her head and made her queen instead of Vashti. 18And the king gave a great banquet, Esther's banquet, for all his nobles and officials. He proclaimed a holiday throughout the provinces and distributed gifts with royal liberality.

Mordecai Uncovers a Conspiracy

19When the virgins were assembled a second time, Mordecai was sitting at the king's gate. 20But Esther had kept secret her family background and nationality just as Mordecai had told her to do, for she continued to follow Mordecai's instructions as she had done when he was bringing her up.

21During the time Mordecai was sitting at the king's gate, Bigthana[a] and Teresh, two of the king's officers who guarded the doorway, became angry and conspired to assassinate King Xerxes. 22But Mordecai found out about the plot and told Queen Esther, who in turn reported it to the king, giving credit to Mordecai. 23And when the report was investigated and found to be true, the two officials were hanged on a gallows.[b] All this was recorded in the book of the annals in the presence of the king.

[a]21 Hebrew *Bigthan,* a variant of *Bigthana*
[b]23 Or *were hung* (or *impaled*) *on poles*; similarly elsewhere in Esther

SHARPEN THE FOCUS

A young mom walks up to the grocery checkout counter, her cart packed with this month's staples. A bell goes off and the manager comes running. She's this month's one-thousandth customer—and her groceries are free!

A seven-year-old casts his line into the water and stands beside Grandpa, waiting. Suddenly he gets a strike, and with a little help, pulls in a record-setting walleye.

Have you ever had the fun of being in the right place at the right time? Esther did. But it must have seemed like anything but fun to her. Imagine, a pious Jewish girl highjacked into the harem of an ungodly king. A king no one dared to disobey.

As we shall see, the Lord gave Esther "the favor of everyone who saw her" (Esther 2:15). The Savior-God who cared for His people stood behind the stage, rewriting Satan's plot to destroy the children of Abraham. Esther didn't know it yet, but the Lord had reserved a role for her in that mighty rescue.

What circumstances in your life look more like a disaster than a delight right now? As you take them to the Lord in prayer, ask Him how He may want to use you *in* them while He takes you safely *through* them.

WEEK 41 • WEDNESDAY

Esther 3:1—4:17

GET THE BIG PICTURE

The book of Esther presents, for the most part, a "bare bones" account of this slice of divine history. It spells out no one's motives. As you read, ask yourself what lay behind Haman's rage, Mordecai's request to Esther, and Esther's decision to act on behalf of her people. If time is short, focus on Esther 4:1–17.

Haman's Plot to Destroy the Jews

3 After these events, King Xerxes
honored Haman son of Hammedatha, the Agagite, elevating him and
giving him a seat of honor higher than
that of all the other nobles. 2All the royal officials at the king's gate knelt down
and paid honor to Haman, for the king
had commanded this concerning him.
But Mordecai would not kneel down or
pay him honor.
3Then the royal officials at the king's
gate asked Mordecai, "Why do you disobey the king's command?" 4Day after
day they spoke to him but he refused to
comply. Therefore they told Haman
about it to see whether Mordecai's behavior would be tolerated, for he had
told them he was a Jew.
5When Haman saw that Mordecai
would not kneel down or pay him
honor, he was enraged. 6Yet having
learned who Mordecai's people were,
he scorned the idea of killing only Mordecai. Instead Haman looked for a way
to destroy all Mordecai's people, the
Jews, throughout the whole kingdom of
Xerxes.
7In the twelfth year of King Xerxes, in
the first month, the month of Nisan,
they cast the *pur* (that is, the lot) in the
presence of Haman to select a day and
month. And the lot fell on[a] the twelfth
month, the month of Adar.
8Then Haman said to King Xerxes,
"There is a certain people dispersed and
scattered among the peoples in all the
provinces of your kingdom whose customs are different from those of all other people and who do not obey the
king's laws; it is not in the king's best
interest to tolerate them. 9If it pleases the
king, let a decree be issued to destroy
them, and I will put ten thousand talents[b]
of silver into the royal treasury for the
men who carry out this business."
10So the king took his signet ring from
his finger and gave it to Haman son of
Hammedatha, the Agagite, the enemy
of the Jews. 11"Keep the money," the
king said to Haman, "and do with the
people as you please."
12Then on the thirteenth day of the
first month the royal secretaries were
summoned. They wrote out in the script
of each province and in the language of
each people all Haman's orders to the
king's satraps, the governors of the various provinces and the nobles of the various peoples. These were written in the
name of King Xerxes himself and sealed
with his own ring. 13Dispatches were
sent by couriers to all the king's provinces with the order to destroy, kill and
annihilate all the Jews—young and old,
women and little children—on a single
day, the thirteenth day of the twelfth
month, the month of Adar, and to plunder their goods. 14A copy of the text of
the edict was to be issued as law in every province and made known to the
people of every nationality so they
would be ready for that day.

[a]7 Septuagint; Hebrew does not have *And the lot fell on.* [b]9 That is, about 375 tons (about 345 metric tons)

[15]Spurred on by the king's command, the couriers went out, and the edict was issued in the citadel of Susa. The king and Haman sat down to drink, but the city of Susa was bewildered.

Mordecai Persuades Esther to Help

4 When Mordecai learned of all that had been done, he tore his clothes, put on sackcloth and ashes, and went out into the city, wailing loudly and bitterly. [2]But he went only as far as the king's gate, because no one clothed in sackcloth was allowed to enter it. [3]In every province to which the edict and order of the king came, there was great mourning among the Jews, with fasting, weeping and wailing. Many lay in sackcloth and ashes.

[4]When Esther's maids and eunuchs came and told her about Mordecai, she was in great distress. She sent clothes for him to put on instead of his sackcloth, but he would not accept them. [5]Then Esther summoned Hathach, one of the king's eunuchs assigned to attend her, and ordered him to find out what was troubling Mordecai and why.

[6]So Hathach went out to Mordecai in the open square of the city in front of the king's gate. [7]Mordecai told him everything that had happened to him, including the exact amount of money Haman had promised to pay into the royal treasury for the destruction of the Jews. [8]He also gave him a copy of the text of the edict for their annihilation, which had been published in Susa, to show to Esther and explain it to her, and he told him to urge her to go into the king's presence to beg for mercy and plead with him for her people.

[9]Hathach went back and reported to Esther what Mordecai had said. [10]Then she instructed him to say to Mordecai, [11]"All the king's officials and the people of the royal provinces know that for any man or woman who approaches the king in the inner court without being summoned the king has but one law: that he be put to death. The only exception to this is for the king to extend the gold scepter to him and spare his life. But thirty days have passed since I was called to go to the king."

[12]When Esther's words were reported to Mordecai, [13]he sent back this answer: "Do not think that because you are in the king's house you alone of all the Jews will escape. [14]For if you remain silent at this time, relief and deliverance for the Jews will arise from another place, but you and your father's family will perish. And who knows but that you have come to royal position for such a time as this?"

[15]Then Esther sent this reply to Mordecai: [16]"Go, gather together all the Jews who are in Susa, and fast for me. Do not eat or drink for three days, night or day. I and my maids will fast as you do. When this is done, I will go to the king, even though it is against the law. And if I perish, I perish."

[17]So Mordecai went away and carried out all of Esther's instructions.

SHARPEN THE FOCUS

"The kingdom of God comes indeed without our prayer, of itself." So begins Martin Luther's explanation of the Second Petition of the Lord's Prayer. His words echo, in a sense, Mordecai's words to Esther in Esther 4:14. Esther could choose to keep her hands unmuddied in the whole sorry mess with Haman. If she did, the Lord would raise up a deliverer from another direction. But Esther would deny herself the privilege of playing a part in that deliverance.

In what ways could your prayers, your note of encouragement, your words of witness, your financial resources be a part of God's plan to bring the Good News of Jesus to those who are lost in a world of hurt and headed toward an eternal hell? Has the Lord perhaps placed you in just the right position to do or say something that could make a difference in someone's destiny?

If selfishness stands in your way, confess it and let your Savior cleanse you from that unrighteousness. If fear has you paralyzed, look to Jesus and let His love give you courage. Then pray. Speak. Act. Give. Use the privilege your Lord has given you to help usher in our Coming King (2 Peter 3:11–12).

WEEK 41 • THURSDAY

Esther 5:1—7:10

Apparently because assassination plots were so common in Persia, no one could approach the throne uninvited. (Xerxes himself later died at an assassin's hand.) But Queen Esther, trusting the Lord, dares to appear in Xerxes' throne room. Filled with pride and obsessed with rage at Mordecai, Haman falls into Esther's trap just as it snaps shut. If time is short, focus on Esther 7:1–10.

Esther's Request to the King

5 On the third day Esther put on
her royal robes and stood in the
inner court of the palace, in front of the
king's hall. The king was sitting on his
royal throne in the hall, facing the entrance. 2When he saw Queen Esther
standing in the court, he was pleased
with her and held out to her the gold
scepter that was in his hand. So Esther
approached and touched the tip of the
scepter.
3Then the king asked, "What is it,
Queen Esther? What is your request?
Even up to half the kingdom, it will be
given you."
4"If it pleases the king," replied Esther,
"let the king, together with Haman,
come today to a banquet I have prepared for him."
5"Bring Haman at once," the king
said, "so that we may do what Esther
asks."
So the king and Haman went to the
banquet Esther had prepared. 6As they
were drinking wine, the king again
asked Esther, "Now what is your petition? It will be given you. And what is
your request? Even up to half the kingdom, it will be granted."
7Esther replied, "My petition and my
request is this: 8If the king regards me
with favor and if it pleases the king to
grant my petition and fulfill my request,
let the king and Haman come tomorrow
to the banquet I will prepare for them.
Then I will answer the king's question."

Haman's Rage Against Mordecai

9Haman went out that day happy and
in high spirits. But when he saw Mordecai at the king's gate and observed that
he neither rose nor showed fear in his
presence, he was filled with rage against
Mordecai. 10Nevertheless, Haman restrained himself and went home.
Calling together his friends and Zeresh, his wife, 11Haman boasted to them
about his vast wealth, his many sons,
and all the ways the king had honored
him and how he had elevated him
above the other nobles and officials.
12"And that's not all," Haman added.
"I'm the only person Queen Esther invited to accompany the king to the banquet she gave. And she has invited me
along with the king tomorrow. 13But all
this gives me no satisfaction as long as
I see that Jew Mordecai sitting at the
king's gate."

[14]His wife Zeresh and all his friends said to him, "Have a gallows built, seventy-five feet[a] high, and ask the king in the morning to have Mordecai hanged on it. Then go with the king to the dinner and be happy." This suggestion delighted Haman, and he had the gallows built.

Mordecai Honored

6 That night the king could not sleep; so he ordered the book of the chronicles, the record of his reign, to be brought in and read to him. [2]It was found recorded there that Mordecai had exposed Bigthana and Teresh, two of the king's officers who guarded the doorway, who had conspired to assassinate King Xerxes.

[3]"What honor and recognition has Mordecai received for this?" the king asked.

"Nothing has been done for him," his attendants answered.

[4]The king said, "Who is in the court?" Now Haman had just entered the outer court of the palace to speak to the king about hanging Mordecai on the gallows he had erected for him.

[5]His attendants answered, "Haman is standing in the court."

"Bring him in," the king ordered.

[6]When Haman entered, the king asked him, "What should be done for the man the king delights to honor?"

Now Haman thought to himself, "Who is there that the king would rather honor than me?" [7]So he answered the king, "For the man the king delights to honor, [8]have them bring a royal robe the king has worn and a horse the king has ridden, one with a royal crest placed on its head. [9]Then let the robe and horse be entrusted to one of the king's most noble princes. Let them robe the man the king delights to honor, and lead him on the horse through the city streets, proclaiming before him, 'This is what is done for the man the king delights to honor!' "

[10]"Go at once," the king commanded Haman. "Get the robe and the horse and do just as you have suggested for Mordecai the Jew, who sits at the king's gate. Do not neglect anything you have recommended."

[11]So Haman got the robe and the horse. He robed Mordecai, and led him on horseback through the city streets, proclaiming before him, "This is what is done for the man the king delights to honor!"

[12]Afterward Mordecai returned to the king's gate. But Haman rushed home, with his head covered in grief, [13]and told Zeresh his wife and all his friends everything that had happened to him.

His advisers and his wife Zeresh said to him, "Since Mordecai, before whom your downfall has started, is of Jewish origin, you cannot stand against him—you will surely come to ruin!" [14]While they were still talking with him, the king's eunuchs arrived and hurried Haman away to the banquet Esther had prepared.

Haman Hanged

7 So the king and Haman went to dine with Queen Esther, [2]and as they were drinking wine on that second day, the king again asked, "Queen Esther, what is your petition? It will be given you. What is your request? Even up to half the kingdom, it will be granted."

[3]Then Queen Esther answered, "If I have found favor with you, O king, and if it pleases your majesty, grant me my life—this is my petition. And spare my people—this is my request. [4]For I and my people have been sold for destruction and slaughter and annihilation. If we had merely been sold as male and female slaves, I would have kept quiet, because no such distress would justify disturbing the king.[b]"

[5]King Xerxes asked Queen Esther, "Who is he? Where is the man who has dared to do such a thing?"

[6]Esther said, "The adversary and enemy is this vile Haman."

[a]14 Hebrew *fifty cubits* (about 23 meters)
[b]4 Or *quiet, but the compensation our adversary offers cannot be compared with the loss the king would suffer*

Then Haman was terrified before the
king and queen. 7The king got up in a
rage, left his wine and went out into the
palace garden. But Haman, realizing
that the king had already decided his
fate, stayed behind to beg Queen Esther
for his life.

8Just as the king returned from the
palace garden to the banquet hall, Haman was falling on the couch where Esther was reclining.

The king exclaimed, "Will he even
molest the queen while she is with me
in the house?"

As soon as the word left the king's
mouth, they covered Haman's face.
9Then Harbona, one of the eunuchs
attending the king, said, "A gallows
seventy-five feet[a] high stands by
Haman's house. He had it made for
Mordecai, who spoke up to help the
king."

The king said, "Hang him on it!" 10So
they hanged Haman on the gallows he
had prepared for Mordecai. Then the
king's fury subsided.

[a]9 Hebrew *fifty cubits* (about 23 meters)

SHARPEN THE FOCUS

"What shall be done for the one the king desires to honor?" In today's reading, we saw the answer Haman gave Xerxes to that question and we saw the honor Xerxes bestowed on Mordecai.

Perhaps you've never thought about it this way before, but *you* are one whom the King, the Lord, desires to honor! Unlike Mordecai who saved Xerxes from a death threat, none of us have earned our King's favor. Just the opposite, in fact. We have, by our sins, earned His wrath and displeasure, death now and forever.

But because of what Jesus did for us on Calvary's cross, we are now the King's favored ones. He delights (Psalm 16:3) in us! And He honors us:

- He has adopted us into His family (Ephesians 1:5). He calls us His own sons and daughters.
- He has given us "everything we need for life and godliness" (2 Peter 1:3).
- He has promised us "a rich welcome into the eternal kingdom of our Lord and Savior Jesus" (2 Peter 1:11).
- Jesus has given us the very same glory the Father gave Him (John 17:22).

Meditate on the honor your Lord has given you. In humble faith, believe it. Then walk today as God's chosen, forgiven, protected, dearly loved child.

WEEK 41 • FRIDAY

Esther 8:1—10:3

GET THE BIG PICTURE

A "law of the Medes and Persians," once sealed by the ruler, could not be revoked. Haman's decree of death to all Jews thus could not be recalled. So, instead, Xerxes gives Esther authority to issue a counter decree, giving her people the right to protect themselves. God's people are saved, and Mordecai receives still greater honor. If time is short, focus on Esther 8:1–17.

The King's Edict in Behalf of the Jews

8 That same day King Xerxes gave
Queen Esther the estate of Haman, the enemy of the Jews. And Mordecai came into the presence of the
king, for Esther had told how he was
related to her. 2The king took off his signet ring, which he had reclaimed from
Haman, and presented it to Mordecai.
And Esther appointed him over Haman's estate.
3Esther again pleaded with the king,
falling at his feet and weeping. She
begged him to put an end to the evil
plan of Haman the Agagite, which he
had devised against the Jews. 4Then the
king extended the gold scepter to Esther
and she arose and stood before him.
5"If it pleases the king," she said, "and
if he regards me with favor and thinks
it the right thing to do, and if he is
pleased with me, let an order be written
overruling the dispatches that Haman
son of Hammedatha, the Agagite, devised and wrote to destroy the Jews in
all the king's provinces. 6For how can I
bear to see disaster fall on my people?
How can I bear to see the destruction of
my family?"
7King Xerxes replied to Queen Esther
and to Mordecai the Jew, "Because Haman attacked the Jews, I have given his
estate to Esther, and they have hanged
him on the gallows. 8Now write another
decree in the king's name in behalf of
the Jews as seems best to you, and seal
it with the king's signet ring—for no
document written in the king's name
and sealed with his ring can be revoked."
9At once the royal secretaries were
summoned—on the twenty-third day
of the third month, the month of Sivan.
They wrote out all Mordecai's orders to
the Jews, and to the satraps, governors
and nobles of the 127 provinces stretching from India to Cush.[a] These orders
were written in the script of each province and the language of each people
and also to the Jews in their own script
and language. 10Mordecai wrote in the
name of King Xerxes, sealed the dispatches with the king's signet ring, and
sent them by mounted couriers, who
rode fast horses especially bred for the
king.
11The king's edict granted the Jews in
every city the right to assemble and protect themselves; to destroy, kill and
annihilate any armed force of any nationality or province that might attack
them and their women and children;
and to plunder the property of their enemies. 12The day appointed for the Jews
to do this in all the provinces of King
Xerxes was the thirteenth day of the
twelfth month, the month of Adar. 13A
copy of the text of the edict was to be
issued as law in every province and
made known to the people of every nationality so that the Jews would be
ready on that day to avenge themselves
on their enemies.
14The couriers, riding the royal horses,
raced out, spurred on by the king's command. And the edict was also issued in
the citadel of Susa.
15Mordecai left the king's presence
wearing royal garments of blue and
white, a large crown of gold and a purple robe of fine linen. And the city of
Susa held a joyous celebration. 16For the
Jews it was a time of happiness and joy,
gladness and honor. 17In every province
and in every city, wherever the edict of
the king went, there was joy and gladness among the Jews, with feasting and
celebrating. And many people of other
nationalities became Jews because fear
of the Jews had seized them.

Triumph of the Jews

9 On the thirteenth day of the
twelfth month, the month of
Adar, the edict commanded by the king

[a]9 That is, the upper Nile region

was to be carried out. On this day the enemies of the Jews had hoped to overpower them, but now the tables were turned and the Jews got the upper hand over those who hated them. [2]The Jews assembled in their cities in all the provinces of King Xerxes to attack those seeking their destruction. No one could stand against them, because the people of all the other nationalities were afraid of them. [3]And all the nobles of the provinces, the satraps, the governors and the king's administrators helped the Jews, because fear of Mordecai had seized them. [4]Mordecai was prominent in the palace; his reputation spread throughout the provinces, and he became more and more powerful.

[5]The Jews struck down all their enemies with the sword, killing and destroying them, and they did what they pleased to those who hated them. [6]In the citadel of Susa, the Jews killed and destroyed five hundred men. [7]They also killed Parshandatha, Dalphon, Aspatha, [8]Poratha, Adalia, Aridatha, [9]Parmashta, Arisai, Aridai and Vaizatha, [10]the ten sons of Haman son of Hammedatha, the enemy of the Jews. But they did not lay their hands on the plunder.

[11]The number of those slain in the citadel of Susa was reported to the king that same day. [12]The king said to Queen Esther, "The Jews have killed and destroyed five hundred men and the ten sons of Haman in the citadel of Susa. What have they done in the rest of the king's provinces? Now what is your petition? It will be given you. What is your request? It will also be granted."

[13]"If it pleases the king," Esther answered, "give the Jews in Susa permission to carry out this day's edict tomorrow also, and let Haman's ten sons be hanged on gallows."

[14]So the king commanded that this be done. An edict was issued in Susa, and they hanged the ten sons of Haman. [15]The Jews in Susa came together on the fourteenth day of the month of Adar, and they put to death in Susa three hundred men, but they did not lay their hands on the plunder.

[16]Meanwhile, the remainder of the Jews who were in the king's provinces also assembled to protect themselves and get relief from their enemies. They killed seventy-five thousand of them but did not lay their hands on the plunder. [17]This happened on the thirteenth day of the month of Adar, and on the fourteenth they rested and made it a day of feasting and joy.

Purim Celebrated

[18]The Jews in Susa, however, had assembled on the thirteenth and fourteenth, and then on the fifteenth they rested and made it a day of feasting and joy.

[19]That is why rural Jews—those living in villages—observe the fourteenth of the month of Adar as a day of joy and feasting, a day for giving presents to each other.

[20]Mordecai recorded these events, and he sent letters to all the Jews throughout the provinces of King Xerxes, near and far, [21]to have them celebrate annually the fourteenth and fifteenth days of the month of Adar [22]as the time when the Jews got relief from their enemies, and as the month when their sorrow was turned into joy and their mourning into a day of celebration. He wrote them to observe the days as days of feasting and joy and giving presents of food to one another and gifts to the poor.

[23]So the Jews agreed to continue the celebration they had begun, doing what Mordecai had written to them. [24]For Haman son of Hammedatha, the Agagite, the enemy of all the Jews, had plotted against the Jews to destroy them and had cast the *pur* (that is, the lot) for their ruin and destruction. [25]But when the plot came to the king's attention,[a] he issued written orders that the evil scheme Haman had devised against the Jews should come back onto his own head, and that he and his sons should be hanged on the gallows. [26](Therefore these days were called Purim, from the

[a]25 Or *when Esther came before the king*

word *pur*.) Because of everything written in this letter and because of what they had seen and what had happened to them, [27]the Jews took it upon themselves to establish the custom that they and their descendants and all who join them should without fail observe these two days every year, in the way prescribed and at the time appointed. [28]These days should be remembered and observed in every generation by every family, and in every province and in every city. And these days of Purim should never cease to be celebrated by the Jews, nor should the memory of them die out among their descendants.

[29]So Queen Esther, daughter of Abihail, along with Mordecai the Jew, wrote with full authority to confirm this second letter concerning Purim. [30]And Mordecai sent letters to all the Jews in the 127 provinces of the kingdom of Xerxes—words of goodwill and assurance— [31]to establish these days of Purim at their designated times, as Mordecai the Jew and Queen Esther had decreed for them, and as they had established for themselves and their descendants in regard to their times of fasting and lamentation. [32]Esther's decree confirmed these regulations about Purim, and it was written down in the records.

The Greatness of Mordecai

10 King Xerxes imposed tribute throughout the empire, to its distant shores. [2]And all his acts of power and might, together with a full account of the greatness of Mordecai to which the king had raised him, are they not written in the book of the annals of the kings of Media and Persia? [3]Mordecai the Jew was second in rank to King Xerxes, preeminent among the Jews, and held in high esteem by his many fellow Jews, because he worked for the good of his people and spoke up for the welfare of all the Jews.

SHARPEN THE FOCUS

Imagine yourself walking into the White House, asking directions to the Oval Office, and heading off down the corridor to see the president. Far fetched? Of course. The Secret Service would nab you before you took your second step. Unless, that is, the president expected you and met you at the front door.

In a sense, that's what happened to Esther in Esther 8:4. Xerxes held out his golden scepter toward her. In doing so, he invited her approach. And it's also what the heavenly Father does for you each time you come to Him in prayer.

In our own right, our own righteousness, we have no claim on God's throne. Our sin disqualifies us from even being in God's holy presence. But through Christ's cross, we who have been God's sworn enemies, rebels in His kingdom, have now become His own dear children. In Christ, God now "extends His golden scepter" toward us as we approach His throne:

> *Let us then approach the throne of grace with confidence, so that we may receive mercy and find grace to help us in our time of need.* (Hebrews 4:16) ☼

JOB

WEEK 41 • SATURDAY

Job 1:1–22

GET THE BIG PICTURE

Why do people, especially God's people, suffer? That's the question the book of Job addresses. Today's reading sets the stage for all that will follow. As you read, keep in mind the fact that Job never hears the conversation that has gone on in heaven between Satan ("the accuser") and God. If time is short, focus on Job 1:1–3, 6–20.

Prologue

1 In the land of Uz there lived a man whose name was Job. This man was blameless and upright; he feared God and shunned evil. [2]He had seven sons and three daughters, [3]and he owned seven thousand sheep, three thousand camels, five hundred yoke of oxen and five hundred donkeys, and had a large number of servants. He was the greatest man among all the people of the East.

[4]His sons used to take turns holding feasts in their homes, and they would invite their three sisters to eat and drink with them. [5]When a period of feasting had run its course, Job would send and have them purified. Early in the morning he would sacrifice a burnt offering for each of them, thinking, "Perhaps my children have sinned and cursed God in their hearts." This was Job's regular custom.

Job's First Test

[6]One day the angels[a] came to present themselves before the LORD, and Satan[b] also came with them. [7]The LORD said to Satan, "Where have you come from?"

Satan answered the LORD, "From roaming through the earth and going back and forth in it."

[8]Then the LORD said to Satan, "Have you considered my servant Job? There is no one on earth like him; he is blameless and upright, a man who fears God and shuns evil."

[9]"Does Job fear God for nothing?" Satan replied. [10]"Have you not put a hedge around him and his household and everything he has? You have blessed the work of his hands, so that his flocks and herds are spread throughout the land. [11]But stretch out your hand and strike everything he has, and he will surely curse you to your face."

[12]The LORD said to Satan, "Very well, then, everything he has is in your hands, but on the man himself do not lay a finger."

Then Satan went out from the presence of the LORD.

[13]One day when Job's sons and daughters were feasting and drinking wine at the oldest brother's house, [14]a messenger came to Job and said, "The oxen were plowing and the donkeys were grazing nearby, [15]and the Sabeans attacked and carried them off. They put the servants to the sword, and I am the

[a]6 Hebrew *the sons of God* [b]6 *Satan* means *accuser.*

only one who has escaped to tell you!"
16While he was still speaking, another
messenger came and said, "The fire of
God fell from the sky and burned up the
sheep and the servants, and I am the
only one who has escaped to tell you!"
17While he was still speaking, another
messenger came and said, "The Chaldeans formed three raiding parties and
swept down on your camels and carried
them off. They put the servants to the
sword, and I am the only one who has
escaped to tell you!"
18While he was still speaking, yet another messenger came and said, "Your
sons and daughters were feasting and
drinking wine at the oldest brother's
house, 19when suddenly a mighty wind
swept in from the desert and struck the
four corners of the house. It collapsed
on them and they are dead, and I am the
only one who has escaped to tell you!"
20At this, Job got up and tore his robe
and shaved his head. Then he fell to the
ground in worship 21and said:

"Naked I came from my mother's
womb,
and naked I will depart.[a]
The LORD gave and the LORD has
taken away;
may the name of the LORD be
praised."

22In all this, Job did not sin by charging God with wrongdoing.

[a]21 Or *will return there*

SHARPEN THE FOCUS

When trouble strikes, people often ask themselves, "What have I done to deserve this?" But as we see in Job 1, maybe we should ask instead, "What have I been doing right?" Job honored God, and still trouble came. Not all our trials spring from personal wrongdoing.

The Scriptures urge us to examine our hearts often. All of us need to confess that we daily sin much and deserve nothing but punishment from God. But God has punished Jesus in our place. All of God's wrath at human sin fell on Christ as He hung on Calvary. God will never punish you or me for our sins. Our debt has been paid in full by our Savior.

No question, Job suffered terribly. But the Scriptures leave no doubt about the source of that suffering. Job suffered Satan's attack, not God's divine retribution for his sins.

So, if you or someone you love is suffering today, know that your Lord is on your side. He has taken your guilt. He wants to comfort you with the Good News of His forgiveness and His limitless love. Let Him do that.

WEEK 42 • MONDAY

Job 2:1—3:26

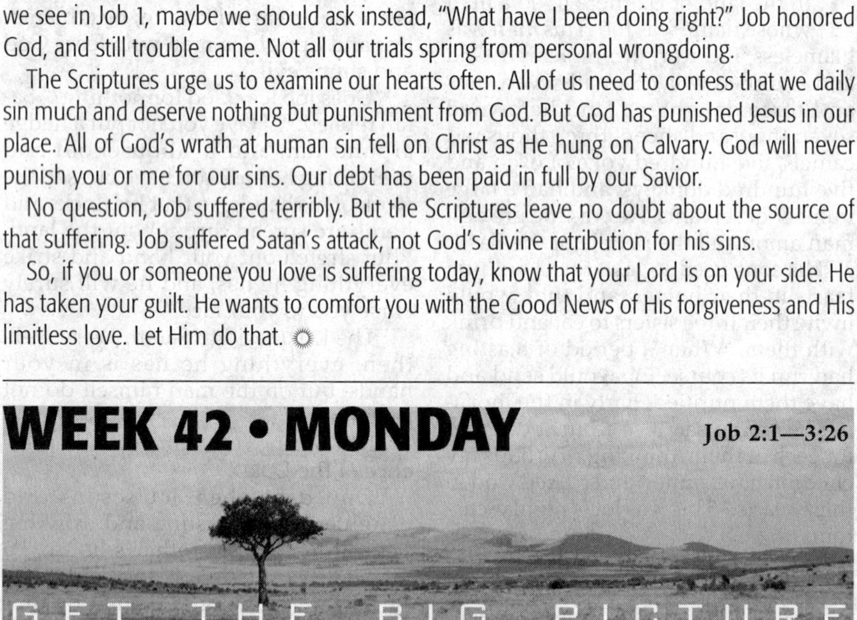

GET THE BIG PICTURE

Jesus once described Satan as a thief who comes only to kill, to steal, and to destroy. (John 10:10). In Job 2, Satan proves the words of Jesus true. As you read today, note the fact that Scripture does not minimize Job's suffering; it was indeed great. Also ask yourself what would have been in your mind and on your heart had you sat in the ash heap with Job and his three friends. If time is short, focus on Job 3:1–25.

Job's Second Test

2 On another day the angels[a] came
to present themselves before the
LORD, and Satan also came with them to
present himself before him. 2And the
LORD said to Satan, "Where have you
come from?"
Satan answered the LORD, "From
roaming through the earth and going
back and forth in it."
3Then the LORD said to Satan, "Have
you considered my servant Job? There
is no one on earth like him; he is blameless and upright, a man who fears God
and shuns evil. And he still maintains
his integrity, though you incited me
against him to ruin him without any
reason."
4"Skin for skin!" Satan replied. "A man
will give all he has for his own life. 5But
stretch out your hand and strike his
flesh and bones, and he will surely curse
you to your face."
6The LORD said to Satan, "Very well,
then, he is in your hands; but you must
spare his life."
7So Satan went out from the presence
of the LORD and afflicted Job with painful sores from the soles of his feet to the
top of his head. 8Then Job took a piece
of broken pottery and scraped himself
with it as he sat among the ashes.
9His wife said to him, "Are you still
holding on to your integrity? Curse God
and die!"
10He replied, "You are talking like a
foolish[b] woman. Shall we accept good
from God, and not trouble?"
In all this, Job did not sin in what he
said.

Job's Three Friends

11When Job's three friends, Eliphaz
the Temanite, Bildad the Shuhite and
Zophar the Naamathite, heard about all
the troubles that had come upon him,
they set out from their homes and met
together by agreement to go and sympathize with him and comfort him.
12When they saw him from a distance,
they could hardly recognize him; they
began to weep aloud, and they tore
their robes and sprinkled dust on their
heads. 13Then they sat on the ground
with him for seven days and seven
nights. No one said a word to him,
because they saw how great his suffering was.

Job Speaks

3 After this, Job opened his mouth
and cursed the day of his birth.
2He said:

3"May the day of my birth perish,
and the night it was said, 'A boy is born!'
4That day—may it turn to darkness;
may God above not care about it;
may no light shine upon it.
5May darkness and deep shadow[c] claim it once more;
may a cloud settle over it;
may blackness overwhelm its light.
6That night—may thick darkness seize it;
may it not be included among the days of the year
nor be entered in any of the months.
7May that night be barren;
may no shout of joy be heard in it.
8May those who curse days[d] curse that day,
those who are ready to rouse Leviathan.
9May its morning stars become dark;
may it wait for daylight in vain
and not see the first rays of dawn,
10for it did not shut the doors of the womb on me
to hide trouble from my eyes.

11"Why did I not perish at birth,
and die as I came from the womb?
12Why were there knees to receive me
and breasts that I might be nursed?
13For now I would be lying down in peace;

[a]1 Hebrew *the sons of God* [b]10 The Hebrew word rendered *foolish* denotes moral deficiency.
[c]5 Or *and the shadow of death* [d]8 Or *the sea*

I would be asleep and at rest
[14] with kings and counselors of the
earth,
who built for themselves places
now lying in ruins,
[15] with rulers who had gold,
who filled their houses with
silver.
[16] Or why was I not hidden in the
ground like a stillborn child,
like an infant who never saw the
light of day?
[17] There the wicked cease from
turmoil,
and there the weary are at rest.
[18] Captives also enjoy their ease;
they no longer hear the slave
driver's shout.
[19] The small and the great are there,
and the slave is freed from his
master.
[20] "Why is light given to those in
misery,
and life to the bitter of soul,
[21] to those who long for death that
does not come,
who search for it more than for
hidden treasure,
[22] who are filled with gladness
and rejoice when they reach the
grave?
[23] Why is life given to a man
whose way is hidden,
whom God has hedged in?
[24] For sighing comes to me instead of
food;
my groans pour out like water.
[25] What I feared has come upon me;
what I dreaded has happened to
me.
[26] I have no peace, no quietness;
I have no rest, but only turmoil."

SHARPEN THE FOCUS

They sat in silence. For a week! So great was Job's suffering. So puzzling were God's ways. No one there had overheard the conversation that occurred in heaven's throne room. No one saw Satan strut or heard his arrogant challenge to the Almighty. And each of them harbored suspicions about God's goodness and about His justice.

Much of what happened to Job and much of what happens to us seems to make no sense. We will not know all the answers until we come to our heavenly home. Between now and then we will at times sail rough seas.

The question for us, as for Job, remains, "Can we trust the Captain of our ship?" Throughout most of the early part of his storm, Job did trust. But by Job 3:23, he begins to waver. As a result, he begins to lose his peace (Job 3:25–26). The voyage grows rockier from there on out.

Sometimes Jesus calms our storms. More often, He reaches out to steady His children while we ride out those storms. If He's reaching out to you like that today, don't push Him away. Let Him hold you in His arms and comfort you. Unlike Job, you've seen your Lord stretched out on Calvary's cross *for you.* Your pain may be a mystery, but your Savior's love *for you* is crystal clear.

WEEK 42 • TUESDAY

Job 4:1—5:27

GET THE BIG PICTURE

In the next chapters, three of Job's friends speak to him about the calamities that have befallen him. The advice they give sounds a lot like much "folk wisdom" today. At the end of the book, God will reprimand these three friends for not speaking the truth about Him (Job 42:7–9). So, read carefully. Ask the Holy Spirit for discernment and true wisdom. If time is short, focus on Job 4:1–21.

Eliphaz

4 Then Eliphaz the Temanite replied:

2 "If someone ventures a word with you, will you be impatient?
But who can keep from speaking?
3 Think how you have instructed many,
how you have strengthened feeble hands.
4 Your words have supported those who stumbled;
you have strengthened faltering knees.
5 But now trouble comes to you, and you are discouraged;
it strikes you, and you are dismayed.
6 Should not your piety be your confidence
and your blameless ways your hope?

7 "Consider now: Who, being innocent, has ever perished?
Where were the upright ever destroyed?
8 As I have observed, those who plow evil
and those who sow trouble reap it.
9 At the breath of God they are destroyed;
at the blast of his anger they perish.
10 The lions may roar and growl,
yet the teeth of the great lions are broken.
11 The lion perishes for lack of prey,
and the cubs of the lioness are scattered.

12 "A word was secretly brought to me,
my ears caught a whisper of it.
13 Amid disquieting dreams in the night,
when deep sleep falls on men,
14 fear and trembling seized me
and made all my bones shake.
15 A spirit glided past my face,
and the hair on my body stood on end.
16 It stopped,
but I could not tell what it was.
A form stood before my eyes,
and I heard a hushed voice:
17 'Can a mortal be more righteous than God?
Can a man be more pure than his Maker?
18 If God places no trust in his servants,
if he charges his angels with error,
19 how much more those who live in houses of clay,
whose foundations are in the dust,
who are crushed more readily than a moth!
20 Between dawn and dusk they are broken to pieces;
unnoticed, they perish forever.

21 Are not the cords of their tent pulled up,
so that they die without wisdom?'[a]

5 "Call if you will, but who will answer you?
To which of the holy ones will you turn?
2 Resentment kills a fool,
and envy slays the simple.
3 I myself have seen a fool taking root,
but suddenly his house was cursed.
4 His children are far from safety,
crushed in court without a defender.
5 The hungry consume his harvest,
taking it even from among thorns,
and the thirsty pant after his wealth.
6 For hardship does not spring from the soil,
nor does trouble sprout from the ground.
7 Yet man is born to trouble
as surely as sparks fly upward.

8 "But if it were I, I would appeal to God;
I would lay my cause before him.
9 He performs wonders that cannot be fathomed,
miracles that cannot be counted.
10 He bestows rain on the earth;
he sends water upon the countryside.
11 The lowly he sets on high,
and those who mourn are lifted to safety.
12 He thwarts the plans of the crafty,
so that their hands achieve no success.
13 He catches the wise in their craftiness,
and the schemes of the wily are swept away.
14 Darkness comes upon them in the daytime;
at noon they grope as in the night.
15 He saves the needy from the sword in their mouth;
he saves them from the clutches of the powerful.
16 So the poor have hope,
and injustice shuts its mouth.

17 "Blessed is the man whom God corrects;
so do not despise the discipline of the Almighty.[b]
18 For he wounds, but he also binds up;
he injures, but his hands also heal.
19 From six calamities he will rescue you;
in seven no harm will befall you.
20 In famine he will ransom you from death,
and in battle from the stroke of the sword.
21 You will be protected from the lash of the tongue,
and need not fear when destruction comes.
22 You will laugh at destruction and famine,
and need not fear the beasts of the earth.
23 For you will have a covenant with the stones of the field,
and the wild animals will be at peace with you.
24 You will know that your tent is secure;
you will take stock of your property and find nothing missing.
25 You will know that your children will be many,
and your descendants like the grass of the earth.
26 You will come to the grave in full vigor,
like sheaves gathered in season.

27 "We have examined this, and it is true.
So hear it and apply it to yourself."

[a] *21* Some interpreters end the quotation after verse 17. [b] *17* Hebrew *Shaddai*; here and throughout Job

SHARPEN THE FOCUS

In the mind of Eliphaz, and still in many people's minds today, "those who plow evil and those who sow trouble reap it" (Job 4:8). While sin does sometimes bring consequences into our lives, not every hardship we face has been caused by a specific, personal sin. Scripture is quite clear on that point.

Eliphaz's error endangers the faith of anyone who believes it, partly because it leads us to believe that the opposite is also true—if life goes well, it's because we've been good enough to earn special favors from our Father (Job 4:6). Yet, if we place our hope in our "blameless ways," we'll soon find ourselves hopeless.

Our hope and confidence in bad times and good must rest in our Lord Jesus. He is our hope. He is our help. Whether you're miserable today or outrageously happy, that truth stands secure. Confess to Him the sins that trouble you, and then relax in the peace of His pardon. All of your guilt has been taken away. All of your sin has been atoned for.

WEEK 42 • WEDNESDAY

Job 6:1—7:21

GET THE BIG PICTURE

Job answers Eliphaz's hints that Job has sinned. He declares himself innocent, and as he talks about his feelings, he describes symptoms most sufferers will recognize—grief, fear, loneliness, the fatigue of sleepless nights, and such a deep desire to be rid of pain that death seems better than life. As you read, think about what Job's friends might have done to bring him better comfort and help. If time is short, focus on Job 6:1–30.

Job

6 Then Job replied:

2 "If only my anguish could be weighed
and all my misery be placed on the scales!
3 It would surely outweigh the sand of the seas—
no wonder my words have been impetuous.
4 The arrows of the Almighty are in me,
my spirit drinks in their poison;
God's terrors are marshaled against me.
5 Does a wild donkey bray when it has grass,
or an ox bellow when it has fodder?
6 Is tasteless food eaten without salt,
or is there flavor in the white of an egg[a]?
7 I refuse to touch it;
such food makes me ill.

8 "Oh, that I might have my request,
that God would grant what I hope for,
9 that God would be willing to crush me,
to let loose his hand and cut me off!

[a]6 The meaning of the Hebrew for this phrase is uncertain.

[10]Then I would still have this
consolation—
my joy in unrelenting pain—
that I had not denied the words of
the Holy One.
[11]"What strength do I have, that I
should still hope?
What prospects, that I should be
patient?
[12]Do I have the strength of stone?
Is my flesh bronze?
[13]Do I have any power to help
myself,
now that success has been driven
from me?
[14]"A despairing man should have the
devotion of his friends,
even though he forsakes the fear
of the Almighty.
[15]But my brothers are as
undependable as
intermittent streams,
as the streams that overflow
[16]when darkened by thawing ice
and swollen with melting snow,
[17]but that cease to flow in the dry
season,
and in the heat vanish from their
channels.
[18]Caravans turn aside from their
routes;
they go up into the wasteland and
perish.
[19]The caravans of Tema look for water,
the traveling merchants of Sheba
look in hope.
[20]They are distressed, because they
had been confident;
they arrive there, only to be
disappointed.
[21]Now you too have proved to be of
no help;
you see something dreadful and
are afraid.
[22]Have I ever said, 'Give something on
my behalf,
pay a ransom for me from your
wealth,
[23]deliver me from the hand of the
enemy,
ransom me from the clutches of
the ruthless'?
[24]"Teach me, and I will be quiet;
show me where I have been
wrong.
[25]How painful are honest words!
But what do your arguments
prove?
[26]Do you mean to correct what I say,
and treat the words of a
despairing man as wind?
[27]You would even cast lots for the
fatherless
and barter away your friend.
[28]"But now be so kind as to look at me.
Would I lie to your face?
[29]Relent, do not be unjust;
reconsider, for my integrity is at
stake.[a]
[30]Is there any wickedness on my lips?
Can my mouth not discern
malice?

7 "Does not man have hard
service on earth?
Are not his days like those of a
hired man?
[2]Like a slave longing for the evening
shadows,
or a hired man waiting eagerly for
his wages,
[3]so I have been allotted months of
futility,
and nights of misery have been
assigned to me.
[4]When I lie down I think, 'How long
before I get up?'
The night drags on, and I toss till
dawn.
[5]My body is clothed with worms and
scabs,
my skin is broken and festering.
[6]"My days are swifter than a
weaver's shuttle,
and they come to an end without
hope.
[7]Remember, O God, that my life is
but a breath;
my eyes will never see happiness
again.
[8]The eye that now sees me will see
me no longer;

[a]29 Or *my righteousness still stands*

you will look for me, but I will be
no more.
9 As a cloud vanishes and is gone,
so he who goes down to the
grave[a] does not return.
10 He will never come to his house
again;
his place will know him no more.

11 "Therefore I will not keep silent;
I will speak out in the anguish of
my spirit,
I will complain in the bitterness of
my soul.
12 Am I the sea, or the monster of the
deep,
that you put me under guard?
13 When I think my bed will comfort
me
and my couch will ease my
complaint,
14 even then you frighten me with
dreams
and terrify me with visions,
15 so that I prefer strangling and death,
rather than this body of mine.
16 I despise my life; I would not live
forever.
Let me alone; my days have no
meaning.
17 "What is man that you make so
much of him,
that you give him so much
attention,
18 that you examine him every
morning
and test him every moment?
19 Will you never look away from me,
or let me alone even for an instant?
20 If I have sinned, what have I done to
you,
O watcher of men?
Why have you made me your
target?
Have I become a burden to you?[b]
21 Why do you not pardon my offenses
and forgive my sins?
For I will soon lie down in the dust;
you will search for me, but I will
be no more."

[a]9 Hebrew *Sheol* [b]20 A few manuscripts of the Masoretic Text, an ancient Hebrew scribal tradition and Septuagint; most manuscripts of the Masoretic Text *I have become a burden to myself.*

SHARPEN THE FOCUS

I'm afraid I'll lose my faith. That may be Job's deepest fear. And as God's people today face pain and loss, we too may find this fear most troubling.

It's true that faith can grow during difficult times. But Scripture shows us that trouble makes people cynical about as often as it makes them stronger. In fact, our outward circumstances, whether good or bad, are pretty much spiritually neutral.

Our Lord clearly tells us how faith is sustained and how it grows. *He* is the one who creates and sustains our faith. *He's* the one who holds on to us; we do not bring ourselves to faith or keep ourselves in the faith.

When trouble hits us hard, when we long for sleep that never comes, when we sit alone in the darkness of a fear-filled future, we can remember that our faithful Lord will sustain us. He comes to us in His Word and in the Holy Supper. He reminds us that our feelings of despair cannot change the fact of His love for us. He will never fail us, nor forsake us.

So when we, ourselves, or those we love suffer, faith cannot be our focus. Instead, we look to Jesus—the one who has given us faith and the one who will keep us in that faith (Hebrews 12:2–3).

WEEK 42 • THURSDAY

Job 8:1—10:22

GET THE BIG PICTURE

Job's second friend, Bildad, takes over from Eliphaz. He, too, assumes Satan's role–as the accuser of God's people. Notice, as you read, how faith and doubt wrestle with each other in Job's heart. If time is short, focus on Job 9:1–22.

Bildad

8 Then Bildad the Shuhite replied:

2 "How long will you say such things?
Your words are a blustering wind.
3 Does God pervert justice?
Does the Almighty pervert what is right?
4 When your children sinned against him,
he gave them over to the penalty of their sin.
5 But if you will look to God
and plead with the Almighty,
6 if you are pure and upright,
even now he will rouse himself on your behalf
and restore you to your rightful place.
7 Your beginnings will seem humble,
so prosperous will your future be.

8 "Ask the former generations
and find out what their fathers learned,
9 for we were born only yesterday
and know nothing,
and our days on earth are but a shadow.
10 Will they not instruct you and tell you?
Will they not bring forth words
from their understanding?
11 Can papyrus grow tall where there is no marsh?
Can reeds thrive without water?
12 While still growing and uncut,
they wither more quickly than grass.
13 Such is the destiny of all who forget God;
so perishes the hope of the godless.
14 What he trusts in is fragile[a];
what he relies on is a spider's web.
15 He leans on his web, but it gives way;
he clings to it, but it does not hold.
16 He is like a well-watered plant in the sunshine,
spreading its shoots over the garden;
17 it entwines its roots around a pile of rocks
and looks for a place among the stones.
18 But when it is torn from its spot,
that place disowns it and says,
'I never saw you.'
19 Surely its life withers away,
and[b] from the soil other plants grow.

20 "Surely God does not reject a blameless man
or strengthen the hands of evildoers.
21 He will yet fill your mouth with laughter
and your lips with shouts of joy.
22 Your enemies will be clothed in shame,
and the tents of the wicked will be no more."

[a]14 The meaning of the Hebrew for this word is uncertain. [b]19 Or *Surely all the joy it has / is that*

Job

9

Then Job replied:

2 "Indeed, I know that this is true.
But how can a mortal be righteous before God?
3 Though one wished to dispute with him,
he could not answer him one time out of a thousand.
4 His wisdom is profound, his power is vast.
Who has resisted him and come out unscathed?
5 He moves mountains without their knowing it
and overturns them in his anger.
6 He shakes the earth from its place
and makes its pillars tremble.
7 He speaks to the sun and it does not shine;
he seals off the light of the stars.
8 He alone stretches out the heavens
and treads on the waves of the sea.
9 He is the Maker of the Bear and Orion,
the Pleiades and the constellations of the south.
10 He performs wonders that cannot be fathomed,
miracles that cannot be counted.
11 When he passes me, I cannot see him;
when he goes by, I cannot perceive him.
12 If he snatches away, who can stop him?
Who can say to him, 'What are you doing?'
13 God does not restrain his anger;
even the cohorts of Rahab cowered at his feet.

14 "How then can I dispute with him?
How can I find words to argue with him?
15 Though I were innocent, I could not answer him;
I could only plead with my Judge for mercy.
16 Even if I summoned him and he responded,
I do not believe he would give me a hearing.
17 He would crush me with a storm
and multiply my wounds for no reason.
18 He would not let me regain my breath
but would overwhelm me with misery.
19 If it is a matter of strength, he is mighty!
And if it is a matter of justice, who will summon him[a]?
20 Even if I were innocent, my mouth would condemn me;
if I were blameless, it would pronounce me guilty.

21 "Although I am blameless,
I have no concern for myself;
I despise my own life.
22 It is all the same; that is why I say,
'He destroys both the blameless and the wicked.'
23 When a scourge brings sudden death,
he mocks the despair of the innocent.
24 When a land falls into the hands of the wicked,
he blindfolds its judges.
If it is not he, then who is it?

25 "My days are swifter than a runner;
they fly away without a glimpse of joy.
26 They skim past like boats of papyrus,
like eagles swooping down on their prey.
27 If I say, 'I will forget my complaint,
I will change my expression, and smile,'
28 I still dread all my sufferings,
for I know you will not hold me innocent.
29 Since I am already found guilty,
why should I struggle in vain?
30 Even if I washed myself with soap[b]
and my hands with washing soda,
31 you would plunge me into a slime pit

[a]*19* See Septuagint; Hebrew *me.* [b]*30* Or *snow*

so that even my clothes would
detest me.

32 "He is not a man like me that I might
answer him,
that we might confront each other
in court.
33 If only there were someone to
arbitrate between us,
to lay his hand upon us both,
34 someone to remove God's rod from
me,
so that his terror would frighten
me no more.
35 Then I would speak up without fear
of him,
but as it now stands with me, I
cannot.

10 "I loathe my very life;
therefore I will give free
rein to my complaint
and speak out in the bitterness of
my soul.
2 I will say to God: Do not condemn
me,
but tell me what charges you have
against me.
3 Does it please you to oppress me,
to spurn the work of your hands,
while you smile on the schemes of
the wicked?
4 Do you have eyes of flesh?
Do you see as a mortal sees?
5 Are your days like those of a mortal
or your years like those of a man,
6 that you must search out my faults
and probe after my sin—
7 though you know that I am not
guilty
and that no one can rescue me
from your hand?

8 "Your hands shaped me and made
me.
Will you now turn and destroy
me?
9 Remember that you molded me like
clay.
Will you now turn me to dust
again?
10 Did you not pour me out like milk
and curdle me like cheese,
11 clothe me with skin and flesh
and knit me together with bones
and sinews?
12 You gave me life and showed me
kindness,
and in your providence watched
over my spirit.

13 "But this is what you concealed in
your heart,
and I know that this was in your
mind:
14 If I sinned, you would be watching
me
and would not let my offense go
unpunished.
15 If I am guilty—woe to me!
Even if I am innocent, I cannot lift
my head,
for I am full of shame
and drowned in[a] my affliction.
16 If I hold my head high, you stalk me
like a lion
and again display your awesome
power against me.
17 You bring new witnesses against me
and increase your anger toward
me;
your forces come against me wave
upon wave.

18 "Why then did you bring me out of
the womb?
I wish I had died before any eye
saw me.
19 If only I had never come into being,
or had been carried straight from
the womb to the grave!
20 Are not my few days almost over?
Turn away from me so I can have
a moment's joy
21 before I go to the place of no return,
to the land of gloom and deep
shadow,[b]
22 to the land of deepest night,
of deep shadow and disorder,
where even the light is like
darkness."

[a]15 Or *and aware of* [b]21 Or *and the shadow of death;* also in verse 22

SHARPEN THE FOCUS

"If you're good enough, and pray hard enough, God will give you a second chance." That, in essence, is Bildad's message (Job 8:5–7). Apparently he believes that Job needs more Law. Job, he thinks, hasn't yet felt sorry enough for his sins. He hasn't thrown himself into prayer sincerely enough.

No doubt Bildad meant well. But Job sees the trap at once. "How can I be righteous enough?" he asks (see Job 9:2). The answer is obvious. He can't be. Neither can we. We can't pray hard enough, or earnestly enough, or purely enough. We can't bring our own "righteous" words and acts to God and expect Him to be impressed.

We would be without hope if it weren't for the fact that we have a merciful Judge. We *do* have the Mediator for whom Job longed (Job 9:33). Jesus Christ is our righteousness. We who sat in our sins wearing the rags of our own supposed goodness have now been clothed in Christ's own robe of righteousness. We can indeed take our case before our Judge and receive the verdict "not guilty."

And because of that, we can take all our other needs to God, too, knowing that He will hear and help, because our Savior Himself pleads for us (Romans 8:34–39).

WEEK 42 • FRIDAY

Job 11:1—12:25

GET THE BIG PICTURE

Job's third friend, Zophar, speaks next. A tone of spiritual smugness oozes from his words: "You might fool us with your protests of purity, Job. But you can't fool God." As you read, notice Zophar's insistence that good things happen to good people and disasters afflict the wicked. Then notice Job's reply—Not always! If time is short, focus on Job 11:1–20.

Zophar

11 Then Zophar the Naamathite replied:

2 "Are all these words to go
unanswered?
Is this talker to be vindicated?
3 Will your idle talk reduce men to
silence?
Will no one rebuke you when you
mock?
4 You say to God, 'My beliefs are
flawless
and I am pure in your sight.'
5 Oh, how I wish that God would
speak,
that he would open his lips
against you
6 and disclose to you the secrets of
wisdom,
for true wisdom has two sides.
Know this: God has even
forgotten some of your sin.

7 "Can you fathom the mysteries of
God?
Can you probe the limits of the
Almighty?

8 They are higher than the heavens—
what can you do?
They are deeper than the depths
of the grave[a]—what can you
know?
9 Their measure is longer than the
earth
and wider than the sea.

10 "If he comes along and confines you
in prison
and convenes a court, who can
oppose him?
11 Surely he recognizes deceitful men;
and when he sees evil, does he
not take note?
12 But a witless man can no more
become wise
than a wild donkey's colt can be
born a man.[b]

13 "Yet if you devote your heart to him
and stretch out your hands to
him,
14 if you put away the sin that is in
your hand
and allow no evil to dwell in your
tent,
15 then you will lift up your face
without shame;
you will stand firm and without
fear.
16 You will surely forget your trouble,
recalling it only as waters gone by.
17 Life will be brighter than noonday,
and darkness will become like
morning.
18 You will be secure, because there is
hope;
you will look about you and take
your rest in safety.
19 You will lie down, with no one to
make you afraid,
and many will court your favor.
20 But the eyes of the wicked will fail,
and escape will elude them;
their hope will become a dying
gasp."

Job

12 Then Job replied:

2 "Doubtless you are the people,
and wisdom will die with you!
3 But I have a mind as well as you;
I am not inferior to you.
Who does not know all these
things?

4 "I have become a laughingstock to
my friends,
though I called upon God and he
answered—
a mere laughingstock, though
righteous and blameless!
5 Men at ease have contempt for
misfortune
as the fate of those whose feet are
slipping.
6 The tents of marauders are
undisturbed,
and those who provoke God are
secure—
those who carry their god in their
hands.[c]

7 "But ask the animals, and they will
teach you,
or the birds of the air, and they
will tell you;
8 or speak to the earth, and it will
teach you,
or let the fish of the sea inform
you.
9 Which of all these does not know
that the hand of the LORD has
done this?
10 In his hand is the life of every
creature
and the breath of all mankind.
11 Does not the ear test words
as the tongue tastes food?
12 Is not wisdom found among the
aged?
Does not long life bring
understanding?

13 "To God belong wisdom and
power;
counsel and understanding are
his.
14 What he tears down cannot be
rebuilt;
the man he imprisons cannot be
released.

[a]8 Hebrew *than Sheol* [b]12 Or *wild donkey can be born tame* [c]6 Or *secure / in what God's hand brings them*

[15]If he holds back the waters, there is drought;
if he lets them loose, they devastate the land.
[16]To him belong strength and victory;
both deceived and deceiver are his.
[17]He leads counselors away stripped
and makes fools of judges.
[18]He takes off the shackles put on by kings
and ties a loincloth[a] around their waist.
[19]He leads priests away stripped
and overthrows men long established.
[20]He silences the lips of trusted advisers
and takes away the discernment of elders.
[21]He pours contempt on nobles
and disarms the mighty.
[22]He reveals the deep things of darkness
and brings deep shadows into the light.
[23]He makes nations great, and destroys them;
he enlarges nations, and disperses them.
[24]He deprives the leaders of the earth of their reason;
he sends them wandering through a trackless waste.
[25]They grope in darkness with no light;
he makes them stagger like drunkards.

[a]18 Or *shackles of kings / and ties a belt*

SHARPEN THE FOCUS

How simple life would be if it worked the way Zophar thought it did. We all would like to draw a straight arrow from obedience to blessings, from sin to hardship. But as Job pointed out, life isn't always so simple. Sometimes those who hate God prosper; sometimes those who love God suffer.

In much of the rest of the book, Job wrestles with this problem as he tries to untangle the knotted mess of his life. For now, it's important for us to acknowledge what Job did. We need to face up to the truth that our Lord doesn't always do things in the way we would wish. He doesn't always act according to our proposed time table.

When the straight arrows tie themselves up into knots, we sometimes panic. When our stomach knots up in fear, when our throat tightens in anger, when our eyes blink back hot tears, just then Satan will tempt us to believe that we can't trust God when we can't understand Him.

But we who have seen Christ's cross and open tomb have a shelter from the storms of guilt and the hurricanes of doubt. Our Savior shares our sorrows just as one day we will, by His grace, share His glory. We can rest in His love, even when we do not understand His ways.

WEEK 42 • SATURDAY

Job 13:1—14:22

GET THE BIG PICTURE

In Job 13, Job denounces the simplistic answers his friends propose. He turns to God in an angry, frustrated prayer. Then, in Job 14, Job muses about his ongoing misery as he longs for death. As you read, note the raw honesty of both his prayers. If time is short, focus on Job 14:1–22.

13 "My eyes have seen all this,
my ears have heard and
understood it.
2 What you know, I also know;
I am not inferior to you.
3 But I desire to speak to the Almighty
and to argue my case with God.
4 You, however, smear me with lies;
you are worthless physicians, all
of you!
5 If only you would be altogether
silent!
For you, that would be wisdom.
6 Hear now my argument;
listen to the plea of my lips.
7 Will you speak wickedly on God's
behalf?
Will you speak deceitfully for
him?
8 Will you show him partiality?
Will you argue the case for God?
9 Would it turn out well if he
examined you?
Could you deceive him as you
might deceive men?
10 He would surely rebuke you
if you secretly showed partiality.
11 Would not his splendor terrify you?
Would not the dread of him fall on
you?
12 Your maxims are proverbs of ashes;
your defenses are defenses of clay.

13 "Keep silent and let me speak;
then let come to me what may.
14 Why do I put myself in jeopardy
and take my life in my hands?
15 Though he slay me, yet will I hope
in him;
I will surely[a] defend my ways to
his face.
16 Indeed, this will turn out for my
deliverance,
for no godless man would dare
come before him!
17 Listen carefully to my words;
let your ears take in what I say.
18 Now that I have prepared my case,
I know I will be vindicated.
19 Can anyone bring charges against
me?
If so, I will be silent and die.

20 "Only grant me these two things,
O God,
and then I will not hide from you:
21 Withdraw your hand far from me,
and stop frightening me with
your terrors.
22 Then summon me and I will answer,
or let me speak, and you reply.
23 How many wrongs and sins have I
committed?
Show me my offense and my sin.
24 Why do you hide your face
and consider me your enemy?
25 Will you torment a windblown leaf?
Will you chase after dry chaff?
26 For you write down bitter things
against me
and make me inherit the sins of
my youth.
27 You fasten my feet in shackles;
you keep close watch on all my
paths

[a]15 Or *He will surely slay me; I have no hope — / yet I will*

by putting marks on the soles of
my feet.
28 "So man wastes away like
something rotten,
like a garment eaten by moths.

14 "Man born of woman
is of few days and full of
trouble.
2 He springs up like a flower and
withers away;
like a fleeting shadow, he does not
endure.
3 Do you fix your eye on such a one?
Will you bring him[a] before you for
judgment?
4 Who can bring what is pure from
the impure?
No one!
5 Man's days are determined;
you have decreed the number of
his months
and have set limits he cannot
exceed.
6 So look away from him and let him
alone,
till he has put in his time like a
hired man.
7 "At least there is hope for a tree:
If it is cut down, it will sprout
again,
and its new shoots will not fail.
8 Its roots may grow old in the ground
and its stump die in the soil,
9 yet at the scent of water it will bud
and put forth shoots like a plant.
10 But man dies and is laid low;
he breathes his last and is no
more.
11 As water disappears from the sea
or a riverbed becomes parched
and dry,
12 so man lies down and does not rise;
till the heavens are no more, men
will not awake
or be roused from their sleep.
13 "If only you would hide me in the
grave[b]
and conceal me till your anger has
passed!
If only you would set me a time
and then remember me!
14 If a man dies, will he live again?
All the days of my hard service
I will wait for my renewal[c] to come.
15 You will call and I will answer you;
you will long for the creature your
hands have made.
16 Surely then you will count my steps
but not keep track of my sin.
17 My offenses will be sealed up in a
bag;
you will cover over my sin.
18 "But as a mountain erodes and
crumbles
and as a rock is moved from its
place,
19 as water wears away stones
and torrents wash away the soil,
so you destroy man's hope.
20 You overpower him once for all, and
he is gone;
you change his countenance and
send him away.
21 If his sons are honored, he does not
know it;
if they are brought low, he does
not see it.
22 He feels but the pain of his own
body
and mourns only for himself."

[a]3 Septuagint, Vulgate and Syriac; Hebrew *me*
[b]13 Hebrew *Sheol* [c]14 Or *release*

SHARPEN THE FOCUS

"If a man dies, will he live again?" (Job 14:14). When the pains and burdens of life in this world grow too heavy, people often start to think about the escape death may provide. In fact, when our struggles grow intense, we may find it easier to trust our Lord to bring us safely through death than to sustain us in our life.

Maybe you've stood at the edge of that cliff. As Job's eyes gazed toward death's horizon, he said to the Lord, "You will call and I will answer You; You will long for the creature Your hands have made" (Job 14:15). Job had no way of knowing what God has now revealed to us in Scripture about our eternal home. But Job knew that the Lord would not abandon him in death. God would, in love, reach out to keep him safe. That confidence amidst death strengthened Job for life, hard as his lot was at that moment.

We too can cling in confidence to our Savior-God in life and in death. Because Jesus' tomb is empty, we know that beyond death is our eternal home. There, our Father reigns forever as King. No pain, death, tears, frustration, hell, or sin will stalk us there. We will live forever free, God's forgiven children, sealed by the power of His cross.

WEEK 43 • MONDAY

Job 15:1—17:16

Eliphaz uses sharper words as he confronts Job the second time with accusations of sin. As you read, notice that Job's doubts have escalated to the point that he now believes that God must hate him, albeit unjustly (Job 16:9). If time is short, focus on Job 16:1–22.

Eliphaz

15 Then Eliphaz the Temanite replied:

2 "Would a wise man answer with empty notions
or fill his belly with the hot east wind?
3 Would he argue with useless words,
with speeches that have no value?
4 But you even undermine piety
and hinder devotion to God.
5 Your sin prompts your mouth;
you adopt the tongue of the crafty.
6 Your own mouth condemns you, not mine;
your own lips testify against you.

7 "Are you the first man ever born?
Were you brought forth before the hills?
8 Do you listen in on God's council?
Do you limit wisdom to yourself?
9 What do you know that we do not know?
What insights do you have that we do not have?
10 The gray-haired and the aged are on our side,
men even older than your father.
11 Are God's consolations not enough for you,
words spoken gently to you?
12 Why has your heart carried you away,
and why do your eyes flash,
13 so that you vent your rage against God
and pour out such words from your mouth?

14 "What is man, that he could be pure,
or one born of woman, that he could be righteous?
15 If God places no trust in his holy ones,
if even the heavens are not pure in his eyes,
16 how much less man, who is vile and corrupt,
who drinks up evil like water!

17 "Listen to me and I will explain to you;
let me tell you what I have seen,
18 what wise men have declared,
hiding nothing received from their fathers
19 (to whom alone the land was given
when no alien passed among them):
20 All his days the wicked man suffers torment,
the ruthless through all the years stored up for him.
21 Terrifying sounds fill his ears;
when all seems well, marauders attack him.
22 He despairs of escaping the darkness;
he is marked for the sword.
23 He wanders about—food for vultures[a];
he knows the day of darkness is at hand.
24 Distress and anguish fill him with terror;
they overwhelm him, like a king poised to attack,
25 because he shakes his fist at God
and vaunts himself against the Almighty,
26 defiantly charging against him
with a thick, strong shield.

27 "Though his face is covered with fat
and his waist bulges with flesh,
28 he will inhabit ruined towns
and houses where no one lives,
houses crumbling to rubble.
29 He will no longer be rich and his wealth will not endure,
nor will his possessions spread over the land.
30 He will not escape the darkness;
a flame will wither his shoots,
and the breath of God's mouth will carry him away.
31 Let him not deceive himself by trusting what is worthless,
for he will get nothing in return.
32 Before his time he will be paid in full,
and his branches will not flourish.
33 He will be like a vine stripped of its unripe grapes,
like an olive tree shedding its blossoms.
34 For the company of the godless will be barren,
and fire will consume the tents of those who love bribes.
35 They conceive trouble and give birth to evil;
their womb fashions deceit."

Job

16

Then Job replied:

2 "I have heard many things like these;
miserable comforters are you all!
3 Will your long-winded speeches never end?
What ails you that you keep on arguing?
4 I also could speak like you,
if you were in my place;
I could make fine speeches against you
and shake my head at you.
5 But my mouth would encourage you;
comfort from my lips would bring you relief.

6 "Yet if I speak, my pain is not relieved;
and if I refrain, it does not go away.
7 Surely, O God, you have worn me out;
you have devastated my entire household.
8 You have bound me—and it has become a witness;
my gauntness rises up and testifies against me.
9 God assails me and tears me in his anger
and gnashes his teeth at me;
my opponent fastens on me his piercing eyes.
10 Men open their mouths to jeer at me;
they strike my cheek in scorn

[a] 23 Or *about, looking for food*

and unite together against me.
[11]God has turned me over to evil men
and thrown me into the clutches of the wicked.
[12]All was well with me, but he shattered me;
he seized me by the neck and crushed me.
He has made me his target;
[13] his archers surround me.
Without pity, he pierces my kidneys
and spills my gall on the ground.
[14]Again and again he bursts upon me;
he rushes at me like a warrior.

[15]"I have sewed sackcloth over my skin
and buried my brow in the dust.
[16]My face is red with weeping,
deep shadows ring my eyes;
[17]yet my hands have been free of violence
and my prayer is pure.

[18]"O earth, do not cover my blood;
may my cry never be laid to rest!
[19]Even now my witness is in heaven;
my advocate is on high.
[20]My intercessor is my friend[a]
as my eyes pour out tears to God;
[21]on behalf of a man he pleads with God
as a man pleads for his friend.

[22]"Only a few years will pass
before I go on the journey of no return.

17

[1]My spirit is broken,
my days are cut short,
the grave awaits me.
[2]Surely mockers surround me;
my eyes must dwell on their hostility.

[3]"Give me, O God, the pledge you demand.
Who else will put up security for me?
[4]You have closed their minds to understanding;
therefore you will not let them triumph.
[5]If a man denounces his friends for reward,
the eyes of his children will fail.

[6]"God has made me a byword to everyone,
a man in whose face people spit.
[7]My eyes have grown dim with grief;
my whole frame is but a shadow.
[8]Upright men are appalled at this;
the innocent are aroused against the ungodly.
[9]Nevertheless, the righteous will hold to their ways,
and those with clean hands will grow stronger.

[10]"But come on, all of you, try again!
I will not find a wise man among you.
[11]My days have passed, my plans are shattered,
and so are the desires of my heart.
[12]These men turn night into day;
in the face of darkness they say, 'Light is near.'
[13]If the only home I hope for is the grave,[b]
if I spread out my bed in darkness,
[14]if I say to corruption, 'You are my father,'
and to the worm, 'My mother' or 'My sister,'
[15]where then is my hope?
Who can see any hope for me?
[16]Will it go down to the gates of death[b]?
Will we descend together into the dust?"

[a]20 Or *My friends treat me with scorn*
[b]13,16 Hebrew *Sheol*

SHARPEN THE FOCUS

It's easy to shout insults at the umpire—until you stand behind home plate, calling the game. It was easy for Job's friends to find fault with him, too. But what if they sat in the ash pile where he sat? That's the gist of Job's comment in Job 16:4. "I also could speak like you, if you were in my place."

All three of his friends must have thought to themselves: "If God could let this happen to Job, then I'm at risk too!" It's no wonder they kept trying to prove Job guilty of some secret, heinous crime. If Job wasn't a wicked scoundrel whom God punished for hidden sins, then Job's fate could befall anyone!

The truth is that we are all vulnerable. All of us, God's people too, live in a fallen world. And while sometimes the Lord may allow troubles to come because we're caught up in sin, most often, trouble is not a sign that we're out of fellowship with the Lord. Given enough pressure, any of us could shake our fist at God as Job did in Job 16:6–14.

The Good News is that God did not give up on Job. Our Savior listened, understood, forgave. Jesus listens, understands, and forgives us, too, especially when we're frustrated beyond words and too worn out even to cry.

WEEK 43 • TUESDAY

Job 18:1—19:29

GET THE BIG PICTURE

Bildad speaks for the second time. His theories about God's ways are, like those of his friends, rooted in fear and in spiritual pride. Job, overcome by isolation from God and from other people, nonetheless moves from the depths of despair to the high ground of faith in his Redeemer. If time is short, focus on Job 19:1–29.

Bildad

18 Then Bildad the Shuhite replied:

2 "When will you end these speeches?
Be sensible, and then we can talk.
3 Why are we regarded as cattle
and considered stupid in your sight?
4 You who tear yourself to pieces in your anger,
is the earth to be abandoned for your sake?
Or must the rocks be moved from their place?

5 "The lamp of the wicked is snuffed out;
the flame of his fire stops burning.
6 The light in his tent becomes dark;
the lamp beside him goes out.
7 The vigor of his step is weakened;
his own schemes throw him down.
8 His feet thrust him into a net
and he wanders into its mesh.
9 A trap seizes him by the heel;
a snare holds him fast.
10 A noose is hidden for him on the ground;
a trap lies in his path.
11 Terrors startle him on every side
and dog his every step.
12 Calamity is hungry for him;
disaster is ready for him when he falls.
13 It eats away parts of his skin;
death's firstborn devours his limbs.

14 He is torn from the security of his tent
and marched off to the king of terrors.
15 Fire resides[a] in his tent;
burning sulfur is scattered over his dwelling.
16 His roots dry up below
and his branches wither above.
17 The memory of him perishes from the earth;
he has no name in the land.
18 He is driven from light into darkness
and is banished from the world.
19 He has no offspring or descendants among his people,
no survivor where once he lived.
20 Men of the west are appalled at his fate;
men of the east are seized with horror.
21 Surely such is the dwelling of an evil man;
such is the place of one who knows not God."

Job

19

Then Job replied:

2 "How long will you torment me
and crush me with words?
3 Ten times now you have reproached me;
shamelessly you attack me.
4 If it is true that I have gone astray,
my error remains my concern alone.
5 If indeed you would exalt yourselves above me
and use my humiliation against me,
6 then know that God has wronged me
and drawn his net around me.

7 "Though I cry, 'I've been wronged!' I get no response;
though I call for help, there is no justice.
8 He has blocked my way so I cannot pass;
he has shrouded my paths in darkness.
9 He has stripped me of my honor
and removed the crown from my head.
10 He tears me down on every side till I am gone;
he uproots my hope like a tree.
11 His anger burns against me;
he counts me among his enemies.
12 His troops advance in force;
they build a siege ramp against me
and encamp around my tent.

13 "He has alienated my brothers from me;
my acquaintances are completely estranged from me.
14 My kinsmen have gone away;
my friends have forgotten me.
15 My guests and my maidservants count me a stranger;
they look upon me as an alien.
16 I summon my servant, but he does not answer,
though I beg him with my own mouth.
17 My breath is offensive to my wife;
I am loathsome to my own brothers.
18 Even the little boys scorn me;
when I appear, they ridicule me.
19 All my intimate friends detest me;
those I love have turned against me.
20 I am nothing but skin and bones;
I have escaped with only the skin of my teeth.[b]

21 "Have pity on me, my friends, have pity,
for the hand of God has struck me.
22 Why do you pursue me as God does?
Will you never get enough of my flesh?

23 "Oh, that my words were recorded,
that they were written on a scroll,
24 that they were inscribed with an iron tool on[c] lead,

[a]15 Or *Nothing he had remains* [b]20 Or *only my gums* [c]24 Or *and*

or engraved in rock forever!
25 I know that my Redeemer[a] lives,
and that in the end he will stand
upon the earth.[b]
26 And after my skin has been
destroyed,
yet[c] in[d] my flesh I will see God;
27 I myself will see him
with my own eyes—I, and not
another.
How my heart yearns within me!

28 "If you say, 'How we will hound
him,
since the root of the trouble lies in
him,'[e]
29 you should fear the sword
yourselves;
for wrath will bring punishment
by the sword,
and then you will know that there
is judgment.[f]"

[a]25 Or *defender* [b]25 Or *upon my grave*
[c]26 Or *And after I awake, / though this* ⌊*body*⌋ *has been destroyed, / then* [d]26 Or */ apart from*
[e]28 Many Hebrew manuscripts, Septuagint and Vulgate; most Hebrew manuscripts *me* [f]29 Or */ that you may come to know the Almighty*

SHARPEN THE FOCUS

Maybe you've fished your favorite lake or stream, a bobber attached to your line. If the stream's current flowed swiftly or the wind made the lake's surface rough, you no doubt saw the bobber disappear under the water, dance above the surface, and then pop beneath the waves again.

Job's faith was a little like that. It bobbed up and down seeming to drown at times, only to resurface again, perhaps brighter than before. Take today's reading. In Job 19:6, Job complains that God has wronged him. But in Job 19:25–27, we read one of the Old Testament's most confident affirmations of the "resurrection of the body and the life everlasting." Job would live forever because of his Redeemer.

And so will we. But we don't always ride along above the waves of discouragement. Sometimes our circumstances can seem to drown our hope. Sometimes, like the great apostle Paul, we "despair of life itself" (2 Corinthians 1:8). But like Job, like Paul, we take comfort in our Redeemer. We rest our hope in His death and resurrection for us. Not even our faithlessness can cancel our Lord's faithful promises to us.

WEEK 43 • WEDNESDAY

Job 20:1—21:34

GET THE BIG PICTURE

Same song. Sixth verse. This time Zophar takes up the chorus. He alters the refrain a bit. "Maybe the wicked *do* briefly prosper, but they don't enjoy it. God rains on their picnic," Zophar sings (see Job 20:23). He sounds a bit like the fox in Aesop's "sour grapes" fable. Job replies by asking a question: "How often *do* the wicked really suffer?" If time is short, focus on Job 21:1–34.

Zophar

20

Then Zophar the Naamathite replied:

[2]"My troubled thoughts prompt me to answer
because I am greatly disturbed.
[3]I hear a rebuke that dishonors me,
and my understanding inspires me to reply.

[4]"Surely you know how it has been from of old,
ever since man[a] was placed on the earth,
[5]that the mirth of the wicked is brief,
the joy of the godless lasts but a moment.
[6]Though his pride reaches to the heavens
and his head touches the clouds,
[7]he will perish forever, like his own dung;
those who have seen him will say, 'Where is he?'
[8]Like a dream he flies away, no more to be found,
banished like a vision of the night.
[9]The eye that saw him will not see him again;
his place will look on him no more.
[10]His children must make amends to the poor;
his own hands must give back his wealth.
[11]The youthful vigor that fills his bones
will lie with him in the dust.

[12]"Though evil is sweet in his mouth
and he hides it under his tongue,
[13]though he cannot bear to let it go
and keeps it in his mouth,
[14]yet his food will turn sour in his stomach;
it will become the venom of serpents within him.
[15]He will spit out the riches he swallowed;
God will make his stomach vomit them up.
[16]He will suck the poison of serpents;
the fangs of an adder will kill him.
[17]He will not enjoy the streams,
the rivers flowing with honey and cream.
[18]What he toiled for he must give back uneaten;
he will not enjoy the profit from his trading.
[19]For he has oppressed the poor and left them destitute;
he has seized houses he did not build.

[20]"Surely he will have no respite from his craving;
he cannot save himself by his treasure.
[21]Nothing is left for him to devour;
his prosperity will not endure.
[22]In the midst of his plenty, distress will overtake him;
the full force of misery will come upon him.
[23]When he has filled his belly,
God will vent his burning anger against him
and rain down his blows upon him.
[24]Though he flees from an iron weapon,
a bronze-tipped arrow pierces him.
[25]He pulls it out of his back,
the gleaming point out of his liver.
Terrors will come over him;
[26] total darkness lies in wait for his treasures.
A fire unfanned will consume him
and devour what is left in his tent.
[27]The heavens will expose his guilt;
the earth will rise up against him.
[28]A flood will carry off his house,
rushing waters[b] on the day of God's wrath.
[29]Such is the fate God allots the wicked,
the heritage appointed for them by God."

Job

21

Then Job replied:

[2]"Listen carefully to my words;

[a]4 Or *Adam* [b]28 Or *The possessions in his house will be carried off, / washed away*

let this be the consolation you
give me.
3 Bear with me while I speak,
and after I have spoken, mock on.

4 "Is my complaint directed to man?
Why should I not be impatient?
5 Look at me and be astonished;
clap your hand over your mouth.
6 When I think about this, I am
terrified;
trembling seizes my body.
7 Why do the wicked live on,
growing old and increasing in
power?
8 They see their children established
around them,
their offspring before their eyes.
9 Their homes are safe and free from
fear;
the rod of God is not upon them.
10 Their bulls never fail to breed;
their cows calve and do not
miscarry.
11 They send forth their children as a
flock;
their little ones dance about.
12 They sing to the music of
tambourine and harp;
they make merry to the sound of
the flute.
13 They spend their years in
prosperity
and go down to the grave[a] in
peace.[b]
14 Yet they say to God, 'Leave us alone!
We have no desire to know your
ways.
15 Who is the Almighty, that we should
serve him?
What would we gain by praying
to him?'
16 But their prosperity is not in their
own hands,
so I stand aloof from the counsel
of the wicked.

17 "Yet how often is the lamp of the
wicked snuffed out?
How often does calamity come
upon them,
the fate God allots in his anger?
18 How often are they like straw before
the wind,
like chaff swept away by a gale?
19 It is said, 'God stores up a man's
punishment for his sons.'
Let him repay the man himself, so
that he will know it!
20 Let his own eyes see his destruction;
let him drink of the wrath of the
Almighty.[c]
21 For what does he care about the
family he leaves behind
when his allotted months come to
an end?

22 "Can anyone teach knowledge to
God,
since he judges even the highest?
23 One man dies in full vigor,
completely secure and at ease,
24 his body[d] well nourished,
his bones rich with marrow.
25 Another man dies in bitterness of
soul,
never having enjoyed anything
good.
26 Side by side they lie in the dust,
and worms cover them both.

27 "I know full well what you are
thinking,
the schemes by which you would
wrong me.
28 You say, 'Where now is the great
man's house,
the tents where wicked men lived?'
29 Have you never questioned those
who travel?
Have you paid no regard to their
accounts—
30 that the evil man is spared from the
day of calamity,
that he is delivered from[e] the day
of wrath?
31 Who denounces his conduct to his
face?
Who repays him for what he has
done?
32 He is carried to the grave,
and watch is kept over his tomb.

[a]13 Hebrew *Sheol* [b]13 Or *in an instant*
[c]17-20 Verses 17 and 18 may be taken as exclamations and 19 and 20 as declarations.
[d]24 The meaning of the Hebrew for this word is uncertain. [e]30 Or *man is reserved for the day of calamity, / that he is brought forth to*

33 The soil in the valley is sweet to him;
all men follow after him,
and a countless throng goes[a]
before him.

34 "So how can you console me with
your nonsense?
Nothing is left of your answers
but falsehood!"

SHARPEN THE FOCUS

As we think about knowing God and His ways, how thankful we can be that the Holy Spirit inspired the book of Romans. There, the apostle Paul lays out clearly and methodically the answer to the question: How does God deal with His sinful human creatures? He points us to our Savior's death in our place, and to the fact that because of Jesus, we are now right with God. What wonderful news!

But how thankful we can also be that the Spirit inspired the book of Job!

Job and Zophar have locked horns over an issue, but it's not their real issue. Job's heart and soul ache. Zophar and the others struggle with hearts filled with fear and frustration, as we do at times. But not one of us will receive from God what we need if we keep on "ministering" to one another by arguing.

Have you ever tried to solve the problem of pain by trying to figure God out? Are you struggling to answer a friend's *why* with logical arguments? Most often when we ask our *whys*, we're not asking our real question. We really mean to say, "Can I trust You, God, even when I don't understand?"

Yes! Because of the truth God has told us in Romans and in Job. In both books, the Holy Spirit welds the Gospel truth to our emptiness to provide the strength and the comfort we need in Christ.

WEEK 43 • THURSDAY

Job 22:1—24:25

GET THE BIG PICTURE

Eliphaz speaks up for the third (and last time). He suggests a specific sin of which Job is probably guilty—cruelty toward the poor and failure to show them compassion. "You thought you could hide it from God," Eliphaz thunders. "But now you're found out." Job seems to shake his head. Not replying to Eliphaz at all, he cries out for justice. "If only we could go to court, I'd sue for peace," Job says. If time is short, focus on Job 23:1–17.

Eliphaz

22 Then Eliphaz the Temanite replied:

2 "Can a man be of benefit to God?
Can even a wise man benefit him?

3 What pleasure would it give the
Almighty if you were
righteous?

[a]33 Or / *as a countless throng went*

What would he gain if your ways
were blameless?

4 "Is it for your piety that he rebukes
you
and brings charges against you?
5 Is not your wickedness great?
Are not your sins endless?
6 You demanded security from your
brothers for no reason;
you stripped men of their
clothing, leaving them
naked.
7 You gave no water to the weary
and you withheld food from the
hungry,
8 though you were a powerful man,
owning land—
an honored man, living on it.
9 And you sent widows away
empty-handed
and broke the strength of the
fatherless.
10 That is why snares are all around
you,
why sudden peril terrifies you,
11 why it is so dark you cannot see,
and why a flood of water covers
you.

12 "Is not God in the heights of
heaven?
And see how lofty are the highest
stars!
13 Yet you say, 'What does God know?
Does he judge through such
darkness?
14 Thick clouds veil him, so he does not
see us
as he goes about in the vaulted
heavens.'
15 Will you keep to the old path
that evil men have trod?
16 They were carried off before their
time,
their foundations washed away by
a flood.
17 They said to God, 'Leave us
alone!
What can the Almighty do to us?'
18 Yet it was he who filled their houses
with good things,
so I stand aloof from the counsel
of the wicked.

19 "The righteous see their ruin and
rejoice;
the innocent mock them, saying,
20 'Surely our foes are destroyed,
and fire devours their wealth.'

21 "Submit to God and be at peace with
him;
in this way prosperity will come
to you.
22 Accept instruction from his mouth
and lay up his words in your
heart.
23 If you return to the Almighty, you
will be restored:
If you remove wickedness far
from your tent
24 and assign your nuggets to the
dust,
your gold of Ophir to the rocks in
the ravines,
25 then the Almighty will be your
gold,
the choicest silver for you.
26 Surely then you will find delight in
the Almighty
and will lift up your face to God.
27 You will pray to him, and he will
hear you,
and you will fulfill your vows.
28 What you decide on will be done,
and light will shine on your ways.
29 When men are brought low and you
say, 'Lift them up!'
then he will save the downcast.
30 He will deliver even one who is not
innocent,
who will be delivered through the
cleanness of your hands."

Job

23

Then Job replied:

2 "Even today my complaint is bitter;
his hand[a] is heavy in spite of[b] my
groaning.
3 If only I knew where to find him;
if only I could go to his dwelling!
4 I would state my case before him
and fill my mouth with
arguments.

[a]2 Septuagint and Syriac; Hebrew / *the hand on me* [b]2 Or *heavy on me in*

[5]I would find out what he would
answer me,
and consider what he would say.
[6]Would he oppose me with great
power?
No, he would not press charges
against me.
[7]There an upright man could present
his case before him,
and I would be delivered forever
from my judge.

[8]"But if I go to the east, he is not there;
if I go to the west, I do not find
him.
[9]When he is at work in the north, I
do not see him;
when he turns to the south, I
catch no glimpse of him.
[10]But he knows the way that I take;
when he has tested me, I will
come forth as gold.
[11]My feet have closely followed his
steps;
I have kept to his way without
turning aside.
[12]I have not departed from the
commands of his lips;
I have treasured the words of his
mouth more than my daily
bread.

[13]"But he stands alone, and who can
oppose him?
He does whatever he pleases.
[14]He carries out his decree against me,
and many such plans he still has
in store.
[15]That is why I am terrified before
him;
when I think of all this, I fear him.
[16]God has made my heart faint;
the Almighty has terrified me.
[17]Yet I am not silenced by the
darkness,
by the thick darkness that covers
my face.

24

"Why does the Almighty
not set times for
judgment?
Why must those who know him
look in vain for such days?
[2]Men move boundary stones;
they pasture flocks they have
stolen.
[3]They drive away the orphan's
donkey
and take the widow's ox in
pledge.
[4]They thrust the needy from the path
and force all the poor of the land
into hiding.
[5]Like wild donkeys in the desert,
the poor go about their labor of
foraging food;
the wasteland provides food for
their children.
[6]They gather fodder in the fields
and glean in the vineyards of the
wicked.
[7]Lacking clothes, they spend the
night naked;
they have nothing to cover
themselves in the cold.
[8]They are drenched by mountain
rains
and hug the rocks for lack of
shelter.
[9]The fatherless child is snatched from
the breast;
the infant of the poor is seized for
a debt.
[10]Lacking clothes, they go about
naked;
they carry the sheaves, but still go
hungry.
[11]They crush olives among the
terraces[a];
they tread the winepresses, yet
suffer thirst.
[12]The groans of the dying rise from
the city,
and the souls of the wounded cry
out for help.
But God charges no one with
wrongdoing.

[13]"There are those who rebel against
the light,
who do not know its ways
or stay in its paths.
[14]When daylight is gone, the
murderer rises up
and kills the poor and needy;

[a]11 Or *olives between the millstones;* the meaning of the Hebrew for this word is uncertain.

in the night he steals forth like a
thief.
15 The eye of the adulterer watches for
dusk;
he thinks, 'No eye will see me,'
and he keeps his face concealed.
16 In the dark, men break into houses,
but by day they shut themselves
in;
they want nothing to do with the
light.
17 For all of them, deep darkness is
their morning[a];
they make friends with the terrors
of darkness.[b]

18 "Yet they are foam on the surface of
the water;
their portion of the land is cursed,
so that no one goes to the
vineyards.
19 As heat and drought snatch away
the melted snow,
so the grave[c] snatches away those
who have sinned.
20 The womb forgets them,
the worm feasts on them;
evil men are no longer remembered
but are broken like a tree.
21 They prey on the barren and
childless woman,
and to the widow show no
kindness.
22 But God drags away the mighty by
his power;
though they become established,
they have no assurance of
life.
23 He may let them rest in a feeling of
security,
but his eyes are on their ways.
24 For a little while they are exalted,
and then they are gone;
they are brought low and
gathered up like all others;
they are cut off like heads of grain.

25 "If this is not so, who can prove me
false
and reduce my words to
nothing?"

[a]17 Or *them, their morning is like the shadow of death* [b]17 Or *of the shadow of death* [c]19 Hebrew *Sheol*

SHARPEN THE FOCUS

In his pain, Job falls back on an old, convincing argument. "This must be God's will," he says in essence (Job 23:14). Fatalism. What will be will be. Disasters that occur in our world are "acts of God." This doctrine is one of Islam's main tenets. But fatalism like this knows no place in Christianity. Case in point: *Who* caused Job's suffering? Not God. But our enemy. And our Lord's enemy.

Yes, God allowed it. Theologians sometimes call this "God's permissive will." But our Lord stands firmly on Job's side, even when Job fails to realize it. Our Lord will bring Job through suffering, *safely* through suffering. And our Lord will use Satan's scheme of hatred for Job's ultimate good. Even in his fear, Job clings to this (Job 23:10).

The same holds true for God's suffering children today. "The thief comes only to steal and kill and destroy," our Savior warns in John 10:10. "I have come that they may have life, and have it to the full."

Satan brings pain and death. Jesus brings joy and life. How could our Lord have said it more plainly? Jesus is our ally. Cling to Him. You can count on Him to bring you through the darkness (compare Job 23:17).

The book of Job begins slowly to move toward resolution from Job 28 onward. While Job still hurts and harbors resentment toward the Lord (Job 27:2), the tone and content of his words shift subtly. As the Holy Spirit works, Job begins to see the limits of his ability to understand God's ways. As you read, look for evidence of this. If time is short, focus on Job 28:1–28.

Bildad

25 Then Bildad the Shuhite replied:

2 "Dominion and awe belong to God;
he establishes order in the heights of heaven.
3 Can his forces be numbered?
Upon whom does his light not rise?
4 How then can a man be righteous before God?
How can one born of woman be pure?
5 If even the moon is not bright
and the stars are not pure in his eyes,
6 how much less man, who is but a maggot—
a son of man, who is only a worm!"

Job

26 Then Job replied:

2 "How you have helped the powerless!
How you have saved the arm that is feeble!
3 What advice you have offered to one without wisdom!
And what great insight you have displayed!
4 Who has helped you utter these words?
And whose spirit spoke from your mouth?

5 "The dead are in deep anguish,
those beneath the waters and all that live in them.
6 Death[a] is naked before God;
Destruction[b] lies uncovered.
7 He spreads out the northern ⌊skies⌋ over empty space;
he suspends the earth over nothing.
8 He wraps up the waters in his clouds,
yet the clouds do not burst under their weight.
9 He covers the face of the full moon,
spreading his clouds over it.
10 He marks out the horizon on the face of the waters
for a boundary between light and darkness.
11 The pillars of the heavens quake,
aghast at his rebuke.
12 By his power he churned up the sea;
by his wisdom he cut Rahab to pieces.
13 By his breath the skies became fair;
his hand pierced the gliding serpent.
14 And these are but the outer fringe of his works;
how faint the whisper we hear of him!
Who then can understand the thunder of his power?"

[a]6 Hebrew *Sheol* [b]6 Hebrew *Abaddon*

27

And Job continued his discourse:

2 "As surely as God lives, who has denied me justice,
the Almighty, who has made me taste bitterness of soul,
3 as long as I have life within me,
the breath of God in my nostrils,
4 my lips will not speak wickedness,
and my tongue will utter no deceit.
5 I will never admit you are in the right;
till I die, I will not deny my integrity.
6 I will maintain my righteousness
and never let go of it;
my conscience will not reproach me as long as I live.

7 "May my enemies be like the wicked,
my adversaries like the unjust!
8 For what hope has the godless when he is cut off,
when God takes away his life?
9 Does God listen to his cry
when distress comes upon him?
10 Will he find delight in the Almighty?
Will he call upon God at all times?

11 "I will teach you about the power of God;
the ways of the Almighty I will not conceal.
12 You have all seen this yourselves.
Why then this meaningless talk?

13 "Here is the fate God allots to the wicked,
the heritage a ruthless man receives from the Almighty:
14 However many his children, their fate is the sword;
his offspring will never have enough to eat.
15 The plague will bury those who survive him,
and their widows will not weep for them.
16 Though he heaps up silver like dust
and clothes like piles of clay,
17 what he lays up the righteous will wear,
and the innocent will divide his silver.
18 The house he builds is like a moth's cocoon,
like a hut made by a watchman.
19 He lies down wealthy, but will do so no more;
when he opens his eyes, all is gone.
20 Terrors overtake him like a flood;
a tempest snatches him away in the night.
21 The east wind carries him off, and he is gone;
it sweeps him out of his place.
22 It hurls itself against him without mercy
as he flees headlong from its power.
23 It claps its hands in derision
and hisses him out of his place.

28

"There is a mine for silver
and a place where gold is refined.
2 Iron is taken from the earth,
and copper is smelted from ore.
3 Man puts an end to the darkness;
he searches the farthest recesses
for ore in the blackest darkness.
4 Far from where people dwell he cuts a shaft,
in places forgotten by the foot of man;
far from men he dangles and sways.
5 The earth, from which food comes,
is transformed below as by fire;
6 sapphires[a] come from its rocks,
and its dust contains nuggets of gold.
7 No bird of prey knows that hidden path,
no falcon's eye has seen it.
8 Proud beasts do not set foot on it,
and no lion prowls there.
9 Man's hand assaults the flinty rock
and lays bare the roots of the mountains.
10 He tunnels through the rock;
his eyes see all its treasures.

[a]6 Or *lapis lazuli*; also in verse 16

[11] He searches[a] the sources of the rivers
and brings hidden things to light.

[12] "But where can wisdom be found?
Where does understanding dwell?
[13] Man does not comprehend its worth;
it cannot be found in the land of the living.
[14] The deep says, 'It is not in me';
the sea says, 'It is not with me.'
[15] It cannot be bought with the finest gold,
nor can its price be weighed in silver.
[16] It cannot be bought with the gold of Ophir,
with precious onyx or sapphires.
[17] Neither gold nor crystal can compare with it,
nor can it be had for jewels of gold.
[18] Coral and jasper are not worthy of mention;
the price of wisdom is beyond rubies.
[19] The topaz of Cush cannot compare with it;
it cannot be bought with pure gold.

[20] "Where then does wisdom come from?
Where does understanding dwell?
[21] It is hidden from the eyes of every living thing,
concealed even from the birds of the air.
[22] Destruction[b] and Death say,
'Only a rumor of it has reached our ears.'
[23] God understands the way to it
and he alone knows where it dwells,
[24] for he views the ends of the earth
and sees everything under the heavens.
[25] When he established the force of the wind
and measured out the waters,
[26] when he made a decree for the rain
and a path for the thunderstorm,
[27] then he looked at wisdom and appraised it;
he confirmed it and tested it.
[28] And he said to man,
'The fear of the Lord—that is wisdom,
and to shun evil is understanding.' "

[a] *11* Septuagint, Aquila and Vulgate; Hebrew *He dams up* [b] 22 Hebrew *Abaddon*

SHARPEN THE FOCUS

Human wisdom relies on reason. Godly wisdom comes from revelation. Only as God comes to us and reveals Himself to us can we know true wisdom. Unless He does that, we'll never experience His victory over the trauma and turmoil that comes into our life.

Human wisdom enables us to do all the things Job lists in Job 28:1–11 and more. But reason has its limits. If we're blessed with a strong intellect, we can sometimes think that we're wrestling with God, when in reality our true enemy is a refusal to trust Him when life seems unreasonable. Our Lord doesn't want us to forget about reason altogether. He gave us our intellectual abilities, and He considers them a good gift. But at some point as we suffer, reason must give way to the relationship our Savior has made possible.

Jesus who suffered the agony of hell on the cross for us has promised to stay with us in our own pain. He will be our light in deep darkness, our strength when we grow weary, and our peace in desperate circumstances.

"When Christ is all you have, you learn that Christ is all you need." Suffering saints down through the ages have testified that it's true. He is our life (Deuteronomy 30:20; Colossians 3:4).

WEEK 43 • SATURDAY

Job speaks the words of these three chapters almost to himself, although he does offer a brief prayer in Job 30:20–23. In Job 31, he examines his heart for specific sins, almost as though he has begun to wonder whether the accusations of his friends might be true. As you read, note the result of that self-examination and notice Job's new plea for a fair trial in heaven's courtroom. If time is short, focus on Job 31:35–40.

29

Job continued his discourse:

2 "How I long for the months gone by,
for the days when God watched over me,
3 when his lamp shone upon my head
and by his light I walked through darkness!
4 Oh, for the days when I was in my prime,
when God's intimate friendship blessed my house,
5 when the Almighty was still with me
and my children were around me,
6 when my path was drenched with cream
and the rock poured out for me streams of olive oil.

7 "When I went to the gate of the city
and took my seat in the public square,
8 the young men saw me and stepped aside
and the old men rose to their feet;
9 the chief men refrained from speaking
and covered their mouths with their hands;
10 the voices of the nobles were hushed,
and their tongues stuck to the roof of their mouths.
11 Whoever heard me spoke well of me,
and those who saw me commended me,
12 because I rescued the poor who cried for help,
and the fatherless who had none to assist him.
13 The man who was dying blessed me;
I made the widow's heart sing.
14 I put on righteousness as my clothing;
justice was my robe and my turban.
15 I was eyes to the blind
and feet to the lame.
16 I was a father to the needy;
I took up the case of the stranger.
17 I broke the fangs of the wicked
and snatched the victims from their teeth.

18 "I thought, 'I will die in my own house,
my days as numerous as the grains of sand.
19 My roots will reach to the water,
and the dew will lie all night on my branches.
20 My glory will remain fresh in me,
the bow ever new in my hand.'

21 "Men listened to me expectantly,
waiting in silence for my counsel.
22 After I had spoken, they spoke no more;
my words fell gently on their ears.
23 They waited for me as for showers
and drank in my words as the spring rain.
24 When I smiled at them, they scarcely believed it;

the light of my face was precious
to them.[a]
25 I chose the way for them and sat as
their chief;
I dwelt as a king among his
troops;
I was like one who comforts
mourners.

30

"But now they mock me,
men younger than I,
whose fathers I would have
disdained
to put with my sheep dogs.
2 Of what use was the strength of
their hands to me,
since their vigor had gone from
them?
3 Haggard from want and hunger,
they roamed[b] the parched land
in desolate wastelands at night.
4 In the brush they gathered salt
herbs,
and their food[c] was the root of the
broom tree.
5 They were banished from their
fellow men,
shouted at as if they were thieves.
6 They were forced to live in the dry
stream beds,
among the rocks and in holes in
the ground.
7 They brayed among the bushes
and huddled in the undergrowth.
8 A base and nameless brood,
they were driven out of the land.

9 "And now their sons mock me in
song;
I have become a byword among
them.
10 They detest me and keep their
distance;
they do not hesitate to spit in my
face.
11 Now that God has unstrung my bow
and afflicted me,
they throw off restraint in my
presence.
12 On my right the tribe[d] attacks;
they lay snares for my feet,
they build their siege ramps
against me.
13 They break up my road;
they succeed in destroying me—
without anyone's helping them.[e]
14 They advance as through a gaping
breach;
amid the ruins they come rolling
in.
15 Terrors overwhelm me;
my dignity is driven away as by
the wind,
my safety vanishes like a cloud.

16 "And now my life ebbs away;
days of suffering grip me.
17 Night pierces my bones;
my gnawing pains never rest.
18 In his great power ⌊God⌋ becomes
like clothing to me[f];
he binds me like the neck of my
garment.
19 He throws me into the mud,
and I am reduced to dust and
ashes.

20 "I cry out to you, O God, but you do
not answer;
I stand up, but you merely look at
me.
21 You turn on me ruthlessly;
with the might of your hand you
attack me.
22 You snatch me up and drive me
before the wind;
you toss me about in the storm.
23 I know you will bring me down to
death,
to the place appointed for all the
living.

24 "Surely no one lays a hand on a
broken man
when he cries for help in his
distress.
25 Have I not wept for those in
trouble?
Has not my soul grieved for the
poor?
26 Yet when I hoped for good, evil
came;

[a]24 The meaning of the Hebrew for this clause is uncertain. [b]3 Or *gnawed* [c]4 Or *fuel* [d]12 The meaning of the Hebrew for this word is uncertain. [e]13 Or *me. / 'No one can help him,' ⌊they say⌋.* [f]18 Hebrew; Septuagint *⌊God⌋ grasps my clothing*

when I looked for light, then came darkness.
27 The churning inside me never stops;
days of suffering confront me.
28 I go about blackened, but not by the sun;
I stand up in the assembly and cry for help.
29 I have become a brother of jackals,
a companion of owls.
30 My skin grows black and peels;
my body burns with fever.
31 My harp is tuned to mourning,
and my flute to the sound of wailing.

31 "I made a covenant with my eyes
not to look lustfully at a girl.
2 For what is man's lot from God above,
his heritage from the Almighty on high?
3 Is it not ruin for the wicked,
disaster for those who do wrong?
4 Does he not see my ways
and count my every step?

5 "If I have walked in falsehood
or my foot has hurried after deceit—
6 let God weigh me in honest scales
and he will know that I am blameless—
7 if my steps have turned from the path,
if my heart has been led by my eyes,
or if my hands have been defiled,
8 then may others eat what I have sown,
and may my crops be uprooted.

9 "If my heart has been enticed by a woman,
or if I have lurked at my neighbor's door,
10 then may my wife grind another man's grain,
and may other men sleep with her.
11 For that would have been shameful,
a sin to be judged.
12 It is a fire that burns to Destruction[a];
it would have uprooted my harvest.

13 "If I have denied justice to my menservants and maidservants
when they had a grievance against me,
14 what will I do when God confronts me?
What will I answer when called to account?
15 Did not he who made me in the womb make them?
Did not the same one form us both within our mothers?

16 "If I have denied the desires of the poor
or let the eyes of the widow grow weary,
17 if I have kept my bread to myself,
not sharing it with the fatherless—
18 but from my youth I reared him as would a father,
and from my birth I guided the widow—
19 if I have seen anyone perishing for lack of clothing,
or a needy man without a garment,
20 and his heart did not bless me
for warming him with the fleece from my sheep,
21 if I have raised my hand against the fatherless,
knowing that I had influence in court,
22 then let my arm fall from the shoulder,
let it be broken off at the joint.
23 For I dreaded destruction from God,
and for fear of his splendor I could not do such things.

24 "If I have put my trust in gold
or said to pure gold, 'You are my security,'
25 if I have rejoiced over my great wealth,
the fortune my hands had gained,

[a] 12 Hebrew *Abaddon*

[26]if I have regarded the sun in its
radiance
or the moon moving in splendor,
[27]so that my heart was secretly
enticed
and my hand offered them a kiss
of homage,
[28]then these also would be sins to be
judged,
for I would have been unfaithful
to God on high.

[29]"If I have rejoiced at my enemy's
misfortune
or gloated over the trouble that
came to him—
[30]I have not allowed my mouth to sin
by invoking a curse against his
life—
[31]if the men of my household have
never said,
'Who has not had his fill of Job's
meat?'—
[32]but no stranger had to spend the
night in the street,
for my door was always open to
the traveler—
[33]if I have concealed my sin as men
do,[a]
by hiding my guilt in my heart
[34]because I so feared the crowd
and so dreaded the contempt of
the clans
that I kept silent and would not go
outside
[35]("Oh, that I had someone to hear
me!
I sign now my defense—let the
Almighty answer me;
let my accuser put his indictment
in writing.
[36]Surely I would wear it on my
shoulder,
I would put it on like a crown.
[37]I would give him an account of my
every step;
like a prince I would approach
him.)—

[38]"if my land cries out against me
and all its furrows are wet with
tears,
[39]if I have devoured its yield without
payment
or broken the spirit of its tenants,
[40]then let briers come up instead of
wheat
and weeds instead of barley."

The words of Job are ended.

[a]33 Or *as Adam did*

SHARPEN THE FOCUS

As Job 31 ends, Job has nothing more to say. He has poured out his heart, saying out loud exactly what he thinks and feels. Some of it has been downright shocking, especially to those of us who have heard Job praised for his patience and faith. He has spewed out a steady stream of bitter words and angry accusations. And mixed in with it have been words of faith in his Lord and desperate trust in God's justice. Even now, Job longs for a legal hearing because he believes that God is just.

Job has hit bottom. From his perspective, it looks like the end–the end of hope, of faith, even of life. But from God's point of view, Job's silence marks a new beginning.

Until Job poured out his pain, this new beginning was impossible. But now the Lord can reach into Job's heart to heal and to help. The Lord says to Job, as He sometimes says to us in our struggling, "Be still, and know that I am God" (Psalm 46:10). In his emptiness, Job is at last ready for the Lord's gracious work.

Until now Elihu, Job's fourth friend and comforter, has kept quiet. But at this point, he finally speaks up. As you read, see if you can spot ways his approach differs from that of the three friends who spoke to Job first. If time is short, focus on Job 33:1–28.

Elihu

32 So these three men stopped answering Job,
because he was righteous in his own
eyes. 2But Elihu son of Barakel the Buzite, of the family of Ram, became very
angry with Job for justifying himself
rather than God. 3He was also angry
with the three friends, because they had
found no way to refute Job, and yet had
condemned him.[a] 4Now Elihu had waited before speaking to Job because they
were older than he. 5But when he saw
that the three men had nothing more to
say, his anger was aroused.

6So Elihu son of Barakel the Buzite
said:

"I am young in years,
and you are old;
that is why I was fearful,
not daring to tell you what I know.
7I thought, 'Age should speak;
advanced years should teach wisdom.'
8But it is the spirit[b] in a man,
the breath of the Almighty, that gives him understanding.
9It is not only the old[c] who are wise,
not only the aged who understand what is right.

10"Therefore I say: Listen to me;
I too will tell you what I know.
11I waited while you spoke,
I listened to your reasoning;
while you were searching for words,
12 I gave you my full attention.
But not one of you has proved Job wrong;
none of you has answered his arguments.
13Do not say, 'We have found wisdom;
let God refute him, not man.'
14But Job has not marshaled his words against me,
and I will not answer him with your arguments.

15"They are dismayed and have no more to say;
words have failed them.
16Must I wait, now that they are silent,
now that they stand there with no reply?
17I too will have my say;
I too will tell what I know.
18For I am full of words,
and the spirit within me compels me;
19inside I am like bottled-up wine,
like new wineskins ready to burst.
20I must speak and find relief;
I must open my lips and reply.
21I will show partiality to no one,
nor will I flatter any man;
22for if I were skilled in flattery,
my Maker would soon take me away.

33 "But now, Job, listen to my words;
pay attention to everything I say.
2I am about to open my mouth;
my words are on the tip of my tongue.

[a]3 Masoretic Text; an ancient Hebrew scribal tradition *Job, and so had condemned God* [b]8 Or *Spirit*; also in verse 18 [c]9 Or *many*; or *great*

3 My words come from an upright heart;
my lips sincerely speak what I know.
4 The Spirit of God has made me;
the breath of the Almighty gives me life.
5 Answer me then, if you can;
prepare yourself and confront me.
6 I am just like you before God;
I too have been taken from clay.
7 No fear of me should alarm you,
nor should my hand be heavy upon you.

8 "But you have said in my hearing—
I heard the very words—
9 'I am pure and without sin;
I am clean and free from guilt.
10 Yet God has found fault with me;
he considers me his enemy.
11 He fastens my feet in shackles;
he keeps close watch on all my paths.'

12 "But I tell you, in this you are not right,
for God is greater than man.
13 Why do you complain to him
that he answers none of man's words[a]?
14 For God does speak—now one way, now another—
though man may not perceive it.
15 In a dream, in a vision of the night,
when deep sleep falls on men
as they slumber in their beds,
16 he may speak in their ears
and terrify them with warnings,
17 to turn man from wrongdoing
and keep him from pride,
18 to preserve his soul from the pit,[b]
his life from perishing by the sword.[c]
19 Or a man may be chastened on a bed of pain
with constant distress in his bones,
20 so that his very being finds food repulsive
and his soul loathes the choicest meal.
21 His flesh wastes away to nothing,
and his bones, once hidden, now stick out.
22 His soul draws near to the pit,[d]
and his life to the messengers of death.[e]

23 "Yet if there is an angel on his side
as a mediator, one out of a thousand,
to tell a man what is right for him,
24 to be gracious to him and say,
'Spare him from going down to the pit[f];
I have found a ransom for him'—
25 then his flesh is renewed like a child's;
it is restored as in the days of his youth.
26 He prays to God and finds favor with him,
he sees God's face and shouts for joy;
he is restored by God to his righteous state.
27 Then he comes to men and says,
'I sinned, and perverted what was right,
but I did not get what I deserved.
28 He redeemed my soul from going down to the pit,[g]
and I will live to enjoy the light.'

29 "God does all these things to a man—
twice, even three times—
30 to turn back his soul from the pit,[h]
that the light of life may shine on him.

31 "Pay attention, Job, and listen to me;
be silent, and I will speak.
32 If you have anything to say, answer me;
speak up, for I want you to be cleared.
33 But if not, then listen to me;
be silent, and I will teach you wisdom."

[a] 13 Or *that he does not answer for any of his actions* [b] 18 Or *preserve him from the grave* [c] 18 Or *from crossing the River* [d] 22 Or *He draws near to the grave* [e] 22 Or *to the dead* [f] 24 Or *grave* [g] 28 Or *redeemed me from going down to the grave* [h] 30 Or *turn him back from the grave*

34

Then Elihu said:

[2]"Hear my words, you wise men;
listen to me, you men of learning.
[3]For the ear tests words
as the tongue tastes food.
[4]Let us discern for ourselves what is right;
let us learn together what is good.

[5]"Job says, 'I am innocent,
but God denies me justice.
[6]Although I am right,
I am considered a liar;
although I am guiltless,
his arrow inflicts an incurable wound.'
[7]What man is like Job,
who drinks scorn like water?
[8]He keeps company with evildoers;
he associates with wicked men.
[9]For he says, 'It profits a man nothing
when he tries to please God.'

[10]"So listen to me, you men of understanding.
Far be it from God to do evil,
from the Almighty to do wrong.
[11]He repays a man for what he has done;
he brings upon him what his conduct deserves.
[12]It is unthinkable that God would do wrong,
that the Almighty would pervert justice.
[13]Who appointed him over the earth?
Who put him in charge of the whole world?
[14]If it were his intention
and he withdrew his spirit[a] and breath,
[15]all mankind would perish together
and man would return to the dust.

[16]"If you have understanding, hear this;
listen to what I say.
[17]Can he who hates justice govern?
Will you condemn the just and mighty One?
[18]Is he not the One who says to kings,
'You are worthless,'
and to nobles, 'You are wicked,'
[19]who shows no partiality to princes
and does not favor the rich over the poor,
for they are all the work of his hands?
[20]They die in an instant, in the middle of the night;
the people are shaken and they pass away;
the mighty are removed without human hand.

[21]"His eyes are on the ways of men;
he sees their every step.
[22]There is no dark place, no deep shadow,
where evildoers can hide.
[23]God has no need to examine men further,
that they should come before him for judgment.
[24]Without inquiry he shatters the mighty
and sets up others in their place.
[25]Because he takes note of their deeds,
he overthrows them in the night
and they are crushed.
[26]He punishes them for their wickedness
where everyone can see them,
[27]because they turned from following him
and had no regard for any of his ways.
[28]They caused the cry of the poor to come before him,
so that he heard the cry of the needy.
[29]But if he remains silent, who can condemn him?
If he hides his face, who can see him?
Yet he is over man and nation alike,
[30]to keep a godless man from ruling,
from laying snares for the people.

[31]"Suppose a man says to God,
'I am guilty but will offend no more.
[32]Teach me what I cannot see;

[a]14 Or *Spirit*

if I have done wrong, I will not do
so again.'
33 Should God then reward you on
your terms,
when you refuse to repent?
You must decide, not I;
so tell me what you know.

34 "Men of understanding declare,
wise men who hear me say to me,
35 'Job speaks without knowledge;
his words lack insight.'
36 Oh, that Job might be tested to the
utmost
for answering like a wicked man!
37 To his sin he adds rebellion;
scornfully he claps his hands
among us
and multiplies his words against
God."

SHARPEN THE FOCUS

Unlike Job's other comforters, Elihu leaves Job's past sins buried. He concerns himself with Job's present attitude, and he focuses there because he sees how that attitude has poisoned Job's heart.

Job has turned his losses and his physical distress from pain into deep suffering. He has cut himself off from his only source of comfort and hope—his Lord.

But Elihu holds out a solution, a remedy. He brings Job the Good News for which Job has longed: Job *has* the Redeemer, the Go-Between for whom he has longed. God has provided someone to bridge the gap between a holy God and His sinful people. This One speaks on Job's behalf—and on ours! "Spare him [or her] from going down to the pit," our Mediator says. "I have found a ransom . . ." (Job 33:24).

In fact, that Mediator Himself became our ransom. He didn't negotiate an installment plan by which we could pay back the debt we owed for our sins. He paid that debt for us with His own bloody death.

Now, in Jesus, we "find favor" with God. We're restored by God to a right standing before Him (Job 33:26). Secure in that relationship, godly sufferers find peace until God grants physical relief.

WEEK 44 • TUESDAY

Job 35:1—37:24

GET THE BIG PICTURE

Elihu continues talking with and counseling Job. As Elihu speaks, he paints a picture of our Lord and of His dealings with us. As you read, note the aspects of God's character Elihu highlights. If time is short, focus on Job 35:1–16.

35

Then Elihu said:

2 "Do you think this is just?
You say, 'I will be cleared by God.[a]'
3 Yet you ask him, 'What profit is it to me,[b]
and what do I gain by not sinning?'

4 "I would like to reply to you
and to your friends with you.
5 Look up at the heavens and see;
gaze at the clouds so high above you.
6 If you sin, how does that affect him?
If your sins are many, what does that do to him?
7 If you are righteous, what do you give to him,
or what does he receive from your hand?
8 Your wickedness affects only a man like yourself,
and your righteousness only the sons of men.

9 "Men cry out under a load of oppression;
they plead for relief from the arm of the powerful.
10 But no one says, 'Where is God my Maker,
who gives songs in the night,
11 who teaches more to us than to[c] the beasts of the earth
and makes us wiser than[d] the birds of the air?'
12 He does not answer when men cry out
because of the arrogance of the wicked.
13 Indeed, God does not listen to their empty plea;
the Almighty pays no attention to it.
14 How much less, then, will he listen
when you say that you do not see him,
that your case is before him
and you must wait for him,
15 and further, that his anger never punishes
and he does not take the least notice of wickedness.[e]
16 So Job opens his mouth with empty talk;
without knowledge he multiplies words."

36

Elihu continued:

2 "Bear with me a little longer and I will show you
that there is more to be said in God's behalf.
3 I get my knowledge from afar;
I will ascribe justice to my Maker.
4 Be assured that my words are not false;
one perfect in knowledge is with you.

5 "God is mighty, but does not despise men;
he is mighty, and firm in his purpose.
6 He does not keep the wicked alive
but gives the afflicted their rights.
7 He does not take his eyes off the righteous;
he enthrones them with kings
and exalts them forever.
8 But if men are bound in chains,
held fast by cords of affliction,
9 he tells them what they have done—
that they have sinned arrogantly.
10 He makes them listen to correction
and commands them to repent of their evil.
11 If they obey and serve him,
they will spend the rest of their days in prosperity
and their years in contentment.
12 But if they do not listen,
they will perish by the sword[f]
and die without knowledge.

13 "The godless in heart harbor resentment;
even when he fetters them, they do not cry for help.
14 They die in their youth,

[a]2 Or *My righteousness is more than God's* [b]3 Or *you* [c]11 Or *teaches us by* [d]11 Or *us wise by* [e]15 Symmachus, Theodotion and Vulgate; the meaning of the Hebrew for this word is uncertain. [f]12 Or *will cross the River*

among male prostitutes of the
shrines.
15 But those who suffer he delivers in
their suffering;
he speaks to them in their affliction.

16 "He is wooing you from the jaws of
distress
to a spacious place free from
restriction,
to the comfort of your table laden
with choice food.
17 But now you are laden with the
judgment due the wicked;
judgment and justice have taken
hold of you.
18 Be careful that no one entices you by
riches;
do not let a large bribe turn you
aside.
19 Would your wealth
or even all your mighty efforts
sustain you so you would not be
in distress?
20 Do not long for the night,
to drag people away from their
homes.[a]
21 Beware of turning to evil,
which you seem to prefer to
affliction.

22 "God is exalted in his power.
Who is a teacher like him?
23 Who has prescribed his ways for
him,
or said to him, 'You have done
wrong'?
24 Remember to extol his work,
which men have praised in song.
25 All mankind has seen it;
men gaze on it from afar.
26 How great is God—beyond our
understanding!
The number of his years is past
finding out.

27 "He draws up the drops of water,
which distill as rain to the
streams[b];
28 the clouds pour down their moisture
and abundant showers fall on
mankind.
29 Who can understand how he
spreads out the clouds,
how he thunders from his
pavilion?
30 See how he scatters his lightning
about him,
bathing the depths of the sea.
31 This is the way he governs[c] the
nations
and provides food in abundance.
32 He fills his hands with lightning
and commands it to strike its
mark.
33 His thunder announces the coming
storm;
even the cattle make known its
approach.[d]

37 "At this my heart pounds
and leaps from its place.
2 Listen! Listen to the roar of his voice,
to the rumbling that comes from
his mouth.
3 He unleashes his lightning beneath
the whole heaven
and sends it to the ends of the
earth.
4 After that comes the sound of his
roar;
he thunders with his majestic
voice.
When his voice resounds,
he holds nothing back.
5 God's voice thunders in marvelous
ways;
he does great things beyond our
understanding.
6 He says to the snow, 'Fall on the
earth,'
and to the rain shower, 'Be a
mighty downpour.'
7 So that all men he has made may
know his work,
he stops every man from his
labor.[e]
8 The animals take cover;
they remain in their dens.
9 The tempest comes out from its
chamber,
the cold from the driving winds.

[a]20 The meaning of the Hebrew for verses 18-20 is uncertain. [b]27 Or *distill from the mist as rain* [c]31 Or *nourishes* [d]33 Or *announces his coming— / the One zealous against evil* [e]7 Or / *he fills all men with fear by his power*

10 The breath of God produces ice,
and the broad waters become frozen.
11 He loads the clouds with moisture;
he scatters his lightning through them.
12 At his direction they swirl around
over the face of the whole earth
to do whatever he commands them.
13 He brings the clouds to punish men,
or to water his earth[a] and show his love.

14 "Listen to this, Job;
stop and consider God's wonders.
15 Do you know how God controls the clouds
and makes his lightning flash?
16 Do you know how the clouds hang poised,
those wonders of him who is perfect in knowledge?
17 You who swelter in your clothes
when the land lies hushed under the south wind,
18 can you join him in spreading out the skies,
hard as a mirror of cast bronze?
19 "Tell us what we should say to him;
we cannot draw up our case
because of our darkness.
20 Should he be told that I want to speak?
Would any man ask to be swallowed up?
21 Now no one can look at the sun,
bright as it is in the skies
after the wind has swept them clean.
22 Out of the north he comes in golden splendor;
God comes in awesome majesty.
23 The Almighty is beyond our reach
and exalted in power;
in his justice and great righteousness, he does not oppress.
24 Therefore, men revere him,
for does he not have regard for all the wise in heart?[b]"

[a]13 Or *to favor them* [b]24 Or *for he does not have regard for any who think they are wise.*

SHARPEN THE FOCUS

Most times, a case argued before the Supreme Court of the United States is not resolved right away. The judges retire to their chambers to deliberate and to debate the case's merit among themselves. Months later, they render a verdict and document their reasoning. No doubt the delay between trial and verdict pains the parties involved in the case. Nonetheless, they must wait.

Job waited, too. His case lay before heaven's throne. Because of the Redeemer whom the Judge Himself had provided, the verdict was never in doubt. Job would receive justice. He had only to wait for it (Job 35:14), and he could wait in hope.

But wait a minute! Didn't Job want mercy? Don't we want mercy, too? Won't justice bring punishment? No. Because Jesus suffered the punishment for all sinners in our place, we now can claim Christ's righteousness. We *are* holy in God's eyes. And in justice, our Judge will render this verdict: not guilty!

We wait, as did Job, for the justice of our cause to be revealed and for the damage of sin to be undone. Our Redeemer lives, and His plan to rescue us cannot be stopped!

WEEK 44 • WEDNESDAY

Job 38:1—41:34

GET THE BIG PICTURE

Throughout the book, Job has longed for his "day in court." He is about to get his hearing! As you read, look for evidence of the Lord's wisdom, power, and authority. If time is short, focus on Job 38:1–7; 40:1–5.

The L*ORD Speaks*

38 Then the LORD answered Job out of the storm. He said:

2 "Who is this that darkens my
counsel
with words without knowledge?
3 Brace yourself like a man;
I will question you,
and you shall answer me.

4 "Where were you when I laid the
earth's foundation?
Tell me, if you understand.
5 Who marked off its dimensions?
Surely you know!
Who stretched a measuring line
across it?
6 On what were its footings set,
or who laid its cornerstone—
7 while the morning stars sang
together
and all the angels[a] shouted for
joy?

8 "Who shut up the sea behind doors
when it burst forth from the
womb,
9 when I made the clouds its garment
and wrapped it in thick darkness,
10 when I fixed limits for it
and set its doors and bars in place,
11 when I said, 'This far you may come
and no farther;
here is where your proud waves
halt'?

12 "Have you ever given orders to the
morning,
or shown the dawn its place,
13 that it might take the earth by the
edges
and shake the wicked out of it?
14 The earth takes shape like clay
under a seal;
its features stand out like those of
a garment.
15 The wicked are denied their light,
and their upraised arm is broken.

16 "Have you journeyed to the springs
of the sea
or walked in the recesses of the
deep?
17 Have the gates of death been shown
to you?
Have you seen the gates of the
shadow of death[b]?
18 Have you comprehended the vast
expanses of the earth?
Tell me, if you know all this.

19 "What is the way to the abode of
light?
And where does darkness reside?
20 Can you take them to their places?
Do you know the paths to their
dwellings?
21 Surely you know, for you were
already born!
You have lived so many years!

22 "Have you entered the storehouses
of the snow
or seen the storehouses of the
hail,
23 which I reserve for times of trouble,
for days of war and battle?

[a]7 Hebrew *the sons of God* [b]17 Or *gates of deep shadows*

24 What is the way to the place where
the lightning is dispersed,
or the place where the east winds
are scattered over the earth?
25 Who cuts a channel for the torrents
of rain,
and a path for the thunderstorm,
26 to water a land where no man lives,
a desert with no one in it,
27 to satisfy a desolate wasteland
and make it sprout with grass?
28 Does the rain have a father?
Who fathers the drops of dew?
29 From whose womb comes the ice?
Who gives birth to the frost from
the heavens
30 when the waters become hard as
stone,
when the surface of the deep is
frozen?

31 "Can you bind the beautiful[a]
Pleiades?
Can you loose the cords of Orion?
32 Can you bring forth the
constellations in their seasons[b]
or lead out the Bear[c] with its cubs?
33 Do you know the laws of the
heavens?
Can you set up ⌞God's[d]⌟ dominion
over the earth?

34 "Can you raise your voice to the
clouds
and cover yourself with a flood of
water?
35 Do you send the lightning bolts on
their way?
Do they report to you, 'Here we
are'?
36 Who endowed the heart[e] with
wisdom
or gave understanding to the
mind[e]?
37 Who has the wisdom to count the
clouds?
Who can tip over the water jars of
the heavens
38 when the dust becomes hard
and the clods of earth stick
together?

39 "Do you hunt the prey for the
lioness
and satisfy the hunger of the lions
40 when they crouch in their dens
or lie in wait in a thicket?
41 Who provides food for the raven
when its young cry out to God
and wander about for lack of
food?

39

"Do you know when the
mountain goats give
birth?
Do you watch when the doe bears
her fawn?
2 Do you count the months till they
bear?
Do you know the time they give
birth?
3 They crouch down and bring forth
their young;
their labor pains are ended.
4 Their young thrive and grow strong
in the wilds;
they leave and do not return.

5 "Who let the wild donkey go free?
Who untied his ropes?
6 I gave him the wasteland as his
home,
the salt flats as his habitat.
7 He laughs at the commotion in the
town;
he does not hear a driver's shout.
8 He ranges the hills for his pasture
and searches for any green thing.

9 "Will the wild ox consent to serve
you?
Will he stay by your manger at
night?
10 Can you hold him to the furrow
with a harness?
Will he till the valleys behind you?
11 Will you rely on him for his great
strength?
Will you leave your heavy work to
him?
12 Can you trust him to bring in your
grain
and gather it to your threshing
floor?

[a]31 Or *the twinkling;* or *the chains of the* [b]32 Or *the morning star in its season* [c]32 Or *out Leo* [d]33 Or *his;* or *their* [e]36 The meaning of the Hebrew for this word is uncertain.

13 "The wings of the ostrich flap joyfully,
but they cannot compare with the pinions and feathers of the stork.
14 She lays her eggs on the ground
and lets them warm in the sand,
15 unmindful that a foot may crush them,
that some wild animal may trample them.
16 She treats her young harshly, as if they were not hers;
she cares not that her labor was in vain,
17 for God did not endow her with wisdom
or give her a share of good sense.
18 Yet when she spreads her feathers to run,
she laughs at horse and rider.

19 "Do you give the horse his strength
or clothe his neck with a flowing mane?
20 Do you make him leap like a locust,
striking terror with his proud snorting?
21 He paws fiercely, rejoicing in his strength,
and charges into the fray.
22 He laughs at fear, afraid of nothing;
he does not shy away from the sword.
23 The quiver rattles against his side,
along with the flashing spear and lance.
24 In frenzied excitement he eats up the ground;
he cannot stand still when the trumpet sounds.
25 At the blast of the trumpet he snorts, 'Aha!'
He catches the scent of battle from afar,
the shout of commanders and the battle cry.

26 "Does the hawk take flight by your wisdom
and spread his wings toward the south?
27 Does the eagle soar at your command
and build his nest on high?
28 He dwells on a cliff and stays there at night;
a rocky crag is his stronghold.
29 From there he seeks out his food;
his eyes detect it from afar.
30 His young ones feast on blood,
and where the slain are, there is he."

40

The LORD said to Job:

2 "Will the one who contends with the Almighty correct him?
Let him who accuses God answer him!"

3 Then Job answered the LORD:

4 "I am unworthy—how can I reply to you?
I put my hand over my mouth.
5 I spoke once, but I have no answer—
twice, but I will say no more."

6 Then the LORD spoke to Job out of the storm:

7 "Brace yourself like a man;
I will question you,
and you shall answer me.

8 "Would you discredit my justice?
Would you condemn me to justify yourself?
9 Do you have an arm like God's,
and can your voice thunder like his?
10 Then adorn yourself with glory and splendor,
and clothe yourself in honor and majesty.
11 Unleash the fury of your wrath,
look at every proud man and bring him low,
12 look at every proud man and humble him,
crush the wicked where they stand.
13 Bury them all in the dust together;
shroud their faces in the grave.
14 Then I myself will admit to you
that your own right hand can save you.

15 "Look at the behemoth,[a]
which I made along with you
and which feeds on grass like an ox.
16 What strength he has in his loins,
what power in the muscles of his belly!
17 His tail[b] sways like a cedar;
the sinews of his thighs are close-knit.
18 His bones are tubes of bronze,
his limbs like rods of iron.
19 He ranks first among the works of God,
yet his Maker can approach him with his sword.
20 The hills bring him their produce,
and all the wild animals play nearby.
21 Under the lotus plants he lies,
hidden among the reeds in the marsh.
22 The lotuses conceal him in their shadow;
the poplars by the stream surround him.
23 When the river rages, he is not alarmed;
he is secure, though the Jordan should surge against his mouth.
24 Can anyone capture him by the eyes,[c]
or trap him and pierce his nose?

41 "Can you pull in the leviathan[d] with a fishhook
or tie down his tongue with a rope?
2 Can you put a cord through his nose
or pierce his jaw with a hook?
3 Will he keep begging you for mercy?
Will he speak to you with gentle words?
4 Will he make an agreement with you
for you to take him as your slave for life?
5 Can you make a pet of him like a bird
or put him on a leash for your girls?
6 Will traders barter for him?
Will they divide him up among the merchants?
7 Can you fill his hide with harpoons
or his head with fishing spears?
8 If you lay a hand on him,
you will remember the struggle
and never do it again!
9 Any hope of subduing him is false;
the mere sight of him is overpowering.
10 No one is fierce enough to rouse him.
Who then is able to stand against me?
11 Who has a claim against me that I must pay?
Everything under heaven belongs to me.

12 "I will not fail to speak of his limbs,
his strength and his graceful form.
13 Who can strip off his outer coat?
Who would approach him with a bridle?
14 Who dares open the doors of his mouth,
ringed about with his fearsome teeth?
15 His back has[e] rows of shields
tightly sealed together;
16 each is so close to the next
that no air can pass between.
17 They are joined fast to one another;
they cling together and cannot be parted.
18 His snorting throws out flashes of light;
his eyes are like the rays of dawn.
19 Firebrands stream from his mouth;
sparks of fire shoot out.
20 Smoke pours from his nostrils
as from a boiling pot over a fire of reeds.
21 His breath sets coals ablaze,
and flames dart from his mouth.
22 Strength resides in his neck;
dismay goes before him.
23 The folds of his flesh are tightly joined;
they are firm and immovable.

[a] *15* Possibly the hippopotamus or the elephant
[b] *17* Possibly trunk [c] *24* Or *by a water hole*
[d] *1* Possibly the crocodile [e] *15* Or *His pride is his*

24 His chest is hard as rock,
hard as a lower millstone.
25 When he rises up, the mighty are terrified;
they retreat before his thrashing.
26 The sword that reaches him has no effect,
nor does the spear or the dart or the javelin.
27 Iron he treats like straw
and bronze like rotten wood.
28 Arrows do not make him flee;
slingstones are like chaff to him.
29 A club seems to him but a piece of straw;
he laughs at the rattling of the lance.
30 His undersides are jagged potsherds,
leaving a trail in the mud like a threshing sledge.
31 He makes the depths churn like a boiling caldron
and stirs up the sea like a pot of ointment.
32 Behind him he leaves a glistening wake;
one would think the deep had white hair.
33 Nothing on earth is his equal—
a creature without fear.
34 He looks down on all that are haughty;
he is king over all that are proud."

SHARPEN THE FOCUS

As long as we live on this sinful earth, we will struggle with the issue of trusting our Lord. He *is* good, but we cannot control Him or direct His infinite power to accomplish our own purposes. Most times, we don't stop to think about that too much. But when we find ourselves in a Job-like dilemma, when the pain boxes us in, we, like Adam and Eve in the garden, want to "be like God."

In grace, the Lord came to Job to convict him of his rebellion and lack of trust. God never does reveal the reasons behind Job's suffering—not to Job, nor for that matter, to us. Instead, He reveals Himself. And for Job, it's enough.

Job admits (Job 40:4–5) to himself and to his Creator that he is unworthy. He will not again presume to correct the all-knowing, all-wise God. Job *sees* (Job 42:5) the Lord in a new way—Job's God is good.

We need to see that, too, as we go through troubled times. We need God to reveal, not His reasons, but Himself. And He has done just that on Calvary's cross. There we see full justice as the One who knew no sin became sin. For us! There we see infinite mercy as all of Jesus' right-standing before God is credited to us (2 Corinthians 5:21).

WEEK 44 • THURSDAY

Job 42:1–17

GET THE BIG PICTURE

Maybe you know the old story about the Sunday School teacher who polled her class for favorite Bible verses. One little girl, steeped in the King James Version, answered, "it came to pass." Her text was out of context, to be sure, but comforting nevertheless. Pain will come, but sooner or later, in God's mercy it will pass. Today you will read the end of Job's story. As you do, note how Job's trials "came to pass." If time is short, focus on Job 42:7–17.

Job

42 Then Job replied to the LORD:

2"I know that you can do all things;
no plan of yours can be thwarted.
3 You asked, 'Who is this that
obscures my counsel without
knowledge?'
Surely I spoke of things I did not
understand,
things too wonderful for me to
know.

4 "You said, 'Listen now, and I will
speak;
I will question you,
and you shall answer me.'
5My ears had heard of you
but now my eyes have seen you.
6Therefore I despise myself
and repent in dust and ashes."

Epilogue

7After the LORD had said these things to Job, he said to Eliphaz the Temanite, "I am angry with you and your two friends, because you have not spoken of me what is right, as my servant Job has.
8So now take seven bulls and seven rams and go to my servant Job and sacrifice a burnt offering for yourselves. My servant Job will pray for you, and I will accept his prayer and not deal with you according to your folly. You have not spoken of me what is right, as my servant Job has."
9So Eliphaz the Temanite, Bildad the Shuhite and Zophar the Naamathite did what the LORD told them; and the LORD accepted Job's prayer.
10After Job had prayed for his friends, the LORD made him prosperous again and gave him twice as much as he had before.
11All his brothers and sisters and everyone who had known him before came and ate with him in his house. They comforted and consoled him over all the trouble the LORD had brought upon him, and each one gave him a piece of silver[a] and a gold ring.
12The LORD blessed the latter part of Job's life more than the first. He had fourteen thousand sheep, six thousand camels, a thousand yoke of oxen and a thousand donkeys.
13And he also had seven sons and three daughters.
14The first daughter he named Jemimah, the second Keziah and the third Keren-Happuch.
15Nowhere in all the land were there found women as beautiful as Job's daughters, and their father granted them an inheritance along with their brothers.
16After this, Job lived a hundred and forty years; he saw his children and their children to the fourth generation.
17And so he died, old and full of years.

[a]11 Hebrew *him a kesitah*; a kesitah was a unit of money of unknown weight and value.

SHARPEN THE FOCUS

What are we to make of Job's story? In some ways, it provokes more questions than it provides answers. What does our Lord want us to carry away from the account?

> *You have heard of Job's perseverance and have seen what the Lord finally brought about. The Lord is full of compassion and mercy.*
> (James 5:11)

At the end (Job 42:8) as at the beginning (Job 1:8), the Lord called Job, "My servant." In the beginning Job was blessed with material blessings, and in the end, doubly so. In the beginning

Job knew God, and in the end, Job saw God's majesty and goodness in an even fuller way (Job 42:5–6). And while Satan seemed to romp through Job's life having his own evil way, the Lord was holding on to Job and even causing Satan's wicked schemes to accomplish a holy purpose.

Can we persevere as Job did? Always. Will Satan's temptations ever be so great that they pull us away from God's love? Never. We have already seen what the Lord brought about in Job's life. We have seen His mercy and compassion for Job and for us in Jesus' nail-scarred hands. Even when we can't answer the *whys* of life, we can be sure of the Lord's ways in our life—ways of mercy and compassion.

PSALMS

The psalms deal with nearly every experience known to human beings. Anger. Disappointment. Delight. Peace. Trouble. Trust. Fear. Seldom does the psalmist give specific details about his situation or problem. Because this is so, we can use the words of the psalms as we lift our own situations and problems to our Lord in prayer. With this in mind, don't simply *read* today's psalms; *pray* them, especially Psalms 4–6. If time is short, focus on Psalm 1.

BOOK I

Psalms 1–41

Psalm 1

1 Blessed is the man
who does not walk in the counsel of the wicked
or stand in the way of sinners
or sit in the seat of mockers.
2 But his delight is in the law of the LORD,
and on his law he meditates day and night.
3 He is like a tree planted by streams of water,
which yields its fruit in season
and whose leaf does not wither.
Whatever he does prospers.

4 Not so the wicked!
They are like chaff
that the wind blows away.
5 Therefore the wicked will not stand in the judgment,
nor sinners in the assembly of the righteous.

6 For the LORD watches over the way of the righteous,
but the way of the wicked will perish.

Psalm 2

1 Why do the nations conspire[a]
and the peoples plot in vain?
2 The kings of the earth take their stand
and the rulers gather together
against the LORD
and against his Anointed One.[b]
3 "Let us break their chains," they say,
"and throw off their fetters."

4 The One enthroned in heaven laughs;
the Lord scoffs at them.
5 Then he rebukes them in his anger
and terrifies them in his wrath, saying,
6 "I have installed my King[c]
on Zion, my holy hill."

7 I will proclaim the decree of the LORD:

He said to me, "You are my Son[d];
today I have become your Father.[e]

[a] 1 Hebrew; Septuagint *rage* [b] 2 Or *anointed one* [c] 6 Or *king* [d] 7 Or *son*; also in verse 12 [e] 7 Or *have begotten you*

8 Ask of me,
and I will make the nations your inheritance,
the ends of the earth your possession.
9 You will rule them with an iron scepter[a];
you will dash them to pieces like pottery."

10 Therefore, you kings, be wise;
be warned, you rulers of the earth.
11 Serve the LORD with fear
and rejoice with trembling.
12 Kiss the Son, lest he be angry
and you be destroyed in your way,
for his wrath can flare up in a moment.
Blessed are all who take refuge in him.

Psalm 3

A psalm of David. When he fled from his son Absalom.

1 O LORD, how many are my foes!
How many rise up against me!
2 Many are saying of me,
"God will not deliver him." *Selah*[b]
3 But you are a shield around me, O LORD;
you bestow glory on me and lift[c] up my head.
4 To the LORD I cry aloud,
and he answers me from his holy hill. *Selah*
5 I lie down and sleep;
I wake again, because the LORD sustains me.
6 I will not fear the tens of thousands
drawn up against me on every side.
7 Arise, O LORD!
Deliver me, O my God!
Strike all my enemies on the jaw;
break the teeth of the wicked.

8 From the LORD comes deliverance.
May your blessing be on your people. *Selah*

Psalm 4

For the director of music. With stringed instruments. A psalm of David.

1 Answer me when I call to you,
O my righteous God.
Give me relief from my distress;
be merciful to me and hear my prayer.

2 How long, O men, will you turn my glory into shame[d]?
How long will you love delusions
and seek false gods[e]? *Selah*
3 Know that the LORD has set apart
the godly for himself;
the LORD will hear when I call to him.
4 In your anger do not sin;
when you are on your beds,
search your hearts and be silent. *Selah*
5 Offer right sacrifices
and trust in the LORD.

6 Many are asking, "Who can show us any good?"
Let the light of your face shine
upon us, O LORD.
7 You have filled my heart with greater joy
than when their grain and new wine abound.
8 I will lie down and sleep in peace,
for you alone, O LORD,
make me dwell in safety.

Psalm 5

For the director of music. For flutes. A psalm of David.

1 Give ear to my words, O LORD,
consider my sighing.
2 Listen to my cry for help,
my King and my God,
for to you I pray.

[a]9 Or *will break them with a rod of iron* [b]2 A word of uncertain meaning, occurring frequently in the Psalms; possibly a musical term [c]3 Or *LORD, / my Glorious One, who lifts* [d]2 Or *you dishonor my Glorious One* [e]2 Or *seek lies*

3 In the morning, O LORD, you hear
my voice;
in the morning I lay my requests
before you
and wait in expectation.
4 You are not a God who takes
pleasure in evil;
with you the wicked cannot dwell.
5 The arrogant cannot stand in your
presence;
you hate all who do wrong.
6 You destroy those who tell lies;
bloodthirsty and deceitful men
the LORD abhors.
7 But I, by your great mercy,
will come into your house;
in reverence will I bow down
toward your holy temple.
8 Lead me, O LORD, in your
righteousness
because of my enemies—
make straight your way before me.
9 Not a word from their mouth can be
trusted;
their heart is filled with
destruction.
Their throat is an open grave;
with their tongue they speak deceit.
10 Declare them guilty, O God!
Let their intrigues be their
downfall.
Banish them for their many sins,
for they have rebelled against you.
11 But let all who take refuge in you be
glad;
let them ever sing for joy.
Spread your protection over them,
that those who love your name
may rejoice in you.
12 For surely, O LORD, you bless the
righteous;
you surround them with your
favor as with a shield.

Psalm 6

For the director of music. With stringed instruments. According to *sheminith*.[a] A psalm of David.

1 O LORD, do not rebuke me in your
anger
or discipline me in your wrath.
2 Be merciful to me, LORD, for I am
faint;
O LORD, heal me, for my bones
are in agony.
3 My soul is in anguish.
How long, O LORD, how long?
4 Turn, O LORD, and deliver me;
save me because of your unfailing
love.
5 No one remembers you when he is
dead.
Who praises you from the grave[b]?
6 I am worn out from groaning;
all night long I flood my bed with
weeping
and drench my couch with tears.
7 My eyes grow weak with sorrow;
they fail because of all my foes.
8 Away from me, all you who do evil,
for the LORD has heard my
weeping.
9 The LORD has heard my cry for
mercy;
the LORD accepts my prayer.
10 All my enemies will be ashamed and
dismayed;
they will turn back in sudden
disgrace.

[a]Title: Probably a musical term [b]5 Hebrew *Sheol*

SHARPEN THE FOCUS

Like a tree. Rooted. Grounded. Secure. Have you ever known someone like that? Someone who seemed unshakable? God wants to create that kind of stable maturity in you. And He does it through His Word.

In His written Word our Lord reveals His will for our lives (Psalm 1:1). But even more important, in His Word our Lord reveals Himself. Knowing God's commands is important; knowing

God is even more important. This kind of knowing involves head, heart, and hands all at once; it transforms our lives and our lifestyle.

Because this is so, it's interesting to notice the connection between Psalm 1 and 2. In Psalm 1, the psalmist ponders God's written Word. In Psalm 2, the psalmist meditates on the Anointed One, the coming King, the Father's final, perfect Word to us poor sinners (Hebrews 1:1–3).

Now that the heavenly Father has given us that Word of grace in Jesus, we can "take refuge in Him" (Psalm 2:12). We can yield fruit (Psalm 1:3), the fruit of righteousness and peace (Hebrews 12:11). We can "serve the LORD with fear and rejoice with trembling" (Psalm 2:11) because we are secure, rooted, stable—in Christ.

In Psalms 7, 9, and 10 the psalmist asks God for the same kind of justice—vindication—for which Job prayed. Psalm 8 is a song of praise to the Lord of creation who silences His enemies. As you pray these psalms, do so with an eye toward the schemes Satan still hatches against Christ's people, Christ's church. If time is short, focus on Psalm 9.

Psalm 7

A *shiggaion*[a] of David, which he sang to the LORD concerning Cush, a Benjamite.

1 O LORD my God, I take refuge in you;
save and deliver me from all who pursue me,
2 or they will tear me like a lion
and rip me to pieces with no one to rescue me.

3 O LORD my God, if I have done this
and there is guilt on my hands—
4 if I have done evil to him who is at peace with me
or without cause have robbed my foe—
5 then let my enemy pursue and overtake me;
let him trample my life to the ground
and make me sleep in the dust.
Selah

6 Arise, O LORD, in your anger;
rise up against the rage of my enemies.
Awake, my God; decree justice.
7 Let the assembled peoples gather around you.
Rule over them from on high;
8 let the LORD judge the peoples.
Judge me, O LORD, according to my righteousness,
according to my integrity, O Most High.
9 O righteous God,
who searches minds and hearts,
bring to an end the violence of the wicked
and make the righteous secure.

10 My shield[b] is God Most High,
who saves the upright in heart.
11 God is a righteous judge,

[a]Title: Probably a literary or musical term
[b]10 Or *sovereign*

a God who expresses his wrath
every day.
12 If he does not relent,
he[a] will sharpen his sword;
he will bend and string his bow.
13 He has prepared his deadly
weapons;
he makes ready his flaming
arrows.

14 He who is pregnant with evil
and conceives trouble gives birth
to disillusionment.
15 He who digs a hole and scoops it out
falls into the pit he has made.
16 The trouble he causes recoils on
himself;
his violence comes down on his
own head.

17 I will give thanks to the LORD
because of his righteousness
and will sing praise to the name of
the LORD Most High.

Psalm 8

For the director of music. According to *gittith.*[b] A psalm of David.

1 O LORD, our Lord,
how majestic is your name in all
the earth!

You have set your glory
above the heavens.
2 From the lips of children and infants
you have ordained praise[c]
because of your enemies,
to silence the foe and the avenger.

3 When I consider your heavens,
the work of your fingers,
the moon and the stars,
which you have set in place,
4 what is man that you are mindful of
him,
the son of man that you care for
him?
5 You made him a little lower than the
heavenly beings[d]
and crowned him with glory and
honor.

6 You made him ruler over the works
of your hands;
you put everything under his feet:
7 all flocks and herds,
and the beasts of the field,
8 the birds of the air,
and the fish of the sea,
all that swim the paths of the seas.

9 O LORD, our Lord,
how majestic is your name in all
the earth!

Psalm 9[e]

For the director of music. To ⌞the tune of⌟ "The Death of the Son." A psalm of David.

1 I will praise you, O LORD, with all
my heart;
I will tell of all your wonders.
2 I will be glad and rejoice in you;
I will sing praise to your name,
O Most High.
3 My enemies turn back;
they stumble and perish before
you.
4 For you have upheld my right and
my cause;
you have sat on your throne,
judging righteously.
5 You have rebuked the nations and
destroyed the wicked;
you have blotted out their name
for ever and ever.
6 Endless ruin has overtaken the
enemy,
you have uprooted their cities;
even the memory of them has
perished.

7 The LORD reigns forever;
he has established his throne for
judgment.
8 He will judge the world in
righteousness;
he will govern the peoples with
justice.

[a]12 Or *If a man does not repent, / God* [b]Title: Probably a musical term [c]2 Or *strength* [d]5 Or *than God* [e]Psalms 9 and 10 may have been originally a single acrostic poem, the stanzas of which begin with the successive letters of the Hebrew alphabet. In the Septuagint they constitute one psalm.

9 The LORD is a refuge for the
oppressed,
a stronghold in times of trouble.
10 Those who know your name will
trust in you,
for you, LORD, have never
forsaken those who seek you.

11 Sing praises to the LORD, enthroned
in Zion;
proclaim among the nations what
he has done.
12 For he who avenges blood
remembers;
he does not ignore the cry of the
afflicted.

13 O LORD, see how my enemies
persecute me!
Have mercy and lift me up from
the gates of death,
14 that I may declare your praises
in the gates of the Daughter of
Zion
and there rejoice in your
salvation.
15 The nations have fallen into the pit
they have dug;
their feet are caught in the net
they have hidden.
16 The LORD is known by his justice;
the wicked are ensnared by the
work of their hands.
Higgaion.[a] *Selah*
17 The wicked return to the grave,[b]
all the nations that forget God.
18 But the needy will not always be
forgotten,
nor the hope of the afflicted ever
perish.

19 Arise, O LORD, let not man
triumph;
let the nations be judged in your
presence.
20 Strike them with terror, O LORD;
let the nations know they are but
men. *Selah*

Psalm 10[c]

1 Why, O LORD, do you stand far off?
Why do you hide yourself in times
of trouble?
2 In his arrogance the wicked man
hunts down the weak,
who are caught in the schemes he
devises.
3 He boasts of the cravings of his
heart;
he blesses the greedy and reviles
the LORD.
4 In his pride the wicked does not
seek him;
in all his thoughts there is no
room for God.
5 His ways are always prosperous;
he is haughty and your laws are
far from him;
he sneers at all his enemies.
6 He says to himself, "Nothing will
shake me;
I'll always be happy and never
have trouble."
7 His mouth is full of curses and lies
and threats;
trouble and evil are under his
tongue.
8 He lies in wait near the villages;
from ambush he murders the
innocent,
watching in secret for his victims.
9 He lies in wait like a lion in cover;
he lies in wait to catch the
helpless;
he catches the helpless and drags
them off in his net.
10 His victims are crushed, they
collapse;
they fall under his strength.
11 He says to himself, "God has
forgotten;
he covers his face and never sees."

12 Arise, LORD! Lift up your hand,
O God.
Do not forget the helpless.
13 Why does the wicked man revile
God?
Why does he say to himself,
"He won't call me to account"?

[a]16 Or *Meditation*; possibly a musical notation
[b]17 Hebrew *Sheol* [c]Psalms 9 and 10 may have been originally a single acrostic poem, the stanzas of which begin with the successive letters of the Hebrew alphabet. In the Septuagint they constitute one psalm.

[14]But you, O God, do see trouble and
grief;
you consider it to take it in hand.
The victim commits himself to you;
you are the helper of the
fatherless.
[15]Break the arm of the wicked and evil
man;
call him to account for his
wickedness
that would not be found out.

[16]The LORD is King for ever and ever;
the nations will perish from his
land.
[17]You hear, O LORD, the desire of the
afflicted;
you encourage them, and you
listen to their cry,
[18]defending the fatherless and the
oppressed,
in order that man, who is of the
earth, may terrify no more.

Psalm 11

For the director of music. Of David.

[1]In the LORD I take refuge.
How then can you say to me:
"Flee like a bird to your mountain.
[2]For look, the wicked bend their
bows;
they set their arrows against the
strings
to shoot from the shadows
at the upright in heart.
[3]When the foundations are being
destroyed,
what can the righteous do[a]?"

[4]The LORD is in his holy temple;
the LORD is on his heavenly
throne.
He observes the sons of men;
his eyes examine them.
[5]The LORD examines the righteous,
but the wicked[b] and those who
love violence
his soul hates.
[6]On the wicked he will rain
fiery coals and burning sulfur;
a scorching wind will be their lot.

[7]For the LORD is righteous,
he loves justice;
upright men will see his face.

[a]3 Or *what is the Righteous One doing* [b]5 Or *The LORD, the Righteous One, examines the wicked, /*

SHARPEN THE FOCUS

The tension between the *now* and the *not yet*—that's where the Lord's people live today. That's where David, too, found himself as he penned Psalm 9. The Lord had promised David that He would judge the wicked. David would not live always in fear of his enemies. So certain, so true was that promise that David burst into a song of praise (Psalm 9:1–2).

Still, we can see from Psalm 9:13–14 and 19–20 that total victory and complete peace had not yet materialized. But as the Lord is faithful, David's hope was sure. David could hope in the *now* as he waited for what had *not yet* come to be.

We, too, cling to our Lord's promises *now* even as we wait for the *not yet.* We expect God to act for us in the future, because we've seen Jesus Christ die and rise again for us in the past.

What promises from God do you most treasure *now*, even though you have not yet seen them fulfilled? Think of these while you pray Psalm 9 again and as you meditate on the faithfulness of our Savior-God.

WEEK 45 • MONDAY

Psalms 12:1—17:15

The enemies of Christ and His cross are the "wicked" described (in Psalm 12) and the "evildoers" (in Psalm 14). Their attitudes and actions contrast sharply with those of the "righteous" of whom Psalm 15 speaks. The ultimate end of the wicked also contrasts sharply with the eternal future the Lord promises those made right with Him through the blood of Christ. As you read, note these contrasts. If time is short, focus on Psalm 17.

Psalm 12

For the director of music. According to *sheminith.*[a] A psalm of David.

1 Help, LORD, for the godly are no more;
the faithful have vanished from among men.
2 Everyone lies to his neighbor;
their flattering lips speak with deception.

3 May the LORD cut off all flattering lips
and every boastful tongue
4 that says, "We will triumph with our tongues;
we own our lips[b]—who is our master?"
5 "Because of the oppression of the weak
and the groaning of the needy,
I will now arise," says the LORD.
"I will protect them from those who malign them."
6 And the words of the LORD are flawless,
like silver refined in a furnace of clay,
purified seven times.

7 O LORD, you will keep us safe
and protect us from such people forever.
8 The wicked freely strut about
when what is vile is honored among men.

Psalm 13

For the director of music.
A psalm of David.

1 How long, O LORD? Will you forget me forever?
How long will you hide your face from me?
2 How long must I wrestle with my thoughts
and every day have sorrow in my heart?
How long will my enemy triumph over me?

3 Look on me and answer, O LORD my God.
Give light to my eyes, or I will sleep in death;
4 my enemy will say, "I have overcome him,"
and my foes will rejoice when I fall.
5 But I trust in your unfailing love;
my heart rejoices in your salvation.
6 I will sing to the LORD,
for he has been good to me.

Psalm 14

For the director of music. Of David.

1 The fool[c] says in his heart,
"There is no God."

[a]Title: Probably a musical term [b]4 Or / *our lips are our plowshares* [c]1 The Hebrew words rendered *fool* in Psalms denote one who is morally deficient.

They are corrupt, their deeds are vile;
there is no one who does good.

2 The LORD looks down from heaven on the sons of men
to see if there are any who understand,
any who seek God.
3 All have turned aside,
they have together become corrupt;
there is no one who does good,
not even one.

4 Will evildoers never learn—
those who devour my people as men eat bread
and who do not call on the LORD?
5 There they are, overwhelmed with dread,
for God is present in the company of the righteous.
6 You evildoers frustrate the plans of the poor,
but the LORD is their refuge.

7 Oh, that salvation for Israel would come out of Zion!
When the LORD restores the fortunes of his people,
let Jacob rejoice and Israel be glad!

Psalm 15

A psalm of David.

1 LORD, who may dwell in your sanctuary?
Who may live on your holy hill?

2 He whose walk is blameless
and who does what is righteous,
who speaks the truth from his heart
3 and has no slander on his tongue,
who does his neighbor no wrong
and casts no slur on his fellowman,
4 who despises a vile man
but honors those who fear the LORD,
who keeps his oath
even when it hurts,
5 who lends his money without usury
and does not accept a bribe
against the innocent.

He who does these things
will never be shaken.

Psalm 16

A *miktam*[a] of David.

1 Keep me safe, O God,
for in you I take refuge.

2 I said to the LORD, "You are my Lord;
apart from you I have no good thing."
3 As for the saints who are in the land,
they are the glorious ones in whom is all my delight.[b]
4 The sorrows of those will increase
who run after other gods.
I will not pour out their libations of blood
or take up their names on my lips.

5 LORD, you have assigned me my portion and my cup;
you have made my lot secure.
6 The boundary lines have fallen for me in pleasant places;
surely I have a delightful inheritance.

7 I will praise the LORD, who counsels me;
even at night my heart instructs me.
8 I have set the LORD always before me.
Because he is at my right hand,
I will not be shaken.

9 Therefore my heart is glad and my tongue rejoices;
my body also will rest secure,
10 because you will not abandon me to the grave,[c]
nor will you let your Holy One[d] see decay.

[a]Title: Probably a literary or musical term [b]3 Or *As for the pagan priests who are in the land / and the nobles in whom all delight, I said:* [c]10 Hebrew *Sheol* [d]10 Or *your faithful one*

11 You have made[a] known to me the
path of life;
you will fill me with joy in your
presence,
with eternal pleasures at your
right hand.

Psalm 17

A prayer of David.

1 Hear, O LORD, my righteous plea;
listen to my cry.
Give ear to my prayer—
it does not rise from deceitful lips.
2 May my vindication come from you;
may your eyes see what is right.

3 Though you probe my heart and
examine me at night,
though you test me, you will find
nothing;
I have resolved that my mouth
will not sin.
4 As for the deeds of men—
by the word of your lips
I have kept myself
from the ways of the violent.
5 My steps have held to your paths;
my feet have not slipped.

6 I call on you, O God, for you will
answer me;
give ear to me and hear my
prayer.
7 Show the wonder of your great love,
you who save by your right hand
those who take refuge in you from
their foes.
8 Keep me as the apple of your eye;
hide me in the shadow of your
wings
9 from the wicked who assail me,
from my mortal enemies who
surround me.

10 They close up their callous hearts,
and their mouths speak with
arrogance.
11 They have tracked me down, they
now surround me,
with eyes alert, to throw me to the
ground.
12 They are like a lion hungry for
prey,
like a great lion crouching in
cover.

13 Rise up, O LORD, confront them,
bring them down;
rescue me from the wicked by
your sword.
14 O LORD, by your hand save me from
such men,
from men of this world whose
reward is in this life.
You still the hunger of those you
cherish;
their sons have plenty,
and they store up wealth for their
children.
15 And I—in righteousness I will see
your face;
when I awake, I will be satisfied
with seeing your likeness.

[a]11 Or *You will make*

SHARPEN THE FOCUS

These longings have always been the longings of God's people: to be like Christ, to be with Christ. Psalm 17:15 expresses the same two yearnings:

And I—in righteousness I will see your face;
when I awake, I will be satisfied with seeing your likeness.

Together, these two concerns keep our outlook balanced between time and eternity. When we long to be *with* Jesus, such longing gives us an eternal perspective. We don't get bogged down in hopelessness or discouragement as we face the problems of day-to-day living.

On the other hand, when we long to be *like* Jesus, such longing motivates us to live productive lives—lives that are Great Commission-oriented, in the present. We rely on our Savior-God for the power we need to share Christ's love and to speak about Christ's love and forgiveness to those around us.

Even now the Holy Spirit works in us, transforming us outwardly into the righteous people He has already made us inwardly through Christ's cross. We see Jesus' humbleness, love, holiness, and care flowing from our lives, and we praise Him for it. Someday we will awaken, fully like our Lord. What a future! What a hope!

Taken together, today's psalms tell us much about the Lord's compassion. He reveals Himself in His creation and in His Word (Psalm 19), but His revelation of Himself shines in all its glory from the cross of His Son. Keep that cross in mind as you read Psalm 22. (Notice the turning point in the psalm as verse 21 ends.) If time is short, focus on Psalm 22.

Psalm 18

For the director of music. Of David the servant of the LORD. He sang to the LORD the words of this song when the LORD delivered him from the hand of all his enemies and from the hand of Saul. He said:

1 I love you, O LORD, my strength.

2 The LORD is my rock, my fortress
and my deliverer;
my God is my rock, in whom I
take refuge.
He is my shield and the horn[a] of
my salvation, my stronghold.
3 I call to the LORD, who is worthy of
praise,
and I am saved from my enemies.

4 The cords of death entangled me;
the torrents of destruction
overwhelmed me.
5 The cords of the grave[b] coiled
around me;
the snares of death confronted me.
6 In my distress I called to the LORD;
I cried to my God for help.
From his temple he heard my voice;
my cry came before him, into his
ears.

7 The earth trembled and quaked,
and the foundations of the
mountains shook;
they trembled because he was
angry.
8 Smoke rose from his nostrils;
consuming fire came from his
mouth,
burning coals blazed out of it.
9 He parted the heavens and came
down;
dark clouds were under his feet.
10 He mounted the cherubim and flew;
he soared on the wings of the
wind.
11 He made darkness his covering, his
canopy around him—
the dark rain clouds of the sky.
12 Out of the brightness of his presence
clouds advanced,

[a]2 *Horn* here symbolizes strength. [b]5 Hebrew *Sheol*

with hailstones and bolts of
lightning.
13 The LORD thundered from heaven;
the voice of the Most High
resounded.[a]
14 He shot his arrows and scattered
⌞the enemies⌟,
great bolts of lightning and routed
them.
15 The valleys of the sea were
exposed
and the foundations of the earth
laid bare
at your rebuke, O LORD,
at the blast of breath from your
nostrils.

16 He reached down from on high and
took hold of me;
he drew me out of deep waters.
17 He rescued me from my powerful
enemy,
from my foes, who were too
strong for me.
18 They confronted me in the day of
my disaster,
but the LORD was my support.
19 He brought me out into a spacious
place;
he rescued me because he
delighted in me.

20 The LORD has dealt with me
according to my
righteousness;
according to the cleanness of my
hands he has rewarded me.
21 For I have kept the ways of the
LORD;
I have not done evil by turning
from my God.
22 All his laws are before me;
I have not turned away from his
decrees.
23 I have been blameless before him
and have kept myself from sin.
24 The LORD has rewarded me
according to my
righteousness,
according to the cleanness of my
hands in his sight.

25 To the faithful you show yourself
faithful,
to the blameless you show
yourself blameless,
26 to the pure you show yourself pure,
but to the crooked you show
yourself shrewd.
27 You save the humble
but bring low those whose eyes
are haughty.
28 You, O LORD, keep my lamp
burning;
my God turns my darkness into
light.
29 With your help I can advance
against a troop[b];
with my God I can scale a wall.

30 As for God, his way is perfect;
the word of the LORD is flawless.
He is a shield
for all who take refuge in him.
31 For who is God besides the LORD?
And who is the Rock except our
God?
32 It is God who arms me with strength
and makes my way perfect.
33 He makes my feet like the feet of a
deer;
he enables me to stand on the
heights.
34 He trains my hands for battle;
my arms can bend a bow of
bronze.
35 You give me your shield of victory,
and your right hand sustains me;
you stoop down to make me
great.
36 You broaden the path beneath me,
so that my ankles do not turn.

37 I pursued my enemies and overtook
them;
I did not turn back till they were
destroyed.
38 I crushed them so that they could
not rise;
they fell beneath my feet.
39 You armed me with strength for
battle;
you made my adversaries bow at
my feet.

[a] *13* Some Hebrew manuscripts and Septuagint (see also 2 Samuel 22:14); most Hebrew manuscripts *resounded, / amid hailstones and bolts of lightning* [b] *29* Or *can run through a barricade*

40 You made my enemies turn their backs in flight,
and I destroyed my foes.
41 They cried for help, but there was no one to save them—
to the LORD, but he did not answer.
42 I beat them as fine as dust borne on the wind;
I poured them out like mud in the streets.

43 You have delivered me from the attacks of the people;
you have made me the head of nations;
people I did not know are subject to me.
44 As soon as they hear me, they obey me;
foreigners cringe before me.
45 They all lose heart;
they come trembling from their strongholds.

46 The LORD lives! Praise be to my Rock!
Exalted be God my Savior!
47 He is the God who avenges me,
who subdues nations under me,
48 who saves me from my enemies.
You exalted me above my foes;
from violent men you rescued me.
49 Therefore I will praise you among the nations, O LORD;
I will sing praises to your name.
50 He gives his king great victories;
he shows unfailing kindness to his anointed,
to David and his descendants forever.

Psalm 19

For the director of music.
A psalm of David.

1 The heavens declare the glory of God;
the skies proclaim the work of his hands.
2 Day after day they pour forth speech;
night after night they display knowledge.
3 There is no speech or language
where their voice is not heard.[a]
4 Their voice[b] goes out into all the earth,
their words to the ends of the world.

In the heavens he has pitched a tent for the sun,
5 which is like a bridegroom coming forth from his pavilion,
like a champion rejoicing to run his course.
6 It rises at one end of the heavens
and makes its circuit to the other;
nothing is hidden from its heat.

7 The law of the LORD is perfect,
reviving the soul.
The statutes of the LORD are trustworthy,
making wise the simple.
8 The precepts of the LORD are right,
giving joy to the heart.
The commands of the LORD are radiant,
giving light to the eyes.
9 The fear of the LORD is pure,
enduring forever.
The ordinances of the LORD are sure
and altogether righteous.
10 They are more precious than gold,
than much pure gold;
they are sweeter than honey,
than honey from the comb.
11 By them is your servant warned;
in keeping them there is great reward.

12 Who can discern his errors?
Forgive my hidden faults.
13 Keep your servant also from willful sins;
may they not rule over me.
Then will I be blameless,
innocent of great transgression.

14 May the words of my mouth and the meditation of my heart

[a]3 Or *They have no speech, there are no words; / no sound is heard from them* [b]4 Septuagint, Jerome and Syriac; Hebrew *line*

be pleasing in your sight,
O LORD, my Rock and my
Redeemer.

Psalm 20

For the director of music.
A psalm of David.

1 May the LORD answer you when
you are in distress;
may the name of the God of Jacob
protect you.
2 May he send you help from the
sanctuary
and grant you support from Zion.
3 May he remember all your sacrifices
and accept your burnt offerings.
Selah
4 May he give you the desire of your
heart
and make all your plans succeed.
5 We will shout for joy when you are
victorious
and will lift up our banners in the
name of our God.
May the LORD grant all your
requests.
6 Now I know that the LORD saves his
anointed;
he answers him from his holy
heaven
with the saving power of his right
hand.
7 Some trust in chariots and some in
horses,
but we trust in the name of the
LORD our God.
8 They are brought to their knees and
fall,
but we rise up and stand firm.
9 O LORD, save the king!
Answer[a] us when we call!

Psalm 21

For the director of music.
A psalm of David.

1 O LORD, the king rejoices in your
strength.
How great is his joy in the
victories you give!
2 You have granted him the desire of
his heart
and have not withheld the request
of his lips. *Selah*
3 You welcomed him with rich
blessings
and placed a crown of pure gold
on his head.
4 He asked you for life, and you gave
it to him—
length of days, for ever and ever.
5 Through the victories you gave, his
glory is great;
you have bestowed on him
splendor and majesty.
6 Surely you have granted him eternal
blessings
and made him glad with the joy of
your presence.
7 For the king trusts in the LORD;
through the unfailing love of the
Most High
he will not be shaken.

8 Your hand will lay hold on all your
enemies;
your right hand will seize your
foes.
9 At the time of your appearing
you will make them like a fiery
furnace.
In his wrath the LORD will swallow
them up,
and his fire will consume them.
10 You will destroy their descendants
from the earth,
their posterity from mankind.
11 Though they plot evil against you
and devise wicked schemes, they
cannot succeed;
12 for you will make them turn their
backs
when you aim at them with
drawn bow.

13 Be exalted, O LORD, in your
strength;
we will sing and praise your
might.

[a]9 Or *save! / O King, answer*

Psalm 22

For the director of music. To ⌞the
tune of⌟ "The Doe of the Morning."
A psalm of David.

1 My God, my God, why have you
forsaken me?
Why are you so far from saving me,
so far from the words of my
groaning?
2 O my God, I cry out by day, but you
do not answer,
by night, and am not silent.

3 Yet you are enthroned as the
Holy One;
you are the praise of Israel.[a]
4 In you our fathers put their trust;
they trusted and you delivered
them.
5 They cried to you and were saved;
in you they trusted and were not
disappointed.

6 But I am a worm and not a man,
scorned by men and despised by
the people.
7 All who see me mock me;
they hurl insults, shaking their
heads:
8 "He trusts in the LORD;
let the LORD rescue him.
Let him deliver him,
since he delights in him."

9 Yet you brought me out of the
womb;
you made me trust in you
even at my mother's breast.
10 From birth I was cast upon you;
from my mother's womb you
have been my God.
11 Do not be far from me,
for trouble is near
and there is no one to help.

12 Many bulls surround me;
strong bulls of Bashan encircle me.
13 Roaring lions tearing their prey
open their mouths wide against
me.
14 I am poured out like water,
and all my bones are out of joint.
My heart has turned to wax;
it has melted away within me.
15 My strength is dried up like a
potsherd,
and my tongue sticks to the roof
of my mouth;
you lay me[b] in the dust of death.
16 Dogs have surrounded me;
a band of evil men has encircled
me,
they have pierced[c] my hands and
my feet.
17 I can count all my bones;
people stare and gloat over me.
18 They divide my garments among
them
and cast lots for my clothing.
19 But you, O LORD, be not far off;
O my Strength, come quickly to
help me.
20 Deliver my life from the sword,
my precious life from the power
of the dogs.
21 Rescue me from the mouth of the
lions;
save[d] me from the horns of the
wild oxen.

22 I will declare your name to my
brothers;
in the congregation I will praise
you.
23 You who fear the LORD, praise him!
All you descendants of Jacob,
honor him!
Revere him, all you descendants
of Israel!
24 For he has not despised or disdained
the suffering of the afflicted one;
he has not hidden his face from him
but has listened to his cry for help.

25 From you comes the theme of my
praise in the great assembly;
before those who fear you[e] will I
fulfill my vows.
26 The poor will eat and be satisfied;
they who seek the LORD will
praise him—

[a]3 Or *Yet you are holy, / enthroned on the praises of Israel* [b]15 Or */ I am laid* [c]16 Some Hebrew manuscripts, Septuagint and Syriac; most Hebrew manuscripts */ like the lion,* [d]21 Or */ you have heard* [e]25 Hebrew *him*

may your hearts live forever!
27 All the ends of the earth
will remember and turn to the
LORD,
and all the families of the nations
will bow down before him,
28 for dominion belongs to the LORD
and he rules over the nations.

29 All the rich of the earth will feast
and worship;
all who go down to the dust will
kneel before him—
those who cannot keep
themselves alive.
30 Posterity will serve him;
future generations will be told
about the Lord.
31 They will proclaim his
righteousness
to a people yet unborn—
for he has done it.

SHARPEN THE FOCUS

Reread Psalm 22 as Christ's prayer on Calvary, for that's what it truly is. Note the words *but* and *yet* as you come to them. These words flag each contrast with which our Savior struggled:

The Father had never abandoned His children.
But He abandoned His Son on Calvary (Psalm 22:1).

The Father had always heard His children's cries.
But He closed His ears to Christ on Calvary (Psalm 22:2).

The Father had always delivered His children from fear and shame (Psalm 22:3–5). *But He turned His back on His dying Son* (Psalm 22:6–16) *as that Son hung naked and ridiculed on Calvary* (Psalm 22:17–18).

Why? As we read Jesus' cries of agony, we too shout the question He Himself hurled at heaven. Lord God, *why?*

Our sins sent God's Son to His cross. Jesus died alone so we need never be alone again. Jesus' prayers fell on deaf ears so that our prayers would always be heard. Jesus endured the pain and shame of hell so that we can now live free from fear and shame forever.

WEEK 45 • WEDNESDAY

Psalms 23:1—28:9

GET THE BIG PICTURE

What do you need from heaven today? You will find it in Christ Jesus who is our shepherd, king, teacher, judge, and rock. Pray Psalms 23–28. Ask for what you need and thank your heavenly Father for those many benefits you have already received from His gracious hand. If time is short, focus on Psalm 24.

Psalm 23

A psalm of David.

1 The LORD is my shepherd, I shall not
be in want.
2 He makes me lie down in green
pastures,
he leads me beside quiet waters,
3 he restores my soul.
He guides me in paths of
righteousness
for his name's sake.
4 Even though I walk
through the valley of the shadow
of death,[a]
I will fear no evil,
for you are with me;
your rod and your staff,
they comfort me.

5 You prepare a table before me
in the presence of my enemies.
You anoint my head with oil;
my cup overflows.
6 Surely goodness and love will follow
me
all the days of my life,
and I will dwell in the house of the
LORD
forever.

Psalm 24

Of David. A psalm.

1 The earth is the LORD's, and
everything in it,
the world, and all who live in it;
2 for he founded it upon the seas
and established it upon the
waters.

3 Who may ascend the hill of the
LORD?
Who may stand in his holy place?
4 He who has clean hands and a pure
heart,
who does not lift up his soul to an
idol
or swear by what is false.[b]
5 He will receive blessing from the
LORD
and vindication from God his
Savior.
6 Such is the generation of those who
seek him,
who seek your face, O God of
Jacob.[c] *Selah*

7 Lift up your heads, O you gates;
be lifted up, you ancient doors,
that the King of glory may come
in.
8 Who is this King of glory?
The LORD strong and mighty,
the LORD mighty in battle.
9 Lift up your heads, O you gates;
lift them up, you ancient doors,
that the King of glory may come in.
10 Who is he, this King of glory?
The LORD Almighty—
he is the King of glory. *Selah*

Psalm 25[d]

Of David.

1 To you, O LORD, I lift up my soul;
2 in you I trust, O my God.
Do not let me be put to shame,
nor let my enemies triumph over
me.
3 No one whose hope is in you
will ever be put to shame,
but they will be put to shame
who are treacherous without
excuse.

4 Show me your ways, O LORD,
teach me your paths;
5 guide me in your truth and teach
me,
for you are God my Savior,
and my hope is in you all day
long.
6 Remember, O LORD, your great
mercy and love,
for they are from of old.
7 Remember not the sins of my youth
and my rebellious ways;
according to your love remember
me,
for you are good, O LORD.

[a]4 Or *through the darkest valley* [b]4 Or *swear falsely*
[c]6 Two Hebrew manuscripts and Syriac (see also Septuagint); most Hebrew manuscripts *face, Jacob*
[d]This psalm is an acrostic poem, the verses of which begin with the successive letters of the Hebrew alphabet.

[8]Good and upright is the LORD;
therefore he instructs sinners in his ways.
[9]He guides the humble in what is right
and teaches them his way.
[10]All the ways of the LORD are loving and faithful
for those who keep the demands of his covenant.
[11]For the sake of your name, O LORD,
forgive my iniquity, though it is great.
[12]Who, then, is the man that fears the LORD?
He will instruct him in the way chosen for him.
[13]He will spend his days in prosperity,
and his descendants will inherit the land.
[14]The LORD confides in those who fear him;
he makes his covenant known to them.
[15]My eyes are ever on the LORD,
for only he will release my feet from the snare.

[16]Turn to me and be gracious to me,
for I am lonely and afflicted.
[17]The troubles of my heart have multiplied;
free me from my anguish.
[18]Look upon my affliction and my distress
and take away all my sins.
[19]See how my enemies have increased
and how fiercely they hate me!
[20]Guard my life and rescue me;
let me not be put to shame,
for I take refuge in you.
[21]May integrity and uprightness protect me,
because my hope is in you.

[22]Redeem Israel, O God,
from all their troubles!

Psalm 26

Of David.

[1]Vindicate me, O LORD,
for I have led a blameless life;
I have trusted in the LORD
without wavering.
[2]Test me, O LORD, and try me,
examine my heart and my mind;
[3]for your love is ever before me,
and I walk continually in your truth.
[4]I do not sit with deceitful men,
nor do I consort with hypocrites;
[5]I abhor the assembly of evildoers
and refuse to sit with the wicked.
[6]I wash my hands in innocence,
and go about your altar, O LORD,
[7]proclaiming aloud your praise
and telling of all your wonderful deeds.
[8]I love the house where you live, O LORD,
the place where your glory dwells.
[9]Do not take away my soul along with sinners,
my life with bloodthirsty men,
[10]in whose hands are wicked schemes,
whose right hands are full of bribes.
[11]But I lead a blameless life;
redeem me and be merciful to me.

[12]My feet stand on level ground;
in the great assembly I will praise the LORD.

Psalm 27

Of David.

[1]The LORD is my light and my salvation—
whom shall I fear?
The LORD is the stronghold of my life—
of whom shall I be afraid?
[2]When evil men advance against me
to devour my flesh,[a]
when my enemies and my foes attack me,
they will stumble and fall.
[3]Though an army besiege me,
my heart will not fear;
though war break out against me,
even then will I be confident.

[a]2 Or *to slander me*

4 One thing I ask of the LORD,
this is what I seek:
that I may dwell in the house of the LORD
all the days of my life,
to gaze upon the beauty of the LORD
and to seek him in his temple.
5 For in the day of trouble
he will keep me safe in his dwelling;
he will hide me in the shelter of his tabernacle
and set me high upon a rock.
6 Then my head will be exalted
above the enemies who surround me;
at his tabernacle will I sacrifice with shouts of joy;
I will sing and make music to the LORD.

7 Hear my voice when I call, O LORD;
be merciful to me and answer me.
8 My heart says of you, "Seek his[a] face!"
Your face, LORD, I will seek.
9 Do not hide your face from me,
do not turn your servant away in anger;
you have been my helper.
Do not reject me or forsake me,
O God my Savior.
10 Though my father and mother forsake me,
the LORD will receive me.
11 Teach me your way, O LORD;
lead me in a straight path
because of my oppressors.
12 Do not turn me over to the desire of my foes,
for false witnesses rise up against me,
breathing out violence.

13 I am still confident of this:
I will see the goodness of the LORD
in the land of the living.
14 Wait for the LORD;
be strong and take heart
and wait for the LORD.

Psalm 28

Of David.

1 To you I call, O LORD my Rock;
do not turn a deaf ear to me.
For if you remain silent,
I will be like those who have gone down to the pit.
2 Hear my cry for mercy
as I call to you for help,
as I lift up my hands
toward your Most Holy Place.

3 Do not drag me away with the wicked,
with those who do evil,
who speak cordially with their neighbors
but harbor malice in their hearts.
4 Repay them for their deeds
and for their evil work;
repay them for what their hands have done
and bring back upon them what they deserve.
5 Since they show no regard for the works of the LORD
and what his hands have done,
he will tear them down
and never build them up again.

6 Praise be to the LORD,
for he has heard my cry for mercy.
7 The LORD is my strength and my shield;
my heart trusts in him, and I am helped.
My heart leaps for joy
and I will give thanks to him in song.

8 The LORD is the strength of his people,
a fortress of salvation for his anointed one.
9 Save your people and bless your inheritance;
be their shepherd and carry them forever.

[a]8 Or *To you, O my heart, he has said, "Seek my*

SHARPEN THE FOCUS

Imagine yourself inside an ancient, walled city, the gates shut up tight against the threat of an enemy army. Now imagine your king riding toward those gates, his standard snapping in the sunlight. Would you open the gate and welcome your king?

When the King of glory, Jesus Christ, arrived on earth in the flesh, His own people rejected Him. Israel—God's outward, visible people in that day and place—refused to recognize Jesus' lordship. They not only slammed their gates down tight, they crucified the Lord of glory (1 Corinthians 2:8).

Still today many in the outward, visible church pay lip service to Christ's lordship but inwardly reject His authority in their lives. They explain away the truth of His Word rather than submitting in repentance and faith.

Our King of glory will return to judge the living and the dead. That day will be full of joy for those who have received from Christ the clean hands and pure heart of Psalm 24:4. We will receive blessings from the Lord into all eternity and the vindication of those made righteous by the blood of the Lamb (Psalms 24:5).

How can this holy hope strengthen you for today's challenges? How might you share it with someone?

WEEK 45 • THURSDAY

Psalms 29:1—34:22

GET THE BIG PICTURE

Today's psalms can bring comfort to children of God who find themselves under pressure. Each psalm holds out hope—that the Lord turns mourning into dancing, destruction into a glorious destiny, shame into honor. While, as the psalmist acknowledges, "a righteous man may have many troubles," it's also true that "the LORD delivers him from them all" (Psalm 34:19). As you pray these psalms, remember that in Christ *you* are "the righteous" to whom these promises belong. If time is short, focus on Psalm 32.

Psalm 29

A psalm of David.

1 Ascribe to the LORD, O mighty ones,
ascribe to the LORD glory and strength.
2 Ascribe to the LORD the glory due his name;
worship the LORD in the splendor of his[a] holiness.

3 The voice of the LORD is over the waters;
the God of glory thunders,
the LORD thunders over the mighty waters.
4 The voice of the LORD is powerful;
the voice of the LORD is majestic.
5 The voice of the LORD breaks the cedars;

[a]2 Or *LORD with the splendor of*

the LORD breaks in pieces the
cedars of Lebanon.
6 He makes Lebanon skip like a calf,
Sirion[a] like a young wild ox.
7 The voice of the LORD strikes
with flashes of lightning.
8 The voice of the LORD shakes the
desert;
the LORD shakes the Desert of
Kadesh.
9 The voice of the LORD twists the
oaks[b]
and strips the forests bare.
And in his temple all cry, "Glory!"
10 The LORD sits[c] enthroned over the
flood;
the LORD is enthroned as King
forever.
11 The LORD gives strength to his
people;
the LORD blesses his people with
peace.

Psalm 30

A psalm. A song. For the dedication of the temple.[d] Of David.

1 I will exalt you, O LORD,
for you lifted me out of the
depths
and did not let my enemies gloat
over me.
2 O LORD my God, I called to you for
help
and you healed me.
3 O LORD, you brought me up from
the grave[e];
you spared me from going down
into the pit.
4 Sing to the LORD, you saints of his;
praise his holy name.
5 For his anger lasts only a moment,
but his favor lasts a lifetime;
weeping may remain for a night,
but rejoicing comes in the
morning.
6 When I felt secure, I said,
"I will never be shaken."
7 O LORD, when you favored me,
you made my mountain[f] stand
firm;
but when you hid your face,
I was dismayed.
8 To you, O LORD, I called;
to the Lord I cried for mercy:
9 "What gain is there in my
destruction,[g]
in my going down into the pit?
Will the dust praise you?
Will it proclaim your faithfulness?
10 Hear, O LORD, and be merciful to
me;
O LORD, be my help."
11 You turned my wailing into dancing;
you removed my sackcloth and
clothed me with joy,
12 that my heart may sing to you and
not be silent.
O LORD my God, I will give you
thanks forever.

Psalm 31

For the director of music.
A psalm of David.

1 In you, O LORD, I have taken refuge;
let me never be put to shame;
deliver me in your righteousness.
2 Turn your ear to me,
come quickly to my rescue;
be my rock of refuge,
a strong fortress to save me.
3 Since you are my rock and my
fortress,
for the sake of your name lead
and guide me.
4 Free me from the trap that is set for
me,
for you are my refuge.
5 Into your hands I commit my spirit;
redeem me, O LORD, the God of
truth.
6 I hate those who cling to worthless
idols;
I trust in the LORD.
7 I will be glad and rejoice in your
love,
for you saw my affliction

[a]6 That is, Mount Hermon [b]9 Or *LORD makes the deer give birth* [c]10 Or *sat* [d]Title: Or *palace* [e]3 Hebrew *Sheol* [f]7 Or *hill country* [g]9 Or *there if I am silenced*

and knew the anguish of my soul.
8 You have not handed me over to the enemy
but have set my feet in a spacious place.

9 Be merciful to me, O LORD, for I am in distress;
my eyes grow weak with sorrow,
my soul and my body with grief.
10 My life is consumed by anguish
and my years by groaning;
my strength fails because of my affliction,[a]
and my bones grow weak.
11 Because of all my enemies,
I am the utter contempt of my neighbors;
I am a dread to my friends—
those who see me on the street
flee from me.
12 I am forgotten by them as though I were dead;
I have become like broken pottery.
13 For I hear the slander of many;
there is terror on every side;
they conspire against me
and plot to take my life.

14 But I trust in you, O LORD;
I say, "You are my God."
15 My times are in your hands;
deliver me from my enemies
and from those who pursue me.
16 Let your face shine on your servant;
save me in your unfailing love.
17 Let me not be put to shame,
O LORD,
for I have cried out to you;
but let the wicked be put to shame
and lie silent in the grave.[b]
18 Let their lying lips be silenced,
for with pride and contempt
they speak arrogantly against the righteous.

19 How great is your goodness,
which you have stored up for those who fear you,
which you bestow in the sight of men
on those who take refuge in you.
20 In the shelter of your presence you hide them
from the intrigues of men;
in your dwelling you keep them safe
from accusing tongues.

21 Praise be to the LORD,
for he showed his wonderful love to me
when I was in a besieged city.
22 In my alarm I said,
"I am cut off from your sight!"
Yet you heard my cry for mercy
when I called to you for help.

23 Love the LORD, all his saints!
The LORD preserves the faithful,
but the proud he pays back in full.
24 Be strong and take heart,
all you who hope in the LORD.

Psalm 32

Of David. A *maskil*.[c]

1 Blessed is he
whose transgressions are forgiven,
whose sins are covered.
2 Blessed is the man
whose sin the LORD does not count against him
and in whose spirit is no deceit.

3 When I kept silent,
my bones wasted away
through my groaning all day long.
4 For day and night
your hand was heavy upon me;
my strength was sapped
as in the heat of summer. *Selah*
5 Then I acknowledged my sin to you
and did not cover up my iniquity.
I said, "I will confess
my transgressions to the LORD"—
and you forgave
the guilt of my sin. *Selah*

6 Therefore let everyone who is godly pray to you
while you may be found;
surely when the mighty waters rise,
they will not reach him.
7 You are my hiding place;
you will protect me from trouble

[a] 10 Or *guilt* [b] 17 Hebrew *Sheol* [c] Title: Probably a literary or musical term

and surround me with songs of
deliverance. *Selah*

8 I will instruct you and teach you in
the way you should go;
I will counsel you and watch over
you.
9 Do not be like the horse or the mule,
which have no understanding
but must be controlled by bit and
bridle
or they will not come to you.
10 Many are the woes of the wicked,
but the LORD's unfailing love
surrounds the man who trusts in
him.
11 Rejoice in the LORD and be glad, you
righteous;
sing, all you who are upright in
heart!

Psalm 33

1 Sing joyfully to the LORD, you
righteous;
it is fitting for the upright to praise
him.
2 Praise the LORD with the harp;
make music to him on the
ten-stringed lyre.
3 Sing to him a new song;
play skillfully, and shout for joy.
4 For the word of the LORD is right
and true;
he is faithful in all he does.
5 The LORD loves righteousness and
justice;
the earth is full of his unfailing
love.
6 By the word of the LORD were the
heavens made,
their starry host by the breath of
his mouth.
7 He gathers the waters of the sea into
jars[a];
he puts the deep into storehouses.
8 Let all the earth fear the LORD;
let all the people of the world
revere him.
9 For he spoke, and it came to be;
he commanded, and it stood firm.
10 The LORD foils the plans of the
nations;
he thwarts the purposes of the
peoples.
11 But the plans of the LORD stand firm
forever,
the purposes of his heart through
all generations.
12 Blessed is the nation whose God is
the LORD,
the people he chose for his
inheritance.
13 From heaven the LORD looks down
and sees all mankind;
14 from his dwelling place he watches
all who live on earth—
15 he who forms the hearts of all,
who considers everything they do.
16 No king is saved by the size of his
army;
no warrior escapes by his great
strength.
17 A horse is a vain hope for
deliverance;
despite all its great strength it
cannot save.
18 But the eyes of the LORD are on
those who fear him,
on those whose hope is in his
unfailing love,
19 to deliver them from death
and keep them alive in famine.
20 We wait in hope for the LORD;
he is our help and our shield.
21 In him our hearts rejoice,
for we trust in his holy name.
22 May your unfailing love rest upon
us, O LORD,
even as we put our hope in you.

Psalm 34[b]

Of David. When he pretended to be
insane before Abimelech,
who drove him away, and he left.

1 I will extol the LORD at all times;
his praise will always be on my
lips.

[a]7 Or *sea as into a heap* [b]This psalm is an acrostic poem, the verses of which begin with the successive letters of the Hebrew alphabet.

[2]My soul will boast in the LORD;
let the afflicted hear and rejoice.
[3]Glorify the LORD with me;
let us exalt his name together.

[4]I sought the LORD, and he answered me;
he delivered me from all my fears.
[5]Those who look to him are radiant;
their faces are never covered with shame.
[6]This poor man called, and the LORD heard him;
he saved him out of all his troubles.
[7]The angel of the LORD encamps around those who fear him,
and he delivers them.

[8]Taste and see that the LORD is good;
blessed is the man who takes refuge in him.
[9]Fear the LORD, you his saints,
for those who fear him lack nothing.
[10]The lions may grow weak and hungry,
but those who seek the LORD lack no good thing.

[11]Come, my children, listen to me;
I will teach you the fear of the LORD.
[12]Whoever of you loves life
and desires to see many good days,
[13]keep your tongue from evil
and your lips from speaking lies.
[14]Turn from evil and do good;
seek peace and pursue it.

[15]The eyes of the LORD are on the righteous
and his ears are attentive to their cry;
[16]the face of the LORD is against those who do evil,
to cut off the memory of them from the earth.

[17]The righteous cry out, and the LORD hears them;
he delivers them from all their troubles.
[18]The LORD is close to the brokenhearted
and saves those who are crushed in spirit.

[19]A righteous man may have many troubles,
but the LORD delivers him from them all;
[20]he protects all his bones,
not one of them will be broken.

[21]Evil will slay the wicked;
the foes of the righteous will be condemned.
[22]The LORD redeems his servants;
no one will be condemned who takes refuge in him.

SHARPEN THE FOCUS

The child who hides a pair of muddy jeans under her bed. The university student who lies his way out of a charge of plagiarism. Police officers who pilfer some of the evidence in a drug case and provide alibis for one another. All of us have too often joined Adam, cowering in the bushes behind a suit of fig leaves.

Perhaps you recall that King David himself stood there. Through an elaborate cover-up scheme of his own, he almost got away with murder in the whole sorry incident with Bathsheba (2 Samuel 11). His self-imposed exile from the Lord lasted possibly for months. In Psalm 32:3–4 David describes the acid of guilt that can eat away at the human soul.

How interesting then to read Psalm 32:1: "Blessed is he . . . whose sins are covered." Fig leaves. Lies. Alibis. None of these will do. Proverbs 28:13 makes it clear: "He who conceals his sins does not prosper, but whoever confesses and renounces them finds mercy." Those who confess will experience mercy. When we try to cover up our own wrong doing, we fool no one but ourselves. But when our sins are covered with the blood of Jesus, we can walk away with both a clean record and a clear conscience. Praise God!

Each of today's psalms speaks about the anguish the psalmist experiences because of the words or actions of the wicked. As you pray these psalms, keep in mind the ultimate enemy of Christ and His church—Satan. And pray for our Lord's return to bring the full victory and peace of heaven. If time is short, focus on Psalm 37:1–11.

Psalm 35

Of David.

1 Contend, O LORD, with those who contend with me;
fight against those who fight against me.
2 Take up shield and buckler;
arise and come to my aid.
3 Brandish spear and javelin[a]
against those who pursue me.
Say to my soul,
"I am your salvation."

4 May those who seek my life
be disgraced and put to shame;
may those who plot my ruin
be turned back in dismay.
5 May they be like chaff before the wind,
with the angel of the LORD driving them away;
6 may their path be dark and slippery,
with the angel of the LORD pursuing them.
7 Since they hid their net for me without cause
and without cause dug a pit for me,
8 may ruin overtake them by surprise—
may the net they hid entangle them,
may they fall into the pit, to their ruin.
9 Then my soul will rejoice in the LORD
and delight in his salvation.
10 My whole being will exclaim,
"Who is like you, O LORD?
You rescue the poor from those too strong for them,
the poor and needy from those who rob them."

11 Ruthless witnesses come forward;
they question me on things I know nothing about.
12 They repay me evil for good
and leave my soul forlorn.
13 Yet when they were ill, I put on sackcloth
and humbled myself with fasting.
When my prayers returned to me unanswered,
14 I went about mourning
as though for my friend or brother.
I bowed my head in grief
as though weeping for my mother.

[a] 3 Or *and block the way*

15 But when I stumbled, they gathered in glee;
attackers gathered against me when I was unaware.
They slandered me without ceasing.
16 Like the ungodly they maliciously mocked[a];
they gnashed their teeth at me.
17 O Lord, how long will you look on?
Rescue my life from their ravages,
my precious life from these lions.
18 I will give you thanks in the great assembly;
among throngs of people I will praise you.

19 Let not those gloat over me
who are my enemies without cause;
let not those who hate me without reason
maliciously wink the eye.
20 They do not speak peaceably,
but devise false accusations
against those who live quietly in the land.
21 They gape at me and say, "Aha! Aha!
With our own eyes we have seen it."

22 O LORD, you have seen this; be not silent.
Do not be far from me, O Lord.
23 Awake, and rise to my defense!
Contend for me, my God and Lord.
24 Vindicate me in your righteousness, O LORD my God;
do not let them gloat over me.
25 Do not let them think, "Aha, just what we wanted!"
or say, "We have swallowed him up."

26 May all who gloat over my distress
be put to shame and confusion;
may all who exalt themselves over me
be clothed with shame and disgrace.
27 May those who delight in my vindication
shout for joy and gladness;
may they always say, "The LORD be exalted,
who delights in the well-being of his servant."
28 My tongue will speak of your righteousness
and of your praises all day long.

Psalm 36

For the director of music.
Of David the servant of the LORD.

1 An oracle is within my heart
concerning the sinfulness of the wicked:[b]
There is no fear of God
before his eyes.
2 For in his own eyes he flatters himself
too much to detect or hate his sin.
3 The words of his mouth are wicked and deceitful;
he has ceased to be wise and to do good.
4 Even on his bed he plots evil;
he commits himself to a sinful course
and does not reject what is wrong.

5 Your love, O LORD, reaches to the heavens,
your faithfulness to the skies.
6 Your righteousness is like the mighty mountains,
your justice like the great deep.
O LORD, you preserve both man and beast.
7 How priceless is your unfailing love!
Both high and low among men
find[c] refuge in the shadow of your wings.
8 They feast on the abundance of your house;
you give them drink from your river of delights.
9 For with you is the fountain of life;
in your light we see light.

[a] 16 Septuagint; Hebrew may mean *ungodly circle of mockers.* [b] 1 Or *heart: / Sin proceeds from the wicked.* [c] 7 Or *love, O God! / Men find*; or *love! / Both heavenly beings and men / find*

[10]Continue your love to those who
know you,
your righteousness to the upright
in heart.
[11]May the foot of the proud not come
against me,
nor the hand of the wicked drive
me away.
[12]See how the evildoers lie fallen—
thrown down, not able to rise!

Psalm 37[a]

Of David.

[1]Do not fret because of evil men
or be envious of those who do
wrong;
[2]for like the grass they will soon
wither,
like green plants they will soon
die away.
[3]Trust in the LORD and do good;
dwell in the land and enjoy safe
pasture.
[4]Delight yourself in the LORD
and he will give you the desires of
your heart.
[5]Commit your way to the LORD;
trust in him and he will do this:
[6]He will make your righteousness
shine like the dawn,
the justice of your cause like the
noonday sun.
[7]Be still before the LORD and wait
patiently for him;
do not fret when men succeed in
their ways,
when they carry out their wicked
schemes.
[8]Refrain from anger and turn from
wrath;
do not fret—it leads only to evil.
[9]For evil men will be cut off,
but those who hope in the LORD
will inherit the land.
[10]A little while, and the wicked will be
no more;
though you look for them, they
will not be found.
[11]But the meek will inherit the land
and enjoy great peace.
[12]The wicked plot against the
righteous
and gnash their teeth at them;
[13]but the Lord laughs at the wicked,
for he knows their day is coming.
[14]The wicked draw the sword
and bend the bow
to bring down the poor and needy,
to slay those whose ways are
upright.
[15]But their swords will pierce their
own hearts,
and their bows will be broken.
[16]Better the little that the righteous
have
than the wealth of many wicked;
[17]for the power of the wicked will be
broken,
but the LORD upholds the
righteous.
[18]The days of the blameless are
known to the LORD,
and their inheritance will endure
forever.
[19]In times of disaster they will not
wither;
in days of famine they will enjoy
plenty.
[20]But the wicked will perish:
The LORD's enemies will be like
the beauty of the fields,
they will vanish—vanish like
smoke.
[21]The wicked borrow and do not
repay,
but the righteous give generously;
[22]those the LORD blesses will inherit
the land,
but those he curses will be cut off.
[23]If the LORD delights in a man's way,
he makes his steps firm;
[24]though he stumble, he will not fall,
for the LORD upholds him with
his hand.

[a]This psalm is an acrostic poem, the stanzas of which begin with the successive letters of the Hebrew alphabet.

25 I was young and now I am old,
yet I have never seen the righteous forsaken
or their children begging bread.
26 They are always generous and lend freely;
their children will be blessed.

27 Turn from evil and do good;
then you will dwell in the land forever.
28 For the LORD loves the just
and will not forsake his faithful ones.

They will be protected forever,
but the offspring of the wicked will be cut off;
29 the righteous will inherit the land
and dwell in it forever.

30 The mouth of the righteous man utters wisdom,
and his tongue speaks what is just.
31 The law of his God is in his heart;
his feet do not slip.

32 The wicked lie in wait for the righteous,
seeking their very lives;
33 but the LORD will not leave them in their power
or let them be condemned when brought to trial.

34 Wait for the LORD
and keep his way.
He will exalt you to inherit the land;
when the wicked are cut off, you will see it.

35 I have seen a wicked and ruthless man
flourishing like a green tree in its native soil,
36 but he soon passed away and was no more;
though I looked for him, he could not be found.

37 Consider the blameless, observe the upright;
there is a future[a] for the man of peace.
38 But all sinners will be destroyed;
the future[b] of the wicked will be cut off.

39 The salvation of the righteous comes from the LORD;
he is their stronghold in time of trouble.
40 The LORD helps them and delivers them;
he delivers them from the wicked and saves them,
because they take refuge in him.

Psalm 38

A psalm of David. A petition.

1 O LORD, do not rebuke me in your anger
or discipline me in your wrath.
2 For your arrows have pierced me,
and your hand has come down upon me.
3 Because of your wrath there is no health in my body;
my bones have no soundness because of my sin.
4 My guilt has overwhelmed me
like a burden too heavy to bear.

5 My wounds fester and are loathsome
because of my sinful folly.
6 I am bowed down and brought very low;
all day long I go about mourning.
7 My back is filled with searing pain;
there is no health in my body.
8 I am feeble and utterly crushed;
I groan in anguish of heart.

9 All my longings lie open before you, O Lord;
my sighing is not hidden from you.
10 My heart pounds, my strength fails me;
even the light has gone from my eyes.
11 My friends and companions avoid me because of my wounds;
my neighbors stay far away.
12 Those who seek my life set their traps,

[a]37 Or *there will be posterity* [b]38 Or *posterity*

those who would harm me talk of
my ruin;
all day long they plot deception.

13 I am like a deaf man, who cannot
hear,
like a mute, who cannot open his
mouth;
14 I have become like a man who does
not hear,
whose mouth can offer no reply.
15 I wait for you, O LORD;
you will answer, O Lord my God.
16 For I said, "Do not let them gloat
or exalt themselves over me when
my foot slips."

17 For I am about to fall,
and my pain is ever with me.
18 I confess my iniquity;
I am troubled by my sin.
19 Many are those who are my
vigorous enemies;
those who hate me without
reason are numerous.
20 Those who repay my good with
evil
slander me when I pursue what is
good.

21 O LORD, do not forsake me;
be not far from me, O my God.
22 Come quickly to help me,
O Lord my Savior.

Psalm 39

For the director of music. For Jeduthun.
A psalm of David.

1 I said, "I will watch my ways
and keep my tongue from sin;
I will put a muzzle on my mouth
as long as the wicked are in my
presence."
2 But when I was silent and still,
not even saying anything good,
my anguish increased.
3 My heart grew hot within me,
and as I meditated, the fire
burned;
then I spoke with my tongue:
4 "Show me, O LORD, my life's end
and the number of my days;
let me know how fleeting is my
life.
5 You have made my days a mere
handbreadth;
the span of my years is as nothing
before you.
Each man's life is but a breath.
Selah

6 Man is a mere phantom as he goes
to and fro:
He bustles about, but only in vain;
he heaps up wealth, not knowing
who will get it.

7 "But now, Lord, what do I look for?
My hope is in you.
8 Save me from all my transgressions;
do not make me the scorn of fools.
9 I was silent; I would not open my
mouth,
for you are the one who has done
this.
10 Remove your scourge from me;
I am overcome by the blow of
your hand.
11 You rebuke and discipline men for
their sin;
you consume their wealth like a
moth—
each man is but a breath. *Selah*

12 "Hear my prayer, O LORD,
listen to my cry for help;
be not deaf to my weeping.
For I dwell with you as an alien,
a stranger, as all my fathers were.
13 Look away from me, that I may
rejoice again
before I depart and am no more."

Psalm 40

For the director of music.
Of David. A psalm.

1 I waited patiently for the LORD;
he turned to me and heard my
cry.
2 He lifted me out of the slimy pit,
out of the mud and mire;
he set my feet on a rock
and gave me a firm place to stand.
3 He put a new song in my mouth,
a hymn of praise to our God.

Many will see and fear
and put their trust in the LORD.

4 Blessed is the man
who makes the LORD his trust,
who does not look to the proud,
to those who turn aside to false gods.[a]
5 Many, O LORD my God,
are the wonders you have done.
The things you planned for us
no one can recount to you;
were I to speak and tell of them,
they would be too many to declare.

6 Sacrifice and offering you did not desire,
but my ears you have pierced[b,c];
burnt offerings and sin offerings
you did not require.
7 Then I said, "Here I am, I have come—
it is written about me in the scroll.[d]
8 I desire to do your will, O my God;
your law is within my heart."

9 I proclaim righteousness in the great assembly;
I do not seal my lips,
as you know, O LORD.
10 I do not hide your righteousness in my heart;
I speak of your faithfulness and salvation.
I do not conceal your love and your truth
from the great assembly.

11 Do not withhold your mercy from me, O LORD;
may your love and your truth
always protect me.
12 For troubles without number
surround me;
my sins have overtaken me, and I cannot see.
They are more than the hairs of my head,
and my heart fails within me.
13 Be pleased, O LORD, to save me;
O LORD, come quickly to help me.

14 May all who seek to take my life
be put to shame and confusion;
may all who desire my ruin
be turned back in disgrace.
15 May those who say to me, "Aha! Aha!"
be appalled at their own shame.
16 But may all who seek you
rejoice and be glad in you;
may those who love your salvation
always say,
"The LORD be exalted!"
17 Yet I am poor and needy;
may the Lord think of me.
You are my help and my deliverer;
O my God, do not delay.

Psalm 41

For the director of music.
A psalm of David.

1 Blessed is he who has regard for the weak;
the LORD delivers him in times of trouble.
2 The LORD will protect him and preserve his life;
he will bless him in the land
and not surrender him to the desire of his foes.
3 The LORD will sustain him on his sickbed
and restore him from his bed of illness.

4 I said, "O LORD, have mercy on me;
heal me, for I have sinned against you."
5 My enemies say of me in malice,
"When will he die and his name perish?"
6 Whenever one comes to see me,
he speaks falsely, while his heart gathers slander;
then he goes out and spreads it abroad.

7 All my enemies whisper together against me;

[a]4 Or *to falsehood* [b]6 Hebrew; Septuagint *but a body you have prepared for me* (see also Symmachus and Theodotion) [c]6 Or *opened* [d]7 Or *come / with the scroll written for me*

they imagine the worst for me,
saying,
8 "A vile disease has beset him;
he will never get up from the
place where he lies."
9 Even my close friend, whom I
trusted,
he who shared my bread,
has lifted up his heel against
me.

10 But you, O LORD, have mercy on
me;
raise me up, that I may repay
them.
11 I know that you are pleased with me,
for my enemy does not triumph
over me.
12 In my integrity you uphold me
and set me in your presence
forever.

13 Praise be to the LORD, the God of
Israel,
from everlasting to everlasting.
Amen and Amen.

SHARPEN THE FOCUS

Most time and money management books begin by asking readers to identify their goals. Until we know what we want to achieve, it's impossible to select a strategy.

Scripture too insists that we clearly identify our priorities for life. "Seek first His kingdom and His righteousness, and all these [material necessities] will be given to you as well" (Matthew 6:33). Psalm 37:4 says, in essence, the same thing:

Delight yourself in the LORD
and He will give you the desires of your heart.

Seeking first the kingdom and delighting oneself in the Lord both involve making God's priorities our own. A person with God's priorities weeps over the lost, feeds the hungry, provides for the homeless, comforts the sick, and participates in proclaiming the Gospel.

For those who died with Christ and rose with Christ (Romans 6:1–14), these things are not what we "have to do," but what we "get to do." Service becomes a possibility and a privilege. Our Lord promises that He will "give [us] the desires of [our] heart"; He will plant in our hearts the seeds of godly desires that will, by His grace, sprout up and grow to produce a harvest of righteous attitudes and actions.

WEEK 45 • SATURDAY

Psalms 42:1—47:9

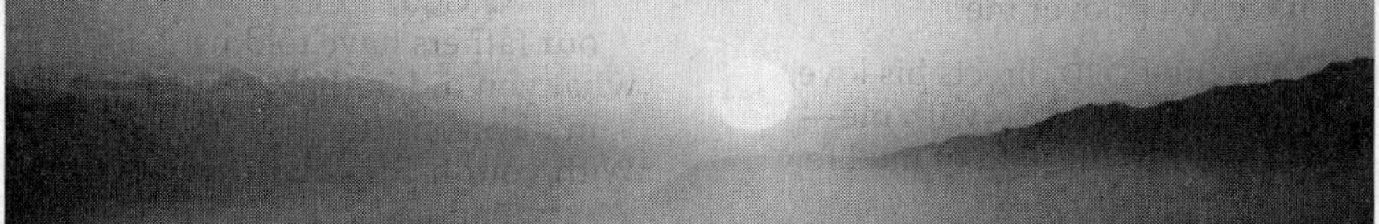

GET THE BIG PICTURE

In two of today's psalms, our Lord is pictured as a great King. As you pray all six psalms, keep in mind Christ's rule over earth for the sake of His people. We are the "city of God" (Psalm 46:4) that will not fall, His holy Christian Church. If time is short, focus on Psalm 46.

BOOK II

Psalms 42–72

Psalm 42[a]

For the director of music.
A *maskil*[b] of the Sons of Korah.

1 As the deer pants for streams of water,
so my soul pants for you, O God.
2 My soul thirsts for God, for the living God.
When can I go and meet with God?
3 My tears have been my food
day and night,
while men say to me all day long,
"Where is your God?"
4 These things I remember
as I pour out my soul:
how I used to go with the multitude,
leading the procession to the house of God,
with shouts of joy and thanksgiving
among the festive throng.

5 Why are you downcast, O my soul?
Why so disturbed within me?
Put your hope in God,
for I will yet praise him,
my Savior and 6 my God.

My[c] soul is downcast within me;
therefore I will remember you
from the land of the Jordan,
the heights of Hermon—from Mount Mizar.
7 Deep calls to deep
in the roar of your waterfalls;
all your waves and breakers
have swept over me.

8 By day the LORD directs his love,
at night his song is with me—
a prayer to the God of my life.

9 I say to God my Rock,
"Why have you forgotten me?
Why must I go about mourning,
oppressed by the enemy?"
10 My bones suffer mortal agony
as my foes taunt me,
saying to me all day long,
"Where is your God?"

11 Why are you downcast, O my soul?
Why so disturbed within me?
Put your hope in God,
for I will yet praise him,
my Savior and my God.

Psalm 43[a]

1 Vindicate me, O God,
and plead my cause against an ungodly nation;
rescue me from deceitful and wicked men.
2 You are God my stronghold.
Why have you rejected me?
Why must I go about mourning,
oppressed by the enemy?
3 Send forth your light and your truth,
let them guide me;
let them bring me to your holy mountain,
to the place where you dwell.
4 Then will I go to the altar of God,
to God, my joy and my delight.
I will praise you with the harp,
O God, my God.

5 Why are you downcast, O my soul?
Why so disturbed within me?
Put your hope in God,
for I will yet praise him,
my Savior and my God.

Psalm 44

For the director of music.
Of the Sons of Korah. A *maskil.*[b]

1 We have heard with our ears, O God;
our fathers have told us
what you did in their days,
in days long ago.
2 With your hand you drove out the nations
and planted our fathers;

[a] In many Hebrew manuscripts Psalms 42 and 43 constitute one psalm. [b] Title: Probably a literary or musical term [c] 5,6 A few Hebrew manuscripts, Septuagint and Syriac; most Hebrew manuscripts *praise him for his saving help.* / [6] *O my God, my*

you crushed the peoples
and made our fathers flourish.
3 It was not by their sword that they won the land,
nor did their arm bring them victory;
it was your right hand, your arm,
and the light of your face, for you loved them.

4 You are my King and my God,
who decrees[a] victories for Jacob.
5 Through you we push back our enemies;
through your name we trample our foes.
6 I do not trust in my bow,
my sword does not bring me victory;
7 but you give us victory over our enemies,
you put our adversaries to shame.
8 In God we make our boast all day long,
and we will praise your name forever. *Selah*

9 But now you have rejected and humbled us;
you no longer go out with our armies.
10 You made us retreat before the enemy,
and our adversaries have plundered us.
11 You gave us up to be devoured like sheep
and have scattered us among the nations.
12 You sold your people for a pittance,
gaining nothing from their sale.

13 You have made us a reproach to our neighbors,
the scorn and derision of those around us.
14 You have made us a byword among the nations;
the peoples shake their heads at us.
15 My disgrace is before me all day long,
and my face is covered with shame
16 at the taunts of those who reproach and revile me,
because of the enemy, who is bent on revenge.

17 All this happened to us,
though we had not forgotten you
or been false to your covenant.
18 Our hearts had not turned back;
our feet had not strayed from your path.
19 But you crushed us and made us a haunt for jackals
and covered us over with deep darkness.

20 If we had forgotten the name of our God
or spread out our hands to a foreign god,
21 would not God have discovered it,
since he knows the secrets of the heart?
22 Yet for your sake we face death all day long;
we are considered as sheep to be slaughtered.

23 Awake, O Lord! Why do you sleep?
Rouse yourself! Do not reject us forever.
24 Why do you hide your face
and forget our misery and oppression?

25 We are brought down to the dust;
our bodies cling to the ground.
26 Rise up and help us;
redeem us because of your unfailing love.

Psalm 45

For the director of music. To ⌞the tune of⌟ "Lilies." Of the Sons of Korah. A *maskil.*[b] A wedding song.

1 My heart is stirred by a noble theme
as I recite my verses for the king;
my tongue is the pen of a skillful writer.

[a] 4 Septuagint, Aquila and Syriac; Hebrew *King, O God; / command* [b] Title: Probably a literary or musical term

[2]You are the most excellent of men
and your lips have been anointed
with grace,
since God has blessed you forever.
[3]Gird your sword upon your side,
O mighty one;
clothe yourself with splendor and
majesty.
[4]In your majesty ride forth
victoriously
in behalf of truth, humility and
righteousness;
let your right hand display
awesome deeds.
[5]Let your sharp arrows pierce the
hearts of the king's enemies;
let the nations fall beneath your
feet.
[6]Your throne, O God, will last for
ever and ever;
a scepter of justice will be the
scepter of your kingdom.
[7]You love righteousness and hate
wickedness;
therefore God, your God, has set
you above your companions
by anointing you with the oil of
joy.
[8]All your robes are fragrant with
myrrh and aloes and cassia;
from palaces adorned with ivory
the music of the strings makes you
glad.
[9]Daughters of kings are among your
honored women;
at your right hand is the royal
bride in gold of Ophir.
[10]Listen, O daughter, consider and
give ear:
Forget your people and your
father's house.
[11]The king is enthralled by your
beauty;
honor him, for he is your lord.
[12]The Daughter of Tyre will come with
a gift,[a]
men of wealth will seek your
favor.
[13]All glorious is the princess within
her chamber;
her gown is interwoven with
gold.
[14]In embroidered garments she is led
to the king;
her virgin companions follow her
and are brought to you.
[15]They are led in with joy and
gladness;
they enter the palace of the king.
[16]Your sons will take the place of your
fathers;
you will make them princes
throughout the land.
[17]I will perpetuate your memory
through all generations;
therefore the nations will praise
you for ever and ever.

Psalm 46

For the director of music. Of the Sons of Korah. According to *alamoth.*[b] A song.

[1]God is our refuge and strength,
an ever-present help in trouble.
[2]Therefore we will not fear, though
the earth give way
and the mountains fall into the
heart of the sea,
[3]though its waters roar and foam
and the mountains quake with
their surging. *Selah*

[4]There is a river whose streams make
glad the city of God,
the holy place where the Most
High dwells.
[5]God is within her, she will not fall;
God will help her at break of day.
[6]Nations are in uproar, kingdoms fall;
he lifts his voice, the earth melts.
[7]The LORD Almighty is with us;
the God of Jacob is our fortress.
Selah

[8]Come and see the works of the
LORD,
the desolations he has brought on
the earth.
[9]He makes wars cease to the ends of
the earth;
he breaks the bow and shatters
the spear,

[a]12 Or *A Tyrian robe is among the gifts* [b]Title: Probably a musical term

he burns the shields[a] with fire.
10 "Be still, and know that I am God;
I will be exalted among the nations,
I will be exalted in the earth."

11 The LORD Almighty is with us;
the God of Jacob is our fortress. *Selah*

Psalm 47

For the director of music.
Of the Sons of Korah. A psalm.

1 Clap your hands, all you nations;
shout to God with cries of joy.
2 How awesome is the LORD Most High,
the great King over all the earth!
3 He subdued nations under us,
peoples under our feet.
4 He chose our inheritance for us,
the pride of Jacob, whom he loved. *Selah*

5 God has ascended amid shouts of joy,
the LORD amid the sounding of trumpets.
6 Sing praises to God, sing praises;
sing praises to our King, sing praises.

7 For God is the King of all the earth;
sing to him a psalm[b] of praise.
8 God reigns over the nations;
God is seated on his holy throne.
9 The nobles of the nations assemble
as the people of the God of Abraham,
for the kings[c] of the earth belong to God;
he is greatly exalted.

[a] 9 Or *chariots* [b] 7 Or *a maskil* (probably a literary or musical term) [c] 9 Or *shields*

SHARPEN THE FOCUS

Again and again the Scriptures speak of the "river" mentioned in Psalm 46:4. The psalmist says this river gladdens the city of God—even while she sits surrounded by the rage of the nations who oppose this city and her great King. This river flows even now, here on earth, so that we will not fall and so that the Gospel will not fail. Jesus Himself identifies this "river":

> *Jesus . . . said . . . "If anyone is thirsty, let him come to Me and drink. Whoever believes in Me, as the Scripture has said, streams of living water will flow from within him." By this He meant the Spirit, whom those who believed in Him were later to receive . . ."* (John 7:37–39)

How are we refreshed by this life-giving water? How do we become channels of refreshment for our brothers and sisters in the faith? Look back at Psalm 1. As we meditate on God's Word, Psalm 1:3 tells us, we become like trees, planted next to channels of water. Rooted in the Word, we need never move away from the riverbank to the spiritual deserts that lie in the distance. No, here the Holy Spirit strengthens us. Here the Spirit soothes and refreshes us. Here we drink deeply and receive the ability to refresh others.

WEEK 46 • MONDAY

Psalms 48:1—53:6

Most of today's psalms touch in one way or another on the theme, "godlessness is foolishness." As you read, note that the psalm writers often referred to the people of God (the invisible church) by using terms like *Zion, Jerusalem, daughters of Judah, Jacob,* and *Israel.* While the outward, visible church includes both believers and unbelievers, "Zion" and its synonyms usually encompass only those who belong to God through faith in the promised Messiah. If time is short, focus on Psalm 48.

Psalm 48

A song. A psalm of the Sons of Korah.

1 Great is the LORD, and most worthy
of praise,
in the city of our God, his holy
mountain.
2 It is beautiful in its loftiness,
the joy of the whole earth.
Like the utmost heights of Zaphon[a]
is Mount Zion,
the[b] city of the Great King.
3 God is in her citadels;
he has shown himself to be her
fortress.

4 When the kings joined forces,
when they advanced together,
5 they saw ⌊her⌋ and were astounded;
they fled in terror.
6 Trembling seized them there,
pain like that of a woman in labor.
7 You destroyed them like ships of
Tarshish
shattered by an east wind.

8 As we have heard,
so have we seen
in the city of the LORD Almighty,
in the city of our God:
God makes her secure forever.
Selah

9 Within your temple, O God,
we meditate on your unfailing
love.
10 Like your name, O God,
your praise reaches to the ends of
the earth;
your right hand is filled with
righteousness.
11 Mount Zion rejoices,
the villages of Judah are glad
because of your judgments.

12 Walk about Zion, go around her,
count her towers,
13 consider well her ramparts,
view her citadels,
that you may tell of them to the
next generation.
14 For this God is our God for ever and
ever;
he will be our guide even to the
end.

Psalm 49

For the director of music.
Of the Sons of Korah. A psalm.

1 Hear this, all you peoples;
listen, all who live in this world,
2 both low and high,
rich and poor alike:
3 My mouth will speak words of
wisdom;
the utterance from my heart will
give understanding.
4 I will turn my ear to a proverb;

[a]2 *Zaphon* can refer to a sacred mountain or the direction north. [b]2 Or *earth, / Mount Zion, on the northern side / of the*

with the harp I will expound my
riddle:
5 Why should I fear when evil days
come,
when wicked deceivers surround
me—
6 those who trust in their wealth
and boast of their great riches?
7 No man can redeem the life of
another
or give to God a ransom for him—
8 the ransom for a life is costly,
no payment is ever enough—
9 that he should live on forever
and not see decay.
10 For all can see that wise men die;
the foolish and the senseless alike
perish
and leave their wealth to others.
11 Their tombs will remain their
houses[a] forever,
their dwellings for endless
generations,
though they had[b] named lands
after themselves.

12 But man, despite his riches, does not
endure;
he is[c] like the beasts that perish.
13 This is the fate of those who trust in
themselves,
and of their followers, who
approve their sayings. *Selah*
14 Like sheep they are destined for the
grave,[d]
and death will feed on them.
The upright will rule over them in
the morning;
their forms will decay in the
grave,[d]
far from their princely mansions.
15 But God will redeem my life[e] from
the grave;
he will surely take me to himself.
Selah

16 Do not be overawed when a man
grows rich,
when the splendor of his house
increases;
17 for he will take nothing with him
when he dies,
his splendor will not descend with
him.
18 Though while he lived he counted
himself blessed—
and men praise you when you
prosper—
19 he will join the generation of his
fathers,
who will never see the light ⌞of
life⌟.

20 A man who has riches without
understanding
is like the beasts that perish.

Psalm 50

A psalm of Asaph.

1 The Mighty One, God, the LORD,
speaks and summons the earth
from the rising of the sun to the
place where it sets.
2 From Zion, perfect in beauty,
God shines forth.
3 Our God comes and will not be
silent;
a fire devours before him,
and around him a tempest rages.
4 He summons the heavens above,
and the earth, that he may judge
his people:
5 "Gather to me my consecrated ones,
who made a covenant with me by
sacrifice."
6 And the heavens proclaim his
righteousness,
for God himself is judge. *Selah*

7 "Hear, O my people, and I will
speak,
O Israel, and I will testify against
you:
I am God, your God.
8 I do not rebuke you for your
sacrifices
or your burnt offerings, which are
ever before me.

[a]*11* Septuagint and Syriac; Hebrew *In their thoughts their houses will remain* [b]*11* Or / *for they have* [c]*12* Hebrew; Septuagint and Syriac read verse 12 the same as verse 20. [d]*14* Hebrew *Sheol*; also in verse 15 [e]*15* Or *soul*

9 I have no need of a bull from your
stall
or of goats from your pens,
10 for every animal of the forest is
mine,
and the cattle on a thousand hills.
11 I know every bird in the mountains,
and the creatures of the field are
mine.
12 If I were hungry I would not tell you,
for the world is mine, and all that
is in it.
13 Do I eat the flesh of bulls
or drink the blood of goats?
14 Sacrifice thank offerings to God,
fulfill your vows to the Most High,
15 and call upon me in the day of
trouble;
I will deliver you, and you will
honor me."

16 But to the wicked, God says:

"What right have you to recite my
laws
or take my covenant on your lips?
17 You hate my instruction
and cast my words behind you.
18 When you see a thief, you join with
him;
you throw in your lot with
adulterers.
19 You use your mouth for evil
and harness your tongue to
deceit.
20 You speak continually against your
brother
and slander your own mother's
son.
21 These things you have done and I
kept silent;
you thought I was altogether[a] like
you.
But I will rebuke you
and accuse you to your face.

22 "Consider this, you who forget God,
or I will tear you to pieces, with
none to rescue:
23 He who sacrifices thank offerings
honors me,
and he prepares the way
so that I may show him[b] the
salvation of God."

Psalm 51

For the director of music.
A psalm of David. When the prophet Nathan came to him after David had committed adultery with Bathsheba.

1 Have mercy on me, O God,
according to your unfailing love;
according to your great compassion
blot out my transgressions.
2 Wash away all my iniquity
and cleanse me from my sin.

3 For I know my transgressions,
and my sin is always before me.
4 Against you, you only, have I sinned
and done what is evil in your
sight,
so that you are proved right when
you speak
and justified when you judge.
5 Surely I was sinful at birth,
sinful from the time my mother
conceived me.
6 Surely you desire truth in the inner
parts[c];
you teach[d] me wisdom in the
inmost place.

7 Cleanse me with hyssop, and I will
be clean;
wash me, and I will be whiter
than snow.
8 Let me hear joy and gladness;
let the bones you have crushed
rejoice.
9 Hide your face from my sins
and blot out all my iniquity.

10 Create in me a pure heart, O God,
and renew a steadfast spirit
within me.
11 Do not cast me from your presence
or take your Holy Spirit from me.
12 Restore to me the joy of your
salvation
and grant me a willing spirit, to
sustain me.

[a] 21 Or *thought the 'I AM' was* [b] 23 Or *and to him who considers his way / I will show* [c] 6 The meaning of the Hebrew for this phrase is uncertain. [d] 6 Or *you desired . . . ; / you taught*

13 Then I will teach transgressors your ways,
and sinners will turn back to you.
14 Save me from bloodguilt, O God,
the God who saves me,
and my tongue will sing of your righteousness.
15 O Lord, open my lips,
and my mouth will declare your praise.
16 You do not delight in sacrifice, or I would bring it;
you do not take pleasure in burnt offerings.
17 The sacrifices of God are[a] a broken spirit;
a broken and contrite heart,
O God, you will not despise.

18 In your good pleasure make Zion prosper;
build up the walls of Jerusalem.
19 Then there will be righteous sacrifices,
whole burnt offerings to delight you;
then bulls will be offered on your altar.

Psalm 52

For the director of music. A *maskil*[b] of David. When Doeg the Edomite had gone to Saul and told him: "David has gone to the house of Ahimelech."

1 Why do you boast of evil, you mighty man?
Why do you boast all day long,
you who are a disgrace in the eyes of God?
2 Your tongue plots destruction;
it is like a sharpened razor,
you who practice deceit.
3 You love evil rather than good,
falsehood rather than speaking the truth. *Selah*
4 You love every harmful word,
O you deceitful tongue!
5 Surely God will bring you down to everlasting ruin:
He will snatch you up and tear you from your tent;
he will uproot you from the land of the living. *Selah*
6 The righteous will see and fear;
they will laugh at him, saying,
7 "Here now is the man
who did not make God his stronghold
but trusted in his great wealth
and grew strong by destroying others!"
8 But I am like an olive tree
flourishing in the house of God;
I trust in God's unfailing love
for ever and ever.
9 I will praise you forever for what you have done;
in your name I will hope, for your name is good.
I will praise you in the presence of your saints.

Psalm 53

For the director of music. According to *mahalath*.[c] A *maskil*[b] of David.

1 The fool says in his heart,
"There is no God."
They are corrupt, and their ways are vile;
there is no one who does good.

2 God looks down from heaven
on the sons of men
to see if there are any who understand,
any who seek God.
3 Everyone has turned away,
they have together become corrupt;
there is no one who does good,
not even one.

4 Will the evildoers never learn—
those who devour my people as men eat bread
and who do not call on God?
5 There they were, overwhelmed with dread,

[a]17 Or *My sacrifice, O God, is* [b]Title: Probably a literary or musical term [c]Title: Probably a musical term

where there was nothing to dread.
God scattered the bones of those
who attacked you;
you put them to shame, for God
despised them.

6 Oh, that salvation for Israel would
come out of Zion!
When God restores the fortunes of
his people,
let Jacob rejoice and Israel be glad!

SHARPEN THE FOCUS

Near the main gate of Busch Stadium in downtown St. Louis stand nine flag poles, each 40 feet tall. Each carries at its base a number: . . . 1964, 1967, 1982 . . . These numbers are, of course, dates—years in which the Cardinals won the World Series. The dates conjure up memories and a sense of pride in even casual Cardinal fans. The dates set in motion a highlight reel starring Stan Musial, Lou Brock, Ozzie Smith, to name only a few.

In ancient times when a particular city won a victory, the citizens erected not a new flag pole, but a new tower. From that point on, residents who saw the tower remembered the heroes, the struggle, the pain, and the triumph of a particular battle.

With this custom in mind, read Psalm 48:12–14. Now, ask yourself about the "towers" surrounding Christ's church. What victories has our Lord won for us? What "towers" stand tall over your individual life? And how will you share the joy of those victories with the next generation? ☼

WEEK 46 • TUESDAY

Psalms 54:1—60:12

GET THE BIG PICTURE

Most of the psalms in today's reading refer to the words spoken by the psalmist's enemies. These words are identified as sinful (59:12), threatening (55:11), and deceptive (55:21). As you read, ask yourself in what ways the enemy, Satan, lies to you. Have you fallen for any of those lies lately? If time is short, focus on Psalm 57.

Psalm 54

For the director of music. With stringed
instruments. A *maskil*[a] of David.
When the Ziphites had gone to Saul
and said, "Is not David hiding among us?"

1 Save me, O God, by your name;
vindicate me by your might.
2 Hear my prayer, O God;
listen to the words of my mouth.

3 Strangers are attacking me;
ruthless men seek my life—
men without regard for God.
Selah

4 Surely God is my help;
the Lord is the one who sustains
me.

5 Let evil recoil on those who slander
me;
in your faithfulness destroy them.

[a]Title: Probably a literary or musical term

[6]I will sacrifice a freewill offering to
you;
I will praise your name, O LORD,
for it is good.
[7]For he has delivered me from all my
troubles,
and my eyes have looked in
triumph on my foes.

Psalm 55

For the director of music. With stringed instruments. A *maskil*[a] of David.

[1]Listen to my prayer, O God,
do not ignore my plea;
[2] hear me and answer me.
My thoughts trouble me and I am
distraught
[3] at the voice of the enemy,
at the stares of the wicked;
for they bring down suffering upon
me
and revile me in their anger.

[4]My heart is in anguish within me;
the terrors of death assail me.
[5]Fear and trembling have beset me;
horror has overwhelmed me.
[6]I said, "Oh, that I had the wings of a
dove!
I would fly away and be at rest—
[7]I would flee far away
and stay in the desert; *Selah*
[8]I would hurry to my place of shelter,
far from the tempest and storm."

[9]Confuse the wicked, O Lord,
confound their speech,
for I see violence and strife in the
city.
[10]Day and night they prowl about on
its walls;
malice and abuse are within it.
[11]Destructive forces are at work in the
city;
threats and lies never leave its
streets.

[12]If an enemy were insulting me,
I could endure it;
if a foe were raising himself against
me,
I could hide from him.
[13]But it is you, a man like myself,
my companion, my close friend,
[14]with whom I once enjoyed sweet
fellowship
as we walked with the throng at
the house of God.

[15]Let death take my enemies by
surprise;
let them go down alive to the
grave,[b]
for evil finds lodging among them.

[16]But I call to God,
and the LORD saves me.
[17]Evening, morning and noon
I cry out in distress,
and he hears my voice.
[18]He ransoms me unharmed
from the battle waged against me,
even though many oppose me.
[19]God, who is enthroned forever,
will hear them and afflict them—
Selah
men who never change their ways
and have no fear of God.

[20]My companion attacks his friends;
he violates his covenant.
[21]His speech is smooth as butter,
yet war is in his heart;
his words are more soothing than oil,
yet they are drawn swords.

[22]Cast your cares on the LORD
and he will sustain you;
he will never let the righteous fall.
[23]But you, O God, will bring down the
wicked
into the pit of corruption;
bloodthirsty and deceitful men
will not live out half their days.

But as for me, I trust in you.

Psalm 56

For the director of music. To ⌊the tune of⌋ "A Dove on Distant Oaks." Of David. A *miktam*.[a] When the Philistines had seized him in Gath.

[1]Be merciful to me, O God, for men
hotly pursue me;

[a]Title: Probably a literary or musical term
[b]15 Hebrew *Sheol*

all day long they press their
attack.
²My slanderers pursue me all day
long;
many are attacking me in their
pride.
³When I am afraid,
I will trust in you.
⁴In God, whose word I praise,
in God I trust; I will not be afraid.
What can mortal man do to me?
⁵All day long they twist my words;
they are always plotting to harm
me.
⁶They conspire, they lurk,
they watch my steps,
eager to take my life.
⁷On no account let them escape;
in your anger, O God, bring down
the nations.
⁸Record my lament;
list my tears on your scroll[a]—
are they not in your record?
⁹Then my enemies will turn back
when I call for help.
By this I will know that God is for
me.
¹⁰In God, whose word I praise,
in the LORD, whose word I
praise—
¹¹in God I trust; I will not be afraid.
What can man do to me?
¹²I am under vows to you, O God;
I will present my thank offerings
to you.
¹³For you have delivered me[b] from
death
and my feet from stumbling,
that I may walk before God
in the light of life.[c]

Psalm 57

For the director of music. ⌊To the tune of⌋ "Do Not Destroy." Of David. A *miktam*.[d] When he had fled from Saul into the cave.

¹Have mercy on me, O God, have
mercy on me,
for in you my soul takes refuge.
I will take refuge in the shadow of
your wings
until the disaster has passed.

²I cry out to God Most High,
to God, who fulfills ⌊his purpose⌋
for me.
³He sends from heaven and saves
me,
rebuking those who hotly pursue
me; *Selah*
God sends his love and his
faithfulness.

⁴I am in the midst of lions;
I lie among ravenous beasts—
men whose teeth are spears and
arrows,
whose tongues are sharp swords.

⁵Be exalted, O God, above the
heavens;
let your glory be over all the
earth.

⁶They spread a net for my feet—
I was bowed down in distress.
They dug a pit in my path—
but they have fallen into it
themselves. *Selah*

⁷My heart is steadfast, O God,
my heart is steadfast;
I will sing and make music.
⁸Awake, my soul!
Awake, harp and lyre!
I will awaken the dawn.

⁹I will praise you, O Lord, among the
nations;
I will sing of you among the
peoples.
¹⁰For great is your love, reaching to
the heavens;
your faithfulness reaches to the
skies.

¹¹Be exalted, O God, above the
heavens;
let your glory be over all the
earth.

[a]8 Or / *put my tears in your wineskin* [b]13 Or *my soul* [c]13 Or *the land of the living* [d]Title: Probably a literary or musical term

Psalm 58

For the director of music.
⌊To the tune of⌋ "Do Not Destroy."
Of David. A *miktam*.[a]

[1]Do you rulers indeed speak
justly?
Do you judge uprightly among
men?
[2]No, in your heart you devise
injustice,
and your hands mete out violence
on the earth.
[3]Even from birth the wicked go
astray;
from the womb they are wayward
and speak lies.
[4]Their venom is like the venom of a
snake,
like that of a cobra that has
stopped its ears,
[5]that will not heed the tune of the
charmer,
however skillful the enchanter
may be.

[6]Break the teeth in their mouths,
O God;
tear out, O LORD, the fangs of the
lions!
[7]Let them vanish like water that
flows away;
when they draw the bow, let their
arrows be blunted.
[8]Like a slug melting away as it moves
along,
like a stillborn child, may they not
see the sun.

[9]Before your pots can feel ⌊the heat of⌋
the thorns—
whether they be green or dry—
the wicked will be swept
away.[b]
[10]The righteous will be glad when
they are avenged,
when they bathe their feet in the
blood of the wicked.
[11]Then men will say,
"Surely the righteous still are
rewarded;
surely there is a God who judges
the earth."

Psalm 59

For the director of music. ⌊To the tune of⌋
"Do Not Destroy." Of David. A *miktam*.[a]
When Saul had sent men to watch David's
house in order to kill him.

[1]Deliver me from my enemies,
O God;
protect me from those who rise up
against me.
[2]Deliver me from evildoers
and save me from bloodthirsty
men.

[3]See how they lie in wait for me!
Fierce men conspire against me
for no offense or sin of mine,
O LORD.
[4]I have done no wrong, yet they are
ready to attack me.
Arise to help me; look on my
plight!
[5]O LORD God Almighty, the God of
Israel,
rouse yourself to punish all the
nations;
show no mercy to wicked traitors.
Selah

[6]They return at evening,
snarling like dogs,
and prowl about the city.
[7]See what they spew from their
mouths—
they spew out swords from their
lips,
and they say, "Who can hear us?"
[8]But you, O LORD, laugh at them;
you scoff at all those nations.

[9]O my Strength, I watch for you;
you, O God, are my fortress, [10]my
loving God.

God will go before me
and will let me gloat over those
who slander me.
[11]But do not kill them, O Lord our
shield,[c]
or my people will forget.

[a]Title: Probably a literary or musical term
[b]9 The meaning of the Hebrew for this verse is uncertain. [c]11 Or *sovereign*

In your might make them wander
about,
and bring them down.
12 For the sins of their mouths,
for the words of their lips,
let them be caught in their pride.
For the curses and lies they utter,
13 consume them in wrath,
consume them till they are no
more.
Then it will be known to the ends of
the earth
that God rules over Jacob. *Selah*

14 They return at evening,
snarling like dogs,
and prowl about the city.
15 They wander about for food
and howl if not satisfied.
16 But I will sing of your strength,
in the morning I will sing of your
love;
for you are my fortress,
my refuge in times of trouble.

17 O my Strength, I sing praise to you;
you, O God, are my fortress, my
loving God.

Psalm 60

For the director of music. To ⌊the tune of⌋ "The Lily of the Covenant." A *miktam*[a] of David. For teaching. When he fought Aram Naharaim[b] and Aram Zobah,[c] and when Joab returned and struck down twelve thousand Edomites in the Valley of Salt.

1 You have rejected us, O God, and
burst forth upon us;
you have been angry—now
restore us!
2 You have shaken the land and torn it
open;
mend its fractures, for it is
quaking.
3 You have shown your people
desperate times;
you have given us wine that
makes us stagger.

4 But for those who fear you, you
have raised a banner
to be unfurled against the bow.
Selah

5 Save us and help us with your right
hand,
that those you love may be
delivered.
6 God has spoken from his sanctuary:
"In triumph I will parcel out
Shechem
and measure off the Valley of
Succoth.
7 Gilead is mine, and Manasseh is
mine;
Ephraim is my helmet,
Judah my scepter.
8 Moab is my washbasin,
upon Edom I toss my sandal;
over Philistia I shout in triumph."

9 Who will bring me to the fortified
city?
Who will lead me to Edom?
10 Is it not you, O God, you who have
rejected us
and no longer go out with our
armies?
11 Give us aid against the enemy,
for the help of man is worthless.
12 With God we will gain the victory,
and he will trample down our
enemies.

[a]Title: Probably a literary or musical term [b]Title: That is, Arameans of Northwest Mesopotamia [c]Title: That is, Arameans of central Syria

SHARPEN THE FOCUS

Armies have always recognized that wars can be lost or won by the morale of the troops. In the days since World War II, propaganda experts have raised their skill to a fine art.

But today's propaganda experts can't hold a candle to Satan and his demons who have been perfecting their skills since well before the time of David. What lies and half-truths does Satan slip into your consciousness?

- That evil is winning in your life, your family, and our world?
- That your Christian influence or witness mean nothing?
- That God doesn't care about you or that He's getting even with you because of your sins?

Satan cannot win unless you listen and begin to believe him. You have a powerful weapon in this war of words–the Word of God! That Word assures us of our Father's love and forgiveness in Christ. That Word promises us strength to fight each battle with temptation.

Look back at the way David wielded this invincible sword in Psalm 57. He did not deny his enemy's power or fall for his scheme. Instead, he told himself the whole truth in opposition to Satan's half-truths. What truth? The truth that the Lord is loving, merciful, forgiving, powerful, and worthy of praise.

WEEK 46 • WEDNESDAY

Psalms 61:1—66:20

GET THE BIG PICTURE

Today's psalms are particularly calming and comforting during times of turmoil and trouble. As you pray them, find in Him your salvation, your rock, your fortress, and your honor (Psalm 62:5–7). If time is short, focus on Psalm 61.

Psalm 61

For the director of music.
With stringed instruments. Of David.

1 Hear my cry, O God;
listen to my prayer.

2 From the ends of the earth I call to you,
I call as my heart grows faint;
lead me to the rock that is higher than I.
3 For you have been my refuge,
a strong tower against the foe.

4 I long to dwell in your tent forever
and take refuge in the shelter of your wings. *Selah*
5 For you have heard my vows, O God;
you have given me the heritage of those who fear your name.

6 Increase the days of the king's life,
his years for many generations.
7 May he be enthroned in God's presence forever;
appoint your love and faithfulness to protect him.

8 Then will I ever sing praise to your name
and fulfill my vows day after day.

Psalm 62

For the director of music.
For Jeduthun. A psalm of David.

1 My soul finds rest in God alone;
my salvation comes from him.

[2]He alone is my rock and my
salvation;
he is my fortress, I will never be
shaken.

[3]How long will you assault a man?
Would all of you throw him
down—
this leaning wall, this tottering
fence?
[4]They fully intend to topple him
from his lofty place;
they take delight in lies.
With their mouths they bless,
but in their hearts they curse. *Selah*

[5]Find rest, O my soul, in God alone;
my hope comes from him.
[6]He alone is my rock and my
salvation;
he is my fortress, I will not be
shaken.
[7]My salvation and my honor depend
on God[a];
he is my mighty rock, my refuge.
[8]Trust in him at all times, O people;
pour out your hearts to him,
for God is our refuge. *Selah*

[9]Lowborn men are but a breath,
the highborn are but a lie;
if weighed on a balance, they are
nothing;
together they are only a breath.
[10]Do not trust in extortion
or take pride in stolen goods;
though your riches increase,
do not set your heart on them.

[11]One thing God has spoken,
two things have I heard:
that you, O God, are strong,
[12]and that you, O Lord, are loving.
Surely you will reward each person
according to what he has done.

Psalm 63

A psalm of David.
When he was in the Desert of Judah.

[1]O God, you are my God,
earnestly I seek you;
my soul thirsts for you,
my body longs for you,
in a dry and weary land
where there is no water.

[2]I have seen you in the sanctuary
and beheld your power and your
glory.
[3]Because your love is better than life,
my lips will glorify you.
[4]I will praise you as long as I live,
and in your name I will lift up my
hands.
[5]My soul will be satisfied as with the
richest of foods;
with singing lips my mouth will
praise you.

[6]On my bed I remember you;
I think of you through the
watches of the night.
[7]Because you are my help,
I sing in the shadow of your
wings.
[8]My soul clings to you;
your right hand upholds me.

[9]They who seek my life will be
destroyed;
they will go down to the depths of
the earth.
[10]They will be given over to the sword
and become food for jackals.

[11]But the king will rejoice in God;
all who swear by God's name will
praise him,
while the mouths of liars will be
silenced.

Psalm 64

For the director of music.
A psalm of David.

[1]Hear me, O God, as I voice my
complaint;
protect my life from the threat of
the enemy.
[2]Hide me from the conspiracy of the
wicked,
from that noisy crowd of
evildoers.

[3]They sharpen their tongues like
swords

[a]7 Or / *God Most High is my salvation and my honor*

and aim their words like deadly arrows.
4 They shoot from ambush at the innocent man;
they shoot at him suddenly, without fear.

5 They encourage each other in evil plans,
they talk about hiding their snares;
they say, "Who will see them[a]?"
6 They plot injustice and say,
"We have devised a perfect plan!"
Surely the mind and heart of man are cunning.

7 But God will shoot them with arrows;
suddenly they will be struck down.
8 He will turn their own tongues against them
and bring them to ruin;
all who see them will shake their heads in scorn.

9 All mankind will fear;
they will proclaim the works of God
and ponder what he has done.
10 Let the righteous rejoice in the LORD
and take refuge in him;
let all the upright in heart praise him!

Psalm 65

For the director of music.
A psalm of David. A song.

1 Praise awaits[b] you, O God, in Zion;
to you our vows will be fulfilled.
2 O you who hear prayer,
to you all men will come.
3 When we were overwhelmed by sins,
you forgave[c] our transgressions.
4 Blessed are those you choose
and bring near to live in your courts!
We are filled with the good things of your house,
of your holy temple.

5 You answer us with awesome deeds of righteousness,
O God our Savior,
the hope of all the ends of the earth
and of the farthest seas,
6 who formed the mountains by your power,
having armed yourself with strength,
7 who stilled the roaring of the seas,
the roaring of their waves,
and the turmoil of the nations.
8 Those living far away fear your wonders;
where morning dawns and evening fades
you call forth songs of joy.

9 You care for the land and water it;
you enrich it abundantly.
The streams of God are filled with water
to provide the people with grain,
for so you have ordained it.[d]
10 You drench its furrows
and level its ridges;
you soften it with showers
and bless its crops.
11 You crown the year with your bounty,
and your carts overflow with abundance.
12 The grasslands of the desert overflow;
the hills are clothed with gladness.
13 The meadows are covered with flocks
and the valleys are mantled with grain;
they shout for joy and sing.

Psalm 66

For the director of music.
A song. A psalm.

1 Shout with joy to God, all the earth!
2 Sing the glory of his name;
make his praise glorious!

[a] 5 Or *us* [b] 1 Or *befits*; the meaning of the Hebrew for this word is uncertain. [c] 3 Or *made atonement for* [d] 9 Or *for that is how you prepare the land*

3 Say to God, "How awesome are your
deeds!
So great is your power
that your enemies cringe before
you.
4 All the earth bows down to you;
they sing praise to you,
they sing praise to your name."
Selah

5 Come and see what God has done,
how awesome his works in man's
behalf!
6 He turned the sea into dry land,
they passed through the waters
on foot—
come, let us rejoice in him.
7 He rules forever by his power,
his eyes watch the nations—
let not the rebellious rise up
against him. *Selah*

8 Praise our God, O peoples,
let the sound of his praise be
heard;
9 he has preserved our lives
and kept our feet from slipping.
10 For you, O God, tested us;
you refined us like silver.
11 You brought us into prison
and laid burdens on our backs.
12 You let men ride over our heads;
we went through fire and water,
but you brought us to a place of
abundance.

13 I will come to your temple with
burnt offerings
and fulfill my vows to you—
14 vows my lips promised and my
mouth spoke
when I was in trouble.
15 I will sacrifice fat animals to you
and an offering of rams;
I will offer bulls and goats. *Selah*

16 Come and listen, all you who fear
God;
let me tell you what he has done
for me.
17 I cried out to him with my mouth;
his praise was on my tongue.
18 If I had cherished sin in my heart,
the Lord would not have
listened;
19 but God has surely listened
and heard my voice in prayer.
20 Praise be to God,
who has not rejected my prayer
or withheld his love from me!

SHARPEN THE FOCUS

Picture yourself walking in a cold rainstorm at night. The raindrops sting your face and hands. You're soaked; you feel chilled to the bone. Your flickering flashlight shines just brightly enough to see a nearby creek rising. You hear it rush wildly as you scramble for higher ground. You're not sure how to find your way to safety—you feel as if you've reached the edge of the earth.

That's the picture painted by the opening verses of Psalm 61. Overwhelmed by circumstances, the psalmist needs to reach high ground and find solid footing. And that's just what the Lord becomes for him—a high rock, a shelter (Psalm 61:2–8). The hymn writer expresses the idea with these words:

Rock of Ages, cleft for me
Let me hide myself in Thee
Let the water and the blood
From Thy riven side which flowed
Be of sin the double cure:
Cleanse me from its guilt and power.
(*Lutheran Worship* 361, stanza 1)

Because of Jesus who is our rock, the guilt of our sins cannot sweep us away. And as God's forgiven children we have received "the heritage of those who fear [His] name" (Psalm 61:5); the God-given ability to live by faith, no matter how loud the roar of dangers and temptations around us. ☼

WEEK 46 • THURSDAY

Psalms 67:1—72:20

GET THE BIG PICTURE

Several of today's psalms speak prophetically about the promised Messiah. As you pray them, keep in mind the work our Lord Jesus has done for us, especially the forgiveness and peace He earned through the blood of His cross. Also note that Psalm 72 in its entirety prophesies about Christ's office and work. He is our King! If time is short, focus on Psalm 72.

Psalm 67

For the director of music.
With stringed instruments.
A psalm. A song.

1 May God be gracious to us and bless
us
and make his face shine upon us,
Selah
2 that your ways may be known on
earth,
your salvation among all nations.

3 May the peoples praise you,
O God;
may all the peoples praise you.
4 May the nations be glad and sing for
joy,
for you rule the peoples justly
and guide the nations of the earth.
Selah
5 May the peoples praise you,
O God;
may all the peoples praise you.

6 Then the land will yield its harvest,
and God, our God, will bless us.
7 God will bless us,
and all the ends of the earth will
fear him.

Psalm 68

For the director of music. Of David.
A psalm. A song.

1 May God arise, may his enemies be
scattered;
may his foes flee before him.
2 As smoke is blown away by the
wind,
may you blow them away;
as wax melts before the fire,
may the wicked perish before
God.
3 But may the righteous be glad
and rejoice before God;
may they be happy and joyful.

4 Sing to God, sing praise to his name,
extol him who rides on the
clouds[a]—
his name is the LORD—
and rejoice before him.
5 A father to the fatherless, a defender
of widows,
is God in his holy dwelling.
6 God sets the lonely in families,[b]
he leads forth the prisoners with
singing;

[a]4 Or / *prepare the way for him who rides through the deserts* [b]6 Or *the desolate in a homeland*

but the rebellious live in a
sun-scorched land.

7 When you went out before your
people, O God,
when you marched through the
wasteland, *Selah*
8 the earth shook,
the heavens poured down rain,
before God, the One of Sinai,
before God, the God of Israel.
9 You gave abundant showers, O God;
you refreshed your weary
inheritance.
10 Your people settled in it,
and from your bounty, O God,
you provided for the poor.
11 The Lord announced the word,
and great was the company of
those who proclaimed it:
12 "Kings and armies flee in haste;
in the camps men divide the
plunder.
13 Even while you sleep among the
campfires,[a]
the wings of ⌞my⌟ dove are
sheathed with silver,
its feathers with shining gold."
14 When the Almighty[b] scattered the
kings in the land,
it was like snow fallen on Zalmon.

15 The mountains of Bashan are
majestic mountains;
rugged are the mountains of
Bashan.
16 Why gaze in envy, O rugged
mountains,
at the mountain where God
chooses to reign,
where the LORD himself will dwell
forever?
17 The chariots of God are tens of
thousands
and thousands of thousands;
the Lord ⌞has come⌟ from Sinai into
his sanctuary.
18 When you ascended on high,
you led captives in your train;
you received gifts from men,
even from[c] the rebellious—
that you,[d] O LORD God, might
dwell there.

19 Praise be to the Lord, to God our
Savior,
who daily bears our burdens.
Selah
20 Our God is a God who saves;
from the Sovereign LORD comes
escape from death.

21 Surely God will crush the heads of
his enemies,
the hairy crowns of those who go
on in their sins.
22 The Lord says, "I will bring them
from Bashan;
I will bring them from the depths
of the sea,
23 that you may plunge your feet in the
blood of your foes,
while the tongues of your dogs
have their share."

24 Your procession has come into view,
O God,
the procession of my God and
King into the sanctuary.
25 In front are the singers, after them
the musicians;
with them are the maidens
playing tambourines.
26 Praise God in the great
congregation;
praise the LORD in the assembly of
Israel.
27 There is the little tribe of Benjamin,
leading them,
there the great throng of Judah's
princes,
and there the princes of Zebulun
and of Naphtali.

28 Summon your power, O God[e];
show us your strength, O God, as
you have done before.
29 Because of your temple at Jerusalem
kings will bring you gifts.
30 Rebuke the beast among the reeds,
the herd of bulls among the calves
of the nations.
Humbled, may it bring bars of silver.

[a]13 Or *saddlebags* [b]14 Hebrew *Shaddai* [c]18 Or *gifts for men, / even* [d]18 Or *they* [e]28 Many Hebrew manuscripts, Septuagint and Syriac; most Hebrew manuscripts *Your God has summoned power for you*

Scatter the nations who delight in
war.
31 Envoys will come from Egypt;
Cush[a] will submit herself to God.

32 Sing to God, O kingdoms of the
earth,
sing praise to the Lord, *Selah*
33 to him who rides the ancient skies
above,
who thunders with mighty voice.
34 Proclaim the power of God,
whose majesty is over Israel,
whose power is in the skies.
35 You are awesome, O God, in your
sanctuary;
the God of Israel gives power and
strength to his people.

Praise be to God!

Psalm 69

For the director of music.
To ⌞the tune of⌟ "Lilies." Of David.

1 Save me, O God,
for the waters have come up to
my neck.
2 I sink in the miry depths,
where there is no foothold.
I have come into the deep waters;
the floods engulf me.
3 I am worn out calling for help;
my throat is parched.
My eyes fail,
looking for my God.
4 Those who hate me without reason
outnumber the hairs of my head;
many are my enemies without
cause,
those who seek to destroy me.
I am forced to restore
what I did not steal.

5 You know my folly, O God;
my guilt is not hidden from you.

6 May those who hope in you
not be disgraced because of me,
O Lord, the LORD Almighty;
may those who seek you
not be put to shame because of
me,
O God of Israel.
7 For I endure scorn for your sake,
and shame covers my face.
8 I am a stranger to my brothers,
an alien to my own mother's sons;
9 for zeal for your house consumes me,
and the insults of those who insult
you fall on me.
10 When I weep and fast,
I must endure scorn;
11 when I put on sackcloth,
people make sport of me.
12 Those who sit at the gate mock me,
and I am the song of the
drunkards.

13 But I pray to you, O LORD,
in the time of your favor;
in your great love, O God,
answer me with your sure
salvation.
14 Rescue me from the mire,
do not let me sink;
deliver me from those who hate me,
from the deep waters.
15 Do not let the floodwaters engulf me
or the depths swallow me up
or the pit close its mouth over me.
16 Answer me, O LORD, out of the
goodness of your love;
in your great mercy turn to me.
17 Do not hide your face from your
servant;
answer me quickly, for I am in
trouble.
18 Come near and rescue me;
redeem me because of my foes.

19 You know how I am scorned,
disgraced and shamed;
all my enemies are before you.
20 Scorn has broken my heart
and has left me helpless;
I looked for sympathy, but there was
none,
for comforters, but I found none.
21 They put gall in my food
and gave me vinegar for my thirst.

22 May the table set before them
become a snare;
may it become retribution and[b] a
trap.

[a]*31* That is, the upper Nile region [b]*22* Or *snare / and their fellowship become*

23 May their eyes be darkened so they
cannot see,
and their backs be bent forever.
24 Pour out your wrath on them;
let your fierce anger overtake
them.
25 May their place be deserted;
let there be no one to dwell in
their tents.
26 For they persecute those you wound
and talk about the pain of those
you hurt.
27 Charge them with crime upon crime;
do not let them share in your
salvation.
28 May they be blotted out of the book
of life
and not be listed with the
righteous.

29 I am in pain and distress;
may your salvation, O God,
protect me.

30 I will praise God's name in song
and glorify him with thanksgiving.
31 This will please the LORD more than
an ox,
more than a bull with its horns
and hoofs.
32 The poor will see and be glad—
you who seek God, may your
hearts live!
33 The LORD hears the needy
and does not despise his captive
people.

34 Let heaven and earth praise him,
the seas and all that move in them,
35 for God will save Zion
and rebuild the cities of Judah.
Then people will settle there and
possess it;
36 the children of his servants will
inherit it,
and those who love his name will
dwell there.

Psalm 70

For the director of music.
Of David. A petition.

1 Hasten, O God, to save me;
O LORD, come quickly to help me.
2 May those who seek my life
be put to shame and confusion;
may all who desire my ruin
be turned back in disgrace.
3 May those who say to me, "Aha!
Aha!"
turn back because of their shame.
4 But may all who seek you
rejoice and be glad in you;
may those who love your salvation
always say,
"Let God be exalted!"

5 Yet I am poor and needy;
come quickly to me, O God.
You are my help and my deliverer;
O LORD, do not delay.

Psalm 71

1 In you, O LORD, I have taken
refuge;
let me never be put to shame.
2 Rescue me and deliver me in your
righteousness;
turn your ear to me and save me.
3 Be my rock of refuge,
to which I can always go;
give the command to save me,
for you are my rock and my
fortress.
4 Deliver me, O my God, from the
hand of the wicked,
from the grasp of evil and cruel
men.

5 For you have been my hope,
O Sovereign LORD,
my confidence since my youth.
6 From birth I have relied on you;
you brought me forth from my
mother's womb.
I will ever praise you.
7 I have become like a portent to
many,
but you are my strong refuge.
8 My mouth is filled with your praise,
declaring your splendor all day
long.

9 Do not cast me away when I am old;
do not forsake me when my
strength is gone.
10 For my enemies speak against me;

those who wait to kill me conspire
together.
11 They say, "God has forsaken him;
pursue him and seize him,
for no one will rescue him."
12 Be not far from me, O God;
come quickly, O my God, to help
me.
13 May my accusers perish in shame;
may those who want to harm me
be covered with scorn and
disgrace.

14 But as for me, I will always have
hope;
I will praise you more and more.
15 My mouth will tell of your
righteousness,
of your salvation all day long,
though I know not its measure.
16 I will come and proclaim your
mighty acts, O Sovereign
LORD;
I will proclaim your
righteousness, yours alone.
17 Since my youth, O God, you have
taught me,
and to this day I declare your
marvelous deeds.
18 Even when I am old and gray,
do not forsake me, O God,
till I declare your power to the next
generation,
your might to all who are to come.

19 Your righteousness reaches to the
skies, O God,
you who have done great things.
Who, O God, is like you?
20 Though you have made me see
troubles, many and bitter,
you will restore my life again;
from the depths of the earth
you will again bring me up.
21 You will increase my honor
and comfort me once again.

22 I will praise you with the harp
for your faithfulness, O my God;
I will sing praise to you with the
lyre,
O Holy One of Israel.
23 My lips will shout for joy
when I sing praise to you—
I, whom you have redeemed.
24 My tongue will tell of your righteous
acts
all day long,
for those who wanted to harm me
have been put to shame and
confusion.

Psalm 72

Of Solomon.

1 Endow the king with your justice,
O God,
the royal son with your
righteousness.
2 He will[a] judge your people in
righteousness,
your afflicted ones with justice.
3 The mountains will bring prosperity
to the people,
the hills the fruit of righteousness.
4 He will defend the afflicted among
the people
and save the children of the
needy;
he will crush the oppressor.

5 He will endure[b] as long as the sun,
as long as the moon, through all
generations.
6 He will be like rain falling on a
mown field,
like showers watering the earth.
7 In his days the righteous will
flourish;
prosperity will abound till the
moon is no more.

8 He will rule from sea to sea
and from the River[c] to the ends of
the earth.[d]
9 The desert tribes will bow before
him
and his enemies will lick the dust.
10 The kings of Tarshish and of distant
shores
will bring tribute to him;
the kings of Sheba and Seba
will present him gifts.

[a]2 Or *May he*; similarly in verses 3-11 and 17 [b]5 Septuagint; Hebrew *You will be feared* [c]8 That is, the Euphrates [d]8 Or *the end of the land*

[11]All kings will bow down to him
and all nations will serve him.

[12]For he will deliver the needy who
cry out,
the afflicted who have no one to
help.
[13]He will take pity on the weak and
the needy
and save the needy from death.
[14]He will rescue them from
oppression and violence,
for precious is their blood in his
sight.

[15]Long may he live!
May gold from Sheba be given
him.
May people ever pray for him
and bless him all day long.
[16]Let grain abound throughout the
land;
on the tops of the hills may it
sway.
Let its fruit flourish like Lebanon;
let it thrive like the grass of the
field.
[17]May his name endure forever;
may it continue as long as the
sun.
All nations will be blessed through
him,
and they will call him blessed.

[18]Praise be to the LORD God, the God
of Israel,
who alone does marvelous
deeds.
[19]Praise be to his glorious name
forever;
may the whole earth be filled with
his glory.
Amen and Amen.

[20]This concludes the prayers of David
son of Jesse.

SHARPEN THE FOCUS

As our Lord Jesus talked with His disciples on Easter evening, He likely quoted parts of Psalm 72. The evangelist Luke tells us:

> *[Jesus] said to them, "This is what I told you while I was still with you: Everything must be fulfilled that is written about Me in the Law of Moses, the Prophets and the Psalms." Then He opened their minds so they could understand the Scriptures.* (Luke 24:44–45)

With that in mind, read Psalm 72 and note all the verbs that describe the holy work our Savior did for us. Pray as you do this. Ask that Jesus will open your mind so that you, too, can "understand the Scriptures."

Then look for a chance today to share the insights you glean with someone who, in the weakness and neediness of sin, needs to see Jesus' salvation:

> *For He will deliver the needy who cry out,*
> *the afflicted who have no one to help.*
> *He will take pity on the weak and the needy*
> *and save the needy from death.*
> *He will rescue them from oppression and violence,*
> *for precious is their blood in His sight.* (Psalm 72:12–14)

In many of the psalms for today, the psalmist struggles with a question that often still torments God's people: "Why do the wicked so often prosper while those who love the LORD suffer?" As Asaph ponders this, he draws some comforting conclusions. Look for these as you pray each psalm. If time is short, focus on Psalm 77.

BOOK III

Psalms 73–89

Psalm 73

A psalm of Asaph.

1 Surely God is good to Israel,
to those who are pure in heart.
2 But as for me, my feet had almost slipped;
I had nearly lost my foothold.
3 For I envied the arrogant
when I saw the prosperity of the wicked.

4 They have no struggles;
their bodies are healthy and strong.[a]
5 They are free from the burdens common to man;
they are not plagued by human ills.
6 Therefore pride is their necklace;
they clothe themselves with violence.
7 From their callous hearts comes iniquity[b];
the evil conceits of their minds know no limits.
8 They scoff, and speak with malice;
in their arrogance they threaten oppression.
9 Their mouths lay claim to heaven,
and their tongues take possession of the earth.
10 Therefore their people turn to them
and drink up waters in abundance.[c]
11 They say, "How can God know?
Does the Most High have knowledge?"

12 This is what the wicked are like—
always carefree, they increase in wealth.

13 Surely in vain have I kept my heart pure;
in vain have I washed my hands in innocence.
14 All day long I have been plagued;
I have been punished every morning.

15 If I had said, "I will speak thus,"
I would have betrayed your children.
16 When I tried to understand all this,
it was oppressive to me
17 till I entered the sanctuary of God;
then I understood their final destiny.

18 Surely you place them on slippery ground;
you cast them down to ruin.
19 How suddenly are they destroyed,
completely swept away by terrors!
20 As a dream when one awakes,
so when you arise, O Lord,
you will despise them as fantasies.

[a]4 With a different word division of the Hebrew; Masoretic Text *struggles at their death; / their bodies are healthy* [b]7 Syriac (see also Septuagint); Hebrew *Their eyes bulge with fat* [c]10 The meaning of the Hebrew for this verse is uncertain.

21 When my heart was grieved
and my spirit embittered,
22 I was senseless and ignorant;
I was a brute beast before you.

23 Yet I am always with you;
you hold me by my right hand.
24 You guide me with your counsel,
and afterward you will take me
into glory.
25 Whom have I in heaven but you?
And earth has nothing I desire
besides you.
26 My flesh and my heart may fail,
but God is the strength of my
heart
and my portion forever.

27 Those who are far from you will
perish;
you destroy all who are unfaithful
to you.
28 But as for me, it is good to be near
God.
I have made the Sovereign LORD
my refuge;
I will tell of all your deeds.

Psalm 74

A *maskil*[a] of Asaph.

1 Why have you rejected us forever,
O God?
Why does your anger smolder
against the sheep of your
pasture?
2 Remember the people you
purchased of old,
the tribe of your inheritance,
whom you redeemed—
Mount Zion, where you dwelt.
3 Turn your steps toward these
everlasting ruins,
all this destruction the enemy has
brought on the sanctuary.

4 Your foes roared in the place where
you met with us;
they set up their standards as
signs.
5 They behaved like men wielding
axes
to cut through a thicket of trees.
6 They smashed all the carved
paneling
with their axes and hatchets.
7 They burned your sanctuary to the
ground;
they defiled the dwelling place of
your Name.
8 They said in their hearts, "We will
crush them completely!"
They burned every place where
God was worshiped in the
land.
9 We are given no miraculous signs;
no prophets are left,
and none of us knows how long
this will be.

10 How long will the enemy mock you,
O God?
Will the foe revile your name
forever?
11 Why do you hold back your hand,
your right hand?
Take it from the folds of your
garment and destroy them!

12 But you, O God, are my king from of
old;
you bring salvation upon the
earth.
13 It was you who split open the sea by
your power;
you broke the heads of the
monster in the waters.
14 It was you who crushed the heads of
Leviathan
and gave him as food to the
creatures of the desert.
15 It was you who opened up springs
and streams;
you dried up the ever flowing
rivers.
16 The day is yours, and yours also the
night;
you established the sun and
moon.
17 It was you who set all the
boundaries of the earth;
you made both summer and
winter.

18 Remember how the enemy has
mocked you, O LORD,

[a] Title: Probably a literary or musical term

how foolish people have reviled
your name.
19 Do not hand over the life of your
dove to wild beasts;
do not forget the lives of your
afflicted people forever.
20 Have regard for your covenant,
because haunts of violence fill the
dark places of the land.
21 Do not let the oppressed retreat in
disgrace;
may the poor and needy praise
your name.
22 Rise up, O God, and defend your
cause;
remember how fools mock you all
day long.
23 Do not ignore the clamor of your
adversaries,
the uproar of your enemies, which
rises continually.

Psalm 75

For the director of music.
⌊To the tune of⌋ "Do Not Destroy."
A psalm of Asaph. A song.

1 We give thanks to you, O God,
we give thanks, for your Name is
near;
men tell of your wonderful deeds.
2 You say, "I choose the appointed
time;
it is I who judge uprightly.
3 When the earth and all its people
quake,
it is I who hold its pillars firm.
Selah
4 To the arrogant I say, 'Boast no
more,'
and to the wicked, 'Do not lift up
your horns.
5 Do not lift your horns against
heaven;
do not speak with outstretched
neck.' "
6 No one from the east or the west
or from the desert can exalt a man.
7 But it is God who judges:
He brings one down, he exalts
another.
8 In the hand of the LORD is a cup
full of foaming wine mixed with
spices;
he pours it out, and all the wicked of
the earth
drink it down to its very dregs.

9 As for me, I will declare this forever;
I will sing praise to the God of
Jacob.
10 I will cut off the horns of all the
wicked,
but the horns of the righteous will
be lifted up.

Psalm 76

For the director of music. With
stringed instruments. A psalm of Asaph.
A song.

1 In Judah God is known;
his name is great in Israel.
2 His tent is in Salem,
his dwelling place in Zion.
3 There he broke the flashing arrows,
the shields and the swords, the
weapons of war. *Selah*

4 You are resplendent with light,
more majestic than mountains
rich with game.
5 Valiant men lie plundered,
they sleep their last sleep;
not one of the warriors
can lift his hands.
6 At your rebuke, O God of Jacob,
both horse and chariot lie still.
7 You alone are to be feared.
Who can stand before you when
you are angry?
8 From heaven you pronounced
judgment,
and the land feared and was
quiet—
9 when you, O God, rose up to judge,
to save all the afflicted of the land.
Selah
10 Surely your wrath against men
brings you praise,
and the survivors of your wrath
are restrained.[a]

[a] 10 Or *Surely the wrath of men brings you praise, / and with the remainder of wrath you arm yourself*

[11] Make vows to the LORD your God
and fulfill them;
let all the neighboring lands
bring gifts to the One to be feared.
[12] He breaks the spirit of rulers;
he is feared by the kings of the
earth.

Psalm 77

For the director of music. For Jeduthun.
Of Asaph. A psalm.

[1] I cried out to God for help;
I cried out to God to hear me.
[2] When I was in distress, I sought the
Lord;
at night I stretched out untiring
hands
and my soul refused to be
comforted.

[3] I remembered you, O God, and I
groaned;
I mused, and my spirit grew faint.
Selah
[4] You kept my eyes from closing;
I was too troubled to speak.
[5] I thought about the former days,
the years of long ago;
[6] I remembered my songs in the
night.
My heart mused and my spirit
inquired:

[7] "Will the Lord reject forever?
Will he never show his favor
again?
[8] Has his unfailing love vanished
forever?
Has his promise failed for all time?
[9] Has God forgotten to be merciful?
Has he in anger withheld his
compassion?" *Selah*

[10] Then I thought, "To this I will
appeal:
the years of the right hand of the
Most High."
[11] I will remember the deeds of the
LORD;
yes, I will remember your miracles
of long ago.
[12] I will meditate on all your works
and consider all your mighty
deeds.

[13] Your ways, O God, are holy.
What god is so great as our God?
[14] You are the God who performs
miracles;
you display your power among
the peoples.
[15] With your mighty arm you
redeemed your people,
the descendants of Jacob and
Joseph. *Selah*

[16] The waters saw you, O God,
the waters saw you and writhed;
the very depths were convulsed.
[17] The clouds poured down water,
the skies resounded with
thunder;
your arrows flashed back and
forth.
[18] Your thunder was heard in the
whirlwind,
your lightning lit up the world;
the earth trembled and quaked.
[19] Your path led through the sea,
your way through the mighty
waters,
though your footprints were not
seen.

[20] You led your people like a flock
by the hand of Moses and Aaron.

SHARPEN THE FOCUS

Has God forgotten me? Not a very pious question. Maybe as you worship or as you teach your Sunday school class, you'd rather that your pastor or your students didn't know you have been asking it. Most of us who know and love God have asked it before. Your pastor might not be shocked nor your students surprised.

When Asaph asked it, the Lord didn't punish or even scold. Instead, the Holy Spirit led Asaph to a conclusion that satisfied him (Psalm 77:10–20), and then led Asaph to record both his questions and his conclusion so that we could find peace during our own times of trouble and doubt.

The questions of Psalm 77:7–9 are very real. Asaph is not a scholar wrestling with a problem of philosophy. He himself, a leader of God's people, is "in distress" (Psalm 77:2). The tone of the psalm begins to change at Psalm 77:10, when Asaph shifts his focus from his own doubts and fears to a meditation on what we might call "God's track record."

Has God failed in the past or ever proven unfaithful to His promises? Has He ever come up against a problem too big for Him? No, no, and no. And projecting the past into the future we, like Asaph, can rely on our Lord's faithful love to continue toward us.

WEEK 46 • SATURDAY

Psalms 78:1—82:8

Many of today's psalms picture the Lord as Israel's shepherd. Though He tended them with gentle care, they continually wandered away from Him, even worshiping other gods. As you pray these psalms, listen for the Lord's voice calling you to repentance and faith. If time is short, focus on Psalm 81.

Psalm 78

A *maskil*[a] of Asaph.

1 O my people, hear my teaching;
listen to the words of my mouth.
2 I will open my mouth in parables,
I will utter hidden things, things from of old—
3 what we have heard and known,
what our fathers have told us.
4 We will not hide them from their children;
we will tell the next generation
the praiseworthy deeds of the LORD,
his power, and the wonders he has done.
5 He decreed statutes for Jacob
and established the law in Israel,
which he commanded our forefathers
to teach their children,
6 so the next generation would know them,
even the children yet to be born,
and they in turn would tell their children.
7 Then they would put their trust in God
and would not forget his deeds
but would keep his commands.
8 They would not be like their forefathers—
a stubborn and rebellious generation,
whose hearts were not loyal to God,
whose spirits were not faithful to him.

9 The men of Ephraim, though armed with bows,
turned back on the day of battle;
10 they did not keep God's covenant
and refused to live by his law.
11 They forgot what he had done,
the wonders he had shown them.

[a]Title: Probably a literary or musical term

[12] He did miracles in the sight of their
fathers
in the land of Egypt, in the region
of Zoan.
[13] He divided the sea and led them
through;
he made the water stand firm like
a wall.
[14] He guided them with the cloud by
day
and with light from the fire all
night.
[15] He split the rocks in the desert
and gave them water as abundant
as the seas;
[16] he brought streams out of a rocky
crag
and made water flow down like
rivers.

[17] But they continued to sin against
him,
rebelling in the desert against the
Most High.
[18] They willfully put God to the test
by demanding the food they
craved.
[19] They spoke against God, saying,
"Can God spread a table in the
desert?
[20] When he struck the rock, water
gushed out,
and streams flowed abundantly.
But can he also give us food?
Can he supply meat for his
people?"
[21] When the LORD heard them, he was
very angry;
his fire broke out against Jacob,
and his wrath rose against Israel,
[22] for they did not believe in God
or trust in his deliverance.
[23] Yet he gave a command to the skies
above
and opened the doors of the
heavens;
[24] he rained down manna for the
people to eat,
he gave them the grain of
heaven.
[25] Men ate the bread of angels;
he sent them all the food they
could eat.
[26] He let loose the east wind from the
heavens
and led forth the south wind by
his power.
[27] He rained meat down on them like
dust,
flying birds like sand on the
seashore.
[28] He made them come down inside
their camp,
all around their tents.
[29] They ate till they had more than
enough,
for he had given them what they
craved.
[30] But before they turned from the
food they craved,
even while it was still in their
mouths,
[31] God's anger rose against them;
he put to death the sturdiest
among them,
cutting down the young men of
Israel.

[32] In spite of all this, they kept on
sinning;
in spite of his wonders, they did
not believe.
[33] So he ended their days in futility
and their years in terror.
[34] Whenever God slew them, they
would seek him;
they eagerly turned to him
again.
[35] They remembered that God was
their Rock,
that God Most High was their
Redeemer.
[36] But then they would flatter him
with their mouths,
lying to him with their tongues;
[37] their hearts were not loyal to him,
they were not faithful to his
covenant.
[38] Yet he was merciful;
he forgave their iniquities
and did not destroy them.
Time after time he restrained his
anger
and did not stir up his full wrath.
[39] He remembered that they were but
flesh,

a passing breeze that does not
return.
40 How often they rebelled against him
in the desert
and grieved him in the wasteland!
41 Again and again they put God to the
test;
they vexed the Holy One of Israel.
42 They did not remember his power—
the day he redeemed them from
the oppressor,
43 the day he displayed his miraculous
signs in Egypt,
his wonders in the region of Zoan.
44 He turned their rivers to blood;
they could not drink from their
streams.
45 He sent swarms of flies that
devoured them,
and frogs that devastated them.
46 He gave their crops to the
grasshopper,
their produce to the locust.
47 He destroyed their vines with hail
and their sycamore-figs with sleet.
48 He gave over their cattle to the hail,
their livestock to bolts of
lightning.
49 He unleashed against them his hot
anger,
his wrath, indignation and
hostility—
a band of destroying angels.
50 He prepared a path for his anger;
he did not spare them from death
but gave them over to the plague.
51 He struck down all the firstborn of
Egypt,
the firstfruits of manhood in the
tents of Ham.
52 But he brought his people out like a
flock;
he led them like sheep through
the desert.
53 He guided them safely, so they were
unafraid;
but the sea engulfed their
enemies.
54 Thus he brought them to the border
of his holy land,
to the hill country his right hand
had taken.
55 He drove out nations before them
and allotted their lands to them as
an inheritance;
he settled the tribes of Israel in
their homes.

56 But they put God to the test
and rebelled against the Most
High;
they did not keep his statutes.
57 Like their fathers they were disloyal
and faithless,
as unreliable as a faulty bow.
58 They angered him with their high
places;
they aroused his jealousy with
their idols.
59 When God heard them, he was very
angry;
he rejected Israel completely.
60 He abandoned the tabernacle of
Shiloh,
the tent he had set up among
men.
61 He sent ⌞the ark of⌟ his might into
captivity,
his splendor into the hands of the
enemy.
62 He gave his people over to the
sword;
he was very angry with his
inheritance.
63 Fire consumed their young men,
and their maidens had no
wedding songs;
64 their priests were put to the sword,
and their widows could not
weep.

65 Then the Lord awoke as from sleep,
as a man wakes from the stupor of
wine.
66 He beat back his enemies;
he put them to everlasting shame.
67 Then he rejected the tents of Joseph,
he did not choose the tribe of
Ephraim;
68 but he chose the tribe of Judah,
Mount Zion, which he loved.
69 He built his sanctuary like the
heights,
like the earth that he established
forever.
70 He chose David his servant

and took him from the sheep
pens;
71 from tending the sheep he brought
him
to be the shepherd of his people
Jacob,
of Israel his inheritance.
72 And David shepherded them with
integrity of heart;
with skillful hands he led them.

Psalm 79

A psalm of Asaph.

1 O God, the nations have invaded
your inheritance;
they have defiled your holy
temple,
they have reduced Jerusalem to
rubble.
2 They have given the dead bodies of
your servants
as food to the birds of the air,
the flesh of your saints to the
beasts of the earth.
3 They have poured out blood like
water
all around Jerusalem,
and there is no one to bury the
dead.
4 We are objects of reproach to our
neighbors,
of scorn and derision to those
around us.
5 How long, O LORD? Will you be
angry forever?
How long will your jealousy burn
like fire?
6 Pour out your wrath on the nations
that do not acknowledge you,
on the kingdoms
that do not call on your name;
7 for they have devoured Jacob
and destroyed his homeland.
8 Do not hold against us the sins of
the fathers;
may your mercy come quickly to
meet us,
for we are in desperate need.
9 Help us, O God our Savior,
for the glory of your name;
deliver us and forgive our sins
for your name's sake.
10 Why should the nations say,
"Where is their God?"
Before our eyes, make known
among the nations
that you avenge the outpoured
blood of your servants.
11 May the groans of the prisoners
come before you;
by the strength of your arm
preserve those condemned to die.
12 Pay back into the laps of our
neighbors seven times
the reproach they have hurled at
you, O Lord.
13 Then we your people, the sheep of
your pasture,
will praise you forever;
from generation to generation
we will recount your praise.

Psalm 80

For the director of music.
To ⌞the tune of⌟ "The Lilies of the Covenant."
Of Asaph. A psalm.

1 Hear us, O Shepherd of Israel,
you who lead Joseph like a flock;
you who sit enthroned between the
cherubim, shine forth
2 before Ephraim, Benjamin and
Manasseh.
Awaken your might;
come and save us.
3 Restore us, O God;
make your face shine upon us,
that we may be saved.
4 O LORD God Almighty,
how long will your anger smolder
against the prayers of your
people?
5 You have fed them with the bread of
tears;
you have made them drink tears
by the bowlful.
6 You have made us a source of
contention to our neighbors,
and our enemies mock us.
7 Restore us, O God Almighty;

make your face shine upon us,
that we may be saved.
8 You brought a vine out of Egypt;
you drove out the nations and planted it.
9 You cleared the ground for it,
and it took root and filled the land.
10 The mountains were covered with its shade,
the mighty cedars with its branches.
11 It sent out its boughs to the Sea,[a]
its shoots as far as the River.[b]
12 Why have you broken down its walls
so that all who pass by pick its grapes?
13 Boars from the forest ravage it
and the creatures of the field feed on it.
14 Return to us, O God Almighty!
Look down from heaven and see!
Watch over this vine,
15 the root your right hand has planted,
the son[c] you have raised up for yourself.
16 Your vine is cut down, it is burned with fire;
at your rebuke your people perish.
17 Let your hand rest on the man at your right hand,
the son of man you have raised up for yourself.
18 Then we will not turn away from you;
revive us, and we will call on your name.
19 Restore us, O LORD God Almighty;
make your face shine upon us,
that we may be saved.

Psalm 81

For the director of music.
According to *gittith.*[d] Of Asaph.

1 Sing for joy to God our strength;
shout aloud to the God of Jacob!
2 Begin the music, strike the tambourine,
play the melodious harp and lyre.
3 Sound the ram's horn at the New Moon,
and when the moon is full, on the day of our Feast;
4 this is a decree for Israel,
an ordinance of the God of Jacob.
5 He established it as a statute for Joseph
when he went out against Egypt,
where we heard a language we did not understand.[e]

6 He says, "I removed the burden from their shoulders;
their hands were set free from the basket.
7 In your distress you called and I rescued you,
I answered you out of a thundercloud;
I tested you at the waters of Meribah. *Selah*
8 "Hear, O my people, and I will warn you—
if you would but listen to me, O Israel!
9 You shall have no foreign god among you;
you shall not bow down to an alien god.
10 I am the LORD your God,
who brought you up out of Egypt.
Open wide your mouth and I will fill it.
11 "But my people would not listen to me;
Israel would not submit to me.
12 So I gave them over to their stubborn hearts
to follow their own devices.

13 "If my people would but listen to me,
if Israel would follow my ways,
14 how quickly would I subdue their enemies

[a]*11* Probably the Mediterranean [b]*11* That is, the Euphrates [c]*15* Or *branch* [d]Title: Probably a musical term [e]*5* Or / *and we heard a voice we had not known*

and turn my hand against their
foes!
15 Those who hate the LORD would
cringe before him,
and their punishment would last
forever.
16 But you would be fed with the finest
of wheat;
with honey from the rock I would
satisfy you."

Psalm 82

A psalm of Asaph.

1 God presides in the great assembly;
he gives judgment among the
"gods":

2 "How long will you[a] defend the
unjust
and show partiality to the wicked?
Selah

3 Defend the cause of the weak and
fatherless;
maintain the rights of the poor
and oppressed.
4 Rescue the weak and needy;
deliver them from the hand of the
wicked.

5 "They know nothing, they
understand nothing.
They walk about in darkness;
all the foundations of the earth are
shaken.

6 "I said, 'You are "gods";
you are all sons of the Most High.'
7 But you will die like mere men;
you will fall like every other
ruler."

8 Rise up, O God, judge the earth,
for all the nations are your
inheritance.

[a]2 The Hebrew is plural.

SHARPEN THE FOCUS

Psalm 81:8, 11, and 13 tell of God's will that His people open their ears and hearts to Him. But, sadly, ancient Israel shut Him and His Word out of their lives most of the time, both in the wilderness and after they had entered the Promised Land.

Psalm 81 was probably written to be sung at the Feast of Tabernacles (Leviticus 23:34–43). During this celebration, all Israel was to camp in hut-like structures made of leafy tree branches. As they camped, they were to remember their roots. They had been slaves, but the Lord had lifted their burdens from their shoulders (Psalm 81:6–7, 10). Now they were His precious sons and daughters.

But they forgot who they were and whose they were. And when they forgot, they wandered like helpless sheep into Satan's clutches. They gave themselves to a new slavery—idolatry.

What would it take to remind you today of where you've come from? What would help you see most clearly where you'd be if not for the cross? Take an hour—or a day—to remember the burdens that the Lord has lifted from your shoulders. Then ask Him for eyes that see clearly, for ears that hear clearly, and for a heart that's totally devoted to Him—your Savior-God.

Each of the psalms you will read today flowed from the pen of someone whose life centered on God. These psalmists viewed all of life's events and each of their interpersonal relationships as an extension of their relationship with Yahweh, their Savior-God. As you pray these psalms, think about the ways you yourself incorporate your faith into the fabric of your own life. If time is short, focus on Psalm 87.

Psalm 83

A song. A psalm of Asaph.

1 O God, do not keep silent;
be not quiet, O God, be not still.
2 See how your enemies are astir,
how your foes rear their heads.
3 With cunning they conspire against
your people;
they plot against those you
cherish.
4 "Come," they say, "let us destroy
them as a nation,
that the name of Israel be
remembered no more."

5 With one mind they plot together;
they form an alliance against
you—
6 the tents of Edom and the
Ishmaelites,
of Moab and the Hagrites,
7 Gebal,[a] Ammon and Amalek,
Philistia, with the people of Tyre.
8 Even Assyria has joined them
to lend strength to the
descendants of Lot. *Selah*

9 Do to them as you did to Midian,
as you did to Sisera and Jabin at
the river Kishon,
10 who perished at Endor
and became like refuse on the
ground.
11 Make their nobles like Oreb and
Zeeb,
all their princes like Zebah and
Zalmunna,
12 who said, "Let us take possession
of the pasturelands of God."

13 Make them like tumbleweed, O my
God,
like chaff before the wind.
14 As fire consumes the forest
or a flame sets the mountains
ablaze,
15 so pursue them with your tempest
and terrify them with your storm.
16 Cover their faces with shame
so that men will seek your name,
O LORD.

17 May they ever be ashamed and
dismayed;
may they perish in disgrace.
18 Let them know that you, whose
name is the LORD—
that you alone are the Most High
over all the earth.

Psalm 84

For the director of music.
According to *gittith*.[b]
Of the Sons of Korah. A psalm.

1 How lovely is your dwelling place,
O LORD Almighty!
2 My soul yearns, even faints,
for the courts of the LORD;

[a]7 That is, Byblos [b]Title: Probably a musical term

my heart and my flesh cry out
for the living God.

3 Even the sparrow has found a
home,
and the swallow a nest for
herself,
where she may have her
young—
a place near your altar,
O LORD Almighty, my King and
my God.
4 Blessed are those who dwell in your
house;
they are ever praising you. *Selah*

5 Blessed are those whose strength is
in you,
who have set their hearts on
pilgrimage.
6 As they pass through the Valley of
Baca,
they make it a place of springs;
the autumn rains also cover it
with pools.[a]
7 They go from strength to strength,
till each appears before God in
Zion.

8 Hear my prayer, O LORD God
Almighty;
listen to me, O God of Jacob.
Selah
9 Look upon our shield,[b] O God;
look with favor on your anointed
one.

10 Better is one day in your courts
than a thousand elsewhere;
I would rather be a doorkeeper in
the house of my God
than dwell in the tents of the
wicked.
11 For the LORD God is a sun and
shield;
the LORD bestows favor and
honor;
no good thing does he withhold
from those whose walk is
blameless.

12 O LORD Almighty,
blessed is the man who trusts in
you.

Psalm 85

For the director of music.
Of the Sons of Korah. A psalm.

1 You showed favor to your land,
O LORD;
you restored the fortunes of
Jacob.
2 You forgave the iniquity of your
people
and covered all their sins. *Selah*
3 You set aside all your wrath
and turned from your fierce
anger.

4 Restore us again, O God our Savior,
and put away your displeasure
toward us.
5 Will you be angry with us forever?
Will you prolong your anger
through all generations?
6 Will you not revive us again,
that your people may rejoice in
you?
7 Show us your unfailing love,
O LORD,
and grant us your salvation.

8 I will listen to what God the LORD
will say;
he promises peace to his people,
his saints—
but let them not return to folly.
9 Surely his salvation is near those
who fear him,
that his glory may dwell in our
land.

10 Love and faithfulness meet together;
righteousness and peace kiss each
other.
11 Faithfulness springs forth from the
earth,
and righteousness looks down
from heaven.
12 The LORD will indeed give what is
good,
and our land will yield its harvest.
13 Righteousness goes before him
and prepares the way for his
steps.

[a]6 Or *blessings* [b]9 Or *sovereign*

Psalm 86

A prayer of David.

[1]Hear, O LORD, and answer me,
for I am poor and needy.
[2]Guard my life, for I am devoted to you.
You are my God; save your servant
who trusts in you.
[3]Have mercy on me, O Lord,
for I call to you all day long.
[4]Bring joy to your servant,
for to you, O Lord,
I lift up my soul.

[5]You are forgiving and good, O Lord,
abounding in love to all who call to you.
[6]Hear my prayer, O LORD;
listen to my cry for mercy.
[7]In the day of my trouble I will call to you,
for you will answer me.

[8]Among the gods there is none like you, O Lord;
no deeds can compare with yours.
[9]All the nations you have made
will come and worship before you, O Lord;
they will bring glory to your name.
[10]For you are great and do marvelous deeds;
you alone are God.

[11]Teach me your way, O LORD,
and I will walk in your truth;
give me an undivided heart,
that I may fear your name.
[12]I will praise you, O Lord my God,
with all my heart;
I will glorify your name forever.
[13]For great is your love toward me;
you have delivered me from the depths of the grave.[a]
[14]The arrogant are attacking me, O God;
a band of ruthless men seeks my life—
men without regard for you.
[15]But you, O Lord, are a compassionate and gracious God,
slow to anger, abounding in love and faithfulness.
[16]Turn to me and have mercy on me;
grant your strength to your servant
and save the son of your maidservant.[b]
[17]Give me a sign of your goodness,
that my enemies may see it and be put to shame,
for you, O LORD, have helped me and comforted me.

Psalm 87

Of the Sons of Korah.
A psalm. A song.

[1]He has set his foundation on the holy mountain;
[2] the LORD loves the gates of Zion
more than all the dwellings of Jacob.
[3]Glorious things are said of you,
O city of God: *Selah*
[4]"I will record Rahab[c] and Babylon
among those who acknowledge me—
Philistia too, and Tyre, along with Cush[d]—
and will say, 'This[e] one was born in Zion.' "

[5]Indeed, of Zion it will be said,
"This one and that one were born in her,
and the Most High himself will establish her."
[6]The LORD will write in the register of the peoples:
"This one was born in Zion." *Selah*

[7]As they make music they will sing,
"All my fountains are in you."

[a]13 Hebrew *Sheol* [b]16 Or *save your faithful son* [c]4 A poetic name for Egypt [d]4 That is, the upper Nile region [e]4 Or *"O Rahab and Babylon, / Philistia, Tyre and Cush, / I will record concerning those who acknowledge me: / 'This*

Psalm 88

A song. A psalm of the Sons of Korah.
For the director of music.
According to *mahalath leannoth.*[a]
A *maskil*[b] of Heman the Ezrahite.

1 O LORD, the God who saves me,
day and night I cry out before you.
2 May my prayer come before you;
turn your ear to my cry.
3 For my soul is full of trouble
and my life draws near the grave.[c]
4 I am counted among those who go down to the pit;
I am like a man without strength.
5 I am set apart with the dead,
like the slain who lie in the grave,
whom you remember no more,
who are cut off from your care.

6 You have put me in the lowest pit,
in the darkest depths.
7 Your wrath lies heavily upon me;
you have overwhelmed me with all your waves. *Selah*
8 You have taken from me my closest friends
and have made me repulsive to them.
I am confined and cannot escape;
9 my eyes are dim with grief.

I call to you, O LORD, every day;
I spread out my hands to you.
10 Do you show your wonders to the dead?
Do those who are dead rise up and praise you? *Selah*
11 Is your love declared in the grave,
your faithfulness in Destruction[d]?
12 Are your wonders known in the place of darkness,
or your righteous deeds in the land of oblivion?

13 But I cry to you for help, O LORD;
in the morning my prayer comes before you.
14 Why, O LORD, do you reject me
and hide your face from me?

15 From my youth I have been afflicted and close to death;
I have suffered your terrors and am in despair.
16 Your wrath has swept over me;
your terrors have destroyed me.
17 All day long they surround me like a flood;
they have completely engulfed me.
18 You have taken my companions and loved ones from me;
the darkness is my closest friend.

Psalm 89

A *maskil*[b] of Ethan the Ezrahite.

1 I will sing of the LORD's great love forever;
with my mouth I will make your faithfulness known through all generations.
2 I will declare that your love stands firm forever,
that you established your faithfulness in heaven itself.

3 You said, "I have made a covenant with my chosen one,
I have sworn to David my servant,
4 'I will establish your line forever
and make your throne firm through all generations.' " *Selah*

5 The heavens praise your wonders, O LORD,
your faithfulness too, in the assembly of the holy ones.
6 For who in the skies above can compare with the LORD?
Who is like the LORD among the heavenly beings?
7 In the council of the holy ones God is greatly feared;
he is more awesome than all who surround him.
8 O LORD God Almighty, who is like you?
You are mighty, O LORD, and your faithfulness surrounds you.

[a]Title: Possibly a tune, "The Suffering of Affliction" [b]Title: Probably a literary or musical term [c]3 Hebrew *Sheol* [d]11 Hebrew *Abaddon*

[9] You rule over the surging sea;
when its waves mount up, you still them.
[10] You crushed Rahab like one of the slain;
with your strong arm you scattered your enemies.
[11] The heavens are yours, and yours also the earth;
you founded the world and all that is in it.
[12] You created the north and the south;
Tabor and Hermon sing for joy at your name.
[13] Your arm is endued with power;
your hand is strong, your right hand exalted.

[14] Righteousness and justice are the foundation of your throne;
love and faithfulness go before you.
[15] Blessed are those who have learned to acclaim you,
who walk in the light of your presence, O LORD.
[16] They rejoice in your name all day long;
they exult in your righteousness.
[17] For you are their glory and strength,
and by your favor you exalt our horn.[a]
[18] Indeed, our shield[b] belongs to the LORD,
our king to the Holy One of Israel.

[19] Once you spoke in a vision,
to your faithful people you said:
"I have bestowed strength on a warrior;
I have exalted a young man from among the people.
[20] I have found David my servant;
with my sacred oil I have anointed him.
[21] My hand will sustain him;
surely my arm will strengthen him.
[22] No enemy will subject him to tribute;
no wicked man will oppress him.
[23] I will crush his foes before him
and strike down his adversaries.
[24] My faithful love will be with him,
and through my name his horn[c] will be exalted.
[25] I will set his hand over the sea,
his right hand over the rivers.
[26] He will call out to me, 'You are my Father,
my God, the Rock my Savior.'
[27] I will also appoint him my firstborn,
the most exalted of the kings of the earth.
[28] I will maintain my love to him forever,
and my covenant with him will never fail.
[29] I will establish his line forever,
his throne as long as the heavens endure.

[30] "If his sons forsake my law
and do not follow my statutes,
[31] if they violate my decrees
and fail to keep my commands,
[32] I will punish their sin with the rod,
their iniquity with flogging;
[33] but I will not take my love from him,
nor will I ever betray my faithfulness.
[34] I will not violate my covenant
or alter what my lips have uttered.
[35] Once for all, I have sworn by my holiness—
and I will not lie to David—
[36] that his line will continue forever
and his throne endure before me like the sun;
[37] it will be established forever like the moon,
the faithful witness in the sky."
Selah

[38] But you have rejected, you have spurned,
you have been very angry with your anointed one.
[39] You have renounced the covenant with your servant
and have defiled his crown in the dust.
[40] You have broken through all his walls

[a] 17 *Horn* here symbolizes strong one. [b] 18 Or *sovereign* [c] 24 *Horn* here symbolizes strength.

and reduced his strongholds to
ruins.
41 All who pass by have plundered
him;
he has become the scorn of his
neighbors.
42 You have exalted the right hand of
his foes;
you have made all his enemies
rejoice.
43 You have turned back the edge of
his sword
and have not supported him in
battle.
44 You have put an end to his
splendor
and cast his throne to the ground.
45 You have cut short the days of his
youth;
you have covered him with a
mantle of shame. *Selah*
46 How long, O LORD? Will you hide
yourself forever?
How long will your wrath burn
like fire?
47 Remember how fleeting is my life.
For what futility you have created
all men!
48 What man can live and not see
death,
or save himself from the power of
the grave[a]? *Selah*
49 O Lord, where is your former great
love,
which in your faithfulness you
swore to David?
50 Remember, Lord, how your servant
has[b] been mocked,
how I bear in my heart the taunts
of all the nations,
51 the taunts with which your enemies
have mocked, O LORD,
with which they have mocked
every step of your anointed
one.

52 Praise be to the LORD forever!
Amen and Amen.

[a]48 Hebrew *Sheol* [b]50 Or *your servants have*

SHARPEN THE FOCUS

To what degree do you value your status as a citizen of your country? What rights of that citizenship do you treasure most? Probably nine out of ten of us don't give it much thought one way or another. We just take the benefits and privileges for granted. We need God's forgiveness for our shallow thankfulness in this regard.

And yet the blessings of political citizenship pale against the backdrop of our spiritual citizenship, our "family of origin"—Zion. Look again at Psalm 87:6:

> *The LORD will write in the register of the peoples: "This one was born in Zion."*

Our Lord knows those who belong to Him. He shed His blood that we might be His own. Make no mistake; He's marked us as His own in our Baptism. We may not see that "rebirth mark," but all the hosts of heaven—and hell—do. We were "born in Zion," citizens of the city of God. For now, we live as aliens and strangers on earth. But one day, soon, we'll find ourselves landing on the shore of our homeland:

> *But our citizenship is in heaven. And we eagerly await a Savior from there, the Lord Jesus Christ.* (Philippians 3:20)

WEEK 47 • TUESDAY

Psalms 90:1—95:11

GET THE BIG PICTURE

As you read today's psalms, you may find several of them familiar. God's people have often counted Psalm 90 and 91 among their favorites. Much of Psalm 95 has found its way into Christian worship. As you pray today's psalms, focus on the majesty of God and praise Him for it. If time is short, focus on Psalm 90.

BOOK IV

Psalms 90–106

Psalm 90

A prayer of Moses the man of God.

1 Lord, you have been our dwelling place
throughout all generations.
2 Before the mountains were born
or you brought forth the earth and the world,
from everlasting to everlasting you are God.

3 You turn men back to dust,
saying, "Return to dust, O sons of men."
4 For a thousand years in your sight
are like a day that has just gone by,
or like a watch in the night.
5 You sweep men away in the sleep of death;
they are like the new grass of the morning—
6 though in the morning it springs up new,
by evening it is dry and withered.

7 We are consumed by your anger
and terrified by your indignation.
8 You have set our iniquities before you,
our secret sins in the light of your presence.
9 All our days pass away under your wrath;
we finish our years with a moan.
10 The length of our days is seventy years—
or eighty, if we have the strength;
yet their span[a] is but trouble and sorrow,
for they quickly pass, and we fly away.

11 Who knows the power of your anger?
For your wrath is as great as the fear that is due you.
12 Teach us to number our days aright,
that we may gain a heart of wisdom.

13 Relent, O LORD! How long will it be?
Have compassion on your servants.
14 Satisfy us in the morning with your unfailing love,
that we may sing for joy and be glad all our days.
15 Make us glad for as many days as you have afflicted us,
for as many years as we have seen trouble.
16 May your deeds be shown to your servants,
your splendor to their children.
17 May the favor[b] of the Lord our God rest upon us;
establish the work of our hands for us—
yes, establish the work of our hands.

[a]10 Or *yet the best of them* [b]17 Or *beauty*

Psalm 91

1 He who dwells in the shelter of the Most High
will rest in the shadow of the Almighty.[a]
2 I will say[b] of the LORD, "He is my refuge and my fortress,
my God, in whom I trust."

3 Surely he will save you from the fowler's snare
and from the deadly pestilence.
4 He will cover you with his feathers,
and under his wings you will find refuge;
his faithfulness will be your shield and rampart.
5 You will not fear the terror of night,
nor the arrow that flies by day,
6 nor the pestilence that stalks in the darkness,
nor the plague that destroys at midday.
7 A thousand may fall at your side,
ten thousand at your right hand,
but it will not come near you.
8 You will only observe with your eyes
and see the punishment of the wicked.

9 If you make the Most High your dwelling—
even the LORD, who is my refuge—
10 then no harm will befall you,
no disaster will come near your tent.
11 For he will command his angels concerning you
to guard you in all your ways;
12 they will lift you up in their hands,
so that you will not strike your foot against a stone.
13 You will tread upon the lion and the cobra;
you will trample the great lion and the serpent.

14 "Because he loves me," says the LORD, "I will rescue him;
I will protect him, for he acknowledges my name.
15 He will call upon me, and I will answer him;
I will be with him in trouble,
I will deliver him and honor him.
16 With long life will I satisfy him
and show him my salvation."

Psalm 92

A psalm. A song. For the Sabbath day.

1 It is good to praise the LORD
and make music to your name, O Most High,
2 to proclaim your love in the morning
and your faithfulness at night,
3 to the music of the ten-stringed lyre
and the melody of the harp.

4 For you make me glad by your deeds, O LORD;
I sing for joy at the works of your hands.
5 How great are your works, O LORD,
how profound your thoughts!
6 The senseless man does not know,
fools do not understand,
7 that though the wicked spring up like grass
and all evildoers flourish,
they will be forever destroyed.

8 But you, O LORD, are exalted forever.

9 For surely your enemies, O LORD,
surely your enemies will perish;
all evildoers will be scattered.
10 You have exalted my horn[c] like that of a wild ox;
fine oils have been poured upon me.
11 My eyes have seen the defeat of my adversaries;
my ears have heard the rout of my wicked foes.

12 The righteous will flourish like a palm tree,
they will grow like a cedar of Lebanon;
13 planted in the house of the LORD,
they will flourish in the courts of our God.

[a] *1* Hebrew *Shaddai* [b] *2* Or *He says* [c] *10 Horn* here symbolizes strength.

14 They will still bear fruit in old age,
they will stay fresh and green,
15 proclaiming, "The LORD is upright;
he is my Rock, and there is no
wickedness in him."

Psalm 93

1 The LORD reigns, he is robed in
majesty;
the LORD is robed in majesty
and is armed with strength.
The world is firmly established;
it cannot be moved.
2 Your throne was established long
ago;
you are from all eternity.

3 The seas have lifted up, O LORD,
the seas have lifted up their voice;
the seas have lifted up their
pounding waves.
4 Mightier than the thunder of the
great waters,
mightier than the breakers of the
sea—
the LORD on high is mighty.

5 Your statutes stand firm;
holiness adorns your house
for endless days, O LORD.

Psalm 94

1 O LORD, the God who avenges,
O God who avenges, shine forth.
2 Rise up, O Judge of the earth;
pay back to the proud what they
deserve.
3 How long will the wicked, O LORD,
how long will the wicked be
jubilant?
4 They pour out arrogant words;
all the evildoers are full of
boasting.
5 They crush your people, O LORD;
they oppress your inheritance.
6 They slay the widow and the alien;
they murder the fatherless.
7 They say, "The LORD does not see;
the God of Jacob pays no heed."

8 Take heed, you senseless ones
among the people;
you fools, when will you become
wise?
9 Does he who implanted the ear not
hear?
Does he who formed the eye not
see?
10 Does he who disciplines nations not
punish?
Does he who teaches man lack
knowledge?
11 The LORD knows the thoughts of
man;
he knows that they are futile.

12 Blessed is the man you discipline,
O LORD,
the man you teach from your law;
13 you grant him relief from days of
trouble,
till a pit is dug for the wicked.
14 For the LORD will not reject his
people;
he will never forsake his
inheritance.
15 Judgment will again be founded on
righteousness,
and all the upright in heart will
follow it.

16 Who will rise up for me against the
wicked?
Who will take a stand for me
against evildoers?
17 Unless the LORD had given me
help,
I would soon have dwelt in the
silence of death.
18 When I said, "My foot is slipping,"
your love, O LORD, supported
me.
19 When anxiety was great within me,
your consolation brought joy to
my soul.

20 Can a corrupt throne be allied with
you—
one that brings on misery by its
decrees?
21 They band together against the
righteous
and condemn the innocent to
death.
22 But the LORD has become my
fortress,

and my God the rock in whom I
take refuge.
23 He will repay them for their sins
and destroy them for their
wickedness;
the LORD our God will destroy
them.

Psalm 95

1 Come, let us sing for joy to the
LORD;
let us shout aloud to the Rock of
our salvation.
2 Let us come before him with
thanksgiving
and extol him with music and
song.

3 For the LORD is the great God,
the great King above all gods.
4 In his hand are the depths of the
earth,
and the mountain peaks belong to
him.
5 The sea is his, for he made it,
and his hands formed the dry
land.

6 Come, let us bow down in worship,
let us kneel before the LORD our
Maker;
7 for he is our God
and we are the people of his
pasture,
the flock under his care.

Today, if you hear his voice,
8 do not harden your hearts as you
did at Meribah,[a]
as you did that day at Massah[b] in
the desert,
9 where your fathers tested and tried
me,
though they had seen what I did.
10 For forty years I was angry with that
generation;
I said, "They are a people whose
hearts go astray,
and they have not known my
ways."
11 So I declared on oath in my anger,
"They shall never enter my rest."

[a]*8 Meribah* means *quarreling.* [b]*8 Massah* means *testing.*

SHARPEN THE FOCUS

Everything we see on this earth has a beginning and an end. Grass sprouts in the spring and blows away on winter winds (Psalm 90:5–6). Buildings that have withstood a century of thunderstorms and blizzards break up and float downstream in the waters of a flood (Psalm 90:5). And how quickly we ourselves learn that one word from God will bring our journey here on earth to an abrupt close.

Our Lord has no beginning and no end. He is God "from everlasting to everlasting" (Psalm 90:2). We cannot fully understand that truth, but we can take comfort in it. He formed us in the womb (Psalm 139:13). And He will take us to Himself when we die.

We can count on His tender mercy even though He's seen every sad detail of our sins (Psalm 90:8). In Jesus, we have a shelter from His anger. Hidden in the cross, we escape the wrath we have coming to us. We receive instead "unfailing love" (Psalm 90:14).

That love fills us with daily joy. We see the changes and decay around us. We realize that we've used up quite a few of the 70 or 80 years allotted to us (Psalm 90:10). Still, we have hope. The Lord, our Savior-God, is our dwelling place. We live with Him now; we will live with Him forever.

WEEK 47 • WEDNESDAY

Psalms 96:1 101:8

Each of today's psalms encourages us to sing, shout, clap, and rejoice in the presence of the Lord. As you pray these psalms of praise, let the Holy Spirit draw you into God's presence. Worship Him with all your heart. If time is short, focus on Psalm 100.

Psalm 96

1 Sing to the LORD a new song;
sing to the LORD, all the earth.
2 Sing to the LORD, praise his name;
proclaim his salvation day after day.
3 Declare his glory among the nations,
his marvelous deeds among all peoples.

4 For great is the LORD and most worthy of praise;
he is to be feared above all gods.
5 For all the gods of the nations are idols,
but the LORD made the heavens.
6 Splendor and majesty are before him;
strength and glory are in his sanctuary.

7 Ascribe to the LORD, O families of nations,
ascribe to the LORD glory and strength.
8 Ascribe to the LORD the glory due his name;
bring an offering and come into his courts.
9 Worship the LORD in the splendor of his[a] holiness;
tremble before him, all the earth.
10 Say among the nations, "The LORD reigns."
The world is firmly established, it cannot be moved;
he will judge the peoples with equity.
11 Let the heavens rejoice, let the earth be glad;
let the sea resound, and all that is in it;
12 let the fields be jubilant, and everything in them.
Then all the trees of the forest will sing for joy;
13 they will sing before the LORD, for he comes,
he comes to judge the earth.
He will judge the world in righteousness
and the peoples in his truth.

Psalm 97

1 The LORD reigns, let the earth be glad;
let the distant shores rejoice.
2 Clouds and thick darkness surround him;
righteousness and justice are the foundation of his throne.
3 Fire goes before him
and consumes his foes on every side.
4 His lightning lights up the world;
the earth sees and trembles.
5 The mountains melt like wax before the LORD,
before the Lord of all the earth.
6 The heavens proclaim his righteousness,
and all the peoples see his glory.
7 All who worship images are put to shame,

[a]9 Or *LORD with the splendor of*

those who boast in idols—
worship him, all you gods!

8 Zion hears and rejoices
and the villages of Judah are glad
because of your judgments,
O LORD.
9 For you, O LORD, are the Most High
over all the earth;
you are exalted far above all gods.

10 Let those who love the LORD hate
evil,
for he guards the lives of his
faithful ones
and delivers them from the hand
of the wicked.
11 Light is shed upon the righteous
and joy on the upright in heart.
12 Rejoice in the LORD, you who are
righteous,
and praise his holy name.

Psalm 98

A psalm.

1 Sing to the LORD a new song,
for he has done marvelous
things;
his right hand and his holy arm
have worked salvation for him.
2 The LORD has made his salvation
known
and revealed his righteousness to
the nations.
3 He has remembered his love
and his faithfulness to the house
of Israel;
all the ends of the earth have seen
the salvation of our God.

4 Shout for joy to the LORD, all the
earth,
burst into jubilant song with
music;
5 make music to the LORD with the
harp,
with the harp and the sound of
singing,
6 with trumpets and the blast of the
ram's horn—
shout for joy before the LORD, the
King.

7 Let the sea resound, and everything
in it,
the world, and all who live in it.
8 Let the rivers clap their hands,
let the mountains sing together
for joy;
9 let them sing before the LORD,
for he comes to judge the earth.
He will judge the world in
righteousness
and the peoples with equity.

Psalm 99

1 The LORD reigns,
let the nations tremble;
he sits enthroned between the
cherubim,
let the earth shake.
2 Great is the LORD in Zion;
he is exalted over all the nations.
3 Let them praise your great and
awesome name—
he is holy.

4 The King is mighty, he loves
justice—
you have established equity;
in Jacob you have done
what is just and right.
5 Exalt the LORD our God
and worship at his footstool;
he is holy.

6 Moses and Aaron were among his
priests,
Samuel was among those who
called on his name;
they called on the LORD
and he answered them.
7 He spoke to them from the pillar of
cloud;
they kept his statutes and the
decrees he gave them.

8 O LORD our God,
you answered them;
you were to Israel[a] a forgiving God,
though you punished their
misdeeds.[b]
9 Exalt the LORD our God

[a]8 Hebrew *them* [b]8 Or / *an avenger of the wrongs done to them*

and worship at his holy mountain,
for the LORD our God is holy.

Psalm 100

A psalm. For giving thanks.

1 Shout for joy to the LORD, all the earth.
2 Worship the LORD with gladness;
come before him with joyful songs.
3 Know that the LORD is God.
It is he who made us, and we are his[a];
we are his people, the sheep of his pasture.

4 Enter his gates with thanksgiving
and his courts with praise;
give thanks to him and praise his name.
5 For the LORD is good and his love endures forever;
his faithfulness continues through all generations.

Psalm 101

Of David. A psalm.

1 I will sing of your love and justice;
to you, O LORD, I will sing praise.
2 I will be careful to lead a blameless life—
when will you come to me?
I will walk in my house
with blameless heart.
3 I will set before my eyes
no vile thing.

The deeds of faithless men I hate;
they will not cling to me.
4 Men of perverse heart shall be far from me;
I will have nothing to do with evil.

5 Whoever slanders his neighbor in secret,
him will I put to silence;
whoever has haughty eyes and a proud heart,
him will I not endure.

6 My eyes will be on the faithful in the land,
that they may dwell with me;
he whose walk is blameless
will minister to me.

7 No one who practices deceit
will dwell in my house;
no one who speaks falsely
will stand in my presence.

8 Every morning I will put to silence
all the wicked in the land;
I will cut off every evildoer
from the city of the LORD.

[a]3 Or *and not we ourselves*

SHARPEN THE FOCUS

Two families prepared to go on vacation. One family planned their route in detail, studying the various Civil War sites they would visit. The other family simply hopped in the car the morning their vacation began. Mom gave Dad the map and asked, "What route should we take to Gettysburg?" Which family will likely get more out of their trip?

People who prepare for an experience and enter into it with open eyes not only enjoy the experience more but are better able to notice and take advantage of happy coincidences that spring up along the way.

Corporate worship is like that, too. The psalmist encourages us, "Enter His gates with thanksgiving and His courts with praise" (Psalm 100:4). We're always welcome in our heavenly Father's house because of Jesus and His cross. But when the Holy Spirit prepares our hearts, when we think ahead of time about the good things for which we want to thank God, when the Lord's praise bubbles up in our hearts, then our worship in church becomes much more meaningful.

Old-time evangelists used to scare people with the words, "Prepare to meet your God!" But we, as Christ's blood-bought brothers and sisters, can rejoice as we prepare weekly to meet and worship Him.

WEEK 47 • THURSDAY

Psalms 102:1—106:48

Most of today's psalms (Psalms 103–106) encourage us to meditate on all God has done, down through time, both for us as individuals and together as His Holy Christian Church. As you pray these psalms, ask yourself what words of praise you would personally want to add to those of the psalmist. If time is short, focus on Psalm 105.

Psalm 102

A prayer of an afflicted man. When he is faint and pours out his lament before the LORD.

1 Hear my prayer, O LORD;
let my cry for help come to you.
2 Do not hide your face from me
when I am in distress.
Turn your ear to me;
when I call, answer me quickly.

3 For my days vanish like smoke;
my bones burn like glowing embers.
4 My heart is blighted and withered like grass;
I forget to eat my food.
5 Because of my loud groaning
I am reduced to skin and bones.
6 I am like a desert owl,
like an owl among the ruins.
7 I lie awake; I have become
like a bird alone on a roof.
8 All day long my enemies taunt me;
those who rail against me use my name as a curse.
9 For I eat ashes as my food
and mingle my drink with tears
10 because of your great wrath,
for you have taken me up and thrown me aside.
11 My days are like the evening shadow;
I wither away like grass.

12 But you, O LORD, sit enthroned forever;
your renown endures through all generations.
13 You will arise and have compassion on Zion,
for it is time to show favor to her;
the appointed time has come.
14 For her stones are dear to your servants;
her very dust moves them to pity.
15 The nations will fear the name of the LORD,
all the kings of the earth will revere your glory.
16 For the LORD will rebuild Zion
and appear in his glory.
17 He will respond to the prayer of the destitute;
he will not despise their plea.

18 Let this be written for a future generation,
that a people not yet created may praise the LORD:
19 "The LORD looked down from his sanctuary on high,
from heaven he viewed the earth,

[20]to hear the groans of the prisoners
and release those condemned to
death."
[21]So the name of the LORD will be
declared in Zion
and his praise in Jerusalem
[22]when the peoples and the kingdoms
assemble to worship the LORD.

[23]In the course of my life[a] he broke my
strength;
he cut short my days.
[24]So I said:
"Do not take me away, O my God,
in the midst of my days;
your years go on through all
generations.
[25]In the beginning you laid the
foundations of the earth,
and the heavens are the work of
your hands.
[26]They will perish, but you remain;
they will all wear out like a
garment.
Like clothing you will change them
and they will be discarded.
[27]But you remain the same,
and your years will never end.
[28]The children of your servants will
live in your presence;
their descendants will be
established before you."

Psalm 103

Of David.

[1]Praise the LORD, O my soul;
all my inmost being, praise his
holy name.
[2]Praise the LORD, O my soul,
and forget not all his benefits—
[3]who forgives all your sins
and heals all your diseases,
[4]who redeems your life from the pit
and crowns you with love and
compassion,
[5]who satisfies your desires with good
things
so that your youth is renewed like
the eagle's.

[6]The LORD works righteousness
and justice for all the oppressed.
[7]He made known his ways to Moses,
his deeds to the people of Israel:
[8]The LORD is compassionate and
gracious,
slow to anger, abounding in love.
[9]He will not always accuse,
nor will he harbor his anger
forever;
[10]he does not treat us as our sins
deserve
or repay us according to our
iniquities.
[11]For as high as the heavens are above
the earth,
so great is his love for those who
fear him;
[12]as far as the east is from the west,
so far has he removed our
transgressions from us.
[13]As a father has compassion on his
children,
so the LORD has compassion on
those who fear him;
[14]for he knows how we are formed,
he remembers that we are dust.
[15]As for man, his days are like grass,
he flourishes like a flower of the
field;
[16]the wind blows over it and it is
gone,
and its place remembers it no
more.
[17]But from everlasting to everlasting
the LORD's love is with those who
fear him,
and his righteousness with their
children's children—
[18]with those who keep his covenant
and remember to obey his
precepts.

[19]The LORD has established his throne
in heaven,
and his kingdom rules over all.
[20]Praise the LORD, you his angels,
you mighty ones who do his
bidding,
who obey his word.
[21]Praise the LORD, all his heavenly
hosts,
you his servants who do his will.

[a]23 Or *By his power*

22 Praise the LORD, all his works
everywhere in his dominion.

Praise the LORD, O my soul.

Psalm 104

1 Praise the LORD, O my soul.

O LORD my God, you are very
great;
you are clothed with splendor and
majesty.
2 He wraps himself in light as with a
garment;
he stretches out the heavens like a
tent
3 and lays the beams of his upper
chambers on their waters.
He makes the clouds his chariot
and rides on the wings of the
wind.
4 He makes winds his messengers,[a]
flames of fire his servants.

5 He set the earth on its foundations;
it can never be moved.
6 You covered it with the deep as with
a garment;
the waters stood above the
mountains.
7 But at your rebuke the waters fled,
at the sound of your thunder they
took to flight;
8 they flowed over the mountains,
they went down into the valleys,
to the place you assigned for
them.
9 You set a boundary they cannot
cross;
never again will they cover the
earth.

10 He makes springs pour water into
the ravines;
it flows between the mountains.
11 They give water to all the beasts of
the field;
the wild donkeys quench their
thirst.
12 The birds of the air nest by the
waters;
they sing among the branches.
13 He waters the mountains from his
upper chambers;
the earth is satisfied by the fruit of
his work.
14 He makes grass grow for the cattle,
and plants for man to cultivate—
bringing forth food from the
earth:
15 wine that gladdens the heart of
man,
oil to make his face shine,
and bread that sustains his heart.
16 The trees of the LORD are well
watered,
the cedars of Lebanon that he
planted.
17 There the birds make their nests;
the stork has its home in the pine
trees.
18 The high mountains belong to the
wild goats;
the crags are a refuge for the
coneys.[b]

19 The moon marks off the seasons,
and the sun knows when to go
down.
20 You bring darkness, it becomes
night,
and all the beasts of the forest
prowl.
21 The lions roar for their prey
and seek their food from God.
22 The sun rises, and they steal away;
they return and lie down in their
dens.
23 Then man goes out to his work,
to his labor until evening.

24 How many are your works, O LORD!
In wisdom you made them all;
the earth is full of your creatures.
25 There is the sea, vast and spacious,
teeming with creatures beyond
number—
living things both large and small.
26 There the ships go to and fro,
and the leviathan, which you
formed to frolic there.

27 These all look to you
to give them their food at the
proper time.

[a]4 Or *angels* [b]18 That is, the hyrax or rock badger

28 When you give it to them,
they gather it up;
when you open your hand,
they are satisfied with good
things.
29 When you hide your face,
they are terrified;
when you take away their breath,
they die and return to the dust.
30 When you send your Spirit,
they are created,
and you renew the face of the
earth.

31 May the glory of the LORD endure
forever;
may the LORD rejoice in his
works—
32 he who looks at the earth, and it
trembles,
who touches the mountains, and
they smoke.

33 I will sing to the LORD all my life;
I will sing praise to my God as
long as I live.
34 May my meditation be pleasing to
him,
as I rejoice in the LORD.
35 But may sinners vanish from the
earth
and the wicked be no more.

Praise the LORD, O my soul.

Praise the LORD.[a]

Psalm 105

1 Give thanks to the LORD, call on his
name;
make known among the nations
what he has done.
2 Sing to him, sing praise to him;
tell of all his wonderful acts.
3 Glory in his holy name;
let the hearts of those who seek
the LORD rejoice.
4 Look to the LORD and his strength;
seek his face always.

5 Remember the wonders he has
done,
his miracles, and the judgments
he pronounced,
6 O descendants of Abraham his
servant,
O sons of Jacob, his chosen ones.
7 He is the LORD our God;
his judgments are in all the earth.

8 He remembers his covenant forever,
the word he commanded, for a
thousand generations,
9 the covenant he made with
Abraham,
the oath he swore to Isaac.
10 He confirmed it to Jacob as a decree,
to Israel as an everlasting
covenant:
11 "To you I will give the land of
Canaan
as the portion you will inherit."

12 When they were but few in number,
few indeed, and strangers in it,
13 they wandered from nation to
nation,
from one kingdom to another.
14 He allowed no one to oppress them;
for their sake he rebuked kings:
15 "Do not touch my anointed ones;
do my prophets no harm."

16 He called down famine on the land
and destroyed all their supplies of
food;
17 and he sent a man before them—
Joseph, sold as a slave.
18 They bruised his feet with shackles,
his neck was put in irons,
19 till what he foretold came to pass,
till the word of the LORD proved
him true.
20 The king sent and released him,
the ruler of peoples set him free.
21 He made him master of his
household,
ruler over all he possessed,
22 to instruct his princes as he pleased
and teach his elders wisdom.

23 Then Israel entered Egypt;
Jacob lived as an alien in the land
of Ham.
24 The LORD made his people very
fruitful;

[a]35 Hebrew *Hallelu Yah;* in the Septuagint this line stands at the beginning of Psalm 105.

he made them too numerous for
their foes,
25 whose hearts he turned to hate his
people,
to conspire against his servants.
26 He sent Moses his servant,
and Aaron, whom he had chosen.
27 They performed his miraculous
signs among them,
his wonders in the land of Ham.
28 He sent darkness and made the land
dark—
for had they not rebelled against
his words?
29 He turned their waters into blood,
causing their fish to die.
30 Their land teemed with frogs,
which went up into the bedrooms
of their rulers.
31 He spoke, and there came swarms of
flies,
and gnats throughout their
country.
32 He turned their rain into hail,
with lightning throughout their
land;
33 he struck down their vines and fig
trees
and shattered the trees of their
country.
34 He spoke, and the locusts came,
grasshoppers without number;
35 they ate up every green thing in
their land,
ate up the produce of their soil.
36 Then he struck down all the
firstborn in their land,
the firstfruits of all their
manhood.

37 He brought out Israel, laden with
silver and gold,
and from among their tribes no
one faltered.
38 Egypt was glad when they left,
because dread of Israel had fallen
on them.
39 He spread out a cloud as a covering,
and a fire to give light at night.
40 They asked, and he brought them
quail
and satisfied them with the bread
of heaven.
41 He opened the rock, and water
gushed out;
like a river it flowed in the desert.
42 For he remembered his holy promise
given to his servant Abraham.
43 He brought out his people with
rejoicing,
his chosen ones with shouts of
joy;
44 he gave them the lands of the
nations,
and they fell heir to what others
had toiled for—
45 that they might keep his precepts
and observe his laws.

Praise the LORD.[a]

Psalm 106

1 Praise the LORD.[b]

Give thanks to the LORD, for he is
good;
his love endures forever.
2 Who can proclaim the mighty acts of
the LORD
or fully declare his praise?
3 Blessed are they who maintain
justice,
who constantly do what is right.
4 Remember me, O LORD, when you
show favor to your people,
come to my aid when you save
them,
5 that I may enjoy the prosperity of
your chosen ones,
that I may share in the joy of your
nation
and join your inheritance in
giving praise.

6 We have sinned, even as our fathers
did;
we have done wrong and acted
wickedly.
7 When our fathers were in Egypt,
they gave no thought to your
miracles;
they did not remember your many
kindnesses,

[a]45 Hebrew *Hallelu Yah* [b]1 Hebrew *Hallelu Yah*; also in verse 48

and they rebelled by the sea, the Red Sea.[a]
8 Yet he saved them for his name's sake,
to make his mighty power known.
9 He rebuked the Red Sea, and it dried up;
he led them through the depths as through a desert.
10 He saved them from the hand of the foe;
from the hand of the enemy he redeemed them.
11 The waters covered their adversaries;
not one of them survived.
12 Then they believed his promises
and sang his praise.

13 But they soon forgot what he had done
and did not wait for his counsel.
14 In the desert they gave in to their craving;
in the wasteland they put God to the test.
15 So he gave them what they asked for,
but sent a wasting disease upon them.

16 In the camp they grew envious of Moses
and of Aaron, who was consecrated to the LORD.
17 The earth opened up and swallowed Dathan;
it buried the company of Abiram.
18 Fire blazed among their followers;
a flame consumed the wicked.

19 At Horeb they made a calf
and worshiped an idol cast from metal.
20 They exchanged their Glory
for an image of a bull, which eats grass.
21 They forgot the God who saved them,
who had done great things in Egypt,
22 miracles in the land of Ham
and awesome deeds by the Red Sea.
23 So he said he would destroy them—
had not Moses, his chosen one,
stood in the breach before him
to keep his wrath from destroying them.

24 Then they despised the pleasant land;
they did not believe his promise.
25 They grumbled in their tents
and did not obey the LORD.
26 So he swore to them with uplifted hand
that he would make them fall in the desert,
27 make their descendants fall among the nations
and scatter them throughout the lands.

28 They yoked themselves to the Baal of Peor
and ate sacrifices offered to lifeless gods;
29 they provoked the LORD to anger by their wicked deeds,
and a plague broke out among them.
30 But Phinehas stood up and intervened,
and the plague was checked.
31 This was credited to him as righteousness
for endless generations to come.
32 By the waters of Meribah they angered the LORD,
and trouble came to Moses because of them;
33 for they rebelled against the Spirit of God,
and rash words came from Moses' lips.[b]
34 They did not destroy the peoples
as the LORD had commanded them,
35 but they mingled with the nations
and adopted their customs.
36 They worshiped their idols,
which became a snare to them.

[a] 7 Hebrew *Yam Suph*; that is, Sea of Reeds; also in verses 9 and 22 [b] 33 Or *against his spirit, / and rash words came from his lips*

37 They sacrificed their sons
and their daughters to demons.
38 They shed innocent blood,
the blood of their sons and
daughters,
whom they sacrificed to the idols of
Canaan,
and the land was desecrated by
their blood.
39 They defiled themselves by what
they did;
by their deeds they prostituted
themselves.

40 Therefore the LORD was angry with
his people
and abhorred his inheritance.
41 He handed them over to the
nations,
and their foes ruled over them.
42 Their enemies oppressed them
and subjected them to their
power.
43 Many times he delivered them,
but they were bent on rebellion
and they wasted away in their sin.

44 But he took note of their distress
when he heard their cry;
45 for their sake he remembered his
covenant
and out of his great love he
relented.
46 He caused them to be pitied
by all who held them captive.

47 Save us, O LORD our God,
and gather us from the nations,
that we may give thanks to your
holy name
and glory in your praise.

48 Praise be to the LORD, the God of
Israel,
from everlasting to everlasting.
Let all the people say, "Amen!"

Praise the LORD.

SHARPEN THE FOCUS

Most world religions could survive without their historical roots. Buddhism, for instance, could continue if someone would prove that Gautama Buddha never lived as an individual.

But Christianity's roots are sunk deep into history. Several times already we've read psalms recounting God's mighty deeds in history. Israel of old watched the Lord act on their behalf, again and again. Today we read two more psalms that tell specifically of God's dealings—in history—with Abraham, Joseph, Moses and Aaron, the people of Israel in the wilderness (Psalms 105–106).

Again and again God's faithless people rebelled against Him. In Psalm 106:15 we see the results. One version translates the last phrase in the verse, "[He] sent leanness into their soul." When we wander from God, our souls shrivel up. We experience spiritual famine.

When we find our souls growing lean and weak, we can remember the Lord who has proven Himself ever faithful to His people. No matter how deep the sin and godlessness into which they had fallen, the Lord always heard their cries for help. He always came to rescue them. And He will come for us, too; Christ's cross guarantees it.

As you zero in on Psalm 110 today, notice its three divisions. Verses 1–2 describe the coming Messiah as our King. Verses 3–4 tell of Him as our great High Priest. Verses 5–7 picture Him as a mighty Warrior. Also keep in mind the kingdom our Messiah rules, serves, and protects—His holy ones, His Church. If time is short, focus on Psalm 110.

BOOK V

Psalms 107–150

Psalm 107

1 Give thanks to the LORD, for he is good;
his love endures forever.
2 Let the redeemed of the LORD say this—
those he redeemed from the hand of the foe,
3 those he gathered from the lands,
from east and west, from north and south.[a]

4 Some wandered in desert wastelands,
finding no way to a city where they could settle.
5 They were hungry and thirsty,
and their lives ebbed away.
6 Then they cried out to the LORD in their trouble,
and he delivered them from their distress.
7 He led them by a straight way
to a city where they could settle.
8 Let them give thanks to the LORD
for his unfailing love
and his wonderful deeds for men,
9 for he satisfies the thirsty
and fills the hungry with good things.

10 Some sat in darkness and the deepest gloom,
prisoners suffering in iron chains,
11 for they had rebelled against the words of God
and despised the counsel of the Most High.
12 So he subjected them to bitter labor;
they stumbled, and there was no one to help.
13 Then they cried to the LORD in their trouble,
and he saved them from their distress.
14 He brought them out of darkness
and the deepest gloom
and broke away their chains.
15 Let them give thanks to the LORD
for his unfailing love
and his wonderful deeds for men,
16 for he breaks down gates of bronze
and cuts through bars of iron.

17 Some became fools through their rebellious ways
and suffered affliction because of their iniquities.
18 They loathed all food
and drew near the gates of death.
19 Then they cried to the LORD in their trouble,
and he saved them from their distress.
20 He sent forth his word and healed them;
he rescued them from the grave.
21 Let them give thanks to the LORD
for his unfailing love
and his wonderful deeds for men.

[a]3 Hebrew *north and the sea*

[22]Let them sacrifice thank offerings
and tell of his works with songs of
joy.

[23]Others went out on the sea in ships;
they were merchants on the
mighty waters.
[24]They saw the works of the LORD,
his wonderful deeds in the deep.
[25]For he spoke and stirred up a
tempest
that lifted high the waves.
[26]They mounted up to the heavens
and went down to the
depths;
in their peril their courage melted
away.
[27]They reeled and staggered like
drunken men;
they were at their wits' end.
[28]Then they cried out to the LORD in
their trouble,
and he brought them out of their
distress.
[29]He stilled the storm to a whisper;
the waves of the sea were
hushed.
[30]They were glad when it grew calm,
and he guided them to their
desired haven.
[31]Let them give thanks to the LORD
for his unfailing love
and his wonderful deeds for men.
[32]Let them exalt him in the assembly
of the people
and praise him in the council of
the elders.

[33]He turned rivers into a desert,
flowing springs into thirsty
ground,
[34]and fruitful land into a salt waste,
because of the wickedness of
those who lived there.
[35]He turned the desert into pools of
water
and the parched ground into
flowing springs;
[36]there he brought the hungry to
live,
and they founded a city where
they could settle.
[37]They sowed fields and planted
vineyards
that yielded a fruitful harvest;
[38]he blessed them, and their numbers
greatly increased,
and he did not let their herds
diminish.

[39]Then their numbers decreased, and
they were humbled
by oppression, calamity and
sorrow;
[40]he who pours contempt on nobles
made them wander in a trackless
waste.
[41]But he lifted the needy out of their
affliction
and increased their families like
flocks.
[42]The upright see and rejoice,
but all the wicked shut their
mouths.

[43]Whoever is wise, let him heed these
things
and consider the great love of the
LORD.

Psalm 108

A song. A psalm of David.

[1]My heart is steadfast, O God;
I will sing and make music with
all my soul.
[2]Awake, harp and lyre!
I will awaken the dawn.
[3]I will praise you, O LORD, among
the nations;
I will sing of you among the
peoples.
[4]For great is your love, higher than
the heavens;
your faithfulness reaches to the
skies.
[5]Be exalted, O God, above the
heavens,
and let your glory be over all the
earth.

[6]Save us and help us with your right
hand,
that those you love may be
delivered.
[7]God has spoken from his sanctuary:
"In triumph I will parcel out
Shechem

and measure off the Valley of
Succoth.
8 Gilead is mine, Manasseh is mine;
Ephraim is my helmet,
Judah my scepter.
9 Moab is my washbasin,
upon Edom I toss my sandal;
over Philistia I shout in triumph."
10 Who will bring me to the fortified
city?
Who will lead me to Edom?
11 Is it not you, O God, you who have
rejected us
and no longer go out with our
armies?
12 Give us aid against the enemy,
for the help of man is worthless.
13 With God we will gain the victory,
and he will trample down our
enemies.

Psalm 109

For the director of music.
Of David. A psalm.

1 O God, whom I praise,
do not remain silent,
2 for wicked and deceitful men
have opened their mouths against
me;
they have spoken against me with
lying tongues.
3 With words of hatred they surround
me;
they attack me without cause.
4 In return for my friendship they
accuse me,
but I am a man of prayer.
5 They repay me evil for good,
and hatred for my friendship.
6 Appoint[a] an evil man[b] to oppose
him;
let an accuser[c] stand at his right
hand.
7 When he is tried, let him be found
guilty,
and may his prayers condemn
him.
8 May his days be few;
may another take his place of
leadership.
9 May his children be fatherless
and his wife a widow.
10 May his children be wandering
beggars;
may they be driven[d] from their
ruined homes.
11 May a creditor seize all he has;
may strangers plunder the fruits
of his labor.
12 May no one extend kindness to him
or take pity on his fatherless
children.
13 May his descendants be cut off,
their names blotted out from the
next generation.
14 May the iniquity of his fathers be
remembered before the
LORD;
may the sin of his mother never
be blotted out.
15 May their sins always remain before
the LORD,
that he may cut off the memory of
them from the earth.
16 For he never thought of doing a
kindness,
but hounded to death the poor
and the needy and the
brokenhearted.
17 He loved to pronounce a curse—
may it[e] come on him;
he found no pleasure in blessing—
may it be[f] far from him.
18 He wore cursing as his garment;
it entered into his body like water,
into his bones like oil.
19 May it be like a cloak wrapped about
him,
like a belt tied forever around
him.
20 May this be the LORD's payment to
my accusers,
to those who speak evil of me.
21 But you, O Sovereign LORD,
deal well with me for your name's
sake;
out of the goodness of your love,
deliver me.

[a]6 Or *They say:* "*Appoint* (with quotation marks at the end of verse 19) [b]6 Or *the Evil One* [c]6 Or *let Satan* [d]10 Septuagint; Hebrew *sought* [e]17 Or *curse, / and it has* [f]17 Or *blessing, / and it is*

[22] For I am poor and needy,
and my heart is wounded within me.
[23] I fade away like an evening shadow;
I am shaken off like a locust.
[24] My knees give way from fasting;
my body is thin and gaunt.
[25] I am an object of scorn to my accusers;
when they see me, they shake their heads.

[26] Help me, O LORD my God;
save me in accordance with your love.
[27] Let them know that it is your hand,
that you, O LORD, have done it.
[28] They may curse, but you will bless;
when they attack they will be put to shame,
but your servant will rejoice.
[29] My accusers will be clothed with disgrace
and wrapped in shame as in a cloak.

[30] With my mouth I will greatly extol the LORD;
in the great throng I will praise him.
[31] For he stands at the right hand of the needy one,
to save his life from those who condemn him.

Psalm 110

Of David. A psalm.

[1] The LORD says to my Lord:
"Sit at my right hand
until I make your enemies
a footstool for your feet."

[2] The LORD will extend your mighty scepter from Zion;
you will rule in the midst of your enemies.
[3] Your troops will be willing
on your day of battle.
Arrayed in holy majesty,
from the womb of the dawn
you will receive the dew of your youth.[a]

[4] The LORD has sworn
and will not change his mind:
"You are a priest forever,
in the order of Melchizedek."

[5] The Lord is at your right hand;
he will crush kings on the day of his wrath.
[6] He will judge the nations, heaping up the dead
and crushing the rulers of the whole earth.
[7] He will drink from a brook beside the way[b];
therefore he will lift up his head.

Psalm 111[c]

[1] Praise the LORD.[d]

I will extol the LORD with all my heart
in the council of the upright and in the assembly.

[2] Great are the works of the LORD;
they are pondered by all who delight in them.
[3] Glorious and majestic are his deeds,
and his righteousness endures forever.
[4] He has caused his wonders to be remembered;
the LORD is gracious and compassionate.
[5] He provides food for those who fear him;
he remembers his covenant forever.
[6] He has shown his people the power of his works,
giving them the lands of other nations.
[7] The works of his hands are faithful and just;
all his precepts are trustworthy.
[8] They are steadfast for ever and ever,
done in faithfulness and uprightness.

[a]3 Or / *your young men will come to you like the dew* [b]7 Or / *The One who grants succession will set him in authority* [c]This psalm is an acrostic poem, the lines of which begin with the successive letters of the Hebrew alphabet. [d]1 Hebrew *Hallelu Yah*

9 He provided redemption for his
people;
he ordained his covenant
forever—
holy and awesome is his name.
10 The fear of the LORD is the
beginning of wisdom;
all who follow his precepts have
good understanding.
To him belongs eternal praise.

Psalm 112[a]

1 Praise the LORD.[b]

Blessed is the man who fears the
LORD,
who finds great delight in his
commands.

2 His children will be mighty in the
land;
the generation of the upright will
be blessed.
3 Wealth and riches are in his house,
and his righteousness endures
forever.
4 Even in darkness light dawns for the
upright,
for the gracious and
compassionate and righteous
man.[c]
5 Good will come to him who is
generous and lends freely,
who conducts his affairs with
justice.
6 Surely he will never be shaken;
a righteous man will be
remembered forever.
7 He will have no fear of bad news;
his heart is steadfast, trusting in
the LORD.
8 His heart is secure, he will have no
fear;
in the end he will look in triumph
on his foes.
9 He has scattered abroad his gifts to
the poor,
his righteousness endures forever;
his horn[d] will be lifted high in
honor.
10 The wicked man will see and be
vexed,
he will gnash his teeth and waste
away;
the longings of the wicked will
come to nothing.

Psalm 113

1 Praise the LORD.[e]

Praise, O servants of the LORD,
praise the name of the LORD.
2 Let the name of the LORD be
praised,
both now and forevermore.
3 From the rising of the sun to the
place where it sets,
the name of the LORD is to be
praised.

4 The LORD is exalted over all the
nations,
his glory above the heavens.
5 Who is like the LORD our God,
the One who sits enthroned on
high,
6 who stoops down to look
on the heavens and the earth?

7 He raises the poor from the dust
and lifts the needy from the ash
heap;
8 he seats them with princes,
with the princes of their people.
9 He settles the barren woman in her
home
as a happy mother of children.

Praise the LORD.

[a] This psalm is an acrostic poem, the lines of which begin with the successive letters of the Hebrew alphabet. [b] 1 Hebrew *Hallelu Yah* [c] 4 Or */ for ⌞the LORD⌟ is gracious and compassionate and righteous* [d] 9 *Horn* here symbolizes dignity. [e] 1 Hebrew *Hallelu Yah;* also in verse 9

SHARPEN THE FOCUS

Nowhere else in all of Scripture do we find such a brief and powerful explanation of these three roles our Lord Jesus fills for us. What comfort each can be. Think of it:

As our King, Christ rules the world–right now–for the benefit of His children and the proclamation of the Gospel (Psalm 110:1–2).

As our High Priest, Christ serves us "arrayed in holy majesty" (Psalm 110:3). The one who hung in naked shame, suffering for our sins, now has clothed Himself with the majesty He once laid aside for our sakes. The glory of the victory He won by sacrificing Himself for us will never, ever fade away. God will never change His mind; Christ is our Mediator forever. No wonder we (Psalm 110:3) serve Him willingly.

As our Protector, Christ sees the injustices Satan and his servants perpetrate against us. He will not overlook their evil-doing forever. Rather, He will come to judge "the living and the dead," as we confess in the Creed. Even as we long for the salvation of the lost, we also hope for the day when all wrongs will be righted, all evil destroyed.

Jesus Christ. King. Priest. Judge. Praise Your Savior right now for His continuing work on your behalf.

WEEK 47 • SATURDAY

Psalms 114:1—118:29

Psalm 115 contrasts the living God, Yahweh, with all other gods. As you pray all of today's psalms, notice the many things the Lord does for His people and thank Him that, unlike all idols, He acts on behalf of those who belong to Him. If time is short, focus on Psalm 115.

Psalm 114

1 When Israel came out of Egypt,
the house of Jacob from a people of foreign tongue,
2 Judah became God's sanctuary,
Israel his dominion.

3 The sea looked and fled,
the Jordan turned back;
4 the mountains skipped like rams,
the hills like lambs.

5 Why was it, O sea, that you fled,
O Jordan, that you turned back,
6 you mountains, that you skipped like rams,
you hills, like lambs?

7 Tremble, O earth, at the presence of the Lord,
at the presence of the God of Jacob,
8 who turned the rock into a pool,
the hard rock into springs of water.

Psalm 115

1 Not to us, O LORD, not to us
but to your name be the glory,
because of your love and faithfulness.

2 Why do the nations say,
"Where is their God?"
3 Our God is in heaven;
he does whatever pleases him.
4 But their idols are silver and gold,
made by the hands of men.
5 They have mouths, but cannot speak,

eyes, but they cannot see;
6 they have ears, but cannot hear,
noses, but they cannot smell;
7 they have hands, but cannot feel,
feet, but they cannot walk;
nor can they utter a sound with their throats.
8 Those who make them will be like them,
and so will all who trust in them.

9 O house of Israel, trust in the LORD—
he is their help and shield.
10 O house of Aaron, trust in the LORD—
he is their help and shield.
11 You who fear him, trust in the LORD—
he is their help and shield.

12 The LORD remembers us and will bless us:
He will bless the house of Israel,
he will bless the house of Aaron,
13 he will bless those who fear the LORD—
small and great alike.

14 May the LORD make you increase,
both you and your children.
15 May you be blessed by the LORD,
the Maker of heaven and earth.

16 The highest heavens belong to the LORD,
but the earth he has given to man.
17 It is not the dead who praise the LORD,
those who go down to silence;
18 it is we who extol the LORD,
both now and forevermore.

Praise the LORD.[a]

Psalm 116

1 I love the LORD, for he heard my voice;
he heard my cry for mercy.
2 Because he turned his ear to me,
I will call on him as long as I live.

3 The cords of death entangled me,
the anguish of the grave[b] came upon me;
I was overcome by trouble and sorrow.
4 Then I called on the name of the LORD:
"O LORD, save me!"

5 The LORD is gracious and righteous;
our God is full of compassion.
6 The LORD protects the simplehearted;
when I was in great need, he saved me.

7 Be at rest once more, O my soul,
for the LORD has been good to you.

8 For you, O LORD, have delivered my soul from death,
my eyes from tears,
my feet from stumbling,
9 that I may walk before the LORD
in the land of the living.
10 I believed; therefore[c] I said,
"I am greatly afflicted."
11 And in my dismay I said,
"All men are liars."

12 How can I repay the LORD
for all his goodness to me?
13 I will lift up the cup of salvation
and call on the name of the LORD.
14 I will fulfill my vows to the LORD
in the presence of all his people.

15 Precious in the sight of the LORD
is the death of his saints.
16 O LORD, truly I am your servant;
I am your servant, the son of your maidservant[d];
you have freed me from my chains.

17 I will sacrifice a thank offering to you
and call on the name of the LORD.
18 I will fulfill my vows to the LORD
in the presence of all his people,
19 in the courts of the house of the LORD—
in your midst, O Jerusalem.

Praise the LORD.[a]

[a] 18,19 Hebrew *Hallelu Yah* [b] 3 Hebrew *Sheol* [c] 10 Or *believed even when* [d] 16 Or *servant, your faithful son*

Psalm 117

1 Praise the LORD, all you nations;
extol him, all you peoples.
2 For great is his love toward us,
and the faithfulness of the LORD endures forever.

Praise the LORD.[a]

Psalm 118

1 Give thanks to the LORD, for he is good;
his love endures forever.

2 Let Israel say:
"His love endures forever."
3 Let the house of Aaron say:
"His love endures forever."
4 Let those who fear the LORD say:
"His love endures forever."

5 In my anguish I cried to the LORD,
and he answered by setting me free.
6 The LORD is with me; I will not be afraid.
What can man do to me?
7 The LORD is with me; he is my helper.
I will look in triumph on my enemies.
8 It is better to take refuge in the LORD
than to trust in man.
9 It is better to take refuge in the LORD
than to trust in princes.

10 All the nations surrounded me,
but in the name of the LORD I cut them off.
11 They surrounded me on every side,
but in the name of the LORD I cut them off.
12 They swarmed around me like bees,
but they died out as quickly as burning thorns;
in the name of the LORD I cut them off.

13 I was pushed back and about to fall,
but the LORD helped me.
14 The LORD is my strength and my song;
he has become my salvation.
15 Shouts of joy and victory
resound in the tents of the righteous:
"The LORD's right hand has done mighty things!
16 The LORD's right hand is lifted high;
the LORD's right hand has done mighty things!"

17 I will not die but live,
and will proclaim what the LORD has done.
18 The LORD has chastened me severely,
but he has not given me over to death.

19 Open for me the gates of righteousness;
I will enter and give thanks to the LORD.
20 This is the gate of the LORD
through which the righteous may enter.
21 I will give you thanks, for you answered me;
you have become my salvation.

22 The stone the builders rejected
has become the capstone;
23 the LORD has done this,
and it is marvelous in our eyes.
24 This is the day the LORD has made;
let us rejoice and be glad in it.

25 O LORD, save us;
O LORD, grant us success.
26 Blessed is he who comes in the name of the LORD.
From the house of the LORD we bless you.[b]
27 The LORD is God,
and he has made his light shine upon us.
With boughs in hand, join in the festal procession
up[c] to the horns of the altar.

[a]2 Hebrew *Hallelu Yah* [b]26 The Hebrew is plural.
[c]27 Or *Bind the festal sacrifice with ropes / and take it*

28 You are my God, and I will give you
thanks;
you are my God, and I will exalt you.

29 Give thanks to the LORD, for he is
good;
his love endures forever.

SHARPEN THE FOCUS

Shortly after World War II, an orphaned girl in Italy happened upon a statue of the Greek goddess, Diana. The girl stood staring in admiration at the statue and came back each day to admire it.

Then she began to arrange her own hair to look like the hair of the goddess. Weeks passed. The girl found work. She bought new clothes and makeup. Still she came to admire the statue every day.

Several years later she sat eating her lunch beside the statue. A soldier walked past and gasped. The girl looked astonishingly like the goddess!

Psalm 115:8 talks about a similar phenomenon. People tend to become like those things they worship. We become like our "gods," as it were.

Which brings us to a personal question: "What do I worship?" Those who, by the Holy Spirit's power, admire Christ our Savior, trust in the pardon He won for them on the cross, worship Him, spend time in His Word and in His presence, become more like Him. But those who admire the wealthy, the famous, the powerful, or the ruthless become like these "gods."

Admire, worship, adore your beautiful Savior as you meditate on Colossians 1:16–20. Ask that He make you more like Himself as you draw strength from Him.

WEEK 48 • MONDAY

Psalm 119:1–176

GET THE BIG PICTURE

As you read today's psalm, note the various ways its author refers to the Word of God: the *law of the LORD*, the *statutes of God*, *God's commands*, and so on. In each case, the phrases refer to the whole Word of God, Law and Gospel, not just the commandments. Look for places in which the "Word of God" could also mean Jesus who is the Word made flesh (John 1:14). If time is short, focus on Psalm 119:89–96.

Psalm 119[a]

א Aleph

1 Blessed are they whose ways are
blameless,
who walk according to the law of
the LORD.
2 Blessed are they who keep his
statutes
and seek him with all their
heart.
3 They do nothing wrong;
they walk in his ways.
4 You have laid down precepts
that are to be fully obeyed.

[a] This psalm is an acrostic poem; the verses of each stanza begin with the same letter of the Hebrew alphabet.

5 Oh, that my ways were steadfast
in obeying your decrees!
6 Then I would not be put to shame
when I consider all your
commands.
7 I will praise you with an upright
heart
as I learn your righteous laws.
8 I will obey your decrees;
do not utterly forsake me.

ב Beth

9 How can a young man keep his way
pure?
By living according to your word.
10 I seek you with all my heart;
do not let me stray from your
commands.
11 I have hidden your word in my
heart
that I might not sin against you.
12 Praise be to you, O LORD;
teach me your decrees.
13 With my lips I recount
all the laws that come from your
mouth.
14 I rejoice in following your statutes
as one rejoices in great riches.
15 I meditate on your precepts
and consider your ways.
16 I delight in your decrees;
I will not neglect your word.

ג Gimel

17 Do good to your servant, and I will
live;
I will obey your word.
18 Open my eyes that I may see
wonderful things in your law.
19 I am a stranger on earth;
do not hide your commands from
me.
20 My soul is consumed with longing
for your laws at all times.
21 You rebuke the arrogant, who are
cursed
and who stray from your
commands.
22 Remove from me scorn and
contempt,
for I keep your statutes.
23 Though rulers sit together and
slander me,
your servant will meditate on
your decrees.
24 Your statutes are my delight;
they are my counselors.

ד Daleth

25 I am laid low in the dust;
preserve my life according to your
word.
26 I recounted my ways and you
answered me;
teach me your decrees.
27 Let me understand the teaching of
your precepts;
then I will meditate on your
wonders.
28 My soul is weary with sorrow;
strengthen me according to your
word.
29 Keep me from deceitful ways;
be gracious to me through your
law.
30 I have chosen the way of truth;
I have set my heart on your laws.
31 I hold fast to your statutes, O LORD;
do not let me be put to shame.
32 I run in the path of your commands,
for you have set my heart free.

ה He

33 Teach me, O LORD, to follow your
decrees;
then I will keep them to the end.
34 Give me understanding, and I will
keep your law
and obey it with all my heart.
35 Direct me in the path of your
commands,
for there I find delight.
36 Turn my heart toward your statutes
and not toward selfish gain.
37 Turn my eyes away from worthless
things;
preserve my life according to your
word.[a]
38 Fulfill your promise to your servant,
so that you may be feared.
39 Take away the disgrace I dread,
for your laws are good.

[a]37 Two manuscripts of the Masoretic Text and Dead Sea Scrolls; most manuscripts of the Masoretic Text *life in your way*

40 How I long for your precepts!
Preserve my life in your righteousness.

ו Waw

41 May your unfailing love come to me, O LORD,
your salvation according to your promise;
42 then I will answer the one who taunts me,
for I trust in your word.
43 Do not snatch the word of truth from my mouth,
for I have put my hope in your laws.
44 I will always obey your law,
for ever and ever.
45 I will walk about in freedom,
for I have sought out your precepts.
46 I will speak of your statutes before kings
and will not be put to shame,
47 for I delight in your commands
because I love them.
48 I lift up my hands to[a] your commands, which I love,
and I meditate on your decrees.

ז Zayin

49 Remember your word to your servant,
for you have given me hope.
50 My comfort in my suffering is this:
Your promise preserves my life.
51 The arrogant mock me without restraint,
but I do not turn from your law.
52 I remember your ancient laws, O LORD,
and I find comfort in them.
53 Indignation grips me because of the wicked,
who have forsaken your law.
54 Your decrees are the theme of my song
wherever I lodge.
55 In the night I remember your name, O LORD,
and I will keep your law.
56 This has been my practice:
I obey your precepts.

ח Heth

57 You are my portion, O LORD;
I have promised to obey your words.
58 I have sought your face with all my heart;
be gracious to me according to your promise.
59 I have considered my ways
and have turned my steps to your statutes.
60 I will hasten and not delay
to obey your commands.
61 Though the wicked bind me with ropes,
I will not forget your law.
62 At midnight I rise to give you thanks
for your righteous laws.
63 I am a friend to all who fear you,
to all who follow your precepts.
64 The earth is filled with your love, O LORD;
teach me your decrees.

ט Teth

65 Do good to your servant
according to your word, O LORD.
66 Teach me knowledge and good judgment,
for I believe in your commands.
67 Before I was afflicted I went astray,
but now I obey your word.
68 You are good, and what you do is good;
teach me your decrees.
69 Though the arrogant have smeared me with lies,
I keep your precepts with all my heart.
70 Their hearts are callous and unfeeling,
but I delight in your law.
71 It was good for me to be afflicted
so that I might learn your decrees.
72 The law from your mouth is more precious to me
than thousands of pieces of silver and gold.

[a]48 Or *for*

י Yodh

73 Your hands made me and formed me;
give me understanding to learn your commands.
74 May those who fear you rejoice when they see me,
for I have put my hope in your word.
75 I know, O LORD, that your laws are righteous,
and in faithfulness you have afflicted me.
76 May your unfailing love be my comfort,
according to your promise to your servant.
77 Let your compassion come to me that I may live,
for your law is my delight.
78 May the arrogant be put to shame for wronging me without cause;
but I will meditate on your precepts.
79 May those who fear you turn to me,
those who understand your statutes.
80 May my heart be blameless toward your decrees,
that I may not be put to shame.

כ Kaph

81 My soul faints with longing for your salvation,
but I have put my hope in your word.
82 My eyes fail, looking for your promise;
I say, "When will you comfort me?"
83 Though I am like a wineskin in the smoke,
I do not forget your decrees.
84 How long must your servant wait?
When will you punish my persecutors?
85 The arrogant dig pitfalls for me,
contrary to your law.
86 All your commands are trustworthy;
help me, for men persecute me without cause.
87 They almost wiped me from the earth,
but I have not forsaken your precepts.
88 Preserve my life according to your love,
and I will obey the statutes of your mouth.

ל Lamedh

89 Your word, O LORD, is eternal;
it stands firm in the heavens.
90 Your faithfulness continues through all generations;
you established the earth, and it endures.
91 Your laws endure to this day,
for all things serve you.
92 If your law had not been my delight,
I would have perished in my affliction.
93 I will never forget your precepts,
for by them you have preserved my life.
94 Save me, for I am yours;
I have sought out your precepts.
95 The wicked are waiting to destroy me,
but I will ponder your statutes.
96 To all perfection I see a limit;
but your commands are boundless.

מ Mem

97 Oh, how I love your law!
I meditate on it all day long.
98 Your commands make me wiser than my enemies,
for they are ever with me.
99 I have more insight than all my teachers,
for I meditate on your statutes.
100 I have more understanding than the elders,
for I obey your precepts.
101 I have kept my feet from every evil path
so that I might obey your word.
102 I have not departed from your laws,
for you yourself have taught me.
103 How sweet are your words to my taste,
sweeter than honey to my mouth!

104 I gain understanding from your
precepts;
therefore I hate every wrong path.

נ Nun

105 Your word is a lamp to my feet
and a light for my path.
106 I have taken an oath and
confirmed it,
that I will follow your righteous
laws.
107 I have suffered much;
preserve my life, O LORD,
according to your word.
108 Accept, O LORD, the willing praise
of my mouth,
and teach me your laws.
109 Though I constantly take my life in
my hands,
I will not forget your law.
110 The wicked have set a snare for me,
but I have not strayed from your
precepts.
111 Your statutes are my heritage
forever;
they are the joy of my heart.
112 My heart is set on keeping your
decrees
to the very end.

ס Samekh

113 I hate double-minded men,
but I love your law.
114 You are my refuge and my shield;
I have put my hope in your word.
115 Away from me, you evildoers,
that I may keep the commands of
my God!
116 Sustain me according to your
promise, and I will live;
do not let my hopes be dashed.
117 Uphold me, and I will be delivered;
I will always have regard for your
decrees.
118 You reject all who stray from your
decrees,
for their deceitfulness is in vain.
119 All the wicked of the earth you
discard like dross;
therefore I love your statutes.
120 My flesh trembles in fear of you;
I stand in awe of your laws.

ע Ayin

121 I have done what is righteous and
just;
do not leave me to my oppressors.
122 Ensure your servant's well-being;
let not the arrogant oppress me.
123 My eyes fail, looking for your
salvation,
looking for your righteous promise.
124 Deal with your servant according to
your love
and teach me your decrees.
125 I am your servant; give me
discernment
that I may understand your
statutes.
126 It is time for you to act, O LORD;
your law is being broken.
127 Because I love your commands
more than gold, more than pure
gold,
128 and because I consider all your
precepts right,
I hate every wrong path.

פ Pe

129 Your statutes are wonderful;
therefore I obey them.
130 The unfolding of your words gives
light;
it gives understanding to the
simple.
131 I open my mouth and pant,
longing for your commands.
132 Turn to me and have mercy on me,
as you always do to those who
love your name.
133 Direct my footsteps according to
your word;
let no sin rule over me.
134 Redeem me from the oppression of
men,
that I may obey your precepts.
135 Make your face shine upon your
servant
and teach me your decrees.
136 Streams of tears flow from my eyes,
for your law is not obeyed.

צ Tsadhe

137 Righteous are you, O LORD,
and your laws are right.

138 The statutes you have laid down are
righteous;
they are fully trustworthy.
139 My zeal wears me out,
for my enemies ignore your
words.
140 Your promises have been
thoroughly tested,
and your servant loves them.
141 Though I am lowly and despised,
I do not forget your precepts.
142 Your righteousness is everlasting
and your law is true.
143 Trouble and distress have come
upon me,
but your commands are my
delight.
144 Your statutes are forever right;
give me understanding that I may
live.

ק Qoph

145 I call with all my heart; answer me,
O LORD,
and I will obey your decrees.
146 I call out to you; save me
and I will keep your statutes.
147 I rise before dawn and cry for help;
I have put my hope in your word.
148 My eyes stay open through the
watches of the night,
that I may meditate on your
promises.
149 Hear my voice in accordance with
your love;
preserve my life, O LORD,
according to your laws.
150 Those who devise wicked schemes
are near,
but they are far from your law.
151 Yet you are near, O LORD,
and all your commands are true.
152 Long ago I learned from your
statutes
that you established them to last
forever.

ר Resh

153 Look upon my suffering and
deliver me,
for I have not forgotten your law.
154 Defend my cause and redeem me;
preserve my life according to your
promise.
155 Salvation is far from the wicked,
for they do not seek out your
decrees.
156 Your compassion is great, O LORD;
preserve my life according to your
laws.
157 Many are the foes who
persecute me,
but I have not turned from your
statutes.
158 I look on the faithless with loathing,
for they do not obey your word.
159 See how I love your precepts;
preserve my life, O LORD,
according to your love.
160 All your words are true;
all your righteous laws are eternal.

ש Sin and Shin

161 Rulers persecute me without cause,
but my heart trembles at your
word.
162 I rejoice in your promise
like one who finds great spoil.
163 I hate and abhor falsehood
but I love your law.
164 Seven times a day I praise you
for your righteous laws.
165 Great peace have they who love
your law,
and nothing can make them
stumble.
166 I wait for your salvation, O LORD,
and I follow your commands.
167 I obey your statutes,
for I love them greatly.
168 I obey your precepts and your
statutes,
for all my ways are known to you.

ת Taw

169 May my cry come before you,
O LORD;
give me understanding according
to your word.
170 May my supplication come before
you;
deliver me according to your
promise.
171 May my lips overflow with praise,
for you teach me your decrees.

172 May my tongue sing of your word,
for all your commands are
righteous.
173 May your hand be ready to
help me,
for I have chosen your precepts.
174 I long for your salvation, O LORD,
and your law is my delight.
175 Let me live that I may praise you,
and may your laws sustain me.
176 I have strayed like a lost sheep.
Seek your servant,
for I have not forgotten your
commands.

SHARPEN THE FOCUS

"What would become of me if not for the Word of God?" That, in essence, expresses the psalmist's thought in Psalm 119:92. We might well ask the same question. Since Psalm 119 is an acrostic—each section beginning with a new letter of the Hebrew alphabet—we can hear the psalmist saying, "God's Word says it all, from A to Z. God's Word is the first and the last word for my life and for how I want to live it."

Without God's Word where would we be? In particular, without Jesus, God's full and final Word, life here on earth would be a series of meaningless moments punctuated by frequent disasters. And life hereafter? Unthinkable.

But because Jesus has claimed us as His own, because He has—by the agony of His cross—saved us (Psalm 119:94), we can in joy seek His precepts. We can delight in them as we receive from Him the grace we need to understand and to obey His word of truth. ☼

WEEK 48 • TUESDAY

Psalms 120:1—125:5

GET THE BIG PICTURE

The city of Jerusalem, and in particular the temple, stood on a hill. When God's people went to Jerusalem, they "went up to Jerusalem." All Jewish males over the age of 12 were required to make this pilgrimage three times a year to celebrate the three great festivals—Passover, Pentecost, and Tabernacles. Psalms 120–134 provided "songs of ascent." Whole families crowded the road as they sang these psalms in praise to God on their way to worship. If time is short, focus on Psalm 122.

Psalm 120

A song of ascents.

1 I call on the LORD in my distress,
and he answers me.
2 Save me, O LORD, from lying
lips
and from deceitful tongues.
3 What will he do to you,
and what more besides,
O deceitful tongue?
4 He will punish you with a warrior's
sharp arrows,
with burning coals of the broom
tree.

5 Woe to me that I dwell in Meshech,
that I live among the tents of
Kedar!

6Too long have I lived
among those who hate peace.
7I am a man of peace;
but when I speak, they are for war.

Psalm 121

A song of ascents.

1I lift up my eyes to the hills—
where does my help come from?
2My help comes from the LORD,
the Maker of heaven and earth.

3He will not let your foot slip—
he who watches over you will not slumber;
4indeed, he who watches over Israel
will neither slumber nor sleep.

5The LORD watches over you—
the LORD is your shade at your right hand;
6the sun will not harm you by day,
nor the moon by night.

7The LORD will keep you from all harm—
he will watch over your life;
8the LORD will watch over your coming and going
both now and forevermore.

Psalm 122

A song of ascents. Of David.

1I rejoiced with those who said to me,
"Let us go to the house of the LORD."
2Our feet are standing
in your gates, O Jerusalem.

3Jerusalem is built like a city
that is closely compacted together.
4That is where the tribes go up,
the tribes of the LORD,
to praise the name of the LORD
according to the statute given to Israel.
5There the thrones for judgment stand,
the thrones of the house of David.

6Pray for the peace of Jerusalem:
"May those who love you be secure.
7May there be peace within your walls
and security within your citadels."
8For the sake of my brothers and friends,
I will say, "Peace be within you."
9For the sake of the house of the LORD our God,
I will seek your prosperity.

Psalm 123

A song of ascents.

1I lift up my eyes to you,
to you whose throne is in heaven.
2As the eyes of slaves look to the hand of their master,
as the eyes of a maid look to the hand of her mistress,
so our eyes look to the LORD our God,
till he shows us his mercy.

3Have mercy on us, O LORD, have mercy on us,
for we have endured much contempt.
4We have endured much ridicule from the proud,
much contempt from the arrogant.

Psalm 124

A song of ascents. Of David.

1If the LORD had not been on our side—
let Israel say—
2if the LORD had not been on our side
when men attacked us,
3when their anger flared against us,
they would have swallowed us alive;
4the flood would have engulfed us,
the torrent would have swept over us,
5the raging waters
would have swept us away.

6Praise be to the LORD,
who has not let us be torn by their teeth.
7We have escaped like a bird

out of the fowler's snare;
the snare has been broken,
and we have escaped.
8 Our help is in the name of the LORD,
the Maker of heaven and earth.

Psalm 125

A song of ascents.

1 Those who trust in the LORD are like Mount Zion,
which cannot be shaken but endures forever.
2 As the mountains surround Jerusalem,
so the LORD surrounds his people
both now and forevermore.

3 The scepter of the wicked will not remain
over the land allotted to the righteous,
for then the righteous might use
their hands to do evil.

4 Do good, O LORD, to those who are good,
to those who are upright in heart.
5 But those who turn to crooked ways
the LORD will banish with the evildoers.

Peace be upon Israel.

SHARPEN THE FOCUS

We enjoy a personal relationship with God because of what Christ has done for us, and we praise Him for it. But the relationship is personal, not private.

Psalm 122 makes that distinction clear. Each of us individually has received from the Lord the clean hands and the pure heart He requires of those who come into His presence (Psalm 24:3–4). Still, when we come to Him, we come with our brothers and sisters in the faith. We don't attend public worship in order to conduct private devotions. We worship together. We pray together. That's precisely why the psalmist enjoins us to pray for peace in "Jerusalem," the Holy Christian Church (Psalm 122:6–9).

All too often Christ's people try to live alone in the family of the Father. We ignore the financial needs of the family that sits ahead of us. We nod with polite coolness toward the widower who stands alone. We kneel at our Lord's Table next to those who are virtual strangers. And then we wonder why we don't "get more out of" public worship.

Confessing your own selfishness, and confident of Christ's forgiveness, pray Psalm 122. Ask the Spirit to open your eyes to the need for "peace [in] Jerusalem."

WEEK 48 • WEDNESDAY

Psalms 126:1—134:3

GET THE BIG PICTURE

The "songs of ascent" continue in today's psalms. As you read them, note both the praises and the concerns God's people bring on their hearts as they come together to worship Him. If time is short, focus on Psalm 133.

Psalm 126

A song of ascents.

[1]When the LORD brought back the
captives to[a] Zion,
we were like men who
dreamed.[b]
[2]Our mouths were filled with
laughter,
our tongues with songs of joy.
Then it was said among the
nations,
"The LORD has done great things
for them."
[3]The LORD has done great things for
us,
and we are filled with joy.

[4]Restore our fortunes,[c] O LORD,
like streams in the Negev.
[5]Those who sow in tears
will reap with songs of joy.
[6]He who goes out weeping,
carrying seed to sow,
will return with songs of joy,
carrying sheaves with him.

Psalm 127

A song of ascents. Of Solomon.

[1]Unless the LORD builds the house,
its builders labor in vain.
Unless the LORD watches over the
city,
the watchmen stand guard in
vain.
[2]In vain you rise early
and stay up late,
toiling for food to eat—
for he grants sleep to[d] those he
loves.

[3]Sons are a heritage from the LORD,
children a reward from him.
[4]Like arrows in the hands of a
warrior
are sons born in one's youth.
[5]Blessed is the man
whose quiver is full of them.
They will not be put to shame
when they contend with their
enemies in the gate.

Psalm 128

A song of ascents.

[1]Blessed are all who fear the LORD,
who walk in his ways.
[2]You will eat the fruit of your labor;
blessings and prosperity will be
yours.
[3]Your wife will be like a fruitful vine
within your house;
your sons will be like olive shoots
around your table.
[4]Thus is the man blessed
who fears the LORD.

[5]May the LORD bless you from Zion
all the days of your life;
may you see the prosperity of
Jerusalem,
[6] and may you live to see your
children's children.

Peace be upon Israel.

Psalm 129

A song of ascents.

[1]They have greatly oppressed me
from my youth—
let Israel say—
[2]they have greatly oppressed me
from my youth,
but they have not gained the
victory over me.
[3]Plowmen have plowed my back
and made their furrows long.
[4]But the LORD is righteous;
he has cut me free from the cords
of the wicked.

[5]May all who hate Zion
be turned back in shame.
[6]May they be like grass on the roof,
which withers before it can grow;
[7]with it the reaper cannot fill his
hands,
nor the one who gathers fill his
arms.
[8]May those who pass by not say,

[a]1 Or *LORD restored the fortunes of* [b]1 Or *men restored to health* [c]4 Or *Bring back our captives* [d]2 Or *eat— / for while they sleep he provides for*

"The blessing of the LORD be upon
you;
we bless you in the name of the
LORD."

Psalm 130

A song of ascents.

1 Out of the depths I cry to you,
O LORD;
2 O Lord, hear my voice.
Let your ears be attentive
to my cry for mercy.

3 If you, O LORD, kept a record of
sins,
O Lord, who could stand?
4 But with you there is forgiveness;
therefore you are feared.

5 I wait for the LORD, my soul waits,
and in his word I put my hope.
6 My soul waits for the Lord
more than watchmen wait for the
morning,
more than watchmen wait for the
morning.

7 O Israel, put your hope in the
LORD,
for with the LORD is unfailing love
and with him is full redemption.
8 He himself will redeem Israel
from all their sins.

Psalm 131

A song of ascents. Of David.

1 My heart is not proud, O LORD,
my eyes are not haughty;
I do not concern myself with great
matters
or things too wonderful for me.
2 But I have stilled and quieted my
soul;
like a weaned child with its
mother,
like a weaned child is my soul
within me.

3 O Israel, put your hope in the LORD
both now and forevermore.

Psalm 132

A song of ascents.

1 O LORD, remember David
and all the hardships he endured.

2 He swore an oath to the LORD
and made a vow to the Mighty
One of Jacob:
3 "I will not enter my house
or go to my bed—
4 I will allow no sleep to my eyes,
no slumber to my eyelids,
5 till I find a place for the LORD,
a dwelling for the Mighty One of
Jacob."

6 We heard it in Ephrathah,
we came upon it in the fields of
Jaar[a,b]:
7 "Let us go to his dwelling place;
let us worship at his footstool—
8 arise, O LORD, and come to your
resting place,
you and the ark of your might.
9 May your priests be clothed with
righteousness;
may your saints sing for joy."

10 For the sake of David your servant,
do not reject your anointed one.

11 The LORD swore an oath to David,
a sure oath that he will not
revoke:
"One of your own descendants
I will place on your throne—
12 if your sons keep my covenant
and the statutes I teach them,
then their sons will sit
on your throne for ever and ever."

13 For the LORD has chosen Zion,
he has desired it for his dwelling:
14 "This is my resting place for ever
and ever;
here I will sit enthroned, for I
have desired it—
15 I will bless her with abundant
provisions;
her poor will I satisfy with food.

[a]6 That is, Kiriath Jearim [b]6 Or *heard of it in Ephrathah, / we found it in the fields of Jaar.* (And no quotes around verses 7-9)

16 I will clothe her priests with
salvation,
and her saints will ever sing for
joy.
17 "Here I will make a horn[a] grow for
David
and set up a lamp for my anointed
one.
18 I will clothe his enemies with shame,
but the crown on his head will be
resplendent."

Psalm 133

A song of ascents. Of David.

1 How good and pleasant it is
when brothers live together in
unity!
2 It is like precious oil poured on the
head,
running down on the beard,
running down on Aaron's beard,
down upon the collar of his robes.
3 It is as if the dew of Hermon
were falling on Mount Zion.
For there the LORD bestows his
blessing,
even life forevermore.

Psalm 134

A song of ascents.

1 Praise the LORD, all you servants of
the LORD
who minister by night in the
house of the LORD.
2 Lift up your hands in the sanctuary
and praise the LORD.

3 May the LORD, the Maker of heaven
and earth,
bless you from Zion.

[a]17 *Horn* here symbolizes strong one, that is, king.

SHARPEN THE FOCUS

People in our culture expect options. College courses, new homes, new cars, and cable TV all offer a dizzying array of options.

It's little wonder that we all, at times, look at Christian unity as just one more option of Christ's church. Our Lord, though, has never considered unity optional. In fact, Jesus Himself lingered in earnest on this issue in His high priestly prayer (John 17).

But what is this unity exactly? Are we just to "go along to get along"? That's not unity. It's compromise, and it's the brand of compromise that will drag us down the road to eternal death. On the other hand, neither can unity coldly demand that everyone else in God's family conform to my tastes in dress code, musical styles, or paving for the church parking lot.

True unity comes as the Holy Spirit unites our hearts in love for one another and for our Savior. It comes as the Spirit teaches us the unshakable truth that each of Christ's people stands forgiven by the Savior's blood under the cross. True unity is the gift of God, given to us by His grace as He works through His Word, and it's one of the most beautiful aspects of Christ's kingdom.

WEEK 48 • THURSDAY

Psalms 135:1—137:9

As you pray today's psalms be especially mindful of the times the psalmist uses God's covenant name, "the LORD". This name comes from a verb form in the Hebrew language that means "to cause to happen." In the context of God's kindness and His promises to His Old Testament people, the name can be translated "The One Who Makes the Good Thing Happen" (Exodus 34:5–7). If time is short, focus on Psalm 136.

Psalm 135

1 Praise the LORD.[a]

Praise the name of the LORD;
praise him, you servants of the LORD,
2 you who minister in the house of the LORD,
in the courts of the house of our God.

3 Praise the LORD, for the LORD is good;
sing praise to his name, for that is pleasant.
4 For the LORD has chosen Jacob to be his own,
Israel to be his treasured possession.

5 I know that the LORD is great,
that our Lord is greater than all gods.
6 The LORD does whatever pleases him,
in the heavens and on the earth,
in the seas and all their depths.
7 He makes clouds rise from the ends of the earth;
he sends lightning with the rain
and brings out the wind from his storehouses.

8 He struck down the firstborn of Egypt,
the firstborn of men and animals.
9 He sent his signs and wonders into your midst, O Egypt,
against Pharaoh and all his servants.
10 He struck down many nations
and killed mighty kings—
11 Sihon king of the Amorites,
Og king of Bashan
and all the kings of Canaan—
12 and he gave their land as an inheritance,
an inheritance to his people Israel.

13 Your name, O LORD, endures forever,
your renown, O LORD, through all generations.
14 For the LORD will vindicate his people
and have compassion on his servants.

15 The idols of the nations are silver and gold,
made by the hands of men.
16 They have mouths, but cannot speak,
eyes, but they cannot see;
17 they have ears, but cannot hear,
nor is there breath in their mouths.
18 Those who make them will be like them,
and so will all who trust in them.

19 O house of Israel, praise the LORD;
O house of Aaron, praise the LORD;

[a]1 Hebrew *Hallelu Yah*; also in verses 3 and 21

[20]O house of Levi, praise the LORD;
you who fear him, praise the LORD.
[21]Praise be to the LORD from Zion,
to him who dwells in Jerusalem.

Praise the LORD.

Psalm 136

[1]Give thanks to the LORD, for he is good.
His love endures forever.
[2]Give thanks to the God of gods.
His love endures forever.
[3]Give thanks to the Lord of lords:
His love endures forever.

[4]to him who alone does great wonders,
His love endures forever.
[5]who by his understanding made the heavens,
His love endures forever.
[6]who spread out the earth upon the waters,
His love endures forever.
[7]who made the great lights—
His love endures forever.
[8]the sun to govern the day,
His love endures forever.
[9]the moon and stars to govern the night;
His love endures forever.

[10]to him who struck down the firstborn of Egypt
His love endures forever.
[11]and brought Israel out from among them
His love endures forever.
[12]with a mighty hand and outstretched arm;
His love endures forever.

[13]to him who divided the Red Sea[a] asunder
His love endures forever.
[14]and brought Israel through the midst of it,
His love endures forever.
[15]but swept Pharaoh and his army into the Red Sea;
His love endures forever.

[16]to him who led his people through the desert,
His love endures forever.
[17]who struck down great kings,
His love endures forever.
[18]and killed mighty kings—
His love endures forever.
[19]Sihon king of the Amorites
His love endures forever.
[20]and Og king of Bashan—
His love endures forever.
[21]and gave their land as an inheritance,
His love endures forever.
[22]an inheritance to his servant Israel;
His love endures forever.

[23]to the One who remembered us in our low estate
His love endures forever.
[24]and freed us from our enemies,
His love endures forever.
[25]and who gives food to every creature.
His love endures forever.

[26]Give thanks to the God of heaven.
His love endures forever.

Psalm 137

[1]By the rivers of Babylon we sat and wept
when we remembered Zion.
[2]There on the poplars
we hung our harps,
[3]for there our captors asked us for songs,
our tormentors demanded songs of joy;
they said, "Sing us one of the songs of Zion!"

[4]How can we sing the songs of the LORD
while in a foreign land?
[5]If I forget you, O Jerusalem,
may my right hand forget ⌞its skill⌟.
[6]May my tongue cling to the roof of my mouth
if I do not remember you,

[a]13 Hebrew *Yam Suph;* that is, Sea of Reeds; also in verse 15

if I do not consider Jerusalem
my highest joy.

7 Remember, O LORD, what the
Edomites did
on the day Jerusalem fell.
"Tear it down," they cried,
"tear it down to its foundations!"

8 O Daughter of Babylon, doomed to
destruction,
happy is he who repays you
for what you have done to
us—
9 he who seizes your infants
and dashes them against the
rocks.

SHARPEN THE FOCUS

Mr. Wrigley had an unusual theory of advertising. "Irritate 'em," he is supposed to have said, "Irritate 'em! They'll soon forget the irritation, but they'll remember your product."

At first, the refrain in Psalm 136 can irritate the reader. "Enough already," we may think, "We know God's love endures forever. Let's move on to the next point."

But there is no "next point." God's steadfast love encompasses our relationship with Him from start to finish. The word the New International Version renders *love* is translated in other Bible versions as *mercy*. *Mercy* refers to a particular kind of love, the love relationship God had promised His people in His covenant with Abraham. In essence when God's Old Testament people prayed, "LORD, have mercy," they were saying, "LORD, remember Your covenant."

That covenant found its fulfillment in Jesus, "The One Who Makes Salvation Happen." Everything we need, we find in Him and in His cross. Were it not for the cross, none of the mighty acts of God listed in Psalm 136 would matter. But through the cross, we see these blessings as the Lord's down-payment that He would keep His best and greatest covenant promise. Oh, give thanks to the Lord!

WEEK 48 • FRIDAY

Psalms 138:1—143:12

GET THE BIG PICTURE

The Lord knows you better than you know yourself. Does that thought comfort you? Frighten you? Challenge you? Do you believe it? Think about these questions as you pray today's psalms, particularly Psalm 139. If time is short, focus on Psalm 139.

Psalm 138

Of David.

1 I will praise you, O LORD, with all
my heart;
before the "gods" I will sing your
praise.
2 I will bow down toward your holy
temple
and will praise your name
for your love and your
faithfulness,
for you have exalted above all things
your name and your word.

[3]When I called, you answered me;
you made me bold and
stouthearted.

[4]May all the kings of the earth praise
you, O LORD,
when they hear the words of your
mouth.
[5]May they sing of the ways of the
LORD,
for the glory of the LORD is great.

[6]Though the LORD is on high, he
looks upon the lowly,
but the proud he knows from afar.
[7]Though I walk in the midst of
trouble,
you preserve my life;
you stretch out your hand against
the anger of my foes,
with your right hand you save me.
[8]The LORD will fulfill ⌞his purpose⌟ for
me;
your love, O LORD, endures
forever—
do not abandon the works of your
hands.

Psalm 139

For the director of music.
Of David. A psalm.

[1]O LORD, you have searched me
and you know me.
[2]You know when I sit and when I
rise;
you perceive my thoughts from
afar.
[3]You discern my going out and my
lying down;
you are familiar with all my ways.
[4]Before a word is on my tongue
you know it completely, O LORD.

[5]You hem me in—behind and before;
you have laid your hand upon
me.
[6]Such knowledge is too wonderful
for me,
too lofty for me to attain.

[7]Where can I go from your Spirit?
Where can I flee from your
presence?
[8]If I go up to the heavens, you are
there;
if I make my bed in the depths,[a]
you are there.
[9]If I rise on the wings of the dawn,
if I settle on the far side of the sea,
[10]even there your hand will guide me,
your right hand will hold me fast.

[11]If I say, "Surely the darkness will
hide me
and the light become night
around me,"
[12]even the darkness will not be dark
to you;
the night will shine like the day,
for darkness is as light to you.
[13]For you created my inmost being;
you knit me together in my
mother's womb.
[14]I praise you because I am fearfully
and wonderfully made;
your works are wonderful,
I know that full well.
[15]My frame was not hidden from you
when I was made in the secret
place.
When I was woven together in the
depths of the earth,
[16] your eyes saw my unformed body.
All the days ordained for me
were written in your book
before one of them came to be.

[17]How precious to[b] me are your
thoughts, O God!
How vast is the sum of them!
[18]Were I to count them,
they would outnumber the grains
of sand.
When I awake,
I am still with you.

[19]If only you would slay the wicked,
O God!
Away from me, you bloodthirsty
men!
[20]They speak of you with evil intent;
your adversaries misuse your
name.
[21]Do I not hate those who hate you,
O LORD,

[a]8 Hebrew *Sheol* [b]17 Or *concerning*

and abhor those who rise up
against you?
22 I have nothing but hatred for them;
I count them my enemies.
23 Search me, O God, and know my
heart;
test me and know my anxious
thoughts.
24 See if there is any offensive way in
me,
and lead me in the way
everlasting.

Psalm 140

For the director of music.
A psalm of David.

1 Rescue me, O LORD, from evil men;
protect me from men of violence,
2 who devise evil plans in their hearts
and stir up war every day.
3 They make their tongues as sharp as
a serpent's;
the poison of vipers is on their
lips. *Selah*
4 Keep me, O LORD, from the hands of
the wicked;
protect me from men of violence
who plan to trip my feet.
5 Proud men have hidden a snare for
me;
they have spread out the cords of
their net
and have set traps for me along
my path. *Selah*
6 O LORD, I say to you, "You are my
God."
Hear, O LORD, my cry for mercy.
7 O Sovereign LORD, my strong
deliverer,
who shields my head in the day of
battle—
8 do not grant the wicked their
desires, O LORD;
do not let their plans succeed,
or they will become proud. *Selah*
9 Let the heads of those who
surround me
be covered with the trouble their
lips have caused.
10 Let burning coals fall upon them;
may they be thrown into the fire,
into miry pits, never to rise.
11 Let slanderers not be established in
the land;
may disaster hunt down men of
violence.
12 I know that the LORD secures justice
for the poor
and upholds the cause of the
needy.
13 Surely the righteous will praise your
name
and the upright will live before
you.

Psalm 141

A psalm of David.

1 O LORD, I call to you; come quickly
to me.
Hear my voice when I call to you.
2 May my prayer be set before you
like incense;
may the lifting up of my hands be
like the evening sacrifice.
3 Set a guard over my mouth,
O LORD;
keep watch over the door of my
lips.
4 Let not my heart be drawn to what
is evil,
to take part in wicked deeds
with men who are evildoers;
let me not eat of their delicacies.
5 Let a righteous man[a] strike me—it is
a kindness;
let him rebuke me—it is oil on my
head.
My head will not refuse it.

Yet my prayer is ever against the
deeds of evildoers;
6 their rulers will be thrown down
from the cliffs,
and the wicked will learn that my
words were well spoken.
7 They will say, "As one plows and
breaks up the earth,

[a]5 Or *Let the Righteous One*

so our bones have been scattered
at the mouth of the grave.[a]"
8 But my eyes are fixed on you,
O Sovereign LORD;
in you I take refuge—do not give
me over to death.
9 Keep me from the snares they have
laid for me,
from the traps set by evildoers.
10 Let the wicked fall into their own
nets,
while I pass by in safety.

Psalm 142

A *maskil*[b] of David.
When he was in the cave. A prayer.

1 I cry aloud to the LORD;
I lift up my voice to the LORD for
mercy.
2 I pour out my complaint before him;
before him I tell my trouble.
3 When my spirit grows faint within
me,
it is you who know my way.
In the path where I walk
men have hidden a snare for me.
4 Look to my right and see;
no one is concerned for me.
I have no refuge;
no one cares for my life.

5 I cry to you, O LORD;
I say, "You are my refuge,
my portion in the land of the
living."
6 Listen to my cry,
for I am in desperate need;
rescue me from those who pursue me,
for they are too strong for me.
7 Set me free from my prison,
that I may praise your name.

Then the righteous will gather about
me
because of your goodness to me.

Psalm 143

A psalm of David.

1 O LORD, hear my prayer,
listen to my cry for mercy;
in your faithfulness and
righteousness
come to my relief.
2 Do not bring your servant into
judgment,
for no one living is righteous
before you.

3 The enemy pursues me,
he crushes me to the ground;
he makes me dwell in darkness
like those long dead.
4 So my spirit grows faint within me;
my heart within me is
dismayed.

5 I remember the days of long ago;
I meditate on all your works
and consider what your hands
have done.
6 I spread out my hands to you;
my soul thirsts for you like a
parched land. *Selah*

7 Answer me quickly, O LORD;
my spirit fails.
Do not hide your face from me
or I will be like those who go
down to the pit.
8 Let the morning bring me word of
your unfailing love,
for I have put my trust in you.
Show me the way I should go,
for to you I lift up my soul.
9 Rescue me from my enemies,
O LORD,
for I hide myself in you.
10 Teach me to do your will,
for you are my God;
may your good Spirit
lead me on level ground.

11 For your name's sake, O LORD,
preserve my life;
in your righteousness, bring me
out of trouble.
12 In your unfailing love, silence my
enemies;
destroy all my foes,
for I am your servant.

[a]7 Hebrew *Sheol* [b]Title: Probably a literary or musical term

SHARPEN THE FOCUS

When did you last praise or thank the Lord for your body? Psalm 139:13–16 impresses us with the fact that each of us has come to exist because God took special care to create us just so. He knitted us together in our mother's womb (Psalm 139:13). He wove our frame together (Psalm 139:15). Like a master artisan, our Lord created us as works of art, as evidence of His kindness, wisdom, and power.

Perhaps you think that overstates the case. Our culture defines beauty with limits so narrow that hardly anyone qualifies. You may think your body leaves a lot to be desired. Or maybe you are contending with a long-term health problem. Or live inside a body under attack by a frightening disease.

St. Peter described his body as a tent that would one day be taken down (2 Peter 1:13–14). Our bodies fray and wear out. The lightning and hail storms of life damage our "tents." Even so, the bodies in which we now live are God's good gifts to us, and they will live forever.

Your body is not a throw-away item. It will one day rise from death, glorified by the power of the God who both created and redeemed you. Your Savior will retrofit your body so that you will be able to enjoy it forever in heaven.

WEEK 48 • SATURDAY

Psalms 144:1—150:6

GET THE BIG PICTURE

The closing hymns of the Psalter extol our Lord for His wisdom, power, majesty, and justice. And they rejoice in His mercy, love, care, forgiveness, and righteousness. Pray these psalms in praise to the Lord, your God. As you do so, remember that He has given you His righteousness as a gift through the finished work of our Lord Jesus. Your God counts you as one of His saints, His righteous ones, and His people. You are a part of Zion, Jerusalem, and Jacob. You belong to Him as His holy child! If time is short, focus on Psalm 145.

Psalm 144

Of David.

1 Praise be to the LORD my Rock,
who trains my hands for war,
my fingers for battle.
2 He is my loving God and my fortress,
my stronghold and my deliverer,
my shield, in whom I take refuge,
who subdues peoples[a] under me.

3 O LORD, what is man that you care
for him,
the son of man that you think of
him?
4 Man is like a breath;
his days are like a fleeting shadow.

5 Part your heavens, O LORD, and
come down;
touch the mountains, so that they
smoke.

[a]2 Many manuscripts of the Masoretic Text, Dead Sea Scrolls, Aquila, Jerome and Syriac; most manuscripts of the Masoretic Text *subdues my people*

6 Send forth lightning and scatter ⌊the
enemies⌋;
shoot your arrows and rout them.
7 Reach down your hand from on
high;
deliver me and rescue me
from the mighty waters,
from the hands of foreigners
8 whose mouths are full of lies,
whose right hands are deceitful.

9 I will sing a new song to you,
O God;
on the ten-stringed lyre I will
make music to you,
10 to the One who gives victory to kings,
who delivers his servant David
from the deadly sword.

11 Deliver me and rescue me
from the hands of foreigners
whose mouths are full of lies,
whose right hands are deceitful.

12 Then our sons in their youth
will be like well-nurtured plants,
and our daughters will be like pillars
carved to adorn a palace.
13 Our barns will be filled
with every kind of provision.
Our sheep will increase by
thousands,
by tens of thousands in our fields;
14 our oxen will draw heavy loads.[a]
There will be no breaching of walls,
no going into captivity,
no cry of distress in our streets.
15 Blessed are the people of whom this
is true;
blessed are the people whose God
is the LORD.

Psalm 145[b]

A psalm of praise. Of David.

1 I will exalt you, my God the King;
I will praise your name for ever
and ever.
2 Every day I will praise you
and extol your name for ever and
ever.

3 Great is the LORD and most worthy
of praise;
his greatness no one can fathom.
4 One generation will commend your
works to another;
they will tell of your mighty acts.
5 They will speak of the glorious
splendor of your majesty,
and I will meditate on your
wonderful works.[c]
6 They will tell of the power of your
awesome works,
and I will proclaim your great
deeds.
7 They will celebrate your abundant
goodness
and joyfully sing of your
righteousness.

8 The LORD is gracious and
compassionate,
slow to anger and rich in love.
9 The LORD is good to all;
he has compassion on all he has
made.
10 All you have made will praise you,
O LORD;
your saints will extol you.
11 They will tell of the glory of your
kingdom
and speak of your might,
12 so that all men may know of your
mighty acts
and the glorious splendor of your
kingdom.
13 Your kingdom is an everlasting
kingdom,
and your dominion endures
through all generations.
The LORD is faithful to all his
promises
and loving toward all he has
made.[d]
14 The LORD upholds all those who fall

[a]14 Or *our chieftains will be firmly established*
[b]This psalm is an acrostic poem, the verses of which (including verse 13b) begin with the successive letters of the Hebrew alphabet.
[c]5 Dead Sea Scrolls and Syriac (see also Septuagint); Masoretic Text *On the glorious splendor of your majesty / and on your wonderful works I will meditate* [d]13 One manuscript of the Masoretic Text, Dead Sea Scrolls and Syriac (see also Septuagint); most manuscripts of the Masoretic Text do not have the last two lines of verse 13.

and lifts up all who are bowed
down.
[15]The eyes of all look to you,
and you give them their food at
the proper time.
[16]You open your hand
and satisfy the desires of every
living thing.

[17]The LORD is righteous in all his ways
and loving toward all he has
made.
[18]The LORD is near to all who call on
him,
to all who call on him in truth.
[19]He fulfills the desires of those who
fear him;
he hears their cry and saves them.
[20]The LORD watches over all who love
him,
but all the wicked he will destroy.

[21]My mouth will speak in praise of the
LORD.
Let every creature praise his holy
name
for ever and ever.

Psalm 146

[1]Praise the LORD.[a]

Praise the LORD, O my soul.
[2] I will praise the LORD all my life;
I will sing praise to my God as
long as I live.

[3]Do not put your trust in princes,
in mortal men, who cannot save.
[4]When their spirit departs, they
return to the ground;
on that very day their plans come
to nothing.

[5]Blessed is he whose help is the God
of Jacob,
whose hope is in the LORD his
God,
[6]the Maker of heaven and earth,
the sea, and everything in them—
the LORD, who remains faithful
forever.
[7]He upholds the cause of the
oppressed
and gives food to the hungry.
The LORD sets prisoners free,
[8] the LORD gives sight to the blind,
the LORD lifts up those who are
bowed down,
the LORD loves the righteous.
[9]The LORD watches over the alien
and sustains the fatherless and the
widow,
but he frustrates the ways of the
wicked.

[10]The LORD reigns forever,
your God, O Zion, for all
generations.

Praise the LORD.

Psalm 147

[1]Praise the LORD.[b]

How good it is to sing praises to our
God,
how pleasant and fitting to praise
him!

[2]The LORD builds up Jerusalem;
he gathers the exiles of Israel.
[3]He heals the brokenhearted
and binds up their wounds.

[4]He determines the number of the
stars
and calls them each by name.
[5]Great is our Lord and mighty in
power;
his understanding has no limit.
[6]The LORD sustains the humble
but casts the wicked to the
ground.

[7]Sing to the LORD with thanksgiving;
make music to our God on the
harp.
[8]He covers the sky with clouds;
he supplies the earth with rain
and makes grass grow on the hills.
[9]He provides food for the cattle
and for the young ravens when
they call.
[10]His pleasure is not in the strength of
the horse,

[a]1 Hebrew *Hallelu Yah*; also in verse 10
[b]1 Hebrew *Hallelu Yah*; also in verse 20

nor his delight in the legs of a
man;
11 the LORD delights in those who fear
him,
who put their hope in his
unfailing love.

12 Extol the LORD, O Jerusalem;
praise your God, O Zion,
13 for he strengthens the bars of your
gates
and blesses your people within
you.
14 He grants peace to your borders
and satisfies you with the finest of
wheat.

15 He sends his command to the earth;
his word runs swiftly.
16 He spreads the snow like wool
and scatters the frost like ashes.
17 He hurls down his hail like pebbles.
Who can withstand his icy blast?
18 He sends his word and melts them;
he stirs up his breezes, and the
waters flow.

19 He has revealed his word to Jacob,
his laws and decrees to Israel.
20 He has done this for no other
nation;
they do not know his laws.

Praise the LORD.

Psalm 148

1 Praise the LORD.[a]

Praise the LORD from the heavens,
praise him in the heights above.
2 Praise him, all his angels,
praise him, all his heavenly hosts.
3 Praise him, sun and moon,
praise him, all you shining stars.
4 Praise him, you highest heavens
and you waters above the skies.
5 Let them praise the name of the
LORD,
for he commanded and they were
created.
6 He set them in place for ever and
ever;
he gave a decree that will never
pass away.

7 Praise the LORD from the earth,
you great sea creatures and all
ocean depths,
8 lightning and hail, snow and clouds,
stormy winds that do his bidding,
9 you mountains and all hills,
fruit trees and all cedars,
10 wild animals and all cattle,
small creatures and flying birds,
11 kings of the earth and all nations,
you princes and all rulers on
earth,
12 young men and maidens,
old men and children.

13 Let them praise the name of the
LORD,
for his name alone is exalted;
his splendor is above the earth
and the heavens.
14 He has raised up for his people a
horn,[b]
the praise of all his saints,
of Israel, the people close to his
heart.

Praise the LORD.

Psalm 149

1 Praise the LORD.[c]

Sing to the LORD a new song,
his praise in the assembly of the
saints.
2 Let Israel rejoice in their Maker;
let the people of Zion be glad in
their King.
3 Let them praise his name with
dancing
and make music to him with
tambourine and harp.
4 For the LORD takes delight in his
people;
he crowns the humble with
salvation.
5 Let the saints rejoice in this honor
and sing for joy on their beds.

6 May the praise of God be in their
mouths

[a] 1 Hebrew *Hallelu Yah;* also in verse 14 [b] 14 *Horn* here symbolizes strong one, that is, king.
[c] 1 Hebrew *Hallelu Yah;* also in verse 9

and a double-edged sword in
their hands,
7 to inflict vengeance on the nations
and punishment on the peoples,
8 to bind their kings with fetters,
their nobles with shackles of iron,
9 to carry out the sentence written
against them.
This is the glory of all his saints.

Praise the LORD.

Psalm 150

1 Praise the LORD.[a]

Praise God in his sanctuary;
praise him in his mighty heavens.
2 Praise him for his acts of power;
praise him for his surpassing
greatness.
3 Praise him with the sounding of the
trumpet,
praise him with the harp and lyre,
4 praise him with tambourine and
dancing,
praise him with the strings and
flute,
5 praise him with the clash of cymbals,
praise him with resounding
cymbals.

6 Let everything that has breath praise
the LORD.

Praise the LORD.

[a]1 Hebrew *Hallelu Yah;* also in verse 6

SHARPEN THE FOCUS

The famous Hot Springs of Arkansas gush about a million gallons of water per day. The water temperature always remains the same: 143 degrees Fahrenheit. Thousands of visitors plan vacations to the Hot Springs each year to bathe in the spas because of the supposed healing properties in the bubbling waters.

Psalm 145:7 speaks about a different kind of bubbling water with healing properties. Literally, the verse could read:

[We] shall bubble forth the memory of Your great goodness,
And shall sing of Your righteousness.

Maybe you know someone you'd describe as "bubbly." The enthusiasm of such people is infectious. We like to spend time with them. We especially enjoy being with those brothers and sisters in the faith whose peace and confidence in the Lord bubble to the surface from the deep river of faith God the Holy Spirit has created in them. Those are healing waters.

Today you will meet people who need our Lord's healing and refreshment. As the Spirit empowers you, you too can "bubble forth the memory of [God's] great goodness." You can be a channel of our Savior's peace in someone else's life. Ask Him for the opportunity and for the grace to recognize and use it. ☼

Proverbs

WEEK 49 • MONDAY

Proverbs 1:1—3:35

In Colossians 2:3, Paul tells us that "in [Christ] are hidden all the treasures of wisdom and knowledge." Keep that very important truth in mind as you read about wisdom in today's chapters. If time is short, focus on Proverbs 3:1–18.

Prologue: Purpose and Theme

1 The proverbs of Solomon son of
David, king of Israel:

2 for attaining wisdom and discipline;
for understanding words of
insight;
3 for acquiring a disciplined and
prudent life,
doing what is right and just and
fair;
4 for giving prudence to the simple,
knowledge and discretion to the
young—
5 let the wise listen and add to their
learning,
and let the discerning get
guidance—
6 for understanding proverbs and
parables,
the sayings and riddles of the
wise.

7 The fear of the LORD is the
beginning of knowledge,
but fools[a] despise wisdom and
discipline.

Exhortations to Embrace Wisdom

Warning Against Enticement

8 Listen, my son, to your father's
instruction
and do not forsake your mother's
teaching.
9 They will be a garland to grace your
head
and a chain to adorn your neck.

10 My son, if sinners entice you,
do not give in to them.
11 If they say, "Come along with us;
let's lie in wait for someone's
blood,
let's waylay some harmless soul;
12 let's swallow them alive, like the
grave,[b]
and whole, like those who go
down to the pit;
13 we will get all sorts of valuable
things
and fill our houses with plunder;
14 throw in your lot with us,
and we will share a common
purse"—
15 my son, do not go along with them,
do not set foot on their paths;
16 for their feet rush into sin,
they are swift to shed blood.
17 How useless to spread a net
in full view of all the birds!
18 These men lie in wait for their own
blood;

[a]7 The Hebrew words rendered *fool* in Proverbs, and often elsewhere in the Old Testament, denote one who is morally deficient.
[b]12 Hebrew *Sheol*

they waylay only themselves!
19 Such is the end of all who go after
ill-gotten gain;
it takes away the lives of those
who get it.

Warning Against Rejecting Wisdom

20 Wisdom calls aloud in the street,
she raises her voice in the public
squares;
21 at the head of the noisy streets[a] she
cries out,
in the gateways of the city she
makes her speech:

22 "How long will you simple ones[b]
love your simple ways?
How long will mockers delight in
mockery
and fools hate knowledge?
23 If you had responded to my rebuke,
I would have poured out my heart
to you
and made my thoughts known to
you.
24 But since you rejected me when I
called
and no one gave heed when I
stretched out my hand,
25 since you ignored all my advice
and would not accept my rebuke,
26 I in turn will laugh at your disaster;
I will mock when calamity
overtakes you—
27 when calamity overtakes you like a
storm,
when disaster sweeps over you
like a whirlwind,
when distress and trouble
overwhelm you.

28 "Then they will call to me but I will
not answer;
they will look for me but will not
find me.
29 Since they hated knowledge
and did not choose to fear the
LORD,
30 since they would not accept my
advice
and spurned my rebuke,
31 they will eat the fruit of their ways
and be filled with the fruit of their
schemes.
32 For the waywardness of the simple
will kill them,
and the complacency of fools will
destroy them;
33 but whoever listens to me will live in
safety
and be at ease, without fear of
harm."

Moral Benefits of Wisdom

2 My son, if you accept my words
and store up my commands
within you,
2 turning your ear to wisdom
and applying your heart to
understanding,
3 and if you call out for insight
and cry aloud for understanding,
4 and if you look for it as for silver
and search for it as for hidden
treasure,
5 then you will understand the fear of
the LORD
and find the knowledge of God.
6 For the LORD gives wisdom,
and from his mouth come
knowledge and
understanding.
7 He holds victory in store for the
upright,
he is a shield to those whose walk
is blameless,
8 for he guards the course of the just
and protects the way of his
faithful ones.

9 Then you will understand what is
right and just
and fair—every good path.
10 For wisdom will enter your heart,
and knowledge will be pleasant to
your soul.
11 Discretion will protect you,
and understanding will guard
you.

12 Wisdom will save you from the ways
of wicked men,
from men whose words are
perverse,

[a]21 Hebrew; Septuagint / *on the tops of the walls*
[b]22 The Hebrew word rendered *simple* in Proverbs generally denotes one without moral direction and inclined to evil.

13 who leave the straight paths
to walk in dark ways,
14 who delight in doing wrong
and rejoice in the perverseness of evil,
15 whose paths are crooked
and who are devious in their ways.

16 It will save you also from the adulteress,
from the wayward wife with her seductive words,
17 who has left the partner of her youth
and ignored the covenant she made before God.[a]
18 For her house leads down to death
and her paths to the spirits of the dead.
19 None who go to her return
or attain the paths of life.

20 Thus you will walk in the ways of good men
and keep to the paths of the righteous.
21 For the upright will live in the land,
and the blameless will remain in it;
22 but the wicked will be cut off from the land,
and the unfaithful will be torn from it.

Further Benefits of Wisdom

3 My son, do not forget my teaching,
but keep my commands in your heart,
2 for they will prolong your life many years
and bring you prosperity.

3 Let love and faithfulness never leave you;
bind them around your neck,
write them on the tablet of your heart.
4 Then you will win favor and a good name
in the sight of God and man.

5 Trust in the LORD with all your heart
and lean not on your own understanding;
6 in all your ways acknowledge him,
and he will make your paths straight.[b]

7 Do not be wise in your own eyes;
fear the LORD and shun evil.
8 This will bring health to your body
and nourishment to your bones.

9 Honor the LORD with your wealth,
with the firstfruits of all your crops;
10 then your barns will be filled to overflowing,
and your vats will brim over with new wine.

11 My son, do not despise the LORD's discipline
and do not resent his rebuke,
12 because the LORD disciplines those he loves,
as a father[c] the son he delights in.

13 Blessed is the man who finds wisdom,
the man who gains understanding,
14 for she is more profitable than silver
and yields better returns than gold.
15 She is more precious than rubies;
nothing you desire can compare with her.
16 Long life is in her right hand;
in her left hand are riches and honor.
17 Her ways are pleasant ways,
and all her paths are peace.
18 She is a tree of life to those who embrace her;
those who lay hold of her will be blessed.

19 By wisdom the LORD laid the earth's foundations,
by understanding he set the heavens in place;
20 by his knowledge the deeps were divided,
and the clouds let drop the dew.

[a]17 Or *covenant of her God* [b]6 Or *will direct your paths* [c]12 Hebrew; Septuagint / *and he punishes*

21 My son, preserve sound judgment
and discernment,
do not let them out of your sight;
22 they will be life for you,
an ornament to grace your neck.
23 Then you will go on your way in
safety,
and your foot will not stumble;
24 when you lie down, you will not be
afraid;
when you lie down, your sleep
will be sweet.
25 Have no fear of sudden disaster
or of the ruin that overtakes the
wicked,
26 for the LORD will be your confidence
and will keep your foot from
being snared.

27 Do not withhold good from those
who deserve it,
when it is in your power to act.
28 Do not say to your neighbor,
"Come back later; I'll give it
tomorrow"—
when you now have it with you.

29 Do not plot harm against your
neighbor,
who lives trustfully near you.
30 Do not accuse a man for no reason—
when he has done you no harm.

31 Do not envy a violent man
or choose any of his ways,
32 for the LORD detests a perverse man
but takes the upright into his
confidence.

33 The LORD's curse is on the house of
the wicked,
but he blesses the home of the
righteous.
34 He mocks proud mockers
but gives grace to the humble.
35 The wise inherit honor,
but fools he holds up to shame.

SHARPEN THE FOCUS

Our experiences and knowledge, new methods and ideas, and all the people we treasure in life come to us as good gifts from our heavenly Father. But we dare not base our security on them. If we do, they will eventually fail us. We will fall, scraping knees and bruising our egos on the rocks of reality. The only sure thing in life is the Lord and His precious promises to us in Jesus.

God wants us to use all the gifts He's given, but none of them can be our ultimate refuge. The alternative? To acknowledge the Lord (Proverbs 3:6) so that He can smooth our path in His own wonderful way. We do this when we acknowledge Him as our guide, and when we, by His grace, follow His lead.

Sometimes what He asks of us will seem pleasant, and we can follow gladly. Sometimes what He asks seems foolish or causes us pain. But even then, we can follow, because we know He wants only the best for us. He proved that once and for all in giving Jesus over to death for our sins.

Do you want a smooth path? Do you want to find the easiest way though the tangled thicket of your circumstances? Acknowledge Christ and follow His leading. Confess your sins, and in the power of God's forgiveness, live a life of repentance.

WEEK 49 • TUESDAY

Proverbs 4:1–27

GET THE BIG PICTURE

As chapter 4 begins, Solomon quotes his father, King David. In fact, the address "my son" punctuates all of Proverbs 1–8. As you read today's chapter, ask yourself what personal experiences equipped David to teach his son, Solomon, these truths. If time is short, focus on Proverbs 4:18–27.

Wisdom Is Supreme

4 Listen, my sons, to a father's
instruction;
pay attention and gain
understanding.
2 I give you sound learning,
so do not forsake my teaching.
3 When I was a boy in my father's
house,
still tender, and an only child of
my mother,
4 he taught me and said,
"Lay hold of my words with all
your heart;
keep my commands and you will
live.
5 Get wisdom, get understanding;
do not forget my words or swerve
from them.
6 Do not forsake wisdom, and she will
protect you;
love her, and she will watch over
you.
7 Wisdom is supreme; therefore get
wisdom.
Though it cost all you have,[a] get
understanding.
8 Esteem her, and she will exalt you;
embrace her, and she will honor
you.
9 She will set a garland of grace on
your head
and present you with a crown of
splendor."

10 Listen, my son, accept what I say,
and the years of your life will be
many.
11 I guide you in the way of wisdom
and lead you along straight paths.
12 When you walk, your steps will not
be hampered;
when you run, you will not
stumble.
13 Hold on to instruction, do not let it
go;
guard it well, for it is your life.
14 Do not set foot on the path of the
wicked
or walk in the way of evil men.
15 Avoid it, do not travel on it;
turn from it and go on your way.
16 For they cannot sleep till they do
evil;
they are robbed of slumber till
they make someone fall.
17 They eat the bread of wickedness
and drink the wine of violence.

18 The path of the righteous is like the
first gleam of dawn,
shining ever brighter till the full
light of day.
19 But the way of the wicked is like
deep darkness;
they do not know what makes
them stumble.

20 My son, pay attention to what I say;
listen closely to my words.
21 Do not let them out of your sight,
keep them within your heart;
22 for they are life to those who find
them
and health to a man's whole body.

[a]7 Or *Whatever else you get*

[23]Above all else, guard your heart,
for it is the wellspring of life.
[24]Put away perversity from your mouth;
keep corrupt talk far from your lips.
[25]Let your eyes look straight ahead,
fix your gaze directly before you.
[26]Make level[a] paths for your feet
and take only ways that are firm.
[27]Do not swerve to the right or the left;
keep your foot from evil.

SHARPEN THE FOCUS

In what direction are you headed? On what paths do your feet take you? When you plan for the week, what goals appear at the top of your list? Why do you get out of bed each morning?

Some of our answers to those questions can and should disturb us. Selfishness dogs the steps of all people, even God's people. Much of the time we live aimlessly; we drift from one obligation, one entertainment, one task to the next. We don't put much thought into walking "the path of the righteous" Solomon describes in Proverbs 4:18.

But think! You already *are* the righteousness of God in Jesus Christ (compare 2 Corinthians 5:21). In the cross of His Son, God has declared it so. He has set your feet on the path of righteousness in your Baptism and given you all the power you need to put one foot in front of the other on that path. You have been given the potential to walk the path of the righteous, which grows brighter and more clear with every passing day (Proverbs 4:18).

So ask yourself, "If Jesus walked in my shoes today, what would He do?" Then, in the Spirit's strength, go do it! Be Christ's person for those around you, for that's who you really are.

WEEK 49 • WEDNESDAY

Proverbs 5:1—6:35

GET THE BIG PICTURE

Some sinful behaviors cause so much pain, so much destruction in *any* culture, at *any* time, that the Holy Spirit has taken special effort to warn His people against them. Adultery is one of these sins. You'll read two of these warnings in Proverbs 5:1–23 and Proverbs 6:20–35. Also note the seven things God hates in Proverbs 6:16–19. If time is short, focus on Proverbs 6:16–19.

Warning Against Adultery

5 My son, pay attention to my wisdom,
listen well to my words of insight,
[2]that you may maintain discretion
and your lips may preserve knowledge.
[3]For the lips of an adulteress drip honey,
and her speech is smoother than oil;
[4]but in the end she is bitter as gall,
sharp as a double-edged sword.
[5]Her feet go down to death;
her steps lead straight to the grave.[b]

[a]26 Or *Consider the* [b]5 Hebrew *Sheol*

6 She gives no thought to the way of
life;
her paths are crooked, but she
knows it not.

7 Now then, my sons, listen to me;
do not turn aside from what I say.
8 Keep to a path far from her,
do not go near the door of her
house,
9 lest you give your best strength to
others
and your years to one who is
cruel,
10 lest strangers feast on your wealth
and your toil enrich another
man's house.
11 At the end of your life you will
groan,
when your flesh and body are
spent.
12 You will say, "How I hated
discipline!
How my heart spurned
correction!
13 I would not obey my teachers
or listen to my instructors.
14 I have come to the brink of utter
ruin
in the midst of the whole
assembly."

15 Drink water from your own cistern,
running water from your own
well.
16 Should your springs overflow in the
streets,
your streams of water in the
public squares?
17 Let them be yours alone,
never to be shared with strangers.
18 May your fountain be blessed,
and may you rejoice in the wife of
your youth.
19 A loving doe, a graceful deer—
may her breasts satisfy you
always,
may you ever be captivated by her
love.
20 Why be captivated, my son, by an
adulteress?
Why embrace the bosom of
another man's wife?

21 For a man's ways are in full view of
the LORD,
and he examines all his paths.
22 The evil deeds of a wicked man
ensnare him;
the cords of his sin hold him fast.
23 He will die for lack of discipline,
led astray by his own great folly.

Warnings Against Folly

6 My son, if you have put up
security for your neighbor,
if you have struck hands in pledge
for another,
2 if you have been trapped by what
you said,
ensnared by the words of your
mouth,
3 then do this, my son, to free
yourself,
since you have fallen into your
neighbor's hands:
Go and humble yourself;
press your plea with your
neighbor!
4 Allow no sleep to your eyes,
no slumber to your eyelids.
5 Free yourself, like a gazelle from the
hand of the hunter,
like a bird from the snare of the
fowler.

6 Go to the ant, you sluggard;
consider its ways and be wise!
7 It has no commander,
no overseer or ruler,
8 yet it stores its provisions in summer
and gathers its food at harvest.

9 How long will you lie there, you
sluggard?
When will you get up from your
sleep?
10 A little sleep, a little slumber,
a little folding of the hands to
rest—
11 and poverty will come on you like a
bandit
and scarcity like an armed man.[a]

12 A scoundrel and villain,
who goes about with a corrupt
mouth,

[a] 11 Or *like a vagrant / and scarcity like a beggar*

13 who winks with his eye,
signals with his feet
and motions with his fingers,
14 who plots evil with deceit in his
heart—
he always stirs up dissension.
15 Therefore disaster will overtake him
in an instant;
he will suddenly be destroyed—
without remedy.

16 There are six things the LORD hates,
seven that are detestable to him:
17 haughty eyes,
a lying tongue,
hands that shed innocent
blood,
18 a heart that devises wicked
schemes,
feet that are quick to rush into
evil,
19 a false witness who pours out
lies
and a man who stirs up
dissension among brothers.

Warning Against Adultery

20 My son, keep your father's
commands
and do not forsake your mother's
teaching.
21 Bind them upon your heart forever;
fasten them around your neck.
22 When you walk, they will guide
you;
when you sleep, they will watch
over you;
when you awake, they will speak
to you.
23 For these commands are a lamp,
this teaching is a light,
and the corrections of discipline
are the way to life,
24 keeping you from the immoral
woman,
from the smooth tongue of the
wayward wife.
25 Do not lust in your heart after her
beauty
or let her captivate you with her
eyes,
26 for the prostitute reduces you to a
loaf of bread,
and the adulteress preys upon
your very life.
27 Can a man scoop fire into his lap
without his clothes being burned?
28 Can a man walk on hot coals
without his feet being scorched?
29 So is he who sleeps with another
man's wife;
no one who touches her will go
unpunished.

30 Men do not despise a thief if he steals
to satisfy his hunger when he is
starving.
31 Yet if he is caught, he must pay
sevenfold,
though it costs him all the wealth
of his house.
32 But a man who commits adultery
lacks judgment;
whoever does so destroys
himself.
33 Blows and disgrace are his lot,
and his shame will never be
wiped away;
34 for jealousy arouses a husband's
fury,
and he will show no mercy when
he takes revenge.
35 He will not accept any
compensation;
he will refuse the bribe, however
great it is.

SHARPEN THE FOCUS

Pride. Deceit. Violence. Eagerness to plan evil and to carry it out. A false witness that hurts an innocent person. Those who stir up quarrels.

Does this list surprise you? If we named the things God hates, based on our own ideas of evil, we would probably choose other, "more outrageous" sins. Maybe that's because we've grown so familiar with the "hateful seven" in ourselves and in others that we hardly bat an eye when these sins invade our lives.

But each of the "hateful seven" is exactly opposite our Lord's character. Our pride affronts His glory. Our deceit contrasts with His truthfulness. Our violent thoughts, words, and actions oppose His kindness. Our plans for evil are at variance with His continual planning to do us good. Our lies subvert His justice. And our gossip and discord keep His family from the complete love He wants us to have for one another.

God's Law has caught us red-handed, and we can offer no excuse. How wonderful then that we can come, openhanded, to God's throne and throw ourselves on the mercy of the court. The one who sits on that throne is our Father. We know that we will receive pardon, richly and fully given in Christ.

WEEK 49 • THURSDAY

Proverbs 7:1–27

GET THE BIG PICTURE

Given King David's personal history, we need not wonder that the advice Solomon quotes from his father, David, includes so many warnings against sexual immorality, especially adultery. As you read this fourth (and final) extended warning (Proverbs 7:6–27), ask yourself what inner safeguards protect God's people from outward sin. If time is short, focus on Proverbs 7:6–7.

Warning Against the Adulteress

7 My son, keep my words
and store up my commands
within you.
2 Keep my commands and you will
live;
guard my teachings as the apple
of your eye.
3 Bind them on your fingers;
write them on the tablet of your
heart.
4 Say to wisdom, "You are my sister,"
and call understanding your
kinsman;
5 they will keep you from the
adulteress,
from the wayward wife with her
seductive words.

6 At the window of my house
I looked out through the lattice.
7 I saw among the simple,
I noticed among the young men,
a youth who lacked judgment.
8 He was going down the street near
her corner,
walking along in the direction of
her house
9 at twilight, as the day was fading,
as the dark of night set in.

10 Then out came a woman to meet
him,
dressed like a prostitute and with
crafty intent.
11 (She is loud and defiant,
her feet never stay at home;
12 now in the street, now in the
squares,
at every corner she lurks.)
13 She took hold of him and kissed him
and with a brazen face she said:

14 "I have fellowship offerings[a] at
home;

[a]14 Traditionally *peace offerings*

today I fulfilled my vows.
15 So I came out to meet you;
I looked for you and have found you!
16 I have covered my bed
with colored linens from Egypt.
17 I have perfumed my bed
with myrrh, aloes and cinnamon.
18 Come, let's drink deep of love till morning;
let's enjoy ourselves with love!
19 My husband is not at home;
he has gone on a long journey.
20 He took his purse filled with money
and will not be home till full moon."

21 With persuasive words she led him astray;
she seduced him with her smooth talk.
22 All at once he followed her
like an ox going to the slaughter,
like a deer[a] stepping into a noose[b]
23 till an arrow pierces his liver,
like a bird darting into a snare,
little knowing it will cost him his life.

24 Now then, my sons, listen to me;
pay attention to what I say.
25 Do not let your heart turn to her ways
or stray into her paths.
26 Many are the victims she has brought down;
her slain are a mighty throng.
27 Her house is a highway to the grave,[c]
leading down to the chambers of death.

[a]22 Syriac (see also Septuagint); Hebrew *fool*
[b]22 The meaning of the Hebrew for this line is uncertain. [c]27 Hebrew *Sheol*

SHARPEN THE FOCUS

Solomon pictures two people in this short drama. The young man is, at best, short-sighted and almost unbelievably foolish. The woman who seduces him is equally foolish and also cunning. Neither seem to have any sense of right and wrong.

Maybe you're reading your life story in these verses. Or perhaps you're comforting yourself with the notion that since you haven't given in to sexual temptation so far, you never could. In either case, Solomon's warning is meant for you personally:

- God's people do sometimes commit adultery. The temptation can catch any of us off guard. If you think you're immune, you're as foolish as the young man. *How prepared are you, in Christ, to confront and overcome sexual temptation?*
- Both people in an adulterous relationship hurt themselves and all the people who know and love them. Your feet will follow where your heart has gone before. *How are you, in Christ, guarding your heart?*
- God's grace covers the sin of adultery, and He will help His repentant children work through the fallout that results from their sin. God, in Christ, forgives. *Will you let Him? Will you, by grace, then extend His forgiveness to those whose actions have hurt you?*

The Lord wants His people to know the wise paths to take and then to take them. He has not hidden these paths from us. In today's reading you will see wisdom personified, standing (Proverbs 8:2–3) in the shopping mall and on the street corner, shouting God's message to all who will listen. As we read, we can't help but see the truth unfold—Jesus Christ Himself *is* God's wisdom. If time is short, focus on Proverbs 8:12–36.

Wisdom's Call

8 Does not wisdom call out?
Does not understanding raise her voice?
2 On the heights along the way,
where the paths meet, she takes her stand;
3 beside the gates leading into the city,
at the entrances, she cries aloud:
4 "To you, O men, I call out;
I raise my voice to all mankind.
5 You who are simple, gain prudence;
you who are foolish, gain understanding.
6 Listen, for I have worthy things to say;
I open my lips to speak what is right.
7 My mouth speaks what is true,
for my lips detest wickedness.
8 All the words of my mouth are just;
none of them is crooked or perverse.
9 To the discerning all of them are right;
they are faultless to those who have knowledge.
10 Choose my instruction instead of silver,
knowledge rather than choice gold,
11 for wisdom is more precious than rubies,
and nothing you desire can compare with her.

12 "I, wisdom, dwell together with prudence;
I possess knowledge and discretion.
13 To fear the LORD is to hate evil;
I hate pride and arrogance,
evil behavior and perverse speech.
14 Counsel and sound judgment are mine;
I have understanding and power.
15 By me kings reign
and rulers make laws that are just;
16 by me princes govern,
and all nobles who rule on earth.[a]
17 I love those who love me,
and those who seek me find me.
18 With me are riches and honor,
enduring wealth and prosperity.
19 My fruit is better than fine gold;
what I yield surpasses choice silver.
20 I walk in the way of righteousness,
along the paths of justice,
21 bestowing wealth on those who love me
and making their treasuries full.

22 "The LORD brought me forth as the first of his works,[b,c]
before his deeds of old;
23 I was appointed[d] from eternity,
from the beginning, before the world began.

[a]16 Many Hebrew manuscripts and Septuagint; most Hebrew manuscripts *and nobles—all righteous rulers* [b]22 Or *way*; or *dominion* [c]22 Or *The LORD possessed me at the beginning of his work*; or *The LORD brought me forth at the beginning of his work* [d]23 Or *fashioned*

24 When there were no oceans, I was
given birth,
when there were no springs
abounding with water;
25 before the mountains were settled in
place,
before the hills, I was given birth,
26 before he made the earth or its
fields
or any of the dust of the world.
27 I was there when he set the heavens
in place,
when he marked out the horizon
on the face of the deep,
28 when he established the clouds
above
and fixed securely the fountains of
the deep,
29 when he gave the sea its boundary
so the waters would not overstep
his command,
and when he marked out the
foundations of the earth.
30 Then I was the craftsman at his
side.
I was filled with delight day after
day,
rejoicing always in his presence,
31 rejoicing in his whole world
and delighting in mankind.

32 "Now then, my sons, listen to me;
blessed are those who keep my
ways.
33 Listen to my instruction and be
wise;
do not ignore it.
34 Blessed is the man who listens to
me,
watching daily at my doors,
waiting at my doorway.
35 For whoever finds me finds life
and receives favor from the LORD.
36 But whoever fails to find me harms
himself;
all who hate me love death."

SHARPEN THE FOCUS

Think of the last time you had to make a tough decision. Maybe you had a job offer. Perhaps you needed to deal with wrong attitudes shown by your child.

Some Christians agonize over knowing and doing the will of God because they believe that He has only one perfect plan for their lives. They think that by making one wrong decision, they can end up in the backwaters of God's will from then on.

Christians like that have an earnest desire to please God. They believe God's "plan" will bring them ultimate fulfillment. Far better for us to seek God's *purpose* for our lives, rather than His plan. You see, the specific circumstances of life matter far less than God's will for our transformation into the image of His Son.

We can ask, "Should I live in Cleveland or Calumet? Should I scold or assign extra chores to my son?" But if we're growing in wisdom, we'll ask instead, "How can I, in this situation, reflect Jesus' wisdom, His compassion, His anger at sin, and His grace toward sinners?" These are the questions that matter most in life. The rest are merely details. We can, in Christian freedom, make those choices as we like, without fear.

WEEK 49 • SATURDAY

Proverbs 9:1–18

You may recognize the picture that begins Proverbs 9. The banquet that wisdom spreads looks a lot like the one the Lord Jesus describes in Luke 14:15–24. As the rest of Proverbs 9 shows, the hosts of both banquets face the pain of rejected invitations. Think about God's banquet as you read. If time is short, focus on Proverbs 9:1–12.

Invitations of Wisdom and of Folly

9 Wisdom has built her house;
she has hewn out its seven pillars.
2 She has prepared her meat and mixed her wine;
she has also set her table.
3 She has sent out her maids, and she calls
from the highest point of the city.
4 "Let all who are simple come in here!"
she says to those who lack judgment.
5 "Come, eat my food
and drink the wine I have mixed.
6 Leave your simple ways and you will live;
walk in the way of understanding.

7 "Whoever corrects a mocker invites insult;
whoever rebukes a wicked man incurs abuse.
8 Do not rebuke a mocker or he will hate you;
rebuke a wise man and he will love you.
9 Instruct a wise man and he will be wiser still;
teach a righteous man and he will add to his learning.

10 "The fear of the LORD is the beginning of wisdom,
and knowledge of the Holy One is understanding.
11 For through me your days will be many,
and years will be added to your life.
12 If you are wise, your wisdom will reward you;
if you are a mocker, you alone will suffer."

13 The woman Folly is loud;
she is undisciplined and without knowledge.
14 She sits at the door of her house,
on a seat at the highest point of the city,
15 calling out to those who pass by,
who go straight on their way.
16 "Let all who are simple come in here!"
she says to those who lack judgment.
17 "Stolen water is sweet;
food eaten in secret is delicious!"
18 But little do they know that the dead are there,
that her guests are in the depths of the grave.[a]

[a]18 Hebrew *Sheol*

SHARPEN THE FOCUS

Come, for all things are now ready! Wisdom invites sinners to receive the good things God has prepared for us in His Word—His promises of mercy, of pardon in Christ, of power to live Christlike lives.

Come, for all things are now ready! The Lord invites sinners to His holy Table to receive the very body and blood with which our Savior has won our salvation. There He seals to us the forgiveness and new life His cross has earned for us.

Come, for all things are now ready! The Lord will one day shout from heaven as He opens for sinners-made-righteous the doors of His heavenly banquet hall where we will feast forever. Together with Him in the presence of His holy angels we will celebrate His goodness, His generosity, His love and kindness in never-ending joy.

Remembering the banquet our Father has spread can take the edge off any sorrow; it can amplify any joy; it can lighten any burden. Meditate on that holy banquet today. As you do so, you might enjoy reading the description of it found in Isaiah 25:6–9.

WEEK 50 • MONDAY

Proverbs 10:1—11:31

GET THE BIG PICTURE

Proverbs 10–15 contains mostly proverbs that contrast the wicked and the righteous. As you read, remember that in Christ's cross *you* are the righteous person of whom these proverbs speak. They describe our Lord's picture of you. If time is short, focus on Proverbs 10:1–32.

Proverbs of Solomon

10 The proverbs of Solomon:

A wise son brings joy to his father,
but a foolish son grief to his mother.

2 Ill-gotten treasures are of no value,
but righteousness delivers from death.

3 The LORD does not let the righteous go hungry
but he thwarts the craving of the wicked.

4 Lazy hands make a man poor,
but diligent hands bring wealth.

5 He who gathers crops in summer is a wise son,
but he who sleeps during harvest is a disgraceful son.

6 Blessings crown the head of the righteous,
but violence overwhelms the mouth of the wicked.[a]

7 The memory of the righteous will be a blessing,
but the name of the wicked will rot.

8 The wise in heart accept commands,
but a chattering fool comes to ruin.

9 The man of integrity walks securely,

[a]6 Or *but the mouth of the wicked conceals violence;* also in verse 11

but he who takes crooked paths
will be found out.

10 He who winks maliciously causes
grief,
and a chattering fool comes to
ruin.

11 The mouth of the righteous is a
fountain of life,
but violence overwhelms the
mouth of the wicked.

12 Hatred stirs up dissension,
but love covers over all wrongs.

13 Wisdom is found on the lips of the
discerning,
but a rod is for the back of him
who lacks judgment.

14 Wise men store up knowledge,
but the mouth of a fool invites
ruin.

15 The wealth of the rich is their
fortified city,
but poverty is the ruin of the
poor.

16 The wages of the righteous bring
them life,
but the income of the wicked
brings them punishment.

17 He who heeds discipline shows the
way to life,
but whoever ignores correction
leads others astray.

18 He who conceals his hatred has
lying lips,
and whoever spreads slander is a
fool.

19 When words are many, sin is not
absent,
but he who holds his tongue is
wise.

20 The tongue of the righteous is
choice silver,
but the heart of the wicked is of
little value.

21 The lips of the righteous nourish
many,
but fools die for lack of judgment.

22 The blessing of the LORD brings
wealth,
and he adds no trouble to it.

23 A fool finds pleasure in evil conduct,
but a man of understanding
delights in wisdom.

24 What the wicked dreads will
overtake him;
what the righteous desire will be
granted.

25 When the storm has swept by, the
wicked are gone,
but the righteous stand firm
forever.

26 As vinegar to the teeth and smoke to
the eyes,
so is a sluggard to those who send
him.

27 The fear of the LORD adds length to
life,
but the years of the wicked are cut
short.

28 The prospect of the righteous is joy,
but the hopes of the wicked come
to nothing.

29 The way of the LORD is a refuge for
the righteous,
but it is the ruin of those who do
evil.

30 The righteous will never be uprooted,
but the wicked will not remain in
the land.

31 The mouth of the righteous brings
forth wisdom,
but a perverse tongue will be cut
out.

32 The lips of the righteous know what
is fitting,
but the mouth of the wicked only
what is perverse.

11 The LORD abhors dishonest
scales,
but accurate weights are his
delight.

2 When pride comes, then comes
disgrace,
but with humility comes wisdom.

3 The integrity of the upright guides them,
but the unfaithful are destroyed by their duplicity.
4 Wealth is worthless in the day of wrath,
but righteousness delivers from death.

5 The righteousness of the blameless makes a straight way for them,
but the wicked are brought down by their own wickedness.
6 The righteousness of the upright delivers them,
but the unfaithful are trapped by evil desires.
7 When a wicked man dies, his hope perishes;
all he expected from his power comes to nothing.
8 The righteous man is rescued from trouble,
and it comes on the wicked instead.
9 With his mouth the godless destroys his neighbor,
but through knowledge the righteous escape.

10 When the righteous prosper, the city rejoices;
when the wicked perish, there are shouts of joy.

11 Through the blessing of the upright a city is exalted,
but by the mouth of the wicked it is destroyed.

12 A man who lacks judgment derides his neighbor,
but a man of understanding holds his tongue.
13 A gossip betrays a confidence,
but a trustworthy man keeps a secret.
14 For lack of guidance a nation falls,
but many advisers make victory sure.
15 He who puts up security for another will surely suffer,
but whoever refuses to strike hands in pledge is safe.
16 A kindhearted woman gains respect,
but ruthless men gain only wealth.

17 A kind man benefits himself,
but a cruel man brings trouble on himself.
18 The wicked man earns deceptive wages,
but he who sows righteousness reaps a sure reward.
19 The truly righteous man attains life,
but he who pursues evil goes to his death.
20 The LORD detests men of perverse heart
but he delights in those whose ways are blameless.
21 Be sure of this: The wicked will not go unpunished,
but those who are righteous will go free.
22 Like a gold ring in a pig's snout
is a beautiful woman who shows no discretion.

23 The desire of the righteous ends only in good,
but the hope of the wicked only in wrath.

24 One man gives freely, yet gains even more;
another withholds unduly, but comes to poverty.

25 A generous man will prosper;
he who refreshes others will himself be refreshed.
26 People curse the man who hoards grain,
but blessing crowns him who is willing to sell.
27 He who seeks good finds goodwill,
but evil comes to him who searches for it.

28 Whoever trusts in his riches will fall,
but the righteous will thrive like a green leaf.

29 He who brings trouble on his family will inherit only wind,
and the fool will be servant to the wise.

30 The fruit of the righteous is a tree of life,
and he who wins souls is wise.

31 If the righteous receive their due on earth,
how much more the ungodly and the sinner!

SHARPEN THE FOCUS

Tornadoes punctuate the month of April in the Midwest most springs. During one recent weekend, thunderstorms spawned over 100 tornadoes, many of them at night. When the sun rose, network news cameras captured the devastation.

Proverbs 10:25 describes just such a scene:

When the storm has swept by, the wicked are gone,
but the righteous stand firm forever.

Tornadoes frighten people, in part, because these storms strike so unpredictably. One trailer explodes; the next stands unharmed. One tree falls, uprooted; the other rustles calmly in the next morning's breeze.

As the proverb shows us, destruction in life's storms is not so whimsical. Jesus' parable of the two builders makes the same point (Matthew 7:24–27). The same storm strikes both houses with equal fierceness; Christians face many of the same problems others face. Even so, those who know Christ, those whose lives are anchored in Him, stand firm now and forever.

What storms roar overhead for you today? Take the winds and waves to the one who knows just how to handle them (Mark 4:39). Rest in Him. Be at peace in Him. Present your needs to Him. He will not let you be swept away.

WEEK 50 • TUESDAY

Proverbs 12:1—13:25

GET THE BIG PICTURE

Today's reading touches a variety of topics, all related to living wisely in a world full of temptations to ignore wisdom. As you read, let the Holy Spirit speak to your heart about any foolish attitudes or actions that have taken root in your life. If time is short, focus on Proverbs 13:1–25.

12 Whoever loves discipline loves knowledge,
but he who hates correction is stupid.

2 A good man obtains favor from the LORD,
but the LORD condemns a crafty man.

3 A man cannot be established
through wickedness,
but the righteous cannot be
uprooted.

4 A wife of noble character is her
husband's crown,
but a disgraceful wife is like decay
in his bones.

5 The plans of the righteous are just,
but the advice of the wicked is
deceitful.

6 The words of the wicked lie in wait
for blood,
but the speech of the upright
rescues them.

7 Wicked men are overthrown and are
no more,
but the house of the righteous
stands firm.

8 A man is praised according to his
wisdom,
but men with warped minds are
despised.

9 Better to be a nobody and yet have a
servant
than pretend to be somebody and
have no food.

10 A righteous man cares for the needs
of his animal,
but the kindest acts of the wicked
are cruel.

11 He who works his land will have
abundant food,
but he who chases fantasies lacks
judgment.

12 The wicked desire the plunder of
evil men,
but the root of the righteous
flourishes.

13 An evil man is trapped by his sinful
talk,
but a righteous man escapes
trouble.

14 From the fruit of his lips a man is
filled with good things
as surely as the work of his hands
rewards him.

15 The way of a fool seems right to
him,
but a wise man listens to advice.

16 A fool shows his annoyance at
once,
but a prudent man overlooks an
insult.

17 A truthful witness gives honest
testimony,
but a false witness tells lies.

18 Reckless words pierce like a sword,
but the tongue of the wise brings
healing.

19 Truthful lips endure forever,
but a lying tongue lasts only a
moment.

20 There is deceit in the hearts of those
who plot evil,
but joy for those who promote
peace.

21 No harm befalls the righteous,
but the wicked have their fill of
trouble.

22 The LORD detests lying lips,
but he delights in men who are
truthful.

23 A prudent man keeps his
knowledge to himself,
but the heart of fools blurts out
folly.

24 Diligent hands will rule,
but laziness ends in slave labor.

25 An anxious heart weighs a man
down,
but a kind word cheers him up.

26 A righteous man is cautious in
friendship,[a]
but the way of the wicked leads
them astray.

27 The lazy man does not roast[b] his
game,
but the diligent man prizes his
possessions.

[a]26 Or *man is a guide to his neighbor* [b]27 The meaning of the Hebrew for this word is uncertain.

[28]In the way of righteousness there is
life;
along that path is immortality.

13 A wise son heeds his
father's instruction,
but a mocker does not listen to
rebuke.

[2]From the fruit of his lips a man
enjoys good things,
but the unfaithful have a craving
for violence.

[3]He who guards his lips guards his
life,
but he who speaks rashly will
come to ruin.

[4]The sluggard craves and gets nothing,
but the desires of the diligent are
fully satisfied.

[5]The righteous hate what is false,
but the wicked bring shame and
disgrace.

[6]Righteousness guards the man of
integrity,
but wickedness overthrows the
sinner.

[7]One man pretends to be rich, yet
has nothing;
another pretends to be poor, yet
has great wealth.

[8]A man's riches may ransom his life,
but a poor man hears no threat.

[9]The light of the righteous shines
brightly,
but the lamp of the wicked is
snuffed out.

[10]Pride only breeds quarrels,
but wisdom is found in those who
take advice.

[11]Dishonest money dwindles away,
but he who gathers money little
by little makes it grow.

[12]Hope deferred makes the heart sick,
but a longing fulfilled is a tree of
life.

[13]He who scorns instruction will pay
for it,
but he who respects a command is
rewarded.

[14]The teaching of the wise is a
fountain of life,
turning a man from the snares of
death.

[15]Good understanding wins favor,
but the way of the unfaithful is
hard.[a]

[16]Every prudent man acts out of
knowledge,
but a fool exposes his folly.

[17]A wicked messenger falls into
trouble,
but a trustworthy envoy brings
healing.

[18]He who ignores discipline comes to
poverty and shame,
but whoever heeds correction is
honored.

[19]A longing fulfilled is sweet to the
soul,
but fools detest turning from evil.

[20]He who walks with the wise grows
wise,
but a companion of fools suffers
harm.

[21]Misfortune pursues the sinner,
but prosperity is the reward of the
righteous.

[22]A good man leaves an inheritance
for his children's children,
but a sinner's wealth is stored up
for the righteous.

[23]A poor man's field may produce
abundant food,
but injustice sweeps it away.

[24]He who spares the rod hates his son,
but he who loves him is careful to
discipline him.

[25]The righteous eat to their hearts'
content,
but the stomach of the wicked
goes hungry.

[a]15 Or *unfaithful does not endure*

SHARPEN THE FOCUS

Physical anorexia can lead to serious disability and even death. But spiritual anorexia does even greater damage. In today's reading from Proverbs, you read about both unnourished and well-nourished souls:

- The unfaithful have a craving for violence (Proverbs 13:2).
- The desires of the diligent are fully satisfied (Proverbs 13:4).
- The righteous eat to their hearts' content, but the stomach of the wicked goes hungry (Proverbs 13:25).

How well-nourished is your soul? Do you feed on violence? on the empty spiritual calories of tabloid news broadcasts? on the spiritual poison prepared by novelists or playwrights who make fun of your Lord and His Word?

Or do you feast on all the truth, all the love, all the goodness your Savior-God has prepared for you in His Word and in the Sacraments? Is your soul healthy, rich, and satisfied?

Talk with your Lord right now. Ask Him to show you any ways in which you may be injuring your soul by taking in too many empty spiritual calories or by ingesting spiritual poison. Confess any sins like these to Him. Then, secure in His forgiveness, plan a balanced spiritual diet.

WEEK 50 • WEDNESDAY

Prov. 14:1—15:33

GET THE BIG PICTURE

These two chapters conclude the antithetical proverbs, those that contrast the wicked and the righteous. As you read, notice this contrast (usually signaled by the word *but*). Also pay attention to the note of humility that graces the description of God's righteous people. If time is short, focus on Proverbs 15:1–33.

14 The wise woman builds her house,
but with her own hands the foolish one tears hers down.

2 He whose walk is upright fears the LORD,
but he whose ways are devious despises him.

3 A fool's talk brings a rod to his back,
but the lips of the wise protect them.

4 Where there are no oxen, the manger is empty,
but from the strength of an ox comes an abundant harvest.

5 A truthful witness does not deceive,
but a false witness pours out lies.

6 The mocker seeks wisdom and finds none,
but knowledge comes easily to the discerning.

7 Stay away from a foolish man,
for you will not find knowledge on his lips.

8 The wisdom of the prudent is to
give thought to their ways,
but the folly of fools is deception.
9 Fools mock at making amends for sin,
but goodwill is found among the
upright.
10 Each heart knows its own bitterness,
and no one else can share its joy.
11 The house of the wicked will be
destroyed,
but the tent of the upright will
flourish.
12 There is a way that seems right to a
man,
but in the end it leads to death.
13 Even in laughter the heart may ache,
and joy may end in grief.
14 The faithless will be fully repaid for
their ways,
and the good man rewarded for
his.
15 A simple man believes anything,
but a prudent man gives thought
to his steps.
16 A wise man fears the LORD and
shuns evil,
but a fool is hotheaded and
reckless.
17 A quick-tempered man does foolish
things,
and a crafty man is hated.
18 The simple inherit folly,
but the prudent are crowned with
knowledge.
19 Evil men will bow down in the
presence of the good,
and the wicked at the gates of the
righteous.
20 The poor are shunned even by their
neighbors,
but the rich have many friends.
21 He who despises his neighbor sins,
but blessed is he who is kind to
the needy.
22 Do not those who plot evil go
astray?
But those who plan what is good
find[a] love and faithfulness.
23 All hard work brings a profit,
but mere talk leads only to
poverty.
24 The wealth of the wise is their
crown,
but the folly of fools yields folly.
25 A truthful witness saves lives,
but a false witness is deceitful.
26 He who fears the LORD has a secure
fortress,
and for his children it will be a
refuge.
27 The fear of the LORD is a fountain of
life,
turning a man from the snares of
death.
28 A large population is a king's glory,
but without subjects a prince is
ruined.
29 A patient man has great
understanding,
but a quick-tempered man
displays folly.
30 A heart at peace gives life to the body,
but envy rots the bones.
31 He who oppresses the poor shows
contempt for their Maker,
but whoever is kind to the needy
honors God.
32 When calamity comes, the wicked
are brought down,
but even in death the righteous
have a refuge.
33 Wisdom reposes in the heart of the
discerning
and even among fools she lets
herself be known.[b]
34 Righteousness exalts a nation,
but sin is a disgrace to any people.
35 A king delights in a wise servant,
but a shameful servant incurs his
wrath.

[a]22 Or *show* [b]33 Hebrew; Septuagint and Syriac / *but in the heart of fools she is not known*

15 A gentle answer turns away
wrath,
but a harsh word stirs up anger.

2 The tongue of the wise commends
knowledge,
but the mouth of the fool gushes
folly.

3 The eyes of the LORD are
everywhere,
keeping watch on the wicked and
the good.

4 The tongue that brings healing is a
tree of life,
but a deceitful tongue crushes the
spirit.

5 A fool spurns his father's discipline,
but whoever heeds correction
shows prudence.

6 The house of the righteous contains
great treasure,
but the income of the wicked
brings them trouble.

7 The lips of the wise spread
knowledge;
not so the hearts of fools.

8 The LORD detests the sacrifice of the
wicked,
but the prayer of the upright
pleases him.

9 The LORD detests the way of the
wicked
but he loves those who pursue
righteousness.

10 Stern discipline awaits him who
leaves the path;
he who hates correction will die.

11 Death and Destruction[a] lie open
before the LORD—
how much more the hearts of men!

12 A mocker resents correction;
he will not consult the wise.

13 A happy heart makes the face
cheerful,
but heartache crushes the spirit.

14 The discerning heart seeks
knowledge,
but the mouth of a fool feeds on
folly.

15 All the days of the oppressed are
wretched,
but the cheerful heart has a
continual feast.

16 Better a little with the fear of the
LORD
than great wealth with turmoil.

17 Better a meal of vegetables where
there is love
than a fattened calf with hatred.

18 A hot-tempered man stirs up
dissension,
but a patient man calms a quarrel.

19 The way of the sluggard is blocked
with thorns,
but the path of the upright is a
highway.

20 A wise son brings joy to his father,
but a foolish man despises his
mother.

21 Folly delights a man who lacks
judgment,
but a man of understanding keeps
a straight course.

22 Plans fail for lack of counsel,
but with many advisers they
succeed.

23 A man finds joy in giving an apt
reply—
and how good is a timely word!

24 The path of life leads upward for the
wise
to keep him from going down to
the grave.[b]

25 The LORD tears down the proud
man's house
but he keeps the widow's
boundaries intact.

26 The LORD detests the thoughts of
the wicked,
but those of the pure are pleasing
to him.

[a]11 Hebrew *Sheol and Abaddon* [b]24 Hebrew *Sheol*

[27]A greedy man brings trouble to his
family,
but he who hates bribes will live.

[28]The heart of the righteous weighs its
answers,
but the mouth of the wicked
gushes evil.

[29]The LORD is far from the wicked
but he hears the prayer of the
righteous.

[30]A cheerful look brings joy to the
heart,
and good news gives health to the
bones.

[31]He who listens to a life-giving
rebuke
will be at home among the wise.

[32]He who ignores discipline despises
himself,
but whoever heeds correction
gains understanding.

[33]The fear of the LORD teaches a man
wisdom,[a]
and humility comes before
honor.

[a]33 Or *Wisdom teaches the fear of the LORD*

SHARPEN THE FOCUS

Someone has commented on the misconceptions many teens have about astronomy: "They think the universe revolves around them." Maybe you know adults like this, too. Maybe you yourself have acted at times as if the universe revolved around you.

Spotting this misbelief in oneself and admitting it takes superhuman insight and courage. The humility to let life revolve around our Lord comes to us as a gift from God Himself. It results as we confess our sins and trust Christ's payment for those sins on His cross. When that kind of humility floods our hearts, we can:

- return the insults of others with grace (Proverbs 15:1).
- offer prayers of faith that delight our Father (Proverbs 15:8).
- enjoy the continual feast of a cheerful heart (Proverbs 15:15).
- find contentment, whatever our financial situation (Proverbs 15:16).
- listen to wise counsel (Proverbs 15:5, 10, 12, 32).
- speak thoughtful words that bless our hearers (Proverbs 15:2, 7, 23, 28).

None of these things can happen in the absence of God-given humility. That's why Proverbs 15:33 can serve as a theme verse for Proverbs 10–15:

> *The fear of the LORD teaches a man wisdom, and humility comes before honor.* (Proverbs 15:33) ☼

WEEK 50 • THURSDAY

Proverbs 16:1—17:28

GET THE BIG PICTURE

Chapter 16 begins the synthetic proverbs—those in which the two parts of each wise saying are linked by the word *and*. The second part of each synthetic proverb in chapters 16–20 adds more information, an explanation, or an example to the first part. As you read today, notice the advice Solomon gives about wise words. If time is short, focus on Proverbs 16:1–33.

16 To man belong the plans of the heart,
but from the LORD comes the reply of the tongue.

2 All a man's ways seem innocent to him,
but motives are weighed by the LORD.

3 Commit to the LORD whatever you do,
and your plans will succeed.

4 The LORD works out everything for his own ends—
even the wicked for a day of disaster.

5 The LORD detests all the proud of heart.
Be sure of this: They will not go unpunished.

6 Through love and faithfulness sin is atoned for;
through the fear of the LORD a man avoids evil.

7 When a man's ways are pleasing to the LORD,
he makes even his enemies live at peace with him.

8 Better a little with righteousness
than much gain with injustice.

9 In his heart a man plans his course,
but the LORD determines his steps.

10 The lips of a king speak as an oracle,
and his mouth should not betray justice.

11 Honest scales and balances are from the LORD;
all the weights in the bag are of his making.

12 Kings detest wrongdoing,
for a throne is established through righteousness.

13 Kings take pleasure in honest lips;
they value a man who speaks the truth.

14 A king's wrath is a messenger of death,
but a wise man will appease it.

15 When a king's face brightens, it means life;
his favor is like a rain cloud in spring.

16 How much better to get wisdom than gold,
to choose understanding rather than silver!

17 The highway of the upright avoids evil;
he who guards his way guards his life.

18 Pride goes before destruction,
a haughty spirit before a fall.

19 Better to be lowly in spirit and among the oppressed
than to share plunder with the proud.

[20]Whoever gives heed to instruction
prospers,
and blessed is he who trusts in the
LORD.

[21]The wise in heart are called
discerning,
and pleasant words promote
instruction.[a]

[22]Understanding is a fountain of life
to those who have it,
but folly brings punishment to
fools.

[23]A wise man's heart guides his mouth,
and his lips promote instruction.[b]

[24]Pleasant words are a honeycomb,
sweet to the soul and healing to
the bones.

[25]There is a way that seems right to a
man,
but in the end it leads to death.

[26]The laborer's appetite works for
him;
his hunger drives him on.

[27]A scoundrel plots evil,
and his speech is like a scorching
fire.

[28]A perverse man stirs up dissension,
and a gossip separates close
friends.

[29]A violent man entices his neighbor
and leads him down a path that is
not good.

[30]He who winks with his eye is
plotting perversity;
he who purses his lips is bent on
evil.

[31]Gray hair is a crown of splendor;
it is attained by a righteous life.

[32]Better a patient man than a warrior,
a man who controls his temper
than one who takes a city.

[33]The lot is cast into the lap,
but its every decision is from the
LORD.

17

Better a dry crust with
peace and quiet
than a house full of feasting,[c] with
strife.

[2]A wise servant will rule over a
disgraceful son,
and will share the inheritance as
one of the brothers.

[3]The crucible for silver and the
furnace for gold,
but the LORD tests the heart.

[4]A wicked man listens to evil lips;
a liar pays attention to a malicious
tongue.

[5]He who mocks the poor shows
contempt for their Maker;
whoever gloats over disaster will
not go unpunished.

[6]Children's children are a crown to
the aged,
and parents are the pride of their
children.

[7]Arrogant[d] lips are unsuited to a
fool—
how much worse lying lips to a
ruler!

[8]A bribe is a charm to the one who
gives it;
wherever he turns, he succeeds.

[9]He who covers over an offense
promotes love,
but whoever repeats the matter
separates close friends.

[10]A rebuke impresses a man of
discernment
more than a hundred lashes a fool.

[11]An evil man is bent only on
rebellion;
a merciless official will be sent
against him.

[12]Better to meet a bear robbed of her
cubs
than a fool in his folly.

[13]If a man pays back evil for good,
evil will never leave his house.

[a]21 Or *words make a man persuasive* [b]23 Or *mouth / and makes his lips persuasive* [c]1 Hebrew *sacrifices* [d]7 Or *Eloquent*

14 Starting a quarrel is like breaching a
dam;
so drop the matter before a
dispute breaks out.

15 Acquitting the guilty and
condemning the innocent—
the LORD detests them both.

16 Of what use is money in the hand of
a fool,
since he has no desire to get
wisdom?

17 A friend loves at all times,
and a brother is born for adversity.

18 A man lacking in judgment strikes
hands in pledge
and puts up security for his
neighbor.

19 He who loves a quarrel loves sin;
he who builds a high gate invites
destruction.

20 A man of perverse heart does not
prosper;
he whose tongue is deceitful falls
into trouble.

21 To have a fool for a son brings grief;
there is no joy for the father of a
fool.

22 A cheerful heart is good
medicine,
but a crushed spirit dries up the
bones.

23 A wicked man accepts a bribe in
secret
to pervert the course of justice.

24 A discerning man keeps wisdom in
view,
but a fool's eyes wander to the
ends of the earth.

25 A foolish son brings grief to his
father
and bitterness to the one who
bore him.

26 It is not good to punish an innocent
man,
or to flog officials for their
integrity.

27 A man of knowledge uses words
with restraint,
and a man of understanding is
even-tempered.

28 Even a fool is thought wise if he
keeps silent,
and discerning if he holds his
tongue.

SHARPEN THE FOCUS

"Even a fool is thought wise if he keeps silent" (Proverbs 17:28). Scripture repeats this thought over and over. Our Lord warns us especially about the harm that gossip and a nit-picking, critical spirit can cause.

There are all kinds of words—juicy, angry, deceitful, or hateful words. How often do your words cause trouble for you or for those around you? Once words like these escape from our lips, we lose control over them. Solomon reminds us that "starting a quarrel is like breaching a dam" (Proverbs 17:14). Angry words may trickle through a crack in a relationship at first, but before long they can cause a flood of retaliation that drowns out all mutual respect and affection.

We cannot tame our tongue on our own. That's why we can rejoice in the words of Proverbs 16:6: "Through love and faithfulness sin is atoned for."

When we were loveless and faithless, Jesus loved us and, faithful to His promise, rescued us. In His love and faithfulness sin is atoned for. In His death we receive pardon, and in His life we receive power to overcome the sins that plague us. He has placed us on the highway of the upright (Proverbs 16:17), and He makes it possible for us to walk that path and speak words of kindness and gentleness to one another.

Many of the proverbs you will read today deal with the care and nurture of relationships—with other people and with the Lord. As you read, ask the Lord what He would like you to see about the relationships He has given you. If time is short, focus on Proverbs 18:1–24.

18 An unfriendly man pursues selfish ends;
he defies all sound judgment.

2 A fool finds no pleasure in understanding
but delights in airing his own opinions.

3 When wickedness comes, so does contempt,
and with shame comes disgrace.

4 The words of a man's mouth are deep waters,
but the fountain of wisdom is a bubbling brook.

5 It is not good to be partial to the wicked
or to deprive the innocent of justice.

6 A fool's lips bring him strife,
and his mouth invites a beating.

7 A fool's mouth is his undoing,
and his lips are a snare to his soul.

8 The words of a gossip are like choice morsels;
they go down to a man's inmost parts.

9 One who is slack in his work
is brother to one who destroys.

10 The name of the LORD is a strong tower;
the righteous run to it and are safe.

11 The wealth of the rich is their fortified city;
they imagine it an unscalable wall.

12 Before his downfall a man's heart is proud,
but humility comes before honor.

13 He who answers before listening—
that is his folly and his shame.

14 A man's spirit sustains him in sickness,
but a crushed spirit who can bear?

15 The heart of the discerning acquires knowledge;
the ears of the wise seek it out.

16 A gift opens the way for the giver
and ushers him into the presence of the great.

17 The first to present his case seems right,
till another comes forward and questions him.

18 Casting the lot settles disputes
and keeps strong opponents apart.

19 An offended brother is more unyielding than a fortified city,
and disputes are like the barred gates of a citadel.

20 From the fruit of his mouth a man's stomach is filled;
with the harvest from his lips he is satisfied.

21 The tongue has the power of life and death,
and those who love it will eat its fruit.

22 He who finds a wife finds what is good
and receives favor from the LORD.

23 A poor man pleads for mercy,
but a rich man answers harshly.

24 A man of many companions may come to ruin,
but there is a friend who sticks closer than a brother.

19 Better a poor man whose walk is blameless
than a fool whose lips are perverse.

2 It is not good to have zeal without knowledge,
nor to be hasty and miss the way.

3 A man's own folly ruins his life,
yet his heart rages against the LORD.

4 Wealth brings many friends,
but a poor man's friend deserts him.

5 A false witness will not go unpunished,
and he who pours out lies will not go free.

6 Many curry favor with a ruler,
and everyone is the friend of a man who gives gifts.

7 A poor man is shunned by all his relatives—
how much more do his friends avoid him!
Though he pursues them with pleading,
they are nowhere to be found.[a]

8 He who gets wisdom loves his own soul;
he who cherishes understanding prospers.

9 A false witness will not go unpunished,
and he who pours out lies will perish.

10 It is not fitting for a fool to live in luxury—
how much worse for a slave to rule over princes!

11 A man's wisdom gives him patience;
it is to his glory to overlook an offense.

12 A king's rage is like the roar of a lion,
but his favor is like dew on the grass.

13 A foolish son is his father's ruin,
and a quarrelsome wife is like a constant dripping.

14 Houses and wealth are inherited from parents,
but a prudent wife is from the LORD.

15 Laziness brings on deep sleep,
and the shiftless man goes hungry.

16 He who obeys instructions guards his life,
but he who is contemptuous of his ways will die.

17 He who is kind to the poor lends to the LORD,
and he will reward him for what he has done.

18 Discipline your son, for in that there is hope;
do not be a willing party to his death.

19 A hot-tempered man must pay the penalty;
if you rescue him, you will have to do it again.

20 Listen to advice and accept instruction,
and in the end you will be wise.

21 Many are the plans in a man's heart,
but it is the LORD's purpose that prevails.

22 What a man desires is unfailing love[b];
better to be poor than a liar.

23 The fear of the LORD leads to life:
Then one rests content,
untouched by trouble.

[a] 7 The meaning of the Hebrew for this sentence is uncertain. [b] 22 Or *A man's greed is his shame*

24 The sluggard buries his hand in the dish;
he will not even bring it back to his mouth!

25 Flog a mocker, and the simple will learn prudence;
rebuke a discerning man, and he will gain knowledge.

26 He who robs his father and drives out his mother
is a son who brings shame and disgrace.

27 Stop listening to instruction, my son,
and you will stray from the words of knowledge.

28 A corrupt witness mocks at justice,
and the mouth of the wicked gulps down evil.

29 Penalties are prepared for mockers,
and beatings for the backs of fools.

SHARPEN THE FOCUS

The Scriptures often condemn the walls we erect between one another to protect ourselves. We do it by lashing out in hate-filled words or spiteful actions or by not caring. We maintain our side of these walls by nursing our grudge or denying we have a problem or avoiding the person whom we've hurt. When a relationship gets to that point, Proverbs 18:19 says, conquering a fortified city takes less effort than winning back our brother or sister.

Proverbs 18:10, in contrast, points us to a tower—a tower of true defense. The name of our Savior-God is our refuge, our place of safety. We can run to Him with our sins and find shelter there from the wrath we deserve. We can hide in the shadow of Christ's cross.

That safety carries with it the courage we need to begin to break down the walls of division that stand between us and our brothers and sisters in the faith. Those walls don't protect us, they imprison us. They keep us from sharing Christ's love with one another.

Do you have a long-standing wall between you and someone else? Removing it probably won't be a one-day job. Walls like that weren't built in a day. But Jesus wants to help you demolish the wall, one brick at a time.

WEEK 50 • SATURDAY

Proverbs 20:1—21:31

GET THE BIG PICTURE

Eating. Drinking. Dealing with public officials. How to bill business transactions. Today's chapters (Proverbs 20–21) cover many practical matters. But more importantly, they address the attitudes of the heart. In particular, they point out the necessity of a pure heart (Proverbs 20:9) and point us toward the only source of righteousness—our Lord Himself. Watch for these accents as you read. If time is short, focus on Proverbs 20:1–12.

20

Wine is a mocker and beer a brawler;
whoever is led astray by them is not wise.

2 A king's wrath is like the roar of a lion;
he who angers him forfeits his life.

3 It is to a man's honor to avoid strife,
but every fool is quick to quarrel.

4 A sluggard does not plow in season;
so at harvest time he looks but finds nothing.

5 The purposes of a man's heart are deep waters,
but a man of understanding draws them out.

6 Many a man claims to have unfailing love,
but a faithful man who can find?

7 The righteous man leads a blameless life;
blessed are his children after him.

8 When a king sits on his throne to judge,
he winnows out all evil with his eyes.

9 Who can say, "I have kept my heart pure;
I am clean and without sin"?

10 Differing weights and differing measures—
the LORD detests them both.

11 Even a child is known by his actions,
by whether his conduct is pure and right.

12 Ears that hear and eyes that see—
the LORD has made them both.

13 Do not love sleep or you will grow poor;
stay awake and you will have food to spare.

14 "It's no good, it's no good!" says the buyer;
then off he goes and boasts about his purchase.

15 Gold there is, and rubies in abundance,
but lips that speak knowledge are a rare jewel.

16 Take the garment of one who puts up security for a stranger;
hold it in pledge if he does it for a wayward woman.

17 Food gained by fraud tastes sweet to a man,
but he ends up with a mouth full of gravel.

18 Make plans by seeking advice;
if you wage war, obtain guidance.

19 A gossip betrays a confidence;
so avoid a man who talks too much.

20 If a man curses his father or mother,
his lamp will be snuffed out in pitch darkness.

21 An inheritance quickly gained at the beginning
will not be blessed at the end.

22 Do not say, "I'll pay you back for this wrong!"
Wait for the LORD, and he will deliver you.

23 The LORD detests differing weights,
and dishonest scales do not please him.

24 A man's steps are directed by the LORD.
How then can anyone understand his own way?

25 It is a trap for a man to dedicate something rashly
and only later to consider his vows.

26 A wise king winnows out the wicked;
he drives the threshing wheel over them.

27 The lamp of the LORD searches the spirit of a man[a];
it searches out his inmost being.

[a]27 Or *The spirit of man is the LORD's lamp*

28 Love and faithfulness keep a king safe;
through love his throne is made secure.

29 The glory of young men is their strength,
gray hair the splendor of the old.

30 Blows and wounds cleanse away evil,
and beatings purge the inmost being.

21 The king's heart is in the hand of the LORD;
he directs it like a watercourse wherever he pleases.

2 All a man's ways seem right to him,
but the LORD weighs the heart.

3 To do what is right and just
is more acceptable to the LORD than sacrifice.

4 Haughty eyes and a proud heart,
the lamp of the wicked, are sin!

5 The plans of the diligent lead to profit
as surely as haste leads to poverty.

6 A fortune made by a lying tongue
is a fleeting vapor and a deadly snare.[a]

7 The violence of the wicked will drag them away,
for they refuse to do what is right.

8 The way of the guilty is devious,
but the conduct of the innocent is upright.

9 Better to live on a corner of the roof
than share a house with a quarrelsome wife.

10 The wicked man craves evil;
his neighbor gets no mercy from him.

11 When a mocker is punished, the simple gain wisdom;
when a wise man is instructed, he gets knowledge.

12 The Righteous One[b] takes note of the house of the wicked
and brings the wicked to ruin.

13 If a man shuts his ears to the cry of the poor,
he too will cry out and not be answered.

14 A gift given in secret soothes anger,
and a bribe concealed in the cloak pacifies great wrath.

15 When justice is done, it brings joy to the righteous
but terror to evildoers.

16 A man who strays from the path of understanding
comes to rest in the company of the dead.

17 He who loves pleasure will become poor;
whoever loves wine and oil will never be rich.

18 The wicked become a ransom for the righteous,
and the unfaithful for the upright.

19 Better to live in a desert
than with a quarrelsome and ill-tempered wife.

20 In the house of the wise are stores of choice food and oil,
but a foolish man devours all he has.

21 He who pursues righteousness and love
finds life, prosperity[c] and honor.

22 A wise man attacks the city of the mighty
and pulls down the stronghold in which they trust.

23 He who guards his mouth and his tongue
keeps himself from calamity.

[a]6 Some Hebrew manuscripts, Septuagint and Vulgate; most Hebrew manuscripts *vapor for those who seek death* [b]12 Or *The righteous man* [c]21 Or *righteousness*

24 The proud and arrogant man—
"Mocker" is his name;
he behaves with overweening
pride.
25 The sluggard's craving will be the
death of him,
because his hands refuse to
work.
26 All day long he craves for more,
but the righteous give without
sparing.
27 The sacrifice of the wicked is
detestable—
how much more so when brought
with evil intent!
28 A false witness will perish,
and whoever listens to him will be
destroyed forever.[a]
29 A wicked man puts up a bold front,
but an upright man gives thought
to his ways.
30 There is no wisdom, no insight, no
plan
that can succeed against the LORD.
31 The horse is made ready for the day
of battle,
but victory rests with the LORD.

[a]28 Or / *but the words of an obedient man will live on*

SHARPEN THE FOCUS

Do you ever see your neighbor yelling at his wife or kicking his dog and shake your head in disgust? Do thoughts like these spring to mind: "I would never do that. He needs to shape up"?

Have you ever listened to a coworker or someone at church complain about the cost of Christmas, about how she's blown her budget but still has half her shopping left? Do thoughts like these spring to mind: "Christmas is so materialistic. I'm glad I'm above the crassness"?

If any of this sounds familiar, you've caught yourself staring at your own self-righteousness. One way we can gauge the degree of spiritual pride in ourselves is to listen to the way we react to other sinners. When we look down on them, we betray the fact that we ourselves deserve God's judgment.

Solomon says, "Many a man claims to have unfailing love, but a faithful man who can find?" (Proverbs 20:6). Does your heart insist on proclaiming your own goodness? Or do you cling in faith to the righteousness Christ won for you on His cross?

You and I can't cleanse our own hearts. But we know the one who can and will cleanse us. Why not talk to Him about that? You may want to use King David's prayer for cleansing from Psalm 51:1–13.

WEEK 51 • MONDAY

Proverbs 22:1—23:35

GET THE BIG PICTURE

We've read the proverbs to youth or fatherly proverbs (Proverbs 1–9), the antithetical proverbs (Proverbs 10–15), and the synthetic proverbs (Proverbs 16–21). Now we turn to the extended proverbs (Proverbs 22–31). These generally deal with their subject matter in more depth. As you read today, look for the Lord's counsel in three areas: parenting, right perspectives on work, and the wise use of money. If time is short, focus on Proverbs 23:1–35.

22

A good name is more desirable than great riches;
to be esteemed is better than silver or gold.

2 Rich and poor have this in common:
The LORD is the Maker of them all.

3 A prudent man sees danger and takes refuge,
but the simple keep going and suffer for it.

4 Humility and the fear of the LORD
bring wealth and honor and life.

5 In the paths of the wicked lie thorns and snares,
but he who guards his soul stays far from them.

6 Train[a] a child in the way he should go,
and when he is old he will not turn from it.

7 The rich rule over the poor,
and the borrower is servant to the lender.

8 He who sows wickedness reaps trouble,
and the rod of his fury will be destroyed.

9 A generous man will himself be blessed,
for he shares his food with the poor.

10 Drive out the mocker, and out goes strife;
quarrels and insults are ended.

11 He who loves a pure heart and whose speech is gracious
will have the king for his friend.

12 The eyes of the LORD keep watch over knowledge,
but he frustrates the words of the unfaithful.

13 The sluggard says, "There is a lion outside!"
or, "I will be murdered in the streets!"

14 The mouth of an adulteress is a deep pit;
he who is under the LORD's wrath will fall into it.

15 Folly is bound up in the heart of a child,
but the rod of discipline will drive it far from him.

16 He who oppresses the poor to increase his wealth
and he who gives gifts to the rich—both come to poverty.

Sayings of the Wise

17 Pay attention and listen to the sayings of the wise;
apply your heart to what I teach,
18 for it is pleasing when you keep them in your heart
and have all of them ready on your lips.
19 So that your trust may be in the LORD,
I teach you today, even you.
20 Have I not written thirty[b] sayings for you,
sayings of counsel and knowledge,
21 teaching you true and reliable words,
so that you can give sound answers
to him who sent you?

22 Do not exploit the poor because they are poor
and do not crush the needy in court,
23 for the LORD will take up their case
and will plunder those who plunder them.

[a]6 Or *Start* [b]20 Or *not formerly written; or not written excellent*

24 Do not make friends with a
hot-tempered man,
do not associate with one easily
angered,
25 or you may learn his ways
and get yourself ensnared.

26 Do not be a man who strikes hands
in pledge
or puts up security for debts;
27 if you lack the means to pay,
your very bed will be snatched
from under you.

28 Do not move an ancient boundary
stone
set up by your forefathers.

29 Do you see a man skilled in his work?
He will serve before kings;
he will not serve before obscure
men.

23 When you sit to dine
with a ruler,
note well what[a] is before you,
2 and put a knife to your throat
if you are given to gluttony.
3 Do not crave his delicacies,
for that food is deceptive.

4 Do not wear yourself out to get rich;
have the wisdom to show
restraint.
5 Cast but a glance at riches, and they
are gone,
for they will surely sprout wings
and fly off to the sky like an eagle.

6 Do not eat the food of a stingy man,
do not crave his delicacies;
7 for he is the kind of man
who is always thinking about the
cost.[b]
"Eat and drink," he says to you,
but his heart is not with you.
8 You will vomit up the little you have
eaten
and will have wasted your
compliments.

9 Do not speak to a fool,
for he will scorn the wisdom of
your words.

10 Do not move an ancient boundary
stone
or encroach on the fields of the
fatherless,
11 for their Defender is strong;
he will take up their case against
you.

12 Apply your heart to instruction
and your ears to words of
knowledge.

13 Do not withhold discipline from a
child;
if you punish him with the rod, he
will not die.
14 Punish him with the rod
and save his soul from death.[c]
15 My son, if your heart is wise,
then my heart will be glad;
16 my inmost being will rejoice
when your lips speak what is
right.

17 Do not let your heart envy sinners,
but always be zealous for the fear
of the LORD.
18 There is surely a future hope for
you,
and your hope will not be cut off.

19 Listen, my son, and be wise,
and keep your heart on the right
path.
20 Do not join those who drink too
much wine
or gorge themselves on meat,
21 for drunkards and gluttons become
poor,
and drowsiness clothes them in
rags.

22 Listen to your father, who gave you
life,
and do not despise your mother
when she is old.
23 Buy the truth and do not sell it;
get wisdom, discipline and
understanding.
24 The father of a righteous man has
great joy;
he who has a wise son delights in
him.

[a]1 Or *who* [b]7 Or *for as he thinks within himself, / so he is*; or *for as he puts on a feast, / so he is*
[c]14 Hebrew *Sheol*

[25]May your father and mother be glad;
may she who gave you birth rejoice!

[26]My son, give me your heart
and let your eyes keep to my ways,
[27]for a prostitute is a deep pit
and a wayward wife is a narrow well.
[28]Like a bandit she lies in wait,
and multiplies the unfaithful among men.

[29]Who has woe? Who has sorrow?
Who has strife? Who has complaints?
Who has needless bruises? Who has bloodshot eyes?
[30]Those who linger over wine,
who go to sample bowls of mixed wine.
[31]Do not gaze at wine when it is red,
when it sparkles in the cup,
when it goes down smoothly!
[32]In the end it bites like a snake
and poisons like a viper.
[33]Your eyes will see strange sights
and your mind imagine confusing things.
[34]You will be like one sleeping on the high seas,
lying on top of the rigging.
[35]"They hit me," you will say, "but I'm not hurt!
They beat me, but I don't feel it!
When will I wake up
so I can find another drink?"

SHARPEN THE FOCUS

Bookstore shelves have exploded in the past 20 years with volumes devoted to success on the job. They deal with everything from how to dress, to the best ways for motivating employees. Some of the ideas work, some do not. But the principles behind those ideas that do work come directly out of God's Word, many from the book of Proverbs. Whether secular writers will admit it or not, all truth is God's truth.

Take the wisdom of Proverbs 23:4–5, for example: "Do not wear yourself out to get rich." This plea comes directly from our Lord's heart. It challenges us to ask ourselves why we do what we do. Whether we earn the minimum wage or pull in a six-figure salary, whether we're unemployed or a college student or a homemaker, we fill the 168 hours of our week somehow.

What is it that will truly fill those hours? What will fulfill us? God says here quite plainly that overworking for wealth falls under the column our Maker labels "foolish." So what are you working for, living for? Think and pray about some of these Scriptures as you ask yourself that question: Proverbs 9:10; 10:22; 11:18; 21:21; 22:17–20; 23:17–18. Then ask your Savior for the forgiveness and strength you need to live more wisely.

WEEK 51 • TUESDAY

Proverbs 24:1—25:28

GET THE BIG PICTURE

Mark Twain once told his publisher, "If I had had more time, I would have written a shorter book." He well knew that tight, powerful writing comes only as a writer crafts each sentence to distill each thought. As the Holy Spirit inspired King Solomon, the king crafted today's proverbs. The wisdom distilled in them works today just as it did in Solomon's time. Pray as you read that the Spirit would impress His wisdom on your heart. If time is short, focus on Proverbs 24:23–34.

24 Do not envy wicked men,
do not desire their company;
2 for their hearts plot violence,
and their lips talk about making trouble.

3 By wisdom a house is built,
and through understanding it is established;
4 through knowledge its rooms are filled
with rare and beautiful treasures.

5 A wise man has great power,
and a man of knowledge increases strength;
6 for waging war you need guidance,
and for victory many advisers.

7 Wisdom is too high for a fool;
in the assembly at the gate he has nothing to say.

8 He who plots evil
will be known as a schemer.
9 The schemes of folly are sin,
and men detest a mocker.

10 If you falter in times of trouble,
how small is your strength!

11 Rescue those being led away to death;
hold back those staggering toward slaughter.
12 If you say, "But we knew nothing about this,"
does not he who weighs the heart perceive it?
Does not he who guards your life know it?
Will he not repay each person
according to what he has done?

13 Eat honey, my son, for it is good;
honey from the comb is sweet to your taste.
14 Know also that wisdom is sweet to your soul;
if you find it, there is a future hope for you,
and your hope will not be cut off.

15 Do not lie in wait like an outlaw
against a righteous man's house,
do not raid his dwelling place;
16 for though a righteous man falls
seven times, he rises again,
but the wicked are brought down
by calamity.

17 Do not gloat when your enemy falls;
when he stumbles, do not let your heart rejoice,
18 or the LORD will see and disapprove
and turn his wrath away from him.

19 Do not fret because of evil men
or be envious of the wicked,
20 for the evil man has no future hope,
and the lamp of the wicked will be snuffed out.

21 Fear the LORD and the king, my son,
and do not join with the rebellious,

22 for those two will send sudden
destruction upon them,
and who knows what calamities
they can bring?

Further Sayings of the Wise

23 These also are sayings of the wise:

To show partiality in judging is not
good:
24 Whoever says to the guilty, "You are
innocent"—
peoples will curse him and
nations denounce him.
25 But it will go well with those who
convict the guilty,
and rich blessing will come upon
them.

26 An honest answer
is like a kiss on the lips.

27 Finish your outdoor work
and get your fields ready;
after that, build your house.

28 Do not testify against your neighbor
without cause,
or use your lips to deceive.
29 Do not say, "I'll do to him as he has
done to me;
I'll pay that man back for what he
did."

30 I went past the field of the sluggard,
past the vineyard of the man who
lacks judgment;
31 thorns had come up everywhere,
the ground was covered with
weeds,
and the stone wall was in ruins.
32 I applied my heart to what I observed
and learned a lesson from what I
saw:
33 A little sleep, a little slumber,
a little folding of the hands to rest—
34 and poverty will come on you like a
bandit
and scarcity like an armed man.[a]

More Proverbs of Solomon

25 These are more proverbs of Solomon, copied by the men of Hezekiah king of Judah:

2 It is the glory of God to conceal a
matter;
to search out a matter is the glory
of kings.

3 As the heavens are high and the
earth is deep,
so the hearts of kings are
unsearchable.

4 Remove the dross from the silver,
and out comes material for[b] the
silversmith;
5 remove the wicked from the king's
presence,
and his throne will be established
through righteousness.

6 Do not exalt yourself in the king's
presence,
and do not claim a place among
great men;
7 it is better for him to say to you,
"Come up here,"
than for him to humiliate you
before a nobleman.

What you have seen with your eyes
8 do not bring[c] hastily to court,
for what will you do in the end
if your neighbor puts you to
shame?

9 If you argue your case with a
neighbor,
do not betray another man's
confidence,
10 or he who hears it may shame you
and you will never lose your bad
reputation.

11 A word aptly spoken
is like apples of gold in settings of
silver.

12 Like an earring of gold or an
ornament of fine gold
is a wise man's rebuke to a
listening ear.

13 Like the coolness of snow at harvest
time
is a trustworthy messenger to
those who send him;

[a] 34 Or *like a vagrant / and scarcity like a beggar*
[b] 4 Or *comes a vessel from* [c] 7,8 Or *nobleman / on whom you had set your eyes. /* [8] *Do not go*

he refreshes the spirit of his
masters.

14 Like clouds and wind without rain
is a man who boasts of gifts he
does not give.

15 Through patience a ruler can be
persuaded,
and a gentle tongue can break a
bone.

16 If you find honey, eat just enough—
too much of it, and you will vomit.
17 Seldom set foot in your neighbor's
house—
too much of you, and he will hate
you.

18 Like a club or a sword or a sharp
arrow
is the man who gives false
testimony against his
neighbor.

19 Like a bad tooth or a lame foot
is reliance on the unfaithful in
times of trouble.

20 Like one who takes away a garment
on a cold day,
or like vinegar poured on soda,
is one who sings songs to a heavy
heart.

21 If your enemy is hungry, give him
food to eat;
if he is thirsty, give him water to
drink.
22 In doing this, you will heap burning
coals on his head,
and the LORD will reward you.

23 As a north wind brings rain,
so a sly tongue brings angry looks.

24 Better to live on a corner of the roof
than share a house with a
quarrelsome wife.

25 Like cold water to a weary soul
is good news from a distant land.

26 Like a muddied spring or a polluted
well
is a righteous man who gives way
to the wicked.

27 It is not good to eat too much honey,
nor is it honorable to seek one's
own honor.

28 Like a city whose walls are broken
down
is a man who lacks self-control.

SHARPEN THE FOCUS

Suppose someone deposited a million dollars in a bank account with your name on it. Unless you knew the money belonged to you, what good would it do you? The same is true with the riches of wisdom our Lord has given us in His Word.

Proverbs 24:23 says, "These also are sayings of the wise." The rest of the chapter goes on to spell out four specific treasures, potentials that belong to us, God's righteous ones in Christ. Through Christ, "in whom are hidden all the treasures of wisdom and knowledge" (Colossians 2:3), we receive both pardon and power so that we can make use of the riches of God's wisdom which Christ has credited to our account.

Think about your own life in relation to these four areas. How will you use these riches of wisdom that are yours in Christ?

- The wise act justly and align their decisions with the revealed will of God (Proverbs 24:23–26).
- The wise put first things first; they set practical priorities (Proverbs 24:27).
- The wise tell the truth about those who hurt them, but leave vengeance to God (Proverbs 24:28–29).
- The wise are diligent to do the work God has given them (Proverbs 24:30–34).

WEEK 51 • WEDNESDAY

Prov. 26:1—27:27

GET THE BIG PICTURE

In a series of extended proverbs, Solomon continues to detail God's wisdom. He shares so many practical hints in so few words that it's easy to miss some of them. Read prayerfully. Ask the Holy Spirit to draw your attention to texts that He wants to personalize to your heart. If time is short, focus on Proverbs 27:1–27.

26 Like snow in summer or rain in harvest,
honor is not fitting for a fool.

2 Like a fluttering sparrow or a darting swallow,
an undeserved curse does not come to rest.

3 A whip for the horse, a halter for the donkey,
and a rod for the backs of fools!

4 Do not answer a fool according to his folly,
or you will be like him yourself.

5 Answer a fool according to his folly,
or he will be wise in his own eyes.

6 Like cutting off one's feet or drinking violence
is the sending of a message by the hand of a fool.

7 Like a lame man's legs that hang limp
is a proverb in the mouth of a fool.

8 Like tying a stone in a sling
is the giving of honor to a fool.

9 Like a thornbush in a drunkard's hand
is a proverb in the mouth of a fool.

10 Like an archer who wounds at random
is he who hires a fool or any passer-by.

11 As a dog returns to its vomit,
so a fool repeats his folly.

12 Do you see a man wise in his own eyes?
There is more hope for a fool than for him.

13 The sluggard says, "There is a lion in the road,
a fierce lion roaming the streets!"

14 As a door turns on its hinges,
so a sluggard turns on his bed.

15 The sluggard buries his hand in the dish;
he is too lazy to bring it back to his mouth.

16 The sluggard is wiser in his own eyes
than seven men who answer discreetly.

17 Like one who seizes a dog by the ears
is a passer-by who meddles in a quarrel not his own.

18 Like a madman shooting firebrands or deadly arrows
19 is a man who deceives his neighbor
and says, "I was only joking!"

20 Without wood a fire goes out;
without gossip a quarrel dies down.

21 As charcoal to embers and as wood to fire,
so is a quarrelsome man for kindling strife.

22 The words of a gossip are like choice morsels;

they go down to a man's inmost
parts.

23 Like a coating of glaze[a] over
earthenware
are fervent lips with an evil heart.

24 A malicious man disguises himself
with his lips,
but in his heart he harbors deceit.

25 Though his speech is charming, do
not believe him,
for seven abominations fill his
heart.

26 His malice may be concealed by
deception,
but his wickedness will be
exposed in the assembly.

27 If a man digs a pit, he will fall into it;
if a man rolls a stone, it will roll
back on him.

28 A lying tongue hates those it hurts,
and a flattering mouth works
ruin.

27 Do not boast about
tomorrow,
for you do not know what a day
may bring forth.

2 Let another praise you, and not your
own mouth;
someone else, and not your own
lips.

3 Stone is heavy and sand a burden,
but provocation by a fool is
heavier than both.

4 Anger is cruel and fury
overwhelming,
but who can stand before jealousy?

5 Better is open rebuke
than hidden love.

6 Wounds from a friend can be
trusted,
but an enemy multiplies kisses.

7 He who is full loathes honey,
but to the hungry even what is
bitter tastes sweet.

8 Like a bird that strays from its nest
is a man who strays from his
home.

9 Perfume and incense bring joy to the
heart,
and the pleasantness of one's
friend springs from his
earnest counsel.

10 Do not forsake your friend and the
friend of your father,
and do not go to your brother's
house when disaster strikes
you—
better a neighbor nearby than a
brother far away.

11 Be wise, my son, and bring joy to
my heart;
then I can answer anyone who
treats me with contempt.

12 The prudent see danger and take
refuge,
but the simple keep going and
suffer for it.

13 Take the garment of one who puts
up security for a stranger;
hold it in pledge if he does it for a
wayward woman.

14 If a man loudly blesses his neighbor
early in the morning,
it will be taken as a curse.

15 A quarrelsome wife is like
a constant dripping on a rainy
day;

16 restraining her is like restraining the
wind
or grasping oil with the hand.

17 As iron sharpens iron,
so one man sharpens another.

18 He who tends a fig tree will eat its
fruit,
and he who looks after his master
will be honored.

19 As water reflects a face,
so a man's heart reflects the man.

20 Death and Destruction[b] are never
satisfied,
and neither are the eyes of man.

[a]23 With a different word division of the Hebrew; Masoretic Text *of silver dross*
[b]20 Hebrew *Sheol and Abaddon*

21 The crucible for silver and the furnace for gold,
but man is tested by the praise he receives.
22 Though you grind a fool in a mortar,
grinding him like grain with a pestle,
you will not remove his folly from him.
23 Be sure you know the condition of your flocks,
give careful attention to your herds;
24 for riches do not endure forever,
and a crown is not secure for all generations.
25 When the hay is removed and new growth appears
and the grass from the hills is gathered in,
26 the lambs will provide you with clothing,
and the goats with the price of a field.
27 You will have plenty of goats' milk
to feed you and your family
and to nourish your servant girls.

SHARPEN THE FOCUS

Today, we seldom hear anyone speak about honor or the importance of a good reputation. Even if our culture discounts honor, we know that nothing can replace our integrity and the confidence others place in us. The "hero" on tonight's family sitcom will never echo Scriptures. Nonetheless, Solomon's words are still true:

> *Man is tested by the praise he receives.* (See Proverbs 27:21; see also Proverbs 22:1.)

If we believe what God says here, how carefully will we guard the reputation of others? How concerned will we be about refusing to repeat gossip? About explaining the actions of others in a kind way?

Most of us must plead guilty to poking holes in the reputation of others. We squirm when we face head-on the true damage this sin causes. It's one of those sins for which we can never make full restitution, no matter how hard we try. So then, as we confess our sin, we treasure ever more deeply the love of our Savior. Jesus willingly laid aside His own glory, the honor due Him as the Son of God. He carried instead our shame and our sins, to His cross. In Him, we find healing and the help we need to tame our hearts and our tongues.

WEEK 51 • THURSDAY

Proverbs 28:1—29:27

GET THE BIG PICTURE

The ideas you will encounter in Proverbs today can serve as a review. Many themes that recur throughout the book appear again here. As you read them, remind yourself of what the Lord has said about His people's relationships with the poor, our decisions about using money and possessions, and His response when we confess our sins. What other themes do you recognize? If time is short, focus on Proverbs 29:1–27.

28 The wicked man flees
though no one pursues,
but the righteous are as bold as a
lion.
2 When a country is rebellious, it has
many rulers,
but a man of understanding and
knowledge maintains order.
3 A ruler[a] who oppresses the poor
is like a driving rain that leaves no
crops.
4 Those who forsake the law praise
the wicked,
but those who keep the law resist
them.
5 Evil men do not understand justice,
but those who seek the LORD
understand it fully.
6 Better a poor man whose walk is
blameless
than a rich man whose ways are
perverse.
7 He who keeps the law is a
discerning son,
but a companion of gluttons
disgraces his father.
8 He who increases his wealth by
exorbitant interest
amasses it for another, who will be
kind to the poor.
9 If anyone turns a deaf ear to the law,
even his prayers are detestable.
10 He who leads the upright along an
evil path
will fall into his own trap,
but the blameless will receive a
good inheritance.
11 A rich man may be wise in his own
eyes,
but a poor man who has
discernment sees through him.
12 When the righteous triumph, there
is great elation;
but when the wicked rise to
power, men go into hiding.
13 He who conceals his sins does not
prosper,
but whoever confesses and
renounces them finds mercy.
14 Blessed is the man who always fears
the LORD,
but he who hardens his heart falls
into trouble.
15 Like a roaring lion or a charging
bear
is a wicked man ruling over a
helpless people.
16 A tyrannical ruler lacks judgment,
but he who hates ill-gotten gain
will enjoy a long life.
17 A man tormented by the guilt of
murder
will be a fugitive till death;
let no one support him.
18 He whose walk is blameless is kept
safe,
but he whose ways are perverse
will suddenly fall.
19 He who works his land will have
abundant food,
but the one who chases fantasies
will have his fill of poverty.
20 A faithful man will be richly
blessed,
but one eager to get rich will not
go unpunished.
21 To show partiality is not good—
yet a man will do wrong for a
piece of bread.
22 A stingy man is eager to get rich
and is unaware that poverty
awaits him.
23 He who rebukes a man will in the
end gain more favor
than he who has a flattering
tongue.
24 He who robs his father or mother
and says, "It's not wrong"—
he is partner to him who destroys.
25 A greedy man stirs up dissension,
but he who trusts in the LORD will
prosper.

[a]3 Or *A poor man*

[26]He who trusts in himself is a fool,
but he who walks in wisdom is kept safe.

[27]He who gives to the poor will lack nothing,
but he who closes his eyes to them receives many curses.

[28]When the wicked rise to power, people go into hiding;
but when the wicked perish, the righteous thrive.

29

A man who remains stiff-necked after many rebukes
will suddenly be destroyed—without remedy.

[2]When the righteous thrive, the people rejoice;
when the wicked rule, the people groan.

[3]A man who loves wisdom brings joy to his father,
but a companion of prostitutes squanders his wealth.

[4]By justice a king gives a country stability,
but one who is greedy for bribes tears it down.

[5]Whoever flatters his neighbor
is spreading a net for his feet.

[6]An evil man is snared by his own sin,
but a righteous one can sing and be glad.

[7]The righteous care about justice for the poor,
but the wicked have no such concern.

[8]Mockers stir up a city,
but wise men turn away anger.

[9]If a wise man goes to court with a fool,
the fool rages and scoffs, and there is no peace.

[10]Bloodthirsty men hate a man of integrity
and seek to kill the upright.

[11]A fool gives full vent to his anger,
but a wise man keeps himself under control.

[12]If a ruler listens to lies,
all his officials become wicked.

[13]The poor man and the oppressor have this in common:
The LORD gives sight to the eyes of both.

[14]If a king judges the poor with fairness,
his throne will always be secure.

[15]The rod of correction imparts wisdom,
but a child left to himself disgraces his mother.

[16]When the wicked thrive, so does sin,
but the righteous will see their downfall.

[17]Discipline your son, and he will give you peace;
he will bring delight to your soul.

[18]Where there is no revelation, the people cast off restraint;
but blessed is he who keeps the law.

[19]A servant cannot be corrected by mere words;
though he understands, he will not respond.

[20]Do you see a man who speaks in haste?
There is more hope for a fool than for him.

[21]If a man pampers his servant from youth,
he will bring grief[a] in the end.

[22]An angry man stirs up dissension,
and a hot-tempered one commits many sins.

[23]A man's pride brings him low,
but a man of lowly spirit gains honor.

[a]*21* The meaning of the Hebrew for this word is uncertain.

24 The accomplice of a thief is his own
enemy;
he is put under oath and dare not
testify.
25 Fear of man will prove to be a snare,
but whoever trusts in the LORD is
kept safe.
26 Many seek an audience with a
ruler,
but it is from the LORD that man
gets justice.
27 The righteous detest the
dishonest;
the wicked detest the upright.

SHARPEN THE FOCUS

Some Christians read one chapter of Proverbs a day each month. The Holy Spirit can use such a practice to drive His wisdom deeply into our hearts.

But regardless of what we read from the Scriptures each day, God's goal for us remains the same: He intends that His Word take root in our hearts and bear fruit in our lives, the fruit of righteous living. In a word: wisdom.

We need to pay attention to our response when our Father corrects us through His Word. When He points out your sins and the corrections He wants to make, how do you react? Proverbs 29:1 describes one response:

A man who remains stiff-necked after many rebukes
will suddenly be destroyed–without remedy.

Those who are stiff-of-neck choose pain and, ultimately, eternal destruction. Are you resisting the Holy Spirit in any area of your life today? How fully are you living out His righteousness in your family? Have you allowed worry or fear to grip your heart? Are you ignoring opportunities to show His compassion toward the poor and needy?

Talk with your Lord about your response to His wisdom. Ask that He keep your heart always soft and open to His correction. Then pray Psalm 143 as a prayer of confession and recommitment.

WEEK 51 • FRIDAY

Proverbs 30:1—31:31

GET THE BIG PICTURE

Extended proverbs fill both of today's chapters, the last two chapters in Proverbs. As you read Proverbs 30:2–16, note the lifestyle described there: self-sufficient, self-righteous, self-satisfied; in short, self-focused. Contrast this with the lifestyle described in Proverbs 31:10–31. Which lifestyle would be easier? More fulfilling? If time is short, focus on Proverbs 31:1–31.

Sayings of Agur

30 The sayings of Agur son of Jakeh—an oracle[a]:

This man declared to Ithiel,
to Ithiel and to Ucal:[b]

2 "I am the most ignorant of men;
I do not have a man's understanding.
3 I have not learned wisdom,
nor have I knowledge of the Holy One.
4 Who has gone up to heaven and come down?
Who has gathered up the wind in the hollow of his hands?
Who has wrapped up the waters in his cloak?
Who has established all the ends of the earth?
What is his name, and the name of his son?
Tell me if you know!

5 "Every word of God is flawless;
he is a shield to those who take refuge in him.
6 Do not add to his words,
or he will rebuke you and prove you a liar.

7 "Two things I ask of you, O LORD;
do not refuse me before I die:
8 Keep falsehood and lies far from me;
give me neither poverty nor riches,
but give me only my daily bread.
9 Otherwise, I may have too much and disown you
and say, 'Who is the LORD?'
Or I may become poor and steal,
and so dishonor the name of my God.

10 "Do not slander a servant to his master,
or he will curse you, and you will pay for it.

11 "There are those who curse their fathers
and do not bless their mothers;
12 those who are pure in their own eyes
and yet are not cleansed of their filth;
13 those whose eyes are ever so haughty,
whose glances are so disdainful;
14 those whose teeth are swords
and whose jaws are set with knives
to devour the poor from the earth,
the needy from among mankind.

15 "The leech has two daughters.
'Give! Give!' they cry.
"There are three things that are never satisfied,
four that never say, 'Enough!':
16 the grave,[c] the barren womb,
land, which is never satisfied with water,
and fire, which never says, 'Enough!'

17 "The eye that mocks a father,
that scorns obedience to a mother,
will be pecked out by the ravens of the valley,
will be eaten by the vultures.

18 "There are three things that are too amazing for me,
four that I do not understand:
19 the way of an eagle in the sky,
the way of a snake on a rock,
the way of a ship on the high seas,
and the way of a man with a maiden.

20 "This is the way of an adulteress:
She eats and wipes her mouth
and says, 'I've done nothing wrong.'

21 "Under three things the earth trembles,
under four it cannot bear up:
22 a servant who becomes king,
a fool who is full of food,
23 an unloved woman who is married,
and a maidservant who displaces her mistress.

[a]1 Or *Jakeh of Massa* [b]1 Masoretic Text; with a different word division of the Hebrew *declared, "I am weary, O God; / I am weary, O God, and faint.* [c]16 Hebrew *Sheol*

24"Four things on earth are small,
yet they are extremely wise:
25Ants are creatures of little strength,
yet they store up their food in the summer;
26coneys[a] are creatures of little power,
yet they make their home in the crags;
27locusts have no king,
yet they advance together in ranks;
28a lizard can be caught with the hand,
yet it is found in kings' palaces.

29"There are three things that are stately in their stride,
four that move with stately bearing:
30a lion, mighty among beasts,
who retreats before nothing;
31a strutting rooster, a he-goat,
and a king with his army around him.[b]

32"If you have played the fool and exalted yourself,
or if you have planned evil,
clap your hand over your mouth!
33For as churning the milk produces butter,
and as twisting the nose produces blood,
so stirring up anger produces strife."

Sayings of King Lemuel

31 The sayings of King Lemuel—an oracle[c] his mother taught him:

2"O my son, O son of my womb,
O son of my vows,[d]
3do not spend your strength on women,
your vigor on those who ruin kings.

4"It is not for kings, O Lemuel—
not for kings to drink wine,
not for rulers to crave beer,
5lest they drink and forget what the law decrees,
and deprive all the oppressed of their rights.
6Give beer to those who are perishing,
wine to those who are in anguish;
7let them drink and forget their poverty
and remember their misery no more.

8"Speak up for those who cannot speak for themselves,
for the rights of all who are destitute.
9Speak up and judge fairly;
defend the rights of the poor and needy."

Epilogue: The Wife of Noble Character

10[e]A wife of noble character who can find?
She is worth far more than rubies.
11Her husband has full confidence in her
and lacks nothing of value.
12She brings him good, not harm,
all the days of her life.
13She selects wool and flax
and works with eager hands.
14She is like the merchant ships,
bringing her food from afar.
15She gets up while it is still dark;
she provides food for her family
and portions for her servant girls.
16She considers a field and buys it;
out of her earnings she plants a vineyard.
17She sets about her work vigorously;
her arms are strong for her tasks.
18She sees that her trading is profitable,
and her lamp does not go out at night.
19In her hand she holds the distaff
and grasps the spindle with her fingers.
20She opens her arms to the poor

[a]26 That is, the hyrax or rock badger
[b]31 Or *king secure against revolt* [c]1 Or *of Lemuel king of Massa, which* [d]2 Or */ the answer to my prayers* [e]10 Verses 10-31 are an acrostic, each verse beginning with a successive letter of the Hebrew alphabet.

and extends her hands to the
needy.
21 When it snows, she has no fear for
her household;
for all of them are clothed in
scarlet.
22 She makes coverings for her bed;
she is clothed in fine linen and
purple.
23 Her husband is respected at the city
gate,
where he takes his seat among the
elders of the land.
24 She makes linen garments and sells
them,
and supplies the merchants with
sashes.
25 She is clothed with strength and
dignity;
she can laugh at the days to come.
26 She speaks with wisdom,
and faithful instruction is on her
tongue.
27 She watches over the affairs of her
household
and does not eat the bread of
idleness.
28 Her children arise and call her
blessed;
her husband also, and he praises
her:
29 "Many women do noble things,
but you surpass them all."
30 Charm is deceptive, and beauty is
fleeting;
but a woman who fears the LORD
is to be praised.
31 Give her the reward she has earned,
and let her works bring her praise
at the city gate.

SHARPEN THE FOCUS

Maybe you've heard the little prayer that goes "Lord, I do not ask for an easy life, but for a strong heart." As we have seen in the book of Proverbs, we can define wisdom as "the ability to live life with skill, to apply to everyday life the knowledge of God and His will."

The selfishness Proverbs 30:11–16 condemns may nonetheless lure us by its promise that a self-focused life will be easy and satisfying. But if that's true, why are the world's emptiest people often those whose arms hold the most toys? The wise woman commended in Proverbs 31 accumulates property and possessions. Scripture never condemns wealth or the leisure to enjoy it. Rather, it condemns the focus on wealth, the myth that anything in creation can fill the place in our hearts our Creator has reserved for Himself.

The woman (or man) who reverences the Lord is the one whose heart can face life's challenges unafraid. That person, forgiven by Christ and righteous in Him, lives a rich, fulfilling life. That person leaves a legacy of Christlike love for others when he or she trades life here for the life hereafter. Let the Lord work out that kind of lifestyle, that kind of legacy, in you.

ECCLESIASTES

WEEK 51 • SATURDAY

Ecclesiastes 1:1—2:26

GET THE BIG PICTURE

The foolish learn through sad experience, if at all. The wise learn by watching the sad experiences of the foolish. (See Proverbs 21:11.) As we read Solomon's story of foolish living from the book of Ecclesiastes, our Lord gives us a chance to learn through Solomon's experiences. As you read, watch for the phrase *under the sun.* It clues us in to the perspective from which the author lived most of the events in this book—the viewpoint of the godless. If time is short, focus on Ecclesiastes 1:1–16.

Everything Is Meaningless

1 The words of the Teacher,[a] son of David, king in Jerusalem:

2 "Meaningless! Meaningless!"
says the Teacher.
"Utterly meaningless!
Everything is meaningless."

3 What does man gain from all his labor
at which he toils under the sun?
4 Generations come and generations go,
but the earth remains forever.
5 The sun rises and the sun sets,
and hurries back to where it rises.
6 The wind blows to the south
and turns to the north;
round and round it goes,
ever returning on its course.
7 All streams flow into the sea,
yet the sea is never full.
To the place the streams come from,
there they return again.
8 All things are wearisome,
more than one can say.
The eye never has enough of seeing,
nor the ear its fill of hearing.
9 What has been will be again,
what has been done will be done again;
there is nothing new under the sun.
10 Is there anything of which one can say,
"Look! This is something new"?
It was here already, long ago;
it was here before our time.
11 There is no remembrance of men of old,
and even those who are yet to come
will not be remembered
by those who follow.

Wisdom Is Meaningless

12 I, the Teacher, was king over Israel in
Jerusalem. 13 I devoted myself to study
and to explore by wisdom all that is
done under heaven. What a heavy burden God has laid on men! 14 I have seen
all the things that are done under the
sun; all of them are meaningless, a chasing after the wind.

[a] 1 Or *leader of the assembly;* also in verses 2 and 12

[15]What is twisted cannot be
straightened;
what is lacking cannot be counted.

[16]I thought to myself, "Look, I have
grown and increased in wisdom more
than anyone who has ruled over Jerusalem before me; I have experienced
much of wisdom and knowledge."
[17]Then I applied myself to the understanding of wisdom, and also of madness and folly, but I learned that this,
too, is a chasing after the wind.

[18]For with much wisdom comes much
sorrow;
the more knowledge, the more
grief.

Pleasures Are Meaningless

2 I thought in my heart, "Come
now, I will test you with pleasure to find out what is good." But that
also proved to be meaningless. [2]"Laughter," I said, "is foolish. And what does
pleasure accomplish?" [3]I tried cheering
myself with wine, and embracing
folly—my mind still guiding me with
wisdom. I wanted to see what was
worthwhile for men to do under heaven
during the few days of their lives.

[4]I undertook great projects: I built
houses for myself and planted vineyards. [5]I made gardens and parks and
planted all kinds of fruit trees in them.
[6]I made reservoirs to water groves of
flourishing trees. [7]I bought male and female slaves and had other slaves who
were born in my house. I also owned
more herds and flocks than anyone in
Jerusalem before me. [8]I amassed silver
and gold for myself, and the treasure of
kings and provinces. I acquired men
and women singers, and a harem[a] as
well—the delights of the heart of man.
[9]I became greater by far than anyone in
Jerusalem before me. In all this my wisdom stayed with me.

[10]I denied myself nothing my eyes
desired;
I refused my heart no pleasure.
My heart took delight in all my
work,
and this was the reward for all my
labor.
[11]Yet when I surveyed all that my
hands had done
and what I had toiled to achieve,
everything was meaningless, a
chasing after the wind;
nothing was gained under the
sun.

Wisdom and Folly Are Meaningless

[12]Then I turned my thoughts to
consider wisdom,
and also madness and folly.
What more can the king's successor
do
than what has already been done?
[13]I saw that wisdom is better than
folly,
just as light is better than
darkness.
[14]The wise man has eyes in his head,
while the fool walks in the
darkness;
but I came to realize
that the same fate overtakes them
both.

[15]Then I thought in my heart,

"The fate of the fool will overtake
me also.
What then do I gain by being
wise?"
I said in my heart,
"This too is meaningless."
[16]For the wise man, like the fool, will
not be long remembered;
in days to come both will be
forgotten.
Like the fool, the wise man too must
die!

Toil Is Meaningless

[17]So I hated life, because the work that
is done under the sun was grievous to
me. All of it is meaningless, a chasing
after the wind. [18]I hated all the things I
had toiled for under the sun, because I
must leave them to the one who comes

[a]*8* The meaning of the Hebrew for this phrase is uncertain.

after me. [19]And who knows whether he
will be a wise man or a fool? Yet he will
have control over all the work into
which I have poured my effort and skill
under the sun. This too is meaningless.
[20]So my heart began to despair over all
my toilsome labor under the sun. [21]For
a man may do his work with wisdom,
knowledge and skill, and then he must
leave all he owns to someone who has
not worked for it. This too is meaningless and a great misfortune. [22]What does
a man get for all the toil and anxious
striving with which he labors under the
sun? [23]All his days his work is pain and
grief; even at night his mind does not
rest. This too is meaningless.
[24]A man can do nothing better than to
eat and drink and find satisfaction in his
work. This too, I see, is from the hand
of God, [25]for without him, who can eat
or find enjoyment? [26]To the man who
pleases him, God gives wisdom, knowledge and happiness, but to the sinner
he gives the task of gathering and storing up wealth to hand it over to the one
who pleases God. This too is meaningless, a chasing after the wind.

SHARPEN THE FOCUS

"What does life mean? What's its point?" Ecclesiastes looks at these questions and at the answers usually given by people who do not acknowledge the Lord.

The author of Ecclesiastes, most likely Solomon, seems to have spent some of his life in a quest for meaning outside a relationship with God. He threw himself into human wisdom and philosophy (Ecclesiastes 1:12–18). He chased after pleasure (Ecclesiastes 2:1–3). He gave himself to accomplishments and to accumulating wealth (Ecclesiastes 2:4–17). He let his work consume him (Ecclesiastes 2:18–23). But each approach to life drew the same verdict—"meaningless."

"How depressing!" you say? Yes, it is. But life "under the sun" is not all we have. As Christ's own blood-bought brothers and sisters, we stand at the mouth of His empty tomb. We, sinners all, stand forgiven and restored to His family. That perspective changes everything.

Knowing our Savior's love, we can take each new day as a gift from Him. We can enjoy life's simple pleasures—eating, drinking, working (Ecclesiastes 2:24). Without Him, true joy escapes us (Ecclesiastes 2:25). But in the sunshine of His smile, even dark days reflect the beauty of His love.

WEEK 52 • MONDAY

Ecclesiastes 3:1—4:16

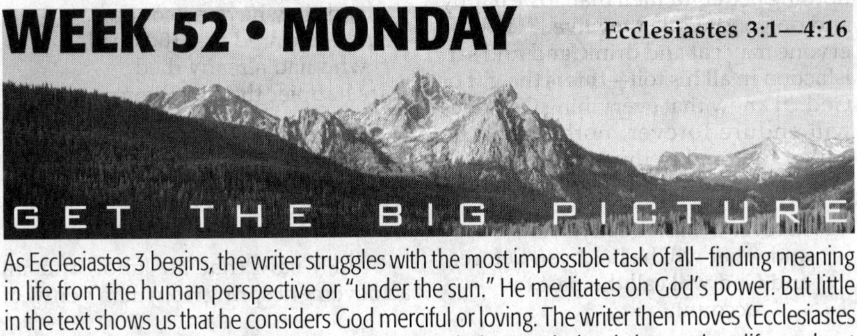

GET THE BIG PICTURE

As Ecclesiastes 3 begins, the writer struggles with the most impossible task of all—finding meaning in life from the human perspective or "under the sun." He meditates on God's power. But little in the text shows us that he considers God merciful or loving. The writer then moves (Ecclesiastes 4) to the implications of a meaningless life. Death, he concludes, is better than life, and not ever having been born would be best of all. If time is short, focus on Ecclesiastes 3:1–22.

A Time for Everything

3 There is a time for everything,
and a season for every activity
under heaven:

2 a time to be born and a time to
die,
a time to plant and a time to
uproot,
3 a time to kill and a time to heal,
a time to tear down and a time to
build,
4 a time to weep and a time to
laugh,
a time to mourn and a time to
dance,
5 a time to scatter stones and a time
to gather them,
a time to embrace and a time to
refrain,
6 a time to search and a time to give
up,
a time to keep and a time to throw
away,
7 a time to tear and a time to mend,
a time to be silent and a time to
speak,
8 a time to love and a time to hate,
a time for war and a time for
peace.

9What does the worker gain from his
toil? 10I have seen the burden God has
laid on men. 11He has made everything
beautiful in its time. He has also set eternity in the hearts of men; yet they cannot fathom what God has done from
beginning to end. 12I know that there is
nothing better for men than to be happy
and do good while they live. 13That everyone may eat and drink, and find satisfaction in all his toil—this is the gift of
God. 14I know that everything God does
will endure forever; nothing can be
added to it and nothing taken from it.
God does it so that men will revere him.

15Whatever is has already been,
and what will be has been before;
and God will call the past to
account.[a]

16And I saw something else under the
sun:

In the place of judgment—
wickedness was there,
in the place of justice—
wickedness was there.

17I thought in my heart,
"God will bring to judgment
both the righteous and the
wicked,
for there will be a time for every
activity,
a time for every deed."

18I also thought, "As for men, God tests
them so that they may see that they are
like the animals. 19Man's fate is like that
of the animals; the same fate awaits
them both: As one dies, so dies the other.
All have the same breath[b]; man has no
advantage over the animal. Everything
is meaningless. 20All go to the same
place; all come from dust, and to dust all
return. 21Who knows if the spirit of man
rises upward and if the spirit of the
animal[c] goes down into the earth?"

22So I saw that there is nothing better
for a man than to enjoy his work, because that is his lot. For who can bring
him to see what will happen after him?

Oppression, Toil, Friendlessness

4 Again I looked and saw all the
oppression that was taking place
under the sun:

I saw the tears of the oppressed—
and they have no comforter;
power was on the side of their
oppressors—
and they have no comforter.
2 And I declared that the dead,
who had already died,
are happier than the living,
who are still alive.
3 But better than both
is he who has not yet been,
who has not seen the evil
that is done under the sun.

4And I saw that all labor and all
achievement spring from man's envy of

[a]15 Or *God calls back the past* [b]19 Or *spirit*
[c]21 Or *Who knows the spirit of man, which rises upward, or the spirit of the animal, which*

his neighbor. This too is meaningless, a chasing after the wind.

5 The fool folds his hands
and ruins himself.
6 Better one handful with
tranquillity
than two handfuls with toil
and chasing after the wind.

7 Again I saw something meaningless under the sun:

8 There was a man all alone;
he had neither son nor brother.
There was no end to his toil,
yet his eyes were not content with
his wealth.
"For whom am I toiling," he asked,
"and why am I depriving myself
of enjoyment?"
This too is meaningless—
a miserable business!

9 Two are better than one,
because they have a good return
for their work:
10 If one falls down,
his friend can help him up.
But pity the man who falls
and has no one to help him up!
11 Also, if two lie down together, they
will keep warm.
But how can one keep warm
alone?
12 Though one may be overpowered,
two can defend themselves.
A cord of three strands is not quickly
broken.

Advancement Is Meaningless

13 Better a poor but wise youth than an
old but foolish king who no longer
knows how to take warning. 14 The
youth may have come from prison to
the kingship, or he may have been born
in poverty within his kingdom. 15 I saw
that all who lived and walked under the
sun followed the youth, the king's successor. 16 There was no end to all the
people who were before them. But
those who came later were not pleased
with the successor. This too is meaningless, a chasing after the wind.

SHARPEN THE FOCUS

Does it sometimes seem that your life has become one long "To Do" list? The first eight verses of Ecclesiastes make even being born and dying one more thing on the list of life's tasks. Life "under the sun," life lived apart from God in Jesus Christ, can bring the shroud of drudgery and meaninglessness even to times of dancing, hugging, and peace.

For those of us who live in the light of the Son of God who came to earth to share our burdens and to die for our sins, life in this world is something of a warm-up activity, a practice run for the grand celebration we will enjoy throughout eternity. Those who do not know Jesus ask, "Is this all there is?" And without Christ, the answer is, "Yes." Hope dies as surely as leaves on an unwatered plant dry up and drop off. We can enjoy life's times to laugh. We can grieve in life's times to mourn. We find meaning in all of life in Jesus, but only in Jesus.

So, what about the children in your neighborhood who don't know the love of Jesus? How about that co-worker at your shop whose family laughs and mourns without Chirst? Pray and think about those you know who need the Gospel. Then plan a winsome witness.

WEEK 52 • TUESDAY

Ecclesiastes 5:1—6:12

How tightly do you hold your toys? As a child, did you share your building blocks or Legos? As a teenager, did you let your sister borrow your favorite sweaters? your best sweater? Who may use your car? your tools? your books? Are your money and your possessions means to an end–or ends in themselves? Ask yourself those questions as you read now. If time is short, focus on Ecclesiastes 5:1–20.

Stand in Awe of God

5 Guard your steps when you go to the house of God. Go near to listen rather than to offer the sacrifice of fools, who do not know that they do wrong.

2 Do not be quick with your mouth,
do not be hasty in your heart
to utter anything before God.
God is in heaven
and you are on earth,
so let your words be few.
3 As a dream comes when there are many cares,
so the speech of a fool when there are many words.

4 When you make a vow to God, do
not delay in fulfilling it. He has no pleasure in fools; fulfill your vow. 5 It is better not to vow than to make a vow and
not fulfill it. 6 Do not let your mouth lead
you into sin. And do not protest to the
⌞temple⌟ messenger, "My vow was a mistake." Why should God be angry at
what you say and destroy the work of
your hands? 7 Much dreaming and
many words are meaningless. Therefore
stand in awe of God.

Riches Are Meaningless

8 If you see the poor oppressed in a
district, and justice and rights denied,
do not be surprised at such things; for
one official is eyed by a higher one, and
over them both are others higher still.
9 The increase from the land is taken by
all; the king himself profits from the
fields.

10 Whoever loves money never has money enough;
whoever loves wealth is never satisfied with his income.
This too is meaningless.

11 As goods increase,
so do those who consume them.
And what benefit are they to the owner
except to feast his eyes on them?

12 The sleep of a laborer is sweet,
whether he eats little or much,
but the abundance of a rich man permits him no sleep.

13 I have seen a grievous evil under the sun:

wealth hoarded to the harm of its owner,
14 or wealth lost through some misfortune,
so that when he has a son
there is nothing left for him.
15 Naked a man comes from his mother's womb,
and as he comes, so he departs.
He takes nothing from his labor
that he can carry in his hand.

16 This too is a grievous evil:

As a man comes, so he departs,
and what does he gain,
since he toils for the wind?

[17] All his days he eats in darkness,
with great frustration, affliction
and anger.

[18] Then I realized that it is good and
proper for a man to eat and drink, and
to find satisfaction in his toilsome labor
under the sun during the few days of
life God has given him—for this is his
lot. [19] Moreover, when God gives any
man wealth and possessions, and enables him to enjoy them, to accept his lot
and be happy in his work—this is a gift
of God. [20] He seldom reflects on the days
of his life, because God keeps him occupied with gladness of heart.

6 I have seen another evil under
the sun, and it weighs heavily on
men: [2] God gives a man wealth, possessions and honor, so that he lacks nothing his heart desires, but God does not
enable him to enjoy them, and a
stranger enjoys them instead. This is
meaningless, a grievous evil.

[3] A man may have a hundred children
and live many years; yet no matter how
long he lives, if he cannot enjoy his
prosperity and does not receive proper
burial, I say that a stillborn child is better off than he. [4] It comes without meaning, it departs in darkness, and in
darkness its name is shrouded. [5] Though
it never saw the sun or knew anything,
it has more rest than does that man—
[6] even if he lives a thousand years twice
over but fails to enjoy his prosperity. Do
not all go to the same place?

[7] All man's efforts are for his mouth,
yet his appetite is never satisfied.
[8] What advantage has a wise man
over a fool?
What does a poor man gain
by knowing how to conduct
himself before others?
[9] Better what the eye sees
than the roving of the appetite.
This too is meaningless,
a chasing after the wind.

[10] Whatever exists has already been
named,
and what man is has been
known;
no man can contend
with one who is stronger than he.
[11] The more the words,
the less the meaning,
and how does that profit anyone?

[12] For who knows what is good for a
man in life, during the few and meaningless days he passes through like a
shadow? Who can tell him what will
happen under the sun after he is gone?

SHARPEN THE FOCUS

"What happened to the food we took them yesterday? We spent nearly $100?" The chairperson of the church social ministry committee shouted the words as if in accusation. Newly concerned about the hunger in a nearby neighborhood, the committee met surprises several times a week. The reason behind this surprise shamed the committee, truth be told. "The neighbors upstairs were hungry, and we had all the food you gave us," the mom explained when she heard the committee's question, "How could we *not* share?" Social workers report it again and again. The poor often share more freely than those of us who have so much. Why? Maybe because they know how hunger feels.

Solomon makes another good point in Ecclesiastes 5:8–20. The more we accumulate and the tighter we cling to it, the less joy we derive from all we own. We will long for more, always more (Ecclesiastes 5:10).

As someone has pointed out, there will always be more requests than resources. And yet, who of us could claim to be innocent of all selfishness, covetousness, and greed? Praise God that our Jesus gave up everything, including His life, to pay for all our sins. And praise Him, too, that He empowers us to live lives of generosity and joy. ☼

WEEK 52 • WEDNESDAY

Eccl. 7:1—8:17

When all was still, and it was midnight,
Your almighty Word, O Lord,
descended from the royal throne.

That's how part of one of the introits appointed for Christmas Eve reads. Today's chapters from Ecclesiastes describe the "midnight" that Jesus Christ came to scatter. As you read, look for evidence that this darkness held all human beings hostage. If time is short, focus on Ecclesiastes 7:19–29.

Wisdom

7 A good name is better than fine
perfume,
and the day of death better than
the day of birth.
2 It is better to go to a house of
mourning
than to go to a house of feasting,
for death is the destiny of every man;
the living should take this to
heart.
3 Sorrow is better than laughter,
because a sad face is good for the
heart.
4 The heart of the wise is in the house
of mourning,
but the heart of fools is in the
house of pleasure.
5 It is better to heed a wise man's
rebuke
than to listen to the song of fools.
6 Like the crackling of thorns under
the pot,
so is the laughter of fools.
This too is meaningless.

7 Extortion turns a wise man into a
fool,
and a bribe corrupts the heart.

8 The end of a matter is better than its
beginning,
and patience is better than pride.
9 Do not be quickly provoked in your
spirit,
for anger resides in the lap of
fools.

10 Do not say, "Why were the old days
better than these?"
For it is not wise to ask such
questions.

11 Wisdom, like an inheritance, is a
good thing
and benefits those who see the sun.
12 Wisdom is a shelter
as money is a shelter,
but the advantage of knowledge is
this:
that wisdom preserves the life of
its possessor.

13 Consider what God has done:

Who can straighten
what he has made crooked?
14 When times are good, be happy;
but when times are bad, consider:
God has made the one
as well as the other.
Therefore, a man cannot discover
anything about his future.

15 In this meaningless life of mine I
have seen both of these:

a righteous man perishing in his
righteousness,
and a wicked man living long in
his wickedness.
16 Do not be overrighteous,

neither be overwise—
why destroy yourself?
17 Do not be overwicked,
and do not be a fool—
why die before your time?
18 It is good to grasp the one
and not let go of the other.
The man who fears God will avoid
all ⌊extremes⌋.[a]
19 Wisdom makes one wise man more
powerful
than ten rulers in a city.
20 There is not a righteous man on
earth
who does what is right and never
sins.

21 Do not pay attention to every word
people say,
or you may hear your servant
cursing you—
22 for you know in your heart
that many times you yourself
have cursed others.

23 All this I tested by wisdom and I
said,

"I am determined to be wise"—
but this was beyond me.
24 Whatever wisdom may be,
it is far off and most profound—
who can discover it?
25 So I turned my mind to understand,
to investigate and to search out
wisdom and the scheme of
things
and to understand the stupidity of
wickedness
and the madness of folly.

26 I find more bitter than death
the woman who is a snare,
whose heart is a trap
and whose hands are chains.
The man who pleases God will
escape her,
but the sinner she will ensnare.

27 "Look," says the Teacher,[b] "this is
what I have discovered:

"Adding one thing to another to
discover the scheme of
things—
28 while I was still searching
but not finding—
I found one ⌊upright⌋ man among a
thousand,
but not one ⌊upright⌋ woman
among them all.
29 This only have I found:
God made mankind upright,
but men have gone in search of
many schemes."

8 Who is like the wise man?
Who knows the explanation of
things?
Wisdom brightens a man's face
and changes its hard appearance.

Obey the King

2 Obey the king's command, I say, because you took an oath before God. 3 Do
not be in a hurry to leave the king's
presence. Do not stand up for a bad
cause, for he will do whatever he
pleases. 4 Since a king's word is supreme,
who can say to him, "What are you doing?"

5 Whoever obeys his command will
come to no harm,
and the wise heart will know the
proper time and procedure.
6 For there is a proper time and
procedure for every matter,
though a man's misery weighs
heavily upon him.

7 Since no man knows the future,
who can tell him what is to come?
8 No man has power over the wind to
contain it[c];
so no one has power over the day
of his death.
As no one is discharged in time of
war,
so wickedness will not release
those who practice it.

9 All this I saw, as I applied my mind
to everything done under the sun.
There is a time when a man lords it over
others to his own[d] hurt. 10 Then too, I saw

[a] 18 Or *will follow them both* [b] 27 Or *leader of the assembly* [c] 8 Or *over his spirit to retain it* [d] 9 Or *to their*

the wicked buried—those who used to
come and go from the holy place and
receive praise[a] in the city where they
did this. This too is meaningless.
[11]When the sentence for a crime is not
quickly carried out, the hearts of the
people are filled with schemes to do
wrong. [12]Although a wicked man commits a hundred crimes and still lives a
long time, I know that it will go better
with God-fearing men, who are reverent before God. [13]Yet because the wicked
do not fear God, it will not go well with
them, and their days will not lengthen
like a shadow.
[14]There is something else meaningless
that occurs on earth: righteous men
who get what the wicked deserve, and
wicked men who get what the righteous
deserve. This too, I say, is meaningless.
[15]So I commend the enjoyment of life,
because nothing is better for a man under the sun than to eat and drink and be
glad. Then joy will accompany him in
his work all the days of the life God has
given him under the sun.
[16]When I applied my mind to know
wisdom and to observe man's labor on
earth—his eyes not seeing sleep day or
night— [17]then I saw all that God has
done. No one can comprehend what
goes on under the sun. Despite all his
efforts to search it out, man cannot
discover its meaning. Even if a wise man
claims he knows, he cannot really comprehend it.

[a]*10* Some Hebrew manuscripts and Septuagint (Aquila); most Hebrew manuscripts *and are forgotten*

SHARPEN THE FOCUS

"I am determined to be wise—but this was beyond me," wrote Solomon (Ecclesiastes 7:23). We sit up and take notice because Solomon said it. Solomon, the statesman, writer, builder. Solomon, whose wisdom spread his fame throughout the ancient world (1 Kings 10:1–13). This Solomon admits that true wisdom lay beyond his grasp.

When we remember what true wisdom is, we see that Solomon's words aren't false modesty. Wisdom, remember, involves the ability to apply to everyday life the knowledge of God and His will. Solomon admits he couldn't do it—neither can we. Ecclesiastes 7:20 reminds us, "There is not a righteous man on earth who does what is right and never sins." None of this is God's fault. He "made [us] upright, but [we] have gone in search of many schemes" (Ecclesiastes 7:29). Solomon could diagnose the problem, but he had no remedy.

We could not achieve wisdom. We could not be right in God's sight. So God's Word, God's Wisdom, God's Righteous One came to us. The Lord Jesus abandoned His robe of glory for a mantle of humility. He exchanged His throne for a manger, then a cross, and then a tomb. For us, He transformed death to life. Rejoice in that, child of God, now and forever!

WEEK 52 • THURSDAY

Ecclesiastes 9:1—10:20

GET THE BIG PICTURE

From where the writer of Ecclesiastes stands, "under the sun," he considers the outcome of individual lives. While wisdom is better than foolishness, the wise and foolish alike are headed for the cemetery at life's end. Much of the time, living wisely keeps a person out of trouble, but not always. As you read, think about what your life would be like without the hope of eternity. If time is short, focus on Ecclesiastes 9:1–18.

A Common Destiny for All

9 So I reflected on all this and concluded that the righteous and
the wise and what they do are in God's
hands, but no man knows whether love
or hate awaits him. 2All share a common
destiny—the righteous and the wicked,
the good and the bad,[a] the clean and the
unclean, those who offer sacrifices and
those who do not.

As it is with the good man,
so with the sinner;
as it is with those who take oaths,
so with those who are afraid to
take them.

3This is the evil in everything that
happens under the sun: The same destiny overtakes all. The hearts of men,
moreover, are full of evil and there is
madness in their hearts while they live,
and afterward they join the dead. 4Any-
one who is among the living has
hope[b]—even a live dog is better off than
a dead lion!

5For the living know that they will
die,
but the dead know nothing;
they have no further reward,
and even the memory of them is
forgotten.
6Their love, their hate
and their jealousy have long since
vanished;
never again will they have a part
in anything that happens under
the sun.

7Go, eat your food with gladness, and
drink your wine with a joyful heart, for
it is now that God favors what you do.
8Always be clothed in white, and always
anoint your head with oil. 9Enjoy life
with your wife, whom you love, all the
days of this meaningless life that God
has given you under the sun— all your
meaningless days. For this is your lot in
life and in your toilsome labor under the
sun. 10Whatever your hand finds to do,
do it with all your might, for in the
grave,[c] where you are going, there is
neither working nor planning nor
knowledge nor wisdom.

11I have seen something else under
the sun:

The race is not to the swift
or the battle to the strong,
nor does food come to the wise
or wealth to the brilliant
or favor to the learned;
but time and chance happen to
them all.

12Moreover, no man knows when his
hour will come:

As fish are caught in a cruel net,
or birds are taken in a snare,
so men are trapped by evil times
that fall unexpectedly upon them.

Wisdom Better Than Folly

13I also saw under the sun this example of wisdom that greatly impressed
me: 14There was once a small city with
only a few people in it. And a powerful
king came against it, surrounded it and
built huge siegeworks against it. 15Now
there lived in that city a man poor but
wise, and he saved the city by his wisdom. But nobody remembered that
poor man. 16So I said, "Wisdom is better
than strength." But the poor man's wisdom is despised, and his words are no
longer heeded.

17The quiet words of the wise are
more to be heeded
than the shouts of a ruler of fools.
18Wisdom is better than weapons of
war,
but one sinner destroys much
good.

[a]2 Septuagint (Aquila), Vulgate and Syriac; Hebrew does not have *and the bad.* [b]4 Or *What then is to be chosen? With all who live, there is hope* [c]10 Hebrew *Sheol*

10 As dead flies give perfume a bad smell,
so a little folly outweighs wisdom and honor.
2 The heart of the wise inclines to the right,
but the heart of the fool to the left.
3 Even as he walks along the road,
the fool lacks sense
and shows everyone how stupid he is.
4 If a ruler's anger rises against you,
do not leave your post;
calmness can lay great errors to rest.

5 There is an evil I have seen under the sun,
the sort of error that arises from a ruler:
6 Fools are put in many high positions,
while the rich occupy the low ones.
7 I have seen slaves on horseback,
while princes go on foot like slaves.

8 Whoever digs a pit may fall into it;
whoever breaks through a wall may be bitten by a snake.
9 Whoever quarries stones may be injured by them;
whoever splits logs may be endangered by them.
10 If the ax is dull
and its edge unsharpened,
more strength is needed
but skill will bring success.

11 If a snake bites before it is charmed,
there is no profit for the charmer.
12 Words from a wise man's mouth are gracious,
but a fool is consumed by his own lips.
13 At the beginning his words are folly;
at the end they are wicked madness—
14 and the fool multiplies words.

No one knows what is coming—
who can tell him what will happen after him?
15 A fool's work wearies him;
he does not know the way to town.

16 Woe to you, O land whose king was a servant[a]
and whose princes feast in the morning.
17 Blessed are you, O land whose king is of noble birth
and whose princes eat at a proper time—
for strength and not for drunkenness.
18 If a man is lazy, the rafters sag;
if his hands are idle, the house leaks.

19 A feast is made for laughter,
and wine makes life merry,
but money is the answer for everything.

20 Do not revile the king even in your thoughts,
or curse the rich in your bedroom,
because a bird of the air may carry your words,
and a bird on the wing may report what you say.

[a]16 Or *king is a child*

SHARPEN THE FOCUS

Cynics and unbelievers have always tried to talk the rest of us out of belief in life after death. They use logical arguments and scientific language. But no society has been able to exist for very long without some kind of hope of life after death. The writer of Ecclesiastes tells us why no one, no matter how influential, has yet erased our "superstitions": God has "set eternity in [our] hearts" (Ecclesiastes 3:11).

Although many people have suppressed that truth, we know that our life story, begun here on earth, will continue without end. But will Judgment Day dawn in a place of pleasure or pain? From a perspective "under the sun," no one can tell. Ecclesiastes 9 makes it clear: we can't judge the truth of God's love for anyone by looking at outward circumstances.

You may be rich or poor. You may be healthy or suffering from a frightening disease. You may have many friends or no friends. Someone looking at your life from the outside cannot tell for sure anything about your eternal destiny or about whether God smiles or frowns upon you right now.

But God wants you to be confident of your place in His eternal home through Jesus. Read 1 John 5:11–13 as you talk to God about eternity. ☼

When human pursuits become ends unto themselves, life seems pointless and unpredictable. But in chapter 12 of Ecclesiastes, the perspective changes. Solomon looks back over the course of his life from a viewpoint above the sun—from the Lord's perspective. As you read, ask yourself what Solomon concludes. If time is short, focus on Ecclesiastes 12:1–14.

Bread Upon the Waters

11 Cast your bread upon the waters,
for after many days you will find it again.
2 Give portions to seven, yes to eight,
for you do not know what disaster may come upon the land.

3 If clouds are full of water,
they pour rain upon the earth.
Whether a tree falls to the south or to the north,
in the place where it falls, there will it lie.
4 Whoever watches the wind will not plant;
whoever looks at the clouds will not reap.

5 As you do not know the path of the wind,
or how the body is formed[a] in a mother's womb,
so you cannot understand the work of God,
the Maker of all things.

6 Sow your seed in the morning,
and at evening let not your hands be idle,
for you do not know which will succeed,
whether this or that,
or whether both will do equally well.

Remember Your Creator While Young

7 Light is sweet,
and it pleases the eyes to see the sun.
8 However many years a man may live,
let him enjoy them all.

[a]5 Or *know how life* (or *the spirit*) / *enters the body being formed*

But let him remember the days of
darkness,
for they will be many.
Everything to come is
meaningless.
[9]Be happy, young man, while you are
young,
and let your heart give you joy in
the days of your youth.
Follow the ways of your heart
and whatever your eyes see,
but know that for all these things
God will bring you to judgment.
[10]So then, banish anxiety from your
heart
and cast off the troubles of your
body,
for youth and vigor are
meaningless.

12 Remember your Creator
in the days of your youth,
before the days of trouble come
and the years approach when you
will say,
"I find no pleasure in them"—
[2]before the sun and the light
and the moon and the stars grow
dark,
and the clouds return after the
rain;
[3]when the keepers of the house
tremble,
and the strong men stoop,
when the grinders cease because
they are few,
and those looking through the
windows grow dim;
[4]when the doors to the street are
closed
and the sound of grinding
fades;
when men rise up at the sound of
birds,
but all their songs grow faint;
[5]when men are afraid of heights
and of dangers in the streets;
when the almond tree blossoms
and the grasshopper drags himself
along
and desire no longer is stirred.
Then man goes to his eternal home
and mourners go about the streets.
[6]Remember him—before the silver
cord is severed,
or the golden bowl is broken;
before the pitcher is shattered at the
spring,
or the wheel broken at the well,
[7]and the dust returns to the ground it
came from,
and the spirit returns to God who
gave it.

[8]"Meaningless! Meaningless!" says
the Teacher.[a]
"Everything is meaningless!"

The Conclusion of the Matter

[9]Not only was the Teacher wise, but
also he imparted knowledge to the
people. He pondered and searched out
and set in order many proverbs. [10]The
Teacher searched to find just the right
words, and what he wrote was upright
and true.
[11]The words of the wise are like goads,
their collected sayings like firmly em-
bedded nails—given by one Shepherd.
[12]Be warned, my son, of anything in addition to them.
Of making many books there is no
end, and much study wearies the body.

[13]Now all has been heard;
here is the conclusion of the
matter:
Fear God and keep his
commandments,
for this is the whole ⌞duty⌟ of man.
[14]For God will bring every deed into
judgment,
including every hidden thing,
whether it is good or evil.

[a]8 Or *the leader of the assembly;* also in verses 9 and 10

SHARPEN THE FOCUS

All the wistful pieces of advice to young people and the amazing description of old age in Ecclesiastes 12:1–7 lead to the conclusion that the writer's life was near its end.

It would seem that in the end the Lord led Solomon to repent of his idolatry and the other sins that grew out of it. Solomon, the king, came at last to see the wisdom of the Shepherd (Ecclesiastes 12:11).

Solomon had at one point in life thrown his father's piety overboard (1 Kings 11:1–40). But now, perhaps, he took comfort in his father's words, his father's God: "The LORD is my shepherd, I shall not be in want . . . Even though I walk through the valley of the shadow of death, I will fear no evil, for You are with me" (Psalm 23:1, 4).

Where are we in relationship to the path of wisdom? We need not wait until we near death to take stock. By God's grace, we can apply His wisdom earlier and with more consistency than Solomon. Let God's Spirit examine your heart today and convict you of any spiritually dangerous attitudes in your heart.

Then, confessing them, receive your Lord's pardon and power. Pray Psalm 23 with confidence as you go about the rest of your day in peace.

SONG OF SONGS

WEEK 52 • SATURDAY

Song of Songs 1:1—3:11

Like a series of snapshots in a young couple's photo album, chapters 1–3 of the Song of Songs show us the courtship of Solomon and his bride. She is a Shulamite, a country girl whose family owns the vineyard in which she and her brothers work. The king falls head-over-heels in love with her, and their wedding procession is a sight to behold (Song of Songs 3:6–11)! If time is short, focus on Song of Songs 1:1–17.

1 Solomon's Song of Songs.

Beloved[a]

2 Let him kiss me with the kisses of his mouth—
for your love is more delightful than wine.
3 Pleasing is the fragrance of your perfumes;
your name is like perfume poured out.
No wonder the maidens love you!
4 Take me away with you—let us hurry!
Let the king bring me into his chambers.

Friends

We rejoice and delight in you[b];
we will praise your love more than wine.

Beloved

How right they are to adore you!

5 Dark am I, yet lovely,
O daughters of Jerusalem,
dark like the tents of Kedar,
like the tent curtains of Solomon.[c]
6 Do not stare at me because I am dark,
because I am darkened by the sun.
My mother's sons were angry with me
and made me take care of the vineyards;
my own vineyard I have neglected.
7 Tell me, you whom I love, where you graze your flock
and where you rest your sheep at midday.
Why should I be like a veiled woman
beside the flocks of your friends?

Friends

8 If you do not know, most beautiful of women,
follow the tracks of the sheep
and graze your young goats
by the tents of the shepherds.

[a]Primarily on the basis of the gender of the Hebrew pronouns used, male and female speakers are indicated in the margins by the captions *Lover* and *Beloved* respectively. The words of others are marked *Friends*. In some instances the divisions and their captions are debatable. [b]4 The Hebrew is masculine singular. [c]5 Or *Salma*

Lover

[9]I liken you, my darling, to a mare
harnessed to one of the chariots of
Pharaoh.
[10]Your cheeks are beautiful with
earrings,
your neck with strings of jewels.
[11]We will make you earrings of gold,
studded with silver.

Beloved

[12]While the king was at his table,
my perfume spread its fragrance.
[13]My lover is to me a sachet of myrrh
resting between my breasts.
[14]My lover is to me a cluster of henna
blossoms
from the vineyards of En Gedi.

Lover

[15]How beautiful you are, my darling!
Oh, how beautiful!
Your eyes are doves.

Beloved

[16]How handsome you are, my lover!
Oh, how charming!
And our bed is verdant.

Lover

[17]The beams of our house are cedars;
our rafters are firs.

Beloved[a]

2 I am a rose[b] of Sharon,
a lily of the valleys.

Lover

[2]Like a lily among thorns
is my darling among the maidens.

Beloved

[3]Like an apple tree among the trees
of the forest
is my lover among the young men.
I delight to sit in his shade,
and his fruit is sweet to my taste.
[4]He has taken me to the banquet hall,
and his banner over me is love.
[5]Strengthen me with raisins,
refresh me with apples,
for I am faint with love.
[6]His left arm is under my head,
and his right arm embraces me.
[7]Daughters of Jerusalem, I charge
you
by the gazelles and by the does of
the field:
Do not arouse or awaken love
until it so desires.
[8]Listen! My lover!
Look! Here he comes,
leaping across the mountains,
bounding over the hills.
[9]My lover is like a gazelle or a young
stag.
Look! There he stands behind our
wall,
gazing through the windows,
peering through the lattice.
[10]My lover spoke and said to me,
"Arise, my darling,
my beautiful one, and come with
me.
[11]See! The winter is past;
the rains are over and gone.
[12]Flowers appear on the earth;
the season of singing has come,
the cooing of doves
is heard in our land.
[13]The fig tree forms its early fruit;
the blossoming vines spread their
fragrance.
Arise, come, my darling;
my beautiful one, come with me."

Lover

[14]My dove in the clefts of the rock,
in the hiding places on the
mountainside,
show me your face,
let me hear your voice;
for your voice is sweet,
and your face is lovely.
[15]Catch for us the foxes,
the little foxes
that ruin the vineyards,
our vineyards that are in bloom.

Beloved

[16]My lover is mine and I am his;
he browses among the lilies.

[a]1 Or *Lover* [b]1 Possibly a member of the crocus family

[17]Until the day breaks
and the shadows flee,
turn, my lover,
and be like a gazelle
or like a young stag
on the rugged hills.[a]

3 All night long on my bed
I looked for the one my heart loves;
I looked for him but did not find him.
[2]I will get up now and go about the city,
through its streets and squares;
I will search for the one my heart loves.
So I looked for him but did not find him.
[3]The watchmen found me
as they made their rounds in the city.
"Have you seen the one my heart loves?"
[4]Scarcely had I passed them
when I found the one my heart loves.
I held him and would not let him go
till I had brought him to my mother's house,
to the room of the one who conceived me.
[5]Daughters of Jerusalem, I charge you
by the gazelles and by the does of the field:
Do not arouse or awaken love
until it so desires.

[6]Who is this coming up from the desert
like a column of smoke,
perfumed with myrrh and incense
made from all the spices of the merchant?
[7]Look! It is Solomon's carriage,
escorted by sixty warriors,
the noblest of Israel,
[8]all of them wearing the sword,
all experienced in battle,
each with his sword at his side,
prepared for the terrors of the night.
[9]King Solomon made for himself the carriage;
he made it of wood from Lebanon.
[10]Its posts he made of silver,
its base of gold.
Its seat was upholstered with purple,
its interior lovingly inlaid
by[b] the daughters of Jerusalem.
[11]Come out, you daughters of Zion,
and look at King Solomon
wearing the crown,
the crown with which his mother crowned him
on the day of his wedding,
the day his heart rejoiced.

[a]17 Or *the hills of Bether* [b]10 Or *its inlaid interior a gift of love / from*

SHARPEN THE FOCUS

A society like ours, confused as it is about sexuality, scoffs at the kind of love Solomon pictures for us. Many in the church are afraid of or embarrassed by sexuality. Many in society are afraid of commitment or are dedicated to using sexuality selfishly. But the Song of Songs challenges all of this.

The Song pictures the love Christ has for His bride, the church. It also paints a portrait of sensual sexuality and the beautiful union our Creator had in mind when He gave Eve to Adam and instituted marriage. Solomon and his bride celebrate their emotional and physical union, their single-minded devotion and faithfulness to each other. God intends marriage to illustrate the oneness of Christ Jesus and His church. The New Testament consistently presents this view of marriage and sexuality, too (see Hebrews 13:4).

If you're married, what would you like to ask your Lord to do in the relationship between you and your spouse—emotionally and sexually? If you're single, what would you like to ask your Lord to do for you—emotionally and sexually? In either case, for what sexual sins do you need your Savior's forgiveness? ☼

WEEK 53 • MONDAY

Song of Songs 4:1—6:13

The wedding over, the Shulamite moves into the royal palace. While Solomon is away, his bride dreams about him knocking at the door, but in her dream she answers him too late (Song of Songs 5:2–6). In a panic, she searches Jerusalem for him (Song of Songs 5:7–8). When he returns to the city, he soothes her fears by repeating his pledges of love and praising her beauty (Song of Songs 6:4–7:10). As you read, think about God's love for His covenant people, Israel, and Christ's love for His bride, the Holy Christian Church. If time is short, focus on Song of Songs 4:1–16.

Lover

4 How beautiful you are, my darling!
Oh, how beautiful!
Your eyes behind your veil are doves.
Your hair is like a flock of goats
descending from Mount Gilead.
2 Your teeth are like a flock of sheep just shorn,
coming up from the washing.
Each has its twin;
not one of them is alone.
3 Your lips are like a scarlet ribbon;
your mouth is lovely.
Your temples behind your veil
are like the halves of a pomegranate.
4 Your neck is like the tower of David,
built with elegance[a];
on it hang a thousand shields,
all of them shields of warriors.
5 Your two breasts are like two fawns,
like twin fawns of a gazelle
that browse among the lilies.
6 Until the day breaks
and the shadows flee,
I will go to the mountain of myrrh
and to the hill of incense.
7 All beautiful you are, my darling;
there is no flaw in you.

8 Come with me from Lebanon, my bride,
come with me from Lebanon.
Descend from the crest of Amana,
from the top of Senir, the summit of Hermon,
from the lions' dens
and the mountain haunts of the leopards.
9 You have stolen my heart, my sister, my bride;
you have stolen my heart
with one glance of your eyes,
with one jewel of your necklace.
10 How delightful is your love, my sister, my bride!
How much more pleasing is your love than wine,
and the fragrance of your perfume than any spice!
11 Your lips drop sweetness as the honeycomb, my bride;

[a]4 The meaning of the Hebrew for this word is uncertain.

milk and honey are under your
tongue.
The fragrance of your garments is
like that of Lebanon.
12 You are a garden locked up, my
sister, my bride;
you are a spring enclosed, a sealed
fountain.
13 Your plants are an orchard of
pomegranates
with choice fruits,
with henna and nard,
14 nard and saffron,
calamus and cinnamon,
with every kind of incense tree,
with myrrh and aloes
and all the finest spices.
15 You are[a] a garden fountain,
a well of flowing water
streaming down from Lebanon.

Beloved

16 Awake, north wind,
and come, south wind!
Blow on my garden,
that its fragrance may spread
abroad.
Let my lover come into his garden
and taste its choice fruits.

Lover

5 I have come into my garden,
my sister, my bride;
I have gathered my myrrh with
my spice.
I have eaten my honeycomb and my
honey;
I have drunk my wine and my
milk.

Friends

Eat, O friends, and drink;
drink your fill, O lovers.

Beloved

2 I slept but my heart was awake.
Listen! My lover is knocking:
"Open to me, my sister, my darling,
my dove, my flawless one.
My head is drenched with dew,
my hair with the dampness of the
night."
3 I have taken off my robe—
must I put it on again?
I have washed my feet—
must I soil them again?
4 My lover thrust his hand through
the latch-opening;
my heart began to pound for him.
5 I arose to open for my lover,
and my hands dripped with
myrrh,
my fingers with flowing myrrh,
on the handles of the lock.
6 I opened for my lover,
but my lover had left; he was
gone.
My heart sank at his departure.[b]
I looked for him but did not find
him.
I called him but he did not answer.
7 The watchmen found me
as they made their rounds in the
city.
They beat me, they bruised me;
they took away my cloak,
those watchmen of the walls!
8 O daughters of Jerusalem, I charge
you—
if you find my lover,
what will you tell him?
Tell him I am faint with love.

Friends

9 How is your beloved better than
others,
most beautiful of women?
How is your beloved better than
others,
that you charge us so?

Beloved

10 My lover is radiant and ruddy,
outstanding among ten thousand.
11 His head is purest gold;
his hair is wavy
and black as a raven.
12 His eyes are like doves
by the water streams,
washed in milk,
mounted like jewels.
13 His cheeks are like beds of spice
yielding perfume.

[a]15 Or *I am* (spoken by the *Beloved*) [b]6 Or *heart had gone out to him when he spoke*

His lips are like lilies
dripping with myrrh.
14 His arms are rods of gold
set with chrysolite.
His body is like polished ivory
decorated with sapphires.[a]
15 His legs are pillars of marble
set on bases of pure gold.
His appearance is like Lebanon,
choice as its cedars.
16 His mouth is sweetness itself;
he is altogether lovely.
This is my lover, this my friend,
O daughters of Jerusalem.

Friends

6 Where has your lover gone,
most beautiful of women?
Which way did your lover turn,
that we may look for him with
you?

Beloved

2 My lover has gone down to his
garden,
to the beds of spices,
to browse in the gardens
and to gather lilies.
3 I am my lover's and my lover is
mine;
he browses among the lilies.

Lover

4 You are beautiful, my darling, as
Tirzah,
lovely as Jerusalem,
majestic as troops with banners.
5 Turn your eyes from me;
they overwhelm me.
Your hair is like a flock of goats
descending from Gilead.
6 Your teeth are like a flock of sheep
coming up from the washing.
Each has its twin,
not one of them is alone.
7 Your temples behind your veil
are like the halves of a
pomegranate.
8 Sixty queens there may be,
and eighty concubines,
and virgins beyond number;
9 but my dove, my perfect one, is
unique,
the only daughter of her mother,
the favorite of the one who bore
her.
The maidens saw her and called her
blessed;
the queens and concubines
praised her.

Friends

10 Who is this that appears like the
dawn,
fair as the moon, bright as the sun,
majestic as the stars in procession?

Lover

11 I went down to the grove of nut trees
to look at the new growth in the
valley,
to see if the vines had budded
or the pomegranates were in
bloom.
12 Before I realized it,
my desire set me among the royal
chariots of my people.[b]

Friends

13 Come back, come back,
O Shulammite;
come back, come back, that we
may gaze on you!

Lover

Why would you gaze on the
Shulammite
as on the dance of Mahanaim?

[a] 14 Or *lapis lazuli* [b] 12 Or *among the chariots of Amminadab*; or *among the chariots of the people of the prince*

SHARPEN THE FOCUS

Like a new bridegroom who sees no flaw in the one he loves, Jesus loves us with unending love. He sees us as beautiful (Song of Songs 4:1); flawless, perfect (Song of Songs 4:7; 5:2);

and unique (Song of Songs 6:9). His cross has made that identity possible for us. If you fully believed these things about yourself, what difference would that truth make in:

- your relationships with others in your family?
- your confidence in God's willingness to hear and answer your prayers?
- your attitudes toward those who don't know Christ?
- the care you take of your body?
- the quality of your worship life?

Solomon arrived home to find his new bride shaken by her dream and somewhat insecure in his love. He swept her off her feet and repeated words of approval and adoration again and again. So our Lord Jesus would assure us of His devotion to us, His commitment of eternal love.

WEEK 53 • TUESDAY

Song of Songs 7:1—8:14

Again today's reading can be understood on two levels. On the surface, we read the love story of Solomon and his bride, the Shulamite. On another level, we read the love of Christ for His church. Nothing can quench this love; no flood can drown it out (Song of Songs 8:7). Neither can anyone buy this love. But our Savior has given it freely to us through His cross and open tomb. As you read, ask your Lord to reveal more of His love to you. If time is short, focus on Song of Songs 7:11–8:14.

7 How beautiful your sandaled
feet,
O prince's daughter!
Your graceful legs are like jewels,
the work of a craftsman's hands.
2 Your navel is a rounded goblet
that never lacks blended wine.
Your waist is a mound of wheat
encircled by lilies.
3 Your breasts are like two fawns,
twins of a gazelle.
4 Your neck is like an ivory tower.
Your eyes are the pools of Heshbon
by the gate of Bath Rabbim.
Your nose is like the tower of
Lebanon
looking toward Damascus.
5 Your head crowns you like Mount
Carmel.
Your hair is like royal tapestry;
the king is held captive by its
tresses.
6 How beautiful you are and how
pleasing,
O love, with your delights!
7 Your stature is like that of the palm,
and your breasts like clusters of
fruit.
8 I said, "I will climb the palm tree;
I will take hold of its fruit."
May your breasts be like the clusters
of the vine,
the fragrance of your breath like
apples,

9 and your mouth like the best
wine.

Beloved

May the wine go straight to my
lover,
flowing gently over lips and
teeth.[a]
10 I belong to my lover,
and his desire is for me.
11 Come, my lover, let us go to the
countryside,
let us spend the night in the
villages.[b]
12 Let us go early to the vineyards
to see if the vines have budded,
if their blossoms have opened,
and if the pomegranates are in
bloom—
there I will give you my love.
13 The mandrakes send out their
fragrance,
and at our door is every delicacy,
both new and old,
that I have stored up for you, my
lover.

8 If only you were to me like a
brother,
who was nursed at my mother's
breasts!
Then, if I found you outside,
I would kiss you,
and no one would despise me.
2 I would lead you
and bring you to my mother's
house—
she who has taught me.
I would give you spiced wine to
drink,
the nectar of my pomegranates.
3 His left arm is under my head
and his right arm embraces me.
4 Daughters of Jerusalem, I charge
you:
Do not arouse or awaken love
until it so desires.

Friends

5 Who is this coming up from the
desert
leaning on her lover?

Beloved

Under the apple tree I roused you;
there your mother conceived you,
there she who was in labor gave
you birth.
6 Place me like a seal over your heart,
like a seal on your arm;
for love is as strong as death,
its jealousy[c] unyielding as the
grave.[d]
It burns like blazing fire,
like a mighty flame.[e]
7 Many waters cannot quench love;
rivers cannot wash it away.
If one were to give
all the wealth of his house for
love,
it[f] would be utterly scorned.

Friends

8 We have a young sister,
and her breasts are not yet grown.
What shall we do for our sister
for the day she is spoken for?
9 If she is a wall,
we will build towers of silver on
her.
If she is a door,
we will enclose her with panels of
cedar.

Beloved

10 I am a wall,
and my breasts are like towers.
Thus I have become in his eyes
like one bringing contentment.
11 Solomon had a vineyard in Baal
Hamon;
he let out his vineyard to tenants.
Each was to bring for its fruit
a thousand shekels[g] of silver.
12 But my own vineyard is mine to give;
the thousand shekels are for you,
O Solomon,
and two hundred[h] are for those
who tend its fruit.

[a] 9 Septuagint, Aquila, Vulgate and Syriac; Hebrew *lips of sleepers* [b] 11 Or *henna bushes* [c] 6 Or *ardor* [d] 6 Hebrew *Sheol* [e] 6 Or / *like the very flame of the* LORD [f] 7 Or *he* [g] 11 That is, about 25 pounds (about 11.5 kilograms); also in verse 12 [h] 12 That is, about 5 pounds (about 2.3 kilograms)

Lover

[13]You who dwell in the
gardens
with friends in attendance,
let me hear your voice!

Beloved

[14]Come away, my lover,
and be like a gazelle
or like a young stag
on the spice-laden mountains.

SHARPEN THE FOCUS

Several times in the Song of Songs we read of the bride pleading for her bridegroom to come to her. In today's reading, you heard her voice another of these pleas (Song of Songs 8:14). In Song of Songs 2:8–14, we read the bride's ecstatic and joyful description of the bridegroom's coming. Look back and reread that now, but as you read it, think about Jesus' second coming. The last day, Judgment Day, when our Lord will return to take His Bride, the Holy Christian Church, to Himself.

As we close each day, month and year of our lives, we can do so by praying, "Come, Lord Jesus" (Revelation 22:20). As we begin each new day, month and year on earth, we can do so clinging to His promise, "Yes, I am coming soon" (Revelation 22:20). Confident in His forgiving love, we await His return with joy and excitement. Come, Lord Jesus!

ISAIAH

WEEK 53 • WEDNESDAY

Isaiah 1:1—2:22

Judah at the time of Isaiah enjoyed many of the same blessings we do. But, much like us, the people of Judah had fallen for the temptation to grab the gifts and forget the Giver. Outwardly religious and financially rich, they were spiritually sick and morally bankrupt. If time is short, focus on Isaiah 1:1–20.

1 The vision concerning Judah and Jerusalem that Isaiah son of Amoz saw during the reigns of Uzziah, Jotham, Ahaz and Hezekiah, kings of Judah.

A Rebellious Nation

2 Hear, O heavens! Listen, O earth!
For the LORD has spoken:
"I reared children and brought them up,
but they have rebelled against me.
3 The ox knows his master,
the donkey his owner's manger,
but Israel does not know,
my people do not understand."
4 Ah, sinful nation,
a people loaded with guilt,
a brood of evildoers,
children given to corruption!
They have forsaken the LORD;
they have spurned the Holy One of Israel
and turned their backs on him.
5 Why should you be beaten anymore?
Why do you persist in rebellion?
Your whole head is injured,
your whole heart afflicted.
6 From the sole of your foot to the top of your head
there is no soundness—
only wounds and welts
and open sores,
not cleansed or bandaged
or soothed with oil.

7 Your country is desolate,
your cities burned with fire;
your fields are being stripped by foreigners
right before you,
laid waste as when overthrown by strangers.
8 The Daughter of Zion is left
like a shelter in a vineyard,
like a hut in a field of melons,
like a city under siege.
9 Unless the LORD Almighty
had left us some survivors,
we would have become like Sodom,
we would have been like Gomorrah.

10 Hear the word of the LORD,
you rulers of Sodom;
listen to the law of our God,
you people of Gomorrah!
11 "The multitude of your sacrifices—
what are they to me?" says the LORD.
"I have more than enough of burnt offerings,

of rams and the fat of fattened
animals;
I have no pleasure
in the blood of bulls and lambs
and goats.
12 When you come to appear before me,
who has asked this of you,
this trampling of my courts?
13 Stop bringing meaningless offerings!
Your incense is detestable to me.
New Moons, Sabbaths and
convocations—
I cannot bear your evil assemblies.
14 Your New Moon festivals and your
appointed feasts
my soul hates.
They have become a burden to me;
I am weary of bearing them.
15 When you spread out your hands in
prayer,
I will hide my eyes from you;
even if you offer many prayers,
I will not listen.
Your hands are full of blood;
16 wash and make yourselves clean.
Take your evil deeds
out of my sight!
Stop doing wrong,
17 learn to do right!
Seek justice,
encourage the oppressed.[a]
Defend the cause of the fatherless,
plead the case of the widow.

18 "Come now, let us reason together,"
says the LORD.
"Though your sins are like scarlet,
they shall be as white as snow;
though they are red as crimson,
they shall be like wool.
19 If you are willing and obedient,
you will eat the best from the
land;
20 but if you resist and rebel,
you will be devoured by the
sword."
For the mouth of the LORD
has spoken.

21 See how the faithful city
has become a harlot!
She once was full of justice;
righteousness used to dwell in
her—
but now murderers!
22 Your silver has become dross,
your choice wine is diluted with
water.
23 Your rulers are rebels,
companions of thieves;
they all love bribes
and chase after gifts.
They do not defend the cause of the
fatherless;
the widow's case does not come
before them.
24 Therefore the Lord, the LORD
Almighty,
the Mighty One of Israel, declares:
"Ah, I will get relief from my foes
and avenge myself on my
enemies.
25 I will turn my hand against you;
I will thoroughly purge away your
dross
and remove all your impurities.
26 I will restore your judges as in days
of old,
your counselors as at the
beginning.
Afterward you will be called
the City of Righteousness,
the Faithful City."

27 Zion will be redeemed with justice,
her penitent ones with
righteousness.
28 But rebels and sinners will both be
broken,
and those who forsake the LORD
will perish.
29 "You will be ashamed because of the
sacred oaks
in which you have delighted;
you will be disgraced because of the
gardens
that you have chosen.
30 You will be like an oak with fading
leaves,
like a garden without water.
31 The mighty man will become
tinder
and his work a spark;
both will burn together,
with no one to quench the fire."

[a]17 Or / *rebuke the oppressor*

The Mountain of the LORD

2 This is what Isaiah son of Amoz saw concerning Judah and Jerusalem:

[2]In the last days
the mountain of the LORD's temple
will be established
as chief among the mountains;
it will be raised above the hills,
and all nations will stream to it.
[3]Many peoples will come and say,
"Come, let us go up to the mountain
of the LORD,
to the house of the God of Jacob.
He will teach us his ways,
so that we may walk in his paths."
The law will go out from Zion,
the word of the LORD from
Jerusalem.
[4]He will judge between the nations
and will settle disputes for many
peoples.
They will beat their swords into
plowshares
and their spears into pruning
hooks.
Nation will not take up sword
against nation,
nor will they train for war
anymore.
[5]Come, O house of Jacob,
let us walk in the light of the LORD.

The Day of the LORD

[6]You have abandoned your people,
the house of Jacob.
They are full of superstitions from
the East;
they practice divination like the
Philistines
and clasp hands with pagans.
[7]Their land is full of silver and gold;
there is no end to their treasures.
Their land is full of horses;
there is no end to their chariots.
[8]Their land is full of idols;
they bow down to the work of
their hands,
to what their fingers have made.
[9]So man will be brought low
and mankind humbled—
do not forgive them.[a]
[10]Go into the rocks,
hide in the ground
from dread of the LORD
and the splendor of his majesty!
[11]The eyes of the arrogant man will be
humbled
and the pride of men brought low;
the LORD alone will be exalted in
that day.
[12]The LORD Almighty has a day in
store
for all the proud and lofty,
for all that is exalted
(and they will be humbled),
[13]for all the cedars of Lebanon, tall
and lofty,
and all the oaks of Bashan,
[14]for all the towering mountains
and all the high hills,
[15]for every lofty tower
and every fortified wall,
[16]for every trading ship[b]
and every stately vessel.
[17]The arrogance of man will be
brought low
and the pride of men humbled;
the LORD alone will be exalted in
that day,
[18] and the idols will totally disappear.
[19]Men will flee to caves in the rocks
and to holes in the ground
from dread of the LORD
and the splendor of his majesty,
when he rises to shake the earth.
[20]In that day men will throw away
to the rodents and bats
their idols of silver and idols of gold,
which they made to worship.
[21]They will flee to caverns in the rocks
and to the overhanging crags
from dread of the LORD
and the splendor of his majesty,
when he rises to shake the earth.
[22]Stop trusting in man,
who has but a breath in his nostrils.
Of what account is he?

[a]9 Or *not raise them up* [b]16 Hebrew *every ship of Tarshish*

Sharpen the Focus

They thought they could fool God. As long as they burned a little incense, mouthed a few prayers, brought a few sacrifices, the Lord would be satisfied. They thought they could pacify Him and then live as they pleased.

They were wrong. He saw through their masks. He knew all along about their deception. Like a bridegroom, madly in love with a childhood sweetheart, the Lord wanted to possess Judah solely. But the evidence had mounted up until no one could deny the truth—the bride was living like a prostitute. And the Bridegroom would not stand for it!

Remember the first commandment. "You shall have no other gods" (Exodus 20:3)? How easily we accuse ancient Israel. How glibly we deny that we bow to "foreign gods." How immediately our Bridegroom sees through our denials. What's first in *your* life? Your job? Pleasure? Your accomplishments? Your house? A dearly loved person? Your ministry? The approval of other people?

Why not accept your Lord's invitation in Isaiah 1:18 as you talk with Him about your relationship with Him right now?

Week 53 • Thursday

Isaiah 3:1—4:6

Get the Big Picture

Ancient Israel ignored her godly kings and disobeyed the priests and prophets God sent. So the Lord let them have the kind of leaders they preferred, and lawlessness multiplied (Isaiah 3:1–15). As you read, look for evidence that the Lord longed to show mercy to Judah despite her sins. If time is short, focus on Isaiah 4:1–6.

Judgment on Jerusalem and Judah

3 See now, the Lord,
the LORD Almighty,
is about to take from Jerusalem and Judah
both supply and support:
all supplies of food and all supplies of water,
2 the hero and warrior,
the judge and prophet,
the soothsayer and elder,
3 the captain of fifty and man of rank,
the counselor, skilled craftsman
and clever enchanter.

4 I will make boys their officials;
mere children will govern them.
5 People will oppress each other—
man against man, neighbor against neighbor.
The young will rise up against the old,
the base against the honorable.

6 A man will seize one of his brothers
at his father's home, and say,
"You have a cloak, you be our leader;
take charge of this heap of ruins!"
7 But in that day he will cry out,
"I have no remedy.
I have no food or clothing in my house;
do not make me the leader of the people."

[8]Jerusalem staggers,
Judah is falling;
their words and deeds are against
the LORD,
defying his glorious presence.
[9]The look on their faces testifies
against them;
they parade their sin like Sodom;
they do not hide it.
Woe to them!
They have brought disaster upon
themselves.

[10]Tell the righteous it will be well with
them,
for they will enjoy the fruit of
their deeds.
[11]Woe to the wicked! Disaster is upon
them!
They will be paid back for what their
hands have done.

[12]Youths oppress my people,
women rule over them.
O my people, your guides lead you
astray;
they turn you from the path.

[13]The LORD takes his place in court;
he rises to judge the people.
[14]The LORD enters into judgment
against the elders and leaders of
his people:
"It is you who have ruined my
vineyard;
the plunder from the poor is in
your houses.
[15]What do you mean by crushing my
people
and grinding the faces of the
poor?"
declares the Lord,
the LORD Almighty.

[16]The LORD says,
"The women of Zion are haughty,
walking along with outstretched
necks,
flirting with their eyes,
tripping along with mincing steps,
with ornaments jingling on their
ankles.
[17]Therefore the Lord will bring sores
on the heads of the women
of Zion;
the LORD will make their scalps
bald."

[18]In that day the Lord will snatch
away their finery: the bangles and
headbands and crescent necklaces, [19]the
earrings and bracelets and veils, [20]the
headdresses and ankle chains and
sashes, the perfume bottles and charms,
[21]the signet rings and nose rings, [22]the
fine robes and the capes and cloaks, the
purses [23]and mirrors, and the linen garments and tiaras and shawls.

[24]Instead of fragrance there will be a
stench;
instead of a sash, a rope;
instead of well-dressed hair, baldness;
instead of fine clothing, sackcloth;
instead of beauty, branding.
[25]Your men will fall by the sword,
your warriors in battle.
[26]The gates of Zion will lament and
mourn;
destitute, she will sit on the ground.

4 In that day seven women
will take hold of one man
and say, "We will eat our own food
and provide our own clothes;
only let us be called by your name.
Take away our disgrace!"

The Branch of the LORD

[2]In that day the Branch of the LORD
will be beautiful and glorious, and the
fruit of the land will be the pride and
glory of the survivors in Israel. [3]Those
who are left in Zion, who remain in Jerusalem, will be called holy, all who are
recorded among the living in Jerusalem.
[4]The Lord will wash away the filth of the
women of Zion; he will cleanse the
bloodstains from Jerusalem by a spirit[a]
of judgment and a spirit[a] of fire. [5]Then
the LORD will create over all of Mount
Zion and over those who assemble
there a cloud of smoke by day and a
glow of flaming fire by night; over all
the glory will be a canopy. [6]It will be a
shelter and shade from the heat of the
day, and a refuge and hiding place from
the storm and rain.

[a]4 Or *the Spirit*

SHARPEN THE FOCUS

We see human history in broad scope in Isaiah 4:2–6. The prophet views God at work from the time of the exodus to the glorious day when the kingdom of heaven comes in its fullness. As we read the words, we see these things with Isaiah:

- Jesus, the Branch of the Lord, the Shoot of Jesse, in all His splendor and love (Isaiah 4:2).
- God's ancient Israel, His remnant of faithful believers, returning to their homeland after exile. They live under His protecting, providing care (Isaiah 4:2, 5–6), purged from their idolatry by His refining, chastening fire (Isaiah 4:4) so that the Messiah can come from Abraham's descendants.
- God's people of every age enjoying the fruit of Christ's saving work (Isaiah 4:2), as we realize the holiness and new life this Branch has won for us on the tree of His cross (Isaiah 4:3).
- Ourselves bearing holy fruit as we remain connected to the Vine (Isaiah 4:2; John 15:1–2).
- Our Father's love providing light, shade, shelter, and refuge for His church in every age from Israel's exodus into all eternity (Isaiah 4:5–6; Exodus 14:19–20).

Do you see yourself in the procession of saints who walk the aisle of history? Do you see yourself as headed toward the marriage supper of the Lamb? ☼

Suppose you planted a garden and for every 100 seeds you planted, you raised an ear of corn with 10 kernels on it? Suppose you invested in the stock market and for every $100 you put in you got only $10 back. How long would you continue your efforts? That's the picture the Lord paints of Judah in Isaiah 5. As you read, look for His expressions of disappointment and for the specific charges He brings against His people. If time is short, focus on Isaiah 5:1–10.

The Song of the Vineyard

5 I will sing for the one I love
a song about his vineyard:
My loved one had a vineyard
on a fertile hillside.
2 He dug it up and cleared it of stones
and planted it with the choicest
vines.
He built a watchtower in it
and cut out a winepress as well.
Then he looked for a crop of good
grapes,
but it yielded only bad fruit.

3 "Now you dwellers in Jerusalem and
men of Judah,

judge between me and my
vineyard.
4 What more could have been done
for my vineyard
than I have done for it?
When I looked for good grapes,
why did it yield only bad?
5 Now I will tell you
what I am going to do to my
vineyard:
I will take away its hedge,
and it will be destroyed;
I will break down its wall,
and it will be trampled.
6 I will make it a wasteland,
neither pruned nor cultivated,
and briers and thorns will grow
there.
I will command the clouds
not to rain on it."

7 The vineyard of the LORD Almighty
is the house of Israel,
and the men of Judah
are the garden of his delight.
And he looked for justice, but saw
bloodshed;
for righteousness, but heard cries
of distress.

Woes and Judgments

8 Woe to you who add house to house
and join field to field
till no space is left
and you live alone in the land.

9 The LORD Almighty has declared in
my hearing:

"Surely the great houses will
become desolate,
the fine mansions left without
occupants.
10 A ten-acre[a] vineyard will produce
only a bath[b] of wine,
a homer[c] of seed only an ephah[d]
of grain."

11 Woe to those who rise early in the
morning
to run after their drinks,
who stay up late at night
till they are inflamed with wine.
12 They have harps and lyres at their
banquets,
tambourines and flutes and wine,
but they have no regard for the
deeds of the LORD,
no respect for the work of his
hands.
13 Therefore my people will go into
exile
for lack of understanding;
their men of rank will die of hunger
and their masses will be parched
with thirst.
14 Therefore the grave[e] enlarges its
appetite
and opens its mouth without
limit;
into it will descend their nobles and
masses
with all their brawlers and
revelers.
15 So man will be brought low
and mankind humbled,
the eyes of the arrogant humbled.
16 But the LORD Almighty will be
exalted by his justice,
and the holy God will show
himself holy by his
righteousness.
17 Then sheep will graze as in their
own pasture;
lambs will feed[f] among the ruins
of the rich.

18 Woe to those who draw sin along
with cords of deceit,
and wickedness as with cart ropes,
19 to those who say, "Let God hurry,
let him hasten his work
so we may see it.
Let it approach,
let the plan of the Holy One of
Israel come,
so we may know it."
20 Woe to those who call evil good
and good evil,
who put darkness for light
and light for darkness,

[a] *10* Hebrew *ten-yoke,* that is, the land plowed by 10 yoke of oxen in one day [b] *10* That is, probably about 6 gallons (about 22 liters) [c] *10* That is, probably about 6 bushels (about 220 liters) [d] *10* That is, probably about 3/5 bushel (about 22 liters) [e] *14* Hebrew *Sheol* [f] *17* Septuagint; Hebrew / *strangers will eat*

who put bitter for sweet
and sweet for bitter.

21 Woe to those who are wise in their own eyes
and clever in their own sight.

22 Woe to those who are heroes at drinking wine
and champions at mixing drinks,
23 who acquit the guilty for a bribe,
but deny justice to the innocent.
24 Therefore, as tongues of fire lick up straw
and as dry grass sinks down in the flames,
so their roots will decay
and their flowers blow away like dust;
for they have rejected the law of the LORD Almighty
and spurned the word of the Holy One of Israel.
25 Therefore the LORD's anger burns against his people;
his hand is raised and he strikes them down.
The mountains shake,
and the dead bodies are like refuse in the streets.

Yet for all this, his anger is not turned away,
his hand is still upraised.

26 He lifts up a banner for the distant nations,
he whistles for those at the ends of the earth.
Here they come,
swiftly and speedily!
27 Not one of them grows tired or stumbles,
not one slumbers or sleeps;
not a belt is loosened at the waist,
not a sandal thong is broken.
28 Their arrows are sharp,
all their bows are strung;
their horses' hoofs seem like flint,
their chariot wheels like a whirlwind.
29 Their roar is like that of the lion,
they roar like young lions;
they growl as they seize their prey
and carry it off with no one to rescue.
30 In that day they will roar over it
like the roaring of the sea.
And if one looks at the land,
he will see darkness and distress;
even the light will be darkened by the clouds.

SHARPEN THE FOCUS

When we invest time and energy in a project, we expect results. After hours behind a hoe or days on hands and knees, who doesn't look forward to taking the first bite of a plump tomato?

Our Lord looks forward with the same kind of anticipation to seeing the fruit of righteousness grow and mature in the lives of His people. Isaiah's parable in Isaiah 5:1–2 makes that point clear. But what does God find in the vineyard called Israel and Judah? Greed (Isaiah 5:8), sensuality and a godless outlook (Isaiah 5:11–12), rebellion against His Law (Isaiah 5:20), pride (Isaiah 5:21), an arrogant attitude toward sin's seriousness (Isaiah 5:22), and injustice (Isaiah 5:23).

We can point an accusing finger at Judah. But who among us can deny that we've accumulated things we didn't really need at the expense of helping the poor? Who can claim never to have taken God's Law or His love lightly? Who has never stretched the truth?

We also deserve to hear the "Woe!" of God's judgment. We can't turn to fruitful living just by wishing or trying. But we can turn to God and turn our need, sin, and guilt over to Him. He gives the gift of repentance. He forgives in Jesus and produces in His repentant people the fruit of the Spirit.

As we have seen so far, Isaiah spoke some of the sternest Law and some of the sweetest Gospel in all of Scripture. But who gave Isaiah, a sinner, the right to speak for a holy God? As you study his commission, focus not on the sinful spokesman, but on the holy God whose Word Isaiah proclaimed. If time is short, focus on Isaiah 6:1–8.

Isaiah's Commission

6 In the year that King Uzziah
died, I saw the Lord seated on a
throne, high and exalted, and the train
of his robe filled the temple. 2Above him
were seraphs, each with six wings: With
two wings they covered their faces, with
two they covered their feet, and with
two they were flying. 3And they were
calling to one another:

"Holy, holy, holy is the LORD
Almighty;
the whole earth is full of his
glory."

4At the sound of their voices the doorposts and thresholds shook and the
temple was filled with smoke.
5"Woe to me!" I cried. "I am ruined!
For I am a man of unclean lips, and I live
among a people of unclean lips, and my
eyes have seen the King, the LORD Almighty."
6Then one of the seraphs flew to me
with a live coal in his hand, which he
had taken with tongs from the altar.
7With it he touched my mouth and said,
"See, this has touched your lips; your
guilt is taken away and your sin atoned
for."
8Then I heard the voice of the Lord
saying, "Whom shall I send? And who
will go for us?"
And I said, "Here am I. Send me!"
9He said, "Go and tell this people:

" 'Be ever hearing, but never
understanding;
be ever seeing, but never
perceiving.'
10Make the heart of this people
calloused;
make their ears dull
and close their eyes.[a]
Otherwise they might see with their
eyes,
hear with their ears,
understand with their hearts,
and turn and be healed."

11Then I said, "For how long, O Lord?"
And he answered:

"Until the cities lie ruined
and without inhabitant,
until the houses are left deserted
and the fields ruined and ravaged,
12until the LORD has sent everyone far
away
and the land is utterly forsaken.
13And though a tenth remains in the
land,
it will again be laid waste.
But as the terebinth and oak
leave stumps when they are cut
down,
so the holy seed will be the stump
in the land."

[a]9,10 Hebrew; Septuagint *'You will be ever hearing, but never understanding; / you will be ever seeing, but never perceiving.' / 10This people's heart has become calloused; / they hardly hear with their ears, / and they have closed their eyes*

SHARPEN THE FOCUS

Most kings who still sit upon royal thrones function mainly as figureheads. And the publicity some monarchs today generate tends to strip away any scrap of respect their subjects may at one time have had for them.

We have almost no experience with human kings and the pomp of a royal court. And so we have a harder time participating in the feelings of Isaiah's original readers. Awesome is, perhaps, the word that comes closest to describing His Majesty, the Lord.

The jolt of being thrust without warning into the holy presence of that majesty threw Isaiah into the deepest dismay (Isaiah 6:5). He fully expected to die—on the spot. He knew his sin and the sins of his people. He knew that holiness incinerates sin the moment sin and holiness meet.

But the Lord is gracious. A live coal purified Isaiah's life and lips (Isaiah 6:6–7). That coal came from heaven's high altar, the place where the holy God watched as His sinless Son poured out His own blood for us on the cross. At that moment Isaiah's sin—and ours—was incinerated forever.

Seeing all this, how can we help but cry out with Isaiah, "Here I am. Send me to serve You!"

WEEK 54 • MONDAY

Isaiah 7:1—8:22

GET THE BIG PICTURE

"Trust Me," God said. But such trust made no earthly sense. And so most of the people in Judah persisted in their self-reliance. As you read Isaiah 7–8, don't get bogged down in the historical details or the Hebrew names. Focus instead on the classic struggle between faith and unbelief. If time is short, focus on Isaiah 8:11–18.

The Sign of Immanuel

7 When Ahaz son of Jotham, the
son of Uzziah, was king of Judah, King Rezin of Aram and Pekah son
of Remaliah king of Israel marched up
to fight against Jerusalem, but they
could not overpower it.
[2]Now the house of David was told,
"Aram has allied itself with[a] Ephraim";
so the hearts of Ahaz and his people
were shaken, as the trees of the forest
are shaken by the wind.
[3]Then the LORD said to Isaiah, "Go
out, you and your son Shear-Jashub,[b] to
meet Ahaz at the end of the aqueduct of
the Upper Pool, on the road to the
Washerman's Field. [4]Say to him, 'Be
careful, keep calm and don't be afraid.
Do not lose heart because of these two
smoldering stubs of firewood—because
of the fierce anger of Rezin and Aram
and of the son of Remaliah. [5]Aram,
Ephraim and Remaliah's son have plotted your ruin, saying, [6]"Let us invade
Judah; let us tear it apart and divide it
among ourselves, and make the son of
Tabeel king over it." [7]Yet this is what the
Sovereign LORD says:

[a]2 Or *has set up camp in* [b]3 *Shear-Jashub* means *a remnant will return.*

" 'It will not take place,
it will not happen,
8 for the head of Aram is Damascus,
and the head of Damascus is only Rezin.
Within sixty-five years
Ephraim will be too shattered to be a people.
9 The head of Ephraim is Samaria,
and the head of Samaria is only Remaliah's son.
If you do not stand firm in your faith,
you will not stand at all.' "

10 Again the LORD spoke to Ahaz,
11 "Ask the LORD your God for a sign,
whether in the deepest depths or in the
highest heights."
12 But Ahaz said, "I will not ask; I will
not put the LORD to the test."
13 Then Isaiah said, "Hear now, you
house of David! Is it not enough to try
the patience of men? Will you try the
patience of my God also? 14 Therefore
the Lord himself will give you[a] a sign:
The virgin will be with child and will
give birth to a son, and[b] will call him
Immanuel.[c] 15 He will eat curds and honey when he knows enough to reject the
wrong and choose the right. 16 But before
the boy knows enough to reject the
wrong and choose the right, the land of
the two kings you dread will be laid
waste. 17 The LORD will bring on you and
on your people and on the house of
your father a time unlike any since
Ephraim broke away from Judah—he
will bring the king of Assyria."
18 In that day the LORD will whistle for
flies from the distant streams of Egypt
and for bees from the land of Assyria.
19 They will all come and settle in the
steep ravines and in the crevices in the
rocks, on all the thornbushes and at all
the water holes. 20 In that day the Lord
will use a razor hired from beyond the
River[d]—the king of Assyria—to shave
your head and the hair of your legs, and
to take off your beards also. 21 In that day,
a man will keep alive a young cow and
two goats. 22 And because of the abundance of the milk they give, he will have
curds to eat. All who remain in the land
will eat curds and honey. 23 In that day,
in every place where there were a thousand vines worth a thousand silver
shekels,[e] there will be only briers and
thorns. 24 Men will go there with bow
and arrow, for the land will be covered
with briers and thorns. 25 As for all the
hills once cultivated by the hoe, you will
no longer go there for fear of the briers
and thorns; they will become places
where cattle are turned loose and where
sheep run.

Assyria, the LORD's Instrument

8 The LORD said to me, "Take a
large scroll and write on it with
an ordinary pen: Maher-Shalal-Hash-
Baz.[f] 2 And I will call in Uriah the priest
and Zechariah son of Jeberekiah as reliable witnesses for me."
3 Then I went to the prophetess, and
she conceived and gave birth to a son.
And the LORD said to me, "Name him
Maher-Shalal-Hash-Baz. 4 Before the boy
knows how to say 'My father' or 'My
mother,' the wealth of Damascus and
the plunder of Samaria will be carried
off by the king of Assyria."
5 The LORD spoke to me again:

6 "Because this people has rejected
the gently flowing waters of Shiloah
and rejoices over Rezin
and the son of Remaliah,
7 therefore the Lord is about to bring against them
the mighty floodwaters of the River[d]—
the king of Assyria with all his pomp.
It will overflow all its channels,
run over all its banks
8 and sweep on into Judah, swirling over it,
passing through it and reaching up to the neck.

[a]14 The Hebrew is plural. [b]14 Masoretic Text; Dead Sea Scrolls *and he* or *and they* [c]14 *Immanuel* means *God with us.* [d]20,7 That is, the Euphrates [e]23 That is, about 25 pounds (about 11.5 kilograms) [f]1 *Maher-Shalal-Hash-Baz* means *quick to the plunder, swift to the spoil*; also in verse 3.

Its outspread wings will cover the
breadth of your land,
O Immanuel[a]!"
9 Raise the war cry,[b] you nations, and
be shattered!
Listen, all you distant lands.
Prepare for battle, and be shattered!
Prepare for battle, and be
shattered!
10 Devise your strategy, but it will be
thwarted;
propose your plan, but it will not
stand,
for God is with us.[c]

Fear God

11 The LORD spoke to me with his strong hand upon me, warning me not to follow the way of this people. He said:

12 "Do not call conspiracy
everything that these people call
conspiracy[d];
do not fear what they fear,
and do not dread it.
13 The LORD Almighty is the one you
are to regard as holy,
he is the one you are to fear,
he is the one you are to dread,
14 and he will be a sanctuary;
but for both houses of Israel he
will be
a stone that causes men to stumble
and a rock that makes them fall.
And for the people of Jerusalem he
will be
a trap and a snare.
15 Many of them will stumble;
they will fall and be broken,
they will be snared and
captured."
16 Bind up the testimony
and seal up the law among my
disciples.
17 I will wait for the LORD,
who is hiding his face from the
house of Jacob.
I will put my trust in him.

18 Here am I, and the children the LORD has given me. We are signs and symbols in Israel from the LORD Almighty, who dwells on Mount Zion.
19 When men tell you to consult mediums and spiritists, who whisper and mutter, should not a people inquire of their God? Why consult the dead on behalf of the living?
20 To the law and to the testimony! If they do not speak according to this word, they have no light of dawn.
21 Distressed and hungry, they will roam through the land; when they are famished, they will become enraged and, looking upward, will curse their king and their God.
22 Then they will look toward the earth and see only distress and darkness and fearful gloom, and they will be thrust into utter darkness.

[a]8 *Immanuel* means *God with us.* [b]9 Or *Do your worst* [c]10 Hebrew *Immanuel* [d]12 Or *Do not call for a treaty / every time these people call for a treaty*

SHARPEN THE FOCUS

Geese flying in formation behind a leader use less energy than when they fly alone. Following the leader cuts wind resistance by 70%!

Jesus says to us, "Follow Me." God's Word patiently explains the spiritual aerodynamics of that command. When we follow, in trust, we receive all our Lord has promised. We can glide on the wind of the Spirit as He exerts the effort necessary to take us safely through this life and into the life to come.

It sounds simple enough. But when the sunshine of favorable circumstances grows dark and the winds of trouble blow, we, like Ahaz and his people, are tempted to strike out on our own. We ignore the Word of our Lord and the sign of His Immanuel and Immanuel's cross.

But our Lord keeps calling to us. "Don't adopt the world's worries. Don't fear their threats. Reverence Me. Fear Me. Let Me be your refuge" (Isaiah 8:12–13).

Many stumble at trusting Christ now or for eternity (Isaiah 8:14–15). Their unbelief destroys them. But we, who by our Savior's grace put our trust in Him have an anchor. When the storms have passed by, we stand with our Savior. We stand as tributes, signs, and wonders, in testimony to our God's love and power to save (Isaiah 8:18; Hebrews 2:11–15).

Hope for the humble; punishment for the proud. Those themes echo back and forth in today's chapters. Note the refrain of judgment in chapter 9. But also note the sweet promises of peace and deliverance for those who rely on Yahweh, the Lord. If time is short, focus on Isaiah 9:1–7; 10:15–27.

To Us a Child Is Born

9 Nevertheless, there will be no more gloom for those who were in distress. In the past he humbled the land of Zebulun and the land of Naphtali, but in the future he will honor Galilee of the Gentiles, by the way of the sea, along the Jordan—

2 The people walking in darkness
have seen a great light;
on those living in the land of the shadow of death[a]
a light has dawned.
3 You have enlarged the nation
and increased their joy;
they rejoice before you
as people rejoice at the harvest,
as men rejoice
when dividing the plunder.
4 For as in the day of Midian's defeat,
you have shattered
the yoke that burdens them,
the bar across their shoulders,
the rod of their oppressor.
5 Every warrior's boot used in battle
and every garment rolled in blood
will be destined for burning,
will be fuel for the fire.
6 For to us a child is born,
to us a son is given,
and the government will be on his shoulders.
And he will be called
Wonderful Counselor,[b] Mighty God,
Everlasting Father, Prince of Peace.
7 Of the increase of his government and peace
there will be no end.
He will reign on David's throne
and over his kingdom,
establishing and upholding it
with justice and righteousness
from that time on and forever.
The zeal of the LORD Almighty
will accomplish this.

The LORD's Anger Against Israel

8 The Lord has sent a message against Jacob;
it will fall on Israel.
9 All the people will know it—
Ephraim and the inhabitants of Samaria—

[a]2 Or *land of darkness* [b]6 Or *Wonderful, Counselor*

who say with pride
and arrogance of heart,
10 "The bricks have fallen down,
but we will rebuild with dressed stone;
the fig trees have been felled,
but we will replace them with cedars."
11 But the LORD has strengthened Rezin's foes against them
and has spurred their enemies on.
12 Arameans from the east and Philistines from the west
have devoured Israel with open mouth.

Yet for all this, his anger is not turned away,
his hand is still upraised.

13 But the people have not returned to him who struck them,
nor have they sought the LORD Almighty.
14 So the LORD will cut off from Israel both head and tail,
both palm branch and reed in a single day;
15 the elders and prominent men are the head,
the prophets who teach lies are the tail.
16 Those who guide this people mislead them,
and those who are guided are led astray.
17 Therefore the Lord will take no pleasure in the young men,
nor will he pity the fatherless and widows,
for everyone is ungodly and wicked,
every mouth speaks vileness.

Yet for all this, his anger is not turned away,
his hand is still upraised.

18 Surely wickedness burns like a fire;
it consumes briers and thorns,
it sets the forest thickets ablaze,
so that it rolls upward in a column of smoke.
19 By the wrath of the LORD Almighty
the land will be scorched
and the people will be fuel for the fire;
no one will spare his brother.
20 On the right they will devour,
but still be hungry;
on the left they will eat,
but not be satisfied.
Each will feed on the flesh of his own offspring[a]:
21 Manasseh will feed on Ephraim,
and Ephraim on Manasseh;
together they will turn against Judah.

Yet for all this, his anger is not turned away,
his hand is still upraised.

10 Woe to those who make unjust laws,
to those who issue oppressive decrees,
2 to deprive the poor of their rights
and withhold justice from the oppressed of my people,
making widows their prey
and robbing the fatherless.
3 What will you do on the day of reckoning,
when disaster comes from afar?
To whom will you run for help?
Where will you leave your riches?
4 Nothing will remain but to cringe among the captives
or fall among the slain.

Yet for all this, his anger is not turned away,
his hand is still upraised.

God's Judgment on Assyria

5 "Woe to the Assyrian, the rod of my anger,
in whose hand is the club of my wrath!
6 I send him against a godless nation,
I dispatch him against a people who anger me,
to seize loot and snatch plunder,
and to trample them down like mud in the streets.
7 But this is not what he intends,

[a]20 Or *arm*

this is not what he has in mind;
his purpose is to destroy,
to put an end to many nations.
8 'Are not my commanders all kings?'
he says.
9 'Has not Calno fared like
Carchemish?
Is not Hamath like Arpad,
and Samaria like Damascus?
10 As my hand seized the kingdoms of
the idols,
kingdoms whose images excelled
those of Jerusalem and
Samaria—
11 shall I not deal with Jerusalem and
her images
as I dealt with Samaria and her
idols?' "

12 When the Lord has finished all his work against Mount Zion and Jerusalem, he will say, "I will punish the king of Assyria for the willful pride of his heart and the haughty look in his eyes.
13 For he says:

" 'By the strength of my hand I have
done this,
and by my wisdom, because I
have understanding.
I removed the boundaries of nations,
I plundered their treasures;
like a mighty one I subdued[a] their
kings.
14 As one reaches into a nest,
so my hand reached for the
wealth of the nations;
as men gather abandoned eggs,
so I gathered all the countries;
not one flapped a wing,
or opened its mouth to chirp.' "

15 Does the ax raise itself above him
who swings it,
or the saw boast against him who
uses it?
As if a rod were to wield him who
lifts it up,
or a club brandish him who is not
wood!
16 Therefore, the Lord, the LORD
Almighty,
will send a wasting disease upon
his sturdy warriors;
under his pomp a fire will be
kindled
like a blazing flame.
17 The Light of Israel will become a
fire,
their Holy One a flame;
in a single day it will burn and
consume
his thorns and his briers.
18 The splendor of his forests and
fertile fields
it will completely destroy,
as when a sick man wastes away.
19 And the remaining trees of his
forests will be so few
that a child could write them
down.

The Remnant of Israel

20 In that day the remnant of Israel,
the survivors of the house of
Jacob,
will no longer rely on him
who struck them down
but will truly rely on the LORD,
the Holy One of Israel.
21 A remnant will return,[b] a remnant of
Jacob
will return to the Mighty God.
22 Though your people, O Israel, be
like the sand by the sea,
only a remnant will return.
Destruction has been decreed,
overwhelming and righteous.
23 The Lord, the LORD Almighty, will
carry out
the destruction decreed upon the
whole land.

24 Therefore, this is what the Lord, the LORD Almighty, says:

"O my people who live in Zion,
do not be afraid of the Assyrians,
who beat you with a rod
and lift up a club against you, as
Egypt did.
25 Very soon my anger against you will
end
and my wrath will be directed to
their destruction."

[a] 13 Or / *I subdued the mighty,* [b] 21 Hebrew *shear-jashub*; also in verse 22

[26]The LORD Almighty will lash them
with a whip,
as when he struck down Midian
at the rock of Oreb;
and he will raise his staff over the
waters,
as he did in Egypt.
[27]In that day their burden will be
lifted from your shoulders,
their yoke from your neck;
the yoke will be broken
because you have grown so fat.[a]
[28]They enter Aiath;
they pass through Migron;
they store supplies at Micmash.
[29]They go over the pass, and say,
"We will camp overnight at Geba."
Ramah trembles;
Gibeah of Saul flees.
[30]Cry out, O Daughter of Gallim!
Listen, O Laishah!
Poor Anathoth!
[31]Madmenah is in flight;
the people of Gebim take cover.
[32]This day they will halt at Nob;
they will shake their fist
at the mount of the Daughter of
Zion,
at the hill of Jerusalem.

[33]See, the Lord, the LORD Almighty,
will lop off the boughs with great
power.
The lofty trees will be felled,
the tall ones will be brought low.
[34]He will cut down the forest thickets
with an ax;
Lebanon will fall before the
Mighty One.

[a]27 Hebrew; Septuagint *broken / from your shoulders*

SHARPEN THE FOCUS

Those who lived through World War II will never forget V-E Day or V-J Day. Later generations remember the choppers lifting off the embassy roof in Saigon, taking the last Americans out of Vietnam. Such beautiful words: The war is over.

That's the message of Isaiah 9:1–7, too. The night has turned into the brightness of noonday (Isaiah 9:2)! Dance and shout in the streets (Isaiah 9:3)! The power of the oppressor is broken (Isaiah 9:4)! Burn the uniforms (Isaiah 9:5)!

It may seem that we're reading about two totally different wars here—the Assyrian invasion against Israel and the war sinners have declared against God. But really it's the same war. "What causes fights and quarrels among you?" the apostle James asks. He answers, "Don't they come from your desires that battle within you?" (James 4:1–2). War grows from the same selfishness that causes bickering in families and hurt feelings in church council meetings.

But Jesus has come as the Prince of Peace. God has forgiven our selfishness and self-sufficient rebellion. We can, in the power of the Holy Spirit, live in peace with ourselves and with others until the perfect peace of Christ's kingdom comes in fullness.

Today's chapters will stretch your imagination. As you read Isaiah 11, try to imagine the wonders of heaven, especially the perfect relationships we will enjoy with our Lord, with one another, and with the "new creation" Christ has promised to give us (2 Peter 3:13; Revelation 21:1). If time is short, focus on Isaiah 12:1–6.

The Branch From Jesse

11 A shoot will come up from the
stump of Jesse;
from his roots a Branch will bear
fruit.
2 The Spirit of the LORD will rest on
him—
the Spirit of wisdom and of
understanding,
the Spirit of counsel and of power,
the Spirit of knowledge and of the
fear of the LORD—
3 and he will delight in the fear of the
LORD.

He will not judge by what he sees
with his eyes,
or decide by what he hears with
his ears;
4 but with righteousness he will judge
the needy,
with justice he will give decisions
for the poor of the earth.
He will strike the earth with the rod
of his mouth;
with the breath of his lips he will
slay the wicked.
5 Righteousness will be his belt
and faithfulness the sash around
his waist.

6 The wolf will live with the lamb,
the leopard will lie down with the
goat,
the calf and the lion and the
yearling[a] together;
and a little child will lead them.
7 The cow will feed with the bear,
their young will lie down
together,
and the lion will eat straw like the
ox.
8 The infant will play near the hole of
the cobra,
and the young child put his hand
into the viper's nest.
9 They will neither harm nor destroy
on all my holy mountain,
for the earth will be full of the
knowledge of the LORD
as the waters cover the sea.

10 In that day the Root of Jesse will
stand as a banner for the peoples; the
nations will rally to him, and his place
of rest will be glorious. 11 In that day the
Lord will reach out his hand a second
time to reclaim the remnant that is left
of his people from Assyria, from Lower
Egypt, from Upper Egypt,[b] from Cush,[c]
from Elam, from Babylonia,[d] from Hamath and from the islands of the sea.

12 He will raise a banner for the
nations
and gather the exiles of Israel;
he will assemble the scattered
people of Judah
from the four quarters of the
earth.
13 Ephraim's jealousy will vanish,
and Judah's enemies[e] will be cut
off;

[a]6 Hebrew; Septuagint *lion will feed* [b]11 Hebrew *from Pathros* [c]11 That is, the upper Nile region [d]11 Hebrew *Shinar* [e]13 Or *hostility*

Ephraim will not be jealous of Judah,
nor Judah hostile toward
Ephraim.
14 They will swoop down on the slopes
of Philistia to the west;
together they will plunder the
people to the east.
They will lay hands on Edom and
Moab,
and the Ammonites will be subject
to them.
15 The LORD will dry up
the gulf of the Egyptian sea;
with a scorching wind he will sweep
his hand
over the Euphrates River.[a]
He will break it up into seven streams
so that men can cross over in
sandals.
16 There will be a highway for the
remnant of his people
that is left from Assyria,
as there was for Israel
when they came up from Egypt.

Songs of Praise

12

In that day you will say:

"I will praise you, O LORD.
Although you were angry with
me,
your anger has turned away
and you have comforted me.
2 Surely God is my salvation;
I will trust and not be afraid.
The LORD, the LORD, is my strength
and my song;
he has become my salvation."
3 With joy you will draw water
from the wells of salvation.

4 In that day you will say:

"Give thanks to the LORD, call on his
name;
make known among the nations
what he has done,
and proclaim that his name is
exalted.
5 Sing to the LORD, for he has done
glorious things;
let this be known to all the
world.
6 Shout aloud and sing for joy, people
of Zion,
for great is the Holy One of Israel
among you."

[a] 15 Hebrew *the River*

SHARPEN THE FOCUS

Isaiah speaks of Jesus often, and the prophet's words reveal much about the Savior whom we worship. Focus on Isaiah 11:2–3, for example:

- Jesus is filled with the Holy Spirit and thus acts in complete unity of purpose with the Godhead.
- Jesus is perfectly wise; He always knows just how to bring good into our lives.
- Jesus understands us fully. He knows what we're going through.
- Jesus is willing and able to counsel us in our times of confusion. He speaks His Word to us in ways we can understand it, find comfort in it, and take courage from it.
- Jesus has the power to help with any problem. He is not only willing to help, He is *able* to help.
- Jesus is anointed with the Spirit of knowledge. Even when we have no idea which way to turn, He knows, quite simply, everything! Nothing takes Him by surprise. We need not worry that He will leave out some important detail as He works with us.

- Jesus delights in the fear of the Lord. He obeyed the Laws of the Lord perfectly in our place, and now He will teach us that same reverent fear for our Savior-God. ☼

WEEK 54 • THURSDAY

Isaiah 13:1—20:6

GET THE BIG PICTURE

In chapters 13–23, Isaiah pronounces the Lord's judgment against many nations that oppose Him. As we read these prophecies today, we can be assured that nothing and no one can stand against God or stop His plan to bring salvation to the world. In justice, God destroys His enemies. And He shares His victory with us. If time is short, focus on Isaiah 14:1–32.

A Prophecy Against Babylon

13 An oracle concerning Babylon that Isaiah son of Amoz saw:

2 Raise a banner on a bare hilltop,
shout to them;
beckon to them
to enter the gates of the nobles.
3 I have commanded my holy ones;
I have summoned my warriors to carry out my wrath—
those who rejoice in my triumph.

4 Listen, a noise on the mountains,
like that of a great multitude!
Listen, an uproar among the kingdoms,
like nations massing together!
The LORD Almighty is mustering
an army for war.
5 They come from faraway lands,
from the ends of the heavens—
the LORD and the weapons of his wrath—
to destroy the whole country.

6 Wail, for the day of the LORD is near;
it will come like destruction from the Almighty.[a]
7 Because of this, all hands will go limp,
every man's heart will melt.
8 Terror will seize them,
pain and anguish will grip them;
they will writhe like a woman in labor.
They will look aghast at each other,
their faces aflame.

9 See, the day of the LORD is coming
—a cruel day, with wrath and fierce anger—
to make the land desolate
and destroy the sinners within it.
10 The stars of heaven and their constellations
will not show their light.
The rising sun will be darkened
and the moon will not give its light.
11 I will punish the world for its evil,
the wicked for their sins.
I will put an end to the arrogance of the haughty
and will humble the pride of the ruthless.
12 I will make man scarcer than pure gold,
more rare than the gold of Ophir.
13 Therefore I will make the heavens tremble;
and the earth will shake from its place

[a] 6 Hebrew *Shaddai*

at the wrath of the LORD Almighty,
in the day of his burning anger.

14 Like a hunted gazelle,
like sheep without a shepherd,
each will return to his own people,
each will flee to his native land.
15 Whoever is captured will be thrust through;
all who are caught will fall by the sword.
16 Their infants will be dashed to pieces before their eyes;
their houses will be looted and their wives ravished.

17 See, I will stir up against them the Medes,
who do not care for silver
and have no delight in gold.
18 Their bows will strike down the young men;
they will have no mercy on infants
nor will they look with compassion on children.
19 Babylon, the jewel of kingdoms,
the glory of the Babylonians'[a] pride,
will be overthrown by God
like Sodom and Gomorrah.
20 She will never be inhabited
or lived in through all generations;
no Arab will pitch his tent there,
no shepherd will rest his flocks there.
21 But desert creatures will lie there,
jackals will fill her houses;
there the owls will dwell,
and there the wild goats will leap about.
22 Hyenas will howl in her strongholds,
jackals in her luxurious palaces.
Her time is at hand,
and her days will not be prolonged.

14 The LORD will have compassion on Jacob;
once again he will choose Israel
and will settle them in their own land.
Aliens will join them
and unite with the house of Jacob.
2 Nations will take them
and bring them to their own place.
And the house of Israel will possess the nations
as menservants and maidservants in the LORD's land.
They will make captives of their captors
and rule over their oppressors.

3 On the day the LORD gives you relief
from suffering and turmoil and cruel
bondage, 4 you will take up this taunt
against the king of Babylon:

How the oppressor has come to an end!
How his fury[b] has ended!
5 The LORD has broken the rod of the wicked,
the scepter of the rulers,
6 which in anger struck down peoples
with unceasing blows,
and in fury subdued nations
with relentless aggression.
7 All the lands are at rest and at peace;
they break into singing.
8 Even the pine trees and the cedars of Lebanon
exult over you and say,
"Now that you have been laid low,
no woodsman comes to cut us down."

9 The grave[c] below is all astir
to meet you at your coming;
it rouses the spirits of the departed
to greet you—
all those who were leaders in the world;
it makes them rise from their thrones—
all those who were kings over the nations.
10 They will all respond,
they will say to you,
"You also have become weak, as we are;

[a]19 Or *Chaldeans'* [b]4 Dead Sea Scrolls, Septuagint and Syriac; the meaning of the word in the Masoretic Text is uncertain. [c]9 Hebrew *Sheol*; also in verses 11 and 15

you have become like us."
11 All your pomp has been brought
down to the grave,
along with the noise of your
harps;
maggots are spread out beneath you
and worms cover you.

12 How you have fallen from heaven,
O morning star, son of the dawn!
You have been cast down to the
earth,
you who once laid low the
nations!
13 You said in your heart,
"I will ascend to heaven;
I will raise my throne
above the stars of God;
I will sit enthroned on the mount of
assembly,
on the utmost heights of the
sacred mountain.[a]
14 I will ascend above the tops of the
clouds;
I will make myself like the Most
High."
15 But you are brought down to the
grave,
to the depths of the pit.

16 Those who see you stare at you,
they ponder your fate:
"Is this the man who shook the
earth
and made kingdoms tremble,
17 the man who made the world a
desert,
who overthrew its cities
and would not let his captives go
home?"

18 All the kings of the nations lie in
state,
each in his own tomb.
19 But you are cast out of your tomb
like a rejected branch;
you are covered with the slain,
with those pierced by the sword,
those who descend to the stones
of the pit.
Like a corpse trampled underfoot,
20 you will not join them in burial,
for you have destroyed your land
and killed your people.

The offspring of the wicked
will never be mentioned again.
21 Prepare a place to slaughter his sons
for the sins of their forefathers;
they are not to rise to inherit the
land
and cover the earth with their
cities.

22 "I will rise up against them,"
declares the LORD Almighty.
"I will cut off from Babylon her
name and survivors,
her offspring and descendants,"
declares the LORD.
23 "I will turn her into a place for owls
and into swampland;
I will sweep her with the broom of
destruction,"
declares the LORD Almighty.

A Prophecy Against Assyria

24 The LORD Almighty has sworn,

"Surely, as I have planned, so it will
be,
and as I have purposed, so it will
stand.
25 I will crush the Assyrian in my land;
on my mountains I will trample
him down.
His yoke will be taken from my
people,
and his burden removed from
their shoulders."

26 This is the plan determined for the
whole world;
this is the hand stretched out over
all nations.
27 For the LORD Almighty has
purposed, and who can
thwart him?
His hand is stretched out, and
who can turn it back?

A Prophecy Against the Philistines

28 This oracle came in the year King
Ahaz died:

29 Do not rejoice, all you Philistines,
that the rod that struck you is
broken;

[a] *13* Or *the north;* Hebrew *Zaphon*

from the root of that snake will
spring up a viper,
its fruit will be a darting,
venomous serpent.
30 The poorest of the poor will find
pasture,
and the needy will lie down in
safety.
But your root I will destroy by
famine;
it will slay your survivors.

31 Wail, O gate! Howl, O city!
Melt away, all you Philistines!
A cloud of smoke comes from the
north,
and there is not a straggler in its
ranks.
32 What answer shall be given
to the envoys of that nation?
"The LORD has established Zion,
and in her his afflicted people will
find refuge."

A Prophecy Against Moab

15 An oracle concerning Moab:

Ar in Moab is ruined,
destroyed in a night!
Kir in Moab is ruined,
destroyed in a night!
2 Dibon goes up to its temple,
to its high places to weep;
Moab wails over Nebo and
Medeba.
Every head is shaved
and every beard cut off.
3 In the streets they wear sackcloth;
on the roofs and in the public
squares
they all wail,
prostrate with weeping.
4 Heshbon and Elealeh cry out,
their voices are heard all the way
to Jahaz.
Therefore the armed men of Moab
cry out,
and their hearts are faint.

5 My heart cries out over Moab;
her fugitives flee as far as Zoar,
as far as Eglath Shelishiyah.
They go up the way to Luhith,
weeping as they go;
on the road to Horonaim
they lament their destruction.
6 The waters of Nimrim are dried up
and the grass is withered;
the vegetation is gone
and nothing green is left.
7 So the wealth they have acquired
and stored up
they carry away over the Ravine
of the Poplars.
8 Their outcry echoes along the
border of Moab;
their wailing reaches as far as
Eglaim,
their lamentation as far as Beer
Elim.
9 Dimon's[a] waters are full of blood,
but I will bring still more upon
Dimon[a]—
a lion upon the fugitives of Moab
and upon those who remain in
the land.

16 Send lambs as tribute
to the ruler of the land,
from Sela, across the desert,
to the mount of the Daughter of
Zion.
2 Like fluttering birds
pushed from the nest,
so are the women of Moab
at the fords of the Arnon.

3 "Give us counsel,
render a decision.
Make your shadow like night—
at high noon.
Hide the fugitives,
do not betray the refugees.
4 Let the Moabite fugitives stay with
you;
be their shelter from the
destroyer."

The oppressor will come to an end,
and destruction will cease;
the aggressor will vanish from the
land.
5 In love a throne will be established;
in faithfulness a man will sit on
it—

[a]9 Masoretic Text; Dead Sea Scrolls, some Septuagint manuscripts and Vulgate *Dibon*

one from the house[a] of David—
one who in judging seeks justice
and speeds the cause of righteousness.
6 We have heard of Moab's pride—
her overweening pride and conceit,
her pride and her insolence—
but her boasts are empty.
7 Therefore the Moabites wail,
they wail together for Moab.
Lament and grieve
for the men[b] of Kir Hareseth.
8 The fields of Heshbon wither,
the vines of Sibmah also.
The rulers of the nations
have trampled down the choicest vines,
which once reached Jazer
and spread toward the desert.
Their shoots spread out
and went as far as the sea.
9 So I weep, as Jazer weeps,
for the vines of Sibmah.
O Heshbon, O Elealeh,
I drench you with tears!
The shouts of joy over your ripened fruit
and over your harvests have been stilled.
10 Joy and gladness are taken away
from the orchards;
no one sings or shouts in the vineyards;
no one treads out wine at the presses,
for I have put an end to the shouting.
11 My heart laments for Moab like a harp,
my inmost being for Kir Hareseth.
12 When Moab appears at her high place,
she only wears herself out;
when she goes to her shrine to pray,
it is to no avail.

13 This is the word the LORD has already spoken concerning Moab. 14 But
now the LORD says: "Within three years,
as a servant bound by contract would
count them, Moab's splendor and all
her many people will be despised, and
her survivors will be very few and
feeble."

An Oracle Against Damascus

17 An oracle concerning Damascus:

"See, Damascus will no longer be a city
but will become a heap of ruins.
2 The cities of Aroer will be deserted
and left to flocks, which will lie down,
with no one to make them afraid.
3 The fortified city will disappear from Ephraim,
and royal power from Damascus;
the remnant of Aram will be
like the glory of the Israelites,"
declares the LORD Almighty.

4 "In that day the glory of Jacob will fade;
the fat of his body will waste away.
5 It will be as when a reaper gathers
the standing grain
and harvests the grain with his arm—
as when a man gleans heads of grain
in the Valley of Rephaim.
6 Yet some gleanings will remain,
as when an olive tree is beaten,
leaving two or three olives on the
topmost branches,
four or five on the fruitful boughs,"
declares the LORD,
the God of Israel.

7 In that day men will look to their Maker
and turn their eyes to the Holy One of Israel.
8 They will not look to the altars,
the work of their hands,
and they will have no regard for the
Asherah poles[c]
and the incense altars their fingers have made.

9 In that day their strong cities, which
they left because of the Israelites, will be

[a] 5 Hebrew *tent* [b] 7 Or *"raisin cakes,"* a wordplay
[c] 8 That is, symbols of the goddess Asherah

like places abandoned to thickets and undergrowth. And all will be desolation.

10 You have forgotten God your Savior;
you have not remembered the Rock, your fortress.
Therefore, though you set out the finest plants
and plant imported vines,
11 though on the day you set them out,
you make them grow,
and on the morning when you plant them, you bring them to bud,
yet the harvest will be as nothing
in the day of disease and incurable pain.

12 Oh, the raging of many nations—
they rage like the raging sea!
Oh, the uproar of the peoples—
they roar like the roaring of great waters!
13 Although the peoples roar like the roar of surging waters,
when he rebukes them they flee far away,
driven before the wind like chaff on the hills,
like tumbleweed before a gale.
14 In the evening, sudden terror!
Before the morning, they are gone!
This is the portion of those who loot us,
the lot of those who plunder us.

A Prophecy Against Cush

18 Woe to the land of whirring wings[a]
along the rivers of Cush,[b]
2 which sends envoys by sea
in papyrus boats over the water.

Go, swift messengers,
to a people tall and smooth-skinned,
to a people feared far and wide,
an aggressive nation of strange speech,
whose land is divided by rivers.

3 All you people of the world,
you who live on the earth,
when a banner is raised on the mountains,
you will see it,
and when a trumpet sounds,
you will hear it.
4 This is what the LORD says to me:
"I will remain quiet and will look on from my dwelling place,
like shimmering heat in the sunshine,
like a cloud of dew in the heat of harvest."
5 For, before the harvest, when the blossom is gone
and the flower becomes a ripening grape,
he will cut off the shoots with pruning knives,
and cut down and take away the spreading branches.
6 They will all be left to the mountain birds of prey
and to the wild animals;
the birds will feed on them all summer,
the wild animals all winter.

7 At that time gifts will be brought to
the LORD Almighty

from a people tall and smooth-skinned,
from a people feared far and wide,
an aggressive nation of strange speech,
whose land is divided by rivers—

the gifts will be brought to Mount Zion, the place of the Name of the LORD Almighty.

A Prophecy About Egypt

19 An oracle concerning Egypt:

See, the LORD rides on a swift cloud
and is coming to Egypt.
The idols of Egypt tremble before him,
and the hearts of the Egyptians melt within them.

2 "I will stir up Egyptian against Egyptian—
brother will fight against brother,
neighbor against neighbor,

[a]1 Or *of locusts* [b]1 That is, the upper Nile region

city against city,
kingdom against kingdom.
3 The Egyptians will lose heart,
and I will bring their plans to nothing;
they will consult the idols and the spirits of the dead,
the mediums and the spiritists.
4 I will hand the Egyptians over
to the power of a cruel master,
and a fierce king will rule over them,"
declares the Lord, the LORD Almighty.

5 The waters of the river will dry up,
and the riverbed will be parched and dry.
6 The canals will stink;
the streams of Egypt will dwindle and dry up.
The reeds and rushes will wither,
7 also the plants along the Nile,
at the mouth of the river.
Every sown field along the Nile
will become parched, will blow away and be no more.
8 The fishermen will groan and lament,
all who cast hooks into the Nile;
those who throw nets on the water
will pine away.
9 Those who work with combed flax will despair,
the weavers of fine linen will lose hope.
10 The workers in cloth will be dejected,
and all the wage earners will be sick at heart.

11 The officials of Zoan are nothing but fools;
the wise counselors of Pharaoh
give senseless advice.
How can you say to Pharaoh,
"I am one of the wise men,
a disciple of the ancient kings"?

12 Where are your wise men now?
Let them show you and make known
what the LORD Almighty
has planned against Egypt.
13 The officials of Zoan have become fools,
the leaders of Memphis[a] are deceived;
the cornerstones of her peoples
have led Egypt astray.
14 The LORD has poured into them
a spirit of dizziness;
they make Egypt stagger in all that she does,
as a drunkard staggers around in his vomit.
15 There is nothing Egypt can do—
head or tail, palm branch or reed.

16 In that day the Egyptians will be like
women. They will shudder with fear at
the uplifted hand that the LORD Almighty raises against them. 17 And the
land of Judah will bring terror to the
Egyptians; everyone to whom Judah is
mentioned will be terrified, because of
what the LORD Almighty is planning
against them.
18 In that day five cities in Egypt will
speak the language of Canaan and
swear allegiance to the LORD Almighty.
One of them will be called the City of
Destruction.[b]
19 In that day there will be an altar to
the LORD in the heart of Egypt, and a
monument to the LORD at its border. 20 It
will be a sign and witness to the LORD
Almighty in the land of Egypt. When
they cry out to the LORD because of their
oppressors, he will send them a savior
and defender, and he will rescue them.
21 So the LORD will make himself known
to the Egyptians, and in that day they
will acknowledge the LORD. They will
worship with sacrifices and grain offerings; they will make vows to the LORD
and keep them. 22 The LORD will strike
Egypt with a plague; he will strike them
and heal them. They will turn to the
LORD, and he will respond to their pleas
and heal them.
23 In that day there will be a highway
from Egypt to Assyria. The Assyrians

[a] 13 Hebrew *Noph* [b] 18 Most manuscripts of the Masoretic Text; some manuscripts of the Masoretic Text, Dead Sea Scrolls and Vulgate *City of the Sun* (that is, Heliopolis)

will go to Egypt and the Egyptians to
Assyria. The Egyptians and Assyrians
will worship together. 24In that day Israel will be the third, along with Egypt
and Assyria, a blessing on the earth.
25The LORD Almighty will bless them,
saying, "Blessed be Egypt my people,
Assyria my handiwork, and Israel my
inheritance."

A Prophecy Against Egypt and Cush

20 In the year that the supreme commander, sent
by Sargon king of Assyria, came to Ashdod and attacked and captured it— 2at
that time the LORD spoke through Isaiah son of Amoz. He said to him, "Take
off the sackcloth from your body and
the sandals from your feet." And he did
so, going around stripped and barefoot.
3Then the LORD said, "Just as my servant Isaiah has gone stripped and
barefoot for three years, as a sign and
portent against Egypt and Cush,[a] 4so the
king of Assyria will lead away stripped
and barefoot the Egyptian captives and
Cushite exiles, young and old, with buttocks bared—to Egypt's shame. 5Those
who trusted in Cush and boasted in
Egypt will be afraid and put to shame.
6In that day the people who live on this
coast will say, 'See what has happened
to those we relied on, those we fled to
for help and deliverance from the king
of Assyria! How then can we escape?' "

[a]3 That is, the upper Nile region; also in verse 5

SHARPEN THE FOCUS

The tower of Babel, on the Plain of Shinar, was earth's first organized rebellion against the Lord and against His Law. In the book of Isaiah, we again encounter this kind of arrogant rebellion in Babylon, also situated on the Plain of Shinar. Babylon reappears in the book of Revelation.

Note the similarities. The people of Babel said, "Let us . . . make a name for ourselves" (Genesis 11:4). The king of Babylon said, "I will ascend to heaven; I will raise my throne above the stars of God" (Isaiah 14:13). The Antichrist who presides over Babylon in the end times demands the worship of all who dwell on earth (Revelation 13:8).

Today's world hates our Lord and His Christ too. It saddens us to see it. And it frightens us to notice that same prideful rebellion often springing up in our own hearts.

At times like that, it's good to know we can take true pride in the one to whom the throne of heaven and earth rightly belong. It's good to remember that the Savior-God who chose Israel, who had mercy on Jacob (Isaiah 14:1) still chooses His church today. His mercy will never end. He has, in Christ's cross, forgiven us. He will, in love, defend us. ☼

WEEK 54 • FRIDAY

Isaiah 21:1—23:18

GET THE BIG PICTURE

Isaiah continues to deliver the indictments heaven's court has handed down against Babylon, against Jerusalem, and against Tyre. Each is an "oracle"—a message that carries a burden, a heavy word of judgment. Look for evidence of this as you read. If time is short, focus on Isaiah 22:1–25.

A Prophecy Against Babylon

21 An oracle concerning the Desert by the Sea:

Like whirlwinds sweeping through
the southland,
an invader comes from the desert,
from a land of terror.

2 A dire vision has been shown to me:
The traitor betrays, the looter
takes loot.
Elam, attack! Media, lay siege!
I will bring to an end all the
groaning she caused.

3 At this my body is racked with pain,
pangs seize me, like those of a
woman in labor;
I am staggered by what I hear,
I am bewildered by what I see.
4 My heart falters,
fear makes me tremble;
the twilight I longed for
has become a horror to me.

5 They set the tables,
they spread the rugs,
they eat, they drink!
Get up, you officers,
oil the shields!

6 This is what the Lord says to me:

"Go, post a lookout
and have him report what he sees.
7 When he sees chariots
with teams of horses,
riders on donkeys
or riders on camels,
let him be alert,
fully alert."

8 And the lookout[a] shouted,

"Day after day, my lord, I stand on
the watchtower;
every night I stay at my post.
9 Look, here comes a man in a chariot
with a team of horses.
And he gives back the answer:
'Babylon has fallen, has fallen!
All the images of its gods
lie shattered on the ground!' "

10 O my people, crushed on the
threshing floor,
I tell you what I have heard
from the LORD Almighty,
from the God of Israel.

A Prophecy Against Edom

11 An oracle concerning Dumah[b]:

Someone calls to me from Seir,
"Watchman, what is left of the
night?
Watchman, what is left of the
night?"
12 The watchman replies,
"Morning is coming, but also the
night.
If you would ask, then ask;
and come back yet again."

A Prophecy Against Arabia

13 An oracle concerning Arabia:

You caravans of Dedanites,
who camp in the thickets of
Arabia,
14 bring water for the thirsty;
you who live in Tema,
bring food for the fugitives.
15 They flee from the sword,
from the drawn sword,
from the bent bow
and from the heat of battle.

16 This is what the Lord says to me:
"Within one year, as a servant bound by
contract would count it, all the pomp of
Kedar will come to an end. 17 The survivors of the bowmen, the warriors of Kedar, will be few." The LORD, the God of
Israel, has spoken.

A Prophecy About Jerusalem

22 An oracle concerning the Valley of Vision:

What troubles you now,
that you have all gone up on the
roofs,

[a] 8 Dead Sea Scrolls and Syriac; Masoretic Text *A lion* [b] 11 *Dumah* means *silence* or *stillness,* a wordplay on *Edom.*

2 O town full of commotion,
O city of tumult and revelry?
Your slain were not killed by the sword,
nor did they die in battle.
3 All your leaders have fled together;
they have been captured without using the bow.
All you who were caught were taken prisoner together,
having fled while the enemy was still far away.
4 Therefore I said, "Turn away from me;
let me weep bitterly.
Do not try to console me
over the destruction of my people."

5 The Lord, the LORD Almighty, has a day
of tumult and trampling and terror
in the Valley of Vision,
a day of battering down walls
and of crying out to the mountains.
6 Elam takes up the quiver,
with her charioteers and horses;
Kir uncovers the shield.
7 Your choicest valleys are full of chariots,
and horsemen are posted at the city gates;
8 the defenses of Judah are stripped away.
And you looked in that day
to the weapons in the Palace of the Forest;
9 you saw that the City of David
had many breaches in its defenses;
you stored up water
in the Lower Pool.
10 You counted the buildings in Jerusalem
and tore down houses to strengthen the wall.
11 You built a reservoir between the two walls
for the water of the Old Pool,
but you did not look to the One who made it,
or have regard for the One who planned it long ago.

12 The Lord, the LORD Almighty,
called you on that day
to weep and to wail,
to tear out your hair and put on sackcloth.
13 But see, there is joy and revelry,
slaughtering of cattle and killing of sheep,
eating of meat and drinking of wine!
"Let us eat and drink," you say,
"for tomorrow we die!"

14 The LORD Almighty has revealed this in my hearing: "Till your dying day this sin will not be atoned for," says the Lord, the LORD Almighty.

15 This is what the Lord, the LORD Almighty, says:

"Go, say to this steward,
to Shebna, who is in charge of the palace:
16 What are you doing here and who gave you permission
to cut out a grave for yourself here,
hewing your grave on the height
and chiseling your resting place in the rock?

17 "Beware, the LORD is about to take firm hold of you
and hurl you away, O you mighty man.
18 He will roll you up tightly like a ball
and throw you into a large country.
There you will die
and there your splendid chariots will remain—
you disgrace to your master's house!
19 I will depose you from your office,
and you will be ousted from your position.

20 "In that day I will summon my servant, Eliakim son of Hilkiah. 21 I will clothe him with your robe and fasten your sash around him and hand your authority over to him. He will be a fa-

ther to those who live in Jerusalem and
to the house of Judah. 22 I will place on
his shoulder the key to the house of David; what he opens no one can shut, and
what he shuts no one can open. 23 I will
drive him like a peg into a firm place; he
will be a seat[a] of honor for the house of
his father. 24 All the glory of his family
will hang on him: its offspring and off-
shoots—all its lesser vessels, from the
bowls to all the jars.

25 "In that day," declares the LORD Almighty, "the peg driven into the firm
place will give way; it will be sheared off
and will fall, and the load hanging on it
will be cut down." The LORD has spoken.

A Prophecy About Tyre

23 An oracle concerning Tyre:

Wail, O ships of Tarshish!
For Tyre is destroyed
and left without house or harbor.
From the land of Cyprus[b]
word has come to them.

2 Be silent, you people of the island
and you merchants of Sidon,
whom the seafarers have enriched.
3 On the great waters
came the grain of the Shihor;
the harvest of the Nile[c] was the
revenue of Tyre,
and she became the marketplace
of the nations.

4 Be ashamed, O Sidon, and you,
O fortress of the sea,
for the sea has spoken:
"I have neither been in labor nor
given birth;
I have neither reared sons nor
brought up daughters."
5 When word comes to Egypt,
they will be in anguish at the
report from Tyre.

6 Cross over to Tarshish;
wail, you people of the island.
7 Is this your city of revelry,
the old, old city,
whose feet have taken her
to settle in far-off lands?
8 Who planned this against Tyre,
the bestower of crowns,
whose merchants are princes,
whose traders are renowned in
the earth?
9 The LORD Almighty planned it,
to bring low the pride of all glory
and to humble all who are
renowned on the earth.

10 Till[d] your land as along the Nile,
O Daughter of Tarshish,
for you no longer have a harbor.
11 The LORD has stretched out his hand
over the sea
and made its kingdoms tremble.
He has given an order concerning
Phoenicia[e]
that her fortresses be destroyed.
12 He said, "No more of your reveling,
O Virgin Daughter of Sidon, now
crushed!

"Up, cross over to Cyprus[b];
even there you will find no rest."
13 Look at the land of the Babylonians,[f]
this people that is now of no
account!
The Assyrians have made it
a place for desert creatures;
they raised up their siege towers,
they stripped its fortresses bare
and turned it into a ruin.

14 Wail, you ships of Tarshish;
your fortress is destroyed!

15 At that time Tyre will be forgotten for
seventy years, the span of a king's life.
But at the end of these seventy years, it
will happen to Tyre as in the song of the
prostitute:

16 "Take up a harp, walk through the
city,
O prostitute forgotten;
play the harp well, sing many a
song,
so that you will be remembered."

[a] 23 Or *throne* [b] 1,12 Hebrew *Kittim*
[c] 2,3 Masoretic Text; one Dead Sea Scroll *Sidon, / who cross over the sea; / your envoys* 3 *are on the great waters. / The grain of the Shihor, / the harvest of the Nile,* [d] 10 Dead Sea Scrolls and some Septuagint manuscripts; Masoretic Text *Go through*
[e] 11 Hebrew *Canaan* [f] 13 Or *Chaldeans*

17At the end of seventy years, the
LORD will deal with Tyre. She will return
to her hire as a prostitute and will ply
her trade with all the kingdoms on the
face of the earth. 18Yet her profit and her
earnings will be set apart for the LORD;
they will not be stored up or hoarded.
Her profits will go to those who live before the LORD, for abundant food and fine clothes.

SHARPEN THE FOCUS

Maybe you've visited a place with a name like "Lookout Peak." Such a vantage point usually juts out from a mountainside or a tall hill and standing there enables you to see for miles.

Isaiah's name for Jerusalem, "The Valley of Vision" (Isaiah 22:1, 5), is ironic. Who goes down into a valley to get a better view?

The people of Jerusalem claimed to see perfectly. Most of them no longer limited their vision by narrowing their minds to worship only one god. They were more sophisticated than that! They had substituted advanced diplomacy and superior weapons systems for the more "primitive" repentance and faith in God that His prophets demanded (Isaiah 22:9–11). They wrongly thought they saw further than their seers, the prophets.

If Isaiah spent a few weeks at your house, if he were to visit a few months at your church, what would God's seer see?

We can have the most well-developed investment plans for retirement. We can follow the latest sociological data as we design an evangelism strategy. We can use the slickest ad agency. But if we fail to "look to the One who made [us], or have regard for the One who planned [His Church] long ago" (Isaiah 22:11), we won't succeed. Look to Him today for His gifts of repentance, pardon, and faith.

WEEK 54 • SATURDAY

Isaiah 24:1—25:12

GET THE BIG PICTURE

When Christians use the word *apocalypse*, we mean the unveiling or revealing of the End Times. The book of Revelation is an apocalypse, for example. So are chapters 24–27 of Isaiah. Both Revelation and Isaiah show God's judgment and the blessings of His coming kingdom. Look for the contrast as you read. If time is short, focus on Isaiah 25:1–12.

The LORD's Devastation of the Earth

24 See, the LORD is going to lay waste the earth
and devastate it;
he will ruin its face
and scatter its inhabitants—
2it will be the same
for priest as for people,
for master as for servant,
for mistress as for maid,
for seller as for buyer,
for borrower as for lender,
for debtor as for creditor.

3 The earth will be completely laid
waste
and totally plundered.
The LORD has spoken
this word.

4 The earth dries up and withers,
the world languishes and withers,
the exalted of the earth languish.
5 The earth is defiled by its people;
they have disobeyed the laws,
violated the statutes
and broken the everlasting
covenant.
6 Therefore a curse consumes the
earth;
its people must bear their guilt.
Therefore earth's inhabitants are
burned up,
and very few are left.
7 The new wine dries up and the vine
withers;
all the merrymakers groan.
8 The gaiety of the tambourines is
stilled,
the noise of the revelers has
stopped,
the joyful harp is silent.
9 No longer do they drink wine with a
song;
the beer is bitter to its drinkers.
10 The ruined city lies desolate;
the entrance to every house is
barred.
11 In the streets they cry out for wine;
all joy turns to gloom,
all gaiety is banished from the
earth.
12 The city is left in ruins,
its gate is battered to pieces.
13 So will it be on the earth
and among the nations,
as when an olive tree is beaten,
or as when gleanings are left after
the grape harvest.
14 They raise their voices, they shout
for joy;
from the west they acclaim the
LORD's majesty.
15 Therefore in the east give glory to
the LORD;
exalt the name of the LORD, the
God of Israel,
in the islands of the sea.
16 From the ends of the earth we hear
singing:
"Glory to the Righteous One."

But I said, "I waste away, I waste
away!
Woe to me!
The treacherous betray!
With treachery the treacherous
betray!"
17 Terror and pit and snare await you,
O people of the earth.
18 Whoever flees at the sound of terror
will fall into a pit;
whoever climbs out of the pit
will be caught in a snare.

The floodgates of the heavens are
opened,
the foundations of the earth
shake.
19 The earth is broken up,
the earth is split asunder,
the earth is thoroughly shaken.
20 The earth reels like a drunkard,
it sways like a hut in the wind;
so heavy upon it is the guilt of its
rebellion
that it falls—never to rise again.

21 In that day the LORD will punish
the powers in the heavens above
and the kings on the earth below.
22 They will be herded together
like prisoners bound in a
dungeon;
they will be shut up in prison
and be punished[a] after many days.
23 The moon will be abashed, the sun
ashamed;
for the LORD Almighty will reign
on Mount Zion and in Jerusalem,
and before its elders, gloriously.

Praise to the LORD

25 O LORD, you are my
God;
I will exalt you and praise your
name,
for in perfect faithfulness
you have done marvelous things,
things planned long ago.

[a]22 Or *released*

[2]You have made the city a heap of
rubble,
the fortified town a ruin,
the foreigners' stronghold a city no
more;
it will never be rebuilt.
[3]Therefore strong peoples will honor
you;
cities of ruthless nations will
revere you.
[4]You have been a refuge for the poor,
a refuge for the needy in his
distress,
a shelter from the storm
and a shade from the heat.
For the breath of the ruthless
is like a storm driving against a
wall
[5] and like the heat of the desert.
You silence the uproar of foreigners;
as heat is reduced by the shadow
of a cloud,
so the song of the ruthless is stilled.

[6]On this mountain the LORD
Almighty will prepare
a feast of rich food for all peoples,
a banquet of aged wine—
the best of meats and the finest of
wines.
[7]On this mountain he will destroy
the shroud that enfolds all
peoples,
the sheet that covers all nations;
[8] he will swallow up death forever.
The Sovereign LORD will wipe away
the tears
from all faces;
he will remove the disgrace of his
people
from all the earth.
The LORD has spoken.

[9]In that day they will say,

"Surely this is our God;
we trusted in him, and he saved
us.
This is the LORD, we trusted in
him;
let us rejoice and be glad in his
salvation."
[10]The hand of the LORD will rest on
this mountain;
but Moab will be trampled under
him
as straw is trampled down in the
manure.
[11]They will spread out their hands in
it,
as a swimmer spreads out his
hands to swim.
God will bring down their pride
despite the cleverness[a] of their
hands.
[12]He will bring down your high
fortified walls
and lay them low;
he will bring them down to the
ground,
to the very dust.

[a]*11* The meaning of the Hebrew for this word is uncertain.

SHARPEN THE FOCUS

God's people have always longed for the end of tyranny. In Genesis 6:4 we read about the multiplication of evil. Martin Luther translated this verse, "In those days there were tyrants on the earth . . ." Heartless. Cruel. Selfish. Wicked. Shameless. We know tyrants today–drug lords, gang leaders, petty dictators. But God promises tyranny and the pain tyrants cause will end (Isaiah 25:1–5).

God's people have always longed for the end of death. In Genesis 4:6–15 we read about Abel's murder. What pain must have stabbed Adam and Eve's hearts as they held the lifeless body of their son. We know death today–murder, heart attacks, cancer, and suicide. But God promises death and the pain death brings will end (Isaiah 25:6–9).

God's people have always longed for the end of pride and human arrogance. In Genesis

6:11–13, we read about the violence and misery caused by those who reject the Lord and refuse to submit to His rule. We know pride and arrogance today—perverted sexuality, covetousness, greed, unbelief, blasphemy. But God promises that pride and the rebellion of the ungodly will end (Isaiah 25:10–12). Let these promises bring you peace in Jesus today.

WEEK 55 • MONDAY

Isaiah 26:1—27:13

"In that day." You will find that short phrase repeated again and again in the book of Isaiah. As you read chapters 26 and 27 now, see if you can discover what particular "day" the prophet is referring to. If time is short, focus on Isaiah 27:1–6.

A Song of Praise

26 In that day this song will be sung in the land of Judah:

We have a strong city;
God makes salvation
its walls and ramparts.
2 Open the gates
that the righteous nation may enter,
the nation that keeps faith.
3 You will keep in perfect peace
him whose mind is steadfast,
because he trusts in you.
4 Trust in the LORD forever,
for the LORD, the LORD, is the Rock eternal.
5 He humbles those who dwell on high,
he lays the lofty city low;
he levels it to the ground
and casts it down to the dust.
6 Feet trample it down—
the feet of the oppressed,
the footsteps of the poor.
7 The path of the righteous is level;
O upright One, you make the way of the righteous smooth.
8 Yes, LORD, walking in the way of your laws,[a]
we wait for you;
your name and renown
are the desire of our hearts.
9 My soul yearns for you in the night;
in the morning my spirit longs for you.
When your judgments come upon the earth,
the people of the world learn righteousness.
10 Though grace is shown to the wicked,
they do not learn righteousness;
even in a land of uprightness they go on doing evil
and regard not the majesty of the LORD.
11 O LORD, your hand is lifted high,
but they do not see it.
Let them see your zeal for your people and be put to shame;
let the fire reserved for your enemies consume them.
12 LORD, you establish peace for us;
all that we have accomplished you have done for us.
13 O LORD, our God, other lords besides you have ruled over us,

[a] 8 Or *judgments*

but your name alone do we honor.
[14]They are now dead, they live no more;
those departed spirits do not rise.
You punished them and brought them to ruin;
you wiped out all memory of them.
[15]You have enlarged the nation, O LORD;
you have enlarged the nation.
You have gained glory for yourself;
you have extended all the borders of the land.

[16]LORD, they came to you in their distress;
when you disciplined them,
they could barely whisper a prayer.[a]
[17]As a woman with child and about to give birth
writhes and cries out in her pain,
so were we in your presence, O LORD.
[18]We were with child, we writhed in pain,
but we gave birth to wind.
We have not brought salvation to the earth;
we have not given birth to people of the world.
[19]But your dead will live;
their bodies will rise.
You who dwell in the dust,
wake up and shout for joy.
Your dew is like the dew of the morning;
the earth will give birth to her dead.

[20]Go, my people, enter your rooms
and shut the doors behind you;
hide yourselves for a little while
until his wrath has passed by.
[21]See, the LORD is coming out of his dwelling
to punish the people of the earth for their sins.
The earth will disclose the blood shed upon her;
she will conceal her slain no longer.

Deliverance of Israel

27 In that day,
the LORD will punish with his sword,
his fierce, great and powerful sword,
Leviathan the gliding serpent,
Leviathan the coiling serpent;
he will slay the monster of the sea.

[2]In that day—

"Sing about a fruitful vineyard:
[3] I, the LORD, watch over it;
I water it continually.
I guard it day and night
so that no one may harm it.
[4] I am not angry.
If only there were briers and thorns confronting me!
I would march against them in battle;
I would set them all on fire.
[5]Or else let them come to me for refuge;
let them make peace with me,
yes, let them make peace with me."

[6]In days to come Jacob will take root,
Israel will bud and blossom
and fill all the world with fruit.

[7]Has ⌊the LORD⌋ struck her
as he struck down those who struck her?
Has she been killed
as those were killed who killed her?
[8]By warfare[b] and exile you contend with her—
with his fierce blast he drives her out,
as on a day the east wind blows.
[9]By this, then, will Jacob's guilt be atoned for,
and this will be the full fruitage of the removal of his sin:
When he makes all the altar stones
to be like chalk stones crushed to pieces,

[a]*16* The meaning of the Hebrew for this clause is uncertain. [b]*8* See Septuagint; the meaning of the Hebrew for this word is uncertain.

no Asherah poles[a] or incense altars
will be left standing.
10 The fortified city stands desolate,
an abandoned settlement,
forsaken like the desert;
there the calves graze,
there they lie down;
they strip its branches bare.
11 When its twigs are dry, they are
broken off
and women come and make fires
with them.
For this is a people without
understanding;
so their Maker has no compassion
on them,
and their Creator shows them no
favor.

12 In that day the LORD will thresh
from the flowing Euphrates[b] to the Wadi
of Egypt, and you, O Israelites, will be
gathered up one by one. 13 And in that
day a great trumpet will sound. Those
who were perishing in Assyria and
those who were exiled in Egypt will
come and worship the LORD on the holy
mountain in Jerusalem.

[a] 9 That is, symbols of the goddess Asherah
[b] 12 Hebrew *River*

SHARPEN THE FOCUS

The "day of the LORD" stands out in the prophets. This "day" is no ordinary day. "In that day," God's people will sing a song of triumph (26:1–6) and Satan will receive God's punishment (Isaiah 27:1–2). "In that day," God's vineyard will be filled with fruit (27:2–6); He will punish His enemies and gather His children one by one (Isaiah 27:12). "In that day," the trumpet will sound and God's people will worship Him on Mt. Zion forever (Isaiah 27:13).

Several individual, earthly days fuse as the Lord brings mercy and justice to His fallen creation. Good Friday, Easter, the day of Christ's return, the day of your Baptism. They all merge into one "day"—Judgment Day. Judgment Day came at Christ's cross as God judged and punished sin, and as the sinless Son of God died in our place. Judgment Day came on Easter as God raised His Son and declared His sacrifice sufficient payment for all our debt. Judgment Day will come as all people stand before God's throne.

Judgment Day came—and passed—for you as you were baptized. You died, were buried, and were raised with Christ at the font. You have been judged and in Christ declared not guilty (Romans 6:1–14).

WEEK 55 • TUESDAY

Isaiah 28:1—29:24

GET THE BIG PICTURE

Isaiah reminds the people of Judah of the judgment that fell on her sister nation, Israel. ("Ephraim," the largest tribe of the Northern Kingdom, is often the name the prophets use as they refer to the whole of that kingdom.) But the people of Judah refuse to repent. Thus Jerusalem brings down on herself the fiery judgment of God. As you read, notice how well the Lord knows His people. If time is short, focus on Isaiah 29:1–23.

Woe to Ephraim

28 Woe to that wreath, the pride of Ephraim's drunkards,
to the fading flower, his glorious beauty,
set on the head of a fertile valley—
to that city, the pride of those laid low by wine!
2 See, the Lord has one who is powerful and strong.
Like a hailstorm and a destructive wind,
like a driving rain and a flooding downpour,
he will throw it forcefully to the ground.
3 That wreath, the pride of Ephraim's drunkards,
will be trampled underfoot.
4 That fading flower, his glorious beauty,
set on the head of a fertile valley,
will be like a fig ripe before harvest—
as soon as someone sees it and takes it in his hand,
he swallows it.

5 In that day the LORD Almighty
will be a glorious crown,
a beautiful wreath
for the remnant of his people.
6 He will be a spirit of justice
to him who sits in judgment,
a source of strength
to those who turn back the battle at the gate.

7 And these also stagger from wine
and reel from beer:
Priests and prophets stagger from beer
and are befuddled with wine;
they reel from beer,
they stagger when seeing visions,
they stumble when rendering decisions.
8 All the tables are covered with vomit
and there is not a spot without filth.

9 "Who is it he is trying to teach?
To whom is he explaining his message?
To children weaned from their milk,
to those just taken from the breast?
10 For it is:
Do and do, do and do,
rule on rule, rule on rule[a];
a little here, a little there."

11 Very well then, with foreign lips and strange tongues
God will speak to this people,
12 to whom he said,
"This is the resting place, let the weary rest";
and, "This is the place of repose"—
but they would not listen.
13 So then, the word of the LORD to them will become:
Do and do, do and do,
rule on rule, rule on rule;
a little here, a little there—
so that they will go and fall backward,
be injured and snared and captured.

14 Therefore hear the word of the LORD, you scoffers
who rule this people in Jerusalem.
15 You boast, "We have entered into a covenant with death,
with the grave[b] we have made an agreement.
When an overwhelming scourge sweeps by,
it cannot touch us,
for we have made a lie our refuge
and falsehood[c] our hiding place."

16 So this is what the Sovereign LORD says:

"See, I lay a stone in Zion,
a tested stone,
a precious cornerstone for a sure foundation;
the one who trusts will never be dismayed.
17 I will make justice the measuring line

[a]10 Hebrew / *sav lasav sav lasav / kav lakav kav lakav* (possibly meaningless sounds; perhaps a mimicking of the prophet's words); also in verse 13 [b]15 Hebrew *Sheol*; also in verse 18 [c]15 Or *false gods*

and righteousness the plumb line;
hail will sweep away your refuge,
the lie,
and water will overflow your
hiding place.
18 Your covenant with death will be
annulled;
your agreement with the grave
will not stand.
When the overwhelming scourge
sweeps by,
you will be beaten down by it.
19 As often as it comes it will carry you
away;
morning after morning, by day
and by night,
it will sweep through."

The understanding of this message
will bring sheer terror.
20 The bed is too short to stretch out
on,
the blanket too narrow to wrap
around you.
21 The LORD will rise up as he did at
Mount Perazim,
he will rouse himself as in the
Valley of Gibeon—
to do his work, his strange work,
and perform his task, his alien
task.
22 Now stop your mocking,
or your chains will become
heavier;
the Lord, the LORD Almighty, has
told me
of the destruction decreed against
the whole land.

23 Listen and hear my voice;
pay attention and hear what I say.
24 When a farmer plows for planting,
does he plow continually?
Does he keep on breaking up and
harrowing the soil?
25 When he has leveled the surface,
does he not sow caraway and
scatter cummin?
Does he not plant wheat in its
place,[a]
barley in its plot,[a]
and spelt in its field?
26 His God instructs him
and teaches him the right way.
27 Caraway is not threshed with a
sledge,
nor is a cartwheel rolled over
cummin;
caraway is beaten out with a rod,
and cummin with a stick.
28 Grain must be ground to make
bread;
so one does not go on threshing it
forever.
Though he drives the wheels of his
threshing cart over it,
his horses do not grind it.
29 All this also comes from the LORD
Almighty,
wonderful in counsel and
magnificent in wisdom.

Woe to David's City

29 Woe to you, Ariel, Ariel,
the city where David
settled!
Add year to year
and let your cycle of festivals go
on.
2 Yet I will besiege Ariel;
she will mourn and lament,
she will be to me like an altar
hearth.[b]
3 I will encamp against you all around;
I will encircle you with towers
and set up my siege works against
you.
4 Brought low, you will speak from
the ground;
your speech will mumble out of
the dust.
Your voice will come ghostlike from
the earth;
out of the dust your speech will
whisper.

5 But your many enemies will become
like fine dust,
the ruthless hordes like blown
chaff.
Suddenly, in an instant,
6 the LORD Almighty will come
with thunder and earthquake and
great noise,

[a]25 The meaning of the Hebrew for this word is uncertain. [b]2 The Hebrew for *altar hearth* sounds like the Hebrew for *Ariel.*

with windstorm and tempest and
flames of a devouring fire.
7 Then the hordes of all the nations
that fight against Ariel,
that attack her and her fortress
and besiege her,
will be as it is with a dream,
with a vision in the night—
8 as when a hungry man dreams that
he is eating,
but he awakens, and his hunger
remains;
as when a thirsty man dreams that
he is drinking,
but he awakens faint, with his
thirst unquenched.
So will it be with the hordes of all
the nations
that fight against Mount Zion.

9 Be stunned and amazed,
blind yourselves and be sightless;
be drunk, but not from wine,
stagger, but not from beer.
10 The LORD has brought over you a
deep sleep:
He has sealed your eyes (the
prophets);
he has covered your heads (the
seers).

11 For you this whole vision is nothing
but words sealed in a scroll. And if you
give the scroll to someone who can read,
and say to him, "Read this, please," he
will answer, "I can't; it is sealed." 12 Or if
you give the scroll to someone who cannot read, and say, "Read this, please," he
will answer, "I don't know how to read."

13 The Lord says:

"These people come near to me with
their mouth
and honor me with their lips,
but their hearts are far from me.
Their worship of me
is made up only of rules taught by
men.[a]
14 Therefore once more I will astound
these people
with wonder upon wonder;
the wisdom of the wise will perish,
the intelligence of the intelligent
will vanish."

15 Woe to those who go to great
depths
to hide their plans from the
LORD,
who do their work in darkness and
think,
"Who sees us? Who will know?"
16 You turn things upside down,
as if the potter were thought to be
like the clay!
Shall what is formed say to him who
formed it,
"He did not make me"?
Can the pot say of the potter,
"He knows nothing"?

17 In a very short time, will not
Lebanon be turned into a
fertile field
and the fertile field seem like a
forest?
18 In that day the deaf will hear the
words of the scroll,
and out of gloom and darkness
the eyes of the blind will see.
19 Once more the humble will rejoice
in the LORD;
the needy will rejoice in the Holy
One of Israel.
20 The ruthless will vanish,
the mockers will disappear,
and all who have an eye for evil
will be cut down—
21 those who with a word make a man
out to be guilty,
who ensnare the defender in
court
and with false testimony deprive
the innocent of justice.

22 Therefore this is what the LORD,
who redeemed Abraham, says to the
house of Jacob:

"No longer will Jacob be ashamed;
no longer will their faces grow
pale.
23 When they see among them their
children,
the work of my hands,
they will keep my name holy;

[a]13 Hebrew; Septuagint *They worship me in vain; / their teachings are but rules taught by men*

they will acknowledge the holiness
of the Holy One of Jacob,
and will stand in awe of the God
of Israel.
24 Those who are wayward in spirit
will gain understanding;
those who complain will accept
instruction."

SHARPEN THE FOCUS

Cecil B. DeMille who gave the world the movie, *The Ten Commandments*, once commented, "It is impossible for us to break the law. We can only break ourselves against the law."

The people of Judah refused to hear Isaiah's message, the message of God's will for His chosen nation. In their prosperity, they didn't want to hear about that day the Lord would withdraw His protecting hand because of their sin.

But no matter how hard Judah tried to ignore God's Law, no matter how hard the people worked at breaking it, it would soon break them instead. The Lord calls this His "strange" work, His "alien" work (Isaiah 28:21b). God longs to show mercy. Grace is His preferred approach to His human creatures. But when His people take grace as only so much babbling, as a "been there, done that" part of their lives, they tread on dangerous turf.

To what degree do you take God's grace for granted? How often do you offer Him only the lip service that Isaiah condemns so harshly in Isaiah 28:13? After you've done a bit of soul-searching, talk to the "LORD, who redeemed Abraham" (Isaiah 29:22). Remember that He has redeemed you, too, in the cross of His Son.

WEEK 55 • WEDNESDAY

Isaiah 30:1—31:9

GET THE BIG PICTURE

Threatened by the Assyrian army, Judah's leaders ignore God's invitation to repent and return to Him. Instead, they forge a political alliance with Egypt. Isaiah speaks God's denunciation, even though the people don't want to hear it. As you read, keep in mind the awful slavery Israel had endured in Egypt. Ask yourself why they would ally themselves with a former slave master. If time is short, focus on Isaiah 30:1–26.

Woe to the Obstinate Nation

30 "Woe to the obstinate
children,"
declares the LORD,
"to those who carry out plans that
are not mine,
forming an alliance, but not by my
Spirit,
heaping sin upon sin;
2 who go down to Egypt
without consulting me;
who look for help to Pharaoh's
protection,
to Egypt's shade for refuge.
3 But Pharaoh's protection will be to
your shame,
Egypt's shade will bring you
disgrace.

[4]Though they have officials in Zoan
and their envoys have arrived in
Hanes,
[5]everyone will be put to shame
because of a people useless to
them,
who bring neither help nor
advantage,
but only shame and disgrace."

[6]An oracle concerning the animals of the Negev:

Through a land of hardship and
distress,
of lions and lionesses,
of adders and darting snakes,
the envoys carry their riches on
donkeys' backs,
their treasures on the humps of
camels,
to that unprofitable nation,
[7] to Egypt, whose help is utterly
useless.
Therefore I call her
Rahab the Do-Nothing.

[8]Go now, write it on a tablet for them,
inscribe it on a scroll,
that for the days to come
it may be an everlasting witness.
[9]These are rebellious people,
deceitful children,
children unwilling to listen to the
LORD's instruction.
[10]They say to the seers,
"See no more visions!"
and to the prophets,
"Give us no more visions of what
is right!
Tell us pleasant things,
prophesy illusions.
[11]Leave this way,
get off this path,
and stop confronting us
with the Holy One of Israel!"

[12]Therefore, this is what the Holy One of Israel says:

"Because you have rejected this
message,
relied on oppression
and depended on deceit,
[13]this sin will become for you
like a high wall, cracked and
bulging,
that collapses suddenly, in an
instant.
[14]It will break in pieces like pottery,
shattered so mercilessly
that among its pieces not a fragment
will be found
for taking coals from a hearth
or scooping water out of a
cistern."

[15]This is what the Sovereign LORD, the Holy One of Israel, says:

"In repentance and rest is your
salvation,
in quietness and trust is your
strength,
but you would have none of it.
[16]You said, 'No, we will flee on
horses.'
Therefore you will flee!
You said, 'We will ride off on swift
horses.'
Therefore your pursuers will be
swift!
[17]A thousand will flee
at the threat of one;
at the threat of five
you will all flee away,
till you are left
like a flagstaff on a mountaintop,
like a banner on a hill."

[18]Yet the LORD longs to be gracious to
you;
he rises to show you compassion.
For the LORD is a God of justice.
Blessed are all who wait for him!

[19]O people of Zion, who live in Jerusalem, you will weep no more. How gracious he will be when you cry for help!
As soon as he hears, he will answer you.
[20]Although the Lord gives you the bread
of adversity and the water of affliction,
your teachers will be hidden no more;
with your own eyes you will see them.
[21]Whether you turn to the right or to the
left, your ears will hear a voice behind
you, saying, "This is the way; walk in it."
[22]Then you will defile your idols overlaid with silver and your images covered with gold; you will throw them

away like a menstrual cloth and say to them, "Away with you!"

[23]He will also send you rain for the seed you sow in the ground, and the food that comes from the land will be rich and plentiful. In that day your cattle will graze in broad meadows. [24]The oxen and donkeys that work the soil will eat fodder and mash, spread out with fork and shovel. [25]In the day of great slaughter, when the towers fall, streams of water will flow on every high mountain and every lofty hill. [26]The moon will shine like the sun, and the sunlight will be seven times brighter, like the light of seven full days, when the LORD binds up the bruises of his people and heals the wounds he inflicted.

[27]See, the Name of the LORD comes
from afar,
with burning anger and dense
clouds of smoke;
his lips are full of wrath,
and his tongue is a consuming
fire.
[28]His breath is like a rushing torrent,
rising up to the neck.
He shakes the nations in the sieve of
destruction;
he places in the jaws of the
peoples
a bit that leads them astray.
[29]And you will sing
as on the night you celebrate a
holy festival;
your hearts will rejoice
as when people go up with flutes
to the mountain of the LORD,
to the Rock of Israel.
[30]The LORD will cause men to hear his
majestic voice
and will make them see his arm
coming down
with raging anger and consuming
fire,
with cloudburst, thunderstorm
and hail.
[31]The voice of the LORD will shatter
Assyria;
with his scepter he will strike
them down.
[32]Every stroke the LORD lays on them
with his punishing rod
will be to the music of tambourines
and harps,
as he fights them in battle with
the blows of his arm.
[33]Topheth has long been prepared;
it has been made ready for the
king.
Its fire pit has been made deep and
wide,
with an abundance of fire and
wood;
the breath of the LORD,
like a stream of burning sulfur,
sets it ablaze.

Woe to Those Who Rely on Egypt

31 Woe to those who go down
to Egypt for help,
who rely on horses,
who trust in the multitude of their
chariots
and in the great strength of their
horsemen,
but do not look to the Holy One of
Israel,
or seek help from the LORD.
[2]Yet he too is wise and can bring
disaster;
he does not take back his words.
He will rise up against the house of
the wicked,
against those who help evildoers.
[3]But the Egyptians are men and not
God;
their horses are flesh and not
spirit.
When the LORD stretches out his
hand,
he who helps will stumble,
he who is helped will fall;
both will perish together.

[4]This is what the LORD says to me:

"As a lion growls,
a great lion over his prey—
and though a whole band of
shepherds
is called together against him,
he is not frightened by their shouts
or disturbed by their clamor—
so the LORD Almighty will come
down

to do battle on Mount Zion and
on its heights.
5 Like birds hovering overhead,
the LORD Almighty will shield
Jerusalem;
he will shield it and deliver it,
he will 'pass over' it and will
rescue it."

6 Return to him you have so greatly revolted against, O Israelites. 7 For in that
day every one of you will reject the idols
of silver and gold your sinful hands
have made.

8 "Assyria will fall by a sword that is
not of man;
a sword, not of mortals, will
devour them.
They will flee before the sword
and their young men will be put
to forced labor.
9 Their stronghold will fall because of
terror;
at sight of the battle standard their
commanders will panic,"
declares the LORD,
whose fire is in Zion,
whose furnace is in Jerusalem.

SHARPEN THE FOCUS

How patiently can you wait? If a crowded doctor's office or long lines at the checkout counter get under your skin, you're not alone. And yet, sometimes in our walk with God, we find ourselves waiting. Take a closer look at Isaiah 30:18.

> *The LORD longs to be gracious to you; He rises to show you compassion. For the LORD is a God of justice. Blessed are all who wait for Him!*

The Lord wanted Judah to return so He could show His people His grace and mercy. But they kept Him waiting. Contrast their endangered state with the blessing of those in Judah who waited in peace for the Lord to act for them.

Perhaps today you find yourself feeling stuck in one way or another. Something needs to happen. Some mountain needs to move. Some attitude needs to change. Some relief needs to come. And it's not happening soon enough to suit you.

If so, ask yourself, "Am I waiting on God? Or is He waiting on me? Am I trying to pull every string, even forging alliances with the ungodly as Judah's leaders did? Or am I by grace doing what God has asked of me and then leaving the outcome in His just and loving hands?"

WEEK 55 • THURSDAY

Isaiah 32:1–20

GET THE BIG PICTURE

God's people have always longed for the day when all of God's priorities will be established. That day will come. But we're not there yet. We wonder when the day will come. But we wonder even more about another question: "Will we make it through? Will we be okay until then?" As you read now, look for the Lord's answer. If time is short, focus on Isaiah 32:12–20.

The Kingdom of Righteousness

32 See, a king will reign in righteousness
and rulers will rule with justice.
2 Each man will be like a shelter from the wind
and a refuge from the storm,
like streams of water in the desert
and the shadow of a great rock in a thirsty land.
3 Then the eyes of those who see will no longer be closed,
and the ears of those who hear will listen.
4 The mind of the rash will know and understand,
and the stammering tongue will be fluent and clear.
5 No longer will the fool be called noble
nor the scoundrel be highly respected.
6 For the fool speaks folly,
his mind is busy with evil:
He practices ungodliness
and spreads error concerning the LORD;
the hungry he leaves empty
and from the thirsty he withholds water.
7 The scoundrel's methods are wicked,
he makes up evil schemes
to destroy the poor with lies,
even when the plea of the needy is just.
8 But the noble man makes noble plans,
and by noble deeds he stands.

The Women of Jerusalem

9 You women who are so complacent,
rise up and listen to me;
you daughters who feel secure,
hear what I have to say!
10 In little more than a year
you who feel secure will tremble;
the grape harvest will fail,
and the harvest of fruit will not come.
11 Tremble, you complacent women;
shudder, you daughters who feel secure!
Strip off your clothes,
put sackcloth around your waists.
12 Beat your breasts for the pleasant fields,
for the fruitful vines
13 and for the land of my people,
a land overgrown with thorns and briers—
yes, mourn for all houses of merriment
and for this city of revelry.
14 The fortress will be abandoned,
the noisy city deserted;
citadel and watchtower will become a wasteland forever,
the delight of donkeys, a pasture for flocks,
15 till the Spirit is poured upon us from on high,
and the desert becomes a fertile field,
and the fertile field seems like a forest.
16 Justice will dwell in the desert
and righteousness live in the fertile field.
17 The fruit of righteousness will be peace;
the effect of righteousness will be quietness and confidence forever.
18 My people will live in peaceful dwelling places,
in secure homes,
in undisturbed places of rest.
19 Though hail flattens the forest
and the city is leveled completely,
20 how blessed you will be,
sowing your seed by every stream,
and letting your cattle and donkeys range free.

SHARPEN THE FOCUS

The mighty forest that had been Assyria (Isaiah 10:33–34) would be shredded in the hailstorm of the Lord's judgment (Isaiah 32:19a). Jerusalem, the city that David and Solomon had built would be razed. The royal palaces of both nations would be forsaken (Isaiah 32:14).

But as God's repentant people then looked ahead to the time of chaos created by human sin, they did not despair. And neither need we. Ancient Judah's faithful remnant believed her Lord would send the King, the Messiah, who would reign in righteousness. We know that King as our Savior. We have seen Him come once—not in judgment, but in mercy to remove our sins. And we know He will come again to take us to Himself in heaven.

Until that Day, He is at work in us, through us, and for us. The same Holy Spirit who strengthened Christ for His mission (Isaiah 11:2) has now been "poured upon us from on high" (Isaiah 32:15). That Spirit makes it possible for our lives to be fruitful fields (Isaiah 32:16), producing by His grace more and more love, joy, peace, patience, and kindness (see Galatians 5:22–23).

Assured of the right standing with our God that comes by faith in Christ, we can face any circumstance with calmness and contentment.

Today's reading provides a mini-vacation, of sorts. It reminds us again of the rest that belongs to the citizens of God's kingdom because of Christ. Many of these blessings are ours right now. Some are yet to come. Look for all of them as you read Isaiah's words of promise. If time is short, focus on Isaiah 35:1–10.

Distress and Help

33 Woe to you, O destroyer,
you who have not been destroyed!
Woe to you, O traitor,
you who have not been betrayed!
When you stop destroying,
you will be destroyed;
when you stop betraying,
you will be betrayed.

2 O LORD, be gracious to us;
we long for you.
Be our strength every morning,
our salvation in time of distress.

3 At the thunder of your voice, the peoples flee;
when you rise up, the nations scatter.
4 Your plunder, O nations, is harvested as by young locusts;
like a swarm of locusts men pounce on it.

5 The LORD is exalted, for he dwells on high;
he will fill Zion with justice and righteousness.
6 He will be the sure foundation for your times,

a rich store of salvation and
wisdom and knowledge;
the fear of the LORD is the key to
this treasure.[a]

7 Look, their brave men cry aloud in
the streets;
the envoys of peace weep bitterly.
8 The highways are deserted,
no travelers are on the roads.
The treaty is broken,
its witnesses[b] are despised,
no one is respected.
9 The land mourns[c] and wastes away,
Lebanon is ashamed and withers;
Sharon is like the Arabah,
and Bashan and Carmel drop
their leaves.

10 "Now will I arise," says the LORD.
"Now will I be exalted;
now will I be lifted up.
11 You conceive chaff,
you give birth to straw;
your breath is a fire that consumes
you.
12 The peoples will be burned as if to
lime;
like cut thornbushes they will be
set ablaze."

13 You who are far away, hear what I
have done;
you who are near, acknowledge
my power!
14 The sinners in Zion are terrified;
trembling grips the godless:
"Who of us can dwell with the
consuming fire?
Who of us can dwell with
everlasting burning?"
15 He who walks righteously
and speaks what is right,
who rejects gain from extortion
and keeps his hand from
accepting bribes,
who stops his ears against plots of
murder
and shuts his eyes against
contemplating evil—
16 this is the man who will dwell on
the heights,
whose refuge will be the
mountain fortress.
His bread will be supplied,
and water will not fail him.

17 Your eyes will see the king in his
beauty
and view a land that stretches afar.
18 In your thoughts you will ponder
the former terror:
"Where is that chief officer?
Where is the one who took the
revenue?
Where is the officer in charge of
the towers?"
19 You will see those arrogant people
no more,
those people of an obscure speech,
with their strange,
incomprehensible tongue.
20 Look upon Zion, the city of our
festivals;
your eyes will see Jerusalem,
a peaceful abode, a tent that will
not be moved;
its stakes will never be pulled up,
nor any of its ropes broken.
21 There the LORD will be our Mighty
One.
It will be like a place of broad
rivers and streams.
No galley with oars will ride them,
no mighty ship will sail them.
22 For the LORD is our judge,
the LORD is our lawgiver,
the LORD is our king;
it is he who will save us.

23 Your rigging hangs loose:
The mast is not held secure,
the sail is not spread.
Then an abundance of spoils will be
divided
and even the lame will carry off
plunder.
24 No one living in Zion will say, "I am
ill";
and the sins of those who dwell
there will be forgiven.

Judgment Against the Nations

34 Come near, you nations,
and listen;

[a]6 Or *is a treasure from him* [b]8 Dead Sea Scrolls; Masoretic Text / *the cities* [c]9 Or *dries up*

pay attention, you peoples!
Let the earth hear, and all that is in it,
the world, and all that comes out of it!
2 The LORD is angry with all nations;
his wrath is upon all their armies.
He will totally destroy[a] them,
he will give them over to slaughter.
3 Their slain will be thrown out,
their dead bodies will send up a stench;
the mountains will be soaked with their blood.
4 All the stars of the heavens will be dissolved
and the sky rolled up like a scroll;
all the starry host will fall
like withered leaves from the vine,
like shriveled figs from the fig tree.
5 My sword has drunk its fill in the heavens;
see, it descends in judgment on Edom,
the people I have totally destroyed.
6 The sword of the LORD is bathed in blood,
it is covered with fat—
the blood of lambs and goats,
fat from the kidneys of rams.
For the LORD has a sacrifice in Bozrah
and a great slaughter in Edom.
7 And the wild oxen will fall with them,
the bull calves and the great bulls.
Their land will be drenched with blood,
and the dust will be soaked with fat.
8 For the LORD has a day of vengeance,
a year of retribution, to uphold Zion's cause.
9 Edom's streams will be turned into pitch,
her dust into burning sulfur;
her land will become blazing pitch!
10 It will not be quenched night and day;
its smoke will rise forever.
From generation to generation it will lie desolate;
no one will ever pass through it again.
11 The desert owl[b] and screech owl[b]
will possess it;
the great owl[b] and the raven will nest there.
God will stretch out over Edom
the measuring line of chaos
and the plumb line of desolation.
12 Her nobles will have nothing there
to be called a kingdom,
all her princes will vanish away.
13 Thorns will overrun her citadels,
nettles and brambles her strongholds.
She will become a haunt for jackals,
a home for owls.
14 Desert creatures will meet with hyenas,
and wild goats will bleat to each other;
there the night creatures will also repose
and find for themselves places of rest.
15 The owl will nest there and lay eggs,
she will hatch them, and care for her young under the shadow of her wings;
there also the falcons will gather,
each with its mate.

16 Look in the scroll of the LORD and read:

None of these will be missing,
not one will lack her mate.
For it is his mouth that has given the order,
and his Spirit will gather them together.
17 He allots their portions;
his hand distributes them by measure.

[a]2 The Hebrew term refers to the irrevocable giving over of things or persons to the LORD, often by totally destroying them; also in verse 5.
[b]11 The precise identification of these birds is uncertain.

They will possess it forever
and dwell there from generation to generation.

Joy of the Redeemed

35 The desert and the parched land will be glad;
the wilderness will rejoice and blossom.
Like the crocus,
2 it will burst into bloom;
it will rejoice greatly and shout for joy.
The glory of Lebanon will be given to it,
the splendor of Carmel and Sharon;
they will see the glory of the LORD,
the splendor of our God.
3 Strengthen the feeble hands,
steady the knees that give way;
4 say to those with fearful hearts,
"Be strong, do not fear;
your God will come,
he will come with vengeance;
with divine retribution
he will come to save you."
5 Then will the eyes of the blind be opened
and the ears of the deaf unstopped.
6 Then will the lame leap like a deer,
and the mute tongue shout for joy.
Water will gush forth in the wilderness
and streams in the desert.
7 The burning sand will become a pool,
the thirsty ground bubbling springs.
In the haunts where jackals once lay,
grass and reeds and papyrus will grow.
8 And a highway will be there;
it will be called the Way of Holiness.
The unclean will not journey on it;
it will be for those who walk in that Way;
wicked fools will not go about on it.[a]
9 No lion will be there,
nor will any ferocious beast get up on it;
they will not be found there.
But only the redeemed will walk there,
10 and the ransomed of the LORD will return.
They will enter Zion with singing;
everlasting joy will crown their heads.
Gladness and joy will overtake them,
and sorrow and sighing will flee away.

[a]8 Or / *the simple will not stray from it*

SHARPEN THE FOCUS

What problems tire you out? What worries rob you of sleep? What concerns so sap your courage that your arms feel heavy and your knees buckle? What would the Lord say to you about those problems, worries, and concerns?

If you cringed at that last question, if you suppose that your Savior would scold or condemn you for fretting and for your lack of faith, you'd be wrong. Look at Isaiah 35:3–4 and read the message the Lord put in the mouth of His spokesman 700 years before Jesus' birth:

> *Strengthen the feeble hands, steady the knees that give way; say to those with fearful hearts, "Be strong, do not fear; your God will come, He will come with vengeance; with divine retribution He will come to save you."*

He will come to save you. Isaiah's readers thought first, perhaps, of the threat from the Assyrian army. And the Lord did deliver Judah from that threat. We think first, perhaps, of the threat from sin and death. And the Lord Jesus did come to deliver all people from that threat, too, on the tree of His cross. Ultimately, our Lord will come to take us to the heavenly Zion, Jerusalem above, where we will be safe forever.

WEEK 55 • SATURDAY

Isaiah 36:1—39:8

Isaiah ministered in Judah under four different kings–Uzziah, Jotham, Ahaz, and Hezekiah (c. 740–680 B.C.). We have read Hezekiah's story twice before, in 2 Kings 18–20 and 2 Chronicles 29–32. Isaiah adds more details and focuses on the cosmic level of Judah's battle, the Lord vs. His enemies. If time is short, focus on Isaiah 38:1–20.

Sennacherib Threatens Jerusalem

36 In the fourteenth year of King Hezekiah's reign, Sennacherib king of Assyria attacked all the fortified cities of Judah and captured them. 2Then the king of Assyria sent his field commander with a large army from Lachish to King Hezekiah at Jerusalem. When the commander stopped at the aqueduct of the Upper Pool, on the road to the Washerman's Field, 3Eliakim son of Hilkiah the palace administrator, Shebna the secretary, and Joah son of Asaph the recorder went out to him.

4The field commander said to them, "Tell Hezekiah,

" 'This is what the great king, the king of Assyria, says: On what are you basing this confidence of yours? 5You say you have strategy and military strength—but you speak only empty words. On whom are you depending, that you rebel against me? 6Look now, you are depending on Egypt, that splintered reed of a staff, which pierces a man's hand and wounds him if he leans on it! Such is Pharaoh king of Egypt to all who depend on him. 7And if you say to me, "We are depending on the LORD our God"—isn't he the one whose high places and altars Hezekiah removed, saying to Judah and Jerusalem, "You must worship before this altar"?

8" 'Come now, make a bargain with my master, the king of Assyria: I will give you two thousand horses—if you can put riders on them! 9How then can you repulse one officer of the least of my master's officials, even though you are depending on Egypt for chariots and horsemen? 10Furthermore, have I come to attack and destroy this land without the LORD? The LORD himself told me to march against this country and destroy it.' "

11Then Eliakim, Shebna and Joah said to the field commander, "Please speak to your servants in Aramaic, since we understand it. Don't speak to us in Hebrew in the hearing of the people on the wall."

12But the commander replied, "Was it only to your master and you that my master sent me to say these things, and

not to the men sitting on the wall—who,
like you, will have to eat their own filth
and drink their own urine?"
13Then the commander stood and
called out in Hebrew, "Hear the words
of the great king, the king of Assyria!
14This is what the king says: Do not let
Hezekiah deceive you. He cannot deliver you! 15Do not let Hezekiah persuade you to trust in the LORD when he
says, 'The LORD will surely deliver us;
this city will not be given into the hand
of the king of Assyria.'
16"Do not listen to Hezekiah. This is
what the king of Assyria says: Make
peace with me and come out to me.
Then every one of you will eat from his
own vine and fig tree and drink water
from his own cistern, 17until I come and
take you to a land like your own—a land
of grain and new wine, a land of bread
and vineyards.
18"Do not let Hezekiah mislead you
when he says, 'The LORD will deliver
us.' Has the god of any nation ever delivered his land from the hand of the
king of Assyria? 19Where are the gods of
Hamath and Arpad? Where are the
gods of Sepharvaim? Have they rescued
Samaria from my hand? 20Who of all the
gods of these countries has been able to
save his land from me? How then can
the LORD deliver Jerusalem from my
hand?"
21But the people remained silent and
said nothing in reply, because the king
had commanded, "Do not answer him."
22Then Eliakim son of Hilkiah the
palace administrator, Shebna the secretary, and Joah son of Asaph the recorder went to Hezekiah, with their clothes
torn, and told him what the field commander had said.

Jerusalem's Deliverance Foretold

37 When King Hezekiah
heard this, he tore his
clothes and put on sackcloth and went
into the temple of the LORD. 2He sent
Eliakim the palace administrator, Shebna the secretary, and the leading priests,
all wearing sackcloth, to the prophet
Isaiah son of Amoz. 3They told him,
"This is what Hezekiah says: This day is
a day of distress and rebuke and disgrace, as when children come to the
point of birth and there is no strength
to deliver them. 4It may be that the LORD
your God will hear the words of the
field commander, whom his master,
the king of Assyria, has sent to ridicule
the living God, and that he will rebuke
him for the words the LORD your God
has heard. Therefore pray for the remnant that still survives."
5When King Hezekiah's officials came
to Isaiah, 6Isaiah said to them, "Tell your
master, 'This is what the LORD says: Do
not be afraid of what you have heard—
those words with which the underlings
of the king of Assyria have blasphemed
me. 7Listen! I am going to put a spirit in
him so that when he hears a certain report, he will return to his own country,
and there I will have him cut down with
the sword.' "
8When the field commander heard
that the king of Assyria had left Lachish,
he withdrew and found the king fighting against Libnah.
9Now Sennacherib received a report
that Tirhakah, the Cushite[a] king ⌞of
Egypt⌟, was marching out to fight
against him. When he heard it, he sent
messengers to Hezekiah with this word:
10"Say to Hezekiah king of Judah: Do
not let the god you depend on deceive
you when he says, 'Jerusalem will not be
handed over to the king of Assyria.'
11Surely you have heard what the kings
of Assyria have done to all the countries,
destroying them completely. And will
you be delivered? 12Did the gods of the
nations that were destroyed by my forefathers deliver them—the gods of Gozan, Haran, Rezeph and the people of
Eden who were in Tel Assar? 13Where is
the king of Hamath, the king of Arpad,
the king of the city of Sepharvaim, or of
Hena or Ivvah?"

Hezekiah's Prayer

14Hezekiah received the letter from
the messengers and read it. Then he

[a]9 That is, from the upper Nile region

went up to the temple of the LORD and
spread it out before the LORD. 15 And
Hezekiah prayed to the LORD: 16 "O
LORD Almighty, God of Israel, enthroned between the cherubim, you alone are God over all the kingdoms of the earth. You have made heaven and
earth. 17 Give ear, O LORD, and hear;
open your eyes, O LORD, and see; listen to all the words Sennacherib has sent to insult the living God.

18 "It is true, O LORD, that the Assyrian
kings have laid waste all these peoples
and their lands. 19 They have thrown
their gods into the fire and destroyed them, for they were not gods but only wood and stone, fashioned by human
hands. 20 Now, O LORD our God, deliver
us from his hand, so that all kingdoms on earth may know that you alone, O LORD, are God.[a]"

Sennacherib's Fall

21 Then Isaiah son of Amoz sent a message to Hezekiah: "This is what the LORD, the God of Israel, says: Because you have prayed to me concerning
Sennacherib king of Assyria, 22 this is the
word the LORD has spoken against him:

"The Virgin Daughter of Zion
despises and mocks you.
The Daughter of Jerusalem
tosses her head as you flee.
23 Who is it you have insulted and
blasphemed?
Against whom have you raised
your voice
and lifted your eyes in pride?
Against the Holy One of Israel!
24 By your messengers
you have heaped insults on the
Lord.
And you have said,
'With my many chariots
I have ascended the heights of the
mountains,
the utmost heights of Lebanon.
I have cut down its tallest cedars,
the choicest of its pines.
I have reached its remotest heights,
the finest of its forests.
25 I have dug wells in foreign lands[b]
and drunk the water there.
With the soles of my feet
I have dried up all the streams of
Egypt.'

26 "Have you not heard?
Long ago I ordained it.
In days of old I planned it;
now I have brought it to pass,
that you have turned fortified
cities
into piles of stone.
27 Their people, drained of power,
are dismayed and put to shame.
They are like plants in the field,
like tender green shoots,
like grass sprouting on the roof,
scorched[c] before it grows up.

28 "But I know where you stay
and when you come and go
and how you rage against me.
29 Because you rage against me
and because your insolence has
reached my ears,
I will put my hook in your nose
and my bit in your mouth,
and I will make you return
by the way you came.

30 "This will be the sign for you, O Hezekiah:

"This year you will eat what grows
by itself,
and the second year what springs
from that.
But in the third year sow and reap,
plant vineyards and eat their fruit.
31 Once more a remnant of the house
of Judah
will take root below and bear fruit
above.
32 For out of Jerusalem will come a
remnant,
and out of Mount Zion a band of
survivors.

[a]20 Dead Sea Scrolls (see also 2 Kings 19:19); Masoretic Text *alone are the LORD* [b]25 Dead Sea Scrolls (see also 2 Kings 19:24); Masoretic Text does not have *in foreign lands.* [c]27 Some manuscripts of the Masoretic Text, Dead Sea Scrolls and some Septuagint manuscripts (see also 2 Kings 19:26); most manuscripts of the Masoretic Text *roof / and terraced fields*

The zeal of the LORD Almighty
will accomplish this.

33"Therefore this is what the LORD
says concerning the king of Assyria:

"He will not enter this city
or shoot an arrow here.
He will not come before it with
shield
or build a siege ramp against it.
34By the way that he came he will
return;
he will not enter this city,"
declares the LORD.
35"I will defend this city and save it,
for my sake and for the sake of
David my servant!"

36Then the angel of the LORD went out
and put to death a hundred and eighty-
five thousand men in the Assyrian
camp. When the people got up the next
morning—there were all the dead bodies! 37So Sennacherib king of Assyria
broke camp and withdrew. He returned
to Nineveh and stayed there.
38One day, while he was worshiping
in the temple of his god Nisroch, his
sons Adrammelech and Sharezer cut
him down with the sword, and they
escaped to the land of Ararat. And Esarhaddon his son succeeded him as king.

Hezekiah's Illness

38 In those days Hezekiah
became ill and was at the
point of death. The prophet Isaiah son
of Amoz went to him and said, "This is
what the LORD says: Put your house in
order, because you are going to die; you
will not recover."
2Hezekiah turned his face to the wall
and prayed to the LORD, 3"Remember, O
LORD, how I have walked before you
faithfully and with wholehearted devotion and have done what is good in your
eyes." And Hezekiah wept bitterly.
4Then the word of the LORD came to
Isaiah: 5"Go and tell Hezekiah, 'This is
what the LORD, the God of your father
David, says: I have heard your prayer
and seen your tears; I will add fifteen
years to your life. 6And I will deliver you
and this city from the hand of the king
of Assyria. I will defend this city.
7" 'This is the LORD's sign to you that
the LORD will do what he has promised:
8I will make the shadow cast by the sun
go back the ten steps it has gone down
on the stairway of Ahaz.' " So the sunlight went back the ten steps it had gone
down.

9A writing of Hezekiah king of Judah
after his illness and recovery:

10I said, "In the prime of my life
must I go through the gates of
death[a]
and be robbed of the rest of my
years?"
11I said, "I will not again see the LORD,
the LORD, in the land of the living;
no longer will I look on mankind,
or be with those who now dwell
in this world.[b]
12Like a shepherd's tent my house
has been pulled down and taken
from me.
Like a weaver I have rolled up my
life,
and he has cut me off from the
loom;
day and night you made an end of
me.
13I waited patiently till dawn,
but like a lion he broke all my
bones;
day and night you made an end of
me.
14I cried like a swift or thrush,
I moaned like a mourning dove.
My eyes grew weak as I looked to
the heavens.
I am troubled; O Lord, come to
my aid!"

15But what can I say?
He has spoken to me, and he
himself has done this.
I will walk humbly all my years
because of this anguish of my
soul.
16Lord, by such things men live;

[a]*10* Hebrew *Sheol* [b]*11* A few Hebrew manuscripts; most Hebrew manuscripts *in the place of cessation*

and my spirit finds life in them
too.
You restored me to health
and let me live.
17 Surely it was for my benefit
that I suffered such anguish.
In your love you kept me
from the pit of destruction;
you have put all my sins
behind your back.
18 For the grave[a] cannot praise you,
death cannot sing your praise;
those who go down to the pit
cannot hope for your faithfulness.
19 The living, the living—they praise
you,
as I am doing today;
fathers tell their children
about your faithfulness.

20 The LORD will save me,
and we will sing with stringed
instruments
all the days of our lives
in the temple of the LORD.

21 Isaiah had said, "Prepare a poultice of figs and apply it to the boil, and he will recover."

22 Hezekiah had asked, "What will be the sign that I will go up to the temple of the LORD?"

Envoys From Babylon

39 At that time Merodach-Baladan son of Baladan king of Babylon sent Hezekiah letters and a gift, because he had heard of his illness and recovery.
2 Hezekiah received
the envoys gladly and showed them what was in his storehouses—the silver, the gold, the spices, the fine oil, his entire armory and everything found among his treasures. There was nothing in his palace or in all his kingdom that Hezekiah did not show them.

3 Then Isaiah the prophet went to King Hezekiah and asked, "What did those men say, and where did they come from?"

"From a distant land," Hezekiah replied. "They came to me from Babylon."

4 The prophet asked, "What did they see in your palace?"

"They saw everything in my palace," Hezekiah said. "There is nothing among my treasures that I did not show them."

5 Then Isaiah said to Hezekiah, "Hear
the word of the LORD Almighty:
6 The
time will surely come when everything in your palace, and all that your fathers have stored up until this day, will be carried off to Babylon. Nothing will be left, says the LORD.
7 And some of
your descendants, your own flesh and blood who will be born to you, will be taken away, and they will become eunuchs in the palace of the king of Babylon."

8 "The word of the LORD you have spoken is good," Hezekiah replied. For he thought, "There will be peace and security in my lifetime."

[a]18 Hebrew *Sheol*

SHARPEN THE FOCUS

When danger approaches, the bridge of the *Enterprise* goes on Red Alert. In the real life Navy and the *Star Trek* science-fiction series, the response to danger is the same—well rehearsed, swift, and certain.

When challenges or dangers, sickness or temptations strike your life, what's *your* first response? Isaiah tells us that King Hezekiah turned to the Lord and to His Word. Hezekiah prayed. The king's response was well-rehearsed, swift, and certain. Why? No doubt Hezekiah had been led by the Holy Spirit to turn to God in every circumstance. We see the king asking for help in time of crisis and returning thanks for that help. He had become convinced that the Lord, the living God, was ready—always ready—to save him (Isaiah 38:20a).

Could it be that out own prayerlessness comes because we're not yet convinced that the

Lord, the living God, is ready—always ready—to save us, too? Why not ask the Holy Spirit to reveal to you those things He would like to do in you to renew your prayer life? He is willing and able because of Jesus' cross to draw you closer to the Father's heart and to lead you into a deeper life of prayer and praise. ☼

WEEK 56 • MONDAY

Isaiah 40:1—41:29

Today's chapters, Isaiah 40 and 41 stand among the most glorious and powerful in all of Scripture. They speak of the Lord's deliverance and power, His reign and mercy. As you read, note the many things your Lord in grace has done and continues to do—for *you*! If time is short, focus on Isaiah 41:1–29.

Comfort for God's People

40 Comfort, comfort my
people,
says your God.
2 Speak tenderly to Jerusalem,
and proclaim to her
that her hard service has been
completed,
that her sin has been paid for,
that she has received from the
LORD's hand
double for all her sins.

3 A voice of one calling:
"In the desert prepare
the way for the LORD[a];
make straight in the wilderness
a highway for our God.[b]
4 Every valley shall be raised up,
every mountain and hill made
low;
the rough ground shall become
level,
the rugged places a plain.
5 And the glory of the LORD will be
revealed,
and all mankind together will see
it.
For the mouth of the LORD
has spoken."

6 A voice says, "Cry out."
And I said, "What shall I cry?"
"All men are like grass,
and all their glory is like the
flowers of the field.
7 The grass withers and the flowers
fall,
because the breath of the LORD
blows on them.
Surely the people are grass.
8 The grass withers and the flowers
fall,
but the word of our God stands
forever."

9 You who bring good tidings to Zion,
go up on a high mountain.
You who bring good tidings to
Jerusalem,[c]
lift up your voice with a shout,
lift it up, do not be afraid;
say to the towns of Judah,
"Here is your God!"
10 See, the Sovereign LORD comes with
power,

[a]3 Or *A voice of one calling in the desert: / "Prepare the way for the LORD* [b]3 Hebrew; Septuagint *make straight the paths of our God* [c]9 Or *O Zion, bringer of good tidings, / go up on a high mountain. / O Jerusalem, bringer of good tidings*

and his arm rules for him.
See, his reward is with him,
and his recompense accompanies him.
11 He tends his flock like a shepherd:
He gathers the lambs in his arms
and carries them close to his heart;
he gently leads those that have young.

12 Who has measured the waters in the hollow of his hand,
or with the breadth of his hand marked off the heavens?
Who has held the dust of the earth in a basket,
or weighed the mountains on the scales
and the hills in a balance?
13 Who has understood the mind[a] of the LORD,
or instructed him as his counselor?
14 Whom did the LORD consult to enlighten him,
and who taught him the right way?
Who was it that taught him knowledge
or showed him the path of understanding?

15 Surely the nations are like a drop in a bucket;
they are regarded as dust on the scales;
he weighs the islands as though they were fine dust.
16 Lebanon is not sufficient for altar fires,
nor its animals enough for burnt offerings.
17 Before him all the nations are as nothing;
they are regarded by him as worthless
and less than nothing.

18 To whom, then, will you compare God?
What image will you compare him to?
19 As for an idol, a craftsman casts it,
and a goldsmith overlays it with gold
and fashions silver chains for it.
20 A man too poor to present such an offering
selects wood that will not rot.
He looks for a skilled craftsman
to set up an idol that will not topple.

21 Do you not know?
Have you not heard?
Has it not been told you from the beginning?
Have you not understood since the earth was founded?
22 He sits enthroned above the circle of the earth,
and its people are like grasshoppers.
He stretches out the heavens like a canopy,
and spreads them out like a tent to live in.
23 He brings princes to naught
and reduces the rulers of this world to nothing.
24 No sooner are they planted,
no sooner are they sown,
no sooner do they take root in the ground,
than he blows on them and they wither,
and a whirlwind sweeps them away like chaff.

25 "To whom will you compare me?
Or who is my equal?" says the Holy One.
26 Lift your eyes and look to the heavens:
Who created all these?
He who brings out the starry host one by one,
and calls them each by name.
Because of his great power and mighty strength,
not one of them is missing.

27 Why do you say, O Jacob,
and complain, O Israel,
"My way is hidden from the LORD;
my cause is disregarded by my God"?

[a]13 Or *Spirit*; or *spirit*

28 Do you not know?
Have you not heard?
The LORD is the everlasting God,
the Creator of the ends of the earth.
He will not grow tired or weary,
and his understanding no one can fathom.
29 He gives strength to the weary
and increases the power of the weak.
30 Even youths grow tired and weary,
and young men stumble and fall;
31 but those who hope in the LORD
will renew their strength.
They will soar on wings like eagles;
they will run and not grow weary,
they will walk and not be faint.

The Helper of Israel

41 "Be silent before me, you islands!
Let the nations renew their strength!
Let them come forward and speak;
let us meet together at the place of judgment.

2 "Who has stirred up one from the east,
calling him in righteousness to his service[a]?
He hands nations over to him
and subdues kings before him.
He turns them to dust with his sword,
to windblown chaff with his bow.
3 He pursues them and moves on unscathed,
by a path his feet have not traveled before.
4 Who has done this and carried it through,
calling forth the generations from the beginning?
I, the LORD—with the first of them
and with the last—I am he."

5 The islands have seen it and fear;
the ends of the earth tremble.
They approach and come forward;
6 each helps the other
and says to his brother, "Be strong!"
7 The craftsman encourages the goldsmith,
and he who smooths with the hammer
spurs on him who strikes the anvil.
He says of the welding, "It is good."
He nails down the idol so it will not topple.

8 "But you, O Israel, my servant,
Jacob, whom I have chosen,
you descendants of Abraham my friend,
9 I took you from the ends of the earth,
from its farthest corners I called you.
I said, 'You are my servant';
I have chosen you and have not rejected you.
10 So do not fear, for I am with you;
do not be dismayed, for I am your God.
I will strengthen you and help you;
I will uphold you with my righteous right hand.

11 "All who rage against you
will surely be ashamed and disgraced;
those who oppose you
will be as nothing and perish.
12 Though you search for your enemies,
you will not find them.
Those who wage war against you
will be as nothing at all.
13 For I am the LORD, your God,
who takes hold of your right hand
and says to you, Do not fear;
I will help you.
14 Do not be afraid, O worm Jacob,
O little Israel,
for I myself will help you," declares the LORD,
your Redeemer, the Holy One of Israel.
15 "See, I will make you into a threshing sledge,
new and sharp, with many teeth.
You will thresh the mountains and crush them,

[a]2 Or / *whom victory meets at every step*

and reduce the hills to chaff.
16 You will winnow them, the wind
will pick them up,
and a gale will blow them away.
But you will rejoice in the LORD
and glory in the Holy One of
Israel.

17 "The poor and needy search for
water,
but there is none;
their tongues are parched with
thirst.
But I the LORD will answer them;
I, the God of Israel, will not
forsake them.
18 I will make rivers flow on barren
heights,
and springs within the valleys.
I will turn the desert into pools of
water,
and the parched ground into
springs.
19 I will put in the desert
the cedar and the acacia, the
myrtle and the olive.
I will set pines in the wasteland,
the fir and the cypress together,
20 so that people may see and know,
may consider and understand,
that the hand of the LORD has done
this,
that the Holy One of Israel has
created it.

21 "Present your case," says the LORD.
"Set forth your arguments," says
Jacob's King.
22 "Bring in ⌊your idols⌋ to tell us
what is going to happen.
Tell us what the former things were,
so that we may consider them
and know their final outcome.
Or declare to us the things to come,
23 tell us what the future holds,
so we may know that you are
gods.
Do something, whether good or
bad,
so that we will be dismayed and
filled with fear.
24 But you are less than nothing
and your works are utterly
worthless;
he who chooses you is detestable.

25 "I have stirred up one from the
north, and he comes—
one from the rising sun who calls
on my name.
He treads on rulers as if they were
mortar,
as if he were a potter treading the
clay.
26 Who told of this from the beginning,
so we could know,
or beforehand, so we could say,
'He was right'?
No one told of this,
no one foretold it,
no one heard any words from
you.
27 I was the first to tell Zion, 'Look,
here they are!'
I gave to Jerusalem a messenger of
good tidings.
28 I look but there is no one—
no one among them to give
counsel,
no one to give answer when I ask
them.
29 See, they are all false!
Their deeds amount to nothing;
their images are but wind and
confusion.

SHARPEN THE FOCUS

You may remember the words of our Lord Jesus:

> *"If you have faith as small as a mustard seed, you can say to this mountain, 'Move from here to there' and it will move. Nothing will be impossible for you."* (Matthew 17:20)

The prophet Isaiah in Isaiah 41:14–16 describes a second mountain-moving technique: Reduce the mountain to dust a little at a time and let the wind blow it away. Either way, the Lord's power and mercy work deliverance on behalf of "Jacob," of "Israel"—God's children.

As we find ourselves up against the mountains in our lives, we can remember God's, "I AM." First spoken to Moses at the burning bush (Exodus 3:14), this name reminds us that God never changes. He'll never grow old, never weaken, never fail us.

Second, we can focus not on the mountain but on the Lord's word of promise, His eternal "I will." Look at Isaiah 41:10:

I will strengthen you and help you;
I will uphold you with My righteous right hand.

Finally, we relax in our Savior-God's command of grace: "Do not fear" (Isaiah 41:10). Because we know what He has done for us in the cross of His Son, we can wait in peace for our mountains to move.

WEEK 56 • TUESDAY

Isaiah 42:1—43:28

GET THE BIG PICTURE

Isaiah's words of comfort grow more powerful as he speaks yet more clearly about the Messiah, the Servant of Yahweh. As you read, note how closely Isaiah ties God's work of creation with His work of redemption. Also note that through redemption the Lord creates Zion, His Israel, His church. If time is short, focus on Isaiah 43:1–28.

The Servant of the LORD

42 "Here is my servant,
whom I uphold,
my chosen one in whom I delight;
I will put my Spirit on him
and he will bring justice to the
nations.
2 He will not shout or cry out,
or raise his voice in the streets.
3 A bruised reed he will not break,
and a smoldering wick he will not
snuff out.
In faithfulness he will bring forth
justice;
4 he will not falter or be discouraged
till he establishes justice on earth.
In his law the islands will put
their hope."

5 This is what God the LORD says—
he who created the heavens and
stretched them out,
who spread out the earth and all
that comes out of it,
who gives breath to its people,
and life to those who walk on it:
6 "I, the LORD, have called you in
righteousness;
I will take hold of your hand.
I will keep you and will make you
to be a covenant for the people
and a light for the Gentiles,
7 to open eyes that are blind,
to free captives from prison
and to release from the
dungeon those who sit in
darkness.

[8]"I am the LORD; that is my name!
I will not give my glory to another
or my praise to idols.
[9]See, the former things have taken
place,
and new things I declare;
before they spring into being
I announce them to you."

Song of Praise to the LORD

[10]Sing to the LORD a new song,
his praise from the ends of the
earth,
you who go down to the sea, and all
that is in it,
you islands, and all who live in
them.
[11]Let the desert and its towns raise
their voices;
let the settlements where Kedar
lives rejoice.
Let the people of Sela sing for joy;
let them shout from the
mountaintops.
[12]Let them give glory to the LORD
and proclaim his praise in the
islands.
[13]The LORD will march out like a
mighty man,
like a warrior he will stir up his
zeal;
with a shout he will raise the battle
cry
and will triumph over his enemies.
[14]"For a long time I have kept silent,
I have been quiet and held myself
back.
But now, like a woman in childbirth,
I cry out, I gasp and pant.
[15]I will lay waste the mountains and
hills
and dry up all their vegetation;
I will turn rivers into islands
and dry up the pools.
[16]I will lead the blind by ways they
have not known,
along unfamiliar paths I will guide
them;
I will turn the darkness into light
before them
and make the rough places
smooth.
These are the things I will do;
I will not forsake them.
[17]But those who trust in idols,
who say to images, 'You are our
gods,'
will be turned back in utter
shame.

Israel Blind and Deaf

[18]"Hear, you deaf;
look, you blind, and see!
[19]Who is blind but my servant,
and deaf like the messenger I
send?
Who is blind like the one committed
to me,
blind like the servant of the
LORD?
[20]You have seen many things, but
have paid no attention;
your ears are open, but you hear
nothing."
[21]It pleased the LORD
for the sake of his righteousness
to make his law great and
glorious.
[22]But this is a people plundered and
looted,
all of them trapped in pits
or hidden away in prisons.
They have become plunder,
with no one to rescue them;
they have been made loot,
with no one to say, "Send them
back."

[23]Which of you will listen to this
or pay close attention in time to
come?
[24]Who handed Jacob over to become
loot,
and Israel to the plunderers?
Was it not the LORD,
against whom we have sinned?
For they would not follow his ways;
they did not obey his law.
[25]So he poured out on them his
burning anger,
the violence of war.
It enveloped them in flames, yet
they did not understand;
it consumed them, but they did
not take it to heart.

Israel's Only Savior

43 But now, this is what the LORD says—
he who created you, O Jacob,
he who formed you, O Israel:
"Fear not, for I have redeemed you;
I have summoned you by name;
you are mine.
2 When you pass through the waters,
I will be with you;
and when you pass through the rivers,
they will not sweep over you.
When you walk through the fire,
you will not be burned;
the flames will not set you ablaze.
3 For I am the LORD, your God,
the Holy One of Israel, your Savior;
I give Egypt for your ransom,
Cush[a] and Seba in your stead.
4 Since you are precious and honored in my sight,
and because I love you,
I will give men in exchange for you,
and people in exchange for your life.
5 Do not be afraid, for I am with you;
I will bring your children from the east
and gather you from the west.
6 I will say to the north, 'Give them up!'
and to the south, 'Do not hold them back.'
Bring my sons from afar
and my daughters from the ends of the earth—
7 everyone who is called by my name,
whom I created for my glory,
whom I formed and made."
8 Lead out those who have eyes but are blind,
who have ears but are deaf.
9 All the nations gather together
and the peoples assemble.
Which of them foretold this
and proclaimed to us the former things?
Let them bring in their witnesses to prove they were right,
so that others may hear and say,
"It is true."
10 "You are my witnesses," declares the LORD,
"and my servant whom I have chosen,
so that you may know and believe me
and understand that I am he.
Before me no god was formed,
nor will there be one after me.
11 I, even I, am the LORD,
and apart from me there is no savior.
12 I have revealed and saved and proclaimed—
I, and not some foreign god among you.
You are my witnesses," declares the LORD, "that I am God.
13 Yes, and from ancient days I am he.
No one can deliver out of my hand.
When I act, who can reverse it?"

God's Mercy and Israel's Unfaithfulness

14 This is what the LORD says—
your Redeemer, the Holy One of Israel:
"For your sake I will send to Babylon
and bring down as fugitives all the Babylonians,[b]
in the ships in which they took pride.
15 I am the LORD, your Holy One,
Israel's Creator, your King."
16 This is what the LORD says—
he who made a way through the sea,
a path through the mighty waters,
17 who drew out the chariots and horses,
the army and reinforcements together,
and they lay there, never to rise again,
extinguished, snuffed out like a wick:

[a]3 That is, the upper Nile region [b]14 Or *Chaldeans*

[18]"Forget the former things;
do not dwell on the past.
[19]See, I am doing a new thing!
Now it springs up; do you not
perceive it?
I am making a way in the desert
and streams in the wasteland.
[20]The wild animals honor me,
the jackals and the owls,
because I provide water in the
desert
and streams in the wasteland,
to give drink to my people, my
chosen,
[21] the people I formed for myself
that they may proclaim my praise.
[22]"Yet you have not called upon me,
O Jacob,
you have not wearied yourselves
for me, O Israel.
[23]You have not brought me sheep for
burnt offerings,
nor honored me with your
sacrifices.
I have not burdened you with grain
offerings
nor wearied you with demands
for incense.
[24]You have not bought any fragrant
calamus for me,
or lavished on me the fat of your
sacrifices.
But you have burdened me with
your sins
and wearied me with your
offenses.

[25]"I, even I, am he who blots out
your transgressions, for my own
sake,
and remembers your sins no
more.
[26]Review the past for me,
let us argue the matter together;
state the case for your innocence.
[27]Your first father sinned;
your spokesmen rebelled against
me.
[28]So I will disgrace the dignitaries of
your temple,
and I will consign Jacob to
destruction[a]
and Israel to scorn.

[a]28 The Hebrew term refers to the irrevocable giving over of things or persons to the LORD, often by totally destroying them.

SHARPEN THE FOCUS

Will the *real* servant please stand up? That may be what we want to say as we study Isaiah 42 and 43. First, the Servant of the Lord is the "Chosen One" of Isaiah 42:1–9. These verses describe the coming Savior. The heavenly Father quotes Isaiah 42:1 as Jesus is baptized (Luke 32:22). Jesus stands there, under the law of God, committing Himself to keep it in our place.

Because He did this and because He gave His life in payment for our sins, we have now become God's chosen children. The heavenly Father now says of each of us: "This is My beloved son, My beloved daughter. With him/her I am well-pleased." We have now become the Savior-God's witnesses, His servants (Isaiah 43:10).

Under the rule of our Lord Jesus, we gather together as His new Israel (Isaiah 43:15). Only He could take sinners and make them saints. Only He could create His church. The Lord created our universe from nothing. The Lord creates His church from the beams of His cross and from the light that streams out of His empty tomb.

We are created (Isaiah 43:7) for His glory. How can we help but serve Him with gladness as we glorify Him still more in words and deeds of love?

WEEK 56 • WEDNESDAY

Isaiah 44:1—45:25

From chapter 40 on, Isaiah has spoken words of special comfort to God's people. This message continues in today's chapters. As you read about Cyrus (Isaiah 44:28–45:7), you may want to review the role this king of Persia played in Judah's history (Ezra 1:1–8). Isaiah foretold all this about 150 years before it actually happened. If time is short, focus on Isaiah 44:1–28.

Israel the Chosen

44 "But now listen,
O Jacob, my servant,
Israel, whom I have chosen.
2 This is what the LORD says—
he who made you, who formed
you in the womb,
and who will help you:
Do not be afraid, O Jacob, my
servant,
Jeshurun, whom I have chosen.
3 For I will pour water on the thirsty
land,
and streams on the dry ground;
I will pour out my Spirit on your
offspring,
and my blessing on your
descendants.
4 They will spring up like grass in a
meadow,
like poplar trees by flowing
streams.
5 One will say, 'I belong to the LORD';
another will call himself by the
name of Jacob;
still another will write on his hand,
'The LORD's,'
and will take the name Israel.

The LORD, Not Idols

6 "This is what the LORD says—
Israel's King and Redeemer, the
LORD Almighty:
I am the first and I am the last;
apart from me there is no God.
7 Who then is like me? Let him
proclaim it.
Let him declare and lay out before
me
what has happened since I
established my ancient
people,
and what is yet to come—
yes, let him foretell what will
come.
8 Do not tremble, do not be afraid.
Did I not proclaim this and foretell
it long ago?
You are my witnesses. Is there any
God besides me?
No, there is no other Rock; I know
not one."

9 All who make idols are nothing,
and the things they treasure are
worthless.
Those who would speak up for them
are blind;
they are ignorant, to their own
shame.
10 Who shapes a god and casts an idol,
which can profit him nothing?
11 He and his kind will be put to
shame;
craftsmen are nothing but men.
Let them all come together and take
their stand;
they will be brought down to
terror and infamy.

12 The blacksmith takes a tool
and works with it in the coals;
he shapes an idol with hammers,
he forges it with the might of his
arm.

He gets hungry and loses his
strength;
he drinks no water and grows
faint.
13 The carpenter measures with a line
and makes an outline with a
marker;
he roughs it out with chisels
and marks it with compasses.
He shapes it in the form of man,
of man in all his glory,
that it may dwell in a shrine.
14 He cut down cedars,
or perhaps took a cypress or oak.
He let it grow among the trees of the
forest,
or planted a pine, and the rain
made it grow.
15 It is man's fuel for burning;
some of it he takes and warms
himself,
he kindles a fire and bakes bread.
But he also fashions a god and
worships it;
he makes an idol and bows down
to it.
16 Half of the wood he burns in the
fire;
over it he prepares his meal,
he roasts his meat and eats his fill.
He also warms himself and says,
"Ah! I am warm; I see the fire."
17 From the rest he makes a god, his
idol;
he bows down to it and worships.
He prays to it and says,
"Save me; you are my god."
18 They know nothing, they
understand nothing;
their eyes are plastered over so
they cannot see,
and their minds closed so they
cannot understand.
19 No one stops to think,
no one has the knowledge or
understanding to say,
"Half of it I used for fuel;
I even baked bread over its coals,
I roasted meat and I ate.
Shall I make a detestable thing from
what is left?
Shall I bow down to a block of
wood?"
20 He feeds on ashes, a deluded heart
misleads him;
he cannot save himself, or say,
"Is not this thing in my right hand
a lie?"

21 "Remember these things, O Jacob,
for you are my servant, O Israel.
I have made you, you are my
servant;
O Israel, I will not forget you.
22 I have swept away your offenses like
a cloud,
your sins like the morning mist.
Return to me,
for I have redeemed you."

23 Sing for joy, O heavens, for the
LORD has done this;
shout aloud, O earth beneath.
Burst into song, you mountains,
you forests and all your trees,
for the LORD has redeemed Jacob,
he displays his glory in Israel.

Jerusalem to Be Inhabited

24 "This is what the LORD says—
your Redeemer, who formed you
in the womb:

I am the LORD,
who has made all things,
who alone stretched out the
heavens,
who spread out the earth by myself,
25 who foils the signs of false prophets
and makes fools of diviners,
who overthrows the learning of the
wise
and turns it into nonsense,
26 who carries out the words of his
servants
and fulfills the predictions of his
messengers,

who says of Jerusalem, 'It shall be
inhabited,'
of the towns of Judah, 'They shall
be built,'
and of their ruins, 'I will restore
them,'
27 who says to the watery deep, 'Be
dry,
and I will dry up your streams,'

[28] who says of Cyrus, 'He is my
shepherd
and will accomplish all that I
please;
he will say of Jerusalem, "Let it be
rebuilt,"
and of the temple, "Let its
foundations be laid." '

45 "This is what the LORD
says to his anointed,
to Cyrus, whose right hand I take
hold of
to subdue nations before him
and to strip kings of their armor,
to open doors before him
so that gates will not be shut:
[2] I will go before you
and will level the mountains[a];
I will break down gates of bronze
and cut through bars of iron.
[3] I will give you the treasures of
darkness,
riches stored in secret places,
so that you may know that I am the
LORD,
the God of Israel, who summons
you by name.
[4] For the sake of Jacob my servant,
of Israel my chosen,
I summon you by name
and bestow on you a title of
honor,
though you do not acknowledge
me.
[5] I am the LORD, and there is no other;
apart from me there is no God.
I will strengthen you,
though you have not
acknowledged me,
[6] so that from the rising of the sun
to the place of its setting
men may know there is none
besides me.
I am the LORD, and there is no
other.
[7] I form the light and create darkness,
I bring prosperity and create
disaster;
I, the LORD, do all these things.

[8] "You heavens above, rain down
righteousness;
let the clouds shower it down.
Let the earth open wide,
let salvation spring up,
let righteousness grow with it;
I, the LORD, have created it.

[9] "Woe to him who quarrels with his
Maker,
to him who is but a potsherd
among the potsherds on the
ground.
Does the clay say to the potter,
'What are you making?'
Does your work say,
'He has no hands'?
[10] Woe to him who says to his father,
'What have you begotten?'
or to his mother,
'What have you brought to birth?'

[11] "This is what the LORD says—
the Holy One of Israel, and its
Maker:
Concerning things to come,
do you question me about my
children,
or give me orders about the work
of my hands?
[12] It is I who made the earth
and created mankind upon it.
My own hands stretched out the
heavens;
I marshaled their starry hosts.
[13] I will raise up Cyrus[b] in my
righteousness:
I will make all his ways straight.
He will rebuild my city
and set my exiles free,
but not for a price or reward,
says the LORD Almighty."

[14] This is what the LORD says:

"The products of Egypt and the
merchandise of Cush,[c]
and those tall Sabeans—
they will come over to you
and will be yours;
they will trudge behind you,
coming over to you in chains.
They will bow down before you

[a]2 Dead Sea Scrolls and Septuagint; the meaning of the word in the Masoretic Text is uncertain.
[b]13 Hebrew *him* [c]14 That is, the upper Nile region

and plead with you, saying,
'Surely God is with you, and there is no other;
there is no other god.'"
15 Truly you are a God who hides himself,
O God and Savior of Israel.
16 All the makers of idols will be put to shame and disgraced;
they will go off into disgrace together.
17 But Israel will be saved by the LORD
with an everlasting salvation;
you will never be put to shame or disgraced,
to ages everlasting.

18 For this is what the LORD says—
he who created the heavens,
he is God;
he who fashioned and made the earth,
he founded it;
he did not create it to be empty,
but formed it to be inhabited—
he says:
"I am the LORD,
and there is no other.
19 I have not spoken in secret,
from somewhere in a land of darkness;
I have not said to Jacob's descendants,
'Seek me in vain.'
I, the LORD, speak the truth;
I declare what is right.

20 "Gather together and come;
assemble, you fugitives from the nations.
Ignorant are those who carry about idols of wood,
who pray to gods that cannot save.
21 Declare what is to be, present it—
let them take counsel together.
Who foretold this long ago,
who declared it from the distant past?
Was it not I, the LORD?
And there is no God apart from me,
a righteous God and a Savior;
there is none but me.

22 "Turn to me and be saved,
all you ends of the earth;
for I am God, and there is no other.
23 By myself I have sworn,
my mouth has uttered in all integrity
a word that will not be revoked:
Before me every knee will bow;
by me every tongue will swear.
24 They will say of me, 'In the LORD alone
are righteousness and strength.'"
All who have raged against him
will come to him and be put to shame.
25 But in the LORD all the descendants of Israel
will be found righteous and will exult.

SHARPEN THE FOCUS

A bit like an editorial cartoonist centuries before his time, the prophet sketches the folly of those who carve idols from stumps and then fall on their faces in worship before them (Isaiah 44:13–20). "Think!" Isaiah says in essence (Isaiah 44:19). "Pick up your idol and look at what you hold in your hand!" (Isaiah 44:20).

Probably not a wooden image. Probably not a bronze Baal. But perhaps a photo of your family? Or the file folder that details your investments? Or the title to your home? Or a certificate of achievement that hangs on your wall or one that you hope to hang there someday? Whatever takes your focus off your Lord, whatever takes priority over spending time with Him in His Word, is an idol just as surely as were Judah's statues of wood and silver.

What are you holding? To what do you cling? Ask the Holy Spirit to reveal your false gods to your heart. Then place them in His hands, asking Him to destroy their hold on you. Ask that you worship the Giver, not His gifts. Then read the Savior's words of absolution—to you—from Isaiah 44:21–23. ☼

WEEK 56 • THURSDAY

Isaiah 46:1—47:15

GET THE BIG PICTURE

Who carries whom? Either the Lord carries us and bears our burdens, or we walk through life burdened by our worries and false gods. That's Isaiah's point in chapter 46. Not only the idols, but the idol worshipers of Babylon will be consumed by the true, living, eternal God when Babylon has fulfilled His purposes. That's the thrust of chapter 47. If time is short, focus on Isaiah 46:1–12.

Gods of Babylon

46 Bel bows down, Nebo
stoops low;
their idols are borne by beasts of
burden.[a]
The images that are carried about
are burdensome,
a burden for the weary.
2 They stoop and bow down together;
unable to rescue the burden,
they themselves go off into
captivity.
3 "Listen to me, O house of Jacob,
all you who remain of the house
of Israel,
you whom I have upheld since you
were conceived,
and have carried since your birth.
4 Even to your old age and gray hairs
I am he, I am he who will sustain
you.
I have made you and I will carry
you;
I will sustain you and I will rescue
you.
5 "To whom will you compare me or
count me equal?
To whom will you liken me that
we may be compared?
6 Some pour out gold from their bags
and weigh out silver on the scales;
they hire a goldsmith to make it into
a god,
and they bow down and worship
it.
7 They lift it to their shoulders and
carry it;
they set it up in its place, and
there it stands.
From that spot it cannot move.
Though one cries out to it, it does
not answer;
it cannot save him from his
troubles.
8 "Remember this, fix it in mind,
take it to heart, you rebels.
9 Remember the former things, those
of long ago;
I am God, and there is no other;
I am God, and there is none like
me.
10 I make known the end from the
beginning,
from ancient times, what is still to
come.
I say: My purpose will stand,
and I will do all that I please.

[a]1 Or *are but beasts and cattle*

11 From the east I summon a bird of prey;
from a far-off land, a man to fulfill my purpose.
What I have said, that will I bring about;
what I have planned, that will I do.
12 Listen to me, you stubborn-hearted,
you who are far from righteousness.
13 I am bringing my righteousness near,
it is not far away;
and my salvation will not be delayed.
I will grant salvation to Zion,
my splendor to Israel.

The Fall of Babylon

47 "Go down, sit in the dust,
Virgin Daughter of Babylon;
sit on the ground without a throne,
Daughter of the Babylonians.[a]
No more will you be called
tender or delicate.
2 Take millstones and grind flour;
take off your veil.
Lift up your skirts, bare your legs,
and wade through the streams.
3 Your nakedness will be exposed
and your shame uncovered.
I will take vengeance;
I will spare no one."

4 Our Redeemer—the LORD Almighty is his name—
is the Holy One of Israel.

5 "Sit in silence, go into darkness,
Daughter of the Babylonians;
no more will you be called
queen of kingdoms.
6 I was angry with my people
and desecrated my inheritance;
I gave them into your hand,
and you showed them no mercy.
Even on the aged
you laid a very heavy yoke.
7 You said, 'I will continue forever—
the eternal queen!'
But you did not consider these things
or reflect on what might happen.

8 "Now then, listen, you wanton creature,
lounging in your security
and saying to yourself,
'I am, and there is none besides me.
I will never be a widow
or suffer the loss of children.'
9 Both of these will overtake you
in a moment, on a single day:
loss of children and widowhood.
They will come upon you in full measure,
in spite of your many sorceries
and all your potent spells.
10 You have trusted in your wickedness
and have said, 'No one sees me.'
Your wisdom and knowledge mislead you
when you say to yourself,
'I am, and there is none besides me.'
11 Disaster will come upon you,
and you will not know how to conjure it away.
A calamity will fall upon you
that you cannot ward off with a ransom;
a catastrophe you cannot foresee
will suddenly come upon you.

12 "Keep on, then, with your magic spells
and with your many sorceries,
which you have labored at since childhood.
Perhaps you will succeed,
perhaps you will cause terror.
13 All the counsel you have received
has only worn you out!
Let your astrologers come forward,
those stargazers who make predictions month by month,
let them save you from what is coming upon you.
14 Surely they are like stubble;
the fire will burn them up.
They cannot even save themselves
from the power of the flame.

[a] 1 Or *Chaldeans*; also in verse 5

Here are no coals to warm anyone;
here is no fire to sit by.
15 That is all they can do for you—
these you have labored with
and trafficked with since
childhood.
Each of them goes on in his error;
there is not one that can save you.

SHARPEN THE FOCUS

The last time I felt lonely was . . .

How would you complete that sentence? Many people can testify to the pain of being alone. Sometimes, though, we can experience loneliness and not recognize it.

There's the loneliness of leadership, the loneliness that comes with the responsibility of making decisions that will affect the lives of others for good or ill in ways we can't foresee. There's the loneliness of grief, of missing someone we loved and lost months, years, or even decades ago. There's the loneliness of leisure, of having nothing meaningful to occupy our hearts or hands. And there's the loneliness of guilt, of feeling we have let down our family or our God.

No matter what lies behind our particular loneliness, no matter how deep or dark our pit, our Lord wants to come to us in it. When He comes, He doesn't come empty-handed. Isaiah 46:12–13 promises that He brings His salvation and His righteousness near. He wants to heal the ache in our hearts and silence the accusations of our conscience.

Think of it! The God of the universe wants to spend time with us. Can you make time for Him today?

What the Lord declares is done, whether or not we believe it. That's the message of Isaiah 48. The chapter ends on a note of Law–the wicked, those who reject the Lord, have no peace. Chapter 49 goes on to describe the one in whom peace can be found–the Messiah. As you read, notice how sweeping that Messiah's mission is. If time is short, focus on Isaiah 49:1–26.

Stubborn Israel

48 "Listen to this, O house
of Jacob,
you who are called by the name of
Israel
and come from the line of Judah,
you who take oaths in the name of
the LORD
and invoke the God of Israel—
but not in truth or
righteousness—
2 you who call yourselves citizens of
the holy city
and rely on the God of Israel—
the LORD Almighty is his name:
3 I foretold the former things long
ago,
my mouth announced them and I
made them known;

then suddenly I acted, and they
came to pass.
4 For I knew how stubborn you were;
the sinews of your neck were iron,
your forehead was bronze.
5 Therefore I told you these things
long ago;
before they happened I
announced them to you
so that you could not say,
'My idols did them;
my wooden image and metal god
ordained them.'
6 You have heard these things; look at
them all.
Will you not admit them?

"From now on I will tell you of new
things,
of hidden things unknown to you.
7 They are created now, and not long
ago;
you have not heard of them
before today.
So you cannot say,
'Yes, I knew of them.'
8 You have neither heard nor
understood;
from of old your ear has not been
open.
Well do I know how treacherous you
are;
you were called a rebel from birth.
9 For my own name's sake I delay my
wrath;
for the sake of my praise I hold it
back from you,
so as not to cut you off.
10 See, I have refined you, though not
as silver;
I have tested you in the furnace of
affliction.
11 For my own sake, for my own sake, I
do this.
How can I let myself be defamed?
I will not yield my glory to
another.

Israel Freed

12 "Listen to me, O Jacob,
Israel, whom I have called:
I am he;
I am the first and I am the last.
13 My own hand laid the foundations
of the earth,
and my right hand spread out the
heavens;
when I summon them,
they all stand up together.

14 "Come together, all of you, and
listen:
Which of the idols has foretold
these things?
The LORD's chosen ally
will carry out his purpose against
Babylon;
his arm will be against the
Babylonians.[a]
15 I, even I, have spoken;
yes, I have called him.
I will bring him,
and he will succeed in his mission.

16 "Come near me and listen to this:
"From the first announcement I have
not spoken in secret;
at the time it happens, I am there."

And now the Sovereign LORD has
sent me,
with his Spirit.

17 This is what the LORD says—
your Redeemer, the Holy One of
Israel:
"I am the LORD your God,
who teaches you what is best for
you,
who directs you in the way you
should go.
18 If only you had paid attention to my
commands,
your peace would have been like a
river,
your righteousness like the waves
of the sea.
19 Your descendants would have been
like the sand,
your children like its numberless
grains;
their name would never be cut off
nor destroyed from before me."

20 Leave Babylon,
flee from the Babylonians!

[a] *14* Or *Chaldeans*; also in verse 20

Announce this with shouts of joy
and proclaim it.
Send it out to the ends of the earth;
say, "The LORD has redeemed his
servant Jacob."
21 They did not thirst when he led
them through the deserts;
he made water flow for them from
the rock;
he split the rock
and water gushed out.

22 "There is no peace," says the LORD,
"for the wicked."

The Servant of the LORD

49 Listen to me, you
islands;
hear this, you distant nations:
Before I was born the LORD called me;
from my birth he has made
mention of my name.
2 He made my mouth like a
sharpened sword,
in the shadow of his hand he hid
me;
he made me into a polished arrow
and concealed me in his quiver.
3 He said to me, "You are my servant,
Israel, in whom I will display my
splendor."
4 But I said, "I have labored to no
purpose;
I have spent my strength in vain
and for nothing.
Yet what is due me is in the LORD's
hand,
and my reward is with my God."

5 And now the LORD says—
he who formed me in the womb
to be his servant
to bring Jacob back to him
and gather Israel to himself,
for I am honored in the eyes of the
LORD
and my God has been my
strength—
6 he says:
"It is too small a thing for you to be
my servant
to restore the tribes of Jacob
and bring back those of Israel I
have kept.
I will also make you a light for the
Gentiles,
that you may bring my salvation
to the ends of the earth."

7 This is what the LORD says—
the Redeemer and Holy One of
Israel—
to him who was despised and
abhorred by the nation,
to the servant of rulers:
"Kings will see you and rise up,
princes will see and bow down,
because of the LORD, who is faithful,
the Holy One of Israel, who has
chosen you."

Restoration of Israel

8 This is what the LORD says:
"In the time of my favor I will
answer you,
and in the day of salvation I will
help you;
I will keep you and will make you
to be a covenant for the people,
to restore the land
and to reassign its desolate
inheritances,
9 to say to the captives, 'Come out,'
and to those in darkness, 'Be free!'

"They will feed beside the roads
and find pasture on every barren
hill.
10 They will neither hunger nor thirst,
nor will the desert heat or the sun
beat upon them.
He who has compassion on them
will guide them
and lead them beside springs of
water.
11 I will turn all my mountains into
roads,
and my highways will be raised
up.
12 See, they will come from afar—
some from the north, some from
the west,
some from the region of Aswan.[a]"

13 Shout for joy, O heavens;
rejoice, O earth;

[a] *12* Dead Sea Scrolls; Masoretic Text *Sinim*

burst into song, O mountains!
For the LORD comforts his people
and will have compassion on his afflicted ones.

14 But Zion said, "The LORD has forsaken me,
the Lord has forgotten me."

15 "Can a mother forget the baby at her breast
and have no compassion on the child she has borne?
Though she may forget,
I will not forget you!
16 See, I have engraved you on the palms of my hands;
your walls are ever before me.
17 Your sons hasten back,
and those who laid you waste depart from you.
18 Lift up your eyes and look around;
all your sons gather and come to you.
As surely as I live," declares the LORD,
"you will wear them all as ornaments;
you will put them on, like a bride.

19 "Though you were ruined and made desolate
and your land laid waste,
now you will be too small for your people,
and those who devoured you will be far away.
20 The children born during your bereavement
will yet say in your hearing,
'This place is too small for us;
give us more space to live in.'
21 Then you will say in your heart,
'Who bore me these?
I was bereaved and barren;
I was exiled and rejected.
Who brought these up?
I was left all alone,
but these—where have they come from?' "

22 This is what the Sovereign LORD says:

"See, I will beckon to the Gentiles,
I will lift up my banner to the peoples;
they will bring your sons in their arms
and carry your daughters on their shoulders.
23 Kings will be your foster fathers,
and their queens your nursing mothers.
They will bow down before you with their faces to the ground;
they will lick the dust at your feet.
Then you will know that I am the LORD;
those who hope in me will not be disappointed."

24 Can plunder be taken from warriors,
or captives rescued from the fierce[a]?

25 But this is what the LORD says:

"Yes, captives will be taken from warriors,
and plunder retrieved from the fierce;
I will contend with those who contend with you,
and your children I will save.
26 I will make your oppressors eat their own flesh;
they will be drunk on their own blood, as with wine.
Then all mankind will know
that I, the LORD, am your Savior,
your Redeemer, the Mighty One of Jacob."

[a]24 Dead Sea Scrolls, Vulgate and Syriac (see also Septuagint and verse 25); Masoretic Text *righteous*

SHARPEN THE FOCUS

In spy novels, an international power sometimes has a secret, invincible weapon. If all else fails, this nation can release the weapon against its enemies. While the victor may suffer setbacks as events unfold, the final outcome is never in doubt.

Isaiah describes the Lord Jesus in terms something like these (Isaiah 49:2). Jesus was God's secret, invincible weapon against sin and the powers of darkness. Satan and his demons did not know the details of the Lord's plan to save His people. The apostle Paul writes:

> *We speak of God's secret wisdom, a wisdom that has been hidden and that God destined for our glory before time began. None of the rulers of this age understood it, for if they had, they would not have crucified the Lord of glory.* (1 Corinthians 2:7–8)

God hid His plan for Jesus, and revealed it at just the right time. Satan celebrated on Good Friday and Holy Saturday. But he awoke on Easter morning to find his power destroyed.

The Holy One of Israel is our Servant-Savior, our King. Today is His Day of Salvation (Isaiah 49:8). Rejoice in His victory.

WEEK 56 • SATURDAY

Isaiah 50:1—52:15

GET THE BIG PICTURE

All three of today's chapters are part of a conversation. As you read, pay attention to the quotation marks and to who is speaking. These texts are packed with the power of God's grace. As you begin, ask the Holy Spirit to reveal the facets of that grace you need most to see. If time is short, focus on Isaiah 52:1–15.

Israel's Sin and the Servant's Obedience

50 This is what the LORD says:

"Where is your mother's certificate
of divorce
with which I sent her away?
Or to which of my creditors
did I sell you?
Because of your sins you were sold;
because of your transgressions
your mother was sent away.
2 When I came, why was there no
one?
When I called, why was there no
one to answer?
Was my arm too short to ransom
you?
Do I lack the strength to rescue
you?
By a mere rebuke I dry up the sea,
I turn rivers into a desert;
their fish rot for lack of water
and die of thirst.
3 I clothe the sky with darkness
and make sackcloth its covering."

4 The Sovereign LORD has given me
an instructed tongue,

to know the word that sustains
the weary.
He wakens me morning by
morning,
wakens my ear to listen like one
being taught.
5 The Sovereign LORD has opened my
ears,
and I have not been rebellious;
I have not drawn back.
6 I offered my back to those who beat
me,
my cheeks to those who pulled
out my beard;
I did not hide my face
from mocking and spitting.
7 Because the Sovereign LORD helps
me,
I will not be disgraced.
Therefore have I set my face like
flint,
and I know I will not be put to
shame.
8 He who vindicates me is near.
Who then will bring charges
against me?
Let us face each other!
Who is my accuser?
Let him confront me!
9 It is the Sovereign LORD who helps
me.
Who is he that will condemn
me?
They will all wear out like a
garment;
the moths will eat them up.

10 Who among you fears the LORD
and obeys the word of his
servant?
Let him who walks in the dark,
who has no light,
trust in the name of the LORD
and rely on his God.
11 But now, all you who light fires
and provide yourselves with
flaming torches,
go, walk in the light of your fires
and of the torches you have set
ablaze.
This is what you shall receive from
my hand:
You will lie down in torment.

Everlasting Salvation for Zion

51 "Listen to me, you who
pursue righteousness
and who seek the LORD:
Look to the rock from which you
were cut
and to the quarry from which you
were hewn;
2 look to Abraham, your father,
and to Sarah, who gave you birth.
When I called him he was but one,
and I blessed him and made him
many.
3 The LORD will surely comfort Zion
and will look with compassion on
all her ruins;
he will make her deserts like Eden,
her wastelands like the garden of
the LORD.
Joy and gladness will be found in
her,
thanksgiving and the sound of
singing.

4 "Listen to me, my people;
hear me, my nation:
The law will go out from me;
my justice will become a light to
the nations.
5 My righteousness draws near
speedily,
my salvation is on the way,
and my arm will bring justice to
the nations.
The islands will look to me
and wait in hope for my arm.
6 Lift up your eyes to the heavens,
look at the earth beneath;
the heavens will vanish like smoke,
the earth will wear out like a
garment
and its inhabitants die like flies.
But my salvation will last forever,
my righteousness will never fail.

7 "Hear me, you who know what is
right,
you people who have my law in
your hearts:
Do not fear the reproach of men
or be terrified by their insults.
8 For the moth will eat them up like a
garment;

the worm will devour them like
wool.
But my righteousness will last
forever,
my salvation through all
generations."

9 Awake, awake! Clothe yourself with
strength,
O arm of the LORD;
awake, as in days gone by,
as in generations of old.
Was it not you who cut Rahab to
pieces,
who pierced that monster
through?
10 Was it not you who dried up the sea,
the waters of the great deep,
who made a road in the depths of
the sea
so that the redeemed might cross
over?
11 The ransomed of the LORD will
return.
They will enter Zion with singing;
everlasting joy will crown their
heads.
Gladness and joy will overtake
them,
and sorrow and sighing will flee
away.

12 "I, even I, am he who comforts you.
Who are you that you fear mortal
men,
the sons of men, who are but
grass,
13 that you forget the LORD your
Maker,
who stretched out the heavens
and laid the foundations of the
earth,
that you live in constant terror every
day
because of the wrath of the
oppressor,
who is bent on destruction?
For where is the wrath of the
oppressor?
14 The cowering prisoners will soon
be set free;
they will not die in their dungeon,
nor will they lack bread.
15 For I am the LORD your God,
who churns up the sea so that its
waves roar—
the LORD Almighty is his name.
16 I have put my words in your mouth
and covered you with the shadow
of my hand—
I who set the heavens in place,
who laid the foundations of the
earth,
and who say to Zion, 'You are my
people.'"

The Cup of the LORD's Wrath

17 Awake, awake!
Rise up, O Jerusalem,
you who have drunk from the hand
of the LORD
the cup of his wrath,
you who have drained to its dregs
the goblet that makes men stagger.
18 Of all the sons she bore
there was none to guide her;
of all the sons she reared
there was none to take her by the
hand.
19 These double calamities have come
upon you—
who can comfort you?—
ruin and destruction, famine and
sword—
who can[a] console you?
20 Your sons have fainted;
they lie at the head of every street,
like antelope caught in a net.
They are filled with the wrath of the
LORD
and the rebuke of your God.

21 Therefore hear this, you afflicted
one,
made drunk, but not with wine.
22 This is what your Sovereign LORD
says,
your God, who defends his
people:
"See, I have taken out of your hand
the cup that made you stagger;
from that cup, the goblet of my
wrath,
you will never drink again.

[a] *19* Dead Sea Scrolls, Septuagint, Vulgate and Syriac; Masoretic Text / *how can I*

[23] I will put it into the hands of your
tormentors,
who said to you,
'Fall prostrate that we may walk
over you.'
And you made your back like the
ground,
like a street to be walked over."

52

Awake, awake, O Zion,
clothe yourself with
strength.
Put on your garments of splendor,
O Jerusalem, the holy city.
The uncircumcised and defiled
will not enter you again.
[2] Shake off your dust;
rise up, sit enthroned,
O Jerusalem.
Free yourself from the chains on
your neck,
O captive Daughter of Zion.

[3] For this is what the LORD says:

"You were sold for nothing,
and without money you will be
redeemed."

[4] For this is what the Sovereign LORD
says:

"At first my people went down to
Egypt to live;
lately, Assyria has oppressed them.

[5] "And now what do I have here?" declares the LORD.

"For my people have been taken
away for nothing,
and those who rule them mock,[a]"
declares the LORD.
"And all day long
my name is constantly
blasphemed.
[6] Therefore my people will know my
name;
therefore in that day they will
know
that it is I who foretold it.
Yes, it is I."

[7] How beautiful on the mountains
are the feet of those who bring
good news,
who proclaim peace,
who bring good tidings,
who proclaim salvation,
who say to Zion,
"Your God reigns!"
[8] Listen! Your watchmen lift up their
voices;
together they shout for joy.
When the LORD returns to Zion,
they will see it with their own eyes.
[9] Burst into songs of joy together,
you ruins of Jerusalem,
for the LORD has comforted his
people,
he has redeemed Jerusalem.
[10] The LORD will lay bare his holy arm
in the sight of all the nations,
and all the ends of the earth will see
the salvation of our God.

[11] Depart, depart, go out from there!
Touch no unclean thing!
Come out from it and be pure,
you who carry the vessels of the
LORD.
[12] But you will not leave in haste
or go in flight;
for the LORD will go before you,
the God of Israel will be your rear
guard.

The Suffering and Glory of the Servant

[13] See, my servant will act wisely[b];
he will be raised and lifted up and
highly exalted.
[14] Just as there were many who were
appalled at him[c]—
his appearance was so disfigured
beyond that of any man
and his form marred beyond
human likeness—
[15] so will he sprinkle many nations,[d]
and kings will shut their mouths
because of him.
For what they were not told, they
will see,
and what they have not heard,
they will understand.

[a] 5 Dead Sea Scrolls and Vulgate; Masoretic Text *wail* [b] 13 Or *will prosper* [c] 14 Hebrew *you*
[d] 15 Hebrew; Septuagint *so will many nations marvel at him*

SHARPEN THE FOCUS

The idols Judah worshiped had such a hypnotic effect on the people that they had nearly lapsed into a spiritual coma (Isaiah 51:17–20). Spiritual death would soon follow. "Wake up!" Isaiah warned repeatedly. Yet Judah need not awaken to judgment. Those who would return to the Lord in repentance and faith would awaken to receive from Him "garments of splendor" (Isaiah 52:1).

We, too, can be so easily lulled to sleep, spiritually speaking. It happens when we forget who we are and whose we are–Jerusalem, Zion, God's own sons and daughters.

When we forget, we find ourselves "playing sidewalk" for Satan (Isaiah 51:23). We find ourselves captive to our former sins. For us, as for the repentant people of ancient Judah, the Lord has a change of clothes. A prayer sometimes offered before the Lord's Supper includes a petition something like this: "Take off from us the spotted garment of . . . our own righteousness and adorn us with the garment of the righteousness purchased with Your blood."

As, by grace, you "wake up and get dressed spiritually" now, thank the Lord Jesus for His cross. Ask that you be alert to opportunities He provides for you to serve Him and others.

WEEK 57 • MONDAY

Isaiah 53:1–12

GET THE BIG PICTURE

Who will believe it? Who can see how powerfully the Lord acted for us in His Messiah and take it all in? Those two questions begin today's chapter. Read it with a heart of worship. Pay special attention to the closing verses. They describe the results of our Savior's sacrifice. If time is short, focus on Isaiah 53:4–11.

53 Who has believed our message
and to whom has the arm of the
LORD been revealed?
2He grew up before him like a tender
shoot,
and like a root out of dry ground.
He had no beauty or majesty to
attract us to him,
nothing in his appearance that we
should desire him.
3He was despised and rejected by
men,
a man of sorrows, and familiar
with suffering.
Like one from whom men hide their
faces
he was despised, and we
esteemed him not.

4Surely he took up our infirmities
and carried our sorrows,
yet we considered him stricken by
God,
smitten by him, and afflicted.
5But he was pierced for our
transgressions,
he was crushed for our iniquities;
the punishment that brought us
peace was upon him,
and by his wounds we are healed.
6We all, like sheep, have gone astray,
each of us has turned to his own
way;

and the LORD has laid on him
the iniquity of us all.

7 He was oppressed and afflicted,
yet he did not open his mouth;
he was led like a lamb to the
slaughter,
and as a sheep before her shearers
is silent,
so he did not open his mouth.
8 By oppression[a] and judgment he
was taken away.
And who can speak of his
descendants?
For he was cut off from the land of
the living;
for the transgression of my people
he was stricken.[b]
9 He was assigned a grave with the
wicked,
and with the rich in his death,
though he had done no violence,
nor was any deceit in his mouth.

10 Yet it was the LORD's will to crush
him and cause him to suffer,
and though the LORD makes[c] his
life a guilt offering,
he will see his offspring and prolong
his days,
and the will of the LORD will
prosper in his hand.
11 After the suffering of his soul,
he will see the light ⌞of life⌟[d] and be
satisfied[e];
by his knowledge[f] my righteous
servant will justify many,
and he will bear their
iniquities.
12 Therefore I will give him a portion
among the great,[g]
and he will divide the spoils with
the strong,[h]
because he poured out his life unto
death,
and was numbered with the
transgressors.
For he bore the sin of many,
and made intercession for the
transgressors.

[a]8 Or *From arrest* [b]8 Or *away. / Yet who of his generation considered / that he was cut off from the land of the living / for the transgression of my people, / to whom the blow was due?* [c]10 Hebrew *though you make* [d]11 Dead Sea Scrolls (see also Septuagint); Masoretic Text does not have *the light ⌞of life⌟.* [e]11 Or (with Masoretic Text) *11He will see the result of the suffering of his soul / and be satisfied* [f]11 Or *by knowledge of him* [g]12 Or *many* [h]12 Or *numerous*

SHARPEN THE FOCUS

Maybe the most emotionally charged phrase used by Christians is "the will of God." The Scriptures often modify the phrase by adding words like "His good, pleasing and perfect will" (Romans 12:2). Perhaps one of the most difficult struggles of the Christian life involves the tension between faith and doubt as we think about the will of God. We know what we've been taught, we know what we should believe, but our hearts can so quickly retreat to skepticism when life goes wrong or Satan tempts us.

Isaiah 53 dampens the fires of doubt as its words flood our being with the assurance of our Lord's love for us. The text does not use the word *love*. Instead, it speaks of the will of God (Isaiah 53:10). It pleased God to punish Jesus instead of you and me, and when Jesus shouted, "It is finished," the will of God—our salvation, our sanctification, our adoption as His children—had become a reality.

> *This is how we know what love is: Jesus Christ laid down His life for us.* (1 John 3:16)

God's love for us and God's will for us are one and the same. Let that forgiving love and perfect will calm your Spirit and drown your doubts today.

The Messiah, God's Servant, paid an infinite price to bring peace between a holy God and His sinful people. Now the Lord offers that peace to everyone. Sadly, not all will receive it. As you read, take joy in all the benefits you receive as an heir of God, a co-heir with Christ. If time is short, focus on Isaiah 55:1–13.

The Future Glory of Zion

54 "Sing, O barren woman,
you who never bore a child;
burst into song, shout for joy,
you who were never in labor;
because more are the children of the desolate woman
than of her who has a husband,"
says the LORD.
2 "Enlarge the place of your tent,
stretch your tent curtains wide,
do not hold back;
lengthen your cords,
strengthen your stakes.
3 For you will spread out to the right and to the left;
your descendants will dispossess nations
and settle in their desolate cities.

4 "Do not be afraid; you will not suffer shame.
Do not fear disgrace; you will not be humiliated.
You will forget the shame of your youth
and remember no more the reproach of your widowhood.
5 For your Maker is your husband—
the LORD Almighty is his name—
the Holy One of Israel is your Redeemer;
he is called the God of all the earth.
6 The LORD will call you back
as if you were a wife deserted and distressed in spirit—
a wife who married young,
only to be rejected," says your God.
7 "For a brief moment I abandoned you,
but with deep compassion I will bring you back.
8 In a surge of anger
I hid my face from you for a moment,
but with everlasting kindness
I will have compassion on you,"
says the LORD your Redeemer.
9 "To me this is like the days of Noah,
when I swore that the waters of Noah would never again cover the earth.
So now I have sworn not to be angry with you,
never to rebuke you again.
10 Though the mountains be shaken
and the hills be removed,
yet my unfailing love for you will not be shaken
nor my covenant of peace be removed,"
says the LORD, who has compassion on you.

11 "O afflicted city, lashed by storms and not comforted,
I will build you with stones of turquoise,[a]

[a] *11* The meaning of the Hebrew for this word is uncertain.

your foundations with sapphires.[a]
12 I will make your battlements of
rubies,
your gates of sparkling jewels,
and all your walls of precious
stones.
13 All your sons will be taught by the
LORD,
and great will be your children's
peace.
14 In righteousness you will be
established:
Tyranny will be far from you;
you will have nothing to fear.
Terror will be far removed;
it will not come near you.
15 If anyone does attack you, it will not
be my doing;
whoever attacks you will
surrender to you.

16 "See, it is I who created the
blacksmith
who fans the coals into flame
and forges a weapon fit for its
work.
And it is I who have created the
destroyer to work havoc;
17 no weapon forged against you
will prevail,
and you will refute every tongue
that accuses you.
This is the heritage of the servants of
the LORD,
and this is their vindication from
me,"
declares the LORD.

Invitation to the Thirsty

55 "Come, all you who are
thirsty,
come to the waters;
and you who have no money,
come, buy and eat!
Come, buy wine and milk
without money and without
cost.
2 Why spend money on what is not
bread,
and your labor on what does not
satisfy?
Listen, listen to me, and eat what is
good,
and your soul will delight in the
richest of fare.
3 Give ear and come to me;
hear me, that your soul may live.
I will make an everlasting covenant
with you,
my faithful love promised to
David.
4 See, I have made him a witness to
the peoples,
a leader and commander of the
peoples.
5 Surely you will summon nations
you know not,
and nations that do not know you
will hasten to you,
because of the LORD your God,
the Holy One of Israel,
for he has endowed you with
splendor."

6 Seek the LORD while he may be
found;
call on him while he is near.
7 Let the wicked forsake his way
and the evil man his thoughts.
Let him turn to the LORD, and he
will have mercy on him,
and to our God, for he will freely
pardon.

8 "For my thoughts are not your
thoughts,
neither are your ways my ways,"
declares the LORD.
9 "As the heavens are higher than the
earth,
so are my ways higher than your
ways
and my thoughts than your
thoughts.
10 As the rain and the snow
come down from heaven,
and do not return to it
without watering the earth
and making it bud and flourish,
so that it yields seed for the sower
and bread for the eater,
11 so is my word that goes out from my
mouth:
It will not return to me empty,
but will accomplish what I desire

[a]11 Or *lapis lazuli*

and achieve the purpose for
which I sent it.
12 You will go out in joy
and be led forth in peace;
the mountains and hills
will burst into song before you,
and all the trees of the field
will clap their hands.
13 Instead of the thornbush will grow
the pine tree,
and instead of briers the myrtle
will grow.
This will be for the LORD's renown,
for an everlasting sign,
which will not be destroyed."

Salvation for Others

56 This is what the LORD says:

"Maintain justice
and do what is right,
for my salvation is close at hand
and my righteousness will soon be
revealed.
2 Blessed is the man who does this,
the man who holds it fast,
who keeps the Sabbath without
desecrating it,
and keeps his hand from doing
any evil."

3 Let no foreigner who has bound
himself to the LORD say,
"The LORD will surely exclude me
from his people."
And let not any eunuch complain,
"I am only a dry tree."

4 For this is what the LORD says:

"To the eunuchs who keep my
Sabbaths,
who choose what pleases me
and hold fast to my covenant—
5 to them I will give within my temple
and its walls
a memorial and a name
better than sons and daughters;
I will give them an everlasting name
that will not be cut off.
6 And foreigners who bind themselves
to the LORD
to serve him,
to love the name of the LORD,
and to worship him,
all who keep the Sabbath without
desecrating it
and who hold fast to my
covenant—
7 these I will bring to my holy
mountain
and give them joy in my house of
prayer.
Their burnt offerings and sacrifices
will be accepted on my altar;
for my house will be called
a house of prayer for all nations."
8 The Sovereign LORD declares—
he who gathers the exiles of Israel:
"I will gather still others to them
besides those already gathered."

God's Accusation Against the Wicked

9 Come, all you beasts of the field,
come and devour, all you beasts of
the forest!
10 Israel's watchmen are blind,
they all lack knowledge;
they are all mute dogs,
they cannot bark;
they lie around and dream,
they love to sleep.
11 They are dogs with mighty
appetites;
they never have enough.
They are shepherds who lack
understanding;
they all turn to their own way,
each seeks his own gain.
12 "Come," each one cries, "let me get
wine!
Let us drink our fill of beer!
And tomorrow will be like today,
or even far better."

57 The righteous perish,
and no one ponders it in
his heart;
devout men are taken away,
and no one understands
that the righteous are taken away
to be spared from evil.
2 Those who walk uprightly
enter into peace;
they find rest as they lie in death.

3 "But you—come here, you sons of a sorceress,
you offspring of adulterers and prostitutes!
4 Whom are you mocking?
At whom do you sneer
and stick out your tongue?
Are you not a brood of rebels,
the offspring of liars?
5 You burn with lust among the oaks
and under every spreading tree;
you sacrifice your children in the ravines
and under the overhanging crags.
6 ⌊The idols⌋ among the smooth stones of the ravines are your portion;
they, they are your lot.
Yes, to them you have poured out drink offerings
and offered grain offerings.
In the light of these things, should I relent?
7 You have made your bed on a high and lofty hill;
there you went up to offer your sacrifices.
8 Behind your doors and your doorposts
you have put your pagan symbols.
Forsaking me, you uncovered your bed,
you climbed into it and opened it wide;
you made a pact with those whose beds you love,
and you looked on their nakedness.
9 You went to Molech[a] with olive oil
and increased your perfumes.
You sent your ambassadors[b] far away;
you descended to the grave[c] itself!
10 You were wearied by all your ways,
but you would not say, 'It is hopeless.'
You found renewal of your strength,
and so you did not faint.

11 "Whom have you so dreaded and feared
that you have been false to me,
and have neither remembered me
nor pondered this in your hearts?
Is it not because I have long been silent
that you do not fear me?
12 I will expose your righteousness and your works,
and they will not benefit you.
13 When you cry out for help,
let your collection ⌊of idols⌋ save you!
The wind will carry all of them off,
a mere breath will blow them away.
But the man who makes me his refuge
will inherit the land
and possess my holy mountain."

Comfort for the Contrite

14 And it will be said:

"Build up, build up, prepare the road!
Remove the obstacles out of the way of my people."
15 For this is what the high and lofty One says—
he who lives forever, whose name is holy:
"I live in a high and holy place,
but also with him who is contrite and lowly in spirit,
to revive the spirit of the lowly
and to revive the heart of the contrite.
16 I will not accuse forever,
nor will I always be angry,
for then the spirit of man would grow faint before me—
the breath of man that I have created.
17 I was enraged by his sinful greed;
I punished him, and hid my face in anger,
yet he kept on in his willful ways.
18 I have seen his ways, but I will heal him;
I will guide him and restore comfort to him,
19 creating praise on the lips of the mourners in Israel.

[a]9 Or *to the king* [b]9 Or *idols* [c]9 Hebrew *Sheol*

Peace, peace, to those far and near,"
says the LORD. "And I will heal
them."
20 But the wicked are like the tossing
sea,
which cannot rest,
whose waves cast up mire and
mud.
21 "There is no peace," says my God,
"for the wicked."

SHARPEN THE FOCUS

We know that Jesus died for the world's people. We know that millions live and die and find themselves in an eternal hell because they have never heard the Good News. We even know unbelieving neighbors and friends who might respond to an authentic witness on our part. We read God's promise that His Word is a powerful Word, a Word that does not fall flat, but accomplishes what He sends it out to do (Isaiah 55:10–11). And still, we often fail to witness.

Yet, despite our selfishness, our lack of urgency, and our hard-heartedness, our Savior-God does not condemn us. Instead, He keeps on assuring us of who we are. He keeps nourishing us with the honey-sweet milk of His Word (Isaiah 55:1–5). We can return to our Lord, knowing that for the sake of His Son, our God will abundantly pardon (Isaiah 55:7). He will pardon even our self-absorption and our lack of concern for His mission.

More than that, He will soften our hearts so that His mission truly becomes our mission, His vision for the world, our vision. Our thoughts and ways will align with His thoughts and ways so that His Word of grace will flow from Him through us to those who need His love so much (Isaiah 55:8–9). Ask that He create that reality anew in you today.

WEEK 57 • WEDNESDAY

Isaiah 58:1—59:21

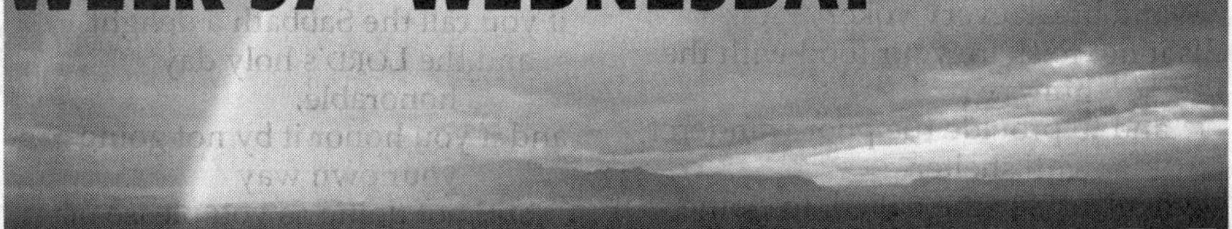

GET THE BIG PICTURE

"I do so much for God. I follow all the prescribed rituals. I make all the prescribed sacrifices. I even fast more often than the law demands. Why hasn't He noticed? What more does He expect?" Those words fell from the lips of Judah's citizens as they listened to Isaiah's preaching. God expected much more. See if you can discover what that was as you read today. If time is short, focus on Isaiah 59:1–21.

True Fasting

58 "Shout it aloud, do not
hold back.
Raise your voice like a trumpet.
Declare to my people their
rebellion
and to the house of Jacob their
sins.
2 For day after day they seek me out;
they seem eager to know my
ways,
as if they were a nation that does
what is right
and has not forsaken the
commands of its God.
They ask me for just decisions
and seem eager for God to come
near them.

3 'Why have we fasted,' they say,
'and you have not seen it?
Why have we humbled ourselves,
and you have not noticed?'

"Yet on the day of your fasting, you do as you please
and exploit all your workers.
4 Your fasting ends in quarreling and strife,
and in striking each other with wicked fists.
You cannot fast as you do today
and expect your voice to be heard on high.
5 Is this the kind of fast I have chosen,
only a day for a man to humble himself?
Is it only for bowing one's head like a reed
and for lying on sackcloth and ashes?
Is that what you call a fast,
a day acceptable to the LORD?

6 "Is not this the kind of fasting I have chosen:
to loose the chains of injustice
and untie the cords of the yoke,
to set the oppressed free
and break every yoke?
7 Is it not to share your food with the hungry
and to provide the poor wanderer with shelter—
when you see the naked, to clothe him,
and not to turn away from your own flesh and blood?
8 Then your light will break forth like the dawn,
and your healing will quickly appear;
then your righteousness[a] will go before you,
and the glory of the LORD will be your rear guard.
9 Then you will call, and the LORD will answer;
you will cry for help, and he will say: Here am I.

"If you do away with the yoke of oppression,
with the pointing finger and malicious talk,
10 and if you spend yourselves in behalf of the hungry
and satisfy the needs of the oppressed,
then your light will rise in the darkness,
and your night will become like the noonday.
11 The LORD will guide you always;
he will satisfy your needs in a sun-scorched land
and will strengthen your frame.
You will be like a well-watered garden,
like a spring whose waters never fail.
12 Your people will rebuild the ancient ruins
and will raise up the age-old foundations;
you will be called Repairer of Broken Walls,
Restorer of Streets with Dwellings.

13 "If you keep your feet from breaking the Sabbath
and from doing as you please on my holy day,
if you call the Sabbath a delight
and the LORD's holy day honorable,
and if you honor it by not going your own way
and not doing as you please or speaking idle words,
14 then you will find your joy in the LORD,
and I will cause you to ride on the heights of the land
and to feast on the inheritance of your father Jacob."
The mouth of the LORD has spoken.

Sin, Confession and Redemption

59 Surely the arm of the LORD is not too short to save,
nor his ear too dull to hear.
2 But your iniquities have separated

[a]8 Or *your righteous One*

you from your God;
your sins have hidden his face from
you,
so that he will not hear.
3 For your hands are stained with
blood,
your fingers with guilt.
Your lips have spoken lies,
and your tongue mutters wicked
things.
4 No one calls for justice;
no one pleads his case with
integrity.
They rely on empty arguments and
speak lies;
they conceive trouble and give
birth to evil.
5 They hatch the eggs of vipers
and spin a spider's web.
Whoever eats their eggs will die,
and when one is broken, an adder
is hatched.
6 Their cobwebs are useless for
clothing;
they cannot cover themselves
with what they make.
Their deeds are evil deeds,
and acts of violence are in their
hands.
7 Their feet rush into sin;
they are swift to shed innocent
blood.
Their thoughts are evil thoughts;
ruin and destruction mark their
ways.
8 The way of peace they do not know;
there is no justice in their paths.
They have turned them into crooked
roads;
no one who walks in them will
know peace.

9 So justice is far from us,
and righteousness does not reach
us.
We look for light, but all is
darkness;
for brightness, but we walk in
deep shadows.
10 Like the blind we grope along the
wall,
feeling our way like men without
eyes.
At midday we stumble as if it were
twilight;
among the strong, we are like the
dead.
11 We all growl like bears;
we moan mournfully like doves.
We look for justice, but find none;
for deliverance, but it is far away.
12 For our offenses are many in your
sight,
and our sins testify against us.
Our offenses are ever with us,
and we acknowledge our
iniquities:
13 rebellion and treachery against the
LORD,
turning our backs on our God,
fomenting oppression and revolt,
uttering lies our hearts have
conceived.
14 So justice is driven back,
and righteousness stands at a
distance;
truth has stumbled in the streets,
honesty cannot enter.
15 Truth is nowhere to be found,
and whoever shuns evil becomes
a prey.

The LORD looked and was
displeased
that there was no justice.
16 He saw that there was no one,
he was appalled that there was no
one to intervene;
so his own arm worked salvation for
him,
and his own righteousness
sustained him.
17 He put on righteousness as his
breastplate,
and the helmet of salvation on his
head;
he put on the garments of
vengeance
and wrapped himself in zeal as in
a cloak.
18 According to what they have done,
so will he repay
wrath to his enemies
and retribution to his foes;
he will repay the islands their
due.

19 From the west, men will fear the
name of the LORD,
and from the rising of the sun,
they will revere his glory.
For he will come like a pent-up flood
that the breath of the LORD drives
along.[a]

20 "The Redeemer will come to Zion,
to those in Jacob who repent of
their sins,"
declares the LORD.

21 "As for me, this is my covenant with
them," says the LORD. "My Spirit, who
is on you, and my words that I have put
in your mouth will not depart from your
mouth, or from the mouths of your
children, or from the mouths of their descendants from this time on and forever," says the LORD.

[a]19 Or *When the enemy comes in like a flood, / the Spirit of the LORD will put him to flight*

SHARPEN THE FOCUS

Maybe you know the story "The Emperor's New Clothes." It concludes with a little boy pointing out the emperor's nakedness, despite the gold he'd given the tailors to create clothes so fine that "only the wise could see them."

Isaiah has had a lot to say about spiritual clothing. In Isaiah 59:6, he uses a word picture quite like the fable of the emperor. "The cobwebs of your own goodness won't cover your sins," he says.

From Genesis through Revelation, the Scriptures warn and remind, scold and plead with us about the dangers of self-righteousness. Those of us who read the Bible every day and go to church every week are not exempt from this sin. In fact, we may be more susceptible to it. "We're good!" we may be tempted to assert before God. But when we think that, we lose the righteousness Christ earned for us on the cross. The cross plus anything equals nothing. That's God's math.

Independent of Christ Jesus, we are all blind and drowning in our sins. But when we admit our condition, we find refuge under the protection of the Saving Warrior described in Isaiah 59:15–20. There we find full release from guilt and from sin's power to harm or enslave us.

WEEK 57 • THURSDAY

Isaiah 60:1—62:12

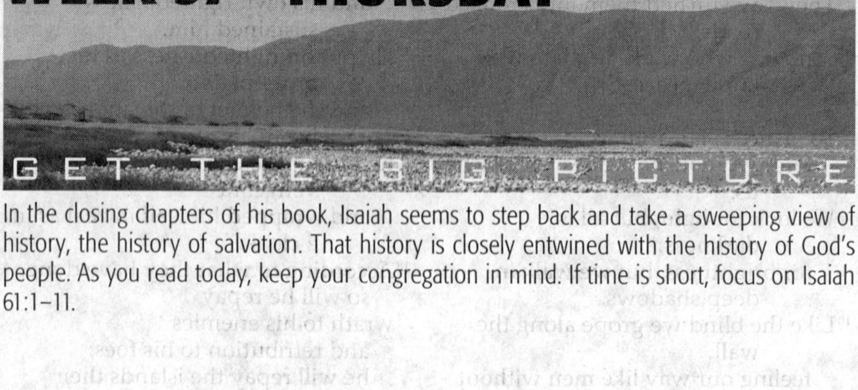

GET THE BIG PICTURE

In the closing chapters of his book, Isaiah seems to step back and take a sweeping view of history, the history of salvation. That history is closely entwined with the history of God's people. As you read today, keep your congregation in mind. If time is short, focus on Isaiah 61:1–11.

The Glory of Zion

60 "Arise, shine, for your light has come,
and the glory of the LORD rises upon you.
2 See, darkness covers the earth
and thick darkness is over the peoples,
but the LORD rises upon you
and his glory appears over you.
3 Nations will come to your light,
and kings to the brightness of your dawn.

4 "Lift up your eyes and look about you:
All assemble and come to you;
your sons come from afar,
and your daughters are carried on the arm.
5 Then you will look and be radiant,
your heart will throb and swell with joy;
the wealth on the seas will be brought to you,
to you the riches of the nations will come.
6 Herds of camels will cover your land,
young camels of Midian and Ephah.
And all from Sheba will come,
bearing gold and incense
and proclaiming the praise of the LORD.
7 All Kedar's flocks will be gathered to you,
the rams of Nebaioth will serve you;
they will be accepted as offerings on my altar,
and I will adorn my glorious temple.

8 "Who are these that fly along like clouds,
like doves to their nests?
9 Surely the islands look to me;
in the lead are the ships of Tarshish,[a]
bringing your sons from afar,
with their silver and gold,
to the honor of the LORD your God,
the Holy One of Israel,
for he has endowed you with splendor.

10 "Foreigners will rebuild your walls,
and their kings will serve you.
Though in anger I struck you,
in favor I will show you compassion.
11 Your gates will always stand open,
they will never be shut, day or night,
so that men may bring you the wealth of the nations—
their kings led in triumphal procession.
12 For the nation or kingdom that will not serve you will perish;
it will be utterly ruined.

13 "The glory of Lebanon will come to you,
the pine, the fir and the cypress together,
to adorn the place of my sanctuary;
and I will glorify the place of my feet.
14 The sons of your oppressors will come bowing before you;
all who despise you will bow down at your feet
and will call you the City of the LORD,
Zion of the Holy One of Israel.

15 "Although you have been forsaken and hated,
with no one traveling through,
I will make you the everlasting pride
and the joy of all generations.
16 You will drink the milk of nations
and be nursed at royal breasts.
Then you will know that I, the LORD, am your Savior,
your Redeemer, the Mighty One of Jacob.
17 Instead of bronze I will bring you gold,
and silver in place of iron.
Instead of wood I will bring you bronze,
and iron in place of stones.

[a] 9 Or *the trading ships*

I will make peace your governor
and righteousness your ruler.
18 No longer will violence be heard in
your land,
nor ruin or destruction within
your borders,
but you will call your walls Salvation
and your gates Praise.
19 The sun will no more be your light
by day,
nor will the brightness of the
moon shine on you,
for the LORD will be your everlasting
light,
and your God will be your glory.
20 Your sun will never set again,
and your moon will wane no
more;
the LORD will be your everlasting
light,
and your days of sorrow will end.
21 Then will all your people be
righteous
and they will possess the land
forever.
They are the shoot I have planted,
the work of my hands,
for the display of my splendor.
22 The least of you will become a
thousand,
the smallest a mighty nation.
I am the LORD;
in its time I will do this swiftly."

The Year of the LORD's Favor

61 The Spirit of the Sovereign
LORD is on me,
because the LORD has anointed
me
to preach good news to the poor.
He has sent me to bind up the
brokenhearted,
to proclaim freedom for the
captives
and release from darkness for the
prisoners,[a]
2 to proclaim the year of the LORD's
favor
and the day of vengeance of our
God,
to comfort all who mourn,
3 and provide for those who grieve
in Zion—
to bestow on them a crown of
beauty
instead of ashes,
the oil of gladness
instead of mourning,
and a garment of praise
instead of a spirit of despair.
They will be called oaks of
righteousness,
a planting of the LORD
for the display of his splendor.
4 They will rebuild the ancient ruins
and restore the places long
devastated;
they will renew the ruined cities
that have been devastated for
generations.
5 Aliens will shepherd your flocks;
foreigners will work your fields
and vineyards.
6 And you will be called priests of the
LORD,
you will be named ministers of
our God.
You will feed on the wealth of
nations,
and in their riches you will boast.

7 Instead of their shame
my people will receive a double
portion,
and instead of disgrace
they will rejoice in their
inheritance;
and so they will inherit a double
portion in their land,
and everlasting joy will be theirs.

8 "For I, the LORD, love justice;
I hate robbery and iniquity.
In my faithfulness I will reward
them
and make an everlasting covenant
with them.
9 Their descendants will be known
among the nations
and their offspring among the
peoples.
All who see them will acknowledge
that they are a people the LORD
has blessed."

[a] *1* Hebrew; Septuagint *the blind*

10 I delight greatly in the LORD;
my soul rejoices in my God.
For he has clothed me with garments of salvation
and arrayed me in a robe of righteousness,
as a bridegroom adorns his head like a priest,
and as a bride adorns herself with her jewels.
11 For as the soil makes the sprout come up
and a garden causes seeds to grow,
so the Sovereign LORD will make righteousness and praise
spring up before all nations.

Zion's New Name

62 For Zion's sake I will not keep silent,
for Jerusalem's sake I will not remain quiet,
till her righteousness shines out like the dawn,
her salvation like a blazing torch.
2 The nations will see your righteousness,
and all kings your glory;
you will be called by a new name
that the mouth of the LORD will bestow.
3 You will be a crown of splendor in the LORD's hand,
a royal diadem in the hand of your God.
4 No longer will they call you Deserted,
or name your land Desolate.
But you will be called Hephzibah,[a]
and your land Beulah[b];
for the LORD will take delight in you,
and your land will be married.
5 As a young man marries a maiden,
so will your sons[c] marry you;
as a bridegroom rejoices over his bride,
so will your God rejoice over you.
6 I have posted watchmen on your walls, O Jerusalem;
they will never be silent day or night.
You who call on the LORD,
give yourselves no rest,
7 and give him no rest till he establishes Jerusalem
and makes her the praise of the earth.
8 The LORD has sworn by his right hand
and by his mighty arm:
"Never again will I give your grain
as food for your enemies,
and never again will foreigners
drink the new wine
for which you have toiled;
9 but those who harvest it will eat it
and praise the LORD,
and those who gather the grapes will drink it
in the courts of my sanctuary."
10 Pass through, pass through the gates!
Prepare the way for the people.
Build up, build up the highway!
Remove the stones.
Raise a banner for the nations.
11 The LORD has made proclamation
to the ends of the earth:
"Say to the Daughter of Zion,
'See, your Savior comes!
See, his reward is with him,
and his recompense accompanies him.'"
12 They will be called the Holy People,
the Redeemed of the LORD;
and you will be called Sought After,
the City No Longer Deserted.

[a]4 *Hephzibah* means *my delight is in her.* [b]4 *Beulah* means *married.* [c]5 Or *Builder*

SHARPEN THE FOCUS

Are you as enthusiastic about God's people as Isaiah was? Zion, our Lord's church, is:

- a crown of splendor and a royal diadem (Isaiah 62:3)
- the Holy People (Isaiah 62:12)
- the one whose righteousness so shines that it becomes a "tourist attraction" for the nations (Isaiah 62:1–2).

"Not my congregation," you may say. And you'd be right. Your church is made up of sinners, you among them. Isaiah recognized and rebuked the sin in the lives of those in Israel in his day.

The descriptions and titles that the Lord through Isaiah gives the church are not wishful thinking. They are God's honest truth. If we try to live in the church on earth as if it were already the church in heaven, we set ourselves up to be hurt. But if we try to live in the church on earth as if it were not God's redeemed Bride headed for heaven, our light won't shine as brightly as it could.

We need continually to remind one another who we are, whose we are, and where we're headed. The Holy One of Israel has redeemed us through the blood of His Son. We are clothed with the garments of the holiness Jesus won for us on Calvary (Isaiah 61:10). Our lives are gardens, bearing the fruit of joy, love, peace, patience, and goodness in the world (Isaiah 61:11).

WEEK 57 • FRIDAY

Isaiah 63:1—66:24

GET THE BIG PICTURE

Stand in the sandals of a citizen of Judah just before the Babylonian's final invasion of your nation. Perhaps you've been one of Judah's few faithful believers. You've heard the prophecies Isaiah made a century earlier—promises of a coming, glorious kingdom. But before it would come, there would be exile and destruction. What would you want to ask the Lord? Isaiah 63–64 includes one such prayer, and the book finishes with God's answer to it. If time is short, focus on Isaiah 66:1–24.

God's Day of Vengeance and Redemption

63 Who is this coming from Edom,
from Bozrah, with his garments stained crimson?
Who is this, robed in splendor,
striding forward in the greatness of his strength?

"It is I, speaking in righteousness, mighty to save."

2 Why are your garments red,
like those of one treading the winepress?

3 "I have trodden the winepress alone;

from the nations no one was with
me.
I trampled them in my anger
and trod them down in my
wrath;
their blood spattered my garments,
and I stained all my clothing.
4 For the day of vengeance was in my
heart,
and the year of my redemption
has come.
5 I looked, but there was no one to
help,
I was appalled that no one gave
support;
so my own arm worked salvation for
me,
and my own wrath sustained me.
6 I trampled the nations in my anger;
in my wrath I made them drunk
and poured their blood on the
ground."

Praise and Prayer

7 I will tell of the kindnesses of the
LORD,
the deeds for which he is to be
praised,
according to all the LORD has
done for us—
yes, the many good things he has
done
for the house of Israel,
according to his compassion and
many kindnesses.
8 He said, "Surely they are my people,
sons who will not be false to me";
and so he became their Savior.
9 In all their distress he too was
distressed,
and the angel of his presence
saved them.
In his love and mercy he redeemed
them;
he lifted them up and carried
them
all the days of old.
10 Yet they rebelled
and grieved his Holy Spirit.
So he turned and became their
enemy
and he himself fought against
them.
11 Then his people recalled[a] the days of
old,
the days of Moses and his
people—
where is he who brought them
through the sea,
with the shepherd of his flock?
Where is he who set
his Holy Spirit among them,
12 who sent his glorious arm of power
to be at Moses' right hand,
who divided the waters before
them,
to gain for himself everlasting
renown,
13 who led them through the depths?
Like a horse in open country,
they did not stumble;
14 like cattle that go down to the plain,
they were given rest by the Spirit
of the LORD.
This is how you guided your people
to make for yourself a glorious
name.
15 Look down from heaven and see
from your lofty throne, holy and
glorious.
Where are your zeal and your
might?
Your tenderness and compassion
are withheld from us.
16 But you are our Father,
though Abraham does not know
us
or Israel acknowledge us;
you, O LORD, are our Father,
our Redeemer from of old is your
name.
17 Why, O LORD, do you make us
wander from your ways
and harden our hearts so we do
not revere you?
Return for the sake of your servants,
the tribes that are your
inheritance.
18 For a little while your people
possessed your holy place,
but now our enemies have
trampled down your
sanctuary.

[a]11 Or *But may he recall*

[19] We are yours from of old;
but you have not ruled over them,
they have not been called by your name.[a]

64

Oh, that you would rend the heavens and come down,
that the mountains would tremble before you!
[2] As when fire sets twigs ablaze
and causes water to boil,
come down to make your name known to your enemies
and cause the nations to quake before you!
[3] For when you did awesome things that we did not expect,
you came down, and the mountains trembled before you.
[4] Since ancient times no one has heard,
no ear has perceived,
no eye has seen any God besides you,
who acts on behalf of those who wait for him.
[5] You come to the help of those who gladly do right,
who remember your ways.
But when we continued to sin against them,
you were angry.
How then can we be saved?
[6] All of us have become like one who is unclean,
and all our righteous acts are like filthy rags;
we all shrivel up like a leaf,
and like the wind our sins sweep us away.
[7] No one calls on your name
or strives to lay hold of you;
for you have hidden your face from us
and made us waste away because of our sins.

[8] Yet, O LORD, you are our Father.
We are the clay, you are the potter;
we are all the work of your hand.
[9] Do not be angry beyond measure, O LORD;
do not remember our sins forever.
Oh, look upon us, we pray,
for we are all your people.
[10] Your sacred cities have become a desert;
even Zion is a desert, Jerusalem a desolation.
[11] Our holy and glorious temple,
where our fathers praised you,
has been burned with fire,
and all that we treasured lies in ruins.
[12] After all this, O LORD, will you hold yourself back?
Will you keep silent and punish us beyond measure?

Judgment and Salvation

65

"I revealed myself to those who did not ask for me;
I was found by those who did not seek me.
To a nation that did not call on my name,
I said, 'Here am I, here am I.'
[2] All day long I have held out my hands
to an obstinate people,
who walk in ways not good,
pursuing their own imaginations—
[3] a people who continually provoke me to my very face,
offering sacrifices in gardens
and burning incense on altars of brick;
[4] who sit among the graves
and spend their nights keeping secret vigil;
who eat the flesh of pigs,
and whose pots hold broth of unclean meat;
[5] who say, 'Keep away; don't come near me,
for I am too sacred for you!'
Such people are smoke in my nostrils,
a fire that keeps burning all day.

[a]19 Or *We are like those you have never ruled, / like those never called by your name*

[6]"See, it stands written before me:
I will not keep silent but will pay back in full;
I will pay it back into their laps—
[7]both your sins and the sins of your fathers,"
says the LORD.
"Because they burned sacrifices on the mountains
and defied me on the hills,
I will measure into their laps
the full payment for their former deeds."

[8]This is what the LORD says:

"As when juice is still found in a cluster of grapes
and men say, 'Don't destroy it,
there is yet some good in it,'
so will I do in behalf of my servants;
I will not destroy them all.
[9]I will bring forth descendants from Jacob,
and from Judah those who will possess my mountains;
my chosen people will inherit them,
and there will my servants live.
[10]Sharon will become a pasture for flocks,
and the Valley of Achor a resting place for herds,
for my people who seek me.
[11]"But as for you who forsake the LORD
and forget my holy mountain,
who spread a table for Fortune
and fill bowls of mixed wine for Destiny,
[12]I will destine you for the sword,
and you will all bend down for the slaughter;
for I called but you did not answer,
I spoke but you did not listen.
You did evil in my sight
and chose what displeases me."

[13]Therefore this is what the Sovereign LORD says:

"My servants will eat,
but you will go hungry;
my servants will drink,
but you will go thirsty;
my servants will rejoice,
but you will be put to shame.
[14]My servants will sing
out of the joy of their hearts,
but you will cry out
from anguish of heart
and wail in brokenness of spirit.
[15]You will leave your name
to my chosen ones as a curse;
the Sovereign LORD will put you to death,
but to his servants he will give another name.
[16]Whoever invokes a blessing in the land
will do so by the God of truth;
he who takes an oath in the land
will swear by the God of truth.
For the past troubles will be forgotten
and hidden from my eyes.

New Heavens and a New Earth

[17]"Behold, I will create
new heavens and a new earth.
The former things will not be remembered,
nor will they come to mind.
[18]But be glad and rejoice forever
in what I will create,
for I will create Jerusalem to be a delight
and its people a joy.
[19]I will rejoice over Jerusalem
and take delight in my people;
the sound of weeping and of crying
will be heard in it no more.
[20]"Never again will there be in it
an infant who lives but a few days,
or an old man who does not live out his years;
he who dies at a hundred
will be thought a mere youth;
he who fails to reach[a] a hundred
will be considered accursed.
[21]They will build houses and dwell in them;
they will plant vineyards and eat their fruit.

[a]20 Or / *the sinner who reaches*

22 No longer will they build houses
and others live in them,
or plant and others eat.
For as the days of a tree,
so will be the days of my people;
my chosen ones will long enjoy
the works of their hands.
23 They will not toil in vain
or bear children doomed to
misfortune;
for they will be a people blessed by
the LORD,
they and their descendants with
them.
24 Before they call I will answer;
while they are still speaking I will
hear.
25 The wolf and the lamb will feed
together,
and the lion will eat straw like the
ox,
but dust will be the serpent's food.
They will neither harm nor destroy
on all my holy mountain,"
says the LORD.

Judgment and Hope

66 This is what the LORD says:

"Heaven is my throne,
and the earth is my footstool.
Where is the house you will build
for me?
Where will my resting place be?
2 Has not my hand made all these
things,
and so they came into being?"
declares the LORD.
"This is the one I esteem:
he who is humble and contrite in
spirit,
and trembles at my word.
3 But whoever sacrifices a bull
is like one who kills a man,
and whoever offers a lamb,
like one who breaks a dog's neck;
whoever makes a grain offering
is like one who presents pig's
blood,
and whoever burns memorial
incense,
like one who worships an idol.
They have chosen their own ways,
and their souls delight in their
abominations;
4 so I also will choose harsh treatment
for them
and will bring upon them what
they dread.
For when I called, no one answered,
when I spoke, no one listened.
They did evil in my sight
and chose what displeases me."
5 Hear the word of the LORD,
you who tremble at his word:
"Your brothers who hate you,
and exclude you because of my
name, have said,
'Let the LORD be glorified,
that we may see your joy!'
Yet they will be put to shame.
6 Hear that uproar from the city,
hear that noise from the temple!
It is the sound of the LORD
repaying his enemies all they
deserve.
7 "Before she goes into labor,
she gives birth;
before the pains come upon her,
she delivers a son.
8 Who has ever heard of such a thing?
Who has ever seen such things?
Can a country be born in a day
or a nation be brought forth in a
moment?
Yet no sooner is Zion in labor
than she gives birth to her
children.
9 Do I bring to the moment of birth
and not give delivery?" says the
LORD.
"Do I close up the womb
when I bring to delivery?" says
your God.
10 "Rejoice with Jerusalem and be glad
for her,
all you who love her;
rejoice greatly with her,
all you who mourn over her.
11 For you will nurse and be satisfied
at her comforting breasts;
you will drink deeply
and delight in her overflowing
abundance."

12 For this is what the LORD says:

"I will extend peace to her like a river,
and the wealth of nations like a flooding stream;
you will nurse and be carried on her arm
and dandled on her knees.
13 As a mother comforts her child,
so will I comfort you;
and you will be comforted over Jerusalem."

14 When you see this, your heart will rejoice
and you will flourish like grass;
the hand of the LORD will be made known to his servants,
but his fury will be shown to his foes.
15 See, the LORD is coming with fire,
and his chariots are like a whirlwind;
he will bring down his anger with fury,
and his rebuke with flames of fire.
16 For with fire and with his sword
the LORD will execute judgment upon all men,
and many will be those slain by the LORD.

17 "Those who consecrate and purify
themselves to go into the gardens, following the one in the midst of[a] those
who eat the flesh of pigs and rats and
other abominable things—they will
meet their end together," declares the
LORD.
18 "And I, because of their actions and
their imaginations, am about to come[b]
and gather all nations and tongues, and
they will come and see my glory.
19 "I will set a sign among them, and I
will send some of those who survive to
the nations—to Tarshish, to the Libyans[c]
and Lydians (famous as archers), to Tubal and Greece, and to the distant islands that have not heard of my fame or
seen my glory. They will proclaim my
glory among the nations.
20 And they
will bring all your brothers, from all the
nations, to my holy mountain in Jerusalem as an offering to the LORD—on
horses, in chariots and wagons, and on
mules and camels," says the LORD.
"They will bring them, as the Israelites
bring their grain offerings, to the temple of the LORD in ceremonially clean
vessels.
21 And I will select some of them
also to be priests and Levites," says the
LORD.

22 "As the new heavens and the new
earth that I make will endure before
me," declares the LORD, "so will your
name and descendants endure.
23 From
one New Moon to another and from
one Sabbath to another, all mankind will
come and bow down before me," says
the LORD.
24 "And they will go out and
look upon the dead bodies of those who
rebelled against me; their worm will
not die, nor will their fire be quenched,
and they will be loathsome to all mankind."

[a]17 Or *gardens behind one of your temples, and*
[b]18 The meaning of the Hebrew for this clause is uncertain. [c]19 Some Septuagint manuscripts *Put* (Libyans); Hebrew *Pul*

SHARPEN THE FOCUS

The green bumper sticker suggested, "Visualize Whirled Peas." Perhaps some would take offense, especially someone whose bumper sports the blue slogan, "Visualize World Peace," parodied by the green one.

Anyone with a blender can produce whirled peas. World peace will not become a reality until the Prince of Peace rules over the new heavens and new earth He will create. Isaiah tells us why. "All our righteous acts are like filthy rags," he confesses (Isaiah 64:6). Even the good things, the "righteous" things we try to do are tainted by self-focus, wrong motives, or the subtle but prideful thought about others, "I'm holier than you" (Isaiah 65:5.)

Peace can come to our world only as the Prince of Peace takes up residence in the sinners for whom He died.

That process is the theme of Isaiah 66: "Can a country be born in a day or a nation be brought forth in a moment?" the prophet asks (Isaiah 66:8). We've seen the answer—on the day of Pentecost. The Lord, the Creator-God, gave all nations great cause for joy.

We who know Christ have come from all nations to see His glory (Isaiah 66:18). Now we pray that the Lord would use us to continue to draw the nations to Christ and His cross.

JEREMIAH

As a young man, perhaps even a teenager, Jeremiah became a seer in Judah. In the 40 year ministry that followed, Jeremiah "saw" more, perhaps, than any human being before or since. Most of what he saw made him weep. As you read today, notice the many word pictures the prophet used to illustrate the shame of Judah's idolatry. If time is short, focus on Jeremiah 1:1–19.

1 The words of Jeremiah son of Hilkiah, one of the priests at Anathoth in the territory of Benjamin. 2The word of the LORD came to him in the thirteenth year of the reign of Josiah son of Amon king of Judah, 3and through the reign of Jehoiakim son of Josiah king of Judah, down to the fifth month of the eleventh year of Zedekiah son of Josiah king of Judah, when the people of Jerusalem went into exile.

The Call of Jeremiah

4The word of the LORD came to me, saying,

5"Before I formed you in the womb I
knew[a] you,
before you were born I set you
apart;
I appointed you as a prophet to
the nations."

6"Ah, Sovereign LORD," I said, "I do not know how to speak; I am only a child."

7But the LORD said to me, "Do not say, 'I am only a child.' You must go to everyone I send you to and say whatever I command you. 8Do not be afraid of them, for I am with you and will rescue you," declares the LORD.

9Then the LORD reached out his hand and touched my mouth and said to me, "Now, I have put my words in your mouth. 10See, today I appoint you over nations and kingdoms to uproot and tear down, to destroy and overthrow, to build and to plant."

11The word of the LORD came to me: "What do you see, Jeremiah?"

"I see the branch of an almond tree," I replied.

12The LORD said to me, "You have seen correctly, for I am watching[b] to see that my word is fulfilled."

13The word of the LORD came to me again: "What do you see?"

"I see a boiling pot, tilting away from the north," I answered.

14The LORD said to me, "From the north disaster will be poured out on all who live in the land. 15I am about to summon all the peoples of the northern kingdoms," declares the LORD.

"Their kings will come and set up
their thrones
in the entrance of the gates of
Jerusalem;

[a]5 Or *chose* [b]12 The Hebrew for *watching* sounds like the Hebrew for *almond tree.*

they will come against all her
surrounding walls
and against all the towns of Judah.
16 I will pronounce my judgments on
my people
because of their wickedness in
forsaking me,
in burning incense to other gods
and in worshiping what their
hands have made.

17 "Get yourself ready! Stand up and
say to them whatever I command you.
Do not be terrified by them, or I will terrify you before them. 18 Today I have
made you a fortified city, an iron pillar
and a bronze wall to stand against the
whole land—against the kings of Judah,
its officials, its priests and the people of
the land. 19 They will fight against you
but will not overcome you, for I am with
you and will rescue you," declares the
LORD.

Israel Forsakes God

2 The word of the LORD came to
me: 2 "Go and proclaim in the
hearing of Jerusalem:

" 'I remember the devotion of your
youth,
how as a bride you loved me
and followed me through the desert,
through a land not sown.
3 Israel was holy to the LORD,
the firstfruits of his harvest;
all who devoured her were held
guilty,
and disaster overtook them,' "
declares the LORD.
4 Hear the word of the LORD,
O house of Jacob,
all you clans of the house of Israel.

5 This is what the LORD says:

"What fault did your fathers find in
me,
that they strayed so far from me?
They followed worthless idols
and became worthless themselves.
6 They did not ask, 'Where is the
LORD,
who brought us up out of Egypt
and led us through the barren
wilderness,
through a land of deserts and rifts,
a land of drought and darkness,[a]
a land where no one travels and
no one lives?'
7 I brought you into a fertile land
to eat its fruit and rich produce.
But you came and defiled my land
and made my inheritance
detestable.
8 The priests did not ask,
'Where is the LORD?'
Those who deal with the law did not
know me;
the leaders rebelled against me.
The prophets prophesied by Baal,
following worthless idols.

9 "Therefore I bring charges against
you again,"
declares the LORD.
"And I will bring charges against
your children's children.
10 Cross over to the coasts of Kittim[b]
and look,
send to Kedar[c] and observe
closely;
see if there has ever been
anything like this:
11 Has a nation ever changed its gods?
(Yet they are not gods at all.)
But my people have exchanged
their[d] Glory
for worthless idols.
12 Be appalled at this, O heavens,
and shudder with great horror,"
declares the LORD.
13 "My people have committed two
sins:
They have forsaken me,
the spring of living water,
and have dug their own cisterns,
broken cisterns that cannot hold
water.
14 Is Israel a servant, a slave by birth?
Why then has he become
plunder?

[a] 6 Or *and the shadow of death* [b] 10 That is, Cyprus and western coastlands [c] 10 The home of Bedouin tribes in the Syro-Arabian desert [d] 11 Masoretic Text; an ancient Hebrew scribal tradition *my*

15 Lions have roared;
they have growled at him.
They have laid waste his land;
his towns are burned and deserted.
16 Also, the men of Memphis[a] and Tahpanhes
have shaved the crown of your head.[b]
17 Have you not brought this on yourselves
by forsaking the LORD your God
when he led you in the way?
18 Now why go to Egypt
to drink water from the Shihor[c]?
And why go to Assyria
to drink water from the River[d]?
19 Your wickedness will punish you;
your backsliding will rebuke you.
Consider then and realize
how evil and bitter it is for you
when you forsake the LORD your God
and have no awe of me,"
declares the Lord,
the LORD Almighty.

20 "Long ago you broke off your yoke
and tore off your bonds;
you said, 'I will not serve you!'
Indeed, on every high hill
and under every spreading tree
you lay down as a prostitute.
21 I had planted you like a choice vine
of sound and reliable stock.
How then did you turn against me
into a corrupt, wild vine?
22 Although you wash yourself with soda
and use an abundance of soap,
the stain of your guilt is still before me,"
declares the Sovereign LORD.
23 "How can you say, 'I am not defiled;
I have not run after the Baals'?
See how you behaved in the valley;
consider what you have done.
You are a swift she-camel
running here and there,
24 a wild donkey accustomed to the desert,
sniffing the wind in her craving—
in her heat who can restrain her?
Any males that pursue her need not tire themselves;
at mating time they will find her.
25 Do not run until your feet are bare
and your throat is dry.
But you said, 'It's no use!
I love foreign gods,
and I must go after them.'

26 "As a thief is disgraced when he is caught,
so the house of Israel is disgraced—
they, their kings and their officials,
their priests and their prophets.
27 They say to wood, 'You are my father,'
and to stone, 'You gave me birth.'
They have turned their backs to me
and not their faces;
yet when they are in trouble, they say,
'Come and save us!'
28 Where then are the gods you made for yourselves?
Let them come if they can save you
when you are in trouble!
For you have as many gods
as you have towns, O Judah.

29 "Why do you bring charges against me?
You have all rebelled against me,"
declares the LORD.
30 "In vain I punished your people;
they did not respond to correction.
Your sword has devoured your prophets
like a ravening lion.

31 "You of this generation, consider the word of the LORD:

"Have I been a desert to Israel
or a land of great darkness?
Why do my people say, 'We are free to roam;
we will come to you no more'?
32 Does a maiden forget her jewelry,

[a]16 Hebrew *Noph* [b]16 Or *have cracked your skull* [c]18 That is, a branch of the Nile [d]18 That is, the Euphrates

a bride her wedding ornaments?
Yet my people have forgotten me,
days without number.
33 How skilled you are at pursuing
love!
Even the worst of women can
learn from your ways.
34 On your clothes men find
the lifeblood of the innocent poor,
though you did not catch them
breaking in.
Yet in spite of all this
35 you say, 'I am innocent;
he is not angry with me.'
But I will pass judgment on you
because you say, 'I have not
sinned.'
36 Why do you go about so much,
changing your ways?
You will be disappointed by Egypt
as you were by Assyria.
37 You will also leave that place
with your hands on your head,
for the LORD has rejected those you
trust;
you will not be helped by them.

SHARPEN THE FOCUS

No doubt Jeremiah watched as each spring for 40 years the almond trees budded. No doubt they reminded him of God's call on his life and of God's promise to keep His word of Law and judgment, grace and mercy.

For the most part, Jeremiah preached God's word of Law. No matter how sternly he thundered, how carefully he crafted his sermons, or how many pointed word pictures he used, the people seemingly ignored him. They turned their backs on the fountain of God's "living water."

The Lord knew how discouraged Jeremiah felt! He knows our tendency toward disappointment, too. When we speak about the Lord Jesus and our friend's eyes glaze over, or when those around us who claim to be Christians disgrace the name of Christ—this can drag us into discouragement. Worse still, we catch ourselves in the sins of spiritual pride or ungodly self-confidence.

Still, no matter what our experiences seem to say, God's Word works to perform His every promise. He has promised to forgive your sins—all of them—for Jesus' sake. And He has promised to empower you as His witness (Acts 1:8). Let these promises fill you with zeal and renewed courage today!

WEEK 58 • MONDAY

Jeremiah 3:1—4:31

GET THE BIG PICTURE

Throughout the book of Jeremiah the Lord will accuse Judah, His bride, of adultery. She has left her first love, the Lord, and has chased after idols. The Lord's pain at this cuts Him deeply. As you read, ask yourself, "How fully do I realize the pain my sin causes my Lord?" If time is short, focus on Jeremiah 4:1–31.

3 "If a man divorces his wife
and she leaves him and marries
another man,
should he return to her again?
Would not the land be completely
defiled?
But you have lived as a prostitute
with many lovers—
would you now return to me?"
declares the LORD.
2 "Look up to the barren heights and
see.
Is there any place where you have
not been ravished?
By the roadside you sat waiting for
lovers,
sat like a nomad[a] in the desert.
You have defiled the land
with your prostitution and
wickedness.
3 Therefore the showers have been
withheld,
and no spring rains have fallen.
Yet you have the brazen look of a
prostitute;
you refuse to blush with shame.
4 Have you not just called to me:
'My Father, my friend from my
youth,
5 will you always be angry?
Will your wrath continue forever?'
This is how you talk,
but you do all the evil you can."

Unfaithful Israel

6 During the reign of King Josiah, the
LORD said to me, "Have you seen what
faithless Israel has done? She has gone
up on every high hill and under every
spreading tree and has committed adultery there. 7 I thought that after she had
done all this she would return to me but
she did not, and her unfaithful sister
Judah saw it. 8 I gave faithless Israel her
certificate of divorce and sent her away
because of all her adulteries. Yet I saw
that her unfaithful sister Judah had no
fear; she also went out and committed
adultery. 9 Because Israel's immorality
mattered so little to her, she defiled the
land and committed adultery with
stone and wood. 10 In spite of all this, her
unfaithful sister Judah did not return to
me with all her heart, but only in pretense," declares the LORD.

11 The LORD said to me, "Faithless Israel is more righteous than unfaithful
Judah. 12 Go, proclaim this message toward the north:

" 'Return, faithless Israel,' declares
the LORD,
'I will frown on you no longer,
for I am merciful,' declares the
LORD,
'I will not be angry forever.
13 Only acknowledge your guilt—
you have rebelled against the
LORD your God,
you have scattered your favors to
foreign gods
under every spreading tree,
and have not obeyed me,' "
declares the LORD.

14 "Return, faithless people," declares
the LORD, "for I am your husband. I will
choose you—one from a town and two
from a clan—and bring you to Zion.
15 Then I will give you shepherds after
my own heart, who will lead you with
knowledge and understanding. 16 In
those days, when your numbers have
increased greatly in the land," declares
the LORD, "men will no longer say, 'The
ark of the covenant of the LORD.' It will
never enter their minds or be remembered; it will not be missed, nor will
another one be made. 17 At that time they
will call Jerusalem The Throne of the
LORD, and all nations will gather in Jerusalem to honor the name of the LORD.
No longer will they follow the stubbornness of their evil hearts. 18 In those days
the house of Judah will join the house
of Israel, and together they will come
from a northern land to the land I gave
your forefathers as an inheritance.

19 "I myself said,

" 'How gladly would I treat you like
sons
and give you a desirable land,
the most beautiful inheritance of
any nation.'
I thought you would call me 'Father'

[a] 2 Or *an Arab*

and not turn away from following
me.
[20]But like a woman unfaithful to her
husband,
so you have been unfaithful to
me, O house of Israel,"
declares the LORD.

[21]A cry is heard on the barren heights,
the weeping and pleading of the
people of Israel,
because they have perverted their
ways
and have forgotten the LORD their
God.

[22]"Return, faithless people;
I will cure you of backsliding."

"Yes, we will come to you,
for you are the LORD our God.
[23]Surely the ⌊idolatrous⌋ commotion on
the hills
and mountains is a deception;
surely in the LORD our God
is the salvation of Israel.
[24]From our youth shameful gods have
consumed
the fruits of our fathers'
labor—
their flocks and herds,
their sons and daughters.
[25]Let us lie down in our shame,
and let our disgrace cover us.
We have sinned against the LORD
our God,
both we and our fathers;
from our youth till this day
we have not obeyed the LORD our
God."

4 "If you will return, O Israel,
return to me,"
declares the LORD.
"If you put your detestable idols out
of my sight
and no longer go astray,
[2]and if in a truthful, just and
righteous way
you swear, 'As surely as the LORD
lives,'
then the nations will be blessed by
him
and in him they will glory."

[3]This is what the LORD says to the men of Judah and to Jerusalem:

"Break up your unplowed ground
and do not sow among thorns.
[4]Circumcise yourselves to the LORD,
circumcise your hearts,
you men of Judah and people of
Jerusalem,
or my wrath will break out and burn
like fire
because of the evil you have
done—
burn with no one to quench it.

Disaster From the North

[5]"Announce in Judah and proclaim in
Jerusalem and say:
'Sound the trumpet throughout
the land!'
Cry aloud and say:
'Gather together!
Let us flee to the fortified cities!'
[6]Raise the signal to go to Zion!
Flee for safety without delay!
For I am bringing disaster from the
north,
even terrible destruction."

[7]A lion has come out of his lair;
a destroyer of nations has set out.
He has left his place
to lay waste your land.
Your towns will lie in ruins
without inhabitant.
[8]So put on sackcloth,
lament and wail,
for the fierce anger of the LORD
has not turned away from us.

[9]"In that day," declares the LORD,
"the king and the officials will lose
heart,
the priests will be horrified,
and the prophets will be
appalled."

[10]Then I said, "Ah, Sovereign LORD, how completely you have deceived this people and Jerusalem by saying, 'You will have peace,' when the sword is at our throats."

[11]At that time this people and Jerusalem will be told, "A scorching wind from the barren heights in the desert blows

toward my people, but not to winnow
or cleanse; [12]a wind too strong for that
comes from me.[a] Now I pronounce my
judgments against them."

[13]Look! He advances like the clouds,
his chariots come like a whirlwind,
his horses are swifter than eagles.
Woe to us! We are ruined!
[14]O Jerusalem, wash the evil from your heart and be saved.
How long will you harbor wicked thoughts?
[15]A voice is announcing from Dan,
proclaiming disaster from the hills of Ephraim.
[16]"Tell this to the nations,
proclaim it to Jerusalem:
'A besieging army is coming from a distant land,
raising a war cry against the cities of Judah.
[17]They surround her like men guarding a field,
because she has rebelled against me,' "
declares the LORD.
[18]"Your own conduct and actions
have brought this upon you.
This is your punishment.
How bitter it is!
How it pierces to the heart!"

[19]Oh, my anguish, my anguish!
I writhe in pain.
Oh, the agony of my heart!
My heart pounds within me,
I cannot keep silent.
For I have heard the sound of the trumpet;
I have heard the battle cry.
[20]Disaster follows disaster;
the whole land lies in ruins.
In an instant my tents are destroyed,
my shelter in a moment.
[21]How long must I see the battle standard
and hear the sound of the trumpet?

[22]"My people are fools;
they do not know me.
They are senseless children;
they have no understanding.
They are skilled in doing evil;
they know not how to do good."

[23]I looked at the earth,
and it was formless and empty;
and at the heavens,
and their light was gone.
[24]I looked at the mountains,
and they were quaking;
all the hills were swaying.
[25]I looked, and there were no people;
every bird in the sky had flown away.
[26]I looked, and the fruitful land was a desert;
all its towns lay in ruins
before the LORD, before his fierce anger.

[27]This is what the LORD says:

"The whole land will be ruined,
though I will not destroy it completely.
[28]Therefore the earth will mourn
and the heavens above grow dark,
because I have spoken and will not relent,
I have decided and will not turn back."

[29]At the sound of horsemen and archers
every town takes to flight.
Some go into the thickets;
some climb up among the rocks.
All the towns are deserted;
no one lives in them.
[30]What are you doing, O devastated one?
Why dress yourself in scarlet
and put on jewels of gold?
Why shade your eyes with paint?
You adorn yourself in vain.
Your lovers despise you;
they seek your life.

[a]12 Or *comes at my command*

31 I hear a cry as of a woman in labor,
a groan as of one bearing her first child—
the cry of the Daughter of Zion
gasping for breath,
stretching out her hands and saying,
"Alas! I am fainting;
my life is given over to murderers."

SHARPEN THE FOCUS

Defense attorneys try hard to script trials for the good of their clients. They plan their strategies down to the nth degree, even taking into account the clothes the client will wear. A sweater–to make him look young and inexperienced? A suit and tie–to indicate respectability? A modest dress–to make her look more vulnerable? But in the day of Judah's judgment, Jeremiah warns, appearances won't count:

Why dress yourself in scarlet
and put on jewels of gold. . . ?
Your lovers . . . seek your life. (Jeremiah 4:30)

For us as for ancient Judah, no amount of makeup, no designer clothes, no collection of fine jewelry will disguise the condition of our hearts. Outward appearance won't mask inward unfaithfulness. That's the truth, and its severity makes our Savior-God's invitation to return to Him that much sweeter.

In love that knows no equal, our Lord says to us, "Come home to Me. Renew your vows to Me. I love you. And by the blood of My Son, I forgive you."

Who can ignore love like that? Who can refuse to respond to love like that?

WEEK 58 • TUESDAY

Jeremiah 5:1—6:30

GET THE BIG PICTURE

"Your shepherds tell you what you want to hear; your spiritual leaders struggle for power just like everyone else. And you love it. But what will you do in the end?" That's the message Jeremiah delivers from the Lord in 5:31. What do *you* expect from your own spiritual leaders? Ask yourself that question as you read today. If time is short, focus on Jeremiah 5:1–31.

Not One Is Upright

5 "Go up and down the streets of Jerusalem,
look around and consider,
search through her squares.
If you can find but one person
who deals honestly and seeks the truth,
I will forgive this city.
2 Although they say, 'As surely as the LORD lives,'
still they are swearing falsely."
3 O LORD, do not your eyes look for truth?
You struck them, but they felt no pain;

you crushed them, but they
refused correction.
They made their faces harder than
stone
and refused to repent.
4 I thought, "These are only the poor;
they are foolish,
for they do not know the way of the
LORD,
the requirements of their God.
5 So I will go to the leaders
and speak to them;
surely they know the way of the
LORD,
the requirements of their God."
But with one accord they too had
broken off the yoke
and torn off the bonds.
6 Therefore a lion from the forest will
attack them,
a wolf from the desert will ravage
them,
a leopard will lie in wait near their
towns
to tear to pieces any who venture
out,
for their rebellion is great
and their backslidings many.
7 "Why should I forgive you?
Your children have forsaken me
and sworn by gods that are not
gods.
I supplied all their needs,
yet they committed adultery
and thronged to the houses of
prostitutes.
8 They are well-fed, lusty stallions,
each neighing for another man's
wife.
9 Should I not punish them for this?"
declares the LORD.
"Should I not avenge myself
on such a nation as this?
10 "Go through her vineyards and
ravage them,
but do not destroy them
completely.
Strip off her branches,
for these people do not belong to
the LORD.
11 The house of Israel and the house of
Judah
have been utterly unfaithful to
me,"
declares the LORD.
12 They have lied about the LORD;
they said, "He will do nothing!
No harm will come to us;
we will never see sword or
famine.
13 The prophets are but wind
and the word is not in them;
so let what they say be done to
them."

14 Therefore this is what the LORD God
Almighty says:

"Because the people have spoken
these words,
I will make my words in your
mouth a fire
and these people the wood it
consumes.
15 O house of Israel," declares the
LORD,
"I am bringing a distant nation
against you—
an ancient and enduring nation,
a people whose language you do
not know,
whose speech you do not
understand.
16 Their quivers are like an open grave;
all of them are mighty warriors.
17 They will devour your harvests and
food,
devour your sons and daughters;
they will devour your flocks and
herds,
devour your vines and fig trees.
With the sword they will destroy
the fortified cities in which you
trust.

18 "Yet even in those days," declares
the LORD, "I will not destroy you completely. 19 And when the people ask,
'Why has the LORD our God done all
this to us?' you will tell them, 'As you
have forsaken me and served foreign
gods in your own land, so now you will
serve foreigners in a land not your own.'

20 "Announce this to the house of Jacob
and proclaim it in Judah:

[21]Hear this, you foolish and senseless
people,
who have eyes but do not see,
who have ears but do not hear:
[22]Should you not fear me?" declares
the LORD.
"Should you not tremble in my
presence?
I made the sand a boundary for the
sea,
an everlasting barrier it cannot
cross.
The waves may roll, but they cannot
prevail;
they may roar, but they cannot
cross it.
[23]But these people have stubborn and
rebellious hearts;
they have turned aside and gone
away.
[24]They do not say to themselves,
'Let us fear the LORD our God,
who gives autumn and spring rains
in season,
who assures us of the regular
weeks of harvest.'
[25]Your wrongdoings have kept these
away;
your sins have deprived you of
good.

[26]"Among my people are wicked men
who lie in wait like men who
snare birds
and like those who set traps to
catch men.
[27]Like cages full of birds,
their houses are full of deceit;
they have become rich and
powerful
[28] and have grown fat and sleek.
Their evil deeds have no limit;
they do not plead the case of the
fatherless to win it,
they do not defend the rights of
the poor.
[29]Should I not punish them for this?"
declares the LORD.
"Should I not avenge myself
on such a nation as this?

[30]"A horrible and shocking thing
has happened in the land:
[31]The prophets prophesy lies,
the priests rule by their own
authority,
and my people love it this way.
But what will you do in the end?

Jerusalem Under Siege

6 "Flee for safety, people of
Benjamin!
Flee from Jerusalem!
Sound the trumpet in Tekoa!
Raise the signal over Beth
Hakkerem!
For disaster looms out of the north,
even terrible destruction.
[2]I will destroy the Daughter of Zion,
so beautiful and delicate.
[3]Shepherds with their flocks will
come against her;
they will pitch their tents around
her,
each tending his own portion."

[4]"Prepare for battle against her!
Arise, let us attack at noon!
But, alas, the daylight is fading,
and the shadows of evening grow
long.
[5]So arise, let us attack at night
and destroy her fortresses!"

[6]This is what the LORD Almighty says:

"Cut down the trees
and build siege ramps against
Jerusalem.
This city must be punished;
it is filled with oppression.
[7]As a well pours out its water,
so she pours out her wickedness.
Violence and destruction resound in
her;
her sickness and wounds are ever
before me.
[8]Take warning, O Jerusalem,
or I will turn away from you
and make your land desolate
so no one can live in it."

[9]This is what the LORD Almighty says:

"Let them glean the remnant of Israel
as thoroughly as a vine;
pass your hand over the branches
again,
like one gathering grapes."

[10]To whom can I speak and give
warning?
Who will listen to me?
Their ears are closed[a]
so they cannot hear.
The word of the LORD is offensive to
them;
they find no pleasure in it.
[11]But I am full of the wrath of the
LORD,
and I cannot hold it in.

"Pour it out on the children in the
street
and on the young men gathered
together;
both husband and wife will be
caught in it,
and the old, those weighed down
with years.
[12]Their houses will be turned over to
others,
together with their fields and their
wives,
when I stretch out my hand
against those who live in the
land,"
declares the LORD.
[13]"From the least to the greatest,
all are greedy for gain;
prophets and priests alike,
all practice deceit.
[14]They dress the wound of my people
as though it were not serious.
'Peace, peace,' they say,
when there is no peace.
[15]Are they ashamed of their
loathsome conduct?
No, they have no shame at all;
they do not even know how to
blush.
So they will fall among the fallen;
they will be brought down when I
punish them,"
says the LORD.

[16]This is what the LORD says:

"Stand at the crossroads and look;
ask for the ancient paths,
ask where the good way is, and
walk in it,
and you will find rest for your
souls.
But you said, 'We will not walk in
it.'
[17]I appointed watchmen over you and
said,
'Listen to the sound of the
trumpet!'
But you said, 'We will not listen.'
[18]Therefore hear, O nations;
observe, O witnesses,
what will happen to them.
[19]Hear, O earth:
I am bringing disaster on this
people,
the fruit of their schemes,
because they have not listened to
my words
and have rejected my law.
[20]What do I care about incense from
Sheba
or sweet calamus from a distant
land?
Your burnt offerings are not
acceptable;
your sacrifices do not please me."

[21]Therefore this is what the LORD
says:

"I will put obstacles before this
people.
Fathers and sons alike will
stumble over them;
neighbors and friends will perish."

[22]This is what the LORD says:

"Look, an army is coming
from the land of the north;
a great nation is being stirred up
from the ends of the earth.
[23]They are armed with bow and
spear;
they are cruel and show no mercy.
They sound like the roaring sea
as they ride on their horses;
they come like men in battle
formation
to attack you, O Daughter of
Zion."

[24]We have heard reports about them,
and our hands hang limp.
Anguish has gripped us,

[a]*10* Hebrew *uncircumcised*

pain like that of a woman in labor.
25 Do not go out to the fields
or walk on the roads,
for the enemy has a sword,
and there is terror on every side.
26 O my people, put on sackcloth
and roll in ashes;
mourn with bitter wailing
as for an only son,
for suddenly the destroyer
will come upon us.

27 "I have made you a tester of metals
and my people the ore,
that you may observe
and test their ways.
28 They are all hardened rebels,
going about to slander.
They are bronze and iron;
they all act corruptly.
29 The bellows blow fiercely
to burn away the lead with fire,
but the refining goes on in vain;
the wicked are not purged out.
30 They are called rejected silver,
because the LORD has rejected them."

SHARPEN THE FOCUS

God's omnipotence and His immeasurable goodness should lead us to bow in reverence, love, and obedience before Him. But people too often turn a cold shoulder and a deaf ear toward God (Jeremiah 5:21, 23).

Perhaps we think we hear every word our heavenly Father speaks. And perhaps we want to believe we've never dawdled in obeying Him. Even so, we have sometimes delayed and often disobeyed, despite both the power and the love He has displayed in our life.

Maybe we've ignored the needs of children whose parents have deserted them or the injustices the poor in our community suffer (Jeremiah 5:28). Maybe we accumulate things, believing they will make us happy (Jeremiah 6:13). Maybe we're in a position of spiritual leadership, but overlook the sins of those whose support we need.

God's Law brings us to the crossroads of Jeremiah 6:16. We can close our ears to our Lord's Word. Or, being led by God's grace, we can in repentance, pray, "Show me the ancient path. Lead me along Your highway, my Savior."

If you can, take a walk today. Have a talk with God about the path you're on and about the path He would have you walk. Listen to His word of comfort and encouragement through our Savior. In Him you will find rest for your soul.

WEEK 58 • WEDNESDAY

Jeremiah 7:1—8:22

GET THE BIG PICTURE

The Lord hates false religion—the outward show of piety that comes forth from hearts made hard by disobedience. As you read today's chapters from Jeremiah ask yourself, "Do I ever cover my own sin with a veneer of religion?" If time is short, focus on Jeremiah 7:1–28.

False Religion Worthless

7 This is the word that came to
Jeremiah from the LORD:
2"Stand at the gate of the LORD's house
and there proclaim this message:
" 'Hear the word of the LORD, all you
people of Judah who come through
these gates to worship the LORD. 3This
is what the LORD Almighty, the God of
Israel, says: Reform your ways and your
actions, and I will let you live in this
place. 4Do not trust in deceptive words
and say, "This is the temple of the LORD,
the temple of the LORD, the temple of
the LORD!" 5If you really change your
ways and your actions and deal with
each other justly, 6if you do not oppress
the alien, the fatherless or the widow
and do not shed innocent blood in this
place, and if you do not follow other
gods to your own harm, 7then I will let
you live in this place, in the land I gave
your forefathers for ever and ever. 8But
look, you are trusting in deceptive
words that are worthless.
9" 'Will you steal and murder, commit
adultery and perjury,[a] burn incense to
Baal and follow other gods you have not
known, 10and then come and stand before me in this house, which bears my
Name, and say, "We are safe"—safe to
do all these detestable things? 11Has this
house, which bears my Name, become
a den of robbers to you? But I have been
watching! declares the LORD.
12" 'Go now to the place in Shiloh
where I first made a dwelling for my
Name, and see what I did to it because
of the wickedness of my people Israel.
13While you were doing all these things,
declares the LORD, I spoke to you again
and again, but you did not listen; I
called you, but you did not answer.
14Therefore, what I did to Shiloh I will
now do to the house that bears my
Name, the temple you trust in, the place
I gave to you and your fathers. 15I will
thrust you from my presence, just as I
did all your brothers, the people of
Ephraim.'
16"So do not pray for this people nor
offer any plea or petition for them; do
not plead with me, for I will not listen
to you. 17Do you not see what they are
doing in the towns of Judah and in the
streets of Jerusalem? 18The children
gather wood, the fathers light the fire,
and the women knead the dough and
make cakes of bread for the Queen of
Heaven. They pour out drink offerings
to other gods to provoke me to anger.
19But am I the one they are provoking?
declares the LORD. Are they not rather
harming themselves, to their own
shame?
20" 'Therefore this is what the Sovereign LORD says: My anger and my
wrath will be poured out on this place,
on man and beast, on the trees of the
field and on the fruit of the ground, and
it will burn and not be quenched.
21" 'This is what the LORD Almighty,
the God of Israel, says: Go ahead, add
your burnt offerings to your other sacrifices and eat the meat yourselves! 22For
when I brought your forefathers out of
Egypt and spoke to them, I did not just
give them commands about burnt offerings and sacrifices, 23but I gave them this
command: Obey me, and I will be your
God and you will be my people. Walk in
all the ways I command you, that it may
go well with you. 24But they did not listen or pay attention; instead, they followed the stubborn inclinations of their
evil hearts. They went backward and
not forward. 25From the time your forefathers left Egypt until now, day after
day, again and again I sent you my servants the prophets. 26But they did not
listen to me or pay attention. They were
stiff-necked and did more evil than their
forefathers.'
27"When you tell them all this, they
will not listen to you; when you call to
them, they will not answer. 28Therefore
say to them, 'This is the nation that has
not obeyed the LORD its God or responded to correction. Truth has perished; it has vanished from their
lips. 29Cut off your hair and throw it
away; take up a lament on the barren
heights, for the LORD has rejected and

[a]9 Or *and swear by false gods*

abandoned this generation that is under his wrath.

The Valley of Slaughter

30" 'The people of Judah have done
evil in my eyes, declares the LORD. They
have set up their detestable idols in the
house that bears my Name and have defiled it. 31They have built the high places
of Topheth in the Valley of Ben Hinnom
to burn their sons and daughters in the
fire—something I did not command,
nor did it enter my mind. 32So beware,
the days are coming, declares the LORD,
when people will no longer call it Topheth or the Valley of Ben Hinnom, but
the Valley of Slaughter, for they will
bury the dead in Topheth until there is
no more room. 33Then the carcasses of
this people will become food for the
birds of the air and the beasts of the
earth, and there will be no one to fright-
en them away. 34I will bring an end to
the sounds of joy and gladness and to
the voices of bride and bridegroom
in the towns of Judah and the streets of
Jerusalem, for the land will become
desolate.

8 " 'At that time, declares the LORD,
the bones of the kings and officials of Judah, the bones of the priests
and prophets, and the bones of the
people of Jerusalem will be removed
from their graves. 2They will be exposed
to the sun and the moon and all the stars
of the heavens, which they have loved
and served and which they have followed and consulted and worshiped.
They will not be gathered up or buried,
but will be like refuse lying on the
ground. 3Wherever I banish them, all
the survivors of this evil nation will prefer death to life, declares the LORD Almighty.'

Sin and Punishment

4"Say to them, 'This is what the LORD
says:

" 'When men fall down, do they not
get up?
When a man turns away, does he
not return?
5Why then have these people turned
away?
Why does Jerusalem always turn
away?
They cling to deceit;
they refuse to return.
6I have listened attentively,
but they do not say what is right.
No one repents of his wickedness,
saying, "What have I done?"
Each pursues his own course
like a horse charging into battle.
7Even the stork in the sky
knows her appointed seasons,
and the dove, the swift and the
thrush
observe the time of their
migration.
But my people do not know
the requirements of the LORD.

8" 'How can you say, "We are wise,
for we have the law of the LORD,"
when actually the lying pen of the
scribes
has handled it falsely?
9The wise will be put to shame;
they will be dismayed and
trapped.
Since they have rejected the word of
the LORD,
what kind of wisdom do they
have?
10Therefore I will give their wives to
other men
and their fields to new owners.
From the least to the greatest,
all are greedy for gain;
prophets and priests alike,
all practice deceit.
11They dress the wound of my people
as though it were not serious.
"Peace, peace," they say,
when there is no peace.
12Are they ashamed of their
loathsome conduct?
No, they have no shame at all;
they do not even know how to
blush.
So they will fall among the fallen;
they will be brought down when
they are punished,
says the LORD.

13 " 'I will take away their harvest,
declares the LORD.
There will be no grapes on the
vine.
There will be no figs on the tree,
and their leaves will wither.
What I have given them
will be taken from them.[a]' "

14 "Why are we sitting here?
Gather together!
Let us flee to the fortified cities
and perish there!
For the LORD our God has doomed
us to perish
and given us poisoned water to
drink,
because we have sinned against
him.
15 We hoped for peace
but no good has come,
for a time of healing
but there was only terror.
16 The snorting of the enemy's horses
is heard from Dan;
at the neighing of their stallions
the whole land trembles.
They have come to devour
the land and everything in it,
the city and all who live there."

17 "See, I will send venomous snakes
among you,
vipers that cannot be charmed,
and they will bite you,"
declares the LORD.

18 O my Comforter[b] in sorrow,
my heart is faint within me.
19 Listen to the cry of my people
from a land far away:
"Is the LORD not in Zion?
Is her King no longer there?"
"Why have they provoked me to
anger with their images,
with their worthless foreign idols?"

20 "The harvest is past,
the summer has ended,
and we are not saved."

21 Since my people are crushed, I am
crushed;
I mourn, and horror grips me.
22 Is there no balm in Gilead?
Is there no physician there?
Why then is there no healing
for the wound of my people?

[a]13 The meaning of the Hebrew for this sentence is uncertain. [b]18 The meaning of the Hebrew for this word is uncertain.

SHARPEN THE FOCUS

Judah believed nothing could happen to her because of her "religion." Whenever an opposing army threatened, the people in Jerusalem repeated these words like a mantra: "We have the temple of the LORD" (Jeremiah 7:4). But her religion was wrong—her trust misplaced.

Since the nation went through the spiritual motions each day, people and priests alike thought they had a license to oppress the poor, worship gods of gold and silver, ignore God's Word, cheat others, lie, and commit any kind of sexual sin (Jeremiah 7:5–9).

They knew the right doctrinal answers, memorized the liturgy, and brought their weekly offerings. In return, they only asked that the Lord keep His nose out of the rest of their lives. They gave God everything He wanted—except their hearts.

That's the reason Jeremiah and all of the Lord's other faithful prophets continually delivered this message: Repent! (Jeremiah 7:13, 25).

We too can easily slip away from our commitment to Christ and substitute ritual for reality. The shift can be very subtle, but it's absolutely deadly. Use the power of your Savior's cross to move away from that today. You might pray Psalm 130 as you do.

WEEK 58 • THURSDAY

Jeremiah 9:1—10:25

GET THE BIG PICTURE

Chapter 9 continues the lament Jeremiah began in Jeremiah 8:18. The prophet weeps for the hurt of his people even as he denounces their sin. Chapter 10, then, ridicules Judah's idols. Such "gods" are a burden, not a blessing. As you read, ask yourself, "Which false gods am I carrying?" If time is short, focus on Jeremiah 10:1–16.

9 1 Oh, that my head were a
spring of water
and my eyes a fountain of tears!
I would weep day and night
for the slain of my people.
2 Oh, that I had in the desert
a lodging place for travelers,
so that I might leave my people
and go away from them;
for they are all adulterers,
a crowd of unfaithful people.

3 "They make ready their tongue
like a bow, to shoot lies;
it is not by truth
that they triumph[a] in the land.
They go from one sin to another;
they do not acknowledge me,"
declares the LORD.
4 "Beware of your friends;
do not trust your brothers.
For every brother is a deceiver,[b]
and every friend a slanderer.
5 Friend deceives friend,
and no one speaks the truth.
They have taught their tongues to
lie;
they weary themselves with
sinning.
6 You[c] live in the midst of deception;
in their deceit they refuse to
acknowledge me,"
declares the LORD.

7 Therefore this is what the LORD Almighty says:

"See, I will refine and test them,
for what else can I do
because of the sin of my people?
8 Their tongue is a deadly arrow;
it speaks with deceit.
With his mouth each speaks
cordially to his neighbor,
but in his heart he sets a trap for
him.
9 Should I not punish them for this?"
declares the LORD.
"Should I not avenge myself
on such a nation as this?"

10 I will weep and wail for the
mountains
and take up a lament concerning
the desert pastures.
They are desolate and untraveled,
and the lowing of cattle is not
heard.
The birds of the air have fled
and the animals are gone.

11 "I will make Jerusalem a heap of
ruins,
a haunt of jackals;
and I will lay waste the towns of
Judah
so no one can live there."

12 What man is wise enough to understand this? Who has been instructed by the LORD and can explain it? Why has the land been ruined and laid waste like a desert that no one can cross?

13 The LORD said, "It is because they

[a]3 Or *lies; / they are not valiant for truth* [b]4 Or *a deceiving Jacob* [c]6 That is, Jeremiah (the Hebrew is singular)

have forsaken my law, which I set before
them; they have not obeyed me or followed my law. 14Instead, they have followed the stubbornness of their hearts;
they have followed the Baals, as their fathers taught them." 15Therefore, this is
what the LORD Almighty, the God of
Israel, says: "See, I will make this people eat bitter food and drink poisoned
water. 16I will scatter them among nations that neither they nor their fathers
have known, and I will pursue them
with the sword until I have destroyed
them."

17This is what the LORD Almighty says:

"Consider now! Call for the wailing
women to come;
send for the most skillful of them.
18 Let them come quickly
and wail over us
till our eyes overflow with tears
and water streams from our
eyelids.
19 The sound of wailing is heard from
Zion:
'How ruined we are!
How great is our shame!
We must leave our land
because our houses are in ruins.' "

20 Now, O women, hear the word of
the LORD;
open your ears to the words of his
mouth.
Teach your daughters how to wail;
teach one another a lament.
21 Death has climbed in through our
windows
and has entered our fortresses;
it has cut off the children from the
streets
and the young men from the
public squares.

22Say, "This is what the LORD declares:

" 'The dead bodies of men will lie
like refuse on the open field,
like cut grain behind the reaper,
with no one to gather them.' "

23This is what the LORD says:

"Let not the wise man boast of his
wisdom
or the strong man boast of his
strength
or the rich man boast of his
riches,
24 but let him who boasts boast about
this:
that he understands and knows
me,
that I am the LORD, who exercises
kindness,
justice and righteousness on
earth,
for in these I delight,"
declares the LORD.

25"The days are coming," declares the
LORD, "when I will punish all who are
circumcised only in the flesh— 26Egypt,
Judah, Edom, Ammon, Moab and all
who live in the desert in distant places.[a]
For all these nations are really uncir-
cumcised, and even the whole house of
Israel is uncircumcised in heart."

God and Idols

10 Hear what the LORD says to
you, O house of Israel. 2This
is what the LORD says:

"Do not learn the ways of the
nations
or be terrified by signs in the sky,
though the nations are terrified by
them.
3 For the customs of the peoples are
worthless;
they cut a tree out of the forest,
and a craftsman shapes it with his
chisel.
4 They adorn it with silver and gold;
they fasten it with hammer and
nails
so it will not totter.
5 Like a scarecrow in a melon patch,
their idols cannot speak;
they must be carried
because they cannot walk.
Do not fear them;
they can do no harm
nor can they do any good."

[a]26 Or *desert and who clip the hair by their foreheads*

6 No one is like you, O LORD;
you are great,
and your name is mighty in power.
7 Who should not revere you,
O King of the nations?
This is your due.
Among all the wise men of the nations
and in all their kingdoms,
there is no one like you.
8 They are all senseless and foolish;
they are taught by worthless wooden idols.
9 Hammered silver is brought from Tarshish
and gold from Uphaz.
What the craftsman and goldsmith have made
is then dressed in blue and purple—
all made by skilled workers.
10 But the LORD is the true God;
he is the living God, the eternal King.
When he is angry, the earth trembles;
the nations cannot endure his wrath.

11 "Tell them this: 'These gods, who did
not make the heavens and the earth,
will perish from the earth and from under the heavens.' "[a]

12 But God made the earth by his power;
he founded the world by his wisdom
and stretched out the heavens by his understanding.
13 When he thunders, the waters in the heavens roar;
he makes clouds rise from the ends of the earth.
He sends lightning with the rain
and brings out the wind from his storehouses.

14 Everyone is senseless and without knowledge;
every goldsmith is shamed by his idols.
His images are a fraud;
they have no breath in them.
15 They are worthless, the objects of mockery;
when their judgment comes, they will perish.
16 He who is the Portion of Jacob is not like these,
for he is the Maker of all things,
including Israel, the tribe of his inheritance—
the LORD Almighty is his name.

Coming Destruction

17 Gather up your belongings to leave the land,
you who live under siege.
18 For this is what the LORD says:
"At this time I will hurl out
those who live in this land;
I will bring distress on them
so that they may be captured."

19 Woe to me because of my injury!
My wound is incurable!
Yet I said to myself,
"This is my sickness, and I must endure it."
20 My tent is destroyed;
all its ropes are snapped.
My sons are gone from me and are no more;
no one is left now to pitch my tent
or to set up my shelter.
21 The shepherds are senseless
and do not inquire of the LORD;
so they do not prosper
and all their flock is scattered.
22 Listen! The report is coming—
a great commotion from the land of the north!
It will make the towns of Judah desolate,
a haunt of jackals.

Jeremiah's Prayer

23 I know, O LORD, that a man's life is not his own;
it is not for man to direct his steps.
24 Correct me, LORD, but only with justice—
not in your anger,
lest you reduce me to nothing.

[a] *11* The text of this verse is in Aramaic.

25 Pour out your wrath on the nations
that do not acknowledge you,
on the peoples who do not call on
your name.
For they have devoured Jacob;
they have devoured him
completely
and destroyed his homeland.

SHARPEN THE FOCUS

Few situations in life have either/or solutions. Usually we can find a way to forge option C apart from options A and B.

Jeremiah sets out a clear either/or situation in today's reading (Jeremiah 10:1–7). Either the Lord, the living God is carrying us, or we're carrying our idols. There is no option C. Does God carry you?

- Do you let Him bear the weight of your financial needs? Or do you carry around the worry of how to provide for yourself?
- Do you place your concerns about your loved ones on Him? Or do you wear yourself out wondering about their spiritual condition, life choices, or their physical or mental health?
- Have you given your worries about your congregation to Him? Or do you plan ways to pull strings and to manipulate people in an effort to help God?

The question is not, "What do you care about?" The question is "Who's carrying those cares?" Remember our Lord's words:

> *I am the LORD, who exercises kindness,*
> *justice and righteousness on earth,*
> *for in these I delight.* (Jeremiah 9:24)

God acts on our behalf. And God forgives, in Christ, even the lack of trust we so often show in Him.

WEEK 58 • FRIDAY

Jeremiah 11:1—12:17

GET THE BIG PICTURE

As Jeremiah goes about His prophetic work, the people of Anathoth—his hometown—conspire to kill him (Jeremiah 11:18–23). In distress, Jeremiah pours out his complaint to the Lord (Jeremiah 12:1–4). And the Lord responds (Jeremiah 12:5–17). As you read, note the complete consistency of God's message. If time is short, focus on Jeremiah 11:1–17.

The Covenant Is Broken

11 This is the word that came to Jeremiah from the LORD: 2"Listen
to the terms of this covenant and tell
them to the people of Judah and to
those who live in Jerusalem. 3Tell them
that this is what the LORD, the God of
Israel, says: 'Cursed is the man who
does not obey the terms of this covenant— 4the terms I commanded your
forefathers when I brought them out of
Egypt, out of the iron-smelting furnace.'
I said, 'Obey me and do everything I
command you, and you will be my
people, and I will be your God. 5Then I
will fulfill the oath I swore to your forefathers, to give them a land flowing with
milk and honey'—the land you possess
today."

I answered, "Amen, LORD."

6The LORD said to me, "Proclaim all
these words in the towns of Judah and
in the streets of Jerusalem: 'Listen to the
terms of this covenant and follow them.
7From the time I brought your forefathers up from Egypt until today, I
warned them again and again, saying,
"Obey me." 8But they did not listen or
pay attention; instead, they followed
the stubbornness of their evil hearts. So
I brought on them all the curses of the
covenant I had commanded them to follow but that they did not keep.' "

9Then the LORD said to me, "There is
a conspiracy among the people of Judah
and those who live in Jerusalem. 10They
have returned to the sins of their forefathers, who refused to listen to my
words. They have followed other gods
to serve them. Both the house of Israel
and the house of Judah have broken the
covenant I made with their forefathers.
11Therefore this is what the LORD says:
'I will bring on them a disaster they cannot escape. Although they cry out to me,
I will not listen to them. 12The towns of
Judah and the people of Jerusalem will
go and cry out to the gods to whom they
burn incense, but they will not help
them at all when disaster strikes. 13You
have as many gods as you have towns,
O Judah; and the altars you have set up
to burn incense to that shameful god
Baal are as many as the streets of Jerusalem.'

14"Do not pray for this people nor offer any plea or petition for them, because I will not listen when they call to
me in the time of their distress.

15"What is my beloved doing in my
temple
as she works out her evil schemes
with many?
Can consecrated meat avert ⌞your
punishment⌟?
When you engage in your
wickedness,
then you rejoice.[a]"

16The LORD called you a thriving olive
tree
with fruit beautiful in form.
But with the roar of a mighty
storm
he will set it on fire,
and its branches will be broken.

17The LORD Almighty, who planted you,
has decreed disaster for you, because
the house of Israel and the house of Judah have done evil and provoked me to
anger by burning incense to Baal.

Plot Against Jeremiah

18Because the LORD revealed their
plot to me, I knew it, for at that time he
showed me what they were doing. 19I
had been like a gentle lamb led to the
slaughter; I did not realize that they had
plotted against me, saying,

"Let us destroy the tree and its fruit;
let us cut him off from the land of
the living,
that his name be remembered no
more."

20But, O LORD Almighty, you who
judge righteously
and test the heart and mind,
let me see your vengeance upon
them,
for to you I have committed my
cause.

[a]15 Or *Could consecrated meat avert your punishment? / Then you would rejoice*

21"Therefore this is what the LORD says about the men of Anathoth who are seeking your life and saying, 'Do not prophesy in the name of the LORD or you will die by our hands'— 22therefore this is what the LORD Almighty says: 'I will punish them. Their young men will die by the sword, their sons and daughters by famine. 23Not even a remnant will be left to them, because I will bring disaster on the men of Anathoth in the year of their punishment.' "

Jeremiah's Complaint

12 You are always righteous, O LORD,
when I bring a case before you.
Yet I would speak with you about your justice:
Why does the way of the wicked prosper?
Why do all the faithless live at ease?
2 You have planted them, and they have taken root;
they grow and bear fruit.
You are always on their lips
but far from their hearts.
3 Yet you know me, O LORD;
you see me and test my thoughts about you.
Drag them off like sheep to be butchered!
Set them apart for the day of slaughter!
4 How long will the land lie parched[a]
and the grass in every field be withered?
Because those who live in it are wicked,
the animals and birds have perished.
Moreover, the people are saying,
"He will not see what happens to us."

God's Answer

5 "If you have raced with men on foot
and they have worn you out,
how can you compete with horses?
If you stumble in safe country,[b]
how will you manage in the thickets by[c] the Jordan?
6 Your brothers, your own family—
even they have betrayed you;
they have raised a loud cry against you.
Do not trust them,
though they speak well of you.

7 "I will forsake my house,
abandon my inheritance;
I will give the one I love
into the hands of her enemies.
8 My inheritance has become to me
like a lion in the forest.
She roars at me;
therefore I hate her.
9 Has not my inheritance become to me
like a speckled bird of prey
that other birds of prey surround and attack?
Go and gather all the wild beasts;
bring them to devour.
10 Many shepherds will ruin my vineyard
and trample down my field;
they will turn my pleasant field
into a desolate wasteland.
11 It will be made a wasteland,
parched and desolate before me;
the whole land will be laid waste
because there is no one who cares.
12 Over all the barren heights in the desert
destroyers will swarm,
for the sword of the LORD will devour
from one end of the land to the other;
no one will be safe.
13 They will sow wheat but reap thorns;
they will wear themselves out but gain nothing.
So bear the shame of your harvest
because of the LORD's fierce anger."

14This is what the LORD says: "As for all my wicked neighbors who seize the inheritance I gave my people Israel, I will uproot them from their lands and I will uproot the house of Judah from

[a]4 Or *land mourn* [b]5 Or *If you put your trust in a land of safety* [c]5 Or *the flooding of*

among them. [15]But after I uproot them, I will again have compassion and will bring each of them back to his own inheritance and his own country. [16]And if they learn well the ways of my people and swear by my name, saying, 'As surely as the LORD lives'—even as they once taught my people to swear by Baal—then they will be established among my people. [17]But if any nation does not listen, I will completely uproot and destroy it," declares the LORD.

SHARPEN THE FOCUS

God had nothing but the purest love for the disobedient people of Judah. He intended Jeremiah's sharp words to shock them into repentance. He has that attitude of love toward you and me too. Remember how He had rescued the children of Abraham, Isaac, and Jacob from slavery in Egypt (Jeremiah 11:4)? He did that so He could give them the land He had promised Abraham and so that He could keep His promise to send the world's Savior as a descendant of Abraham.

In love, the Lord saw His people as "thriving olive trees"—fruitful and lovely (Jeremiah 11:16). He sees you and me in that same way. His people brought Him grief again and again, but He would not abandon His plan, His plan to save us from our slavery to sin and death.

Now think about your own attitude toward those who don't know or believe the Good News. Are you indifferent or hostile toward them? Are you judgmental toward them? Or do you show them the same broken-hearted compassion Jesus shows them?

Ask Him for that kind of compassion if you need it. He will gladly supply it. And He will give you the strength you need to "run with the horses" (Jeremiah 12:5), expending every ounce of the energy He supplies to win souls for Christ.

WEEK 58 • SATURDAY

Jeremiah 13:1—14:22

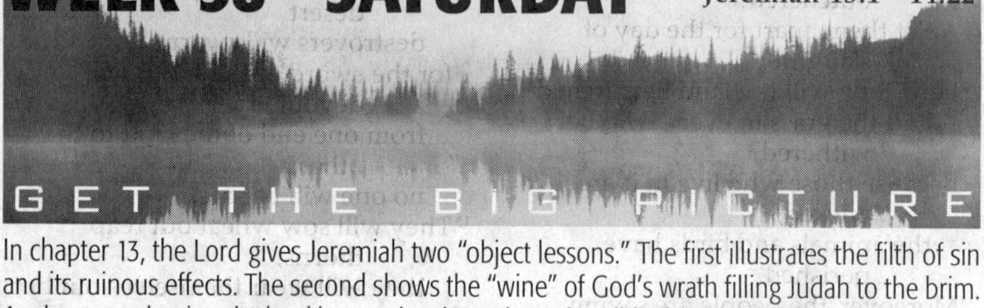

GET THE BIG PICTURE

In chapter 13, the Lord gives Jeremiah two "object lessons." The first illustrates the filth of sin and its ruinous effects. The second shows the "wine" of God's wrath filling Judah to the brim. As chapter 14 begins, the land is experiencing a time of terrible drought. Note Jeremiah's three prayers and the Lord's response to them. If time is short, focus on Jeremiah 13:1–11.

A Linen Belt

13 This is what the LORD said to me: "Go and buy a linen belt and put it around your waist, but do not let it touch water." [2]So I bought a belt, as the LORD directed, and put it around my waist.

[3]Then the word of the LORD came to me a second time: [4]"Take the belt you bought and are wearing around your waist, and go now to Perath[a] and hide it there in a crevice in the rocks." [5]So I

[a]4 Or possibly *the Euphrates;* also in verses 5-7

went and hid it at Perath, as the LORD told me.

[6]Many days later the LORD said to me, "Go now to Perath and get the belt I told you to hide there." [7]So I went to Perath and dug up the belt and took it from the place where I had hidden it, but now it was ruined and completely useless.

[8]Then the word of the LORD came to me: [9]"This is what the LORD says: 'In the same way I will ruin the pride of Judah and the great pride of Jerusalem. [10]These wicked people, who refuse to listen to my words, who follow the stubbornness of their hearts and go after other gods to serve and worship them, will be like this belt—completely useless! [11]For as a belt is bound around a man's waist, so I bound the whole house of Israel and the whole house of Judah to me,' declares the LORD, 'to be my people for my renown and praise and honor. But they have not listened.'

Wineskins

[12]"Say to them: 'This is what the LORD, the God of Israel, says: Every wineskin should be filled with wine.' And if they say to you, 'Don't we know that every wineskin should be filled with wine?' [13]then tell them, 'This is what the LORD says: I am going to fill with drunkenness all who live in this land, including the kings who sit on David's throne, the priests, the prophets and all those living in Jerusalem. [14]I will smash them one against the other, fathers and sons alike, declares the LORD. I will allow no pity or mercy or compassion to keep me from destroying them.' "

Threat of Captivity

[15]Hear and pay attention,
do not be arrogant,
for the LORD has spoken.
[16]Give glory to the LORD your God
before he brings the darkness,
before your feet stumble
on the darkening hills.
You hope for light,
but he will turn it to thick
darkness
and change it to deep gloom.
[17]But if you do not listen,
I will weep in secret
because of your pride;
my eyes will weep bitterly,
overflowing with tears,
because the LORD's flock will be
taken captive.

[18]Say to the king and to the queen
mother,
"Come down from your thrones,
for your glorious crowns
will fall from your heads."
[19]The cities in the Negev will be shut
up,
and there will be no one to open
them.
All Judah will be carried into exile,
carried completely away.

[20]Lift up your eyes and see
those who are coming from the
north.
Where is the flock that was
entrusted to you,
the sheep of which you boasted?
[21]What will you say when ⌞the LORD⌟
sets over you
those you cultivated as your
special allies?
Will not pain grip you
like that of a woman in labor?
[22]And if you ask yourself,
"Why has this happened to
me?"—
it is because of your many sins
that your skirts have been torn off
and your body mistreated.
[23]Can the Ethiopian[a] change his skin
or the leopard its spots?
Neither can you do good
who are accustomed to doing evil.

[24]"I will scatter you like chaff
driven by the desert wind.
[25]This is your lot,
the portion I have decreed for
you,"
declares the LORD,
"because you have forgotten me

[a]23 Hebrew *Cushite* (probably a person from the upper Nile region)

and trusted in false gods.
[26]I will pull up your skirts over your face
that your shame may be seen—
[27]your adulteries and lustful neighings,
your shameless prostitution!
I have seen your detestable acts
on the hills and in the fields.
Woe to you, O Jerusalem!
How long will you be unclean?"

Drought, Famine, Sword

14 This is the word of the LORD to Jeremiah concerning the drought:

[2]"Judah mourns,
her cities languish;
they wail for the land,
and a cry goes up from Jerusalem.
[3]The nobles send their servants for water;
they go to the cisterns
but find no water.
They return with their jars unfilled;
dismayed and despairing,
they cover their heads.
[4]The ground is cracked
because there is no rain in the land;
the farmers are dismayed
and cover their heads.
[5]Even the doe in the field
deserts her newborn fawn
because there is no grass.
[6]Wild donkeys stand on the barren heights
and pant like jackals;
their eyesight fails
for lack of pasture."

[7]Although our sins testify against us,
O LORD, do something for the sake of your name.
For our backsliding is great;
we have sinned against you.
[8]O Hope of Israel,
its Savior in times of distress,
why are you like a stranger in the land,
like a traveler who stays only a night?
[9]Why are you like a man taken by surprise,
like a warrior powerless to save?
You are among us, O LORD,
and we bear your name;
do not forsake us!

[10]This is what the LORD says about
this people:
"They greatly love to wander;
they do not restrain their feet.
So the LORD does not accept them;
he will now remember their wickedness
and punish them for their sins."

[11]Then the LORD said to me, "Do not
pray for the well-being of this people.
[12]Although they fast, I will not listen to
their cry; though they offer burnt offerings and grain offerings, I will not accept them. Instead, I will destroy them
with the sword, famine and plague."
[13]But I said, "Ah, Sovereign LORD, the
prophets keep telling them, 'You will
not see the sword or suffer famine. Indeed, I will give you lasting peace in this
place.' "
[14]Then the LORD said to me, "The
prophets are prophesying lies in my
name. I have not sent them or appointed them or spoken to them. They are
prophesying to you false visions, divinations, idolatries[a] and the delusions of
their own minds. [15]Therefore, this is
what the LORD says about the prophets
who are prophesying in my name: I did
not send them, yet they are saying, 'No
sword or famine will touch this land.'
Those same prophets will perish by
sword and famine. [16]And the people
they are prophesying to will be thrown
out into the streets of Jerusalem because
of the famine and sword. There will be
no one to bury them or their wives, their
sons or their daughters. I will pour out
on them the calamity they deserve.

[17]"Speak this word to them:

" 'Let my eyes overflow with tears
night and day without ceasing;
for my virgin daughter—my people—

[a]14 Or *visions, worthless divinations*

has suffered a grievous wound,
a crushing blow.
18 If I go into the country,
I see those slain by the sword;
if I go into the city,
I see the ravages of famine.
Both prophet and priest
have gone to a land they know
not.' "

19 Have you rejected Judah
completely?
Do you despise Zion?
Why have you afflicted us
so that we cannot be healed?
We hoped for peace
but no good has come,
for a time of healing
but there is only terror.
20 O LORD, we acknowledge our
wickedness
and the guilt of our fathers;
we have indeed sinned against
you.
21 For the sake of your name do not
despise us;
do not dishonor your glorious
throne.
Remember your covenant with us
and do not break it.
22 Do any of the worthless idols of the
nations bring rain?
Do the skies themselves send
down showers?
No, it is you, O LORD our God.
Therefore our hope is in you,
for you are the one who does all
this.

SHARPEN THE FOCUS

The linen of Jeremiah's belt symbolized holiness, purity. The priests' robes were made of linen (Exodus 28:39). Imagine wearing such a belt as you hike 500 or so miles through the wilderness—much of it desert. (The Euphrates lay 500 miles from Jerusalem.) Now imagine burying the belt and walking home. A month or so later, imagine the Lord speaking to you again, this time asking you to go dig the belt up.

No doubt Jeremiah's object lesson caused quite a stir. As he held up the rotting, smelly belt, no one could have missed the prophet's point.

Jeremiah got the point, too. Perhaps his deeper understanding of the Lord's view of human sin led him to confess his own sins and those of his people as he spoke to God in three prayers (Jeremiah 14:7–9, 13, 19–22).

Do you see sin as something that stains, rots, and ruins you? As something that disqualifies you from entering God's presence? If so, you're right. But you're not at the story's end. Like the lost son, you have received a new robe—the robe of Christ's righteousness (Luke 15:22). Like the guests at the wedding supper of the Lamb, you have been given new clothes of fine linen, bright and clean (Revelation 19:8).

So often had Judah's people reneged on their promise to forsake their sinful lifestyle, the Lord grew tired of hearing their confession. Four fates would befall them—death, war, famine, and exile. Jeremiah's lifestyle was to reflect this coming reality (Jeremiah 16:1–13). Even so, a remnant would return to the Promised Land to provide a "cradle for Christ," the Messiah. If time is short, focus on Jeremiah 17:1–18.

15 Then the LORD said to me: "Even if Moses and Samuel
were to stand before me, my heart
would not go out to this people. Send
them away from my presence! Let them
go! 2And if they ask you, 'Where shall
we go?' tell them, 'This is what the LORD
says:

" 'Those destined for death, to death;
those for the sword, to the sword;
those for starvation, to starvation;
those for captivity, to captivity.'

3"I will send four kinds of destroyers
against them," declares the LORD, "the
sword to kill and the dogs to drag away
and the birds of the air and the beasts
of the earth to devour and destroy. 4I
will make them abhorrent to all the
kingdoms of the earth because of what
Manasseh son of Hezekiah king of Judah did in Jerusalem.

5"Who will have pity on you, O Jerusalem?
Who will mourn for you?
Who will stop to ask how you are?
6You have rejected me," declares the LORD.
"You keep on backsliding.
So I will lay hands on you and destroy you;
I can no longer show compassion.
7I will winnow them with a winnowing fork
at the city gates of the land.
I will bring bereavement and destruction on my people,
for they have not changed their ways.
8I will make their widows more numerous
than the sand of the sea.
At midday I will bring a destroyer
against the mothers of their young men;
suddenly I will bring down on them
anguish and terror.
9The mother of seven will grow faint
and breathe her last.
Her sun will set while it is still day;
she will be disgraced and humiliated.
I will put the survivors to the sword
before their enemies,"
declares the LORD.

10Alas, my mother, that you gave me birth,
a man with whom the whole land strives and contends!
I have neither lent nor borrowed,
yet everyone curses me.

11The LORD said,

"Surely I will deliver you for a good purpose;
surely I will make your enemies plead with you
in times of disaster and times of distress.

12"Can a man break iron—
iron from the north—or bronze?
13Your wealth and your treasures
I will give as plunder, without charge,
because of all your sins
throughout your country.
14I will enslave you to your enemies
in[a] a land you do not know,
for my anger will kindle a fire
that will burn against you."

15You understand, O LORD;
remember me and care for me.
Avenge me on my persecutors.
You are long-suffering—do not take me away;
think of how I suffer reproach for your sake.
16When your words came, I ate them;
they were my joy and my heart's delight,

[a]14 Some Hebrew manuscripts, Septuagint and Syriac (see also Jer. 17:4); most Hebrew manuscripts *I will cause your enemies to bring you / into*

for I bear your name,
O LORD God Almighty.
17 I never sat in the company of
revelers,
never made merry with them;
I sat alone because your hand was
on me
and you had filled me with
indignation.
18 Why is my pain unending
and my wound grievous and
incurable?
Will you be to me like a deceptive
brook,
like a spring that fails?

19 Therefore this is what the LORD
says:

"If you repent, I will restore you
that you may serve me;
if you utter worthy, not worthless,
words,
you will be my spokesman.
Let this people turn to you,
but you must not turn to them.
20 I will make you a wall to this people,
a fortified wall of bronze;
they will fight against you
but will not overcome you,
for I am with you
to rescue and save you,"
declares the LORD.
21 "I will save you from the hands of
the wicked
and redeem you from the grasp of
the cruel."

Day of Disaster

16 Then the word of the LORD
came to me: 2 "You must not
marry and have sons or daughters in
this place." 3 For this is what the LORD
says about the sons and daughters born
in this land and about the women who
are their mothers and the men who are
their fathers: 4 "They will die of deadly
diseases. They will not be mourned or
buried but will be like refuse lying on
the ground. They will perish by sword
and famine, and their dead bodies will
become food for the birds of the air and
the beasts of the earth."
5 For this is what the LORD says: "Do
not enter a house where there is a funeral meal; do not go to mourn or show
sympathy, because I have withdrawn
my blessing, my love and my pity from
this people," declares the LORD. 6 "Both
high and low will die in this land. They
will not be buried or mourned, and no
one will cut himself or shave his head
for them. 7 No one will offer food to comfort those who mourn for the dead—not
even for a father or a mother—nor will
anyone give them a drink to console
them.
8 "And do not enter a house where
there is feasting and sit down to eat and
drink. 9 For this is what the LORD Almighty, the God of Israel, says: Before
your eyes and in your days I will bring
an end to the sounds of joy and gladness and to the voices of bride and
bridegroom in this place.
10 "When you tell these people all this
and they ask you, 'Why has the LORD
decreed such a great disaster against us?
What wrong have we done? What sin
have we committed against the LORD
our God?' 11 then say to them, 'It is because your fathers forsook me,' declares
the LORD, 'and followed other gods and
served and worshiped them. They forsook me and did not keep my law. 12 But
you have behaved more wickedly than
your fathers. See how each of you is following the stubbornness of his evil
heart instead of obeying me. 13 So I will
throw you out of this land into a land
neither you nor your fathers have
known, and there you will serve other
gods day and night, for I will show you
no favor.'
14 "However, the days are coming," declares the LORD, "when men will no
longer say, 'As surely as the LORD lives,
who brought the Israelites up out of
Egypt,' 15 but they will say, 'As surely as
the LORD lives, who brought the Israelites up out of the land of the north and
out of all the countries where he had
banished them.' For I will restore them
to the land I gave their forefathers.
16 "But now I will send for many fishermen," declares the LORD, "and they
will catch them. After that I will send for

many hunters, and they will hunt them
down on every mountain and hill and
from the crevices of the rocks. 17My eyes
are on all their ways; they are not hidden from me, nor is their sin concealed
from my eyes. 18I will repay them double
for their wickedness and their sin, because they have defiled my land with
the lifeless forms of their vile images
and have filled my inheritance with
their detestable idols."

19 O LORD, my strength and my
fortress,
my refuge in time of distress,
to you the nations will come
from the ends of the earth and
say,
"Our fathers possessed nothing but
false gods,
worthless idols that did them no
good.
20 Do men make their own gods?
Yes, but they are not gods!"

21 "Therefore I will teach them—
this time I will teach them
my power and might.
Then they will know
that my name is the LORD.

17 "Judah's sin is engraved
with an iron tool,
inscribed with a flint point,
on the tablets of their hearts
and on the horns of their altars.
2 Even their children remember
their altars and Asherah poles[a]
beside the spreading trees
and on the high hills.
3 My mountain in the land
and your[b] wealth and all your
treasures
I will give away as plunder,
together with your high places,
because of sin throughout your
country.
4 Through your own fault you will
lose
the inheritance I gave you.
I will enslave you to your enemies
in a land you do not know,
for you have kindled my anger,
and it will burn forever."

5 This is what the LORD says:

"Cursed is the one who trusts in
man,
who depends on flesh for his
strength
and whose heart turns away from
the LORD.
6 He will be like a bush in the
wastelands;
he will not see prosperity when it
comes.
He will dwell in the parched places
of the desert,
in a salt land where no one lives.

7 "But blessed is the man who trusts
in the LORD,
whose confidence is in him.
8 He will be like a tree planted by the
water
that sends out its roots by the
stream.
It does not fear when heat comes;
its leaves are always green.
It has no worries in a year of
drought
and never fails to bear fruit."

9 The heart is deceitful above all
things
and beyond cure.
Who can understand it?

10 "I the LORD search the heart
and examine the mind,
to reward a man according to his
conduct,
according to what his deeds
deserve."

11 Like a partridge that hatches eggs it
did not lay
is the man who gains riches by
unjust means.
When his life is half gone, they will
desert him,
and in the end he will prove to be
a fool.

12 A glorious throne, exalted from the
beginning,
is the place of our sanctuary.

[a]2 That is, symbols of the goddess Asherah
[b]2,3 Or *hills* / [3]*and the mountains of the land.* / *Your*

13 O LORD, the hope of Israel,
all who forsake you will be put to shame.
Those who turn away from you will be written in the dust
because they have forsaken the LORD,
the spring of living water.

14 Heal me, O LORD, and I will be healed;
save me and I will be saved,
for you are the one I praise.
15 They keep saying to me,
"Where is the word of the LORD?
Let it now be fulfilled!"
16 I have not run away from being your shepherd;
you know I have not desired the day of despair.
What passes my lips is open before you.
17 Do not be a terror to me;
you are my refuge in the day of disaster.
18 Let my persecutors be put to shame,
but keep me from shame;
let them be terrified,
but keep me from terror.
Bring on them the day of disaster;
destroy them with double destruction.

Keeping the Sabbath Holy

19 This is what the LORD said to me:
"Go and stand at the gate of the people,
through which the kings of Judah go in
and out; stand also at all the other gates
of Jerusalem. 20 Say to them, 'Hear the
word of the LORD, O kings of Judah and
all people of Judah and everyone living
in Jerusalem who come through these
gates. 21 This is what the LORD says: Be
careful not to carry a load on the Sabbath day or bring it through the gates of
Jerusalem. 22 Do not bring a load out of
your houses or do any work on the Sabbath, but keep the Sabbath day holy, as
I commanded your forefathers. 23 Yet
they did not listen or pay attention; they
were stiff-necked and would not listen
or respond to discipline. 24 But if you are
careful to obey me, declares the LORD,
and bring no load through the gates of
this city on the Sabbath, but keep the
Sabbath day holy by not doing any
work on it, 25 then kings who sit on
David's throne will come through the
gates of this city with their officials.
They and their officials will come riding
in chariots and on horses, accompanied
by the men of Judah and those living in
Jerusalem, and this city will be inhabited forever. 26 People will come from the
towns of Judah and the villages around
Jerusalem, from the territory of Benjamin and the western foothills, from
the hill country and the Negev, bringing
burnt offerings and sacrifices, grain offerings, incense and thank offerings to
the house of the LORD. 27 But if you do
not obey me to keep the Sabbath day
holy by not carrying any load as you
come through the gates of Jerusalem
on the Sabbath day, then I will kindle
an unquenchable fire in the gates of
Jerusalem that will consume her fortresses.' "

SHARPEN THE FOCUS

For several years, a major clothing manufacturer has sold shirts, hats, and other casual apparel with the slogan, "No Fear." In response, some people have emblazoned, "Fear This" on their bumper stickers and sweatshirts.

Ancient Judah whistled "No Fear" as she walked in the darkness of her sin toward her destruction. The melody couldn't stop the judgment of the Lord who met her brazen impenitence with the might of a very real Babylonian army. "Fear this!" He thundered. And that day, Judah fell to her knees.

But Jeremiah and the faithful remnant, who clung to the Lord even in the dark, escaped by

His grace with their souls. They could whistle "No Fear" when trouble came, and when they did, their Savior backed their words with His power and love.

As you read Jeremiah 17:7–8, put your own name in these verses. By the covenant of grace your Savior-God sealed with you in your Baptism, the promise here belongs to you: You need not fear; you need not worry; and you need never fail to bear spiritual fruit. ☼

WEEK 59 • TUESDAY

Jeremiah 18:1—19:15

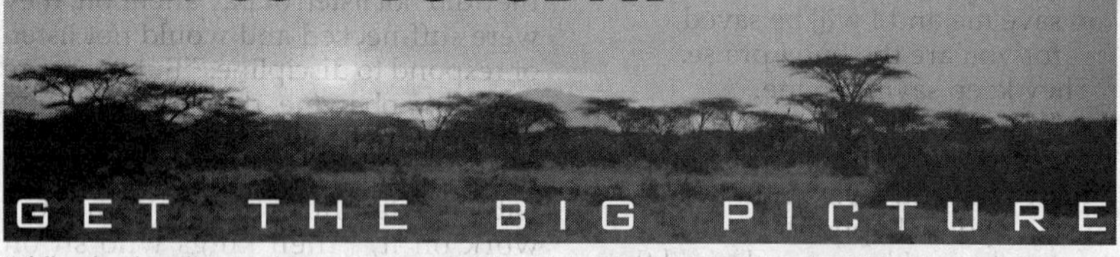

While clay is still wet, the potter can work with it, shaping and forming it into a useful vessel. But once it hardens, imperfections can't be changed. Useless pottery can only be shattered and discarded. Keep these facts in mind as you read the two parables Jeremiah includes in today's reading. If time is short, focus on Jeremiah 18:1–17.

At the Potter's House

18 This is the word that came to
Jeremiah from the LORD:
2"Go down to the potter's house, and
there I will give you my message." 3So I
went down to the potter's house, and I
saw him working at the wheel. 4But the
pot he was shaping from the clay was
marred in his hands; so the potter
formed it into another pot, shaping it as
seemed best to him.

5Then the word of the LORD came to
me: 6"O house of Israel, can I not do with
you as this potter does?" declares the
LORD. "Like clay in the hand of the potter, so are you in my hand, O house of
Israel. 7If at any time I announce that a
nation or kingdom is to be uprooted,
torn down and destroyed, 8and if that
nation I warned repents of its evil, then
I will relent and not inflict on it the disaster I had planned. 9And if at another
time I announce that a nation or kingdom is to be built up and planted, 10and
if it does evil in my sight and does not
obey me, then I will reconsider the good
I had intended to do for it.

11"Now therefore say to the people of
Judah and those living in Jerusalem,
'This is what the LORD says: Look! I am
preparing a disaster for you and devis-
ing a plan against you. So turn from
your evil ways, each one of you, and reform your ways and your actions.' 12But
they will reply, 'It's no use. We will continue with our own plans; each of us
will follow the stubbornness of his evil
heart.' "

13Therefore this is what the LORD
says:

"Inquire among the nations:
Who has ever heard anything like this?
A most horrible thing has been done
by Virgin Israel.
14Does the snow of Lebanon
ever vanish from its rocky slopes?
Do its cool waters from distant sources
ever cease to flow?[a]
15Yet my people have forgotten me;
they burn incense to worthless idols,
which made them stumble in their ways

[a]14 The meaning of the Hebrew for this sentence is uncertain.

and in the ancient paths.
They made them walk in bypaths
and on roads not built up.
16 Their land will be laid waste,
an object of lasting scorn;
all who pass by will be appalled
and will shake their heads.
17 Like a wind from the east,
I will scatter them before their
enemies;
I will show them my back and not
my face
in the day of their disaster."

18 They said, "Come, let's make plans against Jeremiah; for the teaching of the law by the priest will not be lost, nor will counsel from the wise, nor the word from the prophets. So come, let's attack him with our tongues and pay no attention to anything he says."

19 Listen to me, O LORD;
hear what my accusers are saying!
20 Should good be repaid with evil?
Yet they have dug a pit for me.
Remember that I stood before you
and spoke in their behalf
to turn your wrath away from
them.
21 So give their children over to
famine;
hand them over to the power of
the sword.
Let their wives be made childless
and widows;
let their men be put to death,
their young men slain by the
sword in battle.
22 Let a cry be heard from their houses
when you suddenly bring
invaders against them,
for they have dug a pit to capture
me
and have hidden snares for my
feet.
23 But you know, O LORD,
all their plots to kill me.
Do not forgive their crimes
or blot out their sins from your
sight.
Let them be overthrown before you;
deal with them in the time of your
anger.

19 This is what the LORD says:
"Go and buy a clay jar from a
potter. Take along some of the elders of
the people and of the priests
2 and go out
to the Valley of Ben Hinnom, near the
entrance of the Potsherd Gate. There
proclaim the words I tell you,
3 and say,
'Hear the word of the LORD, O kings of
Judah and people of Jerusalem. This is
what the LORD Almighty, the God of Israel, says: Listen! I am going to bring a
disaster on this place that will make the
ears of everyone who hears of it tingle.
4 For they have forsaken me and made
this a place of foreign gods; they have
burned sacrifices in it to gods that neither they nor their fathers nor the kings
of Judah ever knew, and they have filled
this place with the blood of the innocent.
5 They have built the high places of
Baal to burn their sons in the fire as offerings to Baal—something I did not
command or mention, nor did it enter
my mind.
6 So beware, the days are coming, declares the LORD, when people
will no longer call this place Topheth or
the Valley of Ben Hinnom, but the Valley of Slaughter.
7 "'In this place I will ruin[a] the plans
of Judah and Jerusalem. I will make
them fall by the sword before their enemies, at the hands of those who seek
their lives, and I will give their carcasses
as food to the birds of the air and the
beasts of the earth.
8 I will devastate this
city and make it an object of scorn; all
who pass by will be appalled and will
scoff because of all its wounds.
9 I will
make them eat the flesh of their sons
and daughters, and they will eat one
another's flesh during the stress of the
siege imposed on them by the enemies
who seek their lives.'
10 "Then break the jar while those who
go with you are watching,
11 and say to
them, 'This is what the LORD Almighty
says: I will smash this nation and this
city just as this potter's jar is smashed
and cannot be repaired. They will bury
the dead in Topheth until there is no

[a]7 The Hebrew for *ruin* sounds like the Hebrew for *jar* (see verses 1 and 10).

more room. [12]This is what I will do to this
place and to those who live here, declares the LORD. I will make this city like
Topheth. [13]The houses in Jerusalem and
those of the kings of Judah will be defiled
like this place, Topheth—all the houses
where they burned incense on the roofs
to all the starry hosts and poured out
drink offerings to other gods.' "
[14]Jeremiah then returned from Topheth, where the LORD had sent him to
prophesy, and stood in the court of the
LORD's temple and said to all the
people, [15]"This is what the LORD Almighty, the God of Israel, says: 'Listen!
I am going to bring on this city and the
villages around it every disaster I pronounced against them, because they
were stiff-necked and would not listen
to my words.' "

SHARPEN THE FOCUS

"It's no use. This is just how I am. I'll never change." Have you ever heard someone respond to God's Law in this way? Have you ever been tempted to respond this way yourself?

All of us feel discouraged at our failures to obey our Lord. But giving up the struggle will result in hardness of heart. It can drag us down the path to spiritual death. Ancient Judah found that out. How like our own discouragement Judah's discouragement sounds (Jeremiah 18:12). The people of Jeremiah's day used their helplessness as an excuse to wallow in more sin. We've seen the results.

But, praise God, there's an alternative! We can take our struggle to our Father. We can spread out the facts of our sin and our own powerlessness before Him. We can ask and–for the sake of Jesus–receive full forgiveness and access to all of our Savior's mighty power in our struggle with sin and Satan.

We are not victims of our own weakness and of Satan's schemes. We are the adopted sons and daughters of the King of the universe! We are co-heirs with Christ! In His cross, our battle with sin is not useless: it's already won.

How will you pick up the sword of His Word and fight the good fight today?

WEEK 59 • WEDNESDAY

Jer. 20:1—22:30

GET THE BIG PICTURE

Publicly humiliated by Pashhur (Jeremiah 20), Jeremiah was not silenced. This temple official couldn't intimidate God's spokesman. Nor could King Zedekiah (Jeremiah 21) or any of Judah's other rulers (Jeremiah 21). Nevertheless, their incredibly hard hearts discouraged him (Jeremiah 20:7–16). As you read, ask yourself what you do with your own disappointment. If time is short, focus on Jeremiah 20:7–18.

Jeremiah and Pashhur

20 When the priest Pashhur
son of Immer, the chief officer in the temple of the LORD, heard
Jeremiah prophesying these things, [2]he
had Jeremiah the prophet beaten and
put in the stocks at the Upper Gate of
Benjamin at the LORD's temple. [3]The

next day, when Pashhur released him
from the stocks, Jeremiah said to him,
"The LORD's name for you is not Pashhur, but Magor-Missabib.[a] 4For this is
what the LORD says: 'I will make you a
terror to yourself and to all your friends;
with your own eyes you will see them
fall by the sword of their enemies. I will
hand all Judah over to the king of Babylon, who will carry them away to Babylon or put them to the sword. 5I will
hand over to their enemies all the
wealth of this city—all its products, all
its valuables and all the treasures of the
kings of Judah. They will take it away as
plunder and carry it off to Babylon.
6And you, Pashhur, and all who live in
your house will go into exile to Babylon.
There you will die and be buried, you
and all your friends to whom you have
prophesied lies.' "

Jeremiah's Complaint

7O LORD, you deceived[b] me, and I
was deceived[b];
you overpowered me and
prevailed.
I am ridiculed all day long;
everyone mocks me.
8Whenever I speak, I cry out
proclaiming violence and
destruction.
So the word of the LORD has
brought me
insult and reproach all day long.
9But if I say, "I will not mention him
or speak any more in his name,"
his word is in my heart like a fire,
a fire shut up in my bones.
I am weary of holding it in;
indeed, I cannot.
10I hear many whispering,
"Terror on every side!
Report him! Let's report him!"
All my friends
are waiting for me to slip,
saying,
"Perhaps he will be deceived;
then we will prevail over him
and take our revenge on him."

11But the LORD is with me like a
mighty warrior;
so my persecutors will stumble
and not prevail.
They will fail and be thoroughly
disgraced;
their dishonor will never be
forgotten.
12O LORD Almighty, you who examine
the righteous
and probe the heart and mind,
let me see your vengeance upon
them,
for to you I have committed my
cause.

13Sing to the LORD!
Give praise to the LORD!
He rescues the life of the needy
from the hands of the wicked.

14Cursed be the day I was born!
May the day my mother bore me
not be blessed!
15Cursed be the man who brought my
father the news,
who made him very glad, saying,
"A child is born to you—a son!"
16May that man be like the towns
the LORD overthrew without pity.
May he hear wailing in the morning,
a battle cry at noon.
17For he did not kill me in the womb,
with my mother as my grave,
her womb enlarged forever.
18Why did I ever come out of the
womb
to see trouble and sorrow
and to end my days in shame?

God Rejects Zedekiah's Request

21 The word came to Jeremiah
from the LORD when King
Zedekiah sent to him Pashhur son of
Malkijah and the priest Zephaniah son
of Maaseiah. They said: 2"Inquire now
of the LORD for us because Nebuchadnezzar[c] king of Babylon is attacking us.
Perhaps the LORD will perform wonders
for us as in times past so that he will
withdraw from us."
3But Jeremiah answered them, "Tell

[a]3 *Magor-Missabib* means *terror on every side.*
[b]7 Or *persuaded* [c]2 Hebrew *Nebuchadrezzar,* of which *Nebuchadnezzar* is a variant; here and often in Jeremiah and Ezekiel

Zedekiah, 4 "This is what the LORD, the
God of Israel, says: I am about to turn
against you the weapons of war that are
in your hands, which you are using to
fight the king of Babylon and the Babylonians[a] who are outside the wall besieging you. And I will gather them
inside this city. 5 I myself will fight
against you with an outstretched hand
and a mighty arm in anger and fury and
great wrath. 6 I will strike down those
who live in this city—both men and animals—and they will die of a terrible
plague. 7 After that, declares the LORD, I
will hand over Zedekiah king of Judah,
his officials and the people in this city
who survive the plague, sword and
famine, to Nebuchadnezzar king of
Babylon and to their enemies who seek
their lives. He will put them to the
sword; he will show them no mercy or
pity or compassion.'
8 "Furthermore, tell the people, 'This is
what the LORD says: See, I am setting
before you the way of life and the way
of death. 9 Whoever stays in this city will
die by the sword, famine or plague. But
whoever goes out and surrenders to the
Babylonians who are besieging you will
live; he will escape with his life. 10 I have
determined to do this city harm and not
good, declares the LORD. It will be given
into the hands of the king of Babylon,
and he will destroy it with fire.'
11 "Moreover, say to the royal house of
Judah, 'Hear the word of the LORD;
12 O house of David, this is what the
LORD says:

" 'Administer justice every
morning;
rescue from the hand of his
oppressor
the one who has been robbed,
or my wrath will break out and burn
like fire
because of the evil you have
done—
burn with no one to quench it.
13 I am against you, ⌞Jerusalem,⌟
you who live above this valley
on the rocky plateau,
declares the LORD—
you who say, "Who can come
against us?
Who can enter our refuge?"
14 I will punish you as your deeds
deserve,
declares the LORD.
I will kindle a fire in your forests
that will consume everything
around you.' "

Judgment Against Evil Kings

22 This is what the LORD
says: "Go down to the pal-
ace of the king of Judah and proclaim
this message there: 2 'Hear the word of
the LORD, O king of Judah, you who sit
on David's throne—you, your officials
and your people who come through
these gates. 3 This is what the LORD says:
Do what is just and right. Rescue from
the hand of his oppressor the one who
has been robbed. Do no wrong or violence to the alien, the fatherless or the
widow, and do not shed innocent blood
in this place. 4 For if you are careful to
carry out these commands, then kings
who sit on David's throne will come
through the gates of this palace, riding
in chariots and on horses, accompanied
by their officials and their people. 5 But
if you do not obey these commands,
declares the LORD, I swear by myself
that this palace will become a ruin.' "
6 For this is what the LORD says about
the palace of the king of Judah:

"Though you are like Gilead to me,
like the summit of Lebanon,
I will surely make you like a desert,
like towns not inhabited.
7 I will send destroyers against you,
each man with his weapons,
and they will cut up your fine cedar
beams
and throw them into the fire.

8 "People from many nations will pass
by this city and will ask one another,
'Why has the LORD done such a thing
to this great city?' 9 And the answer will
be: 'Because they have forsaken the cov-

[a]4 Or *Chaldeans*; also in verse 9

enant of the LORD their God and have
worshiped and served other gods.' "

10 Do not weep for the dead ⌞king⌟ or
mourn his loss;
rather, weep bitterly for him who
is exiled,
because he will never return
nor see his native land again.

11 For this is what the LORD says about
Shallum[a] son of Josiah, who succeeded
his father as king of Judah but has gone
from this place: "He will never return.
12 He will die in the place where they
have led him captive; he will not see this
land again."

13 "Woe to him who builds his palace
by unrighteousness,
his upper rooms by injustice,
making his countrymen work for
nothing,
not paying them for their labor.
14 He says, 'I will build myself a great
palace
with spacious upper rooms.'
So he makes large windows in it,
panels it with cedar
and decorates it in red.

15 "Does it make you a king
to have more and more cedar?
Did not your father have food and
drink?
He did what was right and just,
so all went well with him.
16 He defended the cause of the poor
and needy,
and so all went well.
Is that not what it means to know
me?"
declares the LORD.
17 "But your eyes and your heart
are set only on dishonest gain,
on shedding innocent blood
and on oppression and
extortion."

18 Therefore this is what the LORD says
about Jehoiakim son of Josiah king of
Judah:

"They will not mourn for him:
'Alas, my brother! Alas, my sister!'
They will not mourn for him:
'Alas, my master! Alas, his
splendor!'
19 He will have the burial of a
donkey—
dragged away and thrown
outside the gates of Jerusalem."

20 "Go up to Lebanon and cry out,
let your voice be heard in Bashan,
cry out from Abarim,
for all your allies are crushed.
21 I warned you when you felt secure,
but you said, 'I will not listen!'
This has been your way from your
youth;
you have not obeyed me.
22 The wind will drive all your
shepherds away,
and your allies will go into exile.
Then you will be ashamed and
disgraced
because of all your wickedness.
23 You who live in 'Lebanon,[b]'
who are nestled in cedar
buildings,
how you will groan when pangs
come upon you,
pain like that of a woman in labor!

24 "As surely as I live," declares the
LORD, "even if you, Jehoiachin[c] son of
Jehoiakim king of Judah, were a signet
ring on my right hand, I would still pull
you off. 25 I will hand you over to those
who seek your life, those you fear—to
Nebuchadnezzar king of Babylon and
to the Babylonians.[d] 26 I will hurl you and
the mother who gave you birth into another country, where neither of you was
born, and there you both will die. 27 You
will never come back to the land you
long to return to."

28 Is this man Jehoiachin a despised,
broken pot,
an object no one wants?
Why will he and his children be
hurled out,
cast into a land they do not know?
29 O land, land, land,

[a] *11* Also called *Jehoahaz* [b] *23* That is, the palace in Jerusalem (see 1 Kings 7:2) [c] *24* Hebrew *Coniah,* a variant of *Jehoiachin;* also in verse 28 [d] *25* Or *Chaldeans*

hear the word of the LORD!
30 This is what the LORD says:
"Record this man as if childless,
a man who will not prosper in his lifetime,
for none of his offspring will prosper,
none will sit on the throne of David
or rule anymore in Judah."

SHARPEN THE FOCUS

As we read Jeremiah's prayer in Jeremiah 20:7–18, we see in his grief the grief of our Lord. The message Jeremiah has delivered—the Word of God—has changed him. It has worked in him the love God has for sinners and the yearning of His heart that they come to Him in repentance. That transformation is not yet complete. We hear Jeremiah lash out at God in words very like those of Job. (Compare Jeremiah 20:14 with Job 3:3.)

You can tell a lot about a person if you know what stirs up anger and grief in that person's heart. You can tell even more by what a person does with anger and grief.

- Do the things that anger God anger you?
- Do the things that grieve God grieve you?
- Do you deny your anger or grief? Do you lash out in anger or grief? Or do you take your anger and grief to the Lord who will share it with you and comfort you in it?

Your Savior understands your hottest anger and deepest grief. He's experienced both. The cross assures us that we need not run from Him when our emotions surge. We can run to Him. His Word will help us ground our feelings in reality. His blood cancels any sins we commit in emotion's grasp. His power makes it possible for us to use our emotions for His glory.

WEEK 59 • THURSDAY

Jeremiah 23:1–40

GET THE BIG PICTURE

From the beginning of Jeremiah's book we have read about the Lord's displeasure with Judah's false prophets. The priests and prophets, who should have warned about sin's consequences, wallowed in sin even more deeply than the people did! As you read, see if you can find your pastor's "job description." If time is short, focus on Jeremiah 23:1–8.

The Righteous Branch

23 "Woe to the shepherds
who are destroying and
scattering the sheep of my pasture!"
declares the LORD. 2 Therefore this is
what the LORD, the God of Israel, says
to the shepherds who tend my people:
"Because you have scattered my flock
and driven them away and have not bestowed care on them, I will bestow punishment on you for the evil you have
done," declares the LORD. 3 "I myself will

gather the remnant of my flock out of all the countries where I have driven them and will bring them back to their pasture, where they will be fruitful and increase in number. 4I will place shepherds over them who will tend them, and they will no longer be afraid or terrified, nor will any be missing," declares the LORD.

5"The days are coming," declares the
LORD,
"when I will raise up to David[a] a
righteous Branch,
a King who will reign wisely
and do what is just and right in
the land.
6In his days Judah will be saved
and Israel will live in safety.
This is the name by which he will be
called:
The LORD Our Righteousness.

7"So then, the days are coming," declares the LORD, "when people will no
longer say, 'As surely as the LORD lives,
who brought the Israelites up out of
Egypt,' 8but they will say, 'As surely as
the LORD lives, who brought the descendants of Israel up out of the land of the north and out of all the countries where he had banished them.' Then they will live in their own land."

Lying Prophets

9Concerning the prophets:

My heart is broken within me;
all my bones tremble.
I am like a drunken man,
like a man overcome by wine,
because of the LORD
and his holy words.
10The land is full of adulterers;
because of the curse[b] the land lies
parched[c]
and the pastures in the desert are
withered.
The ⌞prophets⌟ follow an evil course
and use their power unjustly.

11"Both prophet and priest are
godless;
even in my temple I find their
wickedness,"
declares the LORD.

12"Therefore their path will become
slippery;
they will be banished to darkness
and there they will fall.
I will bring disaster on them
in the year they are punished,"
declares the LORD.

13"Among the prophets of Samaria
I saw this repulsive thing:
They prophesied by Baal
and led my people Israel astray.
14And among the prophets of
Jerusalem
I have seen something horrible:
They commit adultery and live a
lie.
They strengthen the hands of
evildoers,
so that no one turns from his
wickedness.
They are all like Sodom to me;
the people of Jerusalem are like
Gomorrah."

15Therefore, this is what the LORD Almighty says concerning the prophets:

"I will make them eat bitter food
and drink poisoned water,
because from the prophets of
Jerusalem
ungodliness has spread
throughout the land."

16This is what the LORD Almighty says:

"Do not listen to what the
prophets are prophesying to
you;
they fill you with false hopes.
They speak visions from their own
minds,
not from the mouth of the LORD.
17They keep saying to those who
despise me,
'The LORD says: You will have
peace.'
And to all who follow the
stubbornness of their hearts
they say, 'No harm will come to
you.'

[a]5 Or *up from David's line* [b]10 Or *because of these things* [c]10 Or *land mourns*

18 But which of them has stood in the
council of the LORD
to see or to hear his word?
Who has listened and heard his
word?
19 See, the storm of the LORD
will burst out in wrath,
a whirlwind swirling down
on the heads of the wicked.
20 The anger of the LORD will not turn
back
until he fully accomplishes
the purposes of his heart.
In days to come
you will understand it clearly.
21 I did not send these prophets,
yet they have run with their
message;
I did not speak to them,
yet they have prophesied.
22 But if they had stood in my council,
they would have proclaimed my
words to my people
and would have turned them from
their evil ways
and from their evil deeds.

23 "Am I only a God nearby,"
declares the LORD,
"and not a God far away?
24 Can anyone hide in secret places
so that I cannot see him?"
declares the LORD.
"Do not I fill heaven and earth?"
declares the LORD.

25 "I have heard what the prophets say
who prophesy lies in my name. They
say, 'I had a dream! I had a dream!'
26 How long will this continue in the
hearts of these lying prophets, who
prophesy the delusions of their own
minds? 27 They think the dreams they
tell one another will make my people
forget my name, just as their fathers forgot my name through Baal worship.
28 Let the prophet who has a dream tell
his dream, but let the one who has my
word speak it faithfully. For what has
straw to do with grain?" declares the
LORD. 29 "Is not my word like fire," declares the LORD, "and like a hammer
that breaks a rock in pieces?
30 "Therefore," declares the LORD, "I
am against the prophets who steal from
one another words supposedly from
me. 31 Yes," declares the LORD, "I am
against the prophets who wag their
own tongues and yet declare, 'The LORD
declares.' 32 Indeed, I am against those
who prophesy false dreams," declares
the LORD. "They tell them and lead my
people astray with their reckless lies, yet
I did not send or appoint them. They do
not benefit these people in the least,"
declares the LORD.

False Oracles and False Prophets

33 "When these people, or a prophet or
a priest, ask you, 'What is the oracle[a] of
the LORD?' say to them, 'What oracle?[b]
I will forsake you, declares the LORD.'
34 If a prophet or a priest or anyone else
claims, 'This is the oracle of the LORD,' I
will punish that man and his household.
35 This is what each of you keeps on saying to his friend or relative: 'What is the
LORD's answer?' or 'What has the LORD
spoken?' 36 But you must not mention
'the oracle of the LORD' again, because
every man's own word becomes his oracle and so you distort the words of the
living God, the LORD Almighty, our
God. 37 This is what you keep saying to
a prophet: 'What is the LORD's answer
to you?' or 'What has the LORD spoken?'
38 Although you claim, 'This is the oracle
of the LORD,' this is what the LORD says:
You used the words, 'This is the oracle
of the LORD,' even though I told you
that you must not claim, 'This is the
oracle of the LORD.' 39 Therefore, I will
surely forget you and cast you out of my
presence along with the city I gave to
you and your fathers. 40 I will bring upon
you everlasting disgrace—everlasting
shame that will not be forgotten."

[a]33 Or *burden* (see Septuagint and Vulgate)
[b]33 Hebrew; Septuagint and Vulgate *'You are the burden.* (The Hebrew for *oracle* and *burden* is the same.)

SHARPEN THE FOCUS

God's Word is like fire (Jeremiah 23:29). It refines us, melting away our impurities as we see our sins, confess them, and receive the Spirit's power to forsake them.

God's Word is like a hammer (Jeremiah 23:29). Those who harden their hearts to it will one day, the Day of Judgment, be broken by it.

God's Word is like wheat (Jeremiah 23:28). Nourished on the bread of life, our Lord Jesus (John 6:48–51), we grow strong and spiritually healthy.

What a shame, given the Word's power, that we do not always let it have its way with us. When the fire starts to burn, we often back away. When our Lord spreads a banquet before our eyes, we often find ourselves too busy with other things to sit down to feast.

Talk to your Lord about His Word and your response to it today. Remember that Jesus is your righteousness (Jeremiah 23:6). Your confession of sin will not bring God's hammer of wrath down on your head. Rather, you will receive His pardon and compassion.

Jeremiah has something important to say about hearts in chapter 24. The following chapter contains a sermon written during Jeremiah's twenty-third year in ministry. As you read, watch the Lord pour out His cup of wrath on impenitent sinners from one corner of the earth to the other. If time is short, focus on Jeremiah 25:15–29.

Two Baskets of Figs

24 After Jehoiachin[a] son of
Jehoiakim king of Judah
and the officials, the craftsmen and the
artisans of Judah were carried into exile from Jerusalem to Babylon by Nebuchadnezzar king of Babylon, the LORD
showed me two baskets of figs placed in
front of the temple of the LORD. [2]One
basket had very good figs, like those
that ripen early; the other basket had
very poor figs, so bad they could not be
eaten.

[3]Then the LORD asked me, "What do
you see, Jeremiah?"

"Figs," I answered. "The good ones
are very good, but the poor ones are so
bad they cannot be eaten."

[4]Then the word of the LORD came to
me: [5]"This is what the LORD, the God of
Israel, says: 'Like these good figs, I regard as good the exiles from Judah,
whom I sent away from this place to the
land of the Babylonians.[b] [6]My eyes will
watch over them for their good, and I
will bring them back to this land. I will
build them up and not tear them down;
I will plant them and not uproot them.
[7]I will give them a heart to know me,
that I am the LORD. They will be my
people, and I will be their God, for they
will return to me with all their heart.

[8]" 'But like the poor figs, which are so
bad they cannot be eaten,' says the
LORD, 'so will I deal with Zedekiah king
of Judah, his officials and the survivors

[a]1 Hebrew *Jeconiah,* a variant of *Jehoiachin*
[b]5 Or *Chaldeans*

from Jerusalem, whether they remain in this land or live in Egypt. [9]I will make them abhorrent and an offense to all the kingdoms of the earth, a reproach and a byword, an object of ridicule and cursing, wherever I banish them. [10]I will send the sword, famine and plague against them until they are destroyed from the land I gave to them and their fathers.' "

Seventy Years of Captivity

25 The word came to Jeremiah concerning all the people of Judah in the fourth year of Jehoiakim son of Josiah king of Judah, which was the first year of Nebuchadnezzar king of Babylon. [2]So Jeremiah the prophet said to all the people of Judah and to all those living in Jerusalem: [3]For twenty-three years—from the thirteenth year of Josiah son of Amon king of Judah until this very day—the word of the LORD has come to me and I have spoken to you again and again, but you have not listened.

[4]And though the LORD has sent all his servants the prophets to you again and again, you have not listened or paid any attention. [5]They said, "Turn now, each of you, from your evil ways and your evil practices, and you can stay in the land the LORD gave to you and your fathers for ever and ever. [6]Do not follow other gods to serve and worship them; do not provoke me to anger with what your hands have made. Then I will not harm you."

[7]"But you did not listen to me," declares the LORD, "and you have provoked me with what your hands have made, and you have brought harm to yourselves."

[8]Therefore the LORD Almighty says this: "Because you have not listened to my words, [9]I will summon all the peoples of the north and my servant Nebuchadnezzar king of Babylon," declares the LORD, "and I will bring them against this land and its inhabitants and against all the surrounding nations. I will completely destroy[a] them and make them an object of horror and scorn, and an everlasting ruin. [10]I will banish from them the sounds of joy and gladness, the voices of bride and bridegroom, the sound of millstones and the light of the lamp. [11]This whole country will become a desolate wasteland, and these nations will serve the king of Babylon seventy years.

[12]"But when the seventy years are fulfilled, I will punish the king of Babylon and his nation, the land of the Babylonians,[b] for their guilt," declares the LORD, "and will make it desolate forever. [13]I will bring upon that land all the things I have spoken against it, all that are written in this book and prophesied by Jeremiah against all the nations. [14]They themselves will be enslaved by many nations and great kings; I will repay them according to their deeds and the work of their hands."

The Cup of God's Wrath

[15]This is what the LORD, the God of Israel, said to me: "Take from my hand this cup filled with the wine of my wrath and make all the nations to whom I send you drink it. [16]When they drink it, they will stagger and go mad because of the sword I will send among them."

[17]So I took the cup from the LORD's hand and made all the nations to whom he sent me drink it: [18]Jerusalem and the towns of Judah, its kings and officials, to make them a ruin and an object of horror and scorn and cursing, as they are today; [19]Pharaoh king of Egypt, his attendants, his officials and all his people, [20]and all the foreign people there; all the kings of Uz; all the kings of the Philistines (those of Ashkelon, Gaza, Ekron, and the people left at Ashdod); [21]Edom, Moab and Ammon; [22]all the kings of Tyre and Sidon; the kings of the coastlands across the sea; [23]Dedan, Tema, Buz and all who are in distant places[c]; [24]all the kings of Arabia and all the kings of the foreign people who live in the

[a]9 The Hebrew term refers to the irrevocable giving over of things or persons to the LORD, often by totally destroying them. [b]12 Or *Chaldeans* [c]23 Or *who clip the hair by their foreheads*

desert; [25]all the kings of Zimri, Elam and
Media; [26]and all the kings of the north,
near and far, one after the other—all the
kingdoms on the face of the earth. And
after all of them, the king of Sheshach[a]
will drink it too.
[27]"Then tell them, 'This is what the
LORD Almighty, the God of Israel, says:
Drink, get drunk and vomit, and fall to
rise no more because of the sword I will
send among you.' [28]But if they refuse to
take the cup from your hand and drink,
tell them, 'This is what the LORD Almighty says: You must drink it! [29]See, I
am beginning to bring disaster on the
city that bears my Name, and will you
indeed go unpunished? You will not go
unpunished, for I am calling down a
sword upon all who live on the earth,
declares the LORD Almighty.'
[30]"Now prophesy all these words
against them and say to them:

" 'The LORD will roar from on high;
he will thunder from his holy dwelling
and roar mightily against his land.
He will shout like those who tread the grapes,
shout against all who live on the earth.
[31]The tumult will resound to the ends of the earth,
for the LORD will bring charges against the nations;
he will bring judgment on all mankind
and put the wicked to the sword,' "
declares the LORD.

[32]This is what the LORD Almighty
says:

"Look! Disaster is spreading
from nation to nation;
a mighty storm is rising
from the ends of the earth."

[33]At that time those slain by the LORD will be everywhere—from one end of the earth to the other. They will not be mourned or gathered up or buried, but will be like refuse lying on the ground.

[34]Weep and wail, you shepherds;
roll in the dust, you leaders of the flock.
For your time to be slaughtered has come;
you will fall and be shattered like fine pottery.
[35]The shepherds will have nowhere to flee,
the leaders of the flock no place to escape.
[36]Hear the cry of the shepherds,
the wailing of the leaders of the flock,
for the LORD is destroying their pasture.
[37]The peaceful meadows will be laid waste
because of the fierce anger of the LORD.
[38]Like a lion he will leave his lair,
and their land will become desolate
because of the sword[b] of the oppressor
and because of the LORD's fierce anger.

[a]26 *Sheshach* is a cryptogram for Babylon.
[b]38 Some Hebrew manuscripts and Septuagint (see also Jer. 46:16 and 50:16); most Hebrew manuscripts *anger*

SHARPEN THE FOCUS

The Scriptures often picture God's wrath as a cup of foaming, bitter wine. Impenitent sinners have no choice but to drink it. This wine causes, not warmth and relaxation, but the stupor of horror and the numbness of fear. The flip attitude of all the unrepentant will one day melt away. Those who mock God will stand face to face with Him, their Judge.

We shudder when we think of that cup. And we marvel as we remember that our Lord Jesus drained the cup of God's fury at human sin. He drank it to the bitter dregs—for you and for me. Remember what He prayed in the Garden of Gethsemane?

> *My Father, if it is not possible for this cup to be taken away unless I drink it, may Your will be done.* (Matthew 26:42)

Then He rose from prayer to be lifted up on the cross. Now, in place of the cup of the Lord's wrath, we drink the cup of the new covenant (1 Corinthians 11:25). In place of judgment, we receive pardon. In place of punishment, we receive freedom. In place of death, we receive new life, eternal life. In the Lord's Supper, our Savior lifts His cup of grace to our lips.

Thank Him for the Holy Supper and all it means for us as you worship Him now.

WEEK 59 • SATURDAY

Jeremiah 26:1—28:17

So often people put off dealing with problems until they become crises. The low tire becomes a flat. The overcharged credit cards lead to ruined credit and precipitate family crises. That's the way it was in Judah during Jeremiah's ministry. God, in mercy, delayed doom to give His people more time to repent. But doom delayed soon became "doom denied"—the people refused to believe judgment would ever come. If time is short, focus on Jeremiah 28:1–17.

Jeremiah Threatened With Death

26 Early in the reign of Jehoiakim son of Josiah king of
Judah, this word came from the LORD:
[2]"This is what the LORD says: Stand in
the courtyard of the LORD's house and
speak to all the people of the towns of
Judah who come to worship in the
house of the LORD. Tell them everything
I command you; do not omit a word.
[3]Perhaps they will listen and each will
turn from his evil way. Then I will relent
and not bring on them the disaster I was
planning because of the evil they have
done. [4]Say to them, 'This is what the
LORD says: If you do not listen to me
and follow my law, which I have set
before you, [5]and if you do not listen to
the words of my servants the prophets,
whom I have sent to you again and
again (though you have not listened),
[6]then I will make this house like Shiloh
and this city an object of cursing among
all the nations of the earth.' "
[7]The priests, the prophets and all the
people heard Jeremiah speak these
words in the house of the LORD. [8]But as
soon as Jeremiah finished telling all the
people everything the LORD had commanded him to say, the priests, the
prophets and all the people seized him
and said, "You must die! [9]Why do you
prophesy in the LORD's name that this
house will be like Shiloh and this city
will be desolate and deserted?" And all
the people crowded around Jeremiah in
the house of the LORD.
[10]When the officials of Judah heard
about these things, they went up from
the royal palace to the house of the
LORD and took their places at the entrance of the New Gate of the LORD's
house. [11]Then the priests and the prophets said to the officials and all the

people, "This man should be sentenced
to death because he has prophesied
against this city. You have heard it with
your own ears!"
12Then Jeremiah said to all the officials
and all the people: "The LORD sent me
to prophesy against this house and this
city all the things you have heard.
13Now reform your ways and your actions and obey the LORD your God.
Then the LORD will relent and not bring
the disaster he has pronounced against
you. 14As for me, I am in your hands; do
with me whatever you think is good
and right. 15Be assured, however, that if
you put me to death, you will bring the
guilt of innocent blood on yourselves
and on this city and on those who live
in it, for in truth the LORD has sent me
to you to speak all these words in your
hearing."
16Then the officials and all the people
said to the priests and the prophets,
"This man should not be sentenced to
death! He has spoken to us in the name
of the LORD our God."
17Some of the elders of the land
stepped forward and said to the entire
assembly of people, 18"Micah of Moresheth prophesied in the days of Hezekiah
king of Judah. He told all the people of
Judah, 'This is what the LORD Almighty
says:

" 'Zion will be plowed like a field,
Jerusalem will become a heap of
rubble,
the temple hill a mound
overgrown with thickets.'[a]

19"Did Hezekiah king of Judah or anyone else in Judah put him to death? Did
not Hezekiah fear the LORD and seek his
favor? And did not the LORD relent, so
that he did not bring the disaster he pronounced against them? We are about to
bring a terrible disaster on ourselves!"
20(Now Uriah son of Shemaiah from
Kiriath Jearim was another man who
prophesied in the name of the LORD; he
prophesied the same things against this
city and this land as Jeremiah did.
21When King Jehoiakim and all his officers and officials heard his words, the
king sought to put him to death. But
Uriah heard of it and fled in fear to
Egypt. 22King Jehoiakim, however, sent
Elnathan son of Acbor to Egypt, along
with some other men. 23They brought
Uriah out of Egypt and took him to King
Jehoiakim, who had him struck down
with a sword and his body thrown into
the burial place of the common people.)
24Furthermore, Ahikam son of Shaphan supported Jeremiah, and so he
was not handed over to the people to be
put to death.

Judah to Serve Nebuchadnezzar

27 Early in the reign of Zedekiah[b] son of Josiah king of
Judah, this word came to Jeremiah
from the LORD: 2This is what the LORD
said to me: "Make a yoke out of straps
and crossbars and put it on your neck.
3Then send word to the kings of Edom,
Moab, Ammon, Tyre and Sidon through
the envoys who have come to Jerusalem
to Zedekiah king of Judah. 4Give them
a message for their masters and say,
'This is what the LORD Almighty, the
God of Israel, says: "Tell this to your
masters: 5With my great power and outstretched arm I made the earth and its
people and the animals that are on it,
and I give it to anyone I please. 6Now I
will hand all your countries over to my
servant Nebuchadnezzar king of Babylon; I will make even the wild animals
subject to him. 7All nations will serve
him and his son and his grandson until
the time for his land comes; then many
nations and great kings will subjugate
him.
8" ' "If, however, any nation or kingdom will not serve Nebuchadnezzar
king of Babylon or bow its neck under
his yoke, I will punish that nation with
the sword, famine and plague, declares
the LORD, until I destroy it by his hand.
9So do not listen to your prophets, your
diviners, your interpreters of dreams,

[a] *18* Micah 3:12 [b] *1* A few Hebrew manuscripts and Syriac (see also Jer. 27:3, 12 and 28:1); most Hebrew manuscripts *Jehoiakim* (Most Septuagint manuscripts do not have this verse.)

your mediums or your sorcerers who tell you, 'You will not serve the king of Babylon.' 10They prophesy lies to you that will only serve to remove you far from your lands; I will banish you and you will perish. 11But if any nation will bow its neck under the yoke of the king of Babylon and serve him, I will let that nation remain in its own land to till it and to live there, declares the LORD." ' "

12I gave the same message to Zedekiah king of Judah. I said, "Bow your neck under the yoke of the king of Babylon; serve him and his people, and you will live. 13Why will you and your people die by the sword, famine and plague with which the LORD has threatened any nation that will not serve the king of Babylon? 14Do not listen to the words of the prophets who say to you, 'You will not serve the king of Babylon,' for they are prophesying lies to you. 15'I have not sent them,' declares the LORD. 'They are prophesying lies in my name. Therefore, I will banish you and you will perish, both you and the prophets who prophesy to you.' "

16Then I said to the priests and all these people, "This is what the LORD says: Do not listen to the prophets who say, 'Very soon now the articles from the LORD's house will be brought back from Babylon.' They are prophesying lies to you. 17Do not listen to them. Serve the king of Babylon, and you will live. Why should this city become a ruin? 18If they are prophets and have the word of the LORD, let them plead with the LORD Almighty that the furnishings remaining in the house of the LORD and in the palace of the king of Judah and in Jerusalem not be taken to Babylon. 19For this is what the LORD Almighty says about the pillars, the Sea, the movable stands and the other furnishings that are left in this city, 20which Nebuchadnezzar king of Babylon did not take away when he carried Jehoiachin[a] son of Jehoiakim king of Judah into exile from Jerusalem to Babylon, along with all the nobles of Judah and Jerusalem— 21yes, this is what the LORD Almighty, the God of Israel, says about the things that are left in the house of the LORD and in the palace of the king of Judah and in Jerusalem: 22'They will be taken to Babylon and there they will remain until the day I come for them,' declares the LORD. 'Then I will bring them back and restore them to this place.' "

The False Prophet Hananiah

28 In the fifth month of that same year, the fourth year, early in the reign of Zedekiah king of Judah, the prophet Hananiah son of Azzur, who was from Gibeon, said to me in the house of the LORD in the presence of the priests and all the people: 2"This is what the LORD Almighty, the God of Israel, says: 'I will break the yoke of the king of Babylon. 3Within two years I will bring back to this place all the articles of the LORD's house that Nebuchadnezzar king of Babylon removed from here and took to Babylon. 4I will also bring back to this place Jehoiachin[a] son of Jehoiakim king of Judah and all the other exiles from Judah who went to Babylon,' declares the LORD, 'for I will break the yoke of the king of Babylon.' "

5Then the prophet Jeremiah replied to the prophet Hananiah before the priests and all the people who were standing in the house of the LORD. 6He said, "Amen! May the LORD do so! May the LORD fulfill the words you have prophesied by bringing the articles of the LORD's house and all the exiles back to this place from Babylon. 7Nevertheless, listen to what I have to say in your hearing and in the hearing of all the people: 8From early times the prophets who preceded you and me have prophesied war, disaster and plague against many countries and great kingdoms. 9But the prophet who prophesies peace will be recognized as one truly sent by the LORD only if his prediction comes true."

10Then the prophet Hananiah took the yoke off the neck of the prophet Jeremiah and broke it, 11and he said before all the people, "This is what the LORD says: 'In the same way will I break the

[a]20,4 Hebrew *Jeconiah,* a variant of *Jehoiachin*

yoke of Nebuchadnezzar king of Babylon off the neck of all the nations within two years.' " At this, the prophet
Jeremiah went on his way.
12Shortly after the prophet Hananiah
had broken the yoke off the neck of the
prophet Jeremiah, the word of the LORD
came to Jeremiah: 13"Go and tell Hananiah, 'This is what the LORD says: You
have broken a wooden yoke, but in its
place you will get a yoke of iron. 14This
is what the LORD Almighty, the God of
Israel, says: I will put an iron yoke on
the necks of all these nations to make
them serve Nebuchadnezzar king of
Babylon, and they will serve him. I will
even give him control over the wild animals.' "
15Then the prophet Jeremiah said to
Hananiah the prophet, "Listen, Hananiah! The LORD has not sent you, yet you
have persuaded this nation to trust in
lies. 16Therefore, this is what the LORD
says: 'I am about to remove you from
the face of the earth. This very year
you are going to die, because you
have preached rebellion against the
LORD.' "
17In the seventh month of that same
year, Hananiah the prophet died.

SHARPEN THE FOCUS

Jeremiah must have kept the region's gossip mills busy. "You'll never guess what that crazy man has done now," the scoffers in Jerusalem must have muttered to each other.

Take his yoke demonstration, for instance. This was not a one-day object lesson. The prophet walked the countryside for months wearing the kind of yoke–a wooden harness–usually reserved for oxen. Not content to speak only to Judah, Jeremiah demonstrated his message of coming invasion and servitude to five kings whose ambassadors came to Jerusalem to confer with King Zedekiah. It wasn't exactly the kind of publicity Zedekiah needed as he tried to forge an alliance to fend off King Nebuchadnezzar (Jeremiah 27:1–10).

Throughout Jeremiah's ministry, prophets like Hananiah enjoyed much greater popularity. Few in Judah approved of Jeremiah's preaching. But God did. And in the end, that's all that counted.

What counts in our life? To what "audience" do you play? Whose applause matters most to you? Let the Spirit help you answer those questions honestly. Then turn to your Savior for whatever forgiveness and change of heart you need.

WEEK 60 • MONDAY

Jeremiah 29:1–32

GET THE BIG PICTURE

Jeremiah wrote the letters of chapter 29 sometime after Nebuchadnezzar had deported the first exiles to Babylon. Two temptations would assail them there. First, the false prophets would continue to predict a speedy return from exile. Second, the faithful believers among the exiles might despair, believing the Lord had forsaken them. What parts of Jeremiah's letters address each of these temptations? If time is short, focus on Jeremiah 29:1–23.

A Letter to the Exiles

29 This is the text of the letter
that the prophet Jeremiah
sent from Jerusalem to the surviving
elders among the exiles and to the
priests, the prophets and all the other
people Nebuchadnezzar had carried
into exile from Jerusalem to Babylon.
2(This was after King Jehoiachin[a] and
the queen mother, the court officials and
the leaders of Judah and Jerusalem, the
craftsmen and the artisans had gone
into exile from Jerusalem.) 3He entrusted the letter to Elasah son of Shaphan and to Gemariah son of Hilkiah,
whom Zedekiah king of Judah sent to
King Nebuchadnezzar in Babylon. It
said:

4This is what the LORD Almighty,
the God of Israel, says to all those I
carried into exile from Jerusalem to
Babylon: 5"Build houses and settle
down; plant gardens and eat what
they produce. 6Marry and have
sons and daughters; find wives for
your sons and give your daughters
in marriage, so that they too may
have sons and daughters. Increase
in number there; do not decrease.
7Also, seek the peace and prosperity of the city to which I have carried you into exile. Pray to the LORD
for it, because if it prospers, you too
will prosper." 8Yes, this is what the
LORD Almighty, the God of Israel,
says: "Do not let the prophets and
diviners among you deceive you.
Do not listen to the dreams you
encourage them to have. 9They are
prophesying lies to you in my
name. I have not sent them," declares the LORD.

10This is what the LORD says:
"When seventy years are completed for Babylon, I will come to you
and fulfill my gracious promise to
bring you back to this place. 11For I
know the plans I have for you," declares the LORD, "plans to prosper
you and not to harm you, plans to
give you hope and a future. 12Then
you will call upon me and come
and pray to me, and I will listen to
you. 13You will seek me and find me
when you seek me with all your
heart. 14I will be found by you," declares the LORD, "and will bring
you back from captivity.[b] I will
gather you from all the nations and
places where I have banished you,"
declares the LORD, "and will bring
you back to the place from which I
carried you into exile."

15You may say, "The LORD has
raised up prophets for us in Babylon," 16but this is what the LORD
says about the king who sits on
David's throne and all the people
who remain in this city, your countrymen who did not go with you
into exile— 17yes, this is what the
LORD Almighty says: "I will send
the sword, famine and plague
against them and I will make them
like poor figs that are so bad they
cannot be eaten. 18I will pursue
them with the sword, famine and
plague and will make them abhorrent to all the kingdoms of the earth
and an object of cursing and horror,
of scorn and reproach, among all
the nations where I drive them.
19For they have not listened to my
words," declares the LORD, "words
that I sent to them again and again
by my servants the prophets. And
you exiles have not listened either,"
declares the LORD.

20Therefore, hear the word of the
LORD, all you exiles whom I have
sent away from Jerusalem to Babylon. 21This is what the LORD Almighty, the God of Israel, says
about Ahab son of Kolaiah and
Zedekiah son of Maaseiah, who are
prophesying lies to you in my
name: "I will hand them over to
Nebuchadnezzar king of Babylon,
and he will put them to death before your very eyes. 22Because of
them, all the exiles from Judah who
are in Babylon will use this curse:

[a]2 Hebrew *Jeconiah,* a variant of *Jehoiachin*
[b]14 Or *will restore your fortunes*

'The LORD treat you like Zedekiah
and Ahab, whom the king of Babylon burned in the fire.' 23For they
have done outrageous things in Israel; they have committed adultery
with their neighbors' wives and in
my name have spoken lies, which
I did not tell them to do. I know it
and am a witness to it," declares the
LORD.

Message to Shemaiah

24Tell Shemaiah the Nehelamite,
25"This is what the LORD Almighty, the
God of Israel, says: You sent letters in
your own name to all the people in Jerusalem, to Zephaniah son of Maaseiah
the priest, and to all the other priests.
You said to Zephaniah, 26'The LORD has
appointed you priest in place of Jehoiada to be in charge of the house of the
LORD; you should put any madman
who acts like a prophet into the stocks
and neck-irons. 27So why have you not
reprimanded Jeremiah from Anathoth,
who poses as a prophet among you?
28He has sent this message to us in Babylon: It will be a long time. Therefore
build houses and settle down; plant
gardens and eat what they produce.' "

29Zephaniah the priest, however, read
the letter to Jeremiah the prophet.
30Then the word of the LORD came to
Jeremiah: 31"Send this message to all the
exiles: 'This is what the LORD says about
Shemaiah the Nehelamite: Because Shemaiah has prophesied to you, even
though I did not send him, and has led
you to believe a lie, 32this is what the
LORD says: I will surely punish Shemaiah the Nehelamite and his descendants. He will have no one left among
this people, nor will he see the good
things I will do for my people, declares
the LORD, because he has preached rebellion against me.' "

SHARPEN THE FOCUS

"Believe Me," the Lord invites the exiles through His prophet Jeremiah. "You will live in Babylon for 70 years, so settle down. Build yourselves homes. Establish families. I won't forget or forsake you. I won't fail you. I will bring your children back to the land you've left." That, in essence, was God's promise. (Jeremiah 29:10–14)

Do you think of yourself as an exile? Speaking of Abel, Noah, Abraham, Sarah, and many others, the writer to the Hebrews said, "They admitted that they were aliens and strangers on earth . . . They were longing for a better country—a heavenly one. Therefore God is not ashamed to be called their God, for He has prepared a city for them" (Hebrews 11:13, 16).

The Lord used the years of Noah's, Abraham's, and Sarah's "exile," as opportunities to bring them His Word and thereby form in them His own image. He planned the same for Judah in Babylon. His thoughts, hopes, plans, and dreams for His people were for peace.

Are you letting the Lord use the moments, days, and years of your exile here on earth in this way too? He wants to save, protect, teach, and help you to grow up into true Christlikeness. Let Him speak to you through His Word.

The first two chapters from today's reading contain the sweetest Gospel message of Jeremiah's entire book. In the pictures of restoration Jeremiah paints, we see God's grace as the prophet foretells Judah's return from exile, the fruit of the Messiah's finished work, and the glories of the heavenly home God is preparing for us even now. If time is short, focus on Jeremiah 31:1–40.

Restoration of Israel

30 This is the word that came
to Jeremiah from the LORD:
2"This is what the LORD, the God of Israel, says: 'Write in a book all the words
I have spoken to you. 3The days are
coming,' declares the LORD, 'when I will
bring my people Israel and Judah back
from captivity[a] and restore them to the
land I gave their forefathers to possess,'
says the LORD."
4These are the words the LORD spoke
concerning Israel and Judah: 5"This is
what the LORD says:

" 'Cries of fear are heard—
terror, not peace.
6Ask and see:
Can a man bear children?
Then why do I see every strong man
with his hands on his stomach like
a woman in labor,
every face turned deathly pale?
7How awful that day will be!
None will be like it.
It will be a time of trouble for Jacob,
but he will be saved out of it.

8" 'In that day,' declares the LORD
Almighty,
'I will break the yoke off their
necks
and will tear off their bonds;
no longer will foreigners enslave
them.
9Instead, they will serve the LORD
their God
and David their king,
whom I will raise up for them.

10" 'So do not fear, O Jacob my
servant;
do not be dismayed, O Israel,'
declares the LORD.
'I will surely save you out of a
distant place,
your descendants from the land of
their exile.
Jacob will again have peace and
security,
and no one will make him afraid.
11I am with you and will save you,'
declares the LORD.
'Though I completely destroy all the
nations
among which I scatter you,
I will not completely destroy you.
I will discipline you but only with
justice;
I will not let you go entirely
unpunished.'

12"This is what the LORD says:

" 'Your wound is incurable,
your injury beyond healing.
13There is no one to plead your
cause,
no remedy for your sore,
no healing for you.
14All your allies have forgotten you;
they care nothing for you.

[a]3 Or *will restore the fortunes of my people Israel and Judah*

I have struck you as an enemy
would
and punished you as would the
cruel,
because your guilt is so great
and your sins so many.
15 Why do you cry out over your
wound,
your pain that has no cure?
Because of your great guilt and
many sins
I have done these things to you.
16 " 'But all who devour you will be
devoured;
all your enemies will go into exile.
Those who plunder you will be
plundered;
all who make spoil of you I will
despoil.
17 But I will restore you to health
and heal your wounds,'
declares the LORD,
'because you are called an outcast,
Zion for whom no one cares.'

18 "This is what the LORD says:

" 'I will restore the fortunes of
Jacob's tents
and have compassion on his
dwellings;
the city will be rebuilt on her ruins,
and the palace will stand in its
proper place.
19 From them will come songs of
thanksgiving
and the sound of rejoicing.
I will add to their numbers,
and they will not be decreased;
I will bring them honor,
and they will not be disdained.
20 Their children will be as in days of
old,
and their community will be
established before me;
I will punish all who oppress
them.
21 Their leader will be one of their
own;
their ruler will arise from among
them.
I will bring him near and he will
come close to me,
for who is he who will devote
himself
to be close to me?'
declares the LORD.
22 " 'So you will be my people,
and I will be your God.' "

23 See, the storm of the LORD
will burst out in wrath,
a driving wind swirling down
on the heads of the wicked.
24 The fierce anger of the LORD will not
turn back
until he fully accomplishes
the purposes of his heart.
In days to come
you will understand this.

31 "At that time," declares the LORD, "I will be the God of all the clans of Israel, and they will be my people."

2 This is what the LORD says:

"The people who survive the sword
will find favor in the desert;
I will come to give rest to Israel."

3 The LORD appeared to us in the past,[a] saying:

"I have loved you with an
everlasting love;
I have drawn you with
loving-kindness.
4 I will build you up again
and you will be rebuilt, O Virgin
Israel.
Again you will take up your
tambourines
and go out to dance with the
joyful.
5 Again you will plant vineyards
on the hills of Samaria;
the farmers will plant them
and enjoy their fruit.
6 There will be a day when watchmen
cry out
on the hills of Ephraim,
'Come, let us go up to Zion,
to the LORD our God.' "

7 This is what the LORD says:

[a] 3 Or *LORD has appeared to us from afar*

"Sing with joy for Jacob;
shout for the foremost of the nations.
Make your praises heard, and say,
'O LORD, save your people,
the remnant of Israel.'
8 See, I will bring them from the land of the north
and gather them from the ends of the earth.
Among them will be the blind and the lame,
expectant mothers and women in labor;
a great throng will return.
9 They will come with weeping;
they will pray as I bring them back.
I will lead them beside streams of water
on a level path where they will not stumble,
because I am Israel's father,
and Ephraim is my firstborn son.

10 "Hear the word of the LORD,
O nations;
proclaim it in distant coastlands:
'He who scattered Israel will gather them
and will watch over his flock like a shepherd.'
11 For the LORD will ransom Jacob
and redeem them from the hand of those stronger than they.
12 They will come and shout for joy on the heights of Zion;
they will rejoice in the bounty of the LORD—
the grain, the new wine and the oil,
the young of the flocks and herds.
They will be like a well-watered garden,
and they will sorrow no more.
13 Then maidens will dance and be glad,
young men and old as well.
I will turn their mourning into gladness;
I will give them comfort and joy instead of sorrow.
14 I will satisfy the priests with abundance,
and my people will be filled with my bounty,"
declares the LORD.

15 This is what the LORD says:

"A voice is heard in Ramah,
mourning and great weeping,
Rachel weeping for her children
and refusing to be comforted,
because her children are no more."

16 This is what the LORD says:

"Restrain your voice from weeping
and your eyes from tears,
for your work will be rewarded,"
declares the LORD.
"They will return from the land of the enemy.
17 So there is hope for your future,"
declares the LORD.
"Your children will return to their own land.

18 "I have surely heard Ephraim's moaning:
'You disciplined me like an unruly calf,
and I have been disciplined.
Restore me, and I will return,
because you are the LORD my God.
19 After I strayed,
I repented;
after I came to understand,
I beat my breast.
I was ashamed and humiliated
because I bore the disgrace of my youth.'
20 Is not Ephraim my dear son,
the child in whom I delight?
Though I often speak against him,
I still remember him.
Therefore my heart yearns for him;
I have great compassion for him,"
declares the LORD.

21 "Set up road signs;
put up guideposts.
Take note of the highway,
the road that you take.
Return, O Virgin Israel,
return to your towns.
22 How long will you wander,

O unfaithful daughter?
The LORD will create a new thing on
earth—
a woman will surround[a] a man."

[23]This is what the LORD Almighty, the
God of Israel, says: "When I bring them
back from captivity,[b] the people in the
land of Judah and in its towns will once
again use these words: 'The LORD bless
you, O righteous dwelling, O sacred
mountain.' [24]People will live together in
Judah and all its towns—farmers and
those who move about with their flocks.
[25]I will refresh the weary and satisfy the
faint."
[26]At this I awoke and looked around.
My sleep had been pleasant to me.
[27]"The days are coming," declares the
LORD, "when I will plant the house of Israel and the house of Judah with the offspring of men and of animals. [28]Just as I
watched over them to uproot and tear
down, and to overthrow, destroy and
bring disaster, so I will watch over them
to build and to plant," declares the
LORD. [29]"In those days people will no
longer say,

'The fathers have eaten sour grapes,
and the children's teeth are set on
edge.'

[30]Instead, everyone will die for his own
sin; whoever eats sour grapes—his own
teeth will be set on edge.

[31]"The time is coming," declares the
LORD,
"when I will make a new covenant
with the house of Israel
and with the house of Judah.
[32]It will not be like the covenant
I made with their forefathers
when I took them by the hand
to lead them out of Egypt,
because they broke my covenant,
though I was a husband to[c]
them,[d]"
declares the LORD.
[33]"This is the covenant I will make
with the house of Israel
after that time," declares the
LORD.
"I will put my law in their minds
and write it on their hearts.
I will be their God,
and they will be my people.
[34]No longer will a man teach his
neighbor,
or a man his brother, saying,
'Know the LORD,'
because they will all know me,
from the least of them to the
greatest,"
declares the LORD.
"For I will forgive their wickedness
and will remember their sins no
more."

[35]This is what the LORD says,

he who appoints the sun
to shine by day,
who decrees the moon and stars
to shine by night,
who stirs up the sea
so that its waves roar—
the LORD Almighty is his name:
[36]"Only if these decrees vanish from
my sight,"
declares the LORD,
"will the descendants of Israel ever
cease
to be a nation before me."

[37]This is what the LORD says:
"Only if the heavens above can be
measured
and the foundations of the earth
below be searched out
will I reject all the descendants of
Israel
because of all they have done,"
declares the LORD.

[38]"The days are coming," declares the
LORD, "when this city will be rebuilt for
me from the Tower of Hananel to the
Corner Gate. [39]The measuring line will
stretch from there straight to the hill of
Gareb and then turn to Goah. [40]The
whole valley where dead bodies and
ashes are thrown, and all the terraces
out to the Kidron Valley on the east as

[a]22 Or *will go about* ⸤*seeking*⸥; or *will protect*
[b]23 Or *I restore their fortunes* [c]32 Hebrew;
Septuagint and Syriac / *and I turned away from*
[d]32 Or *was their master*

far as the corner of the Horse Gate, will be holy to the LORD. The city will never again be uprooted or demolished."

Jeremiah Buys a Field

32 This is the word that came to Jeremiah from the LORD in the tenth year of Zedekiah king of Judah, which was the eighteenth year of Nebuchadnezzar. [2]The army of the king of Babylon was then besieging Jerusalem, and Jeremiah the prophet was confined in the courtyard of the guard in the royal palace of Judah.

[3]Now Zedekiah king of Judah had imprisoned him there, saying, "Why do you prophesy as you do? You say, 'This is what the LORD says: I am about to hand this city over to the king of Babylon, and he will capture it. [4]Zedekiah king of Judah will not escape out of the hands of the Babylonians[a] but will certainly be handed over to the king of Babylon, and will speak with him face to face and see him with his own eyes. [5]He will take Zedekiah to Babylon, where he will remain until I deal with him, declares the LORD. If you fight against the Babylonians, you will not succeed.' "

[6]Jeremiah said, "The word of the LORD came to me: [7]Hanamel son of Shallum your uncle is going to come to you and say, 'Buy my field at Anathoth, because as nearest relative it is your right and duty to buy it.'

[8]"Then, just as the LORD had said, my cousin Hanamel came to me in the courtyard of the guard and said, 'Buy my field at Anathoth in the territory of Benjamin. Since it is your right to redeem it and possess it, buy it for yourself.'

"I knew that this was the word of the LORD; [9]so I bought the field at Anathoth from my cousin Hanamel and weighed out for him seventeen shekels[b] of silver. [10]I signed and sealed the deed, had it witnessed, and weighed out the silver on the scales. [11]I took the deed of purchase—the sealed copy containing the terms and conditions, as well as the unsealed copy— [12]and I gave this deed to Baruch son of Neriah, the son of Mahseiah, in the presence of my cousin Hanamel and of the witnesses who had signed the deed and of all the Jews sitting in the courtyard of the guard.

[13]"In their presence I gave Baruch these instructions: [14]'This is what the LORD Almighty, the God of Israel, says: Take these documents, both the sealed and unsealed copies of the deed of purchase, and put them in a clay jar so they will last a long time. [15]For this is what the LORD Almighty, the God of Israel, says: Houses, fields and vineyards will again be bought in this land.'

[16]"After I had given the deed of purchase to Baruch son of Neriah, I prayed to the LORD:

[17]"Ah, Sovereign LORD, you have made the heavens and the earth by your great power and outstretched arm. Nothing is too hard for you. [18]You show love to thousands but bring the punishment for the fathers' sins into the laps of their children after them. O great and powerful God, whose name is the LORD Almighty, [19]great are your purposes and mighty are your deeds. Your eyes are open to all the ways of men; you reward everyone according to his conduct and as his deeds deserve. [20]You performed miraculous signs and wonders in Egypt and have continued them to this day, both in Israel and among all mankind, and have gained the renown that is still yours. [21]You brought your people Israel out of Egypt with signs and wonders, by a mighty hand and an outstretched arm and with great terror. [22]You gave them this land you had sworn to give their forefathers, a land flowing with milk and honey. [23]They came in and took possession of it, but they did not obey you or follow your law; they did not do what you commanded them to do.

[a]4 Or *Chaldeans*; also in verses 5, 24, 25, 28, 29 and 43 [b]9 That is, about 7 ounces (about 200 grams)

So you brought all this disaster upon them.

24"See how the siege ramps are built up to take the city. Because of the sword, famine and plague, the city will be handed over to the Babylonians who are attacking it. What you said has happened, as you now see. 25And though the city will be handed over to the Babylonians, you, O Sovereign LORD, say to me, 'Buy the field with silver and have the transaction witnessed.' "

26Then the word of the LORD came to Jeremiah: 27"I am the LORD, the God of all mankind. Is anything too hard for me? 28Therefore, this is what the LORD says: I am about to hand this city over to the Babylonians and to Nebuchadnezzar king of Babylon, who will capture it. 29The Babylonians who are attacking this city will come in and set it on fire; they will burn it down, along with the houses where the people provoked me to anger by burning incense on the roofs to Baal and by pouring out drink offerings to other gods.

30"The people of Israel and Judah have done nothing but evil in my sight from their youth; indeed, the people of Israel have done nothing but provoke me with what their hands have made, declares the LORD. 31From the day it was built until now, this city has so aroused my anger and wrath that I must remove it from my sight. 32The people of Israel and Judah have provoked me by all the evil they have done—they, their kings and officials, their priests and prophets, the men of Judah and the people of Jerusalem. 33They turned their backs to me and not their faces; though I taught them again and again, they would not listen or respond to discipline. 34They set up their abominable idols in the house that bears my Name and defiled it. 35They built high places for Baal in the Valley of Ben Hinnom to sacrifice their sons and daughters[a] to Molech, though I never commanded, nor did it enter my mind, that they should do such a detestable thing and so make Judah sin.

36"You are saying about this city, 'By the sword, famine and plague it will be handed over to the king of Babylon'; but this is what the LORD, the God of Israel, says: 37I will surely gather them from all the lands where I banish them in my furious anger and great wrath; I will bring them back to this place and let them live in safety. 38They will be my people, and I will be their God. 39I will give them singleness of heart and action, so that they will always fear me for their own good and the good of their children after them. 40I will make an everlasting covenant with them: I will never stop doing good to them, and I will inspire them to fear me, so that they will never turn away from me. 41I will rejoice in doing them good and will assuredly plant them in this land with all my heart and soul.

42"This is what the LORD says: As I have brought all this great calamity on this people, so I will give them all the prosperity I have promised them. 43Once more fields will be bought in this land of which you say, 'It is a desolate waste, without men or animals, for it has been handed over to the Babylonians.' 44Fields will be bought for silver, and deeds will be signed, sealed and witnessed in the territory of Benjamin, in the villages around Jerusalem, in the towns of Judah and in the towns of the hill country, of the western foothills and of the Negev, because I will restore their fortunes,[b] declares the LORD."

[a]35 Or *to make their sons and daughters pass through* ⌊*the fire*⌋ [b]44 Or *will bring them back from captivity*

SHARPEN THE FOCUS

A teenaged boy pulls his little sister's sled up the snowy hill time after time. Then he watches as she giggles her way back down.

A rescue worker throws a rope down the cliff to a climber trapped and injured on a ledge far below, a climber who happens to be his wife.

A young mom tramps through the mall choosing birthday gifts for her two-year-old. The youngster toddles along with her, held close by an elastic cord tied to his waist so he won't get lost.

All of these can serve as examples of the "cords of kindness" Jeremiah refers to in Jeremiah 31:3. Here God says, "I have loved you with an everlasting love; I have drawn you with loving-kindness."

We can't see our Lord's cords of kindness. At least, not in the same way we see sled ropes or fire department equipment or bungee cords. But we know that our God has drawn us to Himself in the cross of His Son. Jesus once said, "When I am lifted up from the earth, [I] will draw all men to Myself" (John 12:32). Jesus' death for our sins was the ultimate act of kindness. His love for us is an everlasting love, a love without beginning and without end. He has loved us. He has drawn us to Himself. Praise His unequaled kindness!

WEEK 60 • WEDNESDAY

Jeremiah 33:1–26

GET THE BIG PICTURE

Jeremiah's message of grace continues as the Lord promises not to cancel the covenant He has made with Judah. List the things God promises to do for His people—most of the statements that begin with "I will" indicate these promises. If time is short, focus on Jeremiah 33:14–26.

Promise of Restoration

33 While Jeremiah was still
confined in the courtyard
of the guard, the word of the LORD came
to him a second time: 2"This is what the
LORD says, he who made the earth, the
LORD who formed it and established
it—the LORD is his name: 3'Call to me
and I will answer you and tell you great
and unsearchable things you do not
know.' 4For this is what the LORD, the
God of Israel, says about the houses in
this city and the royal palaces of Judah
that have been torn down to be used
against the siege ramps and the sword
5in the fight with the Babylonians[a]:
'They will be filled with the dead bodies of the men I will slay in my anger
and wrath. I will hide my face from this
city because of all its wickedness.
6" 'Nevertheless, I will bring health
and healing to it; I will heal my people and will let them enjoy abundant
peace and security. 7I will bring Judah
and Israel back from captivity[b] and will
rebuild them as they were before. 8I will
cleanse them from all the sin they have
committed against me and will forgive
all their sins of rebellion against me.
9Then this city will bring me renown,
joy, praise and honor before all nations
on earth that hear of all the good things
I do for it; and they will be in awe and

[a]5 Or *Chaldeans* [b]7 Or *will restore the fortunes of Judah and Israel*

will tremble at the abundant prosperity
and peace I provide for it.'
10"This is what the LORD says: 'You say
about this place, "It is a desolate waste,
without men or animals." Yet in the
towns of Judah and the streets of Jerusalem that are deserted, inhabited by
neither men nor animals, there will be
heard once more 11the sounds of joy and
gladness, the voices of bride and bridegroom, and the voices of those who
bring thank offerings to the house of the
LORD, saying,

"Give thanks to the LORD
Almighty,
for the LORD is good;
his love endures forever."

For I will restore the fortunes of the land
as they were before,' says the LORD.
12"This is what the LORD Almighty
says: 'In this place, desolate and without men or animals—in all its towns
there will again be pastures for shepherds to rest their flocks. 13In the towns
of the hill country, of the western foothills and of the Negev, in the territory
of Benjamin, in the villages around Jerusalem and in the towns of Judah,
flocks will again pass under the hand of
the one who counts them,' says the
LORD.
14" 'The days are coming,' declares the
LORD, 'when I will fulfill the gracious
promise I made to the house of Israel
and to the house of Judah.

15" 'In those days and at that time
I will make a righteous Branch
sprout from David's line;
he will do what is just and right in
the land.
16In those days Judah will be saved
and Jerusalem will live in safety.
This is the name by which it[a] will be
called:
The LORD Our Righteousness.'

17For this is what the LORD says: 'David
will never fail to have a man to sit on the
throne of the house of Israel, 18nor will
the priests, who are Levites, ever fail to
have a man to stand before me continually to offer burnt offerings, to burn
grain offerings and to present sacrifices.' "
19The word of the LORD came to Jeremiah: 20"This is what the LORD says: 'If
you can break my covenant with the
day and my covenant with the night, so
that day and night no longer come at
their appointed time, 21then my covenant with David my servant—and my
covenant with the Levites who are
priests ministering before me—can be
broken and David will no longer have
a descendant to reign on his throne. 22I
will make the descendants of David my
servant and the Levites who minister
before me as countless as the stars of the
sky and as measureless as the sand on
the seashore.' "
23The word of the LORD came to Jeremiah: 24"Have you not noticed that
these people are saying, 'The LORD has
rejected the two kingdoms[b] he chose'?
So they despise my people and no longer regard them as a nation. 25This is what
the LORD says: 'If I have not established
my covenant with day and night and
the fixed laws of heaven and earth,
26then I will reject the descendants of
Jacob and David my servant and will
not choose one of his sons to rule over
the descendants of Abraham, Isaac and
Jacob. For I will restore their fortunes[c]
and have compassion on them.' "

[a]16 Or *he* [b]24 Or *families* [c]26 Or *will bring them back from captivity*

SHARPEN THE FOCUS

For centuries when a couple was married the husband gave his name to his new wife. This tradition helps to unlock the meaning of Jeremiah 33:15–16. Compare these verses with Jeremiah 23:5–6.

In chapter 23, the prophet describes the Bridegroom, Christ Jesus. He's the King who has risen as David's greater Son. He's the Son of God, the Judge who rules in perfect wisdom and who enjoys right standing with God the Father. This King is the only righteous human being who ever lived on earth.

Note the description in Jeremiah 33:16.

In those days Judah will be saved
and Jerusalem will live in safety.
This is the name by which it [Jerusalem] will be called:
The LORD Our Righteousness.

The bride, Jerusalem, the church, receives the Bridegroom's name! Christ Jesus has given us a new identity, a new future, a new life. The guilt, the penalty, and the consequences of our sins have all been canceled. We are, in Christ, citizens of heaven. More than that—we are Jesus' royal bride!

How sure is our new status? If you can stop the sun from shining, if you can stop the sun from setting, then (Jeremiah 33:20) God can break His vows of love to you. Rest secure in your new identity today. The Lord is your righteousness!

WEEK 60 • THURSDAY

Jeremiah 34:1—35:19

King Zedekiah's kingdom now included only three cities—Lachish, Azekah, and Jerusalem. In an act of repentance, Zedekiah led the people to release their Hebrew slaves as per Leviticus 25:39–46. But soon the wealthy reneged on this release, rescinding their repentance. Chapter 35 flashes back in time to the days of King Jehoiakim (609–597 B.C.). What does the Lord say in both chapters about respect for Him and obedience to His Word? If time is short, focus on Jeremiah 35:1–19.

Warning to Zedekiah

34 While Nebuchadnezzar
king of Babylon and all his
army and all the kingdoms and peoples
in the empire he ruled were fighting
against Jerusalem and all its surrounding towns, this word came to Jeremiah
from the LORD: 2"This is what the LORD,
the God of Israel, says: Go to Zedekiah
king of Judah and tell him, 'This is what
the LORD says: I am about to hand this
city over to the king of Babylon, and he
will burn it down. 3You will not escape
from his grasp but will surely be captured and handed over to him. You will
see the king of Babylon with your own
eyes, and he will speak with you face to
face. And you will go to Babylon.
4" 'Yet hear the promise of the LORD,
O Zedekiah king of Judah. This is what
the LORD says concerning you: You will
not die by the sword; 5you will die
peacefully. As people made a funeral
fire in honor of your fathers, the former

kings who preceded you, so they will make a fire in your honor and lament, "Alas, O master!" I myself make this promise, declares the LORD.' "

[6]Then Jeremiah the prophet told all this to Zedekiah king of Judah, in Jerusalem, [7]while the army of the king of Babylon was fighting against Jerusalem and the other cities of Judah that were still holding out—Lachish and Azekah. These were the only fortified cities left in Judah.

Freedom for Slaves

[8]The word came to Jeremiah from the LORD after King Zedekiah had made a covenant with all the people in Jerusalem to proclaim freedom for the slaves. [9]Everyone was to free his Hebrew slaves, both male and female; no one was to hold a fellow Jew in bondage. [10]So all the officials and people who entered into this covenant agreed that they would free their male and female slaves and no longer hold them in bondage. They agreed, and set them free. [11]But afterward they changed their minds and took back the slaves they had freed and enslaved them again.

[12]Then the word of the LORD came to Jeremiah: [13]"This is what the LORD, the God of Israel, says: I made a covenant with your forefathers when I brought them out of Egypt, out of the land of slavery. I said, [14]'Every seventh year each of you must free any fellow Hebrew who has sold himself to you. After he has served you six years, you must let him go free.'[a] Your fathers, however, did not listen to me or pay attention to me. [15]Recently you repented and did what is right in my sight: Each of you proclaimed freedom to his countrymen. You even made a covenant before me in the house that bears my Name. [16]But now you have turned around and profaned my name; each of you has taken back the male and female slaves you had set free to go where they wished. You have forced them to become your slaves again.

[17]"Therefore, this is what the LORD says: You have not obeyed me; you have not proclaimed freedom for your fellow countrymen. So I now proclaim 'freedom' for you, declares the LORD—'freedom' to fall by the sword, plague and famine. I will make you abhorrent to all the kingdoms of the earth. [18]The men who have violated my covenant and have not fulfilled the terms of the covenant they made before me, I will treat like the calf they cut in two and then walked between its pieces. [19]The leaders of Judah and Jerusalem, the court officials, the priests and all the people of the land who walked between the pieces of the calf, [20]I will hand over to their enemies who seek their lives. Their dead bodies will become food for the birds of the air and the beasts of the earth.

[21]"I will hand Zedekiah king of Judah and his officials over to their enemies who seek their lives, to the army of the king of Babylon, which has withdrawn from you. [22]I am going to give the order, declares the LORD, and I will bring them back to this city. They will fight against it, take it and burn it down. And I will lay waste the towns of Judah so no one can live there."

The Recabites

35 This is the word that came to Jeremiah from the LORD during the reign of Jehoiakim son of Josiah king of Judah: [2]"Go to the Recabite family and invite them to come to one of the side rooms of the house of the LORD and give them wine to drink."

[3]So I went to get Jaazaniah son of Jeremiah, the son of Habazziniah, and his brothers and all his sons—the whole family of the Recabites. [4]I brought them into the house of the LORD, into the room of the sons of Hanan son of Igdaliah the man of God. It was next to the room of the officials, which was over that of Maaseiah son of Shallum the doorkeeper. [5]Then I set bowls full of wine and some cups before the men of the Recabite family and said to them, "Drink some wine."

[6]But they replied, "We do not drink

[a]*14* Deut. 15:12

wine, because our forefather Jonadab
son of Recab gave us this command:
'Neither you nor your descendants
must ever drink wine. [7]Also you must
never build houses, sow seed or plant
vineyards; you must never have any of
these things, but must always live in
tents. Then you will live a long time in
the land where you are nomads.' [8]We
have obeyed everything our forefather
Jonadab son of Recab commanded us.
Neither we nor our wives nor our sons
and daughters have ever drunk wine
[9]or built houses to live in or had vineyards, fields or crops. [10]We have lived in
tents and have fully obeyed everything
our forefather Jonadab commanded us.
[11]But when Nebuchadnezzar king of
Babylon invaded this land, we said,
'Come, we must go to Jerusalem to
escape the Babylonian[a] and Aramean
armies.' So we have remained in Jerusalem."

[12]Then the word of the LORD came to
Jeremiah, saying: [13]"This is what the
LORD Almighty, the God of Israel, says:
Go and tell the men of Judah and the
people of Jerusalem, 'Will you not learn
a lesson and obey my words?' declares
the LORD. [14]'Jonadab son of Recab ordered his sons not to drink wine and
this command has been kept. To this day
they do not drink wine, because they
obey their forefather's command. But I
have spoken to you again and again, yet
you have not obeyed me. [15]Again and
again I sent all my servants the prophets to you. They said, "Each of you must
turn from your wicked ways and reform
your actions; do not follow other gods
to serve them. Then you will live in the
land I have given to you and your fathers." But you have not paid attention
or listened to me. [16]The descendants of
Jonadab son of Recab have carried out the
command their forefather gave them,
but these people have not obeyed me.'

[17]"Therefore, this is what the LORD
God Almighty, the God of Israel, says:
'Listen! I am going to bring on Judah
and on everyone living in Jerusalem ev-
ery disaster I pronounced against them.
I spoke to them, but they did not listen;
I called to them, but they did not an-
swer.' "

[18]Then Jeremiah said to the family of
the Recabites, "This is what the LORD Almighty, the God of Israel, says: 'You
have obeyed the command of your forefather Jonadab and have followed all his
instructions and have done everything
he ordered.' [19]Therefore, this is what the
LORD Almighty, the God of Israel, says:
'Jonadab son of Recab will never fail to
have a man to serve me.' "

[a]11 Or *Chaldean*

SHARPEN THE FOCUS

The wealthy and sophisticated in Jerusalem must have looked down their noses at the family of Recab. The Recabites wouldn't build houses, wouldn't engage in agriculture. They lived in tents, possibly as nomads. And, perhaps strangest of all to the social elite of Judah, the Recabites wouldn't drink alcohol, even when tempted.

Why all the self-imposed hardship? Why the hassle and the refusal to accumulate the trappings of wealth? The Recabites had made a promise. They were apparently simple, honest people—people who kept their word, from one generation to the next.

The Lord found their attitude a refreshing contrast with that of His own children. His divine law, backed by centuries of promises made and promises kept, had become for the most part a mere curiosity in Judah. Few held any respect for it. Fewer still obeyed it.

What is your own attitude toward God's Law? Do you see it as a blessing from Him, designed to protect you from harm and to lead you to see your need for our Savior? Or is it an inconvenience, a burden? Only our Lord can change our hearts. Only He can work true repentance and faith. Turn to Him now for whatever you need.

Today's two chapters give us two snapshots of Judah's spiritual condition under two different kings: Jehoiakim (chapter 36) and Zedekiah (chapter 37). In these chapters you will read about incredible courage, incredible disrespect for God's Word, and incredible weakness. Ask yourself, "What does it mean to me that God's Word never changes, no matter how human beings respond to it?" If time is short, focus on Jeremiah 36:1–26.

Jehoiakim Burns Jeremiah's Scroll

36 In the fourth year of Jehoiakim son of Josiah king of
Judah, this word came to Jeremiah from
the LORD: 2"Take a scroll and write on it
all the words I have spoken to you concerning Israel, Judah and all the other
nations from the time I began speaking
to you in the reign of Josiah till now.
3Perhaps when the people of Judah hear
about every disaster I plan to inflict on
them, each of them will turn from his
wicked way; then I will forgive their
wickedness and their sin."
4So Jeremiah called Baruch son of Neriah, and while Jeremiah dictated all the
words the LORD had spoken to him, Baruch wrote them on the scroll. 5Then Jeremiah told Baruch, "I am restricted; I
cannot go to the LORD's temple. 6So you
go to the house of the LORD on a day of
fasting and read to the people from the
scroll the words of the LORD that you
wrote as I dictated. Read them to all the
people of Judah who come in from their
towns. 7Perhaps they will bring their petition before the LORD, and each will
turn from his wicked ways, for the anger and wrath pronounced against this
people by the LORD are great."
8Baruch son of Neriah did everything
Jeremiah the prophet told him to do; at
the LORD's temple he read the words of
the LORD from the scroll. 9In the ninth
month of the fifth year of Jehoiakim son
of Josiah king of Judah, a time of fasting
before the LORD was proclaimed for all
the people in Jerusalem and those who
had come from the towns of Judah.
10From the room of Gemariah son of
Shaphan the secretary, which was in the
upper courtyard at the entrance of the
New Gate of the temple, Baruch read to
all the people at the LORD's temple the
words of Jeremiah from the scroll.
11When Micaiah son of Gemariah, the
son of Shaphan, heard all the words of
the LORD from the scroll, 12he went
down to the secretary's room in the
royal palace, where all the officials were
sitting: Elishama the secretary, Delaiah
son of Shemaiah, Elnathan son of Acbor,
Gemariah son of Shaphan, Zedekiah
son of Hananiah, and all the other officials. 13After Micaiah told them everything he had heard Baruch read to the
people from the scroll, 14all the officials
sent Jehudi son of Nethaniah, the son of
Shelemiah, the son of Cushi, to say to
Baruch, "Bring the scroll from which
you have read to the people and come."
So Baruch son of Neriah went to them

with the scroll in his hand. 15They said
to him, "Sit down, please, and read it
to us."

So Baruch read it to them. 16When
they heard all these words, they looked
at each other in fear and said to Baruch,
"We must report all these words to the
king." 17Then they asked Baruch, "Tell
us, how did you come to write all this?
Did Jeremiah dictate it?"

18"Yes," Baruch replied, "he dictated
all these words to me, and I wrote them
in ink on the scroll."

19Then the officials said to Baruch,
"You and Jeremiah, go and hide. Don't
let anyone know where you are."

20After they put the scroll in the room
of Elishama the secretary, they went to
the king in the courtyard and reported
everything to him. 21The king sent Jehudi to get the scroll, and Jehudi brought
it from the room of Elishama the secretary and read it to the king and all the
officials standing beside him. 22It was
the ninth month and the king was sitting in the winter apartment, with a fire
burning in the firepot in front of him.
23Whenever Jehudi had read three or
four columns of the scroll, the king cut
them off with a scribe's knife and threw
them into the firepot, until the entire
scroll was burned in the fire. 24The king
and all his attendants who heard all
these words showed no fear, nor did
they tear their clothes. 25Even though Elnathan, Delaiah and Gemariah urged
the king not to burn the scroll, he would
not listen to them. 26Instead, the king
commanded Jerahmeel, a son of the
king, Seraiah son of Azriel and Shelemiah son of Abdeel to arrest Baruch the
scribe and Jeremiah the prophet. But
the LORD had hidden them.

27After the king burned the scroll containing the words that Baruch had written at Jeremiah's dictation, the word of
the LORD came to Jeremiah: 28"Take another scroll and write on it all the words
that were on the first scroll, which Jehoiakim king of Judah burned up. 29Also
tell Jehoiakim king of Judah, 'This is
what the LORD says: You burned that
scroll and said, "Why did you write on
it that the king of Babylon would certainly come and destroy this land and
cut off both men and animals from it?"
30Therefore, this is what the LORD says
about Jehoiakim king of Judah: He will
have no one to sit on the throne of David; his body will be thrown out and exposed to the heat by day and the frost
by night. 31I will punish him and his children and his attendants for their wickedness; I will bring on them and those
living in Jerusalem and the people of Judah every disaster I pronounced against
them, because they have not listened.' "

32So Jeremiah took another scroll and
gave it to the scribe Baruch son of Neriah, and as Jeremiah dictated, Baruch
wrote on it all the words of the scroll
that Jehoiakim king of Judah had
burned in the fire. And many similar
words were added to them.

Jeremiah in Prison

37 Zedekiah son of Josiah
was made king of Judah by
Nebuchadnezzar king of Babylon; he
reigned in place of Jehoiachin[a] son of
Jehoiakim. 2Neither he nor his attendants nor the people of the land paid
any attention to the words the LORD
had spoken through Jeremiah the
prophet.

3King Zedekiah, however, sent Jehucal son of Shelemiah with the priest
Zephaniah son of Maaseiah to Jeremiah the prophet with this message:
"Please pray to the LORD our God
for us."

4Now Jeremiah was free to come and
go among the people, for he had not yet
been put in prison. 5Pharaoh's army had
marched out of Egypt, and when the
Babylonians[b] who were besieging Jerusalem heard the report about them, they
withdrew from Jerusalem.

6Then the word of the LORD came to
Jeremiah the prophet: 7"This is what the
LORD, the God of Israel, says: Tell the
king of Judah, who sent you to inquire
of me, 'Pharaoh's army, which has

[a]1 Hebrew *Coniah,* a variant of *Jehoiachin*
[b]5 Or *Chaldeans*; also in verses 8, 9, 13 and 14

marched out to support you, will go
back to its own land, to Egypt. [8]Then the
Babylonians will return and attack this
city; they will capture it and burn it
down.'
[9]"This is what the LORD says: Do not
deceive yourselves, thinking, 'The Babylonians will surely leave us.' They will
not! [10]Even if you were to defeat the entire Babylonian[a] army that is attacking
you and only wounded men were left
in their tents, they would come out and
burn this city down."
[11]After the Babylonian army had
withdrawn from Jerusalem because of
Pharaoh's army, [12]Jeremiah started to
leave the city to go to the territory of
Benjamin to get his share of the property among the people there. [13]But
when he reached the Benjamin Gate,
the captain of the guard, whose name
was Irijah son of Shelemiah, the son of
Hananiah, arrested him and said, "You
are deserting to the Babylonians!"
[14]"That's not true!" Jeremiah said. "I
am not deserting to the Babylonians."
But Irijah would not listen to him;
instead, he arrested Jeremiah and
brought him to the officials. [15]They were
angry with Jeremiah and had him beat-
en and imprisoned in the house of Jonathan the secretary, which they had
made into a prison.
[16]Jeremiah was put into a vaulted cell
in a dungeon, where he remained a
long time. [17]Then King Zedekiah sent
for him and had him brought to the
palace, where he asked him privately,
"Is there any word from the LORD?"
"Yes," Jeremiah replied, "you will be
handed over to the king of Babylon."
[18]Then Jeremiah said to King Zedekiah, "What crime have I committed
against you or your officials or this people, that you have put me in prison?
[19]Where are your prophets who prophesied to you, 'The king of Babylon will
not attack you or this land'? [20]But now,
my lord the king, please listen. Let me
bring my petition before you: Do not
send me back to the house of Jonathan
the secretary, or I will die there."
[21]King Zedekiah then gave orders for
Jeremiah to be placed in the courtyard
of the guard and given bread from the
street of the bakers each day until all the
bread in the city was gone. So Jeremiah
remained in the courtyard of the guard.

[a]*10* Or *Chaldean;* also in verse 11

SHARPEN THE FOCUS

Jehoiakim sat in his palace, warming his feet near a fire. Jeremiah's scribe, Baruch, read the prophet's message—the Word of the Lord—from a scroll. As he finished every few inches, the king took a knife and sliced off the scroll. He threw the scrap on the fire while he listened to the next few paragraphs.

Focus on the contrast between Jehoiakim's contempt for the Lord and His Word and Baruch's love and commitment to both. Baruch could stand in Jehoiakim's presence and proclaim God's Word for only one reason. The Lord had strengthened Baruch through that Word.

Like Zedekiah, we've all collapsed into cowardice at times or wilted in the heat of others' disapproval. Perhaps we've decided to be bold for Christ in our own strength. But self-focused determination like that leads only to a brash bluff. And those around us recognize it.

We need instead the courage that emboldened Baruch—the commitment to our Lord that shines with His love even as it declares His truth. Boldness like that won't always make us popular, but the Savior will work through such a witness to draw some of those around us to Himself. May He work it in us for His glory! ☼

WEEK 60 • SATURDAY

Jeremiah 38:1—40:16

GET THE BIG PICTURE

Did you ever go back to someone in authority to appeal a decision? Perhaps you hoped that *this* time the parent, the judge, the supervisor would have a change of heart. In chapter 38 we read King Zedekiah's third interview with Jeremiah. But God's Word and will had not changed. As you read, ask why Zedekiah went back and forth between wanting to hear God's Word but not wanting to obey it. If time is short, focus on Jeremiah 38:1–28.

Jeremiah Thrown Into a Cistern

38 Shephatiah son of Mattan, Gedaliah son of Pashhur, Jehucal[a] son of Shelemiah, and Pashhur son of Malkijah heard what Jeremiah was telling all the people when he said, 2"This is what the LORD says: 'Whoever stays in this city will die by the sword, famine or plague, but whoever goes over to the Babylonians[b] will live. He will escape with his life; he will live.' 3And this is what the LORD says: 'This city will certainly be handed over to the army of the king of Babylon, who will capture it.' "

4Then the officials said to the king, "This man should be put to death. He is discouraging the soldiers who are left in this city, as well as all the people, by the things he is saying to them. This man is not seeking the good of these people but their ruin."

5"He is in your hands," King Zedekiah answered. "The king can do nothing to oppose you."

6So they took Jeremiah and put him into the cistern of Malkijah, the king's son, which was in the courtyard of the guard. They lowered Jeremiah by ropes into the cistern; it had no water in it, only mud, and Jeremiah sank down into the mud.

7But Ebed-Melech, a Cushite,[c] an official[d] in the royal palace, heard that they had put Jeremiah into the cistern. While the king was sitting in the Benjamin Gate, 8Ebed-Melech went out of the palace and said to him, 9"My lord the king, these men have acted wickedly in all they have done to Jeremiah the prophet. They have thrown him into a cistern, where he will starve to death when there is no longer any bread in the city."

10Then the king commanded Ebed-Melech the Cushite, "Take thirty men from here with you and lift Jeremiah the prophet out of the cistern before he dies."

11So Ebed-Melech took the men with him and went to a room under the treasury in the palace. He took some old rags and worn-out clothes from there and let them down with ropes to Jeremiah in the cistern. 12Ebed-Melech the Cushite said to Jeremiah, "Put these old rags and worn-out clothes under your arms to pad the ropes." Jeremiah did so, 13and they pulled him up with the ropes and lifted him out of the cistern. And Jeremiah remained in the courtyard of the guard.

Zedekiah Questions Jeremiah Again

14Then King Zedekiah sent for Jeremiah the prophet and had him brought to the third entrance to the temple of the LORD. "I am going to ask you some-

[a]1 Hebrew *Jucal,* a variant of *Jehucal* [b]2 Or *Chaldeans*; also in verses 18, 19 and 23
[c]7 Probably from the upper Nile region [d]7 Or *a eunuch*

thing," the king said to Jeremiah. "Do
not hide anything from me."
[15]Jeremiah said to Zedekiah, "If I give
you an answer, will you not kill me?
Even if I did give you counsel, you
would not listen to me."
[16]But King Zedekiah swore this oath
secretly to Jeremiah: "As surely as the
LORD lives, who has given us breath, I
will neither kill you nor hand you over
to those who are seeking your life."
[17]Then Jeremiah said to Zedekiah,
"This is what the LORD God Almighty,
the God of Israel, says: 'If you surrender
to the officers of the king of Babylon,
your life will be spared and this city will
not be burned down; you and your family will live. [18]But if you will not surrender to the officers of the king of Babylon,
this city will be handed over to the Babylonians and they will burn it down;
you yourself will not escape from their
hands.' "
[19]King Zedekiah said to Jeremiah, "I
am afraid of the Jews who have gone
over to the Babylonians, for the Babylonians may hand me over to them and
they will mistreat me."
[20]"They will not hand you over," Jeremiah replied. "Obey the LORD by doing what I tell you. Then it will go well
with you, and your life will be spared.
[21]But if you refuse to surrender, this is
what the LORD has revealed to me: [22]All
the women left in the palace of the king
of Judah will be brought out to the officials of the king of Babylon. Those
women will say to you:

" 'They misled you and overcame
you—
those trusted friends of yours.
Your feet are sunk in the mud;
your friends have deserted you.'

[23]"All your wives and children will be
brought out to the Babylonians. You
yourself will not escape from their
hands but will be captured by the king
of Babylon; and this city will[a] be burned
down."
[24]Then Zedekiah said to Jeremiah,
"Do not let anyone know about this conversation, or you may die. [25]If the officials hear that I talked with you, and
they come to you and say, 'Tell us what
you said to the king and what the king
said to you; do not hide it from us or we
will kill you,' [26]then tell them, 'I was
pleading with the king not to send me
back to Jonathan's house to die there.' "
[27]All the officials did come to Jeremiah and question him, and he told them
everything the king had ordered him to
say. So they said no more to him, for no
one had heard his conversation with the
king.
[28]And Jeremiah remained in the
courtyard of the guard until the day Jerusalem was captured.

The Fall of Jerusalem

39 This is how Jerusalem was
taken: [1]In the ninth year of
Zedekiah king of Judah, in the tenth
month, Nebuchadnezzar king of Babylon marched against Jerusalem with
his whole army and laid siege to it. [2]And
on the ninth day of the fourth month of
Zedekiah's eleventh year, the city wall
was broken through. [3]Then all the officials of the king of Babylon came and
took seats in the Middle Gate: Nergal-
Sharezer of Samgar, Nebo-Sarsekim[b] a
chief officer, Nergal-Sharezer a high official and all the other officials of the
king of Babylon. [4]When Zedekiah king
of Judah and all the soldiers saw them,
they fled; they left the city at night by
way of the king's garden, through the
gate between the two walls, and headed
toward the Arabah.[c]
[5]But the Babylonian[d] army pursued
them and overtook Zedekiah in the
plains of Jericho. They captured him
and took him to Nebuchadnezzar king
of Babylon at Riblah in the land of Hamath, where he pronounced sentence
on him. [6]There at Riblah the king of
Babylon slaughtered the sons of Zedekiah before his eyes and also killed all
the nobles of Judah. [7]Then he put out
Zedekiah's eyes and bound him with

[a]23 Or *and you will cause this city to* [b]3 Or *Nergal-Sharezer, Samgar-Nebo, Sarsekim* [c]4 Or *the Jordan Valley* [d]5 Or *Chaldean*

bronze shackles to take him to Babylon. 8 The Babylonians[a] set fire to the royal palace and the houses of the people and broke down the walls of Jerusalem. 9 Nebuzaradan commander of the imperial guard carried into exile to Babylon the people who remained in the city, along with those who had gone over to him, and the rest of the people. 10 But Nebuzaradan the commander of the guard left behind in the land of Judah some of the poor people, who owned nothing; and at that time he gave them vineyards and fields.

11 Now Nebuchadnezzar king of Babylon had given these orders about Jeremiah through Nebuzaradan commander of the imperial guard: 12 "Take him and look after him; don't harm him but do for him whatever he asks." 13 So Nebuzaradan the commander of the guard, Nebushazban a chief officer, Nergal-Sharezer a high official and all the other officers of the king of Babylon 14 sent and had Jeremiah taken out of the courtyard of the guard. They turned him over to Gedaliah son of Ahikam, the son of Shaphan, to take him back to his home. So he remained among his own people.

15 While Jeremiah had been confined in the courtyard of the guard, the word of the LORD came to him: 16 "Go and tell Ebed-Melech the Cushite, 'This is what the LORD Almighty, the God of Israel, says: I am about to fulfill my words against this city through disaster, not prosperity. At that time they will be fulfilled before your eyes. 17 But I will rescue you on that day, declares the LORD; you will not be handed over to those you fear. 18 I will save you; you will not fall by the sword but will escape with your life, because you trust in me, declares the LORD.' "

Jeremiah Freed

40 The word came to Jeremiah from the LORD after Nebuzaradan commander of the imperial guard had released him at Ramah. He had found Jeremiah bound in chains among all the captives from Jerusalem and Judah who were being carried into exile to Babylon. 2 When the commander of the guard found Jeremiah, he said to him, "The LORD your God decreed this disaster for this place. 3 And now the LORD has brought it about; he has done just as he said he would. All this happened because you people sinned against the LORD and did not obey him. 4 But today I am freeing you from the chains on your wrists. Come with me to Babylon, if you like, and I will look after you; but if you do not want to, then don't come. Look, the whole country lies before you; go wherever you please." 5 However, before Jeremiah turned to go,[b] Nebuzaradan added, "Go back to Gedaliah son of Ahikam, the son of Shaphan, whom the king of Babylon has appointed over the towns of Judah, and live with him among the people, or go anywhere else you please."

Then the commander gave him provisions and a present and let him go. 6 So Jeremiah went to Gedaliah son of Ahikam at Mizpah and stayed with him among the people who were left behind in the land.

Gedaliah Assassinated

7 When all the army officers and their men who were still in the open country heard that the king of Babylon had appointed Gedaliah son of Ahikam as governor over the land and had put him in charge of the men, women and children who were the poorest in the land and who had not been carried into exile to Babylon, 8 they came to Gedaliah at Mizpah—Ishmael son of Nethaniah, Johanan and Jonathan the sons of Kareah, Seraiah son of Tanhumeth, the sons of Ephai the Netophathite, and Jaazaniah[c] the son of the Maacathite, and their men. 9 Gedaliah son of Ahikam, the son of Shaphan, took an oath to reassure them and their men. "Do not be afraid to serve the Babylonians,[d]" he said. "Set-

[a]8 Or *Chaldeans* [b]5 Or *Jeremiah answered*
[c]8 Hebrew *Jezaniah,* a variant of *Jaazaniah*
[d]9 Or *Chaldeans;* also in verse 10

tle down in the land and serve the king
of Babylon, and it will go well with you.
10I myself will stay at Mizpah to represent you before the Babylonians who
come to us, but you are to harvest the
wine, summer fruit and oil, and put
them in your storage jars, and live in the
towns you have taken over."
11When all the Jews in Moab, Ammon,
Edom and all the other countries heard
that the king of Babylon had left a
remnant in Judah and had appointed
Gedaliah son of Ahikam, the son of Shaphan, as governor over them, 12they all
came back to the land of Judah, to Gedaliah at Mizpah, from all the countries
where they had been scattered. And
they harvested an abundance of wine
and summer fruit.
13Johanan son of Kareah and all the
army officers still in the open country
came to Gedaliah at Mizpah 14and said
to him, "Don't you know that Baalis
king of the Ammonites has sent Ishmael son of Nethaniah to take your life?"
But Gedaliah son of Ahikam did not believe them.
15Then Johanan son of Kareah said privately to Gedaliah in Mizpah, "Let me
go and kill Ishmael son of Nethaniah,
and no one will know it. Why should he
take your life and cause all the Jews who
are gathered around you to be scattered
and the remnant of Judah to perish?"
16But Gedaliah son of Ahikam said to
Johanan son of Kareah, "Don't do such
a thing! What you are saying about Ishmael is not true."

SHARPEN THE FOCUS

A sailboat caught in a windstorm will blow back and forth across a lake for as long as the storm lasts. Unless, of course, it capsizes first. Zedekiah's fears concerning the Babylonians and his doubts about God's promises blew him back and forth across a sea of indecision.

Zedekiah was spiritually unstable. He wanted to be sophisticated and skeptical when he sat with his cabinet ministers (Jeremiah 38:4–5). But he knew—deep down—that his ancestor King David had been right to trust Yahweh. Zedekiah was also afraid (Jeremiah 38:19). So he saw Jeremiah in secret. After awhile, the king himself didn't know whether his public self or his private self was the true Zedekiah.

When the winds of fear and of wanting to fit in blow, how far off course do they take you? Are you the same person whether you're on your knees at the Lord's Table or sitting down with your family at the dinner table or drinking coffee with a business associate at a lunch table?

If you need more stability, more integrity, take heart. Your Lord came in Jesus Christ to take your guilt. And He comes to you now in His Word to work true integrity, true stability, in your heart. You need only ask.

WEEK 61 • MONDAY

Jeremiah 41:1—43:13

GET THE BIG PICTURE

Fear suffocates faith. You'll see that happen in today's reading. Nebuchadnezzar left the poorest and least educated people in Judah, but took the rest into exile in Babylon. Those who were left could think of only one thing: getting as far away from Babylon's armies as possible. If time is short, focus on Jeremiah 42:1–22.

41 In the seventh month Ishmael son of Nethaniah, the son of Elishama, who was of royal blood and had been one of the king's officers, came with ten men to Gedaliah son of Ahikam at Mizpah. While they were eating together there, 2Ishmael son of Nethaniah and the ten men who were with him got up and struck down Gedaliah son of Ahikam, the son of Shaphan, with the sword, killing the one whom the king of Babylon had appointed as governor over the land. 3Ishmael also killed all the Jews who were with Gedaliah at Mizpah, as well as the Babylonian[a] soldiers who were there.

4The day after Gedaliah's assassination, before anyone knew about it, 5eighty men who had shaved off their beards, torn their clothes and cut themselves came from Shechem, Shiloh and Samaria, bringing grain offerings and incense with them to the house of the LORD. 6Ishmael son of Nethaniah went out from Mizpah to meet them, weeping as he went. When he met them, he said, "Come to Gedaliah son of Ahikam." 7When they went into the city, Ishmael son of Nethaniah and the men who were with him slaughtered them and threw them into a cistern. 8But ten of them said to Ishmael, "Don't kill us! We have wheat and barley, oil and honey, hidden in a field." So he let them alone and did not kill them with the others. 9Now the cistern where he threw all the bodies of the men he had killed along with Gedaliah was the one King Asa had made as part of his defense against Baasha king of Israel. Ishmael son of Nethaniah filled it with the dead.

10Ishmael made captives of all the rest of the people who were in Mizpah—the king's daughters along with all the others who were left there, over whom Nebuzaradan commander of the imperial guard had appointed Gedaliah son of Ahikam. Ishmael son of Nethaniah took them captive and set out to cross over to the Ammonites.

11When Johanan son of Kareah and all the army officers who were with him heard about all the crimes Ishmael son of Nethaniah had committed, 12they took all their men and went to fight Ishmael son of Nethaniah. They caught up with him near the great pool in Gibeon. 13When all the people Ishmael had with him saw Johanan son of Kareah and the army officers who were with him, they were glad. 14All the people Ishmael had taken captive at Mizpah turned and went over to Johanan son of Kareah. 15But Ishmael son of Nethaniah and eight of his men escaped from Johanan and fled to the Ammonites.

Flight to Egypt

16Then Johanan son of Kareah and all the army officers who were with him led away all the survivors from Mizpah whom he had recovered from Ishmael son of Nethaniah after he had assassinated Gedaliah son of Ahikam: the soldiers, women, children and court officials he had brought from Gibeon. 17And they went on, stopping at Geruth Kimham near Bethlehem on their way to Egypt 18to escape the Babylonians.[b] They were afraid of them because Ishmael son of Nethaniah had killed Gedaliah son of Ahikam, whom the king of Babylon had appointed as governor over the land.

42 Then all the army officers, including Johanan son of Kareah and Jezaniah[c] son of Hoshaiah, and all the people from the least to the greatest approached 2Jeremiah the prophet and said to him, "Please hear our petition and pray to the LORD your God for this entire remnant. For as you now see, though we were once many, now only a few are left. 3Pray that the

[a]3 Or *Chaldean* [b]18 Or *Chaldeans* [c]1 Hebrew; Septuagint (see also 43:2) *Azariah*

LORD your God will tell us where we should go and what we should do."

4"I have heard you," replied Jeremiah the prophet. "I will certainly pray to the LORD your God as you have requested; I will tell you everything the LORD says and will keep nothing back from you."

5Then they said to Jeremiah, "May the LORD be a true and faithful witness against us if we do not act in accordance with everything the LORD your God sends you to tell us. 6Whether it is favorable or unfavorable, we will obey the LORD our God, to whom we are sending you, so that it will go well with us, for we will obey the LORD our God."

7Ten days later the word of the LORD came to Jeremiah. 8So he called together Johanan son of Kareah and all the army officers who were with him and all the people from the least to the greatest. 9He said to them, "This is what the LORD, the God of Israel, to whom you sent me to present your petition, says: 10'If you stay in this land, I will build you up and not tear you down; I will plant you and not uproot you, for I am grieved over the disaster I have inflicted on you. 11Do not be afraid of the king of Babylon, whom you now fear. Do not be afraid of him, declares the LORD, for I am with you and will save you and deliver you from his hands. 12I will show you compassion so that he will have compassion on you and restore you to your land.'

13"However, if you say, 'We will not stay in this land,' and so disobey the LORD your God, 14and if you say, 'No, we will go and live in Egypt, where we will not see war or hear the trumpet or be hungry for bread,' 15then hear the word of the LORD, O remnant of Judah. This is what the LORD Almighty, the God of Israel, says: 'If you are determined to go to Egypt and you do go to settle there, 16then the sword you fear will overtake you there, and the famine you dread will follow you into Egypt, and there you will die. 17Indeed, all who are determined to go to Egypt to settle there will die by the sword, famine and plague; not one of them will survive or escape the disaster I will bring on them.' 18This is what the LORD Almighty, the God of Israel, says: 'As my anger and wrath have been poured out on those who lived in Jerusalem, so will my wrath be poured out on you when you go to Egypt. You will be an object of cursing and horror, of condemnation and reproach; you will never see this place again.'

19"O remnant of Judah, the LORD has told you, 'Do not go to Egypt.' Be sure of this: I warn you today 20that you made a fatal mistake[a] when you sent me to the LORD your God and said, 'Pray to the LORD our God for us; tell us everything he says and we will do it.' 21I have told you today, but you still have not obeyed the LORD your God in all he sent me to tell you. 22So now, be sure of this: You will die by the sword, famine and plague in the place where you want to go to settle."

43 When Jeremiah finished telling the people all the words of the LORD their God—everything the LORD had sent him to tell them— 2Azariah son of Hoshaiah and Johanan son of Kareah and all the arrogant men said to Jeremiah, "You are lying! The LORD our God has not sent you to say, 'You must not go to Egypt to settle there.' 3But Baruch son of Neriah is inciting you against us to hand us over to the Babylonians,[b] so they may kill us or carry us into exile to Babylon."

4So Johanan son of Kareah and all the army officers and all the people disobeyed the LORD's command to stay in the land of Judah. 5Instead, Johanan son of Kareah and all the army officers led away all the remnant of Judah who had come back to live in the land of Judah from all the nations where they had been scattered. 6They also led away all the men, women and children and the king's daughters whom Nebuzaradan commander of the imperial guard had left with Gedaliah son of Ahikam, the son of Shaphan, and Jeremiah the prophet and Baruch son of Neriah. 7So they entered Egypt in disobedience to

[a]20 Or *you erred in your hearts* [b]3 Or *Chaldeans*

the LORD and went as far as Tahpanhes.
8In Tahpanhes the word of the LORD
came to Jeremiah: 9"While the Jews are
watching, take some large stones with
you and bury them in clay in the brick
pavement at the entrance to Pharaoh's
palace in Tahpanhes. 10Then say to them,
'This is what the LORD Almighty, the
God of Israel, says: I will send for my
servant Nebuchadnezzar king of Babylon, and I will set his throne over these
stones I have buried here; he will spread
his royal canopy above them. 11He will
come and attack Egypt, bringing death
to those destined for death, captivity to
those destined for captivity, and the
sword to those destined for the sword.
12He[a] will set fire to the temples of the
gods of Egypt; he will burn their temples and take their gods captive. As a
shepherd wraps his garment around
him, so will he wrap Egypt around himself and depart from there unscathed.
13There in the temple of the sun[b] in
Egypt he will demolish the sacred pillars
and will burn down the temples of the
gods of Egypt.' "

[a]12 Or *I* [b]13 Or *in Heliopolis*

SHARPEN THE FOCUS

Have you ever made a major purchase and then read a glowing review in a consumer magazine? It can make us feel great to learn that our new car or refrigerator gets someone's "seal of approval" for efficiency or durability or owner satisfaction.

The Jews left in the land with Jeremiah wanted a divine seal of approval. They had packed for Egypt. But they wanted the Lord to rubber-stamp their decision. He wasn't about to do that. He knew that Babylon would soon invade Egypt. His people could find safety only by staying in the land He had given to Abraham centuries before. True to form, the people refused to listen to Jeremiah.

Foolish pride led Azariah (Jeremiah 43:2) to denounce Jeremiah as a liar. Foolish pride can con us, too, into trying to get our Lord to rubber-stamp the decisions that we in ignorance or foolishness or stubbornness have already made—without Him.

Maybe you find yourself in that predicament right now. Maybe you've settled on a course of action that seems right to you. There's nothing wrong with asking the Lord's blessing. But ask with a heart made willing by His grace to be changed, if He sees fit to do that.

WEEK 61 • TUESDAY

Jeremiah 44:1—45:5

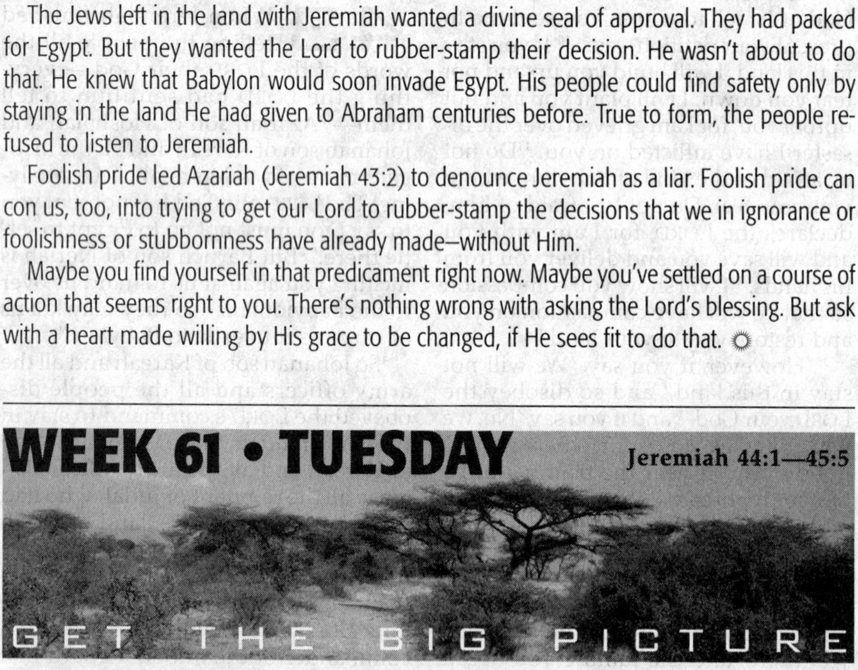

GET THE BIG PICTURE

For 40 or more chapters now the Lord has been telling His people their problem: they *know* but they do not *believe* His Word. Now the people respond in defiance, not repentance (Jeremiah 44:16–17). Note the contrast between this defiance and Baruch's attitude of humility and remorse in chapter 45. If time is short, focus on Jeremiah 44:1–23.

Disaster Because of Idolatry

44 This word came to Jeremiah concerning all the Jews living in Lower Egypt—in Migdol, Tahpanhes and Memphis[a]—and in Upper Egypt[b]: 2"This is what the LORD Almighty, the God of Israel, says: You saw the great disaster I brought on Jerusalem and on all the towns of Judah. Today they lie deserted and in ruins 3because of the evil they have done. They provoked me to anger by burning incense and by worshiping other gods that neither they nor you nor your fathers ever knew. 4Again and again I sent my servants the prophets, who said, 'Do not do this detestable thing that I hate!' 5But they did not listen or pay attention; they did not turn from their wickedness or stop burning incense to other gods. 6Therefore, my fierce anger was poured out; it raged against the towns of Judah and the streets of Jerusalem and made them the desolate ruins they are today.

7"Now this is what the LORD God Almighty, the God of Israel, says: Why bring such great disaster on yourselves by cutting off from Judah the men and women, the children and infants, and so leave yourselves without a remnant? 8Why provoke me to anger with what your hands have made, burning incense to other gods in Egypt, where you have come to live? You will destroy yourselves and make yourselves an object of cursing and reproach among all the nations on earth. 9Have you forgotten the wickedness committed by your fathers and by the kings and queens of Judah and the wickedness committed by you and your wives in the land of Judah and the streets of Jerusalem? 10To this day they have not humbled themselves or shown reverence, nor have they followed my law and the decrees I set before you and your fathers.

11"Therefore, this is what the LORD Almighty, the God of Israel, says: I am determined to bring disaster on you and to destroy all Judah. 12I will take away the remnant of Judah who were determined to go to Egypt to settle there. They will all perish in Egypt; they will fall by the sword or die from famine. From the least to the greatest, they will die by sword or famine. They will become an object of cursing and horror, of condemnation and reproach. 13I will punish those who live in Egypt with the sword, famine and plague, as I punished Jerusalem. 14None of the remnant of Judah who have gone to live in Egypt will escape or survive to return to the land of Judah, to which they long to return and live; none will return except a few fugitives."

15Then all the men who knew that their wives were burning incense to other gods, along with all the women who were present—a large assembly—and all the people living in Lower and Upper Egypt,[c] said to Jeremiah, 16"We will not listen to the message you have spoken to us in the name of the LORD! 17We will certainly do everything we said we would: We will burn incense to the Queen of Heaven and will pour out drink offerings to her just as we and our fathers, our kings and our officials did in the towns of Judah and in the streets of Jerusalem. At that time we had plenty of food and were well off and suffered no harm. 18But ever since we stopped burning incense to the Queen of Heaven and pouring out drink offerings to her, we have had nothing and have been perishing by sword and famine."

19The women added, "When we burned incense to the Queen of Heaven and poured out drink offerings to her, did not our husbands know that we were making cakes like her image and pouring out drink offerings to her?"

20Then Jeremiah said to all the people, both men and women, who were answering him, 21"Did not the LORD remember and think about the incense burned in the towns of Judah and the streets of Jerusalem by you and your fathers, your kings and your officials and the people of the land? 22When the LORD could no longer endure your

[a]1 Hebrew *Noph* [b]1 Hebrew *in Pathros*
[c]15 Hebrew *in Egypt and Pathros*

wicked actions and the detestable things you did, your land became an object of cursing and a desolate waste without inhabitants, as it is today. 23Because you have burned incense and have sinned against the LORD and have not obeyed him or followed his law or his decrees or his stipulations, this disaster has come upon you, as you now see."

24Then Jeremiah said to all the people, including the women, "Hear the word of the LORD, all you people of Judah in Egypt. 25This is what the LORD Almighty, the God of Israel, says: You and your wives have shown by your actions what you promised when you said, 'We will certainly carry out the vows we made to burn incense and pour out drink offerings to the Queen of Heaven.'

"Go ahead then, do what you promised! Keep your vows! 26But hear the word of the LORD, all Jews living in Egypt: 'I swear by my great name,' says the LORD, 'that no one from Judah living anywhere in Egypt will ever again invoke my name or swear, "As surely as the Sovereign LORD lives." 27For I am watching over them for harm, not for good; the Jews in Egypt will perish by sword and famine until they are all destroyed. 28Those who escape the sword and return to the land of Judah from Egypt will be very few. Then the whole remnant of Judah who came to live in Egypt will know whose word will stand—mine or theirs.

29" 'This will be the sign to you that I will punish you in this place,' declares the LORD, 'so that you will know that my threats of harm against you will surely stand.' 30This is what the LORD says: 'I am going to hand Pharaoh Hophra king of Egypt over to his enemies who seek his life, just as I handed Zedekiah king of Judah over to Nebuchadnezzar king of Babylon, the enemy who was seeking his life.' "

A Message to Baruch

45 This is what Jeremiah the prophet told Baruch son of Neriah in the fourth year of Jehoiakim son of Josiah king of Judah, after Baruch had written on a scroll the words Jeremiah was then dictating: 2"This is what the LORD, the God of Israel, says to you, Baruch: 3You said, 'Woe to me! The LORD has added sorrow to my pain; I am worn out with groaning and find no rest.' "

4The LORD said, "Say this to him: 'This is what the LORD says: I will overthrow what I have built and uproot what I have planted, throughout the land. 5Should you then seek great things for yourself? Seek them not. For I will bring disaster on all people, declares the LORD, but wherever you go I will let you escape with your life.' "

SHARPEN THE FOCUS

Throughout his book Jeremiah has referred to the fact that God watches over His Word. Remember the almond branch the prophet saw in the vision of Jeremiah 1:11–12? The Hebrew word for "almond tree" sounds a lot like the word for "watching." Just as the people of Judah would watch closely for almond blossoms as the first sign of spring, so the Lord would watch over His Word to fulfill it.

In Jeremiah 44:27 we read about the watchful eye the Lord keeps on His Word and on His people. This watchfulness is not a comfort, but a threat. Still, it was not the Lord's preferred way to deal with His people. He wanted to watch over them to bless them.

Does the Lord's watchful eye comfort or concern you? If you scoff at God's Word, then you have a right to be concerned. The Lord is watching, and He sees every word and act of defiance.

On the other hand, God has promised:

This is the one I esteem:
he who is humble and contrite in spirit,
and trembles at My Word. (Isaiah 66:2b)

Our Lord, who watched His own Son suffer and die for our sins on the cross, now watches over His repentant sons and daughters. He watches for ways to bless, to comfort, to encourage us.

WEEK 61 • WEDNESDAY

Jer. 46:1—49:39

Jeremiah's book closes with a series of prophecies against the nations that have oppressed Yahweh's chosen people. Despite the Lord's anger at His people's sins, He still has tremendous compassion on and concern for them. As you read, ask yourself whether Jeremiah's ministry to God's people was a success or failure. If time is short, focus on Jeremiah 46:14–28.

A Message About Egypt

46 This is the word of the LORD that came to Jeremiah the prophet concerning the nations:

2 Concerning Egypt:

This is the message against the army of Pharaoh Neco king of Egypt, which was defeated at Carchemish on the Euphrates River by Nebuchadnezzar king of Babylon in the fourth year of Jehoiakim son of Josiah king of Judah:

3 "Prepare your shields, both large
and small,
and march out for battle!
4 Harness the horses,
mount the steeds!
Take your positions
with helmets on!
Polish your spears,
put on your armor!
5 What do I see?
They are terrified,
they are retreating,
their warriors are defeated.
They flee in haste
without looking back,
and there is terror on every side,"
declares the LORD.
6 "The swift cannot flee
nor the strong escape.
In the north by the River Euphrates
they stumble and fall.
7 "Who is this that rises like the Nile,
like rivers of surging waters?
8 Egypt rises like the Nile,
like rivers of surging waters.
She says, 'I will rise and cover the
earth;
I will destroy cities and their
people.'
9 Charge, O horses!
Drive furiously, O charioteers!
March on, O warriors—
men of Cush[a] and Put who carry
shields,
men of Lydia who draw the bow.

[a]9 That is, the upper Nile region

[10]But that day belongs to the Lord, the
LORD Almighty—
a day of vengeance, for vengeance
on his foes.
The sword will devour till it is
satisfied,
till it has quenched its thirst with
blood.
For the Lord, the LORD Almighty,
will offer sacrifice
in the land of the north by the
River Euphrates.

[11]"Go up to Gilead and get balm,
O Virgin Daughter of Egypt.
But you multiply remedies in vain;
there is no healing for you.
[12]The nations will hear of your
shame;
your cries will fill the earth.
One warrior will stumble over
another;
both will fall down together."

[13]This is the message the LORD spoke
to Jeremiah the prophet about the coming of Nebuchadnezzar king of Babylon
to attack Egypt:

[14]"Announce this in Egypt, and
proclaim it in Migdol;
proclaim it also in Memphis[a] and
Tahpanhes:
'Take your positions and get ready,
for the sword devours those
around you.'
[15]Why will your warriors be laid low?
They cannot stand, for the LORD
will push them down.
[16]They will stumble repeatedly;
they will fall over each other.
They will say, 'Get up, let us go back
to our own people and our native
lands,
away from the sword of the
oppressor.'
[17]There they will exclaim,
'Pharaoh king of Egypt is only a
loud noise;
he has missed his opportunity.'
[18]"As surely as I live," declares the
King,
whose name is the LORD
Almighty,
"one will come who is like Tabor
among the mountains,
like Carmel by the sea.
[19]Pack your belongings for exile,
you who live in Egypt,
for Memphis will be laid waste
and lie in ruins without
inhabitant.

[20]"Egypt is a beautiful heifer,
but a gadfly is coming
against her from the north.
[21]The mercenaries in her ranks
are like fattened calves.
They too will turn and flee together,
they will not stand their ground,
for the day of disaster is coming
upon them,
the time for them to be punished.
[22]Egypt will hiss like a fleeing serpent
as the enemy advances in force;
they will come against her with axes,
like men who cut down trees.
[23]They will chop down her forest,"
declares the LORD,
"dense though it be.
They are more numerous than
locusts,
they cannot be counted.
[24]The Daughter of Egypt will be put to
shame,
handed over to the people of the
north."

[25]The LORD Almighty, the God of Israel, says: "I am about to bring punishment on Amon god of Thebes,[b] on
Pharaoh, on Egypt and her gods and
her kings, and on those who rely on
Pharaoh. [26]I will hand them over to
those who seek their lives, to Nebuchadnezzar king of Babylon and his officers. Later, however, Egypt will be
inhabited as in times past," declares the
LORD.

[27]"Do not fear, O Jacob my servant;
do not be dismayed, O Israel.
I will surely save you out of a distant
place,
your descendants from the land of
their exile.

[a]*14* Hebrew *Noph;* also in verse 19
[b]*25* Hebrew *No*

Jacob will again have peace and
security,
and no one will make him afraid.
28 Do not fear, O Jacob my servant,
for I am with you," declares the
LORD.
"Though I completely destroy all the
nations
among which I scatter you,
I will not completely destroy you.
I will discipline you but only with
justice;
I will not let you go entirely
unpunished."

A Message About the Philistines

47 This is the word of the LORD that came to Jeremiah the prophet concerning the Philistines before Pharaoh attacked Gaza:

2 This is what the LORD says:

"See how the waters are rising in the
north;
they will become an overflowing
torrent.
They will overflow the land and
everything in it,
the towns and those who live in
them.
The people will cry out;
all who dwell in the land will
wail
3 at the sound of the hoofs of
galloping steeds,
at the noise of enemy chariots
and the rumble of their wheels.
Fathers will not turn to help their
children;
their hands will hang limp.
4 For the day has come
to destroy all the Philistines
and to cut off all survivors
who could help Tyre and Sidon.
The LORD is about to destroy the
Philistines,
the remnant from the coasts of
Caphtor.[a]
5 Gaza will shave her head in
mourning;
Ashkelon will be silenced.
O remnant on the plain,
how long will you cut yourselves?
6 " 'Ah, sword of the LORD,' ⌞you cry,⌟
'how long till you rest?
Return to your scabbard;
cease and be still.'
7 But how can it rest
when the LORD has commanded
it,
when he has ordered it
to attack Ashkelon and the coast?"

A Message About Moab

48 Concerning Moab:

This is what the LORD Almighty, the God of Israel, says:

"Woe to Nebo, for it will be ruined.
Kiriathaim will be disgraced and
captured;
the stronghold[b] will be disgraced
and shattered.
2 Moab will be praised no more;
in Heshbon[c] men will plot her
downfall:
'Come, let us put an end to that
nation.'
You too, O Madmen,[d] will be
silenced;
the sword will pursue you.
3 Listen to the cries from Horonaim,
cries of great havoc and
destruction.
4 Moab will be broken;
her little ones will cry out.[e]
5 They go up the way to Luhith,
weeping bitterly as they go;
on the road down to Horonaim
anguished cries over the
destruction are heard.
6 Flee! Run for your lives;
become like a bush[f] in the desert.
7 Since you trust in your deeds and
riches,
you too will be taken captive,
and Chemosh will go into exile,
together with his priests and
officials.

[a]4 That is, Crete [b]1 Or / *Misgab* [c]2 The Hebrew for *Heshbon* sounds like the Hebrew for *plot.* [d]2 The name of the Moabite town Madmen sounds like the Hebrew for *be silenced.* [e]4 Hebrew; Septuagint / *proclaim it to Zoar* [f]6 Or *like Aroer*

[8]The destroyer will come against
every town,
and not a town will escape.
The valley will be ruined
and the plateau destroyed,
because the LORD has spoken.
[9]Put salt on Moab,
for she will be laid waste[a];
her towns will become desolate,
with no one to live in them.

[10]"A curse on him who is lax in doing
the LORD's work!
A curse on him who keeps his
sword from bloodshed!

[11]"Moab has been at rest from youth,
like wine left on its dregs,
not poured from one jar to
another—
she has not gone into exile.
So she tastes as she did,
and her aroma is unchanged.
[12]But days are coming,"
declares the LORD,
"when I will send men who pour
from jars,
and they will pour her out;
they will empty her jars
and smash her jugs.
[13]Then Moab will be ashamed of
Chemosh,
as the house of Israel was
ashamed
when they trusted in Bethel.

[14]"How can you say, 'We are warriors,
men valiant in battle'?
[15]Moab will be destroyed and her
towns invaded;
her finest young men will go
down in the slaughter,"
declares the King, whose name is
the LORD Almighty.
[16]"The fall of Moab is at hand;
her calamity will come quickly.
[17]Mourn for her, all who live around
her,
all who know her fame;
say, 'How broken is the mighty
scepter,
how broken the glorious staff!'

[18]"Come down from your glory
and sit on the parched ground,
O inhabitants of the Daughter of
Dibon,
for he who destroys Moab
will come up against you
and ruin your fortified cities.
[19]Stand by the road and watch,
you who live in Aroer.
Ask the man fleeing and the woman
escaping,
ask them, 'What has happened?'
[20]Moab is disgraced, for she is
shattered.
Wail and cry out!
Announce by the Arnon
that Moab is destroyed.
[21]Judgment has come to the
plateau—
to Holon, Jahzah and Mephaath,
[22]to Dibon, Nebo and Beth
Diblathaim,
[23]to Kiriathaim, Beth Gamul and
Beth Meon,
[24]to Kerioth and Bozrah—
to all the towns of Moab, far and
near.
[25]Moab's horn[b] is cut off;
her arm is broken,"
declares the LORD.

[26]"Make her drunk,
for she has defied the LORD.
Let Moab wallow in her vomit;
let her be an object of ridicule.
[27]Was not Israel the object of your
ridicule?
Was she caught among thieves,
that you shake your head in scorn
whenever you speak of her?
[28]Abandon your towns and dwell
among the rocks,
you who live in Moab.
Be like a dove that makes its nest
at the mouth of a cave.

[29]"We have heard of Moab's pride—
her overweening pride and
conceit,
her pride and arrogance
and the haughtiness of her heart.
[30]I know her insolence but it is futile,"
declares the LORD,

[a]9 Or *Give wings to Moab, / for she will fly away*
[b]25 *Horn* here symbolizes strength.

"and her boasts accomplish
nothing.
31 Therefore I wail over Moab,
for all Moab I cry out,
I moan for the men of Kir Hareseth.
32 I weep for you, as Jazer weeps,
O vines of Sibmah.
Your branches spread as far as the
sea;
they reached as far as the sea of
Jazer.
The destroyer has fallen
on your ripened fruit and grapes.
33 Joy and gladness are gone
from the orchards and fields of
Moab.
I have stopped the flow of wine
from the presses;
no one treads them with shouts of
joy.
Although there are shouts,
they are not shouts of joy.

34 "The sound of their cry rises
from Heshbon to Elealeh and
Jahaz,
from Zoar as far as Horonaim and
Eglath Shelishiyah,
for even the waters of Nimrim are
dried up.
35 In Moab I will put an end
to those who make offerings on
the high places
and burn incense to their gods,"
declares the LORD.
36 "So my heart laments for Moab like
a flute;
it laments like a flute for the men
of Kir Hareseth.
The wealth they acquired is gone.
37 Every head is shaved
and every beard cut off;
every hand is slashed
and every waist is covered with
sackcloth.
38 On all the roofs in Moab
and in the public squares
there is nothing but mourning,
for I have broken Moab
like a jar that no one wants,"
declares the LORD.
39 "How shattered she is! How they
wail!
How Moab turns her back in
shame!
Moab has become an object of
ridicule,
an object of horror to all those
around her."

40 This is what the LORD says:

"Look! An eagle is swooping down,
spreading its wings over Moab.
41 Kerioth[a] will be captured
and the strongholds taken.
In that day the hearts of Moab's
warriors
will be like the heart of a woman
in labor.
42 Moab will be destroyed as a nation
because she defied the LORD.
43 Terror and pit and snare await you,
O people of Moab,"
declares the LORD.
44 "Whoever flees from the terror
will fall into a pit,
whoever climbs out of the pit
will be caught in a snare;
for I will bring upon Moab
the year of her punishment,"
declares the LORD.

45 "In the shadow of Heshbon
the fugitives stand helpless,
for a fire has gone out from
Heshbon,
a blaze from the midst of Sihon;
it burns the foreheads of Moab,
the skulls of the noisy boasters.
46 Woe to you, O Moab!
The people of Chemosh are
destroyed;
your sons are taken into exile
and your daughters into captivity.

47 "Yet I will restore the fortunes of
Moab
in days to come,"
declares the LORD.

Here ends the judgment on Moab.

A Message About Ammon

49 Concerning the Ammonites:

[a]41 Or *The cities*

This is what the LORD says:

"Has Israel no sons?
Has she no heirs?
Why then has Molech[a] taken possession of Gad?
Why do his people live in its towns?
[2]But the days are coming,"
declares the LORD,
"when I will sound the battle cry
against Rabbah of the Ammonites;
it will become a mound of ruins,
and its surrounding villages will be set on fire.
Then Israel will drive out
those who drove her out,"
says the LORD.
[3]"Wail, O Heshbon, for Ai is destroyed!
Cry out, O inhabitants of Rabbah!
Put on sackcloth and mourn;
rush here and there inside the walls,
for Molech will go into exile,
together with his priests and officials.
[4]Why do you boast of your valleys,
boast of your valleys so fruitful?
O unfaithful daughter,
you trust in your riches and say,
'Who will attack me?'
[5]I will bring terror on you
from all those around you,"
declares the Lord,
the LORD Almighty.
"Every one of you will be driven away,
and no one will gather the fugitives.

[6]"Yet afterward, I will restore the fortunes of the Ammonites,"
declares the LORD.

A Message About Edom

[7]Concerning Edom:

This is what the LORD Almighty says:

"Is there no longer wisdom in Teman?
Has counsel perished from the prudent?
Has their wisdom decayed?
[8]Turn and flee, hide in deep caves,
you who live in Dedan,
for I will bring disaster on Esau
at the time I punish him.
[9]If grape pickers came to you,
would they not leave a few grapes?
If thieves came during the night,
would they not steal only as much as they wanted?
[10]But I will strip Esau bare;
I will uncover his hiding places,
so that he cannot conceal himself.
His children, relatives and neighbors will perish,
and he will be no more.
[11]Leave your orphans; I will protect their lives.
Your widows too can trust in me."

[12]This is what the LORD says: "If those who do not deserve to drink the cup must drink it, why should you go unpunished? You will not go unpunished, but must drink it. [13]I swear by myself," declares the LORD, "that Bozrah will become a ruin and an object of horror, of reproach and of cursing; and all its towns will be in ruins forever."

[14]I have heard a message from the LORD:
An envoy was sent to the nations to say,
"Assemble yourselves to attack it!
Rise up for battle!"
[15]"Now I will make you small among the nations,
despised among men.
[16]The terror you inspire
and the pride of your heart have deceived you,
you who live in the clefts of the rocks,
who occupy the heights of the hill.
Though you build your nest as high as the eagle's,
from there I will bring you down,"
declares the LORD.
[17]"Edom will become an object of horror;

[a]1 Or *their king*; Hebrew *malcam*; also in verse 3

all who pass by will be appalled
and will scoff
because of all its wounds.
18 As Sodom and Gomorrah were
overthrown,
along with their neighboring
towns,"
says the LORD,
"so no one will live there;
no man will dwell in it.

19 "Like a lion coming up from
Jordan's thickets
to a rich pastureland,
I will chase Edom from its land in an
instant.
Who is the chosen one I will
appoint for this?
Who is like me and who can
challenge me?
And what shepherd can stand
against me?"
20 Therefore, hear what the LORD has
planned against Edom,
what he has purposed against
those who live in Teman:
The young of the flock will be
dragged away;
he will completely destroy their
pasture because of them.
21 At the sound of their fall the earth
will tremble;
their cry will resound to the Red
Sea.[a]
22 Look! An eagle will soar and swoop
down,
spreading its wings over Bozrah.
In that day the hearts of Edom's
warriors
will be like the heart of a woman
in labor.

A Message About Damascus

23 Concerning Damascus:

"Hamath and Arpad are dismayed,
for they have heard bad news.
They are disheartened,
troubled like[b] the restless sea.
24 Damascus has become feeble,
she has turned to flee
and panic has gripped her;
anguish and pain have seized her,
pain like that of a woman in labor.
25 Why has the city of renown not
been abandoned,
the town in which I delight?
26 Surely, her young men will fall in
the streets;
all her soldiers will be silenced in
that day,"
declares the LORD
Almighty.
27 "I will set fire to the walls of
Damascus;
it will consume the fortresses of
Ben-Hadad."

A Message About Kedar and Hazor

28 Concerning Kedar and the kingdoms of Hazor, which Nebuchadnezzar king of Babylon attacked:

This is what the LORD says:

"Arise, and attack Kedar
and destroy the people of the East.
29 Their tents and their flocks will be
taken;
their shelters will be carried off
with all their goods and camels.
Men will shout to them,
'Terror on every side!'

30 "Flee quickly away!
Stay in deep caves, you who live
in Hazor,"
declares the LORD.
"Nebuchadnezzar king of Babylon
has plotted against you;
he has devised a plan against you.

31 "Arise and attack a nation at ease,
which lives in confidence,"
declares the LORD,
"a nation that has neither gates nor
bars;
its people live alone.
32 Their camels will become plunder,
and their large herds will be booty.
I will scatter to the winds those who
are in distant places[c]
and will bring disaster on them
from every side,"
declares the LORD.

[a]21 Hebrew *Yam Suph;* that is, Sea of Reeds
[b]23 Hebrew *on* or *by* [c]32 Or *who clip the hair by their foreheads*

[33] "Hazor will become a haunt of
jackals,
a desolate place forever.
No one will live there;
no man will dwell in it."

A Message About Elam

[34] This is the word of the LORD that came to Jeremiah the prophet concerning Elam, early in the reign of Zedekiah king of Judah:

[35] This is what the LORD Almighty says:

"See, I will break the bow of Elam,
the mainstay of their might.
[36] I will bring against Elam the four
winds
from the four quarters of the
heavens;
I will scatter them to the four
winds,
and there will not be a nation
where Elam's exiles do not go.
[37] I will shatter Elam before their foes,
before those who seek their lives;
I will bring disaster upon them,
even my fierce anger,"
declares the LORD.
"I will pursue them with the sword
until I have made an end of them.
[38] I will set my throne in Elam
and destroy her king and
officials,"
declares the LORD.

[39] "Yet I will restore the fortunes of
Elam
in days to come,"
declares the LORD.

SHARPEN THE FOCUS

In English, a "jeremiad" is a consistent message of doom. Those who speak jeremiads today are no more popular than the prophet from whose name we've derived the word.

Our Lord doesn't measure success by checking the latest poll. Jeremiah's preaching turned many heads, but few hearts. People heard and understood his message. They just didn't care to live it. They—like many people today—had invented their own religion. It suited them to worship "the Queen of Heaven" (Jeremiah 44:17) rather than the true God. Jeremiah complained about their hard-headedness. He even threatened to resign at times (Jeremiah 12:1–4; 20:9).

God in grace counted Jeremiah faithful. The Lord held His prophets responsible to speak His Word. Then He Himself assumed responsibility for the results.

As we witness in Christ's name, we too can count on Him to bring about the results. Still, we would like to see that loved one come to faith—now. We would like our friend or neighbor to enjoy the peace of Christ—today! But God is the world's Savior. We're not.

If you find your service for Jesus growing heavy, take a moment to read Matthew 11:28–30. Ask yourself, "Whose load am I trying to pull?"

WEEK 61 • THURSDAY

Jeremiah 50:1—51:64

GET THE BIG PICTURE

Today's two chapters detail a prophecy against Babylon. Jeremiah evidently sent it along with one of King Zedekiah's officers at a time when Zedekiah paid a state visit to Babylon before that nation invaded Judah. Seraiah was to read and then destroy the scroll. As you read, note the names Jeremiah uses for the Lord and the comfort they provide. If time is short, focus on Jeremiah 50:1–20.

A Message About Babylon

50 This is the word the LORD spoke through Jeremiah the prophet concerning Babylon and the land of the Babylonians[a]:

2 "Announce and proclaim among the nations,
lift up a banner and proclaim it;
keep nothing back, but say,
'Babylon will be captured;
Bel will be put to shame,
Marduk filled with terror.
Her images will be put to shame
and her idols filled with terror.'
3 A nation from the north will attack her
and lay waste her land.
No one will live in it;
both men and animals will flee away.

4 "In those days, at that time,"
declares the LORD,
"the people of Israel and the people of Judah together
will go in tears to seek the LORD their God.
5 They will ask the way to Zion
and turn their faces toward it.
They will come and bind themselves to the LORD
in an everlasting covenant
that will not be forgotten.

6 "My people have been lost sheep;
their shepherds have led them astray
and caused them to roam on the mountains.
They wandered over mountain and hill
and forgot their own resting place.
7 Whoever found them devoured them;
their enemies said, 'We are not guilty,
for they sinned against the LORD, their true pasture,
the LORD, the hope of their fathers.'

8 "Flee out of Babylon;
leave the land of the Babylonians,
and be like the goats that lead the flock.
9 For I will stir up and bring against Babylon
an alliance of great nations from the land of the north.
They will take up their positions against her,
and from the north she will be captured.
Their arrows will be like skilled warriors
who do not return empty-handed.
10 So Babylonia[b] will be plundered;
all who plunder her will have their fill,"
declares the LORD.

[a]1 Or *Chaldeans*; also in verses 8, 25, 35 and 45
[b]10 Or *Chaldea*

[11]"Because you rejoice and are glad,
you who pillage my inheritance,
because you frolic like a heifer
threshing grain
and neigh like stallions,
[12]your mother will be greatly
ashamed;
she who gave you birth will be
disgraced.
She will be the least of the nations—
a wilderness, a dry land, a desert.
[13]Because of the LORD's anger she will
not be inhabited
but will be completely desolate.
All who pass Babylon will be
horrified and scoff
because of all her wounds.

[14]"Take up your positions around
Babylon,
all you who draw the bow.
Shoot at her! Spare no arrows,
for she has sinned against the
LORD.
[15]Shout against her on every side!
She surrenders, her towers fall,
her walls are torn down.
Since this is the vengeance of the
LORD,
take vengeance on her;
do to her as she has done to
others.
[16]Cut off from Babylon the sower,
and the reaper with his sickle at
harvest.
Because of the sword of the
oppressor
let everyone return to his own
people,
let everyone flee to his own land.

[17]"Israel is a scattered flock
that lions have chased away.
The first to devour him
was the king of Assyria;
the last to crush his bones
was Nebuchadnezzar king of
Babylon."

[18]Therefore this is what the LORD Almighty, the God of Israel, says:

"I will punish the king of Babylon
and his land
as I punished the king of Assyria.
[19]But I will bring Israel back to his
own pasture
and he will graze on Carmel and
Bashan;
his appetite will be satisfied
on the hills of Ephraim and
Gilead.
[20]In those days, at that time,"
declares the LORD,
"search will be made for Israel's
guilt,
but there will be none,
and for the sins of Judah,
but none will be found,
for I will forgive the remnant I
spare.

[21]"Attack the land of Merathaim
and those who live in Pekod.
Pursue, kill and completely destroy[a]
them,"
declares the LORD.
"Do everything I have
commanded you.
[22]The noise of battle is in the land,
the noise of great destruction!
[23]How broken and shattered
is the hammer of the whole earth!
How desolate is Babylon
among the nations!
[24]I set a trap for you, O Babylon,
and you were caught before you
knew it;
you were found and captured
because you opposed the LORD.
[25]The LORD has opened his arsenal
and brought out the weapons of
his wrath,
for the Sovereign LORD Almighty
has work to do
in the land of the Babylonians.
[26]Come against her from afar.
Break open her granaries;
pile her up like heaps of grain.
Completely destroy her
and leave her no remnant.
[27]Kill all her young bulls;
let them go down to the slaughter!
Woe to them! For their day has
come,

[a]*21* The Hebrew term refers to the irrevocable giving over of things or persons to the LORD, often by totally destroying them; also in verse 26.

the time for them to be punished.
28 Listen to the fugitives and refugees
from Babylon
declaring in Zion
how the LORD our God has taken
vengeance,
vengeance for his temple.

29 "Summon archers against Babylon,
all those who draw the bow.
Encamp all around her;
let no one escape.
Repay her for her deeds;
do to her as she has done.
For she has defied the LORD,
the Holy One of Israel.
30 Therefore, her young men will fall in
the streets;
all her soldiers will be silenced in
that day,"
declares the LORD.
31 "See, I am against you, O arrogant
one,"
declares the Lord, the LORD
Almighty,
"for your day has come,
the time for you to be punished.
32 The arrogant one will stumble and
fall
and no one will help her up;
I will kindle a fire in her towns
that will consume all who are
around her."

33 This is what the LORD Almighty says:

"The people of Israel are oppressed,
and the people of Judah as well.
All their captors hold them fast,
refusing to let them go.
34 Yet their Redeemer is strong;
the LORD Almighty is his name.
He will vigorously defend their
cause
so that he may bring rest to their
land,
but unrest to those who live in
Babylon.

35 "A sword against the Babylonians!"
declares the LORD—
"against those who live in Babylon
and against her officials and wise
men!
36 A sword against her false prophets!
They will become fools.
A sword against her warriors!
They will be filled with terror.
37 A sword against her horses and
chariots
and all the foreigners in her
ranks!
They will become women.
A sword against her treasures!
They will be plundered.
38 A drought on[a] her waters!
They will dry up.
For it is a land of idols,
idols that will go mad with terror.

39 "So desert creatures and hyenas will
live there,
and there the owl will dwell.
It will never again be inhabited
or lived in from generation to
generation.
40 As God overthrew Sodom and
Gomorrah
along with their neighboring
towns,"
declares the LORD,
"so no one will live there;
no man will dwell in it.

41 "Look! An army is coming from the
north;
a great nation and many kings
are being stirred up from the ends
of the earth.
42 They are armed with bows and
spears;
they are cruel and without mercy.
They sound like the roaring sea
as they ride on their horses;
they come like men in battle
formation
to attack you, O Daughter of
Babylon.
43 The king of Babylon has heard
reports about them,
and his hands hang limp.
Anguish has gripped him,
pain like that of a woman in labor.
44 Like a lion coming up from Jordan's
thickets
to a rich pastureland,

[a]38 Or *A sword against*

I will chase Babylon from its land in
an instant.
Who is the chosen one I will
appoint for this?
Who is like me and who can
challenge me?
And what shepherd can stand
against me?"
45 Therefore, hear what the LORD has
planned against Babylon,
what he has purposed against the
land of the Babylonians:
The young of the flock will be
dragged away;
he will completely destroy their
pasture because of them.
46 At the sound of Babylon's capture
the earth will tremble;
its cry will resound among the
nations.

51

This is what the LORD says:
"See, I will stir up the spirit of a
destroyer
against Babylon and the people of
Leb Kamai.[a]
2 I will send foreigners to Babylon
to winnow her and to devastate
her land;
they will oppose her on every side
in the day of her disaster.
3 Let not the archer string his bow,
nor let him put on his armor.
Do not spare her young men;
completely destroy[b] her army.
4 They will fall down slain in
Babylon,[c]
fatally wounded in her streets.
5 For Israel and Judah have not been
forsaken
by their God, the LORD Almighty,
though their land[d] is full of guilt
before the Holy One of Israel.

6 "Flee from Babylon!
Run for your lives!
Do not be destroyed because of
her sins.
It is time for the LORD's vengeance;
he will pay her what she deserves.
7 Babylon was a gold cup in the
LORD's hand;
she made the whole earth drunk.
The nations drank her wine;
therefore they have now gone
mad.
8 Babylon will suddenly fall and be
broken.
Wail over her!
Get balm for her pain;
perhaps she can be healed.

9 " 'We would have healed Babylon,
but she cannot be healed;
let us leave her and each go to his
own land,
for her judgment reaches to the
skies,
it rises as high as the clouds.'

10 " 'The LORD has vindicated us;
come, let us tell in Zion
what the LORD our God has done.'

11 "Sharpen the arrows,
take up the shields!
The LORD has stirred up the kings of
the Medes,
because his purpose is to destroy
Babylon.
The LORD will take vengeance,
vengeance for his temple.
12 Lift up a banner against the walls of
Babylon!
Reinforce the guard,
station the watchmen,
prepare an ambush!
The LORD will carry out his purpose,
his decree against the people of
Babylon.
13 You who live by many waters
and are rich in treasures,
your end has come,
the time for you to be cut off.
14 The LORD Almighty has sworn by
himself:
I will surely fill you with men, as
with a swarm of locusts,
and they will shout in triumph
over you.

[a]1 *Leb Kamai* is a cryptogram for Chaldea, that is, Babylonia. [b]3 The Hebrew term refers to the irrevocable giving over of things or persons to the LORD, often by totally destroying them. [c]4 Or *Chaldea* [d]5 Or / *and the land* ˌ*of the Babylonians*ˌ

[15]"He made the earth by his power;
he founded the world by his wisdom
and stretched out the heavens by his understanding.
[16]When he thunders, the waters in the heavens roar;
he makes clouds rise from the ends of the earth.
He sends lightning with the rain
and brings out the wind from his storehouses.

[17]"Every man is senseless and without knowledge;
every goldsmith is shamed by his idols.
His images are a fraud;
they have no breath in them.
[18]They are worthless, the objects of mockery;
when their judgment comes, they will perish.
[19]He who is the Portion of Jacob is not like these,
for he is the Maker of all things,
including the tribe of his inheritance—
the LORD Almighty is his name.

[20]"You are my war club,
my weapon for battle—
with you I shatter nations,
with you I destroy kingdoms,
[21]with you I shatter horse and rider,
with you I shatter chariot and driver,
[22]with you I shatter man and woman,
with you I shatter old man and youth,
with you I shatter young man and maiden,
[23]with you I shatter shepherd and flock,
with you I shatter farmer and oxen,
with you I shatter governors and officials.

[24]"Before your eyes I will repay Babylon and all who live in Babylonia[a] for all the wrong they have done in Zion," declares the LORD.

[25]"I am against you, O destroying mountain,
you who destroy the whole earth,"
declares the LORD.
"I will stretch out my hand against you,
roll you off the cliffs,
and make you a burned-out mountain.
[26]No rock will be taken from you for a cornerstone,
nor any stone for a foundation,
for you will be desolate forever,"
declares the LORD.

[27]"Lift up a banner in the land!
Blow the trumpet among the nations!
Prepare the nations for battle against her;
summon against her these kingdoms:
Ararat, Minni and Ashkenaz.
Appoint a commander against her;
send up horses like a swarm of locusts.
[28]Prepare the nations for battle against her—
the kings of the Medes,
their governors and all their officials,
and all the countries they rule.
[29]The land trembles and writhes,
for the LORD's purposes against Babylon stand—
to lay waste the land of Babylon
so that no one will live there.
[30]Babylon's warriors have stopped fighting;
they remain in their strongholds.
Their strength is exhausted;
they have become like women.
Her dwellings are set on fire;
the bars of her gates are broken.
[31]One courier follows another
and messenger follows messenger
to announce to the king of Babylon
that his entire city is captured,
[32]the river crossings seized,
the marshes set on fire,
and the soldiers terrified."

[33]This is what the LORD Almighty, the God of Israel, says:

[a]24 Or *Chaldea;* also in verse 35

"The Daughter of Babylon is like a
threshing floor
at the time it is trampled;
the time to harvest her will soon
come."

34 "Nebuchadnezzar king of Babylon
has devoured us,
he has thrown us into confusion,
he has made us an empty jar.
Like a serpent he has swallowed us
and filled his stomach with our
delicacies,
and then has spewed us out.
35 May the violence done to our flesh[a]
be upon Babylon,"
say the inhabitants of Zion.
"May our blood be on those who
live in Babylonia,"
says Jerusalem.

36 Therefore, this is what the LORD says:

"See, I will defend your cause
and avenge you;
I will dry up her sea
and make her springs dry.
37 Babylon will be a heap of ruins,
a haunt of jackals,
an object of horror and scorn,
a place where no one lives.
38 Her people all roar like young lions,
they growl like lion cubs.
39 But while they are aroused,
I will set out a feast for them
and make them drunk,
so that they shout with laughter—
then sleep forever and not
awake,"
declares the LORD.
40 "I will bring them down
like lambs to the slaughter,
like rams and goats.

41 "How Sheshach[b] will be captured,
the boast of the whole earth
seized!
What a horror Babylon will be
among the nations!
42 The sea will rise over Babylon;
its roaring waves will cover her.
43 Her towns will be desolate,
a dry and desert land,
a land where no one lives,
through which no man travels.
44 I will punish Bel in Babylon
and make him spew out what he
has swallowed.
The nations will no longer stream to
him.
And the wall of Babylon will fall.

45 "Come out of her, my people!
Run for your lives!
Run from the fierce anger of the
LORD.
46 Do not lose heart or be afraid
when rumors are heard in the
land;
one rumor comes this year, another
the next,
rumors of violence in the land
and of ruler against ruler.
47 For the time will surely come
when I will punish the idols of
Babylon;
her whole land will be disgraced
and her slain will all lie fallen
within her.
48 Then heaven and earth and all that
is in them
will shout for joy over Babylon,
for out of the north
destroyers will attack her,"
declares the LORD.
49 "Babylon must fall because of Israel's
slain,
just as the slain in all the earth
have fallen because of Babylon.
50 You who have escaped the sword,
leave and do not linger!
Remember the LORD in a distant
land,
and think on Jerusalem."

51 "We are disgraced,
for we have been insulted
and shame covers our faces,
because foreigners have entered
the holy places of the LORD's
house."

52 "But days are coming," declares the
LORD,

[a]35 Or *done to us and to our children* [b]41 *Sheshach* is a cryptogram for Babylon.

"when I will punish her idols,
and throughout her land
the wounded will groan.
53 Even if Babylon reaches the sky
and fortifies her lofty stronghold,
I will send destroyers against her,"
declares the LORD.

54 "The sound of a cry comes from
Babylon,
the sound of great destruction
from the land of the
Babylonians.[a]
55 The LORD will destroy Babylon;
he will silence her noisy din.
Waves ⌞of enemies⌟ will rage like
great waters;
the roar of their voices will
resound.
56 A destroyer will come against
Babylon;
her warriors will be captured,
and their bows will be broken.
For the LORD is a God of retribution;
he will repay in full.
57 I will make her officials and wise
men drunk,
her governors, officers and
warriors as well;
they will sleep forever and not
awake,"
declares the King, whose name is
the LORD Almighty.

58 This is what the LORD Almighty
says:

"Babylon's thick wall will be leveled
and her high gates set on fire;
the peoples exhaust themselves for
nothing,
the nations' labor is only fuel for
the flames."

59 This is the message Jeremiah gave to
the staff officer Seraiah son of Neriah,
the son of Mahseiah, when he went to
Babylon with Zedekiah king of Judah in
the fourth year of his reign. 60 Jeremiah
had written on a scroll about all the disasters that would come upon Babylon—all that had been recorded
concerning Babylon. 61 He said to Seraiah, "When you get to Babylon, see that
you read all these words aloud. 62 Then
say, 'O LORD, you have said you will destroy this place, so that neither man nor
animal will live in it; it will be desolate
forever.' 63 When you finish reading this
scroll, tie a stone to it and throw it into
the Euphrates. 64 Then say, 'So will Babylon sink to rise no more because of the
disaster I will bring upon her. And her
people will fall.' "

The words of Jeremiah end here.

[a]54 Or *Chaldeans*

SHARPEN THE FOCUS

Jesus said, "Blessed are those who mourn, for they will be comforted" (Matthew 5:4). Our Lord's words speak of a deep grief over sin. Jeremiah paints a similar picture of God's repentant children returning to Him in Jeremiah 50:4–5.

We grieve to different degrees the loss of a job, an opportunity, or a loved one. But how can grief be connected with repentance? Why would one mourn over sin?

God wanted the people of Judah to be like Him, to display His glory so that they could enjoy life in His family and so that others would see His love and come into the family of faith. His purpose for us is much the same.

Unfortunately, our sins rob us of the peace and joy God wants to give. By our wrong words, attitudes, and actions we lose many opportunities to witness for Christ to those who need His saving love. These are losses that can and should produce major grief.

We can grieve these losses because we've heard Jesus' gracious word of peace, of blessing to those who return to the Lord in true repentance. He wants to comfort us, to draw us close to Himself, to assure us that nothing—not even our sin—can separate us from His love. His covenant with us "will not be forgotten" (Jeremiah 50:5).

Most scholars believe chapter 52 was added after Jeremiah's death. Even so, it is still God's inspired Word to us. It's hard to exaggerate the importance of Jerusalem's fall in salvation history. As you read, imagine sitting inside Jerusalem's walls, hungry and fearful, as Nebuchadnezzar knocks on your city's gates. If time is short, focus on Jeremiah 52:1–16.

The Fall of Jerusalem

52 Zedekiah was twenty-one
years old when he became
king, and he reigned in Jerusalem
eleven years. His mother's name was
Hamutal daughter of Jeremiah; she was
from Libnah. 2He did evil in the eyes of
the LORD, just as Jehoiakim had done.
3It was because of the LORD's anger that
all this happened to Jerusalem and Judah, and in the end he thrust them from
his presence.

Now Zedekiah rebelled against the
king of Babylon.

4So in the ninth year of Zedekiah's
reign, on the tenth day of the tenth
month, Nebuchadnezzar king of Babylon marched against Jerusalem with
his whole army. They camped outside
the city and built siege works all around
it. 5The city was kept under siege until
the eleventh year of King Zedekiah.

6By the ninth day of the fourth month
the famine in the city had become so
severe that there was no food for the
people to eat. 7Then the city wall was
broken through, and the whole army
fled. They left the city at night through
the gate between the two walls near the
king's garden, though the Babylonians[a]
were surrounding the city. They fled toward the Arabah,[b] 8but the Babylonian[c]
army pursued King Zedekiah and overtook him in the plains of Jericho. All his
soldiers were separated from him and
scattered, 9and he was captured.

He was taken to the king of Babylon
at Riblah in the land of Hamath, where
he pronounced sentence on him.
10There at Riblah the king of Babylon
slaughtered the sons of Zedekiah before
his eyes; he also killed all the officials of
Judah. 11Then he put out Zedekiah's
eyes, bound him with bronze shackles
and took him to Babylon, where he put
him in prison till the day of his death.

12On the tenth day of the fifth month,
in the nineteenth year of Nebuchadnezzar king of Babylon, Nebuzaradan commander of the imperial guard, who
served the king of Babylon, came to Jerusalem. 13He set fire to the temple of
the LORD, the royal palace and all the
houses of Jerusalem. Every important
building he burned down. 14The whole
Babylonian army under the commander of the imperial guard broke
down all the walls around Jerusalem.
15Nebuzaradan the commander of the
guard carried into exile some of the
poorest people and those who remained in the city, along with the rest
of the craftsmen[d] and those who had

[a]7 Or *Chaldeans*; also in verse 17 [b]7 Or *the Jordan Valley* [c]8 Or *Chaldean*; also in verse 14
[d]15 Or *populace*

gone over to the king of Babylon. [16]But
Nebuzaradan left behind the rest of the
poorest people of the land to work the
vineyards and fields.
[17]The Babylonians broke up the
bronze pillars, the movable stands and
the bronze Sea that were at the temple
of the LORD and they carried all the
bronze to Babylon. [18]They also took
away the pots, shovels, wick trimmers,
sprinkling bowls, dishes and all the
bronze articles used in the temple service. [19]The commander of the imperial
guard took away the basins, censers,
sprinkling bowls, pots, lampstands,
dishes and bowls used for drink offerings—all that were made of pure gold
or silver.
[20]The bronze from the two pillars, the
Sea and the twelve bronze bulls under
it, and the movable stands, which King
Solomon had made for the temple of the
LORD, was more than could be weighed.
[21]Each of the pillars was eighteen cubits
high and twelve cubits in circumference[a]; each was four fingers thick, and
hollow. [22]The bronze capital on top of
the one pillar was five cubits[b] high and
was decorated with a network and
pomegranates of bronze all around. The
other pillar, with its pomegranates, was
similar. [23]There were ninety-six pomegranates on the sides; the total number
of pomegranates above the surrounding network was a hundred.
[24]The commander of the guard took
as prisoners Seraiah the chief priest,
Zephaniah the priest next in rank and
the three doorkeepers. [25]Of those still in
the city, he took the officer in charge of
the fighting men, and seven royal advisers. He also took the secretary who was
chief officer in charge of conscripting
the people of the land and sixty of his
men who were found in the city. [26]Neb-
uzaradan the commander took them all
and brought them to the king of Babylon at Riblah. [27]There at Riblah, in the
land of Hamath, the king had them executed.
So Judah went into captivity, away
from her land. [28]This is the number of
the people Nebuchadnezzar carried
into exile:

in the seventh year, 3,023 Jews;
[29]in Nebuchadnezzar's eighteenth
year,
832 people from Jerusalem;
[30]in his twenty-third year,
745 Jews taken into exile by Nebuzaradan the commander of
the imperial guard.
There were 4,600 people in all.

Jehoiachin Released

[31]In the thirty-seventh year of the exile of Jehoiachin king of Judah, in the
year Evil-Merodach[c] became king of
Babylon, he released Jehoiachin king of
Judah and freed him from prison on the
twenty-fifth day of the twelfth month.
[32]He spoke kindly to him and gave him
a seat of honor higher than those of the
other kings who were with him in Babylon. [33]So Jehoiachin put aside his prison clothes and for the rest of his life ate
regularly at the king's table. [34]Day by
day the king of Babylon gave Jehoiachin
a regular allowance as long as he lived,
till the day of his death.

[a] *21* That is, about 27 feet (about 8.1 meters) high and 18 feet (about 5.4 meters) in circumference
[b] *22* That is, about 7 1/2 feet (about 2.3 meters)
[c] *31* Also called *Amel-Marduk*

SHARPEN THE FOCUS

The Holy Spirit saw fit to record Christ's crucifixion in detail four times in the New Testament. The fact that the same Spirit details Jerusalem's fall four times speaks to its significance. These two events and these alone receive this kind of intense scrutiny.

They are linked in other ways, too. The holy prophets foretold both events repeatedly and for centuries before the fact. In a sense both events came about, just as God had promised, for the same reason: because of the sins of God's people. In both events, the Lord displays His wrath at human sin.

In one important way, though, the two events differ. Jerusalem's citizens felt the wrath of God fall in a measured sense, not to destroy them but to bring them to repentance. At Calvary, God's sinless Son felt the full wrath of God at all human sin. God punished Jesus so that He would never have to punish us.

You and I deserve the horror that fell on faithless Jerusalem. In fact, we deserve the horror that fell on Christ. But because of Christ's sacrifice, we need never experience God's wrath.

Lamentations

The prophet Jeremiah begins the first of his five laments, or funeral dirges, for the city of Jerusalem by painting a word picture of the city, now desolate. As you read, keep in mind the truth of Proverbs 13:15: "The way of the unfaithful is hard." If time is short, focus on Lamentations 1:1–7, 20–22.

1 [a] How deserted lies the city,
once so full of people!
How like a widow is she,
who once was great among the nations!
She who was queen among the provinces
has now become a slave.

2 Bitterly she weeps at night,
tears are upon her cheeks.
Among all her lovers
there is none to comfort her.
All her friends have betrayed her;
they have become her enemies.

3 After affliction and harsh labor,
Judah has gone into exile.
She dwells among the nations;
she finds no resting place.
All who pursue her have overtaken her
in the midst of her distress.

4 The roads to Zion mourn,
for no one comes to her appointed feasts.
All her gateways are desolate,
her priests groan,
her maidens grieve,
and she is in bitter anguish.

5 Her foes have become her masters;
her enemies are at ease.
The LORD has brought her grief
because of her many sins.
Her children have gone into exile,
captive before the foe.

6 All the splendor has departed
from the Daughter of Zion.
Her princes are like deer
that find no pasture;
in weakness they have fled
before the pursuer.

7 In the days of her affliction and wandering
Jerusalem remembers all the treasures
that were hers in days of old.
When her people fell into enemy hands,
there was no one to help her.
Her enemies looked at her
and laughed at her destruction.

8 Jerusalem has sinned greatly
and so has become unclean.
All who honored her despise her,
for they have seen her nakedness;
she herself groans
and turns away.

[a] This chapter is an acrostic poem, the verses of which begin with the successive letters of the Hebrew alphabet.

[9]Her filthiness clung to her skirts;
she did not consider her future.
Her fall was astounding;
there was none to comfort her.
"Look, O LORD, on my affliction,
for the enemy has triumphed."

[10]The enemy laid hands
on all her treasures;
she saw pagan nations
enter her sanctuary—
those you had forbidden
to enter your assembly.

[11]All her people groan
as they search for bread;
they barter their treasures for food
to keep themselves alive.
"Look, O LORD, and consider,
for I am despised."

[12]"Is it nothing to you, all you who pass by?
Look around and see.
Is any suffering like my suffering
that was inflicted on me,
that the LORD brought on me
in the day of his fierce anger?

[13]"From on high he sent fire,
sent it down into my bones.
He spread a net for my feet
and turned me back.
He made me desolate,
faint all the day long.

[14]"My sins have been bound into a yoke[a];
by his hands they were woven together.
They have come upon my neck
and the Lord has sapped my strength.
He has handed me over
to those I cannot withstand.

[15]"The Lord has rejected
all the warriors in my midst;
he has summoned an army against me
to[b] crush my young men.
In his winepress the Lord has trampled
the Virgin Daughter of Judah.

[16]"This is why I weep
and my eyes overflow with tears.
No one is near to comfort me,
no one to restore my spirit.
My children are destitute
because the enemy has prevailed."

[17]Zion stretches out her hands,
but there is no one to comfort her.
The LORD has decreed for Jacob
that his neighbors become his foes;
Jerusalem has become
an unclean thing among them.

[18]"The LORD is righteous,
yet I rebelled against his command.
Listen, all you peoples;
look upon my suffering.
My young men and maidens
have gone into exile.

[19]"I called to my allies
but they betrayed me.
My priests and my elders
perished in the city
while they searched for food
to keep themselves alive.

[20]"See, O LORD, how distressed I am!
I am in torment within,
and in my heart I am disturbed,
for I have been most rebellious.
Outside, the sword bereaves;
inside, there is only death.

[21]"People have heard my groaning,
but there is no one to comfort me.
All my enemies have heard of my distress;
they rejoice at what you have done.
May you bring the day you have announced
so they may become like me.

[22]"Let all their wickedness come before you;
deal with them
as you have dealt with me
because of all my sins.
My groans are many
and my heart is faint."

[a]14 Most Hebrew manuscripts; Septuagint *He kept watch over my sins* [b]15 Or *has set a time for me* / *when he will*

SHARPEN THE FOCUS

Jeremiah preached God's word of warning to Jerusalem for 40 years. Finally, judgment fell. If you or I stood in the prophet's sandals, we might find ourselves feeling vindicated. "At last," we might think.

Instead, Jeremiah's heart aches for God's people. God's enemies have again enslaved them (Lamentations 1:1, 3). God's enemies have trampled through the Most Holy Place of the temple (Lamentations 1:10). Worst of all, Judah knew she had brought the Lord's judgment down on herself by her sin.

Maybe you've felt the sting of that kind of shame and loss. The relationship that ended because you neglected it for too long. The health problem that won't go away because you ignored the lifestyle changes your doctor ordered.

Not every setback in life comes as a result of our sin. But sometimes the logical consequences of our wrongdoing do catch up with us. When that happens, our worst pain often comes from our own accusing conscience.

Our Lord doesn't wag His finger at us then and say, "I told you so." His heart floods with compassion for us just as Jeremiah's did for Judah. Before we speak our words of confession, our Father has already forgiven us for Jesus' sake.

WEEK 62 • MONDAY

Lamentations 2:1—3:66

GET THE BIG PICTURE

Of what are you absolutely sure? Few things in life come with a guarantee. Governments topple. Buildings collapse. Relationships die. Health can fail. Still, God's people can live in confident hope. Look for the reason why as you read today's Scriptures. If time is short, focus on Lamentations 3:22–36.

2 [a] How the Lord has covered the Daughter of Zion
with the cloud of his anger[b]!
He has hurled down the splendor of Israel
from heaven to earth;
he has not remembered his footstool
in the day of his anger.

2 Without pity the Lord has swallowed up
all the dwellings of Jacob;
in his wrath he has torn down
the strongholds of the Daughter of Judah.
He has brought her kingdom and its princes
down to the ground in dishonor.

3 In fierce anger he has cut off
every horn[c] of Israel.
He has withdrawn his right hand
at the approach of the enemy.

[a] This chapter is an acrostic poem, the verses of which begin with the successive letters of the Hebrew alphabet. [b] 1 Or *How the Lord in his anger / has treated the Daughter of Zion with contempt* [c] 3 Or / *all the strength;* or *every king; horn* here symbolizes strength.

He has burned in Jacob like a
flaming fire
that consumes everything around
it.
4 Like an enemy he has strung his
bow;
his right hand is ready.
Like a foe he has slain
all who were pleasing to the eye;
he has poured out his wrath like fire
on the tent of the Daughter of
Zion.
5 The Lord is like an enemy;
he has swallowed up Israel.
He has swallowed up all her palaces
and destroyed her strongholds.
He has multiplied mourning and
lamentation
for the Daughter of Judah.
6 He has laid waste his dwelling like a
garden;
he has destroyed his place of
meeting.
The LORD has made Zion forget
her appointed feasts and her
Sabbaths;
in his fierce anger he has spurned
both king and priest.
7 The Lord has rejected his altar
and abandoned his sanctuary.
He has handed over to the enemy
the walls of her palaces;
they have raised a shout in the
house of the LORD
as on the day of an appointed feast.
8 The LORD determined to tear down
the wall around the Daughter of
Zion.
He stretched out a measuring line
and did not withhold his hand
from destroying.
He made ramparts and walls
lament;
together they wasted away.
9 Her gates have sunk into the
ground;
their bars he has broken and
destroyed.
Her king and her princes are exiled
among the nations,
the law is no more,
and her prophets no longer find
visions from the LORD.
10 The elders of the Daughter of Zion
sit on the ground in silence;
they have sprinkled dust on their
heads
and put on sackcloth.
The young women of Jerusalem
have bowed their heads to the
ground.
11 My eyes fail from weeping,
I am in torment within,
my heart is poured out on the
ground
because my people are destroyed,
because children and infants faint
in the streets of the city.
12 They say to their mothers,
"Where is bread and wine?"
as they faint like wounded men
in the streets of the city,
as their lives ebb away
in their mothers' arms.
13 What can I say for you?
With what can I compare you,
O Daughter of Jerusalem?
To what can I liken you,
that I may comfort you,
O Virgin Daughter of Zion?
Your wound is as deep as the sea.
Who can heal you?
14 The visions of your prophets
were false and worthless;
they did not expose your sin
to ward off your captivity.
The oracles they gave you
were false and misleading.
15 All who pass your way
clap their hands at you;
they scoff and shake their heads
at the Daughter of Jerusalem:
"Is this the city that was called
the perfection of beauty,
the joy of the whole earth?"
16 All your enemies open their
mouths
wide against you;
they scoff and gnash their teeth

and say, "We have swallowed her up.
This is the day we have waited for;
we have lived to see it."

17 The LORD has done what he planned;
he has fulfilled his word,
which he decreed long ago.
He has overthrown you without pity,
he has let the enemy gloat over you,
he has exalted the horn[a] of your foes.

18 The hearts of the people
cry out to the Lord.
O wall of the Daughter of Zion,
let your tears flow like a river
day and night;
give yourself no relief,
your eyes no rest.

19 Arise, cry out in the night,
as the watches of the night begin;
pour out your heart like water
in the presence of the Lord.
Lift up your hands to him
for the lives of your children,
who faint from hunger
at the head of every street.

20 "Look, O LORD, and consider:
Whom have you ever treated like this?
Should women eat their offspring,
the children they have cared for?
Should priest and prophet be killed
in the sanctuary of the Lord?

21 "Young and old lie together
in the dust of the streets;
my young men and maidens
have fallen by the sword.
You have slain them in the day of your anger;
you have slaughtered them without pity.

22 "As you summon to a feast day,
so you summoned against me
terrors on every side.
In the day of the LORD's anger
no one escaped or survived;
those I cared for and reared,
my enemy has destroyed."

3 [b] I am the man who has seen affliction
by the rod of his wrath.
2 He has driven me away and made me walk
in darkness rather than light;
3 indeed, he has turned his hand against me
again and again, all day long.

4 He has made my skin and my flesh grow old
and has broken my bones.
5 He has besieged me and surrounded me
with bitterness and hardship.
6 He has made me dwell in darkness
like those long dead.

7 He has walled me in so I cannot escape;
he has weighed me down with chains.
8 Even when I call out or cry for help,
he shuts out my prayer.
9 He has barred my way with blocks of stone;
he has made my paths crooked.

10 Like a bear lying in wait,
like a lion in hiding,
11 he dragged me from the path and mangled me
and left me without help.
12 He drew his bow
and made me the target for his arrows.

13 He pierced my heart
with arrows from his quiver.
14 I became the laughingstock of all my people;
they mock me in song all day long.
15 He has filled me with bitter herbs
and sated me with gall.

16 He has broken my teeth with gravel;
he has trampled me in the dust.
17 I have been deprived of peace;

[a] 17 *Horn* here symbolizes strength. [b] This chapter is an acrostic poem; the verses of each stanza begin with the successive letters of the Hebrew alphabet, and the verses within each stanza begin with the same letter.

I have forgotten what prosperity
is.
18 So I say, "My splendor is gone
and all that I had hoped from the
LORD."
19 I remember my affliction and my
wandering,
the bitterness and the gall.
20 I well remember them,
and my soul is downcast within
me.
21 Yet this I call to mind
and therefore I have hope:
22 Because of the LORD's great love we
are not consumed,
for his compassions never fail.
23 They are new every morning;
great is your faithfulness.
24 I say to myself, "The LORD is my
portion;
therefore I will wait for him."
25 The LORD is good to those whose
hope is in him,
to the one who seeks him;
26 it is good to wait quietly
for the salvation of the LORD.
27 It is good for a man to bear the yoke
while he is young.
28 Let him sit alone in silence,
for the LORD has laid it on him.
29 Let him bury his face in the dust—
there may yet be hope.
30 Let him offer his cheek to one who
would strike him,
and let him be filled with disgrace.
31 For men are not cast off
by the Lord forever.
32 Though he brings grief, he will show
compassion,
so great is his unfailing love.
33 For he does not willingly bring
affliction
or grief to the children of men.
34 To crush underfoot
all prisoners in the land,
35 to deny a man his rights
before the Most High,
36 to deprive a man of justice—
would not the Lord see such
things?
37 Who can speak and have it happen
if the Lord has not decreed it?
38 Is it not from the mouth of the Most
High
that both calamities and good
things come?
39 Why should any living man
complain
when punished for his sins?
40 Let us examine our ways and test
them,
and let us return to the LORD.
41 Let us lift up our hearts and our
hands
to God in heaven, and say:
42 "We have sinned and rebelled
and you have not forgiven.
43 "You have covered yourself with
anger and pursued us;
you have slain without pity.
44 You have covered yourself with a
cloud
so that no prayer can get through.
45 You have made us scum and refuse
among the nations.
46 "All our enemies have opened their
mouths
wide against us.
47 We have suffered terror and pitfalls,
ruin and destruction."
48 Streams of tears flow from my eyes
because my people are
destroyed.
49 My eyes will flow unceasingly,
without relief,
50 until the LORD looks down
from heaven and sees.
51 What I see brings grief to my soul
because of all the women of my
city.
52 Those who were my enemies
without cause
hunted me like a bird.
53 They tried to end my life in a pit
and threw stones at me;
54 the waters closed over my head,
and I thought I was about to be
cut off.
55 I called on your name, O LORD,
from the depths of the pit.

56 You heard my plea: "Do not close
your ears
to my cry for relief."
57 You came near when I called you,
and you said, "Do not fear."

58 O Lord, you took up my case;
you redeemed my life.
59 You have seen, O LORD, the wrong
done to me.
Uphold my cause!
60 You have seen the depth of their
vengeance,
all their plots against me.

61 O LORD, you have heard their
insults,
all their plots against me—
62 what my enemies whisper and
mutter
against me all day long.
63 Look at them! Sitting or standing,
they mock me in their songs.

64 Pay them back what they deserve,
O LORD,
for what their hands have done.
65 Put a veil over their hearts,
and may your curse be on them!
66 Pursue them in anger and destroy
them
from under the heavens of the
LORD.

SHARPEN THE FOCUS

Most of us are confident that the sun will rise each morning. Jeremiah points us to an even more certain truth in his third lament poem (Lamentations 3:22–24). God's mercies, he says, are new every morning. Our Lord is utterly, absolutely faithful.

Suppose we had to wonder whether God was having a bad day. Or we had to guess whether He'd gotten up on the right side of the bed. Suppose we had to worry about whether we'd offended Him one too many times.

But we need not fear. His compassions (note the plural in Lamentations 3:22) never fail. Human beings often reach the end of their patience. Sooner or later, even a compassionate person will give up on a repeat offender. But our Lord's mercy never, ever runs out.

Confidence in our Lord's mercy comes from His crucified and risen Son. Confidence like that gives us hope (Lamentations 3:24–25), we might say "blazing hope." No matter how dark the long night of our soul grows, Christ remains our light.

Perhaps you face uncertainty today. Jeremiah has some reliable counsel for you: "It is good to wait quietly for the salvation of the LORD" (Lamentations 3:26). As you wait, do so in the sure and certain hope of our Lord's mercy and compassion, afresh each and every day.

WEEK 62 • TUESDAY

Lamentations 4:1—5:22

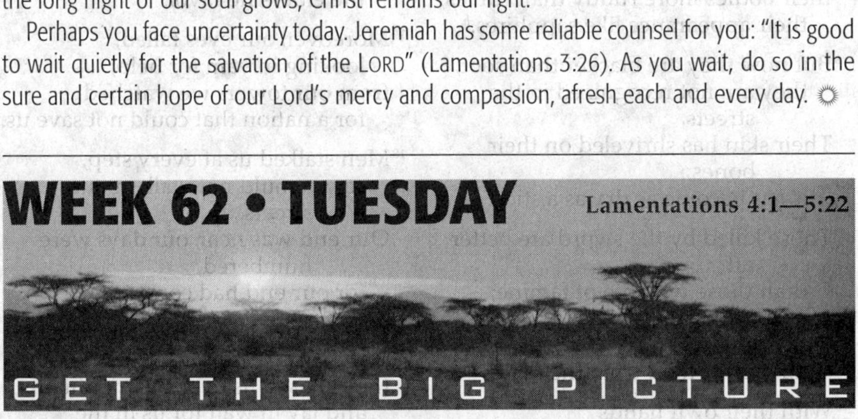

GET THE BIG PICTURE

Jeremiah finishes the book of Lamentations with two final funeral poems. Both mourn the death of the city of Jerusalem, but the dirge of chapter 5 ends on a note of hope: Perhaps the Lord will grant repentance. As you read, ask yourself how repentance and hope fit together. If time is short, focus on Lamentations 5:1–22.

4 [a] How the gold has lost its luster,
the fine gold become dull!
The sacred gems are scattered
at the head of every street.

2 How the precious sons of Zion,
once worth their weight in gold,
are now considered as pots of clay,
the work of a potter's hands!

3 Even jackals offer their breasts
to nurse their young,
but my people have become heartless
like ostriches in the desert.

4 Because of thirst the infant's tongue
sticks to the roof of its mouth;
the children beg for bread,
but no one gives it to them.

5 Those who once ate delicacies
are destitute in the streets.
Those nurtured in purple
now lie on ash heaps.

6 The punishment of my people
is greater than that of Sodom,
which was overthrown in a moment
without a hand turned to help her.

7 Their princes were brighter than snow
and whiter than milk,
their bodies more ruddy than rubies,
their appearance like sapphires.[b]

8 But now they are blacker than soot;
they are not recognized in the streets.
Their skin has shriveled on their bones;
it has become as dry as a stick.

9 Those killed by the sword are better off
than those who die of famine;
racked with hunger, they waste away
for lack of food from the field.

10 With their own hands compassionate women
have cooked their own children,
who became their food
when my people were destroyed.

11 The LORD has given full vent to his wrath;
he has poured out his fierce anger.
He kindled a fire in Zion
that consumed her foundations.

12 The kings of the earth did not believe,
nor did any of the world's people,
that enemies and foes could enter
the gates of Jerusalem.

13 But it happened because of the sins of her prophets
and the iniquities of her priests,
who shed within her
the blood of the righteous.

14 Now they grope through the streets
like men who are blind.
They are so defiled with blood
that no one dares to touch their garments.

15 "Go away! You are unclean!" men cry to them.
"Away! Away! Don't touch us!"
When they flee and wander about,
people among the nations say,
"They can stay here no longer."

16 The LORD himself has scattered them;
he no longer watches over them.
The priests are shown no honor,
the elders no favor.

17 Moreover, our eyes failed,
looking in vain for help;
from our towers we watched
for a nation that could not save us.

18 Men stalked us at every step,
so we could not walk in our streets.
Our end was near, our days were numbered,
for our end had come.

19 Our pursuers were swifter
than eagles in the sky;
they chased us over the mountains
and lay in wait for us in the desert.

[a]This chapter is an acrostic poem, the verses of which begin with the successive letters of the Hebrew alphabet. [b]7 Or *lapis lazuli*

[20]The LORD's anointed, our very life breath,
was caught in their traps.
We thought that under his shadow
we would live among the nations.

[21]Rejoice and be glad, O Daughter of Edom,
you who live in the land of Uz.
But to you also the cup will be passed;
you will be drunk and stripped naked.

[22]O Daughter of Zion, your punishment will end;
he will not prolong your exile.
But, O Daughter of Edom, he will punish your sin
and expose your wickedness.

5 Remember, O LORD, what has happened to us;
look, and see our disgrace.
[2]Our inheritance has been turned over to aliens,
our homes to foreigners.
[3]We have become orphans and fatherless,
our mothers like widows.
[4]We must buy the water we drink;
our wood can be had only at a price.
[5]Those who pursue us are at our heels;
we are weary and find no rest.
[6]We submitted to Egypt and Assyria
to get enough bread.
[7]Our fathers sinned and are no more,
and we bear their punishment.
[8]Slaves rule over us,
and there is none to free us from their hands.
[9]We get our bread at the risk of our lives
because of the sword in the desert.
[10]Our skin is hot as an oven,
feverish from hunger.
[11]Women have been ravished in Zion,
and virgins in the towns of Judah.
[12]Princes have been hung up by their hands;
elders are shown no respect.
[13]Young men toil at the millstones;
boys stagger under loads of wood.
[14]The elders are gone from the city gate;
the young men have stopped their music.
[15]Joy is gone from our hearts;
our dancing has turned to mourning.
[16]The crown has fallen from our head.
Woe to us, for we have sinned!
[17]Because of this our hearts are faint,
because of these things our eyes grow dim
[18]for Mount Zion, which lies desolate,
with jackals prowling over it.

[19]You, O LORD, reign forever;
your throne endures from generation to generation.
[20]Why do you always forget us?
Why do you forsake us so long?
[21]Restore us to yourself, O LORD, that we may return;
renew our days as of old
[22]unless you have utterly rejected us
and are angry with us beyond measure.

SHARPEN THE FOCUS

In Judah, the rich got richer, the poor got poorer. And everyone got more violent and self-centered. Babylon's attack reduced everyone to poverty, but it didn't change the people's lovelessness or violence (Lamentations 4:10).

Our civilization looks a lot like the one Jeremiah condemned. We dismiss those who live in poverty as lazy, while we ignore their needs. We envy the wealthy, while we accuse them of greed. We often enjoy violence disguised as entertainment. We fall far short of Christlike compassion for those who need our love. We deserve God's punishment.

In mercy toward the whole human race, the Savior-God did not completely wipe out the children of Abraham, the line of David. He had promised to send the world's Redeemer through them. And He would keep that promise.

As sin continues to eat away at the framework of our culture, the repentant children of God can still hope in Him. He won't bring us into judgment, because He has drawn us into the kingdom of His mercy for Jesus' sake. In the shadow of the cross, we can pray Jeremiah's prayer of confession, "We have sinned" (Lamentations 5:16). And as we pray that, we can trust our Savior to forgive us and "restore us to Himself" (Lamentations 5:21).

EZEKIEL

WEEK 62 • WEDNESDAY

Ezekiel 1:1—2:10

As a descendant of Aaron, Ezekiel would have begun his duties as a priest in the temple at Jerusalem when he turned 30. Instead, he found himself 1,000 miles away in Babylon. Ezekiel had no hope of returning to his homeland. But the Lord had plans for this young man. He would serve as God's spokesman even though he could not serve at God's altar. As you read the account of Ezekiel's call, note with care the things the Lord revealed about Himself in Ezekiel's vision. If time is short, focus on Ezekiel 1:1–28.

The Living Creatures and the Glory of the LORD

1 In the[a] thirtieth year, in the fourth
month on the fifth day, while I was
among the exiles by the Kebar River, the
heavens were opened and I saw visions
of God.
[2]On the fifth of the month—it was the
fifth year of the exile of King Jehoiachin— [3]the word of the LORD came to
Ezekiel the priest, the son of Buzi,[b] by
the Kebar River in the land of the
Babylonians.[c] There the hand of the
LORD was upon him.
[4]I looked, and I saw a windstorm coming out of the north—an immense cloud
with flashing lightning and surrounded by brilliant light. The center of the
fire looked like glowing metal, [5]and in
the fire was what looked like four living
creatures. In appearance their form was
that of a man, [6]but each of them had
four faces and four wings. [7]Their legs
were straight; their feet were like those
of a calf and gleamed like burnished
bronze. [8]Under their wings on their four
sides they had the hands of a man. All
four of them had faces and wings, [9]and
their wings touched one another. Each
one went straight ahead; they did not
turn as they moved.
[10]Their faces looked like this: Each of
the four had the face of a man, and on
the right side each had the face of a lion,
and on the left the face of an ox; each
also had the face of an eagle. [11]Such
were their faces. Their wings were
spread out upward; each had two
wings, one touching the wing of another creature on either side, and two
wings covering its body. [12]Each one
went straight ahead. Wherever the spirit would go, they would go, without
turning as they went. [13]The appearance
of the living creatures was like burning
coals of fire or like torches. Fire moved
back and forth among the creatures; it
was bright, and lightning flashed out of
it. [14]The creatures sped back and forth
like flashes of lightning.
[15]As I looked at the living creatures, I
saw a wheel on the ground beside each
creature with its four faces. [16]This was
the appearance and structure of the
wheels: They sparkled like chrysolite,
and all four looked alike. Each appeared

[a]1 Or ⌞my⌟ [b]3 Or *Ezekiel son of Buzi the priest*
[c]3 Or *Chaldeans*

to be made like a wheel intersecting a wheel. 17As they moved, they would go in any one of the four directions the creatures faced; the wheels did not turn about[a] as the creatures went. 18Their rims were high and awesome, and all four rims were full of eyes all around.

19When the living creatures moved, the wheels beside them moved; and when the living creatures rose from the ground, the wheels also rose. 20Wherever the spirit would go, they would go, and the wheels would rise along with them, because the spirit of the living creatures was in the wheels. 21When the creatures moved, they also moved; when the creatures stood still, they also stood still; and when the creatures rose from the ground, the wheels rose along with them, because the spirit of the living creatures was in the wheels.

22Spread out above the heads of the living creatures was what looked like an expanse, sparkling like ice, and awesome. 23Under the expanse their wings were stretched out one toward the other, and each had two wings covering its body. 24When the creatures moved, I heard the sound of their wings, like the roar of rushing waters, like the voice of the Almighty,[b] like the tumult of an army. When they stood still, they lowered their wings.

25Then there came a voice from above the expanse over their heads as they stood with lowered wings. 26Above the expanse over their heads was what looked like a throne of sapphire,[c] and high above on the throne was a figure like that of a man. 27I saw that from what appeared to be his waist up he looked like glowing metal, as if full of fire, and that from there down he looked like fire; and brilliant light surrounded him. 28Like the appearance of a rainbow in the clouds on a rainy day, so was the radiance around him.

This was the appearance of the likeness of the glory of the LORD. When I saw it, I fell facedown, and I heard the voice of one speaking.

Ezekiel's Call

2 He said to me, "Son of man, stand up on your feet and I will speak to you." 2As he spoke, the Spirit came into me and raised me to my feet, and I heard him speaking to me.

3He said: "Son of man, I am sending you to the Israelites, to a rebellious nation that has rebelled against me; they and their fathers have been in revolt against me to this very day. 4The people to whom I am sending you are obstinate and stubborn. Say to them, 'This is what the Sovereign LORD says.' 5And whether they listen or fail to listen—for they are a rebellious house—they will know that a prophet has been among them. 6And you, son of man, do not be afraid of them or their words. Do not be afraid, though briers and thorns are all around you and you live among scorpions. Do not be afraid of what they say or terrified by them, though they are a rebellious house. 7You must speak my words to them, whether they listen or fail to listen, for they are rebellious. 8But you, son of man, listen to what I say to you. Do not rebel like that rebellious house; open your mouth and eat what I give you."

9Then I looked, and I saw a hand stretched out to me. In it was a scroll, 10which he unrolled before me. On both sides of it were written words of lament and mourning and woe.

[a]17 Or *aside* [b]24 Hebrew *Shaddai* [c]26 Or *lapis lazuli*

SHARPEN THE FOCUS

What a remarkable vision! As we read Ezekiel's description, we sense his struggle to tell us about it. The greatest artists in history could never have captured this image on canvas.

We can't know for sure exactly what Ezekiel saw, but we can understand something about

God's revelation of Himself in Ezekiel's vision. The light and fire of Ezekiel 1:4–5 speak of His holiness. The wheels that moved supernaturally and the eyes on the wheels symbolize God's omniscience and omnipresence.

Think of it. A God whose holiness burns. A God whose presence fills our universe. A God so powerful that His voice thunders (Ezekiel 1:24). Frightening, isn't it? Frightening, that is, until we see the rainbow (Ezekiel 1:28) above the throne. Our God makes and keeps His covenant with His sinful creatures.

Just as the Lord spared the human race through His rescue of Noah (Genesis 6–10), so He continues to rescue all those who cling in faith to the Savior descended from Noah. Just as He sent Ezekiel to speak His Word to ancient Judah, still He sends His messengers to us today with that word of Law and Gospel, sin and grace.

WEEK 62 • THURSDAY

Ezekiel 3:1—5:17

GET THE BIG PICTURE

Ezekiel often acted out God's message to His people. As you read the four "visual parables" of Ezekiel 4–5, you'll note they all carry the same meaning—God's judgment on the unrepentant. Jerusalem still stood at this time. (Ezekiel had come to Babylon in 597 B.C.; the final collapse of Jerusalem didn't come until 586 B.C.) The exiles still doubted that God would destroy the city. But the Lord always keeps His Word—whether Law or Gospel. If time is short, focus on Ezekiel 3:1–27.

3 And he said to me, "Son of man,
eat what is before you, eat this
scroll; then go and speak to the house
of Israel." 2So I opened my mouth, and
he gave me the scroll to eat.
3Then he said to me, "Son of man, eat
this scroll I am giving you and fill your
stomach with it." So I ate it, and it tasted as sweet as honey in my mouth.
4He then said to me: "Son of man, go
now to the house of Israel and speak my
words to them. 5You are not being sent
to a people of obscure speech and difficult language, but to the house of Israel— 6not to many peoples of obscure
speech and difficult language, whose
words you cannot understand. Surely if
I had sent you to them, they would have
listened to you. 7But the house of Israel
is not willing to listen to you because
they are not willing to listen to me, for
the whole house of Israel is hardened
and obstinate. 8But I will make you as
unyielding and hardened as they are. 9I
will make your forehead like the hardest stone, harder than flint. Do not be
afraid of them or terrified by them,
though they are a rebellious house."
10And he said to me, "Son of man, listen carefully and take to heart all the
words I speak to you. 11Go now to your
countrymen in exile and speak to them.
Say to them, 'This is what the Sovereign
LORD says,' whether they listen or fail to
listen."
12Then the Spirit lifted me up, and I
heard behind me a loud rumbling
sound—May the glory of the LORD be
praised in his dwelling place!— 13the
sound of the wings of the living crea-

tures brushing against each other and the sound of the wheels beside them, a loud rumbling sound. 14The Spirit then lifted me up and took me away, and I went in bitterness and in the anger of my spirit, with the strong hand of the LORD upon me. 15I came to the exiles who lived at Tel Abib near the Kebar River. And there, where they were living, I sat among them for seven days—overwhelmed.

Warning to Israel

16At the end of seven days the word of the LORD came to me: 17"Son of man, I have made you a watchman for the house of Israel; so hear the word I speak and give them warning from me. 18When I say to a wicked man, 'You will surely die,' and you do not warn him or speak out to dissuade him from his evil ways in order to save his life, that wicked man will die for[a] his sin, and I will hold you accountable for his blood. 19But if you do warn the wicked man and he does not turn from his wickedness or from his evil ways, he will die for his sin; but you will have saved yourself.

20"Again, when a righteous man turns from his righteousness and does evil, and I put a stumbling block before him, he will die. Since you did not warn him, he will die for his sin. The righteous things he did will not be remembered, and I will hold you accountable for his blood. 21But if you do warn the righteous man not to sin and he does not sin, he will surely live because he took warning, and you will have saved yourself."

22The hand of the LORD was upon me there, and he said to me, "Get up and go out to the plain, and there I will speak to you." 23So I got up and went out to the plain. And the glory of the LORD was standing there, like the glory I had seen by the Kebar River, and I fell facedown.

24Then the Spirit came into me and raised me to my feet. He spoke to me and said: "Go, shut yourself inside your house. 25And you, son of man, they will tie with ropes; you will be bound so that you cannot go out among the people. 26I will make your tongue stick to the roof of your mouth so that you will be silent and unable to rebuke them, though they are a rebellious house. 27But when I speak to you, I will open your mouth and you shall say to them, 'This is what the Sovereign LORD says.' Whoever will listen let him listen, and whoever will refuse let him refuse; for they are a rebellious house.

Siege of Jerusalem Symbolized

4 "Now, son of man, take a clay tablet, put it in front of you and draw the city of Jerusalem on it. 2Then lay siege to it: Erect siege works against it, build a ramp up to it, set up camps against it and put battering rams around it. 3Then take an iron pan, place it as an iron wall between you and the city and turn your face toward it. It will be under siege, and you shall besiege it. This will be a sign to the house of Israel.

4"Then lie on your left side and put the sin of the house of Israel upon yourself.[b] You are to bear their sin for the number of days you lie on your side. 5I have assigned you the same number of days as the years of their sin. So for 390 days you will bear the sin of the house of Israel.

6"After you have finished this, lie down again, this time on your right side, and bear the sin of the house of Judah. I have assigned you 40 days, a day for each year. 7Turn your face toward the siege of Jerusalem and with bared arm prophesy against her. 8I will tie you up with ropes so that you cannot turn from one side to the other until you have finished the days of your siege.

9"Take wheat and barley, beans and lentils, millet and spelt; put them in a storage jar and use them to make bread for yourself. You are to eat it during the 390 days you lie on your side. 10Weigh out twenty shekels[c] of food to eat each day and eat it at set times. 11Also mea-

[a] *18* Or *in;* also in verses 19 and 20 [b] *4* Or *your side* [c] *10* That is, about 8 ounces (about 0.2 kilogram)

sure out a sixth of a hin[a] of water and
drink it at set times. 12Eat the food as you
would a barley cake; bake it in the sight
of the people, using human excrement
for fuel." 13The LORD said, "In this way
the people of Israel will eat defiled food
among the nations where I will drive
them."

14Then I said, "Not so, Sovereign
LORD! I have never defiled myself. From
my youth until now I have never eaten
anything found dead or torn by wild
animals. No unclean meat has ever entered my mouth."

15"Very well," he said, "I will let you
bake your bread over cow manure instead of human excrement."

16He then said to me: "Son of man, I
will cut off the supply of food in Jerusalem. The people will eat rationed food
in anxiety and drink rationed water in
despair, 17for food and water will be
scarce. They will be appalled at the sight
of each other and will waste away because of[b] their sin.

5 "Now, son of man, take a sharp
sword and use it as a barber's
razor to shave your head and your
beard. Then take a set of scales and divide up the hair. 2When the days of your
siege come to an end, burn a third of the
hair with fire inside the city. Take a third
and strike it with the sword all around
the city. And scatter a third to the wind.
For I will pursue them with drawn
sword. 3But take a few strands of hair
and tuck them away in the folds of your
garment. 4Again, take a few of these and
throw them into the fire and burn them
up. A fire will spread from there to the
whole house of Israel.

5"This is what the Sovereign LORD
says: This is Jerusalem, which I have set
in the center of the nations, with countries all around her. 6Yet in her wickedness she has rebelled against my laws
and decrees more than the nations and
countries around her. She has rejected
my laws and has not followed my decrees.

7"Therefore this is what the Sovereign
LORD says: You have been more unruly
than the nations around you and have
not followed my decrees or kept my
laws. You have not even[c] conformed to the
standards of the nations around you.

8"Therefore this is what the Sovereign
LORD says: I myself am against you, Jerusalem, and I will inflict punishment
on you in the sight of the nations. 9Be-
cause of all your detestable idols, I will
do to you what I have never done before and will never do again. 10Therefore
in your midst fathers will eat their children, and children will eat their fathers.
I will inflict punishment on you and will
scatter all your survivors to the winds.
11Therefore as surely as I live, declares
the Sovereign LORD, because you have
defiled my sanctuary with all your vile
images and detestable practices, I myself will withdraw my favor; I will not
look on you with pity or spare you. 12A
third of your people will die of the
plague or perish by famine inside you;
a third will fall by the sword outside
your walls; and a third I will scatter to
the winds and pursue with drawn
sword.

13"Then my anger will cease and my
wrath against them will subside, and I
will be avenged. And when I have spent
my wrath upon them, they will know
that I the LORD have spoken in my zeal.

14"I will make you a ruin and a reproach among the nations around you,
in the sight of all who pass by. 15You will
be a reproach and a taunt, a warning
and an object of horror to the nations
around you when I inflict punishment
on you in anger and in wrath and with
stinging rebuke. I the LORD have spoken. 16When I shoot at you with my
deadly and destructive arrows of famine, I will shoot to destroy you. I will
bring more and more famine upon you
and cut off your supply of food. 17I will
send famine and wild beasts against
you, and they will leave you childless.
Plague and bloodshed will sweep
through you, and I will bring the sword
against you. I the LORD have spoken."

[a]*11* That is, about 2/3 quart (about 0.6 liter)
[b]*17* Or *away in* [c]*7* Most Hebrew manuscripts; some Hebrew manuscripts and Syriac *You have*

SHARPEN THE FOCUS

Ezekiel ate the scroll in the vision God sent him (Ezekiel 3:1–3). This symbolized the thoroughness with which he was to "digest" the Word of the Lord. That Word would nourish and strengthen him for the work God had called him to do.

How sweet do you find God's Word? If your Scripture reading sometimes seems as tasteless as cardboard or dry as dust, could it be that you're approaching the Word as a dull duty instead of as an opportunity to come face-to-face with the living God? Ancient Judah fell into that trap. They did not take God's Word to heart (Ezekiel 3:10). And they surely did not look for ways to introduce others to their Savior-God.

God wanted to nourish Ezekiel on His sweet Word of life. Then Ezekiel could stand strong against the hardships he would meet in his calling. And he could also share the truth of that Word with those who so needed to hear it (Ezekiel 3:11), regardless of how his audience would respond.

Pray Psalm 119:105–112 before you close your Bible today. Thank God for His Word, especially His promise of pardon in Christ's cross. Then ask Him for a heart that treasures and obeys the Word of life.

While Jeremiah proclaimed doom to the impenitent in Jerusalem, Ezekiel echoed that same message to the refugees in Babylon. In both places, most people closed their ears to the message. Still God's Word would not fail. The words of God's prophets would come true, and those who survived the coming disaster would remember. As you read, look for the phrase, "Then you (they) will know that I am the LORD." If time is short, focus on Ezekiel 6:1–10.

A Prophecy Against the Mountains of Israel

6 The word of the LORD came to
me: 2"Son of man, set your
face against the mountains of Israel; prophesy against them 3and say:
'O mountains of Israel, hear the word of the Sovereign LORD. This is what the Sovereign LORD says to the mountains and hills, to the ravines and valleys: I am about to bring a sword against you, and I will destroy your high places. 4Your
altars will be demolished and your incense altars will be smashed; and I will slay your people in front of your idols.
5I will lay the dead bodies of the Israelites in front of their idols, and I will scatter your bones around your altars.
6Wherever you live, the towns will be laid waste and the high places demolished, so that your altars will be laid waste and devastated, your idols smashed and ruined, your incense altars broken down, and what you have made wiped out. 7Your people will fall slain among you, and you will know that I am the LORD.
8" 'But I will spare some, for some of

you will escape the sword when you are
scattered among the lands and nations.
[9]Then in the nations where they have
been carried captive, those who escape
will remember me—how I have been
grieved by their adulterous hearts,
which have turned away from me, and
by their eyes, which have lusted after
their idols. They will loathe themselves
for the evil they have done and for all
their detestable practices. [10]And they
will know that I am the LORD; I did not
threaten in vain to bring this calamity
on them.
[11]" 'This is what the Sovereign LORD
says: Strike your hands together and
stamp your feet and cry out "Alas!" because of all the wicked and detestable
practices of the house of Israel, for they
will fall by the sword, famine and
plague. [12]He that is far away will die of
the plague, and he that is near will fall
by the sword, and he that survives and
is spared will die of famine. So will I
spend my wrath upon them. [13]And they
will know that I am the LORD, when
their people lie slain among their idols
around their altars, on every high hill
and on all the mountaintops, under
every spreading tree and every leafy
oak—places where they offered fragrant incense to all their idols. [14]And I
will stretch out my hand against them
and make the land a desolate waste
from the desert to Diblah[a]—wherever
they live. Then they will know that I am
the LORD.' "

The End Has Come

7 The word of the LORD came to
me: [2]"Son of man, this is what the
Sovereign LORD says to the land of Israel: The end! The end has come upon
the four corners of the land. [3]The end is
now upon you and I will unleash my
anger against you. I will judge you according to your conduct and repay you
for all your detestable practices. [4]I will
not look on you with pity or spare you;
I will surely repay you for your conduct
and the detestable practices among
you. Then you will know that I am the
LORD.

[5]"This is what the Sovereign LORD
says: Disaster! An unheard-of[b] disaster
is coming. [6]The end has come! The end
has come! It has roused itself against
you. It has come! [7]Doom has come upon
you—you who dwell in the land. The
time has come, the day is near; there is
panic, not joy, upon the mountains. [8]I
am about to pour out my wrath on you
and spend my anger against you; I will
judge you according to your conduct
and repay you for all your detestable
practices. [9]I will not look on you with
pity or spare you; I will repay you in accordance with your conduct and the detestable practices among you. Then you
will know that it is I the LORD who
strikes the blow.
[10]"The day is here! It has come! Doom
has burst forth, the rod has budded, arrogance has blossomed! [11]Violence has
grown into[c] a rod to punish wickedness;
none of the people will be left, none of
that crowd—no wealth, nothing of value. [12]The time has come, the day has arrived. Let not the buyer rejoice nor the
seller grieve, for wrath is upon the
whole crowd. [13]The seller will not recover the land he has sold as long as both
of them live, for the vision concerning
the whole crowd will not be reversed.
Because of their sins, not one of them
will preserve his life. [14]Though they
blow the trumpet and get everything
ready, no one will go into battle, for my
wrath is upon the whole crowd.
[15]"Outside is the sword, inside are
plague and famine; those in the country will die by the sword, and those in
the city will be devoured by famine and
plague. [16]All who survive and escape
will be in the mountains, moaning like
doves of the valleys, each because of his
sins. [17]Every hand will go limp, and every knee will become as weak as water.
[18]They will put on sackcloth and be
clothed with terror. Their faces will be
covered with shame and their heads

[a]*14* Most Hebrew manuscripts; a few Hebrew manuscripts *Riblah* [b]*5* Most Hebrew manuscripts; some Hebrew manuscripts and Syriac *Disaster after* [c]*11* Or *The violent one has become*

will be shaved. 19They will throw their
silver into the streets, and their gold will
be an unclean thing. Their silver and
gold will not be able to save them in the
day of the LORD's wrath. They will not
satisfy their hunger or fill their stomachs
with it, for it has made them stumble
into sin. 20They were proud of their
beautiful jewelry and used it to make
their detestable idols and vile images.
Therefore I will turn these into an unclean thing for them. 21I will hand it all
over as plunder to foreigners and as loot
to the wicked of the earth, and they will
defile it. 22I will turn my face away from
them, and they will desecrate my treasured place; robbers will enter it and
desecrate it.
23"Prepare chains, because the land is
full of bloodshed and the city is full of
violence. 24I will bring the most wicked
of the nations to take possession of their
houses; I will put an end to the pride of
the mighty, and their sanctuaries will be
desecrated. 25When terror comes, they
will seek peace, but there will be none.
26Calamity upon calamity will come,
and rumor upon rumor. They will try to
get a vision from the prophet; the teaching of the law by the priest will be lost,
as will the counsel of the elders. 27The
king will mourn, the prince will be
clothed with despair, and the hands of
the people of the land will tremble. I will
deal with them according to their conduct, and by their own standards I will
judge them. Then they will know that I
am the LORD."

SHARPEN THE FOCUS

Have you ever done something nasty and hated yourself for it later? That's what would happen to the exiles in Babylon when they finally did come to know the Lord (Ezekiel 6:9b). They would "loathe themselves" for their idols. They would realize how much they had hurt their Savior-God by their idolatry.

Usually we think of sin as *offending* our Lord, and it does. But in Ezekiel 6:9, God tells us that the sins of His people also *grieve* Him. He says, "I have been grieved by their adulterous hearts, which have turned away from Me." We deserve death, eternal separation from our Lord (Romans 6:23).

We have turned away from God, but for Jesus' sake He doesn't turn away from us! We can be glad—ecstatic, really—about the "remnant" the Lord promised to return to Judah. From this ragtag group of repatriated exiles, He would fulfill His promises to send the Savior. Jesus would absorb all of God's just anger at our unfaithfulness and in exchange give us His own righteousness. ☼

WEEK 62 • SATURDAY

Ezekiel 8:1—9:11

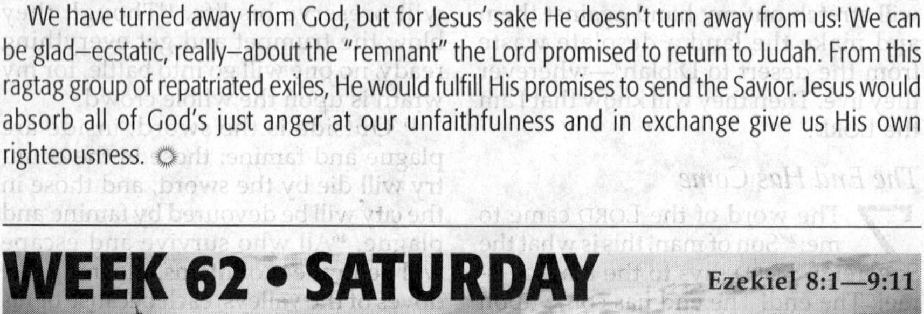

GET THE BIG PICTURE

In the vision you will read today, Ezekiel visits Jerusalem. Though 1,000 miles away in Babylon, the prophet sees what's happening in the inner rooms of the holy temple itself. Everyone—the elders, the women, and even the priests' worship false gods. Judgment falls in chapter 9, but

not before the Lord has marked His own people. In love, He will defend and deliver them. If
time is short, focus on Ezekiel 9:1–11.

Idolatry in the Temple

8 In the sixth year, in the sixth
month on the fifth day, while I
was sitting in my house and the elders
of Judah were sitting before me, the
hand of the Sovereign LORD came
upon me there. 2I looked, and I saw a
figure like that of a man.[a] From what appeared to be his waist down he was like
fire, and from there up his appearance
was as bright as glowing metal. 3He
stretched out what looked like a hand
and took me by the hair of my head. The
Spirit lifted me up between earth and
heaven and in visions of God he took
me to Jerusalem, to the entrance to the
north gate of the inner court, where the
idol that provokes to jealousy stood.
4And there before me was the glory of
the God of Israel, as in the vision I had
seen in the plain.
5Then he said to me, "Son of man,
look toward the north." So I looked, and
in the entrance north of the gate of the
altar I saw this idol of jealousy.
6And he said to me, "Son of man, do
you see what they are doing—the utterly detestable things the house of Israel
is doing here, things that will drive me
far from my sanctuary? But you will see
things that are even more detestable."
7Then he brought me to the entrance
to the court. I looked, and I saw a hole
in the wall. 8He said to me, "Son of man,
now dig into the wall." So I dug into the
wall and saw a doorway there.
9And he said to me, "Go in and see the
wicked and detestable things they are
doing here." 10So I went in and looked,
and I saw portrayed all over the walls all
kinds of crawling things and detestable
animals and all the idols of the house of
Israel. 11In front of them stood seventy
elders of the house of Israel, and Jaazaniah son of Shaphan was standing
among them. Each had a censer in his
hand, and a fragrant cloud of incense
was rising.
12He said to me, "Son of man, have
you seen what the elders of the house
of Israel are doing in the darkness, each
at the shrine of his own idol? They say,
'The LORD does not see us; the LORD has
forsaken the land.' " 13Again, he said,
"You will see them doing things that are
even more detestable."
14Then he brought me to the entrance
to the north gate of the house of the
LORD, and I saw women sitting there,
mourning for Tammuz. 15He said to me,
"Do you see this, son of man? You will
see things that are even more detestable
than this."
16He then brought me into the inner
court of the house of the LORD, and
there at the entrance to the temple, between the portico and the altar, were
about twenty-five men. With their backs
toward the temple of the LORD and their
faces toward the east, they were bowing
down to the sun in the east.
17He said to me, "Have you seen this,
son of man? Is it a trivial matter for the
house of Judah to do the detestable
things they are doing here? Must they
also fill the land with violence and continually provoke me to anger? Look at
them putting the branch to their nose!
18Therefore I will deal with them in anger; I will not look on them with pity or
spare them. Although they shout in my
ears, I will not listen to them."

Idolaters Killed

9 Then I heard him call out in a
loud voice, "Bring the guards of
the city here, each with a weapon in his
hand." 2And I saw six men coming from
the direction of the upper gate, which
faces north, each with a deadly weapon
in his hand. With them was a man
clothed in linen who had a writing kit
at his side. They came in and stood beside the bronze altar.
3Now the glory of the God of Israel
went up from above the cherubim,

[a]2 Or *saw a fiery figure*

where it had been, and moved to the
threshold of the temple. Then the LORD
called to the man clothed in linen who
had the writing kit at his side [4]and said
to him, "Go throughout the city of Jerusalem and put a mark on the foreheads
of those who grieve and lament over
all the detestable things that are done
in it."
[5]As I listened, he said to the others,
"Follow him through the city and kill,
without showing pity or compassion.
[6]Slaughter old men, young men and
maidens, women and children, but do
not touch anyone who has the mark. Begin at my sanctuary." So they began
with the elders who were in front of the
temple.
[7]Then he said to them, "Defile the
temple and fill the courts with the slain.
Go!" So they went out and began killing throughout the city. [8]While they
were killing and I was left alone, I fell
facedown, crying out, "Ah, Sovereign
LORD! Are you going to destroy the entire remnant of Israel in this outpouring
of your wrath on Jerusalem?"
[9]He answered me, "The sin of the
house of Israel and Judah is exceedingly great; the land is full of bloodshed
and the city is full of injustice. They say,
'The LORD has forsaken the land; the
LORD does not see.' [10]So I will not look
on them with pity or spare them, but I
will bring down on their own heads
what they have done."
[11]Then the man in linen with the
writing kit at his side brought back
word, saying, "I have done as you commanded."

SHARPEN THE FOCUS

The Baptismal service has always included words like these: "Receive the sign of the holy cross, both upon the forehead and upon the heart, in token that you have been redeemed by Christ, the crucified."

In Baptism God claims us, adopts us, and marks us as His own. He sets aside both our intellect and our hearts for His holy use. He says to all the angels in heaven and all the demons in hell, "This one is Mine." "The Lord knows those who are His" (2 Timothy 2:19).

The mark by which the Lord sealed His faithful people in Ezekiel's vision (Ezekiel 9:4–6) foreshadowed this. They, like we, would have to endure the pain and trouble of our fallen world. But the Lord would keep His eye on them. He would place His hand of protection over them. Nothing would be able to pull them away from Him.

Our Savior-God keeps His eye on us, too. "Through faith," we are "shielded by God's power until the coming of the salvation that is ready to be revealed in the last time" (1 Peter 1:5). Our Lord has promised to keep us faithful *in* trouble and persecution until He brings us safely *through* it.

WEEK 63 • MONDAY

Ezekiel 10:1—11:25

GET THE BIG PICTURE

Today's chapters contain some of the saddest words in all of Scripture. The Lord's chosen people had turned their backs on Him. They had so defiled His temple with their idols that He could no longer stand to dwell there. The glory-cloud that had led Israel in the exodus and had entered Solomon's temple on the day of dedication now departs. The unbelievers of Jerusalem will face their destruction alone. If time is short, focus on Ezekiel 10:1–22; 11:22–25.

The Glory Departs From the Temple

10 I looked, and I saw the likeness of a throne of sapphire[a] above the expanse that was over the heads of the cherubim. 2The LORD said to the man clothed in linen, "Go in among the wheels beneath the cherubim. Fill your hands with burning coals from among the cherubim and scatter them over the city." And as I watched, he went in.

3Now the cherubim were standing on the south side of the temple when the man went in, and a cloud filled the inner court. 4Then the glory of the LORD rose from above the cherubim and moved to the threshold of the temple. The cloud filled the temple, and the court was full of the radiance of the glory of the LORD. 5The sound of the wings of the cherubim could be heard as far away as the outer court, like the voice of God Almighty[b] when he speaks.

6When the LORD commanded the man in linen, "Take fire from among the wheels, from among the cherubim," the man went in and stood beside a wheel. 7Then one of the cherubim reached out his hand to the fire that was among them. He took up some of it and put it into the hands of the man in linen, who took it and went out. 8(Under the wings of the cherubim could be seen what looked like the hands of a man.)

9I looked, and I saw beside the cherubim four wheels, one beside each of the cherubim; the wheels sparkled like chrysolite. 10As for their appearance, the four of them looked alike; each was like a wheel intersecting a wheel. 11As they moved, they would go in any one of the four directions the cherubim faced; the wheels did not turn about[c] as the cherubim went. The cherubim went in whatever direction the head faced, without turning as they went. 12Their entire bodies, including their backs, their hands and their wings, were completely full of eyes, as were their four wheels. 13I heard the wheels being called "the whirling wheels." 14Each of the cherubim had four faces: One face was that of a cherub, the second the face of a man, the third the face of a lion, and the fourth the face of an eagle.

15Then the cherubim rose upward. These were the living creatures I had seen by the Kebar River. 16When the cherubim moved, the wheels beside them moved; and when the cherubim spread their wings to rise from the ground, the wheels did not leave their side. 17When the cherubim stood still, they also stood still; and when the cherubim rose, they rose with them, because the spirit of the living creatures was in them.

18Then the glory of the LORD departed from over the threshold of the temple and stopped above the cherubim. 19While I watched, the cherubim spread their wings and rose from the ground, and as they went, the wheels went with them. They stopped at the entrance to the east gate of the LORD's house, and the glory of the God of Israel was above them.

20These were the living creatures I had seen beneath the God of Israel by the Kebar River, and I realized that they were cherubim. 21Each had four faces and four wings, and under their wings was what looked like the hands of a man. 22Their faces had the same appearance as those I had seen by the Kebar River. Each one went straight ahead.

Judgment on Israel's Leaders

11 Then the Spirit lifted me up and brought me to the gate of the house of the LORD that faces east. There at the entrance to the gate were twenty-five men, and I saw among them

[a]1 Or *lapis lazuli* [b]5 Hebrew *El-Shaddai* [c]11 Or *aside*

Jaazaniah son of Azzur and Pelatiah son of Benaiah, leaders of the people. 2The LORD said to me, "Son of man, these are the men who are plotting evil and giving wicked advice in this city. 3They say, 'Will it not soon be time to build houses?[a] This city is a cooking pot, and we are the meat.' 4Therefore prophesy against them; prophesy, son of man."

5Then the Spirit of the LORD came upon me, and he told me to say: "This is what the LORD says: That is what you are saying, O house of Israel, but I know what is going through your mind. 6You have killed many people in this city and filled its streets with the dead.

7"Therefore this is what the Sovereign LORD says: The bodies you have thrown there are the meat and this city is the pot, but I will drive you out of it. 8You fear the sword, and the sword is what I will bring against you, declares the Sovereign LORD. 9I will drive you out of the city and hand you over to foreigners and inflict punishment on you. 10You will fall by the sword, and I will execute judgment on you at the borders of Israel. Then you will know that I am the LORD. 11This city will not be a pot for you, nor will you be the meat in it; I will execute judgment on you at the borders of Israel. 12And you will know that I am the LORD, for you have not followed my decrees or kept my laws but have conformed to the standards of the nations around you."

13Now as I was prophesying, Pelatiah son of Benaiah died. Then I fell facedown and cried out in a loud voice, "Ah, Sovereign LORD! Will you completely destroy the remnant of Israel?"

14The word of the LORD came to me: 15"Son of man, your brothers—your brothers who are your blood relatives[b] and the whole house of Israel—are those of whom the people of Jerusalem have said, 'They are[c] far away from the LORD; this land was given to us as our possession.'

Promised Return of Israel

16"Therefore say: 'This is what the Sovereign LORD says: Although I sent them far away among the nations and scattered them among the countries, yet for a little while I have been a sanctuary for them in the countries where they have gone.'

17"Therefore say: 'This is what the Sovereign LORD says: I will gather you from the nations and bring you back from the countries where you have been scattered, and I will give you back the land of Israel again.'

18"They will return to it and remove all its vile images and detestable idols. 19I will give them an undivided heart and put a new spirit in them; I will remove from them their heart of stone and give them a heart of flesh. 20Then they will follow my decrees and be careful to keep my laws. They will be my people, and I will be their God. 21But as for those whose hearts are devoted to their vile images and detestable idols, I will bring down on their own heads what they have done, declares the Sovereign LORD."

22Then the cherubim, with the wheels beside them, spread their wings, and the glory of the God of Israel was above them. 23The glory of the LORD went up from within the city and stopped above the mountain east of it. 24The Spirit lifted me up and brought me to the exiles in Babylonia[d] in the vision given by the Spirit of God.

Then the vision I had seen went up from me, 25and I told the exiles everything the LORD had shown me.

[a]3 Or *This is not the time to build houses.*
[b]15 Or *are in exile with you* (see Septuagint and Syriac) [c]15 Or *those to whom the people of Jerusalem have said, 'Stay* [d]24 Or *Chaldea*

SHARPEN THE FOCUS

When does the Lord's glory abandon a congregation, a group, a person? More to the point, how can I be sure He won't leave me? The answer to those questions depends on your answer to this question: Why do you ask?

If you find yourself concerned about the prestige of your church or worried about your reputation as "God's person of great faith," you're walking down the wrong path. Ancient Judah also clung to the rituals and dismissed the relationship. She needed heart surgery—on an emergency basis (Ezekiel 11:19).

On the other hand, if the thought of losing your relationship with the Lord terrifies you, be at peace. The Lord will be for you a sanctuary (Ezekiel 11:16), a holy place of refuge. When your conscience cringes in fear, when your heart hurts because of the things you've thought and said and done against God's law, you can run to your Savior. You can cling to His cross. You can rest in His love.

In whichever place you find yourself right now, talk to your Lord about it. Express your fears. Confess your sins. Then let Him give you His peace.

WEEK 63 • TUESDAY

Ezekiel 12:1—13:23

GET THE BIG PICTURE

Despite all evidence to the contrary, many exiles clung to the false hope that Jerusalem would never fall. Much like the "magical thinking" of people today who ignore the obvious, the people believed what they wanted to believe. As you read, notice the way they collected false prophets to encourage them in their false faith. If time is short, focus on Ezekiel 12:21–28.

The Exile Symbolized

12 The word of the LORD came
to me: 2"Son of man, you are
living among a rebellious people. They
have eyes to see but do not see and ears
to hear but do not hear, for they are a
rebellious people.
3"Therefore, son of man, pack your
belongings for exile and in the daytime,
as they watch, set out and go from
where you are to another place. Perhaps
they will understand, though they are
a rebellious house. 4During the daytime,
while they watch, bring out your belongings
packed for exile. Then in the
evening, while they are watching, go
out like those who go into exile. 5While
they watch, dig through the wall and
take your belongings out through it.
6Put them on your shoulder as they are
watching and carry them out at dusk.
Cover your face so that you cannot see
the land, for I have made you a sign to
the house of Israel."
7So I did as I was commanded. During
the day I brought out my things
packed for exile. Then in the evening I
dug through the wall with my hands. I
took my belongings out at dusk, carrying
them on my shoulders while they
watched.
8In the morning the word of the LORD

came to me: 9"Son of man, did not that rebellious house of Israel ask you, 'What are you doing?'

10"Say to them, 'This is what the Sovereign LORD says: This oracle concerns the prince in Jerusalem and the whole house of Israel who are there.' 11Say to them, 'I am a sign to you.'

"As I have done, so it will be done to them. They will go into exile as captives.

12"The prince among them will put his things on his shoulder at dusk and leave, and a hole will be dug in the wall for him to go through. He will cover his face so that he cannot see the land. 13I will spread my net for him, and he will be caught in my snare; I will bring him to Babylonia, the land of the Chaldeans, but he will not see it, and there he will die. 14I will scatter to the winds all those around him—his staff and all his troops—and I will pursue them with drawn sword.

15"They will know that I am the LORD, when I disperse them among the nations and scatter them through the countries. 16But I will spare a few of them from the sword, famine and plague, so that in the nations where they go they may acknowledge all their detestable practices. Then they will know that I am the LORD."

17The word of the LORD came to me: 18"Son of man, tremble as you eat your food, and shudder in fear as you drink your water. 19Say to the people of the land: 'This is what the Sovereign LORD says about those living in Jerusalem and in the land of Israel: They will eat their food in anxiety and drink their water in despair, for their land will be stripped of everything in it because of the violence of all who live there. 20The inhabited towns will be laid waste and the land will be desolate. Then you will know that I am the LORD.' "

21The word of the LORD came to me: 22"Son of man, what is this proverb you have in the land of Israel: 'The days go by and every vision comes to nothing'? 23Say to them, 'This is what the Sovereign LORD says: I am going to put an end to this proverb, and they will no longer quote it in Israel.' Say to them, 'The days are near when every vision will be fulfilled. 24For there will be no more false visions or flattering divinations among the people of Israel. 25But I the LORD will speak what I will, and it shall be fulfilled without delay. For in your days, you rebellious house, I will fulfill whatever I say, declares the Sovereign LORD.' "

26The word of the LORD came to me: 27"Son of man, the house of Israel is saying, 'The vision he sees is for many years from now, and he prophesies about the distant future.'

28"Therefore say to them, 'This is what the Sovereign LORD says: None of my words will be delayed any longer; whatever I say will be fulfilled, declares the Sovereign LORD.' "

False Prophets Condemned

13 The word of the LORD came to me: 2"Son of man, prophesy against the prophets of Israel who are now prophesying. Say to those who prophesy out of their own imagination: 'Hear the word of the LORD! 3This is what the Sovereign LORD says: Woe to the foolish[a] prophets who follow their own spirit and have seen nothing! 4Your prophets, O Israel, are like jackals among ruins. 5You have not gone up to the breaks in the wall to repair it for the house of Israel so that it will stand firm in the battle on the day of the LORD. 6Their visions are false and their divinations a lie. They say, "The LORD declares," when the LORD has not sent them; yet they expect their words to be fulfilled. 7Have you not seen false visions and uttered lying divinations when you say, "The LORD declares," though I have not spoken?

8" 'Therefore this is what the Sovereign LORD says: Because of your false words and lying visions, I am against you, declares the Sovereign LORD. 9My hand will be against the prophets who see false visions and utter lying divinations. They will not belong to the coun-

[a]3 Or *wicked*

cil of my people or be listed in the records of the house of Israel, nor will they enter the land of Israel. Then you will know that I am the Sovereign LORD.

10“ ‘Because they lead my people astray, saying, “Peace,” when there is no peace, and because, when a flimsy wall is built, they cover it with whitewash, 11therefore tell those who cover it with whitewash that it is going to fall. Rain will come in torrents, and I will send hailstones hurtling down, and violent winds will burst forth. 12When the wall collapses, will people not ask you, “Where is the whitewash you covered it with?”

13“ ‘Therefore this is what the Sovereign LORD says: In my wrath I will unleash a violent wind, and in my anger hailstones and torrents of rain will fall with destructive fury. 14I will tear down the wall you have covered with whitewash and will level it to the ground so that its foundation will be laid bare. When it[a] falls, you will be destroyed in it; and you will know that I am the LORD. 15So I will spend my wrath against the wall and against those who covered it with whitewash. I will say to you, “The wall is gone and so are those who whitewashed it, 16those prophets of Israel who prophesied to Jerusalem and saw visions of peace for her when there was no peace, declares the Sovereign LORD.” ’

17“Now, son of man, set your face against the daughters of your people who prophesy out of their own imagination. Prophesy against them 18and say, ‘This is what the Sovereign LORD says: Woe to the women who sew magic charms on all their wrists and make veils of various lengths for their heads in order to ensnare people. Will you ensnare the lives of my people but preserve your own? 19You have profaned me among my people for a few handfuls of barley and scraps of bread. By lying to my people, who listen to lies, you have killed those who should not have died and have spared those who should not live.

20“ ‘Therefore this is what the Sovereign LORD says: I am against your magic charms with which you ensnare people like birds and I will tear them from your arms; I will set free the people that you ensnare like birds. 21I will tear off your veils and save my people from your hands, and they will no longer fall prey to your power. Then you will know that I am the LORD. 22Because you disheartened the righteous with your lies, when I had brought them no grief, and because you encouraged the wicked not to turn from their evil ways and so save their lives, 23therefore you will no longer see false visions or practice divination. I will save my people from your hands. And then you will know that I am the LORD.’ ”

[a]14 Or *the city*

SHARPEN THE FOCUS

From Eden onward, Satan has always hissed, “Has God really said . . . ?” The exiles in Babylon listened to his lies gladly. They wanted to believe that since the Lord had delayed their doom, He had probably canceled His verdict of judgment. They even had a proverb about it: “The days go by, and every vision comes to nothing” (Ezekiel 12:22).

The apostle Peter heard Satan planting the same kind of doubts in the minds of Christian people of the first century. “Where is this coming He promised?” (2 Peter 3:4) laugh scoffers in every age. The apostle responds:

> *The Lord is not slow in keeping His promise, as some understand slowness. He is patient with you, not wanting anyone to perish, but everyone to come to repentance.* (2 Peter 3:9)

The Day of Judgment will come as surely as Babylon invaded Judah. In Ezekiel's time, one day, quite unexpectedly, the day of grace ended. The day of justice dawned. Do you await Judgment Day in hope and holy joy? Do you long to see your Savior's face? Do you rest confident in the forgiveness that flows for you from Calvary's cross? You can, you know. Jesus died and rose again for you. ☼

WEEK 63 • WEDNESDAY

Ezekiel 14:1—15:8

GET THE BIG PICTURE

Intrigued by Ezekiel's message, the leaders of the exiles came to hear him quite often. Interested in listening, they had no intention of changing. Ezekiel had only one message for them: Repent! As you read, ask yourself why you come to God to hear His Word. If time is short, focus on Ezekiel 15:1–8.

Idolaters Condemned

14 Some of the elders of Israel
came to me and sat down in
front of me. 2Then the word of the LORD
came to me: 3"Son of man, these men
have set up idols in their hearts and put
wicked stumbling blocks before their
faces. Should I let them inquire of me at
all? 4Therefore speak to them and tell
them, 'This is what the Sovereign LORD
says: When any Israelite sets up idols in
his heart and puts a wicked stumbling
block before his face and then goes to a
prophet, I the LORD will answer him
myself in keeping with his great idolatry.
5I will do this to recapture the hearts
of the people of Israel, who have all deserted me for their idols.'
6"Therefore say to the house of Israel,
'This is what the Sovereign LORD says:
Repent! Turn from your idols and renounce all your detestable practices!
7" 'When any Israelite or any alien living in Israel separates himself from me
and sets up idols in his heart and puts a
wicked stumbling block before his face
and then goes to a prophet to inquire of
me, I the LORD will answer him myself.
8I will set my face against that man and
make him an example and a byword. I
will cut him off from my people. Then
you will know that I am the LORD.
9" 'And if the prophet is enticed to utter a prophecy, I the LORD have enticed
that prophet, and I will stretch out my
hand against him and destroy him from
among my people Israel. 10They will
bear their guilt—the prophet will be as
guilty as the one who consults him.
11Then the people of Israel will no longer stray from me, nor will they defile
themselves anymore with all their sins.
They will be my people, and I will be
their God, declares the Sovereign
LORD.' "

Judgment Inescapable

12The word of the LORD came to me:
13"Son of man, if a country sins against
me by being unfaithful and I stretch out
my hand against it to cut off its food
supply and send famine upon it and kill
its men and their animals, 14even if these
three men—Noah, Daniel[a] and Job—
were in it, they could save only them-

[a]14 Or *Danel*; the Hebrew spelling may suggest a person other than the prophet Daniel; also in verse 20.

selves by their righteousness, declares
the Sovereign LORD.
15“Or if I send wild beasts through that
country and they leave it childless and
it becomes desolate so that no one can
pass through it because of the beasts,
16as surely as I live, declares the Sovereign LORD, even if these three men were
in it, they could not save their own sons
or daughters. They alone would be
saved, but the land would be desolate.
17“Or if I bring a sword against that
country and say, ‘Let the sword pass
throughout the land,’ and I kill its men
and their animals, 18as surely as I live,
declares the Sovereign LORD, even if
these three men were in it, they could
not save their own sons or daughters.
They alone would be saved.
19“Or if I send a plague into that land
and pour out my wrath upon it through
bloodshed, killing its men and their animals, 20as surely as I live, declares the
Sovereign LORD, even if Noah, Daniel
and Job were in it, they could save neither son nor daughter. They would save
only themselves by their righteousness.
21“For this is what the Sovereign LORD
says: How much worse will it be when
I send against Jerusalem my four dreadful judgments—sword and famine and
wild beasts and plague—to kill its men
and their animals! 22Yet there will be
some survivors—sons and daughters
who will be brought out of it. They will
come to you, and when you see their
conduct and their actions, you will be
consoled regarding the disaster I have
brought upon Jerusalem—every disaster I have brought upon it. 23You will be
consoled when you see their conduct
and their actions, for you will know that
I have done nothing in it without cause,
declares the Sovereign LORD.”

Jerusalem, A Useless Vine

15 The word of the LORD came
to me: 2“Son of man, how is
the wood of a vine better than that of a
branch on any of the trees in the forest?
3Is wood ever taken from it to make anything useful? Do they make pegs from
it to hang things on? 4And after it is
thrown on the fire as fuel and the fire
burns both ends and chars the middle,
is it then useful for anything? 5If it was
not useful for anything when it was
whole, how much less can it be made
into something useful when the fire has
burned it and it is charred?
6“Therefore this is what the Sovereign
LORD says: As I have given the wood of
the vine among the trees of the forest as
fuel for the fire, so will I treat the people living in Jerusalem. 7I will set my face
against them. Although they have come
out of the fire, the fire will yet consume
them. And when I set my face against
them, you will know that I am the LORD.
8I will make the land desolate because
they have been unfaithful, declares the
Sovereign LORD.”

SHARPEN THE FOCUS

You probably have never seen furniture built from grapevines. Such vines are too fragile and brittle, and, let’s face it, too ugly to make even cheap furniture. Grapevines have another purpose—bearing fruit.

In Ezekiel’s “parable of the vine,” you see the prophet proclaim the foolishness of trying to find a use for grape vines, much less vines charred by fire. “You are worthless,” the Lord tells His rebellious people. “You have no strength. You bear no fruit. My fire of judgment will burn you up.”

Contrast this with Jesus’ word of grace to His repentant people:

> *I am the vine; you are the branches. If a man remains in Me and I in him, he will bear much fruit; apart from Me you can do nothing.* (John 15:5)

Apart from Christ, we can do nothing; rooted in Christ, our lives bring glory to our Father. We hear God's Word so that through it He can strengthen our attachment to Him. He can supply the nutrients we need to produce lush spiritual fruit. This nourishment is part of the package we call salvation, the blessings that come to us from God in the forgiveness Jesus earned for us on His cross.

WEEK 63 • THURSDAY

Ezekiel 16:1—17:24

You'll better understand both chapters in today's reading with some background of the history of Israel. Chapter 16 reviews that history in broad strokes from the time of Abraham up to the exiles imposed by Assyria and Babylon. Chapter 17 deals with a small slice of that history, mostly the last days of Judah (2 Kings 24:8–20 and Jeremiah 37; 52:1–11). If time is short, focus on Ezekiel 16:3–14.

An Allegory of Unfaithful Jerusalem

16 The word of the LORD came
to me: 2"Son of man, confront
Jerusalem with her detestable practices
3and say, 'This is what the Sovereign
LORD says to Jerusalem: Your ancestry
and birth were in the land of the Canaanites; your father was an Amorite
and your mother a Hittite. 4On the day
you were born your cord was not cut,
nor were you washed with water to
make you clean, nor were you rubbed
with salt or wrapped in cloths. 5No one
looked on you with pity or had compassion enough to do any of these things
for you. Rather, you were thrown out
into the open field, for on the day you
were born you were despised.
6" 'Then I passed by and saw you
kicking about in your blood, and as you
lay there in your blood I said to you,
"Live!"[a] 7I made you grow like a plant of
the field. You grew up and developed
and became the most beautiful of
jewels.[b] Your breasts were formed and
your hair grew, you who were naked
and bare.
8" 'Later I passed by, and when I
looked at you and saw that you were
old enough for love, I spread the corner
of my garment over you and covered
your nakedness. I gave you my solemn
oath and entered into a covenant with
you, declares the Sovereign LORD, and
you became mine.
9" 'I bathed[c] you with water and
washed the blood from you and put
ointments on you. 10I clothed you with
an embroidered dress and put leather
sandals on you. I dressed you in fine linen and covered you with costly garments. 11I adorned you with jewelry: I
put bracelets on your arms and a necklace around your neck, 12and I put a ring
on your nose, earrings on your ears and
a beautiful crown on your head. 13So
you were adorned with gold and silver;
your clothes were of fine linen and costly fabric and embroidered cloth. Your
food was fine flour, honey and olive oil.
You became very beautiful and rose to
be a queen. 14And your fame spread

[a]6 A few Hebrew manuscripts, Septuagint and Syriac; most Hebrew manuscripts *"Live!" And as you lay there in your blood I said to you, "Live!"*
[b]7 Or *became mature* [c]9 Or *I had bathed*

among the nations on account of your beauty, because the splendor I had given you made your beauty perfect, declares the Sovereign LORD.

15" 'But you trusted in your beauty and used your fame to become a prostitute. You lavished your favors on anyone who passed by and your beauty became his.[a] 16You took some of your garments to make gaudy high places, where you carried on your prostitution. Such things should not happen, nor should they ever occur. 17You also took the fine jewelry I gave you, the jewelry made of my gold and silver, and you made for yourself male idols and engaged in prostitution with them. 18And you took your embroidered clothes to put on them, and you offered my oil and incense before them. 19Also the food I provided for you—the fine flour, olive oil and honey I gave you to eat—you offered as fragrant incense before them. That is what happened, declares the Sovereign LORD.

20" 'And you took your sons and daughters whom you bore to me and sacrificed them as food to the idols. Was your prostitution not enough? 21You slaughtered my children and sacrificed them[b] to the idols. 22In all your detestable practices and your prostitution you did not remember the days of your youth, when you were naked and bare, kicking about in your blood.

23" 'Woe! Woe to you, declares the Sovereign LORD. In addition to all your other wickedness, 24you built a mound for yourself and made a lofty shrine in every public square. 25At the head of every street you built your lofty shrines and degraded your beauty, offering your body with increasing promiscuity to anyone who passed by. 26You engaged in prostitution with the Egyptians, your lustful neighbors, and provoked me to anger with your increasing promiscuity. 27So I stretched out my hand against you and reduced your territory; I gave you over to the greed of your enemies, the daughters of the Philistines, who were shocked by your lewd conduct. 28You engaged in prostitution with the Assyrians too, because you were insatiable; and even after that, you still were not satisfied. 29Then you increased your promiscuity to include Babylonia,[c] a land of merchants, but even with this you were not satisfied.

30" 'How weak-willed you are, declares the Sovereign LORD, when you do all these things, acting like a brazen prostitute! 31When you built your mounds at the head of every street and made your lofty shrines in every public square, you were unlike a prostitute, because you scorned payment.

32" 'You adulterous wife! You prefer strangers to your own husband! 33Every prostitute receives a fee, but you give gifts to all your lovers, bribing them to come to you from everywhere for your illicit favors. 34So in your prostitution you are the opposite of others; no one runs after you for your favors. You are the very opposite, for you give payment and none is given to you.

35" 'Therefore, you prostitute, hear the word of the LORD! 36This is what the Sovereign LORD says: Because you poured out your wealth[d] and exposed your nakedness in your promiscuity with your lovers, and because of all your detestable idols, and because you gave them your children's blood, 37therefore I am going to gather all your lovers, with whom you found pleasure, those you loved as well as those you hated. I will gather them against you from all around and will strip you in front of them, and they will see all your nakedness. 38I will sentence you to the punishment of women who commit adultery and who shed blood; I will bring upon you the blood vengeance of my wrath and jealous anger. 39Then I will hand you over to your lovers, and they will tear down your mounds and destroy your lofty shrines. They will strip you of your clothes and take your fine jewelry and

[a] *15* Most Hebrew manuscripts; one Hebrew manuscript (see some Septuagint manuscripts) *by. Such a thing should not happen* [b] 21 Or *and made them pass through ⌊the fire⌋* [c] 29 Or *Chaldea* [d] 36 Or *lust*

leave you naked and bare. [40]They will bring a mob against you, who will stone you and hack you to pieces with their swords. [41]They will burn down your houses and inflict punishment on you in the sight of many women. I will put a stop to your prostitution, and you will no longer pay your lovers. [42]Then my wrath against you will subside and my jealous anger will turn away from you; I will be calm and no longer angry.

[43]" 'Because you did not remember the days of your youth but enraged me with all these things, I will surely bring down on your head what you have done, declares the Sovereign LORD. Did you not add lewdness to all your other detestable practices?

[44]" 'Everyone who quotes proverbs will quote this proverb about you: "Like mother, like daughter." [45]You are a true daughter of your mother, who despised her husband and her children; and you are a true sister of your sisters, who despised their husbands and their children. Your mother was a Hittite and your father an Amorite. [46]Your older sister was Samaria, who lived to the north of you with her daughters; and your younger sister, who lived to the south of you with her daughters, was Sodom. [47]You not only walked in their ways and copied their detestable practices, but in all your ways you soon became more depraved than they. [48]As surely as I live, declares the Sovereign LORD, your sister Sodom and her daughters never did what you and your daughters have done.

[49]" 'Now this was the sin of your sister Sodom: She and her daughters were arrogant, overfed and unconcerned; they did not help the poor and needy. [50]They were haughty and did detestable things before me. Therefore I did away with them as you have seen. [51]Samaria did not commit half the sins you did. You have done more detestable things than they, and have made your sisters seem righteous by all these things you have done. [52]Bear your disgrace, for you have furnished some justification for your sisters. Because your sins were more vile than theirs, they appear more righteous than you. So then, be ashamed and bear your disgrace, for you have made your sisters appear righteous.

[53]" 'However, I will restore the fortunes of Sodom and her daughters and of Samaria and her daughters, and your fortunes along with them, [54]so that you may bear your disgrace and be ashamed of all you have done in giving them comfort. [55]And your sisters, Sodom with her daughters and Samaria with her daughters, will return to what they were before; and you and your daughters will return to what you were before. [56]You would not even mention your sister Sodom in the day of your pride, [57]before your wickedness was uncovered. Even so, you are now scorned by the daughters of Edom[a] and all her neighbors and the daughters of the Philistines—all those around you who despise you. [58]You will bear the consequences of your lewdness and your detestable practices, declares the LORD.

[59]" 'This is what the Sovereign LORD says: I will deal with you as you deserve, because you have despised my oath by breaking the covenant. [60]Yet I will remember the covenant I made with you in the days of your youth, and I will establish an everlasting covenant with you. [61]Then you will remember your ways and be ashamed when you receive your sisters, both those who are older than you and those who are younger. I will give them to you as daughters, but not on the basis of my covenant with you. [62]So I will establish my covenant with you, and you will know that I am the LORD. [63]Then, when I make atonement for you for all you have done, you will remember and be ashamed and never again open your mouth because of your humiliation, declares the Sovereign LORD.' "

[a]57 Many Hebrew manuscripts and Syriac; most Hebrew manuscripts, Septuagint and Vulgate *Aram*

Two Eagles and a Vine

17 The word of the LORD came
to me: 2"Son of man, set forth
an allegory and tell the house of Israel
a parable. 3Say to them, 'This is what the
Sovereign LORD says: A great eagle with
powerful wings, long feathers and full
plumage of varied colors came to Lebanon. Taking hold of the top of a cedar,
4he broke off its topmost shoot and carried it away to a land of merchants,
where he planted it in a city of traders.

5" 'He took some of the seed of your
land and put it in fertile soil. He planted it like a willow by abundant water,
6and it sprouted and became a low,
spreading vine. Its branches turned toward him, but its roots remained under
it. So it became a vine and produced
branches and put out leafy boughs.

7" 'But there was another great eagle
with powerful wings and full plumage.
The vine now sent out its roots toward
him from the plot where it was planted
and stretched out its branches to him for
water. 8It had been planted in good soil
by abundant water so that it would produce branches, bear fruit and become a
splendid vine.'

9"Say to them, 'This is what the Sovereign LORD says: Will it thrive? Will it
not be uprooted and stripped of its fruit
so that it withers? All its new growth
will wither. It will not take a strong arm
or many people to pull it up by the
roots. 10Even if it is transplanted, will it
thrive? Will it not wither completely
when the east wind strikes it—wither
away in the plot where it grew?' "

11Then the word of the LORD came to
me: 12"Say to this rebellious house, 'Do
you not know what these things mean?'
Say to them: 'The king of Babylon went
to Jerusalem and carried off her king
and her nobles, bringing them back
with him to Babylon. 13Then he took a
member of the royal family and made a
treaty with him, putting him under
oath. He also carried away the leading
men of the land, 14so that the kingdom
would be brought low, unable to rise
again, surviving only by keeping his
treaty. 15But the king rebelled against
him by sending his envoys to Egypt to
get horses and a large army. Will he succeed? Will he who does such things escape? Will he break the treaty and yet
escape?

16" 'As surely as I live, declares the Sovereign LORD, he shall die in Babylon, in
the land of the king who put him on the
throne, whose oath he despised and
whose treaty he broke. 17Pharaoh with
his mighty army and great horde will be
of no help to him in war, when ramps
are built and siege works erected to destroy many lives. 18He despised the oath
by breaking the covenant. Because he
had given his hand in pledge and yet
did all these things, he shall not escape.

19" 'Therefore this is what the Sovereign LORD says: As surely as I live, I will
bring down on his head my oath that he
despised and my covenant that he
broke. 20I will spread my net for him,
and he will be caught in my snare. I will
bring him to Babylon and execute judgment upon him there because he was
unfaithful to me. 21All his fleeing troops
will fall by the sword, and the survivors
will be scattered to the winds. Then you
will know that I the LORD have spoken.

22" 'This is what the Sovereign LORD
says: I myself will take a shoot from the
very top of a cedar and plant it; I will
break off a tender sprig from its topmost
shoots and plant it on a high and lofty
mountain. 23On the mountain heights of
Israel I will plant it; it will produce
branches and bear fruit and become a
splendid cedar. Birds of every kind will
nest in it; they will find shelter in the
shade of its branches. 24All the trees of
the field will know that I the LORD bring
down the tall tree and make the low tree
grow tall. I dry up the green tree and
make the dry tree flourish.

" 'I the LORD have spoken, and I will
do it.' "

SHARPEN THE FOCUS

Even if you're not sure about all the historical facts, you can find real and personal meaning, especially in the first parable. As you study Ezekiel 16:3–14 now, think of your own spiritual history and of God's undeserved but incredible love for you in Jesus.

Think of the comparisons based on Ezekiel 16 and your own life and walk with the Lord:

- 16:3–Abraham's parents were sinners, idol-worshipers.
  What are my parents? How did they show (or not show) God's love in their lives?
- 16:4–5–No one considered the Hebrews anything special; Egypt enslaved them. What is special about my family and me? How do others consider us?
- 16:6–8–God chose Israel and gave her life and freedom.
  How has God chosen my family and me? How does He care for us?
- 16:8–10–God washed Israel in the Red Sea and gave her beautiful clothes.
  How has the Lord "washed" me? What is special about that washing?
- 16:11–14–God made Israel prosperous. What has God given me?

Thank God for His greatest gift–forgiveness and eternal life through the death of His Son, Jesus. Then use Ephesians 1:3–4 as a prayer of thanksgiving and praise.

WEEK 63 • FRIDAY

Ezekiel 18:1—19:14

GET THE BIG PICTURE

At times elementary school children can seem obsessed with fairness. A lost kickball game; a low score on a test; a birthday party with cake, but no ice cream–all these lead to the complaint, "It's not fair!" Adults, too, are quick to notice injustice. As you read today, notice the Lord's description of sin and its consequences. Is He fair? If time is short, focus on Ezekiel 18:20–32.

The Soul Who Sins Will Die

18 The word of the LORD came to me: 2"What do you people mean by quoting this proverb about the land of Israel:

" 'The fathers eat sour grapes,
and the children's teeth are set on edge'?

3"As surely as I live, declares the Sovereign LORD, you will no longer quote this proverb in Israel. 4For every living soul belongs to me, the father as well as the son—both alike belong to me. The soul who sins is the one who will die.

5"Suppose there is a righteous man
who does what is just and right.
6He does not eat at the mountain shrines
or look to the idols of the house of Israel.
He does not defile his neighbor's wife

or lie with a woman during her
period.
7 He does not oppress anyone,
but returns what he took in
pledge for a loan.
He does not commit robbery
but gives his food to the hungry
and provides clothing for the
naked.
8 He does not lend at usury
or take excessive interest.[a]
He withholds his hand from doing
wrong
and judges fairly between man
and man.
9 He follows my decrees
and faithfully keeps my laws.
That man is righteous;
he will surely live,
declares the Sovereign
LORD.

10 "Suppose he has a violent son, who
sheds blood or does any of these other
things[b] 11 (though the father has done
none of them):

"He eats at the mountain shrines.
He defiles his neighbor's wife.
12 He oppresses the poor and needy.
He commits robbery.
He does not return what he took in
pledge.
He looks to the idols.
He does detestable things.
13 He lends at usury and takes
excessive interest.

Will such a man live? He will not! Because he has done all these detestable
things, he will surely be put to death
and his blood will be on his own head.

14 "But suppose this son has a son who
sees all the sins his father commits, and
though he sees them, he does not do
such things:

15 "He does not eat at the mountain
shrines
or look to the idols of the house of
Israel.
He does not defile his neighbor's
wife.
16 He does not oppress anyone
or require a pledge for a loan.
He does not commit robbery
but gives his food to the hungry
and provides clothing for the
naked.
17 He withholds his hand from sin[c]
and takes no usury or excessive
interest.
He keeps my laws and follows my
decrees.

He will not die for his father's sin; he
will surely live. 18 But his father will die
for his own sin, because he practiced
extortion, robbed his brother and did
what was wrong among his people.

19 "Yet you ask, 'Why does the son not
share the guilt of his father?' Since the
son has done what is just and right and
has been careful to keep all my decrees,
he will surely live. 20 The soul who sins
is the one who will die. The son will not
share the guilt of the father, nor will the
father share the guilt of the son. The
righteousness of the righteous man will
be credited to him, and the wickedness
of the wicked will be charged against
him.

21 "But if a wicked man turns away
from all the sins he has committed and
keeps all my decrees and does what is
just and right, he will surely live; he will
not die. 22 None of the offenses he has
committed will be remembered against
him. Because of the righteous things he
has done, he will live. 23 Do I take any
pleasure in the death of the wicked? declares the Sovereign LORD. Rather, am I
not pleased when they turn from their
ways and live?

24 "But if a righteous man turns from
his righteousness and commits sin and
does the same detestable things the
wicked man does, will he live? None of
the righteous things he has done will be
remembered. Because of the unfaithfulness he is guilty of and because of the
sins he has committed, he will die.

25 "Yet you say, 'The way of the Lord is
not just.' Hear, O house of Israel: Is my
way unjust? Is it not your ways that are

[a] 8 Or *take interest*; similarly in verses 13 and 17
[b] 10 Or *things to a brother* [c] 17 Septuagint (see also verse 8); Hebrew *from the poor*

unjust? 26If a righteous man turns from
his righteousness and commits sin, he
will die for it; because of the sin he has
committed he will die. 27But if a wicked
man turns away from the wickedness
he has committed and does what is just
and right, he will save his life. 28Because
he considers all the offenses he has committed and turns away from them, he
will surely live; he will not die. 29Yet the
house of Israel says, 'The way of the
Lord is not just.' Are my ways unjust,
O house of Israel? Is it not your ways
that are unjust?

30"Therefore, O house of Israel, I will
judge you, each one according to his
ways, declares the Sovereign LORD. Repent! Turn away from all your offenses;
then sin will not be your downfall. 31Rid
yourselves of all the offenses you have
committed, and get a new heart and a
new spirit. Why will you die, O house
of Israel? 32For I take no pleasure in the
death of anyone, declares the Sovereign
LORD. Repent and live!

A Lament for Israel's Princes

19 "Take up a lament concerning
the princes of Israel 2and say:

" 'What a lioness was your mother
among the lions!
She lay down among the young
lions
and reared her cubs.
3She brought up one of her cubs,
and he became a strong lion.
He learned to tear the prey
and he devoured men.
4The nations heard about him,
and he was trapped in their pit.
They led him with hooks
to the land of Egypt.

5" 'When she saw her hope
unfulfilled,
her expectation gone,
she took another of her cubs
and made him a strong lion.
6He prowled among the lions,
for he was now a strong lion.
He learned to tear the prey
and he devoured men.
7He broke down[a] their strongholds
and devastated their towns.
The land and all who were in it
were terrified by his roaring.
8Then the nations came against him,
those from regions round about.
They spread their net for him,
and he was trapped in their pit.
9With hooks they pulled him into a
cage
and brought him to the king of
Babylon.
They put him in prison,
so his roar was heard no longer
on the mountains of Israel.

10" 'Your mother was like a vine in
your vineyard[b]
planted by the water;
it was fruitful and full of branches
because of abundant water.
11Its branches were strong,
fit for a ruler's scepter.
It towered high
above the thick foliage,
conspicuous for its height
and for its many branches.
12But it was uprooted in fury
and thrown to the ground.
The east wind made it shrivel,
it was stripped of its fruit;
its strong branches withered
and fire consumed them.
13Now it is planted in the desert,
in a dry and thirsty land.
14Fire spread from one of its main[c]
branches
and consumed its fruit.
No strong branch is left on it
fit for a ruler's scepter.'

This is a lament and is to be used as a lament."

[a]7 Targum (see Septuagint); Hebrew *He knew*
[b]10 Two Hebrew manuscripts; most Hebrew
manuscripts *your blood* [c]14 Or *from under its*

SHARPEN THE FOCUS

Ezekiel doesn't explain the term "righteous." From Adam on, we have seen people who believed God and His promise to send a Savior to pay the debt sinners had piled up by their disobedience to God's law. We have seen our Lord declare people right with Him through faith in that coming Savior. Those who know that God has removed their debt live lives rich in the kind of spiritual fruit Ezekiel describes in Ezekiel 18:5–9, 14–17.

On the other hand, those who know God's debt-elimination plan but reject it show their unbelief by their lifestyle too. Ezekiel 18:10–13 describes the violence, injustice, lack of compassion, greed and idolatry of these people. Unbelievers can live outwardly moral lives. Still, if you go beyond the surface, you will soon dig up attitudes and actions that offend our Lord.

Each of us will answer to God someday for what we've done with our lives. We will answer only for ourselves. On that day, the "righteousness of the righteous man will be credited to him" (Ezekiel 18:20). This is good news because our righteousness is the righteousness Jesus has credited to our account. It truly belongs to us, because of His holy life, innocent suffering, and His death on our behalf. ☼

WEEK 63 • SATURDAY

Ezekiel 20:1—21:32

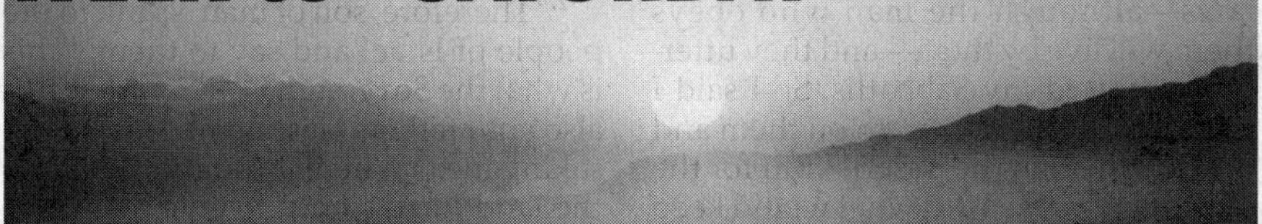

GET THE BIG PICTURE

Ezekiel 20 builds fact upon fact, testifying to Israel's unfaithfulness. Just as the truth of the nation's guilt reaches a crescendo, the Lord stuns us with His grace, His absolute faithfulness to His covenant people. As you read, watch for the contrast between Ezekiel 20:1–43 and 20:44. If time is short, focus on Ezekiel 20:1–44.

Rebellious Israel

20 In the seventh year, in the
fifth month on the tenth
day, some of the elders of Israel came to
inquire of the LORD, and they sat down
in front of me.
2Then the word of the LORD came to
me: 3"Son of man, speak to the elders of
Israel and say to them, 'This is what the
Sovereign LORD says: Have you come to
inquire of me? As surely as I live, I will
not let you inquire of me, declares the
Sovereign LORD.'
4"Will you judge them? Will you
judge them, son of man? Then confront
them with the detestable practices of
their fathers 5and say to them: 'This is
what the Sovereign LORD says: On the
day I chose Israel, I swore with uplifted
hand to the descendants of the house of
Jacob and revealed myself to them in
Egypt. With uplifted hand I said to
them, "I am the LORD your God." 6On
that day I swore to them that I would
bring them out of Egypt into a land I
had searched out for them, a land flowing with milk and honey, the most beautiful of all lands. 7And I said to them,
"Each of you, get rid of the vile images
you have set your eyes on, and do not
defile yourselves with the idols of
Egypt. I am the LORD your God."

8“ 'But they rebelled against me and
would not listen to me; they did not get
rid of the vile images they had set their
eyes on, nor did they forsake the idols
of Egypt. So I said I would pour out my
wrath on them and spend my anger
against them in Egypt. 9But for the sake
of my name I did what would keep it
from being profaned in the eyes of the
nations they lived among and in whose
sight I had revealed myself to the Israelites by bringing them out of Egypt.
10Therefore I led them out of Egypt and
brought them into the desert. 11I gave
them my decrees and made known
to them my laws, for the man who
obeys them will live by them. 12Also I
gave them my Sabbaths as a sign between us, so they would know that I the
LORD made them holy.

13“ 'Yet the people of Israel rebelled
against me in the desert. They did not
follow my decrees but rejected my
laws—although the man who obeys
them will live by them—and they utterly desecrated my Sabbaths. So I said I
would pour out my wrath on them and
destroy them in the desert. 14But for the
sake of my name I did what would keep
it from being profaned in the eyes of the
nations in whose sight I had brought
them out. 15Also with uplifted hand I
swore to them in the desert that I would
not bring them into the land I had given
them—a land flowing with milk and
honey, most beautiful of all lands— 16be-
cause they rejected my laws and did not
follow my decrees and desecrated my
Sabbaths. For their hearts were devoted
to their idols. 17Yet I looked on them with
pity and did not destroy them or put an
end to them in the desert. 18I said to their
children in the desert, "Do not follow
the statutes of your fathers or keep their
laws or defile yourselves with their
idols. 19I am the LORD your God; follow
my decrees and be careful to keep my
laws. 20Keep my Sabbaths holy, that they
may be a sign between us. Then you will
know that I am the LORD your God."

21“ 'But the children rebelled against
me: They did not follow my decrees,
they were not careful to keep my laws—
although the man who obeys them will
live by them—and they desecrated my
Sabbaths. So I said I would pour out my
wrath on them and spend my anger
against them in the desert. 22But I withheld my hand, and for the sake of my
name I did what would keep it from
being profaned in the eyes of the nations in whose sight I had brought
them out. 23Also with uplifted hand I
swore to them in the desert that I would
disperse them among the nations and
scatter them through the countries, 24be-
cause they had not obeyed my laws but
had rejected my decrees and desecrated my Sabbaths, and their eyes ⌊lusted⌋
after their fathers' idols. 25I also gave
them over to statutes that were not
good and laws they could not live by; 26I
let them become defiled through their
gifts—the sacrifice of every firstborn[a]—
that I might fill them with horror so they
would know that I am the LORD.'

27“Therefore, son of man, speak to the
people of Israel and say to them, 'This
is what the Sovereign LORD says: In this
also your fathers blasphemed me by forsaking me: 28When I brought them into
the land I had sworn to give them and
they saw any high hill or any leafy tree,
there they offered their sacrifices, made
offerings that provoked me to anger,
presented their fragrant incense and
poured out their drink offerings. 29Then
I said to them: What is this high place
you go to?' " (It is called Bamah[b] to this
day.)

Judgment and Restoration

30“Therefore say to the house of Israel: 'This is what the Sovereign LORD
says: Will you defile yourselves the way
your fathers did and lust after their vile
images? 31When you offer your gifts—
the sacrifice of your sons in[c] the fire—
you continue to defile yourselves with
all your idols to this day. Am I to let you
inquire of me, O house of Israel? As
surely as I live, declares the Sovereign

[a]26 Or —*making every firstborn pass through ⌊the fire⌋* [b]29 *Bamah* means *high place.* [c]31 Or —*making your sons pass through*

LORD, I will not let you inquire of me.

32" 'You say, "We want to be like the nations, like the peoples of the world, who serve wood and stone." But what you have in mind will never happen. 33As surely as I live, declares the Sovereign LORD, I will rule over you with a mighty hand and an outstretched arm and with outpoured wrath. 34I will bring you from the nations and gather you from the countries where you have been scattered—with a mighty hand and an outstretched arm and with outpoured wrath. 35I will bring you into the desert of the nations and there, face to face, I will execute judgment upon you. 36As I judged your fathers in the desert of the land of Egypt, so I will judge you, declares the Sovereign LORD. 37I will take note of you as you pass under my rod, and I will bring you into the bond of the covenant. 38I will purge you of those who revolt and rebel against me. Although I will bring them out of the land where they are living, yet they will not enter the land of Israel. Then you will know that I am the LORD.

39" 'As for you, O house of Israel, this is what the Sovereign LORD says: Go and serve your idols, every one of you! But afterward you will surely listen to me and no longer profane my holy name with your gifts and idols. 40For on my holy mountain, the high mountain of Israel, declares the Sovereign LORD, there in the land the entire house of Israel will serve me, and there I will accept them. There I will require your offerings and your choice gifts,[a] along with all your holy sacrifices. 41I will accept you as fragrant incense when I bring you out from the nations and gather you from the countries where you have been scattered, and I will show myself holy among you in the sight of the nations. 42Then you will know that I am the LORD, when I bring you into the land of Israel, the land I had sworn with uplifted hand to give to your fathers. 43There you will remember your conduct and all the actions by which you have defiled yourselves, and you will loathe yourselves for all the evil you have done. 44You will know that I am the LORD, when I deal with you for my name's sake and not according to your evil ways and your corrupt practices, O house of Israel, declares the Sovereign LORD.' "

Prophecy Against the South

45The word of the LORD came to me: 46"Son of man, set your face toward the south; preach against the south and prophesy against the forest of the southland. 47Say to the southern forest: 'Hear the word of the LORD. This is what the Sovereign LORD says: I am about to set fire to you, and it will consume all your trees, both green and dry. The blazing flame will not be quenched, and every face from south to north will be scorched by it. 48Everyone will see that I the LORD have kindled it; it will not be quenched.' "

49Then I said, "Ah, Sovereign LORD! They are saying of me, 'Isn't he just telling parables?' "

Babylon, God's Sword of Judgment

21 The word of the LORD came to me: 2"Son of man, set your face against Jerusalem and preach against the sanctuary. Prophesy against the land of Israel 3and say to her: 'This is what the LORD says: I am against you. I will draw my sword from its scabbard and cut off from you both the righteous and the wicked. 4Because I am going to cut off the righteous and the wicked, my sword will be unsheathed against everyone from south to north. 5Then all people will know that I the LORD have drawn my sword from its scabbard; it will not return again.'

6"Therefore groan, son of man! Groan before them with broken heart and bitter grief. 7And when they ask you, 'Why are you groaning?' you shall say, 'Because of the news that is coming. Every heart will melt and every hand go limp; every spirit will become faint and every knee become as weak as water.' It is

[a]40 Or *and the gifts of your firstfruits*

coming! It will surely take place, declares the Sovereign LORD."
8 The word of the LORD came to me:
9 "Son of man, prophesy and say, 'This is
what the Lord says:

" 'A sword, a sword,
sharpened and polished—
10 sharpened for the slaughter,
polished to flash like lightning!
" 'Shall we rejoice in the scepter of my
son ⌞Judah⌟? The sword despises every
such stick.

11 " 'The sword is appointed to be
polished,
to be grasped with the hand;
it is sharpened and polished,
made ready for the hand of the
slayer.
12 Cry out and wail, son of man,
for it is against my people;
it is against all the princes of
Israel.
They are thrown to the sword
along with my people.
Therefore beat your breast.

13 " 'Testing will surely come. And
what if the scepter ⌞of Judah⌟, which the
sword despises, does not continue? declares the Sovereign LORD.'

14 "So then, son of man, prophesy
and strike your hands together.
Let the sword strike twice,
even three times.
It is a sword for slaughter—
a sword for great slaughter,
closing in on them from every
side.
15 So that hearts may melt
and the fallen be many,
I have stationed the sword for
slaughter[a]
at all their gates.
Oh! It is made to flash like lightning,
it is grasped for slaughter.
16 O sword, slash to the right,
then to the left,
wherever your blade is turned.
17 I too will strike my hands together,
and my wrath will subside.
I the LORD have spoken."

18 The word of the LORD came to me:
19 "Son of man, mark out two roads for
the sword of the king of Babylon to take,
both starting from the same country.
Make a signpost where the road
branches off to the city. 20 Mark out one
road for the sword to come against Rabbah of the Ammonites and another
against Judah and fortified Jerusalem.
21 For the king of Babylon will stop at the
fork in the road, at the junction of the
two roads, to seek an omen: He will cast
lots with arrows, he will consult his
idols, he will examine the liver. 22 Into his
right hand will come the lot for Jerusalem, where he is to set up battering
rams, to give the command to slaughter,
to sound the battle cry, to set battering
rams against the gates, to build a ramp
and to erect siege works. 23 It will seem
like a false omen to those who have
sworn allegiance to him, but he will remind them of their guilt and take them
captive.
24 "Therefore this is what the Sovereign LORD says: 'Because you people
have brought to mind your guilt by
your open rebellion, revealing your sins
in all that you do—because you have
done this, you will be taken captive.
25 " 'O profane and wicked prince of Israel, whose day has come, whose time
of punishment has reached its climax,
26 this is what the Sovereign LORD says:
Take off the turban, remove the crown.
It will not be as it was: The lowly will be
exalted and the exalted will be brought
low. 27 A ruin! A ruin! I will make it a
ruin! It will not be restored until he
comes to whom it rightfully belongs; to
him I will give it.'
28 "And you, son of man, prophesy and
say, 'This is what the Sovereign LORD
says about the Ammonites and their insults:

" 'A sword, a sword,
drawn for the slaughter,
polished to consume
and to flash like lightning!
29 Despite false visions concerning you

[a] *15* Septuagint; the meaning of the Hebrew for this word is uncertain.

and lying divinations about you,
it will be laid on the necks
of the wicked who are to be slain,
whose day has come,
whose time of punishment has
reached its climax.
[30]Return the sword to its scabbard.
In the place where you were
created,
in the land of your ancestry,
I will judge you.
[31]I will pour out my wrath upon
you
and breathe out my fiery anger
against you;
I will hand you over to brutal men,
men skilled in destruction.
[32]You will be fuel for the fire,
your blood will be shed in your
land,
you will be remembered no more;
for I the LORD have spoken.'"

SHARPEN THE FOCUS

When North America started to run out of 800 telephone numbers, phone company officials set aside the 888 prefix for use as a toll-free exchange. A shortage of telephone numbers seems impossible until you consider the fact that we set each number aside for the exclusive use of one household. Your phone number is unique.

When the Lord calls His people holy, He means He has set us aside for Himself—exclusively. We belong to Him—exclusively. We exist for the praise of His glory—exclusively.

With that in mind, read Ezekiel 20:12. The Lord set His people aside. He made them holy. They did not—they *could* not—have taken this honor upon themselves. And still today our God is for us "the LORD [who] made them holy."

But how can this be? Our sin has stained us, broken us, and robbed us of the beauty of holiness required in those whom our God uses. Even so, Christ's death has removed the stain of our sin. Christ's resurrection has mended our brokenness. Christ's new life is at work in us even now to restore and preserve the beauty of holy hearts, holy lives.

WEEK 64 • MONDAY

Ezekiel 22:1—23:49

GET THE BIG PICTURE

Ezekiel strikes blow after blow as he tries to hammer home the truth to God's people in exile. The Lord will not spare Jerusalem. Spiritual unfaithfulness will not go unpunished. Judgment will fall. As you read, ask yourself what the Holy Spirit says in these verses about your own lifestyle. If time is short, focus on Ezekiel 22:24–31.

Jerusalem's Sins

22 The word of the LORD
came to me: [2]"Son of man,
will you judge her? Will you judge this
city of bloodshed? Then confront her
with all her detestable practices [3]and
say: 'This is what the Sovereign LORD
says: O city that brings on herself doom
by shedding blood in her midst and defiles herself by making idols, [4]you have

become guilty because of the blood you
have shed and have become defiled by
the idols you have made. You have
brought your days to a close, and the
end of your years has come. Therefore
I will make you an object of scorn to the
nations and a laughingstock to all the
countries. [5]Those who are near and
those who are far away will mock you,
O infamous city, full of turmoil.

[6]" 'See how each of the princes of Israel who are in you uses his power to
shed blood. [7]In you they have treated
father and mother with contempt; in
you they have oppressed the alien and
mistreated the fatherless and the widow. [8]You have despised my holy things
and desecrated my Sabbaths. [9]In you are
slanderous men bent on shedding
blood; in you are those who eat at the
mountain shrines and commit lewd
acts. [10]In you are those who dishonor
their fathers' bed; in you are those who
violate women during their period,
when they are ceremonially unclean.
[11]In you one man commits a detestable
offense with his neighbor's wife, another shamefully defiles his daughter-in-
law, and another violates his sister, his
own father's daughter. [12]In you men accept bribes to shed blood; you take usury and excessive interest[a] and make
unjust gain from your neighbors by extortion. And you have forgotten me, declares the Sovereign LORD.

[13]" 'I will surely strike my hands together at the unjust gain you have made
and at the blood you have shed in your
midst. [14]Will your courage endure or
your hands be strong in the day I deal
with you? I the LORD have spoken, and
I will do it. [15]I will disperse you among
the nations and scatter you through the
countries; and I will put an end to your
uncleanness. [16]When you have been
defiled[b] in the eyes of the nations, you
will know that I am the LORD.' "

[17]Then the word of the LORD came to
me: [18]"Son of man, the house of Israel
has become dross to me; all of them are
the copper, tin, iron and lead left inside
a furnace. They are but the dross of silver. [19]Therefore this is what the Sovereign LORD says: 'Because you have all
become dross, I will gather you into Jerusalem. [20]As men gather silver, copper,
iron, lead and tin into a furnace to melt
it with a fiery blast, so will I gather you
in my anger and my wrath and put you
inside the city and melt you. [21]I will
gather you and I will blow on you with
my fiery wrath, and you will be melted
inside her. [22]As silver is melted in a furnace, so you will be melted inside her,
and you will know that I the LORD have
poured out my wrath upon you.' "

[23]Again the word of the LORD came to
me: [24]"Son of man, say to the land, 'You
are a land that has had no rain or
showers[c] in the day of wrath.' [25]There is
a conspiracy of her princes[d] within her
like a roaring lion tearing its prey; they
devour people, take treasures and precious things and make many widows
within her. [26]Her priests do violence to
my law and profane my holy things;
they do not distinguish between the
holy and the common; they teach that
there is no difference between the unclean and the clean; and they shut their
eyes to the keeping of my Sabbaths, so
that I am profaned among them. [27]Her
officials within her are like wolves tearing their prey; they shed blood and kill
people to make unjust gain. [28]Her
prophets whitewash these deeds for
them by false visions and lying divinations. They say, 'This is what the Sovereign LORD says'—when the LORD has
not spoken. [29]The people of the land
practice extortion and commit robbery;
they oppress the poor and needy and
mistreat the alien, denying them justice.

[30]"I looked for a man among them
who would build up the wall and stand
before me in the gap on behalf of the
land so I would not have to destroy it,
but I found none. [31]So I will pour out my
wrath on them and consume them with
my fiery anger, bringing down on their
own heads all they have done, declares
the Sovereign LORD."

[a]12 Or *usury and interest* [b]16 Or *When I have allotted you your inheritance* [c]24 Septuagint; Hebrew *has not been cleansed or rained on* [d]25 Septuagint; Hebrew *prophets*

Two Adulterous Sisters

23 The word of the LORD
came to me: 2"Son of man,
there were two women, daughters of
the same mother. 3They became prostitutes in Egypt, engaging in prostitution
from their youth. In that land their
breasts were fondled and their virgin
bosoms caressed. 4The older was named
Oholah, and her sister was Oholibah.
They were mine and gave birth to sons
and daughters. Oholah is Samaria, and
Oholibah is Jerusalem.

5"Oholah engaged in prostitution
while she was still mine; and she lusted
after her lovers, the Assyrians—warriors 6clothed in blue, governors and
commanders, all of them handsome
young men, and mounted horsemen.
7She gave herself as a prostitute to all the
elite of the Assyrians and defiled herself
with all the idols of everyone she lusted after. 8She did not give up the prostitution she began in Egypt, when during
her youth men slept with her, caressed
her virgin bosom and poured out their
lust upon her.

9"Therefore I handed her over to her
lovers, the Assyrians, for whom she lusted. 10They stripped her naked, took
away her sons and daughters and killed
her with the sword. She became a byword among women, and punishment
was inflicted on her.

11"Her sister Oholibah saw this, yet in
her lust and prostitution she was more
depraved than her sister. 12She too lusted after the Assyrians—governors and
commanders, warriors in full dress,
mounted horsemen, all handsome
young men. 13I saw that she too defiled
herself; both of them went the same
way.

14"But she carried her prostitution still
further. She saw men portrayed on a
wall, figures of Chaldeans[a] portrayed in
red, 15with belts around their waists and
flowing turbans on their heads; all of
them looked like Babylonian chariot
officers, natives of Chaldea.[b] 16As soon as
she saw them, she lusted after them and
sent messengers to them in Chaldea.
17Then the Babylonians came to her, to
the bed of love, and in their lust they
defiled her. After she had been defiled
by them, she turned away from them in
disgust. 18When she carried on her prostitution openly and exposed her nakedness, I turned away from her in disgust,
just as I had turned away from her sister. 19Yet she became more and more
promiscuous as she recalled the days of
her youth, when she was a prostitute in
Egypt. 20There she lusted after her lovers, whose genitals were like those of
donkeys and whose emission was like
that of horses. 21So you longed for the
lewdness of your youth, when in Egypt
your bosom was caressed and your
young breasts fondled.[c]

22"Therefore, Oholibah, this is what
the Sovereign LORD says: I will stir up
your lovers against you, those you
turned away from in disgust, and I will
bring them against you from every
side— 23the Babylonians and all the
Chaldeans, the men of Pekod and Shoa
and Koa, and all the Assyrians with
them, handsome young men, all of
them governors and commanders, chariot officers and men of high rank, all
mounted on horses. 24They will come
against you with weapons,[d] chariots
and wagons and with a throng of people; they will take up positions against
you on every side with large and small
shields and with helmets. I will turn you
over to them for punishment, and they
will punish you according to their standards. 25I will direct my jealous anger
against you, and they will deal with you
in fury. They will cut off your noses and
your ears, and those of you who are left
will fall by the sword. They will take
away your sons and daughters, and
those of you who are left will be consumed by fire. 26They will also strip you
of your clothes and take your fine jewelry. 27So I will put a stop to the lewdness
and prostitution you began in Egypt.

[a]14 Or *Babylonians* [b]15 Or *Babylonia*; also in verse 16 [c]21 Syriac (see also verse 3); Hebrew *caressed because of your young breasts* [d]24 The meaning of the Hebrew for this word is uncertain.

You will not look on these things with
longing or remember Egypt anymore.
[28]"For this is what the Sovereign LORD
says: I am about to hand you over to
those you hate, to those you turned
away from in disgust. [29]They will deal
with you in hatred and take away everything you have worked for. They will
leave you naked and bare, and the
shame of your prostitution will be exposed. Your lewdness and promiscuity
[30]have brought this upon you, because
you lusted after the nations and defiled
yourself with their idols. [31]You have
gone the way of your sister; so I will put
her cup into your hand.
[32]"This is what the Sovereign LORD
says:

"You will drink your sister's cup,
 a cup large and deep;
it will bring scorn and derision,
 for it holds so much.
[33]You will be filled with drunkenness
 and sorrow,
 the cup of ruin and desolation,
 the cup of your sister Samaria.
[34]You will drink it and drain it dry;
 you will dash it to pieces
 and tear your breasts.

I have spoken, declares the Sovereign
LORD.

[35]"Therefore this is what the Sovereign LORD says: Since you have forgotten me and thrust me behind your back,
you must bear the consequences of your
lewdness and prostitution."
[36]The LORD said to me: "Son of man,
will you judge Oholah and Oholibah?
Then confront them with their detestable practices, [37]for they have committed adultery and blood is on their
hands. They committed adultery with
their idols; they even sacrificed their
children, whom they bore to me,[a] as
food for them. [38]They have also done
this to me: At that same time they defiled my sanctuary and desecrated my
Sabbaths. [39]On the very day they sacrificed their children to their idols, they
entered my sanctuary and desecrated it.
That is what they did in my house.
[40]"They even sent messengers for
men who came from far away, and
when they arrived you bathed yourself
for them, painted your eyes and put on
your jewelry. [41]You sat on an elegant
couch, with a table spread before it on
which you had placed the incense and
oil that belonged to me.
[42]"The noise of a carefree crowd was
around her; Sabeans[b] were brought
from the desert along with men from
the rabble, and they put bracelets on the
arms of the woman and her sister and
beautiful crowns on their heads. [43]Then
I said about the one worn out by adultery, 'Now let them use her as a prostitute, for that is all she is.' [44]And they
slept with her. As men sleep with a prostitute, so they slept with those lewd
women, Oholah and Oholibah. [45]But
righteous men will sentence them to the
punishment of women who commit
adultery and shed blood, because they
are adulterous and blood is on their
hands.
[46]"This is what the Sovereign LORD
says: Bring a mob against them and give
them over to terror and plunder. [47]The
mob will stone them and cut them
down with their swords; they will kill
their sons and daughters and burn
down their houses.
[48]"So I will put an end to lewdness in
the land, that all women may take warning and not imitate you. [49]You will suffer the penalty for your lewdness and
bear the consequences of your sins of
idolatry. Then you will know that I am
the Sovereign LORD."

[a]37 Or *even made the children they bore to me pass through the fire,* [b]42 Or *drunkards*

SHARPEN THE FOCUS

Think about a time in history when personal security depended on the walls that surrounded a city. Imagine that a very wide gap has opened in one of those walls. An enemy army stands poised just outside the breach. Now imagine a group of the city's leaders taking up a position in that opening. They stand in the gap to defend the city.

That's the picture painted in Ezekiel 22:30. Sin has cut a hole in Jerusalem's defense. Rebellion against Yahweh has left Judah's citizens vulnerable to attack by Satan and by Satan's human agents. The Lord looks for a leader to "stand in the gap," to pray for the people.

But He can find no one to fill the role. Princes, prophets, priests—all join in the sins of those whom they are supposed to be leading.

Still today God's people and our leaders often fail to be all our Lord would have us be. We too sometimes rebel against our Lord. We too fail to pray faithfully at times.

How good, then, to view the picture of the Lord Jesus that Isaiah projects in Isaiah 59:16–17. Here our Lord is both our compassionate intercessor and our mighty defender. The one who died for us and rose again "always lives to intercede for [us]" (Hebrews 7:25).

WEEK 64 • TUESDAY

Ezekiel 24:1–27

More than two millenniums before CNN or the Internet, Ezekiel received instant word—from God—that the siege of Jerusalem had begun (Ezekiel 24:2). As you read the "parable of the pot" (Ezekiel 24:1–14), note that the "pot" is Jerusalem and the "pieces of meat" are individual citizens of the city. What do you understand some of the other details to mean? (Compare 2 Kings 25) If time is short, focus on Ezekiel 24:1–14.

The Cooking Pot

24 In the ninth year, in the
tenth month on the tenth
day, the word of the LORD came to me:
2"Son of man, record this date, this very
date, because the king of Babylon has
laid siege to Jerusalem this very day. 3Tell
this rebellious house a parable and say
to them: 'This is what the Sovereign
LORD says:

" 'Put on the cooking pot; put it on
and pour water into it.
4Put into it the pieces of meat,
all the choice pieces—the leg and
the shoulder.
Fill it with the best of these bones;
5 take the pick of the flock.
Pile wood beneath it for the bones;
bring it to a boil
and cook the bones in it.

6" 'For this is what the Sovereign LORD
says:

" 'Woe to the city of bloodshed,
to the pot now encrusted,
whose deposit will not go away!
Empty it piece by piece
without casting lots for them.

7" 'For the blood she shed is in her
midst:
She poured it on the bare rock;
she did not pour it on the ground,
where the dust would cover it.
8To stir up wrath and take revenge
I put her blood on the bare rock,
so that it would not be covered.

[9]" 'Therefore this is what the Sovereign LORD says:

" 'Woe to the city of bloodshed!
I, too, will pile the wood high.
[10]So heap on the wood
and kindle the fire.
Cook the meat well,
mixing in the spices;
and let the bones be charred.
[11]Then set the empty pot on the coals
till it becomes hot and its copper glows
so its impurities may be melted
and its deposit burned away.
[12]It has frustrated all efforts;
its heavy deposit has not been removed,
not even by fire.

[13]" 'Now your impurity is lewdness. Because I tried to cleanse you but you would not be cleansed from your impurity, you will not be clean again until my wrath against you has subsided.

[14]" 'I the LORD have spoken. The time has come for me to act. I will not hold back; I will not have pity, nor will I relent. You will be judged according to your conduct and your actions, declares the Sovereign LORD.' "

Ezekiel's Wife Dies

[15]The word of the LORD came to me:
[16]"Son of man, with one blow I am about to take away from you the delight of your eyes. Yet do not lament or weep or shed any tears. [17]Groan quietly; do not mourn for the dead. Keep your turban fastened and your sandals on your feet; do not cover the lower part of your face or eat the customary food ⌊of mourners⌋."

[18]So I spoke to the people in the morning, and in the evening my wife died. The next morning I did as I had been commanded.

[19]Then the people asked me, "Won't you tell us what these things have to do with us?"

[20]So I said to them, "The word of the LORD came to me: [21]Say to the house of Israel, 'This is what the Sovereign LORD says: I am about to desecrate my sanctuary—the stronghold in which you take pride, the delight of your eyes, the object of your affection. The sons and daughters you left behind will fall by the sword. [22]And you will do as I have done. You will not cover the lower part of your face or eat the customary food ⌊of mourners⌋. [23]You will keep your turbans on your heads and your sandals on your feet. You will not mourn or weep but will waste away because of[a] your sins and groan among yourselves.
[24]Ezekiel will be a sign to you; you will do just as he has done. When this happens, you will know that I am the Sovereign LORD.'

[25]"And you, son of man, on the day I take away their stronghold, their joy and glory, the delight of their eyes, their heart's desire, and their sons and daughters as well— [26]on that day a fugitive will come to tell you the news. [27]At that time your mouth will be opened; you will speak with him and will no longer be silent. So you will be a sign to them, and they will know that I am the LORD."

[a]23 Or *away in*

SHARPEN THE FOCUS

You don't have to be a gambler to understand high stakes. Maybe you've taken a new job and moved your family halfway across the continent to a town in which you know no one. Maybe you've decided to try a new treatment for a fatal disease. All of us take risks sometimes. And sometimes we squirm when we consider the high stakes riding on a decision we've made.

Now consider the stakes at risk in the account you've read for today. The Lord had committed Himself to bring the Savior from Abraham's descendants. That nation had fallen into the grossest kinds of idolatry. Still, God would not back out on His promise. The eternal destiny of the human race depended on it.

And so, the refining fire of God's wrath fell on Jerusalem. He would purify a people for Himself. He would burn up the impurities in their hearts. He would create a cradle into which the Christ would come, a remnant of faithful believers. Worship Him today—the one who is *your* Savior-God in Jesus.

WEEK 64 • WEDNESDAY

Ezekiel 25:1—27:36

When Nebuchadnezzar destroyed Jerusalem, hatreds that had smoldered for centuries burst into flames of spite and celebration (Ezekiel 25:6). Though Judah justly deserved punishment, the Lord grieved when the enemies of His people rejoiced. They, too, were ripe for judgment. As you read, notice the now-familiar refrain: "You will know that I am the LORD." If time is short, focus on Ezekiel 27:1–11, 33–36.

A Prophecy Against Ammon

25 The word of the LORD came to me: 2"Son of man, set your face against the Ammonites and prophesy against them. 3Say to them, 'Hear the word of the Sovereign LORD. This is what the Sovereign LORD says: Because you said "Aha!" over my sanctuary when it was desecrated and over the land of Israel when it was laid waste and over the people of Judah when they went into exile, 4therefore I am going to give you to the people of the East as a possession. They will set up their camps and pitch their tents among you; they will eat your fruit and drink your milk. 5I will turn Rabbah into a pasture for camels and Ammon into a resting place for sheep. Then you will know that I am the LORD. 6For this is what the Sovereign LORD says: Because you have clapped your hands and stamped your feet, rejoicing with all the malice of your heart against the land of Israel, 7therefore I will stretch out my hand against you and give you as plunder to the nations. I will cut you off from the nations and exterminate you from the countries. I will destroy you, and you will know that I am the LORD.' "

A Prophecy Against Moab

8"This is what the Sovereign LORD says: 'Because Moab and Seir said, "Look, the house of Judah has become like all the other nations," 9therefore I will expose the flank of Moab, beginning at its frontier towns—Beth Jeshimoth, Baal Meon and Kiriathaim—the glory of that land. 10I will give Moab along with the Ammonites to the people of the East as a possession, so that the Ammonites will not be remembered among the nations; 11and I will inflict punishment on Moab. Then they will know that I am the LORD.' "

A Prophecy Against Edom

12"This is what the Sovereign LORD says: 'Because Edom took revenge on the house of Judah and became very guilty by doing so, 13therefore this is

what the Sovereign LORD says: I will
stretch out my hand against Edom and
kill its men and their animals. I will lay
it waste, and from Teman to Dedan they
will fall by the sword. [14]I will take vengeance on Edom by the hand of my
people Israel, and they will deal with
Edom in accordance with my anger and
my wrath; they will know my vengeance, declares the Sovereign LORD.' "

A Prophecy Against Philistia

[15]"This is what the Sovereign LORD
says: 'Because the Philistines acted in
vengeance and took revenge with malice in their hearts, and with ancient
hostility sought to destroy Judah,
[16]therefore this is what the Sovereign
LORD says: I am about to stretch out my
hand against the Philistines, and I will
cut off the Kerethites and destroy those
remaining along the coast. [17]I will carry
out great vengeance on them and punish them in my wrath. Then they will
know that I am the LORD, when I take
vengeance on them.' "

A Prophecy Against Tyre

26 In the eleventh year, on
the first day of the month,
the word of the LORD came to me: [2]"Son
of man, because Tyre has said of Jerusalem, 'Aha! The gate to the nations is broken, and its doors have swung open to
me; now that she lies in ruins I will prosper,' [3]therefore this is what the Sovereign LORD says: I am against you,
O Tyre, and I will bring many nations
against you, like the sea casting up its
waves. [4]They will destroy the walls of
Tyre and pull down her towers; I will
scrape away her rubble and make her a
bare rock. [5]Out in the sea she will become a place to spread fishnets, for I
have spoken, declares the Sovereign
LORD. She will become plunder for the
nations, [6]and her settlements on the
mainland will be ravaged by the sword.
Then they will know that I am the LORD.
[7]"For this is what the Sovereign LORD
says: From the north I am going to bring
against Tyre Nebuchadnezzar[a] king of
Babylon, king of kings, with horses and
chariots, with horsemen and a great
army. [8]He will ravage your settlements
on the mainland with the sword; he will
set up siege works against you, build a
ramp up to your walls and raise his
shields against you. [9]He will direct the
blows of his battering rams against your
walls and demolish your towers with
his weapons. [10]His horses will be so
many that they will cover you with
dust. Your walls will tremble at the noise
of the war horses, wagons and chariots
when he enters your gates as men enter a city whose walls have been broken
through. [11]The hoofs of his horses will
trample all your streets; he will kill your
people with the sword, and your strong
pillars will fall to the ground. [12]They will
plunder your wealth and loot your merchandise; they will break down your
walls and demolish your fine houses
and throw your stones, timber and rubble into the sea. [13]I will put an end to
your noisy songs, and the music of your
harps will be heard no more. [14]I will
make you a bare rock, and you will become a place to spread fishnets. You will
never be rebuilt, for I the LORD have
spoken, declares the Sovereign LORD.
[15]"This is what the Sovereign LORD
says to Tyre: Will not the coastlands
tremble at the sound of your fall, when
the wounded groan and the slaughter
takes place in you? [16]Then all the princes
of the coast will step down from their
thrones and lay aside their robes and
take off their embroidered garments.
Clothed with terror, they will sit on the
ground, trembling every moment, appalled at you. [17]Then they will take up
a lament concerning you and say to
you:

" 'How you are destroyed, O city of
renown,
peopled by men of the sea!
You were a power on the seas,
you and your citizens;
you put your terror
on all who lived there.

[a]7 Hebrew *Nebuchadrezzar,* of which *Nebuchadnezzar* is a variant; here and often in Ezekiel and Jeremiah

18 Now the coastlands tremble
on the day of your fall;
the islands in the sea
are terrified at your collapse.'

19 "This is what the Sovereign LORD
says: When I make you a desolate city,
like cities no longer inhabited, and
when I bring the ocean depths over you
and its vast waters cover you, 20 then I
will bring you down with those who go
down to the pit, to the people of long
ago. I will make you dwell in the earth
below, as in ancient ruins, with those
who go down to the pit, and you will
not return or take your place[a] in the land
of the living. 21 I will bring you to a horrible end and you will be no more. You
will be sought, but you will never again
be found, declares the Sovereign LORD."

A Lament for Tyre

27 The word of the LORD
came to me: 2 "Son of man,
take up a lament concerning Tyre. 3 Say
to Tyre, situated at the gateway to the
sea, merchant of peoples on many
coasts, 'This is what the Sovereign LORD
says:

" 'You say, O Tyre,
"I am perfect in beauty."
4 Your domain was on the high seas;
your builders brought your
beauty to perfection.
5 They made all your timbers
of pine trees from Senir[b];
they took a cedar from Lebanon
to make a mast for you.
6 Of oaks from Bashan
they made your oars;
of cypress wood[c] from the coasts of
Cyprus[d]
they made your deck, inlaid with
ivory.
7 Fine embroidered linen from Egypt
was your sail
and served as your banner;
your awnings were of blue and purple
from the coasts of Elishah.
8 Men of Sidon and Arvad were your
oarsmen;
your skilled men, O Tyre, were
aboard as your seamen.
9 Veteran craftsmen of Gebal[e] were on
board
as shipwrights to caulk your
seams.
All the ships of the sea and their
sailors
came alongside to trade for your
wares.

10 " 'Men of Persia, Lydia and Put
served as soldiers in your army.
They hung their shields and helmets
on your walls,
bringing you splendor.
11 Men of Arvad and Helech
manned your walls on every side;
men of Gammad
were in your towers.
They hung their shields around
your walls;
they brought your beauty to
perfection.

12 " 'Tarshish did business with you
because of your great wealth of goods;
they exchanged silver, iron, tin and lead
for your merchandise.

13 " 'Greece, Tubal and Meshech traded with you; they exchanged slaves and
articles of bronze for your wares.

14 " 'Men of Beth Togarmah exchanged
work horses, war horses and mules for
your merchandise.

15 " 'The men of Rhodes[f] traded with
you, and many coastlands were your
customers; they paid you with ivory
tusks and ebony.

16 " 'Aram[g] did business with you because of your many products; they exchanged turquoise, purple fabric,
embroidered work, fine linen, coral and
rubies for your merchandise.

17 " 'Judah and Israel traded with you;
they exchanged wheat from Minnith
and confections,[h] honey, oil and balm
for your wares.

[a]20 Septuagint; Hebrew *return, and I will give glory* [b]5 That is, Hermon [c]6 Targum; the Masoretic Text has a different division of the consonants. [d]6 Hebrew *Kittim* [e]9 That is, Byblos [f]15 Septuagint; Hebrew *Dedan* [g]16 Most Hebrew manuscripts; some Hebrew manuscripts and Syriac *Edom* [h]17 The meaning of the Hebrew for this word is uncertain.

18" 'Damascus, because of your many
products and great wealth of goods, did
business with you in wine from Helbon
and wool from Zahar.
19" 'Danites and Greeks from Uzal
bought your merchandise; they exchanged wrought iron, cassia and calamus for your wares.
20" 'Dedan traded in saddle blankets
with you.
21" 'Arabia and all the princes of Kedar
were your customers; they did business
with you in lambs, rams and goats.
22" 'The merchants of Sheba and Raamah traded with you; for your merchandise they exchanged the finest of all
kinds of spices and precious stones, and
gold.
23" 'Haran, Canneh and Eden and
merchants of Sheba, Asshur and Kilmad
traded with you. 24In your marketplace
they traded with you beautiful garments, blue fabric, embroidered work
and multicolored rugs with cords twisted and tightly knotted.

25" 'The ships of Tarshish serve
as carriers for your wares.
You are filled with heavy cargo
in the heart of the sea.
26 Your oarsmen take you
out to the high seas.
But the east wind will break you to pieces
in the heart of the sea.
27 Your wealth, merchandise and wares,
your mariners, seamen and shipwrights,
your merchants and all your soldiers,
and everyone else on board
will sink into the heart of the sea
on the day of your shipwreck.
28 The shorelands will quake
when your seamen cry out.
29 All who handle the oars
will abandon their ships;
the mariners and all the seamen
will stand on the shore.
30 They will raise their voice
and cry bitterly over you;
they will sprinkle dust on their heads
and roll in ashes.
31 They will shave their heads because of you
and will put on sackcloth.
They will weep over you with anguish of soul
and with bitter mourning.
32 As they wail and mourn over you,
they will take up a lament concerning you:
"Who was ever silenced like Tyre,
surrounded by the sea?"
33 When your merchandise went out on the seas,
you satisfied many nations;
with your great wealth and your wares
you enriched the kings of the earth.
34 Now you are shattered by the sea
in the depths of the waters;
your wares and all your company
have gone down with you.
35 All who live in the coastlands
are appalled at you;
their kings shudder with horror
and their faces are distorted with fear.
36 The merchants among the nations
hiss at you;
you have come to a horrible end
and will be no more.' "

SHARPEN THE FOCUS

Houses paneled with oak. Walls inlaid with ivory. Embroidered tapestries in every room.

Luxury upon luxury. Tyre was wealthy beyond compare.

And still, Tyre was impoverished because she didn't know the Lord. Tyre's glory would fade. In fact, her history would become a horror (Ezekiel 27:36). Who gives Tyre a second thought today?

Many nations on earth now—including our own—enjoy incredible material wealth. But one day all life on this planet will end. The only wealth worth having will be the riches of forgiveness and the eternal life Christ won for us on Calvary.

We live today in our Lord's "day of grace." God gives us material blessings, in part, so we can use them to share His true, eternal riches in Christ. Take a look today at the ways you have invested your time, your money, your talent in our Lord's kingdom. Talk with your Savior about any sins you need to confess and any new opportunities for service He shows you.

WEEK 64 • THURSDAY

Ezekiel 28:1–26

GET THE BIG PICTURE

Today's reading details the arrogance of Tyre's earthly ruler. In that arrogance, we see the rebellion against the Lord and against His Son shown by all ungodly nations of all time. Egged on by Satan, the heathen will continue to oppose God's Word. But our Lord retains control of earth and of earth's rulers. As you read, look for evidence of this. If time is short, focus on Ezekiel 28:1–10.

A Prophecy Against the King of Tyre

28 The word of the LORD came to me: 2"Son of man, say to the ruler of Tyre, 'This is what the Sovereign LORD says:

" 'In the pride of your heart
you say, "I am a god;
I sit on the throne of a god
in the heart of the seas."
But you are a man and not a god,
though you think you are as wise
as a god.
3Are you wiser than Daniel[a]?
Is no secret hidden from you?
4By your wisdom and understanding
you have gained wealth for
yourself
and amassed gold and silver
in your treasuries.
5By your great skill in trading
you have increased your wealth,
and because of your wealth
your heart has grown proud.

6" 'Therefore this is what the Sovereign LORD says:

" 'Because you think you are wise,
as wise as a god,
7I am going to bring foreigners
against you,
the most ruthless of nations;
they will draw their swords against
your beauty and wisdom
and pierce your shining splendor.
8They will bring you down to the pit,
and you will die a violent death
in the heart of the seas.
9Will you then say, "I am a god,"
in the presence of those who kill
you?
You will be but a man, not a god,
in the hands of those who slay
you.
10You will die the death of the
uncircumcised
at the hands of foreigners.

[a]3 Or *Danel*; the Hebrew spelling may suggest a person other than the prophet Daniel.

I have spoken, declares the Sovereign LORD.' "

[11]The word of the LORD came to me:
[12]"Son of man, take up a lament concerning the king of Tyre and say to him: 'This is what the Sovereign LORD says:

" 'You were the model of perfection,
full of wisdom and perfect in beauty.
[13]You were in Eden,
the garden of God;
every precious stone adorned you:
ruby, topaz and emerald,
chrysolite, onyx and jasper,
sapphire,[a] turquoise and beryl.[b]
Your settings and mountings[c] were made of gold;
on the day you were created they were prepared.
[14]You were anointed as a guardian cherub,
for so I ordained you.
You were on the holy mount of God;
you walked among the fiery stones.
[15]You were blameless in your ways
from the day you were created
till wickedness was found in you.
[16]Through your widespread trade
you were filled with violence,
and you sinned.
So I drove you in disgrace from the mount of God,
and I expelled you, O guardian cherub,
from among the fiery stones.
[17]Your heart became proud
on account of your beauty,
and you corrupted your wisdom
because of your splendor.
So I threw you to the earth;
I made a spectacle of you before kings.
[18]By your many sins and dishonest trade
you have desecrated your sanctuaries.
So I made a fire come out from you,
and it consumed you,
and I reduced you to ashes on the ground
in the sight of all who were watching.
[19]All the nations who knew you
are appalled at you;
you have come to a horrible end
and will be no more.' "

A Prophecy Against Sidon

[20]The word of the LORD came to me:
[21]"Son of man, set your face against Sidon; prophesy against her [22]and say: 'This is what the Sovereign LORD says:

" 'I am against you, O Sidon,
and I will gain glory within you.
They will know that I am the LORD,
when I inflict punishment on her
and show myself holy within her.
[23]I will send a plague upon her
and make blood flow in her streets.
The slain will fall within her,
with the sword against her on every side.
Then they will know that I am the LORD.

[24]" 'No longer will the people of Israel have malicious neighbors who are painful briers and sharp thorns. Then they will know that I am the Sovereign LORD.
[25]" 'This is what the Sovereign LORD says: When I gather the people of Israel from the nations where they have been scattered, I will show myself holy among them in the sight of the nations. Then they will live in their own land, which I gave to my servant Jacob. [26]They will live there in safety and will build houses and plant vineyards; they will live in safety when I inflict punishment on all their neighbors who maligned them. Then they will know that I am the LORD their God.' "

[a]13 Or *lapis lazuli* [b]13 The precise identification of some of these precious stones is uncertain. [c]13 The meaning of the Hebrew for this phrase is uncertain.

SHARPEN THE FOCUS

Remember David's outrage at Goliath's taunts? Remember what David said when he heard Goliath insult God's people? "Who is this uncircumcised Philistine that he should defy the armies of the living God?" (1 Samuel 17:26). David's question revealed his faith in the covenant-making God who had sealed His covenant in the Old Testament sacrament of circumcision. Goliath had no covenant with the Lord. That fact—not David's slingshot—destined his defeat.

Again in today's reading this concept appears. The ruler of Tyre would "die the death of the uncircumcised" (Ezekiel 28:10). He had a covenant all right, but a covenant with Satan. He worshiped false gods, and as Deuteronomy 32:15–17 and 1 Corinthians 10:21 make clear, such idolatry amounts to no less than demon worship. His end? Destruction.

Before you close your Bible today, review the covenant God made with you in your Baptism. Use the words of Colossians 2:11–15 to guide your thoughts and prayers. Thank your Lord that He has disarmed the demons, that He has defanged the ancient serpent, Satan, for you. Thank Him that you have a new life, eternal life, and that Christ Jesus is even now at work in you. ☼

WEEK 64 • FRIDAY

Ezekiel 29:1—32:32

GET THE BIG PICTURE

All four of today's chapters (Ezekiel 29–32) foretell the fall of the nation of Egypt. Like a majestic tree cut down and hacked to pieces, Egypt would lose her power and her pride. As you read, look for the benefits for Israel in this downfall of Egypt. If time is short, focus on Ezekiel 31:1–18.

A Prophecy Against Egypt

29 In the tenth year, in the tenth month on the twelfth day, the word of the LORD came to me: 2"Son of man, set your face against Pharaoh king of Egypt and prophesy against him and against all Egypt. 3Speak to him and say: 'This is what the Sovereign LORD says:

" 'I am against you, Pharaoh king of
Egypt,
you great monster lying among
your streams.
You say, "The Nile is mine;
I made it for myself."
4But I will put hooks in your jaws
and make the fish of your streams
stick to your scales.
I will pull you out from among your
streams,
with all the fish sticking to your
scales.
5I will leave you in the desert,
you and all the fish of your
streams.
You will fall on the open field
and not be gathered or picked up.
I will give you as food
to the beasts of the earth and the
birds of the air.

6Then all who live in Egypt will know that I am the LORD.

" 'You have been a staff of reed for the
house of Israel. 7When they grasped you
with their hands, you splintered and
you tore open their shoulders; when
they leaned on you, you broke and their
backs were wrenched.[a]

8" 'Therefore this is what the Sovereign LORD says: I will bring a sword
against you and kill your men and their
animals. 9Egypt will become a desolate
wasteland. Then they will know that I
am the LORD.

" 'Because you said, "The Nile is mine;
I made it," 10therefore I am against you
and against your streams, and I will
make the land of Egypt a ruin and a desolate waste from Migdol to Aswan, as
far as the border of Cush.[b] 11No foot of
man or animal will pass through it; no
one will live there for forty years. 12I will
make the land of Egypt desolate among
devastated lands, and her cities will lie
desolate forty years among ruined cities. And I will disperse the Egyptians
among the nations and scatter them
through the countries.

13" 'Yet this is what the Sovereign
LORD says: At the end of forty years I
will gather the Egyptians from the nations where they were scattered. 14I will
bring them back from captivity and return them to Upper Egypt,[c] the land of
their ancestry. There they will be a lowly kingdom. 15It will be the lowliest of
kingdoms and will never again exalt itself above the other nations. I will make
it so weak that it will never again rule
over the nations. 16Egypt will no longer
be a source of confidence for the people
of Israel but will be a reminder of their
sin in turning to her for help. Then they
will know that I am the Sovereign
LORD.' "

17In the twenty-seventh year, in the
first month on the first day, the word of
the LORD came to me: 18"Son of man,
Nebuchadnezzar king of Babylon drove
his army in a hard campaign against
Tyre; every head was rubbed bare and
every shoulder made raw. Yet he and his
army got no reward from the campaign
he led against Tyre. 19Therefore this is
what the Sovereign LORD says: I am
going to give Egypt to Nebuchadnezzar
king of Babylon, and he will carry off its
wealth. He will loot and plunder the
land as pay for his army. 20I have given
him Egypt as a reward for his efforts
because he and his army did it for me,
declares the Sovereign LORD.

21"On that day I will make a horn[d]
grow for the house of Israel, and I will
open your mouth among them. Then
they will know that I am the LORD."

A Lament for Egypt

30 The word of the LORD
came to me: 2"Son of man,
prophesy and say: 'This is what the Sovereign LORD says:

" 'Wail and say,
"Alas for that day!"
3For the day is near,
the day of the LORD is near—
a day of clouds,
a time of doom for the nations.
4A sword will come against Egypt,
and anguish will come upon
Cush.[e]
When the slain fall in Egypt,
her wealth will be carried away
and her foundations torn down.

5Cush and Put, Lydia and all Arabia,
Libya[f] and the people of the covenant
land will fall by the sword along with
Egypt.

6" 'This is what the LORD says:

" 'The allies of Egypt will fall
and her proud strength will fail.
From Migdol to Aswan
they will fall by the sword within
her,
declares the Sovereign
LORD.
7" 'They will be desolate
among desolate lands,
and their cities will lie
among ruined cities.

[a]7 Syriac (see also Septuagint and Vulgate); Hebrew *and you caused their backs to stand*
[b]10 That is, the upper Nile region [c]14 Hebrew *to Pathros* [d]21 *Horn* here symbolizes strength.
[e]4 That is, the upper Nile region; also in verses 5 and 9 [f]5 Hebrew *Cub*

[8]Then they will know that I am the
LORD,
when I set fire to Egypt
and all her helpers are crushed.

[9]" 'On that day messengers will go out
from me in ships to frighten Cush out
of her complacency. Anguish will take
hold of them on the day of Egypt's
doom, for it is sure to come.

[10]" 'This is what the Sovereign LORD
says:

" 'I will put an end to the hordes of
Egypt
by the hand of Nebuchadnezzar
king of Babylon.
[11]He and his army—the most ruthless
of nations—
will be brought in to destroy the
land.
They will draw their swords against
Egypt
and fill the land with the slain.
[12]I will dry up the streams of the Nile
and sell the land to evil men;
by the hand of foreigners
I will lay waste the land and
everything in it.
I the LORD have spoken.

[13]" 'This is what the Sovereign LORD
says:

" 'I will destroy the idols
and put an end to the images in
Memphis.[a]
No longer will there be a prince in
Egypt,
and I will spread fear throughout
the land.
[14]I will lay waste Upper Egypt,[b]
set fire to Zoan
and inflict punishment on
Thebes.[c]
[15]I will pour out my wrath on
Pelusium,[d]
the stronghold of Egypt,
and cut off the hordes of Thebes.
[16]I will set fire to Egypt;
Pelusium will writhe in agony.
Thebes will be taken by storm;
Memphis will be in constant
distress.
[17]The young men of Heliopolis[e] and
Bubastis[f]
will fall by the sword,
and the cities themselves will go
into captivity.
[18]Dark will be the day at Tahpanhes
when I break the yoke of Egypt;
there her proud strength will
come to an end.
She will be covered with clouds,
and her villages will go into
captivity.
[19]So I will inflict punishment on Egypt,
and they will know that I am the
LORD.' "

[20]In the eleventh year, in the first
month on the seventh day, the word of
the LORD came to me: [21]"Son of man, I
have broken the arm of Pharaoh king of
Egypt. It has not been bound up for
healing or put in a splint so as to become
strong enough to hold a sword. [22]There-
fore this is what the Sovereign LORD
says: I am against Pharaoh king of
Egypt. I will break both his arms, the
good arm as well as the broken one, and
make the sword fall from his hand. [23]I
will disperse the Egyptians among the
nations and scatter them through the
countries. [24]I will strengthen the arms of
the king of Babylon and put my sword
in his hand, but I will break the arms of
Pharaoh, and he will groan before him
like a mortally wounded man. [25]I will
strengthen the arms of the king of Babylon, but the arms of Pharaoh will fall
limp. Then they will know that I am the
LORD, when I put my sword into the
hand of the king of Babylon and he
brandishes it against Egypt. [26]I will disperse the Egyptians among the nations
and scatter them through the countries.
Then they will know that I am the
LORD."

A Cedar in Lebanon

31 In the eleventh year, in the
third month on the first day,

[a]13 Hebrew *Noph;* also in verse 16 [b]14 Hebrew *waste Pathros* [c]14 Hebrew *No;* also in verses 15 and 16 [d]15 Hebrew *Sin;* also in verse 16 [e]17 Hebrew *Awen* (or *On*) [f]17 Hebrew *Pi Beseth*

the word of the LORD came to me: 2"Son
of man, say to Pharaoh king of Egypt
and to his hordes:

" 'Who can be compared with you in
majesty?
3 Consider Assyria, once a cedar in
Lebanon,
with beautiful branches
overshadowing the forest;
it towered on high,
its top above the thick foliage.
4 The waters nourished it,
deep springs made it grow tall;
their streams flowed
all around its base
and sent their channels
to all the trees of the field.
5 So it towered higher
than all the trees of the field;
its boughs increased
and its branches grew long,
spreading because of abundant
waters.
6 All the birds of the air
nested in its boughs,
all the beasts of the field
gave birth under its branches;
all the great nations
lived in its shade.
7 It was majestic in beauty,
with its spreading boughs,
for its roots went down
to abundant waters.
8 The cedars in the garden of God
could not rival it,
nor could the pine trees
equal its boughs,
nor could the plane trees
compare with its branches—
no tree in the garden of God
could match its beauty.
9 I made it beautiful
with abundant branches,
the envy of all the trees of Eden
in the garden of God.

10" 'Therefore this is what the Sovereign LORD says: Because it towered on
high, lifting its top above the thick foliage, and because it was proud of its
height, 11 I handed it over to the ruler of
the nations, for him to deal with according to its wickedness. I cast it aside, 12 and
the most ruthless of foreign nations cut
it down and left it. Its boughs fell on the
mountains and in all the valleys; its
branches lay broken in all the ravines of
the land. All the nations of the earth
came out from under its shade and left
it. 13 All the birds of the air settled on the
fallen tree, and all the beasts of the field
were among its branches. 14 Therefore no
other trees by the waters are ever to
tower proudly on high, lifting their tops
above the thick foliage. No other trees
so well-watered are ever to reach such
a height; they are all destined for death,
for the earth below, among mortal men,
with those who go down to the pit.

15" 'This is what the Sovereign LORD
says: On the day it was brought down
to the grave[a] I covered the deep springs
with mourning for it; I held back its
streams, and its abundant waters were
restrained. Because of it I clothed Lebanon with gloom, and all the trees of the
field withered away. 16 I made the nations tremble at the sound of its fall
when I brought it down to the grave
with those who go down to the pit.
Then all the trees of Eden, the choicest
and best of Lebanon, all the trees that
were well-watered, were consoled in
the earth below. 17 Those who lived in its
shade, its allies among the nations, had
also gone down to the grave with it,
joining those killed by the sword.

18" 'Which of the trees of Eden can be
compared with you in splendor and
majesty? Yet you, too, will be brought
down with the trees of Eden to the earth
below; you will lie among the uncircumcised, with those killed by the
sword.

" 'This is Pharaoh and all his hordes,
declares the Sovereign LORD.' "

A Lament for Pharaoh

32 In the twelfth year, in the
twelfth month on the first
day, the word of the LORD came to me:
2"Son of man, take up a lament concerning Pharaoh king of Egypt and say to
him:

[a]*15* Hebrew *Sheol;* also in verses 16 and 17

" 'You are like a lion among the
nations;
you are like a monster in the seas
thrashing about in your streams,
churning the water with your feet
and muddying the streams.

3" 'This is what the Sovereign LORD
says:

" 'With a great throng of people
I will cast my net over you,
and they will haul you up in my
net.
4I will throw you on the land
and hurl you on the open field.
I will let all the birds of the air settle
on you
and all the beasts of the earth
gorge themselves on you.
5I will spread your flesh on the
mountains
and fill the valleys with your
remains.
6I will drench the land with your
flowing blood
all the way to the mountains,
and the ravines will be filled with
your flesh.
7When I snuff you out, I will cover
the heavens
and darken their stars;
I will cover the sun with a cloud,
and the moon will not give its
light.
8All the shining lights in the heavens
I will darken over you;
I will bring darkness over your
land,
declares the Sovereign
LORD.
9I will trouble the hearts of many
peoples
when I bring about your
destruction among the
nations,
among[a] lands you have not known.
10I will cause many peoples to be
appalled at you,
and their kings will shudder with
horror because of you
when I brandish my sword before
them.
On the day of your downfall
each of them will tremble
every moment for his life.

11" 'For this is what the Sovereign
LORD says:

" 'The sword of the king of Babylon
will come against you.
12I will cause your hordes to fall
by the swords of mighty men—
the most ruthless of all nations.
They will shatter the pride of Egypt,
and all her hordes will be
overthrown.
13I will destroy all her cattle
from beside abundant waters
no longer to be stirred by the foot of
man
or muddied by the hoofs of cattle.
14Then I will let her waters settle
and make her streams flow like oil,
declares the Sovereign
LORD.
15When I make Egypt desolate
and strip the land of everything in
it,
when I strike down all who live
there,
then they will know that I am the
LORD.'

16"This is the lament they will chant
for her. The daughters of the nations
will chant it; for Egypt and all her
hordes they will chant it, declares the
Sovereign LORD."

17In the twelfth year, on the fifteenth
day of the month, the word of the LORD
came to me: 18"Son of man, wail for the
hordes of Egypt and consign to the
earth below both her and the daughters
of mighty nations, with those who go
down to the pit. 19Say to them, 'Are you
more favored than others? Go down
and be laid among the uncircumcised.'
20They will fall among those killed by
the sword. The sword is drawn; let her
be dragged off with all her hordes.
21From within the grave[b] the mighty
leaders will say of Egypt and her allies,

[a]9 Hebrew; Septuagint *bring you into captivity among the nations, / to* [b]21 Hebrew *Sheol*; also in verse 27

'They have come down and they lie with the uncircumcised, with those killed by the sword.'
22"Assyria is there with her whole army; she is surrounded by the graves of all her slain, all who have fallen by the sword. 23Their graves are in the depths of the pit and her army lies around her grave. All who had spread terror in the land of the living are slain, fallen by the sword.
24"Elam is there, with all her hordes around her grave. All of them are slain, fallen by the sword. All who had spread terror in the land of the living went down uncircumcised to the earth below. They bear their shame with those who go down to the pit. 25A bed is made for her among the slain, with all her hordes around her grave. All of them are uncircumcised, killed by the sword. Because their terror had spread in the land of the living, they bear their shame with those who go down to the pit; they are laid among the slain.
26"Meshech and Tubal are there, with all their hordes around their graves. All of them are uncircumcised, killed by the sword because they spread their terror in the land of the living. 27Do they not lie with the other uncircumcised warriors who have fallen, who went down to the grave with their weapons of war, whose swords were placed under their heads? The punishment for their sins rested on their bones, though the terror of these warriors had stalked through the land of the living.
28"You too, O Pharaoh, will be broken and will lie among the uncircumcised, with those killed by the sword.
29"Edom is there, her kings and all her princes; despite their power, they are laid with those killed by the sword. They lie with the uncircumcised, with those who go down to the pit.
30"All the princes of the north and all the Sidonians are there; they went down with the slain in disgrace despite the terror caused by their power. They lie uncircumcised with those killed by the sword and bear their shame with those who go down to the pit.
31"Pharaoh—he and all his army—will see them and he will be consoled for all his hordes that were killed by the sword, declares the Sovereign LORD.
32Although I had him spread terror in the land of the living, Pharaoh and all his hordes will be laid among the uncircumcised, with those killed by the sword, declares the Sovereign LORD."

SHARPEN THE FOCUS

Friedrich Nietzsche once said, "Apart from a knowledge of absolute right and wrong, all human behavior becomes merely a question of power." Unless people have morals, they do whatever they can get away with. Those with the biggest fists, the biggest guns, or the most battleships get their way in such a world.

Egypt, Assyria, Babylon, and Israel lived in a world like that. Might made right. Egypt existed as one of the biggest bullies for centuries. But 70 years after her exile began, Judah would return to her homeland. The Lord wanted His restored people to live in safety. And so He used Babylon and Persia to move Egypt out of the way, just as He had destroyed Assyria at Babylon's hands.

Still today, the Lord "rebuke[s] kings" for the sake of His people (Psalms 105:14). He directs events on earth for the good of His church. He can use bullies like Babylon to thwart the plans of bullies like Egypt. His purpose is to open doors for the Gospel message of His Son. God "wants all . . . to be saved and to come to a knowledge of the truth" (1 Timothy 2:4). Trust Him to work for the good of His kingdom as you pray.

WEEK 64 • SATURDAY

Ezekiel 33:1—34:31

Until now, Ezekiel could speak only when the Lord gave him a message to deliver (3:26–27). Now the prophecy of Ezekiel 24:26–27 is fulfilled; Ezekiel hears of Jerusalem's fall from someone who has escaped the city. The prophet's tongue is then loosed (Ezekiel 33:21–22). The Lord repeats His call to Ezekiel (Ezekiel 33) and gives him a message of comfort (Ezekiel 34). As you read, think of Jesus, our Good Shepherd. If time is short, focus on Ezekiel 34:11–31.

Ezekiel a Watchman

33 The word of the LORD came to me: 2"Son of man, speak to your countrymen and say to them: 'When I bring the sword against a land, and the people of the land choose one of their men and make him their watchman, 3and he sees the sword coming against the land and blows the trumpet to warn the people, 4then if anyone hears the trumpet but does not take warning and the sword comes and takes his life, his blood will be on his own head. 5Since he heard the sound of the trumpet but did not take warning, his blood will be on his own head. If he had taken warning, he would have saved himself. 6But if the watchman sees the sword coming and does not blow the trumpet to warn the people and the sword comes and takes the life of one of them, that man will be taken away because of his sin, but I will hold the watchman accountable for his blood.'

7"Son of man, I have made you a watchman for the house of Israel; so hear the word I speak and give them warning from me. 8When I say to the wicked, 'O wicked man, you will surely die,' and you do not speak out to dissuade him from his ways, that wicked man will die for[a] his sin, and I will hold you accountable for his blood. 9But if you do warn the wicked man to turn from his ways and he does not do so, he will die for his sin, but you will have saved yourself.

10"Son of man, say to the house of Israel, 'This is what you are saying: "Our offenses and sins weigh us down, and we are wasting away because of[b] them. How then can we live?"' 11Say to them, 'As surely as I live, declares the Sovereign LORD, I take no pleasure in the death of the wicked, but rather that they turn from their ways and live. Turn! Turn from your evil ways! Why will you die, O house of Israel?'

12"Therefore, son of man, say to your countrymen, 'The righteousness of the righteous man will not save him when he disobeys, and the wickedness of the wicked man will not cause him to fall when he turns from it. The righteous man, if he sins, will not be allowed to live because of his former righteousness.' 13If I tell the righteous man that he will surely live, but then he trusts in his righteousness and does evil, none of the righteous things he has done will be remembered; he will die for the evil he has done. 14And if I say to the wicked man, 'You will surely die,' but he then turns away from his sin and does what is just and right— 15if he gives back what he took in pledge for a loan, returns what he has stolen, follows the decrees that give life, and does no evil, he will surely live; he will not die. 16None of the sins he has committed will be remembered against him. He has done what is just and right; he will surely live.

[a]*8* Or *in;* also in verse 9 [b]*10* Or *away in*

17"Yet your countrymen say, 'The way of the Lord is not just.' But it is their way that is not just. 18If a righteous man turns from his righteousness and does evil, he will die for it. 19And if a wicked man turns away from his wickedness and does what is just and right, he will live by doing so. 20Yet, O house of Israel, you say, 'The way of the Lord is not just.' But I will judge each of you according to his own ways."

Jerusalem's Fall Explained

21In the twelfth year of our exile, in the tenth month on the fifth day, a man who had escaped from Jerusalem came to me and said, "The city has fallen!" 22Now the evening before the man arrived, the hand of the LORD was upon me, and he opened my mouth before the man came to me in the morning. So my mouth was opened and I was no longer silent.

23Then the word of the LORD came to me: 24"Son of man, the people living in those ruins in the land of Israel are saying, 'Abraham was only one man, yet he possessed the land. But we are many; surely the land has been given to us as our possession.' 25Therefore say to them, 'This is what the Sovereign LORD says: Since you eat meat with the blood still in it and look to your idols and shed blood, should you then possess the land? 26You rely on your sword, you do detestable things, and each of you defiles his neighbor's wife. Should you then possess the land?'

27"Say this to them: 'This is what the Sovereign LORD says: As surely as I live, those who are left in the ruins will fall by the sword, those out in the country I will give to the wild animals to be devoured, and those in strongholds and caves will die of a plague. 28I will make the land a desolate waste, and her proud strength will come to an end, and the mountains of Israel will become desolate so that no one will cross them. 29Then they will know that I am the LORD, when I have made the land a desolate waste because of all the detestable things they have done.'

30"As for you, son of man, your countrymen are talking together about you by the walls and at the doors of the houses, saying to each other, 'Come and hear the message that has come from the LORD.' 31My people come to you, as they usually do, and sit before you to listen to your words, but they do not put them into practice. With their mouths they express devotion, but their hearts are greedy for unjust gain. 32Indeed, to them you are nothing more than one who sings love songs with a beautiful voice and plays an instrument well, for they hear your words but do not put them into practice.

33"When all this comes true—and it surely will—then they will know that a prophet has been among them."

Shepherds and Sheep

34 The word of the LORD came to me: 2"Son of man, prophesy against the shepherds of Israel; prophesy and say to them: 'This is what the Sovereign LORD says: Woe to the shepherds of Israel who only take care of themselves! Should not shepherds take care of the flock? 3You eat the curds, clothe yourselves with the wool and slaughter the choice animals, but you do not take care of the flock. 4You have not strengthened the weak or healed the sick or bound up the injured. You have not brought back the strays or searched for the lost. You have ruled them harshly and brutally. 5So they were scattered because there was no shepherd, and when they were scattered they became food for all the wild animals. 6My sheep wandered over all the mountains and on every high hill. They were scattered over the whole earth, and no one searched or looked for them.

7" 'Therefore, you shepherds, hear the word of the LORD: 8As surely as I live, declares the Sovereign LORD, because my flock lacks a shepherd and so has been plundered and has become food for all the wild animals, and because my shepherds did not search for my flock but cared for themselves rather than for my flock, 9therefore,

O shepherds, hear the word of the
LORD: 10This is what the Sovereign LORD
says: I am against the shepherds and
will hold them accountable for my flock.
I will remove them from tending the
flock so that the shepherds can no
longer feed themselves. I will rescue my
flock from their mouths, and it will no
longer be food for them.

11" 'For this is what the Sovereign
LORD says: I myself will search for my
sheep and look after them. 12As a shepherd looks after his scattered flock when
he is with them, so will I look after my
sheep. I will rescue them from all the
places where they were scattered on a
day of clouds and darkness. 13I will
bring them out from the nations and
gather them from the countries, and I
will bring them into their own land. I
will pasture them on the mountains of
Israel, in the ravines and in all the settlements in the land. 14I will tend them
in a good pasture, and the mountain
heights of Israel will be their grazing
land. There they will lie down in good
grazing land, and there they will feed in
a rich pasture on the mountains of Israel. 15I myself will tend my sheep and
have them lie down, declares the Sovereign LORD. 16I will search for the lost
and bring back the strays. I will bind up
the injured and strengthen the weak,
but the sleek and the strong I will
destroy. I will shepherd the flock with
justice.

17" 'As for you, my flock, this is what
the Sovereign LORD says: I will judge
between one sheep and another, and
between rams and goats. 18Is it not
enough for you to feed on the good
pasture? Must you also trample the rest
of your pasture with your feet? Is it not
enough for you to drink clear water?
Must you also muddy the rest with your
feet? 19Must my flock feed on what you
have trampled and drink what you
have muddied with your feet?

20" 'Therefore this is what the Sovereign LORD says to them: See, I myself
will judge between the fat sheep and
the lean sheep. 21Because you shove
with flank and shoulder, butting all the
weak sheep with your horns until you
have driven them away, 22I will save my
flock, and they will no longer be plundered. I will judge between one sheep
and another. 23I will place over them one
shepherd, my servant David, and he
will tend them; he will tend them and
be their shepherd. 24I the LORD will be
their God, and my servant David will be
prince among them. I the LORD have
spoken.

25" 'I will make a covenant of peace
with them and rid the land of wild
beasts so that they may live in the desert
and sleep in the forests in safety. 26I will
bless them and the places surrounding
my hill.[a] I will send down showers in
season; there will be showers of blessing. 27The trees of the field will yield
their fruit and the ground will yield its
crops; the people will be secure in their
land. They will know that I am the
LORD, when I break the bars of their
yoke and rescue them from the hands
of those who enslaved them. 28They will
no longer be plundered by the nations,
nor will wild animals devour them.
They will live in safety, and no one will
make them afraid. 29I will provide for
them a land renowned for its crops, and
they will no longer be victims of famine
in the land or bear the scorn of the nations. 30Then they will know that I, the
LORD their God, am with them and that
they, the house of Israel, are my people,
declares the Sovereign LORD. 31You my
sheep, the sheep of my pasture, are people, and I am your God, declares the
Sovereign LORD.' "

[a]26 Or *I will make them and the places surrounding my hill a blessing*

SHARPEN THE FOCUS

Few words catch the intensity of feeling parents experience when a child wanders off into the woods, into a blizzard, or down the block in a violent neighborhood. We panic in fear as we imagine what could happen.

And yet those feelings of concern, intense as they are, pale in comparison to the Lord's concern for His lost children. The Good Shepherd watched while sin scattered His flock. The Good Shepherd wept as He saw His sheep wounded and driven into the wilderness by Satan. He saw us, His sheep, frightened and alone, tired and torn.

He saw, and His words thundered from heaven: "I Myself will search for My sheep and look after them" (Ezekiel 34:11)! He came! He came to find us! The Son of God came Himself! He took on a human body and became one of us.

And the hymn says, "The Shepherd died for sheep who loved to wander" (*Lutheran Worship,* 119). Jesus stood between us and Satan on the bloody hill of Calvary. He let death clamp its jaws around His heart.

He suffered alone, abandoned by His Father so we could live forever safe in the Father's family. Now He ever lives to nourish and defend us (Ezekiel 34:23–29). Let yourself relax in his peace and enjoy His love today. ☼

WEEK 65 • MONDAY

Ezekiel 35:1—36:38

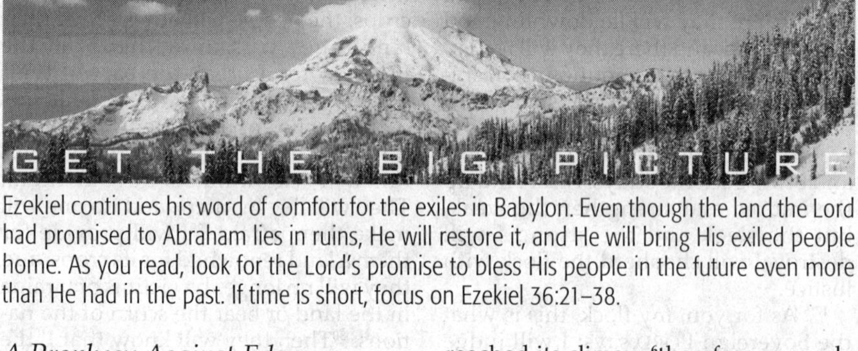

GET THE BIG PICTURE

Ezekiel continues his word of comfort for the exiles in Babylon. Even though the land the Lord had promised to Abraham lies in ruins, He will restore it, and He will bring His exiled people home. As you read, look for the Lord's promise to bless His people in the future even more than He had in the past. If time is short, focus on Ezekiel 36:21–38.

A Prophecy Against Edom

35 The word of the LORD
came to me: 2"Son of man,
set your face against Mount Seir; prophesy against it 3and say: 'This is what the
Sovereign LORD says: I am against you,
Mount Seir, and I will stretch out my
hand against you and make you a desolate waste. 4I will turn your towns into
ruins and you will be desolate. Then
you will know that I am the LORD.
5" 'Because you harbored an ancient
hostility and delivered the Israelites
over to the sword at the time of their
calamity, the time their punishment
reached its climax, 6therefore as surely
as I live, declares the Sovereign LORD, I
will give you over to bloodshed and it
will pursue you. Since you did not hate
bloodshed, bloodshed will pursue you.
7I will make Mount Seir a desolate waste
and cut off from it all who come and go.
8I will fill your mountains with the slain;
those killed by the sword will fall on
your hills and in your valleys and in all
your ravines. 9I will make you desolate
forever; your towns will not be inhabited. Then you will know that I am the
LORD.
10" 'Because you have said, "These

two nations and countries will be ours
and we will take possession of them,"
even though I the LORD was there,
11therefore as surely as I live, declares
the Sovereign LORD, I will treat you in
accordance with the anger and jealousy
you showed in your hatred of them and
I will make myself known among them
when I judge you. 12Then you will know
that I the LORD have heard all the contemptible things you have said against
the mountains of Israel. You said, "They
have been laid waste and have been giv-
en over to us to devour." 13You boasted
against me and spoke against me without restraint, and I heard it. 14This is
what the Sovereign LORD says: While
the whole earth rejoices, I will make you
desolate. 15Because you rejoiced when
the inheritance of the house of Israel became desolate, that is how I will treat
you. You will be desolate, O Mount Seir,
you and all of Edom. Then they will
know that I am the LORD.' "

A Prophecy to the Mountains of Israel

36 "Son of man, prophesy to
the mountains of Israel
and say, 'O mountains of Israel, hear
the word of the LORD. 2This is what the
Sovereign LORD says: The enemy said of
you, "Aha! The ancient heights have
become our possession." ' 3Therefore
prophesy and say, 'This is what the Sovereign LORD says: Because they ravaged
and hounded you from every side so
that you became the possession of the
rest of the nations and the object of
people's malicious talk and slander,
4therefore, O mountains of Israel, hear
the word of the Sovereign LORD: This is
what the Sovereign LORD says to the
mountains and hills, to the ravines and
valleys, to the desolate ruins and the deserted towns that have been plundered
and ridiculed by the rest of the nations
around you— 5this is what the Sovereign LORD says: In my burning zeal I
have spoken against the rest of the nations, and against all Edom, for with
glee and with malice in their hearts they
made my land their own possession so
that they might plunder its pastureland.' 6Therefore prophesy concerning
the land of Israel and say to the mountains and hills, to the ravines and valleys: 'This is what the Sovereign LORD
says: I speak in my jealous wrath because you have suffered the scorn of the
nations. 7Therefore this is what the Sovereign LORD says: I swear with uplifted
hand that the nations around you will
also suffer scorn.

8" 'But you, O mountains of Israel,
will produce branches and fruit for my
people Israel, for they will soon come
home. 9I am concerned for you and will
look on you with favor; you will be
plowed and sown, 10and I will multiply
the number of people upon you, even
the whole house of Israel. The towns
will be inhabited and the ruins rebuilt.
11I will increase the number of men and
animals upon you, and they will be
fruitful and become numerous. I will
settle people on you as in the past and
will make you prosper more than before. Then you will know that I am the
LORD. 12I will cause people, my people
Israel, to walk upon you. They will possess you, and you will be their inheritance; you will never again deprive
them of their children.

13" 'This is what the Sovereign LORD
says: Because people say to you, "You
devour men and deprive your nation of
its children," 14therefore you will no
longer devour men or make your nation
childless, declares the Sovereign LORD.
15No longer will I make you hear the
taunts of the nations, and no longer will
you suffer the scorn of the peoples or
cause your nation to fall, declares the
Sovereign LORD.' "

16Again the word of the LORD came to
me: 17"Son of man, when the people of
Israel were living in their own land,
they defiled it by their conduct and their
actions. Their conduct was like a
woman's monthly uncleanness in my
sight. 18So I poured out my wrath on
them because they had shed blood in
the land and because they had defiled
it with their idols. 19I dispersed them
among the nations, and they were scat-

tered through the countries; I judged
them according to their conduct and
their actions. 20And wherever they went
among the nations they profaned my
holy name, for it was said of them,
'These are the LORD's people, and yet
they had to leave his land.' 21I had concern for my holy name, which the house
of Israel profaned among the nations
where they had gone.

22"Therefore say to the house of Israel, 'This is what the Sovereign LORD
says: It is not for your sake, O house of
Israel, that I am going to do these things,
but for the sake of my holy name, which
you have profaned among the nations
where you have gone. 23I will show the
holiness of my great name, which has
been profaned among the nations, the
name you have profaned among them.
Then the nations will know that I am
the LORD, declares the Sovereign LORD,
when I show myself holy through you
before their eyes.

24" 'For I will take you out of the nations; I will gather you from all the
countries and bring you back into your
own land. 25I will sprinkle clean water
on you, and you will be clean; I will
cleanse you from all your impurities and
from all your idols. 26I will give you a
new heart and put a new spirit in you; I
will remove from you your heart of
stone and give you a heart of flesh.
27And I will put my Spirit in you and
move you to follow my decrees and be
careful to keep my laws. 28You will live
in the land I gave your forefathers; you
will be my people, and I will be your
God. 29I will save you from all your uncleanness. I will call for the grain and
make it plentiful and will not bring famine upon you. 30I will increase the fruit
of the trees and the crops of the field, so
that you will no longer suffer disgrace
among the nations because of famine.
31Then you will remember your evil
ways and wicked deeds, and you will
loathe yourselves for your sins and detestable practices. 32I want you to know
that I am not doing this for your
sake, declares the Sovereign LORD. Be
ashamed and disgraced for your conduct, O house of Israel!

33" 'This is what the Sovereign LORD
says: On the day I cleanse you from all
your sins, I will resettle your towns, and
the ruins will be rebuilt. 34The desolate
land will be cultivated instead of lying
desolate in the sight of all who pass
through it. 35They will say, "This land
that was laid waste has become like the
garden of Eden; the cities that were lying in ruins, desolate and destroyed, are
now fortified and inhabited." 36Then the
nations around you that remain will
know that I the LORD have rebuilt what
was destroyed and have replanted what
was desolate. I the LORD have spoken,
and I will do it.'

37"This is what the Sovereign LORD
says: Once again I will yield to the plea
of the house of Israel and do this for
them: I will make their people as numerous as sheep, 38as numerous as the
flocks for offerings at Jerusalem during
her appointed feasts. So will the ruined
cities be filled with flocks of people.
Then they will know that I am the
LORD."

SHARPEN THE FOCUS

As we began to read Ezekiel, we zeroed in on what the Lord tells us about Himself in the first vision He gave Ezekiel. There, He revealed His holiness, His omniscience, his omnipresence, and above all, His majesty. Today's text, particularly Ezekiel 36:21–38, reveals even more about His glory. We see the following:

- The Lord is merciful (Ezekiel 36:24–25).
- The Lord cleanses His people from sin, washing away our guilt (Ezekiel 36:25, 33).

- The Lord loves to give, to prosper His people (Ezekiel 36:11, 29–30, 35).
- The Lord gives the gift of repentance and fills us with His Holy Spirit (Ezekiel 36:26–27) so that we can honor Him with our lives.

Ezekiel 36:9 sums it up well. God says, "I am concerned for you and will look on you with favor." Imagine that! As the Creator of the universe has taken a personal interest in His people, Israel, so He has taken a personal interest in you! He has shown us His mercy, cleansed us from sin, blessed us beyond measure, and given us the Holy Spirit—all in Christ. He's promised to care for us—body and soul. If God is for us, who can be against us?

WEEK 65 • TUESDAY

Ezekiel 37:1—39:29

GET THE BIG PICTURE

The tear-stained words of Psalm 137 sum up the feelings of the people to whom Ezekiel preached. But Ezekiel brought good news. He promised Judah that she would return to her homeland (Ezekiel 37). Then he comforts the church of all time with this truth: The gates of hell will not prevail against our Lord and His Christ (Ezekiel 38–39). As you read, take your own concerns about the health of His church to your Lord. If time is short, focus on Ezekiel 37:1–14.

The Valley of Dry Bones

37 The hand of the LORD was
upon me, and he brought
me out by the Spirit of the LORD and set
me in the middle of a valley; it was full
of bones. 2He led me back and forth
among them, and I saw a great many
bones on the floor of the valley, bones
that were very dry. 3He asked me, "Son
of man, can these bones live?"

I said, "O Sovereign LORD, you alone
know."

4Then he said to me, "Prophesy to
these bones and say to them, 'Dry
bones, hear the word of the LORD! 5This
is what the Sovereign LORD says to
these bones: I will make breath[a] enter
you, and you will come to life. 6I will
attach tendons to you and make flesh
come upon you and cover you with
skin; I will put breath in you, and you
will come to life. Then you will know
that I am the LORD.' "

7So I prophesied as I was commanded. And as I was prophesying, there was
a noise, a rattling sound, and the bones
came together, bone to bone. 8I looked,
and tendons and flesh appeared on
them and skin covered them, but there
was no breath in them.

9Then he said to me, "Prophesy to the
breath; prophesy, son of man, and say
to it, 'This is what the Sovereign LORD
says: Come from the four winds,
O breath, and breathe into these slain,
that they may live.' " 10So I prophesied
as he commanded me, and breath entered them; they came to life and stood
up on their feet—a vast army.

11Then he said to me: "Son of man,
these bones are the whole house of Israel. They say, 'Our bones are dried up
and our hope is gone; we are cut off.'

[a]5 The Hebrew for this word can also mean *wind* or *spirit* (see verses 6-14).

[12]Therefore prophesy and say to them:
'This is what the Sovereign LORD says:
O my people, I am going to open your
graves and bring you up from them; I
will bring you back to the land of Israel.
[13]Then you, my people, will know that
I am the LORD, when I open your graves
and bring you up from them. [14]I will put
my Spirit in you and you will live, and I
will settle you in your own land. Then
you will know that I the LORD have spoken, and I have done it, declares the
LORD.' "

One Nation Under One King

[15]The word of the LORD came to me:
[16]"Son of man, take a stick of wood and
write on it, 'Belonging to Judah and the
Israelites associated with him.' Then
take another stick of wood, and write on
it, 'Ephraim's stick, belonging to Joseph
and all the house of Israel associated
with him.' [17]Join them together into one
stick so that they will become one in
your hand.

[18]"When your countrymen ask you,
'Won't you tell us what you mean by
this?' [19]say to them, 'This is what the
Sovereign LORD says: I am going to take
the stick of Joseph—which is in Ephraim's hand—and of the Israelite tribes
associated with him, and join it to
Judah's stick, making them a single stick
of wood, and they will become one in
my hand.' [20]Hold before their eyes the
sticks you have written on [21]and say to
them, 'This is what the Sovereign LORD
says: I will take the Israelites out of the
nations where they have gone. I will
gather them from all around and bring
them back into their own land. [22]I will
make them one nation in the land, on
the mountains of Israel. There will be
one king over all of them and they will
never again be two nations or be divided into two kingdoms. [23]They will no
longer defile themselves with their idols
and vile images or with any of their offenses, for I will save them from all their
sinful backsliding,[a] and I will cleanse
them. They will be my people, and I will
be their God.

[24]" 'My servant David will be king
over them, and they will all have one
shepherd. They will follow my laws and
be careful to keep my decrees. [25]They
will live in the land I gave to my servant
Jacob, the land where your fathers lived.
They and their children and their
children's children will live there forever, and David my servant will be their
prince forever. [26]I will make a covenant
of peace with them; it will be an everlasting covenant. I will establish them
and increase their numbers, and I will
put my sanctuary among them forever.
[27]My dwelling place will be with them;
I will be their God, and they will be my
people. [28]Then the nations will know
that I the LORD make Israel holy, when
my sanctuary is among them forever.' "

A Prophecy Against Gog

38 The word of the LORD
came to me: [2]"Son of man,
set your face against Gog, of the land of
Magog, the chief prince of[b] Meshech
and Tubal; prophesy against him [3]and
say: 'This is what the Sovereign LORD
says: I am against you, O Gog, chief
prince of[c] Meshech and Tubal. [4]I will
turn you around, put hooks in your
jaws and bring you out with your whole
army—your horses, your horsemen fully armed, and a great horde with large
and small shields, all of them brandishing their swords. [5]Persia, Cush[d] and Put
will be with them, all with shields and
helmets, [6]also Gomer with all its troops,
and Beth Togarmah from the far north
with all its troops—the many nations
with you.

[7]" 'Get ready; be prepared, you and all
the hordes gathered about you, and
take command of them. [8]After many
days you will be called to arms. In future
years you will invade a land that has
recovered from war, whose people were
gathered from many nations to the
mountains of Israel, which had long
been desolate. They had been brought

[a]23 Many Hebrew manuscripts (see also Septuagint); most Hebrew manuscripts *all their dwelling places where they sinned* [b]2 Or *the prince of Rosh,* [c]3 Or *Gog, prince of Rosh,* [d]5 That is, the upper Nile region

out from the nations, and now all of
them live in safety. 9You and all your
troops and the many nations with you
will go up, advancing like a storm; you
will be like a cloud covering the land.
10" 'This is what the Sovereign LORD
says: On that day thoughts will come
into your mind and you will devise an
evil scheme. 11You will say, "I will invade
a land of unwalled villages; I will attack
a peaceful and unsuspecting people—
all of them living without walls and
without gates and bars. 12I will plunder
and loot and turn my hand against the
resettled ruins and the people gathered
from the nations, rich in livestock and
goods, living at the center of the land."
13Sheba and Dedan and the merchants
of Tarshish and all her villages[a] will say
to you, "Have you come to plunder?
Have you gathered your hordes to loot,
to carry off silver and gold, to take away
livestock and goods and to seize much
plunder?" '
14"Therefore, son of man, prophesy
and say to Gog: 'This is what the Sovereign LORD says: In that day, when my
people Israel are living in safety, will
you not take notice of it? 15You will come
from your place in the far north, you
and many nations with you, all of them
riding on horses, a great horde, a
mighty army. 16You will advance against
my people Israel like a cloud that covers the land. In days to come, O Gog, I
will bring you against my land, so that
the nations may know me when I show
myself holy through you before their
eyes.
17" 'This is what the Sovereign LORD
says: Are you not the one I spoke of in
former days by my servants the prophets of Israel? At that time they prophesied for years that I would bring you
against them. 18This is what will happen
in that day: When Gog attacks the land
of Israel, my hot anger will be aroused,
declares the Sovereign LORD. 19In my
zeal and fiery wrath I declare that at that
time there shall be a great earthquake in
the land of Israel. 20The fish of the sea,
the birds of the air, the beasts of the field,
every creature that moves along the
ground, and all the people on the face
of the earth will tremble at my presence.
The mountains will be overturned, the
cliffs will crumble and every wall will
fall to the ground. 21I will summon a
sword against Gog on all my mountains,
declares the Sovereign LORD. Every
man's sword will be against his brother.
22I will execute judgment upon him with
plague and bloodshed; I will pour down
torrents of rain, hailstones and burning
sulfur on him and on his troops and on
the many nations with him. 23And so I
will show my greatness and my holiness, and I will make myself known in
the sight of many nations. Then they
will know that I am the LORD.'

39

"Son of man, prophesy
against Gog and say: 'This
is what the Sovereign LORD says: I am
against you, O Gog, chief prince of[b]
Meshech and Tubal. 2I will turn you
around and drag you along. I will bring
you from the far north and send you
against the mountains of Israel. 3Then I
will strike your bow from your left hand
and make your arrows drop from your
right hand. 4On the mountains of Israel
you will fall, you and all your troops and
the nations with you. I will give you as
food to all kinds of carrion birds and to
the wild animals. 5You will fall in the
open field, for I have spoken, declares
the Sovereign LORD. 6I will send fire on
Magog and on those who live in safety
in the coastlands, and they will know
that I am the LORD.
7" 'I will make known my holy name
among my people Israel. I will no longer let my holy name be profaned, and
the nations will know that I the LORD
am the Holy One in Israel. 8It is coming!
It will surely take place, declares the
Sovereign LORD. This is the day I have
spoken of.
9" 'Then those who live in the towns
of Israel will go out and use the weapons for fuel and burn them up—the
small and large shields, the bows and
arrows, the war clubs and spears. For
seven years they will use them for fuel.

[a]13 Or *her strong lions* [b]1 Or *Gog, prince of Rosh,*

10They will not need to gather wood
from the fields or cut it from the forests,
because they will use the weapons for
fuel. And they will plunder those who
plundered them and loot those who
looted them, declares the Sovereign
LORD.

11" 'On that day I will give Gog a burial place in Israel, in the valley of those
who travel east toward[a] the Sea.[b] It will
block the way of travelers, because Gog
and all his hordes will be buried there.
So it will be called the Valley of Hamon
Gog.[c]

12" 'For seven months the house of Israel will be burying them in order to
cleanse the land. 13All the people of the
land will bury them, and the day I am
glorified will be a memorable day for
them, declares the Sovereign LORD.

14" 'Men will be regularly employed to
cleanse the land. Some will go throughout the land and, in addition to them,
others will bury those that remain on
the ground. At the end of the seven
months they will begin their search. 15As
they go through the land and one of
them sees a human bone, he will set up
a marker beside it until the gravediggers
have buried it in the Valley of Hamon
Gog. 16(Also a town called Hamonah[d]
will be there.) And so they will cleanse
the land.'

17"Son of man, this is what the Sovereign LORD says: Call out to every kind
of bird and all the wild animals: 'Assemble and come together from all around
to the sacrifice I am preparing for you,
the great sacrifice on the mountains of
Israel. There you will eat flesh and drink
blood. 18You will eat the flesh of mighty
men and drink the blood of the princes
of the earth as if they were rams and
lambs, goats and bulls—all of them fattened animals from Bashan. 19At the sacrifice I am preparing for you, you will
eat fat till you are glutted and drink
blood till you are drunk. 20At my table
you will eat your fill of horses and riders, mighty men and soldiers of every
kind,' declares the Sovereign LORD.

21"I will display my glory among the
nations, and all the nations will see the
punishment I inflict and the hand I lay
upon them. 22From that day forward the
house of Israel will know that I am the
LORD their God. 23And the nations will
know that the people of Israel went into
exile for their sin, because they were
unfaithful to me. So I hid my face from
them and handed them over to their enemies, and they all fell by the sword. 24I
dealt with them according to their uncleanness and their offenses, and I hid
my face from them.

25"Therefore this is what the Sovereign LORD says: I will now bring Jacob
back from captivity[e] and will have compassion on all the people of Israel, and I
will be zealous for my holy name. 26They
will forget their shame and all the unfaithfulness they showed toward me
when they lived in safety in their land
with no one to make them afraid.
27When I have brought them back from
the nations and have gathered them
from the countries of their enemies, I
will show myself holy through them in
the sight of many nations. 28Then they
will know that I am the LORD their God,
for though I sent them into exile among
the nations, I will gather them to their
own land, not leaving any behind. 29I
will no longer hide my face from them,
for I will pour out my Spirit on the
house of Israel, declares the Sovereign
LORD."

[a]11 Or *of* [b]11 That is, the Dead Sea [c]11 *Hamon Gog* means *hordes of Gog.* [d]16 *Hamonah* means *horde.* [e]25 Or *now restore the fortunes of Jacob*

SHARPEN THE FOCUS

The subtle pressure. The angry remark. The prison term or death sentence. Persecution for the sake of Jesus takes many forms. Christians who lived in poverty in communist Eastern Europe can testify to it. But so can the university student whose professor ridicules the Christian faith lecture after lecture.

Seeing persecution outside, we look inside. At the pastor removed for adultery. At a Sunday school teacher arrested for child abuse. At a church treasurer jailed for embezzlement.

What are we to make of this? "Can these dry bones live?" we ask ourselves. Then we remember. Ezekiel's valley of dried bones became a living, breathing army—at the Word of the Lord. That same Word and that same God are still at work in the hearts of His people today. We may feel dried up and despairing, but we need not be. Our Lord Jesus Himself has promised to build His church and to send it—victorious—into battle, a battle He's already won for us (Matthew 16:18).

WEEK 65 • WEDNESDAY

Ezekiel 40:1—42:20

GET THE BIG PICTURE

Ezekiel's temple, described in the three chapters you will read today, has mystified Bible students for centuries. It differs in many significant ways from the temples erected by Solomon and Zerubbabel. In fact, it exists only in Ezekiel's vision. As you read, thank your Lord for making it possible for us, sinners though we are, to approach Him in worship. If time is short, focus on Ezekiel 41:1–4.

The New Temple Area

40 In the twenty-fifth year of
our exile, at the beginning
of the year, on the tenth of the month,
in the fourteenth year after the fall of
the city—on that very day the hand of
the LORD was upon me and he took me
there. 2In visions of God he took me to
the land of Israel and set me on a very
high mountain, on whose south side
were some buildings that looked like a
city. 3He took me there, and I saw a man
whose appearance was like bronze; he
was standing in the gateway with a linen cord and a measuring rod in his
hand. 4The man said to me, "Son of man,
look with your eyes and hear with your
ears and pay attention to everything I
am going to show you, for that is why
you have been brought here. Tell the
house of Israel everything you see."

The East Gate to the Outer Court

5I saw a wall completely surrounding
the temple area. The length of the measuring rod in the man's hand was six
long cubits, each of which was a cubit[a]
and a handbreadth.[b] He measured the
wall; it was one measuring rod thick
and one rod high.

6Then he went to the gate facing east.
He climbed its steps and measured the
threshold of the gate; it was one rod
deep.[c] 7The alcoves for the guards were
one rod long and one rod wide, and the
projecting walls between the alcoves
were five cubits thick. And the threshold of the gate next to the portico facing
the temple was one rod deep.

8Then he measured the portico of the
gateway; 9it[d] was eight cubits deep and
its jambs were two cubits thick. The portico of the gateway faced the temple.

[a]5 The common cubit was about 1 1/2 feet (about 0.5 meter). [b]5 That is, about 3 inches (about 8 centimeters) [c]6 Septuagint; Hebrew *deep, the first threshold, one rod deep* [d]8,9 Many Hebrew manuscripts, Septuagint, Vulgate and Syriac; most Hebrew manuscripts *gateway facing the temple; it was one rod deep. 9Then he measured the portico of the gateway; it*

10Inside the east gate were three alcoves on each side; the three had the
same measurements, and the faces of
the projecting walls on each side had
the same measurements. 11Then he measured the width of the entrance to the
gateway; it was ten cubits and its length
was thirteen cubits. 12In front of each
alcove was a wall one cubit high, and
the alcoves were six cubits square.
13Then he measured the gateway from
the top of the rear wall of one alcove to
the top of the opposite one; the distance
was twenty-five cubits from one parapet opening to the opposite one. 14He
measured along the faces of the projecting walls all around the inside of the
gateway—sixty cubits. The measurement was up to the portico[a] facing the
courtyard.[b] 15The distance from the entrance of the gateway to the far end of
its portico was fifty cubits. 16The alcoves
and the projecting walls inside the gateway were surmounted by narrow parapet openings all around, as was the
portico; the openings all around faced
inward. The faces of the projecting walls
were decorated with palm trees.

The Outer Court

17Then he brought me into the outer
court. There I saw some rooms and a
pavement that had been constructed all
around the court; there were thirty
rooms along the pavement. 18It abutted
the sides of the gateways and was as
wide as they were long; this was the
lower pavement. 19Then he measured
the distance from the inside of the lower gateway to the outside of the inner
court; it was a hundred cubits on the
east side as well as on the north.

The North Gate

20Then he measured the length and
width of the gate facing north, leading
into the outer court. 21Its alcoves—three
on each side—its projecting walls and
its portico had the same measurements
as those of the first gateway. It was fifty
cubits long and twenty-five cubits wide.
22Its openings, its portico and its palm
tree decorations had the same measurements as those of the gate facing east.
Seven steps led up to it, with its portico
opposite them. 23There was a gate to the
inner court facing the north gate, just as
there was on the east. He measured
from one gate to the opposite one; it was
a hundred cubits.

The South Gate

24Then he led me to the south side and
I saw a gate facing south. He measured
its jambs and its portico, and they had
the same measurements as the others.
25The gateway and its portico had narrow openings all around, like the openings of the others. It was fifty cubits long
and twenty-five cubits wide. 26Seven
steps led up to it, with its portico opposite them; it had palm tree decorations
on the faces of the projecting walls on
each side. 27The inner court also had a
gate facing south, and he measured
from this gate to the outer gate on the
south side; it was a hundred cubits.

Gates to the Inner Court

28Then he brought me into the inner
court through the south gate, and he
measured the south gate; it had the
same measurements as the others. 29Its
alcoves, its projecting walls and its portico had the same measurements as the
others. The gateway and its portico had
openings all around. It was fifty cubits
long and twenty-five cubits wide. 30(The
porticoes of the gateways around the
inner court were twenty-five cubits
wide and five cubits deep.) 31Its portico
faced the outer court; palm trees decorated its jambs, and eight steps led up
to it.

32Then he brought me to the inner
court on the east side, and he measured
the gateway; it had the same measurements as the others. 33Its alcoves, its projecting walls and its portico had the
same measurements as the others. The
gateway and its portico had openings
all around. It was fifty cubits long and

[a]14 Septuagint; Hebrew *projecting wall*
[b]14 The meaning of the Hebrew for this verse is uncertain.

twenty-five cubits wide. 34 Its portico
faced the outer court; palm trees decorated the jambs on either side, and eight
steps led up to it.
35 Then he brought me to the north
gate and measured it. It had the same
measurements as the others, 36 as did its
alcoves, its projecting walls and its portico, and it had openings all around. It
was fifty cubits long and twenty-five cubits wide. 37 Its portico[a] faced the outer
court; palm trees decorated the jambs
on either side, and eight steps led up
to it.

The Rooms for Preparing Sacrifices

38 A room with a doorway was by the
portico in each of the inner gateways,
where the burnt offerings were washed.
39 In the portico of the gateway were two
tables on each side, on which the burnt
offerings, sin offerings and guilt offerings were slaughtered. 40 By the outside
wall of the portico of the gateway, near
the steps at the entrance to the north
gateway were two tables, and on the
other side of the steps were two tables.
41 So there were four tables on one side
of the gateway and four on the other—
eight tables in all—on which the sacrifices were slaughtered. 42 There were
also four tables of dressed stone for the
burnt offerings, each a cubit and a half
long, a cubit and a half wide and a cubit high. On them were placed the utensils for slaughtering the burnt offerings
and the other sacrifices. 43 And double-
pronged hooks, each a handbreadth
long, were attached to the wall all
around. The tables were for the flesh of
the offerings.

Rooms for the Priests

44 Outside the inner gate, within the
inner court, were two rooms, one[b] at the
side of the north gate and facing south,
and another at the side of the south[c]
gate and facing north. 45 He said to me,
"The room facing south is for the priests
who have charge of the temple, 46 and
the room facing north is for the priests
who have charge of the altar. These are
the sons of Zadok, who are the only
Levites who may draw near to the LORD
to minister before him."
47 Then he measured the court: It was
square—a hundred cubits long and a
hundred cubits wide. And the altar was
in front of the temple.

The Temple

48 He brought me to the portico of the
temple and measured the jambs of the
portico; they were five cubits wide on
either side. The width of the entrance
was fourteen cubits and its projecting
walls were[d] three cubits wide on either
side. 49 The portico was twenty cubits
wide, and twelve[e] cubits from front to
back. It was reached by a flight of stairs,[f]
and there were pillars on each side of
the jambs.

41 Then the man brought me to
the outer sanctuary and measured the jambs; the width of the jambs
was six cubits[g] on each side.[h] 2 The entrance was ten cubits wide, and the projecting walls on each side of it were five
cubits wide. He also measured the outer sanctuary; it was forty cubits long and
twenty cubits wide.
3 Then he went into the inner sanctuary and measured the jambs of the entrance; each was two cubits wide. The
entrance was six cubits wide, and the
projecting walls on each side of it were
seven cubits wide. 4 And he measured
the length of the inner sanctuary; it was
twenty cubits, and its width was twenty cubits across the end of the outer
sanctuary. He said to me, "This is the
Most Holy Place."
5 Then he measured the wall of the
temple; it was six cubits thick, and each
side room around the temple was four
cubits wide. 6 The side rooms were on
three levels, one above another, thirty

[a] 37 Septuagint (see also verses 31 and 34); Hebrew *jambs* [b] 44 Septuagint; Hebrew *were rooms for singers, which were* [c] 44 Septuagint; Hebrew *east* [d] 48 Septuagint; Hebrew *entrance was* [e] 49 Septuagint; Hebrew *eleven*
[f] 49 Hebrew; Septuagint *Ten steps led up to it*
[g] 1 The common cubit was about 1 1/2 feet (about 0.5 meter). [h] 1 One Hebrew manuscript and Septuagint; most Hebrew manuscripts *side, the width of the tent*

on each level. There were ledges all around the wall of the temple to serve as supports for the side rooms, so that the supports were not inserted into the wall of the temple. [7]The side rooms all around the temple were wider at each successive level. The structure surrounding the temple was built in ascending stages, so that the rooms widened as one went upward. A stairway went up from the lowest floor to the top floor through the middle floor.

[8]I saw that the temple had a raised base all around it, forming the foundation of the side rooms. It was the length of the rod, six long cubits. [9]The outer wall of the side rooms was five cubits thick. The open area between the side rooms of the temple [10]and the ⌞priests'⌟ rooms was twenty cubits wide all around the temple. [11]There were entrances to the side rooms from the open area, one on the north and another on the south; and the base adjoining the open area was five cubits wide all around.

[12]The building facing the temple courtyard on the west side was seventy cubits wide. The wall of the building was five cubits thick all around, and its length was ninety cubits.

[13]Then he measured the temple; it was a hundred cubits long, and the temple courtyard and the building with its walls were also a hundred cubits long. [14]The width of the temple courtyard on the east, including the front of the temple, was a hundred cubits.

[15]Then he measured the length of the building facing the courtyard at the rear of the temple, including its galleries on each side; it was a hundred cubits.

The outer sanctuary, the inner sanctuary and the portico facing the court, [16]as well as the thresholds and the narrow windows and galleries around the three of them—everything beyond and including the threshold was covered with wood. The floor, the wall up to the windows, and the windows were covered. [17]In the space above the outside of the entrance to the inner sanctuary and on the walls at regular intervals all around the inner and outer sanctuary [18]were carved cherubim and palm trees. Palm trees alternated with cherubim. Each cherub had two faces: [19]the face of a man toward the palm tree on one side and the face of a lion toward the palm tree on the other. They were carved all around the whole temple. [20]From the floor to the area above the entrance, cherubim and palm trees were carved on the wall of the outer sanctuary.

[21]The outer sanctuary had a rectangular doorframe, and the one at the front of the Most Holy Place was similar. [22]There was a wooden altar three cubits high and two cubits square[a]; its corners, its base[b] and its sides were of wood. The man said to me, "This is the table that is before the LORD." [23]Both the outer sanctuary and the Most Holy Place had double doors. [24]Each door had two leaves—two hinged leaves for each door. [25]And on the doors of the outer sanctuary were carved cherubim and palm trees like those carved on the walls, and there was a wooden overhang on the front of the portico. [26]On the sidewalls of the portico were narrow windows with palm trees carved on each side. The side rooms of the temple also had overhangs.

Rooms for the Priests

42 Then the man led me northward into the outer court and brought me to the rooms opposite the temple courtyard and opposite the outer wall on the north side. [2]The building whose door faced north was a hundred cubits[c] long and fifty cubits wide. [3]Both in the section twenty cubits from the inner court and in the section opposite the pavement of the outer court, gallery faced gallery at the three levels. [4]In front of the rooms was an inner passageway ten cubits wide and a hundred cubits[d] long. Their doors were on the north. [5]Now the upper rooms were narrower, for the galleries

[a]22 Septuagint; Hebrew *long* [b]22 Septuagint; Hebrew *length* [c]2 The common cubit was about 1 1/2 feet (about 0.5 meter). [d]4 Septuagint and Syriac; Hebrew *and one cubit*

took more space from them than from the rooms on the lower and middle floors of the building. [6]The rooms on the third floor had no pillars, as the courts had; so they were smaller in floor space than those on the lower and middle floors. [7]There was an outer wall parallel to the rooms and the outer court; it extended in front of the rooms for fifty cubits. [8]While the row of rooms on the side next to the outer court was fifty cubits long, the row on the side nearest the sanctuary was a hundred cubits long. [9]The lower rooms had an entrance on the east side as one enters them from the outer court.

[10]On the south side[a] along the length of the wall of the outer court, adjoining the temple courtyard and opposite the outer wall, were rooms [11]with a passageway in front of them. These were like the rooms on the north; they had the same length and width, with similar exits and dimensions. Similar to the doorways on the north [12]were the doorways of the rooms on the south. There was a doorway at the beginning of the passageway that was parallel to the corresponding wall extending eastward, by which one enters the rooms.

[13]Then he said to me, "The north and south rooms facing the temple courtyard are the priests' rooms, where the priests who approach the LORD will eat the most holy offerings. There they will put the most holy offerings—the grain offerings, the sin offerings and the guilt offerings—for the place is holy. [14]Once the priests enter the holy precincts, they are not to go into the outer court until they leave behind the garments in which they minister, for these are holy. They are to put on other clothes before they go near the places that are for the people."

[15]When he had finished measuring what was inside the temple area, he led me out by the east gate and measured the area all around: [16]He measured the east side with the measuring rod; it was five hundred cubits.[b] [17]He measured the north side; it was five hundred cubits[c] by the measuring rod. [18]He measured the south side; it was five hundred cubits by the measuring rod. [19]Then he turned to the west side and measured; it was five hundred cubits by the measuring rod. [20]So he measured the area on all four sides. It had a wall around it, five hundred cubits long and five hundred cubits wide, to separate the holy from the common.

[a]10 Septuagint; Hebrew *Eastward* [b]16 See Septuagint of verse 17; Hebrew *rods*; also in verses 18 and 19. [c]17 Septuagint; Hebrew *rods*

SHARPEN THE FOCUS

We may puzzle over the fact that the almighty God wants to befriend us. The entire Old Testament system of worship points to the fact that the Lord draws people to Himself.

The altars and the sacrifices connected so thoroughly to Old Testament worship remind us again and again that we could not come to God on our own merit. A price had to be paid. More specifically, blood had to be shed. Only bloody, messy death made the Old Testament worshiper acceptable to the Lord.

Awful as that system of symbols must have seemed, its fulfillment, stuns us. Awful. Awesome. Calvary is this and more, all at once. Who could have guessed the lengths to which the Lord would go? Who could have known how precious His human creatures were to Him? But they were. We are.

When Christ came as high priest of the good things that are already here, He went through the greater and more perfect tabernacle that is not man-made, that is to say, not a part of this creation. He did not enter by means of the blood of goats and calves; but He entered the Most Holy Place once for all by His own blood, having obtained eternal redemption. (Hebrews 9:11–12)

Ezekiel's temple was real, but not literal. It showed the exiles the privilege of worship and the God-given sacrificial system they were missing. Through Ezekiel's vision, the Lord hoped to motivate His people to leave Babylon when the time came—for it *would* come. Before you read Ezekiel 43, review Ezekiel 10:18–19; 11:22–25. If time is short, focus on Ezekiel 43:1–12.

The Glory Returns to the Temple

43 Then the man brought
me to the gate facing east,
2 and I saw the glory of the God of Israel
coming from the east. His voice was like
the roar of rushing waters, and the land
was radiant with his glory. 3 The vision I
saw was like the vision I had seen when
he[a] came to destroy the city and like the
visions I had seen by the Kebar River,
and I fell facedown. 4 The glory of the
LORD entered the temple through the
gate facing east. 5 Then the Spirit lifted
me up and brought me into the inner
court, and the glory of the LORD filled
the temple.
6 While the man was standing beside
me, I heard someone speaking to me
from inside the temple. 7 He said: "Son
of man, this is the place of my throne
and the place for the soles of my feet.
This is where I will live among the Israelites forever. The house of Israel will
never again defile my holy name—neither they nor their kings—by their
prostitution[b] and the lifeless idols[c] of
their kings at their high places. 8 When
they placed their threshold next to my
threshold and their doorposts beside
my doorposts, with only a wall between
me and them, they defiled my holy
name by their detestable practices. So I
destroyed them in my anger. 9 Now let
them put away from me their prostitution and the lifeless idols of their kings,
and I will live among them forever.
10 "Son of man, describe the temple to
the people of Israel, that they may be
ashamed of their sins. Let them consider the plan, 11 and if they are ashamed of
all they have done, make known to
them the design of the temple—its arrangement, its exits and entrances—its
whole design and all its regulations[d]
and laws. Write these down before them
so that they may be faithful to its design
and follow all its regulations.
12 "This is the law of the temple: All the
surrounding area on top of the mountain will be most holy. Such is the law of
the temple.

The Altar

13 "These are the measurements of the
altar in long cubits, that cubit being a
cubit[e] and a handbreadth[f]: Its gutter is

[a]3 Some Hebrew manuscripts and Vulgate; most Hebrew manuscripts *I* [b]7 Or *their spiritual adultery*; also in verse 9 [c]7 Or *the corpses*; also in verse 9 [d]11 Some Hebrew manuscripts and Septuagint; most Hebrew manuscripts *regulations and its whole design* [e]13 The common cubit was about 1 1/2 feet (about 0.5 meter). [f]13 That is, about 3 inches (about 8 centimeters)

a cubit deep and a cubit wide, with a rim
of one span[a] around the edge. And this
is the height of the altar: 14From the gutter on the ground up to the lower ledge
it is two cubits high and a cubit wide,
and from the smaller ledge up to the
larger ledge it is four cubits high and a
cubit wide. 15The altar hearth is four cubits high, and four horns project upward from the hearth. 16The altar hearth
is square, twelve cubits long and twelve
cubits wide. 17The upper ledge also is
square, fourteen cubits long and fourteen cubits wide, with a rim of half a
cubit and a gutter of a cubit all around.
The steps of the altar face east."

18Then he said to me, "Son of man,
this is what the Sovereign LORD says:
These will be the regulations for sacrificing burnt offerings and sprinkling
blood upon the altar when it is built:
19You are to give a young bull as a sin
offering to the priests, who are Levites,
of the family of Zadok, who come near
to minister before me, declares the Sovereign LORD. 20You are to take some of
its blood and put it on the four horns of
the altar and on the four corners of the
upper ledge and all around the rim, and
so purify the altar and make atonement
for it. 21You are to take the bull for the sin
offering and burn it in the designated
part of the temple area outside the sanctuary.

22"On the second day you are to offer
a male goat without defect for a sin offering, and the altar is to be purified as
it was purified with the bull. 23When
you have finished purifying it, you are
to offer a young bull and a ram from the
flock, both without defect. 24You are to
offer them before the LORD, and the
priests are to sprinkle salt on them and
sacrifice them as a burnt offering to the
LORD.

25"For seven days you are to provide
a male goat daily for a sin offering; you
are also to provide a young bull and a
ram from the flock, both without defect.
26For seven days they are to make atonement for the altar and cleanse it; thus
they will dedicate it. 27At the end of
these days, from the eighth day on, the
priests are to present your burnt offerings and fellowship offerings[b] on the altar. Then I will accept you, declares the
Sovereign LORD."

[a]13 That is, about 9 inches (about 22 centimeters)
[b]27 Traditionally *peace offerings*

SHARPEN THE FOCUS

The glory of the Lord had left the temple mount. But not forever. The Lord would dwell among His people once again. The returning refugees of Ezra and Nehemiah's time would welcome Him by rebuilding a temple like Solomon's.

But that wasn't the end. God's glory would shine more brightly as Mary and Joseph brought the infant Jesus to Jerusalem's temple to be named and circumcised. They gave Him the name heaven had decreed—Jesus, Savior.

The glory shone brighter still as Jesus entered Jerusalem on Palm Sunday and as He took bread and wine in His hands to give His people the Meal of His new covenant—His body broken and blood shed.

The glory blazed against the blackness that shrouded the sky on Good Friday. There the Lord Jesus lived up to His name. There He saved His people from their sins on the truest altar of burnt offerings as the wrath of God fell like fire on the sinless Son of God.

But the glory burned in all its splendor from Joseph's empty tomb. The Savior rose, defeating death for every one of His people! His story is now our story; His glory is now our glory (John 17:22).

The priests of the old covenant failed God and God's people. We've read much about that failure. (See, for example, Ezekiel 22:26.) But the Lord would provide a Priest—our Lord Jesus—who would offer the sacrifice of Himself on the cross. Think of Him, the perfect Priest, as you read today. If time is short, focus on Ezekiel 44:1–15.

The Prince, the Levites, the Priests

44 Then the man brought
me back to the outer gate
of the sanctuary, the one facing east, and
it was shut. 2The LORD said to me, "This
gate is to remain shut. It must not be
opened; no one may enter through it. It
is to remain shut because the LORD, the
God of Israel, has entered through it.
3The prince himself is the only one who
may sit inside the gateway to eat in the
presence of the LORD. He is to enter by
way of the portico of the gateway and
go out the same way."
4Then the man brought me by way of
the north gate to the front of the temple. I looked and saw the glory of the
LORD filling the temple of the LORD,
and I fell facedown.
5The LORD said to me, "Son of man,
look carefully, listen closely and give attention to everything I tell you concerning all the regulations regarding the
temple of the LORD. Give attention to
the entrance of the temple and all the
exits of the sanctuary. 6Say to the rebellious house of Israel, 'This is what the
Sovereign LORD says: Enough of your
detestable practices, O house of Israel!
7In addition to all your other detestable
practices, you brought foreigners uncircumcised in heart and flesh into my
sanctuary, desecrating my temple while
you offered me food, fat and blood, and
you broke my covenant. 8Instead of carrying out your duty in regard to my
holy things, you put others in charge of
my sanctuary. 9This is what the Sovereign LORD says: No foreigner uncircumcised in heart and flesh is to enter my
sanctuary, not even the foreigners who
live among the Israelites.
10" 'The Levites who went far from me
when Israel went astray and who wandered from me after their idols must
bear the consequences of their sin.
11They may serve in my sanctuary, having charge of the gates of the temple
and serving in it; they may slaughter the
burnt offerings and sacrifices for the
people and stand before the people and
serve them. 12But because they served
them in the presence of their idols and
made the house of Israel fall into sin,
therefore I have sworn with uplifted
hand that they must bear the consequences of their sin, declares the Sovereign LORD. 13They are not to come near
to serve me as priests or come near any
of my holy things or my most holy offerings; they must bear the shame of their
detestable practices. 14Yet I will put them
in charge of the duties of the temple and
all the work that is to be done in it.
15" 'But the priests, who are Levites
and descendants of Zadok and who
faithfully carried out the duties of my
sanctuary when the Israelites went
astray from me, are to come near to minister before me; they are to stand before
me to offer sacrifices of fat and blood,
declares the Sovereign LORD. 16They
alone are to enter my sanctuary; they
alone are to come near my table to minister before me and perform my service.
17" 'When they enter the gates of the

inner court, they are to wear linen
clothes; they must not wear any woolen
garment while ministering at the gates
of the inner court or inside the temple.
[18]They are to wear linen turbans on their
heads and linen undergarments around
their waists. They must not wear anything that makes them perspire. [19]When
they go out into the outer court where
the people are, they are to take off the
clothes they have been ministering in
and are to leave them in the sacred
rooms, and put on other clothes, so that
they do not consecrate the people by
means of their garments.
[20]" 'They must not shave their heads
or let their hair grow long, but they are
to keep the hair of their heads trimmed.
[21]No priest is to drink wine when he enters the inner court. [22]They must not
marry widows or divorced women;
they may marry only virgins of Israelite descent or widows of priests. [23]They
are to teach my people the difference
between the holy and the common and
show them how to distinguish between
the unclean and the clean.
[24]" 'In any dispute, the priests are to
serve as judges and decide it according
to my ordinances. They are to keep my
laws and my decrees for all my appointed feasts, and they are to keep my Sabbaths holy.
[25]" 'A priest must not defile himself by
going near a dead person; however, if
the dead person was his father or mother, son or daughter, brother or unmarried sister, then he may defile himself.
[26]After he is cleansed, he must wait sev-
en days. [27]On the day he goes into the
inner court of the sanctuary to minister
in the sanctuary, he is to offer a sin offering for himself, declares the Sovereign LORD.
[28]" 'I am to be the only inheritance the
priests have. You are to give them no
possession in Israel; I will be their possession. [29]They will eat the grain offerings, the sin offerings and the guilt
offerings; and everything in Israel
devoted[a] to the LORD will belong to
them. [30]The best of all the firstfruits and
of all your special gifts will belong to the
priests. You are to give them the first
portion of your ground meal so that a
blessing may rest on your household.
[31]The priests must not eat anything, bird
or animal, found dead or torn by wild
animals.

[a]29 The Hebrew term refers to the irrevocable giving over of things or persons to the LORD.

SHARPEN THE FOCUS

In the "Flood of '93," the Mississippi River and its tributaries swelled and swept away a record number of bridges. The old saying, "You can't get there from here" literally came true.

As we think about how to get to God from where we stand, we see an even wider chasm. By nature, we not only found ourselves separated from our Creator, but happily so. We wanted nothing to do with Him, even though He was our only source of life, of hope.

And so, God built a bridge from "there" to "here." Jesus became our Mediator, our great High Priest. As priest *and* sacrifice, Jesus Himself is the way, the bridge between a sinful people and a holy God.

No mere human priest could have done all that. The Old Testament priesthood, the Old Testament sacrifices, the rivers of blood that were spilled in the tabernacle and later in the temple, could not dilute, let alone stop the flood of sin that threatened to drown all human beings. But Jesus Christ, true God and true man, came "to do away with sin by the sacrifice of Himself" (Hebrews 9:26). He became our bridge. And now, He offers us peace with God through the forgiveness of all our sins.

WEEK 65 • SATURDAY

Ezekiel 45:1—46:24

Ezekiel's vision continues. The Lord encourages His people by picturing for them an ideal temple district, an ideal system of sacrifice, and an ideal political leader (Ezekiel 46:16–18). None of this was a prescription, but rather a description in pictures of the blessings God wants to give His people in every age. As you read, note the offerings. Think of them in light of the Savior who offered Himself for you. If time is short, focus on Ezekiel 46:1–15.

Division of the Land

45 " 'When you allot the land
as an inheritance, you are
to present to the LORD a portion of the
land as a sacred district, 25,000 cubits
long and 20,000[a] cubits wide; the entire
area will be holy. 2Of this, a section 500
cubits square is to be for the sanctuary,
with 50 cubits around it for open land.
3In the sacred district, measure off a section 25,000 cubits[b] long and 10,000
cubits[c] wide. In it will be the sanctuary,
the Most Holy Place. 4It will be the sacred portion of the land for the priests,
who minister in the sanctuary and who
draw near to minister before the LORD.
It will be a place for their houses as well
as a holy place for the sanctuary. 5An
area 25,000 cubits long and 10,000 cubits
wide will belong to the Levites, who
serve in the temple, as their possession
for towns to live in.[d]

6" 'You are to give the city as its property an area 5,000 cubits wide and 25,000 cubits long, adjoining the sacred portion; it will belong to the whole house of Israel.

7" 'The prince will have the land bordering each side of the area formed by
the sacred district and the property of
the city. It will extend westward from
the west side and eastward from the
east side, running lengthwise from the
western to the eastern border parallel to
one of the tribal portions. 8This land will
be his possession in Israel. And my
princes will no longer oppress my
people but will allow the house of Israel
to possess the land according to their
tribes.

9" 'This is what the Sovereign LORD
says: You have gone far enough,
O princes of Israel! Give up your violence and oppression and do what is
just and right. Stop dispossessing my
people, declares the Sovereign LORD.
10You are to use accurate scales, an accurate ephah[e] and an accurate bath.[f] 11The
ephah and the bath are to be the same
size, the bath containing a tenth of a
homer[g] and the ephah a tenth of a
homer; the homer is to be the standard
measure for both. 12The shekel[h] is to consist of twenty gerahs. Twenty shekels
plus twenty-five shekels plus fifteen
shekels equal one mina.[i]

Offerings and Holy Days

13" 'This is the special gift you are to offer: a sixth of an ephah from each homer of wheat and a sixth of an ephah from each homer of barley. 14The prescribed portion of oil, measured by the bath, is a tenth of a bath from each cor (which consists of ten baths or one ho-

[a]1 Septuagint (see also verses 3 and 5 and 48:9); Hebrew *10,000* [b]3 That is, about 7 miles (about 12 kilometers) [c]3 That is, about 3 miles (about 5 kilometers) [d]5 Septuagint; Hebrew *temple; they will have as their possession 20 rooms* [e]10 An ephah was a dry measure. [f]10 A bath was a liquid measure. [g]11 A homer was a dry measure. [h]12 A shekel weighed about 2/5 ounce (about 11.5 grams). [i]12 That is, 60 shekels; the common mina was 50 shekels.

mer, for ten baths are equivalent to a
homer). 15Also one sheep is to be taken
from every flock of two hundred from
the well-watered pastures of Israel.
These will be used for the grain offerings, burnt offerings and fellowship
offerings[a] to make atonement for the
people, declares the Sovereign LORD.
16All the people of the land will participate in this special gift for the use of the
prince in Israel. 17It will be the duty of
the prince to provide the burnt offerings, grain offerings and drink offerings
at the festivals, the New Moons and the
Sabbaths—at all the appointed feasts of
the house of Israel. He will provide the
sin offerings, grain offerings, burnt offerings and fellowship offerings to make
atonement for the house of Israel.
18" 'This is what the Sovereign LORD
says: In the first month on the first day
you are to take a young bull without defect and purify the sanctuary. 19The
priest is to take some of the blood of the
sin offering and put it on the doorposts
of the temple, on the four corners of the
upper ledge of the altar and on the gate-
posts of the inner court. 20You are to do
the same on the seventh day of the
month for anyone who sins unintentionally or through ignorance; so you
are to make atonement for the temple.
21" 'In the first month on the fourteenth day you are to observe the Passover, a feast lasting seven days, during
which you shall eat bread made without
yeast. 22On that day the prince is to provide a bull as a sin offering for himself
and for all the people of the land. 23Ev-
ery day during the seven days of the
Feast he is to provide seven bulls and
seven rams without defect as a burnt offering to the LORD, and a male goat for
a sin offering. 24He is to provide as a
grain offering an ephah for each bull
and an ephah for each ram, along with
a hin[b] of oil for each ephah.
25" 'During the seven days of the
Feast, which begins in the seventh
month on the fifteenth day, he is to
make the same provision for sin offerings, burnt offerings, grain offerings
and oil.

46

" 'This is what the Sovereign LORD says: The gate
of the inner court facing east is to be
shut on the six working days, but on the
Sabbath day and on the day of the New
Moon it is to be opened. 2The prince is
to enter from the outside through the
portico of the gateway and stand by the
gatepost. The priests are to sacrifice his
burnt offering and his fellowship
offerings.[c] He is to worship at the
threshold of the gateway and then go
out, but the gate will not be shut until
evening. 3On the Sabbaths and New
Moons the people of the land are to
worship in the presence of the LORD at
the entrance to that gateway. 4The burnt
offering the prince brings to the LORD
on the Sabbath day is to be six male
lambs and a ram, all without defect.
5The grain offering given with the ram
is to be an ephah,[d] and the grain offering with the lambs is to be as much as
he pleases, along with a hin[e] of oil for
each ephah. 6On the day of the New
Moon he is to offer a young bull, six
lambs and a ram, all without defect. 7He
is to provide as a grain offering one
ephah with the bull, one ephah with the
ram, and with the lambs as much as he
wants to give, along with a hin of oil
with each ephah. 8When the prince enters, he is to go in through the portico
of the gateway, and he is to come out the
same way.
9" 'When the people of the land come
before the LORD at the appointed feasts,
whoever enters by the north gate to
worship is to go out the south gate; and
whoever enters by the south gate is to
go out the north gate. No one is to return through the gate by which he entered, but each is to go out the opposite
gate. 10The prince is to be among them,
going in when they go in and going out
when they go out.
11" 'At the festivals and the appointed

[a]15 Traditionally *peace offerings*; also in verse 17
[b]24 That is, probably about 4 quarts (about 4 liters)
[c]2 Traditionally *peace offerings*; also in verse 12
[d]5 That is, probably about 3/5 bushel (about 22 liters)
[e]5 That is, probably about 4 quarts (about 4 liters)

feasts, the grain offering is to be an
ephah with a bull, an ephah with a ram,
and with the lambs as much as one
pleases, along with a hin of oil for each
ephah. [12]When the prince provides a
freewill offering to the LORD—whether
a burnt offering or fellowship offerings—the gate facing east is to be
opened for him. He shall offer his burnt
offering or his fellowship offerings as he
does on the Sabbath day. Then he shall
go out, and after he has gone out, the
gate will be shut.
[13]" 'Every day you are to provide a
year-old lamb without defect for a burnt
offering to the LORD; morning by morning you shall provide it. [14]You are also to
provide with it morning by morning a
grain offering, consisting of a sixth of an
ephah with a third of a hin of oil to
moisten the flour. The presenting of this
grain offering to the LORD is a lasting
ordinance. [15]So the lamb and the grain
offering and the oil shall be provided
morning by morning for a regular burnt
offering.
[16]" 'This is what the Sovereign LORD
says: If the prince makes a gift from his
inheritance to one of his sons, it will also
belong to his descendants; it is to be
their property by inheritance. [17]If, however, he makes a gift from his inheritance to one of his servants, the servant
may keep it until the year of freedom;
then it will revert to the prince. His
inheritance belongs to his sons only;
it is theirs. [18]The prince must not take
any of the inheritance of the people,
driving them off their property. He is to
give his sons their inheritance out of his
own property, so that none of my people will be separated from his property.' "
[19]Then the man brought me through
the entrance at the side of the gate to the
sacred rooms facing north, which belonged to the priests, and showed me a
place at the western end. [20]He said to
me, "This is the place where the priests
will cook the guilt offering and the sin
offering and bake the grain offering, to
avoid bringing them into the outer court
and consecrating the people."
[21]He then brought me to the outer
court and led me around to its four corners, and I saw in each corner another
court. [22]In the four corners of the outer
court were enclosed[a] courts, forty cubits
long and thirty cubits wide; each of the
courts in the four corners was the same
size. [23]Around the inside of each of the
four courts was a ledge of stone, with
places for fire built all around under the
ledge. [24]He said to me, "These are the
kitchens where those who minister at
the temple will cook the sacrifices of the
people."

[a]22 The meaning of the Hebrew for this word is uncertain.

SHARPEN THE FOCUS

Imagine an area in the center of your city or town eight miles long and three and a half miles wide. Picture an impressive temple in the center of this district and houses built around the temple for all those who serve the Lord and His people. What would such an arrangement say to you and your fellow citizens? One message that would shout from such a zoning pattern would be the centrality of the Lord and of His Word in our lives.

Why does God want central place? Not because He's petty or egotistic. Instead, it's because He created us for Himself. He knows that true fulfillment and peace come only from trust and commitment to Him. He also knows how close each of us lives to the brink of death. Whether we are 8 or 80 or 108, we live inside fragile bodies. We live in a society far from ideal and full of violence.

When our last hour here comes, our Lord wants us to have a refuge. His Son, Jesus—the crucified and risen Lamb of God–is that refuge. Jesus is the offering that made fellowship, peace with God, possible (Ezekiel 46:2). Why not talk to Him today about any rezoning that needs to happen in your heart?

WEEK 66 • MONDAY

Ezekiel 47:1—48:35

GET THE BIG PICTURE

As Ezekiel's book draws to a close, so does his vision of God's repentant, righteous people. He adds a final feature to the temple we have been studying–a river flows from its threshold to the Dead Sea. Take note of this river's healing, life-giving properties as you read. If time is short, focus on Ezekiel 47:1–12.

The River From the Temple

47 The man brought me
back to the entrance of
the temple, and I saw water coming out
from under the threshold of the temple
toward the east (for the temple faced
east). The water was coming down from
under the south side of the temple,
south of the altar. 2He then brought me
out through the north gate and led me
around the outside to the outer gate facing east, and the water was flowing
from the south side.
3As the man went eastward with a
measuring line in his hand, he measured off a thousand cubits[a] and then
led me through water that was ankle-
deep. 4He measured off another thousand cubits and led me through water
that was knee-deep. He measured off
another thousand and led me through
water that was up to the waist. 5He measured off another thousand, but now it
was a river that I could not cross, because the water had risen and was deep
enough to swim in—a river that no one
could cross. 6He asked me, "Son of man,
do you see this?"
Then he led me back to the bank of
the river. 7When I arrived there, I saw a
great number of trees on each side of the
river. 8He said to me, "This water flows
toward the eastern region and goes
down into the Arabah,[b] where it enters
the Sea.[c] When it empties into the Sea,[c]
the water there becomes fresh. 9Swarms
of living creatures will live wherever the
river flows. There will be large numbers
of fish, because this water flows there
and makes the salt water fresh; so where
the river flows everything will live.
10Fishermen will stand along the shore;
from En Gedi to En Eglaim there will be
places for spreading nets. The fish will
be of many kinds—like the fish of the
Great Sea.[d] 11But the swamps and
marshes will not become fresh; they will
be left for salt. 12Fruit trees of all kinds
will grow on both banks of the river.
Their leaves will not wither, nor will
their fruit fail. Every month they will
bear, because the water from the sanctuary flows to them. Their fruit will
serve for food and their leaves for healing."

[a]3 That is, about 1,500 feet (about 450 meters)
[b]8 Or *the Jordan Valley* [c]8 That is, the Dead Sea [d]10 That is, the Mediterranean; also in verses 15, 19 and 20

The Boundaries of the Land

[13]This is what the Sovereign LORD says: "These are the boundaries by which you are to divide the land for an inheritance among the twelve tribes of Israel, with two portions for Joseph.
[14]You are to divide it equally among them. Because I swore with uplifted hand to give it to your forefathers, this land will become your inheritance.

[15]"This is to be the boundary of the land:

"On the north side it will run from the
Great Sea by the Hethlon road past
Lebo[a] Hamath to Zedad, [16]Bero-
thah[b] and Sibraim (which lies on
the border between Damascus and
Hamath), as far as Hazer Hatticon,
which is on the border of Hauran.
[17]The boundary will extend from
the sea to Hazar Enan,[c] along the
northern border of Damascus, with
the border of Hamath to the north.
This will be the north boundary.
[18]"On the east side the boundary will
run between Hauran and Damas-
cus, along the Jordan between Gilead and the land of Israel, to the
eastern sea and as far as Tamar.[d]
This will be the east boundary.
[19]"On the south side it will run from Tamar as far as the waters of Meribah
Kadesh, then along the Wadi ⌞of
Egypt⌟ to the Great Sea. This will be
the south boundary.
[20]"On the west side, the Great Sea will
be the boundary to a point opposite Lebo[e] Hamath. This will be the
west boundary.

[21]"You are to distribute this land among yourselves according to the tribes of Israel.
[22]You are to allot it as an inheritance for yourselves and for the aliens who have settled among you and who have children. You are to consider them as native-born Israelites; along with you they are to be allotted an inheritance among the tribes of Israel.
[23]In whatever tribe the alien settles, there you are to give him his inheritance," declares the Sovereign LORD.

The Division of the Land

48 "These are the tribes, listed by name: At the northern frontier, Dan will have one portion; it will follow the Hethlon road to Lebo[f] Hamath; Hazar Enan and the northern border of Damascus next to Hamath will be part of its border from the east side to the west side.

[2]"Asher will have one portion; it will border the territory of Dan from east to west.

[3]"Naphtali will have one portion; it will border the territory of Asher from east to west.

[4]"Manasseh will have one portion; it will border the territory of Naphtali from east to west.

[5]"Ephraim will have one portion; it will border the territory of Manasseh from east to west.

[6]"Reuben will have one portion; it will border the territory of Ephraim from east to west.

[7]"Judah will have one portion; it will border the territory of Reuben from east to west.

[8]"Bordering the territory of Judah from east to west will be the portion you are to present as a special gift. It will be 25,000 cubits[g] wide, and its length from east to west will equal one of the tribal portions; the sanctuary will be in the center of it.

[9]"The special portion you are to offer to the LORD will be 25,000 cubits long and 10,000 cubits[h] wide.
[10]This will be the sacred portion for the priests. It will be 25,000 cubits long on the north side, 10,000 cubits wide on the west side, 10,000 cubits wide on the east side and 25,000 cubits long on the south side. In the center of it will be the sanctuary of the LORD.
[11]This will be for the consecrated priests, the Zadokites, who were

[a]15 Or *past the entrance to* [b]15,16 See Septuagint and Ezekiel 48:1; Hebrew *road to go into Zedad, [16]Hamath, Berothah* [c]17 Hebrew *Enon,* a variant of *Enan* [d]18 Septuagint and Syriac; Hebrew *Israel. You will measure to the eastern sea* [e]20 Or *opposite the entrance to* [f]1 Or *to the entrance to* [g]8 That is, about 7 miles (about 12 kilometers) [h]9 That is, about 3 miles (about 5 kilometers)

faithful in serving me and did not go astray as the Levites did when the Israelites went astray. [12]It will be a special gift to them from the sacred portion of the land, a most holy portion, bordering the territory of the Levites.

[13]"Alongside the territory of the priests, the Levites will have an allotment 25,000 cubits long and 10,000 cubits wide. Its total length will be 25,000 cubits and its width 10,000 cubits. [14]They must not sell or exchange any of it. This is the best of the land and must not pass into other hands, because it is holy to the LORD.

[15]"The remaining area, 5,000 cubits wide and 25,000 cubits long, will be for the common use of the city, for houses and for pastureland. The city will be in the center of it [16]and will have these measurements: the north side 4,500 cubits, the south side 4,500 cubits, the east side 4,500 cubits, and the west side 4,500 cubits. [17]The pastureland for the city will be 250 cubits on the north, 250 cubits on the south, 250 cubits on the east, and 250 cubits on the west. [18]What remains of the area, bordering on the sacred portion and running the length of it, will be 10,000 cubits on the east side and 10,000 cubits on the west side. Its produce will supply food for the workers of the city. [19]The workers from the city who farm it will come from all the tribes of Israel. [20]The entire portion will be a square, 25,000 cubits on each side. As a special gift you will set aside the sacred portion, along with the property of the city.

[21]"What remains on both sides of the area formed by the sacred portion and the city property will belong to the prince. It will extend eastward from the 25,000 cubits of the sacred portion to the eastern border, and westward from the 25,000 cubits to the western border. Both these areas running the length of the tribal portions will belong to the prince, and the sacred portion with the temple sanctuary will be in the center of them. [22]So the property of the Levites and the property of the city will lie in the center of the area that belongs to the prince. The area belonging to the prince will lie between the border of Judah and the border of Benjamin.

[23]"As for the rest of the tribes: Benjamin will have one portion; it will extend from the east side to the west side.

[24]"Simeon will have one portion; it will border the territory of Benjamin from east to west.

[25]"Issachar will have one portion; it will border the territory of Simeon from east to west.

[26]"Zebulun will have one portion; it will border the territory of Issachar from east to west.

[27]"Gad will have one portion; it will border the territory of Zebulun from east to west.

[28]"The southern boundary of Gad will run south from Tamar to the waters of Meribah Kadesh, then along the Wadi ⌞of Egypt⌟ to the Great Sea.[a]

[29]"This is the land you are to allot as an inheritance to the tribes of Israel, and these will be their portions," declares the Sovereign LORD.

The Gates of the City

[30]"These will be the exits of the city: Beginning on the north side, which is 4,500 cubits long, [31]the gates of the city will be named after the tribes of Israel. The three gates on the north side will be the gate of Reuben, the gate of Judah and the gate of Levi.

[32]"On the east side, which is 4,500 cubits long, will be three gates: the gate of Joseph, the gate of Benjamin and the gate of Dan.

[33]"On the south side, which measures 4,500 cubits, will be three gates: the gate of Simeon, the gate of Issachar and the gate of Zebulun.

[34]"On the west side, which is 4,500 cubits long, will be three gates: the gate of Gad, the gate of Asher and the gate of Naphtali.

[35]"The distance all around will be 18,000 cubits.

"And the name of the city from that time on will be:

THE LORD IS THERE."

[a] *28* That is, the Mediterranean

SHARPEN THE FOCUS

God can do anything! Remember the beautiful garden he created for our first parents? Adam and Eve enjoyed a beauty, majesty, and peace in creation that we can only vaguely imagine.

God can do anything! As we consider the tragedy, death, and destruction Adam and Eve introduced into God's good creation, we could well weep. We know that we too have added to that tragedy by our own sin. And yet, in Jesus and His cross, our Lord has reversed sin's curse. Despite our sin, god's repentant children enjoy peace, security in His love, and forgiveness.

God can do anything! Paradise lost isn't the end of the story. A sin-stained, tear-stained creation isn't the end of the story. Our life now, blessed as we are by our Savior, isn't the end of the story. One day our Lord will take us to live in His presence forever. Ezekiel paints a picture of that paradise regained in the words you read today. Praise your Lord for His marvelous love!

DANIEL

Deported to Babylon in the first wave of Jewish exiles (605 B.C.), Daniel and his three friends found themselves immersed in an alien culture and surrounded by idols. As you read, note the assaults made on the identity of these four, all probably teenagers. If time is short, focus on Daniel 1:1–7;17–21.

Daniel's Training in Babylon

1 In the third year of the reign of
Jehoiakim king of Judah, Nebuchadnezzar king of Babylon came to
Jerusalem and besieged it. 2And the
Lord delivered Jehoiakim king of Judah
into his hand, along with some of the articles from the temple of God. These he
carried off to the temple of his god in
Babylonia[a] and put in the treasure
house of his god.
3Then the king ordered Ashpenaz,
chief of his court officials, to bring in
some of the Israelites from the royal
family and the nobility— 4young men
without any physical defect, handsome,
showing aptitude for every kind of
learning, well informed, quick to understand, and qualified to serve in the
king's palace. He was to teach them the
language and literature of the Babylonians.[b] 5The king assigned them a daily
amount of food and wine from the
king's table. They were to be trained for
three years, and after that they were to
enter the king's service.
6Among these were some from Judah:
Daniel, Hananiah, Mishael and Azariah.
7The chief official gave them new
names: to Daniel, the name Belteshazzar; to Hananiah, Shadrach; to Mishael, Meshach; and to Azariah, Abednego.
8But Daniel resolved not to defile himself with the royal food and wine, and
he asked the chief official for permission
not to defile himself this way. 9Now God
had caused the official to show favor
and sympathy to Daniel, 10but the official told Daniel, "I am afraid of my lord
the king, who has assigned your[c] food
and drink. Why should he see you looking worse than the other young men
your age? The king would then have my
head because of you."
11Daniel then said to the guard whom
the chief official had appointed over
Daniel, Hananiah, Mishael and Azariah,
12"Please test your servants for ten days:
Give us nothing but vegetables to eat
and water to drink. 13Then compare our
appearance with that of the young men
who eat the royal food, and treat your
servants in accordance with what you
see." 14So he agreed to this and tested
them for ten days.
15At the end of the ten days they
looked healthier and better nourished
than any of the young men who ate the
royal food. 16So the guard took away

[a]2 Hebrew *Shinar* [b]4 Or *Chaldeans* [c]10 The Hebrew for *your* and *you* in this verse is plural.

their choice food and the wine they
were to drink and gave them vegetables
instead.
[17]To these four young men God gave
knowledge and understanding of all
kinds of literature and learning. And
Daniel could understand visions and
dreams of all kinds.
[18]At the end of the time set by the king
to bring them in, the chief official presented them to Nebuchadnezzar. [19]The
king talked with them, and he found
none equal to Daniel, Hananiah, Mishael and Azariah; so they entered the
king's service. [20]In every matter of wisdom and understanding about which
the king questioned them, he found
them ten times better than all the magicians and enchanters in his whole kingdom.
[21]And Daniel remained there until the
first year of King Cyrus.

SHARPEN THE FOCUS

When cadets enter one of the military service academies, no one addresses them by their first names for the entire year. When people enter the federal witness protection program, they receive not only a new address and occupation, but also a new name. How disorienting would it be for you to lose your name?

Daniel and his three friends received new names (Daniel 1:7). Even so, they still considered themselves Daniel, Hananiah, Mishael, and Azariah, not Belteshazzar, Shadrach, Meshach, and Abednego. (Compare Daniel 1:7 with Daniel 1:19.)

Every day our culture assaults our faith and our identity as the baptized children of God. If that weren't enough, our own guilty consciences sometimes rise up to challenge us: "You call yourself a Christian? After what you've done . . . or thought . . . or said?"

But no matter what we do, no matter what anyone does to us, our names are written in heaven. We have that truth on good authority—the Savior who died for us testifies that it's true. And despite all outward circumstances, it brings us great joy (Luke 10:19–20).

WEEK 66 • WEDNESDAY

Daniel 2:1–49

GET THE BIG PICTURE

Nine of the 12 chapters in Daniel revolve around dreams or visions. Today you will read the first of those. It includes a detailed prophecy of world history—the story of Babylon (Daniel 2:37–38), of Persia (Daniel 2:39), and then of Greece under Alexander the Great. Daniel also foresees the rise and fall of the Roman empire (Daniel 2:40–43). But what *is* the great rock that fills the whole earth (Daniel 2:34–35, 44–45)? If time is short, focus on Daniel 2:1–13; 24–45.

Nebuchadnezzar's Dream

2 In the second year of his reign,
Nebuchadnezzar had dreams;
his mind was troubled and he could not
sleep. 2So the king summoned the magicians, enchanters, sorcerers and
astrologers[a] to tell him what he had
dreamed. When they came in and stood
before the king, 3he said to them, "I have
had a dream that troubles me and I
want to know what it means.[b]"

4Then the astrologers answered the
king in Aramaic,[c] "O king, live forever!
Tell your servants the dream, and we
will interpret it."

5The king replied to the astrologers,
"This is what I have firmly decided: If
you do not tell me what my dream was
and interpret it, I will have you cut into
pieces and your houses turned into
piles of rubble. 6But if you tell me the
dream and explain it, you will receive
from me gifts and rewards and great
honor. So tell me the dream and interpret it for me."

7Once more they replied, "Let the
king tell his servants the dream, and we
will interpret it."

8Then the king answered, "I am certain that you are trying to gain time, because you realize that this is what I have
firmly decided: 9If you do not tell me the
dream, there is just one penalty for you.
You have conspired to tell me misleading and wicked things, hoping the situation will change. So then, tell me the
dream, and I will know that you can
interpret it for me."

10The astrologers answered the king,
"There is not a man on earth who can
do what the king asks! No king, however great and mighty, has ever asked
such a thing of any magician or enchanter or astrologer. 11What the king
asks is too difficult. No one can reveal it
to the king except the gods, and they do
not live among men."

12This made the king so angry and furious that he ordered the execution of
all the wise men of Babylon. 13So the decree was issued to put the wise men to
death, and men were sent to look for
Daniel and his friends to put them to
death.

14When Arioch, the commander of the
king's guard, had gone out to put to
death the wise men of Babylon, Daniel
spoke to him with wisdom and tact. 15He
asked the king's officer, "Why did the
king issue such a harsh decree?" Arioch
then explained the matter to Daniel. 16At
this, Daniel went in to the king and
asked for time, so that he might interpret the dream for him.

17Then Daniel returned to his house
and explained the matter to his friends
Hananiah, Mishael and Azariah. 18He
urged them to plead for mercy from the
God of heaven concerning this mystery,
so that he and his friends might not be
executed with the rest of the wise men
of Babylon. 19During the night the mystery was revealed to Daniel in a vision.
Then Daniel praised the God of heaven
20and said:

"Praise be to the name of God for
  ever and ever;
 wisdom and power are his.
21He changes times and seasons;
 he sets up kings and deposes
  them.
He gives wisdom to the wise
 and knowledge to the discerning.
22He reveals deep and hidden
  things;
 he knows what lies in darkness,
 and light dwells with him.
23I thank and praise you, O God of
  my fathers:
 You have given me wisdom and
  power,
you have made known to me what
  we asked of you,
 you have made known to us the
  dream of the king."

Daniel Interprets the Dream

24Then Daniel went to Arioch, whom
the king had appointed to execute the
wise men of Babylon, and said to him,

[a]2 Or *Chaldeans;* also in verses 4, 5 and 10 [b]3 Or *was* [c]4 The text from here through chapter 7 is in Aramaic.

"Do not execute the wise men of Babylon. Take me to the king, and I will interpret his dream for him."

25Arioch took Daniel to the king at
once and said, "I have found a man
among the exiles from Judah who can
tell the king what his dream means."

26The king asked Daniel (also called
Belteshazzar), "Are you able to tell me
what I saw in my dream and interpret it?"

27Daniel replied, "No wise man, enchanter, magician or diviner can explain to the king the mystery he has
asked about, 28but there is a God in
heaven who reveals mysteries. He has
shown King Nebuchadnezzar what will
happen in days to come. Your dream
and the visions that passed through
your mind as you lay on your bed are
these:

29"As you were lying there, O king,
your mind turned to things to come,
and the revealer of mysteries showed
you what is going to happen. 30As for
me, this mystery has been revealed to
me, not because I have greater wisdom
than other living men, but so that you,
O king, may know the interpretation
and that you may understand what
went through your mind.

31"You looked, O king, and there before you stood a large statue—an enormous, dazzling statue, awesome in
appearance. 32The head of the statue
was made of pure gold, its chest and
arms of silver, its belly and thighs of
bronze, 33its legs of iron, its feet partly of
iron and partly of baked clay. 34While
you were watching, a rock was cut out,
but not by human hands. It struck the
statue on its feet of iron and clay and
smashed them. 35Then the iron, the clay,
the bronze, the silver and the gold were
broken to pieces at the same time and
became like chaff on a threshing floor in
the summer. The wind swept them
away without leaving a trace. But the
rock that struck the statue became a
huge mountain and filled the whole
earth.

36"This was the dream, and now
we will interpret it to the king. 37You,
O king, are the king of kings. The God
of heaven has given you dominion and
power and might and glory; 38in your
hands he has placed mankind and the
beasts of the field and the birds of the
air. Wherever they live, he has made
you ruler over them all. You are that
head of gold.

39"After you, another kingdom will
rise, inferior to yours. Next, a third kingdom, one of bronze, will rule over the
whole earth. 40Finally, there will be a
fourth kingdom, strong as iron—for
iron breaks and smashes everything—
and as iron breaks things to pieces, so it
will crush and break all the others. 41Just
as you saw that the feet and toes were
partly of baked clay and partly of iron,
so this will be a divided kingdom; yet it
will have some of the strength of iron in
it, even as you saw iron mixed with clay.
42As the toes were partly iron and partly
clay, so this kingdom will be partly
strong and partly brittle. 43And just as
you saw the iron mixed with baked clay,
so the people will be a mixture and will
not remain united, any more than iron
mixes with clay.

44"In the time of those kings, the God
of heaven will set up a kingdom that
will never be destroyed, nor will it be
left to another people. It will crush all
those kingdoms and bring them to an
end, but it will itself endure forever.
45This is the meaning of the vision of the
rock cut out of a mountain, but not by
human hands—a rock that broke the
iron, the bronze, the clay, the silver and
the gold to pieces.

"The great God has shown the king
what will take place in the future. The
dream is true and the interpretation is
trustworthy."

46Then King Nebuchadnezzar fell
prostrate before Daniel and paid him
honor and ordered that an offering and
incense be presented to him. 47The king
said to Daniel, "Surely your God is the
God of gods and the Lord of kings and
a revealer of mysteries, for you were
able to reveal this mystery."

48Then the king placed Daniel in a
high position and lavished many gifts

on him. He made him ruler over the entire province of Babylon and placed him
in charge of all its wise men. 49Moreover,
at Daniel's request the king appointed
Shadrach, Meshach and Abednego administrators over the province of Babylon, while Daniel himself remained at
the royal court.

SHARPEN THE FOCUS

Alexander. Napoleon. Hitler. Stalin. All fancied themselves world conquerors. All envisioned the day when people of every land, nation, tribe, and language would bow before their authority. All have now become just a few cupsful of dust. No one trembles in their presence now.

Only one kingdom lasts forever. Only one kingdom will never be destroyed or conquered or divided. The Kingdom of God will have no end (Daniel 2:44). Its King has already died—and risen from death to die no more. The citizens of that Kingdom are immortal, too. We will live and reign with Christ, our King, forever.

The stone Nebuchadnezzar dreamed about was cut without human hands. The Kingdom of God has not come about by human effort, but because God—in love—willed it and called it into existence. He welcomes all, granting citizenship freely. But those who refuse His mercy will be crushed by His justice.

Do you treasure your citizenship in that Kingdom? Are you thankful for your King's dominion? Why not praise Him for those things right now, using Daniel's hymn in Daniel 2:20–23.

WEEK 66 • THURSDAY

Daniel 3:1—4:37

GET THE BIG PICTURE

While God intended the exile to humble His people and to break them of their habitual idolatry, He also had the good of Babylon in mind. As you read today, notice the ways in which the Lord's grace called and kept calling the conqueror of His people, Nebuchadnezzar, to repentance and faith. If time is short, focus on Daniel 3:1–30.

The Image of Gold and the Fiery Furnace

3 King Nebuchadnezzar made an
image of gold, ninety feet high
and nine feet[a] wide, and set it up on the
plain of Dura in the province of Babylon. 2He then summoned the satraps,
prefects, governors, advisers, treasurers,
judges, magistrates and all the other
provincial officials to come to the dedication of the image he had set up. 3So
the satraps, prefects, governors, advisers, treasurers, judges, magistrates and
all the other provincial officials assembled for the dedication of the image that
King Nebuchadnezzar had set up, and
they stood before it.
4Then the herald loudly proclaimed,
"This is what you are commanded to do,
O peoples, nations and men of every
language: 5As soon as you hear the
sound of the horn, flute, zither, lyre,

[a]1 Aramaic *sixty cubits high and six cubits wide* (about 27 meters high and 2.7 meters wide)

harp, pipes and all kinds of music, you
must fall down and worship the image
of gold that King Nebuchadnezzar has
set up. 6Whoever does not fall down
and worship will immediately be
thrown into a blazing furnace."

7Therefore, as soon as they heard the
sound of the horn, flute, zither, lyre,
harp and all kinds of music, all the peoples, nations and men of every language
fell down and worshiped the image of
gold that King Nebuchadnezzar had
set up.

8At this time some astrologers[a] came
forward and denounced the Jews.
9They said to King Nebuchadnezzar,
"O king, live forever! 10You have issued
a decree, O king, that everyone who
hears the sound of the horn, flute,
zither, lyre, harp, pipes and all kinds of
music must fall down and worship the
image of gold, 11and that whoever does
not fall down and worship will be
thrown into a blazing furnace. 12But
there are some Jews whom you have set
over the affairs of the province of Babylon—Shadrach, Meshach and Abednego—who pay no attention to you,
O king. They neither serve your gods
nor worship the image of gold you have
set up."

13Furious with rage, Nebuchadnezzar
summoned Shadrach, Meshach and
Abednego. So these men were brought
before the king, 14and Nebuchadnezzar
said to them, "Is it true, Shadrach, Meshach and Abednego, that you do not
serve my gods or worship the image of
gold I have set up? 15Now when you
hear the sound of the horn, flute, zither,
lyre, harp, pipes and all kinds of music,
if you are ready to fall down and worship the image I made, very good. But
if you do not worship it, you will be
thrown immediately into a blazing furnace. Then what god will be able to rescue you from my hand?"

16Shadrach, Meshach and Abednego
replied to the king, "O Nebuchadnezzar, we do not need to defend ourselves
before you in this matter. 17If we are
thrown into the blazing furnace, the
God we serve is able to save us from it,
and he will rescue us from your hand,
O king. 18But even if he does not, we
want you to know, O king, that we will
not serve your gods or worship the image of gold you have set up."

19Then Nebuchadnezzar was furious
with Shadrach, Meshach and Abednego, and his attitude toward them
changed. He ordered the furnace heat-
ed seven times hotter than usual 20and
commanded some of the strongest soldiers in his army to tie up Shadrach,
Meshach and Abednego and throw
them into the blazing furnace. 21So these
men, wearing their robes, trousers, turbans and other clothes, were bound and
thrown into the blazing furnace. 22The
king's command was so urgent and the
furnace so hot that the flames of the fire
killed the soldiers who took up Shadrach, Meshach and Abednego, 23and
these three men, firmly tied, fell into the
blazing furnace.

24Then King Nebuchadnezzar leaped
to his feet in amazement and asked his
advisers, "Weren't there three men that
we tied up and threw into the fire?"

They replied, "Certainly, O king."

25He said, "Look! I see four men walking around in the fire, unbound and unharmed, and the fourth looks like a son
of the gods."

26Nebuchadnezzar then approached
the opening of the blazing furnace and
shouted, "Shadrach, Meshach and
Abednego, servants of the Most High
God, come out! Come here!"

So Shadrach, Meshach and Abedne-
go came out of the fire, 27and the satraps,
prefects, governors and royal advisers
crowded around them. They saw that
the fire had not harmed their bodies,
nor was a hair of their heads singed;
their robes were not scorched, and there
was no smell of fire on them.

28Then Nebuchadnezzar said, "Praise
be to the God of Shadrach, Meshach and
Abednego, who has sent his angel and
rescued his servants! They trusted in
him and defied the king's command
and were willing to give up their lives

[a]*8* Or *Chaldeans*

rather than serve or worship any god
except their own God. 29Therefore I decree that the people of any nation or
language who say anything against the
God of Shadrach, Meshach and Abednego be cut into pieces and their houses
be turned into piles of rubble, for no
other god can save in this way."
30Then the king promoted Shadrach,
Meshach and Abednego in the province
of Babylon.

Nebuchadnezzar's Dream of a Tree

4 King Nebuchadnezzar,

To the peoples, nations and men
of every language, who live in all
the world:

May you prosper greatly!

2It is my pleasure to tell you
about the miraculous signs and
wonders that the Most High God
has performed for me.

3How great are his signs,
how mighty his wonders!
His kingdom is an eternal
kingdom;
his dominion endures from
generation to
generation.

4I, Nebuchadnezzar, was at home
in my palace, contented and prosperous. 5I had a dream that made
me afraid. As I was lying in my bed,
the images and visions that passed
through my mind terrified me. 6So
I commanded that all the wise men
of Babylon be brought before me to
interpret the dream for me. 7When
the magicians, enchanters, astrologers[a] and diviners came, I told them
the dream, but they could not interpret it for me. 8Finally, Daniel came
into my presence and I told him the
dream. (He is called Belteshazzar,
after the name of my god, and the
spirit of the holy gods is in him.)
9I said, "Belteshazzar, chief of the
magicians, I know that the spirit of
the holy gods is in you, and no mystery is too difficult for you. Here is
my dream; interpret it for me.
10These are the visions I saw while
lying in my bed: I looked, and there
before me stood a tree in the
middle of the land. Its height was
enormous. 11The tree grew large
and strong and its top touched the
sky; it was visible to the ends of the
earth. 12Its leaves were beautiful, its
fruit abundant, and on it was food
for all. Under it the beasts of the
field found shelter, and the birds of
the air lived in its branches; from it
every creature was fed.
13"In the visions I saw while lying
in my bed, I looked, and there before me was a messenger,[b] a holy
one, coming down from heaven.
14He called in a loud voice: 'Cut
down the tree and trim off its
branches; strip off its leaves and
scatter its fruit. Let the animals flee
from under it and the birds from its
branches. 15But let the stump and its
roots, bound with iron and bronze,
remain in the ground, in the grass
of the field.

" 'Let him be drenched with the
dew of heaven, and let him live
with the animals among the plants
of the earth. 16Let his mind be
changed from that of a man and
let him be given the mind of an animal, till seven times[c] pass by for
him.
17" 'The decision is announced by
messengers, the holy ones declare
the verdict, so that the living may
know that the Most High is sovereign over the kingdoms of men and
gives them to anyone he wishes and
sets over them the lowliest of men.'
18"This is the dream that I, King
Nebuchadnezzar, had. Now, Belteshazzar, tell me what it means, for
none of the wise men in my kingdom can interpret it for me. But you
can, because the spirit of the holy
gods is in you."

[a]7 Or *Chaldeans* [b]13 Or *watchman;* also in verses 17 and 23 [c]16 Or *years;* also in verses 23, 25 and 32

Daniel Interprets the Dream

19Then Daniel (also called Belteshazzar) was greatly perplexed
for a time, and his thoughts terrified him. So the king said, "Belteshazzar, do not let the dream or its
meaning alarm you."

Belteshazzar answered, "My
lord, if only the dream applied to
your enemies and its meaning to
your adversaries! 20The tree you
saw, which grew large and strong,
with its top touching the sky, visible to the whole earth, 21with beautiful leaves and abundant fruit,
providing food for all, giving shelter to the beasts of the field, and
having nesting places in its
branches for the birds of the air—
22you, O king, are that tree! You
have become great and strong;
your greatness has grown until it
reaches the sky, and your dominion
extends to distant parts of the earth.

23"You, O king, saw a messenger,
a holy one, coming down from
heaven and saying, 'Cut down the
tree and destroy it, but leave the
stump, bound with iron and
bronze, in the grass of the field,
while its roots remain in the
ground. Let him be drenched with
the dew of heaven; let him live like
the wild animals, until seven times
pass by for him.'

24"This is the interpretation,
O king, and this is the decree the
Most High has issued against my
lord the king: 25You will be driven
away from people and will live
with the wild animals; you will eat
grass like cattle and be drenched
with the dew of heaven. Seven
times will pass by for you until you
acknowledge that the Most High is
sovereign over the kingdoms of
men and gives them to anyone he
wishes. 26The command to leave
the stump of the tree with its roots
means that your kingdom will be
restored to you when you acknowledge that Heaven rules. 27There-
fore, O king, be pleased to accept
my advice: Renounce your sins by
doing what is right, and your wickedness by being kind to the oppressed. It may be that then your
prosperity will continue."

The Dream Is Fulfilled

28All this happened to King Nebuchadnezzar. 29Twelve months later,
as the king was walking on the roof
of the royal palace of Babylon, 30he
said, "Is not this the great Babylon
I have built as the royal residence,
by my mighty power and for the
glory of my majesty?"

31The words were still on his lips
when a voice came from heaven,
"This is what is decreed for you,
King Nebuchadnezzar: Your royal
authority has been taken from you.
32You will be driven away from
people and will live with the wild
animals; you will eat grass like cattle. Seven times will pass by for you
until you acknowledge that the
Most High is sovereign over the
kingdoms of men and gives them
to anyone he wishes."

33Immediately what had been
said about Nebuchadnezzar was
fulfilled. He was driven away from
people and ate grass like cattle. His
body was drenched with the dew
of heaven until his hair grew like
the feathers of an eagle and his
nails like the claws of a bird.

34At the end of that time, I, Nebuchadnezzar, raised my eyes toward heaven, and my sanity was
restored. Then I praised the Most
High; I honored and glorified him
who lives forever.

His dominion is an eternal
dominion;
his kingdom endures from
generation to generation.
35All the peoples of the earth
are regarded as nothing.
He does as he pleases
with the powers of heaven

and the peoples of the earth.
No one can hold back his hand
or say to him: "What have you
done?"

[36]At the same time that my sanity was restored, my honor and
splendor were returned to me for
the glory of my kingdom. My advisers and nobles sought me out,
and I was restored to my throne
and became even greater than before. [37]Now I, Nebuchadnezzar,
praise and exalt and glorify the
King of heaven, because everything he does is right and all his
ways are just. And those who walk
in pride he is able to humble.

SHARPEN THE FOCUS

Bow or burn. Not an easy choice. But by God's Spirit of power at work in them, Daniel's three friends chose to die rather than to desert their loyalty to the true God: "[they] were willing to give up their lives rather than serve or worship any god except their own God" (Daniel 3:28). What a remarkable witness they gave. And how remarkably faithful the Lord proved Himself yet again.

Probably no one will ever say to us, "Bow or burn." And yet the apostle Paul urges us, "Offer your bodies as living sacrifices, holy and pleasing to God" (Romans 12:1). He tells us how to do that—"in view of God's mercy." The same Spirit who poured His grace out into Daniel's three friends will also flood us with His mercy to empower our obedience.

As you think of offering your body as a living sacrifice, what comes to mind? Honorable thoughts? Kind words? Gentle acts of concern?

Forgiven by Christ's mercy, yield yourself to His service today—body and soul.

WEEK 66 • FRIDAY

Daniel 5:1–31

GET THE BIG PICTURE

By the time the events of chapter 5 unfold, Daniel may be close to 80. He has seen the Lord raise up Babylon to accomplish His purposes in the nation of Judah, and he is about to see Babylon die—not with a roar, but with barely a whimper. As you read, notice that the God of heaven rules (Daniel 5:18, 28). If time is short, focus on Daniel 5:1–12; 22–31.

The Writing on the Wall

5 King Belshazzar gave a great
banquet for a thousand of his
nobles and drank wine with them.
[2]While Belshazzar was drinking his
wine, he gave orders to bring in the gold
and silver goblets that Nebuchadnezzar
his father[a] had taken from the temple in
Jerusalem, so that the king and his
nobles, his wives and his concubines
might drink from them. [3]So they
brought in the gold goblets that had
been taken from the temple of God in
Jerusalem, and the king and his nobles,
his wives and his concubines drank
from them. [4]As they drank the wine,

[a]2 Or *ancestor;* or *predecessor;* also in verses 11, 13 and 18

they praised the gods of gold and silver,
of bronze, iron, wood and stone.
5Suddenly the fingers of a human
hand appeared and wrote on the plaster of the wall, near the lampstand in the
royal palace. The king watched the
hand as it wrote. 6His face turned pale
and he was so frightened that his knees
knocked together and his legs gave way.
7The king called out for the enchanters, astrologers[a] and diviners to be
brought and said to these wise men of
Babylon, "Whoever reads this writing
and tells me what it means will be
clothed in purple and have a gold chain
placed around his neck, and he will be
made the third highest ruler in the kingdom."
8Then all the king's wise men came in,
but they could not read the writing or
tell the king what it meant. 9So King Belshazzar became even more terrified and
his face grew more pale. His nobles
were baffled.
10The queen,[b] hearing the voices of the
king and his nobles, came into the banquet hall. "O king, live forever!" she
said. "Don't be alarmed! Don't look so
pale! 11There is a man in your kingdom
who has the spirit of the holy gods in
him. In the time of your father he was
found to have insight and intelligence
and wisdom like that of the gods. King
Nebuchadnezzar your father—your father the king, I say—appointed him
chief of the magicians, enchanters, astrologers and diviners. 12This man Daniel, whom the king called Belteshazzar,
was found to have a keen mind and
knowledge and understanding, and
also the ability to interpret dreams, explain riddles and solve difficult problems. Call for Daniel, and he will tell you
what the writing means."
13So Daniel was brought before the
king, and the king said to him, "Are you
Daniel, one of the exiles my father the
king brought from Judah? 14I have
heard that the spirit of the gods is in you
and that you have insight, intelligence
and outstanding wisdom. 15The wise
men and enchanters were brought before me to read this writing and tell me
what it means, but they could not explain it. 16Now I have heard that you are
able to give interpretations and to solve
difficult problems. If you can read this
writing and tell me what it means, you
will be clothed in purple and have a
gold chain placed around your neck,
and you will be made the third highest
ruler in the kingdom."
17Then Daniel answered the king,
"You may keep your gifts for yourself
and give your rewards to someone else.
Nevertheless, I will read the writing for
the king and tell him what it means.
18"O king, the Most High God gave
your father Nebuchadnezzar sover-
eignty and greatness and glory and
splendor. 19Because of the high position
he gave him, all the peoples and nations
and men of every language dreaded
and feared him. Those the king wanted
to put to death, he put to death; those
he wanted to spare, he spared; those he
wanted to promote, he promoted;
and those he wanted to humble, he
humbled. 20But when his heart became
arrogant and hardened with pride, he
was deposed from his royal throne and
stripped of his glory. 21He was driven
away from people and given the mind
of an animal; he lived with the wild
donkeys and ate grass like cattle; and his
body was drenched with the dew of
heaven, until he acknowledged that the
Most High God is sovereign over the
kingdoms of men and sets over them
anyone he wishes.
22"But you his son,[c] O Belshazzar,
have not humbled yourself, though you
knew all this. 23Instead, you have set
yourself up against the Lord of heaven.
You had the goblets from his temple
brought to you, and you and your nobles, your wives and your concubines
drank wine from them. You praised
the gods of silver and gold, of bronze,
iron, wood and stone, which cannot see
or hear or understand. But you did not
honor the God who holds in his hand
your life and all your ways. 24Therefore

[a]7 Or *Chaldeans*; also in verse 11 [b]10 Or *queen mother* [c]22 Or *descendant*; or *successor*

he sent the hand that wrote the inscription.
25"This is the inscription that was written:

MENE, MENE, TEKEL, PARSIN[a]

26"This is what these words mean:

Mene[b]: God has numbered the days of your reign and brought it to an end.
27 *Tekel*[c]: You have been weighed on the scales and found wanting.
28 *Peres*[d]: Your kingdom is divided and given to the Medes and Persians."

29Then at Belshazzar's command,
Daniel was clothed in purple, a gold
chain was placed around his neck, and
he was proclaimed the third highest ruler in the kingdom.
30That very night Belshazzar, king of
the Babylonians,[e] was slain, 31and Darius the Mede took over the kingdom, at
the age of sixty-two.

[a]25 Aramaic *UPARSIN* (that is, *AND PARSIN*)
[b]26 *Mene* can mean *numbered* or *mina* (a unit of money). [c]27 *Tekel* can mean *weighed* or *shekel.*
[d]28 *Peres* (the singular of *Parsin*) can mean *divided* or *Persia* or *a half mina* or *a half shekel.* [e]30 Or *Chaldeans*

SHARPEN THE FOCUS

After World War II, the Soviet Union set up dozens of monuments in the Eastern block countries. Designed to impress, those monuments towered over the countryside. "The U.S.S.R. is invincible!" they proclaimed. Today, visitors who see these behemoths in the clear light of history can smile at the pride, now broken.

Given human nature, we need not be surprised that arrogance often comes with power. In Belshazzar power plus pride plus alcohol proved a volatile mix. His blasphemy (Daniel 5:3–4) provoked God to call a halt then and there to the empire that was Babylon.

No one reading these words rules an empire. But almost all of us exercise authority of some kind. From the school principal who schedules classes to the custodian who locks and unlocks doors. From the father who assigns family chores to the single mom who decides what's for supper. All legitimate authority comes from God.

So how do you use the authority He has entrusted to you? Do you act—even a little bit—in arrogance? Is the good of the people you serve always your top priority? Turn to your Savior today for His gifts of repentance and power to serve those you lead with a pure heart, a humble heart.

WEEK 66 • SATURDAY

Daniel 6:1–28

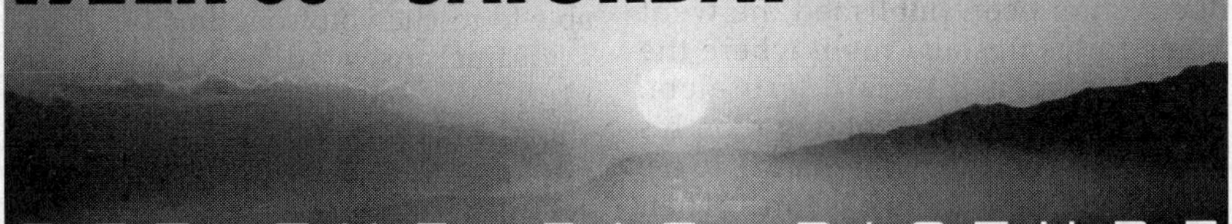

GET THE BIG PICTURE

Which of the two main characters in this chapter would you rather be? Daniel, locked up with roaring hungry lions? Or Darius, wide awake because he is locked up with his guilty conscience? As you read, ask yourself what motivated each of these men. If time is short, focus on Daniel 6:1–23.

Daniel in the Den of Lions

6 It pleased Darius to appoint 120
satraps to rule throughout the
kingdom, 2with three administrators
over them, one of whom was Daniel.
The satraps were made accountable to
them so that the king might not suffer
loss. 3Now Daniel so distinguished himself among the administrators and the
satraps by his exceptional qualities that
the king planned to set him over the
whole kingdom. 4At this, the administrators and the satraps tried to find
grounds for charges against Daniel in
his conduct of government affairs, but
they were unable to do so. They could
find no corruption in him, because he
was trustworthy and neither corrupt
nor negligent. 5Finally these men said,
"We will never find any basis for charges
against this man Daniel unless it has
something to do with the law of his
God."

6So the administrators and the satraps
went as a group to the king and said:
"O King Darius, live forever! 7The royal
administrators, prefects, satraps, advisers and governors have all agreed that
the king should issue an edict and en-
force the decree that anyone who prays
to any god or man during the next thirty
days, except to you, O king, shall be
thrown into the lions' den. 8Now,
O king, issue the decree and put it in
writing so that it cannot be altered—in
accordance with the laws of the Medes
and Persians, which cannot be repealed." 9So King Darius put the decree
in writing.

10Now when Daniel learned that the
decree had been published, he went
home to his upstairs room where the
windows opened toward Jerusalem.
Three times a day he got down on his
knees and prayed, giving thanks to his
God, just as he had done before. 11Then
these men went as a group and found
Daniel praying and asking God for help.
12So they went to the king and spoke to
him about his royal decree: "Did you
not publish a decree that during the
next thirty days anyone who prays to
any god or man except to you, O king,
would be thrown into the lions' den?"

The king answered, "The decree
stands—in accordance with the laws of
the Medes and Persians, which cannot
be repealed."

13Then they said to the king, "Daniel,
who is one of the exiles from Judah,
pays no attention to you, O king, or to
the decree you put in writing. He still
prays three times a day." 14When the
king heard this, he was greatly distressed; he was determined to rescue
Daniel and made every effort until sun-
down to save him.

15Then the men went as a group to the
king and said to him, "Remember,
O king, that according to the law of the
Medes and Persians no decree or edict
that the king issues can be changed."

16So the king gave the order, and they
brought Daniel and threw him into the
lions' den. The king said to Daniel, "May
your God, whom you serve continually,
rescue you!"

17A stone was brought and placed
over the mouth of the den, and the
king sealed it with his own signet ring
and with the rings of his nobles, so
that Daniel's situation might not be
changed. 18Then the king returned to his
palace and spent the night without
eating and without any entertainment
being brought to him. And he could not
sleep.

19At the first light of dawn, the king
got up and hurried to the lions' den.
20When he came near the den, he called
to Daniel in an anguished voice, "Daniel, servant of the living God, has your
God, whom you serve continually, been
able to rescue you from the lions?"

21Daniel answered, "O king, live forever! 22My God sent his angel, and he
shut the mouths of the lions. They have
not hurt me, because I was found innocent in his sight. Nor have I ever done
any wrong before you, O king."

23The king was overjoyed and gave
orders to lift Daniel out of the den. And
when Daniel was lifted from the den, no
wound was found on him, because he
had trusted in his God.

[24]At the king's command, the men who had falsely accused Daniel were brought in and thrown into the lions' den, along with their wives and children. And before they reached the floor of the den, the lions overpowered them and crushed all their bones.

[25]Then King Darius wrote to all the peoples, nations and men of every language throughout the land:

"May you prosper greatly!

[26]"I issue a decree that in every part of my kingdom people must fear and reverence the God of Daniel.

"For he is the living God
and he endures forever;
his kingdom will not be
destroyed,
his dominion will never end.
[27]He rescues and he saves;
he performs signs and wonders
in the heavens and on the earth.
He has rescued Daniel
from the power of the lions."

[28]So Daniel prospered during the reign of Darius and the reign of Cyrus[a] the Persian.

[a]28 Or *Darius, that is, the reign of Cyrus*

SHARPEN THE FOCUS

"Dare to be a Daniel!" we could say. "Stand up for the true God and you'll never be hurt!" we could moralize. But then, how could we explain Isaiah who was probably sawed in two for his faithful testimony (Hebrews 11:37)? Or Stephen who was stoned for his witness (Acts 7:1–60)?

Daniel's story tells us, instead, how to handle persecution, "how to spend the night in the lions' den," as it were.

- The Lord had worked in Daniel daily habits of prayer and thanksgiving (Daniel 6:10–11). When Darius's edict went into effect, Daniel had no decision to make. He could no more stop praying than a fish could sprout legs and live in a tree. (Guess what he did in the den all night.)
- The Lord had worked in Daniel a servant's heart. Daniel knew, by grace, that he never really served Nebuchadnezzar or Darius. Daniel served the living God "continually" (Daniel 6:16, 20). Knowing his true King, Daniel could go in faith wherever the Lord sent him—even to the lions' den.
- The Lord kept Daniel busy with thoughts about His eternal Kingdom, His faithfulness, His might (Daniel 6:26–27). This protected Daniel from bitterness and vengefulness when his ordeal ended.

What do you need the Lord to work in you? Why not ask Him?

WEEK 67 • MONDAY

Daniel 7:1—8:27

From chapter 7 on, the prophet Daniel records a series of prophetic visions. Many people try to pinpoint the date of Christ's second coming from his words, despite the Lord's clear warning against such speculation (Matthew 24:36). As you read today, focus on the over-all truth of these chapters: Our Lord rules all events on earth for the good of His Kingdom, His church. If time is short, focus on Daniel 8:1–27.

Daniel's Dream of Four Beasts

7 In the first year of Belshazzar king of Babylon, Daniel had a dream, and visions passed through his mind as he was lying on his bed. He wrote down the substance of his dream.
2 Daniel said: "In my vision at night I looked, and there before me were the four winds of heaven churning up the great sea.
3 Four great beasts, each different from the others, came up out of the sea.
4 "The first was like a lion, and it had the wings of an eagle. I watched until its wings were torn off and it was lifted from the ground so that it stood on two feet like a man, and the heart of a man was given to it.
5 "And there before me was a second beast, which looked like a bear. It was raised up on one of its sides, and it had three ribs in its mouth between its teeth. It was told, 'Get up and eat your fill of flesh!'
6 "After that, I looked, and there before me was another beast, one that looked like a leopard. And on its back it had four wings like those of a bird. This beast had four heads, and it was given authority to rule.
7 "After that, in my vision at night I looked, and there before me was a fourth beast—terrifying and frightening and very powerful. It had large iron teeth; it crushed and devoured its victims and trampled underfoot whatever was left. It was different from all the former beasts, and it had ten horns.
8 "While I was thinking about the horns, there before me was another horn, a little one, which came up among them; and three of the first horns were uprooted before it. This horn had eyes like the eyes of a man and a mouth that spoke boastfully.
9 "As I looked,

"thrones were set in place,
and the Ancient of Days took his seat.
His clothing was as white as snow;
the hair of his head was white like wool.
His throne was flaming with fire,
and its wheels were all ablaze.
10 A river of fire was flowing,
coming out from before him.
Thousands upon thousands attended him;
ten thousand times ten thousand stood before him.
The court was seated,
and the books were opened.

11 "Then I continued to watch because of the boastful words the horn was speaking. I kept looking until the beast was slain and its body destroyed and thrown into the blazing fire.
12 (The other beasts had been stripped of their authority, but were allowed to live for a period of time.)
13 "In my vision at night I looked, and

there before me was one like a son of
man, coming with the clouds of heaven.
He approached the Ancient of Days and
was led into his presence. 14He was giv-
en authority, glory and sovereign power; all peoples, nations and men of every
language worshiped him. His dominion
is an everlasting dominion that will not
pass away, and his kingdom is one that
will never be destroyed.

The Interpretation of the Dream

15"I, Daniel, was troubled in spirit, and
the visions that passed through my
mind disturbed me. 16I approached one
of those standing there and asked him
the true meaning of all this.

"So he told me and gave me the interpretation of these things: 17'The four
great beasts are four kingdoms that will
rise from the earth. 18But the saints of the
Most High will receive the kingdom and
will possess it forever—yes, for ever and
ever.'

19"Then I wanted to know the true
meaning of the fourth beast, which was
different from all the others and most
terrifying, with its iron teeth and bronze
claws—the beast that crushed and devoured its victims and trampled underfoot whatever was left. 20I also wanted
to know about the ten horns on its head
and about the other horn that came up,
before which three of them fell—the
horn that looked more imposing than
the others and that had eyes and a
mouth that spoke boastfully. 21As I
watched, this horn was waging war
against the saints and defeating them,
22until the Ancient of Days came and
pronounced judgment in favor of the
saints of the Most High, and the time
came when they possessed the kingdom.

23"He gave me this explanation: 'The
fourth beast is a fourth kingdom that
will appear on earth. It will be different
from all the other kingdoms and will
devour the whole earth, trampling it
down and crushing it. 24The ten horns
are ten kings who will come from this
kingdom. After them another king will
arise, different from the earlier ones; he
will subdue three kings. 25He will speak
against the Most High and oppress his
saints and try to change the set times
and the laws. The saints will be handed
over to him for a time, times and half a
time.[a]

26" 'But the court will sit, and his power will be taken away and completely
destroyed forever. 27Then the sover-
eignty, power and greatness of the kingdoms under the whole heaven will be
handed over to the saints, the people of
the Most High. His kingdom will be an
everlasting kingdom, and all rulers will
worship and obey him.'

28"This is the end of the matter. I,
Daniel, was deeply troubled by my
thoughts, and my face turned pale, but
I kept the matter to myself."

Daniel's Vision of a Ram and a Goat

8 In the third year of King
Belshazzar's reign, I, Daniel,
had a vision, after the one that had already appeared to me. 2In my vision I
saw myself in the citadel of Susa in the
province of Elam; in the vision I was
beside the Ulai Canal. 3I looked up, and
there before me was a ram with two
horns, standing beside the canal, and
the horns were long. One of the horns
was longer than the other but grew up
later. 4I watched the ram as he charged
toward the west and the north and the
south. No animal could stand against
him, and none could rescue from his
power. He did as he pleased and became
great.

5As I was thinking about this, suddenly a goat with a prominent horn between his eyes came from the west,
crossing the whole earth without touching the ground. 6He came toward the
two-horned ram I had seen standing
beside the canal and charged at him in
great rage. 7I saw him attack the ram furiously, striking the ram and shattering
his two horns. The ram was powerless
to stand against him; the goat knocked
him to the ground and trampled on

[a]25 Or *for a year, two years and half a year*

him, and none could rescue the ram from his power. 8The goat became very great, but at the height of his power his large horn was broken off, and in its place four prominent horns grew up toward the four winds of heaven.

9Out of one of them came another horn, which started small but grew in power to the south and to the east and toward the Beautiful Land. 10It grew until it reached the host of the heavens, and it threw some of the starry host down to the earth and trampled on them. 11It set itself up to be as great as the Prince of the host; it took away the daily sacrifice from him, and the place of his sanctuary was brought low. 12Because of rebellion, the host ⌊of the saints⌋[a] and the daily sacrifice were given over to it. It prospered in everything it did, and truth was thrown to the ground.

13Then I heard a holy one speaking, and another holy one said to him, "How long will it take for the vision to be fulfilled—the vision concerning the daily sacrifice, the rebellion that causes desolation, and the surrender of the sanctuary and of the host that will be trampled underfoot?"

14He said to me, "It will take 2,300 evenings and mornings; then the sanctuary will be reconsecrated."

The Interpretation of the Vision

15While I, Daniel, was watching the vision and trying to understand it, there before me stood one who looked like a man. 16And I heard a man's voice from the Ulai calling, "Gabriel, tell this man the meaning of the vision."

17As he came near the place where I was standing, I was terrified and fell prostrate. "Son of man," he said to me, "understand that the vision concerns the time of the end."

18While he was speaking to me, I was in a deep sleep, with my face to the ground. Then he touched me and raised me to my feet.

19He said: "I am going to tell you what will happen later in the time of wrath, because the vision concerns the appointed time of the end.[b] 20The two-horned ram that you saw represents the kings of Media and Persia. 21The shaggy goat is the king of Greece, and the large horn between his eyes is the first king. 22The four horns that replaced the one that was broken off represent four kingdoms that will emerge from his nation but will not have the same power.

23"In the latter part of their reign, when rebels have become completely wicked, a stern-faced king, a master of intrigue, will arise. 24He will become very strong, but not by his own power. He will cause astounding devastation and will succeed in whatever he does. He will destroy the mighty men and the holy people. 25He will cause deceit to prosper, and he will consider himself superior. When they feel secure, he will destroy many and take his stand against the Prince of princes. Yet he will be destroyed, but not by human power.

26"The vision of the evenings and mornings that has been given you is true, but seal up the vision, for it concerns the distant future."

27I, Daniel, was exhausted and lay ill for several days. Then I got up and went about the king's business. I was appalled by the vision; it was beyond understanding.

[a]12 Or *rebellion, the armies* [b]19 Or *because the end will be at the appointed time*

SHARPEN THE FOCUS

Many predictors of the end of the world quote Nostradamus, Harry Houdini, and the prophet Daniel, all in the same breath. Their predictions are sensational—after all, sensational sells. And we can expect them to twist the Holy Scriptures into pretzels trying to support their pet theories.

The fact is that much of what Daniel predicted came true decades and centuries after his death. The Medes and Persians (Daniel 7:5; 8:20) ousted Babylon (Daniel 7:4). Alexander the Great replaced the Persian empire with his own in Greece (Daniel 7:6; 8:21). Then the Romans formed the most powerful empire the world had ever seen (Daniel 7:7, 23).

But some of what Daniel wrote in his book still remains veiled in mystery. We, like Daniel himself, find ourselves astonished at the details (Daniel 7:28; 8:27). But our astonishment can't steal our trust in Daniel's main point: The kingdoms of this world have become the kingdom of our Lord and of His Christ (Daniel 7:13–14, 26–27).

WEEK 67 • TUESDAY

Daniel 9:1–27

GET THE BIG PICTURE

As we read the beginning of Daniel 9, we find another clue about what Daniel did during his daily prayer time (Daniel 6:10–11, 9:2). Daniel read the Old Testament scrolls. We don't know how many he had, but we do know the book of the prophet Jeremiah was among them. As you read, notice how Daniel prays God's promises back to Him. If time is short, focus on Daniel 9:1–19.

Daniel's Prayer

9 In the first year of Darius son of
Xerxes[a] (a Mede by descent),
who was made ruler over the Babylonian[b] kingdom— 2in the first year of his
reign, I, Daniel, understood from the
Scriptures, according to the word of the
LORD given to Jeremiah the prophet,
that the desolation of Jerusalem would
last seventy years. 3So I turned to the
Lord God and pleaded with him in
prayer and petition, in fasting, and in
sackcloth and ashes.
4I prayed to the LORD my God and
confessed:

"O Lord, the great and awesome
God, who keeps his covenant of
love with all who love him and
obey his commands, 5we have
sinned and done wrong. We have
been wicked and have rebelled; we
have turned away from your
commands and laws. 6We have not
listened to your servants the prophets, who spoke in your name to our
kings, our princes and our fathers,
and to all the people of the land.
7"Lord, you are righteous, but
this day we are covered with
shame—the men of Judah and people of Jerusalem and all Israel, both
near and far, in all the countries
where you have scattered us because of our unfaithfulness to you.
8O LORD, we and our kings, our
princes and our fathers are covered
with shame because we have
sinned against you. 9The Lord our
God is merciful and forgiving, even
though we have rebelled against
him; 10we have not obeyed the
LORD our God or kept the laws he
gave us through his servants the
prophets. 11All Israel has trans-
gressed your law and turned away,
refusing to obey you.
"Therefore the curses and sworn
judgments written in the Law of
Moses, the servant of God, have

[a]1 Hebrew *Ahasuerus* [b]1 Or *Chaldean*

been poured out on us, because we have sinned against you. 12You have fulfilled the words spoken against us and against our rulers by bringing upon us great disaster. Under the whole heaven nothing has ever been done like what has been done to Jerusalem. 13Just as it is written in the Law of Moses, all this disaster has come upon us, yet we have not sought the favor of the LORD our God by turning from our sins and giving attention to your truth. 14The LORD did not hesitate to bring the disaster upon us, for the LORD our God is righteous in everything he does; yet we have not obeyed him.

15"Now, O Lord our God, who brought your people out of Egypt with a mighty hand and who made for yourself a name that endures to this day, we have sinned, we have done wrong. 16O Lord, in keeping with all your righteous acts, turn away your anger and your wrath from Jerusalem, your city, your holy hill. Our sins and the iniquities of our fathers have made Jerusalem and your people an object of scorn to all those around us.

17"Now, our God, hear the prayers and petitions of your servant. For your sake, O Lord, look with favor on your desolate sanctuary. 18Give ear, O God, and hear; open your eyes and see the desolation of the city that bears your Name. We do not make requests of you because we are righteous, but because of your great mercy. 19O Lord, listen! O Lord, forgive! O Lord, hear and act! For your sake, O my God, do not delay, because your city and your people bear your Name."

The Seventy "Sevens"

20While I was speaking and praying, confessing my sin and the sin of my people Israel and making my request to the LORD my God for his holy hill— 21while I was still in prayer, Gabriel, the man I had seen in the earlier vision, came to me in swift flight about the time of the evening sacrifice. 22He instructed me and said to me, "Daniel, I have now come to give you insight and understanding. 23As soon as you began to pray, an answer was given, which I have come to tell you, for you are highly esteemed. Therefore, consider the message and understand the vision:

24"Seventy 'sevens'[a] are decreed for your people and your holy city to finish[b] transgression, to put an end to sin, to atone for wickedness, to bring in everlasting righteousness, to seal up vision and prophecy and to anoint the most holy.[c]

25"Know and understand this: From the issuing of the decree[d] to restore and rebuild Jerusalem until the Anointed One,[e] the ruler, comes, there will be seven 'sevens,' and sixty-two 'sevens.' It will be rebuilt with streets and a trench, but in times of trouble. 26After the sixty-two 'sevens,' the Anointed One will be cut off and will have nothing.[f] The people of the ruler who will come will destroy the city and the sanctuary. The end will come like a flood: War will continue until the end, and desolations have been decreed. 27He will confirm a covenant with many for one 'seven.'[g] In the middle of the 'seven'[g] he will put an end to sacrifice and offering. And on a wing ⌞of the temple⌟ he will set up an abomination that causes desolation, until the end that is decreed is poured out on him.[h]"[i]

[a]24 Or *'weeks'*; also in verses 25 and 26 [b]24 Or *restrain* [c]24 Or *Most Holy Place*; or *most holy One* [d]25 Or *word* [e]25 Or *an anointed one*; also in verse 26 [f]26 Or *off and will have no one*; or *off, but not for himself* [g]27 Or *'week'* [h]27 Or *it* [i]27 Or *And one who causes desolation will come upon the pinnacle of the abominable ⌞temple⌟, until the end that is decreed is poured out on the desolated ⌞city⌟*

SHARPEN THE FOCUS

"Not because we're good, Lord, but because You are merciful" . . . prayed Daniel (*paraphrase,* Daniel 9:18). Daniel knew that neither he nor his people had any reason for complaint against God. Based on their behavior, the people of Israel deserved only more misery:

> *O LORD, we and our kings, our princes and our fathers are covered with shame because we have sinned against You. The Lord our God is merciful and forgiving, even though we have rebelled against Him.* (Daniel 9:8–9)

Shame belongs to us, every bit as much as it belonged to ancient Israel. We own it, because we've earned it by our sins. We turn away in fear rather than face God with the reality of who we've become in our rebellion. But to the Lord belong mercy and forgiveness. Jesus earned them for us on His cross. Because they belong to Him, He can give them to whomever He wants–*and He wants to give them to you, to me.*

Because His mercy, pardon, and love are now ours, we can ask our Lord for what we need and for what we want. Bold in the righteousness that is ours by faith, we can quote God's promises back to Him in prayer.

What promise do you need your Lord to keep for you today? Go ahead. Ask. He is merciful and forgiving.

WEEK 67 • WEDNESDAY

Daniel 10:1—12:13

GET THE BIG PICTURE

Without a detailed knowledge of ancient history, the prophecies of Daniel 10:1–11:35 are almost impossible to understand. But they did all come true, just as Daniel had foretold. The vision of Daniel 11:37 to the end of the book covers a series of events that have evidently not yet occurred. As you read, look for evidence that even at the end of time, the God of heaven rules (Daniel 4:34–37). If time is short, focus on Daniel 11:36–12:13.

Daniel's Vision of a Man

10 In the third year of Cyrus
king of Persia, a revelation
was given to Daniel (who was called
Belteshazzar). Its message was true and
it concerned a great war.[a] The understanding of the message came to him in
a vision.
2At that time I, Daniel, mourned for
three weeks. 3I ate no choice food; no
meat or wine touched my lips; and I
used no lotions at all until the three
weeks were over.
4On the twenty-fourth day of the first
month, as I was standing on the bank of
the great river, the Tigris, 5I looked up
and there before me was a man dressed
in linen, with a belt of the finest gold
around his waist. 6His body was like
chrysolite, his face like lightning, his

[a]1 Or *true and burdensome*

eyes like flaming torches, his arms and
legs like the gleam of burnished bronze,
and his voice like the sound of a multitude.
[7]I, Daniel, was the only one who saw
the vision; the men with me did not see
it, but such terror overwhelmed them
that they fled and hid themselves. [8]So I
was left alone, gazing at this great vision; I had no strength left, my face
turned deathly pale and I was helpless.
[9]Then I heard him speaking, and as I listened to him, I fell into a deep sleep, my
face to the ground.
[10]A hand touched me and set me
trembling on my hands and knees. [11]He
said, "Daniel, you who are highly esteemed, consider carefully the words I
am about to speak to you, and stand up,
for I have now been sent to you." And
when he said this to me, I stood up
trembling.
[12]Then he continued, "Do not be
afraid, Daniel. Since the first day that
you set your mind to gain understanding and to humble yourself before your
God, your words were heard, and I
have come in response to them. [13]But
the prince of the Persian kingdom resisted me twenty-one days. Then
Michael, one of the chief princes, came
to help me, because I was detained there
with the king of Persia. [14]Now I have
come to explain to you what will happen to your people in the future, for the
vision concerns a time yet to come."
[15]While he was saying this to me, I
bowed with my face toward the ground
and was speechless. [16]Then one who
looked like a man[a] touched my lips, and
I opened my mouth and began to speak.
I said to the one standing before me, "I
am overcome with anguish because of
the vision, my lord, and I am helpless.
[17]How can I, your servant, talk with you,
my lord? My strength is gone and I can
hardly breathe."
[18]Again the one who looked like a
man touched me and gave me strength.
[19]"Do not be afraid, O man highly esteemed," he said. "Peace! Be strong now;
be strong."
When he spoke to me, I was strengthened and said, "Speak, my lord, since
you have given me strength."
[20]So he said, "Do you know why I
have come to you? Soon I will return to
fight against the prince of Persia, and
when I go, the prince of Greece will
come; [21]but first I will tell you what is
written in the Book of Truth. (No one
supports me against them except
11 Michael, your prince. [1]And in
the first year of Darius the Mede,
I took my stand to support and protect
him.)

The Kings of the South and the North

[2]"Now then, I tell you the truth: Three
more kings will appear in Persia, and
then a fourth, who will be far richer than
all the others. When he has gained
power by his wealth, he will stir up everyone against the kingdom of Greece.
[3]Then a mighty king will appear, who
will rule with great power and do as he
pleases. [4]After he has appeared, his empire will be broken up and parceled out
toward the four winds of heaven. It will
not go to his descendants, nor will it
have the power he exercised, because
his empire will be uprooted and given
to others.
[5]"The king of the South will become
strong, but one of his commanders will
become even stronger than he and will
rule his own kingdom with great power.
[6]After some years, they will become allies. The daughter of the king of the
South will go to the king of the North
to make an alliance, but she will not retain her power, and he and his power[b]
will not last. In those days she will be
handed over, together with her royal
escort and her father[c] and the one who
supported her.
[7]"One from her family line will arise
to take her place. He will attack the
forces of the king of the North and enter his fortress; he will fight against
them and be victorious. [8]He will also

[a]*16* Most manuscripts of the Masoretic Text; one manuscript of the Masoretic Text, Dead Sea Scrolls and Septuagint *Then something that looked like a man's hand* [b]*6* Or *offspring* [c]*6* Or *child* (see Vulgate and Syriac)

seize their gods, their metal images and their valuable articles of silver and gold and carry them off to Egypt. For some years he will leave the king of the North alone. [9]Then the king of the North will invade the realm of the king of the South but will retreat to his own country. [10]His sons will prepare for war and assemble a great army, which will sweep on like an irresistible flood and carry the battle as far as his fortress.

[11]"Then the king of the South will march out in a rage and fight against the king of the North, who will raise a large army, but it will be defeated. [12]When the army is carried off, the king of the South will be filled with pride and will slaughter many thousands, yet he will not remain triumphant. [13]For the king of the North will muster another army, larger than the first; and after several years, he will advance with a huge army fully equipped.

[14]"In those times many will rise against the king of the South. The violent men among your own people will rebel in fulfillment of the vision, but without success. [15]Then the king of the North will come and build up siege ramps and will capture a fortified city. The forces of the South will be powerless to resist; even their best troops will not have the strength to stand. [16]The invader will do as he pleases; no one will be able to stand against him. He will establish himself in the Beautiful Land and will have the power to destroy it. [17]He will determine to come with the might of his entire kingdom and will make an alliance with the king of the South. And he will give him a daughter in marriage in order to overthrow the kingdom, but his plans[a] will not succeed or help him. [18]Then he will turn his attention to the coastlands and will take many of them, but a commander will put an end to his insolence and will turn his insolence back upon him. [19]After this, he will turn back toward the fortresses of his own country but will stumble and fall, to be seen no more.

[20]"His successor will send out a tax collector to maintain the royal splendor. In a few years, however, he will be destroyed, yet not in anger or in battle.

[21]"He will be succeeded by a contemptible person who has not been given the honor of royalty. He will invade the kingdom when its people feel secure, and he will seize it through intrigue. [22]Then an overwhelming army will be swept away before him; both it and a prince of the covenant will be destroyed. [23]After coming to an agreement with him, he will act deceitfully, and with only a few people he will rise to power. [24]When the richest provinces feel secure, he will invade them and will achieve what neither his fathers nor his forefathers did. He will distribute plunder, loot and wealth among his followers. He will plot the overthrow of fortresses—but only for a time.

[25]"With a large army he will stir up his strength and courage against the king of the South. The king of the South will wage war with a large and very powerful army, but he will not be able to stand because of the plots devised against him. [26]Those who eat from the king's provisions will try to destroy him; his army will be swept away, and many will fall in battle. [27]The two kings, with their hearts bent on evil, will sit at the same table and lie to each other, but to no avail, because an end will still come at the appointed time. [28]The king of the North will return to his own country with great wealth, but his heart will be set against the holy covenant. He will take action against it and then return to his own country.

[29]"At the appointed time he will invade the South again, but this time the outcome will be different from what it was before. [30]Ships of the western coastlands[b] will oppose him, and he will lose heart. Then he will turn back and vent his fury against the holy covenant. He will return and show favor to those who forsake the holy covenant.

[31]"His armed forces will rise up to desecrate the temple fortress and will abolish the daily sacrifice. Then they will set

[a]17 Or *but she* [b]30 Hebrew *of Kittim*

up the abomination that causes desolation. 32With flattery he will corrupt those who have violated the covenant, but the people who know their God will firmly resist him.

33"Those who are wise will instruct many, though for a time they will fall by the sword or be burned or captured or plundered. 34When they fall, they will receive a little help, and many who are not sincere will join them. 35Some of the wise will stumble, so that they may be refined, purified and made spotless until the time of the end, for it will still come at the appointed time.

The King Who Exalts Himself

36"The king will do as he pleases. He will exalt and magnify himself above every god and will say unheard-of things against the God of gods. He will be successful until the time of wrath is completed, for what has been determined must take place. 37He will show no regard for the gods of his fathers or for the one desired by women, nor will he regard any god, but will exalt himself above them all. 38Instead of them, he will honor a god of fortresses; a god unknown to his fathers he will honor with gold and silver, with precious stones and costly gifts. 39He will attack the mightiest fortresses with the help of a foreign god and will greatly honor those who acknowledge him. He will make them rulers over many people and will distribute the land at a price.[a]

40"At the time of the end the king of the South will engage him in battle, and the king of the North will storm out against him with chariots and cavalry and a great fleet of ships. He will invade many countries and sweep through them like a flood. 41He will also invade the Beautiful Land. Many countries will fall, but Edom, Moab and the leaders of Ammon will be delivered from his hand. 42He will extend his power over many countries; Egypt will not escape. 43He will gain control of the treasures of gold and silver and all the riches of Egypt, with the Libyans and Nubians in submission. 44But reports from the east and the north will alarm him, and he will set out in a great rage to destroy and annihilate many. 45He will pitch his royal tents between the seas at[b] the beautiful holy mountain. Yet he will come to his end, and no one will help him.

The End Times

12 "At that time Michael, the great prince who protects your people, will arise. There will be a time of distress such as has not happened from the beginning of nations until then. But at that time your people—everyone whose name is found written in the book—will be delivered. 2Multitudes who sleep in the dust of the earth will awake: some to everlasting life, others to shame and everlasting contempt. 3Those who are wise[c] will shine like the brightness of the heavens, and those who lead many to righteousness, like the stars for ever and ever. 4But you, Daniel, close up and seal the words of the scroll until the time of the end. Many will go here and there to increase knowledge."

5Then I, Daniel, looked, and there before me stood two others, one on this bank of the river and one on the opposite bank. 6One of them said to the man clothed in linen, who was above the waters of the river, "How long will it be before these astonishing things are fulfilled?"

7The man clothed in linen, who was above the waters of the river, lifted his right hand and his left hand toward heaven, and I heard him swear by him who lives forever, saying, "It will be for a time, times and half a time.[d] When the power of the holy people has been finally broken, all these things will be completed."

8I heard, but I did not understand. So I asked, "My lord, what will the outcome of all this be?"

[a]39 Or *land for a reward* [b]45 Or *the sea and* [c]3 Or *who impart wisdom* [d]7 Or *a year, two years and half a year*

[9]He replied, "Go your way, Daniel, because the words are closed up and sealed until the time of the end. [10]Many will be purified, made spotless and refined, but the wicked will continue to be wicked. None of the wicked will understand, but those who are wise will understand.

[11]"From the time that the daily sacrifice is abolished and the abomination that causes desolation is set up, there will be 1,290 days. [12]Blessed is the one who waits for and reaches the end of the 1,335 days.

[13]"As for you, go your way till the end. You will rest, and then at the end of the days you will rise to receive your allotted inheritance."

SHARPEN THE FOCUS

Christians of another generation used to hang plaques or samplers on their walls that said, "Keep looking up." This was a reminder to believers that Jesus could come at any time.

The words are probably paraphrased from Luke 21:28. Jesus urged His disciples, "When these things begin to take place"—the signs and events of the last days—"stand up and lift up your heads, because your redemption is drawing near."

When did you last stand up, lift your head, and look out the window toward heaven? Do you look up often, anticipating a glimpse of the King of glory as He enters our universe to judge the living and the dead?

When we "keep looking up," our troubles take on a proper perspective; no disaster is permanent. When we "keep looking up," our witness takes on more urgency; more people in more places still need to hear and believe the Gospel before the end comes.

We can keep looking up with joy and hope, because our Judge is our Savior. The one who will render His verdict on our lives has already declared us blameless in the blood of His cross. Every time you see the sky today, pray with the apostle John, "Come, Lord Jesus!" (Revelation 22:20).

HOSEA

WEEK 67 • THURSDAY

Hosea 1:1—2:23

GET THE BIG PICTURE

Isaiah, Jeremiah, Ezekiel, Daniel—all of these prophets at times performed symbolic acts of prophecy. They preached and wrote, but often they acted out their message. Hosea follows in that tradition. As you read, look for his prophetic act and its meaning. If time is short, focus on Hosea 1:1–11.

1 The word of the LORD that came to
Hosea son of Beeri during the
reigns of Uzziah, Jotham, Ahaz and
Hezekiah, kings of Judah, and during
the reign of Jeroboam son of Jehoash[a]
king of Israel:

Hosea's Wife and Children

2When the LORD began to speak
through Hosea, the LORD said to him,
"Go, take to yourself an adulterous wife
and children of unfaithfulness, because
the land is guilty of the vilest adultery
in departing from the LORD." 3So he
married Gomer daughter of Diblaim,
and she conceived and bore him a son.
4Then the LORD said to Hosea, "Call
him Jezreel, because I will soon punish
the house of Jehu for the massacre at
Jezreel, and I will put an end to the kingdom of Israel. 5In that day I will break
Israel's bow in the Valley of Jezreel."
6Gomer conceived again and gave
birth to a daughter. Then the LORD said
to Hosea, "Call her Lo-Ruhamah,[b] for I
will no longer show love to the house of
Israel, that I should at all forgive them.
7Yet I will show love to the house of Judah; and I will save them—not by bow,
sword or battle, or by horses and horsemen, but by the LORD their God."
8After she had weaned Lo-Ruhamah,
Gomer had another son. 9Then the
LORD said, "Call him Lo-Ammi,[c] for you
are not my people, and I am not your
God.
10"Yet the Israelites will be like the
sand on the seashore, which cannot be
measured or counted. In the place
where it was said to them, 'You are not
my people,' they will be called 'sons of
the living God.' 11The people of Judah
and the people of Israel will be reunited, and they will appoint one leader
and will come up out of the land, for
great will be the day of Jezreel.

2 "Say of your brothers, 'My people,' and of your sisters, 'My
loved one.'

Israel Punished and Restored

2"Rebuke your mother, rebuke her,
for she is not my wife,
and I am not her husband.
Let her remove the adulterous look
from her face
and the unfaithfulness from
between her breasts.

[a]1 Hebrew *Joash,* a variant of *Jehoash* [b]6 *Lo-Ruhamah* means *not loved.* [c]9 *Lo-Ammi* means *not my people.*

[3]Otherwise I will strip her naked
and make her as bare as on the
day she was born;
I will make her like a desert,
turn her into a parched land,
and slay her with thirst.
[4]I will not show my love to her
children,
because they are the children of
adultery.
[5]Their mother has been unfaithful
and has conceived them in
disgrace.
She said, 'I will go after my lovers,
who give me my food and my
water,
my wool and my linen, my oil and
my drink.'
[6]Therefore I will block her path with
thornbushes;
I will wall her in so that she
cannot find her way.
[7]She will chase after her lovers but
not catch them;
she will look for them but not find
them.
Then she will say,
'I will go back to my husband as at
first,
for then I was better off than
now.'
[8]She has not acknowledged that I
was the one
who gave her the grain, the new
wine and oil,
who lavished on her the silver and
gold—
which they used for Baal.

[9]"Therefore I will take away my grain
when it ripens,
and my new wine when it is
ready.
I will take back my wool and my
linen,
intended to cover her nakedness.
[10]So now I will expose her lewdness
before the eyes of her lovers;
no one will take her out of my
hands.
[11]I will stop all her celebrations:
her yearly festivals, her New
Moons,
her Sabbath days—all her
appointed feasts.
[12]I will ruin her vines and her fig
trees,
which she said were her pay from
her lovers;
I will make them a thicket,
and wild animals will devour
them.
[13]I will punish her for the days
she burned incense to the Baals;
she decked herself with rings and
jewelry,
and went after her lovers,
but me she forgot,"
declares the LORD.

[14]"Therefore I am now going to allure
her;
I will lead her into the desert
and speak tenderly to her.
[15]There I will give her back her
vineyards,
and will make the Valley of Achor[a]
a door of hope.
There she will sing[b] as in the days of
her youth,
as in the day she came up out of
Egypt.
[16]"In that day," declares the LORD,
"you will call me 'my husband';
you will no longer call me 'my
master.[c]'
[17]I will remove the names of the Baals
from her lips;
no longer will their names be
invoked.
[18]In that day I will make a covenant
for them
with the beasts of the field and the
birds of the air
and the creatures that move along
the ground.
Bow and sword and battle
I will abolish from the land,
so that all may lie down in
safety.
[19]I will betroth you to me forever;
I will betroth you in[d]
righteousness and justice,

[a]15 *Achor* means *trouble*. [b]15 Or *respond*
[c]16 Hebrew *baal* [d]19 Or *with*; also in verse 20

in[a] love and compassion.
20 I will betroth you in faithfulness,
and you will acknowledge the LORD.
21 "In that day I will respond,"
declares the LORD—
"I will respond to the skies,
and they will respond to the earth;
22 and the earth will respond to the grain,
the new wine and oil,
and they will respond to Jezreel.[b]
23 I will plant her for myself in the land;
I will show my love to the one I called 'Not my loved one.[c]'
I will say to those called 'Not my people,[d]' 'You are my people';
and they will say, 'You are my God.' "

[a]19 Or *with* [b]22 *Jezreel* means *God plants.*
[c]23 Hebrew *Lo-Ruhamah* [d]23 Hebrew *Lo-Ammi*

SHARPEN THE FOCUS

The red-light district. XXX-rated movies. Adults only novelty stores. No one would expect to meet her pastor in a place like that. No one would like to think his theology professor spent last Saturday night on a corner in that part of town. But as we round the corner in the seediest part of Samaria we find ourselves face-to-face with God's anointed prophet, Hosea. He's holding hands with his fiancée—the prostitute, Gomer.

An exaggeration? Not really. Hosea begins his book (Hosea 1:2) by repeating the Lord's instructions that he is to propose to a prostitute and marry her. The rest of Hosea's writings will explain the meaning of this prophetic marriage. The Lord chose Israel as His bride, but she prostituted herself with many idols.

Hosea did not write to shame Israel. Rather, the Lord wanted to draw His people back to Himself. Perhaps when they saw in Hosea the depth of God's divine patience and pardon, they would turn back to Him.

Read the promises of Hosea 2:19–20. Think of Christ's cross as you do, for in the cross we see the eternal commitment of love our Lord has made to us. Thank Him for that love.

Despite Hosea's love, Gomer runs away. This time she falls so deeply into prostitution she becomes a slave. Hosea buys her back, just as the Lord commands. In chapter 4 Hosea explains the details of the slavery into which Israel's idols have led them. As you read that chapter, look for all 10 Commandments in the Lord's indictment against His people. If time is short, focus on Hosea 3:1–5.

Hosea's Reconciliation With His Wife

3 The LORD said to me, "Go, show your love to your wife again, though she is loved by another and is an adulteress. Love her as the LORD loves the Israelites, though they turn to other gods and love the sacred raisin cakes."
2So I bought her for fifteen shekels[a] of silver and about a homer and a lethek[b] of barley. 3Then I told her, "You are to live with[c] me many days; you must not be a prostitute or be intimate with any man, and I will live with[c] you."
4For the Israelites will live many days without king or prince, without sacrifice or sacred stones, without ephod or idol.
5Afterward the Israelites will return and seek the LORD their God and David their king. They will come trembling to the LORD and to his blessings in the last days.

The Charge Against Israel

4 Hear the word of the LORD,
you Israelites,
because the LORD has a charge to bring
against you who live in the land:
"There is no faithfulness, no love,
no acknowledgment of God in the land.
2There is only cursing,[d] lying and murder,
stealing and adultery;
they break all bounds,
and bloodshed follows bloodshed.
3Because of this the land mourns,[e]
and all who live in it waste away;
the beasts of the field and the birds of the air
and the fish of the sea are dying.

4"But let no man bring a charge,
let no man accuse another,
for your people are like those
who bring charges against a priest.
5You stumble day and night,
and the prophets stumble with you.
So I will destroy your mother—
6 my people are destroyed from lack of knowledge.

"Because you have rejected knowledge,
I also reject you as my priests;
because you have ignored the law of your God,
I also will ignore your children.
7The more the priests increased,
the more they sinned against me;
they exchanged[f] their[g] Glory for something disgraceful.
8They feed on the sins of my people
and relish their wickedness.
9And it will be: Like people, like priests.
I will punish both of them for their ways
and repay them for their deeds.

10"They will eat but not have enough;
they will engage in prostitution but not increase,
because they have deserted the LORD
to give themselves 11to prostitution,
to old wine and new,
which take away the understanding 12of my people.
They consult a wooden idol
and are answered by a stick of wood.
A spirit of prostitution leads them astray;
they are unfaithful to their God.
13They sacrifice on the mountaintops
and burn offerings on the hills,
under oak, poplar and terebinth,
where the shade is pleasant.
Therefore your daughters turn to prostitution
and your daughters-in-law to adultery.

14"I will not punish your daughters
when they turn to prostitution,
nor your daughters-in-law

[a]2 That is, about 6 ounces (about 170 grams) [b]2 That is, probably about 10 bushels (about 330 liters) [c]3 Or *wait for* [d]2 That is, to pronounce a curse upon [e]3 Or *dries up* [f]7 Syriac and an ancient Hebrew scribal tradition; Masoretic Text *I will exchange* [g]7 Masoretic Text; an ancient Hebrew scribal tradition *my*

when they commit adultery,
because the men themselves consort
with harlots
and sacrifice with shrine
prostitutes—
a people without understanding
will come to ruin!

15 "Though you commit adultery,
O Israel,
let not Judah become guilty.

"Do not go to Gilgal;
do not go up to Beth Aven.[a]
And do not swear, 'As surely as the
LORD lives!'

16 The Israelites are stubborn,
like a stubborn heifer.
How then can the LORD pasture
them
like lambs in a meadow?

17 Ephraim is joined to idols;
leave him alone!

18 Even when their drinks are gone,
they continue their prostitution;
their rulers dearly love shameful
ways.

19 A whirlwind will sweep them away,
and their sacrifices will bring them
shame.

[a]15 *Beth Aven* means *house of wickedness* (a name for Bethel, which means *house of God*).

SHARPEN THE FOCUS

Have you ever approached God for the fourth or fortieth or four-hundredth time to confess the same sin? Selfishness. Greed. Unkindness. Gossip. Whatever the wrongdoing, such confession can be an unsettling experience. Beside the burden of guilt, we also approach God loaded down with shame.

Put yourself in Gomer's sandals. Picture yourself being brutalized by your slave master as you look up to see Hosea approaching. What happens in your heart as you see the love in his eyes? What happens inside you as you watch him hand over a hundred dollars and 10 bushels of barley to buy you back?

Now stand on Calvary as the sun stops shining. Watch as the sinless Son of God pays for your release—not with silver or gold—but with His own blood. Know that your Savior has taken your guilt—all of it. Know that your Lord has removed your shame—all of it.

When you go to Him with current sins, you need not fear He's keeping score. You need not worry about the demerits in your record. You are free—in Jesus. You are forgiven—in Jesus. You are His very own—in Jesus. Live in that power and peace today.

WEEK 67 • SATURDAY

Hosea 5:1—6:11

GET THE BIG PICTURE

Where do you turn when you need spiritual healing? That's the issue Hosea deals with in today's reading. Israel's leaders have torn up themselves and their country with their sin (Hosea 5). But even in the pain and distress of that sin, they have refused to come back to the Lord, their Healer (Hosea 5:13; Exodus 16:28). As you read, ask yourself what spiritual wounds you may be nursing. If time is short, focus on Hosea 6:1–6.

Judgment Against Israel

5 "Hear this, you priests!
Pay attention, you Israelites!
Listen, O royal house!
This judgment is against you:
You have been a snare at Mizpah,
a net spread out on Tabor.
2 The rebels are deep in slaughter.
I will discipline all of them.
3 I know all about Ephraim;
Israel is not hidden from me.
Ephraim, you have now turned to
prostitution;
Israel is corrupt.

4 "Their deeds do not permit them
to return to their God.
A spirit of prostitution is in their
heart;
they do not acknowledge the
LORD.
5 Israel's arrogance testifies against
them;
the Israelites, even Ephraim,
stumble in their sin;
Judah also stumbles with them.
6 When they go with their flocks and
herds
to seek the LORD,
they will not find him;
he has withdrawn himself from
them.
7 They are unfaithful to the LORD;
they give birth to illegitimate
children.
Now their New Moon festivals
will devour them and their fields.

8 "Sound the trumpet in Gibeah,
the horn in Ramah.
Raise the battle cry in Beth Aven[a];
lead on, O Benjamin.
9 Ephraim will be laid waste
on the day of reckoning.
Among the tribes of Israel
I proclaim what is certain.
10 Judah's leaders are like those
who move boundary stones.
I will pour out my wrath on them
like a flood of water.
11 Ephraim is oppressed,
trampled in judgment,
intent on pursuing idols.[b]
12 I am like a moth to Ephraim,
like rot to the people of Judah.

13 "When Ephraim saw his sickness,
and Judah his sores,
then Ephraim turned to Assyria,
and sent to the great king for help.
But he is not able to cure you,
not able to heal your sores.
14 For I will be like a lion to Ephraim,
like a great lion to Judah.
I will tear them to pieces and go
away;
I will carry them off, with no one
to rescue them.
15 Then I will go back to my place
until they admit their guilt.
And they will seek my face;
in their misery they will earnestly
seek me."

Israel Unrepentant

6 "Come, let us return to the
LORD.
He has torn us to pieces
but he will heal us;
he has injured us
but he will bind up our wounds.
2 After two days he will revive us;
on the third day he will restore us,
that we may live in his presence.
3 Let us acknowledge the LORD;
let us press on to acknowledge
him.
As surely as the sun rises,
he will appear;
he will come to us like the winter
rains,
like the spring rains that water the
earth."

4 "What can I do with you, Ephraim?
What can I do with you, Judah?
Your love is like the morning mist,
like the early dew that disappears.
5 Therefore I cut you in pieces with
my prophets,
I killed you with the words of my
mouth;

[a] *8 Beth Aven* means *house of wickedness* (a name for Bethel, which means *house of God*). [b] *11* The meaning of the Hebrew for this word is uncertain.

my judgments flashed like
lightning upon you.
6 For I desire mercy, not sacrifice,
and acknowledgment of God
rather than burnt offerings.
7 Like Adam,[a] they have broken the
covenant—
they were unfaithful to me there.
8 Gilead is a city of wicked men,
stained with footprints of
blood.
9 As marauders lie in ambush for a
man,
so do bands of priests;
they murder on the road to Shechem,
committing shameful crimes.
10 I have seen a horrible thing
in the house of Israel.
There Ephraim is given to
prostitution
and Israel is defiled.

11 "Also for you, Judah,
a harvest is appointed.

"Whenever I would restore the
fortunes of my people,

[a]7 Or *As at Adam*; or *Like men*

SHARPEN THE FOCUS

Sheep often isolate themselves when they are wounded. They find a secluded spot and hide. Once infection and fever set in, dehydration accelerates. Death soon follows.

Especially at a time like that, a sheep needs a shepherd, someone who will come after it, look high and low for it, carry it home, medicate its wounds, bandage them, and protect it while it heals.

When God's children have wounded themselves by their sin, we sometimes move even farther away from our Lord. In shame and fear, we isolate ourselves from Him, the only source of healing. That's why the invitation of Hosea 6:1–2 means so much. Even if we have rejected Him and wandered far from Him, our Lord never rejects us.

Yes, our Good Shepherd does "cut [us] in pieces" with His Word of Law (Hosea 6:5). But He does it so we will recognize the seriousness of sin's infection. He wounds so He can bandage; He tears so He can heal (Hosea 6:1). His Word of Law exposes our need. Then in mercy He brings full restoration through His Word of grace. Reread Hosea 6:1–2 and then talk to your Good Shepherd about your hurts.

WEEK 68 • MONDAY

Hosea 7:1—8:14

GET THE BIG PICTURE

"Come, let us return to the LORD . . . and [He] will heal us"! Hosea invited, implored, and urged God's people in the Northern Kingdom (Hosea 6:1). But as you will see, Israel rejected God's gracious invitation. Note the continuing references to spiritual adultery. If time is short, focus on Hosea 8:1–14.

7 [1]whenever I would heal
Israel,
the sins of Ephraim are exposed
and the crimes of Samaria
revealed.
They practice deceit,
thieves break into houses,
bandits rob in the streets;
[2]but they do not realize
that I remember all their evil
deeds.
Their sins engulf them;
they are always before me.

[3]"They delight the king with their
wickedness,
the princes with their lies.
[4]They are all adulterers,
burning like an oven
whose fire the baker need not stir
from the kneading of the dough
till it rises.
[5]On the day of the festival of our
king
the princes become inflamed with
wine,
and he joins hands with the
mockers.
[6]Their hearts are like an oven;
they approach him with intrigue.
Their passion smolders all night;
in the morning it blazes like a
flaming fire.
[7]All of them are hot as an oven;
they devour their rulers.
All their kings fall,
and none of them calls on me.

[8]"Ephraim mixes with the nations;
Ephraim is a flat cake not turned
over.
[9]Foreigners sap his strength,
but he does not realize it.
His hair is sprinkled with gray,
but he does not notice.
[10]Israel's arrogance testifies against
him,
but despite all this
he does not return to the LORD his
God
or search for him.

[11]"Ephraim is like a dove,
easily deceived and senseless—
now calling to Egypt,
now turning to Assyria.
[12]When they go, I will throw my net
over them;
I will pull them down like birds of
the air.
When I hear them flocking together,
I will catch them.
[13]Woe to them,
because they have strayed from
me!
Destruction to them,
because they have rebelled against
me!
I long to redeem them
but they speak lies against me.
[14]They do not cry out to me from their
hearts
but wail upon their beds.
They gather together[a] for grain and
new wine
but turn away from me.
[15]I trained them and strengthened
them,
but they plot evil against me.
[16]They do not turn to the Most High;
they are like a faulty bow.
Their leaders will fall by the sword
because of their insolent words.
For this they will be ridiculed
in the land of Egypt.

Israel to Reap the Whirlwind

8 "Put the trumpet to your lips!
An eagle is over the house of
the LORD
because the people have broken my
covenant
and rebelled against my law.
[2]Israel cries out to me,
'O our God, we acknowledge
you!'
[3]But Israel has rejected what is good;
an enemy will pursue him.
[4]They set up kings without my
consent;
they choose princes without my
approval.
With their silver and gold
they make idols for themselves

[a]14 Most Hebrew manuscripts; some Hebrew manuscripts and Septuagint *They slash themselves*

to their own destruction.
[5]Throw out your calf-idol,
O Samaria!
My anger burns against them.
How long will they be incapable of
purity?
[6] They are from Israel!
This calf—a craftsman has made it;
it is not God.
It will be broken in pieces,
that calf of Samaria.

[7]"They sow the wind
and reap the whirlwind.
The stalk has no head;
it will produce no flour.
Were it to yield grain,
foreigners would swallow it up.
[8]Israel is swallowed up;
now she is among the nations
like a worthless thing.
[9]For they have gone up to Assyria
like a wild donkey wandering
alone.
Ephraim has sold herself to lovers.
[10]Although they have sold themselves
among the nations,
I will now gather them together.
They will begin to waste away
under the oppression of the
mighty king.

[11]"Though Ephraim built many altars
for sin offerings,
these have become altars for
sinning.
[12]I wrote for them the many things of
my law,
but they regarded them as
something alien.
[13]They offer sacrifices given to me
and they eat the meat,
but the LORD is not pleased with
them.
Now he will remember their
wickedness
and punish their sins:
They will return to Egypt.
[14]Israel has forgotten his Maker
and built palaces;
Judah has fortified many towns.
But I will send fire upon their cities
that will consume their
fortresses."

SHARPEN THE FOCUS

When the nation of Israel split after King Solomon's death, the king of Israel wanted to keep his people from traveling to Judah to worship at the temple in Jerusalem. Fearing that loyalty to the system of worship in Judah would eventually reunite his people with the people in the Southern Kingdom, Jeroboam took steps to prevent that. He set up two calves–one at Dan and one at Bethel. These idols, one on either end of his kingdom, made worship convenient. (See 1 Kings 12 and a good Bible map.)

With this background in mind, read Hosea 8:1–6. Notice the verbs: broken! rebelled! rejected! made idols!

Sinful attitudes (ignoring the covenant, rebellion, and rejecting what God calls good) led to sinful actions in Israel's life. There are no "little" sins; there are no "safe" sins. This truth echoes throughout all of Scripture. The secret attitudes of our hearts sooner or later show up in our lifestyle. Israel "sowed the wind" (Hosea 8:7), and reaped a tornado of judgment.

Prayerfully read Psalm 1 before you close your Bible today. Clinging to Jesus and His cross, ask that the Word that has been sown in your life will result in spiritual stability and a harvest of holy fruit.

WEEK 68 • TUESDAY

Hosea 9:1—10:15

GET THE BIG PICTURE

The laws of the harvest. Today's chapters from Hosea comment on these principles. Israel had planted seeds of faithlessness; she would gather a bumper crop of evil. As you read, ask, "In light of what I'm planting in my life today, will I want a crop failure a few months or years from now?" If time is short, focus on Hosea 10:1–15.

Punishment for Israel

9 Do not rejoice, O Israel;
do not be jubilant like the
other nations.
For you have been unfaithful to
your God;
you love the wages of a prostitute
at every threshing floor.
2 Threshing floors and winepresses
will not feed the people;
the new wine will fail them.
3 They will not remain in the LORD's
land;
Ephraim will return to Egypt
and eat unclean[a] food in Assyria.
4 They will not pour out wine
offerings to the LORD,
nor will their sacrifices please him.
Such sacrifices will be to them like
the bread of mourners;
all who eat them will be unclean.
This food will be for themselves;
it will not come into the temple of
the LORD.

5 What will you do on the day of your
appointed feasts,
on the festival days of the LORD?
6 Even if they escape from
destruction,
Egypt will gather them,
and Memphis will bury them.
Their treasures of silver will be taken
over by briers,
and thorns will overrun their
tents.
7 The days of punishment are coming,
the days of reckoning are at hand.
Let Israel know this.
Because your sins are so many
and your hostility so great,
the prophet is considered a fool,
the inspired man a maniac.
8 The prophet, along with my God,
is the watchman over Ephraim,[b]
yet snares await him on all his paths,
and hostility in the house of his
God.
9 They have sunk deep into
corruption,
as in the days of Gibeah.
God will remember their wickedness
and punish them for their sins.

10 "When I found Israel,
it was like finding grapes in the
desert;
when I saw your fathers,
it was like seeing the early fruit on
the fig tree.
But when they came to Baal Peor,
they consecrated themselves to
that shameful idol
and became as vile as the thing
they loved.
11 Ephraim's glory will fly away like a
bird—
no birth, no pregnancy, no
conception.
12 Even if they rear children,
I will bereave them of every one.
Woe to them
when I turn away from them!

[a]3 That is, ceremonially unclean [b]8 Or *The prophet is the watchman over Ephraim, / the people of my God*

[13] I have seen Ephraim, like Tyre,
planted in a pleasant place.
But Ephraim will bring out
their children to the slayer."

[14] Give them, O LORD—
what will you give them?
Give them wombs that miscarry
and breasts that are dry.

[15] "Because of all their wickedness in Gilgal,
I hated them there.
Because of their sinful deeds,
I will drive them out of my house.
I will no longer love them;
all their leaders are rebellious.
[16] Ephraim is blighted,
their root is withered,
they yield no fruit.
Even if they bear children,
I will slay their cherished offspring."

[17] My God will reject them
because they have not obeyed him;
they will be wanderers among the nations.

10 Israel was a spreading vine;
he brought forth fruit for himself.
As his fruit increased,
he built more altars;
as his land prospered,
he adorned his sacred stones.
[2] Their heart is deceitful,
and now they must bear their guilt.
The LORD will demolish their altars
and destroy their sacred stones.

[3] Then they will say, "We have no king
because we did not revere the LORD.
But even if we had a king,
what could he do for us?"
[4] They make many promises,
take false oaths
and make agreements;
therefore lawsuits spring up
like poisonous weeds in a plowed field.

[5] The people who live in Samaria fear
for the calf-idol of Beth Aven.[a]
Its people will mourn over it,
and so will its idolatrous priests,
those who had rejoiced over its splendor,
because it is taken from them into exile.
[6] It will be carried to Assyria
as tribute for the great king.
Ephraim will be disgraced;
Israel will be ashamed of its wooden idols.[b]
[7] Samaria and its king will float away
like a twig on the surface of the waters.
[8] The high places of wickedness[c] will be destroyed—
it is the sin of Israel.
Thorns and thistles will grow up
and cover their altars.
Then they will say to the mountains,
"Cover us!"
and to the hills, "Fall on us!"

[9] "Since the days of Gibeah, you have sinned, O Israel,
and there you have remained.[d]
Did not war overtake
the evildoers in Gibeah?
[10] When I please, I will punish them;
nations will be gathered against them
to put them in bonds for their double sin.
[11] Ephraim is a trained heifer
that loves to thresh;
so I will put a yoke
on her fair neck.
I will drive Ephraim,
Judah must plow,
and Jacob must break up the ground.
[12] Sow for yourselves righteousness,
reap the fruit of unfailing love,
and break up your unplowed ground;
for it is time to seek the LORD,

[a] 5 *Beth Aven* means *house of wickedness* (a name for Bethel, which means *house of God*). [b] 6 Or *its counsel* [c] 8 Hebrew *aven,* a reference to Beth Aven (a derogatory name for Bethel) [d] 9 Or *there a stand was taken*

until he comes
and showers righteousness on
you.
13 But you have planted wickedness,
you have reaped evil,
you have eaten the fruit of
deception.
Because you have depended on
your own strength
and on your many warriors,
14 the roar of battle will rise against
your people,
so that all your fortresses will be
devastated—
as Shalman devastated Beth Arbel
on the day of battle,
when mothers were dashed to the
ground with their children.
15 Thus will it happen to you,
O Bethel,
because your wickedness is great.
When that day dawns,
the king of Israel will be
completely destroyed.

SHARPEN THE FOCUS

Certain laws cannot be broken. Even someone who refuses to believe in them will find that these laws continue to work. No skeptic can repeal the law of gravity.

The laws of the harvest are like that. You always reap what you sow: No one plants beans and gets corn. Most times, you reap much more than you sow: One hill of cucumber seeds can produce quarts and quarts of dill pickles. And a zucchini seed? Well, you know *that* story!

The laws of the harvest also work in our relationship with the Lord. That's why our Savior-God holds out to us the invitation of Hosea 10:12. "It's time," He says, "to break up the hard places in your heart. It's time to sow the seeds of righteousness there, so I can grow a crop of love in your life." In other words, "Repent!"

We cannot produce the fruit of holy living on our own any more than we can turn a radish seed into a radish. Only God can make the soil productive. Only He can send the rain. Only He can warm our hearts with the life-giving Son-shine of His love. He wants to do that. He wants us to have the joy of harvesting acres and acres of righteousness in our lives.

WEEK 68 • WEDNESDAY

Hosea 11:1—12:14

GET THE BIG PICTURE

Heart-broken, Hosea has wept over unfaithful Gomer. Now he paints a picture of the Lord, even more heart-broken, weeping for unfaithful and unrepentant Israel. As you read, notice the Lord's kindness and care. If time is short, focus on Hosea 11:1–12.

God's Love for Israel

11 "When Israel was a child, I
loved him,
and out of Egypt I called my son.
2 But the more I[a] called Israel,
the further they went from me.[b]
They sacrificed to the Baals
and they burned incense to images.

[a]2 Some Septuagint manuscripts; Hebrew *they*
[b]2 Septuagint; Hebrew *them*

[3]It was I who taught Ephraim to
walk,
taking them by the arms;
but they did not realize
it was I who healed them.
[4]I led them with cords of human
kindness,
with ties of love;
I lifted the yoke from their neck
and bent down to feed them.

[5]"Will they not return to Egypt
and will not Assyria rule over
them
because they refuse to repent?
[6]Swords will flash in their cities,
will destroy the bars of their gates
and put an end to their plans.
[7]My people are determined to turn
from me.
Even if they call to the Most High,
he will by no means exalt them.

[8]"How can I give you up, Ephraim?
How can I hand you over, Israel?
How can I treat you like Admah?
How can I make you like
Zeboiim?
My heart is changed within me;
all my compassion is aroused.
[9]I will not carry out my fierce anger,
nor will I turn and devastate
Ephraim.
For I am God, and not man—
the Holy One among you.
I will not come in wrath.[a]
[10]They will follow the LORD;
he will roar like a lion.
When he roars,
his children will come trembling
from the west.
[11]They will come trembling
like birds from Egypt,
like doves from Assyria.
I will settle them in their homes,"
declares the LORD.

Israel's Sin

[12]Ephraim has surrounded me with
lies,
the house of Israel with deceit.
And Judah is unruly against God,
even against the faithful Holy
One.

12 [1]Ephraim feeds on
the wind;
he pursues the east wind all day
and multiplies lies and violence.
He makes a treaty with Assyria
and sends olive oil to Egypt.
[2]The LORD has a charge to bring
against Judah;
he will punish Jacob[b] according to
his ways
and repay him according to his
deeds.
[3]In the womb he grasped his
brother's heel;
as a man he struggled with God.
[4]He struggled with the angel and
overcame him;
he wept and begged for his favor.
He found him at Bethel
and talked with him there—
[5]the LORD God Almighty,
the LORD is his name of renown!
[6]But you must return to your God;
maintain love and justice,
and wait for your God always.

[7]The merchant uses dishonest
scales;
he loves to defraud.
[8]Ephraim boasts,
"I am very rich; I have become
wealthy.
With all my wealth they will not find
in me
any iniquity or sin."

[9]"I am the LORD your God,
⌞who brought you⌟ out of[c] Egypt;
I will make you live in tents again,
as in the days of your appointed
feasts.
[10]I spoke to the prophets,
gave them many visions
and told parables through them."

[11]Is Gilead wicked?
Its people are worthless!
Do they sacrifice bulls in Gilgal?
Their altars will be like piles of
stones
on a plowed field.

[a]9 Or *come against any city* [b]2 *Jacob* means *he grasps the heel* (figuratively, *he deceives*). [c]9 Or *God / ever since you were in*

12 Jacob fled to the country of Aram[a];
Israel served to get a wife,
and to pay for her he tended sheep.
13 The LORD used a prophet to bring
Israel up from Egypt,
by a prophet he cared for him.
14 But Ephraim has bitterly provoked
him to anger;
his Lord will leave upon him the
guilt of his bloodshed
and will repay him for his
contempt.

SHARPEN THE FOCUS

Imagine a cruel trainer working with an unruly horse. The trainer puts a bit in the animal's mouth, a bit designed to cut and pinch the most tender tissue. An animal treated like this *would* submit to its trainer. But quite likely it would either hate the trainer, or its spirit would be broken.

Hosea has written many chapters calling for Israel to obey the Lord. Still, the prophet knows that forced obedience is no real obedience at all. That's where the pictures of Hosea all fit in.

The Lord loved Israel so much. He called the nation of slaves in Egypt to be His sons, His heirs (Hosea 11:1). He held His people (Hosea 11:3) as they took their first baby-steps to freedom. He removed the cruel bit of slavery, the yoke of bondage. He stooped down and fed them (Hosea 11:4).

What Yahweh did for Israel, He has also done for us. He has called us from sin's slavery to live free as His sons and daughters. He holds our hands as we learn to walk in that freedom. He has taken Satan's bit from our jaw so that our enemy can no longer control us. He's rescued us from the pointless lives people live apart from Christ. Even when we fail our Lord, He remains "the faithful Holy One" (Hosea 11:12).

WEEK 68 • THURSDAY

Hosea 13:1–16

GET THE BIG PICTURE

The wind of God's fury at human sin blows hot across the verses of Hosea 13. This chapter begins with a final indictment and then goes on to reveal God's verdict: Guilty. As you read, look for the oasis in this deadly desert. If time is short, focus on Hosea 13:4–14.

The LORD's Anger Against Israel

13 When Ephraim spoke,
men trembled;
he was exalted in Israel.
But he became guilty of Baal
worship and died.
2 Now they sin more and more;
they make idols for themselves
from their silver,
cleverly fashioned images,
all of them the work of craftsmen.
It is said of these people,
"They offer human sacrifice
and kiss[b] the calf-idols."
3 Therefore they will be like the
morning mist,
like the early dew that disappears,

[a] *12* That is, Northwest Mesopotamia
[b] *2* Or *"Men who sacrifice / kiss*

like chaff swirling from a
threshing floor,
like smoke escaping through a
window.

4 "But I am the LORD your God,
⌊who brought you⌋ out of[a] Egypt.
You shall acknowledge no God but
me,
no Savior except me.
5 I cared for you in the desert,
in the land of burning heat.
6 When I fed them, they were
satisfied;
when they were satisfied, they
became proud;
then they forgot me.
7 So I will come upon them like a lion,
like a leopard I will lurk by the
path.
8 Like a bear robbed of her cubs,
I will attack them and rip them
open.
Like a lion I will devour them;
a wild animal will tear them apart.

9 "You are destroyed, O Israel,
because you are against me,
against your helper.
10 Where is your king, that he may
save you?
Where are your rulers in all your
towns,
of whom you said,
'Give me a king and princes'?
11 So in my anger I gave you a king,
and in my wrath I took him away.
12 The guilt of Ephraim is stored up,
his sins are kept on record.
13 Pains as of a woman in childbirth
come to him,
but he is a child without wisdom;
when the time arrives,
he does not come to the opening
of the womb.

14 "I will ransom them from the power
of the grave[b];
I will redeem them from death.
Where, O death, are your plagues?
Where, O grave,[b] is your
destruction?

"I will have no compassion,
15 even though he thrives among his
brothers.
An east wind from the LORD will
come,
blowing in from the desert;
his spring will fail
and his well dry up.
His storehouse will be plundered
of all its treasures.
16 The people of Samaria must bear
their guilt,
because they have rebelled against
their God.
They will fall by the sword;
their little ones will be dashed to
the ground,
their pregnant women ripped
open."

[a]4 Or *God / ever since you were in* [b]14 Hebrew *Sheol*

SHARPEN THE FOCUS

There's an awful kind of white-hot anger evident in the Lord's judgment on Israel's sin. We may read those words, though, and fail to grasp the connection between Israel's sin and our own. But here the Lord bypasses all our excuses. His Law points a finger directly at our heart as it thunders out the First Commandment (Exodus 20:3): "You shall have no other gods" (see Hosea 13:4).

But we do have other gods. We love our comfort. We trust our financial nest egg. We fear the future. Our hearts cling to all kinds of gods that are not God at all. When we shake our heads in disgust over Israel's foolishness, we agree with God that He is right—and that *we* are unrighteous.

As we begin to prickle under the heat of the Law, though, a breeze from heaven refreshes us. Read the promise of Hosea 13:14. The death that was ours, is ours no longer. The grave that belonged to us, belongs to us no more. That death became Christ's death. That grave became His grave. And His life is now—right now—alive in us by His grace.

Read 1 Corinthians 15:51–58. Praise Jesus for His victory that now belongs to you. And ask Him to show you how He would have you live out 1 Corinthians 15:58.

Have you ever listened in on one side of a conversation? That's the sensation you may experience as you read Hosea 14. The prophet answers a question we haven't heard anyone ask yet: "Suppose we wanted to come back to God, how could we do that?" Listen for the Lord's answer. If time is short, focus on Hosea 14:1–4.

Repentance to Bring Blessing

14 Return, O Israel, to
the LORD your God.
Your sins have been your
downfall!
2 Take words with you
and return to the LORD.
Say to him:
"Forgive all our sins
and receive us graciously,
that we may offer the fruit of our
lips.[a]
3 Assyria cannot save us;
we will not mount war-horses.
We will never again say 'Our gods'
to what our own hands have
made,
for in you the fatherless find
compassion."

4 "I will heal their waywardness
and love them freely,
for my anger has turned away
from them.
5 I will be like the dew to Israel;
he will blossom like a lily.
Like a cedar of Lebanon
he will send down his roots;
6 his young shoots will grow.
His splendor will be like an olive
tree,
his fragrance like a cedar of
Lebanon.
7 Men will dwell again in his shade.
He will flourish like the grain.
He will blossom like a vine,
and his fame will be like the wine
from Lebanon.
8 O Ephraim, what more have I[b] to do
with idols?
I will answer him and care for
him.
I am like a green pine tree;
your fruitfulness comes from me."

9 Who is wise? He will realize these
things.
Who is discerning? He will
understand them.
The ways of the LORD are right;
the righteous walk in them,
but the rebellious stumble in
them.

[a]2 Or *offer our lips as sacrifices of bulls* [b]8 Or *What more has Ephraim*

SHARPEN THE FOCUS

"Home is the place where, when you go there, they have to take you in," observed Mark Twain. As thousands of homeless teens will testify, that's not true any more. Ejected and rejected by the people who have a duty to love and to care, for many young people going home is not an option.

The door to heaven's throne room, though, always stands open. Our Father doesn't *have* to take us in. But He *wants* to. Like the father in Jesus' parable about the prodigal, our Father strains to catch a glimpse of us coming down the road toward the love for which we long.

Like that runaway, we come with empty hands and an empty heart. We bring only words—the words Hosea recommends: "Forgive all our sins and receive us graciously" (Hosea 14:2). We need not try to earn our Father's favor by proving we're sorry enough—we can never be sorry enough. We need not offer to make up for the pain caused—we can never make it up. We simply admit our responsibility and our need.

God will do exactly what He has promised—He will heal us and love us freely (Hosea 14:4). He will refresh us (Hosea 14:5). He will make us beautiful and stable and fruitful (Hosea 14:6–7). What promises! What are you waiting for?

JOEL

WEEK 68 • SATURDAY

Joel 1:1–20

GET THE BIG PICTURE

Movie-makers always include their most exciting scenes in the preview. As Joel opens his book, he describes a recent locust plague and drought in Judah. These preview for his readers the coming main event—the "day of the LORD" (Joel 1:15). As you read, look for Joel's advice to all who survived the preview. If time is short, focus on Joel 1:1–12.

1 The word of the LORD that came to Joel son of Pethuel.

An Invasion of Locusts

2 Hear this, you elders;
listen, all who live in the land.
Has anything like this ever
happened in your days
or in the days of your forefathers?
3 Tell it to your children,
and let your children tell it to their
children,
and their children to the next
generation.
4 What the locust swarm has left
the great locusts have eaten;
what the great locusts have left
the young locusts have eaten;
what the young locusts have left
other locusts[a] have eaten.
5 Wake up, you drunkards, and weep!
Wail, all you drinkers of wine;
wail because of the new wine,
for it has been snatched from your
lips.
6 A nation has invaded my land,
powerful and without number;
it has the teeth of a lion,
the fangs of a lioness.
7 It has laid waste my vines
and ruined my fig trees.
It has stripped off their bark
and thrown it away,
leaving their branches white.
8 Mourn like a virgin[b] in sackcloth
grieving for the husband[c] of her
youth.
9 Grain offerings and drink offerings
are cut off from the house of the
LORD.
The priests are in mourning,
those who minister before the
LORD.
10 The fields are ruined,
the ground is dried up[d];
the grain is destroyed,
the new wine is dried up,
the oil fails.
11 Despair, you farmers,
wail, you vine growers;
grieve for the wheat and the
barley,
because the harvest of the field is
destroyed.
12 The vine is dried up
and the fig tree is withered;

[a]4 The precise meaning of the four Hebrew words used here for locusts is uncertain. [b]8 Or *young woman* [c]8 Or *betrothed* [d]10 Or *ground mourns*

the pomegranate, the palm and the
apple tree—
all the trees of the field—are dried
up.
Surely the joy of mankind
is withered away.

A Call to Repentance

[13] Put on sackcloth, O priests, and
mourn;
wail, you who minister before the
altar.
Come, spend the night in sackcloth,
you who minister before my God;
for the grain offerings and drink
offerings
are withheld from the house of
your God.
[14] Declare a holy fast;
call a sacred assembly.
Summon the elders
and all who live in the land
to the house of the LORD your God,
and cry out to the LORD.

[15] Alas for that day!
For the day of the LORD is near;
it will come like destruction from
the Almighty.[a]
[16] Has not the food been cut off
before our very eyes—
joy and gladness
from the house of our God?
[17] The seeds are shriveled
beneath the clods.[b]
The storehouses are in ruins,
the granaries have been broken
down,
for the grain has dried up.
[18] How the cattle moan!
The herds mill about
because they have no pasture;
even the flocks of sheep are
suffering.

[19] To you, O LORD, I call,
for fire has devoured the open
pastures
and flames have burned up all the
trees of the field.
[20] Even the wild animals pant for you;
the streams of water have dried
up
and fire has devoured the open
pastures.

[a] 15 Hebrew *Shaddai* [b] 17 The meaning of the Hebrew for this word is uncertain.

SHARPEN THE FOCUS

An observer once spotted a cloud of locusts flying over the Red Sea. He estimated the swarm was 2,000 miles long! Locusts travel vast distances by living off fatty tissue stored in their bodies. But once they reach an area with vegetation, they devour every plant in sight.

Such a swarm devastated Judah in Joel's day. Then, in the knockout blow of a one-two punch, a drought hit the land. Judah's people must have thought recovery would never come. "Where can we turn?" they must have wondered. Joel knew. He cried out to the Lord, to Yahweh, to the God who made and kept covenant with Abraham, Isaac, and Jacob.

Despite our technology, human beings prove puny when we come up against the punishing forces of a nature bent by human sin. We may predict disasters, but we can seldom deter them. Where do we go then?

We cry out to Joel's Lord. To the God of Abraham. To our Lord, Jesus Christ. He is forever our help, our hope. The God who forgave us in Christ Jesus will sustain us in all trouble.

WEEK 69 • MONDAY

Joel 2:1–32

GET THE BIG PICTURE

Joel talks often about "the day of the LORD." As you read, keep in mind that this "day" isn't a single, 24-hour period. Instead, it includes the whole of the history in which the Lord is at work. If time is short, focus on Joel 2:12–32.

An Army of Locusts

2 Blow the trumpet in Zion;
sound the alarm on my holy hill.
Let all who live in the land tremble,
for the day of the LORD is coming.
It is close at hand—
2 a day of darkness and gloom,
a day of clouds and blackness.
Like dawn spreading across the mountains
a large and mighty army comes,
such as never was of old
nor ever will be in ages to come.

3 Before them fire devours,
behind them a flame blazes.
Before them the land is like the garden of Eden,
behind them, a desert waste—
nothing escapes them.
4 They have the appearance of horses;
they gallop along like cavalry.
5 With a noise like that of chariots
they leap over the mountaintops,
like a crackling fire consuming stubble,
like a mighty army drawn up for battle.

6 At the sight of them, nations are in anguish;
every face turns pale.
7 They charge like warriors;
they scale walls like soldiers.
They all march in line,
not swerving from their course.
8 They do not jostle each other;
each marches straight ahead.
They plunge through defenses
without breaking ranks.
9 They rush upon the city;
they run along the wall.
They climb into the houses;
like thieves they enter through the windows.

10 Before them the earth shakes,
the sky trembles,
the sun and moon are darkened,
and the stars no longer shine.
11 The LORD thunders
at the head of his army;
his forces are beyond number,
and mighty are those who obey his command.
The day of the LORD is great;
it is dreadful.
Who can endure it?

Rend Your Heart

12 "Even now," declares the LORD,
"return to me with all your heart,
with fasting and weeping and mourning."

13 Rend your heart
and not your garments.
Return to the LORD your God,
for he is gracious and compassionate,
slow to anger and abounding in love,
and he relents from sending calamity.
14 Who knows? He may turn and have pity
and leave behind a blessing—
grain offerings and drink offerings
for the LORD your God.

[15]Blow the trumpet in Zion,
declare a holy fast,
call a sacred assembly.
[16]Gather the people,
consecrate the assembly;
bring together the elders,
gather the children,
those nursing at the breast.
Let the bridegroom leave his room
and the bride her chamber.
[17]Let the priests, who minister before
the LORD,
weep between the temple porch
and the altar.
Let them say, "Spare your people,
O LORD.
Do not make your inheritance an
object of scorn,
a byword among the nations.
Why should they say among the
peoples,
'Where is their God?' "

The LORD's Answer

[18]Then the LORD will be jealous for his
land
and take pity on his people.

[19]The LORD will reply[a] to them:

"I am sending you grain, new wine
and oil,
enough to satisfy you fully;
never again will I make you
an object of scorn to the nations.

[20]"I will drive the northern army far
from you,
pushing it into a parched and
barren land,
with its front columns going into the
eastern sea[b]
and those in the rear into the
western sea.[c]
And its stench will go up;
its smell will rise."

Surely he has done great things.[d]
[21] Be not afraid, O land;
be glad and rejoice.
Surely the LORD has done great
things.
[22] Be not afraid, O wild animals,
for the open pastures are
becoming green.
The trees are bearing their fruit;
the fig tree and the vine yield
their riches.
[23]Be glad, O people of Zion,
rejoice in the LORD your God,
for he has given you
the autumn rains in
righteousness.[e]
He sends you abundant showers,
both autumn and spring rains, as
before.
[24]The threshing floors will be filled
with grain;
the vats will overflow with new
wine and oil.

[25]"I will repay you for the years the
locusts have eaten—
the great locust and the young
locust,
the other locusts and the locust
swarm[f]—
my great army that I sent among
you.
[26]You will have plenty to eat, until you
are full,
and you will praise the name of
the LORD your God,
who has worked wonders for you;
never again will my people be
shamed.
[27]Then you will know that I am in
Israel,
that I am the LORD your God,
and that there is no other;
never again will my people be
shamed.

The Day of the LORD

[28]"And afterward,
I will pour out my Spirit on all
people.
Your sons and daughters will
prophesy,
your old men will dream dreams,
your young men will see visions.

[a]18,19 Or *LORD was jealous . . . / and took pity . . . / [19]The LORD replied* [b]20 That is, the Dead Sea [c]20 That is, the Mediterranean [d]20 Or *rise. / Surely it has done great things."* [e]23 Or / *the teacher for righteousness:* [f]25 The precise meaning of the four Hebrew words used here for locusts is uncertain.

29 Even on my servants, both men and
women,
I will pour out my Spirit in those
days.
30 I will show wonders in the heavens
and on the earth,
blood and fire and billows of
smoke.
31 The sun will be turned to darkness
and the moon to blood
before the coming of the great and
dreadful day of the LORD.
32 And everyone who calls
on the name of the LORD will be
saved;
for on Mount Zion and in Jerusalem
there will be deliverance,
as the LORD has said,
among the survivors
whom the LORD calls.

SHARPEN THE FOCUS

As the stream of life flows by, today is all we have. The moments upstream haven't yet arrived. The moments down stream are passed and gone. We can only step into the current here, now.

As Joel's hearers thought about his words, God's Word, the judgment of Joel 2:1–11 was about to gallop onto the scene. An enemy army would bring horror. That "day" would convince some in Judah that God meant business when He called them to repentance.

At Joel 2:12, the scene shifts. This describes the "day of the Lord" as a day of restoration after repentance. Good Friday made this "day" possible. Possible for Joel and his people. Possible for you and me.

At Joel 2:28, the scene shifts yet again. We step back to see more of the stream: the Lord pouring out His Spirit from Pentecost to the final judgment. And all of this—all of it—is the "day of the LORD."

What's the point? The apostle Paul summarized it well:

[God] says,
"In the time of My favor I heard you,
and in the day of salvation I helped you."
I tell you, now is the time of God's favor, now is the day of salvation.
(2 Corinthians 6:2)

WEEK 69 • TUESDAY

Joel 3:1–21

GET THE BIG PICTURE

Throughout history, most of the world's nations and people have declared war again and again against Christ. As Joel 3 opens, the Lord Himself declares war—against these same rebellious nations. As you read, remember that "Jerusalem," "Zion," and "Judah" often represent God's faithful people of every age—His holy Christian church. If time is short, focus on Joel 3:16–21.

The Nations Judged

3 "In those days and at that time,
when I restore the fortunes of
Judah and Jerusalem,
2 I will gather all nations
and bring them down to the
Valley of Jehoshaphat.[a]
There I will enter into judgment
against them
concerning my inheritance, my
people Israel,
for they scattered my people among
the nations
and divided up my land.
3 They cast lots for my people
and traded boys for prostitutes;
they sold girls for wine
that they might drink.

4 "Now what have you against me,
O Tyre and Sidon and all you regions of
Philistia? Are you repaying me for
something I have done? If you are paying me back, I will swiftly and speedily
return on your own heads what you
have done. 5 For you took my silver and
my gold and carried off my finest treasures to your temples. 6 You sold the people of Judah and Jerusalem to the
Greeks, that you might send them far
from their homeland.
7 "See, I am going to rouse them out of
the places to which you sold them, and
I will return on your own heads what
you have done. 8 I will sell your sons and
daughters to the people of Judah, and
they will sell them to the Sabeans, a nation far away." The LORD has spoken.

9 Proclaim this among the nations:
Prepare for war!
Rouse the warriors!
Let all the fighting men draw near
and attack.
10 Beat your plowshares into swords
and your pruning hooks into
spears.
Let the weakling say,
"I am strong!"
11 Come quickly, all you nations from
every side,
and assemble there.

Bring down your warriors, O LORD!

12 "Let the nations be roused;
let them advance into the Valley of
Jehoshaphat,
for there I will sit
to judge all the nations on every
side.
13 Swing the sickle,
for the harvest is ripe.
Come, trample the grapes,
for the winepress is full
and the vats overflow—
so great is their wickedness!"

14 Multitudes, multitudes
in the valley of decision!
For the day of the LORD is near
in the valley of decision.
15 The sun and moon will be
darkened,
and the stars no longer shine.
16 The LORD will roar from Zion
and thunder from Jerusalem;
the earth and the sky will
tremble.
But the LORD will be a refuge for his
people,
a stronghold for the people of
Israel.

Blessings for God's People

17 "Then you will know that I, the
LORD your God,
dwell in Zion, my holy hill.
Jerusalem will be holy;
never again will foreigners invade
her.

18 "In that day the mountains will drip
new wine,
and the hills will flow with milk;
all the ravines of Judah will run
with water.
A fountain will flow out of the
LORD's house
and will water the valley of
acacias.[b]
19 But Egypt will be desolate,
Edom a desert waste,
because of violence done to the
people of Judah,

[a]2 *Jehoshaphat* means *the LORD judges;* also in verse 12. [b]18 Or *Valley of Shittim*

in whose land they shed innocent
blood.
20 Judah will be inhabited forever
and Jerusalem through all
generations.
21 Their bloodguilt, which I have not
pardoned,
I will pardon."

The LORD dwells in Zion!

SHARPEN THE FOCUS

In the 20th century, more people have endured torture or death for the sake of Christ than in all 19 prior centuries combined. We would like to think of modern culture as "enlightened," but in reality the forces of darkness have never worked more fiercely to destroy the Light of the World and His message of hope.

They will not win. Today's reading makes it clear that the Lord will judge the wicked. Think of it. When God created our world, He *spoke*. His words contained the power that flung the universe into existence. But at the Judgment God will *roar* (Joel 3:16). He will avenge the blood of His saints, from Abel to those faithful martyrs in China and the Middle East being tortured even now. But when He roars, we need not fear. He is our refuge; He is our stronghold (Joel 3:16).

No matter what you face today, remember: the Lord is both *with* and *for* you. He dwells "in Zion" (Joel 3:17). He lives—not on some inaccessible height, but among His people. He has in Jesus pardoned your guilt. Trust Him.

AMOS

Amos takes aim at the nations the Lord will judge. He starts northeast of Israel and Judah and moves in a roughly spiral path around the map until Israel and Judah lie in his crosshairs. As you read, note the refrain: "For three sins . . . even for four" (Amos 1:3). Three plus four is seven, the number of completion or fullness. These nations have broken the Lord's Law and are ripe for judgment. If time is short, focus on Amos 2:6–16.

1 The words of Amos, one of the shepherds of Tekoa—what he saw concerning Israel two years before the earthquake, when Uzziah was king of Judah and Jeroboam son of Jehoash[a] was king of Israel.
2He said:

"The LORD roars from Zion
and thunders from Jerusalem;
the pastures of the shepherds dry up,[b]
and the top of Carmel withers."

Judgment on Israel's Neighbors

3This is what the LORD says:

"For three sins of Damascus,
even for four, I will not turn back
⌞my wrath⌟.
Because she threshed Gilead
with sledges having iron teeth,
4I will send fire upon the house of Hazael
that will consume the fortresses of Ben-Hadad.
5I will break down the gate of Damascus;
I will destroy the king who is in[c]
the Valley of Aven[d]
and the one who holds the scepter
in Beth Eden.
The people of Aram will go into
exile to Kir,"
says the LORD.

6This is what the LORD says:

"For three sins of Gaza,
even for four, I will not turn back
⌞my wrath⌟.
Because she took captive whole communities
and sold them to Edom,
7I will send fire upon the walls of Gaza
that will consume her fortresses.
8I will destroy the king[e] of Ashdod
and the one who holds the scepter
in Ashkelon.
I will turn my hand against Ekron,
till the last of the Philistines is dead,"
says the Sovereign LORD.

9This is what the LORD says:

"For three sins of Tyre,
even for four, I will not turn back
⌞my wrath⌟.

[a]1 Hebrew *Joash,* a variant of *Jehoash* [b]2 Or *shepherds mourn* [c]5 Or *the inhabitants of* [d]5 *Aven* means *wickedness.* [e]8 Or *inhabitants*

Because she sold whole
communities of captives to
Edom,
disregarding a treaty of
brotherhood,
10 I will send fire upon the walls of Tyre
that will consume her fortresses."

11 This is what the LORD says:

"For three sins of Edom,
even for four, I will not turn back
⌊my wrath⌋.
Because he pursued his brother with
a sword,
stifling all compassion,[a]
because his anger raged continually
and his fury flamed unchecked,
12 I will send fire upon Teman
that will consume the fortresses of
Bozrah."

13 This is what the LORD says:

"For three sins of Ammon,
even for four, I will not turn back
⌊my wrath⌋.
Because he ripped open the
pregnant women of Gilead
in order to extend his borders,
14 I will set fire to the walls of Rabbah
that will consume her fortresses
amid war cries on the day of battle,
amid violent winds on a stormy
day.
15 Her king[b] will go into exile,
he and his officials together,"
says the LORD.

2 This is what the LORD says:

"For three sins of Moab,
even for four, I will not turn back
⌊my wrath⌋.
Because he burned, as if to lime,
the bones of Edom's king,
2 I will send fire upon Moab
that will consume the fortresses of
Kerioth.[c]
Moab will go down in great tumult
amid war cries and the blast of the
trumpet.
3 I will destroy her ruler
and kill all her officials with him,"
says the LORD.

4 This is what the LORD says:

"For three sins of Judah,
even for four, I will not turn back
⌊my wrath⌋.
Because they have rejected the law
of the LORD
and have not kept his decrees,
because they have been led astray
by false gods,[d]
the gods[e] their ancestors
followed,
5 I will send fire upon Judah
that will consume the fortresses of
Jerusalem."

Judgment on Israel

6 This is what the LORD says:

"For three sins of Israel,
even for four, I will not turn back
⌊my wrath⌋.
They sell the righteous for silver,
and the needy for a pair of
sandals.
7 They trample on the heads of the
poor
as upon the dust of the ground
and deny justice to the
oppressed.
Father and son use the same girl
and so profane my holy name.
8 They lie down beside every altar
on garments taken in pledge.
In the house of their god
they drink wine taken as fines.

9 "I destroyed the Amorite before
them,
though he was tall as the cedars
and strong as the oaks.
I destroyed his fruit above
and his roots below.

10 "I brought you up out of Egypt,
and I led you forty years in the
desert
to give you the land of the
Amorites.
11 I also raised up prophets from
among your sons

[a]11 Or *sword / and destroyed his allies* [b]15 Or / *Molech*; Hebrew *malcam* [c]2 Or *of her cities* [d]4 Or *by lies* [e]4 Or *lies*

and Nazirites from among your
young men.
Is this not true, people of Israel?"
declares the LORD.
12 "But you made the Nazirites drink
wine
and commanded the prophets not
to prophesy.

13 "Now then, I will crush you
as a cart crushes when loaded
with grain.
14 The swift will not escape,
the strong will not muster their
strength,
and the warrior will not save his
life.
15 The archer will not stand his
ground,
the fleet-footed soldier will not get
away,
and the horseman will not save
his life.
16 Even the bravest warriors
will flee naked on that day,"
declares the LORD.

SHARPEN THE FOCUS

Suppose Amos were to take aim at our society. Look at the specific charges he makes against Israel in chapter 2. How do people in our world commit these same sins today? (see Amos 2:6–8, 12.)

Israel's sins were bad enough. But worse, she committed them despite the Lord's great goodness to her (Amos 2:9–11). Her sins were a slap in the face of the God who had shown her so much tenderness and love.

Look at the list of Israel's sins. Are we any better? When was the last time you paid part of a utility bill for someone who's poor? How have your words or actions at times contributed to the decline of sexual morality? Do you ever worship "idols" of silver and gold? Do you ever despise God's Word by refusing to listen to or obey it?

Amos's charges are as fresh as this morning's E-mail and every bit as personal. The noose that he hung around Israel's neck belongs on yours and mine as well. Thank God for Jesus! Thank God for Good Friday and for Easter! And Lord help us to live holy, kind lives of witness to those around us. ☼

WEEK 69 • THURSDAY

Amos 3:1–15

GET THE BIG PICTURE

Rich in things; poor in soul. Those two short statements about sum up conditions in Israel when the Lord sent Amos to preach to them. As you read, look for evidence of Israel's wealth and her poverty. If time is short, focus on Amos 3:1–8.

Witnesses Summoned Against Israel

3 Hear this word the LORD has spoken against you, O people of Israel—against the whole family I brought up out of Egypt:

[2]"You only have I chosen
of all the families of the earth;
therefore I will punish you
for all your sins."
[3]Do two walk together
unless they have agreed to do so?
[4]Does a lion roar in the thicket
when he has no prey?
Does he growl in his den
when he has caught nothing?
[5]Does a bird fall into a trap on the ground
where no snare has been set?
Does a trap spring up from the earth
when there is nothing to catch?
[6]When a trumpet sounds in a city,
do not the people tremble?
When disaster comes to a city,
has not the LORD caused it?
[7]Surely the Sovereign LORD does nothing
without revealing his plan
to his servants the prophets.

[8]The lion has roared—
who will not fear?
The Sovereign LORD has spoken—
who can but prophesy?

[9]Proclaim to the fortresses of Ashdod
and to the fortresses of Egypt:
"Assemble yourselves on the mountains of Samaria;
see the great unrest within her
and the oppression among her people."

[10]"They do not know how to do right," declares the LORD,
"who hoard plunder and loot in their fortresses."

[11]Therefore this is what the Sovereign LORD says:

"An enemy will overrun the land;
he will pull down your strongholds
and plunder your fortresses."

[12]This is what the LORD says:

"As a shepherd saves from the lion's mouth
only two leg bones or a piece of an ear,
so will the Israelites be saved,
those who sit in Samaria
on the edge of their beds
and in Damascus on their couches.[a]"

[13]"Hear this and testify against the house of Jacob," declares the Lord, the LORD God Almighty.

[14]"On the day I punish Israel for her sins,
I will destroy the altars of Bethel;
the horns of the altar will be cut off
and fall to the ground.
[15]I will tear down the winter house
along with the summer house;
the houses adorned with ivory will be destroyed
and the mansions will be demolished,"
declares the LORD.

[a]*12* The meaning of the Hebrew for this line is uncertain.

SHARPEN THE FOCUS

To understand the ways of God, we need to grasp the dream of His heart—from Eden on, He wanted a family. That's why He called Abram (Genesis 12:1–3). That's why He rescued the people of Israel when they slaved for the Egyptians (Amos 3:1).

Try to envision the Lord's intent. A breathtakingly beautiful planet. An all-powerful Creator-God to watch over and protect His people. Relationships of care, compassion, and joy between all who lived here.

Even as sinners, we can still see how wonderful that kind of family would be. But damaged as we are by sin, we can never, ever reclaim the paradise we've lost. Like Israel of old, we substitute other things. Amos names them—couches, beds, homes—maybe even a winter house and a summer cottage (Amos 3:12, 15)!

Bit by bit the little luxuries of life begin to numb the pain of our loss. Israel's numbness broke God's heart. Our numbness does too.

That's why He sent Jesus to be our Brother. The mansions of heaven were meant from eternity to ring with the laughter of God's children. God's Son died so that Adam's sons and daughters could live forever in joy. In Him, we now have become the family of God (Ephesians 3:14–20).

WEEK 69 • FRIDAY

Amos 4:1—5:27

Amos continues his condemnation of materialism and injustice. He also adds God's disgust at the worship-by-rote His people offer Him. As you read, look for the Lord's radical response to those who fail to worship wholeheartedly. If time is short, focus on Amos 5:1–27.

Israel Has Not Returned to God

4 Hear this word, you cows of
Bashan on Mount Samaria,
you women who oppress the poor
and crush the needy
and say to your husbands, "Bring
us some drinks!"
2 The Sovereign LORD has sworn by
his holiness:
"The time will surely come
when you will be taken away with
hooks,
the last of you with fishhooks.
3 You will each go straight out
through breaks in the wall,
and you will be cast out toward
Harmon,[a]"
declares the LORD.
4 "Go to Bethel and sin;
go to Gilgal and sin yet more.
Bring your sacrifices every morning,
your tithes every three years.[b]
5 Burn leavened bread as a thank
offering
and brag about your freewill
offerings—
boast about them, you Israelites,
for this is what you love to do,"
declares the Sovereign
LORD.

6 "I gave you empty stomachs[c] in
every city
and lack of bread in every town,
yet you have not returned to me,"
declares the LORD.

7 "I also withheld rain from you
when the harvest was still three
months away.
I sent rain on one town,
but withheld it from another.
One field had rain;
another had none and dried up.

[a]3 Masoretic Text; with a different word division of the Hebrew (see Septuagint) *out, O mountain of oppression* [b]4 Or *tithes on the third day* [c]6 Hebrew *you cleanness of teeth*

[8]People staggered from town to town
for water
but did not get enough to drink,
yet you have not returned to me,"
declares the LORD.

[9]"Many times I struck your gardens
and vineyards,
I struck them with blight and
mildew.
Locusts devoured your fig and olive
trees,
yet you have not returned to me,"
declares the LORD.

[10]"I sent plagues among you
as I did to Egypt.
I killed your young men with the
sword,
along with your captured
horses.
I filled your nostrils with the stench
of your camps,
yet you have not returned to me,"
declares the LORD.

[11]"I overthrew some of you
as I[a] overthrew Sodom and
Gomorrah.
You were like a burning stick
snatched from the fire,
yet you have not returned to me,"
declares the LORD.

[12]"Therefore this is what I will do to
you, Israel,
and because I will do this to you,
prepare to meet your God,
O Israel."

[13]He who forms the mountains,
creates the wind,
and reveals his thoughts to man,
he who turns dawn to darkness,
and treads the high places of the
earth—
the LORD God Almighty is his
name.

A Lament and Call to Repentance

5 Hear this word, O house of Israel, this lament I take up concerning you:

[2]"Fallen is Virgin Israel,
never to rise again,
deserted in her own land,
with no one to lift her up."

[3]This is what the Sovereign LORD says:

"The city that marches out a
thousand strong for Israel
will have only a hundred left;
the town that marches out a
hundred strong
will have only ten left."

[4]This is what the LORD says to the house of Israel:

"Seek me and live;
[5] do not seek Bethel,
do not go to Gilgal,
do not journey to Beersheba.
For Gilgal will surely go into exile,
and Bethel will be reduced to
nothing.[b]"

[6]Seek the LORD and live,
or he will sweep through the
house of Joseph like a fire;
it will devour,
and Bethel will have no one to
quench it.

[7]You who turn justice into bitterness
and cast righteousness to the
ground
[8](he who made the Pleiades and
Orion,
who turns blackness into dawn
and darkens day into night,
who calls for the waters of the sea
and pours them out over the face
of the land—
the LORD is his name—
[9]he flashes destruction on the
stronghold
and brings the fortified city to
ruin),
[10]you hate the one who reproves in
court
and despise him who tells the
truth.

[11]You trample on the poor
and force him to give you grain.

[a]11 Hebrew *God* [b]5 Or *grief*; or *wickedness*; Hebrew *aven*, a reference to Beth Aven (a derogatory name for Bethel)

Therefore, though you have built
stone mansions,
you will not live in them;
though you have planted lush
vineyards,
you will not drink their wine.
12 For I know how many are your
offenses
and how great your sins.

You oppress the righteous and take
bribes
and you deprive the poor of
justice in the courts.
13 Therefore the prudent man keeps
quiet in such times,
for the times are evil.

14 Seek good, not evil,
that you may live.
Then the LORD God Almighty will
be with you,
just as you say he is.
15 Hate evil, love good;
maintain justice in the courts.
Perhaps the LORD God Almighty will
have mercy
on the remnant of Joseph.

16 Therefore this is what the Lord, the
LORD God Almighty, says:

"There will be wailing in all the
streets
and cries of anguish in every
public square.
The farmers will be summoned to
weep
and the mourners to wail.
17 There will be wailing in all the
vineyards,
for I will pass through your midst,"
says the LORD.

The Day of the LORD

18 Woe to you who long
for the day of the LORD!
Why do you long for the day of the
LORD?
That day will be darkness, not
light.
19 It will be as though a man fled from
a lion
only to meet a bear,
as though he entered his house
and rested his hand on the wall
only to have a snake bite him.
20 Will not the day of the LORD be
darkness, not light—
pitch-dark, without a ray of
brightness?

21 "I hate, I despise your religious
feasts;
I cannot stand your assemblies.
22 Even though you bring me burnt
offerings and grain offerings,
I will not accept them.
Though you bring choice fellowship
offerings,[a]
I will have no regard for them.
23 Away with the noise of your songs!
I will not listen to the music of
your harps.
24 But let justice roll on like a river,
righteousness like a never-failing
stream!

25 "Did you bring me sacrifices and
offerings
forty years in the desert, O house
of Israel?
26 You have lifted up the shrine of your
king,
the pedestal of your idols,
the star of your god[b]—
which you made for yourselves.
27 Therefore I will send you into exile
beyond Damascus,"
says the LORD, whose name is
God Almighty.

[a]22 Traditionally *peace offerings* [b]26 Or *lifted up Sakkuth your king / and Kaiwan your idols, / your star-gods;* Septuagint *lifted up the shrine of Molech / and the star of your god Rephan, / their idols*

SHARPEN THE FOCUS

The two or three credit reporting agencies in North America almost surely have your name in their files. They know where you live and where you work. They know which credit cards line your wallet, what you owe and to whom you owe it. They even know about that time when you forgot to mail the check to your electric company.

Scary, isn't it? But read Amos 5:12. God says:

> *For I know how many are your offenses and how great your sins.*

Even if you've escaped, somehow, the computer systems of "the great god credit," the Lord has your name in His files. He knows where you live and how much cash you carry in your wallet. More to the point, He knows what you owe—in particular, what you owe Him.

Ancient Israel thought she could buy God off by showing up for worship to nod toward His altar and sing a few songs (Amos 4:4–5; 5:22–23). But the Lord wasn't so easily satisfied. In fact, nothing we can do or say would ever cover our debt. How good, then, to know that our Savior paid the debt we owed Him! He Himself assumed our guilt on Calvary and now our account is paid in full!

WEEK 69 • SATURDAY

Amos 6:1–14

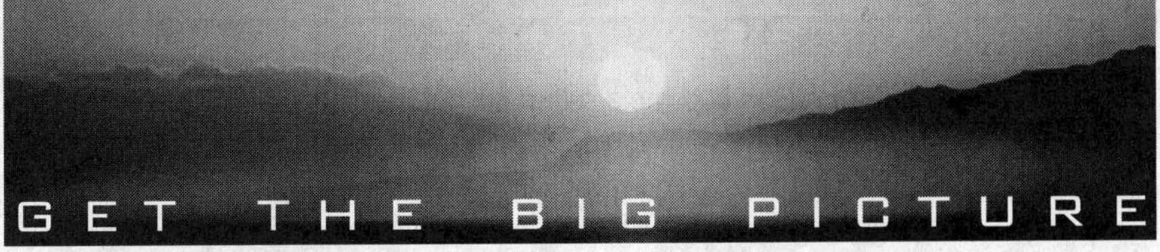

GET THE BIG PICTURE

The Lord wants only good things for His people. He does not begrudge the blessings He gives. But when is it wrong to be at ease or complacent (Amos 6:1)? Think about that as you read today. If time is short, focus on Amos 6:1–10.

Woe to the Complacent

6 Woe to you who are
complacent in Zion,
and to you who feel secure on
Mount Samaria,
you notable men of the foremost
nation,
to whom the people of Israel
come!
2 Go to Calneh and look at it;
go from there to great Hamath,
and then go down to Gath in
Philistia.
Are they better off than your two
kingdoms?
Is their land larger than yours?
3 You put off the evil day
and bring near a reign of terror.
4 You lie on beds inlaid with ivory
and lounge on your couches.
You dine on choice lambs
and fattened calves.
5 You strum away on your harps like
David
and improvise on musical
instruments.
6 You drink wine by the bowlful
and use the finest lotions,
but you do not grieve over the
ruin of Joseph.
7 Therefore you will be among the
first to go into exile;
your feasting and lounging will
end.

The LORD Abhors the Pride of Israel

8 The Sovereign LORD has sworn by himself—the LORD God Almighty declares:

"I abhor the pride of Jacob
and detest his fortresses;
I will deliver up the city
and everything in it."

[9]If ten men are left in one house, they too will die. [10]And if a relative who is to burn the bodies comes to carry them out of the house and asks anyone still hiding there, "Is anyone with you?" and he says, "No," then he will say, "Hush! We must not mention the name of the LORD."

[11]For the LORD has given the
command,
and he will smash the great house
into pieces
and the small house into bits.
[12]Do horses run on the rocky crags?
Does one plow there with oxen?
But you have turned justice into
poison
and the fruit of righteousness into
bitterness—
[13]you who rejoice in the conquest of
Lo Debar[a]
and say, "Did we not take
Karnaim[b] by our own
strength?"

[14]For the LORD God Almighty
declares,
"I will stir up a nation against you,
O house of Israel,
that will oppress you all the way
from Lebo[c] Hamath to the valley
of the Arabah."

[a]13 *Lo Debar* means *nothing.* [b]13 *Karnaim* means *horns; horn* here symbolizes strength.
[c]14 Or *from the entrance to*

SHARPEN THE FOCUS

When does a blessing from God become a selfish luxury? Amos blasts God's people—then and now—for lying "on beds inlaid with ivory," for eating lamb chops and steaks (Amos 6:4), for enjoying good music (Amos 6:5), and savoring life's luxuries (Amos 6:6).

Reading this, we might begin to believe that all luxuries somehow offend God. And yet, He's the one who richly provides us with everything for our enjoyment (1 Timothy 6:17). When *does* a blessing from God become selfish? Look at the rest of what Paul wrote to Timothy (and to us!):

> *Command those who are rich in this present world not to be arrogant nor to put their hope in wealth, which is so uncertain, but to put their hope in God, who richly provides us with everything for our enjoyment. Command them to do good, to be rich in good deeds, and to be generous and willing to share . . . so that they may take hold of the life that is truly life.* (1 Timothy 6:17–19)

Amos' listeners really enjoyed nothing because of their self-centeredness. The children of God Paul describes really enjoy just about everything. At heart, the first set of people are cold and cynical. At heart, the second group are thankful and compassionate. The true life they have in Christ has made this possible.

Jesus has given you this true life, too. Enjoy it today!

WEEK 70 • MONDAY

Amos 7:1–17

Amos earnestly prays for the people of the Lord, yet he is persecuted by them. He wasn't the first prophet to be shabbily treated. Nor was he the last. As you read, think about how you might react. If time is short, focus on Amos 7:14–17.

Locusts, Fire and a Plumb Line

7 This is what the Sovereign LORD
showed me: He was preparing
swarms of locusts after the king's share
had been harvested and just as the second crop was coming up. 2When they
had stripped the land clean, I cried out,
"Sovereign LORD, forgive! How can Jacob survive? He is so small!"
3So the LORD relented.
"This will not happen," the LORD
said.
4This is what the Sovereign LORD
showed me: The Sovereign LORD was
calling for judgment by fire; it dried up
the great deep and devoured the land.
5Then I cried out, "Sovereign LORD, I
beg you, stop! How can Jacob survive?
He is so small!"
6So the LORD relented.
"This will not happen either," the Sovereign LORD said.

7This is what he showed me: The
Lord was standing by a wall that had
been built true to plumb, with a plumb
line in his hand. 8And the LORD asked
me, "What do you see, Amos?"
"A plumb line," I replied.
Then the Lord said, "Look, I am setting a plumb line among my people Israel; I will spare them no longer.

9"The high places of Isaac will be
destroyed
and the sanctuaries of Israel will
be ruined;
with my sword I will rise against
the house of Jeroboam."

Amos and Amaziah

10Then Amaziah the priest of Bethel
sent a message to Jeroboam king of Israel: "Amos is raising a conspiracy
against you in the very heart of Israel.
The land cannot bear all his words. 11For
this is what Amos is saying:

" 'Jeroboam will die by the sword,
and Israel will surely go into
exile,
away from their native land.' "

12Then Amaziah said to Amos, "Get
out, you seer! Go back to the land of Judah. Earn your bread there and do your
prophesying there. 13Don't prophesy
anymore at Bethel, because this is the
king's sanctuary and the temple of the
kingdom."
14Amos answered Amaziah, "I was
neither a prophet nor a prophet's son,
but I was a shepherd, and I also took
care of sycamore-fig trees. 15But the
LORD took me from tending the flock
and said to me, 'Go, prophesy to my
people Israel.' 16Now then, hear the
word of the LORD. You say,

" 'Do not prophesy against Israel,
and stop preaching against the
house of Isaac.'

17"Therefore this is what the LORD
says:

" 'Your wife will become a prostitute
in the city,
and your sons and daughters will
fall by the sword.

Your land will be measured and
divided up,
and you yourself will die in a
pagan[a] country.
And Israel will certainly go into
exile,
away from their native
land.' "

SHARPEN THE FOCUS

Abraham Lincoln. Franklin Roosevelt. Alexander the Great. Albert Einstein. William Shakespeare. Christopher Columbus. The list of people who have shaped the world we now live in goes on and on. For good or evil, those who hold high office or command large armies or have great talent or think new thoughts can change the course of history.

And yet, the power to influence world events belongs most of all to God's children. Do you doubt it? Then read Amos 7:1–6. In brief, the Lord showed His servant a judgment Israel deserved. But Amos prayed and "the LORD relented" (Amos 7:3, 6).

Our Lord could carry on His purposes for our world without us. But in grace He has chosen to make us partners with Himself. He listens—carefully—to what we say. We have influence where it really counts—in the courts of heaven. What an honor! One, of course, that we do not deserve. Still, because of Jesus' death for us, an honor we can claim and use with holy boldness.

Pray today for "Israel," Christ's church. Ask that it grow in both numbers and commitment to our Lord Jesus.

WEEK 70 • TUESDAY

Amos 8:1–14

GET THE BIG PICTURE

When a person believes that money will buy true, unending happiness, no amount of money is large enough. That's one temptation into which most of ancient Israel had fallen. Look for evidence of that as you read. If time is short, focus on Amos 8:9–14.

A Basket of Ripe Fruit

8 This is what the Sovereign LORD
showed me: a basket of ripe fruit.
2 "What do you see, Amos?" he asked.
"A basket of ripe fruit," I answered.
Then the LORD said to me, "The time
is ripe for my people Israel; I will spare
them no longer.
3 "In that day," declares the Sovereign
LORD, "the songs in the temple will turn
to wailing.[b] Many, many bodies—flung
everywhere! Silence!"

4 Hear this, you who trample the
needy
and do away with the poor of the
land,

5 saying,

"When will the New Moon be over
that we may sell grain,
and the Sabbath be ended

[a]17 Hebrew *an unclean* [b]3 Or *"the temple singers will wail*

that we may market wheat?"—
skimping the measure,
boosting the price
and cheating with dishonest
scales,
6 buying the poor with silver
and the needy for a pair of
sandals,
selling even the sweepings with
the wheat.

7 The LORD has sworn by the Pride of
Jacob: "I will never forget anything they
have done.

8 "Will not the land tremble for this,
and all who live in it mourn?
The whole land will rise like the Nile;
it will be stirred up and then sink
like the river of Egypt.

9 "In that day," declares the Sovereign
LORD,

"I will make the sun go down at
noon
and darken the earth in broad
daylight.
10 I will turn your religious feasts into
mourning
and all your singing into weeping.
I will make all of you wear sackcloth
and shave your heads.
I will make that time like mourning
for an only son
and the end of it like a bitter day.

11 "The days are coming," declares the
Sovereign LORD,
"when I will send a famine
through the land—
not a famine of food or a thirst for
water,
but a famine of hearing the words
of the LORD.
12 Men will stagger from sea to sea
and wander from north to east,
searching for the word of the LORD,
but they will not find it.

13 "In that day

"the lovely young women and
strong young men
will faint because of thirst.
14 They who swear by the shame[a] of
Samaria,
or say, 'As surely as your god lives,
O Dan,'
or, 'As surely as the god[b] of
Beersheba lives'—
they will fall,
never to rise again."

[a]14 Or *by Ashima*; or *by the idol* [b]14 Or *power*

SHARPEN THE FOCUS

The worst judgment God can visit on impenitent sinners is to give them what they want. The people of Israel and her leaders wanted Amos to stop proclaiming God's Word (Amos 7:12, 16). They wanted God's silence, and He will soon grant it (Amos 8:11–12).

We want God's silence too sometimes. We want Him to leave us alone with our greed. We want Him to let us put in one more 70-hour work week so we can impress the boss or the client. We want Him to stop stirring our conscience when we check out yet another violent or suggestive movie at the video store. We want Him to keep His ideas about caring for the poor to Himself.

But if we get God's silence, we can be sure we have gotten His harshest judgment. Spiritual famine and thirst lead ultimately to spiritual death. God forbid that we would harden our hearts and close our ears to the point that He leaves us in silence.

The Good News is that our Lord has spoken and continues to speak to us in Jesus, our Savior. He warns us of our sins that hurt us and deny us the joy He wants us to have. But when He speaks, He speaks most of all about His grace toward us. The blood of His Son has washed away all our sins. Knowing this, we can listen—and obey.

WEEK 70 • WEDNESDAY

Amos 9:1–15

GET THE BIG PICTURE

Imagine yourself trapped in a burning building. If you can do that, you have a picture of the panic soon to fall on all Israel. Look for the people's frantic escape attempts as you read. But notice most of all the heart of the Lord, committed to His covenant promise to bring a Savior from the "tent" of David (Amos 9:11). If time is short, focus on Amos 9:8–15.

Israel to Be Destroyed

9 I saw the Lord standing by the altar, and he said:

"Strike the tops of the pillars
so that the thresholds shake.
Bring them down on the heads of all the people;
those who are left I will kill with the sword.
Not one will get away,
none will escape.
2 Though they dig down to the depths of the grave,[a]
from there my hand will take them.
Though they climb up to the heavens,
from there I will bring them down.
3 Though they hide themselves on the top of Carmel,
there I will hunt them down and seize them.
Though they hide from me at the bottom of the sea,
there I will command the serpent to bite them.
4 Though they are driven into exile by their enemies,
there I will command the sword to slay them.
I will fix my eyes upon them
for evil and not for good."

5 The Lord, the LORD Almighty,
he who touches the earth and it melts,
and all who live in it mourn—
the whole land rises like the Nile,
then sinks like the river of Egypt—
6 he who builds his lofty palace[b] in the heavens
and sets its foundation[c] on the earth,
who calls for the waters of the sea
and pours them out over the face of the land—
the LORD is his name.

7 "Are not you Israelites
the same to me as the Cushites[d]?"
declares the LORD.
"Did I not bring Israel up from Egypt,
the Philistines from Caphtor[e]
and the Arameans from Kir?

8 "Surely the eyes of the Sovereign LORD
are on the sinful kingdom.
I will destroy it
from the face of the earth—
yet I will not totally destroy
the house of Jacob,"
declares the LORD.
9 "For I will give the command,
and I will shake the house of Israel
among all the nations
as grain is shaken in a sieve,
and not a pebble will reach the ground.

[a]2 Hebrew *to Sheol* [b]6 The meaning of the Hebrew for this phrase is uncertain. [c]6 The meaning of the Hebrew for this word is uncertain. [d]7 That is, people from the upper Nile region [e]7 That is, Crete

[10]All the sinners among my people
will die by the sword,
all those who say,
'Disaster will not overtake or meet
us.'

Israel's Restoration

[11]"In that day I will restore
David's fallen tent.
I will repair its broken places,
restore its ruins,
and build it as it used to be,
[12]so that they may possess the
remnant of Edom
and all the nations that bear my
name,[a]"
declares the LORD,
who will do these things.

[13]"The days are coming," declares the
LORD,

"when the reaper will be overtaken
by the plowman
and the planter by the one
treading grapes.
New wine will drip from the
mountains
and flow from all the hills.
[14]I will bring back my exiled[b] people
Israel;
they will rebuild the ruined cities
and live in them.
They will plant vineyards and drink
their wine;
they will make gardens and eat
their fruit.
[15]I will plant Israel in their own
land,
never again to be uprooted
from the land I have given them,"
says the LORD your God.

[a]12 Hebrew; Septuagint *so that the remnant of men / and all the nations that bear my name may seek* ⌞*the Lord*⌟ [b]14 Or *will restore the fortunes of my*

SHARPEN THE FOCUS

A missionary who once served in the region below the Sahara Desert tells of the pain of famine. Food would become so scarce, babies' bellies would bloat. Children would grow too weak to cry. In spring the farmers would scatter their seed on the ground, weeping as they went. They needed a crop, but how it hurt to "throw away" grain that could have been cooked to make two or three good meals.

In chapter 8, Amos told about a famine, one in which opportunities to hear the Word of God would dry up. Now he paints a different picture, a picture of abundance. So freely will the fields yield fruit that those who harvest won't be able to finish the task before it's time again to plow and plant (Amos 9:13).

Notice how the prophet connects this abundance to the promise that the Lord will set up David's "tent" (Amos 9:11). God had promised to establish an eternal dynasty through the family of David (1 Chronicles 17:3–14). In the Messiah, Jesus, our God kept that promise. He is the Bread of Life whose coming has brought us, not mere crumbs to sustain us, but a banquet feast of all God's goodness. In Him, our spiritual famine has ended. In Him, the banquet has begun.

OBADIAH

WEEK 70 • THURSDAY

Obadiah 1–21

Because Edom rejoiced when Jerusalem fell, the Lord would bring judgment to Edom. This book, the shortest in the Old Testament, can be read on two levels: First, as we consider the earthly nations of Edom and Judah; second, as we think about all the enemies of Yahweh and of His chosen people. The point remains the same. Look for it when you get to Obadiah 21. If time is short, focus on Obadiah 17–21.

1 The vision of Obadiah.

This is what the Sovereign LORD says
about Edom—

We have heard a message from the
LORD:
An envoy was sent to the nations
to say,
"Rise, and let us go against her for
battle"—
2 "See, I will make you small among
the nations;
you will be utterly despised.
3 The pride of your heart has deceived
you,
you who live in the clefts of the
rocks[a]
and make your home on the
heights,
you who say to yourself,
'Who can bring me down to the
ground?'
4 Though you soar like the eagle
and make your nest among the
stars,
from there I will bring you down,"
declares the LORD.
5 "If thieves came to you,
if robbers in the night—
Oh, what a disaster awaits you—
would they not steal only as much
as they wanted?
If grape pickers came to you,
would they not leave a few
grapes?
6 But how Esau will be ransacked,
his hidden treasures pillaged!
7 All your allies will force you to the
border;
your friends will deceive and
overpower you;
those who eat your bread will set a
trap for you,[b]
but you will not detect it.
8 "In that day," declares the LORD,
"will I not destroy the wise men of
Edom,
men of understanding in the
mountains of Esau?
9 Your warriors, O Teman, will be
terrified,
and everyone in Esau's mountains
will be cut down in the slaughter.
10 Because of the violence against your
brother Jacob,
you will be covered with shame;

[a]3 Or *of Sela* [b]7 The meaning of the Hebrew for this clause is uncertain.

you will be destroyed forever.
11 On the day you stood aloof
while strangers carried off his wealth
and foreigners entered his gates
and cast lots for Jerusalem,
you were like one of them.
12 You should not look down on your brother
in the day of his misfortune,
nor rejoice over the people of Judah
in the day of their destruction,
nor boast so much
in the day of their trouble.
13 You should not march through the gates of my people
in the day of their disaster,
nor look down on them in their calamity
in the day of their disaster,
nor seize their wealth
in the day of their disaster.
14 You should not wait at the crossroads
to cut down their fugitives,
nor hand over their survivors
in the day of their trouble.

15 "The day of the LORD is near
for all nations.
As you have done, it will be done to you;
your deeds will return upon your own head.
16 Just as you drank on my holy hill,
so all the nations will drink continually;
they will drink and drink
and be as if they had never been.
17 But on Mount Zion will be deliverance;
it will be holy,
and the house of Jacob
will possess its inheritance.
18 The house of Jacob will be a fire
and the house of Joseph a flame;
the house of Esau will be stubble,
and they will set it on fire and consume it.
There will be no survivors
from the house of Esau."
The LORD has spoken.

19 People from the Negev will occupy
the mountains of Esau,
and people from the foothills will possess
the land of the Philistines.
They will occupy the fields of Ephraim and Samaria,
and Benjamin will possess Gilead.
20 This company of Israelite exiles who are in Canaan
will possess ⌊the land⌋ as far as Zarephath;
the exiles from Jerusalem who are in Sepharad
will possess the towns of the Negev.
21 Deliverers will go up on[a] Mount Zion
to govern the mountains of Esau.
And the kingdom will be the LORD's.

[a]21 Or *from*

SHARPEN THE FOCUS

When robbers break into a house, they seldom take everything. When the thieves drive away, a few pictures will usually be left hanging on the walls. When farm workers harvest grapes, they don't pick every single grape off the vines. A week or so later, visitors who hike through the field can usually find a snack.

But, thunders Obadiah, not so much as a stick of furniture, not so much as a single dried up grape will remain after God's judgment falls on Judah's arrogant enemies (Obadiah 5–6).

Still today, the wicked rage against God's people. Still today, the "wise" of this world ridicule the Lord's people. But soon, everyone who holds citizenship in Edom will disappear from sight (Obadiah 16). The kingdom is—even now—the Lord's (Obadiah 21). And—even now—there is salvation, deliverance, on Mt. Zion—Christ's holy church.

That's Good News for us, because we once held citizenship in Edom. We were by nature the sworn enemies of the Lord. But our Savior's death made a change of allegiance possible. Now heaven's records say of you and of me by faith in Jesus:

This one and that one were born in [Zion]. (Psalm 87:5)

JONAH

WEEK 70 • FRIDAY

Jonah 1:1—2:10

GET THE BIG PICTURE

The very familiar account of Jonah and the great fish has been told and retold. As you read it now, ask yourself who needed God's gift of repentance more–pagan Nineveh or the Lord's stubborn prophet, Jonah. If time is short, focus on Jonah 1:1–17.

Jonah Flees From the LORD

1 The word of the LORD came to Jonah son of Amittai: 2"Go to the great
city of Nineveh and preach against it,
because its wickedness has come up
before me."
3But Jonah ran away from the LORD
and headed for Tarshish. He went down
to Joppa, where he found a ship bound
for that port. After paying the fare, he
went aboard and sailed for Tarshish to
flee from the LORD.
4Then the LORD sent a great wind on
the sea, and such a violent storm arose
that the ship threatened to break up. 5All
the sailors were afraid and each cried
out to his own god. And they threw the
cargo into the sea to lighten the ship.
But Jonah had gone below deck,
where he lay down and fell into a deep
sleep. 6The captain went to him and
said, "How can you sleep? Get up and
call on your god! Maybe he will take notice of us, and we will not perish."
7Then the sailors said to each other,
"Come, let us cast lots to find out who
is responsible for this calamity." They
cast lots and the lot fell on Jonah.
8So they asked him, "Tell us, who is responsible for making all this trouble for
us? What do you do? Where do you
come from? What is your country? From
what people are you?"
9He answered, "I am a Hebrew and I
worship the LORD, the God of heaven,
who made the sea and the land."
10This terrified them and they asked,
"What have you done?" (They knew he
was running away from the LORD, because he had already told them so.)
11The sea was getting rougher and
rougher. So they asked him, "What
should we do to you to make the sea
calm down for us?"
12"Pick me up and throw me into the
sea," he replied, "and it will become
calm. I know that it is my fault that this
great storm has come upon you."
13Instead, the men did their best to
row back to land. But they could not, for
the sea grew even wilder than before.
14Then they cried to the LORD, "O LORD,
please do not let us die for taking this
man's life. Do not hold us accountable
for killing an innocent man, for you,
O LORD, have done as you pleased."
15Then they took Jonah and threw him
overboard, and the raging sea grew
calm. 16At this the men greatly feared the
LORD, and they offered a sacrifice to the
LORD and made vows to him.
17But the LORD provided a great fish

to swallow Jonah, and Jonah was inside the fish three days and three nights.

Jonah's Prayer

2 From inside the fish Jonah prayed to the LORD his God. [2]He said:

"In my distress I called to the LORD,
and he answered me.
From the depths of the grave[a] I called for help,
and you listened to my cry.
[3]You hurled me into the deep,
into the very heart of the seas,
and the currents swirled about me;
all your waves and breakers
swept over me.
[4]I said, 'I have been banished
from your sight;
yet I will look again
toward your holy temple.'
[5]The engulfing waters threatened me,[b]
the deep surrounded me;
seaweed was wrapped around my head.
[6]To the roots of the mountains I sank down;
the earth beneath barred me in forever.
But you brought my life up from the pit,
O LORD my God.

[7]"When my life was ebbing away,
I remembered you, LORD,
and my prayer rose to you,
to your holy temple.

[8]"Those who cling to worthless idols
forfeit the grace that could be theirs.
[9]But I, with a song of thanksgiving,
will sacrifice to you.
What I have vowed I will make good.
Salvation comes from the LORD."

[10]And the LORD commanded the fish, and it vomited Jonah onto dry land.

[a]2 Hebrew *Sheol* [b]5 Or *waters were at my throat*

SHARPEN THE FOCUS

The sea and the wind obeyed the Lord. So did the fish and the lots the sailors cast. As we shall see, even the hated Assyrians listened to the Word of God, repented, and obeyed.

But when God said, "Go to Nineveh," Jonah set sail for Tarshish, a city several thousand miles in the opposite direction. Only the Lord's "course correction" brought Jonah back into the area of the mission God had set aside for him.

Jonah disobeyed for the same reasons you and I cringe when we hear Jesus tell us to pray for those who hurt us (Matthew 5:43–44): Jonah didn't want to share God's mercy with these cruel foreigners. Jonah knew God would forgive. God would forgive, but Jonah couldn't.

Does resentment restrict your witness in any way? Does a secret wish for vengeance clog up that part of your heart through which the Lord wants to pour out His love to someone who needs it so much?

If you suspect the Lord Jesus would not applaud your answers to these questions, talk to Him about it. Confess your inability to change yourself, and ask for His pardon and power. The Savior-God who showed such tenderness to Jonah despite his stubbornness wants to demonstrate His mercy to you, too.

WEEK 70 • SATURDAY

Jonah 3:1—4:11

In one sense, Jesus' parable of the prodigal son is the story of Jonah. Nineveh—the "lost son"—repents, while Jonah—the "older brother"—refuses to come to the party the heavenly Father gives. Look for that contrast as you read. If time is short, focus on Jonah 4:1–11.

Jonah Goes to Nineveh

3 Then the word of the LORD
came to Jonah a second time:
2"Go to the great city of Nineveh and
proclaim to it the message I give you."
3Jonah obeyed the word of the LORD
and went to Nineveh. Now Nineveh
was a very important city—a visit required three days. 4On the first day, Jonah started into the city. He proclaimed:
"Forty more days and Nineveh will be
overturned." 5The Ninevites believed
God. They declared a fast, and all of
them, from the greatest to the least, put
on sackcloth.
6When the news reached the king of
Nineveh, he rose from his throne, took
off his royal robes, covered himself with
sackcloth and sat down in the dust.
7Then he issued a proclamation in Nineveh:

"By the decree of the king and his
nobles:

> Do not let any man or beast, herd
> or flock, taste anything; do not let
> them eat or drink. 8But let man and
> beast be covered with sackcloth.
> Let everyone call urgently on God.
> Let them give up their evil ways
> and their violence. 9Who knows?
> God may yet relent and with com-
> passion turn from his fierce anger so
> that we will not perish."

10When God saw what they did and
how they turned from their evil ways,
he had compassion and did not bring
upon them the destruction he had
threatened.

Jonah's Anger at the LORD's Compassion

4 But Jonah was greatly displeased and became angry. 2He
prayed to the LORD, "O LORD, is this not
what I said when I was still at home?
That is why I was so quick to flee to Tarshish. I knew that you are a gracious
and compassionate God, slow to anger
and abounding in love, a God who relents from sending calamity. 3Now, O
LORD, take away my life, for it is better
for me to die than to live."
4But the LORD replied, "Have you any
right to be angry?"
5Jonah went out and sat down at a
place east of the city. There he made
himself a shelter, sat in its shade and
waited to see what would happen to the
city. 6Then the LORD God provided a
vine and made it grow up over Jonah to
give shade for his head to ease his dis-
comfort, and Jonah was very happy
about the vine. 7But at dawn the next
day God provided a worm, which
chewed the vine so that it withered.
8When the sun rose, God provided a
scorching east wind, and the sun blazed
on Jonah's head so that he grew faint.
He wanted to die, and said, "It would be
better for me to die than to live."
9But God said to Jonah, "Do you have
a right to be angry about the vine?"
"I do," he said. "I am angry enough to
die."

[10]But the LORD said, "You have been concerned about this vine, though you did not tend it or make it grow. It sprang up overnight and died overnight. [11]But Nineveh has more than a hundred and twenty thousand people who cannot tell their right hand from their left, and many cattle as well. Should I not be concerned about that great city?"

SHARPEN THE FOCUS

Suppose Joseph Stalin had repented, that he had come to faith in Christ on his death bed. Would you be pleased to meet him in heaven? Or suppose Emperor Nero or Jeffrey Dahmer or the executioner who beheaded St. Paul would greet you as you enter paradise. Suppose your place at the Lord's eternal banquet is set next to that neighbor whose habits now drive you to distraction. Suppose your place card at the table would put you across from the supervisor you can't please, or that relative you could never get along with. Would you ask for a new seating assignment?

We are all prone, you see, to Jonah's sins—lovelessness and judgmentalism. Like Jonah, like the older son in Jesus' parable, we often serve the Father reluctantly. And then, as if to minimize our own disobedience of heart, we sometimes look down our noses at others whose sins we see as worse.

How good for us that just as the Lord acted in patience with Jonah, so He acts patiently toward us, too. How good that when we blame and judge and hate, our Savior keeps calling us to repentance, just as He did Jonah. God's forgiveness and favor belong to you in Christ's cross. Fall into your Father's arms and receive them.

MICAH

WEEK 71 • MONDAY

Micah 1:1—2:13

GET THE BIG PICTURE

Micah has been called "Isaiah in Miniature." Both prophets faithfully served the Lord about seven centuries before Christ. Both spoke to similar issues and used similar images. As you read, notice the attitude of Micah's hearers toward the Word of God. If time is short, focus on Micah 2:1–13.

1 The word of the LORD that came to Micah of Moresheth during the reigns of Jotham, Ahaz and Hezekiah, kings of Judah—the vision he saw concerning Samaria and Jerusalem.

2 Hear, O peoples, all of you,
listen, O earth and all who are in it,
that the Sovereign LORD may
witness against you,
the Lord from his holy temple.

Judgment Against Samaria and Jerusalem

3 Look! The LORD is coming from his
dwelling place;
he comes down and treads the
high places of the earth.
4 The mountains melt beneath him
and the valleys split apart,
like wax before the fire,
like water rushing down a slope.
5 All this is because of Jacob's
transgression,
because of the sins of the house of
Israel.
What is Jacob's transgression?
Is it not Samaria?
What is Judah's high place?
Is it not Jerusalem?

6 "Therefore I will make Samaria a
heap of rubble,
a place for planting vineyards.
I will pour her stones into the valley
and lay bare her foundations.
7 All her idols will be broken to pieces;
all her temple gifts will be burned
with fire;
I will destroy all her images.
Since she gathered her gifts from the
wages of prostitutes,
as the wages of prostitutes they
will again be used."

Weeping and Mourning

8 Because of this I will weep and wail;
I will go about barefoot and
naked.
I will howl like a jackal
and moan like an owl.
9 For her wound is incurable;
it has come to Judah.
It[a] has reached the very gate of my
people,
even to Jerusalem itself.
10 Tell it not in Gath[b];
weep not at all.[c]
In Beth Ophrah[d]
roll in the dust.

[a]9 Or *He* [b]10 *Gath* sounds like the Hebrew for *tell.* [c]10 Hebrew; Septuagint may suggest *not in Acco.* The Hebrew for *in Acco* sounds like the Hebrew for *weep.* [d]10 *Beth Ophrah* means *house of dust.*

[11] Pass on in nakedness and shame,
you who live in Shaphir.[a]
Those who live in Zaanan[b]
will not come out.
Beth Ezel is in mourning;
its protection is taken from you.
[12] Those who live in Maroth[c] writhe in pain,
waiting for relief,
because disaster has come from the LORD,
even to the gate of Jerusalem.
[13] You who live in Lachish,[d]
harness the team to the chariot.
You were the beginning of sin
to the Daughter of Zion,
for the transgressions of Israel
were found in you.
[14] Therefore you will give parting gifts
to Moresheth Gath.
The town of Aczib[e] will prove deceptive
to the kings of Israel.
[15] I will bring a conqueror against you
who live in Mareshah.[f]
He who is the glory of Israel
will come to Adullam.
[16] Shave your heads in mourning
for the children in whom you delight;
make yourselves as bald as the vulture,
for they will go from you into exile.

Man's Plans and God's

2 Woe to those who plan iniquity,
to those who plot evil on their beds!
At morning's light they carry it out
because it is in their power to do it.
[2] They covet fields and seize them,
and houses, and take them.
They defraud a man of his home,
a fellowman of his inheritance.

[3] Therefore, the LORD says:

"I am planning disaster against this people,
from which you cannot save yourselves.
You will no longer walk proudly,
for it will be a time of calamity.
[4] In that day men will ridicule you;
they will taunt you with this mournful song:
'We are utterly ruined;
my people's possession is divided up.
He takes it from me!
He assigns our fields to traitors.' "

[5] Therefore you will have no one in the assembly of the LORD
to divide the land by lot.

False Prophets

[6] "Do not prophesy," their prophets say.
"Do not prophesy about these things;
disgrace will not overtake us."
[7] Should it be said, O house of Jacob:
"Is the Spirit of the LORD angry?
Does he do such things?"

"Do not my words do good
to him whose ways are upright?
[8] Lately my people have risen up
like an enemy.
You strip off the rich robe
from those who pass by without a care,
like men returning from battle.
[9] You drive the women of my people
from their pleasant homes.
You take away my blessing
from their children forever.
[10] Get up, go away!
For this is not your resting place,
because it is defiled,
it is ruined, beyond all remedy.
[11] If a liar and deceiver comes and says,
'I will prophesy for you plenty of wine and beer,'
he would be just the prophet for this people!

[a] 11 *Shaphir* means *pleasant*. [b] 11 *Zaanan* sounds like the Hebrew for *come out*. [c] 12 *Maroth* sounds like the Hebrew for *bitter*. [d] 13 *Lachish* sounds like the Hebrew for *team*. [e] 14 *Aczib* means *deception*. [f] 15 *Mareshah* sounds like the Hebrew for *conqueror*.

Deliverance Promised

12 "I will surely gather all of you,
O Jacob;
I will surely bring together the
remnant of Israel.
I will bring them together like sheep
in a pen,
like a flock in its pasture;
the place will throng with people.
13 One who breaks open the way will
go up before them;
they will break through the gate
and go out.
Their king will pass through before
them,
the LORD at their head."

SHARPEN THE FOCUS

Dog trainers know that half the battle involves transferring a simple idea like *sit* or *stay* from your head and into the dog's head so that the dog knows what you expect. The second half of the battle is getting the dog to *want* to obey.

The Lord spoke to His people with absolute consistency throughout the Old Testament. Prophets like Isaiah and Micah sometimes even used the same exact words (compare Micah 4:1–3 and Isaiah 2:2–4).

The concepts the Lord communicated through His prophets were: obey and prosper; repent and believe. The problems God had with Israel and Judah did not stem from a lack of understanding. The problems grew instead from a failure in the people's will. They didn't *want* to obey. And after awhile, they didn't even want to listen (Micah 2:6).

Often we can trace our sin back to the simple fact that our sinful nature doesn't *want* to do what God has said. Like sheep who think the grass is greener in another pasture, we gambol off in our own direction.

Praise God, He comes after us (Micah 2:12–13)! Praise God that in Jesus He brings us back to Himself! Praise God that in the power of the cross He will even change our hearts so that we want what He wants.

WEEK 71 • TUESDAY

Micah 3:1—4:13

GET THE BIG PICTURE

The false prophets in Judah predicted peace—for those who paid them well. The political leaders ruled in favor of those who offered the fattest bribes. Both truth and justice suffered, as you might imagine. That's Micah 3, but Micah's words don't end there. Read on to discover God's Good News in Micah 4. If time is short, focus on Micah 4:1–13.

Leaders and Prophets Rebuked

3 Then I said,
"Listen, you leaders of Jacob,
you rulers of the house of Israel.
Should you not know justice,
2 you who hate good and love evil;
who tear the skin from my people

and the flesh from their bones;
3 who eat my people's flesh,
strip off their skin
and break their bones in pieces;
who chop them up like meat for the pan,
like flesh for the pot?"

4 Then they will cry out to the LORD,
but he will not answer them.
At that time he will hide his face from them
because of the evil they have done.

5 This is what the LORD says:

"As for the prophets
who lead my people astray,
if one feeds them,
they proclaim 'peace';
if he does not,
they prepare to wage war against him.
6 Therefore night will come over you,
without visions,
and darkness, without divination.
The sun will set for the prophets,
and the day will go dark for them.
7 The seers will be ashamed
and the diviners disgraced.
They will all cover their faces
because there is no answer from God."

8 But as for me, I am filled with power,
with the Spirit of the LORD,
and with justice and might,
to declare to Jacob his transgression,
to Israel his sin.
9 Hear this, you leaders of the house of Jacob,
you rulers of the house of Israel,
who despise justice
and distort all that is right;
10 who build Zion with bloodshed,
and Jerusalem with wickedness.
11 Her leaders judge for a bribe,
her priests teach for a price,
and her prophets tell fortunes for money.
Yet they lean upon the LORD and say,
"Is not the LORD among us?
No disaster will come upon us."
12 Therefore because of you,
Zion will be plowed like a field,
Jerusalem will become a heap of rubble,
the temple hill a mound
overgrown with thickets.

The Mountain of the LORD

4 In the last days

the mountain of the LORD's temple
will be established
as chief among the mountains;
it will be raised above the hills,
and peoples will stream to it.

2 Many nations will come and say,

"Come, let us go up to the mountain of the LORD,
to the house of the God of Jacob.
He will teach us his ways,
so that we may walk in his paths."
The law will go out from Zion,
the word of the LORD from Jerusalem.
3 He will judge between many peoples
and will settle disputes for strong nations far and wide.
They will beat their swords into plowshares
and their spears into pruning hooks.
Nation will not take up sword against nation,
nor will they train for war anymore.
4 Every man will sit under his own vine
and under his own fig tree,
and no one will make them afraid,
for the LORD Almighty has spoken.
5 All the nations may walk
in the name of their gods;
we will walk in the name of the LORD
our God for ever and ever.

The LORD's Plan

6 "In that day," declares the LORD,

"I will gather the lame;
I will assemble the exiles

and those I have brought to grief.
7 I will make the lame a remnant,
those driven away a strong nation.
The LORD will rule over them in Mount Zion
from that day and forever.
8 As for you, O watchtower of the flock,
O stronghold[a] of the Daughter of Zion,
the former dominion will be restored to you;
kingship will come to the Daughter of Jerusalem."

9 Why do you now cry aloud—
have you no king?
Has your counselor perished,
that pain seizes you like that of a woman in labor?
10 Writhe in agony, O Daughter of Zion,
like a woman in labor,
for now you must leave the city
to camp in the open field.
You will go to Babylon;
there you will be rescued.
There the LORD will redeem you
out of the hand of your enemies.

11 But now many nations
are gathered against you.
They say, "Let her be defiled,
let our eyes gloat over Zion!"
12 But they do not know
the thoughts of the LORD;
they do not understand his plan,
he who gathers them like sheaves to the threshing floor.

13 "Rise and thresh, O Daughter of Zion,
for I will give you horns of iron;
I will give you hoofs of bronze
and you will break to pieces many nations."
You will devote their ill-gotten gains to the LORD,
their wealth to the Lord of all the earth.

[a]8 Or *hill*

SHARPEN THE FOCUS

Children can sometimes read Mom's mind. Grandma can often anticipate Grandpa's thoughts. Are you close enough to anyone to be able to know what they're thinking before they open their mouth to express it?

Micah 4:12 begins by ridiculing the enemies of the Lord's people. The nations "do not know the thoughts of the LORD." They do not understand His intentions and His fierce loyalty and love for those whom He has redeemed.

Do *you* know the thoughts of the Lord? As you look at world events and even at the sin in the church, can you stay in tune with your Savior's intentions for you and His mercy toward you?

In one sense, the Lord's thoughts transcend our poor ability to understand them. They float as far above us as the sky (Isaiah 55:9). But the Lord has revealed His thoughts to us in the Word of Scripture and in the Word Incarnate, our Lord Jesus. Because He has done this, we can truly know what He's thinking. And we can share those thoughts with the nations—and with individuals—who do not yet know Him and His Word.

WEEK 71 • WEDNESDAY

Micah 5:1–15

God promised that the Messiah would shepherd His people in strength and majesty. He would gather them and protect them. As you read now, look for this flock, His church. Also note the new information Micah adds about this Shepherd in Micah 5:2. If time is short, focus on Micah 5:1–4.

A Promised Ruler From Bethlehem

5 Marshal your troops, O city of
troops,[a]
for a siege is laid against us.
They will strike Israel's ruler
on the cheek with a rod.

2 "But you, Bethlehem Ephrathah,
though you are small among the
clans[b] of Judah,
out of you will come for me
one who will be ruler over Israel,
whose origins[c] are from of old,
from ancient times.[d]"

3 Therefore Israel will be abandoned
until the time when she who is in
labor gives birth
and the rest of his brothers return
to join the Israelites.

4 He will stand and shepherd his flock
in the strength of the LORD,
in the majesty of the name of the
LORD his God.
And they will live securely, for then
his greatness
will reach to the ends of the earth.
5 And he will be their peace.

Deliverance and Destruction

When the Assyrian invades our land
and marches through our
fortresses,
we will raise against him seven
shepherds,
even eight leaders of men.
6 They will rule[e] the land of Assyria
with the sword,
the land of Nimrod with drawn
sword.[f]
He will deliver us from the Assyrian
when he invades our land
and marches into our borders.

7 The remnant of Jacob will be
in the midst of many peoples
like dew from the LORD,
like showers on the grass,
which do not wait for man
or linger for mankind.
8 The remnant of Jacob will be among
the nations,
in the midst of many peoples,
like a lion among the beasts of the
forest,
like a young lion among flocks of
sheep,
which mauls and mangles as it
goes,
and no one can rescue.
9 Your hand will be lifted up in
triumph over your enemies,
and all your foes will be
destroyed.

10 "In that day," declares the LORD,
"I will destroy your horses from
among you
and demolish your chariots.
11 I will destroy the cities of your land
and tear down all your
strongholds.

[a] 1 Or *Strengthen your walls, O walled city* [b] 2 Or *rulers* [c] 2 Hebrew *goings out* [d] 2 Or *from days of eternity* [e] 6 Or *crush* [f] 6 Or *Nimrod in its gates*

12 I will destroy your witchcraft
and you will no longer cast spells.
13 I will destroy your carved images
and your sacred stones from
among you;
you will no longer bow down
to the work of your hands.
14 I will uproot from among you your
Asherah poles[a]
and demolish your cities.
15 I will take vengeance in anger and
wrath
upon the nations that have not
obeyed me."

SHARPEN THE FOCUS

When did you last see the sky—*really* see it? Because we walk beneath it every day, it's easy to miss the sky's remarkable beauty—studded with stars, draped with thunderheads, graced with the vapor trails of jet engines. We tend to overlook even the extraordinary if we've seen it often enough.

Micah 5:2 can lose its luster, too, and for perhaps the same reason. We hear this verse recited each Christmas, mostly as a text to prove Jesus was the Messiah, since He was born in Bethlehem. That point surely is well-taken. But see what else this verse tells us about our Savior.

God, the Father, speaks these words. He says that the Messiah would come out of Bethlehem *for Him*. Jesus came to earth to do the Father's will. He came from God and went back to God (John 13:3). Jesus is the Everlasting One who chose to enter time to rescue us; He was obedient to the Father's call to do so.

God the Father says that the Messiah will be the "ruler over Israel." The Shepherd who died for the sheep now does rule His church, not in harshness or arrogance, but in infinite love and concern. Even now, He continues to gather the lost. How might you participate in that today?

WEEK 71 • THURSDAY

Micah 6:1–16

GET THE BIG PICTURE

Chapter 6 of Micah is a legal transcript, as it were. Here God puts His people on trial. As you read, look for the "jury" He designates, the charges He brings, and the sentence He pronounces. If time is short, focus on Micah 6:1–8.

The LORD's Case Against Israel

6 Listen to what the LORD says:

"Stand up, plead your case before
the mountains;
let the hills hear what you have to
say.
2 Hear, O mountains, the LORD's
accusation;
listen, you everlasting foundations
of the earth.
For the LORD has a case against his
people;
he is lodging a charge against Israel.

3 "My people, what have I done to
you?

[a]*14* That is, symbols of the goddess Asherah

How have I burdened you?
Answer me.
4 I brought you up out of Egypt
and redeemed you from the land
of slavery.
I sent Moses to lead you,
also Aaron and Miriam.
5 My people, remember
what Balak king of Moab counseled
and what Balaam son of Beor
answered.
Remember ⌊your journey⌋ from
Shittim to Gilgal,
that you may know the righteous
acts of the LORD."

6 With what shall I come before the
LORD
and bow down before the exalted
God?
Shall I come before him with burnt
offerings,
with calves a year old?
7 Will the LORD be pleased with
thousands of rams,
with ten thousand rivers of oil?
Shall I offer my firstborn for my
transgression,
the fruit of my body for the sin of
my soul?
8 He has showed you, O man, what
is good.
And what does the LORD require
of you?
To act justly and to love mercy
and to walk humbly with your
God.

Israel's Guilt and Punishment

9 Listen! The LORD is calling to the
city—
and to fear your name is
wisdom—
"Heed the rod and the One who
appointed it.[a]
10 Am I still to forget, O wicked house,
your ill-gotten treasures
and the short ephah,[b] which is
accursed?
11 Shall I acquit a man with dishonest
scales,
with a bag of false weights?
12 Her rich men are violent;
her people are liars
and their tongues speak
deceitfully.
13 Therefore, I have begun to destroy
you,
to ruin you because of your sins.
14 You will eat but not be satisfied;
your stomach will still be empty.[c]
You will store up but save nothing,
because what you save I will give
to the sword.
15 You will plant but not harvest;
you will press olives but not use
the oil on yourselves,
you will crush grapes but not
drink the wine.
16 You have observed the statutes of
Omri
and all the practices of Ahab's
house,
and you have followed their
traditions.
Therefore I will give you over to
ruin
and your people to derision;
you will bear the scorn of the
nations.[d]"

[a]9 The meaning of the Hebrew for this line is uncertain. [b]10 An ephah was a dry measure. [c]14 The meaning of the Hebrew for this word is uncertain. [d]16 Septuagint; Hebrew *scorn due my people*

SHARPEN THE FOCUS

An old idea has begun to re-emerge in current thinking about crime and punishment–restitution. Convicts would work to earn money to repay their victims. The idea merits thought. But most crimes cause such hurt they can never be put right. How do you repay someone who's been raped? or kidnapped? someone whose loved one has been murdered?

When Micah hears the Lord's complaint in Micah 6:1–5, he throws up his hands in despair.

"How can we ever make it up to You, Lord?" he asks in essence. "How many cattle can we slaughter as offerings? How many rivers of oil could we burn? What if we sacrifice our firstborn children?"

Seeing our sins in their enormity throws us on our faces at God's feet. Our feeble attempts to "make it up" to God fall so far short its laughable. Laughable, that is, if our eternal destiny weren't at stake. We haven't and we can't "act justly [and] love mercy [and] walk humbly" with Him (Micah 6:8).

And so He sacrificed His own firstborn Son in our place. He made the restitution we couldn't make so that we could be restored to fellowship with Him and with each other. When we throw ourselves on the mercy of this court, we get just that—mercy.

"Don't trust anyone!" That's Micah's solemn advice as he looks around and sees how thoroughly sin has corrupted his society. But there is Someone we *can* trust. That's what the last part of the chapter is about. If time is short, focus on Micah 7:18–20.

Israel's Misery

7 What misery is mine!
I am like one who gathers summer fruit
at the gleaning of the vineyard;
there is no cluster of grapes to eat,
none of the early figs that I crave.
2 The godly have been swept from the land;
not one upright man remains.
All men lie in wait to shed blood;
each hunts his brother with a net.
3 Both hands are skilled in doing evil;
the ruler demands gifts,
the judge accepts bribes,
the powerful dictate what they desire—
they all conspire together.
4 The best of them is like a brier,
the most upright worse than a thorn hedge.
The day of your watchmen has come,
the day God visits you.
Now is the time of their confusion.
5 Do not trust a neighbor;
put no confidence in a friend.
Even with her who lies in your embrace
be careful of your words.
6 For a son dishonors his father,
a daughter rises up against her mother,
a daughter-in-law against her mother-in-law—
a man's enemies are the members of his own household.

7 But as for me, I watch in hope for the LORD,
I wait for God my Savior;
my God will hear me.

Israel Will Rise

8 Do not gloat over me, my enemy!
Though I have fallen, I will rise.
Though I sit in darkness,
the LORD will be my light.

[9]Because I have sinned against him,
I will bear the LORD's wrath,
until he pleads my case
and establishes my right.
He will bring me out into the light;
I will see his righteousness.
[10]Then my enemy will see it
and will be covered with shame,
she who said to me,
"Where is the LORD your God?"
My eyes will see her downfall;
even now she will be trampled underfoot
like mire in the streets.

[11]The day for building your walls will come,
the day for extending your boundaries.
[12]In that day people will come to you
from Assyria and the cities of Egypt,
even from Egypt to the Euphrates
and from sea to sea
and from mountain to mountain.
[13]The earth will become desolate
because of its inhabitants,
as the result of their deeds.

Prayer and Praise

[14]Shepherd your people with your staff,
the flock of your inheritance,
which lives by itself in a forest,
in fertile pasturelands.[a]
Let them feed in Bashan and Gilead
as in days long ago.
[15]"As in the days when you came out of Egypt,
I will show them my wonders."
[16]Nations will see and be ashamed,
deprived of all their power.
They will lay their hands on their mouths
and their ears will become deaf.
[17]They will lick dust like a snake,
like creatures that crawl on the ground.
They will come trembling out of their dens;
they will turn in fear to the LORD our God
and will be afraid of you.
[18]Who is a God like you,
who pardons sin and forgives the transgression
of the remnant of his inheritance?
You do not stay angry forever
but delight to show mercy.
[19]You will again have compassion on us;
you will tread our sins underfoot
and hurl all our iniquities into the depths of the sea.
[20]You will be true to Jacob,
and show mercy to Abraham,
as you pledged on oath to our fathers
in days long ago.

[a]14 Or *in the middle of Carmel*

SHARPEN THE FOCUS

As human beings down through the ages have made up their own gods, the pictures they have developed have never gotten to the truth. People have seen the gods as vengeful, as mean, as demanding, and as unpredictable. Or they have pictured the gods as indifferent to human beings, like uncaring parents who abandon their children.

That's what lies behind Micah's question in Micah 7:18—"Who is a God like You?" Clearing away all the misinformation, the prophet zeroes in on the main points—God pardons sin; God forgives transgression; God drops His anger; God delights to show mercy—to sinners (Micah 7:18)! God shows us tender compassion; God tramples our offenses in the dirt; God throws our wrongdoing into the ocean of His forgetfulness (Micah 7:19)! Perhaps best of all, God keeps His ancient promise to Abraham—the promise of the Savior (Micah 7:20)!

Down through history, our Lord has consistently done those things. He's never once failed to act in line with His Word. He's always forgiven His penitent people. Yes, who is like Him? To whom can we compare Him? No one!

And so, instead of comparing, we worship. Father. Son. And Holy Spirit. Peerless in majesty. Perfect in mercy.

NAHUM

WEEK 71 • SATURDAY

Nahum 1:1—3:19

GET THE BIG PICTURE

One hundred years or more before Nahum's time, the prophet Jonah preached repentance to the people in the wicked city of Nineveh. The people repented and the Lord forgave. But now Assyria finds itself on trial once again. If time is short, focus on Nahum 1:1–15.

1 An oracle concerning Nineveh. The book of the vision of Nahum the Elkoshite.

The LORD's Anger Against Nineveh

2 The LORD is a jealous and avenging
God;
the LORD takes vengeance and is
filled with wrath.
The LORD takes vengeance on his
foes
and maintains his wrath against
his enemies.
3 The LORD is slow to anger and great
in power;
the LORD will not leave the guilty
unpunished.
His way is in the whirlwind and the
storm,
and clouds are the dust of his feet.
4 He rebukes the sea and dries it up;
he makes all the rivers run dry.
Bashan and Carmel wither
and the blossoms of Lebanon
fade.
5 The mountains quake before him
and the hills melt away.
The earth trembles at his presence,
the world and all who live in it.
6 Who can withstand his indignation?
Who can endure his fierce anger?
His wrath is poured out like fire;
the rocks are shattered before him.

7 The LORD is good,
a refuge in times of trouble.
He cares for those who trust in him,
8 but with an overwhelming flood
he will make an end of ⌞Nineveh⌟;
he will pursue his foes into
darkness.

9 Whatever they plot against the
LORD
he[a] will bring to an end;
trouble will not come a second
time.
10 They will be entangled among
thorns
and drunk from their wine;
they will be consumed like dry
stubble.[b]
11 From you, ⌞O Nineveh,⌟ has one
come forth
who plots evil against the LORD
and counsels wickedness.

12 This is what the LORD says:

"Although they have allies and are
numerous,

[a]9 Or *What do you foes plot against the LORD? / He*
[b]10 The meaning of the Hebrew for this verse is uncertain.

they will be cut off and pass away.
Although I have afflicted you,
⌞O Judah,⌟
I will afflict you no more.
13 Now I will break their yoke from your neck
and tear your shackles away."

14 The LORD has given a command concerning you, ⌞Nineveh⌟:
"You will have no descendants to bear your name.
I will destroy the carved images and cast idols
that are in the temple of your gods.
I will prepare your grave,
for you are vile."

15 Look, there on the mountains,
the feet of one who brings good news,
who proclaims peace!
Celebrate your festivals, O Judah,
and fulfill your vows.
No more will the wicked invade you;
they will be completely destroyed.

Nineveh to Fall

2 An attacker advances against you, ⌞Nineveh⌟.
Guard the fortress,
watch the road,
brace yourselves,
marshal all your strength!

2 The LORD will restore the splendor of Jacob
like the splendor of Israel,
though destroyers have laid them waste
and have ruined their vines.

3 The shields of his soldiers are red;
the warriors are clad in scarlet.
The metal on the chariots flashes
on the day they are made ready;
the spears of pine are brandished.[a]
4 The chariots storm through the streets,
rushing back and forth through the squares.
They look like flaming torches;
they dart about like lightning.

5 He summons his picked troops,
yet they stumble on their way.
They dash to the city wall;
the protective shield is put in place.
6 The river gates are thrown open
and the palace collapses.
7 It is decreed[b] that ⌞the city⌟
be exiled and carried away.
Its slave girls moan like doves
and beat upon their breasts.
8 Nineveh is like a pool,
and its water is draining away.
"Stop! Stop!" they cry,
but no one turns back.
9 Plunder the silver!
Plunder the gold!
The supply is endless,
the wealth from all its treasures!
10 She is pillaged, plundered, stripped!
Hearts melt, knees give way,
bodies tremble, every face grows pale.

11 Where now is the lions' den,
the place where they fed their young,
where the lion and lioness went,
and the cubs, with nothing to fear?
12 The lion killed enough for his cubs
and strangled the prey for his mate,
filling his lairs with the kill
and his dens with the prey.

13 "I am against you,"
declares the LORD Almighty.
"I will burn up your chariots in smoke,
and the sword will devour your young lions.
I will leave you no prey on the earth.
The voices of your messengers
will no longer be heard."

Woe to Nineveh

3 Woe to the city of blood,
full of lies,
full of plunder,

[a]3 Hebrew; Septuagint and Syriac / *the horsemen rush to and fro* [b]7 The meaning of the Hebrew for this word is uncertain.

never without victims!
2 The crack of whips,
the clatter of wheels,
galloping horses
and jolting chariots!
3 Charging cavalry,
flashing swords
and glittering spears!
Many casualties,
piles of dead,
bodies without number,
people stumbling over the corpses—
4 all because of the wanton lust of a harlot,
alluring, the mistress of sorceries,
who enslaved nations by her prostitution
and peoples by her witchcraft.

5 "I am against you," declares the LORD Almighty.
"I will lift your skirts over your face.
I will show the nations your nakedness
and the kingdoms your shame.
6 I will pelt you with filth,
I will treat you with contempt
and make you a spectacle.
7 All who see you will flee from you and say,
'Nineveh is in ruins—who will mourn for her?'
Where can I find anyone to comfort you?"

8 Are you better than Thebes,[a]
situated on the Nile,
with water around her?
The river was her defense,
the waters her wall.
9 Cush[b] and Egypt were her boundless strength;
Put and Libya were among her allies.
10 Yet she was taken captive
and went into exile.
Her infants were dashed to pieces
at the head of every street.
Lots were cast for her nobles,
and all her great men were put in chains.
11 You too will become drunk;
you will go into hiding
and seek refuge from the enemy.

12 All your fortresses are like fig trees
with their first ripe fruit;
when they are shaken,
the figs fall into the mouth of the eater.
13 Look at your troops—
they are all women!
The gates of your land
are wide open to your enemies;
fire has consumed their bars.

14 Draw water for the siege,
strengthen your defenses!
Work the clay,
tread the mortar,
repair the brickwork!
15 There the fire will devour you;
the sword will cut you down
and, like grasshoppers, consume you.
Multiply like grasshoppers,
multiply like locusts!
16 You have increased the number of your merchants
till they are more than the stars of the sky,
but like locusts they strip the land
and then fly away.
17 Your guards are like locusts,
your officials like swarms of locusts
that settle in the walls on a cold day—
but when the sun appears they fly away,
and no one knows where.

18 O king of Assyria, your shepherds[c] slumber;
your nobles lie down to rest.
Your people are scattered on the mountains
with no one to gather them.
19 Nothing can heal your wound;
your injury is fatal.
Everyone who hears the news about you
claps his hands at your fall,
for who has not felt
your endless cruelty?

[a]8 Hebrew *No Amon* [b]9 That is, the upper Nile region [c]18 Or *rulers*

SHARPEN THE FOCUS

"We will bury you!" threatened Nikita Khrushchev in a speech against the United States in the 1960s. Most school children today don't even recognize his name. The memory of the Soviet Union has fast faded into history.

The threat of Nahum 1:14 sounds a lot like that of Khrushchev: "I will prepare your grave," the Lord says to Assyria. Nineveh's citizens lived behind walls 100 feet high. A moat 150 feet wide and 60 feet deep ringed the city. Nineveh's rulers had designed their capital to be able to withstand a 20-year siege. "Prepare *our* graves?" Nineveh's citizens must have sneered.

Nahum's threats weren't bluster. The Lord is "slow to anger," but He is also "great in power" (Nahum 1:3). He was not about to leave the guilty unpunished. Once again we see God's two-sided coin, justice and mercy. By refusing to come to the Lord in repentance and faith, Nineveh rejected mercy. Only justice remained.

For those of us who are in Christ Jesus by faith, the day of justice has passed. In Jesus, we know "The LORD is good, a refuge in times of trouble." We know that "He cares for those who trust in Him" (Nahum 1:7). Take refuge in Him today. He cares for you!

HABAKKUK

WEEK 72 • MONDAY

Habakkuk 1:1—2:20

Have you ever wondered why God lets the wicked "get away with murder"–either literally or figuratively? Habakkuk did. So he asked God. The Holy Spirit chose to include the prophet's questions and the Lord's answers in this little book. As you read today, don't look to the realm of logic. Look instead toward relationship, toward God's assurance that the One who loves us is in control. If time is short, focus on Habakkuk 2:1–20.

1 The oracle that Habakkuk the prophet received.

Habakkuk's Complaint

2 How long, O LORD, must I call for help,
but you do not listen?
Or cry out to you, "Violence!"
but you do not save?
3 Why do you make me look at injustice?
Why do you tolerate wrong?
Destruction and violence are before me;
there is strife, and conflict abounds.
4 Therefore the law is paralyzed,
and justice never prevails.
The wicked hem in the righteous,
so that justice is perverted.

The LORD's Answer

5 "Look at the nations and watch—
and be utterly amazed.
For I am going to do something in your days
that you would not believe,
even if you were told.
6 I am raising up the Babylonians,[a]
that ruthless and impetuous people,
who sweep across the whole earth
to seize dwelling places not their own.
7 They are a feared and dreaded people;
they are a law to themselves
and promote their own honor.
8 Their horses are swifter than leopards,
fiercer than wolves at dusk.
Their cavalry gallops headlong;
their horsemen come from afar.
They fly like a vulture swooping to devour;
9 they all come bent on violence.
Their hordes[b] advance like a desert wind
and gather prisoners like sand.
10 They deride kings
and scoff at rulers.
They laugh at all fortified cities;
they build earthen ramps and capture them.
11 Then they sweep past like the wind and go on—
guilty men, whose own strength is their god."

[a] 6 Or *Chaldeans* [b] 9 The meaning of the Hebrew for this word is uncertain.

Habakkuk's Second Complaint

[12]O LORD, are you not from
everlasting?
My God, my Holy One, we will
not die.
O LORD, you have appointed them
to execute judgment;
O Rock, you have ordained them
to punish.
[13]Your eyes are too pure to look on
evil;
you cannot tolerate wrong.
Why then do you tolerate the
treacherous?
Why are you silent while the
wicked
swallow up those more righteous
than themselves?
[14]You have made men like fish in the
sea,
like sea creatures that have no ruler.
[15]The wicked foe pulls all of them up
with hooks,
he catches them in his net,
he gathers them up in his dragnet;
and so he rejoices and is glad.
[16]Therefore he sacrifices to his net
and burns incense to his dragnet,
for by his net he lives in luxury
and enjoys the choicest food.
[17]Is he to keep on emptying his net,
destroying nations without
mercy?

2 I will stand at my watch
and station myself on the
ramparts;
I will look to see what he will say to
me,
and what answer I am to give to
this complaint.[a]

The LORD's Answer

[2]Then the LORD replied:

"Write down the revelation
and make it plain on tablets
so that a herald[b] may run with it.
[3]For the revelation awaits an
appointed time;
it speaks of the end
and will not prove false.
Though it linger, wait for it;
it[c] will certainly come and will not
delay.

[4]"See, he is puffed up;
his desires are not upright—
but the righteous will live by his
faith[d]—
[5]indeed, wine betrays him;
he is arrogant and never at rest.
Because he is as greedy as the grave[e]
and like death is never satisfied,
he gathers to himself all the nations
and takes captive all the peoples.

[6]"Will not all of them taunt him with
ridicule and scorn, saying,

" 'Woe to him who piles up stolen
goods
and makes himself wealthy by
extortion!
How long must this go on?'
[7]Will not your debtors[f] suddenly
arise?
Will they not wake up and make
you tremble?
Then you will become their
victim.
[8]Because you have plundered many
nations,
the peoples who are left will
plunder you.
For you have shed man's blood;
you have destroyed lands and
cities and everyone in them.

[9]"Woe to him who builds his realm by
unjust gain
to set his nest on high,
to escape the clutches of ruin!
[10]You have plotted the ruin of many
peoples,
shaming your own house and
forfeiting your life.
[11]The stones of the wall will cry out,
and the beams of the woodwork
will echo it.

[12]"Woe to him who builds a city with
bloodshed
and establishes a town by crime!

[a]1 Or *and what to answer when I am rebuked*
[b]2 Or *so that whoever reads it* [c]3 Or *Though he linger, wait for him; / he* [d]4 Or *faithfulness*
[e]5 Hebrew *Sheol* [f]7 Or *creditors*

[13]Has not the LORD Almighty
determined
that the people's labor is only fuel
for the fire,
that the nations exhaust
themselves for nothing?
[14]For the earth will be filled with the
knowledge of the glory of the
LORD,
as the waters cover the sea.

[15]"Woe to him who gives drink to his
neighbors,
pouring it from the wineskin till
they are drunk,
so that he can gaze on their naked
bodies.
[16]You will be filled with shame instead
of glory.
Now it is your turn! Drink and be
exposed[a]!
The cup from the LORD's right hand
is coming around to you,
and disgrace will cover your glory.
[17]The violence you have done to
Lebanon will overwhelm you,
and your destruction of animals
will terrify you.
For you have shed man's blood;
you have destroyed lands and
cities and everyone in them.

[18]"Of what value is an idol, since a
man has carved it?
Or an image that teaches lies?
For he who makes it trusts in his
own creation;
he makes idols that cannot
speak.
[19]Woe to him who says to wood,
'Come to life!'
Or to lifeless stone, 'Wake up!'
Can it give guidance?
It is covered with gold and silver;
there is no breath in it.
[20]But the LORD is in his holy temple;
let all the earth be silent before
him."

[a]*16* Masoretic Text; Dead Sea Scrolls, Aquila, Vulgate and Syriac (see also Septuagint) *and stagger*

SHARPEN THE FOCUS

The *whys* of life can torment the godly. Only the Lord Himself knows how many people have let those *whys* poison their souls with bitterness that became unbelief. Pat answers aren't enough. And those who scold us for our questions miss the fact that God graciously responded to Habakkuk's questions without reproving him for asking. No matter how frustrated or even angry your whys are, your Lord invites you too to keep on asking. Our questions don't intimidate Him.

His answers, by the same token may not satisfy us—at least not our logical selves. The "problem of evil" will remain something of a mystery this side of heaven. Even so, the Lord makes two critical points with Habakkuk:

- Don't give up on God's justice. It's on the way and will arrive at the proper time (Habakkuk 2:3).
- While you wait, trust the Lord. You are righteous by faith; live in faith until you see your Lord act on your behalf (Habakkuk 2:4).

One day, God's judgment will silence all questions—even yours and mine (Habakkuk 2:20). For now, Jesus' cross stills all doubts about His love for us. Certain of that love, we live out the present, hopeful for the future. ☼

As He did for the prophet Job, the Lord revealed Himself to Habakkuk. It was enough. The final answer to all our *whys* rests in God's presence, wisdom, and mercy. As you read, look for evidence of this. If time is short, focus on Habakkuk 3:3–13, 17–19.

Habakkuk's Prayer

3 A prayer of Habakkuk the prophet. On *shigionoth*.[a]

2 LORD, I have heard of your fame;
I stand in awe of your deeds,
O LORD.
Renew them in our day,
in our time make them known;
in wrath remember mercy.

3 God came from Teman,
the Holy One from Mount Paran.
Selah[b]

His glory covered the heavens
and his praise filled the earth.
4 His splendor was like the sunrise;
rays flashed from his hand,
where his power was hidden.
5 Plague went before him;
pestilence followed his steps.
6 He stood, and shook the earth;
he looked, and made the nations
tremble.
The ancient mountains crumbled
and the age-old hills collapsed.
His ways are eternal.
7 I saw the tents of Cushan in distress,
the dwellings of Midian in
anguish.

8 Were you angry with the rivers,
O LORD?
Was your wrath against the
streams?
Did you rage against the sea
when you rode with your horses
and your victorious chariots?
9 You uncovered your bow,
you called for many arrows. *Selah*
You split the earth with rivers;
10 the mountains saw you and
writhed.
Torrents of water swept by;
the deep roared
and lifted its waves on high.

11 Sun and moon stood still in the
heavens
at the glint of your flying arrows,
at the lightning of your flashing
spear.
12 In wrath you strode through the
earth
and in anger you threshed the
nations.
13 You came out to deliver your people,
to save your anointed one.
You crushed the leader of the land of
wickedness,
you stripped him from head to
foot. *Selah*
14 With his own spear you pierced his
head
when his warriors stormed out to
scatter us,
gloating as though about to devour
the wretched who were in hiding.
15 You trampled the sea with your
horses,
churning the great waters.

16 I heard and my heart pounded,
my lips quivered at the sound;
decay crept into my bones,
and my legs trembled.

[a]*1* Probably a literary or musical term [b]*3* A word of uncertain meaning; possibly a musical term; also in verses 9 and 13

Yet I will wait patiently for the day
of calamity
to come on the nation invading
us.
17 Though the fig tree does not bud
and there are no grapes on the
vines,
though the olive crop fails
and the fields produce no food,
though there are no sheep in the
pen
and no cattle in the stalls,
18 yet I will rejoice in the LORD,
I will be joyful in God my Savior.

19 The Sovereign LORD is my strength;
he makes my feet like the feet of a
deer,
he enables me to go on the
heights.

For the director of music. On my
stringed instruments.

SHARPEN THE FOCUS

Take a second look at Habakkuk 3:17–18. How would you recast Habubkkuk's words to fit your own lifestyle?

Could you rejoice if your resources dried up? If you couldn't tell where your next meal would come from? Habakkuk could. Not because He was some holier-than-we-are prophet. Not because trust in the Lord came easier back in those days. No, Habakkuk rejoiced because He had seen the Lord. He knew God's power, and he knew God's mercy. He had seen God act on behalf of His people in the past, and so he took courage from a focus on the Savior-God. Present circumstances faded away in the splendor of the Lord's forgiving love.

If tension or worry grips your heart today, ask your Lord for forgiveness and for a change in focus. Take some time to recall all that He has done for you, especially in Jesus Christ. Then worship Him, that He has remembered mercy (Habakkuk 3:2b).

Zephaniah

Zephaniah shared the prophetic stage with Jeremiah during Judah's last revival (2 Kings 22:1–23:30). The people turned from sin—but only outwardly. When King Josiah died, Judah buried his reforms with him. As you read, notice how thoroughly God judges *all* those who have turned from Him. If time is short, focus on Zephaniah 1:1–18.

1 The word of the LORD that came to Zephaniah son of Cushi, the son of Gedaliah, the son of Amariah, the son of Hezekiah, during the reign of Josiah son of Amon king of Judah:

Warning of Coming Destruction

2 "I will sweep away everything
from the face of the earth,"
declares the LORD.
3 "I will sweep away both men and animals;
I will sweep away the birds of the air
and the fish of the sea.
The wicked will have only heaps of rubble[a]
when I cut off man from the face of the earth,"
declares the LORD.

Against Judah

4 "I will stretch out my hand against Judah
and against all who live in Jerusalem.
I will cut off from this place every remnant of Baal,
the names of the pagan and the idolatrous priests—
5 those who bow down on the roofs
to worship the starry host,
those who bow down and swear by the LORD
and who also swear by Molech,[b]
6 those who turn back from following the LORD
and neither seek the LORD nor inquire of him.
7 Be silent before the Sovereign LORD,
for the day of the LORD is near.
The LORD has prepared a sacrifice;
he has consecrated those he has invited.
8 On the day of the LORD's sacrifice
I will punish the princes
and the king's sons
and all those clad
in foreign clothes.
9 On that day I will punish
all who avoid stepping on the threshold,[c]
who fill the temple of their gods
with violence and deceit.

10 "On that day," declares the LORD,
"a cry will go up from the Fish Gate,
wailing from the New Quarter,

[a]3 The meaning of the Hebrew for this line is uncertain. [b]5 Hebrew *Malcam,* that is, Milcom [c]9 See 1 Samuel 5:5.

and a loud crash from the hills.
11 Wail, you who live in the market
district[a];
all your merchants will be wiped
out,
all who trade with[b] silver will be
ruined.
12 At that time I will search Jerusalem
with lamps
and punish those who are
complacent,
who are like wine left on its dregs,
who think, 'The LORD will do
nothing,
either good or bad.'
13 Their wealth will be plundered,
their houses demolished.
They will build houses
but not live in them;
they will plant vineyards
but not drink the wine.

The Great Day of the LORD

14 "The great day of the LORD is
near—
near and coming quickly.
Listen! The cry on the day of the
LORD will be bitter,
the shouting of the warrior there.
15 That day will be a day of wrath,
a day of distress and anguish,
a day of trouble and ruin,
a day of darkness and gloom,
a day of clouds and blackness,
16 a day of trumpet and battle cry
against the fortified cities
and against the corner towers.
17 I will bring distress on the people
and they will walk like blind
men,
because they have sinned against
the LORD.
Their blood will be poured out like
dust
and their entrails like filth.
18 Neither their silver nor their gold
will be able to save them
on the day of the LORD's wrath.
In the fire of his jealousy
the whole world will be
consumed,
for he will make a sudden end
of all who live in the earth."

2 Gather together, gather together,
O shameful nation,
2 before the appointed time arrives
and that day sweeps on like chaff,
before the fierce anger of the LORD
comes upon you,
before the day of the LORD's
wrath comes upon you.
3 Seek the LORD, all you humble of
the land,
you who do what he commands.
Seek righteousness, seek humility;
perhaps you will be sheltered
on the day of the LORD's anger.

Against Philistia

4 Gaza will be abandoned
and Ashkelon left in ruins.
At midday Ashdod will be emptied
and Ekron uprooted.
5 Woe to you who live by the sea,
O Kerethite people;
the word of the LORD is against you,
O Canaan, land of the Philistines.

"I will destroy you,
and none will be left."

6 The land by the sea, where the
Kerethites[c] dwell,
will be a place for shepherds and
sheep pens.
7 It will belong to the remnant of the
house of Judah;
there they will find pasture.
In the evening they will lie down
in the houses of Ashkelon.
The LORD their God will care for
them;
he will restore their fortunes.[d]

Against Moab and Ammon

8 "I have heard the insults of Moab
and the taunts of the Ammonites,
who insulted my people
and made threats against their
land.
9 Therefore, as surely as I live,"
declares the LORD Almighty, the
God of Israel,

[a]11 Or *the Mortar* [b]11 Or *in* [c]6 The meaning of the Hebrew for this word is uncertain. [d]7 Or *will bring back their captives*

"surely Moab will become like
Sodom,
the Ammonites like Gomorrah—
a place of weeds and salt pits,
a wasteland forever.
The remnant of my people will
plunder them;
the survivors of my nation will
inherit their land."

10 This is what they will get in return
for their pride,
for insulting and mocking the
people of the LORD
Almighty.
11 The LORD will be awesome to them
when he destroys all the gods of
the land.
The nations on every shore will
worship him,
every one in its own land.

Against Cush

12 "You too, O Cushites,[a]
will be slain by my sword."

Against Assyria

13 He will stretch out his hand against
the north
and destroy Assyria,
leaving Nineveh utterly desolate
and dry as the desert.
14 Flocks and herds will lie down there,
creatures of every kind.
The desert owl and the screech owl
will roost on her columns.
Their calls will echo through the
windows,
rubble will be in the doorways,
the beams of cedar will be exposed.
15 This is the carefree city
that lived in safety.
She said to herself,
"I am, and there is none besides
me."
What a ruin she has become,
a lair for wild beasts!
All who pass by her scoff
and shake their fists.

[a]12 That is, people from the upper Nile region

SHARPEN THE FOCUS

Like cockroaches, the enemies of the Lord would try to hide from His judgment. But no one would escape. Notice the warning in Zephaniah 1:12. The Lord would light a lamp and search every dark corner of Jerusalem until He found all those who had offended Him.

Contrast this picture with the parable our Lord Jesus told about another lamp, another search (Luke 15:8–10). A woman loses one of ten silver coins—perhaps her dowry. She drops what she's doing, lights a lamp, sweeps the house, and keeps looking until she finds the coin. She considers it so precious that when she does find it, she invites her neighbors to a block party to celebrate!

You are even more precious to your Savior than that lost coin. The heavenly Father sent Jesus—the Light of life—into our world to search for you. The angels rejoiced when you came to faith in Jesus your Savior. For those who don't know Christ, Judgment Day will be dreadful (Zephaniah 1:15–16). But you can hide behind Christ's cross (Zephaniah 2:3b) while the wrath of God destroys evil.

Into whose life will you shine the light of His love and forgiveness today?

WEEK 72 • THURSDAY

Zephaniah 3:1–20

GET THE BIG PICTURE

Faced with the fury of those who resist the Lord and hate His Christ, God's children can feel intimidated. That fury plus the shame we feel over our sins can shut down our witness. But Zephaniah gives us reason to be bold. Look for that as you read. If time is short, focus on Zephaniah 3:5–20.

The Future of Jerusalem

3 Woe to the city of oppressors,
rebellious and defiled!
2 She obeys no one,
she accepts no correction.
She does not trust in the LORD,
she does not draw near to her
God.
3 Her officials are roaring lions,
her rulers are evening wolves,
who leave nothing for the
morning.
4 Her prophets are arrogant;
they are treacherous men.
Her priests profane the sanctuary
and do violence to the law.
5 The LORD within her is righteous;
he does no wrong.
Morning by morning he dispenses
his justice,
and every new day he does not
fail,
yet the unrighteous know no
shame.
6 "I have cut off nations;
their strongholds are demolished.
I have left their streets deserted,
with no one passing through.
Their cities are destroyed;
no one will be left—no one at all.
7 I said to the city,
'Surely you will fear me
and accept correction!'
Then her dwelling would not be cut
off,
nor all my punishments come
upon her.
But they were still eager
to act corruptly in all they did.
8 Therefore wait for me," declares the
LORD,
"for the day I will stand up to
testify.[a]
I have decided to assemble the
nations,
to gather the kingdoms
and to pour out my wrath on
them—
all my fierce anger.
The whole world will be consumed
by the fire of my jealous anger.
9 "Then will I purify the lips of the
peoples,
that all of them may call on the
name of the LORD
and serve him shoulder to
shoulder.
10 From beyond the rivers of Cush[b]
my worshipers, my scattered
people,
will bring me offerings.
11 On that day you will not be put to
shame
for all the wrongs you have done
to me,
because I will remove from this city
those who rejoice in their pride.
Never again will you be haughty
on my holy hill.
12 But I will leave within you
the meek and humble,

[a] 8 Septuagint and Syriac; Hebrew *will rise up to plunder* [b] 10 That is, the upper Nile region

who trust in the name of the LORD.
13 The remnant of Israel will do no wrong;
they will speak no lies,
nor will deceit be found in their mouths.
They will eat and lie down
and no one will make them afraid."

14 Sing, O Daughter of Zion;
shout aloud, O Israel!
Be glad and rejoice with all your heart,
O Daughter of Jerusalem!
15 The LORD has taken away your punishment,
he has turned back your enemy.
The LORD, the King of Israel, is with you;
never again will you fear any harm.
16 On that day they will say to Jerusalem,
"Do not fear, O Zion;
do not let your hands hang limp.
17 The LORD your God is with you,
he is mighty to save.
He will take great delight in you,
he will quiet you with his love,
he will rejoice over you with singing."

18 "The sorrows for the appointed feasts
I will remove from you;
they are a burden and a reproach to you.[a]
19 At that time I will deal
with all who oppressed you;
I will rescue the lame
and gather those who have been scattered.
I will give them praise and honor
in every land where they were put to shame.
20 At that time I will gather you;
at that time I will bring you home.
I will give you honor and praise
among all the peoples of the earth
when I restore your fortunes[b]
before your very eyes,"
says the LORD.

[a]18 Or *"I will gather you who mourn for the appointed feasts; / your reproach is a burden to you*
[b]20 Or *I bring back your captives*

SHARPEN THE FOCUS

Weight lifters choose weights they can lift 8 to 12 times. The first seven lifts or so come easily. But then the lifter's muscles begin to shake. Finally, they give out altogether. The weight drops. Good trainers push their clients to this point of muscle failure to get the greatest growth in strength.

Like a good coach, Zephaniah shouts encouragement to God's people in Zephaniah 3:14–17. Lifting the hefty burdens of life in our godless society, we may want to "drop the weight," so to speak. We may want to forget about our witness. We may want to insult those who insult us. We may want to fit in with the values of the ungodly rather than choosing to reflect the character of Christ.

But then we hear Zephaniah shouting: "Don't be afraid! Don't let your hands be weak! The Lord is with you! The Mighty One will save you!" (Zephaniah 3:16–17 paraphrased).

Jesus, you see, carried the load of our sins to His cross. Our shame has vanished. Now our God rejoices over us and sings for joy because of us (Zephaniah 3:17). Now by power of the Holy Spirit we can have compassion for those who do not know Christ. In that compassion, we use God's strength to keep on keeping on with the mission our Lord has given us.

HAGGAI

To set the stage for today's reading you may want to skim Ezra 3–4. The people who returned from exile began to rebuild the temple, but let themselves lapse into discouragement when they encountered hardships. For 10 years, the work remained unfinished. Enter Haggai. He encouraged the people to complete their task. As you read look for the reasons he gives them. If time is short, focus on Haggai 2:1–9.

A Call to Build the House of the LORD

1 In the second year of King Darius,
on the first day of the sixth month,
the word of the LORD came through the
prophet Haggai to Zerubbabel son of
Shealtiel, governor of Judah, and to
Joshua[a] son of Jehozadak, the high
priest:
2This is what the LORD Almighty says:
"These people say, 'The time has not yet
come for the LORD's house to be built.' "
3Then the word of the LORD came
through the prophet Haggai: 4"Is it a
time for you yourselves to be living in
your paneled houses, while this house
remains a ruin?"
5Now this is what the LORD Almighty
says: "Give careful thought to your
ways. 6You have planted much, but have
harvested little. You eat, but never have
enough. You drink, but never have your
fill. You put on clothes, but are not
warm. You earn wages, only to put them
in a purse with holes in it."
7This is what the LORD Almighty says:
"Give careful thought to your ways. 8Go
up into the mountains and bring down
timber and build the house, so that I
may take pleasure in it and be honored,"
says the LORD. 9"You expected much,
but see, it turned out to be little. What
you brought home, I blew away. Why?"
declares the LORD Almighty. "Because of
my house, which remains a ruin, while
each of you is busy with his own house.
10Therefore, because of you the heavens
have withheld their dew and the earth
its crops. 11I called for a drought on the
fields and the mountains, on the grain,
the new wine, the oil and whatever the
ground produces, on men and cattle,
and on the labor of your hands."

12Then Zerubbabel son of Shealtiel,
Joshua son of Jehozadak, the high
priest, and the whole remnant of the
people obeyed the voice of the LORD
their God and the message of the
prophet Haggai, because the LORD their
God had sent him. And the people
feared the LORD.
13Then Haggai, the LORD's messenger,
gave this message of the LORD to the
people: "I am with you," declares the
LORD. 14So the LORD stirred up the spirit
of Zerubbabel son of Shealtiel, governor
of Judah, and the spirit of Joshua son of

[a]*1* A variant of *Jeshua*; here and elsewhere in Haggai

Jehozadak, the high priest, and the spirit of the whole remnant of the people. They came and began to work on the house of the LORD Almighty, their God, 15on the twenty-fourth day of the sixth month in the second year of King Darius.

The Promised Glory of the New House

2 On the twenty-first day of the seventh month, the word of the LORD came through the prophet Haggai: 2"Speak to Zerubbabel son of Shealtiel, governor of Judah, to Joshua son of Jehozadak, the high priest, and to the remnant of the people. Ask them, 3'Who of you is left who saw this house in its former glory? How does it look to you now? Does it not seem to you like nothing? 4But now be strong, O Zerubbabel,' declares the LORD. 'Be strong, O Joshua son of Jehozadak, the high priest. Be strong, all you people of the land,' declares the LORD, 'and work. For I am with you,' declares the LORD Almighty. 5'This is what I covenanted with you when you came out of Egypt. And my Spirit remains among you. Do not fear.'

6"This is what the LORD Almighty says: 'In a little while I will once more shake the heavens and the earth, the sea and the dry land. 7I will shake all nations, and the desired of all nations will come, and I will fill this house with glory,' says the LORD Almighty. 8'The silver is mine and the gold is mine,' declares the LORD Almighty. 9'The glory of this present house will be greater than the glory of the former house,' says the LORD Almighty. 'And in this place I will grant peace,' declares the LORD Almighty."

Blessings for a Defiled People

10On the twenty-fourth day of the ninth month, in the second year of Darius, the word of the LORD came to the prophet Haggai: 11"This is what the LORD Almighty says: 'Ask the priests what the law says: 12If a person carries consecrated meat in the fold of his garment, and that fold touches some bread or stew, some wine, oil or other food, does it become consecrated?' "

The priests answered, "No."

13Then Haggai said, "If a person defiled by contact with a dead body touches one of these things, does it become defiled?"

"Yes," the priests replied, "it becomes defiled."

14Then Haggai said, " 'So it is with this people and this nation in my sight,' declares the LORD. 'Whatever they do and whatever they offer there is defiled.

15" 'Now give careful thought to this from this day on[a]—consider how things were before one stone was laid on another in the LORD's temple. 16When anyone came to a heap of twenty measures, there were only ten. When anyone went to a wine vat to draw fifty measures, there were only twenty. 17I struck all the work of your hands with blight, mildew and hail, yet you did not turn to me,' declares the LORD. 18'From this day on, from this twenty-fourth day of the ninth month, give careful thought to the day when the foundation of the LORD's temple was laid. Give careful thought: 19Is there yet any seed left in the barn? Until now, the vine and the fig tree, the pomegranate and the olive tree have not borne fruit.

" 'From this day on I will bless you.' "

Zerubbabel the LORD's Signet Ring

20The word of the LORD came to Haggai a second time on the twenty-fourth day of the month: 21"Tell Zerubbabel governor of Judah that I will shake the heavens and the earth. 22I will overturn royal thrones and shatter the power of the foreign kingdoms. I will overthrow chariots and their drivers; horses and their riders will fall, each by the sword of his brother.

23" 'On that day,' declares the LORD Almighty, 'I will take you, my servant Zerubbabel son of Shealtiel,' declares the LORD, 'and I will make you like my signet ring, for I have chosen you,' declares the LORD Almighty."

[a]15 Or *to the days past*

SHARPEN THE FOCUS

Many major cities have them—roads that go nowhere. The money ran out. Or a lawsuit stopped the bulldozers. The temple reconstruction project led by Zerubbabel met with an even more stubborn block. The builders got discouraged.

Well-begun is half-done, says the old proverb. But half-done is still only half-done. Have you begun well, but failed to finish something your Lord motivated you to tackle? Perhaps you began with zeal to teach a Sunday school class, but now find yourself just coasting along. Perhaps your congregation began to support a missionary family wholeheartedly, but now you find the sacrifice it requires discouraging.

Reread Haggai 2:4–9. God kept His promise to fill Zerubbabel's temple with glory; the Lord Jesus worshiped in the temple Zerubbabel built and Herod later expanded. Crucified and risen, Jesus now rules over the nations for the good of His church. Soon God will shake heaven and earth in judgment. Until then, we have work to do. Immortal souls lie in the balance. God wants them to have the same peace He has given us. Be strong! Get up! Finish the work—by His Spirit alive in you!

ZECHARIAH

WEEK 72 • SATURDAY

Zechariah 1:1—2:13

GET THE BIG PICTURE

Eight visions fill most of the first six chapters of Zechariah. We do not know for sure the meaning of all the details in the visions. But each vision makes a clear point. As you read today, for instance, notice that the Lord promises to protect His people and destroy His enemies. If time is short, focus on Zechariah 1:1–17.

A Call to Return to the LORD

1 In the eighth month of the second
year of Darius, the word of the
LORD came to the prophet Zechariah
son of Berekiah, the son of Iddo:
2"The LORD was very angry with your
forefathers. 3Therefore tell the people:
This is what the LORD Almighty says:
'Return to me,' declares the LORD Almighty, 'and I will return to you,' says
the LORD Almighty. 4Do not be like your
forefathers, to whom the earlier prophets proclaimed: This is what the LORD
Almighty says: 'Turn from your evil
ways and your evil practices.' But they
would not listen or pay attention to me,
declares the LORD. 5Where are your
forefathers now? And the prophets, do
they live forever? 6But did not my words
and my decrees, which I commanded
my servants the prophets, overtake
your forefathers?

"Then they repented and said, 'The
LORD Almighty has done to us what our
ways and practices deserve, just as he
determined to do.' "

The Man Among the Myrtle Trees

7On the twenty-fourth day of the
eleventh month, the month of Shebat,
in the second year of Darius, the word
of the LORD came to the prophet Zechariah son of Berekiah, the son of Iddo.
8During the night I had a vision—and
there before me was a man riding a red
horse! He was standing among the myrtle trees in a ravine. Behind him were
red, brown and white horses.
9I asked, "What are these, my lord?"

The angel who was talking with me
answered, "I will show you what they
are."
10Then the man standing among the
myrtle trees explained, "They are the
ones the LORD has sent to go throughout the earth."
11And they reported to the angel of
the LORD, who was standing among the
myrtle trees, "We have gone throughout
the earth and found the whole world at
rest and in peace."
12Then the angel of the LORD said,
"LORD Almighty, how long will you
withhold mercy from Jerusalem and
from the towns of Judah, which you
have been angry with these seventy
years?" 13So the LORD spoke kind and
comforting words to the angel who
talked with me.
14Then the angel who was speaking to
me said, "Proclaim this word: This is
what the LORD Almighty says: 'I am

very jealous for Jerusalem and Zion, 15but I am very angry with the nations that feel secure. I was only a little angry, but they added to the calamity.'

16"Therefore, this is what the LORD says: 'I will return to Jerusalem with mercy, and there my house will be rebuilt. And the measuring line will be stretched out over Jerusalem,' declares the LORD Almighty.

17"Proclaim further: This is what the LORD Almighty says: 'My towns will again overflow with prosperity, and the LORD will again comfort Zion and choose Jerusalem.' "

Four Horns and Four Craftsmen

18Then I looked up—and there before me were four horns! 19I asked the angel who was speaking to me, "What are these?"

He answered me, "These are the horns that scattered Judah, Israel and Jerusalem."

20Then the LORD showed me four craftsmen. 21I asked, "What are these coming to do?"

He answered, "These are the horns that scattered Judah so that no one could raise his head, but the craftsmen have come to terrify them and throw down these horns of the nations who lifted up their horns against the land of Judah to scatter its people."

A Man With a Measuring Line

2 Then I looked up—and there before me was a man with a measuring line in his hand! 2I asked, "Where are you going?"

He answered me, "To measure Jerusalem, to find out how wide and how long it is."

3Then the angel who was speaking to me left, and another angel came to meet him 4and said to him: "Run, tell that young man, 'Jerusalem will be a city without walls because of the great number of men and livestock in it. 5And I myself will be a wall of fire around it,' declares the LORD, 'and I will be its glory within.'

6"Come! Come! Flee from the land of the north," declares the LORD, "for I have scattered you to the four winds of heaven," declares the LORD.

7"Come, O Zion! Escape, you who live in the Daughter of Babylon!" 8For this is what the LORD Almighty says: "After he has honored me and has sent me against the nations that have plundered you—for whoever touches you touches the apple of his eye— 9I will surely raise my hand against them so that their slaves will plunder them.[a] Then you will know that the LORD Almighty has sent me.

10"Shout and be glad, O Daughter of Zion. For I am coming, and I will live among you," declares the LORD. 11"Many nations will be joined with the LORD in that day and will become my people. I will live among you and you will know that the LORD Almighty has sent me to you. 12The LORD will inherit Judah as his portion in the holy land and will again choose Jerusalem. 13Be still before the LORD, all mankind, because he has roused himself from his holy dwelling."

[a]8,9 Or *says after . . . eye:* 9*"I . . . plunder them."*

SHARPEN THE FOCUS

Tenderness. Compassion. Those words describe the Lord's attitude toward His people in Zechariah 1–2. While we may not understand everything our Lord says to us here, we do see that He has taken up our cause. He is on our side. He has chosen us and He will comfort us (Zechariah 1:17).

Zechariah uses a particular word for "mercy" in Zechariah 1:12 and 16. Related to the Hebrew word for *womb*, this term is not the word meaning "covenant love" we might expect the prophet to use. Instead, this word for mercy conveys the yearning a parent feels when a child hurts. Someone who experiences this kind of mercy cannot help but rush to the rescue. A mother who has carried a child in her womb, close to her heart, longs to soothe that child's fears, comfort that child in pain, protect that child from harm. Our God shows that same kind of mercy toward us, especially in Jesus our Savior.

Such mercy brings us to our knees as we recognize and confess our sins. Such mercy melts the hard and cold places in our hearts and makes it possible for us to forgive others. Such mercy lifts our arms toward God as we worship Him with our whole being for His goodness toward us.

WEEK 73 • MONDAY

Zechariah 3:1–10

Suppose you were to have an audience with an important person. Would you pay attention to your appearance? In today's reading a high priest, Joshua, finds himself whisked into God's presence. But his clothes are filthy. As you read this vision that tells about God's mercy, look for parallels with your own life. If time is short, focus on Zechariah 3:1–5.

Clean Garments for the High Priest

3 Then he showed me Joshua[a] the
high priest standing before the
angel of the LORD, and Satan[b] standing
at his right side to accuse him. 2The
LORD said to Satan, "The LORD rebuke
you, Satan! The LORD, who has chosen
Jerusalem, rebuke you! Is not this man
a burning stick snatched from the fire?"
3Now Joshua was dressed in filthy
clothes as he stood before the angel.
4The angel said to those who were
standing before him, "Take off his filthy
clothes."
Then he said to Joshua, "See, I have
taken away your sin, and I will put rich
garments on you."
5Then I said, "Put a clean turban on
his head." So they put a clean turban on
his head and clothed him, while the angel of the LORD stood by.
6The angel of the LORD gave this
charge to Joshua: 7"This is what the
LORD Almighty says: 'If you will walk in
my ways and keep my requirements,
then you will govern my house and
have charge of my courts, and I will give
you a place among these standing here.
8" 'Listen, O high priest Joshua and
your associates seated before you, who
are men symbolic of things to come: I
am going to bring my servant, the
Branch. 9See, the stone I have set in front
of Joshua! There are seven eyes[c] on that
one stone, and I will engrave an inscription on it,' says the LORD Almighty, 'and
I will remove the sin of this land in a
single day.
10" 'In that day each of you will invite
his neighbor to sit under his vine and fig
tree,' declares the LORD Almighty."

[a]1 A variant of *Jeshua*; here and elsewhere in Zechariah [b]1 *Satan* means *accuser.* [c]9 Or *facets*

SHARPEN THE FOCUS

Maybe Joshua hoped the Lord wouldn't notice him. But Satan—the slanderer—snatched away that hope. Out came a stream of accusations, sins of thought, word, and actions. And from a high priest, no less! Joshua's shame must at some point have taken a back seat to fear. What would the Lord think? What would He do?

But the Savior-God, the One-Who-Makes-the-Good-Thing-Happen, speaks to the accuser, not to Joshua. "I Myself rebuke *you*!" God says in essence to Joshua's enemy. All charges are dismissed with those words. Then, as though with a snap of God's fingers, Joshua's filthy clothes disappear. In their place appear "rich garments" (Zechariah 3:4)—the garments of Christ's righteousness. Joshua begins to relax in the Savior's love. His shame is gone, replaced by the honor the Savior gives those who belong to Him by faith (John 12:26).

What a comfort for those of us who sometimes hesitate to turn to our Lord because of the unworthiness we feel. You, child of God, are Joshua! Wear your "new clothes" with joy today.

WEEK 73 • TUESDAY

Zechariah 4:1–14

GET THE BIG PICTURE

Before you read Zechariah 4 today, turn back to Psalm 119:105 and reread it. That verse, together with Zechariah 4:6a, will help you understand the vision with which today's chapter opens. If time is short, focus on Zechariah 4:1–7.

The Gold Lampstand and the Two Olive Trees

4 Then the angel who talked with
me returned and wakened me,
as a man is wakened from his sleep. 2He
asked me, "What do you see?"

I answered, "I see a solid gold lampstand with a bowl at the top and seven lights on it, with seven channels to the
lights. 3Also there are two olive trees by
it, one on the right of the bowl and the other on its left."

4I asked the angel who talked with me, "What are these, my lord?"

5He answered, "Do you not know what these are?"

"No, my lord," I replied.

6So he said to me, "This is the word of the LORD to Zerubbabel: 'Not by might nor by power, but by my Spirit,' says the LORD Almighty.

7"What[a] are you, O mighty mountain? Before Zerubbabel you will become level ground. Then he will bring out the capstone to shouts of 'God bless it! God bless it!' "

8Then the word of the LORD came to
me: 9"The hands of Zerubbabel have laid the foundation of this temple; his hands will also complete it. Then you will know that the LORD Almighty has sent me to you.

10"Who despises the day of small things? Men will rejoice when they see the plumb line in the hand of Zerubbabel.

[a]7 Or *Who*

"(These seven are the eyes of the LORD,
which range throughout the earth.)"
11Then I asked the angel, "What are
these two olive trees on the right and
the left of the lampstand?"
12Again I asked him, "What are these
two olive branches beside the two
gold pipes that pour out golden oil?"
13He replied, "Do you not know what
these are?"
"No, my lord," I said.
14So he said, "These are the two who
are anointed to[a] serve the Lord of all the
earth."

SHARPEN THE FOCUS

Brick by brick. That's how Zerubbabel and his workers built the temple after God's people returned from exile. Zerubbabel accomplished a lot.

But on another plane, Zerubbabel himself accomplished nothing. His "small things" (Zechariah 4:10) would have stayed small and would soon have blown away, except for the fact that Zerubbabel didn't work alone. The Holy Spirit stood, as it were, on the construction site, too. The Spirit spoke God's Word of encouragement and power through Haggai, through Zechariah, through Ezra, through others of His priests. That Word lighted the way for the people's service. That Word, small though it seemed, accomplished what most people thought impossible.

We too can fall for Satan's temptation to "[despise] the day of small things" (Zechariah 4:10). How powerful, after all, does the Gospel look from a human perspective? Not very. But the power of Almighty God resides in it. The Word that assures us of forgiveness and eternal life will not fail. It will accomplish all that our Savior-God has sent it out to do.

WEEK 73 • WEDNESDAY

Zechariah 5:1–11

GET THE BIG PICTURE

Zechariah's visions continue; chapter 5 contains two new ones. The flying scroll was huge compared to the usual scrolls of Zechariah's day. The Lord doesn't want anyone to miss this message! The woman in the basket represents wickedness, just as Zechariah 5:8 says. As you read, note that the Lord has her under complete control. If time is short, focus on Zechariah 5:1–4.

The Flying Scroll

5 I looked again—and there before
me was a flying scroll!
2He asked me, "What do you see?"
I answered, "I see a flying scroll, thirty feet long and fifteen feet wide.[b]"
3And he said to me, "This is the curse
that is going out over the whole land;
for according to what it says on one side,
every thief will be banished, and according to what it says on the other,
everyone who swears falsely will be
banished. 4The LORD Almighty declares,

[a]14 Or *two who bring oil and* [b]2 Hebrew *twenty cubits long and ten cubits wide* (about 9 meters long and 4.5 meters wide)

'I will send it out, and it will enter the
house of the thief and the house of him
who swears falsely by my name. It will
remain in his house and destroy it, both
its timbers and its stones.' "

The Woman in a Basket

5 Then the angel who was speaking to
me came forward and said to me, "Look
up and see what this is that is appearing."
6 I asked, "What is it?"
He replied, "It is a measuring basket.[a]" And he added, "This is the iniquity[b] of the people throughout the land."
7 Then the cover of lead was raised,
and there in the basket sat a woman!
8 He said, "This is wickedness," and he
pushed her back into the basket and
pushed the lead cover down over its
mouth.
9 Then I looked up—and there before
me were two women, with the wind in
their wings! They had wings like those
of a stork, and they lifted up the basket
between heaven and earth.
10 "Where are they taking the basket?"
I asked the angel who was speaking
to me.
11 He replied, "To the country of Babylonia[c] to build a house for it. When it
is ready, the basket will be set there in
its place."

[a]6 Hebrew *an ephah;* also in verses 7-11 [b]6 Or *appearance* [c]11 Hebrew *Shinar*

SHARPEN THE FOCUS

Have you ever struggled with a tough decision and secretly wished the Lord would hire a skywriter to tell you what to do? That's just what Zechariah seems to see in Zechariah 5:1–4. We might read the scroll, eager for some new, dramatic insight. But instead, we see that Zechariah's banner contains only a curse–a curse on thieves and false witnesses.

Perhaps as we read it, we may be tempted to say, "Big deal!" We may shrug at such spiritual misdemeanors, given the heinous crimes we hear about on the evening news every day. We may shrug; but Zechariah makes it plain that God does not.

Greed and lies. At heart both betray a failure to trust our Lord to meet our needs–in our finances, on the job, or in our earthly relationships. Zechariah's banner should fly high over our heads, following us wherever we go and accusing us of sin. But instead, each of us as God's children can say with Solomon, "He has taken me to the banquet hall, and His banner over me is love" (Song of Songs 2:4). However you picture that banner, the cross of our Lord Jesus surely appears as the central feature!

WEEK 73 • THURSDAY

Zechariah 6:1–15

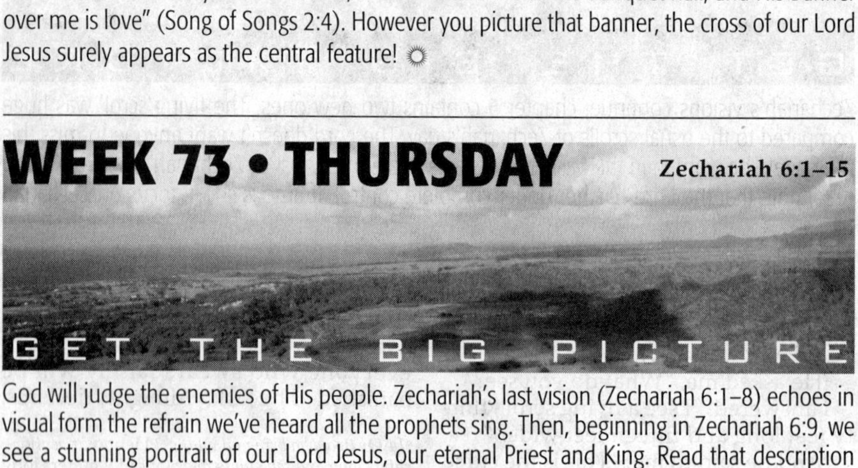

GET THE BIG PICTURE

God will judge the enemies of His people. Zechariah's last vision (Zechariah 6:1–8) echoes in visual form the refrain we've heard all the prophets sing. Then, beginning in Zechariah 6:9, we see a stunning portrait of our Lord Jesus, our eternal Priest and King. Read that description thoughtfully. If time is short, focus on Zechariah 6:9–15.

Four Chariots

6 I looked up again—and there before me were four chariots coming out from between two mountains—
mountains of bronze! 2The first chariot
had red horses, the second black, 3the
third white, and the fourth dappled—
all of them powerful. 4I asked the angel
who was speaking to me, "What are
these, my lord?"
5The angel answered me, "These are
the four spirits[a] of heaven, going out
from standing in the presence of the
Lord of the whole world. 6The one with
the black horses is going toward the
north country, the one with the white
horses toward the west,[b] and the one with
the dappled horses toward the south."
7When the powerful horses went out,
they were straining to go throughout
the earth. And he said, "Go throughout
the earth!" So they went throughout the
earth.
8Then he called to me, "Look, those going toward the north country have given
my Spirit[c] rest in the land of the north."

A Crown for Joshua

9The word of the LORD came to me:
10"Take ⌞silver and gold⌟ from the exiles
Heldai, Tobijah and Jedaiah, who have
arrived from Babylon. Go the same day
to the house of Josiah son of Zephaniah. 11Take the silver and gold and
make a crown, and set it on the head of
the high priest, Joshua son of Jehozadak. 12Tell him this is what the LORD Almighty says: 'Here is the man whose
name is the Branch, and he will branch
out from his place and build the temple
of the LORD. 13It is he who will build the
temple of the LORD, and he will be
clothed with majesty and will sit and
rule on his throne. And he will be a
priest on his throne. And there will be
harmony between the two.' 14The
crown will be given to Heldai,[d] Tobijah,
Jedaiah and Hen[e] son of Zephaniah as
a memorial in the temple of the LORD.
15Those who are far away will come and
help to build the temple of the LORD,
and you will know that the LORD Almighty has sent me to you. This will
happen if you diligently obey the LORD
your God."

[a]5 Or *winds* [b]6 Or *horses after them* [c]8 Or *spirit* [d]14 Syriac; Hebrew *Helem* [e]14 Or *and the gracious one, the*

SHARPEN THE FOCUS

Carpenters choose their tools with great care. Most professional carpenters don't just buy tools, they *invest* in them. In today's reading, we see our Lord Jesus described as a master carpenter. He's the one who will "build the temple of the LORD" (Zechariah 6:12–13). This is no ordinary building. He uses no ordinary tools. Only He could construct this temple. Only He could set its stones in place. In this temple He will rule forever. It will house His throne, His glory (Zechariah 6:13).

The temple Jesus builds is His Holy Christian Church (Matthew 16:18). We, His believers, are the "living stones" (1 Peter 2:5) that the Carpenter fits together so skillfully. His Word of Law chisels and dresses us; His Word of Gospel cements us to Him and to one another in love.

The beams of His cross support this temple; as priest (Zechariah 6:13), Jesus sacrificed Himself for our sins. Now He sits forever enthroned, forever honored, forever glorious as our King. He rules in love those for whom in love He died.

WEEK 73 • FRIDAY

Zechariah 7:1–14

GET THE BIG PICTURE

Motives really do matter—sometimes a lot. In God's kingdom, motives and attitudes count for even more than actions, at least most of the time. Look for evidence of this as you read today. If time is short, focus on Zechariah 7:8–14.

Justice and Mercy, Not Fasting

7 In the fourth year of King Darius, the word of the LORD came to
Zechariah on the fourth day of the ninth
month, the month of Kislev. 2The people
of Bethel had sent Sharezer and Regem-
Melech, together with their men, to entreat the LORD 3by asking the priests of
the house of the LORD Almighty and the
prophets, "Should I mourn and fast in
the fifth month, as I have done for so
many years?"
4Then the word of the LORD Almighty
came to me: 5"Ask all the people of the
land and the priests, 'When you fasted
and mourned in the fifth and seventh
months for the past seventy years, was
it really for me that you fasted? 6And
when you were eating and drinking,
were you not just feasting for yourselves? 7Are these not the words the
LORD proclaimed through the earlier
prophets when Jerusalem and its surrounding towns were at rest and prosperous, and the Negev and the western
foothills were settled?' "
8And the word of the LORD came
again to Zechariah: 9"This is what the
LORD Almighty says: 'Administer true
justice; show mercy and compassion to
one another. 10Do not oppress the
widow or the fatherless, the alien or the
poor. In your hearts do not think evil of
each other.'
11"But they refused to pay attention;
stubbornly they turned their backs
and stopped up their ears. 12They made
their hearts as hard as flint and would
not listen to the law or to the words
that the LORD Almighty had sent by
his Spirit through the earlier prophets. So the LORD Almighty was very
angry.
13" 'When I called, they did not listen;
so when they called, I would not listen,'
says the LORD Almighty. 14'I scattered
them with a whirlwind among all the
nations, where they were strangers. The
land was left so desolate behind them
that no one could come or go. This is
how they made the pleasant land desolate.' "

SHARPEN THE FOCUS

Israel kept repeating its sinful disobedient past. The people "refused to pay attention . . . [They] would not listen to the law or to the words that the LORD Almighty had sent by His Spirit through the earlier prophets. So the LORD Almighty was very angry" (Zechariah 7:11–12).

They *knew*, but didn't *do* God's will. Instead they followed their natural desires. Their stubborn attitudes brought God's anger down on them. Their disobedience carried them away from God.

"But what about the sins *I* repeat?" God's answer depends on why you ask. If you're looking for loopholes, if you hope to have someone tell you that sin doesn't matter and that you can feel free to sin all you want because God loves you, look out! You're developing the hard heart that so damaged ancient Judah.

On the other hand, if you care about your relationship with Jesus, if the Holy Spirit's conviction has left you brokenhearted over your sins, if you feel the burden of having hurt and angered your Lord, be at peace. God, in Christ, has forgiven you. He will keep on working in you until the attitudes and actions that please Him mature in you. ☼

WEEK 73 • SATURDAY

Zechariah 8:1–23

GET THE BIG PICTURE

Human beings may determine to do something, but all kinds of obstacles can prevent them from carrying out their plans. When the Lord determines He will do something, no one can stop Him. As you read today, look for what He says He's determined to do. If time is short, focus on Zechariah 8:1–17.

The LORD Promises to Bless Jerusalem

8 Again the word of the LORD Almighty came to me. 2This is what
the LORD Almighty says: "I am very jealous for Zion; I am burning with jealousy for her."
3This is what the LORD says: "I will return to Zion and dwell in Jerusalem. Then Jerusalem will be called the City of Truth, and the mountain of the LORD Almighty will be called the Holy Mountain."
4This is what the LORD Almighty says: "Once again men and women of ripe old age will sit in the streets of Jerusalem, each with cane in hand because of
his age. 5The city streets will be filled with boys and girls playing there."
6This is what the LORD Almighty says: "It may seem marvelous to the remnant of this people at that time, but will it seem marvelous to me?" declares the LORD Almighty.
7This is what the LORD Almighty says: "I will save my people from the coun-
tries of the east and the west. 8I will bring them back to live in Jerusalem; they will be my people, and I will be faithful and righteous to them as their God."
9This is what the LORD Almighty says: "You who now hear these words spoken by the prophets who were there when the foundation was laid for the house of the LORD Almighty, let your hands be strong so that the temple may be built.
10Before that time there were no wages for man or beast. No one could go about his business safely because of his enemy, for I had turned every man against his
neighbor. 11But now I will not deal with the remnant of this people as I did in the past," declares the LORD Almighty.
12"The seed will grow well, the vine will yield its fruit, the ground will produce its crops, and the heavens will drop their dew. I will give all these things as an inheritance to the remnant
of this people. 13As you have been an object of cursing among the nations, O Judah and Israel, so will I save you, and you will be a blessing. Do not be afraid, but let your hands be strong."

14 This is what the LORD Almighty
says: "Just as I had determined to bring
disaster upon you and showed no pity
when your fathers angered me," says
the LORD Almighty, 15 "so now I have
determined to do good again to Jerusalem and Judah. Do not be afraid. 16 These
are the things you are to do: Speak the
truth to each other, and render true and
sound judgment in your courts; 17 do not
plot evil against your neighbor, and do
not love to swear falsely. I hate all this,"
declares the LORD.

18 Again the word of the LORD Almighty came to me. 19 This is what the
LORD Almighty says: "The fasts of the
fourth, fifth, seventh and tenth months
will become joyful and glad occasions
and happy festivals for Judah. Therefore love truth and peace."

20 This is what the LORD Almighty
says: "Many peoples and the inhabitants of many cities will yet come, 21 and
the inhabitants of one city will go to
another and say, 'Let us go at once to
entreat the LORD and seek the LORD
Almighty. I myself am going.' 22 And
many peoples and powerful nations
will come to Jerusalem to seek the LORD
Almighty and to entreat him."

23 This is what the LORD Almighty
says: "In those days ten men from all
languages and nations will take firm
hold of one Jew by the hem of his robe
and say, 'Let us go with you, because we
have heard that God is with you.' "

SHARPEN THE FOCUS

Just think of it! The Lord is determined to do good things for us, His church (Zechariah 8:15)! He's acted on that determination all along. It's what prompted Him to call Abraham out of idolatry. It's what motivated Him to emancipate Israel from her slave masters in Egypt. It's what led Him to work with King Saul, King David, King Hezekiah, and with all the other sinful rulers down through His people's history. It's what moved Him to send His only Son into our world as a little baby and to stand by while wicked people crucified that grown-up Son.

God is determined to do good things for *you*! Your sins can't stop Him. Your ingratitude can't deter Him. Your indifference won't discourage Him. He chose you from eternity. He counts Jesus' death as your own, and Jesus' holiness now belongs to your account. He's baptized you into His family. He's even now preparing the rooms of the mansion He's planned for you in heaven.

God is determined to do good things for us. If that doesn't bring a smile to your face, nothing will. Live in that joy today. Enjoy the peace it brings. God is on your side. Praise Him!

WEEK 74 • MONDAY

Zechariah 9:1—10:12

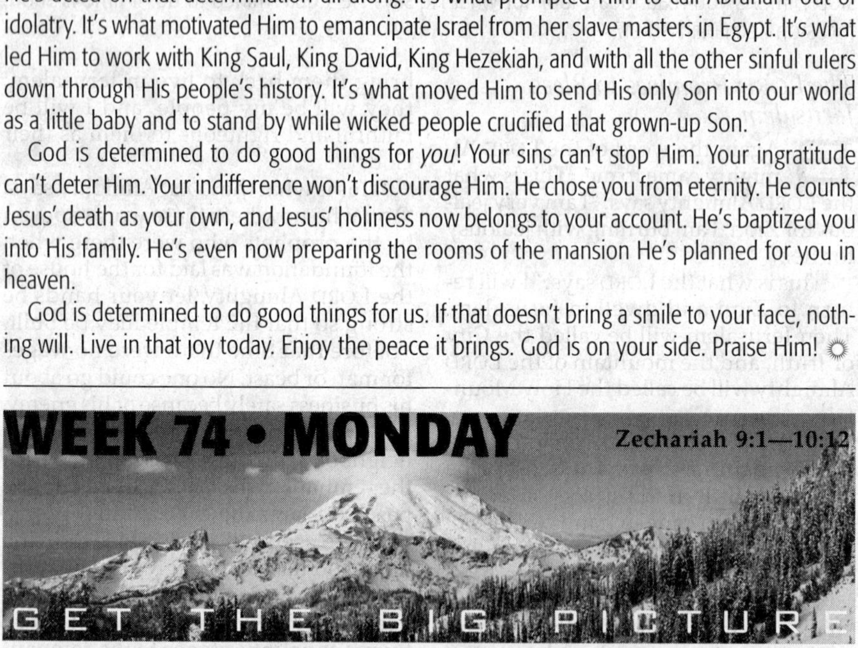

Zechariah describes the Lord camping around His people as a watchman, guarding us against our enemies (Zechariah 9:1–8). He depicts the first and second Advents of our Savior-King (Zechariah 9:9–10); His plan to use His church to tell of the love of Christ (Zechariah 9:11–16); and His grace in gathering those who have been scattered because of sin (Zechariah 10:1–12). Worship your Lord for His love as you read. If time is short, focus on Zechariah 9:1–17.

Judgment on Israel's Enemies

An Oracle

9 The word of the LORD is against
the land of Hadrach
and will rest upon Damascus—
for the eyes of men and all the tribes
of Israel
are on the LORD—[a]
2 and upon Hamath too, which
borders on it,
and upon Tyre and Sidon, though
they are very skillful.
3 Tyre has built herself a stronghold;
she has heaped up silver like dust,
and gold like the dirt of the
streets.
4 But the Lord will take away her
possessions
and destroy her power on the sea,
and she will be consumed by fire.
5 Ashkelon will see it and fear;
Gaza will writhe in agony,
and Ekron too, for her hope will
wither.
Gaza will lose her king
and Ashkelon will be deserted.
6 Foreigners will occupy Ashdod,
and I will cut off the pride of the
Philistines.
7 I will take the blood from their
mouths,
the forbidden food from between
their teeth.
Those who are left will belong to our
God
and become leaders in Judah,
and Ekron will be like the Jebusites.
8 But I will defend my house
against marauding forces.
Never again will an oppressor
overrun my people,
for now I am keeping watch.

The Coming of Zion's King

9 Rejoice greatly, O Daughter of Zion!
Shout, Daughter of Jerusalem!
See, your king[b] comes to you,
righteous and having salvation,
gentle and riding on a donkey,
on a colt, the foal of a donkey.
10 I will take away the chariots from
Ephraim
and the war-horses from
Jerusalem,
and the battle bow will be broken.
He will proclaim peace to the
nations.
His rule will extend from sea to
sea
and from the River[c] to the ends of
the earth.[d]
11 As for you, because of the blood of
my covenant with you,
I will free your prisoners from the
waterless pit.
12 Return to your fortress, O prisoners
of hope;
even now I announce that I will
restore twice as much to you.
13 I will bend Judah as I bend my bow
and fill it with Ephraim.
I will rouse your sons, O Zion,
against your sons, O Greece,
and make you like a warrior's
sword.

The LORD Will Appear

14 Then the LORD will appear over
them;
his arrow will flash like lightning.
The Sovereign LORD will sound the
trumpet;
he will march in the storms of the
south,
15 and the LORD Almighty will shield
them.
They will destroy
and overcome with slingstones.
They will drink and roar as with
wine;
they will be full like a bowl
used for sprinkling[e] the corners of
the altar.
16 The LORD their God will save them
on that day
as the flock of his people.
They will sparkle in his land
like jewels in a crown.
17 How attractive and beautiful they
will be!

[a] 1 Or *Damascus. / For the eye of the LORD is on all mankind, / as well as on the tribes of Israel,* [b] 9 Or *King* [c] 10 That is, the Euphrates [d] 10 Or *the end of the land* [e] 15 Or *bowl, / like*

Grain will make the young men
thrive,
and new wine the young women.

The LORD Will Care for Judah

10 Ask the LORD for rain in the
springtime;
it is the LORD who makes the
storm clouds.
He gives showers of rain to men,
and plants of the field to
everyone.
2 The idols speak deceit,
diviners see visions that lie;
they tell dreams that are false,
they give comfort in vain.
Therefore the people wander like
sheep
oppressed for lack of a shepherd.

3 "My anger burns against the
shepherds,
and I will punish the leaders;
for the LORD Almighty will care
for his flock, the house of Judah,
and make them like a proud horse
in battle.
4 From Judah will come the
cornerstone,
from him the tent peg,
from him the battle bow,
from him every ruler.
5 Together they[a] will be like mighty
men
trampling the muddy streets in
battle.
Because the LORD is with them,
they will fight and overthrow the
horsemen.

6 "I will strengthen the house of Judah
and save the house of Joseph.
I will restore them
because I have compassion on
them.
They will be as though
I had not rejected them,
for I am the LORD their God
and I will answer them.
7 The Ephraimites will become like
mighty men,
and their hearts will be glad as
with wine.
Their children will see it and be
joyful;
their hearts will rejoice in the
LORD.
8 I will signal for them
and gather them in.
Surely I will redeem them;
they will be as numerous as
before.
9 Though I scatter them among the
peoples,
yet in distant lands they will
remember me.
They and their children will
survive,
and they will return.
10 I will bring them back from Egypt
and gather them from Assyria.
I will bring them to Gilead and
Lebanon,
and there will not be room
enough for them.
11 They will pass through the sea of
trouble;
the surging sea will be subdued
and all the depths of the Nile will
dry up.
Assyria's pride will be brought
down
and Egypt's scepter will pass
away.
12 I will strengthen them in the LORD
and in his name they will walk,"
declares the LORD.

[a] 4,5 Or *ruler, all of them together. / 5They*

SHARPEN THE FOCUS

Are you a "prisoner of hope" (Zechariah 9:12)? At first, it can seem like a contradiction in terms. Hope is often the last thing prisoners experience.

When sin held our hearts captive, we too lived in hopelessness. We were "without hope and without God in the world" (Ephesians 2:12). But then, our King came to us. He chose, not a throne of gold, but a cross of wood. When he died in our place and rose again, our chains of guilt and shame fell away.

Now, "in His great mercy [God] has given us new birth into a living hope through the resurrection of Jesus Christ from the dead" (1 Peter 1:3). In Baptism, the Holy Spirit puts His mark of ownership on us. We belong to Him—for now and forever. What fantastic news!

This hope captivates our hearts. It fills us with joy. We've fallen head over heels in love with the Savior who has made our new life possible. We don't *want* to leave Him. Not ever. With the apostle Peter we say, "Lord, to whom shall we go? You have the words of eternal life" (John 6:68).

WEEK 74 • TUESDAY

Zechariah 11:1—12:14

GET THE BIG PICTURE

In chapter 11, Zechariah becomes a kind of "walking billboard." Like many prophets before him, he acts out a message from the Lord. In doing so, he pictures the coming Savior, the Good Shepherd who would be rejected by the sheep for whom He died. As you read, look for ways Zechariah is like Christ. If time is short, focus on Zechariah 12:1–14.

11 Open your doors, O Lebanon,
so that fire may devour your cedars!
2 Wail, O pine tree, for the cedar has fallen;
the stately trees are ruined!
Wail, oaks of Bashan;
the dense forest has been cut down!
3 Listen to the wail of the shepherds;
their rich pastures are destroyed!
Listen to the roar of the lions;
the lush thicket of the Jordan is ruined!

Two Shepherds

4 This is what the LORD my God says:
"Pasture the flock marked for slaughter.
5 Their buyers slaughter them and go
unpunished. Those who sell them say,
'Praise the LORD, I am rich!' Their own
shepherds do not spare them. 6 For I will
no longer have pity on the people of the
land," declares the LORD. "I will hand
everyone over to his neighbor and his
king. They will oppress the land, and I
will not rescue them from their hands."
7 So I pastured the flock marked for
slaughter, particularly the oppressed of
the flock. Then I took two staffs and
called one Favor and the other Union,
and I pastured the flock. 8 In one month
I got rid of the three shepherds.

The flock detested me, and I grew
weary of them 9 and said, "I will not be
your shepherd. Let the dying die, and
the perishing perish. Let those who are
left eat one another's flesh."
10 Then I took my staff called Favor
and broke it, revoking the covenant I
had made with all the nations. 11 It was
revoked on that day, and so the afflicted
of the flock who were watching me
knew it was the word of the LORD.
12 I told them, "If you think it best, give
me my pay; but if not, keep it." So they
paid me thirty pieces of silver.
13 And the LORD said to me, "Throw it

to the potter"—the handsome price at
which they priced me! So I took the thirty pieces of silver and threw them into
the house of the LORD to the potter.
14Then I broke my second staff called
Union, breaking the brotherhood between Judah and Israel.
15Then the LORD said to me, "Take
again the equipment of a foolish shepherd. 16For I am going to raise up a shepherd over the land who will not care for
the lost, or seek the young, or heal the
injured, or feed the healthy, but will eat
the meat of the choice sheep, tearing off
their hoofs.

17"Woe to the worthless shepherd,
who deserts the flock!
May the sword strike his arm and
his right eye!
May his arm be completely
withered,
his right eye totally blinded!"

Jerusalem's Enemies to Be Destroyed

An Oracle

12 This is the word of the LORD
concerning Israel. The LORD,
who stretches out the heavens, who lays
the foundation of the earth, and who
forms the spirit of man within him, declares: 2"I am going to make Jerusalem
a cup that sends all the surrounding
peoples reeling. Judah will be besieged
as well as Jerusalem. 3On that day, when
all the nations of the earth are gathered
against her, I will make Jerusalem an immovable rock for all the nations. All who
try to move it will injure themselves.
4On that day I will strike every horse
with panic and its rider with madness,"
declares the LORD. "I will keep a watchful eye over the house of Judah, but I
will blind all the horses of the nations.
5Then the leaders of Judah will say in
their hearts, 'The people of Jerusalem
are strong, because the LORD Almighty
is their God.'
6"On that day I will make the leaders
of Judah like a firepot in a woodpile, like
a flaming torch among sheaves. They
will consume right and left all the surrounding peoples, but Jerusalem will
remain intact in her place.
7"The LORD will save the dwellings of
Judah first, so that the honor of the
house of David and of Jerusalem's inhabitants may not be greater than that
of Judah. 8On that day the LORD will
shield those who live in Jerusalem, so
that the feeblest among them will be like
David, and the house of David will be
like God, like the Angel of the LORD
going before them. 9On that day I will
set out to destroy all the nations that
attack Jerusalem.

Mourning for the One They Pierced

10"And I will pour out on the house of
David and the inhabitants of Jerusalem
a spirit[a] of grace and supplication. They
will look on[b] me, the one they have
pierced, and they will mourn for him as
one mourns for an only child, and
grieve bitterly for him as one grieves for
a firstborn son. 11On that day the weeping in Jerusalem will be great, like the
weeping of Hadad Rimmon in the plain
of Megiddo. 12The land will mourn, each
clan by itself, with their wives by themselves: the clan of the house of David
and their wives, the clan of the house of
Nathan and their wives, 13the clan of the
house of Levi and their wives, the clan
of Shimei and their wives, 14and all the
rest of the clans and their wives.

[a]10 Or *the Spirit* [b]10 Or *to*

SHARPEN THE FOCUS

Like water roaring over Niagara Falls, the "Spirit of grace and supplication" (Zechariah 12:10) pours out from God's heart into God's people. The first thing the Spirit brings is mourning, the gift of repentance.

Perhaps repentance seems like anything but a gift. In our culture, people worship the great god fun. Who in his right mind wants to lie on his face before God in sorrow over sin? Who in her right mind wants to soak her pillow in the tears of a sleepless night, grieving the loss of holiness?

And yet, Jesus has promised, "Blessed are those who mourn, for they will be comforted" (Matthew 5:4). When we see that our sins–*our* sins–have pierced our Savior, when we see that we indeed were "there when they crucified [our] Lord," then we do mourn. Deeply. From the heart.

But the process of repentance does not end in grief. The Spirit is the Spirit of Grace. He assures us that in our crucified Lord we have forgiveness. He dries our tears with the comfort that we have become, in Jesus, God's own dear sons and daughters.

WEEK 74 • WEDNESDAY

Zechariah 13:1–9

No one enjoys life in the furnace. But impurities cannot be removed from gold in any other way. The trials and challenges of life will come. But as we cling to the Lord and to His Word even in the furnace, we will learn by His grace to say in confidence, "The Lord is [my] God" (Zechariah 13:9). If time is short, focus on Zechariah 13:7–9.

Cleansing From Sin

13 "On that day a fountain will
be opened to the house of
David and the inhabitants of Jerusalem,
to cleanse them from sin and impurity.
2"On that day, I will banish the names
of the idols from the land, and they will
be remembered no more," declares the
LORD Almighty. "I will remove both the
prophets and the spirit of impurity from
the land. 3And if anyone still prophesies,
his father and mother, to whom he was
born, will say to him, 'You must die,
because you have told lies in the LORD's
name.' When he prophesies, his own
parents will stab him.
4"On that day every prophet will be
ashamed of his prophetic vision. He will
not put on a prophet's garment of hair
in order to deceive. 5He will say, 'I am
not a prophet. I am a farmer; the land
has been my livelihood since my
youth.[a]' 6If someone asks him, 'What are
these wounds on your body[b]?' he will
answer, 'The wounds I was given at the
house of my friends.'

The Shepherd Struck, the Sheep Scattered

7"Awake, O sword, against my
shepherd,
against the man who is close to
me!"
declares the LORD Almighty.
"Strike the shepherd,
and the sheep will be scattered,
and I will turn my hand against
the little ones.
8In the whole land," declares the
LORD,
"two-thirds will be struck down
and perish;
yet one-third will be left in it.

[a]5 Or *farmer; a man sold me in my youth* [b]6 Or *wounds between your hands*

9 This third I will bring into the fire;
I will refine them like silver
and test them like gold.
They will call on my name
and I will answer them;
I will say, 'They are my people,'
and they will say, 'The LORD is our
God.' "

SHARPEN THE FOCUS

Come to Calv'ry's holy mountain,
Sinners, ruined by the fall;
Here a pure and healing fountain
Flows for you, for me, for all,
In a full perpetual tide,
Opened when our Savior died.

Take the life that lasts forever;
Trust this soul-renewing flood.
God is faithful; God will never
Break His covenant of blood,
Signed when our Redeemer died,
Sealed when He was glorified.

(James Montgomery)

Zechariah saw that fountain from the distance of nearly five centuries. Nonetheless, he rejoiced in its cleansing power (Zechariah 13:1). You have been washed in it; when you were baptized, you died with Christ (Romans 6:1–14). You are now clean.

The cleansing metaphor appears again and again in Scripture as a picture of forgiveness. See, for instance, how Hebrews 9:14 describes the clean conscience our Lord wants us to enjoy: "the blood of Christ, who through the eternal Spirit offered himself unblemished to God, cleanse[s] our consciences from acts that lead to death, so that we may serve the living God!"

Ask God to assure you of the clean heart He has created in you in Christ Jesus.

WEEK 74 • THURSDAY

Zechariah 14:1–21

GET THE BIG PICTURE

In language strikingly similar to New Testament prophecies, Zechariah describes the coming "day of the LORD." For those who have rejected the Lord and His Messiah, Judgment Day will come with a flood of terror that never ends (Zechariah 14:13). But those who are in Christ will welcome Him and enjoy His presence forever. If time is short, focus on Zechariah 14:1–9.

The LORD Comes and Reigns

14 A day of the LORD is coming when your plunder will be divided among you.

2 I will gather all the nations to Jerusalem to fight against it; the city will be captured, the houses ransacked, and the women raped. Half of the city will go into exile, but the rest of the people will not be taken from the city.

3 Then the LORD will go out and fight against those nations, as he fights in the day of battle. 4 On that day his feet will stand on the Mount of Olives, east of Jerusalem, and the Mount of Olives will be split in two from east to west, forming a great valley, with half of the mountain moving north and half moving south. 5 You will flee by my mountain valley, for it will extend to Azel. You will flee as you fled from the earthquake[a] in the days of Uzziah king of Judah. Then the LORD my God will come, and all the holy ones with him.

6 On that day there will be no light, no cold or frost. 7 It will be a unique day, without daytime or nighttime—a day known to the LORD. When evening comes, there will be light.

8 On that day living water will flow out from Jerusalem, half to the eastern sea[b] and half to the western sea,[c] in summer and in winter.

9 The LORD will be king over the whole earth. On that day there will be one LORD, and his name the only name.

10 The whole land, from Geba to Rimmon, south of Jerusalem, will become like the Arabah. But Jerusalem will be raised up and remain in its place, from the Benjamin Gate to the site of the First Gate, to the Corner Gate, and from the Tower of Hananel to the royal winepresses. 11 It will be inhabited; never again will it be destroyed. Jerusalem will be secure.

12 This is the plague with which the LORD will strike all the nations that fought against Jerusalem: Their flesh will rot while they are still standing on their feet, their eyes will rot in their sockets, and their tongues will rot in their mouths. 13 On that day men will be stricken by the LORD with great panic. Each man will seize the hand of another, and they will attack each other. 14 Judah too will fight at Jerusalem. The wealth of all the surrounding nations will be collected—great quantities of gold and silver and clothing. 15 A similar plague will strike the horses and mules, the camels and donkeys, and all the animals in those camps.

16 Then the survivors from all the nations that have attacked Jerusalem will go up year after year to worship the King, the LORD Almighty, and to celebrate the Feast of Tabernacles. 17 If any of the peoples of the earth do not go up to Jerusalem to worship the King, the LORD Almighty, they will have no rain. 18 If the Egyptian people do not go up and take part, they will have no rain. The LORD[d] will bring on them the plague he inflicts on the nations that do not go up to celebrate the Feast of Tabernacles. 19 This will be the punishment of Egypt and the punishment of all the nations that do not go up to celebrate the Feast of Tabernacles.

20 On that day HOLY TO THE LORD will be inscribed on the bells of the horses, and the cooking pots in the LORD's house will be like the sacred bowls in front of the altar. 21 Every pot in Jerusalem and Judah will be holy to the LORD Almighty, and all who come to sacrifice will take some of the pots and cook in them. And on that day there will no longer be a Canaanite[e] in the house of the LORD Almighty.

[a] 5 Or [5] *My mountain valley will be blocked and will extend to Azel. It will be blocked as it was blocked because of the earthquake* [b] 8 That is, the Dead Sea [c] 8 That is, the Mediterranean [d] 18 Or *part, then the LORD* [e] 21 Or *merchant*

SHARPEN THE FOCUS

Compare Zechariah's version of that day with that of the New Testament writers:

- Jesus will return visibly–Zechariah 14:4
  [Jesus] will come back in the same way you have seen him go into heaven. (Acts 1:11)
- The Day will be marked by a great earthquake–Zechariah 14:4–5
  There was a great earthquake . . . The sky receded like a scroll, rolling up, and every mountain and island was removed from its place. (Revelation 6:12, 14)
- The sun and moon will dim–Zechariah 14:6
  The sun will be darkened, and the moon will not give its light. (Matthew 24:29)
- The Lord will be our eternal light–Zechariah 14:7
  They will not need the light of a lamp or the light of the sun, for the Lord God will give them light. (Revelation 22:5)
- The River of Life will flow through the heavenly Jerusalem–Zechariah 14:8
  The river of the water of life . . . flowing from the throne of God and of the Lamb down the middle of the great street of the city. (Revelation 22:1, 2)

What other comparisons can you suggest? Empowered by God's pardon, look for ways to participate in heaven's highest joy today–Praise your King!

MALACHI

The people of Israel, down through the ages, have treated their Almighty King shabbily and the King is mightily displeased. As you read, look for the offenses with which Malachi charges the descendants of those who had returned from exile. If time is short, focus on Malachi 1:1–14.

1 An oracle: The word of the LORD to
Israel through Malachi.[a]

Jacob Loved, Esau Hated

2"I have loved you," says the LORD.
"But you ask, 'How have you loved
us?'
"Was not Esau Jacob's brother?" the
LORD says. "Yet I have loved Jacob, 3but
Esau I have hated, and I have turned his
mountains into a wasteland and left his
inheritance to the desert jackals."
4Edom may say, "Though we have
been crushed, we will rebuild the ruins."
But this is what the LORD Almighty
says: "They may build, but I will demolish. They will be called the Wicked
Land, a people always under the wrath
of the LORD. 5You will see it with your
own eyes and say, 'Great is the LORD—
even beyond the borders of Israel!'

Blemished Sacrifices

6"A son honors his father, and a servant his master. If I am a father, where
is the honor due me? If I am a master,
where is the respect due me?" says the
LORD Almighty. "It is you, O priests,
who show contempt for my name.
"But you ask, 'How have we shown
contempt for your name?'
7"You place defiled food on my altar.
"But you ask, 'How have we defiled
you?'
"By saying that the LORD's table is
contemptible. 8When you bring blind
animals for sacrifice, is that not wrong?
When you sacrifice crippled or diseased
animals, is that not wrong? Try offering
them to your governor! Would he be
pleased with you? Would he accept
you?" says the LORD Almighty.
9"Now implore God to be gracious to
us. With such offerings from your
hands, will he accept you?"—says the
LORD Almighty.
10"Oh, that one of you would shut the
temple doors, so that you would not
light useless fires on my altar! I am not
pleased with you," says the LORD Almighty, "and I will accept no offering
from your hands. 11My name will be
great among the nations, from the rising to the setting of the sun. In every
place incense and pure offerings will be
brought to my name, because my name
will be great among the nations," says
the LORD Almighty.
12"But you profane it by saying of the
Lord's table, 'It is defiled,' and of its
food, 'It is contemptible.' 13And you say,

[a]*1 Malachi* means *my messenger.*

'What a burden!' and you sniff at it
contemptuously," says the LORD Almighty.
"When you bring injured, crippled or
diseased animals and offer them as sacrifices, should I accept them from your
hands?" says the LORD. 14"Cursed is the
cheat who has an acceptable male in his
flock and vows to give it, but then sacrifices a blemished animal to the Lord.
For I am a great king," says the LORD Almighty, "and my name is to be feared
among the nations.

Admonition for the Priests

2 "And now this admonition is for
you, O priests. 2If you do not listen, and if you do not set your heart to
honor my name," says the LORD Almighty, "I will send a curse upon
you, and I will curse your blessings.
Yes, I have already cursed them, because you have not set your heart to
honor me.
3"Because of you I will rebuke[a] your
descendants[b]; I will spread on your
faces the offal from your festival sacrifices, and you will be carried off with it.
4And you will know that I have sent you
this admonition so that my covenant
with Levi may continue," says the LORD
Almighty. 5"My covenant was with him,
a covenant of life and peace, and I gave
them to him; this called for reverence
and he revered me and stood in awe of
my name. 6True instruction was in his
mouth and nothing false was found on
his lips. He walked with me in peace
and uprightness, and turned many
from sin.
7"For the lips of a priest ought to preserve knowledge, and from his mouth
men should seek instruction—because
he is the messenger of the LORD Almighty. 8But you have turned from the
way and by your teaching have caused
many to stumble; you have violated the
covenant with Levi," says the LORD Almighty. 9"So I have caused you to be despised and humiliated before all the
people, because you have not followed
my ways but have shown partiality in
matters of the law."

Judah Unfaithful

10Have we not all one Father[c]? Did not
one God create us? Why do we profane
the covenant of our fathers by breaking
faith with one another?
11Judah has broken faith. A detestable
thing has been committed in Israel and
in Jerusalem: Judah has desecrated the
sanctuary the LORD loves, by marrying
the daughter of a foreign god. 12As for
the man who does this, whoever he
may be, may the LORD cut him off from
the tents of Jacob[d]—even though he
brings offerings to the LORD Almighty.
13Another thing you do: You flood the
LORD's altar with tears. You weep and
wail because he no longer pays attention to your offerings or accepts them
with pleasure from your hands. 14You
ask, "Why?" It is because the LORD is
acting as the witness between you and
the wife of your youth, because you
have broken faith with her, though she
is your partner, the wife of your marriage covenant.
15Has not ⌞the LORD⌟ made them one?
In flesh and spirit they are his. And why
one? Because he was seeking godly
offspring.[e] So guard yourself in your
spirit, and do not break faith with the
wife of your youth.
16"I hate divorce," says the LORD God
of Israel, "and I hate a man's covering
himself[f] with violence as well as with
his garment," says the LORD Almighty.
So guard yourself in your spirit, and
do not break faith.

The Day of Judgment

17You have wearied the LORD with
your words.
"How have we wearied him?" you ask.
By saying, "All who do evil are good
in the eyes of the LORD, and he is
pleased with them" or "Where is the
God of justice?"

[a]3 Or *cut off* (see Septuagint) [b]3 Or *will blight your grain* [c]10 Or *father* [d]12 Or [12]*May the LORD cut off from the tents of Jacob anyone who gives testimony in behalf of the man who does this* [e]15 Or [15]*But the one ⌞who is our father⌟ did not do this, not as long as life remained in him. And what was he seeking? An offspring from God* [f]16 Or *his wife*

SHARPEN THE FOCUS

Have you ever given less than your best as you sang, praised, and thanked your King in public worship? We've all, at one time or another, gone through the motions of worship without really worshiping.

And since that's true, today's reading from Malachi could scare our socks off: " 'I am a great King,' says the LORD Almighty" (Malachi 1:14). The Commander of heaven's angel army doesn't find our inattention and reluctance amusing. And we have not yet even started to think about our attitudes toward the offerings we bring.

" 'I am not pleased with you,' says the LORD Almighty" (Malachi 1:10). We ought to tremble. We deserve the judgment of those who fail to fear, love, and trust God above everything else. Let's face it. Our inattention grows out of half-hearted love. Our boredom grows out of a picture of God that is far, far too small. Our thanklessness grows out of the pride that claims the ability to take care of ourselves. Is it any wonder our worship is often dead?

But praise God that the curse we've deserved for our sins fell on Jesus at the cross. Assured of His forgiveness, ask Him to fill your heart with a deeper realization of His great goodness.

WEEK 74 • SATURDAY

Malachi 3:1—4:6

GET THE BIG PICTURE

With today's reading we finish the Old Testament. All the writers of the Old Testament attest to the truth of Malachi 3:6—"I the LORD do not change." Look for continued evidence of the Lord's consistent message in today's reading—His message of sin and grace, Law and Gospel. If time is short, focus on Malachi 3:1–18.

3 "See, I will send my messenger, who will prepare the way before me. Then suddenly the Lord you are seeking will come to his temple; the messenger of the covenant, whom you desire, will come," says the LORD Almighty.
2 But who can endure the day of his coming? Who can stand when he appears? For he will be like a refiner's fire or a launderer's soap.
3 He will sit as a refiner and purifier of silver; he will purify the Levites and refine them like gold and silver. Then the LORD will have men who will bring offerings in righteousness,
4 and the offerings of Judah and Jerusalem will be acceptable to the LORD, as in days gone by, as in former years.
5 "So I will come near to you for judgment. I will be quick to testify against sorcerers, adulterers and perjurers, against those who defraud laborers of their wages, who oppress the widows and the fatherless, and deprive aliens of justice, but do not fear me," says the LORD Almighty.

Robbing God

6 "I the LORD do not change. So you, O descendants of Jacob, are not destroyed.
7 Ever since the time of your forefathers you have turned away from my decrees and have not kept them. Re-

turn to me, and I will return to you," says the LORD Almighty.

"But you ask, 'How are we to return?'

8"Will a man rob God? Yet you rob me.

"But you ask, 'How do we rob you?'

"In tithes and offerings. 9You are under a curse—the whole nation of you—because you are robbing me. 10Bring the whole tithe into the storehouse, that there may be food in my house. Test me in this," says the LORD Almighty, "and see if I will not throw open the floodgates of heaven and pour out so much blessing that you will not have room enough for it. 11I will prevent pests from devouring your crops, and the vines in your fields will not cast their fruit," says the LORD Almighty. 12"Then all the nations will call you blessed, for yours will be a delightful land," says the LORD Almighty.

13"You have said harsh things against me," says the LORD.

"Yet you ask, 'What have we said against you?'

14"You have said, 'It is futile to serve God. What did we gain by carrying out his requirements and going about like mourners before the LORD Almighty? 15But now we call the arrogant blessed. Certainly the evildoers prosper, and even those who challenge God escape.' "

16Then those who feared the LORD talked with each other, and the LORD listened and heard. A scroll of remembrance was written in his presence concerning those who feared the LORD and honored his name.

17"They will be mine," says the LORD Almighty, "in the day when I make up my treasured possession.[a] I will spare them, just as in compassion a man spares his son who serves him. 18And you will again see the distinction between the righteous and the wicked, between those who serve God and those who do not.

The Day of the LORD

4 "Surely the day is coming; it will burn like a furnace. All the arrogant and every evildoer will be stubble, and that day that is coming will set them on fire," says the LORD Almighty. "Not a root or a branch will be left to them. 2But for you who revere my name, the sun of righteousness will rise with healing in its wings. And you will go out and leap like calves released from the stall. 3Then you will trample down the wicked; they will be ashes under the soles of your feet on the day when I do these things," says the LORD Almighty.

4"Remember the law of my servant Moses, the decrees and laws I gave him at Horeb for all Israel.

5"See, I will send you the prophet Elijah before that great and dreadful day of the LORD comes. 6He will turn the hearts of the fathers to their children, and the hearts of the children to their fathers; or else I will come and strike the land with a curse."

[a]17 Or *Almighty, "my treasured possession, in the day when I act*

SHARPEN THE FOCUS

Think what a mess we'd be in if our Lord changed—even a little! What if we couldn't be sure He'd forgive us *this* time, take care of us *this* time, hear our prayers *this* time?

Praise God, we can be sure! The covenant of grace our Lord made with Abraham back in Genesis 12 would be fulfilled by the Messenger of the covenant foretold by Malachi (Malachi 3:1). The Lord who revealed Himself as Healer for His people in Exodus 15:26 is the "Sun of Righteousness" who arose for Malachi "with healing in its wings" (Malachi 4:2).

God does not change. His mercy toward us is life's one constant. Therefore, we are not destroyed. Far from it! In Jesus, we are God's treasured possession (Malachi 3:17). Evil will not have its way forever. The wicked will be judged. Death will one day die (Malachi 4:3).

That Day will bring a joy for us unlike any joy we've ever experienced. Like calves, born in a dark barn and never given a chance to stretch our legs, we will one day find ourselves warm and free in the sunshine of our heavenly Father's house. We'll dance and leap for the glory of it (Malachi 4:2). Even so, "Come, Lord Jesus" (Revelation 22:20)!

New Testament

MATTHEW

WEEK 75 • MONDAY

Matthew 1:1—2:23

Matthew links the Old Testament with the New by tracing the "red ribbon of promise" from Abraham, through King David, and on down to Joseph. Note that while Matthew acknowledges Jesus' foster father, he clearly also points to what church has come to call Jesus' "virgin birth." Also note in Matthew 2 the contrasting welcomes the Savior receives. Why so much joy? Why so much fear? If time is short, focus on Matthew 1:18–25.

The Genealogy of Jesus

1 A record of the genealogy of Jesus Christ the son of David, the son of Abraham:

2 Abraham was the father of Isaac,
Isaac the father of Jacob,
Jacob the father of Judah and his brothers,
3 Judah the father of Perez and Zerah, whose mother was Tamar,
Perez the father of Hezron,
Hezron the father of Ram,
4 Ram the father of Amminadab,
Amminadab the father of Nahshon,
Nahshon the father of Salmon,
5 Salmon the father of Boaz, whose mother was Rahab,
Boaz the father of Obed, whose mother was Ruth,
Obed the father of Jesse,
6 and Jesse the father of King David.

David was the father of Solomon, whose mother had been Uriah's wife,
7 Solomon the father of Rehoboam,
Rehoboam the father of Abijah,
Abijah the father of Asa,
8 Asa the father of Jehoshaphat,
Jehoshaphat the father of Jehoram,
Jehoram the father of Uzziah,
9 Uzziah the father of Jotham,
Jotham the father of Ahaz,
Ahaz the father of Hezekiah,
10 Hezekiah the father of Manasseh,
Manasseh the father of Amon,
Amon the father of Josiah,
11 and Josiah the father of Jeconiah[a] and his brothers at the time of the exile to Babylon.

12 After the exile to Babylon:
Jeconiah was the father of Shealtiel,
Shealtiel the father of Zerubbabel,
13 Zerubbabel the father of Abiud,
Abiud the father of Eliakim,
Eliakim the father of Azor,
14 Azor the father of Zadok,
Zadok the father of Akim,
Akim the father of Eliud,
15 Eliud the father of Eleazar,

[a] *11* That is, Jehoiachin; also in verse 12

Eleazar the father of Matthan,
Matthan the father of Jacob,
16 and Jacob the father of Joseph,
the husband of Mary, of whom
was born Jesus, who is called
Christ.

17 Thus there were fourteen generations in all from Abraham to David,
fourteen from David to the exile to Babylon, and fourteen from the exile to the
Christ.[a]

The Birth of Jesus Christ

18 This is how the birth of Jesus Christ
came about: His mother Mary was
pledged to be married to Joseph, but before they came together, she was found
to be with child through the Holy Spirit.
19 Because Joseph her husband was a
righteous man and did not want to expose her to public disgrace, he had in
mind to divorce her quietly.
20 But after he had considered this, an
angel of the Lord appeared to him in a
dream and said, "Joseph son of David,
do not be afraid to take Mary home as
your wife, because what is conceived in
her is from the Holy Spirit. 21 She will
give birth to a son, and you are to give
him the name Jesus,[b] because he will
save his people from their sins."
22 All this took place to fulfill what the
Lord had said through the prophet:
23 "The virgin will be with child and will
give birth to a son, and they will call
him Immanuel"[c]—which means, "God
with us."
24 When Joseph woke up, he did what
the angel of the Lord had commanded
him and took Mary home as his wife.
25 But he had no union with her until she
gave birth to a son. And he gave him the
name Jesus.

The Visit of the Magi

2 After Jesus was born in Bethlehem in Judea, during the time of
King Herod, Magi[d] from the east came
to Jerusalem 2 and asked, "Where is the
one who has been born king of the
Jews? We saw his star in the east[e] and
have come to worship him."
3 When King Herod heard this he was
disturbed, and all Jerusalem with him.
4 When he had called together all the
people's chief priests and teachers of the
law, he asked them where the Christ[f]
was to be born. 5 "In Bethlehem in Judea," they replied, "for this is what the
prophet has written:

6 " 'But you, Bethlehem, in the land of
Judah,
are by no means least among the
rulers of Judah;
for out of you will come a ruler
who will be the shepherd of my
people Israel.'[g]"

7 Then Herod called the Magi secretly
and found out from them the exact time
the star had appeared. 8 He sent them to
Bethlehem and said, "Go and make a
careful search for the child. As soon as
you find him, report to me, so that I too
may go and worship him."
9 After they had heard the king, they
went on their way, and the star they had
seen in the east[h] went ahead of them
until it stopped over the place where the
child was. 10 When they saw the star,
they were overjoyed. 11 On coming to
the house, they saw the child with his
mother Mary, and they bowed down
and worshiped him. Then they opened
their treasures and presented him with
gifts of gold and of incense and of
myrrh. 12 And having been warned in a
dream not to go back to Herod, they returned to their country by another
route.

The Escape to Egypt

13 When they had gone, an angel of the
Lord appeared to Joseph in a dream.
"Get up," he said, "take the child and his
mother and escape to Egypt. Stay there
until I tell you, for Herod is going to
search for the child to kill him."

[a] *17* Or *Messiah.* "The Christ" (Greek) and "the Messiah" (Hebrew) both mean "the Anointed One." [b] *21 Jesus* is the Greek form of *Joshua,* which means *the LORD saves.* [c] 23 Isaiah 7:14 [d] *1* Traditionally *Wise Men* [e] 2 Or *star when it rose* [f] 4 Or *Messiah* [g] 6 Micah 5:2 [h] 9 Or *seen when it rose*

[14]So he got up, took the child and his
mother during the night and left for
Egypt, [15]where he stayed until the death
of Herod. And so was fulfilled what the
Lord had said through the prophet:
"Out of Egypt I called my son."[a]
[16]When Herod realized that he had
been outwitted by the Magi, he was furious,
and he gave orders to kill all the
boys in Bethlehem and its vicinity who
were two years old and under, in accordance
with the time he had learned
from the Magi. [17]Then what was said
through the prophet Jeremiah was fulfilled:

[18]"A voice is heard in Ramah,
weeping and great mourning,
Rachel weeping for her children
and refusing to be comforted,
because they are no more."[b]

The Return to Nazareth

[19]After Herod died, an angel of the
Lord appeared in a dream to Joseph in
Egypt [20]and said, "Get up, take the child
and his mother and go to the land of Israel,
for those who were trying to take
the child's life are dead."
[21]So he got up, took the child and his
mother and went to the land of Israel.
[22]But when he heard that Archelaus was
reigning in Judea in place of his father
Herod, he was afraid to go there. Having
been warned in a dream, he withdrew
to the district of Galilee, [23]and he
went and lived in a town called Nazareth.
So was fulfilled what was said
through the prophets: "He will be called
a Nazarene."

[a]*15* Hosea 11:1 [b]*18* Jer. 31:15

SHARPEN THE FOCUS

Suppose you were to nominate "the greatest sentence in the English language." What words would you pick? A passage from Shakespeare? A line from your favorite poem? Or would you suggest a sentence like one of these:

- You won!
- Welcome home!
- I love you!

If you thought more about it, you might choose the angel's words in Matthew 1:21:

> *. . . give Him the name Jesus, because He will save His people from their sins.*

He will save—rescue, deliver. The word includes so much. Primarily it speaks of release, freedom. In Jesus, we receive freedom from the guilt of sin and freedom from slavery to sin. We need no longer live in shame over who we are or over what we've said or done. We can lay that burden down, trusting that Jesus carried it to His cross where it was destroyed forever.

We need no longer slave for sin either. By the power of the new life at work in us through our Baptism, we can show the love we now want to show our Lord and the people around us.

Where does sin have you loaded down with guilt or trapped in slavery today? Talk to Jesus about it as you meditate on Matthew 1:21.

Like Elijah before him (1 Kings 17:1), John the Baptizer appears out of nowhere to demand repentance. (See Malachi 3:1 and 4:5–6.) Not long after, Jesus Himself picks up John's message. Read today's texts carefully and thoughtfully. What do you learn about Jesus from these chapters? If time is short, focus on Matthew 4:1–11.

John the Baptist Prepares the Way

3 In those days John the Baptist came, preaching in the Desert of Judea 2and saying, "Repent, for the kingdom of heaven is near." 3This is he who was spoken of through the prophet Isaiah:

"A voice of one calling in the desert,
'Prepare the way for the Lord,
make straight paths for him.' "[a]

4John's clothes were made of camel's hair, and he had a leather belt around his waist. His food was locusts and wild honey. 5People went out to him from Jerusalem and all Judea and the whole region of the Jordan. 6Confessing their sins, they were baptized by him in the Jordan River.

7But when he saw many of the Pharisees and Sadducees coming to where he was baptizing, he said to them: "You brood of vipers! Who warned you to flee from the coming wrath? 8Produce fruit in keeping with repentance. 9And do not think you can say to yourselves, 'We have Abraham as our father.' I tell you that out of these stones God can raise up children for Abraham. 10The ax is already at the root of the trees, and every tree that does not produce good fruit will be cut down and thrown into the fire.

11"I baptize you with[b] water for repentance. But after me will come one who is more powerful than I, whose sandals I am not fit to carry. He will baptize you with the Holy Spirit and with fire. 12His winnowing fork is in his hand, and he will clear his threshing floor, gathering his wheat into the barn and burning up the chaff with unquenchable fire."

The Baptism of Jesus

13Then Jesus came from Galilee to the Jordan to be baptized by John. 14But John tried to deter him, saying, "I need to be baptized by you, and do you come to me?"

15Jesus replied, "Let it be so now; it is proper for us to do this to fulfill all righteousness." Then John consented.

16As soon as Jesus was baptized, he went up out of the water. At that moment heaven was opened, and he saw the Spirit of God descending like a dove and lighting on him. 17And a voice from heaven said, "This is my Son, whom I love; with him I am well pleased."

The Temptation of Jesus

4 Then Jesus was led by the Spirit into the desert to be tempted by the devil. 2After fasting forty days and forty nights, he was hungry. 3The tempter came to him and said, "If you are the Son of God, tell these stones to become bread."

4Jesus answered, "It is written: 'Man does not live on bread alone, but on every word that comes from the mouth of God.'[c]"

5Then the devil took him to the holy city and had him stand on the highest point of the temple. 6"If you are the Son

[a]3 Isaiah 40:3 [b]11 Or *in* [c]4 Deut. 8:3

of God," he said, "throw yourself down.
For it is written:

" 'He will command his angels
concerning you,
and they will lift you up in their
hands,
so that you will not strike your foot
against a stone.'[a]"

7 Jesus answered him, "It is also written: 'Do not put the Lord your God to
the test.'[b]"
8 Again, the devil took him to a very
high mountain and showed him all the
kingdoms of the world and their splendor. 9 "All this I will give you," he said, "if
you will bow down and worship me."
10 Jesus said to him, "Away from me,
Satan! For it is written: 'Worship the
Lord your God, and serve him only.'[c]"
11 Then the devil left him, and angels
came and attended him.

Jesus Begins to Preach

12 When Jesus heard that John had
been put in prison, he returned to Galilee. 13 Leaving Nazareth, he went and
lived in Capernaum, which was by the
lake in the area of Zebulun and Naphtali— 14 to fulfill what was said through
the prophet Isaiah:

15 "Land of Zebulun and land of
Naphtali,
the way to the sea, along the
Jordan,
Galilee of the Gentiles—
16 the people living in darkness
have seen a great light;
on those living in the land of the
shadow of death
a light has dawned."[d]

17 From that time on Jesus began to
preach, "Repent, for the kingdom of
heaven is near."

The Calling of the First Disciples

18 As Jesus was walking beside the Sea
of Galilee, he saw two brothers, Simon
called Peter and his brother Andrew.
They were casting a net into the lake, for
they were fishermen. 19 "Come, follow
me," Jesus said, "and I will make you
fishers of men." 20 At once they left their
nets and followed him.
21 Going on from there, he saw two
other brothers, James son of Zebedee
and his brother John. They were in a
boat with their father Zebedee, preparing their nets. Jesus called them, 22 and
immediately they left the boat and their
father and followed him.

Jesus Heals the Sick

23 Jesus went throughout Galilee,
teaching in their synagogues, preaching
the good news of the kingdom, and
healing every disease and sickness
among the people. 24 News about him
spread all over Syria, and people
brought to him all who were ill with various diseases, those suffering severe
pain, the demon-possessed, those having seizures, and the paralyzed, and he
healed them. 25 Large crowds from Galilee, the Decapolis,[e] Jerusalem, Judea and
the region across the Jordan followed
him.

[a] *6* Psalm 91:11,12 [b] *7* Deut. 6:16
[c] *10* Deut. 6:13 [d] *16* Isaiah 9:1,2 [e] *25* That is, the
Ten Cities

SHARPEN THE FOCUS

On one level, we use the term temptation to refer to our desire to eat that piece of pastry. On another level, we know the experience of serious temptation, of being locked in battle with the evil one over whether or not to do God's will. Jesus knew this battle, too. Intimately.

Boiled down, Satan's ploys in Matthew 4 went something like this:

- Did God really say, "You are My Son" (Matthew 4:3; see also Matthew 3:17 and Genesis 3:1)?

- If He said it, prove it's true (Matthew 4:5–6).
- Even though He said it, I can give you what you want, too. Let's do it an easier way (Matthew 4:8–9).

Jesus knows what it's like to fight off questions about God's truthfulness, about God's love, about taking short-cuts to get to a treasured goal. He knows what we go through in the desert times of life when our Baptism seems so long ago and far away and when our heavenly Father's trustworthiness seems open to question.

Jesus wielded the sword of the Spirit, the Word of God (Ephesians 6:17), with precision. He undercut Satan's every temptation, obeying the heavenly Father perfectly in our place. And now He invites us to take up that same powerful sword as we face life's temptations.

WEEK 75 • WEDNESDAY

Matthew 5:1—7:29

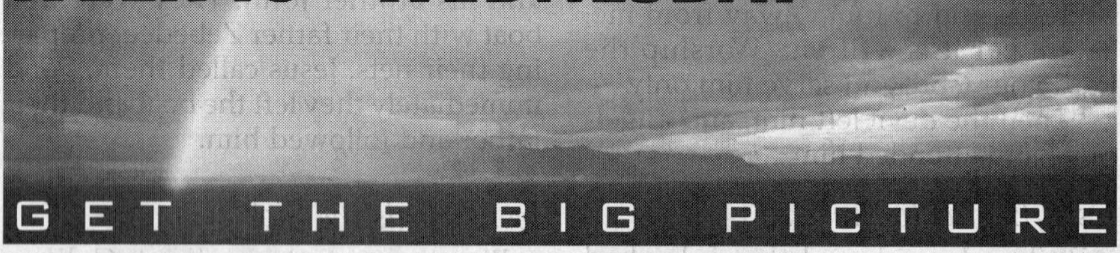

Jesus' entire sermon (Matthew 5–7) can be read aloud in about 15 minutes. And yet we will spend our entire lives mastering our Lord's implications in it. As you read today keep this question in mind: "Now that we've come into the kingdom of God, by His grace, through faith in the Savior, how do we live out our new citizenship?" If time is short, focus on Matthew 5:1–12.

The Beatitudes

5 Now when he saw the crowds, he went up on a mountainside and sat down. His disciples came to him, [2]and he began to teach them, saying:

[3]"Blessed are the poor in spirit,
for theirs is the kingdom of heaven.
[4]Blessed are those who mourn,
for they will be comforted.
[5]Blessed are the meek,
for they will inherit the earth.
[6]Blessed are those who hunger and thirst for righteousness,
for they will be filled.
[7]Blessed are the merciful,
for they will be shown mercy.
[8]Blessed are the pure in heart,
for they will see God.
[9]Blessed are the peacemakers,
for they will be called sons of God.
[10]Blessed are those who are persecuted because of righteousness,
for theirs is the kingdom of heaven.

[11]"Blessed are you when people insult you, persecute you and falsely say all kinds of evil against you because of me.
[12]Rejoice and be glad, because great is your reward in heaven, for in the same way they persecuted the prophets who were before you.

Salt and Light

[13]"You are the salt of the earth. But if the salt loses its saltiness, how can it be made salty again? It is no longer good for anything, except to be thrown out and trampled by men.

[14]"You are the light of the world. A city on a hill cannot be hidden. [15]Neither do people light a lamp and put it under a

bowl. Instead they put it on its stand, and it gives light to everyone in the house. [16]In the same way, let your light shine before men, that they may see your good deeds and praise your Father in heaven.

The Fulfillment of the Law

[17]"Do not think that I have come to abolish the Law or the Prophets; I have not come to abolish them but to fulfill them. [18]I tell you the truth, until heaven and earth disappear, not the smallest letter, not the least stroke of a pen, will by any means disappear from the Law until everything is accomplished. [19]Anyone who breaks one of the least of these commandments and teaches others to do the same will be called least in the kingdom of heaven, but whoever practices and teaches these commands will be called great in the kingdom of heaven. [20]For I tell you that unless your righteousness surpasses that of the Pharisees and the teachers of the law, you will certainly not enter the kingdom of heaven.

Murder

[21]"You have heard that it was said to the people long ago, 'Do not murder,[a] and anyone who murders will be subject to judgment.' [22]But I tell you that anyone who is angry with his brother[b] will be subject to judgment. Again, anyone who says to his brother, 'Raca,[c]' is answerable to the Sanhedrin. But anyone who says, 'You fool!' will be in danger of the fire of hell.

[23]"Therefore, if you are offering your gift at the altar and there remember that your brother has something against you, [24]leave your gift there in front of the altar. First go and be reconciled to your brother; then come and offer your gift.

[25]"Settle matters quickly with your adversary who is taking you to court. Do it while you are still with him on the way, or he may hand you over to the judge, and the judge may hand you over to the officer, and you may be thrown into prison. [26]I tell you the truth, you will not get out until you have paid the last penny.[d]

Adultery

[27]"You have heard that it was said, 'Do not commit adultery.'[e] [28]But I tell you that anyone who looks at a woman lustfully has already committed adultery with her in his heart. [29]If your right eye causes you to sin, gouge it out and throw it away. It is better for you to lose one part of your body than for your whole body to be thrown into hell. [30]And if your right hand causes you to sin, cut it off and throw it away. It is better for you to lose one part of your body than for your whole body to go into hell.

Divorce

[31]"It has been said, 'Anyone who divorces his wife must give her a certificate of divorce.'[f] [32]But I tell you that anyone who divorces his wife, except for marital unfaithfulness, causes her to become an adulteress, and anyone who marries the divorced woman commits adultery.

Oaths

[33]"Again, you have heard that it was said to the people long ago, 'Do not break your oath, but keep the oaths you have made to the Lord.' [34]But I tell you, Do not swear at all: either by heaven, for it is God's throne; [35]or by the earth, for it is his footstool; or by Jerusalem, for it is the city of the Great King. [36]And do not swear by your head, for you cannot make even one hair white or black. [37]Simply let your 'Yes' be 'Yes,' and your 'No,' 'No'; anything beyond this comes from the evil one.

An Eye for an Eye

[38]"You have heard that it was said, 'Eye for eye, and tooth for tooth.'[g] [39]But I tell you, Do not resist an evil person.

[a]*21* Exodus 20:13 [b]*22* Some manuscripts *brother without cause* [c]*22* An Aramaic term of contempt [d]*26* Greek *kodrantes* [e]*27* Exodus 20:14 [f]*31* Deut. 24:1 [g]*38* Exodus 21:24; Lev. 24:20; Deut. 19:21

If someone strikes you on the right cheek, turn to him the other also. [40]And if someone wants to sue you and take your tunic, let him have your cloak as well. [41]If someone forces you to go one mile, go with him two miles. [42]Give to the one who asks you, and do not turn away from the one who wants to borrow from you.

Love for Enemies

[43]"You have heard that it was said, 'Love your neighbor[a] and hate your enemy.' [44]But I tell you: Love your enemies[b] and pray for those who persecute you, [45]that you may be sons of your Father in heaven. He causes his sun to rise on the evil and the good, and sends rain on the righteous and the unrighteous. [46]If you love those who love you, what reward will you get? Are not even the tax collectors doing that? [47]And if you greet only your brothers, what are you doing more than others? Do not even pagans do that? [48]Be perfect, therefore, as your heavenly Father is perfect.

Giving to the Needy

6 "Be careful not to do your 'acts of righteousness' before men, to be seen by them. If you do, you will have no reward from your Father in heaven.

[2]"So when you give to the needy, do not announce it with trumpets, as the hypocrites do in the synagogues and on the streets, to be honored by men. I tell you the truth, they have received their reward in full. [3]But when you give to the needy, do not let your left hand know what your right hand is doing, [4]so that your giving may be in secret. Then your Father, who sees what is done in secret, will reward you.

Prayer

[5]"And when you pray, do not be like the hypocrites, for they love to pray standing in the synagogues and on the street corners to be seen by men. I tell you the truth, they have received their reward in full. [6]But when you pray, go into your room, close the door and pray to your Father, who is unseen. Then your Father, who sees what is done in secret, will reward you. [7]And when you pray, do not keep on babbling like pagans, for they think they will be heard because of their many words. [8]Do not be like them, for your Father knows what you need before you ask him.

[9]"This, then, is how you should pray:

" 'Our Father in heaven,
hallowed be your name,
[10]your kingdom come,
your will be done
on earth as it is in heaven.
[11]Give us today our daily bread.
[12]Forgive us our debts,
as we also have forgiven our debtors.
[13]And lead us not into temptation,
but deliver us from the evil one.[c]'

[14]For if you forgive men when they sin against you, your heavenly Father will also forgive you. [15]But if you do not forgive men their sins, your Father will not forgive your sins.

Fasting

[16]"When you fast, do not look somber as the hypocrites do, for they disfigure their faces to show men they are fasting. I tell you the truth, they have received their reward in full. [17]But when you fast, put oil on your head and wash your face, [18]so that it will not be obvious to men that you are fasting, but only to your Father, who is unseen; and your Father, who sees what is done in secret, will reward you.

Treasures in Heaven

[19]"Do not store up for yourselves treasures on earth, where moth and rust destroy, and where thieves break in and steal. [20]But store up for yourselves treasures in heaven, where moth and rust do not destroy, and where thieves do not break in and steal. [21]For where your treasure is, there your heart will be also.

[a]43 Lev. 19:18 [b]44 Some late manuscripts *enemies, bless those who curse you, do good to those who hate you* [c]13 Or *from evil*; some late manuscripts *one, / for yours is the kingdom and the power and the glory forever. Amen.*

22"The eye is the lamp of the body. If your eyes are good, your whole body will be full of light. 23But if your eyes are bad, your whole body will be full of darkness. If then the light within you is darkness, how great is that darkness!

24"No one can serve two masters. Either he will hate the one and love the other, or he will be devoted to the one and despise the other. You cannot serve both God and Money.

Do Not Worry

25"Therefore I tell you, do not worry about your life, what you will eat or drink; or about your body, what you will wear. Is not life more important than food, and the body more important than clothes? 26Look at the birds of the air; they do not sow or reap or store away in barns, and yet your heavenly Father feeds them. Are you not much more valuable than they? 27Who of you by worrying can add a single hour to his life[a]?

28"And why do you worry about clothes? See how the lilies of the field grow. They do not labor or spin. 29Yet I tell you that not even Solomon in all his splendor was dressed like one of these. 30If that is how God clothes the grass of the field, which is here today and tomorrow is thrown into the fire, will he not much more clothe you, O you of little faith? 31So do not worry, saying, 'What shall we eat?' or 'What shall we drink?' or 'What shall we wear?' 32For the pagans run after all these things, and your heavenly Father knows that you need them. 33But seek first his kingdom and his righteousness, and all these things will be given to you as well. 34Therefore do not worry about tomorrow, for tomorrow will worry about itself. Each day has enough trouble of its own.

Judging Others

7 "Do not judge, or you too will be judged. 2For in the same way you judge others, you will be judged, and with the measure you use, it will be measured to you.

3"Why do you look at the speck of sawdust in your brother's eye and pay no attention to the plank in your own eye? 4How can you say to your brother, 'Let me take the speck out of your eye,' when all the time there is a plank in your own eye? 5You hypocrite, first take the plank out of your own eye, and then you will see clearly to remove the speck from your brother's eye.

6"Do not give dogs what is sacred; do not throw your pearls to pigs. If you do, they may trample them under their feet, and then turn and tear you to pieces.

Ask, Seek, Knock

7"Ask and it will be given to you; seek and you will find; knock and the door will be opened to you. 8For everyone who asks receives; he who seeks finds; and to him who knocks, the door will be opened.

9"Which of you, if his son asks for bread, will give him a stone? 10Or if he asks for a fish, will give him a snake? 11If you, then, though you are evil, know how to give good gifts to your children, how much more will your Father in heaven give good gifts to those who ask him! 12So in everything, do to others what you would have them do to you, for this sums up the Law and the Prophets.

The Narrow and Wide Gates

13"Enter through the narrow gate. For wide is the gate and broad is the road that leads to destruction, and many enter through it. 14But small is the gate and narrow the road that leads to life, and only a few find it.

A Tree and Its Fruit

15"Watch out for false prophets. They come to you in sheep's clothing, but inwardly they are ferocious wolves. 16By their fruit you will recognize them. Do people pick grapes from thornbushes, or figs from thistles? 17Likewise every good tree bears good fruit, but a bad tree bears bad fruit. 18A good tree cannot

[a]27 Or *single cubit to his height*

bear bad fruit, and a bad tree cannot
bear good fruit. 19Every tree that does
not bear good fruit is cut down and
thrown into the fire. 20Thus, by their
fruit you will recognize them.
21"Not everyone who says to me,
'Lord, Lord,' will enter the kingdom of
heaven, but only he who does the will
of my Father who is in heaven. 22Many
will say to me on that day, 'Lord, Lord,
did we not prophesy in your name, and
in your name drive out demons and
perform many miracles?' 23Then I will
tell them plainly, 'I never knew you.
Away from me, you evildoers!'

The Wise and Foolish Builders

24"Therefore everyone who hears
these words of mine and puts them into
practice is like a wise man who built his
house on the rock. 25The rain came
down, the streams rose, and the winds
blew and beat against that house; yet it
did not fall, because it had its foundation on the rock. 26But everyone who
hears these words of mine and does
not put them into practice is like a foolish man who built his house on sand.
27The rain came down, the streams rose,
and the winds blew and beat against
that house, and it fell with a great
crash."

28When Jesus had finished saying
these things, the crowds were amazed
at his teaching, 29because he taught as
one who had authority, and not as their
teachers of the law.

SHARPEN THE FOCUS

One unspoken question frames our Lord's entire sermon: "Where's my heart?"

- Is it broken with grief over my sin (Matthew 5:3–4)?
- Is it committed to a lifestyle designed to bring honor to God and to draw other people to Christ (Matthew 5:16)?
- Is it generous and self-forgetful (Matthew 6:1–4)?
- Is it resting in God's promised provision instead of wrapped up in worry (Matthew 6:25–32)?
- Is it loving and caring in its attitude toward other people (Matthew 7:1–6)?
- Is it completely trusting in the Lord (Matthew 7:7–11)?

You undoubtedly hear the text raising other questions of your heart. Hard questions. Questions you'd rather not hear. Questions you don't want to answer.

Yet the answer to all the questions comes from Jesus Himself in Matthew 6:33. By faith in Jesus, the kingdom of God belongs to us. His righteousness does too. We stand before God blameless and without fault. And that new identity carries with it the power to become—at heart—more and more the people Jesus now says we are because of His cross. We can put His kingdom first. We can live as lights in the world. We can be the salt of the earth. And we can trust Him to supply all our earthly needs as well.

WEEK 75 • THURSDAY

Matthew 8:1—9:38

GET THE BIG PICTURE

King Jesus burst on the scene, teaching with authority in His Sermon on the Mount (Matthew 5–7). Now He demonstrates that authority as He challenges every problem that hurts the sin-racked human race. Watch as He reverses the curse of sin in each incident of Matthew 8 and 9. If time is short, focus on Matthew 9:1–8.

The Man With Leprosy

8 When he came down from the
mountainside, large crowds followed him. 2A man with leprosy[a] came
and knelt before him and said, "Lord, if
you are willing, you can make me
clean."
3Jesus reached out his hand and
touched the man. "I am willing," he
said. "Be clean!" Immediately he was
cured[b] of his leprosy. 4Then Jesus said to
him, "See that you don't tell anyone. But
go, show yourself to the priest and offer the gift Moses commanded, as a testimony to them."

The Faith of the Centurion

5When Jesus had entered Capernaum, a centurion came to him, asking for
help. 6"Lord," he said, "my servant lies
at home paralyzed and in terrible suffering."
7Jesus said to him, "I will go and heal
him."
8The centurion replied, "Lord, I do
not deserve to have you come under my
roof. But just say the word, and my servant will be healed. 9For I myself am a
man under authority, with soldiers under me. I tell this one, 'Go,' and he goes;
and that one, 'Come,' and he comes. I
say to my servant, 'Do this,' and he
does it."
10When Jesus heard this, he was astonished and said to those following
him, "I tell you the truth, I have not
found anyone in Israel with such great
faith. 11I say to you that many will come
from the east and the west, and will take
their places at the feast with Abraham,
Isaac and Jacob in the kingdom of heav-
en. 12But the subjects of the kingdom
will be thrown outside, into the darkness, where there will be weeping and
gnashing of teeth."
13Then Jesus said to the centurion,
"Go! It will be done just as you believed
it would." And his servant was healed
at that very hour.

Jesus Heals Many

14When Jesus came into Peter's house,
he saw Peter's mother-in-law lying in
bed with a fever. 15He touched her hand
and the fever left her, and she got up
and began to wait on him.
16When evening came, many who
were demon-possessed were brought to
him, and he drove out the spirits with a
word and healed all the sick. 17This was
to fulfill what was spoken through the
prophet Isaiah:

"He took up our infirmities
and carried our diseases."[c]

The Cost of Following Jesus

18When Jesus saw the crowd around
him, he gave orders to cross to the other
side of the lake. 19Then a teacher of the
law came to him and said, "Teacher, I
will follow you wherever you go."
20Jesus replied, "Foxes have holes and

[a]2 The Greek word was used for various diseases affecting the skin—not necessarily leprosy.
[b]3 Greek *made clean* [c]17 Isaiah 53:4

birds of the air have nests, but the Son of Man has no place to lay his head."

21 Another disciple said to him, "Lord, first let me go and bury my father."

22 But Jesus told him, "Follow me, and let the dead bury their own dead."

Jesus Calms the Storm

23 Then he got into the boat and his disciples followed him. 24 Without warning, a furious storm came up on the lake, so that the waves swept over the boat. But Jesus was sleeping. 25 The disciples went and woke him, saying, "Lord, save us! We're going to drown!"

26 He replied, "You of little faith, why are you so afraid?" Then he got up and rebuked the winds and the waves, and it was completely calm.

27 The men were amazed and asked, "What kind of man is this? Even the winds and the waves obey him!"

The Healing of Two Demon-possessed Men

28 When he arrived at the other side in the region of the Gadarenes,[a] two demon-possessed men coming from the tombs met him. They were so violent that no one could pass that way. 29 "What do you want with us, Son of God?" they shouted. "Have you come here to torture us before the appointed time?"

30 Some distance from them a large herd of pigs was feeding. 31 The demons begged Jesus, "If you drive us out, send us into the herd of pigs."

32 He said to them, "Go!" So they came out and went into the pigs, and the whole herd rushed down the steep bank into the lake and died in the water. 33 Those tending the pigs ran off, went into the town and reported all this, including what had happened to the demon-possessed men. 34 Then the whole town went out to meet Jesus. And when they saw him, they pleaded with him to leave their region.

Jesus Heals a Paralytic

9 Jesus stepped into a boat, crossed over and came to his own town. 2 Some men brought to him a paralytic, lying on a mat. When Jesus saw their faith, he said to the paralytic, "Take heart, son; your sins are forgiven."

3 At this, some of the teachers of the law said to themselves, "This fellow is blaspheming!"

4 Knowing their thoughts, Jesus said, "Why do you entertain evil thoughts in your hearts? 5 Which is easier: to say, 'Your sins are forgiven,' or to say, 'Get up and walk'? 6 But so that you may know that the Son of Man has authority on earth to forgive sins . . ." Then he said to the paralytic, "Get up, take your mat and go home." 7 And the man got up and went home. 8 When the crowd saw this, they were filled with awe; and they praised God, who had given such authority to men.

The Calling of Matthew

9 As Jesus went on from there, he saw a man named Matthew sitting at the tax collector's booth. "Follow me," he told him, and Matthew got up and followed him.

10 While Jesus was having dinner at Matthew's house, many tax collectors and "sinners" came and ate with him and his disciples. 11 When the Pharisees saw this, they asked his disciples, "Why does your teacher eat with tax collectors and 'sinners'?"

12 On hearing this, Jesus said, "It is not the healthy who need a doctor, but the sick. 13 But go and learn what this means: 'I desire mercy, not sacrifice.'[b] For I have not come to call the righteous, but sinners."

Jesus Questioned About Fasting

14 Then John's disciples came and asked him, "How is it that we and the Pharisees fast, but your disciples do not fast?"

15 Jesus answered, "How can the guests of the bridegroom mourn while

[a] 28 Some manuscripts *Gergesenes;* others *Gerasenes* [b] 13 Hosea 6:6

he is with them? The time will come when the bridegroom will be taken from them; then they will fast.

16"No one sews a patch of unshrunk cloth on an old garment, for the patch will pull away from the garment, making the tear worse. 17Neither do men pour new wine into old wineskins. If they do, the skins will burst, the wine will run out and the wineskins will be ruined. No, they pour new wine into new wineskins, and both are preserved."

A Dead Girl and a Sick Woman

18While he was saying this, a ruler came and knelt before him and said, "My daughter has just died. But come and put your hand on her, and she will live." 19Jesus got up and went with him, and so did his disciples.

20Just then a woman who had been subject to bleeding for twelve years came up behind him and touched the edge of his cloak. 21She said to herself, "If I only touch his cloak, I will be healed."

22Jesus turned and saw her. "Take heart, daughter," he said, "your faith has healed you." And the woman was healed from that moment.

23When Jesus entered the ruler's house and saw the flute players and the noisy crowd, 24he said, "Go away. The girl is not dead but asleep." But they laughed at him. 25After the crowd had been put outside, he went in and took the girl by the hand, and she got up. 26News of this spread through all that region.

Jesus Heals the Blind and Mute

27As Jesus went on from there, two blind men followed him, calling out, "Have mercy on us, Son of David!"

28When he had gone indoors, the blind men came to him, and he asked them, "Do you believe that I am able to do this?"

"Yes, Lord," they replied.

29Then he touched their eyes and said, "According to your faith will it be done to you"; 30and their sight was restored. Jesus warned them sternly, "See that no one knows about this." 31But they went out and spread the news about him all over that region.

32While they were going out, a man who was demon-possessed and could not talk was brought to Jesus. 33And when the demon was driven out, the man who had been mute spoke. The crowd was amazed and said, "Nothing like this has ever been seen in Israel."

34But the Pharisees said, "It is by the prince of demons that he drives out demons."

The Workers Are Few

35Jesus went through all the towns and villages, teaching in their synagogues, preaching the good news of the kingdom and healing every disease and sickness. 36When he saw the crowds, he had compassion on them, because they were harassed and helpless, like sheep without a shepherd. 37Then he said to his disciples, "The harvest is plentiful but the workers are few. 38Ask the Lord of the harvest, therefore, to send out workers into his harvest field."

SHARPEN THE FOCUS

Power and authority go together. A government with authority but no power cannot keep order or prevent rioters from destroying a city. A group of people who use power without authority amounts to no more than a gang of thugs.

Our Lord Jesus had power—to cleanse the lepers, to still the storms, to raise the dead, to forgive sins. And He had the authority from God to do so. Above all, He showed His authority in the sacrifice of love He offered on the cross—authority to lay down His life and authority to take it up again (John 10:18). He revealed His power over sin's curse in His resurrection from the dead. Both power and authority belonged to Him as the sinless Son of God who came to earth to die for the sins of the world.

Our King still wields that power, that authority today. We can "take heart," knowing that our sins are forgiven even now (Matthew 9:2) and knowing that one day we will fully enjoy our Savior's power to reverse sin's destruction in our own bodies and lives.

WEEK 75 • FRIDAY

Matthew 10:1—11:30

GET THE BIG PICTURE

Like the cars of a freight train that carry important cargo, each chapter of Matthew links up with what has gone before. If you uncouple chapter 10 from chapter 9, for instance, you lose part of Matthew's message. Our Lord delegated to His disciples some of the authority and power He has used in announcing the coming of His kingdom. As you read, continue to look for continuity in His message. If time is short, focus on Matthew 10:1–42.

Jesus Sends Out the Twelve

10 He called his twelve disciples
to him and gave them author-
ity to drive out evil[a] spirits and to heal
every disease and sickness.
2These are the names of the twelve
apostles: first, Simon (who is called Peter) and his brother Andrew; James son
of Zebedee, and his brother John; 3Phil-
ip and Bartholomew; Thomas and Matthew the tax collector; James son of
Alphaeus, and Thaddaeus; 4Simon the
Zealot and Judas Iscariot, who betrayed
him.
5These twelve Jesus sent out with the
following instructions: "Do not go
among the Gentiles or enter any town
of the Samaritans. 6Go rather to the lost
sheep of Israel. 7As you go, preach this
message: 'The kingdom of heaven is
near.' 8Heal the sick, raise the dead,
cleanse those who have leprosy,[b] drive
out demons. Freely you have received,
freely give. 9Do not take along any gold
or silver or copper in your belts; 10take
no bag for the journey, or extra tunic, or
sandals or a staff; for the worker is
worth his keep.
11"Whatever town or village you enter, search for some worthy person there
and stay at his house until you leave.
12As you enter the home, give it your
greeting. 13If the home is deserving, let
your peace rest on it; if it is not, let your
peace return to you. 14If anyone will not
welcome you or listen to your words,
shake the dust off your feet when you
leave that home or town. 15I tell you the
truth, it will be more bearable for Sodom and Gomorrah on the day of judgment than for that town. 16I am sending
you out like sheep among wolves.
Therefore be as shrewd as snakes and as
innocent as doves.
17"Be on your guard against men; they
will hand you over to the local councils
and flog you in their synagogues. 18On
my account you will be brought before
governors and kings as witnesses to
them and to the Gentiles. 19But when
they arrest you, do not worry about
what to say or how to say it. At that time

[a]1 Greek *unclean* [b]8 The Greek word was used for various diseases affecting the skin—not necessarily leprosy.

you will be given what to say, 20for it will
not be you speaking, but the Spirit of
your Father speaking through you.
21"Brother will betray brother to
death, and a father his child; children
will rebel against their parents and have
them put to death. 22All men will hate
you because of me, but he who stands
firm to the end will be saved. 23When
you are persecuted in one place, flee to
another. I tell you the truth, you will not
finish going through the cities of Israel
before the Son of Man comes.
24"A student is not above his teacher,
nor a servant above his master. 25It is
enough for the student to be like his
teacher, and the servant like his master.
If the head of the house has been called
Beelzebub,[a] how much more the members of his household!
26"So do not be afraid of them. There
is nothing concealed that will not be disclosed, or hidden that will not be made
known. 27What I tell you in the dark,
speak in the daylight; what is whispered in your ear, proclaim from the
roofs. 28Do not be afraid of those who
kill the body but cannot kill the soul.
Rather, be afraid of the One who can
destroy both soul and body in hell. 29Are
not two sparrows sold for a penny[b]? Yet
not one of them will fall to the ground
apart from the will of your Father. 30And
even the very hairs of your head are all
numbered. 31So don't be afraid; you are
worth more than many sparrows.
32"Whoever acknowledges me before
men, I will also acknowledge him before
my Father in heaven. 33But whoever disowns me before men, I will disown him
before my Father in heaven.
34"Do not suppose that I have come to
bring peace to the earth. I did not come
to bring peace, but a sword. 35For I have
come to turn

" 'a man against his father,
a daughter against her mother,
a daughter-in-law against her
mother-in-law—
36 a man's enemies will be the
members of his own
household.'[c]

37"Anyone who loves his father or
mother more than me is not worthy of
me; anyone who loves his son or daughter more than me is not worthy of me;
38and anyone who does not take his
cross and follow me is not worthy of me.
39Whoever finds his life will lose it, and
whoever loses his life for my sake will
find it.
40"He who receives you receives me,
and he who receives me receives the
one who sent me. 41Anyone who receives a prophet because he is a prophet
will receive a prophet's reward, and
anyone who receives a righteous man
because he is a righteous man will receive a righteous man's reward. 42And if
anyone gives even a cup of cold water
to one of these little ones because he is
my disciple, I tell you the truth, he will
certainly not lose his reward."

Jesus and John the Baptist

11 After Jesus had finished instructing his twelve disciples, he
went on from there to teach and preach
in the towns of Galilee.[d]
2When John heard in prison what
Christ was doing, he sent his disciples
3to ask him, "Are you the one who was
to come, or should we expect someone
else?"
4Jesus replied, "Go back and report to
John what you hear and see: 5The blind
receive sight, the lame walk, those who
have leprosy[e] are cured, the deaf hear,
the dead are raised, and the good news
is preached to the poor. 6Blessed is the
man who does not fall away on account
of me."
7As John's disciples were leaving,
Jesus began to speak to the crowd about
John: "What did you go out into the
desert to see? A reed swayed by the
wind? 8If not, what did you go out to
see? A man dressed in fine clothes? No,
those who wear fine clothes are in

[a]25 Greek *Beezeboul* or *Beelzeboul* [b]29 Greek *an assarion* [c]36 Micah 7:6 [d]1 Greek *in their towns* [e]5 The Greek word was used for various diseases affecting the skin—not necessarily leprosy.

kings' palaces. [9]Then what did you go out to see? A prophet? Yes, I tell you, and more than a prophet. [10]This is the one about whom it is written:

" 'I will send my messenger ahead of you,
who will prepare your way before you.'[a]

[11]I tell you the truth: Among those born of women there has not risen anyone greater than John the Baptist; yet he who is least in the kingdom of heaven is greater than he. [12]From the days of John the Baptist until now, the kingdom of heaven has been forcefully advancing, and forceful men lay hold of it. [13]For all the Prophets and the Law prophesied until John. [14]And if you are willing to accept it, he is the Elijah who was to come. [15]He who has ears, let him hear.

[16]"To what can I compare this generation? They are like children sitting in the marketplaces and calling out to others:

[17]" 'We played the flute for you,
and you did not dance;
we sang a dirge,
and you did not mourn.'

[18]For John came neither eating nor drinking, and they say, 'He has a demon.' [19]The Son of Man came eating and drinking, and they say, 'Here is a glutton and a drunkard, a friend of tax collectors and "sinners." ' But wisdom is proved right by her actions."

Woe on Unrepentant Cities

[20]Then Jesus began to denounce the cities in which most of his miracles had been performed, because they did not repent. [21]"Woe to you, Korazin! Woe to you, Bethsaida! If the miracles that were performed in you had been performed in Tyre and Sidon, they would have repented long ago in sackcloth and ashes. [22]But I tell you, it will be more bearable for Tyre and Sidon on the day of judgment than for you. [23]And you, Capernaum, will you be lifted up to the skies? No, you will go down to the depths.[b] If the miracles that were performed in you had been performed in Sodom, it would have remained to this day. [24]But I tell you that it will be more bearable for Sodom on the day of judgment than for you."

Rest for the Weary

[25]At that time Jesus said, "I praise you, Father, Lord of heaven and earth, because you have hidden these things from the wise and learned, and revealed them to little children. [26]Yes, Father, for this was your good pleasure.

[27]"All things have been committed to me by my Father. No one knows the Son except the Father, and no one knows the Father except the Son and those to whom the Son chooses to reveal him.

[28]"Come to me, all you who are weary and burdened, and I will give you rest. [29]Take my yoke upon you and learn from me, for I am gentle and humble in heart, and you will find rest for your souls. [30]For my yoke is easy and my burden is light."

[a]*10* Mal. 3:1 [b]*23* Greek *Hades*

SHARPEN THE FOCUS

To be like Christ. That's what Jesus' disciples down through the centuries have always wanted. That's what our Lord wants for us, too. As His Spirit continues His holy work in our lives we will be like Jesus:

- in His service to others (Matthew 10:5–11).
- in His persecution by the world (Matthew 10:12–31).
- in His eternal joy and glory (Matthew 10:32–42).

But in our weakness, in our sin, we cannot serve, cannot endure trials, cannot attain joy. And we certainly deserve no glory. How wonderful then to read Matthew's words in Matthew 10:1, "He . . . gave [the disciples] authority . . ." We have our Lord's authorization and His power to do what He would do, to say what He would say, in any situation. And His Spirit will help us know what that is (Matthew 10:18–20).

Take a minute to thoroughly delight in the glorious truth of Matthew 10:32. Jesus will one day acknowledge you before the throne of grace and glory! So how will you, by grace, serve, witness, and rejoice today?

WEEK 75 • SATURDAY

Matthew 12:1—13:58

In Matthew 4 we watched our Lord's first confrontation with the prince of darkness. Chapter 12 is a pivotal chapter in Matthew's gospel, as the kingdom of darkness takes a firmer stand against the kingdom of light. Against the backdrop of that opposition, the parables of chapter 13 are indeed Good News; each in its own way tells of the coming victory for the kingdom of Christ. Watch for that as you read. If time is short, focus on Matthew 12:1–30.

Lord of the Sabbath

12 At that time Jesus went
through the grainfields on
the Sabbath. His disciples were hungry
and began to pick some heads of grain
and eat them. [2]When the Pharisees saw
this, they said to him, "Look! Your disciples are doing what is unlawful on the
Sabbath."

[3]He answered, "Haven't you read
what David did when he and his companions were hungry? [4]He entered the
house of God, and he and his companions ate the consecrated bread—which
was not lawful for them to do, but only
for the priests. [5]Or haven't you read in
the Law that on the Sabbath the priests
in the temple desecrate the day and yet
are innocent? [6]I tell you that one[a] greater than the temple is here. [7]If you had
known what these words mean, 'I desire mercy, not sacrifice,'[b] you would not
have condemned the innocent. [8]For the
Son of Man is Lord of the Sabbath."

[9]Going on from that place, he went
into their synagogue, [10]and a man with
a shriveled hand was there. Looking for
a reason to accuse Jesus, they asked him,
"Is it lawful to heal on the Sabbath?"

[11]He said to them, "If any of you has
a sheep and it falls into a pit on the Sabbath, will you not take hold of it and lift
it out? [12]How much more valuable is a
man than a sheep! Therefore it is lawful to do good on the Sabbath."

[13]Then he said to the man, "Stretch
out your hand." So he stretched it out
and it was completely restored, just as
sound as the other. [14]But the Pharisees
went out and plotted how they might
kill Jesus.

God's Chosen Servant

[15]Aware of this, Jesus withdrew from
that place. Many followed him, and he

[a]6 Or *something;* also in verses 41 and 42
[b]7 Hosea 6:6

healed all their sick, 16warning them not
to tell who he was. 17This was to fulfill
what was spoken through the prophet
Isaiah:

18 "Here is my servant whom I have
chosen,
the one I love, in whom I delight;
I will put my Spirit on him,
and he will proclaim justice to the
nations.
19 He will not quarrel or cry out;
no one will hear his voice in the
streets.
20 A bruised reed he will not break,
and a smoldering wick he will not
snuff out,
till he leads justice to victory.
21 In his name the nations will put
their hope."[a]

Jesus and Beelzebub

22Then they brought him a demon-
possessed man who was blind and
mute, and Jesus healed him, so that he
could both talk and see. 23All the people
were astonished and said, "Could this
be the Son of David?"
24But when the Pharisees heard this,
they said, "It is only by Beelzebub,[b] the
prince of demons, that this fellow drives
out demons."
25Jesus knew their thoughts and said
to them, "Every kingdom divided
against itself will be ruined, and every
city or household divided against itself
will not stand. 26If Satan drives out Satan, he is divided against himself. How
then can his kingdom stand? 27And if I
drive out demons by Beelzebub, by
whom do your people drive them out?
So then, they will be your judges. 28But
if I drive out demons by the Spirit of
God, then the kingdom of God has
come upon you.
29"Or again, how can anyone enter a
strong man's house and carry off his
possessions unless he first ties up the
strong man? Then he can rob his house.
30"He who is not with me is against
me, and he who does not gather with
me scatters. 31And so I tell you, every sin
and blasphemy will be forgiven men,
but the blasphemy against the Spirit will
not be forgiven. 32Anyone who speaks a
word against the Son of Man will be
forgiven, but anyone who speaks
against the Holy Spirit will not be forgiven, either in this age or in the age to
come.
33"Make a tree good and its fruit will
be good, or make a tree bad and its fruit
will be bad, for a tree is recognized by
its fruit. 34You brood of vipers, how can
you who are evil say anything good?
For out of the overflow of the heart the
mouth speaks. 35The good man brings
good things out of the good stored up
in him, and the evil man brings evil
things out of the evil stored up in him.
36But I tell you that men will have to give
account on the day of judgment for every careless word they have spoken.
37For by your words you will be acquitted, and by your words you will be condemned."

The Sign of Jonah

38Then some of the Pharisees and
teachers of the law said to him, "Teacher, we want to see a miraculous sign
from you."
39He answered, "A wicked and adulterous generation asks for a miraculous
sign! But none will be given it except the
sign of the prophet Jonah. 40For as Jonah
was three days and three nights in the
belly of a huge fish, so the Son of Man
will be three days and three nights in
the heart of the earth. 41The men of Nineveh will stand up at the judgment with
this generation and condemn it; for they
repented at the preaching of Jonah, and
now one[c] greater than Jonah is here.
42The Queen of the South will rise at the
judgment with this generation and condemn it; for she came from the ends of
the earth to listen to Solomon's wisdom,
and now one greater than Solomon is
here.
43"When an evil[d] spirit comes out of a
man, it goes through arid places seeking

[a]21 Isaiah 42:1-4 [b]24 Greek *Beezeboul* or *Beelzeboul;* also in verse 27 [c]41 Or *something;* also in verse 42 [d]43 Greek *unclean*

rest and does not find it. 44Then it says,
'I will return to the house I left.' When
it arrives, it finds the house unoccupied,
swept clean and put in order. 45Then it
goes and takes with it seven other spirits more wicked than itself, and they go
in and live there. And the final condition of that man is worse than the first.
That is how it will be with this wicked
generation."

Jesus' Mother and Brothers

46While Jesus was still talking to the
crowd, his mother and brothers stood
outside, wanting to speak to him.
47Someone told him, "Your mother and
brothers are standing outside, wanting
to speak to you."[a]

48He replied to him, "Who is my
mother, and who are my brothers?"
49Pointing to his disciples, he said, "Here
are my mother and my brothers. 50For
whoever does the will of my Father in
heaven is my brother and sister and
mother."

The Parable of the Sower

13 That same day Jesus went out
of the house and sat by the
lake. 2Such large crowds gathered
around him that he got into a boat and
sat in it, while all the people stood on
the shore. 3Then he told them many
things in parables, saying: "A farmer
went out to sow his seed. 4As he was
scattering the seed, some fell along the
path, and the birds came and ate it up.
5Some fell on rocky places, where it did
not have much soil. It sprang up quickly,
because the soil was shallow. 6But when
the sun came up, the plants were
scorched, and they withered because
they had no root. 7Other seed fell
among thorns, which grew up and
choked the plants. 8Still other seed fell
on good soil, where it produced a
crop—a hundred, sixty or thirty times
what was sown. 9He who has ears, let
him hear."

10The disciples came to him and
asked, "Why do you speak to the people
in parables?"

11He replied, "The knowledge of the
secrets of the kingdom of heaven has
been given to you, but not to them.
12Whoever has will be given more, and
he will have an abundance. Whoever
does not have, even what he has will be
taken from him. 13This is why I speak to
them in parables:

"Though seeing, they do not see;
though hearing, they do not hear
or understand.

14In them is fulfilled the prophecy of Isaiah:

" 'You will be ever hearing but never
understanding;
you will be ever seeing but never
perceiving.
15For this people's heart has become
calloused;
they hardly hear with their ears,
and they have closed their eyes.
Otherwise they might see with their
eyes,
hear with their ears,
understand with their hearts
and turn, and I would heal them.'[b]

16But blessed are your eyes because they
see, and your ears because they hear.
17For I tell you the truth, many prophets and righteous men longed to
see what you see but did not see it, and
to hear what you hear but did not
hear it.

18"Listen then to what the parable of
the sower means: 19When anyone hears
the message about the kingdom and
does not understand it, the evil one
comes and snatches away what was
sown in his heart. This is the seed sown
along the path. 20The one who received
the seed that fell on rocky places is the
man who hears the word and at once
receives it with joy. 21But since he has no
root, he lasts only a short time. When
trouble or persecution comes because of
the word, he quickly falls away. 22The
one who received the seed that fell
among the thorns is the man who hears

[a]47 Some manuscripts do not have verse 47.
[b]15 Isaiah 6:9,10

the word, but the worries of this life and the deceitfulness of wealth choke it, making it unfruitful. [23]But the one who received the seed that fell on good soil is the man who hears the word and understands it. He produces a crop, yielding a hundred, sixty or thirty times what was sown."

The Parable of the Weeds

[24]Jesus told them another parable: "The kingdom of heaven is like a man who sowed good seed in his field. [25]But while everyone was sleeping, his enemy came and sowed weeds among the wheat, and went away. [26]When the wheat sprouted and formed heads, then the weeds also appeared.

[27]"The owner's servants came to him and said, 'Sir, didn't you sow good seed in your field? Where then did the weeds come from?'

[28]" 'An enemy did this,' he replied.

"The servants asked him, 'Do you want us to go and pull them up?'

[29]" 'No,' he answered, 'because while you are pulling the weeds, you may root up the wheat with them. [30]Let both grow together until the harvest. At that time I will tell the harvesters: First collect the weeds and tie them in bundles to be burned; then gather the wheat and bring it into my barn.' "

The Parables of the Mustard Seed and the Yeast

[31]He told them another parable: "The kingdom of heaven is like a mustard seed, which a man took and planted in his field. [32]Though it is the smallest of all your seeds, yet when it grows, it is the largest of garden plants and becomes a tree, so that the birds of the air come and perch in its branches."

[33]He told them still another parable: "The kingdom of heaven is like yeast that a woman took and mixed into a large amount[a] of flour until it worked all through the dough."

[34]Jesus spoke all these things to the crowd in parables; he did not say anything to them without using a parable. [35]So was fulfilled what was spoken through the prophet:

"I will open my mouth in parables,
I will utter things hidden since the creation of the world."[b]

The Parable of the Weeds Explained

[36]Then he left the crowd and went into the house. His disciples came to him and said, "Explain to us the parable of the weeds in the field."

[37]He answered, "The one who sowed the good seed is the Son of Man. [38]The field is the world, and the good seed stands for the sons of the kingdom. The weeds are the sons of the evil one, [39]and the enemy who sows them is the devil. The harvest is the end of the age, and the harvesters are angels.

[40]"As the weeds are pulled up and burned in the fire, so it will be at the end of the age. [41]The Son of Man will send out his angels, and they will weed out of his kingdom everything that causes sin and all who do evil. [42]They will throw them into the fiery furnace, where there will be weeping and gnashing of teeth. [43]Then the righteous will shine like the sun in the kingdom of their Father. He who has ears, let him hear.

The Parables of the Hidden Treasure and the Pearl

[44]"The kingdom of heaven is like treasure hidden in a field. When a man found it, he hid it again, and then in his joy went and sold all he had and bought that field.

[45]"Again, the kingdom of heaven is like a merchant looking for fine pearls. [46]When he found one of great value, he went away and sold everything he had and bought it.

The Parable of the Net

[47]"Once again, the kingdom of heaven is like a net that was let down into the

[a]33 Greek *three satas* (probably about 1/2 bushel or 22 liters) [b]35 Psalm 78:2

lake and caught all kinds of fish. [48]When
it was full, the fishermen pulled it up on
the shore. Then they sat down and collected the good fish in baskets, but
threw the bad away. [49]This is how it will
be at the end of the age. The angels will
come and separate the wicked from the
righteous [50]and throw them into the fiery furnace, where there will be weeping and gnashing of teeth.
[51]"Have you understood all these
things?" Jesus asked.
"Yes," they replied.
[52]He said to them, "Therefore every
teacher of the law who has been instructed about the kingdom of heaven
is like the owner of a house who brings
out of his storeroom new treasures as
well as old."

A Prophet Without Honor

[53]When Jesus had finished these
parables, he moved on from there.
[54]Coming to his hometown, he began
teaching the people in their synagogue,
and they were amazed. "Where did this
man get this wisdom and these miraculous powers?" they asked. [55]"Isn't this
the carpenter's son? Isn't his mother's
name Mary, and aren't his brothers
James, Joseph, Simon and Judas?
[56]Aren't all his sisters with us? Where
then did this man get all these things?"
[57]And they took offense at him.
But Jesus said to them, "Only in his
hometown and in his own house is a
prophet without honor."
[58]And he did not do many miracles
there because of their lack of faith.

SHARPEN THE FOCUS

Two newlyweds were talking. She: "Do you love me, John?" He: "Of course, I do." She: "Will you climb the highest mountain for me?" He: "Of course, my pearl." She: "Will you swim the widest oceans?" He: "Of course, my treasure." She: "Will you go to the store and get some ice cream?" He: "Oh, Honey, it's late, and I already took off my shoes."

Jesus' two-verse parable in Matthew 13:45–46 tells about a different kind of love. Here, a merchant sold all that he had to purchase the pearl of his dreams. He's not unlike the main character of Matthew 13:44 who sold all he had to claim the treasure he had found. And they are not unlike our Lord Jesus who gave up His throne in heaven, His eternal glory, and even His life to claim you and me as His own.

Our Lord didn't just promise to love with unending love, He made good on His promise. He loves with extravagant love, love so big we'll never be able to drink it all in. And since He gave His best, we can trust Him not to withhold the rest (Romans 8:32).

WEEK 76 • MONDAY

Matthew 14:1—15:39

GET THE BIG PICTURE

Matthew's first readers included mostly Jews who had come to faith in Jesus as their Messiah. As you read, watch while Jesus moves from one situation to the next in His ministry, demonstrating perfect confidence in both His identity and His authority. In Matthew 15:21–39, notice especially that our Lord reaches out to serve Gentiles, too. Note the irony in Matthew 15:21 as a Gentile woman rightly identifies our Servant-King as the son of David! If time is short, focus on Matthew 14:1–12.

John the Baptist Beheaded

14 At that time Herod the tetrarch heard the reports about Jesus, 2and he said to his attendants, "This is John the Baptist; he has risen from the dead! That is why miraculous powers are at work in him."

3Now Herod had arrested John and bound him and put him in prison because of Herodias, his brother Philip's wife, 4for John had been saying to him: "It is not lawful for you to have her." 5Herod wanted to kill John, but he was afraid of the people, because they considered him a prophet.

6On Herod's birthday the daughter of Herodias danced for them and pleased Herod so much 7that he promised with an oath to give her whatever she asked. 8Prompted by her mother, she said, "Give me here on a platter the head of John the Baptist." 9The king was distressed, but because of his oaths and his dinner guests, he ordered that her request be granted 10and had John beheaded in the prison. 11His head was brought in on a platter and given to the girl, who carried it to her mother. 12John's disciples came and took his body and buried it. Then they went and told Jesus.

Jesus Feeds the Five Thousand

13When Jesus heard what had happened, he withdrew by boat privately to a solitary place. Hearing of this, the crowds followed him on foot from the towns. 14When Jesus landed and saw a large crowd, he had compassion on them and healed their sick.

15As evening approached, the disciples came to him and said, "This is a remote place, and it's already getting late. Send the crowds away, so they can go to the villages and buy themselves some food."

16Jesus replied, "They do not need to go away. You give them something to eat."

17"We have here only five loaves of bread and two fish," they answered.

18"Bring them here to me," he said. 19And he directed the people to sit down on the grass. Taking the five loaves and the two fish and looking up to heaven, he gave thanks and broke the loaves. Then he gave them to the disciples, and the disciples gave them to the people. 20They all ate and were satisfied, and the disciples picked up twelve basketfuls of broken pieces that were left over. 21The number of those who ate was about five thousand men, besides women and children.

Jesus Walks on the Water

22Immediately Jesus made the disciples get into the boat and go on ahead of him to the other side, while he dismissed the crowd. 23After he had dismissed them, he went up on a mountainside by himself to pray. When evening came, he was there alone, 24but the boat was already a considerable distance[a] from land, buffeted by the waves because the wind was against it.

25During the fourth watch of the night Jesus went out to them, walking on the lake. 26When the disciples saw him walking on the lake, they were terrified. "It's a ghost," they said, and cried out in fear.

27But Jesus immediately said to them: "Take courage! It is I. Don't be afraid."

28"Lord, if it's you," Peter replied, "tell me to come to you on the water."

29"Come," he said.

Then Peter got down out of the boat, walked on the water and came toward Jesus. 30But when he saw the wind, he was afraid and, beginning to sink, cried out, "Lord, save me!"

31Immediately Jesus reached out his

[a]24 Greek *many stadia*

hand and caught him. "You of little
faith," he said, "why did you doubt?"
32And when they climbed into the
boat, the wind died down. 33Then those
who were in the boat worshiped him,
saying, "Truly you are the Son of God."
34When they had crossed over, they
landed at Gennesaret. 35And when the
men of that place recognized Jesus, they
sent word to all the surrounding country. People brought all their sick to him
36and begged him to let the sick just
touch the edge of his cloak, and all who
touched him were healed.

Clean and Unclean

15 Then some Pharisees and
teachers of the law came to
Jesus from Jerusalem and asked, 2"Why
do your disciples break the tradition of
the elders? They don't wash their hands
before they eat!"
3Jesus replied, "And why do you break
the command of God for the sake of
your tradition? 4For God said, 'Honor
your father and mother'[a] and 'Anyone
who curses his father or mother must be
put to death.'[b] 5But you say that if a man
says to his father or mother, 'Whatever
help you might otherwise have received
from me is a gift devoted to God,' 6he is
not to 'honor his father[c]' with it. Thus
you nullify the word of God for the sake
of your tradition. 7You hypocrites! Isaiah
was right when he prophesied about
you:

8" 'These people honor me with their
lips,
but their hearts are far from me.
9They worship me in vain;
their teachings are but rules
taught by men.'[d]"

10Jesus called the crowd to him and
said, "Listen and understand. 11What
goes into a man's mouth does not make
him 'unclean,' but what comes out of
his mouth, that is what makes him
'unclean.' "
12Then the disciples came to him and
asked, "Do you know that the Pharisees
were offended when they heard this?"
13He replied, "Every plant that my
heavenly Father has not planted will be
pulled up by the roots. 14Leave them;
they are blind guides.[e] If a blind man
leads a blind man, both will fall into a
pit."
15Peter said, "Explain the parable
to us."
16"Are you still so dull?" Jesus asked
them. 17"Don't you see that whatever
enters the mouth goes into the stomach
and then out of the body? 18But the
things that come out of the mouth come
from the heart, and these make a man
'unclean.' 19For out of the heart come
evil thoughts, murder, adultery, sexual
immorality, theft, false testimony, slander. 20These are what make a man 'unclean'; but eating with unwashed hands
does not make him 'unclean.' "

The Faith of the Canaanite Woman

21Leaving that place, Jesus withdrew
to the region of Tyre and Sidon. 22A Canaanite woman from that vicinity came
to him, crying out, "Lord, Son of David,
have mercy on me! My daughter is suffering terribly from demon-possession."
23Jesus did not answer a word. So his
disciples came to him and urged him,
"Send her away, for she keeps crying
out after us."
24He answered, "I was sent only to the
lost sheep of Israel."
25The woman came and knelt before
him. "Lord, help me!" she said.
26He replied, "It is not right to take the
children's bread and toss it to their
dogs."
27"Yes, Lord," she said, "but even the
dogs eat the crumbs that fall from their
masters' table."
28Then Jesus answered, "Woman, you
have great faith! Your request is granted." And her daughter was healed from
that very hour.

Jesus Feeds the Four Thousand

29Jesus left there and went along the
Sea of Galilee. Then he went up on a

[a]4 Exodus 20:12; Deut. 5:16 [b]4 Exodus 21:17; Lev. 20:9 [c]6 Some manuscripts *father or his mother* [d]9 Isaiah 29:13 [e]14 Some manuscripts *guides of the blind*

mountainside and sat down. 30Great
crowds came to him, bringing the lame,
the blind, the crippled, the mute and
many others, and laid them at his feet;
and he healed them. 31The people were
amazed when they saw the mute speaking, the crippled made well, the lame
walking and the blind seeing. And they
praised the God of Israel.
32Jesus called his disciples to him and
said, "I have compassion for these people; they have already been with me
three days and have nothing to eat. I do
not want to send them away hungry, or
they may collapse on the way."
33His disciples answered, "Where
could we get enough bread in this remote place to feed such a crowd?"
34"How many loaves do you have?"
Jesus asked.
"Seven," they replied, "and a few
small fish."
35He told the crowd to sit down on the
ground. 36Then he took the seven loaves
and the fish, and when he had given
thanks, he broke them and gave them
to the disciples, and they in turn to the
people. 37They all ate and were satisfied. Afterward the disciples picked up
seven basketfuls of broken pieces that
were left over. 38The number of those
who ate was four thousand, besides
women and children. 39After Jesus had
sent the crowd away, he got into the
boat and went to the vicinity of Maga-
dan.

SHARPEN THE FOCUS

The terror of a guilty conscience. What else can explain the paranoia of King Herod in Matthew 14:1–2? He thought his sin had—literally—come back to haunt him.

Does the ghost of a past wrong ever come back to haunt you? Perhaps it's an unconfessed crime. Herod had committed murder. Even Christians have sometimes been guilty of embezzlement. Or infidelity. Or rape. Perhaps it's a rumor you started to secure a promotion for yourself. Perhaps you're an alcoholic, or maybe you've invented credentials no one bothered to check. Perhaps you've fought with a friend, but never obeyed the Holy Spirit's urgings to work toward reconciliation. Maybe you harbor hate.

Whatever your ghost, however long it's haunted your heart, you need not play host to it any more. The Lord Jesus has come—for you—to evict every ghost of guilt. He died so you could live in peace in the present, not in torment over the past. Talk to Him before another hour goes by.

WEEK 76 • TUESDAY

Matthew 16:1—17:27

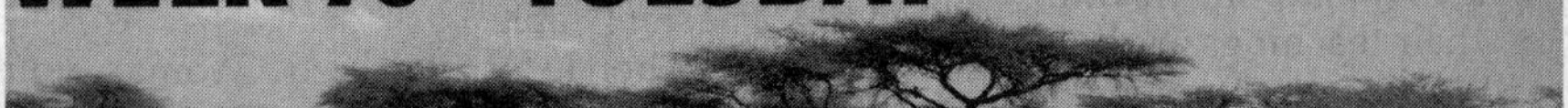

GET THE BIG PICTURE

Is Jesus of Nazareth truly the King whom God the Father had promised to send? That is the question Matthew addresses in Matthew 16 and 17. As you read, pretend you stood in the crowd. What questions would *you* have wanted to ask the Lord? If time is short, focus on Matthew 16:1–12.

SHARPEN THE FOCUS

Few of us would want to live without yeast. Who doesn't enjoy bread warm from the oven or a freshly fried, raised doughnut? Most times, though, Scripture uses yeast as a symbol for something evil. Take Matthew 16:6, 11–12 for example. Here the Lord Jesus urges His disciples to stand guard against the teaching of the Pharisees and Sadducees.

The Pharisees said, "Perfect obedience to God's Law will keep me in God's favor. Someday He will take me to heaven." The Sadducees said, "What heaven?" The Pharisees were legalists. The Sadducees were skeptics. Both groups of leaders led people in the wrong direction—away from faith in a gracious God who acts for our good.

Do a quick heart-scan on yourself. Has the yeast of skepticism kept you from praying in faith lately or from witnessing about Christ and His resurrection? Has the yeast of legalism trapped you into serving God grudgingly or perhaps even into thinking that He owes you something because of your good behavior or great service?

Confess any sins of misbelief you see in yourself. Then ask the Father to reveal to you more fully the truth He revealed to Simon Peter in Matthew 16:13–17.

WEEK 76 • WEDNESDAY

Matt. 18:1—19:30

GET THE BIG PICTURE

The word *kingdom* conjures up pictures of governments and bureaucrats. But today's reading from Matthew 18 makes it clear that Jesus' kingdom consists of individuals bound to Him and to one another in lasting relationships. If time is short, focus on Matthew 18:21–35.

The Greatest in the Kingdom of Heaven

18 At that time the disciples
came to Jesus and asked,
"Who is the greatest in the kingdom of
heaven?"
²He called a little child and had him
stand among them. ³And he said: "I tell
you the truth, unless you change and
become like little children, you will never enter the kingdom of heaven. ⁴There-
fore, whoever humbles himself like this
child is the greatest in the kingdom of
heaven.
⁵"And whoever welcomes a little child
like this in my name welcomes me. ⁶But
if anyone causes one of these little ones
who believe in me to sin, it would be
better for him to have a large millstone
hung around his neck and to be
drowned in the depths of the sea.
⁷"Woe to the world because of the
things that cause people to sin! Such
things must come, but woe to the man
through whom they come! ⁸If your
hand or your foot causes you to sin, cut
it off and throw it away. It is better for
you to enter life maimed or crippled
than to have two hands or two feet and
be thrown into eternal fire. ⁹And if your
eye causes you to sin, gouge it out and
throw it away. It is better for you to enter life with one eye than to have two
eyes and be thrown into the fire of hell.

The Parable of the Lost Sheep

10"See that you do not look down on one of these little ones. For I tell you that their angels in heaven always see the face of my Father in heaven.[a]

12"What do you think? If a man owns a hundred sheep, and one of them wanders away, will he not leave the ninety-nine on the hills and go to look for the one that wandered off? 13And if he finds it, I tell you the truth, he is happier about that one sheep than about the ninety-nine that did not wander off. 14In the same way your Father in heaven is not willing that any of these little ones should be lost.

A Brother Who Sins Against You

15"If your brother sins against you,[b] go and show him his fault, just between the two of you. If he listens to you, you have won your brother over. 16But if he will not listen, take one or two others along, so that 'every matter may be established by the testimony of two or three witnesses.'[c] 17If he refuses to listen to them, tell it to the church; and if he refuses to listen even to the church, treat him as you would a pagan or a tax collector.

18"I tell you the truth, whatever you bind on earth will be[d] bound in heaven, and whatever you loose on earth will be[d] loosed in heaven.

19"Again, I tell you that if two of you on earth agree about anything you ask for, it will be done for you by my Father in heaven. 20For where two or three come together in my name, there am I with them."

The Parable of the Unmerciful Servant

21Then Peter came to Jesus and asked, "Lord, how many times shall I forgive my brother when he sins against me? Up to seven times?"

22Jesus answered, "I tell you, not seven times, but seventy-seven times.[e]

23"Therefore, the kingdom of heaven is like a king who wanted to settle accounts with his servants. 24As he began the settlement, a man who owed him ten thousand talents[f] was brought to him. 25Since he was not able to pay, the master ordered that he and his wife and his children and all that he had be sold to repay the debt.

26"The servant fell on his knees before him. 'Be patient with me,' he begged, 'and I will pay back everything.' 27The servant's master took pity on him, canceled the debt and let him go.

28"But when that servant went out, he found one of his fellow servants who owed him a hundred denarii.[g] He grabbed him and began to choke him. 'Pay back what you owe me!' he demanded.

29"His fellow servant fell to his knees and begged him, 'Be patient with me, and I will pay you back.'

30"But he refused. Instead, he went off and had the man thrown into prison until he could pay the debt. 31When the other servants saw what had happened, they were greatly distressed and went and told their master everything that had happened.

32"Then the master called the servant in. 'You wicked servant,' he said, 'I canceled all that debt of yours because you begged me to. 33Shouldn't you have had mercy on your fellow servant just as I had on you?' 34In anger his master turned him over to the jailers to be tortured, until he should pay back all he owed.

35"This is how my heavenly Father will treat each of you unless you forgive your brother from your heart."

Divorce

19 When Jesus had finished saying these things, he left Galilee and went into the region of Judea to the other side of the Jordan. 2Large crowds followed him, and he healed them there.

[a]10 Some manuscripts *heaven.* 11*The Son of Man came to save what was lost.* [b]15 Some manuscripts do not have *against you.* [c]16 Deut. 19:15
[d]18 Or *have been* [e]22 Or *seventy times seven*
[f]24 That is, millions of dollars [g]28 That is, a few dollars

[3]Some Pharisees came to him to test
him. They asked, "Is it lawful for a man
to divorce his wife for any and every
reason?"
[4]"Haven't you read," he replied, "that
at the beginning the Creator 'made
them male and female,'[a] [5]and said, 'For
this reason a man will leave his father
and mother and be united to his wife,
and the two will become one flesh'[b]? [6]So
they are no longer two, but one. Therefore what God has joined together, let
man not separate."
[7]"Why then," they asked, "did Moses
command that a man give his wife a certificate of divorce and send her away?"
[8]Jesus replied, "Moses permitted you
to divorce your wives because your
hearts were hard. But it was not this
way from the beginning. [9]I tell you that
anyone who divorces his wife, except
for marital unfaithfulness, and marries
another woman commits adultery."
[10]The disciples said to him, "If this is
the situation between a husband and
wife, it is better not to marry."
[11]Jesus replied, "Not everyone can accept this word, but only those to whom
it has been given. [12]For some are eunuchs because they were born that way;
others were made that way by men;
and others have renounced marriage[c]
because of the kingdom of heaven.
The one who can accept this should accept it."

The Little Children and Jesus

[13]Then little children were brought to
Jesus for him to place his hands on them
and pray for them. But the disciples rebuked those who brought them.
[14]Jesus said, "Let the little children
come to me, and do not hinder them, for
the kingdom of heaven belongs to such
as these." [15]When he had placed his
hands on them, he went on from there.

The Rich Young Man

[16]Now a man came up to Jesus and
asked, "Teacher, what good thing must
I do to get eternal life?"
[17]"Why do you ask me about what is
good?" Jesus replied. "There is only One
who is good. If you want to enter life,
obey the commandments."
[18]"Which ones?" the man inquired.
Jesus replied, " 'Do not murder, do
not commit adultery, do not steal, do
not give false testimony, [19]honor your
father and mother,'[d] and 'love your
neighbor as yourself.'[e]"
[20]"All these I have kept," the young
man said. "What do I still lack?"
[21]Jesus answered, "If you want to be
perfect, go, sell your possessions and
give to the poor, and you will have
treasure in heaven. Then come, follow me."
[22]When the young man heard this, he
went away sad, because he had great
wealth.
[23]Then Jesus said to his disciples, "I tell
you the truth, it is hard for a rich man
to enter the kingdom of heaven. [24]Again
I tell you, it is easier for a camel to go
through the eye of a needle than for a
rich man to enter the kingdom of God."
[25]When the disciples heard this, they
were greatly astonished and asked,
"Who then can be saved?"
[26]Jesus looked at them and said, "With
man this is impossible, but with God all
things are possible."
[27]Peter answered him, "We have left
everything to follow you! What then
will there be for us?"
[28]Jesus said to them, "I tell you the
truth, at the renewal of all things, when
the Son of Man sits on his glorious
throne, you who have followed me will
also sit on twelve thrones, judging the
twelve tribes of Israel. [29]And everyone
who has left houses or brothers or sisters or father or mother[f] or children or
fields for my sake will receive a hundred
times as much and will inherit eternal
life. [30]But many who are first will be last,
and many who are last will be first.

[a]4 Gen. 1:27 [b]5 Gen. 2:24 [c]12 Or *have made themselves eunuchs* [d]19 Exodus 20:12-16; Deut. 5:16-20 [e]19 Lev. 19:18 [f]29 Some manuscripts *mother or wife*

SHARPEN THE FOCUS

Contestants in a short-lived TV game show answered questions as in many other game shows. But the winners of this game got a unique prize: financial freedom. If you won, the show's developers paid off all your debts. The winners, you can guess, walked away grinning from ear to ear.

The servant in Jesus' parable (Matthew 18:24) owed the king 10,000 talents (Matthew 18:24). A talent weighed in at 91 pounds. Imagine owing anyone 910,000 pounds of gold! That's a debt bigger than the gross national product of most countries in the world even today! No TV mogul could retire *that* kind of debt. But the king forgave it. He wrote off the loss. He set his servant free.

We are that servant; because of our sin, each of us once owed our Lord an enormous debt. The write-off cost Him—not something cheap like gold or silver; it cost, instead, the life blood of His only Son. Let that truth sink down deeper into the depth of your being today. You are free!

When you realize your freedom, the wrongs others have done to you will seem like pocket change. If you're having trouble forgiving, spend more time in your King's presence, meditating on the freedom He's given you.

WEEK 76 • THURSDAY

Matthew 20:1—21:46

GET THE BIG PICTURE

Jesus' identity as Israel's Messiah shone so clearly from His teaching and His miracles that even the blind could see it (Matthew 20:29–34). But those who should have recognized Him—Israel's religious leaders—failed to see. Even Jesus' own disciples seem remarkably short-sighted at times. As you read today, ask yourself why that may have been so. If time is short, focus on Matthew 21:1–11.

The Parable of the Workers in the Vineyard

20 "For the kingdom of
heaven is like a landowner
who went out early in the morning to
hire men to work in his vineyard.
2He agreed to pay them a denarius
for the day and sent them into his vineyard.
3"About the third hour he went out
and saw others standing in the marketplace doing nothing.
4He told them,
'You also go and work in my vineyard,
and I will pay you whatever is right.' 5So
they went.

"He went out again about the sixth
hour and the ninth hour and did the
same thing.
6About the eleventh hour he
went out and found still others standing around. He asked them, 'Why have
you been standing here all day long doing nothing?'
7"'Because no one has hired us,' they
answered.

"He said to them, 'You also go and
work in my vineyard.'

8"When evening came, the owner of the vineyard said to his foreman, 'Call the workers and pay them their wages, beginning with the last ones hired and going on to the first.'

9"The workers who were hired about the eleventh hour came and each received a denarius. 10So when those came who were hired first, they expected to receive more. But each one of them also received a denarius. 11When they received it, they began to grumble against the landowner. 12'These men who were hired last worked only one hour,' they said, 'and you have made them equal to us who have borne the burden of the work and the heat of the day.'

13"But he answered one of them, 'Friend, I am not being unfair to you. Didn't you agree to work for a denarius? 14Take your pay and go. I want to give the man who was hired last the same as I gave you. 15Don't I have the right to do what I want with my own money? Or are you envious because I am generous?'

16"So the last will be first, and the first will be last."

Jesus Again Predicts His Death

17Now as Jesus was going up to Jerusalem, he took the twelve disciples aside and said to them, 18"We are going up to Jerusalem, and the Son of Man will be betrayed to the chief priests and the teachers of the law. They will condemn him to death 19and will turn him over to the Gentiles to be mocked and flogged and crucified. On the third day he will be raised to life!"

A Mother's Request

20Then the mother of Zebedee's sons came to Jesus with her sons and, kneeling down, asked a favor of him.

21"What is it you want?" he asked.

She said, "Grant that one of these two sons of mine may sit at your right and the other at your left in your kingdom."

22"You don't know what you are asking," Jesus said to them. "Can you drink the cup I am going to drink?"

"We can," they answered.

23Jesus said to them, "You will indeed drink from my cup, but to sit at my right or left is not for me to grant. These places belong to those for whom they have been prepared by my Father."

24When the ten heard about this, they were indignant with the two brothers. 25Jesus called them together and said, "You know that the rulers of the Gentiles lord it over them, and their high officials exercise authority over them. 26Not so with you. Instead, whoever wants to become great among you must be your servant, 27and whoever wants to be first must be your slave— 28just as the Son of Man did not come to be served, but to serve, and to give his life as a ransom for many."

Two Blind Men Receive Sight

29As Jesus and his disciples were leaving Jericho, a large crowd followed him. 30Two blind men were sitting by the roadside, and when they heard that Jesus was going by, they shouted, "Lord, Son of David, have mercy on us!"

31The crowd rebuked them and told them to be quiet, but they shouted all the louder, "Lord, Son of David, have mercy on us!"

32Jesus stopped and called them. "What do you want me to do for you?" he asked.

33"Lord," they answered, "we want our sight."

34Jesus had compassion on them and touched their eyes. Immediately they received their sight and followed him.

The Triumphal Entry

21 As they approached Jerusalem and came to Bethphage on the Mount of Olives, Jesus sent two disciples, 2saying to them, "Go to the village ahead of you, and at once you will find a donkey tied there, with her colt by her. Untie them and bring them to me. 3If anyone says anything to you, tell him that the Lord needs them, and he will send them right away."

4This took place to fulfill what was spoken through the prophet:

5"Say to the Daughter of Zion,
'See, your king comes to you,
gentle and riding on a donkey,
on a colt, the foal of a donkey.' "[a]

6The disciples went and did as Jesus had instructed them. 7They brought the donkey and the colt, placed their cloaks on them, and Jesus sat on them. 8A very large crowd spread their cloaks on the road, while others cut branches from the trees and spread them on the road. 9The crowds that went ahead of him and those that followed shouted,

"Hosanna[b] to the Son of David!"

"Blessed is he who comes in the
name of the Lord!"[c]

"Hosanna[b] in the highest!"

10When Jesus entered Jerusalem, the whole city was stirred and asked, "Who is this?"

11The crowds answered, "This is Jesus, the prophet from Nazareth in Galilee."

Jesus at the Temple

12Jesus entered the temple area and drove out all who were buying and selling there. He overturned the tables of the money changers and the benches of those selling doves. 13"It is written," he said to them, " 'My house will be called a house of prayer,'[d] but you are making it a 'den of robbers.'[e]"

14The blind and the lame came to him at the temple, and he healed them. 15But when the chief priests and the teachers of the law saw the wonderful things he did and the children shouting in the temple area, "Hosanna to the Son of David," they were indignant.

16"Do you hear what these children are saying?" they asked him.

"Yes," replied Jesus, "have you never read,

" 'From the lips of children and
infants
you have ordained praise'[f]?"

17And he left them and went out of the city to Bethany, where he spent the night.

The Fig Tree Withers

18Early in the morning, as he was on his way back to the city, he was hungry. 19Seeing a fig tree by the road, he went up to it but found nothing on it except leaves. Then he said to it, "May you never bear fruit again!" Immediately the tree withered.

20When the disciples saw this, they were amazed. "How did the fig tree wither so quickly?" they asked.

21Jesus replied, "I tell you the truth, if you have faith and do not doubt, not only can you do what was done to the fig tree, but also you can say to this mountain, 'Go, throw yourself into the sea,' and it will be done. 22If you believe, you will receive whatever you ask for in prayer."

The Authority of Jesus Questioned

23Jesus entered the temple courts, and, while he was teaching, the chief priests and the elders of the people came to him. "By what authority are you doing these things?" they asked. "And who gave you this authority?"

24Jesus replied, "I will also ask you one question. If you answer me, I will tell you by what authority I am doing these things. 25John's baptism—where did it come from? Was it from heaven, or from men?"

They discussed it among themselves and said, "If we say, 'From heaven,' he will ask, 'Then why didn't you believe him?' 26But if we say, 'From men'—we are afraid of the people, for they all hold that John was a prophet."

27So they answered Jesus, "We don't know."

Then he said, "Neither will I tell you by what authority I am doing these things.

The Parable of the Two Sons

28"What do you think? There was a man who had two sons. He went to the

[a]5 Zech. 9:9 [b]9 A Hebrew expression meaning "Save!" which became an exclamation of praise; also in verse 15 [c]9 Psalm 118:26 [d]13 Isaiah 56:7 [e]13 Jer. 7:11 [f]16 Psalm 8:2

first and said, 'Son, go and work today
in the vineyard.'
29" 'I will not,' he answered, but later
he changed his mind and went.
30"Then the father went to the other
son and said the same thing. He answered, 'I will, sir,' but he did not go.
31"Which of the two did what his father wanted?"
"The first," they answered.
Jesus said to them, "I tell you the
truth, the tax collectors and the prostitutes are entering the kingdom of God
ahead of you. 32For John came to you to
show you the way of righteousness, and
you did not believe him, but the tax collectors and the prostitutes did. And
even after you saw this, you did not repent and believe him.

The Parable of the Tenants

33"Listen to another parable: There
was a landowner who planted a vineyard. He put a wall around it, dug a
winepress in it and built a watchtower.
Then he rented the vineyard to some
farmers and went away on a journey.
34When the harvest time approached, he
sent his servants to the tenants to collect
his fruit.
35"The tenants seized his servants;
they beat one, killed another, and
stoned a third. 36Then he sent other
servants to them, more than the first
time, and the tenants treated them the
same way. 37Last of all, he sent his son
to them. 'They will respect my son,' he
said.
38"But when the tenants saw the son,
they said to each other, 'This is the heir.
Come, let's kill him and take his inheritance.' 39So they took him and threw
him out of the vineyard and killed him.
40"Therefore, when the owner of the
vineyard comes, what will he do to
those tenants?"
41"He will bring those wretches to a
wretched end," they replied, "and he
will rent the vineyard to other tenants,
who will give him his share of the crop
at harvest time."
42Jesus said to them, "Have you never
read in the Scriptures:

" 'The stone the builders rejected
has become the capstone[a];
the Lord has done this,
and it is marvelous in our eyes'[b]?

43"Therefore I tell you that the kingdom of God will be taken away from
you and given to a people who will produce its fruit. 44He who falls on this
stone will be broken to pieces, but he on
whom it falls will be crushed."[c]
45When the chief priests and the
Pharisees heard Jesus' parables, they
knew he was talking about them. 46They
looked for a way to arrest him, but they
were afraid of the crowd because the
people held that he was a prophet.

[a]42 Or *cornerstone* [b]42 Psalm 118:22,23
[c]44 Some manuscripts do not have verse 44.

SHARPEN THE FOCUS

Picture the prime minister of one of the world's great nations riding to the ceremony in which he receives the authority to govern. Or recall the last inauguration parade in Washington, D.C. Chances are good that the guest of honor—the new prime minister or president—did not sit in the front seat of a Geo Metro. We usually reserve the finest stretch limousines for those who hold high office.

With that in mind, look back at Matthew 21:7. As another son of David—Solomon—took the throne, he rode his father's mule (1 Kings 1:33–34). The kings who followed Solomon chose more appropriate symbols of power. War horses, for instance. But King Jesus followed Solomon's lead.

King Jesus came to ascend, not a throne, but a cross. King Jesus came to battle, not foreign armies, but the powers of darkness. King Jesus came to triumph, to bring us life, by dying in our place. Hosanna to the Son of David! Blessed is He who came to serve and to give His life as a ransom for many (Matthew 20:28).

"God is not interested in your religion." That's the message Jesus tried to hammer home to the Sadducees and Pharisees. They were concerned with performing rituals and proving their worthiness. Listen closely to the seven woes Jesus calls down on the Pharisees and teachers of the law in Matthew 23. Do any of His words hit too close to home? If time is short, focus on Matthew 23:1–39.

The Parable of the Wedding Banquet

22 Jesus spoke to them again
in parables, saying: 2"The
kingdom of heaven is like a king who
prepared a wedding banquet for his
son. 3He sent his servants to those who
had been invited to the banquet to tell
them to come, but they refused to come.
4"Then he sent some more servants
and said, 'Tell those who have been invited that I have prepared my dinner:
My oxen and fattened cattle have been
butchered, and everything is ready.
Come to the wedding banquet.'
5"But they paid no attention and went
off—one to his field, another to his business. 6The rest seized his servants, mistreated them and killed them. 7The king
was enraged. He sent his army and destroyed those murderers and burned
their city.
8"Then he said to his servants, 'The
wedding banquet is ready, but those I
invited did not deserve to come. 9Go to
the street corners and invite to the banquet anyone you find.' 10So the servants
went out into the streets and gathered
all the people they could find, both
good and bad, and the wedding hall
was filled with guests.
11"But when the king came in to see
the guests, he noticed a man there who
was not wearing wedding clothes.
12'Friend,' he asked, 'how did you get in
here without wedding clothes?' The
man was speechless.
13"Then the king told the attendants,
'Tie him hand and foot, and throw him
outside, into the darkness, where there
will be weeping and gnashing of teeth.'
14"For many are invited, but few are
chosen."

Paying Taxes to Caesar

15Then the Pharisees went out and
laid plans to trap him in his words.
16They sent their disciples to him along
with the Herodians. "Teacher," they
said, "we know you are a man of integrity and that you teach the way of God
in accordance with the truth. You aren't
swayed by men, because you pay no attention to who they are. 17Tell us then,
what is your opinion? Is it right to pay
taxes to Caesar or not?"
18But Jesus, knowing their evil intent,
said, "You hypocrites, why are you trying to trap me? 19Show me the coin
used for paying the tax." They brought
him a denarius, 20and he asked them,

"Whose portrait is this? And whose inscription?"
21"Caesar's," they replied.
Then he said to them, "Give to Caesar what is Caesar's, and to God what
is God's."
22When they heard this, they were
amazed. So they left him and went
away.

Marriage at the Resurrection

23That same day the Sadducees, who
say there is no resurrection, came to him
with a question. 24"Teacher," they said,
"Moses told us that if a man dies without having children, his brother must
marry the widow and have children for
him. 25Now there were seven brothers
among us. The first one married and
died, and since he had no children, he
left his wife to his brother. 26The same
thing happened to the second and third
brother, right on down to the seventh.
27Finally, the woman died. 28Now then,
at the resurrection, whose wife will she
be of the seven, since all of them were
married to her?"
29Jesus replied, "You are in error because you do not know the Scriptures or
the power of God. 30At the resurrection
people will neither marry nor be given
in marriage; they will be like the angels
in heaven. 31But about the resurrection
of the dead—have you not read what
God said to you, 32'I am the God of Abraham, the God of Isaac, and the God of
Jacob'[a]? He is not the God of the dead
but of the living."
33When the crowds heard this, they
were astonished at his teaching.

The Greatest Commandment

34Hearing that Jesus had silenced the
Sadducees, the Pharisees got together.
35One of them, an expert in the law, tested him with this question: 36"Teacher,
which is the greatest commandment in
the Law?"
37Jesus replied: " 'Love the Lord your
God with all your heart and with all
your soul and with all your mind.'[b]
38This is the first and greatest commandment. 39And the second is like it: 'Love
your neighbor as yourself.'[c] 40All the
Law and the Prophets hang on these
two commandments."

Whose Son Is the Christ?

41While the Pharisees were gathered
together, Jesus asked them, 42"What do
you think about the Christ[d]? Whose son
is he?"
"The son of David," they replied.
43He said to them, "How is it then that
David, speaking by the Spirit, calls him
'Lord'? For he says,

44" 'The Lord said to my Lord:
"Sit at my right hand
until I put your enemies
under your feet." '[e]

45If then David calls him 'Lord,' how can
he be his son?" 46No one could say a
word in reply, and from that day on
no one dared to ask him any more
questions.

Seven Woes

23 Then Jesus said to the
crowds and to his dis-
ciples: 2"The teachers of the law and the
Pharisees sit in Moses' seat. 3So you
must obey them and do everything they
tell you. But do not do what they do, for
they do not practice what they preach.
4They tie up heavy loads and put them
on men's shoulders, but they themselves are not willing to lift a finger to
move them.
5"Everything they do is done for men
to see: They make their phylacteries[f]
wide and the tassels on their garments
long; 6they love the place of honor at
banquets and the most important seats
in the synagogues; 7they love to be
greeted in the marketplaces and to have
men call them 'Rabbi.'
8"But you are not to be called 'Rabbi,'
for you have only one Master and you
are all brothers. 9And do not call anyone
on earth 'father,' for you have one

[a]32 Exodus 3:6 [b]37 Deut. 6:5 [c]39 Lev. 19:18
[d]42 Or *Messiah* [e]44 Psalm 110:1 [f]5 That is,
boxes containing Scripture verses, worn on
forehead and arm

Father, and he is in heaven. 10Nor are
you to be called 'teacher,' for you have
one Teacher, the Christ.[a] 11The greatest
among you will be your servant. 12For
whoever exalts himself will be humbled,
and whoever humbles himself will be
exalted.
13"Woe to you, teachers of the law and
Pharisees, you hypocrites! You shut the
kingdom of heaven in men's faces. You
yourselves do not enter, nor will you let
those enter who are trying to.[b]
15"Woe to you, teachers of the law and
Pharisees, you hypocrites! You travel
over land and sea to win a single convert, and when he becomes one, you
make him twice as much a son of hell as
you are.
16"Woe to you, blind guides! You say,
'If anyone swears by the temple, it
means nothing; but if anyone swears by
the gold of the temple, he is bound by
his oath.' 17You blind fools! Which is
greater: the gold, or the temple that
makes the gold sacred? 18You also say, 'If
anyone swears by the altar, it means
nothing; but if anyone swears by the gift
on it, he is bound by his oath.' 19You
blind men! Which is greater: the gift, or
the altar that makes the gift sacred?
20Therefore, he who swears by the altar
swears by it and by everything on it.
21And he who swears by the temple
swears by it and by the one who dwells
in it. 22And he who swears by heaven
swears by God's throne and by the one
who sits on it.
23"Woe to you, teachers of the law and
Pharisees, you hypocrites! You give a
tenth of your spices—mint, dill and
cummin. But you have neglected the
more important matters of the law—justice, mercy and faithfulness. You should
have practiced the latter, without neglecting the former. 24You blind guides!
You strain out a gnat but swallow a
camel.
25"Woe to you, teachers of the law and
Pharisees, you hypocrites! You clean
the outside of the cup and dish, but
inside they are full of greed and self-
indulgence. 26Blind Pharisee! First clean
the inside of the cup and dish, and then
the outside also will be clean.
27"Woe to you, teachers of the law and
Pharisees, you hypocrites! You are like
whitewashed tombs, which look beautiful on the outside but on the inside are
full of dead men's bones and everything
unclean. 28In the same way, on the outside you appear to people as righteous
but on the inside you are full of hypocrisy and wickedness.
29"Woe to you, teachers of the law and
Pharisees, you hypocrites! You build
tombs for the prophets and decorate the
graves of the righteous. 30And you say,
'If we had lived in the days of our forefathers, we would not have taken part
with them in shedding the blood of the
prophets.' 31So you testify against yourselves that you are the descendants of
those who murdered the prophets. 32Fill
up, then, the measure of the sin of your
forefathers!
33"You snakes! You brood of vipers!
How will you escape being condemned
to hell? 34Therefore I am sending you
prophets and wise men and teachers.
Some of them you will kill and crucify;
others you will flog in your synagogues
and pursue from town to town. 35And so
upon you will come all the righteous
blood that has been shed on earth, from
the blood of righteous Abel to the blood
of Zechariah son of Berekiah, whom
you murdered between the temple and
the altar. 36I tell you the truth, all this will
come upon this generation.
37"O Jerusalem, Jerusalem, you who
kill the prophets and stone those sent to
you, how often I have longed to gather
your children together, as a hen gathers
her chicks under her wings, but you
were not willing. 38Look, your house is
left to you desolate. 39For I tell you, you
will not see me again until you say,
'Blessed is he who comes in the name of
the Lord.'[c]"

[a]10 Or *Messiah* [b]13 Some manuscripts *to.* 14*Woe to you, teachers of the law and Pharisees, you hypocrites! You devour widows' houses and for a show make lengthy prayers. Therefore you will be punished more severely.* [c]39 Psalm 118:26

SHARPEN THE FOCUS

"Yell the fur off," advises a dog training book that tells how to deal with a pet who appoints himself Official Waste Basket Inspector. If you can catch Inspector Waste Basket on the job, and if you can muster up a blistering-enough lecture, you can sometimes change a pet's behavior.

The Pharisees and teachers of the law had appointed themselves moral watchdogs in Israel. They prided themselves in their obedience to the smallest details of the law but ignored what God wanted most: a heart of mercy toward others, a heart that treats others fairly and with compassion, a heart of integrity.

It's easy to read our Lord's words to the Pharisees and feel smug. After all, *we're* not hypocrites like *they* were. But the moment we think that, we're cornered. We're taking credit for what only God works in our hearts—repentance and faith.

Any mercy in us is there because God has first shown us mercy in Jesus and in His cross. Any integrity in us is there because God has worked it in us by His grace and through His Word. Spiritual pride is deadly; ask your Savior to cleanse it from your heart. He will. He is faithful and merciful.

WEEK 76 • SATURDAY

Matthew 24:1—25:46

GET THE BIG PICTURE

Imagine the Statue of Liberty falling into the ocean and New York City lying in ruins. That's a scenario equal in shock-value to Jesus' words in Matthew 24:1–2 as far as His disciples were concerned. No wonder they asked the questions they did (Matthew 24:3)! As you read His answers, keep in mind that we can't always tell which words refer to the destruction of Jerusalem by the Roman General, Titus, in A.D. 70 and which words refer to Jesus' second coming on Judgment Day. If time is short, focus on Matthew 25:31–46.

Signs of the End of the Age

24 Jesus left the temple and
was walking away when
his disciples came up to him to call his
attention to its buildings. 2"Do you see
all these things?" he asked. "I tell you
the truth, not one stone here will be left
on another; every one will be thrown
down."
3As Jesus was sitting on the Mount of
Olives, the disciples came to him privately. "Tell us," they said, "when will
this happen, and what will be the sign
of your coming and of the end of the
age?"
4Jesus answered: "Watch out that no
one deceives you. 5For many will come
in my name, claiming, 'I am the Christ,[a]'
and will deceive many. 6You will hear of
wars and rumors of wars, but see to it
that you are not alarmed. Such things
must happen, but the end is still to
come. 7Nation will rise against nation,
and kingdom against kingdom. There

[a]5 Or *Messiah;* also in verse 23

will be famines and earthquakes in various places. 8All these are the beginning of birth pains.

9"Then you will be handed over to be persecuted and put to death, and you will be hated by all nations because of me. 10At that time many will turn away from the faith and will betray and hate each other, 11and many false prophets will appear and deceive many people. 12Because of the increase of wickedness, the love of most will grow cold, 13but he who stands firm to the end will be saved. 14And this gospel of the kingdom will be preached in the whole world as a testimony to all nations, and then the end will come.

15"So when you see standing in the holy place 'the abomination that causes desolation,'[a] spoken of through the prophet Daniel—let the reader understand— 16then let those who are in Judea flee to the mountains. 17Let no one on the roof of his house go down to take anything out of the house. 18Let no one in the field go back to get his cloak. 19How dreadful it will be in those days for pregnant women and nursing mothers! 20Pray that your flight will not take place in winter or on the Sabbath. 21For then there will be great distress, unequaled from the beginning of the world until now—and never to be equaled again. 22If those days had not been cut short, no one would survive, but for the sake of the elect those days will be shortened. 23At that time if anyone says to you, 'Look, here is the Christ!' or, 'There he is!' do not believe it. 24For false Christs and false prophets will appear and perform great signs and miracles to deceive even the elect—if that were possible. 25See, I have told you ahead of time.

26"So if anyone tells you, 'There he is, out in the desert,' do not go out; or, 'Here he is, in the inner rooms,' do not believe it. 27For as lightning that comes from the east is visible even in the west, so will be the coming of the Son of Man. 28Wherever there is a carcass, there the vultures will gather.

29"Immediately after the distress of those days

"'the sun will be darkened,
and the moon will not give its light;
the stars will fall from the sky,
and the heavenly bodies will be shaken.'[b]

30"At that time the sign of the Son of Man will appear in the sky, and all the nations of the earth will mourn. They will see the Son of Man coming on the clouds of the sky, with power and great glory. 31And he will send his angels with a loud trumpet call, and they will gather his elect from the four winds, from one end of the heavens to the other.

32"Now learn this lesson from the fig tree: As soon as its twigs get tender and its leaves come out, you know that summer is near. 33Even so, when you see all these things, you know that it[c] is near, right at the door. 34I tell you the truth, this generation[d] will certainly not pass away until all these things have happened. 35Heaven and earth will pass away, but my words will never pass away.

The Day and Hour Unknown

36"No one knows about that day or hour, not even the angels in heaven, nor the Son,[e] but only the Father. 37As it was in the days of Noah, so it will be at the coming of the Son of Man. 38For in the days before the flood, people were eating and drinking, marrying and giving in marriage, up to the day Noah entered the ark; 39and they knew nothing about what would happen until the flood came and took them all away. That is how it will be at the coming of the Son of Man. 40Two men will be in the field; one will be taken and the other left. 41Two women will be grinding with a hand mill; one will be taken and the other left.

42"Therefore keep watch, because you do not know on what day your Lord will come. 43But understand this: If the owner of the house had known at what

[a]*15* Daniel 9:27; 11:31; 12:11 [b]*29* Isaiah 13:10; 34:4 [c]*33* Or *he* [d]*34* Or *race* [e]*36* Some manuscripts do not have *nor the Son.*

time of night the thief was coming, he would have kept watch and would not have let his house be broken into. [44]So you also must be ready, because the Son of Man will come at an hour when you do not expect him.

[45]"Who then is the faithful and wise servant, whom the master has put in charge of the servants in his household to give them their food at the proper time? [46]It will be good for that servant whose master finds him doing so when he returns. [47]I tell you the truth, he will put him in charge of all his possessions. [48]But suppose that servant is wicked and says to himself, 'My master is staying away a long time,' [49]and he then begins to beat his fellow servants and to eat and drink with drunkards. [50]The master of that servant will come on a day when he does not expect him and at an hour he is not aware of. [51]He will cut him to pieces and assign him a place with the hypocrites, where there will be weeping and gnashing of teeth.

The Parable of the Ten Virgins

25 "At that time the kingdom of heaven will be like ten virgins who took their lamps and went out to meet the bridegroom. [2]Five of them were foolish and five were wise. [3]The foolish ones took their lamps but did not take any oil with them. [4]The wise, however, took oil in jars along with their lamps. [5]The bridegroom was a long time in coming, and they all became drowsy and fell asleep.

[6]"At midnight the cry rang out: 'Here's the bridegroom! Come out to meet him!'

[7]"Then all the virgins woke up and trimmed their lamps. [8]The foolish ones said to the wise, 'Give us some of your oil; our lamps are going out.'

[9]" 'No,' they replied, 'there may not be enough for both us and you. Instead, go to those who sell oil and buy some for yourselves.'

[10]"But while they were on their way to buy the oil, the bridegroom arrived. The virgins who were ready went in with him to the wedding banquet. And the door was shut.

[11]"Later the others also came. 'Sir! Sir!' they said. 'Open the door for us!'

[12]"But he replied, 'I tell you the truth, I don't know you.'

[13]"Therefore keep watch, because you do not know the day or the hour.

The Parable of the Talents

[14]"Again, it will be like a man going on a journey, who called his servants and entrusted his property to them. [15]To one he gave five talents[a] of money, to another two talents, and to another one talent, each according to his ability. Then he went on his journey. [16]The man who had received the five talents went at once and put his money to work and gained five more. [17]So also, the one with the two talents gained two more. [18]But the man who had received the one talent went off, dug a hole in the ground and hid his master's money.

[19]"After a long time the master of those servants returned and settled accounts with them. [20]The man who had received the five talents brought the other five. 'Master,' he said, 'you entrusted me with five talents. See, I have gained five more.'

[21]"His master replied, 'Well done, good and faithful servant! You have been faithful with a few things; I will put you in charge of many things. Come and share your master's happiness!'

[22]"The man with the two talents also came. 'Master,' he said, 'you entrusted me with two talents; see, I have gained two more.'

[23]"His master replied, 'Well done, good and faithful servant! You have been faithful with a few things; I will put you in charge of many things. Come and share your master's happiness!'

[24]"Then the man who had received the one talent came. 'Master,' he said, 'I knew that you are a hard man, harvesting where you have not sown and gathering where you have not scattered seed. [25]So I was afraid and went out and

[a]*15* A talent was worth more than a thousand dollars.

hid your talent in the ground. See, here is what belongs to you.'

26"His master replied, 'You wicked, lazy servant! So you knew that I harvest where I have not sown and gather where I have not scattered seed? 27Well then, you should have put my money on deposit with the bankers, so that when I returned I would have received it back with interest.

28" 'Take the talent from him and give it to the one who has the ten talents. 29For everyone who has will be given more, and he will have an abundance. Whoever does not have, even what he has will be taken from him. 30And throw that worthless servant outside, into the darkness, where there will be weeping and gnashing of teeth.'

The Sheep and the Goats

31"When the Son of Man comes in his glory, and all the angels with him, he will sit on his throne in heavenly glory. 32All the nations will be gathered before him, and he will separate the people one from another as a shepherd separates the sheep from the goats. 33He will put the sheep on his right and the goats on his left.

34"Then the King will say to those on his right, 'Come, you who are blessed by my Father; take your inheritance, the kingdom prepared for you since the creation of the world. 35For I was hungry and you gave me something to eat, I was thirsty and you gave me something to drink, I was a stranger and you invited me in, 36I needed clothes and you clothed me, I was sick and you looked after me, I was in prison and you came to visit me.'

37"Then the righteous will answer him, 'Lord, when did we see you hungry and feed you, or thirsty and give you something to drink? 38When did we see you a stranger and invite you in, or needing clothes and clothe you? 39When did we see you sick or in prison and go to visit you?'

40"The King will reply, 'I tell you the truth, whatever you did for one of the least of these brothers of mine, you did for me.'

41"Then he will say to those on his left, 'Depart from me, you who are cursed, into the eternal fire prepared for the devil and his angels. 42For I was hungry and you gave me nothing to eat, I was thirsty and you gave me nothing to drink, 43I was a stranger and you did not invite me in, I needed clothes and you did not clothe me, I was sick and in prison and you did not look after me.'

44"They also will answer, 'Lord, when did we see you hungry or thirsty or a stranger or needing clothes or sick or in prison, and did not help you?'

45"He will reply, 'I tell you the truth, whatever you did not do for one of the least of these, you did not do for me.'

46"Then they will go away to eternal punishment, but the righteous to eternal life."

SHARPEN THE FOCUS

One key word unlocks Jesus description of Judgment Day. If you miss it, you'll misread His meaning altogether. That word? *Inheritance* in Matthew 25:34.

An inheritance differs from a pay check in several key ways. Sometimes a selfish or eccentric person will make her heirs jump through hoops while holding out her estate as a reward, but usually inheritances are unearned. Sometimes they're even a surprise. Then, too, we cannot use an inheritance until the person bestowing it has died.

Now think about the kingdom of God. This kingdom has been set aside for us since our Lord laid the earth's foundations (Matthew 25:34). We have not earned citizenship in it by our brave deeds or right actions. But our place is secure, because the King died for us. Our eternal relationship with Him comes to us as something of a surprise. We know what we deserve by our sins, and it's nothing like what we get through His grace!

With our inheritance, we receive a new title: the righteous ones (Matthew 25:37). And we receive a new eagerness to serve others just as our Savior-King has served us.

Again and again, Matthew has shown us the kind of ruler Jesus is—our Servant-King. Nowhere in Matthew's gospel does this truth shine more clearly than in his account of our Lord's suffering and death. Look for that accent as you read. If time is short, focus on Matthew 27:32–56.

The Plot Against Jesus

26 When Jesus had finished
saying all these things, he
said to his disciples, 2"As you know, the
Passover is two days away—and the
Son of Man will be handed over to be
crucified."
3Then the chief priests and the elders
of the people assembled in the palace of
the high priest, whose name was Caiaphas, 4and they plotted to arrest Jesus in
some sly way and kill him. 5"But not
during the Feast," they said, "or there
may be a riot among the people."

Jesus Anointed at Bethany

6While Jesus was in Bethany in the
home of a man known as Simon the
Leper, 7a woman came to him with an alabaster jar of very expensive perfume,
which she poured on his head as he was
reclining at the table.
8When the disciples saw this, they
were indignant. "Why this waste?" they
asked. 9"This perfume could have been
sold at a high price and the money
given to the poor."
10Aware of this, Jesus said to them,
"Why are you bothering this woman?
She has done a beautiful thing to me.
11The poor you will always have with
you, but you will not always have me.
12When she poured this perfume on my
body, she did it to prepare me for burial. 13I tell you the truth, wherever this
gospel is preached throughout the
world, what she has done will also be
told, in memory of her."

Judas Agrees to Betray Jesus

14Then one of the Twelve—the one
called Judas Iscariot—went to the chief
priests 15and asked, "What are you willing to give me if I hand him over to
you?" So they counted out for him thirty
silver coins. 16From then on Judas
watched for an opportunity to hand
him over.

The Lord's Supper

17On the first day of the Feast of Unleavened Bread, the disciples came to
Jesus and asked, "Where do you want
us to make preparations for you to eat
the Passover?"
18He replied, "Go into the city to a certain man and tell him, 'The Teacher says:
My appointed time is near. I am going
to celebrate the Passover with my disciples at your house.'" 19So the disciples
did as Jesus had directed them and prepared the Passover.

20When evening came, Jesus was reclining at the table with the Twelve.
21And while they were eating, he said,
"I tell you the truth, one of you will betray me."

22They were very sad and began to
say to him one after the other, "Surely
not I, Lord?"

23Jesus replied, "The one who has
dipped his hand into the bowl with me
will betray me. 24The Son of Man will go
just as it is written about him. But woe
to that man who betrays the Son of
Man! It would be better for him if he
had not been born."

25Then Judas, the one who would betray him, said, "Surely not I, Rabbi?"

Jesus answered, "Yes, it is you."[a]

26While they were eating, Jesus took
bread, gave thanks and broke it, and
gave it to his disciples, saying, "Take and
eat; this is my body."

27Then he took the cup, gave thanks
and offered it to them, saying, "Drink
from it, all of you. 28This is my blood of
the[b] covenant, which is poured out for
many for the forgiveness of sins. 29I tell
you, I will not drink of this fruit of the
vine from now on until that day when I
drink it anew with you in my Father's
kingdom."

30When they had sung a hymn, they
went out to the Mount of Olives.

Jesus Predicts Peter's Denial

31Then Jesus told them, "This very
night you will all fall away on account
of me, for it is written:

" 'I will strike the shepherd,
and the sheep of the flock will be
scattered.'[c]

32But after I have risen, I will go ahead
of you into Galilee."

33Peter replied, "Even if all fall away
on account of you, I never will."

34"I tell you the truth," Jesus answered, "this very night, before the
rooster crows, you will disown me three
times."

35But Peter declared, "Even if I have to
die with you, I will never disown you."
And all the other disciples said the
same.

Gethsemane

36Then Jesus went with his disciples to
a place called Gethsemane, and he said
to them, "Sit here while I go over there
and pray." 37He took Peter and the two
sons of Zebedee along with him, and he
began to be sorrowful and troubled.
38Then he said to them, "My soul is overwhelmed with sorrow to the point of
death. Stay here and keep watch with
me."

39Going a little farther, he fell with his
face to the ground and prayed, "My Father, if it is possible, may this cup be
taken from me. Yet not as I will, but as
you will."

40Then he returned to his disciples
and found them sleeping. "Could you
men not keep watch with me for one
hour?" he asked Peter. 41"Watch and
pray so that you will not fall into temptation. The spirit is willing, but the body
is weak."

42He went away a second time and
prayed, "My Father, if it is not possible
for this cup to be taken away unless I
drink it, may your will be done."

43When he came back, he again found
them sleeping, because their eyes were
heavy. 44So he left them and went away
once more and prayed the third time,
saying the same thing.

45Then he returned to the disciples
and said to them, "Are you still sleeping
and resting? Look, the hour is near, and
the Son of Man is betrayed into the
hands of sinners. 46Rise, let us go! Here
comes my betrayer!"

Jesus Arrested

47While he was still speaking, Judas,
one of the Twelve, arrived. With him
was a large crowd armed with swords
and clubs, sent from the chief priests
and the elders of the people. 48Now the
betrayer had arranged a signal with
them: "The one I kiss is the man; arrest

[a]25 Or *"You yourself have said it"* [b]28 Some manuscripts *the new* [c]31 Zech. 13:7

him." 49 Going at once to Jesus, Judas
said, "Greetings, Rabbi!" and kissed
him.
50 Jesus replied, "Friend, do what you
came for."[a]
Then the men stepped forward,
seized Jesus and arrested him. 51 With
that, one of Jesus' companions reached
for his sword, drew it out and struck the
servant of the high priest, cutting off his
ear.
52 "Put your sword back in its place,"
Jesus said to him, "for all who draw the
sword will die by the sword. 53 Do you
think I cannot call on my Father, and he
will at once put at my disposal more
than twelve legions of angels? 54 But how
then would the Scriptures be fulfilled
that say it must happen in this way?"
55 At that time Jesus said to the crowd,
"Am I leading a rebellion, that you have
come out with swords and clubs to capture me? Every day I sat in the temple
courts teaching, and you did not arrest
me. 56 But this has all taken place that the
writings of the prophets might be fulfilled." Then all the disciples deserted
him and fled.

Before the Sanhedrin

57 Those who had arrested Jesus took
him to Caiaphas, the high priest, where
the teachers of the law and the elders had
assembled. 58 But Peter followed him at
a distance, right up to the courtyard of
the high priest. He entered and sat down
with the guards to see the outcome.
59 The chief priests and the whole Sanhedrin were looking for false evidence
against Jesus so that they could put him
to death. 60 But they did not find any,
though many false witnesses came forward.
Finally two came forward 61 and declared, "This fellow said, 'I am able to
destroy the temple of God and rebuild
it in three days.' "
62 Then the high priest stood up and
said to Jesus, "Are you not going to answer? What is this testimony that these
men are bringing against you?" 63 But
Jesus remained silent.
The high priest said to him, "I charge
you under oath by the living God: Tell
us if you are the Christ,[b] the Son of
God."
64 "Yes, it is as you say," Jesus replied.
"But I say to all of you: In the future you
will see the Son of Man sitting at the
right hand of the Mighty One and coming on the clouds of heaven."
65 Then the high priest tore his clothes
and said, "He has spoken blasphemy!
Why do we need any more witnesses?
Look, now you have heard the blasphemy. 66 What do you think?"
"He is worthy of death," they answered.
67 Then they spit in his face and struck
him with their fists. Others slapped him
68 and said, "Prophesy to us, Christ. Who
hit you?"

Peter Disowns Jesus

69 Now Peter was sitting out in the
courtyard, and a servant girl came to
him. "You also were with Jesus of Galilee," she said.
70 But he denied it before them all. "I
don't know what you're talking about,"
he said.
71 Then he went out to the gateway,
where another girl saw him and said to
the people there, "This fellow was with
Jesus of Nazareth."
72 He denied it again, with an oath: "I
don't know the man!"
73 After a little while, those standing
there went up to Peter and said, "Surely
you are one of them, for your accent
gives you away."
74 Then he began to call down curses
on himself and he swore to them, "I
don't know the man!"
Immediately a rooster crowed. 75 Then
Peter remembered the word Jesus had
spoken: "Before the rooster crows, you
will disown me three times." And he
went outside and wept bitterly.

Judas Hangs Himself

27 Early in the morning, all
the chief priests and the

[a]50 Or *"Friend, why have you come?"* [b]63 Or *Messiah;* also in verse 68

elders of the people came to the decision to put Jesus to death. 2They bound him, led him away and handed him over to Pilate, the governor.

3When Judas, who had betrayed him, saw that Jesus was condemned, he was seized with remorse and returned the thirty silver coins to the chief priests and the elders. 4"I have sinned," he said, "for I have betrayed innocent blood."

"What is that to us?" they replied. "That's your responsibility."

5So Judas threw the money into the temple and left. Then he went away and hanged himself.

6The chief priests picked up the coins and said, "It is against the law to put this into the treasury, since it is blood money." 7So they decided to use the money to buy the potter's field as a burial place for foreigners. 8That is why it has been called the Field of Blood to this day. 9Then what was spoken by Jeremiah the prophet was fulfilled: "They took the thirty silver coins, the price set on him by the people of Israel, 10and they used them to buy the potter's field, as the Lord commanded me."[a]

Jesus Before Pilate

11Meanwhile Jesus stood before the governor, and the governor asked him, "Are you the king of the Jews?"

"Yes, it is as you say," Jesus replied.

12When he was accused by the chief priests and the elders, he gave no answer. 13Then Pilate asked him, "Don't you hear the testimony they are bringing against you?" 14But Jesus made no reply, not even to a single charge—to the great amazement of the governor.

15Now it was the governor's custom at the Feast to release a prisoner chosen by the crowd. 16At that time they had a notorious prisoner, called Barabbas. 17So when the crowd had gathered, Pilate asked them, "Which one do you want me to release to you: Barabbas, or Jesus who is called Christ?" 18For he knew it was out of envy that they had handed Jesus over to him.

19While Pilate was sitting on the judge's seat, his wife sent him this message: "Don't have anything to do with that innocent man, for I have suffered a great deal today in a dream because of him."

20But the chief priests and the elders persuaded the crowd to ask for Barabbas and to have Jesus executed.

21"Which of the two do you want me to release to you?" asked the governor.

"Barabbas," they answered.

22"What shall I do, then, with Jesus who is called Christ?" Pilate asked.

They all answered, "Crucify him!"

23"Why? What crime has he committed?" asked Pilate.

But they shouted all the louder, "Crucify him!"

24When Pilate saw that he was getting nowhere, but that instead an uproar was starting, he took water and washed his hands in front of the crowd. "I am innocent of this man's blood," he said. "It is your responsibility!"

25All the people answered, "Let his blood be on us and on our children!"

26Then he released Barabbas to them. But he had Jesus flogged, and handed him over to be crucified.

The Soldiers Mock Jesus

27Then the governor's soldiers took Jesus into the Praetorium and gathered the whole company of soldiers around him. 28They stripped him and put a scarlet robe on him, 29and then twisted together a crown of thorns and set it on his head. They put a staff in his right hand and knelt in front of him and mocked him. "Hail, king of the Jews!" they said. 30They spit on him, and took the staff and struck him on the head again and again. 31After they had mocked him, they took off the robe and put his own clothes on him. Then they led him away to crucify him.

The Crucifixion

32As they were going out, they met a man from Cyrene, named Simon, and they forced him to carry the cross. 33They came to a place called Golgotha

[a] *10* See Zech. 11:12,13; Jer. 19:1-13; 32:6-9.

(which means The Place of the Skull). 34There they offered Jesus wine to drink, mixed with gall; but after tasting it, he refused to drink it. 35When they had crucified him, they divided up his clothes by casting lots.[a] 36And sitting down, they kept watch over him there. 37Above his head they placed the written charge against him: THIS IS JESUS, THE KING OF THE JEWS. 38Two robbers were crucified with him, one on his right and one on his left. 39Those who passed by hurled insults at him, shaking their heads 40and saying, "You who are going to destroy the temple and build it in three days, save yourself! Come down from the cross, if you are the Son of God!"

41In the same way the chief priests, the teachers of the law and the elders mocked him. 42"He saved others," they said, "but he can't save himself! He's the King of Israel! Let him come down now from the cross, and we will believe in him. 43He trusts in God. Let God rescue him now if he wants him, for he said, 'I am the Son of God.'" 44In the same way the robbers who were crucified with him also heaped insults on him.

The Death of Jesus

45From the sixth hour until the ninth hour darkness came over all the land. 46About the ninth hour Jesus cried out in a loud voice, *"Eloi, Eloi,*[b] *lama sabachthani?"*—which means, "My God, my God, why have you forsaken me?"[c]

47When some of those standing there heard this, they said, "He's calling Elijah."

48Immediately one of them ran and got a sponge. He filled it with wine vinegar, put it on a stick, and offered it to Jesus to drink. 49The rest said, "Now leave him alone. Let's see if Elijah comes to save him."

50And when Jesus had cried out again in a loud voice, he gave up his spirit.

51At that moment the curtain of the temple was torn in two from top to bottom. The earth shook and the rocks split. 52The tombs broke open and the bodies of many holy people who had died were raised to life. 53They came out of the tombs, and after Jesus' resurrection they went into the holy city and appeared to many people.

54When the centurion and those with him who were guarding Jesus saw the earthquake and all that had happened, they were terrified, and exclaimed, "Surely he was the Son[d] of God!"

55Many women were there, watching from a distance. They had followed Jesus from Galilee to care for his needs. 56Among them were Mary Magdalene, Mary the mother of James and Joses, and the mother of Zebedee's sons.

The Burial of Jesus

57As evening approached, there came a rich man from Arimathea, named Joseph, who had himself become a disciple of Jesus. 58Going to Pilate, he asked for Jesus' body, and Pilate ordered that it be given to him. 59Joseph took the body, wrapped it in a clean linen cloth, 60and placed it in his own new tomb that he had cut out of the rock. He rolled a big stone in front of the entrance to the tomb and went away. 61Mary Magdalene and the other Mary were sitting there opposite the tomb.

The Guard at the Tomb

62The next day, the one after Preparation Day, the chief priests and the Pharisees went to Pilate. 63"Sir," they said, "we remember that while he was still alive that deceiver said, 'After three days I will rise again.' 64So give the order for the tomb to be made secure until the third day. Otherwise, his disciples may come and steal the body and tell the people that he has been raised from the dead. This last deception will be worse than the first."

65"Take a guard," Pilate answered. "Go, make the tomb as secure as you know how." 66So they went and made the tomb secure by putting a seal on the stone and posting the guard.

[a]35 A few late manuscripts *lots that the word spoken by the prophet might be fulfilled: "They divided my garments among themselves and cast lots for my clothing"* (Psalm 22:18) [b]46 Some manuscripts *Eli, Eli* [c]46 Psalm 22:1 [d]54 Or *a son*

SHARPEN THE FOCUS

Because Satan is "a liar and the father of lies" (John 8:44), we should expect his human agents to also be untruthful. Throughout Jesus' trials they are just that. The chief priests hire false witnesses (Matthew 26:57–61). Pilate looks for a way out of the riot he fears—not a *just* way out, an *easy* way out (Matthew 27:17–24).

Even so, Pilate does manage to proclaim one clear truth. The sign he orders his soldiers to display above Jesus reads: THIS IS JESUS, THE KING OF THE JEWS (Matthew 27:37). Our Lord's crime? Coming to earth not "to be served, but to serve, and to give His life as a ransom for many" (Matthew 20:28).

The cross is a scandal. The cross says, "Throw away your best efforts at serving your King. Tear up the IOU's you think He owes you for trying hard to obey (Isaiah 64:6–9). Stop feeling self-righteous when you witness or pray or give time and money into His kingdom. You cannot save yourself. Throw yourself on the mercy of His Majesty."

That message is a scandal because our sinful nature wants to add something, *anything*, to Jesus' finished work. Instead, we need only to be still, and let our King serve us. There's nothing we can do. There's nothing we need do. ☼

WEEK 77 • TUESDAY

Matthew 28:1–20

GET THE BIG PICTURE

Today's reading, Matthew 28, relates the wondrous fulfillment of God's promises—the resurrection of the Savior, Jesus Christ. Death died when Christ rose. Savor your Savior-King's victory as you read the familiar account of it now. If time is short, focus on Matthew 28:1–15.

The Resurrection

28 After the Sabbath, at dawn
on the first day of the
week, Mary Magdalene and the other
Mary went to look at the tomb.
2There was a violent earthquake, for
an angel of the Lord came down from
heaven and, going to the tomb, rolled
back the stone and sat on it. 3His appearance was like lightning, and his clothes
were white as snow. 4The guards were
so afraid of him that they shook and
became like dead men.
5The angel said to the women, "Do
not be afraid, for I know that you are
looking for Jesus, who was crucified.
6He is not here; he has risen, just as he
said. Come and see the place where he
lay. 7Then go quickly and tell his disciples: 'He has risen from the dead and is
going ahead of you into Galilee. There
you will see him.' Now I have told
you."
8So the women hurried away from
the tomb, afraid yet filled with joy, and
ran to tell his disciples. 9Suddenly Jesus
met them. "Greetings," he said. They
came to him, clasped his feet and worshiped him. 10Then Jesus said to them,
"Do not be afraid. Go and tell my brothers to go to Galilee; there they will
see me."

The Guards' Report

[11]While the women were on their way, some of the guards went into the city and reported to the chief priests everything that had happened.
[12]When the chief priests had met with the elders and devised a plan, they gave the soldiers a large sum of money,
[13]telling them, "You are to say, 'His disciples came during the night and stole him away while we were asleep.'
[14]If this report gets to the governor, we will satisfy him and keep you out of trouble." [15]So the soldiers took the money and did as they were instructed. And this story has been widely circulated among the Jews to this very day.

The Great Commission

[16]Then the eleven disciples went to Galilee, to the mountain where Jesus had told them to go. [17]When they saw him, they worshiped him; but some doubted. [18]Then Jesus came to them and said, "All authority in heaven and on earth has been given to me. [19]Therefore go and make disciples of all nations, baptizing them in[a] the name of the Father and of the Son and of the Holy Spirit, [20]and teaching them to obey everything I have commanded you. And surely I am with you always, to the very end of the age."

[a]19 Or *into*; see Acts 8:16; 19:5; Romans 6:3; 1 Cor. 1:13; 10:2 and Gal. 3:27.

SHARPEN THE FOCUS

Jesus lives! To Him the throne
There above all things is given.
I shall go where He is gone,
Live and reign with Him in heaven.
God is faithful; doubtings, hence!
This shall be my confidence.

Jesus lives! And I am sure
Neither life nor death shall sever
Me from Him. I shall endure
In His love, through death, forever.
God will be my sure defense;
This shall be my confidence.

Jesus lives! And now is death
But the gate of life immortal;
This shall calm my trembling breath
When I pass its gloomy portal.
Faith shall cry, as fails each sense:
Jesus is my confidence!

(Christian F. Gellert)

Jesus Christ really died—for you. Jesus Christ really walked out of His grave, alive forever—for you. Jesus Christ really lives and rules heaven and earth—for you. If you remembered that Good News today, what difference would it make—for you?

MARK

WEEK 77 • WEDNESDAY

Mark 1:1—2:28

Mark's gospel clips along. He uses the word "immediately" 42 times, more than all the other New Testament writers put together. Watch for it as you read. Also note the way Mark presents Jesus—as the Servant come to save. If time is short, focus on Mark 1:1–15.

John the Baptist Prepares the Way

1 The beginning of the gospel about Jesus Christ, the Son of God.[a]

2It is written in Isaiah the prophet:

"I will send my messenger ahead
of you,
who will prepare your way"[b]—
3"a voice of one calling in the desert,
'Prepare the way for the Lord,
make straight paths for him.' "[c]

4And so John came, baptizing in the
desert region and preaching a baptism
of repentance for the forgiveness of sins.
5The whole Judean countryside and all
the people of Jerusalem went out to
him. Confessing their sins, they were
baptized by him in the Jordan River.
6John wore clothing made of camel's
hair, with a leather belt around his waist,
and he ate locusts and wild honey. 7And
this was his message: "After me will
come one more powerful than I, the
thongs of whose sandals I am not worthy to stoop down and untie. 8I baptize
you with[d] water, but he will baptize you
with the Holy Spirit."

The Baptism and Temptation of Jesus

9At that time Jesus came from Nazareth in Galilee and was baptized by John
in the Jordan. 10As Jesus was coming up
out of the water, he saw heaven being
torn open and the Spirit descending on
him like a dove. 11And a voice came from
heaven: "You are my Son, whom I love;
with you I am well pleased."
12At once the Spirit sent him out into
the desert, 13and he was in the desert
forty days, being tempted by Satan. He
was with the wild animals, and angels
attended him.

The Calling of the First Disciples

14After John was put in prison, Jesus
went into Galilee, proclaiming the good
news of God. 15"The time has come," he
said. "The kingdom of God is near. Repent and believe the good news!"
16As Jesus walked beside the Sea of
Galilee, he saw Simon and his brother
Andrew casting a net into the lake, for
they were fishermen. 17"Come, follow
me," Jesus said, "and I will make you
fishers of men." 18At once they left their
nets and followed him.
19When he had gone a little farther, he
saw James son of Zebedee and his
brother John in a boat, preparing their
nets. 20Without delay he called them,
and they left their father Zebedee in

[a]*1* Some manuscripts do not have *the Son of God.*
[b]2 Mal. 3:1 [c]3 Isaiah 40:3 [d]*8* Or *in*

the boat with the hired men and followed him.

Jesus Drives Out an Evil Spirit

21 They went to Capernaum, and when the Sabbath came, Jesus went into the synagogue and began to teach. 22 The people were amazed at his teaching, because he taught them as one who had authority, not as the teachers of the law. 23 Just then a man in their synagogue who was possessed by an evil[a] spirit cried out, 24 "What do you want with us, Jesus of Nazareth? Have you come to destroy us? I know who you are—the Holy One of God!"

25 "Be quiet!" said Jesus sternly. "Come out of him!" 26 The evil spirit shook the man violently and came out of him with a shriek.

27 The people were all so amazed that they asked each other, "What is this? A new teaching—and with authority! He even gives orders to evil spirits and they obey him." 28 News about him spread quickly over the whole region of Galilee.

Jesus Heals Many

29 As soon as they left the synagogue, they went with James and John to the home of Simon and Andrew. 30 Simon's mother-in-law was in bed with a fever, and they told Jesus about her. 31 So he went to her, took her hand and helped her up. The fever left her and she began to wait on them.

32 That evening after sunset the people brought to Jesus all the sick and demon-possessed. 33 The whole town gathered at the door, 34 and Jesus healed many who had various diseases. He also drove out many demons, but he would not let the demons speak because they knew who he was.

Jesus Prays in a Solitary Place

35 Very early in the morning, while it was still dark, Jesus got up, left the house and went off to a solitary place, where he prayed. 36 Simon and his companions went to look for him, 37 and when they found him, they exclaimed: "Everyone is looking for you!"

38 Jesus replied, "Let us go somewhere else—to the nearby villages—so I can preach there also. That is why I have come." 39 So he traveled throughout Galilee, preaching in their synagogues and driving out demons.

A Man With Leprosy

40 A man with leprosy[b] came to him and begged him on his knees, "If you are willing, you can make me clean."

41 Filled with compassion, Jesus reached out his hand and touched the man. "I am willing," he said. "Be clean!" 42 Immediately the leprosy left him and he was cured.

43 Jesus sent him away at once with a strong warning: 44 "See that you don't tell this to anyone. But go, show yourself to the priest and offer the sacrifices that Moses commanded for your cleansing, as a testimony to them." 45 Instead he went out and began to talk freely, spreading the news. As a result, Jesus could no longer enter a town openly but stayed outside in lonely places. Yet the people still came to him from everywhere.

Jesus Heals a Paralytic

2 A few days later, when Jesus again entered Capernaum, the people heard that he had come home. 2 So many gathered that there was no room left, not even outside the door, and he preached the word to them. 3 Some men came, bringing to him a paralytic, carried by four of them. 4 Since they could not get him to Jesus because of the crowd, they made an opening in the roof above Jesus and, after digging through it, lowered the mat the paralyzed man was lying on. 5 When Jesus saw their faith, he said to the paralytic, "Son, your sins are forgiven."

6 Now some teachers of the law were sitting there, thinking to themselves,

[a]23 Greek *unclean*; also in verses 26 and 27
[b]40 The Greek word was used for various diseases affecting the skin—not necessarily leprosy.

[7]"Why does this fellow talk like that? He's blaspheming! Who can forgive sins but God alone?"

[8]Immediately Jesus knew in his spirit that this was what they were thinking in their hearts, and he said to them, "Why are you thinking these things? [9]Which is easier: to say to the paralytic, 'Your sins are forgiven,' or to say, 'Get up, take your mat and walk'? [10]But that you may know that the Son of Man has authority on earth to forgive sins . . ." He said to the paralytic, [11]"I tell you, get up, take your mat and go home." [12]He got up, took his mat and walked out in full view of them all. This amazed everyone and they praised God, saying, "We have never seen anything like this!"

The Calling of Levi

[13]Once again Jesus went out beside the lake. A large crowd came to him, and he began to teach them. [14]As he walked along, he saw Levi son of Alphaeus sitting at the tax collector's booth. "Follow me," Jesus told him, and Levi got up and followed him.

[15]While Jesus was having dinner at Levi's house, many tax collectors and "sinners" were eating with him and his disciples, for there were many who followed him. [16]When the teachers of the law who were Pharisees saw him eating with the "sinners" and tax collectors, they asked his disciples: "Why does he eat with tax collectors and 'sinners'?"

[17]On hearing this, Jesus said to them, "It is not the healthy who need a doctor, but the sick. I have not come to call the righteous, but sinners."

Jesus Questioned About Fasting

[18]Now John's disciples and the Pharisees were fasting. Some people came and asked Jesus, "How is it that John's disciples and the disciples of the Pharisees are fasting, but yours are not?"

[19]Jesus answered, "How can the guests of the bridegroom fast while he is with them? They cannot, so long as they have him with them. [20]But the time will come when the bridegroom will be taken from them, and on that day they will fast.

[21]"No one sews a patch of unshrunk cloth on an old garment. If he does, the new piece will pull away from the old, making the tear worse. [22]And no one pours new wine into old wineskins. If he does, the wine will burst the skins, and both the wine and the wineskins will be ruined. No, he pours new wine into new wineskins."

Lord of the Sabbath

[23]One Sabbath Jesus was going through the grainfields, and as his disciples walked along, they began to pick some heads of grain. [24]The Pharisees said to him, "Look, why are they doing what is unlawful on the Sabbath?"

[25]He answered, "Have you never read what David did when he and his companions were hungry and in need? [26]In the days of Abiathar the high priest, he entered the house of God and ate the consecrated bread, which is lawful only for priests to eat. And he also gave some to his companions."

[27]Then he said to them, "The Sabbath was made for man, not man for the Sabbath. [28]So the Son of Man is Lord even of the Sabbath."

SHARPEN THE FOCUS

What would you be willing to give up to have peace and security? Mark's first readers enjoyed the peace brought by the Roman Empire. They could travel in relative security over the best roads ever built. They didn't need to worry about invasions from their neighbors as had the people of Israel for so long during the time of the Old Testament kings.

Rome freed them from that but kept law and order by force. At the time Mark wrote, the Roman Caesar ruled with an iron fist. In the empire, human life was cheap. Just about everyone with authority in the government used it to make his own life more comfortable—"the arrogance of power."

Now look at the picture Mark paints of the Son of God—

- in humility letting John the Baptizer be the instrument through which the Holy Spirit anoints Him for ministry.
- in humility letting Himself be driven into the wilderness to be tempted.
- in humility caring for the sick and demon-possessed, even *touching* the lepers!

Here, truly, was a gentle man—one who had great strength but who used it in compassion for others and in obedience to the Father; one who would—in strength and humility—even die for us!

WEEK 77 • THURSDAY

Mark 3:1—4:41

GET THE BIG PICTURE

"Is it lawful to love—even on the Sabbath Day?" At heart that's the question with which Mark 3 begins. Jesus answered it in His actions. These actions sparked a clash with the Pharisees and set in motion a series of events in which Jesus revealed the upside-down way a servant looks at relationships, power, and the purpose of life. Be on the lookout for this as you read. If time is short, focus on Mark 3:20–35.

3 Another time he went into the
synagogue, and a man with a
shriveled hand was there. [2]Some of
them were looking for a reason to accuse Jesus, so they watched him closely
to see if he would heal him on the Sabbath. [3]Jesus said to the man with the
shriveled hand, "Stand up in front of everyone."
[4]Then Jesus asked them, "Which is
lawful on the Sabbath: to do good or to
do evil, to save life or to kill?" But they
remained silent.
[5]He looked around at them in anger
and, deeply distressed at their stubborn
hearts, said to the man, "Stretch out
your hand." He stretched it out, and his
hand was completely restored. [6]Then
the Pharisees went out and began to
plot with the Herodians how they
might kill Jesus.

Crowds Follow Jesus

[7]Jesus withdrew with his disciples to
the lake, and a large crowd from Galilee followed. [8]When they heard all he
was doing, many people came to him
from Judea, Jerusalem, Idumea, and the
regions across the Jordan and around
Tyre and Sidon. [9]Because of the crowd
he told his disciples to have a small boat
ready for him, to keep the people from
crowding him. [10]For he had healed
many, so that those with diseases were
pushing forward to touch him. [11]When-
ever the evil[a] spirits saw him, they fell

[a]11 Greek *unclean*; also in verse 30

down before him and cried out, "You
are the Son of God." 12But he gave them
strict orders not to tell who he was.

The Appointing of the Twelve Apostles

13Jesus went up on a mountainside
and called to him those he wanted, and
they came to him. 14He appointed
twelve—designating them apostles[a]—
that they might be with him and that he
might send them out to preach 15and to
have authority to drive out demons.
16These are the twelve he appointed: Simon (to whom he gave the name Peter);
17James son of Zebedee and his brother
John (to them he gave the name Boaner-
ges, which means Sons of Thunder);
18Andrew, Philip, Bartholomew, Matthew, Thomas, James son of Alphaeus,
Thaddaeus, Simon the Zealot 19and Judas Iscariot, who betrayed him.

Jesus and Beelzebub

20Then Jesus entered a house, and
again a crowd gathered, so that he and
his disciples were not even able to eat.
21When his family heard about this, they
went to take charge of him, for they
said, "He is out of his mind."
22And the teachers of the law who
came down from Jerusalem said, "He is
possessed by Beelzebub[b]! By the prince
of demons he is driving out demons."
23So Jesus called them and spoke to
them in parables: "How can Satan drive
out Satan? 24If a kingdom is divided
against itself, that kingdom cannot
stand. 25If a house is divided against itself, that house cannot stand. 26And if
Satan opposes himself and is divided,
he cannot stand; his end has come. 27In
fact, no one can enter a strong man's
house and carry off his possessions unless he first ties up the strong man. Then
he can rob his house. 28I tell you the
truth, all the sins and blasphemies of
men will be forgiven them. 29But whoever blasphemes against the Holy Spirit
will never be forgiven; he is guilty of an
eternal sin."
30He said this because they were saying, "He has an evil spirit."

Jesus' Mother and Brothers

31Then Jesus' mother and brothers arrived. Standing outside, they sent someone in to call him. 32A crowd was sitting
around him, and they told him, "Your
mother and brothers are outside looking for you."
33"Who are my mother and my brothers?" he asked.
34Then he looked at those seated in a
circle around him and said, "Here are
my mother and my brothers! 35Whoever
does God's will is my brother and sister
and mother."

The Parable of the Sower

4 Again Jesus began to teach by
the lake. The crowd that gathered around him was so large that he
got into a boat and sat in it out on the
lake, while all the people were along the
shore at the water's edge. 2He taught
them many things by parables, and in
his teaching said: 3"Listen! A farmer
went out to sow his seed. 4As he was
scattering the seed, some fell along the
path, and the birds came and ate it up.
5Some fell on rocky places, where it did
not have much soil. It sprang up quickly,
because the soil was shallow. 6But when
the sun came up, the plants were
scorched, and they withered because
they had no root. 7Other seed fell
among thorns, which grew up and
choked the plants, so that they did not
bear grain. 8Still other seed fell on good
soil. It came up, grew and produced a
crop, multiplying thirty, sixty, or even a
hundred times."
9Then Jesus said, "He who has ears to
hear, let him hear."
10When he was alone, the Twelve and
the others around him asked him about
the parables. 11He told them, "The secret
of the kingdom of God has been given
to you. But to those on the outside everything is said in parables 12so that,

" 'they may be ever seeing but never
perceiving,

[a]14 Some manuscripts do not have *designating them apostles.* [b]22 Greek *Beezeboul* or *Beelzeboul*

and ever hearing but never
understanding;
otherwise they might turn and be
forgiven!'[a]"

13Then Jesus said to them, "Don't you understand this parable? How then will you understand any parable? 14The farmer sows the word. 15Some people are like seed along the path, where the word is sown. As soon as they hear it, Satan comes and takes away the word that was sown in them. 16Others, like seed sown on rocky places, hear the word and at once receive it with joy. 17But since they have no root, they last only a short time. When trouble or persecution comes because of the word, they quickly fall away. 18Still others, like seed sown among thorns, hear the word; 19but the worries of this life, the deceitfulness of wealth and the desires for other things come in and choke the word, making it unfruitful. 20Others, like seed sown on good soil, hear the word, accept it, and produce a crop—thirty, sixty or even a hundred times what was sown."

A Lamp on a Stand

21He said to them, "Do you bring in a lamp to put it under a bowl or a bed? Instead, don't you put it on its stand? 22For whatever is hidden is meant to be disclosed, and whatever is concealed is meant to be brought out into the open. 23If anyone has ears to hear, let him hear."

24"Consider carefully what you hear," he continued. "With the measure you use, it will be measured to you—and even more. 25Whoever has will be given more; whoever does not have, even what he has will be taken from him."

The Parable of the Growing Seed

26He also said, "This is what the kingdom of God is like. A man scatters seed on the ground. 27Night and day, whether he sleeps or gets up, the seed sprouts and grows, though he does not know how. 28All by itself the soil produces grain—first the stalk, then the head, then the full kernel in the head. 29As soon as the grain is ripe, he puts the sickle to it, because the harvest has come."

The Parable of the Mustard Seed

30Again he said, "What shall we say the kingdom of God is like, or what parable shall we use to describe it? 31It is like a mustard seed, which is the smallest seed you plant in the ground. 32Yet when planted, it grows and becomes the largest of all garden plants, with such big branches that the birds of the air can perch in its shade."

33With many similar parables Jesus spoke the word to them, as much as they could understand. 34He did not say anything to them without using a parable. But when he was alone with his own disciples, he explained everything.

Jesus Calms the Storm

35That day when evening came, he said to his disciples, "Let us go over to the other side." 36Leaving the crowd behind, they took him along, just as he was, in the boat. There were also other boats with him. 37A furious squall came up, and the waves broke over the boat, so that it was nearly swamped. 38Jesus was in the stern, sleeping on a cushion. The disciples woke him and said to him, "Teacher, don't you care if we drown?"

39He got up, rebuked the wind and said to the waves, "Quiet! Be still!" Then the wind died down and it was completely calm.

40He said to his disciples, "Why are you so afraid? Do you still have no faith?"

41They were terrified and asked each other, "Who is this? Even the wind and the waves obey him!"

[a]12 Isaiah 6:9,10

SHARPEN THE FOCUS

God's wisdom is foolishness to human beings. St. Paul makes that fact clear in 1 Corinthians 1:18–30. If that's so, then Jesus *must* have seemed out of His mind (Mark 3:21). Never had anyone spoken and demonstrated the wisdom of God so thoroughly. So far-fetched did His servanthood and humility seem that His friends and family wanted to take Him into custody. His enemies even accused Him of being possessed by the devil.

How thoroughly has God's wisdom infiltrated your heart? When was the last time someone looked at your service for the Lord Jesus and said, "You're out of your mind?"

Jesus lived out a radical lifestyle—radical meaning "from the root" or "getting to the root." He got beyond the showy foliage and down to the core of what it means to care for those whom the Father so loves (John 3:16). That route led Him to the most foolish, most radical, act of all. This is how St. Paul puts it:

> *We preach Christ crucified: a stumbling block to Jews and foolishness to Gentiles, but to those whom God has called, both Jews and Greeks, Christ the power of God and the wisdom of God.* (1 Corinthians 1:23–24)

The dregs of society. That's how the people in Jesus day would have looked at the demon-possessed man (Mark 5:1–20), the little girl (Mark 5:21–24; 35–43), and the woman with the gynecological disorder (Mark 5:25–34). But Jesus sees each of these sufferers as worthy of His attention and help. As you read, look for evidence of our Servant-Savior's compassion. If time is short, focus on Mark 5:25–34.

The Healing of a Demon-possessed Man

5 They went across the lake to the
region of the Gerasenes.[a] 2When
Jesus got out of the boat, a man with an
evil[b] spirit came from the tombs to meet
him. 3This man lived in the tombs, and
no one could bind him any more, not
even with a chain. 4For he had often
been chained hand and foot, but he tore
the chains apart and broke the irons on
his feet. No one was strong enough to
subdue him. 5Night and day among the
tombs and in the hills he would cry out
and cut himself with stones.
6When he saw Jesus from a distance,
he ran and fell on his knees in front of
him. 7He shouted at the top of his voice,
"What do you want with me, Jesus, Son
of the Most High God? Swear to God
that you won't torture me!" 8For Jesus
had said to him, "Come out of this man,
you evil spirit!"

[a]*1* Some manuscripts *Gadarenes*; other manuscripts *Gergesenes* [b]*2* Greek *unclean*; also in verses 8 and 13

9Then Jesus asked him, "What is your name?"

"My name is Legion," he replied, "for we are many." 10And he begged Jesus again and again not to send them out of the area.

11A large herd of pigs was feeding on the nearby hillside. 12The demons begged Jesus, "Send us among the pigs; allow us to go into them." 13He gave them permission, and the evil spirits came out and went into the pigs. The herd, about two thousand in number, rushed down the steep bank into the lake and were drowned.

14Those tending the pigs ran off and reported this in the town and countryside, and the people went out to see what had happened. 15When they came to Jesus, they saw the man who had been possessed by the legion of demons, sitting there, dressed and in his right mind; and they were afraid. 16Those who had seen it told the people what had happened to the demon-possessed man—and told about the pigs as well. 17Then the people began to plead with Jesus to leave their region.

18As Jesus was getting into the boat, the man who had been demon-possessed begged to go with him. 19Jesus did not let him, but said, "Go home to your family and tell them how much the Lord has done for you, and how he has had mercy on you." 20So the man went away and began to tell in the Decapolis[a] how much Jesus had done for him. And all the people were amazed.

A Dead Girl and a Sick Woman

21When Jesus had again crossed over by boat to the other side of the lake, a large crowd gathered around him while he was by the lake. 22Then one of the synagogue rulers, named Jairus, came there. Seeing Jesus, he fell at his feet 23and pleaded earnestly with him, "My little daughter is dying. Please come and put your hands on her so that she will be healed and live." 24So Jesus went with him.

A large crowd followed and pressed around him. 25And a woman was there who had been subject to bleeding for twelve years. 26She had suffered a great deal under the care of many doctors and had spent all she had, yet instead of getting better she grew worse. 27When she heard about Jesus, she came up behind him in the crowd and touched his cloak, 28because she thought, "If I just touch his clothes, I will be healed." 29Immediately her bleeding stopped and she felt in her body that she was freed from her suffering.

30At once Jesus realized that power had gone out from him. He turned around in the crowd and asked, "Who touched my clothes?"

31"You see the people crowding against you," his disciples answered, "and yet you can ask, 'Who touched me?' "

32But Jesus kept looking around to see who had done it. 33Then the woman, knowing what had happened to her, came and fell at his feet and, trembling with fear, told him the whole truth. 34He said to her, "Daughter, your faith has healed you. Go in peace and be freed from your suffering."

35While Jesus was still speaking, some men came from the house of Jairus, the synagogue ruler. "Your daughter is dead," they said. "Why bother the teacher any more?"

36Ignoring what they said, Jesus told the synagogue ruler, "Don't be afraid; just believe."

37He did not let anyone follow him except Peter, James and John the brother of James. 38When they came to the home of the synagogue ruler, Jesus saw a commotion, with people crying and wailing loudly. 39He went in and said to them, "Why all this commotion and wailing? The child is not dead but asleep." 40But they laughed at him.

After he put them all out, he took the child's father and mother and the disciples who were with him, and went in where the child was. 41He took her by the hand and said to her, "*Talitha koum!*" (which means, "Little girl, I say to you,

[a]*20* That is, the Ten Cities

get up!"). [42]Immediately the girl stood up and walked around (she was twelve years old). At this they were completely astonished. [43]He gave strict orders not to let anyone know about this, and told them to give her something to eat.

A Prophet Without Honor

6 Jesus left there and went to his hometown, accompanied by his disciples. [2]When the Sabbath came, he began to teach in the synagogue, and many who heard him were amazed.

"Where did this man get these things?" they asked. "What's this wisdom that has been given him, that he even does miracles! [3]Isn't this the carpenter? Isn't this Mary's son and the brother of James, Joseph,[a] Judas and Simon? Aren't his sisters here with us?" And they took offense at him.

[4]Jesus said to them, "Only in his hometown, among his relatives and in his own house is a prophet without honor." [5]He could not do any miracles there, except lay his hands on a few sick people and heal them. [6]And he was amazed at their lack of faith.

Jesus Sends Out the Twelve

Then Jesus went around teaching from village to village. [7]Calling the Twelve to him, he sent them out two by two and gave them authority over evil[b] spirits.

[8]These were his instructions: "Take nothing for the journey except a staff—no bread, no bag, no money in your belts. [9]Wear sandals but not an extra tunic. [10]Whenever you enter a house, stay there until you leave that town. [11]And if any place will not welcome you or listen to you, shake the dust off your feet when you leave, as a testimony against them."

[12]They went out and preached that people should repent. [13]They drove out many demons and anointed many sick people with oil and healed them.

John the Baptist Beheaded

[14]King Herod heard about this, for Jesus' name had become well known. Some were saying,[c] "John the Baptist has been raised from the dead, and that is why miraculous powers are at work in him."

[15]Others said, "He is Elijah."

And still others claimed, "He is a prophet, like one of the prophets of long ago."

[16]But when Herod heard this, he said, "John, the man I beheaded, has been raised from the dead!"

[17]For Herod himself had given orders to have John arrested, and he had him bound and put in prison. He did this because of Herodias, his brother Philip's wife, whom he had married. [18]For John had been saying to Herod, "It is not lawful for you to have your brother's wife." [19]So Herodias nursed a grudge against John and wanted to kill him. But she was not able to, [20]because Herod feared John and protected him, knowing him to be a righteous and holy man. When Herod heard John, he was greatly puzzled[d]; yet he liked to listen to him.

[21]Finally the opportune time came. On his birthday Herod gave a banquet for his high officials and military commanders and the leading men of Galilee. [22]When the daughter of Herodias came in and danced, she pleased Herod and his dinner guests.

The king said to the girl, "Ask me for anything you want, and I'll give it to you." [23]And he promised her with an oath, "Whatever you ask I will give you, up to half my kingdom."

[24]She went out and said to her mother, "What shall I ask for?"

"The head of John the Baptist," she answered.

[25]At once the girl hurried in to the king with the request: "I want you to give me right now the head of John the Baptist on a platter."

[26]The king was greatly distressed, but because of his oaths and his dinner guests, he did not want to refuse her. [27]So he immediately sent an executioner

[a]3 Greek *Joses*, a variant of *Joseph* [b]7 Greek *unclean* [c]14 Some early manuscripts *He was saying* [d]20 Some early manuscripts *he did many things*

with orders to bring John's head. The man went, beheaded John in the prison, 28and brought back his head on a platter. He presented it to the girl, and she gave it to her mother. 29On hearing of this, John's disciples came and took his body and laid it in a tomb.

Jesus Feeds the Five Thousand

30The apostles gathered around Jesus and reported to him all they had done and taught. 31Then, because so many people were coming and going that they did not even have a chance to eat, he said to them, "Come with me by yourselves to a quiet place and get some rest."

32So they went away by themselves in a boat to a solitary place. 33But many who saw them leaving recognized them and ran on foot from all the towns and got there ahead of them. 34When Jesus landed and saw a large crowd, he had compassion on them, because they were like sheep without a shepherd. So he began teaching them many things.

35By this time it was late in the day, so his disciples came to him. "This is a remote place," they said, "and it's already very late. 36Send the people away so they can go to the surrounding countryside and villages and buy themselves something to eat."

37But he answered, "You give them something to eat."

They said to him, "That would take eight months of a man's wages[a]! Are we to go and spend that much on bread and give it to them to eat?"

38"How many loaves do you have?" he asked. "Go and see."

When they found out, they said, "Five—and two fish."

39Then Jesus directed them to have all the people sit down in groups on the green grass. 40So they sat down in groups of hundreds and fifties. 41Taking the five loaves and the two fish and looking up to heaven, he gave thanks and broke the loaves. Then he gave them to his disciples to set before the people. He also divided the two fish among them all. 42They all ate and were satisfied, 43and the disciples picked up twelve basketfuls of broken pieces of bread and fish. 44The number of the men who had eaten was five thousand.

Jesus Walks on the Water

45Immediately Jesus made his disciples get into the boat and go on ahead of him to Bethsaida, while he dismissed the crowd. 46After leaving them, he went up on a mountainside to pray.

47When evening came, the boat was in the middle of the lake, and he was alone on land. 48He saw the disciples straining at the oars, because the wind was against them. About the fourth watch of the night he went out to them, walking on the lake. He was about to pass by them, 49but when they saw him walking on the lake, they thought he was a ghost. They cried out, 50because they all saw him and were terrified.

Immediately he spoke to them and said, "Take courage! It is I. Don't be afraid." 51Then he climbed into the boat with them, and the wind died down. They were completely amazed, 52for they had not understood about the loaves; their hearts were hardened.

53When they had crossed over, they landed at Gennesaret and anchored there. 54As soon as they got out of the boat, people recognized Jesus. 55They ran throughout that whole region and carried the sick on mats to wherever they heard he was. 56And wherever he went—into villages, towns or countryside—they placed the sick in the marketplaces. They begged him to let them touch even the edge of his cloak, and all who touched him were healed.

[a]37 Greek *take two hundred denarii*

SHARPEN THE FOCUS

Man or woman, anyone who suffered from a discharge in ancient Israel bore the burden of being ceremonially unclean. That person had to observe strict rules about sitting and washing. Anyone who touched an unclean person became unclean also. The rituals for cleansing absorbed much time. The woman who touched Jesus' robe should not have been out in public. (See Leviticus 15:19–33.)

The holiness code may sound to us like just so much rigmarole; but it meant much more than we can go into here. Suffice it to say that the Lord designed it to show His Old Testament people something about the way their sins had defiled them. A holy God could not live among a sinful people. They all needed a Savior.

So why did Jesus call the woman out of the crowd? Why make her explain—in public—what had happened? Jesus wanted her to know that He did not begrudge her healing. He wanted her to leave with His peace (Mark 5:34), not in shame or fear. And He wanted the crowds to see He did not despise the weak.

The woman *heard* of Jesus and *hoped* in Him (Mark 5:27); the One who healed her and who removed her shame, also removed her sin. What do you need from Jesus today?

WEEK 77 • SATURDAY

Mark 7:1—8:38

GET THE BIG PICTURE

Jesus did not stay in one place for any length of time. He and His disciples were always "on the move." The urgency of Jesus' mission carried Him from town to town, region to region, person to person. Mark accents this urgency. Look for it as you read. If time is short, focus on Mark 8:27–38.

Clean and Unclean

7 The Pharisees and some of the
teachers of the law who had
come from Jerusalem gathered around
Jesus and [2]saw some of his disciples
eating food with hands that were "unclean,"
that is, unwashed. [3](The Pharisees
and all the Jews do not eat unless
they give their hands a ceremonial
washing, holding to the tradition of the
elders. [4]When they come from the marketplace
they do not eat unless they
wash. And they observe many other traditions,
such as the washing of cups,
pitchers and kettles.[a])

[5]So the Pharisees and teachers of the
law asked Jesus, "Why don't your disciples
live according to the tradition of
the elders instead of eating their food
with 'unclean' hands?"

[6]He replied, "Isaiah was right when
he prophesied about you hypocrites; as
it is written:

"'These people honor me with their
lips,
but their hearts are far from me.
[7]They worship me in vain;

[a]4 Some early manuscripts *pitchers, kettles and dining couches*

their teachings are but rules
taught by men.'[a]

8You have let go of the commands of God and are holding on to the traditions of men."

9And he said to them: "You have a fine way of setting aside the commands of God in order to observe[b] your own traditions! 10For Moses said, 'Honor your father and your mother,'[c] and, 'Anyone who curses his father or mother must be put to death.'[d] 11But you say that if a man says to his father or mother: 'Whatever help you might otherwise have received from me is Corban' (that is, a gift devoted to God), 12then you no longer let him do anything for his father or mother. 13Thus you nullify the word of God by your tradition that you have handed down. And you do many things like that."

14Again Jesus called the crowd to him and said, "Listen to me, everyone, and understand this. 15Nothing outside a man can make him 'unclean' by going into him. Rather, it is what comes out of a man that makes him 'unclean.'[e]"

17After he had left the crowd and entered the house, his disciples asked him about this parable. 18"Are you so dull?" he asked. "Don't you see that nothing that enters a man from the outside can make him 'unclean'? 19For it doesn't go into his heart but into his stomach, and then out of his body." (In saying this, Jesus declared all foods "clean.")

20He went on: "What comes out of a man is what makes him 'unclean.' 21For from within, out of men's hearts, come evil thoughts, sexual immorality, theft, murder, adultery, 22greed, malice, deceit, lewdness, envy, slander, arrogance and folly. 23All these evils come from inside and make a man 'unclean.'"

The Faith of a Syrophoenician Woman

24Jesus left that place and went to the vicinity of Tyre.[f] He entered a house and did not want anyone to know it; yet he could not keep his presence secret. 25In fact, as soon as she heard about him, a woman whose little daughter was possessed by an evil[g] spirit came and fell at his feet. 26The woman was a Greek, born in Syrian Phoenicia. She begged Jesus to drive the demon out of her daughter.

27"First let the children eat all they want," he told her, "for it is not right to take the children's bread and toss it to their dogs."

28"Yes, Lord," she replied, "but even the dogs under the table eat the children's crumbs."

29Then he told her, "For such a reply, you may go; the demon has left your daughter."

30She went home and found her child lying on the bed, and the demon gone.

The Healing of a Deaf and Mute Man

31Then Jesus left the vicinity of Tyre and went through Sidon, down to the Sea of Galilee and into the region of the Decapolis.[h] 32There some people brought to him a man who was deaf and could hardly talk, and they begged him to place his hand on the man.

33After he took him aside, away from the crowd, Jesus put his fingers into the man's ears. Then he spit and touched the man's tongue. 34He looked up to heaven and with a deep sigh said to him, "*Ephphatha!*" (which means, "Be opened!"). 35At this, the man's ears were opened, his tongue was loosened and he began to speak plainly.

36Jesus commanded them not to tell anyone. But the more he did so, the more they kept talking about it. 37People were overwhelmed with amazement. "He has done everything well," they said. "He even makes the deaf hear and the mute speak."

Jesus Feeds the Four Thousand

8 During those days another large crowd gathered. Since they had nothing to eat, Jesus called his disciples

[a]6,7 Isaiah 29:13 [b]9 Some manuscripts *set up* [c]10 Exodus 20:12; Deut. 5:16 [d]10 Exodus 21:17; Lev. 20:9 [e]15 Some early manuscripts *'unclean.' 16If anyone has ears to hear, let him hear.* [f]24 Many early manuscripts *Tyre and Sidon* [g]25 Greek *unclean* [h]31 That is, the Ten Cities

to him and said, 2"I have compassion for these people; they have already been with me three days and have nothing to eat. 3If I send them home hungry, they will collapse on the way, because some of them have come a long distance."

4His disciples answered, "But where in this remote place can anyone get enough bread to feed them?"

5"How many loaves do you have?" Jesus asked.

"Seven," they replied.

6He told the crowd to sit down on the ground. When he had taken the seven loaves and given thanks, he broke them and gave them to his disciples to set before the people, and they did so. 7They had a few small fish as well; he gave thanks for them also and told the disciples to distribute them. 8The people ate and were satisfied. Afterward the disciples picked up seven basketfuls of broken pieces that were left over. 9About four thousand men were present. And having sent them away, 10he got into the boat with his disciples and went to the region of Dalmanutha.

11The Pharisees came and began to question Jesus. To test him, they asked him for a sign from heaven. 12He sighed deeply and said, "Why does this generation ask for a miraculous sign? I tell you the truth, no sign will be given to it." 13Then he left them, got back into the boat and crossed to the other side.

The Yeast of the Pharisees and Herod

14The disciples had forgotten to bring bread, except for one loaf they had with them in the boat. 15"Be careful," Jesus warned them. "Watch out for the yeast of the Pharisees and that of Herod."

16They discussed this with one another and said, "It is because we have no bread."

17Aware of their discussion, Jesus asked them: "Why are you talking about having no bread? Do you still not see or understand? Are your hearts hardened? 18Do you have eyes but fail to see, and ears but fail to hear? And don't you remember? 19When I broke the five loaves for the five thousand, how many basketfuls of pieces did you pick up?"

"Twelve," they replied.

20"And when I broke the seven loaves for the four thousand, how many basketfuls of pieces did you pick up?"

They answered, "Seven."

21He said to them, "Do you still not understand?"

The Healing of a Blind Man at Bethsaida

22They came to Bethsaida, and some people brought a blind man and begged Jesus to touch him. 23He took the blind man by the hand and led him outside the village. When he had spit on the man's eyes and put his hands on him, Jesus asked, "Do you see anything?"

24He looked up and said, "I see people; they look like trees walking around."

25Once more Jesus put his hands on the man's eyes. Then his eyes were opened, his sight was restored, and he saw everything clearly. 26Jesus sent him home, saying, "Don't go into the village.[a]"

Peter's Confession of Christ

27Jesus and his disciples went on to the villages around Caesarea Philippi. On the way he asked them, "Who do people say I am?"

28They replied, "Some say John the Baptist; others say Elijah; and still others, one of the prophets."

29"But what about you?" he asked. "Who do you say I am?"

Peter answered, "You are the Christ.[b]"

30Jesus warned them not to tell anyone about him.

Jesus Predicts His Death

31He then began to teach them that the Son of Man must suffer many things and be rejected by the elders, chief priests and teachers of the law, and that

[a]26 Some manuscripts *Don't go and tell anyone in the village* [b]29 Or *Messiah.* "The Christ" (Greek) and "the Messiah" (Hebrew) both mean "the Anointed One."

he must be killed and after three days
rise again. 32He spoke plainly about this,
and Peter took him aside and began to
rebuke him.
33But when Jesus turned and looked
at his disciples, he rebuked Peter. "Get
behind me, Satan!" he said. "You do not
have in mind the things of God, but the
things of men."
34Then he called the crowd to him
along with his disciples and said: "If
anyone would come after me, he must
deny himself and take up his cross and
follow me. 35For whoever wants to save
his life[a] will lose it, but whoever loses his
life for me and for the gospel will save
it. 36What good is it for a man to gain the
whole world, yet forfeit his soul? 37Or
what can a man give in exchange for
his soul? 38If anyone is ashamed of me
and my words in this adulterous
and sinful generation, the Son of Man
will be ashamed of him when he comes
in his Father's glory with the holy
angels."

[a]35 The Greek word means either *life* or *soul*; also in verse 36.

SHARPEN THE FOCUS

Suppose you would take a camcorder to a local playground or movie theater or baseball stadium and ask passersby the question Jesus asked in Mark 8:27. What would people say? Probably much the same thing people said back then:

- A great teacher
- A wise man
- Some historical religious leader from long ago
- A miracle-worker

Some might even respond, "Jesus, who?" Nevertheless, the question that concerns us isn't about what other people think of Jesus. Our question is the one the Lord put to Peter: Who do *you* say that I am?

If we answer, from the heart, "You are the Christ" (Mark 8:29), we can have peace. We can rest in the assurance of sins forgiven and in a relationship of love and care with our heavenly Father—now and forever.

But when we answer, from the heart, "You are the Christ," our hearts flood with a sense of urgency. Most of the world's people do not yet know their Savior. Most do not bow before Him in love. Most are still trapped by their sins in a world of hurt and are headed for eternal darkness. Peace and urgency. May the Lord Christ work both in increasing measure in your heart!

WEEK 78 • MONDAY

Mark 9:1–50

After the events of Mark 8, Jesus' main ministry-focus shifts. He has been working with the multitudes. Now he zeroes in on His disciples, preparing them for His suffering and death and also for the work they will carry on in His name when He ascends to heaven. How do the events of Mark 9 reflect this shift? If time is short, focus on Mark 9:30–50.

9 And he said to them, "I tell you the truth, some who are standing here will not taste death before they see the kingdom of God come with power."

The Transfiguration

2After six days Jesus took Peter, James and John with him and led them up a high mountain, where they were all alone. There he was transfigured before them. 3His clothes became dazzling white, whiter than anyone in the world could bleach them. 4And there appeared before them Elijah and Moses, who were talking with Jesus.

5Peter said to Jesus, "Rabbi, it is good for us to be here. Let us put up three shelters—one for you, one for Moses and one for Elijah." 6(He did not know what to say, they were so frightened.)

7Then a cloud appeared and enveloped them, and a voice came from the cloud: "This is my Son, whom I love. Listen to him!"

8Suddenly, when they looked around, they no longer saw anyone with them except Jesus.

9As they were coming down the mountain, Jesus gave them orders not to tell anyone what they had seen until the Son of Man had risen from the dead. 10They kept the matter to themselves, discussing what "rising from the dead" meant.

11And they asked him, "Why do the teachers of the law say that Elijah must come first?"

12Jesus replied, "To be sure, Elijah does come first, and restores all things. Why then is it written that the Son of Man must suffer much and be rejected? 13But I tell you, Elijah has come, and they have done to him everything they wished, just as it is written about him."

The Healing of a Boy With an Evil Spirit

14When they came to the other disciples, they saw a large crowd around them and the teachers of the law arguing with them. 15As soon as all the people saw Jesus, they were overwhelmed with wonder and ran to greet him.

16"What are you arguing with them about?" he asked.

17A man in the crowd answered, "Teacher, I brought you my son, who is possessed by a spirit that has robbed him of speech. 18Whenever it seizes him, it throws him to the ground. He foams at the mouth, gnashes his teeth and becomes rigid. I asked your disciples to drive out the spirit, but they could not."

19"O unbelieving generation," Jesus replied, "how long shall I stay with you? How long shall I put up with you? Bring the boy to me."

20So they brought him. When the spirit saw Jesus, it immediately threw the boy into a convulsion. He fell to the ground and rolled around, foaming at the mouth.

21Jesus asked the boy's father, "How long has he been like this?"

"From childhood," he answered. 22"It has often thrown him into fire or water

to kill him. But if you can do anything,
take pity on us and help us."
23"'If you can'?" said Jesus. "Everything is possible for him who believes."
24Immediately the boy's father exclaimed, "I do believe; help me overcome my unbelief!"
25When Jesus saw that a crowd was
running to the scene, he rebuked the
evil[a] spirit. "You deaf and mute spirit,"
he said, "I command you, come out of
him and never enter him again."
26The spirit shrieked, convulsed him
violently and came out. The boy looked
so much like a corpse that many said,
"He's dead." 27But Jesus took him by the
hand and lifted him to his feet, and he
stood up.
28After Jesus had gone indoors, his
disciples asked him privately, "Why
couldn't we drive it out?"
29He replied, "This kind can come out
only by prayer.[b]"
30They left that place and passed
through Galilee. Jesus did not want anyone to know where they were, 31because
he was teaching his disciples. He said to
them, "The Son of Man is going to be betrayed into the hands of men. They will
kill him, and after three days he will
rise." 32But they did not understand
what he meant and were afraid to ask
him about it.

Who Is the Greatest?

33They came to Capernaum. When he
was in the house, he asked them, "What
were you arguing about on the road?"
34But they kept quiet because on the way
they had argued about who was the
greatest.
35Sitting down, Jesus called the Twelve
and said, "If anyone wants to be first, he
must be the very last, and the servant of
all."
36He took a little child and had him
stand among them. Taking him in his
arms, he said to them, 37"Whoever welcomes one of these little children in my
name welcomes me; and whoever welcomes me does not welcome me but the
one who sent me."

Whoever Is Not Against Us Is for Us

38"Teacher," said John, "we saw a man
driving out demons in your name and
we told him to stop, because he was not
one of us."
39"Do not stop him," Jesus said. "No
one who does a miracle in my name can
in the next moment say anything bad
about me, 40for whoever is not against us
is for us. 41I tell you the truth, anyone
who gives you a cup of water in my
name because you belong to Christ will
certainly not lose his reward.

Causing to Sin

42"And if anyone causes one of these
little ones who believe in me to sin, it
would be better for him to be thrown
into the sea with a large millstone tied
around his neck. 43If your hand causes
you to sin, cut it off. It is better for you
to enter life maimed than with two
hands to go into hell, where the fire never goes out.[c] 45And if your foot causes
you to sin, cut it off. It is better for you
to enter life crippled than to have two
feet and be thrown into hell.[d] 47And if
your eye causes you to sin, pluck it out.
It is better for you to enter the kingdom
of God with one eye than to have two
eyes and be thrown into hell, 48where

"'their worm does not die,
and the fire is not quenched.'[e]

49Everyone will be salted with fire.
50"Salt is good, but if it loses its saltiness, how can you make it salty again?
Have salt in yourselves, and be at peace
with each other."

[a]25 Greek *unclean* [b]29 Some manuscripts *prayer and fasting* [c]43 Some manuscripts *out,* [44]*where* / *" 'their worm does not die,* / *and the fire is not quenched.'* [d]45 Some manuscripts *hell,* [46]*where* / *" 'their worm does not die,* / *and the fire is not quenched.'* [e]48 Isaiah 66:24

SHARPEN THE FOCUS

Think about your circle of friends or the people in your congregation. Whom could you nominate for a "servant's heart award"? Such individuals are all too rare in our me-first culture. If two or three people consistently reflect Jesus' heart of service toward you, God has richly blessed you!

Those with a servant's heart pray and fast as they look for ways to help others (Mark 9:29). Those with a servant's heart often take the back seat so they can spot the child who needs a drink of cold water (Mark 9:41). Those with a servant's heart aren't doormats; they sometimes confront hypocrisy and spiritual pride regardless of what it might do to their status with friend or foe (Mark 9:31, 35, 42–50).

Like those who win the Purple Heart serving in the United States military, those with servant's hearts have been wounded. It goes with the territory. Perhaps that's why so few people adopt this lifestyle. Perhaps it's why we ourselves often shy away from it.

Praise God, our Lord Jesus didn't. He became the Servant who suffered and died in our place. He put us first so we could receive forgiveness and the joy of serving others in His name.

WEEK 78 • TUESDAY

Mark 10:1–52

GET THE BIG PICTURE

Jesus' teachings about divorce reveal His concern for families, particularly women and children who in that culture were usually reduced to grinding poverty and disgrace by divorce. He also reveals His care for children and even infants in a culture that devalued children. His teachings about money and about greatness also conflict with human reasoning. Look for evidence of Jesus tender concern as you read. If time is short, focus on Mark 10:32–45.

Divorce

10 Jesus then left that place and
went into the region of Judea
and across the Jordan. Again crowds of
people came to him, and as was his custom, he taught them.
2Some Pharisees came and tested him
by asking, "Is it lawful for a man to divorce his wife?"
3"What did Moses command you?" he
replied.
4They said, "Moses permitted a man
to write a certificate of divorce and send
her away."
5"It was because your hearts were
hard that Moses wrote you this law,"
Jesus replied. 6"But at the beginning of
creation God 'made them male and
female.'[a] 7'For this reason a man will
leave his father and mother and be united to his wife,[b] 8and the two will become
one flesh.'[c] So they are no longer two,
but one. 9Therefore what God has
joined together, let man not separate."
10When they were in the house again,
the disciples asked Jesus about this. 11He

[a]6 Gen. 1:27 [b]7 Some early manuscripts do not have *and be united to his wife.* [c]8 Gen. 2:24

answered, "Anyone who divorces his
wife and marries another woman commits adultery against her. 12And if she
divorces her husband and marries another man, she commits adultery."

The Little Children and Jesus

13People were bringing little children
to Jesus to have him touch them, but the
disciples rebuked them. 14When Jesus
saw this, he was indignant. He said to
them, "Let the little children come to
me, and do not hinder them, for the
kingdom of God belongs to such as
these. 15I tell you the truth, anyone who
will not receive the kingdom of God like
a little child will never enter it." 16And
he took the children in his arms, put his
hands on them and blessed them.

The Rich Young Man

17As Jesus started on his way, a man
ran up to him and fell on his knees before him. "Good teacher," he asked,
"what must I do to inherit eternal life?"
18"Why do you call me good?" Jesus
answered. "No one is good—except
God alone. 19You know the commandments: 'Do not murder, do not commit
adultery, do not steal, do not give false
testimony, do not defraud, honor your
father and mother.'[a]"
20"Teacher," he declared, "all these I
have kept since I was a boy."
21Jesus looked at him and loved him.
"One thing you lack," he said. "Go, sell
everything you have and give to the
poor, and you will have treasure in
heaven. Then come, follow me."
22At this the man's face fell. He went
away sad, because he had great wealth.
23Jesus looked around and said to his
disciples, "How hard it is for the rich to
enter the kingdom of God!"
24The disciples were amazed at his
words. But Jesus said again, "Children,
how hard it is[b] to enter the kingdom of
God! 25It is easier for a camel to go
through the eye of a needle than for a
rich man to enter the kingdom of God."
26The disciples were even more
amazed, and said to each other, "Who
then can be saved?"
27Jesus looked at them and said, "With
man this is impossible, but not with
God; all things are possible with God."
28Peter said to him, "We have left everything to follow you!"
29"I tell you the truth," Jesus replied,
"no one who has left home or brothers
or sisters or mother or father or children
or fields for me and the gospel 30will fail
to receive a hundred times as much in
this present age (homes, brothers, sisters, mothers, children and fields—and
with them, persecutions) and in the age
to come, eternal life. 31But many who are
first will be last, and the last first."

Jesus Again Predicts His Death

32They were on their way up to Jerusalem, with Jesus leading the way, and
the disciples were astonished, while
those who followed were afraid. Again
he took the Twelve aside and told them
what was going to happen to him. 33"We
are going up to Jerusalem," he said,
"and the Son of Man will be betrayed to
the chief priests and teachers of the law.
They will condemn him to death and
will hand him over to the Gentiles,
34who will mock him and spit on him,
flog him and kill him. Three days later
he will rise."

The Request of James and John

35Then James and John, the sons of
Zebedee, came to him. "Teacher," they
said, "we want you to do for us whatever we ask."
36"What do you want me to do for
you?" he asked.
37They replied, "Let one of us sit at
your right and the other at your left in
your glory."
38"You don't know what you are asking," Jesus said. "Can you drink the cup
I drink or be baptized with the baptism
I am baptized with?"
39"We can," they answered.
Jesus said to them, "You will drink the
cup I drink and be baptized with the
baptism I am baptized with, 40but to sit

[a]*19* Exodus 20:12-16; Deut. 5:16-20 [b]*24* Some manuscripts *is for those who trust in riches*

at my right or left is not for me to grant.
These places belong to those for whom
they have been prepared."
41 When the ten heard about this, they
became indignant with James and John.
42 Jesus called them together and said,
"You know that those who are regarded
as rulers of the Gentiles lord it over
them, and their high officials exercise
authority over them. 43 Not so with you.
Instead, whoever wants to become
great among you must be your servant,
44 and whoever wants to be first must be
slave of all. 45 For even the Son of Man
did not come to be served, but to serve,
and to give his life as a ransom for
many."

Blind Bartimaeus Receives His Sight

46 Then they came to Jericho. As Jesus
and his disciples, together with a large
crowd, were leaving the city, a blind
man, Bartimaeus (that is, the Son of Ti-
maeus), was sitting by the roadside begging. 47 When he heard that it was Jesus
of Nazareth, he began to shout, "Jesus,
Son of David, have mercy on me!"
48 Many rebuked him and told him to
be quiet, but he shouted all the more,
"Son of David, have mercy on me!"
49 Jesus stopped and said, "Call him."
So they called to the blind man,
"Cheer up! On your feet! He's calling
you." 50 Throwing his cloak aside, he
jumped to his feet and came to Jesus.
51 "What do you want me to do for
you?" Jesus asked him.
The blind man said, "Rabbi, I want to
see."
52 "Go," said Jesus, "your faith has
healed you." Immediately he received
his sight and followed Jesus along the
road.

SHARPEN THE FOCUS

When children need medical treatment, someone on staff in the doctor's office will often walk them through it step by step beforehand. The staff person tries to answer questions honestly but without evoking fear. Most children—and we adults too—do better when we know what to expect. When we know that pain is on its way, we can plan ways to deal with it. We're less likely to panic.

Jesus knew that, and so when fear began to rise in the hearts of His followers (Mark 10:32), He took them aside to explain what would happen to Him. His words so shocked them that they seem to have blocked out the truth He told. But Jesus, in compassion, did what He could for them, even though He knew they could not completely receive it.

Jesus knows how to deal with our fears, too. Quite often He tells us just what He told the Twelve: He *was* delivered to be mocked and killed. On the third day, He *did* rise again. And because He did all this for us, we are safe—in life or death. We may not know what the future holds, but we know the One who holds the future, and us, in His care.

"He came to that which was His own, and His own did not receive Him" (John 1:11). Today's reading opens Mark's extended description of Jesus' rejection. As you read, ask yourself what kind of reception Jesus would receive if He came to earth today. If time is short, focus on Mark 11:12–19.

The Triumphal Entry

11 As they approached Jerusalem and came to Bethphage and Bethany at the Mount of Olives, Jesus sent two of his disciples, 2saying to them, "Go to the village ahead of you, and just as you enter it, you will find a colt tied there, which no one has ever ridden. Untie it and bring it here. 3If anyone asks you, 'Why are you doing this?' tell him, 'The Lord needs it and will send it back here shortly.' "

4They went and found a colt outside in the street, tied at a doorway. As they untied it, 5some people standing there asked, "What are you doing, untying that colt?" 6They answered as Jesus had told them to, and the people let them go. 7When they brought the colt to Jesus and threw their cloaks over it, he sat on it. 8Many people spread their cloaks on the road, while others spread branches they had cut in the fields. 9Those who went ahead and those who followed shouted,

"Hosanna![a]"

"Blessed is he who comes in the
name of the Lord!"[b]

10"Blessed is the coming kingdom of
our father David!"

"Hosanna in the highest!"

11Jesus entered Jerusalem and went to the temple. He looked around at everything, but since it was already late, he went out to Bethany with the Twelve.

Jesus Clears the Temple

12The next day as they were leaving Bethany, Jesus was hungry. 13Seeing in the distance a fig tree in leaf, he went to find out if it had any fruit. When he reached it, he found nothing but leaves, because it was not the season for figs. 14Then he said to the tree, "May no one ever eat fruit from you again." And his disciples heard him say it.

15On reaching Jerusalem, Jesus entered the temple area and began driving out those who were buying and selling there. He overturned the tables of the money changers and the benches of those selling doves, 16and would not allow anyone to carry merchandise through the temple courts. 17And as he taught them, he said, "Is it not written:

" 'My house will be called
a house of prayer for all
nations'[c]?

But you have made it 'a den of robbers.'[d]"

18The chief priests and the teachers of the law heard this and began looking for a way to kill him, for they feared him, because the whole crowd was amazed at his teaching.

19When evening came, they[e] went out of the city.

[a]*9* A Hebrew expression meaning "Save!" which became an exclamation of praise; also in verse 10
[b]*9* Psalm 118:25,26 [c]*17* Isaiah 56:7 [d]*17* Jer. 7:11
[e]*19* Some early manuscripts *he*

The Withered Fig Tree

20In the morning, as they went along,
they saw the fig tree withered from the
roots. 21Peter remembered and said to
Jesus, "Rabbi, look! The fig tree you
cursed has withered!"
22"Have[a] faith in God," Jesus answered. 23"I tell you the truth, if anyone
says to this mountain, 'Go, throw yourself into the sea,' and does not doubt in
his heart but believes that what he says
will happen, it will be done for him.
24Therefore I tell you, whatever you ask
for in prayer, believe that you have received it, and it will be yours. 25And
when you stand praying, if you hold
anything against anyone, forgive him,
so that your Father in heaven may forgive you your sins.[b]"

The Authority of Jesus Questioned

27They arrived again in Jerusalem,
and while Jesus was walking in the temple courts, the chief priests, the teachers
of the law and the elders came to him.
28"By what authority are you doing
these things?" they asked. "And who
gave you authority to do this?"
29Jesus replied, "I will ask you one
question. Answer me, and I will tell you
by what authority I am doing these
things. 30John's baptism—was it from
heaven, or from men? Tell me!"
31They discussed it among themselves
and said, "If we say, 'From heaven,' he
will ask, 'Then why didn't you believe
him?' 32But if we say, 'From men'. . ."
(They feared the people, for everyone
held that John really was a prophet.)
33So they answered Jesus, "We don't
know."
Jesus said, "Neither will I tell you by
what authority I am doing these
things."

[a]22 Some early manuscripts *If you have*
[b]25 Some manuscripts *sins.* 26*But if you do not forgive, neither will your Father who is in heaven forgive your sins.*

SHARPEN THE FOCUS

By Passover each spring, the fig trees of Palestine sprout a crop of small figs that are often gathered and sold in the market. (Revelation 6:13 calls this "winter fruit.") Then the trees begin to leaf out and sprout their main crop of figs. When Jesus saw the fig tree with full foliage (Mark 11:13), He assumed He would find "winter fruit" on it. But when He got close enough for a good look, He found nothing but leaves—not even green fruit.

Quite often in Scripture the fig tree symbolizes Israel. In this incident, too, the parallels are clear. The nation had the outward "foliage" of religion. They had plenty of rituals, plenty of rules, plenty of regulations. But when God looked for true spiritual fruit, He found none.

How is it with us? When our Lord Jesus looks for fruit in our lives what does He find? The show of religiosity? Or the love, joy, peace, patience, kindness, and the rest He has promised to work in the hearts of His people (Galatians 5:22–23)?

Thank God for the tree of the cross that made us right with Him. And thank God that the tree of Jesus' cross has made it possible for us to produce the fruit of righteousness.

WEEK 78 • THURSDAY

Mark 12:1—13:37

GET THE BIG PICTURE

Today's reading begins with Jesus telling a parable similar to one in Isaiah 5:1–7–the story of Israel's rejection of the Lord and of His Christ. Notice how the rest of Mark 12 proves Jesus' point. Mark 13 describes the future of those who reject Christ and those who receive Him as Savior. If time is short, focus on Mark 12:28–44.

The Parable of the Tenants

12 He then began to speak to
them in parables: "A man
planted a vineyard. He put a wall
around it, dug a pit for the winepress
and built a watchtower. Then he rented
the vineyard to some farmers and went
away on a journey. 2At harvest time he
sent a servant to the tenants to collect
from them some of the fruit of the vineyard. 3But they seized him, beat him and
sent him away empty-handed. 4Then he
sent another servant to them; they
struck this man on the head and treated
him shamefully. 5He sent still another,
and that one they killed. He sent many
others; some of them they beat, others
they killed.
6"He had one left to send, a son,
whom he loved. He sent him last of all,
saying, 'They will respect my son.'
7"But the tenants said to one another,
'This is the heir. Come, let's kill him, and
the inheritance will be ours.' 8So they
took him and killed him, and threw him
out of the vineyard.
9"What then will the owner of the vineyard do? He will come and kill those
tenants and give the vineyard to others.
10Haven't you read this scripture:

" 'The stone the builders rejected
has become the capstone[a];
11 the Lord has done this,
and it is marvelous in our eyes'[b]?"

12Then they looked for a way to arrest
him because they knew he had spoken
the parable against them. But they were
afraid of the crowd; so they left him and
went away.

Paying Taxes to Caesar

13Later they sent some of the Pharisees and Herodians to Jesus to catch him
in his words. 14They came to him and
said, "Teacher, we know you are a man
of integrity. You aren't swayed by men,
because you pay no attention to who
they are; but you teach the way of God
in accordance with the truth. Is it right
to pay taxes to Caesar or not? 15Should
we pay or shouldn't we?"
But Jesus knew their hypocrisy. "Why
are you trying to trap me?" he asked.
"Bring me a denarius and let me look at
it." 16They brought the coin, and he
asked them, "Whose portrait is this?
And whose inscription?"
"Caesar's," they replied.
17Then Jesus said to them, "Give to
Caesar what is Caesar's and to God
what is God's."
And they were amazed at him.

Marriage at the Resurrection

18Then the Sadducees, who say there
is no resurrection, came to him with a
question. 19"Teacher," they said, "Moses
wrote for us that if a man's brother dies
and leaves a wife but no children, the
man must marry the widow and have
children for his brother. 20Now there
were seven brothers. The first one
married and died without leaving any

[a]*10* Or *cornerstone* [b]*11* Psalm 118:22,23

children. 21 The second one married the widow, but he also died, leaving no child. It was the same with the third. 22 In fact, none of the seven left any children. Last of all, the woman died too. 23 At the resurrection[a] whose wife will she be, since the seven were married to her?"

24 Jesus replied, "Are you not in error because you do not know the Scriptures or the power of God? 25 When the dead rise, they will neither marry nor be given in marriage; they will be like the angels in heaven. 26 Now about the dead rising—have you not read in the book of Moses, in the account of the bush, how God said to him, 'I am the God of Abraham, the God of Isaac, and the God of Jacob'[b]? 27 He is not the God of the dead, but of the living. You are badly mistaken!"

The Greatest Commandment

28 One of the teachers of the law came and heard them debating. Noticing that Jesus had given them a good answer, he asked him, "Of all the commandments, which is the most important?"

29 "The most important one," answered Jesus, "is this: 'Hear, O Israel, the Lord our God, the Lord is one.[c] 30 Love the Lord your God with all your heart and with all your soul and with all your mind and with all your strength.'[d] 31 The second is this: 'Love your neighbor as yourself.'[e] There is no commandment greater than these."

32 "Well said, teacher," the man replied. "You are right in saying that God is one and there is no other but him. 33 To love him with all your heart, with all your understanding and with all your strength, and to love your neighbor as yourself is more important than all burnt offerings and sacrifices."

34 When Jesus saw that he had answered wisely, he said to him, "You are not far from the kingdom of God." And from then on no one dared ask him any more questions.

Whose Son Is the Christ?

35 While Jesus was teaching in the temple courts, he asked, "How is it that the teachers of the law say that the Christ[f] is the son of David? 36 David himself, speaking by the Holy Spirit, declared:

> " 'The Lord said to my Lord:
> "Sit at my right hand
> until I put your enemies
> under your feet." '[g]

37 David himself calls him 'Lord.' How then can he be his son?"

The large crowd listened to him with delight.

38 As he taught, Jesus said, "Watch out for the teachers of the law. They like to walk around in flowing robes and be greeted in the marketplaces, 39 and have the most important seats in the synagogues and the places of honor at banquets. 40 They devour widows' houses and for a show make lengthy prayers. Such men will be punished most severely."

The Widow's Offering

41 Jesus sat down opposite the place where the offerings were put and watched the crowd putting their money into the temple treasury. Many rich people threw in large amounts. 42 But a poor widow came and put in two very small copper coins,[h] worth only a fraction of a penny.[i]

43 Calling his disciples to him, Jesus said, "I tell you the truth, this poor widow has put more into the treasury than all the others. 44 They all gave out of their wealth; but she, out of her poverty, put in everything—all she had to live on."

Signs of the End of the Age

13 As he was leaving the temple, one of his disciples said to him, "Look, Teacher! What massive stones! What magnificent buildings!"

2 "Do you see all these great buildings?" replied Jesus. "Not one stone here will be left on another; every one will be thrown down."

[a]23 Some manuscripts *resurrection, when men rise from the dead,* [b]26 Exodus 3:6 [c]29 Or *the Lord our God is one Lord* [d]30 Deut. 6:4,5 [e]31 Lev. 19:18 [f]35 Or *Messiah* [g]36 Psalm 110:1 [h]42 Greek *two lepta* [i]42 Greek *kodrantes*

3As Jesus was sitting on the Mount of Olives opposite the temple, Peter, James, John and Andrew asked him privately, 4"Tell us, when will these things happen? And what will be the sign that they are all about to be fulfilled?"

5Jesus said to them: "Watch out that no one deceives you. 6Many will come in my name, claiming, 'I am he,' and will deceive many. 7When you hear of wars and rumors of wars, do not be alarmed. Such things must happen, but the end is still to come. 8Nation will rise against nation, and kingdom against kingdom. There will be earthquakes in various places, and famines. These are the beginning of birth pains.

9"You must be on your guard. You will be handed over to the local councils and flogged in the synagogues. On account of me you will stand before governors and kings as witnesses to them. 10And the gospel must first be preached to all nations. 11Whenever you are arrested and brought to trial, do not worry beforehand about what to say. Just say whatever is given you at the time, for it is not you speaking, but the Holy Spirit.

12"Brother will betray brother to death, and a father his child. Children will rebel against their parents and have them put to death. 13All men will hate you because of me, but he who stands firm to the end will be saved.

14"When you see 'the abomination that causes desolation'[a] standing where it[b] does not belong—let the reader understand—then let those who are in Judea flee to the mountains. 15Let no one on the roof of his house go down or enter the house to take anything out. 16Let no one in the field go back to get his cloak. 17How dreadful it will be in those days for pregnant women and nursing mothers! 18Pray that this will not take place in winter, 19because those will be days of distress unequaled from the beginning, when God created the world, until now—and never to be equaled again. 20If the Lord had not cut short those days, no one would survive. But for the sake of the elect, whom he has chosen, he has shortened them. 21At that time if anyone says to you, 'Look, here is the Christ[c]!' or, 'Look, there he is!' do not believe it. 22For false Christs and false prophets will appear and perform signs and miracles to deceive the elect—if that were possible. 23So be on your guard; I have told you everything ahead of time.

24"But in those days, following that distress,

" 'the sun will be darkened,
 and the moon will not give its
 light;
25the stars will fall from the sky,
 and the heavenly bodies will be
 shaken.'[d]

26"At that time men will see the Son of Man coming in clouds with great power and glory. 27And he will send his angels and gather his elect from the four winds, from the ends of the earth to the ends of the heavens.

28"Now learn this lesson from the fig tree: As soon as its twigs get tender and its leaves come out, you know that summer is near. 29Even so, when you see these things happening, you know that it is near, right at the door. 30I tell you the truth, this generation[e] will certainly not pass away until all these things have happened. 31Heaven and earth will pass away, but my words will never pass away.

The Day and Hour Unknown

32"No one knows about that day or hour, not even the angels in heaven, nor the Son, but only the Father. 33Be on guard! Be alert[f]! You do not know when that time will come. 34It's like a man going away: He leaves his house and puts his servants in charge, each with his assigned task, and tells the one at the door to keep watch.

35"Therefore keep watch because you do not know when the owner of the

[a]*14* Daniel 9:27; 11:31; 12:11 [b]*14* Or *he*; also in verse 29 [c]*21* Or *Messiah* [d]*25* Isaiah 13:10; 34:4 [e]*30* Or *race* [f]*33* Some manuscripts *alert and pray*

house will come back—whether in the evening, or at midnight, or when the rooster crows, or at dawn. [36]If he comes suddenly, do not let him find you sleeping. [37]What I say to you, I say to everyone: 'Watch!' "

SHARPEN THE FOCUS

Jesus said that the widow's gift amounted to more than the money put in by all the others.(See Mark 12:43.) The widow gave as an act of worship. As she threw in her coins, she threw herself on the Lord's mercy. He saw. He was watching! She did *not* go hungry; see Psalm 37:25.

Think of all the believers down through history who have read this little story in Mark's gospel (Mark 12:41–44) and have been energized to give themselves into the Lord's care as they worshiped Him with their money. What huge interest has built up on the widow's two copper coins!

We can't duplicate her gift by emptying out our own savings accounts or by signing the deed to all our property over to the church. No, if we want to worship from the heart as we give, we need to turn our hearts over to the Holy Spirit. Only He can renovate them. Only He can assure us of Christ's pardon for our selfishness. Only He can work in us the grace of giving and of worship. To honor God in our giving–what a delight!

WEEK 78 • FRIDAY

Mark 14:1–72

GET THE BIG PICTURE

Mark plunges us into the depth of our Lord's suffering in chapter 14. As you read, remember that our eternal destiny hung in the balance on the fateful night he describes. The kingdom of darkness unleashed its fury on the Son of God. The outcome would change our personal histories forever. If time is short, focus on Mark 14:10–25.

Jesus Anointed at Bethany

14 Now the Passover and the Feast of Unleavened Bread were only two days away, and the chief priests and the teachers of the law were looking for some sly way to arrest Jesus and kill him. [2]"But not during the Feast," they said, "or the people may riot."

[3]While he was in Bethany, reclining at the table in the home of a man known as Simon the Leper, a woman came with an alabaster jar of very expensive perfume, made of pure nard. She broke the jar and poured the perfume on his head.

[4]Some of those present were saying indignantly to one another, "Why this waste of perfume? [5]It could have been sold for more than a year's wages[a] and the money given to the poor." And they rebuked her harshly.

[6]"Leave her alone," said Jesus. "Why are you bothering her? She has done a beautiful thing to me. [7]The poor you will always have with you, and you can help them any time you want. But you will not always have me. [8]She did what she

[a]5 Greek *than three hundred denarii*

could. She poured perfume on my body
beforehand to prepare for my burial. 9I
tell you the truth, wherever the gospel
is preached throughout the world, what
she has done will also be told, in memory of her."
10Then Judas Iscariot, one of the
Twelve, went to the chief priests to betray Jesus to them. 11They were delighted to hear this and promised to give him
money. So he watched for an opportunity to hand him over.

The Lord's Supper

12On the first day of the Feast of Unleavened Bread, when it was customary
to sacrifice the Passover lamb, Jesus' disciples asked him, "Where do you want
us to go and make preparations for you
to eat the Passover?"
13So he sent two of his disciples, telling them, "Go into the city, and a man
carrying a jar of water will meet you.
Follow him. 14Say to the owner of the
house he enters, 'The Teacher asks:
Where is my guest room, where I may
eat the Passover with my disciples?' 15He
will show you a large upper room, furnished and ready. Make preparations
for us there."
16The disciples left, went into the city
and found things just as Jesus had told
them. So they prepared the Passover.
17When evening came, Jesus arrived
with the Twelve. 18While they were reclining at the table eating, he said, "I tell
you the truth, one of you will betray
me—one who is eating with me."
19They were saddened, and one by
one they said to him, "Surely not I?"
20"It is one of the Twelve," he replied,
"one who dips bread into the bowl with
me. 21The Son of Man will go just as it is
written about him. But woe to that man
who betrays the Son of Man! It would be
better for him if he had not been born."
22While they were eating, Jesus took
bread, gave thanks and broke it, and
gave it to his disciples, saying, "Take it;
this is my body."
23Then he took the cup, gave thanks
and offered it to them, and they all
drank from it.
24"This is my blood of the[a] covenant,
which is poured out for many," he said
to them. 25"I tell you the truth, I will not
drink again of the fruit of the vine until
that day when I drink it anew in the
kingdom of God."
26When they had sung a hymn, they
went out to the Mount of Olives.

Jesus Predicts Peter's Denial

27"You will all fall away," Jesus told
them, "for it is written:

" 'I will strike the shepherd,
and the sheep will be scattered.'[b]

28But after I have risen, I will go ahead
of you into Galilee."
29Peter declared, "Even if all fall away,
I will not."
30"I tell you the truth," Jesus answered, "today—yes, tonight—before
the rooster crows twice[c] you yourself
will disown me three times."
31But Peter insisted emphatically,
"Even if I have to die with you, I will
never disown you." And all the others
said the same.

Gethsemane

32They went to a place called Gethsemane, and Jesus said to his disciples,
"Sit here while I pray." 33He took Peter,
James and John along with him, and he
began to be deeply distressed and troubled. 34"My soul is overwhelmed with
sorrow to the point of death," he said to
them. "Stay here and keep watch."
35Going a little farther, he fell to the
ground and prayed that if possible the
hour might pass from him. 36"*Abba*,[d] Father," he said, "everything is possible for
you. Take this cup from me. Yet not what
I will, but what you will."
37Then he returned to his disciples
and found them sleeping. "Simon," he
said to Peter, "are you asleep? Could you
not keep watch for one hour? 38Watch
and pray so that you will not fall into
temptation. The spirit is willing, but the
body is weak."

[a]24 Some manuscripts *the new* [b]27 Zech. 13:7
[c]30 Some early manuscripts do not have *twice.*
[d]36 Aramaic for *Father*

39 Once more he went away and
prayed the same thing. 40 When he came
back, he again found them sleeping, because their eyes were heavy. They did
not know what to say to him.
41 Returning the third time, he said to
them, "Are you still sleeping and resting? Enough! The hour has come. Look,
the Son of Man is betrayed into the
hands of sinners. 42 Rise! Let us go! Here
comes my betrayer!"

Jesus Arrested

43 Just as he was speaking, Judas, one
of the Twelve, appeared. With him was
a crowd armed with swords and clubs,
sent from the chief priests, the teachers
of the law, and the elders.
44 Now the betrayer had arranged a
signal with them: "The one I kiss is the
man; arrest him and lead him away under guard." 45 Going at once to Jesus, Judas said, "Rabbi!" and kissed him. 46 The
men seized Jesus and arrested him.
47 Then one of those standing near drew
his sword and struck the servant of the
high priest, cutting off his ear.
48 "Am I leading a rebellion," said
Jesus, "that you have come out with
swords and clubs to capture me? 49 Every day I was with you, teaching in the
temple courts, and you did not arrest me.
But the Scriptures must be fulfilled."
50 Then everyone deserted him and fled.
51 A young man, wearing nothing but
a linen garment, was following Jesus.
When they seized him, 52 he fled naked,
leaving his garment behind.

Before the Sanhedrin

53 They took Jesus to the high priest,
and all the chief priests, elders and
teachers of the law came together. 54 Peter followed him at a distance, right into
the courtyard of the high priest. There
he sat with the guards and warmed
himself at the fire.
55 The chief priests and the whole Sanhedrin were looking for evidence
against Jesus so that they could put him
to death, but they did not find any.
56 Many testified falsely against him, but
their statements did not agree.
57 Then some stood up and gave
this false testimony against him: 58 "We
heard him say, 'I will destroy this man-
made temple and in three days will
build another, not made by man.'" 59 Yet
even then their testimony did not
agree.
60 Then the high priest stood up before
them and asked Jesus, "Are you not going to answer? What is this testimony
that these men are bringing against
you?" 61 But Jesus remained silent and
gave no answer.
Again the high priest asked him, "Are
you the Christ,[a] the Son of the Blessed
One?"
62 "I am," said Jesus. "And you will see
the Son of Man sitting at the right hand
of the Mighty One and coming on the
clouds of heaven."
63 The high priest tore his clothes.
"Why do we need any more witnesses?"
he asked. 64 "You have heard the blasphemy. What do you think?"
They all condemned him as worthy of
death. 65 Then some began to spit at him;
they blindfolded him, struck him with
their fists, and said, "Prophesy!" And
the guards took him and beat him.

Peter Disowns Jesus

66 While Peter was below in the courtyard, one of the servant girls of the high
priest came by. 67 When she saw Peter
warming himself, she looked closely at
him.
"You also were with that Nazarene,
Jesus," she said.
68 But he denied it. "I don't know or
understand what you're talking about,"
he said, and went out into the entryway.[b]
69 When the servant girl saw him
there, she said again to those standing
around, "This fellow is one of them."
70 Again he denied it.
After a little while, those standing
near said to Peter, "Surely you are one
of them, for you are a Galilean."
71 He began to call down curses on

[a]61 Or *Messiah* [b]68 Some early manuscripts *entryway and the rooster crowed*

himself, and he swore to them, "I don't know this man you're talking about."

72 Immediately the rooster crowed the second time.[a] Then Peter remembered the word Jesus had spoken to him: "Before the rooster crows twice[b] you will disown me three times." And he broke down and wept.

SHARPEN THE FOCUS

For several years funeral directors have been selling a service designed to communicate a person's most important thoughts and words to his or her survivors. An interviewer asks a set of questions, and the interviewee responds while a professional camera operator videotapes the conversation. The tape is kept with the person's will to be viewed by the family after the person's death.

Mark 14 records the last thoughts and words of our Savior before His death. Jesus knew this record would be made, and so we know He chose His actions and words with care. Perhaps none of them meant more to Him than those of Mark 14:22–25. None mean more to us either.

We review these words and thoughts each time we kneel to receive the Holy Supper. Here heaven touches earth. Here Jesus Himself speaks His word of forgiveness and gives us His pardon. Here we not only remember our Savior's death, but we receive the very body and blood that made our salvation possible, and with it the strength we need to live more Christlike lives—lives of courage, gentleness, joy, and love.

WEEK 78 • SATURDAY

Mark 15:1–47

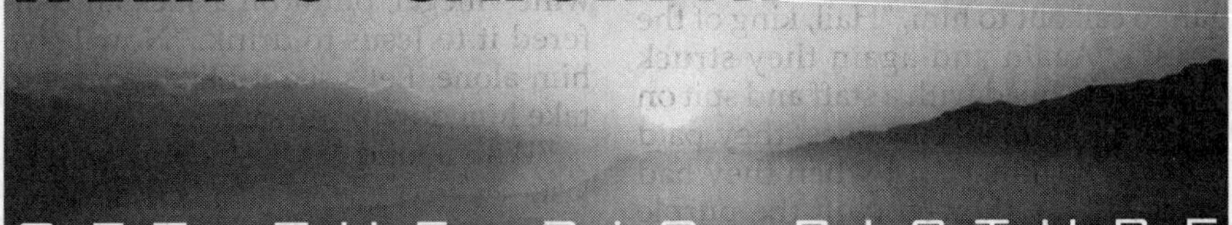

GET THE BIG PICTURE

Absolute and total misery, pain, and rejection. That's what our Lord Jesus endured for you and for me. As you read Mark's account of the crucifixion, find as many aspects of our Lord's suffering as you can. If time is short, focus on Mark 15:24–47.

Jesus Before Pilate

15 Very early in the morning, the chief priests, with the elders, the teachers of the law and the whole Sanhedrin, reached a decision. They bound Jesus, led him away and handed him over to Pilate.

2 "Are you the king of the Jews?" asked Pilate.

"Yes, it is as you say," Jesus replied.

3 The chief priests accused him of many things. 4 So again Pilate asked him, "Aren't you going to answer? See how many things they are accusing you of."

5 But Jesus still made no reply, and Pilate was amazed.

6 Now it was the custom at the Feast to release a prisoner whom the people requested. 7 A man called Barabbas was in prison with the insurrectionists who had committed murder in the uprising. 8 The crowd came up and asked Pilate to do for them what he usually did.

[a]72 Some early manuscripts do not have *the second time.* [b]72 Some early manuscripts do not have *twice.*

9"Do you want me to release to you the king of the Jews?" asked Pilate, 10knowing it was out of envy that the chief priests had handed Jesus over to him. 11But the chief priests stirred up the crowd to have Pilate release Barabbas instead.

12"What shall I do, then, with the one you call the king of the Jews?" Pilate asked them.

13"Crucify him!" they shouted.

14"Why? What crime has he committed?" asked Pilate.

But they shouted all the louder, "Crucify him!"

15Wanting to satisfy the crowd, Pilate released Barabbas to them. He had Jesus flogged, and handed him over to be crucified.

The Soldiers Mock Jesus

16The soldiers led Jesus away into the palace (that is, the Praetorium) and called together the whole company of soldiers. 17They put a purple robe on him, then twisted together a crown of thorns and set it on him. 18And they began to call out to him, "Hail, king of the Jews!" 19Again and again they struck him on the head with a staff and spit on him. Falling on their knees, they paid homage to him. 20And when they had mocked him, they took off the purple robe and put his own clothes on him. Then they led him out to crucify him.

The Crucifixion

21A certain man from Cyrene, Simon, the father of Alexander and Rufus, was passing by on his way in from the country, and they forced him to carry the cross. 22They brought Jesus to the place called Golgotha (which means The Place of the Skull). 23Then they offered him wine mixed with myrrh, but he did not take it. 24And they crucified him. Dividing up his clothes, they cast lots to see what each would get.

25It was the third hour when they crucified him. 26The written notice of the charge against him read: THE KING OF THE JEWS. 27They crucified two robbers with him, one on his right and one on his left.[a] 29Those who passed by hurled insults at him, shaking their heads and saying, "So! You who are going to destroy the temple and build it in three days, 30come down from the cross and save yourself!"

31In the same way the chief priests and the teachers of the law mocked him among themselves. "He saved others," they said, "but he can't save himself! 32Let this Christ,[b] this King of Israel, come down now from the cross, that we may see and believe." Those crucified with him also heaped insults on him.

The Death of Jesus

33At the sixth hour darkness came over the whole land until the ninth hour. 34And at the ninth hour Jesus cried out in a loud voice, *"Eloi, Eloi, lama sabachthani?"*—which means, "My God, my God, why have you forsaken me?"[c]

35When some of those standing near heard this, they said, "Listen, he's calling Elijah."

36One man ran, filled a sponge with wine vinegar, put it on a stick, and offered it to Jesus to drink. "Now leave him alone. Let's see if Elijah comes to take him down," he said.

37With a loud cry, Jesus breathed his last.

38The curtain of the temple was torn in two from top to bottom. 39And when the centurion, who stood there in front of Jesus, heard his cry and[d] saw how he died, he said, "Surely this man was the Son[e] of God!"

40Some women were watching from a distance. Among them were Mary Magdalene, Mary the mother of James the younger and of Joses, and Salome. 41In Galilee these women had followed him and cared for his needs. Many other women who had come up with him to Jerusalem were also there.

[a]27 Some manuscripts *left,* [28]*and the scripture was fulfilled which says, "He was counted with the lawless ones"* (Isaiah 53:12) [b]32 Or *Messiah* [c]34 Psalm 22:1 [d]39 Some manuscripts do not have *heard his cry and* [e]39 Or *a son*

The Burial of Jesus

42It was Preparation Day (that is, the
day before the Sabbath). So as evening
approached, 43Joseph of Arimathea, a
prominent member of the Council, who
was himself waiting for the kingdom of
God, went boldly to Pilate and asked for
Jesus' body. 44Pilate was surprised to
hear that he was already dead. Summoning the centurion, he asked him if
Jesus had already died. 45When he
learned from the centurion that it was
so, he gave the body to Joseph. 46So Joseph bought some linen cloth, took
down the body, wrapped it in the linen,
and placed it in a tomb cut out of rock.
Then he rolled a stone against the entrance of the tomb. 47Mary Magdalene
and Mary the mother of Joses saw
where he was laid.

SHARPEN THE FOCUS

From the loneliness to the scourging to the shame to the agony to the death—Jesus endured it all. But we miss the point unless we see Jesus suffering it in our place. It was my loneliness, my scourging, my shame, my agony, my death that my Lord endured.

He didn't have to do it. At any point along the way He could have called a halt to the whole bloody, agonizing process. But He didn't. He went along. All the way. The hymn writer put it well:

In perfect love He dies
For me. He dies for me!
O all atoning Sacrifice,
I cling by faith to Thee.
(Henry W. Baker)

Theologians have long called this the "vicarious atonement" or "substitutionary atonement." Good words. And true. But until the truth behind them sears our hearts with the fact that Christ's love would not let us go, we miss the point. Until then, Jesus' death remains merely a clinical fact. Our Lord wants it to be a dynamic reality in our lives.

Who else has ever died for you? Who else has ever known you—your most secret sins and all—and still gone on loving you with love that never dims and that will never, ever end? Let that love transform your life forever—starting today.

WEEK 79 • MONDAY

Mark 16:1–20

GET THE BIG PICTURE

Everything had happened just as the Lord Jesus predicted it would—in Mark 9:31; 10:32–34; 14:17–21; and 14:27–30. Now, the last of His predictions would come true, the part the disciples understood least of all, the part about His rising again on the third day. As you read, note Jesus' gentleness, even with their unbelief. If time is short, focus on Mark 16:1–16.

The Resurrection

16 When the Sabbath was over, Mary Magdalene, Mary the mother of James, and Salome bought spices so that they might go to anoint Jesus' body. [2]Very early on the first day of the week, just after sunrise, they were on their way to the tomb [3]and they asked each other, "Who will roll the stone away from the entrance of the tomb?"

[4]But when they looked up, they saw that the stone, which was very large, had been rolled away. [5]As they entered the tomb, they saw a young man dressed in a white robe sitting on the right side, and they were alarmed.

[6]"Don't be alarmed," he said. "You are looking for Jesus the Nazarene, who was crucified. He has risen! He is not here. See the place where they laid him. [7]But go, tell his disciples and Peter, 'He is going ahead of you into Galilee. There you will see him, just as he told you.' "

[8]Trembling and bewildered, the women went out and fled from the tomb. They said nothing to anyone, because they were afraid.

[The earliest manuscripts and some other ancient witnesses do not have Mark 16:9-20.]

[9]When Jesus rose early on the first day of the week, he appeared first to Mary Magdalene, out of whom he had driven seven demons. [10]She went and told those who had been with him and who were mourning and weeping. [11]When they heard that Jesus was alive and that she had seen him, they did not believe it.

[12]Afterward Jesus appeared in a different form to two of them while they were walking in the country. [13]These returned and reported it to the rest; but they did not believe them either.

[14]Later Jesus appeared to the Eleven as they were eating; he rebuked them for their lack of faith and their stubborn refusal to believe those who had seen him after he had risen.

[15]He said to them, "Go into all the world and preach the good news to all creation. [16]Whoever believes and is baptized will be saved, but whoever does not believe will be condemned. [17]And these signs will accompany those who believe: In my name they will drive out demons; they will speak in new tongues; [18]they will pick up snakes with their hands; and when they drink deadly poison, it will not hurt them at all; they will place their hands on sick people, and they will get well."

[19]After the Lord Jesus had spoken to them, he was taken up into heaven and he sat at the right hand of God. [20]Then the disciples went out and preached everywhere, and the Lord worked with them and confirmed his word by the signs that accompanied it.

SHARPEN THE FOCUS

The early church took the world by storm. Those timid disciples hid behind locked doors, afraid to show their faces for fear they'd find themselves on a cross too. But yet, they changed the history of the human race. How?

For one thing, their fear finally gave way to faith. They saw the risen Jesus and believed God had raised Him from the dead! Called by the Servant who had died and risen for them, they began to serve others by sharing the Good News of forgiveness and life in Jesus' name.

Secondly, "the Lord worked with them" (Mark 16:20). He energized their witness and created the faith they could not create.

We, too, can take our world by storm. By God's grace, we too believe Jesus died for all sin and rose again. We, too, can serve others in the name of our suffering and risen Servant, the

Lord Jesus. That same Lord works with us, just as He worked with His early church. He energizes our witness and creates the faith we cannot create. Talk to Jesus today about ways you can be a more faithful witness.

LUKE

WEEK 79 • TUESDAY

Luke 1:1–80

Luke's Gospel displays yet more facets of our Savior's birth, life, death, and resurrection. As you read, notice some of the themes that will recur throughout Luke's book: the trustworthiness of God's Word, the fact that God hears and answers prayer, and above all, the joy God imparts to all the earth in His Son, our Savior. If time is short, focus on Luke 1:26–38.

Introduction

1 Many have undertaken to draw up
an account of the things that have
been fulfilled[a] among us, 2just as they
were handed down to us by those who
from the first were eyewitnesses and
servants of the word. 3Therefore, since
I myself have carefully investigated
everything from the beginning, it
seemed good also to me to write an
orderly account for you, most excellent
Theophilus, 4so that you may know the
certainty of the things you have been
taught.

The Birth of John the Baptist Foretold

5In the time of Herod king of Judea
there was a priest named Zechariah,
who belonged to the priestly division of
Abijah; his wife Elizabeth was also a descendant of Aaron. 6Both of them were
upright in the sight of God, observing
all the Lord's commandments and regulations blamelessly. 7But they had no
children, because Elizabeth was barren;
and they were both well along in years.
8Once when Zechariah's division was
on duty and he was serving as priest before God, 9he was chosen by lot, according to the custom of the priesthood, to
go into the temple of the Lord and burn
incense. 10And when the time for the
burning of incense came, all the assembled worshipers were praying outside.
11Then an angel of the Lord appeared
to him, standing at the right side of the
altar of incense. 12When Zechariah saw
him, he was startled and was gripped
with fear. 13But the angel said to him:
"Do not be afraid, Zechariah; your
prayer has been heard. Your wife Elizabeth will bear you a son, and you are to
give him the name John. 14He will be a
joy and delight to you, and many will
rejoice because of his birth, 15for he will
be great in the sight of the Lord. He is
never to take wine or other fermented
drink, and he will be filled with the Holy
Spirit even from birth.[b] 16Many of the
people of Israel will he bring back to the
Lord their God. 17And he will go on before the Lord, in the spirit and power of
Elijah, to turn the hearts of the fathers
to their children and the disobedient to
the wisdom of the righteous—to make
ready a people prepared for the Lord."
18Zechariah asked the angel, "How
can I be sure of this? I am an old man
and my wife is well along in years."

[a]1 Or *been surely believed* [b]15 Or *from his mother's womb*

19The angel answered, "I am Gabriel. I stand in the presence of God, and I have been sent to speak to you and to tell you this good news. 20And now you will be silent and not able to speak until the day this happens, because you did not believe my words, which will come true at their proper time."

21Meanwhile, the people were waiting for Zechariah and wondering why he stayed so long in the temple. 22When he came out, he could not speak to them. They realized he had seen a vision in the temple, for he kept making signs to them but remained unable to speak.

23When his time of service was completed, he returned home. 24After this his wife Elizabeth became pregnant and for five months remained in seclusion. 25"The Lord has done this for me," she said. "In these days he has shown his favor and taken away my disgrace among the people."

The Birth of Jesus Foretold

26In the sixth month, God sent the angel Gabriel to Nazareth, a town in Galilee, 27to a virgin pledged to be married to a man named Joseph, a descendant of David. The virgin's name was Mary. 28The angel went to her and said, "Greetings, you who are highly favored! The Lord is with you."

29Mary was greatly troubled at his words and wondered what kind of greeting this might be. 30But the angel said to her, "Do not be afraid, Mary, you have found favor with God. 31You will be with child and give birth to a son, and you are to give him the name Jesus. 32He will be great and will be called the Son of the Most High. The Lord God will give him the throne of his father David, 33and he will reign over the house of Jacob forever; his kingdom will never end."

34"How will this be," Mary asked the angel, "since I am a virgin?"

35The angel answered, "The Holy Spirit will come upon you, and the power of the Most High will overshadow you. So the holy one to be born will be called[a] the Son of God. 36Even Elizabeth your relative is going to have a child in her old age, and she who was said to be barren is in her sixth month. 37For nothing is impossible with God."

38"I am the Lord's servant," Mary answered. "May it be to me as you have said." Then the angel left her.

Mary Visits Elizabeth

39At that time Mary got ready and hurried to a town in the hill country of Judea, 40where she entered Zechariah's home and greeted Elizabeth. 41When Elizabeth heard Mary's greeting, the baby leaped in her womb, and Elizabeth was filled with the Holy Spirit. 42In a loud voice she exclaimed: "Blessed are you among women, and blessed is the child you will bear! 43But why am I so favored, that the mother of my Lord should come to me? 44As soon as the sound of your greeting reached my ears, the baby in my womb leaped for joy. 45Blessed is she who has believed that what the Lord has said to her will be accomplished!"

Mary's Song

46And Mary said:

"My soul glorifies the Lord
47 and my spirit rejoices in God my Savior,
48 for he has been mindful
of the humble state of his servant.
From now on all generations will call me blessed,
49 for the Mighty One has done great things for me—
holy is his name.
50 His mercy extends to those who fear him,
from generation to generation.
51 He has performed mighty deeds with his arm;
he has scattered those who are proud in their inmost thoughts.
52 He has brought down rulers from their thrones

[a]35 Or *So the child to be born will be called holy,*

but has lifted up the humble.
53 He has filled the hungry with good things
but has sent the rich away empty.
54 He has helped his servant Israel,
remembering to be merciful
55 to Abraham and his descendants forever,
even as he said to our fathers."

56 Mary stayed with Elizabeth for about three months and then returned home.

The Birth of John the Baptist

57 When it was time for Elizabeth to have her baby, she gave birth to a son.
58 Her neighbors and relatives heard that the Lord had shown her great mercy, and they shared her joy.
59 On the eighth day they came to circumcise the child, and they were going to name him after his father Zechariah,
60 but his mother spoke up and said, "No! He is to be called John."
61 They said to her, "There is no one among your relatives who has that name."
62 Then they made signs to his father, to find out what he would like to name the child.
63 He asked for a writing tablet, and to everyone's astonishment he wrote, "His name is John."
64 Immediately his mouth was opened and his tongue was loosed, and he began to speak, praising God.
65 The neighbors were all filled with awe, and throughout the hill country of Judea people were talking about all these things.
66 Everyone who heard this wondered about it, asking, "What then is this child going to be?" For the Lord's hand was with him.

Zechariah's Song

67 His father Zechariah was filled with the Holy Spirit and prophesied:

68 "Praise be to the Lord, the God of Israel,
because he has come and has redeemed his people.
69 He has raised up a horn[a] of salvation for us
in the house of his servant David
70 (as he said through his holy prophets of long ago),
71 salvation from our enemies
and from the hand of all who hate us—
72 to show mercy to our fathers
and to remember his holy covenant,
73 the oath he swore to our father Abraham:
74 to rescue us from the hand of our enemies,
and to enable us to serve him without fear
75 in holiness and righteousness before him all our days.

76 And you, my child, will be called a prophet of the Most High;
for you will go on before the Lord to prepare the way for him,
77 to give his people the knowledge of salvation
through the forgiveness of their sins,
78 because of the tender mercy of our God,
by which the rising sun will come to us from heaven
79 to shine on those living in darkness
and in the shadow of death,
to guide our feet into the path of peace."

80 And the child grew and became strong in spirit; and he lived in the desert until he appeared publicly to Israel.

[a] *69 Horn* here symbolizes strength.

SHARPEN THE FOCUS

If angels can lose their tempers, Gabriel came close to it as he spoke with Zechariah. We can almost see this holy messenger pull himself up to his full height as he replies to Zechariah's doubt:

I am Gabriel. I stand in the presence of God, and I have been sent to speak to you and to tell you this Good News. (Luke 1:19)

We learn from Scripture that God does not lie, and neither do the angels whom He sends to speak His Word. Zechariah's disbelief robbed him of the joy the Lord wanted him to have in the good news Gabriel brought.

Our own lack of faith often does the same for us. Our Lord has promised never to leave or forsake us. He's promised to provide for all our needs. He's promised to hear our prayers and to keep us safe *in* troubles until He brings us *through* troubles. But like Zechariah, we so often focus on our outward circumstances. We dare to question, "How can I be sure of this?" (Luke 1:18).

Zechariah's unbelief couldn't stop God's holy purpose. Our own lack of faith can't derail God's love toward us either. Zechariah's son, John, would one day point people toward the Lamb of God, come to take away the sin of the world. Zechariah's sin. Your sin. And mine.

Catherine the Great said of her time, "A great wind is blowing, and that gives you either imagination or a headache." The texts you will read today tell of a time when the wind of God's grace blew fresh and clean across the face of the earth. Notice how it ignited the imaginations of God's people, rekindling their hope and joy. If time is short, focus on Luke 3:23–38.

The Birth of Jesus

2 In those days Caesar Augustus issued a decree that a census should be taken of the entire Roman world. 2(This was the first census that took place while Quirinius was governor of Syria.) 3And everyone went to his own town to register.

4So Joseph also went up from the town of Nazareth in Galilee to Judea, to Bethlehem the town of David, because he belonged to the house and line of David. 5He went there to register with Mary, who was pledged to be married to him and was expecting a child. 6While they were there, the time came for the baby to be born, 7and she gave birth to her firstborn, a son. She wrapped him in cloths and placed him in a manger, because there was no room for them in the inn.

The Shepherds and the Angels

8And there were shepherds living out in the fields nearby, keeping watch over their flocks at night. 9An angel of the Lord appeared to them, and the glory of the Lord shone around them, and they were terrified. 10But the angel said to them, "Do not be afraid. I bring you good news of great joy that will be for all the people. 11Today in the town of David a Savior has been born to you; he is Christ[a] the Lord. 12This will be a sign

[a] 11 Or *Messiah.* "The Christ" (Greek) and "the Messiah" (Hebrew) both mean "the Anointed One"; also in verse 26.

to you: You will find a baby wrapped in
cloths and lying in a manger."
13Suddenly a great company of the
heavenly host appeared with the angel,
praising God and saying,

14"Glory to God in the highest,
and on earth peace to men on
whom his favor rests."

15When the angels had left them and
gone into heaven, the shepherds said to
one another, "Let's go to Bethlehem and
see this thing that has happened, which
the Lord has told us about."
16So they hurried off and found Mary
and Joseph, and the baby, who was lying in the manger. 17When they had seen
him, they spread the word concerning
what had been told them about this
child, 18and all who heard it were
amazed at what the shepherds said to
them. 19But Mary treasured up all these
things and pondered them in her heart.
20The shepherds returned, glorifying
and praising God for all the things they
had heard and seen, which were just as
they had been told.

Jesus Presented in the Temple

21On the eighth day, when it was time
to circumcise him, he was named Jesus,
the name the angel had given him before he had been conceived.
22When the time of their purification
according to the Law of Moses had been
completed, Joseph and Mary took him
to Jerusalem to present him to the Lord
23(as it is written in the Law of the Lord,
"Every firstborn male is to be consecrated to the Lord"[a]), 24and to offer a sacrifice in keeping with what is said in the
Law of the Lord: "a pair of doves or two
young pigeons."[b]
25Now there was a man in Jerusalem
called Simeon, who was righteous and
devout. He was waiting for the consolation of Israel, and the Holy Spirit was
upon him. 26It had been revealed to him
by the Holy Spirit that he would not die
before he had seen the Lord's Christ.
27Moved by the Spirit, he went into the
temple courts. When the parents
brought in the child Jesus to do for him
what the custom of the Law required,
28Simeon took him in his arms and
praised God, saying:

29"Sovereign Lord, as you have
promised,
you now dismiss[c] your servant in
peace.
30For my eyes have seen your
salvation,
31 which you have prepared in the
sight of all people,
32a light for revelation to the Gentiles
and for glory to your people
Israel."

33The child's father and mother mar-
veled at what was said about him.
34Then Simeon blessed them and said to
Mary, his mother: "This child is destined
to cause the falling and rising of many
in Israel, and to be a sign that will be
spoken against, 35so that the thoughts of
many hearts will be revealed. And a
sword will pierce your own soul too."
36There was also a prophetess, Anna,
the daughter of Phanuel, of the tribe of
Asher. She was very old; she had lived
with her husband seven years after her
marriage, 37and then was a widow until
she was eighty-four.[d] She never left the
temple but worshiped night and day,
fasting and praying. 38Coming up to
them at that very moment, she gave
thanks to God and spoke about the child
to all who were looking forward to the
redemption of Jerusalem.
39When Joseph and Mary had done
everything required by the Law of the
Lord, they returned to Galilee to their
own town of Nazareth. 40And the child
grew and became strong; he was filled
with wisdom, and the grace of God was
upon him.

The Boy Jesus at the Temple

41Every year his parents went to Jerusalem for the Feast of the Passover.
42When he was twelve years old, they
went up to the Feast, according to the

[a]23 Exodus 13:2,12 [b]24 Lev. 12:8 [c]29 Or *promised, / now dismiss* [d]37 Or *widow for eighty-four years*

custom. 43After the Feast was over, while his parents were returning home, the boy Jesus stayed behind in Jerusalem, but they were unaware of it. 44Thinking he was in their company, they traveled on for a day. Then they began looking for him among their relatives and friends. 45When they did not find him, they went back to Jerusalem to look for him. 46After three days they found him in the temple courts, sitting among the teachers, listening to them and asking them questions. 47Everyone who heard him was amazed at his understanding and his answers. 48When his parents saw him, they were astonished. His mother said to him, "Son, why have you treated us like this? Your father and I have been anxiously searching for you."

49"Why were you searching for me?" he asked. "Didn't you know I had to be in my Father's house?" 50But they did not understand what he was saying to them.

51Then he went down to Nazareth with them and was obedient to them. But his mother treasured all these things in her heart. 52And Jesus grew in wisdom and stature, and in favor with God and men.

John the Baptist Prepares the Way

3 In the fifteenth year of the reign of Tiberius Caesar—when Pontius Pilate was governor of Judea, Herod tetrarch of Galilee, his brother Philip tetrarch of Iturea and Traconitis, and Lysanias tetrarch of Abilene— 2during the high priesthood of Annas and Caiaphas, the word of God came to John son of Zechariah in the desert. 3He went into all the country around the Jordan, preaching a baptism of repentance for the forgiveness of sins. 4As is written in the book of the words of Isaiah the prophet:

"A voice of one calling in the desert,
'Prepare the way for the Lord,
make straight paths for him.
5Every valley shall be filled in,
every mountain and hill made low.
The crooked roads shall become straight,
the rough ways smooth.
6And all mankind will see God's salvation.' "[a]

7John said to the crowds coming out to be baptized by him, "You brood of vipers! Who warned you to flee from the coming wrath? 8Produce fruit in keeping with repentance. And do not begin to say to yourselves, 'We have Abraham as our father.' For I tell you that out of these stones God can raise up children for Abraham. 9The ax is already at the root of the trees, and every tree that does not produce good fruit will be cut down and thrown into the fire."

10"What should we do then?" the crowd asked.

11John answered, "The man with two tunics should share with him who has none, and the one who has food should do the same."

12Tax collectors also came to be baptized. "Teacher," they asked, "what should we do?"

13"Don't collect any more than you are required to," he told them.

14Then some soldiers asked him, "And what should we do?"

He replied, "Don't extort money and don't accuse people falsely—be content with your pay."

15The people were waiting expectantly and were all wondering in their hearts if John might possibly be the Christ.[b] 16John answered them all, "I baptize you with[c] water. But one more powerful than I will come, the thongs of whose sandals I am not worthy to untie. He will baptize you with the Holy Spirit and with fire. 17His winnowing fork is in his hand to clear his threshing floor and to gather the wheat into his barn, but he will burn up the chaff with unquenchable fire." 18And with many other words John exhorted the people and preached the good news to them.

19But when John rebuked Herod the tetrarch because of Herodias, his

[a]6 Isaiah 40:3-5 [b]15 Or *Messiah* [c]16 Or *in*

brother's wife, and all the other evil
things he had done, [20]Herod added
this to them all: He locked John up in
prison.

The Baptism and Genealogy of Jesus

[21]When all the people were being baptized, Jesus was baptized too. And as he
was praying, heaven was opened [22]and
the Holy Spirit descended on him in
bodily form like a dove. And a voice
came from heaven: "You are my Son,
whom I love; with you I am well
pleased."
[23]Now Jesus himself was about thirty
years old when he began his ministry.
He was the son, so it was thought, of
Joseph,

the son of Heli, [24]the son of Matthat,
the son of Levi, the son of Melki,
the son of Jannai, the son of Joseph,
[25]the son of Mattathias, the son of
Amos,
the son of Nahum, the son of Esli,
the son of Naggai, [26]the son of Ma-
ath,
the son of Mattathias, the son of
Semein,
the son of Josech, the son of Joda,
[27]the son of Joanan, the son of
Rhesa,
the son of Zerubbabel, the son of
Shealtiel,
the son of Neri, [28]the son of Melki,
the son of Addi, the son of Cosam,
the son of Elmadam, the son of Er,
[29]the son of Joshua, the son of Eliezer,
the son of Jorim, the son of Matthat,
the son of Levi, [30]the son of Simeon,
the son of Judah, the son of Joseph,
the son of Jonam, the son of Eliakim,
[31]the son of Melea, the son of Men-
na,
the son of Mattatha, the son of Nathan,
the son of David, [32]the son of Jesse,
the son of Obed, the son of Boaz,
the son of Salmon,[a] the son of Nahshon,
[33]the son of Amminadab, the son of
Ram,[b]
the son of Hezron, the son of Perez,
the son of Judah, [34]the son of Jacob,
the son of Isaac, the son of Abraham,
the son of Terah, the son of Nahor,
[35]the son of Serug, the son of Reu,
the son of Peleg, the son of Eber,
the son of Shelah, [36]the son of Cainan,
the son of Arphaxad, the son of
Shem,
the son of Noah, the son of Lamech,
[37]the son of Methuselah, the son of
Enoch,
the son of Jared, the son of Mahalalel,
the son of Kenan, [38]the son of
Enosh,
the son of Seth, the son of Adam,
the son of God.

[a]32 Some early manuscripts *Sala* [b]33 Some manuscripts *Amminadab, the son of Admin, the son of Arni*; other manuscripts vary widely.

SHARPEN THE FOCUS

In the years before Jesus' birth, God's people had known much trouble and sorrow. For centuries, the sins of the nation blew hot across the land, like desert winds. Idolatry. Immorality. Indifference to God's Word and ways. As Luke's gospel opens, 400 years had passed since the last prophet had spoken in Israel. Four centuries of spiritual drought!

Like a cool breeze that blows from an approaching thunderstorm, God began to put in place the final pieces of His plan to rescue the human race. Now the rain of God's pardon and peace had begun to fall. It would fill the earth with the fruit of repentance and faith. (Isaiah 27:2, 6).

Jesus came as the Son of Man, the second Adam (Luke 3:38). He kept all the Old Testament ceremonial laws (Luke 2:39); He grew in grace (Luke 2:40); He respected and learned God's Word, reverencing the Father's house (Luke 2:49); He obeyed all earthly authority (Luke 2:51); He stood in Jordan's baptismal waters (Luke 3:21–22). All this He did *in our place*.

The first Adam left us with sin and death. The second Adam gives us His holy life and right standing with the heavenly Father. Rejoice in that as you read Romans 5:18–19—Good News, fresh from the heart of God!

WEEK 79 • THURSDAY

Luke 4:1—5:39

Jesus Christ was—and is—God's expression of love to a world broken by sin. Today you will walk along with Jesus as He takes the first steps in His earthly ministry. As you read, look for ways He shows the Father's compassion. If time is short, focus on Luke 4:16–37.

The Temptation of Jesus

4 Jesus, full of the Holy Spirit, returned from the Jordan and was
led by the Spirit in the desert, 2where for
forty days he was tempted by the devil.
He ate nothing during those days, and
at the end of them he was hungry.
3The devil said to him, "If you are the
Son of God, tell this stone to become
bread."
4Jesus answered, "It is written: 'Man
does not live on bread alone.'[a]"
5The devil led him up to a high place
and showed him in an instant all the
kingdoms of the world. 6And he said to
him, "I will give you all their authority
and splendor, for it has been given to
me, and I can give it to anyone I want
to. 7So if you worship me, it will all be
yours."
8Jesus answered, "It is written: 'Worship the Lord your God and serve him
only.'[b]"
9The devil led him to Jerusalem and
had him stand on the highest point of
the temple. "If you are the Son of God,"
he said, "throw yourself down from
here. 10For it is written:

" 'He will command his angels
concerning you
to guard you carefully;
11they will lift you up in their hands,
so that you will not strike your
foot against a stone.'[c]"

12Jesus answered, "It says: 'Do not put
the Lord your God to the test.'[d]"
13When the devil had finished all this
tempting, he left him until an opportune time.

Jesus Rejected at Nazareth

14Jesus returned to Galilee in the power of the Spirit, and news about him
spread through the whole countryside.
15He taught in their synagogues, and everyone praised him.
16He went to Nazareth, where he had
been brought up, and on the Sabbath
day he went into the synagogue, as was
his custom. And he stood up to read.
17The scroll of the prophet Isaiah was
handed to him. Unrolling it, he found
the place where it is written:

18"The Spirit of the Lord is on me,
because he has anointed me
to preach good news to the poor.

[a]4 Deut. 8:3 [b]8 Deut. 6:13 [c]11 Psalm 91:11,12
[d]12 Deut. 6:16

He has sent me to proclaim freedom
for the prisoners
and recovery of sight for the
blind,
to release the oppressed,
19 to proclaim the year of the Lord's
favor."[a]

20 Then he rolled up the scroll, gave it
back to the attendant and sat down. The
eyes of everyone in the synagogue were
fastened on him, 21 and he began by saying to them, "Today this scripture is fulfilled in your hearing."
22 All spoke well of him and were
amazed at the gracious words that came
from his lips. "Isn't this Joseph's son?"
they asked.
23 Jesus said to them, "Surely you will
quote this proverb to me: 'Physician,
heal yourself! Do here in your hometown what we have heard that you did
in Capernaum.'"
24 "I tell you the truth," he continued,
"no prophet is accepted in his hometown. 25 I assure you that there were
many widows in Israel in Elijah's time,
when the sky was shut for three and a
half years and there was a severe famine throughout the land. 26 Yet Elijah was
not sent to any of them, but to a widow
in Zarephath in the region of Sidon.
27 And there were many in Israel with
leprosy[b] in the time of Elisha the prophet, yet not one of them was cleansed—
only Naaman the Syrian."
28 All the people in the synagogue
were furious when they heard this.
29 They got up, drove him out of the
town, and took him to the brow of the
hill on which the town was built, in order to throw him down the cliff. 30 But he
walked right through the crowd and
went on his way.

Jesus Drives Out an Evil Spirit

31 Then he went down to Capernaum,
a town in Galilee, and on the Sabbath
began to teach the people. 32 They were
amazed at his teaching, because his
message had authority.
33 In the synagogue there was a man
possessed by a demon, an evil[c] spirit. He
cried out at the top of his voice, 34 "Ha!
What do you want with us, Jesus of
Nazareth? Have you come to destroy
us? I know who you are—the Holy One
of God!"
35 "Be quiet!" Jesus said sternly. "Come
out of him!" Then the demon threw the
man down before them all and came out
without injuring him.
36 All the people were amazed and
said to each other, "What is this teaching? With authority and power he gives
orders to evil spirits and they come out!"
37 And the news about him spread
throughout the surrounding area.

Jesus Heals Many

38 Jesus left the synagogue and went to
the home of Simon. Now Simon's mother-in-law was suffering from a high fever, and they asked Jesus to help her.
39 So he bent over her and rebuked the
fever, and it left her. She got up at once
and began to wait on them.
40 When the sun was setting, the people brought to Jesus all who had various
kinds of sickness, and laying his hands
on each one, he healed them. 41 Moreover, demons came out of many people,
shouting, "You are the Son of God!" But
he rebuked them and would not allow
them to speak, because they knew he
was the Christ.[d]
42 At daybreak Jesus went out to a solitary place. The people were looking for
him and when they came to where he
was, they tried to keep him from leaving them. 43 But he said, "I must preach
the good news of the kingdom of God
to the other towns also, because that is
why I was sent." 44 And he kept on
preaching in the synagogues of Judea.[e]

The Calling of the First Disciples

5 One day as Jesus was standing
by the Lake of Gennesaret,[f] with
the people crowding around him and

[a]*19* Isaiah 61:1,2 [b]*27* The Greek word was used for various diseases affecting the skin—not necessarily leprosy. [c]*33* Greek *unclean;* also in verse 36 [d]*41* Or *Messiah* [e]*44* Or *the land of the Jews;* some manuscripts *Galilee* [f]*1* That is, Sea of Galilee

listening to the word of God, 2he saw at the water's edge two boats, left there by the fishermen, who were washing their nets. 3He got into one of the boats, the one belonging to Simon, and asked him to put out a little from shore. Then he sat down and taught the people from the boat.

4When he had finished speaking, he said to Simon, "Put out into deep water, and let down[a] the nets for a catch."

5Simon answered, "Master, we've worked hard all night and haven't caught anything. But because you say so, I will let down the nets."

6When they had done so, they caught such a large number of fish that their nets began to break. 7So they signaled their partners in the other boat to come and help them, and they came and filled both boats so full that they began to sink.

8When Simon Peter saw this, he fell at Jesus' knees and said, "Go away from me, Lord; I am a sinful man!" 9For he and all his companions were astonished at the catch of fish they had taken, 10and so were James and John, the sons of Zebedee, Simon's partners.

Then Jesus said to Simon, "Don't be afraid; from now on you will catch men." 11So they pulled their boats up on shore, left everything and followed him.

The Man With Leprosy

12While Jesus was in one of the towns, a man came along who was covered with leprosy.[b] When he saw Jesus, he fell with his face to the ground and begged him, "Lord, if you are willing, you can make me clean."

13Jesus reached out his hand and touched the man. "I am willing," he said. "Be clean!" And immediately the leprosy left him.

14Then Jesus ordered him, "Don't tell anyone, but go, show yourself to the priest and offer the sacrifices that Moses commanded for your cleansing, as a testimony to them."

15Yet the news about him spread all the more, so that crowds of people came to hear him and to be healed of their sicknesses. 16But Jesus often withdrew to lonely places and prayed.

Jesus Heals a Paralytic

17One day as he was teaching, Pharisees and teachers of the law, who had come from every village of Galilee and from Judea and Jerusalem, were sitting there. And the power of the Lord was present for him to heal the sick. 18Some men came carrying a paralytic on a mat and tried to take him into the house to lay him before Jesus. 19When they could not find a way to do this because of the crowd, they went up on the roof and lowered him on his mat through the tiles into the middle of the crowd, right in front of Jesus.

20When Jesus saw their faith, he said, "Friend, your sins are forgiven."

21The Pharisees and the teachers of the law began thinking to themselves, "Who is this fellow who speaks blasphemy? Who can forgive sins but God alone?"

22Jesus knew what they were thinking and asked, "Why are you thinking these things in your hearts? 23Which is easier: to say, 'Your sins are forgiven,' or to say, 'Get up and walk'? 24But that you may know that the Son of Man has authority on earth to forgive sins . . ." He said to the paralyzed man, "I tell you, get up, take your mat and go home." 25Immediately he stood up in front of them, took what he had been lying on and went home praising God. 26Everyone was amazed and gave praise to God. They were filled with awe and said, "We have seen remarkable things today."

The Calling of Levi

27After this, Jesus went out and saw a tax collector by the name of Levi sitting at his tax booth. "Follow me," Jesus said to him, 28and Levi got up, left everything and followed him.

29Then Levi held a great banquet for Jesus at his house, and a large crowd of

[a]4 The Greek verb is plural. [b]12 The Greek word was used for various diseases affecting the skin—not necessarily leprosy.

tax collectors and others were eating with them. 30But the Pharisees and the teachers of the law who belonged to their sect complained to his disciples, "Why do you eat and drink with tax collectors and 'sinners'?"

31Jesus answered them, "It is not the healthy who need a doctor, but the sick. 32I have not come to call the righteous, but sinners to repentance."

Jesus Questioned About Fasting

33They said to him, "John's disciples often fast and pray, and so do the disciples of the Pharisees, but yours go on eating and drinking."

34Jesus answered, "Can you make the guests of the bridegroom fast while he is with them? 35But the time will come when the bridegroom will be taken from them; in those days they will fast."

36He told them this parable: "No one tears a patch from a new garment and sews it on an old one. If he does, he will have torn the new garment, and the patch from the new will not match the old. 37And no one pours new wine into old wineskins. If he does, the new wine will burst the skins, the wine will run out and the wineskins will be ruined. 38No, new wine must be poured into new wineskins. 39And no one after drinking old wine wants the new, for he says, 'The old is better.'"

SHARPEN THE FOCUS

Home Town Boy Makes Good. That's how the headlines would have read in Nazareth a few months into Jesus' ministry. As He traveled through the surrounding countryside, everyone praised Him (Luke 4:15). When He returned home, His former playmates greeted Him with chest-swelling pride. He was becoming a homegrown success (Luke 4:22).

And yet, six verses later, those same people became a lynch mob. If they had gotten their way that day, our Savior's ministry would have lasted three months instead of three years (Luke 4:28–29). What accounts for the change in attitude?

Consider this headline: *Home Town Boy Tells the Truth.* Then look at Luke 4:23–27. Jesus begins His sermon by citing two believing Gentiles whom God had blessed. "Your race, your religious heritage, even growing up beside Me don't make you worthy of God's love," He warned by these examples.

Jesus no doubt planned to go on to explain that the heavenly Father wanted to bless them, too, as He had blessed the two Gentiles. He wanted to give them repentance and faith in the Messiah whose life-mission He had read to them from Isaiah (Luke 4:18–19). But the congregation had flown into a rage. The sermon ended as they evicted their preacher.

WEEK 79 • FRIDAY

Luke 6:1–49

GET THE BIG PICTURE

Paul wrote, "It is for freedom that Christ has set us free. Stand firm, then, and do not let yourselves be burdened again by a yoke of slavery" (Galatians 5:1). Notice, as you read today, how Jesus lived and taught the freedom Paul later wrote about. If time is short, focus on Luke 6:1–11.

Lord of the Sabbath

6 One Sabbath Jesus was going through the grainfields, and his disciples began to pick some heads of grain, rub them in their hands and eat the kernels. 2Some of the Pharisees asked, "Why are you doing what is unlawful on the Sabbath?"

3Jesus answered them, "Have you never read what David did when he and his companions were hungry? 4He entered the house of God, and taking the consecrated bread, he ate what is lawful only for priests to eat. And he also gave some to his companions." 5Then Jesus said to them, "The Son of Man is Lord of the Sabbath."

6On another Sabbath he went into the synagogue and was teaching, and a man was there whose right hand was shriveled. 7The Pharisees and the teachers of the law were looking for a reason to accuse Jesus, so they watched him closely to see if he would heal on the Sabbath. 8But Jesus knew what they were thinking and said to the man with the shriveled hand, "Get up and stand in front of everyone." So he got up and stood there.

9Then Jesus said to them, "I ask you, which is lawful on the Sabbath: to do good or to do evil, to save life or to destroy it?"

10He looked around at them all, and then said to the man, "Stretch out your hand." He did so, and his hand was completely restored. 11But they were furious and began to discuss with one another what they might do to Jesus.

The Twelve Apostles

12One of those days Jesus went out to a mountainside to pray, and spent the night praying to God. 13When morning came, he called his disciples to him and chose twelve of them, whom he also designated apostles: 14Simon (whom he named Peter), his brother Andrew, James, John, Philip, Bartholomew, 15Matthew, Thomas, James son of Alphaeus, Simon who was called the Zealot, 16Judas son of James, and Judas Iscariot, who became a traitor.

Blessings and Woes

17He went down with them and stood on a level place. A large crowd of his disciples was there and a great number of people from all over Judea, from Jerusalem, and from the coast of Tyre and Sidon, 18who had come to hear him and to be healed of their diseases. Those troubled by evil[a] spirits were cured, 19and the people all tried to touch him, because power was coming from him and healing them all.

20Looking at his disciples, he said:

"Blessed are you who are poor,
for yours is the kingdom of God.
21Blessed are you who hunger now,
for you will be satisfied.
Blessed are you who weep now,
for you will laugh.
22Blessed are you when men hate you,
when they exclude you and insult you
and reject your name as evil,
because of the Son of Man.

23"Rejoice in that day and leap for joy, because great is your reward in heaven. For that is how their fathers treated the prophets.

24"But woe to you who are rich,
for you have already received your comfort.
25Woe to you who are well fed now,
for you will go hungry.
Woe to you who laugh now,
for you will mourn and weep.
26Woe to you when all men speak well of you,
for that is how their fathers treated the false prophets.

[a]18 Greek *unclean*

Love for Enemies

27"But I tell you who hear me: Love your enemies, do good to those who hate you, 28bless those who curse you, pray for those who mistreat you. 29If someone strikes you on one cheek, turn to him the other also. If someone takes your cloak, do not stop him from taking your tunic. 30Give to everyone who asks you, and if anyone takes what belongs to you, do not demand it back. 31Do to others as you would have them do to you.

32"If you love those who love you, what credit is that to you? Even 'sinners' love those who love them. 33And if you do good to those who are good to you, what credit is that to you? Even 'sinners' do that. 34And if you lend to those from whom you expect repayment, what credit is that to you? Even 'sinners' lend to 'sinners,' expecting to be repaid in full. 35But love your enemies, do good to them, and lend to them without expecting to get anything back. Then your reward will be great, and you will be sons of the Most High, because he is kind to the ungrateful and wicked. 36Be merciful, just as your Father is merciful.

Judging Others

37"Do not judge, and you will not be judged. Do not condemn, and you will not be condemned. Forgive, and you will be forgiven. 38Give, and it will be given to you. A good measure, pressed down, shaken together and running over, will be poured into your lap. For with the measure you use, it will be measured to you."

39He also told them this parable: "Can a blind man lead a blind man? Will they not both fall into a pit? 40A student is not above his teacher, but everyone who is fully trained will be like his teacher.

41"Why do you look at the speck of sawdust in your brother's eye and pay no attention to the plank in your own eye? 42How can you say to your brother, 'Brother, let me take the speck out of your eye,' when you yourself fail to see the plank in your own eye? You hypocrite, first take the plank out of your eye, and then you will see clearly to remove the speck from your brother's eye.

A Tree and Its Fruit

43"No good tree bears bad fruit, nor does a bad tree bear good fruit. 44Each tree is recognized by its own fruit. People do not pick figs from thornbushes, or grapes from briers. 45The good man brings good things out of the good stored up in his heart, and the evil man brings evil things out of the evil stored up in his heart. For out of the overflow of his heart his mouth speaks.

The Wise and Foolish Builders

46"Why do you call me, 'Lord, Lord,' and do not do what I say? 47I will show you what he is like who comes to me and hears my words and puts them into practice. 48He is like a man building a house, who dug down deep and laid the foundation on rock. When a flood came, the torrent struck that house but could not shake it, because it was well built. 49But the one who hears my words and does not put them into practice is like a man who built a house on the ground without a foundation. The moment the torrent struck that house, it collapsed and its destruction was complete."

SHARPEN THE FOCUS

Imagine a fruit tree standing in a fertile, well-watered orchard. Does such a tree ever plot its escape? Does a tree like that worry about a cruel orchard owner who demands that it produce 20 bushels of fruit—or else?

Of course not. It simply soaks up the sunshine and does what comes naturally. You no doubt see the connection to Jesus words in Luke 6:43. We are those "good trees" He talked about.

Rooted in Him by faith, we bear good fruit. We live fruitful, productive lives because we *can* through Christ, because we *get* to. Not because we *have* to.

It's so easy to lose our grip on that truth. It's so easy to live a life of have-tos, of slavery, of guilt. Maybe we forget we already have God's approval in Christ. So we slave away at trying to win it. Or maybe we find ourselves burdened by a need to please other people so we slave at keeping their rules or at trying to get them to keep ours (Luke 6:1–11).

If your life filled with *musts* and *have-tos,* talk to your Lord about it. He'll shift your attitude so that some of those demands become delights. His promises will enable you to drop some of the drudgery. His grace will strengthen you as you rearrange your whole lifestyle.

WEEK 79 • SATURDAY

Luke 7:1—8:56

Luke, long known as "the beloved physician," records summaries of Jesus healing ministry (e.g., Luke 6:17–19; 8:1–2) and also case histories of individual healings (see Luke 7:1–10; 7:11–16). As you read, note Jesus' compassion. Also note all the different kinds of people touched by that compassion. If time is short, focus on Luke 7:36–50.

The Faith of the Centurion

7 When Jesus had finished saying
all this in the hearing of the
people, he entered Capernaum. 2There
a centurion's servant, whom his master
valued highly, was sick and about to die.
3The centurion heard of Jesus and sent
some elders of the Jews to him, asking
him to come and heal his servant.
4When they came to Jesus, they pleaded
earnestly with him, "This man deserves
to have you do this, 5because he loves
our nation and has built our synagogue." 6So Jesus went with them.
He was not far from the house when
the centurion sent friends to say to him:
"Lord, don't trouble yourself, for I do
not deserve to have you come under my
roof. 7That is why I did not even consider myself worthy to come to you. But
say the word, and my servant will be
healed. 8For I myself am a man under
authority, with soldiers under me. I tell
this one, 'Go,' and he goes; and that one,
'Come,' and he comes. I say to my servant, 'Do this,' and he does it."
9When Jesus heard this, he was
amazed at him, and turning to the
crowd following him, he said, "I tell
you, I have not found such great faith
even in Israel." 10Then the men who had
been sent returned to the house and
found the servant well.

Jesus Raises a Widow's Son

11Soon afterward, Jesus went to a
town called Nain, and his disciples and
a large crowd went along with him. 12As
he approached the town gate, a dead
person was being carried out—the only
son of his mother, and she was a widow.
And a large crowd from the town was
with her. 13When the Lord saw her, his
heart went out to her and he said,
"Don't cry."
14Then he went up and touched the
coffin, and those carrying it stood still.
He said, "Young man, I say to you, get

up!" [15]The dead man sat up and began
to talk, and Jesus gave him back to his
mother.

[16]They were all filled with awe and
praised God. "A great prophet has appeared among us," they said. "God has
come to help his people." [17]This news
about Jesus spread throughout Judea[a]
and the surrounding country.

Jesus and John the Baptist

[18]John's disciples told him about all
these things. Calling two of them, [19]he
sent them to the Lord to ask, "Are you
the one who was to come, or should we
expect someone else?"

[20]When the men came to Jesus, they
said, "John the Baptist sent us to you to
ask, 'Are you the one who was to come,
or should we expect someone else?' "

[21]At that very time Jesus cured many
who had diseases, sicknesses and evil
spirits, and gave sight to many who
were blind. [22]So he replied to the messengers, "Go back and report to John
what you have seen and heard: The
blind receive sight, the lame walk, those
who have leprosy[b] are cured, the deaf
hear, the dead are raised, and the good
news is preached to the poor. [23]Blessed
is the man who does not fall away on account of me."

[24]After John's messengers left, Jesus
began to speak to the crowd about John:
"What did you go out into the desert to
see? A reed swayed by the wind? [25]If
not, what did you go out to see? A man
dressed in fine clothes? No, those who
wear expensive clothes and indulge in
luxury are in palaces. [26]But what did you
go out to see? A prophet? Yes, I tell you,
and more than a prophet. [27]This is the
one about whom it is written:

" 'I will send my messenger ahead of
you,
who will prepare your way before
you.'[c]

[28]I tell you, among those born of wom-
en there is no one greater than John; yet
the one who is least in the kingdom of
God is greater than he."

[29](All the people, even the tax collectors, when they heard Jesus' words, acknowledged that God's way was right,
because they had been baptized by
John. [30]But the Pharisees and experts in
the law rejected God's purpose for
themselves, because they had not been
baptized by John.)

[31]"To what, then, can I compare the
people of this generation? What are
they like? [32]They are like children sitting
in the marketplace and calling out to
each other:

" 'We played the flute for you,
and you did not dance;
we sang a dirge,
and you did not cry.'

[33]For John the Baptist came neither eating bread nor drinking wine, and you
say, 'He has a demon.' [34]The Son of Man
came eating and drinking, and you say,
'Here is a glutton and a drunkard, a
friend of tax collectors and "sinners." '
[35]But wisdom is proved right by all her
children."

Jesus Anointed by a Sinful Woman

[36]Now one of the Pharisees invited
Jesus to have dinner with him, so he
went to the Pharisee's house and reclined at the table. [37]When a woman
who had lived a sinful life in that town
learned that Jesus was eating at the
Pharisee's house, she brought an alabaster jar of perfume, [38]and as she stood
behind him at his feet weeping, she began to wet his feet with her tears. Then
she wiped them with her hair, kissed
them and poured perfume on them.

[39]When the Pharisee who had invited
him saw this, he said to himself, "If this
man were a prophet, he would know
who is touching him and what kind of
woman she is—that she is a sinner."

[40]Jesus answered him, "Simon, I have
something to tell you."

"Tell me, teacher," he said.

[41]"Two men owed money to a certain
moneylender. One owed him five hun-

[a]17 Or *the land of the Jews* [b]22 The Greek word was used for various diseases affecting the skin—not necessarily leprosy. [c]27 Mal. 3:1

dred denarii,[a] and the other fifty. 42Neither of them had the money to pay him back, so he canceled the debts of both. Now which of them will love him more?"

43Simon replied, "I suppose the one who had the bigger debt canceled."

"You have judged correctly," Jesus said.

44Then he turned toward the woman and said to Simon, "Do you see this woman? I came into your house. You did not give me any water for my feet, but she wet my feet with her tears and wiped them with her hair. 45You did not give me a kiss, but this woman, from the time I entered, has not stopped kissing my feet. 46You did not put oil on my head, but she has poured perfume on my feet. 47Therefore, I tell you, her many sins have been forgiven—for she loved much. But he who has been forgiven little loves little."

48Then Jesus said to her, "Your sins are forgiven."

49The other guests began to say among themselves, "Who is this who even forgives sins?"

50Jesus said to the woman, "Your faith has saved you; go in peace."

The Parable of the Sower

8 After this, Jesus traveled about from one town and village to another, proclaiming the good news of the kingdom of God. The Twelve were with him, 2and also some women who had been cured of evil spirits and diseases: Mary (called Magdalene) from whom seven demons had come out; 3Joanna the wife of Cuza, the manager of Herod's household; Susanna; and many others. These women were helping to support them out of their own means.

4While a large crowd was gathering and people were coming to Jesus from town after town, he told this parable: 5"A farmer went out to sow his seed. As he was scattering the seed, some fell along the path; it was trampled on, and the birds of the air ate it up. 6Some fell on rock, and when it came up, the plants withered because they had no moisture. 7Other seed fell among thorns, which grew up with it and choked the plants. 8Still other seed fell on good soil. It came up and yielded a crop, a hundred times more than was sown."

When he said this, he called out, "He who has ears to hear, let him hear."

9His disciples asked him what this parable meant. 10He said, "The knowledge of the secrets of the kingdom of God has been given to you, but to others I speak in parables, so that,

"'though seeing, they may not see;
though hearing, they may not
understand.'[b]

11"This is the meaning of the parable: The seed is the word of God. 12Those along the path are the ones who hear, and then the devil comes and takes away the word from their hearts, so that they may not believe and be saved. 13Those on the rock are the ones who receive the word with joy when they hear it, but they have no root. They believe for a while, but in the time of testing they fall away. 14The seed that fell among thorns stands for those who hear, but as they go on their way they are choked by life's worries, riches and pleasures, and they do not mature. 15But the seed on good soil stands for those with a noble and good heart, who hear the word, retain it, and by persevering produce a crop.

A Lamp on a Stand

16"No one lights a lamp and hides it in a jar or puts it under a bed. Instead, he puts it on a stand, so that those who come in can see the light. 17For there is nothing hidden that will not be disclosed, and nothing concealed that will not be known or brought out into the open. 18Therefore consider carefully how you listen. Whoever has will be given more; whoever does not have, even what he thinks he has will be taken from him."

[a]*41* A denarius was a coin worth about a day's wages. [b]*10* Isaiah 6:9

Jesus' Mother and Brothers

19Now Jesus' mother and brothers came to see him, but they were not able to get near him because of the crowd. 20Someone told him, "Your mother and brothers are standing outside, wanting to see you."

21He replied, "My mother and brothers are those who hear God's word and put it into practice."

Jesus Calms the Storm

22One day Jesus said to his disciples, "Let's go over to the other side of the lake." So they got into a boat and set out. 23As they sailed, he fell asleep. A squall came down on the lake, so that the boat was being swamped, and they were in great danger.

24The disciples went and woke him, saying, "Master, Master, we're going to drown!"

He got up and rebuked the wind and the raging waters; the storm subsided, and all was calm. 25"Where is your faith?" he asked his disciples.

In fear and amazement they asked one another, "Who is this? He commands even the winds and the water, and they obey him."

The Healing of a Demon-possessed Man

26They sailed to the region of the Gerasenes,[a] which is across the lake from Galilee. 27When Jesus stepped ashore, he was met by a demon-possessed man from the town. For a long time this man had not worn clothes or lived in a house, but had lived in the tombs. 28When he saw Jesus, he cried out and fell at his feet, shouting at the top of his voice, "What do you want with me, Jesus, Son of the Most High God? I beg you, don't torture me!" 29For Jesus had commanded the evil[b] spirit to come out of the man. Many times it had seized him, and though he was chained hand and foot and kept under guard, he had broken his chains and had been driven by the demon into solitary places.

30Jesus asked him, "What is your name?"

"Legion," he replied, because many demons had gone into him. 31And they begged him repeatedly not to order them to go into the Abyss.

32A large herd of pigs was feeding there on the hillside. The demons begged Jesus to let them go into them, and he gave them permission. 33When the demons came out of the man, they went into the pigs, and the herd rushed down the steep bank into the lake and was drowned.

34When those tending the pigs saw what had happened, they ran off and reported this in the town and countryside, 35and the people went out to see what had happened. When they came to Jesus, they found the man from whom the demons had gone out, sitting at Jesus' feet, dressed and in his right mind; and they were afraid. 36Those who had seen it told the people how the demon-possessed man had been cured. 37Then all the people of the region of the Gerasenes asked Jesus to leave them, because they were overcome with fear. So he got into the boat and left.

38The man from whom the demons had gone out begged to go with him, but Jesus sent him away, saying, 39"Return home and tell how much God has done for you." So the man went away and told all over town how much Jesus had done for him.

A Dead Girl and a Sick Woman

40Now when Jesus returned, a crowd welcomed him, for they were all expecting him. 41Then a man named Jairus, a ruler of the synagogue, came and fell at Jesus' feet, pleading with him to come to his house 42because his only daughter, a girl of about twelve, was dying.

As Jesus was on his way, the crowds almost crushed him. 43And a woman was there who had been subject to bleeding for twelve years,[c] but no

[a]26 Some manuscripts *Gadarenes*; other manuscripts *Gergesenes*; also in verse 37
[b]29 Greek *unclean* [c]43 Many manuscripts *years, and she had spent all she had on doctors*

one could heal her. 44She came up behind him and touched the edge of his
cloak, and immediately her bleeding
stopped.
45"Who touched me?" Jesus asked.
When they all denied it, Peter said,
"Master, the people are crowding and
pressing against you."
46But Jesus said, "Someone touched
me; I know that power has gone out
from me."
47Then the woman, seeing that she
could not go unnoticed, came trembling
and fell at his feet. In the presence of all
the people, she told why she had
touched him and how she had been instantly healed. 48Then he said to her,
"Daughter, your faith has healed you.
Go in peace."
49While Jesus was still speaking,
someone came from the house of Jairus,
the synagogue ruler. "Your daughter is
dead," he said. "Don't bother the teacher any more."
50Hearing this, Jesus said to Jairus,
"Don't be afraid; just believe, and she
will be healed."
51When he arrived at the house of Jairus, he did not let anyone go in with
him except Peter, John and James, and
the child's father and mother. 52Mean-
while, all the people were wailing and
mourning for her. "Stop wailing," Jesus
said. "She is not dead but asleep."
53They laughed at him, knowing that
she was dead. 54But he took her by the
hand and said, "My child, get up!" 55Her
spirit returned, and at once she stood
up. Then Jesus told them to give her
something to eat. 56Her parents were astonished, but he ordered them not to tell
anyone what had happened.

SHARPEN THE FOCUS

Suppose that every day of your life an angel has been following you around with a video camera. Suppose the angel has recorded everything–the chances you've had to say a kind word, but didn't; the times you could have helped, but walked away; the bad-attitude days; the selfishness; the lies; the curses; the thanklessness; the theft.

There is no such angel, of course. Nonetheless, the Lord does know the facts of your life. He knows you, just as He knew the woman who walked into Simon's party uninvited (Luke 7:37).

This woman, Jesus told Simon, had "many" sins. And Jesus knew them all. He knew the toll these sins had taken. The family scandal. The ruined friendships. The lonely hours. The broken heart.

We don't know how this woman heard the Good News. But she did hear it. Somehow she came to faith in Jesus, the friend of sinners (Luke 7:34). Weeping, she worshiped Him for taking her sins–all her many sins–away (Luke 7:38).

The more we realize our sin, the more joy and thankfulness we have in knowing our Savior. Forgiven much, we love much (Luke 7:47). Forgiven, we have Christ's peace (Luke 7:50).

As you read today, stand in the sandals Peter or John or James wore. Imagine yourself seeing for the first time what they saw, doing for the first time what they did. Then ask yourself what fresh insights you've gained. If time is short, focus on Luke 9:37–45.

Jesus Sends Out the Twelve

9 When Jesus had called the
Twelve together, he gave them
power and authority to drive out all
demons and to cure diseases, 2and he
sent them out to preach the kingdom of
God and to heal the sick. 3He told them:
"Take nothing for the journey—no staff,
no bag, no bread, no money, no extra tunic. 4Whatever house you enter, stay
there until you leave that town. 5If
people do not welcome you, shake the
dust off your feet when you leave their
town, as a testimony against them." 6So
they set out and went from village to
village, preaching the gospel and healing people everywhere.
7Now Herod the tetrarch heard about
all that was going on. And he was perplexed, because some were saying that
John had been raised from the dead,
8others that Elijah had appeared, and
still others that one of the prophets of
long ago had come back to life. 9But Herod said, "I beheaded John. Who, then,
is this I hear such things about?" And he
tried to see him.

Jesus Feeds the Five Thousand

10When the apostles returned, they
reported to Jesus what they had done.
Then he took them with him and they
withdrew by themselves to a town
called Bethsaida, 11but the crowds
learned about it and followed him. He
welcomed them and spoke to them
about the kingdom of God, and healed
those who needed healing.
12Late in the afternoon the Twelve
came to him and said, "Send the crowd
away so they can go to the surrounding
villages and countryside and find food
and lodging, because we are in a remote
place here."
13He replied, "You give them something to eat."
They answered, "We have only five
loaves of bread and two fish—unless we
go and buy food for all this crowd."
14(About five thousand men were there.)
But he said to his disciples, "Have
them sit down in groups of about fifty
each." 15The disciples did so, and everybody sat down. 16Taking the five loaves
and the two fish and looking up to
heaven, he gave thanks and broke
them. Then he gave them to the disciples to set before the people. 17They all
ate and were satisfied, and the disciples
picked up twelve basketfuls of broken
pieces that were left over.

Peter's Confession of Christ

18Once when Jesus was praying in private and his disciples were with him, he
asked them, "Who do the crowds say
I am?"
19They replied, "Some say John the
Baptist; others say Elijah; and still others, that one of the prophets of long ago
has come back to life."
20"But what about you?" he asked.
"Who do you say I am?"
Peter answered, "The Christ[a] of God."
21Jesus strictly warned them not to tell
this to anyone. 22And he said, "The Son

[a]20 Or *Messiah*

of Man must suffer many things and be rejected by the elders, chief priests and teachers of the law, and he must be killed and on the third day be raised to life."

[23]Then he said to them all: "If anyone would come after me, he must deny himself and take up his cross daily and follow me. [24]For whoever wants to save his life will lose it, but whoever loses his life for me will save it. [25]What good is it for a man to gain the whole world, and yet lose or forfeit his very self? [26]If anyone is ashamed of me and my words, the Son of Man will be ashamed of him when he comes in his glory and in the glory of the Father and of the holy angels. [27]I tell you the truth, some who are standing here will not taste death before they see the kingdom of God."

The Transfiguration

[28]About eight days after Jesus said this, he took Peter, John and James with him and went up onto a mountain to pray. [29]As he was praying, the appearance of his face changed, and his clothes became as bright as a flash of lightning. [30]Two men, Moses and Elijah, [31]appeared in glorious splendor, talking with Jesus. They spoke about his departure, which he was about to bring to fulfillment at Jerusalem. [32]Peter and his companions were very sleepy, but when they became fully awake, they saw his glory and the two men standing with him. [33]As the men were leaving Jesus, Peter said to him, "Master, it is good for us to be here. Let us put up three shelters—one for you, one for Moses and one for Elijah." (He did not know what he was saying.)

[34]While he was speaking, a cloud appeared and enveloped them, and they were afraid as they entered the cloud. [35]A voice came from the cloud, saying, "This is my Son, whom I have chosen; listen to him." [36]When the voice had spoken, they found that Jesus was alone. The disciples kept this to themselves, and told no one at that time what they had seen.

The Healing of a Boy With an Evil Spirit

[37]The next day, when they came down from the mountain, a large crowd met him. [38]A man in the crowd called out, "Teacher, I beg you to look at my son, for he is my only child. [39]A spirit seizes him and he suddenly screams; it throws him into convulsions so that he foams at the mouth. It scarcely ever leaves him and is destroying him. [40]I begged your disciples to drive it out, but they could not."

[41]"O unbelieving and perverse generation," Jesus replied, "how long shall I stay with you and put up with you? Bring your son here."

[42]Even while the boy was coming, the demon threw him to the ground in a convulsion. But Jesus rebuked the evil[a] spirit, healed the boy and gave him back to his father. [43]And they were all amazed at the greatness of God.

While everyone was marveling at all that Jesus did, he said to his disciples, [44]"Listen carefully to what I am about to tell you: The Son of Man is going to be betrayed into the hands of men." [45]But they did not understand what this meant. It was hidden from them, so that they did not grasp it, and they were afraid to ask him about it.

Who Will Be the Greatest?

[46]An argument started among the disciples as to which of them would be the greatest. [47]Jesus, knowing their thoughts, took a little child and had him stand beside him. [48]Then he said to them, "Whoever welcomes this little child in my name welcomes me; and whoever welcomes me welcomes the one who sent me. For he who is least among you all—he is the greatest."

[49]"Master," said John, "we saw a man driving out demons in your name and we tried to stop him, because he is not one of us."

[50]"Do not stop him," Jesus said, "for whoever is not against you is for you."

[a]42 Greek *unclean*

Samaritan Opposition

51 As the time approached for him to
be taken up to heaven, Jesus resolutely
set out for Jerusalem. 52 And he sent messengers on ahead, who went into a Samaritan village to get things ready for
him; 53 but the people there did not welcome him, because he was heading for
Jerusalem. 54 When the disciples James
and John saw this, they asked, "Lord, do
you want us to call fire down from
heaven to destroy them[a]?" 55 But Jesus
turned and rebuked them, 56 and[b] they
went to another village.

The Cost of Following Jesus

57 As they were walking along the
road, a man said to him, "I will follow
you wherever you go."
58 Jesus replied, "Foxes have holes and
birds of the air have nests, but the Son
of Man has no place to lay his head."
59 He said to another man, "Follow
me."

But the man replied, "Lord, first let
me go and bury my father."
60 Jesus said to him, "Let the dead bury
their own dead, but you go and proclaim the kingdom of God."
61 Still another said, "I will follow you,
Lord; but first let me go back and say
good-by to my family."
62 Jesus replied, "No one who puts his
hand to the plow and looks back is fit for
service in the kingdom of God."

[a]54 Some manuscripts *them, even as Elijah did*
[b]55,56 Some manuscripts *them. And he said, "You do not know what kind of spirit you are of, for the Son of Man did not come to destroy men's lives, but to save them."* [56]*And*

SHARPEN THE FOCUS

It takes a lot to impress some people. A bored few can even view the Grand Canyon or Niagara Falls with a "been there, done that" attitude.

Those of us familiar with the Holy Scriptures can find ourselves a bit jaded as we read the gospels, too. Many of us have heard these words dozens or even hundreds of times. But the crowds who followed Jesus around and who saw first-hand the things He did "were all amazed at the greatness of God" (Luke 9:43).

Luke notes this and in the very next verse reports Jesus' prediction about the greatest thing He will do—the greatest work of God. Read Luke 9:44.

When you remember Christ's cross, do you marvel at the majesty of God? Above all else God's glory *is* His grace—His unconditional love toward us who by our sins have declared ourselves to be His enemies, rebels and traitors in His kingdom.

In Christ's cross we find not only forgiveness but also the power to live out Christlike greatness. Not by jockeying for position (Luke 9:46–50). Not by calling fire from heaven down on our enemies (Luke 9:51–56). But by following our Savior, by His grace, step-by-step in humble service.

WEEK 80 • TUESDAY

Luke 10:1–42

GET THE BIG PICTURE

Joy is one of Luke's key words. Joy glowed warm and bright over baby Jesus' manger bed. Joy filled the hearts and minds of those whom Jesus healed. Joy would flow from our Savior's garden tomb and flood the whole earth. Today you will read of an event in which both Jesus and His followers experienced great joy. If time is short, focus on Luke 10:1–24.

Jesus Sends Out the Seventy-two

10 After this the Lord appointed
seventy-two[a] others and sent
them two by two ahead of him to every
town and place where he was about to
go. 2He told them, "The harvest is plentiful, but the workers are few. Ask the
Lord of the harvest, therefore, to send
out workers into his harvest field. 3Go!
I am sending you out like lambs among
wolves. 4Do not take a purse or bag or
sandals; and do not greet anyone on the
road.
5"When you enter a house, first say,
'Peace to this house.' 6If a man of peace
is there, your peace will rest on him; if
not, it will return to you. 7Stay in that
house, eating and drinking whatever
they give you, for the worker deserves
his wages. Do not move around from
house to house.
8"When you enter a town and are
welcomed, eat what is set before you.
9Heal the sick who are there and tell
them, 'The kingdom of God is near you.'
10But when you enter a town and are not
welcomed, go into its streets and say,
11'Even the dust of your town that sticks
to our feet we wipe off against you. Yet
be sure of this: The kingdom of God is
near.' 12I tell you, it will be more bearable
on that day for Sodom than for that
town.
13"Woe to you, Korazin! Woe to you,
Bethsaida! For if the miracles that were
performed in you had been performed
in Tyre and Sidon, they would have repented long ago, sitting in sackcloth and
ashes. 14But it will be more bearable for
Tyre and Sidon at the judgment than for
you. 15And you, Capernaum, will you be
lifted up to the skies? No, you will go
down to the depths.[b]
16"He who listens to you listens to me;
he who rejects you rejects me; but he
who rejects me rejects him who
sent me."
17The seventy-two returned with joy
and said, "Lord, even the demons submit to us in your name."
18He replied, "I saw Satan fall like
lightning from heaven. 19I have given
you authority to trample on snakes and
scorpions and to overcome all the power of the enemy; nothing will harm you.
20However, do not rejoice that the spirits submit to you, but rejoice that your
names are written in heaven."
21At that time Jesus, full of joy through
the Holy Spirit, said, "I praise you, Father, Lord of heaven and earth, because
you have hidden these things from the
wise and learned, and revealed them to
little children. Yes, Father, for this was
your good pleasure.
22"All things have been committed to
me by my Father. No one knows who
the Son is except the Father, and no one
knows who the Father is except the Son
and those to whom the Son chooses to
reveal him."
23Then he turned to his disciples and
said privately, "Blessed are the eyes that
see what you see. 24For I tell you that

[a] 1 Some manuscripts *seventy;* also in verse 17
[b] 15 Greek *Hades*

many prophets and kings wanted to see what you see but did not see it, and to hear what you hear but did not hear it."

The Parable of the Good Samaritan

[25]On one occasion an expert in the law stood up to test Jesus. "Teacher," he asked, "what must I do to inherit eternal life?"

[26]"What is written in the Law?" he replied. "How do you read it?"

[27]He answered: " 'Love the Lord your God with all your heart and with all your soul and with all your strength and with all your mind'[a]; and, 'Love your neighbor as yourself.'[b]"

[28]"You have answered correctly," Jesus replied. "Do this and you will live."

[29]But he wanted to justify himself, so he asked Jesus, "And who is my neighbor?"

[30]In reply Jesus said: "A man was going down from Jerusalem to Jericho, when he fell into the hands of robbers. They stripped him of his clothes, beat him and went away, leaving him half dead. [31]A priest happened to be going down the same road, and when he saw the man, he passed by on the other side. [32]So too, a Levite, when he came to the place and saw him, passed by on the other side. [33]But a Samaritan, as he traveled, came where the man was; and when he saw him, he took pity on him. [34]He went to him and bandaged his wounds, pouring on oil and wine. Then he put the man on his own donkey, took him to an inn and took care of him. [35]The next day he took out two silver coins[c] and gave them to the innkeeper. 'Look after him,' he said, 'and when I return, I will reimburse you for any extra expense you may have.'

[36]"Which of these three do you think was a neighbor to the man who fell into the hands of robbers?"

[37]The expert in the law replied, "The one who had mercy on him."

Jesus told him, "Go and do likewise."

At the Home of Martha and Mary

[38]As Jesus and his disciples were on their way, he came to a village where a woman named Martha opened her home to him. [39]She had a sister called Mary, who sat at the Lord's feet listening to what he said. [40]But Martha was distracted by all the preparations that had to be made. She came to him and asked, "Lord, don't you care that my sister has left me to do the work by myself? Tell her to help me!"

[41]"Martha, Martha," the Lord answered, "you are worried and upset about many things, [42]but only one thing is needed.[d] Mary has chosen what is better, and it will not be taken away from her."

[a]27 Deut. 6:5 [b]27 Lev. 19:18 [c]35 Greek *two denarii* [d]42 Some manuscripts *but few things are needed—or only one*

SHARPEN THE FOCUS

Down through the centuries Christians have made two kinds of errors when it comes to dealing with Satan. Some have made the devil out to be a comic character, dressed in long, red underwear and carrying a pitchfork. Satan, to them, has no power and, indeed, probably doesn't exist in any true sense at all. Other Christians have taken Satan too seriously. They elevate him in their mind's eye to a position of power equal to that of our Lord.

How about us? Do we ever ignore Satan? When we do, we're setting ourselves up to be flattened by the steamroller of temptation. Are we ever afraid of Satan, seeing a demon behind every bush and crediting the devil for all our sins and troubles? Then we're poised at the edge of another deadly cliff, living as victims instead of as the overcomers Christ says we are in Him (John 16:33; 1 John 5:4).

So then what attitude does our Lord want us to have?

- A sure and certain knowledge that our Savior has ousted our accuser from heaven's courtroom (Luke 10:18);
- A sure and certain joy that our names are inscribed in heaven with all God's saints;
- And a watchful reliance on Jesus for strength during times of temptation.

WEEK 80 • WEDNESDAY

Luke 11:1—12:59

As Jesus' ministry picked up momentum, He began to draw larger and larger crowds (Luke 12:1). And the more He taught, the greater grew His opposition. As you read today, notice the harsh words of judgment the Savior speaks to the Pharisees and teachers of the law. Why did He treat them as He did? If time is short, focus on Luke 11:1–13.

Jesus' Teaching on Prayer

11 One day Jesus was praying in a
certain place. When he finished,
one of his disciples said to him, "Lord,
teach us to pray, just as John taught his
disciples."
2He said to them, "When you pray,
say:

" 'Father,[a]
hallowed be your name,
your kingdom come.[b]
3Give us each day our daily bread.
4Forgive us our sins,
for we also forgive everyone who
sins against us.[c]
And lead us not into temptation.[d]' "

5Then he said to them, "Suppose one
of you has a friend, and he goes to him
at midnight and says, 'Friend, lend me
three loaves of bread, 6because a friend
of mine on a journey has come to me,
and I have nothing to set before him.'
7"Then the one inside answers, 'Don't
bother me. The door is already locked,
and my children are with me in bed. I
can't get up and give you anything.' 8I
tell you, though he will not get up and
give him the bread because he is his
friend, yet because of the man's boldness[e] he will get up and give him as
much as he needs.
9"So I say to you: Ask and it will be
given to you; seek and you will find;
knock and the door will be opened to
you. 10For everyone who asks receives;
he who seeks finds; and to him who
knocks, the door will be opened.
11"Which of you fathers, if your son
asks for[f] a fish, will give him a snake instead? 12Or if he asks for an egg, will give
him a scorpion? 13If you then, though
you are evil, know how to give good
gifts to your children, how much more
will your Father in heaven give the Holy
Spirit to those who ask him!"

Jesus and Beelzebub

14Jesus was driving out a demon that
was mute. When the demon left, the

[a]2 Some manuscripts *Our Father in heaven*
[b]2 Some manuscripts *come. May your will be done on earth as it is in heaven.* [c]4 Greek *everyone who is indebted to us* [d]4 Some manuscripts *temptation but deliver us from the evil one* [e]8 Or *persistence*
[f]11 Some manuscripts *for bread, will give him a stone; or if he asks for*

man who had been mute spoke, and the crowd was amazed. 15But some of them said, "By Beelzebub,[a] the prince of demons, he is driving out demons." 16Others tested him by asking for a sign from heaven.

17Jesus knew their thoughts and said to them: "Any kingdom divided against itself will be ruined, and a house divided against itself will fall. 18If Satan is divided against himself, how can his kingdom stand? I say this because you claim that I drive out demons by Beelzebub. 19Now if I drive out demons by Beelzebub, by whom do your followers drive them out? So then, they will be your judges. 20But if I drive out demons by the finger of God, then the kingdom of God has come to you.

21"When a strong man, fully armed, guards his own house, his possessions are safe. 22But when someone stronger attacks and overpowers him, he takes away the armor in which the man trusted and divides up the spoils.

23"He who is not with me is against me, and he who does not gather with me, scatters.

24"When an evil[b] spirit comes out of a man, it goes through arid places seeking rest and does not find it. Then it says, 'I will return to the house I left.' 25When it arrives, it finds the house swept clean and put in order. 26Then it goes and takes seven other spirits more wicked than itself, and they go in and live there. And the final condition of that man is worse than the first."

27As Jesus was saying these things, a woman in the crowd called out, "Blessed is the mother who gave you birth and nursed you."

28He replied, "Blessed rather are those who hear the word of God and obey it."

The Sign of Jonah

29As the crowds increased, Jesus said, "This is a wicked generation. It asks for a miraculous sign, but none will be given it except the sign of Jonah. 30For as Jonah was a sign to the Ninevites, so also will the Son of Man be to this generation. 31The Queen of the South will rise at the judgment with the men of this generation and condemn them; for she came from the ends of the earth to listen to Solomon's wisdom, and now one[c] greater than Solomon is here. 32The men of Nineveh will stand up at the judgment with this generation and condemn it; for they repented at the preaching of Jonah, and now one greater than Jonah is here.

The Lamp of the Body

33"No one lights a lamp and puts it in a place where it will be hidden, or under a bowl. Instead he puts it on its stand, so that those who come in may see the light. 34Your eye is the lamp of your body. When your eyes are good, your whole body also is full of light. But when they are bad, your body also is full of darkness. 35See to it, then, that the light within you is not darkness. 36Therefore, if your whole body is full of light, and no part of it dark, it will be completely lighted, as when the light of a lamp shines on you."

Six Woes

37When Jesus had finished speaking, a Pharisee invited him to eat with him; so he went in and reclined at the table. 38But the Pharisee, noticing that Jesus did not first wash before the meal, was surprised.

39Then the Lord said to him, "Now then, you Pharisees clean the outside of the cup and dish, but inside you are full of greed and wickedness. 40You foolish people! Did not the one who made the outside make the inside also? 41But give what is inside ⌞the dish⌟[d] to the poor, and everything will be clean for you.

42"Woe to you Pharisees, because you give God a tenth of your mint, rue and all other kinds of garden herbs, but you neglect justice and the love of God. You should have practiced the latter without leaving the former undone.

[a]15 Greek *Beezeboul* or *Beelzeboul;* also in verses 18 and 19 [b]24 Greek *unclean* [c]31 Or *something;* also in verse 32 [d]41 Or *what you have*

43"Woe to you Pharisees, because you love the most important seats in the synagogues and greetings in the marketplaces.

44"Woe to you, because you are like unmarked graves, which men walk over without knowing it."

45One of the experts in the law answered him, "Teacher, when you say these things, you insult us also."

46Jesus replied, "And you experts in the law, woe to you, because you load people down with burdens they can hardly carry, and you yourselves will not lift one finger to help them.

47"Woe to you, because you build tombs for the prophets, and it was your forefathers who killed them. 48So you testify that you approve of what your forefathers did; they killed the prophets, and you build their tombs. 49Because of this, God in his wisdom said, 'I will send them prophets and apostles, some of whom they will kill and others they will persecute.' 50Therefore this generation will be held responsible for the blood of all the prophets that has been shed since the beginning of the world, 51from the blood of Abel to the blood of Zechariah, who was killed between the altar and the sanctuary. Yes, I tell you, this generation will be held responsible for it all.

52"Woe to you experts in the law, because you have taken away the key to knowledge. You yourselves have not entered, and you have hindered those who were entering."

53When Jesus left there, the Pharisees and the teachers of the law began to oppose him fiercely and to besiege him with questions, 54waiting to catch him in something he might say.

Warnings and Encouragements

12 Meanwhile, when a crowd of many thousands had gathered, so that they were trampling on one another, Jesus began to speak first to his disciples, saying: "Be on your guard against the yeast of the Pharisees, which is hypocrisy. 2There is nothing concealed that will not be disclosed, or hidden that will not be made known. 3What you have said in the dark will be heard in the daylight, and what you have whispered in the ear in the inner rooms will be proclaimed from the roofs.

4"I tell you, my friends, do not be afraid of those who kill the body and after that can do no more. 5But I will show you whom you should fear: Fear him who, after the killing of the body, has power to throw you into hell. Yes, I tell you, fear him. 6Are not five sparrows sold for two pennies[a]? Yet not one of them is forgotten by God. 7Indeed, the very hairs of your head are all numbered. Don't be afraid; you are worth more than many sparrows.

8"I tell you, whoever acknowledges me before men, the Son of Man will also acknowledge him before the angels of God. 9But he who disowns me before men will be disowned before the angels of God. 10And everyone who speaks a word against the Son of Man will be forgiven, but anyone who blasphemes against the Holy Spirit will not be forgiven.

11"When you are brought before synagogues, rulers and authorities, do not worry about how you will defend yourselves or what you will say, 12for the Holy Spirit will teach you at that time what you should say."

The Parable of the Rich Fool

13Someone in the crowd said to him, "Teacher, tell my brother to divide the inheritance with me."

14Jesus replied, "Man, who appointed me a judge or an arbiter between you?" 15Then he said to them, "Watch out! Be on your guard against all kinds of greed; a man's life does not consist in the abundance of his possessions."

16And he told them this parable: "The ground of a certain rich man produced a good crop. 17He thought to himself, 'What shall I do? I have no place to store my crops.'

18"Then he said, 'This is what I'll do. I

[a]6 Greek *two assaria*

will tear down my barns and build bigger ones, and there I will store all my grain and my goods. 19And I'll say to myself, "You have plenty of good things laid up for many years. Take life easy; eat, drink and be merry." '

20"But God said to him, 'You fool! This very night your life will be demanded from you. Then who will get what you have prepared for yourself?'

21"This is how it will be with anyone who stores up things for himself but is not rich toward God."

Do Not Worry

22Then Jesus said to his disciples: "Therefore I tell you, do not worry about your life, what you will eat; or about your body, what you will wear. 23Life is more than food, and the body more than clothes. 24Consider the ravens: They do not sow or reap, they have no storeroom or barn; yet God feeds them. And how much more valuable you are than birds! 25Who of you by worrying can add a single hour to his life[a]? 26Since you cannot do this very little thing, why do you worry about the rest?

27"Consider how the lilies grow. They do not labor or spin. Yet I tell you, not even Solomon in all his splendor was dressed like one of these. 28If that is how God clothes the grass of the field, which is here today, and tomorrow is thrown into the fire, how much more will he clothe you, O you of little faith! 29And do not set your heart on what you will eat or drink; do not worry about it. 30For the pagan world runs after all such things, and your Father knows that you need them. 31But seek his kingdom, and these things will be given to you as well.

32"Do not be afraid, little flock, for your Father has been pleased to give you the kingdom. 33Sell your possessions and give to the poor. Provide purses for yourselves that will not wear out, a treasure in heaven that will not be exhausted, where no thief comes near and no moth destroys. 34For where your treasure is, there your heart will be also.

Watchfulness

35"Be dressed ready for service and keep your lamps burning, 36like men waiting for their master to return from a wedding banquet, so that when he comes and knocks they can immediately open the door for him. 37It will be good for those servants whose master finds them watching when he comes. I tell you the truth, he will dress himself to serve, will have them recline at the table and will come and wait on them. 38It will be good for those servants whose master finds them ready, even if he comes in the second or third watch of the night. 39But understand this: If the owner of the house had known at what hour the thief was coming, he would not have let his house be broken into. 40You also must be ready, because the Son of Man will come at an hour when you do not expect him."

41Peter asked, "Lord, are you telling this parable to us, or to everyone?"

42The Lord answered, "Who then is the faithful and wise manager, whom the master puts in charge of his servants to give them their food allowance at the proper time? 43It will be good for that servant whom the master finds doing so when he returns. 44I tell you the truth, he will put him in charge of all his possessions. 45But suppose the servant says to himself, 'My master is taking a long time in coming,' and he then begins to beat the menservants and maidservants and to eat and drink and get drunk. 46The master of that servant will come on a day when he does not expect him and at an hour he is not aware of. He will cut him to pieces and assign him a place with the unbelievers.

47"That servant who knows his master's will and does not get ready or does not do what his master wants will be beaten with many blows. 48But the one who does not know and does things deserving punishment will be beaten with few blows. From everyone who has been given much, much will be

[a]25 Or *single cubit to his height*

demanded; and from the one who has
been entrusted with much, much more
will be asked.

Not Peace but Division

49 "I have come to bring fire on the
earth, and how I wish it were already
kindled! 50 But I have a baptism to undergo, and how distressed I am until it is
completed! 51 Do you think I came to
bring peace on earth? No, I tell you, but
division. 52 From now on there will be
five in one family divided against each
other, three against two and two against
three. 53 They will be divided, father
against son and son against father,
mother against daughter and daughter
against mother, mother-in-law against
daughter-in-law and daughter-in-law
against mother-in-law."

Interpreting the Times

54 He said to the crowd: "When you
see a cloud rising in the west, immediately you say, 'It's going to rain,' and it
does. 55 And when the south wind blows,
you say, 'It's going to be hot,' and it is.
56 Hypocrites! You know how to interpret the appearance of the earth and the
sky. How is it that you don't know how
to interpret this present time?

57 "Why don't you judge for yourselves what is right? 58 As you are going
with your adversary to the magistrate,
try hard to be reconciled to him on the
way, or he may drag you off to the
judge, and the judge turn you over to
the officer, and the officer throw you
into prison. 59 I tell you, you will not get
out until you have paid the last penny.[a]"

[a]59 Greek *lepton*

SHARPEN THE FOCUS

Why pray? Our heavenly Father already knows what we need. Why, then ask Him for anything?

How would you answer those questions if a friend asked them? For one thing, you might point out the obvious–prayer involves much besides laying a wish list before God. We pray prayers of thanks, of adoration, and of praise too.

But that truth won't take us off the hook when we think about intercession (praying for others) and petition (asking God for personal needs). Why pray those kinds of prayers?

For one thing, Jesus tells us to ask. He urges us to bring our own needs and the needs of others to Him in prayer. Christ commands that we pray. Second, God knows our burdens are too big for us. He invites us to bring the worries and troubles of this life to Him so He can, in turn, give us His peace.

Finally, our Lord has, in grace, chosen to make us His co-workers in bringing His mercy into the lives of others. He could act without our prayers, but He gives us the high honor of participating in His holy work here on earth. So, approach God's throne today in bold confidence!

WEEK 80 • THURSDAY

Luke 13:1–35

GET THE BIG PICTURE

Jesus is headed toward Jerusalem to die for our sins (Luke 13:22). He stops often along the way to teach about the coming kingdom and to heal the sick. His ministry brings joy (Luke

13:17) to His followers and shame to His enemies. As you read, look for evidence that the Lord offers salvation freely to all alike. Only faith in Jesus counts, and He gives us that faith as a free gift. If time is short focus on Luke 13:22–30.

Repent or Perish

13 Now there were some present at that time who told Jesus about the Galileans whose blood Pilate had mixed with their sacrifices. 2Jesus answered, "Do you think that these Galileans were worse sinners than all the other Galileans because they suffered this way? 3I tell you, no! But unless you repent, you too will all perish. 4Or those eighteen who died when the tower in Siloam fell on them—do you think they were more guilty than all the others living in Jerusalem? 5I tell you, no! But unless you repent, you too will all perish."

6Then he told this parable: "A man had a fig tree, planted in his vineyard, and he went to look for fruit on it, but did not find any. 7So he said to the man who took care of the vineyard, 'For three years now I've been coming to look for fruit on this fig tree and haven't found any. Cut it down! Why should it use up the soil?'

8" 'Sir,' the man replied, 'leave it alone for one more year, and I'll dig around it and fertilize it. 9If it bears fruit next year, fine! If not, then cut it down.' "

A Crippled Woman Healed on the Sabbath

10On a Sabbath Jesus was teaching in one of the synagogues, 11and a woman was there who had been crippled by a spirit for eighteen years. She was bent over and could not straighten up at all. 12When Jesus saw her, he called her forward and said to her, "Woman, you are set free from your infirmity." 13Then he put his hands on her, and immediately she straightened up and praised God.

14Indignant because Jesus had healed on the Sabbath, the synagogue ruler said to the people, "There are six days for work. So come and be healed on those days, not on the Sabbath."

15The Lord answered him, "You hypocrites! Doesn't each of you on the Sabbath untie his ox or donkey from the stall and lead it out to give it water? 16Then should not this woman, a daughter of Abraham, whom Satan has kept bound for eighteen long years, be set free on the Sabbath day from what bound her?"

17When he said this, all his opponents were humiliated, but the people were delighted with all the wonderful things he was doing.

The Parables of the Mustard Seed and the Yeast

18Then Jesus asked, "What is the kingdom of God like? What shall I compare it to? 19It is like a mustard seed, which a man took and planted in his garden. It grew and became a tree, and the birds of the air perched in its branches."

20Again he asked, "What shall I compare the kingdom of God to? 21It is like yeast that a woman took and mixed into a large amount[a] of flour until it worked all through the dough."

The Narrow Door

22Then Jesus went through the towns and villages, teaching as he made his way to Jerusalem. 23Someone asked him, "Lord, are only a few people going to be saved?"

He said to them, 24"Make every effort to enter through the narrow door, because many, I tell you, will try to enter and will not be able to. 25Once the owner of the house gets up and closes the door, you will stand outside knocking and pleading, 'Sir, open the door for us.'

"But he will answer, 'I don't know you or where you come from.'

26"Then you will say, 'We ate and drank with you, and you taught in our streets.'

27"But he will reply, 'I don't know you

[a]21 Greek *three satas* (probably about 1/2 bushel or 22 liters)

or where you come from. Away from
me, all you evildoers!'
28"There will be weeping there, and
gnashing of teeth, when you see Abraham, Isaac and Jacob and all the prophets in the kingdom of God, but you
yourselves thrown out. 29People will
come from east and west and north and
south, and will take their places at the
feast in the kingdom of God. 30Indeed
there are those who are last who will be
first, and first who will be last."

Jesus' Sorrow for Jerusalem

31At that time some Pharisees came to
Jesus and said to him, "Leave this place
and go somewhere else. Herod wants to
kill you."
32He replied, "Go tell that fox, 'I will
drive out demons and heal people today and tomorrow, and on the third day
I will reach my goal.' 33In any case, I
must keep going today and tomorrow
and the next day—for surely no prophet
can die outside Jerusalem!
34"O Jerusalem, Jerusalem, you who
kill the prophets and stone those sent to
you, how often I have longed to gather
your children together, as a hen gathers
her chicks under her wings, but you
were not willing! 35Look, your house is
left to you desolate. I tell you, you will
not see me again until you say, 'Blessed
is he who comes in the name of the
Lord.'[a]"

[a] 35 Psalm 118:26

SHARPEN THE FOCUS

Atlases have one of the shortest shelf lives among the many books in a library. Boundaries change. Capitol cities change. Those who publish atlases and globes have quite a time keeping up.

But think about this: The Kingdom of God can't be mapped at all! Its boundaries continue to expand daily as more and more people come to know their Savior-King and their life's true meaning.

In ancient times, people understood the capitol of a kingdom to be wherever the king resided. When the king moved, so did the capitol. Whenever our Lord Jesus takes up residence in the heart of a believer, there He plants the kingdom of God. Person by person. Heart by heart. Our King conquers the world with His love.

Astronauts often comment that from space they cannot see political boundaries. In the heavenly Father's eyes, boundaries drop away, too. Jesus died for all. He has earned citizenship in the kingdom of heaven for us all.

Jesus' sermons and the stories He told cut to the recesses of the human heart where pride, hypocrisy, and greed hide. There, in the dark places no one sees, grow the most dangerous of sins. Think about that as you read today. If time is short, focus on Luke 14:25–35.

Jesus at a Pharisee's House

14 One Sabbath, when Jesus went to eat in the house of a prominent Pharisee, he was being carefully watched. 2There in front of him was a man suffering from dropsy. 3Jesus asked the Pharisees and experts in the law, "Is it lawful to heal on the Sabbath or not?" 4But they remained silent. So taking hold of the man, he healed him and sent him away.

5Then he asked them, "If one of you has a son[a] or an ox that falls into a well on the Sabbath day, will you not immediately pull him out?" 6And they had nothing to say.

7When he noticed how the guests picked the places of honor at the table, he told them this parable: 8"When someone invites you to a wedding feast, do not take the place of honor, for a person more distinguished than you may have been invited. 9If so, the host who invited both of you will come and say to you, 'Give this man your seat.' Then, humiliated, you will have to take the least important place. 10But when you are invited, take the lowest place, so that when your host comes, he will say to you, 'Friend, move up to a better place.' Then you will be honored in the presence of all your fellow guests. 11For everyone who exalts himself will be humbled, and he who humbles himself will be exalted."

12Then Jesus said to his host, "When you give a luncheon or dinner, do not invite your friends, your brothers or relatives, or your rich neighbors; if you do, they may invite you back and so you will be repaid. 13But when you give a banquet, invite the poor, the crippled, the lame, the blind, 14and you will be blessed. Although they cannot repay you, you will be repaid at the resurrection of the righteous."

The Parable of the Great Banquet

15When one of those at the table with him heard this, he said to Jesus, "Blessed is the man who will eat at the feast in the kingdom of God."

16Jesus replied: "A certain man was preparing a great banquet and invited many guests. 17At the time of the banquet he sent his servant to tell those who had been invited, 'Come, for everything is now ready.'

18"But they all alike began to make excuses. The first said, 'I have just bought a field, and I must go and see it. Please excuse me.'

19"Another said, 'I have just bought five yoke of oxen, and I'm on my way to try them out. Please excuse me.'

20"Still another said, 'I just got married, so I can't come.'

21"The servant came back and reported this to his master. Then the owner of the house became angry and ordered his servant, 'Go out quickly into the streets and alleys of the town and bring in the poor, the crippled, the blind and the lame.'

22" 'Sir,' the servant said, 'what you ordered has been done, but there is still room.'

23"Then the master told his servant, 'Go out to the roads and country lanes and make them come in, so that my house will be full. 24I tell you, not one of those men who were invited will get a taste of my banquet.' "

The Cost of Being a Disciple

25Large crowds were traveling with Jesus, and turning to them he said: 26"If anyone comes to me and does not hate his father and mother, his wife and children, his brothers and sisters—yes, even his own life—he cannot be my disciple. 27And anyone who does not carry his cross and follow me cannot be my disciple.

28"Suppose one of you wants to build a tower. Will he not first sit down and estimate the cost to see if he has enough money to complete it? 29For if he lays the foundation and is not able to finish it, everyone who sees it will ridicule him, 30saying, 'This fellow began to build and was not able to finish.'

31"Or suppose a king is about to go to

[a]5 Some manuscripts *donkey*

war against another king. Will he not
first sit down and consider whether he
is able with ten thousand men to oppose the one coming against him with
twenty thousand? 32If he is not able, he
will send a delegation while the other is
still a long way off and will ask for terms
of peace. 33In the same way, any of you
who does not give up everything he has
cannot be my disciple.
34"Salt is good, but if it loses its saltl-
ness, how can it be made salty again? 35It
is fit neither for the soil nor for the manure pile; it is thrown out.
"He who has ears to hear, let him
hear."

SHARPEN THE FOCUS

All of us exaggerate at times to make a point. Advertisers use this technique, too. There's even a name for it–*hyperbole*. For instance, we might say, "I'd rather die than see him again." Or a billboard might use letters 12 feet tall to proclaim, "Every Customer a Satisfied Customer."

The words of Luke 14:26 at first seem puzzling, even shocking. We know our Lord is not teaching us to hate the members of our own family, because elsewhere in the gospels He commands that we love one another, even our enemies (Luke 6:35).

So then what point does Jesus' hyperbole make? Simply this: He wants first place in our hearts and lives. Nothing else, no one else can claim our highest loyalty. Family and friends come to us as gifts of God, but they cannot be gods in our lives.

Look at your calendar or think through your plans for this weekend and for the week ahead. Could someone who didn't know you tell that time with Jesus is your first priority? Talk with Him about any false "gods" you recognize. Then pray Psalm 32 as a prayer of confession. Know that the forgiveness the psalmist writes about belongs to you in the cross of Christ.

WEEK 80 • SATURDAY

Luke 15:1–16:31

GET THE BIG PICTURE

Luke records more of Jesus' parables than any other Gospel writer does. Today you will read several favorite parables and one quite difficult parable. As you read, look for the central point in each. Also watch for the joy that is one of Luke's hallmarks. If time is short, focus on Luke 15:11–32.

The Parable of the Lost Sheep

15 Now the tax collectors and
"sinners" were all gathering
around to hear him. 2But the Pharisees
and the teachers of the law muttered,
"This man welcomes sinners and eats
with them."
3Then Jesus told them this parable:
4"Suppose one of you has a hundred
sheep and loses one of them. Does he
not leave the ninety-nine in the open
country and go after the lost sheep until he finds it? 5And when he finds it, he
joyfully puts it on his shoulders 6and
goes home. Then he calls his friends and
neighbors together and says, 'Rejoice

with me; I have found my lost sheep.' [7]I tell you that in the same way there will be more rejoicing in heaven over one sinner who repents than over ninety-nine righteous persons who do not need to repent.

The Parable of the Lost Coin

[8]"Or suppose a woman has ten silver coins[a] and loses one. Does she not light a lamp, sweep the house and search carefully until she finds it? [9]And when she finds it, she calls her friends and neighbors together and says, 'Rejoice with me; I have found my lost coin.' [10]In the same way, I tell you, there is rejoicing in the presence of the angels of God over one sinner who repents."

The Parable of the Lost Son

[11]Jesus continued: "There was a man who had two sons. [12]The younger one said to his father, 'Father, give me my share of the estate.' So he divided his property between them.

[13]"Not long after that, the younger son got together all he had, set off for a distant country and there squandered his wealth in wild living. [14]After he had spent everything, there was a severe famine in that whole country, and he began to be in need. [15]So he went and hired himself out to a citizen of that country, who sent him to his fields to feed pigs. [16]He longed to fill his stomach with the pods that the pigs were eating, but no one gave him anything.

[17]"When he came to his senses, he said, 'How many of my father's hired men have food to spare, and here I am starving to death! [18]I will set out and go back to my father and say to him: Father, I have sinned against heaven and against you. [19]I am no longer worthy to be called your son; make me like one of your hired men.' [20]So he got up and went to his father.

"But while he was still a long way off, his father saw him and was filled with compassion for him; he ran to his son, threw his arms around him and kissed him.

[21]"The son said to him, 'Father, I have sinned against heaven and against you. I am no longer worthy to be called your son.[b]'

[22]"But the father said to his servants, 'Quick! Bring the best robe and put it on him. Put a ring on his finger and sandals on his feet. [23]Bring the fattened calf and kill it. Let's have a feast and celebrate. [24]For this son of mine was dead and is alive again; he was lost and is found.' So they began to celebrate.

[25]"Meanwhile, the older son was in the field. When he came near the house, he heard music and dancing. [26]So he called one of the servants and asked him what was going on. [27]'Your brother has come,' he replied, 'and your father has killed the fattened calf because he has him back safe and sound.'

[28]"The older brother became angry and refused to go in. So his father went out and pleaded with him. [29]But he answered his father, 'Look! All these years I've been slaving for you and never disobeyed your orders. Yet you never gave me even a young goat so I could celebrate with my friends. [30]But when this son of yours who has squandered your property with prostitutes comes home, you kill the fattened calf for him!'

[31]" 'My son,' the father said, 'you are always with me, and everything I have is yours. [32]But we had to celebrate and be glad, because this brother of yours was dead and is alive again; he was lost and is found.' "

The Parable of the Shrewd Manager

16 Jesus told his disciples: "There was a rich man whose manager was accused of wasting his possessions. [2]So he called him in and asked him, 'What is this I hear about you? Give an account of your management, because you cannot be manager any longer.'

[3]"The manager said to himself, 'What shall I do now? My master is taking away my job. I'm not strong enough to

[a]8 Greek *ten drachmas,* each worth about a day's wages [b]21 Some early manuscripts *son. Make me like one of your hired men.*

dig, and I'm ashamed to beg— [4]I know what I'll do so that, when I lose my job here, people will welcome me into their houses.'

[5]"So he called in each one of his master's debtors. He asked the first, 'How much do you owe my master?'

[6]" 'Eight hundred gallons[a] of olive oil,' he replied.

"The manager told him, 'Take your bill, sit down quickly, and make it four hundred.'

[7]"Then he asked the second, 'And how much do you owe?'

" 'A thousand bushels[b] of wheat,' he replied.

"He told him, 'Take your bill and make it eight hundred.'

[8]"The master commended the dishonest manager because he had acted shrewdly. For the people of this world are more shrewd in dealing with their own kind than are the people of the light. [9]I tell you, use worldly wealth to gain friends for yourselves, so that when it is gone, you will be welcomed into eternal dwellings.

[10]"Whoever can be trusted with very little can also be trusted with much, and whoever is dishonest with very little will also be dishonest with much. [11]So if you have not been trustworthy in handling worldly wealth, who will trust you with true riches? [12]And if you have not been trustworthy with someone else's property, who will give you property of your own?

[13]"No servant can serve two masters. Either he will hate the one and love the other, or he will be devoted to the one and despise the other. You cannot serve both God and Money."

[14]The Pharisees, who loved money, heard all this and were sneering at Jesus. [15]He said to them, "You are the ones who justify yourselves in the eyes of men, but God knows your hearts. What is highly valued among men is detestable in God's sight.

Additional Teachings

[16]"The Law and the Prophets were proclaimed until John. Since that time, the good news of the kingdom of God is being preached, and everyone is forcing his way into it. [17]It is easier for heaven and earth to disappear than for the least stroke of a pen to drop out of the Law.

[18]"Anyone who divorces his wife and marries another woman commits adultery, and the man who marries a divorced woman commits adultery.

The Rich Man and Lazarus

[19]"There was a rich man who was dressed in purple and fine linen and lived in luxury every day. [20]At his gate was laid a beggar named Lazarus, covered with sores [21]and longing to eat what fell from the rich man's table. Even the dogs came and licked his sores.

[22]"The time came when the beggar died and the angels carried him to Abraham's side. The rich man also died and was buried. [23]In hell,[c] where he was in torment, he looked up and saw Abraham far away, with Lazarus by his side. [24]So he called to him, 'Father Abraham, have pity on me and send Lazarus to dip the tip of his finger in water and cool my tongue, because I am in agony in this fire.'

[25]"But Abraham replied, 'Son, remember that in your lifetime you received your good things, while Lazarus received bad things, but now he is comforted here and you are in agony. [26]And besides all this, between us and you a great chasm has been fixed, so that those who want to go from here to you cannot, nor can anyone cross over from there to us.'

[27]"He answered, 'Then I beg you, father, send Lazarus to my father's house, [28]for I have five brothers. Let him warn them, so that they will not also come to this place of torment.'

[29]"Abraham replied, 'They have Moses and the Prophets; let them listen to them.'

[30]" 'No, father Abraham,' he said, 'but

[a]6 Greek *one hundred batous* (probably about 3 kiloliters) [b]7 Greek *one hundred korous* (probably about 35 kiloliters) [c]23 Greek *Hades*

if someone from the dead goes to them,
they will repent.'
31"He said to him, 'If they do not listen to Moses and the Prophets, they will
not be convinced even if someone rises
from the dead.'"

SHARPEN THE FOCUS

In a broad sense, repentance includes:

- deep sorrow when confronted with God's Law and our need
- God's grace at work to turn us from sin and create heartfelt trust and God-pleasing desires.

Notice how the younger son in Jesus' parable illustrates both facets. He first realizes his guilt and just how deep his need really is. He remembers his father and his home, and he recognizes that his father has the resources to help him (Luke 15:18).

When he sees his father running—yes, running, even though no nobleman would be caught in such an undignified gait—the son's heart melts. He drops the payback scheme he had planned to propose (Luke 15:18, 21). He relaxes in his father's unconditional, forgiving love (Luke 15:22–24).

Jesus doesn't tell us what happened the next day. Knowing the power of sin as we do, we can't believe the son led a perfect life from that moment on. But knowing the power of grace as we do, we can't believe the son consistently abused his newly restored relationship, either.

Think about your own life. Reflect upon the rhythm of repentance and faith, rejoicing that God's grace is at work in both. Then ask God to move you farther down the road by His grace.

WEEK 81 • MONDAY

Luke 17:1—18:43

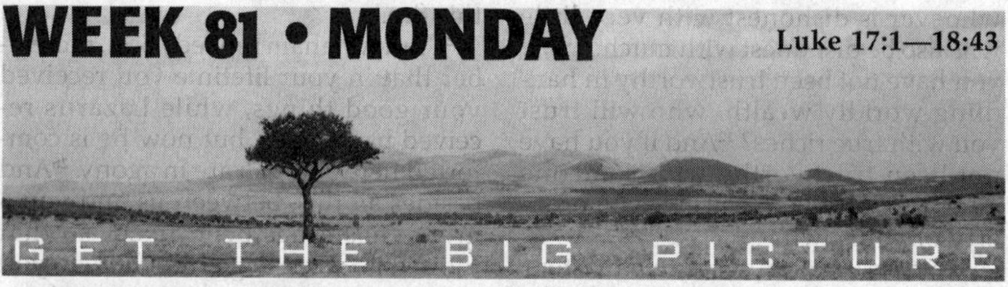

GET THE BIG PICTURE

As you read Luke 17–18, keep in mind that Jesus is on the road to Jerusalem to suffer and die for our sins. As He travels, He makes the most of every opportunity to teach His disciples what they'll need to know to continue His ministry after His ascension. What light does this context shed on His words and actions? If time is short, focus on Luke 18:1–8.

Sin, Faith, Duty

17 Jesus said to his disciples:
"Things that cause people to
sin are bound to come, but woe to that
person through whom they come. 2It
would be better for him to be thrown into
the sea with a millstone tied around his
neck than for him to cause one of these
little ones to sin. 3So watch yourselves.
"If your brother sins, rebuke him, and
if he repents, forgive him. 4If he sins
against you seven times in a day, and
seven times comes back to you and says,
'I repent,' forgive him."
5The apostles said to the Lord, "Increase our faith!"
6He replied, "If you have faith as small
as a mustard seed, you can say to this

mulberry tree, 'Be uprooted and planted in the sea,' and it will obey you.
7"Suppose one of you had a servant
plowing or looking after the sheep.
Would he say to the servant when he
comes in from the field, 'Come along
now and sit down to eat'? 8Would he not
rather say, 'Prepare my supper, get yourself ready and wait on me while I eat
and drink; after that you may eat and
drink'? 9Would he thank the servant
because he did what he was told to do?
10So you also, when you have done everything you were told to do, should
say, 'We are unworthy servants; we
have only done our duty.'"

Ten Healed of Leprosy

11Now on his way to Jerusalem, Jesus
traveled along the border between Samaria and Galilee. 12As he was going
into a village, ten men who had leprosy[a]
met him. They stood at a distance 13and
called out in a loud voice, "Jesus, Master, have pity on us!"
14When he saw them, he said, "Go,
show yourselves to the priests." And as
they went, they were cleansed.
15One of them, when he saw he was
healed, came back, praising God in a
loud voice. 16He threw himself at Jesus'
feet and thanked him—and he was a
Samaritan.
17Jesus asked, "Were not all ten
cleansed? Where are the other nine?
18Was no one found to return and give
praise to God except this foreigner?"
19Then he said to him, "Rise and go;
your faith has made you well."

The Coming of the Kingdom of God

20Once, having been asked by the
Pharisees when the kingdom of God
would come, Jesus replied, "The kingdom of God does not come with your
careful observation, 21nor will people
say, 'Here it is,' or 'There it is,' because
the kingdom of God is within[b] you."
22Then he said to his disciples, "The
time is coming when you will long to
see one of the days of the Son of Man,
but you will not see it. 23Men will tell
you, 'There he is!' or 'Here he is!' Do not
go running off after them. 24For the Son
of Man in his day[c] will be like the lightning, which flashes and lights up the
sky from one end to the other. 25But first
he must suffer many things and be rejected by this generation.
26"Just as it was in the days of Noah,
so also will it be in the days of the Son
of Man. 27People were eating, drinking,
marrying and being given in marriage
up to the day Noah entered the ark. Then
the flood came and destroyed them all.
28"It was the same in the days of Lot.
People were eating and drinking, buying and selling, planting and building.
29But the day Lot left Sodom, fire and
sulfur rained down from heaven and
destroyed them all.
30"It will be just like this on the day the
Son of Man is revealed. 31On that day no
one who is on the roof of his house, with
his goods inside, should go down to get
them. Likewise, no one in the field
should go back for anything. 32Remem-
ber Lot's wife! 33Whoever tries to keep
his life will lose it, and whoever loses his
life will preserve it. 34I tell you, on that
night two people will be in one bed; one
will be taken and the other left. 35Two
women will be grinding grain together;
one will be taken and the other left.[d]"
37"Where, Lord?" they asked.
He replied, "Where there is a dead
body, there the vultures will gather."

The Parable of the Persistent Widow

18 Then Jesus told his disciples
a parable to show them that
they should always pray and not give
up. 2He said: "In a certain town there
was a judge who neither feared God nor
cared about men. 3And there was a
widow in that town who kept coming
to him with the plea, 'Grant me justice
against my adversary.'
4"For some time he refused. But finally he said to himself, 'Even though I

[a]12 The Greek word was used for various diseases affecting the skin—not necessarily leprosy. [b]21 Or *among* [c]24 Some manuscripts do not have *in his day.* [d]35 Some manuscripts *left.* 36*Two men will be in the field; one will be taken and the other left.*

don't fear God or care about men, 5yet
because this widow keeps bothering
me, I will see that she gets justice, so that
she won't eventually wear me out with
her coming!' "

6And the Lord said, "Listen to what
the unjust judge says. 7And will not God
bring about justice for his chosen ones,
who cry out to him day and night? Will
he keep putting them off? 8I tell you, he
will see that they get justice, and quickly.
However, when the Son of Man comes,
will he find faith on the earth?"

The Parable of the Pharisee and the Tax Collector

9To some who were confident of their
own righteousness and looked down on
everybody else, Jesus told this parable:
10"Two men went up to the temple to
pray, one a Pharisee and the other a tax
collector. 11The Pharisee stood up and
prayed about[a] himself: 'God, I thank
you that I am not like other men—robbers, evildoers, adulterers—or even like
this tax collector. 12I fast twice a week
and give a tenth of all I get.'

13"But the tax collector stood at a distance. He would not even look up to
heaven, but beat his breast and said,
'God, have mercy on me, a sinner.'

14"I tell you that this man, rather than
the other, went home justified before
God. For everyone who exalts himself
will be humbled, and he who humbles
himself will be exalted."

The Little Children and Jesus

15People were also bringing babies to
Jesus to have him touch them. When the
disciples saw this, they rebuked them.
16But Jesus called the children to him
and said, "Let the little children come to
me, and do not hinder them, for the
kingdom of God belongs to such as
these. 17I tell you the truth, anyone who
will not receive the kingdom of God like
a little child will never enter it."

The Rich Ruler

18A certain ruler asked him, "Good
teacher, what must I do to inherit eternal life?"

19"Why do you call me good?" Jesus
answered. "No one is good—except God
alone. 20You know the commandments:
'Do not commit adultery, do not murder,
do not steal, do not give false testimony, honor your father and mother.'[b]"

21"All these I have kept since I was a
boy," he said.

22When Jesus heard this, he said to
him, "You still lack one thing. Sell everything you have and give to the poor, and
you will have treasure in heaven. Then
come, follow me."

23When he heard this, he became very
sad, because he was a man of great
wealth. 24Jesus looked at him and said,
"How hard it is for the rich to enter the
kingdom of God! 25Indeed, it is easier for
a camel to go through the eye of a needle than for a rich man to enter the kingdom of God."

26Those who heard this asked, "Who
then can be saved?"

27Jesus replied, "What is impossible
with men is possible with God."

28Peter said to him, "We have left all
we had to follow you!"

29"I tell you the truth," Jesus said to
them, "no one who has left home or wife
or brothers or parents or children for the
sake of the kingdom of God 30will fail to
receive many times as much in this age
and, in the age to come, eternal life."

Jesus Again Predicts His Death

31Jesus took the Twelve aside and told
them, "We are going up to Jerusalem,
and everything that is written by the
prophets about the Son of Man will be
fulfilled. 32He will be handed over to the
Gentiles. They will mock him, insult
him, spit on him, flog him and kill him.
33On the third day he will rise again."

34The disciples did not understand
any of this. Its meaning was hidden
from them, and they did not know what
he was talking about.

A Blind Beggar Receives His Sight

35As Jesus approached Jericho, a blind
man was sitting by the roadside beg-

[a]*11* Or *to* [b]*20* Exodus 20:12-16; Deut. 5:16-20

ging. 36When he heard the crowd going
by, he asked what was happening.
37They told him, "Jesus of Nazareth is
passing by."
38He called out, "Jesus, Son of David,
have mercy on me!"
39Those who led the way rebuked him
and told him to be quiet, but he shouted
all the more, "Son of David, have mercy
on me!"
40Jesus stopped and ordered the man
to be brought to him. When he came
near, Jesus asked him, 41"What do you
want me to do for you?"
"Lord, I want to see," he replied.
42Jesus said to him, "Receive your
sight; your faith has healed you." 43Im-
mediately he received his sight and followed Jesus, praising God. When all the
people saw it, they also praised God.

SHARPEN THE FOCUS

The parable of the persistent widow pivots on a contrast. How unlike the unjust judge our heavenly Father is! The judge in Jesus' story cared only about himself. Public opinion didn't sway him. Upholding justice didn't matter. He acted on the widow's case only to get away from under her persistent nagging.

As Jesus finishes His story, He asks, "Will not God bring about justice for His chosen ones, who cry out to Him day and night?" (Luke 18:7).

Think of it! You are His chosen one in Christ Jesus. Your heavenly Father Himself will hear your case, not some uncaring stranger. He's invited, even commanded, you to petition His court. Go ahead; cry out to Him day and night! Bring your needs, your hurts, your sins to Him. He will hear. He will help. He will forgive.

Fervent, persistent prayer requires faith, which is, of course, a gift from God. Ask Him for that, too, even as you begin to pray. ☼

WEEK 81 • TUESDAY

Luke 19:1—20:47

GET THE BIG PICTURE

Unseen by human eyes, the armies of light and of darkness are assembling to view the battle of the ages. Jesus nears Jerusalem. As the crowds thicken to cheer, Jesus' enemies gather to plot His death. Watch the clash between the kingdom of light and the kingdom of darkness as you read. If time is short, focus on Luke 19:11–27.

Zacchaeus the Tax Collector

19 Jesus entered Jericho and was
passing through. 2A man was
there by the name of Zacchaeus; he was
a chief tax collector and was wealthy.
3He wanted to see who Jesus was, but
being a short man he could not, because
of the crowd. 4So he ran ahead and
climbed a sycamore-fig tree to see him,
since Jesus was coming that way.
5When Jesus reached the spot, he
looked up and said to him, "Zacchaeus,
come down immediately. I must stay at
your house today." 6So he came down at
once and welcomed him gladly.
7All the people saw this and began to

mutter, "He has gone to be the guest of
a 'sinner.'"
8But Zacchaeus stood up and said to
the Lord, "Look, Lord! Here and now I
give half of my possessions to the poor,
and if I have cheated anybody out of
anything, I will pay back four times the
amount."
9Jesus said to him, "Today salvation
has come to this house, because this
man, too, is a son of Abraham. 10For the
Son of Man came to seek and to save
what was lost."

The Parable of the Ten Minas

11While they were listening to this, he
went on to tell them a parable, because
he was near Jerusalem and the people
thought that the kingdom of God was
going to appear at once. 12He said: "A
man of noble birth went to a distant
country to have himself appointed king
and then to return. 13So he called ten of
his servants and gave them ten minas.[a]
'Put this money to work,' he said, 'until
I come back.'
14"But his subjects hated him and sent
a delegation after him to say, 'We don't
want this man to be our king.'
15"He was made king, however, and
returned home. Then he sent for the servants to whom he had given the money, in order to find out what they had
gained with it.
16"The first one came and said, 'Sir,
your mina has earned ten more.'
17" 'Well done, my good servant!' his
master replied. 'Because you have been
trustworthy in a very small matter, take
charge of ten cities.'
18"The second came and said, 'Sir,
your mina has earned five more.'
19"His master answered, 'You take
charge of five cities.'
20"Then another servant came and
said, 'Sir, here is your mina; I have kept
it laid away in a piece of cloth. 21I was
afraid of you, because you are a hard
man. You take out what you did not put
in and reap what you did not sow.'
22"His master replied, 'I will judge you
by your own words, you wicked servant! You knew, did you, that I am a
hard man, taking out what I did not
put in, and reaping what I did not
sow? 23Why then didn't you put my
money on deposit, so that when I came
back, I could have collected it with interest?'
24"Then he said to those standing by,
'Take his mina away from him and give
it to the one who has ten minas.'
25" 'Sir,' they said, 'he already has ten!'
26"He replied, 'I tell you that to everyone who has, more will be given, but as
for the one who has nothing, even what
he has will be taken away. 27But those
enemies of mine who did not want me
to be king over them—bring them here
and kill them in front of me.' "

The Triumphal Entry

28After Jesus had said this, he went on
ahead, going up to Jerusalem. 29As he
approached Bethphage and Bethany at
the hill called the Mount of Olives, he
sent two of his disciples, saying to them,
30"Go to the village ahead of you, and as
you enter it, you will find a colt tied
there, which no one has ever ridden.
Untie it and bring it here. 31If anyone
asks you, 'Why are you untying it?' tell
him, 'The Lord needs it.'"
32Those who were sent ahead went
and found it just as he had told them.
33As they were untying the colt, its owners asked them, "Why are you untying
the colt?"
34They replied, "The Lord needs it."
35They brought it to Jesus, threw their
cloaks on the colt and put Jesus on it.
36As he went along, people spread their
cloaks on the road.
37When he came near the place where
the road goes down the Mount of Olives, the whole crowd of disciples began
joyfully to praise God in loud voices for
all the miracles they had seen:

38"Blessed is the king who comes in
the name of the Lord!"[b]

"Peace in heaven and glory in the
highest!"

[a]*13* A mina was about three months' wages.
[b]*38* Psalm 118:26

39Some of the Pharisees in the crowd
said to Jesus, "Teacher, rebuke your
disciples!"
40"I tell you," he replied, "if they keep
quiet, the stones will cry out."
41As he approached Jerusalem and
saw the city, he wept over it 42and said,
"If you, even you, had only known on
this day what would bring you peace—
but now it is hidden from your eyes.
43The days will come upon you when
your enemies will build an embank-
ment against you and encircle you and
hem you in on every side. 44They will
dash you to the ground, you and the
children within your walls. They will
not leave one stone on another, because
you did not recognize the time of God's
coming to you."

Jesus at the Temple

45Then he entered the temple area
and began driving out those who were
selling. 46"It is written," he said to them,
" 'My house will be a house of prayer'[a];
but you have made it 'a den of robbers.'[b]"
47Every day he was teaching at the
temple. But the chief priests, the teachers of the law and the leaders among
the people were trying to kill him. 48Yet
they could not find any way to do it,
because all the people hung on his
words.

The Authority of Jesus Questioned

20 One day as he was teaching the people in the
temple courts and preaching the gospel,
the chief priests and the teachers of the
law, together with the elders, came up
to him. 2"Tell us by what authority you
are doing these things," they said. "Who
gave you this authority?"
3He replied, "I will also ask you a
question. Tell me, 4John's baptism—was
it from heaven, or from men?"
5They discussed it among themselves
and said, "If we say, 'From heaven,' he
will ask, 'Why didn't you believe him?'
6But if we say, 'From men,' all the people will stone us, because they are persuaded that John was a prophet."
7So they answered, "We don't know
where it was from."
8Jesus said, "Neither will I tell you by
what authority I am doing these
things."

The Parable of the Tenants

9He went on to tell the people this
parable: "A man planted a vineyard,
rented it to some farmers and went
away for a long time. 10At harvest time
he sent a servant to the tenants so they
would give him some of the fruit of the
vineyard. But the tenants beat him and
sent him away empty-handed. 11He sent
another servant, but that one also they
beat and treated shamefully and sent
away empty-handed. 12He sent still a
third, and they wounded him and
threw him out.
13"Then the owner of the vineyard
said, 'What shall I do? I will send my
son, whom I love; perhaps they will respect him.'
14"But when the tenants saw him,
they talked the matter over. 'This is the
heir,' they said. 'Let's kill him, and the
inheritance will be ours.' 15So they threw
him out of the vineyard and killed him.
"What then will the owner of the
vineyard do to them? 16He will come
and kill those tenants and give the vineyard to others."
When the people heard this, they
said, "May this never be!"
17Jesus looked directly at them and
asked, "Then what is the meaning of
that which is written:

" 'The stone the builders rejected
has become the capstone'[c][d]?

18Everyone who falls on that stone will
be broken to pieces, but he on whom it
falls will be crushed."
19The teachers of the law and the chief
priests looked for a way to arrest him
immediately, because they knew he had
spoken this parable against them. But
they were afraid of the people.

[a]46 Isaiah 56:7 [b]46 Jer. 7:11 [c]17 Or *cornerstone*
[d]17 Psalm 118:22

Paying Taxes to Caesar

[20]Keeping a close watch on him, they sent spies, who pretended to be honest. They hoped to catch Jesus in something he said so that they might hand him over to the power and authority of the governor. [21]So the spies questioned him: "Teacher, we know that you speak and teach what is right, and that you do not show partiality but teach the way of God in accordance with the truth. [22]Is it right for us to pay taxes to Caesar or not?"

[23]He saw through their duplicity and said to them, [24]"Show me a denarius. Whose portrait and inscription are on it?"

[25]"Caesar's," they replied.

He said to them, "Then give to Caesar what is Caesar's, and to God what is God's."

[26]They were unable to trap him in what he had said there in public. And astonished by his answer, they became silent.

The Resurrection and Marriage

[27]Some of the Sadducees, who say there is no resurrection, came to Jesus with a question. [28]"Teacher," they said, "Moses wrote for us that if a man's brother dies and leaves a wife but no children, the man must marry the widow and have children for his brother. [29]Now there were seven brothers. The first one married a woman and died childless. [30]The second [31]and then the third married her, and in the same way the seven died, leaving no children. [32]Finally, the woman died too. [33]Now then, at the resurrection whose wife will she be, since the seven were married to her?"

[34]Jesus replied, "The people of this age marry and are given in marriage. [35]But those who are considered worthy of taking part in that age and in the resurrection from the dead will neither marry nor be given in marriage, [36]and they can no longer die; for they are like the angels. They are God's children, since they are children of the resurrection. [37]But in the account of the bush, even Moses showed that the dead rise, for he calls the Lord 'the God of Abraham, and the God of Isaac, and the God of Jacob.'[a] [38]He is not the God of the dead, but of the living, for to him all are alive."

[39]Some of the teachers of the law responded, "Well said, teacher!" [40]And no one dared to ask him any more questions.

Whose Son Is the Christ?

[41]Then Jesus said to them, "How is it that they say the Christ[b] is the Son of David? [42]David himself declares in the Book of Psalms:

" 'The Lord said to my Lord:
"Sit at my right hand
[43]until I make your enemies
a footstool for your feet." '[c]

[44]David calls him 'Lord.' How then can he be his son?"

[45]While all the people were listening, Jesus said to his disciples, [46]"Beware of the teachers of the law. They like to walk around in flowing robes and love to be greeted in the marketplaces and have the most important seats in the synagogues and the places of honor at banquets. [47]They devour widows' houses and for a show make lengthy prayers. Such men will be punished most severely."

[a]37 Exodus 3:6 [b]41 Or *Messiah* [c]43 Psalm 110:1

SHARPEN THE FOCUS

How do you picture your Lord? As a stern, hateful judge with fire in His eyes? As a stingy miser who has to be begged before He'll help?

The Parable of the Minas (Luke 19:11–27) paints a portrait very different from that. The king in Jesus' story trusted His servants. When he returned, he called them together to find out what they had gained. He expected to reward them! The rewards he gave far exceeded the profit even the most diligent servant had gained.

But one of the servants had never gotten to know his master. He saw his lord as harsh and punitive (Luke 19:21). He acted in fear, not faith.

Our King has entrusted each of us with the treasure of His Gospel. The Good News of pardon, peace, and new life through Jesus' cross has the power to change hearts. When we share it, it will do just that. Our Lord will return one day soon to reward us for it. Think of that. He will reward *us* for what He Himself has done in us and through us. How generous He is! We need never dread Him or His return.

So now with happy hearts we can "put His Gospel to work" until He returns.

WEEK 81 • WEDNESDAY

Luke 21:1—22:71

As Jesus taught His disciples, their conversations often centered on the cross. He warned them about the cross that lay ahead for Him. He told them, too, of the cross of persecution they would carry because they belonged to him. Keep the cross in mind as you read now. If time is short, focus on Luke 21:5–36.

The Widow's Offering

21 As he looked up, Jesus saw
the rich putting their gifts
into the temple treasury. 2He also saw a
poor widow put in two very small copper coins.[a] 3"I tell you the truth," he said,
"this poor widow has put in more than
all the others. 4All these people gave
their gifts out of their wealth; but she
out of her poverty put in all she had to
live on."

Signs of the End of the Age

5Some of his disciples were remarking
about how the temple was adorned
with beautiful stones and with gifts
dedicated to God. But Jesus said, 6"As for
what you see here, the time will come
when not one stone will be left on another; every one of them will be thrown
down."

7"Teacher," they asked, "when will
these things happen? And what will be
the sign that they are about to take
place?"

8He replied: "Watch out that you are
not deceived. For many will come in my
name, claiming, 'I am he,' and, 'The time
is near.' Do not follow them. 9When you
hear of wars and revolutions, do not be
frightened. These things must happen
first, but the end will not come right
away."

10Then he said to them: "Nation will
rise against nation, and kingdom
against kingdom. 11There will be great
earthquakes, famines and pestilences in
various places, and fearful events and
great signs from heaven.

12"But before all this, they will lay
hands on you and persecute you. They
will deliver you to synagogues and prisons, and you will be brought before
kings and governors, and all on account

[a]2 Greek *two lepta*

of my name. [13]This will result in your being witnesses to them. [14]But make up your mind not to worry beforehand how you will defend yourselves. [15]For I will give you words and wisdom that none of your adversaries will be able to resist or contradict. [16]You will be betrayed even by parents, brothers, relatives and friends, and they will put some of you to death. [17]All men will hate you because of me. [18]But not a hair of your head will perish. [19]By standing firm you will gain life.

[20]"When you see Jerusalem being surrounded by armies, you will know that its desolation is near. [21]Then let those who are in Judea flee to the mountains, let those in the city get out, and let those in the country not enter the city. [22]For this is the time of punishment in fulfillment of all that has been written. [23]How dreadful it will be in those days for pregnant women and nursing mothers! There will be great distress in the land and wrath against this people. [24]They will fall by the sword and will be taken as prisoners to all the nations. Jerusalem will be trampled on by the Gentiles until the times of the Gentiles are fulfilled.

[25]"There will be signs in the sun, moon and stars. On the earth, nations will be in anguish and perplexity at the roaring and tossing of the sea. [26]Men will faint from terror, apprehensive of what is coming on the world, for the heavenly bodies will be shaken. [27]At that time they will see the Son of Man coming in a cloud with power and great glory. [28]When these things begin to take place, stand up and lift up your heads, because your redemption is drawing near."

[29]He told them this parable: "Look at the fig tree and all the trees. [30]When they sprout leaves, you can see for yourselves and know that summer is near. [31]Even so, when you see these things happening, you know that the kingdom of God is near.

[32]"I tell you the truth, this generation[a] will certainly not pass away until all these things have happened. [33]Heaven and earth will pass away, but my words will never pass away.

[34]"Be careful, or your hearts will be weighed down with dissipation, drunkenness and the anxieties of life, and that day will close on you unexpectedly like a trap. [35]For it will come upon all those who live on the face of the whole earth. [36]Be always on the watch, and pray that you may be able to escape all that is about to happen, and that you may be able to stand before the Son of Man."

[37]Each day Jesus was teaching at the temple, and each evening he went out to spend the night on the hill called the Mount of Olives, [38]and all the people came early in the morning to hear him at the temple.

Judas Agrees to Betray Jesus

22 Now the Feast of Unleavened Bread, called the Passover, was approaching, [2]and the chief priests and the teachers of the law were looking for some way to get rid of Jesus, for they were afraid of the people. [3]Then Satan entered Judas, called Iscariot, one of the Twelve. [4]And Judas went to the chief priests and the officers of the temple guard and discussed with them how he might betray Jesus. [5]They were delighted and agreed to give him money. [6]He consented, and watched for an opportunity to hand Jesus over to them when no crowd was present.

The Last Supper

[7]Then came the day of Unleavened Bread on which the Passover lamb had to be sacrificed. [8]Jesus sent Peter and John, saying, "Go and make preparations for us to eat the Passover."

[9]"Where do you want us to prepare for it?" they asked.

[10]He replied, "As you enter the city, a man carrying a jar of water will meet you. Follow him to the house that he enters, [11]and say to the owner of the house, 'The Teacher asks: Where is the guest room, where I may eat the Passover with my disciples?' [12]He will show

[a]32 Or *race*

you a large upper room, all furnished.
Make preparations there."
13They left and found things just as
Jesus had told them. So they prepared
the Passover.
14When the hour came, Jesus and his
apostles reclined at the table. 15And he
said to them, "I have eagerly desired to
eat this Passover with you before I suffer. 16For I tell you, I will not eat it again
until it finds fulfillment in the kingdom
of God."
17After taking the cup, he gave thanks
and said, "Take this and divide it among
you. 18For I tell you I will not drink again
of the fruit of the vine until the kingdom
of God comes."
19And he took bread, gave thanks and
broke it, and gave it to them, saying,
"This is my body given for you; do this
in remembrance of me."
20In the same way, after the supper he
took the cup, saying, "This cup is the
new covenant in my blood, which is
poured out for you. 21But the hand of
him who is going to betray me is with
mine on the table. 22The Son of Man will
go as it has been decreed, but woe to
that man who betrays him." 23They began
to question among themselves which of
them it might be who would do this.
24Also a dispute arose among them as
to which of them was considered to be
greatest. 25Jesus said to them, "The kings
of the Gentiles lord it over them; and
those who exercise authority over them
call themselves Benefactors. 26But you
are not to be like that. Instead, the greatest among you should be like the
youngest, and the one who rules like
the one who serves. 27For who is greater,
the one who is at the table or the one
who serves? Is it not the one who is at
the table? But I am among you as one
who serves. 28You are those who have
stood by me in my trials. 29And I confer
on you a kingdom, just as my Father
conferred one on me, 30so that you may
eat and drink at my table in my kingdom and sit on thrones, judging the
twelve tribes of Israel.
31"Simon, Simon, Satan has asked to
sift you[a] as wheat. 32But I have prayed
for you, Simon, that your faith may not
fail. And when you have turned back,
strengthen your brothers."
33But he replied, "Lord, I am ready to
go with you to prison and to death."
34Jesus answered, "I tell you, Peter, before the rooster crows today, you will
deny three times that you know me."
35Then Jesus asked them, "When I
sent you without purse, bag or sandals,
did you lack anything?"
"Nothing," they answered.
36He said to them, "But now if you
have a purse, take it, and also a bag; and
if you don't have a sword, sell your
cloak and buy one. 37It is written: 'And
he was numbered with the transgressors'[b]; and I tell you that this must be
fulfilled in me. Yes, what is written
about me is reaching its fulfillment."
38The disciples said, "See, Lord, here
are two swords."
"That is enough," he replied.

Jesus Prays on the Mount of Olives

39Jesus went out as usual to the Mount
of Olives, and his disciples followed
him. 40On reaching the place, he said to
them, "Pray that you will not fall into
temptation." 41He withdrew about a
stone's throw beyond them, knelt down
and prayed, 42"Father, if you are willing,
take this cup from me; yet not my will,
but yours be done." 43An angel from
heaven appeared to him and strengthened him. 44And being in anguish, he
prayed more earnestly, and his sweat
was like drops of blood falling to the
ground.[c]
45When he rose from prayer and went
back to the disciples, he found them
asleep, exhausted from sorrow. 46"Why
are you sleeping?" he asked them. "Get
up and pray so that you will not fall into
temptation."

Jesus Arrested

47While he was still speaking a crowd
came up, and the man who was called

[a] *31* The Greek is plural. [b] *37* Isaiah 53:12
[c] *44* Some early manuscripts do not have verses 43 and 44.

Judas, one of the Twelve, was leading
them. He approached Jesus to kiss him,
48but Jesus asked him, "Judas, are you
betraying the Son of Man with a kiss?"
49When Jesus' followers saw what was
going to happen, they said, "Lord,
should we strike with our swords?"
50And one of them struck the servant of
the high priest, cutting off his right ear.
51But Jesus answered, "No more of
this!" And he touched the man's ear and
healed him.
52Then Jesus said to the chief priests,
the officers of the temple guard, and the
elders, who had come for him, "Am I
leading a rebellion, that you have come
with swords and clubs? 53Every day
I was with you in the temple courts,
and you did not lay a hand on me. But
this is your hour—when darkness
reigns."

Peter Disowns Jesus

54Then seizing him, they led him
away and took him into the house of the
high priest. Peter followed at a distance.
55But when they had kindled a fire in the
middle of the courtyard and had sat
down together, Peter sat down with
them. 56A servant girl saw him seated
there in the firelight. She looked closely
at him and said, "This man was with
him."
57But he denied it. "Woman, I don't
know him," he said.
58A little later someone else saw him
and said, "You also are one of them."
"Man, I am not!" Peter replied.
59About an hour later another asserted, "Certainly this fellow was with him,
for he is a Galilean."
60Peter replied, "Man, I don't know
what you're talking about!" Just as he
was speaking, the rooster crowed. 61The
Lord turned and looked straight at Peter. Then Peter remembered the word
the Lord had spoken to him: "Before the
rooster crows today, you will disown me
three times." 62And he went outside and
wept bitterly.

The Guards Mock Jesus

63The men who were guarding Jesus
began mocking and beating him. 64They
blindfolded him and demanded,
"Prophesy! Who hit you?" 65And they
said many other insulting things to him.

Jesus Before Pilate and Herod

66At daybreak the council of the elders
of the people, both the chief priests and
teachers of the law, met together, and
Jesus was led before them. 67"If you are
the Christ,[a]" they said, "tell us."
Jesus answered, "If I tell you, you will
not believe me, 68and if I asked you, you
would not answer. 69But from now on,
the Son of Man will be seated at the
right hand of the mighty God."
70They all asked, "Are you then the
Son of God?"
He replied, "You are right in saying
I am."
71Then they said, "Why do we need
any more testimony? We have heard it
from his own lips."

[a]67 Or *Messiah*

SHARPEN THE FOCUS

As the earth rolls along toward the Day of Judgment, unbelievers continue to deny Christ's claims on their lives and Christ's return to hold them accountable for their sins. They are ill-prepared to stand before the Lord of heaven and earth.

But as Jesus tells his disciples about the coming judgment, He also warns them to be prepared. He urges them to guard against two dangers: hedonism and worry (Luke 21:34). If we live only for the pleasures, the thrills, the toys of this life, the judgment may fall on us like a trap snapping shut. If we focus only on the troubles, fears, and problems of this life, the judgment may find us just as ill-prepared as those who live for the great god "fun."

Instead of worry, instead of materialism or hedonism, Jesus urges us to watch and to pray. We watch with joy because we know the true pleasures that await us when we set foot on heaven's shores. We pray with courage because we can trust our Lord to meet our needs and to keep us safe from the forces of evil.

WEEK 81 • THURSDAY

Luke 23:1—24:53

All Old Testament history pointed forward to the events you will read about today. All New Testament history finds its anchor in the events recorded here. As you read, keep these three words in mind: *in my place.* Jesus suffered, died, and rose again as your substitute. If time is short, focus on Luke 23:26–56; 24:13–32.

23 Then the whole assembly
rose and led him off to Pilate. 2And they began to accuse him,
saying, "We have found this man sub-
verting our nation. He opposes payment of taxes to Caesar and claims to be
Christ,[a] a king."
3So Pilate asked Jesus, "Are you the
king of the Jews?"
"Yes, it is as you say," Jesus replied.
4Then Pilate announced to the chief
priests and the crowd, "I find no basis
for a charge against this man."
5But they insisted, "He stirs up the
people all over Judea[b] by his teaching.
He started in Galilee and has come all
the way here."
6On hearing this, Pilate asked if the
man was a Galilean. 7When he learned
that Jesus was under Herod's jurisdic-
tion, he sent him to Herod, who was
also in Jerusalem at that time.
8When Herod saw Jesus, he was
greatly pleased, because for a long time
he had been wanting to see him. From
what he had heard about him, he hoped
to see him perform some miracle. 9He
plied him with many questions, but
Jesus gave him no answer. 10The chief
priests and the teachers of the law were
standing there, vehemently accusing
him. 11Then Herod and his soldiers ridiculed and mocked him. Dressing him
in an elegant robe, they sent him back
to Pilate. 12That day Herod and Pilate
became friends—before this they had
been enemies.
13Pilate called together the chief
priests, the rulers and the people, 14and
said to them, "You brought me this man
as one who was inciting the people to
rebellion. I have examined him in your
presence and have found no basis for
your charges against him. 15Neither has
Herod, for he sent him back to us; as you
can see, he has done nothing to deserve
death. 16Therefore, I will punish him
and then release him.[c]"
18With one voice they cried out, "Away
with this man! Release Barabbas to us!"
19(Barabbas had been thrown into prison
for an insurrection in the city, and for
murder.)
20Wanting to release Jesus, Pilate appealed to them again. 21But they kept
shouting, "Crucify him! Crucify him!"

[a]2 Or *Messiah;* also in verses 35 and 39 [b]5 Or *over the land of the Jews* [c]16 Some manuscripts *him."* [17]*Now he was obliged to release one man to them at the Feast.*

22 For the third time he spoke to them: "Why? What crime has this man committed? I have found in him no grounds for the death penalty. Therefore I will have him punished and then release him."

23 But with loud shouts they insistently demanded that he be crucified, and their shouts prevailed. 24 So Pilate decided to grant their demand. 25 He released the man who had been thrown into prison for insurrection and murder, the one they asked for, and surrendered Jesus to their will.

The Crucifixion

26 As they led him away, they seized Simon from Cyrene, who was on his way in from the country, and put the cross on him and made him carry it behind Jesus. 27 A large number of people followed him, including women who mourned and wailed for him. 28 Jesus turned and said to them, "Daughters of Jerusalem, do not weep for me; weep for yourselves and for your children. 29 For the time will come when you will say, 'Blessed are the barren women, the wombs that never bore and the breasts that never nursed!' 30 Then

" 'they will say to the mountains,
"Fall on us!"
and to the hills, "Cover us!" '[a]

31 For if men do these things when the tree is green, what will happen when it is dry?"

32 Two other men, both criminals, were also led out with him to be executed. 33 When they came to the place called the Skull, there they crucified him, along with the criminals—one on his right, the other on his left. 34 Jesus said, "Father, forgive them, for they do not know what they are doing."[b] And they divided up his clothes by casting lots.

35 The people stood watching, and the rulers even sneered at him. They said, "He saved others; let him save himself if he is the Christ of God, the Chosen One."

36 The soldiers also came up and mocked him. They offered him wine vinegar 37 and said, "If you are the king of the Jews, save yourself."

38 There was a written notice above him, which read: THIS IS THE KING OF THE JEWS.

39 One of the criminals who hung there hurled insults at him: "Aren't you the Christ? Save yourself and us!"

40 But the other criminal rebuked him. "Don't you fear God," he said, "since you are under the same sentence? 41 We are punished justly, for we are getting what our deeds deserve. But this man has done nothing wrong."

42 Then he said, "Jesus, remember me when you come into your kingdom.[c]"

43 Jesus answered him, "I tell you the truth, today you will be with me in paradise."

Jesus' Death

44 It was now about the sixth hour, and darkness came over the whole land until the ninth hour, 45 for the sun stopped shining. And the curtain of the temple was torn in two. 46 Jesus called out with a loud voice, "Father, into your hands I commit my spirit." When he had said this, he breathed his last.

47 The centurion, seeing what had happened, praised God and said, "Surely this was a righteous man." 48 When all the people who had gathered to witness this sight saw what took place, they beat their breasts and went away. 49 But all those who knew him, including the women who had followed him from Galilee, stood at a distance, watching these things.

Jesus' Burial

50 Now there was a man named Joseph, a member of the Council, a good and upright man, 51 who had not consented to their decision and action. He came from the Judean town of Arimathea and he was waiting for the kingdom of God. 52 Going to Pilate, he asked for Jesus' body. 53 Then he took it down,

[a] *30* Hosea 10:8 [b] *34* Some early manuscripts do not have this sentence. [c] *42* Some manuscripts *come with your kingly power*

wrapped it in linen cloth and placed it in a tomb cut in the rock, one in which no one had yet been laid. 54It was Preparation Day, and the Sabbath was about to begin.

55The women who had come with Jesus from Galilee followed Joseph and saw the tomb and how his body was laid in it. 56Then they went home and prepared spices and perfumes. But they rested on the Sabbath in obedience to the commandment.

The Resurrection

24 On the first day of the week, very early in the morning, the women took the spices they had prepared and went to the tomb. 2They found the stone rolled away from the tomb, 3but when they entered, they did not find the body of the Lord Jesus. 4While they were wondering about this, suddenly two men in clothes that gleamed like lightning stood beside them. 5In their fright the women bowed down with their faces to the ground, but the men said to them, "Why do you look for the living among the dead? 6He is not here; he has risen! Remember how he told you, while he was still with you in Galilee: 7'The Son of Man must be delivered into the hands of sinful men, be crucified and on the third day be raised again.' " 8Then they remembered his words.

9When they came back from the tomb, they told all these things to the Eleven and to all the others. 10It was Mary Magdalene, Joanna, Mary the mother of James, and the others with them who told this to the apostles. 11But they did not believe the women, because their words seemed to them like nonsense. 12Peter, however, got up and ran to the tomb. Bending over, he saw the strips of linen lying by themselves, and he went away, wondering to himself what had happened.

On the Road to Emmaus

13Now that same day two of them were going to a village called Emmaus, about seven miles[a] from Jerusalem. 14They were talking with each other about everything that had happened. 15As they talked and discussed these things with each other, Jesus himself came up and walked along with them; 16but they were kept from recognizing him.

17He asked them, "What are you discussing together as you walk along?"

They stood still, their faces downcast. 18One of them, named Cleopas, asked him, "Are you only a visitor to Jerusalem and do not know the things that have happened there in these days?"

19"What things?" he asked.

"About Jesus of Nazareth," they replied. "He was a prophet, powerful in word and deed before God and all the people. 20The chief priests and our rulers handed him over to be sentenced to death, and they crucified him; 21but we had hoped that he was the one who was going to redeem Israel. And what is more, it is the third day since all this took place. 22In addition, some of our women amazed us. They went to the tomb early this morning 23but didn't find his body. They came and told us that they had seen a vision of angels, who said he was alive. 24Then some of our companions went to the tomb and found it just as the women had said, but him they did not see."

25He said to them, "How foolish you are, and how slow of heart to believe all that the prophets have spoken! 26Did not the Christ[b] have to suffer these things and then enter his glory?" 27And beginning with Moses and all the Prophets, he explained to them what was said in all the Scriptures concerning himself.

28As they approached the village to which they were going, Jesus acted as if he were going farther. 29But they urged him strongly, "Stay with us, for it is nearly evening; the day is almost over." So he went in to stay with them.

30When he was at the table with them, he took bread, gave thanks, broke it and

[a]*13* Greek *sixty stadia* (about 11 kilometers)
[b]*26* Or *Messiah;* also in verse 46

began to give it to them. 31Then their
eyes were opened and they recognized
him, and he disappeared from their
sight. 32They asked each other, "Were
not our hearts burning within us while
he talked with us on the road and
opened the Scriptures to us?"
33They got up and returned at once to
Jerusalem. There they found the Eleven
and those with them, assembled together 34and saying, "It is true! The Lord
has risen and has appeared to Simon."
35Then the two told what had happened
on the way, and how Jesus was recognized by them when he broke the bread.

Jesus Appears to the Disciples

36While they were still talking about
this, Jesus himself stood among them
and said to them, "Peace be with you."
37They were startled and frightened,
thinking they saw a ghost. 38He said
to them, "Why are you troubled, and
why do doubts rise in your minds?
39Look at my hands and my feet. It is I
myself! Touch me and see; a ghost does
not have flesh and bones, as you see I
have."
40When he had said this, he showed
them his hands and feet. 41And while
they still did not believe it because of joy
and amazement, he asked them, "Do
you have anything here to eat?" 42They
gave him a piece of broiled fish, 43and he
took it and ate it in their presence.
44He said to them, "This is what I told
you while I was still with you: Everything must be fulfilled that is written
about me in the Law of Moses, the
Prophets and the Psalms."
45Then he opened their minds so they
could understand the Scriptures. 46He
told them, "This is what is written: The
Christ will suffer and rise from the dead
on the third day, 47and repentance and
forgiveness of sins will be preached in
his name to all nations, beginning at Jerusalem. 48You are witnesses of these
things. 49I am going to send you what
my Father has promised; but stay in the
city until you have been clothed with
power from on high."

The Ascension

50When he had led them out to the vicinity of Bethany, he lifted up his hands
and blessed them. 51While he was blessing them, he left them and was taken up
into heaven. 52Then they worshiped
him and returned to Jerusalem with
great joy. 53And they stayed continually
at the temple, praising God.

SHARPEN THE FOCUS

As Jesus hung dying on the cross in the darkness that bleak Friday afternoon, the angel armies of heaven and hell stood at attention, watching. The demons delighted in our Lord's agony. The heavenly host waited, hoping to hear the cry for help that never came. Our Lord Jesus, obedient to the Father's will, endured to the end.

The demons no doubt cheered loudly when He died. Satan, no doubt, shouted in exuberant victory. But that victory was short-lived. In heaven, preparations had already begun for the glorious Easter Day Celebration and for Christ's triumphant Ascension Day return to rule both heaven and earth.

You and I share in that victory. Jesus suffered in your and my place. Jesus died in your and my place. Jesus walked out of the tomb in your and my place. Dead, buried, and risen with Him in Baptism, you and I share in His victory (Romans 6:1–14).

JOHN

WEEK 81 • FRIDAY

John 1:1—2:25

GET THE BIG PICTURE

The apostle John begins his gospel by introducing several simple, but key words that reappear again and again. Each word carries much meaning. Look for these words as you read: *life, light, Word, hour* or *time, and sign*. Look for these words as you read today. If time is short, focus on John 1:29–51.

The Word Became Flesh

1 In the beginning was the Word, and
the Word was with God, and the
Word was God. 2 He was with God in the
beginning.
3 Through him all things were made;
without him nothing was made that has
been made. 4 In him was life, and that life
was the light of men. 5 The light shines
in the darkness, but the darkness has
not understood[a] it.
6 There came a man who was sent
from God; his name was John. 7 He came
as a witness to testify concerning that
light, so that through him all men might
believe. 8 He himself was not the light;
he came only as a witness to the light.
9 The true light that gives light to every
man was coming into the world.[b]
10 He was in the world, and though the
world was made through him, the
world did not recognize him. 11 He came
to that which was his own, but his own
did not receive him. 12 Yet to all who received him, to those who believed in his
name, he gave the right to become children of God— 13 children born not of
natural descent,[c] nor of human decision
or a husband's will, but born of God.
14 The Word became flesh and made
his dwelling among us. We have seen
his glory, the glory of the One and
Only,[d] who came from the Father, full of
grace and truth.
15 John testifies concerning him. He
cries out, saying, "This was he of whom
I said, 'He who comes after me has
surpassed me because he was before
me.' " 16 From the fullness of his grace we
have all received one blessing after another. 17 For the law was given through
Moses; grace and truth came through
Jesus Christ. 18 No one has ever seen
God, but God the One and Only,[d,e] who
is at the Father's side, has made him
known.

John the Baptist Denies Being the Christ

19 Now this was John's testimony
when the Jews of Jerusalem sent priests
and Levites to ask him who he was. 20 He
did not fail to confess, but confessed
freely, "I am not the Christ.[f]"

[a]5 Or *darkness, and the darkness has not overcome*
[b]9 Or *This was the true light that gives light to every man who comes into the world*
[c]13 Greek *of bloods*
[d]14,18 Or *the Only Begotten*
[e]18 Some manuscripts *but the only* (or *only begotten*) *Son*
[f]20 Or *Messiah.* "The Christ" (Greek) and "the Messiah" (Hebrew) both mean "the Anointed One"; also in verse 25.

21 They asked him, "Then who are you? Are you Elijah?"

He said, "I am not."

"Are you the Prophet?"

He answered, "No."

22 Finally they said, "Who are you? Give us an answer to take back to those who sent us. What do you say about yourself?"

23 John replied in the words of Isaiah the prophet, "I am the voice of one calling in the desert, 'Make straight the way for the Lord.' "[a]

24 Now some Pharisees who had been sent 25 questioned him, "Why then do you baptize if you are not the Christ, nor Elijah, nor the Prophet?"

26 "I baptize with[b] water," John replied, "but among you stands one you do not know. 27 He is the one who comes after me, the thongs of whose sandals I am not worthy to untie."

28 This all happened at Bethany on the other side of the Jordan, where John was baptizing.

Jesus the Lamb of God

29 The next day John saw Jesus coming toward him and said, "Look, the Lamb of God, who takes away the sin of the world! 30 This is the one I meant when I said, 'A man who comes after me has surpassed me because he was before me.' 31 I myself did not know him, but the reason I came baptizing with water was that he might be revealed to Israel."

32 Then John gave this testimony: "I saw the Spirit come down from heaven as a dove and remain on him. 33 I would not have known him, except that the one who sent me to baptize with water told me, 'The man on whom you see the Spirit come down and remain is he who will baptize with the Holy Spirit.' 34 I have seen and I testify that this is the Son of God."

Jesus' First Disciples

35 The next day John was there again with two of his disciples. 36 When he saw Jesus passing by, he said, "Look, the Lamb of God!"

37 When the two disciples heard him say this, they followed Jesus. 38 Turning around, Jesus saw them following and asked, "What do you want?"

They said, "Rabbi" (which means Teacher), "where are you staying?"

39 "Come," he replied, "and you will see."

So they went and saw where he was staying, and spent that day with him. It was about the tenth hour.

40 Andrew, Simon Peter's brother, was one of the two who heard what John had said and who had followed Jesus. 41 The first thing Andrew did was to find his brother Simon and tell him, "We have found the Messiah" (that is, the Christ). 42 And he brought him to Jesus.

Jesus looked at him and said, "You are Simon son of John. You will be called Cephas" (which, when translated, is Peter[c]).

Jesus Calls Philip and Nathanael

43 The next day Jesus decided to leave for Galilee. Finding Philip, he said to him, "Follow me."

44 Philip, like Andrew and Peter, was from the town of Bethsaida. 45 Philip found Nathanael and told him, "We have found the one Moses wrote about in the Law, and about whom the prophets also wrote—Jesus of Nazareth, the son of Joseph."

46 "Nazareth! Can anything good come from there?" Nathanael asked.

"Come and see," said Philip.

47 When Jesus saw Nathanael approaching, he said of him, "Here is a true Israelite, in whom there is nothing false."

48 "How do you know me?" Nathanael asked.

Jesus answered, "I saw you while you were still under the fig tree before Philip called you."

49 Then Nathanael declared, "Rabbi, you are the Son of God; you are the King of Israel."

50 Jesus said, "You believe[d] because I

[a] 23 Isaiah 40:3 [b] 26 Or *in*; also in verses 31 and 33 [c] 42 Both *Cephas* (Aramaic) and *Peter* (Greek) mean *rock*. [d] 50 Or *Do you believe . . . ?*

told you I saw you under the fig tree.
You shall see greater things than that."
[51]He then added, "I tell you[a] the truth,
you[a] shall see heaven open, and the angels of God ascending and descending
on the Son of Man."

Jesus Changes Water to Wine

2 On the third day a wedding took
place at Cana in Galilee. Jesus'
mother was there, [2]and Jesus and his
disciples had also been invited to the
wedding. [3]When the wine was gone,
Jesus' mother said to him, "They have
no more wine."
[4]"Dear woman, why do you involve
me?" Jesus replied. "My time has not yet
come."
[5]His mother said to the servants, "Do
whatever he tells you."
[6]Nearby stood six stone water jars, the
kind used by the Jews for ceremonial
washing, each holding from twenty to
thirty gallons.[b]
[7]Jesus said to the servants, "Fill the
jars with water"; so they filled them to
the brim.
[8]Then he told them, "Now draw some
out and take it to the master of the
banquet."
They did so, [9]and the master of the
banquet tasted the water that had been
turned into wine. He did not realize
where it had come from, though the servants who had drawn the water knew.
Then he called the bridegroom aside
[10]and said, "Everyone brings out the
choice wine first and then the cheaper
wine after the guests have had too
much to drink; but you have saved the
best till now."
[11]This, the first of his miraculous signs,
Jesus performed at Cana in Galilee. He
thus revealed his glory, and his disciples
put their faith in him.

Jesus Clears the Temple

[12]After this he went down to Capernaum with his mother and brothers and
his disciples. There they stayed for a few
days.
[13]When it was almost time for the Jewish Passover, Jesus went up to Jerusalem.
[14]In the temple courts he found men selling cattle, sheep and doves, and others
sitting at tables exchanging money. [15]So
he made a whip out of cords, and drove
all from the temple area, both sheep and
cattle; he scattered the coins of the money changers and overturned their tables. [16]To those who sold doves he said,
"Get these out of here! How dare you
turn my Father's house into a market!"
[17]His disciples remembered that it is
written: "Zeal for your house will consume me."[c]
[18]Then the Jews demanded of him,
"What miraculous sign can you show us
to prove your authority to do all this?"
[19]Jesus answered them, "Destroy this
temple, and I will raise it again in three
days."
[20]The Jews replied, "It has taken for-
ty-six years to build this temple, and you
are going to raise it in three days?" [21]But
the temple he had spoken of was his
body. [22]After he was raised from the
dead, his disciples recalled what he had
said. Then they believed the Scripture
and the words that Jesus had spoken.
[23]Now while he was in Jerusalem at
the Passover Feast, many people saw
the miraculous signs he was doing and
believed in his name.[d] [24]But Jesus would
not entrust himself to them, for he knew
all men. [25]He did not need man's testimony about man, for he knew what was
in a man.

[a]51 The Greek is plural. [b]6 Greek *two to three metretes* (probably about 75 to 115 liters)
[c]17 Psalm 69:9 [d]23 Or *and believed in him*

SHARPEN THE FOCUS

What one or two events in your life stand out in such a way that you recall the details as if the event happened yesterday? Do you recall the time of day you graduated from high school? The time your wedding began? The hour your first child was born?

The apostle John wrote his Gospel perhaps 50 years or so after the events he records actually happened. Still, he remembers the exact time and place he first met Jesus (John 1:39).

Meeting Jesus changed his life. Has it changed yours? Many people today find it fashionable to respect Jesus as a great teacher or as one of many prophets. Jesus surely was both a teacher and a prophet. But He was much more than that.

He was and is the bridge, the mediator, the go-between who links sinful human beings with the holy God. His life, death, and resurrection make it possible for us to have life—eternal life. He is "the Lamb of God, who takes away the sin of the world" (John 1:29).

That Lamb, that Life, that Light changes everything.

As John the Baptizer wraps up his ministry, Jesus picks up John's message. Under the blessing of God, the Baptizer has done his work well. Those in Israel who are spiritually hungry and thirsty begin to come to Jesus. You will read about one such person today. As you do that, notice again the simple words the apostle John sprinkles throughout the account: *life, light, truth, sign.* If time is short, focus on John 3:1–21.

Jesus Teaches Nicodemus

3 Now there was a man of the
Pharisees named Nicodemus, a
member of the Jewish ruling council.
2 He came to Jesus at night and said,
"Rabbi, we know you are a teacher who
has come from God. For no one could
perform the miraculous signs you are
doing if God were not with him."
3 In reply Jesus declared, "I tell you the
truth, no one can see the kingdom of
God unless he is born again.[a]"
4 "How can a man be born when he is
old?" Nicodemus asked. "Surely he
cannot enter a second time into his
mother's womb to be born!"
5 Jesus answered, "I tell you the truth,
no one can enter the kingdom of God
unless he is born of water and the Spirit.
6 Flesh gives birth to flesh, but the Spirit[b]
gives birth to spirit. 7 You should not be
surprised at my saying, 'You[c] must be
born again.' 8 The wind blows wherever
it pleases. You hear its sound, but you
cannot tell where it comes from or
where it is going. So it is with everyone
born of the Spirit."
9 "How can this be?" Nicodemus
asked.
10 "You are Israel's teacher," said Jesus,
"and do you not understand these
things? 11 I tell you the truth, we speak
of what we know, and we testify to what
we have seen, but still you people do
not accept our testimony. 12 I have spoken to you of earthly things and you do
not believe; how then will you believe
if I speak of heavenly things? 13 No one
has ever gone into heaven except the
one who came from heaven—the Son
of Man.[d] 14 Just as Moses lifted up
the snake in the desert, so the Son of
Man must be lifted up, 15 that everyone

[a]3 Or *born from above;* also in verse 7 [b]6 Or *but spirit* [c]7 The Greek is plural. [d]13 Some manuscripts *Man, who is in heaven*

who believes in him may have eternal life.[a]

16“For God so loved the world that he gave his one and only Son,[b] that whoever believes in him shall not perish but have eternal life. 17For God did not send his Son into the world to condemn the world, but to save the world through him. 18Whoever believes in him is not condemned, but whoever does not believe stands condemned already because he has not believed in the name of God’s one and only Son.[c] 19This is the verdict: Light has come into the world, but men loved darkness instead of light because their deeds were evil. 20Everyone who does evil hates the light, and will not come into the light for fear that his deeds will be exposed. 21But whoever lives by the truth comes into the light, so that it may be seen plainly that what he has done has been done through God.”[d]

John the Baptist’s Testimony About Jesus

22After this, Jesus and his disciples went out into the Judean countryside, where he spent some time with them, and baptized. 23Now John also was baptizing at Aenon near Salim, because there was plenty of water, and people were constantly coming to be baptized. 24(This was before John was put in prison.) 25An argument developed between some of John’s disciples and a certain Jew[e] over the matter of ceremonial washing. 26They came to John and said to him, “Rabbi, that man who was with you on the other side of the Jordan—the one you testified about—well, he is baptizing, and everyone is going to him.”

27To this John replied, “A man can receive only what is given him from heaven. 28You yourselves can testify that I said, ‘I am not the Christ[f] but am sent ahead of him.’ 29The bride belongs to the bridegroom. The friend who attends the bridegroom waits and listens for him, and is full of joy when he hears the bridegroom’s voice. That joy is mine, and it is now complete. 30He must become greater; I must become less.

31“The one who comes from above is above all; the one who is from the earth belongs to the earth, and speaks as one from the earth. The one who comes from heaven is above all. 32He testifies to what he has seen and heard, but no one accepts his testimony. 33The man who has accepted it has certified that God is truthful. 34For the one whom God has sent speaks the words of God, for God[g] gives the Spirit without limit. 35The Father loves the Son and has placed everything in his hands. 36Whoever believes in the Son has eternal life, but whoever rejects the Son will not see life, for God’s wrath remains on him.”[h]

[a]15 Or *believes may have eternal life in him* [b]16 Or *his only begotten Son* [c]18 Or *God’s only begotten Son* [d]21 Some interpreters end the quotation after verse 15. [e]25 Some manuscripts *and certain Jews* [f]28 Or *Messiah* [g]34 Greek *he* [h]36 Some interpreters end the quotation after verse 30.

SHARPEN THE FOCUS

A second-grader once asked his science teacher, “Where does the darkness go when I turn on the light?” An interesting question, isn’t it? As frightening and even powerful as darkness may seem at times, it disappears at the flick of a switch or with one lighted match.

When Jesus came to live on this earth, He entered a world shrouded in the darkness of sin. We know what it was like, because our world lies in that darkness, too. The darkness suits some people just fine. If we’re honest, we can probably think of times in our own lives when we’ve wanted to pull a thick blanket of darkness over those thoughts or words or acts of which we are ashamed (John 3:19).

Jesus came into our world to scatter the darkness. He didn’t turn on the light; He *is* the Light.

We need not be afraid that He will expose our guilt, that He will shame us for our misdeeds. Not at all. He came not to condemn us, but to save us (John 3:17). Sin and shame melt away in the light that shines from His cross.

WEEK 82 • MONDAY

John 4:1–54

GET THE BIG PICTURE

To understand today's reading, you need to recall the ancient hatreds that festered between Jews and Samaritans. Jesus broke custom simply by walking through Samaria, not to mention sitting down to talk with a Samaritan. Second, remember that few rabbis would give a woman the time of day. If time is short, focus on John 4:1–42.

Jesus Talks With a Samaritan Woman

4 The Pharisees heard that Jesus
was gaining and baptizing more
disciples than John, 2although in fact it
was not Jesus who baptized, but his disciples. 3When the Lord learned of this,
he left Judea and went back once more
to Galilee.
4Now he had to go through Samaria.
5So he came to a town in Samaria called
Sychar, near the plot of ground Jacob
had given to his son Joseph. 6Jacob's
well was there, and Jesus, tired as he
was from the journey, sat down by the
well. It was about the sixth hour.
7When a Samaritan woman came to
draw water, Jesus said to her, "Will you
give me a drink?" 8(His disciples had
gone into the town to buy food.)
9The Samaritan woman said to him,
"You are a Jew and I am a Samaritan
woman. How can you ask me for a
drink?" (For Jews do not associate with
Samaritans.[a])
10Jesus answered her, "If you knew
the gift of God and who it is that asks
you for a drink, you would have asked
him and he would have given you living water."
11"Sir," the woman said, "you have
nothing to draw with and the well is
deep. Where can you get this living water? 12Are you greater than our father
Jacob, who gave us the well and drank
from it himself, as did also his sons and
his flocks and herds?"
13Jesus answered, "Everyone who
drinks this water will be thirsty again,
14but whoever drinks the water I give
him will never thirst. Indeed, the water
I give him will become in him a spring
of water welling up to eternal life."
15The woman said to him, "Sir, give
me this water so that I won't get thirsty
and have to keep coming here to draw
water."
16He told her, "Go, call your husband
and come back."
17"I have no husband," she replied.
Jesus said to her, "You are right when
you say you have no husband. 18The fact
is, you have had five husbands, and the
man you now have is not your husband.
What you have just said is quite true."
19"Sir," the woman said, "I can see that
you are a prophet. 20Our fathers worshiped on this mountain, but you Jews
claim that the place where we must
worship is in Jerusalem."

[a]9 Or *do not use dishes Samaritans have used*

21Jesus declared, "Believe me, woman,
a time is coming when you will worship
the Father neither on this mountain nor
in Jerusalem. 22You Samaritans worship
what you do not know; we worship
what we do know, for salvation is from
the Jews. 23Yet a time is coming and has
now come when the true worshipers
will worship the Father in spirit and
truth, for they are the kind of worshipers the Father seeks. 24God is spirit, and
his worshipers must worship in spirit
and in truth."

25The woman said, "I know that Messiah" (called Christ) "is coming. When
he comes, he will explain everything
to us."

26Then Jesus declared, "I who speak to
you am he."

The Disciples Rejoin Jesus

27Just then his disciples returned and
were surprised to find him talking with
a woman. But no one asked, "What do
you want?" or "Why are you talking
with her?"

28Then, leaving her water jar, the
woman went back to the town and said
to the people, 29"Come, see a man who
told me everything I ever did. Could
this be the Christ[a]?" 30They came out of
the town and made their way toward
him.

31Meanwhile his disciples urged him,
"Rabbi, eat something."

32But he said to them, "I have food to
eat that you know nothing about."

33Then his disciples said to each other,
"Could someone have brought him
food?"

34"My food," said Jesus, "is to do the
will of him who sent me and to finish his
work. 35Do you not say, 'Four months
more and then the harvest'? I tell you,
open your eyes and look at the fields!
They are ripe for harvest. 36Even now
the reaper draws his wages, even now
he harvests the crop for eternal life, so
that the sower and the reaper may be
glad together. 37Thus the saying 'One
sows and another reaps' is true. 38I sent
you to reap what you have not worked
for. Others have done the hard work,
and you have reaped the benefits of
their labor."

Many Samaritans Believe

39Many of the Samaritans from that
town believed in him because of the
woman's testimony, "He told me everything I ever did." 40So when the Samaritans came to him, they urged him to
stay with them, and he stayed two days.
41And because of his words many more
became believers.

42They said to the woman, "We no
longer believe just because of what you
said; now we have heard for ourselves,
and we know that this man really is the
Savior of the world."

Jesus Heals the Official's Son

43After the two days he left for Galilee.
44(Now Jesus himself had pointed out
that a prophet has no honor in his own
country.) 45When he arrived in Galilee,
the Galileans welcomed him. They had
seen all that he had done in Jerusalem
at the Passover Feast, for they also had
been there.

46Once more he visited Cana in Galilee, where he had turned the water into
wine. And there was a certain royal official whose son lay sick at Capernaum.
47When this man heard that Jesus had
arrived in Galilee from Judea, he went
to him and begged him to come and
heal his son, who was close to death.

48"Unless you people see miraculous
signs and wonders," Jesus told him,
"you will never believe."

49The royal official said, "Sir, come
down before my child dies."

50Jesus replied, "You may go. Your son
will live."

The man took Jesus at his word and
departed. 51While he was still on the
way, his servants met him with the
news that his boy was living. 52When he
inquired as to the time when his son got
better, they said to him, "The fever left
him yesterday at the seventh hour."

53Then the father realized that this

[a]29 Or *Messiah*

was the exact time at which Jesus had
said to him, "Your son will live." So he
and all his household believed.

[54]This was the second miraculous sign
that Jesus performed, having come from
Judea to Galilee.

SHARPEN THE FOCUS

When conversations grow too uncomfortable, human beings often change the subject. Look at John 4:18–20. Do you see how skillfully the woman flipped the topic of conversation away from her sin? "Let's argue religion," she seems to say to this Prophet sitting before her.

But Jesus brings her back to God's Law, to God's requirement that His people worship Him "in spirit and in truth" (John 4:24). The life she was living did not align itself with that truth. Her unrepented sin kept her from worshiping from her heart, her spirit. As she listened, God gave her His gift of repentance and faith.

When the Holy Spirit begins to converse with you about your sins, do you change the subject? It's easy to do that, especially when He points out lifestyle sins—overwork, laziness, not taking good care of our bodies, living as though accumulating things will make us happy. If you've been avoiding one of these topics, finish talking with your Lord about it now. Remember, in Jesus He is "compassionate and gracious, slow to anger, abounding in love" (Psalm 103:8).

WEEK 82 • TUESDAY

John 5:1—6:71

GET THE BIG PICTURE

In John 5 and 6 the Holy Spirit spreads out a rich banquet of comfort and encouragement for believers. In John 5, count the witnesses whom Jesus says testify to Him as the Son of God. (There are at least four.) In John 6:26–66, note the many times Jesus promises to give the gift of eternal life to those who believe in Him. (There are at least 10.) If time is short, focus on John 6:25–58.

The Healing at the Pool

5 Some time later, Jesus went up to
Jerusalem for a feast of the Jews.
[2]Now there is in Jerusalem near the
Sheep Gate a pool, which in Aramaic is
called Bethesda[a] and which is surrounded by five covered colonnades.
[3]Here a great number of disabled people
used to lie—the blind, the lame, the
paralyzed.[b] [5]One who was there had
been an invalid for thirty-eight years.
[6]When Jesus saw him lying there and
learned that he had been in this condition for a long time, he asked him, "Do
you want to get well?"
[7]"Sir," the invalid replied, "I have no
one to help me into the pool when the
water is stirred. While I am trying to get

[a]2 Some manuscripts *Bethzatha*; other manuscripts *Bethsaida* [b]3 Some less important manuscripts *paralyzed—and they waited for the moving of the waters.* [4]*From time to time an angel of the Lord would come down and stir up the waters. The first one into the pool after each such disturbance would be cured of whatever disease he had.*

in, someone else goes down ahead
of me."
[8]Then Jesus said to him, "Get up! Pick
up your mat and walk." [9]At once the
man was cured; he picked up his mat
and walked.
The day on which this took place was
a Sabbath, [10]and so the Jews said to the
man who had been healed, "It is the
Sabbath; the law forbids you to carry
your mat."
[11]But he replied, "The man who made
me well said to me, 'Pick up your mat
and walk.' "
[12]So they asked him, "Who is this
fellow who told you to pick it up and
walk?"
[13]The man who was healed had no
idea who it was, for Jesus had slipped
away into the crowd that was there.
[14]Later Jesus found him at the temple
and said to him, "See, you are well
again. Stop sinning or something worse
may happen to you." [15]The man went
away and told the Jews that it was Jesus
who had made him well.

Life Through the Son

[16]So, because Jesus was doing these
things on the Sabbath, the Jews persecuted him. [17]Jesus said to them, "My Father is always at his work to this very
day, and I, too, am working." [18]For this
reason the Jews tried all the harder to
kill him; not only was he breaking the
Sabbath, but he was even calling God
his own Father, making himself equal
with God.
[19]Jesus gave them this answer: "I tell
you the truth, the Son can do nothing
by himself; he can do only what he sees
his Father doing, because whatever the
Father does the Son also does. [20]For the
Father loves the Son and shows him all
he does. Yes, to your amazement he will
show him even greater things than
these. [21]For just as the Father raises the
dead and gives them life, even so the
Son gives life to whom he is pleased to
give it. [22]Moreover, the Father judges no
one, but has entrusted all judgment to
the Son, [23]that all may honor the Son just
as they honor the Father. He who does
not honor the Son does not honor the
Father, who sent him.
[24]"I tell you the truth, whoever hears
my word and believes him who sent me
has eternal life and will not be condemned; he has crossed over from
death to life. [25]I tell you the truth, a time
is coming and has now come when the
dead will hear the voice of the Son of
God and those who hear will live. [26]For
as the Father has life in himself, so he
has granted the Son to have life in himself. [27]And he has given him authority to
judge because he is the Son of Man.
[28]"Do not be amazed at this, for a time
is coming when all who are in their
graves will hear his voice [29]and come
out—those who have done good will
rise to live, and those who have done
evil will rise to be condemned. [30]By myself I can do nothing; I judge only as I
hear, and my judgment is just, for I seek
not to please myself but him who
sent me.

Testimonies About Jesus

[31]"If I testify about myself, my testimony is not valid. [32]There is another
who testifies in my favor, and I know
that his testimony about me is valid.
[33]"You have sent to John and he has
testified to the truth. [34]Not that I accept
human testimony; but I mention it that
you may be saved. [35]John was a lamp
that burned and gave light, and you
chose for a time to enjoy his light.
[36]"I have testimony weightier than
that of John. For the very work that the
Father has given me to finish, and
which I am doing, testifies that the Father has sent me. [37]And the Father who
sent me has himself testified concerning
me. You have never heard his voice nor
seen his form, [38]nor does his word dwell
in you, for you do not believe the one
he sent. [39]You diligently study[a] the
Scriptures because you think that by
them you possess eternal life. These are
the Scriptures that testify about me, [40]yet
you refuse to come to me to have life.
[41]"I do not accept praise from men,

[a]39 Or *Study diligently* (the imperative)

42but I know you. I know that you do not
have the love of God in your hearts. 43I
have come in my Father's name, and
you do not accept me; but if someone
else comes in his own name, you will
accept him. 44How can you believe if
you accept praise from one another, yet
make no effort to obtain the praise that
comes from the only God[a]?

45"But do not think I will accuse you
before the Father. Your accuser is Moses,
on whom your hopes are set. 46If you believed Moses, you would believe me, for
he wrote about me. 47But since you do
not believe what he wrote, how are you
going to believe what I say?"

Jesus Feeds the Five Thousand

6 Some time after this, Jesus
crossed to the far shore of the Sea
of Galilee (that is, the Sea of Tiberias),
2and a great crowd of people followed
him because they saw the miraculous
signs he had performed on the sick.
3Then Jesus went up on a mountainside
and sat down with his disciples. 4The
Jewish Passover Feast was near.

5When Jesus looked up and saw a
great crowd coming toward him, he said
to Philip, "Where shall we buy bread for
these people to eat?" 6He asked this only
to test him, for he already had in mind
what he was going to do.

7Philip answered him, "Eight months'
wages[b] would not buy enough bread for
each one to have a bite!"

8Another of his disciples, Andrew, Simon Peter's brother, spoke up, 9"Here is
a boy with five small barley loaves and
two small fish, but how far will they go
among so many?"

10Jesus said, "Have the people sit
down." There was plenty of grass in that
place, and the men sat down, about five
thousand of them. 11Jesus then took the
loaves, gave thanks, and distributed to
those who were seated as much as they
wanted. He did the same with the fish.

12When they had all had enough to
eat, he said to his disciples, "Gather the
pieces that are left over. Let nothing be
wasted." 13So they gathered them and
filled twelve baskets with the pieces of
the five barley loaves left over by those
who had eaten.

14After the people saw the miraculous
sign that Jesus did, they began to say,
"Surely this is the Prophet who is to
come into the world." 15Jesus, knowing
that they intended to come and make
him king by force, withdrew again to a
mountain by himself.

Jesus Walks on the Water

16When evening came, his disciples
went down to the lake, 17where they got
into a boat and set off across the lake for
Capernaum. By now it was dark, and
Jesus had not yet joined them. 18A
strong wind was blowing and the waters grew rough. 19When they had
rowed three or three and a half miles,[c]
they saw Jesus approaching the boat,
walking on the water; and they were
terrified. 20But he said to them, "It is I;
don't be afraid." 21Then they were willing to take him into the boat, and immediately the boat reached the shore
where they were heading.

22The next day the crowd that had
stayed on the opposite shore of the lake
realized that only one boat had been
there, and that Jesus had not entered it
with his disciples, but that they had
gone away alone. 23Then some boats
from Tiberias landed near the place
where the people had eaten the bread
after the Lord had given thanks. 24Once
the crowd realized that neither Jesus
nor his disciples were there, they got
into the boats and went to Capernaum
in search of Jesus.

Jesus the Bread of Life

25When they found him on the other
side of the lake, they asked him, "Rabbi,
when did you get here?"

26Jesus answered, "I tell you the truth,
you are looking for me, not because you
saw miraculous signs but because you ate
the loaves and had your fill. 27Do not work

[a]44 Some early manuscripts *the Only One*
[b]7 Greek *two hundred denarii* [c]19 Greek
rowed twenty-five or thirty stadia (about 5 or 6
kilometers)

for food that spoils, but for food that endures to eternal life, which the Son of Man will give you. On him God the Father has placed his seal of approval."

28Then they asked him, "What must we do to do the works God requires?"

29Jesus answered, "The work of God is this: to believe in the one he has sent."

30So they asked him, "What miraculous sign then will you give that we may see it and believe you? What will you do? 31Our forefathers ate the manna in the desert; as it is written: 'He gave them bread from heaven to eat.'[a]"

32Jesus said to them, "I tell you the truth, it is not Moses who has given you the bread from heaven, but it is my Father who gives you the true bread from heaven. 33For the bread of God is he who comes down from heaven and gives life to the world."

34"Sir," they said, "from now on give us this bread."

35Then Jesus declared, "I am the bread of life. He who comes to me will never go hungry, and he who believes in me will never be thirsty. 36But as I told you, you have seen me and still you do not believe. 37All that the Father gives me will come to me, and whoever comes to me I will never drive away. 38For I have come down from heaven not to do my will but to do the will of him who sent me. 39And this is the will of him who sent me, that I shall lose none of all that he has given me, but raise them up at the last day. 40For my Father's will is that everyone who looks to the Son and believes in him shall have eternal life, and I will raise him up at the last day."

41At this the Jews began to grumble about him because he said, "I am the bread that came down from heaven." 42They said, "Is this not Jesus, the son of Joseph, whose father and mother we know? How can he now say, 'I came down from heaven'?"

43"Stop grumbling among yourselves," Jesus answered. 44"No one can come to me unless the Father who sent me draws him, and I will raise him up at the last day. 45It is written in the Prophets: 'They will all be taught by God.'[b] Everyone who listens to the Father and learns from him comes to me. 46No one has seen the Father except the one who is from God; only he has seen the Father. 47I tell you the truth, he who believes has everlasting life. 48I am the bread of life. 49Your forefathers ate the manna in the desert, yet they died. 50But here is the bread that comes down from heaven, which a man may eat and not die. 51I am the living bread that came down from heaven. If anyone eats of this bread, he will live forever. This bread is my flesh, which I will give for the life of the world."

52Then the Jews began to argue sharply among themselves, "How can this man give us his flesh to eat?"

53Jesus said to them, "I tell you the truth, unless you eat the flesh of the Son of Man and drink his blood, you have no life in you. 54Whoever eats my flesh and drinks my blood has eternal life, and I will raise him up at the last day. 55For my flesh is real food and my blood is real drink. 56Whoever eats my flesh and drinks my blood remains in me, and I in him. 57Just as the living Father sent me and I live because of the Father, so the one who feeds on me will live because of me. 58This is the bread that came down from heaven. Your forefathers ate manna and died, but he who feeds on this bread will live forever." 59He said this while teaching in the synagogue in Capernaum.

Many Disciples Desert Jesus

60On hearing it, many of his disciples said, "This is a hard teaching. Who can accept it?"

61Aware that his disciples were grumbling about this, Jesus said to them, "Does this offend you? 62What if you see the Son of Man ascend to where he was before! 63The Spirit gives life; the flesh counts for nothing. The words I have spoken to you are spirit[c] and they are life. 64Yet there are some of you who do not believe." For Jesus had known from

[a]*31* Exodus 16:4; Neh. 9:15; Psalm 78:24,25
[b]*45* Isaiah 54:13 [c]*63* Or *Spirit*

the beginning which of them did not believe and who would betray him. [65]He
went on to say, "This is why I told you
that no one can come to me unless the
Father has enabled him."
[66]From this time many of his disciples
turned back and no longer followed
him.
[67]"You do not want to leave too, do
you?" Jesus asked the Twelve.
[68]Simon Peter answered him, "Lord,
to whom shall we go? You have the
words of eternal life. [69]We believe and
know that you are the Holy One of
God."
[70]Then Jesus replied, "Have I not chosen you, the Twelve? Yet one of you is a
devil!" [71](He meant Judas, the son of Simon Iscariot, who, though one of the
Twelve, was later to betray him.)

SHARPEN THE FOCUS

"If I've told you once, I've told you a hundred times . . ." Parental lectures often begin with this sentence. Parents often repeat and repeat and repeat instructions they want their children to understand and act upon.

We've seen the Lord repeat Himself again and again in Scripture, but nowhere does He do that quite so often in such few verses as in John 6. Here our Savior promises eternal life to those who believe in him. That life belongs to us here and now by faith.

Jesus' listeners had asked life's most important question: "What must we do to do the works God requires?" (John 6:28). Our sinful nature yearns, at times even demands, that God show us how to earn His love, His forgiveness. But Jesus points us away from ourselves and our efforts. He directs us toward relationship—the intimate relationship of faith which He gives us as a free gift through His death. In His death, we have life, now and forever.

WEEK 82 • WEDNESDAY

John 7:1—8:59

GET THE BIG PICTURE

As John 7 opens, we see Jesus going to Jerusalem for the Feast of Tabernacles as the law of Moses required (Leviticus 23:33–44). Each morning of the feast a priest would walk to the fountain of Siloam, fill a pitcher with water, and walk back to pour the water and a pitcher of wine into two bowls on the altar of burnt sacrifice. This ceremony reminded the people of God's provision for their ancestors in the wilderness. If time is short, focus on John 7:37–53.

Jesus Goes to the Feast of Tabernacles

7 After this, Jesus went around in
Galilee, purposely staying away
from Judea because the Jews there were
waiting to take his life. [2]But when the
Jewish Feast of Tabernacles was near,
[3]Jesus' brothers said to him, "You ought
to leave here and go to Judea, so that
your disciples may see the miracles you
do. [4]No one who wants to become a
public figure acts in secret. Since you are
doing these things, show yourself to the
world." [5]For even his own brothers did
not believe in him.
[6]Therefore Jesus told them, "The right

time for me has not yet come; for you any time is right. [7]The world cannot hate you, but it hates me because I testify that what it does is evil. [8]You go to the Feast. I am not yet[a] going up to this Feast, because for me the right time has not yet come." [9]Having said this, he stayed in Galilee.

[10]However, after his brothers had left for the Feast, he went also, not publicly, but in secret. [11]Now at the Feast the Jews were watching for him and asking, "Where is that man?"

[12]Among the crowds there was widespread whispering about him. Some said, "He is a good man."

Others replied, "No, he deceives the people." [13]But no one would say anything publicly about him for fear of the Jews.

Jesus Teaches at the Feast

[14]Not until halfway through the Feast did Jesus go up to the temple courts and begin to teach. [15]The Jews were amazed and asked, "How did this man get such learning without having studied?"

[16]Jesus answered, "My teaching is not my own. It comes from him who sent me. [17]If anyone chooses to do God's will, he will find out whether my teaching comes from God or whether I speak on my own. [18]He who speaks on his own does so to gain honor for himself, but he who works for the honor of the one who sent him is a man of truth; there is nothing false about him. [19]Has not Moses given you the law? Yet not one of you keeps the law. Why are you trying to kill me?"

[20]"You are demon-possessed," the crowd answered. "Who is trying to kill you?"

[21]Jesus said to them, "I did one miracle, and you are all astonished. [22]Yet, because Moses gave you circumcision (though actually it did not come from Moses, but from the patriarchs), you circumcise a child on the Sabbath. [23]Now if a child can be circumcised on the Sabbath so that the law of Moses may not be broken, why are you angry with me for healing the whole man on the Sabbath? [24]Stop judging by mere appearances, and make a right judgment."

Is Jesus the Christ?

[25]At that point some of the people of Jerusalem began to ask, "Isn't this the man they are trying to kill? [26]Here he is, speaking publicly, and they are not saying a word to him. Have the authorities really concluded that he is the Christ[b]? [27]But we know where this man is from; when the Christ comes, no one will know where he is from."

[28]Then Jesus, still teaching in the temple courts, cried out, "Yes, you know me, and you know where I am from. I am not here on my own, but he who sent me is true. You do not know him, [29]but I know him because I am from him and he sent me."

[30]At this they tried to seize him, but no one laid a hand on him, because his time had not yet come. [31]Still, many in the crowd put their faith in him. They said, "When the Christ comes, will he do more miraculous signs than this man?"

[32]The Pharisees heard the crowd whispering such things about him. Then the chief priests and the Pharisees sent temple guards to arrest him.

[33]Jesus said, "I am with you for only a short time, and then I go to the one who sent me. [34]You will look for me, but you will not find me; and where I am, you cannot come."

[35]The Jews said to one another, "Where does this man intend to go that we cannot find him? Will he go where our people live scattered among the Greeks, and teach the Greeks? [36]What did he mean when he said, 'You will look for me, but you will not find me,' and 'Where I am, you cannot come'?"

[37]On the last and greatest day of the Feast, Jesus stood and said in a loud voice, "If anyone is thirsty, let him come to me and drink. [38]Whoever believes in me, as[c] the Scripture has said, streams of

[a] 8 Some early manuscripts do not have *yet*.
[b] 26 Or *Messiah*; also in verses 27, 31, 41 and 42
[c] 37,38 Or / *If anyone is thirsty, let him come to me. / And let him drink,* [38]*who believes in me.* / As

living water will flow from within him."
39By this he meant the Spirit, whom
those who believed in him were later to
receive. Up to that time the Spirit had
not been given, since Jesus had not yet
been glorified.
40On hearing his words, some of the
people said, "Surely this man is the
Prophet."
41Others said, "He is the Christ."
Still others asked, "How can the
Christ come from Galilee? 42Does not the
Scripture say that the Christ will come
from David's family[a] and from Bethlehem, the town where David lived?"
43Thus the people were divided because
of Jesus. 44Some wanted to seize him,
but no one laid a hand on him.

Unbelief of the Jewish Leaders

45Finally the temple guards went back
to the chief priests and Pharisees, who
asked them, "Why didn't you bring
him in?"
46"No one ever spoke the way this
man does," the guards declared.
47"You mean he has deceived you
also?" the Pharisees retorted. 48"Has any
of the rulers or of the Pharisees believed
in him? 49No! But this mob that knows
nothing of the law—there is a curse on
them."
50Nicodemus, who had gone to Jesus
earlier and who was one of their own
number, asked, 51"Does our law condemn anyone without first hearing him
to find out what he is doing?"
52They replied, "Are you from Galilee,
too? Look into it, and you will find that
a prophet[b] does not come out of Galilee."

[The earliest manuscripts and many other ancient witnesses do not have John 7:53–8:11.]

53Then each went to his own home.

8 But Jesus went to the Mount of
Olives. 2At dawn he appeared
again in the temple courts, where all the
people gathered around him, and he sat
down to teach them. 3The teachers of
the law and the Pharisees brought in a
woman caught in adultery. They made
her stand before the group 4and said to
Jesus, "Teacher, this woman was caught
in the act of adultery. 5In the Law Moses commanded us to stone such
women. Now what do you say?" 6They
were using this question as a trap, in
order to have a basis for accusing him.
But Jesus bent down and started to
write on the ground with his finger.
7When they kept on questioning him,
he straightened up and said to them, "If
any one of you is without sin, let him be
the first to throw a stone at her." 8Again
he stooped down and wrote on the
ground.
9At this, those who heard began to go
away one at a time, the older ones first,
until only Jesus was left, with the woman still standing there. 10Jesus straightened up and asked her, "Woman, where
are they? Has no one condemned you?"
11"No one, sir," she said.
"Then neither do I condemn you,"
Jesus declared. "Go now and leave your
life of sin."

The Validity of Jesus' Testimony

12When Jesus spoke again to the
people, he said, "I am the light of the
world. Whoever follows me will never
walk in darkness, but will have the light
of life."
13The Pharisees challenged him,
"Here you are, appearing as your own
witness; your testimony is not valid."
14Jesus answered, "Even if I testify on
my own behalf, my testimony is valid,
for I know where I came from and
where I am going. But you have no idea
where I come from or where I am going.
15You judge by human standards; I pass
judgment on no one. 16But if I do judge,
my decisions are right, because I am not
alone. I stand with the Father, who sent
me. 17In your own Law it is written that

[a]42 Greek *seed* [b]52 Two early manuscripts *the Prophet*

the testimony of two men is valid. [18]I am
one who testifies for myself; my other
witness is the Father, who sent me."
[19]Then they asked him, "Where is
your father?"
"You do not know me or my Father,"
Jesus replied. "If you knew me, you
would know my Father also." [20]He
spoke these words while teaching in the
temple area near the place where the offerings were put. Yet no one seized him,
because his time had not yet come.
[21]Once more Jesus said to them, "I am
going away, and you will look for me,
and you will die in your sin. Where I go,
you cannot come."
[22]This made the Jews ask, "Will he kill
himself? Is that why he says, 'Where I
go, you cannot come'?"
[23]But he continued, "You are from
below; I am from above. You are of this
world; I am not of this world. [24]I told you
that you would die in your sins; if you
do not believe that I am ⌞the one I claim
to be⌟,[a] you will indeed die in your sins."
[25]"Who are you?" they asked.
"Just what I have been claiming all
along," Jesus replied. [26]"I have much to
say in judgment of you. But he who sent
me is reliable, and what I have heard
from him I tell the world."
[27]They did not understand that he
was telling them about his Father. [28]So
Jesus said, "When you have lifted up the
Son of Man, then you will know that I
am ⌞the one I claim to be⌟ and that I do
nothing on my own but speak just what
the Father has taught me. [29]The one who
sent me is with me; he has not left me
alone, for I always do what pleases
him." [30]Even as he spoke, many put
their faith in him.

The Children of Abraham

[31]To the Jews who had believed him,
Jesus said, "If you hold to my teaching,
you are really my disciples. [32]Then you
will know the truth, and the truth will
set you free."
[33]They answered him, "We are
Abraham's descendants[b] and have never been slaves of anyone. How can you
say that we shall be set free?"
[34]Jesus replied, "I tell you the truth,
everyone who sins is a slave to sin.
[35]Now a slave has no permanent place
in the family, but a son belongs to it forever. [36]So if the Son sets you free, you
will be free indeed. [37]I know you are
Abraham's descendants. Yet you are
ready to kill me, because you have no
room for my word. [38]I am telling you
what I have seen in the Father's presence, and you do what you have heard
from your father.[c]"
[39]"Abraham is our father," they
answered.
"If you were Abraham's children,"
said Jesus, "then you would[d] do the
things Abraham did. [40]As it is, you are
determined to kill me, a man who has
told you the truth that I heard from
God. Abraham did not do such things.
[41]You are doing the things your own father does."
"We are not illegitimate children,"
they protested. "The only Father we
have is God himself."

The Children of the Devil

[42]Jesus said to them, "If God were
your Father, you would love me, for I
came from God and now am here. I
have not come on my own; but he sent
me. [43]Why is my language not clear to
you? Because you are unable to hear
what I say. [44]You belong to your father,
the devil, and you want to carry out
your father's desire. He was a murderer
from the beginning, not holding to the
truth, for there is no truth in him. When
he lies, he speaks his native language,
for he is a liar and the father of lies. [45]Yet
because I tell the truth, you do not believe me! [46]Can any of you prove me
guilty of sin? If I am telling the truth,
why don't you believe me? [47]He who belongs to God hears what God says. The
reason you do not hear is that you do
not belong to God."

[a]24 Or *I am he*; also in verse 28 [b]33 Greek *seed*; also in verse 37 [c]38 Or *presence. Therefore do what you have heard from the Father.* [d]39 Some early manuscripts *"If you are Abraham's children," said Jesus, "then*

The Claims of Jesus About Himself

48 The Jews answered him, "Aren't we
right in saying that you are a Samaritan
and demon-possessed?"
49 "I am not possessed by a demon,"
said Jesus, "but I honor my Father and
you dishonor me. 50 I am not seeking glory for myself; but there is one who seeks
it, and he is the judge. 51 I tell you the
truth, if anyone keeps my word, he will
never see death."
52 At this the Jews exclaimed, "Now we
know that you are demon-possessed!
Abraham died and so did the prophets,
yet you say that if anyone keeps your
word, he will never taste death. 53 Are
you greater than our father Abraham?
He died, and so did the prophets. Who
do you think you are?"
54 Jesus replied, "If I glorify myself,
my glory means nothing. My Father,
whom you claim as your God, is the one
who glorifies me. 55 Though you do not
know him, I know him. If I said I did
not, I would be a liar like you, but I do
know him and keep his word. 56 Your
father Abraham rejoiced at the thought
of seeing my day; he saw it and was
glad."
57 "You are not yet fifty years old," the
Jews said to him, "and you have seen
Abraham!"
58 "I tell you the truth," Jesus answered, "before Abraham was born, I
am!" 59 At this, they picked up stones
to stone him, but Jesus hid himself, slipping away from the temple
grounds.

SHARPEN THE FOCUS

One hot summer a national chain of convenience store franchises sent banners to all their outlets. The banners read, "87 Ways to Quench Your Thirst!" The marketers in that company knew that the majority of people in our culture today value choice. The more options, the better.

Sad to say when it comes to spiritual thirst, most people sincerely believe that in this situation, they also have 87 or more options from which to choose. Many feel free to invent their own god, their own rituals, their own faith, their own definitions of right and wrong.

But Jesus didn't leave that option open. "If anyone is thirsty," He says, "let him come to *Me* and drink" (John 7:37, emphasis added). Only in Jesus will we find the living water that truly will quench our thirsty souls. Only the Good News of His cross and empty tomb will refresh us and give us life, eternal life.

Are you in a "dry place" in your walk with the Lord today? Take your thirst to Him. Pray Psalm 84 as you let your Savior's love and forgiveness wash over you.

WEEK 82 • THURSDAY

John 9:1—10:42

GET THE BIG PICTURE

Matthew, Mark, Luke, and John all document the opposition Jesus faced from the Pharisees and the teachers of the law. In John 9 the opposition grows into something close to hatred, a hatred that blinds Jesus' enemies to the truth He proclaims. As you read, notice the words of

Law our Lord speaks to the impenitent and the sweet grace He speaks to those who recognize their sin and their need for the Savior. If time is short, focus on John 10:1–30.

Jesus Heals a Man Born Blind

9 As he went along, he saw a man blind from birth. [2]His disciples asked him, "Rabbi, who sinned, this man or his parents, that he was born blind?"

[3]"Neither this man nor his parents sinned," said Jesus, "but this happened so that the work of God might be displayed in his life. [4]As long as it is day, we must do the work of him who sent me. Night is coming, when no one can work. [5]While I am in the world, I am the light of the world."

[6]Having said this, he spit on the ground, made some mud with the saliva, and put it on the man's eyes. [7]"Go," he told him, "wash in the Pool of Siloam" (this word means Sent). So the man went and washed, and came home seeing.

[8]His neighbors and those who had formerly seen him begging asked, "Isn't this the same man who used to sit and beg?" [9]Some claimed that he was.

Others said, "No, he only looks like him."

But he himself insisted, "I am the man."

[10]"How then were your eyes opened?" they demanded.

[11]He replied, "The man they call Jesus made some mud and put it on my eyes. He told me to go to Siloam and wash. So I went and washed, and then I could see."

[12]"Where is this man?" they asked him.

"I don't know," he said.

The Pharisees Investigate the Healing

[13]They brought to the Pharisees the man who had been blind. [14]Now the day on which Jesus had made the mud and opened the man's eyes was a Sabbath. [15]Therefore the Pharisees also asked him how he had received his sight. "He put mud on my eyes," the man replied, "and I washed, and now I see."

[16]Some of the Pharisees said, "This man is not from God, for he does not keep the Sabbath."

But others asked, "How can a sinner do such miraculous signs?" So they were divided.

[17]Finally they turned again to the blind man, "What have you to say about him? It was your eyes he opened."

The man replied, "He is a prophet."

[18]The Jews still did not believe that he had been blind and had received his sight until they sent for the man's parents. [19]"Is this your son?" they asked. "Is this the one you say was born blind? How is it that now he can see?"

[20]"We know he is our son," the parents answered, "and we know he was born blind. [21]But how he can see now, or who opened his eyes, we don't know. Ask him. He is of age; he will speak for himself." [22]His parents said this because they were afraid of the Jews, for already the Jews had decided that anyone who acknowledged that Jesus was the Christ[a] would be put out of the synagogue. [23]That was why his parents said, "He is of age; ask him."

[24]A second time they summoned the man who had been blind. "Give glory to God,[b]" they said. "We know this man is a sinner."

[25]He replied, "Whether he is a sinner or not, I don't know. One thing I do know. I was blind but now I see!"

[26]Then they asked him, "What did he do to you? How did he open your eyes?"

[27]He answered, "I have told you already and you did not listen. Why do you want to hear it again? Do you want to become his disciples, too?"

[28]Then they hurled insults at him and said, "You are this fellow's disciple! We are disciples of Moses! [29]We know that God spoke to Moses, but as for this fellow, we don't even know where he comes from."

[a]22 Or *Messiah* [b]24 A solemn charge to tell the truth (see Joshua 7:19)

30 The man answered, "Now that is remarkable! You don't know where he
comes from, yet he opened my eyes.
31 We know that God does not listen to
sinners. He listens to the godly man
who does his will. 32 Nobody has ever
heard of opening the eyes of a man born
blind. 33 If this man were not from God,
he could do nothing."

34 To this they replied, "You were
steeped in sin at birth; how dare you lecture us!" And they threw him out.

Spiritual Blindness

35 Jesus heard that they had thrown
him out, and when he found him, he
said, "Do you believe in the Son of
Man?"

36 "Who is he, sir?" the man asked. "Tell
me so that I may believe in him."

37 Jesus said, "You have now seen him;
in fact, he is the one speaking with you."

38 Then the man said, "Lord, I believe,"
and he worshiped him.

39 Jesus said, "For judgment I have
come into this world, so that the blind
will see and those who see will become
blind."

40 Some Pharisees who were with him
heard him say this and asked, "What?
Are we blind too?"

41 Jesus said, "If you were blind, you
would not be guilty of sin; but now
that you claim you can see, your guilt
remains.

The Shepherd and His Flock

10 "I tell you the truth, the man
who does not enter the sheep
pen by the gate, but climbs in by some
other way, is a thief and a robber. 2 The
man who enters by the gate is the shepherd of his sheep. 3 The watchman
opens the gate for him, and the sheep
listen to his voice. He calls his own
sheep by name and leads them out.
4 When he has brought out all his own,
he goes on ahead of them, and his sheep
follow him because they know his voice.
5 But they will never follow a stranger;
in fact, they will run away from him
because they do not recognize a
stranger's voice." 6 Jesus used this figure
of speech, but they did not understand
what he was telling them.

7 Therefore Jesus said again, "I tell you
the truth, I am the gate for the sheep.
8 All who ever came before me were
thieves and robbers, but the sheep did
not listen to them. 9 I am the gate; whoever enters through me will be saved.[a]
He will come in and go out, and find
pasture. 10 The thief comes only to steal
and kill and destroy; I have come that
they may have life, and have it to the
full.

11 "I am the good shepherd. The good
shepherd lays down his life for the
sheep. 12 The hired hand is not the shepherd who owns the sheep. So when he
sees the wolf coming, he abandons the
sheep and runs away. Then the wolf attacks the flock and scatters it. 13 The man
runs away because he is a hired hand
and cares nothing for the sheep.

14 "I am the good shepherd; I know my
sheep and my sheep know me— 15 just
as the Father knows me and I know the
Father—and I lay down my life for the
sheep. 16 I have other sheep that are not
of this sheep pen. I must bring them
also. They too will listen to my voice,
and there shall be one flock and one
shepherd. 17 The reason my Father loves
me is that I lay down my life—only to
take it up again. 18 No one takes it from
me, but I lay it down of my own accord.
I have authority to lay it down and authority to take it up again. This command I received from my Father."

19 At these words the Jews were again
divided. 20 Many of them said, "He is demon-possessed and raving mad. Why
listen to him?"

21 But others said, "These are not the
sayings of a man possessed by a demon.
Can a demon open the eyes of the
blind?"

The Unbelief of the Jews

22 Then came the Feast of Dedication[b]
at Jerusalem. It was winter, 23 and Jesus
was in the temple area walking in Solomon's Colonnade. 24 The Jews gathered

[a] 9 Or *kept safe* [b] 22 That is, Hanukkah

around him, saying, "How long will you
keep us in suspense? If you are the
Christ,[a] tell us plainly."
25 Jesus answered, "I did tell you, but
you do not believe. The miracles I do in
my Father's name speak for me, 26 but
you do not believe because you are not
my sheep. 27 My sheep listen to my voice;
I know them, and they follow me. 28 I
give them eternal life, and they shall
never perish; no one can snatch them
out of my hand. 29 My Father, who has
given them to me, is greater than all[b]; no
one can snatch them out of my Father's
hand. 30 I and the Father are one."
31 Again the Jews picked up stones to
stone him, 32 but Jesus said to them, "I
have shown you many great miracles
from the Father. For which of these do
you stone me?"
33 "We are not stoning you for any of
these," replied the Jews, "but for blasphemy, because you, a mere man, claim
to be God."
34 Jesus answered them, "Is it not written in your Law, 'I have said you are
gods'[c]? 35 If he called them 'gods,' to
whom the word of God came—and the
Scripture cannot be broken— 36 what
about the one whom the Father set
apart as his very own and sent into the
world? Why then do you accuse me of
blasphemy because I said, 'I am God's
Son'? 37 Do not believe me unless I do
what my Father does. 38 But if I do it,
even though you do not believe me, believe the miracles, that you may know
and understand that the Father is in me,
and I in the Father." 39 Again they tried
to seize him, but he escaped their grasp.
40 Then Jesus went back across the Jordan to the place where John had been
baptizing in the early days. Here he
stayed 41 and many people came to him.
They said, "Though John never performed a miraculous sign, all that John
said about this man was true." 42 And in
that place many believed in Jesus.

[a]24 Or *Messiah* [b]29 Many early manuscripts *What my Father has given me is greater than all*
[c]34 Psalm 82:6

SHARPEN THE FOCUS

Some people just seem to have a knack for giving great gifts, gifts the receiver loves to unwrap and use. Maybe you have a friend like that, someone who knows you well and whose gifts match your interests exactly.

Think about the most wonderful earthly gift you've ever received. Then read John 10:28–29. To follow Jesus' logic here, we need to read backwards a bit. We are the gift given to Jesus by His heavenly Father (John 10:29). We, in turn, receive a gift from Jesus—eternal life. Would the Father give His dearly loved Son something shabby off the discount rack? Surely not!

Make no mistake: We once were sinners who hated God and who rejected His love. But even then, while we lived as our Father's enemies, He loved us. He wanted us to live in His family forever (Romans 5:8). And so He sent His Son to earth to die for us, to gather us, and to bring us home to Himself in repentance and faith.

So precious are we to Jesus that He stands guard over us constantly. He promises that no one will snatch us out of His hand. Neither He nor our Father will allow it (John 10:28, 29).

Our Lord never intended that we read his Word in the same way we read a philosophy text or a home-improvement magazine. The Holy Scriptures are the record of God acting in love to save His people from sin and from sin's fallout. The Bible is both God's love letter to the world and the account of our family's roots, the history of God's family. Read today with this in mind. If time is short, focus on John 11:1–53.

The Death of Lazarus

11 Now a man named Lazarus was
sick. He was from Bethany, the
village of Mary and her sister Martha.
[2]This Mary, whose brother Lazarus now
lay sick, was the same one who poured
perfume on the Lord and wiped his feet
with her hair. [3]So the sisters sent word
to Jesus, "Lord, the one you love is sick."
[4]When he heard this, Jesus said, "This
sickness will not end in death. No, it is
for God's glory so that God's Son may
be glorified through it." [5]Jesus loved
Martha and her sister and Lazarus. [6]Yet
when he heard that Lazarus was sick, he
stayed where he was two more days.
[7]Then he said to his disciples, "Let us
go back to Judea."
[8]"But Rabbi," they said, "a short while
ago the Jews tried to stone you, and yet
you are going back there?"
[9]Jesus answered, "Are there not
twelve hours of daylight? A man who
walks by day will not stumble, for he
sees by this world's light. [10]It is when
he walks by night that he stumbles, for
he has no light."
[11]After he had said this, he went on to
tell them, "Our friend Lazarus has fallen
asleep; but I am going there to wake
him up."
[12]His disciples replied, "Lord, if he
sleeps, he will get better." [13]Jesus had
been speaking of his death, but his disciples thought he meant natural sleep.
[14]So then he told them plainly, "Lazarus is dead, [15]and for your sake I am glad
I was not there, so that you may believe.
But let us go to him."
[16]Then Thomas (called Didymus) said
to the rest of the disciples, "Let us also
go, that we may die with him."

Jesus Comforts the Sisters

[17]On his arrival, Jesus found that Lazarus had already been in the tomb for
four days. [18]Bethany was less than two
miles[a] from Jerusalem, [19]and many Jews
had come to Martha and Mary to comfort them in the loss of their brother.
[20]When Martha heard that Jesus was
coming, she went out to meet him, but
Mary stayed at home.
[21]"Lord," Martha said to Jesus, "if you
had been here, my brother would not
have died. [22]But I know that even now
God will give you whatever you ask."
[23]Jesus said to her, "Your brother will
rise again."
[24]Martha answered, "I know he will
rise again in the resurrection at the last
day."
[25]Jesus said to her, "I am the resurrection and the life. He who believes in me
will live, even though he dies; [26]and
whoever lives and believes in me will
never die. Do you believe this?"
[27]"Yes, Lord," she told him, "I believe
that you are the Christ,[b] the Son of God,
who was to come into the world."
[28]And after she had said this, she went
back and called her sister Mary aside.

[a]18 Greek *fifteen stadia* (about 3 kilometers)
[b]27 Or *Messiah*

"The Teacher is here," she said, "and is
asking for you." 29When Mary heard
this, she got up quickly and went to
him. 30Now Jesus had not yet entered
the village, but was still at the place
where Martha had met him. 31When the
Jews who had been with Mary in the
house, comforting her, noticed how
quickly she got up and went out, they
followed her, supposing she was going
to the tomb to mourn there.
32When Mary reached the place
where Jesus was and saw him, she fell
at his feet and said, "Lord, if you had
been here, my brother would not have
died."
33When Jesus saw her weeping, and
the Jews who had come along with her
also weeping, he was deeply moved in
spirit and troubled. 34"Where have you
laid him?" he asked.
"Come and see, Lord," they replied.
35Jesus wept.
36Then the Jews said, "See how he
loved him!"
37But some of them said, "Could not
he who opened the eyes of the blind
man have kept this man from dying?"

Jesus Raises Lazarus From the Dead

38Jesus, once more deeply moved,
came to the tomb. It was a cave with a
stone laid across the entrance. 39"Take
away the stone," he said.
"But, Lord," said Martha, the sister of
the dead man, "by this time there is
a bad odor, for he has been there four
days."
40Then Jesus said, "Did I not tell you
that if you believed, you would see the
glory of God?"
41So they took away the stone. Then
Jesus looked up and said, "Father, I
thank you that you have heard me. 42I
knew that you always hear me, but I
said this for the benefit of the people
standing here, that they may believe
that you sent me."
43When he had said this, Jesus called
in a loud voice, "Lazarus, come out!"
44The dead man came out, his hands and
feet wrapped with strips of linen, and a
cloth around his face.
Jesus said to them, "Take off the grave
clothes and let him go."

The Plot to Kill Jesus

45Therefore many of the Jews who
had come to visit Mary, and had seen
what Jesus did, put their faith in him.
46But some of them went to the Pharisees and told them what Jesus had
done. 47Then the chief priests and the
Pharisees called a meeting of the Sanhedrin.
"What are we accomplishing?" they
asked. "Here is this man performing
many miraculous signs. 48If we let him
go on like this, everyone will believe in
him, and then the Romans will come
and take away both our place[a] and our
nation."
49Then one of them, named Caiaphas,
who was high priest that year, spoke up,
"You know nothing at all! 50You do not
realize that it is better for you that one
man die for the people than that the
whole nation perish."
51He did not say this on his own, but
as high priest that year he prophesied
that Jesus would die for the Jewish nation, 52and not only for that nation but
also for the scattered children of God, to
bring them together and make them
one. 53So from that day on they plotted
to take his life.
54Therefore Jesus no longer moved
about publicly among the Jews. Instead
he withdrew to a region near the desert,
to a village called Ephraim, where he
stayed with his disciples.
55When it was almost time for the Jewish Passover, many went up from the
country to Jerusalem for their ceremonial cleansing before the Passover.
56They kept looking for Jesus, and as
they stood in the temple area they asked
one another, "What do you think? Isn't
he coming to the Feast at all?" 57But the
chief priests and Pharisees had given
orders that if anyone found out where
Jesus was, he should report it so that
they might arrest him.

[a]48 Or *temple*

Jesus Anointed at Bethany

12 Six days before the Passover,
Jesus arrived at Bethany,
where Lazarus lived, whom Jesus had
raised from the dead. 2Here a dinner
was given in Jesus' honor. Martha
served, while Lazarus was among those
reclining at the table with him. 3Then
Mary took about a pint[a] of pure nard, an
expensive perfume; she poured it on
Jesus' feet and wiped his feet with her
hair. And the house was filled with the
fragrance of the perfume.

4But one of his disciples, Judas Iscariot, who was later to betray him, objected, 5"Why wasn't this perfume sold and
the money given to the poor? It was
worth a year's wages.[b]" 6He did not say
this because he cared about the poor but
because he was a thief; as keeper of the
money bag, he used to help himself to
what was put into it.

7"Leave her alone," Jesus replied. "⌊It
was intended⌋ that she should save this
perfume for the day of my burial. 8You
will always have the poor among you,
but you will not always have me."

9Meanwhile a large crowd of Jews
found out that Jesus was there and
came, not only because of him but also
to see Lazarus, whom he had raised
from the dead. 10So the chief priests
made plans to kill Lazarus as well, 11for
on account of him many of the Jews
were going over to Jesus and putting
their faith in him.

The Triumphal Entry

12The next day the great crowd that
had come for the Feast heard that Jesus
was on his way to Jerusalem. 13They
took palm branches and went out to
meet him, shouting,

"Hosanna![c]"

"Blessed is he who comes in the
name of the Lord!"[d]

"Blessed is the King of Israel!"

14Jesus found a young donkey and sat
upon it, as it is written,

15"Do not be afraid, O Daughter of
Zion;
see, your king is coming,
seated on a donkey's colt."[e]

16At first his disciples did not understand all this. Only after Jesus was glorified did they realize that these things
had been written about him and that
they had done these things to him.

17Now the crowd that was with him
when he called Lazarus from the tomb
and raised him from the dead continued
to spread the word. 18Many people, because they had heard that he had given
this miraculous sign, went out to meet
him. 19So the Pharisees said to one another, "See, this is getting us nowhere.
Look how the whole world has gone after him!"

Jesus Predicts His Death

20Now there were some Greeks
among those who went up to worship
at the Feast. 21They came to Philip, who
was from Bethsaida in Galilee, with a request. "Sir," they said, "we would like to
see Jesus." 22Philip went to tell Andrew;
Andrew and Philip in turn told Jesus.

23Jesus replied, "The hour has come
for the Son of Man to be glorified. 24I tell
you the truth, unless a kernel of wheat
falls to the ground and dies, it remains
only a single seed. But if it dies, it produces many seeds. 25The man who loves
his life will lose it, while the man who
hates his life in this world will keep it for
eternal life. 26Whoever serves me must
follow me; and where I am, my servant
also will be. My Father will honor the
one who serves me.

27"Now my heart is troubled, and
what shall I say? 'Father, save me from
this hour'? No, it was for this very reason I came to this hour. 28Father, glorify
your name!"

Then a voice came from heaven, "I
have glorified it, and will glorify it

[a]3 Greek *a litra* (probably about 0.5 liter)
[b]5 Greek *three hundred denarii* [c]*13* A Hebrew expression meaning "Save!" which became an exclamation of praise [d]*13* Psalm 118:25,26
[e]*15* Zech. 9:9

again.” 29The crowd that was there and
heard it said it had thundered; others
said an angel had spoken to him.
30Jesus said, “This voice was for your
benefit, not mine. 31Now is the time for
judgment on this world; now the prince
of this world will be driven out. 32But I,
when I am lifted up from the earth, will
draw all men to myself.” 33He said this
to show the kind of death he was going
to die.
34The crowd spoke up, “We have
heard from the Law that the Christ[a] will
remain forever, so how can you say, ‘The
Son of Man must be lifted up’? Who is
this ‘Son of Man’?”
35Then Jesus told them, “You are going to have the light just a little while
longer. Walk while you have the light,
before darkness overtakes you. The
man who walks in the dark does not
know where he is going. 36Put your trust
in the light while you have it, so that
you may become sons of light.” When
he had finished speaking, Jesus left and
hid himself from them.

The Jews Continue in Their Unbelief

37Even after Jesus had done all these
miraculous signs in their presence, they
still would not believe in him. 38This was
to fulfill the word of Isaiah the prophet:

“Lord, who has believed our
message
and to whom has the arm of the
Lord been revealed?”[b]

39For this reason they could not believe, because, as Isaiah says elsewhere:

40“He has blinded their eyes
and deadened their hearts,
so they can neither see with their
eyes,
nor understand with their hearts,
nor turn—and I would heal
them.”[c]

41Isaiah said this because he saw Jesus’
glory and spoke about him.
42Yet at the same time many even
among the leaders believed in him. But
because of the Pharisees they would not
confess their faith for fear they would be
put out of the synagogue; 43for they
loved praise from men more than praise
from God.
44Then Jesus cried out, “When a man
believes in me, he does not believe in me
only, but in the one who sent me.
45When he looks at me, he sees the one
who sent me. 46I have come into the
world as a light, so that no one who believes in me should stay in darkness.
47“As for the person who hears my
words but does not keep them, I do not
judge him. For I did not come to judge
the world, but to save it. 48There is a
judge for the one who rejects me and
does not accept my words; that very
word which I spoke will condemn him
at the last day. 49For I did not speak of
my own accord, but the Father who sent
me commanded me what to say and
how to say it. 50I know that his command leads to eternal life. So whatever
I say is just what the Father has told me
to say.”

[a]34 Or *Messiah* [b]38 Isaiah 53:1 [c]40 Isaiah 6:10

SHARPEN THE FOCUS

One word. That’s all it took. Jesus called Lazarus’ name (John 11:32) and His friend awoke from death. It wasn’t that Lazarus’ name had such power. No, Lazarus awoke because of the One who spoke that name.

One day Jesus will speak your name, my name, too, and we will rise from the dust of death. It won’t matter how long we’ve been dead. It won’t matter whether our bodies are in a grave or lost at sea or scattered as ashes to the four winds. Jesus will speak, and our bodies will at that instant be reunited with our souls.

Mary and Martha invited Jesus to a celebration of Lazarus’ new life (John 12:1–2). We will celebrate, too, at the Marriage Supper of the Lamb (Revelation 19:7–10). Imagine a family reunion, a victory celebration, and a homecoming party, all rolled into one. Forever we will sing and cheer Jesus' love and His triumph over sin, Satan, and death. What a day that will be!

Whenever someone speaks your name today, let it remind you of the Day you will hear the voice of your Lord Jesus.

WEEK 82 • SATURDAY

John 13:1—14:31

Words spoken from one's deathbed usually carry a lot of weight. People who know they are dying most often choose their words carefully. Jesus knew what lay ahead of Him as He spent Holy Thursday evening with His disciples. He chose His words carefully. Read them with care, too. If time is short, focus on John 14:1–31.

Jesus Washes His Disciples' Feet

13 It was just before the Passover
Feast. Jesus knew that the
time had come for him to leave this
world and go to the Father. Having
loved his own who were in the world,
he now showed them the full extent of
his love.[a]
2The evening meal was being served,
and the devil had already prompted
Judas Iscariot, son of Simon, to betray
Jesus. 3Jesus knew that the Father had
put all things under his power, and that
he had come from God and was returning to God; 4so he got up from the
meal, took off his outer clothing, and
wrapped a towel around his waist. 5Af-
ter that, he poured water into a basin
and began to wash his disciples' feet,
drying them with the towel that was
wrapped around him.
6He came to Simon Peter, who said
to him, "Lord, are you going to wash
my feet?"
7Jesus replied, "You do not realize
now what I am doing, but later you will
understand."
8"No," said Peter, "you shall never
wash my feet."
Jesus answered, "Unless I wash you,
you have no part with me."
9"Then, Lord," Simon Peter replied,
"not just my feet but my hands and my
head as well!"
10Jesus answered, "A person who has
had a bath needs only to wash his feet;
his whole body is clean. And you are
clean, though not every one of you."
11For he knew who was going to betray
him, and that was why he said not every one was clean.
12When he had finished washing their
feet, he put on his clothes and returned
to his place. "Do you understand what
I have done for you?" he asked them.
13"You call me 'Teacher' and 'Lord,' and
rightly so, for that is what I am. 14Now
that I, your Lord and Teacher, have
washed your feet, you also should wash
one another's feet. 15I have set you an
example that you should do as I have
done for you. 16I tell you the truth, no
servant is greater than his master, nor is
a messenger greater than the one who
sent him. 17Now that you know these
things, you will be blessed if you do
them.

[a]1 Or *he loved them to the last*

Jesus Predicts His Betrayal

18"I am not referring to all of you; I
know those I have chosen. But this is to
fulfill the scripture: 'He who shares my
bread has lifted up his heel against me.'[a]
19"I am telling you now before it happens, so that when it does happen you
will believe that I am He. 20I tell you the
truth, whoever accepts anyone I send
accepts me; and whoever accepts me accepts the one who sent me."
21After he had said this, Jesus was
troubled in spirit and testified, "I tell you
the truth, one of you is going to betray me."
22His disciples stared at one another,
at a loss to know which of them he
meant. 23One of them, the disciple
whom Jesus loved, was reclining next to
him. 24Simon Peter motioned to this disciple and said, "Ask him which one he
means."
25Leaning back against Jesus, he asked
him, "Lord, who is it?"
26Jesus answered, "It is the one to
whom I will give this piece of bread
when I have dipped it in the dish."
Then, dipping the piece of bread, he
gave it to Judas Iscariot, son of Simon.
27As soon as Judas took the bread, Satan
entered into him.
"What you are about to do, do quickly," Jesus told him, 28but no one at the
meal understood why Jesus said this to
him. 29Since Judas had charge of the
money, some thought Jesus was telling
him to buy what was needed for the
Feast, or to give something to the poor.
30As soon as Judas had taken the bread,
he went out. And it was night.

Jesus Predicts Peter's Denial

31When he was gone, Jesus said,
"Now is the Son of Man glorified and
God is glorified in him. 32If God is glorified in him,[b] God will glorify the Son in
himself, and will glorify him at once.
33"My children, I will be with you only
a little longer. You will look for me, and
just as I told the Jews, so I tell you now:
Where I am going, you cannot come.
34"A new command I give you: Love
one another. As I have loved you, so you
must love one another. 35By this all men
will know that you are my disciples, if
you love one another."
36Simon Peter asked him, "Lord,
where are you going?"
Jesus replied, "Where I am going, you
cannot follow now, but you will follow
later."
37Peter asked, "Lord, why can't I follow you now? I will lay down my life for
you."
38Then Jesus answered, "Will you
really lay down your life for me? I tell
you the truth, before the rooster crows,
you will disown me three times!

Jesus Comforts His Disciples

14 "Do not let your hearts be
troubled. Trust in God[c]; trust
also in me. 2In my Father's house are
many rooms; if it were not so, I would
have told you. I am going there to prepare a place for you. 3And if I go and
prepare a place for you, I will come back
and take you to be with me that you also
may be where I am. 4You know the way
to the place where I am going."

Jesus the Way to the Father

5Thomas said to him, "Lord, we don't
know where you are going, so how can
we know the way?"
6Jesus answered, "I am the way and
the truth and the life. No one comes to
the Father except through me. 7If you
really knew me, you would know[d] my
Father as well. From now on, you do
know him and have seen him."
8Philip said, "Lord, show us the Father and that will be enough for us."
9Jesus answered: "Don't you know
me, Philip, even after I have been
among you such a long time? Anyone
who has seen me has seen the Father.
How can you say, 'Show us the Father'?
10Don't you believe that I am in the Father, and that the Father is in me? The

[a]*18* Psalm 41:9 [b]*32* Many early manuscripts do not have *If God is glorified in him.* [c]*1* Or *You trust in God* [d]*7* Some early manuscripts *If you really have known me, you will know*

words I say to you are not just my own.
Rather, it is the Father, living in me, who
is doing his work. [11]Believe me when I
say that I am in the Father and the Father is in me; or at least believe on the
evidence of the miracles themselves. [12]I
tell you the truth, anyone who has faith
in me will do what I have been doing.
He will do even greater things than
these, because I am going to the Father.
[13]And I will do whatever you ask in my
name, so that the Son may bring glory
to the Father. [14]You may ask me for anything in my name, and I will do it.

Jesus Promises the Holy Spirit

[15]"If you love me, you will obey what
I command. [16]And I will ask the Father,
and he will give you another Counselor
to be with you forever— [17]the Spirit of
truth. The world cannot accept him, because it neither sees him nor knows
him. But you know him, for he lives
with you and will be[a] in you. [18]I will not
leave you as orphans; I will come to you.
[19]Before long, the world will not see me
anymore, but you will see me. Because
I live, you also will live. [20]On that day
you will realize that I am in my Father,
and you are in me, and I am in you.
[21]Whoever has my commands and
obeys them, he is the one who loves me.
He who loves me will be loved by my
Father, and I too will love him and show
myself to him."
[22]Then Judas (not Judas Iscariot) said,
"But, Lord, why do you intend to show
yourself to us and not to the world?"
[23]Jesus replied, "If anyone loves me,
he will obey my teaching. My Father
will love him, and we will come to him
and make our home with him. [24]He who
does not love me will not obey my
teaching. These words you hear are not
my own; they belong to the Father who
sent me.
[25]"All this I have spoken while still
with you. [26]But the Counselor, the Holy
Spirit, whom the Father will send in
my name, will teach you all things
and will remind you of everything I
have said to you. [27]Peace I leave with
you; my peace I give you. I do not give
to you as the world gives. Do not let
your hearts be troubled and do not be
afraid.
[28]"You heard me say, 'I am going away
and I am coming back to you.' If you
loved me, you would be glad that I am
going to the Father, for the Father is
greater than I. [29]I have told you now before it happens, so that when it does
happen you will believe. [30]I will not
speak with you much longer, for the
prince of this world is coming. He has
no hold on me, [31]but the world must
learn that I love the Father and that I
do exactly what my Father has commanded me.
"Come now; let us leave.

[a]*17* Some early manuscripts *and is*

SHARPEN THE FOCUS

Their Friend was about to die. The disciples' dreams of a glorious earthly destiny would die with Him. Fear flooded their hearts. Jesus knew. He understood. And so He spoke to them about their fears. Tender words. Encouraging words.

"Stop letting your hearts be upset," He says in essence (John 14:1). How were they to do that? The last part of the verse explains: "Keep on trusting in God; keep on trusting in Me." As long as they could see Jesus, as long as He walked and talked and taught them, trust wouldn't be too tough. But once He was crucified, once He died, once He arose and ascended into heaven, their human eyes would not see Him. Would they trust Him even then, even when it looked like they were on their own?

Yes, they would. Yes, as by the power of the Holy Spirit they kept their focus on Jesus and on the heavenly Father whom Jesus had revealed to them.

What upsets or worries you today? You need not let your heart be troubled or afraid. Focus on Jesus, on His Word, on His death and resurrection for you. Trustingly, throw yourself into the Father's arms. He will keep you safe here until He comes to take you home to Himself.

WEEK 83 • MONDAY

John 15:1—16:33

Jesus continues His last instructions to His disciples on the night before He is to die. His words are not only instructive, they are also comforting and encouraging. Read slowly and think about our Lord's words. They are short and look simple, yet they are truly, deeply profound. If time is short, focus on John 16:1–33.

The Vine and the Branches

15 "I am the true vine, and my
Father is the gardener. 2He
cuts off every branch in me that bears no
fruit, while every branch that does bear
fruit he prunes[a] so that it will be even
more fruitful. 3You are already clean
because of the word I have spoken to
you. 4Remain in me, and I will remain
in you. No branch can bear fruit by itself; it must remain in the vine. Neither
can you bear fruit unless you remain
in me.

5"I am the vine; you are the branches.
If a man remains in me and I in him, he
will bear much fruit; apart from me you
can do nothing. 6If anyone does not
remain in me, he is like a branch that is
thrown away and withers; such
branches are picked up, thrown into the
fire and burned. 7If you remain in me
and my words remain in you, ask whatever you wish, and it will be given you.
8This is to my Father's glory, that you
bear much fruit, showing yourselves to
be my disciples.

9"As the Father has loved me, so have
I loved you. Now remain in my love.
10If you obey my commands, you will
remain in my love, just as I have obeyed
my Father's commands and remain in
his love. 11I have told you this so that my
joy may be in you and that your joy may
be complete. 12My command is this:
Love each other as I have loved you.
13Greater love has no one than this, that
he lay down his life for his friends. 14You
are my friends if you do what I command. 15I no longer call you servants,
because a servant does not know his
master's business. Instead, I have called
you friends, for everything that I
learned from my Father I have made
known to you. 16You did not choose me,
but I chose you and appointed you to go
and bear fruit—fruit that will last. Then
the Father will give you whatever you
ask in my name. 17This is my command:
Love each other.

The World Hates the Disciples

18"If the world hates you, keep in
mind that it hated me first. 19If you belonged to the world, it would love you
as its own. As it is, you do not belong to
the world, but I have chosen you out of
the world. That is why the world hates
you. 20Remember the words I spoke to
you: 'No servant is greater than his
master.'[b] If they persecuted me, they will

[a]2 The Greek for *prunes* also means *cleans*.
[b]20 John 13:16

persecute you also. If they obeyed my
teaching, they will obey yours also.
[21]They will treat you this way because of
my name, for they do not know the One
who sent me. [22]If I had not come and
spoken to them, they would not be
guilty of sin. Now, however, they have
no excuse for their sin. [23]He who hates
me hates my Father as well. [24]If I had not
done among them what no one else did,
they would not be guilty of sin. But now
they have seen these miracles, and yet
they have hated both me and my Father.
[25]But this is to fulfill what is written in
their Law: 'They hated me without
reason.'[a]

[26]"When the Counselor comes, whom
I will send to you from the Father, the
Spirit of truth who goes out from the
Father, he will testify about me. [27]And
you also must testify, for you have been
with me from the beginning.

16 "All this I have told you so
that you will not go astray.
[2]They will put you out of the synagogue; in fact, a time is coming when
anyone who kills you will think he is offering a service to God. [3]They will do
such things because they have not
known the Father or me. [4]I have told
you this, so that when the time comes
you will remember that I warned you. I
did not tell you this at first because I was
with you.

The Work of the Holy Spirit

[5]"Now I am going to him who sent
me, yet none of you asks me, 'Where are
you going?' [6]Because I have said these
things, you are filled with grief. [7]But I
tell you the truth: It is for your good that
I am going away. Unless I go away, the
Counselor will not come to you; but if I
go, I will send him to you. [8]When he
comes, he will convict the world of
guilt[b] in regard to sin and righteousness
and judgment: [9]in regard to sin, because
men do not believe in me; [10]in regard to
righteousness, because I am going to the
Father, where you can see me no longer;
[11]and in regard to judgment, because
the prince of this world now stands condemned.

[12]"I have much more to say to you,
more than you can now bear. [13]But
when he, the Spirit of truth, comes, he
will guide you into all truth. He will not
speak on his own; he will speak only
what he hears, and he will tell you what
is yet to come. [14]He will bring glory to
me by taking from what is mine and
making it known to you. [15]All that belongs to the Father is mine. That is why
I said the Spirit will take from what is
mine and make it known to you.

[16]"In a little while you will see me no
more, and then after a little while you
will see me."

The Disciples' Grief Will Turn to Joy

[17]Some of his disciples said to one another, "What does he mean by saying,
'In a little while you will see me no
more, and then after a little while you
will see me,' and 'Because I am going to
the Father'?" [18]They kept asking, "What
does he mean by 'a little while'? We
don't understand what he is saying."

[19]Jesus saw that they wanted to ask
him about this, so he said to them, "Are
you asking one another what I meant
when I said, 'In a little while you will see
me no more, and then after a little while
you will see me'? [20]I tell you the truth,
you will weep and mourn while the
world rejoices. You will grieve, but your
grief will turn to joy. [21]A woman giving
birth to a child has pain because her
time has come; but when her baby is
born she forgets the anguish because of
her joy that a child is born into the
world. [22]So with you: Now is your time
of grief, but I will see you again and you
will rejoice, and no one will take away
your joy. [23]In that day you will no longer
ask me anything. I tell you the truth, my
Father will give you whatever you ask
in my name. [24]Until now you have not
asked for anything in my name. Ask and
you will receive, and your joy will be
complete.

[25]"Though I have been speaking figuratively, a time is coming when I will no

[a]25 Psalms 35:19; 69:4 [b]8 Or *will expose the guilt of the world*

longer use this kind of language but
will tell you plainly about my Father.
26In that day you will ask in my name.
I am not saying that I will ask the Father on your behalf. 27No, the Father
himself loves you because you have
loved me and have believed that I
came from God. 28I came from the Father
and entered the world; now I am leaving the world and going back to the
Father."
29Then Jesus' disciples said, "Now you
are speaking clearly and without figures
of speech. 30Now we can see that you
know all things and that you do not
even need to have anyone ask you
questions. This makes us believe that
you came from God."
31"You believe at last!"[a] Jesus answered. 32"But a time is coming, and has
come, when you will be scattered, each
to his own home. You will leave me all
alone. Yet I am not alone, for my Father
is with me.
33"I have told you these things, so that
in me you may have peace. In this world
you will have trouble. But take heart! I
have overcome the world."

[a]31 Or *"Do you now believe?"*

SHARPEN THE FOCUS

On this last night of His earthly life, Jesus shared with His disciples some of the deepest mysteries of our faith, talking with them about His love for them and about the ways the Father and the Holy Spirit are working with Him to bring about our salvation.

Think of it! As those joined by faith to Jesus we have:

- The assurance we are cleansed from our sins; Jesus has given us His Word on it (John 15:3).
- An invitation from our Savior to abide in Him by faith now and forever (John 15:9).
- Power from Christ to bear a bumper crop of spiritual fruit (John 15:5).
- The fullness of Christ's joy (John 15:11).
- Friendship with Jesus (John 15:15).
- The sustaining presence of the Holy Spirit (John 15:26), sent from the heavenly Father.

Think of some more of the fantastic promises Jesus left as His legacy to His disciples and to us. Then pray, thanking your God for all the benefits that are yours through the death and resurrection of His Son.

WEEK 83 • TUESDAY

John 17:1–26

GET THE BIG PICTURE

As we read John 17, we're listening in on one of the last conversations Jesus had with His heavenly Father while our Savior lived on earth. The Holy Spirit inspired John to record this prayer for our comfort and encouragement. As you read it, remember that as our Great High Priest, Jesus continues to intercede for us, asking for many of the same blessings for which He prayed on Holy Thursday evening. If time is short, focus on John 17:20–26.

Jesus Prays for Himself

17 After Jesus said this, he
looked toward heaven and
prayed:
"Father, the time has come. Glorify your Son, that your Son may
glorify you. 2For you granted him
authority over all people that he
might give eternal life to all those
you have given him. 3Now this is
eternal life: that they may know
you, the only true God, and Jesus
Christ, whom you have sent. 4I
have brought you glory on earth by
completing the work you gave me
to do. 5And now, Father, glorify me
in your presence with the glory I
had with you before the world began.

Jesus Prays for His Disciples

6"I have revealed you[a] to those
whom you gave me out of the
world. They were yours; you gave
them to me and they have obeyed
your word. 7Now they know that
everything you have given me
comes from you. 8For I gave them
the words you gave me and they
accepted them. They knew with
certainty that I came from you, and
they believed that you sent me. 9I
pray for them. I am not praying for
the world, but for those you have
given me, for they are yours. 10All I
have is yours, and all you have is
mine. And glory has come to me
through them. 11I will remain in the
world no longer, but they are still in
the world, and I am coming to you.
Holy Father, protect them by the
power of your name—the name
you gave me—so that they may be
one as we are one. 12While I was
with them, I protected them and
kept them safe by that name you
gave me. None has been lost except
the one doomed to destruction so
that Scripture would be fulfilled.
13"I am coming to you now, but I
say these things while I am still in
the world, so that they may have
the full measure of my joy within
them. 14I have given them your
word and the world has hated
them, for they are not of the world
any more than I am of the world.
15My prayer is not that you take
them out of the world but that you
protect them from the evil one.
16They are not of the world, even as
I am not of it. 17Sanctify[b] them by
the truth; your word is truth. 18As
you sent me into the world, I have
sent them into the world. 19For
them I sanctify myself, that they too
may be truly sanctified.

Jesus Prays for All Believers

20"My prayer is not for them
alone. I pray also for those who will
believe in me through their message, 21that all of them may be one,
Father, just as you are in me and I
am in you. May they also be in us
so that the world may believe that
you have sent me. 22I have given
them the glory that you gave me,
that they may be one as we are one:
23I in them and you in me. May they
be brought to complete unity to let
the world know that you sent me
and have loved them even as you
have loved me.
24"Father, I want those you have
given me to be with me where I am,
and to see my glory, the glory you
have given me because you loved
me before the creation of the world.
25"Righteous Father, though the
world does not know you, I know

[a]6 Greek *your name*; also in verse 26
[b]17 Greek *hagiazo (set apart for sacred use* or *make holy)*; also in verse 19

you, and they know that you have
sent me. [26]I have made you known
to them, and will continue to make
you known in order that the love
you have for me may be in them
and that I myself may be in them."

SHARPEN THE FOCUS

Grace to be kept in faith (John 17:11). Unity of heart and purpose with God and with each other (John 17:11b). Joy (John 17:13). Safety from Satan (John 17:15). Sanctification (John 17:17). A powerful witness in the world (John 17:23). A place in the heavenly home forever (John 17:24). Love as pure and intense as the Father's love for Jesus (John 17:26).

Wow! What a list of blessings. Jesus asked all these things for us and more. Have you ever asked them for yourself? You can, you know. How could we be more sure of God's will for us than to hear our Lord Jesus ask the Father for these things on our behalf?

But Jesus' prayer reveals even more. For instance, read John 17:7–8. Jesus says of His disciples, "They knew with certainty that I came from You." True enough, the Twelve had moments of clarity. But more often than not, they saw failures of faith litter the dusty roads of Palestine along which they walked. How could Jesus say this of them?

In the same way, of course, that He says it of us and of all His saints. He had deleted the record of their failures—and ours. He has expunged their record—and ours. In a few short hours, the Lord would bleed and agonize and die in the disciples' place—and in ours.

WEEK 83 • WEDNESDAY

John 18:1—19:42

GET THE BIG PICTURE

As we read the passion accounts from all four evangelists, we can't help but be impressed that Jesus suffered and died willingly. As you read today, keep in mind that Jesus is the Good Shepherd who, in love for us and obedience to His Father, laid down His life for us all. If time is short, focus on John 18:1–11.

Jesus Arrested

18 When he had finished praying, Jesus left with his disciples and crossed the Kidron Valley. On
the other side there was an olive grove,
and he and his disciples went into it.
[2]Now Judas, who betrayed him, knew
the place, because Jesus had often met
there with his disciples. [3]So Judas came
to the grove, guiding a detachment of
soldiers and some officials from the
chief priests and Pharisees. They were
carrying torches, lanterns and weapons.
[4]Jesus, knowing all that was going to
happen to him, went out and asked
them, "Who is it you want?"
[5]"Jesus of Nazareth," they replied.
"I am he," Jesus said. (And Judas the
traitor was standing there with them.)
[6]When Jesus said, "I am he," they drew
back and fell to the ground.
[7]Again he asked them, "Who is it you
want?"
And they said, "Jesus of Nazareth."

8"I told you that I am he," Jesus answered. "If you are looking for me, then let these men go." 9This happened so that the words he had spoken would be fulfilled: "I have not lost one of those you gave me."[a]

10Then Simon Peter, who had a sword, drew it and struck the high priest's servant, cutting off his right ear. (The servant's name was Malchus.)

11Jesus commanded Peter, "Put your sword away! Shall I not drink the cup the Father has given me?"

Jesus Taken to Annas

12Then the detachment of soldiers with its commander and the Jewish officials arrested Jesus. They bound him 13and brought him first to Annas, who was the father-in-law of Caiaphas, the high priest that year. 14Caiaphas was the one who had advised the Jews that it would be good if one man died for the people.

Peter's First Denial

15Simon Peter and another disciple were following Jesus. Because this disciple was known to the high priest, he went with Jesus into the high priest's courtyard, 16but Peter had to wait outside at the door. The other disciple, who was known to the high priest, came back, spoke to the girl on duty there and brought Peter in.

17"You are not one of his disciples, are you?" the girl at the door asked Peter.

He replied, "I am not."

18It was cold, and the servants and officials stood around a fire they had made to keep warm. Peter also was standing with them, warming himself.

The High Priest Questions Jesus

19Meanwhile, the high priest questioned Jesus about his disciples and his teaching.

20"I have spoken openly to the world," Jesus replied. "I always taught in synagogues or at the temple, where all the Jews come together. I said nothing in secret. 21Why question me? Ask those who heard me. Surely they know what I said."

22When Jesus said this, one of the officials nearby struck him in the face. "Is this the way you answer the high priest?" he demanded.

23"If I said something wrong," Jesus replied, "testify as to what is wrong. But if I spoke the truth, why did you strike me?" 24Then Annas sent him, still bound, to Caiaphas the high priest.[b]

Peter's Second and Third Denials

25As Simon Peter stood warming himself, he was asked, "You are not one of his disciples, are you?"

He denied it, saying, "I am not."

26One of the high priest's servants, a relative of the man whose ear Peter had cut off, challenged him, "Didn't I see you with him in the olive grove?" 27Again Peter denied it, and at that moment a rooster began to crow.

Jesus Before Pilate

28Then the Jews led Jesus from Caiaphas to the palace of the Roman governor. By now it was early morning, and to avoid ceremonial uncleanness the Jews did not enter the palace; they wanted to be able to eat the Passover. 29So Pilate came out to them and asked, "What charges are you bringing against this man?"

30"If he were not a criminal," they replied, "we would not have handed him over to you."

31Pilate said, "Take him yourselves and judge him by your own law."

"But we have no right to execute anyone," the Jews objected. 32This happened so that the words Jesus had spoken indicating the kind of death he was going to die would be fulfilled.

33Pilate then went back inside the palace, summoned Jesus and asked him, "Are you the king of the Jews?"

34"Is that your own idea," Jesus asked, "or did others talk to you about me?"

35"Am I a Jew?" Pilate replied. "It was

[a]9 John 6:39 [b]24 Or *(Now Annas had sent him, still bound, to Caiaphas the high priest.)*

your people and your chief priests who handed you over to me. What is it you have done?"

36 Jesus said, "My kingdom is not of this world. If it were, my servants would fight to prevent my arrest by the Jews. But now my kingdom is from another place."

37 "You are a king, then!" said Pilate.

Jesus answered, "You are right in saying I am a king. In fact, for this reason I was born, and for this I came into the world, to testify to the truth. Everyone on the side of truth listens to me."

38 "What is truth?" Pilate asked. With this he went out again to the Jews and said, "I find no basis for a charge against him. 39 But it is your custom for me to release to you one prisoner at the time of the Passover. Do you want me to release 'the king of the Jews'?"

40 They shouted back, "No, not him! Give us Barabbas!" Now Barabbas had taken part in a rebellion.

Jesus Sentenced to Be Crucified

19 Then Pilate took Jesus and had him flogged. 2 The soldiers twisted together a crown of thorns and put it on his head. They clothed him in a purple robe 3 and went up to him again and again, saying, "Hail, king of the Jews!" And they struck him in the face.

4 Once more Pilate came out and said to the Jews, "Look, I am bringing him out to you to let you know that I find no basis for a charge against him." 5 When Jesus came out wearing the crown of thorns and the purple robe, Pilate said to them, "Here is the man!"

6 As soon as the chief priests and their officials saw him, they shouted, "Crucify! Crucify!"

But Pilate answered, "You take him and crucify him. As for me, I find no basis for a charge against him."

7 The Jews insisted, "We have a law, and according to that law he must die, because he claimed to be the Son of God."

8 When Pilate heard this, he was even more afraid, 9 and he went back inside the palace. "Where do you come from?" he asked Jesus, but Jesus gave him no answer. 10 "Do you refuse to speak to me?" Pilate said. "Don't you realize I have power either to free you or to crucify you?"

11 Jesus answered, "You would have no power over me if it were not given to you from above. Therefore the one who handed me over to you is guilty of a greater sin."

12 From then on, Pilate tried to set Jesus free, but the Jews kept shouting, "If you let this man go, you are no friend of Caesar. Anyone who claims to be a king opposes Caesar."

13 When Pilate heard this, he brought Jesus out and sat down on the judge's seat at a place known as the Stone Pavement (which in Aramaic is Gabbatha). 14 It was the day of Preparation of Passover Week, about the sixth hour.

"Here is your king," Pilate said to the Jews.

15 But they shouted, "Take him away! Take him away! Crucify him!"

"Shall I crucify your king?" Pilate asked.

"We have no king but Caesar," the chief priests answered.

16 Finally Pilate handed him over to them to be crucified.

The Crucifixion

So the soldiers took charge of Jesus. 17 Carrying his own cross, he went out to the place of the Skull (which in Aramaic is called Golgotha). 18 Here they crucified him, and with him two others—one on each side and Jesus in the middle.

19 Pilate had a notice prepared and fastened to the cross. It read: JESUS OF NAZARETH, THE KING OF THE JEWS. 20 Many of the Jews read this sign, for the place where Jesus was crucified was near the city, and the sign was written in Aramaic, Latin and Greek. 21 The chief priests of the Jews protested to Pilate, "Do not write 'The King of the Jews,' but that this man claimed to be king of the Jews."

22 Pilate answered, "What I have written, I have written."

23 When the soldiers crucified Jesus,
they took his clothes, dividing them into
four shares, one for each of them, with
the undergarment remaining. This garment was seamless, woven in one piece
from top to bottom.
24 "Let's not tear it," they said to one
another. "Let's decide by lot who will
get it."
This happened that the scripture
might be fulfilled which said,

"They divided my garments among
them
and cast lots for my clothing."[a]

So this is what the soldiers did.
25 Near the cross of Jesus stood his
mother, his mother's sister, Mary the
wife of Clopas, and Mary Magdalene.
26 When Jesus saw his mother there, and
the disciple whom he loved standing
nearby, he said to his mother, "Dear
woman, here is your son," 27 and to the
disciple, "Here is your mother." From
that time on, this disciple took her into
his home.

The Death of Jesus

28 Later, knowing that all was now
completed, and so that the Scripture
would be fulfilled, Jesus said, "I am
thirsty." 29 A jar of wine vinegar was
there, so they soaked a sponge in it, put
the sponge on a stalk of the hyssop
plant, and lifted it to Jesus' lips. 30 When
he had received the drink, Jesus said, "It
is finished." With that, he bowed his
head and gave up his spirit.
31 Now it was the day of Preparation,
and the next day was to be a special Sabbath. Because the Jews did not want
the bodies left on the crosses during the
Sabbath, they asked Pilate to have the
legs broken and the bodies taken down.
32 The soldiers therefore came and broke
the legs of the first man who had been
crucified with Jesus, and then those of
the other. 33 But when they came to Jesus
and found that he was already dead,
they did not break his legs. 34 Instead,
one of the soldiers pierced Jesus' side
with a spear, bringing a sudden flow of
blood and water. 35 The man who saw it
has given testimony, and his testimony
is true. He knows that he tells the truth,
and he testifies so that you also may
believe. 36 These things happened so that
the scripture would be fulfilled: "Not
one of his bones will be broken,"[b] 37 and,
as another scripture says, "They will
look on the one they have pierced."[c]

The Burial of Jesus

38 Later, Joseph of Arimathea asked
Pilate for the body of Jesus. Now Joseph
was a disciple of Jesus, but secretly
because he feared the Jews. With Pilate's
permission, he came and took the body
away. 39 He was accompanied by Nicodemus, the man who earlier had visited Jesus at night. Nicodemus brought a
mixture of myrrh and aloes, about seventy-five pounds.[d] 40 Taking Jesus' body,
the two of them wrapped it, with the
spices, in strips of linen. This was in accordance with Jewish burial customs.
41 At the place where Jesus was crucified,
there was a garden, and in the garden a
new tomb, in which no one had ever
been laid. 42 Because it was the Jewish
day of Preparation and since the tomb
was nearby, they laid Jesus there.

[a] *24* Psalm 22:18 [b] *36* Exodus 12:46; Num. 9:12; Psalm 34:20 [c] *37* Zech. 12:10 [d] *39* Greek *a hundred litrai* (about 34 kilograms)

SHARPEN THE FOCUS

Even before the malignant force of sin slipped into God's good creation, ruining it, Calvary was written on the pages of history. For thousands of years Satan looked for ways to erase, to stop, to derail God's planned salvation. He failed.

Satan failed because God had promised to crush the ancient serpent's head (Genesis 3:15). Satan failed because "it was the LORD'S will to crush [Jesus] and cause Him to suffer "for our sins (Isaiah 53:10).

Jesus' death could not be stopped, because Jesus' love cannot be stopped. People may say to us, "You made your bed; now lie in it." Jesus says, "I don't care where you've been sleeping. I gave My life to free you from the burden of your sin. Come home. I will give you rest."

Because Jesus willingly laid down on the cross, we can in peace close our eyes in death. Because He lay in the tomb, the grave is not our eternal bed. As the Easter hymn says, "Made like Him, like Him we rise, ours the cross, the grave, the skies!"

Good Friday. Holy Saturday. Easter Sunday. These three days changed the course of human history forever. They also changed your personal history and mine. As you read, think about ways your life is different because you can say with Job of old, "I know that my Redeemer lives!" (Job 19:25). If time is short, focus on John 20:1–18.

The Empty Tomb

20 Early on the first day of
the week, while it was still
dark, Mary Magdalene went to the
tomb and saw that the stone had been
removed from the entrance. 2So she
came running to Simon Peter and the
other disciple, the one Jesus loved, and
said, "They have taken the Lord out of
the tomb, and we don't know where
they have put him!"
3So Peter and the other disciple started for the tomb. 4Both were running,
but the other disciple outran Peter and
reached the tomb first. 5He bent over
and looked in at the strips of linen lying
there but did not go in. 6Then Simon Peter, who was behind him, arrived and
went into the tomb. He saw the strips of
linen lying there, 7as well as the burial
cloth that had been around Jesus' head.
The cloth was folded up by itself, separate from the linen. 8Finally the other
disciple, who had reached the tomb
first, also went inside. He saw and believed. 9(They still did not understand
from Scripture that Jesus had to rise
from the dead.)

Jesus Appears to Mary Magdalene

10Then the disciples went back to their
homes, 11but Mary stood outside the
tomb crying. As she wept, she bent over
to look into the tomb 12and saw two
angels in white, seated where Jesus'
body had been, one at the head and the
other at the foot.
13They asked her, "Woman, why are
you crying?"
"They have taken my Lord away," she
said, "and I don't know where they
have put him." 14At this, she turned
around and saw Jesus standing there,
but she did not realize that it was Jesus.
15"Woman," he said, "why are you crying? Who is it you are looking for?"
Thinking he was the gardener, she
said, "Sir, if you have carried him away,
tell me where you have put him, and I
will get him."
16Jesus said to her, "Mary."
She turned toward him and cried out
in Aramaic, "Rabboni!" (which means
Teacher).
17Jesus said, "Do not hold on to me, for
I have not yet returned to the Father. Go
instead to my brothers and tell them, 'I

am returning to my Father and your
Father, to my God and your God.'"

18 Mary Magdalene went to the disciples with the news: "I have seen the
Lord!" And she told them that he had
said these things to her.

Jesus Appears to His Disciples

19 On the evening of that first day of
the week, when the disciples were together, with the doors locked for fear of
the Jews, Jesus came and stood among
them and said, "Peace be with you!"
20 After he said this, he showed them his
hands and side. The disciples were overjoyed when they saw the Lord.

21 Again Jesus said, "Peace be with you!
As the Father has sent me, I am sending
you." 22 And with that he breathed on
them and said, "Receive the Holy Spirit.
23 If you forgive anyone his sins, they are
forgiven; if you do not forgive them,
they are not forgiven."

Jesus Appears to Thomas

24 Now Thomas (called Didymus), one
of the Twelve, was not with the disciples
when Jesus came. 25 So the other disciples told him, "We have seen the Lord!"

But he said to them, "Unless I see the
nail marks in his hands and put my finger where the nails were, and put my
hand into his side, I will not believe it."

26 A week later his disciples were in the
house again, and Thomas was with
them. Though the doors were locked,
Jesus came and stood among them and
said, "Peace be with you!" 27 Then he said
to Thomas, "Put your finger here; see
my hands. Reach out your hand and
put it into my side. Stop doubting and
believe."

28 Thomas said to him, "My Lord and
my God!"

29 Then Jesus told him, "Because you
have seen me, you have believed;
blessed are those who have not seen
and yet have believed."

30 Jesus did many other miraculous
signs in the presence of his disciples,
which are not recorded in this book.
31 But these are written that you may[a]
believe that Jesus is the Christ, the Son
of God, and that by believing you may
have life in his name.

Jesus and the Miraculous Catch of Fish

21 Afterward Jesus appeared
again to his disciples, by the
Sea of Tiberias.[b] It happened this way:
2 Simon Peter, Thomas (called Didymus),
Nathanael from Cana in Galilee, the
sons of Zebedee, and two other disciples were together. 3 "I'm going out to
fish," Simon Peter told them, and they
said, "We'll go with you." So they went
out and got into the boat, but that night
they caught nothing.

4 Early in the morning, Jesus stood on
the shore, but the disciples did not realize that it was Jesus.

5 He called out to them, "Friends,
haven't you any fish?"

"No," they answered.

6 He said, "Throw your net on the
right side of the boat and you will find
some." When they did, they were unable to haul the net in because of the
large number of fish.

7 Then the disciple whom Jesus loved
said to Peter, "It is the Lord!" As soon as
Simon Peter heard him say, "It is the
Lord," he wrapped his outer garment
around him (for he had taken it off) and
jumped into the water. 8 The other disciples followed in the boat, towing the
net full of fish, for they were not far
from shore, about a hundred yards.[c]
9 When they landed, they saw a fire of
burning coals there with fish on it, and
some bread.

10 Jesus said to them, "Bring some of
the fish you have just caught."

11 Simon Peter climbed aboard and
dragged the net ashore. It was full of
large fish, 153, but even with so many
the net was not torn. 12 Jesus said to
them, "Come and have breakfast." None
of the disciples dared ask him, "Who are
you?" They knew it was the Lord.
13 Jesus came, took the bread and gave it

[a]31 Some manuscripts *may continue to* [b]1 That is, Sea of Galilee [c]8 Greek *about two hundred cubits* (about 90 meters)

to them, and did the same with the fish. [14]This was now the third time Jesus appeared to his disciples after he was raised from the dead.

Jesus Reinstates Peter

[15]When they had finished eating, Jesus said to Simon Peter, "Simon son of John, do you truly love me more than these?"

"Yes, Lord," he said, "you know that I love you."

Jesus said, "Feed my lambs."

[16]Again Jesus said, "Simon son of John, do you truly love me?"

He answered, "Yes, Lord, you know that I love you."

Jesus said, "Take care of my sheep."

[17]The third time he said to him, "Simon son of John, do you love me?"

Peter was hurt because Jesus asked him the third time, "Do you love me?" He said, "Lord, you know all things; you know that I love you."

Jesus said, "Feed my sheep. [18]I tell you the truth, when you were younger you dressed yourself and went where you wanted; but when you are old you will stretch out your hands, and someone else will dress you and lead you where you do not want to go." [19]Jesus said this to indicate the kind of death by which Peter would glorify God. Then he said to him, "Follow me!"

[20]Peter turned and saw that the disciple whom Jesus loved was following them. (This was the one who had leaned back against Jesus at the supper and had said, "Lord, who is going to betray you?") [21]When Peter saw him, he asked, "Lord, what about him?"

[22]Jesus answered, "If I want him to remain alive until I return, what is that to you? You must follow me." [23]Because of this, the rumor spread among the brothers that this disciple would not die. But Jesus did not say that he would not die; he only said, "If I want him to remain alive until I return, what is that to you?"

[24]This is the disciple who testifies to these things and who wrote them down. We know that his testimony is true.

[25]Jesus did many other things as well. If every one of them were written down, I suppose that even the whole world would not have room for the books that would be written.

SHARPEN THE FOCUS

The Old Testament prophets saw the Savior's victory from afar. They spoke of His resurrection in words filled with joy. Isaiah, for example, described Jesus' agony and death in his eloquent chapter 53. But Isaiah's eyes saw past the tomb. The Lord says about Christ:

After the suffering of His soul,
He will see the light of life and be satisfied;
by His knowledge My righteous Servant will justify many,
and He will bear their iniquities.
Therefore I will give Him a portion among the great,
and He will divide the spoils with the strong. (Isaiah 53:11–12)

Jesus did indeed see the light of life. God raised his righteous Servant from the dead. Now our Savior divides the "spoils" of His victory with us. In Him, we are "the strong" who now rejoice in freedom from guilt, power over Satan's accusations and temptations, and the sure and certain hope of eternal life. His victory is our victory!

ACTS

In what we might call Volume 1 of his work, his gospel, Dr. Luke told us about how Jesus began to serve and to teach. Now in Volume 2, Acts, Luke will explain the many ways our Lord continued that ministry—through His people. This chapter sets the tone of excitement, joy, and anticipation that will fill all of Acts. Catch a sense of that tone as you read. If time is short focus on Acts 1:1–14.

Jesus Taken Up Into Heaven

1 In my former book, Theophilus, I wrote about all that Jesus began to do and to teach [2]until the day he was taken up to heaven, after giving instructions through the Holy Spirit to the apostles he had chosen. [3]After his suffering, he showed himself to these men and gave many convincing proofs that he was alive. He appeared to them over a period of forty days and spoke about the kingdom of God. [4]On one occasion, while he was eating with them, he gave them this command: "Do not leave Jerusalem, but wait for the gift my Father promised, which you have heard me speak about. [5]For John baptized with[a] water, but in a few days you will be baptized with the Holy Spirit."

[6]So when they met together, they asked him, "Lord, are you at this time going to restore the kingdom to Israel?"

[7]He said to them: "It is not for you to know the times or dates the Father has set by his own authority. [8]But you will receive power when the Holy Spirit comes on you; and you will be my witnesses in Jerusalem, and in all Judea and Samaria, and to the ends of the earth."

[9]After he said this, he was taken up before their very eyes, and a cloud hid him from their sight.

[10]They were looking intently up into the sky as he was going, when suddenly two men dressed in white stood beside them. [11]"Men of Galilee," they said, "why do you stand here looking into the sky? This same Jesus, who has been taken from you into heaven, will come back in the same way you have seen him go into heaven."

Matthias Chosen to Replace Judas

[12]Then they returned to Jerusalem from the hill called the Mount of Olives, a Sabbath day's walk[b] from the city. [13]When they arrived, they went upstairs to the room where they were staying. Those present were Peter, John, James and Andrew; Philip and Thomas, Bartholomew and Matthew; James son of Alphaeus and Simon the Zealot, and Judas son of James. [14]They all joined together constantly in prayer, along with the women and Mary the mother of Jesus, and with his brothers.

[a]5 Or *in* [b]12 That is, about 3/4 mile (about 1,100 meters)

15In those days Peter stood up among
the believers[a] (a group numbering
about a hundred and twenty) 16and said,
"Brothers, the Scripture had to be fulfilled which the Holy Spirit spoke long
ago through the mouth of David concerning Judas, who served as guide for
those who arrested Jesus— 17he was one
of our number and shared in this ministry."
18(With the reward he got for his wickedness, Judas bought a field; there he
fell headlong, his body burst open and
all his intestines spilled out. 19Everyone
in Jerusalem heard about this, so they
called that field in their language Akel-
dama, that is, Field of Blood.)
20"For," said Peter, "it is written in the
book of Psalms,

" 'May his place be deserted;
let there be no one to dwell in it,'[b]

and,

" 'May another take his place of
leadership.'[c]

21Therefore it is necessary to choose one
of the men who have been with us the
whole time the Lord Jesus went in and
out among us, 22beginning from John's
baptism to the time when Jesus was
taken up from us. For one of these must
become a witness with us of his resurrection."
23So they proposed two men: Joseph
called Barsabbas (also known as Justus)
and Matthias. 24Then they prayed,
"Lord, you know everyone's heart.
Show us which of these two you have
chosen 25to take over this apostolic ministry, which Judas left to go where he belongs." 26Then they cast lots, and the lot
fell to Matthias; so he was added to the
eleven apostles.

[a]15 Greek *brothers* [b]20 Psalm 69:25
[c]20 Psalm 109:8

SHARPEN THE FOCUS

Vision without action amounts to only so much daydreaming. Action without vision will produce only random results.

Before Jesus ascended into heaven, He gave His followers both a vision and a specific assignment. Acts 1:8 records both:

> *You will receive power when the Holy Spirit comes on you; and you will be My witnesses in Jerusalem, and in all Judea and Samaria, and to the ends of the earth.*

Waves of believers would move out from the then spiritual epicenter of the universe—Jerusalem. Filled to overflowing with the Holy Spirit, wave after wave of Christ's followers would invade every corner of the earth with the Good News that streams from Christ's cross and open tomb.

Whether you know it or not, you belong to that mighty army of witnesses. Believe it or not, the same Spirit who empowered Peter, John, and the rest now empowers you. Act on it or not, the mandate they received from Jesus has been passed down to you.

WEEK 83 • SATURDAY

Acts 2:1–47

GET THE BIG PICTURE

What do Matthew 3:11, Mark 1:8, Luke 3:16, John 1:33, Acts 1:5, and Joel 2:28 have in common? All six foretell the coming of the Holy Spirit at Pentecost. As you read, ask yourself what benefits have come to you because the Holy Spirit has taken up residence in you, God's redeemed and forgiven child. If time is short, focus on Acts 2:1–21.

The Holy Spirit Comes at Pentecost

2 When the day of Pentecost came,
they were all together in one
place. [2]Suddenly a sound like the blowing of a violent wind came from heaven
and filled the whole house where they
were sitting. [3]They saw what seemed to
be tongues of fire that separated and
came to rest on each of them. [4]All of
them were filled with the Holy Spirit
and began to speak in other tongues[a] as
the Spirit enabled them.
[5]Now there were staying in Jerusalem
God-fearing Jews from every nation
under heaven. [6]When they heard this
sound, a crowd came together in bewilderment, because each one heard them
speaking in his own language. [7]Utterly
amazed, they asked: "Are not all these
men who are speaking Galileans? [8]Then
how is it that each of us hears them in
his own native language? [9]Parthians,
Medes and Elamites; residents of Mesopotamia, Judea and Cappadocia, Pontus and Asia, [10]Phrygia and Pamphylia,
Egypt and the parts of Libya near
Cyrene; visitors from Rome [11](both
Jews and converts to Judaism); Cretans
and Arabs—we hear them declaring
the wonders of God in our own
tongues!" [12]Amazed and perplexed,
they asked one another, "What does this
mean?"
[13]Some, however, made fun of them
and said, "They have had too much
wine.[b]"

Peter Addresses the Crowd

[14]Then Peter stood up with the Elev-
en, raised his voice and addressed the
crowd: "Fellow Jews and all of you who
live in Jerusalem, let me explain this to
you; listen carefully to what I say.
[15]These men are not drunk, as you suppose. It's only nine in the morning! [16]No,
this is what was spoken by the prophet
Joel:

[17]" 'In the last days, God says,
I will pour out my Spirit on all
people.
Your sons and daughters will
prophesy,
your young men will see visions,
your old men will dream dreams.
[18]Even on my servants, both men and
women,
I will pour out my Spirit in those
days,
and they will prophesy.
[19]I will show wonders in the heaven
above
and signs on the earth below,
blood and fire and billows of
smoke.
[20]The sun will be turned to darkness
and the moon to blood
before the coming of the great and
glorious day of the Lord.
[21]And everyone who calls
on the name of the Lord will be
saved.'[c]

[a]4 Or *languages*; also in verse 11 [b]13 Or *sweet wine* [c]21 Joel 2:28-32

22"Men of Israel, listen to this: Jesus of
Nazareth was a man accredited by God
to you by miracles, wonders and signs,
which God did among you through
him, as you yourselves know. 23This
man was handed over to you by God's
set purpose and foreknowledge; and
you, with the help of wicked men,[a] put
him to death by nailing him to the cross.
24But God raised him from the dead,
freeing him from the agony of death,
because it was impossible for death to
keep its hold on him. 25David said about
him:

" 'I saw the Lord always before me.
Because he is at my right hand,
I will not be shaken.
26Therefore my heart is glad and my
tongue rejoices;
my body also will live in hope,
27because you will not abandon me to
the grave,
nor will you let your Holy One
see decay.
28You have made known to me the
paths of life;
you will fill me with joy in your
presence.'[b]

29"Brothers, I can tell you confidently
that the patriarch David died and was
buried, and his tomb is here to this day.
30But he was a prophet and knew that
God had promised him on oath that he
would place one of his descendants on
his throne. 31Seeing what was ahead, he
spoke of the resurrection of the Christ,[c]
that he was not abandoned to the grave,
nor did his body see decay. 32God has
raised this Jesus to life, and we are all
witnesses of the fact. 33Exalted to the
right hand of God, he has received from
the Father the promised Holy Spirit and
has poured out what you now see and
hear. 34For David did not ascend to heav-
en, and yet he said,

" 'The Lord said to my Lord:
"Sit at my right hand
35until I make your enemies
a footstool for your feet." '[d]

36"Therefore let all Israel be assured of
this: God has made this Jesus, whom
you crucified, both Lord and Christ."
37When the people heard this, they
were cut to the heart and said to Peter
and the other apostles, "Brothers, what
shall we do?"
38Peter replied, "Repent and be baptized, every one of you, in the name of
Jesus Christ for the forgiveness of your
sins. And you will receive the gift of the
Holy Spirit. 39The promise is for you and
your children and for all who are far
off—for all whom the Lord our God will
call."
40With many other words he warned
them; and he pleaded with them, "Save
yourselves from this corrupt generation." 41Those who accepted his message
were baptized, and about three thousand were added to their number that
day.

The Fellowship of the Believers

42They devoted themselves to the
apostles' teaching and to the fellowship,
to the breaking of bread and to prayer.
43Everyone was filled with awe, and
many wonders and miraculous signs
were done by the apostles. 44All the
believers were together and had everything in common. 45Selling their possessions and goods, they gave to anyone as
he had need. 46Every day they continued to meet together in the temple
courts. They broke bread in their homes
and ate together with glad and sincere
hearts, 47praising God and enjoying the
favor of all the people. And the Lord
added to their number daily those who
were being saved.

[a] 23 Or *of those not having the law* (that is, Gentiles) [b] 28 Psalm 16:8-11 [c] 31 Or *Messiah.* "The Christ" (Greek) and "the Messiah" (Hebrew) both mean "the Anointed One"; also in verse 36. [d] 35 Psalm 110:1

SHARPEN THE FOCUS

Notice what the Holy Spirit did on the day of Pentecost:

- First, He prompted the believers to declare the wonders of God (Acts 2:11). He filled their hearts and mouths with praise.
- Second, He emboldened Peter and the other apostles to preach the Word of God, both Law and Gospel, with power (Acts 2:14–39).
- Third, He brought 3,000 people to faith as a result of the apostle's testimony. These new believers came into a living relationship with their Savior and with one another as a result of the Spirit's work that day (Acts 2:41–43).
- He created a bond of love and unity that turned all the believers' priorities and values upside down. Love reigned supreme (Acts 2:44–47). This led—daily—to more conversions.

As you pray today, think about what the Holy Spirit did for His people on Pentecost. Think about what you and the people in your congregation need from Him. Then ask that, in grace, He give it to you as together you continue the Word and Sacrament ministry of the early church in Christ's name.

WEEK 84 • MONDAY

Acts 3:1—4:37

GET THE BIG PICTURE

Thunderstruck. That's the only word to describe the people's reaction to the healing miracle you'll read about today. Not only did the beggar walk, he leaped and ran—things he had never, ever done. Forty years of muscle atrophy were reversed in one moment (Acts 3:2; 4:22). As you read, look for the *other* miracles in the story, especially for changes in the hearts of the apostles and those who sat under the apostles' teaching. If time is short, focus on Acts 3:1–26.

Peter Heals the Crippled Beggar

3 One day Peter and John were going up to the temple at the time
of prayer—at three in the afternoon.
[2]Now a man crippled from birth was
being carried to the temple gate called
Beautiful, where he was put every day
to beg from those going into the temple
courts. [3]When he saw Peter and John
about to enter, he asked them for money. [4]Peter looked straight at him, as did
John. Then Peter said, "Look at us!" [5]So
the man gave them his attention, expecting to get something from them.
[6]Then Peter said, "Silver or gold I do
not have, but what I have I give you. In
the name of Jesus Christ of Nazareth,
walk." [7]Taking him by the right hand, he
helped him up, and instantly the man's
feet and ankles became strong. [8]He
jumped to his feet and began to walk.
Then he went with them into the
temple courts, walking and jumping,
and praising God. [9]When all the people

saw him walking and praising God,
10they recognized him as the same man
who used to sit begging at the temple
gate called Beautiful, and they were
filled with wonder and amazement at
what had happened to him.

Peter Speaks to the Onlookers

11While the beggar held on to Peter
and John, all the people were astonished and came running to them in the
place called Solomon's Colonnade.
12When Peter saw this, he said to them:
"Men of Israel, why does this surprise
you? Why do you stare at us as if by our
own power or godliness we had made
this man walk? 13The God of Abraham,
Isaac and Jacob, the God of our fathers,
has glorified his servant Jesus. You
handed him over to be killed, and you
disowned him before Pilate, though he
had decided to let him go. 14You disowned the Holy and Righteous One
and asked that a murderer be released
to you. 15You killed the author of life, but
God raised him from the dead. We are
witnesses of this. 16By faith in the name
of Jesus, this man whom you see and
know was made strong. It is Jesus' name
and the faith that comes through him
that has given this complete healing to
him, as you can all see.

17"Now, brothers, I know that you acted in ignorance, as did your leaders.
18But this is how God fulfilled what he
had foretold through all the prophets,
saying that his Christ[a] would suffer.
19Repent, then, and turn to God, so that
your sins may be wiped out, that times
of refreshing may come from the Lord,
20and that he may send the Christ, who
has been appointed for you—even
Jesus. 21He must remain in heaven until
the time comes for God to restore everything, as he promised long ago through
his holy prophets. 22For Moses said, 'The
Lord your God will raise up for you a
prophet like me from among your own
people; you must listen to everything
he tells you. 23Anyone who does not listen to him will be completely cut off
from among his people.'[b]

24"Indeed, all the prophets from Samuel on, as many as have spoken, have
foretold these days. 25And you are heirs
of the prophets and of the covenant
God made with your fathers. He said to
Abraham, 'Through your offspring all
peoples on earth will be blessed.'[c]
26When God raised up his servant, he
sent him first to you to bless you by
turning each of you from your wicked
ways."

Peter and John Before the Sanhedrin

4 The priests and the captain of
the temple guard and the Sadducees came up to Peter and John while
they were speaking to the people. 2They
were greatly disturbed because the
apostles were teaching the people and
proclaiming in Jesus the resurrection of
the dead. 3They seized Peter and John,
and because it was evening, they put
them in jail until the next day. 4But
many who heard the message believed,
and the number of men grew to about
five thousand.

5The next day the rulers, elders and
teachers of the law met in Jerusalem.
6Annas the high priest was there, and so
were Caiaphas, John, Alexander and the
other men of the high priest's family.
7They had Peter and John brought before them and began to question them:
"By what power or what name did you
do this?"

8Then Peter, filled with the Holy Spirit, said to them: "Rulers and elders of the
people! 9If we are being called to account today for an act of kindness
shown to a cripple and are asked how
he was healed, 10then know this, you
and all the people of Israel: It is by the
name of Jesus Christ of Nazareth, whom
you crucified but whom God raised
from the dead, that this man stands before you healed. 11He is

" 'the stone you builders rejected,
which has become the capstone.[d]'[e]

12Salvation is found in no one else, for

[a]*18* Or *Messiah;* also in verse 20
[b]*23* Deut. 18:15,18,19 [c]*25* Gen. 22:18; 26:4
[d]*11* Or *cornerstone* [e]*11* Psalm 118:22

there is no other name under heaven
given to men by which we must be
saved."
13When they saw the courage of Peter
and John and realized that they were
unschooled, ordinary men, they were
astonished and they took note that
these men had been with Jesus. 14But
since they could see the man who had
been healed standing there with them,
there was nothing they could say. 15So
they ordered them to withdraw from
the Sanhedrin and then conferred together. 16"What are we going to do with
these men?" they asked. "Everybody
living in Jerusalem knows they have
done an outstanding miracle, and we
cannot deny it. 17But to stop this thing
from spreading any further among the
people, we must warn these men to
speak no longer to anyone in this
name."
18Then they called them in again and
commanded them not to speak or teach
at all in the name of Jesus. 19But Peter
and John replied, "Judge for yourselves
whether it is right in God's sight to obey
you rather than God. 20For we cannot
help speaking about what we have seen
and heard."
21After further threats they let them
go. They could not decide how to punish them, because all the people were
praising God for what had happened.
22For the man who was miraculously
healed was over forty years old.

The Believers' Prayer

23On their release, Peter and John
went back to their own people and reported all that the chief priests and elders had said to them. 24When they
heard this, they raised their voices together in prayer to God. "Sovereign
Lord," they said, "you made the heaven
and the earth and the sea, and everything in them. 25You spoke by the Holy
Spirit through the mouth of your servant, our father David:

" 'Why do the nations rage
and the peoples plot in vain?
26The kings of the earth take their
stand
and the rulers gather together
against the Lord
and against his Anointed One.'[a][b]

27Indeed Herod and Pontius Pilate met
together with the Gentiles and the people[c] of Israel in this city to conspire
against your holy servant Jesus, whom
you anointed. 28They did what your
power and will had decided beforehand
should happen. 29Now, Lord, consider
their threats and enable your servants
to speak your word with great boldness.
30Stretch out your hand to heal and perform miraculous signs and wonders
through the name of your holy servant
Jesus."
31After they prayed, the place where
they were meeting was shaken. And
they were all filled with the Holy Spirit
and spoke the word of God boldly.

The Believers Share Their Possessions

32All the believers were one in heart
and mind. No one claimed that any of
his possessions was his own, but they
shared everything they had. 33With
great power the apostles continued to
testify to the resurrection of the Lord
Jesus, and much grace was upon them
all. 34There were no needy persons
among them. For from time to time
those who owned lands or houses sold
them, brought the money from the sales
35and put it at the apostles' feet, and it
was distributed to anyone as he had
need.
36Joseph, a Levite from Cyprus, whom
the apostles called Barnabas (which
means Son of Encouragement), 37sold a
field he owned and brought the money
and put it at the apostles' feet.

[a]26 That is, Christ or Messiah [b]26 Psalm 2:1,2
[c]27 The Greek is plural.

SHARPEN THE FOCUS

An old story begins with Satan ordering his junior demons to devise a strategy to win the world for the kingdom of darkness.

The first demon to answer the challenge says, "Let's tell people there is no god." Satan scoffs and replies, "Ineffective for the mass of humankind. We've never been able to make that lie convincing."

The second demon then speaks up. "Let's tell people there's no heaven and no hell." Satan frowns and dismisses the idea, saying, "It will never work. Eternity is written on the souls of all human creatures."

The third demon then raises his hand. "I know," he says. "Let's tell Christians there's no hurry." At that, Satan beams and hell explodes in applause.

Peter, John, and Barnabas believed the Lord Jesus would appear in the sky with His heavenly hosts at any moment. That faith energized their witness. But 2,000 years later, some of us have lost that sense of urgency. If this describes you at times, too, go to your Savior in repentance and faith. Let His pardon fill you with renewed zeal for the Great-Commission work He's privileged you to do.

WEEK 84 • TUESDAY

Acts 5:1-42

GET THE BIG PICTURE

No one could miss the message: the early believers had somehow tapped into a power source well beyond human invention or effort. As you read, look for contrasts between the servants of Christ in this chapter and those who sought to serve themselves. If time is short, focus on Acts 5:1–32.

Ananias and Sapphira

5 Now a man named Ananias, together with his wife Sapphira,
also sold a piece of property. 2With his
wife's full knowledge he kept back part
of the money for himself, but brought
the rest and put it at the apostles' feet.
3Then Peter said, "Ananias, how is it
that Satan has so filled your heart that
you have lied to the Holy Spirit and
have kept for yourself some of the
money you received for the land?
4Didn't it belong to you before it was
sold? And after it was sold, wasn't the
money at your disposal? What made
you think of doing such a thing? You
have not lied to men but to God."
5When Ananias heard this, he fell
down and died. And great fear seized all
who heard what had happened. 6Then
the young men came forward, wrapped
up his body, and carried him out and
buried him.
7About three hours later his wife came
in, not knowing what had happened.
8Peter asked her, "Tell me, is this the price
you and Ananias got for the land?"
"Yes," she said, "that is the price."
9Peter said to her, "How could you
agree to test the Spirit of the Lord?

Look! The feet of the men who buried
your husband are at the door, and they
will carry you out also."
[10]At that moment she fell down at his
feet and died. Then the young men
came in and, finding her dead, carried
her out and buried her beside her husband. [11]Great fear seized the whole
church and all who heard about these
events.

The Apostles Heal Many

[12]The apostles performed many miraculous signs and wonders among the
people. And all the believers used to
meet together in Solomon's Colonnade.
[13]No one else dared join them, even
though they were highly regarded by
the people. [14]Nevertheless, more and
more men and women believed in the
Lord and were added to their number.
[15]As a result, people brought the sick
into the streets and laid them on beds
and mats so that at least Peter's shadow
might fall on some of them as he passed
by. [16]Crowds gathered also from the
towns around Jerusalem, bringing their
sick and those tormented by evil[a] spirits, and all of them were healed.

The Apostles Persecuted

[17]Then the high priest and all his associates, who were members of the party of the Sadducees, were filled with
jealousy. [18]They arrested the apostles
and put them in the public jail. [19]But
during the night an angel of the Lord
opened the doors of the jail and brought
them out. [20]"Go, stand in the temple
courts," he said, "and tell the people the
full message of this new life."
[21]At daybreak they entered the temple
courts, as they had been told, and began
to teach the people.

When the high priest and his associates arrived, they called together the
Sanhedrin—the full assembly of the elders of Israel—and sent to the jail for the
apostles. [22]But on arriving at the jail, the
officers did not find them there. So they
went back and reported, [23]"We found
the jail securely locked, with the guards
standing at the doors; but when we
opened them, we found no one inside."
[24]On hearing this report, the captain of
the temple guard and the chief priests
were puzzled, wondering what would
come of this.
[25]Then someone came and said,
"Look! The men you put in jail are
standing in the temple courts teaching
the people." [26]At that, the captain went
with his officers and brought the apostles. They did not use force, because
they feared that the people would stone
them.
[27]Having brought the apostles, they
made them appear before the Sanhedrin to be questioned by the high priest.
[28]"We gave you strict orders not to teach
in this name," he said. "Yet you have
filled Jerusalem with your teaching and
are determined to make us guilty of this
man's blood."
[29]Peter and the other apostles replied:
"We must obey God rather than men!
[30]The God of our fathers raised Jesus
from the dead—whom you had killed
by hanging him on a tree. [31]God exalted
him to his own right hand as Prince and
Savior that he might give repentance
and forgiveness of sins to Israel. [32]We are
witnesses of these things, and so is the
Holy Spirit, whom God has given to
those who obey him."
[33]When they heard this, they were furious and wanted to put them to death.
[34]But a Pharisee named Gamaliel, a
teacher of the law, who was honored by
all the people, stood up in the Sanhedrin and ordered that the men be put
outside for a little while. [35]Then he addressed them: "Men of Israel, consider
carefully what you intend to do to these
men. [36]Some time ago Theudas appeared, claiming to be somebody, and
about four hundred men rallied to him.
He was killed, all his followers were
dispersed, and it all came to nothing.
[37]After him, Judas the Galilean appeared
in the days of the census and led a band
of people in revolt. He too was killed,
and all his followers were scattered.
[38]Therefore, in the present case I advise

[a]16 Greek *unclean*

you: Leave these men alone! Let them
go! For if their purpose or activity is of
human origin, it will fail. [39]But if it is
from God, you will not be able to stop
these men; you will only find yourselves fighting against God."
[40]His speech persuaded them. They
called the apostles in and had them
flogged. Then they ordered them not to
speak in the name of Jesus, and let
them go.
[41]The apostles left the Sanhedrin, rejoicing because they had been counted
worthy of suffering disgrace for the
Name. [42]Day after day, in the temple
courts and from house to house, they
never stopped teaching and proclaiming
the good news that Jesus is the Christ.[a]

SHARPEN THE FOCUS

Tense. Angry. Insecure. Troubled. The Sadducees and their leaders were all this and worse. They couldn't produce Jesus' body. The apostles had pronounced them guilty of His death. No Sadducees believed in miracles, let alone in the resurrection, but recent events had left their theology in shambles. These men stood on the edge of the cliff marked "desperation."

Confident. Peaceful. Secure. Focused. The new believers and their leaders were all this and more. They drew strength from the teachings of Jesus and from the love and unity the Holy Spirit continued to pour out on them. Beaten and harangued by the priests, they shrugged off the temptation to bitterness. Instead, they rejoiced "because they had been counted worthy of suffering disgrace for the Name" (Acts 5:41). The Name? *Jesus,* of course. Savior. Crucified and risen and reigning.

Just think what could happen in your corner of our Lord's harvest fields if God's people there would more consistently live with the same security, the same peace, the same confident hope and witness that the Holy Spirit empowered His first century believers to maintain. He wants to do that, you know. For you and in you.

WEEK 84 • WEDNESDAY

Acts 6:1—8:40

GET THE BIG PICTURE

Blessed by the Holy Spirit, the early church continued to mushroom. But opposition grew as well. As you read the sermon Stephen preached, the sermon that led to his martyrdom, note the two points he makes to the religious leaders: *You and your ancestors have always resisted God,* and *the temple has become your idol.* If time is short, focus on Acts 6:1–15.

The Choosing of the Seven

6 In those days when the number
of disciples was increasing, the
Grecian Jews among them complained
against the Hebraic Jews because their
widows were being overlooked in the
daily distribution of food. [2]So the Twelve
gathered all the disciples together and

[a]42 Or *Messiah*

said, "It would not be right for us to neglect the ministry of the word of God in order to wait on tables. [3]Brothers, choose seven men from among you who are known to be full of the Spirit and wisdom. We will turn this responsibility over to them [4]and will give our attention to prayer and the ministry of the word."

[5]This proposal pleased the whole group. They chose Stephen, a man full of faith and of the Holy Spirit; also Philip, Procorus, Nicanor, Timon, Parmenas, and Nicolas from Antioch, a convert to Judaism. [6]They presented these men to the apostles, who prayed and laid their hands on them.

[7]So the word of God spread. The number of disciples in Jerusalem increased rapidly, and a large number of priests became obedient to the faith.

Stephen Seized

[8]Now Stephen, a man full of God's grace and power, did great wonders and miraculous signs among the people. [9]Opposition arose, however, from members of the Synagogue of the Freedmen (as it was called)—Jews of Cyrene and Alexandria as well as the provinces of Cilicia and Asia. These men began to argue with Stephen, [10]but they could not stand up against his wisdom or the Spirit by whom he spoke.

[11]Then they secretly persuaded some men to say, "We have heard Stephen speak words of blasphemy against Moses and against God."

[12]So they stirred up the people and the elders and the teachers of the law. They seized Stephen and brought him before the Sanhedrin. [13]They produced false witnesses, who testified, "This fellow never stops speaking against this holy place and against the law. [14]For we have heard him say that this Jesus of Nazareth will destroy this place and change the customs Moses handed down to us."

[15]All who were sitting in the Sanhedrin looked intently at Stephen, and they saw that his face was like the face of an angel.

Stephen's Speech to the Sanhedrin

7 Then the high priest asked him, "Are these charges true?"

[2]To this he replied: "Brothers and fathers, listen to me! The God of glory appeared to our father Abraham while he was still in Mesopotamia, before he lived in Haran. [3]'Leave your country and your people,' God said, 'and go to the land I will show you.'[a]

[4]"So he left the land of the Chaldeans and settled in Haran. After the death of his father, God sent him to this land where you are now living. [5]He gave him no inheritance here, not even a foot of ground. But God promised him that he and his descendants after him would possess the land, even though at that time Abraham had no child. [6]God spoke to him in this way: 'Your descendants will be strangers in a country not their own, and they will be enslaved and mistreated four hundred years. [7]But I will punish the nation they serve as slaves,' God said, 'and afterward they will come out of that country and worship me in this place.'[b] [8]Then he gave Abraham the covenant of circumcision. And Abraham became the father of Isaac and circumcised him eight days after his birth. Later Isaac became the father of Jacob, and Jacob became the father of the twelve patriarchs.

[9]"Because the patriarchs were jealous of Joseph, they sold him as a slave into Egypt. But God was with him [10]and rescued him from all his troubles. He gave Joseph wisdom and enabled him to gain the goodwill of Pharaoh king of Egypt; so he made him ruler over Egypt and all his palace.

[11]"Then a famine struck all Egypt and Canaan, bringing great suffering, and our fathers could not find food. [12]When Jacob heard that there was grain in Egypt, he sent our fathers on their first visit. [13]On their second visit, Joseph told his brothers who he was, and Pharaoh learned about Joseph's family. [14]After this, Joseph sent for his father Jacob and his whole family, seventy-five in all.

[a]3 Gen. 12:1 [b]7 Gen. 15:13,14

15Then Jacob went down to Egypt,
where he and our fathers died. 16Their
bodies were brought back to Shechem
and placed in the tomb that Abraham
had bought from the sons of Hamor at
Shechem for a certain sum of money.
17"As the time drew near for God to
fulfill his promise to Abraham, the number of our people in Egypt greatly increased. 18Then another king, who knew
nothing about Joseph, became ruler of
Egypt. 19He dealt treacherously with our
people and oppressed our forefathers
by forcing them to throw out their newborn babies so that they would die.
20"At that time Moses was born, and he
was no ordinary child.[a] For three
months he was cared for in his father's
house. 21When he was placed outside,
Pharaoh's daughter took him and
brought him up as her own son. 22Mo-
ses was educated in all the wisdom of
the Egyptians and was powerful in
speech and action.
23"When Moses was forty years old,
he decided to visit his fellow Israelites.
24He saw one of them being mistreated
by an Egyptian, so he went to his defense and avenged him by killing the
Egyptian. 25Moses thought that his own
people would realize that God was using him to rescue them, but they did
not. 26The next day Moses came upon
two Israelites who were fighting. He
tried to reconcile them by saying, 'Men,
you are brothers; why do you want to
hurt each other?'
27"But the man who was mistreating
the other pushed Moses aside and said,
'Who made you ruler and judge over
us? 28Do you want to kill me as you
killed the Egyptian yesterday?'[b] 29When
Moses heard this, he fled to Midian,
where he settled as a foreigner and had
two sons.
30"After forty years had passed, an
angel appeared to Moses in the flames
of a burning bush in the desert near
Mount Sinai. 31When he saw this, he
was amazed at the sight. As he went
over to look more closely, he heard the
Lord's voice: 32'I am the God of your fathers, the God of Abraham, Isaac and
Jacob.'[c] Moses trembled with fear and
did not dare to look.
33"Then the Lord said to him, 'Take off
your sandals; the place where you are
standing is holy ground. 34I have indeed
seen the oppression of my people in
Egypt. I have heard their groaning and
have come down to set them free. Now
come, I will send you back to Egypt.'[d]
35"This is the same Moses whom they
had rejected with the words, 'Who
made you ruler and judge?' He was sent
to be their ruler and deliverer by God
himself, through the angel who appeared to him in the bush. 36He led them
out of Egypt and did wonders and miraculous signs in Egypt, at the Red Sea[e]
and for forty years in the desert.
37"This is that Moses who told the Israelites, 'God will send you a prophet
like me from your own people.'[f] 38He
was in the assembly in the desert, with
the angel who spoke to him on Mount
Sinai, and with our fathers; and he received living words to pass on to us.
39"But our fathers refused to obey
him. Instead, they rejected him and in
their hearts turned back to Egypt.
40They told Aaron, 'Make us gods who
will go before us. As for this fellow Moses who led us out of Egypt—we don't
know what has happened to him!'[g]
41That was the time they made an idol
in the form of a calf. They brought sacrifices to it and held a celebration in
honor of what their hands had made.
42But God turned away and gave them
over to the worship of the heavenly
bodies. This agrees with what is written
in the book of the prophets:

" 'Did you bring me sacrifices and
offerings
forty years in the desert, O house
of Israel?
43You have lifted up the shrine of
Molech
and the star of your god Rephan,
the idols you made to worship.

[a]20 Or *was fair in the sight of God* [b]28 Exodus 2:14
[c]32 Exodus 3:6 [d]34 Exodus 3:5,7,8,10
[e]36 That is, Sea of Reeds [f]37 Deut. 18:15
[g]40 Exodus 32:1

Therefore I will send you into exile'[a]
beyond Babylon.

44"Our forefathers had the tabernacle of the Testimony with them in the desert. It had been made as God directed Moses, according to the pattern he had seen. 45Having received the tabernacle, our fathers under Joshua brought it with them when they took the land from the nations God drove out before them. It remained in the land until the time of David, 46who enjoyed God's favor and asked that he might provide a dwelling place for the God of Jacob.[b] 47But it was Solomon who built the house for him.

48"However, the Most High does not live in houses made by men. As the prophet says:

49" 'Heaven is my throne,
and the earth is my footstool.
What kind of house will you build
for me?
says the Lord.
Or where will my resting place
be?
50Has not my hand made all these
things?'[c]

51"You stiff-necked people, with uncircumcised hearts and ears! You are just like your fathers: You always resist the Holy Spirit! 52Was there ever a prophet your fathers did not persecute? They even killed those who predicted the coming of the Righteous One. And now you have betrayed and murdered him— 53you who have received the law that was put into effect through angels but have not obeyed it."

The Stoning of Stephen

54When they heard this, they were furious and gnashed their teeth at him. 55But Stephen, full of the Holy Spirit, looked up to heaven and saw the glory of God, and Jesus standing at the right hand of God. 56"Look," he said, "I see heaven open and the Son of Man standing at the right hand of God."

57At this they covered their ears and, yelling at the top of their voices, they all rushed at him, 58dragged him out of the city and began to stone him. Meanwhile, the witnesses laid their clothes at the feet of a young man named Saul.

59While they were stoning him, Stephen prayed, "Lord Jesus, receive my spirit." 60Then he fell on his knees and cried out, "Lord, do not hold this sin against them." When he had said this, he fell asleep.

8 And Saul was there, giving approval to his death.

The Church Persecuted and Scattered

On that day a great persecution broke out against the church at Jerusalem, and all except the apostles were scattered throughout Judea and Samaria. 2Godly men buried Stephen and mourned deeply for him. 3But Saul began to destroy the church. Going from house to house, he dragged off men and women and put them in prison.

Philip in Samaria

4Those who had been scattered preached the word wherever they went. 5Philip went down to a city in Samaria and proclaimed the Christ[d] there. 6When the crowds heard Philip and saw the miraculous signs he did, they all paid close attention to what he said. 7With shrieks, evil[e] spirits came out of many, and many paralytics and cripples were healed. 8So there was great joy in that city.

Simon the Sorcerer

9Now for some time a man named Simon had practiced sorcery in the city and amazed all the people of Samaria. He boasted that he was someone great, 10and all the people, both high and low, gave him their attention and exclaimed, "This man is the divine power known as the Great Power." 11They followed him because he had amazed them for a long time with his magic. 12But when they believed Philip as he preached the good

[a]43 Amos 5:25-27 [b]46 Some early manuscripts *the house of Jacob* [c]50 Isaiah 66:1,2 [d]5 Or *Messiah* [e]7 Greek *unclean*

news of the kingdom of God and the
name of Jesus Christ, they were baptized, both men and women. 13Simon
himself believed and was baptized. And
he followed Philip everywhere, astonished by the great signs and miracles he
saw.
14When the apostles in Jerusalem
heard that Samaria had accepted the
word of God, they sent Peter and John
to them. 15When they arrived, they
prayed for them that they might receive
the Holy Spirit, 16because the Holy Spirit
had not yet come upon any of them;
they had simply been baptized into[a] the
name of the Lord Jesus. 17Then Peter and
John placed their hands on them, and
they received the Holy Spirit.
18When Simon saw that the Spirit was
given at the laying on of the apostles'
hands, he offered them money 19and
said, "Give me also this ability so that
everyone on whom I lay my hands may
receive the Holy Spirit."
20Peter answered: "May your money
perish with you, because you thought
you could buy the gift of God with money! 21You have no part or share in this
ministry, because your heart is not right
before God. 22Repent of this wickedness
and pray to the Lord. Perhaps he will
forgive you for having such a thought
in your heart. 23For I see that you are full
of bitterness and captive to sin."
24Then Simon answered, "Pray to the
Lord for me so that nothing you have
said may happen to me."
25When they had testified and proclaimed the word of the Lord, Peter and
John returned to Jerusalem, preaching
the gospel in many Samaritan villages.

Philip and the Ethiopian

26Now an angel of the Lord said to
Philip, "Go south to the road—the
desert road—that goes down from Jerusalem to Gaza." 27So he started out, and
on his way he met an Ethiopian[b] eunuch, an important official in charge of
all the treasury of Candace, queen of the
Ethiopians. This man had gone to
Jerusalem to worship, 28and on his way
home was sitting in his chariot reading
the book of Isaiah the prophet. 29The
Spirit told Philip, "Go to that chariot and
stay near it."
30Then Philip ran up to the chariot
and heard the man reading Isaiah the
prophet. "Do you understand what you
are reading?" Philip asked.
31"How can I," he said, "unless someone explains it to me?" So he invited
Philip to come up and sit with him.
32The eunuch was reading this passage of Scripture:

"He was led like a sheep to the
slaughter,
and as a lamb before the shearer is
silent,
so he did not open his mouth.
33In his humiliation he was deprived
of justice.
Who can speak of his
descendants?
For his life was taken from the
earth."[c]

34The eunuch asked Philip, "Tell me,
please, who is the prophet talking
about, himself or someone else?" 35Then
Philip began with that very passage of
Scripture and told him the good news
about Jesus.
36As they traveled along the road,
they came to some water and the eunuch said, "Look, here is water. Why
shouldn't I be baptized?"[d] 38And he gave
orders to stop the chariot. Then both
Philip and the eunuch went down into
the water and Philip baptized him.
39When they came up out of the water,
the Spirit of the Lord suddenly took
Philip away, and the eunuch did not see
him again, but went on his way rejoicing. 40Philip, however, appeared at Azo-
tus and traveled about, preaching the
gospel in all the towns until he reached
Caesarea.

[a]16 Or *in* [b]27 That is, from the upper Nile region [c]33 Isaiah 53:7,8 [d]36 Some late manuscripts *baptized?" 37Philip said, "If you believe with all your heart, you may." The eunuch answered, "I believe that Jesus Christ is the Son of God."*

SHARPEN THE FOCUS

Sometimes success seems to bring more problems than failure. Had the church at Jerusalem not grown so fast, the believers and their leaders might have been ignored. Had Stephen not proven such a Spirit-empowered leader and speaker, he might have led an easy life and died in bed.

But no one in the early church aspired to be merely respectable in the community. None of the leaders simply wanted to blend into the background of first-century Jerusalem. The fire of God burned in their hearts. Zeal for the Lord's honor consumed them. They had Good News to share!

The message of forgiveness and the eternal life that comes through faith in Jesus exploded like firecrackers of joy in household after household. The enemies of the cross had no ammunition. How do you intimidate someone who says in all confidence, "For to me, to live is Christ and to die is gain" (Philippians 1:21)? Paul wrote it, but the early Christians lived it.

And so can we. God wants to work in us through His Word that same confidence, that same courage. Let His joy well up and bubble over in your life today, too, as you trust Him to direct your steps, your witness. ☼

WEEK 84 • THURSDAY

Acts 9:1–43

GET THE BIG PICTURE

Any task goes more smoothly if the worker can reach into the tool box and select just the right tool. Saul (a.k.a. Paul) was God's chosen tool to carry the message of the cross to the far corners of the Roman Empire (Acts 9:15). As you read, watch God, the Master Craftsman, at work. If time is short, focus on Acts 9:1–22.

Saul's Conversion

9 Meanwhile, Saul was still breathing out murderous threats
against the Lord's disciples. He went to
the high priest 2and asked him for letters to the synagogues in Damascus, so
that if he found any there who belonged
to the Way, whether men or women, he
might take them as prisoners to Jerusalem. 3As he neared Damascus on his
journey, suddenly a light from heaven
flashed around him. 4He fell to the
ground and heard a voice say to him,
"Saul, Saul, why do you persecute
me?"
5"Who are you, Lord?" Saul asked.

"I am Jesus, whom you are persecuting," he replied. 6"Now get up and go
into the city, and you will be told what
you must do."
7The men traveling with Saul stood
there speechless; they heard the sound
but did not see anyone. 8Saul got up
from the ground, but when he opened
his eyes he could see nothing. So they
led him by the hand into Damascus. 9For
three days he was blind, and did not eat
or drink anything.
10In Damascus there was a disciple
named Ananias. The Lord called to him
in a vision, "Ananias!"
"Yes, Lord," he answered.

11The Lord told him, "Go to the house of Judas on Straight Street and ask for a man from Tarsus named Saul, for he is praying. 12In a vision he has seen a man named Ananias come and place his hands on him to restore his sight."

13"Lord," Ananias answered, "I have heard many reports about this man and all the harm he has done to your saints in Jerusalem. 14And he has come here with authority from the chief priests to arrest all who call on your name."

15But the Lord said to Ananias, "Go! This man is my chosen instrument to carry my name before the Gentiles and their kings and before the people of Israel. 16I will show him how much he must suffer for my name."

17Then Ananias went to the house and entered it. Placing his hands on Saul, he said, "Brother Saul, the Lord—Jesus, who appeared to you on the road as you were coming here—has sent me so that you may see again and be filled with the Holy Spirit." 18Immediately, something like scales fell from Saul's eyes, and he could see again. He got up and was baptized, 19and after taking some food, he regained his strength.

Saul in Damascus and Jerusalem

Saul spent several days with the disciples in Damascus. 20At once he began to preach in the synagogues that Jesus is the Son of God. 21All those who heard him were astonished and asked, "Isn't he the man who raised havoc in Jerusalem among those who call on this name? And hasn't he come here to take them as prisoners to the chief priests?" 22Yet Saul grew more and more powerful and baffled the Jews living in Damascus by proving that Jesus is the Christ.[a]

23After many days had gone by, the Jews conspired to kill him, 24but Saul learned of their plan. Day and night they kept close watch on the city gates in order to kill him. 25But his followers took him by night and lowered him in a basket through an opening in the wall.

26When he came to Jerusalem, he tried to join the disciples, but they were all afraid of him, not believing that he really was a disciple. 27But Barnabas took him and brought him to the apostles. He told them how Saul on his journey had seen the Lord and that the Lord had spoken to him, and how in Damascus he had preached fearlessly in the name of Jesus. 28So Saul stayed with them and moved about freely in Jerusalem, speaking boldly in the name of the Lord. 29He talked and debated with the Grecian Jews, but they tried to kill him. 30When the brothers learned of this, they took him down to Caesarea and sent him off to Tarsus.

31Then the church throughout Judea, Galilee and Samaria enjoyed a time of peace. It was strengthened; and encouraged by the Holy Spirit, it grew in numbers, living in the fear of the Lord.

Aeneas and Dorcas

32As Peter traveled about the country, he went to visit the saints in Lydda. 33There he found a man named Aeneas, a paralytic who had been bedridden for eight years. 34"Aeneas," Peter said to him, "Jesus Christ heals you. Get up and take care of your mat." Immediately Aeneas got up. 35All those who lived in Lydda and Sharon saw him and turned to the Lord.

36In Joppa there was a disciple named Tabitha (which, when translated, is Dorcas[b]), who was always doing good and helping the poor. 37About that time she became sick and died, and her body was washed and placed in an upstairs room. 38Lydda was near Joppa; so when the disciples heard that Peter was in Lydda, they sent two men to him and urged him, "Please come at once!"

39Peter went with them, and when he arrived he was taken upstairs to the room. All the widows stood around him, crying and showing him the robes and other clothing that Dorcas had made while she was still with them.

40Peter sent them all out of the room;

[a]22 Or *Messiah* [b]36 Both *Tabitha* (Aramaic) and *Dorcas* (Greek) mean *gazelle.*

then he got down on his knees and
prayed. Turning toward the dead woman, he said, "Tabitha, get up." She
opened her eyes, and seeing Peter she
sat up. 41He took her by the hand and
helped her to her feet. Then he called
the believers and the widows and presented her to them alive. 42This became
known all over Joppa, and many people
believed in the Lord. 43Peter stayed in
Joppa for some time with a tanner
named Simon.

SHARPEN THE FOCUS

Do you remember the parable of the two debtors Jesus told to Simon the Pharisee (Luke 7:40–43)? One man owed 500 days' wages. The other owed 50. The creditor forgave both debts. Jesus asked Simon, "Which of these will love the creditor more?"

Throughout the rest of his life after his conversion, Saul of Tarsus saw himself as the first debtor in Jesus' parable (1 Timothy 1:15). Forgiven much, Paul loved much. And he served Christ with the zeal of a heart set ablaze by divine love.

Here we see a remedy when our own love for Jesus cools. Here we see an antidote for our own times of apathy. We can ask our Lord to help us remember where we've come from. We can think about the massive debt of sin He retired for us in His death. We can recall and rejoice in the new spiritual wealth, the new peace, the new right-standing with the Father that are now ours. Forgiven much, we, too, can love much.

WEEK 84 • FRIDAY

Acts 10:1—11:30

GET THE BIG PICTURE

The rings of witness rippled out further and further from Jerusalem. As Greek-speaking Jews and Samaritans and then even Gentiles began to come to faith, God stretched the comfort zone of the Jewish believers. As you read, ask yourself about ways your Lord might like to enlarge your own comfort zone to accomplish His mission in your community. If time is short, focus on Acts 11:1–18.

Cornelius Calls for Peter

10 At Caesarea there was a man
named Cornelius, a centu-
rion in what was known as the Italian
Regiment. 2He and all his family were
devout and God-fearing; he gave generously to those in need and prayed to
God regularly. 3One day at about three
in the afternoon he had a vision. He dis-
tinctly saw an angel of God, who came
to him and said, "Cornelius!"
4Cornelius stared at him in fear.
"What is it, Lord?" he asked.
The angel answered, "Your prayers
and gifts to the poor have come up as a
memorial offering before God. 5Now
send men to Joppa to bring back a man
named Simon who is called Peter. 6He is
staying with Simon the tanner, whose
house is by the sea."
7When the angel who spoke to him
had gone, Cornelius called two of his

servants and a devout soldier who was
one of his attendants. 8He told them everything that had happened and sent
them to Joppa.

Peter's Vision

9About noon the following day as
they were on their journey and approaching the city, Peter went up on the
roof to pray. 10He became hungry and
wanted something to eat, and while the
meal was being prepared, he fell into a
trance. 11He saw heaven opened and
something like a large sheet being let
down to earth by its four corners. 12It
contained all kinds of four-footed animals, as well as reptiles of the earth and
birds of the air. 13Then a voice told him,
"Get up, Peter. Kill and eat."
14"Surely not, Lord!" Peter replied. "I
have never eaten anything impure or
unclean."
15The voice spoke to him a second
time, "Do not call anything impure that
God has made clean."
16This happened three times, and immediately the sheet was taken back to
heaven.
17While Peter was wondering about
the meaning of the vision, the men
sent by Cornelius found out where
Simon's house was and stopped at the
gate. 18They called out, asking if Simon
who was known as Peter was staying
there.
19While Peter was still thinking about
the vision, the Spirit said to him, "Simon, three[a] men are looking for you.
20So get up and go downstairs. Do not
hesitate to go with them, for I have sent
them."
21Peter went down and said to the
men, "I'm the one you're looking for.
Why have you come?"
22The men replied, "We have come
from Cornelius the centurion. He is a
righteous and God-fearing man, who
is respected by all the Jewish people.
A holy angel told him to have you
come to his house so that he could hear
what you have to say." 23Then Peter invited the men into the house to be his
guests.

Peter at Cornelius's House

The next day Peter started out with
them, and some of the brothers from
Joppa went along. 24The following day
he arrived in Caesarea. Cornelius
was expecting them and had called together his relatives and close friends.
25As Peter entered the house, Cornelius met him and fell at his feet in reverence. 26But Peter made him get up.
"Stand up," he said, "I am only a man
myself."
27Talking with him, Peter went inside
and found a large gathering of people.
28He said to them: "You are well aware
that it is against our law for a Jew to associate with a Gentile or visit him. But
God has shown me that I should not call
any man impure or unclean. 29So when
I was sent for, I came without raising
any objection. May I ask why you sent
for me?"
30Cornelius answered: "Four days ago
I was in my house praying at this hour,
at three in the afternoon. Suddenly a
man in shining clothes stood before me
31and said, 'Cornelius, God has heard
your prayer and remembered your gifts
to the poor. 32Send to Joppa for Simon
who is called Peter. He is a guest in the
home of Simon the tanner, who lives by
the sea.' 33So I sent for you immediately, and it was good of you to come. Now
we are all here in the presence of God
to listen to everything the Lord has
commanded you to tell us."
34Then Peter began to speak: "I now
realize how true it is that God does not
show favoritism 35but accepts men from
every nation who fear him and do what
is right. 36You know the message God
sent to the people of Israel, telling the
good news of peace through Jesus
Christ, who is Lord of all. 37You know
what has happened throughout Judea,
beginning in Galilee after the baptism
that John preached— 38how God
anointed Jesus of Nazareth with the
Holy Spirit and power, and how he
went around doing good and healing all

[a]19 One early manuscript *two*; other manuscripts do not have the number.

who were under the power of the devil, because God was with him.

39"We are witnesses of everything he did in the country of the Jews and in Jerusalem. They killed him by hanging him on a tree, 40but God raised him from the dead on the third day and caused him to be seen. 41He was not seen by all the people, but by witnesses whom God had already chosen—by us who ate and drank with him after he rose from the dead. 42He commanded us to preach to the people and to testify that he is the one whom God appointed as judge of the living and the dead. 43All the prophets testify about him that everyone who believes in him receives forgiveness of sins through his name."

44While Peter was still speaking these words, the Holy Spirit came on all who heard the message. 45The circumcised believers who had come with Peter were astonished that the gift of the Holy Spirit had been poured out even on the Gentiles. 46For they heard them speaking in tongues[a] and praising God.

Then Peter said, 47"Can anyone keep these people from being baptized with water? They have received the Holy Spirit just as we have." 48So he ordered that they be baptized in the name of Jesus Christ. Then they asked Peter to stay with them for a few days.

Peter Explains His Actions

11 The apostles and the brothers throughout Judea heard that the Gentiles also had received the word of God. 2So when Peter went up to Jerusalem, the circumcised believers criticized him 3and said, "You went into the house of uncircumcised men and ate with them."

4Peter began and explained everything to them precisely as it had happened: 5"I was in the city of Joppa praying, and in a trance I saw a vision. I saw something like a large sheet being let down from heaven by its four corners, and it came down to where I was. 6I looked into it and saw four-footed animals of the earth, wild beasts, reptiles, and birds of the air. 7Then I heard a voice telling me, 'Get up, Peter. Kill and eat.'

8"I replied, 'Surely not, Lord! Nothing impure or unclean has ever entered my mouth.'

9"The voice spoke from heaven a second time, 'Do not call anything impure that God has made clean.' 10This happened three times, and then it was all pulled up to heaven again.

11"Right then three men who had been sent to me from Caesarea stopped at the house where I was staying. 12The Spirit told me to have no hesitation about going with them. These six brothers also went with me, and we entered the man's house. 13He told us how he had seen an angel appear in his house and say, 'Send to Joppa for Simon who is called Peter. 14He will bring you a message through which you and all your household will be saved.'

15"As I began to speak, the Holy Spirit came on them as he had come on us at the beginning. 16Then I remembered what the Lord had said: 'John baptized with[b] water, but you will be baptized with the Holy Spirit.' 17So if God gave them the same gift as he gave us, who believed in the Lord Jesus Christ, who was I to think that I could oppose God?"

18When they heard this, they had no further objections and praised God, saying, "So then, God has granted even the Gentiles repentance unto life."

The Church in Antioch

19Now those who had been scattered by the persecution in connection with Stephen traveled as far as Phoenicia, Cyprus and Antioch, telling the message only to Jews. 20Some of them, however, men from Cyprus and Cyrene, went to Antioch and began to speak to Greeks also, telling them the good news about the Lord Jesus. 21The Lord's hand was with them, and a great number of people believed and turned to the Lord.

22News of this reached the ears of the

[a]46 Or *other languages* [b]16 Or *in*

church at Jerusalem, and they sent Barnabas to Antioch. [23]When he arrived
and saw the evidence of the grace of
God, he was glad and encouraged them
all to remain true to the Lord with all
their hearts. [24]He was a good man, full
of the Holy Spirit and faith, and a great
number of people were brought to the
Lord.
[25]Then Barnabas went to Tarsus to
look for Saul, [26]and when he found him,
he brought him to Antioch. So for a
whole year Barnabas and Saul met with
the church and taught great numbers of
people. The disciples were called Christians first at Antioch.
[27]During this time some prophets
came down from Jerusalem to Antioch.
[28]One of them, named Agabus, stood up
and through the Spirit predicted that a
severe famine would spread over the
entire Roman world. (This happened
during the reign of Claudius.) [29]The disciples, each according to his ability, decided to provide help for the brothers
living in Judea. [30]This they did, sending
their gift to the elders by Barnabas and
Saul.

SHARPEN THE FOCUS

Commentators call the Sunday morning worship service "the most segregated hour of the week." Sociologists who study racial prejudice fail to find much difference between Christians and unbelievers. We might say that racial hatred is one sin that doesn't discriminate.

The early church ran into this problem in the first few years after Jesus ascended. Jewish believers had a hard time believing non-Jews could have a place in Christ's church. The Lord had to give Peter a vision to open his eyes to the fact that all people stand on level ground beneath the cross.

What prejudices keep you from reaching out to others with Christ's love? What ugly thoughts or words have offended your Lord and compromised your witness? Talk with your Savior about these questions, confident that He will forgive and bring about heartfelt repentance—a turn-around—in your heart and life. Then carefully read the words of Cornelius in Acts 10:33. What an open door the Lord set before Peter! He will do the same for us!

WEEK 84 • SATURDAY

Acts 12:1–25

GET THE BIG PICTURE

First Stephen. Then James. As Peter sat in Herod's jail, he no doubt expected to die the next day. But the Lord had other plans. As you read, take special note of the peace the Lord worked in Peter's heart. Ask yourself what accounted for it. If time is short, focus on Acts 12:1–19.

Peter's Miraculous Escape From Prison

12 It was about this time that
King Herod arrested some
who belonged to the church, intending
to persecute them. [2]He had James, the
brother of John, put to death with the
sword. [3]When he saw that this pleased
the Jews, he proceeded to seize Peter
also. This happened during the Feast of

Unleavened Bread. 4After arresting him,
he put him in prison, handing him over
to be guarded by four squads of four soldiers each. Herod intended to bring him
out for public trial after the Passover.
5So Peter was kept in prison, but the
church was earnestly praying to God for
him.
6The night before Herod was to bring
him to trial, Peter was sleeping between
two soldiers, bound with two chains,
and sentries stood guard at the entrance. 7Suddenly an angel of the Lord
appeared and a light shone in the cell.
He struck Peter on the side and woke
him up. "Quick, get up!" he said, and
the chains fell off Peter's wrists.
8Then the angel said to him, "Put on
your clothes and sandals." And Peter
did so. "Wrap your cloak around you
and follow me," the angel told him. 9Peter followed him out of the prison, but
he had no idea that what the angel was
doing was really happening; he thought
he was seeing a vision. 10They passed
the first and second guards and came to
the iron gate leading to the city. It
opened for them by itself, and they
went through it. When they had walked
the length of one street, suddenly the
angel left him.
11Then Peter came to himself and said,
"Now I know without a doubt that the
Lord sent his angel and rescued me
from Herod's clutches and from everything the Jewish people were anticipating."
12When this had dawned on him, he
went to the house of Mary the mother
of John, also called Mark, where many
people had gathered and were praying.
13Peter knocked at the outer entrance,
and a servant girl named Rhoda came
to answer the door. 14When she recognized Peter's voice, she was so overjoyed she ran back without opening it
and exclaimed, "Peter is at the door!"
15"You're out of your mind," they told
her. When she kept insisting that it was
so, they said, "It must be his angel."
16But Peter kept on knocking, and
when they opened the door and saw
him, they were astonished. 17Peter motioned with his hand for them to be quiet and described how the Lord had
brought him out of prison. "Tell James
and the brothers about this," he said,
and then he left for another place.
18In the morning, there was no small
commotion among the soldiers as to
what had become of Peter. 19After Herod had a thorough search made for him
and did not find him, he cross-examined the guards and ordered that they
be executed.

Herod's Death

Then Herod went from Judea to
Caesarea and stayed there a while. 20He
had been quarreling with the people of
Tyre and Sidon; they now joined together and sought an audience with
him. Having secured the support of
Blastus, a trusted personal servant of
the king, they asked for peace, because
they depended on the king's country
for their food supply.
21On the appointed day Herod, wearing his royal robes, sat on his throne and
delivered a public address to the people.
22They shouted, "This is the voice of a
god, not of a man." 23Immediately, because Herod did not give praise to God,
an angel of the Lord struck him down,
and he was eaten by worms and died.
24But the word of God continued to
increase and spread.
25When Barnabas and Saul had finished their mission, they returned from[a]
Jerusalem, taking with them John, also
called Mark.

[a]25 Some manuscripts *to*

SHARPEN THE FOCUS

Maybe you know someone who can sleep through anything: typhoons; sirens; the Marine Corps marching band. Even so, such a person might have trouble dropping off to sleep if he or she lay on a cot on death row the night before his or her own execution.

With that in mind, read Acts 12:6–7. Imagine the peace with which the Spirit of peace had surrounded Peter! So relaxed was he that the angel had to hit him to wake him up!

Remember Isaiah 26:3?

> *You will keep in perfect peace him whose mind is steadfast, because he trusts in You.*

Did you get a good night's sleep last night? Or did worries rob you of the rest your Lord wants you to have? What disturbs you? A troubled son or daughter? A mess at work? Medical or credit card bills?

If Satan has succeeded in stealing your peace for any reason, you can take it back. How? By confessing your worries as sin and asking your Savior for a renewed sense of His care—His care for you personally. He is, you know, the Prince of Peace (Isaiah 9:6), the one in whom you rest from the burden of your sin (Hebrews 4:9) and through whom you can come boldly to God's throne to find help in every time of need (Hebrews 4:16).

WEEK 85 • MONDAY

Acts 13:1—14:28

GET THE BIG PICTURE

Barnabas, John Mark, and Paul leave from Antioch with the express purpose of sharing the Good News of Jesus—crucified, risen, and reigning—with the world. As you read, notice Paul's practice of preaching first in the synagogue of a town; then, later he meets with Gentiles outside the synagogue. Notice too the opposition Satan raises. If time if short, focus on Acts 13:1–43.

Barnabas and Saul Sent Off

13 In the church at Antioch
there were prophets and
teachers: Barnabas, Simeon called Niger,
Lucius of Cyrene, Manaen (who had
been brought up with Herod the tetrarch) and Saul. 2While they were worshiping the Lord and fasting, the Holy
Spirit said, "Set apart for me Barnabas
and Saul for the work to which I have
called them." 3So after they had fasted
and prayed, they placed their hands on
them and sent them off.

On Cyprus

4The two of them, sent on their way
by the Holy Spirit, went down to Seleu-
cia and sailed from there to Cyprus.
5When they arrived at Salamis, they
proclaimed the word of God in the Jewish synagogues. John was with them as
their helper.

6They traveled through the whole island until they came to Paphos. There
they met a Jewish sorcerer and false
prophet named Bar-Jesus, 7who was an
attendant of the proconsul, Sergius Pau-

lus. The proconsul, an intelligent man,
sent for Barnabas and Saul because he
wanted to hear the word of God. 8But
Elymas the sorcerer (for that is what his
name means) opposed them and tried
to turn the proconsul from the faith.
9Then Saul, who was also called Paul,
filled with the Holy Spirit, looked
straight at Elymas and said, 10"You are a
child of the devil and an enemy of everything that is right! You are full of all
kinds of deceit and trickery. Will you
never stop perverting the right ways of
the Lord? 11Now the hand of the Lord
is against you. You are going to be blind,
and for a time you will be unable to see
the light of the sun."

Immediately mist and darkness came
over him, and he groped about, seeking
someone to lead him by the hand.
12When the proconsul saw what had
happened, he believed, for he was
amazed at the teaching about the Lord.

In Pisidian Antioch

13From Paphos, Paul and his companions sailed to Perga in Pamphylia, where
John left them to return to Jerusalem.
14From Perga they went on to Pisidian
Antioch. On the Sabbath they entered
the synagogue and sat down. 15After the
reading from the Law and the Prophets,
the synagogue rulers sent word to
them, saying, "Brothers, if you have a
message of encouragement for the
people, please speak."

16Standing up, Paul motioned with his
hand and said: "Men of Israel and you
Gentiles who worship God, listen to me!
17The God of the people of Israel chose
our fathers; he made the people prosper
during their stay in Egypt, with mighty
power he led them out of that country,
18he endured their conduct[a] for about
forty years in the desert, 19he overthrew
seven nations in Canaan and gave their
land to his people as their inheritance.
20All this took about 450 years.

"After this, God gave them judges
until the time of Samuel the prophet.
21Then the people asked for a king, and
he gave them Saul son of Kish, of the
tribe of Benjamin, who ruled forty
years. 22After removing Saul, he made
David their king. He testified concerning him: 'I have found David son of Jesse a man after my own heart; he will do
everything I want him to do.'

23"From this man's descendants God
has brought to Israel the Savior Jesus, as
he promised. 24Before the coming of
Jesus, John preached repentance and
baptism to all the people of Israel. 25As
John was completing his work, he said:
'Who do you think I am? I am not that
one. No, but he is coming after me,
whose sandals I am not worthy to untie.'

26"Brothers, children of Abraham, and
you God-fearing Gentiles, it is to us that
this message of salvation has been sent.
27The people of Jerusalem and their rulers did not recognize Jesus, yet in condemning him they fulfilled the words of
the prophets that are read every Sabbath. 28Though they found no proper
ground for a death sentence, they asked
Pilate to have him executed. 29When
they had carried out all that was written about him, they took him down
from the tree and laid him in a tomb.
30But God raised him from the dead,
31and for many days he was seen by
those who had traveled with him from
Galilee to Jerusalem. They are now his
witnesses to our people.

32"We tell you the good news: What
God promised our fathers 33he has ful-
filled for us, their children, by raising up
Jesus. As it is written in the second
Psalm:

" 'You are my Son;
today I have become your
Father.[b] '[c]

34The fact that God raised him from the
dead, never to decay, is stated in these
words:

" 'I will give you the holy and sure
blessings promised to
David.'[d]

35So it is stated elsewhere:

[a]18 Some manuscripts *and cared for them*
[b]33 Or *have begotten you* [c]33 Psalm 2:7
[d]34 Isaiah 55:3

"'You will not let your Holy One see
decay.'[a]

36"For when David had served God's purpose in his own generation, he fell asleep; he was buried with his fathers and his body decayed. 37But the one whom God raised from the dead did not see decay.

38"Therefore, my brothers, I want you to know that through Jesus the forgiveness of sins is proclaimed to you. 39Through him everyone who believes is justified from everything you could not be justified from by the law of Moses. 40Take care that what the prophets have said does not happen to you:

41" 'Look, you scoffers,
wonder and perish,
for I am going to do something in
your days
that you would never believe,
even if someone told you.'[b]"

42As Paul and Barnabas were leaving the synagogue, the people invited them to speak further about these things on the next Sabbath. 43When the congregation was dismissed, many of the Jews and devout converts to Judaism followed Paul and Barnabas, who talked with them and urged them to continue in the grace of God.

44On the next Sabbath almost the whole city gathered to hear the word of the Lord. 45When the Jews saw the crowds, they were filled with jealousy and talked abusively against what Paul was saying.

46Then Paul and Barnabas answered them boldly: "We had to speak the word of God to you first. Since you reject it and do not consider yourselves worthy of eternal life, we now turn to the Gentiles. 47For this is what the Lord has commanded us:

" 'I have made you[c] a light for the
Gentiles,
that you[c] may bring salvation to
the ends of the earth.'[d]"

48When the Gentiles heard this, they were glad and honored the word of the Lord; and all who were appointed for eternal life believed.

49The word of the Lord spread through the whole region. 50But the Jews incited the God-fearing women of high standing and the leading men of the city. They stirred up persecution against Paul and Barnabas, and expelled them from their region. 51So they shook the dust from their feet in protest against them and went to Iconium. 52And the disciples were filled with joy and with the Holy Spirit.

In Iconium

14 At Iconium Paul and Barnabas went as usual into the Jewish synagogue. There they spoke so effectively that a great number of Jews and Gentiles believed. 2But the Jews who refused to believe stirred up the Gentiles and poisoned their minds against the brothers. 3So Paul and Barnabas spent considerable time there, speaking boldly for the Lord, who confirmed the message of his grace by enabling them to do miraculous signs and wonders. 4The people of the city were divided; some sided with the Jews, others with the apostles. 5There was a plot afoot among the Gentiles and Jews, together with their leaders, to mistreat them and stone them. 6But they found out about it and fled to the Lycaonian cities of Lystra and Derbe and to the surrounding country, 7where they continued to preach the good news.

In Lystra and Derbe

8In Lystra there sat a man crippled in his feet, who was lame from birth and had never walked. 9He listened to Paul as he was speaking. Paul looked directly at him, saw that he had faith to be healed 10and called out, "Stand up on your feet!" At that, the man jumped up and began to walk.

11When the crowd saw what Paul had done, they shouted in the Lycaonian

[a]35 Psalm 16:10 [b]41 Hab. 1:5 [c]47 The Greek is singular. [d]47 Isaiah 49:6

language, "The gods have come down to us in human form!" [12]Barnabas they called Zeus, and Paul they called Hermes because he was the chief speaker. [13]The priest of Zeus, whose temple was just outside the city, brought bulls and wreaths to the city gates because he and the crowd wanted to offer sacrifices to them.

[14]But when the apostles Barnabas and Paul heard of this, they tore their clothes and rushed out into the crowd, shouting: [15]"Men, why are you doing this? We too are only men, human like you. We are bringing you good news, telling you to turn from these worthless things to the living God, who made heaven and earth and sea and everything in them. [16]In the past, he let all nations go their own way. [17]Yet he has not left himself without testimony: He has shown kindness by giving you rain from heaven and crops in their seasons; he provides you with plenty of food and fills your hearts with joy." [18]Even with these words, they had difficulty keeping the crowd from sacrificing to them.

[19]Then some Jews came from Antioch and Iconium and won the crowd over. They stoned Paul and dragged him outside the city, thinking he was dead. [20]But after the disciples had gathered around him, he got up and went back into the city. The next day he and Barnabas left for Derbe.

The Return to Antioch in Syria

[21]They preached the good news in that city and won a large number of disciples. Then they returned to Lystra, Iconium and Antioch, [22]strengthening the disciples and encouraging them to remain true to the faith. "We must go through many hardships to enter the kingdom of God," they said. [23]Paul and Barnabas appointed elders[a] for them in each church and, with prayer and fasting, committed them to the Lord, in whom they had put their trust. [24]After going through Pisidia, they came into Pamphylia, [25]and when they had preached the word in Perga, they went down to Attalia.

[26]From Attalia they sailed back to Antioch, where they had been committed to the grace of God for the work they had now completed. [27]On arriving there, they gathered the church together and reported all that God had done through them and how he had opened the door of faith to the Gentiles. [28]And they stayed there a long time with the disciples.

[a]23 Or *Barnabas ordained elders;* or *Barnabas had elders elected*

SHARPEN THE FOCUS

No one (except Jonah) had ever done it before. No one (not even Jonah) had *wanted* to do it before. But the church in Antioch didn't know that. They fasted and prayed and when God spoke, they obeyed. Barnabas and Paul, touched by the grace and power of God, set sail for the mission field—the Gentile world.

Ever since, God has blessed the world through other pioneers.

- Those who saw the power of radio and television to share the Gospel—even when many Christians sincerely considered these inventions as "tools of the devil."
- Those who endured harsh northern winters to bring the Gospel by circuit rider to the sand hills of the Midwest and the prairies of central Canada.
- Those who now dream and work through ways to baptize the World Wide Web and Pentium chips for the kingdom of heaven.

Pray today for those who innovate—not for their own financial gain, but for the glory of Christ and for the eternal salvation of those who do not know their Savior.

WEEK 85 • TUESDAY

Acts 15:1–41

GET THE BIG PICTURE

Must a Gentile become a Jew before he or she can become a Christian? That question caused no small stir in the early Christian church. Jews who had grown up steeped in the Old Testament laws wanted to retain their culture. Many Gentiles resisted. As you read, watch how the decision of the council came down on the side of grace, not of law. If time is short, focus on Acts 15:1, 6–31.

The Council at Jerusalem

15 Some men came down from
Judea to Antioch and were
teaching the brothers: "Unless you are
circumcised, according to the custom
taught by Moses, you cannot be saved."
2This brought Paul and Barnabas into
sharp dispute and debate with them. So
Paul and Barnabas were appointed,
along with some other believers, to go
up to Jerusalem to see the apostles and
elders about this question. 3The church
sent them on their way, and as they
traveled through Phoenicia and Samaria, they told how the Gentiles had been
converted. This news made all the
brothers very glad. 4When they came to
Jerusalem, they were welcomed by the
church and the apostles and elders, to
whom they reported everything God
had done through them.
5Then some of the believers who belonged to the party of the Pharisees
stood up and said, "The Gentiles must
be circumcised and required to obey the
law of Moses."
6The apostles and elders met to consider this question. 7After much discussion, Peter got up and addressed them:
"Brothers, you know that some time ago
God made a choice among you that the
Gentiles might hear from my lips the
message of the gospel and believe.
8God, who knows the heart, showed
that he accepted them by giving the
Holy Spirit to them, just as he did to us.
9He made no distinction between us
and them, for he purified their hearts by
faith. 10Now then, why do you try to test
God by putting on the necks of the disciples a yoke that neither we nor our fathers have been able to bear? 11No! We
believe it is through the grace of our
Lord Jesus that we are saved, just as
they are."
12The whole assembly became silent
as they listened to Barnabas and Paul
telling about the miraculous signs and
wonders God had done among the
Gentiles through them. 13When they finished, James spoke up: "Brothers, listen
to me. 14Simon[a] has described to us how
God at first showed his concern by taking from the Gentiles a people for himself. 15The words of the prophets are in
agreement with this, as it is written:

16" 'After this I will return
and rebuild David's fallen tent.
Its ruins I will rebuild,
and I will restore it,
17that the remnant of men may seek
the Lord,

[a]14 Greek *Simeon*, a variant of *Simon*; that is, Peter

and all the Gentiles who bear my
name,
says the Lord, who does these
things'[a]
18 that have been known for ages.[b]

[19]"It is my judgment, therefore, that we should not make it difficult for the Gentiles who are turning to God. [20]Instead we should write to them, telling them to abstain from food polluted by idols, from sexual immorality, from the meat of strangled animals and from blood. [21]For Moses has been preached in every city from the earliest times and is read in the synagogues on every Sabbath."

The Council's Letter to Gentile Believers

[22]Then the apostles and elders, with the whole church, decided to choose some of their own men and send them to Antioch with Paul and Barnabas. They chose Judas (called Barsabbas) and Silas, two men who were leaders among the brothers. [23]With them they sent the following letter:

The apostles and elders, your brothers,

To the Gentile believers in Antioch, Syria and Cilicia:

Greetings.

[24]We have heard that some went out from us without our authorization and disturbed you, troubling your minds by what they said. [25]So we all agreed to choose some men and send them to you with our dear friends Barnabas and Paul—[26]men who have risked their lives for the name of our Lord Jesus Christ. [27]Therefore we are sending Judas and Silas to confirm by word of mouth what we are writing. [28]It seemed good to the Holy Spirit and to us not to burden you with anything beyond the following requirements: [29]You are to abstain from food sacrificed to idols, from blood, from the meat of strangled animals and from sexual immorality. You will do well to avoid these things.

Farewell.

[30]The men were sent off and went down to Antioch, where they gathered the church together and delivered the letter. [31]The people read it and were glad for its encouraging message. [32]Judas and Silas, who themselves were prophets, said much to encourage and strengthen the brothers. [33]After spending some time there, they were sent off by the brothers with the blessing of peace to return to those who had sent them.[c] [35]But Paul and Barnabas remained in Antioch, where they and many others taught and preached the word of the Lord.

Disagreement Between Paul and Barnabas

[36]Some time later Paul said to Barnabas, "Let us go back and visit the brothers in all the towns where we preached the word of the Lord and see how they are doing." [37]Barnabas wanted to take John, also called Mark, with them, [38]but Paul did not think it wise to take him, because he had deserted them in Pamphylia and had not continued with them in the work. [39]They had such a sharp disagreement that they parted company. Barnabas took Mark and sailed for Cyprus, [40]but Paul chose Silas and left, commended by the brothers to the grace of the Lord. [41]He went through Syria and Cilicia, strengthening the churches.

[a]17 Amos 9:11,12 [b]17,18 Some manuscripts *things'— / [18]known to the Lord for ages is his work*
[c]33 Some manuscripts *them, [34]but Silas decided to remain there*

SHARPEN THE FOCUS

From the time of the apostles on, people have tried to change the clear, simple Gospel message by adding one law or another. The Gospel says, "Christ died for our sins. Believe and be saved." Legalism says, "Yes, but . . .

- . . . you have to go to church."
- . . . you have to stop swearing or playing the lottery."
- . . . you have to tithe or be a better parent."

Who knows how many ways the "but you have to" sentence can end. Most often the endings refer to commendable activities. It's good for us to avoid swearing, to go to church, and the rest. Even so, any "but you have to . . ." ruins the Gospel, turns it from Good News to bad.

God led the council at Jerusalem to see this trap. They urged the Gentile believers to show love to Jewish believers by refusing to eat bloody meat and animals killed in a nonkosher way (Acts 15:20b). For the sake of the Gentiles and their families, the apostles reminded all the believers of the dangers of idol worship and sexual immorality (including pagan temple prostitution; Acts 15:20a). But no new laws came into being; everyone rejoiced in their Christ-given freedom (Acts 15:31).

WEEK 85 • WEDNESDAY

Acts 16:1–40

GET THE BIG PICTURE

With today's reading, we begin Paul's second missionary journey. Trouble, harassment from Satan, and even sin marked this mission. Even so, the Lord blessed it mightily. Read Acts 13:13 to get the background for Acts 15:36–40. Also as you read, ask yourself what accounts for the remarkable strength and growth of the holy Christian church in the first century. If time is short, focus on Acts 15:36–41.

Timothy Joins Paul and Silas

16 He came to Derbe and then
to Lystra, where a disciple
named Timothy lived, whose mother
was a Jewess and a believer, but whose
father was a Greek. 2The brothers at
Lystra and Iconium spoke well of him.
3Paul wanted to take him along on the
journey, so he circumcised him because
of the Jews who lived in that area, for
they all knew that his father was a
Greek. 4As they traveled from town to
town, they delivered the decisions
reached by the apostles and elders in
Jerusalem for the people to obey. 5So the
churches were strengthened in the faith
and grew daily in numbers.

Paul's Vision of the Man of Macedonia

6Paul and his companions traveled
throughout the region of Phrygia and
Galatia, having been kept by the Holy
Spirit from preaching the word in the
province of Asia. 7When they came to
the border of Mysia, they tried to enter

Bithynia, but the Spirit of Jesus would not allow them to. [8]So they passed by Mysia and went down to Troas. [9]During the night Paul had a vision of a man of Macedonia standing and begging him, "Come over to Macedonia and help us." [10]After Paul had seen the vision, we got ready at once to leave for Macedonia, concluding that God had called us to preach the gospel to them.

Lydia's Conversion in Philippi

[11]From Troas we put out to sea and sailed straight for Samothrace, and the next day on to Neapolis. [12]From there we traveled to Philippi, a Roman colony and the leading city of that district of Macedonia. And we stayed there several days.

[13]On the Sabbath we went outside the city gate to the river, where we expected to find a place of prayer. We sat down and began to speak to the women who had gathered there. [14]One of those listening was a woman named Lydia, a dealer in purple cloth from the city of Thyatira, who was a worshiper of God. The Lord opened her heart to respond to Paul's message. [15]When she and the members of her household were baptized, she invited us to her home. "If you consider me a believer in the Lord," she said, "come and stay at my house." And she persuaded us.

Paul and Silas in Prison

[16]Once when we were going to the place of prayer, we were met by a slave girl who had a spirit by which she predicted the future. She earned a great deal of money for her owners by fortune-telling. [17]This girl followed Paul and the rest of us, shouting, "These men are servants of the Most High God, who are telling you the way to be saved." [18]She kept this up for many days. Finally Paul became so troubled that he turned around and said to the spirit, "In the name of Jesus Christ I command you to come out of her!" At that moment the spirit left her.

[19]When the owners of the slave girl realized that their hope of making money was gone, they seized Paul and Silas and dragged them into the marketplace to face the authorities. [20]They brought them before the magistrates and said, "These men are Jews, and are throwing our city into an uproar [21]by advocating customs unlawful for us Romans to accept or practice."

[22]The crowd joined in the attack against Paul and Silas, and the magistrates ordered them to be stripped and beaten. [23]After they had been severely flogged, they were thrown into prison, and the jailer was commanded to guard them carefully. [24]Upon receiving such orders, he put them in the inner cell and fastened their feet in the stocks.

[25]About midnight Paul and Silas were praying and singing hymns to God, and the other prisoners were listening to them. [26]Suddenly there was such a violent earthquake that the foundations of the prison were shaken. At once all the prison doors flew open, and everybody's chains came loose. [27]The jailer woke up, and when he saw the prison doors open, he drew his sword and was about to kill himself because he thought the prisoners had escaped. [28]But Paul shouted, "Don't harm yourself! We are all here!"

[29]The jailer called for lights, rushed in and fell trembling before Paul and Silas. [30]He then brought them out and asked, "Sirs, what must I do to be saved?"

[31]They replied, "Believe in the Lord Jesus, and you will be saved—you and your household." [32]Then they spoke the word of the Lord to him and to all the others in his house. [33]At that hour of the night the jailer took them and washed their wounds; then immediately he and all his family were baptized. [34]The jailer brought them into his house and set a meal before them; he was filled with joy because he had come to believe in God—he and his whole family.

[35]When it was daylight, the magistrates sent their officers to the jailer with the order: "Release those men." [36]The jailer told Paul, "The magistrates have ordered that you and Silas be released. Now you can leave. Go in peace."

37But Paul said to the office[...] beat us publicly without a t[...] though we are Roman citiz[...] threw us into prison. And no[...] want to get rid of us quietly[...] them come themselves and es[...] out."
38The officers reported this to the magistrates, and when they heard that

SHARPEN THE F[...]

Speaking to His redeemed people, the Lord gave this promise:

Enlarge the place of your tent,
stretch your tent curtains wide, do not hold back;
lengthen your cords,
strengthen your stakes.
For you will spread out to the right and to the left;
your descendants will dispossess nations and settle in their desolate cities.
(Isaiah 54:2–3)

The early church grew despite the arguments and sins of her leaders and despite the opposition of her enemies. She drove her stakes deep into the grace of God in Christ. She made the "tent" bigger and bigger, not by compromising, but by preaching Christ crucified to thousands who had not heard it. As the Spirit had promised, the church—His church—prospered. She "dispossess[ed] the nations."

Isaiah's promise, God's promise, still belongs to us, His people today. What will you ask God's Spirit to do for your congregation?

WEEK 85 • THURSDAY

Acts 17:1—18:22

GET THE BIG PICTURE

Today you will finish reading the account of Paul's second missionary journey. You may recognize the names of some of the places he visited; he later wrote letters to the churches in many of these cities. As you read, study Paul's tactics. If time is short, focus on Acts 17:16–34.

In Thessalonica

17 When they had passed through Amphipolis and Apollonia, they came to Thessalonica, where there was a Jewish synagogue.
2As his custom was, Paul went into the synagogue, and on three Sabbath days he reasoned with them from the Scrip-

...the
...ing to
...ne of the
...joined Paul
...umber of God-
...a few prominent

...were jealous; so they
...me bad characters from
...place, formed a mob and
...riot in the city. They rushed to
...s house in search of Paul and
...s in order to bring them out to
...e crowd.[b] 6But when they did not
find them, they dragged Jason and
some other brothers before the city
officials, shouting: "These men who
have caused trouble all over the world
have now come here, 7and Jason has
welcomed them into his house. They
are all defying Caesar's decrees, saying
that there is another king, one called
Jesus." 8When they heard this, the
crowd and the city officials were thrown
into turmoil. 9Then they made Jason
and the others post bond and let
them go.

In Berea

10As soon as it was night, the brothers
sent Paul and Silas away to Berea. On arriving there, they went to the Jewish
synagogue. 11Now the Bereans were of
more noble character than the Thessalonians, for they received the message
with great eagerness and examined the
Scriptures every day to see if what Paul
said was true. 12Many of the Jews believed, as did also a number of prominent Greek women and many Greek
men.
13When the Jews in Thessalonica
learned that Paul was preaching the
word of God at Berea, they went there
too, agitating the crowds and stirring
them up. 14The brothers immediately
sent Paul to the coast, but Silas and Timothy stayed at Berea. 15The men who
escorted Paul brought him to Athens
and then left with instructions for Silas
and Timothy to join him as soon as possible.

In Athens

16While Paul was waiting for them in
Athens, he was greatly distressed to see
that the city was full of idols. 17So he reasoned in the synagogue with the Jews
and the God-fearing Greeks, as well as
in the marketplace day by day with
those who happened to be there. 18A
group of Epicurean and Stoic philoso-
phers began to dispute with him. Some
of them asked, "What is this babbler trying to say?" Others remarked, "He
seems to be advocating foreign gods."
They said this because Paul was preaching the good news about Jesus and the
resurrection. 19Then they took him and
brought him to a meeting of the Areopagus, where they said to him, "May we
know what this new teaching is that
you are presenting? 20You are bringing
some strange ideas to our ears, and we
want to know what they mean." 21(All
the Athenians and the foreigners who
lived there spent their time doing nothing but talking about and listening to
the latest ideas.)
22Paul then stood up in the meeting of
the Areopagus and said: "Men of Athens! I see that in every way you are very
religious. 23For as I walked around and
looked carefully at your objects of worship, I even found an altar with this inscription: TO AN UNKNOWN GOD. Now
what you worship as something unknown I am going to proclaim to you.
24"The God who made the world and
everything in it is the Lord of heaven
and earth and does not live in temples
built by hands. 25And he is not served by
human hands, as if he needed anything,
because he himself gives all men life and
breath and everything else. 26From one
man he made every nation of men, that
they should inhabit the whole earth;
and he determined the times set for
them and the exact places where they
should live. 27God did this so that men
would seek him and perhaps reach out
for him and find him, though he is not
far from each one of us. 28'For in him we
live and move and have our being.' As

[a]3 Or *Messiah* [b]5 Or *the assembly of the people*

wrote to the disciples there to welcome him. On arriving, he was a great help to those who by grace had believed. 28For he vigorously refuted the Jews in public debate, proving from the Scriptures that Jesus was the Christ.

Paul in Ephesus

19 While Apollos was at Corinth, Paul took the road through the interior and arrived at Ephesus. There he found some disciples 2and asked them, "Did you receive the Holy Spirit when[a] you believed?"

They answered, "No, we have not even heard that there is a Holy Spirit."

3So Paul asked, "Then what baptism did you receive?"

"John's baptism," they replied.

4Paul said, "John's baptism was a baptism of repentance. He told the people to believe in the one coming after him, that is, in Jesus." 5On hearing this, they were baptized into[b] the name of the Lord Jesus. 6When Paul placed his hands on them, the Holy Spirit came on them, and they spoke in tongues[c] and prophesied. 7There were about twelve men in all.

8Paul entered the synagogue and spoke boldly there for three months, arguing persuasively about the kingdom of God. 9But some of them became obstinate; they refused to believe and publicly maligned the Way. So Paul left them. He took the disciples with him and had discussions daily in the lecture hall of Tyrannus. 10This went on for two years, so that all the Jews and Greeks who lived in the province of Asia heard the word of the Lord.

11God did extraordinary miracles through Paul, 12so that even handkerchiefs and aprons that had touched him were taken to the sick, and their illnesses were cured and the evil spirits left them.

13Some Jews who went around driving out evil spirits tried to invoke the name of the Lord Jesus over those who were demon-possessed. They would say, "In the name of Jesus, whom Paul preaches, I command you to come out." 14Seven sons of Sceva, a Jewish chief priest, were doing this. 15⌞One day⌟ the evil spirit answered them, "Jesus I know, and I know about Paul, but who are you?" 16Then the man who had the evil spirit jumped on them and overpowered them all. He gave them such a beating that they ran out of the house naked and bleeding.

17When this became known to the Jews and Greeks living in Ephesus, they were all seized with fear, and the name of the Lord Jesus was held in high honor. 18Many of those who believed now came and openly confessed their evil deeds. 19A number who had practiced sorcery brought their scrolls together and burned them publicly. When they calculated the value of the scrolls, the total came to fifty thousand drachmas.[d] 20In this way the word of the Lord spread widely and grew in power.

21After all this had happened, Paul decided to go to Jerusalem, passing through Macedonia and Achaia. "After I have been there," he said, "I must visit Rome also." 22He sent two of his helpers, Timothy and Erastus, to Macedonia, while he stayed in the province of Asia a little longer.

The Riot in Ephesus

23About that time there arose a great disturbance about the Way. 24A silversmith named Demetrius, who made silver shrines of Artemis, brought in no little business for the craftsmen. 25He called them together, along with the workmen in related trades, and said: "Men, you know we receive a good income from this business. 26And you see and hear how this fellow Paul has convinced and led astray large numbers of people here in Ephesus and in practically the whole province of Asia. He says that man-made gods are no gods at all. 27There is danger not only that our trade will lose its good name, but also that the temple of the great

[a]2 Or *after* [b]5 Or *in* [c]6 Or *other languages*
[d]19 A drachma was a silver coin worth about a day's wages.

goddess Artemis will be discredited,
and the goddess herself, who is worshiped throughout the province of Asia
and the world, will be robbed of her divine majesty."
28When they heard this, they were furious and began shouting: "Great is Artemis of the Ephesians!" 29Soon the
whole city was in an uproar. The people
seized Gaius and Aristarchus, Paul's
traveling companions from Macedonia,
and rushed as one man into the theater.
30Paul wanted to appear before the
crowd, but the disciples would not let
him. 31Even some of the officials of the
province, friends of Paul, sent him a
message begging him not to venture
into the theater.
32The assembly was in confusion:
Some were shouting one thing, some
another. Most of the people did not even
know why they were there. 33The Jews
pushed Alexander to the front, and
some of the crowd shouted instructions
to him. He motioned for silence in order
to make a defense before the people.
34But when they realized he was a Jew,
they all shouted in unison for about two
hours: "Great is Artemis of the Ephesians!"
35The city clerk quieted the crowd and
said: "Men of Ephesus, doesn't all the
world know that the city of Ephesus is
the guardian of the temple of the great
Artemis and of her image, which fell
from heaven? 36Therefore, since these
facts are undeniable, you ought to be
quiet and not do anything rash. 37You
have brought these men here, though
they have neither robbed temples nor
blasphemed our goddess. 38If, then, Demetrius and his fellow craftsmen have
a grievance against anybody, the courts
are open and there are proconsuls. They
can press charges. 39If there is anything
further you want to bring up, it must be
settled in a legal assembly. 40As it is, we
are in danger of being charged with ri-
oting because of today's events. In that
case we would not be able to account for
this commotion, since there is no reason
for it." 41After he had said this, he dismissed the assembly.

Through Macedonia and Greece

20 When the uproar had
ended, Paul sent for the
disciples and, after encouraging them,
said good-by and set out for Macedonia.
2He traveled through that area, speaking many words of encouragement to
the people, and finally arrived in
Greece, 3where he stayed three months.
Because the Jews made a plot against
him just as he was about to sail for Syria,
he decided to go back through Macedonia. 4He was accompanied by Sopater
son of Pyrrhus from Berea, Aristarchus
and Secundus from Thessalonica, Gaius
from Derbe, Timothy also, and Tychicus
and Trophimus from the province of
Asia. 5These men went on ahead and
waited for us at Troas. 6But we sailed
from Philippi after the Feast of Unleavened Bread, and five days later joined
the others at Troas, where we stayed
seven days.

Eutychus Raised From the Dead at Troas

7On the first day of the week we came
together to break bread. Paul spoke to
the people and, because he intended to
leave the next day, kept on talking until
midnight. 8There were many lamps in
the upstairs room where we were meeting. 9Seated in a window was a young
man named Eutychus, who was sinking
into a deep sleep as Paul talked on and
on. When he was sound asleep, he fell
to the ground from the third story and
was picked up dead. 10Paul went down,
threw himself on the young man and
put his arms around him. "Don't be
alarmed," he said. "He's alive!" 11Then
he went upstairs again and broke bread
and ate. After talking until daylight, he
left. 12The people took the young man
home alive and were greatly comforted.

Paul's Farewell to the Ephesian Elders

13We went on ahead to the ship and
sailed for Assos, where we were going
to take Paul aboard. He had made this
arrangement because he was going

there on foot. [14]When he met us at Assos, we took him aboard and went on to
Mitylene. [15]The next day we set sail from
there and arrived off Kios. The day after that we crossed over to Samos, and
on the following day arrived at Miletus.
[16]Paul had decided to sail past Ephesus
to avoid spending time in the province
of Asia, for he was in a hurry to reach
Jerusalem, if possible, by the day of Pentecost.

[17]From Miletus, Paul sent to Ephesus
for the elders of the church. [18]When they
arrived, he said to them: "You know
how I lived the whole time I was with
you, from the first day I came into the
province of Asia. [19]I served the Lord
with great humility and with tears, although I was severely tested by the
plots of the Jews. [20]You know that I have
not hesitated to preach anything that
would be helpful to you but have taught
you publicly and from house to house.
[21]I have declared to both Jews and
Greeks that they must turn to God in
repentance and have faith in our Lord
Jesus.

[22]"And now, compelled by the Spirit, I
am going to Jerusalem, not knowing
what will happen to me there. [23]I only
know that in every city the Holy Spirit
warns me that prison and hardships are
facing me. [24]However, I consider my life
worth nothing to me, if only I may finish the race and complete the task the
Lord Jesus has given me—the task of
testifying to the gospel of God's grace.

[25]"Now I know that none of you
among whom I have gone about
preaching the kingdom will ever see me
again. [26]Therefore, I declare to you today that I am innocent of the blood of
all men. [27]For I have not hesitated to
proclaim to you the whole will of God.
[28]Keep watch over yourselves and all the
flock of which the Holy Spirit has made
you overseers.[a] Be shepherds of the
church of God,[b] which he bought with
his own blood. [29]I know that after I
leave, savage wolves will come in
among you and will not spare the flock.
[30]Even from your own number men will
arise and distort the truth in order to
draw away disciples after them. [31]So be
on your guard! Remember that for three
years I never stopped warning each of
you night and day with tears.

[32]"Now I commit you to God and to
the word of his grace, which can build
you up and give you an inheritance
among all those who are sanctified. [33]I
have not coveted anyone's silver or gold
or clothing. [34]You yourselves know that
these hands of mine have supplied my
own needs and the needs of my companions. [35]In everything I did, I showed
you that by this kind of hard work we
must help the weak, remembering the
words the Lord Jesus himself said: 'It is
more blessed to give than to receive.' "

[36]When he had said this, he knelt
down with all of them and prayed.
[37]They all wept as they embraced him
and kissed him. [38]What grieved them
most was his statement that they would
never see his face again. Then they accompanied him to the ship.

On to Jerusalem

21 After we had torn ourselves
away from them, we put out
to sea and sailed straight to Cos. The
next day we went to Rhodes and from
there to Patara. [2]We found a ship crossing over to Phoenicia, went on board
and set sail. [3]After sighting Cyprus and
passing to the south of it, we sailed on
to Syria. We landed at Tyre, where our
ship was to unload its cargo. [4]Finding
the disciples there, we stayed with them
seven days. Through the Spirit they
urged Paul not to go on to Jerusalem.
[5]But when our time was up, we left and
continued on our way. All the disciples
and their wives and children accompanied us out of the city, and there on the
beach we knelt to pray. [6]After saying
good-by to each other, we went aboard
the ship, and they returned home.

[7]We continued our voyage from Tyre
and landed at Ptolemais, where we
greeted the brothers and stayed with
them for a day. [8]Leaving the next day,

[a]28 Traditionally *bishops* [b]28 Many manuscripts *of the Lord*

we reached Caesarea and stayed at the
house of Philip the evangelist, one of
the Seven. 9He had four unmarried
daughters who prophesied.
10After we had been there a number
of days, a prophet named Agabus came
down from Judea. 11Coming over to us,
he took Paul's belt, tied his own hands
and feet with it and said, "The Holy Spirit says, 'In this way the Jews of Jerusalem will bind the owner of this belt and
will hand him over to the Gentiles.'"
12When we heard this, we and the
people there pleaded with Paul not to
go up to Jerusalem. 13Then Paul answered, "Why are you weeping and
breaking my heart? I am ready not only
to be bound, but also to die in Jerusalem
for the name of the Lord Jesus." 14When
he would not be dissuaded, we gave up
and said, "The Lord's will be done."
15After this, we got ready and went up
to Jerusalem. 16Some of the disciples
from Caesarea accompanied us and
brought us to the home of Mnason,
where we were to stay. He was a man
from Cyprus and one of the early disciples.

SHARPEN THE FOCUS

When you get to heaven, which person from Bible times do you most want to meet? St. Paul? Sarah? Moses? Ruth? Good choices all.

But perhaps you'd like to think also about shaking hands with Apollos. Apollos was cultured, learned. He had "a thorough knowledge of the Scriptures" (Acts 18:24). He was fervent about his faith. When Apollos taught, people listened, learned, and came to faith. But perhaps most importantly, Apollos was teachable. He didn't get offended when Aquila and Priscilla took him aside to correct some of his misconceptions (Acts 18:26). He wasn't a Mr. Know-It-All.

Would the people who know you consider you teachable? It takes true humility, godly humility, to admit our blind spots, ignorance, or misconceptions. The Lord had, by grace, given that humility to Apollos. And He will give it to us as well. We need only confess our need and let Him draw us to His cross.

The correction Apollos received from his friends made it possible for him to be a "great help" to the believers in Achaia (Acts 18:27). That's our Lord's desire for you, too—that your life blesses those lives it touches—always, of course, by His power and grace at work in you.

WEEK 85 • SATURDAY

Acts 21:17—23:35

GET THE BIG PICTURE

With plot shifts as exciting as any movie, the pace of Luke's narrative picks up. Paul's arrest opens the way for him to proclaim the Good News of salvation to several groups and individuals. Watch to see how each responds. If time is short, focus on Acts 21:17–22:23.

Paul's Arrival at Jerusalem

17When we arrived at Jerusalem, the
brothers received us warmly. 18The next
day Paul and the rest of us went to see
James, and all the elders were present.
19Paul greeted them and reported in de-

tail what God had done among the Gentiles through his ministry.
[20]When they heard this, they praised
God. Then they said to Paul: "You see,
brother, how many thousands of Jews
have believed, and all of them are zealous for the law. [21]They have been informed that you teach all the Jews who
live among the Gentiles to turn away
from Moses, telling them not to circumcise their children or live according to
our customs. [22]What shall we do? They
will certainly hear that you have come,
[23]so do what we tell you. There are four
men with us who have made a vow.
[24]Take these men, join in their purification rites and pay their expenses, so that
they can have their heads shaved. Then
everybody will know there is no truth
in these reports about you, but that you
yourself are living in obedience to the
law. [25]As for the Gentile believers, we
have written to them our decision that
they should abstain from food sacrificed
to idols, from blood, from the meat of
strangled animals and from sexual immorality."
[26]The next day Paul took the men and
purified himself along with them. Then
he went to the temple to give notice of
the date when the days of purification
would end and the offering would be
made for each of them.

Paul Arrested

[27]When the seven days were nearly
over, some Jews from the province of
Asia saw Paul at the temple. They stirred
up the whole crowd and seized him,
[28]shouting, "Men of Israel, help us! This
is the man who teaches all men everywhere against our people and our law
and this place. And besides, he has
brought Greeks into the temple area
and defiled this holy place." [29](They had
previously seen Trophimus the Ephesi-
an in the city with Paul and assumed
that Paul had brought him into the temple area.)
[30]The whole city was aroused, and the
people came running from all directions. Seizing Paul, they dragged him
from the temple, and immediately the
gates were shut. [31]While they were trying to kill him, news reached the commander of the Roman troops that the
whole city of Jerusalem was in an uproar. [32]He at once took some officers and
soldiers and ran down to the crowd.
When the rioters saw the commander
and his soldiers, they stopped beating
Paul.
[33]The commander came up and arrested him and ordered him to be
bound with two chains. Then he asked
who he was and what he had done.
[34]Some in the crowd shouted one thing
and some another, and since the commander could not get at the truth because of the uproar, he ordered that
Paul be taken into the barracks. [35]When
Paul reached the steps, the violence of
the mob was so great he had to be
carried by the soldiers. [36]The crowd that
followed kept shouting, "Away with
him!"

Paul Speaks to the Crowd

[37]As the soldiers were about to take
Paul into the barracks, he asked the commander, "May I say something to you?"
"Do you speak Greek?" he replied.
[38]"Aren't you the Egyptian who started
a revolt and led four thousand terrorists
out into the desert some time ago?"
[39]Paul answered, "I am a Jew, from Tarsus in Cilicia, a citizen of no ordinary
city. Please let me speak to the people."
[40]Having received the commander's
permission, Paul stood on the steps and
motioned to the crowd. When they
were all silent, he said to them in Ara
22 maic[a]: [1]"Brothers and fathers, listen now to my
defense."
[2]When they heard him speak to them
in Aramaic, they became very quiet.
Then Paul said: [3]"I am a Jew, born in
Tarsus of Cilicia, but brought up in this
city. Under Gamaliel I was thoroughly
trained in the law of our fathers and was
just as zealous for God as any of you are
today. [4]I persecuted the followers of this
Way to their death, arresting both men

[a]40 Or possibly *Hebrew;* also in 22:2

and women and throwing them into prison, 5as also the high priest and all the Council can testify. I even obtained letters from them to their brothers in Damascus, and went there to bring these people as prisoners to Jerusalem to be punished.

6"About noon as I came near Damascus, suddenly a bright light from heaven flashed around me. 7I fell to the ground and heard a voice say to me, 'Saul! Saul! Why do you persecute me?'

8" 'Who are you, Lord?' I asked.

" 'I am Jesus of Nazareth, whom you are persecuting,' he replied. 9My companions saw the light, but they did not understand the voice of him who was speaking to me.

10" 'What shall I do, Lord?' I asked.

" 'Get up,' the Lord said, 'and go into Damascus. There you will be told all that you have been assigned to do.' 11My companions led me by the hand into Damascus, because the brilliance of the light had blinded me.

12"A man named Ananias came to see me. He was a devout observer of the law and highly respected by all the Jews living there. 13He stood beside me and said, 'Brother Saul, receive your sight!' And at that very moment I was able to see him.

14"Then he said: 'The God of our fathers has chosen you to know his will and to see the Righteous One and to hear words from his mouth. 15You will be his witness to all men of what you have seen and heard. 16And now what are you waiting for? Get up, be baptized and wash your sins away, calling on his name.'

17"When I returned to Jerusalem and was praying at the temple, I fell into a trance 18and saw the Lord speaking. 'Quick!' he said to me. 'Leave Jerusalem immediately, because they will not accept your testimony about me.'

19" 'Lord,' I replied, 'these men know that I went from one synagogue to another to imprison and beat those who believe in you. 20And when the blood of your martyr[a] Stephen was shed, I stood there giving my approval and guarding the clothes of those who were killing him.'

21"Then the Lord said to me, 'Go; I will send you far away to the Gentiles.' "

Paul the Roman Citizen

22The crowd listened to Paul until he said this. Then they raised their voices and shouted, "Rid the earth of him! He's not fit to live!"

23As they were shouting and throwing off their cloaks and flinging dust into the air, 24the commander ordered Paul to be taken into the barracks. He directed that he be flogged and questioned in order to find out why the people were shouting at him like this. 25As they stretched him out to flog him, Paul said to the centurion standing there, "Is it legal for you to flog a Roman citizen who hasn't even been found guilty?"

26When the centurion heard this, he went to the commander and reported it. "What are you going to do?" he asked. "This man is a Roman citizen."

27The commander went to Paul and asked, "Tell me, are you a Roman citizen?"

"Yes, I am," he answered.

28Then the commander said, "I had to pay a big price for my citizenship."

"But I was born a citizen," Paul replied.

29Those who were about to question him withdrew immediately. The commander himself was alarmed when he realized that he had put Paul, a Roman citizen, in chains.

Before the Sanhedrin

30The next day, since the commander wanted to find out exactly why Paul was being accused by the Jews, he released him and ordered the chief priests and all the Sanhedrin to assemble. Then he brought Paul and had him stand before them.

23 Paul looked straight at the Sanhedrin and said, "My

[a]20 Or *witness*

brothers, I have fulfilled my duty to God
in all good conscience to this day." 2At
this the high priest Ananias ordered
those standing near Paul to strike him
on the mouth. 3Then Paul said to him,
"God will strike you, you whitewashed
wall! You sit there to judge me according to the law, yet you yourself violate
the law by commanding that I be
struck!"

4Those who were standing near Paul
said, "You dare to insult God's high
priest?"

5Paul replied, "Brothers, I did not realize that he was the high priest; for it
is written: 'Do not speak evil about the
ruler of your people.'[a]"

6Then Paul, knowing that some of
them were Sadducees and the others
Pharisees, called out in the Sanhedrin,
"My brothers, I am a Pharisee, the son
of a Pharisee. I stand on trial because of
my hope in the resurrection of the
dead." 7When he said this, a dispute
broke out between the Pharisees and
the Sadducees, and the assembly was
divided. 8(The Sadducees say that there
is no resurrection, and that there are
neither angels nor spirits, but the Pharisees acknowledge them all.)

9There was a great uproar, and some
of the teachers of the law who were
Pharisees stood up and argued vigorously. "We find nothing wrong with this
man," they said. "What if a spirit or an
angel has spoken to him?" 10The dispute
became so violent that the commander
was afraid Paul would be torn to pieces
by them. He ordered the troops to go
down and take him away from them
by force and bring him into the barracks.

11The following night the Lord stood
near Paul and said, "Take courage! As
you have testified about me in Jerusalem, so you must also testify in Rome."

The Plot to Kill Paul

12The next morning the Jews formed
a conspiracy and bound themselves
with an oath not to eat or drink until
they had killed Paul. 13More than forty
men were involved in this plot. 14They
went to the chief priests and elders and
said, "We have taken a solemn oath not
to eat anything until we have killed
Paul. 15Now then, you and the Sanhedrin petition the commander to bring
him before you on the pretext of wanting more accurate information about his
case. We are ready to kill him before he
gets here."

16But when the son of Paul's sister
heard of this plot, he went into the barracks and told Paul.

17Then Paul called one of the centurions and said, "Take this young man to
the commander; he has something to
tell him." 18So he took him to the commander.

The centurion said, "Paul, the prisoner, sent for me and asked me to bring
this young man to you because he has
something to tell you."

19The commander took the young
man by the hand, drew him aside and
asked, "What is it you want to tell me?"

20He said: "The Jews have agreed to
ask you to bring Paul before the Sanhedrin tomorrow on the pretext of wanting more accurate information about
him. 21Don't give in to them, because
more than forty of them are waiting in
ambush for him. They have taken an
oath not to eat or drink until they have
killed him. They are ready now, waiting
for your consent to their request."

22The commander dismissed the
young man and cautioned him, "Don't
tell anyone that you have reported this
to me."

Paul Transferred to Caesarea

23Then he called two of his centurions
and ordered them, "Get ready a detachment of two hundred soldiers, seventy
horsemen and two hundred spearmen[b]
to go to Caesarea at nine tonight. 24Pro-
vide mounts for Paul so that he may be
taken safely to Governor Felix."

25He wrote a letter as follows:

26Claudius Lysias,

[a]5 Exodus 22:28 [b]23 The meaning of the Greek for this word is uncertain.

To His Excellency, Governor Felix:
Greetings.

[27]This man was seized by the
Jews and they were about to kill
him, but I came with my troops and
rescued him, for I had learned that
he is a Roman citizen. [28]I wanted to
know why they were accusing him,
so I brought him to their Sanhedrin. [29]I found that the accusation
had to do with questions about
their law, but there was no charge
against him that deserved death or
imprisonment. [30]When I was informed of a plot to be carried out
against the man, I sent him to you
at once. I also ordered his accusers
to present to you their case against
him.

[31]So the soldiers, carrying out their orders, took Paul with them during the
night and brought him as far as Antipa-
tris. [32]The next day they let the cavalry
go on with him, while they returned to
the barracks. [33]When the cavalry arrived
in Caesarea, they delivered the letter to
the governor and handed Paul over to
him. [34]The governor read the letter and
asked what province he was from.
Learning that he was from Cilicia, [35]he
said, "I will hear your case when your
accusers get here." Then he ordered that
Paul be kept under guard in Herod's
palace.

SHARPEN THE FOCUS

It was a miscarriage of justice. Anyone today jailed and held as Paul was would no doubt sue for false arrest. And yet, Paul saw all of it not as an interruption in his service for the Lord, but as an open door of witness. He was the tool chosen by the Lord to carry the Gospel to many, even to the Gentiles and their kings (Acts 7:15). From heaven's perspective, Paul was exactly where he needed to be.

Perhaps today you find yourself cruising life's highway. But maybe instead you lie bogged down in what appears to be a senseless detour. Job loss. Money problems. Chronic illness. Relationship challenges. Depression or anxiety. Maybe, like Paul, you did nothing to cause your difficulties. Or perhaps you did, and now guilt feelings pile themselves on your stack of burdens, too.

In any case, let the Savior that Paul proclaimed comfort and encourage you. You do not struggle alone. The God who forgives for Jesus' sake also strengthens. Secure in that truth, you can with confidence look for doors of witness your Savior may open.

WEEK 86 • MONDAY

Acts 24:1—26:32

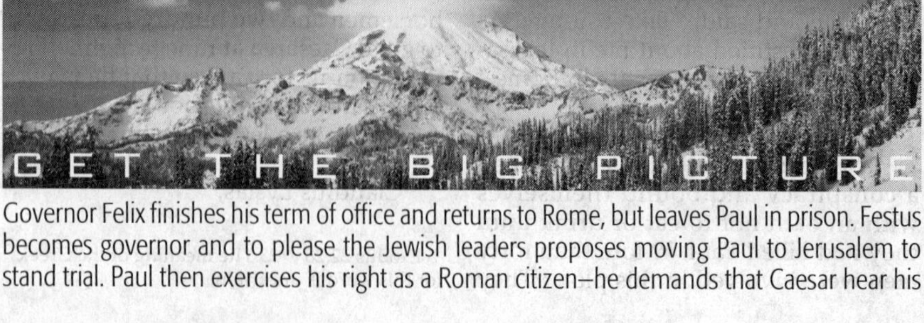

GET THE BIG PICTURE

Governor Felix finishes his term of office and returns to Rome, but leaves Paul in prison. Festus becomes governor and to please the Jewish leaders proposes moving Paul to Jerusalem to stand trial. Paul then exercises his right as a Roman citizen—he demands that Caesar hear his case. Consulting with King Herod Agrippa II, Festus puzzles over what crime to name on Paul's indictment. If time is short, focus on Acts 26:1–32.

The Trial Before Felix

24 Five days later the high priest Ananias went down to Caesarea with some of the elders and a lawyer named Tertullus, and they brought their charges against Paul before the governor. [2]When Paul was called in, Tertullus presented his case before Felix: "We have enjoyed a long period of peace under you, and your foresight has brought about reforms in this nation. [3]Everywhere and in every way, most excellent Felix, we acknowledge this with profound gratitude. [4]But in order not to weary you further, I would request that you be kind enough to hear us briefly.

[5]"We have found this man to be a troublemaker, stirring up riots among the Jews all over the world. He is a ringleader of the Nazarene sect [6]and even tried to desecrate the temple; so we seized him. [8]By[a] examining him yourself you will be able to learn the truth about all these charges we are bringing against him."

[9]The Jews joined in the accusation, asserting that these things were true.

[10]When the governor motioned for him to speak, Paul replied: "I know that for a number of years you have been a judge over this nation; so I gladly make my defense. [11]You can easily verify that no more than twelve days ago I went up to Jerusalem to worship. [12]My accusers did not find me arguing with anyone at the temple, or stirring up a crowd in the synagogues or anywhere else in the city. [13]And they cannot prove to you the charges they are now making against me. [14]However, I admit that I worship the God of our fathers as a follower of the Way, which they call a sect. I believe everything that agrees with the Law and that is written in the Prophets, [15]and I have the same hope in God as these men, that there will be a resurrection of both the righteous and the wicked. [16]So I strive always to keep my conscience clear before God and man.

[17]"After an absence of several years, I came to Jerusalem to bring my people gifts for the poor and to present offerings. [18]I was ceremonially clean when they found me in the temple courts doing this. There was no crowd with me, nor was I involved in any disturbance. [19]But there are some Jews from the province of Asia, who ought to be here before you and bring charges if they have anything against me. [20]Or these who are here should state what crime they found in me when I stood before the Sanhedrin— [21]unless it was this one thing I shouted as I stood in their presence: 'It is concerning the resurrection of the dead that I am on trial before you today.' "

[22]Then Felix, who was well acquainted with the Way, adjourned the proceedings. "When Lysias the commander comes," he said, "I will decide your case." [23]He ordered the centurion to keep Paul under guard but to give him some freedom and permit his friends to take care of his needs.

[24]Several days later Felix came with his wife Drusilla, who was a Jewess. He sent for Paul and listened to him as he spoke about faith in Christ Jesus. [25]As Paul discoursed on righteousness, self-control and the judgment to come, Felix was afraid and said, "That's enough for now! You may leave. When I find it convenient, I will send for you." [26]At the same time he was hoping that Paul would offer him a bribe, so he sent for him frequently and talked with him.

[27]When two years had passed, Felix was succeeded by Porcius Festus, but because Felix wanted to grant a favor to the Jews, he left Paul in prison.

[a]*6-8* Some manuscripts *him and wanted to judge him according to our law. [7]But the commander, Lysias, came and with the use of much force snatched him from our hands [8]and ordered his accusers to come before you. By*

The Trial Before Festus

25 Three days after arriving
in the province, Festus
went up from Caesarea to Jerusalem,
2where the chief priests and Jewish leaders appeared before him and presented
the charges against Paul. 3They urgently
requested Festus, as a favor to them, to
have Paul transferred to Jerusalem, for
they were preparing an ambush to kill
him along the way. 4Festus answered,
"Paul is being held at Caesarea, and I
myself am going there soon. 5Let some
of your leaders come with me and press
charges against the man there, if he has
done anything wrong."
6After spending eight or ten days with
them, he went down to Caesarea, and
the next day he convened the court and
ordered that Paul be brought before
him. 7When Paul appeared, the Jews
who had come down from Jerusalem
stood around him, bringing many serious charges against him, which they
could not prove.
8Then Paul made his defense: "I have
done nothing wrong against the law of
the Jews or against the temple or against
Caesar."
9Festus, wishing to do the Jews a favor, said to Paul, "Are you willing to go
up to Jerusalem and stand trial before
me there on these charges?"
10Paul answered: "I am now standing
before Caesar's court, where I ought to
be tried. I have not done any wrong to
the Jews, as you yourself know very
well. 11If, however, I am guilty of doing
anything deserving death, I do not refuse to die. But if the charges brought
against me by these Jews are not true,
no one has the right to hand me over to
them. I appeal to Caesar!"
12After Festus had conferred with his
council, he declared: "You have appealed to Caesar. To Caesar you will
go!"

Festus Consults King Agrippa

13A few days later King Agrippa and
Bernice arrived at Caesarea to pay their
respects to Festus. 14Since they were
spending many days there, Festus discussed Paul's case with the king. He
said: "There is a man here whom Felix
left as a prisoner. 15When I went to Jerusalem, the chief priests and elders of the
Jews brought charges against him and
asked that he be condemned.
16"I told them that it is not the Roman
custom to hand over any man before he
has faced his accusers and has had an
opportunity to defend himself against
their charges. 17When they came here
with me, I did not delay the case, but
convened the court the next day and ordered the man to be brought in. 18When
his accusers got up to speak, they did
not charge him with any of the crimes I
had expected. 19Instead, they had some
points of dispute with him about their
own religion and about a dead man
named Jesus who Paul claimed was
alive. 20I was at a loss how to investigate
such matters; so I asked if he would be
willing to go to Jerusalem and stand trial
there on these charges. 21When Paul
made his appeal to be held over for the
Emperor's decision, I ordered him held
until I could send him to Caesar."
22Then Agrippa said to Festus, "I
would like to hear this man myself."
He replied, "Tomorrow you will hear
him."

Paul Before Agrippa

23The next day Agrippa and Bernice
came with great pomp and entered the
audience room with the high ranking
officers and the leading men of the city.
At the command of Festus, Paul was
brought in. 24Festus said: "King Agrippa,
and all who are present with us, you see
this man! The whole Jewish community
has petitioned me about him in Jerusalem and here in Caesarea, shouting that
he ought not to live any longer. 25I found
he had done nothing deserving of
death, but because he made his appeal
to the Emperor I decided to send him to
Rome. 26But I have nothing definite to
write to His Majesty about him. Therefore I have brought him before all of
you, and especially before you, King
Agrippa, so that as a result of this

investigation I may have something to write. 27For I think it is unreasonable to send on a prisoner without specifying the charges against him."

26 Then Agrippa said to Paul, "You have permission to speak for yourself."

So Paul motioned with his hand and began his defense: 2"King Agrippa, I consider myself fortunate to stand before you today as I make my defense against all the accusations of the Jews, 3and especially so because you are well acquainted with all the Jewish customs and controversies. Therefore, I beg you to listen to me patiently.

4"The Jews all know the way I have lived ever since I was a child, from the beginning of my life in my own country, and also in Jerusalem. 5They have known me for a long time and can testify, if they are willing, that according to the strictest sect of our religion, I lived as a Pharisee. 6And now it is because of my hope in what God has promised our fathers that I am on trial today. 7This is the promise our twelve tribes are hoping to see fulfilled as they earnestly serve God day and night. O king, it is because of this hope that the Jews are accusing me. 8Why should any of you consider it incredible that God raises the dead?

9"I too was convinced that I ought to do all that was possible to oppose the name of Jesus of Nazareth. 10And that is just what I did in Jerusalem. On the authority of the chief priests I put many of the saints in prison, and when they were put to death, I cast my vote against them. 11Many a time I went from one synagogue to another to have them punished, and I tried to force them to blaspheme. In my obsession against them, I even went to foreign cities to persecute them.

12"On one of these journeys I was going to Damascus with the authority and commission of the chief priests. 13About noon, O king, as I was on the road, I saw a light from heaven, brighter than the sun, blazing around me and my companions. 14We all fell to the ground, and I heard a voice saying to me in Aramaic,[a] 'Saul, Saul, why do you persecute me? It is hard for you to kick against the goads.'

15"Then I asked, 'Who are you, Lord?'

" 'I am Jesus, whom you are persecuting,' the Lord replied. 16'Now get up and stand on your feet. I have appeared to you to appoint you as a servant and as a witness of what you have seen of me and what I will show you. 17I will rescue you from your own people and from the Gentiles. I am sending you to them 18to open their eyes and turn them from darkness to light, and from the power of Satan to God, so that they may receive forgiveness of sins and a place among those who are sanctified by faith in me.'

19"So then, King Agrippa, I was not disobedient to the vision from heaven. 20First to those in Damascus, then to those in Jerusalem and in all Judea, and to the Gentiles also, I preached that they should repent and turn to God and prove their repentance by their deeds. 21That is why the Jews seized me in the temple courts and tried to kill me. 22But I have had God's help to this very day, and so I stand here and testify to small and great alike. I am saying nothing beyond what the prophets and Moses said would happen— 23that the Christ[b] would suffer and, as the first to rise from the dead, would proclaim light to his own people and to the Gentiles."

24At this point Festus interrupted Paul's defense. "You are out of your mind, Paul!" he shouted. "Your great learning is driving you insane."

25"I am not insane, most excellent Festus," Paul replied. "What I am saying is true and reasonable. 26The king is familiar with these things, and I can speak freely to him. I am convinced that none of this has escaped his notice, because it was not done in a corner. 27King Agrippa, do you believe the prophets? I know you do."

28Then Agrippa said to Paul, "Do you

[a]14 Or *Hebrew* [b]23 Or *Messiah*

think that in such a short time you can
persuade me to be a Christian?"
29Paul replied, "Short time or long—I
pray God that not only you but all who
are listening to me today may become
what I am, except for these chains."
30The king rose, and with him the
governor and Bernice and those sitting
with them. 31They left the room, and
while talking with one another, they
said, "This man is not doing anything that deserves death or imprisonment."
32Agrippa said to Festus, "This man
could have been set free if he had not
appealed to Caesar."

SHARPEN THE FOCUS

Luke records three accounts of Paul's conversion (Acts 9:1–19; 22:3–21; and 26:8–18). Each account adds different details to flesh out the bare bones facts of the conversion. When we've read all three, we realize how truly gracious our Lord was to Paul and to all of us whose lives have been changed through Paul's ministry.

Much of the rest of what we will read from the New Testament in the next few months flowed from Paul's pen. Our Lord has definite goals He wants to accomplish in us as we read these inspired texts. Acts 26:18 specifies five of these. Personalize each for yourself and jot them on a piece of paper. Your list may read something like this:

- that my eyes will be open to God's truth;
- that I will be turned from darkness to light;
- that I will be turned from the power of Satan to God,
- that I will receive forgiveness of sins;
- that I will receive a place among those who are sanctified by faith in Christ.

Now pray the list you just made. Ask God to continue to do these things in you through His Word for the sake of Jesus and His cross. ☼

WEEK 86 • TUESDAY

Acts 27:1—28:31

GET THE BIG PICTURE

The Lord had told Paul he would get a chance to witness in Rome (Acts 23:11). Today you will read how that came about. Notice throughout the reading that Paul takes charge. He knows whose he is and whom he serves (Acts 27:23), and it fills him with a holy boldness. If time is short, focus on Acts 27:1–44.

Paul Sails for Rome

27 When it was decided that
we would sail for Italy,
Paul and some other prisoners were
handed over to a centurion named
Julius, who belonged to the Imperial
Regiment. 2We boarded a ship from
Adramyttium about to sail for ports

along the coast of the province of Asia,
and we put out to sea. Aristarchus, a
Macedonian from Thessalonica, was
with us.
3The next day we landed at Sidon;
and Julius, in kindness to Paul, allowed
him to go to his friends so they might
provide for his needs. 4From there we
put out to sea again and passed to the
lee of Cyprus because the winds were
against us. 5When we had sailed across
the open sea off the coast of Cilicia and
Pamphylia, we landed at Myra in Lyc-
ia. 6There the centurion found an Alexandrian ship sailing for Italy and put us
on board. 7We made slow headway for
many days and had difficulty arriving
off Cnidus. When the wind did not allow us to hold our course, we sailed to
the lee of Crete, opposite Salmone. 8We
moved along the coast with difficulty
and came to a place called Fair Havens,
near the town of Lasea.
9Much time had been lost, and sailing
had already become dangerous because
by now it was after the Fast.[a] So Paul
warned them, 10"Men, I can see that our
voyage is going to be disastrous and
bring great loss to ship and cargo, and
to our own lives also." 11But the centurion, instead of listening to what Paul
said, followed the advice of the pilot and
of the owner of the ship. 12Since the harbor was unsuitable to winter in, the
majority decided that we should sail on,
hoping to reach Phoenix and winter
there. This was a harbor in Crete, facing
both southwest and northwest.

The Storm

13When a gentle south wind began to
blow, they thought they had obtained
what they wanted; so they weighed anchor and sailed along the shore of Crete.
14Before very long, a wind of hurricane
force, called the "northeaster," swept
down from the island. 15The ship was
caught by the storm and could not head
into the wind; so we gave way to it and
were driven along. 16As we passed to the
lee of a small island called Cauda, we
were hardly able to make the lifeboat
secure. 17When the men had hoisted it
aboard, they passed ropes under the
ship itself to hold it together. Fearing
that they would run aground on the
sandbars of Syrtis, they lowered the sea
anchor and let the ship be driven along.
18We took such a violent battering from
the storm that the next day they began
to throw the cargo overboard. 19On the
third day, they threw the ship's tackle
overboard with their own hands.
20When neither sun nor stars appeared
for many days and the storm continued
raging, we finally gave up all hope of
being saved.
21After the men had gone a long time
without food, Paul stood up before
them and said: "Men, you should have
taken my advice not to sail from Crete;
then you would have spared yourselves
this damage and loss. 22But now I urge
you to keep up your courage, because
not one of you will be lost; only the ship
will be destroyed. 23Last night an angel
of the God whose I am and whom I
serve stood beside me 24and said, 'Do
not be afraid, Paul. You must stand trial
before Caesar; and God has graciously
given you the lives of all who sail with
you.' 25So keep up your courage, men,
for I have faith in God that it will happen just as he told me. 26Nevertheless,
we must run aground on some island."

The Shipwreck

27On the fourteenth night we were
still being driven across the Adriatic[b]
Sea, when about midnight the sailors
sensed they were approaching land.
28They took soundings and found that
the water was a hundred and twenty
feet[c] deep. A short time later they took
soundings again and found it was
ninety feet[d] deep. 29Fearing that we
would be dashed against the rocks, they
dropped four anchors from the stern
and prayed for daylight. 30In an attempt
to escape from the ship, the sailors let
the lifeboat down into the sea, pretend-

[a]9 That is, the Day of Atonement (Yom Kippur)
[b]27 In ancient times the name referred to an area extending well south of Italy. [c]28 Greek *twenty orguias* (about 37 meters) [d]28 Greek *fifteen orguias* (about 27 meters)

ing they were going to lower some anchors from the bow. 31Then Paul said to
the centurion and the soldiers, "Unless
these men stay with the ship, you cannot be saved." 32So the soldiers cut the
ropes that held the lifeboat and let it fall
away.

33Just before dawn Paul urged them
all to eat. "For the last fourteen days," he
said, "you have been in constant suspense and have gone without food—
you haven't eaten anything. 34Now I
urge you to take some food. You need it
to survive. Not one of you will lose a
single hair from his head." 35After he
said this, he took some bread and gave
thanks to God in front of them all. Then
he broke it and began to eat. 36They
were all encouraged and ate some food
themselves. 37Altogether there were 276
of us on board. 38When they had eaten
as much as they wanted, they lightened
the ship by throwing the grain into the
sea.

39When daylight came, they did not
recognize the land, but they saw a bay
with a sandy beach, where they decided
to run the ship aground if they could.
40Cutting loose the anchors, they left
them in the sea and at the same time
untied the ropes that held the rudders.
Then they hoisted the foresail to the
wind and made for the beach. 41But the
ship struck a sandbar and ran aground.
The bow stuck fast and would not
move, and the stern was broken to
pieces by the pounding of the surf.

42The soldiers planned to kill the prisoners to prevent any of them from
swimming away and escaping. 43But the
centurion wanted to spare Paul's life
and kept them from carrying out their
plan. He ordered those who could swim
to jump overboard first and get to land.
44The rest were to get there on planks or
on pieces of the ship. In this way everyone reached land in safety.

Ashore on Malta

28 Once safely on shore, we
found out that the island
was called Malta. 2The islanders showed
us unusual kindness. They built a fire
and welcomed us all because it was rain-
ing and cold. 3Paul gathered a pile of
brushwood and, as he put it on the fire,
a viper, driven out by the heat, fastened
itself on his hand. 4When the islanders
saw the snake hanging from his hand,
they said to each other, "This man must
be a murderer; for though he escaped
from the sea, Justice has not allowed
him to live." 5But Paul shook the snake
off into the fire and suffered no ill effects. 6The people expected him to
swell up or suddenly fall dead, but after waiting a long time and seeing nothing unusual happen to him, they
changed their minds and said he was a
god.

7There was an estate nearby that belonged to Publius, the chief official of
the island. He welcomed us to his home
and for three days entertained us hos-
pitably. 8His father was sick in bed, suffering from fever and dysentery. Paul
went in to see him and, after prayer,
placed his hands on him and healed
him. 9When this had happened, the rest
of the sick on the island came and were
cured. 10They honored us in many
ways and when we were ready to sail,
they furnished us with the supplies we
needed.

Arrival at Rome

11After three months we put out to sea
in a ship that had wintered in the island.
It was an Alexandrian ship with the fig-
urehead of the twin gods Castor and
Pollux. 12We put in at Syracuse and
stayed there three days. 13From there we
set sail and arrived at Rhegium. The
next day the south wind came up, and
on the following day we reached Pute-
oli. 14There we found some brothers
who invited us to spend a week with
them. And so we came to Rome. 15The
brothers there had heard that we were
coming, and they traveled as far as the
Forum of Appius and the Three Taverns
to meet us. At the sight of these men
Paul thanked God and was encouraged.
16When we got to Rome, Paul was allowed to live by himself, with a soldier
to guard him.

Paul Preaches at Rome Under Guard

[17]Three days later he called together the leaders of the Jews. When they had assembled, Paul said to them: "My brothers, although I have done nothing against our people or against the customs of our ancestors, I was arrested in Jerusalem and handed over to the Romans. [18]They examined me and wanted to release me, because I was not guilty of any crime deserving death. [19]But when the Jews objected, I was compelled to appeal to Caesar—not that I had any charge to bring against my own people. [20]For this reason I have asked to see you and talk with you. It is because of the hope of Israel that I am bound with this chain."

[21]They replied, "We have not received any letters from Judea concerning you, and none of the brothers who have come from there has reported or said anything bad about you. [22]But we want to hear what your views are, for we know that people everywhere are talking against this sect."

[23]They arranged to meet Paul on a certain day, and came in even larger numbers to the place where he was staying. From morning till evening he explained and declared to them the kingdom of God and tried to convince them about Jesus from the Law of Moses and from the Prophets. [24]Some were convinced by what he said, but others would not believe. [25]They disagreed among themselves and began to leave after Paul had made this final statement: "The Holy Spirit spoke the truth to your forefathers when he said through Isaiah the prophet:

[26]" 'Go to this people and say,
"You will be ever hearing but never understanding;
you will be ever seeing but never perceiving."
[27]For this people's heart has become calloused;
they hardly hear with their ears,
and they have closed their eyes.
Otherwise they might see with their eyes,
hear with their ears,
understand with their hearts
and turn, and I would heal them.'[a]

[28]"Therefore I want you to know that God's salvation has been sent to the Gentiles, and they will listen!"[b]

[30]For two whole years Paul stayed there in his own rented house and welcomed all who came to see him. [31]Boldly and without hindrance he preached the kingdom of God and taught about the Lord Jesus Christ.

[a]27 Isaiah 6:9,10 [b]28 Some manuscripts *listen!"* [29]*After he said this, the Jews left, arguing vigorously among themselves.*

SHARPEN THE FOCUS

It was autumn. October. The seas were unpredictable, and the ship in which Paul and the others sailed was no bigger than today's average church fellowship hall. When the northeaster hit, the sailors must have heaved a sigh of desperation.

They undergirded the ship with cables; they took some sails down (Acts 27:17). They jettisoned their tackle (Acts 27:18–19). They couldn't see the stars and, because of that, they didn't know where they were (Acts 27:20). The storm howled for 14 long days and nights (Acts 27:27). Then the ship hit a reef and began to take on water (Acts 27:27, 41). It was every man for himself (Acts 27:43–44).

But not really. Surely it seemed that way to the sailors and to the Roman soldiers aboard. But the Lord had promised that for Paul's sake not one of the 276 people aboard would be lost (Acts 27:24). And they weren't (Acts 27:44).

Regardless of the "storms" you face today, you can do what you need to do with confidence. The God whose you are and whom you serve has promised to keep you safe in life and in death. He will do it for your Savior's sake.

ROMANS

WEEK 86 • WEDNESDAY

Romans 1:1—2:29

In his letter to the Christians at Rome, Paul outlines God's plan of love to save the world. He writes with the precision of a legal expert, laying out human need and God's plan to meet it. Read slowly and pray about the text as you do so. The Holy Spirit did not waste a word when He inspired the book of Romans! If time is short, focus on Acts 1:1–23.

1 Paul, a servant of Christ Jesus,
called to be an apostle and set apart
for the gospel of God— 2the gospel he
promised beforehand through his
prophets in the Holy Scriptures 3regard-
ing his Son, who as to his human nature
was a descendant of David, 4and who
through the Spirit[a] of holiness was declared with power to be the Son of God[b]
by his resurrection from the dead: Jesus
Christ our Lord. 5Through him and for
his name's sake, we received grace and
apostleship to call people from among
all the Gentiles to the obedience that
comes from faith. 6And you also are
among those who are called to belong
to Jesus Christ.

7To all in Rome who are loved by God
and called to be saints:

Grace and peace to you from God our Father and from the Lord Jesus Christ.

Paul's Longing to Visit Rome

8First, I thank my God through Jesus
Christ for all of you, because your faith
is being reported all over the world.
9God, whom I serve with my whole
heart in preaching the gospel of his Son,
is my witness how constantly I remember you 10in my prayers at all times; and
I pray that now at last by God's will the
way may be opened for me to come to
you.

11I long to see you so that I may impart to you some spiritual gift to make
you strong— 12that is, that you and I
may be mutually encouraged by each
other's faith. 13I do not want you to be
unaware, brothers, that I planned many
times to come to you (but have been
prevented from doing so until now) in
order that I might have a harvest among
you, just as I have had among the other
Gentiles.

14I am obligated both to Greeks and
non-Greeks, both to the wise and the
foolish. 15That is why I am so eager to
preach the gospel also to you who are
at Rome.

16I am not ashamed of the gospel, because it is the power of God for the salvation of everyone who believes: first
for the Jew, then for the Gentile. 17For in
the gospel a righteousness from God is
revealed, a righteousness that is by faith
from first to last,[c] just as it is written:
"The righteous will live by faith."[d]

[a]4 Or *who as to his spirit* [b]4 Or *was appointed to be the Son of God with power* [c]17 Or *is from faith to faith* [d]17 Hab. 2:4

God's Wrath Against Mankind

18 The wrath of God is being revealed from heaven against all the godlessness and wickedness of men who suppress the truth by their wickedness, 19 since what may be known about God is plain to them, because God has made it plain to them. 20 For since the creation of the world God's invisible qualities—his eternal power and divine nature—have been clearly seen, being understood from what has been made, so that men are without excuse.

21 For although they knew God, they neither glorified him as God nor gave thanks to him, but their thinking became futile and their foolish hearts were darkened. 22 Although they claimed to be wise, they became fools 23 and exchanged the glory of the immortal God for images made to look like mortal man and birds and animals and reptiles.

24 Therefore God gave them over in the sinful desires of their hearts to sexual impurity for the degrading of their bodies with one another. 25 They exchanged the truth of God for a lie, and worshiped and served created things rather than the Creator—who is forever praised. Amen.

26 Because of this, God gave them over to shameful lusts. Even their women exchanged natural relations for unnatural ones. 27 In the same way the men also abandoned natural relations with women and were inflamed with lust for one another. Men committed indecent acts with other men, and received in themselves the due penalty for their perversion.

28 Furthermore, since they did not think it worthwhile to retain the knowledge of God, he gave them over to a depraved mind, to do what ought not to be done. 29 They have become filled with every kind of wickedness, evil, greed and depravity. They are full of envy, murder, strife, deceit and malice. They are gossips, 30 slanderers, God-haters, insolent, arrogant and boastful; they invent ways of doing evil; they disobey their parents; 31 they are senseless, faithless, heartless, ruthless. 32 Although they know God's righteous decree that those who do such things deserve death, they not only continue to do these very things but also approve of those who practice them.

God's Righteous Judgment

2 You, therefore, have no excuse, you who pass judgment on someone else, for at whatever point you judge the other, you are condemning yourself, because you who pass judgment do the same things. 2 Now we know that God's judgment against those who do such things is based on truth. 3 So when you, a mere man, pass judgment on them and yet do the same things, do you think you will escape God's judgment? 4 Or do you show contempt for the riches of his kindness, tolerance and patience, not realizing that God's kindness leads you toward repentance?

5 But because of your stubbornness and your unrepentant heart, you are storing up wrath against yourself for the day of God's wrath, when his righteous judgment will be revealed. 6 God "will give to each person according to what he has done."[a] 7 To those who by persistence in doing good seek glory, honor and immortality, he will give eternal life. 8 But for those who are self-seeking and who reject the truth and follow evil, there will be wrath and anger. 9 There will be trouble and distress for every human being who does evil: first for the Jew, then for the Gentile; 10 but glory, honor and peace for everyone who does good: first for the Jew, then for the Gentile. 11 For God does not show favoritism.

12 All who sin apart from the law will also perish apart from the law, and all who sin under the law will be judged by the law. 13 For it is not those who hear the law who are righteous in God's sight, but it is those who obey the law who will be declared righteous. 14 (Indeed, when Gentiles, who do not have the law, do by nature things required by the

[a]6 Psalm 62:12; Prov. 24:12

law, they are a law for themselves, even though they do not have the law, [15]since they show that the requirements of the law are written on their hearts, their consciences also bearing witness, and their thoughts now accusing, now even defending them.) [16]This will take place on the day when God will judge men's secrets through Jesus Christ, as my gospel declares.

The Jews and the Law

[17]Now you, if you call yourself a Jew; if you rely on the law and brag about your relationship to God; [18]if you know his will and approve of what is superior because you are instructed by the law; [19]if you are convinced that you are a guide for the blind, a light for those who are in the dark, [20]an instructor of the foolish, a teacher of infants, because you have in the law the embodiment of knowledge and truth— [21]you, then, who teach others, do you not teach yourself? You who preach against stealing, do you steal? [22]You who say that people should not commit adultery, do you commit adultery? You who abhor idols, do you rob temples? [23]You who brag about the law, do you dishonor God by breaking the law? [24]As it is written: "God's name is blasphemed among the Gentiles because of you."[a]

[25]Circumcision has value if you observe the law, but if you break the law, you have become as though you had not been circumcised. [26]If those who are not circumcised keep the law's requirements, will they not be regarded as though they were circumcised? [27]The one who is not circumcised physically and yet obeys the law will condemn you who, even though you have the[b] written code and circumcision, are a lawbreaker.

[28]A man is not a Jew if he is only one outwardly, nor is circumcision merely outward and physical. [29]No, a man is a Jew if he is one inwardly; and circumcision is circumcision of the heart, by the Spirit, not by the written code. Such a man's praise is not from men, but from God.

[a]24 Isaiah 52:5; Ezek. 36:22 [b]27 Or *who, by means of a*

SHARPEN THE FOCUS

A husband caught in adultery asks his distraught wife, "What can I do to make it right?"

A daughter who has wrecked the family's only car, driving it while drunk asks, "What can I do to make it right?"

Even on a human scale, questions like these have no easy answers. Cars can, of course, be replaced. But ruined relationships are another matter.

Now think about the problem of human sin from God's perspective. Like a malignant, fatal disease, the sinful nature was passed down from generation to generation. This nature held all human beings prisoner, forcing us to act like the sinners we were. Our relationship with a holy God and our relationships with one another lay in ruins. What could we do to make things right? Nothing. And what's more, we didn't even want to.

So God made a way in Jesus to make *us* right, righteous. From prologue to postscript, Romans unfolds the story of God's salvation, first revealed to Israel, but now to the whole world.

Read Romans 1:16–17 several times. As you do, think of the cross which stands at the very center of the Gospel about which Paul boasted. Then praise God for His overwhelming love.

All are guilty under the Law. But in Romans 3:19 we get our first inkling of hope: the Law—and its condemnation—apply only to those who are under it. Those who are right with God by faith in His Son have been freed from the penalties we deserve. As you read, watch Paul build his case for *your* righteousness. If time is short, focus on Romans 3:21-31.

God's Faithfulness

3 What advantage, then, is there in
being a Jew, or what value is
there in circumcision? [2]Much in every
way! First of all, they have been entrusted with the very words of God.
[3]What if some did not have faith? Will
their lack of faith nullify God's faithfulness? [4]Not at all! Let God be true, and
every man a liar. As it is written:

"So that you may be proved right
when you speak
and prevail when you judge."[a]

[5]But if our unrighteousness brings out
God's righteousness more clearly, what
shall we say? That God is unjust in
bringing his wrath on us? (I am using a
human argument.) [6]Certainly not! If
that were so, how could God judge the
world? [7]Someone might argue, "If my
falsehood enhances God's truthfulness
and so increases his glory, why am I still
condemned as a sinner?" [8]Why not
say—as we are being slanderously reported as saying and as some claim that
we say—"Let us do evil that good may
result"? Their condemnation is deserved.

No One Is Righteous

[9]What shall we conclude then? Are
we any better[b]? Not at all! We have already made the charge that Jews and
Gentiles alike are all under sin. [10]As it is
written:

"There is no one righteous, not even
one;
[11] there is no one who understands,
no one who seeks God.
[12] All have turned away,
they have together become
worthless;
there is no one who does good,
not even one."[c]
[13] "Their throats are open graves;
their tongues practice deceit."[d]
"The poison of vipers is on their
lips."[e]
[14] "Their mouths are full of cursing
and bitterness."[f]
[15] "Their feet are swift to shed blood;
[16] ruin and misery mark their ways,
[17] and the way of peace they do not
know."[g]
[18] "There is no fear of God before
their eyes."[h]

[19]Now we know that whatever the
law says, it says to those who are under
the law, so that every mouth may be silenced and the whole world held accountable to God. [20]Therefore no one
will be declared righteous in his sight by
observing the law; rather, through the
law we become conscious of sin.

Righteousness Through Faith

[21]But now a righteousness from God,
apart from law, has been made known,
to which the Law and the Prophets testify. [22]This righteousness from God
comes through faith in Jesus Christ to all

[a]4 Psalm 51:4 [b]9 Or *worse* [c]12 Psalms 14:1-3; 53:1-3; Eccles. 7:20 [d]13 Psalm 5:9 [e]13 Psalm 140:3 [f]14 Psalm 10:7 [g]17 Isaiah 59:7,8 [h]18 Psalm 36:1

who believe. There is no difference, [23]for all have sinned and fall short of the glory of God, [24]and are justified freely by his grace through the redemption that came by Christ Jesus. [25]God presented him as a sacrifice of atonement,[a] through faith in his blood. He did this to demonstrate his justice, because in his forbearance he had left the sins committed beforehand unpunished— [26]he did it to demonstrate his justice at the present time, so as to be just and the one who justifies those who have faith in Jesus.

[27]Where, then, is boasting? It is excluded. On what principle? On that of observing the law? No, but on that of faith. [28]For we maintain that a man is justified by faith apart from observing the law. [29]Is God the God of Jews only? Is he not the God of Gentiles too? Yes, of Gentiles too, [30]since there is only one God, who will justify the circumcised by faith and the uncircumcised through that same faith. [31]Do we, then, nullify the law by this faith? Not at all! Rather, we uphold the law.

Abraham Justified by Faith

4 What then shall we say that Abraham, our forefather, discovered in this matter? [2]If, in fact, Abraham was justified by works, he had something to boast about—but not before God. [3]What does the Scripture say? "Abraham believed God, and it was credited to him as righteousness."[b]

[4]Now when a man works, his wages are not credited to him as a gift, but as an obligation. [5]However, to the man who does not work but trusts God who justifies the wicked, his faith is credited as righteousness. [6]David says the same thing when he speaks of the blessedness of the man to whom God credits righteousness apart from works:

[7]"Blessed are they
 whose transgressions are forgiven,
 whose sins are covered.
[8]Blessed is the man
 whose sin the Lord will never
 count against him."[c]

[9]Is this blessedness only for the circumcised, or also for the uncircumcised? We have been saying that Abraham's faith was credited to him as righteousness. [10]Under what circumstances was it credited? Was it after he was circumcised, or before? It was not after, but before! [11]And he received the sign of circumcision, a seal of the righteousness that he had by faith while he was still uncircumcised. So then, he is the father of all who believe but have not been circumcised, in order that righteousness might be credited to them. [12]And he is also the father of the circumcised who not only are circumcised but who also walk in the footsteps of the faith that our father Abraham had before he was circumcised.

[13]It was not through law that Abraham and his offspring received the promise that he would be heir of the world, but through the righteousness that comes by faith. [14]For if those who live by law are heirs, faith has no value and the promise is worthless, [15]because law brings wrath. And where there is no law there is no transgression.

[16]Therefore, the promise comes by faith, so that it may be by grace and may be guaranteed to all Abraham's offspring—not only to those who are of the law but also to those who are of the faith of Abraham. He is the father of us all. [17]As it is written: "I have made you a father of many nations."[d] He is our father in the sight of God, in whom he believed—the God who gives life to the dead and calls things that are not as though they were.

[18]Against all hope, Abraham in hope believed and so became the father of many nations, just as it had been said to him, "So shall your offspring be."[e] [19]Without weakening in his faith, he faced the fact that his body was as good as dead—since he was about a hundred years old—and that Sarah's womb was also dead. [20]Yet he did not waver

[a]25 Or *as the one who would turn aside his wrath, taking away sin* [b]3 Gen. 15:6; also in verse 22 [c]8 Psalm 32:1,2 [d]17 Gen. 17:5 [e]18 Gen. 15:5

through unbelief regarding the promise
of God, but was strengthened in his
faith and gave glory to God, [21]being
fully persuaded that God had power to
do what he had promised. [22]This is why
"it was credited to him as righteousness." [23]The words "it was credited to
him" were written not for him alone,
[24]but also for us, to whom God will
credit righteousness—for us who believe in him who raised Jesus our Lord
from the dead. [25]He was delivered over
to death for our sins and was raised to
life for our justification.

SHARPEN THE FOCUS

Diplomatic immunity has protected spies for many years. Diplomats have used this immunity to avoid being penalized for everything from parking violations to multiple murder. If a nation chooses to grant a foreign service agent this immunity, the host country can expel the agent, but that's all. Such an agent is immune from prosecution.

In one sense, that's what has happened to us. God has given us diplomatic immunity in heaven's court. When we came to faith in Jesus, we received Christ's own righteousness as a gift. With this right-standing before God, came release from sin's guilt and its penalties. We don't deserve this release, but in Christ it is ours. We don't deserve freedom from guilt, but in Christ we are free. We are right with God through His grace in Jesus. All the charges that stood against us have been dropped—all of them.

We could study the first 11 verses of Romans 5 each day into eternity and still not fully grasp the enormous truths Paul captures for us. *Life may be hard, but our God is infinitely good.* Keep this central thought in mind as you read, asking the Holy Spirit to open your heart to more fully comprehend all the treasures that are yours in Christ Jesus. If time is short, focus on Romans 5:1–11.

Peace and Joy

5 Therefore, since we have been
justified through faith, we[a] have
peace with God through our Lord Jesus
Christ, [2]through whom we have gained
access by faith into this grace in which
we now stand. And we[a] rejoice in the
hope of the glory of God. [3]Not only so,
but we[a] also rejoice in our sufferings,
because we know that suffering produces perseverance; [4]perseverance,
character; and character, hope. [5]And
hope does not disappoint us, because
God has poured out his love into our
hearts by the Holy Spirit, whom he has
given us.
[6]You see, at just the right time, when
we were still powerless, Christ died for
the ungodly. [7]Very rarely will anyone
die for a righteous man, though for a
good man someone might possibly dare

[a]1,2,3 Or *let us*

to die. [8]But God demonstrates his own love for us in this: While we were still sinners, Christ died for us.

[9]Since we have now been justified by his blood, how much more shall we be saved from God's wrath through him! [10]For if, when we were God's enemies, we were reconciled to him through the death of his Son, how much more, having been reconciled, shall we be saved through his life! [11]Not only is this so, but we also rejoice in God through our Lord Jesus Christ, through whom we have now received reconciliation.

Death Through Adam, Life Through Christ

[12]Therefore, just as sin entered the world through one man, and death through sin, and in this way death came to all men, because all sinned— [13]for before the law was given, sin was in the world. But sin is not taken into account when there is no law. [14]Nevertheless, death reigned from the time of Adam to the time of Moses, even over those who did not sin by breaking a command, as did Adam, who was a pattern of the one to come.

[15]But the gift is not like the trespass. For if the many died by the trespass of the one man, how much more did God's grace and the gift that came by the grace of the one man, Jesus Christ, overflow to the many! [16]Again, the gift of God is not like the result of the one man's sin: The judgment followed one sin and brought condemnation, but the gift followed many trespasses and brought justification. [17]For if, by the trespass of the one man, death reigned through that one man, how much more will those who receive God's abundant provision of grace and of the gift of righteousness reign in life through the one man, Jesus Christ.

[18]Consequently, just as the result of one trespass was condemnation for all men, so also the result of one act of righteousness was justification that brings life for all men. [19]For just as through the disobedience of the one man the many were made sinners, so also through the obedience of the one man the many will be made righteous.

[20]The law was added so that the trespass might increase. But where sin increased, grace increased all the more, [21]so that, just as sin reigned in death, so also grace might reign through righteousness to bring eternal life through Jesus Christ our Lord.

SHARPEN THE FOCUS

"We rejoice in the hope of the glory of God" (Romans 5:2). Ten short words, but so encouraging!

Israel of old saw God's glory on Mount Sinai–and their hearts melted in fear (Exodus 20:18–19).

We have seen God's glory on Mount Calvary–and our hearts have melted in wonder and love at the gift God gave (John 1:14; 3:16).

But there's even more! We who were once condemned sinners will one day share in God's own glory! It sounds too good to be true, doesn't it? We sin every day. We often dishonor God. But the Bible is very clear. In John 17:22 we hear our Lord Jesus Himself tell the Father about that glory. The Father gave it to Jesus, and Jesus has given it to us!

Even now, if we could see ourselves through heaven's eyes, we would see that we have received a down payment of this glory. And we have God's sure and certain word that we will one day receive its fullness, and so "we rejoice in the hope of the glory of God!"

WEEK 86 • SATURDAY

Romans 6:1–23

GET THE BIG PICTURE

Grace. Righteousness. Justification. Paul writes on, piling one life-changing idea on top of the next. In chapter 6 we come to one of the key teachings on Baptism in all of Scripture. As you read, ask yourself what impact your own Baptism has each and every day of your life. If time is short, focus on Romans 6:1–14.

Dead to Sin, Alive in Christ

6 What shall we say, then? Shall
we go on sinning so that grace
may increase? [2]By no means! We died to
sin; how can we live in it any longer?
[3]Or don't you know that all of us who
were baptized into Christ Jesus were
baptized into his death? [4]We were therefore buried with him through baptism
into death in order that, just as Christ
was raised from the dead through the
glory of the Father, we too may live a
new life.

[5]If we have been united with him like
this in his death, we will certainly also
be united with him in his resurrection.
[6]For we know that our old self was crucified with him so that the body of sin
might be done away with,[a] that we
should no longer be slaves to sin— [7]be-
cause anyone who has died has been
freed from sin.

[8]Now if we died with Christ, we believe that we will also live with him. [9]For
we know that since Christ was raised
from the dead, he cannot die again;
death no longer has mastery over him.
[10]The death he died, he died to sin once
for all; but the life he lives, he lives to
God.

[11]In the same way, count yourselves
dead to sin but alive to God in Christ
Jesus. [12]Therefore do not let sin reign in
your mortal body so that you obey its
evil desires. [13]Do not offer the parts of
your body to sin, as instruments of
wickedness, but rather offer yourselves
to God, as those who have been brought
from death to life; and offer the parts of
your body to him as instruments of
righteousness. [14]For sin shall not be your
master, because you are not under law,
but under grace.

Slaves to Righteousness

[15]What then? Shall we sin because we
are not under law but under grace? By
no means! [16]Don't you know that when
you offer yourselves to someone to
obey him as slaves, you are slaves to
the one whom you obey—whether
you are slaves to sin, which leads to
death, or to obedience, which leads
to righteousness? [17]But thanks be to
God that, though you used to be slaves
to sin, you wholeheartedly obeyed the
form of teaching to which you were entrusted. [18]You have been set free from
sin and have become slaves to righteousness.

[19]I put this in human terms because
you are weak in your natural selves. Just
as you used to offer the parts of your
body in slavery to impurity and to ever-
increasing wickedness, so now offer
them in slavery to righteousness leading to holiness. [20]When you were slaves
to sin, you were free from the control of
righteousness. [21]What benefit did you
reap at that time from the things you are
now ashamed of? Those things result in
death! [22]But now that you have been set

[a]6 Or *be rendered powerless*

free from sin and have become slaves to
God, the benefit you reap leads to holi-
ness, and the result is eternal life. [23]For
the wages of sin is death, but the gift of
God is eternal life in[a] Christ Jesus our
Lord.

SHARPEN THE FOCUS

The verb in Romans 6:11 illuminates one more facet on the gemstone of salvation. In English, we read the word *count*. But the word in Greek comes out of the world of finance. It's as if Paul were saying, "Write it down in your ledger. Use it as you balance the books of your life. Count yourselves dead to sin, but alive to God in Christ."

Here we see a wonderful truth. The new life you have received from Christ is as real and certain as the math your accountant uses. In God's ledger, your debt is wiped out. The sinful person you once were died on Calvary with Christ. That person was buried with Christ in Baptism. Now you have been raised with Christ from the dead. You have a whole new life, a fresh start. In your Baptism, it's a new day—every day!

That "old us" could do nothing *but* sin. The "new us," the baptized and resurrected us, now wants only and always to please Jesus, the one who died for us and rose again. That's what counts with God—and He's done it for us and in us!

WEEK 87 • MONDAY

Romans 7:1–25

GET THE BIG PICTURE

If all that Paul wrote in Romans 6 is true—and it is—then why do we go on sinning after we've come to faith and been baptized? Paul himself asked about that (and answered it). Look for the inspired answer in Romans 7. If time is short, focus on Romans 7:7–25.

An Illustration From Marriage

7 Do you not know, brothers—for
I am speaking to men who know
the law—that the law has authority over
a man only as long as he lives? [2]For example, by law a married woman is
bound to her husband as long as he is
alive, but if her husband dies, she is released from the law of marriage. [3]So
then, if she marries another man while
her husband is still alive, she is called an
adulteress. But if her husband dies, she
is released from that law and is not an
adulteress, even though she marries
another man.
[4]So, my brothers, you also died to the
law through the body of Christ, that you
might belong to another, to him who
was raised from the dead, in order that
we might bear fruit to God. [5]For when
we were controlled by the sinful nature,[b] the sinful passions aroused by
the law were at work in our bodies, so
that we bore fruit for death. [6]But now,
by dying to what once bound us, we
have been released from the law so that
we serve in the new way of the Spirit,
and not in the old way of the written
code.

[a]23 Or *through* [b]5 Or *the flesh;* also in verse 25

Struggling With Sin

7What shall we say, then? Is the law sin? Certainly not! Indeed I would not have known what sin was except through the law. For I would not have known what coveting really was if the law had not said, "Do not covet."[a] 8But sin, seizing the opportunity afforded by the commandment, produced in me every kind of covetous desire. For apart from law, sin is dead. 9Once I was alive apart from law; but when the commandment came, sin sprang to life and I died. 10I found that the very commandment that was intended to bring life actually brought death. 11For sin, seizing the opportunity afforded by the commandment, deceived me, and through the commandment put me to death. 12So then, the law is holy, and the commandment is holy, righteous and good.

13Did that which is good, then, become death to me? By no means! But in order that sin might be recognized as sin, it produced death in me through what was good, so that through the commandment sin might become utterly sinful.

14We know that the law is spiritual; but I am unspiritual, sold as a slave to sin. 15I do not understand what I do. For what I want to do I do not do, but what I hate I do. 16And if I do what I do not want to do, I agree that the law is good. 17As it is, it is no longer I myself who do it, but it is sin living in me. 18I know that nothing good lives in me, that is, in my sinful nature.[b] For I have the desire to do what is good, but I cannot carry it out. 19For what I do is not the good I want to do; no, the evil I do not want to do—this I keep on doing. 20Now if I do what I do not want to do, it is no longer I who do it, but it is sin living in me that does it.

21So I find this law at work: When I want to do good, evil is right there with me. 22For in my inner being I delight in God's law; 23but I see another law at work in the members of my body, waging war against the law of my mind and making me a prisoner of the law of sin at work within my members. 24What a wretched man I am! Who will rescue me from this body of death? 25Thanks be to God—through Jesus Christ our Lord!

So then, I myself in my mind am a slave to God's law, but in the sinful nature a slave to the law of sin.

[a]7 Exodus 20:17; Deut. 5:21 [b]18 Or *my flesh*

SHARPEN THE FOCUS

Maybe you've seen a cartoon drawn to depict temptation. On one shoulder of the person being tempted sits a red demon with horns and a pitchfork tail. On the other sits a halo-crowned angel. Will sin or righteousness win? In the cartoon, that's anyone's guess.

Sometimes believers get the idea that this cartoon version of temptation is reality. True enough, each Christian is at the same time saint and sinner. Paul tells us that in Romans 7. But he in no way implies that the two forces are equal in power or that God has left the outcome in doubt. God ultimately wins the victory for us, His saints, His holy ones in Christ Jesus (Romans 7:24–25)! No question.

Therefore, Paul the saint desires to do what is good (Romans 7:18). Paul the saint delights in God's law (Romans 7:22). Paul the saint serves God's law as God's slave (Romans 7:25). And, because of what God has worked in you in your Baptism, so do you!

Yes, like Paul you will wage war with your sinful nature each day of your earthly life. But in God's eyes, you are already holy, blameless, righteous. Confident in that, be who you are today.

WEEK 87 • TUESDAY

Romans 8:1–39

GET THE BIG PICTURE

Ask any group of Christians to name their favorite Bible chapter and, no doubt, Romans 8 will spring to many minds. Romans 8 provides comfort and courage in life's darkest hours. Even if the words you read today are very familiar, approach them as though you were reading them for the first time. Let God's love *for you* sink down deep into your heart. If time is short, focus on Romans 8:1–17.

Life Through the Spirit

8 Therefore, there is now no condemnation for those who are in
Christ Jesus,[a] 2 because through Christ
Jesus the law of the Spirit of life set me
free from the law of sin and death. 3 For
what the law was powerless to do in
that it was weakened by the sinful
nature,[b] God did by sending his own
Son in the likeness of sinful man to be a
sin offering.[c] And so he condemned sin
in sinful man,[d] 4 in order that the righteous requirements of the law might be
fully met in us, who do not live according to the sinful nature but according to
the Spirit.
5 Those who live according to the sinful nature have their minds set on what
that nature desires; but those who live
in accordance with the Spirit have their
minds set on what the Spirit desires.
6 The mind of sinful man[e] is death, but
the mind controlled by the Spirit is life
and peace; 7 the sinful mind[f] is hostile to
God. It does not submit to God's law,
nor can it do so. 8 Those controlled by the
sinful nature cannot please God.
9 You, however, are controlled not by
the sinful nature but by the Spirit, if the
Spirit of God lives in you. And if anyone
does not have the Spirit of Christ, he
does not belong to Christ. 10 But if Christ
is in you, your body is dead because of
sin, yet your spirit is alive because of
righteousness. 11 And if the Spirit of him
who raised Jesus from the dead is living
in you, he who raised Christ from the
dead will also give life to your mortal
bodies through his Spirit, who lives in
you.
12 Therefore, brothers, we have an obligation—but it is not to the sinful nature, to live according to it. 13 For if you
live according to the sinful nature, you
will die; but if by the Spirit you put to
death the misdeeds of the body, you will
live, 14 because those who are led by the
Spirit of God are sons of God. 15 For you
did not receive a spirit that makes you
a slave again to fear, but you received
the Spirit of sonship.[g] And by him we
cry, "*Abba*,[h] Father." 16 The Spirit himself
testifies with our spirit that we are God's
children. 17 Now if we are children, then
we are heirs—heirs of God and co-heirs
with Christ, if indeed we share in his
sufferings in order that we may also
share in his glory.

Future Glory

18 I consider that our present sufferings are not worth comparing with the
glory that will be revealed in us. 19 The
creation waits in eager expectation for
the sons of God to be revealed. 20 For the

[a]1 Some later manuscripts *Jesus, who do not live according to the sinful nature but according to the Spirit,* [b]3 Or *the flesh;* also in verses 4, 5, 8, 9, 12 and 13 [c]3 Or *man, for sin* [d]3 Or *in the flesh* [e]6 Or *mind set on the flesh* [f]7 Or *the mind set on the flesh* [g]15 Or *adoption* [h]15 Aramaic for *Father*

creation was subjected to frustration,
not by its own choice, but by the will of
the one who subjected it, in hope 21that[a]
the creation itself will be liberated from
its bondage to decay and brought into
the glorious freedom of the children of
God.
22We know that the whole creation
has been groaning as in the pains of
childbirth right up to the present time.
23Not only so, but we ourselves, who
have the firstfruits of the Spirit, groan
inwardly as we wait eagerly for our
adoption as sons, the redemption of our
bodies. 24For in this hope we were saved.
But hope that is seen is no hope at all.
Who hopes for what he already has?
25But if we hope for what we do not yet
have, we wait for it patiently.
26In the same way, the Spirit helps us
in our weakness. We do not know what
we ought to pray for, but the Spirit himself intercedes for us with groans that
words cannot express. 27And he who
searches our hearts knows the mind of
the Spirit, because the Spirit intercedes
for the saints in accordance with God's
will.

More Than Conquerors

28And we know that in all things God
works for the good of those who love
him,[b] who[c] have been called according
to his purpose. 29For those God foreknew he also predestined to be conformed to the likeness of his Son, that
he might be the firstborn among many
brothers. 30And those he predestined, he
also called; those he called, he also justified; those he justified, he also glorified.
31What, then, shall we say in response
to this? If God is for us, who can be
against us? 32He who did not spare his
own Son, but gave him up for us all—
how will he not also, along with him,
graciously give us all things? 33Who will
bring any charge against those whom
God has chosen? It is God who justifies.
34Who is he that condemns? Christ
Jesus, who died—more than that, who
was raised to life—is at the right hand
of God and is also interceding for us.
35Who shall separate us from the love of
Christ? Shall trouble or hardship or persecution or famine or nakedness or danger or sword? 36As it is written:

"For your sake we face death all day
long;
we are considered as sheep to be
slaughtered."[d]

37No, in all these things we are more
than conquerors through him who
loved us. 38For I am convinced that neither death nor life, neither angels nor
demons,[e] neither the present nor the
future, nor any powers, 39neither height
nor depth, nor anything else in all creation, will be able to separate us from
the love of God that is in Christ Jesus our
Lord.

[a]20,21 Or *subjected it in hope.* 21*For* [b]28 Some manuscripts *And we know that all things work together for good to those who love God*
[c]28 Or *works together with those who love him to bring about what is good—with those who*
[d]36 Psalm 44:22 [e]38 Or *nor heavenly rulers*

SHARPEN THE FOCUS

Suppose that Jesus were to appear visibly across the table or next to your chair right now, this instant. How would you react? Would you cover your face in embarrassment? begin confessing that particular sin that causes you so much shame? look for a way to leave the room? Or would you feel confident in His presence? Would you with Mary at the garden tomb want to hold Him, to hug Him (John 20:16–17)?

Romans 8:1 tells us in no uncertain terms that for those who are in Christ Jesus, for those who abide in Him by faith, there is no condemnation. There is *now* no condemnation.

When Jesus shouted from the cross, "It is finished" (John 19 :30), your salvation was complete. Your guilt was taken away; your sin was atoned for (Isaiah 6:7). At this moment, nothing stands between you and a holy God. Right now—this instant—you are free from guilt. And because that's true, your Lord also wants you to be free from guilt feelings. He wants you to walk away from any shame that imprisons you and steals your joy. You can in confidence lay those things at the foot of his cross and let Him remove them from you forever. There is *now no* condemnation!

The Gospel Paul communicates in Romans 6, 7, and 8 is so good that Paul yearns for everyone to know what God has done, most especially his fellow Jews. But many of them have rejected their Messiah. How could that be? In Romans 9–11 Paul reasons it out. As you read, keep this question in mind: "Who is—and always was—the *true* Israel?" If time is short, focus on Romans 10:1–21.

God's Sovereign Choice

9 I speak the truth in Christ—I am
not lying, my conscience confirms it in the Holy Spirit—2I have great
sorrow and unceasing anguish in my
heart. 3For I could wish that I myself
were cursed and cut off from Christ for
the sake of my brothers, those of my
own race, 4the people of Israel. Theirs is
the adoption as sons; theirs the divine
glory, the covenants, the receiving of the
law, the temple worship and the promises. 5Theirs are the patriarchs, and from
them is traced the human ancestry of
Christ, who is God over all, forever
praised![a] Amen.
6It is not as though God's word had
failed. For not all who are descended
from Israel are Israel. 7Nor because they
are his descendants are they all Abraham's children. On the contrary, "It is
through Isaac that your offspring will
be reckoned."[b] 8In other words, it is
not the natural children who are God's
children, but it is the children of the
promise who are regarded as Abraham's offspring. 9For this was how the
promise was stated: "At the appointed
time I will return, and Sarah will have a
son."[c]
10Not only that, but Rebekah's children had one and the same father, our
father Isaac. 11Yet, before the twins were
born or had done anything good or
bad—in order that God's purpose in
election might stand: 12not by works but
by him who calls—she was told, "The
older will serve the younger."[d] 13Just as
it is written: "Jacob I loved, but Esau I
hated."[e]
14What then shall we say? Is God unjust? Not at all! 15For he says to Moses,

"I will have mercy on whom I have
mercy,
and I will have compassion on
whom I have compassion."[f]

16It does not, therefore, depend on
man's desire or effort, but on God's mercy. 17For the Scripture says to Pharaoh:

[a]5 Or *Christ, who is over all. God be forever praised!* Or *Christ. God who is over all be forever praised!*
[b]7 Gen. 21:12 [c]9 Gen. 18:10,14 [d]12 Gen. 25:23
[e]13 Mal. 1:2,3 [f]15 Exodus 33:19

"I raised you up for this very purpose,
that I might display my power in you
and that my name might be proclaimed
in all the earth."[a] [18]Therefore God has
mercy on whom he wants to have
mercy, and he hardens whom he wants
to harden.

[19]One of you will say to me: "Then
why does God still blame us? For who
resists his will?" [20]But who are you,
O man, to talk back to God? "Shall
what is formed say to him who formed
it, 'Why did you make me like this?' "[b]
[21]Does not the potter have the right to
make out of the same lump of clay some
pottery for noble purposes and some for
common use?

[22]What if God, choosing to show his
wrath and make his power known, bore
with great patience the objects of his
wrath—prepared for destruction?
[23]What if he did this to make the riches
of his glory known to the objects of his
mercy, whom he prepared in advance
for glory— [24]even us, whom he also
called, not only from the Jews but also
from the Gentiles? [25]As he says in Hosea:

"I will call them 'my people' who are
not my people;
and I will call her 'my loved one'
who is not my loved one,"[c]

[26]and,

"It will happen that in the very place
where it was said to them,
'You are not my people,'
they will be called 'sons of the living
God.' "[d]

[27]Isaiah cries out concerning Israel:

"Though the number of the
Israelites be like the sand by
the sea,
only the remnant will be saved.
[28]For the Lord will carry out
his sentence on earth with speed
and finality."[e]

[29]It is just as Isaiah said previously:

"Unless the Lord Almighty
had left us descendants,
we would have become like Sodom,
we would have been like
Gomorrah."[f]

Israel's Unbelief

[30]What then shall we say? That the
Gentiles, who did not pursue righteousness, have obtained it, a righteousness
that is by faith; [31]but Israel, who pursued
a law of righteousness, has not attained
it. [32]Why not? Because they pursued it
not by faith but as if it were by works.
They stumbled over the "stumbling
stone." [33]As it is written:

"See, I lay in Zion a stone that causes
men to stumble
and a rock that makes them fall,
and the one who trusts in him will
never be put to shame."[g]

10 Brothers, my heart's desire
and prayer to God for the Israelites is that they may be saved. [2]For I
can testify about them that they are
zealous for God, but their zeal is not
based on knowledge. [3]Since they did
not know the righteousness that comes
from God and sought to establish their
own, they did not submit to God's righteousness. [4]Christ is the end of the law
so that there may be righteousness for
everyone who believes.

[5]Moses describes in this way the righteousness that is by the law: "The man
who does these things will live by
them."[h] [6]But the righteousness that is by
faith says: "Do not say in your heart,
'Who will ascend into heaven?'[i]" (that
is, to bring Christ down) [7]"or 'Who will
descend into the deep?'[j]" (that is, to
bring Christ up from the dead). [8]But
what does it say? "The word is near you;
it is in your mouth and in your heart,"[k]
that is, the word of faith we are proclaiming: [9]That if you confess with your
mouth, "Jesus is Lord," and believe in
your heart that God raised him from the
dead, you will be saved. [10]For it is with
your heart that you believe and are jus-

[a] *17* Exodus 9:16 [b] *20* Isaiah 29:16; 45:9
[c] *25* Hosea 2:23 [d] *26* Hosea 1:10
[e] *28* Isaiah 10:22,23 [f] *29* Isaiah 1:9
[g] *33* Isaiah 8:14; 28:16 [h] *5* Lev. 18:5 [i] *6* Deut. 30:12
[j] *7* Deut. 30:13 [k] *8* Deut. 30:14

tified, and it is with your mouth that you confess and are saved. 11As the Scripture says, "Anyone who trusts in him will never be put to shame."[a] 12For there is no difference between Jew and Gentile—the same Lord is Lord of all and richly blesses all who call on him, 13for, "Everyone who calls on the name of the Lord will be saved."[b]

14How, then, can they call on the one they have not believed in? And how can they believe in the one of whom they have not heard? And how can they hear without someone preaching to them? 15And how can they preach unless they are sent? As it is written, "How beautiful are the feet of those who bring good news!"[c]

16But not all the Israelites accepted the good news. For Isaiah says, "Lord, who has believed our message?"[d] 17Consequently, faith comes from hearing the message, and the message is heard through the word of Christ. 18But I ask: Did they not hear? Of course they did:

> "Their voice has gone out into all the earth,
> their words to the ends of the world."[e]

19Again I ask: Did Israel not understand? First, Moses says,

> "I will make you envious by those who are not a nation;
> I will make you angry by a nation that has no understanding."[f]

20And Isaiah boldly says,

> "I was found by those who did not seek me;
> I revealed myself to those who did not ask for me."[g]

21But concerning Israel he says,

> "All day long I have held out my hands
> to a disobedient and obstinate people."[h]

The Remnant of Israel

11 I ask then: Did God reject his people? By no means! I am an Israelite myself, a descendant of Abraham, from the tribe of Benjamin. 2God did not reject his people, whom he foreknew. Don't you know what the Scripture says in the passage about Elijah—how he appealed to God against Israel: 3"Lord, they have killed your prophets and torn down your altars; I am the only one left, and they are trying to kill me"[i]? 4And what was God's answer to him? "I have reserved for myself seven thousand who have not bowed the knee to Baal."[j] 5So too, at the present time there is a remnant chosen by grace. 6And if by grace, then it is no longer by works; if it were, grace would no longer be grace.[k]

7What then? What Israel sought so earnestly it did not obtain, but the elect did. The others were hardened, 8as it is written:

> "God gave them a spirit of stupor,
> eyes so that they could not see
> and ears so that they could not hear,
> to this very day."[l]

9And David says:

> "May their table become a snare and a trap,
> a stumbling block and a retribution for them.
> 10May their eyes be darkened so they cannot see,
> and their backs be bent forever."[m]

Ingrafted Branches

11Again I ask: Did they stumble so as to fall beyond recovery? Not at all! Rather, because of their transgression, salvation has come to the Gentiles to make Israel envious. 12But if their transgression means riches for the world, and their loss means riches for the Gentiles,

[a] *11* Isaiah 28:16 [b] *13* Joel 2:32
[c] *15* Isaiah 52:7 [d] *16* Isaiah 53:1 [e] *18* Psalm 19:4
[f] *19* Deut. 32:21 [g] *20* Isaiah 65:1 [h] *21* Isaiah 65:2
[i] *3* 1 Kings 19:10,14 [j] *4* 1 Kings 19:18 [k] *6* Some manuscripts *by grace. But if by works, then it is no longer grace; if it were, work would no longer be work.* [l] *8* Deut. 29:4; Isaiah 29:10
[m] *10* Psalm 69:22,23

how much greater riches will their fullness bring!

13I am talking to you Gentiles. Inasmuch as I am the apostle to the Gentiles, I make much of my ministry 14in the hope that I may somehow arouse my own people to envy and save some of them. 15For if their rejection is the reconciliation of the world, what will their acceptance be but life from the dead? 16If the part of the dough offered as firstfruits is holy, then the whole batch is holy; if the root is holy, so are the branches.

17If some of the branches have been broken off, and you, though a wild olive shoot, have been grafted in among the others and now share in the nourishing sap from the olive root, 18do not boast over those branches. If you do, consider this: You do not support the root, but the root supports you. 19You will say then, "Branches were broken off so that I could be grafted in." 20Granted. But they were broken off because of unbelief, and you stand by faith. Do not be arrogant, but be afraid. 21For if God did not spare the natural branches, he will not spare you either.

22Consider therefore the kindness and sternness of God: sternness to those who fell, but kindness to you, provided that you continue in his kindness. Otherwise, you also will be cut off. 23And if they do not persist in unbelief, they will be grafted in, for God is able to graft them in again. 24After all, if you were cut out of an olive tree that is wild by nature, and contrary to nature were grafted into a cultivated olive tree, how much more readily will these, the natural branches, be grafted into their own olive tree!

All Israel Will Be Saved

25I do not want you to be ignorant of this mystery, brothers, so that you may not be conceited: Israel has experienced a hardening in part until the full number of the Gentiles has come in. 26And so all Israel will be saved, as it is written:

> "The deliverer will come from Zion;
> he will turn godlessness away
> from Jacob.
> 27And this is[a] my covenant with them
> when I take away their sins."[b]

28As far as the gospel is concerned, they are enemies on your account; but as far as election is concerned, they are loved on account of the patriarchs, 29for God's gifts and his call are irrevocable. 30Just as you who were at one time disobedient to God have now received mercy as a result of their disobedience, 31so they too have now become disobedient in order that they too may now[c] receive mercy as a result of God's mercy to you. 32For God has bound all men over to disobedience so that he may have mercy on them all.

Doxology

> 33Oh, the depth of the riches of the
> wisdom and[d] knowledge of
> God!
> How unsearchable his
> judgments,
> and his paths beyond tracing
> out!
> 34"Who has known the mind of the
> Lord?
> Or who has been his counselor?"[e]
> 35"Who has ever given to God,
> that God should repay him?"[f]
> 36For from him and through him and
> to him are all things.
> To him be the glory forever!
> Amen.

[a]27 Or *will be* [b]27 Isaiah 59:20,21; 27:9; Jer. 31:33,34 [c]31 Some manuscripts do not have *now.* [d]33 Or *riches and the wisdom and the* [e]34 Isaiah 40:13 [f]35 Job 41:11

SHARPEN THE FOCUS

In Greek mythology, the Sirens were creatures who had the heads of women but bodies like birds. By their haunting songs the Sirens lured mariners to their deaths.

Our sinful nature tends to hear God's Law as a kind of siren song. Our old nature wants to believe that the Law shows us the way to heaven—by trying hard to be good. But this misbelief lures people to eternal destruction.

The Lord never intended that His Law serve as a ladder by which we could clamber to heaven if only we would try hard enough. No, Paul has already explained why God gave the Law—to show us our sin (Romans 3:20) and our helplessness (Romans 5:20). But many in ancient Israel, like many people in our world today, insisted on racing after right-standing with God on their own terms. Sad to say, no one ever attained it (Romans 9:30–32; 10:3).

But those in Israel who trusted God's covenant promises *did* attain it, and so have we! Not by keeping the Law, but by believing in Christ who fulfilled the law for us. The Law is now for us a mirror, a useful tool to show us our continuing need for Christ. The Law also shows us the direction God would have us walk. The Law of God is His good gift. But we praise Him even more fervently for the Gospel.

WEEK 87 • THURSDAY

Romans 12:1–21

GET THE BIG PICTURE

If you miss the point of Romans 12:1–2, Romans 12 (and 13–16, too) can seem to be a laundry list of attitudes and behaviors which God demands and which we, in our sinful weakness, cannot attain. So, read Romans 12:1–2 carefully; note in particular Paul's accent on God's mercy. If time is short, focus on Romans 12:1–2.

Living Sacrifices

12 Therefore, I urge you, brothers, in view of God's mercy, to
offer your bodies as living sacrifices,
holy and pleasing to God—this is your
spiritual[a] act of worship. 2Do not conform any longer to the pattern of this
world, but be transformed by the re-
newing of your mind. Then you will be
able to test and approve what God's will
is—his good, pleasing and perfect will.
3For by the grace given me I say to every one of you: Do not think of yourself
more highly than you ought, but rather
think of yourself with sober judgment,
in accordance with the measure of faith
God has given you. 4Just as each of us
has one body with many members, and
these members do not all have the same
function, 5so in Christ we who are many
form one body, and each member belongs to all the others. 6We have different gifts, according to the grace given
us. If a man's gift is prophesying, let him
use it in proportion to his[b] faith. 7If it is
serving, let him serve; if it is teaching,
let him teach; 8if it is encouraging, let
him encourage; if it is contributing to
the needs of others, let him give generously; if it is leadership, let him govern
diligently; if it is showing mercy, let him
do it cheerfully.

Love

9Love must be sincere. Hate what is
evil; cling to what is good. 10Be devoted

[a]1 Or *reasonable* [b]6 Or *in agreement with the*

to one another in brotherly love. Honor
one another above yourselves. [11]Never
be lacking in zeal, but keep your spiritual fervor, serving the Lord. [12]Be joyful
in hope, patient in affliction, faithful in
prayer. [13]Share with God's people who
are in need. Practice hospitality.
[14]Bless those who persecute you; bless
and do not curse. [15]Rejoice with those
who rejoice; mourn with those who
mourn. [16]Live in harmony with one another. Do not be proud, but be willing
to associate with people of low position.[a] Do not be conceited.
[17]Do not repay anyone evil for evil. Be
careful to do what is right in the eyes of
everybody. [18]If it is possible, as far as it
depends on you, live at peace with everyone. [19]Do not take revenge, my
friends, but leave room for God's wrath,
for it is written: "It is mine to avenge; I
will repay,"[b] says the Lord. [20]On the contrary:

"If your enemy is hungry, feed him;
if he is thirsty, give him something to drink.
In doing this, you will heap burning coals on his head."[c]

[21]Do not be overcome by evil, but overcome evil with good.

[a]*16* Or *willing to do menial work* [b]*19* Deut. 32:35
[c]*20* Prov. 25:21,22

SHARPEN THE FOCUS

"Offer your bodies as living sacrifices" (Romans 12:1), writes Paul. Commenting on these words, Martin Luther wrote, "[Our life in Christ] is not a static thing, but in movement from good to better, just as a sick man proceeds from sickness to health."

We were, at one time, not just spiritually sick, but actually dead in sin (Ephesians 2:1). Christ has worked in us new life, eternal life, through His cross and open tomb. And He now continues to work in us, renovating our attitudes, thoughts, and desires so that our lives more and more reflect His own attitudes and actions. God's mercy has begun to work this in us, and His work will continue until we go home to live with the Lord forever.

An apt picture might be that of a mud turtle who somehow learns to fly and eventually turns into an eagle. No turtle could transform itself in such a dramatic way. And neither can we. But the mercies of God have infinite transformative power!

WEEK 87 • FRIDAY

Romans 13:1—14:23

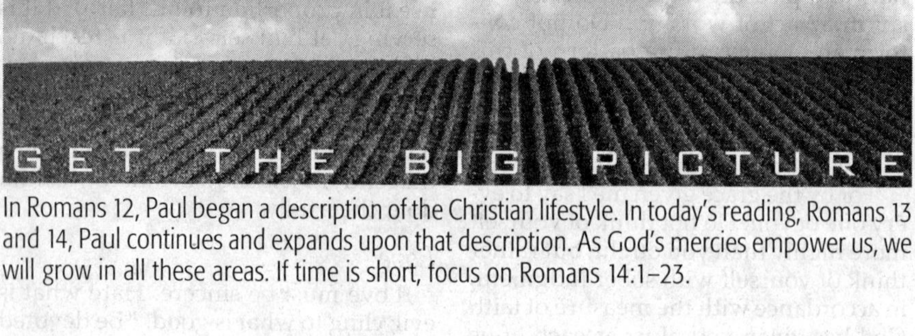

GET THE BIG PICTURE

In Romans 12, Paul began a description of the Christian lifestyle. In today's reading, Romans 13 and 14, Paul continues and expands upon that description. As God's mercies empower us, we will grow in all these areas. If time is short, focus on Romans 14:1–23.

Submission to the Authorities

13 Everyone must submit himself to the governing authori-
ties, for there is no authority except that
which God has established. The authorities that exist have been established
by God. 2Consequently, he who rebels
against the authority is rebelling against
what God has instituted, and those who
do so will bring judgment on themselves. 3For rulers hold no terror for
those who do right, but for those who
do wrong. Do you want to be free from
fear of the one in authority? Then do
what is right and he will commend you.
4For he is God's servant to do you good.
But if you do wrong, be afraid, for he
does not bear the sword for nothing. He
is God's servant, an agent of wrath to
bring punishment on the wrongdoer.
5Therefore, it is necessary to submit to
the authorities, not only because of possible punishment but also because of
conscience.
6This is also why you pay taxes, for
the authorities are God's servants, who
give their full time to governing. 7Give
everyone what you owe him: If you
owe taxes, pay taxes; if revenue, then
revenue; if respect, then respect; if
honor, then honor.

Love, for the Day Is Near

8Let no debt remain outstanding, except the continuing debt to love one another, for he who loves his fellowman
has fulfilled the law. 9The commandments, "Do not commit adultery," "Do
not murder," "Do not steal," "Do not
covet,"[a] and whatever other commandment there may be, are summed up in
this one rule: "Love your neighbor as
yourself."[b] 10Love does no harm to its
neighbor. Therefore love is the fulfillment of the law.
11And do this, understanding the
present time. The hour has come for
you to wake up from your slumber, because our salvation is nearer now than
when we first believed. 12The night is
nearly over; the day is almost here. So
let us put aside the deeds of darkness
and put on the armor of light. 13Let us
behave decently, as in the daytime, not
in orgies and drunkenness, not in sexual
immorality and debauchery, not in dissension and jealousy. 14Rather, clothe
yourselves with the Lord Jesus Christ,
and do not think about how to gratify
the desires of the sinful nature.[c]

The Weak and the Strong

14 Accept him whose faith is
weak, without passing judg-
ment on disputable matters. 2One man's
faith allows him to eat everything, but
another man, whose faith is weak, eats
only vegetables. 3The man who eats
everything must not look down on him
who does not, and the man who does
not eat everything must not condemn
the man who does, for God has accepted him. 4Who are you to judge someone
else's servant? To his own master he
stands or falls. And he will stand, for the
Lord is able to make him stand.
5One man considers one day more sacred than another; another man considers every day alike. Each one should be
fully convinced in his own mind. 6He
who regards one day as special, does so
to the Lord. He who eats meat, eats to
the Lord, for he gives thanks to God;
and he who abstains, does so to the Lord
and gives thanks to God. 7For none of us
lives to himself alone and none of us
dies to himself alone. 8If we live, we live
to the Lord; and if we die, we die to the
Lord. So, whether we live or die, we
belong to the Lord.
9For this very reason, Christ died and
returned to life so that he might be the
Lord of both the dead and the living.
10You, then, why do you judge your
brother? Or why do you look down on
your brother? For we will all stand before God's judgment seat. 11It is written:

" 'As surely as I live,' says the Lord,
'every knee will bow before me;
every tongue will confess to
God.' "[d]

[a]*9* Exodus 20:13-15,17; Deut. 5:17-19,21
[b]*9* Lev. 19:18 [c]*14* Or *the flesh* [d]*11* Isaiah 45:23

12So then, each of us will give an account
of himself to God.
13Therefore let us stop passing judgment on one another. Instead, make up
your mind not to put any stumbling
block or obstacle in your brother's
way. 14As one who is in the Lord Jesus,
I am fully convinced that no food[a]
is unclean in itself. But if anyone
regards something as unclean, then for
him it is unclean. 15If your brother is
distressed because of what you eat,
you are no longer acting in love.
Do not by your eating destroy your
brother for whom Christ died. 16Do not
allow what you consider good to be
spoken of as evil. 17For the kingdom
of God is not a matter of eating and
drinking, but of righteousness, peace
and joy in the Holy Spirit, 18because
anyone who serves Christ in this way
is pleasing to God and approved by
men.
19Let us therefore make every effort to
do what leads to peace and to mutual
edification. 20Do not destroy the work of
God for the sake of food. All food is
clean, but it is wrong for a man to eat
anything that causes someone else to
stumble. 21It is better not to eat meat or
drink wine or to do anything else that
will cause your brother to fall.
22So whatever you believe about these
things keep between yourself and God.
Blessed is the man who does not condemn himself by what he approves.
23But the man who has doubts is condemned if he eats, because his eating is
not from faith; and everything that does
not come from faith is sin.

[a]14 Or *that nothing*

SHARPEN THE FOCUS

We hear a lot today about ethics. We hear a lot, too, about lawsuits and how to avoid them. But in all this talk, we hear little about conscience.

In Romans 14, Paul warns believers three times about offending their own consciences (Romans 14:14, 20, and 23). He urges them to let their consciences guide them. He says that when we do something we believe to be wrong that act is for us sin, whether or not it is sinful in and of itself.

Our Lord truly does want our conscience to be a reliable compass. When you study the Scriptures, the Spirit works in your conscience to make you more and more sensitive to God's will for you. He wants your conscience to be as trustworthy as Jesus' conscience was when He lived here on earth.

When we ignore our conscience, we numb it a bit. When we repeatedly ignore its warnings, we run the risk Paul warns of in 1 Timothy 4:2. We eventually can wind up with a conscience "seared as with a hot iron," insensitive to God's will and an unreliable guide for everyday life.

God forgives for Jesus' sake even the sins we commit against our conscience. And He will use His Word to resensitize our hearts, to repair the damage we've caused. We need only ask.

As Paul closes his letter to the Roman Christians, he discloses his heart—his reasons for writing and his affection for the saints who live in Rome. As you read, note the prayers he prays and the prayer requests he makes. If time is short, focus on Romans 15:1–21.

15 We who are strong ought to
bear with the failings of the
weak and not to please ourselves. [2]Each
of us should please his neighbor for his
good, to build him up. [3]For even Christ
did not please himself but, as it is written: "The insults of those who insult you
have fallen on me."[a] [4]For everything that
was written in the past was written to
teach us, so that through endurance and
the encouragement of the Scriptures we
might have hope.
[5]May the God who gives endurance
and encouragement give you a spirit of
unity among yourselves as you follow
Christ Jesus, [6]so that with one heart and
mouth you may glorify the God and Father of our Lord Jesus Christ.
[7]Accept one another, then, just as
Christ accepted you, in order to bring
praise to God. [8]For I tell you that Christ
has become a servant of the Jews[b] on behalf of God's truth, to confirm the promises made to the patriarchs [9]so that the
Gentiles may glorify God for his mercy,
as it is written:

"Therefore I will praise you among
the Gentiles;
I will sing hymns to your name."[c]

[10]Again, it says,

"Rejoice, O Gentiles, with his
people."[d]

[11]And again,

"Praise the Lord, all you Gentiles,
and sing praises to him, all you
peoples."[e]

[12]And again, Isaiah says,

"The Root of Jesse will spring up,
one who will arise to rule over the
nations;
the Gentiles will hope in him."[f]

[13]May the God of hope fill you with all
joy and peace as you trust in him, so
that you may overflow with hope by the
power of the Holy Spirit.

Paul the Minister to the Gentiles

[14]I myself am convinced, my brothers,
that you yourselves are full of goodness,
complete in knowledge and competent
to instruct one another. [15]I have written
you quite boldly on some points, as if to
remind you of them again, because of
the grace God gave me [16]to be a minister of Christ Jesus to the Gentiles with
the priestly duty of proclaiming the gospel of God, so that the Gentiles might
become an offering acceptable to God,
sanctified by the Holy Spirit.
[17]Therefore I glory in Christ Jesus in
my service to God. [18]I will not venture
to speak of anything except what Christ
has accomplished through me in leading the Gentiles to obey God by what I
have said and done— [19]by the power of
signs and miracles, through the power
of the Spirit. So from Jerusalem all the
way around to Illyricum, I have fully
proclaimed the gospel of Christ. [20]It has

[a] *3* Psalm 69:9 [b] *8* Greek *circumcision*
[c] *9* 2 Samuel 22:50; Psalm 18:49
[d] *10* Deut. 32:43 [e] *11* Psalm 117:1
[f] *12* Isaiah 11:10

always been my ambition to preach the
gospel where Christ was not known, so
that I would not be building on someone else's foundation. 21Rather, as it is
written:

"Those who were not told about him
will see,
and those who have not heard
will understand."[a]

22This is why I have often been hindered
from coming to you.

Paul's Plan to Visit Rome

23But now that there is no more place
for me to work in these regions, and
since I have been longing for many
years to see you, 24I plan to do so when
I go to Spain. I hope to visit you while
passing through and to have you assist
me on my journey there, after I have
enjoyed your company for a while.
25Now, however, I am on my way to Jerusalem in the service of the saints
there. 26For Macedonia and Achaia were
pleased to make a contribution for the
poor among the saints in Jerusalem.
27They were pleased to do it, and indeed
they owe it to them. For if the Gentiles
have shared in the Jews' spiritual blessings, they owe it to the Jews to share
with them their material blessings. 28So
after I have completed this task and
have made sure that they have received
this fruit, I will go to Spain and visit you
on the way. 29I know that when I come
to you, I will come in the full measure
of the blessing of Christ.

30I urge you, brothers, by our Lord
Jesus Christ and by the love of the Spirit, to join me in my struggle by praying
to God for me. 31Pray that I may be rescued from the unbelievers in Judea and
that my service in Jerusalem may be acceptable to the saints there, 32so that by
God's will I may come to you with joy
and together with you be refreshed.
33The God of peace be with you all.
Amen.

Personal Greetings

16 I commend to you our sister
Phoebe, a servant[b] of the
church in Cenchrea. 2I ask you to receive
her in the Lord in a way worthy of the
saints and to give her any help she may
need from you, for she has been a great
help to many people, including me.

3 Greet Priscilla[c] and Aquila, my fellow workers in Christ Jesus. 4They risked their lives for me. Not only I but all the churches of the Gentiles are grateful to them.
5 Greet also the church that meets at their house.

Greet my dear friend Epenetus, who was the first convert to Christ in the province of Asia.
6 Greet Mary, who worked very hard for you.
7 Greet Andronicus and Junias, my relatives who have been in prison with me. They are outstanding among the apostles, and they were in Christ before I was.
8 Greet Ampliatus, whom I love in the Lord.
9 Greet Urbanus, our fellow worker in Christ, and my dear friend Stachys.
10 Greet Apelles, tested and approved in Christ.

Greet those who belong to the household of Aristobulus.
11 Greet Herodion, my relative.

Greet those in the household of Narcissus who are in the Lord.
12 Greet Tryphena and Tryphosa, those women who work hard in the Lord.

Greet my dear friend Persis, another woman who has worked very hard in the Lord.
13 Greet Rufus, chosen in the Lord, and his mother, who has been a mother to me, too.
14 Greet Asyncritus, Phlegon, Hermes, Patrobas, Hermas and the brothers with them.
15 Greet Philologus, Julia, Nereus and his sister, and Olympas and all the saints with them.
16 Greet one another with a holy kiss.

[a]21 Isaiah 52:15 [b]1 Or *deaconess* [c]3 Greek *Prisca*, a variant of *Priscilla*

All the churches of Christ send greetings.

[17]I urge you, brothers, to watch out for those who cause divisions and put obstacles in your way that are contrary to the teaching you have learned. Keep away from them. [18]For such people are not serving our Lord Christ, but their own appetites. By smooth talk and flattery they deceive the minds of naive people. [19]Everyone has heard about your obedience, so I am full of joy over you; but I want you to be wise about what is good, and innocent about what is evil.

[20]The God of peace will soon crush Satan under your feet.

The grace of our Lord Jesus be with you.

[21]Timothy, my fellow worker, sends his greetings to you, as do Lucius, Jason and Sosipater, my relatives.

[22]I, Tertius, who wrote down this letter, greet you in the Lord.

[23]Gaius, whose hospitality I and the whole church here enjoy, sends you his greetings.

Erastus, who is the city's director of public works, and our brother Quartus send you their greetings.[a]

[25]Now to him who is able to establish you by my gospel and the proclamation of Jesus Christ, according to the revelation of the mystery hidden for long ages past, [26]but now revealed and made known through the prophetic writings by the command of the eternal God, so that all nations might believe and obey him— [27]to the only wise God be glory forever through Jesus Christ! Amen.

[a]23 Some manuscripts *their greetings.* [24]*May the grace of our Lord Jesus Christ be with all of you. Amen.*

SHARPEN THE FOCUS

Endurance plus the encouragement of the Scriptures produces hope (Romans 15:4). What an equation! And how often we need to use this "holy math!"

It can seem at times as though all in hell and all on earth have joined forces to punch holes in our hope. Requests outnumber resources. Trouble piles on top of trouble. Worries distract us all day and keep us awake all night.

We need endurance. Not the bravery of children who whistle past the cemetery, pretending they're not afraid. Not the despairing gut-it-out endurance that leaves us bitter and weaker. We need instead the endurance that God alone gives. He *is,* after all, "the God who gives endurance" (Romans 15:5).

And in Him we receive endurance as the Scriptures encourage our hearts. In the Scriptures we read what He has done for His people in the past. In the Scriptures we see His promises to us in the present, all His splendid promises!

As He makes endurance possible for us, as He encourages us in His Word, a holy hope pours into our hearts, refreshing us and those around us.

1 CORINTHIANS

WEEK 88 • MONDAY

1 Corinthians 1:1—2:16

Noted for its debauchery, Corinth's culture had much in common with ours today, and Corinthian Christians wrestled with temptations most of us will recognize. Paul planted the church in Corinth, but soon too much of Corinth began to grow in the church. Still, Paul addresses these believers as saints and recognizes God's mighty work in them. Note this as you read. If time is short, focus on 1 Corinthians 1:1–24.

1 Paul, called to be an apostle of
Christ Jesus by the will of God, and
our brother Sosthenes,

[2]To the church of God in Corinth, to
those sanctified in Christ Jesus and
called to be holy, together with all those
everywhere who call on the name of
our Lord Jesus Christ—their Lord and
ours:

[3]Grace and peace to you from God
our Father and the Lord Jesus Christ.

Thanksgiving

[4]I always thank God for you because
of his grace given you in Christ Jesus.
[5]For in him you have been enriched in
every way—in all your speaking and in
all your knowledge— [6]because our testimony about Christ was confirmed in
you. [7]Therefore you do not lack any
spiritual gift as you eagerly wait for our
Lord Jesus Christ to be revealed. [8]He
will keep you strong to the end, so that
you will be blameless on the day of our
Lord Jesus Christ. [9]God, who has called
you into fellowship with his Son Jesus
Christ our Lord, is faithful.

Divisions in the Church

[10]I appeal to you, brothers, in the
name of our Lord Jesus Christ, that
all of you agree with one another so
that there may be no divisions among
you and that you may be perfectly united in mind and thought. [11]My brothers,
some from Chloe's household have informed me that there are quarrels
among you. [12]What I mean is this: One
of you says, "I follow Paul"; another,
"I follow Apollos"; another, "I follow Cephas[a]"; still another, "I follow
Christ."

[13]Is Christ divided? Was Paul crucified
for you? Were you baptized into[b] the
name of Paul? [14]I am thankful that I did
not baptize any of you except Crispus
and Gaius, [15]so no one can say that you
were baptized into my name. [16](Yes, I
also baptized the household of Stephanas; beyond that, I don't remember if I
baptized anyone else.) [17]For Christ did
not send me to baptize, but to preach
the gospel—not with words of human
wisdom, lest the cross of Christ be emptied of its power.

[a]*12* That is, Peter [b]*13* Or *in*; also in verse 15

Christ the Wisdom and Power of God

[18]For the message of the cross is foolishness to those who are perishing, but
to us who are being saved it is the power of God. [19]For it is written:

"I will destroy the wisdom of the wise;
the intelligence of the intelligent I
will frustrate."[a]

[20]Where is the wise man? Where is the
scholar? Where is the philosopher of
this age? Has not God made foolish the
wisdom of the world? [21]For since in the
wisdom of God the world through
its wisdom did not know him, God was
pleased through the foolishness of what
was preached to save those who believe.
[22]Jews demand miraculous signs and
Greeks look for wisdom, [23]but we
preach Christ crucified: a stumbling
block to Jews and foolishness to Gentiles, [24]but to those whom God has
called, both Jews and Greeks, Christ
the power of God and the wisdom of
God. [25]For the foolishness of God is wiser than man's wisdom, and the weakness of God is stronger than man's
strength.

[26]Brothers, think of what you were
when you were called. Not many of you
were wise by human standards; not
many were influential; not many were
of noble birth. [27]But God chose the foolish things of the world to shame the
wise; God chose the weak things of the
world to shame the strong. [28]He chose
the lowly things of this world and the
despised things—and the things that
are not—to nullify the things that are,
[29]so that no one may boast before him.
[30]It is because of him that you are in
Christ Jesus, who has become for us
wisdom from God—that is, our righteousness, holiness and redemption.
[31]Therefore, as it is written: "Let him
who boasts boast in the Lord."[b]

2 When I came to you, brothers, I
did not come with eloquence or
superior wisdom as I proclaimed to you
the testimony about God.[c] [2]For I resolved to know nothing while I was
with you except Jesus Christ and him
crucified. [3]I came to you in weakness
and fear, and with much trembling. [4]My
message and my preaching were not
with wise and persuasive words, but
with a demonstration of the Spirit's
power, [5]so that your faith might not
rest on men's wisdom, but on God's
power.

Wisdom From the Spirit

[6]We do, however, speak a message of
wisdom among the mature, but not the
wisdom of this age or of the rulers of this
age, who are coming to nothing. [7]No,
we speak of God's secret wisdom, a wisdom that has been hidden and that God
destined for our glory before time began. [8]None of the rulers of this age understood it, for if they had, they would
not have crucified the Lord of glory.
[9]However, as it is written:

"No eye has seen,
no ear has heard,
no mind has conceived
what God has prepared for those
who love him"[d]—

[10]but God has revealed it to us by his
Spirit.

The Spirit searches all things, even
the deep things of God. [11]For who
among men knows the thoughts of a
man except the man's spirit within him?
In the same way no one knows the
thoughts of God except the Spirit of
God. [12]We have not received the spirit of
the world but the Spirit who is from
God, that we may understand what
God has freely given us. [13]This is what
we speak, not in words taught us by
human wisdom but in words taught by
the Spirit, expressing spiritual truths in
spiritual words.[e] [14]The man without the
Spirit does not accept the things that
come from the Spirit of God, for they are
foolishness to him, and he cannot un-

[a]19 Isaiah 29:14 [b]31 Jer. 9:24 [c]1 Some manuscripts *as I proclaimed to you God's mystery* [d]9 Isaiah 64:4 [e]13 Or *Spirit, interpreting spiritual truths to spiritual men*

derstand them, because they are spiritually discerned. 15The spiritual man
makes judgments about all things, but
he himself is not subject to any man's
judgment:

16"For who has known the mind of the
Lord
that he may instruct him?"[a]

But we have the mind of Christ.

SHARPEN THE FOCUS

The Peterkin Papers, a children's book, describes the exploits of an English family notable for their foolishness. In chapter after chapter one or another family member puts salt instead of sugar in her coffee. And almost always one or another family member "visits the lady from Philadelphia" who proposes a wise solution like, "Pour a new cup of coffee." Only after every compound in the chemist's shop has failed to remove the saltiness does the family take her advice.

Blinded as unbelievers are by sin, the only real answer to their guilt escapes them. They just can't grasp it. Down through history, people have tried every "wise" solution they can devise—education, philosophy, pleasure, drugs, even suicide. But this earth's wisdom is foolishness; sooner or later it will fail.

That's why we can be so glad that Jesus "has become for us wisdom from God—that is, our righteousness, holiness, and redemption" (1 Corinthians 1:30). Meditate today on that, and let it bring you joy.

WEEK 88 • TUESDAY

1 Corinthians 3:1—4:21

GET THE BIG PICTURE

Many in Corinth challenged Paul's authority. Factions grew up, threatening to split the church into "followers of Apollos," "followers of Cephas," and so on. You read about some of this last time (1 Corinthians 1:10–17). Today's reading encourages a balanced attitude toward spiritual leaders. Look for that as you compare 1 Corinthians 3 with 1 Corinthians 4. If time is short, focus on 1 Corinthians 4:1–21.

On Divisions in the Church

3 Brothers, I could not address you
as spiritual but as worldly—mere
infants in Christ. 2I gave you milk, not
solid food, for you were not yet ready
for it. Indeed, you are still not ready.
3You are still worldly. For since there is
jealousy and quarreling among you, are
you not worldly? Are you not acting like
mere men? 4For when one says, "I follow Paul," and another, "I follow Apollos," are you not mere men?
5What, after all, is Apollos? And what
is Paul? Only servants, through whom
you came to believe—as the Lord has assigned to each his task. 6I planted the
seed, Apollos watered it, but God made
it grow. 7So neither he who plants nor

[a]*16* Isaiah 40:13

he who waters is anything, but only God, who makes things grow. [8]The man who plants and the man who waters have one purpose, and each will be rewarded according to his own labor. [9]For we are God's fellow workers; you are God's field, God's building.

[10]By the grace God has given me, I laid a foundation as an expert builder, and someone else is building on it. But each one should be careful how he builds. [11]For no one can lay any foundation other than the one already laid, which is Jesus Christ. [12]If any man builds on this foundation using gold, silver, costly stones, wood, hay or straw, [13]his work will be shown for what it is, because the Day will bring it to light. It will be revealed with fire, and the fire will test the quality of each man's work. [14]If what he has built survives, he will receive his reward. [15]If it is burned up, he will suffer loss; he himself will be saved, but only as one escaping through the flames.

[16]Don't you know that you yourselves are God's temple and that God's Spirit lives in you? [17]If anyone destroys God's temple, God will destroy him; for God's temple is sacred, and you are that temple.

[18]Do not deceive yourselves. If any one of you thinks he is wise by the standards of this age, he should become a "fool" so that he may become wise. [19]For the wisdom of this world is foolishness in God's sight. As it is written: "He catches the wise in their craftiness"[a]; [20]and again, "The Lord knows that the thoughts of the wise are futile."[b] [21]So then, no more boasting about men! All things are yours, [22]whether Paul or Apollos or Cephas[c] or the world or life or death or the present or the future—all are yours, [23]and you are of Christ, and Christ is of God.

Apostles of Christ

4 So then, men ought to regard us as servants of Christ and as those entrusted with the secret things of God. [2]Now it is required that those who have been given a trust must prove faithful. [3]I care very little if I am judged by you or by any human court; indeed, I do not even judge myself. [4]My conscience is clear, but that does not make me innocent. It is the Lord who judges me. [5]Therefore judge nothing before the appointed time; wait till the Lord comes. He will bring to light what is hidden in darkness and will expose the motives of men's hearts. At that time each will receive his praise from God.

[6]Now, brothers, I have applied these things to myself and Apollos for your benefit, so that you may learn from us the meaning of the saying, "Do not go beyond what is written." Then you will not take pride in one man over against another. [7]For who makes you different from anyone else? What do you have that you did not receive? And if you did receive it, why do you boast as though you did not?

[8]Already you have all you want! Already you have become rich! You have become kings—and that without us! How I wish that you really had become kings so that we might be kings with you! [9]For it seems to me that God has put us apostles on display at the end of the procession, like men condemned to die in the arena. We have been made a spectacle to the whole universe, to angels as well as to men. [10]We are fools for Christ, but you are so wise in Christ! We are weak, but you are strong! You are honored, we are dishonored! [11]To this very hour we go hungry and thirsty, we are in rags, we are brutally treated, we are homeless. [12]We work hard with our own hands. When we are cursed, we bless; when we are persecuted, we endure it; [13]when we are slandered, we answer kindly. Up to this moment we have become the scum of the earth, the refuse of the world.

[14]I am not writing this to shame you, but to warn you, as my dear children. [15]Even though you have ten thousand guardians in Christ, you do not have many fathers, for in Christ Jesus I became your father through the gospel. [16]Therefore I urge you to imitate me.

[a]*19* Job 5:13 [b]*20* Psalm 94:11 [c]*22* That is, Peter

[17]For this reason I am sending to you
Timothy, my son whom I love, who is
faithful in the Lord. He will remind you
of my way of life in Christ Jesus, which
agrees with what I teach everywhere in
every church.
[18]Some of you have become arrogant,
as if I were not coming to you. [19]But I
will come to you very soon, if the Lord
is willing, and then I will find out not
only how these arrogant people are
talking, but what power they have. [20]For
the kingdom of God is not a matter of
talk but of power. [21]What do you prefer?
Shall I come to you with a whip, or in
love and with a gentle spirit?

SHARPEN THE FOCUS

Does your pastor live in a pressure cooker? From the outside looking in, a pastor's life can sometimes seem quite cushy. But too many pastors today live with pressures not unlike those Paul describes in 1 Corinthians. Unjust criticism and infighting can make a pastor's life miserable. Worse still, Satan can use it to suck the heart out of a ministry, a congregation.

We dare not expect of our spiritual leaders what God does not expect. Certainly, pastors are responsible for shepherding the flock, for feeding us on the green pastures of the pure Word of Christ, and for living out a Christlike lifestyle.

But God and God alone gives the growth—in our life, in our pastor's life, and in our congregation. Pray that the Holy Spirit will empower your pastor to serve God faithfully, for your good and for Christ's glory.

WEEK 88 • WEDNESDAY

1 Cor. 5:1—6:20

GET THE BIG PICTURE

Divisions. Dissension. These plagued the church at Corinth. But they weren't the only problems. You'll read about two more today. Specific individuals were sinning, but so was the congregation. As you read, look for the congregation's sin of omission. If time is short, focus on 1 Corinthians 5:1–13.

Expel the Immoral Brother!

5 It is actually reported that there
is sexual immorality among you,
and of a kind that does not occur even
among pagans: A man has his father's
wife. [2]And you are proud! Shouldn't
you rather have been filled with grief
and have put out of your fellowship the
man who did this? [3]Even though I am
not physically present, I am with you in
spirit. And I have already passed judgment on the one who did this, just as if
I were present. [4]When you are assembled in the name of our Lord Jesus
and I am with you in spirit, and the
power of our Lord Jesus is present,
[5]hand this man over to Satan, so that the
sinful nature[a] may be destroyed and his
spirit saved on the day of the Lord.
[6]Your boasting is not good. Don't you
know that a little yeast works through
the whole batch of dough? [7]Get rid of

[a]5 Or *that his body*; or *that the flesh*

the old yeast that you may be a new batch without yeast—as you really are. For Christ, our Passover lamb, has been sacrificed. 8Therefore let us keep the Festival, not with the old yeast, the yeast of malice and wickedness, but with bread without yeast, the bread of sincerity and truth.

9I have written you in my letter not to associate with sexually immoral people— 10not at all meaning the people of this world who are immoral, or the greedy and swindlers, or idolaters. In that case you would have to leave this world. 11But now I am writing you that you must not associate with anyone who calls himself a brother but is sexually immoral or greedy, an idolater or a slanderer, a drunkard or a swindler. With such a man do not even eat.

12What business is it of mine to judge those outside the church? Are you not to judge those inside? 13God will judge those outside. "Expel the wicked man from among you."[a]

Lawsuits Among Believers

6 If any of you has a dispute with another, dare he take it before the ungodly for judgment instead of before the saints? 2Do you not know that the saints will judge the world? And if you are to judge the world, are you not competent to judge trivial cases? 3Do you not know that we will judge angels? How much more the things of this life! 4Therefore, if you have disputes about such matters, appoint as judges even men of little account in the church![b] 5I say this to shame you. Is it possible that there is nobody among you wise enough to judge a dispute between believers? 6But instead, one brother goes to law against another—and this in front of unbelievers!

7The very fact that you have lawsuits among you means you have been completely defeated already. Why not rather be wronged? Why not rather be cheated? 8Instead, you yourselves cheat and do wrong, and you do this to your brothers.

9Do you not know that the wicked will not inherit the kingdom of God? Do not be deceived: Neither the sexually immoral nor idolaters nor adulterers nor male prostitutes nor homosexual offenders 10nor thieves nor the greedy nor drunkards nor slanderers nor swindlers will inherit the kingdom of God. 11And that is what some of you were. But you were washed, you were sanctified, you were justified in the name of the Lord Jesus Christ and by the Spirit of our God.

Sexual Immorality

12"Everything is permissible for me"—but not everything is beneficial. "Everything is permissible for me"—but I will not be mastered by anything. 13"Food for the stomach and the stomach for food"—but God will destroy them both. The body is not meant for sexual immorality, but for the Lord, and the Lord for the body. 14By his power God raised the Lord from the dead, and he will raise us also. 15Do you not know that your bodies are members of Christ himself? Shall I then take the members of Christ and unite them with a prostitute? Never! 16Do you not know that he who unites himself with a prostitute is one with her in body? For it is said, "The two will become one flesh."[c] 17But he who unites himself with the Lord is one with him in spirit.

18Flee from sexual immorality. All other sins a man commits are outside his body, but he who sins sexually sins against his own body. 19Do you not know that your body is a temple of the Holy Spirit, who is in you, whom you have received from God? You are not your own; 20you were bought at a price. Therefore honor God with your body.

[a] *13* Deut. 17:7; 19:19; 21:21; 22:21,24; 24:7 [b] *4* Or *matters, do you appoint as judges men of little account in the church?* [c] *16* Gen. 2:24

SHARPEN THE FOCUS

If you grew up in a Christian home, perhaps you played church at one time or another. Maybe you preached a sermon to the dog or baptized the cat or even collected an offering from the neighbor's children.

The Christians in Corinth forgot that they weren't just playing church. They forgot that together they were God's temple, that God's Spirit lived in them (1 Corinthians 3:16). They forgot that when they gathered in the name of our Lord Jesus, His power was there (1 Corinthians 5:4). They forgot they were accountable to one another in Him. They forgot that Jesus had called them together in His body, the church, to pray for one another and to warn one another about Satan's schemes. And because they forgot, sexual immorality and greed slipped into the fellowship.

How about us? Do we see our congregation as just another human organization? Or do we see ourselves as an essential part of a living organism—the body of Christ? Do we encourage one another? Do we pay attention when other believers point out the temptations and sins that endanger us? Lord God, make it so!

WEEK 88 • THURSDAY

1 Corinthians 7:1–40

GET THE BIG PICTURE

Jesus was unmarried. Paul likely remained unmarried. Remaining unmarried has its advantages when it comes to living a Christian lifestyle. Still, marriage is God's good gift. Marriage has its advantages when it comes to living a Christian lifestyle. Whether you're married or unmarried, listen to God's counsel as you read today. If time is short, focus on 1 Corinthians 7:1–24.

Marriage

7 Now for the matters you wrote
about: It is good for a man not to
marry.[a] [2]But since there is so much immorality, each man should have his own
wife, and each woman her own husband. [3]The husband should fulfill his
marital duty to his wife, and likewise
the wife to her husband. [4]The wife's
body does not belong to her alone but
also to her husband. In the same way,
the husband's body does not belong to
him alone but also to his wife. [5]Do not
deprive each other except by mutual
consent and for a time, so that you may
devote yourselves to prayer. Then come
together again so that Satan will not
tempt you because of your lack of self-
control. [6]I say this as a concession, not
as a command. [7]I wish that all men were
as I am. But each man has his own gift
from God; one has this gift, another has
that.
[8]Now to the unmarried and the widows I say: It is good for them to stay un-

[a]1 Or *"It is good for a man not to have sexual relations with a woman."*

married, as I am. 9But if they cannot control themselves, they should marry, for
it is better to marry than to burn with
passion.
10To the married I give this command
(not I, but the Lord): A wife must not
separate from her husband. 11But if
she does, she must remain unmarried
or else be reconciled to her husband.
And a husband must not divorce his
wife.
12To the rest I say this (I, not the Lord):
If any brother has a wife who is not a believer and she is willing to live with him,
he must not divorce her. 13And if a
woman has a husband who is not a believer and he is willing to live with her,
she must not divorce him. 14For the unbelieving husband has been sanctified
through his wife, and the unbelieving
wife has been sanctified through her
believing husband. Otherwise your
children would be unclean, but as it is,
they are holy.
15But if the unbeliever leaves, let him
do so. A believing man or woman is
not bound in such circumstances; God
has called us to live in peace. 16How do
you know, wife, whether you will save
your husband? Or, how do you know,
husband, whether you will save your
wife?
17Nevertheless, each one should retain the place in life that the Lord assigned to him and to which God has
called him. This is the rule I lay down
in all the churches. 18Was a man already
circumcised when he was called? He
should not become uncircumcised. Was
a man uncircumcised when he was
called? He should not be circumcised.
19Circumcision is nothing and uncircumcision is nothing. Keeping God's
commands is what counts. 20Each one
should remain in the situation which
he was in when God called him. 21Were
you a slave when you were called?
Don't let it trouble you—although if
you can gain your freedom, do so.
22For he who was a slave when he was
called by the Lord is the Lord's freed-
man; similarly, he who was a free man
when he was called is Christ's slave.
23You were bought at a price; do not
become slaves of men. 24Brothers, each
man, as responsible to God, should
remain in the situation God called
him to.
25Now about virgins: I have no command from the Lord, but I give a judgment as one who by the Lord's mercy is
trustworthy. 26Because of the present
crisis, I think that it is good for you to
remain as you are. 27Are you married?
Do not seek a divorce. Are you unmarried? Do not look for a wife. 28But if you
do marry, you have not sinned; and if a
virgin marries, she has not sinned. But
those who marry will face many troubles in this life, and I want to spare you
this.
29What I mean, brothers, is that the
time is short. From now on those who
have wives should live as if they had
none; 30those who mourn, as if they did
not; those who are happy, as if they
were not; those who buy something, as
if it were not theirs to keep; 31those who
use the things of the world, as if not en-
grossed in them. For this world in its
present form is passing away.
32I would like you to be free from concern. An unmarried man is concerned
about the Lord's affairs—how he can
please the Lord. 33But a married man is
concerned about the affairs of this
world—how he can please his wife—
34and his interests are divided. An unmarried woman or virgin is concerned
about the Lord's affairs: Her aim is to be
devoted to the Lord in both body and
spirit. But a married woman is concerned about the affairs of this world—
how she can please her husband. 35I am
saying this for your own good, not to
restrict you, but that you may live in a
right way in undivided devotion to the
Lord.
36If anyone thinks he is acting improp-
erly toward the virgin he is engaged to,
and if she is getting along in years
and he feels he ought to marry, he
should do as he wants. He is not sinning. They should get married. 37But
the man who has settled the matter in
his own mind, who is under no com-

pulsion but has control over his own
will, and who has made up his mind
not to marry the virgin—this man also
does the right thing. 38 So then, he who
marries the virgin does right, but he
who does not marry her does even
better.[a]
39 A woman is bound to her husband
as long as he lives. But if her husband
dies, she is free to marry anyone she
wishes, but he must belong to the Lord.
40 In my judgment, she is happier if she
stays as she is—and I think that I too
have the Spirit of God.

[a]36-38 Or [36]*If anyone thinks he is not treating his daughter properly, and if she is getting along in years, and he feels she ought to marry, he should do as he wants. He is not sinning. He should let her get married.* [37]*But the man who has settled the matter in his own mind, who is under no compulsion but has control over his own will, and who has made up his mind to keep the virgin unmarried—this man also does the right thing.* [38]*So then, he who gives his virgin in marriage does right, but he who does not give her in marriage does even better.*

SHARPEN THE FOCUS

"[God] knows how we are formed, He remembers that we are dust," so says the psalmist (Psalm 103:14). We are weak. But in love, our Lord does not despise that weakness. Instead, He helps us in it.

Love underlies all of 1 Corinthians 7. Our Savior-God is not looking for a way to make our lives difficult. No, He wants to spare us any hurt and defend us against any temptation.

And so Paul lays before us the gift of marriage. With it comes companionship in times of loneliness, safeguards against sexual temptations, and the opportunity Christian husbands and wives have to encourage one another in the faith (1 Corinthians 7:1–7).

Then the apostle lays before us the gift of being unmarried. With it comes freedom from the many troubles and entanglements common to marriage, the opportunity to honor Christ by exercising His gift of self-control, and the blessing of being able to serve Christ with undivided devotion (1 Corinthians 7:8–9, 25–35).

Need help in your marriage? Need help in your unmarriedness? Either way, Jesus wants to provide what you need. Pardon? Peace? Power? Ask!

WEEK 88 • FRIDAY

1 Corinthians 8:1—9:27

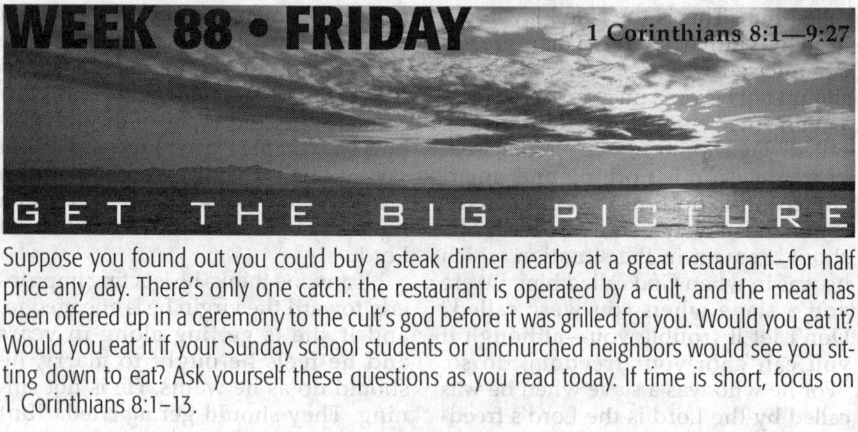

GET THE BIG PICTURE

Suppose you found out you could buy a steak dinner nearby at a great restaurant—for half price any day. There's only one catch: the restaurant is operated by a cult, and the meat has been offered up in a ceremony to the cult's god before it was grilled for you. Would you eat it? Would you eat it if your Sunday school students or unchurched neighbors would see you sitting down to eat? Ask yourself these questions as you read today. If time is short, focus on 1 Corinthians 8:1–13.

Food Sacrificed to Idols

8 Now about food sacrificed to idols: We know that we all possess knowledge.[a] Knowledge puffs up, but love builds up. 2The man who thinks he knows something does not yet know as he ought to know. 3But the man who loves God is known by God.

4So then, about eating food sacrificed to idols: We know that an idol is nothing at all in the world and that there is no God but one. 5For even if there are so-called gods, whether in heaven or on earth (as indeed there are many "gods" and many "lords"), 6yet for us there is but one God, the Father, from whom all things came and for whom we live; and there is but one Lord, Jesus Christ, through whom all things came and through whom we live.

7But not everyone knows this. Some people are still so accustomed to idols that when they eat such food they think of it as having been sacrificed to an idol, and since their conscience is weak, it is defiled. 8But food does not bring us near to God; we are no worse if we do not eat, and no better if we do.

9Be careful, however, that the exercise of your freedom does not become a stumbling block to the weak. 10For if anyone with a weak conscience sees you who have this knowledge eating in an idol's temple, won't he be emboldened to eat what has been sacrificed to idols? 11So this weak brother, for whom Christ died, is destroyed by your knowledge. 12When you sin against your brothers in this way and wound their weak conscience, you sin against Christ. 13Therefore, if what I eat causes my brother to fall into sin, I will never eat meat again, so that I will not cause him to fall.

The Rights of an Apostle

9 Am I not free? Am I not an apostle? Have I not seen Jesus our Lord? Are you not the result of my work in the Lord? 2Even though I may not be an apostle to others, surely I am to you! For you are the seal of my apostleship in the Lord.

3This is my defense to those who sit in judgment on me. 4Don't we have the right to food and drink? 5Don't we have the right to take a believing wife along with us, as do the other apostles and the Lord's brothers and Cephas[b]? 6Or is it only I and Barnabas who must work for a living?

7Who serves as a soldier at his own expense? Who plants a vineyard and does not eat of its grapes? Who tends a flock and does not drink of the milk? 8Do I say this merely from a human point of view? Doesn't the Law say the same thing? 9For it is written in the Law of Moses: "Do not muzzle an ox while it is treading out the grain."[c] Is it about oxen that God is concerned? 10Surely he says this for us, doesn't he? Yes, this was written for us, because when the plowman plows and the thresher threshes, they ought to do so in the hope of sharing in the harvest. 11If we have sown spiritual seed among you, is it too much if we reap a material harvest from you? 12If others have this right of support from you, shouldn't we have it all the more?

But we did not use this right. On the contrary, we put up with anything rather than hinder the gospel of Christ. 13Don't you know that those who work in the temple get their food from the temple, and those who serve at the altar share in what is offered on the altar? 14In the same way, the Lord has commanded that those who preach the gospel should receive their living from the gospel.

15But I have not used any of these rights. And I am not writing this in the hope that you will do such things for me. I would rather die than have anyone deprive me of this boast. 16Yet when I preach the gospel, I cannot boast, for I am compelled to preach. Woe to me if I do not preach the gospel! 17If I preach voluntarily, I have a reward; if not voluntarily, I am simply discharging the trust committed to me. 18What then is

[a]1 Or *"We all possess knowledge," as you say*
[b]5 That is, Peter [c]9 Deut. 25:4

my reward? Just this: that in preaching the gospel I may offer it free of charge, and so not make use of my rights in preaching it.

[19]Though I am free and belong to no man, I make myself a slave to everyone, to win as many as possible. [20]To the Jews I became like a Jew, to win the Jews. To those under the law I became like one under the law (though I myself am not under the law), so as to win those under the law. [21]To those not having the law I became like one not having the law (though I am not free from God's law but am under Christ's law), so as to win those not having the law. [22]To the weak I became weak, to win the weak. I have become all things to all men so that by all possible means I might save some. [23]I do all this for the sake of the gospel, that I may share in its blessings.

[24]Do you not know that in a race all the runners run, but only one gets the prize? Run in such a way as to get the prize. [25]Everyone who competes in the games goes into strict training. They do it to get a crown that will not last; but we do it to get a crown that will last forever. [26]Therefore I do not run like a man running aimlessly; I do not fight like a man beating the air. [27]No, I beat my body and make it my slave so that after I have preached to others, I myself will not be disqualified for the prize.

SHARPEN THE FOCUS

Christian freedom and Christian love, a difficult balancing act, one Paul applies with care to a big issue in Corinth—should believers eat meat offered to idols?

And Paul's words apply to our own big issues, too. In Jesus, we are free. Unless God has specifically forbidden something, we can do it or not, use it or not. No one can legitimately enslave us or limit our freedom in any way.

But, Paul says, sometimes we voluntarily limit ourselves. We don't have to, but in love we *want* to. Sometimes, like Paul, we lay aside our rights, our freedom. We do it out of concern for those whose faith is weak. We forego that drink. We decide against seeing that movie. We do the work without submitting a bill. Our motive? Love for Christ and Christ's people.

We can lay aside our rights and give up our Christian freedom because Jesus did that for us—in full. He laid aside not just His throne, but even His right to life! He gave it up on the cross for our sin. See Philippians 2:5–11.

WEEK 88 • SATURDAY

1 Corinthians 10:1–33

GET THE BIG PICTURE

Paul had a joy even greater than that of exercising his Christian freedom—the joy of seeing the lost found. Concerned that the Corinthians lose neither their salvation nor their freedom in Christ, Paul goes on to warn them—and us—about that. If time is short, focus on 1 Corinthians 10:14–33.

Warnings From Israel's History

10 For I do not want you to be ignorant of the fact, brothers, that our forefathers were all under the cloud and that they all passed through the sea. 2They were all baptized into Moses in the cloud and in the sea. 3They all ate the same spiritual food 4and drank the same spiritual drink; for they drank from the spiritual rock that accompanied them, and that rock was Christ. 5Nevertheless, God was not pleased with most of them; their bodies were scattered over the desert.

6Now these things occurred as examples[a] to keep us from setting our hearts on evil things as they did. 7Do not be idolaters, as some of them were; as it is written: "The people sat down to eat and drink and got up to indulge in pagan revelry."[b] 8We should not commit sexual immorality, as some of them did—and in one day twenty-three thousand of them died. 9We should not test the Lord, as some of them did—and were killed by snakes. 10And do not grumble, as some of them did—and were killed by the destroying angel.

11These things happened to them as examples and were written down as warnings for us, on whom the fulfillment of the ages has come. 12So, if you think you are standing firm, be careful that you don't fall! 13No temptation has seized you except what is common to man. And God is faithful; he will not let you be tempted beyond what you can bear. But when you are tempted, he will also provide a way out so that you can stand up under it.

Idol Feasts and the Lord's Supper

14Therefore, my dear friends, flee from idolatry. 15I speak to sensible people; judge for yourselves what I say. 16Is not the cup of thanksgiving for which we give thanks a participation in the blood of Christ? And is not the bread that we break a participation in the body of Christ? 17Because there is one loaf, we, who are many, are one body, for we all partake of the one loaf.

18Consider the people of Israel: Do not those who eat the sacrifices participate in the altar? 19Do I mean then that a sacrifice offered to an idol is anything, or that an idol is anything? 20No, but the sacrifices of pagans are offered to demons, not to God, and I do not want you to be participants with demons. 21You cannot drink the cup of the Lord and the cup of demons too; you cannot have a part in both the Lord's table and the table of demons. 22Are we trying to arouse the Lord's jealousy? Are we stronger than he?

The Believer's Freedom

23"Everything is permissible"—but not everything is beneficial. "Everything is permissible"—but not everything is constructive. 24Nobody should seek his own good, but the good of others.

25Eat anything sold in the meat market without raising questions of conscience, 26for, "The earth is the Lord's, and everything in it."[c]

27If some unbeliever invites you to a meal and you want to go, eat whatever is put before you without raising questions of conscience. 28But if anyone says to you, "This has been offered in sacrifice," then do not eat it, both for the sake of the man who told you and for conscience' sake[d]— 29the other man's conscience, I mean, not yours. For why should my freedom be judged by another's conscience? 30If I take part in the meal with thankfulness, why am I denounced because of something I thank God for?

31So whether you eat or drink or whatever you do, do it all for the glory of God. 32Do not cause anyone to stumble, whether Jews, Greeks or the church of God— 33even as I try to please everybody in every way. For I am not seeking my own good but the good of many, so that they may be saved.

[a]6 Or *types;* also in verse 11 [b]7 Exodus 32:6 [c]26 Psalm 24:1 [d]28 Some manuscripts *conscience' sake, for "the earth is the Lord's and everything in it"*

SHARPEN THE FOCUS

As the *Titanic* steamed out of England in 1912, the officials of the White Star Line believed her to be unsinkable. So great was their faith that the ship had less than half the number of lifeboats needed for the crew and passengers. When the time came to escape, 1,513 of those on board were left behind to drown.

Contrast their plight with 1 Corinthians 10:13–14. Many in Corinth needed a way to escape the icy waters of sin. God had provided the perfect way to escape temptation. But Paul feared they would not use it, that they would fall overboard despite the Savior's provision. "God has made a way out," Paul says in essence in 1 Corinthians 10:13. "Use it," he urges in 1 Corinthians 10:14.

For the Corinthians this meant avoiding anything that might drag them back to idol worship. For us it means walking—or even running—away from any person or circumstance that might lure us into sin. We are free to do what we want, but by grace we want to use our freedom wisely (1 Corinthians 10:23).

1 Corinthians 10:31 summarizes our Christian freedom and the principles behind it. Because our Lord Jesus died for our sins and rose again, we live as God's forgiven children, free to honor Him in all we do.

WEEK 89 • MONDAY

1 Corinthians 11:1—12:31

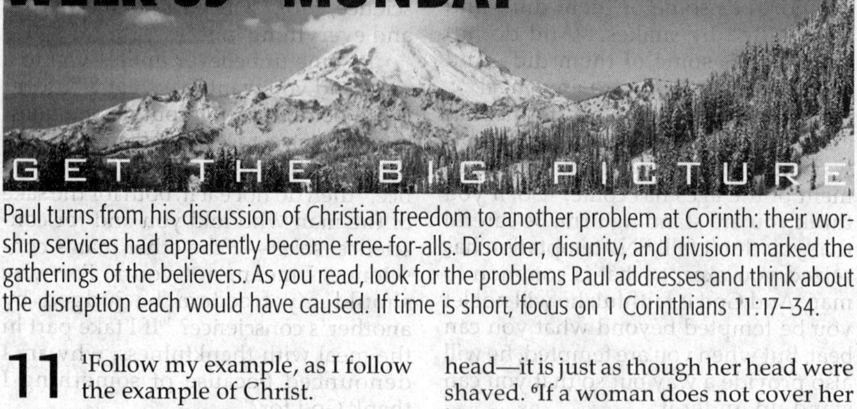

GET THE BIG PICTURE

Paul turns from his discussion of Christian freedom to another problem at Corinth: their worship services had apparently become free-for-alls. Disorder, disunity, and division marked the gatherings of the believers. As you read, look for the problems Paul addresses and think about the disruption each would have caused. If time is short, focus on 1 Corinthians 11:17–34.

11 [1]Follow my example, as I follow
the example of Christ.

Propriety in Worship

[2]I praise you for remembering me in
everything and for holding to the teachings,[a] just as I passed them on to you.
[3]Now I want you to realize that the
head of every man is Christ, and
the head of the woman is man, and the
head of Christ is God. [4]Every man who
prays or prophesies with his head covered dishonors his head. [5]And every
woman who prays or prophesies with
her head uncovered dishonors her
head—it is just as though her head were
shaved. [6]If a woman does not cover her
head, she should have her hair cut off;
and if it is a disgrace for a woman to
have her hair cut or shaved off, she
should cover her head. [7]A man ought
not to cover his head,[b] since he is the

[a]2 Or *traditions* [b]4-7 Or [4]*Every man who prays or prophesies with long hair dishonors his head.* [5]*And every woman who prays or prophesies with no covering ⌊of hair⌋ on her head dishonors her head—she is just like one of the "shorn women."* [6]*If a woman has no covering, let her be for now with short hair, but since it is a disgrace for a woman to have her hair shorn or shaved, she should grow it again.* [7]*A man ought not to have long hair*

image and glory of God; but the woman
is the glory of man. 8For man did not
come from woman, but woman from
man; 9neither was man created for
woman, but woman for man. 10For this
reason, and because of the angels, the
woman ought to have a sign of authority on her head.
11In the Lord, however, woman is not
independent of man, nor is man independent of woman. 12For as woman
came from man, so also man is born of
woman. But everything comes from
God. 13Judge for yourselves: Is it proper
for a woman to pray to God with her
head uncovered? 14Does not the very
nature of things teach you that if a man
has long hair, it is a disgrace to him, 15but
that if a woman has long hair, it is her
glory? For long hair is given to her as a
covering. 16If anyone wants to be con-
tentious about this, we have no other
practice—nor do the churches of God.

The Lord's Supper

17In the following directives I have no
praise for you, for your meetings do
more harm than good. 18In the first
place, I hear that when you come together as a church, there are divisions
among you, and to some extent I believe
it. 19No doubt there have to be differences among you to show which of you
have God's approval. 20When you come
together, it is not the Lord's Supper you
eat, 21for as you eat, each of you goes
ahead without waiting for anybody
else. One remains hungry, another gets
drunk. 22Don't you have homes to eat
and drink in? Or do you despise the
church of God and humiliate those who
have nothing? What shall I say to you?
Shall I praise you for this? Certainly not!
23For I received from the Lord what I
also passed on to you: The Lord Jesus,
on the night he was betrayed, took
bread, 24and when he had given thanks,
he broke it and said, "This is my body,
which is for you; do this in remembrance of me." 25In the same way, after
supper he took the cup, saying, "This
cup is the new covenant in my blood; do
this, whenever you drink it, in remembrance of me." 26For whenever you eat
this bread and drink this cup, you proclaim the Lord's death until he comes.
27Therefore, whoever eats the bread
or drinks the cup of the Lord in an unworthy manner will be guilty of sinning
against the body and blood of the Lord.
28A man ought to examine himself before he eats of the bread and drinks of
the cup. 29For anyone who eats and
drinks without recognizing the body of
the Lord eats and drinks judgment on
himself. 30That is why many among you
are weak and sick, and a number of you
have fallen asleep. 31But if we judged
ourselves, we would not come under
judgment. 32When we are judged by the
Lord, we are being disciplined so that
we will not be condemned with the
world.
33So then, my brothers, when you
come together to eat, wait for each other. 34If anyone is hungry, he should eat
at home, so that when you meet together it may not result in judgment.
And when I come I will give further
directions.

Spiritual Gifts

12 Now about spiritual gifts,
brothers, I do not want you to
be ignorant. 2You know that when you
were pagans, somehow or other you
were influenced and led astray to mute
idols. 3Therefore I tell you that no one
who is speaking by the Spirit of God
says, "Jesus be cursed," and no one can
say, "Jesus is Lord," except by the Holy
Spirit.
4There are different kinds of gifts, but
the same Spirit. 5There are different
kinds of service, but the same Lord.
6There are different kinds of working,
but the same God works all of them in
all men.
7Now to each one the manifestation of
the Spirit is given for the common good.
8To one there is given through the Spirit
the message of wisdom, to another the
message of knowledge by means of
the same Spirit, 9to another faith by the
same Spirit, to another gifts of healing
by that one Spirit, 10to another miracu-

lous powers, to another prophecy, to another distinguishing between spirits, to another speaking in different kinds of tongues,[a] and to still another the interpretation of tongues.[a] 11All these are the work of one and the same Spirit, and he gives them to each one, just as he determines.

One Body, Many Parts

12The body is a unit, though it is made up of many parts; and though all its parts are many, they form one body. So it is with Christ. 13For we were all baptized by[b] one Spirit into one body—whether Jews or Greeks, slave or free—and we were all given the one Spirit to drink.

14Now the body is not made up of one part but of many. 15If the foot should say, "Because I am not a hand, I do not belong to the body," it would not for that reason cease to be part of the body. 16And if the ear should say, "Because I am not an eye, I do not belong to the body," it would not for that reason cease to be part of the body. 17If the whole body were an eye, where would the sense of hearing be? If the whole body were an ear, where would the sense of smell be? 18But in fact God has arranged the parts in the body, every one of them, just as he wanted them to be. 19If they were all one part, where would the body be? 20As it is, there are many parts, but one body.

21The eye cannot say to the hand, "I don't need you!" And the head cannot say to the feet, "I don't need you!" 22On the contrary, those parts of the body that seem to be weaker are indispensable, 23and the parts that we think are less honorable we treat with special honor. And the parts that are unpresentable are treated with special modesty, 24while our presentable parts need no special treatment. But God has combined the members of the body and has given greater honor to the parts that lacked it, 25so that there should be no division in the body, but that its parts should have equal concern for each other. 26If one part suffers, every part suffers with it; if one part is honored, every part rejoices with it.

27Now you are the body of Christ, and each one of you is a part of it. 28And in the church God has appointed first of all apostles, second prophets, third teachers, then workers of miracles, also those having gifts of healing, those able to help others, those with gifts of administration, and those speaking in different kinds of tongues. 29Are all apostles? Are all prophets? Are all teachers? Do all work miracles? 30Do all have gifts of healing? Do all speak in tongues[c]? Do all interpret? 31But eagerly desire[d] the greater gifts.

Love

And now I will show you the most excellent way.

[a]10 Or *languages*; also in verse 28 [b]13 Or *with*; or *in* [c]30 Or *other languages* [d]31 Or *But you are eagerly desiring*

SHARPEN THE FOCUS

Scripture nowhere prescribes an order of service for New Testament worship. Our Lord leaves that to us in Christian freedom. But the holy writers do give us principles to guide us. For one thing, in-fighting and disunity do not impress God. Nor does lovelessness, especially not as we come to the Lord's Table.

In Christ, all believers are "one body" (1 Corinthians 10:17). Crucified with Jesus, dead, buried, and raised with Him, we belong to one another. But the Corinthians had found ways to downplay their unity, to accent their differences.

In pride, the rich lorded it over the poor (1 Corinthians 11:21). Those who arrived early refused to wait for late arrivals (1 Corinthians 11:33). And most came to the table carelessly, not thinking through what Jesus had done for them, not remembering with reverence what He in the Sacrament was giving them (1 Corinthians 11:27–29).

Think about your attitude toward fellow believers in your congregation. How much love do you show? How inclusive are you—especially toward those who differ from you? Talk to the Lord Jesus about these questions before you commune next time. Ask for any forgiveness you need. Then rely on Him to create true love and a genuine unity in your congregation.

WEEK 89 • TUESDAY

1 Corinthians 13:1—14:40

GET THE BIG PICTURE

Paul wrote 1 Corinthians 13 as the vital link between chapters 12 and 14. Believers in Corinth, mightily gifted by God, had begun to use their gifts selfishly and in arrogance. "You are gifted," Paul says to them (1 Corinthians 12:1–31). "Now use those gifts for Christ and His people" (1 Corinthians 14:1–40). The key is love (1 Corinthians 13:1–13). God says the same things to us. Listen as you read! If time is short, focus on 1 Corinthians 13:1–13.

13 If I speak in the tongues[a] of men and of angels, but have not love, I am only a resounding gong or a clanging cymbal. 2 If I have the gift of prophecy and can fathom all mysteries and all knowledge, and if I have a faith that can move mountains, but have not love, I am nothing. 3 If I give all I possess to the poor and surrender my body to the flames,[b] but have not love, I gain nothing.

4 Love is patient, love is kind. It does not envy, it does not boast, it is not proud. 5 It is not rude, it is not self-seeking, it is not easily angered, it keeps no record of wrongs. 6 Love does not delight in evil but rejoices with the truth. 7 It always protects, always trusts, always hopes, always perseveres.

8 Love never fails. But where there are prophecies, they will cease; where there are tongues, they will be stilled; where there is knowledge, it will pass away. 9 For we know in part and we prophesy in part, 10 but when perfection comes, the imperfect disappears. 11 When I was a child, I talked like a child, I thought like a child, I reasoned like a child. When I became a man, I put childish ways behind me. 12 Now we see but a poor reflection as in a mirror; then we shall see face to face. Now I know in part; then I shall know fully, even as I am fully known.

13 And now these three remain: faith, hope and love. But the greatest of these is love.

Gifts of Prophecy and Tongues

14 Follow the way of love and eagerly desire spiritual gifts, especially the gift of prophecy. 2 For anyone who speaks in a tongue[c] does not speak to men but to God. Indeed, no one understands him; he utters mysteries with his spirit.[d] 3 But everyone who prophesies speaks to men for their strengthening, encouragement and comfort. 4 He who speaks in a tongue edifies himself, but he who prophesies edifies the church. 5 I would like every

[a]1 Or *languages* [b]3 Some early manuscripts *body that I may boast* [c]2 Or *another language;* also in verses 4, 13, 14, 19, 26 and 27 [d]2 Or *by the Spirit*

one of you to speak in tongues,[a] but I
would rather have you prophesy. He
who prophesies is greater than one who
speaks in tongues,[a] unless he interprets,
so that the church may be edified.
[6]Now, brothers, if I come to you and
speak in tongues, what good will I be to
you, unless I bring you some revelation
or knowledge or prophecy or word of
instruction? [7]Even in the case of lifeless
things that make sounds, such as the
flute or harp, how will anyone know
what tune is being played unless there
is a distinction in the notes? [8]Again, if
the trumpet does not sound a clear call,
who will get ready for battle? [9]So it is
with you. Unless you speak intelligible
words with your tongue, how will anyone know what you are saying? You will
just be speaking into the air. [10]Undoubt-
edly there are all sorts of languages in
the world, yet none of them is without
meaning. [11]If then I do not grasp the
meaning of what someone is saying, I
am a foreigner to the speaker, and he is
a foreigner to me. [12]So it is with you.
Since you are eager to have spiritual
gifts, try to excel in gifts that build up
the church.
[13]For this reason anyone who speaks
in a tongue should pray that he may interpret what he says. [14]For if I pray in a
tongue, my spirit prays, but my mind is
unfruitful. [15]So what shall I do? I will
pray with my spirit, but I will also pray
with my mind; I will sing with my spirit,
but I will also sing with my mind. [16]If
you are praising God with your spirit,
how can one who finds himself among
those who do not understand[b] say
"Amen" to your thanksgiving, since he
does not know what you are saying? [17]You
may be giving thanks well enough, but
the other man is not edified.
[18]I thank God that I speak in tongues
more than all of you. [19]But in the church
I would rather speak five intelligible
words to instruct others than ten thousand words in a tongue.
[20]Brothers, stop thinking like children.
In regard to evil be infants, but in your
thinking be adults. [21]In the Law it is
written:

"Through men of strange tongues
and through the lips of foreigners
I will speak to this people,
but even then they will not listen
to me,"[c]
says the Lord.

[22]Tongues, then, are a sign, not for believers but for unbelievers; prophecy,
however, is for believers, not for unbelievers. [23]So if the whole church comes
together and everyone speaks in tongues, and some who do not understand[d] or some unbelievers come in, will
they not say that you are out of your
mind? [24]But if an unbeliever or someone
who does not understand[e] comes in
while everybody is prophesying, he will
be convinced by all that he is a sinner
and will be judged by all, [25]and the secrets of his heart will be laid bare. So he
will fall down and worship God, ex-
claiming, "God is really among you!"

Orderly Worship

[26]What then shall we say, brothers?
When you come together, everyone has
a hymn, or a word of instruction, a revelation, a tongue or an interpretation.
All of these must be done for the
strengthening of the church. [27]If anyone
speaks in a tongue, two—or at the most
three—should speak, one at a time, and
someone must interpret. [28]If there is no
interpreter, the speaker should keep
quiet in the church and speak to himself
and God.
[29]Two or three prophets should speak,
and the others should weigh carefully
what is said. [30]And if a revelation comes
to someone who is sitting down, the
first speaker should stop. [31]For you can
all prophesy in turn so that everyone
may be instructed and encouraged.
[32]The spirits of prophets are subject to
the control of prophets. [33]For God is not
a God of disorder but of peace.
As in all the congregations of the
saints, [34]women should remain silent in

[a]5 Or *other languages;* also in verses 6, 18, 22, 23 and 39 [b]16 Or *among the inquirers*
[c]21 Isaiah 28:11,12 [d]23 Or *some inquirers*
[e]24 Or *or some inquirer*

the churches. They are not allowed to
speak, but must be in submission, as the
Law says. 35If they want to inquire about
something, they should ask their own
husbands at home; for it is disgraceful
for a woman to speak in the church.
36Did the word of God originate with
you? Or are you the only people it has
reached? 37If anybody thinks he is a
prophet or spiritually gifted, let him
acknowledge that what I am writing
to you is the Lord's command. 38If he
ignores this, he himself will be ignored.[a]
39Therefore, my brothers, be eager to
prophesy, and do not forbid speaking in
tongues. 40But everything should be
done in a fitting and orderly way.

SHARPEN THE FOCUS

Think about a child who loves to make paper airplanes and then grows up to become an aeronautical engineer. Think about a child who loves to finger paint and then grows up to become Monet or Renoir.

That's the parallel Paul makes in 1 Corinthians 13:11. God has revealed much about Himself in the Holy Scriptures and especially in the Word made flesh, our Lord Jesus. Still, our knowledge of Him remains incomplete. While we live here on earth, we must be satisfied with seeing His truth as though we were looking "through a mirror in an enigma." (That, in fact, is the literal Greek of 1 Corinthians 13:12a.)

But when we arrive on heaven's shores, we will see our Savior face to face. Life's riddles will vanish. Doubts and fears will evaporate in the light of His love. That love, revealed in Christ's death for our sins, overwhelms us even now. But He has an even clearer, brighter revelation in store for us!

He invites us to let His love flow through us to our brothers and sisters in the faith. He gifts us to build them up. How could you do that in your congregation this week?

WEEK 89 • WEDNESDAY

1 Cor. 15:1–58

As we have seen, many problems troubled the infant congregation in Corinth. Perhaps none posed as great a danger as the one Paul addresses in today's chapter. Some so-called teachers there had begun to deny the resurrection! As you read, note the zeal in Paul's words as he emphasizes the certainty of our resurrection hope. If time is short, focus on 1 Corinthians 15:35–58.

The Resurrection of Christ

15 Now, brothers, I want to remind you of the gospel I
preached to you, which you received
and on which you have taken your
stand. 2By this gospel you are saved, if
you hold firmly to the word I preached

[a]38 Some manuscripts *If he is ignorant of this, let him be ignorant*

to you. Otherwise, you have believed in vain.

3For what I received I passed on to you as of first importance[a]: that Christ died for our sins according to the Scriptures, 4that he was buried, that he was raised on the third day according to the Scriptures, 5and that he appeared to Peter,[b] and then to the Twelve. 6After that, he appeared to more than five hundred of the brothers at the same time, most of whom are still living, though some have fallen asleep. 7Then he appeared to James, then to all the apostles, 8and last of all he appeared to me also, as to one abnormally born.

9For I am the least of the apostles and do not even deserve to be called an apostle, because I persecuted the church of God. 10But by the grace of God I am what I am, and his grace to me was not without effect. No, I worked harder than all of them—yet not I, but the grace of God that was with me. 11Whether, then, it was I or they, this is what we preach, and this is what you believed.

The Resurrection of the Dead

12But if it is preached that Christ has been raised from the dead, how can some of you say that there is no resurrection of the dead? 13If there is no resurrection of the dead, then not even Christ has been raised. 14And if Christ has not been raised, our preaching is useless and so is your faith. 15More than that, we are then found to be false witnesses about God, for we have testified about God that he raised Christ from the dead. But he did not raise him if in fact the dead are not raised. 16For if the dead are not raised, then Christ has not been raised either. 17And if Christ has not been raised, your faith is futile; you are still in your sins. 18Then those also who have fallen asleep in Christ are lost. 19If only for this life we have hope in Christ, we are to be pitied more than all men.

20But Christ has indeed been raised from the dead, the firstfruits of those who have fallen asleep. 21For since death came through a man, the resurrection of the dead comes also through a man. 22For as in Adam all die, so in Christ all will be made alive. 23But each in his own turn: Christ, the firstfruits; then, when he comes, those who belong to him. 24Then the end will come, when he hands over the kingdom to God the Father after he has destroyed all dominion, authority and power. 25For he must reign until he has put all his enemies under his feet. 26The last enemy to be destroyed is death. 27For he "has put everything under his feet."[c] Now when it says that "everything" has been put under him, it is clear that this does not include God himself, who put everything under Christ. 28When he has done this, then the Son himself will be made subject to him who put everything under him, so that God may be all in all.

29Now if there is no resurrection, what will those do who are baptized for the dead? If the dead are not raised at all, why are people baptized for them? 30And as for us, why do we endanger ourselves every hour? 31I die every day—I mean that, brothers—just as surely as I glory over you in Christ Jesus our Lord. 32If I fought wild beasts in Ephesus for merely human reasons, what have I gained? If the dead are not raised,

> "Let us eat and drink,
> for tomorrow we die."[d]

33Do not be misled: "Bad company corrupts good character." 34Come back to your senses as you ought, and stop sinning; for there are some who are ignorant of God—I say this to your shame.

The Resurrection Body

35But someone may ask, "How are the dead raised? With what kind of body will they come?" 36How foolish! What you sow does not come to life unless it dies. 37When you sow, you do not plant the body that will be, but just a seed, perhaps of wheat or of something else. 38But God gives it a body as he has determined, and to each kind of seed he

[a]3 Or *you at the first* [b]5 Greek *Cephas*
[c]27 Psalm 8:6 [d]32 Isaiah 22:13

gives its own body. 39All flesh is not the
same: Men have one kind of flesh, animals have another, birds another and
fish another. 40There are also heavenly
bodies and there are earthly bodies; but
the splendor of the heavenly bodies is
one kind, and the splendor of the earthly bodies is another. 41The sun has one
kind of splendor, the moon another and
the stars another; and star differs from
star in splendor.

42So will it be with the resurrection of
the dead. The body that is sown is perishable, it is raised imperishable; 43it is
sown in dishonor, it is raised in glory; it
is sown in weakness, it is raised in power; 44it is sown a natural body, it is raised
a spiritual body.

If there is a natural body, there is also
a spiritual body. 45So it is written: "The
first man Adam became a living being"[a];
the last Adam, a life-giving spirit. 46The
spiritual did not come first, but the natural, and after that the spiritual. 47The
first man was of the dust of the earth, the
second man from heaven. 48As was
the earthly man, so are those who are of
the earth; and as is the man from heav-
en, so also are those who are of heaven.
49And just as we have borne the likeness
of the earthly man, so shall we[b] bear the
likeness of the man from heaven.

50I declare to you, brothers, that flesh
and blood cannot inherit the kingdom
of God, nor does the perishable inherit
the imperishable. 51Listen, I tell you a
mystery: We will not all sleep, but we
will all be changed— 52in a flash, in the
twinkling of an eye, at the last trumpet.
For the trumpet will sound, the dead
will be raised imperishable, and we will
be changed. 53For the perishable must
clothe itself with the imperishable, and
the mortal with immortality. 54When the
perishable has been clothed with the
imperishable, and the mortal with immortality, then the saying that is written
will come true: "Death has been swallowed up in victory."[c]

55"Where, O death, is your victory?
Where, O death, is your sting?"[d]

56The sting of death is sin, and the power of sin is the law. 57But thanks be to
God! He gives us the victory through
our Lord Jesus Christ.

58Therefore, my dear brothers, stand
firm. Let nothing move you. Always
give yourselves fully to the work of the
Lord, because you know that your labor
in the Lord is not in vain.

[a]*45* Gen. 2:7 [b]*49* Some early manuscripts *so let us* [c]*54* Isaiah 25:8 [d]*55* Hosea 13:14

SHARPEN THE FOCUS

"If Christ rose from the dead, then . . ." How would you finish this sentence? The implications of our Lord's resurrection stagger human imagination.

- If Christ rose from the dead, then He is who He claimed to be—this world's Savior from sin (1 Corinthians 15:3).
- If Christ rose from the dead, then our faith in Him is vindicated and our sins are gone (1 Corinthians 15:17).
- If Christ rose from the dead, then our believing loved ones are not lost (1 Corinthians 15:18).
- If Christ rose from the dead, then we too will rise (1 Corinthians 15:20).
- If Christ rose from the dead, then one day death itself will die (1 Corinthians 15:26).
- If Christ rose from the dead, that fact calls us to live for Him even now, here on this earth (1 Corinthians 15:34, 58).

No wonder Satan has tried to trample the truth of the Savior's resurrection underfoot! But despite his lies, we can live with the sound of that "last trumpet" ringing in our ears. Muted though it may at times seem, the sound cannot be silenced by our troubles, by our fears, by our doubts.

Christ has risen. And we will one day rise to eternal life with Him. We will one day bear His image; by His grace we will be like Him forever! Let that truth empower your service today.

WEEK 89 • THURSDAY

1 Corinthians 16:1–24

Affection. That note graces Paul's concluding remarks in his first letter to the believers in Corinth. Despite the stern words of correction he has written, the apostle loves these people. Look for evidence of that as you read. If time is short, focus on 1 Corinthians 16:1–9.

The Collection for God's People

16 Now about the collection for
God's people: Do what I told
the Galatian churches to do. 2On the
first day of every week, each one of you
should set aside a sum of money in
keeping with his income, saving it up,
so that when I come no collections will
have to be made. 3Then, when I arrive,
I will give letters of introduction to the
men you approve and send them with
your gift to Jerusalem. 4If it seems advisable
for me to go also, they will accompany
me.

Personal Requests

5After I go through Macedonia, I will
come to you—for I will be going
through Macedonia. 6Perhaps I will stay
with you awhile, or even spend the winter,
so that you can help me on my journey,
wherever I go. 7I do not want to see
you now and make only a passing visit; I
hope to spend some time with you, if the
Lord permits. 8But I will stay on at Ephesus
until Pentecost, 9because a great door
for effective work has opened to me,
and there are many who oppose me.

10If Timothy comes, see to it that he
has nothing to fear while he is with you,
for he is carrying on the work of the
Lord, just as I am. 11No one, then, should
refuse to accept him. Send him on his
way in peace so that he may return to
me. I am expecting him along with the
brothers.

12Now about our brother Apollos: I
strongly urged him to go to you with
the brothers. He was quite unwilling to
go now, but he will go when he has the
opportunity.

13Be on your guard; stand firm in the
faith; be men of courage; be strong. 14Do
everything in love.

15You know that the household of
Stephanas were the first converts in
Achaia, and they have devoted themselves
to the service of the saints. I urge
you, brothers, 16to submit to such as
these and to everyone who joins in the
work, and labors at it. 17I was glad when
Stephanas, Fortunatus and Achaicus arrived,
because they have supplied what
was lacking from you. 18For they refreshed
my spirit and yours also. Such
men deserve recognition.

Final Greetings

[19]The churches in the province of Asia
send you greetings. Aquila and Priscilla[a]
greet you warmly in the Lord, and so
does the church that meets at their
house. [20]All the brothers here send you
greetings. Greet one another with a holy
kiss.
[21]I, Paul, write this greeting in my own
hand.
[22]If anyone does not love the Lord—
a curse be on him. Come, O Lord[b]!
[23]The grace of the Lord Jesus be with
you.
[24]My love to all of you in Christ Jesus.
Amen.[c]

[a]19 Greek *Prisca,* a variant of *Priscilla* [b]22 In Aramaic the expression *Come, O Lord* is *Marana tha.* [c]24 Some manuscripts do not have *Amen.*

SHARPEN THE FOCUS

Most of the believers in Corinth wouldn't meet the Christians in Jerusalem until they gathered in the glories of heaven. Still, these brothers and sisters in Christ cared—deeply—about their fellow believers. They cared enough to give. When they heard about financial need in Jerusalem, they began a collection.

In 1 Corinthians 16:1–4, Paul gives some direction to the gift they were planning. He asks that it be:

- planned;
- proportional;
- practiced.

Planned in the sense that each giver would think through his or her situation and then decide what to give.

Proportional in the sense that those who could afford more would give more, those who had less financial prosperity would give less.

Practiced in the sense that each Sunday the givers would bring the fruit of that week's work. Week by week they would remember God's gifts and respond to the Giver by giving.

2 CORINTHIANS

Sometimes Christians today look at the problems in the church and find themselves shocked or dismayed. But we need not be. The New Testament never hides the fact that the church on earth has struggled with controversies and divisions from the beginning. Even the great apostle Paul found it necessary to defend the call he had received from the Lord. As you read, watch for Paul's perspective on these troubles. If time is short, focus on 2 Corinthians 2:1–17.

1 Paul, an apostle of Christ Jesus by
the will of God, and Timothy our
brother,

To the church of God in Corinth, together with all the saints throughout Achaia:

2Grace and peace to you from God
our Father and the Lord Jesus Christ.

The God of All Comfort

3Praise be to the God and Father of
our Lord Jesus Christ, the Father of compassion and the God of all comfort,
4who comforts us in all our troubles, so
that we can comfort those in any trouble with the comfort we ourselves have
received from God. 5For just as the sufferings of Christ flow over into our lives,
so also through Christ our comfort overflows. 6If we are distressed, it is for your
comfort and salvation; if we are comforted, it is for your comfort, which produces in you patient endurance of the
same sufferings we suffer. 7And our
hope for you is firm, because we know
that just as you share in our sufferings,
so also you share in our comfort.
8We do not want you to be uninformed, brothers, about the hardships
we suffered in the province of Asia. We
were under great pressure, far beyond
our ability to endure, so that we despaired even of life. 9Indeed, in our
hearts we felt the sentence of death. But
this happened that we might not rely on
ourselves but on God, who raises the
dead. 10He has delivered us from such a
deadly peril, and he will deliver us. On
him we have set our hope that he will
continue to deliver us, 11as you help us
by your prayers. Then many will give
thanks on our[a] behalf for the gracious
favor granted us in answer to the
prayers of many.

Paul's Change of Plans

12Now this is our boast: Our conscience testifies that we have conducted
ourselves in the world, and especially in
our relations with you, in the holiness
and sincerity that are from God. We
have done so not according to worldly
wisdom but according to God's grace.
13For we do not write you anything you
cannot read or understand. And I hope
that, 14as you have understood us in
part, you will come to understand fully

[a]*11* Many manuscripts *your*

that you can boast of us just as we will boast of you in the day of the Lord Jesus.

[15]Because I was confident of this, I planned to visit you first so that you might benefit twice. [16]I planned to visit you on my way to Macedonia and to come back to you from Macedonia, and then to have you send me on my way to Judea. [17]When I planned this, did I do it lightly? Or do I make my plans in a worldly manner so that in the same breath I say, "Yes, yes" and "No, no"?

[18]But as surely as God is faithful, our message to you is not "Yes" and "No." [19]For the Son of God, Jesus Christ, who was preached among you by me and Silas[a] and Timothy, was not "Yes" and "No," but in him it has always been "Yes." [20]For no matter how many promises God has made, they are "Yes" in Christ. And so through him the "Amen" is spoken by us to the glory of God. [21]Now it is God who makes both us and you stand firm in Christ. He anointed us, [22]set his seal of ownership on us, and put his Spirit in our hearts as a deposit, guaranteeing what is to come.

[23]I call God as my witness that it was in order to spare you that I did not return to Corinth. [24]Not that we lord it over your faith, but we work with you for your joy, because it is by faith you

2 stand firm. [1]So I made up my mind that I would not make another painful visit to you. [2]For if I grieve you, who is left to make me glad but you whom I have grieved? [3]I wrote as I did so that when I came I should not be distressed by those who ought to make me rejoice. I had confidence in all of you, that you would all share my joy. [4]For I wrote you out of great distress and anguish of heart and with many tears, not to grieve you but to let you know the depth of my love for you.

Forgiveness for the Sinner

[5]If anyone has caused grief, he has not so much grieved me as he has grieved all of you, to some extent—not to put it too severely. [6]The punishment inflicted on him by the majority is sufficient for him. [7]Now instead, you ought to forgive and comfort him, so that he will not be overwhelmed by excessive sorrow. [8]I urge you, therefore, to reaffirm your love for him. [9]The reason I wrote you was to see if you would stand the test and be obedient in everything. [10]If you forgive anyone, I also forgive him. And what I have forgiven—if there was anything to forgive—I have forgiven in the sight of Christ for your sake, [11]in order that Satan might not outwit us. For we are not unaware of his schemes.

Ministers of the New Covenant

[12]Now when I went to Troas to preach the gospel of Christ and found that the Lord had opened a door for me, [13]I still had no peace of mind, because I did not find my brother Titus there. So I said good-by to them and went on to Macedonia.

[14]But thanks be to God, who always leads us in triumphal procession in Christ and through us spreads everywhere the fragrance of the knowledge of him. [15]For we are to God the aroma of Christ among those who are being saved and those who are perishing. [16]To the one we are the smell of death; to the other, the fragrance of life. And who is equal to such a task? [17]Unlike so many, we do not peddle the word of God for profit. On the contrary, in Christ we speak before God with sincerity, like men sent from God.

[a]19 Greek *Silvanus*, a variant of *Silas*

SHARPEN THE FOCUS

When Roman generals returned victorious from battle, they entered the city gates in a parade called a "triumph." All the prisoners they had taken followed them, often caged in wagons. Citizens cheered and burned spices along the parade route in honor of the conquering commanders.

Paul imports this image into his description of the church's mission (2 Corinthians 2:14–16). Rome's generals smelled the spices and smiled at the thought of victory. But to Rome's prisoners, the scent was anything but sweet. It signaled their coming execution.

The message of the Gospel lightens our steps and thrills our hearts. It's the fragrance of life and victory through the death and rising again of our dear Lord Jesus. But those in the world who have closed their ears and their hearts to the Gospel receive only the scent of impending doom.

Who needs to hear the sweet words of forgiveness and peace from you today? How will you speak them?

WEEK 89 • SATURDAY

2 Corinthians 3:1—4:18

GET THE BIG PICTURE

Most of the people you spot in a worship service wouldn't impress the world's rich and powerful. The teen who dragged himself to church without washing his face. The elderly couple who long ago stopped trying to make a fashion statement. Maybe even the pastor is too short or too chubby or lacks polish. Given all this, how *does* the church keep on changing people's lives? Ask yourself that question as you read today. If time is short, focus on 2 Corinthians 3:6–18.

3 Are we beginning to commend
ourselves again? Or do we need,
like some people, letters of recommen-
dation to you or from you? 2You yourselves are our letter, written on our
hearts, known and read by everybody.
3You show that you are a letter from
Christ, the result of our ministry, written not with ink but with the Spirit of
the living God, not on tablets of stone
but on tablets of human hearts.
4Such confidence as this is ours
through Christ before God. 5Not that we
are competent in ourselves to claim anything for ourselves, but our competence
comes from God. 6He has made us competent as ministers of a new covenant—
not of the letter but of the Spirit; for the
letter kills, but the Spirit gives life.

The Glory of the New Covenant

7Now if the ministry that brought
death, which was engraved in letters on
stone, came with glory, so that the Israelites could not look steadily at the face
of Moses because of its glory, fading
though it was, 8will not the ministry of
the Spirit be even more glorious? 9If the
ministry that condemns men is glorious,
how much more glorious is the ministry that brings righteousness! 10For what
was glorious has no glory now in comparison with the surpassing glory. 11And
if what was fading away came with
glory, how much greater is the glory of
that which lasts!
12Therefore, since we have such a
hope, we are very bold. 13We are not like
Moses, who would put a veil over his
face to keep the Israelites from gazing at
it while the radiance was fading away.
14But their minds were made dull, for to
this day the same veil remains when the
old covenant is read. It has not been removed, because only in Christ is it tak-
en away. 15Even to this day when Moses
is read, a veil covers their hearts. 16But
whenever anyone turns to the Lord, the

veil is taken away. 17Now the Lord is the Spirit, and where the Spirit of the Lord is, there is freedom. 18And we, who with unveiled faces all reflect[a] the Lord's glory, are being transformed into his likeness with ever-increasing glory, which comes from the Lord, who is the Spirit.

Treasures in Jars of Clay

4 Therefore, since through God's mercy we have this ministry, we do not lose heart. 2Rather, we have renounced secret and shameful ways; we do not use deception, nor do we distort the word of God. On the contrary, by setting forth the truth plainly we commend ourselves to every man's conscience in the sight of God. 3And even if our gospel is veiled, it is veiled to those who are perishing. 4The god of this age has blinded the minds of unbelievers, so that they cannot see the light of the gospel of the glory of Christ, who is the image of God. 5For we do not preach ourselves, but Jesus Christ as Lord, and ourselves as your servants for Jesus' sake. 6For God, who said, "Let light shine out of darkness,"[b] made his light shine in our hearts to give us the light of the knowledge of the glory of God in the face of Christ.

7But we have this treasure in jars of clay to show that this all-surpassing power is from God and not from us. 8We are hard pressed on every side, but not crushed; perplexed, but not in despair; 9persecuted, but not abandoned; struck down, but not destroyed. 10We always carry around in our body the death of Jesus, so that the life of Jesus may also be revealed in our body. 11For we who are alive are always being given over to death for Jesus' sake, so that his life may be revealed in our mortal body. 12So then, death is at work in us, but life is at work in you.

13It is written: "I believed; therefore I have spoken."[c] With that same spirit of faith we also believe and therefore speak, 14because we know that the one who raised the Lord Jesus from the dead will also raise us with Jesus and present us with you in his presence. 15All this is for your benefit, so that the grace that is reaching more and more people may cause thanksgiving to overflow to the glory of God.

16Therefore we do not lose heart. Though outwardly we are wasting away, yet inwardly we are being renewed day by day. 17For our light and momentary troubles are achieving for us an eternal glory that far outweighs them all. 18So we fix our eyes not on what is seen, but on what is unseen. For what is seen is temporary, but what is unseen is eternal.

[a]*18* Or *contemplate* [b]*6* Gen. 1:3
[c]*13* Psalm 116:10

SHARPEN THE FOCUS

What made Paul competent to serve the church at Corinth? Was he handsome? Probably just the opposite. Was he famous? His contemporaries would probably have used the adjective *infamous* instead. Was he a great orator? Even he denies that (1 Corinthians 2:1, 4).

Paul did not come to Corinth boasting about his own credentials. Rather, he preached Christ crucified, and he relied on God to convert and transform human hearts. His competence, he wrote, came from God (2 Corinthians 3:5). The Lord who called him also equipped him (2 Corinthians 1:1; 3:6).

Perhaps you think the world of your pastor. Or maybe you can't name anything he's ever done right. Wherever you fall along this satisfaction spectrum, talk to your Lord about it now. Pray for your pastor, and also pray for yourself. Ask that your heart (and his) be more open to the transforming power of Christ's forgiveness and love. Then look for ways to be an encourager, a positive influence for good in your congregation.

WEEK 90 • MONDAY

2 Corinthians 5:1–21

GET THE BIG PICTURE

What makes your life worthwhile? What motivates you to keep on living and witnessing for Christ? In 2 Corinthians 4:16–5:21, Paul spells out five truths that empower him. See if you can find them as you read. If time is short, focus on 2 Corinthians 5:14–21.

Our Heavenly Dwelling

5 Now we know that if the earthly
tent we live in is destroyed, we
have a building from God, an eternal
house in heaven, not built by human
hands. [2]Meanwhile we groan, longing
to be clothed with our heavenly dwelling, [3]because when we are clothed, we
will not be found naked. [4]For while we
are in this tent, we groan and are burdened, because we do not wish to be
unclothed but to be clothed with our
heavenly dwelling, so that what is mortal may be swallowed up by life. [5]Now
it is God who has made us for this very
purpose and has given us the Spirit as a
deposit, guaranteeing what is to come.
[6]Therefore we are always confident
and know that as long as we are at home
in the body we are away from the Lord.
[7]We live by faith, not by sight. [8]We are
confident, I say, and would prefer to be
away from the body and at home with
the Lord. [9]So we make it our goal to
please him, whether we are at home in
the body or away from it. [10]For we must
all appear before the judgment seat of
Christ, that each one may receive what
is due him for the things done while in
the body, whether good or bad.

The Ministry of Reconciliation

[11]Since, then, we know what it is to
fear the Lord, we try to persuade men.
What we are is plain to God, and I hope
it is also plain to your conscience. [12]We
are not trying to commend ourselves to
you again, but are giving you an opportunity to take pride in us, so that you can
answer those who take pride in what is
seen rather than in what is in the heart.
[13]If we are out of our mind, it is for the
sake of God; if we are in our right mind,
it is for you. [14]For Christ's love compels
us, because we are convinced that one
died for all, and therefore all died. [15]And
he died for all, that those who live
should no longer live for themselves but
for him who died for them and was
raised again.
[16]So from now on we regard no one
from a worldly point of view. Though
we once regarded Christ in this way, we
do so no longer. [17]Therefore, if anyone
is in Christ, he is a new creation; the old
has gone, the new has come! [18]All this is
from God, who reconciled us to himself
through Christ and gave us the ministry of reconciliation: [19]that God was rec-
onciling the world to himself in Christ,
not counting men's sins against them.
And he has committed to us the message of reconciliation. [20]We are therefore
Christ's ambassadors, as though God
were making his appeal through us. We
implore you on Christ's behalf: Be reconciled to God. [21]God made him who
had no sin to be sin[a] for us, so that in him
we might become the righteousness of
God.

[a]21 Or *be a sin offering*

SHARPEN THE FOCUS

Architects who dream about the not-so-distant future talk about "smart homes." Such dwellings will be wired for computer control. Theoretically, the owner could phone home to ask the house to draw a hot bath, to make ice cubes for tonight's party, and to adjust the heat to 69 degrees. A new home like that has a lot to recommend it!

Most people like new things—new cars, new clothes, new carpets. The newness Paul describes in 2 Corinthians 5:17 has wonderful appeal too. This "new you" is a gift to you from God through Christ (2 Corinthians 5:18). He didn't just patch up the tatters of your sinful self. Your sin had thoroughly ruined you. And so He thoroughly recreated you; you are His new creation in Christ, Paul says. Yes, the old nature still rears its ugly head at times to pull you back to sin. But you no longer have to slave for it.

The new you can claim Christ's own righteousness (2 Corinthians 5:21). And you can live your new life thinking right thoughts, saying right words, doing right acts (2 Corinthians 5:15). Praise the God who does such wonderful things for us!

WEEK 90 • TUESDAY

2 Corinthians 6:1—7:16

GET THE BIG PICTURE

After Paul wrote 1 Corinthians, he had to sit back and leave the results of his words of reprimand to God. His concern for the believers in Corinth caused him great anguish. But then Titus arrived with a report about the Corinthian congregation. Look for the details of that as you read. If time is short, focus on 2 Corinthians 7:1–16.

6 As God's fellow workers we urge
you not to receive God's grace in
vain. [2]For he says,

"In the time of my favor I heard you,
and in the day of salvation I
helped you."[a]

I tell you, now is the time of God's favor, now is the day of salvation.

Paul's Hardships

[3]We put no stumbling block in
anyone's path, so that our ministry will
not be discredited. [4]Rather, as servants
of God we commend ourselves in every
way: in great endurance; in troubles,
hardships and distresses; [5]in beatings,
imprisonments and riots; in hard work,
sleepless nights and hunger; [6]in purity,
understanding, patience and kindness;
in the Holy Spirit and in sincere love; [7]in
truthful speech and in the power of
God; with weapons of righteousness in
the right hand and in the left; [8]through
glory and dishonor, bad report and
good report; genuine, yet regarded as
impostors; [9]known, yet regarded as unknown;
dying, and yet we live on; beaten,
and yet not killed; [10]sorrowful, yet
always rejoicing; poor, yet making
many rich; having nothing, and yet possessing everything.

[11]We have spoken freely to you, Corinthians, and opened wide our hearts

[a]2 Isaiah 49:8

to you. [12]We are not withholding our
affection from you, but you are withholding yours from us. [13]As a fair
exchange—I speak as to my children—
open wide your hearts also.

Do Not Be Yoked With Unbelievers

[14]Do not be yoked together with unbelievers. For what do righteousness
and wickedness have in common? Or
what fellowship can light have with
darkness? [15]What harmony is there between Christ and Belial[a]? What does a
believer have in common with an unbeliever? [16]What agreement is there between the temple of God and idols? For
we are the temple of the living God. As
God has said: "I will live with them and
walk among them, and I will be their
God, and they will be my people."[b]

[17]"Therefore come out from them
  and be separate,
    says the Lord.
Touch no unclean thing,
  and I will receive you."[c]
[18]"I will be a Father to you,
  and you will be my sons and
    daughters,
      says the Lord Almighty."[d]

7 Since we have these promises,
dear friends, let us purify ourselves from everything that contami-
nates body and spirit, perfecting
holiness out of reverence for God.

Paul's Joy

[2]Make room for us in your hearts. We
have wronged no one, we have corrupted no one, we have exploited no one. [3]I
do not say this to condemn you; I have
said before that you have such a place
in our hearts that we would live or die
with you. [4]I have great confidence in
you; I take great pride in you. I am
greatly encouraged; in all our troubles
my joy knows no bounds.
[5]For when we came into Macedonia,
this body of ours had no rest, but we
were harassed at every turn—conflicts
on the outside, fears within. [6]But God,
who comforts the downcast, comforted
us by the coming of Titus, [7]and not only
by his coming but also by the comfort
you had given him. He told us about
your longing for me, your deep sorrow,
your ardent concern for me, so that my
joy was greater than ever.
[8]Even if I caused you sorrow by my
letter, I do not regret it. Though I did
regret it—I see that my letter hurt you,
but only for a little while— [9]yet now I
am happy, not because you were made
sorry, but because your sorrow led you
to repentance. For you became sorrowful as God intended and so were not
harmed in any way by us. [10]Godly sorrow brings repentance that leads to
salvation and leaves no regret, but
worldly sorrow brings death. [11]See what
this godly sorrow has produced in you:
what earnestness, what eagerness to
clear yourselves, what indignation,
what alarm, what longing, what concern, what readiness to see justice done.
At every point you have proved yourselves to be innocent in this matter. [12]So
even though I wrote to you, it was not
on account of the one who did the
wrong or of the injured party, but rather that before God you could see for
yourselves how devoted to us you are.
[13]By all this we are encouraged.
In addition to our own encouragement, we were especially delighted to
see how happy Titus was, because his
spirit has been refreshed by all of you.
[14]I had boasted to him about you, and
you have not embarrassed me. But just
as everything we said to you was true,
so our boasting about you to Titus has
proved to be true as well. [15]And his affection for you is all the greater when he
remembers that you were all obedient,
receiving him with fear and trembling.
[16]I am glad I can have complete confidence in you.

[a] *15* Greek *Beliar*, a variant of *Belial*
[b] *16* Lev. 26:12; Jer. 32:38; Ezek. 37:27
[c] *17* Isaiah 52:11; Ezek. 20:34,41
[d] *18* 2 Samuel 7:14; 7:8

SHARPEN THE FOCUS

I'm sorry. When did you last speak these words? What did you mean by them? In today's reading, Paul points out the difference between "godly sorrow" and "worldly sorrow" (2 Corinthians 7:9–12).

Worldly sorrow regrets getting caught. Worldly sorrow blushes as it sits on the curb waiting for the ticket the traffic officer is writing. Worldly sorrow fumes at the F it will receive for cheating on this morning's test. Worldly sorrow resolves to sin smarter next time.

Godly sorrow, on the other hand, is the true contrition produced by the Holy Spirit in the hearts of God's children. Godly sorrow acknowledges wrongdoing without excuse-making. Godly sorrow receives God's pardon in Jesus and His cross, relying fully on God's grace alone. Godly sorrow then looks high and low by grace for ways to repair damaged relationships.

You can guess which kind of sorrow, of penitence, pleases our Lord. Ask Him to continually work it in your heart for His glory and your good.

WEEK 90 • WEDNESDAY

2 Cor. 8:1—9:15

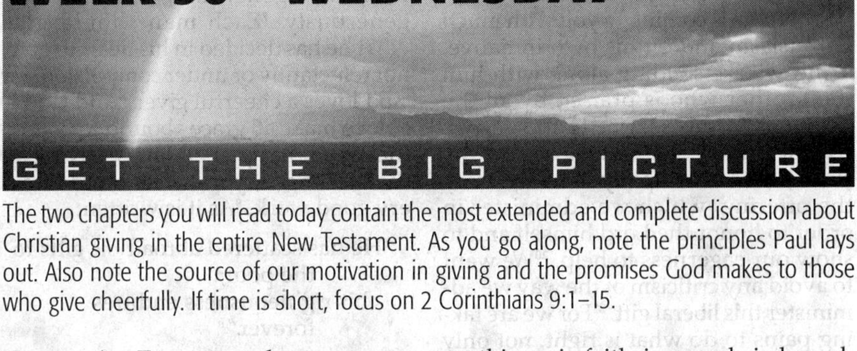

GET THE BIG PICTURE

The two chapters you will read today contain the most extended and complete discussion about Christian giving in the entire New Testament. As you go along, note the principles Paul lays out. Also note the source of our motivation in giving and the promises God makes to those who give cheerfully. If time is short, focus on 2 Corinthians 9:1–15.

Generosity Encouraged

8 And now, brothers, we want you
to know about the grace that
God has given the Macedonian
churches. 2Out of the most severe trial,
their overflowing joy and their extreme
poverty welled up in rich generosity.
3For I testify that they gave as much as
they were able, and even beyond their
ability. Entirely on their own, 4they urgently pleaded with us for the privilege
of sharing in this service to the saints.
5And they did not do as we expected,
but they gave themselves first to the
Lord and then to us in keeping with
God's will. 6So we urged Titus, since he
had earlier made a beginning, to bring
also to completion this act of grace on
your part. 7But just as you excel in everything—in faith, in speech, in knowledge, in complete earnestness and in
your love for us[a]—see that you also excel in this grace of giving.
8I am not commanding you, but I
want to test the sincerity of your love by
comparing it with the earnestness of
others. 9For you know the grace of our
Lord Jesus Christ, that though he was
rich, yet for your sakes he became poor,
so that you through his poverty might
become rich.
10And here is my advice about what is
best for you in this matter: Last year
you were the first not only to give but
also to have the desire to do so. 11Now
finish the work, so that your eager

[a]7 Some manuscripts *in our love for you*

willingness to do it may be matched by your completion of it, according to your means. [12]For if the willingness is there, the gift is acceptable according to what one has, not according to what he does not have.

[13]Our desire is not that others might be relieved while you are hard pressed, but that there might be equality. [14]At the present time your plenty will supply what they need, so that in turn their plenty will supply what you need. Then there will be equality, [15]as it is written: "He who gathered much did not have too much, and he who gathered little did not have too little."[a]

Titus Sent to Corinth

[16]I thank God, who put into the heart of Titus the same concern I have for you. [17]For Titus not only welcomed our appeal, but he is coming to you with much enthusiasm and on his own initiative. [18]And we are sending along with him the brother who is praised by all the churches for his service to the gospel. [19]What is more, he was chosen by the churches to accompany us as we carry the offering, which we administer in order to honor the Lord himself and to show our eagerness to help. [20]We want to avoid any criticism of the way we administer this liberal gift. [21]For we are taking pains to do what is right, not only in the eyes of the Lord but also in the eyes of men.

[22]In addition, we are sending with them our brother who has often proved to us in many ways that he is zealous, and now even more so because of his great confidence in you. [23]As for Titus, he is my partner and fellow worker among you; as for our brothers, they are representatives of the churches and an honor to Christ. [24]Therefore show these men the proof of your love and the reason for our pride in you, so that the churches can see it.

9 There is no need for me to write to you about this service to the saints. [2]For I know your eagerness to help, and I have been boasting about it to the Macedonians, telling them that since last year you in Achaia were ready to give; and your enthusiasm has stirred most of them to action. [3]But I am sending the brothers in order that our boasting about you in this matter should not prove hollow, but that you may be ready, as I said you would be. [4]For if any Macedonians come with me and find you unprepared, we—not to say anything about you—would be ashamed of having been so confident. [5]So I thought it necessary to urge the brothers to visit you in advance and finish the arrangements for the generous gift you had promised. Then it will be ready as a generous gift, not as one grudgingly given.

Sowing Generously

[6]Remember this: Whoever sows sparingly will also reap sparingly, and whoever sows generously will also reap generously. [7]Each man should give what he has decided in his heart to give, not reluctantly or under compulsion, for God loves a cheerful giver. [8]And God is able to make all grace abound to you, so that in all things at all times, having all that you need, you will abound in every good work. [9]As it is written:

> "He has scattered abroad his gifts to
> the poor;
> his righteousness endures
> forever."[b]

[10]Now he who supplies seed to the sower and bread for food will also supply and increase your store of seed and will enlarge the harvest of your righteousness. [11]You will be made rich in every way so that you can be generous on every occasion, and through us your generosity will result in thanksgiving to God.

[12]This service that you perform is not only supplying the needs of God's people but is also overflowing in many expressions of thanks to God. [13]Because of the service by which you have proved yourselves, men will praise God for the obedience that accompanies your confession of the gospel of Christ, and for

[a]*15* Exodus 16:18 [b]*9* Psalm 112:9

your generosity in sharing with them
and with everyone else. 14And in their
prayers for you their hearts will go out
to you, because of the surpassing grace
God has given you. 15Thanks be to God
for his indescribable gift!

SHARPEN THE FOCUS

Carefully read 9:8–11, pen and paper close at hand. Note each *all* and *every* you find. What did you discover?

The text surely points to a God who gives and who enjoys giving. Our Lord is generous by nature. And He wants us, His children, to find joy in generosity too.

Did you notice that this text does not limit itself to promises about giving money (although that's the context)? When we give others our time, when we use our abilities for the benefit of others, when we make a casserole, or rake some leaves, or provide respite care for a weary parent or spouse, God is honored. God is praised. God is thanked (2 Corinthians 9:11–12).

So much does God desire generous giving from His children that He surrounds His commands with promises of great blessings. We do not give in order to manipulate our Lord into some kind of "debt repayment plan." He owes us nothing, and what's more, the ability to give is in itself a gift from His gracious hand, not a way we can make the King of the universe indebted to us.

Even so, our Lord promises to enrich us, heart, mind, and soul as we give. And He promises to provide for our needs in such a way that we always have the ability to give to others.

WEEK 90 • THURSDAY

2 Cor. 10:1—11:33

GET THE BIG PICTURE

Paul had been the first to preach the Gospel in Corinth, and many had come to faith. That faith, worked by the Holy Spirit, testified to Paul's true apostleship (2 Corinthians 3:2–3). But after Paul left, self-styled "super-apostles" wormed their way into the flock. They undermined the pure Gospel and belittled Paul. You will read Paul's answer to their challenge today and tomorrow. If time is short focus on 2 Corinthians 10:1–18.

Paul's Defense of His Ministry

10 By the meekness and gentleness of Christ, I appeal to
you—I, Paul, who am "timid" when face
to face with you, but "bold" when away!
2I beg you that when I come I may not
have to be as bold as I expect to be toward some people who think that we
live by the standards of this world. 3For
though we live in the world, we do not
wage war as the world does. 4The weapons we fight with are not the weapons
of the world. On the contrary, they have
divine power to demolish strongholds.
5We demolish arguments and every pre-
tension that sets itself up against the
knowledge of God, and we take captive
every thought to make it obedient to

Christ. [6]And we will be ready to punish every act of disobedience, once your obedience is complete.

[7]You are looking only on the surface of things.[a] If anyone is confident that he belongs to Christ, he should consider again that we belong to Christ just as much as he. [8]For even if I boast somewhat freely about the authority the Lord gave us for building you up rather than pulling you down, I will not be ashamed of it. [9]I do not want to seem to be trying to frighten you with my letters. [10]For some say, "His letters are weighty and forceful, but in person he is unimpressive and his speaking amounts to nothing." [11]Such people should realize that what we are in our letters when we are absent, we will be in our actions when we are present.

[12]We do not dare to classify or compare ourselves with some who commend themselves. When they measure themselves by themselves and compare themselves with themselves, they are not wise. [13]We, however, will not boast beyond proper limits, but will confine our boasting to the field God has assigned to us, a field that reaches even to you. [14]We are not going too far in our boasting, as would be the case if we had not come to you, for we did get as far as you with the gospel of Christ. [15]Neither do we go beyond our limits by boasting of work done by others.[b] Our hope is that, as your faith continues to grow, our area of activity among you will greatly expand, [16]so that we can preach the gospel in the regions beyond you. For we do not want to boast about work already done in another man's territory. [17]But, "Let him who boasts boast in the Lord."[c] [18]For it is not the one who commends himself who is approved, but the one whom the Lord commends.

Paul and the False Apostles

11 I hope you will put up with a little of my foolishness; but you are already doing that. [2]I am jealous for you with a godly jealousy. I promised you to one husband, to Christ, so that I might present you as a pure virgin to him. [3]But I am afraid that just as Eve was deceived by the serpent's cunning, your minds may somehow be led astray from your sincere and pure devotion to Christ. [4]For if someone comes to you and preaches a Jesus other than the Jesus we preached, or if you receive a different spirit from the one you received, or a different gospel from the one you accepted, you put up with it easily enough. [5]But I do not think I am in the least inferior to those "super-apostles." [6]I may not be a trained speaker, but I do have knowledge. We have made this perfectly clear to you in every way.

[7]Was it a sin for me to lower myself in order to elevate you by preaching the gospel of God to you free of charge? [8]I robbed other churches by receiving support from them so as to serve you. [9]And when I was with you and needed something, I was not a burden to anyone, for the brothers who came from Macedonia supplied what I needed. I have kept myself from being a burden to you in any way, and will continue to do so. [10]As surely as the truth of Christ is in me, nobody in the regions of Achaia will stop this boasting of mine. [11]Why? Because I do not love you? God knows I do! [12]And I will keep on doing what I am doing in order to cut the ground from under those who want an opportunity to be considered equal with us in the things they boast about.

[13]For such men are false apostles, deceitful workmen, masquerading as apostles of Christ. [14]And no wonder, for Satan himself masquerades as an angel of light. [15]It is not surprising, then, if his servants masquerade as servants of righteousness. Their end will be what their actions deserve.

[a]7 Or *Look at the obvious facts* [b]13-15 Or [13]*We, however, will not boast about things that cannot be measured, but we will boast according to the standard of measurement that the God of measure has assigned us—a measurement that relates even to you.* [14] . . . [15]*Neither do we boast about things that cannot be measured in regard to the work done by others.*
[c]17 Jer. 9:24

Paul Boasts About His Sufferings

[16]I repeat: Let no one take me for a fool. But if you do, then receive me just as you would a fool, so that I may do a little boasting. [17]In this self-confident boasting I am not talking as the Lord would, but as a fool. [18]Since many are boasting in the way the world does, I too will boast. [19]You gladly put up with fools since you are so wise! [20]In fact, you even put up with anyone who enslaves you or exploits you or takes advantage of you or pushes himself forward or slaps you in the face. [21]To my shame I admit that we were too weak for that!

What anyone else dares to boast about—I am speaking as a fool—I also dare to boast about. [22]Are they Hebrews? So am I. Are they Israelites? So am I. Are they Abraham's descendants? So am I. [23]Are they servants of Christ? (I am out of my mind to talk like this.) I am more. I have worked much harder, been in prison more frequently, been flogged more severely, and been exposed to death again and again. [24]Five times I received from the Jews the forty lashes minus one. [25]Three times I was beaten with rods, once I was stoned, three times I was shipwrecked, I spent a night and a day in the open sea, [26]I have been constantly on the move. I have been in danger from rivers, in danger from bandits, in danger from my own countrymen, in danger from Gentiles; in danger in the city, in danger in the country, in danger at sea; and in danger from false brothers. [27]I have labored and toiled and have often gone without sleep; I have known hunger and thirst and have often gone without food; I have been cold and naked. [28]Besides everything else, I face daily the pressure of my concern for all the churches. [29]Who is weak, and I do not feel weak? Who is led into sin, and I do not inwardly burn?

[30]If I must boast, I will boast of the things that show my weakness. [31]The God and Father of the Lord Jesus, who is to be praised forever, knows that I am not lying. [32]In Damascus the governor under King Aretas had the city of the Damascenes guarded in order to arrest me. [33]But I was lowered in a basket from a window in the wall and slipped through his hands.

SHARPEN THE FOCUS

It's easy to mistake meekness for weakness (2 Corinthians 10:1). Paul's enemies had seen his gentleness and had evidently concluded they could usurp his authority in Corinth. They looked good on the outside, but they tried to replace the power of the Gospel in the same way outwardly religious people always have—by substituting a long to-do list.

"Sure, Jesus died for you," they said, but . . .

- you must follow the traditions."
- you must try to keep the commandments."
- you must tithe."

Our sinful nature wants to believe that we have something worthwhile to offer God. Our service, our obedience, our worship all *do* please Him, but these things do not create or sustain our relationship with Him. Only Jesus' death and resurrection for us could do that. And it *has* done that! That's the true Good News. That's the pure Gospel.

Meek and gentle though Paul was, he would defend that Gospel. His weapons weren't weak and limited (2 Corinthians 10:4). No, he wielded the sword of the Spirit, the mighty Word of God (Ephesians 6:17). The Corinthians could stand firm by faith in that Word, in that Gospel (2 Corinthians 1:24).

And so can we.

WEEK 90 • FRIDAY

2 Corinthians 12:1—13:14

GET THE BIG PICTURE

People will usually overlook weaknesses and flaws in their spiritual leaders if they believe those leaders care about them. No one in Corinth could doubt Paul's care and concern, especially after hearing the words you will read today. What evidence of that concern do you see? If time is short, focus on 2 Corinthians 12:1–10.

Paul's Vision and His Thorn

12 I must go on boasting. Although there is nothing to be
gained, I will go on to visions and revelations from the Lord. [2]I know a man in
Christ who fourteen years ago was
caught up to the third heaven. Whether it was in the body or out of the body
I do not know—God knows. [3]And I
know that this man—whether in the
body or apart from the body I do not
know, but God knows— [4]was caught up
to paradise. He heard inexpressible
things, things that man is not permitted
to tell. [5]I will boast about a man like that,
but I will not boast about myself, except
about my weaknesses. [6]Even if I should
choose to boast, I would not be a fool,
because I would be speaking the truth.
But I refrain, so no one will think more
of me than is warranted by what I do or
say.

[7]To keep me from becoming conceited because of these surpassingly great
revelations, there was given me a thorn
in my flesh, a messenger of Satan, to torment me. [8]Three times I pleaded with
the Lord to take it away from me. [9]But
he said to me, "My grace is sufficient for
you, for my power is made perfect in
weakness." Therefore I will boast all the
more gladly about my weaknesses, so
that Christ's power may rest on me.
[10]That is why, for Christ's sake, I delight
in weaknesses, in insults, in hardships,
in persecutions, in difficulties. For when
I am weak, then I am strong.

Paul's Concern for the Corinthians

[11]I have made a fool of myself, but you
drove me to it. I ought to have been
commended by you, for I am not in the
least inferior to the "super-apostles,"
even though I am nothing. [12]The things
that mark an apostle—signs, wonders
and miracles—were done among you
with great perseverance. [13]How were
you inferior to the other churches, except that I was never a burden to you?
Forgive me this wrong!

[14]Now I am ready to visit you for the
third time, and I will not be a burden to
you, because what I want is not your
possessions but you. After all, children
should not have to save up for their parents, but parents for their children. [15]So
I will very gladly spend for you everything I have and expend myself as well.
If I love you more, will you love me less?
[16]Be that as it may, I have not been a burden to you. Yet, crafty fellow that I am,
I caught you by trickery! [17]Did I exploit
you through any of the men I sent you?
[18]I urged Titus to go to you and I sent
our brother with him. Titus did not
exploit you, did he? Did we not act in the
same spirit and follow the same course?

[19]Have you been thinking all along
that we have been defending ourselves
to you? We have been speaking in the
sight of God as those in Christ; and everything we do, dear friends, is for your
strengthening. [20]For I am afraid that
when I come I may not find you as I
want you to be, and you may not find

me as you want me to be. I fear that
there may be quarreling, jealousy, out-
bursts of anger, factions, slander, gossip,
arrogance and disorder. 21I am afraid
that when I come again my God will
humble me before you, and I will be
grieved over many who have sinned
earlier and have not repented of the impurity, sexual sin and debauchery in
which they have indulged.

Final Warnings

13 This will be my third visit to
you. "Every matter must be
established by the testimony of two or
three witnesses."[a] 2I already gave you a
warning when I was with you the second time. I now repeat it while absent:
On my return I will not spare those who
sinned earlier or any of the others, 3since
you are demanding proof that Christ is
speaking through me. He is not weak
in dealing with you, but is powerful
among you. 4For to be sure, he was crucified in weakness, yet he lives by God's
power. Likewise, we are weak in him,
yet by God's power we will live with
him to serve you.
5Examine yourselves to see whether
you are in the faith; test yourselves. Do
you not realize that Christ Jesus is in
you—unless, of course, you fail the test?
6And I trust that you will discover that
we have not failed the test. 7Now we
pray to God that you will not do anything wrong. Not that people will see
that we have stood the test but that you
will do what is right even though we
may seem to have failed. 8For we cannot
do anything against the truth, but only
for the truth. 9We are glad whenever we
are weak but you are strong; and our
prayer is for your perfection. 10This is
why I write these things when I am absent, that when I come I may not have
to be harsh in my use of authority—the
authority the Lord gave me for building
you up, not for tearing you down.

Final Greetings

11Finally, brothers, good-by. Aim for
perfection, listen to my appeal, be of one
mind, live in peace. And the God of love
and peace will be with you.
12Greet one another with a holy kiss.
13All the saints send their greetings.
14May the grace of the Lord Jesus
Christ, and the love of God, and the
fellowship of the Holy Spirit be with
you all.

[a] *1* Deut. 19:15

SHARPEN THE FOCUS

Sports Illustrated hardly ever interviews the body builder who takes last place in this month's weight-lifting contest. Marathon runners try to forget their slowest races.

How odd, then, to read Paul's boast in 2 Corinthians 12:5, 9b. Who boasts about weakness? The great apostle Paul, that's who. And if we're wise, he implies, so will we.

Why? Simply because when we are weak, then we are strong (2 Corinthians 12:10b). At first reading, this seems like an oxymoron, a concept that contradicts itself. But if we dig a bit deeper, we see the truth. Once we acknowledge our own weakness, then by God's grace we access Christ's infinite resources:

- We confess our sins; we receive Christ's own righteousness.
- We admit our powerlessness to obey God; we receive Christ's own love and power.
- We acknowledge our inadequacy to serve as Christ's ambassadors in the world; we receive the commission, the credentials, and the competence from our Lord Himself.

The light of Christ shines forth most clearly from clay jars (2 Corinthians 4:7). What weaknesses could you offer up to your Lord right now?

GALATIANS

WEEK 90 • SATURDAY

Galatians 1:1—2:21

GET THE BIG PICTURE

Medicine adulterated with arsenic can kill those who take it. Paul writes to warn the Galatians about another kind of adulteration–adulteration of the Gospel. Corinth wasn't the only place in which the Judaizers tried to destroy the peace and freedom of God's faithful people. As you read today, look for evidence that Paul, by the power of the Holy Spirit, passed on the pure Gospel to the church in Galatia–and to us! If time is short, focus on Galatians 1:1–24.

1 Paul, an apostle—sent not from
men nor by man, but by Jesus Christ
and God the Father, who raised him
from the dead— [2]and all the brothers
with me,

To the churches in Galatia:

[3]Grace and peace to you from God
our Father and the Lord Jesus Christ,
[4]who gave himself for our sins to rescue
us from the present evil age, according
to the will of our God and Father, [5]to
whom be glory for ever and ever. Amen.

No Other Gospel

[6]I am astonished that you are so
quickly deserting the one who called
you by the grace of Christ and are turning to a different gospel— [7]which is really no gospel at all. Evidently some
people are throwing you into confusion
and are trying to pervert the gospel of
Christ. [8]But even if we or an angel from
heaven should preach a gospel other
than the one we preached to you, let
him be eternally condemned! [9]As we
have already said, so now I say again: If
anybody is preaching to you a gospel
other than what you accepted, let him
be eternally condemned!

[10]Am I now trying to win the approval of men, or of God? Or am I trying to please men? If I were still trying
to please men, I would not be a servant
of Christ.

Paul Called by God

[11]I want you to know, brothers, that
the gospel I preached is not something
that man made up. [12]I did not receive it
from any man, nor was I taught it; rather, I received it by revelation from Jesus
Christ.

[13]For you have heard of my previous
way of life in Judaism, how intensely I
persecuted the church of God and tried
to destroy it. [14]I was advancing in Judaism beyond many Jews of my own age
and was extremely zealous for the traditions of my fathers. [15]But when God,
who set me apart from birth[a] and called
me by his grace, was pleased [16]to reveal
his Son in me so that I might preach him
among the Gentiles, I did not consult
any man, [17]nor did I go up to Jerusalem
to see those who were apostles before I
was, but I went immediately into Arabia and later returned to Damascus.

[a]15 Or *from my mother's womb*

[18]Then after three years, I went up to Jerusalem to get acquainted with Peter[a] and stayed with him fifteen days. [19]I saw none of the other apostles—only James, the Lord's brother. [20]I assure you before God that what I am writing you is no lie. [21]Later I went to Syria and Cilicia. [22]I was personally unknown to the churches of Judea that are in Christ. [23]They only heard the report: "The man who formerly persecuted us is now preaching the faith he once tried to destroy." [24]And they praised God because of me.

Paul Accepted by the Apostles

2 Fourteen years later I went up again to Jerusalem, this time with Barnabas. I took Titus along also. [2]I went in response to a revelation and set before them the gospel that I preach among the Gentiles. But I did this privately to those who seemed to be leaders, for fear that I was running or had run my race in vain. [3]Yet not even Titus, who was with me, was compelled to be circumcised, even though he was a Greek. [4]⌞This matter arose⌟ because some false brothers had infiltrated our ranks to spy on the freedom we have in Christ Jesus and to make us slaves. [5]We did not give in to them for a moment, so that the truth of the gospel might remain with you.

[6]As for those who seemed to be important—whatever they were makes no difference to me; God does not judge by external appearance—those men added nothing to my message. [7]On the contrary, they saw that I had been entrusted with the task of preaching the gospel to the Gentiles,[b] just as Peter had been to the Jews.[c] [8]For God, who was at work in the ministry of Peter as an apostle to the Jews, was also at work in my ministry as an apostle to the Gentiles. [9]James, Peter[d] and John, those reputed to be pillars, gave me and Barnabas the right hand of fellowship when they recognized the grace given to me. They agreed that we should go to the Gentiles, and they to the Jews. [10]All they asked was that we should continue to remember the poor, the very thing I was eager to do.

Paul Opposes Peter

[11]When Peter came to Antioch, I opposed him to his face, because he was clearly in the wrong. [12]Before certain men came from James, he used to eat with the Gentiles. But when they arrived, he began to draw back and separate himself from the Gentiles because he was afraid of those who belonged to the circumcision group. [13]The other Jews joined him in his hypocrisy, so that by their hypocrisy even Barnabas was led astray.

[14]When I saw that they were not acting in line with the truth of the gospel, I said to Peter in front of them all, "You are a Jew, yet you live like a Gentile and not like a Jew. How is it, then, that you force Gentiles to follow Jewish customs?

[15]"We who are Jews by birth and not 'Gentile sinners' [16]know that a man is not justified by observing the law, but by faith in Jesus Christ. So we, too, have put our faith in Christ Jesus that we may be justified by faith in Christ and not by observing the law, because by observing the law no one will be justified.

[17]"If, while we seek to be justified in Christ, it becomes evident that we ourselves are sinners, does that mean that Christ promotes sin? Absolutely not! [18]If I rebuild what I destroyed, I prove that I am a lawbreaker. [19]For through the law I died to the law so that I might live for God. [20]I have been crucified with Christ and I no longer live, but Christ lives in me. The life I live in the body, I live by faith in the Son of God, who loved me and gave himself for me. [21]I do not set aside the grace of God, for if righteousness could be gained through the law, Christ died for nothing!"[e]

[a] *18* Greek *Cephas* [b] *7* Greek *uncircumcised*
[c] *7* Greek *circumcised*; also in verses 8 and 9
[d] *9* Greek *Cephas*; also in verses 11 and 14
[e] *21* Some interpreters end the quotation after verse 14.

SHARPEN THE FOCUS

The heart of the giver makes the gift precious. Never has this proverb proven more true than in Jesus Christ,

> *who gave Himself for our sins to rescue us from the present evil age, according to the will of our God and Father, to whom be glory for ever and ever. Amen.* (Galatians 1:4–5)

Sometimes as we paddle through the troubled waters of life, we wish we could read God's mind. We want to know what He's up to, what His plans for us might be.

But Paul's opening words in his letter to the believers in Galatia make it clear that even when we can't read God's mind, we can know His heart, His heart of love toward us. Our precious Savior "gave Himself . . . to rescue us."

People often make great sacrifices for worthy causes. But we needed to be rescued because we had formed a willing partnership with this "present evil age" (Galatians 1:4). Nonetheless, God loved the world—each of us—so much that He sent Jesus to die for us anyway. Despite our sin, He has delivered us. To Him be glory for ever and ever! Amen.

WEEK 91 • MONDAY

Galatians 3:1–29

GET THE BIG PICTURE

Maybe you've seen a circus sideshow in which the performer hypnotized someone from the audience. We laugh as we watch a dignified adult sit on his haunches and bark like a dog. The believers in Galatia acted even more foolishly. "Are you under a spell?" Paul asks. Note the reason for Paul's astonishment as you read. If time is short, focus on Galatians 3:1–14.

Faith or Observance of the Law

3 You foolish Galatians! Who has
bewitched you? Before your
very eyes Jesus Christ was clearly portrayed as crucified. [2]I would like to learn
just one thing from you: Did you receive
the Spirit by observing the law, or by believing what you heard? [3]Are you so
foolish? After beginning with the Spirit,
are you now trying to attain your goal
by human effort? [4]Have you suffered so
much for nothing—if it really was for
nothing? [5]Does God give you his Spirit
and work miracles among you because
you observe the law, or because you believe what you heard?

[6]Consider Abraham: "He believed
God, and it was credited to him as righteousness."[a] [7]Understand, then, that
those who believe are children of Abraham. [8]The Scripture foresaw that God
would justify the Gentiles by faith, and
announced the gospel in advance to
Abraham: "All nations will be blessed
through you."[b] [9]So those who have faith
are blessed along with Abraham, the
man of faith.

[10]All who rely on observing the law
are under a curse, for it is written:
"Cursed is everyone who does not con-

[a]6 Gen. 15:6 [b]8 Gen. 12:3; 18:18; 22:18

tinue to do everything written in the
Book of the Law."[a] [11]Clearly no one is
justified before God by the law, because,
"The righteous will live by faith."[b] [12]The
law is not based on faith; on the contrary, "The man who does these things
will live by them."[c] [13]Christ redeemed us
from the curse of the law by becoming
a curse for us, for it is written: "Cursed
is everyone who is hung on a tree."[d]
[14]He redeemed us in order that the
blessing given to Abraham might come
to the Gentiles through Christ Jesus, so
that by faith we might receive the promise of the Spirit.

The Law and the Promise

[15]Brothers, let me take an example
from everyday life. Just as no one can set
aside or add to a human covenant that
has been duly established, so it is in this
case. [16]The promises were spoken to
Abraham and to his seed. The Scripture
does not say "and to seeds," meaning
many people, but "and to your seed,"[e]
meaning one person, who is Christ.
[17]What I mean is this: The law, introduced 430 years later, does not set aside
the covenant previously established by
God and thus do away with the promise. [18]For if the inheritance depends on
the law, then it no longer depends on a
promise; but God in his grace gave it to
Abraham through a promise.
[19]What, then, was the purpose of the
law? It was added because of transgressions until the Seed to whom the promise referred had come. The law was put
into effect through angels by a mediator. [20]A mediator, however, does not represent just one party; but God is one.
[21]Is the law, therefore, opposed to the
promises of God? Absolutely not! For if
a law had been given that could impart
life, then righteousness would certainly
have come by the law. [22]But the Scripture declares that the whole world is a
prisoner of sin, so that what was promised, being given through faith in Jesus
Christ, might be given to those who believe.
[23]Before this faith came, we were held
prisoners by the law, locked up until
faith should be revealed. [24]So the law
was put in charge to lead us to Christ[f]
that we might be justified by faith.
[25]Now that faith has come, we are no
longer under the supervision of the law.

Sons of God

[26]You are all sons of God through faith
in Christ Jesus, [27]for all of you who were
baptized into Christ have clothed yourselves with Christ. [28]There is neither Jew
nor Greek, slave nor free, male nor female, for you are all one in Christ Jesus.
[29]If you belong to Christ, then you are
Abraham's seed, and heirs according to
the promise.

[a]*10* Deut. 27:26 [b]*11* Hab. 2:4 [c]*12* Lev. 18:5
[d]*13* Deut. 21:23 [e]*16* Gen. 12:7; 13:15; 24:7
[f]*24* Or *charge until Christ came*

SHARPEN THE FOCUS

Slaves have endured unspeakable, cruel things down through history. And yet, no one has ever slaved for a crueler master than the slave-master about which Paul writes in Galatians 3.

The Law torments its slaves day and night. It always accuses those slaves of not doing enough, not trying hard enough, not having attitudes that are pure enough, not thinking thoughts that are loving enough. The curse of the Law includes most of all the terrible burden of trying to keep it (Galatians 3:10)! No matter how hard we slave for the Law, it's never, ever enough.

Who would willingly submit to that kind of slave master? How foolish! But that's exactly what we ourselves do anytime we let ourselves be tricked into thinking that we can make ourselves more right with God by trying harder.

Take a close look at Galatians 3:2–3. We began our faith-walk as God's Spirit came, by grace, to create faith in us and indwell us, bringing His gifts. Rest assured that God will not leave us on our own to complete the rest of our journey, our sanctification.

WEEK 91 • TUESDAY

Galatians 4:1–31

GET THE BIG PICTURE

As we saw last time, the Galatian Christians had begun to believe a clever, demonic lie. It's a bill of goods Satan still peddles—with great success—today. But the truth of grace is so much more inviting! Would you rather be a slave or an heir? Free or in bondage? Ask yourself those questions as you read. If time is short, focus on Galatians 4:1–20.

4 What I am saying is that as long
as the heir is a child, he is no different from a slave, although he owns
the whole estate. 2He is subject to guardians and trustees until the time set by his
father. 3So also, when we were children,
we were in slavery under the basic principles of the world. 4But when the time
had fully come, God sent his Son, born
of a woman, born under law, 5to redeem
those under law, that we might receive
the full rights of sons. 6Because you are
sons, God sent the Spirit of his Son into
our hearts, the Spirit who calls out,
"Abba,[a] Father." 7So you are no longer a
slave, but a son; and since you are a son,
God has made you also an heir.

Paul's Concern for the Galatians

8Formerly, when you did not know
God, you were slaves to those who by
nature are not gods. 9But now that you
know God—or rather are known by
God—how is it that you are turning
back to those weak and miserable principles? Do you wish to be enslaved by
them all over again? 10You are observing
special days and months and seasons
and years! 11I fear for you, that somehow
I have wasted my efforts on you.

12I plead with you, brothers, become
like me, for I became like you. You have
done me no wrong. 13As you know, it
was because of an illness that I first
preached the gospel to you. 14Even
though my illness was a trial to you, you
did not treat me with contempt or scorn.
Instead, you welcomed me as if I were
an angel of God, as if I were Christ Jesus
himself. 15What has happened to all
your joy? I can testify that, if you could
have done so, you would have torn out
your eyes and given them to me. 16Have
I now become your enemy by telling
you the truth?

17Those people are zealous to win you
over, but for no good. What they want
is to alienate you ⌊from us⌋, so that you
may be zealous for them. 18It is fine to be
zealous, provided the purpose is good,
and to be so always and not just when I
am with you. 19My dear children, for
whom I am again in the pains of childbirth until Christ is formed in you, 20how
I wish I could be with you now and
change my tone, because I am perplexed about you!

Hagar and Sarah

21Tell me, you who want to be under
the law, are you not aware of what the
law says? 22For it is written that Abra-

[a]6 Aramaic for *Father*

ham had two sons, one by the slave
woman and the other by the free woman. [23]His son by the slave woman was
born in the ordinary way; but his son by
the free woman was born as the result
of a promise.
[24]These things may be taken figuratively, for the women represent two
covenants. One covenant is from Mount
Sinai and bears children who are to be
slaves: This is Hagar. [25]Now Hagar
stands for Mount Sinai in Arabia and
corresponds to the present city of Jerusalem, because she is in slavery with her
children. [26]But the Jerusalem that is
above is free, and she is our mother. [27]For
it is written:

"Be glad, O barren woman,
who bears no children;
break forth and cry aloud,
you who have no labor pains;
because more are the children of the
desolate woman
than of her who has a husband."[a]

[28]Now you, brothers, like Isaac, are
children of promise. [29]At that time the
son born in the ordinary way persecuted the son born by the power of the
Spirit. It is the same now. [30]But what
does the Scripture say? "Get rid of the
slave woman and her son, for the slave
woman's son will never share in the inheritance with the free woman's son."[b]
[31]Therefore, brothers, we are not children of the slave woman, but of the free
woman.

[a]27 Isaiah 54:1 [b]30 Gen. 21:10

SHARPEN THE FOCUS

The book of Galatians is the Christian's glorious Emancipation Proclamation. It's our copy of the last will and testament that names us heirs of all heaven's riches.

"You want to be Abraham's children?" Paul asks in Galatians 4:21–31. "Then remember that Abraham had *two* sons: One born to the slave, Hagar (Genesis 16), and one born to his wife, Sarah (Genesis 21). Only Sarah's son, Isaac, inherited Abraham's estate. Only Isaac carried God's covenant promises."

Paul's argument is this: not everyone born with Abraham's genes can call himself or herself a descendant of Abraham. Only those who are the "children of promise" (Galatians 4:28). In Jesus, by faith in Jesus, all that God promised to Abraham belongs to us. With believing Isaac, we are God's adopted children (Galatians 4:5), Abraham's descendants, heirs of the promises God has made to His family (Galatians 3:29, 4:7).

When we remember all that our Lord has done for us, His heirs and children, we can face all of life with joy—that deep down contentment and peace that never leaves, not even in times of trouble.

WEEK 91 • WEDNESDAY

Galatians 5:1—6:18

GET THE BIG PICTURE

What does Christian freedom look like once we leave the church and re-enter everyday life? In the last two chapters of Galatians Paul answers that question. He does not propose a prescription. Instead, he lays out a description of the Christian lifestyle. What pictures come to mind as you read it? If time is short, focus on Galatians 5:1–25.

Freedom in Christ

5 It is for freedom that Christ has set us free. Stand firm, then, and do not let yourselves be burdened again by a yoke of slavery.

2Mark my words! I, Paul, tell you that if you let yourselves be circumcised, Christ will be of no value to you at all. 3Again I declare to every man who lets himself be circumcised that he is obligated to obey the whole law. 4You who are trying to be justified by law have been alienated from Christ; you have fallen away from grace. 5But by faith we eagerly await through the Spirit the righteousness for which we hope. 6For in Christ Jesus neither circumcision nor uncircumcision has any value. The only thing that counts is faith expressing itself through love.

7You were running a good race. Who cut in on you and kept you from obeying the truth? 8That kind of persuasion does not come from the one who calls you. 9"A little yeast works through the whole batch of dough." 10I am confident in the Lord that you will take no other view. The one who is throwing you into confusion will pay the penalty, whoever he may be. 11Brothers, if I am still preaching circumcision, why am I still being persecuted? In that case the offense of the cross has been abolished. 12As for those agitators, I wish they would go the whole way and emasculate themselves!

13You, my brothers, were called to be free. But do not use your freedom to indulge the sinful nature[a]; rather, serve one another in love. 14The entire law is summed up in a single command: "Love your neighbor as yourself."[b] 15If you keep on biting and devouring each other, watch out or you will be destroyed by each other.

Life by the Spirit

16So I say, live by the Spirit, and you will not gratify the desires of the sinful nature. 17For the sinful nature desires what is contrary to the Spirit, and the Spirit what is contrary to the sinful nature. They are in conflict with each other, so that you do not do what you want. 18But if you are led by the Spirit, you are not under law.

19The acts of the sinful nature are obvious: sexual immorality, impurity and debauchery; 20idolatry and witchcraft; hatred, discord, jealousy, fits of rage, selfish ambition, dissensions, factions 21and envy; drunkenness, orgies, and the like. I warn you, as I did before, that those who live like this will not inherit the kingdom of God.

22But the fruit of the Spirit is love, joy, peace, patience, kindness, goodness, faithfulness, 23gentleness and self-control. Against such things there is no law. 24Those who belong to Christ Jesus have crucified the sinful nature with its passions and desires. 25Since we live by the Spirit, let us keep in step with the Spirit. 26Let us not become conceited, provoking and envying each other.

Doing Good to All

6 Brothers, if someone is caught in a sin, you who are spiritual should restore him gently. But watch yourself, or you also may be tempted. 2Carry each other's burdens, and in this way you will fulfill the law of Christ. 3If anyone thinks he is something when he is nothing, he deceives himself. 4Each one should test his own actions. Then he can take pride in himself, without comparing himself to somebody else, 5for each one should carry his own load.

6Anyone who receives instruction in the word must share all good things with his instructor.

7Do not be deceived: God cannot be mocked. A man reaps what he sows. 8The one who sows to please his sinful nature, from that nature[c] will reap de-

[a]13 Or *the flesh;* also in verses 16, 17, 19 and 24
[b]14 Lev. 19:18 [c]8 Or *his flesh, from the flesh*

struction; the one who sows to please the Spirit, from the Spirit will reap eternal life. [9]Let us not become weary in doing good, for at the proper time we will reap a harvest if we do not give up. [10]Therefore, as we have opportunity, let us do good to all people, especially to those who belong to the family of believers.

Not Circumcision but a New Creation

[11]See what large letters I use as I write to you with my own hand!

[12]Those who want to make a good impression outwardly are trying to compel you to be circumcised. The only reason they do this is to avoid being persecuted for the cross of Christ. [13]Not even those who are circumcised obey the law, yet they want you to be circumcised that they may boast about your flesh. [14]May I never boast except in the cross of our Lord Jesus Christ, through which[a] the world has been crucified to me, and I to the world. [15]Neither circumcision nor uncircumcision means anything; what counts is a new creation. [16]Peace and mercy to all who follow this rule, even to the Israel of God.

[17]Finally, let no one cause me trouble, for I bear on my body the marks of Jesus.

[18]The grace of our Lord Jesus Christ be with your spirit, brothers. Amen.

[a]14 Or *whom*

SHARPEN THE FOCUS

Life lived in slavery to the Law is like a forced march with a hundred-pound knapsack over rough terrain. Never joyful or easy, it quickly becomes impossible.

Life in the Spirit, life lived under the Gospel, frees us for joy, for peace, for giving and receiving love. This kind of walk is more of a dance, a thing of grace and tireless beauty.

Ballroom dancing has experienced a resurgence in popularity in recent years. That kind of dancing has certain defined movements, but no one follows rules. No one keeps score. There are no losers. The object is to move gracefully, keeping in step with your partner and enjoying the activity together. The more experience a couple has, the less they think about where to move next. Instead, they begin to flow together, to move instinctively as one along the floor.

So with us. In grace, God has called us to life in the Spirit. As we grow in faith, our Father continues to form the image of Christ in us (Galatians 4:19). And we, by grace, begin to flow in line with the will of God for our lives. We keep in step with God's Spirit, not by trying hard, but simply doing God's will as His forgiven, dearly-loved, Spirit-empowered children.

EPHESIANS

WEEK 91 • THURSDAY

Ephesians 1:1–23

GET THE BIG PICTURE

In Christ. You will read that phrase or something equivalent to it nearly thirty-five times in this letter to the Ephesians. As you study Chapter 1, see if you can figure out what it means to be "in Christ." If time is short, focus on Ephesians 1:1–14.

1 Paul, an apostle of Christ Jesus by the will of God,

To the saints in Ephesus,[a] the faithful[b] in Christ Jesus:

2 Grace and peace to you from God our Father and the Lord Jesus Christ.

Spiritual Blessings in Christ

3 Praise be to the God and Father of our Lord Jesus Christ, who has blessed us in the heavenly realms with every spiritual blessing in Christ. 4 For he chose us in him before the creation of the world to be holy and blameless in his sight. In love 5 he[c] predestined us to be adopted as his sons through Jesus Christ, in accordance with his pleasure and will— 6 to the praise of his glorious grace, which he has freely given us in the One he loves. 7 In him we have redemption through his blood, the forgiveness of sins, in accordance with the riches of God's grace 8 that he lavished on us with all wisdom and understanding. 9 And he[d] made known to us the mystery of his will according to his good pleasure, which he purposed in Christ, 10 to be put into effect when the times will have reached their fulfillment—to bring all things in heaven and on earth together under one head, even Christ.

11 In him we were also chosen,[e] having been predestined according to the plan of him who works out everything in conformity with the purpose of his will, 12 in order that we, who were the first to hope in Christ, might be for the praise of his glory. 13 And you also were included in Christ when you heard the word of truth, the gospel of your salvation. Having believed, you were marked in him with a seal, the promised Holy Spirit, 14 who is a deposit guaranteeing our inheritance until the redemption of those who are God's possession—to the praise of his glory.

Thanksgiving and Prayer

15 For this reason, ever since I heard about your faith in the Lord Jesus and your love for all the saints, 16 I have not stopped giving thanks for you, remembering you in my prayers. 17 I keep asking that the God of our Lord Jesus Christ, the glorious Father, may give you the Spirit[f] of wisdom and revelation, so that you may know him better. 18 I pray also that the eyes of your heart may be

[a] 1 Some early manuscripts do not have *in Ephesus.* [b] 1 Or *believers who are* [c] 4,5 Or *sight in love.* [5] *He* [d] 8,9 Or *us. With all wisdom and understanding,* [9] *he* [e] 11 Or *were made heirs* [f] 17 Or *a spirit*

enlightened in order that you may
know the hope to which he has called
you, the riches of his glorious inheritance in the saints, [19]and his incompara-
bly great power for us who believe. That
power is like the working of his mighty
strength, [20]which he exerted in Christ
when he raised him from the dead and
seated him at his right hand in the heavenly realms, [21]far above all rule and authority, power and dominion, and every
title that can be given, not only in the
present age but also in the one to come.
[22]And God placed all things under his
feet and appointed him to be head over
everything for the church, [23]which is his
body, the fullness of him who fills everything in every way.

SHARPEN THE FOCUS

Have you ever found yourself so excited that when you met a friend, you blurted out all your good news in one breath?

That's the feeling behind Ephesians 1. Paul is just bursting to tell the believers in Ephesus all God has done for them—and for all His people of every time and place. Our Lord has:

- blessed and chosen us (Ephesians 1:3–4);
- loved and adopted us (Ephesians 1:4–5);
- redeemed and forgiven us (Ephesians 1:7);
- lavished His grace on us (Ephesians 1:8);
- revealed to us His mystery, His plan to create the church and unite it with Himself (Ephesians 1:9–10);
- sealed us with the Holy Spirit and guaranteed to us our heavenly inheritance (Ephesians 1:13–14).

Any one of those things would be enough to make us burst out in praise. This list of benefits outdoes anything available anywhere else in the universe! Considering what we really deserve for our sins, God's goodness revealed here should make us eternally thankful.

And still, the sin that clings to us keeps us from the joy our Lord would create in us. As you examine your own attitude today, ask the Holy Spirit to point out and cut away any hardness in your heart. Then read Ephesians 1:3–14 as God's absolution and re-affirmation of His love—for you!

WEEK 91 • FRIDAY

Ephesians 2:1–22

GET THE BIG PICTURE

Paul plunges headlong into God's grace in Ephesians 2. The first seven verses are one sentence in the original text. The grace of God so moves the apostle that he barely pauses to take a breath as he proclaims it. Note the "before" and "after" comparisons he makes in this chapter. If time is short, focus on Ephesians 2:1–10.

Made Alive in Christ

2 As for you, you were dead in
your transgressions and sins, 2in
which you used to live when you followed the ways of this world and of the
ruler of the kingdom of the air, the spirit
who is now at work in those who are
disobedient. 3All of us also lived among
them at one time, gratifying the cravings of our sinful nature[a] and following
its desires and thoughts. Like the rest,
we were by nature objects of wrath. 4But
because of his great love for us, God,
who is rich in mercy, 5made us alive with
Christ even when we were dead in
transgressions—it is by grace you have
been saved. 6And God raised us up with
Christ and seated us with him in the
heavenly realms in Christ Jesus, 7in order that in the coming ages he might
show the incomparable riches of his
grace, expressed in his kindness to us in
Christ Jesus. 8For it is by grace you have
been saved, through faith—and this not
from yourselves, it is the gift of God—
9not by works, so that no one can boast.
10For we are God's workmanship, created in Christ Jesus to do good works,
which God prepared in advance for us
to do.

One in Christ

11Therefore, remember that formerly
you who are Gentiles by birth and called
"uncircumcised" by those who call
themselves "the circumcision" (that
done in the body by the hands of
men)— 12remember that at that time
you were separate from Christ, excluded from citizenship in Israel and
foreigners to the covenants of the promise, without hope and without God in
the world. 13But now in Christ Jesus you
who once were far away have been
brought near through the blood of
Christ.

14For he himself is our peace, who has
made the two one and has destroyed
the barrier, the dividing wall of hostility, 15by abolishing in his flesh the law
with its commandments and regulations. His purpose was to create in himself one new man out of the two, thus
making peace, 16and in this one body to
reconcile both of them to God through
the cross, by which he put to death their
hostility. 17He came and preached peace
to you who were far away and peace to
those who were near. 18For through him
we both have access to the Father by
one Spirit.

19Consequently, you are no longer foreigners and aliens, but fellow citizens
with God's people and members of
God's household, 20built on the foundation of the apostles and prophets, with
Christ Jesus himself as the chief cornerstone. 21In him the whole building is
joined together and rises to become a
holy temple in the Lord. 22And in him
you too are being built together to become a dwelling in which God lives by
his Spirit.

[a]3 Or *our flesh*

SHARPEN THE FOCUS

In ancient times, kings who fought and won great battles would set up a pillar for each victory. The story of each victory would be inscribed on its own pillar. Each pillar thus honored the victor and presumably elevated him in the eyes of his subjects—friend and foe alike.

Our Savior-God has inscribed the story of His victories, too, but not on stone pillars. Each of us, His children, carries the mark of that victory. He has inscribed the story of His love on our lives. He has redeemed, restored, and forgiven us in Jesus, giving us new life:

> *in order that in the coming ages He might show [display, demonstrate] the incomparable riches of His grace, expressed in His kindness to us in Christ Jesus.* (Ephesians 2:7)

Throughout eternity, we will be living, breathing, walking reminders to one another and to all the angels of heaven (and hell) of God's mercy.

Even so, we need not wait until then. Right now, today, you can declare the glory of your Savior and His victory over sin and death. Think about what you say and about what you do in that light as you interact with others today. ☼

WEEK 91 • SATURDAY

Ephesians 3:1–21

God created us for community, for relationship. No one in the early church would have understood the "just Jesus and me" attitude that infects much North American Christianity today. Read to see how Paul elaborates on the "mystery," the church, in Ephesians 3. If time is short, focus on Ephesians 3:1–13.

Paul the Preacher to the Gentiles

3 For this reason I, Paul, the prisoner of Christ Jesus for the sake
of you Gentiles—
2Surely you have heard about the administration of God's grace that was
given to me for you, 3that is, the mystery
made known to me by revelation, as I
have already written briefly. 4In reading
this, then, you will be able to understand my insight into the mystery of
Christ, 5which was not made known to
men in other generations as it has now
been revealed by the Spirit to God's
holy apostles and prophets. 6This mystery is that through the gospel the Gentiles are heirs together with Israel,
members together of one body, and
sharers together in the promise in Christ
Jesus.
7I became a servant of this gospel by
the gift of God's grace given me through
the working of his power. 8Although I
am less than the least of all God's people, this grace was given me: to preach
to the Gentiles the unsearchable riches
of Christ, 9and to make plain to everyone the administration of this mystery,
which for ages past was kept hidden in
God, who created all things. 10His intent
was that now, through the church, the
manifold wisdom of God should be
made known to the rulers and authorities in the heavenly realms, 11according
to his eternal purpose which he accomplished in Christ Jesus our Lord. 12In
him and through faith in him we may
approach God with freedom and confidence. 13I ask you, therefore, not to be
discouraged because of my sufferings
for you, which are your glory.

A Prayer for the Ephesians

14For this reason I kneel before the
Father, 15from whom his whole family[a]
in heaven and on earth derives its name.
16I pray that out of his glorious riches he
may strengthen you with power
through his Spirit in your inner being,
17so that Christ may dwell in your hearts
through faith. And I pray that you, being rooted and established in love,
18may have power, together with all
the saints, to grasp how wide and
long and high and deep is the love of
Christ, 19and to know this love that

[a]15 Or *whom all fatherhood*

surpasses knowledge—that you may be
filled to the measure of all the fullness
of God.
20 Now to him who is able to do immea-
surably more than all we ask or imagine,
according to his power that is at work
within us, 21 to him be glory in the
church and in Christ Jesus throughout
all generations, for ever and ever!
Amen.

SHARPEN THE FOCUS

It may not seem like much of a mystery to us. Many Christians have even committed this summary of it to memory: "[God] wants all men to be saved and to come to a knowledge of the truth" (1 Timothy 2:4).

Under the old covenant, this truth shone only as a faint glow on the horizon (Ephesians 3:5). Many in Old Testament Israel, in fact, excluded all Gentiles as they thought about God's chosen people. Truth be told, God never hid His love for those outside Israel. But few in Israel wanted to see it.

As Paul meditated on the church, though, the Holy Spirit revealed God's mystery in all its blazing glory (Ephesians 3:4–5). Paul saw that our Lord sets aside all racial and ethnic distinctions as He creates His family in Christ.

When we come to our Father's throne in prayer (Ephesians 2:18; 3:12), we do not come alone. All Christians stand together there on level ground. We all receive the same forgiveness for our sins. We all wear the same robe of righteousness Jesus purchased for us by His perfect life and bloody death. We all need our brothers and sisters to comfort us, challenge us, encourage us, and cheer us on. We all—together—bring God glory (Ephesians 3:21).

WEEK 92• MONDAY

Ephesians 4:1–32

GET THE BIG PICTURE

All the truth Paul has proclaimed so far in Ephesians carries marvelous implications. Since all these things are true, now what? That's the question he answers in Ephesians 4, 5, and 6. As you read today, notice once again the new identity we have received in Christ. If time is short, focus on Ephesians 4:17–32.

Unity in the Body of Christ

4 As a prisoner for the Lord, then,
I urge you to live a life worthy
of the calling you have received. 2 Be
completely humble and gentle; be patient, bearing with one another in love.
3 Make every effort to keep the unity of
the Spirit through the bond of peace.
4 There is one body and one Spirit—just
as you were called to one hope when
you were called— 5 one Lord, one faith,
one baptism; 6 one God and Father of all,
who is over all and through all and in
all.
7 But to each one of us grace has been
given as Christ apportioned it. 8 This is
why it[a] says:

[a] 8 Or *God*

"When he ascended on high,
  he led captives in his train
  and gave gifts to men."[a]

9(What does "he ascended" mean except that he also descended to the lower, earthly regions[b]? 10He who descended is the very one who ascended higher than all the heavens, in order to fill the whole universe.) 11It was he who gave some to be apostles, some to be prophets, some to be evangelists, and some to be pastors and teachers, 12to prepare God's people for works of service, so that the body of Christ may be built up 13until we all reach unity in the faith and in the knowledge of the Son of God and become mature, attaining to the whole measure of the fullness of Christ.

14Then we will no longer be infants, tossed back and forth by the waves, and blown here and there by every wind of teaching and by the cunning and craftiness of men in their deceitful scheming. 15Instead, speaking the truth in love, we will in all things grow up into him who is the Head, that is, Christ. 16From him the whole body, joined and held together by every supporting ligament, grows and builds itself up in love, as each part does its work.

Living as Children of Light

17So I tell you this, and insist on it in the Lord, that you must no longer live as the Gentiles do, in the futility of their thinking. 18They are darkened in their understanding and separated from the life of God because of the ignorance that is in them due to the hardening of their hearts. 19Having lost all sensitivity, they have given themselves over to sensuality so as to indulge in every kind of impurity, with a continual lust for more.

20You, however, did not come to know Christ that way. 21Surely you heard of him and were taught in him in accordance with the truth that is in Jesus. 22You were taught, with regard to your former way of life, to put off your old self, which is being corrupted by its deceitful desires; 23to be made new in the attitude of your minds; 24and to put on the new self, created to be like God in true righteousness and holiness.

25Therefore each of you must put off falsehood and speak truthfully to his neighbor, for we are all members of one body. 26"In your anger do not sin"[c]: Do not let the sun go down while you are still angry, 27and do not give the devil a foothold. 28He who has been stealing must steal no longer, but must work, doing something useful with his own hands, that he may have something to share with those in need.

29Do not let any unwholesome talk come out of your mouths, but only what is helpful for building others up according to their needs, that it may benefit those who listen. 30And do not grieve the Holy Spirit of God, with whom you were sealed for the day of redemption. 31Get rid of all bitterness, rage and anger, brawling and slander, along with every form of malice. 32Be kind and compassionate to one another, forgiving each other, just as in Christ God forgave you.

[a]8 Psalm 68:18 [b]9 Or *the depths of the earth*
[c]26 Psalm 4:4

SHARPEN THE FOCUS

No one would expect to find the Queen of England dressed in full royal robes and crown crawling out from under her limousine after having changed the oil. Yet, as Paul points out in Ephesians 4, something very like that can happen in our walk with the Savior.

Paul insists (Ephesians 4:17) that we no longer follow the lifestyle of those who don't know Christ (Ephesians 4:18–19). We have been taught the truth. When we came to faith, "we put off [our] old self" (Ephesians 4:22) once and for all. By God's grace through faith in Jesus we have become new.

In our Baptism, God draped the royal robe of righteousness across our shoulders. We have been re-created "to be like God in true righteousness and holiness" (Ephesians 4:24). Since that is true, why would we want to act as though we still wore the rags of our old life? Why would we flirt with the things that will stain us—dishonesty, bitterness, gossip, or slander?

We are the children of God, sons and daughters of the King! We no longer want to indulge in any kind of impurity. God creates in us a longing to be like Jesus and continually works in our hearts through His Word to fill that longing.

WEEK 92• TUESDAY

Ephesians 5:1—6:24

GET THE BIG PICTURE

The further north of the equator you live, the greater the chances you've noticed the amount of daylight decreasing in early fall. Residents of the far north, for instance Alaska, lose about 11 minutes of daylight each day that time of year. Paul has a lot to say about another kind of light and darkness in Ephesians 5 and 6. Notice that word-picture as you read. If time is short, focus on Ephesians 5:1–21.

5 Be imitators of God, therefore, as
dearly loved children [2]and live a
life of love, just as Christ loved us and
gave himself up for us as a fragrant offering and sacrifice to God.
[3]But among you there must not be
even a hint of sexual immorality, or of
any kind of impurity, or of greed, because these are improper for God's holy
people. [4]Nor should there be obscenity,
foolish talk or coarse joking, which are
out of place, but rather thanksgiving.
[5]For of this you can be sure: No immoral, impure or greedy person—such a
man is an idolater—has any inheritance
in the kingdom of Christ and of God.[a]
[6]Let no one deceive you with empty
words, for because of such things God's
wrath comes on those who are disobedient. [7]Therefore do not be partners
with them.
[8]For you were once darkness, but now
you are light in the Lord. Live as children of light [9](for the fruit of the light
consists in all goodness, righteousness
and truth) [10]and find out what pleases
the Lord. [11]Have nothing to do with the
fruitless deeds of darkness, but rather
expose them. [12]For it is shameful even to
mention what the disobedient do in secret. [13]But everything exposed by the
light becomes visible, [14]for it is light that
makes everything visible. This is why it
is said:

"Wake up, O sleeper,
rise from the dead,
and Christ will shine on you."

[15]Be very careful, then, how you
live—not as unwise but as wise, [16]mak-
ing the most of every opportunity, because the days are evil. [17]Therefore do
not be foolish, but understand what the
Lord's will is. [18]Do not get drunk on
wine, which leads to debauchery. Instead, be filled with the Spirit. [19]Speak
to one another with psalms, hymns
and spiritual songs. Sing and make
music in your heart to the Lord, [20]always
giving thanks to God the Father for ev-

[a]5 Or *kingdom of the Christ and God*

erything, in the name of our Lord Jesus
Christ.
[21]Submit to one another out of reverence for Christ.

Wives and Husbands

[22]Wives, submit to your husbands as
to the Lord. [23]For the husband is the
head of the wife as Christ is the head of
the church, his body, of which he is the
Savior. [24]Now as the church submits to
Christ, so also wives should submit to
their husbands in everything.
[25]Husbands, love your wives, just as
Christ loved the church and gave himself up for her [26]to make her holy,
cleansing[a] her by the washing with water through the word, [27]and to present
her to himself as a radiant church, without stain or wrinkle or any other blemish, but holy and blameless. [28]In this
same way, husbands ought to love their
wives as their own bodies. He who loves
his wife loves himself. [29]After all, no one
ever hated his own body, but he feeds
and cares for it, just as Christ does the
church— [30]for we are members of his
body. [31]"For this reason a man will leave
his father and mother and be united to
his wife, and the two will become one
flesh."[b] [32]This is a profound mystery—
but I am talking about Christ and the
church. [33]However, each one of you
also must love his wife as he loves himself, and the wife must respect her husband.

Children and Parents

6 Children, obey your parents in
the Lord, for this is right.
[2]"Honor your father and mother"—
which is the first commandment with a
promise— [3]"that it may go well with
you and that you may enjoy long life on
the earth."[c]
[4]Fathers, do not exasperate your children; instead, bring them up in the
training and instruction of the Lord.

Slaves and Masters

[5]Slaves, obey your earthly masters
with respect and fear, and with sincerity of heart, just as you would obey
Christ. [6]Obey them not only to win their
favor when their eye is on you, but like
slaves of Christ, doing the will of God
from your heart. [7]Serve wholeheartedly,
as if you were serving the Lord, not
men, [8]because you know that the Lord
will reward everyone for whatever
good he does, whether he is slave or
free.
[9]And masters, treat your slaves in the
same way. Do not threaten them, since
you know that he who is both their Master and yours is in heaven, and there is
no favoritism with him.

The Armor of God

[10]Finally, be strong in the Lord and in
his mighty power. [11]Put on the full armor of God so that you can take your
stand against the devil's schemes. [12]For
our struggle is not against flesh and
blood, but against the rulers, against the
authorities, against the powers of this
dark world and against the spiritual
forces of evil in the heavenly realms.
[13]Therefore put on the full armor of
God, so that when the day of evil comes,
you may be able to stand your ground,
and after you have done everything, to
stand. [14]Stand firm then, with the belt of
truth buckled around your waist, with
the breastplate of righteousness in
place, [15]and with your feet fitted with
the readiness that comes from the gospel of peace. [16]In addition to all this, take
up the shield of faith, with which you
can extinguish all the flaming arrows of
the evil one. [17]Take the helmet of salvation and the sword of the Spirit, which
is the word of God. [18]And pray in the
Spirit on all occasions with all kinds of
prayers and requests. With this in mind,
be alert and always keep on praying for
all the saints.
[19]Pray also for me, that whenever I
open my mouth, words may be given
me so that I will fearlessly make known
the mystery of the gospel, [20]for which I
am an ambassador in chains. Pray that
I may declare it fearlessly, as I should.

[a]26 Or *having cleansed* [b]31 Gen. 2:24
[c]3 Deut. 5:16

Final Greetings

[21]Tychicus, the dear brother and faithful servant in the Lord, will tell you everything, so that you also may know how I am and what I am doing. [22]I am sending him to you for this very purpose, that you may know how we are, and that he may encourage you.

[23]Peace to the brothers, and love with faith from God the Father and the Lord Jesus Christ. [24]Grace to all who love our Lord Jesus Christ with an undying love.

SHARPEN THE FOCUS

God's Word is a "lamp for [our] feet and a light for [our] path" (Psalm 119:105). Especially in Jesus, the Word made flesh, the Light of the world, we receive the insight and power we need so that we can avoid stumbling around in ungodliness.

Ephesians 5:18–21 has a lot to say about the process by which we plug into that power. "Keep on letting yourselves be filled in spirit"—that's one way Ephesians 5:18b could be translated.

Many people in the world try to fill their own emptiness by getting drugged or drunk. But our Lord urges us to let Him fill us to overflowing. His love and peace are more than enough to ease the ache of emptiness, the pain of loneliness.

As we open the Scripture, as we kneel at the Lord's Table, as we hear God's Word spoken by our brothers and sisters in Christ, God's Spirit keeps on filling us. When that happens, we can watch God's love overflow from our hearts into the lives of others as we "speak to one another with psalms, hymns, and spiritual songs," as we "sing and make music in [our] heart to the Lord," and as we give "thanks to God the Father for everything, in the name of our Lord Jesus Christ" (Ephesians 5:19–20).

PHILIPPIANS

WEEK 92 • WEDNESDAY

Philippians 1:1–30

When Solomon wrote Ecclesiastes, he expressed the hopelessness and futility of life lived "under the sun." That kind of life, lived without the Lord, remains empty and becomes meaningless. Solomon wrote from a palace; Paul wrote to the Philippians from a prison cell. But Philippians resounds with hope and joy. As you read, note this contrast and look for the reason Paul could live above his circumstances. If time is short, focus on Philippians 1:1–24.

1 Paul and Timothy, servants of
Christ Jesus,

To all the saints in Christ Jesus at Philippi, together with the overseers[a] and
deacons:

[2]Grace and peace to you from God
our Father and the Lord Jesus Christ.

Thanksgiving and Prayer

[3]I thank my God every time I remember you. [4]In all my prayers for all of you,
I always pray with joy [5]because of your
partnership in the gospel from the first
day until now, [6]being confident of this,
that he who began a good work in you
will carry it on to completion until the
day of Christ Jesus.

[7]It is right for me to feel this way
about all of you, since I have you in my
heart; for whether I am in chains or defending and confirming the gospel, all
of you share in God's grace with me.
[8]God can testify how I long for all of you
with the affection of Christ Jesus.

[9]And this is my prayer: that your love
may abound more and more in knowledge and depth of insight, [10]so that you
may be able to discern what is best and
may be pure and blameless until the day
of Christ, [11]filled with the fruit of righteousness that comes through Jesus
Christ—to the glory and praise of God.

Paul's Chains Advance the Gospel

[12]Now I want you to know, brothers,
that what has happened to me has
really served to advance the gospel. [13]As
a result, it has become clear throughout
the whole palace guard[b] and to everyone else that I am in chains for Christ.
[14]Because of my chains, most of the
brothers in the Lord have been encouraged to speak the word of God more
courageously and fearlessly.

[15]It is true that some preach Christ out
of envy and rivalry, but others out of
goodwill. [16]The latter do so in love,
knowing that I am put here for the defense of the gospel. [17]The former preach
Christ out of selfish ambition, not sincerely, supposing that they can stir up
trouble for me while I am in chains.[c]
[18]But what does it matter? The important thing is that in every way, whether
from false motives or true, Christ is

[a]*1* Traditionally *bishops* [b]*13* Or *whole palace*
[c]*16,17* Some late manuscripts have verses 16 and 17 in reverse order.

preached. And because of this I rejoice.
Yes, and I will continue to rejoice, [19]for
I know that through your prayers and
the help given by the Spirit of Jesus
Christ, what has happened to me will
turn out for my deliverance.[a] [20]I eagerly
expect and hope that I will in no way be
ashamed, but will have sufficient courage so that now as always Christ will be
exalted in my body, whether by life or
by death. [21]For to me, to live is Christ
and to die is gain. [22]If I am to go on living in the body, this will mean fruitful
labor for me. Yet what shall I choose? I
do not know! [23]I am torn between the
two: I desire to depart and be with
Christ, which is better by far; [24]but it is
more necessary for you that I remain in
the body. [25]Convinced of this, I know
that I will remain, and I will continue
with all of you for your progress and joy
in the faith, [26]so that through my being
with you again your joy in Christ Jesus
will overflow on account of me.
[27]Whatever happens, conduct yourselves in a manner worthy of the gospel
of Christ. Then, whether I come and see
you or only hear about you in my absence, I will know that you stand firm
in one spirit, contending as one man for
the faith of the gospel [28]without being
frightened in any way by those who oppose you. This is a sign to them that they
will be destroyed, but that you will be
saved—and that by God. [29]For it has
been granted to you on behalf of Christ
not only to believe on him, but also to
suffer for him, [30]since you are going
through the same struggle you saw I
had, and now hear that I still have.

[a]19 Or *salvation*

SHARPEN THE FOCUS

No matter what happens, I'll be okay. No matter what! That's the faith Paul expresses in Philippians 1:19–20. Can you say that, too? Can you say it as you look at the struggles in your family? As you consider the challenges you face on the job? As you look at the financial needs you face, both now and in the future? As you stare into the teeth of death?

Without Christ, where would we be as we walked through life? Even the most exotic palace can't shelter us from what Shakespeare called "the slings and arrows of outrageous fortune." But with Paul we live in Christ. He is our refuge. With Paul we too can say:

> *I know that through [the prayers of the saints] and the help given by the Spirit of Jesus Christ, what has happened to me will turn out for my deliverance. I eagerly expect and hope that I will in no way be ashamed, but will have sufficient courage so that now as always Christ will be exalted in my body, whether by life or by death.*
> (Philippians 1:19–20)

Paul's thank-you note to the believers in Philippi, begun in chapter 1, continues. Paul encourages the Philippians to remain united with Christ and with one another. Notice how humility undergirds their unity in the faith. If time is short, focus on Philippians 2:1–18.

Imitating Christ's Humility

2 If you have any encouragement
from being united with Christ, if
any comfort from his love, if any fellowship with the Spirit, if any tenderness
and compassion, [2]then make my joy
complete by being like-minded, having
the same love, being one in spirit and
purpose. [3]Do nothing out of selfish ambition or vain conceit, but in humility
consider others better than yourselves.
[4]Each of you should look not only to
your own interests, but also to the interests of others.
[5]Your attitude should be the same as
that of Christ Jesus:

[6]Who, being in very nature[a] God,
did not consider equality with
God something to be
grasped,
[7]but made himself nothing,
taking the very nature[b] of a
servant,
being made in human likeness.
[8]And being found in appearance as a
man,
he humbled himself
and became obedient to death—
even death on a cross!
[9]Therefore God exalted him to the
highest place
and gave him the name that is
above every name,
[10]that at the name of Jesus every knee
should bow,
in heaven and on earth and under
the earth,
[11]and every tongue confess that Jesus
Christ is Lord,
to the glory of God the Father.

Shining as Stars

[12]Therefore, my dear friends, as you
have always obeyed—not only in my
presence, but now much more in my absence—continue to work out your salvation with fear and trembling, [13]for it
is God who works in you to will and to
act according to his good purpose.
[14]Do everything without complaining
or arguing, [15]so that you may become
blameless and pure, children of God
without fault in a crooked and depraved
generation, in which you shine like stars
in the universe [16]as you hold out[c] the
word of life—in order that I may boast
on the day of Christ that I did not run
or labor for nothing. [17]But even if I am
being poured out like a drink offering
on the sacrifice and service coming from
your faith, I am glad and rejoice with all
of you. [18]So you too should be glad and
rejoice with me.

Timothy and Epaphroditus

[19]I hope in the Lord Jesus to send
Timothy to you soon, that I also may be
cheered when I receive news about you.
[20]I have no one else like him, who takes
a genuine interest in your welfare. [21]For
everyone looks out for his own interests, not those of Jesus Christ. [22]But you

[a]6 Or *in the form of* [b]7 Or *the form*
[c]16 Or *hold on to*

know that Timothy has proved himself,
because as a son with his father he has
served with me in the work of the gospel. 23I hope, therefore, to send him as
soon as I see how things go with me.
24And I am confident in the Lord that I
myself will come soon.
25But I think it is necessary to send
back to you Epaphroditus, my brother,
fellow worker and fellow soldier, who
is also your messenger, whom you
sent to take care of my needs. 26For he
longs for all of you and is distressed
because you heard he was ill. 27Indeed
he was ill, and almost died. But God had
mercy on him, and not on him only but
also on me, to spare me sorrow upon
sorrow. 28Therefore I am all the more
eager to send him, so that when you
see him again you may be glad and I
may have less anxiety. 29Welcome him in
the Lord with great joy, and honor men
like him, 30because he almost died for
the work of Christ, risking his life to
make up for the help you could not
give me.

SHARPEN THE FOCUS

As Paul makes clear in Philippians 2, self-forgetfulness is the essence of humility. Christ Jesus saw the mortal danger we had placed ourselves in by our sins. Without thinking about Himself or what He would be giving up, He threw aside His rights as the Son of God. He gave up the glories of heaven and stripped Himself of the absolute powers that rightly belonged to Him.

"He humbled Himself and became obedient to death" (Philippians 2:8). We can almost hear Paul gasp in wonder at the words he adds next: "even death on a cross!" Those who lived in the first century Roman Empire knew much better than we the agony and shame of crucifixion.

And yet, self-forgetful for our sakes, Jesus endured it so that we would be united with Him now and forever. That unity makes possible another unity—the oneness of mind and purpose Paul describes in Philippians 2:1–4.

Christ's love flowing to us emboldens us to believe God will meet our needs. That faith frees us then to go about meeting the needs of one another. We focus, by grace, on serving others and find in that service true joy flooding our own lives.

Many countries of the world operate under a parliamentary form of government. In such a system, the parliament occasionally passes judgment on the prime minister's record. If parliament votes "no confidence," the government dissolves and new national elections must be held. Today you will read Paul's "no confidence" vote (Philippians 3:3). As you read ask yourself where you put your confidence. If time is short, focus on Philippians 3:1–16.

No Confidence in the Flesh

3 Finally, my brothers, rejoice in the Lord! It is no trouble for me to write the same things to you again, and it is a safeguard for you.

2 Watch out for those dogs, those men who do evil, those mutilators of the flesh. 3 For it is we who are the circumcision, we who worship by the Spirit of God, who glory in Christ Jesus, and who put no confidence in the flesh— 4 though I myself have reasons for such confidence.

If anyone else thinks he has reasons to put confidence in the flesh, I have more: 5 circumcised on the eighth day, of the people of Israel, of the tribe of Benjamin, a Hebrew of Hebrews; in regard to the law, a Pharisee; 6 as for zeal, persecuting the church; as for legalistic righteousness, faultless.

7 But whatever was to my profit I now consider loss for the sake of Christ. 8 What is more, I consider everything a loss compared to the surpassing greatness of knowing Christ Jesus my Lord, for whose sake I have lost all things. I consider them rubbish, that I may gain Christ 9 and be found in him, not having a righteousness of my own that comes from the law, but that which is through faith in Christ—the righteousness that comes from God and is by faith. 10 I want to know Christ and the power of his resurrection and the fellowship of sharing in his sufferings, becoming like him in his death, 11 and so, somehow, to attain to the resurrection from the dead.

Pressing on Toward the Goal

12 Not that I have already obtained all this, or have already been made perfect, but I press on to take hold of that for which Christ Jesus took hold of me. 13 Brothers, I do not consider myself yet to have taken hold of it. But one thing I do: Forgetting what is behind and straining toward what is ahead, 14 I press on toward the goal to win the prize for which God has called me heavenward in Christ Jesus.

15 All of us who are mature should take such a view of things. And if on some point you think differently, that too God will make clear to you. 16 Only let us live up to what we have already attained.

17 Join with others in following my example, brothers, and take note of those who live according to the pattern we gave you. 18 For, as I have often told you before and now say again even with tears, many live as enemies of the cross of Christ. 19 Their destiny is destruction, their god is their stomach, and their glory is in their shame. Their mind is on earthly things. 20 But our citizenship is in heaven. And we eagerly await a Savior from there, the Lord Jesus Christ, 21 who, by the power that enables him to bring everything under his control, will transform our lowly bodies so that they will be like his glorious body.

SHARPEN THE FOCUS

Paul had many achievements to recommend his life to the judgment of heaven. But he preempts that vote by voting "no confidence" in his flesh, in his own human efforts to please God. Instead, he throws every one of his human achievements in the trash (Philippians 3:7) and puts all his confidence instead in Christ's death and resurrection (Philippians 3:9–10).

Notice that Paul does this not only as he thinks about his need to be justified, acquitted, made right with God, but *also* as he thinks about becoming more like Christ (Philippians 3:12–14). Whether we talk about justification or sanctification, our vote must be the same. Along with our brother Paul, we have no confidence in our flesh, our own effort and achievements.

Our Lord justifies us by grace through faith. And He sanctifies us in that same way. He deserves and rightly receives all the glory. The more we grow up into Christ, the clearer this truth will become to us. May our Lord grant us the insight He gave Paul!

WEEK 92 • SATURDAY

Philippians 4:1–23

GET THE BIG PICTURE

The note of joy that has rung out from Philippians all along rings again as Paul concludes. Listen for that note and ask your Lord to show you how you might incorporate more joy into your own lifestyle. If time is short, focus on Philippians 4:1–19.

4 Therefore, my brothers, you
whom I love and long for, my
joy and crown, that is how you should
stand firm in the Lord, dear friends!

Exhortations

[2]I plead with Euodia and I plead with
Syntyche to agree with each other in the
Lord. [3]Yes, and I ask you, loyal yoke-
fellow,[a] help these women who have
contended at my side in the cause of the
gospel, along with Clement and the rest
of my fellow workers, whose names are
in the book of life.

[4]Rejoice in the Lord always. I will say
it again: Rejoice! [5]Let your gentleness be
evident to all. The Lord is near. [6]Do not
be anxious about anything, but in everything, by prayer and petition, with
thanksgiving, present your requests to
God. [7]And the peace of God, which
transcends all understanding, will
guard your hearts and your minds in
Christ Jesus.

[8]Finally, brothers, whatever is true,
whatever is noble, whatever is right,
whatever is pure, whatever is lovely, whatever is admirable—if anything
is excellent or praiseworthy—think
about such things. [9]Whatever you have
learned or received or heard from me,
or seen in me—put it into practice. And
the God of peace will be with you.

Thanks for Their Gifts

[10]I rejoice greatly in the Lord that at last
you have renewed your concern for me.
Indeed, you have been concerned, but
you had no opportunity to show it. [11]I am
not saying this because I am in need, for I
have learned to be content whatever the
circumstances. [12]I know what it is to be in
need, and I know what it is to have plenty. I have learned the secret of being content in any and every situation, whether
well fed or hungry, whether living in
plenty or in want. [13]I can do everything
through him who gives me strength.

[14]Yet it was good of you to share in my
troubles. [15]Moreover, as you Philippians
know, in the early days of your acquain-
tance with the gospel, when I set out
from Macedonia, not one church shared
with me in the matter of giving and receiving, except you only; [16]for even
when I was in Thessalonica, you sent
me aid again and again when I was in
need. [17]Not that I am looking for a gift,
but I am looking for what may be credited to your account. [18]I have received
full payment and even more; I am am-
ply supplied, now that I have received
from Epaphroditus the gifts you sent.
They are a fragrant offering, an acceptable sacrifice, pleasing to God. [19]And my

[a]3 Or *loyal Syzygus*

God will meet all your needs according
to his glorious riches in Christ Jesus.
[20]To our God and Father be glory for
ever and ever. Amen.

Final Greetings

[21]Greet all the saints in Christ Jesus.
The brothers who are with me send
greetings. [22]All the saints send you
greetings, especially those who belong
to Caesar's household.
[23]The grace of the Lord Jesus Christ be
with your spirit. Amen.[a]

[a]23 Some manuscripts do not have *Amen*.

SHARPEN THE FOCUS

When other people panic and then blame us for their problems, we tend to lose our own peace, too. Joy becomes a casualty in the kind of blaming-wars that can follow.

The apostle Paul shows us the heart and mind of God toward our anxieties. Note that vv. 6 and 7 do not urge us to try hard to be at peace. Our own efforts will accomplish nothing; at the end of the day, we will have added anxiety about our anxiety to our list of worries!

Instead, our Lord here gives us a direction and a promise. When anxious thoughts hold us hostage, we can take every single worry to our Lord (verse 6). We can ask for what we need, and we can thank Him for taking care of us even before we see how He plans to do that.

Then, He promises (verse 7), His peace will stand guard at the door of our heart like a fully armed Roman sentry. God's Spirit will flood our minds with the true, noble, right, pure, lovely, excellent things of His Word (verse 8). These things will be the peace-keepers in our souls.

What sins, worries, concerns, and fears do you need to talk to your Savior about right now?

COLOSSIANS

WEEK 93 • MONDAY

Colossians 1:1–29

What a truly big picture today's reading paints! A big picture of Christ. A big picture of God's grace toward us in Christ. Human words cannot contain or fully explain the glory of either Christ or His grace. Read slowly as you marvel at the refreshing truths in Colossians 1. If time is short, focus on Colossians 1:15–23.

1 Paul, an apostle of Christ Jesus by
the will of God, and Timothy our
brother,

2To the holy and faithful[a] brothers in
Christ at Colosse:

Grace and peace to you from God our
Father.[b]

Thanksgiving and Prayer

3We always thank God, the Father of
our Lord Jesus Christ, when we pray for
you, 4because we have heard of your
faith in Christ Jesus and of the love you
have for all the saints— 5the faith and
love that spring from the hope that is
stored up for you in heaven and that
you have already heard about in the
word of truth, the gospel 6that has come
to you. All over the world this gospel is
bearing fruit and growing, just as it has
been doing among you since the day
you heard it and understood God's
grace in all its truth. 7You learned it from
Epaphras, our dear fellow servant, who
is a faithful minister of Christ on our[c]
behalf, 8and who also told us of your
love in the Spirit.

9For this reason, since the day we
heard about you, we have not stopped
praying for you and asking God to fill
you with the knowledge of his will
through all spiritual wisdom and understanding. 10And we pray this in order
that you may live a life worthy of the
Lord and may please him in every way:
bearing fruit in every good work, growing in the knowledge of God, 11being
strengthened with all power according
to his glorious might so that you may
have great endurance and patience, and
joyfully 12giving thanks to the Father,
who has qualified you[d] to share in the
inheritance of the saints in the kingdom
of light. 13For he has rescued us from the
dominion of darkness and brought us
into the kingdom of the Son he loves,
14in whom we have redemption,[e] the
forgiveness of sins.

The Supremacy of Christ

15He is the image of the invisible God,
the firstborn over all creation. 16For by
him all things were created: things in
heaven and on earth, visible and invisible, whether thrones or powers or rulers or authorities; all things were
created by him and for him. 17He is be-

[a]2 Or *believing* [b]2 Some manuscripts *Father and the Lord Jesus Christ* [c]7 Some manuscripts *your* [d]12 Some manuscripts *us* [e]14 A few late manuscripts *redemption through his blood*

fore all things, and in him all things hold together. [18]And he is the head of the body, the church; he is the beginning and the firstborn from among the dead, so that in everything he might have the supremacy. [19]For God was pleased to have all his fullness dwell in him, [20]and through him to reconcile to himself all things, whether things on earth or things in heaven, by making peace through his blood, shed on the cross.

[21]Once you were alienated from God and were enemies in your minds because of[a] your evil behavior. [22]But now he has reconciled you by Christ's physical body through death to present you holy in his sight, without blemish and free from accusation— [23]if you continue in your faith, established and firm, not moved from the hope held out in the gospel. This is the gospel that you heard and that has been proclaimed to every creature under heaven, and of which I, Paul, have become a servant.

Paul's Labor for the Church

[24]Now I rejoice in what was suffered for you, and I fill up in my flesh what is still lacking in regard to Christ's afflictions, for the sake of his body, which is the church. [25]I have become its servant by the commission God gave me to present to you the word of God in its fullness— [26]the mystery that has been kept hidden for ages and generations, but is now disclosed to the saints. [27]To them God has chosen to make known among the Gentiles the glorious riches of this mystery, which is Christ in you, the hope of glory.

[28]We proclaim him, admonishing and teaching everyone with all wisdom, so that we may present everyone perfect in Christ. [29]To this end I labor, struggling with all his energy, which so powerfully works in me.

[a]21 Or *minds, as shown by*

SHARPEN THE FOCUS

Imagine yourself kidnapped by a madman who buries you alive. He's planted a speaker in your coffin. Through it, he shouts lies all day long, every day. He tells you your family hates you; they've forgotten you; they couldn't care less what happens to you. After weeks in the dark, in your fear, in your hunger, you begin to believe the propaganda.

Now imagine the sounds of digging above your casket. Imagine the lid popping off and the sunlight flooding in to reveal your brother's face. Imagine him telling you that your father sent him to pay the ransom and to rescue you, to deliver you from living death to life, from darkness to light, from fear to love.

The words St. Paul uses in Colossians 1 to picture Christ's work on our behalf fit just this kind of analogy. Satan had us just where he wanted us, trapped in a living death by our sins. He lied to us, and we believed his words. The darkness was spiritual darkness, but very real nonetheless.

And Christ's rescue (Colossians 1:13–14) is very real, too. Our plight was *that* serious but Jesus' death accomplished a *full* rescue. Realizing that, no wonder God's people would pray (Colossians 1:9–12) for one another. Make it your prayer today, too.

Paul doesn't waste time with superfluous words and phrases. He packs every sentence in Colossians with meaning. Again today, read slowly. Think about all the treasure that belongs to you because you are in Christ by faith. If time is short, focus on Colossians 2:1–10.

2 I want you to know how much I
am struggling for you and for
those at Laodicea, and for all who have
not met me personally. [2]My purpose is
that they may be encouraged in heart
and united in love, so that they may
have the full riches of complete understanding, in order that they may know
the mystery of God, namely, Christ, [3]in
whom are hidden all the treasures of
wisdom and knowledge. [4]I tell you this
so that no one may deceive you by fine-
sounding arguments. [5]For though I am
absent from you in body, I am present
with you in spirit and delight to see how
orderly you are and how firm your faith
in Christ is.

Freedom From Human Regulations Through Life With Christ

[6]So then, just as you received Christ
Jesus as Lord, continue to live in him,
[7]rooted and built up in him, strengthened in the faith as you were taught,
and overflowing with thankfulness.

[8]See to it that no one takes you captive through hollow and deceptive philosophy, which depends on human
tradition and the basic principles of this
world rather than on Christ.

[9]For in Christ all the fullness of the
Deity lives in bodily form, [10]and you
have been given fullness in Christ, who
is the head over every power and authority. [11]In him you were also circumcised, in the putting off of the sinful
nature,[a] not with a circumcision done by
the hands of men but with the circumcision done by Christ, [12]having been
buried with him in baptism and raised
with him through your faith in the
power of God, who raised him from the
dead.

[13]When you were dead in your sins
and in the uncircumcision of your sinful nature,[b] God made you[c] alive with
Christ. He forgave us all our sins, [14]hav-
ing canceled the written code, with its
regulations, that was against us and that
stood opposed to us; he took it away,
nailing it to the cross. [15]And having disarmed the powers and authorities, he
made a public spectacle of them, tri-
umphing over them by the cross.[d]

[16]Therefore do not let anyone judge
you by what you eat or drink, or with
regard to a religious festival, a New
Moon celebration or a Sabbath day.
[17]These are a shadow of the things that
were to come; the reality, however, is
found in Christ. [18]Do not let anyone
who delights in false humility and the
worship of angels disqualify you for the
prize. Such a person goes into great detail about what he has seen, and his unspiritual mind puffs him up with idle
notions. [19]He has lost connection with
the Head, from whom the whole body,
supported and held together by its lig-
aments and sinews, grows as God
causes it to grow.

[20]Since you died with Christ to the basic principles of this world, why, as
though you still belonged to it, do you

[a]11 Or *the flesh* [b]13 Or *your flesh* [c]13 Some manuscripts *us* [d]15 Or *them in him*

submit to its rules: [21]"Do not handle! Do
not taste! Do not touch!"? [22]These are all
destined to perish with use, because
they are based on human commands
and teachings. [23]Such regulations indeed have an appearance of wisdom,
with their self-imposed worship, their
false humility and their harsh treatment
of the body, but they lack any value in
restraining sensual indulgence.

SHARPEN THE FOCUS

Have you ever watched a building go up? The work starts below ground as the foundation is poured. Then board by board, brick by brick, the first, second, third, and fourth stories take shape. The structure becomes more and more the building that the architect intended.

In Colossians 3:6–7 Paul uses this picture to show what our life in Christ is like. A tap root (Colossians 2:7) sinks deeper into the soil as it grows. A building rises higher according to the architect's plan. And we as God's children grow up more and more into Christ's image.

Paul says, "Just as you received Christ Jesus as Lord, continue to live in Him" (Colossians 2:6). How did we receive Christ? By grace! God worked in us a relationship with Himself through the saving, forgiving work of Christ. And just as we received Him by grace, so we continue to live and to grow by grace.

As we confess the sins He shows us day by day, and receive His full forgiveness in Christ, we receive also with that forgiveness the power we need to overcome Satan's temptations and the leanings of our old sinful self. ☼

WEEK 93 • WEDNESDAY

Col. 3:1—4:18

GET THE BIG PICTURE

We serve a glorious Christ! He has done tremendous things for us. Colossians 1 and 2 unpacked the treasures of His power and grace. But in Scripture, truth always has practical application. Wisdom involves putting into practice in everyday life the truths God has taught us. That's what Colossians 3–4 will help us do. If time is short, focus on Colossians 3:1–17.

Rules for Holy Living

3 Since, then, you have been raised
with Christ, set your hearts on
things above, where Christ is seated at
the right hand of God. [2]Set your minds
on things above, not on earthly things.
[3]For you died, and your life is now hidden with Christ in God. [4]When Christ,
who is your[a] life, appears, then you also
will appear with him in glory.
[5]Put to death, therefore, whatever belongs to your earthly nature: sexual immorality, impurity, lust, evil desires and
greed, which is idolatry. [6]Because of
these, the wrath of God is coming.[b] [7]You
used to walk in these ways, in the life
you once lived. [8]But now you must rid
yourselves of all such things as these:
anger, rage, malice, slander, and filthy

[a]4 Some manuscripts *our* [b]6 Some early manuscripts *coming on those who are disobedient*

language from your lips. 9Do not lie to each other, since you have taken off your old self with its practices 10and have put on the new self, which is being renewed in knowledge in the image of its Creator. 11Here there is no Greek or Jew, circumcised or uncircumcised, barbarian, Scythian, slave or free, but Christ is all, and is in all.

12Therefore, as God's chosen people, holy and dearly loved, clothe yourselves with compassion, kindness, humility, gentleness and patience. 13Bear with each other and forgive whatever grievances you may have against one another. Forgive as the Lord forgave you. 14And over all these virtues put on love, which binds them all together in perfect unity.

15Let the peace of Christ rule in your hearts, since as members of one body you were called to peace. And be thankful. 16Let the word of Christ dwell in you richly as you teach and admonish one another with all wisdom, and as you sing psalms, hymns and spiritual songs with gratitude in your hearts to God. 17And whatever you do, whether in word or deed, do it all in the name of the Lord Jesus, giving thanks to God the Father through him.

Rules for Christian Households

18Wives, submit to your husbands, as is fitting in the Lord.

19Husbands, love your wives and do not be harsh with them.

20Children, obey your parents in everything, for this pleases the Lord.

21Fathers, do not embitter your children, or they will become discouraged.

22Slaves, obey your earthly masters in everything; and do it, not only when their eye is on you and to win their favor, but with sincerity of heart and reverence for the Lord. 23Whatever you do, work at it with all your heart, as working for the Lord, not for men, 24since you know that you will receive an inheritance from the Lord as a reward. It is the Lord Christ you are serving. 25Anyone who does wrong will be repaid for his wrong, and there is no favoritism.

4 Masters, provide your slaves with what is right and fair, because you know that you also have a Master in heaven.

Further Instructions

2Devote yourselves to prayer, being watchful and thankful. 3And pray for us, too, that God may open a door for our message, so that we may proclaim the mystery of Christ, for which I am in chains. 4Pray that I may proclaim it clearly, as I should. 5Be wise in the way you act toward outsiders; make the most of every opportunity. 6Let your conversation be always full of grace, seasoned with salt, so that you may know how to answer everyone.

Final Greetings

7Tychicus will tell you all the news about me. He is a dear brother, a faithful minister and fellow servant in the Lord. 8I am sending him to you for the express purpose that you may know about our[a] circumstances and that he may encourage your hearts. 9He is coming with Onesimus, our faithful and dear brother, who is one of you. They will tell you everything that is happening here.

10My fellow prisoner Aristarchus sends you his greetings, as does Mark, the cousin of Barnabas. (You have received instructions about him; if he comes to you, welcome him.) 11Jesus, who is called Justus, also sends greetings. These are the only Jews among my fellow workers for the kingdom of God, and they have proved a comfort to me. 12Epaphras, who is one of you and a servant of Christ Jesus, sends greetings. He is always wrestling in prayer for you, that you may stand firm in all the will of God, mature and fully assured. 13I vouch for him that he is working hard for you and for those at Laodicea and Hierapolis. 14Our dear friend Luke, the doctor, and Demas send greetings. 15Give my greetings to the brothers at

[a]8 Some manuscripts *that he may know about your*

Laodicea, and to Nympha and the church in her house.
16After this letter has been read to you, see that it is also read in the church of the Laodiceans and that you in turn read the letter from Laodicea.
17Tell Archippus: "See to it that you complete the work you have received in the Lord."
18I, Paul, write this greeting in my own hand. Remember my chains. Grace be with you.

SHARPEN THE FOCUS

Religion always contradicts and undermines Christianity. The false teachers Paul warned the Colossians about made rules about what to eat, what to touch, what holy days to observe (Colossians 2:16–23). These rules provided an outward show of humility, of self-denial. But they had no power. They did no one any good!

Contrast these regulations and ceremonies with the change of heart and lifestyle Paul describes in chapters 3–4! By comparison, the religious rituals show themselves to be what they are—mere shells, empty shells.

The apostle James, concerned about Christians who had begun to drift spiritually wrote:

> *Religion that God our Father accepts as pure and faultless is this: to look after orphans and widows in their distress and to keep oneself from being polluted by the world.* (James 1:27)

In Christ, rules are transformed into relationships—a relationship with God and relationships with other believers. In Him we receive power for pure religion.

1 THESSALONIANS

To serve and to wait. Hard to do–but still, this describes the life to which we in Christ have been called. As you read today, ask yourself whom you are to serve and for what you are to wait. If time is short, focus on 1 Thessalonians 1:1–4.

1 Paul, Silas[a] and Timothy,

To the church of the Thessalonians in
God the Father and the Lord Jesus
Christ:

Grace and peace to you.[b]

Thanksgiving for the Thessalonians' Faith

[2]We always thank God for all of you,
mentioning you in our prayers. [3]We
continually remember before our God
and Father your work produced by
faith, your labor prompted by love, and
your endurance inspired by hope in our
Lord Jesus Christ.
[4]For we know, brothers loved by God,
that he has chosen you, [5]because our
gospel came to you not simply with
words, but also with power, with the
Holy Spirit and with deep conviction.
You know how we lived among you for
your sake. [6]You became imitators of us
and of the Lord; in spite of severe suffering, you welcomed the message with
the joy given by the Holy Spirit. [7]And so
you became a model to all the believers
in Macedonia and Achaia. [8]The Lord's
message rang out from you not only in
Macedonia and Achaia—your faith in
God has become known everywhere.
Therefore we do not need to say anything about it, [9]for they themselves report what kind of reception you gave
us. They tell how you turned to God
from idols to serve the living and true
God, [10]and to wait for his Son from
heaven, whom he raised from the
dead—Jesus, who rescues us from the
coming wrath.

[a]1 Greek *Silvanus*, a variant of *Silas* [b]1 Some early manuscripts *you from God our Father and the Lord Jesus Christ*

SHARPEN THE FOCUS

Most of us have heard the insult, "He's too heavenly-minded to be any earthly good." That proverb has a corollary: "She's too earthly-minded to be any heavenly good."

If we ignore the needs around us because we're too wrapped up in our own piety or too single-mindedly focused on speculations about Christ's return, we miss God's purpose for us.

But if we live forgetful of Christ's return and turn Christianity into merely a philosophy of doing good for others, of eliminating injustice and poverty here on earth, we also miss God's purpose.

How balanced is your lifestyle as you hold it up beside Paul's description of our calling "to serve the living and true God, and to wait for His Son from heaven" (1 Thessalonians 1:9b-10a)?

Think that question through. Confess any imbalances you see to your Savior. Then, confident of His forgiveness, ask Him to help you rebalance as you need to. Look for a specific way "to serve the living and true God" by helping someone who is carrying a heavy burden. And set aside some time to meditate on Christ's promise to return (see Revelation 22).

WEEK 93 • FRIDAY

1 Thessalonians 2:1–20

In Paul's day as in ours, charlatans found ways to profit from the spiritual hunger of others. Paul bent over backwards to avoid giving even the slightest hint that he fleeced the flock of God. Today's reading illustrates this. If time is short, focus on 1 Thessalonians 2:1–13.

Paul's Ministry in Thessalonica

2 You know, brothers, that our visit
to you was not a failure. 2We had
previously suffered and been insulted
in Philippi, as you know, but with the
help of our God we dared to tell you his
gospel in spite of strong opposition. 3For
the appeal we make does not spring
from error or impure motives, nor are
we trying to trick you. 4On the contrary,
we speak as men approved by God to
be entrusted with the gospel. We are not
trying to please men but God, who tests
our hearts. 5You know we never used
flattery, nor did we put on a mask to
cover up greed—God is our witness.
6We were not looking for praise from
men, not from you or anyone else.
As apostles of Christ we could have
been a burden to you, 7but we were gentle among you, like a mother caring for
her little children. 8We loved you so
much that we were delighted to share
with you not only the gospel of God but
our lives as well, because you had become so dear to us. 9Surely you remember, brothers, our toil and hardship; we
worked night and day in order not to be
a burden to anyone while we preached
the gospel of God to you.
10You are witnesses, and so is God, of
how holy, righteous and blameless we
were among you who believed. 11For
you know that we dealt with each of
you as a father deals with his own children, 12encouraging, comforting and
urging you to live lives worthy of God,
who calls you into his kingdom and
glory.
13And we also thank God continually
because, when you received the word of
God, which you heard from us, you accepted it not as the word of men, but as
it actually is, the word of God, which is
at work in you who believe. 14For you,
brothers, became imitators of God's
churches in Judea, which are in Christ
Jesus: You suffered from your own
countrymen the same things those
churches suffered from the Jews, 15who

killed the Lord Jesus and the prophets
and also drove us out. They displease
God and are hostile to all men [16]in their
effort to keep us from speaking to the
Gentiles so that they may be saved. In
this way they always heap up their sins
to the limit. The wrath of God has come
upon them at last.[a]

Paul's Longing to See the Thessalonians

[17]But, brothers, when we were torn
away from you for a short time (in
person, not in thought), out of our intense longing we made every effort to
see you. [18]For we wanted to come to
you—certainly I, Paul, did, again and
again—but Satan stopped us. [19]For what
is our hope, our joy, or the crown in
which we will glory in the presence of
our Lord Jesus when he comes? Is it not
you? [20]Indeed, you are our glory and
joy.

[a]16 Or *them fully*

SHARPEN THE FOCUS

In *A Letter to Garcia,* Elbert Hubbard told a story from the Spanish American War. In the story, the U. S. President needed to get a message to the leader of a guerrilla force deep in the Cuban jungles.

"A fellow by the name of Rowan" took the letter, sealed it in an oilskin pouch, strapped it over his heart, and disappeared into the jungle. Three weeks later he emerged on the opposite side of the island having done what he had been asked to do—take a letter to Garcia. Nothing had stopped him.

Hubbard went on to bemoan the lack of trustworthiness in the overwhelming majority of the people of his day. We still recognize Hubbard's complaints. The people of the first century were no different. Yet God saw fit to entrust the greatest message of all—the Gospel—with Paul (1 Thessalonians 2:4). He could do this because He had packed the Word Paul proclaimed with the power to create trustworthiness in Paul's life.

How faithful are you to pray and speak and give support to the Gospel message God has entrusted to His church? If you're not happy with your answer to that question remember that *God* is faithful to forgive all your unfaithfulness and to create trustworthiness in you.

WEEK 93 • SATURDAY

1 Thessalonians 3:1–13

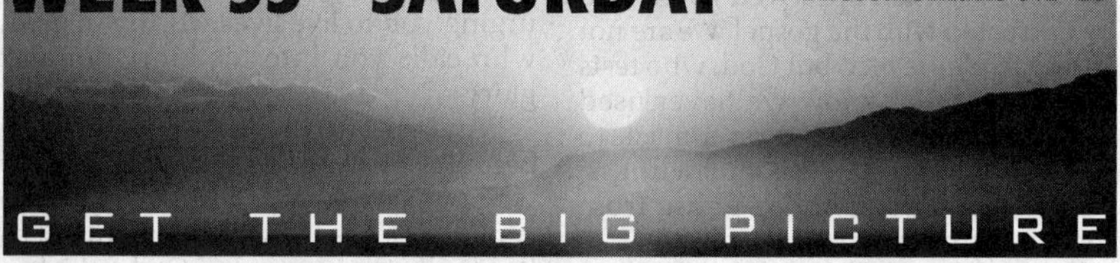

GET THE BIG PICTURE

Those who write ad copy focus on a given product's benefits. From that perspective, Paul really blew his presentation in Thessalonica. He promised his listeners that they would be persecuted for their faith! And that promise came true. As you read, ask yourself how Paul's approach paid off. If time is short, focus on 1 Thessalonians 3:1–10.

3 So when we could stand it no
longer, we thought it best to be
left by ourselves in Athens. 2We sent
Timothy, who is our brother and God's
fellow worker[a] in spreading the gospel
of Christ, to strengthen and encourage
you in your faith, 3so that no one would
be unsettled by these trials. You know
quite well that we were destined for
them. 4In fact, when we were with you,
we kept telling you that we would be
persecuted. And it turned out that way,
as you well know. 5For this reason, when
I could stand it no longer, I sent to find
out about your faith. I was afraid that in
some way the tempter might have
tempted you and our efforts might have
been useless.

Timothy's Encouraging Report

6But Timothy has just now come to us
from you and has brought good news
about your faith and love. He has told
us that you always have pleasant memories of us and that you long to see us,
just as we also long to see you. 7There-
fore, brothers, in all our distress and
persecution we were encouraged about
you because of your faith. 8For now we
really live, since you are standing firm
in the Lord. 9How can we thank God
enough for you in return for all the joy
we have in the presence of our God because of you? 10Night and day we pray
most earnestly that we may see you
again and supply what is lacking in
your faith.

11Now may our God and Father himself and our Lord Jesus clear the way for
us to come to you. 12May the Lord make
your love increase and overflow for
each other and for everyone else, just as
ours does for you. 13May he strengthen
your hearts so that you will be blameless and holy in the presence of our God
and Father when our Lord Jesus comes
with all his holy ones.

[a]2 Some manuscripts *brother and fellow worker*; other manuscripts *brother and God's servant*

SHARPEN THE FOCUS

"It was all for nothing." Perhaps no sadder words exist in English.

- Someone comes in fourth after training for the Olympics for years.
- Someone prepares a gourmet meal for loved ones who don't show up.
- Someone carries her baby to term and endures labor only to have that baby stillborn.

Disappointment of the bitterest kind comes wrapped in experiences like these. That's the kind of disappointment Paul feared. Like Paul, the Christians in Thessalonica faced opposition from their "own countrymen" (1 Thessalonians 2:14). Separated from their mentor in Christ, the new converts were easy prey for false teachers. So Paul sent Timothy to check on these young believers, to "strengthen and encourage" them in their faith. Timothy returned with good news. God had in grace preserved the work He had begun. He had done what Paul could not do.

What witnessing have you done that seems to have fallen on sterile soil? Talk to God about those concerns. Then trust Him to finish what He has begun. Let Him comfort you with His forgiving love for you and for those you love.

WEEK 94 • MONDAY

1 Thessalonians 4:1–18

Some in the first-century church fully expected the Lord Jesus returning in glory to judge and deliver them at any time. When that didn't happen right away, many began to worry about practical points of doctrine. Today and tomorrow you will read Paul's comforting words regarding those who die in the Lord. If time is short, focus on 1 Thessalonians 4:13–18.

Living to Please God

4 Finally, brothers, we instructed you how to live in order to please God, as in fact you are living. Now we ask you and urge you in the Lord Jesus to do this more and more. [2]For you know what instructions we gave you by the authority of the Lord Jesus.

[3]It is God's will that you should be sanctified: that you should avoid sexual immorality; [4]that each of you should learn to control his own body[a] in a way that is holy and honorable, [5]not in passionate lust like the heathen, who do not know God; [6]and that in this matter no one should wrong his brother or take advantage of him. The Lord will punish men for all such sins, as we have already told you and warned you. [7]For God did not call us to be impure, but to live a holy life. [8]Therefore, he who rejects this instruction does not reject man but God, who gives you his Holy Spirit.

[9]Now about brotherly love we do not need to write to you, for you yourselves have been taught by God to love each other. [10]And in fact, you do love all the brothers throughout Macedonia. Yet we urge you, brothers, to do so more and more.

[11]Make it your ambition to lead a quiet life, to mind your own business and to work with your hands, just as we told you, [12]so that your daily life may win the respect of outsiders and so that you will not be dependent on anybody.

The Coming of the Lord

[13]Brothers, we do not want you to be ignorant about those who fall asleep, or to grieve like the rest of men, who have no hope. [14]We believe that Jesus died and rose again and so we believe that God will bring with Jesus those who have fallen asleep in him. [15]According to the Lord's own word, we tell you that we who are still alive, who are left till the coming of the Lord, will certainly not precede those who have fallen asleep. [16]For the Lord himself will come down from heaven, with a loud command, with the voice of the archangel and with the trumpet call of God, and the dead in Christ will rise first. [17]After that, we who are still alive and are left will be caught up together with them in the clouds to meet the Lord in the air. And so we will be with the Lord forever. [18]Therefore encourage each other with these words.

[a]4 Or *learn to live with his own wife;* or *learn to acquire a wife*

SHARPEN THE FOCUS

If we think of hope as primarily a feeling, circumstances in life will lead us around by the nose. Good news will inflate our hope; bad news will burst our bubble. But Christian hope does not rest on circumstances. Paul wrote about that in his letter to the Romans:

> *Hope that is seen is no hope at all. Who hopes for what he already has? But if we hope for what we do not yet have, we wait for it patiently.* (Romans 8:24–25)

Christian hope rests on the promises of God. Even though we do not yet see a given promise unfolding in our lives, we know with utter certainty that it will unfold. God is true to His Word.

That's why Paul could say what he said to the anxious Thessalonians in 1 Thessalonians 4:13. We do grieve loved ones who die. But even in our grief, we have hope. We rest in the sure and certain truth of the resurrection—both Christ's resurrection and our own. Read 1 Thessalonians 4:13–18 and rejoice in the hope that belongs to you in Christ.

WEEK 94 • TUESDAY

1 Thessalonians 5:1–28

GET THE BIG PICTURE

The class that goofs off when the teacher leaves the room. The employees who give their level best—but only while the boss is watching. The Christian who forgets about Christ's return and lives a lifestyle incompatible with the new identity that is ours in Christ. All these people share a similar problem. Think about them—and about yourself—as you read today. If time is short, focus on 1 Thessalonians 5:1–11, 23–24.

5 Now, brothers, about times and
dates we do not need to write to
you, [2]for you know very well that the
day of the Lord will come like a thief in
the night. [3]While people are saying,
"Peace and safety," destruction will
come on them suddenly, as labor pains
on a pregnant woman, and they will not
escape.
[4]But you, brothers, are not in darkness
so that this day should surprise you like
a thief. [5]You are all sons of the light and
sons of the day. We do not belong to the
night or to the darkness. [6]So then, let us
not be like others, who are asleep, but
let us be alert and self-controlled. [7]For
those who sleep, sleep at night, and
those who get drunk, get drunk at
night. [8]But since we belong to the day,
let us be self-controlled, putting on
faith and love as a breastplate, and the
hope of salvation as a helmet. [9]For
God did not appoint us to suffer wrath
but to receive salvation through our
Lord Jesus Christ. [10]He died for us so
that, whether we are awake or asleep,
we may live together with him. [11]There-
fore encourage one another and build
each other up, just as in fact you are
doing.

Final Instructions

[12]Now we ask you, brothers, to respect those who work hard among you,
who are over you in the Lord and who
admonish you. [13]Hold them in the highest regard in love because of their work.
Live in peace with each other. [14]And we
urge you, brothers, warn those who are
idle, encourage the timid, help the
weak, be patient with everyone. [15]Make
sure that nobody pays back wrong for
wrong, but always try to be kind to each
other and to everyone else.
[16]Be joyful always; [17]pray continually;
[18]give thanks in all circumstances, for
this is God's will for you in Christ Jesus.
[19]Do not put out the Spirit's fire; [20]do
not treat prophecies with contempt.
[21]Test everything. Hold on to the good.
[22]Avoid every kind of evil.
[23]May God himself, the God of peace,
sanctify you through and through. May
your whole spirit, soul and body be kept
blameless at the coming of our Lord
Jesus Christ. [24]The one who calls you is
faithful and he will do it.

[25]Brothers, pray for us. [26]Greet all the
brothers with a holy kiss. [27]I charge you
before the Lord to have this letter read
to all the brothers.
[28]The grace of our Lord Jesus Christ be
with you.

SHARPEN THE FOCUS

Watch while you wait! Christ can return at any moment. While some ignore that fact, and many fear it, we need not. "He died for us," Paul says (1 Thessalonians 5:10), "so that, whether we are awake or asleep"—physically dead or alive when He returns—"we may live together with Him." Jesus endured the wrath of God's judgment in our place. Because He did, we can await His coming on tiptoe, longing for it with hearts filled with joy.

Shine while you serve! We are "sons of the light and sons of the day" (1 Thessalonians 5:5). We "do not belong to the night or to the darkness" (1 Thessalonians 5:5). Malignant and aggressive, the darkness of this world tries to snuff out the truth. But the truth shines on from both our lips and our lives, as Jesus Himself empowers it. The darkness does not understand it, but neither will the darkness ever extinguish the truth of the Gospel (see John 1:5).

Find a brother or sister in the faith today and encourage him or her with the truth of 1 Thessalonians 5. Share especially verse 11, and urge your friend to pass the encouragement on.

2 THESSALONIANS

WEEK 94 • WEDNESDAY

2 Thess. 1:1–12

GET THE BIG PICTURE

Suffering for their faith, the believers in Thessalonica longed for Christ's return. They endured Satan's attacks, his questions about the reality of the Lord's love. Then as now believers ask, "Where is God when it hurts?" Paul points all of us to our Lord's mercy in Christ and to His justice. Let Paul's words encourage your heart as you read. If time is short, focus on 2 Thessalonians 1:1–10.

1 Paul, Silas[a] and Timothy,

To the church of the Thessalonians in
God our Father and the Lord Jesus
Christ:

[2]Grace and peace to you from God the
Father and the Lord Jesus Christ.

Thanksgiving and Prayer

[3]We ought always to thank God for
you, brothers, and rightly so, because
your faith is growing more and more,
and the love every one of you has for
each other is increasing. [4]Therefore,
among God's churches we boast about
your perseverance and faith in all the
persecutions and trials you are enduring.

[5]All this is evidence that God's judgment is right, and as a result you will be
counted worthy of the kingdom of God,
for which you are suffering. [6]God is just:
He will pay back trouble to those who
trouble you [7]and give relief to you who
are troubled, and to us as well. This will
happen when the Lord Jesus is revealed
from heaven in blazing fire with his
powerful angels. [8]He will punish those
who do not know God and do not obey
the gospel of our Lord Jesus. [9]They will
be punished with everlasting destruction and shut out from the presence of
the Lord and from the majesty of his
power [10]on the day he comes to be glorified in his holy people and to be mar-
veled at among all those who have
believed. This includes you, because
you believed our testimony to you.

[11]With this in mind, we constantly
pray for you, that our God may count
you worthy of his calling, and that by
his power he may fulfill every good purpose of yours and every act prompted
by your faith. [12]We pray this so that the
name of our Lord Jesus may be glorified
in you, and you in him, according to the
grace of our God and the Lord Jesus
Christ.[b]

[a]*1* Greek *Silvanus*, a variant of *Silas* [b]*12* Or *God and Lord, Jesus Christ*

SHARPEN THE FOCUS

Down through history, the Lord has often used the fires of persecution to refine His church. Hypocrites don't stay around long when the world turns up the heat.

The true believers in Thessalonica had, by God's grace, come through the fire. Their faith, like gold, had become more and more pure as God continued to strengthen and support them. Sins like jealousy, materialism, greed, and gossip had melted away. The Holy Spirit testifies through Paul that their faith was growing and their love was increasing (2 Thessalonians 1:3), all this in spite of–and perhaps even because of–the persecution. Thrown on the mercy of Christ, they found that mercy sufficient to keep them in the faith.

We may never have to give up the title to our house because we believe in Jesus. We may never have to choose between a career and our love for Christ. We may never face death for our relationship with our Savior. Or we may.

Either way, the mercy that has called us to saving faith is big enough to keep us in that faith. The one who died for us will make it possible for us to live or to die for His glory. And He will continue to burn away sin's impurities. Why not talk to him about that right now?

WEEK 94 • THURSDAY

2 Thess. 2:1—3:18

GET THE BIG PICTURE

Your dad left without you. Can you think of a crueler lie any child could tell another? The fear of being left behind, of being abandoned, can chill even adult hearts. The Thessalonians struggled under the burden of that kind of fear. Look for the lie and for the Lord's response to it as you read today. If time is short, focus on 2 Thessalonians 2:1–17.

The Man of Lawlessness

2 Concerning the coming of our
Lord Jesus Christ and our being
gathered to him, we ask you, brothers,
2not to become easily unsettled or
alarmed by some prophecy, report or
letter supposed to have come from us,
saying that the day of the Lord has already come. 3Don't let anyone deceive
you in any way, for ⌞that day will not
come⌟ until the rebellion occurs and the
man of lawlessness[a] is revealed, the man
doomed to destruction. 4He will oppose
and will exalt himself over everything
that is called God or is worshiped, so
that he sets himself up in God's temple,
proclaiming himself to be God.

5Don't you remember that when I
was with you I used to tell you these
things? 6And now you know what is
holding him back, so that he may be
revealed at the proper time. 7For the
secret power of lawlessness is already at
work; but the one who now holds it
back will continue to do so till he is
taken out of the way. 8And then the
lawless one will be revealed, whom
the Lord Jesus will overthrow with the
breath of his mouth and destroy by the
splendor of his coming. 9The coming of
the lawless one will be in accordance
with the work of Satan displayed in all
kinds of counterfeit miracles, signs and
wonders, 10and in every sort of evil that
deceives those who are perishing. They
perish because they refused to love the
truth and so be saved. 11For this reason
God sends them a powerful delusion so

[a]3 Some manuscripts *sin*

that they will believe the lie 12 and so that all will be condemned who have not believed the truth but have delighted in wickedness.

Stand Firm

13 But we ought always to thank God for you, brothers loved by the Lord, because from the beginning God chose you[a] to be saved through the sanctifying work of the Spirit and through belief in the truth. 14 He called you to this through our gospel, that you might share in the glory of our Lord Jesus Christ. 15 So then, brothers, stand firm and hold to the teachings[b] we passed on to you, whether by word of mouth or by letter.

16 May our Lord Jesus Christ himself and God our Father, who loved us and by his grace gave us eternal encouragement and good hope, 17 encourage your hearts and strengthen you in every good deed and word.

Request for Prayer

3 Finally, brothers, pray for us that the message of the Lord may spread rapidly and be honored, just as it was with you. 2 And pray that we may be delivered from wicked and evil men, for not everyone has faith. 3 But the Lord is faithful, and he will strengthen and protect you from the evil one. 4 We have confidence in the Lord that you are doing and will continue to do the things we command. 5 May the Lord direct your hearts into God's love and Christ's perseverance.

Warning Against Idleness

6 In the name of the Lord Jesus Christ, we command you, brothers, to keep away from every brother who is idle and does not live according to the teaching[c] you received from us. 7 For you yourselves know how you ought to follow our example. We were not idle when we were with you, 8 nor did we eat anyone's food without paying for it. On the contrary, we worked night and day, laboring and toiling so that we would not be a burden to any of you. 9 We did this, not because we do not have the right to such help, but in order to make ourselves a model for you to follow. 10 For even when we were with you, we gave you this rule: "If a man will not work, he shall not eat."

11 We hear that some among you are idle. They are not busy; they are busybodies. 12 Such people we command and urge in the Lord Jesus Christ to settle down and earn the bread they eat. 13 And as for you, brothers, never tire of doing what is right.

14 If anyone does not obey our instruction in this letter, take special note of him. Do not associate with him, in order that he may feel ashamed. 15 Yet do not regard him as an enemy, but warn him as a brother.

Final Greetings

16 Now may the Lord of peace himself give you peace at all times and in every way. The Lord be with all of you.

17 I, Paul, write this greeting in my own hand, which is the distinguishing mark in all my letters. This is how I write.

18 The grace of our Lord Jesus Christ be with you all.

[a] *13* Some manuscripts *because God chose you as his firstfruits* [b] *15* Or *traditions* [c] *6* Or *tradition*

SHARPEN THE FOCUS

Evil has always wormed its way into the events, decisions, and institutions of earth. Ever since Adam and Eve opened the door by their disobedience, the "secret power of lawlessness" has been at work (2 Thessalonians 2:7).

Evil wears no neon sign that flashes the warning, "Stay away." Rather, evil has a certain appeal. It can sound so reasonable. It can look so legitimate, so beautiful, so noble.

Toward the time of the end, evil's allure will grow even more intense. Paul tells us that Satan's opposition to Christ will one day gel in one person, the "lawless one" (2 Thessalonians 2:8). Satan will throw all of his power behind this Antichrist—so much so that the world will stand in awe of the miracles, signs, and wonders the lawless one will perform (2 Thessalonians 2:9).

The miracles will seem so good, the wonders so beautiful. But they will be counterfeit, produced by the father of lies (John 8:44).

How can we be sure we will not be led astray? In 2 Thessalonians 2:15 Paul urges us to cling to the truths Scripture teaches, in particular, the truth of Jesus our Savior from sin. Standing firm on the truth, we will be able to avoid falling for Satan's lies. God will keep us, encourage us and strengthen us (2 Thessalonians 2:16–17).

1 Timothy

Paul mentored several young pastors during the course of his ministry, Timothy among them. This, Paul's first letter to Timothy, contains many encouragements and instructions. As you read 1 Timothy 1, look carefully at the connection between pure teaching and holy living. If time is short, focus on 1 Timothy 1:1–11.

1 Paul, an apostle of Christ Jesus by
the command of God our Savior
and of Christ Jesus our hope,

2To Timothy my true son in the faith:

Grace, mercy and peace from God the
Father and Christ Jesus our Lord.

Warning Against False Teachers of the Law

3As I urged you when I went into
Macedonia, stay there in Ephesus so
that you may command certain men not
to teach false doctrines any longer 4nor
to devote themselves to myths and endless genealogies. These promote controversies rather than God's work—which
is by faith. 5The goal of this command is
love, which comes from a pure heart
and a good conscience and a sincere
faith. 6Some have wandered away from
these and turned to meaningless talk.
7They want to be teachers of the law, but
they do not know what they are talking
about or what they so confidently affirm.

8We know that the law is good if one
uses it properly. 9We also know that law[a]
is made not for the righteous but for
lawbreakers and rebels, the ungodly
and sinful, the unholy and irreligious;
for those who kill their fathers or mothers, for murderers, 10for adulterers and
perverts, for slave traders and liars and
perjurers—and for whatever else is contrary to the sound doctrine 11that con-
forms to the glorious gospel of the
blessed God, which he entrusted to me.

The Lord's Grace to Paul

12I thank Christ Jesus our Lord, who
has given me strength, that he considered me faithful, appointing me to his
service. 13Even though I was once a blasphemer and a persecutor and a violent
man, I was shown mercy because I acted
in ignorance and unbelief. 14The grace of
our Lord was poured out on me abundantly, along with the faith and love
that are in Christ Jesus.

15Here is a trustworthy saying that deserves full acceptance: Christ Jesus came
into the world to save sinners—of
whom I am the worst. 16But for that very
reason I was shown mercy so that in me,
the worst of sinners, Christ Jesus might

[a]9 Or *that the law*

display his unlimited patience as an example for those who would believe on
him and receive eternal life. [17]Now to
the King eternal, immortal, invisible, the
only God, be honor and glory for ever
and ever. Amen.
[18]Timothy, my son, I give you this instruction in keeping with the prophecies once made about you, so that by following them you may fight the good
fight, [19]holding on to faith and a good
conscience. Some have rejected these
and so have shipwrecked their faith.
[20]Among them are Hymenaeus and Alexander, whom I have handed over to
Satan to be taught not to blaspheme.

SHARPEN THE FOCUS

A thorn bush doesn't produce grapes. A thistle doesn't bear figs. When Jesus used this word picture, He wasn't giving lessons to Palestine's farmers. Pure teaching produces wholesome spiritual fruit in those who teach and then in those who hear. This was our Lord's point in Matthew 7:16–17.

Paul makes the same observation. The goal of Christian doctrine is "love, which comes from a pure heart and a good conscience and a sincere faith" (1 Timothy 1:5). None of us is perfect, of course, this side of heaven. We all need our Savior's cross and the blood He shed for our sins. But once Jesus' love has touched our hearts, our lifestyle begins to change. The focus of our life is then Jesus' mission and the trend in our life is toward increasing godliness.

In contrast, Paul points out the dangers of straying from the Gospel. Then as now false teachers focused on tangents—"myths" and "genealogies" (1 Timothy 1:4). This "meaningless talk" (1 Timothy 1:6) diverted the hearts of God's people from God's will for them: an intimate relationship with Christ and continuing progress in becoming like Him. Some had shipwrecked their faith by their speculations that had eventually become blasphemies. May God preserve us from that fate! ☼

WEEK 94 • SATURDAY

1 Timothy 2:1–15

GET THE BIG PICTURE

Pastor Timothy carried a heavy load of responsibilities for a person so young. Paul had tutored him, modeled ministry for him, and then sent him to the church at Ephesus. Paul kept in touch with his protégé. Watch for the practical, pastoral points Paul makes in chapter 2. If time is short, focus on 1 Timothy 2:1–8.

Instructions on Worship

2 I urge, then, first of all, that requests, prayers, intercession and
thanksgiving be made for everyone—
[2]for kings and all those in authority, that
we may live peaceful and quiet lives in
all godliness and holiness. [3]This is good,
and pleases God our Savior, [4]who wants
all men to be saved and to come to a
knowledge of the truth. [5]For there is one

God and one mediator between God
and men, the man Christ Jesus, 6who
gave himself as a ransom for all men—
the testimony given in its proper time.
7And for this purpose I was appointed
a herald and an apostle—I am telling the
truth, I am not lying—and a teacher of
the true faith to the Gentiles.
8I want men everywhere to lift up
holy hands in prayer, without anger or
disputing.
9I also want women to dress modestly,
with decency and propriety, not with
braided hair or gold or pearls or expensive clothes, 10but with good deeds, appropriate for women who profess to
worship God.
11A woman should learn in quietness
and full submission. 12I do not permit a
woman to teach or to have authority
over a man; she must be silent. 13For
Adam was formed first, then Eve. 14And
Adam was not the one deceived; it was
the woman who was deceived and
became a sinner. 15But women[a] will be
saved[b] through childbearing—if they
continue in faith, love and holiness with
propriety.

[a]15 Greek *she* [b]15 Or *restored*

SHARPEN THE FOCUS

Get an ice cube from the freezer and float it in a glass of water. Go ahead. Really do it! Now look at it carefully. What proportion stays above the water? What part is submerged?

From lowly ice cubes to ice floes to icebergs, this proportion does not vary. Two-thirds of any block of ice–whatever its size–floats below the surface of the glass or lake or ocean in which it finds itself.

Now think about the work of Christ's church. Where does the bulk of that work go on– above or below the surface? Worship services. Sermons. Evangelism calls. Sunday school. All these things happen in public. And all are important. Paul devoted much of 1 Timothy 1 to a discussion about the public teaching of the Word.

But much of the church's most important work happens beneath the surface, where no one but our Lord will ever see it. That work happens as the people of Christ approach God's throne on behalf of others.

Take a look at the way Paul links the intercession in 1 Timothy 2:1 with the Gospel proclamation in 1 Timothy 2:3–6. God uses our prayers to create peace among the nations on earth, and to enable His people to live godly lives. That pleases Him (1 Timothy 2:3) *and* opens doors for the Gospel (1 Timothy 2:4).

WEEK 95 • MONDAY

1 Timothy 3:1–16

GET THE BIG PICTURE

Today's text talks about "overseers," "deacons," and "wives" (or "women"; perhaps deaconesses or wives of deacons). We can equate the office of overseer with the pastoral office today. Perhaps deacons and deaconesses correspond with our other church workers. In any case, notice that most of the standards Paul sets apply equally well to lay people. Can you find the exceptions? If time is short, focus on 1 Timothy 3:1–13.

Overseers and Deacons

3 Here is a trustworthy saying: If anyone sets his heart on being an overseer,[a] he desires a noble task. 2 Now the overseer must be above reproach, the husband of but one wife, temperate, self-controlled, respectable, hospitable, able to teach, 3 not given to drunkenness, not violent but gentle, not quarrelsome, not a lover of money. 4 He must manage his own family well and see that his children obey him with proper respect. 5 (If anyone does not know how to manage his own family, how can he take care of God's church?) 6 He must not be a recent convert, or he may become conceited and fall under the same judgment as the devil. 7 He must also have a good reputation with outsiders, so that he will not fall into disgrace and into the devil's trap.

8 Deacons, likewise, are to be men worthy of respect, sincere, not indulging in much wine, and not pursuing dishonest gain. 9 They must keep hold of the deep truths of the faith with a clear conscience. 10 They must first be tested; and then if there is nothing against them, let them serve as deacons.

11 In the same way, their wives[b] are to be women worthy of respect, not malicious talkers but temperate and trustworthy in everything.

12 A deacon must be the husband of but one wife and must manage his children and his household well. 13 Those who have served well gain an excellent standing and great assurance in their faith in Christ Jesus.

14 Although I hope to come to you soon, I am writing you these instructions so that, 15 if I am delayed, you will know how people ought to conduct themselves in God's household, which is the church of the living God, the pillar and foundation of the truth. 16 Beyond all question, the mystery of godliness is great:

He[c] appeared in a body,[d]
was vindicated by the Spirit,
was seen by angels,
was preached among the nations,
was believed on in the world,
was taken up in glory.

[a]1 Traditionally *bishop*; also in verse 2
[b]11 Or *way, deaconesses* [c]16 Some manuscripts *God* [d]16 Or *in the flesh*

SHARPEN THE FOCUS

This part of Paul's letter to Timothy has been diced, sliced, and boiled countless times in an effort to understand what the Holy Spirit says to His church today about the pastoral office. That discussion is important. But in it, two of the text's key points can easily get lost. Those points? The respect God asks His people to show those who serve them in Jesus' name and the humility of heart God asks of pastors and other workers who serve His people.

Nothing in the text even hints at the "hire 'em and fire 'em" mentality we sometimes see in the church as she deals with those who serve her today. Rather, the text conveys honor, nobility, and calling. Pastors and other workers are not employees of the congregation. They are servants of Christ, His gifts to us.

By the same token, Paul assumes that church workers have servants' hearts. Nothing here hints at sloughing off responsibilities or ignoring needs or lording it over the flock. Just the opposite, in fact.

In whatever position you serve Christ today, let the Holy Spirit touch you with the truths of this text, absolve you by the power of Christ's cross, and adjust your attitudes as He sees fit.

WEEK 95 • TUESDAY

1 Timothy 4:1–16

GET THE BIG PICTURE

Do you thank God for your food before you eat it? Today's reading encourages that practice and gives us a reason to do so. Pay special attention also to the continuing, practical advice Paul gives to young Pastor Timothy. If time is short, focus on 1 Timothy 4:1–10.

Instructions to Timothy

4 The Spirit clearly says that in later times some will abandon the faith and follow deceiving spirits and things taught by demons. [2]Such teachings come through hypocritical liars, whose consciences have been seared as with a hot iron. [3]They forbid people to marry and order them to abstain from certain foods, which God created to be received with thanksgiving by those who believe and who know the truth. [4]For everything God created is good, and nothing is to be rejected if it is received with thanksgiving, [5]because it is consecrated by the word of God and prayer.

[6]If you point these things out to the brothers, you will be a good minister of Christ Jesus, brought up in the truths of the faith and of the good teaching that you have followed. [7]Have nothing to do with godless myths and old wives' tales; rather, train yourself to be godly. [8]For physical training is of some value, but godliness has value for all things, holding promise for both the present life and the life to come.

[9]This is a trustworthy saying that deserves full acceptance [10](and for this we labor and strive), that we have put our hope in the living God, who is the Savior of all men, and especially of those who believe.

[11]Command and teach these things. [12]Don't let anyone look down on you because you are young, but set an example for the believers in speech, in life, in love, in faith and in purity. [13]Until I come, devote yourself to the public reading of Scripture, to preaching and to teaching. [14]Do not neglect your gift, which was given you through a prophetic message when the body of elders laid their hands on you.

[15]Be diligent in these matters; give yourself wholly to them, so that everyone may see your progress. [16]Watch your life and doctrine closely. Persevere in them, because if you do, you will save both yourself and your hearers.

SHARPEN THE FOCUS

Many people in our culture pick and choose what to believe, what rituals to practice, what groups to join.

When this philosophy is taken to the extreme, doctrine is rooted not in objective fact but in whatever warm thoughts an individual wants to believe. Our Lord makes it clear where the confusion comes from:

> *The Spirit clearly says that in later times some will abandon the faith and follow deceiving spirits and things taught by demons.*
> (1 Timothy 4:1)

Note those words. Those who "abandon the faith" once believed it! Such people did not wake up one morning deciding to walk away from the Lord Jesus. Chances are they drifted away slowly, like a boat loosened from its moorings.

Perhaps they grew too busy for worship and Bible study. Or they experienced some tragedy and got angry at God but were afraid to tell Him about their feelings. Maybe they committed a sin that caused so much shame, they convinced themselves they were no longer welcome in His presence.

If any of these descriptions fit you—even a little bit—don't delay. Run home to your Father. Tell Him about your hurt, your sin, and your need. Let Christ's cross comfort you and keep you in faith.

WEEK 95 • WEDNESDAY

1 Timothy 5:1–25

The world loves glitzy charities: the multi-million dollar university endowment, the food airlift to the millions starving in a far-off place with an unpronounceable name. Of course, we applaud such efforts. But as Paul makes clear, the good deeds our Lord asks of us are sometimes much closer to home. If time is short, focus on 1 Timothy 5:1–16.

Advice About Widows,
Elders and Slaves

5 Do not rebuke an older man
harshly, but exhort him as if he
were your father. Treat younger men as
brothers, 2older women as mothers, and
younger women as sisters, with absolute purity.
3Give proper recognition to those
widows who are really in need. 4But if
a widow has children or grandchildren,
these should learn first of all to put their
religion into practice by caring for their
own family and so repaying their parents and grandparents, for this is pleasing to God. 5The widow who is really in
need and left all alone puts her hope in
God and continues night and day to
pray and to ask God for help. 6But the
widow who lives for pleasure is dead
even while she lives. 7Give the people
these instructions, too, so that no one
may be open to blame. 8If anyone does
not provide for his relatives, and especially for his immediate family, he has
denied the faith and is worse than an
unbeliever.
9No widow may be put on the list of
widows unless she is over sixty, has
been faithful to her husband,[a] 10and is
well known for her good deeds, such as
bringing up children, showing hospitality, washing the feet of the saints, helping those in trouble and devoting
herself to all kinds of good deeds.
11As for younger widows, do not put
them on such a list. For when their sensual desires overcome their dedication
to Christ, they want to marry. 12Thus
they bring judgment on themselves, because they have broken their first
pledge. 13Besides, they get into the habit
of being idle and going about from
house to house. And not only do they

[a]9 Or *has had but one husband*

become idlers, but also gossips and
busybodies, saying things they ought
not to. 14So I counsel younger widows
to marry, to have children, to manage
their homes and to give the enemy no
opportunity for slander. 15Some have
in fact already turned away to follow
Satan.

16If any woman who is a believer has
widows in her family, she should help
them and not let the church be burdened with them, so that the church can
help those widows who are really in
need.

17The elders who direct the affairs of
the church well are worthy of double
honor, especially those whose work is
preaching and teaching. 18For the Scripture says, "Do not muzzle the ox while
it is treading out the grain,"[a] and "The
worker deserves his wages."[b] 19Do not
entertain an accusation against an elder
unless it is brought by two or three
witnesses. 20Those who sin are to be rebuked publicly, so that the others may
take warning.

21I charge you, in the sight of God and
Christ Jesus and the elect angels, to keep
these instructions without partiality,
and to do nothing out of favoritism.

22Do not be hasty in the laying on of
hands, and do not share in the sins of
others. Keep yourself pure.

23Stop drinking only water, and use a
little wine because of your stomach and
your frequent illnesses.

24The sins of some men are obvious,
reaching the place of judgment ahead of
them; the sins of others trail behind
them. 25In the same way, good deeds are
obvious, and even those that are not
cannot be hidden.

[a]*18* Deut. 25:4 [b]*18* Luke 10:7

SHARPEN THE FOCUS

In loving God and showing love to one another, we will one day find heaven's best and highest joy. But we need not reserve that joy for heaven. Our Lord urges us throughout Scripture to begin now, here on earth.

Love didn't start with us or in us. In our natural state—our sinful nature—love was impossible. Jesus came as "the Savior of all" (1 Timothy 4:10) to heal that flaw and to make our love possible. Because "God so loved" and gave His Son (John 3:16), we can now act in love toward Him and other people.

All this sounds so simple in theory. But then the Holy Spirit shows us specific ways to put it into practice. Take 1 Timothy 5:4, for instance. If we're honest, we must admit that some elderly parents are cantankerous. Some grandparents are alone because they are mean or cross or unpleasant to be around for some other reason.

We cannot make ourselves love them. On our own we cannot even *want* to show them love. That's why only God's people can do the kind of ministry our Lord here asks. We know what it's like to be loved when we we're unlovable. That's what Jesus has done for us, and in Him we can find strength, compassion, and yes, even joy in showing love to others.

Peace. Everyone longs for it, but it can often be elusive. As God's children, peace is one of the crown jewels of our faith. One facet of peace is contentment. As you read today, look for reasons you personally can be content. If time is short, focus on 1 Timothy 6:3–19.

6 All who are under the yoke of
slavery should consider their
masters worthy of full respect, so that
God's name and our teaching may not
be slandered. 2Those who have believing masters are not to show less respect
for them because they are brothers. Instead, they are to serve them even better, because those who benefit from
their service are believers, and dear to
them. These are the things you are to
teach and urge on them.

Love of Money

3If anyone teaches false doctrines and
does not agree to the sound instruction
of our Lord Jesus Christ and to godly
teaching, 4he is conceited and understands nothing. He has an unhealthy interest in controversies and quarrels
about words that result in envy, strife,
malicious talk, evil suspicions 5and constant friction between men of corrupt
mind, who have been robbed of the
truth and who think that godliness is a
means to financial gain.
6But godliness with contentment is
great gain. 7For we brought nothing into
the world, and we can take nothing out
of it. 8But if we have food and clothing,
we will be content with that. 9People
who want to get rich fall into temptation
and a trap and into many foolish and
harmful desires that plunge men into
ruin and destruction. 10For the love of
money is a root of all kinds of evil. Some
people, eager for money, have wandered from the faith and pierced themselves with many griefs.

Paul's Charge to Timothy

11But you, man of God, flee from all
this, and pursue righteousness, godliness, faith, love, endurance and gentleness. 12Fight the good fight of the faith.
Take hold of the eternal life to which
you were called when you made your
good confession in the presence of
many witnesses. 13In the sight of God,
who gives life to everything, and of
Christ Jesus, who while testifying before
Pontius Pilate made the good confession, I charge you 14to keep this command without spot or blame until the
appearing of our Lord Jesus Christ,
15which God will bring about in his own
time—God, the blessed and only Ruler,
the King of kings and Lord of lords,
16who alone is immortal and who lives
in unapproachable light, whom no one
has seen or can see. To him be honor and
might forever. Amen.

17Command those who are rich in this
present world not to be arrogant nor to
put their hope in wealth, which is so uncertain, but to put their hope in God,
who richly provides us with everything
for our enjoyment. 18Command them to
do good, to be rich in good deeds,
and to be generous and willing to
share. 19In this way they will lay up
treasure for themselves as a firm foundation for the coming age, so that they

may take hold of the life that is truly life.
[20]Timothy, guard what has been entrusted to your care. Turn away from godless chatter and the opposing ideas of what is falsely called knowledge,
[21]which some have professed and in so doing have wandered from the faith.

Grace be with you.

SHARPEN THE FOCUS

"Simplify!" preached Henry David Thoreau. No doubt many in his day considered him something of a nut case. But today several best-selling books and at least one monthly magazine proclaim the same message and give dozens of practical ways to accomplish it.

Clutter can get in the way of contentment. But so does greed. And even more so, the belief that collecting things and amassing money will make us happy.

Look around you. See what God has given! The sky. The leaves. Today's lunch. The clothes you wear. His Son.

God is a giver. It's His nature. Even when we disobey Him, even when we live unthankful lives, He goes on loving and forgiving us, for Jesus' sake. He will keep on giving us what we need until the day we die. And then He will give us all the riches of His heavenly mansions.

Knowing this, we can be content. We can be rich in good works, generous and willing to share (1 Timothy 6:18). We can enjoy the gifts we receive each day from our Father's hand (1 Timothy 6:17), especially His peace and contentment in Jesus, our Savior.

2 TIMOTHY

Paul begins his second letter to Timothy by pointing out that God has been at work, bringing Timothy to faith and then keeping him faithful. Paul points out that the Gospel is not "do" but "done!" Look for evidence of that as you read now. If time is short, focus on 2 Timothy 1:6–10.

1 Paul, an apostle of Christ Jesus by
the will of God, according to the
promise of life that is in Christ Jesus,

2To Timothy, my dear son:

Grace, mercy and peace from God the Father and Christ Jesus our Lord.

Encouragement to Be Faithful

3I thank God, whom I serve, as my
forefathers did, with a clear conscience,
as night and day I constantly remember
you in my prayers. 4Recalling your tears,
I long to see you, so that I may be filled
with joy. 5I have been reminded of your
sincere faith, which first lived in your
grandmother Lois and in your mother
Eunice and, I am persuaded, now lives
in you also. 6For this reason I remind
you to fan into flame the gift of God,
which is in you through the laying on
of my hands. 7For God did not give us a
spirit of timidity, but a spirit of power,
of love and of self-discipline.

8So do not be ashamed to testify about
our Lord, or ashamed of me his prisoner.
But join with me in suffering for the gospel, by the power of God, 9who has
saved us and called us to a holy life—
not because of anything we have done
but because of his own purpose and
grace. This grace was given us in Christ
Jesus before the beginning of time, 10but
it has now been revealed through the
appearing of our Savior, Christ Jesus,
who has destroyed death and has
brought life and immortality to light
through the gospel. 11And of this gospel
I was appointed a herald and an apostle
and a teacher. 12That is why I am suffering as I am. Yet I am not ashamed, because I know whom I have believed,
and am convinced that he is able to
guard what I have entrusted to him for
that day.

13What you heard from me, keep as
the pattern of sound teaching, with
faith and love in Christ Jesus. 14Guard
the good deposit that was entrusted to
you—guard it with the help of the Holy
Spirit who lives in us.

15You know that everyone in the province of Asia has deserted me, including
Phygelus and Hermogenes.

16May the Lord show mercy to the
household of Onesiphorus, because he
often refreshed me and was not
ashamed of my chains. 17On the contrary, when he was in Rome, he
searched hard for me until he found me.
18May the Lord grant that he will find
mercy from the Lord on that day! You
know very well in how many ways he
helped me in Ephesus.

SHARPEN THE FOCUS

The truth that the Son of God became true man for us fills our hearts with comfort and with joy.

Paul would know. As he wrote 2 Timothy, he sat in a cold, stone prison cell awaiting the executioner's sword. Most of his friends, afraid for their lives, had abandoned him. If anyone needed comfort, it was Paul. If anyone needed a reason to be joyful, it was Paul.

And yet his words ring out with both comfort and joy. Read 2 Timothy 1:8. Paul actually invites Timothy to join him—to share in suffering for the Gospel! But note—note it well—*not* in his own strength. No, "by the power of God," he says. Look what that great God has done for us (2 Timothy 1:9–10):

- saved by His grace
- called us to a holy life by His grace
- given us grace, His undeserved love, before time began
- revealed that grace in Jesus Christ
- destroyed death
- brought us new life and immortality

And what God has given, He will guard and keep (2 Timothy 1:12). He will preserve us steadfast in faith until He returns to take us home.

Paul was not timid in witnessing to this Gospel nor in trusting God to do what He had promised (2 Timothy 1:7). We need not be either. The Gospel is our comfort and our joy.

WEEK 95 • SATURDAY

2 Timothy 2:1–26

GET THE BIG PICTURE

Soldiers. Athletes. Farmers. Today's text talks about all three. Ask yourself what they have in common. Also ask why Paul chose these models for those in Christian ministry. If time is short, focus on 2 Timothy 2:1–13.

2 You then, my son, be strong in
the grace that is in Christ Jesus.
2And the things you have heard me say
in the presence of many witnesses entrust to reliable men who will also be
qualified to teach others. 3Endure hardship with us like a good soldier of Christ
Jesus. 4No one serving as a soldier gets
involved in civilian affairs—he wants to
please his commanding officer. 5Similarly, if anyone competes as an athlete,
he does not receive the victor's crown
unless he competes according to the
rules. 6The hardworking farmer should
be the first to receive a share of the
crops. 7Reflect on what I am saying, for
the Lord will give you insight into all
this.

8Remember Jesus Christ, raised from
the dead, descended from David. This
is my gospel, 9for which I am suffering
even to the point of being chained like
a criminal. But God's word is not
chained. 10Therefore I endure everything for the sake of the elect, that they
too may obtain the salvation that is in
Christ Jesus, with eternal glory.
11Here is a trustworthy saying:

If we died with him,
  we will also live with him;
12if we endure,
  we will also reign with him.
If we disown him,
  he will also disown us;
13if we are faithless,
  he will remain faithful,
  for he cannot disown himself.

A Workman Approved by God

14Keep reminding them of these
things. Warn them before God against
quarreling about words; it is of no value, and only ruins those who listen. 15Do
your best to present yourself to God as
one approved, a workman who does
not need to be ashamed and who correctly handles the word of truth. 16Avoid
godless chatter, because those who indulge in it will become more and more
ungodly. 17Their teaching will spread
like gangrene. Among them are Hymenaeus and Philetus, 18who have wandered away from the truth. They say
that the resurrection has already taken
place, and they destroy the faith of
some. 19Nevertheless, God's solid foundation stands firm, sealed with this inscription: "The Lord knows those who
are his,"[a] and, "Everyone who confesses
the name of the Lord must turn away
from wickedness."
20In a large house there are articles not
only of gold and silver, but also of wood
and clay; some are for noble purposes
and some for ignoble. 21If a man cleanses
himself from the latter, he will be an instrument for noble purposes, made
holy, useful to the Master and prepared
to do any good work.
22Flee the evil desires of youth, and
pursue righteousness, faith, love and
peace, along with those who call on the
Lord out of a pure heart. 23Don't have
anything to do with foolish and stupid
arguments, because you know they
produce quarrels. 24And the Lord's servant must not quarrel; instead, he must
be kind to everyone, able to teach, not
resentful. 25Those who oppose him he
must gently instruct, in the hope that
God will grant them repentance leading
them to a knowledge of the truth, 26and
that they will come to their senses and
escape from the trap of the devil, who
has taken them captive to do his will.

[a] *19* Num. 16:5 (see Septuagint)

SHARPEN THE FOCUS

Paul did not sugarcoat the truth about Timothy's service for Christ. Like every faithful pastor before or since, Timothy would encounter opposition. Not everything God asked of him would come easily nor every decision draw applause. Sometimes ministry would seem to grind on, mile after mile, like the training course of a marathon runner.

But God would grant a harvest (2 Timothy 2:6). The hardworking farmer would one day see fruit filling the trees of the orchard. Until then, Timothy could keep his eyes on the prize instead of on the problems. He could remember the Son of God who took on the flesh and blood of human beings, the Son of David who died and rose again to save sinners (2 Timothy 2:8). And he could focus on "the elect" (2 Timothy 2:10), those whom God chose from all eternity to inherit a place in His family. What a privilege to serve them!

Whether you are a pastor or a parishioner, ask yourself what you and your congregation are focused on. Is the Gospel central in your life? As you serve Christ, whom do you encourage? To whom can you turn for encouragement? Talk about these questions with your Lord in prayer before you go back to the "war," the "marathon," the "field."

WEEK 96 • MONDAY

2 Timothy 3:1—4:22

When someone sits down to write your obituary, what do you hope they include? The chapters you will read today stand like an epitaph over Paul's life. Why do you suppose he included the things he did? If time is short, focus on 2 Timothy 3:1–17.

Godlessness in the Last Days

3 But mark this: There will be terrible times in the last days.
2People will be lovers of themselves, lovers of money, boastful, proud, abusive,
disobedient to their parents, ungrateful,
unholy, 3without love, unforgiving,
slanderous, without self-control, brutal,
not lovers of the good, 4treacherous,
rash, conceited, lovers of pleasure rather
than lovers of God— 5having a form of
godliness but denying its power. Have
nothing to do with them.
6They are the kind who worm their
way into homes and gain control over
weak-willed women, who are loaded
down with sins and are swayed by all
kinds of evil desires, 7always learning
but never able to acknowledge the
truth. 8Just as Jannes and Jambres opposed Moses, so also these men oppose
the truth—men of depraved minds,
who, as far as the faith is concerned, are
rejected. 9But they will not get very far
because, as in the case of those men,
their folly will be clear to everyone.

Paul's Charge to Timothy

10You, however, know all about my
teaching, my way of life, my purpose,
faith, patience, love, endurance, 11per-
secutions, sufferings—what kinds of
things happened to me in Antioch, Iconium and Lystra, the persecutions I endured. Yet the Lord rescued me from all
of them. 12In fact, everyone who wants
to live a godly life in Christ Jesus will be
persecuted, 13while evil men and impostors will go from bad to worse, deceiving and being deceived. 14But as for you,
continue in what you have learned and
have become convinced of, because you
know those from whom you learned it,
15and how from infancy you have
known the holy Scriptures, which are
able to make you wise for salvation
through faith in Christ Jesus. 16All Scripture is God-breathed and is useful for
teaching, rebuking, correcting and
training in righteousness, 17so that the
man of God may be thoroughly
equipped for every good work.

4 In the presence of God and of
Christ Jesus, who will judge the
living and the dead, and in view of his
appearing and his kingdom, I give you
this charge: 2Preach the Word; be prepared in season and out of season; correct, rebuke and encourage—with great
patience and careful instruction. 3For
the time will come when men will not
put up with sound doctrine. Instead,
to suit their own desires, they will gather around them a great number of

teachers to say what their itching ears
want to hear. [4]They will turn their ears
away from the truth and turn aside to
myths. [5]But you, keep your head in all
situations, endure hardship, do the
work of an evangelist, discharge all the
duties of your ministry.

[6]For I am already being poured out
like a drink offering, and the time has
come for my departure. [7]I have fought
the good fight, I have finished the race,
I have kept the faith. [8]Now there is in
store for me the crown of righteousness,
which the Lord, the righteous Judge,
will award to me on that day—and not
only to me, but also to all who have
longed for his appearing.

Personal Remarks

[9]Do your best to come to me quickly,
[10]for Demas, because he loved this
world, has deserted me and has gone to
Thessalonica. Crescens has gone to Galatia, and Titus to Dalmatia. [11]Only Luke
is with me. Get Mark and bring him
with you, because he is helpful to me in
my ministry. [12]I sent Tychicus to Ephesus. [13]When you come, bring the cloak
that I left with Carpus at Troas, and my
scrolls, especially the parchments.

[14]Alexander the metalworker did me
a great deal of harm. The Lord will repay him for what he has done. [15]You too
should be on your guard against him,
because he strongly opposed our message.

[16]At my first defense, no one came to
my support, but everyone deserted me.
May it not be held against them. [17]But
the Lord stood at my side and gave me
strength, so that through me the message might be fully proclaimed and all
the Gentiles might hear it. And I was delivered from the lion's mouth. [18]The
Lord will rescue me from every evil attack and will bring me safely to his
heavenly kingdom. To him be glory for
ever and ever. Amen.

Final Greetings

[19]Greet Priscilla[a] and Aquila and the
household of Onesiphorus. [20]Erastus
stayed in Corinth, and I left Trophimus
sick in Miletus. [21]Do your best to get
here before winter. Eubulus greets you,
and so do Pudens, Linus, Claudia and
all the brothers.

[22]The Lord be with your spirit. Grace
be with you.

[a]19 Greek *Prisca*, a variant of *Priscilla*

SHARPEN THE FOCUS

Suppose a trusted friend gave you the keys to a condo in a resort area. Imagine he provided you with a map that gave detailed directions about where to get free meals and gasoline. Few of us would argue about the map. We would simply use it.

In 2 Timothy 3:15–17, our Lord states most clearly the total trustworthiness of the Holy Scriptures. He goes on to tell us how to use them. We believe His Word is infallible truth. But believing, we also act on that truth. We use God's Word as He intended:

- For "teaching"—God's Word tells us all we need to know about the salvation that is ours in Jesus' death and resurrection.
- For "rebuking"—God's Word refutes the demonic lies that undermine the fact of Christ's work on our behalf.
- For "correcting"—God's Word sets us on our feet when we fall into sin.
- For "training in righteousness"—God's Word educates us about the favorable verdict already rendered because of Jesus. We are *righteous,* right with God.

As Scripture continues to work these things in our hearts, God equips us through it for every good work (2 Timothy 3:17). We receive the willingness and ability to be Christ's witnesses, partners in the Gospel.

TITUS

"If you talk the talk, then walk the walk." That's what Paul says to the false teachers in Crete. Faith—true saving faith—works. Or, as the reformer Martin Luther put it, "Faith alone saves, but faith is never alone." If time is short, focus on Titus 1:1–4.

1 Paul, a servant of God and an apostle of Jesus Christ for the faith of
God's elect and the knowledge of the
truth that leads to godliness— 2a faith
and knowledge resting on the hope of
eternal life, which God, who does not
lie, promised before the beginning of
time, 3and at his appointed season he
brought his word to light through the
preaching entrusted to me by the command of God our Savior,

4To Titus, my true son in our common
faith:

Grace and peace from God the Father and Christ Jesus our Savior.

Titus's Task on Crete

5The reason I left you in Crete was
that you might straighten out what was
left unfinished and appoint[a] elders in
every town, as I directed you. 6An elder
must be blameless, the husband of but
one wife, a man whose children believe
and are not open to the charge of being
wild and disobedient. 7Since an overseer[b] is entrusted with God's work, he
must be blameless—not overbearing,
not quick-tempered, not given to
drunkenness, not violent, not pursuing
dishonest gain. 8Rather he must be hospitable, one who loves what is good,
who is self-controlled, upright, holy and
disciplined. 9He must hold firmly to the
trustworthy message as it has been
taught, so that he can encourage others
by sound doctrine and refute those who
oppose it.

10For there are many rebellious people, mere talkers and deceivers, especially those of the circumcision group.
11They must be silenced, because they
are ruining whole households by teaching things they ought not to teach—and
that for the sake of dishonest gain.
12Even one of their own prophets has
said, "Cretans are always liars, evil
brutes, lazy gluttons." 13This testimony
is true. Therefore, rebuke them sharply,
so that they will be sound in the faith
14and will pay no attention to Jewish
myths or to the commands of those who
reject the truth. 15To the pure, all things
are pure, but to those who are corrupted and do not believe, nothing is
pure. In fact, both their minds and consciences are corrupted. 16They claim to
know God, but by their actions they
deny him. They are detestable, disobedient and unfit for doing anything
good.

[a]5 Or *ordain* [b]7 Traditionally *bishop*

SHARPEN THE FOCUS

A slave's clothes, time, body—all these belong to that slave's master. With that in mind, think about the fact that Paul calls himself "a [slave] of God" (Titus 1:1). "Slave" is the literal meaning of the Greek word most English versions translate as "servant." Paul uses this word to describe his life in Titus and in several of his other letters too.

Early readers of the New Testament would have opened their eyes wider as they read this word. No one alive at that time would have chosen life as a slave, and surely no one in pleasure-drenched Crete would have volunteered for that position. But Paul treasures it, boasts of it even. He belongs to God.

The slave Paul is also the "apostle" Paul (Titus 1:1). Sent by Jesus Christ, he serves as an ambassador of heaven. As such, he invites everyone to share in the riches of hope, security, forgiveness, peace, wholeness, and eternal life Jesus died to earn for us.

While none of us today can claim the title "apostle," we do belong totally to Christ. He purchased us with His own blood. We serve our gracious Savior with all that we are and all that we have. And we witness to the goodness of our Master.

Serve today in joy!

WEEK 96 • WEDNESDAY

Titus 2:1–15

GET THE BIG PICTURE

Teach what is true; do what is right. So Paul instructs Titus, again calling attention to the importance of integrity of faith and life. Think about the link between your own faith talk and faith walk as you read today. If time is short, focus on Titus 2:11–15.

What Must Be Taught to Various Groups

2 You must teach what is in accord
with sound doctrine. 2Teach the
older men to be temperate, worthy of
respect, self-controlled, and sound in
faith, in love and in endurance.
3Likewise, teach the older women to
be reverent in the way they live, not to
be slanderers or addicted to much wine,
but to teach what is good. 4Then they
can train the younger women to love
their husbands and children, 5to be self-
controlled and pure, to be busy at home,
to be kind, and to be subject to their
husbands, so that no one will malign
the word of God.
6Similarly, encourage the young men
to be self-controlled. 7In everything set
them an example by doing what is
good. In your teaching show integrity,
seriousness 8and soundness of speech
that cannot be condemned, so that
those who oppose you may be ashamed
because they have nothing bad to say
about us.
9Teach slaves to be subject to their
masters in everything, to try to please
them, not to talk back to them, 10and not
to steal from them, but to show that they

can be fully trusted, so that in every way
they will make the teaching about God
our Savior attractive.
11For the grace of God that brings salvation has appeared to all men. 12It
teaches us to say "No" to ungodliness
and worldly passions, and to live self-
controlled, upright and godly lives
in this present age, 13while we wait
for the blessed hope—the glorious
appearing of our great God and Savior,
Jesus Christ, 14who gave himself for
us to redeem us from all wickedness
and to purify for himself a people that
are his very own, eager to do what is
good.
15These, then, are the things you
should teach. Encourage and rebuke
with all authority. Do not let anyone despise you.

SHARPEN THE FOCUS

In every era those who oppose the Christian faith justify their opposition by pointing to bad behavior by Christians. Paul, Peter, John, and James all call Christ's followers to lead exemplary lives—not just because holy lives please God, but also "so that in every way [we] will make the teaching about God our Savior attractive" (Titus 2:10).

"The whole world is watching!" Protesters have screamed these words at police officers during all kinds of demonstrations in the recent past as TV cameras beamed both words and pictures around the globe.

The "whole world" may not be watching you, but someone is! Your son or daughter. Your neighbor up the street. The other spectators at the football game you attend. The waiter at that restaurant you frequent. Would these people say they're attracted to your Savior and His teaching because of what they see in you?

Of course, none of us lives with 100% Christian consistency. When we examine our motives, our attitudes, our words, how glad we can be for our Savior and His cross. And how powerfully His love and pardon work in our lives to motivate and equip us to live in such a way that others are drawn to Him.

WEEK 96 • THURSDAY

Titus 3:1–15

GET THE BIG PICTURE

Again in Titus, chapter 3, Paul ties a Christlike lifestyle with a clear understanding of God's grace in Christ and reliance on that grace. Look for that important connection as you read. If time is short, focus on Titus 3:1–8.

Doing What Is Good

3 Remind the people to be subject
to rulers and authorities, to be
obedient, to be ready to do whatever is
good, 2to slander no one, to be peaceable
and considerate, and to show true humility toward all men.
3At one time we too were foolish, disobedient, deceived and enslaved by all
kinds of passions and pleasures. We

lived in malice and envy, being hated
and hating one another. 4But when the
kindness and love of God our Savior appeared, 5he saved us, not because of
righteous things we had done, but because of his mercy. He saved us through
the washing of rebirth and renewal by
the Holy Spirit, 6whom he poured out
on us generously through Jesus Christ
our Savior, 7so that, having been justified by his grace, we might become heirs
having the hope of eternal life. 8This is
a trustworthy saying. And I want you to
stress these things, so that those who
have trusted in God may be careful to
devote themselves to doing what is
good. These things are excellent and
profitable for everyone.
9But avoid foolish controversies and
genealogies and arguments and quarrels about the law, because these are unprofitable and useless. 10Warn a divisive
person once, and then warn him a second time. After that, have nothing to do
with him. 11You may be sure that such a
man is warped and sinful; he is self-
condemned.

Final Remarks

12As soon as I send Artemas or Tychicus to you, do your best to come to me
at Nicopolis, because I have decided to
winter there. 13Do everything you can to
help Zenas the lawyer and Apollos on
their way and see that they have everything they need. 14Our people must
learn to devote themselves to doing
what is good, in order that they may
provide for daily necessities and not live
unproductive lives.
15Everyone with me sends you greetings. Greet those who love us in the
faith.

Grace be with you all.

SHARPEN THE FOCUS

The field of medical risk assessment came into being because government officials, industry, and insurance companies wanted ways to measure the damage done by specific environmental hazards.

As the experts work, they have come to some uncomfortable conclusions. The biggest risks we face each day are of our own making. Unhealthy diets, tobacco use, lack of exercise, and failure to wear seat belts pose huge risks when compared with all the air and water pollution and the chemical exposures of modern living combined!

Most people get out of their bodies pretty much what they put into them. This is true in our spiritual lives, too. Yes, we want to avoid exposure to the pollution of false doctrine. But far more critical is the truth that God works a healthy Christian life and lifestyle in us as we take in a healthy portion of the pure Gospel each day of our lives.

"I want you to stress these things," Paul says, referring to the Good News of God's grace toward us in Christ, "*so that* those who have trusted in God may be careful to devote themselves to doing what is good" (Titus 3:8). When the Gospel continually acts on our hearts, godly living will establish itself in us.

PHILEMON

WEEK 96 • FRIDAY

Philemon 1–25

Onesimus, whose name means "useful," belonged to Philemon. This slave escaped and met up somehow with someone Philemon knew well–the apostle Paul. Through this contact, Onesimus came to faith. Paul then sent him back to Philemon–a personal letter in hand. If you were Philemon, how would you have responded?

[1]Paul, a prisoner of Christ Jesus, and
Timothy our brother,

To Philemon our dear friend and fellow worker, [2]to Apphia our sister, to Archippus our fellow soldier and to the
church that meets in your home:

[3]Grace to you and peace from God
our Father and the Lord Jesus Christ.

Thanksgiving and Prayer

[4]I always thank my God as I remember you in my prayers, [5]because I hear
about your faith in the Lord Jesus and
your love for all the saints. [6]I pray that
you may be active in sharing your faith,
so that you will have a full understanding of every good thing we have in
Christ. [7]Your love has given me great joy
and encouragement, because you,
brother, have refreshed the hearts of
the saints.

Paul's Plea for Onesimus

[8]Therefore, although in Christ I could
be bold and order you to do what you
ought to do, [9]yet I appeal to you on the
basis of love. I then, as Paul—an old man
and now also a prisoner of Christ
Jesus— [10]I appeal to you for my son
Onesimus,[a] who became my son while
I was in chains. [11]Formerly he was useless to you, but now he has become useful both to you and to me.

[12]I am sending him—who is my very
heart—back to you. [13]I would have liked
to keep him with me so that he could
take your place in helping me while I
am in chains for the gospel. [14]But I did
not want to do anything without your
consent, so that any favor you do will be
spontaneous and not forced. [15]Perhaps
the reason he was separated from you
for a little while was that you might
have him back for good— [16]no longer as
a slave, but better than a slave, as a dear
brother. He is very dear to me but even
dearer to you, both as a man and as a
brother in the Lord.

[17]So if you consider me a partner, welcome him as you would welcome me.
[18]If he has done you any wrong or owes
you anything, charge it to me. [19]I, Paul,
am writing this with my own hand. I
will pay it back—not to mention that
you owe me your very self. [20]I do wish,
brother, that I may have some benefit
from you in the Lord; refresh my heart

[a]10 *Onesimus* means *useful.*

in Christ. 21Confident of your obedience, I write to you, knowing that you will do even more than I ask.

22And one thing more: Prepare a guest room for me, because I hope to be restored to you in answer to your prayers.

23Epaphras, my fellow prisoner in Christ Jesus, sends you greetings. 24And so do Mark, Aristarchus, Demas and Luke, my fellow workers.

25The grace of the Lord Jesus Christ be with your spirit.

SHARPEN THE FOCUS

Onesimus had committed a capital offense. If Philemon forgave, what might his neighbors think?

Philemon may never have thought of Onesimus as a human being before—slaves had zero status. But now Paul was calling Onesimus a brother! How could Philemon enslave a fellow Christian?

We will never face Philemon's dilemma. But we all encounter situations in which others ask for our forgiveness. Most times, their offenses have truly hurt us. Perhaps we've suffered economic setbacks because of what someone has done. Or our status at work or in the community has lost some of its glow. Maybe we've never really thought much about the offender. Or maybe we've been close friends. Either way, the offender asks for forgiveness. Do we set him free or make him pay?

Knowing we *should* forgive and *wanting* to forgive are often two different things. But not one "should" appears in Paul's letter. Instead, Paul points Philemon back to the Gospel, back to God's love in Jesus Christ. Philemon's ability to forgive—and ours too—begins there. When we have trouble tearing up the IOUs we have collected from others, we need to go back to stand for a while at the foot of the cross. There, Christ's love to us will melt our unforgiving hearts.

HEBREWS

WEEK 96 • SATURDAY

Hebrews 1:1–14

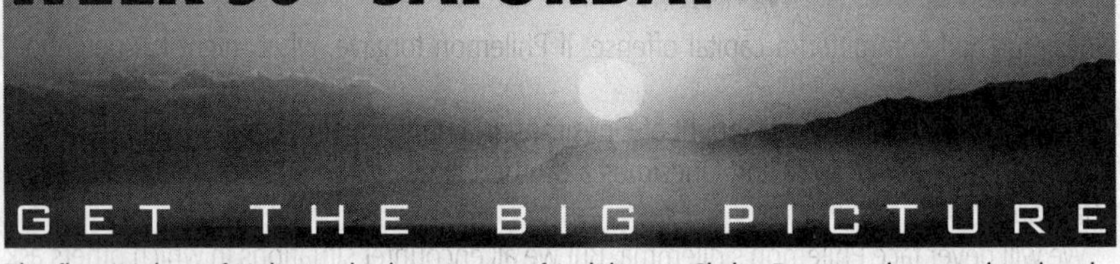

The first readers of Hebrews had come out of Judaism to Christ. But now, harassed and anticipating even more severe persecution, some of them had begun to think of going back to their Jewish faith. Are you ever tempted to walk away from Christ? If so, where will you go? If time is short, focus on Hebrews 1:1–4.

The Son Superior to Angels

1 In the past God spoke to our forefathers through the prophets at
many times and in various ways, 2but in
these last days he has spoken to us by
his Son, whom he appointed heir of all
things, and through whom he made the
universe. 3The Son is the radiance of
God's glory and the exact representa-
tion of his being, sustaining all things by
his powerful word. After he had provided purification for sins, he sat down at
the right hand of the Majesty in heav-
en. 4So he became as much superior to
the angels as the name he has inherited
is superior to theirs.

5For to which of the angels did God ever say,

> "You are my Son;
> today I have become your
> Father[a]"[b]?

Or again,

> "I will be his Father,
> and he will be my Son"[c]?

6And again, when God brings his firstborn into the world, he says,

> "Let all God's angels worship him."[d]

7In speaking of the angels he says,

> "He makes his angels winds,
> his servants flames of fire."[e]

8But about the Son he says,

> "Your throne, O God, will last for
> ever and ever,
> and righteousness will be the
> scepter of your kingdom.
> 9You have loved righteousness and
> hated wickedness;
> therefore God, your God, has set
> you above your companions
> by anointing you with the oil of
> joy."[f]

10He also says,

> "In the beginning, O Lord, you laid
> the foundations of the earth,
> and the heavens are the work of
> your hands.
> 11They will perish, but you remain;
> they will all wear out like a
> garment.
> 12You will roll them up like a robe;

[a]5 Or *have begotten you* [b]5 Psalm 2:7
[c]5 2 Samuel 7:14; 1 Chron. 17:13 [d]6 Deut. 32:43 (see Dead Sea Scrolls and Septuagint)
[e]7 Psalm 104:4 [f]9 Psalm 45:6,7

like a garment they will be
changed.
But you remain the same,
and your years will never end."[a]

[13]To which of the angels did God ever
say,

"Sit at my right hand
until I make your enemies
a footstool for your feet"[b]?

[14]Are not all angels ministering spirits
sent to serve those who will inherit salvation?

SHARPEN THE FOCUS

If you change your will, you'll find your lawyer including language at the beginning of the new document to certify it as your "*last* will and testament." By signing it, you revoke any and all previous wills. You want your heirs and the probate court to hear your final word on who inherits what.

In a similar way Hebrews 1 makes it clear that Jesus is the Father's final, perfect Word toward us poor sinners. God spoke through the prophets, to be sure (Hebrews 1:1). But now He has spoken through His Son!

In Jesus, we hear from God the word of grace. In Jesus, we hear from God the word of pardon and of peace. In Jesus, God Himself provided purification for our sins (Hebrews 1:3). Now this Word occupies heaven's high throne as Savior, as King, as Preserver of the universe, and as our soon-coming Judge.

This final Word of God did not revoke what the prophets said and wrote. Jesus didn't contradict the prophets' words. Jesus fulfilled them. God's first revelation of His will to Adam and Eve in the garden agrees fully with God's revelation of Himself in Christ. Jesus is God's Word of love—to you!

WEEK 97 • MONDAY

Hebrews 2:1–18

GET THE BIG PICTURE

Chapter 2 begins with the first of five explicit warnings to the readers of Hebrews: *Don't drift away!* As you read what writer has to say to the Hebrews, think about times in the past when you *have* drifted. What led to that? If time is short, focus on Hebrews 2:5–18.

Warning to Pay Attention

2 We must pay more careful attention, therefore, to what we have
heard, so that we do not drift away. [2]For
if the message spoken by angels was
binding, and every violation and disobedience received its just punishment,
[3]how shall we escape if we ignore such
a great salvation? This salvation, which
was first announced by the Lord, was
confirmed to us by those who heard
him. [4]God also testified to it by signs,
wonders and various miracles, and gifts
of the Holy Spirit distributed according
to his will.

[a]12 Psalm 102:25-27 [b]13 Psalm 110:1

Jesus Made Like His Brothers

[5]It is not to angels that he has subjected the world to come, about which we are speaking. [6]But there is a place where someone has testified:

> "What is man that you are mindful
> of him,
> the son of man that you care for
> him?
> [7]You made him a little[a] lower than
> the angels;
> you crowned him with glory and
> honor
> [8] and put everything under his
> feet."[b]

In putting everything under him, God left nothing that is not subject to him. Yet at present we do not see everything subject to him. [9]But we see Jesus, who was made a little lower than the angels, now crowned with glory and honor because he suffered death, so that by the grace of God he might taste death for everyone.

[10]In bringing many sons to glory, it was fitting that God, for whom and through whom everything exists, should make the author of their salvation perfect through suffering. [11]Both the one who makes men holy and those who are made holy are of the same family. So Jesus is not ashamed to call them brothers. [12]He says,

> "I will declare your name to my
> brothers;
> in the presence of the
> congregation I will sing your
> praises."[c]

[13]And again,

> "I will put my trust in him."[d]

And again he says,

> "Here am I, and the children God
> has given me."[e]

[14]Since the children have flesh and blood, he too shared in their humanity so that by his death he might destroy him who holds the power of death—that is, the devil— [15]and free those who all their lives were held in slavery by their fear of death. [16]For surely it is not angels he helps, but Abraham's descendants. [17]For this reason he had to be made like his brothers in every way, in order that he might become a merciful and faithful high priest in service to God, and that he might make atonement for[f] the sins of the people. [18]Because he himself suffered when he was tempted, he is able to help those who are being tempted.

[a]7 Or *him for a little while*; also in verse 9
[b]8 Psalm 8:4-6 [c]12 Psalm 22:22
[d]13 Isaiah 8:17 [e]13 Isaiah 8:18
[f]17 Or *and that he might turn aside God's wrath, taking away*

SHARPEN THE FOCUS

Rust ruins neglected tools. Neglecting our faith-life leads just as surely to ruin. When we neglect our faith we soon begin to drift away from our spiritual mooring–Christ's cross.

At the cross, Christ secured for us "a great salvation" (Hebrews 2:3)–our *only* salvation. There, He "taste[d] death" for us (Hebrews 2:9). The bitterness of that death should have remained on our lips forever. It belonged to us because of our sins. Asaph wrote about God's cup of anger and judgment:

> *In the hand of the LORD there is a cup*
> *full of foaming wine mixed with spices;*
> *He pours it out, and all the wicked of the earth*
> *drink it down to its very dregs.* (Psalm 75:8)

Jesus drank the bitter dregs of God's fury. Jesus "taste[d] death" (Hebrews 2:9) for us. He now holds out to us the sweet cup of His salvation (Psalm 116:13). At the Lord's Table, we receive a foretaste of the salvation that will be ours to enjoy fully—one day soon—in heaven.

No wonder Jesus is now "crowned with glory and honor" (Hebrews 2:9)! Thank God for His grace today, grace that both humbled and exalted Christ so that you can live free from the fear of death (Hebrews 2:15) and the power of the devil (Hebrews 2:14). ☼

WEEK 97 • TUESDAY

Hebrews 3:1–19

GET THE BIG PICTURE

Remember the days of Israel's desert wanderings? Remember the grumbling, the unbelief, and the rebellion of the people against Moses and against God? As you think about the sins of ancient Israel, are you ever tempted to say, "I would never act like they did?" Ask God to reveal His truth to your heart as you read now the second of five explicit warnings in Hebrews. If time is short, focus on Hebrews 3:1–13.

Jesus Greater Than Moses

3 Therefore, holy brothers, who
share in the heavenly calling, fix
your thoughts on Jesus, the apostle and
high priest whom we confess. 2He was
faithful to the one who appointed him,
just as Moses was faithful in all God's
house. 3Jesus has been found worthy of
greater honor than Moses, just as the
builder of a house has greater honor
than the house itself. 4For every house
is built by someone, but God is the
builder of everything. 5Moses was faithful as a servant in all God's house, testifying to what would be said in the
future. 6But Christ is faithful as a son
over God's house. And we are his
house, if we hold on to our courage and
the hope of which we boast.

Warning Against Unbelief

7So, as the Holy Spirit says:

"Today, if you hear his voice,
8 do not harden your hearts
as you did in the rebellion,
during the time of testing in the
desert,
9 where your fathers tested and tried
me
and for forty years saw what I did.
10 That is why I was angry with that
generation,
and I said, 'Their hearts are always
going astray,
and they have not known my
ways.'
11 So I declared on oath in my anger,
'They shall never enter my rest.' "[a]

12See to it, brothers, that none of you
has a sinful, unbelieving heart that turns
away from the living God. 13But encourage one another daily, as long as it is
called Today, so that none of you may be
hardened by sin's deceitfulness. 14We
have come to share in Christ if we hold
firmly till the end the confidence we
had at first. 15As has just been said:

"Today, if you hear his voice,
do not harden your hearts
as you did in the rebellion."[b]

[a]11 Psalm 95:7-11 [b]15 Psalm 95:7,8

[16]Who were they who heard and rebelled? Were they not all those Moses
led out of Egypt? [17]And with whom was
he angry for forty years? Was it not with
those who sinned, whose bodies fell in
the desert? [18]And to whom did God
swear that they would never enter his
rest if not to those who disobeyed[a]? [19]So
we see that they were not able to enter,
because of their unbelief.

SHARPEN THE FOCUS

How gullible are you? None of us likes to think we'd fall for the line a con man feeds us or for the latest version of a get-rich-quick pyramid scheme. Today's text describes a much more frightening prospect—being taken in by "sin's deceitfulness" (Hebrews 3:13).

The Israelites in the desert didn't plan to fall into any of the tar pits of sin that eventually trapped them. They were just thirsty. Or hungry. Or tired. Or bored. Or hot. Or frightened. And one thing led to another. Satan put a hook in their noses and led them to destruction. They didn't even notice—until it was too late.

Sin is tricky. Satan is crafty. God in love still warns us today, "Do not harden your hearts" (Hebrews 3:8, 15). When our feet go astray, we can be sure they're following a path paved first in our hearts (Hebrews 3:10).

How glad we can be, then, that we have the faithful High Priest described in Hebrews 3:1–4. Remember Jesus words to Peter? "I have prayed for you, . . . that your faith may not fail" (Luke 22:32). Jesus prays for us too. You can commit yourself to His safekeeping, confident that He will strengthen you and keep you faithful to the end. (See 1 Thessalonians 5:23–24.)

WEEK 97 • WEDNESDAY

Hebrews 4:1–16

GET THE BIG PICTURE

Joshua led God's people into their Promised Land. (Joshua 4:1–24). Even so, Joshua did not give them rest. The earthly Canaan was a place of war, temptation, and eventually, for many, apostasy. Nonetheless, God provided the Sabbath-rest He had promised—in Jesus. As you read, rest—in your Savior. If time is short, focus on Hebrews 4:9–16.

A Sabbath-Rest for the People of God

4 Therefore, since the promise of
entering his rest still stands, let
us be careful that none of you be found
to have fallen short of it. [2]For we also
have had the gospel preached to us, just
as they did; but the message they heard
was of no value to them, because those
who heard did not combine it with
faith.[b] [3]Now we who have believed enter that rest, just as God has said,

"So I declared on oath in my anger,
'They shall never enter my rest.' "[c]

[a]18 Or *disbelieved* [b]2 Many manuscripts *because they did not share in the faith of those who obeyed* [c]3 Psalm 95:11; also in verse 5

And yet his work has been finished since the creation of the world. [4]For somewhere he has spoken about the seventh day in these words: "And on the seventh day God rested from all his work."[a] [5]And again in the passage above he says, "They shall never enter my rest."

[6]It still remains that some will enter that rest, and those who formerly had the gospel preached to them did not go in, because of their disobedience.
[7]Therefore God again set a certain day, calling it Today, when a long time later he spoke through David, as was said before:

"Today, if you hear his voice,
do not harden your hearts."[b]

[8]For if Joshua had given them rest, God would not have spoken later about another day. [9]There remains, then, a Sabbath-rest for the people of God; [10]for anyone who enters God's rest also rests from his own work, just as God did from his. [11]Let us, therefore, make every effort to enter that rest, so that no one will fall by following their example of disobedience.

[12]For the word of God is living and active. Sharper than any double-edged sword, it penetrates even to dividing soul and spirit, joints and marrow; it judges the thoughts and attitudes of the heart. [13]Nothing in all creation is hidden from God's sight. Everything is uncovered and laid bare before the eyes of him to whom we must give account.

Jesus the Great High Priest

[14]Therefore, since we have a great high priest who has gone through the heavens,[c] Jesus the Son of God, let us hold firmly to the faith we profess. [15]For we do not have a high priest who is unable to sympathize with our weaknesses, but we have one who has been tempted in every way, just as we are—yet was without sin. [16]Let us then approach the throne of grace with confidence, so that we may receive mercy and find grace to help us in our time of need.

[a]4 Gen. 2:2 [b]7 Psalm 95:7,8 [c]14 Or *gone into heaven*

SHARPEN THE FOCUS

John Grisham, author of *The Client* and *The Chamber,* paints the everyday life of lawyers as stressed, overloaded almost beyond belief. His characters regularly work 80–100 hours each week. Anyone whose job demands that kind of output doubtless needs more rest than he or she is getting.

And yet, there's one job even more demanding still. That's the assignment of trying to win salvation by our own efforts. A person could work 168 hours every week and still not come close to making up for sin.

So God, in compassion, sent His own Son to be our Sabbath-rest (Hebrews 4:9). Jesus has taken the burden of trying to please God, of trying to save ourselves, out of our hands. We rest—fully and forever—in Him.

When our hearts are weighed down with guilt, when our arms carry a load of failure, Jesus "sympathizes" (Hebrews 4:15—literally, "suffers with us in our weaknesses"). He knows what temptation is like; He's been tempted. He knows how crushing a burden guilt can be; our guilt crushed Him at the cross. This Jesus, crucified and now risen, meets us in His Word and in the Sacrament. We can come to Him—in confidence—to "receive mercy and find grace to help us" (Hebrews 4:16) in every time of need.

WEEK 97 • THURSDAY

Hebrews 5:1–14

GET THE BIG PICTURE

To be a priest in Old Testament Israel, a person had to (a) be born into the tribe of Levi; (b) be a descendant of Aaron; (c) offer sacrifices, not just for the people, but also for his own sins. As you read Hebrews 5, look for ways the Lord Jesus, our great High Priest, is superior to all the priests from the line of Aaron. If time is short, focus on Hebrews 5:1–10.

5 Every high priest is selected from
among men and is appointed to
represent them in matters related to
God, to offer gifts and sacrifices for sins.
2He is able to deal gently with those who
are ignorant and are going astray, since
he himself is subject to weakness. 3This
is why he has to offer sacrifices for his
own sins, as well as for the sins of the
people.
4No one takes this honor upon himself; he must be called by God, just as
Aaron was. 5So Christ also did not take
upon himself the glory of becoming a
high priest. But God said to him,

"You are my Son;
today I have become your
Father.[a]"[b]

6And he says in another place,

"You are a priest forever,
in the order of Melchizedek."[c]

7During the days of Jesus' life on
earth, he offered up prayers and petitions with loud cries and tears to the one
who could save him from death, and he
was heard because of his reverent submission. 8Although he was a son, he
learned obedience from what he suffered 9and, once made perfect, he became the source of eternal salvation for
all who obey him 10and was designated
by God to be high priest in the order of
Melchizedek.

Warning Against Falling Away

11We have much to say about this, but
it is hard to explain because you are
slow to learn. 12In fact, though by this
time you ought to be teachers, you need
someone to teach you the elementary
truths of God's word all over again. You
need milk, not solid food! 13Anyone who
lives on milk, being still an infant, is not
acquainted with the teaching about
righteousness. 14But solid food is for the
mature, who by constant use have
trained themselves to distinguish good
from evil.

[a]5 Or *have begotten you* [b]5 Psalm 2:7
[c]6 Psalm 110:4

SHARPEN THE FOCUS

How can perfection be improved? A golfer who aces all 18 holes on the course could boast a perfect score. A place kicker whose attempts all sail over the goal posts at dead center couldn't do a better job.

If you have examples like these in mind, Hebrews 5:8–9 may trouble you. How could Jesus be "made perfect"?

These words don't refer to Christ's character, but to His office as our Redeemer and High Priest. Instead of "made perfect," we might say instead, "made complete." The Greek verb is related to Jesus' cry of triumph from His cross: "It is finished" (John 19:30).

As Jesus walked step by step to His cross, He learned from personal experience the price of obedience to the Father's will. He gained a direct hands-on knowledge of what the human struggle with sin and Satan are like. Now, as our High Priest, our Lord Jesus is "able to deal gently" with us (Hebrews 5:2), just as the Old Testament priests could with those whom they served.

Jesus completely obeyed the heavenly Father in our place, and by suffering the full, complete, and total punishment for our sins has become "the source of eternal salvation" (Hebrews 5:9) for all who turn to Him in repentance and faith.

Hebrews 6 focuses on a third warning the writer to the Hebrews issues. As you read, keep in mind that the original recipients of this letter had already undergone persecution for their faith and would undergo more. Considering these circumstances, how would you summarize the warning? If time is short, focus on Hebrews 6:9–20.

6 Therefore let us leave the elementary teachings about Christ and go on to maturity, not laying again the foundation of repentance from acts that lead to death,[a] and of faith in God, [2]instruction about baptisms, the laying on of hands, the resurrection of the dead, and eternal judgment. [3]And God permitting, we will do so.

[4]It is impossible for those who have once been enlightened, who have tasted the heavenly gift, who have shared in the Holy Spirit, [5]who have tasted the goodness of the word of God and the powers of the coming age, [6]if they fall away, to be brought back to repentance, because[b] to their loss they are crucifying the Son of God all over again and subjecting him to public disgrace.

[7]Land that drinks in the rain often falling on it and that produces a crop useful to those for whom it is farmed receives the blessing of God. [8]But land that produces thorns and thistles is worthless and is in danger of being cursed. In the end it will be burned.

[9]Even though we speak like this, dear friends, we are confident of better things in your case—things that accompany salvation. [10]God is not unjust; he will not forget your work and the love you have shown him as you have helped his people and continue to help them. [11]We want each of you to show this same diligence to the very end, in order to make your hope sure. [12]We do not want you to become lazy, but to imitate those who through faith and patience inherit what has been promised.

[a]1 Or *from useless rituals* [b]6 Or *repentance while*

The Certainty of God's Promise

[13]When God made his promise to
Abraham, since there was no one greater for him to swear by, he swore by himself, [14]saying, "I will surely bless you and
give you many descendants."[a] [15]And so
after waiting patiently, Abraham received what was promised.
[16]Men swear by someone greater than
themselves, and the oath confirms what
is said and puts an end to all argument.
[17]Because God wanted to make the unchanging nature of his purpose very
clear to the heirs of what was promised,
he confirmed it with an oath. [18]God did
this so that, by two unchangeable things
in which it is impossible for God to lie,
we who have fled to take hold of the
hope offered to us may be greatly encouraged. [19]We have this hope as an
anchor for the soul, firm and secure. It
enters the inner sanctuary behind the
curtain, [20]where Jesus, who went before
us, has entered on our behalf. He has become a high priest forever, in the order
of Melchizedek.

[a]*14* Gen. 22:17

SHARPEN THE FOCUS

What could make God swear? A startling question, one that perhaps you've never considered before. But Hebrews 6:13–20 talks at length about God's oath, about His determination that we know He will not change His mind about His love and forgiveness for us.

Our Lord had "no one greater . . . to swear by" (Hebrews 6:13). So He swore by Himself that He would keep His promise to bless Abraham—and "all peoples on earth" (Genesis 12:3)—through Abraham's "Seed," our Lord Jesus (Galatians 3:6–19). God will not renege on His oath; God will not take back His promise. God's oath and God's promise both stand in unchanging testimony to His faithfulness (Hebrews 6:18).

That faithfulness gives us hope and courage (Hebrews 6:18). It anchors us, no matter what storms pound hard against our lives. Even if persecution comes for the name of Jesus, we stand on firm ground as we trust His grace toward us.

Flee for refuge to Him! Take hold of the hope He offers you! Live in great courage! You are His for now and forever.

WEEK 97 • SATURDAY

Hebrews 7:1–28

GET THE BIG PICTURE

Unlike the priests descended from Aaron, Jesus remains a priest forever. Since death did not hold Him, we can be sure He will never be replaced. That's one argument the writer makes in Hebrews 7 for the superiority of Christ's priesthood. Can you find at least two more? If time is short, focus on Hebrews 7:20–28.

Melchizedek the Priest

7 This Melchizedek was king of Salem and priest of God Most High. He met Abraham returning from the defeat of the kings and blessed him, [2]and Abraham gave him a tenth of everything. First, his name means "king of righteousness"; then also, "king of Salem" means "king of peace." [3]Without father or mother, without genealogy, without beginning of days or end of life, like the Son of God he remains a priest forever.

[4]Just think how great he was: Even the patriarch Abraham gave him a tenth of the plunder! [5]Now the law requires the descendants of Levi who become priests to collect a tenth from the people—that is, their brothers—even though their brothers are descended from Abraham. [6]This man, however, did not trace his descent from Levi, yet he collected a tenth from Abraham and blessed him who had the promises. [7]And without doubt the lesser person is blessed by the greater. [8]In the one case, the tenth is collected by men who die; but in the other case, by him who is declared to be living. [9]One might even say that Levi, who collects the tenth, paid the tenth through Abraham, [10]because when Melchizedek met Abraham, Levi was still in the body of his ancestor.

Jesus Like Melchizedek

[11]If perfection could have been attained through the Levitical priesthood (for on the basis of it the law was given to the people), why was there still need for another priest to come—one in the order of Melchizedek, not in the order of Aaron? [12]For when there is a change of the priesthood, there must also be a change of the law. [13]He of whom these things are said belonged to a different tribe, and no one from that tribe has ever served at the altar. [14]For it is clear that our Lord descended from Judah, and in regard to that tribe Moses said nothing about priests. [15]And what we have said is even more clear if another priest like Melchizedek appears, [16]one who has become a priest not on the basis of a regulation as to his ancestry but on the basis of the power of an indestructible life. [17]For it is declared:

"You are a priest forever,
in the order of Melchizedek."[a]

[18]The former regulation is set aside because it was weak and useless [19](for the law made nothing perfect), and a better hope is introduced, by which we draw near to God.

[20]And it was not without an oath! Others became priests without any oath, [21]but he became a priest with an oath when God said to him:

"The Lord has sworn
and will not change his mind:
'You are a priest forever.' "[a]

[22]Because of this oath, Jesus has become the guarantee of a better covenant.

[23]Now there have been many of those priests, since death prevented them from continuing in office; [24]but because Jesus lives forever, he has a permanent priesthood. [25]Therefore he is able to save completely[b] those who come to God through him, because he always lives to intercede for them.

[26]Such a high priest meets our need—one who is holy, blameless, pure, set apart from sinners, exalted above the heavens. [27]Unlike the other high priests, he does not need to offer sacrifices day after day, first for his own sins, and then for the sins of the people. He sacrificed for their sins once for all when he offered himself. [28]For the law appoints as high priests men who are weak; but the oath, which came after the law, appointed the Son, who has been made perfect forever.

[a] *17,21* Psalm 110:4 [b] *25* Or *forever*

SHARPEN THE FOCUS

When Jesus was inaugurated as our High Priest, the heavenly Father took an oath about Christ's office. He swore never to remove Jesus from that office. He swore that the Lord Christ will serve as our High Priest forever.

The priests who served in the order of Aaron had weaknesses. They sinned (Hebrews 7:27). They died (Hebrews 7:23). And when they died, they stayed dead; they did not return to earth to resume their priestly duties. The sacrifices made by priests in the order of Aaron had to be repeated again and again and again. Those sacrifices couldn't remove sin. They only covered it.

For all these reasons, we sinners needed not just a new priest, but a priest of a different order. We needed a better priest. That's why God sent Jesus—not in the order of Aaron, but in the "order of Melchizedek" (Hebrews 7:17, 21).

The priests of Aaron's order died; Jesus' life is indestructible (Hebrews 7:16). The priests of Aaron's order sinned; Jesus is "holy, blameless, pure, set apart from sinners" (Hebrews 7:26). The priests of Aaron's order had to offer repeated sacrifices (Hebrews 7:27). Jesus offered Himself—"once for all" (Hebrews 7:27). He is able to save us completely (Hebrews 7:25).

WEEK 98 • MONDAY

Hebrews 8:1–13

GET THE BIG PICTURE

A better ministry. A better covenant. Better promises. Jesus brings us all these. As you read, ask yourself why the old covenant had to be replaced. Was it flawed? Or was there some other reason? If time is short, focus on Hebrews 8:7–13.

The High Priest of a New Covenant

8 The point of what we are saying
is this: We do have such a high
priest, who sat down at the right hand
of the throne of the Majesty in heaven,
2 and who serves in the sanctuary, the
true tabernacle set up by the Lord, not
by man.
3 Every high priest is appointed to offer both gifts and sacrifices, and so it was
necessary for this one also to have something to offer.
4 If he were on earth, he
would not be a priest, for there are already men who offer the gifts prescribed by the law.
5 They serve at a
sanctuary that is a copy and shadow of
what is in heaven. This is why Moses
was warned when he was about to build
the tabernacle: "See to it that you make
everything according to the pattern
shown you on the mountain."[a]
6 But the
ministry Jesus has received is as superi-
or to theirs as the covenant of which he
is mediator is superior to the old one,
and it is founded on better promises.
7 For if there had been nothing wrong
with that first covenant, no place would
have been sought for another.
8 But God
found fault with the people and said[b]:

"The time is coming, declares the
Lord,

[a]5 Exodus 25:40 [b]8 Some manuscripts may be translated *fault and said to the people.*

when I will make a new covenant
with the house of Israel
and with the house of Judah.
9 It will not be like the covenant
I made with their forefathers
when I took them by the hand
to lead them out of Egypt,
because they did not remain faithful
to my covenant,
and I turned away from them,
declares the Lord.
10 This is the covenant I will make with
the house of Israel
after that time, declares the Lord.
I will put my laws in their minds
and write them on their hearts.
I will be their God,
and they will be my people.
11 No longer will a man teach his
neighbor,
or a man his brother, saying,
'Know the Lord,'
because they will all know me,
from the least of them to the
greatest.
12 For I will forgive their wickedness
and will remember their sins no
more."[a]

13 By calling this covenant "new," he
has made the first one obsolete; and
what is obsolete and aging will soon disappear.

[a] *12* Jer. 31:31-34

SHARPEN THE FOCUS

Imagine a puppy that has run away from home during a thunderstorm. One last, loud crack of lightning and he's off into the woods. Imagine him wandering, lost and hungry for two weeks. Then imagine his owner finally finding him, limping and exhausted. If you can picture the puppy, you can picture misery. If you can picture the owner's tears, you can picture pity and joy.

In Hebrews 8:12, the holy writer quotes our Lord saying, "I will forgive their wickedness." God took pity on us in the misery of our sins. When we wandered far from Him, lost, exhausted, and totally unable to find our way home, He came to get us. He came to bring us back to Himself.

He had to come to us; we could not go to Him. The old covenant wasn't flawed; *we* were. We could not keep God's commandments. We could not even *want* to do that. So in grace our Lord set up a new covenant. One with a better priest—Jesus! One founded on better promises (Hebrews 8:6, 10–12).

How will you celebrate God's new and better covenant with you today?

WEEK 98 • TUESDAY

Hebrews 9:1–28

GET THE BIG PICTURE

Architects sometimes build scale models of the structures they design. Children sometimes put sticks or strings on the ground to represent the walls of a house or a castle. In a similar way, the place of sacrifice and the people who offered the sacrifices of the old covenant only represented the reality. These earthly structures and ceremonies were not the real thing. A much deeper reality existed—in heaven. Watch for that reality as you read. If time is short, focus on Hebrews 9:11–28.

Worship in the Earthly Tabernacle

9 Now the first covenant had regulations for worship and also an earthly sanctuary. [2]A tabernacle was set up. In its first room were the lampstand, the table and the consecrated bread; this was called the Holy Place. [3]Behind the second curtain was a room called the Most Holy Place, [4]which had the golden altar of incense and the gold-covered ark of the covenant. This ark contained the gold jar of manna, Aaron's staff that had budded, and the stone tablets of the covenant. [5]Above the ark were the cherubim of the Glory, overshadowing the atonement cover.[a] But we cannot discuss these things in detail now.

[6]When everything had been arranged like this, the priests entered regularly into the outer room to carry on their ministry. [7]But only the high priest entered the inner room, and that only once a year, and never without blood, which he offered for himself and for the sins the people had committed in ignorance. [8]The Holy Spirit was showing by this that the way into the Most Holy Place had not yet been disclosed as long as the first tabernacle was still standing. [9]This is an illustration for the present time, indicating that the gifts and sacrifices being offered were not able to clear the conscience of the worshiper. [10]They are only a matter of food and drink and various ceremonial washings—external regulations applying until the time of the new order.

The Blood of Christ

[11]When Christ came as high priest of the good things that are already here,[b] he went through the greater and more perfect tabernacle that is not man-made, that is to say, not a part of this creation. [12]He did not enter by means of the blood of goats and calves; but he entered the Most Holy Place once for all by his own blood, having obtained eternal redemption. [13]The blood of goats and bulls and the ashes of a heifer sprinkled on those who are ceremonially unclean sanctify them so that they are outwardly clean. [14]How much more, then, will the blood of Christ, who through the eternal Spirit offered himself unblemished to God, cleanse our consciences from acts that lead to death,[c] so that we may serve the living God!

[15]For this reason Christ is the mediator of a new covenant, that those who are called may receive the promised eternal inheritance—now that he has died as a ransom to set them free from the sins committed under the first covenant.

[16]In the case of a will,[d] it is necessary to prove the death of the one who made it, [17]because a will is in force only when somebody has died; it never takes effect while the one who made it is living. [18]This is why even the first covenant was not put into effect without blood. [19]When Moses had proclaimed every commandment of the law to all the people, he took the blood of calves, together with water, scarlet wool and branches of hyssop, and sprinkled the scroll and all the people. [20]He said, "This is the blood of the covenant, which God has commanded you to keep."[e] [21]In the same way, he sprinkled with the blood both the tabernacle and everything used in its ceremonies. [22]In fact, the law requires that nearly everything be cleansed with blood, and without the shedding of blood there is no forgiveness.

[23]It was necessary, then, for the copies of the heavenly things to be purified with these sacrifices, but the heavenly things themselves with better sacrifices than these. [24]For Christ did not enter a man-made sanctuary that was only a copy of the true one; he entered heaven itself, now to appear for us in God's presence. [25]Nor did he enter heaven to offer himself again and again, the way the high priest enters the Most Holy Place every year with blood that is not his own. [26]Then Christ would have had to suffer many times since the creation

[a]5 Traditionally *the mercy seat* [b]11 Some early manuscripts *are to come* [c]14 Or *from useless rituals* [d]16 Same Greek word as *covenant*; also in verse 17 [e]20 Exodus 24:8

of the world. But now he has appeared
once for all at the end of the ages to do
away with sin by the sacrifice of himself.
27 Just as man is destined to die once, and
after that to face judgment, 28 so Christ
was sacrificed once to take away the sins
of many people; and he will appear a
second time, not to bear sin, but to bring
salvation to those who are waiting for
him.

SHARPEN THE FOCUS

Hebrews 9 contrasts the old and new covenants in detail:

- In the old covenant, the High Priest enters the Most Holy Place on earth (Hebrews 9:7–8); in the new covenant, Jesus enters heaven itself (Hebrews 9:24).
- In the old covenant, the consciences of worshipers still accuse them (Hebrews 9:9); in the new covenant, consciences are cleaned from acts that lead to death—sin (Hebrews 9:14).
- In the old covenant, the priest offers blood of goats and calves (Hebrews 9:12); in the new covenant, Jesus offered His own blood as a perfect sacrifice (Hebrews 9:12).
- In the old covenant, the result was outward cleansing (Hebrews 9:13); in the new covenant, the result was in Jesus eternal redemption for all sinners (Hebrews 9:12).

The "ashes of a heifer" mentioned in Hebrews 9:13 were used in a ceremony described in Numbers 19:1–22. Mixed in water, they were used to purify God's people from the defilement of death. As you can see, this picture sprang to reality in Jesus' death—and resurrection—for us!

WEEK 98 • WEDNESDAY

Hebrews 10:1–18

GET THE BIG PICTURE

Would it help to show a sick person a photograph of the medicine she needs? Would it help to show a drowning person a picture of a life jacket? No. And neither could the "pictures" or "shadows" of the old covenant have any real or lasting effect on sin. But Jesus' sacrifice could and did. Look for that accent as you read. If time is short, focus on Hebrews 10:11–18.

Christ's Sacrifice Once for All

10 The law is only a shadow of
the good things that are coming—not the realities themselves. For
this reason it can never, by the same sacrifices repeated endlessly year after year,
make perfect those who draw near to
worship. 2 If it could, would they not
have stopped being offered? For the
worshipers would have been cleansed

once for all, and would no longer have felt guilty for their sins. [3]But those sacrifices are an annual reminder of sins, [4]because it is impossible for the blood of bulls and goats to take away sins.

[5]Therefore, when Christ came into the world, he said:

"Sacrifice and offering you did not desire,
but a body you prepared for me;
[6]with burnt offerings and sin offerings
you were not pleased.
[7]Then I said, 'Here I am—it is written about me in the scroll—
I have come to do your will, O God.' "[a]

[8]First he said, "Sacrifices and offerings, burnt offerings and sin offerings you did not desire, nor were you pleased with them" (although the law required them to be made). [9]Then he said, "Here I am, I have come to do your will." He sets aside the first to establish the second. [10]And by that will, we have been made holy through the sacrifice of the body of Jesus Christ once for all.

[11]Day after day every priest stands and performs his religious duties; again and again he offers the same sacrifices, which can never take away sins. [12]But when this priest had offered for all time one sacrifice for sins, he sat down at the right hand of God. [13]Since that time he waits for his enemies to be made his footstool, [14]because by one sacrifice he has made perfect forever those who are being made holy.

[15]The Holy Spirit also testifies to us about this. First he says:

[16]"This is the covenant I will make with them
after that time, says the Lord.
I will put my laws in their hearts,
and I will write them on their minds."[b]

[17]Then he adds:

"Their sins and lawless acts
I will remember no more."[c]

[18]And where these have been forgiven, there is no longer any sacrifice for sin.

[a]*7* Psalm 40:6-8 (see Septuagint) [b]*16* Jer. 31:33 [c]*17* Jer. 31:34

SHARPEN THE FOCUS

How would you define *holy?* Or *sanctified?* Both words mean, in part, "set aside for God's unique use" or "designated as belonging to God for His purposes." So then, are you *already* sanctified, holy? Or are you *being* sanctified?

Yes. And yes.

The Bible uses both the past tense and an ongoing, present tense as it describes our sanctification. Compare, for example, Hebrews 10:10 with Hebrews 10:14:

> *We have been made holy through the sacrifice of the body of Jesus Christ once for all.* (Hebrews 10:10)

> *By one sacrifice He has made perfect forever those who are being made holy.* (Hebrews 10:14)

God has declared us holy; He has set us aside for Himself once and for all time. And we are even now being made holy as the new life He gives us works in us. Notice that these are two inseparable parts of God's saving work, a work that begins and concludes in the sacrifice Jesus made on His cross.

The declaration that we are righteous in Christ works in us to transform our lifestyle. And all of this is made possible because of Christ's self-sacrifice on the cross. How can you live as God's holy, unique servant today? ☼

We have access to God's throne (Hebrews 10:19–20). We have Jesus who serves as our High Priest, interceding for us and having redeemed us (Hebrews 10:21). Now, based on those unshakable truths, the writer draws five powerful conclusions (Hebrews 10:22–25). Why would these be important to Christians enduring persecution? Why are they important to *you?* If time is short, focus on Hebrews 10:19–35.

A Call to Persevere

[19]Therefore, brothers, since we have
confidence to enter the Most Holy
Place by the blood of Jesus, [20]by a new
and living way opened for us through
the curtain, that is, his body, [21]and
since we have a great priest over the
house of God, [22]let us draw near to God
with a sincere heart in full assurance
of faith, having our hearts sprinkled
to cleanse us from a guilty conscience
and having our bodies washed with
pure water. [23]Let us hold unswervingly
to the hope we profess, for he who
promised is faithful. [24]And let us consider how we may spur one another
on toward love and good deeds. [25]Let
us not give up meeting together, as
some are in the habit of doing, but let
us encourage one another—and all
the more as you see the Day approaching.
[26]If we deliberately keep on sinning
after we have received the knowledge
of the truth, no sacrifice for sins is left,
[27]but only a fearful expectation of judgment and of raging fire that will consume the enemies of God. [28]Anyone
who rejected the law of Moses died
without mercy on the testimony of two
or three witnesses. [29]How much more
severely do you think a man deserves to
be punished who has trampled the Son
of God under foot, who has treated as
an unholy thing the blood of the covenant that sanctified him, and who has
insulted the Spirit of grace? [30]For we
know him who said, "It is mine to
avenge; I will repay,"[a] and again, "The
Lord will judge his people."[b] [31]It is a
dreadful thing to fall into the hands of
the living God.
[32]Remember those earlier days after
you had received the light, when you
stood your ground in a great contest in
the face of suffering. [33]Sometimes you
were publicly exposed to insult and persecution; at other times you stood side
by side with those who were so treated.
[34]You sympathized with those in prison
and joyfully accepted the confiscation of
your property, because you knew that
you yourselves had better and lasting
possessions.
[35]So do not throw away your confidence; it will be richly rewarded. [36]You
need to persevere so that when you
have done the will of God, you will re-

[a]*30* Deut. 32:35 [b]*30* Deut. 32:36; Psalm 135:14

ceive what he has promised. 37For in just
a very little while,

"He who is coming will come and
will not delay.
38 But my righteous one[a] will live by
faith.
And if he shrinks back,
I will not be pleased with him."[b]

39But we are not of those who shrink
back and are destroyed, but of those
who believe and are saved.

SHARPEN THE FOCUS

Maybe you've sung the words: *Soon and very soon, we are going to see the King.* This gospel song encourages us to look up from the frustrations, persecutions, and problems of this life to recall our Savior's promise to split the sky one day as He returns on the clouds of heaven to take us home.

Hebrews 10:35–39 makes a similar point: "In just a very little while" (Hebrews 10:37), the writer promises, our wait will end. Jesus will come. "Hold on," he urges. "Don't give up now. Don't throw away everything you've been waiting for. You can be confident your Savior will keep His promise. Endure!"

Probably some of those who first read this book would soon face the executioner's sword. We may not. Nonetheless, circumstances in our lives can tempt us to give up on God's promised deliverance too. You know the personal issues that Satan uses most often to steal your confidence. Things may get worse for us, even as they got tougher for the first-century Christians. Still, the same grace that brings God's people to faith also keeps us in that faith.

Live in that confidence. The grace that sustains us—think of it—will soon reward us (Hebrews 10:35)!

Today's reading, Hebrews 11, gives a brief history of the Jewish nation as they followed God through the centuries. Some have called this chapter "The Honor Roll of Heroes" or "The Hall of Fame." A better title would be "The Hall of Faith." Can you see why? If time is short, focus on Hebrews 11:1–31.

By Faith

11 Now faith is being sure of what
we hope for and certain of what
we do not see. 2This is what the ancients
were commended for.
3By faith we understand that the universe was formed at God's command, so
that what is seen was not made out of
what was visible.
4By faith Abel offered God a better
sacrifice than Cain did. By faith he was

[a]38 One early manuscript *But the righteous*
[b]38 Hab. 2:3,4

commended as a righteous man, when
God spoke well of his offerings. And by
faith he still speaks, even though he is
dead.
[5]By faith Enoch was taken from this
life, so that he did not experience death;
he could not be found, because God had
taken him away. For before he was tak-
en, he was commended as one who
pleased God. [6]And without faith it is
impossible to please God, because anyone who comes to him must believe that
he exists and that he rewards those who
earnestly seek him.
[7]By faith Noah, when warned about
things not yet seen, in holy fear built an
ark to save his family. By his faith he
condemned the world and became heir
of the righteousness that comes by faith.
[8]By faith Abraham, when called to go
to a place he would later receive as his
inheritance, obeyed and went, even
though he did not know where he was
going. [9]By faith he made his home in
the promised land like a stranger in a
foreign country; he lived in tents, as did
Isaac and Jacob, who were heirs with
him of the same promise. [10]For he was
looking forward to the city with foundations, whose architect and builder is
God.
[11]By faith Abraham, even though he
was past age—and Sarah herself was
barren—was enabled to become a father
because he[a] considered him faithful
who had made the promise. [12]And so
from this one man, and he as good as
dead, came descendants as numerous
as the stars in the sky and as countless
as the sand on the seashore.
[13]All these people were still living by
faith when they died. They did not receive the things promised; they only
saw them and welcomed them from a
distance. And they admitted that they
were aliens and strangers on earth.
[14]People who say such things show that
they are looking for a country of their
own. [15]If they had been thinking of the
country they had left, they would have
had opportunity to return. [16]Instead,
they were longing for a better country—
a heavenly one. Therefore God is not
ashamed to be called their God, for he
has prepared a city for them.
[17]By faith Abraham, when God tested
him, offered Isaac as a sacrifice. He who
had received the promises was about to
sacrifice his one and only son, [18]even
though God had said to him, "It is
through Isaac that your offspring[b] will
be reckoned."[c] [19]Abraham reasoned that
God could raise the dead, and figuratively speaking, he did receive Isaac
back from death.
[20]By faith Isaac blessed Jacob and Esau
in regard to their future.
[21]By faith Jacob, when he was dying,
blessed each of Joseph's sons, and worshiped as he leaned on the top of his
staff.
[22]By faith Joseph, when his end was
near, spoke about the exodus of the Israelites from Egypt and gave instructions about his bones.
[23]By faith Moses' parents hid him for
three months after he was born, because
they saw he was no ordinary child, and
they were not afraid of the king's edict.
[24]By faith Moses, when he had grown
up, refused to be known as the son of
Pharaoh's daughter. [25]He chose to be
mistreated along with the people of
God rather than to enjoy the pleasures
of sin for a short time. [26]He regarded
disgrace for the sake of Christ as of
greater value than the treasures of
Egypt, because he was looking ahead to
his reward. [27]By faith he left Egypt, not
fearing the king's anger; he persevered
because he saw him who is invisible.
[28]By faith he kept the Passover and the
sprinkling of blood, so that the destroyer of the firstborn would not touch
the firstborn of Israel.
[29]By faith the people passed through
the Red Sea[d] as on dry land; but when
the Egyptians tried to do so, they were
drowned.
[30]By faith the walls of Jericho fell, after the people had marched around
them for seven days.

[a]*11* Or *By faith even Sarah, who was past age, was enabled to bear children because she* [b]*18* Greek *seed* [c]*18* Gen. 21:12 [d]*29* That is, Sea of Reeds

[31]By faith the prostitute Rahab, because she welcomed the spies, was not killed with those who were disobedient.[a]

[32]And what more shall I say? I do not have time to tell about Gideon, Barak, Samson, Jephthah, David, Samuel and the prophets, [33]who through faith conquered kingdoms, administered justice, and gained what was promised; who shut the mouths of lions, [34]quenched the fury of the flames, and escaped the edge of the sword; whose weakness was turned to strength; and who became powerful in battle and routed foreign armies. [35]Women received back their dead, raised to life again. Others were tortured and refused to be released, so that they might gain a better resurrection. [36]Some faced jeers and flogging, while still others were chained and put in prison. [37]They were stoned[b]; they were sawed in two; they were put to death by the sword. They went about in sheepskins and goatskins, destitute, persecuted and mistreated— [38]the world was not worthy of them. They wandered in deserts and mountains, and in caves and holes in the ground.

[39]These were all commended for their faith, yet none of them received what had been promised. [40]God had planned something better for us so that only together with us would they be made perfect.

[a]31 Or *unbelieving* [b]37 Some early manuscripts *stoned; they were put to the test;*

SHARPEN THE FOCUS

Suppose God kept a family photo album. What snapshots might He include? Hebrews 11 gives us some broad hints. The chapter reads a little like what we might expect of a proud parent who keeps careful records of his children's achievements: athletic ribbons, newspaper clippings, certificates of scholarship:

- God "spoke well" of Abel's offerings (Hebrews 11:4).
- Enoch "pleased God" (Hebrews 11:5).
- Noah became an "heir of the righteousness that comes by faith" (Hebrews 11:7).
- Abraham "obeyed" (Hebrews 11:8).
- Jacob "worshiped" (Hebrews 11:21).

And on it goes. Snapshot after snapshot, each displaying God's pride and the joy He finds in His children.

But we know these "children"—and there's more to the story! Where are the photos of Noah's drunkenness (Genesis 9:20–21) or Abraham's lies (Genesis 12:11–20; 20:1–18)? Where are the news clippings that detail Jacob's cowardice? If all the facts were in, this chapter would be a "hall of shame."

But all the facts are in. Jesus' death on Calvary destroyed sin's power to accuse those who belong to God by faith. You see, God did not just sweep human guilt under the rug. He atoned for it at the cross. Noah's sins are forgiven! Abraham's sins are forgiven! Your sins and my sins are forgiven! Hebrews 11 is an accurate record of the lives lived by these people made perfect by faith (Hebrews 10:14).

Using an image familiar to athletes, the Holy Spirit pictures for us what He wants to accomplish in us during times of hardship, especially persecution. Watch carefully for His purposes as you read. If time is short, focus on Hebrews 12:1–13.

God Disciplines His Sons

12 Therefore, since we are surrounded by such a great
cloud of witnesses, let us throw off everything that hinders and the sin that so
easily entangles, and let us run with perseverance the race marked out for us.
2Let us fix our eyes on Jesus, the author
and perfecter of our faith, who for the
joy set before him endured the cross,
scorning its shame, and sat down at the
right hand of the throne of God. 3Consider him who endured such opposition
from sinful men, so that you will not
grow weary and lose heart.
4In your struggle against sin, you
have not yet resisted to the point of
shedding your blood. 5And you have
forgotten that word of encouragement
that addresses you as sons:

"My son, do not make light of the
Lord's discipline,
and do not lose heart when he
rebukes you,
6because the Lord disciplines those
he loves,
and he punishes everyone he
accepts as a son."[a]

7Endure hardship as discipline; God
is treating you as sons. For what son is
not disciplined by his father? 8If you are
not disciplined (and everyone undergoes discipline), then you are illegitimate children and not true sons.
9Moreover, we have all had human fathers who disciplined us and we respected them for it. How much more
should we submit to the Father of our
spirits and live! 10Our fathers disciplined
us for a little while as they thought best;
but God disciplines us for our good, that
we may share in his holiness. 11No discipline seems pleasant at the time, but
painful. Later on, however, it produces
a harvest of righteousness and peace for
those who have been trained by it.
12Therefore, strengthen your feeble
arms and weak knees. 13"Make level
paths for your feet,"[b] so that the lame
may not be disabled, but rather healed.

Warning Against Refusing God

14Make every effort to live in peace
with all men and to be holy; without
holiness no one will see the Lord. 15See
to it that no one misses the grace of God
and that no bitter root grows up to cause
trouble and defile many. 16See that no
one is sexually immoral, or is godless
like Esau, who for a single meal sold his
inheritance rights as the oldest son. 17Afterward, as you know, when he wanted
to inherit this blessing, he was rejected.
He could bring about no change of
mind, though he sought the blessing
with tears.
18You have not come to a mountain
that can be touched and that is burning
with fire; to darkness, gloom and storm;
19to a trumpet blast or to such a voice
speaking words that those who heard it
begged that no further word be spoken
to them, 20because they could not bear
what was commanded: "If even an animal touches the mountain, it must be

[a]6 Prov. 3:11,12 [b]13 Prov. 4:26

stoned."[a] [21]The sight was so terrifying that Moses said, "I am trembling with fear."[b]

[22]But you have come to Mount Zion, to the heavenly Jerusalem, the city of the living God. You have come to thousands upon thousands of angels in joyful assembly, [23]to the church of the firstborn, whose names are written in heaven. You have come to God, the judge of all men, to the spirits of righteous men made perfect, [24]to Jesus the mediator of a new covenant, and to the sprinkled blood that speaks a better word than the blood of Abel.

[25]See to it that you do not refuse him who speaks. If they did not escape when they refused him who warned them on earth, how much less will we, if we turn away from him who warns us from heaven? [26]At that time his voice shook the earth, but now he has promised, "Once more I will shake not only the earth but also the heavens."[c] [27]The words "once more" indicate the removing of what can be shaken—that is, created things—so that what cannot be shaken may remain.

[28]Therefore, since we are receiving a kingdom that cannot be shaken, let us be thankful, and so worship God acceptably with reverence and awe, [29]for our "God is a consuming fire."[d]

[a]20 Exodus 19:12,13 [b]21 Deut. 9:19
[c]26 Haggai 2:6 [d]29 Deut. 4:24

SHARPEN THE FOCUS

No one would run an Olympic tryout in an overcoat or galoshes. Nor would an athlete race with a backpack full of rocks slung over her shoulder. That's the picture in v. 1. The excess baggage the holy writer advises us to drop isn't just sin; it refers to anything that weighs us down, that keeps us from running the race of life freely and in as much joy as our Lord would have us run it.

Owning a beautiful home isn't wrong; it can be a gift from God. But if we spend every waking moment cleaning and maintaining it, we crowd other, God-pleasing activities out of our lives. We may have little time to disciple our children or little money to feed the poor.

Enrolling our children in sports or gymnastics isn't wrong; it can promote social growth and physical health. But if the resulting schedule makes finding time for a devotional life or public worship a burden, we can start to feel like we're running the race of life in snow boots.

What hindrances keep you from more steady progress in your faith-walk? Why not ask your Coach to show you any entanglements He would like to free you from right now? Remember He's your Father; He has your best interests at heart.

WEEK 99 • MONDAY

Hebrews 13:1–25

GET THE BIG PICTURE

Each exhortation you will read today holds special importance for people facing persecution for their Lord's name. Keep this background in mind as you read. Ask yourself which of the exhortations you need to take most to heart right now. If time is short, focus on Hebrews 13:1–8, 10–21.

Concluding Exhortations

13 Keep on loving each other as
brothers. 2Do not forget to entertain strangers, for by so doing some
people have entertained angels without
knowing it. 3Remember those in prison
as if you were their fellow prisoners,
and those who are mistreated as if you
yourselves were suffering.
4Marriage should be honored by all,
and the marriage bed kept pure, for God
will judge the adulterer and all the sexually immoral. 5Keep your lives free
from the love of money and be content
with what you have, because God has
said,

"Never will I leave you;
never will I forsake you."[a]

6So we say with confidence,

"The Lord is my helper; I will not be
afraid.
What can man do to me?"[b]

7Remember your leaders, who spoke
the word of God to you. Consider the
outcome of their way of life and imitate
their faith. 8Jesus Christ is the same yesterday and today and forever.
9Do not be carried away by all kinds
of strange teachings. It is good for our
hearts to be strengthened by grace, not
by ceremonial foods, which are of no
value to those who eat them. 10We have
an altar from which those who minister
at the tabernacle have no right to eat.
11The high priest carries the blood of
animals into the Most Holy Place as a sin
offering, but the bodies are burned outside the camp. 12And so Jesus also suffered outside the city gate to make the
people holy through his own blood.
13Let us, then, go to him outside the
camp, bearing the disgrace he bore. 14For
here we do not have an enduring city,
but we are looking for the city that is to
come.
15Through Jesus, therefore, let us continually offer to God a sacrifice of
praise—the fruit of lips that confess his
name. 16And do not forget to do good
and to share with others, for with such
sacrifices God is pleased.
17Obey your leaders and submit to
their authority. They keep watch over
you as men who must give an account.
Obey them so that their work will be a
joy, not a burden, for that would be of
no advantage to you.
18Pray for us. We are sure that we have
a clear conscience and desire to live
honorably in every way. 19I particularly
urge you to pray so that I may be restored to you soon.
20May the God of peace, who through
the blood of the eternal covenant
brought back from the dead our Lord
Jesus, that great Shepherd of the sheep,
21equip you with everything good for
doing his will, and may he work in us
what is pleasing to him, through Jesus
Christ, to whom be glory for ever and
ever. Amen.

22Brothers, I urge you to bear with my
word of exhortation, for I have written
you only a short letter.
23I want you to know that our brother
Timothy has been released. If he arrives
soon, I will come with him to see you.
24Greet all your leaders and all God's
people. Those from Italy send you their
greetings.
25Grace be with you all.

[a]*5* Deut. 31:6 [b]*6* Psalm 118:6,7

SHARPEN THE FOCUS

We have a hard time realizing the impact Hebrews 13:11–13 would have made on first-century readers. Those who lived under the threat of crucifixion understood its disgrace. Our Lord Jesus—condemned, tormented, and naked for all to see—endured the most shameful death imaginable, especially for a Jew, a son of the covenant. We might refer to a blizzard-swept prairie as "God forsaken." But no place on earth deserves that adjective to the degree Jesus' cross did.

Disgraced. Deserted. Despised. Our Savior suffered all this—and more—"outside the camp" (Hebrews 13:11) for us. And because He did, we now are at peace with God. In fact, God is now for us "the God of peace" (Hebrews 13:20). He brought Jesus back from death and in doing so declared that His demands for justice had been fully satisfied at the cross. Our sins are gone. Our Savior is now our Good Shepherd.

JAMES

The book of James could be titled "People of Faith and How We Live." James writes to believers, introducing his main topics in summary form in chapter 1. Chapters 2–5 then circle back around these themes, further explaining and expanding them. As you read today, look for the themes James introduces. If time is short, focus on James 1:13–18.

1 James, a servant of God and of the
Lord Jesus Christ,
To the twelve tribes scattered among
the nations:
Greetings.

Trials and Temptations

2Consider it pure joy, my brothers,
whenever you face trials of many kinds,
3because you know that the testing of
your faith develops perseverance. 4Per-
severance must finish its work so that
you may be mature and complete, not
lacking anything. 5If any of you lacks
wisdom, he should ask God, who gives
generously to all without finding fault,
and it will be given to him. 6But when
he asks, he must believe and not doubt,
because he who doubts is like a wave of
the sea, blown and tossed by the wind.
7That man should not think he will receive anything from the Lord; 8he is a
double-minded man, unstable in all he
does.
9The brother in humble circumstances
ought to take pride in his high position.
10But the one who is rich should take
pride in his low position, because he
will pass away like a wild flower. 11For
the sun rises with scorching heat and
withers the plant; its blossom falls and
its beauty is destroyed. In the same way,
the rich man will fade away even while
he goes about his business.
12Blessed is the man who perseveres
under trial, because when he has stood
the test, he will receive the crown of life
that God has promised to those who
love him.
13When tempted, no one should say,
"God is tempting me." For God cannot
be tempted by evil, nor does he tempt
anyone; 14but each one is tempted
when, by his own evil desire, he is
dragged away and enticed. 15Then, after
desire has conceived, it gives birth to
sin; and sin, when it is full-grown, gives
birth to death.
16Don't be deceived, my dear brothers. 17Every good and perfect gift is from
above, coming down from the Father of
the heavenly lights, who does not
change like shifting shadows. 18He
chose to give us birth through the word
of truth, that we might be a kind of firstfruits of all he created.

Listening and Doing

19My dear brothers, take note of this:
Everyone should be quick to listen, slow
to speak and slow to become angry, 20for

man's anger does not bring about the
righteous life that God desires. 21 Therefore, get rid of all moral filth and the evil
that is so prevalent and humbly accept
the word planted in you, which can
save you.
22 Do not merely listen to the word,
and so deceive yourselves. Do what it
says. 23 Anyone who listens to the word
but does not do what it says is like a man
who looks at his face in a mirror 24 and,
after looking at himself, goes away and
immediately forgets what he looks like.
25 But the man who looks intently into
the perfect law that gives freedom, and
continues to do this, not forgetting what
he has heard, but doing it—he will be
blessed in what he does.
26 If anyone considers himself religious
and yet does not keep a tight rein on his
tongue, he deceives himself and his religion is worthless. 27 Religion that God
our Father accepts as pure and faultless
is this: to look after orphans and widows in their distress and to keep oneself
from being polluted by the world.

SHARPEN THE FOCUS

James warns us against the tendency to believe temptation comes from God. "Don't be deceived," he says (James 1:16). Then he declares that God gives only good gifts. We need not fear that He will change His mind about wanting to bless His very own children (James 1:17–18)!

James said all this because then as now our sinful flesh and Satan, too, lie to us about God's goodness. Some Christians believe that God deliberately puts them into situations that may compromise their faith to see whether or not they will fall into sin.

But God teaches us through His Word! And God knows everything; He doesn't have to devise tests like your high school chemistry teacher to find out how much truth you've internalized. Temptation comes from our own desires (James 1:14). It also comes when we're "enticed" (James 1:14). Who does this enticing? Scripture is clear: Satan.

Everything evil in life comes from the devil and from our own sinful nature. Everything good comes from God through Christ.

> *God anointed Jesus of Nazareth with the Holy Spirit and power, and [He] went around doing good and healing all who were under the power of the devil, because God was with Him.* (Acts 10:38)

WEEK 99 • WEDNESDAY

James 2:1–26

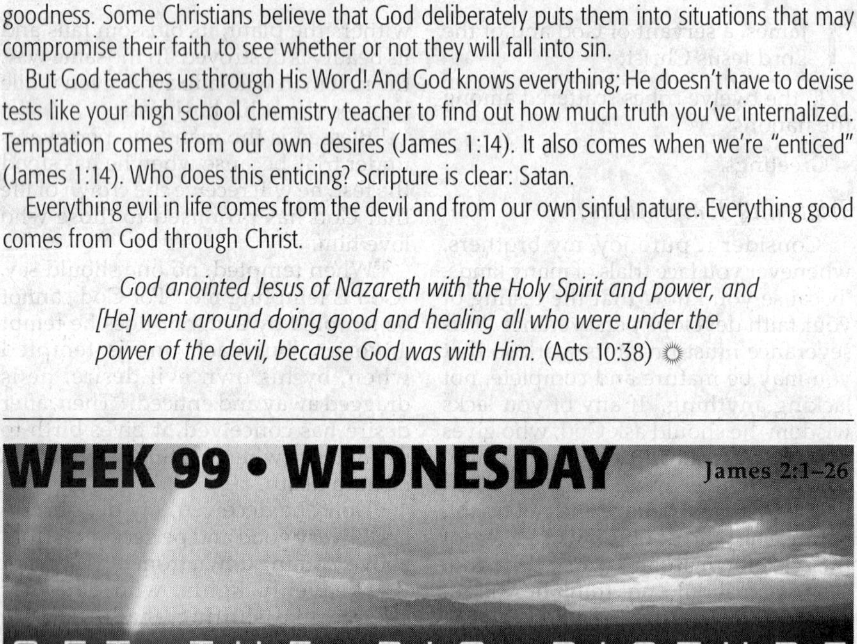

GET THE BIG PICTURE

As chapter 2 begins, James circles back to the ideas he introduced in James 1:9–11. Discrimination based on social status has no place in the church of Jesus Christ. Neither does the kind of "faith" that amounts to nothing more than dead, intellectual assent. Look for these two ideas as you read. If time is short, focus on James 2:14–26.

Favoritism Forbidden

2 My brothers, as believers in our glorious Lord Jesus Christ, don't show favoritism. 2Suppose a man comes into your meeting wearing a gold ring and fine clothes, and a poor man in shabby clothes also comes in. 3If you show special attention to the man wearing fine clothes and say, "Here's a good seat for you," but say to the poor man, "You stand there" or "Sit on the floor by my feet," 4have you not discriminated among yourselves and become judges with evil thoughts?

5Listen, my dear brothers: Has not God chosen those who are poor in the eyes of the world to be rich in faith and to inherit the kingdom he promised those who love him? 6But you have insulted the poor. Is it not the rich who are exploiting you? Are they not the ones who are dragging you into court? 7Are they not the ones who are slandering the noble name of him to whom you belong?

8If you really keep the royal law found in Scripture, "Love your neighbor as yourself,"[a] you are doing right. 9But if you show favoritism, you sin and are convicted by the law as lawbreakers. 10For whoever keeps the whole law and yet stumbles at just one point is guilty of breaking all of it. 11For he who said, "Do not commit adultery,"[b] also said, "Do not murder."[c] If you do not commit adultery but do commit murder, you have become a lawbreaker.

12Speak and act as those who are going to be judged by the law that gives freedom, 13because judgment without mercy will be shown to anyone who has not been merciful. Mercy triumphs over judgment!

Faith and Deeds

14What good is it, my brothers, if a man claims to have faith but has no deeds? Can such faith save him? 15Suppose a brother or sister is without clothes and daily food. 16If one of you says to him, "Go, I wish you well; keep warm and well fed," but does nothing about his physical needs, what good is it? 17In the same way, faith by itself, if it is not accompanied by action, is dead.

18But someone will say, "You have faith; I have deeds."

Show me your faith without deeds, and I will show you my faith by what I do. 19You believe that there is one God. Good! Even the demons believe that—and shudder.

20You foolish man, do you want evidence that faith without deeds is useless[d]? 21Was not our ancestor Abraham considered righteous for what he did when he offered his son Isaac on the altar? 22You see that his faith and his actions were working together, and his faith was made complete by what he did. 23And the scripture was fulfilled that says, "Abraham believed God, and it was credited to him as righteousness,"[e] and he was called God's friend. 24You see that a person is justified by what he does and not by faith alone.

25In the same way, was not even Rahab the prostitute considered righteous for what she did when she gave lodging to the spies and sent them off in a different direction? 26As the body without the spirit is dead, so faith without deeds is dead.

[a] *8* Lev. 19:18 [b] *11* Exodus 20:14; Deut. 5:18
[c] *11* Exodus 20:13; Deut. 5:17 [d] *20* Some early manuscripts *dead* [e] *23* Gen. 15:6

SHARPEN THE FOCUS

In old cowboy movies, outlaws sometimes tried to find out if a wounded sheriff was dead by putting a mirror under his nose. Breath was evidence of life. James uses the word "spirit" in v. 26 in a similar way. In fact, the Greek word here *could* be translated "breath."

Just as a body that doesn't breathe is dead, James writes, "so faith without works is likewise dead." Does that conclusion frighten you? It can, especially if we start asking questions like these: "How many good works does it take?" "Have I done enough?" Questions like that grow out of the mistaken notion that we *could* do enough to make ourselves worthy in God's eyes. We can't, of course.

Instead, as we read passages like this one in James, we remember this truth about our identity: Who we are as God's redeemed, baptized children shows up in what we do. Someone who's alive spiritually lives in Christlike ways. Jesus is alive in us. His new nature can't help but show. Not because we force it or because we're keeping track, but because by God's grace, we can't stop it. We're just being who we now—in Christ—are.

WEEK 99 • THURSDAY

James 3:1–18

James circles back around another time to define true wisdom and to elaborate on his statements in James 1:19 about being quick to hear, slow to speak, and slow to anger. What effect *does* our Christian faith have on our words and attitudes? Ask yourself that as you read. If time is short, focus on James 3:13–18.

Taming the Tongue

3 Not many of you should presume to be teachers, my brothers,
because you know that we who teach
will be judged more strictly. 2We all
stumble in many ways. If anyone is
never at fault in what he says, he is a
perfect man, able to keep his whole
body in check.
3When we put bits into the mouths of
horses to make them obey us, we can
turn the whole animal. 4Or take ships as
an example. Although they are so large
and are driven by strong winds, they are
steered by a very small rudder wherever the pilot wants to go. 5Likewise the
tongue is a small part of the body, but it
makes great boasts. Consider what a
great forest is set on fire by a small
spark. 6The tongue also is a fire, a world
of evil among the parts of the body. It
corrupts the whole person, sets the
whole course of his life on fire, and is
itself set on fire by hell.
7All kinds of animals, birds, reptiles
and creatures of the sea are being tamed
and have been tamed by man, 8but no
man can tame the tongue. It is a restless
evil, full of deadly poison.
9With the tongue we praise our Lord
and Father, and with it we curse men,
who have been made in God's likeness.
10Out of the same mouth come praise
and cursing. My brothers, this should
not be. 11Can both fresh water and salt[a]
water flow from the same spring? 12My
brothers, can a fig tree bear olives, or a
grapevine bear figs? Neither can a salt
spring produce fresh water.

Two Kinds of Wisdom

13Who is wise and understanding
among you? Let him show it by his good
life, by deeds done in the humility that
comes from wisdom. 14But if you harbor
bitter envy and selfish ambition in your
hearts, do not boast about it or deny the
truth. 15Such "wisdom" does not come
down from heaven but is earthly, un-

[a]11 Greek *bitter* (see also verse 14)

spiritual, of the devil. [16]For where you have envy and selfish ambition, there you find disorder and every evil practice.

[17]But the wisdom that comes from heaven is first of all pure; then peace-loving, considerate, submissive, full of mercy and good fruit, impartial and sincere. [18]Peacemakers who sow in peace raise a harvest of righteousness.

SHARPEN THE FOCUS

If you could paint a picture titled "Peace," what would it look like? Perhaps the word brings to mind a quiet stream on a warm spring day. Or perhaps you see an infant sleeping on Dad's shoulder. Or maybe the prophet's picture in Micah 4:4 captures the essence of *peace* for you.

James connects wisdom with peace and then with righteousness. If we tease out his line of reasoning in James 3, it might go something like this: Our faith in Jesus makes it possible for us to act wisely by avoiding gossip, envy, and selfish ambition. Instead, we can sow seeds of peace and harmony in our families and in our churches. These seeds sprout and grow to produce a harvest of righteousness—acts of Christlike love—among our family members and between individuals in our congregations.

A harvest of righteousness! What a legacy! And yet, too often, we sow just the opposite of peace—discord, envy, rumor, innuendo. How we need the Prince of peace each and every day! How thankful we can be for God's wisdom—wisdom that sent Jesus to the cross for us. And how wonderful to know that in Jesus we can start each day afresh, forgiven, and empowered to walk in the wisdom that "comes from heaven" (James 3:17). ☼

WEEK 99 • FRIDAY

James 4:1–17

GET THE BIG PICTURE

Why are there wars? That simple but profound question begins today's Bible reading of James 4. The rest of the chapter goes on to answer it and to offer an alternative to war—the grace of God. If time is short, focus on James 4:1–12.

Submit Yourselves to God

4 What causes fights and quarrels among you? Don't they come from your desires that battle within you? [2]You want something but don't get it. You kill and covet, but you cannot have what you want. You quarrel and fight. You do not have, because you do not ask God. [3]When you ask, you do not receive, because you ask with wrong motives, that you may spend what you get on your pleasures.

[4]You adulterous people, don't you know that friendship with the world is hatred toward God? Anyone who chooses to be a friend of the world becomes an enemy of God. [5]Or do you think Scripture says without reason that the spirit he caused to live in us envies intensely?[a] [6]But he gives us more grace. That is why Scripture says:

[a]5 Or *that God jealously longs for the spirit that he made to live in us;* or *that the Spirit he caused to live in us longs jealously*

"God opposes the proud
but gives grace to the humble."[a]

7Submit yourselves, then, to God. Resist the devil, and he will flee from you.
8Come near to God and he will come
near to you. Wash your hands, you sinners, and purify your hearts, you double-minded. 9Grieve, mourn and wail.
Change your laughter to mourning and
your joy to gloom. 10Humble yourselves
before the Lord, and he will lift you up.
11Brothers, do not slander one another. Anyone who speaks against his
brother or judges him speaks against
the law and judges it. When you judge
the law, you are not keeping it, but sitting in judgment on it. 12There is only
one Lawgiver and Judge, the one who
is able to save and destroy. But you—
who are you to judge your neighbor?

Boasting About Tomorrow

13Now listen, you who say, "Today or
tomorrow we will go to this or that city,
spend a year there, carry on business
and make money." 14Why, you do not
even know what will happen tomorrow. What is your life? You are a mist
that appears for a little while and then
vanishes. 15Instead, you ought to say, "If
it is the Lord's will, we will live and do
this or that." 16As it is, you boast and
brag. All such boasting is evil. 17Anyone,
then, who knows the good he ought to
do and doesn't do it, sins.

[a]6 Prov. 3:34

SHARPEN THE FOCUS

"Be on your guard against all kinds of greed," Jesus warned. "A man's life does not consist in the abundance of his possessions" (Luke 12:15). James accents temptations like greed in James 1:9–11. He touches on the dangers of showing preference to the wealthy in James 2:1–9. Now, in James 4:1–5, he comes back around to highlight another facet of our relationship to earthly wealth. Covetousness leads to quarrels and, ultimately, to war.

Maybe you've seen this in action as heirs divided your neighbor's estate. (That kind of situation prompted the Lord's warning about greed you just read.) Or maybe the urge to be rich occupies much of your own thought-life and has begun to cause you trouble of one sort or another—sleepless nights focused on the health of your investments or quarrels with your spouse over what to spend when.

What's the alternative? The grace of God (James 4:6)! That grace enables us to submit in peace to God's will and to resist Satan's temptations (James 4:7). That grace gives us the gifts of repentance and faith (James 4:8–9). And as we confess our misplaced priorities—really our sins of idolatry—God lifts us out of our despair and draws us to Himself (James 4:10).

WEEK 99 • SATURDAY

James 5:1–20

GET THE BIG PICTURE

Patience. Persistence. Prayer. These themes round out James 5. As you read, notice how James touches on several ideas we've encountered previously in his letter, broadening them still further. Also ask yourself how patience and perseverance pay off in true wealth. If time is short, focus on James 5:7–18.

Warning to Rich Oppressors

5 Now listen, you rich people,
weep and wail because of the
misery that is coming upon you. [2]Your
wealth has rotted, and moths have
eaten your clothes. [3]Your gold and silver
are corroded. Their corrosion will testify
against you and eat your flesh like fire.
You have hoarded wealth in the last
days. [4]Look! The wages you failed to
pay the workmen who mowed your
fields are crying out against you. The
cries of the harvesters have reached the
ears of the Lord Almighty. [5]You have
lived on earth in luxury and self-indul-
gence. You have fattened yourselves in
the day of slaughter.[a] [6]You have condemned and murdered innocent men,
who were not opposing you.

Patience in Suffering

[7]Be patient, then, brothers, until the
Lord's coming. See how the farmer
waits for the land to yield its valuable
crop and how patient he is for the autumn and spring rains. [8]You too, be patient and stand firm, because the Lord's
coming is near. [9]Don't grumble against
each other, brothers, or you will be
judged. The Judge is standing at the
door!

[10]Brothers, as an example of patience
in the face of suffering, take the prophets who spoke in the name of the Lord.
[11]As you know, we consider blessed
those who have persevered. You have
heard of Job's perseverance and have
seen what the Lord finally brought
about. The Lord is full of compassion
and mercy.

[12]Above all, my brothers, do not
swear—not by heaven or by earth or
by anything else. Let your "Yes" be yes,
and your "No," no, or you will be condemned.

The Prayer of Faith

[13]Is any one of you in trouble? He
should pray. Is anyone happy? Let him
sing songs of praise. [14]Is any one of you
sick? He should call the elders of the
church to pray over him and anoint him
with oil in the name of the Lord. [15]And
the prayer offered in faith will make the
sick person well; the Lord will raise him
up. If he has sinned, he will be forgiven.
[16]Therefore confess your sins to each
other and pray for each other so that
you may be healed. The prayer of a righteous man is powerful and effective.

[17]Elijah was a man just like us. He
prayed earnestly that it would not rain,
and it did not rain on the land for three
and a half years. [18]Again he prayed, and
the heavens gave rain, and the earth
produced its crops.

[19]My brothers, if one of you should
wander from the truth and someone
should bring him back, [20]remember this:
Whoever turns a sinner from the error
of his way will save him from death and
cover over a multitude of sins.

[a]5 Or *yourselves as in a day of feasting*

SHARPEN THE FOCUS

Sometimes it can seem that God's "soon" isn't soon enough. Job felt that way. Satan's attacks brought on his grumbling despite God's compassionate and merciful purpose (James 5:11). The Christians being cheated in the ways described in James 5:1–6 no doubt had trouble waiting for the Lord's promised vindication (James 5:7–8). That's why James encourages them to wait in patience.

We, like the saints who have gone before us, sometimes must endure wrong while we wait for God to act. In times like that we can easily fall prey to the temptations of short-temperedness and fault-finding (James 5:8–9).

But we need not wallow in the muck at the bottom of that pit. Instead, we can let our Lord remind us that even now He stands at the door as Judge (James 5:9). We may wait for now, but we will not wait forever. We can remember the lives of faith lived by those who have gone before us (James 5:11). We can comfort our hearts with the truth that the God who took them safely through life's trials will bring us safely through them too.

And we can pray—for relief (James 5:13); for healing (James 5:14–15); for forgiveness (James 5:16)—for whatever we need as we press on in faith by God's grace.

1 PETER

WEEK 100 • MONDAY

1 Peter 1:1–25

GET THE BIG PICTURE

How do you define *hope?* While some in our culture frame the word in terms of wishful thinking, the Bible uses it to refer to certainties we have not yet received. List a few examples of biblical hope on a slip of paper before you read 1 Peter 1. If time is short, focus on 1 Peter 1:1–21.

1 Peter, an apostle of Jesus Christ,

To God's elect, strangers in the world, scattered throughout Pontus, Galatia, Cappadocia, Asia and Bithynia, [2]who have been chosen according to the foreknowledge of God the Father, through the sanctifying work of the Spirit, for obedience to Jesus Christ and sprinkling by his blood:

Grace and peace be yours in abundance.

Praise to God for a Living Hope

[3]Praise be to the God and Father of our Lord Jesus Christ! In his great mercy he has given us new birth into a living hope through the resurrection of Jesus Christ from the dead, [4]and into an inheritance that can never perish, spoil or fade—kept in heaven for you, [5]who through faith are shielded by God's power until the coming of the salvation that is ready to be revealed in the last time. [6]In this you greatly rejoice, though now for a little while you may have had to suffer grief in all kinds of trials. [7]These have come so that your faith—of greater worth than gold, which perishes even though refined by fire—may be proved genuine and may result in praise, glory and honor when Jesus Christ is revealed. [8]Though you have not seen him, you love him; and even though you do not see him now, you believe in him and are filled with an inexpressible and glorious joy, [9]for you are receiving the goal of your faith, the salvation of your souls.

[10]Concerning this salvation, the prophets, who spoke of the grace that was to come to you, searched intently and with the greatest care, [11]trying to find out the time and circumstances to which the Spirit of Christ in them was pointing when he predicted the sufferings of Christ and the glories that would follow. [12]It was revealed to them that they were not serving themselves but you, when they spoke of the things that have now been told you by those who have preached the gospel to you by the Holy Spirit sent from heaven. Even angels long to look into these things.

Be Holy

[13]Therefore, prepare your minds for action; be self-controlled; set your hope fully on the grace to be given you when Jesus Christ is revealed. [14]As obedient children, do not conform to the evil desires you had when you lived in igno-

rance. 15But just as he who called you is
holy, so be holy in all you do; 16for it is
written: "Be holy, because I am holy."[a]
17Since you call on a Father who
judges each man's work impartially, live
your lives as strangers here in reverent
fear. 18For you know that it was not with
perishable things such as silver or gold
that you were redeemed from the
empty way of life handed down to you
from your forefathers, 19but with the
precious blood of Christ, a lamb without
blemish or defect. 20He was chosen before the creation of the world, but was
revealed in these last times for your
sake. 21Through him you believe in God,
who raised him from the dead and glorified him, and so your faith and hope
are in God.
22Now that you have purified yourselves by obeying the truth so that you
have sincere love for your brothers, love
one another deeply, from the heart.[b]
23For you have been born again, not of
perishable seed, but of imperishable,
through the living and enduring word
of God. 24For,

"All men are like grass,
and all their glory is like the
flowers of the field;
the grass withers and the flowers
fall,
25 but the word of the Lord stands
forever."[c]

And this is the word that was preached
to you.

[a]*16* Lev. 11:44,45; 19:2; 20:7 [b]22 Some early manuscripts *from a pure heart* [c]25 Isaiah 40:6-8

SHARPEN THE FOCUS

It may surprise you to know that your whole life story appears in the Bible. In fact, you just read it! 1 Peter 1 gives the biography of every Christian who has ever lived on earth. This is your story and mine:

- Before creation, God chose you (1 Peter 1:2)—elected you (1 Peter 1:1)—to belong to Him. Your real home is with God; you live here on earth as a stranger (1 Peter 1:1).
- God sent the prophets for your sake, so you could hear and believe the Gospel (1 Peter 1:10–12).
- God has worked new life, spiritual life, in you, and He has written your name into His will. You have become, in Jesus, His child and heir (1 Peter 1:3–4).
- Right now you are enduring various kinds of trials. These bring you grief, but God is keeping you in faith (1 Peter 1:5–7).
- Despite your hardships, you live in the joy He gives you—a joy too full for words (1 Peter 1:8).
- When Jesus returns, your life experiences and faith-walk will bring praise, glory, and honor to Him (1 Peter 1:7).

Aren't those the important pieces of your life story? Life is Christ. The rest is only details.

WEEK 100 • TUESDAY

1 Peter 2:1–25

GET THE BIG PICTURE

Peter carefully lays out who Christ is and who we have become in Christ. Then he goes on to spell out the implications of these truths for daily living. Watch carefully to see how he connects our Christian witness with godly submission in 1 Peter 2:11–25. If time is short, focus on 1 Peter 2:1–10.

2 Therefore, rid yourselves of all
malice and all deceit, hypocrisy,
envy, and slander of every kind. [2]Like
newborn babies, crave pure spiritual
milk, so that by it you may grow up in
your salvation, [3]now that you have
tasted that the Lord is good.

The Living Stone and a Chosen People

[4]As you come to him, the living
Stone—rejected by men but chosen by
God and precious to him— [5]you also,
like living stones, are being built into a
spiritual house to be a holy priesthood,
offering spiritual sacrifices acceptable to
God through Jesus Christ. [6]For in Scripture it says:

"See, I lay a stone in Zion,
a chosen and precious cornerstone,
and the one who trusts in him
will never be put to shame."[a]

[7]Now to you who believe, this stone is
precious. But to those who do not believe,

"The stone the builders rejected
has become the capstone,[b]"[c]

[8]and,

"A stone that causes men to stumble
and a rock that makes them fall."[d]

They stumble because they disobey the
message—which is also what they were
destined for.

[9]But you are a chosen people, a royal
priesthood, a holy nation, a people belonging to God, that you may declare
the praises of him who called you out of
darkness into his wonderful light.
[10]Once you were not a people, but now
you are the people of God; once you
had not received mercy, but now you
have received mercy.

[11]Dear friends, I urge you, as aliens
and strangers in the world, to abstain
from sinful desires, which war against
your soul. [12]Live such good lives among
the pagans that, though they accuse you
of doing wrong, they may see your
good deeds and glorify God on the day
he visits us.

Submission to Rulers and Masters

[13]Submit yourselves for the Lord's
sake to every authority instituted
among men: whether to the king, as
the supreme authority, [14]or to governors, who are sent by him to punish
those who do wrong and to commend
those who do right. [15]For it is God's will
that by doing good you should silence
the ignorant talk of foolish men. [16]Live
as free men, but do not use your freedom as a cover-up for evil; live as servants of God. [17]Show proper respect to
everyone: Love the brotherhood of believers, fear God, honor the king.

[18]Slaves, submit yourselves to your
masters with all respect, not only to
those who are good and considerate,
but also to those who are harsh. [19]For it

[a]6 Isaiah 28:16 [b]7 Or *cornerstone*
[c]7 Psalm 118:22 [d]8 Isaiah 8:14

is commendable if a man bears up under the pain of unjust suffering because
he is conscious of God. 20But how is it to
your credit if you receive a beating for
doing wrong and endure it? But if you
suffer for doing good and you endure
it, this is commendable before God. 21To
this you were called, because Christ suffered for you, leaving you an example,
that you should follow in his steps.

22"He committed no sin,
and no deceit was found in his
mouth."[a]

23When they hurled their insults at him,
he did not retaliate; when he suffered,
he made no threats. Instead, he entrusted himself to him who judges
justly. 24He himself bore our sins in his
body on the tree, so that we might die
to sins and live for righteousness; by his
wounds you have been healed. 25For
you were like sheep going astray, but
now you have returned to the Shepherd
and Overseer of your souls.

[a]22 Isaiah 53:9

SHARPEN THE FOCUS

Have you ever tried to quiet a hungry baby? A hungry infant can't be distracted for long by a favorite toy or lulled to sleep by even the sweetest song. Hungry babies have one thing on their minds. Only warm milk will satisfy them.

Peter urges us to recognize and act on the same kind of craving—a craving for the "pure spiritual milk" of God's Word (1 Peter 2:2). We've tasted that milk as we've enjoyed the sweet grace and goodness of our Lord (1 Peter 2:3). Once our souls have savored that grace, nothing else will satisfy us or distract us. We want more! That milk not only satisfies, it stimulates spiritual growth (1 Peter 2:2). In fact, only God's Word can nourish our souls so that we grow up in Christ.

All of us as God's people need the kind of spiritual maturity that renounces malice, deceit, hypocrisy, envy, and slander (1 Peter 2:1). Only as we grow in Christ, feeding on His Gospel, will that kind of maturity become ours. All of us need the kind of spiritual maturity that submits in joy to the government (1 Peter 2:13–17), to those who supervise us on the job (1 Peter 2:18–20), and even to persecution for Christ's sake (1 Peter 2:21–24). That kind of maturity comes only as our Lord nourishes us with His Word of life.

WEEK 100 • WEDNESDAY

1 Peter 3:1—4:19

GET THE BIG PICTURE

What a witness a congregation full of believers like the ones Peter describes would be—even today, especially today! But no matter how exemplary our conduct, it will not exempt us from persecution by the enemies of the cross. But we can bring honor to our Lord, even in times of trial. Read to see how that happens. If time is short, focus on 1 Peter 3:18–22.

Wives and Husbands

3 Wives, in the same way be submissive to your husbands so
that, if any of them do not believe the
word, they may be won over without
words by the behavior of their wives,
2when they see the purity and reverence
of your lives. 3Your beauty should not
come from outward adornment, such as
braided hair and the wearing of gold
jewelry and fine clothes. 4Instead, it
should be that of your inner self, the
unfading beauty of a gentle and quiet
spirit, which is of great worth in God's
sight. 5For this is the way the holy
women of the past who put their hope
in God used to make themselves beautiful. They were submissive to their own
husbands, 6like Sarah, who obeyed
Abraham and called him her master. You
are her daughters if you do what is right
and do not give way to fear.

7Husbands, in the same way be considerate as you live with your wives,
and treat them with respect as the
weaker partner and as heirs with you of
the gracious gift of life, so that nothing
will hinder your prayers.

Suffering for Doing Good

8Finally, all of you, live in harmony
with one another; be sympathetic, love
as brothers, be compassionate and humble. 9Do not repay evil with evil or insult
with insult, but with blessing, because
to this you were called so that you may
inherit a blessing. 10For,

"Whoever would love life
and see good days
must keep his tongue from evil
and his lips from deceitful speech.
11 He must turn from evil and do good;
he must seek peace and pursue it.
12 For the eyes of the Lord are on the
righteous
and his ears are attentive to their
prayer,
but the face of the Lord is against
those who do evil."[a]

13Who is going to harm you if you are
eager to do good? 14But even if you
should suffer for what is right, you are
blessed. "Do not fear what they fear[b]; do
not be frightened."[c] 15But in your hearts
set apart Christ as Lord. Always be prepared to give an answer to everyone
who asks you to give the reason for the
hope that you have. But do this with
gentleness and respect, 16keeping a clear
conscience, so that those who speak
maliciously against your good behavior
in Christ may be ashamed of their slander. 17It is better, if it is God's will, to suffer for doing good than for doing evil.
18For Christ died for sins once for all, the
righteous for the unrighteous, to bring
you to God. He was put to death in the
body but made alive by the Spirit,
19through whom[d] also he went and
preached to the spirits in prison 20who
disobeyed long ago when God waited
patiently in the days of Noah while the
ark was being built. In it only a few
people, eight in all, were saved through
water, 21and this water symbolizes baptism that now saves you also—not the
removal of dirt from the body but the
pledge[e] of a good conscience toward
God. It saves you by the resurrection of
Jesus Christ, 22who has gone into heav-
en and is at God's right hand—with angels, authorities and powers in submission to him.

Living for God

4 Therefore, since Christ suffered
in his body, arm yourselves also
with the same attitude, because he who
has suffered in his body is done with
sin. 2As a result, he does not live the rest
of his earthly life for evil human desires,
but rather for the will of God. 3For you
have spent enough time in the past
doing what pagans choose to do—living in debauchery, lust, drunkenness,
orgies, carousing and detestable idolatry. 4They think it strange that you do
not plunge with them into the same
flood of dissipation, and they heap
abuse on you. 5But they will have to give

[a]12 Psalm 34:12-16 [b]14 Or *not fear their threats*
[c]14 Isaiah 8:12 [d]18,19 Or *alive in the spirit,*
19through which [e]21 Or *response*

account to him who is ready to judge the living and the dead. [6]For this is the reason the gospel was preached even to those who are now dead, so that they might be judged according to men in regard to the body, but live according to God in regard to the spirit.

[7]The end of all things is near. Therefore be clear minded and self-controlled so that you can pray. [8]Above all, love each other deeply, because love covers over a multitude of sins. [9]Offer hospitality to one another without grumbling. [10]Each one should use whatever gift he has received to serve others, faithfully administering God's grace in its various forms. [11]If anyone speaks, he should do it as one speaking the very words of God. If anyone serves, he should do it with the strength God provides, so that in all things God may be praised through Jesus Christ. To him be the glory and the power for ever and ever. Amen.

Suffering for Being a Christian

[12]Dear friends, do not be surprised at the painful trial you are suffering, as though something strange were happening to you. [13]But rejoice that you participate in the sufferings of Christ, so that you may be overjoyed when his glory is revealed. [14]If you are insulted because of the name of Christ, you are blessed, for the Spirit of glory and of God rests on you. [15]If you suffer, it should not be as a murderer or thief or any other kind of criminal, or even as a meddler. [16]However, if you suffer as a Christian, do not be ashamed, but praise God that you bear that name. [17]For it is time for judgment to begin with the family of God; and if it begins with us, what will the outcome be for those who do not obey the gospel of God? [18]And,

"If it is hard for the righteous to be
saved,
what will become of the ungodly
and the sinner?"[a]

[19]So then, those who suffer according to God's will should commit themselves to their faithful Creator and continue to do good.

[a]*18* Prov. 11:31

SHARPEN THE FOCUS

Imagine meeting your pastor on the street. Imagine him asking you, "How's your conscience?" Would you be taken off guard? Or suppose God Himself would ask you that question. What would you reply?

The apostle Peter promises Christ's people something that many of the world's rich and famous can only dream about—"the pledge of a good conscience" (1 Peter 3:21). A good conscience belongs to us in our Baptism. Baptism's water didn't wipe dirt or smudges off our bodies, Peter says. Instead it connected us to the resurrection of Jesus Christ—and, by implication, to His death as well.

Dead and buried and raised with Christ, we emerge from Baptism's waters whole, saved, right with God, and with our conscience cleansed from all accusations. If your conscience bothers you right now, reread 1 Peter 3:21–22 and meditate on 1 John 3:19–20. Then live today in the freedom Christ's peace brings.

WEEK 100 • THURSDAY

1 Peter 5:1–14

GET THE BIG PICTURE

Many countries celebrate a national day of thanksgiving. Quite often most of the expressions of thanks are for physical things—food, house, health, and so on. Today read 1 Peter 5 with an eye toward the *spiritual* blessings for which you want to thank your Lord. If time is short, focus on 1 Peter 5:5–14.

To Elders and Young Men

5 To the elders among you, I appeal as a fellow elder, a witness
of Christ's sufferings and one who also
will share in the glory to be revealed: 2Be
shepherds of God's flock that is under
your care, serving as overseers—not because you must, but because you are
willing, as God wants you to be; not
greedy for money, but eager to serve;
3not lording it over those entrusted to
you, but being examples to the flock.
4And when the Chief Shepherd appears, you will receive the crown of
glory that will never fade away.
5Young men, in the same way be submissive to those who are older. All of
you, clothe yourselves with humility toward one another, because,

"God opposes the proud
but gives grace to the humble."[a]

6Humble yourselves, therefore, under
God's mighty hand, that he may lift you
up in due time. 7Cast all your anxiety on
him because he cares for you.
8Be self-controlled and alert. Your enemy the devil prowls around like a roaring lion looking for someone to devour.
9Resist him, standing firm in the faith,
because you know that your brothers
throughout the world are undergoing
the same kind of sufferings.
10And the God of all grace, who called
you to his eternal glory in Christ, after
you have suffered a little while, will
himself restore you and make you
strong, firm and steadfast. 11To him be
the power for ever and ever. Amen.

Final Greetings

12With the help of Silas,[b] whom I regard as a faithful brother, I have written
to you briefly, encouraging you and testifying that this is the true grace of God.
Stand fast in it.
13She who is in Babylon, chosen together with you, sends you her greetings, and so does my son Mark. 14Greet
one another with a kiss of love.
Peace to all of you who are in Christ.

[a]5 Prov. 3:34 [b]12 Greek *Silvanus*, a variant of *Silas*

SHARPEN THE FOCUS

Today's reading repeats the truths about humility you read in James 4 less than a week ago. Peter and James quote the same Old Testament verse (Proverbs 3:34). Both writers also urge us to humble ourselves, and they assure us this will result in God exalting us, lifting us up. (See James 4:6, 10.) Both also speak in almost the same breath about humility and about resisting Satan.

True, godly humility comes to us as God's gift of grace. When His Word leads us to see our helplessness, our sinfulness, our need for Jesus, we're on the road toward humility. When we—by grace—focus on Christ, when we cling to Him as our only hope, we are exactly where God wants us to be. When we trust in Christ's pardon alone as the remedy for our sin, then God can lift us up. He gives us—us!—the very righteousness of Christ.

This right-standing with God undercuts Satan's schemes for us. A focus on Christ protects us from self-absorption, selfishness, and self-confidence. And in that God-given humility is our peace and hope—even in times of suffering.

2 PETER

Grace. Glory. Goodness. Godliness. These and more belong to us as God's children in Christ. That's the point of 2 Peter 1. Destruction. Shame. Greed. Arrogance. These and more belong to Satan and his human agents. That's the point of 2 Peter 2. As you read, note the stark contrasts, particularly the final outcome of each belief system and lifestyle. If time is short, focus on 2 Peter 2:1–22.

1 Simon Peter, a servant and apostle
of Jesus Christ,

To those who through the righteousness of our God and Savior Jesus Christ
have received a faith as precious as ours:

2Grace and peace be yours in abundance through the knowledge of God
and of Jesus our Lord.

Making One's Calling and Election Sure

3His divine power has given us everything we need for life and godliness
through our knowledge of him who
called us by his own glory and goodness. 4Through these he has given us his
very great and precious promises, so
that through them you may participate
in the divine nature and escape the
corruption in the world caused by evil
desires.

5For this very reason, make every
effort to add to your faith goodness; and
to goodness, knowledge; 6and to knowledge, self-control; and to self-control,
perseverance; and to perseverance,
godliness; 7and to godliness, brotherly
kindness; and to brotherly kindness,
love. 8For if you possess these qualities
in increasing measure, they will keep
you from being ineffective and unproductive in your knowledge of our Lord
Jesus Christ. 9But if anyone does not
have them, he is nearsighted and blind,
and has forgotten that he has been
cleansed from his past sins.

10Therefore, my brothers, be all the
more eager to make your calling and
election sure. For if you do these things,
you will never fall, 11and you will receive
a rich welcome into the eternal kingdom of our Lord and Savior Jesus
Christ.

Prophecy of Scripture

12So I will always remind you of these
things, even though you know them
and are firmly established in the truth
you now have. 13I think it is right to refresh your memory as long as I live in
the tent of this body, 14because I know
that I will soon put it aside, as our Lord
Jesus Christ has made clear to me. 15And
I will make every effort to see that after
my departure you will always be able to
remember these things.

16We did not follow cleverly invented
stories when we told you about the
power and coming of our Lord Jesus

Christ, but we were eyewitnesses of his majesty. 17 For he received honor and glory from God the Father when the voice came to him from the Majestic Glory, saying, "This is my Son, whom I love; with him I am well pleased."[a] 18 We ourselves heard this voice that came from heaven when we were with him on the sacred mountain.

19 And we have the word of the prophets made more certain, and you will do well to pay attention to it, as to a light shining in a dark place, until the day dawns and the morning star rises in your hearts. 20 Above all, you must understand that no prophecy of Scripture came about by the prophet's own interpretation. 21 For prophecy never had its origin in the will of man, but men spoke from God as they were carried along by the Holy Spirit.

False Teachers and Their Destruction

2 But there were also false prophets among the people, just as there will be false teachers among you. They will secretly introduce destructive heresies, even denying the sovereign Lord who bought them—bringing swift destruction on themselves. 2 Many will follow their shameful ways and will bring the way of truth into disrepute. 3 In their greed these teachers will exploit you with stories they have made up. Their condemnation has long been hanging over them, and their destruction has not been sleeping.

4 For if God did not spare angels when they sinned, but sent them to hell,[b] putting them into gloomy dungeons[c] to be held for judgment; 5 if he did not spare the ancient world when he brought the flood on its ungodly people, but protected Noah, a preacher of righteousness, and seven others; 6 if he condemned the cities of Sodom and Gomorrah by burning them to ashes, and made them an example of what is going to happen to the ungodly; 7 and if he rescued Lot, a righteous man, who was distressed by the filthy lives of lawless men 8 (for that righteous man, living among them day after day, was tormented in his righteous soul by the lawless deeds he saw and heard)— 9 if this is so, then the Lord knows how to rescue godly men from trials and to hold the unrighteous for the day of judgment, while continuing their punishment.[d] 10 This is especially true of those who follow the corrupt desire of the sinful nature[e] and despise authority.

Bold and arrogant, these men are not afraid to slander celestial beings; 11 yet even angels, although they are stronger and more powerful, do not bring slanderous accusations against such beings in the presence of the Lord. 12 But these men blaspheme in matters they do not understand. They are like brute beasts, creatures of instinct, born only to be caught and destroyed, and like beasts they too will perish.

13 They will be paid back with harm for the harm they have done. Their idea of pleasure is to carouse in broad daylight. They are blots and blemishes, reveling in their pleasures while they feast with you.[f] 14 With eyes full of adultery, they never stop sinning; they seduce the unstable; they are experts in greed—an accursed brood! 15 They have left the straight way and wandered off to follow the way of Balaam son of Beor, who loved the wages of wickedness. 16 But he was rebuked for his wrongdoing by a donkey—a beast without speech—who spoke with a man's voice and restrained the prophet's madness.

17 These men are springs without water and mists driven by a storm. Blackest darkness is reserved for them. 18 For they mouth empty, boastful words and, by appealing to the lustful desires of sinful human nature, they entice people who are just escaping from those who live in error. 19 They promise them freedom, while they themselves are slaves of depravity—for a man is a slave to whatever has mastered him. 20 If they

[a] 17 Matt. 17:5; Mark 9:7; Luke 9:35 [b] 4 Greek *Tartarus* [c] 4 Some manuscripts *into chains of darkness* [d] 9 Or *unrighteous for punishment until the day of judgment* [e] 10 Or *the flesh* [f] 13 Some manuscripts *in their love feasts*

have escaped the corruption of the
world by knowing our Lord and Savior
Jesus Christ and are again entangled in
it and overcome, they are worse off at
the end than they were at the beginning. [21]It would have been better for
them not to have known the way of
righteousness, than to have known it
and then to turn their backs on the sacred command that was passed on to
them. [22]Of them the proverbs are true:
"A dog returns to its vomit,"[a] and, "A sow
that is washed goes back to her wallowing in the mud."

SHARPEN THE FOCUS

Peter minces no words. Destructive teaching leads to a destructive lifestyle which results ultimately in destruction at the Day of Judgment (2 Peter 2:1–3). Not a pretty picture. Not a truth we enjoy hearing. But we need Peter's warnings today just as much or more than did the apostle's first readers.

Still today many in our world try to assure us that "Scripture is, after all, simply a matter of your own interpretation." But Peter thunders in reply:

> *Above all, you must understand that no prophecy of Scripture came about by the prophet's own interpretation. . . . but men spoke from God as they were carried along by the Holy Spirit.* (2 Peter 1:20–21)

If not even the prophet's own interpretation counted, how much less can we, the prophet's readers, invent our own interpretations! No, Scripture interprets Scripture. The more Scripture we know, the more certain God's Spirit makes us of its clarity and truth, especially about the precious faith we have received through the "righteousness of our God and Savior Jesus Christ" (2 Peter 1:1).

One foot in eternity. That's how Peter urges us to live. If you always remembered that Jesus could return at any moment, how would it affect your thoughts, your attitudes, and your decisions? Ask yourself that as you read the last chapter of 2 Peter. If time is short, focus on 2 Peter 3:1–13.

The Day of the Lord

3 Dear friends, this is now my second letter to you. I have written
both of them as reminders to stimulate
you to wholesome thinking. [2]I want you
to recall the words spoken in the past by
the holy prophets and the command
given by our Lord and Savior through
your apostles.
[3]First of all, you must understand that
in the last days scoffers will come, scoffing and following their own evil desires.

[a]22 Prov. 26:11

[4]They will say, "Where is this 'coming' he promised? Ever since our fathers died, everything goes on as it has since the beginning of creation." [5]But they deliberately forget that long ago by God's word the heavens existed and the earth was formed out of water and by water. [6]By these waters also the world of that time was deluged and destroyed. [7]By the same word the present heavens and earth are reserved for fire, being kept for the day of judgment and destruction of ungodly men.

[8]But do not forget this one thing, dear friends: With the Lord a day is like a thousand years, and a thousand years are like a day. [9]The Lord is not slow in keeping his promise, as some understand slowness. He is patient with you, not wanting anyone to perish, but everyone to come to repentance.

[10]But the day of the Lord will come like a thief. The heavens will disappear with a roar; the elements will be destroyed by fire, and the earth and everything in it will be laid bare.[a]

[11]Since everything will be destroyed in this way, what kind of people ought you to be? You ought to live holy and godly lives [12]as you look forward to the day of God and speed its coming.[b] That day will bring about the destruction of the heavens by fire, and the elements will melt in the heat. [13]But in keeping with his promise we are looking forward to a new heaven and a new earth, the home of righteousness.

[14]So then, dear friends, since you are looking forward to this, make every effort to be found spotless, blameless and at peace with him. [15]Bear in mind that our Lord's patience means salvation, just as our dear brother Paul also wrote you with the wisdom that God gave him. [16]He writes the same way in all his letters, speaking in them of these matters. His letters contain some things that are hard to understand, which ignorant and unstable people distort, as they do the other Scriptures, to their own destruction.

[17]Therefore, dear friends, since you already know this, be on your guard so that you may not be carried away by the error of lawless men and fall from your secure position. [18]But grow in the grace and knowledge of our Lord and Savior Jesus Christ. To him be glory both now and forever! Amen.

[a]10 Some manuscripts *be burned up* [b]12 Or *as you wait eagerly for the day of God to come*

SHARPEN THE FOCUS

Nothing ever changes. Life goes on. It never has changed, and it never will. The "scoffers" Peter refers to in 2 Peter 3:3–4 take great comfort in their view of world history as a continual replay of business as usual. They hope never to encounter any radical change, especially not one like the arrival of Christ in judgment!

Peter demolishes their comfort by denying the premise on which it rests. God can indeed destroy the world as we know it; in fact He's done it once before—in the great flood (2 Peter 3:5–6). And God will one day roll up the sky and ignite our planet with a fire hot enough to melt the elements that compose it (2 Peter 3:10). Whether we're ready or not, the Lord of glory will appear to call an end to this present creation. Everything will simply melt away.

Will you awaken to that morning in peace (2 Peter 3:14)? Will you greet that day as the one you've looked forward to all your life? You can. The true riches of the life to come belong to you even now; Christ's righteousness and the peace it brings are yours in His cross. You'll live forever in "the home of righteousness" (2 Peter 3:13). What a future! What a hope!

1 JOHN

WEEK 101 • MONDAY

1 John 1:1–10

GET THE BIG PICTURE

John uses simple, familiar words in his letters as he did in his gospel. It's easy reading—perhaps too easy. We can skim the chapters, reading the words and missing the truths the Holy Spirit wants to impress on our hearts. Slow down enough to catch what God wants to say to you in His Word today. If time is short, focus on 1 John 1:5–10.

The Word of Life

1 That which was from the beginning, which we have heard, which
we have seen with our eyes, which we
have looked at and our hands have
touched—this we proclaim concerning
the Word of life. [2]The life appeared; we
have seen it and testify to it, and we proclaim to you the eternal life, which was
with the Father and has appeared to us.
[3]We proclaim to you what we have seen
and heard, so that you also may have
fellowship with us. And our fellowship
is with the Father and with his Son,
Jesus Christ. [4]We write this to make our[a]
joy complete.

Walking in the Light

[5]This is the message we have heard
from him and declare to you: God is
light; in him there is no darkness at all.
[6]If we claim to have fellowship with him
yet walk in the darkness, we lie and do
not live by the truth. [7]But if we walk in
the light, as he is in the light, we have
fellowship with one another, and the
blood of Jesus, his Son, purifies us from
all[b] sin.
[8]If we claim to be without sin, we deceive ourselves and the truth is not in
us. [9]If we confess our sins, he is faithful
and just and will forgive us our sins and
purify us from all unrighteousness. [10]If
we claim we have not sinned, we make
him out to be a liar and his word has no
place in our lives.

[a]4 Some manuscripts *your* [b]7 Or *every*

SHARPEN THE FOCUS

Stumbling around in the dark leads to stubbed toes and bruised shins. That's the metaphor John uses to describe life without a relationship with God. On the other hand, to know God in Christ is to walk in the light.

That kind of walk can never be the "just Jesus and me" kind of faith to which some Christians fall prey. Read 1 John 1:7. When we walk in the light of the Gospel we walk not only with our Lord, but also with other believers.

That path isn't always smooth. Even the first-century church saw its fellowship disrupted by hypocrisy, greed, selfishness, and other sins—sins we in the church today surely recognize and regret in our own lives. That's why John ties fellowship with other believers so tightly to the cleansing blood of Jesus Christ. How we need His continual pardon and His continual cleansing!

Are you "out of step" with anyone in your congregation today? Ask the Holy Spirit to reveal His truth about any dark places in your own heart. Then, refreshed by God's forgiveness in Christ's cross, seek out your brother or sister in the faith and do what you can do to restore your fellowship.

WEEK 101 • TUESDAY

1 John 2:1–29

GET THE BIG PICTURE

1 John 2 covers a lot of ground—from forgiveness in the redeeming blood of Jesus to following Him to growing up in faith to the deception of the Antichrist. Read with care. You'll not want to miss the important truths recorded here. If time is short, focus on 1 John 2:1–17.

2 My dear children, I write this to
you so that you will not sin. But
if anybody does sin, we have one who
speaks to the Father in our defense—
Jesus Christ, the Righteous One. 2 He is
the atoning sacrifice for our sins, and
not only for ours but also for[a] the sins
of the whole world.
3 We know that we have come to know
him if we obey his commands. 4 The man
who says, "I know him," but does not do
what he commands is a liar, and the
truth is not in him. 5 But if anyone obeys
his word, God's love[b] is truly made complete in him. This is how we know we
are in him: 6 Whoever claims to live in
him must walk as Jesus did.
7 Dear friends, I am not writing you a
new command but an old one, which
you have had since the beginning. This
old command is the message you have
heard. 8 Yet I am writing you a new command; its truth is seen in him and you,
because the darkness is passing and the
true light is already shining.
9 Anyone who claims to be in the light
but hates his brother is still in the darkness. 10 Whoever loves his brother lives
in the light, and there is nothing in him[c]
to make him stumble. 11 But whoever
hates his brother is in the darkness and
walks around in the darkness; he does
not know where he is going, because
the darkness has blinded him.

12 I write to you, dear children,
because your sins have been
forgiven on account of his
name.
13 I write to you, fathers,
because you have known him
who is from the beginning.
I write to you, young men,
because you have overcome the
evil one.
I write to you, dear children,
because you have known the
Father.
14 I write to you, fathers,
because you have known him
who is from the beginning.

[a]2 Or *He is the one who turns aside God's wrath, taking away our sins, and not only ours but also* [b]5 Or *word, love for God* [c]10 Or *it*

I write to you, young men,
because you are strong,
and the word of God lives in you,
and you have overcome the evil
one.

Do Not Love the World

15Do not love the world or anything
in the world. If anyone loves the world,
the love of the Father is not in him. 16For
everything in the world—the cravings
of sinful man, the lust of his eyes and the
boasting of what he has and does—
comes not from the Father but from the
world. 17The world and its desires pass
away, but the man who does the will of
God lives forever.

Warning Against Antichrists

18Dear children, this is the last hour;
and as you have heard that the antichrist is coming, even now many antichrists have come. This is how we know
it is the last hour. 19They went out from
us, but they did not really belong to us.
For if they had belonged to us, they
would have remained with us; but their
going showed that none of them belonged to us.
20But you have an anointing from the
Holy One, and all of you know the
truth.[a] 21I do not write to you because
you do not know the truth, but because
you do know it and because no lie
comes from the truth. 22Who is the liar?
It is the man who denies that Jesus is the
Christ. Such a man is the antichrist—he
denies the Father and the Son. 23No one
who denies the Son has the Father;
whoever acknowledges the Son has the
Father also.
24See that what you have heard from
the beginning remains in you. If it does,
you also will remain in the Son and in
the Father. 25And this is what he promised us—even eternal life.
26I am writing these things to you
about those who are trying to lead you
astray. 27As for you, the anointing
you received from him remains in you,
and you do not need anyone to teach
you. But as his anointing teaches you
about all things and as that anointing is
real, not counterfeit—just as it has
taught you, remain in him.

Children of God

28And now, dear children, continue in
him, so that when he appears we may
be confident and unashamed before
him at his coming.
29If you know that he is righteous, you
know that everyone who does what is
right has been born of him.

[a]20 Some manuscripts *and you know all things*

SHARPEN THE FOCUS

In the early 1970s Dr. Kenneth Cooper started what came to be known as "the aerobic revolution." Dr. Cooper offered convincing, even overwhelming, evidence to prove the health benefits of exercising at between 70% and 85% of one's maximum heart rate for 20 minutes four or five times each week.

People read Cooper's research and listened to him speak, and hordes of them took his message to heart. Following his suggestions, they bought walking or jogging shoes and hit the road. Others signed on at health clubs to use treadmills, stationery bikes, steppers, or rowing machines.

After a while many dropped out, but many continued in their new-found lifestyle. Some of us are still at it 20 or more years later. We have "obeyed" or "kept" Cooper's teachings in the sense John uses this word in his first letter.

For God's "dear children" (1 John 2:2), such obedience or keeping of God's commands isn't coerced. It isn't done through gritted teeth or against our better judgment. By God's grace, we follow Jesus because we want to. We've become convinced by the power of His Holy Spirit that life lived apart from Christ or in disobedience to Him isn't worth living.

WEEK 101 • WEDNESDAY

1 John 3:1–24

Many verses in today's reading of 1 John 3 could be punctuated with exclamation points; they shout out the Christian hope loud and clear. Look for the verses that especially encourage you as you read. If time is short, focus on 1 John 3:13–24.

3 How great is the love the Father
has lavished on us, that we
should be called children of God! And
that is what we are! The reason the
world does not know us is that it did not
know him. 2Dear friends, now we are
children of God, and what we will be
has not yet been made known. But we
know that when he appears,[a] we shall
be like him, for we shall see him as he
is. 3Everyone who has this hope in him
purifies himself, just as he is pure.
4Everyone who sins breaks the law; in
fact, sin is lawlessness. 5But you know
that he appeared so that he might take
away our sins. And in him is no sin. 6No
one who lives in him keeps on sinning.
No one who continues to sin has either
seen him or known him.
7Dear children, do not let anyone lead
you astray. He who does what is right
is righteous, just as he is righteous. 8He
who does what is sinful is of the devil,
because the devil has been sinning from
the beginning. The reason the Son of
God appeared was to destroy the devil's
work. 9No one who is born of God will
continue to sin, because God's seed remains in him; he cannot go on sinning,
because he has been born of God. 10This
is how we know who the children of
God are and who the children of the
devil are: Anyone who does not do
what is right is not a child of God; nor
is anyone who does not love his brother.

Love One Another

11This is the message you heard from
the beginning: We should love one another. 12Do not be like Cain, who belonged to the evil one and murdered his
brother. And why did he murder him?
Because his own actions were evil and
his brother's were righteous. 13Do not be
surprised, my brothers, if the world
hates you. 14We know that we have
passed from death to life, because we
love our brothers. Anyone who does not
love remains in death. 15Anyone who
hates his brother is a murderer, and you
know that no murderer has eternal life
in him.
16This is how we know what love is:
Jesus Christ laid down his life for us.
And we ought to lay down our lives for
our brothers. 17If anyone has material
possessions and sees his brother in need
but has no pity on him, how can the love
of God be in him? 18Dear children, let us
not love with words or tongue but with
actions and in truth. 19This then is how
we know that we belong to the truth,
and how we set our hearts at rest in his
presence 20whenever our hearts con-

[a]2 Or *when it is made known*

demn us. For God is greater than our
hearts, and he knows everything.
[21]Dear friends, if our hearts do not
condemn us, we have confidence before
God [22]and receive from him anything
we ask, because we obey his commands
and do what pleases him. [23]And this is
his command: to believe in the name of
his Son, Jesus Christ, and to love one
another as he commanded us. [24]Those
who obey his commands live in him,
and he in them. And this is how we
know that he lives in us: We know it by
the Spirit he gave us.

SHARPEN THE FOCUS

The zombies portrayed in *Night of the Living Dead* walk around as the "undead"; they feel nothing, sense little, and think not at all. In some ways these pitiful creatures illustrate the condition of people without Christ. Look carefully at 1 John 3:14 once more. With these words John shows us that death is the minute-by-minute existence of those who don't know Jesus as Savior. Like the "undead" of horror movies, they can't wake themselves up or warm others by their love. They don't even *want* to awaken, let alone love in the way Christ loved.

Thank God that He has, in grace, transferred us from the kingdom of death to give us a place in His very own family, a family of life (Colossians 1:13). With Christ's empowering presence in our lives, we can grow in living the Christian life. We begin to love more and more as He loves—self-sacrificially. We do "what is right" (1 John 3:7), following the example of Christ (John 13:15).

Physical death can no longer chill us, because we know the moment of death will mark our entrance into heaven. As we enter God's presence, we will know and love even as we are now known and loved by God (1 John 3:2; see also 1 Corinthians 13:12).

WEEK 101 • THURSDAY

1 John 4:1–21

GET THE BIG PICTURE

John makes some strong statements in today's reading. By today's standards, his words might even be judged "intolerant." But in truth he writes the most loving words he could possibly write. How do you explain this seeming contradiction? If time is short, focus on 1 John 4:1–6.

Test the Spirits

4 Dear friends, do not believe every spirit, but test the spirits to
see whether they are from God, because
many false prophets have gone out into
the world. [2]This is how you can recognize the Spirit of God: Every spirit that
acknowledges that Jesus Christ has
come in the flesh is from God, [3]but every
spirit that does not acknowledge Jesus
is not from God. This is the spirit of the
antichrist, which you have heard is
coming and even now is already in the
world.
[4]You, dear children, are from God and
have overcome them, because the one
who is in you is greater than the one
who is in the world. [5]They are from the

world and therefore speak from the
viewpoint of the world, and the world
listens to them. [6]We are from God, and
whoever knows God listens to us; but
whoever is not from God does not listen to us. This is how we recognize the
Spirit[a] of truth and the spirit of falsehood.

God's Love and Ours

[7]Dear friends, let us love one another,
for love comes from God. Everyone
who loves has been born of God and
knows God. [8]Whoever does not love
does not know God, because God is
love. [9]This is how God showed his love
among us: He sent his one and only
Son[b] into the world that we might live
through him. [10]This is love: not that we
loved God, but that he loved us and sent
his Son as an atoning sacrifice for[c] our
sins. [11]Dear friends, since God so loved
us, we also ought to love one another.
[12]No one has ever seen God; but if we
love one another, God lives in us and his
love is made complete in us.
[13]We know that we live in him and he
in us, because he has given us of his
Spirit. [14]And we have seen and testify
that the Father has sent his Son to be the
Savior of the world. [15]If anyone acknowledges that Jesus is the Son of God,
God lives in him and he in God. [16]And
so we know and rely on the love God
has for us.
God is love. Whoever lives in love
lives in God, and God in him. [17]In this
way, love is made complete among us so
that we will have confidence on the day
of judgment, because in this world we
are like him. [18]There is no fear in love.
But perfect love drives out fear, because
fear has to do with punishment. The
one who fears is not made perfect in
love.
[19]We love because he first loved us. [20]If
anyone says, "I love God," yet hates his
brother, he is a liar. For anyone who does
not love his brother, whom he has seen,
cannot love God, whom he has not
seen. [21]And he has given us this command: Whoever loves God must also
love his brother.

[a]6 Or *spirit* [b]9 Or *his only begotten Son* [c]10 Or *as the one who would turn aside his wrath, taking away*

SHARPEN THE FOCUS

Our Lord Jesus once asked His followers *the* diagnostic question of the ages:

What about you? . . . Who do you say I am? (Matthew 16:15)

Peter, of course, answered well. God Himself had revealed that answer to Peter:

You are the Christ, the Son of the living God. (Matthew 16:16)

John certainly heard Peter's answer. And in chapter 4 of his first letter, John confirmed it and elaborated on it. Look carefully at John's words now. You will find at least four specific facts about our Lord Jesus and His holy work:

- Jesus Christ came in the flesh, from God (1 John 4:2).
- Jesus was sent into the world that we might live through Him (1 John 4:9).
- Jesus was sent to be the Savior of the world (1 John 4:14).
- Because of Jesus' love, we can have confidence on the day of judgment (1 John 4:17).

Now think about your own answer to your Lord's question. Can you say what Peter said in Matthew 16:16? Can you say with conviction what John said to you just now in 1 John 4? If you can, it's because God, in grace, has taken up residence in your heart. He abides in you and you in Him (1 John 4:13). Jesus is the Savior of the world, to be sure (1 John 4:14). But He is *your* Savior too.

Do you live fully assured that eternal life belongs to you? That assurance is the foundation on which a growing faith is built. Personalize this very basic truth of the Gospel as you read today. If time is short, focus on 1 John 5:1–13.

Faith in the Son of God

5 Everyone who believes that
Jesus is the Christ is born of God,
and everyone who loves the father
loves his child as well. 2This is how we
know that we love the children of God:
by loving God and carrying out his commands. 3This is love for God: to obey his
commands. And his commands are not
burdensome, 4for everyone born of God
overcomes the world. This is the victory
that has overcome the world, even our
faith. 5Who is it that overcomes the
world? Only he who believes that Jesus
is the Son of God.
6This is the one who came by water
and blood—Jesus Christ. He did not
come by water only, but by water and
blood. And it is the Spirit who testifies,
because the Spirit is the truth. 7For there
are three that testify: 8the[a] Spirit, the
water and the blood; and the three are
in agreement. 9We accept man's testimony, but God's testimony is greater because it is the testimony of God, which
he has given about his Son. 10Anyone
who believes in the Son of God has this
testimony in his heart. Anyone who
does not believe God has made him out
to be a liar, because he has not believed
the testimony God has given about his
Son. 11And this is the testimony: God has
given us eternal life, and this life is in his
Son. 12He who has the Son has life; he
who does not have the Son of God does
not have life.

Concluding Remarks

13I write these things to you who believe in the name of the Son of God so
that you may know that you have eternal life. 14This is the confidence we have
in approaching God: that if we ask anything according to his will, he hears us.
15And if we know that he hears us—
whatever we ask—we know that we
have what we asked of him.
16If anyone sees his brother commit a
sin that does not lead to death, he
should pray and God will give him life.
I refer to those whose sin does not lead
to death. There is a sin that leads to
death. I am not saying that he should
pray about that. 17All wrongdoing is sin,
and there is sin that does not lead to
death.
18We know that anyone born of God
does not continue to sin; the one who
was born of God keeps him safe, and
the evil one cannot harm him. 19We
know that we are children of God, and

[a]7,8 Late manuscripts of the Vulgate *testify in heaven: the Father, the Word and the Holy Spirit, and these three are one.* [8]*And there are three that testify on earth: the* (not found in any Greek manuscript before the sixteenth century)

that the whole world is under the
control of the evil one. 20We know also
that the Son of God has come and has
given us understanding, so that we may
know him who is true. And we are in
him who is true—even in his Son Jesus
Christ. He is the true God and eternal
life.
21Dear children, keep yourselves from
idols.

SHARPEN THE FOCUS

The caffeine you may have had in your coffee this morning probably helped wake you up. That's why many of us spend the first minutes of each day, cup in hand.

But caffeine's effects soon wear off. We may find ourselves soon craving more help in overcoming the fog of drowsiness.

Overcoming. It's a key word in 1 John. Like all the writers of Holy Scripture, John chose his words carefully:

> *Everyone born of God overcomes the world. This is the victory that has overcome the world, even our faith.* (1 John 5:4)

We have, in Jesus, already overcome the pull of the world. That pull would drag us down into the meaninglessness and despair of rebellion against our Father. The victory Jesus gives *has overcome* the world–already now!

And this victory is still at work in our lives. Everyone who lives in Christ *overcomes the world.* As long as we live here on earth, we will encounter temptation after temptation, trouble after trouble. But Jesus lives in us; His cross and life have become our death and new life in our Baptism. We are–right now–in the process of overcoming the worst the world can throw at us. Where do you see Jesus' victory at work in you right now? Thank Him for it!

2 JOHN

WEEK 101 • SATURDAY

2 John 1–13

GET THE BIG PICTURE

Tradition places John in Ephesus during the last years of his life. Released from exile on the island of Patmos, John was revered as an elder in the congregation at Ephesus until he died. In 2 John he commands us to love one another. But he also warns that love has its limits. Look for those limits as you read today. If time is short, focus on 2 John 1–6.

1 The elder,

To the chosen lady and her children,
whom I love in the truth—and not I
only, but also all who know the truth—
2 because of the truth, which lives in us
and will be with us forever:

3 Grace, mercy and peace from God
the Father and from Jesus Christ, the
Father's Son, will be with us in truth
and love.

4 It has given me great joy to find some
of your children walking in the truth,
just as the Father commanded us. 5 And
now, dear lady, I am not writing you a
new command but one we have had
from the beginning. I ask that we love
one another. 6 And this is love: that we
walk in obedience to his commands. As
you have heard from the beginning, his
command is that you walk in love.
7 Many deceivers, who do not acknowledge Jesus Christ as coming in the
flesh, have gone out into the world. Any
such person is the deceiver and the antichrist. 8 Watch out that you do not lose
what you have worked for, but that you
may be rewarded fully. 9 Anyone who
runs ahead and does not continue in the
teaching of Christ does not have God;
whoever continues in the teaching has
both the Father and the Son. 10 If anyone
comes to you and does not bring this
teaching, do not take him into your
house or welcome him. 11 Anyone who
welcomes him shares in his wicked
work.
12 I have much to write to you, but I
do not want to use paper and ink. Instead, I hope to visit you and talk with
you face to face, so that our joy may be
complete.

13 The children of your chosen sister
send their greetings.

SHARPEN THE FOCUS

One story tells of a time the aged John was invited to speak to the congregation in Ephesus. He struggled slowly to his feet. "Little children," he said, "let us love one another." Then he sat down. The love of Christ was John's legacy. The "Son of Thunder" who had wanted to burn up a Samaritan village for rejecting Jesus had become the apostle of love (Mark 3:17; Luke 9:51–56).

Even so, John urges Christ's people of all time to stand steadfast against "deceivers," against false teachers who deny Christ and His sacrifice for our sins. Such a person, John says, "does not have God" (2 John 9).

John's warnings do not justify hateful words or the hate crimes that have been defended down through history as "a concern for pure doctrine." We care—deeply—about those who live apart from Christ. Jesus died for them too! What a waste, what a tragedy if they refuse His free gift of eternal life.

Still, our concern and Christian love do not dictate that we invite false teachers to lead classes or worship in our church. The Good Shepherd would not want us to open the door of His sheepfold to wolves in the name of "love" (2 John 10–11).

3 JOHN

WEEK 102 • MONDAY

3 John 1–14

GET THE BIG PICTURE

In his first epistle, John described the fellowship with God that Jesus earned for us in His life, death, and rising again. In his second epistle, John forbids fellowship with false teachers. Now, in the third letter, John describes and commends true fellowship among believers; he uses Gaius as an example of that fellowship. As you read look for the contrasts between Gaius and Diotrephes. If time is short, focus on 3 John 1–8.

1The elder,

To my dear friend Gaius, whom I love
in the truth.

2Dear friend, I pray that you may enjoy good health and that all may go well
with you, even as your soul is getting
along well. 3It gave me great joy to have
some brothers come and tell about your
faithfulness to the truth and how you
continue to walk in the truth. 4I have no
greater joy than to hear that my children are walking in the truth.
5Dear friend, you are faithful in what
you are doing for the brothers, even
though they are strangers to you. 6They
have told the church about your love.
You will do well to send them on their
way in a manner worthy of God. 7It was
for the sake of the Name that they went
out, receiving no help from the pagans.
8We ought therefore to show hospitality
to such men so that we may work together for the truth.
9I wrote to the church, but Diotrephes, who loves to be first, will have
nothing to do with us. 10So if I come, I
will call attention to what he is doing,
gossiping maliciously about us. Not satisfied with that, he refuses to welcome
the brothers. He also stops those who
want to do so and puts them out of the
church.
11Dear friend, do not imitate what is
evil but what is good. Anyone who does
what is good is from God. Anyone who
does what is evil has not seen God. 12De-
metrius is well spoken of by everyone—
and even by the truth itself. We also
speak well of him, and you know that
our testimony is true.
13I have much to write you, but I do
not want to do so with pen and ink. 14I
hope to see you soon, and we will talk
face to face.

Peace to you. The friends here send
their greetings. Greet the friends there
by name.

SHARPEN THE FOCUS

What in the world got into Diotrephes? A good question, and phrased in a way that points to part of the answer. The world's desire for recognition had gotten into Diotrephes. The world's plan for winning by intimidation had gotten into Diotrephes. The world's myth that if you're not number one you're no one had gotten into Diotrephes.

These worldly notions had inflamed Diotrephes' own sinful nature and had led him to reject the authority of the apostle John (3 John 9), to slander John and his teaching (3 John 10a), and to persecute those who did honor John as a representative of our Savior (3 John 10b).

The world still creeps into the church of our day too. In fact, we ourselves can be sucked into the kind of foolish pride that undid Diotrephes. Ask yourself these questions:

- Do I respect—from the heart—those whom my Lord has placed in spiritual authority over me?
- Do I speak well of all who serve the Lord Christ, particularly those in public ministry in His church?
- Do I see the service I give in Christ's name as a chance to love others self-sacrificially? Or do I enjoy power and position for their own sake?

If your Lord would not approve of your attitudes in any of these examples, run to His cross. There you will find mercy and grace to help you in your need.

JUDE

WEEK 102 • TUESDAY

Jude 1–25

GET THE BIG PICTURE

Jude, probably a half-brother of our Lord, wrote the last of the general epistles. Like Peter and John, Jude warns against false teachers. But he refers to false teachers of a particular kind. What error lies at the root of their particular heresy? If time is short, focus on Jude 17–25.

1Jude, a servant of Jesus Christ and a
brother of James,

To those who have been called, who
are loved by God the Father and kept
by[a] Jesus Christ:

2Mercy, peace and love be yours in
abundance.

The Sin and Doom of Godless Men

3Dear friends, although I was very eager to write to you about the salvation
we share, I felt I had to write and urge
you to contend for the faith that was
once for all entrusted to the saints. 4For
certain men whose condemnation was
written about[b] long ago have secretly
slipped in among you. They are godless
men, who change the grace of our God
into a license for immorality and deny
Jesus Christ our only Sovereign and
Lord.

5Though you already know all this, I
want to remind you that the Lord[c] delivered his people out of Egypt, but later
destroyed those who did not believe.
6And the angels who did not keep their
positions of authority but abandoned
their own home—these he has kept in
darkness, bound with everlasting
chains for judgment on the great Day.
7In a similar way, Sodom and Gomorrah
and the surrounding towns gave themselves up to sexual immorality and perversion. They serve as an example of
those who suffer the punishment of
eternal fire.

8In the very same way, these dream-
ers pollute their own bodies, reject authority and slander celestial beings. 9But
even the archangel Michael, when he
was disputing with the devil about the
body of Moses, did not dare to bring a
slanderous accusation against him, but
said, "The Lord rebuke you!" 10Yet these
men speak abusively against whatever
they do not understand; and what
things they do understand by instinct,
like unreasoning animals—these are the
very things that destroy them.

11Woe to them! They have taken the
way of Cain; they have rushed for profit
into Balaam's error; they have been destroyed in Korah's rebellion.

12These men are blemishes at your
love feasts, eating with you without the
slightest qualm—shepherds who feed
only themselves. They are clouds without rain, blown along by the wind;
autumn trees, without fruit and uprooted—twice dead. 13They are wild waves

[a]1 Or *for*; or *in* [b]4 Or *men who were marked out for condemnation* [c]5 Some early manuscripts *Jesus*

of the sea, foaming up their shame; wandering stars, for whom blackest darkness has been reserved forever.

[14]Enoch, the seventh from Adam, prophesied about these men: "See, the Lord is coming with thousands upon thousands of his holy ones [15]to judge everyone, and to convict all the ungodly of all the ungodly acts they have done in the ungodly way, and of all the harsh words ungodly sinners have spoken against him." [16]These men are grumblers and faultfinders; they follow their own evil desires; they boast about themselves and flatter others for their own advantage.

A Call to Persevere

[17]But, dear friends, remember what the apostles of our Lord Jesus Christ foretold. [18]They said to you, "In the last times there will be scoffers who will follow their own ungodly desires." [19]These are the men who divide you, who follow mere natural instincts and do not have the Spirit.

[20]But you, dear friends, build yourselves up in your most holy faith and pray in the Holy Spirit. [21]Keep yourselves in God's love as you wait for the mercy of our Lord Jesus Christ to bring you to eternal life.

[22]Be merciful to those who doubt; [23]snatch others from the fire and save them; to others show mercy, mixed with fear—hating even the clothing stained by corrupted flesh.

Doxology

[24]To him who is able to keep you from falling and to present you before his glorious presence without fault and with great joy— [25]to the only God our Savior be glory, majesty, power and authority, through Jesus Christ our Lord, before all ages, now and forevermore! Amen.

SHARPEN THE FOCUS

Freedom that becomes license is no longer freedom, but a new slavery. Jude warns against those who "change the grace of our God into a license for immorality" (Jude 4). Then he gives examples:

- The Israelites who by God's grace found themselves miraculously freed from the clay pits of Egypt, but who grumbled and rebelled against the God who had freed them (Jude 5).
- The evil angels who once enjoyed all the glories of heaven and who stood in the very presence of the Lord Himself; yet they would not content themselves with being His creatures but tried to usurp the authority of their Creator (Jude 6).
- The people of Sodom who enjoyed the most pleasant and fertile setting of Canaan, but who instead of being thankful to God perverted their sexuality and became violent rebels (Jude 7).

Ask your Lord to show you today if you are taking His grace for granted in any facet of your life. Then ask for His gifts of repentance, pardon, and power to live free from the slavery to selfishness Jude describes.

REVELATION

Christ revealed—that's what the book of Revelation is all about! Those who try to read it as some kind of Christian horoscope or as "planet earth's future revealed" will miss God's point. As you read Revelation ask the Holy Spirit to reveal to you more about your Savior-God. If time is short, focus on Revelation 1:1–8.

Prologue

1 The revelation of Jesus Christ,
which God gave him to show his
servants what must soon take place. He
made it known by sending his angel to
his servant John, 2who testifies to everything he saw—that is, the word of God
and the testimony of Jesus Christ.
3Blessed is the one who reads the words
of this prophecy, and blessed are those
who hear it and take to heart what is
written in it, because the time is near.

Greetings and Doxology

4John,

To the seven churches in the province of Asia:

Grace and peace to you from him who is, and who was, and who is to come, and from the seven spirits[a] before
his throne, 5and from Jesus Christ, who is the faithful witness, the firstborn from the dead, and the ruler of the kings of the earth.

To him who loves us and has freed us
from our sins by his blood, 6and has
made us to be a kingdom and priests to serve his God and Father—to him be glory and power for ever and ever! Amen.

7Look, he is coming with the clouds,
and every eye will see him,
even those who pierced him;
and all the peoples of the earth
will mourn because of him.
So shall it be! Amen.

8"I am the Alpha and the Omega," says the Lord God, "who is, and who was, and who is to come, the Almighty."

One Like a Son of Man

9I, John, your brother and companion
in the suffering and kingdom and patient endurance that are ours in Jesus, was on the island of Patmos because of the word of God and the testimony of
Jesus. 10On the Lord's Day I was in the
Spirit, and I heard behind me a loud
voice like a trumpet, 11which said:
"Write on a scroll what you see and send it to the seven churches: to Ephesus, Smyrna, Pergamum, Thyatira, Sardis, Philadelphia and Laodicea."
12I turned around to see the voice that
was speaking to me. And when I turned

[a]4 Or *the sevenfold Spirit*

I saw seven golden lampstands, [13]and
among the lampstands was someone
"like a son of man,"[a] dressed in a robe
reaching down to his feet and with a
golden sash around his chest. [14]His head
and hair were white like wool, as white
as snow, and his eyes were like blazing
fire. [15]His feet were like bronze glowing
in a furnace, and his voice was like the
sound of rushing waters. [16]In his right
hand he held seven stars, and out of his
mouth came a sharp double-edged
sword. His face was like the sun shining
in all its brilliance.
[17]When I saw him, I fell at his feet as
though dead. Then he placed his right
hand on me and said: "Do not be afraid.
I am the First and the Last. [18]I am the
Living One; I was dead, and behold I
am alive for ever and ever! And I hold
the keys of death and Hades.
[19]"Write, therefore, what you have
seen, what is now and what will take
place later. [20]The mystery of the seven
stars that you saw in my right hand and
of the seven golden lampstands is this:
The seven stars are the angels[b] of the
seven churches, and the seven lampstands are the seven churches.

[a]*13* Daniel 7:13 [b]*20* Or *messengers*

SHARPEN THE FOCUS

In a debate, most contenders like to have the last word. That's true even for children fighting on the playground. Having the last word implies that you've silenced all comers, that no foe can refute your arguments.

In Revelation 1:17, our Lord Jesus reveals Himself as "the First and the Last," the A and the Z. He spoke the first word—His creative word—and by it laid the earth's foundations and set the thresholds of the oceans in place (see Proverbs 8:22–31).

And when earth's end comes, our Lord Jesus will have the last word as well. Evil will not. Satan will not. Pain will not. Death will not. The keys of hell and of death belong to our Savior. He will say to all who have longed for His appearing, "Come, you who are blessed by My Father; take your inheritance, the kingdom prepared for you since the creation of the world" (Matthew 25:34).

The first word was His. The last word will be His. He *is* the Word of God to us sinners—God's Word of grace. Worship Him!

WEEK 102 • THURSDAY

Revelation 2:1–29

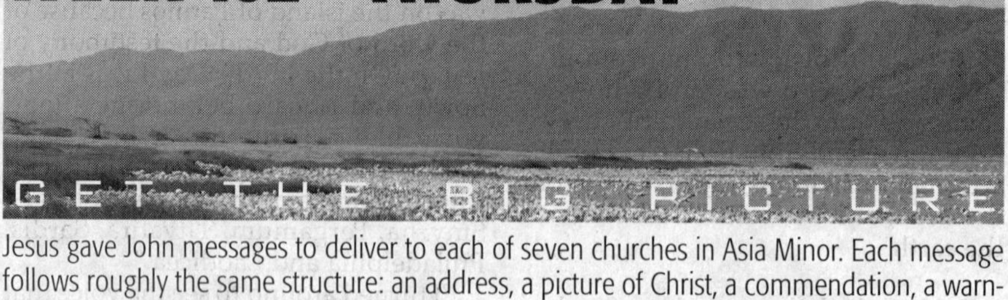

GET THE BIG PICTURE

Jesus gave John messages to deliver to each of seven churches in Asia Minor. Each message follows roughly the same structure: an address, a picture of Christ, a commendation, a warning, and a promise or encouragement. Pay particular attention to the pictures of Christ you will read in Revelation 2:1, 8, 12, and 18. If time is short, focus on Revelation 2:1–7.

To the Church in Ephesus

2 "To the angel[a] of the church in
Ephesus write:

These are the words of him who
holds the seven stars in his right
hand and walks among the seven
golden lampstands: 2I know your
deeds, your hard work and your
perseverance. I know that you cannot tolerate wicked men, that you
have tested those who claim to be
apostles but are not, and have
found them false. 3You have persevered and have endured hardships
for my name, and have not grown
weary.
4Yet I hold this against you: You
have forsaken your first love. 5Re-
member the height from which you
have fallen! Repent and do the
things you did at first. If you do not
repent, I will come to you and remove your lampstand from its
place. 6But you have this in your
favor: You hate the practices of the
Nicolaitans, which I also hate.
7He who has an ear, let him hear
what the Spirit says to the
churches. To him who overcomes,
I will give the right to eat from the
tree of life, which is in the paradise
of God.

To the Church in Smyrna

8"To the angel of the church in Smyrna
write:

These are the words of him who
is the First and the Last, who died
and came to life again. 9I know your
afflictions and your poverty—yet
you are rich! I know the slander of
those who say they are Jews and
are not, but are a synagogue of
Satan. 10Do not be afraid of what
you are about to suffer. I tell you,
the devil will put some of you in
prison to test you, and you will
suffer persecution for ten days.
Be faithful, even to the point of
death, and I will give you the
crown of life.
11He who has an ear, let him hear
what the Spirit says to the
churches. He who overcomes will
not be hurt at all by the second
death.

To the Church in Pergamum

12"To the angel of the church in Pergamum write:

These are the words of him who
has the sharp, double-edged
sword. 13I know where you live—
where Satan has his throne. Yet you
remain true to my name. You did
not renounce your faith in me,
even in the days of Antipas, my
faithful witness, who was put to
death in your city—where Satan
lives.
14Nevertheless, I have a few
things against you: You have people there who hold to the teaching
of Balaam, who taught Balak to entice the Israelites to sin by eating
food sacrificed to idols and by committing sexual immorality. 15Like-
wise you also have those who hold
to the teaching of the Nicolaitans.
16Repent therefore! Otherwise, I
will soon come to you and will fight
against them with the sword of my
mouth.
17He who has an ear, let him hear
what the Spirit says to the
churches. To him who overcomes,
I will give some of the hidden manna. I will also give him a white
stone with a new name written
on it, known only to him who receives it.

To the Church in Thyatira

18"To the angel of the church in Thyatira write:

These are the words of the Son of
God, whose eyes are like blazing
fire and whose feet are like burnished bronze. 19I know your
deeds, your love and faith, your
service and perseverance, and that

[a]1 Or *messenger*; also in verses 8, 12 and 18

you are now doing more than you
did at first.
[20]Nevertheless, I have this
against you: You tolerate that woman Jezebel, who calls herself a
prophetess. By her teaching she
misleads my servants into sexual
immorality and the eating of food
sacrificed to idols. [21]I have given her
time to repent of her immorality,
but she is unwilling. [22]So I will cast
her on a bed of suffering, and I will
make those who commit adultery
with her suffer intensely, unless
they repent of her ways. [23]I will
strike her children dead. Then all
the churches will know that I am he
who searches hearts and minds,
and I will repay each of you according to your deeds. [24]Now I say to
the rest of you in Thyatira, to you
who do not hold to her teaching
and have not learned Satan's so-
called deep secrets (I will not impose any other burden on you):
[25]Only hold on to what you have
until I come.
[26]To him who overcomes and
does my will to the end, I will give
authority over the nations—

[27]'He will rule them with an iron
scepter;
he will dash them to pieces
like pottery'[a]—

just as I have received authority
from my Father. [28]I will also give
him the morning star. [29]He who has
an ear, let him hear what the Spirit
says to the churches.

[a]27 Psalm 2:9

SHARPEN THE FOCUS

As you read the messages in Revelation 2, take a step back from them and consider for a moment what these messages—together—tell us about our Savior. Would you agree they show the following?

- That the resurrected, ascended Jesus knows—in detail—what's going on in His church on earth.
- That Jesus cares—deeply—about the assaults of persecution and false teachings we endure.
- That Jesus urges and commands us to live with an attitude of openness toward both His correction and His gift of repentance.
- That our Savior loves us—with His whole heart—and will do whatever is necessary to preserve His bride, the church, for everlasting life.

Perhaps you can draw more conclusions than those above. But all of them will point to the fact that we are not alone and we are not forgotten. Let these truths comfort and encourage you today.

WEEK 102 • FRIDAY

Revelation 3:1–22

The three messages you will read in Revelation 3 today follow the general pattern established in Revelation 2. One of the three includes no word of warning or rebuke. Which one? Why? One has no commendation. Which one? Why? If time is short, focus on Revelation 3:14–22.

To the Church in Sardis

3 "To the angel[a] of the church in
Sardis write:

These are the words of him who
holds the seven spirits[b] of God and
the seven stars. I know your deeds;
you have a reputation of being
alive, but you are dead. 2Wake up!
Strengthen what remains and is
about to die, for I have not found
your deeds complete in the sight of
my God. 3Remember, therefore,
what you have received and heard;
obey it, and repent. But if you do
not wake up, I will come like a thief,
and you will not know at what time
I will come to you.

4Yet you have a few people in Sardis who have not soiled their
clothes. They will walk with me,
dressed in white, for they are worthy. 5He who overcomes will, like
them, be dressed in white. I will
never blot out his name from the
book of life, but will acknowledge
his name before my Father and his
angels. 6He who has an ear, let him
hear what the Spirit says to the
churches.

To the Church in Philadelphia

7"To the angel of the church in Philadelphia write:

These are the words of him who
is holy and true, who holds the key
of David. What he opens no one
can shut, and what he shuts no one
can open. 8I know your deeds. See,
I have placed before you an open
door that no one can shut. I know
that you have little strength, yet
you have kept my word and have
not denied my name. 9I will make
those who are of the synagogue of
Satan, who claim to be Jews though
they are not, but are liars—I will
make them come and fall down at
your feet and acknowledge that I
have loved you. 10Since you have
kept my command to endure patiently, I will also keep you from the
hour of trial that is going to come
upon the whole world to test those
who live on the earth.

11I am coming soon. Hold on to
what you have, so that no one will
take your crown. 12Him who overcomes I will make a pillar in the
temple of my God. Never again will
he leave it. I will write on him the
name of my God and the name of
the city of my God, the new Jerusalem, which is coming down out
of heaven from my God; and I
will also write on him my new
name. 13He who has an ear, let him
hear what the Spirit says to the
churches.

To the Church in Laodicea

14"To the angel of the church in Laodicea write:

These are the words of the
Amen, the faithful and true wit-

[a]1 Or *messenger*; also in verses 7 and 14 [b]1 Or *the sevenfold Spirit*

ness, the ruler of God's creation. [15]I
know your deeds, that you are neither cold nor hot. I wish you were
either one or the other! [16]So, because you are lukewarm—neither
hot nor cold—I am about to spit
you out of my mouth. [17]You say, 'I
am rich; I have acquired wealth
and do not need a thing.' But you
do not realize that you are
wretched, pitiful, poor, blind and
naked. [18]I counsel you to buy from
me gold refined in the fire, so
you can become rich; and white
clothes to wear, so you can cover
your shameful nakedness; and
salve to put on your eyes, so you
can see.

[19]Those whom I love I rebuke
and discipline. So be earnest, and
repent. [20]Here I am! I stand at the
door and knock. If anyone hears
my voice and opens the door, I will
come in and eat with him, and he
with me.

[21]To him who overcomes, I will
give the right to sit with me on my
throne, just as I overcame and sat
down with my Father on his
throne. [22]He who has an ear, let him
hear what the Spirit says to the
churches."

SHARPEN THE FOCUS

Asia Minor was quite geologically active in ancient times. The city of Hierapolis, for instance, enjoyed hot springs that became famous for their healing properties. The city of Colosse enjoyed drinking water that gushed from a cold, refreshing spring.

Though Laodicea lay close to both Hierapolis and Colosse, its water came from a lukewarm, brackish spring, one that nauseated rather than healed or refreshed.

That's the background for our Lord's words about lukewarmness in Revelation 3:15–16. The church in Laodicea offered neither healing nor refreshment to weary and burdened sinners. Their attitude was that of self-sufficiency (Revelation 3:17). They did not see their need, so they did not treasure their Savior. They compromised their witness to the point it became tepid, even nauseating!

How about our witness today? Does the Gospel flow from our lips and from our lives like a cold, refreshing stream in the desert? Does the Good News of forgiveness in Jesus bring healing and wholeness to others?

Talk with your Savior about your own witness and about what clouds or compromises it. Then read Jesus' pardon and promise to you in Revelation 3:18–21.

WEEK 102 • SATURDAY

Revelation 4:1—5:14

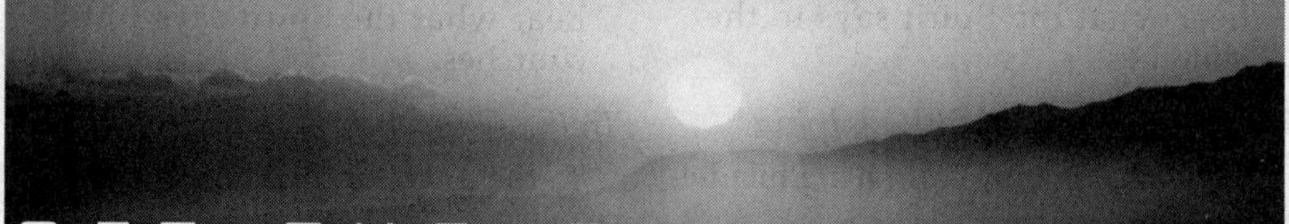

GET THE BIG PICTURE

Revelation 4–5 lifts us from earth to the very presence of God in all His majesty! We fall on our faces with the church of every age and every place to worship the Lord. Pray that the Holy Spirit will draw you into that worship as you read. Our God is an awesome God of glory and of grace! If time is short, focus on Revelation 5:1–14.

The Throne in Heaven

4 After this I looked, and there before me was a door standing open in heaven. And the voice I had first heard speaking to me like a trumpet said, "Come up here, and I will show you what must take place after this." [2]At once I was in the Spirit, and there before me was a throne in heaven with someone sitting on it. [3]And the one who sat there had the appearance of jasper and carnelian. A rainbow, resembling an emerald, encircled the throne. [4]Surrounding the throne were twenty-four other thrones, and seated on them were twenty-four elders. They were dressed in white and had crowns of gold on their heads. [5]From the throne came flashes of lightning, rumblings and peals of thunder. Before the throne, seven lamps were blazing. These are the seven spirits[a] of God. [6]Also before the throne there was what looked like a sea of glass, clear as crystal.

In the center, around the throne, were four living creatures, and they were covered with eyes, in front and in back. [7]The first living creature was like a lion, the second was like an ox, the third had a face like a man, the fourth was like a flying eagle. [8]Each of the four living creatures had six wings and was covered with eyes all around, even under his wings. Day and night they never stop saying:

"Holy, holy, holy
is the Lord God Almighty,
who was, and is, and is to come."

[9]Whenever the living creatures give glory, honor and thanks to him who sits on the throne and who lives for ever and ever, [10]the twenty-four elders fall down before him who sits on the throne, and worship him who lives for ever and ever. They lay their crowns before the throne and say:

[11]"You are worthy, our Lord and God,
to receive glory and honor and
power,
for you created all things,
and by your will they were
created
and have their being."

The Scroll and the Lamb

5 Then I saw in the right hand of him who sat on the throne a scroll with writing on both sides and sealed with seven seals. [2]And I saw a mighty angel proclaiming in a loud voice, "Who is worthy to break the seals and open the scroll?" [3]But no one in heaven or on earth or under the earth could open the scroll or even look inside it. [4]I wept and wept because no one was found who was worthy to open the scroll or look inside. [5]Then one of the elders said to me, "Do not weep! See, the Lion of the tribe of Judah, the Root of David, has triumphed. He is able to open the scroll and its seven seals."

[6]Then I saw a Lamb, looking as if it had been slain, standing in the center of the throne, encircled by the four living creatures and the elders. He had seven horns and seven eyes, which are the seven spirits[a] of God sent out into all the earth. [7]He came and took the scroll from the right hand of him who sat on the throne. [8]And when he had taken it, the four living creatures and the twenty-four elders fell down before the Lamb. Each one had a harp and they were holding golden bowls full of incense, which are the prayers of the saints. [9]And they sang a new song:

"You are worthy to take the scroll
and to open its seals,
because you were slain,
and with your blood you
purchased men for God
from every tribe and language
and people and nation.
[10]You have made them to be a
kingdom and priests to serve
our God,
and they will reign on the earth."

[11]Then I looked and heard the voice of many angels, numbering thousands upon thousands, and ten thousand

[a]5,6 Or *the sevenfold Spirit*

times ten thousand. They encircled the
throne and the living creatures and the
elders. 12In a loud voice they sang:

"Worthy is the Lamb, who was
slain,
to receive power and wealth and
wisdom and strength
and honor and glory and praise!"

13Then I heard every creature in heav-
en and on earth and under the earth
and on the sea, and all that is in them,
singing:

"To him who sits on the throne and
to the Lamb
be praise and honor and glory and
power,
for ever and ever!"

14The four living creatures said, "Amen,"
and the elders fell down and worshiped.

SHARPEN THE FOCUS

The worship service described in Revelation 4–5 is still going on. The church, represented by the 24 elders (12 tribes of the Old Testament plus 12 apostles of the New Testament), continues to fall before the throne of God in reverence (Revelation 4:10). The living creatures continue day and night to shout, "Holy, holy, holy" (Revelation 4:6–8). The prayers of the saints continue to rise like sweet-smelling incense (Revelation 5:8).

Whenever we lift our voices in prayer or praise, we join the chorus of the saints. Especially when we meet together with other Christians around Christ's banquet table of Word and Sacrament, we enter the cathedral of God's holy presence.

Choose one of the praise choruses from today's reading (Revelation 4:8, 11; 5:9–10, 12, or 13). Use it right now as you offer the praise of your heart to our Savior-God. Then use it again as part of your preparation for worship in God's house this weekend. The Lamb who was slain for our sins is truly worthy to be praised!

WEEK 103 • MONDAY

Revelation 6:1—8:5

Today's reading presents the first cycle of visions telling about God's judgment on human sin. As you read, note how the scene shifts back and forth between earth and heaven. Also remember that "the great tribulation" (Revelation 7:14) encompasses the sufferings of all God's saints for His name from the beginning of time to its end.

The Seals

6 I watched as the Lamb opened
the first of the seven seals. Then
I heard one of the four living creatures
say in a voice like thunder, "Come!" 2I
looked, and there before me was a white
horse! Its rider held a bow, and he was
given a crown, and he rode out as a conqueror bent on conquest.

3When the Lamb opened the second
seal, I heard the second living creature
say, "Come!" 4Then another horse came

out, a fiery red one. Its rider was given power to take peace from the earth and to make men slay each other. To him was given a large sword.

5When the Lamb opened the third seal, I heard the third living creature say, "Come!" I looked, and there before me was a black horse! Its rider was holding a pair of scales in his hand. 6Then I heard what sounded like a voice among the four living creatures, saying, "A quart[a] of wheat for a day's wages,[b] and three quarts of barley for a day's wages,[b] and do not damage the oil and the wine!"

7When the Lamb opened the fourth seal, I heard the voice of the fourth living creature say, "Come!" 8I looked, and there before me was a pale horse! Its rider was named Death, and Hades was following close behind him. They were given power over a fourth of the earth to kill by sword, famine and plague, and by the wild beasts of the earth.

9When he opened the fifth seal, I saw under the altar the souls of those who had been slain because of the word of God and the testimony they had maintained. 10They called out in a loud voice, "How long, Sovereign Lord, holy and true, until you judge the inhabitants of the earth and avenge our blood?" 11Then each of them was given a white robe, and they were told to wait a little longer, until the number of their fellow servants and brothers who were to be killed as they had been was completed.

12I watched as he opened the sixth seal. There was a great earthquake. The sun turned black like sackcloth made of goat hair, the whole moon turned blood red, 13and the stars in the sky fell to earth, as late figs drop from a fig tree when shaken by a strong wind. 14The sky receded like a scroll, rolling up, and every mountain and island was removed from its place.

15Then the kings of the earth, the princes, the generals, the rich, the mighty, and every slave and every free man hid in caves and among the rocks of the mountains. 16They called to the mountains and the rocks, "Fall on us and hide us from the face of him who sits on the throne and from the wrath of the Lamb! 17For the great day of their wrath has come, and who can stand?"

144,000 Sealed

7 After this I saw four angels standing at the four corners of the earth, holding back the four winds of the earth to prevent any wind from blowing on the land or on the sea or on any tree. 2Then I saw another angel coming up from the east, having the seal of the living God. He called out in a loud voice to the four angels who had been given power to harm the land and the sea: 3"Do not harm the land or the sea or the trees until we put a seal on the foreheads of the servants of our God." 4Then I heard the number of those who were sealed: 144,000 from all the tribes of Israel.

5 From the tribe of Judah 12,000
were sealed,
from the tribe of Reuben 12,000,
from the tribe of Gad 12,000,
6 from the tribe of Asher 12,000,
from the tribe of Naphtali 12,000,
from the tribe of Manasseh 12,000,
7 from the tribe of Simeon 12,000,
from the tribe of Levi 12,000,
from the tribe of Issachar 12,000,
8 from the tribe of Zebulun 12,000,
from the tribe of Joseph 12,000,
from the tribe of Benjamin 12,000.

The Great Multitude in White Robes

9After this I looked and there before me was a great multitude that no one could count, from every nation, tribe, people and language, standing before the throne and in front of the Lamb. They were wearing white robes and were holding palm branches in their hands. 10And they cried out in a loud voice:

"Salvation belongs to our God,
who sits on the throne,
and to the Lamb."

[a]6 Greek *a choinix* (probably about a liter)
[b]6 Greek *a denarius*

11All the angels were standing around
the throne and around the elders and
the four living creatures. They fell down
on their faces before the throne and
worshiped God, 12saying:

"Amen!
Praise and glory
and wisdom and thanks and honor
and power and strength
be to our God for ever and ever.
Amen!"

13Then one of the elders asked me,
"These in white robes—who are they,
and where did they come from?"
14I answered, "Sir, you know."
And he said, "These are they who
have come out of the great tribulation;
they have washed their robes and made
them white in the blood of the Lamb.
15Therefore,

"they are before the throne of God
and serve him day and night in
his temple;
and he who sits on the throne will
spread his tent over them.
16Never again will they hunger;
never again will they thirst.
The sun will not beat upon them,
nor any scorching heat.
17For the Lamb at the center of the
throne will be their
shepherd;
he will lead them to springs of
living water.
And God will wipe away every tear
from their eyes."

The Seventh Seal and the Golden Censer

8 When he opened the seventh
seal, there was silence in heaven
for about half an hour.
2And I saw the seven angels who
stand before God, and to them were giv-
en seven trumpets.
3Another angel, who had a golden
censer, came and stood at the altar. He
was given much incense to offer, with
the prayers of all the saints, on the gold-
en altar before the throne. 4The smoke
of the incense, together with the prayers
of the saints, went up before God from
the angel's hand. 5Then the angel took
the censer, filled it with fire from the altar, and hurled it on the earth; and there
came peals of thunder, rumblings,
flashes of lightning and an earthquake.

SHARPEN THE FOCUS

The Old Testament prophets wrote over and over again about the Day of the Lord. That "day" was, is, and will be a day of judgment on human sin and a day of deliverance for those who cling to Christ as Savior. That day will arrive fully with the angel army of heaven that escorts the Judge of all the earth as He returns in glory to declare His verdict on both the righteous and the unrighteous.

Revelation pictures several features of that prophetic "day." In Revelation 6, for example, we see a false messiah (Revelation 6:1–2); war (Revelation 6:3–4); famine (Revelation 6:5–6); death and hell (Revelation 6:7–8) unleashed on the earth. And yet, sinners continue in their hatred and rebellion against God (Revelation 6:15–17).

But the God who has called His saints to faith has also sealed us in that faith (Revelation 7:3). He preserves us steadfast in His Word despite the pressures the enemies of the cross raise against us. And so, our cry throughout all eternity will be "salvation belongs to our God, who sits on the throne, and to the Lamb" (Revelation 7:10).

Today's reading describes a second cycle of judgment on human sin and unbelief. It repeats the first cycle, but in an intensified way. Still, despite the revelation of God's power and His wrath, the ungodly plunge ever more deeply into rebellion. If time is short, focus on Revelation 9:13–21.

The Trumpets

[6]Then the seven angels who had the
seven trumpets prepared to sound
them.
[7]The first angel sounded his trumpet,
and there came hail and fire mixed with
blood, and it was hurled down upon the
earth. A third of the earth was burned
up, a third of the trees were burned up,
and all the green grass was burned up.
[8]The second angel sounded his trumpet, and something like a huge mountain, all ablaze, was thrown into the sea.
A third of the sea turned into blood, [9]a
third of the living creatures in the sea
died, and a third of the ships were destroyed.
[10]The third angel sounded his trumpet, and a great star, blazing like a torch,
fell from the sky on a third of the rivers
and on the springs of water— [11]the
name of the star is Wormwood.[a] A third
of the waters turned bitter, and many
people died from the waters that had
become bitter.
[12]The fourth angel sounded his trumpet, and a third of the sun was struck, a
third of the moon, and a third of the
stars, so that a third of them turned
dark. A third of the day was without
light, and also a third of the night.
[13]As I watched, I heard an eagle that
was flying in midair call out in a loud
voice: "Woe! Woe! Woe to the inhabitants of the earth, because of the trumpet blasts about to be sounded by the
other three angels!"

9 The fifth angel sounded his
trumpet, and I saw a star that
had fallen from the sky to the earth. The
star was given the key to the shaft of the
Abyss. [2]When he opened the Abyss,
smoke rose from it like the smoke from
a gigantic furnace. The sun and sky
were darkened by the smoke from the
Abyss. [3]And out of the smoke locusts
came down upon the earth and were
given power like that of scorpions of the
earth. [4]They were told not to harm the
grass of the earth or any plant or tree,
but only those people who did not have
the seal of God on their foreheads.
[5]They were not given power to kill
them, but only to torture them for five
months. And the agony they suffered
was like that of the sting of a scorpion
when it strikes a man. [6]During those
days men will seek death, but will not
find it; they will long to die, but death
will elude them.
[7]The locusts looked like horses prepared for battle. On their heads they
wore something like crowns of gold,
and their faces resembled human faces.
[8]Their hair was like women's hair, and
their teeth were like lions' teeth. [9]They
had breastplates like breastplates of
iron, and the sound of their wings was
like the thundering of many horses and
chariots rushing into battle. [10]They had
tails and stings like scorpions, and in
their tails they had power to torment

[a]*11* That is, Bitterness

people for five months. 11They had as
king over them the angel of the Abyss,
whose name in Hebrew is Abaddon,
and in Greek, Apollyon.[a]
12The first woe is past; two other woes
are yet to come.
13The sixth angel sounded his trumpet, and I heard a voice coming from the
horns[b] of the golden altar that is before
God. 14It said to the sixth angel who had
the trumpet, "Release the four angels
who are bound at the great river Euphrates." 15And the four angels who had
been kept ready for this very hour
and day and month and year were released to kill a third of mankind. 16The
number of the mounted troops was
two hundred million. I heard their number.
17The horses and riders I saw in my vision looked like this: Their breastplates
were fiery red, dark blue, and yellow as
sulfur. The heads of the horses resembled the heads of lions, and out of their
mouths came fire, smoke and sulfur. 18A
third of mankind was killed by the three
plagues of fire, smoke and sulfur that
came out of their mouths. 19The power
of the horses was in their mouths and
in their tails; for their tails were like
snakes, having heads with which they
inflict injury.
20The rest of mankind that were not
killed by these plagues still did not repent of the work of their hands; they
did not stop worshiping demons, and
idols of gold, silver, bronze, stone and
wood—idols that cannot see or hear or
walk. 21Nor did they repent of their murders, their magic arts, their sexual immorality or their thefts.

[a]*11 Abaddon* and *Apollyon* mean *Destroyer.*
[b]*13* That is, projections

SHARPEN THE FOCUS

Horror. Terror. Grief. Disaster. All these words and more fail to fully communicate the destruction depicted by Revelation 8–9. The ecological havoc, the devastation described here, move almost beyond our ability to imagine them.

In what are obviously symbolic terms, John struggles to tell us what he has seen. Human beings apparently bring much of their own punishment down around their own ears. But, as Revelation 9:11–19 make clear, Satan himself eventually compounds the global disaster. The Destroyer lives up to his name–in full! (See John 10:10.)

Even in all the mayhem, though, God's own children will be protected. We have been sealed by His grace (Revelation 7:3–4; 9:4). Satan and his agents cannot ultimately harm us. We need not "be afraid of those who kill the body but cannot kill the soul" (Matthew 10:28).

Instead, as the darkness thickens around us, we can continue to offer the incense of our prayers before heaven's high throne (Revelation 8:3–5). We can continue to intercede for the coming of Christ's kingdom to the ends of the earth. Those prayers, never fear, will be answered. That kingdom, never doubt it, will come!

WEEK 103 • WEDNESDAY

Rev. 10:1–11

GET THE BIG PICTURE

Down through the pages of Scripture, God honored His prophets. But He also gave the prophets heavy responsibility. Their tasks were often distasteful, even bitter. Look for evidence of this in John's experience. If time is short, focus on Revelation 10:5–11.

The Angel and the Little Scroll

10 Then I saw another mighty
angel coming down from
heaven. He was robed in a cloud, with
a rainbow above his head; his face was
like the sun, and his legs were like fiery
pillars. 2He was holding a little scroll,
which lay open in his hand. He planted
his right foot on the sea and his left foot
on the land, 3and he gave a loud shout
like the roar of a lion. When he shouted,
the voices of the seven thunders spoke.
4And when the seven thunders spoke, I
was about to write; but I heard a voice
from heaven say, "Seal up what the seven thunders have said and do not write
it down."

5Then the angel I had seen standing
on the sea and on the land raised his
right hand to heaven. 6And he swore by
him who lives for ever and ever, who
created the heavens and all that is in
them, the earth and all that is in it, and
the sea and all that is in it, and said,
"There will be no more delay! 7But in the
days when the seventh angel is about to
sound his trumpet, the mystery of God
will be accomplished, just as he announced to his servants the prophets."

8Then the voice that I had heard from
heaven spoke to me once more: "Go,
take the scroll that lies open in the hand
of the angel who is standing on the sea
and on the land."

9So I went to the angel and asked him
to give me the little scroll. He said to me,
"Take it and eat it. It will turn your
stomach sour, but in your mouth it
will be as sweet as honey." 10I took the
little scroll from the angel's hand
and ate it. It tasted as sweet as honey
in my mouth, but when I had eaten it,
my stomach turned sour. 11Then I was
told, "You must prophesy again about
many peoples, nations, languages and
kings."

SHARPEN THE FOCUS

No one today serves as a prophet in quite the same way as did Moses or Isaiah or the apostle John. The canon of Scripture is, for all practical purposes, closed. God's revelation of Himself in His Book and in His Son are complete.

But our Lord is still at work fulfilling the Word He spoke through His prophets. As the seventh angel sounds his trumpet (Revelation 10:6–7), God sets in motion the events that will bring to pass everything He has promised through "His servants the prophets." Like Ezekiel before him (Ezekiel 3:1–11), John digested the Lord's message. The Law's message of judgment and condemnation on sin turned John's stomach. But he had to speak it; it was God's truth.

When God's spokesmen today declare God's Law to you, how do you respond? We can make the ministries of the Lord's servants sour or a joy depending upon our response. Repentance. Rebellion. God's Law can provoke either in us. But how blessed we will be as God's Word of Law and Gospel produces in us repentance and faith.

WEEK 103 • THURSDAY

Revelation 11:1–19

GET THE BIG PICTURE

Revelation 11 includes many symbols that seem very strange, unless we remember that apocalyptic writing is surrealistic. Here are a few keys for interpretation. The temple of God likely refers to the church on earth—true believers in the inner court, hypocrites and unbelievers in the outer court. The two witnesses probably are the true church, the invisible church—God's people who witness in the spirit and power of Moses and Elijah. If time is short, focus on Revelation 11:1–14.

The Two Witnesses

11 I was given a reed like a measuring rod and was told, "Go and
measure the temple of God and the altar, and count the worshipers there. 2But
exclude the outer court; do not measure
it, because it has been given to the Gentiles. They will trample on the holy city
for 42 months. 3And I will give power to
my two witnesses, and they will prophesy for 1,260 days, clothed in sackcloth." 4These are the two olive trees and
the two lampstands that stand before
the Lord of the earth. 5If anyone tries to
harm them, fire comes from their
mouths and devours their enemies. This
is how anyone who wants to harm them
must die. 6These men have power to
shut up the sky so that it will not rain
during the time they are prophesying;
and they have power to turn the waters
into blood and to strike the earth with
every kind of plague as often as they
want.
7Now when they have finished their
testimony, the beast that comes up from
the Abyss will attack them, and overpower and kill them. 8Their bodies will
lie in the street of the great city, which
is figuratively called Sodom and Egypt,
where also their Lord was crucified. 9For
three and a half days men from every
people, tribe, language and nation will
gaze on their bodies and refuse them
burial. 10The inhabitants of the earth will
gloat over them and will celebrate by
sending each other gifts, because these
two prophets had tormented those who
live on the earth.
11But after the three and a half days a
breath of life from God entered them,
and they stood on their feet, and terror
struck those who saw them. 12Then they
heard a loud voice from heaven saying
to them, "Come up here." And they
went up to heaven in a cloud, while
their enemies looked on.
13At that very hour there was a severe
earthquake and a tenth of the city collapsed. Seven thousand people were
killed in the earthquake, and the survivors were terrified and gave glory to the
God of heaven.
14The second woe has passed; the
third woe is coming soon.

The Seventh Trumpet

15The seventh angel sounded his
trumpet, and there were loud voices in
heaven, which said:

"The kingdom of the world has
become the kingdom of our
Lord and of his Christ,
and he will reign for ever and
ever."

16 And the twenty-four elders, who were seated on their thrones before God, fell on their faces and worshiped God, 17 saying:

"We give thanks to you, Lord God
Almighty,
the One who is and who was,
because you have taken your great
power
and have begun to reign.
18 The nations were angry;
and your wrath has come.
The time has come for judging the
dead,
and for rewarding your servants
the prophets
and your saints and those who
reverence your name,
both small and great—
and for destroying those who
destroy the earth."

19 Then God's temple in heaven was opened, and within his temple was seen the ark of his covenant. And there came flashes of lightning, rumblings, peals of thunder, an earthquake and a great hailstorm.

SHARPEN THE FOCUS

Much of the symbolism of Revelation 11 comes directly from Zechariah 4. The prophet Zechariah turns on the light for us as we struggle to understand John's imagery.

God gave Zechariah a vision in which two olive trees on either side of a lampstand represented the "sons of fresh oil" (literal translation, Zechariah 4:14) who would one day serve the Lord in righteousness and in the power of the Holy Spirit.

Ultimately, Zechariah's vision was fulfilled in Jesus, the Anointed One, the only Son of fresh oil whom the Holy Spirit filled beyond measure (Psalm 45:7). Then, through what Jesus did, God made all believers kings and priests (Revelation 1:6). Anointed with the oil of the Spirit, we serve Christ as His witnesses.

The world hates our witness. Throughout history Satan has fanned this hatred into a fire storm of persecution (Revelation 11:7). And yet, the enemies of the church will never prevail against our Lord and His Christ. He will reign for ever and ever (Revelation 11:15).

WEEK 103 • FRIDAY

Revelation 12:1–17

GET THE BIG PICTURE

The book of Revelation could have ended at Revelation 11:19 with the church triumphant praising God forever in heaven. But the Holy Spirit continues His revelation of Christ and His victory. In Revelation 12–22 God uses new symbols and new imagery, but the message is the same: God's people triumph in the end. Look for this theme in Revelation 12. If time is short, focus on Revelation 12:7–17.

The Woman and the Dragon

12 A great and wondrous sign
appeared in heaven: a
woman clothed with the sun, with the
moon under her feet and a crown of
twelve stars on her head. 2She was pregnant and cried out in pain as she was
about to give birth. 3Then another sign
appeared in heaven: an enormous red
dragon with seven heads and ten horns
and seven crowns on his heads. 4His tail
swept a third of the stars out of the sky
and flung them to the earth. The dragon
stood in front of the woman who was
about to give birth, so that he might devour her child the moment it was born.
5She gave birth to a son, a male child,
who will rule all the nations with an
iron scepter. And her child was snatched
up to God and to his throne. 6The
woman fled into the desert to a place
prepared for her by God, where she
might be taken care of for 1,260 days.
7And there was war in heaven. Michael and his angels fought against the
dragon, and the dragon and his angels
fought back. 8But he was not strong
enough, and they lost their place in
heaven. 9The great dragon was hurled
down—that ancient serpent called the
devil, or Satan, who leads the whole
world astray. He was hurled to the
earth, and his angels with him.
10Then I heard a loud voice in heaven
say:

"Now have come the salvation and
the power and the kingdom
of our God,
and the authority of his Christ.
For the accuser of our brothers,
who accuses them before our God
day and night,
has been hurled down.
11They overcame him
by the blood of the Lamb
and by the word of their testimony;
they did not love their lives so much
as to shrink from death.
12Therefore rejoice, you heavens
and you who dwell in them!
But woe to the earth and the sea,
because the devil has gone down
to you!
He is filled with fury,
because he knows that his time is
short."

13When the dragon saw that he had
been hurled to the earth, he pursued the
woman who had given birth to the male
child. 14The woman was given the two
wings of a great eagle, so that she might
fly to the place prepared for her in the
desert, where she would be taken care
of for a time, times and half a time, out
of the serpent's reach. 15Then from his
mouth the serpent spewed water like a
river, to overtake the woman and sweep
her away with the torrent. 16But the
earth helped the woman by opening its
mouth and swallowing the river that the
dragon had spewed out of his mouth.
17Then the dragon was enraged at the
woman and went off to make war against
the rest of her offspring—those who
obey God's commandments and hold to
the testimony of Jesus.

SHARPEN THE FOCUS

"World History in a Nutshell." That could be the title of Revelation 12. Satan pursued, hounded, tempted, and tried to destroy God's people of the old covenant (the woman of Revelation 12:1–2), so that the promised Savior could not come.

But despite the fury of Egypt's Pharaoh, of Babylon's Nebuchadnezzar, of Rome's Herod, Jesus Christ did live and die, rise again and ascend to heaven—all for us and for our salvation. Now Satan can no longer prance before the throne of God to accuse us. Neither he nor his accusations get a hearing any longer in heaven's court. He has been thrown out (Revelation 12:9). We are righteous before God in Jesus forever!

Still, the ancient serpent continues to vent his fury on God's people. He will war with us until the end of time (Revelation 12:17). Even so, he cannot win. God both nourishes and protects us (Revelation 12:14). That *doesn't* mean we will be spared hardship for the name of Christ; it *does* mean we can stand up boldly for His name. We can remember the identity of our true enemy—Satan. We can pray for the human beings who, deceived by him, play out his schemes. And we can continue to testify that the blood of Jesus cleanses from all sin (Revelation 12:11; 1 John 1:7).

WEEK 103 • SATURDAY

Revelation 13:1–18

Together with the dragon, the "beast coming out of the sea" (Revelation 13:1) and the "beast coming out of the earth" (Revelation 13:11) form an unholy trinity. They use brute force and the power of persuasive propaganda against Christ and His church. Today's reading may chill your heart, but rejoice, your name is written in the Lamb's book of life (Revelation 13:8). If time is short, focus on Revelation 13:1–10.

13 1And the dragon[a] stood on
the shore of the sea.

The Beast out of the Sea

And I saw a beast coming out of the
sea. He had ten horns and seven heads,
with ten crowns on his horns, and on
each head a blasphemous name. 2The
beast I saw resembled a leopard, but
had feet like those of a bear and a mouth
like that of a lion. The dragon gave the
beast his power and his throne and
great authority. 3One of the heads of the
beast seemed to have had a fatal
wound, but the fatal wound had been
healed. The whole world was astonished and followed the beast. 4Men
worshiped the dragon because he had
given authority to the beast, and they
also worshiped the beast and asked,
"Who is like the beast? Who can make
war against him?"
5The beast was given a mouth to utter proud words and blasphemies and
to exercise his authority for forty-two
months. 6He opened his mouth to blaspheme God, and to slander his name
and his dwelling place and those who
live in heaven. 7He was given power to
make war against the saints and to conquer them. And he was given authority
over every tribe, people, language and
nation. 8All inhabitants of the earth will
worship the beast—all whose names
have not been written in the book of life
belonging to the Lamb that was slain
from the creation of the world.[b]
9He who has an ear, let him hear.

10If anyone is to go into captivity,
into captivity he will go.
If anyone is to be killed[c] with the
sword,
with the sword he will be killed.

This calls for patient endurance and
faithfulness on the part of the saints.

[a]1 Some late manuscripts *And I* [b]8 Or *written from the creation of the world in the book of life belonging to the Lamb that was slain* [c]10 Some manuscripts *anyone kills*

The Beast out of the Earth

[11]Then I saw another beast, coming
out of the earth. He had two horns like
a lamb, but he spoke like a dragon. [12]He
exercised all the authority of the first
beast on his behalf, and made the earth
and its inhabitants worship the first
beast, whose fatal wound had been
healed. [13]And he performed great and
miraculous signs, even causing fire to
come down from heaven to earth in full
view of men. [14]Because of the signs he
was given power to do on behalf of the
first beast, he deceived the inhabitants
of the earth. He ordered them to set up
an image in honor of the beast who was
wounded by the sword and yet lived.
[15]He was given power to give breath to
the image of the first beast, so that it
could speak and cause all who refused
to worship the image to be killed. [16]He
also forced everyone, small and great,
rich and poor, free and slave, to receive
a mark on his right hand or on his forehead, [17]so that no one could buy or sell
unless he had the mark, which is the
name of the beast or the number of his
name.

[18]This calls for wisdom. If anyone has
insight, let him calculate the number of
the beast, for it is man's number. His
number is 666.

SHARPEN THE FOCUS

Christians in Iran, in Egypt, in Sudan, in China stare down the throat of the "beast coming out of the sea." Backed by Satan, the governments that rule these countries hound God's children, threatening their very lives for the sake of the Savior.

Christians in other countries of the world face the "beast coming out of the earth." This "beast" looks less fierce (Revelation 13:1–2, 11), but it is just as dangerous. It has "two horns like a lamb"; its ideals may resemble those of Christianity and of *the* Lamb. But its teachings are counterfeit—and spiritually deadly.

Sometimes the two beasts work in concert, sometimes alone. But always the dragon—Satan—stands behind them, using whatever means at his disposal to undermine the authority of Christ and to steal the worship that rightly belongs to our Lord alone.

And yet "the Lamb that was slain from the creation of the world" (Revelation 13:8) is also our Good Shepherd. Despite all the ranting and raving of the beasts, Jesus has the keys of hell and death (Revelation 13:18). The hardships we face for Christ's sake won't last forever. Outward circumstances, no matter how fearsome, cannot overpower us. Jesus rules—and He loves us!

WEEK 104 • MONDAY

Revelation 14:1–20

GET THE BIG PICTURE

Despite the great tribulation, those whom God has sealed all make it safely to His heavenly home. (Compare Revelation 14:1 with Revelation 7:3–4.) God's love for unbelievers cannot be stopped; He sends three angels—probably the church—to warn them. When the message has been delivered, judgment begins. If time is short, focus on Revelation 14:1–5.

The Lamb and the 144,000

14 Then I looked, and there before me was the Lamb,
standing on Mount Zion, and with him
144,000 who had his name and his
Father's name written on their foreheads. 2And I heard a sound from
heaven like the roar of rushing waters
and like a loud peal of thunder. The
sound I heard was like that of harpists
playing their harps. 3And they sang a
new song before the throne and before
the four living creatures and the elders.
No one could learn the song except the
144,000 who had been redeemed from
the earth. 4These are those who did not
defile themselves with women, for they
kept themselves pure. They follow the
Lamb wherever he goes. They were
purchased from among men and offered as firstfruits to God and the Lamb.
5No lie was found in their mouths; they
are blameless.

The Three Angels

6Then I saw another angel flying in
midair, and he had the eternal gospel to
proclaim to those who live on the
earth—to every nation, tribe, language
and people. 7He said in a loud voice,
"Fear God and give him glory, because
the hour of his judgment has come.
Worship him who made the heavens,
the earth, the sea and the springs of
water."

8A second angel followed and said,
"Fallen! Fallen is Babylon the Great,
which made all the nations drink the
maddening wine of her adulteries."

9A third angel followed them and said
in a loud voice: "If anyone worships the
beast and his image and receives his
mark on the forehead or on the hand,
10he, too, will drink of the wine of God's
fury, which has been poured full
strength into the cup of his wrath. He
will be tormented with burning sulfur
in the presence of the holy angels and
of the Lamb. 11And the smoke of their
torment rises for ever and ever. There is
no rest day or night for those who worship the beast and his image, or for anyone who receives the mark of his name."
12This calls for patient endurance on the
part of the saints who obey God's commandments and remain faithful to
Jesus.

13Then I heard a voice from heaven
say, "Write: Blessed are the dead who
die in the Lord from now on."

"Yes," says the Spirit, "they will rest
from their labor, for their deeds will follow them."

The Harvest of the Earth

14I looked, and there before me was a
white cloud, and seated on the cloud
was one "like a son of man"[a] with a
crown of gold on his head and a sharp
sickle in his hand. 15Then another angel
came out of the temple and called in a
loud voice to him who was sitting on the
cloud, "Take your sickle and reap, because the time to reap has come, for the
harvest of the earth is ripe." 16So he who
was seated on the cloud swung his sickle over the earth, and the earth was harvested.

17Another angel came out of the temple in heaven, and he too had a sharp
sickle. 18Still another angel, who had
charge of the fire, came from the altar
and called in a loud voice to him who
had the sharp sickle, "Take your sharp
sickle and gather the clusters of grapes
from the earth's vine, because its grapes
are ripe." 19The angel swung his sickle
on the earth, gathered its grapes and
threw them into the great winepress of
God's wrath. 20They were trampled in
the winepress outside the city, and
blood flowed out of the press, rising as
high as the horses' bridles for a distance
of 1,600 stadia.[b]

[a]*14* Daniel 7:13 [b]*20* That is, about 180 miles (about 300 kilometers)

SHARPEN THE FOCUS

What's your favorite hymn or Christian song? After you've answered that question, answer this one: Could a choir of unbelievers learn it and sing it?

In one sense, yes. The melody and lyrics you treasure could, no doubt, be added to the repertoire of any credible choir, whether the members of that choir know Jesus or not. In a deeper sense, though, the answer is no. A hymn of praise amounts to much more than simply a melody and a set of lyrics. It includes most of all the worship that flows from our hearts.

That's really what Revelation 14:3 means when it says that only God's human children ("the 144,000") can learn the new song of the Lamb. Surely the angels could master the melody and lyrics of such a song. But they, never having been redeemed, cannot fully comprehend—or offer—the praise that flows from hearts forgiven, cleansed, and given the righteousness of Christ as His free gift.

You need not wait for heaven to offer that kind of praise from a heart transformed by grace. Why not join the heavenly chorus right now? ☼

WEEK 104 • TUESDAY

Revelation 15:1–8

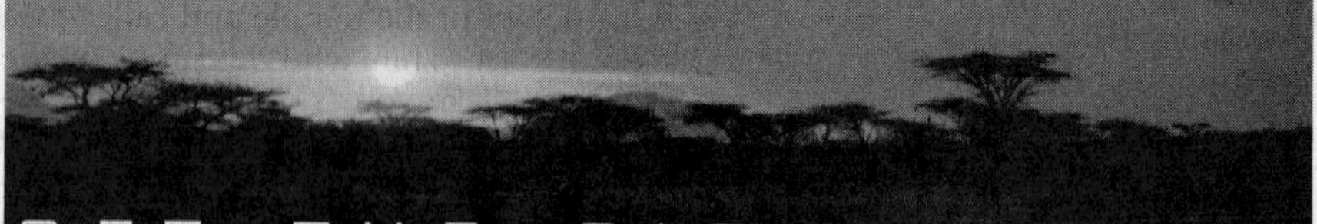

GET THE BIG PICTURE

John will soon watch as the third and final cycle of the Lord's judgment falls on a sinful earth and on Satan himself. John is in heaven as it were. The Lord wants John—and us—to be sure of these facts: Christ is victorious, and He shares His victory with us. With what situation in life do you personally need the reassurances of Revelation 15 today? If time is short, focus on Revelation 15:1–4.

Seven Angels With Seven Plagues

15 I saw in heaven another great
and marvelous sign: seven
angels with the seven last plagues—last,
because with them God's wrath is completed. 2And I saw what looked like a sea
of glass mixed with fire and, standing
beside the sea, those who had been victorious over the beast and his image and
over the number of his name. They held
harps given them by God 3and sang the
song of Moses the servant of God and
the song of the Lamb:

"Great and marvelous are your
deeds,
Lord God Almighty.
Just and true are your ways,
King of the ages.
4Who will not fear you, O Lord,
and bring glory to your name?
For you alone are holy.
All nations will come
and worship before you,
for your righteous acts have been
revealed."

5After this I looked and in heaven the
temple, that is, the tabernacle of the Testimony, was opened. 6Out of the temple
came the seven angels with the seven
plagues. They were dressed in clean,
shining linen and wore golden sashes
around their chests. 7Then one of the

four living creatures gave to the seven
angels seven golden bowls filled with
the wrath of God, who lives for ever and
ever. 8And the temple was filled with
smoke from the glory of God and from
his power, and no one could enter the
temple until the seven plagues of the
seven angels were completed.

SHARPEN THE FOCUS

Thousands of first-century believers suffered persecution for the faith. Anyone persecuted for Christ's sake gained the title "martyr." After a while, this word came to mean someone who had endured death for the name of Jesus. The believers left behind began to commemorate the day each martyr died as that martyr's "Day of Victory."

We can see echoes of that idea in Revelation 15:2. Here John describes God's saints in heaven as those who have been victorious

- over the beast;
- over his image;
- over the number of his name.

These victors in Christ had triumphed over the Antichrist and over all the false gods, false philosophies of life, and false values he erects. Satan himself, of course, stands behind all these falsehoods. We are victorious in Christ even now. And we will receive victory in full from the nail-pierced hands of our Savior in eternity.

What a gift! Why not use Revelation 15:3–4 as a hymn of praise right now?

WEEK 104 • WEDNESDAY

Rev. 16:1–21

GET THE BIG PICTURE

Revelation 16 summarizes the last judgment cycle in John's vision. The horror of the seals and trumpets is described from a third viewpoint and in a more intensified way. Nature is in upheaval (Revelation 16:1–11), the dragon, the beast from the sea, and the beast from the earth unleash all their powers of darkness (Revelation 16:13–14; compare Revelation 13). Even so, those who watch and await Christ's coming are blessed (Revelation 16:15). If time is short, focus on Revelation 16:1–16.

The Seven Bowls of God's Wrath

16 Then I heard a loud voice
from the temple saying to the
seven angels, "Go, pour out the seven
bowls of God's wrath on the earth."
2The first angel went and poured out
his bowl on the land, and ugly and painful sores broke out on the people who
had the mark of the beast and worshiped his image.
3The second angel poured out his
bowl on the sea, and it turned into blood
like that of a dead man, and every living thing in the sea died.

4 The third angel poured out his bowl
on the rivers and springs of water, and
they became blood. 5 Then I heard the
angel in charge of the waters say:

"You are just in these judgments,
you who are and who were, the
Holy One,
because you have so judged;
6 for they have shed the blood of your
saints and prophets,
and you have given them blood to
drink as they deserve."

7 And I heard the altar respond:

"Yes, Lord God Almighty,
true and just are your judgments."

8 The fourth angel poured out his
bowl on the sun, and the sun was given
power to scorch people with fire. 9 They
were seared by the intense heat and
they cursed the name of God, who had
control over these plagues, but they refused to repent and glorify him.
10 The fifth angel poured out his bowl
on the throne of the beast, and his kingdom was plunged into darkness. Men
gnawed their tongues in agony 11 and
cursed the God of heaven because
of their pains and their sores, but they
refused to repent of what they had
done.
12 The sixth angel poured out his bowl
on the great river Euphrates, and its water was dried up to prepare the way for
the kings from the East. 13 Then I saw
three evil[a] spirits that looked like frogs;
they came out of the mouth of the dragon, out of the mouth of the beast and
out of the mouth of the false prophet.
14 They are spirits of demons performing
miraculous signs, and they go out to the
kings of the whole world, to gather
them for the battle on the great day of
God Almighty.
15 "Behold, I come like a thief! Blessed
is he who stays awake and keeps his
clothes with him, so that he may not go
naked and be shamefully exposed."
16 Then they gathered the kings together to the place that in Hebrew is
called Armageddon.
17 The seventh angel poured out his
bowl into the air, and out of the temple
came a loud voice from the throne, saying, "It is done!" 18 Then there came
flashes of lightning, rumblings, peals of
thunder and a severe earthquake. No
earthquake like it has ever occurred
since man has been on earth, so tremendous was the quake. 19 The great city split
into three parts, and the cities of the
nations collapsed. God remembered
Babylon the Great and gave her the cup
filled with the wine of the fury of his
wrath. 20 Every island fled away and the
mountains could not be found. 21 From
the sky huge hailstones of about a hundred pounds each fell upon men. And
they cursed God on account of the
plague of hail, because the plague was
so terrible.

[a]13 Greek *unclean*

SHARPEN THE FOCUS

Armageddon. You know *that* name! But take notice of this most important truth as you read. The "Battle of Armageddon" never takes place!

Oh, sure enough, puny human beings gather. They ally themselves against the Lord and His Christ (Revelation 16:16). But as soon as they do, the seventh angel pours out his bowl and a voice from heaven's throne pronounces the end: "It is done!" (Revelation 16:17). Then Babylon—all the enemies of the Lord and His people—fall in a great destruction.

Not a very uplifting reading? In one sense not. We who know firsthand what our King has done for us shudder to see others—others for whom Jesus came and lived and died—reject Him and thus perish in their sins.

On the other hand, we who celebrate Christ's first coming long for His second advent. We await Him every bit as anxiously as God's old covenant believers awaited the first advent of the Messiah. And while we wait, we invite our unbelieving family members and friends to know and trust in Him. We pray His kingdom will dawn in their hearts. ☼

If at times we feel oppressed by the idolatry of materialism and the scoffing of the unbelief around us, it's no wonder. The system of the Antichrist that has invaded our world is no insignificant enemy. Satan and the world system he has created sit bloated and arrogant in triumph (Revelation 17:3–6). But the Lamb and those who are with Him will overcome. Look for that hope as you read. If time is short, focus on Revelation 18:1–8.

The Woman on the Beast

17 One of the seven angels who
had the seven bowls came
and said to me, "Come, I will show you
the punishment of the great prostitute,
who sits on many waters. 2With her the
kings of the earth committed adultery
and the inhabitants of the earth were
intoxicated with the wine of her adulteries."
3Then the angel carried me away in
the Spirit into a desert. There I saw a
woman sitting on a scarlet beast that
was covered with blasphemous names
and had seven heads and ten horns.
4The woman was dressed in purple and
scarlet, and was glittering with gold,
precious stones and pearls. She held a
golden cup in her hand, filled with
abominable things and the filth of her
adulteries. 5This title was written on her
forehead:

MYSTERY
BABYLON THE GREAT
THE MOTHER OF PROSTITUTES
AND OF THE ABOMINATIONS OF THE
EARTH.

6I saw that the woman was drunk with
the blood of the saints, the blood of
those who bore testimony to Jesus.

When I saw her, I was greatly astonished. 7Then the angel said to me: "Why
are you astonished? I will explain to you
the mystery of the woman and of the
beast she rides, which has the seven
heads and ten horns. 8The beast, which
you saw, once was, now is not, and will
come up out of the Abyss and go to his
destruction. The inhabitants of the earth
whose names have not been written in
the book of life from the creation of the
world will be astonished when they see
the beast, because he once was, now is
not, and yet will come.
9"This calls for a mind with wisdom.
The seven heads are seven hills on
which the woman sits. 10They are also
seven kings. Five have fallen, one is, the
other has not yet come; but when he
does come, he must remain for a little
while. 11The beast who once was, and
now is not, is an eighth king. He belongs
to the seven and is going to his destruction.
12"The ten horns you saw are ten
kings who have not yet received a kingdom, but who for one hour will receive
authority as kings along with the beast.
13They have one purpose and will give
their power and authority to the beast.
14They will make war against the Lamb,

but the Lamb will overcome them because he is Lord of lords and King of kings—and with him will be his called, chosen and faithful followers."
[15]Then the angel said to me, "The waters you saw, where the prostitute sits, are peoples, multitudes, nations and languages. [16]The beast and the ten horns you saw will hate the prostitute. They will bring her to ruin and leave her naked; they will eat her flesh and burn her with fire. [17]For God has put it into their hearts to accomplish his purpose by agreeing to give the beast their power to rule, until God's words are fulfilled. [18]The woman you saw is the great city that rules over the kings of the earth."

The Fall of Babylon

18 After this I saw another angel coming down from heaven. He had great authority, and the earth was illuminated by his splendor. [2]With a mighty voice he shouted:

"Fallen! Fallen is Babylon the Great!
She has become a home for demons
and a haunt for every evil[a] spirit,
a haunt for every unclean and detestable bird.
[3]For all the nations have drunk
the maddening wine of her adulteries.
The kings of the earth committed adultery with her,
and the merchants of the earth grew rich from her excessive luxuries."

[4]Then I heard another voice from heaven say:

"Come out of her, my people,
so that you will not share in her sins,
so that you will not receive any of her plagues;
[5]for her sins are piled up to heaven,
and God has remembered her crimes.
[6]Give back to her as she has given;
pay her back double for what she has done.
Mix her a double portion from her own cup.
[7]Give her as much torture and grief
as the glory and luxury she gave herself.
In her heart she boasts,
'I sit as queen; I am not a widow,
and I will never mourn.'
[8]Therefore in one day her plagues will overtake her:
death, mourning and famine.
She will be consumed by fire,
for mighty is the Lord God who judges her.

[a]2 Greek *unclean*

SHARPEN THE FOCUS

"In one day" (Revelation 18:8) the world system Scripture calls "Babylon" will fall. Down through history the arrogant and rebellious forces of evil have persecuted God's people. But God has remembered Babylon's iniquities (Revelation 18:5). And though it may not seem like it right now, the "one day" of Babylon's fall is closer than ever before.

That "one day" began in Eden with God's promise to crush the serpent's head (Genesis 3:15). That "one day" continued in glory on the night the angels split the sky to announce our Savior's birth (Luke 2:8–13). That "one day" roared with the earthquake that tore the curtain of the Holy of Holies on the afternoon Christ died and gave us poor sinners direct access to the very throne room of our God (Matthew 27:50–51). That "one day" shouted with a triumph that echoes even now the glory of our Lord's resurrection (Matthew 28:2–7).

Soon, very soon, the angel army of heaven will split the sky one last time as our strong Lord (Revelation 18:8) comes to destroy His enemies and to gather His saints. On that day, we will join the eternal song of praise to God and to the Lamb.

The earth that receives the returning Christ is a world steeped in wealth, luxury, culture, and trade. In short, an earth very much like our own. Still, the rich and powerful exploit the poor—trafficking in human "bodies and souls" (Revelation 18:13). These sins and others have made the "city of Babylon" a ticking time bomb, liable to blow up at any moment. Think about this morning's news as you read Revelation 18. If time is short, focus on Revelation 18:20–24.

9"When the kings of the earth who
committed adultery with her and
shared her luxury see the smoke of her
burning, they will weep and mourn
over her. 10Terrified at her torment, they
will stand far off and cry:

" 'Woe! Woe, O great city,
O Babylon, city of power!
In one hour your doom has come!'

11"The merchants of the earth will
weep and mourn over her because no
one buys their cargoes any more—12car-
goes of gold, silver, precious stones and
pearls; fine linen, purple, silk and scarlet cloth; every sort of citron wood, and
articles of every kind made of ivory,
costly wood, bronze, iron and marble;
13cargoes of cinnamon and spice, of incense, myrrh and frankincense, of wine
and olive oil, of fine flour and wheat;
cattle and sheep; horses and carriages;
and bodies and souls of men.
14"They will say, 'The fruit you longed
for is gone from you. All your riches and
splendor have vanished, never to be recovered.' 15The merchants who sold
these things and gained their wealth
from her will stand far off, terrified
at her torment. They will weep and
mourn 16and cry out:

" 'Woe! Woe, O great city,
dressed in fine linen, purple and
scarlet,
and glittering with gold, precious
stones and pearls!
17In one hour such great wealth has
been brought to ruin!'

"Every sea captain, and all who travel
by ship, the sailors, and all who earn
their living from the sea, will stand far
off. 18When they see the smoke of her
burning, they will exclaim, 'Was there
ever a city like this great city?' 19They
will throw dust on their heads, and with
weeping and mourning cry out:

" 'Woe! Woe, O great city,
where all who had ships on the sea
became rich through her wealth!
In one hour she has been brought to
ruin!
20Rejoice over her, O heaven!
Rejoice, saints and apostles and
prophets!
God has judged her for the way she
treated you.' "

21Then a mighty angel picked up a
boulder the size of a large millstone and
threw it into the sea, and said:

"With such violence
the great city of Babylon will be
thrown down,
never to be found again.
22The music of harpists and musicians,
flute players and trumpeters,
will never be heard in you again.
No workman of any trade
will ever be found in you again.
The sound of a millstone
will never be heard in you again.

23 The light of a lamp
will never shine in you again.
The voice of bridegroom and bride
will never be heard in you again.
Your merchants were the world's
great men.
By your magic spell all the nations
were led astray.
24 In her was found the blood of
prophets and of the saints,
and of all who have been killed on
the earth."

SHARPEN THE FOCUS

In his poem *Ozymandias,* Percy Bysshe Shelley describes a grandiose monument lying broken in the desert sand. The pedestal of that monument is inscribed:

> My name is Ozymandias, King of Kings:
> Look on my works, ye Almighty, and despair!

Then Shelley adds:

> Nothing besides remains. Round the decay
> Of that colossal wreck, boundless and bare
> The lone and level sands stretch far away.

Shelley's poem could well be the epitaph of the system of the Antichrist. Pride. Idolatry. Selfish lovelessness. These three sins in particular mark that system for destruction.

Human nature run amok and egged on by Satan always stumbles into these transgressions. Even we as God's people can find our clothes stained by the filth that is Babylon. But because of what Jesus did for us on His cross, no human being need fall into eternal destruction with Babylon.

The true King of kings does not want "anyone to perish, but everyone to come to repentance" (2 Peter 3:9). That's why the complete collapse of Babylon has not yet occurred. The Lord is being patient—with the citizens of "Babylon" and with us, those whom He has entrusted to share the Gospel with every creature (Mark 16:15).

WEEK 104 • SATURDAY

Revelation 19:1–21

GET THE BIG PICTURE

Today's reading announces the fall of Babylon yet again and the eternal, glorious celebration of heaven at Jesus' great victory. Read carefully—the story of that celebration and victory are *your* story too. Do you see yourself in this picture? If time is short, focus on Revelation 19:1–10.

Hallelujah!

19 After this I heard what
sounded like the roar of a
great multitude in heaven shouting:

"Hallelujah!
Salvation and glory and power
belong to our God,
2 for true and just are his
judgments.
He has condemned the great
prostitute
who corrupted the earth by her
adulteries.
He has avenged on her the blood of
his servants."

3 And again they shouted:

"Hallelujah!
The smoke from her goes up for
ever and ever."

4 The twenty-four elders and the four
living creatures fell down and worshiped God, who was seated on the
throne. And they cried:

"Amen, Hallelujah!"

5 Then a voice came from the throne,
saying:

"Praise our God,
all you his servants,
you who fear him,
both small and great!"

6 Then I heard what sounded like a
great multitude, like the roar of rushing
waters and like loud peals of thunder,
shouting:

"Hallelujah!
For our Lord God Almighty
reigns.
7 Let us rejoice and be glad
and give him glory!
For the wedding of the Lamb has
come,
and his bride has made herself
ready.
8 Fine linen, bright and clean,
was given her to wear."
(Fine linen stands for the righteous acts
of the saints.)

9 Then the angel said to me, "Write:
'Blessed are those who are invited to the
wedding supper of the Lamb!' " And he
added, "These are the true words of
God."

10 At this I fell at his feet to worship
him. But he said to me, "Do not do it!
I am a fellow servant with you and
with your brothers who hold to the testimony of Jesus. Worship God! For the
testimony of Jesus is the spirit of prophecy."

The Rider on the White Horse

11 I saw heaven standing open and
there before me was a white horse,
whose rider is called Faithful and True.
With justice he judges and makes war.
12 His eyes are like blazing fire, and on his
head are many crowns. He has a name
written on him that no one knows but
he himself. 13 He is dressed in a robe
dipped in blood, and his name is the
Word of God. 14 The armies of heaven
were following him, riding on white
horses and dressed in fine linen, white
and clean. 15 Out of his mouth comes a
sharp sword with which to strike down
the nations. "He will rule them with an
iron scepter."[a] He treads the winepress
of the fury of the wrath of God Almighty. 16 On his robe and on his thigh
he has this name written:

KING OF KINGS AND LORD OF LORDS.

17 And I saw an angel standing in the
sun, who cried in a loud voice to all the
birds flying in midair, "Come, gather together for the great supper of God, 18 so
that you may eat the flesh of kings, generals, and mighty men, of horses and
their riders, and the flesh of all people,
free and slave, small and great."

19 Then I saw the beast and the kings
of the earth and their armies gathered
together to make war against the rider
on the horse and his army. 20 But the
beast was captured, and with him
the false prophet who had performed
the miraculous signs on his behalf. With
these signs he had deluded those who

[a] *15* Psalm 2:9

had received the mark of the beast and worshiped his image. The two of them were thrown alive into the fiery lake of burning sulfur. 21The rest of them were killed with the sword that came out of the mouth of the rider on the horse, and all the birds gorged themselves on their flesh.

SHARPEN THE FOCUS

Remember that the purpose of the book of Revelation is to reveal Jesus Christ in all His glory. Today's chapter certainly does that! In particular, it reveals Jesus as the Lover of the church. It also reveals us—God's people—as the bride of Christ.

From all eternity, God planned to give His church to His Son in an eternal, perfect union.

Jesus loves the church. He has always loved us. That love led to a huge scandal—the cross. Like all husbands-to-be in the culture of the Near East, Jesus offered a "bride price," a dowry, to win us for Himself. He offered not the trinkets and trash of worldly wealth. No, He purchased us with His own blood and death.

He is our ever faithful, ever true Lord (Revelation 19:11). He has given us His very own holiness and the power to act in holy obedience to God—symbolized by the white linen in Revelation 19:8 and 14. Worship Him!

WEEK 105 • MONDAY

Revelation 20:1–15

GET THE BIG PICTURE

The first part of today's chapter sweeps through history from the time of Christ to the end of time as we know it. While some details here may seem mysterious, the overall message is crystal clear: We win—in Christ. If time is short, focus on Revelation 20:11–15.

The Thousand Years

20 And I saw an angel coming down out of heaven, having the key to the Abyss and holding in his hand a great chain. 2He seized the dragon, that ancient serpent, who is the devil, or Satan, and bound him for a thousand years. 3He threw him into the Abyss, and locked and sealed it over him, to keep him from deceiving the nations anymore until the thousand years were ended. After that, he must be set free for a short time.

4I saw thrones on which were seated those who had been given authority to judge. And I saw the souls of those who had been beheaded because of their testimony for Jesus and because of the word of God. They had not worshiped the beast or his image and had not received his mark on their foreheads or their hands. They came to life and reigned with Christ a thousand years. 5(The rest of the dead did not come to life until the thousand years were ended.) This is the first resurrection. 6Blessed and holy are those who have part in the first resurrection. The second death has no power over them, but they will be priests of God and of Christ and

will reign with him for a thousand
years.

Satan's Doom

7When the thousand years are over,
Satan will be released from his prison
8and will go out to deceive the nations
in the four corners of the earth—Gog
and Magog—to gather them for battle.
In number they are like the sand on the
seashore. 9They marched across the
breadth of the earth and surrounded
the camp of God's people, the city he
loves. But fire came down from heaven
and devoured them. 10And the devil,
who deceived them, was thrown into
the lake of burning sulfur, where the
beast and the false prophet had been
thrown. They will be tormented day
and night for ever and ever.

The Dead Are Judged

11Then I saw a great white throne and
him who was seated on it. Earth and sky
fled from his presence, and there was no
place for them. 12And I saw the dead,
great and small, standing before the
throne, and books were opened. Another book was opened, which is the book
of life. The dead were judged according
to what they had done as recorded in
the books. 13The sea gave up the dead
that were in it, and death and Hades
gave up the dead that were in them, and
each person was judged according to
what he had done. 14Then death and
Hades were thrown into the lake of fire.
The lake of fire is the second death. 15If
anyone's name was not found written
in the book of life, he was thrown into
the lake of fire.

SHARPEN THE FOCUS

Someone has said, "When Satan taunts you with your past, remind him of his future." Great advice. Satan, after all, is the one who has incited wicked people to torture the saints for their faith down through time. He's the one who foments war and who applauds slaughter and pain and famine and plague. He's the one who has deceived the nations (Revelation 20:3) and in that deception led millions to reject God's gracious gift of eternal life in our Savior Jesus.

He's also the one who continually accuses God's children of wrongdoing and who tries to convince us that God hates us for our sin. He uses the crowbar of fear and doubt to pry us out of our Father's arms and to drive us into the cold night of despair.

But he's also the one destined for the "lake of burning sulfur" (Revelation 20:10). From there, he will never escape. We, on the other hand, are by God's grace destined for glory. Your name—right now—shines in golden letters on one of the pages in the Lamb's book of life (Revelation 20:12). Christ's death and rising again made that inscription possible. Nothing Satan can do, no charge he can level, will cause God to take His eraser to your page in His book. In Jesus, you are His child, alive forever!

Heave a sigh of relief. The war between God and Satan has ended as Revelation 21 begins. There's no more Antichrist, no more judgment, no more death or pain or persecution to read about. Instead, we can revel in the beauty of heaven. To what do you most fervently look forward? If time is short, focus on Revelation 21:1–7.

The New Jerusalem

21 Then I saw a new heaven and
a new earth, for the first
heaven and the first earth had passed
away, and there was no longer any sea.
2I saw the Holy City, the new Jerusalem,
coming down out of heaven from God,
prepared as a bride beautifully dressed
for her husband. 3And I heard a loud
voice from the throne saying, "Now the
dwelling of God is with men, and he
will live with them. They will be his
people, and God himself will be with
them and be their God. 4He will wipe
every tear from their eyes. There will be
no more death or mourning or crying or
pain, for the old order of things has
passed away."
5He who was seated on the throne
said, "I am making everything new!"
Then he said, "Write this down, for
these words are trustworthy and true."
6He said to me: "It is done. I am the
Alpha and the Omega, the Beginning
and the End. To him who is thirsty I will
give to drink without cost from the
spring of the water of life. 7He who overcomes will inherit all this, and I will be
his God and he will be my son. 8But the
cowardly, the unbelieving, the vile, the
murderers, the sexually immoral, those
who practice magic arts, the idolaters
and all liars—their place will be in the
fiery lake of burning sulfur. This is the
second death."
9One of the seven angels who had the
seven bowls full of the seven last
plagues came and said to me, "Come, I
will show you the bride, the wife of the
Lamb." 10And he carried me away in the
Spirit to a mountain great and high, and
showed me the Holy City, Jerusalem,
coming down out of heaven from God.
11It shone with the glory of God, and its
brilliance was like that of a very precious
jewel, like a jasper, clear as crystal. 12It
had a great, high wall with twelve gates,
and with twelve angels at the gates. On
the gates were written the names of the
twelve tribes of Israel. 13There were
three gates on the east, three on the
north, three on the south and three on
the west. 14The wall of the city had
twelve foundations, and on them were
the names of the twelve apostles of the
Lamb.
15The angel who talked with me had
a measuring rod of gold to measure the
city, its gates and its walls. 16The city was
laid out like a square, as long as it was
wide. He measured the city with the rod
and found it to be 12,000 stadia[a] in
length, and as wide and high as it is
long. 17He measured its wall and it was
144 cubits[b] thick,[c] by man's measurement, which the angel was using. 18The
wall was made of jasper, and the city of
pure gold, as pure as glass. 19The foundations of the city walls were decorated
with every kind of precious stone. The

[a]*16* That is, about 1,400 miles (about 2,200 kilometers) [b]*17* That is, about 200 feet (about 65 meters) [c]*17* Or *high*

first foundation was jasper, the second
sapphire, the third chalcedony, the
fourth emerald, [20]the fifth sardonyx, the
sixth carnelian, the seventh chrysolite,
the eighth beryl, the ninth topaz, the
tenth chrysoprase, the eleventh jacinth,
and the twelfth amethyst.[a] [21]The twelve
gates were twelve pearls, each gate
made of a single pearl. The great street
of the city was of pure gold, like trans-
parent glass.
[22]I did not see a temple in the city, because the Lord God Almighty and the
Lamb are its temple. [23]The city does not
need the sun or the moon to shine on it,
for the glory of God gives it light, and
the Lamb is its lamp. [24]The nations will
walk by its light, and the kings of the
earth will bring their splendor into it.
[25]On no day will its gates ever be shut,
for there will be no night there. [26]The
glory and honor of the nations will be
brought into it. [27]Nothing impure will
ever enter it, nor will anyone who does
what is shameful or deceitful, but only
those whose names are written in the
Lamb's book of life.

[a]20 The precise identification of some of these precious stones is uncertain.

SHARPEN THE FOCUS

Forever with the Lord. That's how I want my epitaph to read. How about you? We can only guess at the architecture of the heavenly city in which we will spend eternity. We can only speculate about the brilliance and beauty we will see there. Surely, it will be wonderful.

But there's one element that will be gloriously familiar—the Lord's presence. The same Savior who held us while we wept on earth will dry our tears in heaven (Revelation 21:4). The same Lord who fed us at His Table and in His Word on earth will nourish us in heaven. The same Father who whispered words of love to us again and again on earth will shout of that love for us as the angels explode their applause.

The words of v. 3 will one day come true for each of us:

> *Now the dwelling of God is with men, and He will live with them. They will be His people, and God Himself will be with them and be their God.*

As He is with us now, so He will be with us forever. In Jesus, He is for us Immanuel—God with us. Forever.

WEEK 105 • WEDNESDAY

Rev. 22:1–21

GET THE BIG PICTURE

Is today a day of joy for you? Of nostalgia? Of regrets? Of reflection? Of grief? Whatever fills your heart today, take some time right now to meditate on the past and on the future as you pray about Revelation 22. If time is short, focus on Revelation 22:1–17.

The River of Life

22 Then the angel showed
me the river of the water
of life, as clear as crystal, flowing from
the throne of God and of the Lamb
2down the middle of the great street of
the city. On each side of the river stood
the tree of life, bearing twelve crops of
fruit, yielding its fruit every month. And
the leaves of the tree are for the healing
of the nations. 3No longer will there be
any curse. The throne of God and of the
Lamb will be in the city, and his servants
will serve him. 4They will see his face,
and his name will be on their foreheads.
5There will be no more night. They will
not need the light of a lamp or the light
of the sun, for the Lord God will give
them light. And they will reign for ever
and ever.
6The angel said to me, "These words
are trustworthy and true. The Lord, the
God of the spirits of the prophets, sent
his angel to show his servants the things
that must soon take place."

Jesus Is Coming

7"Behold, I am coming soon! Blessed
is he who keeps the words of the prophecy in this book."

8I, John, am the one who heard and
saw these things. And when I had heard
and seen them, I fell down to worship
at the feet of the angel who had been
showing them to me. 9But he said to me,
"Do not do it! I am a fellow servant with
you and with your brothers the prophets and of all who keep the words of this
book. Worship God!"
10Then he told me, "Do not seal up the
words of the prophecy of this book,
because the time is near. 11Let him who
does wrong continue to do wrong; let
him who is vile continue to be vile; let
him who does right continue to do
right; and let him who is holy continue
to be holy."

12"Behold, I am coming soon! My reward is with me, and I will give to everyone according to what he has done.
13I am the Alpha and the Omega, the
First and the Last, the Beginning and
the End.
14"Blessed are those who wash their
robes, that they may have the right to
the tree of life and may go through
the gates into the city. 15Outside are the
dogs, those who practice magic arts,
the sexually immoral, the murderers,
the idolaters and everyone who loves
and practices falsehood.
16"I, Jesus, have sent my angel to give
you[a] this testimony for the churches. I
am the Root and the Offspring of David,
and the bright Morning Star."

17The Spirit and the bride say, "Come!"
And let him who hears say, "Come!"
Whoever is thirsty, let him come; and
whoever wishes, let him take the free
gift of the water of life.

18I warn everyone who hears the
words of the prophecy of this book: If
anyone adds anything to them, God will
add to him the plagues described in this
book. 19And if anyone takes words away
from this book of prophecy, God will
take away from him his share in the tree
of life and in the holy city, which are
described in this book.
20He who testifies to these things says,
"Yes, I am coming soon."
Amen. Come, Lord Jesus.
21The grace of the Lord Jesus be with
God's people. Amen.

[a] *16* The Greek is plural.

SHARPEN THE FOCUS

From beginning to end Revelation reveals Jesus to us. He is:

- the Lamb (Revelation 22:1) who occupies heaven's high throne and who has cancelled the curse of sin and death for us (Revelation 22:3).

- the A and the Z of our existence, the Beginning and the End, the First and the Last (Revelation 22:13). As we began this day—and our lives—in His grace, so we can continue through all our days in that same grace.
- the Root and the Offpsring of David (Revelation 22:16), the Anointed One—Christ—whom the Father had promised through all His holy prophets and who has fulfilled their prophecies to the letter.
- the bright Morning Star (Revelation 22:16), the Light of the world (John 8:12).

Jesus is truly our Lord, our Savior, our Messiah, and our soon-coming King. Praise Him, for in Him you have the peace of sin forgiven and the joy that anticipates His return.

Amen. Come, Lord Jesus! (Revelation 22:20)

Table of Weights and Measures

The figures of the table are calculated on the basis of a shekel equaling 11.5 grams, a cubit equaling 18 inches and an ephah equaling 22 liters. The quart referred to is either a dry quart (slightly larger than a liter) or a liquid quart (slightly smaller than a liter), whichever is applicable. The ton referred to in the footnotes is the American ton of 2,000 pounds.

This table is based upon the best available information, but it is not intended to be mathematically precise; like the measurement equivalents in the footnotes, it merely gives approximate amounts and distances. Weights and measures differed somewhat at various times and places in the ancient world. There is uncertainty particularly about the ephah and the bath; further discoveries may shed more light on these units of capacity.

		BIBLICAL UNIT	APPROXIMATE AMERICAN EQUIVALENT	APPROXIMATE METRIC EQUIVALENT
WEIGHTS	talent	(60 minas)	75 pounds	34 kilograms
	mina	(50 shekels)	1¼ pounds	0.6 kilogram
	shekel	(2 bekas)	⅖ ounce	11.5 grams
	pim	(⅔ shekel)	⅓ ounce	7.6 grams
	beka	(10 gerahs)	⅕ ounce	5.5 grams
	gerah		1/50 ounce	0.6 gram
LENGTH	cubit		18 inches	0.5 meter
	span		9 inches	23 centimeters
	handbreadth		3 inches	8 centimeters
CAPACITY				
Dry Measure	cor [homer]	(10 ephahs)	6 bushels	220 liters
	lethek	(5 ephahs)	3 bushels	110 liters
	ephah	(10 omers)	⅗ bushel	22 liters
	seah	(⅓ ephah)	7 quarts	7.3 liters
	omer	(1/10 ephah)	2 quarts	2 liters
	cab	(1/18 ephah)	1 quart	1 liter
Liquid Measure	bath	(1 ephah)	6 gallons	22 liters
	hin	(⅙ bath)	4 quarts	4 liters
	log	(1/72 bath)	⅓ quart	0.3 liter

Reading Plan for the Today's Light Bible

This reading plan will guide you through the Bible in two years. You don't have to start at the beginning of the year, you can start today with Week One. Two years from today, you will have read the entire Bible. May God bless your study of His Word.

Week 1

- ❐ Monday .... Genesis 1:1—2:25
- ❐ Tuesday .... Genesis 3:1–24
- ❐ Wednesday .... Genesis 4:1—6:8
- ❐ Thursday .... Genesis 6:9—8:22
- ❐ Friday .... Genesis 9:1—10:32
- ❐ Saturday .... Genesis 11:1—12:9

Week 2

- ❐ Monday .... Genesis 12:10—13:18
- ❐ Tuesday .... Genesis 14:1—15:21
- ❐ Wednesday .... Genesis 16:1—17:27
- ❐ Thursday .... Genesis 18:1—19:38
- ❐ Friday .... Genesis 20:1—21:33
- ❐ Saturday .... Genesis 22:1–23

Week 3

- ❐ Monday .... Genesis 23:1—24:66
- ❐ Tuesday .... Genesis 25:1—26:35
- ❐ Wednesday .... Genesis 27:1—28:22
- ❐ Thursday .... Genesis 29:1—30:43
- ❐ Friday .... Genesis 31:1—33:20
- ❐ Saturday .... Genesis 34:1—35:29

Week 4

- ❐ Monday .... Genesis 36:1—37:36
- ❐ Tuesday .... Genesis 38:1—39:23
- ❐ Wednesday .... Genesis 40:1–23
- ❐ Thursday .... Genesis 41:1–40
- ❐ Friday .... Genesis 41:41–57
- ❐ Saturday .... Genesis 42:1—44:34

Week 5

- ❒ Monday .... Genesis 45:1—46:34
- ❒ Tuesday .... Genesis 47:1—48:22
- ❒ Wednesday .... Genesis 49:1—50:26
- ❒ Thursday .... Exodus 1:1–22
- ❒ Friday .... Exodus 2:1–25
- ❒ Saturday .... Exodus 3:1—4:31

Week 6

- ❒ Monday .... Exodus 5:1—6:29
- ❒ Tuesday .... Exodus 7:1–24
- ❒ Wednesday .... Exodus 8:1—9:35
- ❒ Thursday .... Exodus 10:1–29
- ❒ Friday .... Exodus 11:1—12:51
- ❒ Saturday .... Exodus 13:1–22

Week 7

- ❒ Monday .... Exodus 14:1–31
- ❒ Tuesday .... Exodus 15:1–27
- ❒ Wednesday .... Exodus 16:1—17:16
- ❒ Thursday .... Exodus 18:1–27
- ❒ Friday .... Exodus 19:1—20:26
- ❒ Saturday .... Exodus 21:1—22:31

Week 8

- ❒ Monday .... Exodus 23:1—24:18
- ❒ Tuesday .... Exodus 25:1—27:20
- ❒ Wednesday .... Exodus 28:1—29:46
- ❒ Thursday .... Exodus 30:1—31:18
- ❒ Friday .... Exodus 32:1–35
- ❒ Saturday .... Exodus 33:1–23

Week 9

- ❒ Monday .... Exodus 34:1–35
- ❒ Tuesday .... Exodus 35:1—36:38
- ❒ Wednesday .... Exodus 37:1—38:30
- ❒ Thursday .... Exodus 39:1—40:38
- ❒ Friday .... Leviticus 1:1–17
- ❒ Saturday .... Leviticus 2:1—3:17

Week 10

- ❒ Monday .... Leviticus 4:1—6:30
- ❒ Tuesday .... Leviticus 7:1—9:24
- ❒ Wednesday .... Leviticus 10:1—11:47
- ❒ Thursday .... Leviticus 12:1—15:33
- ❒ Friday .... Leviticus 16:1—17:16
- ❒ Saturday .... Leviticus 18:1—19:37

Week 11

- ❒ Monday .... Leviticus 20:1—22:33
- ❒ Tuesday .... Leviticus 23:1—25:55
- ❒ Wednesday .... Leviticus 26:1—27:34
- ❒ Thursday .... Numbers 1:1—3:51
- ❒ Friday .... Numbers 4:1—6:27
- ❒ Saturday .... Numbers 7:1—8:26

Week 12

- ❒ Monday .... Numbers 9:1—10:36
- ❒ Tuesday .... Numbers 11:1—12:16
- ❒ Wednesday .... Numbers 13:1—15:41
- ❒ Thursday .... Numbers 16:1—18:32
- ❒ Friday .... Numbers 19:1—20:29
- ❒ Saturday .... Numbers 21:1–35

Week 13

- ❒ Monday .... Numbers 22:1—25:18
- ❒ Tuesday .... Numbers 26:1—27:23
- ❒ Wednesday .... Numbers 28:1—30:16
- ❒ Thursday .... Numbers 31:1–54
- ❒ Friday .... Numbers 32:1—34:29
- ❒ Saturday .... Numbers 35:1—36:13

Week 14

- ❒ Monday .... Deuteronomy 1:1–46
- ❒ Tuesday .... Deuteronomy 2:1–37
- ❒ Wednesday .... Deuteronomy 3:1–29
- ❒ Thursday .... Deuteronomy 4:1–49
- ❒ Friday .... Deuteronomy 5:1–33
- ❒ Saturday .... Deuteronomy 6:1–25

Week 15
- ❒ Monday .... Deuteronomy 7:1–26
- ❒ Tuesday .... Deuteronomy 8:1–20
- ❒ Wednesday .... Deuteronomy 9:1—10:22
- ❒ Thursday .... Deuteronomy 11:1—12:32
- ❒ Friday .... Deuteronomy 13:1–18
- ❒ Saturday .... Deuteronomy 14:1—15:23

Week 16
- ❒ Monday .... Deuteronomy 16:1—17:20
- ❒ Tuesday .... Deuteronomy 18:1—19:21
- ❒ Wednesday .... Deuteronomy 20:1—21:23
- ❒ Thursday .... Deuteronomy 22:1—23:25
- ❒ Friday .... Deuteronomy 24:1–22
- ❒ Saturday .... Deuteronomy 25:1—26:19

Week 17
- ❒ Monday .... Deuteronomy 27:1–26
- ❒ Tuesday .... Deuteronomy 28:1–68
- ❒ Wednesday .... Deuteronomy 29:1–29
- ❒ Thursday .... Deuteronomy 30:1–20
- ❒ Friday .... Deuteronomy 31:1–30
- ❒ Saturday .... Deuteronomy 32:1–52

Week 18
- ❒ Monday .... Deuteronomy 33:1–29
- ❒ Tuesday .... Deuteronomy 34:1–12
- ❒ Wednesday .... Joshua 1:1–18
- ❒ Thursday .... Joshua 2:1—3:17
- ❒ Friday .... Joshua 4:1—5:12
- ❒ Saturday .... Joshua 5:13—7:26

Week 19
- ❒ Monday .... Joshua 8:1—9:27
- ❒ Tuesday .... Joshua 10:1–43
- ❒ Wednesday .... Joshua 11:1—12:24
- ❒ Thursday .... Joshua 13:1—15:63
- ❒ Friday .... Joshua 16:1—17:18
- ❒ Saturday .... Joshua 18:1—19:51

Week 20

- ❒ Monday .... Joshua 20:1—21:45
- ❒ Tuesday .... Joshua 22:1–34
- ❒ Wednesday .... Joshua 23:1–16
- ❒ Thursday .... Joshua 24:1–33
- ❒ Friday .... Judges 1:1–36
- ❒ Saturday .... Judges 2:1–23

Week 21

- ❒ Monday .... Judges 3:1–31
- ❒ Tuesday .... Judges 4:1—5:31
- ❒ Wednesday .... Judges 6:1—8:34
- ❒ Thursday .... Judges 9:1—10:18
- ❒ Friday .... Judges 11:1—12:15
- ❒ Saturday .... Judges 13:1—16:31

Week 22

- ❒ Monday .... Judges 17:1—18:31
- ❒ Tuesday .... Judges 19:1—20:48
- ❒ Wednesday .... Judges 21:1–25
- ❒ Thursday .... Ruth 1:1—2:23
- ❒ Friday .... Ruth 3:1—4:22
- ❒ Saturday .... 1 Samuel 1:1–28

Week 23

- ❒ Monday .... 1 Samuel 2:1–36
- ❒ Tuesday .... 1 Samuel 3:1–21
- ❒ Wednesday .... 1 Samuel 4:1–22
- ❒ Thursday .... 1 Samuel 5:1—6:21
- ❒ Friday .... 1 Samuel 7:1–17
- ❒ Saturday .... 1 Samuel 8:1–22

Week 24

- ❒ Monday .... 1 Samuel 9:1—10:27
- ❒ Tuesday .... 1 Samuel 11:1–15
- ❒ Wednesday .... 1 Samuel 12:1–25
- ❒ Thursday .... 1 Samuel 13:1–22
- ❒ Friday .... 1 Samuel 14:1–52
- ❒ Saturday .... 1 Samuel 15:1–35

Week 25

- ❐ Monday .... 1 Samuel 16:1–23
- ❐ Tuesday .... 1 Samuel 17:1–58
- ❐ Wednesday .... 1 Samuel 18:1—19:24
- ❐ Thursday .... 1 Samuel 20:1—21:15
- ❐ Friday .... 1 Samuel 22:1–23
- ❐ Saturday .... 1 Samuel 23:1–29

Week 26

- ❐ Monday .... 1 Samuel 24:1–22
- ❐ Tuesday .... 1 Samuel 25:1–44
- ❐ Wednesday .... 1 Samuel 26:1–25
- ❐ Thursday .... 1 Samuel 27:1—29:11
- ❐ Friday .... 1 Samuel 30:1–31
- ❐ Saturday .... 1 Samuel 31:1–13

Week 27

- ❐ Monday .... 2 Samuel 1:1—2:32
- ❐ Tuesday .... 2 Samuel 3:1—4:12
- ❐ Wednesday .... 2 Samuel 5:1–25
- ❐ Thursday .... 2 Samuel 6:1–23
- ❐ Friday .... 2 Samuel 7:1–29
- ❐ Saturday .... 2 Samuel 8:1—10:19

Week 28

- ❐ Monday .... 2 Samuel 11:1—12:31
- ❐ Tuesday .... 2 Samuel 13:1—14:24
- ❐ Wednesday .... 2 Samuel 14:25—16:23
- ❐ Thursday .... 2 Samuel 17:1—18:33
- ❐ Friday .... 2 Samuel 19:1—20:26
- ❐ Saturday .... 2 Samuel 21:1—22:51

Week 29

- ❐ Monday .... 2 Samuel 23:1–39
- ❐ Tuesday .... 2 Samuel 24:1–25
- ❐ Wednesday .... 1 Kings 1:1—2:46
- ❐ Thursday .... 1 Kings 3:1—4:34
- ❐ Friday .... 1 Kings 5:1—7:51
- ❐ Saturday .... 1 Kings 8:1–66

Week 30

- ❒ Monday .... 1 Kings 9:1—10:29
- ❒ Tuesday .... 1 Kings 11:1–43
- ❒ Wednesday .... 1 Kings 12:1–33
- ❒ Thursday .... 1 Kings 13:1—14:31
- ❒ Friday .... 1 Kings 15:1—16:34
- ❒ Saturday .... 1 Kings 17:1—18:46

Week 31

- ❒ Monday .... 1 Kings 19:1–21
- ❒ Tuesday .... 1 Kings 20:1–43
- ❒ Wednesday .... 1 Kings 21:1—22:53
- ❒ Thursday .... 2 Kings 1:1—2:25
- ❒ Friday .... 2 Kings 3:1—4:44
- ❒ Saturday .... 2 Kings 5:1–27

Week 32

- ❒ Monday .... 2 Kings 6:1—7:20
- ❒ Tuesday .... 2 Kings 8:1–29
- ❒ Wednesday .... 2 Kings 9:1—10:36
- ❒ Thursday .... 2 Kings 11:1—12:21
- ❒ Friday .... 2 Kings 13:1—14:29
- ❒ Saturday .... 2 Kings 15:1—16:20

Week 33

- ❒ Monday .... 2 Kings 17:1–41
- ❒ Tuesday .... 2 Kings 18:1—19:37
- ❒ Wednesday .... 2 Kings 20:1–21
- ❒ Thursday .... 2 Kings 21:1–26
- ❒ Friday .... 2 Kings 22:1—23:37
- ❒ Saturday .... 2 Kings 24:1—25:30

Week 34

- ❒ Monday .... 1 Chronicles 1:1—4:43
- ❒ Tuesday .... 1 Chronicles 5:1—8:40
- ❒ Wednesday .... 1 Chronicles 9:1—12:40
- ❒ Thursday .... 1 Chronicles 13:1—14:17
- ❒ Friday .... 1 Chronicles 15:1—16:43
- ❒ Saturday .... 1 Chronicles 17:1–27

Week 35

- ❒ Monday .... 1 Chronicles 18:1—20:8
- ❒ Tuesday .... 1 Chronicles 21:1–30
- ❒ Wednesday .... 1 Chronicles 22:1–19
- ❒ Thursday .... 1 Chronicles 23:1—27:34
- ❒ Friday .... 1 Chronicles 28:1–21
- ❒ Saturday .... 1 Chronicles 29:1–30

Week 36

- ❒ Monday .... 2 Chronicles 1:1—2:18
- ❒ Tuesday .... 2 Chronicles 3:1—5:14
- ❒ Wednesday .... 2 Chronicles 6:1—7:22
- ❒ Thursday .... 2 Chronicles 8:1—9:31
- ❒ Friday .... 2 Chronicles 10:1—11:23
- ❒ Saturday .... 2 Chronicles 12:1–16

Week 37

- ❒ Monday .... 2 Chronicles 13:1—14:15
- ❒ Tuesday .... 2 Chronicles 15:1—16:14
- ❒ Wednesday .... 2 Chronicles 17:1—18:34
- ❒ Thursday .... 2 Chronicles 19:1—20:37
- ❒ Friday .... 2 Chronicles 21:1—22:12
- ❒ Saturday .... 2 Chronicles 23:1—24:27

Week 38

- ❒ Monday .... 2 Chronicles 25:1—26:23
- ❒ Tuesday .... 2 Chronicles 27:1—28:27
- ❒ Wednesday .... 2 Chronicles 29:1–36
- ❒ Thursday .... 2 Chronicles 30:1—31:21
- ❒ Friday .... 2 Chronicles 32:1–33
- ❒ Saturday .... 2 Chronicles 33:1–25

Week 39

- ❒ Monday .... 2 Chronicles 34:1—35:27
- ❒ Tuesday .... 2 Chronicles 36:1–23
- ❒ Wednesday .... Ezra 1:1—2:70
- ❒ Thursday .... Ezra 3:1—4:24
- ❒ Friday .... Ezra 5:1—6:22
- ❒ Saturday .... Ezra 7:1—8:36

Week 40

- ❒ Monday .... Ezra 9:1—10:44
- ❒ Tuesday .... Nehemiah 1:1–11
- ❒ Wednesday .... Nehemiah 2:1—3:32
- ❒ Thursday .... Nehemiah 4:1—6:19
- ❒ Friday .... Nehemiah 7:1—8:18
- ❒ Saturday .... Nehemiah 9:1—10:39

Week 41

- ❒ Monday .... Nehemiah 11:1—13:31
- ❒ Tuesday .... Esther 1:1—2:23
- ❒ Wednesday .... Esther 3:1—4:17
- ❒ Thursday .... Esther 5:1—7:10
- ❒ Friday .... Esther 8:1—10:3
- ❒ Saturday .... Job 1:1–22

Week 42

- ❒ Monday .... Job 2:1—3:26
- ❒ Tuesday .... Job 4:1—5:27
- ❒ Wednesday .... Job 6:1—7:21
- ❒ Thursday .... Job 8:1—10:22
- ❒ Friday .... Job 11:1—12:25
- ❒ Saturday .... Job 13:1—14:22

Week 43

- ❒ Monday .... Job 15:1—17:16
- ❒ Tuesday .... Job 18:1—19:29
- ❒ Wednesday .... Job 20:1—21:34
- ❒ Thursday .... Job 22:1—24:25
- ❒ Friday .... Job 25:1—28:28
- ❒ Saturday .... Job 29:1—31:40

Week 44

- ❒ Monday .... Job 32:1—34:37
- ❒ Tuesday .... Job 35:1—37:24
- ❒ Wednesday .... Job 38:1—41:34
- ❒ Thursday .... Job 42:1–17
- ❒ Friday .... Psalms 1:1—6:10
- ❒ Saturday .... Psalms 7:1—11:7

Week 45

- ❒ Monday .... Psalms 12:1—17:15
- ❒ Tuesday .... Psalms 18:1—22:31
- ❒ Wednesday .... Psalms 23:1—28:9
- ❒ Thursday .... Psalms 29:1—34:22
- ❒ Friday .... Psalms 35:1—41:13
- ❒ Saturday .... Psalms 42:1—47:9

Week 46

- ❒ Monday .... Psalms 48:1—53:6
- ❒ Tuesday .... Psalms 54:1—60:12
- ❒ Wednesday .... Psalms 61:1—66:20
- ❒ Thursday .... Psalms 67:1—72:20
- ❒ Friday .... Psalms 73:1—77:20
- ❒ Saturday .... Psalms 78:1—82:8

Week 47

- ❒ Monday .... Psalms 83:1—89:52
- ❒ Tuesday .... Psalms 90:1—95:11
- ❒ Wednesday .... Psalms 96:1—101:8
- ❒ Thursday .... Psalms 102:1—106:48
- ❒ Friday .... Psalms 107:1—113:9
- ❒ Saturday .... Psalms 114:1—118:29

Week 48

- ❒ Monday .... Psalm 119:1–176
- ❒ Tuesday .... Psalms 120:1—125:5
- ❒ Wednesday .... Psalms 126:1—134:3
- ❒ Thursday .... Psalms 135:1—137:9
- ❒ Friday .... Psalms 138:1—143:12
- ❒ Saturday .... Psalm 144:1—150:6

Week 49

- ❒ Monday .... Proverbs 1:1—3:35
- ❒ Tuesday .... Proverbs 4:1–27
- ❒ Wednesday .... Proverbs 5:1—6:35
- ❒ Thursday .... Proverbs 7:1–27
- ❒ Friday .... Proverbs 8:1–36
- ❒ Saturday .... Proverbs 9:1–18

Week 50

- ❐ Monday .... Proverbs 10:1—11:31
- ❐ Tuesday .... Proverbs 12:1—13:25
- ❐ Wednesday .... Proverbs 14:1—15:33
- ❐ Thursday .... Proverbs 16:1—17:28
- ❐ Friday .... Proverbs 18:1—19:29
- ❐ Saturday .... Proverbs 20:1—21:31

Week 51

- ❐ Monday .... Proverbs 22:1—23:35
- ❐ Tuesday .... Proverbs 24:1—25:28
- ❐ Wednesday .... Proverbs 26:1—27:27
- ❐ Thursday .... Proverbs 28:1—29:27
- ❐ Friday .... Proverbs 30:1—31:31
- ❐ Saturday .... Ecclesiastes 1:1—2:26

Week 52

- ❐ Monday .... Ecclesiastes 3:1—4:16
- ❐ Tuesday .... Ecclesiastes 5:1—6:12
- ❐ Wednesday .... Ecclesiastes 7:1—8:17
- ❐ Thursday .... Ecclesiastes 9:1—10:20
- ❐ Friday .... Ecclesiastes 11:1—12:14
- ❐ Saturday .... Song of Songs 1:1—3:11

Week 53

- ❐ Monday .... Song of Songs 4:1—6:13
- ❐ Tuesday .... Song of Songs 7:1—8:14
- ❐ Wednesday .... Isaiah 1:1—2:22
- ❐ Thursday .... Isaiah 3:1—4:6
- ❐ Friday .... Isaiah 5:1–30
- ❐ Saturday .... Isaiah 6:1–13

Week 54

- ❐ Monday .... Isaiah 7:1—8:22
- ❐ Tuesday .... Isaiah 9:1—10:34
- ❐ Wednesday .... Isaiah 11:1—12:6
- ❐ Thursday .... Isaiah 13:1—20:6
- ❐ Friday .... Isaiah 21:1—23:18
- ❐ Saturday .... Isaiah 24:1—25:12

Week 55

- ❐ Monday .... Isaiah 26:1—27:13
- ❐ Tuesday .... Isaiah 28:1—29:24
- ❐ Wednesday .... Isaiah 30:1—31:9
- ❐ Thursday .... Isaiah 32:1–20
- ❐ Friday .... Isaiah 33:1—35:10
- ❐ Saturday .... Isaiah 36:1—39:8

Week 56

- ❐ Monday .... Isaiah 40:1—41:29
- ❐ Tuesday .... Isaiah 42:1—43:28
- ❐ Wednesday .... Isaiah 44:1—45:25
- ❐ Thursday .... Isaiah 46:1—47:15
- ❐ Friday .... Isaiah 48:1—49:26
- ❐ Saturday .... Isaiah 50:1—52:15

Week 57

- ❐ Monday .... Isaiah 53:1–12
- ❐ Tuesday .... Isaiah 54:1—57:21
- ❐ Wednesday .... Isaiah 58:1—59:21
- ❐ Thursday .... Isaiah 60:1—62:12
- ❐ Friday .... Isaiah 63:1—66:24
- ❐ Saturday .... Jeremiah 1:1—2:37

Week 58

- ❐ Monday .... Jeremiah 3:1—4:31
- ❐ Tuesday .... Jeremiah 5:1—6:30
- ❐ Wednesday .... Jeremiah 7:1—8:22
- ❐ Thursday .... Jeremiah 9:1—10:25
- ❐ Friday .... Jeremiah 11:1—12:17
- ❐ Saturday .... Jeremiah 13:1—14:22

Week 59

- ❐ Monday .... Jeremiah 15:1—17:27
- ❐ Tuesday .... Jeremiah 18:1—19:15
- ❐ Wednesday .... Jeremiah 20:1—22:30
- ❐ Thursday .... Jeremiah 23:1–40
- ❐ Friday .... Jeremiah 24:1—25:38
- ❐ Saturday .... Jeremiah 26:1—28:17

Week 60

- ❐ Monday .... Jeremiah 29:1–32
- ❐ Tuesday .... Jeremiah 30:1—32:44
- ❐ Wednesday .... Jeremiah 33:1–26
- ❐ Thursday .... Jeremiah 34:1—35:19
- ❐ Friday .... Jeremiah 36:1—37:21
- ❐ Saturday .... Jeremiah 38:1—40:16

Week 61

- ❐ Monday .... Jeremiah 41:1—43:13
- ❐ Tuesday .... Jeremiah 44:1—45:5
- ❐ Wednesday .... Jeremiah 46:1—49:39
- ❐ Thursday .... Jeremiah 50:1—51:64
- ❐ Friday .... Jeremiah 52:1–34
- ❐ Saturday .... Lamentations 1:1–22

Week 62

- ❐ Monday .... Lamentations 2:1—3:66
- ❐ Tuesday .... Lamentations 4:1—5:22
- ❐ Wednesday .... Ezekiel 1:1—2:10
- ❐ Thursday .... Ezekiel 3:1—5:17
- ❐ Friday .... Ezekiel 6:1—7:27
- ❐ Saturday .... Ezekiel 8:1—9:11

Week 63

- ❐ Monday .... Ezekiel 10:1—11:25
- ❐ Tuesday .... Ezekiel 12:1—13:23
- ❐ Wednesday .... Ezekiel 14:1—15:8
- ❐ Thursday .... Ezekiel 16:1—17:24
- ❐ Friday .... Ezekiel 18:1—19:14
- ❐ Saturday .... Ezekiel 20:1—21:32

Week 64

- ❐ Monday .... Ezekiel 22:1—23:49
- ❐ Tuesday .... Ezekiel 24:1–27
- ❐ Wednesday .... Ezekiel 25:1—27:36
- ❐ Thursday .... Ezekiel 28:1–26
- ❐ Friday .... Ezekiel 29:1—32:32
- ❐ Saturday .... Ezekiel 33:1—34:31

Week 65

- ❒ Monday .... Ezekiel 35:1—36:38
- ❒ Tuesday .... Ezekiel 37:1—39:29
- ❒ Wednesday .... Ezekiel 40:1—42:20
- ❒ Thursday .... Ezekiel 43:1–27
- ❒ Friday .... Ezekiel 44:1–31
- ❒ Saturday .... Ezekiel 45:1—46:24

Week 66

- ❒ Monday .... Ezekiel 47:1—48:35
- ❒ Tuesday .... Daniel 1:1–21
- ❒ Wednesday .... Daniel 2:1–49
- ❒ Thursday .... Daniel 3:1—4:37
- ❒ Friday .... Daniel 5:1–31
- ❒ Saturday .... Daniel 6:1–28

Week 67

- ❒ Monday .... Daniel 7:1—8:27
- ❒ Tuesday .... Daniel 9:1–27
- ❒ Wednesday .... Daniel 10:1—12:13
- ❒ Thursday .... Hosea 1:1—2:23
- ❒ Friday .... Hosea 3:1—4:19
- ❒ Saturday .... Hosea 5:1—6:11

Week 68

- ❒ Monday .... Hosea 7:1—8:14
- ❒ Tuesday .... Hosea 9:1—10:15
- ❒ Wednesday .... Hosea 11:1—12:14
- ❒ Thursday .... Hosea 13:1–16
- ❒ Friday .... Hosea 14:1–9
- ❒ Saturday .... Joel 1:1–20

Week 69

- ❒ Monday .... Joel 2:1–32
- ❒ Tuesday .... Joel 3:1–21
- ❒ Wednesday .... Amos 1:1—2:16
- ❒ Thursday .... Amos 3:1–15
- ❒ Friday .... Amos 4:1—5:27
- ❒ Saturday .... Amos 6:1–14

Week 70

- ❒ Monday .... Amos 7:1–17
- ❒ Tuesday .... Amos 8:1–14
- ❒ Wednesday .... Amos 9:1–15
- ❒ Thursday .... Obadiah 1–21
- ❒ Friday .... Jonah 1:1—2:10
- ❒ Saturday .... Jonah 3:1—4:11

Week 71

- ❒ Monday .... Micah 1:1—2:13
- ❒ Tuesday .... Micah 3:1—4:13
- ❒ Wednesday .... Micah 5:1–15
- ❒ Thursday .... Micah 6:1–16
- ❒ Friday .... Micah 7:1–20
- ❒ Saturday .... Nahum 1:1—3:19

Week 72

- ❒ Monday .... Habakkuk 1:1—2:20
- ❒ Tuesday .... Habakkuk 3:1–19
- ❒ Wednesday .... Zephaniah 1:1—2:15
- ❒ Thursday .... Zephaniah 3:1–20
- ❒ Friday .... Haggai 1:1—2:23
- ❒ Saturday .... Zechariah 1:1—2:13

Week 73

- ❒ Monday .... Zechariah 3:1–10
- ❒ Tuesday .... Zechariah 4:1–14
- ❒ Wednesday .... Zechariah 5:1–11
- ❒ Thursday .... Zechariah 6:1–15
- ❒ Friday .... Zechariah 7:1–14
- ❒ Saturday .... Zechariah 8:1–23

Week 74

- ❒ Monday .... Zechariah 9:1—10:12
- ❒ Tuesday .... Zechariah 11:1—12:14
- ❒ Wednesday .... Zechariah 13:1–9
- ❒ Thursday .... Zechariah 14:1–21
- ❒ Friday .... Malachi 1:1—2:17
- ❒ Saturday .... Malachi 3:1—4:6

Week 75

- ❒ Monday .... Matthew 1:1—2:23
- ❒ Tuesday .... Matthew 3:1—4:25
- ❒ Wednesday .... Matthew 5:1—7:29
- ❒ Thursday .... Matthew 8:1—9:38
- ❒ Friday .... Matthew 10:1—11:30
- ❒ Saturday .... Matthew 12:1—13:58

Week 76

- ❒ Monday .... Matthew 14:1—15:39
- ❒ Tuesday .... Matthew 16:1—17:27
- ❒ Wednesday .... Matthew 18:1—19:30
- ❒ Thursday .... Matthew 20:1—21:46
- ❒ Friday .... Matthew 22:1—23:39
- ❒ Saturday .... Matthew 24:1—25:46

Week 77

- ❒ Monday .... Matthew 26:1—27:66
- ❒ Tuesday .... Matthew 28:1–20
- ❒ Wednesday .... Mark 1:1—2:28
- ❒ Thursday .... Mark 3:1—4:41
- ❒ Friday .... Mark 5:1—6:56
- ❒ Saturday .... Mark 7:1—8:38

Week 78

- ❒ Monday .... Mark 9:1–50
- ❒ Tuesday .... Mark 10:1–52
- ❒ Wednesday .... Mark 11:1–33
- ❒ Thursday .... Mark 12:1—13:37
- ❒ Friday .... Mark 14:1–72
- ❒ Saturday .... Mark 15:1–47

Week 79

- ❒ Monday .... Mark 16:1–20
- ❒ Tuesday .... Luke 1:1–80
- ❒ Wednesday .... Luke 2:1—3:38
- ❒ Thursday .... Luke 4:1—5:39
- ❒ Friday .... Luke 6:1–49
- ❒ Saturday .... Luke 7:1—8:56

Week 80
- ❒ Monday .... Luke 9:1–62
- ❒ Tuesday .... Luke 10:1–42
- ❒ Wednesday .... Luke 11:1—12:59
- ❒ Thursday .... Luke 13:1–35
- ❒ Friday .... Luke 14:1–35
- ❒ Saturday .... Luke 15:1–16:31

Week 81
- ❒ Monday .... Luke 17:1—18:43
- ❒ Tuesday .... Luke 19:1—20:47
- ❒ Wednesday .... Luke 21:1—22:71
- ❒ Thursday .... Luke 23:1—24:53
- ❒ Friday .... John 1:1—2:25
- ❒ Saturday .... John 3:1–36

Week 82
- ❒ Monday .... John 4:1–54
- ❒ Tuesday .... John 5:1—6:71
- ❒ Wednesday .... John 7:1—8:59
- ❒ Thursday .... John 9:1—10:42
- ❒ Friday .... John 11:1—12:50
- ❒ Saturday .... John 13:1—14:31

Week 83
- ❒ Monday .... John 15:1—16:33
- ❒ Tuesday .... John 17:1–26
- ❒ Wednesday .... John 18:1—19:42
- ❒ Thursday .... John 20:1—21:25
- ❒ Friday .... Acts 1:1–26
- ❒ Saturday .... Acts 2:1–47

Week 84
- ❒ Monday .... Acts 3:1—4:37
- ❒ Tuesday .... Acts 5:1–42
- ❒ Wednesday .... Acts 6:1—8:40
- ❒ Thursday .... Acts 9:1–43
- ❒ Friday .... Acts 10:1—11:30
- ❒ Saturday .... Acts 12:1–25

Week 85

- ❒ Monday .... Acts 13:1—14:28
- ❒ Tuesday .... Acts 15:1–35
- ❒ Wednesday .... Acts 15:36—16:40
- ❒ Thursday .... Acts 17:1—18:22
- ❒ Friday .... Acts 18:23—21:16
- ❒ Saturday .... Acts 21:17—23:35

Week 86

- ❒ Monday .... Acts 24:1—26:32
- ❒ Tuesday .... Acts 27:1—28:31
- ❒ Wednesday .... Romans 1:1—2:29
- ❒ Thursday .... Romans 3:1—4:25
- ❒ Friday .... Romans 5:1–21
- ❒ Saturday .... Romans 6:1–23

Week 87

- ❒ Monday .... Romans 7:1–25
- ❒ Tuesday .... Romans 8:1–39
- ❒ Wednesday .... Romans 9:1—11:36
- ❒ Thursday .... Romans 12:1–21
- ❒ Friday .... Romans 13:1—14:23
- ❒ Saturday .... Romans 15:1—16:27

Week 88

- ❒ Monday .... 1 Corinthians 1:1—2:16
- ❒ Tuesday .... 1 Corinthians 3:1—4:21
- ❒ Wednesday .... 1 Corinthians 5:1—6:20
- ❒ Thursday .... 1 Corinthians 7:1–40
- ❒ Friday .... 1 Corinthians 8:1—9:27
- ❒ Saturday .... 1 Corinthians 10:1–33

Week 89

- ❒ Monday .... 1 Corinthians 11:1—12:31
- ❒ Tuesday .... 1 Corinthians 13:1—14:40
- ❒ Wednesday .... 1 Corinthians 15:1–58
- ❒ Thursday .... 1 Corinthians 16:1–24
- ❒ Friday .... 2 Corinthians 1:1—2:17
- ❒ Saturday .... 2 Corinthians 3:1—4:18

Week 90

- ❒ Monday .... 2 Corinthians 5:1–21
- ❒ Tuesday .... 2 Corinthians 6:1—7:16
- ❒ Wednesday .... 2 Corinthians 8:1—9:15
- ❒ Thursday .... 2 Corinthians 10:1—11:33
- ❒ Friday .... 2 Corinthians 12:1—13:14
- ❒ Saturday .... Galatians 1:1—2:21

Week 91

- ❒ Monday .... Galatians 3:1–29
- ❒ Tuesday .... Galatians 4:1–31
- ❒ Wednesday .... Galatians 5:1—6:18
- ❒ Thursday .... Ephesians 1:1–23
- ❒ Friday .... Ephesians 2:1–22
- ❒ Saturday .... Ephesians 3:1–21

Week 92

- ❒ Monday .... Ephesians 4:1–32
- ❒ Tuesday .... Ephesians 5:1—6:24
- ❒ Wednesday .... Philippians 1:1–30
- ❒ Thursday .... Philippians 2:1–30
- ❒ Friday .... Philippians 3:1–21
- ❒ Saturday .... Philippians 4:1–23

Week 93

- ❒ Monday .... Colossians 1:1–29
- ❒ Tuesday .... Colossians 2:1–23
- ❒ Wednesday .... Colossians 3:1—4:18
- ❒ Thursday .... 1 Thessalonians 1:1–10
- ❒ Friday .... 1 Thessalonians 2:1–20
- ❒ Saturday .... 1 Thessalonians 3:1–13

Week 94

- ❒ Monday .... 1 Thessalonians 4:1–18
- ❒ Tuesday .... 1 Thessalonians 5:1–28
- ❒ Wednesday .... 2 Thessalonians 1:1–12
- ❒ Thursday .... 2 Thessalonians 2:1—3:18
- ❒ Friday .... 1 Timothy 1:1–20
- ❒ Saturday .... 1 Timothy 2:1–15

Week 95

- ❒ Monday .... 1 Timothy 3:1–16
- ❒ Tuesday .... 1 Timothy 4:1–16
- ❒ Wednesday .... 1 Timothy 5:1–25
- ❒ Thursday .... 1 Timothy 6:1–21
- ❒ Friday .... 2 Timothy 1:1–18
- ❒ Saturday .... 2 Timothy 2:1–26

Week 96

- ❒ Monday .... 2 Timothy 3:1—4:22
- ❒ Tuesday .... Titus 1:1–16
- ❒ Wednesday .... Titus 2:1–15
- ❒ Thursday .... Titus 3:1–15
- ❒ Friday .... Philemon 1–25
- ❒ Saturday .... Hebrews 1:1–14

Week 97

- ❒ Monday .... Hebrews 2:1–18
- ❒ Tuesday .... Hebrews 3:1–19
- ❒ Wednesday .... Hebrews 4:1–16
- ❒ Thursday .... Hebrews 5:1–14
- ❒ Friday .... Hebrews 6:1–20
- ❒ Saturday .... Hebrews 7:1–28

Week 98

- ❒ Monday .... Hebrews 8:1–13
- ❒ Tuesday .... Hebrews 9:1–28
- ❒ Wednesday .... Hebrews 10:1–18
- ❒ Thursday .... Hebrews 10:19–39
- ❒ Friday .... Hebrews 11:1–40
- ❒ Saturday .... Hebrews 12:1–29

Week 99

- ❒ Monday .... Hebrews 13:1–25
- ❒ Tuesday .... James 1:1–27
- ❒ Wednesday .... James 2:1–26
- ❒ Thursday .... James 3:1–18
- ❒ Friday .... James 4:1–17
- ❒ Saturday .... James 5:1–20

Week 100

- ❒ Monday .... 1 Peter 1:1–25
- ❒ Tuesday .... 1 Peter 2:1–25
- ❒ Wednesday .... 1 Peter 3:1—4:19
- ❒ Thursday .... 1 Peter 5:1–14
- ❒ Friday .... 2 Peter 1:1—2:22
- ❒ Saturday .... 2 Peter 3:1–18

Week 101

- ❒ Monday .... 1 John 1:1–10
- ❒ Tuesday .... 1 John 2:1–29
- ❒ Wednesday .... 1 John 3:1–24
- ❒ Thursday .... 1 John 4:1–21
- ❒ Friday .... 1 John 5:1–21
- ❒ Saturday .... 2 John 1–13

Week 102

- ❒ Monday .... 3 John 1–14
- ❒ Tuesday .... Jude 1–25
- ❒ Wednesday .... Revelation 1:1–20
- ❒ Thursday .... Revelation 2:1–29
- ❒ Friday .... Revelation 3:1–22
- ❒ Saturday .... Revelation 4:1—5:14

Week 103

- ❒ Monday .... Revelation 6:1—8:5
- ❒ Tuesday .... Revelation 8:6—9:21
- ❒ Wednesday .... Revelation 10:1–11
- ❒ Thursday .... Revelation 11:1–19
- ❒ Friday .... Revelation 12:1–17
- ❒ Saturday .... Revelation 13:1–18

Week 104

- ❒ Monday .... Revelation 14:1–20
- ❒ Tuesday .... Revelation 15:1–8
- ❒ Wednesday .... Revelation 16:1–21
- ❒ Thursday .... Revelation 17:1—18:8
- ❒ Friday .... Revelation 18:9–24
- ❒ Saturday .... Revelation 19:1–21

Week 105

- ❐ Monday .... Revelation 20:1–15
- ❐ Tuesday .... Revelation 21:1–27
- ❐ Wednesday .... Revelation 22:1–21

Notes

NOTES